20°E
40°E
60°E
80°E
100°E
120°E
140°E
160°E
180°
80°N
ARCTIC OCEAN
60°N
40°N
Tropic of Cancer
20°N
0°
20°S
Tropic of Capricorn
60°S
Antarctic Circle
80°S
180°

EUROPE
ALPS
URAL MTS.
Volga
Ob
ASIA
GOBI DESERT
HINDU KUSH
HIMALAYA MTS.
Indus
Ganges
Yangzi
SYRIAN DESERT
DECCAN PLATEAU
SAHARA
Nile
AFRICA
PACIFIC OCEAN
INDIAN OCEAN
GREAT SANDY DESERT
AUSTRALIA
NAMIB DESERT
KALAHARI DESERT
Cape of Good Hope

0 1000 2000 3000 Km.
0 1000 2000 3000 Mi.

ANTARCTICA

# A HISTORY OF WORLD SOCIETIES

# A HISTORY OF WORLD SOCIETIES

SIXTH EDITION

JOHN P. McKAY
University of Illinois at Urbana-Champaign

BENNETT D. HILL
Georgetown University

JOHN BUCKLER
University of Illinois at Urbana-Champaign

PATRICIA BUCKLEY EBREY
University of Washington

HOUGHTON MIFFLIN COMPANY
Boston New York

**Publisher:** Charles Hartford
**Editor-in-Chief:** Jean L. Woy
**Senior Sponsoring Editor:** Nancy Blaine
**Development Editor:** Julie Dunn
**Senior Project Editor:** Christina M. Horn
**Editorial Assistant:** Talia M. Kingsbury
**Senior Production/Design Coordinator:** Jennifer Meyer Dare
**Senior Manufacturing Coordinator:** Marie Barnes
**Senior Marketing Manager:** Sandra McGuire

Text credits appear on page I-72.

**Cover image:** Ming Emperor Ch'eng-tsu (Yung-Lo). Ink and color on silk by an anonymous painter. National Palace Museum, Taipei/Laurie Platt Winfrey, Inc.



Printed in the U.S.A.

Library of Congress Control Number: 2002117257

ISBN: 0-618-30195-X

5 6 7 8 9-VH-09 08 07 06 05

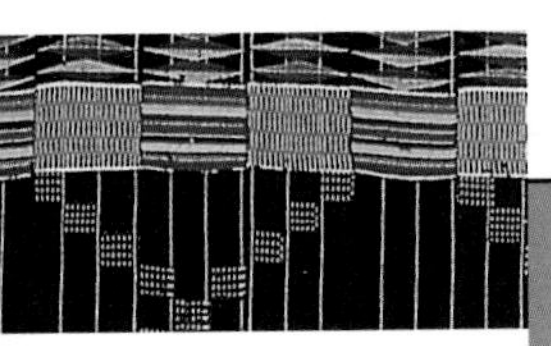

# ABOUT THE AUTHORS

**JOHN P. McKAY** Born in St. Louis, Missouri, John P. McKay received his B.A. from Wesleyan University (1961) and his Ph.D. from the University of California, Berkeley (1968). He began teaching history at the University of Illinois in 1966 and became a professor there in 1976. John won the Herbert Baxter Adams Prize for his book *Pioneers for Profit: Foreign Entrepreneurship and Russian Industrialization, 1885–1913* (1970). He has translated Jules Michelet's *The People* (1973) and has written *Tramways and Trolleys: The Rise of Urban Mass Transport in Europe* (1976), as well as more than a hundred articles, book chapters, and reviews, which have appeared in numerous publications. His research has been supported by fellowships from the Ford Foundation, the Guggenheim Foundation, the National Endowment for the Humanities, and IREX. Recently, he contributed extensively to C. Stewart and P. Fritzsche, eds., *Imagining the Twentieth Century* (1997).

**BENNETT D. HILL** A native of Philadelphia, Bennett D. Hill earned advanced degrees from Harvard (A.M., 1958) and Princeton (Ph.D., 1963). He taught history at the University of Illinois at Urbana, where he was department chairman from 1978 to 1981. He has published *English Cistercian Monasteries and Their Patrons in the Twelfth Century* (1968), *Church and State in the Middle Ages* (1970), and articles in *Analecta Cisterciensia, The New Catholic Encyclopaedia, The American Benedictine Review,* and *The Dictionary of the Middle Ages.* His reviews have appeared in *The American Historical Review, Speculum,* and the *Journal of World History.* He is one of the contributing editors to *The Encyclopedia of World History* (2001). He has been a Fellow of the American Council of Learned Societies and served as vice president of the American Catholic Historical Association (1995–1996). A Benedictine monk of St. Anselm's Abbey in Washington, D.C., he is also a Visiting Professor at Georgetown University.

**JOHN BUCKLER** Born in Louisville, Kentucky, John Buckler received his B.A. (summa cum laude) from the University of Louisville (1967) and his Ph.D. from Harvard University (1973). From 1984 to 1986 he was an Alexander von Humboldt Fellow at the Institut für Alte Geschichte, University of Munich. He has lectured at the Fondation Hardt at the University of Geneva and at the University of Freiburg. He is currently a professor of Greek history at the University of Illinois. In 1980 Harvard University Press published his *Theban Hegemony, 371–362 B.C.* He has also published *Philip II and the Sacred War* (Leiden 1989) and co-edited *BOIOTIKA: Vorträge vom 5. Internationalen Böotien-Kolloquium* (Munich 1989). He has contributed articles to *The American Historical Association's Guide to Historical Literature* (Oxford 1995), *The Oxford Classical Dictionary* (Oxford 1996), and *Encyclopedia of Greece and the Hellenic Tradition* (London 1999).

**PATRICIA BUCKLEY EBREY** Born in Hasbrouck Heights, New Jersey, Patricia Ebrey received her A.B. from the University of Chicago in 1968 and her M.A. and Ph.D. from Columbia University in 1970 and 1975. Formerly a faculty member at the University of Illinois, she now teaches at the University of Washington. Her books include *The Aristocratic Families of Early Imperial China* (1978), *Family and Property in Sung China* (1984), *Confucianism and Family Rituals in Imperial China* (1991), *The Inner Quarters: Marriage and the Lives of Chinese Women in the Sung Period* (1993), and *The Cambridge Illustrated History of China* (1996), which has been translated into four languages, including Chinese and Korean. *The Inner Quarters* was awarded the Levenson Prize of the Association for Asian Studies. She has also edited or coedited several important works, most notably *Chinese Civilization: A Sourcebook* (1981, 1993).

# BRIEF CONTENTS

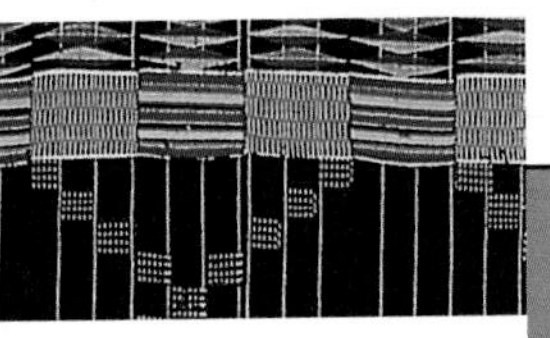

# CONTENTS

## CHAPTER 13

## EUROPE IN THE MIDDLE AGES 363



## CHAPTER 14

## CIVILIZATIONS OF THE AMERICAS, CA 400–1500 417

## CHAPTER 34



## CHAPTER 35



## CHAPTER 36

# MAPS

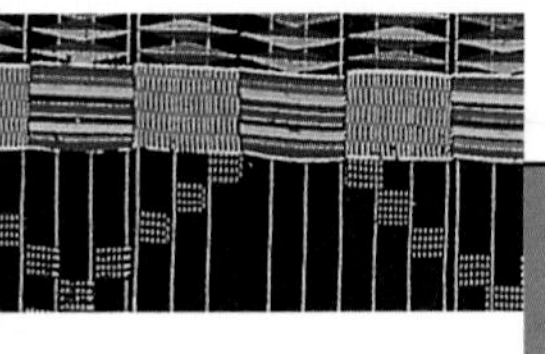

# LISTENING TO THE PAST

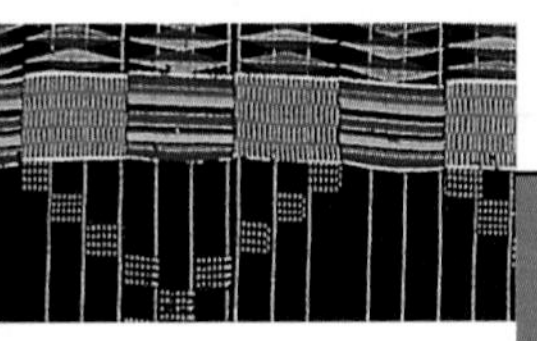

# PREFACE

In this age of a global environment and global warming, of a global economy and global banking, of global migration and rapid global travel, of global sports and global popular culture, the study of world history becomes more urgent. Surely, an appreciation of other, and earlier, societies helps us to understand better our own and to cope more effectively in pluralistic cultures worldwide. The large numbers of Turks living in Germany, of Italians, Hungarians, and Slavic peoples living in Australia, of Japanese living in Peru and Argentina, and of Arabs, Mexicans, Chinese, and Filipinos living in the United States—to mention just a few obvious examples—represent diversity on a global scale. The movement of large numbers of peoples from one continent to another goes back thousands of years, at least as far back as the time when Asian peoples migrated across the Bering Strait to North America. Swift air travel and the Internet have accelerated these movements, and they testify to the incredible technological changes the world has experienced in the last half of the twentieth century.

For most peoples, the study of history has traditionally meant the study of their own national, regional, and ethnic pasts. Fully appreciating the great differences among various societies and the complexity of the historical problems surrounding these cultures, we have wondered if the study of local or national history is sufficient for people who will spend most of their lives in the twenty-first century on one small interconnected planet. The authors of this book believe the study of world history in a broad and comparative context is an exciting, important, and highly practical pursuit.

It is our conviction, based on considerable experience in introducing large numbers of students to the broad sweep of civilization, that a book reflecting current trends can excite readers and inspire a renewed interest in history and the human experience. Our strategy has been twofold.

First, we have made social history the core element of our work. We not only incorporate recent research by social historians but also seek to re-create the life of ordinary people in appealing human terms. A strong social element seems especially appropriate in a world history text, for identification with ordinary people of the past allows today's reader to reach an empathetic understanding of different cultures and civilizations. At the same time we have been mindful of the need to give great economic, political, intellectual, and cultural developments the attention they deserve. We want to give individual students and instructors a balanced, integrated perspective so that they can pursue on their own or in the classroom those themes and questions that they find particularly exciting and significant.

Second, we have made every effort to strike an effective global balance. We are acutely aware of the great drama of our times—the passing of the era of Western dominance and the simultaneous rise of Asian and African peoples in world affairs. Increasingly, the whole world interacts, and to understand that interaction and what it means for today's citizens, we must study the whole world's history. Thus we have adopted a comprehensive yet manageable global perspective. We study all geographical areas and the world's main civilizations, conscious of their separate identities and unique contributions. We also stress the links among civilizations, for it is these links that have been transforming multicentered world history into the complex interactive process of different continents, peoples, and cultures that we see today.

## CHANGES IN THE SIXTH EDITION

In preparing the Sixth Edition of this book, we have worked hard to keep our book up-to-date and to strengthen our distinctive yet balanced approach.

### Organizational Changes

In order to give greater depth to our world focus, major organizational changes again proved essential. In preparing the Fifth Edition of this book, the fortunate addition of a distinguished Asian specialist, Patricia Buckley Ebrey, to our author team enabled us to expand coverage of Asian developments and to concentrate on those historical problems that scholars today consider most current. In revising the text for this Sixth Edition, Professor Ebrey's contributions on Asian civilizations have broadened. Chapters 7 and 12 now cover only East Asia, rather than all of Asia, allowing for greater in-depth treatment. The old Chapter 11 on Asia, 800–1400, has been split into two separate chapters on South and East Asia, now Chapters 11 and 12.

Other broad organizational changes include the combination of the old Chapters 12 and 13 on the Middle Ages into one chapter, now Chapter 13. The old Chapter 27, "Africa and Asia in the Era of Western Industrialization, 1800–1914," has been split into two separate chapters: one on West Asia and Africa, now Chapter 26, and one on Asia, now Chapter 27. In keeping with our general goal of expanding coverage of non-Western parts of the world, we have incorporated material on the "Changing Life of the People in Europe," formerly in Chapter 19, into the revised Chapter 18. And, together with a reduction of European material, the section on the United States in Chapter 31 has been cut back.

## "Global Trade" Feature

The Sixth Edition introduces a new feature on trade. In the form of four two-page essays, each focused on a particular commodity, the authors explore world trade in that commodity, the social and economic impact of the commodity, and the cultural influence the commodity has had. Each essay is accompanied by a detailed map showing the trade routes of the commodity. The essays deal with the international trade in pottery in the Greek and Roman worlds (Chapter 6), tea in the medieval and early modern worlds (Chapter 12), slaves in the early modern, modern, and contemporary worlds (Chapter 19), and oil in the modern world (Chapter 33). We believe that careful attention to these essays will enable the student to appreciate the ways in which trade has connected the various parts of the world.

## Expanded Ethnic and Geographic Scope

In the Sixth Edition we have added significantly more discussion of groups and regions that are often shortchanged in the general histories of world civilizations. This expanded scope is, we feel, an important improvement. It reflects the renewed awareness within the profession of the enormous diversity of the world's peoples, and of those peoples' efforts (or lack thereof) to understand others' regional, ethnic, and cultural identities. Examples of this enlarged scope include new material on Muslim attitudes toward blacks (Chapter 9) and on the Mongols and other peoples of Central Asia (Chapter 11); a broadened treatment of Europe's frontier regions—Iberia, Ireland, Scotland, eastern Europe, and the Baltic region (Chapter 13); the peoples of the Indian Ocean—of the Malay archipelago and the Philippines (Chapter 16); and a completely fresh discussion of twentieth-century eastern Europe (Chapters 29 and 33). Our broader treatment of Jewish history has been integrated in the text, with stimulating material on anti-Semitism during the Crusades (Chapter 13), during the Spanish Inquisition (Chapter 15), Jewish Enlightenment thought in Germany (Chapter 18), and the unfolding of the Holocaust during the Second World War (Chapter 32). Just as the Fifth Edition developed our treatment of the history of women and gender, so in this Sixth Edition significant issues of gender are explored with respect to Native American peoples (Chapter 14) and Indian Ocean peoples (Chapter 16). Overall, an expanded treatment of non-European societies and cultures has been achieved by reducing detailed coverage of Europe.

## Incorporation of Recent Scholarship

As in previous revisions, we have made a strenuous effort to keep our book up-to-date with new and important scholarship. Because the authors are committed to a balanced approach that reflects the true value of history, we have continued to incorporate significant new findings on political, cultural, and intellectual developments in this Sixth Edition. The treatment of Paleolithic and Neolithic civilizations in Chapter 1 has been revised, including a discussion of Stonehenge as an example of Neolithic civilization. Material on the Phoenicians and early Judaism in Chapter 2 has been revised, again, and fresh information on the Greek gods and heroes added in Chapter 5. Recent scholarship on the role of the army in Muslim expansion and on the formative period of Muslim theology and law has been incorporated into Chapter 9, as well as new material on Sufism. Likewise, the treatment of Bantu-speaking people in Africa and of the role of Islam in East Africa has been revised in Chapter 10. The Mongols receive a much more extensive treatment in Chapter 11, which complements discussion of them in the Islamic chapters, 9 and 20. The role of war in Aztec society, along with a detailed analysis of an actual battle, provides a fuller treatment of indigenous peoples of the Americas in Chapter 14, as does a new section on the mound builders of North America.

Moreover, the Sixth Edition gives more attention to the role of spices in the transmission of cultures (Chapter 16) and to the evolution of coffee drinking in the Ottoman world (Chapter 20). New scholarship has been added on the French Revolution in Chapter 22 and on nationalism in Chapter 24. Chapter 27 on Asia in the nineteenth century offers much greater coverage of colonial India and a completely new section on the Philippines. In Chapter 34, the coverage of South Asia and the Muslim world has been split to allow for greater treatment of each. Material on the Middle East—most notably on the Arab-Israeli conflict, Iraq, and Iran—has been considerably expanded. Finally, in addition to a new treatment of Jewish emancipation in the nineteenth century (Chapter 25) and expanded coverage of eastern Europe in several chapters, the last chapter, 36, brings international relations up to the present and includes a new discussion on terrorism.

### Revised Full-Color Art and Map Program

Finally, the illustrative component of our work has been carefully revised. We have added many new illustrations to our extensive art program, which includes over three hundred color reproductions, letting great art and important events come alive. Illustrations have been selected to support and complement the text, and, wherever possible, illustrations are contemporaneous with the textual material discussed. Considerable research went into many of the captions in order to make them as informative as possible. We have reflected on the observation that "there are more valid facts and details in works of art than there are in history books," and we would modify it to say that art is "a history book." Artwork remains an integral part of our book; the past can speak in pictures as well as in words. The use of full color serves to clarify the maps and graphs and to enrich the textual material. The maps and map captions have been updated to correlate directly to the text, and several new maps have been added, as in Chapters 3, 8, 9, 11, 12, 14, 19, and 33.

## DISTINCTIVE FEATURES

In addition to the new "Global Trade" essays, distinctive features from earlier editions guide the reader in the process of historical understanding. Many of these features also show how historians sift through and evaluate evidence. Our goal is to suggest how historians actually work and think. We want the reader to think critically and to realize that history is neither a list of cut-and-dried facts nor a senseless jumble of conflicting opinions. To help students and instructors realize this goal, we include a substantial discussion of "what is history" in Chapter 1.

### "Individuals in Society" Feature

In each chapter of the Fifth Edition we added a short study of a fascinating man or woman or group of people, which is carefully integrated into the main discussion in the text. This "Individuals in Society" feature grew out of our long-standing focus on people's lives and the varieties of historical experience, and we believe that readers will empathize with these flesh-and-blood human beings as they themselves seek to define their own identities today. The spotlighting of individuals, both famous and obscure, carries forward the greater attention to cultural and intellectual developments that we have used to invigorate our social history, and it reflects changing interests within the historical profession as well as the development of "micro history."

The men and women we have selected represent a wide range of careers and personalities. Several are well-known historical or present-day figures, such as Queen Cratesicleia, the Hellenistic queen who allowed herself to be held as a hostage for Sparta (Chapter 5); Theodora, the Byzantine empress (Chapter 8); Ibn Battuta, the Muslim world-traveler (Chapter 9); Leonardo da Vinci, the great Renaissance artist and polymath (Chapter 15); Olaudah Equiano, the black slave, entrepreneur, and navigator (Chapter 19); Theodor Herzl, the Zionist leader (Chapter 25); Gustav Stresemann, the German foreign minister (Chapter 31); and Kofi Annan, secretary general of the United Nations (Chapter 36). Other individuals, some perhaps less well-known, illuminate aspects of their times: Mukhali, a Mongol army officer (Chapter 11); Zheng He, a Muslim admiral in the service of the Chinese emperor (Chapter 16); Madame du Coudray, the pioneering French midwife (Chapter 18); Hurrem, wife of Suleiman the Magnificent (Chapter 20); Shen Gua, a widely traveled Chinese official who wrote extensively on medicine and mathematics (Chapter 27); and the Sioux warrior Crazy Horse (Chapter 28). Creative artists and intellectuals include the ancient Egyptian scholar-bureaucrat Wen-Amon (Chapter 2); the Chinese poet Tao Qian (Chapter 7); an unknown West African artist from Djenné (Chapter 10); the prolific Japanese artist Hokusai (Chapter 21); and the influential romantic writer Germaine de Staël (Chapter 24).

## Revised Primary Source Feature

A two-page excerpt from a primary source concludes each chapter. This important feature, entitled "Listening to the Past," extends and illuminates a major historical issue considered in the chapter, and it has been well received by instructors and students. In the Sixth Edition we have reviewed our selections and made judicious substitutions. For example, in Chapter 5 the Seleucid emperor Antiochus III bestows benefits on the Jews; in Chapter 9 an eleventh-century physician provides a guide for buying slaves; in Chapter 11 a Sanskrit inscription in stone praises the capital city of Delhi in India; in Chapter 15 the Protestant reformer Martin Luther presents his concept of liberty; in Chapter 18 the French philosophe Jean-Jacques Rousseau discusses gendered education; in Chapter 26 the French statesman Jules Ferry defends French imperialism; and in Chapter 31 the English writer George Orwell analyzes British unemployment during the Great Depression. Several primary source readings new to the Fifth Edition, such as the Portuguese Barbosa's description of the Swahili city-states in Chapter 19, the weighing of Shah Jahan in Mughal India in Chapter 20, and the Polish Solidarity activist Adam Michnik's defense of nonviolent resistance in Chapter 33, have proved stimulating for student discussions.

Each primary source opens with a problem-setting introduction and closes with "Questions for Analysis" that invite students to evaluate the evidence as historians would. Drawn from a range of writings addressing a variety of social, cultural, political, and intellectual issues, these sources promote active involvement and critical interpretation. Selected for their interest and importance and carefully fitted into their historical context, these sources do indeed allow the student to "listen to the past" and to observe how history has been shaped by individual men and women, some of them great aristocrats, others ordinary folk.

## Improved Chapter Features

Other distinctive features from earlier editions have been reviewed and improved in the Sixth Edition. To help guide the reader toward historical understanding, we pose specific historical questions at the beginning of each chapter. These questions are then answered in the course of the chapter, and each chapter concludes with a concise summary of its findings. All of the questions and summaries have been re-examined and frequently revised in order to maximize the usefulness of this popular feature.

A list of Key Terms concludes each chapter, another new feature of the Sixth Edition. These terms are highlighted in boldface in the text. The student may use these terms to test his or her understanding of the chapter's material.

In addition to posing chapter-opening questions and presenting more problems in historical interpretation, we have quoted extensively from a wide variety of primary sources in the narrative, demonstrating in our use of these quotations how historians evaluate evidence. Thus primary sources are examined as an integral part of the narrative as well as presented in extended form in the "Listening to the Past" chapter feature. We believe that such an extensive program of both integrated and separate primary source excerpts will help readers learn to interpret and think critically.

Each chapter concludes with carefully selected suggestions for further reading. These suggestions are briefly described to help readers know where to turn to continue thinking and learning about the world. Also, chapter bibliographies have been thoroughly revised and updated to keep them current with the vast amount of new work being done in many fields.

## Revised Timelines

New comparative timelines now begin each chapter. These timelines organize historical events into three categories: political/military, social/economic, and intellectual/religious. In addition, the topic-specific timelines appearing in earlier editions have been revised for this edition. Once again we provide a unified timeline in an appendix at the end of the book. Comprehensive and easy to locate, this useful timeline allows students to compare simultaneous political, economic, social, cultural, intellectual, and scientific developments over the centuries.

## Flexible Format

World history courses differ widely in chronological structure from one campus to another. To accommodate the various divisions of historical time into intervals that fit a two-quarter, three-quarter, or two-semester period, *A History of World Societies* is published in three versions that embrace the complete work:

- One-volume hardcover edition: *A History of World Societies*
- Two-volume paperback edition: *Volume I: To 1715* (Chapters 1–17); and *Volume II: Since 1500* (Chapters 16–36)
- Three-volume paperback edition: *Volume A: From Antiquity to 1500* (Chapters 1–14); *Volume B: From*

*800 to 1815* (Chapters 13–22); and *Volume C: From 1775 to the Present* (Chapters 22–36)

Overlapping chapters in two-volume and three-volume editions facilitate matching the appropriate volume with the opening and closing dates of a specific course.

## ANCILLARIES

Our learning and teaching ancillaries enhance the usefulness of the textbook:

- *GeoQuest™ World CD-ROM*
- *@history website*
- *Study Guide*
- *Instructor's Resource Manual*
- *Test Items*
- *HM ClassPrep with HM Testing* (contains PowerPoint maps and other presentation materials)
- *Blackboard™ and WebCT™ course cartridges*
- *Website for instructors and students*
- *Map Transparencies*

A CD-ROM, *GeoQuest™ World,* features thirty interactive maps that illuminate world history events from the days of the Persian Empire to the present. Each map is accompanied by exercises with answers and essay questions. The four different types of interactivity allow students to move at their own pace through each section.

Houghton Mifflin's *@history website* provides the finest text-based materials available for students and instructors. For students, this site offers primary sources, text-specific self-tests, and gateways to relevant history sites. Additional resources are provided for instructors.

The excellent *Study Guide* has been thoroughly revised by Professor James Schmiechen of Central Michigan University. Professor Schmiechen has been a tower of strength ever since he critiqued our initial prospectus, and he has continued to give us many valuable suggestions as well as his warmly appreciated support. His *Study Guide* contains learning objectives, chapter summaries, chapter outlines, review questions, extensive multiple-choice exercises, self-check lists of important concepts and events, and a variety of study aids and suggestions. The Sixth Edition also retains the study-review exercises on the interpretation of visual sources and major political ideas as well as suggested issues for discussion and essay, chronology reviews, and sections on studying effectively. To enable both students and instructors to use the *Study Guide* with the greatest possible flexibility, the guide is available in two volumes, with considerable overlapping of chapters. Instructors and students who use only Volumes A and B of the textbook have all the pertinent study materials in a single volume, *Study Guide,* Volume I (Chapters 1–22). Those who use only Volumes B and C of the textbook also have all the necessary materials in one volume, *Study Guide,* Volume II (Chapters 13–36).

The *Instructor's Resource Manual,* prepared by John Reisbord of Vassar College, contains instructional objectives, annotated chapter outlines, suggestions for lectures and discussion, paper and class activity topics, primary source exercises, map activities, and lists of audio-visual resources. The accompanying *Test Items,* by Professor Matthew Lenoe of Assumption College, offer identification, multiple-choice, map, and essay questions for a total of approximately two thousand test items. These test items are available to adopters in a computerized version, with editing capabilities.

New to this edition is *HM ClassPrep with HM Testing,* the latest comprehensive instructor's resource in computerized testing, which includes electronic versions of the *Instructor's Resource Manual* and *Test Items,* as well as PowerPoint maps, timelines, and chronologies from the text.

Course material is offered in both Blackboard™ and Web CT™ formats.

The text-specific website has been thoroughly revised and expanded for this edition. It now includes web activities, links to web resources, interactive exercises on the "Individuals in Society" and "Global Trade" features, chronological ordering exercises, and the ACE self-testing quiz program.

In addition, a set of full-color *Map Transparencies* of all the maps in the textbook is available on adoption.

## ACKNOWLEDGMENTS

It is a pleasure to thank the many instructors who have read and critiqued the manuscript through its development:

Calvin W. Allen, Jr.
*University of Memphis*

David H. Anthony
*University of California, Santa Cruz*

Major Peter K. Bacon
*United States Military Academy*

Eva Semien Baham
*Southern University*

Richard B. Barnett
*University of Virginia*

Roger B. Beck
*Eastern Illinois University*

Major Arnold A. Bennett
*United States Military Academy*

Paul Brians
*Washington State University*

James W. Brodman
*University of Central Arkansas*

Clarence B. Davis
*Marian College of Fond du Lac*

Charles T. Evans
*Northern Virginia Community College*

Michael A. Gomez
*New York University*

Sumit Guha
*Brown University*

Kenda Mutongi
*Williams College*

Peter von Sivers
*University of Utah*

It is also a pleasure to thank our many editors at Houghton Mifflin for their efforts over many years. To Christina Horn, who guided production in the ever-more intensive email age, and to Julie Dunn, our development editor, we express our admiration and special appreciation. And we thank Carole Frohlich for her contributions in photo research and selection.

Many of our colleagues at the University of Illinois and at Georgetown University continued to provide information and stimulation, often without even knowing it. We thank them for it. John McKay wishes to thank and acknowledge Professor Charles Crouch of Georgia Southern University for his valuable contribution to the revision of Chapters 17–19, 23–26, and 29–30 in the Fifth Edition. He also happily acknowledges the fine research assistance provided by Patricia Clark and Bryan Ganaway and thanks them for it. Finally, he also expresses his deep appreciation to Jo Ann McKay for her sharp-eyed editorial support and unfailing encouragement. Bennett Hill wishes to thank Alice Croft for her technical assistance and Donald Franklin for his patience, understanding, and support.

Each of us has benefited from the criticism of his or her coauthors, although each of us assumes responsibility for what he or she has written. John Buckler has written Chapters 1–2 and 5–6; Patricia Buckley Ebrey has contributed Chapters 3, 4, 7, 11, 12, and 27; Bennett Hill has continued the narrative in Chapters 8–10, 13–16, 19–21, and 28; and John McKay has written Chapters 17, 18, 22–26, and 29–36. Finally, we continue to welcome the many comments and suggestions that have come from our readers, for they have helped us greatly in this ongoing endeavor.

**J. P. M.  B. D. H.  J. B.  P. B. E.**

# A HISTORY OF WORLD SOCIETIES

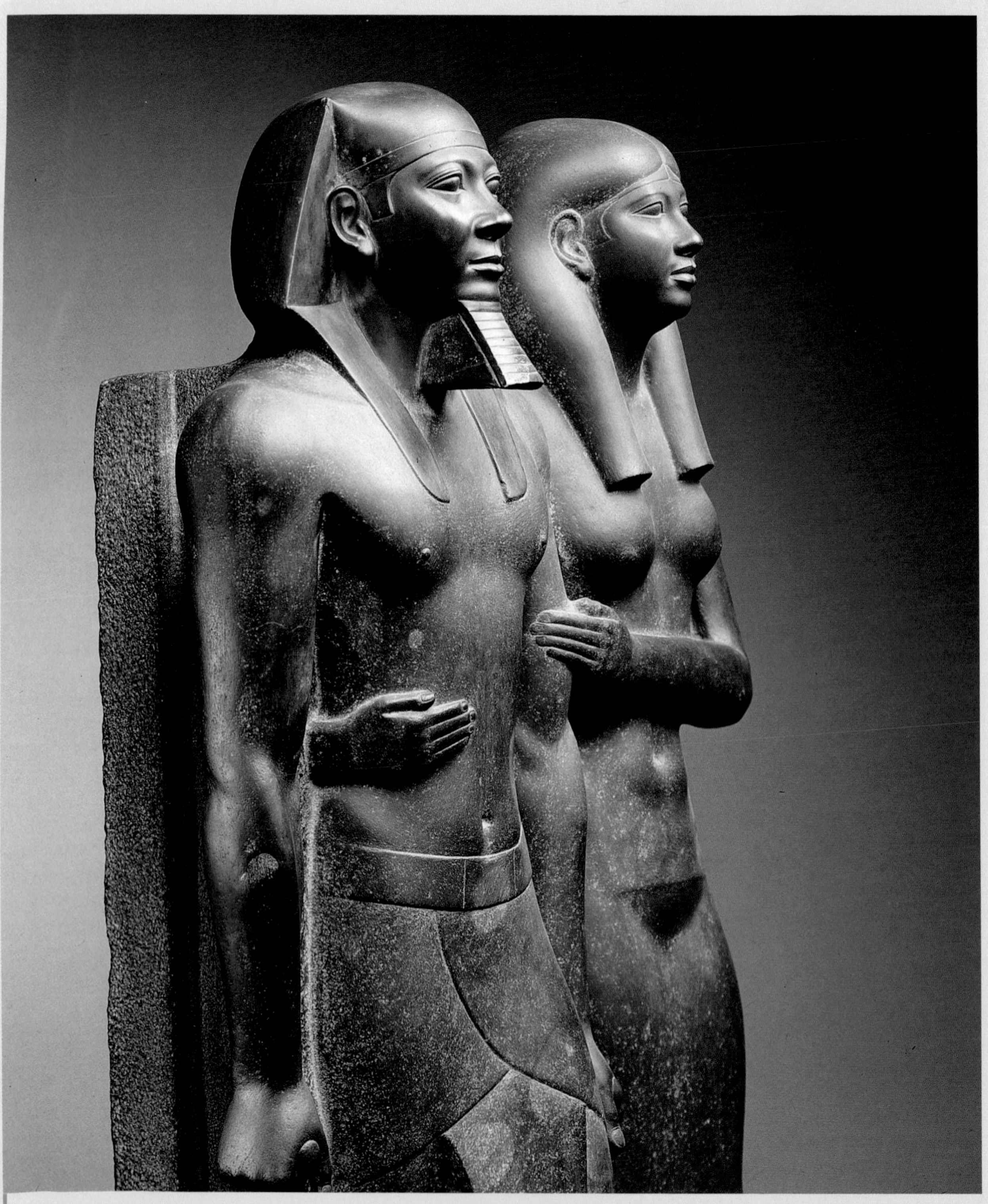

King Menkaure and Queen. The pharaoh and his wife represent all the magnificence, serenity, and grandeur of Egypt. *(Old Kingdom, Dynasty 4, reign of Mycerinus, 2532–2510 B.C.E.; Greywacke; H × W × D: 54¹¹⁄₁₆ × 22⅜ × 21⁵⁄₁₆ in. (139 × 57 × 54 cm). Harvard University—Museum of Fine Arts Expedition, 11.1738. Museum of Fine Arts, Boston.)*

CHAPTER

# 1 ORIGIN OF CIVILIZATIONS IN WEST ASIA AND NORTH AFRICA

## CHAPTER OUTLINE

- What Is History and Why?
- From Caves to Towns
- Mesopotamian Civilization
- The Spread of Mesopotamian Culture
- Egypt, the Land of the Pharaohs (3100–1200 B.C.E.)
- The Hittites
- The Fall of Empires and the Survival of Cultures (ca 1200 B.C.E.)

The civilization and cultures of the modern Western world, like great rivers, have many sources. These sources have flowed from many places and directions. Peoples in western Europe developed numerous communities uniquely their own but also sharing some common features. They mastered such diverse subjects as astronomy, mathematics, geometry, trigonometry, engineering, religious practices, and social organization. Yet the earliest of these peoples did not record their learning and lore in systems of writing. Their lives and customs are consequently largely lost to us.

In the East, however, other early peoples confronted many of the same basic challenges as those in the West. They also made progress, but they took the important step of recording their experiences in writing. The most enduring innovations occurred in the ancient Near East, a region that includes the lands bordering the Mediterranean's eastern shore, the Arabian peninsula, parts of northeastern Africa, and perhaps above all Mesopotamia, the area of modern Iraq. Fundamental to the development of Western civilization and culture was the invention of writing by the Sumerians, which allowed knowledge of the past to be preserved. It also facilitated the spread and accumulation of learning, science, and literature. Ancient Near Eastern civilizations also produced the first written law codes, as well as religious concepts that still permeate daily life. Writing is the primary reason modern people look to the East as the richest sources of their origins.

But how do we know and understand these things? Before embarking on the study of history, it is necessary to ask, "What is it?" Only then can the peoples and events of tens of thousands of years be placed into a coherent whole. Once the nature of history is understood, further questions can be asked and reasonably answered. Specifically for this chapter,

- What were the fundamental Neolithic contributions to the rise of Western civilization?
- What caused Mesopotamian culture to become predominate in most of the ancient Near East?
- How did the Egyptians contribute to this vast story?

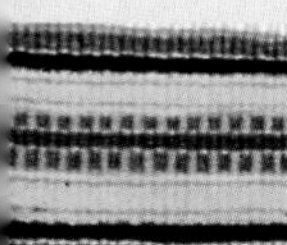

- What did the arrival of the Hittites on the frontiers of Mesopotamia and Egypt mean to the more advanced cultures of their new neighbors?

These are the questions we will explore in this chapter.

## WHAT IS HISTORY AND WHY?

History is the effort to reconstruct the past to discover what people thought, what they did, and how their beliefs and actions continue to influence human life. In order to appreciate the past fully, we must put it into perspective so that we can understand the factors that have helped to shape us as individuals, the society in which we live, and the nature of other peoples' societies. Why else should we study civilizations as separated from ours through time, distance, and culture as classical Greece, medieval Germany, and modern Russia? Although many of the people involved in these epochs are long dead, what they did has touched everyone alive today.

To answer the questions above, historians examine primary sources, the firsthand accounts of people who lived through the events, people in the best position to know what happened. Historians normally use a variety of evidence in their search for an accurate understanding of the past. Most important are documents written by people who recorded their experiences and analyzed the significance of them. They investigated what happened, who was responsible for it, why it happened, and what it meant. Another written historical source is the chronicle. Writers of chronicles noted events in their chronological order (therefore the name) and sometimes added a brief explanation of the events.

Historians also rely on other, nonliterary evidence. In nearly all periods of early history, people inscribed laws, treaties with other states, and honors to individuals in stone. Governments still engrave similar documents in bronze. Even today, one cannot visit a Civil War battlefield without encountering a plaque giving information about what happened there. In the medieval period scribes produced thousands of documents giving detailed accounts of agricultural life on manors—how they were run, what the local customs were, and how society actually functioned. These scribes, many of them Christian monks, also left a record of religious and political affairs.

With the modern period has come an explosion of information. In addition to the traditional sources of historical knowledge, we have official statistics covering virtually everything from the annual number of deaths in automobile accidents to the daily results of the stock market. Public and private archives preserve a wealth of material that is useful in understanding governments, corporations, and private people. All these materials are the raw resources of historians.

In the face of the evidence, historians must determine what is accurate and what is false or biased. They do so by taking the earliest information first. They compare various versions of particular events or large trends with one another. Some people who have left us with evidence of the past were more intelligent or better informed than others. Therefore, their testimony is preferred and indeed strengthened by other writers who independently reported the same things. When two or more dependable sources record the same thing in the same way, historians conclude that they present an accurate account of events.

Once historians have determined which sources are reliable, they use this information to conclude that they have established a fact or that they are in a position to understand the significance of the information. Understanding the past does not necessarily come easily, which is one of the joys and frustrations of history. Unlike the more exact physical sciences, history cannot reproduce experiments under controlled conditions, because no two historical events are precisely alike. People cannot be put into test tubes, and they are not as predictable as atoms or hydrocarbons. That is hardly surprising, for history is about people, the most complex organisms on this planet.

To complicate matters, for many epochs of history only the broad outlines are known, so interpretation is especially difficult. For example, historians know that the Hittite Empire collapsed at the height of its power, but interpretations of the causes of the catastrophe are still speculative. On the other end of the spectrum, some developments are so vast and complex that historians must master mountains of data before they can even begin to interpret them properly. Events as diverse as the end of the western Roman Empire, the origins of the Industrial Revolution, and the causes of the French Revolution are very complicated because so many people brought so many different forces to bear for so many reasons. In such cases, there is never one simple explanation that will satisfy everyone, which testifies to the complexity of life in developed societies.

Still another matter complicates an accurate understanding of the past. The attempt to understand history is uniquely human. Interpretations of the past sometimes change because people's points of view change in the course of life. The values and attitudes of one generation may not be shared by another. Despite such differences in interpretation, the efforts of historians to examine and

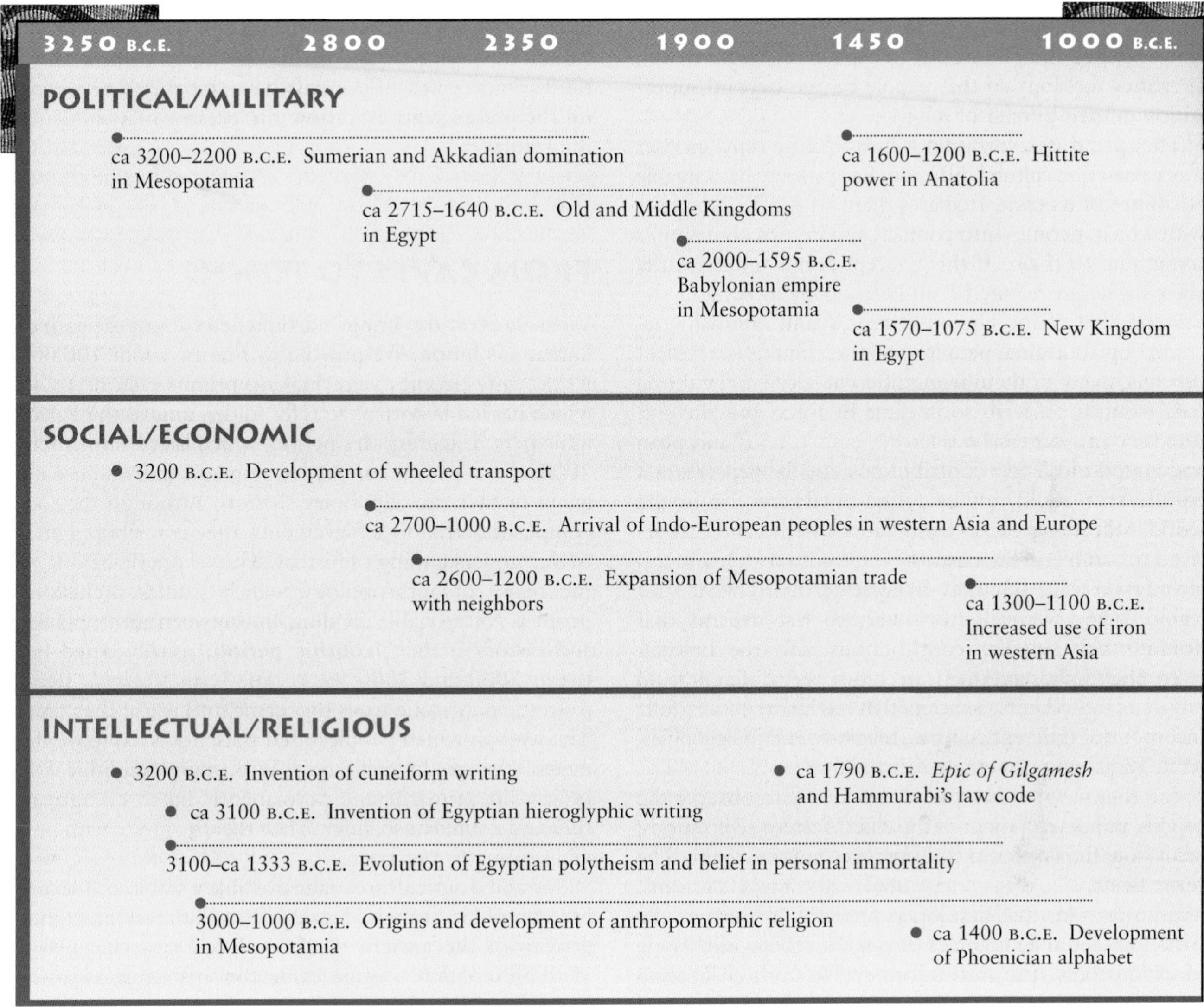


understand the past can give them a perspective that is valuable to the present. It is through this process of analysis and interpretation of evidence that historians come to understand not only the past but its relation to life today.

3250 B.C.E.
2800
2350
1900
1450
1000 B.C.E.
POLITICAL/MILITARY
ca 3200–2200 B.C.E. Sumerian and Akkadian domination in Mesopotamia
ca 2715–1640 B.C.E. Old and Middle Kingdoms in Egypt
ca 2000–1595 B.C.E. Babylonian empire in Mesopotamia
ca 1600–1200 B.C.E. Hittite power in Anatolia
ca 1570–1075 B.C.E. New Kingdom in Egypt
SOCIAL/ECONOMIC
3200 B.C.E. Development of wheeled transport
ca 2700–1000 B.C.E. Arrival of Indo-European peoples in western Asia and Europe
ca 2600–1200 B.C.E. Expansion of Mesopotamian trade with neighbors
ca 1300–1100 B.C.E. Increased use of iron in western Asia
INTELLECTUAL/RELIGIOUS
3200 B.C.E. Invention of cuneiform writing
ca 3100 B.C.E. Invention of Egyptian hieroglyphic writing
3100–ca 1333 B.C.E. Evolution of Egyptian polytheism and belief in personal immortality
3000–1000 B.C.E. Origins and development of anthropomorphic religion in Mesopotamia
ca 1790 B.C.E. Epic of Gilgamesh and Hammurabi's law code
ca 1400 B.C.E. Development of Phoenician alphabet

Social history, an important subject of this book, is itself an example of the historian's reappraisal of the meaning of the past. For centuries people took the basic facts, details, and activities of life for granted. Obviously, people lived in certain types of houses, ate certain foods that they either raised or bought, and reared families. These matters seemed so ordinary that few serious historians gave them much thought. Yet within this generation a growing number of scholars have demonstrated that studies of the ways in which people have lived over the years deserve as much attention as the reigns of monarchs, the careers of great political figures, and the outcomes of big battles.

The topics of history and human societies lead to the question, "What is civilization?" *Civilization* is a word easier to describe than to define. It comes from the Latin adjective *civilis,* which refers to a citizen. Citizens willingly and mutually bind themselves in political, economic, and social organizations in which individuals merge themselves, their energies, and their interests in a larger community.

Civilization, however, goes far beyond politics. It also includes an advanced stage of social development, which entails enlightenment and education. Civilized society is refined, possessing the notion of law to govern the conduct of its members. It includes a code of manners and social conduct that creates an atmosphere of harmony and peace within the community. It creates art and generates science and philosophy to explain the larger world. It creates theology so that people can go beyond superstition in their pursuit of religion.

The spread of civilization is in one sense only another way to describe cultural diffusion. Each society has valuable attributes of its own. It shares them with other societies with which it comes into contact, and in turn contributes something to them. If this concept seems unnecessarily abstract, it can readily be understood by looking at the development of the United States. A land originally occupied by aboriginal peoples saw the coming of the Europeans, many of them from different social and cultural backgrounds. Africans soon came by force, but the culture they encountered was already a mixture of European and American. Their contributions also helped create a culture that could not be found anywhere else in the world. Still later, peoples from Latin America and Asia arrived to assimilate the customs and traditions they found already existing, but they likewise fertilized what they found. They were all from start to last streams that poured their singular contributions into the broader river. The result is an American culture very different from any of its ingredients, a society that has rather successfully incorporated different cultures, religions, and philosophies, while remaining nonetheless distinctive.

Another way to understand this idea is to observe the origins and development of the chief Western civilizations, analyzing similarities and differences among them. The term *Western* in this context means the ideas, customs, and institutions that developed primarily in Europe, the Americas, and their colonies throughout the world. These ideas, customs, and institutions set Western civilization apart from other civilizations, such as the African and Asian, that developed their unique way of life as a result of different demands, challenges, and opportunities, both human and geographical. Yet even the term *Western* has its irony. Some of the roots of this civilization lie in western Asia and northern Africa. Mesopotamia, and to a lesser extent Egypt, created concepts that are basic to Western thought and conduct. The term *Western* in this context means the ideas, customs, and institutions that set Western civilization apart from others. Yet no civilization stands alone. Each influences its neighbors, all the while preserving the essentials that make it distinctive.

At the fundamental level, the similarities of Western civilization are greater than the differences. Almost all people in Europe and the Americas share some values, even though they may live far apart, speak different languages, and have different religions and political and social systems. These values are the bonds that hold a civilization together. By studying these shared cultural values, which stretch through time and across distance, we can see how the various events of the past have left their impression on the present and even how the present may influence the future.

## FROM CAVES TO TOWNS

Virtually every day brings startling news about the path of human evolution. We now know that by about 400,000 B.C.E. early peoples were making primitive stone tools, which has led historians to refer to this time as the Paleolithic period. During this period, which lasted until about 7000 B.C.E., people survived as nomadic hunters, usually living in caves or temporary shelters. Although they accomplished striking achievements, they contributed little to our understanding of history. They properly belong to the realm of anthropology, which studies prehistoric peoples. A reasonable dividing line between anthropology and history is the **Neolithic period,** usually dated between 7000 and 3000 B.C.E. The term *Neolithic* stems from the new stone tools that came into use at that time. The ways in which peoples used these tools led to fundamental changes in civilization. With them Neolithic folk built a life primarily and permanently based on agriculture and animal husbandry. They thereby broke with previous nomadic practices.

Sustained agriculture made possible a stable and secure life. Neolithic farmers developed the primary economic activity of the ancient world and one still vital today. With this settled routine came the evolution of towns and eventually of cities. Neolithic farmers usually raised more food than they could consume, so their surpluses permitted larger, healthier populations. Population growth in turn created an even greater reliance on settled farming, as only systematic agriculture could sustain the increased numbers of people. Since surpluses of food could also be bartered for other commodities, the Neolithic era witnessed the beginnings of the large-scale exchange of goods. Neolithic farmers also improved their tools and agricultural techniques. They domesticated bigger, stronger animals to work for them, invented the plow, and developed new mutations of seeds. By 3000 B.C.E. they had invented the wheel. Agricultural surpluses also made possible the division of labor. It freed some people to become craftsmen and artisans, who made tools, pottery vessels, woven baskets, clothing, and jewelry. In short, these advances resulted in a wealthier, more comfortable, and more complex life.

**Return of the Iceman** This scene captures the discovery of a Neolithic herdsman who was trapped in the ice about 5,300 years ago. The discovery was made by chance in September 1991. In an ancient accident, he was sealed in ice with all of his tools, thus providing modern scholars with a unique view of the past. The discovery is so important that scientists have not yet done an autopsy on the corpse. *(Paul Hanny/Gamma)*

These developments generally led to the further evolution of towns and a whole new way of life. People not necessarily related to one another created rudimentary governments that transcended the family. These governments, led by a recognized central authority, made decisions that channeled the shared wisdom, physical energy, and resources of the whole population toward a common goal. These societies made their decisions according to custom, the generally accepted norms of traditional conduct. Here was the beginning of law. Towns also meant life in individual houses or groups of them, which led to greater personal independence. Growing wealth and the need for communal cooperation prompted people to erect public buildings and religious monuments. These groups also protected their possessions and themselves by raising walls.

Many scholars consider walled towns the basic feature of Neolithic society. Yet numerous examples prove that some Neolithic towns existed without stone or mudbrick walls. For instance, at Stonehenge in England the natives erected wooden palisades for safety. At Unteruhldingen in Germany the community established its unwalled town just offshore on a lake. They let nature defend them. The most concentrated collection of walled towns is found in Mesopotamia. This fact presents a historical problem. Since generations of archaeologists and historians have concentrated their attention on this region, they have considered it typical. Yet they have failed to appreciate properly circumstances elsewhere. The fundamental points about this period are that these folk created stable communities based on agriculture. They defended their towns in various ways by common consent and effort. This organized communal effort is far more important than the types of defenses they built.

The simplest way to support these conclusions is to examine briefly Stonehenge now and Mesopotamia afterward, each in its own unique context. A mute but engaging glimpse of a particular Neolithic society can readily be seen today in industrial England. Between 4700 and 2000 B.C.E. arose the Stonehenge people, named after the famous stone circle on Salisbury Plain. Though named after a single spot, this culture spread throughout Great Britain, Ireland, and Brittany in France. Circles like Stonehenge sometimes contained the houses of permanent settlers. Some were fortified enclosures, in which the inhabitants established a safe haven for themselves. Both were proto-urban centers. Some of these sites have yielded burial remains. Others were dedicated to religious rituals. They provided magical, not military, protection. They all served diverse social functions, another testimony to Neolithic creativity. Stonehenge and neighboring sites reveal the existence of prosperous, well-organized, and centrally led communities. They also provide evidence for cooperation among similarly constituted societies. None of them individually could have built the circle. By pooling their resources, human and material,

**Stonehenge** Seen in regal isolation, Stonehenge sits among the stars and in April 1997 along the path of the comet Hale-Bopp. Long before Druids existed, a Neolithic society laboriously built this circle to mark the passing of the seasons. *(Jim Burgess)*

they raised it. Thus Stonehenge itself testifies to contact and cohesion among stable groups that cooperated toward a common goal. These factors alone prove the widening horizon of these Neolithic peoples.

Stonehenge offers another insight into this Neolithic culture. It indicates an intellectual world that encompassed astronomy, the environment, and religion. The circle is oriented toward the midwinter sunset and the midsummer sunrise. Stonehenge thus marked the clocklike celestial change of the seasons. This silent evidence proves the existence of a society prosperous enough to endure over long periods during which lore about heaven and earth could be preserved and passed along to successive generations. It also demonstrates that these communities considered themselves members of a wider world that they amiably shared with the deities of nature and the broader universe. Even the magnificent Stonehenge, however, cannot lead to history. The Stonehenge people achieved wonders, but they lacked the literacy to spread their legacy to others beyond their own culture. That breakthrough came in Mesopotamia.

## MESOPOTAMIAN CIVILIZATION

In the East peoples faced many challenges similar to those of their Western contemporaries. In western Asia this process can easily be seen in Mesopotamia, the Greek name for the land between the Euphrates and Tigris Rivers. There the arid climate confronted the peoples with the hard problem of farming with scant water supplies. In the East farmers learned to irrigate their land and later to drain it to prevent the buildup of salt in the soil. **Irrigation** on a large scale, like building stone circles in the West, demanded organized group effort. That in turn underscored the need for strong central authority to direct it. In the East, as in the West, this corporate spirit led to governments in which individuals participated in the whole community while subordinating some of their particular concerns to its broader interests. These factors made urban life possible in a demanding environment. By about 3000 B.C.E. the Sumerians, whose origins are mysterious, established a number of cities in the south-

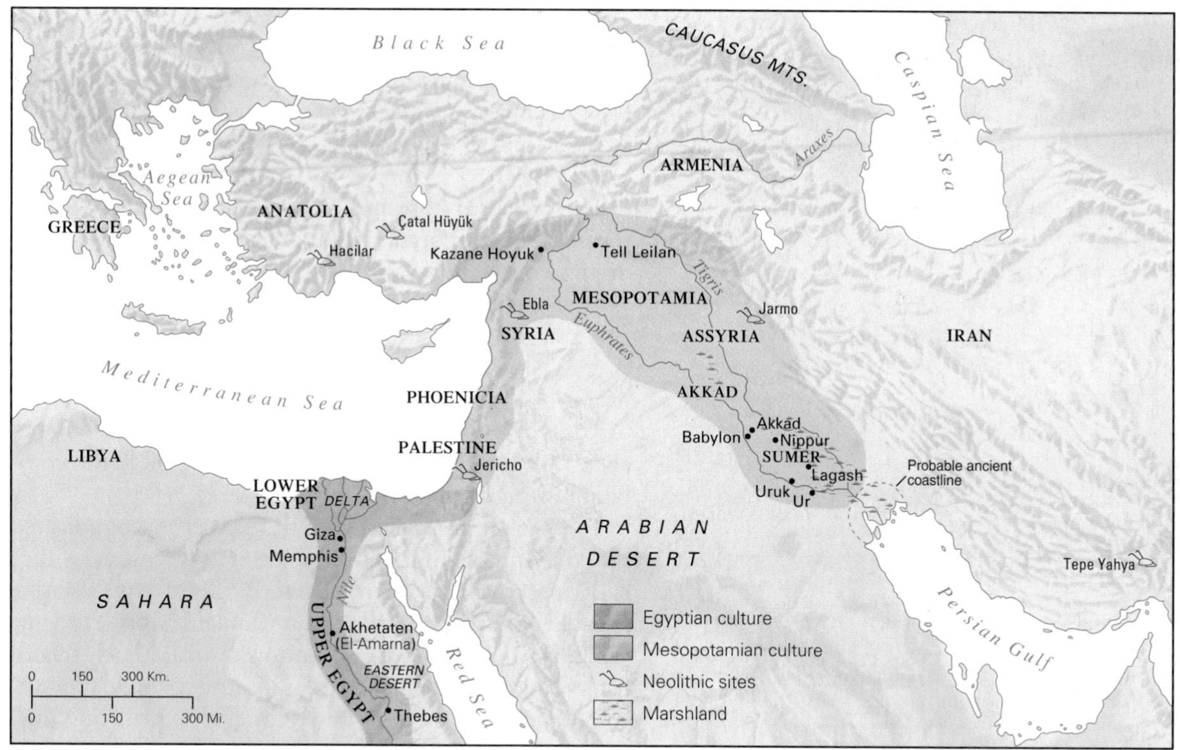


**MAP 1.1 Spread of Cultures in the Ancient Near East** This map illustrates the spread of the Mesopotamian and Egyptian cultures through a semicircular stretch of land often called the Fertile Crescent. From this area knowledge and use of agriculture spread throughout the western part of Asia Minor.

ernmost part of Mesopotamia, which became known as Sumer. The Sumerians soon turned the region into what generations have called the "cradle of civilization" (see Map 1.1). Some might argue that this phrase should be honorably retired, for civilization was advancing by various degrees from England to Mesopotamia. No one, however, can deny that the fundamental innovation of the Sumerians was the creation of writing, which helped unify this society culturally and opened it to the broader world that we still share today.

## The Invention of Writing and the First Schools

The origins of writing probably go back to the ninth millennium B.C.E., when Near Eastern peoples used clay tokens as counters for record keeping. By the fourth millennium people had realized that drawing pictures of the tokens on clay was simpler than making tokens. This breakthrough in turn suggested that more information could be conveyed by adding pictures of still other objects. The result was a complex system of pictographs, in which each sign pictured an object. These pictographs were the forerunners of a Sumerian form of writing known as **cuneiform,** from the Latin term for "wedge-shaped," used to describe the strokes of the stylus.

How did this pictographic system work, and how did it evolve into cuneiform writing? At first, if a scribe wanted to indicate a star, he simply drew a picture of it (line A of Figure 1.1) on a wet clay tablet, which became rock-hard when baked. Anyone looking at the picture would know what it meant and would think of the word for star. This complicated and laborious system had serious limitations. It could not represent abstract ideas or combinations of ideas. For instance, how could it depict a slave woman?

The solution appeared when the scribe discovered that signs could be combined to express meaning. To refer to a slave woman the scribe used the sign for woman (line B) and the sign for mountain (line C)—literally, "mountain woman" (line D). Because the Sumerians regularly obtained their slave women from the mountains, this combination of signs was easily understandable.

| | MEANING | PICTOGRAPH | IDEOGRAM | PHONETIC SIGN |
|---|---|---|---|---|
| A | Star | | | |
| B | Woman | | | |
| C | Mountain | | | |
| D | Slave woman | | | |
| E | Water In | | | |

**FIGURE 1.1 Sumerian Writing** *(Source: Excerpted from S. N. Kramer,* The Sumerians: Their History, Culture and Character, *University of Chicago Press, Chicago, 1963, pp. 302–306. Reprinted by permission.)*

The next step was to simplify the system. Instead of drawing pictures, the scribe made conventionalized signs that were generally understood to represent ideas. Thus the signs became *ideograms:* they symbolized ideas. The sign for star could also be used to indicate heaven, sky, or even god.

The real breakthrough came when the scribe learned to use signs to represent sounds. For instance, the scribe drew two parallel wavy lines to indicate the word *a* or "water" (line E). Besides water, the word *a* in Sumerian also meant "in." The word *in* expresses a relationship that is very difficult to represent pictorially. Instead of trying to invent a sign to mean "in," some clever scribe used the sign for water because the two words sounded alike. This phonetic use of signs made possible the combining of signs to convey abstract ideas.

The Sumerian system of writing was so complicated that only professional scribes mastered it, and even they had to study it for many years. By 2500 B.C.E. scribal schools flourished throughout Sumer. Most students came from wealthy families and were male. Each school had a master, teachers, and monitors. Discipline was strict, and students were caned for sloppy work and mis-

**Aerial View of Ur** This photograph gives a good idea of the size and complexity of Ur, one of the most powerful cities in Mesopotamia. In the lower right-hand corner stands the massive ziggurat of Umammu. *(Georg Gerster/ Photo Researchers)*

behavior. One graduate of a scribal school had few fond memories of the joy of learning:

*My headmaster read my tablet, said:*
*"There is something missing," caned me.*
. . . .
*The fellow in charge of silence said:*
*"Why did you talk without permission," caned me.*
*The fellow in charge of the assembly said:*
*"Why did you stand at ease without permission," caned me.*[1]

The Sumerian system of schooling set the educational standards for Mesopotamian culture, and the Akkadians and, later, the Babylonians adopted its practices and techniques. Mesopotamian education always had a practical side because of the economic and administrative importance of scribes. Most scribes took administrative positions in the temple or palace, where they kept records of business transactions, accounts, and inventories. But scribal schools did not limit their curriculum to business affairs. They were also centers of culture and scholarship. Topics of study included mathematics, botany, and linguistics. Advanced students copied and studied the classics of Sumerian literature. Talented students and learned scribes wrote compositions of their own. As a result, many literary, mathematical, and religious texts survive today, giving a full picture of Mesopotamian intellectual and spiritual life.

## Mesopotamian Thought and Religion

The Mesopotamians made significant and sophisticated advances in mathematics using a numerical system based on units of sixty, ten, and six. They developed the concept of place value—that the value of a number depends on where it stands in relation to other numbers. The Mesopotamians did not consider mathematics a purely theoretical science. The building of cities, palaces, temples, and canals demanded practical knowledge of geometry and trigonometry.

Mesopotamian medicine was a combination of magic, prescriptions, and surgery. Mesopotamians believed that demons and evil spirits caused sickness and that magic spells could drive them out. Or, they believed, the physician could force the demon out by giving the patient a foul-tasting prescription. As medical knowledge grew, some prescriptions were found to work and thus were true medicines. In this slow but empirical fashion medicine grew from superstition to an early form of rational treatment.

Mesopotamian thought had a profound impact in theology and religion. The Sumerians originated many beliefs, and their successors added to them. The Mesopotamians believed that many gods run the world, but they did not consider all gods and goddesses equal. Some deities had very important jobs, taking care of music, law, sex, and victory, while others had lesser tasks, overseeing leatherworking and basketweaving. The god in charge of metalworking was hardly the equal of the god of wisdom.

Mesopotamian gods lived their lives much as human beings lived theirs. The gods were anthropomorphic, or human in form. Unlike men and women, they were powerful and immortal and could make themselves invisible. Otherwise, Mesopotamian gods and goddesses were very human: they celebrated with food and drink, and they raised families. They enjoyed their own "Garden of Eden," a green and fertile place. They could be irritable, vindictive, and irresponsible.

The Mesopotamians did not worship their deities because the gods were benevolent. Human beings were too insignificant to pass judgment on the conduct of the gods, and the gods were too superior to honor human morals. Rather, the Mesopotamians worshiped the gods because they were mighty. Likewise, it was not the place of men and women to understand the gods. The Sumerian equivalent to the biblical Job once complained to his god:

*The man of deceit has conspired against me,*
*And you, my god, do not thwart him,*
*You carry off my understanding.*[2]

The motives of the gods were not always clear. In times of affliction one could only pray and offer sacrifices to appease them.

The Mesopotamians had many myths to account for the creation of the universe. According to one Sumerian myth (echoed in Genesis, the first book of the Bible), only the primeval sea existed at first. The sea produced heaven and earth, which were united. Heaven and earth gave birth to Enlil, who separated them and made possible the creation of the other gods. Babylonian beliefs were similar. In the beginning was the primeval sea, the goddess Tiamat, who gave birth to the gods. When Tiamat tried to destroy the gods, Marduk, the chief god of the Babylonians, proceeded to kill her and divide her body and thus created the sky and earth. These myths are the earliest known attempts to answer the question, "How did it all begin?" The Mesopotamians obviously thought about these matters, as about the gods, in human terms. They never organized their beliefs into a philosophy, but their myths offered understandable explanations of natural phenomena. The myths were emotionally satisfying, and that was their greatest appeal.

**Votive Dog** Many Sumerian dedications to their gods were as artistic as this statuette of a dog that dates from 1900 B.C.E. The body of the dog bears a cuneiform inscription that informs the viewer and the goddess Ninisinna of the nature of the donor's prayer. *(Réunion des Musées Nationaux/Art Resource, NY)*

In addition to myths, the Sumerians produced the first epic poem, the *Epic of Gilgamesh,* which evolved as a reworking of at least five earlier myths. An epic poem is a narration of the achievements, labors, and sometimes the failures of heroes that embodies a people's or a nation's conception of its own past. Historians can use epic poems to learn about various aspects of a society, and to that extent epics can be used as historical sources. The Sumerian epic recounts the wanderings of Gilgamesh—the semihistorical king of Uruk—and his companion Enkidu, their fatal meeting with the goddess Ishtar, after which Enkidu dies, and Gilgamesh's subsequent search for eternal life. During his search Gilgamesh learns that life after death is so dreary that he returns to Uruk, where he becomes a good king and ends his life happily. The *Epic of Gilgamesh* is not only an excellent piece of literature but also an intellectual triumph. It shows the Sumerians grappling with such enduring questions as life and death, humankind and deity, and immortality. Despite its great antiquity, it addresses questions of importance to people today. (See the feature "Listening to the Past: A Quest for Immortality" on pages 28–29.)

## Sumerian Society

Their harsh environment fostered a grim, even pessimistic, spirit among the Mesopotamians. The Sumerians sought to please and calm the gods, especially the patron deity of the city. Encouraged and directed by the traditional priesthood, which was dedicated to understanding the ways of the gods, the people erected shrines in the center of each city and then built their houses around them. The best way to honor the gods was to make the shrine as grand and as impressive as possible, for gods who had a splendid temple might think twice about sending floods to destroy the city.

Sumerian society was a complex arrangement of freedom and dependence, and its members were divided into four categories: nobles, free clients of the nobility, commoners, and slaves. **Nobles** consisted of the king and his family, the chief priests, and high palace officials. Generally, the king rose to power as a war leader, elected by the citizenry, who established a regular army, trained it, and led it into battle. The might of the king and the frequency of warfare quickly made him the supreme figure in the city, and kingship soon became hereditary. The symbol of royal status was the palace, which rivaled the temple in grandeur.

The king and the lesser nobility held extensive tracts of land that were, like the estates of the temple, worked by slaves and clients. **Clients** were free men and women who were dependent on the nobility. In return for their labor, the clients received small plots of land to work for themselves. Although this arrangement assured the clients of a livelihood, the land they worked remained the possession of the nobility or the temple. Thus not only did the nobility control most—and probably the best—land, they also commanded the obedience of a huge segment of society. They were the dominant force in Mesopotamian society.

Commoners were free citizens. They were independent of the nobility; however, they could not rival the nobility in social status and political power. Commoners belonged to large patriarchal families who owned land in their own right. Commoners could sell their land, if the family approved, but even the king could not legally take their land without their approval. Commoners had a voice in the political affairs of the city and full protection under the law.

Until comparatively recent times, slavery has been a fact of life throughout the history of Western society. Some Sumerian slaves were foreigners and prisoners of war. Some were criminals who had lost their freedom as punishment for their crimes. Still others served as slaves to repay debts. These were more fortunate than the others, because the law required that they be freed after three years. But all slaves were subject to whatever treatment their owners might mete out. They could be beaten and even branded. Yet they were not considered dumb beasts. Slaves engaged in trade and made profits. Indeed, many slaves were able to buy their freedom. They could borrow money and received at least some legal protection.

## THE SPREAD OF MESOPOTAMIAN CULTURE

The Sumerians established the basic social, economic, and intellectual patterns of Mesopotamia, but the Semites played a large part in spreading Sumerian culture far beyond the boundaries of Mesopotamia. The interaction of the Sumerians and Semites, in fact, gives one of the very first glimpses of a phenomenon that can still be seen today. History provides abundant evidence of peoples of different origins coming together, usually on the borders of an established culture. The result was usually cultural change, outweighing any hostility, for each side learned from the other. The outcome in these instances was the evolution of a new culture that consisted of two or more old parts. Although the older culture almost invariably looked on the newcomers as inferior, the new just as invariably contributed something valuable to the old. So it was in 2331 B.C.E. The Semitic chieftain Sargon conquered Sumer and created a new empire. The symbol of his triumph was a new capital, the city of Akkad. Sargon, the first "world conqueror," led his armies to the Mediterranean Sea. Although his empire lasted only a few generations, it spread Mesopotamian culture throughout the Fertile Crescent, the belt of rich farmland that extends from Mesopotamia in the east up through Syria in the north and down to Egypt in the west (see Map 1.1).

The question to answer is why Mesopotamian culture had such an immediate and wide appeal. In the first place it was successful and enjoyed the prestige of its success. Newcomers wanted to find a respectable place in this old and venerated culture. It also provided an easy means of communication among people on a broad scale. The Eblaites (a Semitic people) could efficiently deal with the Mesopotamians and others who embraced this culture in ways that all could understand. Culture ignores borders. Despite local variations, so much common ground existed that similar political and economic institutions, exchange of ideas and religious beliefs, methods of writing, and a shared etiquette served as links among all who embraced Mesopotamian culture.

### The Triumph of Babylon

Although the empire of Sargon was extensive, it was short-lived. The Akkadians, too, failed to solve the problems posed by Mesopotamia's geography and population pattern. It was left to the Babylonians to unite Mesopotamia politically and culturally. The Babylonians were Amorites, a Semitic people who had migrated from Arabia and settled on the site of Babylon along the middle Euphrates, where that river runs close to the Tigris. Babylon enjoyed an excellent geographical position and was ideally suited to be the capital of Mesopotamia. It dominated trade on the Tigris and Euphrates Rivers: all commerce to and from Sumer and Akkad had to pass by its walls. It also looked beyond Mesopotamia. Babylonian merchants followed the Tigris north to Assyria and Anatolia. The Euphrates led merchants to Syria, Palestine, and the Mediterranean. The city grew great because of its commercial importance and soundly based power.

Babylon was also fortunate to have a farseeing and able king, Hammurabi (r. 1792–1750 B.C.E.). Hammurabi set out to do three things: make Babylon secure, unify Mesopotamia, and win for the Babylonians a place in Mesopotamian civilization. The first two he accomplished by conquering Assyria in the north and Sumer and Akkad in the south. Then he turned to his third goal.

Politically, Hammurabi joined in his kingship the Semitic concept of the tribal chieftain and the Sumerian idea of urban kingship. Culturally, he encouraged the spread of myths that explained how Marduk, the god of Babylon, had been elected king of the gods by the other Mesopotamian deities. Hammurabi's success in making Marduk the god of all Mesopotamians made Babylon the

**Law Code of Hammurabi** Hammurabi ordered his code to be inscribed on a stone pillar and set up in public. At the top of the pillar Hammurabi is depicted receiving the scepter of authority from the god Shamash. *(Hirmer Verlag München)*

religious center of Mesopotamia. Through Hammurabi's genius the Babylonians made their own contribution to Mesopotamian culture—a culture vibrant enough to maintain its identity while assimilating new influences. Hammurabi's conquests and the activity of Babylonian merchants spread this enriched culture north to Anatolia and west to Syria and Palestine.

## Life Under Hammurabi

One of Hammurabi's most memorable accomplishments was the proclamation of a **law code** that offers a wealth of information about daily life in Mesopotamia. Hammurabi's was not the first law code in Mesopotamia; indeed, the earliest goes back to about 2100 B.C.E. Like earlier lawgivers, Hammurabi proclaimed that he issued his laws on divine authority "to establish law and justice in the language of the land, thereby promoting the welfare of the people." Hammurabi's code inflicted such penalties as mutilation, whipping, and burning. Despite its severity, a spirit of justice and a sense of responsibility pervade the code. Hammurabi genuinely felt that his duty was to govern the Mesopotamians as righteously as possible. He tried to regulate the relations of his people so that they could live together in harmony.

The practical impact of Hammurabi's code is much debated. There is much disagreement about whether it recorded laws already established, promulgated new laws, or simply proclaimed what was just and proper. It is also unknown whether Hammurabi's proclamation, like others before it, was legally binding on the courts. At the very least, Hammurabi pronounced to the world what principles of justice he encouraged, while giving everyone visible evidence of his intentions as ruler of Babylonia.

The Code of Hammurabi has two striking characteristics. First, the law differed according to the social status of the offender. Aristocrats were not punished as harshly as commoners, nor commoners as harshly as slaves. Second, the code demanded that the punishment fit the crime. It called for "an eye for an eye, and a tooth for a tooth," at least among equals. However, an aristocrat who destroyed the eye of a commoner or slave could pay a fine instead of losing his own eye. Otherwise, as long as criminal and victim shared the same social status, the victim could demand exact vengeance.

Hammurabi's code began with legal procedure. There were no public prosecutors or district attorneys, so individuals brought their own complaints before the court. Each side had to produce written documents or witnesses to support its case. In cases of murder, the accuser had to prove the defendant guilty; any accuser who failed to do so was put to death. This strict law was designed to prevent people from lodging groundless charges. The Mesopotamians were very worried about witchcraft and sorcery. Anyone accused of witchcraft, even if the charges were not proved, underwent an ordeal by water. The gods themselves would decide the case. The defendant was thrown into the Euphrates, which was considered the instrument of the gods. A defendant who sank was guilty; a defendant who floated was innocent. Another procedural regulation covered the conduct of judges. Once a judge had rendered a verdict, he could not change it. Any judge who did so was fined heavily and deposed. In short, the code tried to guarantee a fair trial and a just verdict.

Consumer protection is not a modern idea; it goes back to Hammurabi's day. Merchants and businessmen had to guarantee the quality of their goods and services. A boat builder who did sloppy work had to repair the boat at his own expense. A boatman who lost the owner's boat or sank someone else's boat replaced it and its cargo. House builders guaranteed their work with their lives. Careless work could result in the collapse of a house and the death of its inhabitants. If that happened, the builder was put to death. A merchant who tried to increase the interest rate on a loan forfeited the entire amount. Hammurabi's laws tried to ensure that consumers got what they paid for and paid a just price.

Because farming was essential to Mesopotamian life, Hammurabi's code dealt extensively with agriculture. Tenant farming was widespread, and tenants rented land on a yearly basis. Instead of money they paid a portion of their crops as rent. Unless the land was carefully cultivated, it quickly reverted to wasteland. Therefore, tenants faced severe penalties for neglecting the land or not working it at all. Since irrigation was essential to grow crops, tenants had to keep the canals and ditches in good repair. Otherwise the land would be subject to floods and farmers would face crippling losses. Anyone whose neglect of the canals resulted in damaged crops had to bear all the expense of the lost crops. Those tenants who could not pay the costs were forced into slavery.

Hammurabi gave careful attention to marriage and the family. As elsewhere in the Near East, marriage had aspects of a business agreement. The prospective groom and the father of the future bride arranged everything. The man offered the father a bridal gift, usually money. If the man and his bridal gift were acceptable, the father provided his daughter with a dowry. After marriage the dowry belonged to the woman (although the husband normally administered it) and was a means of protecting her rights and status. Once the two men agreed on financial matters, they drew up a contract; no marriage was considered legal without one. Either party could break off the marriage, but not without paying a stiff penalty. Fathers often contracted marriages while their children were still young. The girl either continued to live in her father's house until she reached maturity or went to live in the house of her father-in-law. During this time she was legally considered a wife. Once she and her husband came of age, they set up their own house.

The wife was expected to be rigorously faithful. The penalty for adultery was death. According to Hammurabi's code: "If the wife of a man has been caught while lying with another man, they shall bind them and throw them into the water."[3] The husband had the power to spare his wife by obtaining a pardon for her from the king. He could, however, accuse his wife of adultery even if he had not caught her in the act. In such a case she could try to clear herself before the city council that investigated the charge. If she was found innocent, she could take her dowry and leave her husband. If a woman decided to take the direct approach and kill her husband, she was impaled.

The husband had virtually absolute power over his household. He could even sell his wife and children into slavery to pay debts. Sons did not lightly oppose their fathers, and any son who struck his father could have his hand cut off. A father was free to adopt children and include them in his will. Artisans sometimes adopted children to teach them the family trade. Although the father's power was great, he could not disinherit a son without just cause. Cases of disinheritance became matters for the city to decide, and the code ordered the courts to forgive a son for his first offense. Only if a son wronged his father a second time could he be disinherited.

Law codes, preoccupied as they are with the problems of society, provide a bleak view of things. Other Mesopotamian documents give a happier glimpse of life. Although Hammurabi's code dealt with marriage in a hard-fisted fashion, a Mesopotamian poem tells of two people meeting secretly in the city. Their parting is delightfully romantic:

*Come now, set me free, I must go home,*
*Kuli-Enlil . . . set me free, I must go home.*
*What can I say to deceive my mother?*[4]

Countless wills and testaments show that husbands habitually left their estates to their wives, who in turn willed the property to their children. All this suggests happy family life. Hammurabi's code restricted married women from commercial pursuits, but financial documents prove that many women engaged in business without hindrance. Some carried on the family business, while others became wealthy landowners in their own right. Mesopotamians found their lives lightened by holidays and religious festivals. Traveling merchants brought news of the outside world and swapped marvelous tales. Despite their pessimism, the Mesopotamians enjoyed a vibrant and creative culture, a culture that left its mark on the entire Near East.

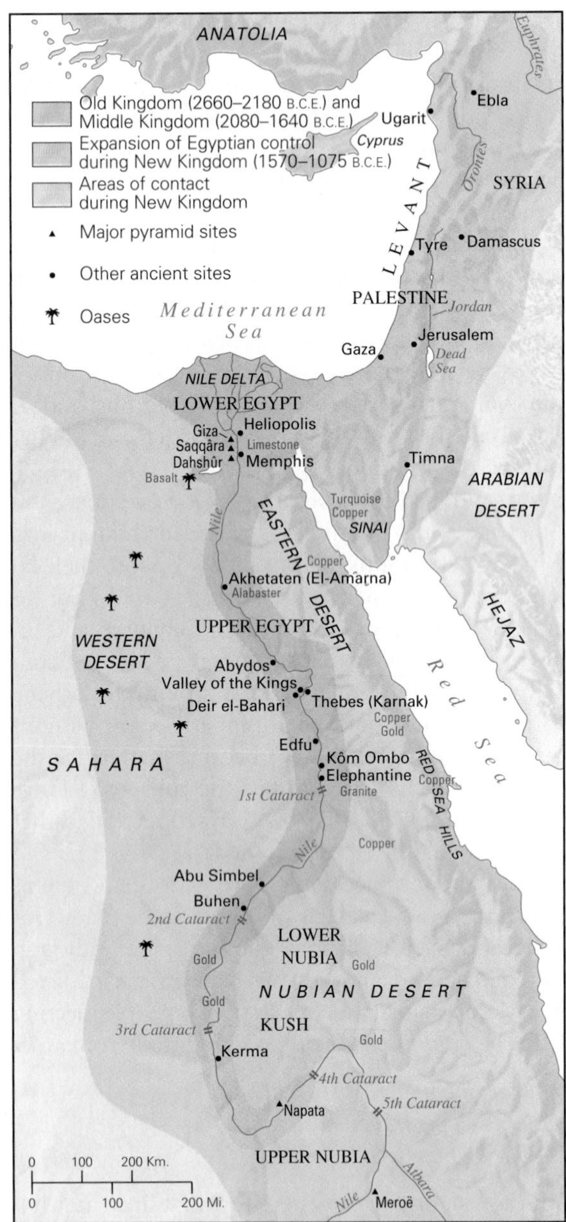


**MAP 1.2 Ancient Egypt** Geography and natural resources provided Egypt with centuries of peace and abundance.

## EGYPT, THE LAND OF THE PHARAOHS (3100–1200 B.C.E.)

The Greek historian and traveler Herodotus in the fifth century B.C.E. called Egypt the "gift of the Nile." No other single geographical factor had such a fundamental and profound impact on the shaping of Egyptian life, society, and history as the Nile (see Map 1.2). Unlike the rivers of Mesopotamia, it rarely brought death and destruction by devastating entire cities. The river was primarily a creative force. The Egyptians never feared the relatively tame Nile in the way the Mesopotamians feared the Tigris. Instead, they sang its praises:

*Hail to thee, O Nile, that issues from the earth and comes to keep Egypt alive! . . .*
*He that waters the meadows which Re [Ra] created,*
*He that makes to drink the desert . . .*
*He who makes barley and brings emmer [wheat] into being . . .*
*He who brings grass into being for the cattle . . .*
*He who makes every beloved tree to grow . . .*
*O Nile, verdant art thou, who makest man and cattle to live.*[5]

In the mind of the Egyptians, the Nile was the supreme fertilizer and renewer of the land. Each September the Nile floods its valley, transforming it into a huge area of marsh or lagoon. By the end of November the water retreats, leaving behind a thin covering of fertile mud ready to be planted with crops.

The annual flood made the growing of abundant crops almost effortless, especially in southern Egypt. Herodotus, used to the rigors of Greek agriculture, was amazed by the ease with which the Egyptians raised crops:

*For indeed without trouble they obtain crops from the land more easily than all other men. . . . They do not labor to dig furrows with the plough or hoe or do the work which other men do to raise grain. But when the river by itself inundates the fields and the water recedes, then each man, having sown his field, sends pigs into it. When the pigs trample down the seed, he waits for the harvest. Then when the pigs thresh the grain, he gets his crop.*[6]

The extraordinary fertility of the Nile Valley made it easy to produce an annual agricultural surplus, which in turn sustained a growing and prosperous population. The Nile also unified Egypt. The river was the region's principal highway, promoting easy communication throughout the valley.

Egypt was fortunate in that it was nearly self-sufficient. Besides the fertility of its soil, Egypt possessed enormous quantities of stone, which served as the raw material of architecture and sculpture. Abundant clay was available for pottery, as was gold for jewelry and ornaments. The raw materials that Egypt lacked were close at hand. The Egyptians could obtain copper from Sinai and timber from Lebanon. They had little cause to look to the outside world for their essential needs, a fact that helps to explain the insular quality of Egyptian life.

## The God-King of Egypt

Geographical unity quickly gave rise to political unification of the country under the authority of a king whom the Egyptians called "pharaoh." The precise details of this process have been lost. The Egyptians themselves told of a great king, Menes, who united Upper and Lower Egypt into a single kingdom around 3100 B.C.E. Thereafter the Egyptians divided their history into dynasties, or families of kings. For modern historical purposes, however, it is more useful to divide Egyptian history into periods (see page 18). The political unification of Egypt ushered in the period known as the Old Kingdom (2660–2180 B.C.E.), an era remarkable for prosperity, artistic flowering, and the evolution of religious beliefs.

In religion, the Egyptians developed complex, often contradictory, ideas of their gods. They were polytheistic in that they worshiped many gods, some mightier than others. Their beliefs were all rooted in the environment and human ecology. The most powerful of these gods was Amon, a primeval sky-god, and Ra, the sun-god. Amon created the entire cosmos by his thoughts. He caused the Nile to make its annual inundations and the northern wind to blow. He brought life to the land and its people, and he sustained both. The Egyptians cherished Amon because he championed fairness and honesty, especially for the common people. The Egyptians called him the "vizier of the humble" and the "voice of the poor." He was also a magician and physician who cured ills, protected people from natural dangers, and protected travelers. The Egyptians considered Ra the creator of life. He commanded the sky, earth, and underworld. This giver of life could also take it without warning. Ra was associated with the falcon-god Horus, the "lord of the sky," who served as the symbol of divine kingship. Horus united Egypt and bestowed divinity on the pharaoh. The obvious similarities between Amon and Ra eventually led the Egyptians to combine them into one god, **Amon-Ra.** Yet the Egyptians never fashioned a

**Ra and Horus** The god Ra appears on the left in a form associated with Horus, the falcon-god. The red circle over Ra's head identifies him as the sun-god. In this scene Ra also assumes characteristics of Osiris, god of the underworld. He stands in judgment of the dead woman on the right. She meets the god with respect but without fear, as he will guide her safely to a celestial heaven. *(Egyptian Museum, Cairo)*

## PERIODS OF EGYPTIAN HISTORY

| PERIOD | DATES | SIGNIFICANT EVENTS |
|---|---|---|
| Archaic | 3100–2660 B.C.E. | Unification of Egypt |
| Old Kingdom | 2715–2180 B.C.E. | Construction of the pyramids |
| First Intermediate | 2180–2080 B.C.E. | Political chaos |
| Middle Kingdom | 2080–1640 B.C.E. | Recovery and political stability |
| Second Intermediate | 1640–1570 B.C.E. | Hyksos "invasion" |
| New Kingdom | 1570–1075 B.C.E. | Creation of an Egyptian empire<br>Akhenaten's religious policy |

formal theology to resolve these differences. Instead they worshiped these gods as different aspects of the same celestial phenomena.

The Egyptians likewise developed views of an afterlife that reflected the world around them. The dry air of Egypt preserves much that would decay in other climates. Thus there was a sense of permanence about Egypt: the past was never far from the present. The dependable rhythm of the seasons also shaped the fate of the dead. According to the Egyptians, Osiris, a fertility god associated with the Nile, died each year, and each year his wife, Isis, brought him back to life. Osiris eventually became king of the dead, and he weighed human beings' hearts to determine whether they had lived justly enough to deserve everlasting life. Osiris's care of the dead was shared by Anubis, the jackal-headed god who annually helped Isis to resuscitate Osiris. Anubis was the god of mummification, so essential to Egyptian funerary rites. The Egyptians preserved these ideas in the ***Book of the Dead,*** which explained that after death the soul left the body to become part of the divine. It entered gladly through the gate of heaven and remained in the presence of Aton (a sun-god) and the stars. Thus the Egyptians did not draw a firm boundary between the human and the divine, and life did not end with death.

**Anubis and the Underworld** In this scene from a coffin, Anubis embalms a body. The jars containing the corpse's internal organs are lined up beneath the bier. The heads on the jars represent the sons of Horus, who like their father tended the dead. The remains will all be buried together for eternity. *(Egyptian Museum, Cairo)*

The focal point of religious and political life in the Old Kingdom was the **pharaoh,** who commanded the wealth, resources, and people of all Egypt. The pharaoh's power was such that the Egyptians considered him to be Horus in human form. The link between the pharaoh and Horus was doubly important. In Egyptian religion Horus was the son of Osiris, which meant that the pharaoh, a living god on earth, became one with Osiris after death. The pharaoh was not simply the mediator between the gods and the Egyptian people. Above all, he was the power that achieved the integration between gods and human beings, between nature and society, that ensured peace

**Pyramids of Giza** Giza was the burial place of the pharaohs of the Old Kingdom and of their aristocracy, whose smaller rectangular tombs surround the two foremost pyramids. The small pyramid probably belonged to a pharaoh's wife. *(© John Ross)*

and prosperity for the land of the Nile. The pharaoh was thus a guarantee to his people, a pledge that the gods of Egypt (strikingly unlike those of Mesopotamia) cared for their people.

The king's surroundings had to be worthy of a god. Only a magnificent palace was suitable for his home; in fact, the very word *pharaoh* means "great house." Only later, in the Eighteenth Dynasty (see page 21), did it come to mean "king." Just as the pharaoh occupied a great house in life, so he reposed in a great **pyramid** after death. The massive tomb contained all the things needed by the pharaoh in his afterlife. The walls of the burial chamber were inscribed with religious texts and spells relating to the king's journeys after death. Contrary to common belief, no curses for violation of the pyramid have been found. The pyramid also symbolized the king's power and his connection with the sun-god. After burial the entrance was blocked and concealed to ensure the pharaoh's undisturbed peace. To this day the great pyramids at Giza near Cairo bear silent but magnificent testimony to the god-kings of Egypt.

## The Pharaoh's People

Because the common folk stood at the bottom of the social and economic scale, they were always at the mercy of grasping officials. The arrival of the tax collector was never a happy occasion. One Egyptian scribe described the worst that could happen:

> *And now the scribe lands on the river-bank and is about to register the harvest-tax. The janitors carry staves and the Nubians rods of palm, and they say, Hand over the corn, though there is none. The cultivator is beaten all over, he is bound and thrown into a well, soused and dipped head downwards. His wife has been bound in his presence and his children are in fetters.*[7]

That was an extreme situation. Nonetheless, taxes might amount to 20 percent of the harvest, and tax collection could be brutal.

The regularity of the climate meant that the agricultural year was also routine and dependable. For the Egyptian peasants who formed the bulk of the population, the

**Hippopotamus Hunt** This wall painting depicts the success of two men in a small boat who have killed a hippopotamus, seen in the lower right-hand corner. Behind the hippopotamus swims a crocodile hoping for a snack. *(Egyptian Museum SMPK, Berlin/Bildarchiv Preussischer Kulturbesitz)*

agricultural year normally began in July, when the mud of the Nile covered the land. The waters receded four months later, and then the land was plowed and sowed. This was a particularly busy time, for the crop had to be planted before the land dried. The next period, from mid-March to July, saw the harvesting of crops. Farmers also nurtured a large variety of fruit trees, vegetables, and vines. They tended cattle and poultry, and when time permitted, they hunted and fished in the marshlands of the Nile. People could routinely depend on these aspects of life. This very regularity gave a sense of calm and order to Egypt that was not found in Mesopotamia or later in Greece.

Egyptian society seems to have been a curious mixture of freedom and constraint. Slavery did not become widespread until the New Kingdom (1570–1200 B.C.E.). There was neither a caste system nor a color bar, and humble people could rise to the highest positions if they possessed talent. On the other hand, most ordinary folk were probably little more than serfs who could not easily leave the land of their own free will. Peasants were also subject to forced labor, including work on the pyramids and canals. Young men were drafted into the pharaoh's army, which served both as a fighting force and as a labor corps.

The vision of thousands of people straining to build the pyramids and countless artists adorning the pharaoh's tomb brings to the modern mind a distasteful picture of oriental despotism. Indeed, the Egyptian view of life and society is alien to those raised on the Western concepts of individual freedom and human rights. To ancient Egyptians the pharaoh embodied justice and order—harmony among human beings, nature, and the divine. If the pharaoh was weak or allowed anyone to challenge his unique position, he opened the way to chaos. Twice in Egyptian history the pharaoh failed to maintain rigid centralization. During those two eras, known as the First and Second Intermediate Periods, Egypt was exposed to civil war and invasion. Yet the monarchy survived, and in each period a strong pharaoh arose to crush the rebels or expel the invaders and restore order.

## The Hyksos in Egypt (1640–1570 B.C.E.)

While Egyptian civilization flourished behind its bulwark of sand and sea, momentous changes were taking place in the ancient Near East, changes that would leave their mark even on rich, insular Egypt. These changes involved enormous and remarkable movements, especially of peoples who spoke Semitic tongues.

The original home of the Semites was perhaps the Arabian peninsula. Some tribes moved into northern

Mesopotamia, others into Syria and Palestine, and still others into Egypt. Shortly after 1800 B.C.E. people whom the Egyptians called **Hyksos,** which means "Rulers of the Uplands," began to settle in the Nile Delta. The movements of the Hyksos were part of a larger pattern of migration of peoples during this period. The history of Mesopotamia records many such wanderings of people in search of better homes for themselves. Such nomads normally settled in and accommodated themselves with the native cultures. The process was mutual, for each group had something to give and to learn from the other.

So it was in Egypt, but Egyptian tradition, as later recorded by the priest Manetho in the third century B.C.E., depicted the coming of the Hyksos as a brutal invasion:

*In the reign of Toutimaios—I do not know why—the wind of god blew against us. Unexpectedly from the regions of the east men of obscure race, looking forward confidently to victory, invaded our land, and without a battle easily seized it all by sheer force. Having subdued those in authority in the land, they then barbarously burned our cities and razed to the ground the temples of the gods. They fell upon all the natives in an entirely hateful fashion, slaughtering them and leading both their children and wives into slavery. At last they made one of their people king, whose name was Salitis. This man resided at Memphis, leaving in Upper and Lower Egypt tax collectors and garrisons in strategic places.*[8]

The Hyksos created a capital city at Avaris, located in the northeastern Nile Delta, but they probably exerted direct rule no farther south.

Although the Egyptians portrayed the Hyksos as a conquering horde, they were probably no more than nomads looking for good land. Their entry into the delta was probably gradual and generally peaceful. The Hyksos brought with them the method of making bronze and casting it into tools and weapons that became standard in Egypt. They thereby brought Egypt fully into the **Bronze Age** culture of the Mediterranean world, a culture in which the production and use of bronze implements became basic to society. Bronze tools made farming more efficient than ever before because they were sharper and more durable than the copper tools they replaced. The Hyksos' use of bronze armor and weapons as well as horse-drawn chariots and the composite bow, made of laminated wood and horn and far more powerful than the simple wooden bow, revolutionized Egyptian warfare. However much the Egyptians learned from the Hyksos, Egyptian culture eventually absorbed the newcomers. The Hyksos came to worship Egyptian gods and modeled their monarchy on the pharaonic system.

## The New Kingdom: Revival and Empire (1570–1075 B.C.E.)

Politically, Egypt was only in eclipse. The Egyptian sun shone again when a remarkable line of kings, the pharaohs of the Eighteenth Dynasty, arose to challenge the Hyksos. These pharaohs pushed the Hyksos out of the delta, subdued Nubia in the south, and conquered Palestine and parts of Syria in the northeast. In this way, Egyptian warrior-pharaohs inaugurated the New Kingdom—a period in Egyptian history characterized by enormous wealth and conscious imperialism. During this period, probably for the first time, widespread slavery became a feature of Egyptian life. The pharaoh's armies returned home leading hordes of slaves, who constituted a new labor force for imperial building projects.

The kings of the Eighteenth Dynasty created the first Egyptian empire. They ruled Palestine and Syria through their officers and incorporated into the kingdom of Egypt the neighboring region of Nubia. Egyptian religion and customs flourished in Nubia, making a huge impact on African culture there and in neighboring areas. The warrior-kings celebrated their success with monuments on a scale unparalleled since the pharaohs of the Old Kingdom had built the pyramids. Even today the colossal granite statues of these pharaohs and the rich tomb objects of Tutankhamon ("King Tut") testify to the might and splendor of the New Kingdom.

One of the most extraordinary of this unusual line of kings was Akhenaten (r. 1367–1350 B.C.E.), a pharaoh more concerned with religion than with conquest. Nefertiti, his wife and queen, encouraged his religious bent. (See the feature "Individuals in Society: Nefertiti, the 'Great Wife.'") The precise nature of Akhenaten's religious beliefs remains debatable. The problem began during his own lifetime. His religion was often unpopular among the people and the traditional priesthood, and its practice declined in the later years of his reign. After his death, it was condemned and denounced; consequently, not much is known about it. Most historians, however, agree that Akhenaten and Nefertiti were monotheists; that is, they believed that the sun-god Aton, whom they worshiped, was universal, the only god. They considered all other Egyptian gods and goddesses frauds and disregarded their worship. Yet their belief suffered from an obvious flaw. The pharaoh himself was considered the son of god, and monotheism obviously cannot have two gods. What Akhenaten meant by **monotheism** is that only Aton among the traditional Egyptian deities was god.

Akhenaten's monotheism, imposed from above, failed to find a place among the people. The prime reason for

**Tutankhamon as Pharaoh** This painted casket depicts the pharaoh as the defender of the kingdom repulsing its invaders. Tutankhamon rides into battle under the signs of the sun-disk and the vulture-goddess, indicating that he and Egypt enjoy the protection of the gods. *(Egyptian Museum, Cairo)*

Akhenaten's failure is that his god had no connection with the past of the Egyptian people, who trusted the old gods and felt comfortable praying to them. Average Egyptians were no doubt distressed and disheartened when their familiar gods were outlawed, for those gods were the heavenly powers that had made Egypt powerful and unique. The fanaticism and persecution that accompanied the new monotheism were in complete defiance of the Egyptian tradition of tolerant **polytheism,** or worship of several gods. Thus, when Akhenaten died, his religion died with him.

## THE HITTITES

About the time the Hyksos entered the Nile Delta, the Hittites, who had long been settled in Anatolia (modern Turkey), became a major power in that region and began to expand eastward (see Map 1.3). The Hittites were an Indo-European people. The term **Indo-European** refers to a large family of languages that includes English, most of the languages of modern Europe, Greek, Latin, Persian, and Sanskrit, the sacred tongue of ancient India. During the eighteenth and nineteenth centuries European scholars learned that peoples who spoke related languages had spread as far west as Ireland and as far east as Central Asia. Archaeologists were able to date the migrations roughly and put them into their historical context.

The rise of the Hittites to prominence in Anatolia is reasonably clear. During the nineteenth century B.C.E. the native kingdoms in the area engaged in suicidal warfare that left most of Anatolia's once-flourishing towns in ashes and rubble. In this climate of exhaustion the Hittite king Hattusilis I built a hill citadel at Hattusas, the modern Boghazköy, from which he led his Hittites against neighboring kingdoms. Hattusilis's grandson and successor,

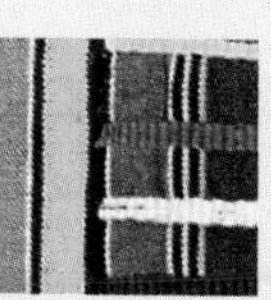

## NEFERTITI, THE "GREAT WIFE"

The Egyptians always named the pharaoh's wife the "great wife," somewhat in the way that Americans refer to the president's wife as the "first lady." The great wife legitimized her husband's exercise of power through religious beliefs. The Egyptians believed that she was divinely born and that Amon took the human form of her husband, impregnated her, oversaw the development of the child in her womb, and ensured a healthy delivery. Thus the child was the offspring of both the god and the pharaoh. The great wife could not legally be pharaoh, for only a male could exercise that power. Yet only she could make legitimate a man's right to power. The Egyptians literally and formally considered hers the throne of power, although her power was passive rather than active. Egyptian artists usually depicted the great wife with as much care and dignity as they did the pharaoh. They stylized her body as that of the ideal woman, and her portrait was more idealized than realistic.

So stood things until Nefertiti, who was an exceptional great wife. Unlike her predecessors, she was not content to play a passive role in Egyptian life. Like her husband, Akhenaten, she passionately embraced the worship of Aton. She used her position to support her husband's zeal to spread the god's worship. Together they built a new palace at Akhetaten, the present Amarna, away from the old centers of power. There they developed and promulgated the cult of Aton to the exclusion of the traditional deities. Nearly the only literary survival of their religious belief is the "Hymn to Aton," which declares Aton to be the only god. It also mentions Nefertiti as "the great royal consort whom he !Akhenaten! loves, the mistress of the Two Lands !Upper and Lower Egypt!"

Yet something mysterious and unexplained later occurred at the royal court. Akhenaten stripped Nefertiti of her crown name, which was the equivalent of divorce, and exiled her to a palace in the northernmost part of Amarna. It is quite possible, but beyond proof, that Akhenaten wanted a reconciliation with the old gods and their priests. The cult of Aton was so unpopular among the Egyptians that many considered it sacrilegious. Unwilling to alienate the Egyptian people and their religious leaders any longer, Akhenaten may have dropped or at least softened his insistence on Aton's divine position. Nefertiti in that case may have held true to her religious faith and been punished accordingly. At the death of Akhenaten his memory and that of Nefertiti were cursed, and their palace at Amarna was abandoned. This abandonment (and the fact that Amarna was recovered only in the twentieth century) accounts for the little that is now known of the royal couple. Nonetheless, no queen before Nefertiti had played such an active part in Egyptian religious life.

*Nefertiti, queen of Egypt.* (Staatliche Muzeen zu Berlin/ Bildarchiv Preussischer Kulturbesitz. Photo: Margarete Busing)

Nefertiti likewise played a novel role in Egyptian art. In funerary and temple art she is usually depicted with Akhenaten and their daughters. This practice went against the tradition of presenting the royal couple as austere and aloof. Instead, Nefertiti and Akhenaten were portrayed as an ordinary family. Their daughters often appear playing on their parents' laps or with one another. Even Nefertiti's own appearance in Egyptian art was a departure from tradition. As the illustration here shows, the famous bust of her is a realistic, not an idealized, portrait. The face is one of grace, beauty, and dignity. It is the portrait of an individual, not a type.

Nefertiti's bust has its own story. When Akhenaten's successor abandoned the palace at Amarna, the site was ignored, except as a source for building materials. Nefertiti's bust remained in the sculptor's workroom, which eventually caved in. There it lay, undamaged, for more than three thousand years. On December 6, 1912, a German archaeological team discovered it intact and sent it to Germany. After World War II, the bust was moved to its current home outside Berlin, where Nefertiti can still be admired today.

### QUESTIONS FOR ANALYSIS

1. Did Nefertiti's individualism have any effect on Egyptian society?
2. Did she have a more profound and philosophical concept of divinity, or were her beliefs purely personal?

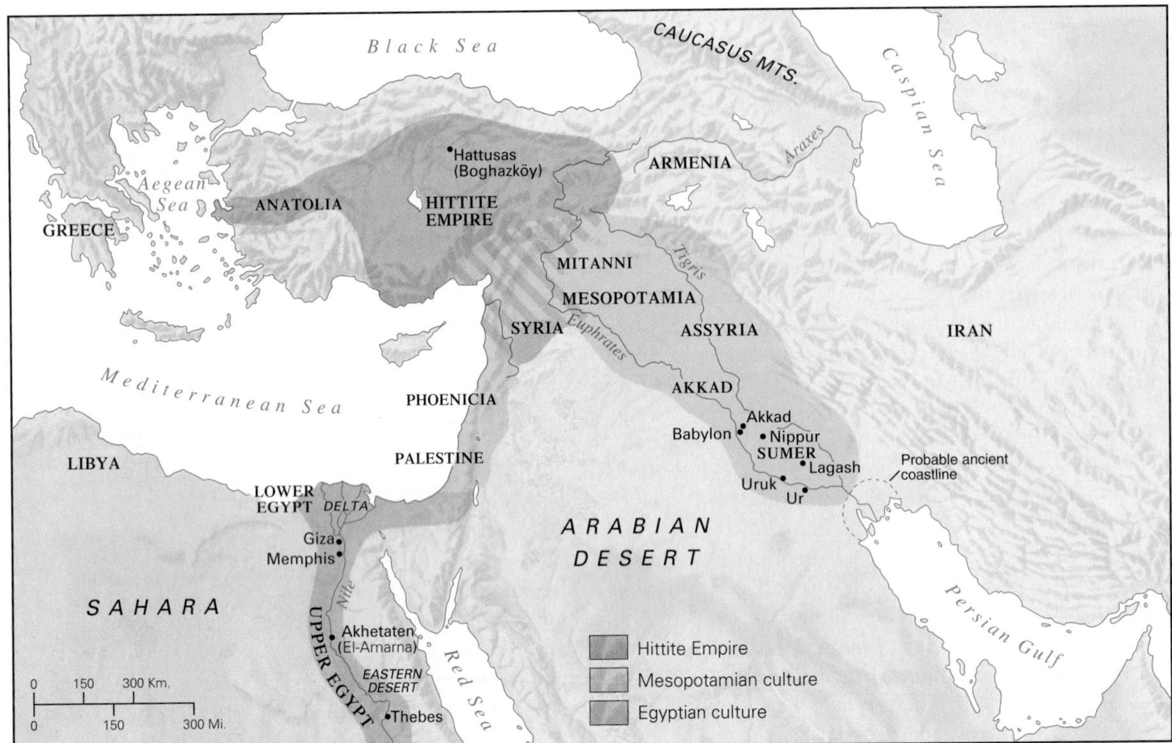


**MAP 1.3 Balance of Power in the Near East** This map shows the regions controlled by the Hittites and Egyptians at the height of their power. The striped area represents the part of Mesopotamia conquered by the Hittites during their expansion eastward.

Mursilis I (r. ca 1595 B.C.E.), extended the Hittite conquests as far as Babylon. Upon his return home, the victorious Mursilis was assassinated by members of his own family, an act that plunged the kingdom into confusion and opened the door to foreign invasion. Mursilis's career is representative of the success and weakness of the Hittites. They were extremely vulnerable to attack by vigilant and tenacious enemies. Yet once they were united behind a strong king, the Hittites were a power to be reckoned with.

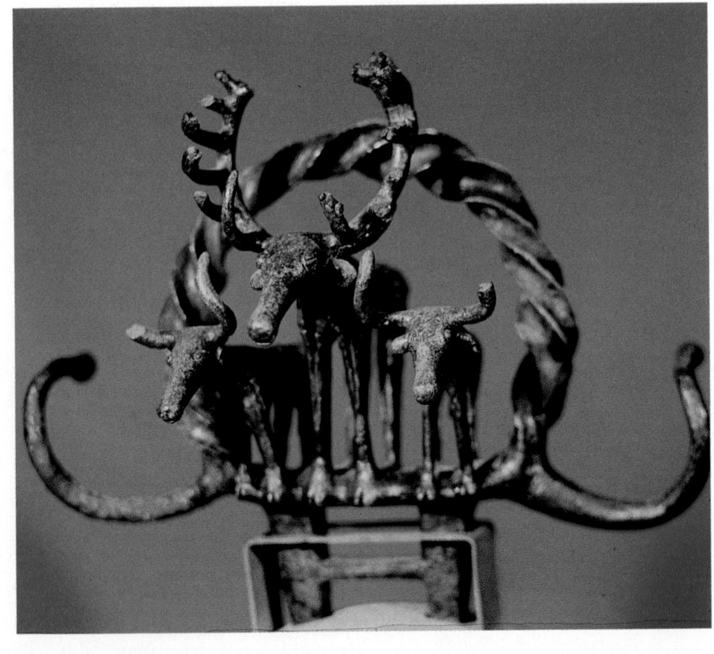

**Hittite Solar Disk** This cult standard represents Hittite concepts of fertility and prosperity. The circle surrounding the animals is the sun, beneath which stands a stag flanked by two bulls. Stylized bull's horns spread from the base of the disk. The symbol is also one of might and protection from outside harm. *(Museum of Anatolian Civilizations, Ankara)*

The Hittites, like the Egyptians of the New Kingdom, produced an energetic and able line of kings who built a powerful empire. Perhaps their major contribution was the introduction of iron into war and agriculture in the form of weapons and tools. Around 1300 B.C.E. the Hittites stopped the Egyptian army of Rameses II at the Battle of Kadesh in Syria. Having fought each other to a standstill, the Hittites and Egyptians first made peace, then an alliance. Alliance was followed by friendship, and friendship by active cooperation. The two greatest powers of the early Near East tried to make war between them impossible.

They next included the Babylonians in their diplomacy. All three empires developed an official etiquette in which they treated one another as "brothers." They made alliances for offensive and defensive protection, and swore to uphold one another's authority. These contacts facilitated the exchange of ideas throughout the Near East. Furthermore, the Hittites passed much knowledge and lore from the Near East to the newly arrived Greeks in Europe. The details of Hittite contact with the Greeks are unknown, but enough literary themes and physical objects exist to prove the connection.

## THE FALL OF EMPIRES AND THE SURVIVAL OF CULTURES (CA 1200 B.C.E.)

The height of Hittite and Egyptian power came to a tumultuous end, but the achievements of these peoples lasted long after their governments had been overthrown or diminished in power. New political alignments appeared, but to some degree they all adopted and adapted the examples of their predecessors. They likewise embraced the cultures of those whom they had replaced on the political map.

### Political Chaos

Like the Hittite kings, Rameses II (r. ca 1290–1224 B.C.E.) used the peace after the Battle of Kadesh to promote the prosperity of his own kingdom. Free from the expense and waste of warfare, he concentrated the income from the natural wealth and the foreign trade of Egypt on internal affairs. In many ways, he was the last great pharaoh of Egypt.

This stable and generally peaceful situation endured until the late thirteenth century B.C.E., when both the Hittite and the Egyptian empires were destroyed by invaders. The most famous of these marauders, called the **Sea Peoples** by the Egyptians, remain one of the puzzles of ancient history. Despite much new work, modern archaeology is still unable to identify the Sea Peoples satisfactorily. The reason for this uncertainty is that the Sea Peoples were a collection of peoples who went their own, individual ways after their attacks on the Hittites and Egyptians. It is known, however, that their incursions were part of a larger movement of peoples. Although there is serious doubt about whether the Sea Peoples alone overthrew the Hittites, they did deal both the Hittites and the Egyptians a hard blow, making the Hittites vulnerable to overland invasion from the north and driving the Egyptians back to the Nile Delta. The Hittites fell under the external blows, but the Egyptians, shaken and battered, retreated to the delta and held on.

### Cultural Endurance and Dissemination

The Egyptians and Mesopotamians established basic social, economic, and cultural patterns in the ancient Near East. Moreover, they spread them far beyond their homelands. Egypt exerted vast influence in Palestine and Syria, while Mesopotamia was influential in southern Anatolia (modern Turkey). Yet it is a mistake to think that these older civilizations moved into a cultural vacuum.

In Palestine and southern Syria the Egyptians found Semitic peoples living in small walled towns. Municipal life was quite advanced, with towns that included urban centers and small outlying hamlets. Although these societies were primarily based on agriculture, there is ample evidence of international trade. In short, both Palestine and Syria possessed an extensive political, social, and religious organization even before the arrival of the Egyptians. Contact had begun as early as the Bronze Age, when the Egyptians had moved along the eastern Mediterranean coast. The contact immediately led to trade. The Egyptians exploited the turquoise and copper trade in the area, and exported local pottery and other goods. Sometimes the Egyptians traded peacefully, but at other times they resorted to military invasion.

Farther north the Egyptians made maritime contact with the Phoenicians, most clearly seen from the excavations at Byblos. The two peoples exchanged not only goods but also technological knowledge. The Egyptians learned many shipbuilding techniques, their own boats being better designed for the Nile than the open sea. The Phoenicians in turn adopted aspects of Egyptian technology. Yet the cultural exchange between the two peoples was by far more important. The Phoenicians honored some Egyptian gods and adopted Egyptian artistic motifs. They learned the Egyptian script and became acquainted with some Egyptian myths. At the same time some deities of Byblos made their appearance in Egypt. Despite armed conflict, trade, not warfare, generally characterized relations in the area.

The situation in northern Syria was similar to that in southern Syria and Palestine. Cities were common, normally ruled by royal families. The families usually shared power and dealt jointly with foreign affairs. They often left the internal administration of the cities to local elders. The cities were primarily mercantile centers but also rich in agricultural produce, timber, and metal deposits. The need for record keeping soon led to the development of writing. These northern Semites adopted Sumerian writing in order to understand their neighbors to the east, but they also adapted it to write their own northern Semitic language. Their texts provide a wealth of information about the life of northern Syria. In the process, northern Syrians gained a solid knowledge of Mesopotamian literature, mathematics, and culture. Both local and Sumerian deities were honored. Despite Mesopotamian influence, northern Syria maintained its native traditions. The cultural exchange was a mixture of adoption, adaptation, contrast, and finally balance, as the two cultures came to understand each other.

Southern Anatolia presented a somewhat similar picture. Human settlement there consisted of trading colonies and small agricultural communities. Thousands of cuneiform tablets testify to commercial and cultural exchanges with Mesopotamia. In Anatolia kingship and temple were closely allied, but the government was not a **theocracy** (rule by a priestly order). A city assembly worked together with the king, and provincial cities were administered by a prince. The political and social organization was one of a firmly established native culture that gladly received foreign ideas while keeping its own identity.

A pattern emerged in Palestine, Syria, and Anatolia. In these areas native cultures established themselves during the prehistoric period. Upon coming into contact with the Egyptian and Mesopotamian civilizations, they adopted many aspects of these cultures, adapting them to their own traditional customs. Yet they also contributed to the advance of Egyptian and Mesopotamian cultures by introducing new technologies and religious ideas. The result was the emergence of a huge group of communities stretching from Egypt in the south to Anatolia in the north and from the Levant in the west to Mesopotamia in the east. Each enjoyed its own individual character, while at the same time sharing many common features with its neighbors.

## SUMMARY

For thousands of years Paleolithic peoples roamed this planet seeking game. Only in the Neolithic era—with the invention of new stone tools, a reliance on sustained agriculture, and the domestication of animals—did people begin to live in permanent locations. These villages evolved into towns, where people began to create new social bonds and political organizations. The result was economic prosperity.

The earliest area where these developments led to genuine urban societies is Mesopotamia. Here the Sumerians and then other Mesopotamians developed writing, which enabled their culture to be passed on to others. The wealth of the Mesopotamians made it possible for them to devote time to history, astronomy, urban planning, medicine, and other arts and sciences. Mesopotamian culture was so rich and advanced that neighboring peoples eagerly adopted it, thereby spreading it through much of the Near East.

Nor were the Mesopotamians alone in advancing the civilization of the day. In Egypt another strong culture developed, one that made an impact in Africa, the Near East, and, later, in Greece. The Egyptians too enjoyed such prosperity that they developed writing of their own, mathematical skills, and religious beliefs that influenced the lives of their neighbors. Into this world came the Hittites, an Indo-European people who were culturally less advanced than the Mesopotamians and Egyptians. The Hittites learned from their neighbors and rivals, but they also introduced their own sophisticated political system for administering their empire, a system that in some ways influenced both their contemporaries and later peoples.

## KEY TERMS

Neolithic period
irrigation
cuneiform
nobles
clients
law code
Amon-Ra
*Book of the Dead*
pharaoh
pyramid
Hyksos
Bronze Age
monotheism
polytheism
Indo-European
Sea Peoples
theocracy

## NOTES

1. Quoted in S. N. Kramer, *The Sumerians* (Chicago: University of Chicago Press, 1963), p. 238. John Buckler is the translator of all uncited quotations from a foreign language in Chapter 1.
2. J. B. Pritchard, ed., *Ancient Near Eastern Texts,* 3d ed. (Princeton, N.J.: Princeton University Press, 1969), p. 590. Hereafter called ANET.
3. Ibid., p. 171.
4. Kramer, p. 251.
5. ANET, p. 372.
6. Herodotus, *The Histories* 2.14.
7. Quoted in A. H. Gardiner, "Ramesside Texts Relating to the Taxation and Transport of Corn," *Journal of Egyptian Archaeology* 27 (1941): 19–20.
8. Manetho, *History of Egypt,* frag. 42.75–77.

## SUGGESTED READING

Some very illuminating general studies of Near Eastern developments have been published. A broad-ranging work, A. Kuhrt, *The Ancient Near East,* 2 vols. (1995), covers the region from the earliest time to Alexander's conquest, as does C. Snell, *Life in the Ancient Near East, 3100–332 B.C.E.*, which also covers social history. Most welcome is D. Schmandt-Besserat's two-volume work on the origins of writing, *Before Writing,* vol. 1 (1992), which explores the origins of writing, and vol. 2 (1992), which provides actual evidence on the topic. G. Visicato, *The Power of Writing* (2000), studies the practical importance of early Mesopotamian scribes. For the Stonehenge people A. Burl, the leading expert on the topic, provides *The Stonehenge People* (1987) and *Great Stone Circles* (1999), which examine the people and their monuments.

D. T. Potts, *Mesopotamian Civilization* (1996), presents a view of Mesopotamians from their material remains but is not purely architectural. H. W. F. Saggs, *The Babylonians* (2000), treats all the eras of Mesopotamian history. G. Stein and M. S. Rothman, *Chiefdoms and Early States in the Near East* (1994), provides a clear view of the political evolution of the region. An ambitious work is M. Hudson and B. Levine, *Privatization in the Ancient Near East and the Classical World* (1996), which treats the concept of private property. A very ambitious and thoughtful book, G. Algaze, *The Uruk World System* (1993), examines how the early Mesopotamians expanded their civilization.

K. Mysliwiec, *The Twilight of Ancient Egypt* (2000), provides a history of Egypt in the first millennium B.C.E. D. P. Silverman, *Ancient Egypt* (1997), also gives a good general account of the region. S. Donadoni, ed., *The Egyptians* (1997), treats various aspects of Egyptian history and life. A. G. McDowell, *Village Life in Ancient Egypt* (1999), is a readable study of the basic social and economic factors of the entire period. D. Meeks and C. Favard-Meeks, *Daily Life of the Egyptian Gods* (1996), with a learned and original point of view, discusses how the Egyptian gods are sometimes treated in literature as an ethnic group not so very different from human beings. A. R. David, *Pyramid Builders of Ancient Egypt,* 2d ed. (1996), studies the lives of the people who actually labored to build the pyramids for their pharaohs. A. Blackman, *Gods, Priests and Men* (1993), is a series of studies in the religion of pharaonic Egypt. Z. Hawass, *Silent Images: Women in Pharaonic Egypt* (2000), blends text and pictures to draw a history of ancient Egyptian women. W. L. Moran, *The Amarna Letters* (1992), is a translation of the Egyptian documents so important to the understanding of the events of the New Kingdom. E. D. Oren, *The Hyksos* (1997), concentrates on the archaeological evidence for them.

The coming of the Indo-Europeans receives the attention of M. R. Dexter and K. Jones-Bley, eds., *The Kurgan Culture and the Indo-Europeanization of Europe* (1997), a controversial work that explores the homeland of the Indo-Europeans and the nature of their movements. Less challenging but perhaps more useful is A. Harding, *European Societies in the Bronze Age* (2000), a comprehensive survey of developments in Europe. Often and unfortunately neglected, the Hittites have received relatively little new attention. Dated but solid is O. R. Gurney, *The Hittites,* 2d ed. (1954), a fine introduction by an eminent scholar. Good also is J. G. MacQueen, *The Hittites and Their Contemporaries in Asia Minor,* 2d ed. (1986). The Sea Peoples have been studied by T. and M. Dothan, *People of the Sea* (1992), who concentrate their work on the Philistines.

A truly excellent study of ancient religions, from Sumer to the late Roman Empire, is M. Eliade, ed., *Religions of Antiquity* (1989), which treats concisely but amply all of the religions mentioned in Chapters 1, 2, 5, and 6.

# LISTENING TO THE PAST

## A Quest for Immortality

*The human desire to escape the grip of death, to achieve immortality, is one of the oldest wishes of all peoples. The Sumerian* Epic of Gilgamesh *is the earliest recorded treatment of this topic. The oldest elements of the epic go back at least to the third millennium B.C.E. According to tradition, Gilgamesh was a king of Uruk whom the Sumerians, Babylonians, and Assyrians considered a hero-king and a god. In the story Gilgamesh and his friend Enkidu set out to attain immortality and join the ranks of the gods. They attempt to do so by performing wondrous feats against fearsome agents of the gods, who are determined to thwart them.*

*During their quest Enkidu dies. Gilgamesh, more determined than ever to become immortal, begins seeking anyone who might tell him how to do so. His journey involves the effort not only to escape from death but also to reach an understanding of the meaning of life.*

*The passage begins with Enkidu speaking of a dream that foretells his own death.*

Listen, my friend [Gilgamesh], this is the dream I dreamed last night. The heavens roared, and earth rumbled back an answer; between them I stood before an awful being, the sombre-faced man-bird; he had directed on me his purpose. His was a vampire face, his foot was a lion's foot, his hand was an eagle's talon. He fell on me and his claws were in my hair, he held me fast and I smothered; then he transformed me so that my arms became wings covered with feathers. He turned his stare towards me, and he led me away to the palace of Irkalla, the Queen of Darkness [the goddess of the underworld; in other words, an agent of death], to the house from which none who enters ever returns, down the road from which there is no coming back.

*At this point Enkidu dies, whereupon Gilgamesh sets off on his quest for the secret of immortality. During his travels he meets with Siduri, the wise and good-natured goddess of wine, who gives him the following advice.*

Gilgamesh, where are you hurrying to? You will never find that life for which you are looking. When the gods created man they allotted to him death, but life they retained in their own keeping. As for you, Gilgamesh, fill your belly with good things; day and night, night and day, dance and be merry, feast and rejoice. Let your clothes be fresh, bathe yourself in water, cherish the little child that holds your hand, and make your wife happy in your embrace; for this too is the lot of man.

*Ignoring Siduri's advice, Gilgamesh continues his journey, until he finds Utnapishtim. Meeting Utnapishtim is especially important because, like Gilgamesh, he was once a mortal, but the gods so favored him that they put him in an eternal paradise. Gilgamesh puts to Utnapishtim the question that is the reason for his quest.*

Oh, father Utnapishtim, you who have entered the assembly of the gods, I wish to question you concerning the living and the dead, how shall I find the life for which I am searching?

Utnapishtim said, "There is no permanence. Do we build a house to stand forever, do we seal a contract to hold for all time? Do brothers divide an inheritance to keep forever, does the flood-time of rivers endure? . . . What is there between the master and the servant when both have fulfilled their doom? When the Anunnaki [the gods of the underworld], the judges, come together, and Mammetun [the goddess of fate] the mother of destinies, together they decree the fates of men. Life and death they allot but the day of death they do not disclose.

Gilgamesh, from decorative panel of a lyre unearthed at Ur. *(The University Museum, University of Pennsylvania, neg. T4-108)*

Then Gilgamesh said to Utnapishtim the Faraway, "I look at you now, Utnapishtim, and your appearance is no different from mine; there is nothing strange in your features. I thought I should find you like a hero prepared for battle, but you lie here taking your ease on your back. Tell me truly, how was it that you came to enter the company of the gods and to possess everlasting life?" Utnapishtim said to Gilgamesh, "I shall reveal to you a mystery, I shall tell you a secret of the gods."

*Utnapishtim then tells Gilgamesh of a time when the great god Enlil had become angered with the Sumerians and encouraged the other gods to wipe out humanity. The god Ea, however, warned Utnapishtim about the gods' decision to send a great flood to destroy the Sumerians. He commanded Utnapishtim to build a boat big enough to hold his family, various artisans, and all animals in order to survive the flood that was to come. Although Enlil was infuriated by the Sumerians' survival, Ea rebuked him. Then Enlil relented and blessed Utnapishtim with eternal paradise. After telling the story, Utnapishtim foretells Gilgamesh's fate.*

Utnapishtim said, ". . . The destiny was fulfilled which the father of the gods, Enlil of the mountain, had decreed for Gilgamesh: In nether-earth the darkness will show him a light: of mankind, all that are known, none will leave a monument for generations to compare with his. The heroes, the wise men, like the new moon have their waxing and waning. Men will say, Who has ever ruled with might and power like his? As in the dark month, the month of shadows, so without him there is no light. O Gilgamesh, this was the meaning of your dream [of immortality]. You were given the kingship, such was your destiny, everlasting life was not your destiny. Because of this do not be sad at heart, do not be grieved or oppressed; he [Enlil] has given you power to bind and to loose, to be the darkness and the light of mankind. He has given unexampled supremacy over the people, victory in battle from which no fugitive returns, in forays and assaults from which there is no going back. But do not abuse this power, deal justly with your servants in the palace, deal justly before the face of the Sun."

## QUESTIONS FOR ANALYSIS

1. What does the *Epic of Gilgamesh* reveal about Sumerian attitudes toward the gods and human beings?
2. At the end of his quest, did Gilgamesh achieve immortality? If so, what was the nature of that immortality?
3. What does the epic tell us about Sumerian views of the nature of human life? Where do human beings fit into the cosmic world?

*Source: The Epic of Gilgamesh,* translated by N. K. Sanders. Penguin Classics 1960, Second revised edition, 1972, pp. 91–119. 

Reconstruction of the "Ishtar Gate," Babylon, early sixth century B.C.E. Located in the Berlin Museum. *(Staatliche Museen zu Berlin/Bildarchiv Preussicher Kulturbesitz)*

CHAPTER 2

# SMALL KINGDOMS AND MIGHTY EMPIRES IN THE NEAR EAST

## CHAPTER OUTLINE

- Recovery and Diffusion
- A Shattered Egypt and a Rising Phoenicia
- The Children of Israel
- Assyria, the Military Monarchy
- The Empire of the Persian Kings

The migratory invasions that brought down the Hittites and stunned the Egyptians in the late thirteenth century B.C.E. ushered in an era of confusion and weakness. Although much was lost in the chaos, the old cultures of the ancient Near East survived to nurture new societies. In the absence of powerful empires, the Phoenicians, Hebrews, and many other peoples carved out small independent kingdoms, until the Near East was a patchwork of them. During this period Hebrew culture and religion evolved under the influence of urbanism, kings, and prophets.

In the ninth century B.C.E. this jumble of small states gave way to an empire that for the first time embraced the entire Near East. Yet the very ferocity of the Assyrian Empire led to its downfall only two hundred years later. In 550 B.C.E. the Persians and Medes, who had migrated into Iran, created a "world empire" stretching from Anatolia in the west to the Indus Valley in the east. For over two hundred years the Persians gave the ancient Near East peace and stability.

- How did Egypt, its political greatness behind it, pass on its cultural heritage to its African neighbors?
- How did the Hebrew state evolve, and what was daily life like in Hebrew society?
- What forces helped to shape Hebrew religious thought, still powerfully influential in today's world?
- What enabled the Assyrians to overrun their neighbors, and how did their cruelty finally cause their undoing?
- Last, how did Iranian nomads create the Persian Empire?

This chapter will look at these questions.

## RECOVERY AND DIFFUSION

If the fall of empires was a time of massive political disruption, it also ushered in a period of cultural diffusion, an expansion of what had already blossomed in the broad region. Even though empires expired, many small kingdoms survived, along with a largely shared culture. These small states and local societies had

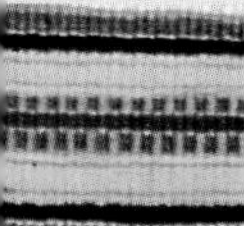

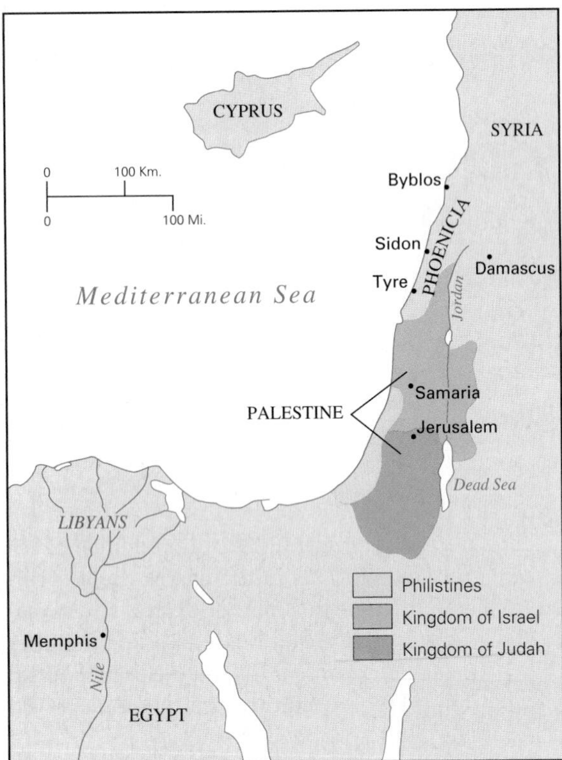


**MAP 2.1 Small Kingdoms of the Near East** This map illustrates the political fragmentation of the Near East after the great wave of invasions that occurred during the thirteenth century B.C.E.

learned much from the great powers, but they nonetheless retained their own lore and native traditions, which they passed on to their neighbors, thus diffusing a Near Eastern culture that was slowly becoming common in nature. The best-known examples can be found along the coast of the eastern Mediterranean, where various peoples—some of them newcomers—created homes and petty kingdoms in Phoenicia and Palestine. After the Sea Peoples raided Egypt, a branch of them, known in the Bible as Philistines, settled along the coast of Palestine (see Map 2.1). Establishing themselves in five cities somewhat inland from the sea, the Philistines set about farming and raising flocks.

## A SHATTERED EGYPT AND A RISING PHOENICIA

The invasions of the Sea Peoples brought the great days of Egyptian power to an end. The long wars against invaders weakened and impoverished Egypt, causing political upheaval and economic chaos. One scribe left behind a somber portrait of Egypt stunned and leaderless:

*The land of Egypt was abandoned and every man was a law to himself. During many years there was no leader who could speak for others. Central government lapsed, small officials and headmen took over the whole land. Any man, great or small, might kill his neighbor. In the distress and vacuum that followed . . . men banded together to plunder one another. They treated the gods no better than men, and cut off the temple revenues.*[1]

No longer able to dream of foreign conquests, Egypt looked to its own security from foreign invasion. Egyptians suffered a four-hundred-year period of political fragmentation, a new dark age known to Egyptian specialists as the Third Intermediate Period (eleventh to seventh centuries B.C.E.). (See the feature "Individuals in Society: Wen-Amon" on page 35.)

The decline of Egypt was especially sharp in foreign affairs. Whereas the pharaohs of the Eighteenth Dynasty had held sway as far abroad as Syria, their weak successors found it unsafe to venture far from home. In the wake of the Sea Peoples, numerous small kingdoms sprang up in the Near East, each fiercely protective of its own independence. To them Egypt was a memory. Disrupted at home and powerless abroad, Egypt fell prey to invasion by its African neighbors. From 950 to 730 B.C.E. northern Egypt was ruled by Libyan pharaohs, who had come from North Africa. The Libyans built cities, and for the first time a sturdy urban life grew up in the Nile Delta. Although the Libyans changed the face of the delta, they genuinely admired Egyptian culture and eagerly adopted Egypt's religion and way of life.

In southern Egypt, meanwhile, the pharaoh's decline opened the way to the energetic Nubians, who extended their authority northward throughout the Nile Valley. Since the imperial days of the Eighteenth Dynasty (see pages 21–22), the Nubians, too, had adopted many features of Egyptian culture. Now Nubian kings and aristocrats embraced Egyptian culture wholesale. Thus the Nubians and the Libyans repeated an old Near Eastern phenomenon: new peoples conquered old centers of political and military power but were assimilated into the older culture.

The reunification of Egypt occurred late and unexpectedly. With Egypt distracted and disorganized by foreign invasions, an independent African state, the kingdom of Kush, grew up in the region of modern Sudan with its capital at Nepata. Like the Libyans, the Kushites worshiped Egyptian gods and used Egyptian hieroglyphs. In the eighth century B.C.E. their king, Piankhy, swept through the entire Nile Valley from Nepata in the south to the delta in the north. United once again, Egypt enjoyed a brief

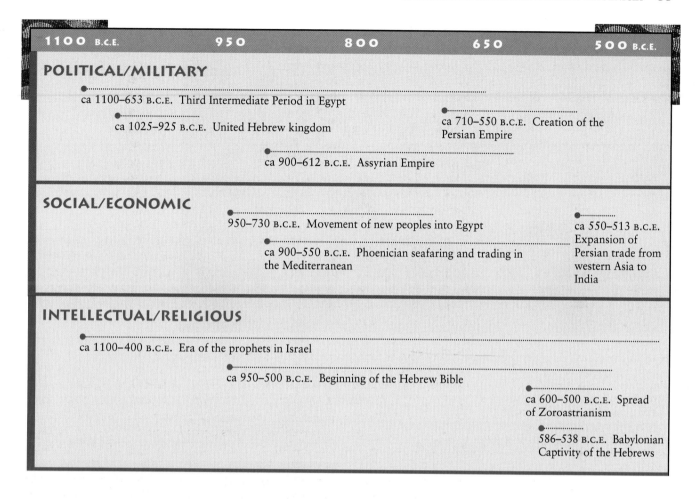

| 1100 B.C.E. | 950 | 800 | 650 | 500 B.C.E. |
|---|---|---|---|---|

**POLITICAL/MILITARY**

- ca 1100–653 B.C.E. Third Intermediate Period in Egypt
- ca 1025–925 B.C.E. United Hebrew kingdom
- ca 900–612 B.C.E. Assyrian Empire
- ca 710–550 B.C.E. Creation of the Persian Empire

**SOCIAL/ECONOMIC**

- 950–730 B.C.E. Movement of new peoples into Egypt
- ca 900–550 B.C.E. Phoenician seafaring and trading in the Mediterranean
- ca 550–513 B.C.E. Expansion of Persian trade from western Asia to India

**INTELLECTUAL/RELIGIOUS**

- ca 1100–400 B.C.E. Era of the prophets in Israel
- ca 950–500 B.C.E. Beginning of the Hebrew Bible
- ca 600–500 B.C.E. Spread of Zoroastrianism
- 586–538 B.C.E. Babylonian Captivity of the Hebrews

period of peace during which the Egyptians continued to assimilate their conquerors. Nonetheless, reunification of the realm did not lead to a new Egyptian empire.

Yet Egypt's legacy to its African neighbors remained vibrant and rich. By trading and exploring southward along the coast of the Red Sea, the Egyptians introduced their goods and ideas as far south as the land of Punt, probably a region on the Somali coast. Egypt was the primary civilizing force in Nubia, which became another version of the pharaoh's realm, complete with royal pyramids and

**Life Goes On** Although the Egyptians suffered political defeat, much of their society continued without interruption. Here a farmer and two oxen still plow their field as usual. In many instances, a change of rule did not greatly affect the lives of ordinary people. *(Archaeological site, Luxor/Erich Lessing/Art Resource, NY)*

**Nubian Pyramids** The Nubians adopted many aspects of Egyptian culture and customs. The pyramids shown here are not as magnificent as their Egyptian predecessors, but they served the same purpose of honoring the dead king. Their core was constructed of bricks, which were then covered with stone blocks. At the doors of the pyramids stood monumental gates to the interiors of the tombs. *(Michael Yamashita)*

Egyptian deities. Egyptian religion penetrated as far south as Ethiopia.

One of the sturdy peoples who rose to prominence were the Phoenicians, a Semitic-speaking people who had long inhabited several cities along the coast of modern Lebanon. They had lived under the shadow of the Hittites and Egyptians, but in this period the Phoenicians enjoyed full independence. Unlike the Philistine newcomers, who turned from seafaring to farming, the Phoenicians took to the sea and became outstanding merchants and explorers. They played a predominate role in international trade, manufacturing many goods. The most valued products were purple and blue textiles, from which originated their Greek name, Phoenicians, meaning **"Purple People."** They also worked metals, which they shipped processed or as ore. They imported rare goods and materials from Persia in the East and from their neighbors to the south. Their exported wares went to Egypt, as far west as North Africa and Spain, and even into the Atlantic. The variety and quality of their exports generally made them welcome visitors. Although their goal was trade, not colonization, they nevertheless founded Carthage in 813 B.C.E., a city that would one day struggle with Rome for domination of the western

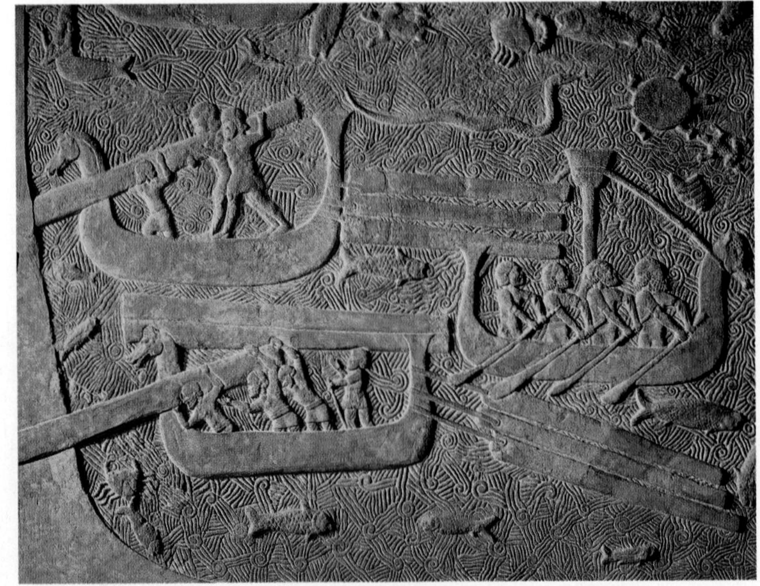

**Phoenician Maritime Trade** In this Assyrian relief dating from the eighth century B.C.E., Phoenician ships tow hewn logs for building purposes to a foreign port. Phoenician ships like these not only plied the eastern Aegean but also ventured into the western Mediterranean. *(Louvre/Erich Lessing/Art Resource, NY)*

# INDIVIDUALS IN SOCIETY

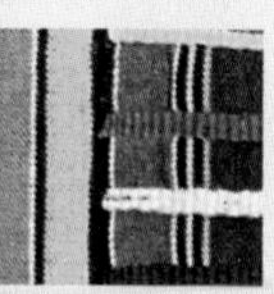

## WEN-AMON

Surprising as it may sound, the life of a bureaucrat is not always easy. Wen-Amon, an official of the temple of Amon-Ra at Karnak in Egypt, learned that on an authorized mission to Phoenicia. He left his own narrative of his travels, which date to sometime in the eleventh century B.C.E. Egypt, the shattered kingdom, could no longer exert the authority that it had enjoyed under the pharaohs of the New Kingdom. Despite this political disruption, Egyptian officials continued to expect the traditional respect of the people whom they called "Asiatics." These Asiatics, however, had begun to doubt the power of Egypt and expressed their independence by openly opposing its authority.

Wen-Amon personally experienced this changed atmosphere when he was sent to Byblos in Phoenicia to obtain lumber for Amon-Ra's ceremonial barge. Wen-Amon's detailed account of his experiences comes in the form of an official report to the chief priest of the temple.

Entrusted with ample funds in silver to pay for the lumber, Wen-Amon set out on his voyage. He docked at Dor, in modern Israel, which was independent of the pharaoh, but the local prince received him graciously. While his ship was at anchor, one of Wen-Amon's own sailors vanished with the silver. Wen-Amon immediately reported the robbery to the prince and demanded that he investigate the theft. Wen-Amon pointed out that the silver belonged to Amon-Ra and the great men of Egypt. The prince flatly told Wen-Amon that he did not care whether Wen-Amon and the others were important men. He pointed out that an Egyptian, one of Wen-Amon's own men, had stolen the silver. It was not the prince's problem. No earlier Asian prince would have dared speak to a high Egyptian official in such terms.

Although rebuffed, Wen-Amon found a ship from Byblos and robbed it of an equivalent amount of silver. When he left Dor and entered the harbor of Byblos, the prince there, who had learned of the theft, ordered him to leave. For twenty-nine days there was an impasse. Each day that Wen-Amon remained, the prince told him to get out, but respect both for the great days of Egypt and for Amon-Ra kept the prince from laying hands on Wen-Amon. Finally, the prince sent for Wen-Amon and asked for his papers. A heated argument ensued, with the prince shouting, "I am not your servant. I am not the servant of him who sent you either." Then he asked Wen-Amon what silly voyage he was making. By this time the Egyptian was greatly annoyed, and he reminded the prince of the greatness of Amon-Ra. He flatly stated that unless the prince honored the great god, he and his land would have neither health nor prosperity. When the two calmed down, the prince agreed to send the timber to Egypt.

*Pillars of the great temple of Amon at Karnak, New Kingdom.* (Marc Bernheim/Woodfin Camp & Associates)

After the timber was loaded aboard his ship, Wen-Amon saw eleven enemy ships entering the harbor. They anchored, and those in charge reported to the prince of Byblos that they had come for the Egyptians. He refused to hand them over, saying that he would never arrest a messenger of Amon-Ra. He agreed, however, to send Wen-Amon away first and allow the enemy ships to pursue the Egyptians. Stormy seas blew the Egyptian ship into Hittite territory. When Wen-Amon landed there, Queen Heteb granted him protection and asylum.

The papyrus breaks off at this point, but it is obvious that Wen-Amon weathered his various storms to return safely to Egypt. The document illustrates the presumption of power by Wen-Amon and his bluster at the lack of respect shown him. It also shows how Egypt's neighbors no longer feared Egyptian power. Finally, it illustrates the impact of Egyptian culture and religion on the peoples living along the coast of the Levant. Although Egyptian political power was in eclipse, its cultural legacy endured.

### QUESTIONS FOR ANALYSIS

1. What do Wen-Amon's experiences tell us about political conditions in the eastern Mediterranean?
2. Since Wen-Amon could no longer depend upon the majesty of Egypt for respect, how did he fulfill his duty?

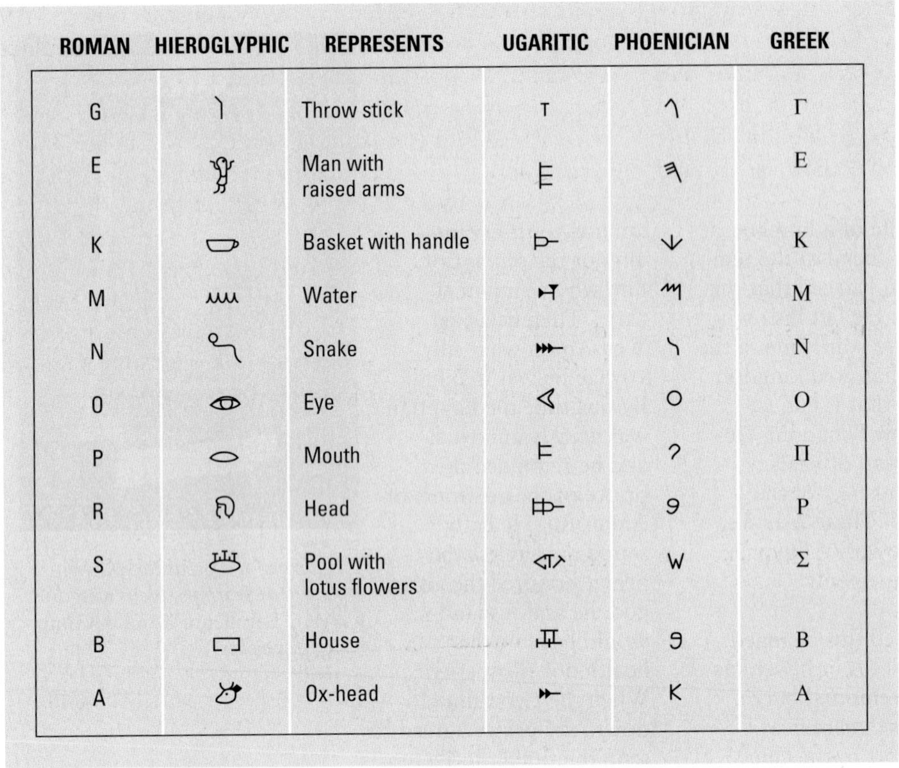

| ROMAN | HIEROGLYPHIC | REPRESENTS | UGARITIC | PHOENICIAN | GREEK |
|---|---|---|---|---|---|
| G | 𓌙 | Throw stick | 𐎂 | 𐤂 | Γ |
| E | 𓀠 | Man with raised arms | 𐎅 | 𐤄 | E |
| K | 𓎡 | Basket with handle | 𐎋 | 𐤊 | K |
| M | 𓈖 | Water | 𐎎 | 𐤌 | M |
| N | 𓆓 | Snake | 𐎐 | 𐤍 | N |
| O | 𓁹 | Eye | 𐎓 | 𐤏 | O |
| P | 𓂋 | Mouth | 𐎔 | 𐤐 | Π |
| R | 𓁶 | Head | 𐎗 | 𐤓 | P |
| S | 𓆷 | Pool with lotus flowers | 𐎌 | 𐤔 | Σ |
| B | 𓉐 | House | 𐎁 | 𐤁 | B |
| A | 𓃾 | Ox-head | 𐎀 | 𐤀 | A |

**FIGURE 2.1 Origins of the Alphabet** List of Roman, hieroglyphic, Ugaritic, Phoenician, and Greek sign forms. *(Source: A. B. Knapp,* The History and Culture of Ancient Western Asia and Egypt, *Dorsey Press, Chicago, 1988, p. 191. Reprinted by permission of Wadsworth, a division of Thomson Learning.)*

Mediterranean. Their voyages naturally brought them into contact with the Greeks, to whom they introduced the older cultures of the Near East. Indeed, their enduring significance lay in their spreading the experiences of the East throughout the western Mediterranean.

Phoenician culture was urban, based on the prosperous commercial centers of Tyre, Sidon, and Byblos. The Phoenicians' overwhelming cultural achievement was the development of an alphabet (see Figure 2.1): they, unlike other literate peoples, used one letter to designate one sound, a system that vastly simplified writing and reading. The Greeks modified this alphabet and then used it to write their own language.

## THE CHILDREN OF ISRAEL

The fall of the Hittite Empire and Egypt's collapse created a vacuum of power in the western Near East that allowed for the rise of numerous small states. South of Phoenicia arose a small kingdom, the land of the ancient Jews or Hebrews. It is difficult to say precisely who the Hebrews were and what brought them to this area, because virtually the only source for much of their history is the Bible, which is essentially a religious document. Even though it contains much historical material, it also contains many Hebrew myths and legends. Moreover, it was compiled at different times, with the earliest parts dating to between about 950 and 800 B.C.E.

Earlier Mesopotamian and Egyptian sources refer to people called the **Hapiru,** which seems to mean homeless, independent **nomads.** These nomads led roaming lives, always in search of pasturage for their flocks. According to Hebrew tradition, the followers of Abraham migrated from Mesopotamia, but Egyptian documents record Hapiru already in Syria and Palestine in the second millennium B.C.E. The Hebrews were probably a part of them. Together with other seminomadic peoples, they probably migrated into the Nile Delta seeking good land. According to the Bible the Egyptians enslaved them. One group, however, under the leadership of Moses, perhaps a semimythical figure, left Egypt in what the Hebrews remembered as the Exodus. From Egypt they wandered in the Sinai Peninsula, until they settled in Palestine in the thirteenth century B.C.E.

In Palestine the Hebrews encountered the Philistines; the Amorites, relatives of Hammurabi's Babylonians; and the Semitic-speaking Canaanites. Despite numerous wars, contact between the Hebrews and their new neighbors was not always hostile. The Hebrews freely mingled with the Canaanites, and some went so far as to worship **Baal,** an ancient Semitic fertility god represented as a golden calf. Archaeological research supports the biblical account of these developments. In 1990 an expedition sponsored by Harvard University discovered a statue of a golden calf in its excavations of Ashkelon in modern Israel. Despite the anger expressed in the Bible over Hebrew worship of Baal, there is nothing surprising about the phenomenon. Once again, newcomers adapted themselves to the culture of an older, well-established people.

The greatest danger to the Hebrews came from the Philistines, whose superior technology and military organization at first made them invincible. In Saul (ca 1000 B.C.E.), a farmer of the tribe of Benjamin, the Hebrews found a champion and a spirited leader. In the biblical account Saul carried the war to the Philistines, often without success. Yet in the meantime he established a monarchy over the twelve Hebrew tribes.

Saul's work was carried on by David of Bethlehem, who in his youth had followed Saul into battle against the Philistines. Through courage and cunning, David pushed back the Philistines and waged war against his other neighbors. To give his kingdom a capital, he captured the city of Jerusalem, which he enlarged, fortified, and made the religious and political center of his realm. David's military successes won the Hebrews unprecedented security, and his forty-year reign was a period of vitality and political consolidation. His work in consolidating the monarchy and enlarging the kingdom paved the way for his son Solomon.

Solomon (ca 965–925 B.C.E.) applied his energies to creating a nation out of a collection of tribes ruled by a king. He divided the kingdom into twelve territorial districts cutting across the old tribal borders. To bring his kingdom up to the level of its more sophisticated neighbors, he set about a building program to make Israel a respectable Near Eastern state. Work was begun on a magnificent temple in Jerusalem and on cities, palaces, fortresses, and roads. Solomon dedicated the temple in grand style and made it the home of the Ark of the Covenant, the cherished chest that contained the holiest of Hebrew religious articles. The temple in Jerusalem was intended to be the religious heart of the kingdom and the symbol of Hebrew unity. Solomon turned a rude kingdom into a state with broad commercial horizons and greater knowledge of the outside world. At his death, the Hebrews broke into two political halves (see Map 2.1). The northern part of the kingdom of David and Solomon became Israel, with its capital at Samaria. The southern half was Judah, and Jerusalem remained its center. With political division went a religious rift: Israel, the northern kingdom, established rival sanctuaries for gods other than Yahweh. The Hebrew nation was divided, but at least it was divided into two far more sophisticated political units than before the time of Solomon. Nonetheless, war soon broke out between them, as recorded in the Bible. Unexpected and independent evidence of this warfare came to light in August 1993, when an Israeli archaeologist found an inscription that refers to the "House of David," the royal line of Israel. The stone celebrates an Israelite victory from the early ninth century B.C.E. This discovery is the first mention of King David's royal family outside

**The Golden Calf** According to the Hebrew Bible, Moses descended from Mount Sinai, where he had received the Ten Commandments, to find the Hebrews worshiping a golden calf, which was against Yahweh's laws. In July 1990 an American archaeological team found this model of a gilded calf inside a pot. The figurine, which dates to about 1550 B.C.E., is strong evidence for the existence of the cult represented by the calf in Palestine. *(Courtesy of the Leon Levy Expedition to Ashkelon. Photo: Carl Andrews)*

**Megiddo** This aerial view shows the substantial fortress of Megiddo, in modern Israel, which was a stronghold on the frontiers of Syria and Egypt. Standing atop a small plateau, it was heavily fortified and commanded a fertile plain. It also stood astride the major road between Egypt and the north, making it strategically valuable. It was the scene of a major battle in which the Egyptians routed a Canaanite army. *(Rolf Michael Kneller)*

the Bible and helps to confirm the biblical account of the fighting between the two kingdoms.

Eventually, the northern kingdom of Israel was wiped out by the Assyrians, but the southern kingdom of Judah survived numerous calamities until the Babylonians crushed it in 587 B.C.E. The survivors were sent into exile in Babylonia, a period commonly known as the **Babylonian Captivity.** In 538 B.C.E. the Persians, under their king, Cyrus the Great, permitted some forty thousand exiles to return to Jerusalem. During and especially after the Babylonian Captivity, the exiles redefined their beliefs and practices, and thus established what they believed was the law of Yahweh. Those who lived by these precepts can be called *Jews*.

## The Evolution of Jewish Religion

Hand in hand with their political evolution from fierce nomads to urban dwellers, the Hebrews were evolving spiritual ideas that still permeate Western society. Their chief literary product, the Hebrew Bible, has fundamentally influenced both Christianity and Islam and still exerts a compelling force on the modern world.

Fundamental to an understanding of Jewish religion is the concept of the **Covenant,** a formal agreement between Yahweh and the Hebrew people. According to the Bible, the god **Yahweh,** who in medieval Latin became "Jehovah," appeared to Moses on Mount Sinai. There Yahweh made a covenant with the Hebrews that was in fact a contract: if the Hebrews worshiped Yahweh as their only god, he would consider them his chosen people and protect them from their enemies. The Hebrews believed that Yahweh had led them out of bondage in Egypt and had helped them to conquer their new land, the Promised Land. In return, the Hebrews worshiped Yahweh alone and obeyed his Ten Commandments, an ethical code of conduct revealed to them by Moses.

At first Yahweh was probably viewed as no more than the god of the Hebrews, who sometimes faced competition from Baal and other gods in Palestine. Enlil, Marduk, Amon-Ra, and the others sufficed for foreigners. In time, however, the Hebrews came to regard Yahweh as the only god. This was the beginning of true monotheism.

Unlike Akhenaten's monotheism, Hebrew monotheism became the religion of a whole people, deeply felt and cherished. Some might fall away from Yahweh's worship, and various holy men had to exhort the Hebrews to honor the Covenant, but on the whole the people clung to Yahweh. Yet the Hebrews did not consider it their duty to spread the belief in the one god, as later Christians did. As the chosen people, their chief duty was to maintain the worship of Yahweh as he demanded. That worship was embodied in the Ten Commandments, which forbade the Hebrews to steal, murder, lie, or commit adultery. The Covenant was a constant force in Hebrew life (see the feature "Listening to the Past: The Covenant Between Yahweh and the Hebrews" on pages 50–51), and the Old Testament records one occasion when the entire nation formally reaffirmed it:

*And the king [of the Jews] stood by a pillar, and made a covenant before the lord, to walk after the lord, and to keep his commandments and his testimonies and his statutes with all their heart and all their soul, to perform the words of this covenant that were written in this book [Deuteronomy]. And all the people stood to the covenant.*[2]

From the Ten Commandments evolved Hebrew law, a code of law and custom originating with Moses and built on by priests and prophets. The earliest part of this code, the **Torah** or Mosaic law, was often as harsh as Hammurabi's code, which had a powerful impact on it. Later tradition, largely the work of prophets who lived from the eleventh to the fifth centuries B.C.E., was more humanitarian. The work of the prophet Jeremiah (ca 626 B.C.E.) exemplifies this gentler spirit. According to Jeremiah, Yahweh demanded righteousness from his people and protection for the weak and helpless.

The uniqueness of this phenomenon can be seen by comparing the essence of Hebrew monotheism with the religious outlook of the Mesopotamians. Whereas the Mesopotamians considered their gods capricious, the Hebrews knew what Yahweh expected. The Hebrews believed that their god would protect them and make them prosper if they obeyed his commandments. The Mesopotamians thought human beings insignificant compared to the gods, so insignificant that the gods might even be indifferent to them. The Hebrews, too, considered themselves puny in comparison to Yahweh. Yet they were Yahweh's chosen people, whom he had promised never to abandon. Finally, though the Mesopotamians believed that the gods generally preferred good to evil, their religion did not demand ethical conduct. The Hebrews could please their god only by living up to high moral standards as well as worshiping him.

## Daily Life in Israel

The nomadic Hebrews first entered modern Palestine as tribes, numerous families who thought of themselves as all related to one another. At first, good farmland, pastureland, and water spots were held in common by the tribe. Common use of land was—and still is—characteristic of nomadic peoples. Typically each family or group of families in the tribe drew lots every year to determine who worked which fields. But as formerly nomadic peoples turned increasingly to settled agriculture, communal use of land gave way to family ownership. In this respect the experience of the ancient Hebrews seems typical of that of many early peoples. Slowly the shift from nomad to farmer affected far more than just how people fed themselves. Family relationships reflected evolving circumstances. With the transition to settled agriculture, the tribe gradually became less important than the extended family. With the advent of village life and finally full-blown urban life, the extended family in turn gave way to the nuclear family.

For women, however, the evolution of Jewish society led to less freedom of action, especially in religious life. At first women served as priestesses in festivals and religious cults. Some were considered prophetesses of Yahweh, although they never conducted his official rituals. In the course of time, however, the worship of Yahweh became more male-oriented and male-dominated. Increasingly, he also became the god of holiness, and to worship him people must be pure in mind and body. Women were seen as ritually impure because of menstruation and childbirth. Because of these "impurities," women now played a much reduced role in religion. Even when they did participate in religious rites, they were segregated from the men. For the most part, women were largely confined to the home and the care of the family.

Marriage was one of the most important and joyous events in Hebrew family life. The typical marriage in ancient Israel was monogamous, and a virtuous wife was revered and honored.

As in most other societies, in ancient Israel the early education of children was in the mother's hands. She taught her children right from wrong and gave them their first instruction in the moral values of society. As boys grew older, they received education from their fathers in religion and the history of their people. Many children were taught to read and write, and the head of each family was probably able to write. Fathers also taught sons the family craft or trade. Boys soon learned that inattention could be painful, for Jewish custom advised fathers to be strict: "He that spareth his rod hateth his son: but he that loveth him chasteneth him betimes."[3]

The land was precious to the family, not simply because it provided a living, but also because it was a link to the past. Ironically, the success of the first Hebrew kings endangered the future of many family farms. With peace, more settled conditions, and increasing prosperity, some Jews began to amass larger holdings by buying out poor and struggling farmers. Far from discouraging this development, the kings created their own huge estates. In many cases slaves, both Jewish and foreign, worked these large farms and estates shoulder to shoulder with paid free men. In still later times, rich landowners rented plots of land to poor, free families; the landowners provided the renters with seed and livestock and normally took half the yield as rent. Although many Bible prophets denounced the destruction of the family farm, the trend continued toward large estates that were worked by slaves and hired free men.

The development of urban life among the Jews created new economic opportunities, especially in crafts and trades. People specialized in certain occupations, such as milling flour, baking bread, making pottery, weaving, and carpentry. All these crafts were family trades. Sons worked with their father, daughters with their mother. If the business prospered, the family might be assisted by a few paid workers or slaves. The practitioners of a craft usually lived in a particular section of town, a custom still prevalent in the Middle East today. Commerce and trade developed later than crafts. Trade with neighboring countries was handled by foreigners, usually Phoenicians. Jews dealt mainly in local trade, and in most instances craftsmen and farmers sold directly to their customers.

These social and economic developments also left their mark on daily life by prompting the compilation of two significant works, the Torah and the Talmud. The Torah is basically the Mosaic law, or the first five books of the Bible. The Talmud is a later work composed during the period between the Roman destruction of the second temple in 70 C.E. to the Arab conquest of 636 C.E. The **Talmud** records civil and ceremonial law and Jewish legend. The dietary rules of the Jews provide an excellent example of both the relationship between the Torah and the Talmud and their effect on ordinary life and culture. According to the Torah, people were not to eat meat that they found in the field. This very sensible prohibition protected them from eating dangerous food. Yet if meat from the countryside could not be eaten, some rules were needed for meat in the city. The solution found in the Talmud was a set of regulations for the proper way to conduct ritual slaughter. Together these two works regulated and codified Jewish dietary customs.

## ASSYRIA, THE MILITARY MONARCHY

Small kingdoms like those of the Phoenicians and the Hebrews could exist only in the absence of a major power. The beginning of the ninth century B.C.E. saw the rise of such a power: the Assyrians of northern Mesopotamia, whose chief capital was at Nineveh on the Tigris River. The Assyrians were a Semitic-speaking people heavily influenced, like so many other peoples of the Near East, by the Mesopotamian culture of Babylon to the south. They were also one of the most warlike peoples in history, largely because throughout their history they were threatened by neighboring folk. Living in an open, exposed land, the Assyrians experienced frequent and devastating attacks by the wild, war-loving tribes to their north and east and by the Babylonians to the south. The constant threat to survival experienced by the Assyrians promoted political cohesion and military might. Yet they were also a mercantile people who had long pursued commerce with both the Babylonians in the south and other peoples in the north.

### The Power of Assyria

For over two hundred years the Assyrians labored to dominate the Near East. In 859 B.C.E. the new Assyrian king, Shalmaneser, unleashed the first of a long series of attacks on the peoples of Syria and Palestine. Year after relentless year, Assyrian armies hammered at the peoples of the West. These ominous events inaugurated two turbulent centuries marked by Assyrian military campaigns, constant efforts by Syria and the two Jewish kingdoms to maintain or recover their independence, and eventual Assyrian conquest

**Surrender of the Jews** The Jewish king Jahu finally surrendered to the Assyrians. Here his envoy kneels before the Assyrian king Shalmaneser III in total defeat. Although the Assyrian king treated Jahu well, his people were led off into slavery. *(British Museum/ Michael Holford)*

of Babylonia and northern Egypt. In addition, periodic political instability occurred in Assyria itself, which prompted stirrings of freedom throughout the Near East.

Under the Assyrian kings Tiglath-pileser III (774–727 B.C.E.) and Sargon II (r. 721–705 B.C.E.), both mighty warriors, the Near East trembled as never before under the blows of Assyrian armies. The Assyrians stepped up their attacks on Anatolia, Syria, and Palestine. The kingdom of Israel and many other states fell; others, like the kingdom of Judah, became subservient to the warriors from the Tigris. In 717 to 716 B.C.E., Sargon led his army in a sweeping attack along the Philistine coast, where he defeated the pharaoh. Sargon also lashed out at Assyria's traditional enemies to the north and then turned south against a renewed threat in Babylonia. By means of almost constant warfare, Tiglath-pileser III and Sargon carved out an Assyrian empire that stretched from east and north of the Tigris River to central Egypt (see Map 2.2). Revolt

**Siege of a City** Art here serves to glorify horror. The Assyrian king Tiglath-pileser III launches an assault on a fortified city. The impaled bodies shown at center demonstrate the cruelty of Assyrian warfare. Also noticeable are the various weapons and means of attack used against the city. *(Courtesy of the Trustees of the British Museum)*

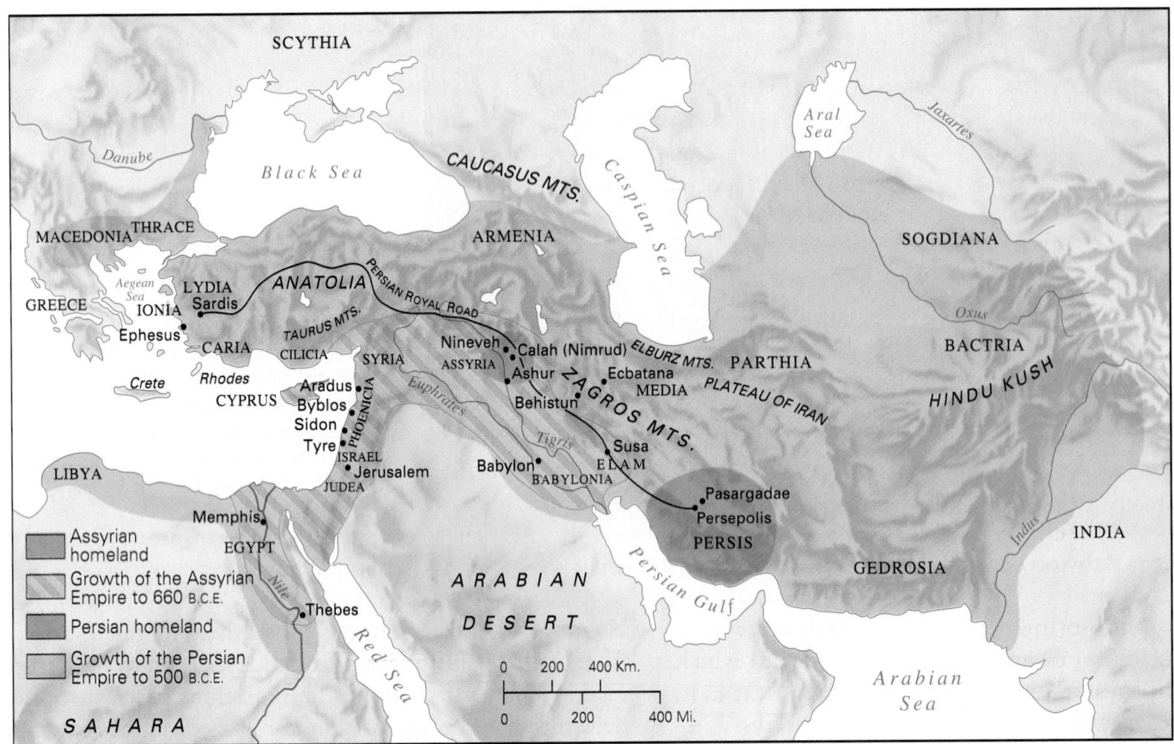


**MAP 2.2 The Assyrian and Persian Empires** The Assyrian Empire at its height (ca 650 B.C.E.) included almost all of the old centers of power in the ancient Near East. By 513 B.C.E., however, the Persian Empire not only included more of that area but also extended as far east as western India. With the rise of the Medes and Persians, the balance of power in the Near East shifted east of Mesopotamia for the first time.

against the Assyrians inevitably promised the rebels bloody battles and cruel sieges.

Though atrocity and terrorism struck unspeakable fear into Assyria's subjects, Assyria's success was actually due to sophisticated, farsighted, and effective military organization. By Sargon's time the Assyrians had invented the mightiest military machine the ancient Near East had ever seen. The mainstay of the Assyrian army was the infantryman armed with spear and sword and protected by helmet and armor. The Assyrian army also featured archers, some on foot, others on horseback, still others in chariots—the latter ready to wield lances once they had expended their supply of arrows. Some infantry archers wore heavy armor. These soldiers served as a primitive field artillery, whose job was to sweep the enemy's walls of defenders so that others could storm the defenses. Slingers also served as artillery in pitched battles. For mobility on the battlefield, the Assyrians organized a corps of chariots.

Assyrian military genius was remarkable for the development of a wide variety of siege machinery and techniques, including excavation to undermine city walls and battering rams to knock down walls and gates. Never before in the Near East had anyone applied such technical knowledge to warfare. The Assyrians even invented the concept of a corps of engineers, who bridged rivers with pontoons or provided soldiers with inflatable skins for swimming. And the Assyrians knew how to coordinate their efforts, both in open battle and in siege warfare. King Sennacherib's account of his siege of Jerusalem in 701 B.C.E. is a vivid portrait of the Assyrian war machine:

*As to Hezekiah, the Jew, he did not submit to my yoke, I laid siege to 46 of his strong cities, walled forts and to the countless small villages in their vicinity, and conquered them by means of well-stamped earth-ramps, and battering rams brought thus near to the walls combined with the attack by foot soldiers, using mines, breaches as well as sapper work. . . . Himself I made prisoner in Jerusalem, his royal residence, like a bird in a cage. I surrounded him with earthwork in order to molest those who were leaving his city's gate.*[4]

## Assyrian Rule and Culture

Not only did the Assyrians know how to win battles, but they also knew how to use their victories. As early as the reign of Tiglath-pileser III, the Assyrian kings began to organize their conquered territories into an empire. The lands closest to Assyria became provinces governed by Assyrian officials. Kingdoms beyond the provinces were not annexed but became dependent states that followed Assyria's lead. The Assyrian king chose their rulers either by regulating the succession of native kings or by supporting native kings who appealed to him. Against more distant states the Assyrian kings waged frequent war in order to conquer them outright or make the dependent states secure.

In the seventh century B.C.E. Assyrian power seemed firmly established. Yet the downfall of Assyria was swift and complete. Babylon finally won its independence in 626 B.C.E. and joined forces with a newly aggressive people, the Medes, an Indo-European-speaking folk from Iran. Together the Babylonians and the Medes destroyed the Assyrian Empire in 612 B.C.E., paving the way for the rise of the Persians. The Hebrew prophet Nahum spoke for many when he asked: "Nineveh is laid waste: who will bemoan her?"[5] Their cities destroyed and their power shattered, the Assyrians disappeared from history, remembered only as a cruel people of the Old Testament who oppressed the Hebrews. Two hundred years later, when the Greek adventurer and historian Xenophon passed by the ruins of Nineveh, he marveled at the extent of the former city but knew nothing of the Assyrians. The glory of their empire was forgotten.

Yet modern archaeology has brought the Assyrians out of obscurity. In 1839 the intrepid English archaeologist and traveler A. H. Layard began the most noteworthy excavations of Nineveh, then a mound of debris beside the Tigris. His findings electrified the world. Layard's workers unearthed masterpieces, including monumental sculpted figures—huge winged bulls, human-headed lions, and sphinxes—as well as brilliantly sculpted friezes. Equally valuable were the numerous Assyrian cuneiform documents, which ranged from royal accounts of mighty military campaigns to simple letters by common people.

Among the most renowned of Layard's finds were the Assyrian palace reliefs, whose number was increased by the discoveries of twentieth-century archaeologists. Assyrian kings delighted in scenes of war, which their artists depicted in graphic detail. By the time of Ashurbanipal (r. 668–633 B.C.E.), Assyrian artists had hit on the idea of portraying a series of episodes—in fact, a visual narrative of

**Royal Lion Hunt** This relief from the palace of Ashurbanipal at Nineveh, which shows the king fighting a lion, is a typical representation of the energy and artistic brilliance of Assyrian sculptors. The lion hunt, portrayed in a series of episodes, was a favorite theme of Assyrian palace reliefs. *(Courtesy of the Trustees of the British Museum)*

events that had actually taken place. Scene followed scene in a continuous frieze, so that the viewer could follow the progress of a military campaign from the time the army marched out until the enemy was conquered.

Assyrian art fared better than Assyrian military power. The techniques of Assyrian artists influenced the Persians, who adapted them to gentler scenes. In fact, many Assyrian innovations, military and political as well as artistic, were taken over wholesale by the Persians. Although the memory of Assyria was hateful throughout the Near East, the fruits of Assyrian organizational genius helped enable the Persians to bring peace and stability to the same regions where Assyrian armies had spread terror.

## THE EMPIRE OF THE PERSIAN KINGS

Like the Hittites before them, the Iranians were Indo-Europeans from central Europe and southern Russia. They migrated into the land to which they have given their name, the area between the Caspian Sea and the Persian Gulf. Like the Hittites, they then fell under the spell of the more sophisticated cultures of their Mesopotamian neighbors. Yet the Iranians went on to create one of the greatest empires of antiquity, one that encompassed scores of peoples and cultures. The Persians, the most important of the Iranian peoples, had a farsighted conception of empire. Though as conquerors they willingly used force to accomplish their ends, they normally preferred to depend on diplomacy to rule. They usually respected their subjects and allowed them to practice their native customs and religions. Thus the Persians gave the Near East both political unity and cultural diversity. Never before had Near Eastern people viewed empire in such intelligent and humane terms.

### The Land of Mountains and Plateau

Persia—the modern country of Iran—is a stark land of towering mountains and flaming deserts, with a broad central plateau in the heart of the country (see Map 2.2). Iran stretches from the Caspian Sea in the north to the Persian Gulf in the south. Between the Tigris-Euphrates Valley in the west and the Indus Valley in the east rises an immense plateau, surrounded on all sides by lofty mountains that cut off the interior from the sea.

At the center of the plateau lies an enormous depression—a forbidding region devoid of water and vegetation, so glowing hot in summer that it is virtually impossible to cross. This depression forms two distinct grim and burning salt deserts, perhaps the most desolate spots on earth.

Iran's geographical position and topography explain its traditional role as the highway between East and West. Throughout history wild, nomadic peoples migrating from the broad steppes of Russia and Central Asia have streamed into Iran. The very harshness of the geography urged them to continue in search of new and more hospitable lands. Confronting the uncrossable salt deserts, most have turned either eastward or westward, moving on until they reached the advanced and wealthy urban centers of Mesopotamia and India. When cities emerged along the natural lines of East-West communication, Iran became the area where nomads met urban dwellers, a meeting ground of unique significance for the civilizations of both East and West.

### The Coming of the Medes and Persians

The Iranians entered this land around 1000 B.C.E. They were part of the vast movement of Indo-European-speaking peoples whose wanderings led them into Europe, the Near East, and India in many successive waves (see page 22). These Iranians were nomads who migrated with their flocks and herds. Like their kinsmen the Aryans, who moved into India, they were also horse breeders, and the horse gave them a decisive military advantage over the prehistoric peoples of Iran. The Iranians rode into battle in horse-drawn chariots or on horseback and easily swept the natives before them. Yet, because the influx of Iranians went on for centuries, there continued to be constant cultural interchange between conquering newcomers and conquered natives.

The Iranians initially created a patchwork of tiny kingdoms, of which Siyalk was one. The chieftain or petty king was basically a warlord who depended on fellow warriors for aid and support. This band of noble warriors formed the fighting strength of the army. The king owned estates that supported him and his nobles; for additional income the king levied taxes, which were paid in kind and not in cash. He also demanded labor services from the peasants. Below the king and his warrior nobles were free people who held land and others who owned nothing. Artisans produced the various goods needed to keep society running. At the bottom of the social scale were slaves—probably both natives and newcomers—to whom fell the drudgery of hard labor and household service to king and nobles.

Gradually two groups of Iranians began coalescing into larger units. The Persians had settled in Persia, the modern region of Fars, in southern Iran. Their kinsmen the Medes occupied Media in the north, with their capital at

Ecbatana, the modern Hamadan. The Medes were exposed to attack by nomads from the north, but their greatest threat was the frequent raids of the Assyrian army. Even though distracted by grave pressures from their neighbors, the Medes united under one king around 710 B.C.E. and extended their control over the Persians in the south. In 612 B.C.E. the Medes were strong enough to join the Babylonians in overthrowing the Assyrian Empire. With the rise of the Medes, the balance of power in the Near East shifted for the first time east of Mesopotamia.

## The Creation of the Persian Empire

In 550 B.C.E. Cyrus the Great (r. 559–530 B.C.E.), king of the Persians and one of the most remarkable statesmen of antiquity, threw off the yoke of the Medes by conquering them and turning their country into his first *satrapy,* or province. In the space of a single lifetime, Cyrus created one of the greatest empires of antiquity. Two characteristics lift Cyrus above the common level of warrior-kings. First, he thought of Iran, not just Persia and Media, as a state. His concept has survived a long, complex, and often turbulent history to play its part in the contemporary world.

Second, Cyrus held an enlightened view of empire. Many of the civilizations and cultures that fell to his armies were, he realized, far older, more advanced, and more sophisticated than his. Free of the narrow-minded snobbery of the Egyptians, the religious exclusiveness of the Hebrews, and the calculated cruelty of the Assyrians, Cyrus gave Near Eastern peoples and their cultures his respect, toleration, and protection. Conquered peoples continued to enjoy their institutions, religions, languages, and ways of life under the Persians. The Persian Empire, which Cyrus created, became a political organization sheltering many different civilizations. To rule such a vast area and so many diverse peoples demanded talent, intelligence, sensitivity, and a cosmopolitan view of the world. These qualities Cyrus and many of his successors possessed in abundance. Though the Persians were sometimes harsh, especially with those who rebelled against them, they were for the most part enlightened rulers. Consequently, the Persians gave the ancient Near East over two hundred years of peace, prosperity, and security.

Cyrus showed his magnanimity at the outset of his career. Once the Medes had fallen to him, Cyrus united them with his Persians. Persepolis became a Persian seat of power. Medes were honored with important military and political posts and thenceforth helped the Persians to rule the expanding empire. Cyrus's conquest of the Medes resulted not in slavery and slaughter but in the union of Iranian peoples.

With Iran united, Cyrus looked at the broader world. He set out to achieve two goals. First, he wanted to win control of the west and thus of the terminal ports of the great trade routes that crossed Iran and Anatolia. Second, Cyrus strove to secure eastern Iran from the pressure of nomadic invaders. In 550 B.C.E. neither goal was easy to accomplish. To the northwest was the young

**Tomb of Cyrus** For all of his greatness Cyrus retained a sense of perspective. His tomb, though monumental in size, is rather simple and unostentatious. Greek writers reported that it bore the following epitaph: "O man, I am Cyrus the son of Cambyses. I established the Persian Empire and was king of Asia. Do not begrudge me my memorial." *(The Oriental Institute, University of Chicago)*

kingdom of Lydia in Anatolia, whose king Croesus was proverbial for his wealth. To the west was Babylonia, enjoying a new period of power now that the Assyrian Empire had been crushed. To the southwest was Egypt, still weak but sheltered behind its bulwark of sand and sea. To the east ranged tough, mobile nomads, capable of massive and destructive incursions deep into Iranian territory.

Cyrus turned first to Croesus's Lydian kingdom, which fell to him around 546 B.C.E. He established a garrison at Sardis, the capital of Lydia, and ordered his generals to subdue the Greek cities along the coast of Anatolia. Cyrus had thus gained the important ports that looked out to the Mediterranean world. In addition, for the first time the Persians came into direct contact with the Greeks, a people with whom their later history was to be intimately connected.

From Lydia, Cyrus next marched to the far eastern corners of Iran. In a brilliant campaign he conquered the regions of Parthia and Bactria. All of Iran was now Persian, from Mesopotamia in the west to the western slopes of the Hindu Kush in the east. In 540 B.C.E. Cyrus moved against Babylonia, now isolated from outside help. When Persian soldiers marched quietly into Babylon the next year, the Babylonians welcomed Cyrus as a liberator. Cyrus won the hearts of the Babylonians with humane treatment, toleration of their religion, and support of their efforts to refurbish their capital.

Cyrus was equally generous toward the Jews. He allowed them to return to Palestine, from which they had been deported by the Babylonians. He protected them, gave them back the sacred items they used in worship, and rebuilt the temple of Yahweh in Jerusalem. The Old Testament sings the praises of Cyrus, whom the Jews considered the shepherd of Yahweh, the lord's anointed. Rarely have conquered peoples shown such gratitude to their conquerors. Cyrus's benevolent policy created a Persian Empire in which the cultures and religions of its members were respected and honored. Seldom have conquerors been as wise, sensitive, and farsighted as Cyrus and his Persians.

## Thus Spake Zarathustra

Iranian religion was originally simple and primitive. **Ahuramazda**, the chief god, was the creator and benefactor of all living creatures. Yet, unlike Yahweh, he was not a lone god. The Iranians were polytheistic. Mithra, the sun-god, whose cult would later spread throughout the Roman Empire, saw to justice and redemption. Other Iranian deities personified the natural elements: moon, earth, water, and wind. As in ancient India, fire was a particularly important god. The sacred fire consumed the blood sacrifices that the early Iranians offered to all of their deities.

Early Iranian religion was close to nature and unencumbered by ponderous theological beliefs. A priestly class, the **Magi,** developed among the Medes to officiate at sacrifices, chant prayers to the gods, and tend the sacred flame. In time the Iranians built fire temples for these sacrifices. As late as the nineteenth century, fire was still worshiped in Baku, a major city on the Russian-Iranian border.

Around 600 B.C.E. the religious thinking of Zarathustra—Zoroaster, as he is better known—breathed new meaning into Iranian religion. So little is known of Zoroaster that even the date of his birth is unknown, but it cannot be earlier than around 1100 B.C.E. The most reliable information about Zoroaster comes from the *Zend Avesta,* a collection of hymns and poems, the earliest part of which treats Zoroaster and primitive Persian religion. Zoroaster preached a novel concept of divinity and human life. Life, he taught, is a constant battleground for two opposing forces, good and evil. Ahuramazda embodied good and truth but was opposed by Ahriman, a hateful spirit who stood for evil and falsehood. Ahuramazda and Ahriman were locked together in a cosmic battle for the human race, a battle that stretched over thousands of years.

Zoroaster emphasized the individual's responsibility to choose between good and evil. He taught that people possessed the free will to decide between Ahuramazda and Ahriman and that they must rely on their own conscience to guide them through life. Their decisions were crucial, Zoroaster warned, for there would be a time of reckoning. He promised that Ahuramazda would eventually triumph over evil and lies, and that at death each person would stand before the tribunal of good. Ahuramazda, like the Egyptian god Osiris, would judge whether the dead had lived righteously and on that basis would weigh their lives in the balance. In short, Zoroaster taught the concept of a Last Judgment at which Ahuramazda would decide each person's eternal fate.

In Zoroaster's thought the Last Judgment was linked to the notion of a divine kingdom after death for those who had lived according to good and truth. Liars and the wicked, denied this blessed immortality, would be condemned to eternal pain, darkness, and punishment. Thus Zoroaster preached a Last Judgment that led to a heaven or a hell.

Though tradition has it that Zoroaster's teachings originally met with opposition and coldness, his thought converted Darius (r. 521–486 B.C.E.), one of the most energetic men ever to sit on the Persian throne. The Persian royal family adopted **Zoroastrianism** but did not try

**The Impact of Zoroastrianism** The Persian kings embraced Zoroastrianism as the religion of the realm. This rock carving at Behistun records the bond. King Darius I is seen trampling on one rebel with others behind him. Above is the sign of Ahuramazda, the god of truth and guardian of the Persian king. *(Robert Harding Picture Library)*

to impose it on others. Under the protection of the Persian kings, Zoroastrianism swept through Iran, winning converts and sinking roots that sustained healthy growth for centuries. Zoroastrianism survived the fall of the Persian Empire to influence liberal Judaism, Christianity, and early Islam, largely because of its belief in an afterlife that satisfied the longings of most people. Good behavior in the world, even though unrecognized at the time, would be amply rewarded in the hereafter. Evil, no matter how powerful in life, would be punished after death. Zoroastrianism presented the ideal of a fair god who would honor the good with a happy life in heaven. It had a profound impact on Manichaeism, a religion that was to pose a significant challenge to Christianity and to spread through the Byzantine Empire. In some form or another Zoroastrian concepts still pervade the major religions of the West and every part of the world touched by Islam. A handful of the faithful still follow the teachings of Zoroaster, whose vision of divinity and human life has long outlived him.

## Persia's World Empire

Cyrus's successors rounded out the Persian conquest of the ancient Near East. In 525 B.C.E. Cyrus's son Cambyses (r. 530–522 B.C.E.) subdued Egypt. Darius (r. 521–486 B.C.E.) and his son Xerxes (r. 486–464 B.C.E.) invaded Greece but were forced to retreat (see page 116); the Persians never won a permanent foothold in Europe. Yet Darius carried Persian arms into India. Around 513 B.C.E. western India became the Persian satrapy of Hindush, which included the valley of the Indus River. Thus within thirty-seven years (550–513 B.C.E.) the Persians transformed themselves from a subject people to the rulers of an empire that included Anatolia, Egypt, Mesopotamia, Iran, and western India. They had created a **world empire** encompassing all of the oldest and most honored kingdoms and peoples of the ancient Near East. Never before had the Near East been united in one such vast political organization (see Map 2.2).

The Persians knew how to use the peace they had won on the battlefield. Unlike the Assyrians, they did not resort to royal terrorism to keep order. Like the Assyrians, however, they employed a number of bureaucratic techniques to bind the empire together. The sheer size of the empire made it impossible for one man to rule it effectively. Consequently, the Persians divided the empire into some twenty huge satrapies measuring hundreds of square miles apiece, many of them kingdoms in themselves. Each satrapy had a governor, usually drawn from the Median and Persian nobility and often a relative of the king; the governor, or **satrap,** was directly responsible to the king. Others were local dynasts subject to the Persian king. An army officer, also responsible to the

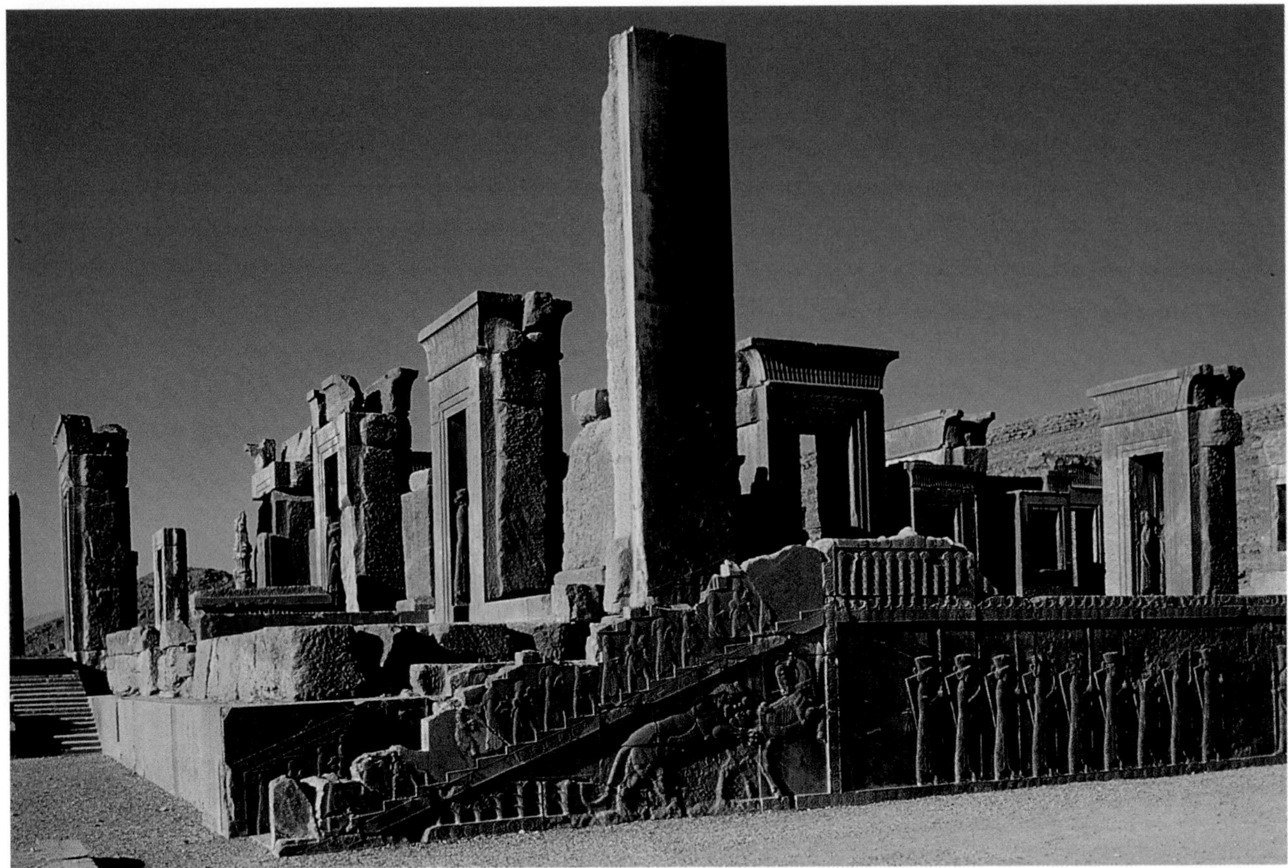

**The Royal Palace at Persepolis** King Darius began and King Xerxes finished building a grand palace worthy of the glory of the Persian Empire. Pictured here is the monumental audience hall, where the king dealt with ministers of state and foreign envoys. *(George Holton/Photo Researchers)*

king, commanded the military forces stationed in the satrapy. Still another official collected the taxes. Moreover, the king sent out royal inspectors to watch the satraps and other officials, a method of surveillance later used by the medieval king Charlemagne.

Effective rule of the empire demanded good communications. To meet this need the Persians established a network of roads. The main highway, known as the **Royal Road,** spanned some 1,677 miles from the Greek city of Ephesus on the coast of Asia Minor to Susa in western Iran. The distance was broken into 111 post stations, each equipped with fresh horses for the king's messengers. Other roads branched out to link all parts of the empire from the coast of Asia Minor to the valley of the Indus River. This system of communications enabled the Persian king to keep in intimate touch with his subjects and officials. He was able to rule efficiently, keep his ministers in line, and protect the rights of the peoples under his control.

## SUMMARY

During the centuries following the Sea Peoples' invasions, Egypt was overrun by its African neighbors, but its long and rich traditions and culture, its firmly established religion, and its administrative techniques became the heritage of these conquerors. The defeat of Egypt also led to conditions that allowed the Hebrews to create their own state. A series of strong leaders fighting hard wars won the Hebrews independence and security. In this atmosphere Hebrew religion evolved and flourished, thanks to priests, prophets, and common piety among the people. Daily life involved the transition from nomad to farmer, and people's lives revolved around the religious and agricultural year.

In the eighth century B.C.E. the Hebrews and others in the ancient Near East fell to the onslaught of Assyria, a powerful Mesopotamian kingdom. The Assyrians combined administrative skills, economic acumen, and wealth with military organization to create an aggressive military state. Yet the Assyrians' military ruthlessness and cruelty raised powerful enemies against them. The most important of these enemies were the Iranians, who created the Persian Empire. The Persians had migrated into Iran, settled the land, and entered the cultural orbit of the Near East. The result was rapid progress in culture, economic prosperity, and increase in population, which enabled them to create the largest empire yet seen in the Near East. Unlike the Assyrians, however, they ruled mildly and gave the Near East a long period of peace.

## KEY TERMS

"Purple People"
Hapiru
nomads
Baal
Babylonian Captivity
Covenant
Yahweh
Torah
Talmud
Ahuramazda
Magi
Zoroastrianism
world empire
satrap
Royal Road

## NOTES

1. James H. Breasted, *Ancient Records of Egypt,* vol. 4 (Chicago: University of Chicago Press, 1907), para. 398.
2. 2 Kings 23:3.
3. Proverbs 13:24.
4. J. B. Pritchard, ed., *Ancient Near Eastern Texts,* 3d ed. (Princeton, N.J.: Princeton University Press, 1969), p. 288.
5. Nahum 3:7.

## SUGGESTED READING

Although late Egyptian history is still largely a specialist's field, K. A. Kitchen, *The Third Intermediate Period in Egypt* (1973), is a sturdy synthesis of the period from 1100 to 650 B.C.E. D. B. Redford, *Egypt, Canaan, and Israel in Ancient Times* (1992), is an excellent study of relations among the three states. D. O'Connor, *Ancient Nubia* (1994), which is well illustrated, gives the freshest treatment of that region and points to its importance in African developments.

R. G. Morkot, *The Black Pharaohs* (2000), examines the growth of the Kushite kingdom and its rule over pharaonic Egypt in the eighth century B.C.E. G. Herm, *The Phoenicians* (1975), treats Phoenician seafaring and commercial enterprises, as does the more recent G. E. Markoe, *The Phoenicians* (2000), a fresh investigation of these sailors at home and abroad in the western Mediterranean. Similarly, M. Gil, *A History of Palestine* (1997), provides the most recent treatment of that region.

The Jews have been one of the best-studied people in the ancient world, so the reader can easily find many good treatments of Jewish history and society. A rewarding approach is J. Bartlett, ed., *Archaeology and Biblical Interpretation* (1997). More general is W. R. F. Browning, ed., *Oxford Dictionary of the Bible* (1996), which is very rich in a variety of topics. Similar is R. S. Zwi Werblowsky and G. Wigoder, eds., *The Oxford Dictionary of the Jewish Religion* (1997). For the Jews in Egypt, two good studies have appeared: J. K. Hoffmeier, *Israel in Egypt* (1997), which discusses the evidence for the authenticity of the tradition concerning the Exodus; and J. Assmann, *Moses the Egyptian* (1997), which is a study in monotheism. B. N. Porter, ed., *One God or Many?* (2000), explores the concept of monotheism in Assyrian and Jewish religion. A broader interpretation of Jewish religious developments can be found in S. Niditch, *Ancient Israelite Religion* (1997). G. Alon, *The Jews in Their Land* (1989), covers the Talmudic age. H. Shanks, ed., *The Rise of Ancient Israel* (1991), is a collection of papers that treat numerous aspects of the period. R. Tappy, *The Archaeology of Israelite Samaria* (1993), studies the archaeological remains of the period. S. Niditch, *War in the Hebrew Bible* (1992), addresses the ethics of violence in the Bible. H. W. Attridge, ed., *Of Scribes and Scrolls* (1990), gives a fascinating study of the Hebrew Bible and of Christian origins. Turning to politics, M. Smith, *Palestinian Parties and Politics That Shaped the Old Testament,* 2d ed. (1987), takes a practical look at events. W. D. Davis et al., *The Cambridge History of Judaism,* vol. 1 (1984), begins an important synthesis with work on Judaism in the Persian period. R. Hachlili, *Ancient Jewish Art and Archaeology in the Land of Israel* (1988), attempts to trace the development and meaning of Jewish art in its archaeological context.

The Assyrians, despite their achievements, have not attracted the scholarly attention that other Near Eastern peoples have. Even though woefully outdated, A. T. Olmstead, *History of Assyria* (1928), has the merit of being soundly based in the original sources. H. W. F. Saggs, *Everyday Life in Babylonia and Assyria,* rev. ed. (1987), offers a general and well-illustrated survey of Mesopotamian history from 3000 to 300 B.C.E. M. T. Larsen, *The Conquest of Assyria* (1996), gives a fascinating account of the modern discovery of the Assyrians. Those who appreciate the vitality of Assyrian art should start with the masterful work of R. D. Barnett and W. Forman, *Assyrian Palace Reliefs,* 2d ed. (1970), an exemplary combination of fine photographs and learned, but not difficult, discussion.

A comprehensive survey of Persian history is given by one of the leading scholars in the field, R. N. Frye, *History of Ancient Iran* (1984). I. Gershevitch, ed., *The Cambridge History of Iran,* vol. 2 (1985), provides the reader with a full account of ancient Persian history, but many of the chapters are out-of-date. E. Herzfeld, *Iran in the Ancient East* (1987), puts Persian history in a broad context. Most welcome is M. A. Dandamaev, *A Political History of the Achaemenid Empire* (1989), which discusses in depth the history of the Persians and the organization of their empire. Finally, M. Boyce, a leading scholar in the field, provides a sound and readable treatment of the essence of Zoroastrianism in her *Zoroastrianism* (1979).

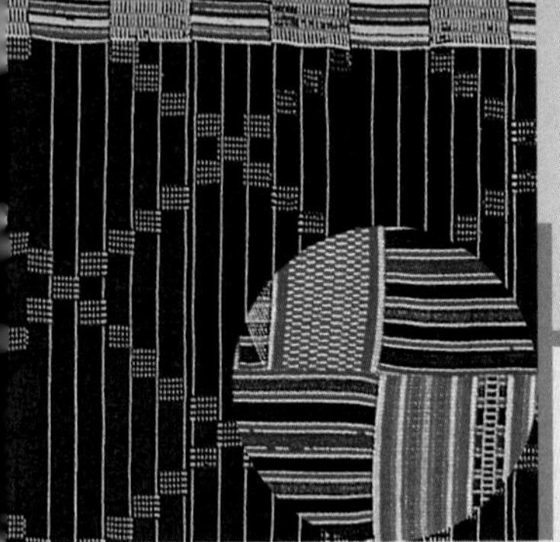

LISTENING TO THE PAST

# The Covenant Between Yahweh and the Hebrews

*These passages from the Hebrew Bible address two themes important to Hebraic thinking. The first is the meaning of kingship; the second is the nature of the Covenant between the Hebrews and the Lord, Yahweh. The selection also raises the difficult question of how much of the Hebrew Bible can be accepted historically. As we discussed in this chapter, the Hebrew Bible is not a document that we may accept as literal truth, but it does tell us a great deal about the people who created it. From the following passages we may discern what the Hebrews thought about their own past and religion.*

*The background of the excerpt is a political crisis that has some archaeological support. The war with the Philistines put a huge strain on Hebrew society. The passage below describes one such incident when Nahash, the king of the Ammonites, threatens to destroy the Hebrews. A new and effective political and military leadership was needed to meet the situation. The elders of the tribes had previously chosen judges to lead the community only in times of crisis. The Hebrews, however, demanded that a kingship be established, even though Yahweh was their king. They turned to Samuel, the last of the judges, who anointed Saul as the first Hebrew king. In this excerpt Samuel reviews the political, military, and religious situation confronting the Hebrews, reminding them of their obligation to honor the Covenant and expressing hesitation in naming a king.*

Then Nahash the Ammonite came up and encamped against Jabeshgilead: and all the men of Jabesh said unto Nahash, Make a covenant with us, and we will serve thee. And Nahash the Ammonite answered them, On this condition will I make a covenant with you, that I may thrust out all your right eyes, and lay it for a reproach upon all Israel. And the elders of Jabesh said unto him, Give us seven days' respite, that we may send messengers unto all the coasts of Israel: and then, if there be no man to save us, we will come out to thee.

Then came the messengers to Gibeah of Saul, and told the tidings in the ears of the people: and all the people lifted up their voices, and wept. And, behold, Saul came after the herd out of the field; and Saul said, What aileth the people that they weep? And they told him the tidings of the men of Jabesh. And the Spirit of God came upon Saul when he heard those tidings, and his anger was kindled greatly. And he took a yoke of oxen, and hewed them in pieces, and sent them throughout all the coasts of Israel by the hands of messengers, saying, Whosoever cometh not forth after Saul and after Samuel, so shall it be done unto his oxen. And the fear of the Lord fell on the people, and they came out with one consent. And when he numbered them in Bezek, the children of Israel were three hundred thousand, and the men of Judah thirty thousand. And they said unto the messengers that came, Thus shall ye say unto the men of Jabeshgilead, To morrow, by that time the sun be hot, ye shall have help. And the messengers came and shewed it to the men of Jabesh; and they were glad. Therefore the men of Jabesh said, To morrow we will come out unto you, and ye shall do with us all that seemeth good unto you. And it was so on the morrow, that Saul put the people in three companies; and they came into the midst of the host in the morning watch, and slew the Ammonites until the heat of the day: and it came to pass, that they which remained were scattered, so that two of them were not left together.

And the people said unto Samuel, Who is he that said, Shall Saul reign over us? bring the men, that we may put them to death. And Saul said, There shall not a man be put to death this day: for to day the Lord hath wrought salvation in Israel. Then said Samuel to the people, Come, and let us go to Gilgal, and renew the kingdom there. And

Ark of the Covenant, depicted in a relief from Capernaum Synagogue, second century C.E. *(Ancient Art & Architecture Collection)*

all the people went to Gilgal; and there they made Saul king before the Lord in Gilgal; and there they sacrificed sacrifices of peace offerings before the Lord; and there Saul and all the men of Israel rejoiced greatly.

And Samuel said unto all Israel, Behold, I have hearkened unto your voice in all that you said to me, and have made a king over you. And now, behold, the king walks before you; and I am old and gray-headed; and behold, my sons are with you: and I have walked before you from my childhood until this day. Behold, here I am: witness against me before the Lord, and before his anointed: whose ox have I taken? or whose ass have I taken? or whom have I defrauded? whom have I oppressed? or of whose hand have I received any bribe to blind my eyes with it? and I will restore it to you.

And they said, You have not defrauded us, nor oppressed us, neither have you taken anything from any man's hand. And he said to them, the Lord is witness against you, and his anointed is witness this day, that you have not found anything in my hand. And they answered, he is witness. And Samuel said unto the people, It is the Lord that advanced Moses and Aaron, and that brought your fathers up out of the land of Egypt. Now therefore stand still, that I may reason with you before the Lord of all the righteous acts of the Lord, which he did to you and your fathers.

*At this point Samuel reminds the Hebrews of their Covenant with Yahweh. He lists the times when they had broken that Covenant, the times when they had served other gods. He also reminds them of Yahweh's punishment for their backsliding. He tells them frankly that they are wrong to demand a king to rule over them, for Yahweh was their lord, god, and king. Nonetheless, Samuel gives way to their demands.*

Now therefore behold the king whom you have chosen, and whom you have desired! and behold, the Lord has set a king over you. If you will fear the Lord, and serve him, and obey his voice, and not rebel against the commandment of the Lord, then shall both you and also the king who reigns over you continue following the Lord your God: But if you will not obey the voice of the Lord, but rebel against the commandment of the Lord, then shall the hand of the Lord be against you, as it was against your fathers. Now therefore stand and see this great thing, which the Lord will do before your eyes. Is it not wheat harvest today? I will call to the Lord, and he shall send thunder and rain; that you may perceive and see that your wickedness is great, which you have done in the sight of the Lord, in asking you a king. So Samuel called to the Lord; and the Lord sent thunder and rain that day: and all the people greatly feared the Lord and Samuel. And all the people said to Samuel, pray for your servants to the Lord your God, so that we will not die: for we have added to all of our sins this evil, to ask us for a king. And Samuel said to the people, Fear not: you have done all this wickedness; yet turn not aside from following the Lord, but serve the Lord with all your heart; And do not turn aside; for then should you go after vain things, which cannot profit nor deliver; for they are vain. For the Lord will not forsake his people for his great name's sake: because it pleases the Lord to make you his people. Moreover, as for me, God forbid that I should sin against the Lord in ceasing to pray for you: but I will teach you the good and the right way: Only fear the Lord, and serve him in truth with all your heart: for consider how great things he has done for you. But if you shall still act wickedly, you will be consumed, both you and your king.

## QUESTIONS FOR ANALYSIS

1. How did Samuel explain his anointment of a king?
2. What was Samuel's attitude toward kingship?
3. What were the duties of the Hebrews toward Yahweh?
4. Might those duties conflict with those toward the secular king? If so, in what ways, and how might the Hebrews avoid the conflict?

*Source:* 1 Samuel 11:1–15, 12:1–7, 13–25. Abridged and adapted from *The Holy Bible,* King James Version.

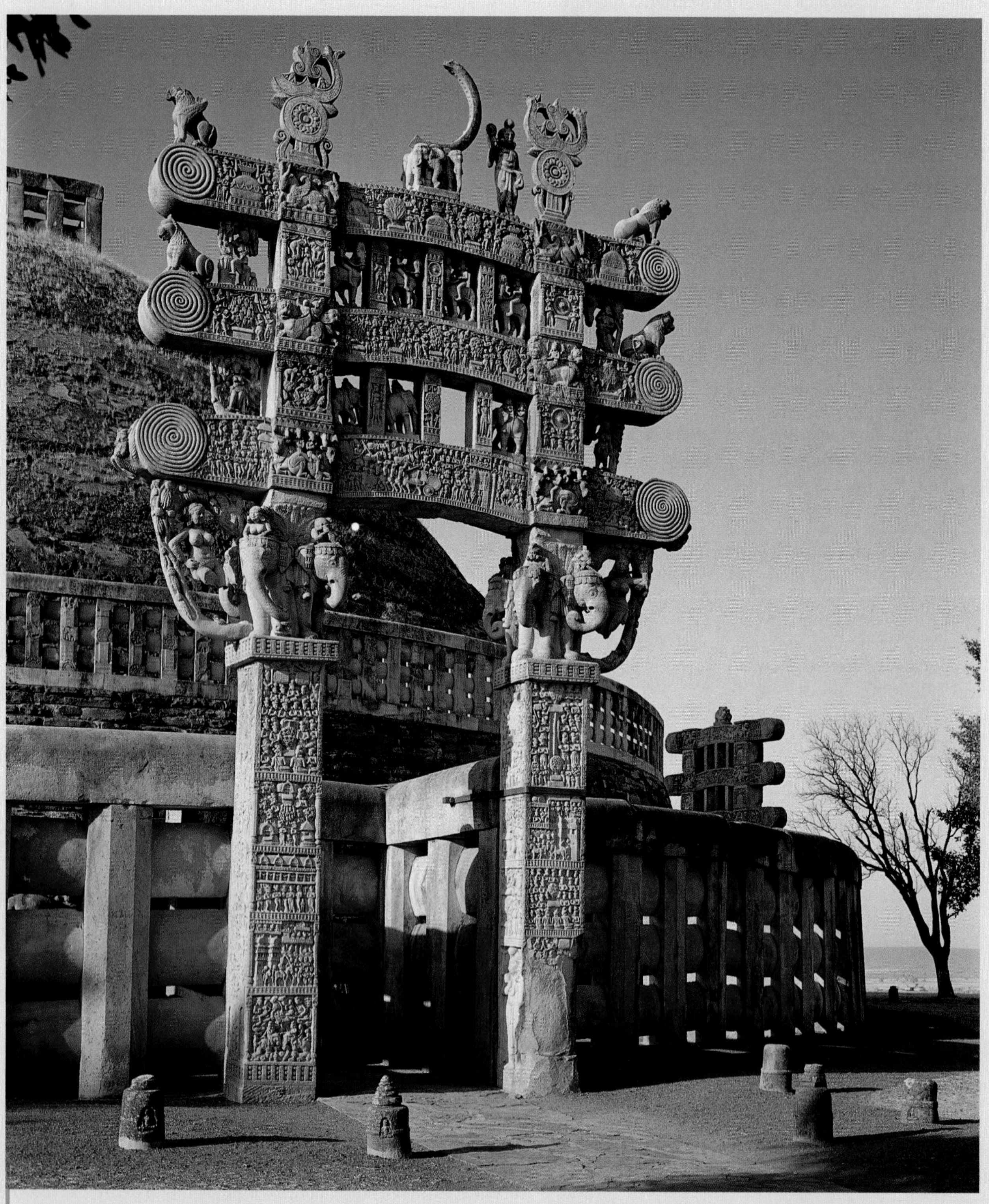

The North Gate is one of four ornately carved gates guarding the Buddhist memorial shrine at Sanchi, Madhya Pradesh. Satavahana, second century B.C.E. *(Jean-Louis Nou)*

CHAPTER

# 3 THE FOUNDATION OF INDIAN SOCIETY, TO 300 C.E.

## CHAPTER OUTLINE

- The Land and Its First Settlers (ca 3000–1500 B.C.E.)
- The Aryans and the Vedic Age (ca 1500–500 B.C.E.)
- India's Great Religions
- India and the West (ca 513–298 B.C.E.)
- The Mauryan Empire (ca 322–185 B.C.E.)
- Regional Developments (200 B.C.E.–300 C.E.)

During the centuries when the peoples of ancient Mesopotamia and Egypt were developing urban civilizations, people in India were wrestling with the same challenges—making the land yield food, improving agricultural techniques, building cities and urban cultures, grappling with the political administration of large tracts of land, and asking basic questions about human life and the cosmos.

Like the civilizations of the Middle East, the earliest Indian civilization centered on a great river, the Indus. From about 2800 to 1800 B.C.E., this Indus, or Harappan, culture thrived, and numerous cities were built over a huge area. A very different Indian society emerged after the decline of this civilization. It was dominated by the Aryans, warriors who spoke an early version of Sanskrit. The Indian caste system and the Hindu religion, key features of Indian society into modern times, had their origins in early Aryan society. The earliest Indian literature consists of the epics and religious texts of these Aryan tribes.

By the middle of the first millennium B.C.E., the Aryans had set up numerous small kingdoms throughout north India. This was the great age of Indian religious creativity, when Buddhism and Jainism were founded and the early Brahmanic religion of the Aryans developed into Hinduism. Alexander the Great invaded north India in 326 B.C.E., and after his army withdrew, the first major Indian empire was created by the Mauryan dynasty (ca 322–ca 180 B.C.E.), which unified most of north India. This dynasty reached its peak under the great king Ashoka (r. ca 269–232 B.C.E.), who actively promoted Buddhism both within his realm and beyond it. Not long afterward, however, the dynasty broke up, and for several centuries India was politically divided.

- What does archaeology tell us about the earliest civilization in India?
- What kind of social and political organization developed in India?
- What intellectual and religious values did this society generate?
- How were developments in India linked to developments outside it?
- Which features of ancient Indian culture and society shaped later developments most profoundly?

These questions are the central concerns of this chapter.

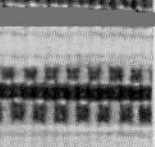

## THE LAND AND ITS FIRST SETTLERS (CA 3000–1500 B.C.E.)

The subcontinent of India, a landmass as large as western Europe, juts southward into the warm waters of the Indian Ocean. Today this region is divided into the separate countries of Pakistan, Nepal, India, Bangladesh, and Sri Lanka, but these divisions are recent, and for premodern times the entire subcontinent will be called India here.

In India, as elsewhere, the possibilities for both agriculture and communication have always been strongly shaped by geography (see Map 3.1). Some regions are among the wettest on earth; others are arid deserts and scrubland. The lower reaches of the Himalaya Mountains in the northeast are covered by some of India's densest forests, sustained by heavy rainfall. Immediately to the south, the land drops away to the fertile valleys of the Indus and Ganges Rivers. These lowland plains, which stretch all the way across the subcontinent, over time were tamed for agriculture, and India's great empires were centered there. To the west of them are the great deserts of Rajasthan and southeastern Pakistan, historically important in part because their flat terrain enabled invaders to sweep into India from the northwest. South of the great river valleys rise the jungle-clad Vindhya Mountains and the dry, hilly Deccan Plateau. In this part of India, only along the coasts do the hills give way to narrow plains where crop agriculture flourished. Throughout much of antiquity, the Indian Ocean served to keep out invaders on India's south coast while fostering maritime trade both with the Near East and with China and Southeast Asia. Thus India's geography ensured that it would never be an isolated civilization and channeled contact in certain directions.

**MAP 3.1 India from ca 2500 B.C.E. to 300 C.E.** The earliest civilization in India developed in the Indus River valley in the west of the subcontinent. The Ganges River valley was the heart of the later Mauryan Empire. Although India is protected from the cold by mountains in the north, mountain passes in the northwest allowed both migration and invasion.

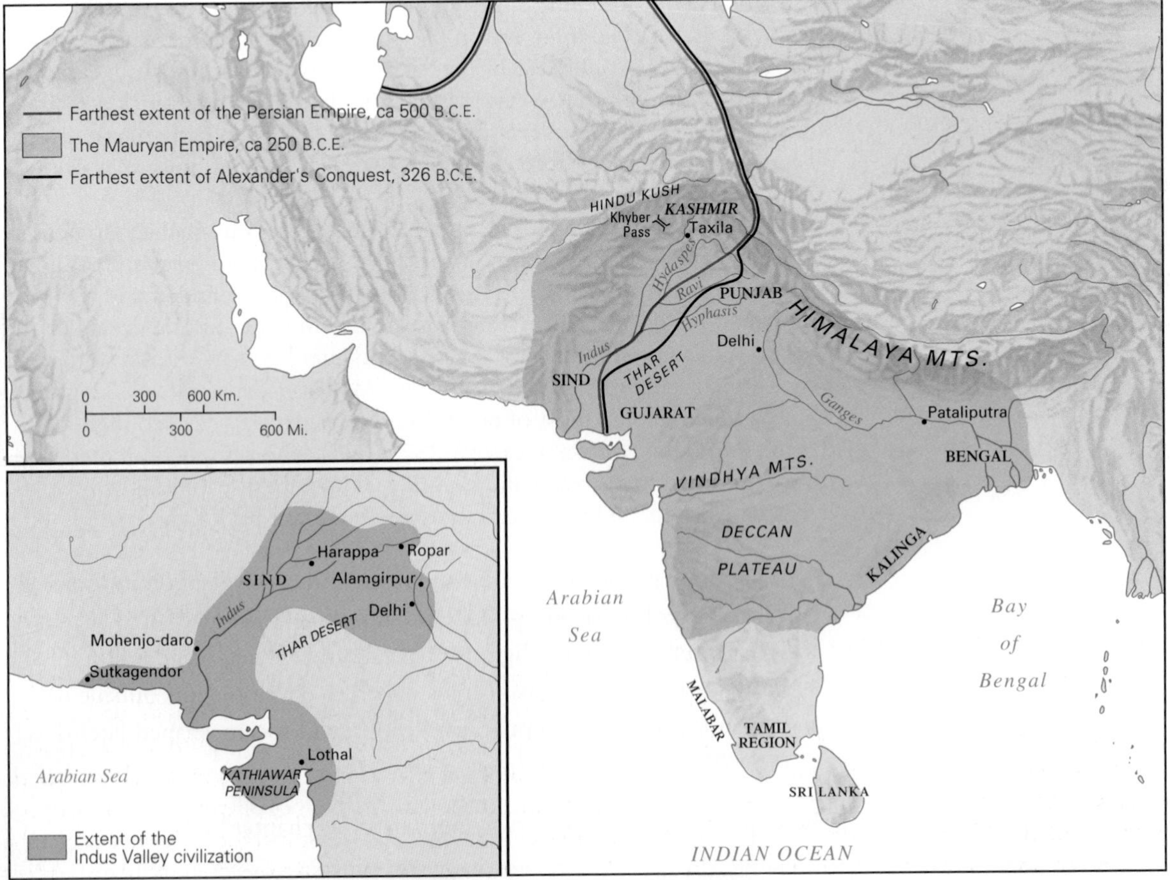

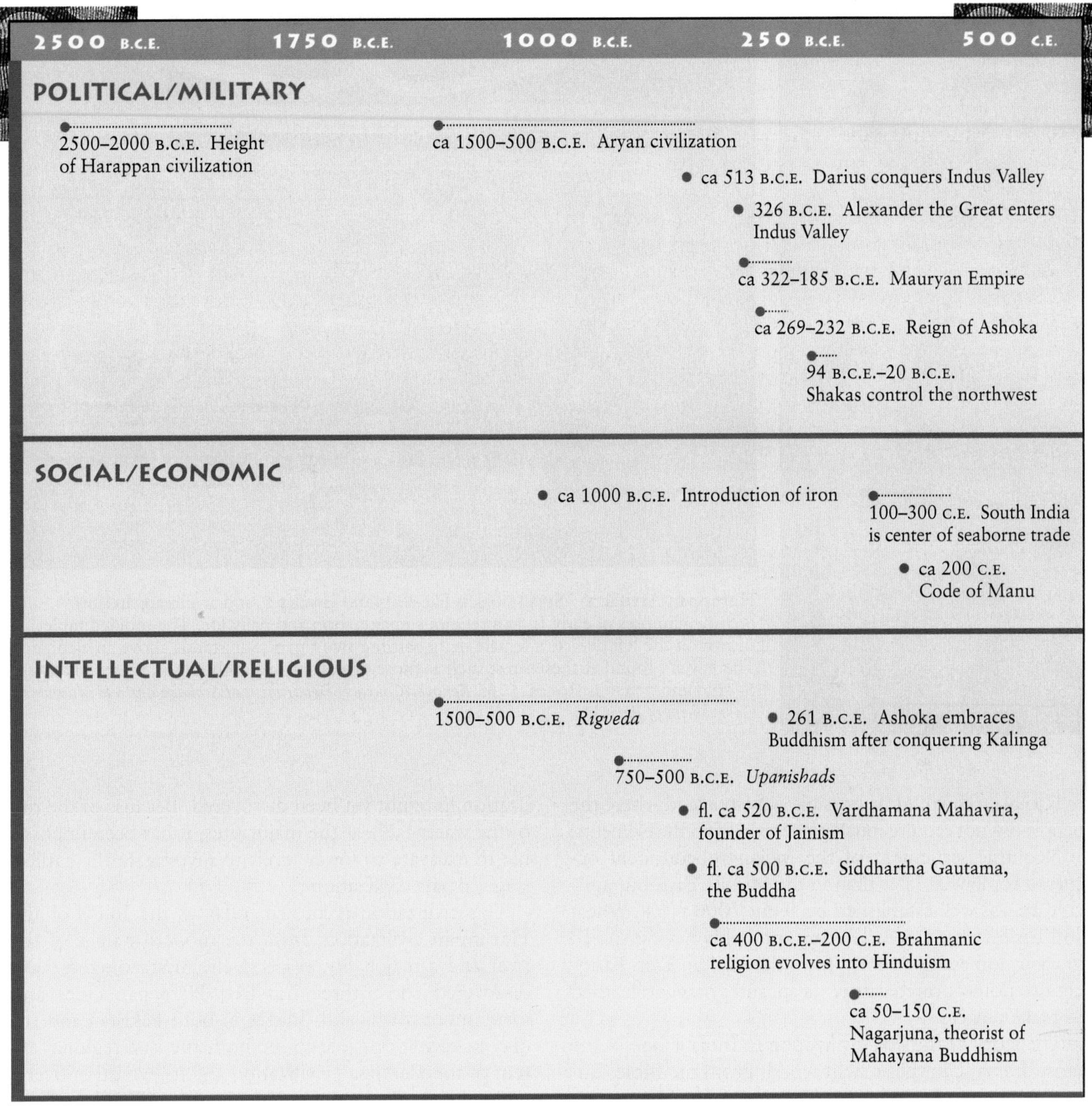


India's climate is shaped by the ocean and mountains. The Himalayas shield the subcontinent from the northern cold. Most areas are warm all year, with temperatures over 100°F common. Average temperatures range from 79°F in the north to 85°F in the south. The mountains also hold in the monsoon rains that sweep northward from the Indian Ocean each summer. The monsoons and the melting snows of the Himalayas provide India with most of its water. In some areas the resulting moisture has created vast tracts of jungle and swamp. The Ganges, for example, was in ancient times a particularly forbidding region, and only gradually did settlers move there from the tamer west and clear it for agriculture. India's climate has shaped not only its agriculture but also its religions. Given the heat and regular rainfall characteristic of the Indian heartland, it is not surprising that both fire and water came to play central roles in Indian religions. Moreover, the extreme ascetic practices of many Indian

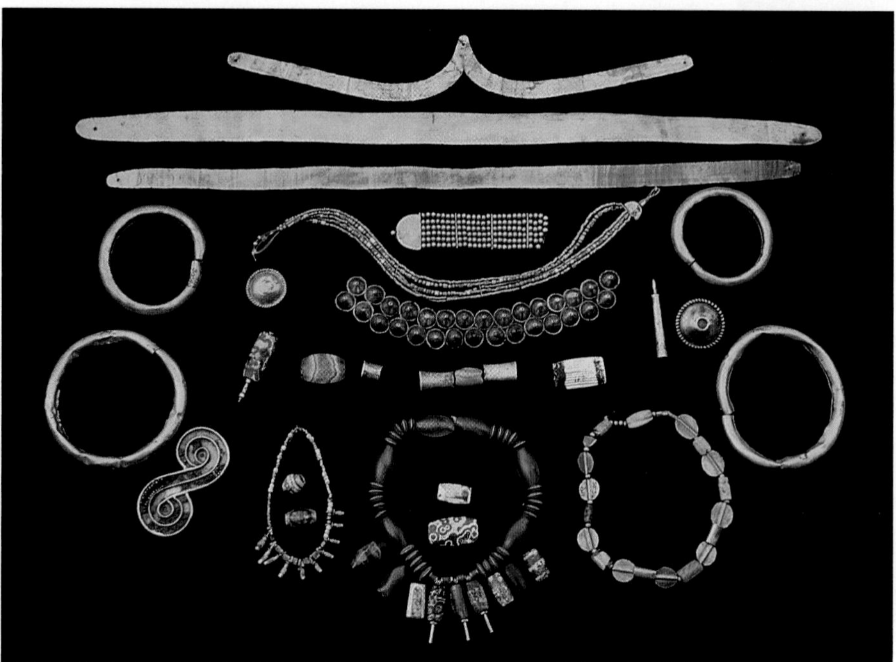

**Harappan Artifacts** Small objects like seals and jewelry found at Harappan sites provide glimpses of early Indian religious imagination and daily life. The molded tablet shown on the left depicts a female deity battling two tigers. She stands above an elephant. The jewelry found at these sites, such as those pieces shown on the right, makes much use of gold and precious stones. *(J. M. Kenoyer/Courtesy Department of Archaeology and Museums, Government of Pakistan)*

religious sects would be possible only in a land where the people did not require much protection from the elements.

Neolithic settlement of the Indian subcontinent occurred somewhat later than in the Middle East, but agriculture was well established by about 7000 B.C.E. Wheat and barley were the early crops, probably having spread in their domesticated form from the Middle East. Farmers also domesticated cattle, sheep, and goats and learned to make pottery.

The story of the first civilization in India is one of the most dramatic in the ancient world. From the Bible, Europeans knew about ancient Egypt and Ur, but no one knew about the ancient cities of the Indus Valley until 1921, when archaeologists found astonishing evidence of a thriving and sophisticated Bronze Age urban culture dating to about 2500 B.C.E. at Mohenjo-daro in what is now Pakistan. This city had obviously been planned and built before being settled; it had straight streets, uniform houses, and underground sewers. To some the advanced culture of this site suggested that a powerful state had moved into the area or sent colonists there, but it is also possible that early stages of the development of this civilization have not yet been discovered. Because of the rise of the water table at the major sites, it has been impossible to excavate to lower levels to investigate the earliest stages of the civilization.

This civilization is known today as the Indus or the **Harappan** civilization, from the modern names of the river and a major city, respectively. Archaeologists have discovered some three hundred Harappan cities and many more towns and villages in both Pakistan and India, making it possible to see both the vast regional extent of the Harappan civilization and its evolution over a period of nearly a millennium. It was a literate civilization, like those of Egypt and Mesopotamia, but no one has been able to decipher the more than four hundred symbols inscribed on stone seals and copper tablets. Its most flourishing period was 2500 to 2000 B.C.E.

The Indus civilization extended over nearly 500,000 square miles in the Indus Valley, making it more than twice as large as the territories of the ancient Egyptian and Sumerian civilizations. Numerous sites are still being excavated, but it is already clear that the Harappan civilization was marked by a striking uniformity. Through-

**Mohenjo-daro**
Mohenjo-daro was a planned city, built of fired mud brick. Its streets were straight, and covered drain-pipes were installed to carry away waste. From sites like this, we know that the early Indian political elite had the power and technical expertise to organize large, coordinated building projects. *(Josephine Powell)*

out the region, for instance, even in small villages, bricks were made to standard proportions of 4:2:1. Standardized weights have been found at all sites as well as at ports along the Arabian Sea. Figurines of pregnant women, believed to represent fertility goddesses, have been found throughout the area, suggesting common religious ideas and practices. Yet compared to archaeological sites in Egypt and Sumer, relatively few graves have been found at Harappan sites. Thus the luxury goods of the rich and powerful have not been preserved to the extent that they have been in other early civilizations. Bronze objects have been found throughout the Harrapan region, but they are usually utilitarian tools rather than the highly decorated vessels and jewelry found in Egyptian and Sumerian tombs.

Like Mesopotamian cities, Harappan cities were centers for crafts and trade surrounded by extensive farmland. Fine ceramics were made on the potter's wheel and decorated with geometric designs. Cotton was used to make cloth (the earliest anywhere) and was so abundant that goods were wrapped in it for shipment. Trade was extensive. As early as the reign of Sargon of Akkad in the third millennium B.C.E., trade between India and Mesopotamia carried goods and ideas between the two cultures, probably by way of the Persian Gulf. The port of Lothal had a stone dock seven hundred feet long, next to which were massive granaries and beadmaking factories. Hundreds of seals were found there, some of Persian Gulf origin, indicating that Lothal was a major port of exit and entry.

The best-known cities of the Harappan civilization are Mohenjo-daro, in southern Pakistan, and Harappa, some four hundred miles to the north in the Punjab region of Pakistan. Both cities were huge, more than three miles in circumference, and housed populations estimated at thirty-five thousand to forty thousand. Three other cities of similar size have been identified but have not yet been excavated.

Built of fired mud brick, Mohenjo-daro and Harappa were both defended by great citadels that towered forty

**Figurine from Mohenjo-daro** This small stone figure, about seven inches tall, is thought to depict a priest-king. The man's beard is carefully trimmed and his upper lip shaved. The headband and armband have circular ornaments, probably once filled with colored paste. His robe with its trefoil designs was probably also filled with colors to suggest the fabric more vividly. *(National Museum, Karachi)*

to fifty feet above the surrounding plain and may have had walls surrounding them, though only small sections survive. Both cities were logically planned from the outset, not the outcomes of villages that grew and sprawled haphazardly. In both, blocks of houses were laid out on a grid plan, centuries before the Greeks or Chinese used this method of urban design. Streets were straight and varied from nine to thirty-four feet in width. The houses were substantial—many two stories tall, some perhaps three—and their brick exteriors were unadorned. The focal point of the houses was a central courtyard onto which the rooms opened, much like many houses today in both rural and urban India.

Perhaps the most surprising aspect of the elaborate planning of these cities is their complex system of drainage, well preserved at Mohenjo-daro. Each house had a bathroom with a drain connected to brick-lined drains located under the major streets. Openings allowed the refuse to be collected, probably to be used as fertilizer on nearby fields. No other ancient city had such an advanced sanitation system.

Both cities also contained numerous large structures, which excavators think were public buildings. One of the most important was the large ventilated storehouse for the community's grain. Moreover, a set of tenement buildings next to a series of round work areas near the granary at Harappa suggests that the central government dominated the storage and processing of the city's cereal crops. Near the citadel at Mohenjo-daro were a marketplace or place of assembly, a palace, and a huge bath featuring a pool some thirty-nine feet long by twenty-three feet wide and eight feet deep. The bath resembles the later Roman baths in that it is an intricate structure with spacious dressing rooms for the bathers. Because the Great Bath at Mohenjo-daro resembles the ritual purification pools of later Indian society, some scholars have speculated that power was in the hands of a priest-king and that the Great Bath played a role in the religious rituals of the city.

The prosperity of the Indus civilization depended on constant and intensive cultivation of the rich river valley. Although rainfall seems to have been greater then than in recent times, the Indus, like the Nile, flowed through a relatively dry region, made fertile by annual floods and irrigation. And as in Egypt, agriculture was aided by a long growing season of high temperatures and near constant sunshine. Besides growing wheat, barley, vegetables, and cotton, the Indus people domesticated cattle, water buffalo, fowl, and possibly pigs and asses. Their efforts led to agricultural surpluses that they traded with Mesopotamia. They also traded with peoples to the south for gold and to the north for lapis lazuli.

Because the written language of the Harappan people has not been deciphered, their political, intellectual, and religious life is largely unknown. There clearly was a political structure with the authority to organize city planning and facilitate trade, but we do not even know whether there were hereditary kings. There are clear connections between Harappan civilization and Sumerian, but just as clear differences. For instance, the Harappan script was incised on clay tablets and seals, as it was at Sumer, but the script has no connection to Sumerian cuneiform, and the artistic style of the seals also is distinct. There are many signs of continuity with later Indian civilization, ranging from the sorts of pottery ovens used to some of the images of gods. A three-headed figure surrounded by animals that was found at Mohenjo-daro closely resembles later depictions of Shiva, a major

Hindu god. There are also many female figurines and other signs of fertility cults. Because of evidence like this, some scholars think that the people of Harappa may have been the ancestors of the Dravidian-speaking peoples of modern south India. Analysis of skeletons, however, indicates that the population of the Indus Valley in ancient times was very similar to the modern population of the same region.

The decline of Harappan civilization, which began soon after 2000 B.C.E., cannot be attributed to the arrival of powerful invaders, as was once thought. Rather the decline was internally generated. The port of Lothal was abandoned by about 1900 B.C.E., and other major centers came to house only a fraction of their earlier populations. Scholars have offered many explanations for the mystery of the abandonment of these cities. Perhaps an earthquake led to a shift in the course of the river, or perhaps rainfall and snowmelt decreased and the rivers dried up. Perhaps the long-term practice of irrigation led to the buildup of salts and alkalines in the soil until they reached levels toxic to plants. Perhaps long-distance commerce collapsed, leading to an economic depression. Perhaps the population fell prey to diseases, such as malaria, that led people to flee the cities. Even though the Harappan population apparently lived on after scattering to villages, they were not able to retain key features of the high culture of the Indus civilization. For the next thousand years, there were no large cities, no kiln-fired bricks, and no written language in India.

## THE ARYANS AND THE VEDIC AGE (CA 1500–500 B.C.E.)

After the decline of the Indus Valley civilization, a people who called themselves **Aryans** became dominant in north India. They were speakers of an early form of Sanskrit, which was an Indo-European language closely related to ancient Persian and more distantly related to Latin, Greek, Celtic, and their modern descendants, such as English. The Sanskrit *nava,* "ship," is related to the English word *naval; deva,* "god," to *divine; raja,* "ruler," to *regal;* and so on. The word *Aryan* itself comes from *Arya,* "noble" or "pure" in Sanskrit, and has the same root as Iran and Eire.

Until relatively recently, the dominant theory was that the Aryans came into India from outside, perhaps as a part of the same movements of people that led to the Hittites occupying parts of Anatolia, the Achaeans entering Greece, and the Kassites conquering Sumer—all in the period from about 1900 to 1750 B.C.E. (see Chapter 1). Some scholars, however, have proposed that the Indo-European languages spread to this area much earlier; to them it is possible that the Harappan people were speakers of an early Indo-European language. If that was the case, the Aryans would just be one of the groups descended from this early population.

Modern politics complicates analysis of the appearance of the Aryans and their role in India's history. It was Europeans in the eighteenth and nineteenth century who developed the concept of Indo-European languages, and they did it in an age both highly conscious of race and in the habit of identifying races with languages. The racist potential of the concept was fully exploited by the Nazis, with their glorification of the Aryans as a superior race. But even in less politicized contexts, the notion of a group of people who entered India from outside and made themselves its rulers is troubling to many. Does it mean that the non-Aryans are the true Indians? Or, to the contrary, does it add legitimacy to those who in later times conquered India from outside? Does it justify or undermine the caste system? One of the difficulties faced by scholars who wish to take a dispassionate view of these issues is that the evidence for the earlier Harappan culture is entirely archaeological and the evidence for the Aryans is almost entirely based on linguistic analysis of modern languages and orally transmitted texts of uncertain date.

The central source for the early Aryans is the ***Rigveda,*** the earliest of the Vedas, a collection of hymns, ritual texts, and philosophical treatises composed between 1500 and 500 B.C.E. in Sanskrit. Like Homer's epics in Greece, these texts were transmitted orally and are in verse. Since writing was not used in the early Vedic period, events in early Indian history can be dated only approximately.

The *Rigveda* portrays the Aryans as warrior tribes who glorified military skill and heroism; loved to drink, hunt, race, and dance; and counted their wealth in cattle. They looked down on the short, dark-skinned indigenous people, whom they did their best to subjugate. The Aryans did not sweep across India in a quick campaign, nor were they a disciplined army led by one conqueror. Rather they were a collection of tribes who frequently fought with each other and only over the course of several centuries came to dominate north India.

Those the Aryans fought often lived in fortified towns and put up a strong defense against them. The key to the Aryans' success probably lay in their superior military technology: they had fast two-wheeled chariots, horses, and bronze swords and spears. Their epics, however, present the struggle in religious terms: their chiefs were godlike heroes, their opponents irreligious savages who did not perform the proper sacrifices. In time, however, the Aryans clearly absorbed much from those they conquered.

At the head of each Aryan tribe was a chief, or **raja,** who led his followers in battle and ruled them in peacetime. The warriors in the tribe elected the chief for his military skills. Next in importance to the chief was the priest, entrusted with sacrifices to the gods and the knowledge of sacred rituals. In time, as Aryan society put increasing emphasis on proper performance of the religious rituals, priests evolved into a distinct class possessing precise knowledge of the complex rituals and of the invocations and formulas that accompanied them, rather like the priest classes in ancient Egypt, Mesopotamia, and Persia. The warrior nobility rode into battle in chariots and perhaps on horseback; they met at assemblies to reach decisions and advise the raja. The common tribesmen tended herds and in time worked the land. To the conquered non-Aryans fell the drudgery of menial tasks. It is difficult to define precisely their social status. Though probably not slaves, they were certainly subordinate to the Aryans and worked for them in return for protection.

**Bronze Sword** A striking example of the quality of Aryan arms is this bronze sword, with its rib in the middle of the blade for strength. Native Indians lacked comparable weapons. *(Courtesy of the Trustees of the British Museum)*

Over the course of several centuries, the Aryans pushed farther east into the valley of the Ganges River, at that time a land of thick jungle populated by aboriginal forest peoples. The jungle was as stubborn an enemy as its inhabitants. The tremendous challenge of clearing it was made somewhat easier by the introduction of iron around 1000 B.C.E. Iron made it possible to produce strong axes and knives relatively cheaply. During this time the Aryans and those they displaced or conquered undoubtedly borrowed cultural elements from each other. Rice, for instance, was grown in the Ganges Valley, apparently introduced from Southeast Asia, where it had been cultivated since at least 5000 B.C.E. Rice, in time, became a central element of the Indian diet.

The Aryans did not gain dominance over the entire Indian subcontinent. South of the Vindhya range, people speaking Dravidian languages maintained their control. In the great Aryan epics the *Ramayana* and *Mahabharata,* the people of the south and Sri Lanka are spoken of as dark-skinned savages and demons who resisted the Aryans' conquests. Still, in time these epics became part of the common cultural heritage of all of India.

## Early Indian Society, 1000–500 B.C.E.

As Aryan rulers came to dominate large settled populations, the style of political organization changed from tribal chieftainship to territorial kingship. In other words, the ruler controlled an area whose people might change, not a nomadic tribe who might move as a group. Moreover, kings no longer needed to be elected by the tribe; it was enough to be invested by priests and to perform the splendid royal ceremonies they designed. The priests, or **Brahmans,** supported the growth of royal power in return for royal confirmation of their own religious rights, power, and status. The Brahmans also served as advisers to the kings. In the face of this royal-priestly alliance, the old tribal assemblies of warriors withered away. By the time Persian armies reached the Indus around 513 B.C.E., there were sixteen major kingdoms in north India.

Early Aryan society had distinguished among the warrior elite, the priests, ordinary tribesmen, and conquered subjects. These distinctions gradually evolved into the **caste system.** Society was conceived in terms of four hierarchical strata that do not eat with each other or marry each other. These strata (called **varna**) are *Brahman* (priests), *Kshatriya* (warriors and officials), *Vaishya* (merchants and artisans), and *Shudra* (peasants and laborers). The lowest level probably evolved out of the efforts of the numerically outnumbered Aryans to maintain their dominance over their subjects and not be absorbed by them. The three upper varnas probably accounted for no more than 30 percent of the population. Social and religious attitudes entered into these distinctions as well. Aryans considered the work of artisans impure. They left all such work to the local people, who were probably superior to them in these arts anyway. Trade, by contrast, was not viewed as demeaning, and Aryans would practice it. Brahmanic texts of the period refer to trade as equal in value to farming, serving the king, or serving as a priest.

In the *Rigveda,* the caste system is attributed to the gods:

*When they divided the [primeval] Man into how many parts did they divide him?*
*What was his mouth, what were his arms, what were his thighs and his feet called?*
*The Brahman was his mouth, of his arms was made the warrior.*
*His thighs became the Vaishya, of his feet the Shudra was born.*[1]

Those without places in this tidy social division—that is, those who entered it later than the others or who had lost their caste status through violations of ritual—were **outcastes.** That simply meant that they belonged to no caste. In time, some of these people became "untouchables," because they were "impure." They were scorned because they earned their living by performing such "polluting" jobs as slaughtering animals and dressing skins.

Slavery was also a feature of early Indian social life, as it was in Egypt, Mesopotamia, and elsewhere in antiquity. Slaves were often people captured in battle, but these captives could be ransomed by their families. Later, slavery was less connected with warfare and became more of an economic and social institution. As in ancient Mesopotamia, a free man might sell himself and his family into slavery because he could not pay his debts. And, as in Hammurabi's Mesopotamia, he could, if clever, hard-working, or fortunate, buy his and his family's way out of slavery. At birth, slave children automatically became the slaves of their parents' masters. Indian slaves could be bought, used as collateral, or even given away.

Slaves in India performed tasks similar to those of slaves in other societies. Like Joseph in ancient Egypt, a man might serve as a royal counselor, having more actual authority than many a free man. Otherwise slaves served in their masters' fields, mines, or houses. Whatever their economic function, socially they were members of their masters' households, and Indian masters were required to perform the customary duties necessary for the welfare of the soul of a deceased slave. Indian law forbade a master from abandoning his slaves in their old age; it also recommended manumission of slaves as an act of piety. Nonetheless, in Indian literature there is ample evidence of the abuse of slaves, for in India as in other societies—both ancient and modern—laws and social injunctions were not always obeyed.

Women's lives in early India varied according to their social status, much as men's did. Like most nomadic tribes, the Aryans were patrilineal and patriarchal (tracing descent through males and placing power over family members in the senior men of the family). Thus women in Aryan society probably had more subordinate roles than did women among the local Dravidian population, many of whom were matrilineal. But even in Aryan society, women were treated somewhat more favorably than in later Indian society. They were not yet given in child-marriage, and widows had the right to remarry. In the epics such as the *Ramayana,* women are often portrayed as forceful personalities, able to achieve their goals both by feminine ploys of cajoling men and by more direct action. (See the feature "Listening to the Past: Rama and Sita" on pages 76–77.)

## Brahmanism

The gods of the Aryans shared some features with the gods of other early Indo-European societies such as the Persians and Greeks. Some of them were great brawling figures, such as Agni, the god of fire; Indra, wielder of the thunderbolt and god of war, who each year slew a dragon to release the monsoon rains; and Rudra, the divine archer who spread disaster and disease by firing his arrows at people. Others were shadowy figures, such as Dyaus, the father of the gods, related to the Greek Zeus and the Roman Jupiter. Varuna, the god of order in the universe, was a hard god, quick to punish those who sinned and thus upset the balance of nature. Ushas, the goddess of dawn, was a refreshingly gentle deity who welcomed the birds, gave delight to human beings, and warded off evil spirits.

The core of the Aryans' religion was its focus on sacrifice. By giving valued things to the gods, people strengthened them and established relationships with them. As in ancient Persia, the fire-god Agni was a particularly important god. Agni had three forms: fire, lightning, and the sun. In his capacity as the sacrificial fire of the priests, he served as a liaison between human beings and the gods, carrying to the gods the offerings made by the Brahman priests. The fire sacrifice was the most elaborate of the sacrifices, but all the Aryan gods enjoyed having offerings made to them. Gradually, under the priestly monopoly of the Brahmans, correct sacrifice and proper ritual became so important that most Brahmans believed that a properly performed ritual would force a god to grant a worshiper's wish.

The *Upanishads* record speculations about the mystical meaning of sacrificial rites and about cosmological questions of man's relationship to the universe. They document a gradual shift from the mythical world-view of the early Vedic age to a deeply philosophical one. Associated with this shift was a movement toward *asceticism*—severe self-discipline and self-denial. In search of wisdom, some men retreated to the forests. These ascetics concluded that disciplined meditation on the ritual sacrifice could produce the same results as the physical ritual itself. Thus they reinterpreted ritual sacrifices as symbolic gestures with mystical meanings.

These Brahmanic thinkers also developed ideas about the nature of the cosmos. Ancient Indian cosmology focused not on a creator who made the universe out of nothing, but rather on endlessly repeating cycles. Key ideas were **samsara,** the transmigration of souls by a continual process of rebirth, and **karma,** the tally of good and bad deeds that determined the status of an individual's next life. Good deeds led to better future lives, evil deeds to worse future lives—even to reincarnation as an animal. Thus gradually arose the concept of a wheel of life that included human beings, animals, and even gods. Reward and punishment worked automatically; there was no all-knowing god who judged people and could be petitioned to forgive a sin, and each individual was responsible for his or her own destiny in a just and impartial world.

To most people, especially those on the low end of the economic and social scale, these concepts were attractive. All existence, no matter how harsh and bitter, could lead to better things. By living righteously and doing good deeds, people could improve their lot in the next life. Yet there was another side to these ideas: the wheel of life could be seen as a treadmill, giving rise to a yearning for release from the relentless cycle of birth and death. One solution offered in the *Upanishads* was **moksha,** or release from the wheel of life. Brahmanic mystics claimed that life in the world was actually an illusion, and the only way to escape it and the wheel of life was to realize that the ultimate reality was unchanging.

This unchanging, ultimate reality was called **brahman.** The multitude of things in the world were all fleeting; the only true reality was brahman. Even the individual soul or self, *atman,* is ultimately the same substance as the universal brahman, in the same way that each spark is in substance the same as a large fire. Equating the individual self with the ultimate reality suggested that the apparent duality in the world is in some sense unreal. At the same time it conveyed that all people had in themselves an eternal truth, which corresponded to an identical but greater all-encompassing reality. The profound and subtle teaching of the connections between brahman and atman was summed up in the *Upanishads* in one sentence: "Thou art That." The *Chandogya Upanishad* tells the story of a father explaining this sentence to his son:

*"Believe me, my son, an invisible and subtle essence is the Spirit of the whole universe. That is Reality. That is Atman. THOU ART THAT."*

*"Explain more to me, father," said Svetaketu.*

*"So be it, my son.*

*"Place this salt in water and come to me tomorrow morning."*

*Svetaketu did as he was commanded, and in the morning his father said to him: "Bring me the salt you put into the water last night."*

*Svetaketu looked into the water, but could not find it, for it had dissolved.*

*His father then said: "Taste the water from this side. How is it?"*

*"It is salt."*

*"Taste it from the middle. How is it?"*

*"It is salt."*

*"Taste it from that side. How is it?"*

*"It is salt."*

*"Look for the salt again and come again to me."*

*The son did so, saying: "I cannot see the salt. I only see water."*

*His father then said: "In the same way, O my son, you cannot see the Spirit. But in truth he is here.*

*"An invisible and subtle essence is the Spirit of the whole universe. That is Reality. That is Truth. THOU ART THAT."*[2]

The *Upanishads* gave the Brahmans a high status to which the poor and lowly could aspire in a future life. Consequently, the Brahmans greeted the concepts presented in these works and those who taught them with tolerance and understanding and made a place for them in traditional religious practice. The rulers of Indian society also encouraged the new trends, since the doctrines of samsara and karma encouraged the poor and oppressed to labor peacefully and dutifully. In other words, although the new doctrines were intellectually revolutionary, in social and political terms they supported the existing power structure.

## INDIA'S GREAT RELIGIONS

By the sixth and fifth centuries B.C.E., cities had reappeared in India, and merchants and trade were thriving. Bricks were again baked in kilns and used to build ramparts around cities. The center of population had shifted to the Ganges Valley. One particular kingdom, Magadha, had become much more powerful than any of the other states in the Ganges plain, defeating its enemies by using war elephants and catapults for hurling stones. Written language had by this point reappeared.

This was a period of intellectual ferment throughout Eurasia—the period of the early Greek philosophers, the Hebrew prophets, Zoroaster in Persia, Confucius and the early Daoists in China. In India it led to numerous sects that rejected various elements of Brahmanic teachings. (See the feature "Individuals in Society: Gosala.") The two most important in world-historical terms were Jainism and Buddhism. Their founders were contemporaries, both living in east India in minor states of the Ganges plain. Hinduism emerged in response to these new religions but at the same time was the most direct descendant of the old Brahmanic religion.

### Jainism

The key figure of Jainism, Vardhamana Mahavira (fl. ca 520 B.C.E.), was the son of the chief of a petty state. Like many ascetics of the period, he left home to become a holy man (a wandering mendicant ascetic), and for twelve years, from ages thirty to forty-two, he wandered through the Ganges Valley until he found enlightenment and became a "completed soul." Mahavira taught his doctrines for about thirty years, founding a disciplined order of monks and gaining the support of many lay followers, male and female.

Mahavira accepted the doctrines of karma and rebirth but developed these ideas in new directions. He argued that human beings, animals, plants, and even inanimate objects and natural phenomena all have living souls enmeshed in matter, accumulated through the workings of karma. Even a rock has a soul locked inside it, enchained by matter but capable of suffering if someone kicks it. Unlike the earlier concept of atman, which referred to immaterial and infinite souls, the souls conceived by the Jains have finite dimensions. They float or sink depending on the amount of matter with which they are enmeshed. The ascetic, who willingly undertakes suffering, can dissipate some of the karma accumulated and make progress toward liberation. If a soul at last escapes from all the matter weighing it down, it becomes lighter than ordinary objects and floats to the top of the universe, where it remains forever in inactive bliss.

**Jain Ascetic** The most extreme of Jain ascetics not only endured the elements without the help of clothes but were also generally indifferent to bodily comfort. The Jain saint depicted in this eighth-century cave temple has maintained his yogic posture for so long that vines have grown up around him. *(Courtesy, Robert Fisher)*

Mahavira's followers pursued salvation by living lives of asceticism and avoiding evil thoughts and actions. The Jains considered all life sacred and tried to live without destroying other life. Some early Jains went to the extreme of starving themselves to death, since it is impossible to eat without destroying at least plants, but most took the less extreme step of distinguishing between different levels of life. The most sacred life forms were human beings, followed by animals, plants, and inanimate objects. A Jain who wished to avoid violence to life became a vegetarian and took pains not to kill any creature, even tiny insects in the air and soil. Farming was impossible for Jains, who tended instead to take up trade. Among the most conservative, priests practiced nudity, for clinging to clothes, even a loincloth, was a form of attachment. Lay Jains could pursue Jain teachings by practicing nonviolence and purity through more moderate means of self-control. They wore clothes but did not eat meat. The Jains' radical nonviolence was motivated by a desire to escape the karmic consequences of causing harm to a life. In other words, violence had to be avoided above all because it harms the person who commits it.

For the first century after Mahavira's death, the Jains were a comparatively small and unimportant sect. Jainism began to flourish under the Mauryan dynasty (ca 322–ca 180 B.C.E.; see pages 70–72), and Jain tradition claims the Mauryan Empire's founder, Chandragupta, as a major patron. About 300 B.C.E. the Jain scriptures were recorded, and the religion split into two sects, one maintaining the tradition of total nudity, the other choosing to wear white robes, on the grounds that clothes were an insignificant external sign, unrelated to true liberation. Over the next few centuries, Jain monks were particularly important in spreading northern culture into the Deccan and Tamil regions of south India.

Although Jainism never took hold as widely as Hinduism and Buddhism, it has been an influential strand in Indian thought and has several million adherents in India today. Fasting and nonviolence as spiritual practices in India owe much to Jain teachings. Mahatma Gandhi was influenced by these ideas through his mother, and Dr. Martin Luther King, Jr., was influenced by Gandhi.

## Siddhartha Gautama and Buddhism

Siddhartha Gautama (fl. ca 500 B.C.E.), also called Shakyamuni ("sage of the Shakya tribe"), is best known as the Buddha ("enlightened one"). He was a contemporary of Mahavira and came from the same social class (that is, warrior, not Brahman). He was born the son of a chief of one of the tribes in the Himalayan foothills in what is now Nepal. At age twenty-nine, unsatisfied with his life of comfort and troubled by the suffering he saw around him, he left home to become a wandering ascetic. He traveled south to the kingdom of Magadha, where he studied with yoga masters, but later took up extreme asceticism. According to tradition, he reached enlightenment while meditating under a bo tree at Bodh Gaya, gaining perfect insight into the processes of the universe. After several weeks of meditation, he preached his first sermon, urging a "middle way" between asceticism and worldly life. For the next forty-five years, the Buddha traveled through the Ganges Valley, propounding his ideas, refuting his adversaries, making converts, and attracting followers. These followers can be called monks, members of a religious community much like others of the time in India, including the Jains. To reach as wide an audience as possible, the Buddha preached in the local language, Magadhi, rather than Sanskrit, which was already becoming a priestly language. Probably because he refused to recognize the divine authority of the Vedas and dismissed sacrifices, he attracted followers mostly from among merchants, artisans, and farmers, rather than Brahmans.

In his first sermon, the Buddha outlined his main message, summed up in the **Four Noble Truths** and the **Eightfold Path.** The truths are as follows: (1) pain and suffering, frustration and anxiety, are ugly but inescapable parts of human life; (2) suffering and anxiety are caused by human desires and attachments; (3) people can understand these weaknesses and triumph over them; and (4) this triumph is made possible by following a simple code of conduct, the Eightfold Path. The basic insight of Buddhism is thus psychological. The deepest human longings can never be satisfied, and even those things that seem to give pleasure cause anxiety because we are afraid of losing them. Attachment to people and things causes sorrow at their loss.

The Buddha offered an optimistic message, however, because everyone can set out on the Eightfold Path toward liberation. All they have to do is take steps such as recognizing the universality of suffering, deciding to free themselves from it, and choosing "right conduct," "right speech," "right livelihood," and "right endeavor." For instance, they should abstain from taking life. The seventh step is "right awareness," constant contemplation of one's deeds and words, giving full thought to their importance and whether they lead to enlightenment. "Right contemplation," the last step, entails deep meditation on the impermanence of everything in the world. Those who achieve liberation are freed from the cycle of birth and death and enter the state called **nirvana,** a kind of blissful nothingness and freedom from reincarnation.

# INDIVIDUALS IN SOCIETY

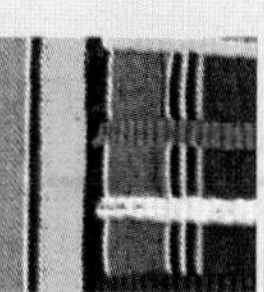

## GOSALA

Texts that survive from early India are rich in religious and philosophical speculation and tales of gods and heroes, but not in history of the sort written by the early Chinese and Greeks. Because Indian writers and thinkers of antiquity found little interest in recording the actions of rulers or accounting for the rise and decline of different states, few people's lives are known in any detail.

Religious literature, however, does sometimes include details of the lives of followers and adversaries. The life of Gosala, for instance, is known primarily from early Buddhist and Jain scriptures. He was a contemporary of both Mahavira, the founder of the Jains, and Gautama, the Buddha, and both saw him as one of their most pernicious rivals.

According to the Jain account, Gosala was born in the north Indian kingdom of Magadha, the son of a professional mendicant. The name Gosala, which means "cowshed," alluded to the fact that he was born in a cowshed where his parents had taken refuge during the rainy season. The Buddhist account adds that he became a naked wandering ascetic when he fled from his enraged master after breaking an oil vessel. As a mendicant, he soon fell in with Mahavira, who had recently commenced his life as an ascetic. After accompanying Mahavira on his travels for at least six years, Gosala came to feel that he was spiritually more advanced than his master and left to undertake the practice of austerities on his own. After he gained magic powers, he challenged his master and gathered his own disciples.

Both the Jain and Buddhist sources agree that Gosala taught a form of fatalism that they saw as dangerously wrong. A Buddhist source says that he taught that people are good or bad not because of their own efforts but because of fate. No matter how wise or righteous a person, he or she can do nothing about his or her karma or alter the course of transmigration. "Just as a ball of string, when it is cast forth, will spread out just as far and no farther than it can unwind, so both fools and wise alike, wandering in transmigration exactly for the allotted term, shall then, and only then, make an end of pain."* Some people reach perfection, but not by their own efforts; rather they are individuals who have through the course of numerous rebirths over hundreds of thousands of years rid themselves of bad karma.

*Ascetics of many sects in early India saw clothing as a comfort to be renounced.* (Dinodia Picture Agency)

The Jains claimed that Gosala lived with a potter woman, violating the celibacy expected of ascetics and moreover teaching that sexual relations were not sinful. The followers of Gosala, a Buddhist source stated, wore no clothing and were very particular about the food they accepted, refusing food specially prepared for them, food in a cooking pan, and food from couples or women with children. Like other ascetics, Gosala's followers owned no property, carrying the principle further than the Jains, who allowed the possession of a food bowl. Instead they made a bowl from the palms of their hands, giving them the name "hand lickers."

Jain sources report that after sixteen years of separation, Mahavira happened to come to the town where Gosala lived. When Gosala heard that Mahavira spoke contemptuously of him, he and his followers went to Mahavira's lodgings, and the two sides came to blows. Soon thereafter Gosala became unhinged, gave up all ascetic restraint, and after six months of singing, dancing, drinking, and other riotous living died, though not before telling his disciples, the Jains report, that Mahavira was right. Doubt is cast on this version of his end by the fact that for centuries to come, Gosala's followers, called the Ajivikas, were an important sect in several parts of India. Ashoka honored them among other sects and dedicated some caves to them.

### QUESTIONS FOR ANALYSIS

1. How would Gosala's own followers have described his life? What sorts of distortions are likely in a life known primarily from the writings of rivals?
2. How would the early Indian economy have been affected by the presence of ascetic mendicants?

*A. F. R. Hoernle, "Ajivikas," in *Encyclopedia of Religion and Ethics,* vol. 1, ed. James Hastings (Edinburgh: T. & T. Clark, 1908), p. 262.

Although he accepted the Indian idea of reincarnation, the Buddha denied the integrity of the individual self or soul. He saw human beings as a collection of parts, physical and mental. As long as the parts remain combined, that combination can be called "I." When that combination changes, as at death, the various parts remain in existence, ready to become the building blocks of different combinations. According to Buddhist teaching, life is passed from person to person as a flame is passed from candle to candle.

The success of Buddhism was aided by the Buddha's teaching that everyone, noble and peasant, educated and ignorant, male and female, could follow the Eightfold Path. Buddhism differed from Brahmanism and later Hinduism in that it in effect ignored the caste system. Moreover, the Buddha was extraordinarily undogmatic. Convinced that each person must achieve enlightenment on his or her own, he emphasized that the path was important only because it led the traveler to enlightenment, not for its own sake. He compared it to a raft, essential to cross a river but useless once on the far shore. There was no harm in honoring local gods or observing traditional ceremonies, as long as one remembered the goal of enlightenment and did not let sacrifices become snares or attachments.

Like Mahavira, the Buddha formed a circle of disciples, primarily men but including some women as well. He continually reminded them that each person must reach ultimate fulfillment by individual effort, but he also recognized the value of a group of people striving together for the same goal.

The Buddha's followers transmitted his teachings orally

**Men Worshiping at a Stupa** The frieze on this pillar from the first century C.E. depicts a stupa (the round building in the center). Stupas housed relics of the Buddha and attracted pilgrims and worshipers. Here both humans and winged heavenly beings are praying, bringing offerings, and making music. *(Eliot Elisofon Collection, Harry Ransom Humanities Center, University of Texas, Austin)*

until they were written down in the second or first century B.C.E. as sutras. The form of monasticism that developed among the Buddhists was less strict than that of the Jains. Buddhist monks moved about for eight months of the year (except the rainy season), consuming only one meal a day obtained by begging, but they could bathe and wear clothes. Within a few centuries, Buddhist monks began to overlook the rule that they should travel. They set up permanent monasteries, generally on land donated by kings or other patrons. Orders of nuns also appeared, giving women the opportunity to seek truth in ways men had traditionally done. The main ritual that monks and nuns performed in their monastic establishments was the communal recitation of the sutras. Lay Buddhists could aid the spread of the Buddhist teachings by providing food for monks and support for their monasteries, and could pursue their own spiritual progress by adopting practices such as abstaining from meat and alcohol.

Because there was no ecclesiastical authority like that developed by early Christian communities, early Buddhist communities developed several divergent traditions and came to stress different sutras. One of the most important of these, associated with the monk-philosopher Nagarjuna (fl. ca 150–250 C.E.), is called **Mahayana,** or "Great Vehicle," because it is a more inclusive form of the religion. It drew on a set of discourses allegedly given by the Buddha and kept hidden by his followers for centuries. One branch of Mahayana taught that reality is "empty" (that is, nothing exists independently, of itself). Another branch held that ultimate reality is consciousness, that everything is produced by the mind.

Just as important as the metaphysical literature of Mahayana Buddhism was its devotional side, influenced by the religions then prevalent in Central Asia. The Buddha became deified and placed at the head of an expanding pantheon of other Buddhas and bodhisattvas. Bodhisattvas were Buddhas-to-be who had stayed in the world after enlightenment to help others on the path to salvation. These Buddhas and bodhisattvas became objects of veneration, especially the Buddha Amitabha and the bodhisattva Avalokitesvara (Guanyin in Chinese, Kannon in Japanese). With the growth of Mahayana, Buddhism attracted more and more laypeople.

Buddhism remained an important religion in India until about 1200 C.E., but thereafter it declined, and the number of Buddhists in India today is small. In Sri Lanka and Nepal, however, Buddhism never lost its hold. Moreover, many elements of Buddhist philosophy were absorbed into Indian thought.

**Queen Maya's Dream** The stupa erected at Bharhut in the second century B.C.E. depicts stories of the Buddha's previous lives and events in his life as Shakyamuni. Depicted in this nineteen-inch-tall panel is the legend of his conception. As a lamp flickers at Queen Maya's bedside, a large white elephant hovers above her before descending into her side. *(Government of India, Department of Archaeology)*

## Hinduism

Both Buddhism and Jainism were direct challenges to the old Brahmanic religion. Both rejected animal sacrifice, which by then was a central element in Brahmanic power. Although Buddhist and Jain monks still had Brahmans perform life cycle rituals for them, their teachings did not place much weight on these rituals. Even more important, both religions tacitly rejected the caste system, accepting people of any caste into their ranks. In response to this challenge, over the next several centuries (ca 400 B.C.E.–200 C.E.) the Brahmanic religion evolved in a more devotional direction, today commonly called Hinduism. In Hinduism Brahmans retained their high social status, but it became possible for individual worshipers to have more direct contact with the gods, showing their devotion to them without the aid of priests as intermediaries. The bedrock of Hinduism is the belief that the Vedas are sacred revelations and that a specific caste system is implicitly prescribed in them. Hinduism assumes that there are innumerable legitimate ways of worshiping the supreme principle of life. Consequently, it readily incorporates new sects, doctrines, beliefs, rites, and deities.

Hinduism is a guide to life, the goal of which is to reach union with brahman, the ground of all being. There are four steps in this search, progressing from study of the Vedas in youth to complete asceticism in old age. In their quest for brahman, people are to observe **dharma,** the moral law. Dharma stipulates the legitimate pursuits of Hindus: material gain, as long as it is honestly and honorably achieved; pleasure and love, for the perpetuation of the family; and *moksha,* release from the wheel of life and unity with brahman. Hinduism, recognizing the need for material gain and pleasure, allows a joyful embracing of life.

After the third century B.C.E., Hinduism began to emphasize the roles and personalities of thousands of powerful gods. Brahma, the creator; Shiva, the cosmic dancer who both creates and destroys; and Vishnu, the preserver and sustainer of creation, are three main male deities. Female deities included Lakshmi, goddess of wealth, and Saraswati, goddess of learning and music. People could reach brahman by devotion to personal gods, usually represented by images. A worshiper's devotion to one god did

**Shiva** One of the three most important Vedic gods, Shiva represented both destruction and procreation. Here Shiva, mounted on a bull and carrying a spear, attacks the demon Andhaka. Shiva is seen as a fierce and bloodthirsty warrior. *(C. M. Dixon/Photo Resources)*

not entail denial of other deities; ultimately all were manifestations of the divine force that pervades the universe.

A central ethical text of Hinduism is the *Bhagavad Gita,* a part of the world's longest ancient epic, the *Mahabharata.* The *Bhagavad Gita* offers guidance on the most serious problem facing a Hindu—how to live in the world and yet honor dharma and thus achieve release. The heart of the *Bhagavad Gita* is the spiritual conflict confronting Arjuna, a human hero about to ride into battle against his kinsmen. As he surveys the battlefield, struggling with the grim notion of killing his relatives, Arjuna voices his doubts to his charioteer, none other than the god Krishna. When at last Arjuna refuses to spill his family's blood, Krishna instructs him, as he has instructed generations of Hindus, on the true meaning of Hinduism.

*You grieve for those beyond grief,*
*and you speak words of insight;*
*but learned men do not grieve*
*for the dead or the living.*

*Never have I not existed,*
*nor you, nor these kings;*
*and never in the future*
*shall we cease to exist.*

*Just as the embodied self*
*enters childhood, youth, and old age,*
*so does it enter another body;*
*this does not confound a steadfast man.*

*Contacts with matter make us feel*
*heat and cold, pleasure and pain.*
*Arjuna, you must learn to endure*
*fleeting things—they come and go!*

*When these cannot torment a man,*
*when suffering and joy are equal*
*for him and he has courage,*
*he is fit for immortality.*

*Nothing of nonbeing comes to be,*
*nor does being cease to exist;*
*the boundary between these two*
*is seen by men who see reality.*

*Indestructible is the presence*
*that pervades all this;*
*no one can destroy*
*this unchanging reality.*

*Our bodies are known to end,*
*but the embodied self is enduring,*
*indestructible, and immeasurable;*
*therefore, Arjuna, fight the battle!*

*He who thinks this self a killer*
*and he who thinks it killed,*
*both fail to understand;*
*it does not kill, nor is it killed.*

*It is not born,*
*it does not die;*
*having been,*
*it will never not be;*
*unborn, enduring,*
*constant, and primordial,*
*it is not killed*
*when the body is killed.*[3]

Krishna then clarifies the relationship between human reality and the eternal spirit. He explains compassionately to Arjuna the duty to act—to live in the world and carry out his duties as a warrior. Indeed, the *Bhagavad Gita* emphasizes the necessity of action, which is essential for the welfare of the world. Arjuna makes it the warrior's duty to wage war in compliance with his dharma. Only those who live within the divine law without complaint will be released from rebirth. One person's dharma may be different from another's, but both must follow their own dharmas.

Early in India's history, Hinduism provided a complex and sophisticated philosophy of life and a religion of enormous emotional appeal. Hinduism also inspired the preservation, in Sanskrit and the major regional languages of India, of literary masterpieces. Among these are the *Puranas,* which are stories of the gods and great warrior clans, and the *Mahabharata* and *Ramayana,* which are verse epics of India's early kings. Hinduism also validated the caste system, adding to the stability of everyday village life, since people all knew where they stood in society.

## INDIA AND THE WEST (CA 513–298 B.C.E.)

In the late sixth century B.C.E., west India was swept up in events that were changing the face of the ancient Near East. During this period the Persians were creating an empire that stretched from the west coast of Anatolia to the Indus River (see pages 47–48). India became involved in these events when the Persian emperor Darius conquered the Indus Valley and Kashmir about 513 B.C.E.

Persian control did not reach eastward beyond the Punjab. Even so, it fostered increased contact between India and the Middle East and led to the introduction of new ideas, techniques, and materials into India. From

Persian administrators Indians learned more about how to rule large tracts of land and huge numbers of people. They also learned the technique of minting silver coins, and they adopted the Persian monetary standard to facilitate trade with other parts of the empire. Even states in the Ganges Valley, which were never part of the Persian Empire, adopted the use of coinage.

Another result of contact with Persia was introduction of the Aramaic script, used to write the official language of the Persian Empire. To keep records and publish proclamations just as the Persians did, Indians in northwest India adapted the Aramaic script for writing several local languages (elsewhere, Indians developed the Brahmi script, the ancestor of the script used for modern Hindi). In time the sacred texts of the Buddhists and the Jains, as well as the epics and other literary works, all came to be recorded.

The Persian Empire in turn succumbed to Alexander the Great, and in 326 B.C.E. Alexander led his Macedonian and Greek troops through the Khyber Pass into the Indus Valley (see page 125). The India that Alexander encountered was composed of many rival states. He defeated some of these states in the northwest and heard reports of others. Porus, king of west Punjab, fought Alexander with a battalion of two thousand war elephants and after being defeated agreed to become a subordinate king under Alexander. Alexander had heard of the sophistication of Indian philosophers and summoned some to instruct him or debate with him.

The Greeks were impressed with Taxila, a major center of trade in the Punjab (see Map 3.1), and described it as "a city great and prosperous, the biggest of those between the Indus River and the Hydaspes [the modern Jhelum River]—a region not inferior to Egypt in size, with especially good pastures and rich in fine fruits."[4] From Taxila, Alexander followed the Indus River south, hoping to find the end of the world. His men, however, mutinied and refused to continue. When Alexander turned back, he left generals in charge of the regions he had conquered; Seleucus was put in charge of the eastern region.

## THE MAURYAN EMPIRE (CA 322–185 B.C.E.)

The one to benefit most from Alexander's invasion was Chandragupta, the ruler of a growing state in the Ganges Valley. He took advantage of the crisis caused by Alexander's invasion to expand his territories, and by 322 B.C.E. he had made himself sole master of north India. In 304 B.C.E. he defeated the forces of Seleucus. In the wake of this battle, Seleucus surrendered the easternmost provinces to Chandragupta, who in return gave him five hundred war elephants and concluded a treaty of alliance with him. In this way Chandragupta not only defeated one of the mightiest of Alexander's lieutenants (see Chapter 5) but also entered the world of Hellenistic politics.

The Mauryan Empire founded by Chandragupta stretched from the Punjab in the west to Bengal in the east. With stunning effectiveness, Chandragupta applied the lessons learned from Persian rule. He adopted the Persian practice of dividing the area into provinces. Each province was assigned a governor, most of whom were drawn from Chandragupta's own family. He established a complex bureaucracy to see to the operation of the state and a bureaucratic taxation system that financed public services through taxes on agriculture. He also built a regular army, complete with departments for everything from naval matters to the collection of supplies.

From his capital at Pataliputra in the Ganges Valley (now Patna in Bihar), Chandragupta sent agents to the provinces to oversee the workings of government and to keep him informed of conditions in his realm. For the first time in Indian history, one man governed most of the subcontinent, exercising control through delegated power. In designing his bureaucratic system, Chandragupta enjoyed the able assistance of his great minister Kautilya, who wrote a treatise on how a king should seize, hold, and manipulate power, rather like the Legalist treatises produced in China later that century (see Chapter 4). The king was urged to use propaganda to gain support, for instance, to disguise secret agents to look like gods so that people would be awed when they saw him in their company. The king was also alerted to the fact that all his immediate neighbors were his enemies but the princes directly beyond them were his natural friends. When a neighboring prince was in trouble, that was the perfect time to attack him. Interstate relations were likened to the law of the fish: the large swallow the small.

Megasthenes, a Greek ambassador sent by Seleucus to Chandragupta's court at Pataliputra, left a lively description of life there. He described the city as square and surrounded by wooden walls, 22 miles on each side, with 570 towers and 64 gates. It had a university, a library, and magnificent palaces, temples, gardens, and parks. The king personally presided over court sessions where legal cases were heard and petitions received. The king claimed for the state all mines and forests, and there were large state farms, granaries, shipyards, and spinning and weaving factories. Even prostitution was controlled by the state.

Megasthenes described Chandragupta as afraid of treachery, especially assassination. According to Megasthenes:

*Attendance on the king's person is the duty of women, who indeed are bought from their fathers. Outside the gates of the palace stand the bodyguards and the rest of the soldiers. . . . Nor does the king sleep during the day, and at night he is forced at various hours to change his bed because of those plotting against him. Of his non-military departures from the palace one is to the courts, in which he passes the day hearing cases to the end, even if the hour arrives for attendance on his person. . . . When he leaves to hunt, he is thickly surrounded by a circle of women, and on the outside by spear-carrying bodyguards. The road is fenced off with ropes, and to anyone who passes within the ropes as far as the women death is the penalty.*[5]

Those measures apparently worked, and Chandragupta lived a long life. According to Jain tradition, Chandragupta became a Jain ascetic and died a peaceful death in 298 B.C.E. Although he personally adopted a nonviolent philosophy, he left behind a kingdom with the military might to maintain order and defend India from invasion.

## The Reign of Ashoka (ca 269–232 B.C.E.)

The years after Chandragupta's death were an epoch of political greatness, thanks largely to Ashoka, one of India's most remarkable figures. The grandson of Chandragupta, Ashoka extended the Mauryan Empire to its farthest limits. The era of Ashoka was enormously important in the religious history of the world, because Ashoka embraced Buddhism, helped to establish it as an important religion in India, and promoted its spread beyond India.

As a young prince, Ashoka served as governor of two prosperous provinces where Buddhism flourished. At the death of his father about 274 B.C.E., Ashoka rebelled against his older brother, the rightful king, and after four years of fighting succeeded in his bloody bid for the throne. Crowned king, Ashoka ruled intelligently and energetically. He was equally serious about his pleasures, especially those of the banquet hall and harem.

In the ninth year of his reign, 261 B.C.E., Ashoka conquered Kalinga, the modern state of Orissa, on the east coast of India. In a grim and savage campaign, Ashoka reduced Kalinga by wholesale slaughter. As Ashoka himself admitted, "One hundred and fifty thousand were forcibly abducted from their homes, 100,000 were killed in battle, and many more died later on."[6] Instead of exulting like a conqueror, however, Ashoka was consumed with remorse and revulsion at the horror of war. He embraced Buddhism and used the machinery of his empire to spread Buddhist teachings throughout India. He supported the doctrine of not hurting humans or animals, then spreading among religious people of all sects, and banned animal sacrifices and any killing of certain species. In place of hunting expeditions, he took pilgrimages. Two years after his conversion, he undertook a 256-day pilgrimage to all the holy sites of Buddhism, and on his return he began his missionary activity, sending missionaries to all known countries. Buddhist tradition also credits him with erecting throughout India 84,000 stupas (Buddhist reliquary mounds), among which the ashes or other bodily remains of the Buddha were distributed, beginning the association of Buddhism with monumental art and architecture.

Ashoka's remarkable crisis of conscience, like the later conversion to Christianity of the Roman emperor Constantine (see pages 174–175), affected the way he ruled. He emphasized compassion, nonviolence, and adherence to dharma. He appointed officials to oversee the moral welfare of the realm and required local officials to govern humanely. He may have perceived dharma as a kind of civic virtue, a universal ethical model capable of uniting the diverse peoples of his extensive empire. Ashoka erected stone pillars, on the Persian model, with inscriptions to inform the people of his policies. He also had long inscriptions carved into large rock surfaces near trade routes. In one inscription he spoke to his people like a father:

*Whatever good I have done has indeed been accomplished for the progress and welfare of the world. By these shall grow virtues namely: proper support of mother and father, regard for preceptors and elders, proper treatment of Brahmans and ascetics, of the poor and the destitute, slaves and servants.*[7]

These inscriptions are the earliest fully dated Indian texts. (Until the script in which they were written was deciphered in 1837, nothing was known of Ashoka's achievements.) The pillars on which they are inscribed are also the first examples of Indian art to survive since the end of the Indus civilization.

Ashoka felt the need to protect his new religion and to keep it pure. Warning Buddhist monks that he would not tolerate *schism*—divisions based on differences of opinion about doctrine or ritual—he threw his support to religious orthodoxy. According to Buddhist tradition, a great council of Buddhist monks was held at Pataliputra,

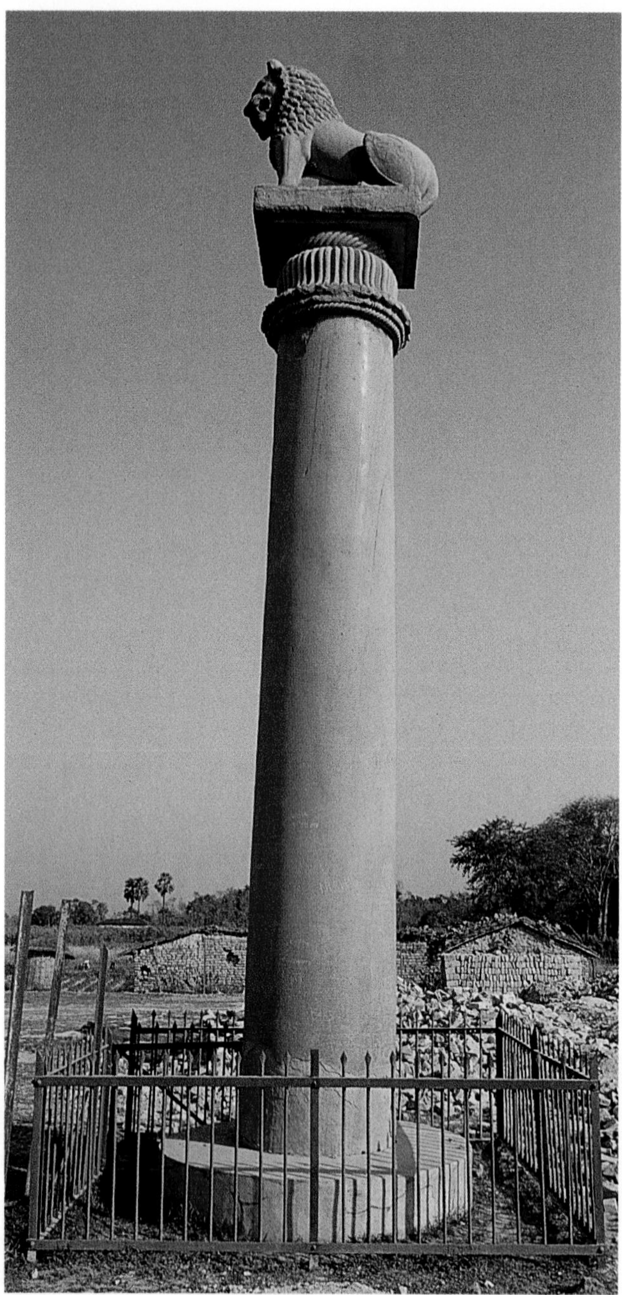

**Ashokan Pillar** The best preserved of the pillars that King Ashoka erected in about 240 B.C.E. is this one in the Bihar region, near Nepal. The solid shaft of polished sandstone rises thirty-two feet in the air. It weighs about fifty tons, making its erection a remarkable feat of engineering. Like other Ashokan pillars, it is inscribed with accounts of Ashoka's political achievements and instructions to his subjects on proper behavior. These pillars are the earliest extant examples of Indian writing and a major historical source for the Mauryan period. *(Borromeo/Art Resource, NY)*

where the earliest canon of Buddhist texts was codified. At the same time, Ashoka honored India's other religions, even building shrines for Hindu and Jain worshipers. In one edict he banned rowdy popular fairs, allowing only religious gatherings.

Despite his devotion to Buddhism, Ashoka never neglected his duties as emperor. He tightened the central government of the empire and kept a close check on local officials. He also built roads and rest spots to improve communication within the realm. Ashoka himself described this work: "On the highways Banyan trees have been planted so that they may afford shade to men and animals; mango-groves have been planted; watering-places have been established for the benefit of animals and men."[8] These measures also facilitated the march of armies and the armed enforcement of Ashoka's authority. Ashoka's efforts were eminently successful: during his reign India enjoyed peace, prosperity, and humane rule.

Ashoka's inscriptions indirectly tell us much about the Mauryan Empire. He directly administered the central part of the empire, focusing on Magadha. Beyond it were four large provinces, under princes who served as viceroys, each with its own sets of smaller districts and officials. The interior of south India was described as inhabited by undefeated forest tribes. Farther south, along the coasts, were peoples Ashoka maintained friendly relations with but did not rule, such as the Cholas and Pandyas. Relations with Sri Lanka were especially close under Ashoka, and the king sent a branch of the tree under which the Buddha gained enlightenment to the Sri Lankan king. According to Buddhist legend, Ashoka's son Mahinda traveled to Sri Lanka to convert the people there.

Ashoka ruled for thirty-seven years. After he died in about 232 B.C.E., the Mauryan dynasty went into decline, and India broke up into smaller units, much like those in existence before Alexander's invasion. Even though Chandragupta had instituted bureaucratic methods of centralized political control and Ashoka had vigorously pursued the political and cultural integration of the empire, the institutions they created were not entrenched enough to survive periods with weaker kings. For much of subsequent Indian history, political unity would be the exception rather than the rule. By this time, however, key elements of Indian culture—the caste system; the religious traditions of Hinduism, Buddhism, and Jainism; and the great epics and legends—had given India a cultural unity strong enough to endure even without political unity.

## REGIONAL DEVELOPMENTS (200 B.C.E.–300 C.E.)

After the Mauryan dynasty collapsed in 184 B.C.E., a series of foreign powers dominated the Indus Valley and adjoining regions. The first were hybrid Indo-Greek states, ruled by the inheritors of Alexander's defunct empire stationed in what is now Afghanistan. King Menander (fl. 160–135 B.C.E.) is remembered because a profound conversation between him and the Buddhist monk Nagasena was recorded as the *Questions of King Milenda.* The city of Taxila became a major center of trade, culture, and education, fusing elements of Greek and Indian culture.

The great, slow movement of nomadic peoples out of East Asia that brought the Scythians to the Middle East brought the Shakas to northwest India. They controlled the region from about 94 to 20 B.C.E., when they were displaced by a new nomadic invader, the Kushans, who ruled the region of today's Afghanistan, Pakistan, and west India as far south as Gujarat. Their king Kanishka (r. ca 78–ca 103 C.E.) is known from Buddhist sources. The famous silk trade from China to Rome passed through his territory.

We know less about what was happening in east and south India in this period, but it is apparent that political division into competing states in India did not lead to cultural or economic decline. During the Kushan period, Greek culture had a considerable impact on Indian art. Indo-Greek artists and sculptors working in India adorned Buddhist shrines, modeling the earliest representation of the Buddha on Hellenistic statues of Apollo. Another contribution from the Indo-Greek states was coins cast with images of the king, which came to be widely adopted by Indian rulers, aiding commerce and adding evidence to the historical record. Cultural exchange also went in the other direction as well. Old Indian animal folktales were translated into Syriac and Greek, and from that source eventually made their way to Europe as well.

During these centuries there were significant advances in science, mathematics, and philosophy. Nagarjuna (fl. ca 50–150 C.E.) was a major theorist of Mahayana Buddhism, who developed sophisticated theories of the nature of reality and debated them directly with Brahman priests. This was also the period when Indian law was codified. The **Code of Manu,** which lays down family, caste, and commercial law, was compiled in the second or third century C.E.

Regional cultures tend to flourish when there is no dominant, unifying state. In south India the third century B.C.E. to the third century C.E. is considered the classical period of Tamil culture, when many great works of literature were written under the patronage of the regional kings. Some of these poems take a hard look at war.

**Kushan Girl** The young woman on this second-century C.E. stone sculpture wears bracelets, necklaces, and earrings. She is carrying a platter of food, perhaps for a feast. *(Courtesy, Archaeological Museum, Mathura)*

*Harvest of War*

*Great king*
*you shield your men from ruin,*
*so your victories, your greatness*
*are bywords.*

*Loose chariot wheels*
*lie about the battleground*
*with the long white tusks*
*of bull-elephants.*

*Flocks of male eagles*
*eat carrion*
*with their mates.*

*Headless bodies*
*dance about*
*before they fall*
*to the ground.*

*Blood glows,*
*like the sky before nightfall,*
*in the red center*
*of the battlefield.*

*Demons dance there.*
*And your kingdom*
*is an unfailing harvest*
*of victorious wars.*[9]

South India in this period was also the center of active seaborne trade, with networks reaching all the way to Rome. Indian sailing technology was highly advanced, and much of this trade was in the hands of Indian merchants. Roman traders based in Egypt followed the routes already used by Arab traders, sailing with the monsoon from the Red Sea to the west coast of India in about two weeks, returning about six months later when the direction of the winds reversed. In the second half of the first century C.E. a Greek merchant involved in this trade reported that the traders sold coins, topaz, coral, crude glass, copper, tin, and lead and bought pearls, ivory, silk (probably originally from China), jewels of many sorts (probably many from Southeast Asia), and above all cinnamon and pepper. More Roman gold coins of the first and second centuries C.E. have been found near the southern tip of India than in any other area. The local rulers had slits made across the image of the Roman emperor to show that his sovereignty was not recognized, but they had no objection to the coins circulating. (By contrast, the Kushan rulers in the north had Roman coins melted down to use to make coins with their own images on them.)

Even after the fall of Rome, many of the traders on the southwest coast of India remained. These diasporic communities of Christians and Jews lived in the coastal cities into modern times. When Vasco da Gama, the Portuguese explorer, reached Calicut in 1498, he found a local Jewish merchant who was able to interpret for him.

## SUMMARY

Many of the cultural elements that unify India date to the ancient period discussed in this chapter. Although India never had a single language and only periodically had a centralized government, certain ideas and cultural practices gave India a distinct identity. These included the core ideas of Brahmanism, the caste system, and the story cycles recorded in the great epics. These cultural elements spread through trade and other contact, even when the subcontinent was divided into hostile kingdoms. India also was in contact with the outside world from the time of the Indus civilization on. Just as India came to absorb some Persian bureaucratic techniques and Greek artistic styles, other regions borrowed crops, textiles, inventions, and religious ideas from India.

## KEY TERMS

Harappan
Aryans
*Rigveda*
raja
Brahmans
caste system
varna
outcastes
samsara
karma
moksha
brahman
Four Noble Truths
Eightfold Path
nirvana
Mahayana
dharma
Code of Manu

## NOTES

1. *Rigveda* 10.90, translated by A. L. Basham, in *The Wonder That Was India* (New York: Grove Press, 1954), p. 241.
2. J. Mascaro, trans., *The Upanishads* (London: Penguin Books, 1965), pp. 117–118.
3. B. S. Miller, trans., *The Bhagavad-gita: Krishna's Counsel in Time of War* (New York: Columbia University Press, 1986), pp. 31–32.
4. Arrian, *Anabasis* 5.8.2; Plutarch, *Alexander* 59.1. Translated by John Buckler.
5. *Strabo,* 15.1.55. Translated by John Buckler.
6. Quoted in H. Kulke and D. Rothermund, *A History of India,* 3d ed. (London: Routledge, 1998), p. 62.
7. Quoted in B. G. Gokhale, *Asoka Maurya* (New York: Twayne Publishers, 1966), p. 169.
8. Quoted ibid., pp. 168–169.
9. A. K. Ramanujan, ed. and trans., *Poems of Love and War: From the Eight Anthologies and the Ten Long Poems of Classical Tamil* (New York: Columbia University Press, 1985), p. 115.

## SUGGESTED READING

Much splendid work has been done on the geographical background of ancient Indian society. See, in particular, G. Johnson, *Cultural Atlas of India* (1996), and J. Schwartzberg, ed., *An Historical Atlas of South Asia* (1978), the epitome of what a historical atlas should be. The contents of both range well into contemporary times. Useful general reference works on India include A. T. Embree, ed., *Encyclopedia of Asian History* (1989), and F. Robinson, ed., *The Cambridge Encyclopedia of India* (1989). On Indian art, see S. L. Huntington, *The Art of Ancient India* (1985); J. C. Harle, *The Art and Architecture of the Indian Subcontinent* (1986); and V. Dehejia, *Indian Art* (1997). Good translations of Indian literature discussed in the chapter are listed in the Notes. For an overview of Indian literature, see E. Dimock, Jr., et al., *The Literatures of India* (1974).

Among the best general histories of India are H. Kulke and D. Rothermund, *A History of India,* 3d ed. (1998); A. L. Basham, *The Wonder That Was India,* 3d rev. ed. (1968); R. Thapar, *History of India* (1966); and B. Stein, *A History of India* (1998). Also rewarding are R. Thapar, *Ancient Indian Social History* (1978); Z. Liu, *Ancient India and Ancient China* (1988); S. F. Mahmud, *A Concise History of Indo-Pakistan,* 2d ed. (1988); H. Scharff, *The State in Indian Tradition* (1989), which covers the period from the Aryans to the Muslims; and N. N. Bhattacharya, *Ancient Indian History and Civilization* (1988), which focuses on India before 1000 C.E.

Work on the Indus civilization continues at a rapid pace. See G. L. Possehl, ed., *Harappan Civilization: A Recent Perspective* (1993); G. L. Possehl and M. H. Ravel, *Harappan Civilization and Rojdi* (1989); and J. M. Kenoyer, *Ancient Cities of the Indus Valley Civilization* (1998). Trade between the Indus and Mesopotamian civilizations is treated in E. C. L. During Caspers, "Sumer, Coastal Arabia and the Indus Valley in Protoliterate and Early Dynastic Eras," *Journal of Economic and Social History of the Orient* 22 (1979): 121–135, and S. Ratnagar, *Encounters: The Westerly Trade of the Harappa Civilization* (1981).

For the Aryans and the Vedic period, see N. R. Banerjee, *The Iron Age in India* (1965), and C. Chakraborty, *Common Life in the Rig-veda and Atharvaveda* (1977). D. K. Chakrabarti, *The Early Use of Iron in India* (1992), uses archaeological evidence to prove that the ancient Indians used iron far earlier than previously thought. The question of the origins of the Aryans is analyzed in depth in C. Renfew, *Archaeology and Language: The Puzzle of Indo-European Origins* (1987). The polemical side of the debate can be seen from K. Elst, *Update on the Aryan Invasion Debate* (1999).

An excellent introduction to Indian religion, philosophy, and intellectual history is A. Embree, ed., *Sources of Indian Tradition,* 2d ed. (1988), which provides translations of major sources. Another excellent source of translated documents is D. Lopez, ed., *Religions of India in Practice* (1998). A broad overview of Indian religion is provided by J. Koller, *The Indian Way* (1982). P. S. Jaini, *The Jaina Path of Purification* (1979), and T. Hopkins, *Hindu Religious Tradition* (1971), cover two of the major religions, to which should be added K. K. Klostermaier, *A Survey of Hinduism* (1989), and K. H. Potter, *Guide to Indian Philosophy* (1988).

Buddhism is such a popular topic that the bibliography is virtually endless. H. Akira, *A History of Indian Buddhism* (1990), treats the early history of the Buddha and his followers. R. Robinson and W. Johnson, *The Buddhist Religion,* 4th ed. (1996), offers a comprehensive overview. See also D. Lopez, *The Story of the Buddha: A Concise Guide to Its History and Teachings* (2001). Still unsurpassed for its discussion of the relations between Buddhism and Hinduism is the grand work of C. N. Eliot, *Hinduism and Buddhism,* 3 vols. (reprint 1954), which traces the evolution of theistic ideas in both religions. C. Humphreys has written extensively about Buddhism. The student may wish to consult his *Buddhism* (1962), *Exploring Buddhism* (1975), or *The Wisdom of Buddhism,* rev. ed. (1979). More recent is D. Fox, *The Heart of Buddhist Wisdom* (1985). A well-illustrated volume is H. Bechert and R. Gombrich, ed., *The World of Buddhism* (1984).

Among the numerous works describing India's relations with the Persian Empire and Alexander the Great are several titles cited in the Suggested Reading for Chapters 2 and 5. P. H. L. Eggermont, *Alexander's Campaigns in Sind and Baluchistan* (1975), focuses solely on Alexander's activities in India. A. J. Dani, *The Historic City of Taxila* (1988), uses anthropological and historic evidence to study this important city and its influence.

On the reigns of Chandragupta and Ashoka, see R. K. Mookerji, *Chandragupta Maurya and His Times,* rev. ed. (1966), and R. Thapar, *Asoka and the Decline of the Mauryas* (1961), as well as her *Mauryas Revisited* (1987). J. C. Heesterman, "Kautilya and the Ancient Indian State," *Wiener Zeitschrift* 15 (1971): 5–22, analyzes the work and thought of Chandragupta's great minister of state.

For the Gupta period, see O. P. Singh Bhatia, trans., *The Imperial Guptas* (1962), and B. Smith, ed., *Essays on Gupta Culture* (1983). In a series of works, S. K. Maity covers many facets of the period: *Gupta Civilization: A Study* (1974), *The Imperial Guptas and Their Times* (1975), and *Economic Life in North India in the Gupta Period* (1975). Good treatments of Indian society and daily life in this period can be found in J. Auboyer, *Daily Life in Ancient India from Approximately 200 B.C. to A.D. 700* (1965).

# LISTENING TO THE PAST

## RAMA AND SITA

*The* Ramayana, *an epic poem of about fifty thousand verses, is attributed to the third-century B.C.E. poet Valmiki. Its main character, Rama, the oldest son of a king, is an incarnation of the great god Vishnu. As a young man, he wins the princess Sita as his wife when he alone among her suitors proves strong enough to bend a huge bow. Rama and Sita love each other deeply, but court intrigue disturbs their happy life. After the king announces that he will retire and consecrate Rama as his heir, his beautiful junior wife, wishing to advance her own son, reminds the king that he has promised her a favor of her choice. She then asks to have him appoint her son heir and to have Rama sent into the wilderness for fourteen years. The king is forced to consent, and Rama obeys his father.*

*The passage below gives the conversations between Rama and Sita after Rama learns he must leave. In subsequent parts of the very long epic, the lovers undergo many other tribulations, including Sita's abduction by the lord of the demons, the ten-headed Ravana, and her eventual recovery by Rama with the aid of monkeys.*

*The* Ramayana *eventually appeared in numerous versions in all the major languages of India. Hearing it recited was said to bring religious merit. Sita, passionate in her devotion to her husband, has remained the favorite Indian heroine. Rama, Sita, and the monkey Hanuman are cult figures in Hinduism, with temples devoted to their worship.*

"For fourteen years I must live in Dandaka, while my father will appoint Bharata prince regent. I have come to see you before I leave for the desolate forest. You are never to boast of me in the presence of Bharata. Men in power cannot bear to hear others praised, and so you must never boast of my virtues in front of Bharata. . . . When I have gone to the forest where sages make their home, my precious, blameless wife, you must earnestly undertake vows and fasts. You must rise early and worship the gods according to custom and then pay homage to my father Dasaratha, lord of men. And my aged mother Kausalya, who is tormented by misery, deserves your respect as well, for she has subordinated all to righteousness. The rest of my mothers, too, must always receive your homage. . . . My beloved, I am going to the great forest, and you must stay here. You must do as I tell you, my lovely, and not give offense to anyone."

So Rama spoke, and Sita, who always spoke kindly to her husband and deserved kindness from him, grew angry just because she loved him, and said, "My lord, a man's father, his mother, brother, son, or daughter-in-law all experience the effects of their own past deeds and suffer an individual fate. But a wife, and she alone, bull among men, must share her husband's fate. Therefore I, too, have been ordered to live in the forest. It is not her father or mother, not her son or friends or herself, but her husband, and he alone, who gives a woman permanent refuge in this world and after death. If you must leave this very day for the trackless forest, Rama, I will go in front of you, softening the thorns and sharp *kusa* grass. Cast out your anger and resentment, like so much water left after drinking one's fill. Do not be reluctant to take me, my mighty husband. There is no evil in me. The shadow of a husband's feet in any circumstances surpasses the finest mansions, an aerial chariot, or even flying through the sky. . . . O Rama, bestower of honor, you have the power to protect any other person in the forest. Why then not me? . . .

"If I were to be offered a place to live in heaven itself, Rama, tiger among men, I would refuse it if you were not there. I will go to the trackless forest teeming with deer, monkeys, and elephants, and live there as in my father's house, clinging to your feet alone, in strict self-discipline. I love no one else; my heart is so attached to you that were we to be parted I am resolved to die. Take me, oh please grant my request. I shall not be a burden to you." . . .

When Sita finished speaking, the righteous prince, who knew what was right and cherished it, attempted to dissuade her. . . .

"Sita, give up this notion of living in the forest. The name 'forest' is given only to wild regions where hardships abound. . . . There are lions that live in mountain caves; their roars are redoubled by mountain torrents and are a painful thing to hear—the forest is a place of pain. At night worn with fatigue, one must sleep upon the ground on a bed of leaves, broken off of themselves—the forest is a place of utter pain. And one has to fast, Sita, to the limit of one's endurance, wear clothes of barkcloth and bear the burden of matted hair. . . . There are many creeping creatures, of every size and shape, my lovely, ranging aggressively over the ground. . . . Moths, scorpions, worms, gnats, and flies continually harass one, my frail Sita—the forest is wholly a place of pain. . . ."

Sita was overcome with sorrow when she heard what Rama said. With tears trickling down her face, she answered him in a faint voice. . . . "If from feelings of love I follow you, my pure-hearted husband, I shall have no sin to answer for, because my husband is my deity. My union with you is sacred and shall last even beyond death. . . . If you refuse to take me to the forest despite the sorrow that I feel, I shall have no recourse but to end my life by poison, fire, or water."

Though she pleaded with him in this and every other way to be allowed to go, great-armed Rama would not consent to taking her to the desolate forest. And when he told her as much, Sita fell to brooding, and drenched the ground, it seemed, with the hot tears that fell from her eyes. . . . She was nearly insensible with sorrow when Rama took her in his arms and comforted her. . . . "Without knowing your true feelings, my lovely, I could not consent to your living in the wilderness, though I am perfectly capable of protecting you. Since you are determined to live with me in the forest, Sita, I could no sooner abandon you than a self-respecting man his reputation. . . . My father keeps to the path of righteousness and truth, and I wish to act just as he instructs me. That is the eternal way of righteousness. Follow me, my timid one, be my companion in righteousness. Go now and bestow precious objects on the brahmans, give food to the mendicants and all who ask for it. Hurry, there is no time to waste."

Finding that her husband had acquiesced in her going, the lady was elated and set out at once to make the donations.

Rama and Sita in the forest, from a set of miniature paintings done in about 1600. *(National Museum, New Delhi)*

## QUESTIONS FOR ANALYSIS

1. What can you infer about early Indian family life and social relations from this story?
2. What do Sita's words and actions indicate about women's roles in Indian society of the time?
3. What do you think accounts for the continuing popularity of the story of Rama throughout Indian history?

*Source: The Ramayana of Valmiki: An Epic of India,* vol. 2: *Ayodhyakanda,* trans. Sheldon I. Pollock, ed. Robert P. Goldman (Princeton, N.J.: Princeton University Press, 1986), pp. 134–142, modified slightly. 

This nearly foot-tall ivory cup is inlaid with turquoise from the tomb (ca 1200 B.C.E.) of a Shang royal consort. *(© Cultural Relics Data Center of China)*

CHAPTER

# 4 CHINA'S CLASSICAL AGE, TO 256 B.C.E.

## CHAPTER OUTLINE

- The Land and Its Challenge
- China's Earliest Civilizations, to 1050 B.C.E.
- The Zhou Dynasty (ca 1050–256 B.C.E.)
- The Golden Age of Chinese Philosophy

The early development of China's civilization occurred with little contact with the other early civilizations of Eurasia. The reasons for China's relative isolation were geographic: communication between the Middle East or India and East Asia was very difficult, impeded by high mountains and vast deserts. Thus, in comparison to India and the ancient Middle East, there was less cross-fertilization through trade and other contact with other comparably advanced civilizations. Moreover, there were no cultural breaks comparable to the rise of the Aryans in India or the Assyrians in the Middle East; there were no new peoples and no new languages.

The impact of early China's relative isolation is found in many distinctive or unique features of its culture. Perhaps the most important of these is its writing system. Unlike the other major societies of Eurasia, China retained a logographic writing system, with a separate symbol for each word. This writing system shaped not only Chinese literature and thought but also key social and political processes, such as the nature of the ruling class and the way Chinese interacted with non-Chinese.

Chinese history is discussed in terms of a succession of dynasties. The Shang Dynasty (ca 1500–ca 1050 B.C.E.) was the first to have writing, metalworking, cities, and chariots. The Shang kings played priestly roles, serving as intermediaries with both their royal ancestors and the high god Di. The Shang were overthrown by one of their vassal states, the Zhou (ca 1050–256 B.C.E.). The Zhou rulers set up a decentralized, feudal governmental structure. After several centuries, this structure evolved into a multistate system. As warfare between the states intensified from the sixth century B.C.E. on, social and cultural change also quickened. Aristocratic privileges declined, and China entered one of its most creative periods, when the philosophies of Confucianism, Daoism, and Legalism were developed.

- How did China's geography influence its development?
- In what ways did ancient and classical China resemble other early civilizations?
- What effects did China's retaining a logographic writing system have on its culture?
- What were the key contributions of the ancient and classical periods to the later development of Chinese civilization?

These are the questions addressed in this chapter.

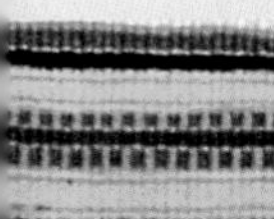

## THE LAND AND ITS CHALLENGE

The term *China,* like the term *India,* does not refer to the same geographical entity at all points in history. But the historical China, also called China proper, was smaller than present-day China, not larger like the historical India. The contemporary People's Republic of China includes territories like Tibet, Inner Mongolia, Turkestan, and Manchuria that were not in premodern times inhabited by Chinese or ruled directly by Chinese states (see Map 4.1).

China proper, about a thousand miles north to south and east to west, occupies much of the temperate zone of East Asia. The northern part, drained by the Yellow River, is colder, flatter, and more arid than the south. Rainfall in many areas is less than twenty inches a year, making it well suited to crops like wheat and millet. The dominant soil is **loess**—fine wind-driven earth that is fertile and easy to work even with primitive tools. Because so much of the loess ends up as silt in the Yellow River, the riverbed rises, and the river has to be diked and easily floods. Drought is another perennial problem for farmers in the north. The Yangzi River is the dominant feature of the warmer, wetter, and more lush south, a region well suited to rice cultivation and double cropping. The Yangzi and its many tributaries are navigable, so boats were traditionally the preferred means of transportation in the south.

Mountains, deserts, and grasslands separated China proper from other early civilizations. Between China and India lay Tibet, with its vast mountain ranges and high plateaus. North of Tibet are great expanses of desert

**MAP 4.1 China Under the Shang and Zhou Dynasties** Chinese civilization developed in the temperate regions drained by the Yellow and Yangzi Rivers. The early Zhou government controlled larger areas than the Shang did, but the independent states of the Warring States Period were more aggressive about pushing out their frontiers, greatly extending the geographical boundaries of Chinese civilization.

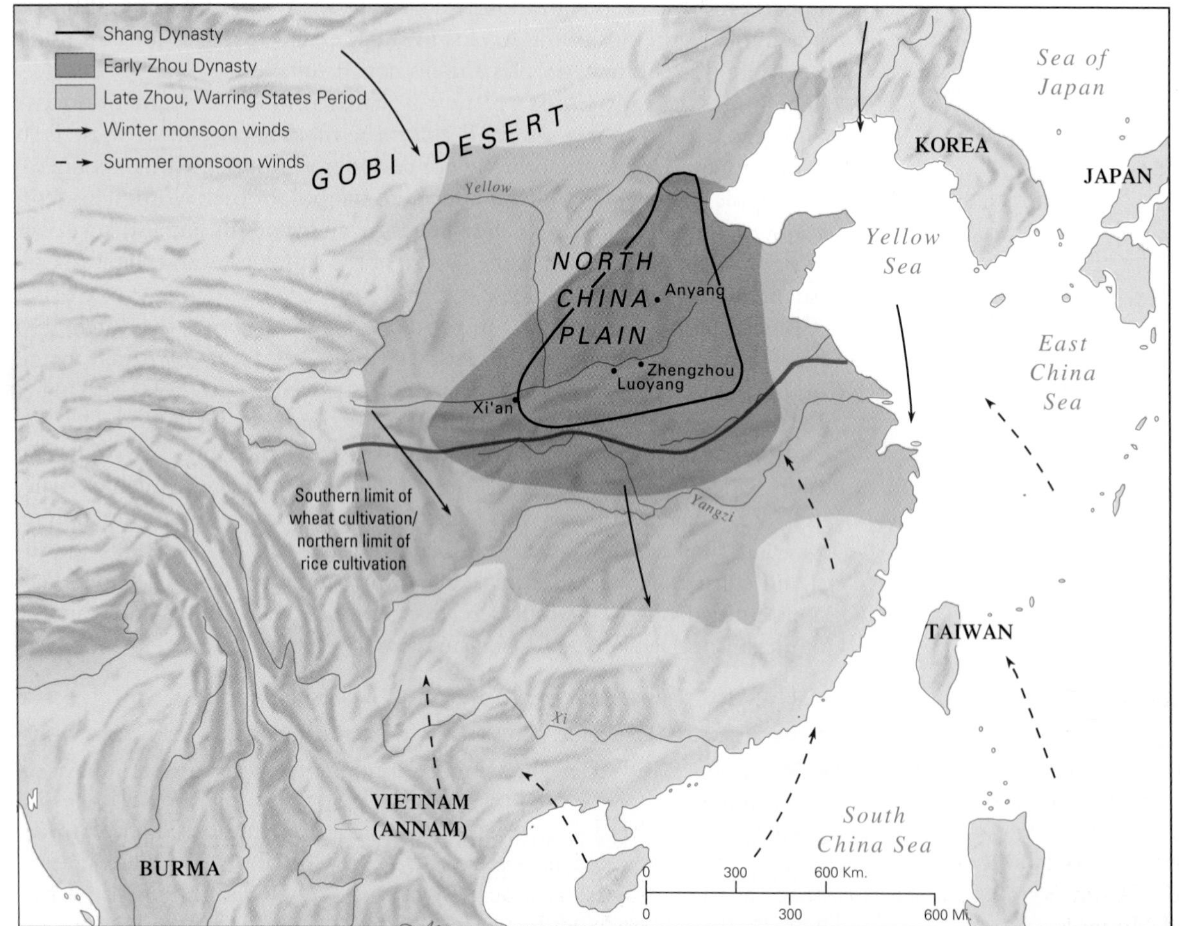

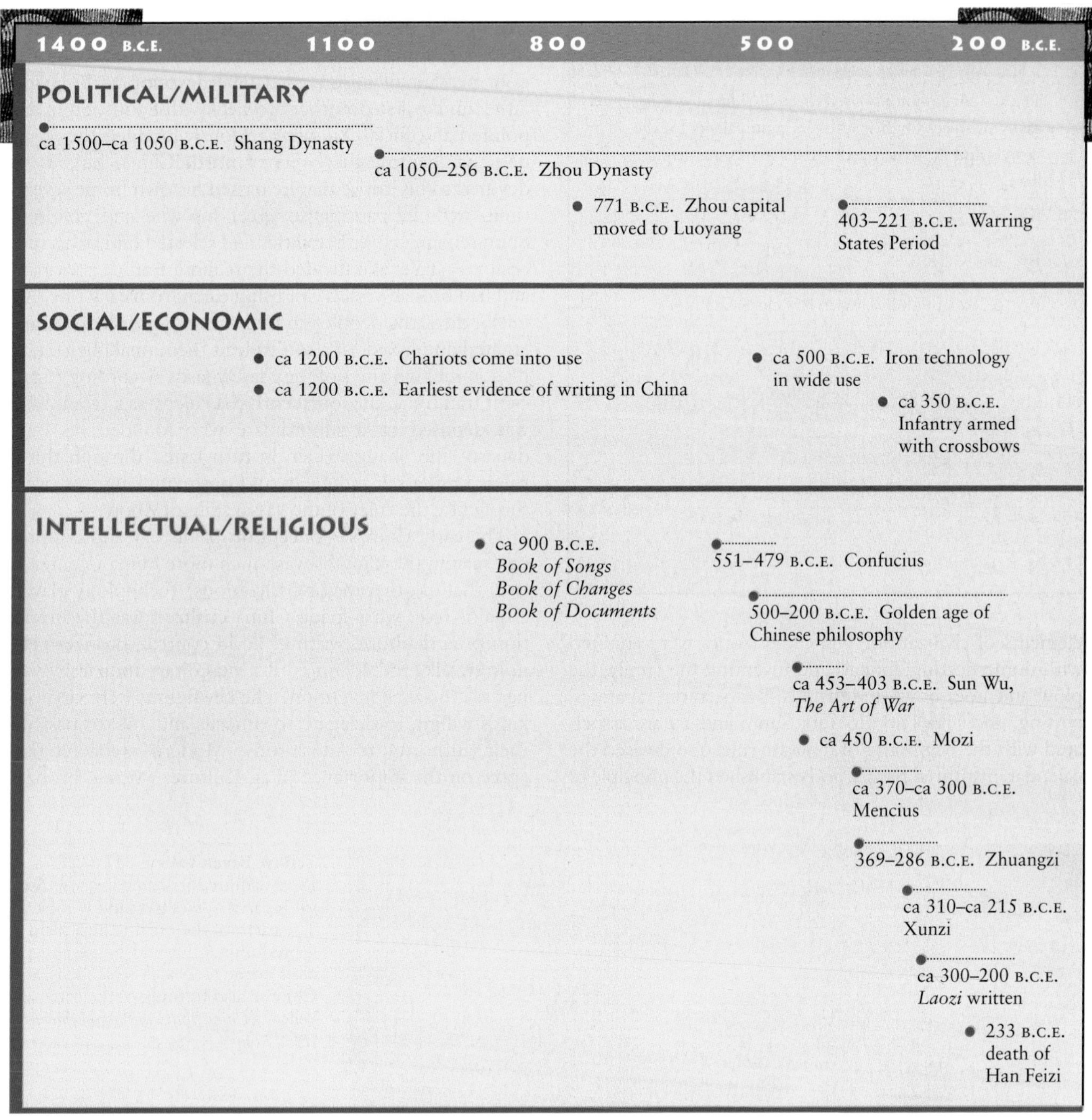


where nothing grows except in rare oases, and north of them stretch grasslands from Ukraine to eastern Siberia. Chinese civilization did not spread into any of these Inner Asian regions, above all because they were not suited to crop agriculture. Inner Asia, where raising animals is a more productive use of land than planting crops, became the heartland of China's traditional enemies, such as the **Xiongnu** and Mongols.

## CHINA'S EARLIEST CIVILIZATIONS, TO 1050 B.C.E.

Chinese myths and legends, like those of other early civilizations, reveal what the Chinese considered to be their central and distinctive values. In the form in which these myths have been preserved, China was fashioned not by gods but by brilliant human beings who invented the key

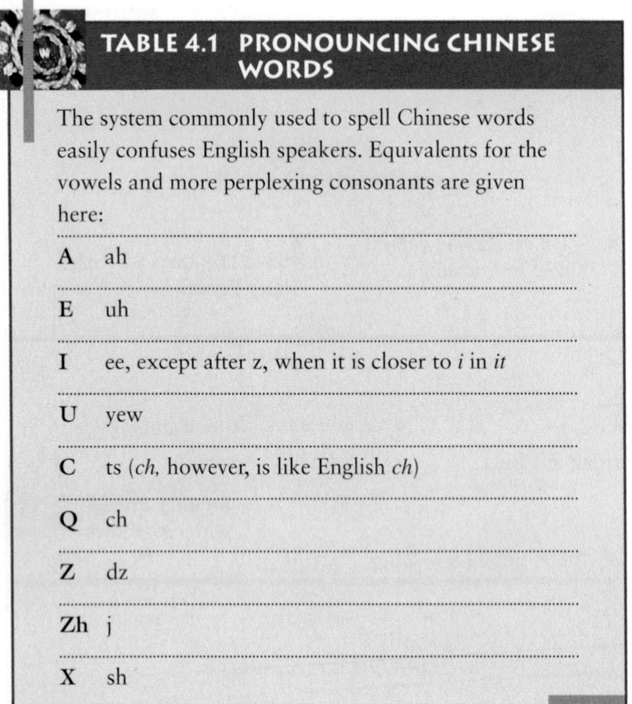

**TABLE 4.1 PRONOUNCING CHINESE WORDS**

The system commonly used to spell Chinese words easily confuses English speakers. Equivalents for the vowels and more perplexing consonants are given here:

| | |
|---|---|
| **A** | ah |
| **E** | uh |
| **I** | ee, except after z, when it is closer to *i* in *it* |
| **U** | yew |
| **C** | ts (*ch,* however, is like English *ch*) |
| **Q** | ch |
| **Z** | dz |
| **Zh** | j |
| **X** | sh |

elements of civilization. The earliest ones were credited with domesticating animals and inventing the family, the plow and hoe, bows and arrows, boats, carts, ceramics, writing, and silk. The trio Yao, Shun, and Yu are associated with the beginning of dynastic rule. Yao devised the calendar, instituted rituals, and established the principle of rule by the worthy: when it was time to turn over power, he bypassed his own less worthy son in favor of Shun, a poor peasant of unsurpassed filial devotion to his blind father and evil stepmother. To deal with floods, Shun appointed an official, Yu, who zealously dredged the channels that became the rivers of north China. Yu was so devoted to his duties that he passed his own home several times without pausing to greet his wife and children. Shun recognized Yu's abilities and selected him as his successor. As ruler, Yu divided the realm into nine provinces and had bronze vessels cast using earth from each one. After Yu died, the people ignored the successor he had designated and asked Yu's son to lead them, making Yu and his son the two kings of the Xia Dynasty. According to ancient traditions, the fourteenth Xia ruler was a tyrant who was deposed by a subordinate who founded his own dynasty, the Shang, which in turn lasted through thirty rulers until a self-indulgent and obstinate king was overthrown by the ruler of the vassal state of Zhou.

The early Chinese conception of history and cosmology seen in these myths was much more human-centered than that of other major civilizations. Technology played a major role: what made China civilized was the invention of agriculture, writing, flood control, bronze technology, silk, and ceramics. But hereditary monarchy was just as crucial an invention. The key figures were virtuous kings willing to delegate to officials and able to pass on their authority to their sons. Modern archaeologists agree on the importance of agriculture, writing, bronze,

**Yellow River Valley** The Yellow River acquired its name because the silt it carries gives it a muddy look. The earth of the north China plain is predominantly wind-borne and river-borne loess soil, which led early Chinese also to think of the earth as yellow. *(China Tourism Photo Library, Hong Kong)*

**Painted Pottery Figure** The Neolithic cultures of northwest China in the third millennium B.C.E. decorated pottery with red and black paint. Most of the finds are jars decorated with geometric designs, but there are occasionally images of human beings, animals, and fish. Some scholars speculate that this image depicts a shaman wearing face paint. Note the snake depicted climbing the back of its head. *(© Museum of Far Eastern Antiquities)*

and state formation to the story of Chinese civilization but also give weight to ritual and religion. Moreover, rather than concentrate narrowly on the direct predecessors of the Shang kings, they have shown that both in Shang times and in the millennium before them, China proper was home to many distinct cultures, all of which played a part in the evolution of Chinese civilization.

## The Neolithic Age

From about 10,000 B.C.E. agriculture was practiced in China, apparently originating independently of somewhat earlier developments in Egypt and Mesopotamia, but perhaps influenced by developments in Southeast Asia, where rice cultivation began earlier than in China. By 5000 B.C.E. there were Neolithic village settlements in several regions of China. The primary Neolithic crops were drought-resistant millet, grown in the loess soils of the region drained by the Yellow River, and rice, grown in the wetlands of the lower reaches of the Yangzi River, where it was supplemented by fish. In both areas pigs, dogs, and cattle were domesticated, and by 3000 B.C.E. sheep had become important in the north and water buffalo in the south.

Over the course of the fifth to third millennia B.C.E., many distinct regional Neolithic cultures emerged. For instance, in the northwest during the fourth and third millennia B.C.E., people made fine red pottery vessels decorated in black pigment with bold designs, including spirals, sawtooth lines, and zoomorphic stick figures. At the same time in the east, pottery was rarely painted but was made into distinctive shapes, including three-legged, deep-bodied tripods. Jade ornaments, blades, and ritual objects, sometimes of extraordinary craftsmanship, have been found in several eastern sites but are rare in western ones.

Over time Neolithic cultures came to share more by way of material culture and social and cultural practices. Many practices related to treatment of the dead spread out of their original area, including use of coffins, ramped chambers, large numbers of grave goods, and divination based on interpreting cracks induced by heat in cattle bones. Fortified walls, made of rammed earth, came to be built around settlements in many areas, suggesting not only increased contact but also increased conflict.

## The Shang Dynasty (ca 1500–ca 1050 B.C.E.)

After 2000 B.C.E. a Bronze Age civilization appeared in north China with the traits found in Bronze Age civilizations elsewhere, such as writing, metalworking, domestication of the horse, class stratification, and cult centers. Perhaps the first stage of this transition should be identified as the Xia Dynasty, traditionally said to precede the Shang, but no sites from that period have yielded written documents. The Shang Dynasty, however, is well documented in the divination texts excavated from Shang royal tombs.

Shang civilization was not as densely urban as Mesopotamia, but Shang kings ruled from large settlements. The best excavated is **Anyang,** from which the Shang kings ruled for more than two centuries. At the center of Anyang were large palaces, temples, and altars. These buildings were constructed on rammed-earth foundations (a feature of Chinese building practice that would last for centuries). Outside the central core were industrial areas where bronzeworkers, potters, stone carvers, and other artisans lived and worked. Many homes were built partly below ground level, probably as a way to conserve heat. Beyond these urban settlements were farming areas and large forests. Deer, bears, tigers, wild boars, elephants, and rhinoceros were still plentiful in north China in this era.

The divinatory texts found in the royal tombs outside Anyang show that Shang kings—the ones posing the questions in these texts—were military chieftains. The king regularly sent out armies of three thousand to five thousand men on campaigns, and when not at war they would go on hunts lasting for months. They fought rebellious vassals and foreign tribes, but the situation constantly changed as vassals became enemies and enemies accepted offers of alliance. War booty was an important source of the king's revenue, especially the war captives who could be made into slaves. Captives not needed as slaves might end up as sacrificial victims—or perhaps the demands of the gods and ancestors for sacrifices were a motive for going to war.

Bronze technology gave Shang warriors improved weapons. Bronze-tipped spears and halberds were widely used. Bronze was also used for the fittings of the chariots that came into use around 1200 B.C.E., probably as a result of diffusion across Asia. The chariot provided commanders with a mobile station from which they could supervise their troops; it also gave archers and soldiers armed with long halberds increased mobility.

Shang power did not rest solely on military supremacy. The Shang king was also the high priest, the one best qualified to offer sacrifices to the royal ancestors and the high god Di. Royal ancestors were viewed as able to intervene with Di, send curses, produce dreams, assist the king in battle, and so on. The king communicated with his ancestors by interpreting the cracks made in heated cattle bones or tortoise shells, prepared for him by professional diviners.

Shang palaces were undoubtedly splendid but were constructed of perishable material like wood, and nothing of them remains today, unlike the stone buildings and monuments so characteristic of the ancient West. What

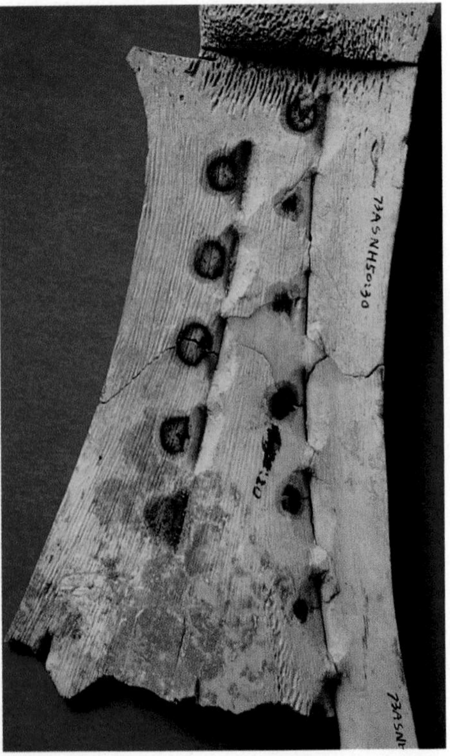

**Shang Oracle Bone**
To communicate with their ancestors or the high gods, Shang kings employed diviners. After the ruler posed a yes or no question, the diviner applied a hot point to a prepared bone, usually a cattle scapula bone. The direction of the cracks indicated whether the god's answer was yes or no. Sometimes the diviners, to keep records, would record the question and answer on the other side of the bone. On the bone shown here, the question related to a hunt. Other questions commonly posed concerned weather, travel, illness, and dreams. *(Lowell Georgia/Photo Researchers)*

**Royal Tomb at Anyang** Eleven large tombs and more than a thousand small graves have been excavated at the royal burial ground at Anyang. This grave, about sixty feet deep and three hundred feet long, would have taken thousands of laborers many months to complete. But even more wealth was expended to fill it with bronze, stone, pottery, jade, and textile grave goods. Human victims were also placed in it. *(Academia Sinica, Taiwan)*

has survived are the lavish underground tombs built for Shang kings and their consorts. The one royal tomb not to have been robbed before it was excavated was for Lady Hao, one of the many wives of the king Wu Ding (ca 1200 B.C.E.). Although one of the smaller royal tombs (about 13 by 18 feet at the mouth and about 25 feet deep) and not in the main royal cemetery, it was nonetheless filled with an extraordinary array of sacrificial goods. Human beings were sacrificed at her tomb (the 16 human skeletons included both males and females, children and adults), but not on as great a scale as at some of the larger tombs. Rather it was the burial of a profusion of valuable objects that was the most striking feature of this tomb, which contained 460 bronze objects (including more than 200 ritual vessels, more than 130 weapons, 23 bells, 27 knives, 4 mirrors, and 4 tigers or tiger heads), nearly 750 jade objects, some 70 stone sculptures, nearly 500 bone hairpins, more than 20 bone arrowheads, and 3 ivory carvings. Others, however, were apparently tribute sent to the capital from distant places. More than 20 different types of ritual vessels were buried in the tomb, of which about 60 had Lady Hao's name inscribed on them. The weapons found in this tomb are only one sign that Lady Hao took an interest in military affairs. From inscribed bones found elsewhere at Anyang, we know that she led military campaigns, once with 13,000 troops against the Qiang to the west, at other times against the Fu Fang in the northwest, the Ba Fang in the southwest, and the Yi in the east.

In addition to objects of value or practical use, the Shang interred human beings in royal tombs, sometimes dozens of them. Many were war captives, offered as sacrifices. Others were the king's followers, retainers, and servants, who had voluntarily decided to accompany him in death. Early Shang graves rarely had more than three victims or followers accompanying the main occupant, but over time the practice grew. The late Shang tomb for the king who reigned about 1200 B.C.E. contained the

**Owl-Shaped Shang Bronze** This 18-inch-tall bronze vessel in the shape of an owl was one of more than two hundred bronze ritual vessels buried in about 1200 B.C.E. in the tomb of Lady Hao, a consort of the Shang king Wu Ding. *(© Cultural Relics Data Center of China)*

**Jade Figure** Among the valuables placed in royal Shang tombs were many jade objects, such as this figure, 2¾ inches tall. Since Neolithic times, jade has had the place in China occupied by gold in many other cultures: it is valued for its beauty, rarity, and endurance. This figure was one of seven hundred jade pieces in the tomb of Lady Hao (see page 85). *(© Cultural Relics Data Center of China)*

remains of 90 followers, 74 human sacrifices, 12 horses, and 11 dogs. The sacrificial victims are recognizable because they were decapitated, cut at the waist, or otherwise put to death by mutilation. Those who voluntarily followed their king to the grave generally had their own ornaments and might also have had coffins and grave goods such as weapons.

Shang rulers had to have the ability to mobilize thousands of laborers to dig the 30- to 40-foot pits for these tombs, then later fill in the site by ramming earth. Ramming earth was also used to construct city walls. It has been estimated that even with 10,000 laborers working to move and ram the earth, the 60-foot-wide and 30-foot-high wall at Zhengzhou would not have been completed in less than 10 years.

Shang society was marked by sharp status distinctions. The Shang royal family and aristocracy lived in large houses built on huge platforms of rammed earth. The king and other noble families had family and clan names transmitted along patrilineal lines, from father to son. Kingship similarly passed along patrilines, from elder to younger brother and father to son, but never to or through sisters or daughters. The kings and the aristocracy owned slaves, many of whom had been captured in war. In the urban centers there were substantial numbers of craftsmen who worked in stone, bone, and bronze.

Shang farmers were essentially serfs of the aristocrats. Their life was not that different from that of their Neolithic ancestors, and they worked the fields with similar stone tools. They usually lived in small, compact villages surrounded by fields. Some new crops became common in Shang times, most notably wheat, which had spread from West Asia. Shang farmers themselves probably deserve the credit for discovering how to make silk from the cocoons of silkworms, which liked to feed on mulberry trees. Because of its beauty, strength, and light weight, silk became an important item of long-distance trade even in ancient times. Recently silk from Shang China was discovered in an Egyptian tomb.

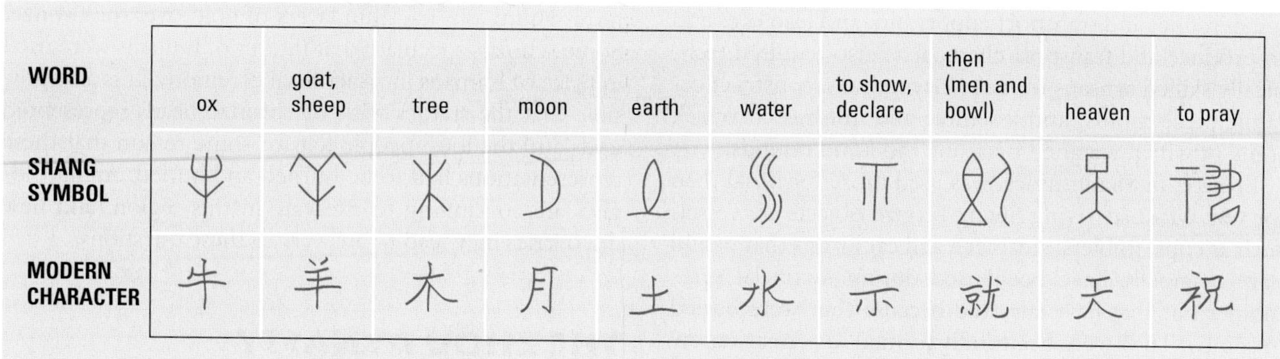


**FIGURE 4.1 The Origins of Chinese Writing** The modern Chinese writing system (bottom row) evolved from the script employed by diviners in the Shang period (upper row). *(Source: Adapted from Patricia Buckley Ebrey,* The Cambridge Illustrated History of China *[Cambridge: Cambridge University Press, 1996], p. 26. Reprinted by permission of Cambridge University Press.)*

**Writing** The survival of divination texts inscribed on bones from Shang tombs demonstrates that writing was already a major element in Chinese culture by 1200 B.C.E. Writing must have been developed earlier, but the early stages cannot be traced, probably because writing was done on perishable materials like wood, bamboo, or silk. The earliest possible signs of writing are the symbols or emblems inscribed on late Neolithic pots and the symbols cast into early Shang bronzes. Not until the oracle bones from the late Shang period, however, is there evidence of full sentences.

Once writing was invented, it had profound effects on China's culture and government. A written language made possible a bureaucracy capable of keeping records and conducting correspondence with commanders and governors far from the palace. Hence literacy became the ally of royal rule, facilitating communication with and effective control over the realm. Literacy also preserved the learning, lore, and experience of early Chinese society and facilitated the development of abstract thought.

The Chinese script was **logographic,** like ancient Egyptian and Sumerian, meaning that each word was represented by a single symbol. In the Chinese case, some of these symbols were pictures, but for the names of abstract concepts other methods were adopted. Sometimes the symbol for a different word was borrowed because the two words were pronounced alike. Sometimes two different symbols were combined; for instance, to represent different types of trees, the symbol for tree could be combined with another symbol borrowed for its pronunciation (see Figure 4.1).

In western Eurasia logographic scripts were eventually modified or replaced by phonetic scripts, but that never happened in China (although, because of changes in the spoken language, today many words are represented by two or three characters rather than a single one). Because China retained its early logographic writing system, many years were required to gain full mastery of reading and writing, which added to the prestige of education.

Why did China retain a logographic writing system, even after encounters with phonetic ones? Although phonetic systems have many real advantages, especially with respect to ease of learning to read, there are some costs to dropping a logographic system. Those who learned to read Chinese could communicate with a wider range of people than those who read scripts based on speech. Since characters did not change when the pronunciation changed, educated Chinese could read texts written centuries earlier without the need for them to be translated. Moreover, as the Chinese language developed regional variants, readers of Chinese could read books and letters by contemporaries whose oral language they could not comprehend. Thus the Chinese script played a large role in holding China together and fostering a sense of connection with the past. In addition, many of China's neighbors (Japan, Korea, and Vietnam, in particular) adopted the Chinese script, allowing communication through writing between people whose languages were totally unrelated. In this regard, the Chinese language was like Arabic numerals, which have the same meaning however they are read.

**Bronzes** As in Egypt, Mesopotamia, and India, the development of more complex forms of social organization in Shang China coincided with the mastery of metalworking, specifically bronze. The bronze industry required central coordination of a large labor force to mine, refine, and transport copper, tin, and lead ores and to produce and transport charcoal. It also required technically skilled artisans to make clay models, construct ceramic piece molds, and assemble and finish each vessel, some of which weighed over one thousand pounds.

Bronze, in Shang times, was used more for ritual than for war. Most surviving Shang bronze objects are vessels such as cups, goblets, steamers, and cauldrons that would have originally have been used during sacrificial ceremonies but that have survived because they were buried in tombs. They were beautifully formed in a great variety of shapes and sizes. Complex designs were achieved through mold casting and prefabrication of parts. For instance, legs, handles, and other protruding members were cast first before the body was cast onto them.

The decoration on Shang bronzes seems to say something interesting about Shang culture, but scholars cannot agree just what it says. In the art of ancient Egypt, Assyria, and Babylonia, representations of agriculture (domesticated plants and animals) and of social hierarchy (kings, priests, scribes, and slaves) are very common, matching our understandings of the social, political, and economic development of those societies. In Shang China, by contrast, images of wild animals predominate. Some animal images readily suggest possible meanings. Jade cicadas were sometimes found in the mouths of the dead, and images of cicadas on bronzes are easy to interpret as images evocative of rebirth in the realm of ancestral spirits, as cicadas spend years underground before emerging. Birds, similarly, suggest to many the idea of messengers that can communicate with other realms, especially ones in the sky. More problematic is the most common image, the stylized animal face called the **taotie.** To some it is a monster—a fearsome image that would scare away evil forces. Others imagine a dragon—an animal whose vast powers had more positive associations. Some hypothesize that it reflects masks used in rituals. Others associate it with animal sacrifices, totemism, or shamanism. Still others see these images as hardly more than designs.

Bronze technology spread beyond Shang territories into areas the Shang would have considered enemy lands. A striking example was discovered in 1986 in the western province of Sichuan. There a bronze-producing culture contemporaneous with the late Shang had markedly different religious and artistic practices. This culture did not practice human sacrifice, but two sacrificial pits contained the burned remains of elephant tusks and a wide range of gold, bronze, jade, and stone objects. Among them were a life-size statue and many life-size bronze heads, all with angular facial features and enormous eyes. The heads may have been used to top wood or clay statues. Some of the heads and masks had thin layers of gold over the bronze. Some scholars speculate that figures of humans were used in place of humans in a sacrificial ceremony. It is also possible that the statues with the bronze heads represented gods and the local people felt for some reason that these representations had to be burned and buried. Archaeologists are continuing to excavate in this region, and new discoveries may lead to answers to these questions.

## THE ZHOU DYNASTY (CA 1050–256 B.C.E.)

The Shang campaigned constantly against enemies. To the west were the fierce Qiang, considered barbarian tribesmen by the Shang and perhaps speaking an early form of Tibetan. Between the Shang capital and the Qiang was a frontier state called Zhou, which seems to have both inherited cultural traditions from the Neolithic cultures of the northwest and absorbed most of the material culture of the Shang. In about 1050 B.C.E., the Zhou rose against the Shang and defeated them in battle.

### Zhou Politics

The early Zhou period is the first one for which transmitted texts exist in some abundance. The ***Book of Documents*** describes the Zhou conquest of the Shang as the victory of just and noble warriors over decadent courtiers who were led by a dissolute, sadistic king. At the same time, these documents show that the Zhou recognized the Shang as occupying the center of the world, were eager to succeed to that role rather than dispute it, and saw history as a major way to legitimate power. Thus, like many of the invaders in Mesopotamia, the Zhou built on the accomplishments of their predecessors. The three early Zhou rulers who are given the most praise are King Wen (the "cultured" or "literate" king), who expanded the Zhou domain; his son King Wu (the "martial" king), who conquered the Shang; and Wu's brother, the Duke of Zhou, who consolidated the conquest and served as loyal regent for Wu's heir. Besides these transmitted texts, hundreds of inscriptions on ritual bronzes have survived, some of which record benefactions from the king and mention the services that had earned the king's favor.

Like the Shang kings, the Zhou kings sacrificed to their ancestors, but they also sacrificed to Heaven. The *Book of Documents* assumes a close relationship between Heaven and the king, who was called the Son of Heaven. Heaven gives the king a mandate to rule only as long as he rules in the interests of the people. Thus it was because the last king of the Shang had been decadent and cruel that Heaven took the mandate away from him and entrusted it to the virtuous Zhou kings. Humanity needs such a king to mediate between it and Heaven. Because this theory of the **Mandate of Heaven** does not seem to have had any place in Shang cosmology, it may have been elaborated by the early Zhou rulers as a kind of propaganda to win over the conquered subjects of the Shang. Whatever its origins, it remained a central feature of Chinese political ideology from the early Zhou period on.

Rather than attempt to rule all of their territories directly, the early Zhou rulers set up a decentralized, feudal system. They sent out relatives and trusted subordinates with troops to establish walled garrisons in the conquered territories. These vassals were generally able to pass their positions on to a son, so that in time the domains became hereditary fiefs. By 800 B.C.E. there were about two hundred lords with domains large and small, of which only about twenty-five were large enough to matter much in interstate politics. Each lord appointed officers to serve him in ritual, administrative, or military capacities. These posts and their associated titles tended to become hereditary as well. Each domain thus came to have noble families with patrimonies in offices and associated lands.

The decentralized rule of the early Zhou period had from the beginning carried within it the danger that the regional lords would become so powerful that they would no longer obey the commands of the king. As generations passed and ties of loyalty and kinship grew more distant, this indeed happened. In 771 B.C.E. the Zhou king was killed by an alliance of Rong tribesmen and Zhou vassals. One of his sons was put on the throne, and then for safety's sake the capital was moved east out of the Wei River valley to modern Luoyang, just south of the Yellow River in the heart of the central plains (see Map 4.1).

The revived Zhou Dynasty never fully regained control over its vassals, and China entered a prolonged period without a strong central authority. For a couple of centuries a code of chivalrous or sportsmanlike conduct still regulated warfare between the states: one state would not attack another while it was in mourning for its ruler; during battles one side would not attack before the other side had time to line up; ruling houses were not wiped out, so that a successor could continue to sacrifice to their ancestors; and so on. Thereafter, however, such niceties were abandoned and China entered a period of nearly constant conflict called the **Warring States Period** (403–221 B.C.E.). By the third century B.C.E. there were only seven important states remaining. These states were much more centralized than their early Zhou predecessors. The kings of these states had eliminated indirect control through vassals and in its place had dispatched royal officials to remote cities, controlling them from a distance through the transmission of documents and dismissing them at will.

## Zhou Society

Over the course of the eight centuries of the Zhou Dynasty, Chinese society underwent radical changes. Early Zhou rule was highly aristocratic. Inherited ranks placed people in a hierarchy ranging from the king to the rulers of states with titles like duke and marquis, the hereditary lords of the individual states, the hereditary great officials of the states, the lower ranks of the aristocracy (men who could serve either in military or civil capacities, known as **shi**), and finally to the ordinary people (the farmers, craftsmen, and traders). Patrilineal family ties were very important in this society, and at the upper reaches at least, sacrifices to ancestors were one of the key rituals that were used to forge social ties.

Glimpses of what life was like at various social levels in the early Zhou Dynasty can be found in the ***Book of Songs,*** which contains the earliest Chinese poetry. Some of the songs are hymns used in court religious ceremonies, such as offerings to ancestors, and reveal aspects of religious practice, such as the use of a grandson of the deceased to impersonate him during the ceremony. Others clearly had their origins in folk songs. Some of these folk songs depict farmers at work clearing fields, plowing and planting, gathering mulberry leaves for silkworms, spinning and weaving. The seasons set the pace for rural life, and the songs contain many references to seasonal changes, such as the appearance of insects like grasshoppers and crickets. Farming life involved not merely the cultivation of crops like millet, hemp (for cloth), beans, and vegetables, but also hunting small animals and collecting grasses and rushes to make rope and baskets.

Many of the folk songs are love songs that depict a more informal pattern of courtship than prevailed in later China. One stanza reads:

*Please, Zhongzi,*
*Do not leap over our wall,*
*Do not break our mulberry trees.*
*It's not that I begrudge the mulberries,*
*But I fear my brothers.*
*You I would embrace,*
*But my brothers' words—those I dread.*[1]

There were also songs of complaint, such as this one in which soldiers protest:

*Which plant is not brown?*
*Which man is not sad?*
*Have pity on us soldiers,*
*Treated as though we were not men!*[2]

Other songs in this collection are court odes that reveal attitudes of the aristocrats. One such ode expresses a deep distrust of women's involvement in politics:

*Clever men build cities,*
*Clever women topple them.*
*Beautiful, these clever women may be*
*But they are owls and kites.*
*Women have long tongues*
*That lead to ruin.*
*Disorder does not come down from heaven;*
*It is produced by women.*[3]

Part of the reason for distrust of women in politics was the practice of concubinage. Rulers regularly demonstrated their power and wealth by accumulating large numbers of concubines and thus would have children by several women. In theory, succession went to the eldest son of the wife, then younger sons by her, and only in their absence sons of concubines, but in actual practice, the ruler of a state or head of a powerful ministerial family could select a son of a concubine to be his heir if he wished. This led to much scheming for favor among the various sons and their mothers and the common perception that women were incapable of taking a disinterested view of the larger good.

The economic growth of the Zhou period is evident in the appearance of cities all over north China. Thick earthen walls were built around the palaces and ancestral temples of the ruler and other aristocrats, and often an outer wall was added to protect the artisans, merchants, and farmers who lived outside the inner wall. Accounts of

**Bronze Relief of Hunters** Hunting provided an important source of food in the Zhou period, and hunters were often depicted on inlaid bronzes of the period. *(The Avery Brundage Collection/Laurie Platt Winfrey, Inc.)*

sieges launched against these walled citadels, with scenes of the scaling of walls and the storming of gates, are central to descriptions of military confrontations in this period.

By the Warring States Period, the old aristocratic social structure of the Zhou was being undermined by the effects of intense competition between the states and advances in military technology. Large, well-drilled infantry armies also became a potent military force in this period, able to withstand and defeat chariot-led forces. By 300 B.C.E. states were sending out armies of a couple hundred thousand drafted foot soldiers, usually accompanied by horsemen. Adding to the effectiveness of armies of drafted foot soldiers was the development of the **crossbow.** The trigger of a crossbow is an intricate bronze mechanism that allowed a foot soldier to shoot farther than a horseman carrying a light bow. One text of the period reports that a skilled soldier with a powerful crossbow and a sharp sword was the match of a hundred ordinary men. To defend against crossbows, soldiers began wearing armor and helmets. Most of the armor was made of leader strips tied with cords. Helmets were sometimes made of iron.

The introduction of cavalry in this period also reduced the need for a chariot-riding aristocracy. Shooting bows and arrows from horseback was first perfected by non-Chinese peoples to the north of China proper, who at that time were making the transition to a nomadic pastoral economy. The northern state of Jin, to defend itself from the attacks of these horsemen, developed its own cavalry armies. Once it started using them against other Chinese states, they naturally had to master the new technology in turn. From this time on, acquiring and pasturing horses was a key component of military preparedness.

Because these developments made commoners and craftsmen central to the success of their armies, rulers of the warring states tried to find ways to increase their populations. To increase agricultural output, they brought new land into cultivation, drained marshes, and dug irrigation channels. By the sixth century B.C.E. rulers were surveying their land and beginning to try to tax farmers. They wanted to undermine the power of lords over their subjects in order to get direct access to the peasants' labor power. Serfdom thus gradually declined. Registering populations led to the extension of family names to commoners at an earlier date than anywhere else in the world.

To encourage trade, rulers began casting coins. The development of iron technology in the early Zhou Dynasty also promoted economic expansion. By the fifth century iron was being widely used for both farm tools and weapons. By the third century the largest smelters employed two hundred or more workmen. A new powerful group also emerged in society—the rich who had acquired their wealth through trade or industry rather than inheritance or political favor. Merchants were another important new group in society, and late Zhou texts frequently mention cross-regional trade in objects such as furs, copper, dyes, hemp, salt, and horses.

Within elite strata as well, social mobility increased in this period. Rulers more often sent out their own officials rather than delegate authority to hereditary lesser lords. This trend toward centralized bureaucratic control created opportunities for social advancement for those on the lower end of the old aristocracy (the shi), valued for their ability more than their birth. Competition among such men guaranteed rulers a ready supply of able and willing subordinates, and competition among rulers for talent meant that ambitious men could be selective in deciding where to offer their services. (See the feature "Individuals in Society: Guan Zhong.")

The development of infantry armies also created the need for a new type of general, and rulers became less willing to let men lead troops merely because of aristocratic birth. Treatises on the art of war described the ideal general as a master of maneuver, illusion, and deception. *The Art of War,* attributed to Sun Wu, is thought to have appeared between 453 and 403 B.C.E. Master Sun analyzed battle tactics and ways to win wars without combat by deceiving the enemy. He argued that heroism is a useless virtue that leads to needless deaths. But discipline is essential, and he insisted that the entire army had to be trained to follow the orders of its commanders without questioning them.

Archaeology provides ample evidence of changes in material and religious culture throughout Zhou times. The practice of burying the living with the dead steadily declined, but a ruler who died in 433 B.C.E. still had his female musicians buried with him, and not until 384 B.C.E. did the king of Qin outlaw the practice in his state. Bronze ritual vessels continued to be buried in the tombs of rulers, but their styles had radically changed. Music played a major role in court entertainment, and bells are among the most impressive bronze objects of the period.

Social groups that had been considered barbarian or semibarbarian among the early Zhou were more and more brought into the cultural sphere of the Central States, the core region of China. These were the states on the periphery, with room to expand. By the fourth and third centuries B.C.E., they were the most powerful of the states. For instance, the southern state of Chu expanded rapidly in the Yangzi Valley, defeating and absorbing fifty

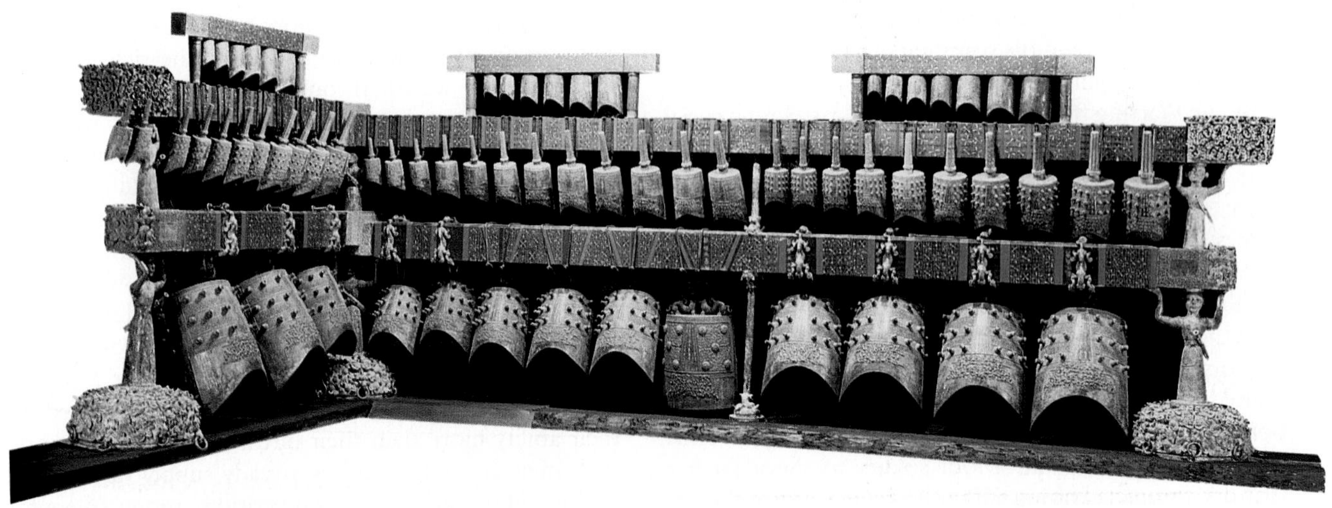

**Bells of the Marquis of Yi** Music played a central role in court life in ancient China. The tomb of a minor ruler who died about 400 B.C.E. contained 124 musical instruments, including drums, flutes, mouth organs, pan pipes, zithers, a set of 32 chime stones, and this 64-piece bell set. The bells bear inscriptions that name the two tones each bell could make, depending on where it was struck. Five men, using poles and mallets, and standing on either side of the set of bells, would have played the bells by hitting them from outside. *(© Cultural Relics Data Center of China)*

or more small states as it extended its reach north to the heartland of Zhou and east to absorb the old states of Wu and Yue. By the late Zhou period, Chu was on the forefront of cultural innovation and produced the greatest literary masterpieces of the era, the *Songs of Chu,* a collection of fantastical poems full of images of elusive deities and shamans who can fly through the spirit world.

## THE GOLDEN AGE OF CHINESE PHILOSOPHY

Known as the time when the "Hundred Schools of Thought" contended, the late Zhou period was one of intellectual flowering. During the same period in which Indian sages and mystics were developing religious speculation about karma, souls, and eons of time, Chinese thinkers were arguing about the ideal forms of social and political organization and man's connections to nature.

The constant warfare of the period helped rather than hindered intellectual creativity. People wanted solutions to the disorder they saw around them. Rulers and high officials took advantage of the destruction of states to recruit newly unemployed men to serve as their advisers and court assistants. Lively debate often resulted as these strategists proposed court policies and defended their ideas against challengers. Followers took to recording their teachers' ideas, and the circulation of these "books" (rolls of silk, or strips of wood or bamboo tied together) served further to stimulate debate.

### Confucius and His Followers

Confucius (traditional dates, 551–479 B.C.E.) was the first and most important of the men of ideas seeking to influence the rulers of the day. As a young man, Confucius served in the court of his home state of Lu without gaining much influence. After leaving Lu, he set out with a small band of students and wandered through neighboring states in search of a ruler who would take his advice. Although he yearned for a ruler to serve devotedly, he spent most of his life teaching the sons of the aristocracy.

Confucius's ideas are known to us primarily through the sayings recorded by his disciples in the *Analects.* The thrust of his thought was ethical rather than theoretical or metaphysical. He talked repeatedly of an ideal age in the early Zhou Dynasty, which he conceived of as a perfect society in which everyone was devoted to fulfilling his or her role: superiors looked after those dependent on them, inferiors devoted themselves to the service of their superiors, parents and children, husbands and wives, all wholeheartedly embraced what was expected of them.

# INDIVIDUALS IN SOCIETY

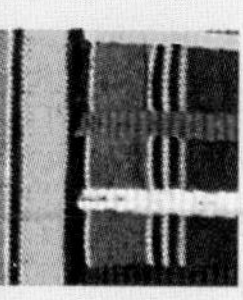

## GUAN ZHONG

By the time of Confucius, the success of states was often credited more to the lord's astute advisers than to the lord himself. To Confucius, the most praiseworthy political adviser was Guan Zhong (ca 720–645 B.C.E.), the genius behind the rise of the state of Qi, in eastern China.

The earliest historical sources to recount Guan Zhong's accomplishments are the "commentaries" compiled in the Warring States Period to elaborate on the dry chronicle known as the *Spring and Autumn Annals*. The *Zuo Commentary,* for instance, tells us that in the year 660 B.C.E. Guan Zhong advised Duke Huan to aid the small state of Xing, then under attack by the non-Chinese Rong tribes: "The Rong and the Di are wolves who cannot be satiated. The Xia (Chinese) states are kin who should not be abandoned." In 652 B.C.E., it tells us, Guan Zhong urged the duke to maintain the respect of the other states by refusing the offer of the son of a recently defeated state's ruler to ally himself with Qi if Qi would help him depose his father. Because the duke regularly listened to Guan Zhong's sound advice, Qi brought the other states under its sway and the duke came to be recognized as the first *hegemon,* or leader of the alliance of states.

Guan Zhong was also credited with strengthening the duke's internal administration. He encouraged the employment of officials on the basis of their moral character and ability rather than their birth. He introduced a system of drafting commoners for military service. In the history of China written by Sima Qian in about 100 B.C.E., Guan Zhong is also given credit for enriching Qi by promoting trade, issuing coins, and standardizing merchants' scales. He was credited with the statement, "When the granaries are full, the people will understand ritual and moderation. When they have enough food and clothing, they will understand honor and disgrace."

Sima Qian's biography of Guan Zhong emphasizes his early poverty and the key role played by a friend, Bao Shuya, who recognized his worth. As young men, both Bao and Guan Zhong served brothers of the duke of Qi. When this duke was killed and a messy succession struggle followed, Bao's patron won out and became the next duke, while Guan Zhong's patron had to flee and in the end was killed. Bao, however, recommended Guan Zhong to the new duke, Duke Huan, and Guan Zhong took up a post under him.

*The inlaid decoration on bronze vessels of the Warring States Period often shows people engaged in warfare, hunting, preparing food, performing rituals, and making music.* (© Courtesy, Sichuan Museum)

In the *Analects,* one of Confucius's disciples thought that Guan Zhong's lack of loyalty to his first lord made him a man unworthy of respect: "When Duke Huan killed his brother Jiu, Guan Zhong was unable to die with Jiu but rather became prime minister to Duke Huan." Confucius disagreed: "Guan Zhong became prime minister to Duke Huan and made him hegemon among the lords, uniting and reforming all under Heaven. The people, down to the present, continued to receive benefits from this. Were it not for Guan Zhong our hair would hang unbound and we would fold our robes on the left [that is, live as barbarians]."*

A book of the teachings associated with Guan Zhong, the *Guanzi,* was in circulation by the late Warring States Period. Although it is today not thought to reflect the teachings of the historical Guan Zhong, the fact that later statecraft thinkers would borrow his name is an indication of his fame as a great statesman.

### QUESTIONS FOR ANALYSIS

1. How did the form of government promoted by Guan Zhong differ from the early Zhou political system?
2. What can one infer about Chinese notions of loyalty from the story of Guan Zhong and his friend Bao Shuya?
3. Did Guan Zhong and Confucius share similar understandings of the differences between Chinese and barbarians?

**Analects,* 14.18. Translated by Patricia Ebrey.

Confucius considered the family the basic unit of society. He extolled **filial piety,** which to him meant more than just reverent obedience of children toward their parents.

*The Master said, "You can be of service to your father and mother by remonstrating with them tactfully. If you perceive that they do not wish to follow your advice, then continue to be reverent toward them without offending or disobeying them; work hard and do not murmur against them."*[4]

The relationship between father and son was one of the five cardinal relationships stressed by Confucius. The others were between ruler and subject, husband and wife, elder and younger brother, and friend and friend. Mutual obligations of a hierarchical sort underlay the first four of these relationships—the senior leads and protects, the junior supports and obeys. The exception was the relationship between friends, which was conceived in terms of the mutual obligations between equals.

A man of moderation, Confucius was an earnest advocate of gentlemanly conduct. He redefined the term *gentleman* (*junzi*) to mean a man of moral cultivation rather than a man of noble birth. He repeatedly urged his followers to aspire to be gentlemen of integrity and duty, rather than petty men intent on personal gain. The gentleman, he said, "feels bad when his capabilities fall short of the task. He does not feel bad when people fail to recognize him."[5] Confucius did not advocate social equality, but his teachings minimized the importance of class distinctions and opened the way for intelligent and talented people to rise in the social scale.

The Confucian gentleman found his calling in service to the ruler. Loyal advisers should encourage their rulers to govern through ritual, virtue, and concern for the welfare of their subjects, and much of the *Analects* concerns the way to govern well.

*The Master said, "Lead the people by means of government policies and regulate them through punishments, and they will be evasive and have no sense of shame. Lead them by means of virtue and regulate them through rituals and they will have a sense of shame and moreover have standards."*[6]

To Confucius the ultimate virtue was **ren,** a term that has been translated as perfect goodness, benevolence, humanity, human-heartedness, and nobility. A person of ren cares about others and acts accordingly.

*Zhonggong asked about humanity. The Master said, "When you go out, treat everyone as if you were welcoming a great guest. Employ people as though you were conducting a great sacrifice. Do not do unto others what you would not have them do unto you. Then neither in your country nor in your family will there be complaints against you."*[7]

In the Confucian tradition, studying texts came to be valued over speculation, meditation, and mystical identification with deities. Confucius encouraged the men who came to study with him to master the poetry, rituals, and historical traditions that we know today as Confucian classics. Many passages in the *Analects* reveal Confucius's confidence in the power of study:

*The Master said, "I am not someone who was born wise. I am someone who loves the ancients and tries to learn from them."*

*The Master said, "I once spent a whole day without eating and a whole night without sleeping in order to think. It was of no use. It is better to study."*[8]

The eventual success of Confucian ideas owes much to Confucius's followers in the two centuries following his death, the most important of whom were Mencius (ca 370–ca 300 B.C.E.) and Xunzi (ca 310–ca 215 B.C.E.).

Mencius, like Confucius, traveled around offering advice to rulers of various states. (See the feature "Listening to the Past: The Book of Mencius" on pages 102–103.) Over and over he tried to convert them to the view that the ruler able to win over the people through benevolent government would succeed in unifying "all under Heaven." Mencius proposed concrete political and financial measures for easing tax burdens and otherwise improving the people's lot. Men willing to serve an unworthy ruler earned his contempt, especially when they worked hard to fill his coffers or expand his territory. With his disciples and fellow philosophers, Mencius also discussed other issues in moral philosophy, arguing strongly, for instance, that human nature is fundamentally good, as everyone is born with the capacity to recognize what is right and act on it.

Xunzi, a half century later, took the opposite view of human nature, arguing that people are born selfish and that it is only through education and ritual that they learn to put moral principle above their own interest. Much of what is desirable is not inborn but must be taught.

*When a son yields to his father, or a younger brother yields to his elder brother, or when a son takes on the work for his father or a younger brother for his elder brother, their actions go against their natures and run counter to their feelings.*

*And yet these are the way of the filial son and the principles of ritual and morality.*[9]

Neither Confucius nor Mencius had had much actual political or administrative experience, but Xunzi had worked for many years in the court of his home state. Not surprisingly, he showed more consideration than either Confucius or Mencius for the difficulties a ruler might face in trying to rule through ritual and virtue. Xunzi was also a more rigorous thinker than his predecessors and developed the philosophical foundations of many ideas merely outlined by Confucius or Mencius. Confucius, for instance, had declined to discuss gods, portents, and anomalies, and had spoken of sacrificing as if the spirits were present. Xunzi went further and explicitly argued that Heaven does not intervene in human affairs. Praying to Heaven or to gods, he asserted, does not induce them to act. "Why does it rain after a prayer for rain? In my opinion, for no reason. It is the same as raining when you had not prayed."[10]

Even though he did not think praying could bring rain or other benefits from Heaven, Xunzi did not propose abandoning traditional rituals. In contrast to Daoists and Mohists (discussed below), who saw rituals as unnatural or extravagant, Xunzi saw them as an efficient way to attain order in society. Rulers and educated men should continue traditional ritual practices such as complex funeral protocols because the rites themselves have positive effects on performers and observers. Not only do they let people express feelings and satisfy desires in an orderly way, but because they specify graduated ways to perform the rites according to social rank, ritual traditions sustain the social hierarchy. Xunzi compared and contrasted ritual and music: music shapes people's emotions and creates feelings of solidarity, while ritual shapes people's sense of duty and creates social differentiation.

The Confucian vision of personal ethics and public service found a small but ardent following in late Zhou times. In later centuries, rulers came to see men educated in Confucian virtues as ideal advisers and officials. Neither revolutionaries nor toadies, Confucian scholar-officials opposed bad government and upheld the best ideals of statecraft. Confucian political ideals shaped Chinese society into the twentieth century.

The Confucian vision also provided the moral basis for the Chinese family into modern times. Repaying parents and ancestors came to be seen as a sacred duty. Because people owe their very existence to their parents, they should reciprocate by respecting them, making efforts to please them, honoring their memories, and placing the interests of the family line above personal preferences. Since this family line is a patrilineal line from father to son to grandson, placing great importance on it has had the effect of devaluing women.

## Mozi

Not long after Confucius died, his ideas were challenged by a man who did not come from the aristocracy but rather, it would seem, from among the master craftsmen. Mozi (ca 450 B.C.E.), perhaps an expert in constructing siege engines, did not talk of the distinction between gentlemen and vulgar "petty men," but rather of "concern for everyone." He also argued strongly for the merit principle, that rulers should choose their advisers on the basis of their ability, not their birth.

The book ascribed to Mozi proposes that every idea be evaluated on the basis of its utility: does it benefit the people and the state? The Confucian stress on ritual and filial piety led to prolonged mourning for parents, which Mozi rejected because it interrupts work, injures health, and thus impoverishes the people and weakens the state. Music, too, Mozi saw as a wasteful extravagance.

Mozi made a similar case against aggressive war, seeing no glory in expansion for its own sake and pointing to the huge losses in weapons, horses, and human lives it causes. The capture of a city, he argued, is not worth the loss of thousands of men. But Mozi was for strong government, and in particular for respect for superiors. He argued that disorder could be eliminated if everyone conformed his beliefs to those of his superior, with the king conforming to Heaven. He believed that Confucius's reference to fate and his failure to discuss gods undermined popular morality.

Mozi had many followers over the next couple of centuries, but his school eventually lost its distinct identity. Certain ideas, such as support for the merit principle and the critique of extravagance, in later centuries were absorbed into Confucian thought. Confucians, however, never accepted Mohist ideas about treating everyone equally, unnatural in their minds, or of applying rigidly utilitarian tests to ritual and music, whose value they saw in very different terms.

## Daoism

Confucius and his followers believed in moral effort and statecraft. They thought men of virtue should devote themselves to making the government work to the benefit of the people. Those who came to be labeled Daoists disagreed. They thought striving to make things better generally makes them worse. Daoists defended private life and wanted the rulers to leave the people alone. They sought to go beyond everyday concerns and let their minds wander freely. Rather than making human beings and human actions the center of concern, they focused on the larger scheme of things, the whole natural order identified as **the Way,** or Dao.

Early Daoist teachings are known from two surviving books, the *Laozi* and the *Zhuangzi,* both dating to the third century B.C.E. Laozi, the putative author of the *Laozi,* may not be a historical figure, but the text ascribed to him has been of enduring importance. A recurrent theme in this brief, aphoristic text is the mystical superiority of yielding over assertion and silence over words: "The Way that can be discussed is not the constant Way."[11] The highest good is like water: "Water benefits all creatures but does not compete. It occupies the places people disdain and thus comes near to the Way."[12]

Because purposeful action is counterproductive, the ruler should let people return to a natural state of ignorance and contentment.

*Do not honor the worthy,*
*And the people will not compete.*
*Do not value rare treasures,*
*And the people will not steal.*
*Do not display what others want,*
*And the people will not have their hearts confused.*
*A sage governs this way:*
*He empties people's minds and fills their bellies.*
*He weakens their wills and strengthens their bones.*
*Keep the people always without knowledge and without desires,*
*For then the clever will not dare act.*
*Engage in no action and order will prevail.*[13]

In the philosophy of the *Laozi,* the people would be better off if they knew less, gave up tools, renounced writing, stopped envying their neighbors, and lost their desire to travel or engage in war.

Zhuangzi (369–286 B.C.E.), the author of the book of the same name, was a historical figure who shared many of the central ideas of the *Laozi,* such as the usefulness of the useless and the relativity of ordinary distinctions. He was proud of his disinterest in politics. In one of his many anecdotes, he reported that the king of Chu once sent an envoy to invite him to take over the government of his

**Book Written on Silk** This text of the *Laozi* was excavated from a second-century B.C.E. tomb. *(© Cultural Relics Data Center of China)*

realm. In response Zhuangzi asked the envoy whether a tortoise that had been held as sacred for three thousand years would prefer to be dead with its bones venerated or alive with its tail dragging in the mud. When the envoy agreed that life was preferable, Zhuangzi told the envoy to leave. He preferred to drag his tail in the mud.

The *Zhuangzi* is filled with parables, flights of fancy, and fictional encounters between historical figures, including Confucius and his disciples. A more serious strain of Zhuangzi's thought concerned death. He questioned whether we can be sure life is better than death. People fear what they do not know, the same way a captive girl will be terrified when she learns she is to become the king's concubine. Perhaps people will discover that death has as many delights as life in the palace.

When a friend expressed shock that Zhuangzi was not weeping at his wife's death but rather singing, Zhuangzi explained:

*When she first died, how could I have escaped feeling the loss? Then I looked back to the beginning before she had life. Not only before she had life, but before she had form. Not only before she had form, but before she had vital energy. In this confused amorphous realm, something changed and vital energy appeared; when the vital energy was changed, form appeared; with changes in form, life began. Now there is another change bringing death. This is like the progression of the four seasons of spring and fall, winter and summer. Here she was lying down to sleep in a huge room and I followed her, sobbing and wailing. When I realized my actions showed I hadn't understood destiny, I stopped.*[14]

Zhuangzi was similarly iconoclastic in his political ideas. In one parable a wheelwright insolently tells a duke that books are useless since all they contain are the dregs of men long dead. The duke, insulted, threatens to execute him if he cannot give an adequate explanation of his remark. The wheelwright replies:

*I see things in terms of my own work. When I chisel at a wheel, if I go slow, the chisel slides and does not stay put; if I hurry, it jams and doesn't move properly. When it is neither too slow nor too fast, I can feel it in my hand and respond to it from my heart. My mouth cannot describe it in words, but there is something there. I cannot teach it to my son, and my son cannot learn it from me. So I have gone on for seventy years, growing old chiseling wheels. The men of old died in possession of what they could not transmit. So it follows that what you are reading are their dregs.*[15]

To put this another way, truly skilled craftsmen respond to situations spontaneously; they do not analyze or reason or even keep in mind the rules they have mastered. This strain of Daoist thought denies the validity of verbal reasoning and the sorts of knowledge conveyed through words.

Daoism can be seen as a response to Confucianism, a rejection of many of its basic premises. Nevertheless, over the course of Chinese history, many people felt the pull of both Confucian and Daoist ideas and studied the writings of both schools. Even Confucian scholars who had devoted much of their lives to public service might find that the teachings of the *Laozi* or *Zhuangzi* helped to put their frustrations in perspective. Whereas Confucianism often seems sternly masculine, Daoism is more accepting of feminine principles and even celebrates passivity and yielding. Those drawn to the arts were also often drawn to Daoism, with its validation of spontaneity and freedom. Rulers, too, were drawn to the Daoist notion of the ruler who can have great power simply by being himself without instituting anything.

## Legalism

Over the course of the fourth and third centuries B.C.E., the number of surviving states dwindled as one small state after another was conquered. Rulers fearful that their states might be next were ready to listen to political theorists who claimed expertise in the accumulation of power. These theorists, labeled **Legalists** because of their emphasis on the need for rigorous laws, argued that strong government depended not on the moral qualities of the ruler and his officials, as Confucians claimed, but on establishing effective laws and procedures. Legalism, though eventually discredited, laid the basis for China's later bureaucratic government.

In the fourth century B.C.E. the state of Qin, under the leadership of its chief minister, Lord Shang (d. 338 B.C.E.), adopted many Legalist policies. It abolished the aristocracy. Social distinctions were to be based on military ranks determined by the objective criterion of the number of enemy heads cut off in battle. In place of the old fiefs, Qin divided the country into counties and appointed officials to govern them according to the laws decreed at court. To increase the population, migrants were recruited from other states with offers of land and houses. To encourage farmers to work hard and improve their land, they were allowed to buy and sell it. Ordinary farmers were thus freed from serflike obligations to the local nobility, but direct control by the state could be even more onerous. Taxes and labor service obligations were heavy. Travel required a permit, and vagrants could be forced into penal labor service. All families were grouped into mutual responsibility groups of five and ten families; whenever anyone in the group committed a crime, all the others were equally liable unless they reported it.

A book ascribed to Lord Shang heaped scorn on respect for tradition and urged the ruler not to hesitate to institute changes that would strengthen his state: "Wise people create laws while ignorant ones are controlled by them; the worthy alter the rites while the unworthy are held fast by them."[16]

In the century after Lord Shang, Legalism found its greatest exponent in Han Feizi (d. 233 B.C.E.). Han Feizi had studied with the Confucian master Xunzi but had little interest in Confucian values of goodness or ritual. In his writings he warned rulers of the political pitfalls awaiting them. They had to be careful where they placed their trust, for "when the ruler trusts someone, he falls under that person's control."[17] This is true even of wives and concubines, who think of the interests of their sons. Given subordinates' propensities to pursue their own selfish interests, the ruler should keep them ignorant of his intentions and control them by manipulating competition among them. Warmth, affection, or candor could have no place in his relationships with others.

Han Feizi saw the Confucian notion that government could be based on virtue as naive.

*Think of parents' relations to their children. They congratulate each other when a son is born, but complain to each other when a daughter is born. Why do parents have these divergent responses when both are equally their offspring? It is because they calculate their long-term advantage. Since even parents deal with their children in this calculating way, what can one expect where there is no parent-child bond? When present-day scholars counsel rulers, they all tell them to rid themselves of thoughts of profit and follow the path of mutual love. This is expecting rulers to go further than parents.*[18]

If rulers would make the laws and prohibitions clear and the rewards and punishments automatic, then the officials and common people would be easy to govern. Uniform laws get people to do things they would not

**Embroidered Silk** From ancient times, silk was one of China's most famous products. Women traditionally did most of the work involved in making silk, from feeding mulberry leaves to the silkworms, to reeling and twisting the fibers, to weaving and embroidering. The embroidered silk depicted here is from a robe found in a fourth-century B.C.E. tomb in central China. The flowing, curvilinear design incorporates dragons, phoenixes, and tigers. *(Jingzhou Museum)*

otherwise be inclined to do, such as work hard and fight wars, essential to the goal of establishing hegemony over all the other states.

The laws of the Legalists were designed as much to constrain officials as to regulate the common people. The third century B.C.E. tomb of a Qin official has yielded statutes detailing the rules for keeping accounts, supervising subordinates, managing penal labor, conducting investigations, and many other responsibilities. Infractions were generally punishable through the imposition of fines.

Legalism saw no value in intellectual debate or private opinion. Divergent views of right and wrong lead to weakness and disorder. The ruler should not allow others to undermine his laws by questioning them. In Legalism, there were no laws above or independent of the wishes of the rulers, ones that might set limits on rulers' actions in the way that natural or divine laws did in Greek thought. Indeed, a ruler's right to exercise the law as he sees fit is demonstrated in the violent deaths of the two leading Legalist thinkers: Lord Shang was drawn and quartered by chariots in 338 B.C.E., and Han Feizi was imprisoned and forced to drink poison in 233 B.C.E.

Rulers of several states adopted some Legalist ideas, but only the state of Qin systematically followed them. The extraordinary but brief success Qin had with these policies is discussed in Chapter 7.

**Dagger Depicting Taiyi** Recent archaeological excavations of manuscripts from the Warring States Period have given us a much clearer understanding of religious beliefs and practices in early China. The deity Taiyi ("Grand One"), depicted on this late-fourth-century B.C.E. dagger, was the god of the pole star. Sacrifices were made to Taiyi to avert evil or gain his protection in battle. *(From Michael Loewe and Edward Shaughnessy, eds.,* Cambridge History of Ancient China *[New York: Cambridge University Press, 1999])*

## Other Schools of Thought

Confucians, Mohists, Daoists, and Legalists had the greatest long-term impact on Chinese civilization, but the late Zhou "Hundred Schools of Thought" also included everything from logicians, hedonists, and utopians, to agriculturalists who argued that no one should eat who does not farm, and hermits who justified withdrawal from social life.

Cosmological speculation formed one important strain of early Chinese thought. The concepts of **yin and yang** are found in early form in the divination manual the *Book of Changes,* but late Zhou theorists developed much more elaborate theories based on them. Yin is the feminine, dark, receptive, yielding, negative, and weak; yang is the masculine, bright, assertive, creative, positive, and strong. Yin and yang are complementary poles rather than distinct entities or opposing forces. The movement of yin and yang accounts for the transition from day to night and from summer to winter. These models based on observation of nature were extended to explain not only phenomena we might classify as natural, such as illness, storms, or earthquakes, but also social phenomena, such as the rise and fall of states or conflict in families. In all these realms, when the balance between yin and yang gets disturbed, unwanted things happen.

In recent decades archaeologists have further complicated our understanding of early Chinese thought by unearthing records of the popular religion of the time—astrological manuals, handbooks of lucky and unlucky days, medical prescriptions, exercises, and ghost stories. The tomb of an official who died in 316 B.C.E. has records of divinations showing that illness was seen as the result of unsatisfied spirits or malevolent demons, best dealt with through exorcisms or offering sacrifices to the god Taiyi (Grand One). Taiyi was an astral deity, sometimes depicted on weapons of the period as well.

## SUMMARY

By 200 B.C.E. Chinese civilization had passed through several distinct phases. After a long Neolithic period, China entered the Bronze Age with the Shang Dynasty. In Shang times, the kings served also as priests, and great wealth was invested in extraordinarily complex bronze ritual vessels. From Shang times on, the Chinese language has been written in a logographic script, which shaped the ways people have become educated and the value assigned to education.

The Zhou Dynasty, which overthrew the Shang in about 1050 B.C.E., parceled out their territory to lords in a feudal manner. These fiefs gradually came to act like independent states, so by 500 B.C.E. China is best thought of as a multistate society. Social and cultural change was particularly rapid under these conditions of intense competition.

The period from 500 to 200 B.C.E. was the golden age of Chinese philosophy. Confucius and his followers advocated a deeply moral view of the way to achieve order through the cultivation of virtues by everyone from the ruler on down. Mozi contended that every idea should be evaluated on the basis of its utility for the common good and objected to hereditary privilege and aggressive warfare on these grounds. Daoists like Laozi and Zhuangzi looked beyond the human realm to the entire cosmos and spoke of the relativity of concepts such as good and bad and life and death. The Legalists were hardheaded men who heaped ridicule on the idea that a ruler could get his people to be good by being good himself and proposed instead clear laws with strict rewards and punishments. Chinese thought in later centuries was profoundly shaped by the ideas espoused by these early thinkers.

## KEY TERMS

loess
Xiongnu
Anyang
logographic
taotie
*Book of Documents*
Mandate of Heaven
Warring States Period
shi
*Book of Songs*
crossbow
filial piety
ren
the Way
Legalists
yin and yang

## NOTES

1. Patricia Buckley Ebrey, ed., *Chinese Civilization: A Sourcebook,* 2d ed. (New York: Free Press/Macmillan, 1993), p. 11.
2. Ibid., p. 13.
3. Patricia Buckley Ebrey, *The Cambridge Illustrated History of China* (Cambridge: Cambridge University Press, 1996), p. 34.
4. Ebrey, *Chinese Civilization,* p. 21.
5. Ibid., p. 19.
6. Ibid., p. 21.
7. Ibid.
8. *Analects* 7.19, 15.30. Translated by Patricia Ebrey.
9. Ebrey, *Chinese Civilization,* p. 26.
10. Ibid., p. 24, modified.
11. Ibid., p. 27.
12. Ibid., p. 28, modified.
13. Ibid., p. 28.
14. Ibid., p. 31.
15. Ibid.
16. Ibid., p. 33.
17. Ibid.
18. Ibid., p. 35.

## SUGGESTED READING

Among the most interesting and accessible general histories of China are R. Huang's lively, interpretive *China: A Macro History* (1988), J. Gernet's solid *A History of Chinese Civilization* (1989), C. Schirokaur's popular and balanced textbook *A Brief History of Chinese Civilization* (1991), C. Hucker's *China's Imperial Past* (1975), and P. Ebrey's attractive *Cambridge Illustrated History of China* (1996). For premodern history, see also V. Hansen, *The Open Empire: A History of China to 1600* (2000). P. Ropp, ed., *Heritage of China: Contemporary Perspectives on Chinese Civilization* (1990), offers readers essays on religion, thought, family, art, and other topics. For translations of Chinese writings providing insights into Chinese society and culture, see P. Ebrey, *Chinese Civilization: A Sourcebook* (1993) and W. de Bary and I. Bloom, *Sources of Chinese Tradition* (1999). An introduction to Chinese history through biographies of key individuals is provided by J. Wills, Jr., *Mountain of Fame: Portraits in Chinese History* (1994). A recent well-illustrated topical volume is E. Shaunhessey, *China: Empire and Civilization* (2000).

Useful reference works for China include B. Hook and D. Twitchett, eds., *The Cambridge Encyclopedia of China* (1991); H. T. Zurndorfer, *China Bibliography* (1995); and A. Embree, ed., *Encyclopedia of Asian History* (1988). For historical maps and well-illustrated topical essays, see C. Blunden and M. Elvin, *Cultural Atlas of China* (1983). Many fine surveys of art are available, including L. Sickman and A. Soper, *The Art and Architecture of China* (1978);

J. Rawson, ed., *The British Museum Book of Chinese Art* (1992), and, most recently, R. Thorp and R. Vinograd, *Chinese Art and Culture* (2001).

For early China, the most authoritative volume is M. Loewe and E. Shaunhessey, *The Cambridge History of Ancient China: From the Origins of Civilization to 221 B.C.* (1999). The journal *Early China* often reports on important new archaeological finds. The foremost authority on the archaeology of early China is K. C. Chang. See his *Archeology of Ancient China,* 4th ed. (1986), *Shang Civilization* (1986), and *Art, Myth, and Ritual: The Path to Political Authority in Ancient China* (1983). For the development of the Chinese writing system, see W. Boltz, *The Origin and Early Development of the Chinese Writing System* (1994). For a comparative perspective on prehistory and the ancient period, see Gina L. Barnes, *The Rise of Civilization in East Asia* (1993). Sarah Allan examines Shang cosmology and Zhou myths in *The Shape of the Turtle: Myth, Art, and Cosmology in Early China* (1991). For ancient art and technology, see W. Fong's lavishly illustrated *Great Bronze Age of China* (1980) and Jessica Rawson's *Ancient China: Art and Archeology* (1980).

For the Zhou period, see M. Lewis, *Sanctioned Violence in Early China* (1990); C. Hsu and K. Linduff, *Western Chou Civilization* (1988); and X. Li, *Eastern Zhou and Qin Civilizations* (1985).

Good overviews of the intellectual flowering of the Warring States Period include A. C. Graham, *Disputers of the Tao: Philosophical Argument in Ancient China* (1989); Benjamin Schwartz, *The World of Thought in Ancient China* (1985); M. Lewis, *Writing and Authority in Early China* (1999); and, more briefly, F. W. Mote, *Intellectual Foundations of China* (1989). James Legge did a complete translation of *The Chinese Classics,* 5 vols. (1960), in the nineteenth century. More recent translators include A. Waley, D. C. Lau, and B. Watson. For Waley, see *Analects of Confucius* (1938) and *Book of Songs* (1937). Lau translated *Confucius: The Analects* (1979), *Tao Te Ching: Chinese Classics* (1982), and *Mencius* (1970). Watson has published *The Tso Chuan: Selections from China's Oldest Narrative History* (1989), *The Complete Works of Chuang Tzu* (1968), and *Basic Writings of Mo Tzu, Hsun Tzu, and Han Fei Tzu* (1967). For military thinking, see R. Ames, trans., *Sun-tzu: The Art of War* (1993).

# LISTENING TO THE PAST

## The Book of Mencius

*The book that records the teachings of Mencius (ca 370–ca 300 B.C.E.) was modeled on the* Analects *of Confucius. It presents, in no particular order, conversations between Mencius and several rulers, philosophers, and disciples. Unlike the* Analects, *however, the* Book of Mencius *includes extended discussions of particular points, suggesting that Mencius had a hand in recording the conversations.*

Mencius had an audience with King Hui of Liang. The king said, "Sir, you did not consider a thousand *li* too far to come. You must have some ideas about how to benefit my state."

Mencius replied, "Why must Your Majesty use the word 'benefit'? All I am concerned with are the benevolent and the right. If Your Majesty says, 'How can I benefit my state?' your officials will say, 'How can I benefit my family,' and officers and common people will say, 'How can I benefit myself?' Once superiors and inferiors are competing for benefit, the state will be in danger.

"When the head of a state of ten thousand chariots is murdered, the assassin is invariably a noble with a fief of a thousand chariots. When the head of a fief of a thousand chariots is murdered, the assassin is invariably head of a subfief of a hundred chariots. Those with a thousand out of ten thousand, or a hundred out of a thousand, had quite a bit. But when benefit is put before what is right, they are not satisfied without snatching it all. By contrast, there has never been a benevolent person who neglected his parents or a righteous person who put his lord last. Your Majesty perhaps will now also say, 'All I am concerned with are the benevolent and the right.' Why mention 'benefit'?"

After seeing King Xiang of Liang, Mencius said to someone, "When I saw him from a distance, he did not look like a ruler, and when I got closer, I saw nothing to command respect. But he asked, 'How can the realm be settled?'

"I answered, 'It can be settled through unity.'

"'Who can unify it?' he asked.

"I answered, 'Someone not fond of killing people.'

"'Who could give it to him?'

"I answered, 'Everyone in the world will give it to him. Your Majesty knows what rice plants are? If there is a drought in the seventh and eighth months, the plants wither, but if moisture collects in the sky and forms clouds and rain falls in torrents, the plants suddenly revive. This is the way it is; no one can stop the process. In the world today there are no rulers disinclined toward killing. If there were a ruler who did not like to kill people, everyone in the world would crane their necks to catch sight of him. This is really true. The people would flow toward him the way water flows down. No one would be able to repress them.'"

After an incident between Zou and Lu, Duke Mu asked, "Thirty-three of my officials died but no common people died. I could punish them, but I could not punish them all. I could refrain from punishing them, but they did angrily watch their superiors die without saving them. What would be the best course for me to follow?"

Mencius answered, "When the harvest failed, even though your granaries were full, nearly a thousand of your subjects were lost—the old and weak among them dying in the gutters, the able-bodied scattering in all directions. Your officials never reported the situation, a case of superiors callously inflicting suffering on their subordinates. Zengzi said, 'Watch out, watch out! What you do will be done to you.' This was the first chance the people had to pay them back. You should not resent them. If Your Highness practices benevolent government, the common people will love their superiors and die for those in charge of them."

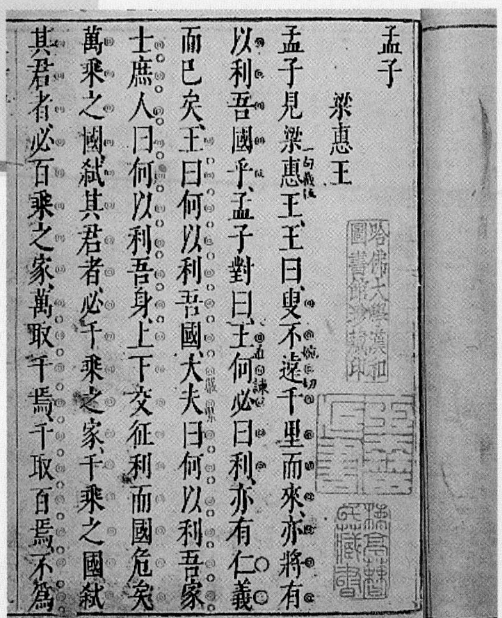

孟子
梁惠王
孟子見梁惠王王曰叟不遠千里而來亦將有
以利吾國乎孟子對曰王何必曰利亦有仁義
而已矣王曰何以利吾國大夫曰何以利吾家
士庶人曰何以利吾身上下交征利而國危矣
萬乘之國弒其君者必千乘之家千乘之國弒
其君者必百乘之家萬取千焉千取百焉不為

Opening page of a 1617 edition of the *Book of Mencius. (Rare Books Collections, Harvard-Yenching Library, Harvard University)*

King Xuan of Qi asked, "Is it true that Tang banished Jie and King Wu took up arms against Zhou?"

Mencius replied, "That is what the records say."

"Then is it permissible for a subject to assassinate his lord?"

Mencius said, "Someone who does violence to the good we call a villain; someone who does violence to the right we call a criminal. A person who is both a villain and a criminal we call a scoundrel. I have heard that the scoundrel Zhou was killed, but have not heard that a lord was killed."

King Xuan of Qi asked about ministers.

Mencius said, "What sort of ministers does Your Majesty mean?"

The king said, "Are there different kinds of ministers?"

"There are. There are noble ministers related to the ruler and ministers of other surnames."

The king said, "I'd like to hear about noble ministers."

Mencius replied, "When the ruler makes a major error, they point it out. If he does not listen to their repeated remonstrations, then they put someone else on the throne."

The king blanched. Mencius continued, "Your Majesty should not be surprised at this. Since you asked me, I had to tell you truthfully."

After the king regained his composure, he asked about unrelated ministers. Mencius said, "When the king makes an error, they point it out. If he does not heed their repeated remonstrations, they quit their posts."

Bo Gui said, "I'd like a tax of one part in twenty. What do you think?"

Mencius said, "Your way is that of the northern tribes. Is one potter enough for a state with ten thousand households?"

"No, there would not be enough wares."

"The northern tribes do not grow all the five grains, only millet. They have no cities or houses, no ritual sacrifices. They do not provide gifts or banquets for feudal lords, and do not have a full array of officials. Therefore, for them, one part in twenty is enough. But we live in the central states. How could we abolish social roles and do without gentlemen? If a state cannot do without potters, how much less can it do without gentlemen. Those who want to make government lighter than it was under Yao and Shun are to some degree barbarians. Those who wish to make government heavier than it was under Yao and Shun are to some degree [tyrants like] Jie."

Gaozi said, "Human nature is like whirling water. When an outlet is opened to the east, it flows east; when an outlet is opened to the west, it flows west. Human nature is no more inclined to good or bad than water is inclined to east or west."

Mencius responded, "Water, it is true, is not inclined to either east or west, but does it have no preference for high or low? Goodness is to human nature like flowing downward is to water. There are no people who are not good and no water that does not flow down. Still, water, if splashed, can go higher than your head; if forced, it can be brought up a hill. This isn't the nature of water; it is the specific circumstances. Although people can be made to be bad, their natures are not changed."

## QUESTIONS FOR ANALYSIS

1. Does Mencius give consistent advice to the kings he talks to?
2. Do you see a link between Mencius's views on human nature and his views on the true king?
3. What role does Mencius see for ministers?

*Source:* Patricia Buckley Ebrey, ed., *Chinese Civilization: A Sourcebook,* 2d ed. (New York: Free Press/Macmillan, 1993), pp. 22–24. 

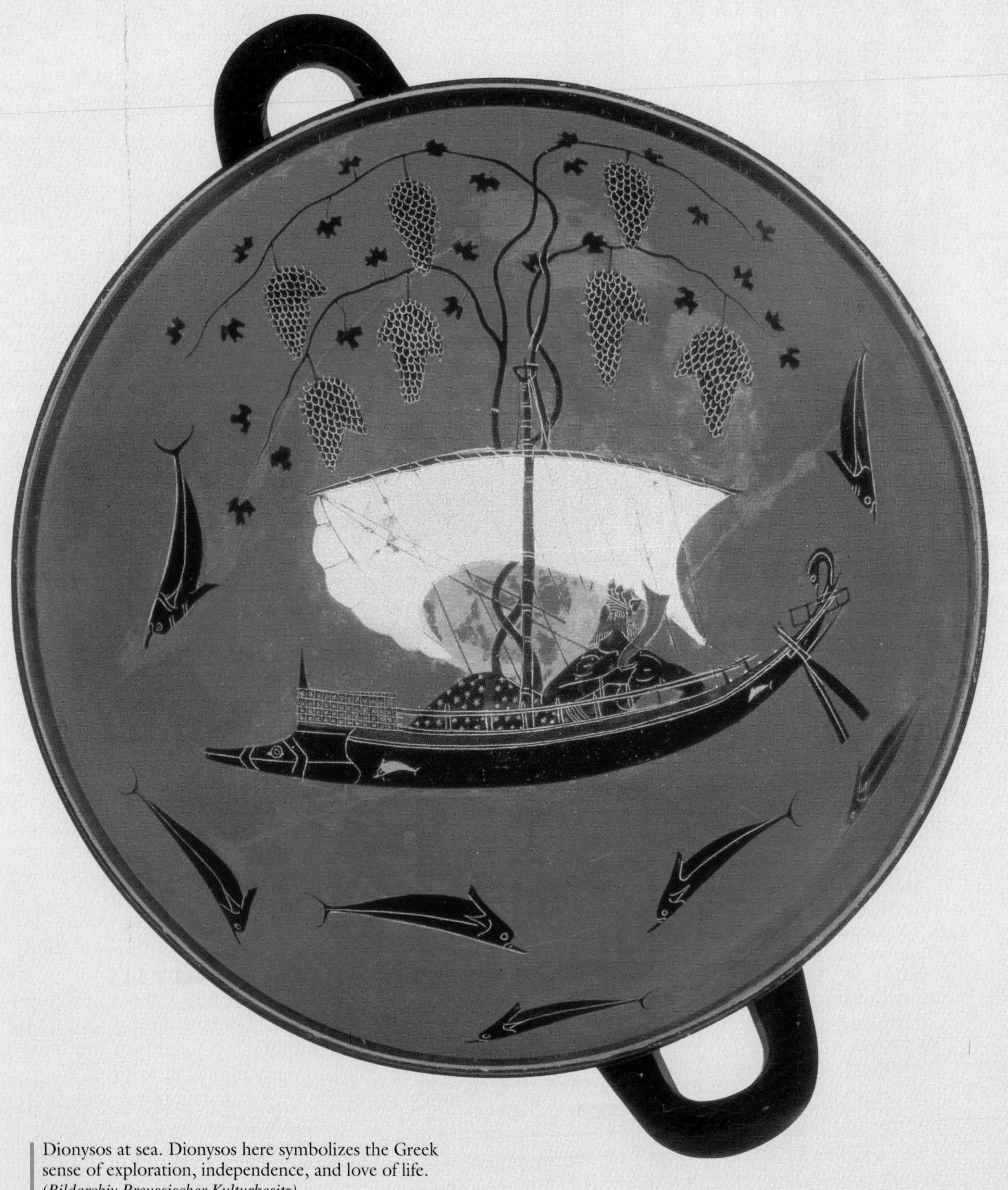

Dionysos at sea. Dionysos here symbolizes the Greek sense of exploration, independence, and love of life. *(Bildarchiv Preussischer Kulturbesitz)*

CHAPTER

# 5 THE GREEK EXPERIENCE

## CHAPTER OUTLINE

- Hellas: The Land
- The Polis
- The Archaic Age (800–500 B.C.E.)
- The Classical Period (500–338 B.C.E.)
- The Spread of Hellenism
- The Economic Scope of the Hellenistic World
- Religion in the Hellenistic World
- Hellenistic Thought

The rocky peninsula of Greece was the home of the civilization that fundamentally shaped Western civilization and nurtured a culture that eventually spread its essence, concepts, and values throughout the world. The Greeks explored questions that continue to concern people to this day. Going beyond mythmaking and religion, the Greeks strove to understand in logical, rational terms both the universe and the place of human beings in it.

The history of the Greeks and their culture is divided into two broad periods. The first is the Hellenic, roughly the time between the arrival of the Greeks (approximately 2000 B.C.E.) and the victory of Philip of Macedon over them in 338 B.C.E. The second is the Hellenistic, the years beginning with the reign of Alexander the Great (336–323 B.C.E.) and ending with the Roman conquest of the Hellenistic East (200–146 B.C.E.).

During the first of these periods, the Greeks developed and spread their culture and people beyond Greece to West Asia, North Africa, and southern Europe. The greatest monuments of the Greeks were profound thoughts set down in terms as fresh and immediate today as they were some twenty-four hundred years ago.

The Hellenistic period saw this civilization burst upon a larger world. In the footsteps of Alexander came others spreading all aspects of Greek culture deeper into western and Central Asia and into western Europe. In the process the Greeks shared their heritage with both emerging societies in Europe and venerable cultures in Asia.

- How did the Greeks develop basic political forms, as different as democracy and tyranny, that have influenced all of later history?
- What did the Greek intellectual triumph entail, and what were its effects?
- What did the spread of Hellenism mean to the Greeks and to the peoples of Asia, Africa, and Europe?
- What did the meeting of West and East hold for the development of economics, religion, philosophy, women's concerns, science, and medicine?

These are the questions we will explore in this chapter.

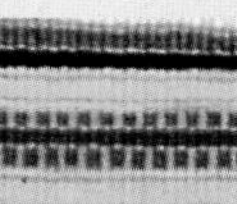

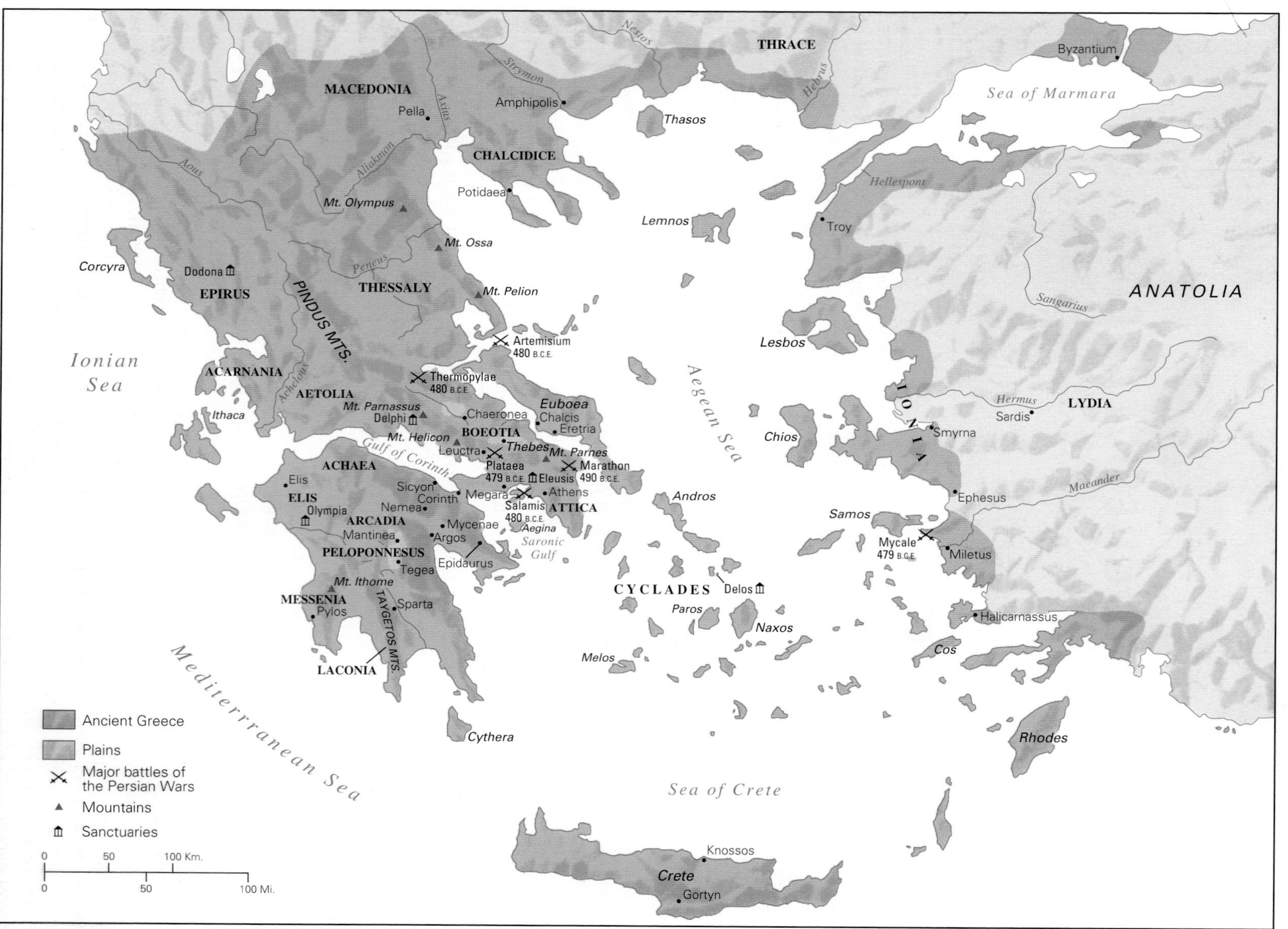


**MAP 5.1 Ancient Greece** In antiquity the home of the Greeks included the islands of the Aegean and the western shore of Turkey as well as the Greek peninsula itself.

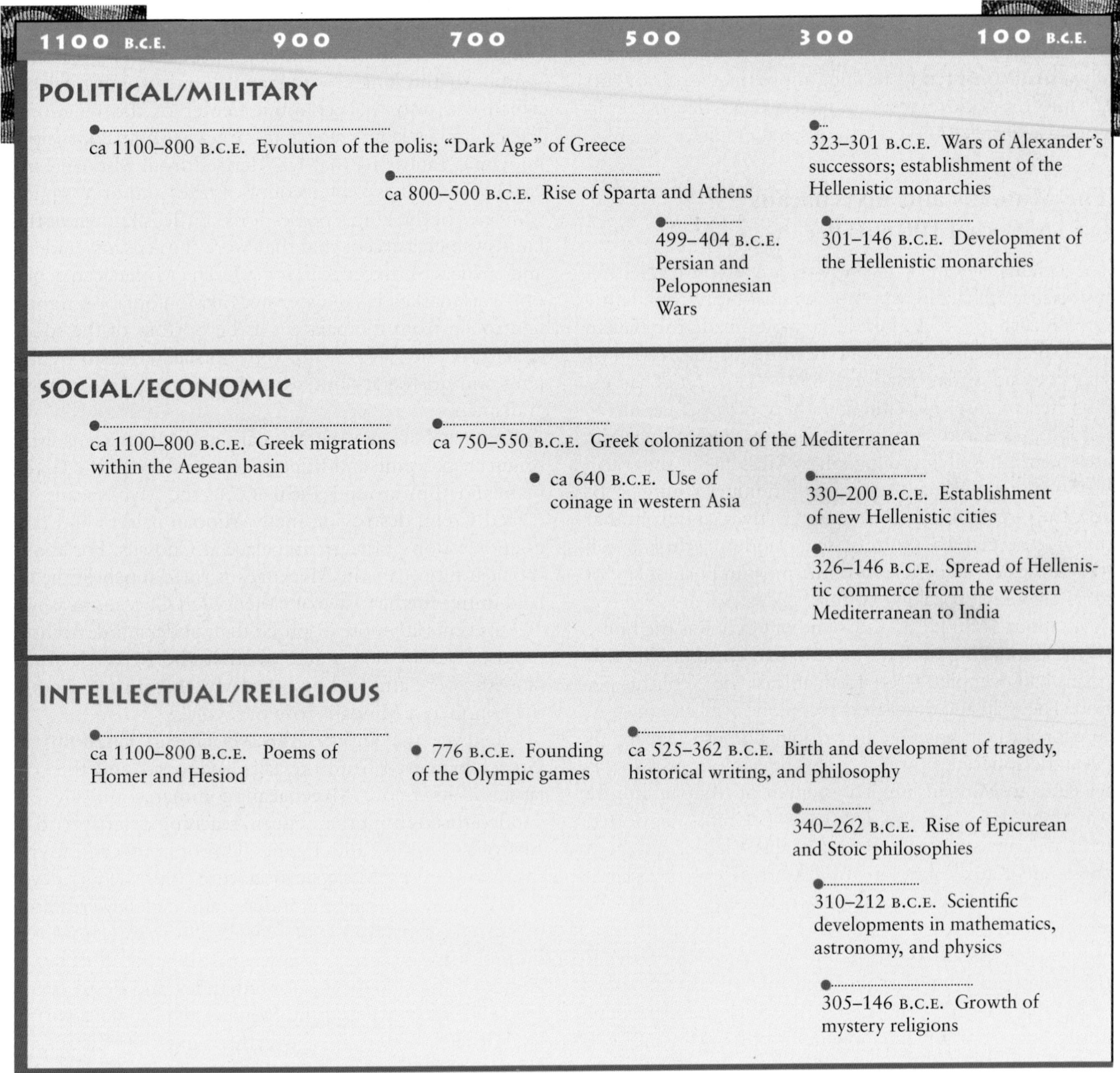

1100 B.C.E.
900
700
500
300
100 B.C.E.
POLITICAL/MILITARY
ca 1100–800 B.C.E. Evolution of the polis; "Dark Age" of Greece
ca 800–500 B.C.E. Rise of Sparta and Athens
499–404 B.C.E. Persian and Peloponnesian Wars
323–301 B.C.E. Wars of Alexander's successors; establishment of the Hellenistic monarchies
301–146 B.C.E. Development of the Hellenistic monarchies
SOCIAL/ECONOMIC
ca 1100–800 B.C.E. Greek migrations within the Aegean basin
ca 750–550 B.C.E. Greek colonization of the Mediterranean
ca 640 B.C.E. Use of coinage in western Asia
330–200 B.C.E. Establishment of new Hellenistic cities
326–146 B.C.E. Spread of Hellenistic commerce from the western Mediterranean to India
INTELLECTUAL/RELIGIOUS
ca 1100–800 B.C.E. Poems of Homer and Hesiod
776 B.C.E. Founding of the Olympic games
ca 525–362 B.C.E. Birth and development of tragedy, historical writing, and philosophy
340–262 B.C.E. Rise of Epicurean and Stoic philosophies
310–212 B.C.E. Scientific developments in mathematics, astronomy, and physics
305–146 B.C.E. Growth of mystery religions


## HELLAS: THE LAND

Hellas, as the Greeks call their land, encompassed the Aegean Sea and its islands as well as the Greek peninsula (see Map 5.1). The Greek peninsula itself, stretching in the direction of Egypt and the Near East, is an extension of the Balkan system of mountains. The rivers of Greece are never more than creeks, and most of them go dry in the summer. Greece is, however, a land blessed with good harbors, the most important of which look to the east. The islands of the Aegean serve as steppingstones between the peninsula and Asia Minor.

Despite the beauty of the region, geography acts as an enormously divisive force in Greek life. The mountains of Greece dominate the landscape, cutting the land into many small pockets and isolating areas of habitation. Innumerable small peninsulas open to the sea, which is dotted with islands, most of them small and many uninhabitable. The geographical fragmentation of Greece encouraged political fragmentation. Furthermore, communications were extraordinarily poor. Rocky tracks were far more common than roads, and the few roads were unpaved. Usually a road consisted of nothing more than a pair of ruts cut into the rock to accommodate wheels. These conditions discouraged the growth of great empires.

## The Minoans and Mycenaeans (ca 1650–ca 1100 B.C.E.)

The origins of Greek civilization are obscure. Neither historians, archaeologists, nor linguists can confidently establish when Greek-speaking peoples made the Balkan Peninsula of Greece their homeland. All that can now safely be said is that by about 1650 B.C.E. Greeks had established themselves at the great city of Mycenae in the Peloponnesus and elsewhere in Greece. Before then, the area from Thessaly in the north to Messenia in the south was inhabited by small farming communities. Quite probably the Greeks merged with these natives, and from that union emerged the society that modern scholars call "Mycenaean," after Mycenae, the most important site of this new Greek-speaking culture.

By about 1650 B.C.E. the island of Crete was the home of the flourishing and vibrant Minoan culture. The Minoans had occupied Crete from at least the Neolithic period. They had also developed a script, now called Linear A, to express their language in writing. Because Linear A is yet undeciphered, however, only archaeology and art offer clues to Minoan life. The symbol of Minoan culture was the palace. Around 1650 B.C.E. Crete was dotted with palaces, such as those at Mallia on the northern coast and Kato Zakro on the eastern tip of the island. Towering above all others in importance was the palace at Cnossus.

Few specifics are known about Minoan society except that at its head stood a king and his nobles, who governed the lives and toil of Crete's farmers, sailors, shepherds, and artisans. The implements of the Minoans, like those of the Mycenaeans, were bronze, so archaeologists have named this period the Bronze Age. Minoan society was wealthy and, to judge from the absence of fortifications on the island, peaceful. Enthusiastic sailors and merchants, the Minoans traded with Egypt and the cities of the area known today as the Middle East, or Levant. They also established trading posts throughout the Aegean Sea, which brought them into contact with the Mycenaeans on the Greek peninsula.

By about 1650 B.C.E. Greek-speakers were firmly settled at Mycenae, which became a major city and trading center. Later, other Mycenaean palaces and cities developed at Thebes, Athens, Tiryns, and Pylos. As in Crete, the political unit was the kingdom. The king and his warrior aristocracy stood at the top of society. The seat and symbol of the king's power and wealth was his palace, which was also the economic center of the kingdom. Palace scribes kept records in Greek with a script (now known as Linear B) that was derived from Minoan Linear A. The scribes kept account of taxes and drew up inventories of the king's possessions. Little is known of the king's subjects except that they were the artisans, traders, and farmers of Mycenaean society. The Mycenaean economy was marked by an extensive division of labor, tightly controlled from the palace. At the bottom of the social scale were the slaves, who were normally owned by the king and aristocrats but who also worked for ordinary craftsmen.

Contacts between the Minoans and Mycenaeans were originally peaceful, and Minoan culture flooded the Greek mainland. But around 1450 B.C.E. the Mycenaeans attacked Crete, destroying many Minoan palaces and taking possession of the grand palace at Cnossus. For about the next fifty years the Mycenaeans ruled much of the island until a further wave of violence left Cnossus in ashes. These events are more disputed than understood. Archaeologists cannot determine whether the Mycenaeans at Cnossus were attacked by other Mycenaeans or whether the conquered Minoans rose in revolt.

Whatever the answer, the Mycenaean kingdoms in Greece benefited from the fall of Cnossus and the collapse of its trade. Mycenaean commerce quickly expanded throughout the Aegean, reaching as far abroad as Anatolia, Cyprus, and Egypt. Throughout central and southern Greece Mycenaean culture flourished as never before. Palaces became grander, and citadels were often protected by mammoth stone walls. Prosperity, however, did not bring peace, and between 1300 and 1000 B.C.E. kingdom after kingdom suffered attack and destruction.

Later Greeks accused the Dorians, who spoke a particular dialect of Greek, of overthrowing the Mycenaean kingdoms. Yet some modern linguists argue that the Dorians dwelt in Greece during the Mycenaean period. Archaeologists generally conclude that the Dorians, if not already present, could have entered Greece only long after the era of destruction. Furthermore, not one alien artifact has been found at any of these sites; thus there is no archaeological evidence for outside invaders. Normally, foreign invaders leave traces of themselves—for example, broken pottery and weapons—that are different from those of the attacked. We can conclude, therefore, that no outside intrusion destroyed the Mycenaean world. In fact, the legends preserved by later Greeks tell of grim wars between Mycenaean kingdoms and of the fall of

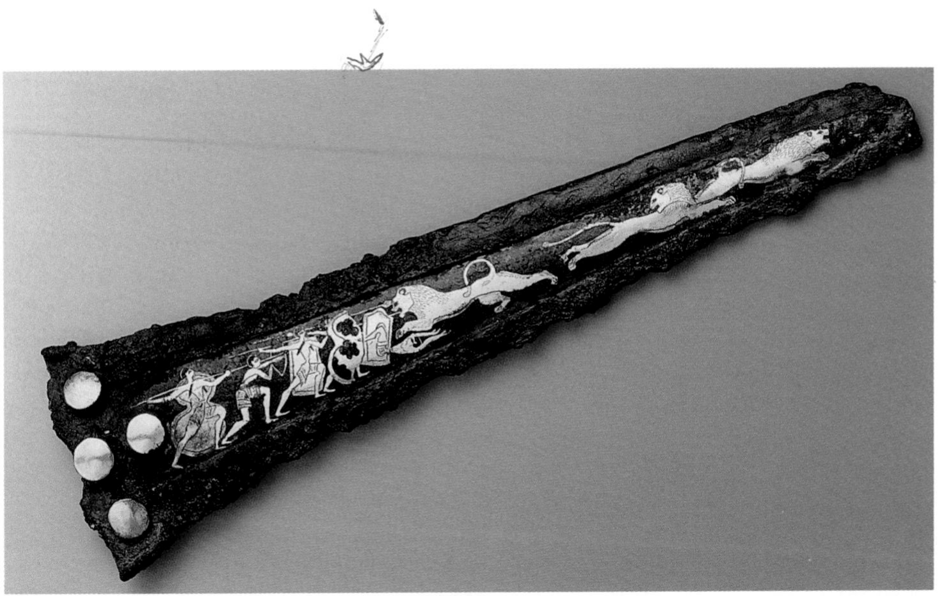

**Mycenaean Lion Hunt**
The Mycenaeans were a robust, warlike people who enjoyed the thrill and the danger of hunting. This scene on the blade of a dagger depicts hunters armed with spears and protected by shields defending themselves against charging lions. *(National Archaeological Museum/Archaeological Receipts Fund)*

great royal families. Apparently, Mycenaean Greece destroyed itself in a long series of internecine wars, a pattern that later Greeks would repeat.

The fall of the Mycenaean kingdoms ushered in a period of such poverty, disruption, and backwardness that historians usually call it the "Dark Age" of Greece (ca 1100–800 B.C.E.). Even literacy, which was not widespread in any case, was a casualty of the chaos. Nonetheless, the Greeks survived the storm to preserve their culture and civilization. Greece remained Greek; nothing essential was swept away. Greek religious cults remained vital to the people, and basic elements of social organization continued to function effectively. It was a time of change and challenge, but not of utter collapse.

This period also saw a development of enormous importance for the course of Western civilization. The disruption of Mycenaean societies caused the widespread movement of Greek peoples. Some Greeks sailed to Crete, where they established new communities. The most important line of immigration was east to the shores of Asia Minor. The Greeks arrived during a time when the traditional states and empires had collapsed. Economic hardship was common, and various peoples wandered for years. The age saw both the displacement of peoples throughout the region and ethnic intermixing. Whereas the Sea Peoples (see page 25) had eventually dissolved into their various parts and gone their separate ways, the Greeks spread the culture of their homeland throughout the eastern Mediterranean.

Upon landing in Asia Minor, the Greeks encountered peoples who had been influenced by the older cultures of the region. Furthermore, the Greeks themselves had had long associations with these peoples. Thus they were hardly strangers, nor was Greek culture alien or unknown to the natives. By the end of the Dark Age of Greece, the Greeks had established a string of settlements along a coast already accustomed to them. Their arrival resulted in the spread of Greek culture throughout the area, not through force of arms but because of its freedom of ideas, the right of individuals to express them, and the vitality of Greek social life.

## Homer, Hesiod, and the Heroic Past (1100–800 B.C.E.)

The Greeks, unlike the Hebrews, had no sacred book that chronicled their past. Instead they had the *Iliad* and the *Odyssey* to describe a time when gods still walked the earth. And they learned the origin and descent of the gods from the *Theogony,* an epic poem by Hesiod (ca 700 B.C.E.). Instead of authentic history the poems of Homer and Hesiod offered the Greeks an ideal past, a largely legendary Heroic Age. These poems contain scraps of information about the Bronze Age, much about the early Dark Age, and some about the poets' own era. Chronologically, the Heroic Age falls mainly in the period between the collapse of the Mycenaean world and the rebirth of literacy.

The *Iliad* recounts an expedition of Mycenaeans, whom Homer called "Achaeans," to besiege the city of Troy in Asia Minor. The heart of the *Iliad,* however, concerns the quarrel between Agamemnon, the king of Mycenae, and Achilles, the tragic hero of the poem, and how their anger and pride brought suffering to the

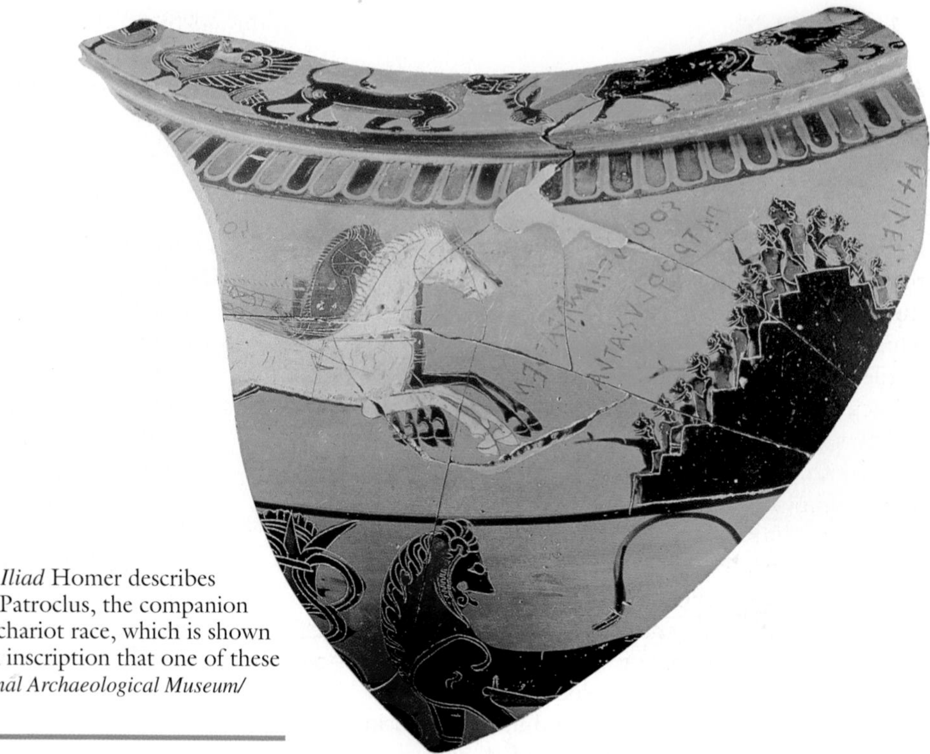

**Funeral Games** At the end of the *Iliad* Homer describes the funeral games given in honor of Patroclus, the companion of Achilles. The main event was the chariot race, which is shown here. The painter states in the Greek inscription that one of these chariots belonged to Achilles. *(National Archaeological Museum/Archaeological Receipts Fund)*

Achaeans. The *Odyssey,* probably composed later than the *Iliad,* narrates the adventures of Odysseus, one of the Achaean heroes who fought at Troy, during his voyage home from the fighting.

The splendor of these poems does not lie in their plots, although the *Odyssey* is a marvelous adventure story. Rather, both poems portray engaging but often flawed characters who are larger than life and yet typically human. Homer was also strikingly successful in depicting the great gods, who generally sit on Mount Olympus and watch the fighting at Troy like spectators at a baseball game, although they sometimes participate in the action. Homer's deities are reminiscent of Mesopotamian gods and goddesses. Hardly a decorous lot, the Olympians are raucous, petty, deceitful, and splendid. In short, they are human.

Homer at times portrayed the gods in a serious vein, but he never treated them in a systematic fashion, as did Hesiod, who lived somewhat later than Homer. Hesiod's epic poem, the *Theogony,* traces the descent of Zeus. Hesiod was influenced by Mesopotamian myths, which the Hittites had adopted and spread to the Aegean. Like the Hebrews, however, Hesiod envisaged his *cosmogony*—his account of the way the universe developed—in moral terms. Cronus, the son of Earth and Heaven, like the Mesopotamian Enlil, separated the two and became king of the gods. Zeus, the son of Cronus, defeated his evil father and took his place as king of the gods. He then sired Lawfulness, Right, Peace, and other powers of light and beauty. Thus, in Hesiod's conception, Zeus was the god of righteousness, who loved justice and hated wrongdoing.

In another epic poem, *Works and Days,* Hesiod wrote of his own time and his own village of Ascra in Boeotia, a scenic place set between beautiful mountains and fertile plains. In his will, Hesiod's father had divided his lands between Hesiod and his brother, Perses. Perses bribed the aristocratic authorities to give him the larger part of the inheritance and then squandered his wealth. Undaunted by the injustice of the powerful, Hesiod thundered back:

*Bribe-devouring lords, make straight your decisions,*
*Forget entirely crooked judgments.*
*He who causes evil to another harms himself.*
*Evil designs are most evil to the plotter.*[1]

Hesiod did not receive justice from the political authorities of the day, but he fully expected divine vindication. Hesiod spoke of Zeus as Jeremiah had spoken of Yahweh, warning that Zeus would see that justice was done and injustice punished. He cautioned his readers that Zeus was angered by those who committed adultery, harmed orphans, and offended the aged.

## THE POLIS

After the upheavals that ended the Mycenaean period and the slow recovery of prosperity during the Dark Age, the Greeks developed their basic political and institutional unit, the **polis,** or city-state. Only three city-states were able to muster the resources of an entire region behind them (see Map 5.1): Sparta, which dominated the regions of Laconia and Messenia; Athens, which united the large peninsula of Attica under its rule; and Thebes, which in several periods marshaled the resources of the fertile region of Boeotia. Otherwise, the political pattern of ancient Greece was one of many small city-states, few of which were much stronger or richer than their neighbors.

Physically the term *polis* designated a city or town and its surrounding countryside. The people of a typical polis lived in a compact group of houses within a city. The city's water supply came from public fountains and cisterns. By the fifth century B.C.E. the city was generally surrounded by a wall. The city contained a point, usually elevated, called the **acropolis,** and a public square or marketplace, the *agora.* On the acropolis, which in the early period was a place of refuge, stood the temples, altars, public monuments, and various dedications to the gods of the polis. The agora was originally the place where the warrior assembly met, but it became the political center of the polis. In the agora were porticoes, shops, and public buildings and courts.

The unsettled territory of the polis—arable land, pastureland, and wasteland—was typically its source of wealth. Farmers left the city each morning to work their fields or tend their flocks of sheep and goats, and they returned at night. On the wasteland men often quarried stone or mined for precious metals. Thus the polis was the scene of both urban and agrarian life.

The size of the polis varied according to geographical circumstances. Population figures for Greece are mostly guesswork, because most city-states were too small to need a census. But regardless of its size or wealth, the polis was fundamental to Greek life. The intimacy of the polis was an important factor. The smallness of the polis enabled Greeks to see how the individual fitted into the

**Polis of Argos** This view of modern Argos remarkably illustrates the structure of an ancient polis. Atop the hill in the background are the remains of the ancient acropolis. At its foot to the right are foundations of ancient public and private buildings, spreading beyond which are modern houses, situated where ancient houses were located. The trees and cut grain in the foreground were also major features of the *chora,* the agricultural basis of the polis. *(John Buckler)*

overall system—how the human parts made up the social whole. These simple facts go far to explain why the Greek polis was fundamentally different from the great empires of Persia and China. The Greeks knew their leaders and elected them to limited terms of office. They were unlike the subjects of the Mauryan Empire or the Han Dynasty, who might spend their entire lives without ever seeing their emperors. One result of these factors was the absence in Greek politics of a divine emperor. Another was the lack of an extensive imperial bureaucracy and a standing army. The ancient Greeks were their own magistrates, administrators, and soldiers.

Instead of a standing army, the average polis relied on its own citizens for protection. Very rich citizens often served as cavalry. However, the heavily armed infantry was the backbone of the army. The foot soldiers, or **hoplites,** provided their own equipment and were basically amateurs. When in battle, they stood in several dense lines, in which cohesion and order became as valuable as courage.

The polis could be governed in any of several ways. In a **monarchy,** a term derived from the Greek for "the rule of one man," a king represented the community, reigning according to law and respecting the rights of the citizens. Or the **aristocracy** could govern the state. A literal political translation of this term means "power in the hands of the best." Or the running of the polis could be the duty and prerogative of an **oligarchy,** which literally means "the rule of a few"—in this case a small group of wealthy citizens, not necessarily of aristocratic birth. Or the polis could be governed as a **democracy,** through the rule of the people, a concept that in Greece meant that all citizens, regardless of birth or wealth, administered the workings of government. How a polis was governed depended on who had the upper hand. When the wealthy held power, they usually instituted oligarchies; when the people could break the hold of the rich, they established democracies. Still another form of Greek government was **tyranny,** rule by a tyrant, a man who had seized power by extralegal means, generally by using his wealth to gain a political following that could topple the existing government.

Because the bonds that held the polis together were so intimate, Greeks were extremely reluctant to allow foreigners to share fully in its life. An alien, even someone Greek by birth, could almost never expect to be made a citizen. Nor could women play a political role. Women participated in the civic cults and served as priestesses, but the polis had no room for them in state affairs. This exclusiveness doomed the polis to a limited horizon.

Although each polis was jealous of its independence, some Greeks banded together to create leagues of city-states. Here was the birth of Greek federalism, a political system in which several states formed a central government while remaining independent in their internal affairs. United in a league, a confederation of city-states was far stronger than any of the individual members and better able to withstand external attack.

**Early Greek Warfare** Before the hoplites became the backbone of the army, wealthy warriors rode into battle in a chariot, dismounted, and engaged the enemy. This scene, almost a photograph, shows on the left the warrior protecting the chariot before it returns to the rear. The painter has caught the lead horses already beginning the turn. *(Courtesy of the Ure Museum of Greek Archaeology, University of Reading)*

The passionate individualism of the polis proved to be another serious weakness. The citizens of each polis were determined to remain free and autonomous. Rarely were the Greeks willing to unite in larger political bodies. The political result in Greece, as in Sumer, was almost constant warfare. The polis could dominate, but unlike Rome it could not incorporate.

# THE ARCHAIC AGE (800–500 B.C.E.)

The maturation of the polis coincided with one of the most vibrant periods of Greek history, an era of extraordinary expansion geographically, artistically, and politically. Greeks ventured as far east as the Black Sea and as far west as Spain (see Map 5.2). With the rebirth of literacy, this period also witnessed a tremendous literary flowering as poets broke away from the heroic tradition and wrote about their own lives. Politically these were the years when Sparta and Athens—the two poles of the Greek experience—rose to prominence.

## Overseas Expansion

Between 1100 and 800 B.C.E. the Greeks not only recovered from the breakdown of the Mycenaean world but also grew in wealth and numbers. This new prosperity brought with it new problems. Greece is a small and not especially fertile country. The increase in population meant that many men and their families had very little land or none at all. Land hunger and the resulting social and political tensions drove many Greeks to seek new homes outside Greece (see Map 5.2).

From about 750 to 550 B.C.E., Greeks from the mainland and Asia Minor traveled throughout the Mediterranean and even into the Atlantic Ocean in their quest for new land. They sailed in the greatest numbers to Sicily and southern Italy, where there was ample space for expansion. They also sailed farther west to Sardinia, southern France and Spain, and even the Canary Islands. In Sicily they found the Sicels, who had already adopted many Carthaginian customs, including a nascent urban culture. Fiercely independent, they greeted the coming of the Greeks just as they had the arrival of the Carthaginians. They welcomed Greek culture but not Greek

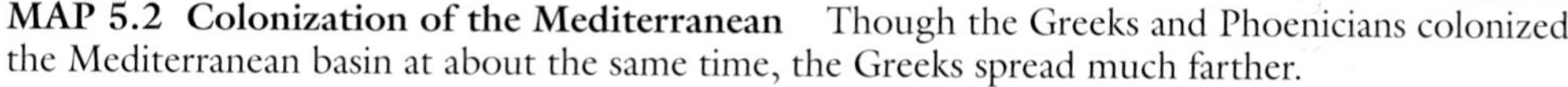

**MAP 5.2 Colonization of the Mediterranean** Though the Greeks and Phoenicians colonized the Mediterranean basin at about the same time, the Greeks spread much farther.

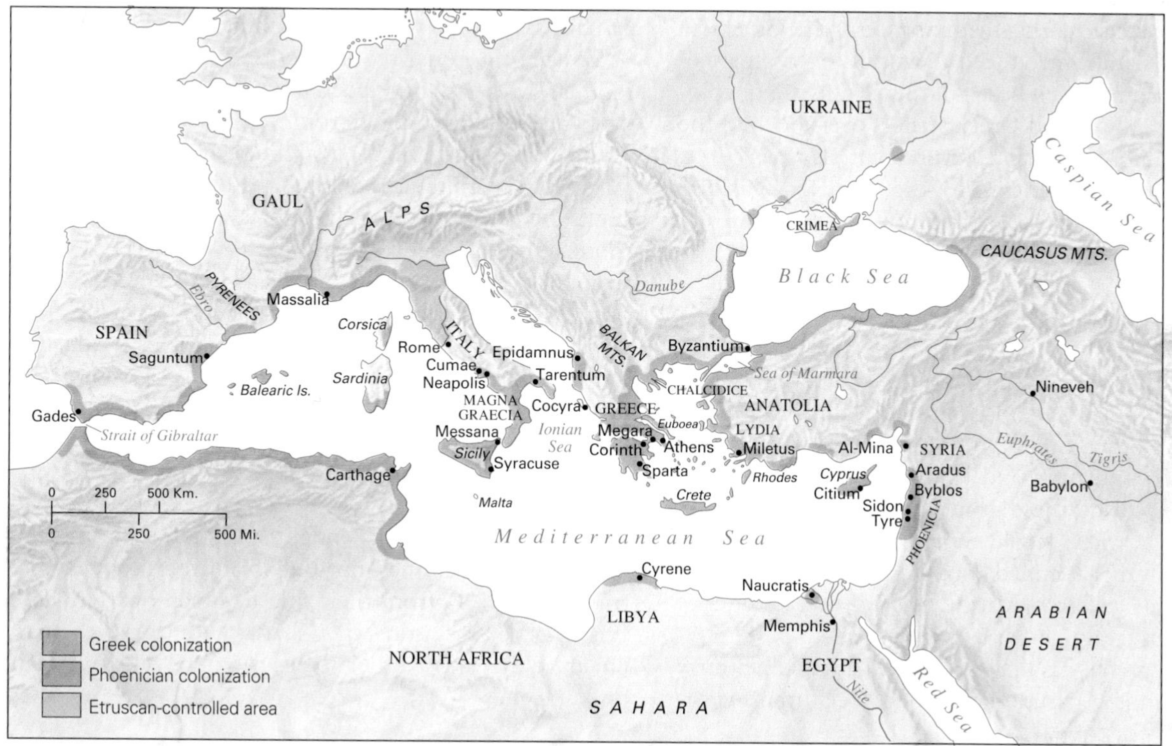

demands for their land. Nonetheless, the two peoples made a somewhat uneasy accommodation. There was enough land in Sicily for Greeks and Sicels alike, so both flourished, albeit not always peacefully.

In southern Italy the Greeks encountered a number of Indo-European peoples. They were for the most part rural and enjoyed few material comforts. Some of their villages were evolving into towns, but in the mountains looser tribal units prevailed. They both welcomed Greek culture, and the Greeks found it easy to establish prosperous cities without facing significant local hostility.

Some adventurous Greeks sailed to Sardinia and the southern coast of modern France. In Sardinia they established outposts that were originally trading ports, meant primarily for bartering with the natives. Commerce was so successful that some Greeks established permanent towns there. Greek influence, in terms of physical remains and the ideas that they reflect, was far stronger on the island than was recognized even a few years ago. From these new outposts Greek influence extended to southern France. The modern city of Marseilles began as a Greek colony and later sent settlers to southern Spain.

One of the most remarkable aspects of the sense of adventure of the Greeks is seen from their remains on the Canary Islands in the Atlantic Ocean. Their settlements on some of the islands took their culture beyond the Mediterranean for the first time. The presence of these pioneers widened the geographical and intellectual horizons of the Greek world. In the process, the Greeks of the Canary Islands introduced their culture to a part of Africa that had not even heard of them. This era of colonization not only spread Greek settlers over much of the western Mediterranean and beyond but also passed on the Hellenic legacy to the rest of the Mediterranean and even to a part of western Africa. Above all, Rome would later fall heir to this heritage.

## The Growth of Sparta

During the Lyric Age the Spartans expanded the boundaries of their polis and made it the leading power in Greece. Like other Greeks, the Spartans faced the problems of overpopulation and land hunger. Unlike other Greeks, they solved these problems by conquest, taking control of the rich, fertile region of Messenia after a twenty-year war that ended about 715 B.C.E. They made the Messenians *helots,* or state serfs, who after decades of harsh Spartan treatment rose in revolt.

When the revolt was finally squashed after some thirty years of fighting, Sparta underwent a social transformation. Non-nobles demanded rights equal to those of the nobility. The aristocrats agreed to remodel the state in a pattern called the Lycurgan regimen after Lycurgus, a legendary lawgiver. Politically, all Spartan men were given equal rights. Two kings ruled, assisted by a council of nobles. Executive power lay in the hands of five overseers elected by the people. Economically, the helots did all the work of the polis; Spartan citizens were supposed to devote their time exclusively to military training.

In the Lycurgan system every citizen owed primary allegiance to Sparta. Suppression of the individual together with emphasis on military prowess led to a barracks state. Family life itself was sacrificed to the polis. Once Spartan boys reached the age of twelve, they were enrolled in separate companies with other boys their age. They slept outside on reed mats and underwent rugged physical and military training until age twenty-four, when they became frontline soldiers. For the rest of their lives, Spartan men kept themselves prepared for combat. Their military training never ceased, and the older men were expected to be models of endurance, frugality, and sturdiness to the younger men. In battle Spartans were supposed to stand and die rather than retreat. An anecdote about one Spartan mother sums up Spartan military values. As her son was setting off to battle, the mother handed him his shield and advised him to come back either victorious, carrying the shield, or dead, being carried on it. In the Lycurgan regimen Spartan men were expected to train vigorously, disdain luxury and wealth, do with little, and like it.

Similar rigorous requirements applied to Spartan women, who may have been unique in all of Greek society. They were prohibited from wearing jewelry or ornate clothes. They too exercised strenuously in the belief that hard physical training promoted the birth of healthy children. Yet they were hardly oppressed. They enjoyed a more active and open public life than most other Greek women, even though they could neither vote nor hold office. They were far more emancipated than many other Greek women in part because Spartan society felt that mothers and wives had to be as hardy as their sons and husbands. Sparta was not a place for weaklings, male or female. Spartan women saw it as their privilege to be the wives and mothers of victorious warriors, and on several occasions their own courage became legendary. They had a reputation for an independent spirit and self-assertion. This position stemmed not only from their genuine patriotism but also from their title to much Spartan land. For all of these reasons, they shared a footing with Spartan men that most other Greek women lacked in their own societies.

Along with the emphasis on military values for both sexes, the Lycurgan regimen had another purpose as well: it served to instill in society the civic virtues of dedication to the state and a code of moral conduct. These aspects of the Spartan system were generally admired throughout the Greek world.

### The Evolution of Athens

Like Sparta, Athens faced serious social and economic problems, but it responded in a very different way by creating one of the most thoroughgoing democracies of ancient Greece. In the early sixth century B.C.E. the aristocracy was governing Athens oppressively. Noble landowners had all the best land and governed the polis. They used their power to seize the land of smaller landowners, selling debtors into slavery or sending them to exile. Solon, himself an aristocrat, grew alarmed by these trends. With the respect of both nobles and peasants, he was elected by the nobles as chief magistrate around 594 B.C.E. and given broad powers to reform the state.

Solon freed those who had been enslaved for debt, recalled the exiles, canceled debts for land, and banned enslavement for debtors. He allowed all citizens to join the aristocratic assembly that elected leaders and then, refusing the offer to take power as tyrant, left Athens.

Solon's reforms did not completely solve social problems in Athens. It was not until 508 B.C.E. that Cleisthenes further reorganized the state and created Athenian democracy. He did so with the full approval of the Athenian people; he presented every innovation to the assembly for discussion and ratification.

Cleisthenes created the **deme,** a local unit, to serve as the basis of his political system. Citizenship was tightly linked to the deme, for each deme kept the roll of those within its jurisdiction who were admitted to citizenship. Cleisthenes grouped all the demes into ten tribes, which thus formed the link between the demes and the central government. The central government included an assembly of all citizens and a new council of five hundred members.

The democracy functioned on the idea that all full citizens, the *demos,* were sovereign. Yet not all citizens could take time from work to participate in government. Therefore, they delegated their power to other citizens by creating various offices to run the democracy. The most prestigious of them was the board of ten archons, who were charged with handling legal and military matters. Legislation was in the hands of two bodies, the *boule,* or council, composed of five hundred members, and the *ecclesia,* the assembly of all citizens. The boule was perhaps the major institution of the democracy. By supervising the various committees of government and proposing bills to the assembly, it guided Athenian political life and held the democracy together. The ecclesia, however, had the final word. Open to all male citizens over eighteen years of age, this assembly could accept, amend, or reject bills put before it. Every member could express his opinion on any subject on the agenda. A simple majority vote was needed to pass or reject a bill.

Athenian democracy was to prove an inspiring model by demonstrating that a large group of people, not just a few, could efficiently run the affairs of state. Yet it must not be thought of in modern terms. While any citizen could theoretically enjoy political power, most important offices were held by aristocrats. Furthermore, the polis denied citizenship rights to many people, including women and slaves. Nevertheless, Athenian democracy has proved an inspiring model in that every citizen was expected to vote and to serve. The people were the government. It is this idea that the state exists for the good of the citizen, whose duty it is to serve it well, that has made Athenian democracy so compelling.

Yet Athenian democracy also had a dark side. Because comparatively few people actually exercised power, they could sometimes take advantage of their positions to dominate Athens. In periods of crisis some unscrupulous politicians suppressed political rights and even freedom of speech. These situations were rare, but the ancient Athenians, like modern Americans, balanced the desire for liberty with the need for security.

## THE CLASSICAL PERIOD (500–338 B.C.E.)

In the years from 500 to 338 B.C.E. Greek civilization reached its highest peak in politics, thought, and art. In this period the Greeks beat back the armies of the Persian Empire. Then, turning their spears against one another, they destroyed their own political system in a century of warfare. Some thoughtful Greeks felt prompted to record and analyze these momentous events; the result was the creation of history. This era also saw the flowering of philosophy, as Greek thinkers began to ponder the nature and meaning of the universe and human experience. The Greeks also invented drama, and Greek architects reached the zenith of their art. Because Greek intellectual and artistic efforts attained their fullest and finest expression in these years, this age is called the classical period.

## The Deadly Conflicts (499–404 B.C.E.)

One of the hallmarks of the classical period was warfare. In 499 B.C.E. the Greeks of West Asia, with the feeble help of Athens, rebelled against the Persian Empire. In 490 B.C.E. the Persians struck back at Athens but were beaten off at the Battle of Marathon, a small plain in Attica (see Map 5.1). In 480 B.C.E. the Persian king Xerxes retaliated with a mighty invasion force. Facing this emergency, many of the Greeks united to resist the invaders. The Spartans provided the overall leadership and commanded the Greek armies. The Athenians, led by the wily Themistocles, provided the heart of the naval forces.

In a series of hard-fought battles at the pass of Thermopylae and in the waters off Artemisium in 480 B.C.E., the Greeks retreated after heavy losses, but that autumn they decisively defeated the enemy at the naval battle of Salamis. In 479 B.C.E. they routed the last Persian forces at Plataea. These victories meant that the Greeks remained free to develop their particular genius. Their political forms and intellectual concepts would be the heritage of the West.

In 478 B.C.E. the victorious Athenians and their allies formed the **Delian League,** a grand naval alliance aimed at liberating Ionia from Persian rule. But Athenian success had a sinister side. While the Athenians drove the Persians out of the Aegean, they also became increasingly imperialistic, even to the point of turning the Delian League into an Athenian empire. Under their great leader Pericles (ca 494–429 B.C.E.), the Athenians grew so powerful and aggressive that they alarmed Sparta and its allies. A short war ending in 445 B.C.E. settled nothing, and in 431 B.C.E. Athenian imperialism finally drove Sparta to another conflict. At the outbreak of this conflict, the Peloponnesian War, a Spartan ambassador warned the Athenians: "This day will be the beginning of great evils for the Greeks." Few have ever spoken more prophetically. The Peloponnesian War lasted a generation (431–404 B.C.E.) and brought in its wake fearful plagues, famines, civil wars, widespread destruction, and huge loss of life. Finally, in 404 B.C.E. the Athenians surrendered, but by then the war had dealt Greek civilization a serious blow.

One positive development stemming from these events was the beginning of historical writing in the West. Just as Sima Qian during the Han Dynasty wrote a comprehensive history of China (see page 187), so Herodotus (ca 485–425 B.C.E.) and Thucydides (ca 460–ca 399 B.C.E.) left vivid, generally accurate accounts of Greek events. Their writings were not the chronicles or king lists of the Near East but analyses of what happened and why, with great emphasis on cause and effect and the role of individuals in important events. For the first time in the West, some men felt that the deeds of human beings were important enough to be recorded, understood, and instructive to others.

## Athenian Arts in the Age of Pericles

In the last half of the fifth century B.C.E. Pericles turned Athens into the showplace of Greece by turning the Acropolis into a monument for all time. The planning of the architects and the skill of the workmen who erected these buildings were both very sophisticated. Visitors approaching the Acropolis first saw the Propylaea, the ceremonial gateway, a building of complicated layout and grand design whose Doric columns seemed to hold up the sky. On the right was the small temple of Athena Nike, whose dimensions harmonized with those of the Propylaea. The temple was built to commemorate the victory over the Persians, and the Ionic frieze above its columns depicted the struggle between the Greeks and the Persians. Here for all the world to see was a tribute to Athenian and Greek valor—and a reminder of Athens's part in the victory.

To the left of the visitors, as they passed through the Propylaea, stood the Erechtheum, an Ionic temple that housed several ancient shrines. On its southern side was the famous Portico of the Caryatids, a porch whose roof was supported by statues of Athenian maidens. As visitors walked on, they obtained a full view of the Parthenon, thought by many to be the perfect Doric temple. The Parthenon was the chief monument to Athena and her city. The sculptures that adorned the temple portrayed the greatness of Athens and its goddess.

In many ways the Athenian Acropolis is the epitome of Greek art and its spirit. Although the buildings were dedicated to the gods and most of the sculptures portrayed gods, these works nonetheless express the Greek fascination with the human and the rational. Greek deities were anthropomorphic, and Greek artists portrayed them as human beings. While honoring the gods, Greek artists were thus celebrating human beings. They captured the noblest aspects of human beings: their reason, dignity, and promise.

Other aspects of Athenian cultural life were as rooted in the life of the polis as were the architecture and sculpture of the Acropolis. The development of drama was tied to the religious festivals of the city. The Athenian dramatists were the first artists in Western society to examine such basic questions as the rights of the individual, the demands of society on the individual, and the nature of good and evil. Conflict is a constant element in Athen-

**The Acropolis of Athens** These buildings embody the noblest spirit of Greek architecture. At the right rises the Parthenon, the temple that honored Athena and Athens alike. The Erechtheum stands next to it and to its left the Propylaea and the small temple of Athena Nike. Despite the ravages of time, they abide today in their silent grandeur. *(Spyros Spyrou Photo Gallery, Aegina)*

ian drama. The dramatists used their art to portray, understand, and resolve life's basic conflicts.

Aeschylus (525–456 B.C.E.), the first of the great Athenian dramatists, was also the first to express the agony of the individual caught in conflict. In his trilogy of plays, *The Oresteia,* Aeschylus deals with the themes of betrayal, murder, and reconciliation, urging that reason and justice be applied to reconcile fundamental conflicts. The final play concludes with a prayer that civil dissension never be allowed to destroy the city and that the life of the city be one of harmony and grace.

Sophocles (496–406 B.C.E.) also dealt with matters personal and political. In *Antigone* he expresses the precedence of divine law over human defects and touches on the need for recognition of the law and adherence to it as a prerequisite for a tranquil state.

Sophocles' masterpieces have inspired generations of playwrights. Perhaps his most famous plays are *Oedipus the King* and its sequel, *Oedipus at Colonus. Oedipus the King* is the ironic story of a man doomed by the gods to kill his father and marry his mother. Try as he might to avoid his fate, Oedipus's every action brings him closer to its fulfillment. When at last he realizes that he has carried out the decree of the gods, Oedipus blinds himself and flees into exile. In *Oedipus at Colonus* Sophocles dramatizes the last days of the broken king, whose patient suffering and uncomplaining piety win him an exalted position. In the end the gods honor him for his virtue. The interpretation of these two plays has been hotly debated, but Sophocles seems to be saying that human beings should obey the will of the gods, even without fully understanding it, for the gods stand for justice and order.

Euripides (ca 480–406 B.C.E.), the last of the three great Greek tragic dramatists, also explored the theme of personal conflict within the polis and sounded the depths of the individual. With Euripides drama entered a new, and in many ways more personal, phase. To him the gods were far less important than human beings. The essence of Euripides' tragedy is the flawed character—men and women who bring disaster on themselves and their loved ones because their passions overwhelm reason. Although Euripides' plays were less popular in his lifetime than were those of Aeschylus and Sophocles, Euripides was a dramatist of genius whose work later had a significant impact on Roman drama.

Writers of comedy treated the affairs of the polis bawdily and often coarsely. Even so, their plays too were performed at religious festivals. The comic playwrights dealt primarily with the political affairs of the polis and the conduct of its leading politicians. Best known are the comedies of Aristophanes (ca 445–386 B.C.E.), an ardent lover of his city and a merciless critic of cranks and quacks. He lampooned eminent generals, at times depicting them as morons. He commented snidely on Pericles, poked fun at Socrates, and hooted at Euripides. Like Aeschylus, Sophocles, and Euripides, Aristophanes used his art to dramatize his ideas on the right conduct of the citizen and the value of the polis.

Perhaps never were art and political life so intimately and congenially bound together as at Athens. Athenian art was the product of deep and genuine love of the polis. It was aimed at bettering the lives of the citizens and the quality of life in the state.

## Daily Life in Periclean Athens

In sharp contrast with the rich intellectual and cultural life of Periclean Athens stands the simplicity of its material life. The Athenians—and in this respect they were typical of Greeks in general—lived very happily with comparatively few material possessions. In the first place, there were very few material goods to own. The thousands of machines, tools, and gadgets considered essential for modern life had no counterparts in Athenian life. Common items of the Greek home included pottery, metal utensils for cooking, tools, luxury goods such as jewelry, and a few other things. These items they had to buy from craftsmen. Whatever else they needed, such as clothes and blankets, they produced at home.

The Athenian house was rather simple. Whether large or small, the typical house consisted of a series of rooms built around a central courtyard, with doors opening onto the courtyard. Many houses had bedrooms on an upper floor. Artisans and craftsmen often set aside a room to use as a shop or work area. The two principal rooms were the men's dining room and the room where the women worked wool. Other rooms included the kitchen and bathroom. By modern standards there was not much furniture. In the men's dining room were couches, a sideboard, and small tables. Cups and other pottery were often hung on the wall from pegs.

In the courtyard were the well, a small altar, and a washbasin. If the family lived in the country, the stalls of the animals faced the courtyard. Country dwellers kept oxen for plowing, pigs for slaughtering, sheep for wool, goats for cheese, and mules and donkeys for transportation. Even in the city chickens and perhaps a goat or two roamed the courtyard together with dogs and cats.

Cooking, done over a hearth in the house, provided welcome warmth in the winter. Baking and roasting were done in ovens. Food consisted primarily of various grains, especially wheat and barley, as well as lentils, olives, figs, and grapes. Garlic and onion were popular garnishes, and wine was always on hand. These foods were stored at home in large jars; with them the Greek family sometimes ate fish, chicken, and vegetables. Women ground wheat into flour, baked it into bread, and on special occasions made honey or sesame cakes. The Greeks used olive oil for cooking, as families still do in modern Greece; they also used it as an unguent and as lamp fuel.

By American standards the Greeks did not eat much meat. On special occasions, such as important religious festivals, the family ate the animal sacrificed to the god and gave the god the exquisite delicacy of the thighbone wrapped in fat. The only Greeks who consistently ate meat were the Spartan warriors. They received a small portion of meat each day, together with the infamous Spartan black broth, a ghastly concoction of pork cooked in blood, vinegar, and salt. One Greek, after tasting the broth, commented that he could easily understand why the Spartans were so willing to die.

In the city a man might support himself as a craftsman—a potter, bronzesmith, sailmaker, or tanner—or he could contract with the polis to work on public buildings, such as the Parthenon and Erechtheum. Men without skills worked as paid laborers but competed with slaves for work. Slaves were usually foreigners and often barbarians. By "barbarians" the Greeks meant people whose native language was not Greek. Citizens, slaves, and barbarians were paid the same amount for their work.

Slavery was commonplace in Greece, as it was throughout history. In its essentials Greek slavery resembled Mesopotamian slavery. Slaves received some protection under the law and could buy their freedom. On the other hand, masters could mistreat or neglect their slaves, although killing them was illegal. Most slaves in Athens served as domestics and performed light labor around the house. Nurses for children, teachers of reading and writing, and guardians for young men were often slaves.

The lives of these slaves were much like those of their owners. Other slaves were skilled workers, who could be found working on public buildings or in small workshops.

The importance of slavery in Athens must not be exaggerated. Athenians did not own huge gangs of slaves as did Roman owners of large estates. Slave labor competed with free labor and kept wages down, but it never replaced the free labor that was the mainstay of the Athenian economy.

Most Athenians supported themselves by agriculture, but unless the family was fortunate enough to possess holdings in a plain more fertile than most of the land, they found it difficult to reap a good crop from the soil. Many people must have consumed nearly everything they raised. Attic farmers were free and, though hardly prosperous, by no means destitute. They could usually expect yields of five bushels of wheat and ten of barley per acre for every bushel of grain sown. A bad harvest meant a lean year. Farmers usually grew more barley than wheat because of the nature of the soil. Wherever possible farmers also cultivated vines and olive trees.

The social condition of Athenian women has been the subject of much debate and little agreement. One of the difficulties is the fragmentary nature of the evidence. Women appear frequently in literature and art, often in idealized roles, but seldom in historical contexts of a wider and more realistic nature. This is due in part to the fact that most Greek historians of the time recounted primarily the political, diplomatic, and military events of the day, events in which women seldom played a notable part. Yet that does not mean that women were totally invisible in the life of the polis. It indicates instead that ancient sources provide only a glimpse of how women affected the society in which they lived. Greek wives, for example, played an important economic and social role by their management of the household. Perhaps the best way to describe the position of the free woman in Greek society is to use the anthropologist's term *liminal,* which means in this case that although women lacked official power, they nonetheless played a vital role in shaping the society in which they lived. The same situation had existed in Hammurabi's Babylonia, and it would later recur in the Hellenistic period. The mere fact that Athenian and other Greek women did not sit in the assembly does not mean that they did not influence public affairs.

The status of a free woman of the citizen class was strictly protected by law. Only her children, not those of foreigners or slaves, could be citizens. Only she was in charge of the household and the family's possessions. Yet the law protected her primarily to protect her husband's interests. Raping a free woman was a lesser crime than seducing her, because seduction involved the winning of her affections. This law was concerned not with the husband's feelings but with ensuring that he need not doubt the legitimacy of his children.

Women in Athens and elsewhere in Greece received a certain amount of social and legal protection from their dowries. Upon marriage, the bride's father gave the couple a gift of land or money, which the husband administered. However, it was never his, and in the rare cases of divorce, it returned to the wife's domain. The same is often true in Greece today among the upper class.

Ideally, respectable women lived a secluded life in which the only men they saw were relatives. How far this ideal was actually put into practice is impossible to say. At least Athenian women seem to have enjoyed a social circle of other women of their own class. They also attended public festivals, sacrifices, and funerals. Nonetheless, prosperous and respectable women probably spent much of their time in the house. A white complexion—a sign that a woman did not have to work in the fields—was valued highly.

Courtesans lived the freest lives of all Athenian women. Although some courtesans were simply prostitutes, others added intellectual accomplishments to physical beauty. In constant demand, cultured courtesans moved freely in male society. Their artistic talents and intellectual abilities appealed to men who wanted more than sex.

A woman's main functions were to raise the children, oversee the domestic slaves and hired labor, and together with her maids work wool into cloth. The women washed the wool in the courtyard and then brought it into the women's room, where the loom stood. They spun the wool into thread and wove the thread into cloth. They also dyed wool at home and decorated the cloth by weaving in colors and designs. The woman of the household either did the cooking herself or directed her maids. In a sense, poor women lived freer lives than did wealthier women. They performed manual labor in the fields or sold goods in the agora, going about their affairs much as men did.

A distinctive feature of Athenian life and of Greek life in general was acceptance of homosexuality. The Greeks accepted the belief that both homosexual and heterosexual practices were normal parts of life. They did not think that homosexual practices created any particular problems for those who engaged in them.

No one has satisfactorily explained how the Greek attitude toward homosexual love developed or determined how common homosexual behavior was. Homosexuality was probably far more common among the aristocracy

## PERIODS OF GREEK HISTORY

| PERIOD | SIGNIFICANT EVENTS | MAJOR WRITERS |
|---|---|---|
| Bronze Age<br>1650–1100 B.C.E. | Arrival of the Greeks in Greece<br>Rise and fall of the Mycenaean kingdoms | |
| Dark Age<br>1100–800 B.C.E. | Greek migrations within the Aegean basin<br>Social and political recovery<br>Evolution of the polis<br>Rebirth of literacy | Homer<br>Hesiod |
| Archaic Age<br>800–500 B.C.E. | Rise of Sparta and Athens<br>Colonization of the Mediterranean basin<br>Flowering of lyric poetry<br>Development of philosophy and science in Ionia | Archilochus<br>Sappho<br>Tyrtaeus<br>Solon<br>Anaximander<br>Heraclitus |
| Classical Period<br>500–338 B.C.E. | Persian wars<br>Growth of the Athenian Empire<br>Peloponnesian War<br>Rise of drama and historical writing<br>Flowering of Greek philosophy<br>Spartan and Theban hegemonies<br>Conquest of Greece by Philip of Macedonia | Herodotus<br>Thucydides<br>Aeschylus<br>Sophocles<br>Euripides<br>Aristophanes<br>Plato<br>Aristotle |

than among the lower classes. Even among the aristocracy attitudes toward homosexuality were complex and sometimes conflicting. Most people saw homosexual love affairs among the young as a stage in the development of a mature heterosexual life. Warrior aristocracies generally emphasized the physical side of the relationship in the belief that warriors who were also lovers would fight all the harder to impress and to protect each other. Whatever their intellectual content, homosexual love affairs were also overtly sexual.

## Greek Religion

Greek religion is extremely difficult for modern people to understand, largely because of the great differences between Greek and modern cultures. In the first place, it is not even easy to talk about "Greek religion," since the Greeks had no uniform faith or creed. Although the Greeks usually worshiped the same deities—Zeus, Hera, Apollo, Athena, and others—the cults of these gods and goddesses varied from polis to polis. The Greeks had no sacred books such as the Bible, and Greek religion was often a matter more of ritual than of belief. Nor did cults impose an ethical code of conduct. Greeks did not have to follow any particular rule of life, practice certain virtues, or even live decent lives in order to participate. Unlike the Egyptians and Hebrews, the Greeks lacked a priesthood as the modern world understands the term. In Greece priests and priestesses existed to care for temples and sacred property and to conduct the proper rituals, but not to make religious rules or doctrines, much less to enforce them. In short, there existed in Greece no central ecclesiastical authority and no organized creed.

Although temples to the gods were common, they were unlike modern churches or synagogues in that they were not normally places where a congregation met to worship as a spiritual community. Instead, the individual Greek either visited the temple occasionally on matters of private concern or walked in a procession to a particular temple to celebrate a particular festival. In Greek religion the altar, which stood outside the temple, was important; when the Greeks sought the favor of the gods, they offered them sacrifices. Greek religious observances were generally cheerful. Festivals and sacrifices were frequently times for people to meet together socially, times of high spirits and conviviality rather than of pious gloom. By offering the gods parts of the sacrifice while consuming the rest themselves, worshipers forged a bond with the gods.

The most important members of the Greek pantheon were Zeus, the king of the gods, and his consort, Hera. Although they were the mightiest and most honored of the deities who lived on Mount Olympus, their divine children were closer to ordinary people. Apollo was especially popular. He represented the epitome of youth, beauty, benevolence, and athletic skill. He was also the god of music and culture and in many ways symbolized the best of Greek culture. His sister Athena, who patronized women's crafts such as weaving, was also a warrior-goddess. Best known for her cult at Athens, to which she gave her name, she was highly revered throughout Greece, even in Sparta, which eventually became a fierce enemy of Athens. Artemis was Apollo's elder sister. A virgin and a huntress, she oversaw women's passage from virginity to marriage. Paradoxically, though a huntress, she also protected wildlife. There was something wild and free about her. Other divinities watched over every aspect of human life.

The Greeks also honored some heroes. A hero was born of a union of a god and a mortal and was an intermediate between the divine and the human. A hero displayed his divine origins by performing deeds beyond the ability of human beings. Herakles (or Hercules) was easily the greatest of them. He successfully fulfilled twelve labors, all of which pitted him against mythical opponents or tasks. Like other heroes, he protected mortals from supernatural dangers. The Greeks created other divinities with various purposes and powers, but in the hero, they believed, human beings could partake of divinity.

Besides the Olympian gods, each polis had its own minor deities, each with his or her own local cult. In many instances Greek religion involved the official gods and goddesses of the polis and their cults. The polis administered the cults and festivals, and all were expected to participate in this civic religion, regardless of whether they even believed in the deities being worshiped. Participating unbelievers, who seem to have been a small minority, were not considered hypocrites. Rather, they were seen as patriotic, loyal citizens who in honoring the gods also honored the polis. If this attitude seems contradictory, an analogy may help. Before baseball games Americans stand at the playing of the national anthem, whether they are Democrats, Republicans, or neither, and whether they agree or disagree with the policies of the current administration. They honor their nation as represented by its flag, in somewhat the same way an ancient Greek honored the polis and demonstrated solidarity with it by participating in the state cults.

Some Greeks turned to mystery religions like those of the Eleusinian mysteries in Attica and of Trophonios in Boeotia. These mystery religions in some ways foreshadowed aspects of early Christian practices by their rites of initiation, their acceptance of certain doctrines, and generally their promise of life after death. The basic concept of these cults was to unite individuals in an exclusive religious society with particular deities. Those who joined them went through a period of preparation in which they learned the essential beliefs of the cult and its necessary rituals. Once they had successfully undergone initiation, they were forbidden to reveal the secrets of the cult. Consequently, modern scholars know comparatively little about their tenets. Although the mystery religions were popular until the coming of Christianity in the Roman Empire, relatively few except the wealthy could afford the luxuries of time and money to join them.

For most Greeks religion was quite simple and close to nature. They believed in the supernatural. The religion of the common people was a rich combination of myth, ritual, folklore, and cult. They believed in a world of deities who were all around them. A single example can give an idea of the essence of this religion, its bond with nature, and its sense of ethics and propriety. Whereas no one today would think much about wading across a stream, Hesiod would have considered it sacrilegious. He advises the traveler who encounters a stream:

*Never cross the beautifully flowing water of an overflowing*
*river on foot,*
*until having looked into the lovely stream and having*
*washed your hands in the very lovely, clear waters,*
*you offer a prayer. Whoever crosses a river and with hands*
*unwashed of evil,*
*to him the gods will wreak vengeance and will give him*
*pain.*[2]

Though Greek religion in general was individual or related to the polis, the Greeks also shared some Pan-Hellenic festivals, the chief of which were held at Olympia in honor of Zeus and at Delphi in honor of Apollo. The festivities at Olympia included the famous games, athletic contests that have inspired the modern Olympic games. Held every four years, these games were for the glory of Zeus. They attracted visitors from all over the Greek world and lasted well into Christian times. The Pythian games at Delphi were also held every four years, but these contests differed from the Olympic games by including musical and literary contests. Both the Olympic and the Pythian games were unifying factors in Greek life, bringing Greeks together culturally as well as religiously.

## The Flowering of Philosophy

The myths and epics of the Mesopotamians, Aryans, and others provide ample testimony that speculation about the origin of the universe and of humankind did not begin with the Greeks. The signal achievement of the Greeks was the willingness of some to treat these questions in rational rather than mythological terms. Although Greek philosophy did not fully flower until the classical period, Ionian thinkers had already begun to ask what the universe was made of. These men are called the Pre-Socratics, for their work preceded the philosophical revolution begun by the Athenian Socrates. Taking individual facts, they wove them into general theories. Despite appearances, they concluded, the universe was actually simple and subject to natural laws. Drawing on their observations, they speculated about the basic building blocks of the universe.

The first of these Pre-Socratic thinkers, Thales (ca 600 B.C.E.), differed from wise men elsewhere because he concluded that natural phenomena could be explained in natural terms, not by the actions of gods. He sought a basic element of the universe from which all else sprang. He surmised that it was water. Although he was wrong, the way in which he asked the question was momentous: it was the beginning of the scientific method. Other Pre-Socratics continued Thales' work. Anaximander was the first to use general concepts, which are essential to abstract thought. He concluded that the basic element of the universe was the "boundless"—something infinite and indestructible. Heraclitus (ca 500 B.C.E.) declared the primal element to be fire, which is ever changing and eternal. Democritus (ca 460 B.C.E.) created the atomic theory that the universe is made up of invisible, indestructible particles. The culmination of Pre-Socratic thought was the theory that four simple substances make up the universe: fire, air, earth, and water.

With this impressive heritage behind them, the philosophers of the classical period ventured into new areas of speculation. This development was partly due to the work of Hippocrates (second half of the fifth century B.C.E.), the father of medicine. Like Thales, Hippocrates sought natural explanations for natural phenomena. Basing his opinions on empirical knowledge, not on religion or magic, he taught that natural means could be employed to fight disease. But Hippocrates broke away from the mainstream of Ionian speculation by declaring that medicine was a separate craft—just as ironworking was—that had its own principles.

The distinction between natural science and philosophy on which Hippocrates insisted was also promoted by the Sophists, who traveled the Greek world teaching young men. Despite differences of opinion on philosophical matters, the Sophists all agreed that human beings were the proper subject of study. They also believed that excellence could be taught, and they used philosophy and rhetoric to prepare young men for life in the polis. The Sophists laid great emphasis on logic and the meanings of words. They criticized traditional beliefs, religion, rituals, and myth and even questioned the laws of the polis. In essence, they argued that nothing is absolute, that everything is relative.

One of those whom contemporaries thought was a Sophist was Socrates (ca 470–399 B.C.E.), who sprang from the class of small artisans. Socrates spent his life in investigation and definition. Not, strictly speaking, a Sophist, because he never formally taught or collected fees from anyone, Socrates shared the Sophists' belief that human beings and their environment are the essential subjects of philosophical inquiry. His approach when posing ethical questions and defining concepts was to start with a general topic or problem and to narrow the matter to its essentials. He did so by continuous questioning, conducting a running dialogue with his listeners. Never did he lecture. Socrates thought that by constantly pursuing excellence, an essential part of which was knowledge, human beings could approach the supreme good and thus find true happiness. Yet in 399 B.C.E. Socrates was brought to trial, convicted, and executed on charges of corrupting the youth of the city and introducing new gods.

Socrates' student Plato (427–347 B.C.E.) carried on his master's search for the truth. Unlike Socrates, Plato wrote down his thoughts and theories and founded a philosophical school, the Academy. Most people rightly think of Plato as a philosopher. Yet his writings were also literary essays of great charm. They drew out characters, locales, and scenes from ordinary life that otherwise would have been lost to posterity. In addition, Plato used satire, irony, and comedy to relay his thoughts. Behind the elegance of his literary style, however, stand the profound thoughts of a brilliant mind grappling with the problems of his own day and the eternal realities of life. The destruction and chaos of the Peloponnesian War prompted him to ask new and different questions about the nature of human society. He pondered where, why, and how the polis had gone wrong. He gave serious thought to the form that it should take. In these considerations Plato was not only a philosopher but a political scientist and a utopian.

Plato tried to show that a life of ignorance was wretched. From education, he believed, came the possibility of determining an all-comprising unity of virtues that would lead to an intelligent, moral, and ethical life. Plato concluded that only divine providence could guide people to virtue. In his opinion, divine providence was one intelligible and individualistic being. In short, he equated god with the concept of good.

Plato developed the theory that all visible, tangible things are unreal and temporary, copies of "forms" or "ideas" that are constant and indestructible. Only the mind, not the senses, can perceive eternal forms. In Plato's view the highest form is the idea of good. He discussed these ideas in two works. In *The Republic* Plato applied his theory of forms to politics in an effort to describe the ideal polis. His perfect polis was utopian; it aimed at providing the greatest good and happiness to all its members. Plato thought that the ideal polis could exist only if its rulers were philosophers and were devoted to educating their people. He divided society into rulers, guardians of the polis, and workers. The role of individuals in each category would be decided by their education, wisdom, and ability. In Plato's republic men and women would be equal to one another, and women could become rulers. The utopian polis would be a balance, with each individual doing what he or she could to support the state and with each receiving from the state his or her just due. In *The Laws,* however, Plato drew a more authoritarian picture of government and society, one not so very different from that of twentieth-century dictatorship.

A student of Plato, Aristotle (384–322 B.C.E.) went far beyond him in striving to understand the universe. The range of Aristotle's thought is staggering. Everything in human experience was fit subject for his inquiry. In *Politics* Aristotle followed Plato's lead by writing about the ideal polis, approaching the question more realistically than Plato had done. In *Politics* and elsewhere, Aristotle stressed moderation, concluding that the balance of the ideal state depended on people of talent and education who could avoid extremes.

Aristotle was both a philosopher and a scientist. He became increasingly interested in the observation and explanation of natural phenomena. He used logic as his method of scientific discussion, and he attempted to bridge the gap that Plato had created between abstract truth and concrete perception. He argued that the universe was finite, spherical, and eternal. He discussed an immaterial being that was his conception of god. Yet his god neither created the universe nor guided it. The inconsistencies of Aristotle on these matters are obvious. His god was without purpose. Yet for him scientific endeavor, the highest attainable form of living, reached the divine.

Aristotle expressed the heart of his philosophy in *Physics* and *Metaphysics.* In those masterful works he combined empiricism, or observation, and speculative method. In *Physics* he tried to explain how natural physical phenomena interact and how their interactions lead to the results that people see around them daily. He postulated four principles: matter, form, movement, and goal. A seed, for example, possesses both matter and an encoded form. Form determines whether a plant will be a rose or poison ivy. Growth represents movement, and the mature plant the goal of the seed. Although Aristotle considered nature impersonal, he felt that it had its own purposes. In a sense, this notion is a rudimentary ancestor of the concept of evolution.

In *On the Heaven* Aristotle took up the thread of Ionian speculation. His theory of cosmology added ether to air, fire, water, and earth as building blocks of the universe. He concluded that the universe revolves and that it is spherical and eternal. He wrongly thought that the earth is the center of the universe and that the stars and planets revolve around it.

Aristotle possessed one of history's keenest and most curious philosophical minds. While rethinking the old topics explored by the Pre-Socratics, he created whole new areas of study. In short, he tried to learn everything possible about the universe and everything in it.

## From Polis to Monarchy (404–323 B.C.E.)

Immediately after the Peloponnesian War, with Athens humbled, Sparta began striving for empire over the Greeks. The arrogance and imperialism of the Spartans turned their former allies against them. Even with Persian help Sparta could not maintain its hold on Greece. In 371 B.C.E. on the plain of Leuctra in Boeotia, a Theban army under the command of Epaminondas destroyed the flower of the Spartan army on a single summer day. But the Thebans were unable to bring peace to Greece. In 362 B.C.E. Epaminondas was killed in battle, and a period of stalemate set in. The Greek states were virtually exhausted.

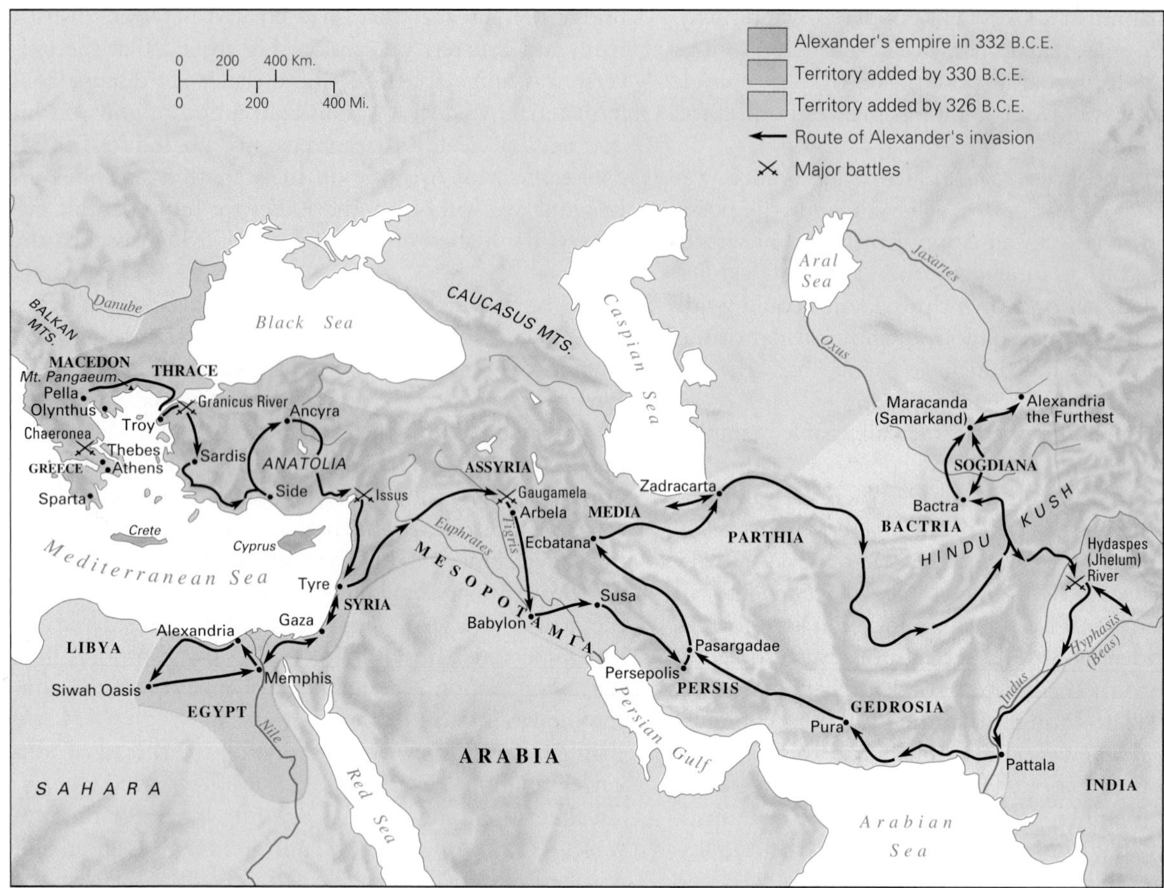


**MAP 5.3 Alexander's Conquests** This map shows the course of Alexander's invasion of the Persian Empire and the speed of his progress. More important than the great success of his military campaigns was his founding of Hellenistic cities in the East.

The man who turned the situation to his advantage was Philip II, king of Macedonia (359–336 B.C.E.). Throughout most of Greek history Macedonia, which bordered Greece in the north (see Map 5.3), had been a backward, disunited kingdom, but Philip's genius and courage turned it into a major power. One of the ablest statesmen of antiquity, Philip united his powerful kingdom, built a redoubtable army, and pursued his ambition with drive and determination. His horizon was not limited to Macedonia, for he realized that he could turn the rivalry and exhaustion of the Greek states to his own purposes. By clever use of his wealth and superb army, Philip won control of the northern Aegean and awakened fear in Athens, which had vital interests there. A comic playwright depicted one of Philip's ambassadors warning the Athenians:

*Do you know that your battle will be with men*
*Who dine on sharpened swords,*
*And gulp burning firebrands for wine?*
*Then immediately after dinner the slave*
*Brings us dessert—Cretan arrows*
*Or pieces of broken spears.*
*We have shields and breastplates for*
*Cushions and at our feet slings and arrows,*
*And we are crowned with catapults.*[3]

In 338 B.C.E. a combined Theban-Athenian army met Philip's veterans at the Boeotian city of Chaeronea. Philip's army won a hard-fought victory: he had conquered Greece and put an end to Greek freedom. Because the Greeks could not put aside their quarrels, they fell to an invader.

**Alexander at the Battle of Issus** At left, Alexander the Great, bareheaded and wearing a breastplate, charges King Darius, who is standing in a chariot. The moment marks the turning point of the battle, as Darius turns to flee from the attack. *(National Museum, Naples/Alinari/Art Resource, NY)*

Philip used his victory to unite the Greek states with his Macedonian kingdom to form the League of Corinth. He hoped to bring unity and harmony to both Greeks and Macedonians for the first time in history. He also proclaimed that the mission of this union was to liberate the Greeks of Asia from Persian control. Although Greeks and Macedonians alike prepared for a massive invasion of the Persian Empire, Philip fell to an assassin's dagger in 336 B.C.E. His young son Alexander, soon to be known as "the Great," ascended the Macedonian throne and vowed to carry on Philip's mission. Alexander proclaimed to all that the invasion of Persian territory was to be a great crusade, a mighty act of revenge for the Persian invasion of Greece in 480 B.C.E. Despite his youth, Alexander was well prepared to lead the attack. In 334 B.C.E. he led an army of Macedonians and Greeks into western Asia. In the next three years he won three major battles—at the Granicus River, at Issus, and at Gaugamela—victories that stand almost as road signs marking his march to the east (see Map 5.3). Having overthrown the Persian Empire, he crossed the Indus River in 326 B.C.E. and entered India, where he saw hard fighting. Finally, at the Hyphasis River his troops refused to go farther. Still eager to explore the limits of the world, Alexander turned south to the Arabian Sea and then west. In 324 B.C.E. a long, hard march brought him back to his camp at Susa. The great crusade was over, and Alexander himself died the next year in Babylon.

The political result of Alexander's premature death was chaos. Since several of the chief Macedonian officers aspired to Alexander's position as emperor and others opposed these ambitions, civil war lasting forty-three years tore Alexander's empire apart. By the end of this conflict, the most successful generals had carved out their own small and more or less stable monarchies.

Ptolemy immediately seized Egypt and transformed the native system of administration by appointing Greeks and Macedonians to the chief bureaucratic positions. Meanwhile, Seleucus won the bulk of Alexander's empire; his monarchy extended from western Asia to India. In the third century B.C.E., however, the eastern parts of Seleucus's monarchy gained their independence: the

**Theater of Stratos** Excavation of this theater in Stratos, a major city in northwestern Greece, began only in 1994. Not a city in the mainstream of Greek affairs, Stratos nevertheless shared the love and appreciation of the arts that stamped all of Greek culture. Even in its partially excavated state, the theater boasts the remains of a stone building in the foreground, the orchestra, and behind it the seats. Beyond its many architectural refinements, the theater is of interest because most Greek plays were staged in small theaters such as this. *(John Buckler)*

Parthians came to power in Iran, and the Greeks created a monarchy of their own in Bactria. Antigonus maintained control of the Macedonian monarchy in Europe. Until the arrival of the Romans in the eastern Mediterranean in the second century B.C.E., these great monarchies were often at war with one another, but without winning any significant political or military advantage. In that respect, the Hellenistic monarchy was no improvement on the Greek polis.

Despite the disintegration of his empire, Alexander was instrumental in changing the face of politics in the eastern Mediterranean. His campaign swept away the Persian Empire, which had ruled the East for over two hundred years. In its place he established a Macedonian monarchy. More important in the long run was his founding of new cities and military colonies, which scattered Greeks and Macedonians throughout the East (see Map 5.3). Thus the practical result of Alexander's campaign was to open the East to the tide of Hellenism.

# THE SPREAD OF HELLENISM

When the Greeks and Macedonians entered Asia Minor, Egypt, and the more remote East, they encountered civilizations older than their own. In some ways the Eastern cultures were more advanced than the Greek, in others less so. Thus this third great tide of Greek migration differed from preceding waves, which had spread over land that was uninhabited or inhabited by less-developed peoples.

How did Hellenism and the cultures of the East affect one another? What did the meeting of East and West entail for the history of the world?

## Cities and Kingdoms

A major development of the Hellenistic kingdoms, the resurgence of monarchy had many repercussions. For most Greeks, monarchs were something out of the heroic past, something found in Homer's *Iliad* but not in daily life.

Most Hellenistic kingdoms encompassed numerous different peoples who had little in common. Hellenistic kings thus attempted to create a ruler cult that linked the king's authority with that of the gods and to establish an easily understandable symbol of political and religious unity within the kingdom.

Monarchy included royal women, who began to play an active part in political and diplomatic life. Some of them did so in their own right, others by manipulating their husbands. Many Hellenistic queens have been depicted as willful or ruthless, especially in power struggles over the throne. In some cases, those charges are accurate. Yet for the most part, queens served as examples that women were as capable of shouldering vast responsibilities and performing them successfully as men were. (See the feature "Individuals in Society: Queen Cratesicleia's Sacrifice.")

Hellenistic kings needed large numbers of Greeks to run their kingdoms. Without them, royal business would have ground to a halt, and the conquerors would soon have been swallowed up by the far more numerous conquered population. Obviously, then, the kings had to encourage Greeks to immigrate and build new homes. Since Greek civilization was urban, the kings continued Alexander's policy of establishing cities throughout their kingdoms in order to entice Greeks to immigrate. Yet the creation of these cities posed a serious political problem that the Hellenistic kings failed to solve.

To the Greeks civilized life was unthinkable without the polis, which was far more than a mere city. The Greek polis was by definition **sovereign.** It was an independent, autonomous state run by its citizens, free of any outside power or restraint. Hellenistic kings, however, refused to grant sovereignty to their cities. They gave their cities all the external trappings of a polis. Each had an assembly of citizens, a council to prepare legislation, and a board of magistrates to conduct the city's political business. But these cities could not pursue their own foreign policy, wage their own wars, or govern their own affairs without interference from the king, who often placed his own officials in the cities to see that his decrees were followed. There were no constitutional links between city and king. The city was simply his possession. Its citizens had no voice in how the kingdom was run and no rights except for those the king granted.

In many respects the Hellenistic city resembled a modern city. It was a cultural center with theaters, temples,

**The Main Street of Pergamum** No matter where in old Greece they had come from, all Greeks would immediately feel at home walking along this main street in Pergamum. They would all see familiar sights. To the left is the top of the theater where they could watch the plays of the great dramatists, climb farther to the temple, and admire the fortifications on the right. *(Fatih Cimok/A Turizm Yayinlari Ltd.)*

and libraries—a seat of learning and a place where people could find amusement. The Hellenistic city was also an economic center—a marketplace, a scene of trade and manufacturing. In short, the Hellenistic city offered cultural and economic opportunities but did not foster a sense of united, integrated enterprise.

Hellenistic kings tried to make the kingdom the political focus of citizens' allegiance. If the king could secure the frontiers of his kingdom, he could give it a geographical identity. He could then hope that his subjects would direct their primary loyalty to the kingdom rather than to a particular city. However, the kings' efforts to fix their borders led only to sustained warfare, and rule by force became the chief political principle of the Hellenistic world (see Map 5.4).

Border wars were frequent and exhausting. The Seleucids and Ptolemies, for instance, waged five wars for the possession of southern Syria. Other kings followed Alexander's example and waged wars to reunify his empire under their own authority. By the third century B.C.E., a weary balance of power was reached, but only as the result of stalemate, not any political principle.

The Hellenistic city remained the basic social and political unit in the Hellenistic East until the sixth century C.E. Cities were the chief agents of Hellenization, and their influence spread far beyond their walls. Roman rule in the Hellenistic East would later be based on this urban culture. In broad terms, Hellenistic cities were remarkably successful.

## The Greeks and the Opening of the East

If the Hellenistic kings failed to satisfy the Greeks' political yearnings, they nonetheless succeeded in giving them unequaled economic and social opportunities. The ruling dynasties of the Hellenistic world were Macedonian,

**MAP 5.4 The Hellenistic World** After Alexander's death, no single commander could hold his vast conquests together, resulting in the empire's breakup into several kingdoms and leagues.

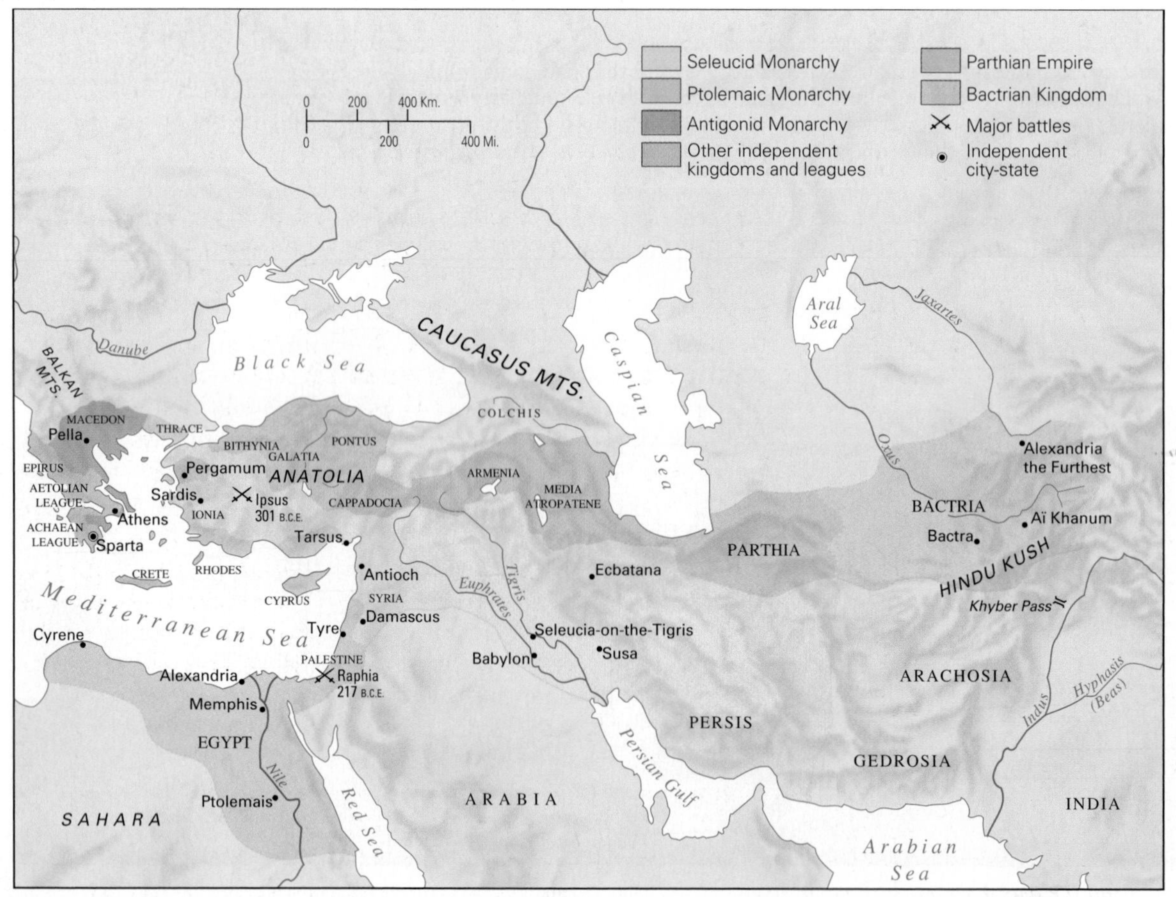

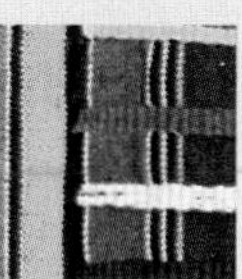

## QUEEN CRATESICLEIA'S SACRIFICE

Hellenistic queens were hardly ordinary women, but they were women nonetheless. The Spartan Cratesicleia combined in herself the duties of queen mother to her homeland and mother of her own family. Her finest hour came in 225 B.C.E., when Sparta tried to reassert itself as a major power. As was seen on page 123, Epaminondas and the Thebans had shattered Spartan might. Yet in the late third century B.C.E., Cratesicleia's son, King Cleomenes, made a valiant effort to restore Sparta's fortunes. He tried to win control of the Peloponnesus and stoutly opposed King Antigonus of Macedonia, who drove him back to Sparta. At this point Ptolemy, son of the Macedonian Lagus and king of Egypt, offered to help, but at a high and humiliating price.

*Now, Ptolemy the king of Egypt promised Cleomenes aid and assistance, but demanded his mother [Cratesicleia] and his children as hostages. For a long time, therefore, he was ashamed to tell his mother, and though he often went to her and was at the very point of letting her know, he held his peace, so that she on her part became suspicious and enquired of his friends whether there was not something that he wished to tell her but hesitated to do so. Finally, when Cleomenes plucked up courage to speak to the matter, his mother burst into a hearty laugh and said: "Was this the thing that you often had a mind to tell me but lost your courage? Hurry, put me on board a ship, and send this frail body wheresoever you think it will be of most use to Sparta, before old age destroys it sitting idly here."*

*Accordingly, when all things were ready, they came to Taenarus [a harbor in Laconia] by land, while the army escorted them under arms. And as Cratesicleia was about to embark, she drew Cleomenes aside by himself into the temple of Poseidon, and after embracing and kissing him in his anguish and deep trouble, said: "Come, king of the Spartans, when we go forth let no one see us weeping or doing anything unworthy of Sparta. For this lies in our power, and this alone; but as for the issues of Tyche [Fortune], we shall have what the deity may grant." After saying this, she composed herself and proceeded to the ship with her little grandson, and bade the captain to put to sea with all speed. And when she arrived in Egypt, and learned that Ptolemy was receiving embassies and proposals from Antigonus, and heard that although the Achaeans invited Cleomenes to make peace with them, he was afraid on her account to end the war without the consent of Ptolemy, she sent word to him that he must do what was fitting and advantageous for Sparta, and not, because of one old woman and a little boy, be ever in fear of Ptolemy.*

*From Corone (shown here in an 1829 sketch) Cratesicleia did her duty by sailing as a hostage to Egypt.* (Boccuet in *Expédition scientifique de Moree*)

With the time and the military support bought in large part by Cratesicleia's sacrifice, Cleomenes renewed the war against the Macedonians. Yet at the Battle of Sellasia in 222 B.C.E., Antigonus defeated him, forcing him to flee to Ptolemy in Egypt. There in defeat and disgrace, he died the victim of a palace plot. Plutarch recounts Ptolemy's response:

*When Ptolemy learned of these events, he gave orders that the body of Cleomenes should be flayed and hung up, and that his children, his mother, and the women who were with her, should be killed. . . . And Cratesicleia herself was not one bit dismayed at death, but asked only one favor, that she might die before the children died. However, when they arrived at the place of execution, first the children were murdered before her eyes, and then Cratesicleia herself was killed, making only this one cry at sorrows so great: "O children, where have you gone?"*

Though horrified, she nonetheless met her death with dignity and without fear. Plutarch ends the story by observing: "Virtue cannot be outraged by the might of Tyche," or, it can be said, by human barbarity.

### QUESTIONS FOR ANALYSIS

1. Was Cratesicleia's valor any greater or less than that of Spartan soldiers who defended the state on the battlefield?
2. What does this episode tell us about the tradition of Spartan patriotism?
3. Was Cleomenes justified in putting his family in such jeopardy?

*Source:* Quotations reprinted by permission of the publishers and Trustees of the Loeb Classical Library from *Plutarch: Vol. X—Plutarch Lives,* trans. B. Perrin (Cambridge, Mass.: Harvard University Press, 1921). The Loeb Classical Library® is a registered trademark of the President and Fellows of Harvard College.

**Ladies Chatting** In the Hellenistic period, art gracefully embraced the ordinary. This terra-cotta group has captured two well-dressed ladies in intimate conversation. This small piece is realistic in depicting the women, the styles of their clothes, and even their varied colors. *(British Museum/Michael Holford)*

and Greeks filled all important political, military, and diplomatic positions. They constituted an upper class that sustained Hellenism. Besides building Greek cities, Hellenistic kings offered Greeks land and money as lures to further immigration.

The Hellenistic monarchy, unlike the Greek polis, did not depend solely on its citizens to fulfill its political needs. Talented Greeks could expect to rise quickly in the government bureaucracy. Appointed by the king, these administrators held their jobs year after year and had ample time to evolve new administrative techniques. The needs of the Hellenistic monarchy and the opportunities it offered thus gave rise to a professional corps of Greek administrators.

Greeks and Macedonians also found ready employment in the armies and navies of the Hellenistic monarchies. Alexander had proved the Greco-Macedonian style of warfare to be far superior to that of the Easterners, and Alexander's successors, themselves experienced officers, realized the importance of trained Greek and Macedonian soldiers. Moreover, Hellenistic kings were extremely reluctant to allow the native populations to serve in the army, fearing military rebellions among their conquered subjects. The result was the emergence of professional armies and navies consisting entirely of Greeks and Macedonians.

Greeks were able to dominate other professions as well. The kingdoms and cities recruited Greek writers and artists to bring Greek culture to Asian soil. Architects, engineers, and skilled craftsmen found their services in great demand. If Hellenistic kingdoms were to have Greek cities, those cities needed Greek buildings—temples, porticoes, gymnasia, theaters, fountains, and houses. Architects and engineers were sometimes commissioned to design and build whole cities, which they laid out in checkerboard fashion. An enormous wave of construction took place under the Hellenistic monarchs.

New opportunities opened for women as well, owing in part to the examples of the queens. More women than ever before received educations that enabled them to enter medicine and other professions. Literacy among women increased dramatically, and their options expanded accordingly. Some won fame as poets, while others studied with philosophers and contributed to the intellectual life of the age. Women also began to participate in politics on a limited basis. They served in civil capacities, for which they often received public acknowledgment. A few women received honorary citizenship from foreign cities because of aid given in times of crisis. As a rule, however, these developments touched only wealthy women, and not all of them. Although some poor women were literate, most were not.

The major reason for the new prominence of women was their increased participation in economic affairs. During the Hellenistic period some women took part in commercial transactions. They still lived under legal handicaps. In Egypt, for example, a Greek woman needed a male guardian to buy, sell, or lease land, to borrow money, and to represent her in other transactions. Yet often the guardian was present only to fulfill the letter of the law. The woman was the real agent and handled the business being transacted. In Hellenistic Sparta, women accumulated large fortunes and vast amounts of land. Spartan women, however, were exceptional. In most other areas, even women who were wealthy in their own right were formally under the protection of their male relatives.

Despite the opportunities they offered, the Hellenistic monarchies were hampered by their artificial origins. Their failure to win the political loyalty of their Greek subjects and their policy of wooing Greeks with lucrative positions encouraged a feeling of uprootedness and self-serving individualism among Greek immigrants. Once a Greek had left home to take service with, for instance, the army or the bureaucracy of the Ptolemies, he had no incentive beyond his pay and the comforts of life in Egypt to keep him there. If the Seleucid king offered him more money or a promotion, he might well accept it and take his talents to Asia Minor, where he could find the same sort of life and environment.

As long as Greeks continued to replenish their professional ranks, the Hellenistic kingdoms remained strong. In the process they drew an immense amount of talent from the Greek peninsula, draining the vitality of the Greek homeland. However, the Hellenistic monarchies could not keep recruiting Greeks forever, in spite of their wealth and willingness to spend lavishly. In time, the huge surge of immigration slowed greatly. Even then, the Hellenistic monarchs were reluctant to recruit Easterners to fill posts normally held by Greeks. The result was at first the stagnation of the Hellenistic world and finally, after 202 B.C.E., its collapse in the face of the young and vigorous Roman republic.

## Greeks and Easterners

The Greeks in the East were a minority, but Hellenistic monarchies were remarkably successful in at least partially Hellenizing Easterners and spreading a uniform culture throughout the East. Indeed, the Near East had seen nothing comparable since the days when Mesopotamian culture had spread throughout the area. The spread of Greek culture, however, was wider than it was deep. At best it was a veneer, thicker in some places than in others. Hellenistic kingdoms were never entirely unified in language, customs, and thought. Greek culture took firmest hold along the shores of the Mediterranean, but in the Far East, in Persia and Bactria, it eventually gave way to Eastern cultures.

The Ptolemies in Egypt made no effort to spread Greek culture, and unlike other Hellenistic kings they were not city builders. Indeed, they founded only the city of Ptolemais near Thebes. At first the native Egyptian population, the descendants of the pharaoh's people, retained their traditional language, outlook, religion, and way of life. Initially untouched by Hellenism, the natives continued to be the foundation of the state: they fed it by their labor in the fields and financed its operations with their taxes.

**Greek Influence Abroad** This stunning gold comb is a remarkable combination of Greek and Eastern details. The art is almost purely Greek. The mounted horseman is clothed with largely Greek armor, but he attacks an Eastern enemy. The horseman's companion is also Eastern. This splendid piece of art testifies to the exchange of artistic motifs and styles in the eastern Mediterranean basin. *(Hermitage, Leningrad)*

## SPREAD OF HELLENISM

| | |
|---|---|
| 338 B.C.E. | Battle of Chaeronea: Philip II of Macedonia conquers Greece |
| 336 B.C.E. | Alexander the Great inherits Macedonian crown |
| 334–330 B.C.E. | Alexander overthrows the Persian Empire |
| 330–326 B.C.E. | Alexander conquers Bactria |
| 326 B.C.E. | Alexander enters India; troops mutiny at the Hyphasis River |
| 323 B.C.E. | Alexander dies in Babylon at the age of thirty-two |
| 323–275 B.C.E. | Alexander's empire divided: new dynasties founded by Ptolemy I (Egypt), Antigonus Gonatar (Macedonia, Asia Minor), and Seleucus I (Mesopotamia) |
| 3d century B.C.E. | Development of the Hellenistic city |
| ca 300–250 B.C.E. | Diffusion of philosophy; new schools founded by Epicurus and Zeno |
| ca 300–200 B.C.E. | Scientific advances by Euclid, Archimedes, Eratosthenes, and Aristarchus of Samos |

The bureaucracy of the Ptolemies was ruthlessly efficient, and the native population was viciously and cruelly exploited. Even in times of hardship the king's taxes came first, although payment might mean starvation for the natives. Their desperation was summed up by one Egyptian, who scrawled the warning: "We are worn out; we will run away."[4]

Throughout the third century B.C.E., the Greek upper class in Egypt had little to do with the native population. But in the second century B.C.E., Greeks and native Egyptians began to intermarry and mingle their cultures and languages. Some natives adopted Greek customs and language and began to play a role in the administration of the kingdom and even to serve in the army. While many Greeks and Egyptians remained aloof from each other, the overall result was the evolution of a widespread Greco-Egyptian culture.

Meanwhile, the Seleucid kings established many cities and military colonies in western Asia Minor and along the banks of the Tigris and Euphrates Rivers in order to nurture a vigorous and large Greek population. The Seleucids had no elaborate plan for Hellenizing the native population, but the arrival of so many Greeks was bound to have an impact. Seleucid military colonies were generally founded near native villages, thus exposing Easterners to all aspects of Greek life. In Asia Minor and Syria, numerous native villages and towns developed along Greek lines, and some of them became Hellenized cities. Farther east, the Greek kings who replaced the Seleucids in the third century B.C.E. spread Greek culture to their neighbors, even into the Indian subcontinent.

For Easterners the prime advantage of Greek culture was its very pervasiveness. The Greek language became the common speech of the East. A common dialect called **koine** even influenced the speech of peninsular Greece itself. Greek became the speech of the royal court, bureaucracy, and army, and any Easterner who wanted to compete in business had to learn it. As early as the third century B.C.E., some Greek cities were giving citizenship to Hellenized natives.

The vast majority of Hellenized Easterners, however, took only the externals of Greek culture while retaining the essentials of their own way of life. A prime illustration is the impact of Greek culture on the Jews. Jews in Hellenistic cities were allowed to attend to their religious and internal affairs without interference from the Greek municipal government. They obeyed the king's commands, but there was virtually no royal interference with the Jewish religion. Indeed, the Greeks were always reluctant to tamper with anyone's religion. (See the feature "Listening to the Past: Antiochus III Meets the Jews" on pages 140–141.)

Some Jews were given the right to become full citizens of Hellenistic cities, but few exercised that right. Citizenship would have obligated them to worship the gods of the city—a practice few Jews chose to follow. But Jews living in Hellenistic cities often embraced a good deal of Hellenism. So many Jews learned Greek, especially in Alexandria, that the Old Testament was translated into Greek. Yet no matter how much of Greek culture or its externals Jews borrowed, most remained attached to their religion. Thus, in spite of Hellenistic trappings, Hellenized Jews remained Jews at heart.

Though Greeks and Easterners adapted to each other's ways, there was never a true fusion of cultures. Nonetheless, each found useful things in the civilization of the other, and the two fertilized each other. This mingling of Greek and Eastern elements is what makes Hellenistic culture unique.

### Developments in the Western Mediterranean

While Hellenism made new and broader strides in the East, far more complicated and imperfectly understood developments occurred in the western Mediterranean. A survey of the region reveals a wealth of peoples and cultures, some already settled in the area and others moving into it. One group of peoples usually called Berbers were Libyans, Numidians, and Moors, who settled the area of modern Algeria, Morocco, and Tunisia. They also made contact with Sicily and Spain to the north. Even by today's standards the western Mediterranean was a small world. Into this world had come the Phoenicians from the east, planting trading stations and spreading their customs primarily along the coast. To the north the Iberians, Celtiberians, and Celts, all Indo-European-speakers, moved into modern Spain and Portugal. In the eighth century B.C.E. they began mining the rich mineral deposits of these regions, which soon attracted the Phoenicians and later the Greeks. In southern France Ligurian and Celto-Ligurian peoples arrived from the east, sometimes in organized confederations. As early as the seventh century B.C.E. they extended contact beyond their immediate neighbors to the Greeks in southern Italy.

In Italy a pre-Indo-European people first occupied the land, but little is known of them. The arrival of Italic folk, who spoke a variety of related dialects, occurred perhaps as early as 1000 B.C.E. They overwhelmed the native population and transformed the way of life of the peninsula. In the process they encountered the Etruscans, one of the most mysterious peoples of antiquity, and came into contact with the Greeks, who had long established themselves in the south. For historical purposes the importance of these social contacts can be best understood by treating them in the context of the rise of Rome (see Chapter 6). Here it is sufficient to recognize that even at this early period, the Mediterranean world was drawing closer together.

## THE ECONOMIC SCOPE OF THE HELLENISTIC WORLD

The Hellenistic period did not see a revolution in the way people lived and worked. The material demands of Hellenistic society remained as simple as those of Athenian society in the fifth century B.C.E. Clothes and furniture were essentially unchanged, as were household goods, tools, and jewelry. Yet Alexander and his successors brought the East fully into the sphere of Greek economics, linking East and West in a broad commercial network. The spread of Greeks throughout the East created new markets and stimulated trade. The economic unity of the Hellenistic world, like its cultural bonds, would later prove valuable to the Romans.

### Commerce

Alexander's conquest of the Persian Empire had immediate effects on trade. In the Persian capitals Alexander had found vast sums of gold, silver, and other treasure. This wealth financed the creation of new cities, the building of roads, and the development of harbors. Most of the great monarchies coined their money on the Attic standard. Traders were less in need of moneychangers than in the days when each major power coined money on a different standard of value. As a result of Alexander's conquests, geographical knowledge of the East increased dramatically. The Greeks spread their law and methods of transacting business throughout the East. In bazaars, ports, and trading centers Greeks learned of Eastern customs and traditions while spreading knowledge of their own culture.

The Seleucid and Ptolemaic dynasties traded as far afield as India, Arabia, and sub-Saharan Africa. Overland trade with India and Arabia was conducted by caravan and was largely in the hands of Easterners. The caravan trade never dealt in bulk items or essential commodities; only luxury goods could be transported in this very expensive fashion. Once the goods reached the Hellenistic monarchies, Greek merchants took a hand in the trade.

The caravan trade linked China to the Mediterranean world. Goods flowed into Egypt and the excellent harbors of Palestine, Phoenicia, and Syria and from there to Greece, Italy, and Spain. Over these routes came luxury goods that were light, rare, and expensive, including gold, silver, ivory, precious stones, spices, and a host of other goods. Most important were tea and, especially, silk, which is why the route came to be called the **Great Silk Road.** The Greeks and Macedonians sent east manufactured goods, especially metal weapons, cloth, wine, and olive oil. These routes actually date to earlier times, but they became more prominent—and business practices became more standard—in the Hellenistic period. The importance of the trade is demonstrated by the fact that it continued even in the chaos that followed Alexander's death.

In the early Hellenistic period, the Seleucids and Ptolemies ensured that the caravan trade proceeded efficiently. Later in the period—a time of increased war and confusion—they left the caravans unprotected. Taking advantage of this situation, Palmyra in the Syrian Desert and Nabataean Petra in Arabia arose as caravan states. Such states protected the caravans from bandits and marauders and served as dispersal areas for caravan goods.

The Ptolemies discovered how to use monsoon winds to establish direct contact with India. One hardy merchant left a firsthand account of sailing this important maritime route:

*Hippalos, the pilot, observing the position of the ports and the conditions of the sea, first discovered how to sail across the ocean. Concerning the winds of the ocean in this region, when with us the Etesian winds begin, in India a wind between southwest and south, named for Hippalos, sets in from the open sea. From then until now some mariners set forth from Kanes and some from the Cape of Spices. Those sailing to Dimurikes [in southern India] throw the bow of the ship farther out to sea. Those bound for Barygaza and the realm of the Sakas [in northern India] hold to the land no more than three days; and if the wind remains favorable, they hold the same course through the outer sea, and they sail along past the previously mentioned gulfs.*[5]

Although this sea route never replaced overland caravan traffic, it kept direct relations between East and West alive, stimulating the exchange of ideas as well as goods.

More economically important than the exotic caravan trade were commercial dealings in essential commodities like raw materials, grain, and industrial products. The Hellenistic monarchies usually raised enough grain for their own needs as well as a surplus for export. For the cities of Greece and the Aegean this trade in grain was essential, because many of them could not grow enough.

The large-scale wars of the Hellenistic period often interrupted both the production and the distribution of grain. In addition, natural calamities, such as excessive rain or drought, frequently damaged harvests. Throughout the Hellenistic period, famine or severe food shortage remained a grim possibility.

The Greek cities paid for their grain by exporting olive oil and wine. Another significant commodity was fish, which for export was salted, pickled, or dried. This trade was doubly important because fish provided poor people with an essential element of their diet. Also important was the trade in honey, dried fruit, nuts, and vegetables. Of raw materials, wood was high in demand, but little trade occurred in manufactured goods.

Slaves were a staple of Hellenistic trade. The wars provided prisoners for the slave market; to a lesser extent, so did kidnapping and capture by pirates. The number of slaves involved cannot be estimated, but there is no doubt that slavery flourished. Both old Greek states and new Hellenistic kingdoms were ready slave markets, as was Rome when it emerged triumphant from the Second Punic War (see page 149). Only the Ptolemies discouraged both the trade and slavery itself, and they did so only for economic reasons. Their system had no room for slaves, who would only have competed with free labor. Otherwise, slave labor was to be found in the cities and temples of the Hellenistic world, in the factories and fields, and in the homes of wealthy people. Slaves were vitally important to the Hellenistic economy.

## Industry and Agriculture

Although demand for goods increased during the Hellenistic period, no new techniques of production appear to have developed. Manual labor, not machinery, continued to turn out the agricultural produce, raw materials, and few manufactured goods the Hellenistic world used. Nowhere was this truer than in mining.

Invariably miners were slaves, criminals, or forced laborers. The conditions under which they worked were frightful. The Ptolemies ran their gold mines along typically harsh lines. One historian gives a grim picture of the miners' lives:

*The kings of Egypt condemn [to the mines] those found guilty of wrong-doing and those taken prisoner in war, those who were victims of false accusations and were put into jail because of royal anger. . . . The condemned—and they are very many—all of them are put in chains, and they work persistently and continually, both by day and throughout the night, getting no rest, and carefully cut off from escape.*[6]

The Ptolemies even condemned women and children to work in the mines. The strongest men lived and died swinging iron sledgehammers to break up the gold-bearing quartz rock. Others worked underground, following the seams of quartz; laboring with lamps bound to their foreheads, they were whipped by overseers if they slacked off. Once the diggers had cut out blocks of quartz, young boys gathered up the blocks and carried them outside. All of them—men, women, and boys—worked until they died.

Apart from gold and silver, which were used primarily for coins and jewelry, iron was the most important metal and saw the most varied use. Even so, the method of its production never became very sophisticated.

Although new techniques of production and wider use of machinery did not develop, the volume of goods produced increased in the Hellenistic period. Small manufacturing establishments existed in nearly all parts of the Hellenistic world.

Just as all kings concerned themselves with trade and industry, they also paid special attention to agriculture. Much of their revenue was derived from the produce of royal lands, rents paid by the tenants of royal lands, and taxation of agricultural lands. Some Hellenistic kings even sought out and supported agricultural experts. The Ptolemies, who made the greatest strides in agriculture, sponsored experiments to improve seed grain. Hellenistic authors wrote handbooks discussing how farms and large estates could most profitably be run. Whether these efforts had any impact on the average farmer is difficult to determine, and there is no evidence that agricultural productivity increased.

## RELIGION IN THE HELLENISTIC WORLD

In religion the Greeks and Easterners shared their traditions without one dominating the other. They noticed similarities among their respective deities and assumed that they were worshiping the same gods in different garb. The tendency toward religious universalism and personal immortality would prove significant when the Hellenistic world was united politically under the sway of Rome.

At first the Hellenistic period saw the spread of Greek religious cults throughout the East. When Hellenistic kings founded cities, they built temples and established new cults and priesthoods for the old Olympian gods. These cults enjoyed the prestige of being the religion of the conquerors, and they were supported by public money. Still, the Greek cults were attractive only to those socially aspiring Easterners who adopted Greek culture for personal advancement. Indeed, the Greeks themselves felt little genuine attachment to the new cults.

Greek cults suffered from some severe shortcomings. They were primarily concerned with ritual, and participation in them did not even require belief. As a result they could not satisfy deep religious feelings or spiritual yearnings. Educated and thoughtful Greeks turned, at first, to philosophy as a guide for life. Others turned to superstition, magic, or astrology. Still others spoke of *Tyche,* which means "fate," "chance," "doom"—a capricious and sometimes malevolent force.

By the second century B.C.E., after a century of exposure to Eastern religions, Greeks began to adopt one of the Eastern "mystery religions," so called because they featured a body of ritual not to be divulged to anyone not initiated into the cult. These mystery cults incorporated aspects of both Greek and Eastern religions and had a broad appeal to people of both groups. Since the Greeks were already familiar with old mystery cults, such as the Eleusinian Mysteries in Attica, the new cults did not strike them as alien or barbarian. And these new religions enjoyed one tremendous advantage over the old Greek mystery cults. The Greek cults had been tied to one place, forcing people to make pilgrimages to the sacred site to become initiated. The new religions were spread throughout the Hellenistic world.

The mystery religions all claimed to save their adherents from the worst that fate could do and promised life for the soul after death. They all shared the belief that by means of rites of initiation, devotees became united with a particular god, who had died and risen from the dead. The god's sacrifice and victory over death saved the devotee from eternal death. Like the old Greek cults, these religions required a period of preparation and then a ritual initiation that was usually of great emotional intensity.

The two Eastern cults that took the Hellenistic world by storm were the Egyptian cults of Serapis and Isis. Serapis, invented by King Ptolemy, combined elements of the Egyptian god Osiris with aspects of the Greek gods Zeus, Pluto (prince of the underworld), and Asclepius (god of medicine). Serapis was believed to be the judge of souls, who rewarded virtuous and righteous people with eternal life. Many Hellenistic Greeks thought of him as Zeus. The cult of Isis enjoyed even wider appeal. Isis, wife of Osiris, was claimed to have conquered Tyche and promised to save any mortal who came to her. She became the most important goddess in the Hellenistic world, and her worship was very popular among women due to her role as goddess of marriage, conception, and childbirth. Her priests claimed that she had bestowed on humanity the gift of civilization and had founded law and literature.

**Tyche** This statue depicts Tyche as the city-goddess of Antioch, a new Hellenistic foundation of the Seleucid king Antiochus. Some Hellenistic Greeks worshiped Tyche in the hope that she would be kind to them. Philosophers tried to free people from her whimsies. Antiochus tried to win her favor by honoring her. *(Photo Vatican Museums)*

## HELLENISTIC THOUGHT

The Hellenistic world was a time of uncertainty and instability, and the growing popularity of the mystery religions reflected a desire for a spiritual answer to the problem of Tyche. These same trends left their mark on the thinking of the period, as new schools of philosophy tried to develop their own answers to the questions of how humans relate to the world and to one another. At the same time, the meeting of Greek and Eastern thinking contributed to a surge in scientific knowledge.

### Philosophy

Philosophy during the Hellenic period had been the exclusive province of the wealthy, for only they had had leisure enough to pursue philosophical study. During the Hellenistic period, however, philosophy reached out to touch the lives of more men and women than ever before. One reason was that, with the decline of the ideal of the polis, politics no longer offered people an intellectual outlet. Second, much of Hellenistic life, especially in the new cities of the East, seemed unstable and without venerable traditions. Many people in search of something permanent turned to philosophy. Finally, the decline of traditional religion and the growing belief in Tyche led many Greeks to look to philosophy to protect them against the worst that Tyche could do.

Philosophers became more numerous, and they developed several different schools of thought. Although these philosophers felt a good deal of rivalry, all shared the idea that people could be truly happy—could deal successfully with Tyche—only when they had turned their backs on the world and focused their full attention on one enduring thing. They differed chiefly on what that enduring thing was.

Epicurus (340–270 B.C.E.) based his view of life on scientific theories and put forward a naturalistic theory of the universe. The gods, he said, had no effect on human life. He argued that the principal good of human life is pleasure, which is the absence of pain. Hardly a promoter of drunken revels or sexual dissipation, Epicurus taught that individuals can most easily attain peace and serenity by rejecting the world and examining their personal feelings. He urged people to ignore politics, which could cause emotional upheaval that would disturb the soul.

Zeno (335–262 B.C.E.) founded a school of thought called **Stoicism** that rejected the passivity of the Epicureans. Zeno and his followers thought that people could be happy only if they lived in accordance with nature. They also said that people should participate in politics, but they did not advocate attempts to change the political order. Rather, the Stoic, like an actor in a play, plays an assigned part but does not try to change the play. What matters is not what a person achieves in life, but whether he or she lives a virtuous life. Stoics believed that all people are brothers and all are governed by one natural law. Rome adopted this Stoic concept of a universal state governed by natural law.

## Hellenistic Science

Hellenistic culture achieved its greatest triumphs in science, and these achievements resulted from contributions by both East and West. The Babylonians, who had scanned the skies for centuries, provided the foundation of Hellenistic astronomy. The most notable Hellenistic astronomer was Aristarchus of Samos (ca 310–230 B.C.E.), who concluded that the sun is far larger than the earth and the stars are exceedingly distant. Breaking with Aristotle, his teacher, he said that the sun, not the earth, was the center of the solar system. In the second century C.E., however, mathematician and astronomer Claudius Ptolemy accepted Aristotle's view, and the earth-centered universe prevailed for the next fourteen hundred years.

In geometry Hellenistic thinkers discovered little that was new, but Euclid (ca 300 B.C.E.) compiled a valuable textbook of existing knowledge. *The Elements of Geometry* became the standard introduction to the field.

The greatest thinker of the period was Archimedes (ca 287–212 B.C.E.), also a skilled inventor. From his home in Syracuse in Sicily, he watched Rome rise as a power. To thwart the Roman conquest of his city, he invented a catapult that hurled rocks large enough to sink ships and grappling devices that lifted ships out of the water. In peacetime he invented the Archimedean screw to raise water from a lower to a higher level and a compound pulley to lift heavy weights. His chief interest, however, lay in pure mathematics, and he researched and wrote in many areas, including mechanics. He also founded the science of hydrostatics and discovered the principle that the weight of a solid floating in a liquid is equal to the weight of the liquid displaced by the solid.

One of Archimedes' colleagues, Eratosthenes (285–ca 204 B.C.E.), served as librarian of the great royal library in Alexandria, Egypt. While there he calculated the circumference of the earth at about 24,675 miles—only 185 miles off the actual circumference. Interested in geography, he argued that a ship could sail from Spain either around Africa or directly westward and eventually reach India. Not until the fifteenth century C.E. was this idea proved.

The study of botany also originated in the Hellenistic period when Theophrastus (ca 372–288 B.C.E.), another student of Aristotle, studied the botanical information made available by Alexander's penetration into the East. In his two books he classified plants and accurately described their parts. He detected the process of germination and realized the importance of climate and soil to plants. Some of his findings made their way into agricultural handbooks, but for the most part Hellenistic science did not carry botany any further.

In fact Hellenistic science did not exploit many of its remarkable discoveries. Although scientists of the period invented machines such as an air gun, a water organ, and even a steam engine, they did not develop them as labor-saving devices. The explanation may be that they saw no need for such machines since slave labor was abundant. Still, later scientists preserved the discoveries of Hellenistic science for modern times.

One practical area in which Hellenistic science did flourish was medicine. Herophilus, who lived in the first half of the third century B.C.E., approached the study of medicine in a systematic fashion. He dissected dead bod-

**An Unsuccessful Delivery** This funeral stele depicts a mother who has perhaps lost her own life as well as her baby's. Maternal and infant mortality were quite common in antiquity. A similar stele elsewhere bears the heartbreaking words attributed to the mother by her grieving family: "All my labor could not bring the child forth; he lies in my womb, among the dead." *(National Archaeological Museum, Athens/Archaeological Receipts Fund)*

ies and measured what he observed. He discovered the nervous system and studied the brain. His work and that of his Dogmatic school of medicine improved knowledge of anatomy, which led to better surgical tools and techniques. Another school of medicine, the Pragmatists, arose in opposition. They concentrated on the observation and cure of illnesses and put more emphasis on the use of drugs and medicines.

Despite these medical advances, Hellenistic medicine had its dark side. Many physicians were moneygrubbers, fools, or quacks. Still others claimed to cure illness through incantations and magic.

## SUMMARY

In a comparatively brief span of time the Greeks progressed from a primitive folk—backward and rude compared with their Near Eastern neighbors—to one of the most influential peoples of history. These originators of science and philosophy asked penetrating questions about the nature of life and society and came up with deathless responses to many of their own questions. Greek achievements range from the development of sophisticated political institutions to the creation of a stunningly rich literature.

Greek civilization was in full bloom when Alexander the Great launched his crusade against the Persian Empire in 334 B.C.E. Though bent on military conquest alone, Alexander nonetheless opened the cultural world of the ancient Near East to the Greeks and Macedonians as never before. They poured into Egypt and into western and even Central Asia. Not only did West meet East, but the two also combined to create a new cosmopolitan world that mingled political, social, and religious ideas. Further Greek exploration to the west pushed back the physical and intellectual frontiers until the Hellenistic world in its broadest sense stretched from Gibraltar to India. For the first time in history, vast reaches of the globe shared at least some aspects of the same culture.

## KEY TERMS

polis
acropolis
hoplites
monarchy
aristocracy
oligarchy
democracy
tyranny
deme
Delian League
sovereign
koine
Great Silk Road
Stoicism

## NOTES

1. Hesiod, *Works and Days* 263–266. John Buckler is the translator of all uncited quotations from foreign languages in Chapter 5.
2. Ibid., 737–741.
3. J. M. Edmonds, *The Fragments of Attic Comedy* (Leiden: E. J. Brill, 1971), 2.366–369, Mnesimachos frag. 7.
4. Quoted in W. W. Tarn and G. T. Griffith, *Hellenistic Civilisation*, 3d ed. (London: Edward Arnold, 1959), p. 199.
5. *Periplous of the Erythraian Sea* 57.
6. Diodoros 3.12.2–3.

## SUGGESTED READING

Translations of the most important writings of the Greeks and Romans can be found in the Loeb Classical Library published by Harvard University Press. Paperback editions of the major Greek and Latin authors are available in the Penguin Classics. Translations of documents include C. Fornara, *Translated Documents of Greece and Rome*, vol. 1 (1977); P. Harding, vol. 2 (1985); S. M. Burstein, vol. 3 (1985); and M. M. Austin, *The Hellenistic World from Alexander to the Roman Conquest* (1985).

Among the general treatments of the period is J. Boardman et al., *The Cambridge Ancient History*, vols. 3–7 (1982–1994), which covers both the classical and Hellenistic periods. More general are J. K. Davies, *Democracy and Classical Greece* (1993), and F. W. Walbank, *The Hellenistic World*, rev. ed. (1993).

Books on early Greece include C. G. Thomas, *Myth Becomes History* (1993), an excellent treatment of early Greece and modern attitudes toward it. R. Osborne, *Greece in the Making* (1996), surveys developments from 1200 to 479 B.C.E. S. Nelson, *God and the Land* (1998), explores the economic and religious significance of agriculture. R. Gotshalk, *Homer and Hesiod* (2000), provides a good account of their poetry and purposes in writing. L. H. Wilson, *Sappho's Sweetbitter Songs* (1996), deals with female and male relations in terms of her poetry. Some of the most original and substantial recent work on the polis appears in M. H. Hansen and K. Raaflaub, eds., *Studies in the Ancient Greek Polis* (1995) and *More Studies in the Ancient Greek Polis* (1996). Related is F. de Polignac, *Cults, Territory, and the Origins of the Greek State* (1995). A. J. Graham, *Colony and Mother City in Ancient Greece*, rev. ed. (1984), gives a good but somewhat dated account of Greek colonization. C. Roebuck, *Economy and Society in the Early Greek World* (1984), though also dated, is still a reliable treatment of the topic. W. Burkert, *The Orientalizing Revolution* (1992), is a masterful discussion of Near Eastern influence on early Greek culture. A good survey of early Sparta is S. Hodkinson, *Property and Wealth in Classical Sparta* (2000), which discusses many aspects of Spartan life. The Athenian democracy has become an overworked and sterile subject, but the best treatments are M. Ostwald, *From Popular Sovereignty to the Sovereignty of Law* (1986), and especially M. H. Hansen, *The Athenian Democracy in the Age of Demosthenes* (1991).

Useful studies of fifth-century B.C. Greece include M. McGregor, *The Athenians and Their Empire* (1987); M. C. Miller, *Athens and Persia in the Fifth Century B.C.* (1997); and E. Badian, *From Plataea to Potidaea* (1993), a challenging collection of essays on major aspects of the period. The fourth century B.C.E. has been one of the most fertile fields of recent research. P. Cartledge, *Agesilaos and the Crisis of Sparta* (1987), treats Spartan government and society in its period of greatness and collapse. J. Buckler, *The Theban Hegemony, 371–362 B.C.* (1980), examines the period of the Theban ascendancy, and his *Philip II and the Sacred War* (1989) studies the ways in which Philip of Macedonia used Greek politics to his own ends. J. Cargill, *The Second Athenian League* (1981), traces Athens's generally successful foreign policy during the century. G. Cawkwell, *Philip of Macedon* (1978), provides the best study of the king, and A. B. Bosworth, *Conquest and Empire* (1988), is a magisterial study of Alexander the Great, which reveals a ruthless but brilliant conqueror. F. L. Holt, *Alexander the Great and Bactria* (1988), discusses the formation of a Greco-Macedonian frontier in Central Asia.

Greek social life is a recent theme of continuing interest among classical scholars. R. Just, *Women in Athenian Law and Life* (1988), explores topics such as daily life, the family, and women's role in society, as do C. B. Patterson, *The Family in Greek History* (1998), and S. B. Pomeroy, *Families in Classical and Hellenistic Greece* (1997). M. Golden, *Children and Childhood in Ancient Athens* (1993), studies a neglected topic, as does Z. H. Archibald et al., *Hellenistic Economics* (2001). M. Golden, *Sport and Society in Ancient Greece* (1998), places athletics in its social context, and Y. Garlan, *Slavery in Ancient Greece* (1988), gives a balanced interpretation of this difficult subject.

Much new work has focused on the spread of Hellenism throughout the Near East. Very extensive is A. Kuhrt and S. Sherwin-White, eds., *Hellenism in the East* (1988), which treats a broad range of topics, including biblical studies, Christianity, and Islam. A. E. Samuel, *The Promise of the West* (1988), studies connections among Greek, Roman, and Jewish culture. A. K. Bowman, *Egypt After the Pharaohs* (1986), gives an account of the Greeks' and Macedonians' impact on Egyptian society. R. A. Billows, *Antigonus the One-Eyed and the Creation of the Hellenistic State* (1990), examines the career of the one man who most nearly reunited Alexander's empire, and G. M. Cohen, *The Hellenistic Settlements in Europe, the Islands, and Asia Minor* (1996), ably studies the impact of the Greeks on the world around them.

Studies of Greek religion in general are P. N. Hunt, ed., *Encyclopedia of Classical Mystery Religions* (1993), which includes more than a thousand entries on mystery religions. J. D. Mikalson, *Athenian Popular Religion* (reprint 1987), opens an avenue to Greek popular religion in general, and his *Religion in Hellenistic Society* (1998) extends his studies into later Greek society. W. Burkert, *Greek Religion* (1987), is a masterful study of the topic. A. W. Bulloch et al., *Images and Ideologies* (1993), is a broad-ranging treatment of all important intellectual aspects of Hellenistic history. S. K. Heyob, *The Cult of Isis Among Women in the Graeco-Roman World* (1975), and J. G. Griffiths, *The Origins of Osiris and His Cult* (1980), treat this influential pair of deities. L. H. Feldman, *Jew and Gentile in the Ancient World* (1993), argues that the pagan response to Judaism was not as negative as is often thought. Lastly, P. Franklin, *Magic in the Ancient World* (1997), is a fresh treatment of a neglected subject.

G. Vlastos, *Studies in Greek Philosophy*, vols. 1 and 2 (1995–1996), covers philosophy from the Pre-Socratics to Plato. R. W. Sharples, *Stoics, Epicureans, Sceptics* (1996), provides a good synthesis of these three major philosophies. P. Kingsley, *Ancient Philosophy* (1996), studies the effects of myth and magic on the development of Greek philosophy. A novel approach to the topic is J. K. Ward, ed., *Feminism in Ancient Philosophy* (1996). G. E. R. Lloyd, *Greek Science After Aristotle* (1963), is a solid survey of Hellenistic science.

# LISTENING TO THE PAST

## Antiochus III Meets the Jews

*Ever since the days of the pharaohs and the Hittites the Levant, the area known today as the Middle East, has served as a battleground between the Egyptians and any major power to their north. The peoples in this area were perennially caught between their more powerful neighbors on either side. Nothing changed in the Hellenistic period. Around 200 B.C.E. Antiochus III, king of the Seleucid empire, drove the Ptolemies from Syria and Palestine. In his victory he encountered the Jews, a people theretofore unfamiliar to him. The Jews, who had long been discontented with Ptolemaic rule, eagerly welcomed Antiochus, and he responded to them with equal enthusiasm. The Hellenized Jewish historian Josephus (37/38–100 C.E.), in his work* Jewish Antiquities *(12.138–153), preserves three royal documents in which Antiochus officially instructs his governor of the area, also named Ptolemy, of the benefits that he had conferred on the Jews and his reasons for having done so.*

"King Antiochus [III] to Ptolemy, greetings. Since the Jews, when we entered their country, at once displayed their enthusiasm for us, and when we arrived at their city received us magnificently and came to meet us with their senate, and have provided abundant supplies to our soldiers and elephants, and assisted us in expelling the Egyptian garrison in the citadel, we thought it right on our part to repay them for these services and to restore their city which had been destroyed by the accidents of war, and to repeople it by bringing back to it those who have been scattered abroad. In the first place we have decided because of their piety to provide them with an allowance for sacrifices consisting of sacrificial animals, wine, olive oil and frankincense, to the value of 20,000 silver pieces, and sacred artabas of finest flour in accordance with their native law, and 1,460 medimni of wheat, and 375 medimni of salt. I wish these grants to be made to them in accordance with my instructions, and the work on the Temple to be completed together with the stoas and anything else which needs to be built. The timber required for the woodwork shall be brought from Judaea itself, from the other nations and from Lebanon, and no one shall charge any duty on it. Similarly for the other materials needed for repairing the Temple in a more splendid way. All the people of the nation shall govern themselves in accordance with their ancestral laws, and the senate, the priests, the scribes of the Temple and the Temple-singers shall be exempted from the poll-tax, the crown-tax and the salt-tax. To hasten the repeopling of the city, I grant to the present inhabitants and to those who come back before the month of Hyperberetaeus [ca October] freedom from taxes for three years. We also remit for the future one third of their taxes to make good the injuries they have sustained. As for all those who were carried away from their city and are now slaves, I grant their freedom to them and to their children, and order the restoration of their property to them."

Such was the content of the letter. And out of respect for the Temple he issued a proclamation throughout the whole kingdom in the following terms: "No foreigner shall be allowed to enter the precinct of the Temple which is forbidden to the Jews, except for those who are accustomed to doing so after purifying themselves in accordance with ancestral custom. Nor shall anyone bring into the city the flesh of horses, mules, wild or tame asses, leopards, foxes, and hares, and generally of any of the animals forbidden to the Jews. Nor is it allowed to bring in their skins, nor even to rear any of these animals in the city. Only the sacrificial animals used by their ancestors,

Coin of Antiochus III. *(British Museum/ Michael Holford)*

necessary for a propitious sacrifice to God, shall they be allowed to use. Whoever transgresses any of these rules shall pay to the priests a fine of 3,000 drachmas of silver."

He also gave witness to our piety and good faith when during his stay in the upper satrapies he heard of the revolt of Phrygia and Lydia, and wrote to Zeuxis, his general and one of his closest "friends," with instructions to send some of our people from Babylon to Phrygia. He writes as follows: "King Antiochus to Zeuxis, his father, greetings. If you are in good health, it is well; I too am in good health. On hearing that the people in Lydia and Phrygia are in revolt, I thought this required great attention on my part, and after discussing with my friends what ought to be done, I resolved to move 2,000 Jewish families with their chattels from Mesopotamia and Babylonia to the strongholds and the most strategic places. For I am convinced that they will be loyal guardians of our interests because of their piety to God, and I know that my ancestors have given witness to their loyalty and eagerness for what they are asked to do. I wish therefore to transfer them, although this is a laborious task, with the promise that they shall use their own laws. When you have brought them to the places I have mentioned, you will give them each a place to build a house and a plot of land to cultivate and plant vines, and you will grant them exemption from taxes on agricultural produce for ten years. Until such time as they obtain produce from the soil, corn shall be measured out to them to feed their servants. To those who perform services [?] shall be provided everything they need, so that by receiving this favour from us they might show themselves more devoted to our interests. Show concern for their people as much as possible, so that it may not be troubled by anyone." Concerning the friendliness of Antiochus the Great towards the Jews let the proofs we have given suffice.

## QUESTIONS FOR ANALYSIS

1. What were the principal reasons for Antiochus's kindness to the Jews?
2. Did his actions show genuine respect for Jewish religion and tradition?
3. Did Antiochus use the Jews as political pawns, or was he sincerely concerned for them as loyal subjects?

*Source:* Reprinted by permission of the publishers and the Trustees of the Loeb Classical Library from *Josephus: Volume IX—Jewish Antiquities,* Loeb Classical Library Volume L 365, trans. Ralph Marcus (Cambridge, Mass.: Harvard University Press, 1943, 1998). The Loeb Classical Library® is a registered trademark of the President and Fellows of Harvard College.

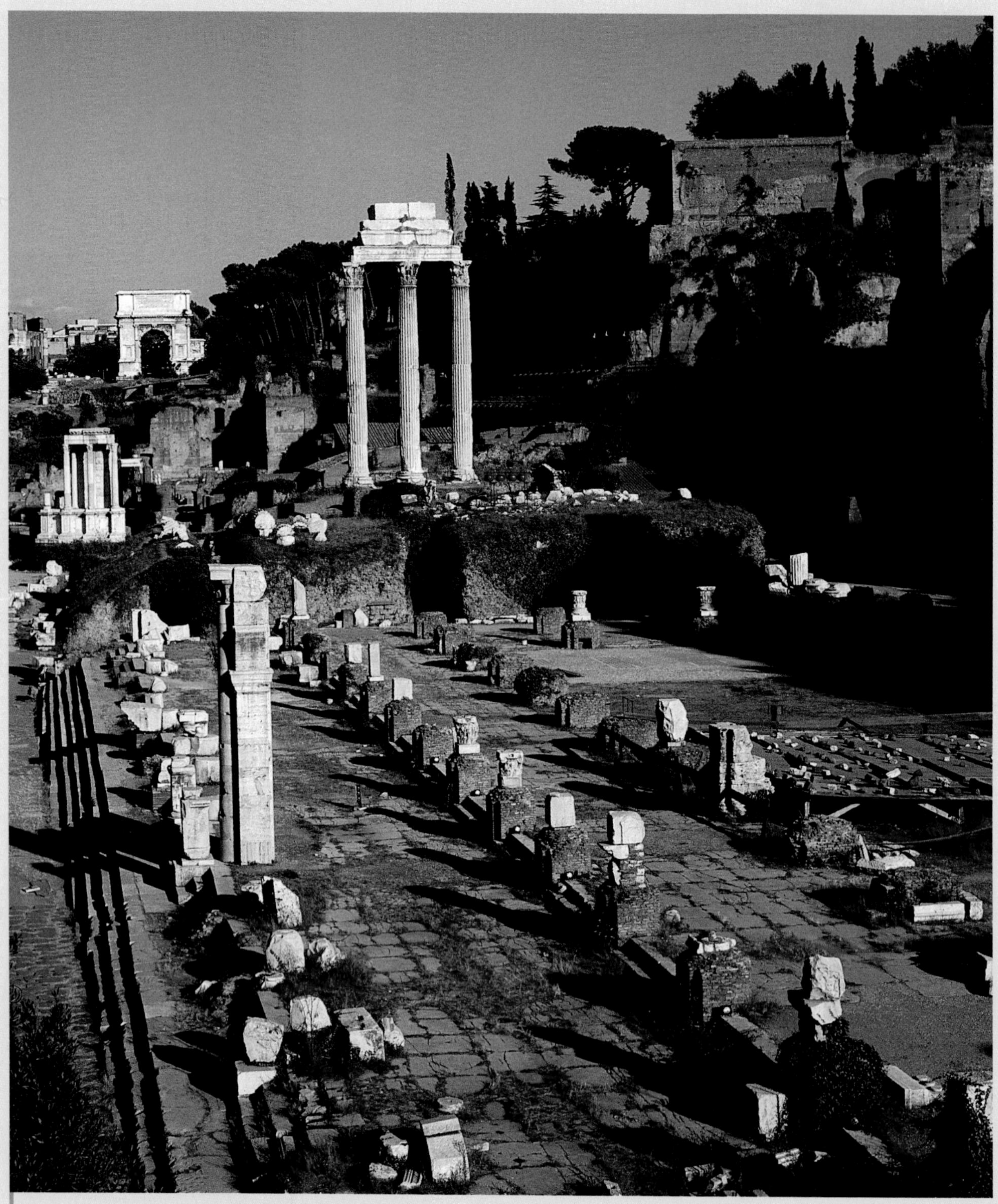

The Roman Forum. *(Josephine Powell)*

CHAPTER

# 6 THE GLORY OF ROME

## CHAPTER OUTLINE

- The Land and the Sea
- The Etruscans and the Roman Conquest of Italy (750–290 B.C.E.)
- The Roman Republic
- The Pax Romana
- The Coming of Christianity
- The Golden Age
- Life in the Golden Age: Imperial Rome and the Provinces
- Rome and the East
- The Empire in Crisis

"Who is so thoughtless and lazy that he does not want to know in what way and with what kind of government the Romans in less than 53 years conquered nearly the entire inhabited world and brought it under their rule—an achievement previously unheard of?"[1] This question was first asked by Polybius, a Greek historian who lived in the second century B.C.E. With keen awareness Polybius realized that the Romans were achieving something unique in world history.

What was that achievement? Rome was not the first to create a huge empire. The Persians and the Han emperors had done the same thing. Chandragupta and his successors had likewise brought many peoples under their rule. The Romans themselves admitted that in matters of art, literature, philosophy, and culture they learned from the Greeks. Rome's achievement lay in the ability of the Romans not only to conquer peoples but to incorporate them into the Roman system. Rome succeeded where the Greek polis had failed. Unlike the Greeks, who refused to share citizenship, the Romans extended their citizenship first to the Italians and later to the peoples of the provinces. With that citizenship went Roman government and law. Rome created a world state that embraced the entire Mediterranean area. For the first and second centuries C.E. the lot of the Mediterranean world was the Roman peace—the pax Romana, a period of security, order, harmony, flourishing culture, and expanding economy. It was a period that saw the wilds of Gaul, Spain, Germany, and eastern Europe introduced to Greco-Roman culture.

Nor was Rome's achievement limited to the ancient world. By the third century C.E., when the empire began to give way to the medieval world, the greatness of Rome and its culture had left an indelible mark on the ages to come. Rome's law, language, and administrative practices were a precious heritage to medieval and modern Europe.

- How did Rome rise to greatness?
- What effects did the conquest of the Mediterranean have on the Romans themselves?
- How did the Roman emperors govern the empire, and how did they spread Roman influence into northern Europe?
- Why did Christianity, originally a minor local religion, sweep across the Roman world to change it fundamentally?

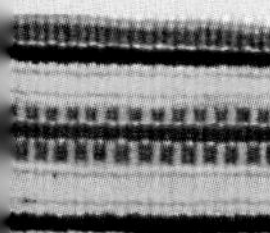

- How did the Roman Empire meet the grim challenge of barbarian invasion and subsequent economic decline?

These are the questions we will answer in this chapter.

## THE LAND AND THE SEA

To the west of Greece the boot-shaped peninsula of Italy, with Sicily at its toe, occupies the center of the Mediterranean basin. As Map 6.1 shows, Italy and Sicily thrust southward toward Africa: the distance between southwestern Sicily and the northern African coast is at one point only about a hundred miles. Italy and Sicily literally divide the Mediterranean into two basins and form the focal point between the halves.

Like Greece and other Mediterranean lands, Italy enjoys a genial, almost subtropical climate. The winters are rainy, but the summer months are dry. Because of the climate the rivers of Italy usually carry little water during the summer, and some go entirely dry. Thus Italian rivers never became major thoroughfares for commerce and communication.

In the north of Italy the Apennine Mountains break off from the Alps and form a natural barrier. The Apennines hindered but did not prevent peoples from invading Italy from the north. North of the Apennines lies the Po Valley, an important part of modern Italy. In antiquity this valley did not become Roman territory until late in the history of the republic. From the north the Apennines run southward the entire length of the Italian boot; they virtually cut off access to the Adriatic Sea, inducing Italy to look west to Spain and Carthage rather than east to Greece.

Even though most of the land is mountainous, the hill country is not as inhospitable as are the Greek highlands. In antiquity the general fertility of the soil provided the basis for a large population. Nor did the mountains of Italy so carve up the land as to prevent the development of political unity. Geography proved kinder to Italy than to Greece.

In their southward course the Apennines leave two broad and fertile plains, those of Latium and Campania. These plains attracted settlers and invaders from the time when peoples began to move into Italy. Among these peoples were the Romans, who established their city on the Tiber River in Latium. The Tiber provided Rome with a constant source of water. Located at an easy crossing point on the Tiber, Rome stood astride the main avenue of communication between northern and southern Italy. The seven hills of Rome were defensible and safe from the floods of the Tiber. Rome was in an excellent position to develop the resources of Latium and maintain contact with the rest of Italy.

## THE ETRUSCANS AND THE ROMAN CONQUEST OF ITALY (750–290 B.C.E.)

According to Roman legend, Romulus and Remus founded Rome in 753 B.C.E. From then until 509 B.C.E. the Romans lived under the rule of Etruscan kings and embraced many Etruscan customs. They adopted the

**Sarcophagus of Lartie Seianti** The woman portrayed on this lavish sarcophagus is the noble Etruscan Lartie Seianti. Although the sarcophagus is her place of burial, she is portrayed as in life, comfortable and at rest. The influence of Greek art on Etruscan is apparent in almost every feature of the sarcophagus. *(Archaeological Museum, Florence/Nimatallah/Art Resource, NY)*

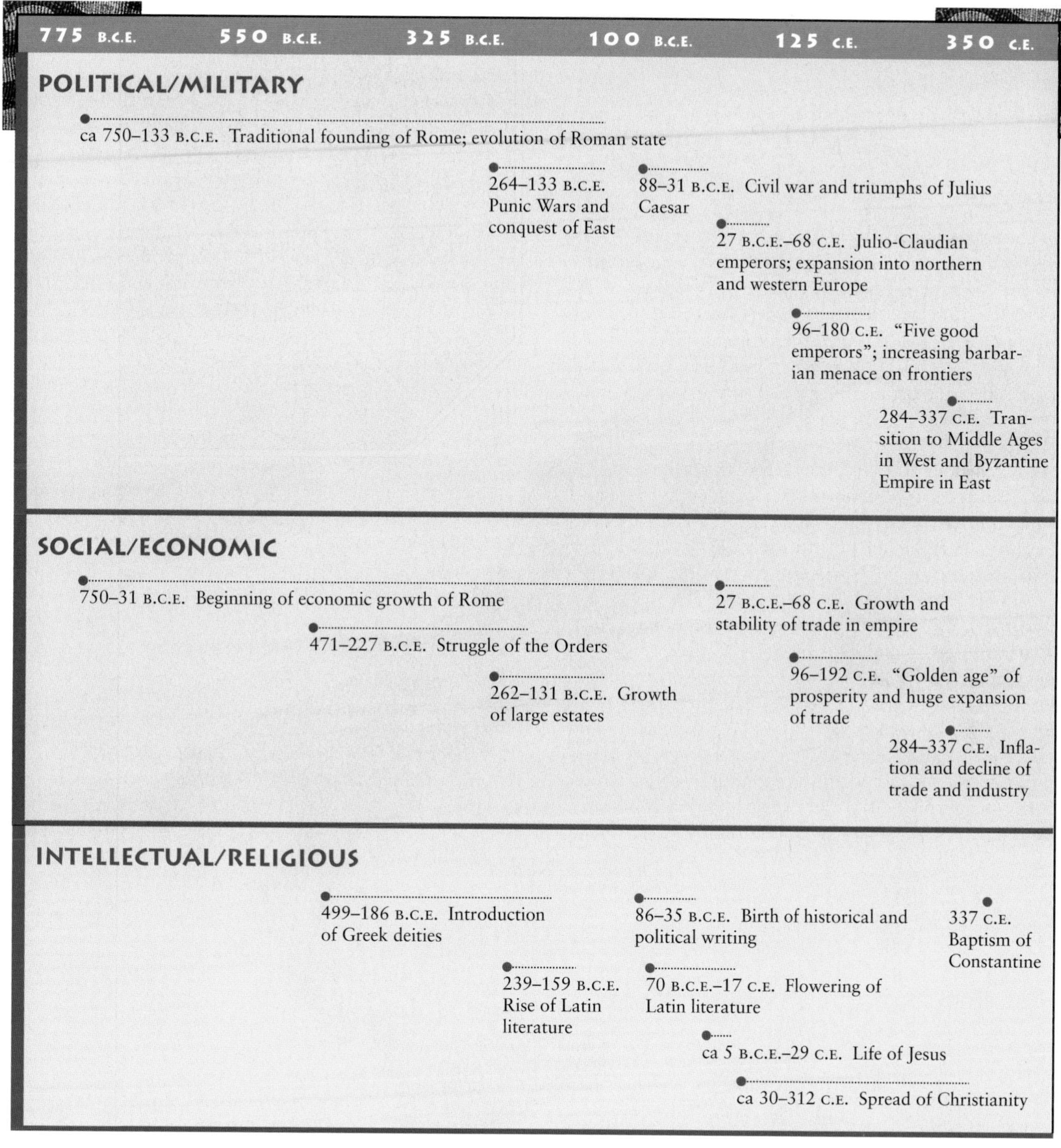


Etruscan alphabet, which the Etruscans themselves had adopted from the Greeks and which the Romans later passed on to medieval Europe. In this period Rome enjoyed contacts with the larger Mediterranean world, including trade in metalwork and Greek vases. The city began to grow, and between 575 and 550 B.C.E. temples and public buildings began to grace the city. The temple of Jupiter Optimus Maximus (Jupiter the Best and Greatest) became the religious center of the city. The Forum, on the site of a former cemetery, began to serve as a public meeting place, like a Greek agora. The Etruscans had found Rome a collection of villages and made it a city.

According to tradition, in 509 B.C.E. the Romans expelled an Etruscan king from the city and founded the

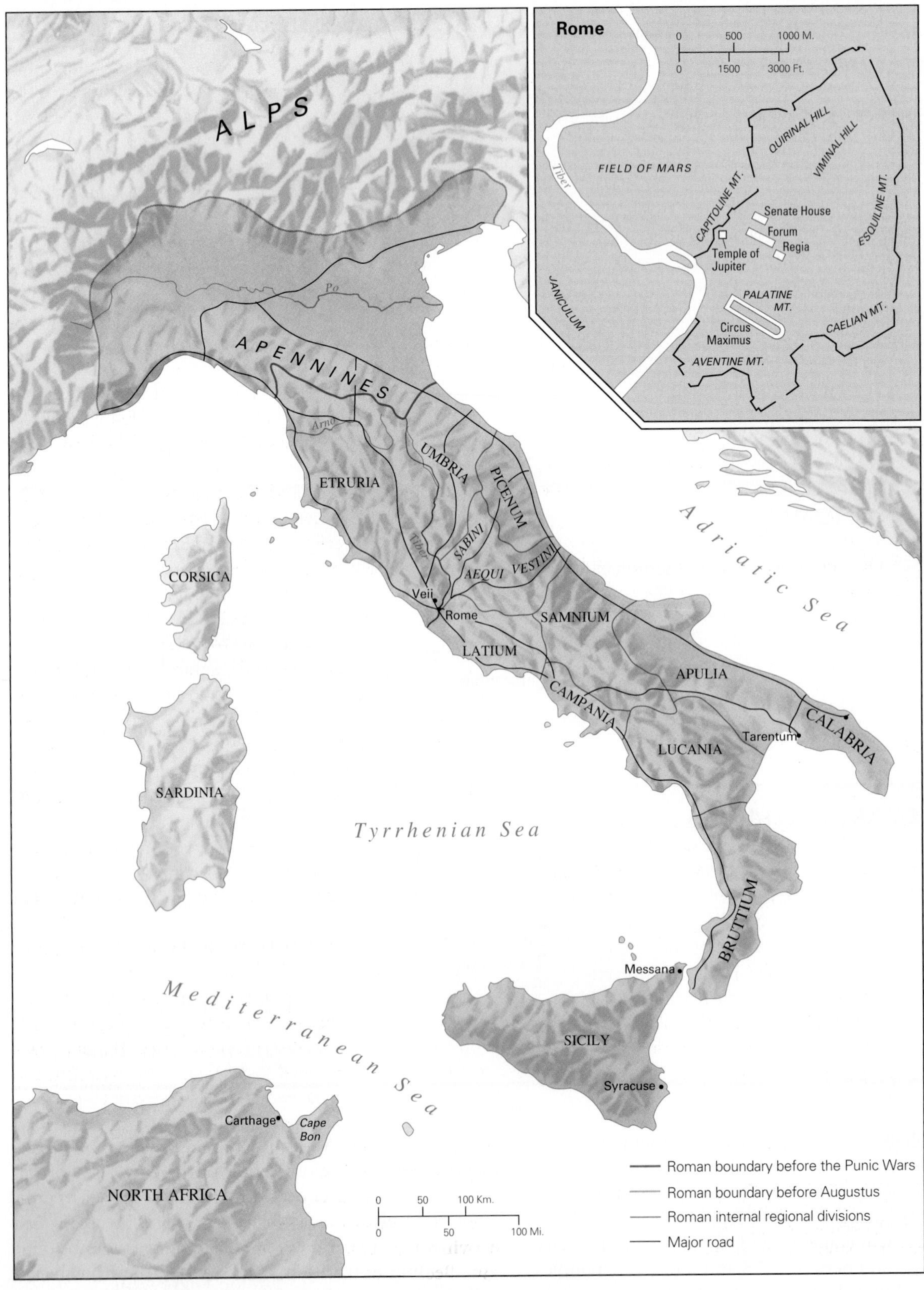

Rome
0 500 1000 M.
0 1500 3000 Ft.
FIELD OF MARS
QUIRINAL HILL
VIMINAL HILL
CAPITOLINE MT.
ESQUILINE MT.
Tiber
Senate House
Forum
Regia
Temple of Jupiter
JANICULUM
PALATINE MT.
Circus Maximus
CAELIAN MT.
AVENTINE MT.
ALPS
Po
APENNINES
Arno
ETRURIA
UMBRIA
PICENUM
SABINI
AEQUI
VESTINI
Tiber
CORSICA
Veii
Rome
SAMNIUM
LATIUM
Adriatic Sea
APULIA
CAMPANIA
CALABRIA
Tarentum
LUCANIA
SARDINIA
Tyrrhenian Sea
BRUTTIUM
Messana
Mediterranean Sea
SICILY
Syracuse
Carthage
Cape Bon
NORTH AFRICA
0 50 100 Km.
0 50 100 Mi.
Roman boundary before the Punic Wars
Roman boundary before Augustus
Roman internal regional divisions
Major road

republic. In the years that followed, the Romans expanded throughout the Italian peninsula as a result of their tenacious fighting and their skillful diplomacy. The growth of Roman power was slow. It took a century to drive the Etruscans fully out of Latium. Around 390 B.C.E. the Romans suffered a setback when a new people, the Celts—or Gauls, as the Romans called them—swept aside a Roman army and sacked Rome. They agreed to abandon the city in return for a thousand pounds of gold.

From 390 to 290 B.C.E. the Romans regrouped and began their drive to empire. They reorganized their army to create the mobile legion, a flexible unit capable of fighting on either broken or open ground. First they brought Latium and their Latin allies fully under their control (see Map 6.1). Then they defeated the Samnites after a long conflict and gained southern Italy.

In this expansion Rome's success in diplomacy and politics was vitally important. Like Cyrus the Persian and unlike the Greeks, they proved generous victors. They shared with other Italian cities political power and degrees of citizenship. While all allied peoples were not given the right to vote or hold office, they were allowed to run local affairs, and Latin allies could gain full citizenship by moving to Rome. The unwillingness of the Greek polis to share its citizenship condemned it to a limited horizon. By contrast, the extension of Roman citizenship gave Rome additional manpower and wealth.

## THE ROMAN REPUBLIC

The Romans summed up their political existence in a single phrase: *senatus populusque Romanus,* "the Roman senate and the people." The real genius of the Romans lay in the fields of politics and law. Unlike the Greeks, they did not often speculate on the ideal state or on political forms. Instead, they realistically met actual challenges and created institutions, magistracies, and legal concepts to deal with practical problems. Change was consequently commonplace in Roman political life; thus the constitution of 509 B.C.E. was far simpler than that of 27 B.C.E. Moreover, the Roman constitution was not a single written document but a set of traditional beliefs, customs, and laws.

**MAP 6.1 Italy and the City of Rome** The geographical configuration of the Italian peninsula shows how Rome stood astride north-south communication routes and how the state that united Italy stood poised to move into Sicily and northern Africa.

### The Roman State and Social Conflict

In the early republic social divisions determined the shape of politics. Political power was in the hands of the aristocracy—the **patricians,** who were wealthy landowners. Patrician families formed clans, as did aristocrats in early Greece. They dominated the affairs of state, provided military leadership in times of war, and monopolized knowledge of law and legal procedure. The common people of Rome, the **plebeians,** had few of the patricians' advantages. Some plebeians formed their own clans and rivaled the patricians in wealth, but most plebeians were poor. They were the artisans, small farmers, and landless urban dwellers. The plebeians, rich and poor alike, were free citizens with a voice in politics. Nonetheless, they were overshadowed by the patricians.

Perhaps the greatest institution of the republic was the **senate,** which had originated under the Etruscans as a council of noble elders who advised the king. During the republic the senate advised the consuls and other magistrates. Because the senate sat year after year, while magistrates changed annually, it provided stability and continuity. It also served as a reservoir of experience and knowledge. Technically, the senate could not pass legislation; it could only offer its advice. But increasingly, because of the senate's prestige, its advice came to have the force of law.

The Romans created several assemblies through which the people elected magistrates and passed legislation. Patricians generally dominated, but in 471 B.C.E. the plebeians won the right to meet in an assembly of their own, the *concilium plebis,* and to pass ordinances.

The chief magistrates of the republic were two consuls, elected for one-year terms. At first the consulship was open only to patricians. The consuls commanded the army in battle, administered state business, and supervised financial affairs. In effect, they and the senate ran the state.

In 366 B.C.E. the Romans created the office of **praetor,** and in 227 B.C.E. the number of praetors was increased to four. When the consuls were away from Rome, the praetors could act in their place. The praetors dealt primarily with the administration of justice. When a praetor took office, he issued a proclamation declaring the principles by which he would interpret the law. These proclamations became very important because they usually covered areas where the law was vague and thus helped clarify the law.

After the age of overseas conquest (see pages 149–151), the Romans divided the Mediterranean area into **provinces** governed by former consuls and former praetors. Because of their experience in Roman politics, they

## THE ROMAN REPUBLIC

| | |
|---|---|
| 509 B.C.E. | Founding of the Roman republic |
| 471 B.C.E. | Plebeians win official recognition of their assembly, the *concilium plebis* |
| ca 450 B.C.E. | Law of the Twelve Tables |
| 390 B.C.E. | Gauls sack Rome |
| 390–290 B.C.E. | Rebuilding of Rome<br>Reorganization of the army<br>Roman expansion in Italy |
| 287 B.C.E. | Legislation of the *concilium plebis* made binding on entire population |
| 264–241 B.C.E. | First Punic War: Rome defeats Carthage, acquires Sicily |
| 218–202 B.C.E. | Second Punic War: Scipio defeats Hannibal<br>Rome dominates the western Mediterranean |
| 200–148 B.C.E. | Rome conquers the Hellenistic East |
| 149–146 B.C.E. | Third Punic War: destruction of Carthage and Corinth |
| 133–121 B.C.E. | The Gracchi introduce land reform but are murdered |
| 107 B.C.E. | Marius becomes consul and begins the professionalization of the army |
| 91–88 B.C.E. | War with Rome's Italian allies |
| 88–27 B.C.E. | Era of civil war |
| 45 B.C.E. | Julius Caesar defeats Pompey's forces and becomes dictator |
| 44 B.C.E. | Assassination of Julius Caesar |
| 31 B.C.E. | Augustus defeats Antony and Cleopatra at Actium |

were well suited to administer the affairs of the provincials and to fit Roman law and custom into new contexts.

The development of law was one of the Romans' most splendid achievements. Roman law began as a set of rules that regulated the lives and relations of citizens. This civil law, or **ius civile,** consisted of statutes, customs, and forms of procedure. Roman assemblies added to the body of law, and praetors interpreted it. The spirit of the law aimed at protecting the property, lives, and reputations of citizens; redressing wrongs; and giving satisfaction to victims of injustice.

As the Romans came into more frequent contact with foreigners, they had to devise laws to deal with disputes between Romans and foreigners and between foreigners living under Roman jurisdiction. In these instances, where there was no precedent to guide the Romans, the legal decisions of the praetors proved of immense importance. The praetors adopted aspects of other legal systems and resorted to the law of equity—what they thought was right and just to all parties. Free, in effect, to determine law, the praetors enjoyed a great deal of flexibility. This situation illustrates the practicality and the genius of the Romans. By addressing specific, actual circumstances the praetors developed a body of law, the *ius gentium,* "law of peoples," that applied to Romans and foreigners and that laid the foundation for a universal conception of law. By the time of the late republic, Roman jurists were reaching decisions on the basis of the

Stoic concept of **ius naturale,** "natural law," a universal law that could be applied to all societies.

Another important aspect of early Roman history was a great social conflict, usually known as the **Struggle of the Orders,** which developed between patricians and plebeians. What the plebeians wanted was real political representation and safeguards against patrician domination. The plebeians' efforts to obtain recognition of their rights are the crux of the Struggle of the Orders.

Rome's early wars gave the plebeians the leverage they needed: Rome's survival depended on the army, and the army needed the plebeians. The first showdown between plebeians and patricians came, according to tradition, in 494 B.C.E. To force the patricians to grant concessions, the plebeians seceded from the state; they literally walked out of Rome and refused to serve in the army. The plebeians' general strike worked. Because of it the patricians made important concessions. One of these was social. In 445 B.C.E. the patricians passed a law, the *lex Canuleia,* that for the first time allowed patricians and plebeians to marry each other. Furthermore, the patricians recognized the right of plebeians to elect their own officials, the **tribunes.** The tribunes in turn had the right to protect the plebeians from the arbitrary conduct of patrician magistrates. The tribunes brought plebeian grievances to the senate for resolution. The plebeians were not bent on undermining the state. Rather, they used their gains only to win full equality under the law.

The law itself was the plebeians' next target. Only the patricians knew what the law was, and only they could argue cases in court. All too often they had used the law for their own benefit. The plebeians wanted the law codified and published. The result of their agitation was the Law of the Twelve Tables. Later still, the plebeians forced the patricians to publish legal procedures as well. The plebeians had broken the patricians' legal monopoly and henceforth enjoyed full protection under the law.

The decisive plebeian victory came in 367 B.C.E. after rich plebeians joined the poor to mount a sweeping assault on patrician privilege. Wealthy plebeians demanded that the patricians allow them access to all the magistracies of the state. The senate did approve a law that stipulated that one of the two consuls had to be a plebeian. Though decisive, this victory did not automatically end the Struggle of the Orders. That happened only in 287 B.C.E. with the passage of a law, the *lex Hortensia,* that gave the resolutions of the concilium plebis the force of law for patricians and plebeians alike.

The Struggle of the Orders resulted in a Rome stronger and better united than before. It could have led to class warfare and anarchy, but again certain Roman traits triumphed. The values fostered by their social structure predisposed the Romans to compromise, especially in the face of common danger. Important, too, were Roman patience, tenacity, and a healthy sense of the practical. These qualities enabled both sides to keep working until they had resolved the crisis. The Struggle of the Orders ended in 287 B.C.E. with a new concept of Roman citizenship. All citizens shared equally under the law. Theoretically, all could aspire to the highest political offices. Patrician or plebeian, rich or poor, Roman citizenship was equal for all.

## The Age of Overseas Conquest (282–146 B.C.E.)

In 282 B.C.E. Rome embarked on a series of wars that left it ruler of the Mediterranean world. These wars did not result from a grandiose strategy for world conquest. In many instances the Romans did not even initiate military action; they simply responded to events. Although they sometimes declared war reluctantly, they always felt a need to dominate, to eliminate any threat.

After Rome won the Samnite wars, the Greek city of Tarentum felt threatened by growing Roman power. Tarentum invited help from Pyrrhus, the king of Epirus in Greece. He won two furious battles against the Romans but suffered heavy losses (hence the phrase "Pyrrhic victory") and was finally driven out by the Roman army.

The next battleground for Rome was nearby Sicily, long the target of the Phoenician city of Carthage in North Africa (see Map 6.2). The struggle for control of Sicily produced the First Punic War, which lasted for twenty-three years (264–241 B.C.E.). The Romans quickly learned that they could not conquer Sicily unless they controlled the sea. Although they lacked a fleet and hated the sea, the Romans, with grim resolution, built a navy and then won six of seven major naval battles against the Carthaginians. In 241 B.C.E. Rome took control of Sicily, which became its first real province. Rome's resources, manpower, and determination had proved decisive.

But the First Punic War was a beginning, not an end. Carthage, still a formidable enemy, expanded its army led by a brilliant general, Hannibal (ca 247–183 B.C.E.). Realizing the advantage of swift mobile forces and an innovator in tactics, Hannibal moved against Rome. During the Second Punic War, in 218 B.C.E. he led his troops—infantry, cavalry, and elephants—on a thousand-mile march across southern France and over the Alps to carry the fighting to the gates of Rome. He won three major victories, inflicting some forty thousand casualties on Rome's army at the Battle of Cannae in 216 B.C.E. He

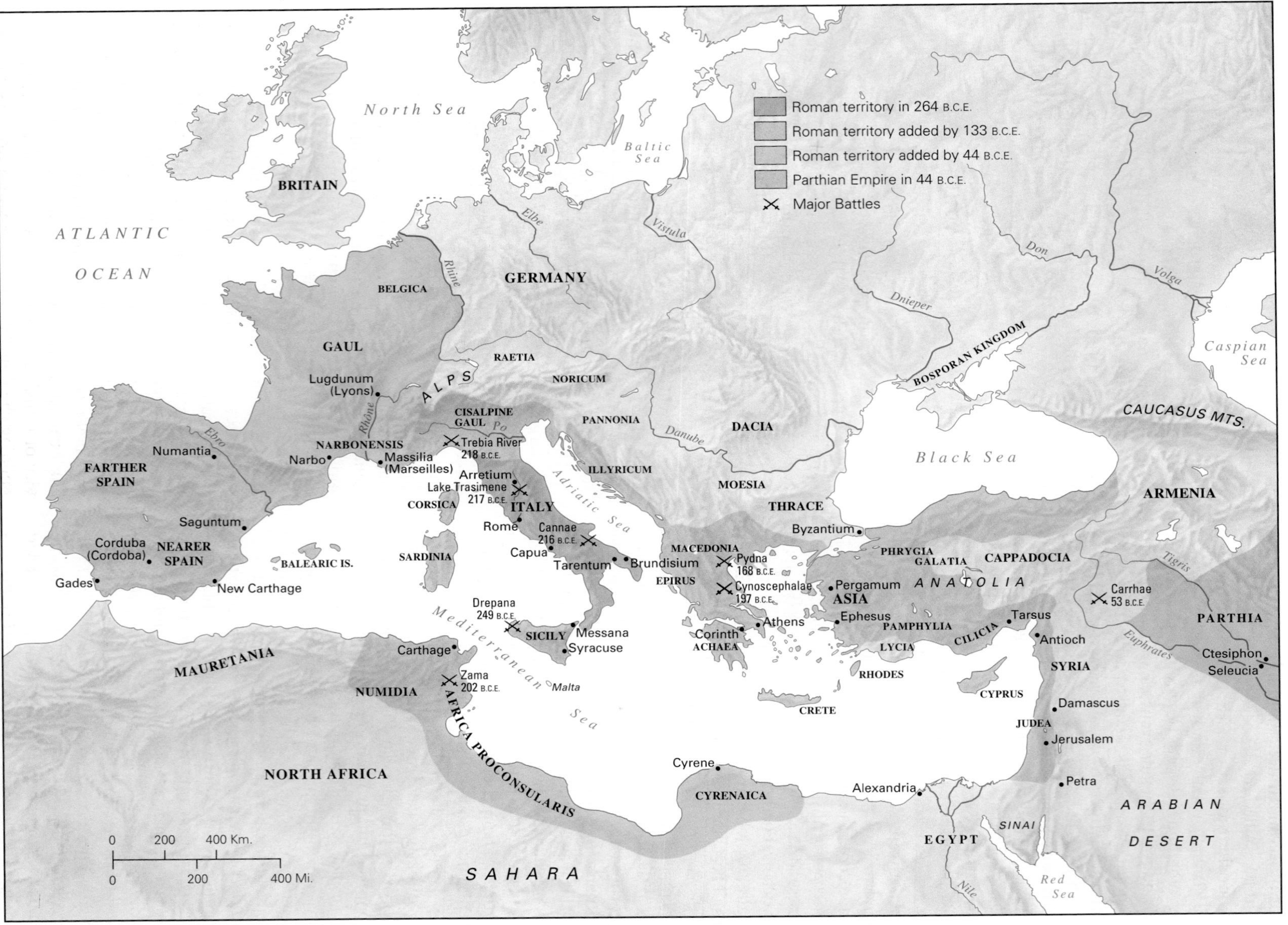


**MAP 6.2 Roman Expansion During the Republic** The main spurt of Roman expansion occurred between 264 and 133 B.C.E., when most of the Mediterranean fell to Rome, followed by the conquest of Gaul and the eastern Mediterranean by 44 B.C.E.

also spread devastation across the Italian countryside. But he could not break Rome's iron circle of Latium, Etruria, and Samnium, and Rome and its Italian allies fought back.

The Roman general Scipio Africanus (ca 236–ca 183 B.C.E.) copied Hannibal's mobile warfare to wrest Spain from Carthage's control. The Roman fleet dominated the seas, preventing Carthage from sending reinforcements to Hannibal in Italy. Then Scipio landed in North Africa and threatened Carthage itself. Hannibal hurried back, and in 202 B.C.E., near the town of Zama, Scipio defeated Hannibal in one of history's most decisive battles. Scipio's victory ensured that Rome's heritage would be passed on to the Western world.

One more conflict between Rome and Carthage remained. The Third Punic War ended in 146 B.C.E. when Scipio's grandson destroyed Carthage. When Rome took complete control of Spain in 133 B.C.E., it dominated the western Mediterranean.

Even in the midst of this bitter series of conflicts, the Romans began to reach to the east. During the Second Punic War, the king of Macedonia had made an alliance with Carthage. Roman legions moved east to settle accounts and quickly conquered Macedonia, Greece, and the Seleucid monarchy. By 146 B.C.E. the Romans stood unchallenged in the eastern Mediterranean and had turned many states into provinces. (See the feature "Listening to the Past: Titus Flamininus and the Liberty of the Greeks" on pages 178–179.) In 133 B.C.E. the king of Pergamum in Asia Minor willed his kingdom to Rome when he died. The Ptolemies of Egypt meekly obeyed Roman wishes. The Mediterranean had become *mare nostrum,* "our sea."

**Triumphal Column of Caius Duilius** This curious monument celebrates Rome's first naval victory in the First Punic War. In the battle Caius Duilius destroyed fifty Carthaginian ships. He then celebrated his success by erecting this column that portrays the prows of the enemy ships projecting from the column. *(Alinari/Art Resource, NY)*

## Old Values and Greek Culture

Rome had conquered the Mediterranean world, but some Romans considered that victory a misfortune. The historian Sallust (86–34 B.C.E.), writing from hindsight, complained that the acquisition of an empire was the beginning of Rome's troubles:

*But when through labor and justice our Republic grew powerful, great kings defeated in war, fierce nations and mighty peoples subdued by force, when Carthage the rival of the Roman people was wiped out root and branch, all the seas and lands lay open, then fortune began to be harsh and to throw everything into confusion. The Romans had easily borne labor, danger, uncertainty, and hardship. To them leisure, riches—otherwise desirable—proved to be burdens and torments. So at first money, then desire for power, grew great. These things were a sort of cause of all evils.*[2]

Sallust was not alone in his feelings. At the time, some senators had opposed the destruction of Carthage on the grounds that fear of their old rival would keep the Romans in check. In the second century B.C.E. the Romans learned that they could not return to what they fondly considered a simple life. They were world rulers. The responsibilities they faced were complex and awesome. They had to change their institutions, social patterns, and way of thinking to meet the new era. They were in fact building the foundations of a great imperial system.

How did the Romans of the day meet these challenges? How did they lead their lives and cope with these momentous changes? Obviously there are as many answers to these questions as there were Romans. Yet two attitudes represent the major trends of the second century B.C.E. One was a longing for the good old days and an idealized view of the traditional agrarian way of life. The other was an embracing of the new urban life, with its eager acceptance of Greek culture.

In Roman society ties within the family were very strong. The head of the family was the **paterfamilias,** a term that means far more than merely "father." The paterfamilias was the oldest dominant male of the family. He held nearly absolute power over the lives of his wife and children as long as he lived. He could legally kill his wife for adultery or divorce her at will. He could kill his children or sell them into slavery. He could force them to marry against their will. Until the paterfamilias died, his sons could not legally own property. At his death, the wife and children of the paterfamilias inherited his property.

Despite his immense power, the paterfamilias did not necessarily act alone or arbitrarily. To deal with important family matters, he usually called a council of the adult males. In this way the leading members of the family aired their views. In these councils the women of the family had no formal part, but it can safely be assumed that they played an important role behind the scenes. Although the possibility of serious conflicts between a paterfamilias and his grown sons is obvious, no one in ancient Rome ever complained about the institution. Perhaps in practice the paterfamilias preferred to be lenient rather than absolute.

In the traditional Roman family, the wife was the matron of the family, a position of authority and respect. The virtues expected of a Roman matron were fidelity, chastity, modesty, and dedication to the family. She ran the household. She supervised the domestic slaves, planned the meals, and devoted a good deal of attention to her children. In wealthy homes during this period, the matron had begun to employ a slave as a wet nurse, but most ordinary Roman women nursed their babies and bathed and swaddled them daily. After the age of seven, sons—and in many wealthy households daughters too—began to undertake formal education.

The agricultural year followed the sun and the stars—the farmer's calendar. Farmers used oxen and donkeys to pull the plow, collecting the dung of the animals for fertilizer. The main money crops, at least for rich soils, were wheat and flax. Forage crops included clover, vetch, and alfalfa. Prosperous farmers raised olive trees chiefly for the oil. They also raised grapevines for the production of wine. Harvests varied depending on the soil, but farmers could usually expect yields of 5½ bushels of wheat or 10½ bushels of barley per acre.

An influx of slaves came about from Rome's wars and conquests. Prisoners from Spain, Africa, and the Hellenistic East and even some blacks and other prisoners from Hannibal's army came to Rome as the spoils of war. The Roman attitude toward slaves and slavery had little in common with modern views. To the Romans slavery was a misfortune that befell some people, but it did not entail any racial theories. Races were not enslaved because the Romans thought them inferior. The black African slave was treated no worse—and no better—than

**Scene of the Life of a Child** This scene depicts the life of Marcus Cornelius from infancy to playing with his ponies to death. The entire scene suggests a pleasant and loving, if brief, childhood. *(Giraudon/Art Resource, NY)*

the Spaniard. Indeed, some slaves were valued because of their physical distinctiveness: black Africans and blond Germans were particular favorites. For the talented slave, the Romans always held out the hope of eventual freedom. **Manumission**—the freeing of individual slaves by their masters—became so common that it had to be limited by law. Not even Christians questioned the institution of slavery. It was just a fact of life.

For most Romans, religion played an important part in life. Originally the Romans thought of the gods as invisible, shapeless natural forces. Only through Etruscan and Greek influence did Roman deities take on human form. Jupiter, the sky-god, and his wife, Juno, became equivalent to the Greek Zeus and Hera. Mars was the god of war but also guaranteed the fertility of the farm and protected it from danger. The gods of the Romans were not loving and personal. They were stern, powerful, and aloof. But as long as the Romans honored the cults of their gods, they could expect divine favor.

In addition to the great gods, the Romans believed in spirits who haunted fields, forests, crossroads, and even the home itself. Some of the deities were hostile; only magic could ward them off. The spirits of the dead, like ghosts in modern horror films, frequented places where they had lived. They, too, had to be placated but were ordinarily benign. As the poet Ovid (43 B.C.E.–17 C.E.) put it:

*The spirits of the dead ask for little.*
*They are more grateful for piety than for an*
*expensive gift—*
*Not greedy are the gods who haunt the Styx below.*
*A rooftile covered with a sacrificial crown,*
*Scattered kernels, a few grains of salt,*
*Bread dipped in wine, and loose violets—*
*These are enough.*
*Put them in a potsherd and leave them in the middle of*
*the road.*[3]

A good deal of Roman religion consisted of rituals such as those Ovid describes. These practices lived on long after the Romans had lost interest in the great gods. Even Christianity could not entirely wipe them out. Instead, Christianity was to incorporate many of these rituals into its own style of worship.

By the second century B.C.E. the ideals of traditional Roman society came into conflict with a new spirit of wealth and leisure. The conquest of the Mediterranean world and the spoils of war made Rome a great city. Roman life, especially in the cities, was changing and becoming less austere. The spoils of war went to build baths, theaters, and other places of amusement. Simultaneously, the new responsibilities of governing the world produced in Rome a sophisticated society. Romans developed new tastes and a liking for Greek culture and literature. They began to learn the Greek language. Hellenism dominated the cultural life of Rome.

The new Hellenism profoundly stimulated the growth and development of Roman art and literature. After conquering the Hellenistic East, the Romans brought back Greek paintings and sculptures to grace temples, public buildings, and private homes. Roman artists copied many aspects of Greek art, but their emphasis on realistic portraiture carried on a native tradition. Similarly, Roman writers such as Plautus (ca 254–184 B.C.E.) and Terence (ca 195–159 B.C.E.) followed Greek models for their plays but put their own Roman stamp on them. All of early Roman literature was derived from the Greeks, but it managed in time to flourish in its own voice because it had something of its own to say.

The conquest of the Mediterranean world brought the Romans leisure, and Hellenism influenced how they

**African Acrobat** Conquest and prosperity brought exotic pleasure to Rome. Every feature of this sculpture is exotic. The young African woman and her daring gymnastic pose would catch anyone's attention. To add to the spice of her act, she performs using a live crocodile as her platform. Americans would have loved it. *(Courtesy of the Trustees of the British Museum)*

**Roman Table Manners** This mosaic is a floor that can never be swept clean. It whimsically suggests what a dining room floor looked like after a lavish dinner and also tells something about the menu: a chicken head, a wishbone, and remains of various seafood, vegetables, and fruit are easily recognizable. *(Museo Gregoriano Profano, Vatican Museums/Scala/Art Resource, NY)*

**Dressing of the Bride** Preparing for a wedding was an occasion for fun and ceremony. On the night before the event the bride tried on her wedding dress for a favorable omen. The next morning she was fastidiously dressed by her mother or under her mother's supervision. Here a sister or maid arranges the bride's hair, over which was later placed her veil, normally crowned with flowers that the girl had picked herself. *(Erich Lessing/Art Resource, NY)*

spent their free time. During the second century B.C.E. the Greek custom of bathing became a Roman passion and an important part of the day. In the early republic Romans had bathed infrequently, especially in the winter. Now large buildings containing pools and exercise rooms went up in great numbers, and the baths became an essential part of the Roman city. Architects built intricate systems of aqueducts to supply the bathing establishments with water. Conservatives railed at this Greek custom, calling it a waste of time and an encouragement to idleness. But the baths were socially important places where men and women went to see and be seen. Social climbers tried to talk to the "right people" and wangle invitations to dinner; politicians took advantage of the occasion to discuss the affairs of the day.

Did Hellenism and new social customs corrupt the Romans? Perhaps the best answer is this: the Roman state and the empire it ruled continued to exist for six more centuries. Rome did not collapse; the state continued to prosper. The golden age of Roman literature was still before it. The high tide of Roman prosperity still lay in the future. The Romans did not like change but took it in stride. That was part of their practical turn of mind and their strength.

## The Late Republic (133–31 B.C.E.)

The wars of conquest created serious problems for the Romans. Some of the most pressing were political. The republican constitution had suited the needs of a simple city-state but was inadequate to meet the requirements of Rome's new position in international affairs (see Map 6.2). Sweeping changes and reforms were necessary to make it serve the demands of empire. A system of provincial administration had to be established. Armies had to be provided for defense, and a system of tax collection had to be created.

Other political problems were equally serious. During the wars Roman generals commanded huge numbers of troops for long periods of time. Men such as Scipio Aemilianus were on the point of becoming too mighty for the state to control. Although Rome's Italian allies had borne much of the burden of the fighting, they received fewer rewards than did Roman officers and soldiers. Italians began to agitate for full Roman citizenship and a voice in politics.

There were serious economic problems, too. Hannibal's operations and the warfare in Italy had left the countryside a shambles. The movements of numerous armies had disrupted agriculture. The prolonged fighting had also drawn untold numbers of Roman and Italian men away from their farms for long periods. The families of these soldiers could not keep the land under full cultivation. The people who defended Rome and conquered the world for Rome became impoverished for having done their duty. These problems, complex and explosive, largely account for the turmoil of the closing years of the republic.

When the legionaries returned home, they found that their farms looked like those of the people they had conquered. Many chose to sell their land; they found ready buyers in those who had become incredibly rich through the wars of conquest. These wealthy men created huge estates called **latifundia.** Landless veterans moved to the cities, especially Rome, but most could find no work. Those who did work received meager pay kept low by competition from slave labor. These changes threatened Rome's army, as landless men were forbidden to serve.

The landless veterans were willing to follow any leader who promised help. Tiberius Gracchus (163–133 B.C.E.) emerged. An aristocrat, Tiberius was appalled that Rome's soldiers "fight and die to support others in luxury" and decried the fact that "they are styled masters of the world, [but] they have not a single clod of earth that is their own."[4] Elected tribune of the people in 133 B.C.E., Tiberius proposed dividing public land among the poor, but his sensible plan was thwarted by wealthy aristocrats. A group of senators murdered Tiberius, launching a long era of political violence that would destroy the republic.

Still, Tiberius's land bill became law, and his brother Gaius Gracchus (153–121 B.C.E.) led the fight for further reforms. He passed a law providing the urban poor with cheap grain and urged that poor Romans be sent to colonize southern Italy. When he proposed giving full citizenship rights to all Italians, senators once again tried to stem the tide of reform by murder.

The next reforming leader was Gaius Marius, who unlike the Gracchus brothers was not part of the traditional Roman aristocracy. In 107 B.C.E. he recruited the landless into the army he needed to campaign against a rebel king in North Africa. When the soldiers returned home, they expected Marius to deliver on the land he had promised them. The senate, however, refused to enact Marius's bill. From then on, Roman soldiers looked to their commanders, not the senate or the state, to protect their interests.

Soon after, in 91 B.C.E., a bitter war erupted between the Romans and their allies over the issue of full citizenship for Italians. In 88 B.C.E. the Roman general Sulla ended the war and made himself dictator. Although he stepped down nine years later and tried to restore the republican constitution, it was too late. Once the senate and other institutions of the Roman state had failed to meet the needs of the empire, once they had lost control of their generals and armies, and once the soldiers had put their faith in generals rather than the state, the republic was doomed.

The history of the late republic is the story of the power struggles of some of Rome's most famous figures: Julius Caesar, Pompey, Augustus, Marc Antony, and Cicero. (See the feature "Individuals in Society: Cicero.") A man of boundless ambition, Pompey used military success in Spain to force the senate to allow him to run for consul. In 59 B.C.E. he was joined in a political alliance called the **First Triumvirate** by Crassus, another ambitious politician, and Julius Caesar (100–44 B.C.E.). Born of a noble family, Caesar was a cultivated man, an able general, and a brilliant politician with unbridled ambition. Recognizing that military service was the road to power, Caesar led an army in Spain, winning the respect and affection of his troops with his courage. Brave,

**Julius Caesar** This realistic bust of Caesar captures all of the power, intensity, and brilliance of the man. It is a study of determination and an excellent example of Roman portraiture. *(National Archaeological Museum, Naples/Alinari/Art Resource, NY)*

tireless, and a superb strategist, he moved next to conquer all of Gaul (modern France). By 49 B.C.E. the First Triumvirate had collapsed. Crassus had died in battle, and Caesar and Pompey, each suspecting the other of treachery, were engaged in a bloody civil war. Pompey had the official support of the government, but Caesar defeated him in 45 B.C.E.

Making himself dictator, Caesar was determined to enact basic reforms. He extended citizenship to many of the provincials (people outside Italy) who had supported him. To relieve the pressure of Rome's growing population, he sent eighty thousand poor and jobless people to plant colonies in Gaul, Spain, and North Africa. These new communities—formed of Roman citizens, not subjects—helped spread Roman culture.

In 44 B.C.E. a group of conspirators assassinated Caesar and set off another round of civil war. His grandnephew and heir, the eighteen-year-old Octavian, joined with two of Caesar's followers, Marc Antony and Lepidus, in the Second Triumvirate. They defeated Caesar's murderers but soon had a falling-out. Octavian forced Lepidus out of office and waged war against Antony, who had become allied with Cleopatra, queen of Egypt. In 31 B.C.E., with the might of Rome at his back, Octavian met and defeated the combined forces of Antony and Cleopatra at the Battle of Actium in Greece. His victory ended an age of civil war that had lasted since the days of Sulla. For this success the senate in 27 B.C.E. voted Octavian the name *Augustus*.

## THE PAX ROMANA

When Augustus put an end to the civil wars that had raged since 88 B.C.E., he faced monumental problems of reconstruction. He could easily have declared himself dictator, as Caesar had done, but the thought was repugnant to him. Augustus was neither an autocrat nor a revolutionary. His solution, as he put it, was to restore the republic. But was that possible? Some eighteen years of anarchy and civil war had shattered the republican constitution. From 29 to 23 B.C.E., Augustus toiled to heal Rome's wounds. The first problem facing him was to rebuild the constitution and the organs of government. Next he had to demobilize much of the army and care for the welfare of the provinces. Then he had to meet the danger of barbarians at Rome's European frontiers. Augustus was highly successful in meeting these challenges. The world came to know this era as the **pax Romana,** the Roman peace. His gift of peace to a war-torn world sowed the seeds of the empire's golden age.

### Augustus's Settlement (31 B.C.E.–14 C.E.)

Augustus claimed that in restoring constitutional government he was also restoring the republic. Typically Roman, he preferred not to create anything new; he intended instead to modify republican forms and offices to meet new circumstances. Augustus expected the senate to administer some of the provinces, continue to be the chief deliberative body of the state, and act as a court of law. But he did not give the senate enough power to become his partner in government. As a result, the senate could not live up to the responsibilities that Augustus assigned. Many of its prerogatives shifted by default to Augustus and his successors.

Augustus's own position in the restored republic was something of an anomaly. He could not simply surrender the reins of power, for someone else would have seized them. But how was he to fit into a republican constitution? Again Augustus had his own answer. He became **princeps civitatis,** the "First Citizen of the State." This prestigious title carried no power; it indicated only that

# INDIVIDUALS IN SOCIETY

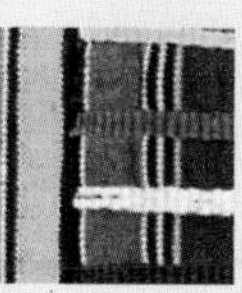

## CICERO

*Bust of Cicero from the first century* B.C.E. (Alinari/Art Resource, NY)

In republican Rome entry of a "new man" into the exalted rank of senator was possible but also difficult and infrequent. The families that had traditional hold on power in the senate formed an exclusive circle, jealous of their power and proud of their prestige. They provided the leadership of the republic and were very reluctant to allow social inferiors to join their ranks. Few men from the lower classes were admitted. Those few who were ultimately accepted into this rarefied air needed outstanding ability, wealth, a good education, social graces, and a noble patron. Cicero was one of those who possessed all of these advantages.

Marcus Tullius Cicero was born on January 3, 106 B.C.E., in Arpinum, southwest of Rome. He was of equestrian rank, which means that his social standing was inferior to that of the senators. Furthermore, not having been born in Rome, he was an outsider. Yet his father was intelligent, ambitious, and foresighted. He sent Cicero and his brother to Rome for an education. Rome was the place to make a reputation, and Cicero made good use of the opportunity. He studied philosophy and rhetoric there and laid the foundations of his later career.

From 90 to 89 B.C.E. he served in the Roman army, which gave him firsthand knowledge of military affairs. Although the dream of military glory remained with him always, his martial ability was that of a subordinate, not a leader.

After his military service Cicero turned to the study of law, which was a lucrative avenue to a political career. He won his first case in 81 B.C.E. and immediately earned a reputation for knowledge of the law, reasoned argument, and eloquent speaking. His victory may have annoyed Sulla, because it legally demonstrated the weakness of his dictatorship. In 79 B.C.E. Cicero traveled first to Athens and then to Rhodes to continue his study of philosophy and oratory. He was honing the skills that would establish his reputation and make his career.

Cicero returned to Rome to enter politics after Sulla's death in 78 B.C.E. Success was immediate. He became praetor of Sicily in 66 B.C.E., which gave him direct experience with Roman administration. He also earned a reputation as a man who honored Rome's traditional values. He was politically conservative and thus acceptable to many senators. The height of his political career came in 63 B.C.E., when he was elected consul. He was the first *novus homo* (new man) to be elected to the consulship in thirty-one years.

Cicero took no active part in the revolution that brought down the republic. Instead, he tried to stop it. He urged peace and a return to the traditional government, what he called "concord of the orders," an attempt to reconcile the warring factions. His plan fell on deaf ears. Events had escalated beyond him, and now only politicians with armies could decide the fate of the republic. He took no part in Caesar's assassination but nonetheless made several influential enemies. One of them, Marc Antony, ordered his execution. Cicero made a halfhearted attempt to escape, but Roman soldiers caught him and murdered him on December 7, 43 B.C.E. He died with dignity and courage.

Cicero exhibited little military talent, fair but not brilliant administrative skills, and mediocre political abilities. Why does history remember him? Most Romans respected him for his dedication to Rome and its laws. Posterity has honored him for his writings, which have endured. He was a literary genius whose Latin prose was never equaled, even in antiquity. His essays on politics and philosophy explore the nature and functioning of proper, stable government and an attempt to understand the universe and people's place in it. The finest tribute to him was one he never heard. The emperor Augustus once called him "a learned man . . . and a lover of his country."

### QUESTIONS FOR ANALYSIS

1. Was Cicero's ideal of "concord of the orders" a realistic ideal in his day?
2. For all of his fame and talent, how successful was Cicero in practical politics, and what did he achieve?

**MAP 6.3 Roman Expansion Under the Empire** Following Roman expansion during the republic, Augustus added vast tracts of Europe to the Roman Empire, which the emperor Hadrian later enlarged by assuming control over parts of central Europe, the Near East, and North Africa.

Augustus was the most distinguished of all Roman citizens. In effect, it designated Augustus as the first among equals—a little "more equal" than anyone else. His real power resided in the multiple magistracies he held and in the powers granted him by the senate. As consul he had no more constitutional and legal power than his fellow consuls, but he was consul every year. In addition, Augustus held many magistracies that his fellow consuls did not. The senate also voted him the full power of the tribunes, giving him the right to call the senate into session, present legislation to the people, and defend their rights. Along with all these other powers, Augustus had control of the army, which he made a permanent, standing organization. Although he carefully kept this power in the background, it was there. Augustus did not restore the republic, but he did create a constitutional monarchy. Without saying so, he created the office of emperor.

Augustus's title as commander of the Roman army was *imperator,* the title with which Rome customarily honored a general after a major victory, and it came to mean "emperor" in the modern sense of the term. Augustus governed the provinces where troops were needed for defense. The frontiers were his special concern. There Roman legionaries held the German barbarians at arm's length. Augustus made sure that Rome went to war only at his command. He controlled deployment of the Roman army and paid its wages. He granted it bonuses and gave veterans retirement benefits. To employ Rome's surplus of soldiers, he also founded at least forty new colonies, which, like Julius Caesar's, were a significant tool in the spread of Roman culture. Thus he avoided the problems with the army that the old senate had created for itself. Augustus never shared control of the army, and no Roman found it easy to defy him militarily.

Augustus, however, failed to solve a momentous problem. He never found a way to institutionalize his position with the army. The ties between the princeps and the army were always personal. The army was loyal to the princeps but not necessarily to the state. The Augustan principate worked well at first, but by the third century C.E. the army would make and break emperors at will. Nonetheless, it is a measure of Augustus's success that his settlement survived as long and as well as it did.

## Administration and Expansion Under Augustus

In the areas under his immediate jurisdiction, Augustus put provincial administration on an orderly basis and improved its functioning. Believing that the cities of the empire should look after their own affairs, he encouraged local self-government and urbanism. Augustus respected local customs and ordered his governors to do the same.

As a spiritual bond between the provinces and Rome, Augustus encouraged the cult of Roma, goddess and guardian of the state. In the Hellenistic East, where king worship was an established custom, the cult of *Roma et Augustus* (Rome and Augustus) grew and spread rapidly. Augustus then introduced it in the West. By the time of his death in 14 C.E., nearly every province in the empire could boast an altar or a shrine to Roma et Augustus. In the West it was not the person of the emperor who was worshiped but his *genius*—his guardian spirit. In praying for the good health and welfare of the emperor, Romans and provincials were praying for the empire itself. The cult became a symbol of Roman unity.

For the history of Western civilization, one of the most momentous aspects of Augustus's reign was Roman expansion into the wilderness of northern and western Europe (see Map 6.3). Carrying on Caesar's work, Augustus pushed Rome's frontier into the region of modern Germany.

Augustus began his work in the west and north by completing the conquest of Spain. In Gaul, apart from minor campaigns, most of his work was peaceful. He founded twelve new towns, and the Roman road system linked new settlements with one another and with Italy. But the German frontier, along the Rhine River, was the scene of hard fighting. In 12 B.C.E. Augustus ordered a major invasion of Germany beyond the Rhine. In 9 C.E. Augustus's general Varus lost some twenty thousand troops at the Battle of the Teutoburger Forest. Thereafter the Rhine remained the Roman frontier.

Meanwhile more successful generals extended the Roman standards as far as the Danube. Roman legions penetrated the area of modern Austria, southern Bavaria, and western Hungary. The regions of modern Serbia, Bulgaria, and Romania fell. Within this area the legionaries built fortified camps. Roads linked these camps with one another, and settlements grew up around the camps. Amid the vast expanse of forests, Roman towns, trade, language, and law began to exert a civilizing influence on the barbarians. Many military camps became towns, and many modern European cities owe their origins to the forts of the Roman army. For the first time, the barbarian north came into direct, immediate, and continuous contact with Mediterranean culture. The arrival of the Romans often provoked resistance from barbarian tribes that simply wanted to be left alone. In other cases the prosperity and wealth of the new Roman towns lured

**Boscoreale Cup** The central scene lavishly depicted on the side of a silver cup shows Augustus seated in majesty. In his right hand he holds an orb that represents his position as master of the world. The scroll in his left hand symbolizes his authority as lawgiver. On his right is a group of divinities who support his efforts, on his left a group of barbarians who have submitted to Rome. *(Louvre/R.M.N./Art Resource, NY)*

barbarians eager for plunder. The Romans maintained peaceful relations with the barbarians whenever possible, but Roman legions remained on the frontier to repel hostile barbarians. The result was the evolution of a consistent, systematic frontier policy.

### Literary Flowering

The Augustan settlement's gift of peace inspired a literary flowering unparalleled in Roman history. The tone and ideal of Roman literature, like that of the Greeks, was humanistic and worldly. Roman poets and prose writers celebrated the dignity of humanity and the range of its accomplishments. They stressed the physical and emotional joys of a comfortable, peaceful life.

Virgil (70–19 B.C.E.), Rome's greatest poet, wrote the *Aeneid,* an epic poem that is the equivalent of the *Iliad* and *Odyssey* of Greece. The poem marries the traditional Roman tradition of the founding of Rome by Romulus with the legend of Aeneas, a Trojan hero who escaped to Italy at the fall of Troy. In doing so he connected Rome with Greece's heroic past.

Livy's history of Rome is the prose counterpart of the *Aeneid.* Livy (59 B.C.E.–17 C.E.) received training in Latin literature, rhetoric, and philosophy. He loved and admired the heroes and great deeds of the republic, but he was also a friend of Augustus and a supporter of the principate. He especially approved of Augustus's efforts to restore republican virtues.

The poet Horace (65–8 B.C.E.) rose from humble beginnings to friendship with Augustus—who, along with many of his friends, actively encouraged the writers who created this literary flowering. One of his finest odes commemorates Augustus's victory over Antony and Cleopatra at Actium in 31 B.C.E.

## THE COMING OF CHRISTIANITY

During the reign of Tiberius (14–37 C.E.), perhaps in 29 C.E., Pontius Pilate, prefect of Judaea—the Roman province formed of the old kingdom of Judah—condemned Jesus of Nazareth to death. Jesus lived in a troubled time when Roman rule aroused hatred and unrest among the Jews. This climate of hostility formed the backdrop of his ministry.

The Roman civil wars had touched the eastern Mediterranean world, as local populations—including the Jews—took sides in the fighting and both caused and suffered damage. Augustus's peace was less celebrated here than in Rome, as the Jews resented the embrace of Greek culture by his handpicked king, Herod (ca 73–4 B.C.E.). When Herod died, civil war erupted, and the Roman army was needed to restore order. Augustus then put a Roman official, a prefect who reported directly to him, in charge of the province. Resentment of Roman troops and tax collectors sharpened.

Two movements spread among the Jews. First was the rise of the Zealots, resolute in the worship of Yahweh and savage in their attempts to throw off the Roman yoke. Second was the rise of a militant apocalyptic sentiment. The old Jewish belief in the coming of the **Messiah** became more fervent and widespread. People believed that this savior would destroy the Roman Empire and usher in a period of happiness and plenty for the Jews. One who prophesied the coming of the Messiah was John the Baptist. At the same time, the sect described in the Dead Sea Scrolls, probably the Essenes, prepared themselves for the end of the world.

The spiritual ferment of the time extended beyond Judaea. Roman pagans—those who believed in the Greco-Roman gods—were undergoing a turbulent

**Pontius Pilate and Jesus** This Byzantine mosaic from Ravenna illustrates a dramatic moment in Jesus' trial and crucifixion. Jesus stands accused before Pilate, but Pilate symbolically washes his hands of the whole affair. *(Scala/Art Resource, NY)*

time as well. Paganism at the time of Jesus' birth can be divided into three broad types: the official state religion of Rome, the traditional Roman cults of hearth and countryside, and the new mystery religions that flowed from the Hellenistic East. The formal state religion, full of ritual and grand spectacle, reflected a bond between the gods and the people, a religious contract for the well-being of the empire, but it provided little emotional or spiritual comfort. Many Romans turned to the old cults of home and countryside. These popular cults brought Romans back in touch with nature but did not satisfy the need for a religion that was more immediate and personal. Many people in the Roman Empire found that need met by the Hellenistic mystery cults (see pages 135–136). While these religions met people's spiritual needs, none was truly international and open to everyone, as each excluded some people for various reasons.

Into this climate of Roman religious yearning, political severity, fanatical Zealotry, and Messianic hope came Jesus of Nazareth (ca 5 B.C.E.–29 C.E.). He was raised in Galilee, stronghold of the Zealots. Yet Jesus himself was a man of peace. Jesus urged his listeners to love God as their father and one another as God's children.

Jesus' teachings were Jewish. He declared that he would change not one jot of the Jewish law. His major deviation from orthodoxy was his insistence that he taught in his own name, not in the name of Yahweh. Was he then the Messiah? A small band of followers thought so, and Jesus claimed that he was. But Jesus had his own conception of the Messiah. Jesus would not destroy the Roman Empire. He told his disciples flatly that they were to "render unto Caesar the things that are Caesar's." Jesus would establish a spiritual kingdom, not an earthly one. Repeatedly he told his disciples that his kingdom was "not of this world," but one of eternal happiness in a life after death.

Of Jesus' life and teachings the prefect Pontius Pilate knew little and cared even less. All that concerned him was the maintenance of peace and order. The crowds following Jesus at the time of the Passover, a highly emotional time in the Jewish year, alarmed Pilate, who faced a volatile situation. To avert riot and bloodshed, Pilate condemned Jesus to death. After being scourged, he was hung from a cross until he died in the sight of family, friends, enemies, and the merely curious.

Once Pilate's soldiers had carried out the sentence, the entire matter seemed to be closed. Then on the third day after Jesus' crucifixion, an odd rumor began to circulate in Jerusalem. Some of Jesus' followers were saying he had risen from the dead, while others accused them of having stolen his body. For the earliest Christians and for generations to come, the resurrection of Jesus became a central element of faith—and more than that, a promise: Jesus had triumphed over death, and his resurrection promised all Christians immortality.

The memory of Jesus and his teachings sturdily survived. Believers in his divinity met in small assemblies or congregations, often in each other's homes to discuss the meaning of Jesus' message. These meetings always took place outside the synagogue. They included such orthodox Jews as the Pharisees. These earliest Christians were clearly defining their faith to fit the life of Jesus into an orthodox Jewish context. Only later did these congregations evolve into what can be called a church with a formal organization and set of beliefs. One of the first significant events occurred in Jerusalem on the Jewish festival of Pentecost, when Jesus' followers assembled. They were joined by Jews from many parts of the world, including some from as far away as Parthia to the east, Crete to the west, Rome, and Ethiopia. These early followers were Hellenized Jews, many of them rich merchants. They were in an excellent position to spread the Word throughout the known world.

The catalyst in the spread of Jesus' teachings and the formation of the Christian church was Paul of Tarsus, a Hellenized Jew who was comfortable in both the Roman and Jewish worlds. He had begun by persecuting the new sect, but on the road to Damascus he was converted to belief in Jesus. He was the single most important figure responsible for changing Christianity from a Jewish sect into a separate religion. Paul was familiar with Greek philosophy, and he had actually discussed the tenets of the new religion with Epicurean and Stoic philosophers in Athens. Indeed, one of his seminal ideas may have stemmed from the Stoic concept of the unity of mankind. He proclaimed that the mission of Christianity was "to make one of all the folk of men." His vision was to include all the kindred of the earth. That concept meant that he urged the Jews to include non-Jews in the faith. He was the first to voice a universal message of Christianity.

Paul's vision was both bold and successful. When he traveled abroad, he first met with the leaders of the local synagogue, then went among the people. He applied himself especially to the Greco-Romans, whom he did not consider common or unclean because they were not Jews. He went so far as to say that there were no differences between Jews and Gentiles, which in orthodox Jewish thought was not only revolutionary but also heresy. Paul found a ready audience among the Gentiles, who converted to the new religion with surprising enthusiasm. A significant part of this process was the acceptance of Gentile women into the faith. The reasons for this were several. First, intermarriage between Greeks and Jews was common. More important, Christianity gave women more rights than they could expect from either paganism or Judaism. For women Christianity was a source of liberation.

Christianity was attractive to many because it gave the Roman world a cause. Hellenistic philosophy had attempted to make men and women self-sufficient: people who became indifferent to the outside world could no longer be hurt by it. That goal alone ruled out any cause except the attainment of serenity. The Romans, never innovators in philosophy, merely elaborated this lonely and austere message. Instead of passivity, Christianity stressed the ideal of striving for a goal. Each and every Christian, no matter how poor or humble, supposedly worked to realize the triumph of Christianity on earth. This was God's will, a sacred duty for every Christian. By spreading the Word of Christ, Christians played their part in God's plan. No matter how small, the part each Christian played was important. Since this duty was God's will, Christians believed that the goal would be achieved. The

**The Catacombs of Rome** The early Christians used underground crypts and rock chambers to bury their dead. The bodies were placed in these galleries and then sealed up. The catacombs became places of pilgrimage, and in this way the dead continued to be united with the living. *(Catacombe di Priscilla, Rome/Scala/Art Resource, NY)*

Christian was not discouraged by temporary setbacks, believing Christianity to be invincible.

Christianity gave its devotees a sense of community. No Christian was alone. All members of the Christian community strove toward the same goal of fulfilling God's plan. Each individual community was in turn a member of a greater community. And that community, the Church General, was indestructible.

So Christianity's attractions were many, from forgiveness of sin to an exalted purpose for each individual. Its insistence on the individual's importance gave solace and encouragement, especially to the poor and meek. Its claim to divine protection fed hope in the eventual success of the Christian community. Christianity made participation in the universal possible for everyone. The ultimate reward promised by Christianity was eternal bliss after death.

## THE GOLDEN AGE

For fifty years after Augustus's death the dynasty that he established—known as the Julio-Claudians because all were members of the Julian and Claudian clans—provided the emperors of Rome. Two, Caligula and Nero, were weak and frivolous men who exercised their power stupidly and brought misery to the empire. But two others, Tiberius and Claudius, were sound rulers and able administrators, and during their reigns the empire largely prospered. One of their most momentous achievements was Claudius's creation of an imperial bureaucracy of professional administrators. The numerous duties and immense reponsibilities of the emperor prompted Claudius to delegate power. He created a simple, workable system that enabled him and later emperors to rule more easily and efficiently.

In 68 C.E. Nero's inept rule led to military rebellion and his death, followed by widespread disruption. The next year four men claimed the position of emperor, and several armies marched on Rome to back their claims. The winner was Vespasian, who entered Rome in 70 and restored order.

By establishing the Flavian dynasty (named after his clan), Vespasian turned the principate into an open and admitted monarchy. The Flavians (69–96 C.E.) carried on Augustus's work on the frontiers, gave the Roman world peace, and kept the legions in line. Their work paved the way for the era of the **five good emperors,** the golden age of the empire (96–180 C.E.).

Beginning in the second century C.E., the era of the five good emperors was a period of almost unparalleled prosperity for the empire. Wars generally ended in victories and were confined to the frontiers. The five good emperors—Nerva, Trajan, Hadrian, Antoninus Pius, and Marcus Aurelius—were among the noblest, most dedicated, ablest men in Roman history.

Under the Flavians the principate became a full-blown monarchy, and by the time of the five good emperors the principate was an office with definite rights, powers, and prerogatives. In the years between Augustus and the era of the five good emperors, the emperor had become an indispensable part of the imperial machinery. In short, without the emperor the empire would quickly have fallen to pieces. Augustus had been monarch in fact but not in theory; during their reigns, the five good emperors were monarchs in both.

The five good emperors were not power-hungry autocrats. The concentration of power was the result of empire. The easiest and most efficient way to run the Roman Empire was to invest the emperor with vast powers. Furthermore, Roman emperors on the whole proved to be effective rulers and administrators. As capable and efficient emperors took on new tasks and functions, the emperor's hand was felt in more areas of life and government. The five good emperors were benevolent and exercised their power intelligently, but they were absolute kings all the same. Lesser men would later throw off the façade of constitutionality and use this same power in a despotic fashion.

One of the most significant changes in Roman government since Augustus's day was the enormous growth of the imperial bureaucracy created by Claudius. Hadrian, who became emperor in 117 C.E., reformed this system by putting the bureaucracy on an organized, official basis. He established imperial administrative departments to handle the work formerly done by imperial freedmen. Hadrian also separated civil service from military service. Men with little talent or taste for the army could instead serve the state as administrators. Hadrian's bureaucracy demanded professionalism from its members. Administrators made a career of the civil service. These innovations made for more efficient running of the empire and increased the authority of the emperor—the ruling power of the bureaucracy.

The Roman army had also changed since Augustus's time. The Roman legion had once been a mobile unit, but its duties under the empire no longer called for mobility. The successors of Augustus generally called a halt to further conquests. The army was expected to defend what had already been won. Under the Flavian emperors the frontiers became firmly fixed. Forts and watch stations guarded the borders. Behind the forts the Romans built a system of roads that allowed the forts to be quickly supplied and reinforced in times of trouble. The army had evolved into a garrison force, with legions guarding specific areas for long periods.

The personnel of the legions was also changing. Italy could no longer supply all the recruits needed for the army. Increasingly, only the officers came from Italy and from the more Romanized provinces. The legionaries were mostly drawn from the less civilized provinces, especially the ones closest to the frontiers. In the third century C.E. the barbarization of the army would result in an army indifferent to Rome and its traditions. In the era of the five good emperors, however, the army was still a source of economic stability and a Romanizing agent. Men from the provinces and even barbarians joined the army to learn a trade and to gain Roman citizenship. Even so, the signs were ominous. Veterans from Julius Caesar's campaigns would hardly have recognized Hadrian's troops as Roman legionaries.

## LIFE IN THE GOLDEN AGE: IMPERIAL ROME AND THE PROVINCES

Many people, both ancient and modern, have considered these years one of the happiest epochs in Western history. But popular accounts have also portrayed Rome as already decadent by the time of the five good emperors. If Rome was decadent, who kept the empire running? For that matter, can life in Rome itself be taken as representative of life in other parts of the empire? Rome was unique and must be seen as such. Rome no more resembled a provincial city like Cologne than New York resembles Keokuk, Iowa. Only when the uniqueness of Rome is understood in its own right can one turn to the provinces to obtain a full and reasonable picture of the empire under the five good emperors.

Rome was truly an extraordinary city, especially by ancient standards. It was enormous, with a population somewhere between 500,000 and 750,000. Although it could boast of stately palaces, noble buildings, and beautiful residential areas, most people lived in jerrybuilt apartment houses. Fire and crime were perennial problems even after Augustus created fire and urban police forces. Streets were narrow, and drainage was inadequate. During the republic sanitation had been a common problem. Numerous inscriptions record prohibitions against dumping human refuse and even cadavers on the grounds of sanctuaries and cemeteries. Under the empire this situation improved. By comparison with medieval and early modern European cities, Rome was a healthy enough place to live.

Rome was such a huge city that the surrounding countryside could not feed it. Because of the danger of starvation, the emperor, following republican practice, provided the citizen population with free grain for bread and, later, oil and wine. By feeding the citizenry, the emperor prevented bread riots caused by shortages and high prices. For the rest of the urban population who did not enjoy the rights of citizenship, the emperor provided grain at low prices. This measure was designed to prevent speculators from forcing up grain prices in times of crisis. By maintaining the grain supply, the emperor kept the favor of the people and ensured that Rome's poor and idle did not starve.

The emperor also entertained the Roman populace, often at vast expense. The most popular forms of public entertainment were gladiatorial contests and chariot racing. Gladiatorial fighting was originally an Etruscan funerary custom, a blood sacrifice for the dead. Many **gladiators** were criminals; some were the slaves of gladiatorial trainers; others were prisoners of war. Still others were free men who volunteered for the arena. Even women at times engaged in gladiatorial combat. Although some Romans protested gladiatorial fighting, most delighted in it. Not until the fifth century did Christianity put a stop to it.

The Romans were even more addicted to chariot racing than to gladiatorial shows. Two-horse and four-horse chariots ran a course of seven laps, about five miles. Four permanent teams, each with its own color, competed against each other. Some Romans claimed that people cared more about their favorite team than the race itself, but champion drivers won wide accolades. One, who won 1,462 of his 4,257 races, was honored by an inscription that proclaimed him champion of all charioteers.

Ordinary Romans left their own messages for posterity in the inscriptions that grace their graves. They were proud of their work and accomplishments, affectionate toward their families and friends, and eager to be remembered after death. Paprius Vitalis wrote an engaging inscription for his wife: "If there is anything good in the lower regions—I, however, finish a poor life without you—be happy there too, sweetest Thalassia."[5] Other inscriptions reflect individuals' personal philosophies: "All we who are dead below have become bones and ashes, but nothing else"[6] or "I was, I am not, I don't care." Though fond of brutal spectacles, the Romans, like people of all ages, had their loves and dreams.

In the provinces and even on the frontiers, the era of the five good emperors was one of extensive prosperity, especially in western Europe. The Roman army had beaten back the barbarians and exposed them to the civilizing effects of Roman traders. The resulting peace and security opened Britain, Gaul, Germany, and the lands of the Danube to immigration. Agriculture flourished as large tracts of land came under cultivation. Most of this land was in the hands of free tenant farmers. From the

**Gladiatorial Games** Though hardly games, these gaudy spectacles often pitted gladiators against rare animals. Many of them, like the lion shown here, were formidable foes. Others, like the ostrich in the background, were probably not too ferocious. *(Galleria Borghese, Rome/Scala/Art Resource, NY)*

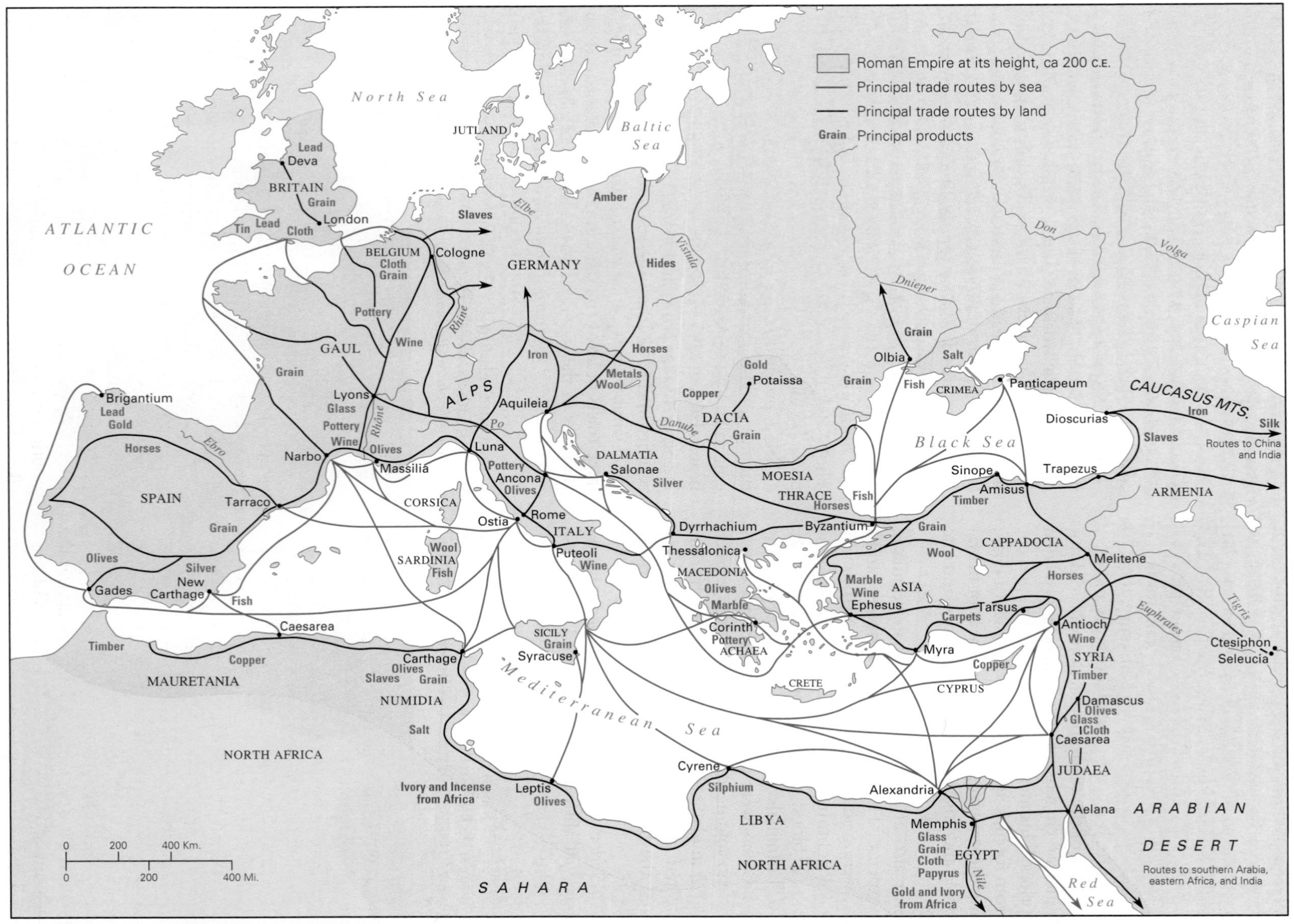


**MAP 6.4 The Economic Aspect of the Pax Romana** The Roman Empire was not merely a political and military organization but also an intricate economic network through which goods from Armenia and Syria were traded for Western products from as far away as Spain and Britain.

time of Augustus slavery had declined in the empire, as had the growth of latifundia (see page 155). Augustus and his successors encouraged the rise of free farmers. Under the five good emperors this trend continued, and the holders of small parcels of land thrived as never before. The emperors provided loans on easy terms to farmers, enabling them to rent land previously worked by slaves. They also permitted them to cultivate the new lands that were being opened up. Consequently, the small tenant farmer was becoming the backbone of Roman agriculture.

In continental Europe the army was largely responsible for the new burst of expansion. The areas where legions were stationed readily became Romanized. When legionaries retired from the army, they often settled where they had served. Since they had usually learned a trade in the army, they brought essential skills to areas that badly needed trained men. These veterans took their retirement pay and used it to set themselves up in business.

The eastern part of the empire also participated in the boom. The Roman navy had swept the sea of pirates, and Eastern merchants traded throughout the Mediterranean. The flow of goods and produce in the East matched that of the West. Venerable cities like Corinth, Antioch, and Ephesus flourished as rarely before. The cities of the East built extensively, bedecking themselves with new amphitheaters, temples, fountains, and public buildings. For the East this age was the heyday of the city. Life there grew ever richer and more comfortable.

Trade among the provinces increased dramatically. Britain and Belgium became prime grain producers, much of their harvests going to the armies of the Rhine. Britain's wool industry probably got its start under the Romans. Italy and southern Gaul produced wine in huge quantities. Roman colonists introduced the olive to southern Spain and northern Africa, an experiment so successful that these regions produced most of the oil consumed in the western empire. In the East Syrian farmers continued to cultivate the olive, and oil production reached an all-time high. Egypt was the prime grain producer of the East, and tons of Egyptian wheat went to feed the Roman populace. The Roman army in Mesopotamia consumed a high percentage of the raw materials and manufactured products of Syria and Asia Minor. The spread of trade meant the end of isolated and self-contained economies. By the time of the five good emperors, the empire had become an economic as well as a political reality (see Map 6.4).

One of the most striking features of this period was the growth of industry in the provinces. Cities in Gaul and Germany eclipsed the old Mediterranean manufacturing centers. Italian cities were particularly hard hit by this development. Cities like Arretium and Capua had dominated the production of glass, pottery, and bronze ware. Yet in the second century C.E. Gaul and Germany took over the pottery market. Lyons in Gaul, and later Cologne, became the new center of the glassmaking industry. The cities of Gaul were nearly unrivaled in the manufacture of bronze and brass. For the first time in history, northern Europe was able to rival the Mediterranean as a producer of manufactured goods. Europe had entered fully into the economic and cultural life of the Mediterranean world.

The age of the five good emperors was generally one of peace, progress, and prosperity. The work of the Romans in northern and western Europe was a permanent contribution to the history of Western society. This period was also one of consolidation. Roads and secure sea-lanes linked the empire in one vast web. The empire had become a commonwealth of cities, and urban life was its hallmark.

## ROME AND THE EAST

Their march to empire and their growing interest in foreign peoples brought the Romans into contact with a world much larger than Europe and the Mediterranean. As early as the late republic, Roman commanders in the East encountered peoples who created order out of the chaos left by Alexander the Great and his Hellenistic successors. This meeting of West and East had two immediate effects. The first was a long military confrontation between the Romans and their Iranian neighbors. Second, Roman military expansion to the east coincided with Chinese expansion to the west, and the surprising result was a period when the major ancient civilizations of the world were in touch with one another (see "China and Rome," pages 189–190).

### Romans Versus Iranians

When Roman armies moved into Mesopotamia in 92 B.C.E., they encountered the Parthians, a people who had entered the Iranian Plateau from Central Asia in the time of the Persian kings. The disintegration of Alexander's eastern holdings enabled them to reap the harvest of his victory. They created an empire that once stretched from Armenia and Babylonia in the west to the Hellenistic kingdom of Bactria in the east. They divided their realm into large provinces, or *satrapies,* and created a flexible political organization to administer their holdings. Unlike China, however, Parthia never had a sophisticated

## ROMAN HISTORY AFTER AUGUSTUS

| PERIOD | IMPORTANT EMPERORS | SIGNIFICANT EVENTS |
|---|---|---|
| **Julio-Claudians**<br>27 B.C.E.–68 C.E. | Augustus, 27 B.C.E.–14 C.E.<br>Tiberius, 14–37<br>Caligula, 37–41<br>Claudius, 41–54<br>Nero, 54–68 | Augustan settlement<br>Beginning of the principate<br>Birth and death of Jesus<br>Expansion into northern and western Europe<br>Creation of the imperial bureaucracy |
| **Year of the Four Emperors**<br>69 | Nero<br>Galba<br>Otho<br>Vitellius | Civil war<br>Major breakdown of the concept of the principate |
| **Flavians**<br>69–96 | Vespasian, 69–79<br>Titus, 79–81<br>Domitian, 81–96 | Growing trend toward the concept of monarchy<br>Defense and further consolidation of the European frontiers |
| **Antonines**<br>96–192 | Nerva, 96–98<br>Trajan, 98–117<br>Hadrian, 117–138<br>Antoninus Pius, 138–161<br>Marcus Aurelius, 161–180<br>Commodus, 180–192 | The "golden age"—the era of the "five good emperors"<br>Economic prosperity<br>Trade and growth of cities in northern Europe<br>Beginning of barbarian menace on the frontiers |
| **Severi**<br>193–235 | Septimius Severus, 193–211<br>Caracalla, 198–217<br>Elagabalus, 218–222<br>Severus Alexander, 222–235 | Military monarchy<br>All free men within the empire given Roman citizenship |
| **"Barracks Emperors"**<br>235–284 | Twenty-two emperors in forty-nine years | Civil war<br>Breakdown of the empire<br>Barbarian invasions<br>Severe economic decline |
| **Tetrarchy**<br>284–337 | Diocletian, 284–305<br>Constantine, 306–337 | Political recovery<br>Autocracy<br>Legalization of Christianity<br>Transition to the Middle Ages in the West<br>Birth of the Byzantine Empire in the East |

bureaucracy. Nonetheless, the loose provincial organization enabled the Parthians to govern the many different peoples who inhabited their realm. The Romans marveled at Parthia's success, as the Greek geographer Strabo (ca 65 B.C.E.–19 C.E.) attests: "and now they rule so much territory and so many people that they have become in a way rivals of the Romans in the greatness of their empire."[7] In the process the Parthians won their place in history as the heirs of the Persian Empire.

Although Augustus sought peace with the Parthians, later Roman emperors, beginning with Nero in 58 C.E., struggled to wrest Armenia and Mesopotamia from them. Until their downfall in 226, the Parthians met the Roman advance to the east with iron and courage.

The Romans found nothing to celebrate in the eclipse of the Parthians, for their place was immediately taken by the Sasanids, a people indigenous to southern Iran. As early as 230 the Sasanids launched a campaign to the west, which the Romans blunted. The setback was only temporary, for in 256 the great Persian king Shapur overran Mesopotamia and the Roman province of Syria. Four years later Shapur defeated the legions of the emperor Valerian, whom he took prisoner. Thereafter the Romans and Sasanids fought long, bitter, and destructive wars in western Asia as the Romans battled to save their eastern provinces. Not until the reigns of Diocletian and Constantine was Roman rule again firmly established in western Asia.

### Trade and Contact

Although warfare between Roman emperors and Iranian kings disrupted western Asia, it did not prevent the East-West trade that had become firmly established in Hellenistic times (see pages 133–134). Iran served as the crossroads of East and West, and the Parthians eagerly filled the role of middlemen. Chinese merchants sold their wares to the Parthians at the Stone Tower, located in modern Tashkurghan in Afghanistan. The Parthians then carried the goods overland to Mesopotamia or Egypt, where they were shipped throughout the Roman Empire. Silk was still a major shipment from East to West, along with such luxuries as gems, gold, silver, spices, and perfumes. The Romans traded glassware, statuettes, and slaves trained as jugglers and acrobats. The Parthians added exotic fruits, rare birds, ostrich eggs, and other dainties desired in China. (See the feature "Global Trade: Pottery" on pages 170–171.)

Rarely did a merchant travel the entire distance from China to Mesopotamia. The Parthians tried to prevent the Chinese and Romans from making direct contact—and thus learning how large a cut the Parthians took in commercial transactions. The trade fostered urban life in Parthia, as cities arose and prospered. The Parthians themselves became important consumers of goods, contributing to the volume of trade and reinforcing East-West commercial ties.

More than goods passed along these windswept roads. Ideas, religious lore, and artistic inspiration also traveled the entire route. A fine example of how ideas and artistic influence spread across long distances is a Parthian coin that caught the fancy of an artist in China. The coin bore an inscription—a practice the Parthians had adopted from the Greeks—and although the artist could not read it, he used the lettering as a motif on a bronze vessel. Similarly, thoughts, ideas, and literary works found ready audiences; Greek plays were performed at the court of the Parthian king. At a time when communication was difficult and often dangerous, trade routes were important avenues for the spread of knowledge about other societies.

This was also an era of exciting maritime exploration. Roman ships sailed from Egyptian ports to the mouth of the Indus River, where they traded local merchandise and wares imported by the Parthians. Merchants who made the voyage had to contend with wind, shoal waters, and pirates. Despite such dangers and discomforts, hardy mariners pushed into the Indian Ocean and beyond, reaching Malaya, Sumatra, and Java.

Direct maritime trade between China and the West began in the second century C.E. The period of this contact coincided with the era of Han greatness in China. It was the Han emperor Wu Ti who took the momentous step of opening the Silk Road to the Parthian empire. Indeed, a later Han emperor sent an ambassador directly to the Roman Empire by sea. The ambassador, Kan Ying, sailed to the Roman province of Syria, where during the reign of the Roman emperor Nerva (96–98) he became the first Chinese official to have a firsthand look at the Greco-Roman world. Kan Ying enjoyed himself thoroughly, and in 97 delivered a fascinating report of his travels to his emperor:

*The inhabitants of that country are tall and well-proportioned, somewhat like the Chinese, whence they are called* Ta-ts'in. *The country contains much gold, silver, and rare precious stones . . . corals, amber, glass . . . gold embroidered rugs and thin silk-cloth and asbestos cloth. All the rare gems of other foreign countries come from there. They make coins of gold and silver. Ten units of silver are worth one of gold. They traffic by sea with An-hsi (Parthia) and Tien-chu (India), the profit of which trade is ten-fold. They are honest in their transactions and there are no double prices. Cereals are always cheap. . . . Their kings always desired to send embassies to China, but the An-hsi (Parthians) wished to carry on trade with them in Chinese silks, and it is for this reason that they were cut off from communication.*[8]

## THE EMPIRE IN CRISIS

The era of the five good emperors gave way to a period of chaos and stress. During the third century C.E. the Roman Empire was stunned by civil wars and barbarian invasions. By the time peace was restored, the economy was shattered, cities had shrunk in size, and agriculture was becoming manorial. In the disruption of the third century and the reconstruction of the fourth, the medieval world had its origins.

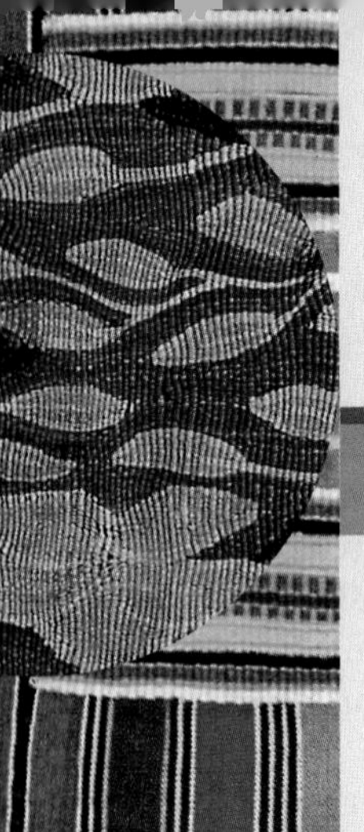

# GLOBAL TRADE

## POTTERY

Today we often consider pottery in utilitarian and decorative terms, but it served a surprisingly large number of purposes in the ancient world. Families used earthen pottery for cooking and tableware, for storing grains and liquids, and for lamps. On a larger scale pottery was used for the transportation and protection of goods traded overseas.

The creation of pottery dates back to the Neolithic period. Pottery required few resources to make, as potters needed only abundant sources of good clay and wheels upon which to throw their vessels. Once made, the pots were baked in specially constructed kilns. Although the whole process was relatively simple, skilled potters formed groups that made utensils for entire communities. Later innovations occurred when the artisans learned to glaze their pots by applying a varnish before baking them in a kiln.

The earliest potters focused on coarse ware: plain plates, cups, and cooking pots that remained virtually unchanged throughout antiquity. Increasingly, however, potters began to decorate these pieces with simple designs. In this way pottery became both functional and decorative. One of the most popular pieces was the amphora, a large two-handled jar with

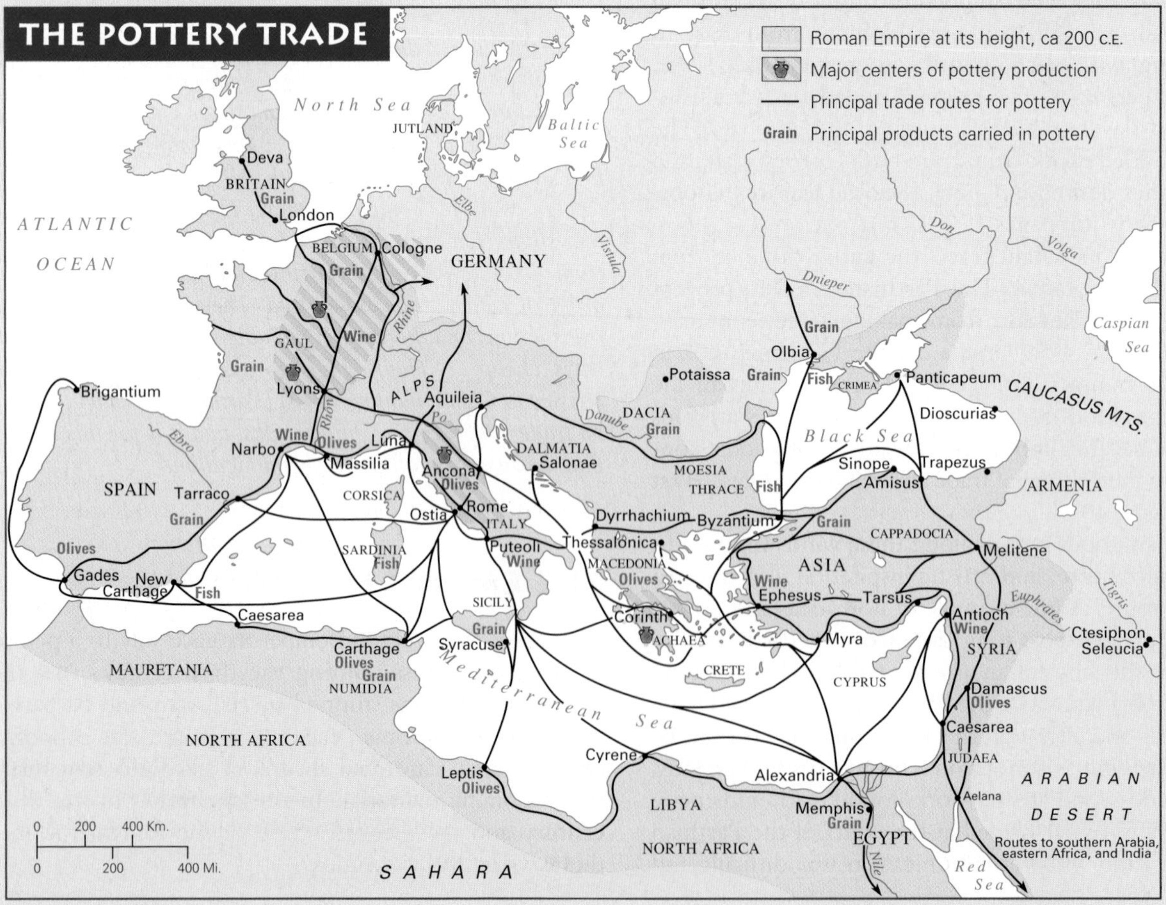

### THE POTTERY TRADE

Roman Empire at its height, ca 200 C.E.

Major centers of pottery production

Principal trade routes for pottery

Grain — Principal products carried in pottery

*The Greeks captured Troy by concealing themselves in a wooden horse, which the Trojans pulled into the city. On this piece from a pot found in Mykonos, probably dating to the seventh century* B.C.E., *Greeks have just launched their attack from inside the horse.* (Archaeological Receipts Fund, Athens)

a wide mouth, a round belly, and a base. It became the workhorse of maritime shipping because it protected contents from water and rodents, was easy and cheap to produce, and could be reused. Amphoras contained goods as different as wine and oil, spices and unguents, dried fish and pitch. The amphora's dependability and versatility kept it in use from the fourth century B.C.E. to the beginning of the Middle Ages.

In classical Greece individual potters sold their wares directly to local customers or traders; manufacturer and buyer alone determined the quantity of goods for sale and their price. In the Hellenistic and Roman periods amphoras became common throughout the Mediterranean and carried goods eastward to the Black Sea, Persian Gulf, and Red Sea. The Ptolemies of Egypt sent amphoras and their contents even farther, to Arabia, eastern Africa, and India. Thus merchants and mariners who had never seen the Mediterranean depended on these containers.

Other pots proved as useful as the amphora, and all became a medium of decorative art. By the eighth century B.C.E. Greek potters and artists began to decorate their wares by painting them with patterns and scenes from mythology, legend, and daily life. They portrayed episodes such as the chariot race at Patroclus's funeral (see page 110) or battles from the *Iliad* (see page 112). Some portrayed the gods, such as Dionysos at sea (see page 104). These images widely spread knowledge of Greek religion and culture. In the West, especially the Etruscans in Italy and the Carthaginians in North Africa eagerly welcomed the pots, their decoration, and their ideas. The Hellenistic kings shipped these pots as far east as China. Pottery thus served as a cultural exchange among people scattered across huge portions of the globe.

The Romans took the manufacture of pottery to an advanced stage by introducing a wider range of vessels for new purposes. The Roman ceramic trade spread from Italy throughout the Mediterranean. The Roman army provides the best example of how this ordinary industry affected the broader culture. Especially on the European frontiers the army used its soldiers to produce the pottery it needed. These soldiers made their own Italian *terra sigallata,* which was noted for its smooth red glaze. Native potters immediately copied this style, thus giving rise to local industries. Indeed, terra sigallata remained the dominate pottery style in northern Europe until the seventh century C.E. When Roman soldiers retired, they often settled where they had served, especially if they could continue their trades. Such ordinary Romans added local ideas to their craft. This exchange resulted in a culture that was becoming European, rather than just Roman, and extended into Britain, France, the Low Countries, and southern Germany.

## Civil Wars and Invasions in the Third Century

After the death of Marcus Aurelius, the last of the five good emperors, his son Commodus, a man totally unsuited to govern the empire, came to the throne. His misrule led to his murder and a renewal of civil war. After a brief but intense spasm of fighting, the African general Septimius Severus defeated other rival commanders and established the Severan dynasty (193–235 C.E.). Although Septimius Severus was able to stabilize the empire, his successors proved incapable of disciplining the legions. When the last of the Severi was killed by one of his own soldiers, the empire plunged into still another grim, destructive, and this time prolonged round of civil war.

Over twenty different emperors ascended the throne in the forty-nine years between 235 and 284, and many rebels died in the attempt to seize power. So many military commanders seized rule that the middle of the third century has become known as the age of the barracks emperors. The Augustan principate had become a military monarchy, and that monarchy was nakedly autocratic.

The first and most disastrous result of the civil wars was trouble on the frontiers. It was Rome's misfortune that this era of anarchy coincided with immense movements of barbarian peoples, still another example of the effects of mass migrations in ancient history, this time against one of the best organized empires of antiquity. Historians still dispute the precise reason for these migrations, though their immediate cause was pressure from tribes moving westward across Asia. In the sixth century C.E. Jordanes, a Christianized Goth, preserved the memory of innumerable wars among the barbarians in his *History of the Goths.* Goths fought Vandals; Huns fought Goths. Steadily the defeated and displaced tribes moved toward the Roman frontiers. Finally, like "a swarm of bees"—to use Jordanes's image—the Goths burst into Europe in 258 C.E.

When the barbarians reached the Rhine and Danube frontiers, they often found huge gaps in the Roman defenses. During much of the third century C.E. bands of Goths devastated the Balkans as far south as Greece. The Alamanni, a Germanic people, at one point entered Italy and reached Milan before they were beaten back. Meanwhile, the Franks, still another Germanic folk, invaded eastern and central Gaul and northeastern Spain. Saxons from Scandinavia sailed into the English Channel in search of loot. In the East the Sasanids overran Mesopotamia. If the Roman army had been guarding the borders instead of creating and destroying emperors, none of these invasions would have been possible. The barracks emperors should be credited with one accomplishment, however: they fought barbarians when they were not fighting one other. Only that kept the empire from total ruin.

## Reconstruction Under Diocletian and Constantine (284–337 C.E.)

At the close of the third century C.E. the emperor Diocletian (r. 284–305) put an end to the period of turmoil. Repairing the damage done in the third century was the major work of the emperor Constantine (r. 306–337) in the fourth. But the price was high.

Under Diocletian, the princeps became *dominus*—"lord." The emperor claimed that he was "the elect of God"—that he ruled because of God's favor. Constantine even claimed to be the equal of Jesus' first twelve followers.

No mere soldier but rather an adroit administrator, Diocletian gave serious thought to the empire's ailments. He recognized that the empire and its difficulties had become too great for one man to handle. He also realized that during the third century provincial governors had frequently used their positions to foment or participate in rebellions. To solve the first of these problems, Diocletian divided the empire into a western and an eastern half. Diocletian assumed direct control of the eastern part; he gave the rule of the western part to a colleague, along with the title *augustus,* which had become synonymous with *emperor.* Diocletian and his fellow augustus further delegated power by appointing two men to assist them. Each man was given the title *caesar* to indicate his exalted rank. Although this system is known as the **Tetrarchy** because four men ruled the empire, Diocletian was clearly the senior partner and final source of authority.

Each half of the empire was further split into two prefectures, each governed by a prefect responsible to an augustus. Diocletian reduced the power of the old provincial governors by dividing provinces into smaller units. He organized the prefectures into small administrative units called *dioceses,* which were in turn subdivided into small provinces. Provincial governors were also deprived of their military power, retaining only their civil and administrative duties.

Diocletian's political reforms were a momentous step. The Tetrarchy soon failed, but Diocletian's division of the empire into two parts became permanent. Constantine and later emperors tried hard but unsuccessfully to keep the empire together. Throughout the fourth century C.E. the eastern and the western sections drifted apart. In later centuries the western part witnessed the

**The Arch of Constantine** To celebrate the victory that made him emperor, Constantine built his triumphal arch in Rome. Rather than decorate the arch with the inferior work of his own day, Constantine plundered other Roman monuments, including those of Trajan and Marcus Aurelius. *(C. M. Dixon/Photo Resources)*

fall of Roman government and the rise of barbarian kingdoms, while the eastern empire evolved into the majestic Byzantine Empire.

The most serious immediate matters confronting Diocletian and Constantine were economic, social, and religious. They needed additional revenues to support the army and the imperial court. Yet the wars and the barbarian invasions had caused widespread destruction and poverty. The fighting had struck a serious blow to Roman agriculture, which the emperors tried to revive. Christianity had become too strong either to ignore or to crush. The responses to these problems by Diocletian, Constantine, and their successors helped create the economic and social patterns that medieval Europe inherited.

The barracks emperors had dealt with economic hardship by depreciating the currency, cutting the silver content of coins until money was virtually worthless. As a result, the entire monetary system fell into ruin. In Egypt governors had to order bankers to accept imperial money. The immediate result was crippling inflation throughout the empire.

The empire was less capable of recovery than in earlier times. Wars and invasions had disrupted normal commerce and the means of production and had hit the cities especially hard. Markets were disrupted, and travel became dangerous. Craftsmen, artisans, and traders rapidly left devastated regions. Cities were no longer places where trade and industry thrived. The devastation of the countryside increased the difficulty of feeding and supplying the cities. So extensive was the destruction that many wondered whether the ravages could be repaired at all.

The response of Diocletian and Constantine to these problems was marked by compulsion, rigidity, and loss of individual freedom. Diocletian's attempt to curb inflation illustrates the methods of absolute monarchy. In a move unprecedented in Roman history, he issued an edict that fixed maximum prices and wages throughout the empire. The measure proved a failure because it was unrealistic as well as unenforceable.

With the monetary system in ruins, most imperial taxes became payable in kind—that is, in goods or produce instead of money. The major drawback of payment in kind is its demands on transportation. Goods have to be moved from where they are grown or manufactured to where they are needed. Accordingly, the emperors locked into their occupations all people involved in the growing, preparation, and transportation of food and essential commodities. A baker or shipper could not go into any other business, and his son took up the trade at his death. The late Roman Empire had a place for everyone, and everyone had a place.

The late Roman heritage to medieval Europe is most evident in agriculture. During the third century C.E. many free tenant farmers were killed or abandoned farms that had been ravaged in the fighting. Consequently, large tracts of land lay deserted. Great landlords with ample resources began to reclaim land and amass the huge estates that were the forerunners of medieval manors. In return for the protection and security that landlords could offer, free men and their families became the landlords' clients. To ensure a steady supply of labor for themselves, the landlords bound the free men to the soil. Henceforth they worked their patrons' land, not their own, and could not move elsewhere. Free men and women were in effect becoming serfs.

## The Acceptance of Christianity

In religious affairs Constantine took the decisive step of recognizing Christianity as a legitimate religion. No longer would Christians suffer persecution for their beliefs as they had occasionally experienced earlier. Constantine himself died a Christian in 337. Why had the pagans persecuted Christians in the first place? Polytheism is by nature tolerant of new gods and accommodating in religious matters. Why was Christianity singled out for violence? These questions are still matters of scholarly debate, but some broad answers can be given.

A splendid approach to these problems has come from the eminent Italian scholar Marta Sordi.[9] Confronting a very complicated topic, she offers evidence that the Christians exaggerated the degree of pagan hostility to them and that most of the gory stories about the martyrs are fictitious. There were indeed some cases of pagan persecution of the Christians, but with few exceptions they were local and sporadic. Even Nero's notorious persecution was temporary and limited to Rome. No constant persecution of Christians occurred. Instead, pagans and Christians alike enjoyed long periods of tolerance and even friendship. Nonetheless, some pagans thought that Christians were atheists because they scorned the traditional pagan gods. Christians in fact either denied the existence of pagan gods or called them evil spirits. They went so far as to urge people not to worship pagan gods. In turn pagans, who believed in their gods as fervently as the Christians believed in their one god, feared that the gods would withdraw their favor from the Roman Empire because of Christian blasphemy.

At first many pagans genuinely misunderstood Christian practices and rites. Even educated and cultured people like the historian Tacitus opposed Christianity because they saw it as a bizarre new sect. Tacitus believed that Christians hated the whole human race. As a rule, early Christians kept to themselves. Romans distrusted and feared their exclusiveness, which seemed unsociable and even subversive. They thought the Lord's Supper, at which Christians said that they ate and drank the body and blood of Jesus, was an act of cannibalism. Pagans also thought that Christians indulged in immoral and indecent rituals. They considered Christianity one of the worst of the Eastern mystery cults, for one of the hallmarks of many of those cults was disgusting rituals.

Another source of misunderstanding was that the pagans did not demand that Christians *believe* in pagan gods. Greek and Roman religion was never a matter of belief or ethics. It was purely a religion of ritual. One of the clearest statements of pagan theological attitudes comes from the Roman senator Symmachus in the later fourth century C.E.: "We watch the same stars; heaven is the same for us all; the same universe envelops us: what importance is it in what way anyone looks for truth? It is impossible to arrive by one route at such a great secret."[10] Yet Roman religion was inseparable from the state. An attack on one was an attack on the other. The Romans were being no more fanatical or intolerant than the eighteenth-century English judge who declared the Christian religion part of the law of the land. All the pagans expected was performance of the ritual act, a small token of sacrifice. Those Christians who sacrificed went free, no matter what they personally believed.

As time went on, pagan hostility decreased. Pagans realized that Christians were not working to overthrow the state and that Jesus was no rival of Caesar. The emperor Trajan forbade his governors to hunt down Christians. Trajan admitted that he thought Christianity an abomination, but he preferred to leave Christians in peace.

The stress of the third century, however, seemed to some emperors the punishment of the gods. What else could account for such anarchy? With the empire threatened on every side, a few emperors thought that one way to appease the gods was by offering them the proper sacrifices. Such sacrifices would be a sign of loyalty to the empire, a show of Roman solidarity and religious piety. Consequently, a new wave of persecutions began out of desperation. Although the Christians depicted the emperor Diocletian as a fiend, he persecuted them in the hope that the gods would restore their blessings on Rome. Yet even these persecutions were never very widespread or long-lived; most pagans were not greatly sympathetic to the new round of persecutions. Pagan and Christian alike must have been relieved when Constantine legalized the Christian religion.

In time the Christian triumph would be complete. In 380 the emperor Theodosius made Christianity the official religion of the Roman Empire. At that point Christians began to persecute the pagans for their beliefs. History had come full circle.

## The Construction of Constantinople

The triumph of Christianity was not the only event that made Constantine's reign a turning point in Roman history. Constantine took the bold step of building a new capital for the empire. Constantinople, the New Rome, was constructed on the site of Byzantium, an old Greek city on the Bosporus. Throughout the third century, emperors had found Rome and the West hard to defend. The eastern part of the empire was more easily defensible and escaped the worst of the barbarian devastation. It was wealthy and its urban life still vibrant. Moreover Christianity was more widespread in the East than in the West, and the city of Constantinople was intended to be a Christian center.

## Late Antiquity

Recent scholars have identified the period from the third to the eighth centuries C.E. as "late antiquity," arguing that in this time the Mediterranean world witnessed tremendous religious, social, political, and intellectual ferment. The world of the pax Romana, over which Augustus had extended order, harmony, and security, clustered around the Mediterranean Sea. An aristocracy of uniform culture, taste, and language governed that world.

By about 500 C.E., however, a clear political, geographical, and cultural division existed between East and West. The East remained Mediterranean-centered, ruled by a Roman—that is, a Byzantine—emperor (see Chapter 8). It was primarily urban, and the sophisticated life of the populous cities was maintained by a lively trade. In the West Roman imperial power decayed, as did both commerce and cities. Economic life meant agriculture, and the increasingly isolated urban villa was the typical form of organized life.

The most important socioeconomic feature of late antiquity was the enormous and widening gulf between rich and poor. The western senatorial aristocracy, though still open to rising talent from below, was five times more wealthy than senators in the first century. In the East the average senator earned 120,000 gold pieces a year, but a merchant earned only 200 and a peasant a mere 5. An oppressive tax system forced many poor farmers to sell their farms, and fewer and fewer people accumulated more and more land.

The growth of Christianity was another major difference in the world of late antiquity. The religion grew in terms of both numbers of adherents and imperial acceptance. Christians offered a strong sense of community by maintaining their services in the third century, when traditional Roman public ceremonies were declining. Further, church leaders began to play larger roles in civil society. Between 200 and 500, as Roman civil officials neglected or were unable to perform their duties, or as they retreated from the cities for the luxury of their rural estates, Christian officials assumed public responsibilities. They ensured that pipes and aqueducts were repaired, arranged for relief when famine struck, and even organized defenses against barbarian attacks.

The Christianization of the Roman world left its mark on intellectual life as well. The aristocratic culture of late antiquity had sought leisure to develop the mind. By 600 the pagan, educated, senatorial elite had all but disappeared—or become church leaders. These leaders were busy, with little time for leisure. Nor did they wish for their followers to study pagan writers, lest they learn pagan superstitions. In 529 the emperor Justinian (see page 225) prohibited pagans from holding positions in public education. As a result the Academy of Athens, since its founding by Plato a center of education in the eastern Mediterranean, was closed.

## SUMMARY

The Romans conquered the Mediterranean world only to find that conquest required them to change their way of life. Politically, their city-state constitution broke down and expired in the wars of the republic. Even so, men like Caesar and later Augustus sought new solutions to the problems confronting Rome. The result was a system of government capable of administering an empire with justice and fairness. Out of the failure of the republic arose the pax Romana of the empire.

The Roman Empire created by Augustus nearly collapsed before being restored by Diocletian and Constantine. Constantine's legalization and patronage of Christianity and his shift of the capital from Rome to Constantinople marked a new epoch in Western history as the ancient world gave way to the medieval. In the process the Roman Empire came into direct contact with its Asian neighbors, sometimes in anger but more often in peace. The force of Rome did not end with its political eclipse. The period known as late antiquity preserved the essence of Greco-Roman civilization and its assimilation of Judeo-Christian culture for the European Middle Ages and ultimately for the world.

The true heritage of Rome is its long tradition of law and freedom. Under Roman law and government, the empire enjoyed relative peace and security for extensive periods of time. Through Rome the best of ancient thought and culture was preserved to make its contribution to modern life. Perhaps no better epitaph for Rome can be found than the words of Virgil:

*While rivers shall run to the sea,*
*While shadows shall move across the valleys of mountains,*
*While the heavens shall nourish the stars,*
*Always shall your honor and your name and your fame endure.*[11]

## KEY TERMS

patricians
plebeians
senate
praetor
provinces
ius civile (civil law)
ius naturale (natural law)
Struggle of the Orders
tribunes
paterfamilias
manumission
latifundia
pax Romana
First Triumvirate
princeps civitatis
Messiah
five good emperors
gladiators
Tetrarchy

## NOTES

1. Polybius, *The Histories* 1.1.5. John Buckler is the translator of all uncited quotations from foreign languages in Chapter 6.
2. Sallust, *War with Catiline* 10.1–3.
3. Ovid, *Fasti* 2.535–539.
4. Plutarch, *Life of Tiberius Gracchus* 9.5–6.
5. *Corpus Inscriptionum Latinarum,* vol. 6 (Berlin: G. Reimer, 1882), no. 9792.
6. Ibid., vol. 6, no. 14672.
7. Strabo, 11.9.2.
8. Quoted in W. H. Schoff, *The Periplus of the Erythraean Sea* (London: Longmans, Green, 1912), p. 276.
9. See M. Sordi, *The Christians and the Roman Empire,* trans. A. Bedini (Norman: University of Oklahoma Press, 1986).
10. Symmachus, *Relations* 3.10.
11. Virgil, *Aeneid* 1.607–609.

## SUGGESTED READING

H. H. Scullard gives a broad account of Roman history in *A History of the Roman World, 753–146 B.C.,* 4th ed. (1993). For the Etruscan place in Italian history, a good starting place is H. Barker and T. Rasmussen, *The Etruscans* (1997), and J. F. Hall, ed., *Etruscan Italy* (1998). Various works treat aspects of early Roman history, notably C. J. Smith, *Early Rome and Latium: Economy and Society, c. 1000 to 500 B.C.* (1996), and A. Gtandazzi, *The Foundation of Rome* (1997), which explores the mythology and history of Rome's origins. D. J. Gargola, *Lands, Laws, and Gods* (1995), examines how Roman magistrates regulated the public lands of Rome. Similar is N. Morley, *Metropolis and Hinterland* (1996), a study of how Romans and Italians integrated their economies between 200 B.C.E. and 200 C.E. Military aspects of this development are the concern of A. K. Goldsworthy, *The Roman Army at War, 100 B.C.–A.D. 200* (1996), and C. Brunn, ed., *The Roman Middle Republic, ca. 400–133 B.C.* (2000), though unfortunately many of the chapters in the latter are in foreign languages.

On Roman political developments, the place to start is A. N. Sherwin-White, *Roman Citizenship,* 2d ed. (1973), still a classic work. J. F. Gardner, *Being a Roman Citizen* (1993), is a broad work that includes material on ex-slaves, the lower classes, and much else. E. S. Gruen explores the effects of Greek ideas, literature, and learning on Roman life in *Studies in Greek Culture and Roman Policy* (1996). The topic of Roman intellectual and cultural growth has become a very popular pursuit and is the subject of E. Fantham, *Roman Literary Culture* (1996), and D. Feeney, *Literature and Religion at Rome* (1997).

Some good general treatments of the empire include J. Wacher, ed., *The Roman World,* 2 vols. (1987), and R. MacMullen, *Enemies of the Roman Order* (1993), which treats the ways in which the Romans dealt with aliens and sometimes hostile behavior within the empire. MacMullen's

*Romanization in the Time of Augustus* (2000) analyzes how the emperor spread Roman concepts throughout the empire. D. Noy, *Foreigners at Rome* (2000), studies the mingling of visitors and natives in the city. D. J. Breeze and B. Dobson, *Roman Officers and Frontiers* (1993), analyzes the careers of officers in the defense of the empire. A. Goldsworthy, *Roman Warfare* (2000), concisely treats warfare from republican to imperial times. B. Isaac, *The Near East Under Roman Rule* (1997), and H. Wolfram, *The Roman Empire and Its Germanic Peoples* (1997), deal with specific but broad parts of the empire.

K. D. White, *Roman Farming* (1970), remains the best treatment of the basic economic activity of most Romans. Work on Roman social history is quickly expanding and producing a wealth of material, including S. Treggiari, *Roman Marriage* (1991); B. Rawson and P. Weaver, *The Roman Family in Italy* (1997); R. A. Baumann, *Women and Politics in Ancient Rome* (1992); and E. Eyben, *Restless Youth in Ancient Rome* (1993). G. A. Williams, *Roman Homosexuality* (1999), is the first systematic study of the subject. Still the best treatment of economics and society combined is M. Rostovtzeff, *The Economic and Social History of the Roman Empire,* 2 vols., rev. ed. (1957).

Social aspects of the empire are the subject of L. A. Thompson, *Romans and Blacks* (1989), while J. Humphrey, *Roman Circuses and Chariot Racing* (1985), covers a favorite Roman sport. C. A. Barton, *The Sorrows of the Ancient Romans* (1993), makes a valiant attempt at explaining the Roman fascination with gladiatorial games. K. R. Bradley, *Slaves and Masters in the Roman Empire* (1988), discusses social controls in a slaveholding society.

Christianity, paganism, Judaism, and their relations have received great attention. The place to start is N. Hyldahl, *The History of Early Christianity* (1997). Other works include J. D. Crossen, *The Historical Jesus* (1992), and J. Meier, *A Marginal Jew* (1992), which examines the Jewish origins of Jesus. On the Gospels and early Christianity, the following works are among the most challenging: J. E. Powell, *The Evolution of the Gospel* (1994), and B. L. Mack, *The Lost Gospel of Q* (1993), which traces the earliest elements of the Gospels. Both S. G. Burnett, *From Christian Hebraism to Jewish Studies* (1996), and J. H. Hexter, *The Judaeo-Christian Tradition,* 2d ed. (1995), deal with Judaism and Christianity in their mutual impact. B. W. Winter, *After Paul Left Corinth* (2001), treats Paul's wider missionary work in the Roman world. L. V. Rutgers, *Subterranean Rome* (2000), serves as a guide to the catacombs. For early Christian society, see D. F. Sawyer, *Women and Religion in the First Christian Centuries* (1996); R. S. Kraemer et al., *Women and Christian Origins* (1998); and H. Moxnes, ed., *Constructing Early Christian Families* (1997).

On Constantine, the man and his significance, see R. MacMullen, *Constantine* (1988), and H. A. Pohlsander, *The Emperor Constantine* (1997). Good introductions to late antiquity are provided by P. Brown, *The World of Late Antiquity, A.D. 150–750* (1989), and R. L. Webste and M. Brown, eds., *The Transformation of the Roman World, A.D. 400–900* (1997).

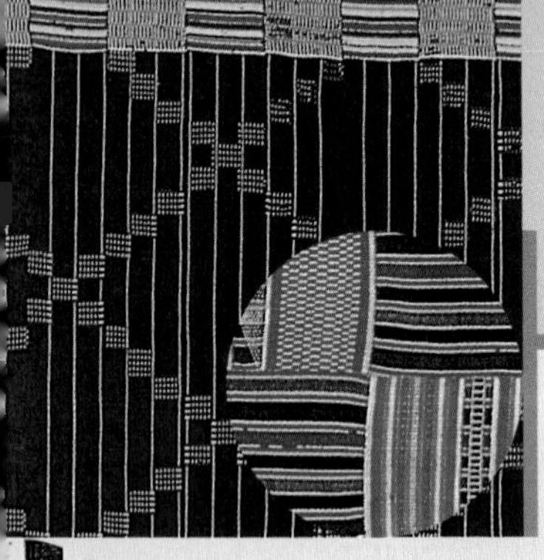

# LISTENING TO THE PAST

## Titus Flamininus and the Liberty of the Greeks

*After his arrival in Greece in 197 B.C.E., Titus Flamininus defeated the Macedonians in Thessaly. He next sent his recommendations to the Roman senate on the terms of the peace agreement. The following year the senate sent him ten commissioners, who agreed with his ideas. The year 196 B.C.E. was also the occasion when the great Pan-Hellenic Isthmian games were regularly celebrated near Corinth. Many of the dignitaries and the most prominent people of the Hellenistic world were present. Among them was Flamininus, who came neither as a participant in the games nor solely as a spectator of them. Instead, he took the occasion to make a formal announcement about Roman policy. There in Isthmia he officially announced that Rome granted freedom to the Greeks. He assured his audience that Rome had not come as a conqueror. The eminent Greek biographer Plutarch has left a vivid account of the general response to this pronouncement.*

Accordingly, at the Isthmian games, where a great throng of people were sitting in the stadium and watching the athletic contests (since, indeed, after many years Greece had at last ceased from wars waged in hopes of freedom, and was now holding festival in time of assured peace), the trumpet signalled a general silence, and the herald, coming forward into the midst of the spectators, made proclamation that the Roman senate and Titus Quintius Flamininus proconsular general, having conquered King Philip and the Macedonians, restored to freedom, without garrisons and without imposts, and to the enjoyment of their ancient laws, the Corinthians, the Locrians, the Phocians, the Euboeans, the Achaeans of Phthiotis, the Magnesians, the Thessalians, and the Perrhaebians. At first, then, the proclamation was by no means generally or distinctly heard, but there was a confused and tumultuous movement in the stadium of people who wondered what had been said, and asked one another questions about it, and called out to have the proclamation made again; but when silence had been restored, and the herald in tones that were louder than before and reached the ears of all, had recited the proclamation, a shout of joy arose, so incredibly loud that it reached the sea. The whole audience rose to their feet, and no heed was paid to the contending athletes, but all were eager to spring forward and greet and hail the saviour and champion of Greece.

And that which is often said of the volume and power of the human voice was then apparent to the eye. For ravens which chanced to be flying overhead fell down into the stadium. The cause of this was the rupture of the air; for when the voice is borne aloft loud and strong, the air is rent asunder by it and will not support flying creatures, but lets them fall, as if they were over a vacuum, unless, indeed, they are transfixed by a sort of blow, as of a weapon, and fall down dead. It is possible, too, that in such cases there is a whirling motion of the air, which becomes like a waterspout at sea with a refluent flow of the surges caused by their very volume.

Be that as it may, had not Titus, now that the spectacle was given up, at once foreseen the rush and press of the throng and taken himself away, it would seem that he could hardly have survived the concourse of so many people about him at once and from all sides. But when they were tired of shouting about his tent, and night was already come, then, with greetings and embraces for any friends and fellow citizens whom they saw, they betook themselves to banqueting and carousing with one another. And here, their pleasure naturally increasing, they moved to reason and discourse about Greece, saying that although she had waged many wars for the sake of her freedom, she had not yet obtained a more secure or more delightful exercise of it than now, when others had striven in her behalf, and she herself, almost without a drop of blood or a pang of grief, had borne away the fairest and most enviable of prizes. Verily, they would say, valour and wisdom are rare things among men, but the rarest of all blessings is the just man. For men like Agesilaüs, or Lysander, or Nicias, or Alcibiades could indeed conduct wars well, and understood how to be victorious commanders in battles by land and sea, but they would not use their successes so as to win legitimate favour and promote the right. Indeed, if one excepts the action at Marathon, the sea-fight at Salamis, Plataea, Thermopylae, and the achievements of Cimon at the Eurymedon and about Cyprus, Greece has fought all her battles to bring servitude upon herself, and every one of her trophies stands as a memorial of her own calamity and disgrace, since she owed her overthrow chiefly to the baseness and contentiousness of her leaders. Whereas men of another race, who were thought to have only slight sparks and insignificant traces of a common remote ancestry, from whom it was astonishing that any helpful word or purpose should be vouchsafed to Greece—these men underwent the greatest perils and hardships in order to rescue Greece and set her free from cruel despots and tyrants.

So ran the thoughts of the Greeks; and the acts of Titus were consonant with his proclamations. For at once he sent Lentulus to Asia to set Bargylia free, and Stertinius to Thrace to deliver the cities and islands there from Philip's garrisons. Moreover, Publius Villius sailed to have a conference with Antiochus concerning the freedom of the Greeks who were under his sway. Titus himself also paid a visit to Chalcis, and then sailed from there to Magnesia, removing their garrisons and restoring to the peoples their constitutions. He was also appointed master of ceremonies for the Nemeian games at Argos, where he conducted the festival in the best possible manner, and once more publicly proclaimed freedom to the Greeks. Then he visited the different cities, establishing among them law and order, abundant justice, concord, and mutual friendliness. He quieted their factions and restored their exiles, and plumed himself on

This coin provides a contemporary profile of Titus Flamininus, which also illustrates Roman realism in portraiture. *(Courtesy of the Trustees of the British Museum)*

his persuading and reconciling the Greeks more than on his conquest of the Macedonians, so that their freedom presently seemed to them the least of his benefactions. . . .

. . . In the case of Titus and the Romans, . . . gratitude for their benefactions to the Greeks brought them, not merely praises, but also confidence among all men and power, and justly too. For men not only received the officers appointed by them, but actually sent for them and invited them and put themselves in their hands. And this was true not only of peoples and cities, nay, even kings who had been wronged by other kings fled for refuge into the hands of Roman officials, so that in a short time—and perhaps there was also divine guidance in this—everything became subject to them. But Titus himself took most pride in his liberation of Greece.

## QUESTIONS FOR ANALYSIS

1. Did Titus Flamininus really want peace for the Greeks, or was this a cynical propaganda gesture?
2. What caused Greek political difficulties in the first place?
3. Was the Greek response to Titus Flamininus's proclamation genuine and realistic?

*Source:* Reprinted by permission of the publishers and the Trustees of the Loeb Classical Library from *Plutarch: Volume X—Parallel Lives.* Loeb Classical Library Volume L 102, trans. B. Perrin (Cambridge, Mass.: Harvard University Press, 1921). The Loeb Classical Library® is a registered trademark of the President and Fellows of Harvard College.

The cave temples of Dunhuang are among the richest depositories of Buddhist art. These three clay statues, which attend the main Buddha in Cave 45 (eighth century C.E.), represent the Buddha's disciple Ananda, a bodhisattva, and a heavenly king. *(© Cultural Relics Data Center of China)*

CHAPTER

# 7 EAST ASIA AND THE SPREAD OF BUDDHISM, CA 200 B.C.E.–800 C.E.

## CHAPTER OUTLINE

- The Age of Empire in China
- The Spread of Buddhism Out of India
- The Second Chinese Empire: Sui (581–618) and Tang (618–907)
- The East Asian Cultural Sphere

East Asia was transformed over the millennium from 200 B.C.E. to 800 C.E. In 200 B.C.E. there was only one advanced civilization in the region that had writing, iron technology, large cities, and complex state organizations. Over the course of the next several centuries, this situation changed dramatically as war, trade, diplomacy, missionary activity, and pursuit of learning brought increased contact among the peoples of the region. Buddhism came to provide a common set of ideas and visual images for the entire area. Chinese was widely used as an international language outside its native area.

Increased communication stimulated state formation in Central Asia, Tibet, Korea, Manchuria, and Japan. The new states usually adopted political models from China. Nevertheless, by 800 each of these regions was well on its way to developing a distinct political and cultural identity. Ancient China was treated in Chapter 4, but this is the first chapter to treat Korea and Japan.

- What were the consequences of long periods of strong centralized government in China to its own people and to their neighbors?
- How did elements of the cultures of China spread to neighboring lands?
- In what ways was the spread of Buddhism similar to the spread of other world religions?

These questions are addressed in this chapter.

## THE AGE OF EMPIRE IN CHINA

In much the same period in which Rome created a huge empire, the Qin and Han rulers in China created an empire on a similar scale. Like the Roman Empire, the Chinese empire was put together through force of arms and held in place by sophisticated centralized administrative machinery.

### The Qin Unification (221–206 B.C.E.)

The year 221 B.C.E. marks the beginning of the Chinese empire and has been called "by far the most important single date in Chinese history."[1] That year the state of Qin, the state that had adopted Legalist policies (see

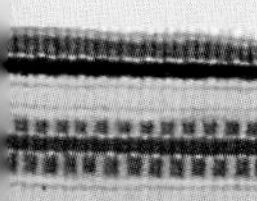

**Army of the First Emperor** The thousands of life-size ceramic soldiers buried in pits about a half mile from the First Emperor's tomb help us imagine the Qin military machine. It was the Qin emperor's concern with the afterlife that led him to construct such a lifelike guard. The soldiers were orginally painted in bright colors, and they held real bronze weapons. *(Robert Harding Picture Library)*

pages 98–99), succeeded in defeating the last of its rivals, thus unifying China for the first time in many centuries. The king of Qin decided that the title "king" was not grand enough and invented the title "emperor" (*huangdi*). He called himself the First Emperor (Shihuangdi) in anticipation of a long line of successors.

The victory of the Qin state owed much to the program of Legalist administrative, economic, and military reforms that had been in place since the mid-fourth century B.C.E. Within Qin the power of the old nobility and the patriarchal family had been undermined to create instead a direct relationship between the ruler and his subjects, based on uniformly enforced laws and punishments.

Once Qin ruled all of China, the First Emperor and his shrewd Legalist minister Li Si embarked on a sweeping program of centralization that touched the lives of nearly everyone in China. To cripple the nobility of the defunct states, the First Emperor ordered them to leave their lands and move to the capital, Xianyang (near modern Xi'an). To administer the territory that had been seized, he dispatched officials, then controlled them through a mass of regulations, reporting requirements, and penalties for inadequate performance. These officials owed their power and positions entirely to the favor of the emperor and had no hereditary rights to their offices.

To harness the enormous human resources of his people, the First Emperor ordered a census of the population. Census information helped the imperial bureaucracy to plan its activities—to estimate the costs of public works, the tax revenues needed to pay for them, and the labor force available for military service and building projects. To make it easier to administer all regions uniformly,

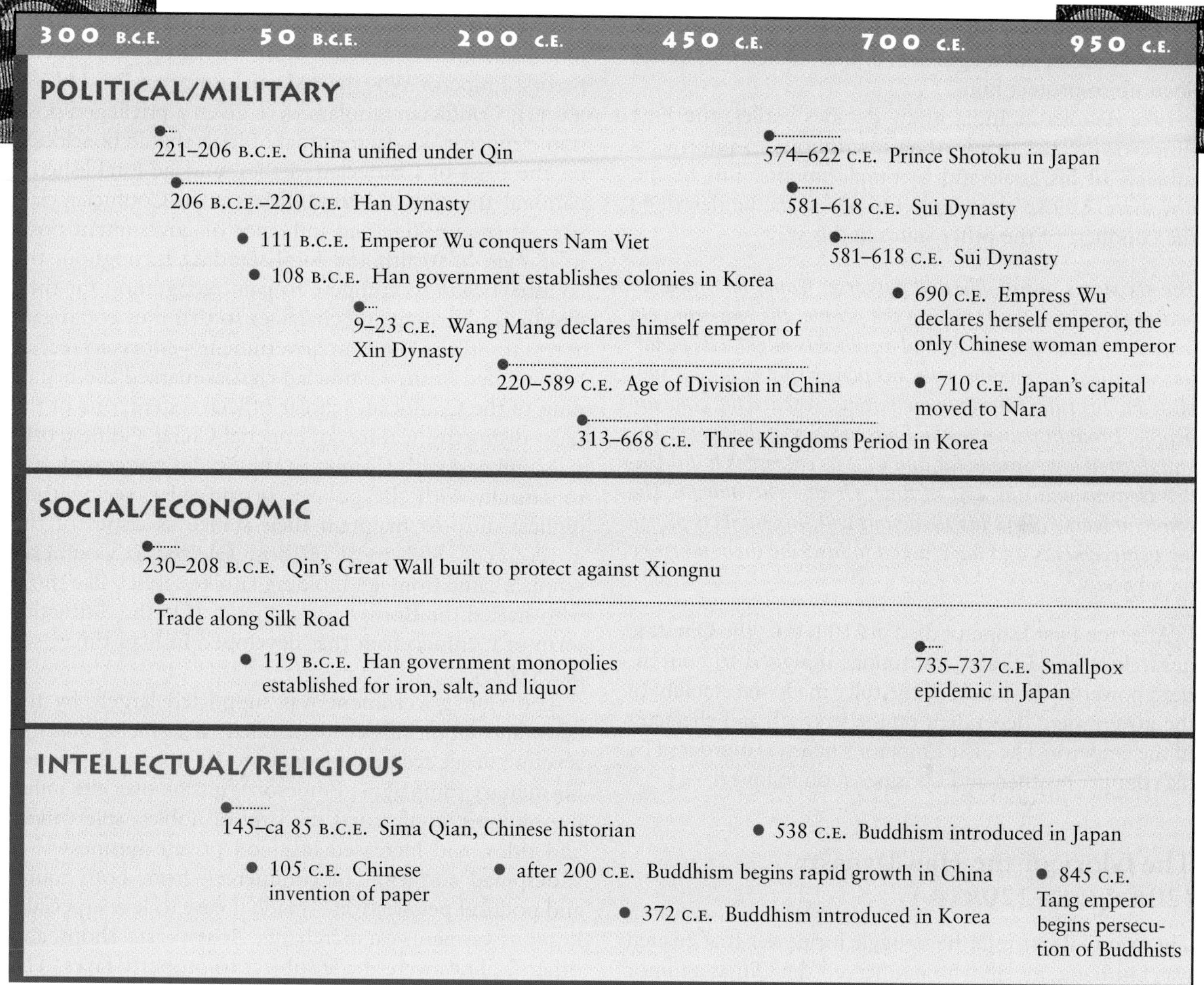


the script was standardized, along with weights, measures, coinage, even the axle lengths of carts. Private possession of arms was outlawed in order to make it more difficult for subjects to rebel. To make it easier for Qin armies to move rapidly, thousands of miles of roads were built. Investment was also made in canals that could connect rivers, making it possible to travel long distances by boat. Most of the labor on these projects came from peasants performing required corvée labor or convicts working their sentences.

300 B.C.E.
50 B.C.E.
200 C.E.
450 C.E.
700 C.E.
950 C.E.
POLITICAL/MILITARY
221–206 B.C.E. China unified under Qin
206 B.C.E.–220 C.E. Han Dynasty
111 B.C.E. Emperor Wu conquers Nam Viet
108 B.C.E. Han government establishes colonies in Korea
9–23 C.E. Wang Mang declares himself emperor of Xin Dynasty
220–589 C.E. Age of Division in China
313–668 C.E. Three Kingdoms Period in Korea
574–622 C.E. Prince Shotoku in Japan
581–618 C.E. Sui Dynasty
581–618 C.E. Sui Dynasty
690 C.E. Empress Wu declares herself emperor, the only Chinese woman emperor
710 C.E. Japan's capital moved to Nara
SOCIAL/ECONOMIC
230–208 B.C.E. Qin's Great Wall built to protect against Xiongnu
Trade along Silk Road
119 B.C.E. Han government monopolies established for iron, salt, and liquor
735–737 C.E. Smallpox epidemic in Japan
INTELLECTUAL/RELIGIOUS
145–ca 85 B.C.E. Sima Qian, Chinese historian
105 C.E. Chinese invention of paper
after 200 C.E. Buddhism begins rapid growth in China
372 C.E. Buddhism introduced in Korea
538 C.E. Buddhism introduced in Japan
845 C.E. Tang emperor begins persecution of Buddhists

Some twentieth-century Chinese historians glorified the First Emperor as a bold conqueror who let no obstacle stop him, but the traditional evaluation of him was almost entirely negative. For centuries Chinese historians castigated him as a cruel, arbitrary, impetuous, suspicious, and superstitious megalomaniac. Hundreds of thousands of subjects were drafted to build the **Great Wall,** a rammed-earth fortification along the northern border between the Qin realm and the land controlled by the nomadic Xiongnu. After Li Si complained that scholars used records of the past to denigrate the emperor's achievements and undermine popular support, the emperor had all writings other than useful manuals on topics such as agriculture, medicine, and divination collected and burned. As a result of this massive book burning, many ancient texts were lost and others could be only partly reconstructed.

Three times assassins tried to kill the First Emperor, and perhaps in consequence he became obsessed with discovering the secrets of immortality. He spent lavishly on a tomb designed to protect him in the afterlife. Although the central chambers have not yet been excavated, archaeologists have unearthed in nearby pits thousands of life-size terra-cotta figures of armed soldiers and horses lined up to protect him.

Like Ashoka in India a few decades earlier, the First Emperor erected many stone inscriptions to inform his subjects of his goals and accomplishments. But he did not share Ashoka's modesty. On one stone he described the conquest of the other states in this way:

*The six states, insatiable and perverse, would not make an end of slaughter, until, pitying the people, the emperor sent troops to punish the wicked and display his might. His penalties were just, his actions true, his power spread far, all submitted to his rule. He wiped out tyrants, rescued the common people, brought peace to the four corners of the earth. His enlightened laws spread far and wide as examples to All Under Heaven until the end of time. Great is he indeed! The whole universe obeys his sagacious will; his subjects praise his achievements and have asked to inscribe them on stone for posterity.*[2]

After the First Emperor died in 210 B.C.E., the Qin state unraveled. The Legalist institutions designed to concentrate power in the hands of the ruler made the stability of the government dependent on the strength and character of the emperor. The First Emperor's heir was murdered by his younger brother, and uprisings soon followed.

## The Glory of the Han Dynasty (206 B.C.E.–220 C.E.)

The eventual victor in the struggle for power that ensued was Liu Bang, a man who had served the Qin as a minor local official. Liu Bang (known in history as Emperor Gaozu, r. 202–195 B.C.E.) did not disband the centralized government created by the Qin, but he did remove its most unpopular features. Harsh laws were abrogated, taxes were sharply reduced, and a policy of laissez faire was adopted in an effort to promote economic recovery. At first large and nearly autonomous fiefs were given out to the new emperor's relatives, but by the middle of the second century B.C.E. most of these kingdoms had been eliminated, and almost all Han territory was under direct imperial rule. With policies of this sort, relative peace, and the extension of China's frontiers, the Chinese population grew rapidly in the first two centuries of the Han Dynasty. The census of 2 C.E. recorded a population of 58 million, the earliest indication of the large size of China's population.

In contrast to the Qin promotion of Legalism, the Han came to promote Confucianism and recruit officials on the basis of their Confucian learning or Confucian moral qualities. Under the most activist of the Han emperors, Emperor Wu (the "Martial Emperor," r. 141–87 B.C.E.), Confucian scholars were given a privileged position. Emperor Wu decreed that officials should be selected on the basis of Confucian virtues, and he established a national university to train officials in the Confucian classics. As the prestige and influence of government posts rose, men of wealth and local standing throughout the country began to compete to gain recognition for their Confucian learning and character so that they could gain access to office. The Han government's efforts to recruit men trained in the Confucian classics marked the beginning of the Confucian scholar-official system, one of the most distinctive features of imperial China. Chinese officials, imbued with Confucian values, did not comply automatically with the policies of the ruler, seeing their highest duty to maintain their stance as critics of the government. Still, most of those selected as Confucian scholars came from landholding families, much like those who staffed the Roman government. (On the distinctive form of Confucianism that developed in Han times, see page 187.)

The Han government was supported largely by the taxes and labor service demanded of farmers, but this revenue never seemed adequate to its needs. To pay for his military campaigns, Emperor Wu took over the minting of coins, confiscated the land of nobles, sold offices and titles, and increased taxes on private businesses. A widespread suspicion of commerce—from both moral and political perspectives—made it easy to levy especially heavy assessments on merchants. Boats, carts, shops, and other facilities were made subject to property taxes. The worst blow to businessmen, however, was the government's decision to enter into market competition with them by selling the commodities that had been collected as taxes. In 119 B.C.E. government monopolies were established in the production of iron, salt, and liquor. These enterprises had previously been sources of great profit for private entrepreneurs. Large-scale grain dealing also had been a profitable business, which the government now took over under the guise of equitable marketing. Grain was to be bought where it was plentiful and its price low and to be either stored in granaries or transported to areas of scarcity. This procedure was supposed to eliminate speculation in grain, provide more constant prices, and bring profit to the government.

One weakness in the Han system of government lay in the institution of hereditary succession of the throne from father to son. During the last decades of the first century B.C.E., this pattern of succession led to a series of child emperors. **Regents,** generally selected from the families of the boys' mothers, were appointed to rule in their place. One of these regents, Wang Mang, ended up deposing an infant emperor and declared himself emperor of the Xin (New) Dynasty (9–23 C.E.). Though condemned as a usurper, Wang Mang was a learned Confucian scholar who wished to implement policies described in the classics. He renamed offices, asserted state ownership of forests and swamps, built ritual halls, revived public granaries, outlawed slavery, limited private landholdings, and cut court expenses. Some of his policies, such as issuing new coins and nationalizing gold, led to economic turmoil. Matters were made worse when the Yellow River broke through its dikes and shifted course from north to south, driving millions of peasants from their homes as huge regions were flooded. Rebellion broke out, and in the ensuing warfare a Han imperial clansman succeeded in re-establishing the Han Dynasty.

## Inner Asia and the Silk Road

The difficulty of defending against the nomadic pastoral peoples to the north is a major reason China came to favor a centralized bureaucratic form of government. From the third century B.C.E. on, China needed a government capable of massive defense.

Beginning long before the Han Dynasty, China's contacts with its northern neighbors had involved both trade and military conflict. China's neighbors sought Chinese products such as silk and lacquer ware. When they did not have goods to trade or trading relations were disrupted, raiding was considered an acceptable alternative in the tribal cultures of the region. Chinese sources speak of defending against raids of "barbarians" from Shang times (ca 1500–ca 1050 B.C.E. ) on, but not until the rise of nomadism in the mid-Zhou period (fifth–fourth centuries B.C.E.) did the horsemen of the north become China's main military threat.

The economy of these nomads was based on raising sheep, goats, camels, and horses. Families lived in tents that could be taken down and moved north in summer and south in winter as groups of families moved in search of pasture. Herds were tended on horseback, and everyone learned to ride from a young age. Especially awesome from the Chinese perspective was the ability of nomad horsemen to shoot arrows while riding horseback. The typical social structure of the steppe nomads was fluid, with family and clan units linked through loyalty to tribal chiefs selected for their military prowess. Charismatic tribal leaders could form large coalitions and mobilize the entire society for war.

**Xiongnu Metalwork** The metal ornaments of the Xiongnu provide convincing evidence that they were in contact with nomadic pastoralists farther west in Asia, such as the Scythians, who also fashioned metal plaques and buckles in animal designs. This buckle or ornament is made of gold and is about three inches tall. *(The Metropolitan Museum of Art, Gift of J. Pierpont Morgan, 1917. [17.190.1672] Photograph © 1981 The Metropolitan Museum of Art)*

Chinese farmers and Inner Asian herders had such different modes of life that it is not surprising that they had little respect for each other. For most of the imperial period, Chinese farmers looked on the northern non-Chinese horsemen as gangs of bullies who thought robbing was easier than working for a living. The nomads identified glory with military might and viewed farmers as contemptible weaklings.

In the late third century B.C.E. the Xiongnu (known in the West as the Huns) formed the first great confederation of nomadic tribes (see Map 7.1). The Qin's Great Wall was built to defend against them, and the Qin sent out huge armies against them. The early Han emperors tried to make peace with them, offering generous gifts of silk, rice, cash, and even imperial princesses as brides. But these policies were controversial, since critics thought they merely strengthened the enemy. Certainly Xiongnu power did not decline, and in 166 B.C.E. 140,000 Xiongnu raided to within a hundred miles of the Chinese capital.

Emperor Wu decided that China had to push the Xiongnu back. He sent several armies of 100,000 to

300,000 troops deep into Xiongnu territory. These costly campaigns were of limited value since the Xiongnu were a moving target: fighting nomads was not like attacking walled cities. If the Xiongnu did not want to fight the Chinese troops, they simply moved their camps. To try to find allies and horses, Emperor Wu turned his attention west, toward Central Asia. From the envoy he sent into Bactria, Parthia, and Ferghana in 139 B.C.E., the Chinese learned for the first time of other civilized states comparable to China (see Map 7.1). The envoy described Ferghana as an urban society ten thousand li (about three thousand miles) west of China, where grapes were grown for wine and the horses were particularly fine. Concerning Parthia, he was impressed by the use of silver coins stamped with the image of the king's face. These regions, he reported, were familiar with Chinese products, especially silk, and did a brisk trade in them.

Emperor Wu sent an army into Ferghana and gained recognition of Chinese overlordship in the area, thus obtaining control over the trade routes across Central Asia, commonly called the **Silk Road.** The city-states along this route did not resist the Chinese presence. They could carry out the trade on which they depended more conveniently with Chinese garrisons to protect them than with rival tribes raiding them.

At the same time, Emperor Wu sent troops into northern Korea to establish military districts that would flank the Xiongnu on their eastern border. By 111 B.C.E. the Han government also had extended its rule south into what is now northern Vietnam. Thus during Emperor

**MAP 7.1 The Han Empire** The Han Dynasty asserted sovereignty over vast regions from Korea in the east to Central Asia in the west and Vietnam in the south. Once garrisons were established, traders were quick to follow, leading to considerable spread of Chinese material culture in East Asia. Chinese goods, especially silk, were in demand far beyond East Asia, promoting long-distance trade across Eurasia.

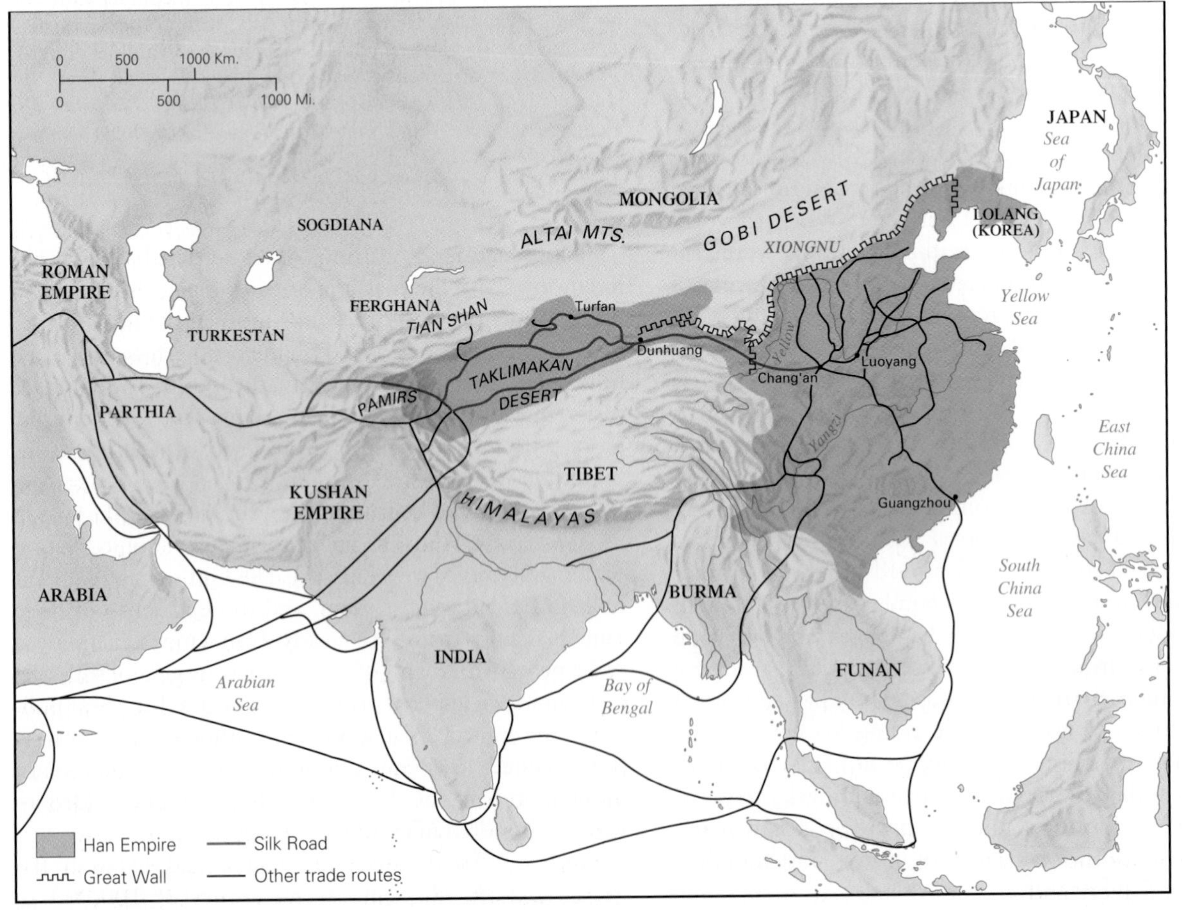

Wu's reign, the territorial reach of the Han state was vastly extended.

During the Han Dynasty, China developed a **tributary system** to regulate contact with foreign powers. States and tribes beyond its borders sent envoys bearing gifts and received gifts in return. Over the course of the dynasty the Han government's outlay on these gifts was huge, perhaps as much as 10 percent of state revenue. In 25 B.C.E., for instance, the government gave tributary states twenty thousand rolls of silk cloth and about twenty thousand pounds of silk floss. Although the tribute system was a financial burden to the Chinese, it reduced the cost of defense and offered China confirmation that it was the center of the civilized world.

The silk given to the Xiongnu and other northern tributaries often entered the trading networks of Sogdian, Parthian, and Indian merchants, who carried it by caravans all the way to Rome. There was a market both for skeins of silk thread and for silk cloth woven in Chinese or Syrian workshops. Caravans returning to China carried gold, horses, and occasionally handicrafts of West Asian origin, such as glass beads and cups. Through the trade along the Silk Road, the Chinese learned of new foodstuffs, including walnuts, pomegranates, sesame, and coriander, all of which came to be grown in China. This trade was largely carried by the two-humped Bactrian camel, which had been bred in Central Asia since the first century B.C.E. With a heavy coat of hair to withstand the bitter cold of winter, each camel could carry about five hundred pounds of cargo.

Maintaining a military presence so far from the center of China threatened to bankrupt the Han government. It tried all sorts of cost-saving policies, such as setting up self-supporting military colonies and recruiting Xiongnu tribes to serve as auxiliary forces, but none of these measures solved the government's financial problems. Vast government horse farms tried to supply the army with horses, but the number of horses was never adequate.

## Han Intellectual and Cultural Life

Confucianism made a comeback during the Han Dynasty, but it was a changed Confucianism. Although Confucian texts had fed the First Emperor's bonfires, some dedicated scholars had hidden their books, and others had memorized whole works: one ninety-year-old man was able to recite two books virtually in their entirety. The ancient books recovered in this way came to be regarded as **Confucian classics,** or canonical scriptures, containing the wisdom of the past. Scholars studied them with piety and attempted to make them more useful as sources of moral guidance by writing commentaries on them. Many Confucian scholars specialized in a single classic, with teachers passing on to their disciples their understanding of each sentence in the work. Other Han Confucians went to the opposite extreme, developing comprehensive cosmological theories that explained the world in terms of cyclical flows of yin and yang and the five phases (fire, water, earth, metal, and wood). Some used these theories to elevate the role of the emperor, who alone had the capacity to link the realms of Heaven, earth, and man. Natural disasters such as floods or earthquakes were viewed as portents that the emperor had failed in his role to maintain the proper balance among the forces of Heaven and earth.

Another important intellectual accomplishment of the Han Dynasty was the development of historical writing. The Chinese, like the Greeks, conceived of history as broader and more complex than the mere chronicling of events. Sima Qian (145–ca 85 B.C.E.) wrote a comprehensive history of China from the time of the mythical sage-kings of high antiquity to his own day, dividing his account into a chronology recounting political events, biographies of key individuals, and treatises on subjects such as geography, taxation, and court rituals. Like the Greek Thucydides (see page 116), Sima Qian believed fervently in visiting the sites where history was made, examining artifacts, and questioning people about events. He was also interested in China's geographical variations, local customs, and local history. As an official of the emperor, he had access to important people and documents and to the imperial library. The result of his research, ten years in the making, was ***Records of the Grand Historian,*** a massive work of literary and historical genius.

Sima Qian's work set the standard for Chinese historical writing, although most of the histories modeled after it covered only a single dynasty. The first of these was the work of three members of the Ban family in the first century C.E. The Ban family included China's first woman historian and scholar, Ban Zhao, who not only helped compile the history but also wrote poems and essays, notably *Admonitions for Women,* on the education of girls.

Han men of letters often had varied interests. Zhang Heng (78–139 C.E.), like the Hellenistic philosopher Eratosthenes, delved deeply into astronomy and concluded that the world is round, not flat as many of his contemporaries assumed. Not content to speculate, Zhang Heng built models to test his theories. He even designed a seismograph capable of discerning the direction in which an earthquake was taking place, though not its severity.

Perhaps the most momentous product of Han imagination was the invention of paper, which the Chinese traditionally date to 105 C.E. Scribes had previously written on strips of bamboo and wood. Fine books for the wealthy were written on silk rolls. Cai Lun, to whom the Chinese attribute the invention of paper, worked the fibers of rags, hemp, bark, and other scraps into sheets of paper. Though much less durable than wood, paper was far cheaper than silk and became a convenient means of conveying the written word. By the fifth century paper was in common use, preparing the way for the invention of printing.

Han art and literature reveal a fascination with omens, portents, spirits, immortals, and occult forces. Emperor Wu tried to make contact with the world of gods and immortals through elaborate sacrifices, and welcomed astrologers, alchemists, seers, and shamans to his court. He marveled at stories of the paradise of the Queen Mother of the West and the exploits of the Yellow Emperor, who had taken his entire court with him when he ascended to the realm of the immortals. When Wang Mang was consolidating his power, his allies kept discovering portents that a major change was to take place, an indication that they assumed most people believed in messages from Heaven. Much of this interest in immortality and communicating with the spirit world was absorbed into the emerging religion of Daoism, which also drew on the philosophical ideas of Laozi and Zhuangzi.

## Daily Life in Han China

How were ordinary people's lives affected by the creation of a huge bureaucratic empire? The lucky ones who lived in Chang'an or Luoyang, the great cities of the empire, got to enjoy the material benefits of increased long-distance trade and a boom in the production of luxury goods.

The government did not promote trade per se. The Confucian elite, like ancient Hebrew wise men, considered trade necessary but lowly. Agriculture and crafts were more honorable because they produced something, but merchants merely took advantage of others' shortages to make profits as middlemen. This attitude justified the government's takeover of the grain, iron, and salt businesses. Still, the government indirectly promoted commerce by building cities and roads. Cities attracted merchants, who set up shop in stalls in the markets, grouped together according to their wares. All the butchers, for example, congregated in one part of the market, each trying to outsell the others. The markets were also the haunts of entertainers and fortunetellers. People flocked to puppet shows and performances of jugglers and acrobats. Magic shows dazzled the impressionable, and cockfighting appealed to bloody tastes. The markets also were used for the execution of criminals, to serve as a warning to the onlooking crowd.

Government patronage helped maintain the quality of craftsmanship in the cities. By the beginning of the first century C.E., China had about fifty state-run ironworking factories. These factories smelted iron ore into ingots before turning it over to the craftsmen, who worked it into tools and other articles. Han workmen turned out iron plowshares, agricultural tools with wooden handles, and weapons and armor. Han metalsmiths were mass-producing superb crossbows long before the crossbow was dreamed of in Europe.

Iron was replacing bronze in tools, but bronzeworkers still turned out a host of goods. Bronze was prized for jewelry, mirrors, dishes, and spoons. Bronze was also used for minting coins and for precision tools such as carpenters' rules and adjustable wrenches. Surviving bronze gear-and-cog wheels bear eloquent testimony to the sophistication of Han machinery. Han craftsmen also developed lacquer work to a fine art. Because **lacquer** (made from the sap of the lac tree) creates a hard surface that withstands water, it was ideal for cups, dishes, toilet articles, and even parts of carriages.

The bulk of the population in Han times and even into the twentieth century consisted of peasants living in villages of a few hundred households. Since the Han empire, much like the contemporaneous Roman Empire, drew its strength from a large population of free peasants who contributed both taxes and labor services to the state, the government had to try to keep peasants independent and productive. The economic insecurity of small holders was described by one official in 178 B.C.E. in terms that could well have been repeated in most later dynasties:

*They labor at plowing in the spring and hoeing in the summer, harvesting in the autumn and storing foodstuff in winter, cutting wood, performing labour service for the local government, all the while exposed to the dust of spring, the heat of summer, the storms of autumn, and the chill of winter. Through all four seasons they never get a day off. They need funds to cover such obligations as entertaining guests, burying the dead, visiting the sick, caring for orphans, and bringing up the young. No matter how hard they work they can be ruined by floods or droughts, or cruel and arbitrary officials who impose taxes at the wrong times or keep changing their orders. When taxes fall due, those with produce have to sell it at half price [to raise the needed cash], and those without [anything to sell] have to borrow [at such high rates] they will have to pay back twice what they borrowed. Some as a consequence sell their lands and houses, even their children and grandchildren.*[3]

To fight peasant poverty, the government kept land taxes low, provided relief, aided migration, and promoted improvements in agriculture, such as planting two crops in alternate rows and planting a succession of carefully timed crops. Still, many peasants were left to choose between migration to areas where new lands could be opened and quasi-servile status as the dependents of a magnate. Throughout the Han period, Chinese migrants in search of land to till pushed into frontier areas, expanding Chinese domination at the expense of other ethnic groups, especially in central and south China.

Pressure on small farmers also encouraged technical innovation. The new and more effective plow introduced during the Han period was fitted with two plowshares, guided by a pair of handles, and typically pulled by a pair of oxen. Farmers used fans to blow the chaff from kernels of grain, and they used either mortars and pestles or hand mills to grind grain into flour. The Chinese also developed an elaborate system using long hammers to mill grain and pound earth. Eventually, the hammers were driven by waterpower, long before waterpower was put to this use in Europe. Irrigation was aided by brick-faced wells and pumping devices ranging from a simple pole with an attached bucket and counterweight to a sophisticated machine worked by foot. Chinese metalworking was the most advanced in the world at the time. In contrast to Roman blacksmiths, who hammered heated iron to make wrought iron tools, the Chinese knew how to liquefy iron and pour it into molds, producing tools with a higher carbon content that were harder and more durable.

Smaller and smaller farms were in part a product of the inheritance system. By Han times the common practice in China was equal division of family property among all sons, even if the resulting plots of land were tiny. This was a major change from the primogeniture of the Zhou period, when a single heir, generally the eldest son, succeeded to both aristocratic titles and responsibility to maintain ancestral rites. As free buying and selling of land spread, dividing family property became customary, making downward social mobility due to declining farm sizes quite common.

The Chinese family in Han times was much like the Roman one (see page 152) and the Indian one (see pages 314–315). In all three societies, senior males had great authority, marriages were arranged by parents, and brides normally joined their husbands' families. In Han times the Confucian virtue of filial piety was glorified to an exceptional degree, and the brief *Classic of Filial Piety,* which claimed that filial piety was the root of all virtue, gained wide circulation. The virtues of loyal wives and devoted mothers were extolled in the *Biographies of Exemplary Women,* which told the stories of women from China's past who were notable for giving their husbands good advice, knowing how to educate their sons, and sacrificing themselves when forced to choose between their fathers and husbands. The book also contained a few cautionary tales of scheming, jealous, manipulative women who brought destruction to all around them. Another notable text on women's education was written by the woman scholar Ban Zhao. Her *Admonitions for Women* urged girls to master the seven virtues appropriate to women: humility, resignation, subservience, self-abasement, obedience, cleanliness, and industry.

**Plowing with Oxen** Farmers in Han times began to use animal-drawn plows, as depicted here in a stone relief. Improvements in agricultural technology in Han times aided the geographical expansion of Chinese civilization and the growth of the Chinese population. *(From Patricia Buckley Ebrey,* The Cambridge Illustrated History of China, *1996)*

## China and Rome

The empires of China and Rome have often been compared. Both were large, complex states governed by monarchs, bureaucracies, and standing armies. Both reached directly to the people through taxation and conscription policies. Both invested in infrastructure such as roads and waterworks. Both had to work hard to keep land from becoming too concentrated in the hands of wealthy magnates, which would threaten the empires' tax base. In both empires people in areas that came under political domination were attracted to the conquerors' material goods, productive techniques, and other cultural products, which led to gradual cultural assimilation. Both China and Rome had similar frontier problems and tried similar solutions, such as using "barbarian" auxiliaries and settling soldier-colonists.

Nevertheless, the differences between Rome and Han China are worth as much notice as the similarities. The Roman Empire was linguistically and culturally more diverse than China. In China there was only one written language, but in the Roman Empire people still wrote in Greek and several other languages, and people from the East could claim more ancient civilizations. Politically, the dynastic principle was stronger in China than in Rome. Han emperors were never chosen by the army or any institution comparable to the Roman senate, nor were there any republican ideals in China. In contrast to the exclusive notion of the Roman citizen, all those in conquered areas who were willing to assimilate were encouraged to do so. The social and economic structures also differed in the two empires. In Rome slavery was much more important than in China, and merchants were more favored. Over time these differences put Chinese and Roman social and political development on rather different trajectories.

## The Fall of the Han and the Age of Division

In the second century C.E. the Han government suffered a series of blows. The succession of child emperors allowed maternal relatives of the emperors to dominate the court. Emperors turned to eunuch palace servants for help in ousting the consort families, only to find that the **eunuchs** were just as difficult to control. In 166 and 169 scholars who had denounced the eunuchs were arrested, killed, or banished from the capital and official life. Then in 184 a millenarian religious sect rose in massive revolt. The armies raised to suppress the rebels soon took to fighting among themselves. In 189 one general slaughtered two thousand eunuchs in the palace and took the Han emperor captive. After years of fighting, a stalemate was reached, with three warlords each controlling distinct territories—one in the north, one in the southeast, and one in the southwest. In 220 one of them forced the last of the Han emperors to abdicate, formally ending the Han Dynasty.

The period after the fall of the Han Dynasty is often referred to as the **Age of Division** (220–589). A brief reunification from 280 to 316 came to an end when non-Chinese who had been settling in north China since Han times seized the opportunity afforded by the political turmoil to take power. For the next two and a half centuries north China was ruled by one or more non-Chinese dynasties (the Northern Dynasties), while the south was ruled by a sequence of four short-lived Chinese dynasties, all of which were centered in the area of the present-day city of Nanjing (the Southern Dynasties).

One difficulty the rulers of the south faced was that a hereditary aristocracy entrenched itself in the higher reaches of officialdom. These families judged themselves and others on the basis of their ancestors, intermarried only with families of equivalent pedigree, and compiled lists and genealogies of the most eminent families. They saw themselves as maintaining the high culture of the Han, and many excelled in writing poetry or engaging in witty conversation. At the same time many were able to build up great landed estates worked by destitute refugees from the north. At court they often looked on the emperors of the successive dynasties as upstarts—as military men rather than men of culture. (See the feature "Individuals in Society: Tao Qian.")

Constructing a capital at Nanjing, south of the Yangzi River, had a beneficial effect on the economic development of the south. To pay for an army and to support the imperial court and aristocracy in a style that matched their pretensions, the government had to expand the area of taxable agricultural land, whether through settling migrants or converting the local inhabitants into taxpayers. The south, with its temperate climate and ample supply of water, offered nearly unlimited possibilities for such development.

In the north none of the states set up by non-Chinese lasted very long until the Xianbei set up the Northern Wei Dynasty (386–534). During the second half of the fifth century, the Northern Wei rulers adopted a series of policies designed to strengthen the state. To promote agricultural production, they instituted an "equal-field" system to distribute land to peasants. The capital was moved from the northern border near the Great Wall to the ancient city of Luoyang. Chinese-style clothing and customs were adopted at court, and Chinese was made the official language. The tribesmen, who still formed the main military force, saw themselves marginalized by these policies and rebelled in 524. For the next fifty years north China was torn apart by struggles for power.

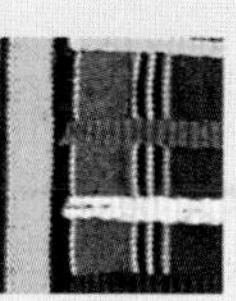

## TAO QIAN

One of China's best-loved poets, Tao Qian (365–427), lived during the turbulent period of the Age of Division. Like others of his social class, he was expected to take a post with the government. For a few years Tao worked for two or three of the generals who were busy putting down rebellions in this unsettled period, but he found the work distasteful. After a period at home to mourn his mother according to Confucian norms, he accepted an appointment as magistrate of the county of Pengce, but he held it for only eighty-two days. He is reported to have quit his post rather than entertain a visiting inspector, saying, "How could I bend my waist to this village buffoon for five pecks of rice!"

By the age of forty Tao Qian quit government service altogether and supported himself by farming. Over the next twenty-two years he experienced all the hardships of a farmer's life: the backbreaking work in the fields, crop failure through drought or insect pests, hunger for himself and his family, and, as he grew older, periods of sickness. He was not just any farmer, however, and he maintained social relations with men of education and rank, exchanging visits and poems with them.

In his poems Tao Qian celebrates the quiet life and the pleasures of books, music, and wine:

*I try a cup and all my concerns become remote.*
*Another cup and suddenly I forget even Heaven.*
*But is Heaven really far from this state?*
*Nothing is better than to trust your true self.**

Tao Qian also idealized the farming life, describing its pleasures as a genuine alternative to public service. In his poems he portrays himself as a happy rustic:

*Since youth I have not fit the common mold,*
*Instinctively loving the mountains and hills.*
*By mistake I fell into the dusty net*
*And was gone from home for thirty years.*
*A bird in a cage yearns for its native woods;*
*A fish in a pond remembers its old mountain pool.*
*Now I shall clear some land at the edge of the southern wild*
*And, clinging to the simple life, return to garden and field,*
*To my two-acre lot,*
*My thatched cottage of eight or nine rooms*
*With elms and willows shading the back*
*And peach and plum trees growing in a row in the front.*†

*Tao Qian (detail), by Chen Hongshou (1599–1652).*
(Honolulu Academy of Arts, Purchase 1954 [1912.1])

Tao also wrote a eulogy for himself to be read at his funeral:

*My rice bin and wine gourd have often been empty. I have worn thin clothing in winter. Yet I have gone happily to draw water from the spring and have sung with a load of firewood on my back. In my humble thatched hut, I performed my chores day and night. As spring and autumn alternated, I busied myself in the fields. I sowed, I plowed. Things grew and multiplied. I pleased myself with the seven string zither. In winter I soaked in the sun, and in summer I bathed in the springs. I have had little rest from my work, yet my mind has always been at leisure. I enjoyed Heaven's gifts and accepted my lot, until I lived out my years.*‡

### QUESTIONS FOR ANALYSIS

1. Does Tao Qian seem more Confucian or more Daoist?
2. Does Tao reveal much of his personality in his writings? Which traits would have made him appealing to an educated audience?

* From "Drinking Alone in the Rainy Season." Translated by Patricia Ebrey.

† From "On Returning to My Garden and Fields." Translated by Patricia Ebrey.

‡ William H. Nienhauser, Jr., ed., *The Indiana Companion to Traditional Chinese Literature* (Bloomington: Indiana University Press, 1986), p. 676.

For the ordinary person, the Age of Division was notable for the spread of Buddhism, discussed in the following section, and for an increasing proportion of people who were not fully free (slaves, serfs, and the like). The governments after the Han dynasty were not very successful in curbing the tendencies that pushed the poor to accept demeaned status as serfs or soldiers in private armies. In addition, it had long been the custom of the northern pastoral tribes to enslave those they captured; the Northern Wei Dynasty and its successors sometimes enslaved the residents of entire cities. In 554, when the city of Jiangling was taken, 100,000 civilians were enslaved and distributed to generals and officials.

## THE SPREAD OF BUDDHISM OUT OF INDIA

In much the same period that Christianity was spreading out of its original home in ancient Israel, Buddhism was spreading beyond India. And just as Christianity was shaped by its contact with cultures in the different areas into which it spread, leading to several distinct forms of Christianity, the forms of Buddhism that spread via Central Asia to China, Korea, and Japan are distinct from those that spread from India to Sri Lanka, Tibet, and Southeast Asia.

Central Asia is a loose term used to refer to the vast area between the ancient civilizations of Persia, India, and China. Modern political borders, in fact, are a product of competition among the British, Russians, and Chinese for empire in the mid-nineteenth century and have relatively little to do with the earlier history of the region. Through most of recorded history, the region was ethnically and culturally diverse; it was home to both urban centers, especially at the oases along the Silk Road, and pastoralists in the mountains and grasslands (see Map 7.2).

Under Ashoka (see pages 71–72) Buddhism began to spread to Central Asia. This continued under the Kushan empire (ca 50–250 C.E.), especially under their greatest king, Kanishka I (ca 100 C.E.). In this region, where the influence of Greek art was strong, artists began to depict the Buddha in human form. Over the next several centuries most of the city-states of Central Asia became centers of Buddhism, from Bamiyan, northwest of Kabul, to Kucha, Khotan, Loulan, Turfan, and Dunhuang (see Map 7.2). Because the remarkable Buddhist civilization of Central Asia was later supplanted by Islam, it was not until early in the twentieth century that European archaeologists discovered its traces. The main sites yielded not only numerous Buddhist paintings but also thousands of texts in a variety of languages. In Khotan, for instance, an Indian language was used for administrative purposes long after the fall of the Kushan empire. Other texts were in various Persian languages, showing the cultural mix of the region.

The form of Buddhism that spread from Central Asia to China, Japan, and Korea was called Mahayana, which means "Great Vehicle" (see page 67), reflecting the claims of its adherents to a more inclusive form of the religion. One branch of Mahayana taught that reality is "empty" (that is, nothing exists independently, of itself). Emptiness was seen as an absolute, underlying all phenomena, which are themselves transient and illusory. Another branch held that ultimate reality is consciousness, that everything is produced by the mind.

But more important than the metaphysical literature of Mahayana Buddhism was its devotional side, influenced by the Iranian religions then prevalent in Central Asia. The Buddha came to be treated as a god, the head of an expanding pantheon of other Buddhas and bodhisattvas (Buddhas-to-be). These Buddhas and bodhisattvas became objects of worship, especially the Buddha Amitabha and the bodhisattva Avalokitesvara (Guanyin in Chinese, Kannon in Japanese). With the growth of this pantheon, Buddhism became as much a religion for laypeople as for monks and nuns.

The first translators of Buddhist texts into Chinese were not Indians but Parthians, Sogdians, and Kushans from Central Asia. For instance, one of the major interpreters of Buddhism in China was the eminent Central Asian monk Kumarajiva (350–413), from Kucha, who settled in Chang'an and directed several thousand monks in the translation of Buddhist texts.

Why did Buddhism find so many adherents in China during the three centuries after the fall of the Han Dynasty in 220? There were no forced conversions, but still the religion spread rapidly, having something to offer everyone. To Chinese scholars the Buddhist concepts of the transmigration of souls, karma, and nirvana posed a stimulating intellectual challenge. To rulers the Buddhist religion offered a source of magical power and a political tool to unite Chinese and non-Chinese. To the middle and lower classes Buddhism's egalitarianism came as a breath of fresh air. The lower orders of society had as much chance as the elite to live according to the Buddha's precepts, and faith and devotion alone could lead to salvation. For many, regardless of their social status, Buddhism's promise of eternal bliss as the reward for a just and upright life was deeply comforting. In a rough

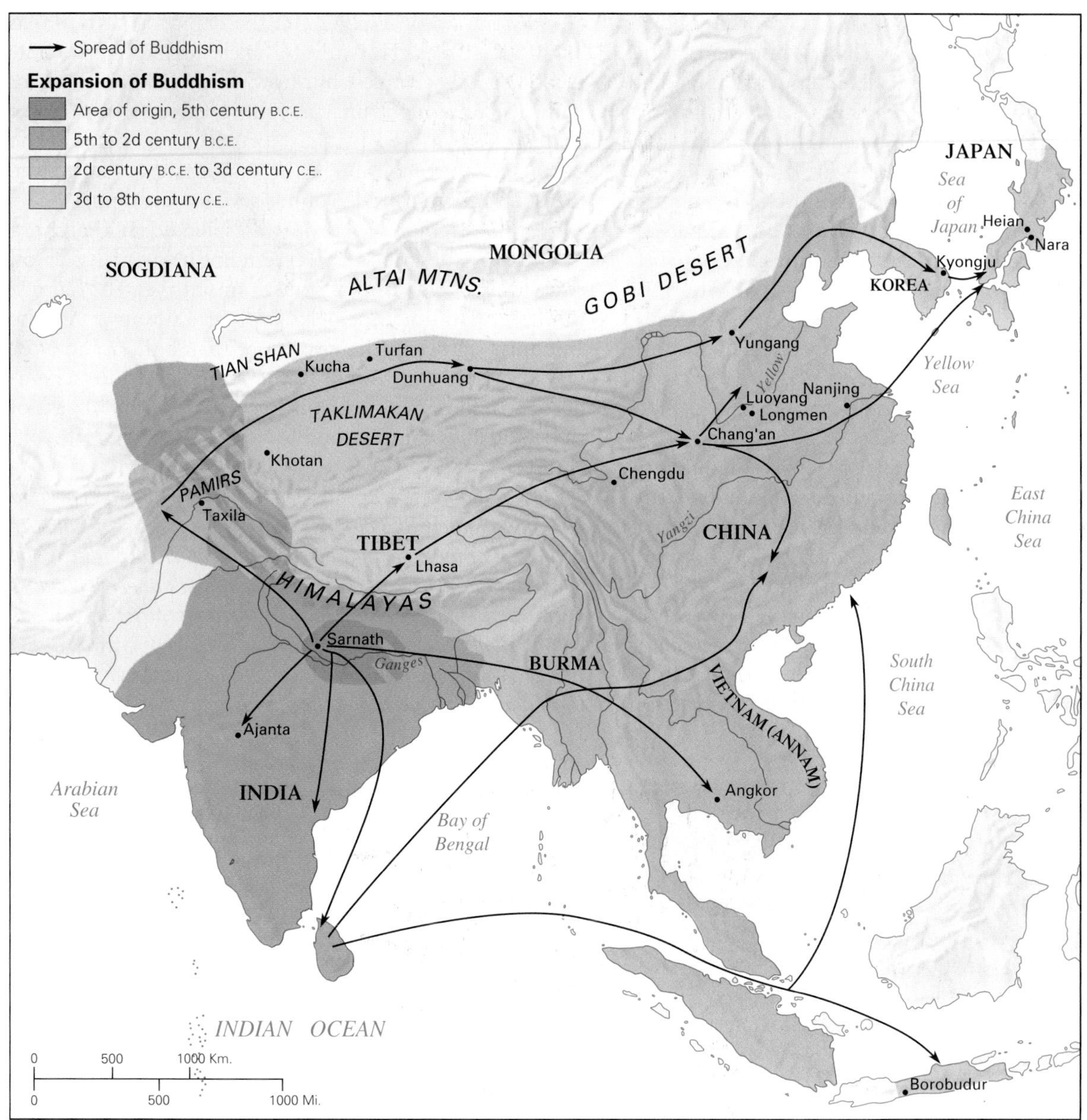


**MAP 7.2 The Spread of Buddhism** Buddhism spread throughout India in Ashoka's time and beyond India in later centuries. The different forms of Buddhism found in Asia today reflect this history. The Mahayana Buddhism of Japan came via Central Asia, China, and Korea, with a secondary later route through Tibet. The Theravada Buddhism of Southeast Asia came directly from India and indirectly through Sri Lanka.

and tumultuous age Buddhism's emphasis on kindness, charity, and the value of human life offered hope of a better life on earth. As in India, Buddhism posed no threat to the social order, and the elite who were drawn to Buddhism encouraged its spread to people of all classes. (See the feature "Listening to the Past: Copying Buddhist Sutras" on pages 206–207.)

The monastic establishment grew rapidly in China. Like their Christian counterparts in medieval Europe, Buddhist monasteries played an active role in social, economic, and political life. By 477 there were said to be 6,478 Buddhist temples and 77,258 monks and nuns in the north. Some decades later south China had 2,846 temples and 82,700 clerics. Given the importance of family lines in China, becoming a monk was a big step, since a man had to give up his surname and take a vow of celibacy, thus cutting himself off from the ancestral cult. Those not ready to become monks or nuns could pursue Buddhist goals as pious laypeople by performing devotional acts and making contributions toward the construction or beautification of temples. Among the most generous patrons were rulers in both north and south.

In China women turned to Buddhism as readily as men. Although incarnation as a female was considered lower than incarnation as a male, it was also viewed as temporary, and women were encouraged to pursue salvation on terms nearly equal to men. Joining a nunnery became an alternative for women who did not want to marry or did not want to stay with their husbands' families in widowhood.

Buddhism had an enormous impact on the visual arts in China, especially sculpture and painting. The merchants and missionaries from Central Asia who brought Buddhism to China also brought ideas about the construction and decoration of temples and the depiction of Buddhas and bodhisattvas. The earlier Chinese had not set up statues of gods in temples, but now they decorated temples with a profusion of images. The great cave temples at Yungang, sponsored by the Northern Wei rulers in the fifth century, contain huge Buddha figures in stone, the tallest a standing Buddha about seventy feet high.

Buddhist temples were just as splendid in the cities. One author described the ceremony held each year on the seventh day of the fourth month at the largest monastery in the northern capital, Luoyang. All the Buddhist statues in the city, more than a thousand altogether, would be brought to the monastery, and the emperor would come in person to scatter flowers as part of the Great Blessing ceremony.

*The gold and the flowers dazzled in the sun, and the jewelled canopies floated like clouds; there were forests of banners and a fog of incense, and the Buddhist music of India shook heaven and earth. All kinds of entertainers and trick riders performed shoulder to shoulder. Virtuous hosts of famous monks came, carrying their staves; there were crowds of the Buddhist faithful, holding flowers; horsemen and carriages were packed beside each other in an endless mass.*[4]

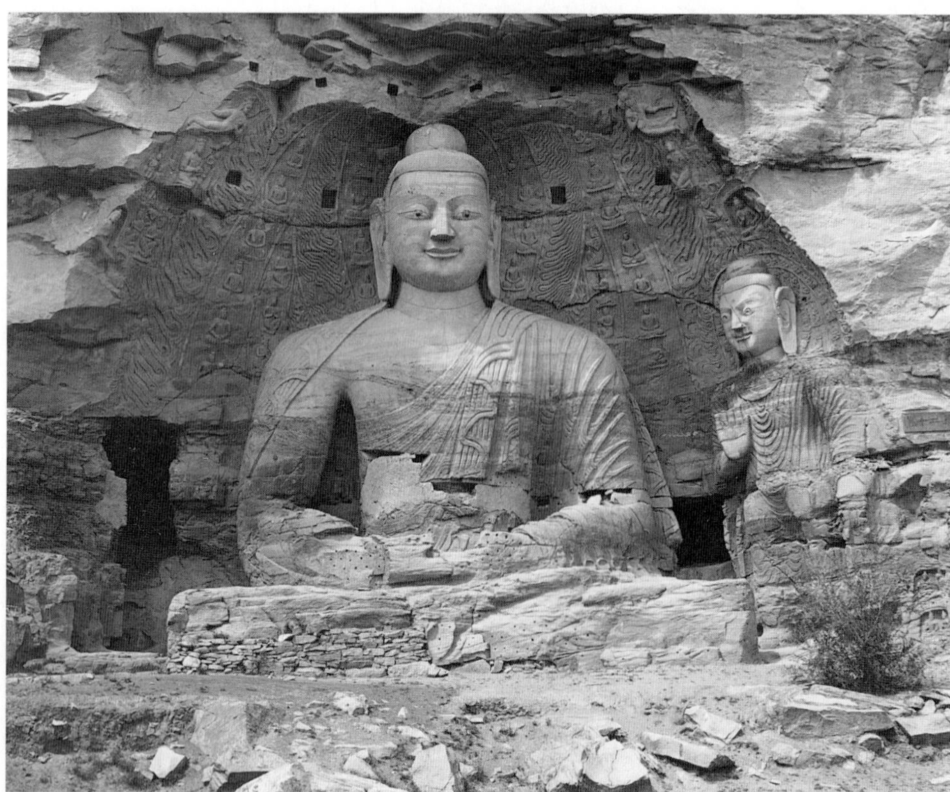

**The Great Buddha** This huge Buddha at Yungang in north China is about forty-five feet tall. It is the most massive of some 51,000 Buddhist images carved into the surface of a cliff that extends for over half a mile. Buddhist missionaries from northern India and Afghanistan brought to China the idea of carving images of the Buddha into stone cliffs. The arrival of Buddhism greatly enriched Chinese art traditions, especially sculpture. *(Werner Forman/Art Resource, NY)*

Not everyone was won over by Buddhist teachings. Critics of Buddhism labeled it immoral, unsuited to China, and a threat to the state since monastery land was not taxed. Twice in the north orders were issued to close monasteries and force monks and nuns to return to lay life, but these suppressions did not last long, and no attempt was made to suppress private Buddhist belief.

# THE SECOND CHINESE EMPIRE: SUI (581–618) AND TANG (618–907)

In the 570s and 580s, the long period of division in China was brought to an end under the leadership of the Sui Dynasty. Yang Jian, who both founded the Sui Dynasty and oversaw the reunification of China, was from a Chinese family that had intermarried with the non-Chinese elite of the north. He and his successor were both activists. The conquest of the south involved naval as well as land attacks, with thousands of ships on both sides contending for control of the Yangzi River. The Sui reasserted Chinese control over northern Vietnam and campaigned into Korea and against the new force on the steppe, the Turks. The Sui tried to strengthen central control of the government by curtailing the power of local officials to appoint their own subordinates and by instituting competitive written examinations for the selection of officials. Although only a few officials were selected through examinations during the Sui Dynasty, the groundwork was laid for the civil service examinations that came to dominate the lives of educated men in later centuries.

The crowning achievement of the Sui Dynasty was the **Grand Canal,** which connected the Yellow and Yangzi Rivers. The canal facilitated the shipping of tax grain from the recently developed Yangzi Delta to the centers of political and military power in north China. Henceforth the rice-growing Yangzi Valley and south China played an ever more influential role in the country's economic and political life, strengthening China's internal cohesion. Accordingly, maritime trade with Southeast Asia, India, and areas farther west became more important to the Chinese economy and culture.

Despite these accomplishments, the Sui Dynasty lasted for only two reigns. The ambitious projects of the two Sui emperors led to exhaustion and unrest, and in the ensuing warfare Li Yuan, a Chinese from the same northwest aristocratic circles as the founder of the Sui, seized the throne.

## The Tang Dynasty (618–907)

The dynasty founded by Li Yuan, the Tang, was one of the high points of traditional Chinese civilization. Especially during this dynasty's first century, China and its capital, Chang'an, were the cultural centers of East Asia, drawing in merchants, pilgrims, missionaries, and students to a degree never matched before or after. This position of strength gave the Chinese the confidence to be open to what they could learn from the outside world, leading to a more cosmopolitan culture than in any other period before the twentieth century.

The first two Tang rulers, Taizu (r. 618–626) and Taizong (r. 626–649), were able monarchs. They extended the equal-field and militia systems of the Northern Dynasties. Using the militia plus auxiliary troops composed of Turks, Tanguts, Khitans, and other non-Chinese led by their own chieftains, they campaigned into Korea, Vietnam, and Central Asia. In 630 the Chinese turned against their former allies the Turks, gaining territory from them and winning for Taizong the title of Great Khan, so that he was for a short period simultaneously head of both the Chinese and the Inner Asian empires.

In the civil sphere Tang accomplishments far outstripped anything known in Europe until the growth of national states in the seventeenth century. Tang emperors subdivided the administration of the empire into departments, much like the numerous agencies of modern governments. They built on Sui precedent, using examinations to select officials. Although only about thirty men were recruited this way each year, the prestige of passing the examinations became so great that more and more men attempted them. Candidates had to master the Confucian classics and the rules of poetry, and they had to be able to discuss practical administrative and political matters. Government schools were founded to prepare the sons of officials and other young men for service as officials.

The mid-Tang Dynasty saw two women—Empress Wu and Consort Yang Guifei—rise to positions of great political power through their hold on rulers. Empress Wu was the consort of the weak and sickly Emperor Gaozong. After Gaozong suffered a stroke in 660, she took full charge. She continued to rule after Gaozong's death, summarily deposing her own two sons and dealing harshly with all opponents. In 690 she proclaimed herself emperor, the only woman who took that title in Chinese history. To gain support, she circulated a Buddhist sutra that predicted the imminent reincarnation of the Buddha Maitreya as a female monarch, during whose reign the world would be free of illness, worry, and disaster. Although despised by later historians as an evil usurper,

Empress Wu was an effective leader who suppressed rebellions, organized aggressive military campaigns, and brought new groups into the bureaucracy. It was not until she was over eighty that members of the court were able to force her out in favor of her son.

Her grandson, the emperor Xuanzong (r. 713–756), in his early years presided over a brilliant court. In his later years, however, after he became enamored of his consort Yang Guifei, he let things slide. This was a period when ample and rounded proportions were much admired in women, and Yang was said to be such a full-figured beauty. The emperor allowed her to place friends and relatives in important positions in the government. One of her favorites was the able general An Lushan, who after getting into a quarrel with Yang's brother over control of the government, rebelled in 755. Xuanzong had to flee the capital, and the troops that accompanied him forced him to have Yang Guifei executed.

But more lay behind this crisis than imperial foolishness. The Tang had outgrown the institutions of the Northern Dynasties, such as the equal-field system. As a result of population growth, in many areas individual allotment holders received only a fraction of the land they were due but still had to pay the standard per capita tax. Peasants fled their allotments, thereby reducing government income. Moreover, as defense problems grew, especially warfare with the Turks and Tibetans, the militia system proved inadequate. A system of military districts had to be established along the borders, and defense was entrusted to professional armies and non-Chinese auxiliary troops. It was because An Lushan commanded one of these armies that he was able to launch an attack on the central government.

The rebellion of An Lushan was devastating to the Tang Dynasty. Peace was restored only by calling on the Uighurs, a Turkish people allied with the Tang, who looted the capital after taking it from the rebels. After the rebellion was finally suppressed in 763, the central government never regained control of the military provinces on the frontiers and had to keep meeting the extortionate demands of the Uighurs. Abandoning the equal-field system and instituting taxes based on actual landholdings helped restore the government's finances, but many military governors came to treat their provinces as hereditary kingdoms and withheld tax returns from the central government. In addition, eunuchs gained increasing power at court and were able to prevent both the emperors and Confucian officials from doing much about them.

## Tang Culture

A vibrant, outward-looking culture flourished under the conditions created by reuniting north and south China. The Tang capital cities of Chang'an and Luoyang became great metropolises, with Chang'an and its suburbs growing to more than 2 million inhabitants. The cities

**Urban Planning** Chang'an in Tang times attracted merchants, pilgrims, and students from all over East Asia. The city was laid out on a square grid (*left*) and divided into walled wards, the gates to which were closed at night. Temples were found throughout the city, but trade was limited to two government-supervised markets. In the eighth and ninth centuries the Japanese copied the general plan of Chang'an in designing their capitals—first at Nara, then at Heian, shown on the right. *(From* Cradles of Civilization: China *[Weldon Owen Pty Limited, Australia])*

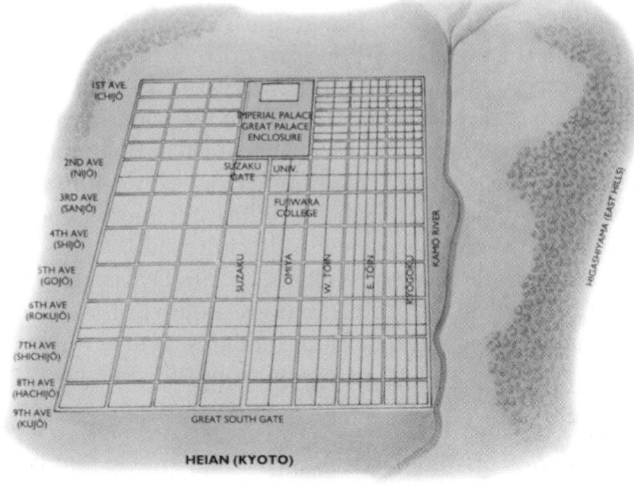

were laid out in rectangular grids and contained a hundred-odd "blocks" inside their walls. Each block was a mini-city divided by many lanes and surrounded by a wall. Like the gates of the city, the gates of each block were locked at night.

In these cosmopolitan cities, knowledge of the outside world was stimulated by the presence of envoys, merchants, and pilgrims who came from the neighboring states in Central Asia, Japan, Korea, and Tibet. Because of the presence of foreign merchants, many religions were practiced, including Nestorian Christianity, Manichaeism, Zoroastrianism, Judaism, and Islam, although none of them spread into the Chinese population the way Buddhism had a few centuries earlier. Foreign fashions in hair and clothing were often copied, and foreign amusements such as polo found followings among the well-to-do. The introduction of new instruments and tunes from India, Iran, and Central Asia brought about a major transformation in Chinese music.

The Tang Dynasty was the great age of Chinese poetry. Skill in composing poetry was tested in the civil service examinations, and educated men had to be able to compose poems at social gatherings. The pain of parting, the joys of nature, and the pleasures of wine and friendship were all common poetic topics. One of Li Bo's (701–762) most famous poems describes an evening of drinking with only the moon and his shadow for company:

*A cup of wine, under the flowering trees;*
*I drink alone, for no friend is near.*
*Raising my cup I beckon the bright moon,*
*For he, with my shadow, will make three men.*
*The moon, alas, is no drinker of wine;*
*Listless, my shadow creeps about at my side.*
. . .
*Now we are drunk, each goes his way.*
*May we long share our odd, inanimate feast,*
*And we meet at last on the cloudy River of the sky.*[5]

Less cheerful but no less talented was Bo Juyi (772–846). He felt the weight of his responsibilities as governor of several small provinces and sympathized with the people whom he governed. At times Bo Juyi worried about whether he was doing his job justly and well:

*From these high walls I look at the town below*
*Where the natives of Pa cluster like a swarm of flies.*
*How can I govern these people and lead them aright?*
*I cannot even understand what they say.*
*But at least I am glad, now that the taxes are in,*
*To learn that in my province there is no discontent.*[6]

In Tang times Buddhism fully penetrated Chinese daily life. Stories of Buddhist origin became widely known, and Buddhist festivals, such as the festival for feeding hungry ghosts in the summer, became among the most popular holidays.

**Woman Playing Polo** Notions of what makes women attractive have changed over the course of Chinese history. The figurines found in Tang tombs reveal that active women, even ones playing polo on horseback like the one shown here, were viewed as appealing. In earlier and later periods, female beauty was identified with slender waists and delicate faces, but in Tang times women were admired for their plump bodies and full faces. *(Chinese. Equestrienne [tomb figure], buff earthenware with traces of polychromy, first half 8th cent., 56.2 × 48.2 cm. Gift of Mrs. Pauline Palmer Wood, 1970.1073. Photograph © 1998, The Art Institute of Chicago)*

Buddhist monasteries had become an important part of everyday life. They ran schools for children. In remote areas they provided lodging for travelers, and in towns they offered literati places to gather for social occasions such as going-away parties. Merchants entrusted their money and wares to monasteries for safekeeping, in effect transforming the monasteries into banks and warehouses. The wealthy often donated money or land to support temples and monasteries, making monasteries among the largest landlords. Formidable in wealth and number, monasteries became influential participants in politics, rivaling the power of the traditional Chinese landed families.

At the intellectual and religious level, Buddhism was developing in a distinctly Chinese direction. Two schools that thrived were Pure Land and Chan. **Pure Land** appealed to laypeople. The simple act of paying homage to the Buddha Amitabha and his chief helper, the compassionate bodhisattva Guanyin, could lead to rebirth in Amitabha's paradise, the Pure Land. Among the educated elite the **Chan** school (known in Japan as Zen) gained popularity. Chan teachings rejected the authority of the sutras and claimed the superiority of mind-to-mind transmission of Buddhist truths. The "northern" tradition emphasized meditation and monastic discipline. The "southern" tradition was even more iconoclastic, holding that enlightenment could be achieved suddenly through insight into one's own true nature, even without prolonged meditation.

In the late Tang period, opposition to Buddhism reemerged. In addition to concerns about the fiscal impact of removing so much land from the tax rolls and so many men from the labor service force, there were concerns about Buddhism's foreign origins. Probably as China's international position weakened, xenophobia emerged. In 845 the Tang emperor began a full-scale persecution. More than 4,600 monasteries and 40,000 temples and shrines were destroyed, and more than 260,000 Buddhist monks and nuns were forced to return to secular life. Other religious groups were also brought under state control. Although this ban was lifted after a few years, the monastic establishment never fully recovered. Among laypeople Buddhism retained a strong hold, and basic Buddhist ideas like karma and reincarnation had become fully incorporated into everyday Chinese thinking. But Buddhism was never again as central to Chinese life.

## THE EAST ASIAN CULTURAL SPHERE

During the millennium from 200 B.C.E. to 800 C.E. China exerted a powerful influence on its immediate neighbors, who began forming states of their own. By Tang times China was surrounded by independent states in Korea, Manchuria, Tibet, the area that is now Yunnan province, Vietnam, and Japan. All of these states were much smaller than China in area and population, making China by far the dominant force politically and culturally until the late nineteenth century. Nevertheless, each of these separate states developed a strong sense of uniqueness and independent identity.

The earliest information about each of these countries is found in Chinese sources. The expansionist tendencies of the Han Dynasty began the process of bringing the knowledge of Chinese civilization to both Korea and Vietnam, but even in those cases much cultural borrowing was entirely voluntary as the elite, merchants, and craftsmen of surrounding areas adopted the techniques, ideas, and practices they found appealing. In Japan much of the process of absorbing elements of Chinese culture was mediated via Korea. In Korea, Japan, and Vietnam the fine arts—painting, architecture, and ceramics, in particular—were all strongly influenced by Chinese models. Tibet, though a thorn in the side of Tang China, was as much in the Indian sphere of influence as the Chinese and thus followed a somewhat different trajectory. Most significant, it never adopted Chinese characters as its written language, nor was it as influenced by Chinese artistic styles as other areas. Moreover the form of Buddhism that became dominant in Tibet came directly from India, not through Central Asia and China.

In each area literate, Chinese-style culture was at first an upper-level overlay over an indigenous cultural base, but in time many products and ideas adopted from China became incorporated into everyday life, ranging from written language to chopsticks and soy sauce. By the eighth century the Chinese language was a written lingua franca among educated people throughout East Asia. Vietnamese, Koreans, and Japanese could communicate in writing when they could not understand each other's spoken languages, and envoys to Chang'an could carry out "brush conversations" with each other. The books that educated people read included the Chinese classics, histories, and poetry, as well as Buddhist texts translated into Chinese.

### Korea

Korea is a mountainous peninsula some 600 miles long and 125 to 200 miles wide extending south from Manchuria and Siberia. At its tip it is about 120 miles from Japan (see Map 7.3). Archaeological, linguistic, and anthropological evidence indicates that the Korean people share a common ethnic origin with other peoples of North Asia, including those of Manchuria, Siberia, and Japan. Linguistically they are not related to the Chinese.

Bronze and iron technology spread from China in the Zhou period, and Korean mythology reflects links to China. According to one myth, a royal refugee from the Shang Dynasty founded a dynasty in Korea. During the Warring States Period in China (403–221 B.C.E.), the state of Yan extended into southern Manchuria and a bit of what is now Korea. Through this contact features of China's material culture, such as iron technology, spread to Korea. In about 194 B.C.E. Wiman, an unsuccessful rebel against the Han Dynasty, fled to Korea and set up a state called Choson in what is now northwest Korea and southern Manchuria. In 108 B.C.E. this state was overthrown by the armies of the Han emperor Wu. Four military districts were established there, and Chinese officials were dispatched to govern them.

The Chinese colonies founded at that time served as outposts of Chinese civilization and survived nearly a century after the fall of the Han Dynasty, to 313 C.E. The impact of the Chinese military districts in Korea was similar to that of the contemporary Roman colonies in Britain. Even though the later Korean states were not the direct heirs of the colonies, they retained much that had been introduced by the Chinese. Among the many aspects of Chinese culture that penetrated deeply in this period were names: Korean place names and personal names use Chinese characters.

The Chinese never controlled the entire Korean peninsula. They coexisted with the native Korean kingdom of Koguryo, founded in the first century B.C.E. Chinese sources describe this kingdom as a society of aristocratic tribal warriors who had under them a mass of serfs and slaves, mostly from conquered tribes. After the Chinese colonies were finally overthrown, the kingdoms of Paekche and Silla emerged in the third and fourth centuries C.E. farther south on the peninsula. In all three Korean kingdoms Chinese was used as the language of government and learning.

Buddhism was officially introduced in Koguryo from China in 372 and in the other states not long after. Buddhism placed Korea in a pan-Asian cultural context. Buddhist monks went back and forth between China and Korea. One even made the journey to India and back, and others traveled on to Japan to aid in the spread of Buddhism there.

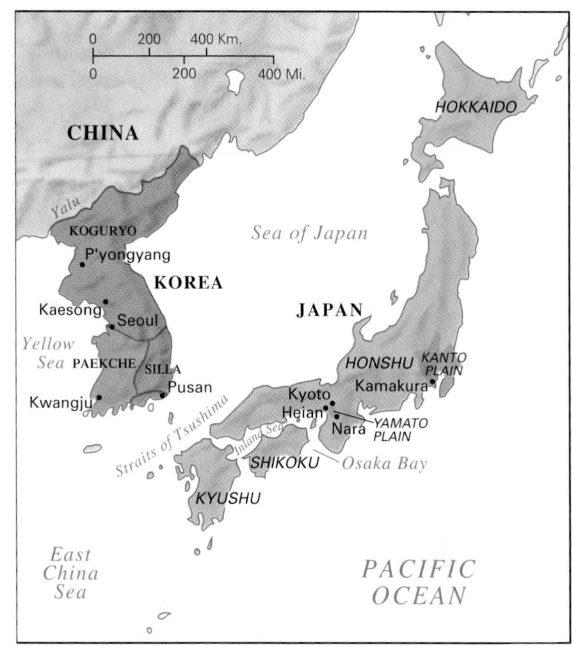


**MAP 7.3 Korea and Japan, ca 600** Korea and Japan are of similar latitude, but Korea's climate is more continental, with harsher winters. Of Japan's four islands, Kyushu is closest to Korea and mainland Asia.

Each of the three main Korean kingdoms had hereditary kings, but their power was curbed by the existence of very strong hereditary elites. For instance, Silla had a Council of Nobles, which made important decisions, and a system of "bone ranks" that determined hereditary status.

When the Sui Dynasty finally reunified China in 589, it attempted to take Korea to re-establish the sort of empire the Han had fashioned. But the Korean kingdoms were

### KOREA TO CA 700 C.E.

| | |
|---|---|
| 194 B.C.E. | Wiman establishes Choson |
| 108 B.C.E.–313 C.E. | Chinese colonies in Korea |
| 313–668 C.E. | Three Kingdoms period (Silla, Paekche, and Koguryo) |
| 372 C.E. | Buddhism introduced |
| 668 C.E. | Unification under Silla<br>Chinese models widely adopted |

**Hunters** The Korean elite of the late fifth to early sixth century—the date of this tomb mural—were warriors who took pleasure in hunting. Here men on horses are depicted hunting tigers and deer. The skill and artistry of the painters also testify to the high level attained by Korean artists of the period. *(Courtesy, Yushin Yoo)*

much stronger than their predecessors in Han times, and they repeatedly repulsed Chinese attacks. The Tang government then tried allying itself with one state to fight another. Silla and Tang jointly destroyed Paekche in 660 and Koguryo in 668. With its new resources Silla was able to repel Tang efforts to make Korea a colony but acceded to vassal status. This marks the first political unification of Korea.

For the next century Silla embarked on a policy of wholesale borrowing of Chinese culture and institutions. Annual embassies were sent to Chang'an, and large numbers of students studied in China. The Silla government was modeled on the Tang, although modifications were made to accommodate Korea's more aristocratic social structure.

As in Japan, a powerful force in promoting cultural borrowing from China was the tremendous appeal of Buddhism, known primarily through Chinese texts. The Silla kings spent lavishly on Buddhist monasteries. The stone and brick pagodas and temples built in this period, as well as the stone and bronze Buddhist images, are exceptionally fine. Many Buddhist monks studied in China, and books written by Korean monks were read by Chinese monks as well. The Buddhist master Wonhyo (617–686), for instance, wrote a commentary on the *Awakening of Faith* that was influential in China, and his biography was included in the Chinese collection *Lives of Eminent Monks.*

## Vietnam

Vietnam is today classed with the countries to its west as part of Southeast Asia, but its ties are at least as strong to China. The Vietnamese language is part of the Sino-Tibetan family, distantly related to Chinese. Communication between the Guangdong (Canton) region in southernmost China and the Hanoi region and farther south in Vietnam was easy along the coast, even in early times.

The Vietnamese appear in Chinese sources as a people of south China called the Yue, who gradually migrated farther south as the Chinese state expanded. From both Chinese sources and archaeological findings, it is known that the people of the Red River valley in northern Vietnam had achieved a relatively advanced level of Bronze Age civilization by the first century B.C.E. They had learned how to irrigate their rice fields by using the tides that backed up the rivers, but plows and water buffalo as draft animals were still unknown. The bronze heads of their arrows often were dipped in poison to facilitate killing large animals such as elephants, whose tusks were traded to China for iron. Power was held by hereditary tribal chiefs who served as civil, religious, and military leaders, with the king as the most powerful chief.

The collapse of the Qin Dynasty in 206 B.C.E. had an impact on this area because a former Qin general, Zhao Tuo (Trieu Da in Vietnamese), finding himself in the far south, set up his own kingdom of Nam Viet (Nan Yue in Chinese). This kingdom covered much of south China and was ruled by Trieu Da from his capital near the present site of Canton. Its population consisted chiefly of the Viet people. After killing all officials loyal to the Chinese emperor, Trieu Da adopted the customs of the Viet and made himself the ruler of a vast state that extended as far south as modern-day Da Nang.

After almost a hundred years of diplomatic and military duels between the Han Dynasty and Trieu Da and his successors, Nam Viet was conquered in 111 B.C.E. by the Chinese emperor Wu. As in Korea, Chinese administrators were imported to replace the local landed nobility. Chinese political institutions were imposed, and Confucianism became the official ideology. The Chinese language was introduced as the medium of official and literary expression, and Chinese ideographs were adopted as the written form for the Vietnamese spoken language. The Chinese built roads, waterways, and harbors to facilitate communication within the region and to ensure that they maintained administrative and military control over it. Chinese art, architecture, and music had a powerful impact on their Vietnamese counterparts.

Chinese innovations that were beneficial to the Vietnamese were readily integrated into the indigenous culture, but the local elite were not reconciled to Chinese political domination. The most famous early revolt took place in 39 C.E., when two widows of local aristocrats, the Trung sisters, led an uprising against foreign rule. They gathered together the tribal chiefs and their armed followers, attacked and overwhelmed the Chinese strongholds, and had themselves proclaimed queens of an independent Vietnamese kingdom. Three years later a powerful army sent by the Han emperor re-established Chinese rule. The local aristocracy was deprived of all power, Vietnam was given a centralized Chinese administration, and Chinese influence was resumed.

China retained at least nominal control over northern Vietnam through the Tang Dynasty, and there were no real borders between China proper and Vietnam during this time. The local elite became culturally dual, serving as brokers between the Chinese governors and the native people.

## Japan

Japan does not touch China as do Korea, Tibet, and Vietnam. The heart of Japan is four mountainous islands off the coast of Korea (see Map 7.3). Japan's climate ranges from subtropical in the south, which the Pacific bathes in warm currents, to cold winters in the north. Rainfall is abundant, favoring rice production. The long seacoast favors fishing.

Since the land is rugged and lacking in navigable waterways, the Inland Sea, like the Aegean in Greece, was the easiest avenue of communication in early times. Hence the land bordering the Inland Sea developed as the political and cultural center of early Japan. Geography also blessed Japan with a moat—the Korea Strait and the Sea of Japan. Consequently, the Japanese for long periods were free to develop their way of life without external interference.

Japan's creation myths, at least in the form they have been preserved, center on the divine origins of the Japanese imperial family. A divine brother and sister, **Izanagi and Izanami,** came to earth and created the Japanese islands and other gods. Izanami died after giving birth to the god of fire, and Izanagi, like the Greek Orpheus, followed her to the world of the dead. Repelled by her putrifying body, he went to a stream to purify himself, where he gave birth to more deities, above all the sun-goddess,

### JAPAN TO CA 800 C.E.

| | |
|---|---|
| **3d century** C.E. | Creation of the Yamato state |
| 538 | Introduction of Buddhism |
| 604 | Shotoku's "Seventeen Article Constitution" |
| 646 | Taika Reforms |
| 710 | Establishment of Nara as Japan's first capital and first city |
| 710–794 | Nara era |

Amaterasu, and the storm-god, Susanoo. Their union gave birth to a new generation of gods, but they eventually quarreled, and Susanoo moved to Izumo, where he became the progenitor of a line of rulers who were in constant conflict with the line descended from Amaterasu, the line that became the Japanese imperial family.

From archaeology, however, it is evident that Japan's early development was closely tied to that of the mainland, especially to Korea. Physical anthropologists have discerned several major waves of immigrants into Japan. Wet-field rice was introduced by about 350 B.C.E. During the Han Dynasty in China, some objects of Chinese or Korean manufacture found their way into Japan, an indication that people were traveling back and forth as well.

A Chinese historian wrote one of the earliest reliable descriptions of Japanese life in 297 C.E.:

*The land of Wa [Japan] is warm and mild. In winter as in summer the people live on raw vegetables and go barefooted. They live in houses; father and mother, elder and younger, sleep separately. They smear their bodies with pink and scarlet, just as the Chinese use powder. They serve food on bamboo and wooden trays, helping themselves with their fingers.*[7]

The society that Chinese sources portray was based on agriculture and dominated by a warrior aristocracy organized into clans, much like Korea. Clad in helmet and armor, these warriors wielded swords and battle-axes and often bows. Some of them rode into battle on horseback.

Each aristocratic clan dominated a particular territory, and the ordinary villagers in the area were treated as subordinates to the warriors. Each clan had its own chieftain, who marshaled clansmen for battle and served as chief priest. Over time these clans fought with each other, and their numbers were gradually reduced through conquest and alliance. By the fifth century or so the chief of the clan that claimed descent from the sun-goddess, located in the Yamato plain around modern Osaka, had come to occupy the position of Great King.

Clans that recognized Yamato dominion continued to exercise local authority, and some clans were given specific military or religious functions to fulfill. In an effort to further centralize the administration of the state, the king created a council of chieftains, who were treated as though they were appointed officials.

The Yamato rulers also used their religion to subordinate the gods of their supporters, much as Hammurabi had used Marduk in Babylonia (see page 13). They established the chief shrine of the sun-goddess near the seacoast, where she could catch the first rays of the rising sun. Cults to other gods also were supported, as long as they were viewed as subordinate to the sun-goddess. This native religion was called **Shinto,** the Way of the Gods. Much of Shinto's appeal rose from the fact that it was a happy religion. Its rituals celebrated the beauty of nature instead of invoking the hazards of fate or divine wrath, and its festivals were marked by wine, song, and good cheer. Shinto emphasized ritual cleanliness, a form of spiritual purification common in many other religions.

In the fifth and sixth centuries Korea played a major role as the avenue through which Chinese influence reached Japan. Following the Korean example, the Japanese adapted the Chinese systems of writing and record keeping, which allowed for bureaucratic administration along Chinese lines and set the stage for literature, philosophy, and written history.

Buddhism entered Japan this way as well. In 538 a Korean king sent the Yamato court Buddhist images and scriptures. The new religion immediately became a political football. One faction of the ruling clan favored its official adoption, and other factions opposed it. The resulting turmoil, both religious and political, ended only in 587, when members of the pro-Buddhist group defeated their opponents on the battlefield.

The victorious pro-Buddhist faction undertook a sweeping reform of the state, designed to strengthen Yamato rule by introducing Chinese political and bureaucratic practices. The architect of this effort was Prince Shotoku (574–622), the author of the "Seventeen Article Constitution." Issued in 604, this political manifesto upheld the rights of the ruler and commanded his subjects to obey him. It recommended an intricate bureaucracy similar to China's, admonished the nobility to avoid strife and opposition, and urged adherence to Buddhist precepts.

Prince Shotoku was a generous patron of Buddhist temples, sponsoring the magnificent Horyuji Temple and staffing it with clergy from Korea. He also opened direct relations with China, recently unified by the Sui. The Sui emperor was not amused to receive a letter "from the emperor of the sunrise country to the emperor of the sunset country," but during the brief Sui Dynasty Japan sent four missions to China.

Even after Prince Shotoku's death, his policies were pursued. In 645 his supporters gained supremacy, and the following year they proclaimed the Taika Reforms, a bold effort to create a complete imperial and bureaucratic system like that of the Tang empire, down to outlawing private ownership of land and instituting the equal-field system and per capita taxes. The symbol of this new political awareness was the establishment in 710 of Japan's first true city, at **Nara,** north of modern Osaka.

**Prince Shotoku** Not only did Prince Shotoku introduce many features of Chinese-style bureaucratic government, but he also sponsored four missions to China. Here he is depicted, along with two attendants, wearing Chinese-style robes and holding the Chinese symbol of office. *(Imperial Household Collection, Kyoto)*

**Horyuji Temple** Japanese Buddhist temples, like those in China and Korea, consisted of several buildings within a walled compound. The buildings of the Horyuji Temple (built 670–711; Prince Shotoku's original temple burned down) include the oldest wooden structures in the world and house some of the best early Buddhist sculpture in Japan. The three main buildings depicted here are the pagoda, housing relics; the main hall, with the temple's principal images; and the lecture hall, for sermons. The five-story pagoda could be seen from far away, much like the steeples of cathedrals in medieval Europe. *(The Orion Press)*

Nara, which was modeled on the Tang capital, gave its name to an era that lasted until 794, an era characterized by the avid importation of Chinese ideas and methods. Seven times missions with five hundred to six hundred men were sent on the difficult journey to Chang'an. Chinese and Korean craftsmen were often brought back to Japan, especially to help with the decoration of the many Buddhist temples then under construction. Increased contact with the mainland had unwanted effects as well, such as the great smallpox epidemic of 735–737, which is thought to have reduced the population by 30 percent. (Smallpox did not become an endemic childhood disease in Japan until the tenth or eleventh century.)

The Buddhist monasteries that ringed Nara were both religious centers and wealthy landlords, and the monks were active in the political life of the capital. Copying the policy of the Tang Dynasty in China, the government ordered that every province establish a Buddhist temple with twenty monks and ten nuns to chant sutras and perform other ceremonies on behalf of the emperor and the state.

Many of the temples built during the Nara period still stand, the wood, clay, and bronze statues in them exceptionally well preserved. The largest of these temples was the Todaiji, with its huge (fifty-three feet tall) bronze statue of the Buddha, made from more than a million pounds of metal. When the temple and statue were completed in 752, an Indian monk painted the eyes, and the ten thousand monks present for the celebration had a magnificent vegetarian feast. Objects from the dedication ceremony were placed in a special storehouse, the Shosoin, and about ten thousand of them are still there, including books, weapons, mirrors, screens, and objects of gold, lacquer, and glass, most made in China but some coming via the Silk Road from Central Asia and Persia.

As part of a culture-building process, the Japanese also began writing their own history and poetry. Some books were written entirely in Chinese; others were written in the Japanese language but using Chinese characters to represent each sound, since there was no alphabet. The masterpiece among these books is the *Manyoshu,* a collection of 4,500 mostly short Japanese poems written in Chinese characters borrowed for their sound. Because rhyming is so easy in Japanese, it was not an important feature of poetry, which instead stressed the number of syllables per line. The dominant form was the **tanka,** with thirty-one syllables in five lines of 5-7-5-7-7. The poet Kakinomoto Hitomaro wrote a tanka on the prospect of his own death:

*Not knowing I am pillowed*
*Among the crags of Kamo Mountain*
*My wife must still be waiting for my return.*

When his wife learned of his death, she also wrote a poem:

*Never again to meet him in the flesh—*
*Rise, oh clouds, and spread*
*Over Ishi River,*
*That, gazing on you,*
*I may remember him.*[8]

## SUMMARY

During the millennium from 200 B.C.E. to 800 C.E., China and India came into contact with each other via the kingdoms of Central Asia. Throughout Asia Buddhism became a major religion, usually coexisting with other religions, including Daoism in China and Shinto in Japan. China's neighbors, notably including Korea, Japan, and Vietnam, began to adopt elements of China's material, political, and religious culture.

In some cases, culture and social forms were spread by force of arms. The Qin, Han, and Tang armies moved into northern Korea, Central Asia, south China, and even northern Vietnam. But military might was not the primary means by which culture spread in this period. Buddhism was not spread by conquest in the way that Christianity and Islam so often were. Moreover Korea and Japan sought out Chinese expertise, believing it to be to their advantage to adopt the most advanced political and economic technologies. Perhaps as a consequence, they could pick and choose, using those elements of the more advanced cultures that suited them, and retaining features of their earlier cultures that they believed superior, in the process developing distinctive national styles.

## KEY TERMS

Great Wall
regents
Silk Road
tributary system
Confucian classics
*Records of the Grand Historian*
lacquer
eunuchs
Age of Division
Grand Canal
Pure Land
Chan
Izanagi and Izanami
Shinto
Nara
tanka

## NOTES

1. Derk Bodde, "The State and Empire of Ch'in," in M. Loewe and D. Twitchett, eds., *The Cambridge History of China,* vol. 1 (New York: Cambridge University Press, 1986), p. 20.

2. Li Yuning, ed., *The First Emperor of China* (White Plains, N.Y.: International Arts and Sciences Press, 1975), pp. 275–276, slightly modified.
3. Patricia Buckley Ebrey, *The Cambridge Illustrated History of China* (Cambridge: Cambridge University Press, 1996), p. 74.
4. W. F. Jenner, *Memories of Loyang: Yang Hsüan-chih and the Lost Capital (493–534)* (Oxford: Clarendon Press, 1981), p. 208.
5. A. Waley, trans., *More Translations from the Chinese* (New York: Knopf, 1919), p. 27.
6. Ibid., p. 71.
7. R. Tsunoda et al., *Sources of the Japanese Tradition* (New York: Columbia University Press, 1958), p. 6.
8. Martin Collcott, Marius Jansen, and Isao Kumakura, *Cultural Atlas of Japan* (New York: Facts on File, 1988), p. 65.

## SUGGESTED READING

Good general histories of China are listed in the Suggested Reading for Chapter 4. For China's relations with the Xiongnu, Xianbei, Turks, and other northern neighbors, see T. Barfield, *Perilous Frontier: Nomadic Empires and China, 221 B.C.–A.D. 1757* (1989), and N. DiCosmo, *Ancient China and Its Enemies: The Rise of Nomadic Power in East Asia* (2002). The nature of the Qin and later empires is analyzed from a fiscal and military standpoint in M. Elvin, *The Pattern of the Chinese Past* (1973). The political and military success of the Qin is the subject of D. Bodde, *China's First Unifier: A Study of the Ch'in Dynasty as Seen in the Life of Li Ssu (280?–208 B.C.)* (1958).

B. Watson has provided two good studies of Sima Qian and his historical work: *Records of the Grand Historian of China* (1961) and *Ssu-ma Ch'ien: Grand Historian of China* (1958). China's most important woman scholar is the subject of N. L. Swann, *Pan Chao: Foremost Woman Scholar of China* (1950). M. Loewe, *Everyday Life in Early Imperial China* (1968), paints a vibrant picture of ordinary life during the Han period, a portrayal that attempts to include all segments of Han society. See also Y. Yu, *Trade and Expansion in Han China: A Study in the Structure of Sino-Barbarian Economic Relations* (1967), and M. Perazzoli-t'Serstevens, *The Han Dynasty,* trans. Janet Seligman (1982). For religion, see Mu-chou Poo, *In Search of Personal Welfare: A View of Ancient Chinese Religion* (1998).

Current scholarship on the turbulent Age of Division after the fall of the Han can be sampled in A. Dien, ed., *State and Society in Early Medieval China* (1990). Also recommended is A. Wright's gracefully written *The Sui Dynasty* (1978). The best short introduction to the topic of Buddhism in China remains Wright's brief *Buddhism in Chinese History* (1959). See also K. Ch'en, *The Chinese Transformation of Buddhism* (1973). E. O. Reischauer provides a glimpse into the social and cultural aspects of Tang Buddhism in his translation, *Ennin's Diary: The Record of a Pilgrimage to China in Search of the Law*, and the companion volume, *Ennin's Travels in T'ang China* (both 1955).

Diverse aspects of the Tang period are explored in two collections of essays: A. Wright and D. Twitchett, eds., *Perspectives on the T'ang* (1973), and J. Perry and B. Smith, eds., *Essays on T'ang Society: The Interplay of Social, Political, and Economic Forces* (1976). On Tang rulership, see H. Wechsler, *Mirror to the Son of Heaven: Wei Cheng at the Court of T'ang T'ai-tsung* (1974). R. W. L. Guisso analyzes the career of China's only empress in *Wu Tse-t'ien and the Politics of Legitimization in T'ang China* (1978). A thorough examination of the economic, political, and military conditions of the early eighth century is found in E. Pulleyblank, *The Background of the Rebellion of An Lu-shan* (1955). For an introduction to Tang poetry, see S. Owen, *The Great Age of Chinese Poetry: The High T'ang* (1981), or one of the many biographies of Tang poets, such as W. Hung, *Tu Fu: China's Greatest Poet* (1952); A. Waley, *The Life and Times of Po Chu-i, 772–846 A.D.* (1949); or C. Hartman, *Han Yü and the T'ang Search for Unity* (1985). For other features of Tang culture, see E. Schafer, *The Golden Peaches of Samarkand* (1963), and J. Gernet, *Buddhism in Chinese Society: An Economic History of the Fifth to the Tenth Centuries* (1995).

On the interconnections among the societies of East Asia, see C. Holcomb, *The Genesis of East Asia, 221 B.C.–A.D. 907* (2001), and W. Cohen, *East Asia at the Center* (2000). For early Korean history, see A. Nahm, *Introduction to Korean History and Culture* (1993), and K. Kim, *A New History of Korea* (1964). P. Lee, ed., *Sourcebook of Korean Civilization* (1993), offers an excellent selection of primary sources.

Good general histories of Japan include P. Varley, *Japanese Culture* (1984); C. Totman, *A History of Japan* (1999); and J. Hall, *Japan from Prehistory to Modern Times* (1970). Still of value is G. Samson, *Japan: A Short Cultural History* (1952). An attractive volume that covers more than history and geography is M. Collcott, M. Jansen, and I. Kumakura, *Cultural Atlas of Japan* (1988). For primary sources, see W. T. de Bary et al., *Sources of Japanese Tradition* (2001), and D. Lu, *Japan: A Documentary History* (1996). The six-volume *Cambridge History of Japan,* ed. J. Hall et al. (1988–1999), offers authoritative accounts of all periods.

W. G. Aston, trans., *Nihongi: Chronicles of Japan from Earliest Times to A.D. 697* (1896, reprint 1990), despite its age, is still the only English translation of the earliest historical chronicle. J. P. Maas, *Antiquity and Anachronism in Japanese History* (1992), makes the bold suggestion that an exaggerated history of antiquity led to a distorted perception of the past. Quite readable is the well-illustrated J. E. Kidder, *Early Buddhist Japan* (1972). J. M. Kitagawa, *Religion in Japanese History* (1966), discusses both Shinto and Buddhism. J. Piggott, *The Emergence of Japanese Kingship* (1999), draws on both archaeology and chronicles to examine the sacred quality of early Japanese rulers.

# LISTENING TO THE PAST

## Copying Buddhist Sutras

*Buddhism was not merely a set of ideas but also a set of practices. In Chinese, Japanese, and Korean monasteries, as in Western ones, monks and nuns, under the direction of the abbot or abbess, would read and copy scriptures as an act of devotion. Pious laypeople might pay to have sutras copied as a means of earning religious merit. Sometimes a copyist attached a statement at the end of a sutra explaining the circumstances that had surrounded the act of copying. Below are two such statements, one from a sutra found in Dunhuang, on the northwest fringe of China proper, dated 550, and the other from Korea, dated 755.*

**1.**

Happiness is not fortuitous: pray for it and it will be found. Results are not born of thin air: pay heed to causes and results will follow. This explains how the Buddhist disciple and nun Daorong—because her conduct in her previous life was not correct—came to be born in her present form, a woman, vile and unclean.

Now if she does not honor the awesome decree of Buddha, how can future consequences be favorable for her? Therefore, having cut down her expenditures on food and clothing, she reverently has had the *Nirvana sutra* copied once. She prays that those who read it carefully will be exalted in mind to the highest realms and that those who communicate its meaning will cause others to be so enlightened.

She also prays that in her present existence she will have no further sickness or suffering, that her parents in seven other incarnations (who have already died or will die in the future) and her present family and close relatives may experience joy in the four elements [earth, water, fire, and air], and that whatever they seek may indeed come to pass. Finally, she prays that all those endowed with knowledge may be included within this prayer. Dated the 29th day of the fourth month of 550.

**2.**

The copying began on the first day of the eighth month of 754, and was completed on the fourteenth day of the second month of the following year.

One who made a vow to copy the scripture is Dharma master Yongi of Hwangnyong Monastery. His purposes were to repay the love of his parents and to pray for all living beings in the dharma realm to attain the path of the Buddha.

The scripture is made as follows: First scented water is sprinkled around the roots of a paperbark mulberry tree to quicken its growth; the bark is then peeled and pounded to make paper with a clean surface. The copyists, the artisans who make the centerpiece of the scroll, and the painters who draw the images of buddhas and bodhisattvas all receive the bodhisattva ordination and observe abstinence. After relieving themselves, sleeping, eating, or drinking, they take a bath in scented water before returning to the work. Copyists are adorned with new pure garments, loose trousers, a coarse crown, and a deva crown. Two azure-clad boys sprinkle water on their heads and . . . azure-clad boys and musicians perform music. The processions to the copying site are headed by one who sprinkles scented water on their path, another who scatters flowers, a dharma master who carries a censer, and another dharma master who chants Buddhist verses. Each of the copyists carries incense and flowers and invokes the name of the Buddha as he progresses.

This gilt bronze image of Maitreya, not quite three feet tall, was made in Korea in about 600. It depicts the Buddha Maitreya, the Future Buddha who presides over Tushita Heaven. The rounded face, slender body, and gracefully draped robe help convey the idea that the Buddha is neither male nor female, but beyond such distinctions. *(Courtesy, Yushin Yoo)*

Upon reaching the site, all take refuge in the three Jewels (the Buddha, the Dharma, and the Order), make three bows, and offer the *Flower Garland Scripture* and others to buddhas and bodhisattvas. Then they sit down and copy the scripture, make the centerpiece of the scroll, and paint the buddhas and bodhisattvas. Thus, azure-clad boys and musicians cleanse everything before a piece of relic is placed in the center.

Now I make a vow that the copied scripture will not break till the end of the future—even when a major chilicosm [millions of universes] is destroyed by the three calamities, this scripture shall be intact as the void. If all living things rely on this scripture, they shall witness the Buddha, listen to his dharma, worship the relic, aspire to enlightenment without backsliding, cultivate the vows of the Universally Worthy Bodhisattva, and achieve Buddhahood.

## QUESTIONS FOR ANALYSIS

1. What common Buddhist beliefs are expressed in both of these statements?
2. What do you make of the emphasis on rituals surrounding copying the sutra in the second statement?

*Sources:* Patricia Buckley Ebrey, ed., *Chinese Civilization: A Sourcebook* (New York: Free Press, 1993), pp. 102–103; Peter H. Lee, ed., *Sourcebook of Korean Civilization* (New York: Columbia University Press, 1993), pp. 201–202, modified.

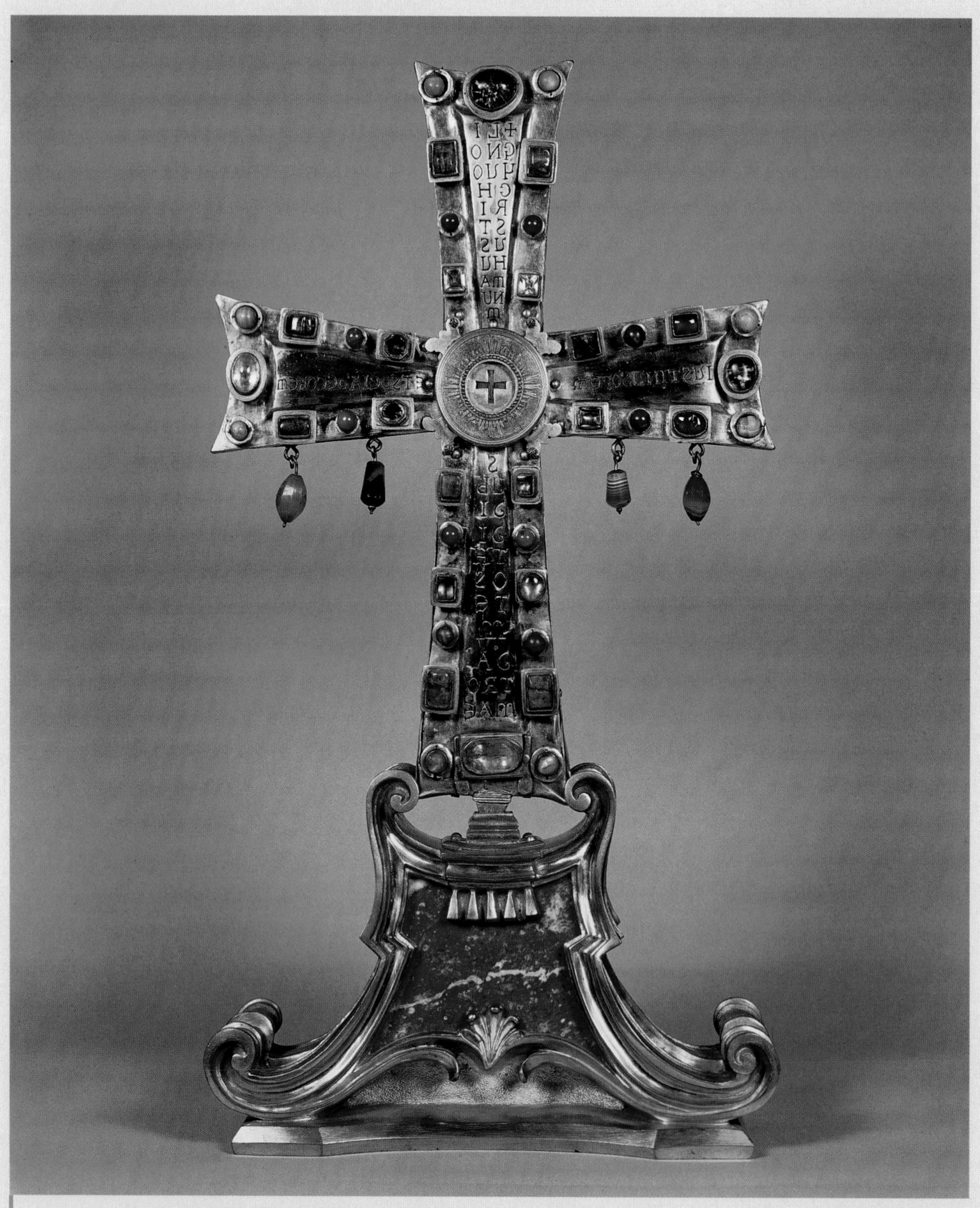

Byzantine cross. Justin II gave this cross to Pope John III; it was one of a very few not destroyed in the sack of Rome in 1527. *(Scala/Art Resource, NY)*

CHAPTER

# 8 THE MAKING OF EUROPE

## CHAPTER OUTLINE

- The Growth of the Christian Church
- Christian Attitudes Toward Classical Culture
- Christian Monasticism
- The Migration of the Germanic Peoples
- Germanic Society
- The Byzantine East (ca 400–788)

The centuries between approximately 400 and 900 present a paradox. On the one hand, they witnessed the disintegration of the western Roman Empire, which had been one of humanity's great political and cultural achievements. On the other hand, these five centuries were a creative and seminal period, during which Europeans laid the foundations for medieval and modern Europe. It is not too much to say that this period saw the making of Europe.

The idea of Europe—with the geographical and cultural implications that we in the twenty-first century attach to the word—is actually a fairly recent notion. Classical geographers used the term *Europe* to distinguish it from Africa and Asia, the only other landmasses they knew, and medieval scholars imitated and followed the ancients. Only in the sixteenth century did the word *Europe* enter the common language of educated peoples living in the western parts of the Eurasian landmass and did the continent we call Europe gain a map-based frame of reference.[1] The vision of almost everyone else was provincial, limited by the boundaries of their province or even village. While the peoples living there did not define themselves as European for centuries, a European identity began to be forged in late antiquity and the early medieval period.

The basic ingredients that went into the making of a distinctly European civilization were the cultural legacy of Greece and Rome, the customs and traditions of the Germanic peoples, and the Christian faith. The most important of these was Christianity, because it absorbed and assimilated the other two. It reinterpreted the classics in a Christian sense. It instructed the Germanic peoples and gave them new ideals of living and social behavior. Christianity became the cement that held European society together. As a result, people's understanding of themselves shifted from a social or political one (German, Celt, Roman) to a religious one.

During this period, the Byzantine Empire, centered at Constantinople, served as a protective buffer between Europe and peoples to the east. The Byzantine Greeks preserved the philosophical and scientific texts of the ancient world, which later formed the basis for study in science and medicine, and produced a great synthesis of Roman law, the Justinian *Code.* In the urbane and sophisticated life led at Constantinople, the Greeks set a standard far above the primitive existence of the West.

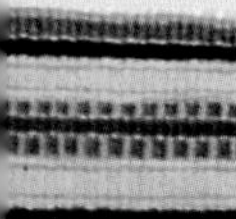

The civilization later described as European resulted from the fusion of the Greco-Roman heritage, Germanic traditions, Christian faith, and significant elements of Islamic culture (see Chapter 9).

- How did these components act on one another?
- How did they lead to the making of Europe?
- What influence did Byzantine culture have on the making of Europe?

This chapter will focus on these questions.

## THE GROWTH OF THE CHRISTIAN CHURCH

In doctrine Christianity was a **syncretic faith.** That is, it absorbed and adopted many of the religious ideas of the eastern Mediterranean world. From Judaism came the concept, unique in the ancient world, of monotheism, belief in one God, together with the rich ethical and moral precepts of the Old Testament Scriptures. From Orphism, a set of sixth-century B.C.E. religious ideas, came the belief that the body is the prison of the soul. From Hellenistic thought derived the notion of the superiority of spirit over matter. Likewise, scholars have noticed the similarity between the career of Jesus and that of the gods of Eastern mystery cults such as Mithra, who died and rose from the dead, and whose followers had a ceremony of communion in which the god's flesh was symbolically eaten. All of these ideas played a part in the formulation of Christian doctrine and in attracting people to it.

With the support of the emperors, the institutional church gradually established an orthodox set of beliefs and adopted a system of organization based on that of the Roman state. Moreover, the church possessed able leaders who launched a dynamic missionary policy. Finally, the church slowly succeeded in assimilating, or adapting, pagan peoples, both Germanic and Roman, to Christianity. These factors help explain the growth of the church in the face of repeated Germanic invasions.

### The Church and the Roman Emperors

The church benefited considerably from the emperors' support. In return, the emperors expected the support of the Christian church in maintaining order and unity. After legalizing its practice, Constantine encouraged Christianity throughout his reign. In 380 the emperor Theodosius went further than Constantine and made Christianity the official religion of the empire. Theodosius stripped Roman pagan temples of statues, made the practice of the old Roman state religion a treasonable offense, and persecuted Christians who dissented from orthodox doctrine. Most significant, he allowed the church to establish its own courts. Church courts began to develop their own body of law, called *canon law.* These courts, not the Roman government, had jurisdiction over the clergy and ecclesiastical disputes.

In the fourth century, theological disputes frequently and sharply divided the Christian community. Some disagreements had to do with the nature of Christ. For example, **Arianism,** which originated with Arius (ca 250–336), a priest of Alexandria, denied that Christ was divine and co-eternal with God the Father—two propositions of Orthodox Christian belief. Arius held that God the Father was by definition uncreated and unchangeable. Jesus, however, was born of Mary, grew in wisdom, and suffered punishment and death. Jesus was created by the will of the Father and thus was not co-eternal with the Father. Therefore, Arius reasoned, Jesus the Son must be less than or inferior to the Unbegotten Father, who is incapable of suffering and did not die. This argument implies that Jesus stands somewhere between God the Creator and humanity in need of redemption. Orthodox theologians branded Arius's position a *heresy*—denial of a basic doctrine of faith.

Arianism enjoyed such popularity and provoked such controversy that Constantine, to whom religious disagreement meant civil disorder, interceded. In 325 he summoned a council of church leaders to Nicaea in Asia Minor and presided over it personally. The council produced the Nicene Creed, which defined the Orthodox position that Christ is "eternally begotten of the Father" and of the same substance as the Father. Arius and those who refused to accept the creed were banished, the first case of civil punishment for heresy. This participation of the emperor in a theological dispute within the church paved the way for later emperors to claim that they could do the same.

So active was the emperor Theodosius's participation in church matters that he eventually came to loggerheads with Bishop Ambrose of Milan (339–397). Theodosius ordered Ambrose to hand over his cathedral church to the emperor. Ambrose's response had important consequences for the future:

*At length came the command, "Deliver up the Basilica"; I reply, "It is not lawful for us to deliver it up, nor for your Majesty to receive it. . . . It is asserted that all things are*

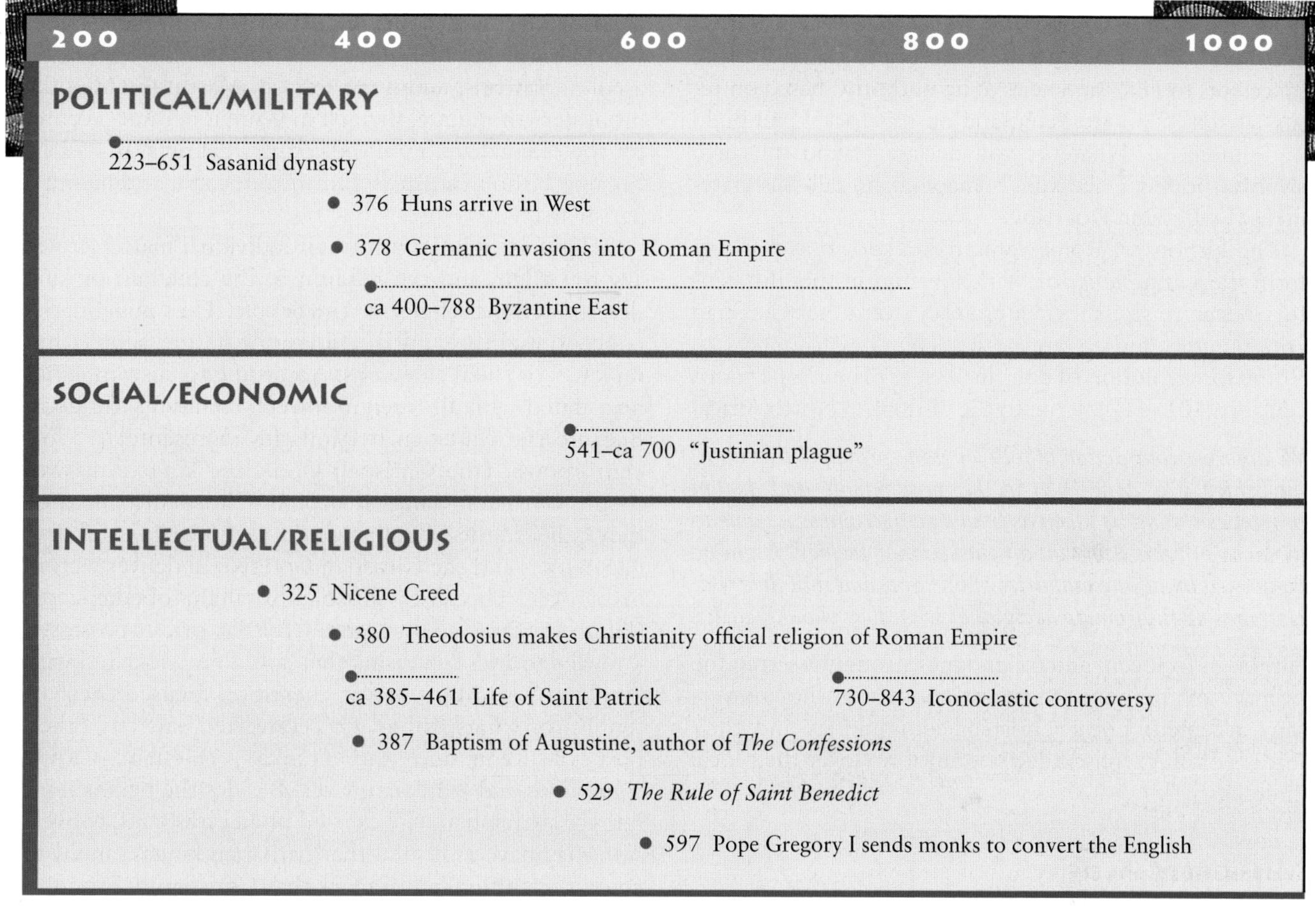


*lawful to the Emperor, that all things are his. But do not burden your conscience with the thought that you have any right as Emperor over sacred things. . . . It is written, God's to God and Caesar's to Caesar. The palace is the Emperor's, the Churches are the Bishop's. To you is committed jurisdiction over public, not over sacred buildings."*[2]

Throughout the Middle Ages, theologians, canonists, and propagandists repeatedly cited Ambrose's position as the basis for relations between the two powers.

## Administration and Leadership

The early church benefited from the administrative abilities of some church leaders and the identification of the authority and dignity of the bishop of Rome with the imperial traditions of the city. The early church organized itself along the lines of the Roman Empire. During the reign of Diocletian (284–305), the empire had been divided for administrative purposes into geographical units called *dioceses.* Christian bishops made their headquarters, or *sees,* in the urban centers of the old Roman dioceses. A bishop's jurisdiction gradually extended throughout his diocese. The center of his authority was his cathedral, a word deriving from the Latin *cathedra,* meaning "chair."

With imperial power weak, educated people joined and worked for the church in the belief that it was the one institution capable of providing leadership. Bishop Ambrose, the son of the Roman prefect of Gaul, was a trained lawyer and governor of a province. He was typical of Roman aristocrats who held high public office before joining the church and becoming bishops.

After the removal of the imperial capital and the emperor to Constantinople, the bishop of Rome exercised considerable influence in the West, in part because he had no real competitor there. In addition, successive bishops of Rome stressed the special role of that see. They pointed to the importance that Rome had enjoyed in the framework of the old empire. Moreover, according to tradition,

Peter, the chief of Christ's first twelve followers, had lived and been executed in Rome. The popes claimed to be successors to Peter and heirs to his authority, based on Jesus' words: "You are Peter, and on this rock I will build my church. . . . Whatever you declare bound on earth shall be bound in heaven." Theologians call this statement the **Petrine Doctrine.**

The bishops of Rome came to be known as popes—from the Latin *papa,* for "father"—and in the fifth century began to stress their supremacy over other Christian communities and to urge other churches to appeal to Rome for resolution of doctrinal issues. Thus Pope Innocent I (r. 401–417) wrote to the bishops of North Africa:

*We approve your action in following the principle that nothing which was done even in the most remote and distant provinces should be taken as finally settled unless it came to the notice of this See, that any just pronouncement might be confirmed by all the authority of this See, and that the other churches might from thence gather what they should teach.*[3]

Although Innocent and other popes strongly asserted the primacy of the pope, those assertions were not universally accepted. Local Christian communities and their leaders often exercised decisive authority over their local churches.

## Missionary Activity

The word *catholic* derives from a Greek word meaning "general," "universal," or "worldwide." Christ had said that his teaching was for all peoples, and Christians sought to make their faith catholic—that is, believed everywhere. This could be accomplished only through missionary activity. As Saint Paul had written to the Christian community at Colossae in Asia Minor:

*You have stripped off your old behavior with your old self, and you have put on a new self which will progress towards true knowledge the more it is renewed in the image of its creator; and in that image there is no room for distinction between Greek and Jew, between the circumcised or the uncircumcised, or between barbarian or Scythian, slave and free man. There is only Christ; he is everything and he is in everything.*[4]

Paul urged Christians to bring the "good news" of Christ to all peoples. The Mediterranean served as the highway over which Christianity spread to the cities of the empire (see Map 8.1).

Christian communities were scattered throughout Gaul and Britain during the Roman occupation. The effective beginnings of Christianity in Gaul can be traced to Saint Martin of Tours (ca 316–397), a Roman soldier who, after giving half of his cloak to a naked beggar, had a vision of Christ and was baptized. Martin founded the monastery of Ligugé, the first in Gaul; it became a center for the evangelization of the country districts. In 372 he became bishop of Tours and introduced a rudimentary parish system.

Religion was not a private or individual matter; it was a social affair, and the religion of the chieftain or king determined the religion of the people. Thus missionaries concentrated their initial efforts not on the people, but on kings or tribal chieftains. According to custom, kings negotiated with all foreign powers, including the gods. Because the Christian missionaries represented a "foreign" power (the Christian God), the king dealt with them. Germanic kings accepted Christianity because they believed the Christian God was more powerful than pagan ones and the Christian God would deliver victory in battle; or because Christianity taught obedience to (kingly) authority; or because Christian priests possessed knowledge and a charisma that could be associated with kingly power. Missionaries, therefore, focused their attention on kings. Kings who converted, such as Ethelbert of Kent and the Frankish chieftain Clovis, sometimes had Christian wives. Besides the personal influence a Christian wife exerted on her husband, conversion may have indicated that barbarian kings wanted to enjoy the cultural advantages that Christianity brought,

**Ardagh Silver Chalice** This chalice (ca 800) formed part of the treasure of Ardagh Cathedral in County Limerick, Ireland. It has been called "one of the most sumptuous pieces of ecclesiastical metalwork to survive from early medieval Europe." The circular filigree decoration resembles that of Irish manuscript illumination. *(National Museum of Ireland)*

such as literate assistants and an ideological basis for their rule.

Tradition identifies the conversion of Ireland with Saint Patrick (ca 385–461). Born in western England to a Christian family of Roman citizenship, Patrick was captured and enslaved by Irish raiders and taken to Ireland, where he worked for six years as a herdsman. He escaped and returned to England, where a vision urged him to Christianize Ireland. In preparation, Patrick studied in Gaul and in 432 was consecrated a bishop. Patrick's missionary activities followed the existing social pattern: he converted the Irish tribe by tribe, first baptizing the king. In 445, with the approval of Pope Leo I, Patrick established his see in Armagh.

The Christianization of the English really began in 597, when Pope Gregory I sent a delegation of monks under the Roman Augustine to Britain to convert the English. The conversion of the English had far-reaching consequences because Britain later served as a base for the Christianization of the European continent (see Map 8.1). Between the fifth and tenth centuries, the great majority of peoples living on the European continent and the nearby islands accepted the Christian religion—that is, they received baptism, though baptism in itself did not automatically transform people into Christians.

The Germanic peoples were warriors who idealized the military virtues of physical strength, ferocity in battle, and loyalty to the leader. Victors in battle enjoyed the spoils of success and plundered the vanquished. The greater the fighter, the more trophies and material goods he collected. Thus the Germans had trouble accepting the Christian precepts of "love your enemies" and "turn the other cheek," and they found the Christian notions

**MAP 8.1 The Spread of Christianity** Originating in Judaea, the southern part of modern Israel and Jordan, Christianity spread throughout the Roman world. Roman sea-lanes and roads facilitated the expansion.

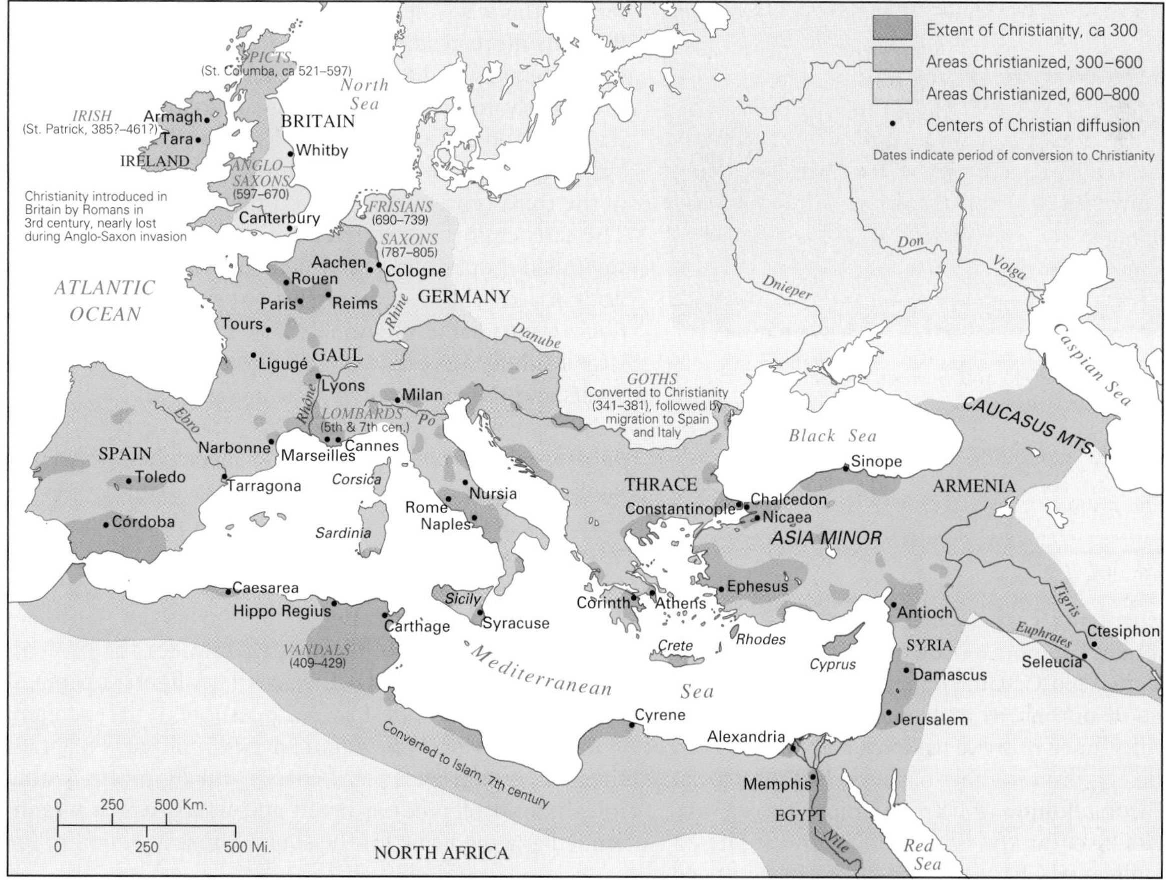

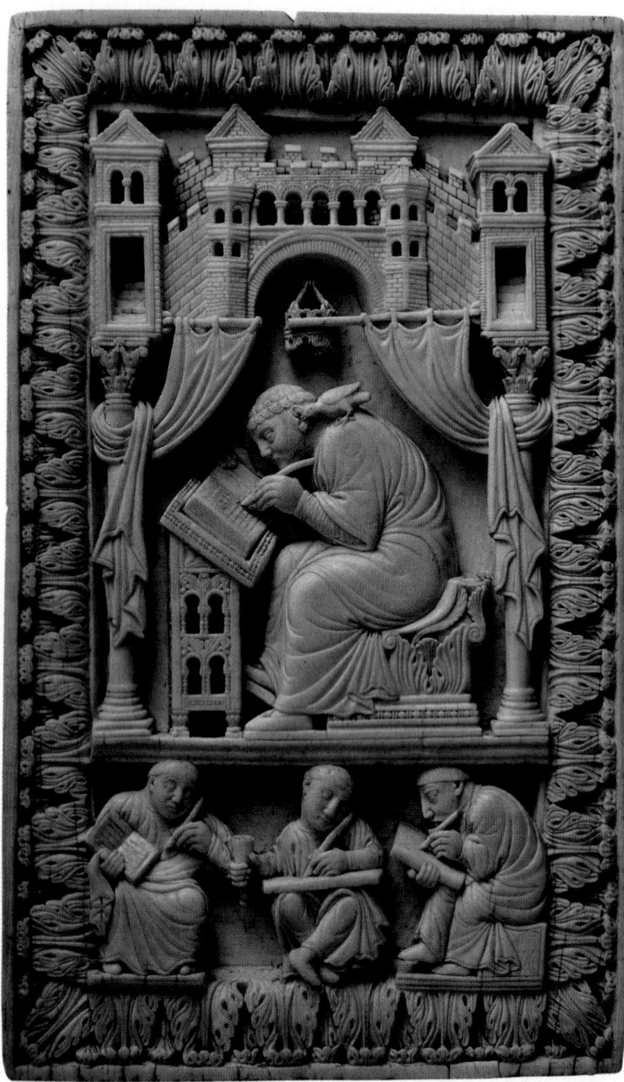

**Pope Gregory I (590–604) and Scribes** One of the four "Doctors" (or Learned Fathers) of the Latin church, Gregory is shown in this tenth-century ivory book cover writing at his desk while the Holy Spirit, in the form of a dove, whispers in his ear. Below, scribes copy Gregory's works. *(Kunsthistorisches Museum, Vienna/Art Resource, NY)*

of sin and repentance virtually incomprehensible. Sin in Christian thought meant disobedience to the will of God as revealed in the Ten Commandments and the teaching of Christ. Good or "moral" behavior to the barbarians meant the observance of tribal customs and practices. In Germanic society, dishonorable behavior brought social ostracism. The inculcation of Christian ideals took a very long time.

## Conversion and Assimilation

In Christian theology, conversion involves a turning toward God—that is, a conscious effort to live according to the Gospel message. How did missionaries and priests get masses of pagan and illiterate peoples to understand and live by Christian ideals and teachings? Through preaching, through assimilation, and through the penitential system.

Preaching aimed at instruction and edification. Instruction presented the basic teachings of Christianity. Edification was intended to strengthen the newly baptized in their faith through stories about the lives of Christ and the saints. Deeply ingrained pagan customs and practices, however, could not be stamped out by words alone or even by imperial edicts. Christian missionaries often pursued a policy of assimilation, easing the conversion of pagan men and women by stressing similarities between their customs and beliefs and those of Christianity. A letter from Pope Gregory I to Augustine of Canterbury in 601 illustrates this policy. The pope instructed Augustine not to tear down the pagan English temples but to destroy the idols and then cleanse the temples with holy water. "In this way," he wrote, "we hope that the people . . . flocking more readily to their accustomed resorts, may come to know and adore the true God."[5]

Similarly, the church joined pagan holidays with Christian occasions. There were two Roman Christians named Valentine, both of whom were martyred for their beliefs in the third century C.E. around the middle of February. The early church converted a mid-February Roman festival called Lupercalia—at which the Romans asked the gods for fertility for themselves, their fields, and their flocks—into Saint Valentine's Day. (It was not until the later Middle Ages that the day became associated with lovers and the exchange of messages and gifts.)

In the early church, confession meant that the sinner *publicly* acknowledged charges laid against him or her and *publicly* carried out the penitential works that the priest or bishop prescribed. For example, an adulterer might have to stand outside the church before services, wearing a sign naming his or her sin and asking for the prayers of everyone who entered. Beginning in the late sixth century, Irish and English missionaries brought the penitential system to continental Europe. The illiterate penitent knelt before the priest, who questioned the penitent about the sins he or she might have committed. The priest then imposed a penance. Penance usually meant fasting for a period of time on bread and water, which was intended as a medicine for the soul. Here is a section of the penitential prepared by Archbishop Theodore of Canterbury (668–690), which circulated widely at the time:

*If anyone commits fornication with a virgin he shall do penance for one year. If with a married woman, he shall do penance for four years, two of these entire. . . .*

*A male who commits fornication with a male shall do penance for three years. . . .*

*Whoever has often committed theft, seven years is his penance, or such a sentence as his priest shall determine, that is, according to what can be arranged with those whom he has wronged. . . .*

*If a layman slays another with malice aforethought, if he will not lay aside his arms, he shall do penance for seven years; without flesh and wine, three years. . . .*

*Women who commit abortion before [the fetus] has life, shall do penance for one year or for the three forty-day periods or for forty days, according to the nature of the offense; and if later, that is, more than forty days after conception, they shall do penance as murderesses.*[6]

As this sample suggests, writers of penitentials were preoccupied with sexual transgressions.

**Penitentials** provide an enormous amount of information about the ascetic ideals of early Christianity and about the crime-ridden realities of Celtic and Germanic societies. Penitentials also reveal the ecclesiastical foundations of some modern attitudes toward sex, birth control, and abortion. Unlike the earlier public penances, Celtic forms permitted the repeated reconciliation of the same sinner in a *private* situation involving only the priest and penitent. We do not know whether these severe penances were actually enforced; some scholars believe they were not. In any case, the penitential system contributed to the growth of a different attitude toward religion: formerly public, corporate, and social, religious observances became private, personal, and individual.[7]

## CHRISTIAN ATTITUDES TOWARD CLASSICAL CULTURE

Probably the major dilemma the early Christian church faced concerned Greco-Roman culture. In Greek philosophy, art, and architecture, and in Roman law, literature, education, and engineering, the legacy of a great civilization continued. The Christian religion had begun and spread within this intellectual and psychological milieu. What was to be the attitude of Christians to the Greco-Roman world of ideas?

### Adjustment

Christians in the first and second centuries believed that Christ would soon fulfill his promise to return and that the end of the world was near. Thus they considered knowledge useless and learning a waste of time, and they preached the duty of Christians to prepare for the Second Coming of the Lord. Good Christians who sought the Kingdom of Heaven by imitating Christ believed they had to disassociate themselves from the "filth" that Roman culture embodied.

Saint Paul (5?–67? C.E.) had written, "The wisdom of the world is foolishness, we preach Christ crucified." And about a century and a half later, Tertullian (ca 160–220), an influential African Christian writer, condemned all secular literature as foolishness in the eyes of God. "What has Athens to do with Jerusalem," he demanded, "the Academy with the Church? We have no need for curiosity since Jesus Christ, nor for inquiry since the gospel."

On the other hand, Christianity encouraged adjustment to the ideas and institutions of the Roman world. Some biblical texts urged Christians to accept the existing social, economic, and political establishment. Specifically addressing Christians living among non-Christians in the hostile environment of Rome, the author of the First Letter of Peter had written about the obligations of Christians:

*Always behave honorably among pagans, so that they can see your good works for themselves and, when the day of reckoning comes, give thanks to God for the things which now make them denounce you as criminals. . . .*

*Accept the authority of every social institution: the emperor, as the supreme authority, and the governors as commissioned by him to punish criminals and praise good citizenship. . . . Have respect for everyone and love for your community; fear God and honour the emperor.*[8]

Christians really had little choice. Jewish and Roman cultures were the only cultures early Christians knew; they had to adapt their Roman education to their Christian beliefs. Even Saint Paul believed that there was a good deal of truth in pagan thought, as long as it was correctly understood. The result was compromise, as evidenced by Saint Jerome (340–419). He thought that Christians should study the best of ancient thought because it would direct their minds to God.

The early Christians' adoption of the views of their contemporary world is evidenced as well in Christian attitudes toward women and homosexuality. Jesus considered women the equal of men in his plan of salvation. He

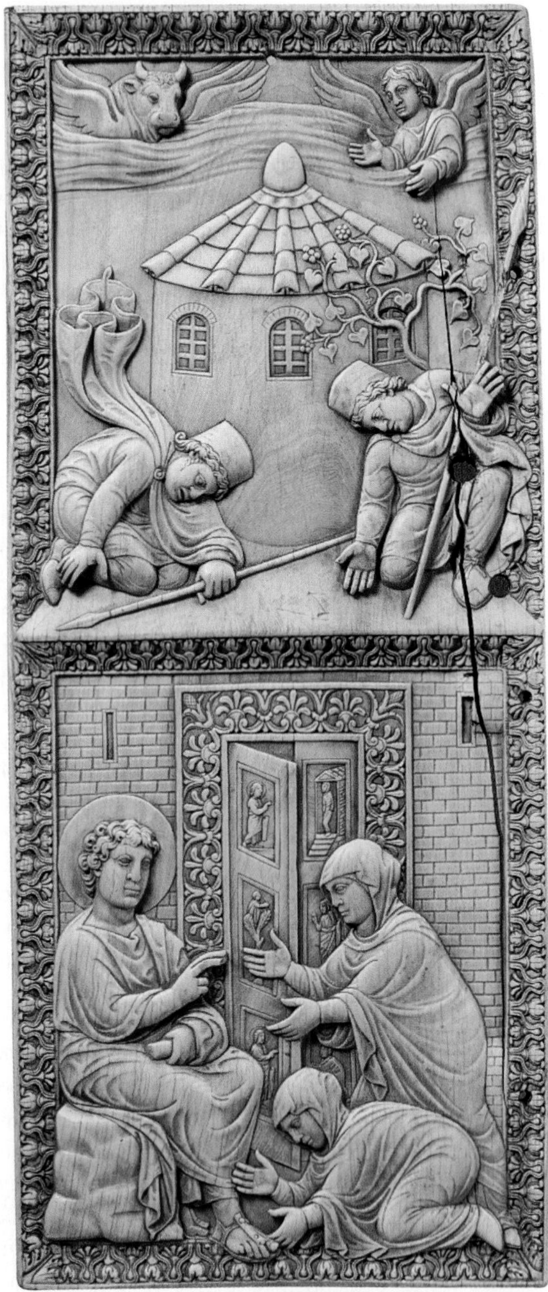

**The Marys at the Sepulcher** This late-fourth-century ivory panel tells the story (Matthew 28:1–6) of Mary Magdalene and another Mary (*lower*), who went to Jesus' tomb to discover the stone at the entrance rolled away; that an angel had descended from heaven; and in shock the guards assigned (*upper*) to watch the tomb "trembled and became like dead men." The angel told the women that Jesus had risen. The blend of Roman artistic style—in spacing, drapery, men's hair fashion—and Christian subject matter shows the assimilation of classical form and Christian teaching. *(Castello Sforzesco/ Scala/Art Resource, NY)*

attributed no disreputable qualities to women, made no comment on the wiles of women, made no reference to them as inferior creatures. On the contrary, women were among his earliest and most faithful converts. He discussed his mission with them (John 4:21–25), he accepted the ministrations of a reformed prostitute, and women were the first persons to whom he revealed himself after his resurrection (Matthew 28:9–10). The influence of Jewish and Christian writers on the formation of medieval (and modern) attitudes toward women, however, was greater than Jesus' influence.

Jesus' message emphasized love for God and for one's fellow human beings. Later writers tended to stress Christianity as a religion of renunciation and asceticism. Their views derive from Platonic-Hellenistic ideas of the contemporary Mediterranean world. The Hellenistic Jewish philosopher Philo of Alexandria (ca 20 B.C.E.–ca 50 C.E.), for example, held that since the female represented sense perception and the male the higher, rational soul, the female was inferior to the male. Female beauty may come from God, who created everything, the African church father Tertullian wrote, but it should be feared. Women should wear veils, he warned; otherwise, men would be endangered by the sight of them.[9]

The church fathers acknowledged that God had established marriage for the generation of children, but they believed marriage was a concession to weak people who could not bear celibacy. Saint Augustine (see below) considered sexual intercourse a great threat to spiritual freedom. In daily life every act of intercourse was evil, he taught; every child was conceived by a sinful act and came into the world tainted with original sin. Celibacy was the highest good, intercourse little more than animal lust.

Women were considered incapable of writing on the subject, so we have none of their views. The church fathers, by definition, were men. Because many of them experienced physical desire when in the presence of women, misogyny (hatred of women) entered Christian thought. Although early Christian writers believed women the spiritual equals of men, and although Saint Melania, Saint Scholastica (see page 220), and some other women exercised influence as teachers and charismatic leaders, Christianity became a male-centered and sex-negative religion. "The Church Fathers regarded sex as at best something to be tolerated, an evil whose only good was procreation."[10] Until perhaps very recently, this attitude dominated religious thinking on human sexuality.

Toward homosexuality, according to a controversial study, Christians of the first three or four centuries simply imbibed the attitude of the world in which they lived. Many Romans indulged in homosexual activity, and contemporaries did not consider such behavior (or inclinations to it) immoral, bizarre, or harmful. Early Christians, too, considered homosexuality a conventional expression of physical desire and were no more susceptible to antihomosexual prejudices than pagans were. Some prominent Christians experienced loving same-gender relationships that probably had a sexual element. What eventually led to a change in public and Christian attitudes toward sexual behavior was the shift from the sophisticated urban culture of the Greco-Roman world to the rural culture of medieval Europe.[11]

## Synthesis: Saint Augustine

The finest representative of the blending of classical and Christian ideas, and indeed one of the most brilliant thinkers in the history of the Western world, was Saint Augustine of Hippo (354–430). Aside from the scriptural writers, no one else has had a greater impact on Christian thought in succeeding centuries. Saint Augustine was born into an urban family in what is now Algeria in North Africa. His father was a pagan; his mother, Monica, a devout Christian.

Augustine received his basic education in the local school. By modern and even medieval standards, that education was extremely narrow: textual study of the writings of the poet Virgil, the orator-politician Cicero, the historian Sallust, and the playwright Terence. As in the Islamic (see page 266) and Chinese worlds, learning in the Christian West meant memorization. Education in the late Roman world aimed at appreciation of words, particularly those of renowned and eloquent orators.

At the age of seventeen, Augustine went to nearby Carthage to continue his education. There he took a mistress with whom he lived for fifteen years. At Carthage, Augustine began an intellectual and spiritual pilgrimage that led him through experiments with several philosophies and heretical Christian sects. In 383 he traveled to Rome, where he endured not only illness but also disappointment in his teaching: his students fled when their bills were due.

Finally, in Milan in 387, Augustine received Christian baptism. He later became bishop of the seacoast city of Hippo Regius in his native North Africa. He was a renowned preacher to Christians there, a vigorous defender of orthodox Christianity, and the author of over ninety-three books and treatises.

Augustine's autobiography, *The Confessions,* is one of the most influential books in the history of Europe. Written in the form of a prayer, *The Confessions* describes Augustine's moral struggle: the conflict between his spiritual and intellectual aspirations and his sensual and material self.

*The Confessions,* written in the rhetorical style and language of late Roman antiquity, marks the synthesis of Greco-Roman forms and Christian thought. Many Greek and Roman philosophers had taught that knowledge and virtue are the same—that a person who really knows what is right will do what is right. Augustine rejected this idea. He believed that a person may know what is right but fail to act righteously because of the innate weakness of the human will. He pointed out that people do not always act on the basis of rational knowledge. A learned person can be corrupt and evil.

Augustine's ideas on sin, grace, and redemption became the foundation of all subsequent Christian theology, Protestant as well as Catholic. He wrote that the basic or dynamic force in any individual is the *will,* which he defined as "the power of the soul to hold on to or to obtain an object without constraint." The end or goal of the will determines the moral character of the individual. When Adam ate the fruit forbidden by God in the garden of Eden (Genesis 3:6), he committed "the original sin" and corrupted the will. By concupiscence, or sexual desire, which all humans have, Adam's sin has been passed on by hereditary transmission through the flesh to all humanity. Original sin thus became a common social stain. Because Adam disobeyed God and fell, so all human beings have an innate tendency to sin: their will is weak. But, according to Augustine, God restores the strength of the will through grace (his love, assistance, support), which is transmitted through the sacraments, such as penance, or reconciliation, by the action of the Spirit.

When the Visigothic chieftain Alaric conquered Rome in 410, horrified pagans blamed the disaster on the Christians. In response, Augustine wrote *City of God.* This profoundly original work contrasts Christianity with the secular society in which it existed. *City of God* presents a moral interpretation of the Roman government—in fact, of all history. Filled with references to ancient history and mythology, it remained for centuries the standard statement of the Christian philosophy of history.

According to Augustine, history is the account of God acting in time. Human history reveals that there are two kinds of people: those who live according to the flesh in the City of Babylon and those who live according to the spirit in the City of God. The former will endure eternal hellfire, the latter eternal bliss.

Augustine maintained that states came into existence as the result of Adam's fall and people's inclination to sin. The state is a necessary evil, but it can work for the good by providing the peace, justice, and order that Christians need in order to pursue their pilgrimage to the City of God. The particular form of government—whether monarchy, aristocracy, or democracy—is basically irrelevant. Any civil government that fails to provide justice is no more than a band of gangsters.

Although the state results from a moral lapse—from sin—the church (the Christian community) is not entirely free from sin. The church is certainly not equivalent to the City of God. But the church, which is concerned with salvation, is responsible for everyone, including Christian rulers. Churches in the Middle Ages used Augustine's theory to defend their belief in the ultimate superiority of the spiritual power over the temporal.

## CHRISTIAN MONASTICISM

Christianity began and spread as a city religion. Since the first century, however, some especially pious Christians had felt that the only alternative to the decadence of urban life was complete separation from the world. The fourth century witnessed a significant change in the relationship between Christianity and the broader society. Until Constantine's legalization of Christianity, Christians were a persecuted minority. Some were tortured and killed. Christians greatly revered these martyrs, who, like Jesus, suffered and died for their faith. When Christianity was legalized and the persecutions ended, a new problem arose.

Whereas Christians had been a suffering minority, now they came to be identified with the state: non-Christians could not advance in the imperial service. But if Christianity had triumphed, so had "the world," for secular attitudes and values pervaded the church. The church of martyrs no longer existed. Some scholars believe the monasteries provided a way of life for those Christians who wanted to make a total response to Christ's teachings—people who wanted more than a lukewarm Christianity. The monks became the new martyrs. Saint Anthony of Egypt (d. 356), the first monk for whom there is concrete evidence and the person later considered the father of monasticism, went to Alexandria during the last persecution in the hope of gaining martyrdom. Christians believed that monks, like the martyrs before them, could speak to God and that their prayers had special influence with him.

### Western Monasticism

Monasticism began in Egypt in the third century. At first individuals and small groups withdrew from cities and organized society to seek God through prayer in caves and shelters in the desert or mountains. Gradually large colonies of monks emerged in the deserts of Upper Egypt. They were called hermits, from the Greek word *eremos,* meaning "desert." Many devout women also were attracted to the monastic life. Although monks (and nuns) led isolated lives and the monastic movement represented the antithesis of the ancient ideal of an urban social existence, ordinary people soon recognized the monks and nuns as holy people and sought them as spiritual guides.

Church leaders did not really approve of **eremitical** life. Hermits sometimes claimed to have mystical experiences—direct communications with God. If hermits could communicate directly with the Lord, what need had they for the priest and the institutional church? The scholarly bishop Basil of Caesarea in Cappadocia in Asia Minor argued that the eremitical life posed the danger of excessive concern with the self and did not provide the opportunity for the exercise of charity, the first virtue of any Christian. Saint Basil and the church hierarchy encouraged **coenobitic monasticism,** communal living in monasteries, which provided an environment for training the aspirant in the virtues of charity, poverty, and freedom from self-deception.

In the fourth, fifth, and sixth centuries, many experiments in communal monasticism were made in Gaul, Italy, Spain, Anglo-Saxon England, and Ireland. The abbey or monastery of Lérins on the Mediterranean Sea near Cannes (ca 410) encouraged the severely penitential and extremely ascetic behavior common in the East, such as long hours of prayer, fasting, and self-flagellation. The Roman-British monk Saint Patrick carried this tradition of harsh self-mortification from Lérins to Ireland in the fifth century, and Irish monastic life followed the ascetic Eastern form. Around 540 the former Roman senator Cassiodorus established a monastery, the Vivarium, on his estate in Italy. Cassiodorus enlisted highly educated and sophisticated men to copy both sacred and secular manuscripts, intending this to be their sole occupation. Cassiodorus started the association of monasticism with scholarship and learning. This developed into a great tradition in the medieval and modern worlds.

### The *Rule* of Benedict

In 529 Benedict of Nursia (480–543), who had experimented with both the eremitical and the communal forms of monastic life, wrote a brief set of regulations for the monks who had gathered around him at Monte Cassino between Rome and Naples. Benedict's *Rule* proved highly adaptable and slowly replaced all others.

**Saint Benedict** Holding his *Rule* in his left hand, the seated and cowled patriarch of Western monasticism blesses a monk with his right hand. His monastery, Monte Cassino, is in the background. *(Biblioteca Apostolica Vaticana)*

*The Rule of Saint Benedict* has influenced all forms of organized religious life in the Roman church.

Saint Benedict conceived of his *Rule* as a simple code for ordinary men. It outlined a monastic life of regularity, discipline, and moderation. Each monk had ample food and adequate sleep. Self-destructive acts of mortification were forbidden. In an atmosphere of silence, the monk spent part of the day in formal prayer, which Benedict called the "Work of God." This consisted of chanting psalms and other prayers from the Bible. The rest of the day was passed in study and manual labor. After a year of probation, the monk made three vows.

First, the monk vowed stability: he promised to live his entire life in the monastery of his profession. The object of this vow was to prevent the wandering so common in Saint Benedict's day. Second, the monk vowed conversion of manners—that is, to strive to improve himself and to come closer to God. Third, he promised obedience to the abbot, or head of the monastery.

*The Rule of Saint Benedict* expresses the assimilation of the Roman spirit into Western monasticism. It reveals the logical mind of its creator and the Roman concern for order, organization, and respect for law. Its spirit of moderation and flexibility is reflected in the patience, wisdom, and understanding with which the abbot is to govern and, indeed, with which life is to be led.

Saint Benedict's *Rule* implies that a person who wants to become a monk or nun need have no previous ascetic experience or even a particularly strong bent toward the religious life. Thus it allowed for the admission of newcomers with different backgrounds and personalities. From Chapter 59, "The Offering of Sons by Nobles or by the Poor," and from Benedict's advice to the abbot—"The abbot should avoid all favoritism in the monastery. . . . A man born free is not to be given higher rank than a slave who becomes a monk" (Chapter 2)—we know that men of different social classes belonged to his monastery. This flexibility helps to explain the attractiveness of Benedictine monasticism throughout the centuries.

The monastic life as conceived by Saint Benedict did not lean too heavily in any one direction. With its division of the day into prayer, study, and manual labor, it struck a balance between asceticism and idleness. It thus provided opportunities for persons of entirely different abilities and talents—from mechanics to gardeners to literary scholars. Benedict's *Rule* contrasts sharply with Cassiodorus's narrow concept of the monastery as a place for aristocratic bibliophiles.

Benedictine monasticism also suited the social circumstances of early medieval society. The Germanic invasions had fragmented European life: the self-sufficient rural estate replaced the city as the basic unit of civilization. A monastery, too, had to be economically self-sufficient. It was supposed to produce from its lands and properties all that was needed for food, clothing, shelter, and liturgical service of the altar. The monastery fitted in—indeed, represented—the trend toward localism. The Benedictine form of religious life also proved congenial to women. Five miles from Monte Cassino at Plombariola, Benedict's twin sister Scholastica (480–543) adapted the *Rule* for the use of her community of nuns. Many other convents for nuns were established in the early Middle Ages.

Benedictine monasticism also succeeded partly because it was so materially successful. In the seventh and eighth centuries, monasteries pushed back forest and wasteland, drained swamps, and experimented with crop rotation. Such Benedictine houses made a significant contribution to the agricultural development of Europe, earning immense wealth in the process. The communal nature of their organization, whereby property was held in common and profits were pooled and reinvested, made this contribution possible.

Finally, monasteries conducted schools for local young people. Some learned about prescriptions and herbal remedies and went on to provide medical treatment for their localities. A few copied manuscripts and wrote books. This training did not go unappreciated in a society desperately in need of it. Local and royal governments drew on the services of the literate men and able administrators the monasteries produced.

### Eastern Monasticism

From Egypt, Christian monasticism also spread to the Greek provinces of Syria and Palestine and to Constantinople itself. With financial assistance from the emperor Justinian I (527–565) and from wealthy nobles, monasteries soon spread throughout the empire, with seventy abbeys erected in Constantinople alone. Justinian granted the monks the right to inherit property from private citizens and the right to receive **solemnia,** or annual gifts, from the imperial treasury or from the taxes of certain provinces, and he prohibited lay confiscation of monastic estates. Beginning in the tenth century, the monasteries acquired fields, pastures, livestock, mills, saltworks, and urban rental properties, as well as cash and precious liturgical vessels. The exemption of Byzantine monasteries from state taxes also served to increase monastic wealth.

Monasticism in the Greek Orthodox world differed in fundamental ways from the monasticism that evolved in western Europe. First, while *The Rule of Saint Benedict* gradually became the universal guide for all western European monasteries, each individual house in the Byzantine world developed its own **typikon,** or set of rules for organization and behavior. The *typika* contain regulations about novitiate, diet, clothing, liturgical functions, commemorative services for benefactors, and the election of officials, such as the *hegoumenos,* or superior of the house. Second, while stability in the monastery eventually characterized Western monasticism, many Orthodox monks "moved frequently from one monastery to another or alternated between a coenobitic monastery and a hermit's kellion [cell]."[12] Finally, unlike the West, where monasteries often established schools for the education of the youth of the neighborhood, education never became a central feature of the Greek houses. Monks and nuns had to be literate to perform the services of the choir, and children destined for the monastic life were taught to read and write. In the monasteries where monks or nuns devoted themselves to study and writing, their communities sometimes played important roles in the development of theology and in the intellectual life of the empire. But those houses were very few, and no monastery assumed responsibility for the general training of the local young. Since bishops and patriarchs of the Greek church were recruited only from the monasteries, Greek houses did, however, exercise a cultural influence.

## THE MIGRATION OF THE GERMANIC PEOPLES

The migration of peoples from one area to another has been a dominant and continuing feature of world history. The causes of early migrations varied and are not thoroughly understood by scholars. But there is no question that they profoundly affected both the regions to which peoples moved and the regions they left behind.

The *Völkerwanderungen,* or migrations of the Germanic peoples, were important in the decline of the western Roman Empire and in the making of European civilization. Since about 150, Germanic tribes from the regions of the northern Rhine, Elbe, and Oder Rivers had pressed along the Rhine-Danube frontier of the Roman Empire. Some tribes, such as the Visigoths and Ostrogoths, led a settled existence, engaged in agriculture and trade, and accepted Arian Christianity. Other tribes, such as the Angles, Saxons, and Huns, led a nomadic life unaffected by Roman influences.

Why did the Germans migrate? Although many twentieth-century scholars have tried to answer this question, the answer is not known. Perhaps overpopulation and the resulting food shortages caused migration. Perhaps victorious tribes forced the vanquished to move southward. Probably "the primary stimulus for this gradual migration was the Roman frontier, which increasingly offered service in the army and work for pay around the camps."[13]

## The Idea of the Barbarian

The Greeks and Romans invented the idea of the **barbarian.** The Romans labeled all peoples living outside the frontiers of the Roman Empire (except the Persians) as barbarians. Geography, rather than ethnic background, determined a people's classification. The Romans also held that peoples outside the empire had no history and were touched by history only when they entered the Roman Empire.

The modern study of ethnography (writing about the formation of ethnic groups) involves the systematic recording of the major characteristics of different human cultures. Scholars today identify three models of ethnic formation among the Germanic peoples who came in contact with the Romans and whom the Romans called barbarians.

First, there were those Germanic peoples whose identity was shaped by a militarily successful or "royal" family. For example, the Salian Franks, Lombards, and Goths attracted and controlled followers from other peoples by getting them to adhere to the cultural traditions of the leading family. Followers assimilated the "kernel family's" legendary traditions and myths, which traced their origins to a family or individual of divine ancestry. The kernel family led these followers from their original territory, won significant victories over other peoples, and settled someplace within the Roman world.

A second model of ethnic formation derives from Central Asian steppe peoples such as the Huns, Avars, and Alans. These were polyethnic, seminomadic, and sedentary groups led by a small body of steppe commanders. (The term *steppe* refers to the vast semiarid plain in Russian Siberia.) These peoples constituted large confederations, whose success depended on constant expansion by military victory or the use of terror. Defeat in battle or the death of a leader could lead to the disintegration of the confederation.

The Alamanni and the Slavs represented a third model of barbarian ethnic formation. Because no evidence of collective legends, genealogies, or traditions among these peoples survives, we do not know whether they had a consciousness of collective identity. They were loosely organized, short-lived bands of peoples who lacked centralized leadership. Because the Slavs intermingled with Turko-Tartar, Finnic, Germanic, and Mongol peoples, the early Slavs possessed no ethnic identity.

One fundamental trait characterizes all barbarian peoples: the formation of ethnic groups did not represent a single historical event. Rather, the formation of such peoples was a continuous and changing process extending over long periods of time.[14]

## Romanization and Barbarization

By the late third century, a large percentage of military recruits came from the Germanic peoples. Besides army recruits, several types of barbarian peoples entered the empire and became affiliated with Roman government. The *laeti,* refugees or prisoners of war, were settled with their families in areas of Gaul and Italy under the supervision of Roman prefects and landowners. Generally isolated from the local Roman population, the laeti farmed regions depopulated by plague. The men had to serve in the Roman army.

Free barbarian units called **foederati,** stationed near major provincial cities, were a second type of affiliated barbarian group. Research has suggested that rather than giving them land, the Romans assigned the foederati shares of the tax revenues from the region.[15] Living close to Roman communities, the foederati quickly assimilated into Roman culture. In fact, in the fourth century, some foederati rose to the highest ranks of the army and moved in the most cultured and aristocratic circles.

The arrival of the Huns in the West in 376 precipitated the entry of entire peoples, the *gentes,* into the Roman Empire. Pressured by defeat in battle, starvation, or the movement of other peoples, tribes such as the Ostrogoths and Visigoths entered in large numbers, perhaps as many as twenty thousand men, women, and children.[16] Once the Visigoths were inside the empire, Roman authorities exploited their hunger by forcing them to sell

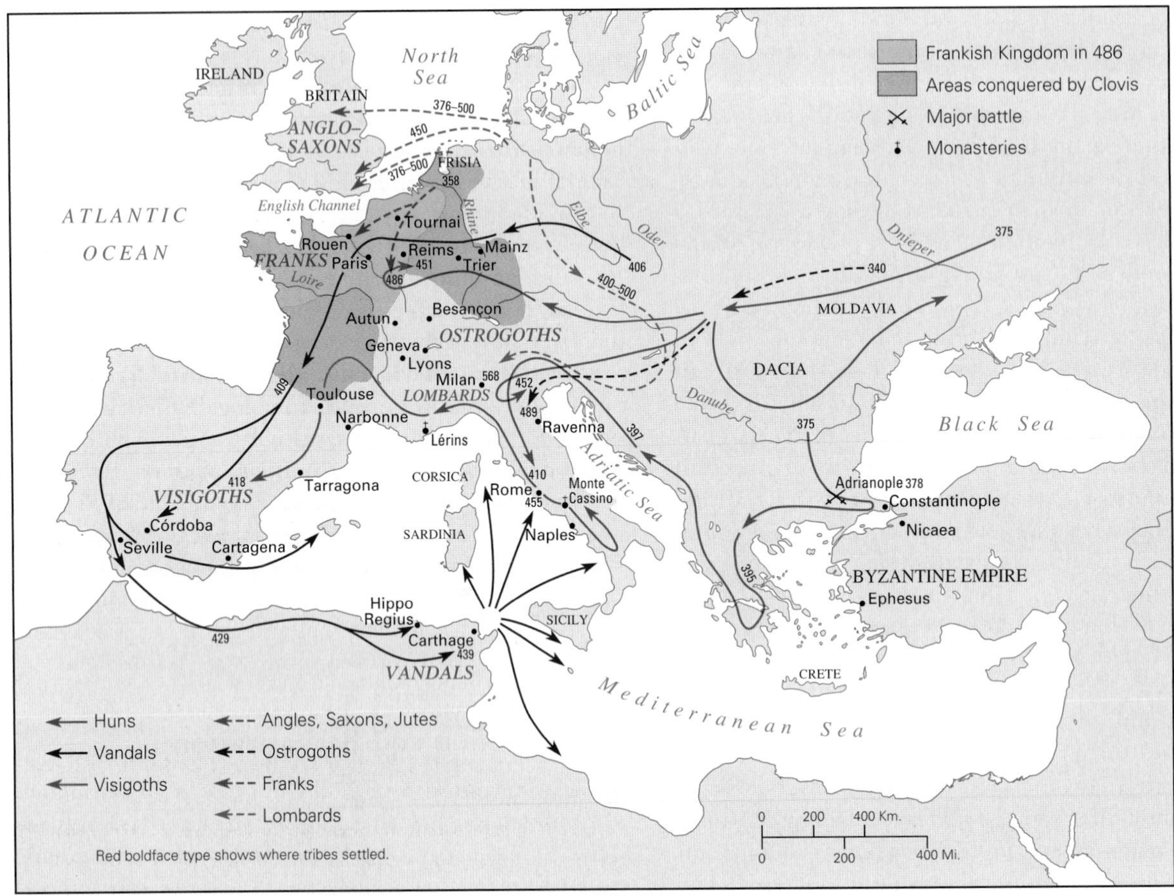


**MAP 8.2 The Germanic Migrations** The Germanic tribes infiltrated and settled in all parts of western Europe. The Huns, who were not German ethnically, originated in Central Asia. The Huns' victory over the Ostrogoths led the emperor to allow the Visigoths to settle within the empire, a decision that proved disastrous for Rome.

their own people in exchange for dog flesh: "the going rate was one dog for one Goth." The bitterness of those enslaved was aggravated by the arrival of the Ostrogoths. A huge rebellion erupted, and the Goths crushed the Roman army at Adrianople on August 9, 378.[17] This date marks the beginning of massive Germanic invasions into the empire (see Map 8.2).

Except for the Lombards, whose conquests of Italy persisted into the mid-eighth century, the movements of Germanic peoples on the European continent ended about 600. Between 450 and 565, the Germans established a number of kingdoms, but none except the Frankish kingdom lasted very long. Unlike modern nation-states, the Germanic kingdoms did not have definite geographical boundaries. The Visigoths overran much of southwestern Gaul. Establishing their headquarters at Toulouse, they exercised a weak domination over Spain until a great Muslim victory at Guadalete in 711 ended Visigothic rule. The Vandals, whose destructive ways are commemorated in the word *vandal,* settled in North Africa. In northern and western Europe in the sixth century, the Burgundians established rule over lands roughly circumscribed by old Roman army camps at Lyons, Besançon, Geneva, and Autun.

In northern Italy, the Ostrogothic king Theodoric (r. 471–526) established his capital at Ravenna and gradually won control of all Italy, Sicily, and the territory north and east of the upper Adriatic. Though attached to the customs of his people, Theodoric pursued a policy of assimilation between Germans and Romans. He maintained close relations with the emperor at Constantinople and attracted to his administration able scholars such

**Germanic Bracteate (Gold Leaf) Pendant** This late-fifth-century piece, with the head of Rome above a wolf suckling Romulus and Remus, reflects Germanic assimilation of Roman legend and artistic design. *(Courtesy of the Trustees of the British Museum)*

as Cassiodorus (see page 218). Theodoric's accomplishments were significant, but after his death his administration fell apart.

The most enduring Germanic kingdom was established by the Frankish chieftain Clovis (r. 481–511). Originally only a petty chieftain in northwestern Gaul (modern Belgium), Clovis began to expand his territories in 486. His Catholic wife Clothild worked to convert her husband and supported the founding of churches and monasteries. Clothild typifies the role women played in the Christianization and Romanization of the Germanic kingdoms. Clovis's conversion to orthodox Christianity in 496 won him the crucial support of the papacy and the bishops of Gaul. (See the feature "Listening to the Past: The Conversion of Clovis" on pages 236–237.) As the defender of Roman Catholicism against heretical Germanic tribes, Clovis went on to conquer the Visigoths, extending his domain as far as the Pyrenees and making Paris his headquarters. Because he was descended from the half-legendary chieftain Merovech, the dynasty that Clovis founded has been called Merovingian (see pages 364–365).

The island of Britain, conquered by Rome during the reign of Claudius, shared fully in the life of the Roman Empire during the first four centuries of the Christian era. A military aristocracy governed, and the official religion was the cult of the emperor. Towns were planned in the Roman fashion, with temples, public baths, theaters, and amphitheaters. In the countryside, large manors controlled the surrounding lands. Roman merchants brought Eastern luxury goods and religions—including Christianity—into Britain. The native Britons, a peaceful Celtic people, became thoroughly Romanized. Their language was Latin; their lifestyle was Roman.

After the Roman defeat at Adrianople, however, Roman troops were withdrawn from Britain, leaving it unprotected. The savage Picts from Scotland harassed the north. Teutonic tribes from modern-day Norway, Sweden, and Denmark—the Angles, Saxons, and Jutes—stepped up their assaults. Germans took over the best lands and humbled the Britons. Germanic tribes never subdued Scotland, where the Picts remained strong, or Wales, where the Celts and native Britons continued to put up stubborn resistance.

## GERMANIC SOCIETY

After the Germans replaced the Romans, Germanic customs and traditions shaped European society for centuries. What sorts of social, political, and economic life did the Germans have? Scholars are hampered in answering such questions because the Germans did not write and thus kept no written records before their conversion to Christianity. The earliest information about them comes from moralistic accounts by Romans such as the historian Tacitus (see page 174), who was acquainted only with the tribes living closest to the borders of the Roman Empire and imposed Greco-Roman categories of tribes and nations on the Germanic peoples he described.

### Kinship, Class, and Law

The Germans had no notion of the state as we use the term; they thought in social, not political, terms. The basic Germanic social unit was the tribe, or *folk.* Members of the folk believed that they were all descended from a common ancestor. Blood united them. Kinship protected them. Law was custom—unwritten and handed down by word of mouth from generation to generation. Custom regulated everything. Members were subject to their tribe's customary law wherever they went, and friendly tribes respected one another's laws.

Germanic tribes were led by kings or tribal chieftains. The chief, recognized as the strongest and bravest in battle, was elected from among the male members of the strongest family. He led the tribe in war, settled disputes among its members, conducted negotiations with outside powers, and offered sacrifices to the gods.

Closely associated with the chief in some southern tribes was the **comitatus,** or "war band." Writing at the end of the first century, Tacitus described the war band as the bravest young men in the tribe. They swore loyalty to the chief, fought with him in battle, and were not supposed to leave the battlefield without him; to do so implied cowardice and disloyalty and resulted in social disgrace. Social egalitarianism existed among members of the war band.

During the migrations of the third and fourth centuries, and as a result of constant warfare, the war band was transformed into a system of stratified ranks. Armbands, first obtained through contact with the Romans, came to be coveted as marks of rank, especially the gold ones reserved for the "royal families." During the Ostrogothic conquest of Italy under Theodoric, warrior-nobles also sought to acquire land, both as a mark of prestige and as a means to power. As land and wealth came into the hands of a small elite class, social inequalities emerged and gradually grew stronger.[18] These inequalities help to explain the origins of the European noble class (see page 396).

As long as custom determined all behavior, the early Germans had no need for written law. Beginning in the late sixth century, however, German tribal chieftains began to collect, write, and publish lists of their customs. Why then? The Christian missionaries who were slowly converting the Germans to Christianity wanted to read about German ways in order to assimilate the tribes to Christianity, and they encouraged German rulers to write their customs down. Moreover, by the sixth century the German rulers needed regulations that applied to the Romans under their jurisdiction as well as to their own people.

Today, if a person holds up a bank, American law maintains that the robber attacks both the bank and the state in which it exists—a sophisticated notion involving the abstract idea of the state. In early Germanic law, all crimes were regarded as crimes against a person.

According to the code of the Salian Franks, every person had a particular monetary value to the tribe. This value was called the **wergeld,** which literally means "man-money" or "money to buy off the spear." Men of fighting age had the highest wergeld, then women of childbearing age, then children, and finally the aged. If a person accused of a crime agreed to pay the wergeld and if the victim and his or her family accepted the payment, there was peace. If the accused refused to pay the wergeld or if the victim's family refused to accept it, a blood feud ensued. Individuals depended on their kin for protection, and kinship served as a force of social control.

The early law codes are patchwork affairs studded with additions made in later centuries. The law code of the Salian Franks issued by Clovis offers a general picture of Germanic life and problems in the early Middle Ages and is typical of the law codes of other tribes. The **Salic Law** is not really a code of law at all, but a list of tariffs or fines for particular offenses.

*If any person strike another on the head so that the brain appears, and the three bones which lie above the brain shall project, he shall be sentenced to 1200 denars, which make 300 shillings. . . .*

*If any one have killed a free woman after she has begun bearing children, he shall be sentenced to 2400 denars, which make 600 shillings. . . .*

*If any one shall have drawn a harrow through another's harvest after it has sprouted, or shall have gone through it with a wagon where there was no road, he shall be sentenced to 120 denars, which make 30 shillings.*[19]

Germanic law aimed at the prevention or reduction of violence. It was not concerned with abstract justice.

Germanic law differed considerably from Roman law. By the time of the Germanic migrations, Roman law consisted of a mass of imperial edicts, judicial decisions, senatorial enactments, and commentaries of jurists. Roman law included public law, which concerned affairs of the state, and private law, which related to the interests of individuals. It dealt with issues of marriage and the family, commerce and trade, property rights and criminal acts. It was written down. It regulated a complex and sophisticated society, and it involved abstract ideas such as the state and justice. Germanic law was unwritten; it was custom passed down by oral tradition from one generation to the next. Legislation did not consist of new laws issued by a king or chief or made by an assembly. Rather, Germanic law was found in the collective memory of the customs of the folk, and that custom was then applied to a particular situation. Germanic law was attached to the individual person, not to any territory, and the person took his law wherever he went.

As German kings accepted Christianity and as Romans and Germans increasingly intermarried, the distinction between Germanic and Roman law blurred and, in the course of the seventh and eighth centuries, disappeared. The result would be the new feudal law.

## Germanic Life

The Germans usually resided in small villages. Climate and geography determined the basic patterns of agricultural and pastoral life. In the flat or open coastal regions, men engaged in animal husbandry, especially cattle raising. Many tribes lived in small settlements on the edges of clearings where they raised barley, wheat, oats, peas, and beans. They tilled their fields with a simple wooden scratch plow and harvested their grains with a small iron sickle. Women ground the kernels of grain with a grindstone and made the resulting flour into a dough that they shaped into flat cakes and baked on clay trays. Much of the grain was fermented into a strong, thick beer. Women performed the heavy work of raising, grinding, and preserving cereals, a mark, some scholars believe, of their low status in a male-dominated society. Women were also responsible for weaving and spinning.

Within the small villages, there were great differences in wealth and status. Free men constituted the largest class. The number of cattle a man possessed indicated his wealth and determined his social status. "Cattle were so much the quintessential indicator of wealth in traditional society that the modern English term 'fee' (meaning cost of goods or services), which developed from the medieval term 'fief,' had its origin in the Germanic term *fihu* . . . , meaning cattle, chattels, and hence, in general, wealth."[20] Free men also shared in tribal warfare. Slaves (prisoners of war) worked as farm laborers, herdsmen, or household servants.

Germanic society was patriarchal: within each household the father had authority over his wives, children, and slaves. The Germans practiced polygamy, and men who could afford them had more than one wife.

Did the Germans produce goods for trade and exchange? Ironworking was the most advanced craft of the Germanic peoples. Much of northern Europe had iron deposits at or near the earth's surface, and the dense forests provided wood for charcoal. Most villages had an oven and smiths who produced agricultural tools and instruments of war—one-edged swords, arrowheads, and shields. In the first two centuries C.E., the quantity and quality of German goods increased dramatically, and the first steel swords were superior to the weapons of Roman troops. German goods, however, were produced for war and the subsistence economy, not for trade. Goods were also used for gift giving, a social custom that conferred status on the giver. Gift giving showed the higher (economic) status of the giver, cemented friendship, and placed the receiver in the giver's debt.[21] Goods that could not be produced in the village were acquired by raiding and warfare rather than by commercial exchanges. Raids between tribes brought the victors booty; captured cattle and slaves were traded or given as gifts. Warfare determined the economy and the individual's status within Germanic society.

What was the position of women in Germanic society? Did they have, as some scholars contend, a higher status than they were to have later in the Middle Ages? The law codes provide the best evidence. The codes show societies that regarded women as family property. A marriageable daughter went to the highest bidder. A woman of childbearing years had a very high wergeld. The codes also protected the virtue of women. For example, the Salic Law of the Franks fined a man a large amount if he pressed the hand of a woman and even more if he touched her above the elbow. But heavy fines did not stop injury, rape, or abduction. Widows were sometimes seized on the battlefields where their dead husbands lay and were forced to marry the victors.

A few slaves and peasant women used their beauty and their intelligence to advance their positions. The slave Fredegunda, for whom King Chilperic murdered his Visigothic wife, became a queen and held her position after her husband's death.[22]

# THE BYZANTINE EAST (CA 400–788)

Constantine (r. 306–337) and later emperors tried to maintain the unity of the Roman Empire, but during the fifth and sixth centuries the western and eastern halves drifted apart. Justinian (r. 527–565) waged long and hard-fought wars against the Ostrogoths and temporarily regained Italy and North Africa. But his conquests had disastrous consequences. Justinian's wars exhausted the resources of the Byzantine state, destroyed Italy's economy, and killed a large part of Italy's population. The wars paved the way for the easy conquest of Italy by the Lombards shortly after Justinian's death. In the late sixth century, the territory of the western Roman Empire came under Germanic sway, while in the East the Byzantine Empire (see Map 8.3) continued the traditions and institutions of the caesars.

Latin Christian culture was only one legacy the Roman Empire bequeathed to the Western world. The Byzantine culture centered at Constantinople was another. The

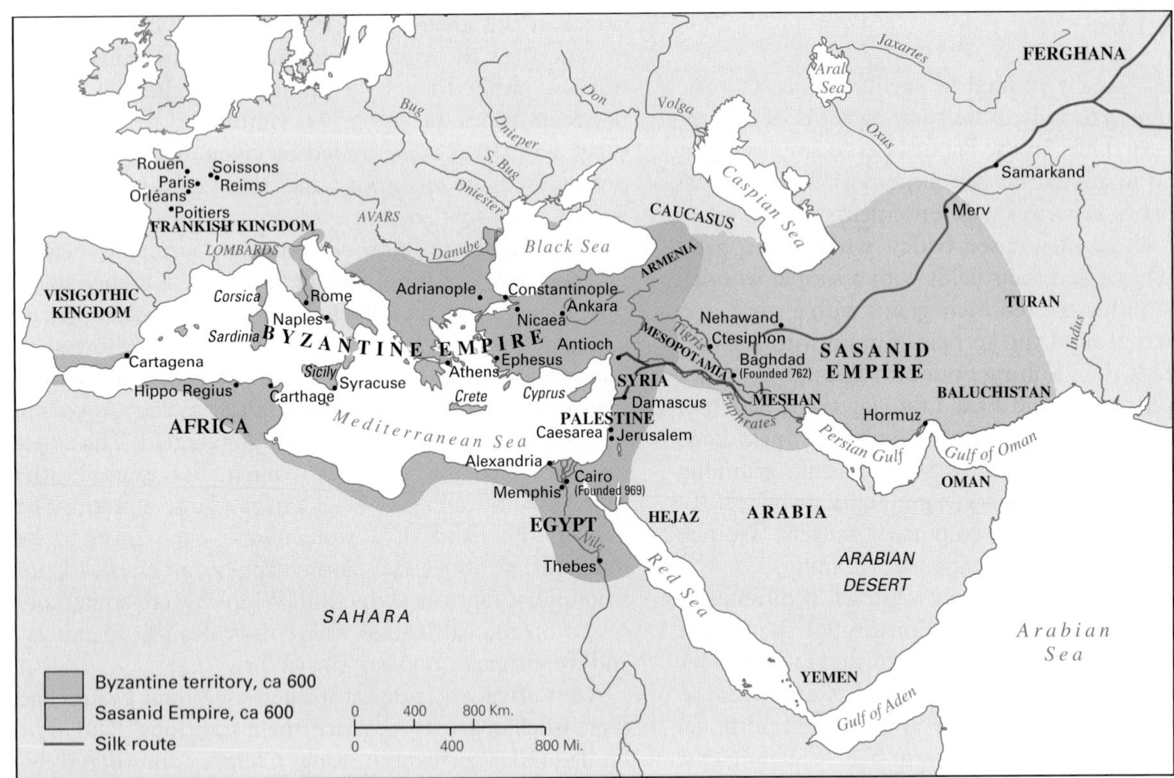


**MAP 8.3 The Byzantine Empire, ca 600** The Sasanid kingdom of Persia spanned much of central Asia, while the Byzantine Empire straddled Asia and Europe. The series of wars between the two powers brought neither of them lasting territorial acquisitions; the strife weakened them and paved the way for Islamic conquest in the seventh century.

Byzantine Empire maintained a high standard of living, and for centuries the Greeks were the most civilized people in the Western world. The Byzantine Empire held at bay barbarian peoples who otherwise could have wreaked additional devastation on western Europe, retarding its development. Most important, however, is the role of the Byzantines, together with the Muslims (see pages 232, 268–269), as preservers of the wisdom of the ancient world. Throughout the long years when barbarians in western Europe trampled down the old and then painfully built something new, Byzantium protected the intellectual heritage of Greco-Roman civilization.

While the western parts of the Roman Empire gradually succumbed to Germanic invaders, the eastern or Roman-Byzantine Empire survived Germanic, Persian, and Arab attacks. In 540 the Huns and Bulgars raided Greece. In 559 a force of Huns and Slavs reached the gates of Constantinople. In 583 the Avars, a mounted Mongol people who had swept across Russia and southeastern Europe, seized Byzantine forts along the Danube and also reached the walls of Constantinople. Between 572 and 630 the Greeks were repeatedly at war with the Sasanid Persians (see below). Beginning in 632, the Arabs pressured the Greek empire. Why didn't one or a combination of these enemies capture Constantinople, as the Germans had taken Rome?

The answer lies in the strong military leadership the Greeks possessed, and even more in the city's location and its excellent fortifications. Under the skillful leadership of General Priskos (d. 612), Byzantine armies inflicted a severe defeat on the Avars in 601. Then, after a long war, the well-organized emperor Heraclius I (r. 610–641), helped by dynastic disputes among the Persians and Muslim pressures on them, crushed the Persians at Nineveh in Iraq. The Muslim Arabs now posed the greatest threat to the Byzantines. Why didn't they conquer the city? As a recent scholar explains, "If in the fourth century Constantine had chosen Antioch, Alexandria or Palestinian Caesarea as a capital there could be little doubt that the Roman empire would have gone as swiftly (to the Muslims) as the Persian."[23] The site of Constantinople was not absolutely impregnable—as the Venetians demonstrated in 1204 (see page 375) and as the Ottoman Turks showed in 1453. But it was almost so. Constantinople had the most powerful defenses in the ancient world. Massive triple walls, built by Constantine and Theodosius II (r. 408–450) and kept in good repair, protected the city from sea invasion. Within the walls huge cisterns provided water, and vast gardens and grazing areas supplied vegetables and meat. Such strong fortifications and provisions meant that if attacked by sea, a defending people could hold out far longer than a besieging army.

The site chosen for the imperial capital in the fourth century enabled Constantinople to survive in the eighth century. Because the city survived, the empire, though reduced in territory, endured.[24]

## The Sasanid Kingdom of Persia and Byzantium

In 226, Ardashir I (r. 226–243), a member of the Sasanid family indigenous to southern Persia and a vassal of the Parthian king Artabanus V, defeated Artabanus at Hormuz. Ardashir assumed authority over Parthian territories, received the submission of the Kushans and of Turan (modern Pakistan and Baluchistan) in the east and of Merv in the northeast, and founded the Sasanid dynasty, which lasted until 651, when it was overthrown by the Muslims. On the death of the Roman emperor Alexander Severus in 235, Ardashir absorbed the Roman province of Mesopotamia.

Centered in the fertile Tigris-Euphrates Valley, but with access to the Persian Gulf and extending south to Meshan (modern Kuwait), the Sasanid kingdom's economic prosperity rested on agriculture; its location also proved well suited for commerce. A lucrative caravan trade from Ctesiphon north to Merv and then east to Samarkand linked the Sasanid kingdom to the Silk Road and China (see page 186). Persian metalwork, textiles, and glass were exchanged for Chinese silks, and these goods brought about considerable cultural contact between the Sasanids and the Chinese.

**Sasanid Persian Plate** Hunting scenes enjoyed great popularity in Sasanid art. This image of King Shapur II (r. 309–379), depicting the ruler with a full beard and elaborately styled hair while hunting lions on horseback, seems reminiscent of ancient Assyrian art (see page 43). Carried across the Central Asian Silk Road and exchanged for Chinese silk, this gilded silver plate came into the possession of a Tang Dynasty official. Chinese desire for things Persian mirrored Western passion for Chinese silk. *(Courtesy of the Middle Eastern Culture Center in Japan)*

Whereas the Parthians had tolerated many religions, the Sasanid Persians made Zoroastrianism the official state religion. Religion and the state were inextricably tied together. The king's power rested on the support of nobles and Zoroastrian **magi** (priests), who monopolized positions in the court and in the imperial bureaucracy. A highly elaborate court ceremonial and ritual exalted the status of the king and emphasized his semidivine pre-eminence over his subjects. (The Byzantine monarchy, the Roman papacy, and the Muslim caliphate subsequently copied aspects of this Persian ceremonial.) Zoroastrianism promoted hostility toward Christians because of what was perceived as their connections to Rome and Constantinople, and the sizable Jewish population in Mesopotamia after the **diaspora** (dispersion of the Jews from Jerusalem between 132 and 135) suffered intermittent persecution.

An expansionist foreign policy brought Persia into frequent conflict with the Roman Empire. Between 337 and 376, the Persians and Romans engaged in three indecisive wars. After the shift of the Roman capital to Constantinople, war repeatedly erupted between the Persians and Byzantines, partly because of Persian persecution of Christians, whom the Greeks sought to defend, and partly because both Persia and Byzantium had interests in Syria and Armenia. Neither side was able to achieve a clear-cut victory. The long wars, financed by higher taxation, on top of the arrival of the bubonic plague (see page 233), compounded discontent in both Byzantine and Persian societies. Political instability, characterized by palace coups, weakened both regimes. Finally, Byzantine persecution of Monophysites and Persian persecution of Christians and Jews created bitterness in those minorities. Thus domestic infirmities eased the way for the Arab sweep across the Persian plains and defeat of the imperial Sasanid army in 642 at Nihawand. The execution of Yazdgird III (r. 632–651) brought an end to the Sasanid dynasty. Persian territories were then absorbed into the Islamic caliphate (see page 244).

## Byzantine East and Germanic West

As imperial authority disintegrated in the West during the fifth century, civic functions were performed first by church leaders and then by German chieftains. Meanwhile, in the East, the Byzantines preserved the forms and traditions of the old Roman Empire and even called themselves Romans. Byzantine emperors traced their lines back past Constantine to the emperor Augustus. The senate that sat in Constantinople carried on the traditions and preserved the glory of the old Roman senate. The army that defended the empire was the direct descendant of the old Roman legions. Even the chariot factions of the Roman Empire lived on under the Greeks, who cheered their favorites as enthusiastically as had the Romans of Hadrian's day.

The position of the church differed considerably in the Byzantine East and the Germanic West. The fourth-century emperors Constantine and Theodosius had wanted the church to act as a unifying force within the empire, but the Germanic invasions made that impossible. The bishops of Rome repeatedly called on the emperors at Constantinople for military support against the invaders, but rarely could the emperors send it. The church in the West steadily grew away from the empire and became involved in social and political affairs. Nevertheless, until the eighth century, the popes, who were often selected by the clergy of Rome, continued to send announcements of their election to the emperors at Constantinople—a sign that the popes long saw themselves as bishops of the Roman Empire.

Because the Western church concentrated on its missionary function, it took centuries for the clergy to be organized. Most church theology in the West came from the East, and the overwhelming majority of popes were of Eastern origin.

We have seen that Ambrose of Milan presented a view typical of the church in the West: that spiritual authority rested with church officials. Such an assertion was virtually unheard-of in the East, where the emperor's jurisdiction over the church was fully acknowledged. The emperor in Constantinople nominated the *patriarch,* as the highest prelate of the Eastern church was called. The Eastern emperor looked on religion as a branch of the state. Religion was such a vital aspect of the social life of the people that the emperor devoted considerable attention to it. He considered it his duty to protect the faith, not only against heathen enemies but also against heretics within the empire. In case of doctrinal disputes, the emperor, following Constantine's example at Nicaea, summoned councils of bishops and theologians to settle problems.

## External Threats and Internal Conflicts

The wars of Justinian's reign left the Byzantine Empire economically and demographically weakened. Over the next two centuries, two additional troubles threatened its very survival: foreign invasions and internal theological disputes.

From these foreign invasions certain benefits did result. First, the territories lost to the empire contained peoples of very diverse ethnic origins, languages, and religions. The territories that continued under imperial authority gradually achieved a strong cultural unity. They were Greek in culture and administration, orthodox in religion.

Second, foreign invasions created the need for internal reorganization. The emperors militarized the administration, dividing the empire into **themes,** or military districts, governed by *strategoi,* or generals, who held both civil and military authority. The strategoi were directly responsible to the emperor. This reorganization brought into being a new peasant army. Foreign invasions had broken up the great landed estates of the empire, and the estate land was distributed to peasant soldiers, who equipped and supported themselves from the profits of the land. Formerly, the Byzantine state had relied on foreign mercenaries. Now each theme had an army of native soldiers with a permanent (landed) interest in the preservation of the empire. The government saved the costs of hiring troops and was assured the loyalty of native soldiers.

In addition, some scholars maintain that the military disasters of the period led to an increase in popular piety and devotion to *icons*—images or representations in painting, bas-relief, or mosaic of God the Father, Jesus, the Virgin, or the saints. Since the third century, the church had allowed people to venerate icons. Although all prayer had to be directed to God the Father, Christian teaching held that icons representing the saints fostered reverence and that Jesus and the saints could most effectively plead a cause to God the Father. *Iconoclasts,* those who favored the destruction of icons, argued that people were worshiping the image itself rather than what it signified. This, they claimed, constituted *idolatry,* a violation of the Mosaic prohibition of graven images in the Ten Commandments.

The result of the controversy over icons was a terrible theological conflict that split the Byzantine world for a century. In 730 the emperor Leo III (r. 717–741) ordered the destruction of the images. The removal of icons from Byzantine churches provoked a violent reaction: entire provinces revolted, and the empire and Roman papacy severed relations. Since Eastern monasteries were the fiercest defenders of icons, Leo's son Constantine V (r. 741–775), nicknamed "Copronymous" ("Dung-name") by his enemies, took the war to the monasteries. He seized their property, executed some of the monks, and forced others into the army. Theological disputes and civil disorder over the icons continued intermittently until 843, when the icons were restored.

The implications of the **iconoclastic controversy** extended far beyond strictly theological issues. Iconoclasm raised the question of the right of the emperor to intervene in religious disputes—a central problem in the relations of church and state. Iconoclasm antagonized the pope and served to encourage him in his quest for an alliance with the Frankish monarchy (see page 365). Iconoclasm thus contributed to the end of Byzantine political influence in central Italy. Arab control of the Mediterranean in the seventh and eighth centuries furthered the separation of the Roman and Byzantine churches by dividing the two parts of Christendom. Separation bred isolation. Isolation, combined with prejudice on both sides, bred hostility.

In 1054 a theological disagreement led the bishop of Rome and the patriarch of Constantinople to excommunicate each other. The outcome was a continuing **schism,** or split, between the Roman Catholic and the Greek Orthodox churches. The bitterness generated by iconoclasm contributed to that schism. Finally, the acceptance of icons profoundly influenced subsequent religious art. That art rejected the Judaic and Islamic prohibition of figural representation and continued in the Greco-Roman tradition of human representation.

The Byzantines spread their views to the East by civilizing the Slavs in the Balkans and in Russia. Byzantine missionaries spread the Word of Christ, and one of their triumphs was the conversion of the Russians in the tenth century. The Byzantine missionary Cyril invented a Slavic alphabet using Greek characters, and this script (called the Cyrillic alphabet) is still in use today. Cyrillic script made possible the birth of Russian literature. Similarly, Byzantine art and architecture became the basis and inspiration for Russian forms. The Byzantines were so successful that the Russians claimed to be the successors of the Byzantine Empire. For a time, Moscow was even known as the "Third Rome" (the second Rome being Constantinople).

## The Law Code of Justinian

One of the most splendid achievements of the Byzantine emperors was the preservation of Roman law for the medieval and modern worlds. Roman law had developed from many sources—decisions by judges, edicts of the emperors, legislation passed by the senate, and the opinions of jurists expert in the theory and practice of law. By the fourth century, Roman law had become a huge, bewildering mass. Its sheer bulk made it almost unusable. Some laws had become outdated; some repeated or contradicted others.

**Justinian and His Attendants** This mosaic detail is composed of thousands of tiny cubes of colored glass or stone called *tessarae,* which are set in plaster against a blazing golden background. Some attempt has been made at naturalistic portraiture. *(Scala/Art Resource, NY)*

The emperor Justinian appointed a committee of eminent jurists to sort through and organize the laws. The result was the *Code,* which distilled the legal genius of the Romans into a coherent whole, eliminated outmoded laws and contradictions, and clarified the law itself.

Justinian next set about bringing order to the equally huge body of Roman *jurisprudence,* the science or philosophy of law. To harmonize the often differing opinions of Roman jurists, Justinian directed his jurists to clear up disputed points and to issue definitive rulings. Accordingly, in 533 his lawyers published the *Digest,* which codified Roman legal thought. Then Justinian's lawyers compiled a handbook of civil law, the *Institutes.*

These three works—the *Code, Digest,* and *Institutes*—are the backbone of the **corpus juris civilis,** the "body of civil law," which is the foundation of law for nearly every modern European nation.

## Byzantine Intellectual Life

Among the Byzantines, education was highly prized, and because of them many masterpieces of ancient Greek literature survived to influence the intellectual life of the modern world. The literature of the Byzantine Empire was predominately Greek, although Latin was long spoken by top politicians, scholars, and lawyers. Among members of the large reading public, history was a favorite subject. Generations of Byzantines read the historical works of Herodotus, Thucydides, and Polybius.

The most remarkable Byzantine historian was Procopius (ca 500–ca 562), who left a rousing account of Justinian's reconquest of North Africa and Italy. Procopius's *Secret History,* however, is a vicious and uproarious attack on Justinian and his wife, the empress Theodora. (See the feature "Individuals in Society: Theodora of Constantinople.")

# INDIVIDUALS IN SOCIETY

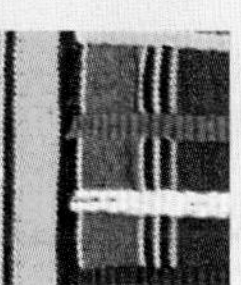

## THEODORA OF CONSTANTINOPLE

The most notorious woman in Byzantine history, daughter of a circus bear trainer in the hippodrome, Theodora (ca 497–548) grew up in what contemporaries considered a morally corrupt atmosphere. Heredity gave her intelligence, wit, charm, and beauty, which she put to use as a striptease artist and actress. Modern scholars question the tales spread by the historian Procopius's *Secret History* (ca 550) about Theodora's insatiable sexual appetite, but the legend of her sensuality has often influenced interpretations of her.

Theodora gave up her stage career and passed her time spinning wool and discussing theological issues. When Justinian first saw her, he was so impressed by her beauty and wit, he brought her to the court, raised her to the *patriciate* (high nobility), and in 525 married her. When he was proclaimed co-emperor with his uncle Justin on April 1, 527, Theodora received the rare title of *augusta,* empress. Thereafter her name was always linked with Justinian's in the exercise of imperial power.

We know a fair amount about Theodora's public life. With four thousand attendants, she processed through the streets of Constantinople to attend Mass and celebrations thanking God for deliverance from the plague. She presided at imperial receptions for Arab sheiks, Persian ambassadors, Gothic princesses from the West, and barbarian chieftains from southern Russia. Her endowment of hospitals, orphanages, houses for the rehabilitation of prostitutes, and Monophysite churches gave her a reputation for piety and charity. But her private life remains hidden. She spent her days in the silken luxury of the *gynaceum* (women's quarters) among her female attendants and eunuch guards. She took the waters at the sulfur springs in Bithynia, and spent the hot summer months at her palace at Hieron, a small town on the Asiatic shore of the Bosporus. Justinian is reputed to have consulted her every day about all aspects of state policy.

One conciliar occasion stands out. In 532 various elements combined to provoke a massive revolt against the emperor. Shouting N-I-K-A (Victory), rioters swept through the city burning and looting. Justinian's counselors urged flight, but Theodora rose and declared:

*For one who has reigned, it is intolerable to be an exile. . . . If you wish, O Emperor, to save yourself, there is no difficulty: we have ample funds and there are the ships. Yet reflect whether, when you have once escaped to a place of security, you will not prefer death to safety. I agree with an old saying that the purple is a fair winding sheet.*

*The Empress Theodora, with a halo—symbolic of power in Eastern art.*
(Scala/Art Resource, NY)

Justinian rallied, had the rioters driven into the hippodrome, and ordered between thirty-five thousand and forty thousand men and women executed. The revolt was crushed. When the bubonic plague hit Justinian in 532, Theodora took over his duties. Her influence over her husband and her power in the Byzantine state continued until she died of cancer.

How do we assess this highly complicated woman who played so many roles, who could be ruthless and merciless, political realist and yet visionary, totally loyal to those she loved? As striptease artist? Actress? Politician? Pious philanthropist? Did she learn survival in the brutal world of the hippodrome? To jump from striptease artist and the stage all the way to the imperial throne suggests enormous intelligence. Is Theodora a symbol of that manipulation of beauty and cleverness by which some women (and men) in every age have attained position and power? Were her many charitable works, especially the houses for the rehabilitation of prostitutes, the result of compassion for a profession she knew well? Or were those benefactions only what her culture expected of the rich and famous? With twenty years service to Justinian and the state, is it fair to brand her as "notorious" for what may only have been youthful indiscretions?

### QUESTIONS FOR ANALYSIS

1. How would you assess the importance of ceremony in Byzantine life?
2. Since Theodora's name was always linked with Justinian's, was she a co-ruler?

The Byzantines are often depicted as dull and lifeless, but such opinions are hard to defend in the face of Procopius's description of Justinian's character:

*For he was at once villainous and amenable; as people say colloquially, a moron. He was never truthful with anyone, but always guileful in what he said and did, yet easily hoodwinked by any who wanted to deceive him. His nature was an unnatural mixture of folly and wickedness.*[25]

How much of this is true, how much the hostility of a sanctimonious hypocrite relishing the gossip he spreads, we will never know. Certainly *The Secret History* is robust reading.

In mathematics and geometry, the Byzantines discovered little that was new. Yet they were exceptionally important as catalysts, for they passed Greco-Roman learning on to the Arabs, who assimilated it and made remarkable advances with it. The Byzantines were equally uncreative in astronomy and natural science, but at least they faithfully learned what the ancients had to teach.

Only when science could be put to military use did the Byzantines make advances. The best-known Byzantine scientific discovery was chemical—"Greek fire" or "liquid fire," an explosive compound made of crude oil mixed with resin and sulfur, which was heated and propelled by a pump through a bronze tube. As the liquid jet left the tube, it was ignited. The Byzantines zealously guarded details of Greek fire's composition. The equivalent of a modern flamethrower, it saved Constantinople from Arab assault in 678. In mechanics the Byzantines continued the work of Hellenistic and Roman inventors of artillery and siege machinery.

The Byzantines devoted a great deal of attention to medicine, and the general level of medical competence was far higher in the Byzantine Empire than it was in the medieval West. The Byzantines assimilated the discoveries of Hellenic and Hellenistic medicine but added very few of their own. The basis of their medical theory was Hippocrates' concept of the four humors. Byzantine physicians emphasized the importance of diet and rest

**Anicia Juliana (462?–528?)** Daughter of a Byzantine emperor and great benefactor of the church and of the arts, Anicia Juliana commissioned a manuscript of the works of the physician Dioscorides (fl. first century) on herbal medicines, which remained the standard reference work on the subject for centuries. She is shown here seated between two Virtues, Magnanimity and Patience. *(Osterreichische Nationalbibliothek)*

and relied heavily on herbal drugs. Perhaps their chief weakness was excessive use of bleeding and burning, which often succeeded only in further weakening an already feeble patient.

Greek medical science, however, could not cope with the terrible disease, often called "the Justinian plague," that swept through the Byzantine Empire, Italy, southern France, Iberia, and the Rhine Valley between 541 and approximately 700. Probably originating in northwestern India and carried to the Mediterranean region by ships, the disease was similar to modern forms of bubonic plague. Characterized by high fevers, chills, delirium, and enlarged lymph nodes, or by inflammation of the lungs that caused hemorrhages of black blood, the plague carried off tens of thousands of people. It reappeared in eight- or twelve-year cycles (558–561, 580–582, 599–600, and so on) but killed fewer people each time.

The epidemic had profound political as well as social consequences. It weakened Justinian's military resources, thus hampering his efforts to restore unity to the Mediterranean world (see page 225). Losses from the plague also further weakened Byzantine and Persian forces that had badly damaged each other, contributing to their inability to offer more than token opposition to the Muslim armies when the Arabs swarmed out of Arabia in 634[26] (see page 245).

Still, by the ninth or tenth century, most major Greek cities had hospitals for the care of the sick. The hospital operated by the Pantokrator monastery in Constantinople possessed fifty beds divided into five wards for different illnesses. A female gynecologist practiced in the women's ward. The hospital staff also included an ophthalmologist (specialist in the functions and diseases of the eye), a surgeon who performed hernia repairs, and two general practitioners. The imperial Byzantine government bore the costs of this hospital and others.

## Constantinople: The Second Rome

In the tenth century, Constantinople was the greatest city in the Christian world: the seat of the imperial court and administration, a large population center, and the pivot of a large volume of international trade. As a natural geographical entrepôt between East and West, the city's markets offered goods from many parts of the world. About 1060 the Spanish Jew Benjamin of Tudela reported that Constantinople had merchant communities from Babylon, Canaan, Egypt, Hungary, Persia, Russia, Sennar (in the Sudan), and Spain, plus two thousand Jews.

But Constantinople did not enjoy constant political stability. Between the accession of Heraclius in 610 and the fall of the city to Western Crusaders in 1204 (see page 375), four separate dynasties ruled at Constantinople. Imperial government involved such intricate court intrigue, assassinations, and military revolts that the word *byzantine* is sometimes used in English to mean extremely entangled and complicated politics. For example, in 963 the emperor Nicephorus I Phocas married Theophano, the widow of the emperor Romanus II. In 969 Nicephorus was murdered and replaced by his nephew John I Tzimisces, Theophano's lover and an exceptionally able general.

Jewish, Muslim, and Italian merchants controlled most foreign trade. Among the Greeks, commerce faced ancient prejudices, and aristocrats and monasteries usually invested their wealth in real estate, which involved little risk but brought little gain. As in the medieval West and early modern China, rural ideals permeated Byzantine society. The landed aristocracy always held the dominant social position. Merchants and craftsmen, even when they acquired considerable wealth, never won social prominence.

Behind the public life of the imperial court with its assassinations and complicated politics, beyond the noise and bustle of the marketplaces thronged with Venetian and Eastern merchants, and behind the monastery walls enclosing the sophisticated theological debates of the monks, what do we know of the private life of the Greeks in Constantinople? Recent research has revealed a fair amount about the Byzantine *oikos,* or household. The Greek household included family members and servants, some of whom were slaves. Artisans lived and worked in their shops. Clerks, civil servants, minor officials, business people—those who today would be called middle class—commonly dwelt in multistory buildings perhaps comparable to the apartment complexes of modern American cities. Wealthy aristocrats resided in freestanding mansions that frequently included interior courts, galleries, large reception halls, small sleeping rooms, reading and writing rooms, baths, and *oratories,* chapels where all members of the household met for religious services. A complicated system of locks protected most houses from intrusion.

In the homes of the upper classes, the segregation of women seems to have been the first principle of interior design. Private houses contained a *gynaceum,* or women's apartment, where women were kept strictly separated from the outside world (the Muslim harem, discussed on page 256, probably derives from this Greek institution). The fundamental reason for this segregation was the family's honor: "An unchaste daughter is guilty of harming not only herself but also her parents and relatives. That is why you should keep your daughters under lock and key, as if proven guilty or imprudent, in order to avoid venomous bites," as an eleventh-century Byzantine writer put it.[27] Women did not receive outside guests, at least in theory. Although they were allowed at family banquets, they could not attend if wine was served or questionable entertainment was given. To do so gave a husband grounds for divorce.

Marriage served as part of a family's strategy for social advancement. The family and the entire kinship group participated in the selection of brides and grooms. Wealth and social connections were the chief qualities sought in potential candidates. Weddings could take place at home, in the oratory of the bride's house, or in the local church.

## SUMMARY

Saint Augustine died in 430 as the Vandals approached the coastal city of Hippo. Scholars have sometimes described Augustine as standing with one foot in the ancient world and one in the Middle Ages. Indeed, Augustine represents the end of ancient culture and the birth of what has been called the Middle Ages. A new and different kind of society was gestating in the mid-fifth century.

The world of the Middle Ages combined Germanic practices and institutions, classical ideas and patterns of thought, Christianity, and a significant dash of Islam (see Chapter 9). Christianity, because it creatively and energetically fashioned the Germanic and classical legacies, was the most powerful agent in the making of Europe. Saint Augustine of Hippo, dogmatic thinker and Christian bishop, embodied the coming world-view. In the Byzantine Empire, a vigorous intellectual life, which preserved Greek scientific and medical knowledge and Roman law, flourished.

## KEY TERMS

- syncretic faith
- Arianism
- Petrine Doctrine
- penitentials
- eremitical
- coenobitic monasticism
- solemnia
- typikon
- barbarian
- foederati
- comitatus
- wergeld
- Salic Law
- magi
- diaspora
- themes
- iconoclastic controversy
- schism
- corpus juris civilis

## NOTES

1. See J. Hale, *The Civilization of Europe in the Renaissance* (New York: Atheneum, 1994), pp. xix, 3–5.
2. R. C. Petry, ed., *A History of Christianity: Readings in the History of Early and Medieval Christianity* (Englewood Cliffs, N.J.: Prentice-Hall, 1962), p. 70.
3. H. Bettenson, ed., *Documents of the Christian Church* (Oxford: Oxford University Press, 1947), p. 113.
4. Colossians 3:9–11.
5. L. Sherley-Price, trans., *Bede: A History of the English Church and People* (Baltimore: Penguin Books, 1962), pp. 86–87.
6. J. T. McNeill and H. Gamer, trans., *Medieval Handbooks of Penance* (New York: Octagon Books, 1965), pp. 184–197.
7. L. White, "The Life of the Silent Majority," in *Life and Thought in the Early Middle Ages,* ed. R. S. Hoyt (Minneapolis: University of Minnesota Press, 1967), p. 100.
8. 1 Peter 2:11–20.
9. Quoted in V. L. Bullough, *The Subordinate Sex: A History of Attitudes Toward Women* (Urbana: University of Illinois Press, 1973), p. 114.
10. Ibid., pp. 118–119.
11. See J. Boswell, *Christianity, Social Tolerance, and Homosexuality: Gay People in Western Europe from the Beginning of the Christian Era to the Fourteenth Century* (Chicago: University of Chicago Press, 1980), Chaps. 3 and 5, esp. pp. 87, 127–131.
12. A. Talbot, "Monasteries," in *The Oxford Dictionary of Byzantium,* vol. 2, ed. A. P. Kazhdan (New York: Oxford University Press, 1991), p. 1393.
13. T. Burns, *A History of the Ostrogoths* (Bloomington: Indiana University Press, 1984), pp. 18, 21.
14. See Patrick J. Geary, "Barbarians and Ethnicity," in *Late Antiquity: A Guide to the Postclassical World,* ed. G. W. Bowerstock, P. Brown, and O. Grabar (Cambridge, Mass.: Harvard University Press, 1999), pp. 107–129, esp. 107–113.
15. See W. Goffart, *Barbarians and Romans: The Techniques of Accommodation* (Princeton, N.J.: Princeton University Press, 1980), Chap. 3, and esp. Conclusion, pp. 211–230.
16. See P. J. Geary, *Before France and Germany: The Creation and Transformation of the Merovingian World* (New York: Oxford University Press, 1988), pp. 18–25.
17. Ibid., p. 24.
18. Ibid., pp. 108–112.
19. E. F. Henderson, ed., *Select Historical Documents of the Middle Ages* (London: G. Bell & Sons, 1912), pp. 176–189.
20. Geary, *Before France and Germany,* p. 46.
21. Ibid., p. 50.
22. See S. F. Wemple, "Sanctity and Power: The Dual Pursuit of Early Medieval Women," in *Becoming Visible: Women in European History,* 2d ed., ed. R. Bridenthal et al. (Boston: Houghton Mifflin, 1987), pp. 133–136.
23. M. Whittow, *The Making of Byzantium, 600–1025* (Berkeley: University of California Press, 1996), p. 99.
24. Ibid., pp. 99–103.
25. R. Atwater, trans., *Procopius: The Secret History* (Ann Arbor: University of Michigan Press, 1963), bk. 8.
26. W. H. McNeill, *Plagues and Peoples* (New York: Doubleday, 1976), pp. 127–128.

27. Quoted in E. Patlagean, "Byzantium in the Tenth and Eleventh Centuries," in *A History of Private Life.* Vol. 1: *From Pagan Rome to Byzantium,* ed. P. Ariès and G. Duby (Cambridge, Mass.: Harvard University Press, 1987), p. 573.

## SUGGESTED READING

J. Herrin's *The Formation of Christendom* (1987) is a fine synthesis of the history of the early Middle Ages. P. Brown, *The World of Late Antiquity,* A.D. *150–750,* rev. ed. (1989), which stresses social and cultural change, is a lavishly illustrated and lucidly written introduction to the period. J. Pelikan, *The Excellent Empire: The Fall of Rome and the Triumph of the Church* (1987), describes how interpretations of the fall of Rome have influenced our understanding of Western culture.

J. Pelikan, *Jesus Through the Centuries: His Place in the History of Culture* (1985), discusses the image of Jesus held by various cultures over the centuries. F. Oakley, *The Medieval Experience: Foundations of Western Cultural Singularity* (1974), emphasizes the Christian roots of Western cultural uniqueness. W. Meeks, *The First Urban Christians: The Social World of the Apostle Paul* (1983), provides fascinating material and shows that early Christians came from all social classes. For a solid appreciation of Christian life in a non-Christian society, see M. Mullin, *Called to Be Saints: Christian Living in First Century Rome* (1992). For the conversion of the Germans and other pagan peoples, see R. Fletcher, *The Barbarian Conversion: From Paganism to Christianity* (1997), and R. MacMullen, *Christianity and Paganism in the Fourth to Eighth Centuries* (1997). Students seeking to understand early Christian attitudes on sexuality and how they replaced Roman ones should consult the magisterial work of P. Brown, *The Body and Society: Men, Women, and Sexual Renunciation in Early Christianity* (1988). The profound study of J. Cohen, *"Be Fertile and Increase, Fill the Earth and Master It": The Ancient and Medieval Career of a Biblical Text* (1992), gives a lucid analysis of the church fathers' views on marriage.

The best biography of Saint Augustine is P. Brown, *Augustine of Hippo* (1967), which treats him as a symbol of change. J. B. Russell, *Dissent and Order in the Middle Ages: The Search for Legitimate Authority* (1992), offers a provocative discussion of orthodoxy and heresy.

For the Germans, see, in addition to Burns's work cited in the Notes, H. Wolfram, *History of the Goths,* trans. T. J. Dunlop (1988), which explores Germanic tribal formation and places Gothic history within the context of late Roman society and institutions. F. Lot, *The End of the Ancient World* (1965), emphasizes the economic and social causes of Rome's decline. E. Amt, ed., *Women's Lives in Medieval Europe: A Sourcebook* (1993), is perhaps the best available collection of primary materials on women from biblical times through the thirteenth century.

The phenomenon of monasticism has attracted interest throughout the centuries. The best modern edition of the document is T. Fry et al., eds., *RB 1980: The Rule of St. Benedict in Latin and English with Notes* (1981), which contains a history of Western monasticism and a scholarly commentary on the *Rule.* Especially useful for students is O. Chadwick, *The Making of the Benedictine Ideal* (1981), a short but profound essay that emphasizes the personality of Saint Benedict in the development of the Benedictine ideal. G. Constable, *Medieval Monasticism: A Select Bibliography* (1976), is a useful research tool.

For Byzantium, see J. J. Norwich, *Byzantium: The Early Centuries* (1989), an elegantly written sketch; E. Patlagean, "Byzantium in the Tenth and Eleventh Centuries," in *A History of Private Life.* Vol. 1: *From Pagan Rome to Byzantium* (1987); J. Hussey, *The Byzantine World* (1961); S. Runciman, *Byzantine Civilization* (1956); and A. Bridge, *Theodora: Portrait in a Byzantine Landscape* (1984), a romantic and amusing biography of the courtesan who became empress. A. Harvey, *Economic Expansion in the Byzantine Empire, 900–1200* (1989), should prove useful for research on social and economic change.

# LISTENING TO THE PAST

## THE CONVERSION OF CLOVIS

*Modern Christian doctrine holds that conversion is a process, the gradual turning toward Jesus and the teachings of the Christian Gospels. But in the early medieval world, conversion was perceived more as a one-time event determined by the tribal chieftain. If he accepted baptism, the mass conversion of his people followed. The selection here about the Frankish king Clovis is from* The History of the Franks *by Gregory, bishop of Tours (ca 504–594), written about a century after the events it describes.*

The first child which Clotild bore for Clovis was a son. She wanted to have her baby baptized, and she kept urging her husband to agree to this. "The gods whom you worship are no good," she would say. "They haven't even been able to help themselves, let alone others. . . . Take your Saturn, for example, who ran away from his own son to avoid being exiled from his kingdom, or so they say; and Jupiter, that obscene perpetrator of all sorts of mucky deeds, who couldn't keep his hands off other men, who had his fun with all his female relatives and couldn't even refrain from intercourse with his own sister. . . .

"You ought instead to worship Him who created at a word and out of nothing heaven, and earth, the sea and all that therein is, who made the sun to shine, who lit the sky with stars, who peopled the water with fish, the earth with beasts, the sky with flying creatures, by whose hand the race of man was made, by whose gift all creation is constrained to serve in deference and devotion the man He made." However often the Queen said this, the King came no nearer to belief. . . .

The Queen, who was true to her faith, brought her son to be baptized. . . . The child was baptized; he was given the name Ingomer; but no sooner had he received baptism than he died in his white robes. Clovis was extremely angry. He began immediately to reproach his Queen. "If he had been dedicated in the name of my gods," he said, "he would have lived without question; but now that he has been baptized in the name of your God he has not been able to live a single day!"

"I give thanks to Almighty God," replied Clotild, "the Creator of all things who has not found me completely unworthy, for He has deigned to welcome into his Kingdom a child conceived in my womb. . . ."

Some time later Clotild bore a second son. He was baptized Chlodomer. He began to ail and Clovis said, "What else do you expect? It will happen to him as it happened to his brother: no sooner is he baptized in the name of your Christ than he will die!" Clotild prayed to the Lord and at His commands the baby recovered.

Queen Clotild continued to pray that her husband might recognize the true God and give up his idol-worship. Nothing could persuade him to accept Christianity. Finally war broke out against the Alamanni and in this conflict he was forced by necessity to accept what he had refused of his own free will. It so turned out that when the two armies met on the battlefield there was a great slaughter and the troops of Clovis were rapidly being annihilated. He raised his eyes to heaven when he saw this, felt compunction in his heart and was moved to tears. "Jesus Christ," he said, "you who Clotild maintains to be the Son of the living God, you who deign to give help to those in travail and victory to those who trust in you, in faith I beg the glory of your help. If you will give me victory over my enemies, and if I may have evidence to that miraculous power which the people dedicated to your name say that they have experienced, then I will believe in you and I will be baptized in your name. I have called upon my own gods, but, as I see only too clearly, they have no intention of helping me. I therefore cannot believe that they possess any power for they do not come to the assistance of those who trust them. I now call upon you. I want to believe in you, but I must first be saved from my enemies." Even as he said this the Alamanni turned their backs and began to run away. As soon as they saw that their King was killed, they submitted to Clovis. "We beg you," they said, "to put an end to this slaughter. We are prepared to obey you." Clovis stopped the war. He made a speech in which he called for peace. Then he went home. He told the Queen how he had won a victory by calling on the name of Christ. This happened in the fifteenth year of his reign (496).

The Queen then ordered Saint Remigius, Bishop of the town of Rheims, to be summoned in secret. She begged him to impart the word of salvation to the King. The Bishop asked Clovis to meet him in private and began to urge him to believe in the true God, Maker of heaven and earth, and to forsake his idols, which were powerless to help him or anyone else. The King replied: "I have listened to you willingly, holy father. There remains one obstacle. The people under my command will not agree to forsake their gods. I will go and put to them what you have just said to me." He arranged a meeting with his people, but God in his power had preceded him, and before he could say a word all those present shouted in unison: "We will give up worshipping our mortal gods, pious King, and we are prepared to follow the immortal God about whom Remigius preaches." This news was reported to the Bishop. He was greatly pleased and he ordered the baptismal pool to be made ready. . . . The baptistry was prepared, sticks of incense gave off clouds of perfume, sweet-smelling candles gleamed bright and the holy place of baptism was filled with divine fragrance. God filled the hearts of all present with such grace that they imagined themselves to have been transported to some perfumed paradise. King Clovis asked that he might be baptized first by the Bishop. Like some new Constantine he stepped forward to the baptismal pool, ready to wash away the sores of his old leprosy and to be cleansed in flowing water from the sordid stains which he had borne so long.

Ninth-century ivory carving showing Clovis being baptized by Saint Remi. *(Musée Condé, Chantilly/ Laurie Platt Winfrey, Inc.)*

King Clovis confessed his belief in God Almighty, three in one. He was baptized in the name of the Father, the Son and the Holy Ghost, and marked in holy chrism [an anointing oil] with the sign of the Cross of Christ. More than three thousand of his army were baptized at the same time.

## QUESTIONS FOR ANALYSIS

1. Who took the initiative in urging Clovis's conversion? What can we deduce from that?
2. According to this account, why did Clovis ultimately accept Christianity?
3. For the Salian Franks, what was the best proof of divine power?
4. On the basis of this selection, do you consider *The History of the Franks* reliable history? Why or why not?

*Sources:* L. Thorpe, trans., *The History of the Franks by Gregory of Tours* (Harmondsworth, England: Penguin, 1974), p. 159; P. J. Geary, ed., *Readings in Medieval History* (Peterborough, Ontario: Broadview Press, 1991), pp. 165–166.

Arch before the *mihrab* (small niche) in the beautiful mosque of Córdoba, which was begun by Abd al-Rahman I in 795. *(Institut Amatller d'Art Hispanic)*

CHAPTER

# 9 THE ISLAMIC WORLD, CA 600–1400

## CHAPTER OUTLINE

- The Arabs Before Islam
- Muhammad and the Faith of Islam
- The Expansion of Islam
- Beginnings of the Islamic State
- Decentralization
- The Life of the People

Historians have traditionally explained the origins and beginnings of Islam in terms of central Arabia, the region of Mecca and Medina, also known as the Hijaz. Thus, according to Islamic tradition, the background and the impetus for the growth and spread of the religion lies in the Hijaz. Recent research, however, stresses that although Islam traces its geographical beginnings to Arabia, it underwent essential development and achieved distinct form outside Arabia. Historians seek to separate the tradition or legend that grew up around a person or event, which may be widely believed and accepted as truth, from information that is verifiable and provable, which legend sometimes is not.

According to tradition, around 610, in the city of Mecca in what is now Saudi Arabia, a merchant called Muhammad began to have religious experiences. By the time he died in 632, most of Arabia had accepted his creed. A century later, his followers controlled Syria, Palestine, Egypt, Iraq, Persia (present-day Iran), northern India, North Africa, Spain, and part of France. Within another century, Muhammad's beliefs had been carried across Central Asia to the borders of China. In the ninth, tenth, and eleventh centuries, the Muslims created a brilliant civilization centered at Baghdad in Iraq, a culture that profoundly influenced the development of both Eastern and Western civilizations.

- Who were the Arabs?
- What are the main tenets of the Muslim faith?
- What factors account for the remarkable spread of Islam?
- How did the Muslims govern the vast territories they conquered?
- Why did the Shi'ite Muslim tradition arise, and how did the split between Shi'ites and Sunnis affect the course of Islam?
- What position did women hold in Muslim society?
- What features characterized the societies of the great Muslim cities of Baghdad and Córdoba?
- How did the Muslims view Western society and culture?

This chapter explores these questions.

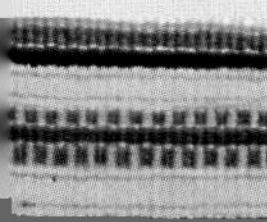

## THE ARABS BEFORE ISLAM

The Arabian peninsula, perhaps a third of the size of Europe or the United States, covers about a million square miles. Ancient Greek geographers named the peninsula *Arabia* after the Bedouin Arabs, nomads who grazed their animals in the sparse patches of grass that dotted the vast, semiarid land. Thus *Arab* originally meant a native of Arabia. After Islam spread and peoples of various ethnic backgrounds attached themselves to or intermarried with the Arabs, they assumed an Arab identity. Today, the term *Arab* refers to an ethnic identity; *Arabic* means a linguistic and cultural heritage.

In the sixth century C.E., most Arabs were not nomads; most led a settled existence. In the southwestern mountain valleys of the Arabian peninsula, plentiful rainfall and sophisticated irrigation techniques resulted in highly productive agriculture that supported fairly dense population settlements. In other areas scattered throughout the peninsula, oasis towns based on the cultivation of date palms grew up around underground sources of water. Some oasis towns sustained sizable populations including artisans, merchants, and religious leaders. Some, such as Mecca, according to tradition served as important trading outposts. The presence of the **Ka'ba**, a temple containing a black stone thought to be a god's dwelling place, also attracted pilgrims and enabled Mecca to become the metropolis of western Arabia. Mecca served economic and religious/cultic functions.

Thinly spread over the entire peninsula, the nomadic Bedouins migrated from place to place, grazing their sheep, goats, and camels. Though always small in number, Bedouins were the most important political and military force in the region because of their toughness, solidarity, fighting traditions, possession of horses, and ability to control trade and lines of communication. Between the peoples settled in oasis towns and the Bedouin nomads were seminomads. As the agricultural conditions around them fluctuated, they practiced either settled agriculture or nomadic pastoralism.

For all Arabs, the basic social unit was the *tribe*—a group of blood relations that descended in the male line. The tribe provided protection and support and in turn received members' total loyalty. Like the Germanic peoples in the age of their migrations (see pages 220–221), Arab tribes were not static entities but continually evolving groups. A particular tribe might include both nomadic and sedentary members.

Strong economic links joined all Arab peoples. Nomads and seminomads depended on the agriculturally productive communities for food they could not produce, cloth, metal products, and weapons. Nomads paid for these goods with the livestock, milk and milk products, hides, and hair wanted by oasis towns. Nomads acquired income by serving as desert guides and as guards for caravans. Plundering caravans and extorting protection money also yielded funds.

In northern and central Arabia, tribal confederations dominated by a warrior elite characterized Arab political organization. In the southern parts of the peninsula in the early seventh century, religious aristocracies tended to hold political power. Many oasis or market towns contained members of one holy family who claimed to be servants or priests of the deity who resided in the town, and they served as guardians of the deity's shrine, or *haram*. At the haram, a *mansib*, or cultic leader, adjudicated disputes and tried to get agreements among warrior tribes. All Arabs respected the harams because they feared retribution if the gods' shrines were desecrated and because the harams served as neutral places for arbitration among warring tribes.

The power of the northern warrior class rested on its fighting skills. The southern religious aristocracy, by contrast, depended on its cultic and economic power. Located in agricultural areas that were also commercial centers, the religious aristocracy had a stronger economic base than the warrior-aristocrats. Scholarship has shown that the arbitrator role of the mansib marks a step toward a society governed by law.[1] The political genius of Muhammad was to bind together these different tribal groups into a strong unified state.

## MUHAMMAD AND THE FAITH OF ISLAM

No contemporary biography of Muhammad (ca 570–632) survives. The earliest account of his life, by Ibn Ishaq (d. 767), was edited in 833 and based on oral tradition. It was not concerned with factual accuracy as historians today understand that phrase. Rather, the biography sought to provide a model of Muhammad, an example that the Muslim believer should imitate. (Similarly, the sources of information about Jesus—the Christian Gospels and the letters of Saint Paul—were written fifty to seventy-five years after Jesus' death. They represent views traditional in Christian communities at the time they were written, and they had as their purpose the building up of Christian faith and Christian churches, or communities.)

Orphaned at the age of six, Muhammad was brought up by his paternal uncle. As a young man, he became a

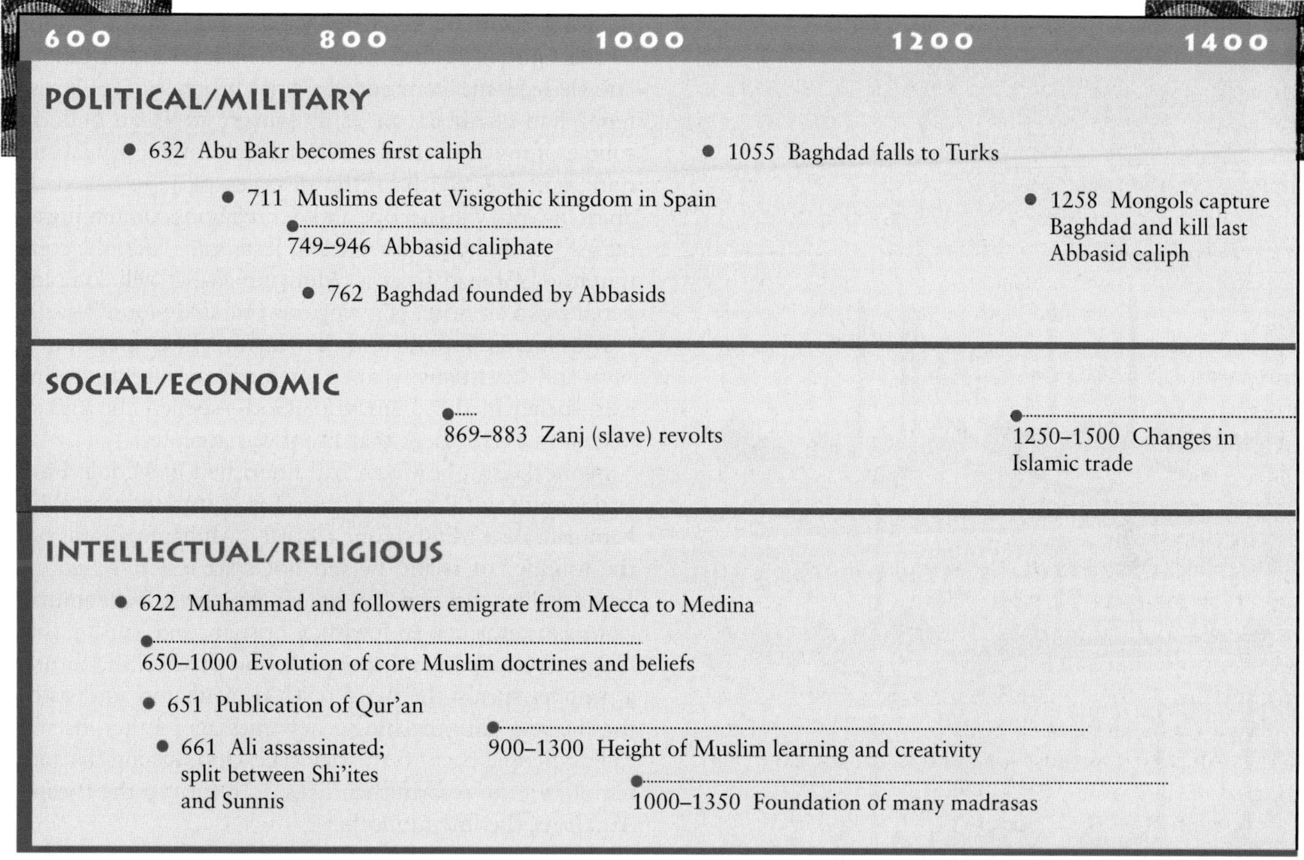


merchant in the caravan trade. Later he entered the service of a wealthy widow, Khadija, and their subsequent marriage brought him financial security while she lived. Muhammad apparently was extremely pious, self-disciplined, and devoted to contemplation. At about forty, in a cave in the hills near Mecca where he was accustomed to pray, Muhammad had a profound religious experience. In a vision, an angelic being (whom Muhammad later interpreted to be Gabriel, God's messenger) commanded him to preach the revelations that God would be sending him. Muhammad began to preach to the people of Mecca, urging them to give up their idols and submit to the one indivisible God. During his lifetime, Muhammad's followers jotted down his revelations haphazardly. After his death, scribes organized the revelations into chapters. In 651 they published the version of them that Muslims consider authoritative, the **Qur'an** (from an Arabic word meaning "reading" or "recitation"). Muslims revere the Qur'an for its sacred message and for the beauty of its Arabic language.

600
800
1000
1200
1400
POLITICAL/MILITARY
632 Abu Bakr becomes first caliph
1055 Baghdad falls to Turks
711 Muslims defeat Visigothic kingdom in Spain
1258 Mongols capture Baghdad and kill last Abbasid caliph
749–946 Abbasid caliphate
762 Baghdad founded by Abbasids
SOCIAL/ECONOMIC
869–883 Zanj (slave) revolts
1250–1500 Changes in Islamic trade
INTELLECTUAL/RELIGIOUS
622 Muhammad and followers emigrate from Mecca to Medina
650–1000 Evolution of core Muslim doctrines and beliefs
651 Publication of Qur'an
661 Ali assassinated; split between Shi'ites and Sunnis
900–1300 Height of Muslim learning and creativity
1000–1350 Foundation of many madrasas

After the death of Muhammad, two or three centuries passed before Islam emerged as a fixed religious system, before the emergence of a distinct Muslim identity. Some writers call this early period the Age of Arab Monotheism. Islam had to be differentiated from the other Middle Eastern monotheistic religions, Judaism and Christianity, as the Dome of the Rock mosque in Jerusalem attempts to do in architecture. Theological issues, such as the oneness of God, the role of angels, the prophets, the Scriptures, and Judgment Day, as well as political issues, such as the authority of Muhammad and that of the **caliph** (successor to Muhammad, representative or deputy of God), all had to be worked out. Likewise, legal issues relating to the **hadith,** collections of the sayings of or anecdotes about Muhammad, required investigation. The hadith were organized according to legal topics and communicated by Muhammad's close companions to later transmitters. Muhammad's example as revealed in the hadith became the legal basis for the conduct or behavior of every Muslim. The life of Muhammad, who is also known as the Prophet, provides the "normative example," or *sunna,* for the Muslim believer. Once Islamic theology and law had evolved into a religious system, Muhammad was revealed as the perfect

**Qur'an with Kufic Script** Kufic takes its name from the town of Kufa, south of Baghdad in Iraq, at one time a major center of Muslim learning. Kufic scripts were angular and derived from inscriptions on stone monuments. *(Mashed Shrine Library, Iran/Robert Harding Picture Library)*

man, the embodiment of the will of God. The Muslim way of life rests on Muhammad's example. It follows that if Muhammad's life represents the perfect embodiment of God's will, criticism of Muhammad is by implication criticism of the Muslim way of life, "at least in its idealized conception."[2]

Islam, the strict monotheistic faith that is based on the teachings of Muhammad, rests on the principle of the absolute unity and omnipotence of Allah, God. The word *Islam* means "submission to God," and *Muslim* means "a person who submits." Thus the community of Muslims consists of people who have submitted to God by accepting his teachings as revealed by Muhammad. Muslims believe that Muhammad was the last of the prophets, completing the work begun by Abraham, Moses, and Jesus. According to the Qur'an, both Jewish and Christian authorities acknowledged the coming of a final prophet. The Jewish rabbi Kab al-Ahbar, an early convert to Islam and the source of much of the Jewish material in the early Islamic tradition, asserted that "the disciples of Jesus asked, O Spirit of God, will there be another religious community after us?" And, the rabbi reported, Jesus said: "Yes, the community of Ahmad [that is, Muhammad]. It will comprise people who are wise, knowing, devout, and pious."[3]

Muslims believe that they worship the same God as Jews and Christians. Islam's uncompromising monotheism—belief in the oneness of God—spelled the end of paganism everywhere that Islam was accepted.

Monotheism, however, had flourished in Middle Eastern Semitic and Persian cultures for centuries before Muhammad. According to one scholar, "Muhammad was not the founder of Islam; he did not start a new religion." Instead, like the Old Testament prophets, Muhammad came as a reformer. In Jewish, Christian, and Muslim theology, a prophet is not someone who predicts the future; a prophet speaks the word of God. Muhammad insisted that he was not preaching a new message; rather, he was calling people back to the one true God, urging his contemporaries to reform their lives, to return to the faith of Abraham, the first monotheist.[4]

Muhammad's social and political views are inseparable from his religious ideas. Muhammad displayed genius as both political strategist and religious teacher. He gave Arabs the idea of a unique and unified **umma,** or community, which consisted of all those whose primary identity and bond was a common religious faith and commitment, not a tribal tie. The umma was to be a religious and political community led by Muhammad for the achievement of God's will on earth.

In the early seventh century, the southern Arab tribal confederations, which centered on sacred enclaves, lacked cohesiveness and unity and were constantly warring; they recognized no single higher authority. The Islamic notion of an absolute higher authority transcended the boundaries of individual tribal units and fostered the political consolidation of the tribal confederations. All authority came from God *through Muhammad.* Within the umma, the law of God was discerned and applied through Muhammad. Thus Islam centralized authority, both political and religious, in Muhammad's hands.[5]

The Qur'an prescribes a strict code of moral behavior. A Muslim must recite the profession of faith in God and in Muhammad as his prophet: "There is no God but God, and Muhammad is his Prophet." A believer must also pray five times a day, fast and pray during the sacred

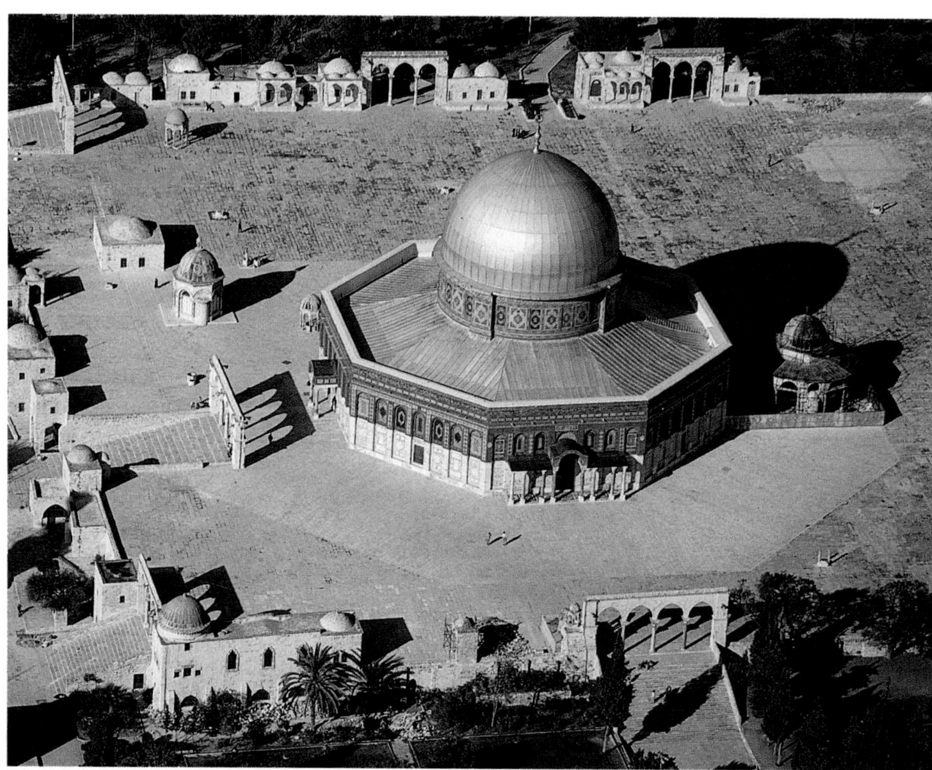

**Dome of the Rock, Jerusalem** The Syrian (Muslim) architects intended to assert the theological principle that Islam was victorious, completing the revelation of the earlier monotheistic faiths, Judaism and Christianity. They sought to distinguish the octagonal dome from Jewish and Christian shrines but used Byzantine and Sasanid designs. The seven hundred feet of carefully selected Qur'anic inscriptions and vegetal motifs, however, represent distinctly Arabic features. Completed in 691 and revered by Muslims as the site where Muhammad ascended to Heaven, the Dome of the Rock is the oldest surviving Islamic sanctuary and, after Mecca and Medina, the holiest place in Islam. *(Sonia Halliday)*

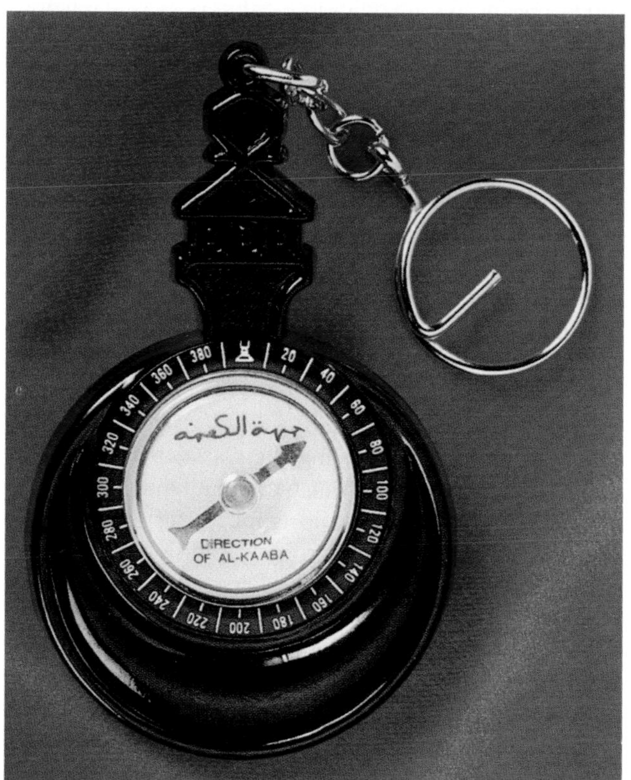


**Qibla Compass** Religious precepts inspired Muslims to considerable scientific knowledge. For example, the Second Pillar of Islam requires them to pray five times a day facing the Ka'ba in Mecca. To determine the direction of Mecca, called the *qibla,* Muslims advanced the science of astronomy. Modern worshipers still use the qibla compass. *(Robert Selkowitz)*

month of Ramadan, make a pilgrimage to the holy city of Mecca once during his or her lifetime, and give alms to the Muslim poor. These fundamental obligations are known as the **Five Pillars of Islam,** and they distinguish Islam from Christianity and Judaism.

Islam forbids alcoholic beverages and gambling. It condemns usury in business—that is, lending money and charging the borrower interest—and taking advantage of market demand for products by charging high prices. Some foods, such as pork, are forbidden, a dietary regulation probably adopted from the Mosaic law of the Hebrews.

Most scholars hold that compared with earlier Arab standards, the Qur'an set forth an austere sexual code. Muslim jurisprudence condemned licentious behavior by both men and women, and the status of women improved. About marriage, illicit intercourse, and inheritance, the Qur'an states:

*Of . . . women who seem good in your eyes, marry but two, three, or four; and if ye still fear that ye shall not act equitably, then only one. . . .*

*The whore and the fornicator: whip each of them a hundred times. . . .*

*The fornicator shall not marry other than a whore; and the whore shall not marry other than a fornicator.*[6]

By contrast, Frankish law tended to punish prostitutes, not their clients.

Islam warns about Judgment Day and the importance of the life to come. The Islamic Judgment Day bears a striking resemblance to the Christian one: on that day God will separate the saved and the damned. The Qur'an describes in detail the frightful tortures with which God will punish the damned: scourgings, beatings with iron clubs, burnings, and forced drinking of boiling water. Muhammad's accounts of the heavenly rewards of the saved and the blessed are equally graphic but are different in kind from those of Western Christian theology. The Muslim vision of Heaven features lush green gardens surrounded by refreshing streams. There the saved, clothed in rich silks, lounge on brocade couches, nibbling ripe fruits, sipping delicious beverages, and enjoying the companionship of physically attractive people.

How do those of the Muslim faithful merit the rewards of Heaven? Salvation is by God's grace and choice alone. Because God is all-powerful, he knows from the moment of conception whether a person will be saved. But predestination does not mean that believers have no reason to try to achieve Heaven. Muslims who suffer and die for the faith in battle are ensured the rewards of Heaven. For others, the Qur'anic precepts mark the path to salvation.

## THE EXPANSION OF ISLAM

According to Muslim tradition, Muhammad's preaching at first did not appeal to many people. Legend has it that for the first three years he attracted only fourteen believers. Muhammad's teaching constituted social revolution. He preached a revelation that opposed the undue accumulation of wealth and social stratification and that held all men as brothers within a social order ordained by God. Moreover, he urged the destruction of the idols in the Ka'ba at Mecca, a site that drew thousands of devout Arabs annually and thus brought important revenue to the city. The bankers and merchants of Mecca fought him. The townspeople turned against him, and he and his followers were forced to flee to Medina. This *hijra,* or emigration, occurred in 622, and Muslims later dated the beginning of their era from that event. At Medina, Muhammad attracted increasing numbers of believers, and his teachings began to have an impact.

### Expansion to the East and the West

By the time Muhammad died in 632, he had welded together all the Bedouin tribes. The crescent of Islam, the Muslim symbol, controlled most of the Arabian peninsula (see Map 9.1). After the Prophet's death, Islam eventually emerged not only as a religious faith but also as a gradually expanding culture of worldwide significance. The roots of that development lay in the geopolitics of the ancient Middle Eastern world.

In the sixth century, two powerful empires divided the Middle East: the Greek-Byzantine empire centered at Constantinople and the Persian-Sasanid empire concentrated at the Ctesiphon (near Baghdad in present-day Iraq). The Byzantine Empire stood for Hellenistic culture and championed Christianity. The Sasanid empire espoused Persian cultural traditions and favored the religious faith known as Zoroastrianism. Although each empire maintained an official state religion, neither possessed religious unity. Both had sizable Jewish populations, and within Byzantium sects whom Orthodox Greeks considered heretical—Monophysites and Nestorians—served as a politically divisive force. Between the fourth and sixth centuries, these two empires had fought each other fiercely to expand their territories and to control (tax) the rich trade coming from Arabia and the Indian Ocean region.

The second and third successors of Muhammad, Umar (r. 634–644) and Uthman (r. 644–656; see page 248), launched a two-pronged attack. One force moved north from Arabia against the Byzantine provinces of Syria and Palestine. The Greek armies there could not halt them (see page 228). From Syria, the Muslims conquered the rich province of Egypt, taking the commercial and intellectual hub of Alexandria in 642. Simultaneously, Arab armies swept into the Sasanid empire, crushing the Persians at al-Qadisiyah (modern-day Kadisiya in southern Iraq). The Muslim defeat of the Persians at Nihawand in 642 signaled the collapse of the Sasanid empire.[7]

The Muslims continued their drive eastward. In the mid-seventh century, they occupied the province of Khurasan, where the city of Merv became the center of Muslim control over eastern Persia and the base for campaigns farther east. By 700 the Muslims had crossed the

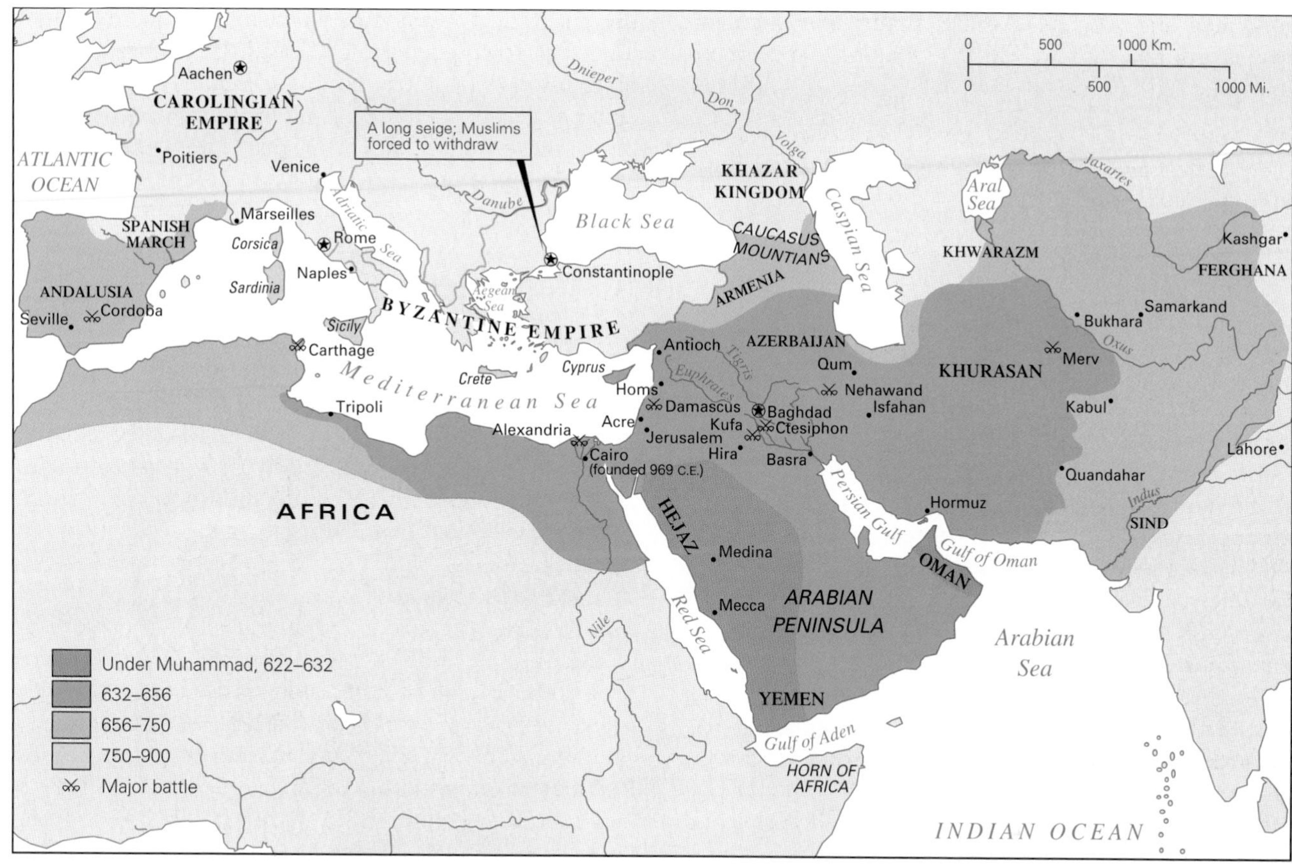


**MAP 9.1 The Islamic World, ca 900** The rapid expansion of Islam in a relatively short span of time testifies to the Arabs' superior fighting skills, religious zeal, economic ambition, as well as to their enemies' weakness. Plague, famine, and political troubles in Sasanid Persia contributed to Muslim victory there.

Oxus River and swept toward Kabul, today the capital of Afghanistan. They penetrated Kazakhstan and then seized Tashkent, one of the oldest cities in Central Asia. The clash of Muslim horsemen with a Chinese army at the Talas River in 751 marked the farthest Islamic penetration into Central Asia.

From Makran in southern Persia, a Muslim force marched into the Indus Valley in northern India and in 713 founded an Islamic community at Multan. Beginning in the eleventh century, Muslim dynasties from Ghazni in Afghanistan carried Islam deeper into the Indian subcontinent.

Likewise to the west, Arab forces moved across North Africa, crossed the Strait of Gibraltar, and in 711 at the Guadalete River easily defeated the Visigothic kingdom of Spain. A few Christian princes supported by Merovingian rulers held out in the Cantabrian Mountains, but the Muslims controlled most of Spain until the thirteenth century. From one perspective, the history of the Iberian Peninsula in the Middle Ages is the account of the coexistence and intermingling of Muslims, Christians, and Jews. From another perspective, that history is the story of the *reconquista,* the Christian reconquest of the area (see Map 13.3 on page 378).

## Reasons for the Spread of Islam

By the beginning of the eleventh century, the crescent of Islam flew from the Iberian heartlands to northern India. How can this rapid and remarkable expansion be explained? Muslim historians attribute Islamic victories to God's support for the Islamic faith. True, the Arabs

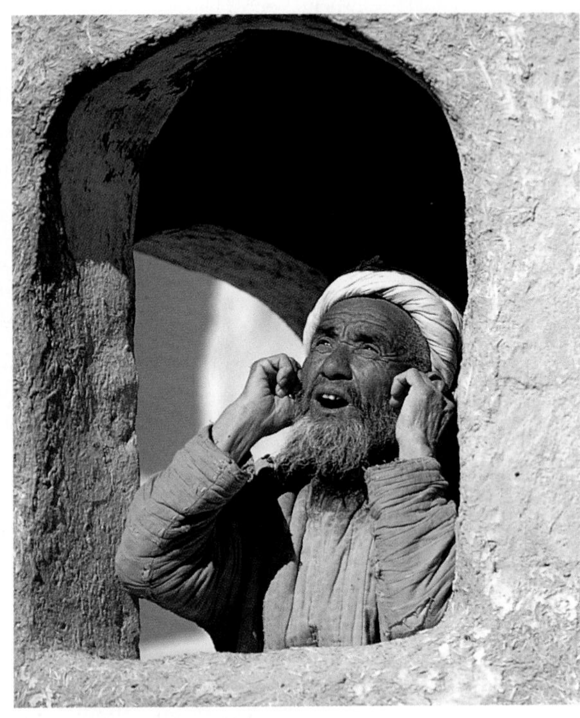

**Muezzin Calling People to Prayer** A mosque is usually surrounded by an open courtyard containing a fountain for ritual ablutions and a *minaret,* or lofty tower (*left*) surrounded by projecting balconies from which an official, the *muezzin,* summons the faithful to prayer. *(left: Ian Graham; right: R & S Michaud/Woodfin Camp & Associates)*

possessed a religious fervor that their enemies could not equal. Perhaps they were convinced of the necessity of the **jihad,** or holy war. The Qur'an does not precisely explain the concept. Thus modern Islamicists, as well as early Muslims, have debated the meaning of jihad, sometimes called the sixth pillar of Islam. Some students hold that it signifies the *individual* struggle against sin and toward perfection on "the straight path" of Islam. Other scholars claim that jihad has a *social and communal* implication—a militancy as part of a holy war against unbelievers living in territories outside the control of the Muslim community. The Qur'an states, "Fight those in the way of God who fight you. . . . Fight those wheresoever you find them, and expel them from the place they had turned you out from. . . . Fight until sedition comes to an end and the law of God [prevails]." Similarly, according to the Qur'an, "We shall bestow on who fights in the way of God, whether he is killed or is victorious, a glorious reward" (Qur'an 4:74–76).[8] Since the Qur'an suggests that God sent the Prophet to establish justice on earth, it would follow that justice will take effect only where Islam triumphs. Just as Christians have a missionary duty to spread their faith, so Muslims have the obligation, as individuals and as a community, to extend the power of Islam. For some Islam came to mean the struggle to expand Islam, and those involved in that struggle were assured happiness in the world to come.

The Muslim practice of establishing garrison cities or camps facilitated expansion. Rather than scattering as landlords of peasant farmers over conquered lands, Arab soldiers remained together in garrison cities, where their Arab ethnicity, tribal organization, religion, and military success set them apart from defeated peoples. Situated on the edge of the desert, which afforded a place for quick retreat in case of trouble, new garrison cities such as Al-Fustat in Egypt, Kufa and Basra in Iraq, and Qayrawan (now Kairouan) in North Africa, and old cities such as Merv in Khurasan adapted for garrison use, fostered the development of Muslim identity and society. From a garrison city, armies could be sent forth for further expansion or to crush revolts.

Garrison cities were army camps, the outposts of Muslim society. Gradually, Muslim society became identical with Arab armies. The Muslim surge originated from Medina in Arabia. As Arabs left their homes in Arabia and emigrated to garrison cities to serve Allah as soldiers, the cities grew in size. Muslim society came to mean "the community set up by Arabs in the conquered Middle East, rather than the Arabs who stayed behind in Arabia." Muslims were emigrants, while those who stayed behind were "bedouins," regardless of whether they were pastoralists, agriculturalists, or business people.[9] Garrison cities forged a distinct Muslim identity and served as springboards for future expansion.

All soldiers were registered in the **diwan,** an administrative device adopted from the Persians or Byzantines meaning "register." Soldiers received a monthly ration of food for themselves and their families and an annual cash stipend. In return, they had to be available for military service. Fixed salaries, regular pay, and the lure of battlefield booty attracted more rugged tribesmen from Arabia. Except for the Berbers of North Africa, whom the Arabs could not pacify, Muslim armies initially did not seek to convert or recruit warriors from conquered peoples.[10] Instead, conquered peoples became slaves. In later campaigns, to the east, many recruits were recent converts to Islam from Christian, Persian, and Berber backgrounds. The assurance of army wages secured the loyalty of these very diverse men. Here is an eleventh-century description of the Egyptian army (medieval numbers were always greatly exaggerated):

*Each corps has its own name and designation. One group are called Kitamis [a Berber tribe]. These came from Qayrawan in the service of al-Mu'izz li-Din Allah. They are said to number 20,000 horsemen. . . . Another group is called Masmudis. They are blacks from the land of the Masmudis and said to number 20,000 men. Another group are called the Easterners, consisting of Turks and Persians. They are so-called because they are not of Arab origin. Though most of them were born in Egypt, their name derives from their origin. They are said to number 10,000 powerfully built men. Another group are called the slaves by purchase. . . . They are slaves bought for money and are said to number 30,000 men. Another group are called Bedouin. They are from the Hijaz [Hejaz] and are all armed with spears. They are said to number 50,000 horsemen.*[11]

Still, in the first two centuries of Muslim expansion, Arab military victories probably resulted more from their enemies' (the Sasanid Persians and the Byzantines; see page 228) weakness than from Arab strength.

Some scholars speculate that the Muslim outburst from Arabia had economic and political, as well as religious and military, causes. The Arab surge may have reflected the economic needs of a people squeezed into a semibarren, overpopulated area and the desire to share in the rich life of the Fertile Crescent. Arab expansion in the seventh and eighth centuries, these scholars argue, was another phase of the infiltration that had taken the ancient Hebrews to the other end of the Fertile Crescent (see Map 1.1 on page 9).

The Muslim conquest of Syria may provide an example of several motives that propelled early Muslim expansion. Situated to the north of the Arabian peninsula, Syria had been under Byzantine-Christian or Roman rule for centuries. Arab caravans knew the market towns of southern Syria and the rich commercial centers of the north, such as Edessa, Aleppo, and Damascus. Syria's economic prosperity may have attracted the Muslims, and perhaps Muhammad saw the land as a potential means of support for the poor who flooded Medina. Syria also contained sites important to the faith: Jerusalem, where Jesus and other prophets mentioned in the Qur'an had lived and preached, and Hebron, the traditional burial place of Abraham, the father of monotheism.[12]

How did conquered peoples perceive the motives of the Muslims? How did the defeated make sense of their new subordinate situations? Defeated peoples almost never commented on the actions and motives of the Arabs. Jews and Christians both tried to minimize the damage done to their former status and played down the gains of their new masters. A scripturally rooted people, they sought explanation in the Bible. Christians regarded the conquering Arabs as God's punishment for their sins, while Jews saw the Arabs as instruments for their deliverance from Greek and Sasanid persecution.[13]

## BEGINNINGS OF THE ISLAMIC STATE

Although centered in towns, Islam arose within a tribal society that lacked stable governing institutions. When Muhammad died in 632, he left a large Muslim umma, but this community stood in danger of disintegrating into separate tribal groups. Some tribespeople even attempted to elect new chiefs for their tribes. What provisions did Muhammad make for the religious and political organization of his followers? How was the vast empire that came into existence within one hundred years of his death to be governed?

### The Caliphate

Muhammad fulfilled his prophetic mission, but his religious work remained. The Muslim umma had to be maintained and Islam carried to the rest of the world. To achieve these goals, political and military power had to be exercised. But neither the Qur'an nor the Sunna, the account of the Prophet's sayings and conduct in particular situations, offered guidance for the succession (see page 241).

In this crisis, according to tradition, a group of Muhammad's ablest followers elected Abu Bakr (573–634), a close supporter of the Prophet and his father-in-law, and hailed him as *khalifa,* or caliph, an Arabic term combining the ideas of leader, successor, and deputy (of the Prophet). This election marked the victory of the concept of a universal community of Muslim believers. The goals of the Muslim umma were set down in the Qur'an to make the faith revealed to Muhammad the cornerstone of Muslim law, government, and personal behavior.

Because the law of the Qur'an was to guide the community, there had to be an authority to enforce the law. Muslim teaching held that the law was paramount. God is the sole source of the law, and the ruler is bound to obey the law. Government exists not to make law but to enforce it. Muslim teaching also maintained that there is no distinction between the temporal and spiritual domains: social law is a basic strand in the fabric of comprehensive religious law. Thus religious belief and political power are inextricably intertwined: the first sanctifies the second, and the second sustains the first.[14] The creation of Islamic law in an institutional sense took three or four centuries and is one of the great achievements of medieval Islam.

In the two years of his rule (632–634), Abu Bakr governed on the basis of his personal prestige within the Muslim umma. He sent out military expeditions, collected taxes, dealt with tribes on behalf of the entire community, and led the community in prayer. Gradually, under Abu Bakr's first three successors, Umar (r. 634–644), Uthman (r. 644–656), and Ali (r. 656–661), the caliphate emerged as an institution. Umar succeeded in exerting his authority over the Bedouin tribes involved in ongoing conquests. Uthman asserted the right of the caliph to protect the economic interests of the entire umma. Uthman's publication of the definitive text of the Qur'an showed his concern for the unity of the umma. But Uthman's enemies accused him of nepotism—of using his position to put his family in powerful and lucrative jobs—and of unnecessary cruelty. Opposition coalesced around Ali, and when Uthman was assassinated in 656, Ali was chosen to succeed him.

The issue of responsibility for Uthman's murder raised the question of whether Ali's accession was legitimate. Uthman's cousin Mu'awiya, a member of the Umayyad family, who had built a power base as governor of Syria, refused to recognize Ali as caliph. In the ensuing civil war, Ali was assassinated, and Mu'awiya (r. 661–680) assumed the caliphate. Mu'awiya founded the Umayyad Dynasty and shifted the capital of the Islamic state from Medina in Arabia to Damascus in Syria.

When the Umayyad family assumed the leadership of Islam, there was no Muslim state, no formal impersonal institutions of government exercising jurisdiction over a very wide area. Rather, there was "only a federation of regional armies, each one of which was recruited and employed within its own region, maintained from its own revenues, and administered by such local bureaucrats as it contained."[15] Familiar only with tribal relationships with people they knew, the Umayyads depended for governmental services on personal connections, reinforced by marriage alliances, with tribal chiefs. "This preference for personal networks over formal institutions was to become a standard feature of Muslim society."[16]

The first four caliphs were elected by their peers, and the theory of an elected caliphate remained the Islamic legal ideal. Three of the four "patriarchs," as they were called, were murdered, however, and civil war ended the elective caliphate. Beginning with Mu'awiya, the office of caliph was in fact, but never in theory, dynastic. Two successive dynasties, the Umayyad (661–750) and the Abbasid (750–1258), held the caliphate.

From its inception with Abu Bakr, the caliphate rested on the theoretical principle that Muslim political and religious unity transcended tribalism. But tribal connections remained very strong. Mu'awiya sought to enhance the power of the caliphate by making the tribal leaders dependent on him for concessions and special benefits.

At the same time, his control of a loyal and well-disciplined army enabled him to develop the caliphate in an authoritarian direction. Through intimidation he forced the tribal leaders to accept his son Yazid as his heir—thereby establishing the dynastic principle of succession. By distancing himself from a simple life within the umma and withdrawing into the palace that he built at Damascus, and by surrounding himself with symbols and ceremony, Mu'awiya laid the foundations for an elaborate caliphal court. Many of Mu'awiya's innovations were designed to protect him from assassination. A new official, the *hajib,* or chamberlain, restricted access to the caliph, who received visitors seated on a throne surrounded by bodyguards. Beginning with Mu'awiya, the Umayyad caliphs developed court ritual into a grand spectacle.

The assassination of Ali and the assumption of the caliphate by Mu'awiya had another profound consequence. It gave rise to a fundamental division in the umma and in Muslim theology. Ali had claimed the caliphate on the basis of family ties—he was Muhammad's cousin and son-in-law. When Ali was murdered, his followers argued—partly because of the blood tie, partly because Muhammad had designated Ali **imam,** or leader in community prayer—that Ali had been the Prophet's designated successor. These supporters of Ali were called **Shi'ites,** or *Shi'at Ali,* or simply *Shi'a*—Arabic terms all meaning "supporters" or "partisans" of Ali. In succeeding generations, opponents of the Umayyad Dynasty emphasized their blood descent from Ali and claimed to possess divine knowledge that Muhammad had given them as his heirs.

Other Muslims adhered to the practice and beliefs of the umma, based on the precedents of the Prophet. They were called **Sunnis,** which derived from *Sunna.* When a situation arose for which the Qur'an offered no solution, Sunni scholars searched for a precedent in the Sunna, which gained an authority comparable to the Qur'an itself.

What basically distinguished Sunni and Shi'ite Muslims was the Shi'ite doctrine of the *imamate.* According to the Sunnis, the caliph, the elected successor of the Prophet, possessed political and military leadership but not Muhammad's religious authority. In contrast, according to the

**Woven Silk Fragment** This tenth-century piece from Khurasan, in northern Iran, shows elephants used as pack animals and an elegant Kufic border inscription reading "Glory and prosperity to Qa'id Abu-l-Mansur Bakht-tegin, may Allah perpetuate his happiness," which identifies the original owner. *(Louvre © Photo R.M.N./Art Resource, NY)*

Shi'ites, the imam (leader) is directly descended from the Prophet and is the sinless, divinely inspired political leader and religious guide of the community. Put another way, both Sunnis and Shi'ites maintain that authority within Islam lies first in the Qur'an and then in the Sunna. Who interprets these sources? Shi'ites claim that the imam does, for he is invested with divine grace and insight. Sunnis insist that interpretation comes from the consensus of the **ulama,** a group of religious scholars.

The Umayyad caliphs were Sunnis, and throughout the Umayyad period the Shi'ites constituted a major source of discontent. Shi'ite rebellions expressed religious opposition in political terms. The Shi'ites condemned the Umayyads as worldly and sensual rulers, in contrast to the pious and true "successors" of Muhammad.

The Abbasid clan, which based its claim to the caliphate on the descent of Abbas, Muhammad's uncle, exploited the situation. The Abbasids agitated the Shi'ites, encouraged dissension among tribal factions, and contrasted Abbasid piety with the pleasure-loving style of the Umayyads.

## The Abbasid Caliphate

In 747 Abu' al-Abbas led a rebellion against the Umayyads, and in 750 he won general recognition as caliph. Damascus had served as the headquarters of Umayyad rule over the eastern Mediterranean countries and the Hijaz, the region of Mecca and Medina in Arabia. Abu' al-Abbas's successor, al-Mansur (r. 754–775), founded the city of Baghdad and made it his capital. Thus the geographical center of the caliphate shifted eastward to former Sasanid territories: southern Iraq, parts of Persia (modern Iran), and Khurasan. The first three Abbasid caliphs crushed their opponents, eliminated their Shi'ite supporters, and created a new ruling elite drawn from newly converted Persian families that had traditionally served the ruler. The Abbasid revolution established a basis for rule and citizenship more cosmopolitan and Islamic than the narrow, elitist, and Arab basis that had characterized Umayyad government. The Abbasids worked to identify their rule with Islam. They patronized the ulama, built mosques, and supported the development of Islamic scholarship. Moreover, under the Umayyads the Muslim state had been a federation of regional and tribal armies; during the Abbasid caliphate, provincial governors gradually won semi-independent power. Although at first Muslims represented only a small minority of the conquered peoples, Abbasid rule provided the religious-political milieu in which Islam gained, over time, the allegiance of the vast majority of the populations from Spain to Afghanistan.

The Abbasids also borrowed heavily from Persian culture. Following Persian tradition, the Abbasid caliphs claimed to rule by divine right, as reflected in the change of their title from "successor of the Prophet" to "deputy of God." A magnificent palace with hundreds of attendants and elaborate court ceremonial deliberately isolated the caliph from the people he ruled. Subjects had to bow before the caliph, kissing the ground, a symbol of his absolute power.[17]

Baghdad came to represent the political ideals of the new dynasty. Located on both banks of the Tigris River and linked by canals to rich agricultural lands, the city had easy access to a plentiful food supply. It also had strong commercial potential, attracting business people who could be taxed for governmental revenues. Baghdad was designed to reflect the splendor and distance of the caliph: the walled palace, the army barracks, and the state bureaucracy staffed largely by Persians sat on the west bank of the Tigris; outside the walls were the markets, bazaars, mosques, and residences of the ordinary people.

Under the third caliph, Harun al-Rashid (r. 786–809), Baghdad emerged as a flourishing commercial, artistic, and scientific center—the greatest city in Islam and one of the most cosmopolitan cities in the world. Its population of about one million people—an astoundingly large size in preindustrial times—represented a huge demand for goods and services. Baghdad served as an entrepôt for textiles, slaves, and foodstuffs coming from Oman, East Africa, and India. Harun al-Rashid established a library, the Bayt al-Hikma (House of Wisdom), that translated Greek medical and philosophical texts. The scholar Hunayn ib Ishaq al-Ibadi (808–873) translated Galen's medical works into Arabic and made Baghdad a center for the study and practice of medicine. Likewise, under the caliph al-Mamun (r. 813–833), impetus was given to the study of astronomy, and through a program of astronomical observations, Muslim astronomers sought to correct and complement Ptolemaic astronomy. Above all, studies in Qur'anic textual analysis, history, poetry, law, and philosophy—all in Arabic—reflected the development of a distinctly Islamic literary and scientific culture.

The Abbasids made one other significant innovation. The caliph al-Mu'taşim (r. 833–842) recruited a retinue of several thousand Turkish soldiers. They were bought as slaves, converted to Islam, and often freed for military service. Islamicists call them "slave soldiers" because they were or had been slaves. Why this change? Scholars have speculated that the use of slave soldiers was a response to a manpower shortage; that as heavy cavalry with expertise as horse archers, the Turks had military skills superior to those of the Arabs and other peoples; and that al-Mu'taşim felt he could trust the Turks more than the Arabs, Persians, Khurasans, and other recruits. In any case, slave soldiers—later Slavs, Indians, and sub-Saharan blacks—were a standard feature of Muslim armies in the Middle East down to the twentieth century.[18]

## Administration of Islamic Territories

The Islamic conquests brought into being a new imperial system that dominated southwestern Asia and North Africa. The Muslims adopted the patterns of administration used by the Byzantines in Egypt and Syria and by the Sasanids in Persia. Arab **emirs,** or governors, were appointed and given overall responsibility for good order, maintenance of the armed forces, and tax collecting. Below them, experienced native officials—Greeks, Syrians, Copts (Egyptian Christians)—remained in office. Thus there was continuity with previous administrations.

The Umayyad caliphate witnessed the further development of the imperial administration. At the head stood the caliph, who led the holy war against unbelievers. Theoretically, he had the ultimate responsibility for the interpretation of the sacred law. In practice, the ulama interpreted the law as revealed in the Qur'an and in the Sunna. In the course of time, the ulama's interpretations constituted a rich body of law, the **shari'a,** which covered social, criminal, political, commercial, and ritualistic matters. The ulama enjoyed great prestige in the Muslim community and was consulted by the caliph on difficult legal and spiritual matters. The **qadis,** or judges, who were well versed in the sacred law, carried out the judicial functions of the state. Nevertheless, Muslim law prescribed that all people have access to the caliph, and he set aside special times for hearing petitions and for the direct redress of grievances.

The central administrative organ was the diwan, which collected the taxes that paid soldiers' salaries (see page 247) and financed charitable and public works that the caliph undertook, such as aid to the poor (as the Qur'an prescribed) and the construction of mosques, irrigation works, and public baths.

As Arab conquests extended into Spain, Central Asia, and Afghanistan, lines of communication had to be kept open. Emirs and other officials, remote from the capital at Damascus and later Baghdad, might revolt. Thus a relay network known as the *barid* was established to convey letters and intelligence reports between the capital and the various outposts. The barid employed a special technical vocabulary, as similar networks used by the Byzantine and Sasanid empires had done.

The early Abbasid period witnessed considerable economic expansion and population growth, so the work of government became more complicated. New and specialized departments emerged, each with a hierarchy of officials. The most important new official was the **vizier,** a position that the Abbasids adopted from the Persians. The vizier was the caliph's chief assistant, advising the caliph on matters of general policy, supervising the bureaucratic administration, and, under the caliph, overseeing the army, the provincial governors, and relations with foreign governments. As the caliphs withdrew from leading Friday prayers and other routine functions, the viziers gradually assumed power. But the authority and power of the vizier usually depended on the caliph's personality and direct involvement in state affairs. Many viziers used their offices for personal gain and wealth. Although some careers ended with the vizier's execution, there were always candidates seeking the job.

In theory, the caliph and his central administration governed the whole empire. In practice, the many parts of the empire enjoyed considerable local independence; and as long as public order was maintained and taxes were forwarded to the diwan, the central government rarely interfered. In theory, Muslim towns did not possess the chartered self-governing status of the towns and cities of medieval Europe (see pages 385–386). In practice, although a capable governor kept a careful eye on municipal activities, wealthy merchants and property owners had broad local autonomy.

# DECENTRALIZATION

The Umayyad state comprised virtually all Islamic provinces and territories. Under the Abbasids, decentralization began nearly from the start of the dynasty. In 755 an Umayyad prince who had escaped death at the hands of the triumphant Abbasids and fled to Spain set up an independent regime at Córdoba (see Map 9.1). In 800 the emir in Tunisia in North Africa set himself up as an independent ruler and refused to place the caliph's name on the local coinage. In 820 Tahir, the son of a slave, was rewarded with the governorship of Khurasan because he had supported the caliphate. Once there, Tahir ruled independently of Baghdad, not even mentioning the caliph's name in the traditional Friday prayers in recognition of caliphal authority.

Likewise, in 969 the Fatimids, a Shi'ite dynasty who claimed descent from Muhammad's daughter Fatima, conquered the Abbasid province of Egypt. The Fatimids founded the city of Cairo as their capital. Later the

Ayyubid Dynasty replaced the Fatimids, and in 1250 the Mamluks replaced the Ayyubids and ruled Egypt until the Ottoman conquest in 1517.

This sort of decentralization occurred all over the Muslim world. The enormous distance separating many provinces from the imperial capital enabled the provinces to throw off the caliph's jurisdiction. Particularism and ethnic or tribal tendencies, combined with strength and fierce ambition, led to the creation of local dynasties. Incompetent caliphs at Baghdad were unable to enforce their authority over distant and strong local rulers. This pattern led to the decline of the Abbasids and invasion by foreign powers.

## Decline of the Abbasids

In the later ninth century, rebellions shook Arabia, Syria, and Persia, and a slave revolt devastated Iraq (see page 257). These disorders hurt agricultural productivity and in turn cut tax receipts. Having severely taxed the urban mercantile groups, the caliphate had already alienated the commercial classes. Disorder and disintegration threatened the Muslim state.

First, the inordinately large military salaries paid to Turkish troops severely strained the financial resources of the caliphate. Then, the luxury and extravagance of the caliphal court imposed another heavy burden. In the caliph's palace complexes, maintained by staffs numbering in the tens of thousands, an important visitor would be conducted through elaborate rituals and confronted with indications of the caliph's majesty and power: rank upon rank of lavishly appointed guards, pages, servants, slaves, and other retainers; lush parks full of exotic wild beasts; fantastic arrays of gold and silver objects, ornamented furniture, precious carpets and tapestries, pools of mercury, and ingenious mechanical devices. The most famous of the mechanical devices was a gold and silver tree with leaves that rustled, branches that swayed, and mechanical birds that sang as the breezes blew.[19]

Some caliphs in the early tenth century worked to halt the process of decay. But in 945 the Ayyubids, a Shi'ite clan originating in Daylam, the mountainous region on the southern shores of the Caspian Sea, overran Iraq and occupied Baghdad. The caliph, al-Mu'taşim, was forced to recognize the Ayyubid leader as *amir al-umara* (commander-in-chief) and to allow the celebration of Shi'ite festivals—though the caliph and most of the people were Sunnis. A year later, the caliph was accused of plotting against his new masters, snatched from his throne, dragged through the streets, and blinded. Blinding was a practice that the Ayyubids adopted from the Byzantines as a way of rendering a ruler incapable of carrying out his duties. This incident marks the practical collapse of the Abbasid caliphate. Abbasid caliphs, however, remained as puppets of successive Ayyubid leaders and symbols of Muslim unity until the Mongols killed the last Abbasid in 1258.

## The Assault of the Turks and Mongols

In the mid-tenth century, the Seljuk Turks began to besiege the Islamic world. Originating in Turkestan in Central Asia and displaying great physical endurance and mobility, the Turks surged westward. They accepted Sunni Islam near Bukhara (then a great Persian commercial and intellectual center), swarmed over the rest of Persia, and pushed through Iraq and Syria. Baghdad fell to them on December 18, 1055, and the caliph became a puppet of the Turkish *sultan*—literally, "he with authority." The sultans replaced the Ayyubids as masters of the Abbasid caliphate. The Turks did not acquire all of the former Abbasid state. To the west, the Shi'ite Fatimids had conquered present-day central Algeria, Sicily, and, in 969, Egypt.

In the early thirteenth century appeared the Mongols, a nomadic people from the vast plains of Central Asia (see pages 319–328). In 1206 their leader, Chinggis Khan (1162–1227), having welded Mongol and related Turkish tribes into a strong confederation, began to sweep westward, leaving a trail of blood and destruction. The Mongols used terror as a weapon, and out of fear the rich commercial centers of Central Asia—Khwarazm, Bukhara (whose mosques were turned into stables), Herat, Samarkand, and Baikal (whose people were all slaughtered or enslaved)—fell before them. When Chinggis Khan died, his empire stretched from northern China and Korea to the Caspian Sea and from the Danube River to the Arctic. Throughout the 1200s, the Mongols extended their conquests to include Russia, China, and the Abbasid Empire.

Chinggis Khan's grandson Hulagu (1217–1265) led the attack on the Abbasids. His armies sacked and burned Baghdad and killed the last Abbasid caliph in 1258. Two years later, they took Damascus, and only a major defeat at Ayn Jalut in Syria saved Egypt and the Muslim lands in North Africa and perhaps Spain.

Hulagu tried to eradicate Muslim culture, but his descendant Ghazan embraced Islam in 1295 and worked for the revival of Muslim culture. As the Turks had done earlier, the Mongols, once converted, injected new vigor into the faith and spirit of Islam. In the Middle East, the Mongols governed through Persian viziers and native financial officials.

**Jonah and the Whale** When the Mongol ruler Ghazan asked his chief minister, the remarkable Persian polymath Rashid al-Din—a Jew by birth who converted to Islam, a physician by training—to write a history of the Mongols in Persia, he responded with the *Collection of Histories,* which treats China, India, the Jews, Muhammad and the caliphs, pre- and post-Islamic Persia, even the Franks (Europeans). To explain the section on the Jews, a Chinese artist inserted this illustration of the Old Testament prophet Jonah; the story represents divine mercy for those who reform. The Chinese artist had never seen a whale, but he possessed imagination and mastery of movement. The artist testifies to the considerable Chinese migration to Persia in the early fourteenth century. *(Courtesy of Edinburgh University Library, Or Ms 20, fol 23N)*

## THE LIFE OF THE PEOPLE

When the Prophet appeared, Arab society consisted of independent Bedouin tribal groups loosely held together by loyalty to a strong leader and by the belief that all members of a tribe were descended from a common ancestor. Heads of families elected the *sheik,* or tribal chief. He was usually chosen from among elite warrior families whose members had a strong sense of their superiority. Birth determined aristocracy.

According to the Qur'an, however, birth counted for nothing; zeal for Islam was the only criterion for honor: "O ye folk, verily we have created you male and female. . . . Verily the most honourable of you in the sight of God is the most pious of you."[20] The idea of social equality founded on piety was a basic Muslim doctrine.

When Muhammad defined social equality, he was thinking about equality among Muslims alone. But even among Muslims, a sense of pride in ancestry could not be destroyed by a stroke of the pen. Claims of birth remained strong among the first Muslims, and after Islam spread outside of Arabia, full-blooded Arab tribesmen regarded themselves as superior to foreign converts.

### The Classes of Society

In the Umayyad period, Muslim society consisted of several classes. At the top were the caliph's household and the ruling Arab Muslims. Descended from Bedouin tribespeople and composed of warriors, veterans, governing officials, and town settlers, this class constituted the ruling elite. Because birth continued to determine membership, it was more a caste than a class. It was also a relatively small group, greatly outnumbered by Muslim villagers and country people.

Converts constituted the second class in Islamic society. Converts to Islam had to attach themselves to one of the Arab tribes as clients. For economic, social, and cultural reasons, they greatly resented having to do this. They believed they represented a culture superior to the culture of the Arab tribespeople. From the Muslim converts eventually came the members of the commercial and learned professions—merchants, traders, teachers, doctors, artists, and interpreters of the shari'a. Second-class citizenship led some Muslim converts to adopt Shi'ism (see page 249) and other unorthodox doctrines inimical to the state. Over the centuries, Berber, Copt, Persian, Aramaean, and other converts to Islam intermarried with their Muslim conquerors. Gradually, assimilation united peoples of various ethnic and "national" backgrounds. However, in the words of one scholar, "an Arabian remained a native of the peninsula, but an Arab became one who professed Islam and spoke Arabic, regardless of national origin."[21]

**Dhimmis,** or "protected peoples"—Jews, Christians, and Zoroastrians—formed the third class. They were allowed to practice their religions, maintain their houses of worship, and conduct their business affairs, as long as they gave unequivocal recognition to Muslim political supremacy and paid a small tax. Here is a formula drawn up in the ninth century as a pact between Muslims and their nonbelieving subjects:

*I accord to you and to the Christians of the city of so-and-so that which is accorded to the dhimmis . . . safe-conduct . . . namely:*

*You will be subject to the authority of Islam and to no contrary authority. You will not refuse to carry out any obligation which we think fit to impose upon you by virtue of this authority.*

**Lustre Dish: Prince Khusraw Discovers Shirin Bathing** Major Persian pottery centers at Rayy and Kashan produced ceramic masterpieces, often in styles influenced by Chinese artists or by imported Chinese porcelains. The subjects are derived from Persian literature. *(Courtesy of the Freer Gallery of Art, Smithsonian Institution, Washington, D.C., 41.11)*

*If any one of you speaks improperly of Muhammed, may God bless and save him, the Book of God, or of His religion, he forfeits the protection [dhimma] of God, of the Commander of the Faithful, and of all the Muslims; his property and his life are at the disposal of the Commander of the Faithful. . . .*

*If any one of them commits fornication with a Muslim woman or goes through a form of marriage with her or robs a Muslim on the highway or subverts a Muslim from his religion or aids those who made war against the Muslims by fighting with them or by showing them the weak points of the Muslims, or by harboring their spies, he has contravened his pact . . . and his life and his property are at the disposal of the Muslims. . . .*

*You may not display crosses in Muslim cities, nor proclaim polytheism, nor build churches or meeting places for your prayers . . . nor proclaim your polytheistic beliefs on the subject of Jesus [beliefs relating to the Trinity]. . . .*

*Every adult male of sound mind among you shall have to pay a poll tax [jizya] of one dinar, in good coin, at the beginning of each year.*[22]

Restrictions placed on Christians and Jews were not severe, and both groups seem to have thrived under Muslim rule. Rare outbursts of violence against Christians and Jews occurred only when Muslims felt that the dhimmis had stepped out of line and broken the agreement. The social position of the "protected peoples" deteriorated during the Crusades (see pages 375–376) and the Mongol invasions, when there was a general rise of religious loyalties. At those times, Muslims suspected the dhimmis, often rightly, of collaborating with the enemies of Islam.

What was the fate of Jews living under Islam? How does their experience compare with that of Jews living in Christian Europe? Recent scholarship shows that in Europe, Jews were first marginalized in the Christian social order, then completely expelled from it (see pages 374–376). In Islam, though marginalized, Jews participated fully in commercial and professional activities, some attaining an economic equality with their Muslim counterparts. Why? The 17th Sura (chapter) of the Qur'an, titled Bani Isra'il, "The Children of Israel," accords to the Jews a special respect because they were "the people of the Book." Scriptural admonitions of the Qur'an carried over into social and political legislation, and "the relative stability over time of the basic law regarding their (Jews') legal status assured them a considerable degree of continuity."[23] In contrast, Western Christian legislation about the Jews fluctuated, making their legal position more ambiguous, tenuous, and insecure. Also, Islamic culture was an urban and commercial culture that gave the merchant considerable respect; medieval Christian culture was basically rural and agricultural; it did not revere the business person.

By the beginning of the tenth century, Islamic society had undergone significant change. The courtier al-Fadl b. Yahya, writing in 903, divided humankind into four classes:

*Firstly, rulers elevated to office by their deserts; secondly, viziers, distinguished by their wisdom and understanding; thirdly, the upper classes, elevated by their wealth; and fourthly, the middle classes to which belong men marked by their culture. The remainder are filthy refuse, a torrent of scum, base cattle, none of whom thinks of anything but his food and sleep.*[24]

The last category hardly reflects compassion for the poor and unfortunate. However, it is clear that birth as a sign of social distinction had yielded to wealth and talent.

## Slavery

At the bottom of the social scale were slaves. Slavery had long existed in the ancient Middle East, and Islam accepted it as a natural institution. The Qur'anic acceptance of slavery parallels that of the Old and New Testaments. But the Qur'an prescribes a just and humane treatment of slaves. A master is not to treat his slaves contemptuously. He should feed and clothe his slaves adequately; give them moderate, not excessive, work; and not punish them severely. The Qur'an also explicitly encourages the freeing of slaves and urges owners whose slaves ask for their freedom to give them the opportunity to buy it.[25]

Muslim expansion ensured a steady flow of slaves. Prisoners of war or people captured in raids or purchased in markets, slaves constituted very large numbers in the Islamic world. (See the feature "Listening to the Past: A Treatise on Buying Slaves" on pages 276–277.) The great Muslim commander Musa ibn Nusayr, himself the son of a Christian enslaved in Iraq, is reputed to have taken 300,000 prisoners of war in his North African campaigns (708–818) and 30,000 virgins from the Visigothic nobility of Spain. (These numbers are surely greatly inflated, as most medieval numbers are.) Every soldier, from general to private, had a share of slaves from captured prisoners. Tradition holds that one of the Prophet's ten closest companions, 'Abd al Rahman bin 'Awf, freed 30,000 slaves at his death in 652.

How were slaves employed? A great household required slaves for many purposes. Women worked as cooks, cleaners, laundresses, and nursemaids. A few performed as

**Slave Market at Zabid, Yemen** During the thirteenth century, this market offered slaves of many races—women and children for domestic purposes and for harems, boys to be trained for military and administrative service. Manumission (encouraged by the Qur'an) and the promotion of some slaves to high positions worked against the growth of class consciousness. *(Bibliothèque nationale de France)*

singers, musicians, dancers, and reciters of poetry. Many women also served as concubines, and Muslim society did not consider their sexual services degrading. Not only rulers but high officials and rich merchants owned many concubines. Down the economic ladder, artisans and tradesmen often had a few concubines who assumed domestic tasks as well as sexual ones.

According to tradition, the seclusion of women in the harem protected their virtue (see page 261), and when men had the means the harem was secured by eunuch guards. The use of eunuch guards seems to have been a practice Muslims adopted from the Byzantines and Persians. Early Muslim law forbade castration, so in the early Islamic period Muslims secured European eunuchs from the slave markets at Prague (in the modern Czech Republic) and Verdun in northeastern France; Central Asian eunuchs from Kharazon in the Caspian Sea region; and African eunuchs from Bornu (in modern Nigeria). After the seventeenth century, Baghirmi, a region southeast of Lake Chad in Africa, produced eunuchs for the Islamic world. Because of the insatiable demand for eunuch guards, the cost of eunuchs was very high, perhaps seven times that of uncastrated male slaves.

Muslims also employed eunuchs as secretaries, tutors, and commercial agents, possibly because unlike men with ordinary desires, eunuchs were said to be more tractable and dependable. In the tenth century, the caliph of Baghdad had seven thousand black eunuchs and four thousand white ones in his palace.

Besides administrative, business, or domestic services, male slaves, eunuchs or not, were also set to work as longshoremen on the docks, as oarsmen on ships, in construction crews, in factories, and in gold and silver mines. The existence of large numbers of male slaves led to another aspect of Islamic culture: the strict seclusion of upper-class women, the financial inability of young Muslims to marry or buy concubines, and the glorification of aggressively virile and macho attitudes in a military society led to homosexual activity. According to one authority, "sex between men entered pervasively into the ethic of the upper classes. . . . The Muslim stereotype of such sexual relations answered the idea of the sex act as an act of domination."[26]

Male slaves also fought as soldiers. Any free person could buy a slave, but only a ruler could own military slaves. In the ninth century, the rulers of Tunisia formed a special corps of black military slaves, and at the end of that century the Tulunid rulers of Egypt built an army of 24,000 white and 45,000 black slaves. The Fatimid rulers of Egypt (969–1171) raised large black battalions, and a Persian visitor to Cairo between 1046 and 1049 estimated an army of 100,000 slaves, of whom 30,000 were black soldiers. Likewise, the trans-Saharan slave trade (see page 288) afforded the Almoravid rulers of Morocco and parts of Spain the opportunity to use black soldiers until they were defeated by insurgent Al-mohad forces also using black slave soldiers.

Slavery in the Islamic world differed in at least two fundamental ways from the slavery later practiced in South and North America. First, Muslims did not identify slavery with blackness as Europeans did in the Americas. The general and widespread use of Caucasian slaves in Islamic societies made that connection impossible. Second, slavery in the Islamic world was not the virtual equivalent of commercial plantation agriculture as practiced in the southern United States, the Caribbean, and Brazil in the eighteenth and nineteenth centuries. True, in the tenth century, large numbers of black slaves worked on the date plantations in northeastern Arabia. But massive revolts of black slaves from East Africa called Zanj, provoked by mercilessly harsh labor conditions in the salt flats and on the sugar and cotton plantations of southwestern Persia, erupted in 869. Gathering momentum, the Zanj captured the rich cities of Ahwaz, Basra, and Wasit and threatened Baghdad. Only the strenuous efforts of the commander of the caliph's armies, which were composed of Turkish slaves and included naval as well as land forces, halted and gradually crushed the Zanj in 883. The long and destructive Zanj revolt ended the Muslim experiment of plantation agriculture.[27]

## Race

From ancient times to very recently, most peoples used the term *race* to designate an ethnic or a national group defined by language, culture, or religion, such as "the Irish race," "the Jewish race," or "the Japanese race." Since about 1950, however, the American usage of the word to denote major divisions among peoples according to perceived physical differences—Asian, black, white—has spread to other countries. Physical traits, rather than linguistic, historical, or cultural features, now seem to determine "race." While ancient and medieval peoples often looked on outsiders with hostility and prejudice, that prejudice existed because the foreigners spoke a different language, practiced a different religion, and had different dietary, marriage, or social customs. Thus the ancient Greeks considered outsiders "barbarians," Jews considered Gentiles "heathens," and Romans had contempt for all non-Romans.

The rise and spread of Islam changed this attitude. By conquest and conversion, and by a single religious culture, Islam attempted to create a universal civilization, incorporating very different peoples such as Chinese, East Indians, sub-Saharan blacks, and white Europeans, all bound by one religious-political text, the Qur'an. The Qur'an stresses that there are no superior and inferior races; it shows no color prejudice, emphasizes that piety is more important than race, and condemns those who claim social distinction on the basis of birth. It is indifferent to what we label racial differences. Scholars have taken the Qur'an at face value. Thus a distinguished British historian, Arnold Toynbee, wrote:

*The Arabs and all other white Muslims have always been free of colour-prejudice vis-à-vis the non-white races; and at the present day, Muslims still make the dichotomy of the human family which Western Christians used to make in the Middle Ages. They (Muslims) divide mankind into Believers and Unbelievers who are all potentially Believers. . . . This liberality is more remarkable to White Muslims than it was in White Western Christianity in our Middle Ages.*[28]

Views of authorities like Toynbee, which rested entirely on the study of the Qur'an, have shaped interpretations of race in the Muslim world. But the Qur'an, like the Judeo-Christian Scriptures, sets forth religious ideals, not actual social practice. Literary and social evidence suggests that scholars' assumptions rest more on myth and imagination than on the historical facts.

The very first story of the folklore classic *The Thousand and One Nights* relates the tale of King Shahzaman, who returns home unexpectedly to find his wife asleep in the arms of a black male slave. Enraged, Shahzaman kills them both with his sword. He then visits his brother, Shahriyar, ruler of a neighboring kingdom. Sitting at a palace window overlooking a garden, Shahzaman sees

*a door open in the palace through which came twenty slave girls and twenty Negroes. In their midst was his brother's queen, a woman of surpassing beauty. . . . The king's wife called out: "O Messood" and there promptly came to her a black slave who mounted her after smothering her with embraces and kisses. So also did the Negroes with the slave girls.*

When Shahriyar heard of this, he imposed the same death penalty as his brother had. This story poses problems: Did these kings react as any man would on discovering his wife having sex with another man? Or were the kings especially resentful of the blacks' supposed sexual prowess?

Another tale in the *Nights* describes a black slave who led a life of exemplary piety and virtue. As his reward, he turned white at the moment of his death. Isn't this tale suggestive of relative Muslim attitudes toward the races? All the slaves, black and white, in *The Thousand and One Nights* worked as household servants, porters, nannies for children, or attendants at the public baths.[29]

In the centuries of the classical Islamic period, a significant difference existed between white and black slaves. Islamic law declared that the offspring of a free male and a slave woman were free, because lineage was in the paternal line. Many Muslims took slave women as concubines, and a few black women gained wealth and influence as concubines and court musicians. Almost no black male slaves did so. In the tenth century, the Nubian slave Abu'l-Misk Kafur (from a region of modern northern Sudan) became regent of Egypt, which contemporary Muslim writers found extraordinary. He seems to have been the exception that proved the rule. The millions of other black slaves never rose above menial positions. The obvious explanation is racial discrimination.

Enlightenment philosophers in the eighteenth century and nineteenth-century abolitionists developed the notion that complete social harmony existed in Islamic society—that it was free of color prejudice. This was a myth, an ideological stick used by the opponents of slavery in the Western Hemisphere, and later of apartheid in South Africa, to flail the defenders of slavery and the advocates of the separation of the races. The evidence shows that the toleration of blacks varied considerably in time and place; suspicion, hostility, and discrimination were often the norm.[30] Even so, many caliphs were the sons of Turkish, Greek, Slavic, or black slave women.

**An Interracial Couple Scolded** Black people appear in many Islamic paintings but rarely in an erotic situation. Here a Mughal painting (1629) illustrates the story by the Persian painter Sadi of a black man and an Indian girl chastised for flirting. She seems to be sitting on his lap, and he seems to protest the old man's correction. In a multiracial society, such relationships were virtually inevitable. *(British Library)*

## Women in Classical Islamic Society

Arab tribal law gave women virtually no legal status. At birth girls could be buried alive by their fathers. They were sold into marriage by their guardians for a price. Their husbands could terminate the union at will. And women had virtually no property or succession rights. The Qur'an sought to improve the social position of women.

The hadith—records of what Muhammad said and did, and what believers in the first two centuries after his death believed he said and did (see page 241)—also provide information about his wives. (Scholars dispute the number of those wives, though most hadith traditions put the number at fourteen, nine of whom were alive when he died. The Qur'an limits the number of wives for Muslims to four, but classical interpreters held that the Prophet had the right to unrestricted polygamy, a prerogative God's sunna gave to all prophets as his spokesmen on earth.) Some hadith portray the Prophet's wives as subject to common human frailties, such as jealousy; other hadith report miraculous events in their lives. Most hadith describe the wives as "mothers of the believers"—models of piety and righteousness, whose every act illustrates their commitment to promoting God's order on earth by personal example.

Muhammad's wives also became examplars of juridic norms. They and other prominent women sometimes exercised political influence in the succession struggles that followed Muhammad's death. For example, Aisha, daughter of Abu Bakr (the first caliph) and probably Muhammad's favorite wife, played a "leading role" in rallying support for the movement opposing Ali, who succeeded Uthman in 656 (see page 248). Likewise, Umm Salama, member of a wealthy and prominent clan in Mecca, at first supported Ali, then switched sides and supported the Umayyads. Although the hadith usually depict women in terms of moral virtue, domesticity, and saintly ideals, the hadith also show some prominent women in "public" and political roles.[31]

The Qur'an, like the religious writings of all traditions, represents moral precept rather than social practice, and the texts are open to different interpretations. Yet modern scholars tend to agree that the Islamic sacred book intended women as the spiritual and sexual equals of men and gave women considerable economic rights. In the early Umayyad period, moreover, women played an active role in the religious, economic, and political life of the community. They owned property. They had freedom of movement and traveled widely. Women participated with men in the public religious rituals and observances. But this Islamic ideal of women and men of equal value to the community did not last.[32] As Islamic society changed, the precepts of the Qur'an were interpreted to meet different circumstances.

In the later Umayyad period, the status of women declined. The rapid conquest of vast territories led to the influx of large numbers of slave women. As wealth replaced birth as the criterion of social status, scholars speculate, men more and more viewed women as possessions, as a form of wealth. The increasingly inferior status of women is revealed in three ways: in the relationship of women to their husbands, in the practice of veiling women, and in the seclusion of women in harems (see page 261).

On the rights and duties of a husband to his wife, the Qur'an states that "men are in charge of women because Allah hath made the one to excel the other, and because they (men) spend of their property (for the support of women). So good women are obedient, guarding in secret that which Allah hath guarded."[33] A tenth-century interpreter, Abu Ja'far Muhammad ibn-Jarir al-Tabari, commented on that passage in this way:

*Men are in charge of their women with respect to disciplining (or chastising) them, and to providing them with restrictive guidance concerning their duties toward God and themselves (i.e., the men), by virtue of that by which God has given excellence (or preference) to the men over their wives: i.e., the payment of their dowers to them, spending of their wealth on them, and providing for them in full.*[34]

A thirteenth-century commentator on the same Qur'anic passage goes into more detail and argues that women are incapable of and unfit for any public duties, such as participating in religious rites, giving evidence in the law courts, or being involved in any public political decisions.[35] Muslim society fully accepted this view, and later interpreters further categorized the ways in which men were superior to women.

The Sunni aphorism "There shall be no monkery Islam" captures the importance of marriage in Muslim culture and the Muslim belief that a sexually frustrated person is dangerous to the community. Islam vehemently discourages sexual abstinence. Islam expects that every man and woman, unless physically incapable or financially unable, will marry: marriage is a safeguard of chastity, essential to the stability both of the family and of society. Marriage in Muslim society is a sacred contract between two families.

As in medieval Europe and in Ming China, marriage in Muslim society was considered too important an undertaking to be left to the romantic emotions of the young. Families or guardians, not the prospective bride and groom, identified suitable partners and finalized the contract. The official wedding ceremony consisted of an offer and its acceptance by representatives of the bride's and groom's parents at a meeting before witnesses. A wedding banquet at which men and women feasted separately followed; the quality of the celebration, of the gifts, and of the food depended on the relative wealth of the two families. Because it was absolutely essential that the bride be a virgin, marriages were arranged shortly after the onset of the girl's menarche at age twelve or thirteen. Husbands were perhaps ten to fifteen years older. Youthful marriages ensured a long period of fertility.

A wife's responsibilities depended on the financial status of her husband. A farmer's wife helped in the fields, ground the corn, carried water, prepared food, and did the myriad tasks necessary in rural life. Shopkeepers' wives in the cities sometimes helped in business. In an upper-class household, the lady supervised servants, looked after all domestic arrangements, and did whatever was needed for her husband's comfort.

In every case, children were the wife's special domain. A mother exercised authority over her children and enjoyed their respect. A Muslim tradition asserts that "Paradise is at the mother's feet." Thus, as in Chinese culture, the prestige of the young wife depended on the production of children—especially sons—as rapidly as possible. A wife's failure to have children was one of the main reasons for a man to take a second wife or to divorce his wife entirely.

Like the Jewish tradition, Muslim law permits divorce, but the Qur'an seeks to preserve the union and to protect a possible child's paternity. The law prescribes that if a man intends to divorce his wife, he should avoid hasty action and not have intercourse with her for three months; hopefully, they will reconcile. If the woman becomes pregnant during that period, the father can be identified:

> *Women who are divorced have to wait for three monthly periods (before remarriage), and if they believe in God and the Last Day, they must not hide unlawfully what God has formed within their wombs. Their (ex-)husbands would do well to take them back in that period, if they wish to be reconciled. Women also have recognized rights as men have, though men are over them in rank.*[36]

Some interpreters of the Islamic traditions on divorce show a marked similarity to the Christian attitude. For example, some Pharisees asked Jesus whether it was permissible for a man to divorce his wife. When the Pharisees quoted the Mosaic Law as allowing divorce, Jesus discussed the Mosaic Law as a concession to human weakness, arguing that what God has joined together no one should separate. In other words, Jesus held that divorce is wrong, whatever the law does to regulate it (Mark 10:2–9). Likewise, the commentator Ibn Urnan reported the Prophet as saying, "The lawful thing which God hates most is divorce."[37]

Interpretations of the Qur'an's statements on polygamy give an example of the declining status of women in Muslim society. The Qur'an permits a man to have four wives, provided "that all are treated justly. . . . Marry of the women who seem good to you, two or three or four; and if ye fear that you cannot do justice (to so many) then one (only) or the captives that your right hand possess."[38] Muslim jurists interpreted the statement as having legal force. The Prophet's emphasis on justice to the several wives, however, was understood as a mere recommendation.[39] Although the Qur'an allows polygamy, only very wealthy men could afford several wives. The vast majority of Muslim males were monogamous because women could not earn money and men had difficulty enough supporting one wife.

In contrast to the Christian view of sexual activity as something inherently shameful and even within marriage only a cure for concupiscence, Islam maintains a healthy acceptance of sexual pleasure for both males and females. Islam holds that sexual satisfaction for both partners in marriage is necessary to prevent extramarital activity. Men, however, are entitled to as many as four legal partners. Women have to be content with one. Because satisfaction of the sexual impulse for males allows polygamy,

> *one can speculate that fear of its inverse—one woman with four husbands—might explain the assumption of women's insatiability, which is at the core of the Muslim concept of female sexuality. Since Islam assumes that a sexually frustrated individual is a very problematic believer and a troublesome citizen, . . . the distrust of women is even greater.*[40]

Modern sociologists contend that polygamy affects individuals' sense of identity. It supports men's self-images as primarily sexual beings. And, by emphasizing wives' inability to satisfy their husbands, it undermines women's confidence in their sexuality. The function of polygamy as a device to humiliate women is evident in an aphorism from Moroccan folklore: "Debase a woman by bringing in (the house) another one."[41]

In many present-day Muslim cultures, few issues are more sensitive than those of the veiling and the seclusion of women. These practices have their roots in pre-Islamic times, and they took firm hold in classical Islamic society. The head veil seems to have been the mark of freeborn urban women; wearing the veil distinguished free women from slave women. Country and desert women did not wear veils because they interfered with work. Probably of Byzantine or Persian origin, the veil indicated respectability and modesty. As the Arab conquerors subjugated various peoples, they adopted some of the vanquished peoples' customs, one of which was veiling. The Qur'an contains no specific rule about the veil, but its few vague references have been interpreted as sanctioning the practice. Gradually, all parts of a woman's body were considered *pudendal* (shameful because they are capable of arousing sexual desire) and were not allowed to be seen in public.

Even more restrictive of the freedom of women than veiling was the practice of *purdah,* literally seclusion behind a screen or curtain—the **harem** system. The English word *harem* comes from the Arabic *haram,* meaning "forbidden" or "sacrosanct," which the women's quarters of a house or palace were considered to be. The practice of secluding women in a harem also derives from Arabic contacts with other Eastern cultures. Scholars do not know precisely when the harem system began, but within "one-and-a-half centuries after the death of the Prophet, the (harem) system was fully established. . . . Amongst the richer classes, the women were shut off from the rest of the household."[42] The harem became another symbol of male prestige and prosperity, as well as a way to distinguish upper-class women from peasants.

## Trade and Commerce

Islam had a highly positive disposition toward profit-making enterprises. In the period from 1000 to 1500, there was less ideological resistance to the striving for profit in trade and commerce in the Muslim world than there was in the Christian West. Christianity tended to condemn the acquisition of wealth beyond one's basic needs. "For Islam, the stress is laid rather upon the good use to be made of one's possessions, the merit that lies in expending them intelligently and distributing them with generosity—an attitude more favourable to economic expansion than that of the Christian theologians."[43]

Since Muslim theology and law were fully compatible with profitable economic activity, trade and commerce played a prominent role in the Islamic world. Muhammad had earned his living in business as a representative of the city of Mecca, which carried on a brisk trade from southern Palestine to southwestern Arabia. Although Bedouin nomads were among the first converts to Islam, Islam arose in a mercantile, not an agricultural, setting. The merchant had a respectable place in Muslim society. According to the sayings of the Prophet:

*The honest, truthful Muslim merchant will stand with the martyrs on the Day of Judgment.*

*I commend the merchants to you, for they are the couriers of the horizons and God's trusted servants on earth.*[44]

In contrast to the social values of the medieval West and of Confucian China, Muslims tended to look with disdain on agricultural labor and to hold trade in esteem. The Qur'an, moreover, has no prohibition against trade with Christians or other unbelievers.

Western scholars have tended to focus attention on the Mediterranean Sea as the source of Islamic mercantile influence on Europe in the Middle Ages. From the broad perspective of Muslim commerce, however, the Mediterranean held a position much subordinate to other waterways: the Black Sea; the Caspian Sea and the Volga River, which gave access deep into Russia; the Aral Sea, from which caravans departed for China; the Gulf of Aden; and the Arabian Sea and the Indian Ocean, which linked the Arabian gulf region with eastern Africa, the Indian subcontinent, and eventually Indonesia and the Philippines. These served as the main commercial seaways of the Islamic world (see Map 9.2).

Cairo was the major Mediterranean entrepôt for intercontinental trade. An Egyptian official, the *wakil-al-tryjar,* served as the legal representative of foreign merchants from Central Asia, Persia, Iraq, northern Europe (especially Venice), the Byzantine Empire, and Spain. They or their agents sailed up the Nile to the Aswan region, traveled east from Aswan by caravan to the Red Sea, and sailed down the Red Sea to Aden, whence they crossed the Indian Ocean to India. They exchanged textiles, glass, gold, silver, and copper for Asian spices, dyes, and drugs and for Chinese silks and porcelains. Muslim and Jewish merchants dominated the trade with India; both spoke and wrote Arabic. Their commercial practices included the *sakk,* an Arabic word that is the root of the English *check,* an order to a banker to pay money held on account to a third party; the practice can be traced to Roman Palestine. Muslims originated other business devices, such as the bill of exchange, a written order from one person to another to pay a specified sum of money to a designated person or party; and the idea of the joint stock company, an arrangement that lets a group of people invest in a venture and share its profits (and losses) in proportion to the amount each has invested.

Between 1250 and 1500, Islamic trade changed markedly. In maritime technology, the adoption from the Chinese of the magnetic compass, an instrument for determining directions at sea by means of a magnetic needle turning on a pivot, allowed greater reconnaissance of

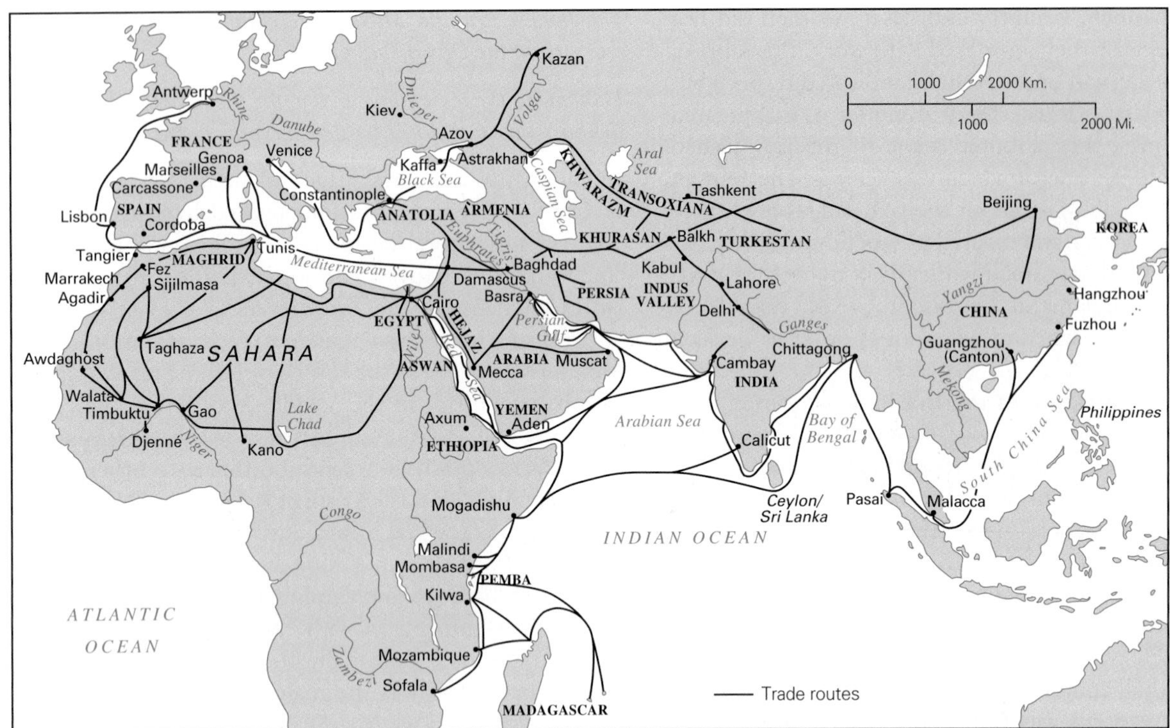


**MAP 9.2 Major Trade Routes of the Thirteenth and Fourteenth Centuries** Muslim merchants carried on extensive trade in Southeast Asia, Central Asia, southern Europe, Africa, and the Indian Ocean long before the arrival (in the last area) of Europeans.

the Arabian Sea and the Indian Ocean. The construction of larger ships led to a shift in long-distance cargoes from luxury goods such as pepper, spices, and drugs to bulk goods such as sugar, rice, and timber. Venetian galleys sailing the Mediterranean came to carry up to 250 tons of cargo, but the *dhows* plying the Indian Ocean were built to carry even more, up to 400 tons. The teak forests of western India supplied the wood for Arab ships.

Commercial routes also shifted. The Mongol invasions, culminating in the capture of Baghdad and the fall of the Abbasid caliphate (see page 252), led to the decline of Iraq and the rise of Egypt as the center of Muslim trade. In the fourteenth century, Persian and Arab seamen sailed down the east coast of Africa and established trading towns between Somalia and Sofala (see page 298). These thirty to fifty urban centers—each merchant controlled, fortified, and independent—linked Zimbabwe in southern Africa (see page 300) with the Indian Ocean trade and the Middle Eastern trade. The overland route, through Persia and Central Asia, to China and the Persian Gulf route both declined in importance.[45]

A private ninth-century list mentions a great variety of commodities transported into and through the Islamic world by land and by sea:

*Imported from India: tigers, leopards, elephants, leopard skins, red rubies, white sandalwood, ebony, and coconuts*

*From China: aromatics, silk, porcelain, paper, ink, peacocks, fiery horses, saddles, felts, cinnamon*

*From the Byzantines: silver and gold vessels, embroidered cloths, fiery horses, slave girls, rare articles in red copper, strong locks, lyres, water engineers, specialists in plowing and cultivation, marble workers, and eunuchs*

*From Arabia: Arab horses, ostriches, thoroughbred she-camels, and tanned hides*

*From Barbary and Maghrib (the Arabic name for northwest Africa, an area that included Morocco, Algeria, and Tunisia): leopards, acacia, felts, and black falcons*

*From Egypt: ambling donkeys, fine cloths, papyrus, balsam oil, and, from its mines, high-quality topaz*

**Arab Trade and Commerce** A mariner's compass determines direction at sea. Arab traders brought this Chinese south-pointing compass (*left*) to the West, probably in the twelfth century. In 1984, archaeologists unearthed these coins (*right*) on the island of Pemba, off the coast of modern Kenya. Deriving from Tunisian, Egyptian, and Syrian mints, and bearing Arabic scripts, the coins testify to Muslim trade with the Swahili city-states. *(left: Ontario Science Center, Toronto; right: Ashmolean Museum, Oxford)*

*From the Khazars (a people living on the northern shore of the Black Sea): slaves, slave women, armor, helmets, and hoods of mail*

*From Samarkand: paper*

*From Ahwaz (a city in southwestern Persia): sugar, silk brocades, castanet players and dancing girls, kinds of dates, grape molasses, and candy.*[46]

Camels made long-distance land transportation possible. Stubborn and vicious, camels nevertheless proved more efficient for desert transportation than horses or oxen. The use of the camel to carry heavy and bulky freight facilitated the development of world commerce.

Vigorous long-distance trade had significant consequences. Commodities produced in one part of the world became available in many other places, providing a uniformity of consumer goods among diverse peoples living over a vast area. Trade promoted technological advances in navigation, shipbuilding, and cartography. All this trade obviously generated very great wealth.

Did Muslim economic activity amount to a kind of capitalism? If by capitalism is meant private (not state) ownership of the means of production, the production of goods for market sale, profit as the main motive for economic activity, competition, a money economy, and the lending of money at interest, then, unquestionably, the medieval Muslim economy had capitalistic features. Students of Muslim economic life have not made a systematic and thorough investigation of Muslims' industries, businesses, and seaports, but the impressionistic evidence is overwhelming: "Not only did the Muslim world know a capitalist sector, but this sector was apparently the most extensive in history before the establishment of the world market created by the Western European bourgeoisie, and this did not outstrip it in importance until the sixteenth century."[47]

**Design for a Water Clock, Egypt** From a book describing the construction of various mechanical devices, this clock from the Mamluk period (1354) was to be run by water and operated by a system of reservoirs, pulleys, and floats. Below the arcade with signs of the zodiac (*top*) stand twelve doorways. A figure emerges from one of these doorways on every daylight hour. During the night, one of the circles in the lower arch lights up on every hour. *(Museum of Fine Arts, Boston. Francis Bartlett Donation of 1912 and Picture Fund 14.533)*

## Urban Centers

Long-distance trade provided the wealth that made possible a gracious and sophisticated culture in the cities of the Muslim world. (See the feature "Individuals in Society: Abu 'Abdallah Ibn Battuta.") Although cities and mercantile centers dotted the entire Islamic world, the cities of Baghdad and Córdoba at their peak in the tenth century stand out as the finest examples of cosmopolitan Muslim civilization. On Baghdad's streets thronged a kaleidoscope of races, creeds, costumes, and cultures, an almost infinite variety of peoples: returning travelers, administrative officials, slaves, visitors, merchants from Asia, Africa, and Europe. Shops and marketplaces offered the rich and extravagant a dazzling and exotic array of goods from all over the world.

The caliph Harun al-Rashid (r. 786–809) presided over a glamorous court. He invited writers, dancers, musicians, poets, and artists to live in Baghdad, and he is reputed to have rewarded one singer with a hundred thousand silver pieces for a single song. This brilliant era provided the background for the tales that appear in *The Thousand and One Nights* (see page 257).

The central plot of the fictional tales involves the efforts of Scheherazade to keep her husband, Schariar, legendary king of Samarkand, from killing her. She entertains him

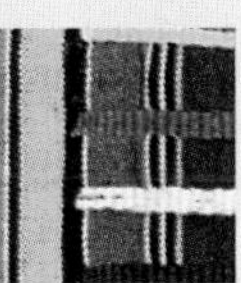

# ABU 'ABDALLAH IBN BATTUTA

*A traveler, perhaps Ibn Battuta, as depicted on a 1375 European map.*
(Bibliothèque nationale de France)

In 1354 the sultan of Morocco appointed a scribe to write an account of the travels of Ibn Battuta (1304–1368), who between 1325 and 1354 had traveled through most of the Islamic world. The two men collaborated. The result was a *Rihla,* or travel book, written in Arabic for educated people and later hailed as the richest eyewitness account of fourteenth-century Islamic culture. It has often been compared to the Venetian Marco Polo's *Travels* (see page 330).

Ibn Battuta was born in Tangiers to a family of legal scholars. As a youth, he studied Muslim legal sciences, gained fluency in Arabic, and acquired the qualities considered essential for a civilized Muslim gentleman: courtesy, manners, the social polish that eases relations among people.

At age twenty-one, he left Tangiers to make the *hajii* (pilgrimage) to Mecca. He crossed North Africa and visited Alexandria, Cairo, Damascus, and Medina. Reaching Mecca in October 1326, he immediately praised God for his safe journey, kissed the Holy Stone at the Ka'ba, and recited the ritual prayers. There he decided to see more of the world.

In the next four years, he traveled to Iraq and to Basra and Baghdad in Persia, then returned to Mecca before sailing down the coast of Africa as far as modern Tanzania. On the return voyage, he visited Oman and the Persian Gulf region, then traveled by land across central Arabia to Mecca. Strengthened by his stay in the holy city, he decided to go to India by way of Egypt, Syria, and Anatolia; across the Black Sea to the plains of western Central Asia, detouring to see Constantinople; back to the Asian steppe; east to Khurasan and Afghanistan; and down to Delhi in northern India.

For eight years, Ibn Battuta served as a *qadi,* or judge, in the service of the sultan of Delhi. In 1341 the sultan chose him to lead a diplomatic mission to China; the expedition was shipwrecked off the southeastern coast of India. Ibn Battuta used the disaster to travel through southern India, Ceylon (Sri Lanka), and the Maldive Islands. Thence he went on his own to China, stopping in Bengal and Sumatra before reaching the southern coast of China. Returning to Mecca in 1346, he set off for home, getting to Fez in Morocco in 1349. After a brief trip across the Strait of Gibraltar to Granada, he undertook his last journey, by camel caravan across the Sahara to Mali in the West African Sudan (see page 292), returning home in 1354. Scholars estimate that he had traveled about seventy-five thousand miles. He retired to a provincial Moroccan town, where he held a judicial post until he died.

Ibn Battuta had a driving intellectual curiosity to see and understand the world. At every stop, he sought out the learned jurists and pious men at the mosques and madrasas. He marveled at the Lighthouse of Alexandria, eighteen hundred years old in his day; at the vast harbor at Kaffa (modern Feodosiya), in southern Ukraine on the Black Sea, whose two hundred Genoese ships were loaded with silks and slaves for the markets at Venice, Cairo, and Damascus; and at the elephants in the sultan's procession in Delhi, which carried machines that tossed gold and silver coins to the crowds.

He must have had an iron constitution. Besides walking long distances on his land trips, he endured fevers, dysentery, malaria, the scorching heat of the Sahara, and the freezing cold of the steppe. His thirst for adventure was stronger than his fear of nomadic warriors and bandits on land and the dangers of storms and pirates at sea.

## QUESTIONS FOR ANALYSIS

1. Trace the routes of Ibn Battuta's travels on a map.
2. How did a common Muslim culture facilitate his travels?

*Source:* R. E. Dunn, *The Adventures of Ibn Battuta: A Muslim Traveler of the Fourteenth Century* (Berkeley: University of California Press, 1986).

with one tale a night for 1,001 nights. The best-known tales are "Aladdin and His Lamp," "Sinbad the Sailor," and "Ali Baba and the Forty Thieves." Also known as *The Arabian Nights,* this book offers a sumptuous collection of caliphs, viziers, and genies, varieties of sexual experiences, and fabulous happenings. *The Arabian Nights,* though folklore, has provided many of the images that Europeans have used since the eighteenth century to describe the Islamic world.

Córdoba in southern Spain competed with Baghdad for the cultural leadership of the Islamic world. In the tenth century, no city in Asia or Europe could equal dazzling Córdoba. Its streets were well paved and lighted, and the city had an abundant supply of fresh water. With a population of about 1 million, Córdoba contained 1,600 mosques, 900 public baths, 213,177 houses for ordinary people, and 60,000 mansions for generals, officials, and the wealthy. In its 80,455 shops, 13,000 weavers produced silks, woolens, and brocades that were internationally famous. The English language has memorialized the city's leather with the word *cordovan.* Córdoba utilized the Syrian process of manufacturing crystal. It was a great educational center with 27 free schools and a library containing 400,000 volumes. (By contrast, the great Benedictine abbey of Saint-Gall in Switzerland had about 600 books. The use of paper—whose manufacture the Muslims had learned from the Chinese—instead of vellum, gave rise to this great disparity.) Through Iran and Córdoba, the Indian game of chess entered western Europe. Córdoba's scholars made contributions in chemistry, medicine and surgery, music, philosophy, and mathematics. Its fame was so great it is no wonder that the contemporary Saxon nun Hrosthwita of Gandersheim (d. 1000) described the city as the "ornament of the world."[48]

## Education and Intellectual Life

Urban and sophisticated Muslim culture possessed a strong educational foundation. Recent scholarly research provides exciting information about medieval Muslim education. Muslim culture placed extraordinary emphasis on knowledge, especially religious knowledge; indeed, knowledge and learning were esteemed above every other human activity. Knowledge provided the guidelines by which men and women should live. What kinds of educational institutions existed in the Muslim world? What was the method of instruction? What social or practical purposes did Muslim education serve?

Islam is a religion of the law, and the institution for instruction in Muslim jurisprudence was the **madrasa,** the school for the study of Muslim law and religious science. The Arabic noun *madrasa* derives from a verb meaning "to study." The first madrasas were probably established in Khurasan in northeastern Persia. By 1193 thirty madrasas existed in Damascus; between 1200 and 1250, sixty more were established there. Aleppo, Jerusalem, Alexandria, and above all Cairo also witnessed the foundation of madrasas.

Schools were urban phenomena. Wealthy merchants endowed these schools, providing salaries for the teachers, stipends for students, and living accommodations for both. The *sheik,* or teacher, served as a guide to the correct path of living. All Islamic higher education rested on a close relationship between teacher and students, so in selecting a teacher, the student (or his father) considered the character and intellectual reputation of the sheik, not that of any institution. Students built their subsequent careers on the reputation of their teachers.

Learning depended heavily on memorization. In primary school, which was often attached to the institution of higher learning, a boy began his education by memorizing the entire Qur'an. Normally, he achieved this feat by the time he was seven or eight! In adolescence a student learned by heart an introductory work in one of the branches of knowledge, such as jurisprudence or grammar. Later he analyzed the texts in detail. Because the hadith laid great stress on memory, students learned the entire texts through memory and willpower. Memorizing four hundred to five hundred lines a day was considered outstanding. Every class day, the sheik examined the student on the previous day's learning and determined whether the student fully understood what he had memorized. Students of course learned to write, for they had to write down the teacher's commentary on a particular text. But the overwhelming emphasis was on the oral transmission of knowledge.

Because Islamic education focused on particular books or texts, when the student had mastered that text to his teacher's satisfaction, the teacher issued the student an *ijaza,* or license, certifying that he had studied a book or collection of traditions with his teacher. The ijaza allowed the student to transmit on the authority of his teacher a text to the next generation. The ijaza legalized the transmission of sacred knowledge.[49]

Apart from the fundamental goal of preparing men to live wisely and in accordance with God's law, Muslim higher education aimed at preparing men to perform religious and legal functions in the umma, or community: as Qur'an- or hadith-readers; as preachers in the mosques; as professors, educators, copyists; and especially as judges. Judges issued *fatwas,* or legal opinions, in the public

**Mechanical Hand Washer** Building on the work of the Greek engineer and inventor Archimedes (see page 137), the Arab scientist ibn al-Razzaz al-Raziri (ca 1200) designed practical devices to serve general social needs and illustrated them in a mechanical engineering handbook. In this diagram, a device in the form of a servant pours water with his right hand and offers a towel with his left. The device resembles a modern faucet that releases water when hands are held under it. *(Courtesy of the Freer Gallery of Art, Smithsonian Institution, Washington, D.C. Purchase, F1930.75a)*

courts; their training was in the Qur'an, hadith, or some text forming part of the shari'a. Islam did not know the division between religious and secular knowledge characteristic of the modern Western world.

What about women—what educational opportunities were available to them? Although tradition holds that Muhammad said, "The seeking of knowledge is a duty of every Muslim," Islamic culture was ambivalent on the issue of female education. Because of the basic Islamic principle, "Men are the guardians of women, because God has set the one over the other," the law excluded women from participation in the legal, religious, or civic occupations for which the madrasa prepared young men. Moreover, educational theorists insisted that men should study in a sexually isolated environment because feminine allure would distract male students. Rich evidence shows that no woman studied or held a professorship in the schools of Cairo, for example. Nevertheless, many young women received substantial educations from their parents or family members; the initiative invariably rested with their fathers or older brothers. The daughter of Ali ibn Muhammad al-Diruti al Mahalli, for example, memorized the Qur'an, learned to write, and received instruction in several sacred works. One biographical dictionary containing the lives of 1,075 women reveals that 411 had memorized the Qur'an, studied with a particular teacher, and received the ijaza. After marriage, responsibility for a woman's education belonged to her husband.[50]

How does Islamic higher education compare with that available in medieval Europe (see pages 389–390) or Ming

China? There are some striking similarities and some major differences. In the Christian West and in China, primary and higher education was institutional. The church operated schools and universities in Europe. Local villages or towns ran schools in China. In contrast, in the Islamic world the transmission of knowledge depended overwhelmingly on the personal relationship of teacher and student: though dispensed through the madrasa, education was not institutional. In Europe, the reward for satisfactory completion of a course of study was a degree granted by the university. In Muslim culture, it was not the school but the individual teacher who granted the ijaza. In China, the imperial civil service examination tested candidates' knowledge and rewarded achievement with appointments in the state bureaucracy.

In all three cultures, education rested heavily on the study of basic religious, legal, or philosophical texts: the Old and New Testaments or the Justinian *Code* in Europe; the ethical writings of Confucian philosophy in China; the Qur'an, hadith, and legal texts deriving from these in the Muslim world. Also in all three cultures, memorization played a large role in the acquisition and transmission of information. In the European university, however, the professor lectured on biblical text or passages of the *Code,* and in the Muslim madrasa the sheik commented on a section of the Qur'an or hadith. Both professors and sheiks sometimes disagreed fiercely about the correct interpretations of a particular text, forcing students to question, to think critically, and to choose between divergent opinions. Such does not appear to be the case in Ming China; there critical thinking and individual imagination were discouraged.

Finally, educated people in each culture shared the same broad literary and religious or ethical culture, giving that culture cohesion and stability. Just as a man who took a degree at Cambridge University in England shared the Latin language and general philosophical outlook of someone with a degree from Montpellier in France or Naples in Italy, so a Muslim gentleman from Cairo spoke and read the same Arabic and knew the same hadith as a man from Baghdad or Samarkand. Such education as women received in Christian Europe, the Islamic world, or Ming China began and usually ended in the home and with the family.

In the Muslim world, the spread of the Arabic language, not only among the educated classes but also among all people, was the decisive element in the creation of a common means of communication and a universal culture. Recent scholarship demonstrates that after the establishment of the Islamic empire, the major influence in the cultural transformation of the Byzantine–Sasanid–North African and the Central Asian worlds was language. The Arabic language proved more important than religion in this regard. Whereas conversion to Islam was gradual, linguistic conversion went much faster. Arabic became the official language of the state and its bureaucracies in former Byzantine and Sasanid territories. Muslim conquerors forbade Persian-speaking people to use their native language. Islamic rulers required tribute from monotheistic peoples—the Persians and Greeks—but they did not force them to change their religions. Instead, conquered peoples were compelled to submit to a linguistic conversion—to adopt the Arabic language.[51] In time Arabic produced a cohesive and "international" culture over a large part of the Eurasian world.

The cosmopolitan nature of the Muslim world gave rise to a period of intellectual vitality. In spite of schism, warfare, and dynastic conflicts, the sacred Arabic language and dedication to scholarship and learning combined Semitic, Hellenic, and Persian knowledge. "A scholar might publish in Samarkand the definitive work on arithmetic used in the religious schools of Cairo. Or, in a dialogue with colleagues in Baghdad and Hamadan, he could claim to have recovered the unalloyed teachings of Aristotle in the libraries of Fez and Cordoba."[52] Modern scholars consider Muslim creativity and vitality from about 900 to 1300 one of the most brilliant periods in the world's history.

The Persian scholar al-Khwarizmi (d. ca 850) harmonized Greek and Indian findings to produce astronomical tables that formed the basis for later Eastern and Western research. Al-Khwarizmi also studied mathematics, and his textbook on algebra (from the Arabic *al-Jabr*) was the first work in which the word *algebra* is used to mean the "transposing of negative terms in an equation to the opposite side."

Muslim medical knowledge far surpassed that of the West. The Baghdad physician al-Razi (865–925) produced an encyclopedic treatise on medicine that was translated into Latin and circulated widely in the West. Al-Razi was the first physician to make the clinical distinction between measles and smallpox. The great surgeon of Córdoba, al-Zahrawi (d. 1013), produced an important work in which he discussed the cauterization of wounds (searing with a branding iron) and the crushing of stones in the bladder. In Ibn Sina of Bukhara (980–1037), known in the West as Avicenna, Muslim science reached its peak. His *al-Qanun* codified all Greco-Arabic medical thought, described the contagious nature of tuberculosis and the spreading of diseases, and listed 760 pharmaceutical drugs. Muslim scholars also wrote works on geography and jurisprudence.

Likewise, in philosophy the Muslims made significant contributions. Although the majority of the ulama considered philosophy incompatible with jurisprudence and theology, a minority of them obviously did not. Al-Kindi (d. ca 870) was the first Muslim thinker to try to harmonize Greek philosophy and the religious precepts of the Qur'an. He sought to integrate Islamic concepts of human beings and their relations to God and the universe with the principles of ethical and social conduct discussed by Plato and Aristotle.

Inspired by Plato's *Republic* and Aristotle's *Politics,* the distinguished philosopher al-Farabi (d. 950) wrote a political treatise describing an ideal city whose ruler is morally and intellectually perfect and who has as his goal the citizens' complete happiness. Avicenna maintained that the truths found by human reason cannot conflict with the truths of revelation as given in the Qur'an. Ibn Rushid, or Averroës (1126–1198), of Córdoba, a judge in Seville and later royal court physician, paraphrased and commented on the works of Aristotle. He insisted on the right to subject all knowledge, except the dogmas of faith, to the test of reason and on the essential harmony between religion and philosophy.

At the start of the fourteenth century, Islamic learning as revealed in astronomy, mathematics, medicine, architecture, and philosophical investigation was highly advanced, perhaps the most creative in the world. In the development and transmission of ancient Egyptian, Persian, and Greek wisdom, Muslims played a vital role. They also incorporated into their studies

**Pharmacist Preparing Drugs** The translation of Greek scientific treatises into Arabic, combined with considerable botanical experimentation, gave Muslims virtually unrivaled medical knowledge. Treatment for many ailments was by prescription drugs. In this thirteenth-century illustration, a pharmacist prepares a drug in a cauldron over a brazier. It has been said that the pharmacy as an institution is an Islamic invention. *(The Metropolitan Museum of Art, Bequest of Cora Timkin Burnett Collection of Persian Miniatures and Other Persian Art Objects, Bequest of Cora Timken Burnett, 1957 [57.51.21]. Photograph © 1991 The Metropolitan Museum of Art)*

new information from China and India. And they not only preserved and transmitted ancient wisdom "in the medieval Middle East," but they also "developed an approach rarely used by the ancients—experiment. Through this and other means, they brought major advances in virtually all the sciences."[53]

## Sufism

Like the world's other major religions—Buddhism, Hinduism, Judaism, and Christianity—Islam also developed a mystical tradition. It arose as a popular movement in the ninth and tenth centuries as a reaction to what some especially devout individuals perceived as the materialism of the Umayyad regime. These people were called *Sufis,* an Arabic term deriving from *suf* (wool), a reference to the woolen garments worn by early Muslim ascetics. Sufis wanted a personal union with God—divine love and knowledge through intuition rather than through rational deduction and study of the shari'a. They followed an ascetic routine (denial of physical desires to gain a spiritual goal), dedicating themselves to fasting, prayer, meditation on the Qur'an, and the avoidance of sin. These practices are summarized in the word *zuhd,* meaning "renunciation."

The woman mystic Rabia (d. 801) epitomized this combination of renunciation and devotionalism. An attractive woman who refused marriage so that nothing would distract her from a total commitment to God, Rabia attracted followers, whom she served as a spiritual guide. Her poem in the form of prayer captures her deep devotion: "O my lord, if I worship thee from fear of hell, and if I worship thee in hope of paradise, exclude me thence, but if I worship thee for thine own sake, then withhold not from me thine eternal beauty."

In the twelfth century, groups of Sufis gathered around sheiks (teachers), and the term *tariqa,* which originally meant "spiritual path," came to designate the skeiks' ritual system and the fraternity or brotherhood of a particular community or order. A member of a Sufi order was called a *dervish.* The ritual of Sufi brotherhoods directed the dervish to a hypnotic or ecstatic trance, either through the constant repetition of certain prayers or through physical exertions such as whirling or dancing (hence the English phrase "whirling dervish" for one who dances with abandonment). Some Sufis acquired reputations as charismatic holy men to whom ordinary Muslims came seeking spiritual consolation, healing, charity, or political mediation between tribal and factional rivals.

Probably the most famous medieval Sufi was the Spanish mystic-philosopher Ibn al-'Arabi (1165–1240). Born in Valencia and educated in Seville, then a leading center of Islamic culture, Ibn al-'Arabi traveled widely in Spain, North Africa, and Arabia seeking masters of Sufism. He visited Mecca, where he received a "divine commandment" to begin his major work, *The Meccan Revelation,* which evolved into a personal encyclopedia of 560 chapters. At Mecca the wisdom of a beautiful young girl inspired him to write a collection of love poems, *The Interpreter of Desires,* for which he composed a mystical commentary. In 1223, after visits to Egypt, Anatolia, Baghdad, and Aleppo, Ibn al-'Arabi concluded his pilgrimage through the Islamic world at Damascus, where he produced *The Bezels [Edges] of Wisdom,* considered one of the greatest works of Sufism.

## The Muslim View of the West

What did early Muslims think of Jesus? Of Europeans? Jesus is mentioned in ninety-three verses of the Qur'an, which affirms that he was born of Mary the Virgin. He is described as a righteous prophet who performed miracles and continued the work of Abraham and Moses, and he was a sign of the coming Judgment Day. But Muslims held that Jesus was only an apostle, not God, and those (that is, Christians) who called Jesus divine committed blasphemy, showing contempt for God. Muslims esteemed the Judeo-Christian Scriptures as part of God's revelation, although they believed that Christian communities had corrupted the Scriptures and that the Qur'an superseded them. The Christian doctrine of the Trinity—that there is one God in three persons, Father, Son, and Holy Spirit—posed a powerful obstacle to Muslim-Christian understanding because of Islam's total and uncompromising monotheism.[54]

Europeans and Muslims of the Middle East were geographical neighbors. The two peoples shared a common cultural heritage from the Judeo-Christian past. But a thick psychological iron curtain restricted contact between them. The Muslim assault on Christian Europe in the eighth and ninth centuries—villages were burned, monasteries sacked, and Christians sold into slavery (see page 370)—left a legacy of bitter hostility. Europeans' fierce intolerance also helped buttress the barrier between the two peoples. Christians felt threatened by a faith that acknowledged God as creator of the universe but denied the doctrine of the Trinity; that accepted Christ as a prophet but denied his divinity; that believed in the Judgment Day but seemed to describe Heaven in sensuous terms. Popes preached against the Muslims;

**Sufi Collective Ritual** Collective or group rituals, in which Sufis tried through ecstatic experiences to come closer to God, have always fascinated outsiders, including non-Sufi Muslims. Here the sixteenth-century Persian painter Sultan Muhammad illustrates the writing of the fourteenth-century lyric poet Hafiz. Just as Hafiz's poetry moved back and forth between profane and mystical themes, so it is difficult to determine whether the ecstasy achieved here is alcoholic or spiritual. Many figures seem to enjoy wine. Notice the various musical instruments and the delicate floral patterns so characteristic of Persian art. *(Courtesy of the Arthur M. Sackler Museum, Harvard University Art Museums. Promised gift of Mr. and Mrs. Stuart Cary Welch, Jr. Partially owned by the Metropolitan Museum of Art and the Arthur M. Sackler Museum, Harvard University, 1988. In honor of the students of Harvard University and Radcliffe College. Photo by Rick Stafford. © President and Fellows of Harvard College)*

theologians penned tracts against them; and church councils condemned them. Europeans' perception of Islam as a menace helped inspire the Crusades of the eleventh through thirteenth centuries (see pages 374–376). The knightly class believed that it had a sacred obligation to fight the Muslims. As a popular song during the Second Crusade put it: "God has brought before you his suit against the Turks and Saracens [Crusaders' hostile term for Muslims], who have done him great despite [injury]. They have seized his fiefs, where God was first served [that is, the holy places in Palestine] and recognized as Lord."[55]

During the Crusades, Europeans imposed Christianity on any lands they conquered from Islam, and at times they compelled Muslims to choose among conversion, exile, and death. By the thirteenth century, Western literature, such as the Florentine poet Dante's *Divine Comedy,* portrayed the Muslims as the most dreadful of Europe's enemies, guilty of every kind of crime.

Muslims had a strong aversion to travel in Europe. They were quite willing to trade with Europeans, but they rejected European culture. Medieval Europe had no resident Muslim communities where a traveler could find the mosques, food, or other things needed for the Muslim way of life. Muslims generally had a horror of going among those they perceived as infidels, and often when compelled to make diplomatic or business contacts, they preferred to send Jewish or Christian intermediaries, the dhimmis. Commercially, from the Muslim perspective, Europe had very little to offer, apart from fine English woolens, which Muslims admired, and the slaves from southern Russia and central and southeastern Europe.

Did Western culture have any impact on Islam? Muslims considered Christianity to be a flawed religion superseded by Islam. "For the Muslim, Christ was a precursor, for the Christian Muhammad was an impostor. For the Muslim, Christianity was an early, incomplete, and obsolete form of the true religion."[56] Religion dominated the Islamic perception of Europe. Muslims understood Europe not as Western, European, or white but as Christian. And the fact that European culture was Christian immediately discredited it in Muslim eyes. Christians were presumed to be hostile to Islam and were thought to be culturally inferior. Thus Muslims had no interest in them.

An enormous quantity of Muslim historical writing survives from the period between about 800 and 1600. Although the material reflects some knowledge of European geography, it shows an almost total lack of interest among Muslim scholars in European languages, life, and culture. Before the nineteenth century, not a single grammar book or dictionary of any Western language existed in the Muslim world. By contrast, Western scholarship on the Middle East steadily advanced. By the early seventeenth century, a curious European student could find an extensive literature on the history, religion, and culture of the Muslim peoples. In 1633 a professorship in Arabic studies was founded at Cambridge University in England.[57]

As in language and literature, so in science, engineering, and medicine: the medieval West had no influence on the Muslim world. Muslims had only contempt for Western science. Western art, however, attracted and influenced Muslim artists. At least from the time of the visit of the Venetian artist Gentile Bellini to the court of Sultan Mehmet II in Istanbul (1479–1481), Turkish, Persian, and Indian artists seemed fascinated by Western techniques, materials, and subject matter, and Muslim artists imitated them.

Muslims also showed interest in European knowledge of the art of warfare. During the Crusades, the Muslims adopted Frankish weapons and methods of fortification. Islam, however, distinguished between Byzantium, which was held in fair regard as a realm of culture, and "the land of the Franks," or western Europe, which was perceived as backward and barbaric, and Europeans as "ignorant infidels."[58]

## SUMMARY

Islam represents a powerful phenomenon in world history. Its universal monotheistic creed helps to explain its initial attractiveness to Bedouin tribes. Driven by the religious zeal of the jihad, Muslims carried their faith from the Arabian peninsula through the Middle East to North Africa, Spain, and southern France in the west and to the borders of China and northern India in the east—within the short span of one hundred years. Economic need, the political weaknesses of their enemies, strong military organization, and the practice of establishing army cities in newly conquered territories account for their expansion.

Two successive dynasties—the Umayyad, centered at Damascus in Syria, and the Abbasid, located at Baghdad in Iraq—governed the Islamic state. A large imperial bureaucracy headed by a vizier supervised the administration of the state. All government agencies evolved from the diwan. As provincial governors acquired independent power, which the caliphs could not check, centralized authority within the Islamic state disintegrated.

Commerce and trade also spread the faith of Muhammad. Although its first adherents were nomads, Islam developed and flourished in a mercantile milieu. By land and sea, Muslim merchants transported a rich variety of goods across Asia, the Middle East, Africa, and western Europe. Muslim business procedures and terminology greatly influenced the West.

On the basis of the wealth that trade generated, a gracious, sophisticated, and cosmopolitan culture developed with centers at Baghdad and Córdoba. In the tenth and eleventh centuries, the Islamic world witnessed enormous intellectual vitality and creativity. Muslim scholars produced important work in many disciplines, especially mathematics, medicine, and philosophy. Muslim civilization in the Middle Ages was far in advance of that of Christian Europe, and Muslims, with some justification, looked on Europeans as ignorant barbarians.

## KEY TERMS

Ka'ba
Qur'an
caliph
hadith
umma
Five Pillars of Islam
jihad
diwan
imam
Shi'ites
Sunnis
ulama
emirs
shari'a
qadis
vizier
dhimmis
harem
madrasa

## NOTES

1. F. M. Donner, *The Early Islamic Conquests* (Princeton, N.J.: Princeton University Press, 1981), pp. 14–37.
2. See A. Rippin, *Muslims: Their Religious Beliefs and Practices.* Vol. 1: *The Formative Period* (New York: Routledge, 1990), pp. 30–40.
3. Quoted in F. E. Peters, *A Reader on Classical Islam* (Princeton, N.J.: Princeton University Press, 1994), p. 47.
4. J. L. Esposito, *Islam: The Straight Path* (New York: Oxford University Press, 1988), pp. 6–17; the quotation is on p. 15.
5. Donner, *The Early Islamic Conquests,* pp. 57–60.
6. Quoted in J. O'Faolain and L. Martines, eds., *Not in God's Image: Women in History from the Greeks to the Victorians* (New York: Harper & Row, 1973), pp. 108–115.
7. See F. M. Donner, "Muhammad and the Caliphate," in *The Oxford History of Islam,* ed. J. L. Esposito (New York: Oxford University Press, 1999), pp. 3–13.
8. Quoted in Peters, *A Reader on Classical Islam,* pp. 154–155; the quotations are on p. 155.
9. See P. Crone, "The Early Islamic World," in *War and Society in the Ancient and Medieval Worlds: Asia, the Mediterranean, Europe, and Meso-America,* ed. K. Raaflaub and N. Rosenstein (Cambridge, Mass.: Harvard University Press, 1999), p. 312.
10. Ibid., pp. 312–313.
11. Quoted in Donner, *The Early Islamic Conquests,* p. 217.
12. Donner, *The Early Islamic Conquests,* pp. 92–101.
13. R. G. Hoyland, ed., *Seeing Islam as Others Saw It: A Survey and Evaluation of Christian, Jewish and Zoroastrian Writings on Early Islam* (Princeton, N.J.: Darwin Press, 1997), pp. 524–525.
14. G. E. von Grunebaum, *Medieval Islam: A Study in Cultural Orientation* (Chicago: University of Chicago Press, 1954), pp. 142–150.
15. Crone, "The Early Islamic World," p. 324.
16. Ibid., p. 325.
17. Esposito, *Islam,* pp. 57–58; A. Hourani, *A History of the Arab Peoples* (Cambridge, Mass.: Harvard University Press, 1991), p. 36.
18. Crone, "The Early Islamic World," pp. 319, 321.
19. L. I. Conrad, "Caliphate," in *Dictionary of the Middle Ages,* vol. 3, ed. J. R. Strayer (New York: Scribner's, 1983), p. 49.
20. Quoted in R. Levy, *The Social Structure of Islam,* 2d ed. (Cambridge: Cambridge University Press, 1957), p. 56.
21. P. K. Hitti, *The Near East in History* (Princeton, N.J.: Van Nostrand, 1961), p. 229.
22. B. Lewis, ed. and trans., *Islam: From the Prophet Muhammad to the Capture of Constantinople.* Vol. 2: *Religion and Society* (New York: Harper & Row, 1975), pp. 219–221.
23. M. R. Cohen, *Under Crescent and Cross: The Jews in the Middle Ages* (Princeton, N.J.: Princeton University Press, 1994), Chap. 4; the quotation is on p. 74.
24. Quoted in Levy, *The Social Structure of Islam,* p. 67.
25. R. Segal, *Islam's Black Slaves* (New York: Farrar, Straus and Giroux, 2001), p. 35; see also Esposito, *Islam,* p. 45.
26. M. G. S. Hodgson, quoted in Segal, *Islam's Black Slaves,* pp. 41–42.
27. Segal, *Islam's Black Slaves,* p. 44.
28. Quoted in B. Lewis, *Race and Slavery in the Middle East* (New York: Oxford University Press, 1990), p. 19.
29. Ibid., p. 20. This section leans on Lewis's book on race.
30. Ibid., pp. 54–71.
31. See B. F. Stowasser, *Women in the Qur'an, Tradition, and Interpretation* (New York: Oxford University Press, 1994), pp. 94–118.
32. N. Coulson and D. Hinchcliffe, "Women and Law Reform in Contemporary Islam," in *Women in the Muslim World,* ed. L. Beck and N. Keddie (Cambridge, Mass.: Harvard University Press, 1982), p. 37.
33. Quoted in B. F. Stowasser, "The Status of Women in Early Islam," in *Muslim Women,* ed. F. Hussain (New York: St. Martin's Press, 1984), p. 25.
34. Quoted ibid., pp. 25–26.
35. Ibid., p. 26.
36. Peters, *A Reader on Classical Islam,* pp. 249–250; the quotation is on p. 250.
37. Ibid.
38. Ibid., p. 16.
39. G. Nashat, "Women in Pre-Revolutionary Iran: A Historical Overview," in *Women and Revolution in Iran,* ed. G. Nashat (Boulder, Colo.: Westview Press, 1983), pp. 47–48.
40. F. Mernissi, *Beyond the Veil: Male-Female Dynamics in Modern Muslim Society* (New York: Schenkman, 1975), p. 16.
41. Ibid.

42. Quoted in D. J. Gerner, "Roles in Transition: The Evolving Position of Women in Arab Islamic Countries," in *Muslim Women,* ed. F. Hussain (New York: St. Martin's Press, 1984), p. 73.
43. Quoted in Cohen, *Under Crescent and Cross,* p. 90.
44. Quoted in Lewis, *Religion and Society,* p. 126.
45. S. D. Curtin, *Cross-Cultural Trade in World History* (Cambridge: Cambridge University Press, 1986), pp. 113–115.
46. Adapted from Lewis, *Religion and Society,* pp. 154–157.
47. M. Rodinson, *Islam and Capitalism,* trans. Brian Pearce (Austin: University of Texas Press, 1981), p. 56.
48. R. Hillenbrand, "Cordoba," in *Dictionary of the Middle Ages,* vol. 3, ed. J. R. Strayer (New York: Scribner's, 1983), pp. 597–601.
49. I have leaned heavily here on the important study of J. Berkey, *The Transmission of Knowledge in Medieval Cairo: A Social History of Islamic Education* (Princeton, N.J.: Princeton University Press, 1992), pp. 22–43.
50. Ibid., pp. 161–181; the quotation is on p. 161.
51. A. Dallal, "Science, Medicine, and Technology: The Making of a Scientific Culture," in *The Oxford History of Islam,* ed. J. L. Esposito (New York: Oxford University Press, 1999), pp. 158–159.
52. P. Brown, "Understanding Islam," *New York Review of Books,* February 22, 1979, pp. 30–33.
53. B. Lewis, *What Went Wrong? Western Impact and Middle Eastern Response* (New York: Oxford University Press, 2002), pp. 78–79.
54. See J. I. Smith, "Islam and Christianity: Historical, Cultural and Religious Interaction from the Seventh to the Fifteenth Centuries," in *The Oxford History of Islam,* ed. J. L. Esposito (New York: Oxford University Press, 1999), pp. 317–321.
55. Quoted in R. W. Southern, *The Making of the Middle Ages* (New Haven, Conn.: Yale University Press, 1961), p. 55.
56. B. Lewis, *The Muslim Discovery of Europe* (New York: W. W. Norton, 1982), p. 297.
57. Ibid., pp. 296–297.
58. Ibid., p. 222.

## SUGGESTED READING

The titles by Peters and Cohen cited in the Notes are especially useful: Peters for its rich collection of documents on many facets of the culture of classical Islam, Cohen for the study of Jews and Christians living in Muslim societies. C. Lindholm, *The Anthropology of Islam* (1995), argues that Islam is the most egalitarian of the Middle Eastern religions. Perhaps the best introduction to Shi'ism is Y. Richard, *Shi'ite Islam* (1994). For the social, commercial, and political significance of the obligatory Muslim pilgrimage to Mecca, see F. E. Peters, *The Haji: The Muslim Pilgrimage to Mecca and the Holy Places* (1994). For general surveys, the curious student may consult A. Hourani, *A History of the Arab Peoples* (1991), a readable and important synthesis, and S. Fisher and W. Ochsenwald, *The Middle East: A History* (1990), which has helpful bibliographical material. "Peoples of the Book: Muslim and Jewish Thought," in M. L. Colish's splendid synthesis *Medieval Foundations of the Western Intellectual Tradition, 400–1400* (1997), treats many aspects of the intellectual history discussed in this chapter. For the Prophet, see W. M. Watt, *Muhammad at Mecca* (1953) and *Muhammad at Medina* (1956), and M. Rodinson, *Mohammed,* trans. A. Carter (1971). M. G. S. Hodgson, *The Venture of Islam.* Vol. 1: *The Classical Age of Islam* (1964), is comprehensive but for the specialist. K. Cragg and R. M. G. Speight, eds., *Islam from Within: Anthology of a Religion* (1980), offers a fine collection of primary materials on the beginnings of Islam. For the cultural impact of Islam, G. E. von Grunebaum, *Classical Islam: A History 600–1258,* trans. K. Watson (1970), remains valuable. B. Lewis, *A Middle East Mosaic: Fragments of Life, Letters, and History* (2000), is a rich source for many aspects of Islamic life, culture, and prejudices.

The best starting point for the study of Muslim expansion is P. Crone, "The Early Islamic World," in *War and Society in the Ancient and Medieval Worlds,* ed. K. Raaflaub and N. Rosenstein (1999); the thesis here should be compared with that of F. M. Donner, *The Early Islamic Conquests* (1981). For the ways in which the Arabs came to terms with non-Muslim peoples of their conquered territories, see the studies in C. E. Bosworth, *The Arabs, Byzantium, and Iran* (1996). For the early evolution of Muslim religious beliefs and practices, see the title by Rippin cited in the Notes. For law and religious authority, in addition to the title by Berkey cited in the Notes, see N. J. Coulson, *A History of Islamic Law* (1964); J. N. D. Anderson, *Islamic Law in the Modern World* (1959); R. P. Mottahedeh, *Loyalty and Leadership in Early Islamic Society* (1986); and S. D. Gottein, *Studies in Islamic History and Institutions* (1966).

For Muslim trade and commerce, see the excellent study by O. R. Constable, *Trade and Traders in Muslim Spain: The Commercial Realignment of the Iberian Peninsula, 900–1500* (1994). The older study by A. L. Udovich, *Partnership and Profit in Medieval Islam* (1970), is still helpful but should be compared with the work by Rodinson cited in the Notes. For agricultural practices, see A. M. Watson, *Agricultural Innovation in the Early Islamic World* (1983), and the fascinating material in T. F. Glick, *Islamic and Christian Spain in the Early Middle Ages* (1979). For slavery in the Arab world, see B. Lewis, *Race and Slavery in the Middle East* (1990), which demythologizes the Western view of the Middle East as free of racial prejudice, and G. Murray, *Slavery in the Arab World* (1989), which explains the persistence of slavery in Muslim societies in sexual, not economic, terms. W. M. Watson, *Islam and the Integration of Society* (1961), provides an important sociological interpretation of factors that led to the unity of very diverse peoples.

In the avalanche of material on women and gender in Islamic societies, J. Tucker, *Gender and Islamic History* (1993), which offers a broad sketch and an excellent introduction to the many problems in the study of gender, is especially recommended. B. F. Stowasser, *Women in the Qur'an: Traditions and Interpretation* (1994), gives a fine analysis of the

Qur'an's statement on women. The following studies contain fascinating and important discussions: L. Ahmed, *Women and Gender in Islam: Historical Roots of a Modern Debate* (1992); D. Kandiyoti, "Islam and Patriarchy: A Comparative Perspective," in *Women in Middle Eastern History,* ed. B. Baron and N. Keddie (1991); J. F. Tucker, "The Arab Family in History: 'Otherness' and the Study of the Family," in *Arab Women: Old Boundaries, New Frontiers,* ed. J. F. Tucker (1993), which, although focusing on the period since 1800, will interest students of any period; N. Hijab, *Woman-power* (1988); and G. Nashat, "Women in the Middle East, 8000 B.C.–A.D. 1800," in *Restoring Women to History* (1988).

For Islamic art, see the stunning achievement of S. S. Blair and J. M. Bloom, *The Art and Architecture of Islam, 1250–1800* (1994), which authoritatively treats the trends in Islamic art and discusses virtually all the masterpieces in Islamic lands. The older studies by O. Grabar, *The Formation of Islamic Art* (1987), and D. Talbot Rice, *Islamic Art,* rev. ed. (1985), provide valuable material.

On the Mongols, see P. Ratchnevsky, *Genghis Khan* (1993), which is based on Chinese, Mongol, and Persian sources, as well as European ones, to give a balanced account of the great world conqueror; M. Rossabi, *Khubilai Khan: His Life and Times* (1988); and D. Morgan, *The Mongols* (1986), an especially readable study. R. E. Dunn, *The Adventures of Ibn Battuta: A Muslim Traveler of the Fourteenth Century* (1987), gives a fascinating account of Asian and African societies by a Muslim world traveler.

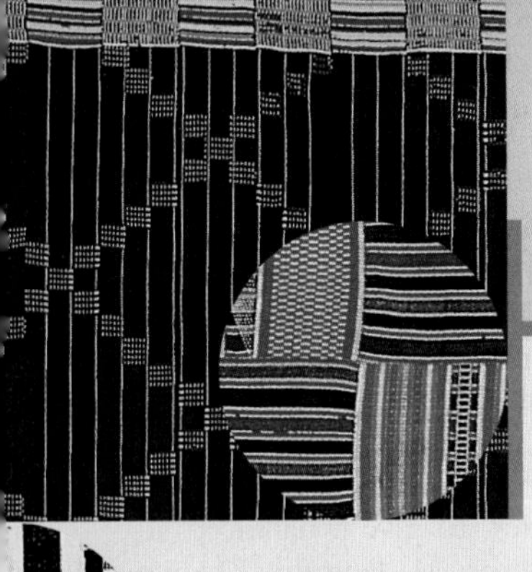

# LISTENING TO THE PAST

## A Treatise on Buying Slaves

*Ibn Butlan (d. 1066) was a Christian who practiced medicine in Baghdad. He wrote an important scientific treatise on the importance of good hygiene and diet, but his most popular work was his "Treatise on Buying Slaves, A Consumer's Guide," a section of which is reprinted here.*

The Turkish women combine beauty and whiteness and grace. Their faces tend to look sullen, but their eyes, though small, are sweet. They have a smooth brownness and their stature is between medium and short. There are very few tall ones among them. The beautiful ones are extremely beautiful and the ugly ones exceptional. They are treasure houses for children, gold mines for generation. It very rarely happens that their children are ugly or badly formed. They are clean and refined. . . . Bad breath is hardly ever found among them, nor any with large buttocks, but they have some nasty characteristics and are of little loyalty.

The women of Daylam [in northern Iran] are both outwardly and inherently beautiful, but they have the worst characters of all and the coarsest natures. They can endure hardship . . . in every respect.

The women of the Alans [a people of the northern Caucasus] are reddish-white and well-fleshed. The cold humor predominates in their temperaments. They are better suited for service than for pleasure since they have good characters in that they are trustworthy and honest and are both reliant and compliant. Also, they are far from licentious.

The Greek women are blond, with straight hair and blue eyes. As slaves they are obedient, adaptable, serviceable, well meaning, loyal, trustworthy and reliable. They are good as treasurers because they are meticulous and not very generous. Sometimes they are skilled in some fine handicraft.

The Armenians would be beautiful were it not for their peculiarly ugly feet, though they are well built, energetic and strong. Chastity is rare or absent among them and thievery widespread. Avarice is very rare among them, but they are coarse in nature and speech. Cleanliness is not in their language. They are slaves for hard work and service. . . . This race is untrustworthy even when they are contented, not to speak of when they are angry. Their women are useless for pleasure. In fine, the Armenians are the worst of the whites as the Zanj are the worst of the blacks. And how much do they resemble one another in the strength of their bodies, their great wickedness, and their coarse natures!

### QUESTIONS FOR ANALYSIS

1. How valid are broad generalizations about ethnic and racial characteristics?
2. How do assumptions about race, ethnic origins, and social status influence perceptions of beauty?
3. According to this guide, what physical and character traits were most desirable in female slaves? What is meant by the phrase "gold mines for generation"?

*Source:* Excerpts from *The Travels of Ibn Battuta,* vols I, II, and III, trans. H. A. R. Gibb (London: The Hakluyt Society, 1958). Reprinted in Bernard Lewis, *A Middle East Mosaic: Fragments of Life, Letters, and History* (New York: Random House, 2000), pp. 187–188. Used by permission of David Higham Associates.

Female slaves of many ethnic and racial backgrounds in the Aurat Bazaar, Istanbul, 1838. *(From Bernard Lewis,* What Went Wrong. *© 2002 by Bernard Lewis. Used by permission of Oxford University Press.)*

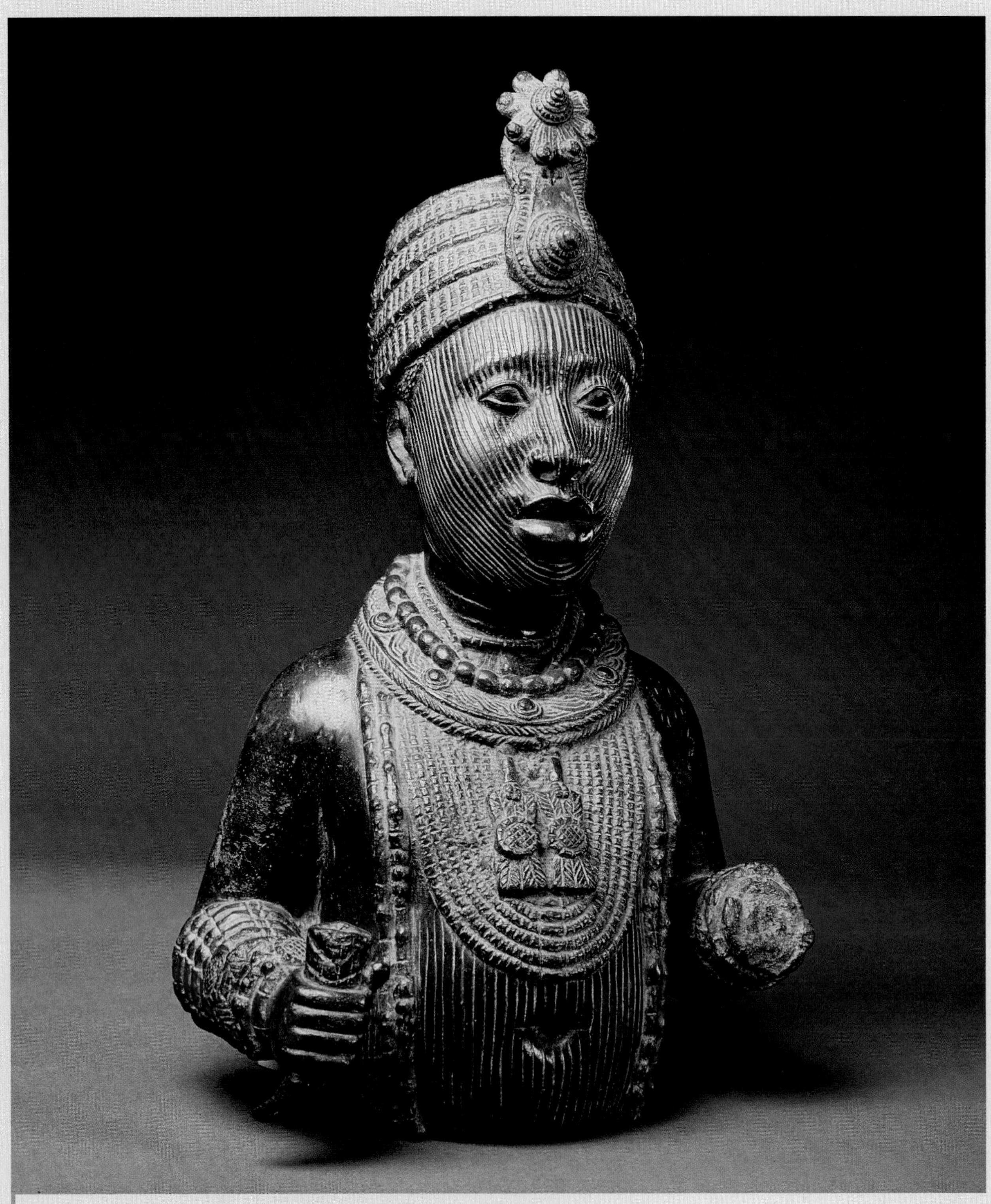

Bronze striated head (marked with stripes, grooves, or ridges in parallel lines) showing an Oni of Ife, thirteenth to fourteenth century. *(© Jerry Thompson)*

CHAPTER

# 10 AFRICAN SOCIETIES AND KINGDOMS, CA 400–1450

## CHAPTER OUTLINE

- The Land and Peoples of Africa
- African Kingdoms and Empires (ca 800–1450)

Between about 400 and 1500, Africa witnessed the development of some centralized, bureaucratized, and socially stratified civilizations alongside a spectrum of communities with a more attenuated form of social organization that functioned at the level of lineage or descent groups. Until fairly recently, ethnocentrism, Eurocentrism, and white racism have limited what Asians, Europeans, and Americans have known about Africa. The more that historians, sociologists, and anthropologists have learned about early African civilizations, the more they have come to appreciate the richness, diversity, and dynamism of those cultures.

- What patterns of social and political organization prevailed among the peoples of Africa?
- What types of agriculture and commerce did Africans engage in?
- What values do Africans' art, architecture, and religions express?

In a discussion of the major civilizations of Africa before 1500, these are the questions this chapter explores.

## THE LAND AND PEOPLES OF AFRICA

Africa is immense. The world's second largest continent (after Asia), it is three times as big as Europe and covers 20 percent of the earth's land surface. The coastal regions of Africa have most felt the impact of other cultures, and African peoples in turn have influenced European, Middle Eastern, and Asian societies. African peoples have never been isolated from other peoples. Five climatic zones roughly divide the continent (see Map 10.1). Fertile land with unpredictable rainfall borders parts of the Mediterranean coast in the north and the southwestern coast of the Cape of Good Hope in the south. Inland from these areas lies dry steppe country with little plant life. The southern fringe of this area is called the Sahel. The steppe gradually gives way to Africa's great deserts: the Sahara in the north and the Namib and Kalahari in the south. The vast Sahara—3.5 million square miles—takes its name from the Arabic word for "tan," the color of the desert. (Folk etymology ascribes the word *Sahara* to an ancient Arabic word that sounds like a parched man's gasp

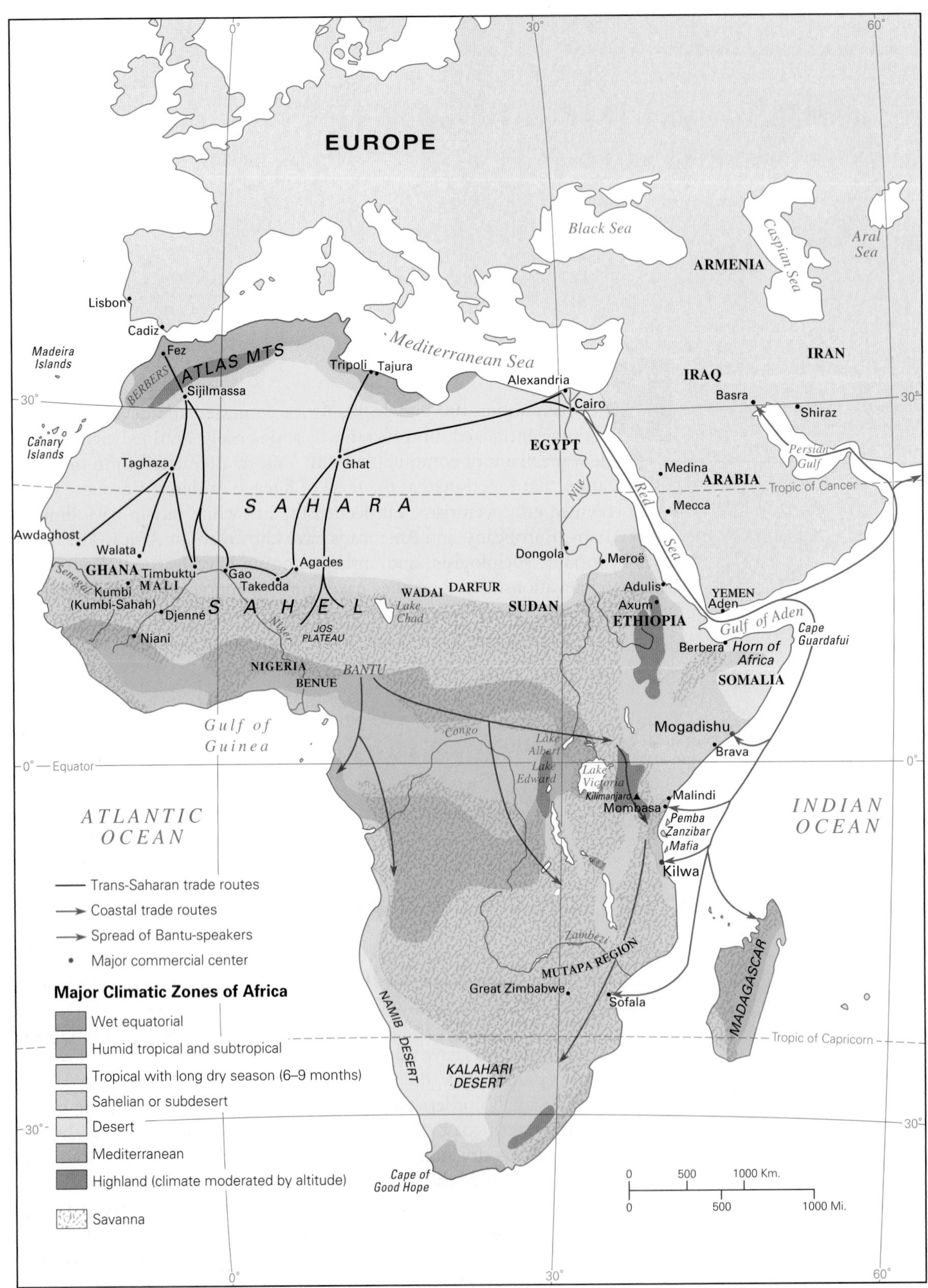
EUROPE
Black Sea
Caspian Sea
Aral Sea
ARMENIA
IRAN
IRAQ
Basra
Shiraz
Persian Gulf
Mediterranean Sea
Lisbon
Cadiz
Madeira Islands
Canary Islands
Fez
ATLAS MTS
BERBERS
Sijilmassa
Tripoli
Tajura
Alexandria
Cairo
EGYPT
Taghaza
Ghat
Medina
ARABIA
Tropic of Cancer
Mecca
Nile
Red Sea
S A H A R A
Awdaghost
Walata
Agades
Dongola
Meroë
GHANA
Timbuktu
Gao
Takedda
Senegal
Kumbi
(Kumbi-Sahah)
MALI
Djenné
Niani
S A H E L
Niger
Lake Chad
JOS PLATEAU
WADAI
DARFUR
SUDAN
Adulis
Axum
ETHIOPIA
YEMEN
Aden
Gulf of Aden
Cape Guardafui
Berbera
Horn of Africa
SOMALIA
NIGERIA
BENUE
BANTU
Gulf of Guinea
Congo
Lake Albert
Lake Edward
Lake Victoria
Kilimanjaro
Mogadishu
Brava
Equator
Malindi
Mombasa
Pemba
Zanzibar
Mafia
Kilwa
ATLANTIC OCEAN
INDIAN OCEAN
Zambezi
MUTAPA REGION
Great Zimbabwe
Sofala
MADAGASCAR
NAMIB DESERT
KALAHARI DESERT
Tropic of Capricorn
Cape of Good Hope
Trans-Saharan trade routes
Coastal trade routes
Spread of Bantu-speakers
Major commercial center
Major Climatic Zones of Africa
Wet equatorial
Humid tropical and subtropical
Tropical with long dry season (6–9 months)
Sahelian or subdesert
Desert
Mediterranean
Highland (climate moderated by altitude)
Savanna
0 500 1000 Km.
0 500 1000 Mi.
0°
30°
60°
30°
0°
30°

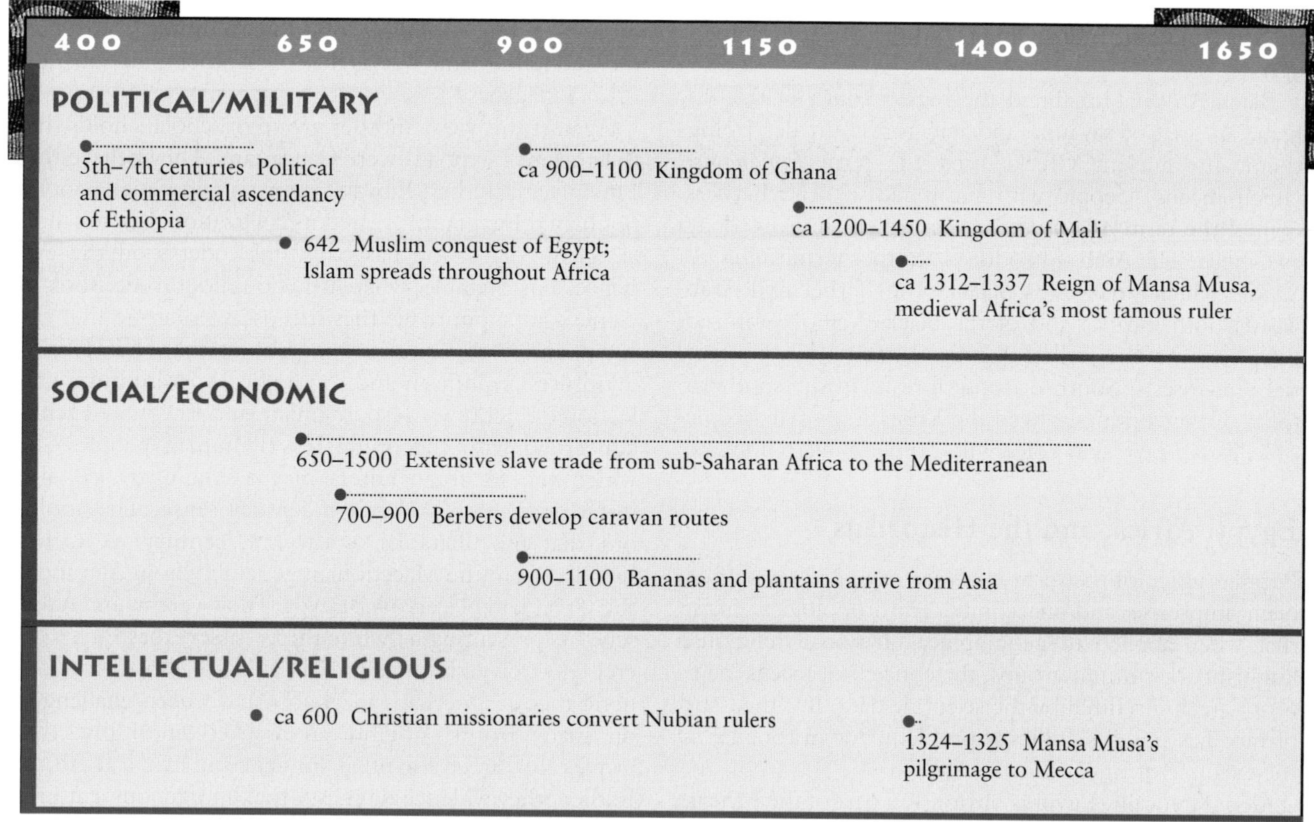


for water.) The Savanna—flat grassland—extends in a swath across the widest part of the continent, as well as across parts of south-central Africa and along the eastern coast. One of the richest habitats in the world and accounting for perhaps 55 percent of the African continent, the Savanna has always invited migration and cultural contacts. Thus it is the most important region of West Africa historically. Dense, humid, tropical rain forests stretch along coastal West Africa and on both sides of the equator in central Africa until they are stopped by volcanic mountains two-thirds of the way across the continent.

400
650
900
1150
1400
1650
POLITICAL/MILITARY
5th–7th centuries Political and commercial ascendancy of Ethiopia
642 Muslim conquest of Egypt; Islam spreads throughout Africa
ca 900–1100 Kingdom of Ghana
ca 1200–1450 Kingdom of Mali
ca 1312–1337 Reign of Mansa Musa, medieval Africa's most famous ruler
SOCIAL/ECONOMIC
650–1500 Extensive slave trade from sub-Saharan Africa to the Mediterranean
700–900 Berbers develop caravan routes
900–1100 Bananas and plantains arrive from Asia
INTELLECTUAL/RELIGIOUS
ca 600 Christian missionaries convert Nubian rulers
1324–1325 Mansa Musa's pilgrimage to Mecca

The climate in most of Africa is tropical. Subtropical climates are limited to the northern and southern coasts and to regions of high elevation. Rainfall is seasonal in most parts of the continent and is very sparse in desert and semidesert areas.

**MAP 10.1 Africa Before 1500** For centuries trade linked West Africa with Mediterranean and Asian societies. Note the various climatic zones, the trans-Saharan trade routes, and the trade routes along the coast of East Africa.

Geography and climate have shaped the economic development of the peoples of Africa just as they have shaped the lives of people everywhere else. In the eastern African plains, the earliest humans hunted wild animals. The drier steppe regions favored the development of herding. Wetter Savanna regions, like the Nile Valley, encouraged the rise of grain-based agriculture. The tropical forests favored hunting and gathering and, later, root-based agriculture. Regions around rivers and lakes supported economies based on fishing.

The peoples of Africa are as diverse as the topography of the continent. In North Africa, contacts with Asian and European civilizations date back to the ancient Phoenicians, Greeks, and Romans. The native Berbers, who lived along the Mediterranean, intermingled with many different peoples—with Muslim Arabs, who first conquered the region of North Africa in the seventh and eighth centuries C.E.; with Spanish Muslims and Jews, many of whom settled in North Africa after their expulsion from Spain in 1492 (see pages 466–467); and with sub-Saharan blacks.[1] The peoples living along the east, or Swahili, coast developed a maritime civilization and had rich commercial contacts with southern Arabia, the Persian Gulf, India, China, and the Malay Archipelago.

Black Africans inhabited the region south of the Sahara, an area of savanna and rain forest. In describing them, the ancient Greeks used the term *Ethiopians,* which means "people with burnt faces." The Berbers coined the term *Akal-n-Iquinawen,* which survives today as *Guinea.* The Arabs introduced another term, *Bilad al-Sudan,* which survives as *Sudan.* The Berber and Arab words both mean "land of the blacks." Short-statured peoples sometimes called Pygmies inhabited the equatorial rain forests. South of those forests, in the southern third of the continent, lived the Khoisan, a small people of yellow-brown skin color who primarily were hunters.

## Egypt, Africa, and the Historians

Popular usage of the term *race* (see page 257) has often been imprecise and inaccurate. Anthropologists insist that when applied to geographical, national, religious, linguistic, or cultural groups, the concept of race is inappropriate and refuted by the scientific data. But the issue of race has posed significant problems for historians, as the example of Egypt shows.

Geographically, Egypt is obviously a part of the African continent. But from the days of the ancient Greek historian Herodotus of Halicarnassus, who visited Egypt (see page 16), down to the present, scholars have vigorously, even violently, debated whether racially and culturally Egypt is part of the Mediterranean world or part of the African world. The notion of race poses an important but very complicated problem for students of all civilizations. Unfortunately, the application of general characteristics and patterns of behavior to peoples based on perceptions of physical differences is one of the legacies of imperialism and colonialism. Were Egyptians of the first century B.C.E. black people who made enormous contributions to the Western world in architecture (the pyramids), mathematics, philosophy (the ideas of Socrates), science, and religion (the idea of divine kingship)? A Senegalese scholar, Cheikh Anta Diop, argues that much Western historical writing since the eighteenth century has been a "European racist plot" to destroy the evidence that the people of the pharaohs belonged to the Negro world. Diop and his followers in Africa and the United States have amassed architectural and linguistic evidence, as well as a small mountain of quotations from Greek and Roman writers and from the Bible, to insist that the ancient Egyptians belonged to the black race. Diop claims to have examined the skin of ancient Egyptian mummies and says that on the basis of "infallible scientific techniques . . . the epidermis of those mummies was pigmented in the same way as that of all other (sub-Saharan) African negroes."[2]

Against this view, another group of scholars holds that the ancient Egyptians were Caucasians. They believe that Phoenician, Berber, Libyan, Hebrew, and Greek peoples populated Egypt and created its civilization. These scholars claim that Diop has badly misunderstood the evidence. For example, whereas Diop relies on the Book of Genesis to support his thesis, those who argue that the Egyptians were Caucasians point out that the Hebrew Scriptures are not an anthropological treatise but a collection of Hebrew, Mesopotamian, and Egyptian legends concerned with the origins of all human peoples—by which the Hebrew writers meant ethnic groups, not racial ones in the twentieth-century sense. They point out that the pharaohs of the first century B.C.E. descended from the Macedonian generals whom Alexander the Great had placed over Egypt. They were white. A few scholars presenting a "white thesis" assert that Egypt exercised a "civilizing mission" in sub-Saharan Africa. Genetic theories, perhaps inevitably, have been challenged on many fronts, notably an archaeological one that proves no direct Egyptian influence in tropical Africa. Rather, the evidence suggests that indigenous cultures south of the Sahara developed independently, without any Egyptian influence. Both the "black thesis" and the "white thesis" are extremist.

A third proposition, perhaps the most plausible, holds that ancient Egypt, at the crossroads of three continents, was a melting pot of different cultures and peoples. To attribute Egyptian civilization to any one group is blatant racism. The great achievements of Egyptian culture resulted from the contributions of many diverse peoples. Moderate scholars believe that there were black Africans in ancient Egypt, primarily in Upper Egypt (south of what is now Cairo), but that other racial groups constituted the majority of the population.[3] On this complex issue, the jury is still out.

In the seventh and early eighth centuries, the Arabs conquered all of North Africa, taking control of Egypt between 639 and 642 (see page 244); ever since Egypt has been an integral part of the Muslim world. Egypt's strategic location and commercial importance made it a logical target for Crusaders in the Middle Ages. In 1250 the Mamluks, a military warrior caste that originated in Anatolia, took over Egypt. With their slave soldiers, the Mamluks ruled until they were overthrown by the Ottoman Turks in 1517. The Mamluk tradition of cavalry soldiers fighting with swords and shields proved no match for Turkish artillery.

## Early African Societies

Africa was one of the sites where agriculture began. Archaeological investigations suggest that knowledge of cultivation moved west from ancient Judaea (southern Palestine) and arrived in the Nile Delta in Egypt about the fifth millennium before Christ. Settled agriculture then traveled down the Nile Valley and moved west across the southern edge of the Sahara to the central and western Sudan. By the first century B.C.E., settled agriculture existed in West Africa. From there it spread to the equatorial forests. African farmers learned to domesticate plants, including millet, sorghum, and yams. Cereal-growing people probably taught forest people to plant regular fields. Gradually African farmers also learned to clear land by burning. They evolved a sedentary way of life: living in villages, clearing fields, relying on root crops, and fishing.

Between 1500 and 1000 B.C.E., settled agriculture also spread southward from Ethiopia along the Rift Valley of present-day Kenya and Tanzania. Archaeological evidence reveals that the peoples of this region grew cereals, raised cattle, and used tools made of wood and stone. Cattle raising spread more quickly than did planting. Early African peoples prized cattle highly. Many trading agreements, marriage alliances, political compacts, and treaties were negotiated in terms of cattle.

Cereals such as millet and sorghum are indigenous to Africa. Scholars speculate that traders brought bananas, taros (a type of yam), sugar cane, and coconut palms to Africa from Southeast Asia. Because tropical forest conditions were ideal for banana trees, their cultivation spread rapidly; they were easier to raise than cereal grains. Donkeys, pigs, chickens, geese, and ducks were also domesticated.

The evolution to a settled life had profound effects. In contrast to nomadic conditions, settled societies made shared or common needs more apparent, and those needs strengthened ties among extended families. Population also increased:

**Tassili Rock Painting** This scene of cattle grazing near the group of huts (represented on the left by stylized white ovals) reflects the domestication of animals and the development of settled pastoral agriculture. Women and children seem to perform most of the domestic chores. Tassili is a mountainous region in the Sahara. *(Henri Lhote, Montrichard, France)*

**Nok Woman** Hundreds of terra-cotta sculptures such as the head of this woman survive from the Nok culture, which originated in the central plateau of northern Nigeria in the first millennium B.C.E. *(National Museum, Lagos, Nigeria/Werner Forman Archive/Art Resource, NY)*

*The change from a hunter-gatherer economy to a settled farming economy affected population numbers. . . . What remains uncertain is whether in the agricultural economy there were more people, better fed, or more people, less well fed. . . . In precolonial Africa agricultural and pastoral populations may not have increased steadily over time, but fluctuated cyclically, growing and declining, though overall slowly growing.*[4]

Scholars dispute the route by which ironworking spread to sub-Saharan Africa. Some believe that the Phoenicians brought the technique for smelting iron to northwestern Africa and that from the north it spread southward. Others insist that it spread from the Meroe region on the Nile westward. Most of West Africa had acquired knowledge of ironworking by 250 B.C.E., and archaeologists believe that Meroe achieved pre-eminence as an iron-smelting center only in the first century B.C.E. Thus a stronger case can probably be made for the Phoenicians. The great trans-Saharan trade routes may have carried ironworking south from the Mediterranean coast. In any case, ancient iron tools found at the village of Nok on the Jos Plateau in present-day Nigeria seem to prove a knowledge of ironworking in West Africa. The Nok culture, which enjoys enduring fame for its fine terra-cotta (baked clay) sculptures, flourished from about 800 B.C.E. to 200 C.E.

## Bantu Migrations

The spread of ironworking seems to be linked to the migrations of the **Bantu** people. Today the overwhelming majority of the 70 million people living south of the Congo River speak a Bantu language. Because very few Muslims or Europeans penetrated beyond the east coast, very few written sources for the early history of the region survive. Lacking written sources, modern scholars have tried to reconstruct the history of the Bantu-speakers on the basis of linguistics, oral traditions (rarely reliable beyond three hundred years back), and archaeology. The word *Bantu* is a linguistic classification, and on the basis of linguistics (the study of the nature, structure, and modification of human speech), students have been able to explain the migratory patterns of African peoples east and south of the equatorial forest. There are hundreds of Bantu languages, including Zulu, Sotho, and Xhosa, which are part of the southern African linguistic and cultural nexus. Swahili is spoken in eastern, and to a limited extent central, Africa.

Bantu-speaking peoples originated in the Benue region, the borderlands of modern Cameroon and Nigeria. In the second millennium B.C.E. they began to spread south and east into the forest zone of equatorial Africa. From there, groups moved onto the Savanna along the lower Congo River. Since they had words for fishing, fishhooks, fish traps, dugout canoes, paddles, yams, and goats, linguists assume that they were fishermen and that they cultivated roots. Because initially they lacked words for grains and cattle herding, they probably were not involved in those activities.

During the next fifteen hundred years, Bantu-speakers migrated throughout the Savanna, adopted mixed agriculture, and learned ironworking. Mixed agriculture (cultivating cereals and raising livestock) and ironworking were practiced in western East Africa (the region of modern Burundi) in the first century before Christ. In the first millennium C.E., Bantu-speakers migrated into eastern and southern Africa. They did not displace earlier peoples, but assimilated with them. The earlier inhabitants gradually adopted a form of Bantu speech.

The settled cultivation of cereals and the keeping of livestock, together with intermarriage with indigenous peoples, apparently led over a long time to considerable population increases and the need to migrate further. The so-called Bantu migrations should not be seen as a single movement of cultivating, ironworking, Bantu-speaking black people sweeping across Africa from west to east and displacing all peoples in their path. Rather, those migrations were "a series of interrelated diffusions and syntheses, as small groups of Bantu-speakers interacted with preexisting peoples and new technical developments to produce a range of distinct cultural syntheses across the southern half of Africa."[5]

Thus Bantu expansion and the settlement of the lands of eastern and southern Africa provides the dominant theme during the first millennium and a half C.E. Enormous differences in the quality of the environment conditioned settlement. Some regions were well watered; others were very arid. This situation resulted in very uneven population distribution. The largest concentration of people seems to have been in the region bounded on the west by the Congo River and on the north, south, and east by Lakes Edward, Victoria, and Kilimanjaro, comprising parts of modern Uganda, Rwanda, and Tanzania. There the agricultural system rested on the cultivation of sorghum and yams. Between 900 and 1100, bananas and plantains (a starchy form of the banana) arrived from Asia. Because little effort was needed for their cultivation and the yield was much higher than for yams, bananas soon became the staple crop. The Bantu population greatly expanded, and Bantu villages multiplied, leading to further migration southward and eastward.[6] By the eighth century, Bantu-speaking people had reached the region of present-day Zimbabwe. By the fifteenth century, they had reached the southeastern coast of Africa.

## Kingdoms of the Western Sudan, ca 1000 B.C.E.–200 C.E.

The region bounded on the north by the Sahara, on the south by the Gulf of Guinea, on the west by the Atlantic Ocean, and on the east by the mountains of Ethiopia is known as the **Sudan.** In the Savanna of the western Sudan—where the Bantu migrations originated—a series of dynamic kingdoms emerged in the millennium before European intrusion.

Between 1000 B.C.E. and 200 C.E., the peoples of the western Sudan made the momentous shift from nomadic hunting to settled agriculture. The rich Savanna proved ideally suited to the production of cereals, especially rice, millet, and sorghum, and people situated near the Senegal River and Lake Chad supplemented their diet with fish. Food supply tends to affect population, and the peoples of the region—known as the Mande-speakers and the Chadic-speakers, or Sao—increased dramatically in number. By 400 C.E. the entire Savanna, particularly the areas around Lake Chad, the Niger River bend, and present-day central Nigeria (see Map 10.1), had a large population.

Families and clans affiliated by blood kinship lived together in villages or small city-states. The basic social unit was the extended family. A chief, in consultation with a council of elders, governed a village. Some villages seem to have formed kingdoms. Village chiefs were responsible to regional heads, who answered to provincial governors, who in turn were responsible to a king. The chiefs and their families formed an aristocracy.

Kingship in the Sudan may have emerged from the priesthood, whose members were believed to make rain and to have contact with spirit powers. African kings always had religious sanction or support for their authority and were often considered divine. In this respect, early African kingship bears a strong resemblance to Germanic kingship of the same period: the authority of the king rested in part on the ruler's ability to negotiate with outside powers, such as the gods.

African religions were animistic and polytheistic. Most people believed that a supreme being had created the universe and was the source of all life. The supreme being breathed spirit into all living things, and the *anima,* or spirit, residing in such things as trees, water, and earth had to be appeased. In the cycle of the agricultural year, for example, all the spirits had to be propitiated from the time of clearing the land through sowing the seed to the final harvest. Because special ceremonies were necessary to satisfy the spirits, special priests with the knowledge and power to communicate with them through sacred rituals were needed. Thus the heads of families and villages were likely to be priests. The head of each family was responsible for maintaining the family ritual cults—ceremonies honoring the dead and living members of the family.[7]

In sum, the most prominent feature of early African society was a strong sense of community, based on the blood relationship and on religion. (See the feature "Individuals in Society: An Unknown Artist of Djenné.") Extended families made up the villages that collectively formed small kingdoms. What spurred the expansion of these small kingdoms into formidable powers controlling sizable territory was the development of long-distance trade. And what made long-distance or trans-Saharan trade possible was the camel.

## The Trans-Saharan Trade

The expression "trans-Saharan trade" refers to the north-south trade across the Sahara (see Map 10.1). The camel had an impact on this trade comparable to the impact of the horse on European agriculture (see pages 393–394). Although scholars dispute exactly when the camel was introduced from Central Asia—first into North Africa, then into the Sahara and the Sudan—they agree that it was before 200 C.E. Camels can carry about five hundred pounds as far as twenty-five miles a day and can go for days without drinking, living on the water stored in their stomachs. Sometimes stupid and vicious, camels had to be loaded on a daily, sometimes twice-daily, basis. And much of the cargo for a long trip was provisions for the journey itself. Nevertheless, camels proved more efficient for desert transportation than horses or oxen, and the use of this beast to carry heavy and bulky freight not only brought economic and social change to Africa but also affected the development of world commerce.

Sometime in the fifth century, the North African **Berbers** fashioned a saddle for use on the camel. This saddle had no direct effect on commercial operations, for a merchant usually walked and guided the camel on foot. But the saddle gave the Berbers and later the Arabian inhabitants of the region maneuverability on the animal and thus a powerful political and military advantage: they came to dominate the desert and to create lucrative routes across it. The Berbers determined who could enter the desert, and they extracted large sums of protection money from merchant caravans in exchange for a safe trip.

Between 700 and 900 C.E., the Berbers developed a network of caravan routes between the Mediterranean coast and the Sudan (see Map 10.1). The Morocco-Niger route ran from Fez to Sijilmassa on the edge of the desert and then south by way of Taghaza and Walata and back to Fez. Another route originated at Sijilmassa and extended due south to Timbuktu with a stop at Taghaza. A third route ran south from Tripoli to Lake Chad. A fourth ran from Egypt to Gao by way of the Saharan oases of Ghat and Agades and then on to Takedda.

The long expedition across the Sahara testifies to the spirit of the traders and to their passion for wealth. Because of the blistering sun and daytime temperatures of 110 degrees, the caravan drivers preferred to travel at night, when the temperature might drop to the low 20s. Ibn Battuta, an Arab traveler who made the journey in the fourteenth century when trans-Saharan traffic was at its height, wrote an account of the experience (see page 265).

Nomadic raiders, the Tuareg Berbers, posed a serious threat. The Tuaregs lived in the desert uplands and preyed on the caravans as a way of life. Thus merchants made safe-conduct agreements with them and selected guides from among them. Caravans of twelve thousand camels were reported in the fourteenth century. Large numbers of merchants crossed the desert together to discourage attack. Blinding sandstorms often isolated part of a line of camels and on at least one occasion buried alive some camels and drivers. Water was the biggest problem. The Tuaregs sometimes poisoned wells to wipe out caravans and steal their goods. To satisfy normal thirst and to compensate for constant sweating, a gallon of water a day per person was required. Desperate thirst sometimes forced the traders to kill camels and drink the foul, brackish water in their stomachs. It took Ibn Battuta twenty-five days to travel from Sijilmassa to the oasis of Taghaza and another sixty-five days to travel from Taghaza to the important market town of Walata.

The Arab-Berber merchants from North Africa who controlled the caravan trade carried manufactured goods—silk and cotton cloth, beads, mirrors—as well as dates and salt (essential in tropical climates to replace the loss from perspiration) from the Saharan oases and mines to the Sudan. These products were exchanged for the much-coveted commodities of the West African savanna—gold, ivory, gum, kola nuts (eaten as a stimulant), and captive slaves.

The steady growth of trans-Saharan trade had three important effects on West African society. The trade stimulated gold mining and the search for slaves. Parts of modern-day Senegal, Nigeria, and Ghana contained rich veins of gold. Both sexes shared in mining it. Men sank the shafts and hacked out gold-bearing rocks and crushed them, separating the gold from the soil. Women washed the gold in gourds. Alluvial gold (mixed with soil, sand, or gravel) was separated from the soil by panning. Scholars estimate that by the eleventh century nine tons were exported to Europe annually—a prodigious amount for the time, since even with modern machinery and sophisticated techniques, the total gold exports from the same region in 1937 amounted to only twenty-one tons. A large percentage of this metal went to Egypt. From there it was transported down the Red Sea and eventually to India (see Map 10.3 on page 296) to pay for the spices and silks demanded by Mediterranean commerce. West African gold proved "absolutely vital for the monetization of the medieval Mediterranean economy and for the maintenance of its balance of payments with South Asia."[8] African gold linked the entire world, exclusive of the Western Hemisphere.

Slaves were West Africa's second most valuable export (after gold). African slaves, like their early European and

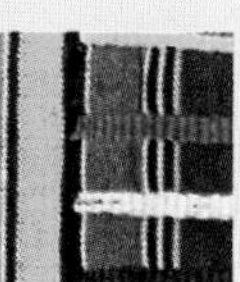

## AN UNKNOWN ARTIST OF DJENNÉ

In the thirteenth century, the market in slaves, gold, and salt at Djenné on the Niger River delta attracted Berber, Muslim, and black traders and brought the region considerable economic prosperity. After accepting Islam, the ruler built a mosque said to be more imposing than the Ka'ba at Mecca (see page 240). A cultural center, Djenné supported mosques and madrasas, scholars and artists.

About 1975, when severe drought caused the Niger's water level to drop, archaeologists discovered a fragment of terra-cotta sculpture (right). Terra cotta is a hard, waterproof, usually brownish orange ceramic clay that is shaped, fired over low heat, and left unglazed. This 18¾-inch figure, composed of geometric shapes (cylinders and cones), is kneeling. It has long graceful arms, each bearing ten bracelets, and elongated fingers. Two serpents coil around the arms. One serpent's head lies like a pendant on the figure's chest, below which is a triangular navel, in keeping with the overall geometric approach to depicting human anatomy characteristic of delta artists. The head is missing, and time has eroded the original shape of the legs. The figure rests on a terra-cotta base.

Who was the artist who made the kneeling figure? What was its purpose? What significance do the coiled snakes have? As in the court cultures of Mughal India and Renaissance Italy (see page 454), artists in many African societies produced works on the specific commissions of princes, merchants, or rulers. Artists did not work to convey their own personal messages. When a work was completed, the patron's name, not the artist's, was associated with it. The bracelets on this figure's arms suggest gold, indicating that the model was very rich. The figure is either a portrait of a royal person or a representation of a protective family spirit.

Serpent cults played an important role in the cultural myths and legends of early West African peoples, just as they did among the Aztec of Central America (see page 427). Serpents were thought to possess supernatural powers, with which kings wanted to be associated. Serpents also were thought to embody the spirits and qualities of ancestors. In Djenné, West Africa, the snake cult lent a special mystique to the ruler. Coiling around his arms, the snake gave him strength in battle, an important trait since the first duty of any king was to protect his people. The serpent's head lying on his chest implies that the wisdom and experience of his ancestors were close to his heart.

*Kneeling figure with entwined serpents (18¾ inches high), from Mali, eleventh to fourteenth century.*
(Maurice D. Galleher, Ada Turnbull Hertle, Laura T. Magnuson funds, 1983.917. Photograph © 1988, The Art Institute of Chicago)

Why would a ruler who had accepted Islam retain such a powerful pagan symbol? For practical political reasons. While many royal courts adopted the faith of Muhammad, it did not make deep inroads among ordinary people. A wise ruler might no doubt feel he must continue his people's traditions if he wanted to keep their loyalty. Perhaps like some early Roman and Germanic chieftains who accepted Christianity, the king shown here was quite willing to accept divine assistance from wherever it came; he "put his money on both horses."

Like most African tribal artifacts, the kneeling figure had a particular ritual or ceremonial purpose. As an individual (not a group) image, it was believed to embody the spirits of the dead and perpetuate the essence of the tribe's ancestry. Although we can tell more about the patron of this work of art than about the artist who made it, the artist has provided us with some valuable information about his society.

### QUESTIONS FOR ANALYSIS

1. How would you describe the kneeling terra-cotta figure?
2. What does it tell us about Djenné, one early West African society?

*Source: The Art Institute of Chicago: The Essential Guide* (1933). The authors especially wish to thank curator Amy M. Mooney.

**TABLE 10.1 ESTIMATED MAGNITUDE OF TRANS-SAHARAN SLAVE TRADE, 650–1500**

| YEARS | ANNUAL AVERAGE OF SLAVES TRADED | TOTAL |
|---|---|---|
| 650–800 | 1,000 | 150,000 |
| 800–900 | 3,000 | 300,000 |
| 900–1100 | 8,700 | 1,740,000 |
| 1100–1400 | 5,500 | 1,650,000 |
| 1400–1500 | 4,300 | 430,000 |

*Source: From R. A. Austen, "The Trans-Saharan Slave Trade: A Tentative Census," in* The Uncommon Market: Essays in the Economic History of the Atlantic Slave Trade, *ed. H. A. Gemery and J. S. Hogendorn (New York: Academic Press, 1979). Used with permission.*

Asian counterparts, seem to have been peoples captured in war. In the Muslim cities of North Africa, southern Europe, and southwestern Asia, the demand for household slaves was high among the elite. Slaves were also needed to work the gold and salt mines. Recent research suggests, moreover, that large numbers of black slaves were recruited through the trans-Saharan trade for Muslim military service. High death rates from disease, manumission, and the assimilation of some blacks into Muslim society meant that the demand for slaves remained high for centuries. Table 10.1 shows one scholar's tentative conclusions, based on many kinds of evidence, about the scope of the trans-Saharan slave trade. The total number of blacks enslaved over an 850-year period may be tentatively estimated at over 4 million.[9]

Slavery in Muslim societies, as in European and Asian countries before the fifteenth century, was not based on skin color. Muslims also enslaved Caucasians who had been purchased, seized in war, or kidnapped from Europe. The households of wealthy Muslims in Córdoba, Alexandria, or Tunis often included slaves of a number of races, all of whom had been completely cut off from their cultural roots. Likewise, West African kings who sold blacks to traders from the north also bought a few white slaves—Slavic, British, and Turkish—for their domestic needs. Race had little to do with the phenomenon of slavery.[10]

The trans-Saharan trade also stimulated the development of vigorous urban centers in West Africa. Scholars date the growth of African cities from around the beginning of the ninth century. Families that had profited from trade tended to congregate in the border zones between the Savanna and the Sahara. They acted as middlemen between the miners to the south and Muslim merchants from the north. By the early thirteenth century, these families had become powerful black merchant dynasties. Muslim traders from the Mediterranean settled permanently in the trading depots, from which they organized the trans-Saharan caravans. The concentration of people stimulated agriculture and the craft industries. Gradually cities of sizable population emerged. Djenné, Gao, and Timbuktu, which enjoyed commanding positions on the Niger River bend, became centers of the export-import trade. Sijilmassa grew into a thriving market center. Kumbi, with between fifteen thousand and twenty thousand inhabitants, was probably the largest city in the western Sudan in the twelfth century. (By European standards, Kumbi was a metropolis; London and Paris achieved its size only in the late thirteenth century.) Between 1100 and 1400, these cities played a dynamic role in the commercial life of West Africa and Europe and became centers of intellectual creativity.

Perhaps the most influential consequence of the trans-Saharan trade was the introduction of Islam to West African society. After the Muslim conquest of Egypt in 642 (see page 244), Islam spread southward from Egypt up the Nile Valley and west to Darfur and Wadai. This Muslim penetration came not by military force but, as in the trans-Saharan trade routes in West Africa, by gradual commercial passage. Muslim expansion from the Arabian peninsula across the Red Sea to the Horn of Africa, then southward along the coast of East Africa represents a third direction of Islam's growth in Africa. From ports on the Red Sea and the Gulf of Aden, maritime trade carried the Prophet's teachings to East Africa and the Indian Ocean. Muslims founded the port city of **Mogadishu,** today the capital of Somalia, between the eighth and tenth centuries. In the twelfth century, Mogadishu developed into a Muslim sultanate, a monarchy that employed a slave military corps against foreign and domestic enemies. Archaeological evidence, confirmed by Arabic sources, reveals a rapid Islamic expansion along Africa's east coast in the thirteenth century. Many settlers came from Yemen in the southern Arabian peninsula, and one family set up the Abul-Mawahib dynasty in Kilwa.[11] When Ibn Battuta visited Kilwa in 1331, he discovered a center for the discovery of Islamic law.

By the tenth century, Muslim Berbers controlled the north-south trade routes to the Savanna. By the eleventh century, African rulers of Gao and Timbuktu had accepted

Islam. The king of Ghana was also influenced by Islam. Muslims quickly became integral to West African government and society.

Conversion to Islam introduced West Africans to a rich and sophisticated culture. By the late eleventh century, Muslims were guiding the ruler of Ghana in the operation of his administrative machinery. The king of Ghana adopted the Muslim diwan, the agency for keeping financial records (see page 251). Because efficient government depends on the preservation of records, the arrival of Islam in West Africa marked the advent of written documents there. Arab Muslims also taught the rulers of Ghana how to manufacture bricks, and royal palaces and mosques began to be built of brick. African rulers corresponded with Muslim architects, theologians, and other intellectuals, who advised them on statecraft and religion. Islam accelerated the development of the African empires of the ninth through fifteenth centuries.

## African Kingdoms and Empires (ca 800–1450)

All African societies shared one basic feature: a close relationship between political and social organization. Ethnic or blood ties bound clan members together. What scholars call **stateless societies** were culturally homogeneous ethnic societies. The smallest ones numbered fewer than a hundred people and were nomadic hunting groups. Larger stateless societies of perhaps several thousand people lived a settled and often agricultural or herding life.

The period from about 800 to 1450 witnessed the flowering of several powerful African states. In the western Sudan, the large empires of Ghana and Mali developed, complete with large royal bureaucracies. On the east coast emerged powerful city-states based on sophisticated mercantile activities and, like Sudan, very much influenced by Islam. In Ethiopia, in central East Africa, kings relied on the Christian faith of their people to strengthen political authority. In South Africa, the empire of Great Zimbabwe, built on the gold trade with the east coast, flourished.

### The Kingdom of Ghana (ca 900–1100)

So remarkable was the kingdom of **Ghana** during the age of Africa's great empires that writers throughout the medieval world, such as the fourteenth-century Muslim historian Ibn Khaldun, praised it as a model for other rulers. Medieval Ghana also holds a central place in the historical consciousness of the modern state of Ghana. Since this former British colony attained independence in 1957, its political leaders have hailed the medieval period as a glorious heritage. The name of the modern republic of Ghana—which in fact lies far from the site of the old kingdom—was selected to signify the rebirth of an age of gold in black Africa.

The nucleus of the territory that became the kingdom of Ghana was inhabited by Soninke people who called their ruler **ghana,** or war chief. By the late eighth century, Muslim traders and other foreigners applied the word to the region where the Soninke lived, the black kingdom south of the Sahara. The Soninke themselves called their land "Aoukar" or "Awkar," by which they meant the region north of the Senegal and Niger Rivers. Only the southern part of Aoukar received enough rainfall to be agriculturally productive, and it was in this area that the civilization of Ghana developed. Skillful farming and an efficient system of irrigation led to the production of abundant crops, which eventually supported a population of as many as 200,000.

The Soninke name for their king—war chief—aptly describes the king's major preoccupation in the tenth century. In 992 Ghana captured the Berber town of Awdaghost, strategically situated on the trans-Saharan trade route (see Map 10.1). Thereafter Ghana controlled the southern portion of a major caravan route. Before the year 1000, the rulers of Ghana had extended their influence almost to the Atlantic coast and had captured a number of small kingdoms in the south and east. By the beginning of the eleventh century, the king exercised sway over a territory approximately the size of Texas. No other power in the West African region could successfully challenge him.

Throughout this vast West African area, all authority sprang from the king. Religious ceremonies and court rituals emphasized the king's sacredness and were intended to strengthen his authority. The king's position was hereditary in the matrilineal line—that is, the heir of the ruling king was one of the king's sister's sons (presumably the eldest or fittest for battle). According to the eleventh-century Spanish Muslim geographer al-Bakri (1040?–1094), "This is their custom . . . the kingdom is inherited only by the son of the king's sister. He the king has no doubt that his successor is a son of his sister, while he is not certain that his son is in fact his own."[12]

A council of ministers assisted the king in the work of government, and from the ninth century on, most of these ministers were Muslims. Detailed evidence about the early Ghanaian bureaucracy has not survived, but scholars suspect that separate agencies were responsible for taxation, royal property, foreigners, forests, and the

**The Great Friday Mosque, Djenné** The mosque at Djenné was built in the form of a parallelogram. Inside, nine long rows of adobe columns run along a north-south axis and support a flat roof of palm logs. A pointed arch links each column to the next in its row, forming nine east-west archways facing the *mihrab,* the niche indicating the direction of Mecca and from which the *imam* (prayer leader) speaks. This mosque (rebuilt in 1907 on a thirteenth-century model) testifies to the considerable wealth, geometrical knowledge, and manpower of the region. *(Copyright Carollee Pelos. From* Spectacular Vernacular: The Adobe Tradition, *Chapter 11, "Histories of the Great Mosques of Djenné" [New York: Aperture, 1996])*

army. The royal administration was well served by Muslim ideas, skills, and especially literacy. The king and his people, however, clung to their ancestral religion, and the basic cultural institutions of Ghana remained tribal.

The king of Ghana held his court in **Kumbi.** Al-Bakri provides a valuable picture of the city in the eleventh century:

*The city of Ghana consists of two towns lying on a plain, one of which is inhabited by Muslims and is large, possessing twelve mosques—one of which is a congregational mosque for Friday prayer; each has its imam, its muezzin and paid reciters of the Quran. The town possesses a large number of jurisconsults and learned men.*[13]

Either for their own protection or to preserve their special identity, the Muslims lived separate from the African artisans and tradespeople. The Muslim community in Ghana must have been large and prosperous to have supported twelve mosques. The *imam* was the religious leader who conducted the ritual worship, especially the main prayer service on Fridays. The *muezzin* led the prayer responses after the imam; he needed a strong voice so that those at a distance and the women in the harems, or enclosures, could hear. Muslim religious leaders exercised civil authority over their coreligionists. Their presence and that of other learned Muslims also suggests vigorous intellectual activity.

Al-Bakri describes the town where the king lived and the royal court:

*The town inhabited by the king is six miles from the Muslim one and is called Al Ghana. . . . The residence of the king consists of a palace and a number of dome-shaped dwellings, all of them surrounded by a strong enclosure, like a city wall. In the town . . . is a mosque, where Muslims who come on diplomatic missions to the king pray. The town where the king lives is surrounded by domed huts, woods, and copses where priest-magicians live; in these woods also are the religious idols and tombs of the kings. Special guards protect this area and prevent anyone from entering it so that no foreigners know what is inside. Here also are the king's prisons, and if anyone is imprisoned there, nothing more is heard of him.*[14]

*The king adorns himself, as do the women here, with necklaces and bracelets; on their heads they wear caps decorated with gold, sewn on material of fine cotton stuffing. When he holds court in order to hear the people's complaints and to do justice, he sits in a pavilion around which stand ten horses wearing golden trappings; behind him ten pages stand, holding shields and swords decorated with gold; at his right are the sons of the chiefs of the country, splendidly dressed and with their hair sprinkled with gold. The governor of the city sits on the ground in front of the king with other officials likewise sitting around him. Excellently pedigreed dogs guard the door of the pavilion. . . . The noise of a sort-of drum, called a daba, and made from a long hollow log, announces the start of the royal audience. When the king's coreligionists appear before him, they fall on their knees and toss dust on their heads—this is their way of greeting their sovereign. Muslims show respect by clapping their hands.*[15]

What sort of juridical system did Ghana have? How was the guilt or innocence of an accused person determined? Justice derived from the king, who heard cases at court or on his travels throughout his kingdom. As al-Bakri recounts:

*When a man is accused of denying a debt or of having shed blood or some other crime, a headman (village chief) takes a thin piece of wood, which is sour and bitter to taste, and pours upon it some water which he then gives to the defendant to drink. If the man vomits, his innocence is recognized and he is congratulated. If he does not vomit and the drink remains in his stomach, the accusation is accepted as justified.*[16]

This appeal to the supernatural for judgment was very similar to the justice by ordeal that prevailed among the Germanic peoples of western Europe at the same time. Complicated cases in Ghana seem to have been appealed to the king, who often relied on the advice of Muslim legal experts.

The king's elaborate court, the administrative machinery he built, and the extensive territories he governed were all expensive. The king of Ghana needed a lot of money, and he apparently had four main sources of support. The royal estates—some hereditary, others conquered in war—produced annual revenue, mostly in the form of foodstuffs for the royal household. The king also received tribute annually from subordinate chieftains (lack of evidence prevents an estimate of the value of this tax). Customs duties on goods entering and leaving the country generated revenues. Salt was the largest import. Berber merchants paid a tax to the king on the cloth, metalwork, weapons, and other goods that they brought into the country from North Africa; in return these traders received royal protection from bandits. African traders bringing gold into Ghana from the south also paid the customs duty.

Finally, the royal treasury held a monopoly on the export of gold. The gold industry was undoubtedly the king's largest source of income. It was on gold that the fame of medieval Ghana rested. The ninth-century geographer al-Ya-qubi wrote, "Its king is mighty, and in his lands are gold mines. Under his authority are various other kingdoms—and in all this region there is gold."[17]

The governing aristocracy—the king, his court, and Muslim administrators—occupied the highest rung on the Ghanaian social ladder. On the next rung stood the merchant class. Considerably below the merchants stood the farmers, cattle breeders, supervisors of the gold mines, and skilled craftsmen and weavers—what today might be called the middle class. Some merchants and miners must have enjoyed great wealth, but, as in all aristocratic societies, money alone did not suffice. High status was based on blood and royal service. At the bottom of the social ladder were slaves, who worked in households, on farms, and in the mines. As in Asian and European societies of the time, slaves accounted for only a small percentage of the population.

Apart from these social classes stood the army. According to al-Bakri, "the king of Ghana can put 200,000 warriors in the field, more than 40,000 being armed with bow and arrow."[18] Like most medieval estimates, this is probably a gross exaggeration. Even a modern industrialized state with sophisticated means of transportation, communication, and supply lines would have enormous difficulty mobilizing so many men for battle. The king of Ghana, however, was not called "war chief" for nothing. He maintained at his palace a crack standing force of a thousand men, comparable to the Roman Praetorian Guard. These thoroughly disciplined, well-armed, totally loyal troops protected the king and the royal court. They lived in special compounds, enjoyed the favor of the king, and sometimes acted as his personal ambassadors to subordinate rulers. In wartime, this regular army was augmented by levies of soldiers from conquered peoples and by the use of slaves and free reserves. The force that the king could field was sizable, if not as huge as al-Bakri estimated.

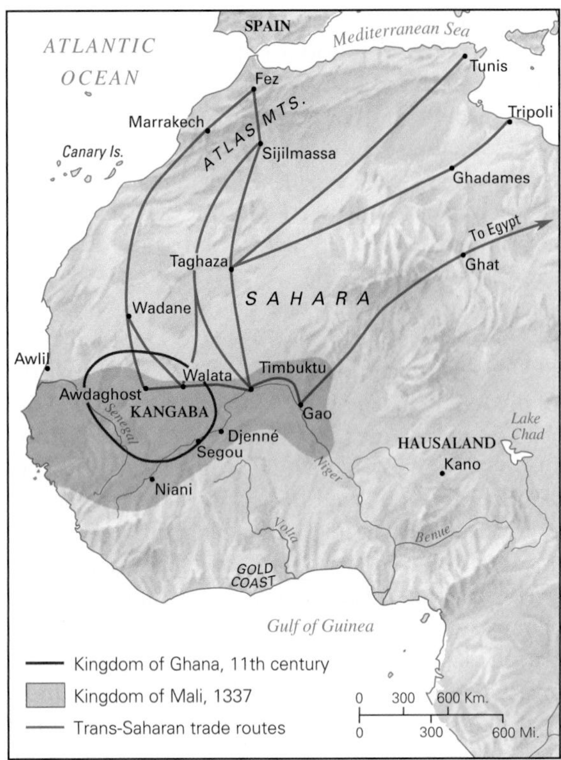


**MAP 10.2 The Kingdom of Mali** The economic strength of the kingdom of Mali rested heavily on the trans-Saharan trade.

## The Kingdom of Mali (ca 1200–1450)

During the century after the collapse of Kumbi, a cloud of obscurity hung over the western Sudan. The kingdom of Ghana split into several small kingdoms that feuded among themselves. One people, the Mandinke, lived in the kingdom of Kangaba on the upper Niger River. The Mandinke had long been part of the Ghanaian empire, and the Mandinke and Soninke belonged to the same language group. Kangaba formed the core of the new empire of Mali. Building on Ghanaian foundations, Mali developed into a better-organized and more powerful state than Ghana.

The kingdom of Mali (see Map 10.2) owed its greatness to two fundamental assets. First, its strong agricultural and commercial base provided for a large population and enormous wealth. Second, Mali had two rulers, Sundiata and Mansa Musa, who combined military success with exceptionally creative personalities. (See the feature "Listening to the Past: The Epic of Old Mali" on pages 304–305.)

The earliest surviving evidence about the Mandinke, dating from the early eleventh century, indicates that they were extremely successful at agriculture. Consistently large harvests throughout the twelfth and thirteenth centuries meant a plentiful supply of food, which encouraged steady population growth. The geographical location of Kangaba also placed the Mandinke in an ideal position in West African trade. Earlier, during the period of Ghanaian hegemony, the Mandinke had acted as middlemen in the gold and salt traffic flowing north and south. In the thirteenth century, Mandinke traders formed companies, traveled widely, and gradually became a major force in the entire West African trade.

Sundiata (r. ca 1230–1255) set up his capital at Niani, transforming the city into an important financial and trading center. He then embarked on a policy of imperial expansion. Through a series of military victories, Sundiata and his successors absorbed into Mali other territories of the former kingdom of Ghana and established hegemony over the trading cities of Gao, Djenné, and Walata.

These expansionist policies were continued in the fourteenth century by Sundiata's descendant Mansa Musa (r. ca 1312–1337), early Africa's most famous ruler. In the language of the Mandinke, *mansa* means "emperor." Mansa Musa fought many campaigns and checked every attempt at rebellion. Ultimately his influence extended northward to several Berber cities in the Sahara, eastward to Timbuktu and Gao, and westward as far as the Atlantic Ocean. Throughout his territories, he maintained strict royal control over the rich trans-Saharan trade. Thus this empire, roughly twice the size of the Ghanaian kingdom and containing perhaps 8 million people, brought Mansa Musa fabulous wealth.

Mansa Musa built on the foundations of his predecessors. The stratified aristocratic structure of Malian society perpetuated the pattern set in Ghana, as did the system of provincial administration and annual tribute. The emperor took responsibility for the territories that formed the heart of the empire and appointed governors to rule the outlying provinces or dependent kingdoms. But Mansa Musa made a significant innovation: in a practice strikingly similar to a system used in both China and France at that time, he appointed members of the royal family as provincial governors. He could count on their loyalty, and they received valuable experience in the work of government.

In another aspect of administration, Mansa Musa also differed from his predecessors. He became a devout Muslim. Although most of the Mandinke clung to their ancestral animism, Islamic practices and influences in Mali multiplied.

The most celebrated event of Mansa Musa's reign was his pilgrimage to Mecca in 1324–1325, during which he paid a state visit to the sultan of Egypt. Mansa Musa's entrance into Cairo was magnificent. Preceded by five hundred slaves, each carrying a six-pound staff of gold, he followed with a huge host of retainers, including one hundred elephants each bearing one hundred pounds of gold. The emperor lavished his wealth on the citizens of the Egyptian capital. Writing twelve years later, al-Omari, one of the sultan's officials, recounts:

*This man Mansa Musa spread upon Cairo the flood of his generosity: there was no person, officer of the court, or holder of any office of the Sultanate who did not receive a sum of gold from him. The people of Cairo earned incalculable sums from him, whether by buying and selling or by gifts. So much gold was current in Cairo that it ruined the value of money.*[19]

Mansa Musa's gold brought about terrible inflation throughout Egypt. For the first time, the Mediterranean world gained concrete knowledge of the wealth and power of the black kingdom of Mali, and it began to be known as one of the great empires of the world. Mali retained this international reputation into the fifteenth century.

Musa's pilgrimage also had significant consequences within Mali. He gained some understanding of the Mediterranean countries and opened diplomatic relations with the Muslim rulers of Morocco and Egypt. His zeal for the Muslim faith and Islamic culture increased. Musa brought back from Arabia the distinguished architect al-Saheli, whom he commissioned to build new mosques at Timbuktu and other cities. These mosques served as centers for the conversion of Africans. Musa employed Muslim engineers to build in brick. He also encouraged Malian merchants and traders to wear the distinctive flowing robes and turbans of Muslim males.

**Timbuktu** began as a campsite for desert nomads. Under Mansa Musa, it grew into a thriving entrepôt, attracting merchants and traders from North Africa and all parts of the Mediterranean world. These people brought with them cosmopolitan attitudes and ideas. In the fifteenth century, Timbuktu developed into a great center for scholarship and learning. Architects, astronomers, poets, lawyers, mathematicians, and theologians flocked there. One hundred fifty schools were devoted to the study of the Qur'an. The school of Islamic law enjoyed a distinction in Africa comparable to the prestige of the school at Cairo (see page 266). A vigorous trade in books flourished in Timbuktu. Leo Africanus, a sixteenth-century Muslim traveler and writer who later converted to Christianity, recounts that around 1500 Timbuktu had a

*great store of doctors, judges, priests, and other learned men that are bountifully maintained at the king's cost and charges. And hitherto are brought diverse manuscripts or written books out of Barbarie the north African states, from Egypt to the Atlantic Ocean which are sold for more money than any other merchandise.*

**Dogon Couple** This seated couple, made of wood and metal, tells us a great deal about the culture of the people who lived in the Dogon region at the bend of the Niger River in West Africa, in what is now Mali. The man's right arm circles the woman's shoulder and rests on her breast; his left hand points toward his genitals. He carries a quiver on his back; she bears an infant on hers. The mutually dependent figures indicate that the man is progenitor, protector, and provider; the woman is childbearer and nurturer. Dogon society was strongly patrilineal and famous for its artwork. This piece was done between the sixteenth and twentieth centuries. *(The Metropolitan Museum of Art, Gift of Lester Wunderman, 1977 [1977.394.15]. Photograph © 1993 The Metropolitan Museum of Art)*

It is easy to understand why the university at Timbuktu was called by a contemporary writer "the Queen of the Sudan." Timbuktu's tradition and reputation for African scholarship lasted until the eighteenth century.

Moreover, in the fourteenth and fifteenth centuries, many Muslim intellectuals and Arab traders married native African women. These unions brought into being a group of racially mixed people. The necessity of living together harmoniously, the traditional awareness of diverse cultures, and the cosmopolitan atmosphere of Timbuktu all contributed to a rare degree of racial toleration and understanding. After visiting the court of Mansa Musa's successor in 1352–1353, Ibn Battuta observed that

> *the Negroes possess some admirable qualities. They are seldom unjust, and have a greater abhorrence of injustice than any other people. Their sultan shows no mercy to anyone who is guilty of the least act of it. There is complete security in their country. Neither traveler nor inhabitant in it has anything to fear from robbers. . . . They do not confiscate the property of any white man who dies in their country, even if it be uncounted wealth. On the contrary, they give it into the charge of some trustworthy person among the whites, until the rightful heir takes possession of it.*[20]

## Ethiopia: The Christian Kingdom of Axum

Egyptian culture exerted a profound influence on the sub-Saharan kingdom of Nubia in northeastern Africa (see Map 10.3). Nubia's capital was at Meroe; thus the country is often referred to as the Nubian kingdom of Meroe. As part of the Roman Empire, Egypt was naturally subject to Hellenistic and Roman cultural forces, and it became an early center of Christianity. Nubia, however, was never part of the Roman Empire; its people clung to ancient Egyptian religious ideas. Christian missionaries went to the Upper Nile region and succeeded in converting the Nubian rulers around 600 C.E. By that time, there were three separate Nubian states, of which the kingdom of Nobatia, centered at Dongola, was the strongest. The Christian rulers of Nobatia had close ties with **Ethiopia.**

According to Ethiopian oral tradition, the queen of Sheba visited the Hebrew king Solomon (r. 961–922 B.C.E.) in Jerusalem to acquire some of his wisdom. They slept together, and the queen conceived a son. When the boy reached maturity, he returned to Israel, received Solomon's blessing, and was crowned king of Ethiopia as Menelik I. Except for a period in the twelfth and thirteenth centuries, all rulers of Ethiopia supposedly descended from Menelik. Because of the vast treasure of gold, spices, and precious stones that the queen of Sheba took to Solomon's court (1 Kings 10, 2 Chronicles 9), modern scholars believe that she actually headed a trade mission. Although these scholars also identify the land of Sheba with modern Yemen, artists usually portray the queen as a black woman. The legend suggests ancient contacts between Ethiopia and western Asia.

Tradition ascribes to Frumentius (ca 300–380 C.E.), a Syrian Christian trader, the introduction of Christianity into Ethiopia. Kidnapped en route from India to Tyre (now a town in southern Lebanon), Frumentius was taken to **Axum** and appointed tutor to the future king, Ezana. Later, Frumentius went to Alexandria in Egypt, where he was consecrated the first bishop of Axum. Thus Christianity came to Ethiopia from Egypt in the Monophysite form. Shortly after members of the royal court accepted Christianity, it became the Ethiopian state religion. The future of Ethiopia was to be inextricably tied up with Christianity, a unique situation in black Africa.

Ethiopia's acceptance of Christianity led to the production of ecclesiastical documents and royal chronicles, making Ethiopia the first black African society that can be studied from written records. The Scriptures were translated into Ge'ez, the language of Axum; pagan temples were dedicated to Christian saints; and, as in early medieval Ireland (see page 218) and in the Orthodox church of the Byzantine world, the monasteries were the main cultural institutions of the Christian faith in Ethiopia. From the monasteries, monks went out to preach and convert the people, who resorted to the monasteries in times of need. As the Ethiopian state expanded, vibrant monasteries made daughter foundations, as in medieval Europe (see pages 372–374).

Monastic records provide fascinating information about early Ethiopian society. Settlements were made on the warm and moist plateau lands, not in the arid lowlands or the river valleys. Farmers used a scratch plow (unique in sub-Saharan Africa) to cultivate wheat and barley and to rotate those cereals. Plentiful rainfall seems to have helped produce abundant crops, which in turn led to population growth. In contrast to most of sub-Saharan Africa, both sexes probably married young. Because of ecclesiastical opposition to polygyny, monogamy was the norm, except for kings and the very rich. The abundance of land meant that young couples could establish independent households, and widely scattered farms, with the parish church as the central social unit, seem to have been the usual pattern of existence.

Above the broad class of peasant farmers stood warrior-nobles. Their wealth and status derived from their fighting skills, which kings rewarded with grants of estates and

**Aerial View of Church of Saint George, Lalibela** The cross is the basic Christian symbol. When the capital of Ethiopia was moved south from Axum to Lalibela, this church was carved out of volcanic rock and dedicated to the third-century Palestinian martyr Saint George, who had a large cult in Ethiopia. Concentric Greek crosses, formed of four equal arms and symbolizing the universal Christian church, composed the roof. *(Kal Muller/Woodfin Camp & Associates)*

with the right to collect tribute from the peasants. To acquire lands and to hold warriors' loyalty, Ethiopian kings had to pursue a policy of constant territorial expansion. Nobles maintained order in their regions, supplied kings with fighting men, and displayed their superior status by the size of their households and their generosity to the poor.

The Solomonid kings of Ethiopia (so called because of their theoretical descent from King Solomon and the queen of Sheba) exerted their authority by constant travel to oversee and overawe their peoples and to extend their kingdoms. Until the fifteenth century, they had no truly permanent capital, but ruled from itinerant military camps. Amda Siyon (r. 1314–1344), who defeated the Muslims at Ifat and spread his kingdom to the south and west, proved to be Ethiopia's greatest ruler.[21]

From the fifth through seventh centuries, Axum was an important and cosmopolitan center, whose mercantile activities played a part in international commerce. Its military and political power was the dominant influence in East Africa. The expansion of Islam in the eighth century reduced Axum's trading contacts with the Byzantine Empire and ended its control of the Red Sea trade routes.

Ethiopia's high mountains encouraged an inward concentration of attention and hindered access from the outside. Twelfth-century Crusaders returning from the

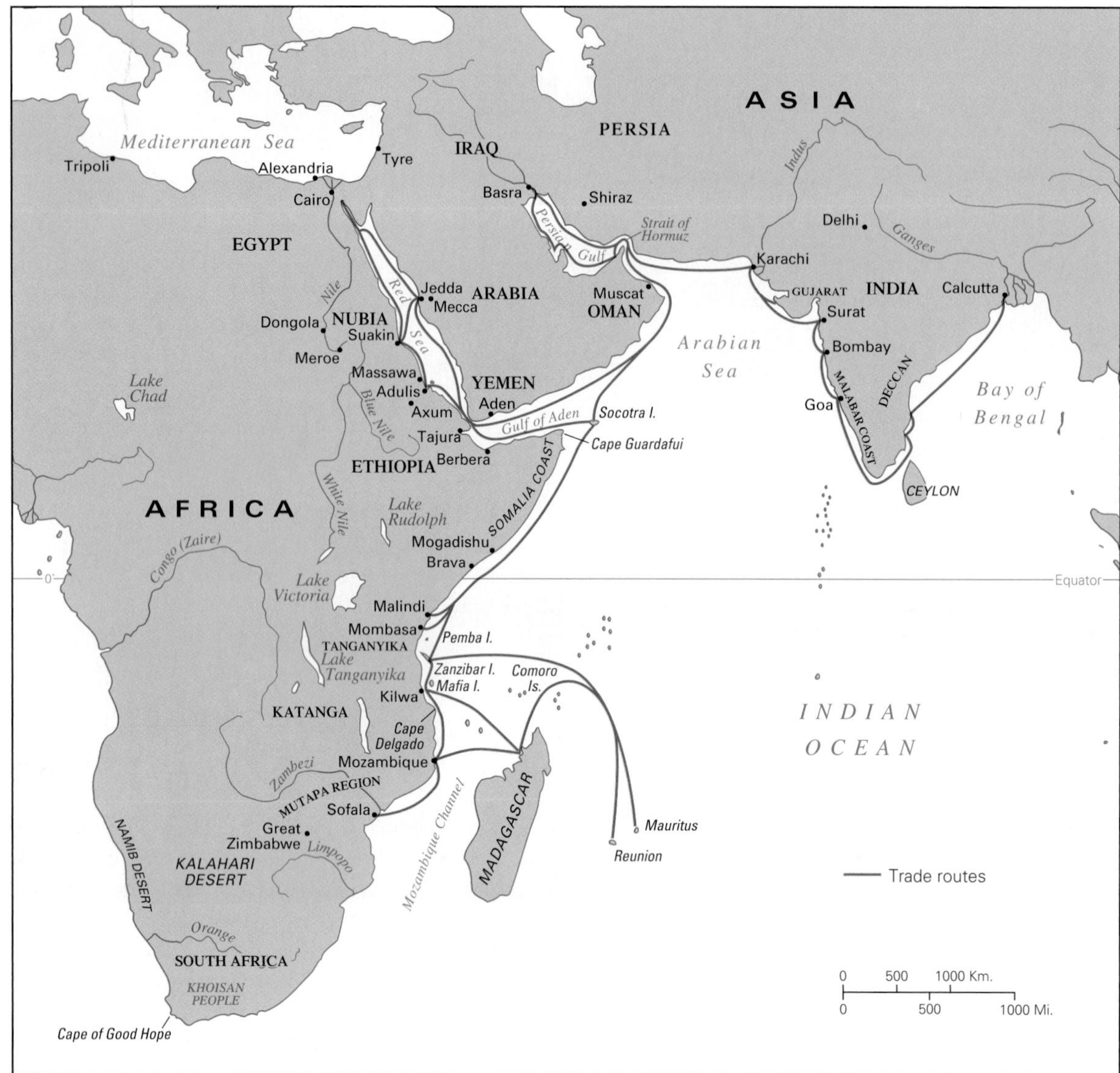


**MAP 10.3 Trade Routes Between East Africa and India** The Indian Ocean, controlled by the Muslim merchant fleet until the arrival of the Portuguese in the late fifteenth century, was of far greater importance to world trade than the Mediterranean. Gold from Great Zimbabwe passed through the cities on the East African coast before shipment north to the Middle East and east to India and China.

Middle East told of a powerful Christian ruler, Prester John, whose lands lay behind Muslim lines and who was eager to help restore the Holy Land to Christian control. Europeans identified that kingdom with Ethiopia. In the later thirteenth century, the dynasty of the Solomonid kings witnessed a literary and artistic renaissance particularly notable for works of hagiography (biographies of saints), biblical exegesis, and manuscript illumination. The most striking feature of Ethiopian society in the period from 500 to 1500 was the close relationship between the church and the state. Christianity inspired a fierce devotion and tended to equate doctrinal heresy with political rebellion, thus reinforcing central monarchical power.

**Emperor Yekuno Amlak** The Ethiopian emperor's claim of possessing Solomon's blood won him considerable popular support in his war against the decaying Zagwe dynasty, which he overthrew in 1270. Here he receives Muslim ambassadors while slaves attend him. *(British Library)*

## The East African City-States

In the first century C.E., a merchant seaman from Alexandria in Egypt sailed down the Red Sea and out into the Indian Ocean. Along the coasts of East Africa and India, he found seaports. He took careful notes on all he observed, and the result, *Periplus of the Erythraean Sea* (as the Greeks called the Indian Ocean), is the earliest surviving literary evidence of the city-states of the East African coast. Although primarily preoccupied with geography and navigation, the *Periplus* includes accounts of the local peoples and their commercial activities. Even in the days of the Roman emperors, the *Periplus* testifies, the East African coast had strong commercial links with India and the Mediterranean.

Greco-Roman ships traveled from Adulis on the Red Sea around the tip of the Gulf of Aden and down the African coast that the Greeks called "Azania," in modern-day Kenya and Tanzania (see Map 10.3). These ships carried manufactured goods—cotton cloth, copper and brass, iron tools, and gold and silver plate. At the African coastal emporiums, Mediterranean merchants exchanged these goods for cinnamon, myrrh and frankincense, captive slaves, and animal byproducts such as ivory, rhinoceros horns, and tortoise shells. Somewhere around Cape Guardafui on the Horn of Africa, the ships caught the monsoon winds eastward to India, where ivory was in great demand.

An omission in the *Periplus* has created a debate over the racial characteristics of the native peoples in East Africa and the dates of Bantu migrations into the area. The author, writing in the first century, did not describe the natives; apparently he did not find their skin color striking enough to comment on. Yet in the fifth century, there are references to these peoples as "Ethiopians." Could this mean that migrating black Bantu-speakers reached the east coast between the first and fifth centuries? Possibly. The distinguished archaeologist Neville Chittick, however, thinks not: "The writer of the *Periplus* made few comments on the physical nature of the inhabitants of the countries which he described . . . therefore nothing can be based on the mere omission of any mention of skin color."[22]

In the first few centuries of the Christian era, many merchants and seamen from the Mediterranean settled in East African coastal towns. Succeeding centuries saw the arrival of more traders. The great emigration from Arabia after the death of Muhammad accelerated Muslim penetration of the area, which the Arabs called the *Zanj,* "land of the blacks." Arabic Muslims established along the coast small trading colonies whose local peoples were ruled by kings and practiced various animistic religions.

Eventually—whether through Muslim political hegemony or gradual assimilation—the coastal peoples slowly converted to Islam. Indigenous African religions, however, remained strong in the interior of the continent.

Beginning in the late twelfth century, fresh waves of Arabs and of Persians from Shiraz poured down the coast, first settling at Mogadishu, then pressing southward to Kilwa (see Map 10.3). Everywhere they landed, they introduced Islamic culture to the indigenous population. Similarly, from the earliest Christian centuries through the Middle Ages, Indonesians crossed the Indian Ocean and settled on the African coast and on the large island of Madagascar, or Malagasy, an Indonesian name. All these immigrants intermarried with Africans, and the resulting society combined Asian, African, and especially Islamic traits. The East African coastal culture was called **Swahili,** after a Bantu language whose vocabulary and poetic forms exhibit a strong Arabic influence. The thirteenth-century Muslim mosque at Mogadishu and the fiercely Muslim populations of Mombasa and Kilwa in the fourteenth century attest to strong Muslim influence.

By the late thirteenth century, **Kilwa** had become the most powerful city on the coast, exercising political hegemony as far north as Pemba and as far south as Sofala (see Map 10.3). In the fourteenth and fifteenth centuries, the coastal cities were great commercial empires comparable to Venice and Genoa (see page 387). Like those Italian city-states, Kilwa, Mombasa, and Mafia were situated on offshore islands. The tidal currents that isolated them from the mainland also protected them from landside attack.

Much current knowledge about life in the East African trading societies rests on the account of Ibn Battuta. When he arrived at Kilwa, he found, in the words of a modern historian,

*the city large and elegant, its buildings, as was typical along the coast, constructed of stone and coral rag [roofing slate].*

**Great Mosque at Kilwa** Built between the thirteenth and fifteenth centuries to serve the Muslim commercial aristocracy of Kilwa on the Indian Ocean, the mosque attests to the wealth and power of the East African city-states. *(Marc & Evelyn Bernheim/Woodfin Camp & Associates)*

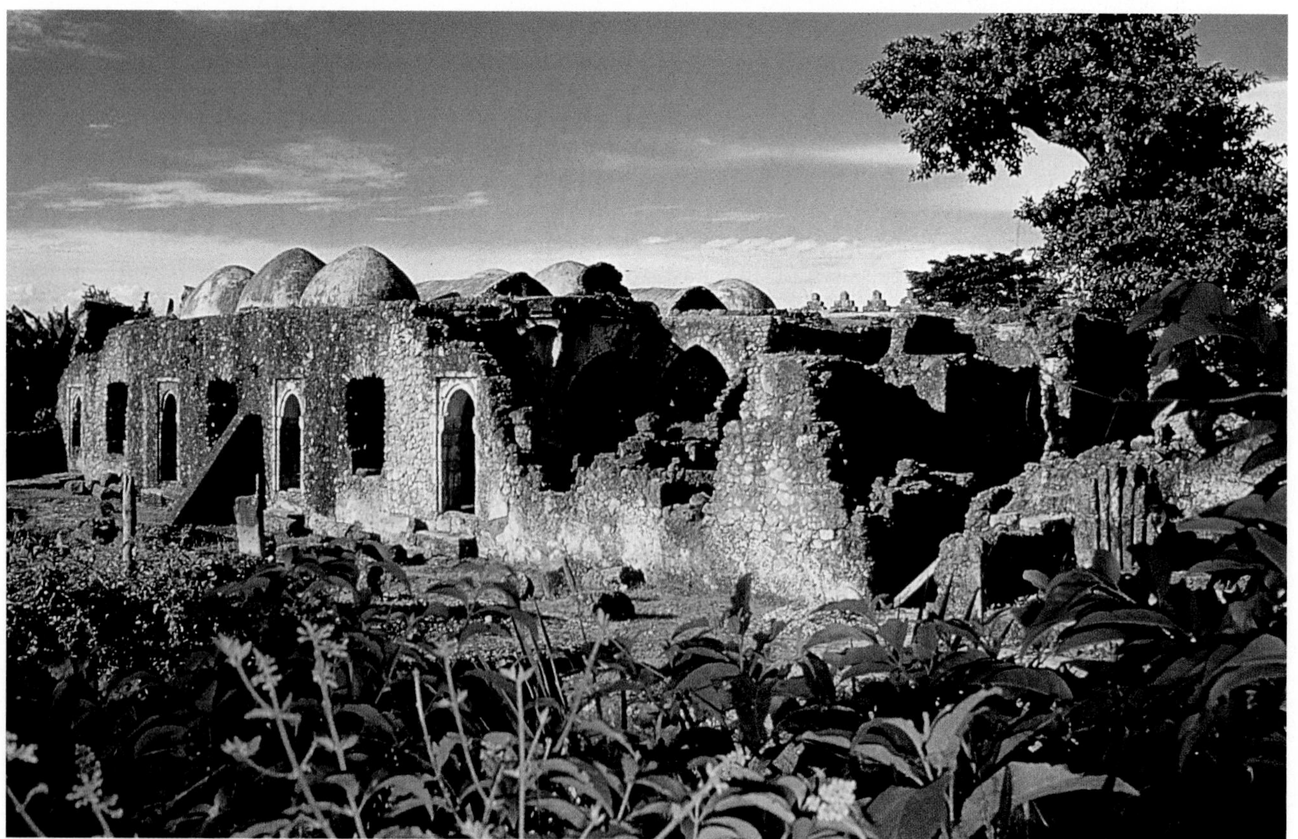

*Houses were generally single storied, consisting of a number of small rooms separated by thick walls supporting heavy stone roofing slabs laid across mangrove poles. Some of the more formidable structures contained second and third stories, and many were embellished with cut stone decorative borders framing the entranceways. Tapestries and ornamental niches covered the walls and the floors were carpeted. Of course, such appointments were only for the wealthy; the poorer classes occupied the timeless mud and straw huts of Africa, their robes a simple loincloth, their dinner a millet porridge.*[23]

On the mainland were fields and orchards of rice, millet, oranges, mangoes, and bananas, and pastures and yards for cattle, sheep, and poultry. Yields were apparently high; Ibn Battuta noted that the rich enjoyed three enormous meals a day and were very fat.

From among the rich mercantile families that controlled the coastal cities arose a ruler who by the fourteenth century had taken the Arabic title *sheik.* The sheik governed both the island city and the nearby mainland. Farther inland, tribal chiefs ruled with the advice of councils of elders.

The Portuguese, approaching the East African coastal cities in the late fifteenth century, were astounded at their enormous wealth and prosperity. This wealth rested on monopolistic control of all trade in the area. Some coastal cities manufactured goods for export: Mogadishu produced cloth for the Egyptian market; Mombasa and Malindi processed iron tools; and Sofala made cottons for the interior trade. The bulk of the cities' exports, however, consisted of animal products—leopard skins, tortoise shell, ambergris, ivory—and gold. The gold originated in the Mutapa region south of the Zambezi River, where the Bantu mined it. As in tenth-century Ghana, gold was a royal monopoly in the fourteenth-century coastal city-states. The Mutapa kings received it as annual tribute, prohibited outsiders from entering the mines or participating in the trade, and controlled shipments down the Zambezi to the coastal markets. The prosperity of Kilwa rested on its traffic in gold.

African goods satisfied the widespread aristocratic demand for luxury goods. In Arabia, leopard skins were made into saddles, shells were made into combs, and ambergris was used in the manufacture of perfumes. Because the tusks of African elephants were larger and more durable than the tusks of Indian elephants, African ivory was in great demand in India for sword and dagger handles, carved decorative objects, and the ceremonial bangles used in Hindu marriage rituals. In China, the wealthy valued African ivory for use in the construction of sedan chairs.

**Copper Coin from Mogadishu, Twelfth Century** Islamic proscriptions against representation of the human form, combined with a deep veneration for writing, prevented the use of rulers' portraits on coinage, as the Romans, Byzantines, and Sasanids had. Instead, Islamic coins since the Umayyad period were decorated exclusively with writing. Sultan Haran ibn Sulayman of Kilwa on the east African coast minted this coin, a symbol of the region's Muslim culture and of its rich maritime trade. *(Courtesy of the Trustees of the British Museum)*

In exchange for these natural products, the Swahili cities bought pottery, glassware and beads, and many varieties of cloth. Swahili kings imposed enormous duties on imports, perhaps more than 80 percent of the value of the goods themselves. Even so, traders who came to Africa made fabulous profits.

Slaves were another export from the East African coast. Reports of slave trading began with the *Periplus.* The trade accelerated with the establishment of Muslim settlements in the eighth century and continued down to the arrival of the Portuguese in the late fifteenth century. In fact, the East African coastal trade in slaves persisted at least to the beginning of the twentieth century.

As in West Africa, traders obtained slaves primarily through raids and kidnapping. As early as the tenth century, Arabs from Oman enticed hungry children with dates. When the children accepted the sweet fruits, they were abducted and enslaved. Profit was the traders' motive.

The Arabs called the northern Somalia coast *Ras Assir* (Cape of Slaves). From there, Arab traders transported slaves northward up the Red Sea to the markets of Arabia, Persia, and Iraq. Muslim dealers also shipped blacks from the region of Zanzibar across the Indian Ocean to markets in India. Rulers of the Deccan Plateau in central India used large numbers of black slave soldiers in their military campaigns. Slaves also worked on the docks and *dhows* (typical Arab lateen-rigged ships) in the Muslim-controlled Indian Ocean and as domestic servants and concubines throughout South and East Asia.

As early as the tenth century, sources mention persons with "lacquer-black bodies" in the possession of wealthy families in Song China.[24] In 1178 a Chinese official noted in a memorial to the emperor that Arab traders were shipping thousands of blacks from East Africa to the Chinese port of Guangzhou (Canton) by way of the Malay Archipelago. The Chinese employed these slaves as household servants, as musicians, and, because East Africans were often expert swimmers, as divers to caulk the leaky seams of ships below the water line.

By the thirteenth century, Africans living in many parts of South and East Asia had made significant economic and cultural contributions to their societies. Neither Asian nor Western scholars have adequately explored this subject. It appears, however, that in Indian, Chinese, and East African markets, slaves were never as valuable a commodity as ivory. Thus the volume of the Eastern slave trade did not approach that of the trans-Saharan trade.[25]

## South Africa

South Africa, the region bordered on the northwest by tropical grasslands and on the northeast by the Zambezi River (see Map 10.3), enjoys a mild and temperate climate. Desert conditions prevail along the Atlantic coast, which gets less than five inches of annual rainfall. Eastward, rainfall increases, though some areas receive less than twenty inches a year. Although the Limpopo Valley in the east is very dry, temperate grasslands characterize the highlands to the north and northwest (the region of the modern Orange Free State, the Transvaal, and Zimbabwe). Considerable variations in climate occur throughout much of South Africa from year to year.

Located at the southern extremity of the Afro-Eurasian landmass, South Africa has a history that is very different from the histories of West Africa, the Nile Valley, and the east coast. Over the centuries, North and West Africa felt the influences of Phoenician, Greek, Roman, and Muslim cultures; the Nile Valley experienced the impact of major Egyptian, Assyrian, Persian, and Muslim civilizations; and the coast of East Africa had important contacts across the Indian Ocean with southern and eastern Asia and across the Red Sea with Arabia and Persia. South Africa, however, remained far removed from the outside world until the arrival of the Portuguese in the late fifteenth century—with one important exception. Bantu-speaking people reached South Africa in the eighth century. They brought with them skills in ironworking and mixed farming (settled crop production plus cattle and sheep raising) and an immunity to the kinds of diseases that later decimated the Amerindians of South America (see pages 525–527).

The earliest residents of South Africa were hunters and gatherers. In the first millennium after the birth of Christ, new farming techniques from the north arrived. A lack of water and timber (which were needed to produce the charcoal used in iron smelting) slowed the spread of iron technology and tools and thus of crop production in western South Africa. These advances, however, reached the western coastal region by 1500. By that date, Khoisan-speakers were farming in the arid western regions. To the east, descendants of Bantu immigrants grew sorghum, raised sheep and cattle, and fought with iron-headed spears. They practiced polygamy and traced their descent in the male line.

In 1871 a German explorer discovered the ruined city of **Great Zimbabwe** southeast of what is now Nyanda in Zimbabwe. Archaeologists consider Great Zimbabwe the most powerful monument in Africa south of the Nile Valley and the Ethiopian highlands. The ruins consist of two vast complexes of dry-stone buildings, a fortress, and an elliptically shaped enclosure commonly called the Temple. Stone carvings, gold and copper ornaments, and Asian ceramics once decorated the buildings. The ruins extend over sixty acres and are encircled by a massive wall. The entire city was built from local granite between the eleventh and fifteenth centuries without any outside influence.

These ruins tell a remarkable story. Great Zimbabwe was the political and religious capital of a vast empire. During the first millennium C.E., settled crop cultivation, cattle raising, and work in metal led to a steady buildup in population in the Zambezi-Limpopo region. The area also contained a rich gold-bearing belt. Gold ore lay near the surface; alluvial gold lay in the Zambezi River tributaries. In the tenth century, the inhabitants collected the alluvial gold by panning and washing; after the year 1000, the gold was worked in open mines with iron picks. Traders shipped the gold eastward to Sofala (see Map 10.3). The wealth and power of Great Zimbabwe rested on this gold trade.[26]

Great Zimbabwe declined in the fifteenth century, perhaps because the area had become agriculturally exhausted and could no longer support the large popula-

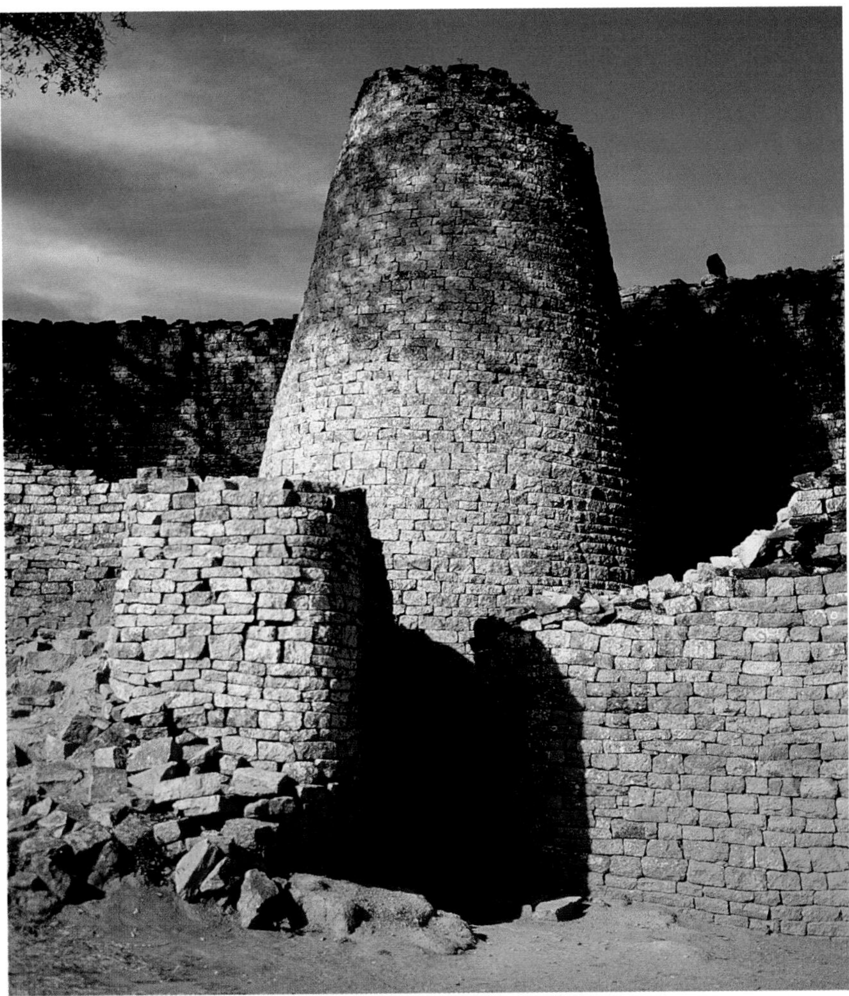

**Ruins of Great Zimbabwe** Considered the most impressive monument in the African interior south of the Ethiopian highlands, these ruins of Great Zimbabwe consist of two complexes of dry-stone buildings, some surrounded by a massive serpentine wall thirty-two feet high and seventeen feet thick at its maximum. Great Zimbabwe was the center of a state whose wealth rested on gold. Towers were probably used for defensive purposes. *(Robert Aberman/Barbara Heller/Werner Forman Archive/Art Resource, NY)*

**Bird at Top of Monolith, 14½ inches, Great Zimbabwe, ca 1200–1400 C.E.** The walls and buildings at Great Zimbabwe seem intended to reflect the wealth and power of the ruler. Among the archaeological finds there are monoliths crowned by soapstone birds; this one also appears to have an alligator-like creature on the side of the monolith. Scholars debate the significance of these birds: were they symbols of royal power? eagles? messengers from the spiritual world to the terrestrial? And what does the alligator mean? *(Courtesy of the National Archives of Zimbabwe)*

tion. Some people migrated northward and settled in the valley of the Mazoe River, a tributary of the Zambezi. This region also contained gold, and there the settlers built a new empire in the tradition of Great Zimbabwe. Rulers of this empire were called "Mwene Mutapa," and their power too was based on the gold trade carried on by means of the Zambezi River and Indian Ocean ports. It was this gold that the Portuguese sought when they arrived on the East African coast in the late fifteenth century.

## SUMMARY

In the fifteenth century, the African continent contained a number of very different societies and civilizations and many diverse ethnic groups. All of North Africa, from Morocco in the west to Egypt in the east, was part of the Muslim world. In West Africa, Mali continued the brisk trade in salt, gold, and slaves that had originated many centuries earlier. Islam, which had spread to sub-Saharan Africa through the caravan trade, had a tremendous influence on the peoples of the western Sudan, their governmental bureaucracies, and their vibrant urban centers. The kings of Ethiopia ruled a uniquely Christian kingdom, partly by right of their Solomonic blood, frequently by force of arms. The impact of the Islamic faith was also felt in East Africa, whose bustling port cities were in touch with the cultures of the Indian Ocean and the Mediterranean Sea. While the city-states of the eastern coast—Kilwa, Mombasa, and Mogadishu—conducted complicated mercantile activities with foreign societies, the mountain-protected kingdom of Ethiopia increasingly led an isolated, inward-looking existence. In South Africa, the vast empire of Great Zimbabwe was yielding to yet another kingdom whose power was based on precious gold.

The student beginning the study of African history should bear in mind the enormous diversity of African peoples and cultures, a diversity both within and across regions. It is, therefore, difficult and often dangerous to make broad generalizations about African life. Statements such as "African culture is . . . " or "African peoples are . . . " are virtually meaningless. African peoples are not now and never have been homogeneous. This rich diversity helps explain why the study of African history is so exciting and challenging.

## KEY TERMS

| | |
|---|---|
| Bantu | Kumbi |
| Sudan | Timbuktu |
| Berbers | Ethiopia |
| Mogadishu | Axum |
| stateless societies | Swahili |
| Ghana | Kilwa |
| ghana | Great Zimbabwe |

## NOTES

1. J. Hiernaux, *The People of Africa* (New York: Scribner's, 1975), pp. 46–48.
2. C. A. Diop, "The African Origins of Western Civilization," and R. Mauny, "A Review of Diop," in *Problems in African History: The Precolonial Centuries,* ed. R. O. Collins et al. (New York: Markus Weiner Publishing, 1994), pp. 32–40, 41–49; the quotations are on p. 42.
3. Mauny, "A Review of Diop." For contrasting views of Afrocentrism in American higher education, see T. Martin, *The Jewish Onslaught: Despatches from the Wellesley Battlefront* (Dover, Mass.: The Majority Press, 1993), and M. Lefkowitz, *Not out of Africa: How Afrocentrism Became an Excuse to Teach Myth as History* (New York: Basic Books, 1996).
4. "African Historical Demography," in *Proceedings of a Seminar Held in the Centre of African Studies,* University of Edinburgh, April 29–30, 1977, p. 3.
5. T. Spear, "Bantu Migrations," in *Problems in African History: The Precolonial Centuries,* ed. R. O. Collins et al. (New York: Markus Weiner Publishing, 1994), p. 98.
6. J. Iliffe, *Africans: The History of a Continent* (Cambridge: Cambridge University Press, 1995), pp. 105–111; J. L. Newman, *The Peopling of Africa: A Geographic Interpretation* (New Haven, Conn.: Yale University Press, 1995), pp. 140–147.
7. J. S. Trimingham, *Islam in West Africa* (Oxford: Oxford University Press, 1959), pp. 6–9.
8. R. A. Austen, *Africa in Economic History* (London: James Currey/ Heinemann, 1987), p. 36.
9. R. A. Austen, "The Trans-Saharan Slave Trade: A Tentative Census," in *The Uncommon Market: Essays in the Economic History of the Atlantic Slave Trade,* ed. H. A. Gemery and J. S. Hogendorn (New York: Academic Press, 1979), pp. 1–71, esp. p. 66.
10. R. N. July, *Precolonial Africa: An Economic and Social History* (New York: Scribner's, 1975), pp. 124–129.
11. See N. Levtzion, "Islam in Africa to 1800: Merchants, Chiefs, and Saints," in *The Oxford History of Islam,* ed. J. L. Esposito (New York: Oxford University Press, 1999), pp. 502–504.
12. Quoted in J. O. Hunwick, "Islam in West Africa, A.D. 1000–1800," in *A Thousand Years of West African History,* ed. J. F. Ade Ajayi and I. Espie (New York: Humanities Press, 1972), pp. 244–245.
13. Quoted in A. A. Boahen, "Kingdoms of West Africa, c. A.D. 500–1600," in *The Horizon History of Africa* (New York: American Heritage, 1971), p. 183.
14. Al-Bakri, *Kitab al-mughrib fdhikr bilad Ifriqiya wa'l-Maghrib (Description de l'Afrique Septentrionale),* trans. De Shane (Paris: Adrien-Maisonneuve, 1965), pp. 328–329.
15. Quoted in R. Oliver and C. Oliver, eds., *Africa in the Days of Exploration* (Englewood Cliffs, N.J.: Prentice-Hall, 1965), p. 10.
16. Quoted in Boahen, "Kingdoms of West Africa, c. A.D. 500–1600," p. 184.
17. Quoted in E. J. Murphy, *History of African Civilization* (New York: Delta, 1972), p. 109.
18. Quoted ibid., p. 111.
19. Quoted ibid., p. 120.
20. Quoted in Oliver and Oliver, *Africa in the Days of Exploration,* p. 18.
21. Iliffe, *Africans,* pp. 57–61.
22. H. N. Chittick, "The Peopling of the East African Coast," in *East Africa and the Orient: Cultural Syntheses in Pre-Colonial Times,* ed. H. N. Chittick and R. I. Rotberg (New York: Africana Publishing, 1975), p. 19.
23. July, *Precolonial Africa,* p. 209.
24. Austen, "The Trans-Saharan Slave Trade," p. 65; J. H. Harris, *The African Presence in Asia* (Evanston, Ill.: Northwestern University

Press, 1971), pp. 3–6, 27–30; and P. Wheatley, "Analecta Sino-Africana Recensa," in Chittick and Rotberg, *East Africa and the Orient,* p. 109.

25. I. Hrbek, ed., *General History of Africa.* Vol. 3: *Africa from the Seventh to the Eleventh Century* (Berkeley: University of California Press; New York: UNESCO, 1991), pp. 294–295, 346–347.
26. P. Curtin et al., *African History,* rev. ed. (New York: Longman, 1984), pp. 284–287.

## SUGGESTED READING

Perhaps the best starting point for the study of early African history is J. Iliffe, *Africans: The History of a Continent* (1995), which has colonization and population as its main themes; although the peoples of Africa are studied with rare sensitivity, the style is not always clear. J. L. Newman, *The Peopling of Africa: A Geographic Interpretation* (1995), uses many types of evidence to explore population distribution and technological change down to the beginning of European colonization in the late nineteenth century. M. A. Ogutu and S. S. Kenyanchui, *An Introduction to African History* (1991), offers a useful sketch from a strongly Afrocentric point of view. J. Reader, *Africa: A Biography of a Continent* (1997), is a well-researched, exciting, and popular account with considerable material on Africa before 1450. The titles by Austen, Chittick, Curtin et al., Hiernaux, Hrbek, and Wheatley listed in the Notes represent some of the most reliable scholarship on early African history, and they are especially recommended. Most contain useful bibliographies. The enterprising student should also see B. Davidson, *African Civilization Revisited* (1991), a useful collection of primary documents with material on all parts of Africa; R. O. Collins, ed., *Problems in African History: The Precolonial Centuries* (1993), another collection of sources; and V. B. Khapoya, *The African Experience* (1994), and R. Oliver, *The African Experience* (1991), both of which offer broad interpretations.

For specific topics in early African history, see, in addition to the topics in the Notes, J. Suret-Canale, "The Traditional Societies in Tropical Africa and the Concept of the 'Asiatic Production,'" in J. Suret-Canale, *Essays on African History* (1988), which explores a Marxist understanding of precolonial African societies. For the east coast, see J. de Vere Allen, *Swahili Origins* (1993), a study of the problem of Swahili identity; R. Oliver and G. Mathews, eds., *History of East Africa* (1963), perhaps still the standard general work on this part of the continent; and G. S. P. Freeman-Grenville, *The East African Coast: Select Documents from the First to the Earlier Nineteenth Century* (1962), which has valuable material from Arabic, Chinese, and Portuguese perspectives. The works of J. S. Trimingham, *A History of Islam in West Africa* (1970) and *Islam in East Africa* (1974), remain standard studies on the important issue of Islam. J. Kritzeck and W. H. Lewis, eds., *Islam in Africa* (1969), and M. Lombard, *The Golden Age of Islam* (1975), are also helpful. For the importance of the camel to African trade, R. W. Bulliet, *The Camel and the Wheel* (1975), is basic. For southern Africa, see Chapter 1 of L. Thompson, *A History of South Africa,* rev. ed. (1995).

Students interested in the art of early Africa will find the following titles provocative and attractively produced: K. Ezra, *Royal Art of Benin* (1992); E. Eyo and F. Willett, *Treasures of Ancient Nigeria* (1980); and P. Ben-Amos, *The Art of Benin* (1980), which describes the political, social, and religious significance of Benin art through beautiful illustrations. C. Beckwith and A. Fisher, *African Art: People and Ancient Culture of Ethiopia and the Horn of Africa* (1990), is a splendidly illustrated appreciation of Ethiopian art and culture.

# LISTENING TO THE PAST

## The Epic of Old Mali

*Just as the Greek epic poems the* Iliad *and the* Odyssey *serve as essential sources for the early history of ancient Greece, so the testimony of African griots (storytellers) provides information about early West African societies. There were three classes of griots. Musician-entertainers in the service of nobles formed the lowest group. In the middle group were griots who acted as praise-singers of kings and as their advisers. "Traditionalists" who were attached to a royal household and whose function was to recite from memory in sung poems the royal family's historic traditions and to stress the family's rights and precedence constituted the highest-ranking griots. The Mandinke griot Djeli Mamadou Kouyate was a member of this third group. This selection is from the beginning of his account of old Mali, which is an important source for the early history of the kingdom of Mali.*

I am a griot. It is I, Djeli Mamadou Kouyate, son of Bintou Kouyate and Djeli Kediane Kouyate, master in the art of eloquence. Since time immemorial the Kouyates have been in the service of the Keita princes of Mali; we are vessels of speech, we are the repositories which harbor secrets many centuries old. The art of eloquence has no secrets for us; without us the names of kings would vanish into oblivion, we are the memory of mankind; by the spoken word we bring to life the deeds and exploits of kings for younger generations. . . . I know the list of all the sovereigns who succeeded to the throne of Mali. . . . I teach kings the history of their ancestors so that the lives of the ancients might serve them as an example, for the world is old, but the future springs from the past. . . . Listen to my word, you who want to know; by my mouth you will learn the history of Mali. . . . Listen to the story of the Buffalo. I am going to tell you of Maghan Sundiata, of Mari-Djata, of Sogolon Djata, of Nare Maghan Djata: the man of many names against whom sorcery could avail nothing. . . . Listen then, sons of Mali, children of the black people, listen to my word, for I am going to tell you of Sundiata, the father of the Bright Country, of the savanna land, the ancestor of those who draw the bow, the master of a hundred vanished kings.

### QUESTIONS FOR ANALYSIS

1. How did Djeli Mamadou Kouyate secure his position as a griot?
2. What did Kouyate understand his social function to be?
3. According to Kouyate, what purpose does history serve among the Mali? Does this purpose resemble that among any other people you have studied, such as the Christians, Muslims, or Chinese?
4. Consider the value of oral history for the modern historian.

*Source:* B. Davidson, *African Civilization Revisited* (Trenton, N.J.: Africa World Press, 1991), p. 90.

A griot retells the history of his people. *(Bibliothèque nationale de France)*

Mongol army attacking a walled city, from a Persian manuscript. Note the use of catapults on both sides. (*Staatsbibliothek zu Berlin/Bildarchiv Preussischer Kulturbesitz. Foto: Ruth Schacht, 1979*)

CHAPTER

# 11 SOUTHERN AND CENTRAL ASIA TO THE RISE OF THE MONGOLS, CA 300–1400

## CHAPTER OUTLINE

- India, 300–1400
- Southeast Asia, to 1400
- Central Asia, to 1400
- East-West Communication During the Mongol Era

The large chunks of Asia treated in this chapter underwent profound changes during the eleven centuries examined here. In the Indian subcontinent regional cultures flourished and the area had its first encounter with Islam. Southeast Asia developed several distinct cultures, most of them borrowing ideas and techniques from India. The Central Asian grasslands gave birth to nomadic confederations capable of dominating major states—first the Turks, then later, even more spectacularly, the Mongols.

Ancient India was covered in Chapter 3, but this is the first chapter to treat Southeast Asia or to look at Central Asia on its own terms rather than as a problem for nearby agricultural societies.

- What impact did India's political division have on its cultural and economic development?
- How did trade contribute to the development of states in Southeast Asia?
- What gave the nomadic pastoralists military advantages over the settled civilizations?
- How was the world changed by the Mongol unification of much of Eurasia?

This chapter will explore these questions.

## INDIA, 300–1400

Chapter 3 traced the early development of Indian civilization, including the emergence of the principal religious traditions of Hinduism, Buddhism, and Jainism; the impact of the Persian and Greek invasions; and the Mauryan dynasty, with its great pro-Buddhist king, Ashoka. As discussed at the end of that chapter, after the Mauryan dynasty broke apart in 184 B.C.E., India was politically divided into small kingdoms for several centuries. Northwest India fell to the Shakas, a nomadic group from the Central Asian grasslands.

## The Gupta Empire (ca 320–480)

In the early fourth century a state emerged in the Ganges plain that was able to bring large parts of north India under its control. The rulers of this Indian empire, the Guptas, consciously modeled their rule after that of the Mauryan Empire, and the founder took the name of the founder of that dynasty, Chandragupta. Although the Guptas never controlled as much territory as the Mauryans had, they united north India and received tribute from states in Nepal and the Indus Valley, thus giving large parts of India a period of peace and political unity.

The real creator of the Gupta Empire was Chandragupta's son Samudragupta (r. ca 335–375). Samudragupta once issued gold coins with the legend, "After conquering the earth the Great King of Kings with the strength of an invincible hero is going to conquer the heavens."[1] By means of military conquest and shrewd alliances, Samudragupta brought much of India, from the Himalayas in the north to the Vindhya Mountains in the south, under his government.

Under Samudragupta's son Chandragupta II (r. ca 375–415), the glory of the Guptas reached its highest point. Perhaps Chandragupta's most significant exploit was the overthrow of the Shakas in west India. As a result, the busy trade between west India and the Middle East and China came under the protection of the Guptas. Indian agricultural cash crops, especially sugar, cotton, pepper, and cinnamon, were in great demand elsewhere.

The great crisis of the Gupta Empire was the invasion of the Huns. The migration of these nomads from Central Asia shook much of Eurasia. Around 450 a group of them known as the White Huns thundered into India. Mustering his full might, the ruler Skandagupta (r. ca 455–467) threw back the invaders. Although the Huns failed to uproot the Gupta Empire, they dealt the dynasty a fatal blow.

The Guptas' administrative system was not as centralized as the Mauryans'. In the central regions they drew their revenue from a tax on agriculture of one-quarter of the harvest and maintained monopolies on key products such as metals and salt (reminiscent of Chinese practice). They also exacted labor service for the construction and upkeep of roads, wells, and irrigation systems. More distant areas were assigned to governors allowed considerable leeway, and governorships often became hereditary. Areas still farther away were encouraged to become vassal states, able to participate in the splendor of the capital and royal court in subordinate roles and to engage in profitable trade, but not required to turn over much in the way of revenue.

The Gupta kings were patrons of the arts. During their ascendancy, Sanskrit masterpieces were preserved, and traditional epic poems and verses on mythological themes were reworked and polished. Poets composed epics for the courts of the Gupta kings, and other writers experimented with prose romances and popular tales.

The Gupta period also saw the rise of Indian drama. India's greatest poet, Kalidasa (ca 380–450), like Shakespeare, wrote poems as well as plays in verse. His most highly esteemed play, *Shakuntala,* concerns a daughter of a hermit who enthralls a king out hunting. The king sets up house with her, then returns to his court and owing to a curse forgets her. Only much later does he acknowledge their child as his true heir. Equally loved is Kalidasa's one-hundred-verse poem "The Cloud Messenger," about a demigod who asks a passing cloud to carry a message to his wife, from whom he has long been separated. At one point he instructs the cloud to tell her:

*I see your body in the sinuous creeper, your gaze in the startled eyes of deer,*
*your cheek in the moon, your hair in the plumage of peacocks,*
*and in the tiny ripples of the river I see your sidelong glances,*
*but alas, my dearest, nowhere do I see your whole likeness.*[2]

In mathematics, too, the Gupta period could boast of impressive intellectual achievements. The so-called Arabic numerals were actually of Indian origin. Indian mathematicians developed place-value notation that was far more efficient than the numerical systems of the Egyptians, Greeks, and Romans. It was a base ten system, with separate columns for ones, tens, and hundreds, as well as a zero sign to indicate the absence of units in a given column. This system greatly facilitated calculation and spread to the rest of Eurasia by the seventh century.

The Gupta rulers were Hindus but tolerated all faiths. Buddhist pilgrims from other areas of Asia reported that Buddhist monasteries with hundreds or even thousands of monks and nuns flourished in the cities. The Chinese Buddhist pilgrim Faxian, during his six years in Gupta India, found the Buddhist monasteries flourishing but also noted the popularity of the many gods of Hinduism. He described India as a peaceful land, where people could move about freely without needing passports and where the upper castes were vegetarians. He was the first to make explicit reference to "untouchables," remarking that they hovered around the margins of Indian society, carrying gongs to warn upper-caste people of their polluting presence.

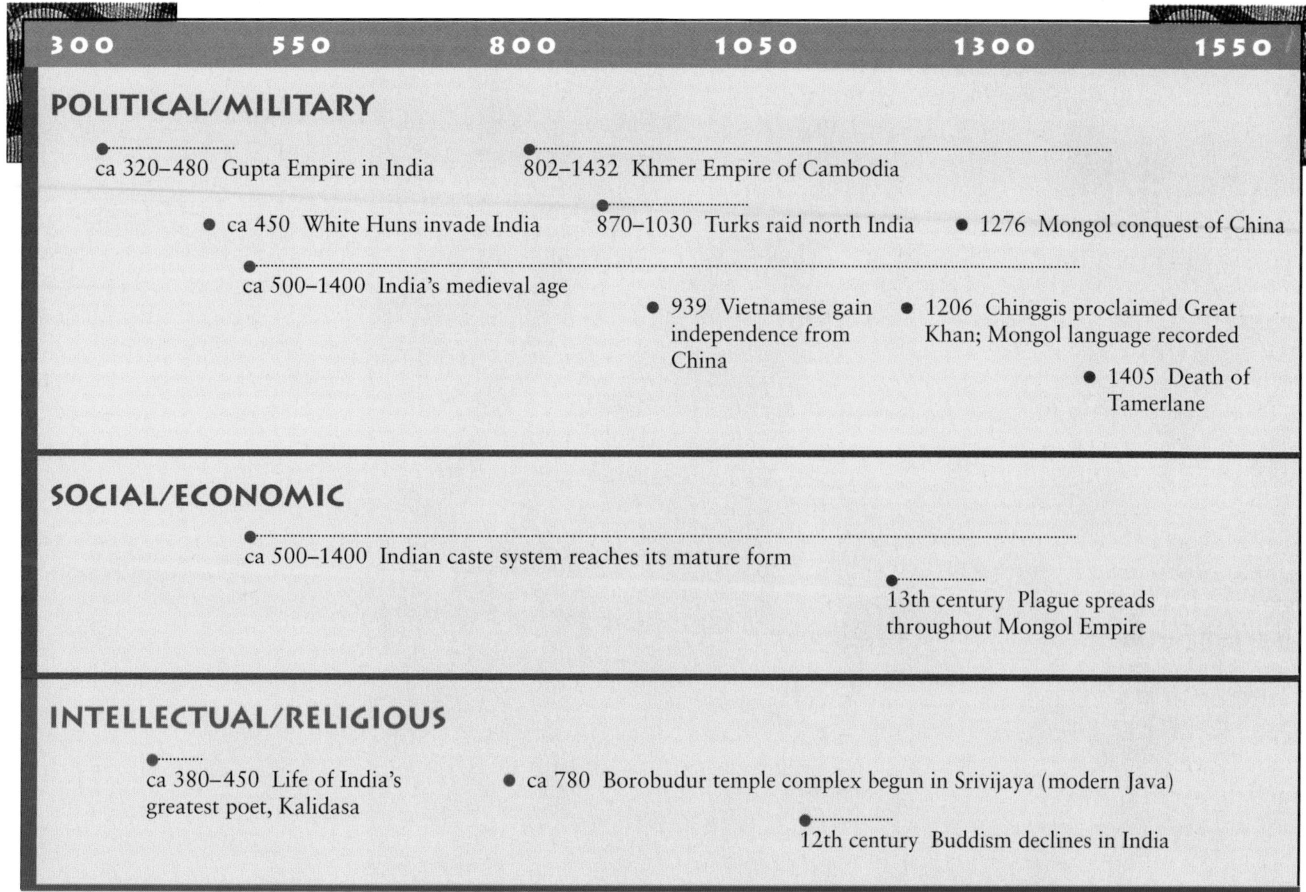

300
550
800
1050
1300
1550
POLITICAL/MILITARY
ca 320–480 Gupta Empire in India
802–1432 Khmer Empire of Cambodia
ca 450 White Huns invade India
870–1030 Turks raid north India
1276 Mongol conquest of China
ca 500–1400 India's medieval age
939 Vietnamese gain independence from China
1206 Chinggis proclaimed Great Khan; Mongol language recorded
1405 Death of Tamerlane
SOCIAL/ECONOMIC
ca 500–1400 Indian caste system reaches its mature form
13th century Plague spreads throughout Mongol Empire
INTELLECTUAL/RELIGIOUS
ca 380–450 Life of India's greatest poet, Kalidasa
ca 780 Borobudur temple complex begun in Srivijaya (modern Java)
12th century Buddism declines in India


## India's Medieval Age (ca 500–1400) and the First Encounter with Islam

After the decline of the Gupta Empire, India once again broke into separate kingdoms that were frequently at war with each other. Most of the dynasties were short-lived, but a balance of power was maintained between the four major regions of India, with none gaining enough of an advantage to conquer the others. Particularly notable are the Cholas, who dominated the southern tip of the peninsula, Sri Lanka, and much of the eastern Indian Ocean to the twelfth century (see Map 11.1).

Political division fostered the development of regional cultures. Literature came to be written in regional languages, among them Marathi, Bengali, and Assamese. Commerce continued as before, and the coasts of India remained important in the sea trade of the Indian Ocean.

The first encounters with Islam occurred in this period. In 711, after pirates had plundered a richly laden Arab ship near the mouth of the Indus, the Ummayad governor of Iraq sent a force with six thousand horses and six thousand camels to seize the Sind area. The western part of India remained a part of the caliphate for centuries, but Islam did not spread much beyond this foothold. During the ninth and tenth centuries tribes of Turkish-speaking herdsmen and warriors from Central Asia moved into the region of today's northeastern Iran and western Afghanistan, then known as Khurasan. Converts to Islam, they first served as military forces for the caliphate in Baghdad, but as its authority weakened (see page 252), they made themselves rulers of an effectively independent Khurasan and frequently sent raiding parties into north India. Beginning in 997, Mahmud of Ghazni (r. 997–1030) led seventeen annual forays into India from his base in modern Afghanistan. His goal was plunder to finance his wars against other Muslim rulers in Central Asia. Toward this end, he systematically looted Indian palaces and temples, viewing religious statues as infidels' idols. His court chronicler, undoubtedly exaggerating, reported that in 1025 the Hindu inhabitants of one town on his route calmly watched as his troops reached the walls of their temple to Shiva, confident that

**Mriga Jataka** The fifth-century Buddhist caves at Ajanta contain the most important wall paintings from the Gupta period. This painting is an illustration of one of the 547 Jatakas (legends of the Buddha's life), and shows a royal servant with a dog on a leash. *(Satish Pavashav/Dinodia Picture Agency)*

Shiva would protect his worshipers. The Turkish soldiers, undeterred, seized more than 2 million dinars' worth of gold and jewels and killed fifty thousand Hindus. Eventually even the Arab conquerors of the Sind fell to the Turks. By 1030 the Indus Valley, the Punjab, and the rest of northwest India were in the grip of the Turks.

The new rulers encouraged the spread of Islam, but the Indian caste system made it difficult to convert higher-caste Indians. Al-Biruni (d. 1048), a Persian scholar who spent much of his later life at the court of Mahmud and learned Sanskrit, gave some thought to the obstacles to Hindu-Muslim communication. The most basic barrier, he wrote, was language, but the religious gulf was also fundamental:

*They totally differ from us in religion, as we believe in nothing in which they believe, and vice versa. On the whole, there is very little disputing about theological topics among them; at the utmost they fight with words, but they will never stake their soul or body or property on religious controversy. . . .*

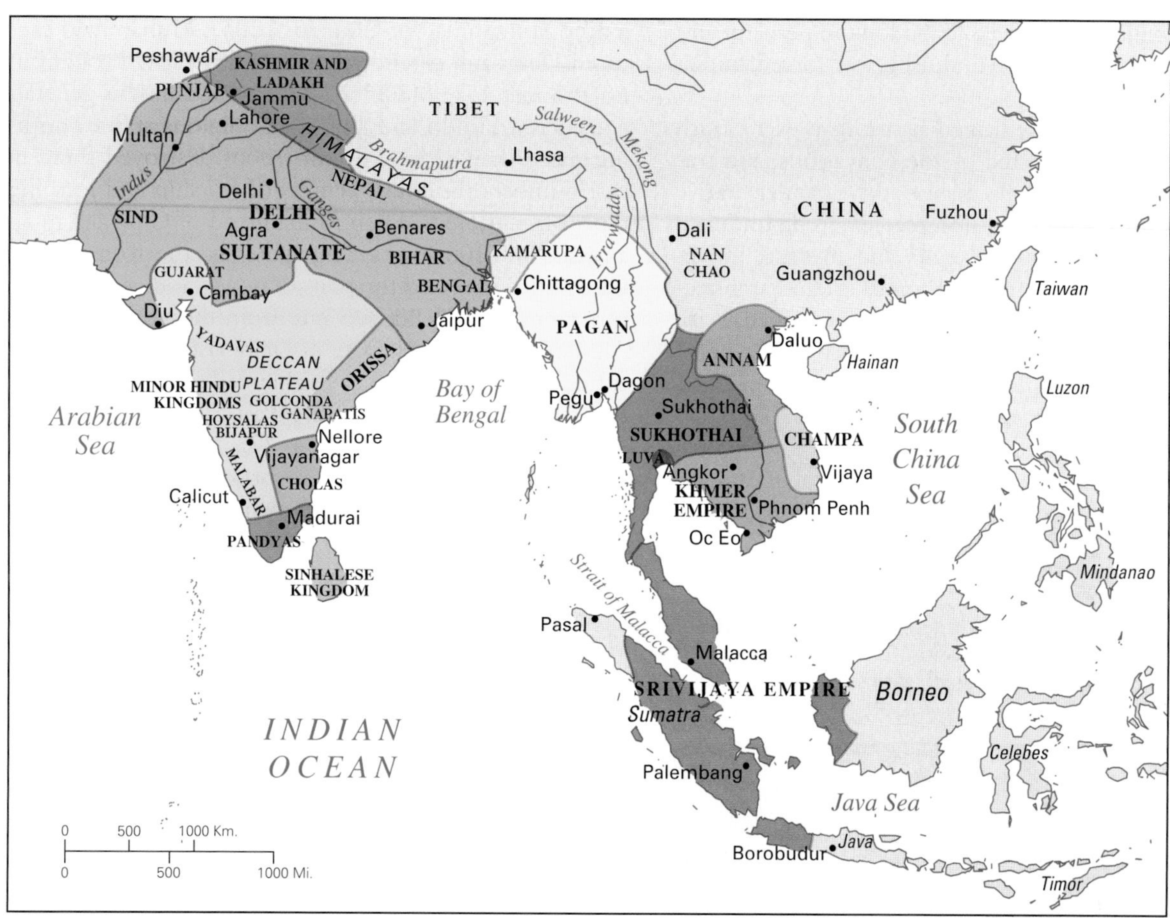


**MAP 11.1 South and Southeast Asia in the Thirteenth Century** The extensive coastlines of South and Southeast Asia and the predictable monsoon winds aided seafaring in this region. Note the Strait of Malacca, through which most east-west sea trade passed.

*They call foreigners impure and forbid having any connection with them, be it by intermarriage or any kind of relationship, or by sitting, eating, and drinking with them, because thereby, they think, they would be polluted.*[3]

After the initial period of raids and destruction of temples, the Muslim Turks came to an accommodation with the Hindus, who were classed as a **protected people,** like the Christians and Jews, and allowed to follow their religion. They had to pay a special tax but did not have to perform military service. Local chiefs and rajas were often allowed to remain in control of their domains as long as they paid tribute. Most Indians looked on the Muslim conquerors as a new ruling caste, capable of governing and taxing them but otherwise peripheral to their lives. The myriad castes largely governed themselves, isolating the newcomers. Nevertheless, over the course of several centuries Islam gained a strong hold on north India, especially in the Indus Valley (modern Pakistan) and in Bengal at the mouth of the Ganges River (modern Bangladesh). Moreover, the sultanate seems to have had a positive effect on the economy. Much of the wealth confiscated from temples was put to more productive use, and India's first truly large cities emerged. The Turks also were eager to employ skilled workers, giving new opportunities to low-caste manual and artisan labor.

The Muslim rulers were much more hostile to Buddhism than to Hinduism, seeing Buddhism as a competitive proselytizing religion. In 1193 a Turkish raiding party destroyed the great Buddhist university at Nalanda in Bihar. Buddhist monks were killed or forced to flee to Buddhist centers in Southeast Asia, Nepal, and Tibet.

Buddhism, which had thrived for so long in peaceful and friendly competition with Hinduism, was forced out of its native land.

Hinduism, however, remained as strong as ever. South India was largely unaffected by these invasions, and traditional Hindu culture flourished there under native kings ruling small kingdoms. Temple-centered Hinduism flourished, as did devotional cults and mystical movements. This was a great age of religious art and architecture in India. Extraordinary temples, covered with elaborate bas-relief, were built in many areas. Sexual passion and the union of men and women were frequently depicted, symbolically representing passion for and union with the temple god.

Mahmud and his successors had their capital in Afghanistan. After them a new line of Turkish rulers arose there, led by Muhammad of Ghur (d. 1206). Muhammad captured Delhi and extended his control nearly throughout north India. Like Mahmud, Muhammad and his generals considered Hindu and Buddhist religious statues nothing more than idols; Muslim troops destroyed them in vast numbers. Buddhist centers of worship and learning especially suffered. When Muhammad of Ghur fell to an assassin in 1206, one of his generals, the former slave Qutb-ud-din, seized the reins of power and established a government at Delhi, separate from the government in Afghanistan. This sultanate of Delhi lasted for three centuries, even though dynasties changed several times. (See the feature "Listening to the Past: To Commemorate Building a Well" on pages 334–335.)

**Hindu Temple** Medieval Hindu temples were frequently decorated with scenes of sexual passion. Here Vishnu caresses Lakshami at the Parshvinath Temple. *(Richard Ashworth/Robert Harding Picture Library)*

The North African Muslim world traveler Ibn Battuta (1304–1368) (see page 265), who journeyed through Africa and Asia from 1325 to 1354, served for several years as a judge at the court of one of the Delhi sultans. He praised the sultan for his insistence on the observance of ritual prayers and many acts of generosity to those in need, but he also considered the sultan overly violent. Here is just one of many examples he offered of how quick the sultan was to execute:

> *During the years of the famine, the Sultan had given orders to dig wells outside the capital, and have grain crops sown in those parts. He provided the cultivators with the seed, as well as with all that was necessary for cultivation in the way of money and supplies, and required them to cultivate these crops for the [royal] grain-store. When the jurist 'Afif al-Din heard of this, he said, "This crop will not produce what is hoped for." Some informer told the Sultan what he had said, so the Sultan jailed him, and said to him, "What reason have you to meddle with the government's business?" Some time later he released him, and as 'Afif al-Din went to his house he was met on the way by two friends of his, also jurists, who said to him, "Praise be to God for your release," to which our jurist replied, "Praise be to God who has delivered us from the evildoers." They then separated, but they had not reached their houses before this was reported to the Sultan, and he commanded all three to be fetched and brought before him. "Take out this fellow," he said, referring to 'Afif al-Din, "and cut off his head baldrickwise," that is, the head is cut off along with an arm and part of the chest, "and behead the other two." They said to him, "He deserves punishment, to be sure, for what he said, but in our case for what crime are you killing us?" He replied, "You heard what he said and did not disavow it, so you as good as agreed with it." So they were all put to death, God Most High have mercy on them.*[4]

A major accomplishment of the Delhi sultanate was holding off the Mongols. Chinggis Khan and his troops entered the Indus Valley in 1221 in pursuit of the shah of Khurasan. The sultan wisely kept out of the way, and when Chinggis left some troops in the area, the sultan made no attempt to challenge them. Two generations later, in 1299, a Mongol khan launched a campaign into India with 200,000 men, but the sultan of the time was able to defeat them. Two years later the Mongols returned and camped at Delhi for two months, but they eventually left without taking the sultan's fort. Another Mongol raid in 1306–1307 also was successfully repulsed.

Although the Turks by this time were highly cosmopolitan, they had retained their martial skills and understanding of steppe warfare. They were expert horsemen, and horses thrived in northwest India. The south and east of India, like the south of China, were less hospitable to raising horses and generally had to import them. In India's case, though, the climate of the south and east was well suited to elephants, which had been used as weapons of war in India since early times. Rulers in the northwest imported elephants from more tropical regions. The Delhi sultanate is said to have had as many as one thousand war elephants at its height. After one of his victories, the sultan arranged for his court to watch as thousands of Mongol prisoners were trampled to death by elephants.

During the fourteenth century, however, the Delhi sultanate was in decline and proved unable to ward off the armies of Tamerlane (see page 328), who took Delhi in 1398. Tamerlane's chronicler reported that when the troops drew up for battle outside Delhi, the sultanate had 10,000 horsemen, 20,000 foot soldiers, and 120 war elephants, with archers riding in the structures on the elephants' backs. Although Tamerlane's men were alarmed at the sight of the elephants, he dug trenches to trap them and also shot at their drivers. The sultan fled, leaving the city to surrender. Tamerlane took as booty all of the elephants, loading them with treasures seized from the city. Ruy Gonzalez de Clavijo, an ambassador from the king of Castile who arrived in Samarkand in 1403, was greatly impressed by these well-trained elephants. "When all the elephants together charged abreast, it seemed as though the solid earth itself shook at their onrush," he observed, noting that he thought each elephant was worth a thousand foot soldiers in battle.[5]

## Daily Life in Medieval India

For the overwhelming majority of people in medieval India, it did not matter much how large a territory was controlled by their king. Local institutions played a much larger role in their lives than the state. Guilds oversaw conditions of work and trade; local councils handled law and order at the town or village level; religious sects gave members a sense of belonging and identity, as did local castes.

Like peasant societies elsewhere, including China, Japan, and Southeast Asia, in India agricultural life ordinarily meant village life. The average farmer worked a small plot of land outside the village, aided by the efforts of the extended family. All the family members pooled their resources—human, animal, and material—under the direction of the head of the family. Joint struggles strengthened family solidarity.

The agricultural year began with spring plowing. The ancient plow, drawn by two oxen wearing yokes and collars, had an iron-tipped share and a handle with which the farmer guided it. Rice, the most important and popular grain, was sown at the beginning of the long rainy season. Beans, lentils, and peas were the farmer's friends, for they grew during the cold season and were harvested in the spring when fresh food was scarce. Cereal crops such as wheat, barley, and millet, grown twice a year, provided carbohydrates and other nutrients. Sugar cane was another important crop. Some families cultivated vegetables, spices, and flowers in their gardens. Village orchards kept people supplied with fruit, and the inhabitants of well-situated villages could eat their fill of fresh and dried fruit and sell the surplus at a nearby town.

Indian farmers raised livestock. Most highly valued were cattle. They were used for plowing and esteemed for their milk, hides, and horns, but Hindus did not slaughter them for meat. Like the Islamic and Jewish prohibition on the consumption of pork, the eating of beef was forbidden among Hindus.

Farmers fortunate enough to raise surpluses found ready markets in towns and cities. There they came into contact with merchants and traders, some of whom dealt in local commodities and others in East-West trade. Like their Roman counterparts, Indian merchants enjoyed a respectable place in society. There were huge profits to be made in foreign commerce. Daring Indian sailors founded new trading centers along the coasts of Southeast Asia and in the process spread Indian culture. Other Indian merchants specialized in the caravan trade that linked China, Iran, India, and the West.

Local craftsmen and tradesmen lived and worked in specific parts of a town or village. They were frequently organized into guilds, corresponding mostly with castes, with guild heads and guild rules. The textile industries were particularly well developed. Silk (which had entered India from China), muslin, calico, linen, wool, and cotton were produced in large quantities and traded throughout India. The cutting and polishing of precious stones was an industry associated more with foreign trade.

In the cities shops were open to the street; families lived on the floors above. The busiest tradesmen dealt in milk and cheese, oil, spices, and perfumes. Equally prominent but disreputable were tavern keepers. Indian taverns were haunts of criminals and con artists, and in the worst of them fighting was as common as drinking. In addition to these tradesmen and merchants, a host of peddlers shuffled through towns and villages selling everything from needles to freshly cut flowers.

Leatherworkers were economically important but were considered outcastes, as Indian religious and social customs condemned those who made a living handling the skins of dead animals. Masons, carpenters, and brickmakers were more highly respected. As in all agricultural societies, blacksmiths were essential, though of low caste.

Villages were often walled, as in north China and the Middle East, and the typical village was divided into quarters by two main streets that intersected at the center of the village. The streets were unpaved, and the rainy season turned them into a muddy soup. Cattle and sheep roamed as freely as people. Some families kept pets, such as cats or parrots. Half-wild mongooses served as effective protection against snakes. The pond outside the village served as its main source of water and also as a spawning ground for fish, birds, and mosquitoes. Women drawing water frequently encountered water buffalo wallowing in the shallows. After the farmers returned from the fields in the evening, the village gates were closed until morning.

In this period the caste system reached its mature form. Within the broad division into the four *varna* (strata) of Brahman, Kshatriya, Vaishya, and Shudra, the population was subdivided into numerous castes, or **jati.** Each caste had a proper occupation. In addition, its members married only within the caste and ate only with other members. Members of high-status castes feared pollution from contact with lower-caste individuals and had to undertake rituals of purification to remove the taint. Eventually Indian society comprised perhaps as many as three thousand castes. Each caste had its own governing body, which enforced the rules of the caste. Those incapable of living up to the rules were expelled, becoming outcastes. These unfortunates lived hard lives, performing tasks that others considered unclean or lowly.

The life of the well-to-do is described in the *Kamasutra* (Book on the Art of Love). Comfortable surroundings provided a place for men to enjoy poetry, painting, and music in the company of like-minded friends. Well-trained courtesans added to the pleasures of the wealthy, but it was also acceptable for a man to have several wives. Those who did were advised not to let one speak ill of the other and to try to keep each of them happy by taking them to gardens, giving them presents, telling them secrets, and loving them well.

For all members of Indian society, regardless of caste, marriage and the family were the focus of life. As in China, the joint family was under the authority of the eldest male, who might take several wives. The family affirmed its solidarity by the religious ritual of honoring its dead ancestors—a ritual that linked the living and the dead, much like ancestor worship in China. People commonly lived in extended families: grandparents, uncles and aunts, cousins, and nieces and nephews all lived together in the same house or compound.

Children were viewed as a great source of happiness. The poet Kalidasa depicts children as the greatest joy of their father's life:

*With their teeth half-shown in causeless laughter,*
*and their efforts at talking so sweetly uncertain,*
*when children ask to sit on his lap*
*a man is blessed, even by the dirt on their bodies.*[6]

Children in poor households worked as soon as they were able. Children in wealthier households faced the age-old irritations of reading, writing, and arithmetic. Less attention was paid to daughters, though in the most prosperous families they were often literate.

Boys of the three upper varnas underwent a religious initiation, the sacred thread investiture, symbolizing a second birth. Ideally, they then entered into a period of religious training at the hands of *gurus,* Brahman teachers with whom the boys boarded. In reality, relatively few went through this expensive education. Having completed their education, young men were ready to lead adult lives, the first and foremost step in which was marriage.

Women's situations seem to have deteriorated since the Vedic age. They could no longer own or inherit property and were barred from participating in many rituals. Because girls who had lost their virginity could seldom hope to find good husbands, and thus would become financial burdens and social disgraces to their families, daughters were customarily married before their first menstrual periods, with consummation delayed until the girl reached puberty.

As in China, in India women ideally spent their entire lives, from childhood to old age, under the authority of men. Indian law was blunt: "A woman is not independent, the males are her masters. . . . Their fathers protect them in childhood, their husbands protect them in youth, and their sons protect them in age; a woman is never fit for independence."[7]

**Two Indian Women**
Indian women not only applied cosmetics but also adorned themselves with a wide variety of jewelry. The scene here was engraved on the ivory top of a chest or stool. *(National Museum of Afghanistan, Kabul. Drawing by Frances Mortimer Price)*

Women of high rank rarely left the house, and then only with a chaperone. Wives' bonds with their husbands were so strong that it was felt a wife should have no life apart from her husband. Widows were expected to lead the hard life of the ascetic, sleeping on the ground; eating only one simple meal a day, without meat, wine, salt, or honey; wearing plain undyed clothes without jewelry; and shaving their heads. A widow was viewed as inauspicious to everyone but her children, and she did not attend family festivals. Among high-caste Hindus, a widow would be praised for throwing herself on her husband's funeral pyre. Buddhist sects objected to this practice, called **sati,** but some writers declared that by self-immolation a widow could expunge both her own and her husband's sins, so that both would enjoy eternal bliss in Heaven.

Within the home the position of a wife often depended chiefly on her own intelligence and strength of character. Wives were traditionally supposed to be humble, cheerful, and diligent even toward worthless husbands. As in other patriarchal societies, however, occasionally a woman ruled the roost. An Indian verse paints a vivid picture of what a henpecked husband could expect:

*But when she has him in her clutches*
*it's all housework and errands!*
*"Fetch a knife to cut this gourd!"*
*"Get me some fresh fruit!"*
*"We want wood to boil the greens,*
*and for a fire in the evening!"*
*"Now paint my feet!"*
*"Come and massage my back!"*
*So . . . resist the wiles of women,*
*avoid their friendship and company.*
*The little pleasure you get from them*
*will only lead you into trouble.*[8]

The most eagerly desired event was the birth of a child. Before consummating their marriage, newlyweds repeated traditional prayers for the wife to become pregnant immediately. While pregnant, the wife was nearly suffocated with affection and attention and rigorously circumscribed by religious ritual. At labor and birth, while the women of the household prepared for the birth, the husband performed rituals intended to guarantee an easy delivery and a healthy child. After the birth the parents performed rituals intended to bring the baby happiness, prosperity, and desirable intellectual, physical, and moral qualities. Infants were pampered until they reached the age of schooling and preparation for the adult world.

For women who did not want to accept the strictures of married life, the main way out was to join a Buddhist or Jain religious community.

## SOUTHEAST ASIA, TO 1400

Much as Roman culture spread to Europe and Chinese culture spread to Korea, Japan, and Vietnam, in the first millennium C.E. Indian learning, technology, and material culture spread to Southeast Asia, both mainland and insular.

Southeast Asia is a tropical region that is more like India than China, with temperatures hovering around 80°F and rain falling dependably throughout the year. The topography of mainland Southeast Asia is marked by several mountain ranges that extend from south China to the Bay of Bengal or the South China Sea (see Map 11.1). Between these north-south ranges are the valleys of the major rivers—the Irrawaddy and the Salween in Burma, the Chao Phraya in Thailand, and the Red and Mekong in Vietnam. It was easy for people to migrate south along these rivers but harder for them to cross the heavily forested mountains, which divided the region into areas that had limited contact with each other. The indigenous population was originally mostly Malay, but migrations over the centuries brought many other peoples, including speakers of Austro-Asiatic, Austronesian, and Sino-Tibetan-Burmese languages, some of whom moved on to the islands of the Pacific.

The northern part of modern Vietnam was under Chinese political control off and on from the second century B.C.E. to the tenth century C.E. (see pages 200–201), but for the rest of Southeast Asia, Indian influence was of much greater significance. The first state to appear in Southeast Asia, called **Funan** by Chinese visitors, had its capital in southern Vietnam. In the first to sixth centuries C.E. Funan extended its control over much of Indochina and the Malay Peninsula, so that it could dominate trade at the key point of the Isthmus of Kra. Merchants from northwest India would offload their goods and carry them across the narrow strip of land. The ports of Funan offered food and lodging to the merchants as they waited for the winds to shift to continue their voyages. Brahman priests and Buddhist monks from India settled along with the traders, serving the Indian population and attracting local converts. Rulers often invited Indian priests and monks to serve under them, using them as foreign experts knowledgeable about law, government, architecture, and other fields.

Sixth-century Chinese sources report that the Funan king lived in a multistory palace and the common people lived in houses built on piles with roofs of bamboo leaves. The king rode about on an elephant, but a more important means of transportation was narrow boats measuring up to ninety feet long. The people enjoyed both cockfighting and pig fighting. Instead of drawing water from wells, as the Chinese did, they made pools, from which dozens of nearby families would draw water. When in mourning, people would shave their hair and beards. They worshiped a variety of deities represented by bronze statues, some with multiple arms and heads.

After the decline of Funan, maritime trade continued to grow, and petty kingdoms appeared in many places. Indian traders frequently established small settlements, generally located on the coast and stretching from modern Thailand in the west to the Mekong Delta of modern Vietnam. Contact with the local populations led to intermarriage and the creation of hybrid cultures. Local rulers often adopted Indian customs and values, embraced Hinduism and Buddhism, and learned **Sanskrit,** India's classical literary language. Sanskrit gave different peoples a common mode of written expression, much as Chinese did in East Asia and Latin did in Europe.

Outside the courts of the rulers, native societies maintained their own cultural identities even when they assimilated various Indian customs. For instance, the Javanese took up the *Ramayana,* the Indian epic poem describing the deeds of the Vedic heroes, but they added to it native Javanese legends, thus creating a work that did not belong solely to either culture.

When the Indians entered mainland Southeast Asia, they encountered both long-settled peoples and migrants moving southward from the frontiers of China. As in other such extensive migrations, the newcomers fought one another as often as they fought the native populations. In 939 the Vietnamese finally became independent of China and extended their power southward along the coast of present-day Vietnam. The Thais had long lived in what is today southwest China and north Burma. In the eighth century the Thai tribes united in a confederacy and even expanded northward against Tang China. Like China, however, the Thai confederacy fell to the Mongols in 1253. Still farther west another tribal people, the Burmese, migrated to the area of modern Burma in the eighth century. They also established a state, which they ruled from their capital, Pagan, and came into contact with India and Sri Lanka.

The most important mainland state was the Khmer Empire of Cambodia, which controlled the heart of the

**Angkor Wat** The Khmer rulers built both Buddhist and Hindu temples, the most elaborate of which is the twelfth-century Angkor Wat, dedicated to the Hindu god Shiva and decorated with bas-relief carvings of Indian legends and Khmer history. *(Robert Harding Picture Library)*

region. The Khmers were indigenous to the area. Their empire, founded in 802, eventually extended south to the sea and the northeast Malay Peninsula. Indian influence was pervasive; the impressive temple complex at Angkor Wat was dedicated to the Hindu god Vishnu. Social organization, however, was not modeled on the Indian caste system but on indigenous traditions. A large part of the population was of servile status, many descended from non-Khmer mountain tribes defeated by the Khmers. Generally successful in a long series of wars with the Vietnamese, the Khmers reached the peak of their power in 1219 and then declined.

Far different from these land-based states was the maritime empire of **Srivijaya,** which from the sixth century on held the important Strait of Malacca, through which most of the sea traffic between China and India passed. Based on the island of Sumatra, the Srivijayan navy ruled the waters around Sumatra, Borneo, and Java, and the empire came to control the southern part of the Malay Peninsula as well. This state, held together as much by alliances as direct rule, was in many ways like the Gupta state in India, securing its prominence and binding its vassals/allies through its splendor and promise of riches through trade.

Much as the Korean and Japanese rulers adapted Chinese models, the Srivijayan rulers drew on Indian traditions to justify their rule and organize their state. The Sanskrit writing system was used for government documents, and Indians were often employed as priests, scribes, and administrators. Sanskrit also broke down the barriers raised by the many different native languages of the region. Indian mythology took hold, as did Indian architecture and sculpture. Kings and their courts, the first to embrace Indian culture, consciously spread it to their subjects. The Chinese Buddhist monk Yixing (d. 727) stopped at Srivijaya for six months in 671 on his way to India to study Sanskrit grammar and for four years on his return journey. He found there a thousand monks, some of whom helped him translate Sanskrit texts.

Borobudur, the most magnificent Buddhist temple complex, was begun around 780. This stone monument depicts the ten tiers of Buddhist cosmology. When pilgrims made the three-mile-long winding ascent, they passed numerous sculpted reliefs depicting the journey from ignorance to enlightenment.

After several centuries of prosperity, Srivijaya suffered a stunning blow in 1025. The Chola state in south India launched a large naval raid and captured the Srivijaya king and capital. Unable to hold their gains, the Indians retreated, but the Srivijaya Empire never regained its vigor. By the mid-thirteenth century the arrival of Chinese traders had further weakened the empire, and eventually it fell to local rivals.

Buddhism became progressively more dominant in Southeast Asia after 800. Mahayana Buddhism became important in Srivijaya, but Theravada Buddhism, closer to the original Buddhism of early India, became the dominant form in mainland Southeast Asia. Buddhist missionaries from India and Sri Lanka played a prominent role in these developments. Local converts continued the process by making pilgrimages to India and Sri Lanka to worship and to observe Indian life for themselves.

### The Spread of Indian Culture in Comparative Perspective

The social, cultural, and political systems developed in India, China, and Rome all had enormous impact on neighboring peoples whose cultures were originally not as advanced. Some of the mechanisms for cultural spread were similar in all three cases, but differences were important as well.

In the case of Rome and both Han and Tang China, strong states came to rule directly outlying regions, bringing their civilizations with them. India's states, even its largest empires, such as the Mauryan and Gupta, did not have comparable centralized bureaucracies administered by professional officeholders. Outlying areas tended to be in the hands of local lords who had consented to recognize the overlordship of the stronger state, and most of the time India was politically divided.

The expansion of Indian culture into Southeast Asia thus came not from conquest and extending direct political control, but from the extension of trading networks, with missionaries following along. This made it closer to the way Japan adopted features of Chinese culture, often through the intermediary of Korea. In both cases, the cultural exchange was largely voluntary, as the Japanese or Southeast Asians sought to adopt more up-to-date technologies (such as writing) or were persuaded of the truth of religious ideas they learned from foreigners.

## CENTRAL ASIA, TO 1400

One experience Rome, India, China, and the Middle East all shared was conflict with **nomads** who came from the very broad region referred to as Central Asia. This broad region was dominated by the arid **grasslands** (called the steppe) that stretched from Hungary, through southern Russia and across Central Asia (today's Tajikistan, Turkmenistan, Kazakhstan, Kyrgyzstan, and Uzbekistan), to Mongolia and parts of north China. The grasslands are easily crossed by horses but not suited to crop agriculture. They can support only a thin population of nomadic herders.

This common ecology also led to common forms of social and political organization based on families, clans, tribes, and sometimes tribal confederations. In their search for water and good pastures, nomadic groups often came into conflict with other nomadic groups pursuing the same resources, which the two would then fight over, as there was normally no higher political authority able to settle differences of this sort. Groups on the losing end, especially if they were small, faced the threat of extermination or slavery, which prompted them to make alliances with other groups or move far away. Thus, over the centuries, the ethnic groups living in particular sections of the grasslands would change. Groups on the winning end of intertribal conflicts could exact tribute from those they defeated, sometimes so much that they could devote themselves entirely to war, leaving to their slaves and vassals the work of tending herds.

To get the products of the agricultural societies nearby, especially grain, woven textiles, iron, tea, and wood, nomadic herders would trade their own products, such as horses and furs. When trade was difficult, they would turn to raiding to seize what they needed. Much of the time nomadic herders raided other nomads, but relatively nearby agricultural settlements also were often targets. The nomads' skill as horsemen and archers made it difficult for farmers or townsmen to oppose them. It was largely to defend against the raids of the Xiongnu nomads, for example, that the Chinese built the Great Wall.

Political organization among nomadic herders was generally very simple. Clans had chiefs, as did tribes (which were coalitions of clans, often related to each other). Leadership within a group was based on military prowess and often settled by fighting. Occasionally a charismatic leader would emerge who was able to extend alliances to form confederations of tribes. From the point of view of the settled societies, which have left most of the records about these nomadic groups, large confederations were much more of a threat, since they could plan coordinated attacks on cities and towns. Large confederations rarely lasted more than a century or so, however, and when they broke up, tribes again spent much of their time fighting with each other, relieving some of the pressure on their settled neighbors.

The three most wide-ranging and successful confederations were those of the Xiongnu/Huns, who emerged in the third century B.C.E. in the area near China; the Turks, who had their origins in the same area in the fourth and fifth centuries C.E.; and the Mongols, who did not become important until the late twelfth century. In all three cases, the entire grasslands area was eventually swept up in the movement of peoples and armies.

The might of the Xiongnu caused rival groups to move west, resulting in the arrival of the Shakas and Kushans in Afghanistan and north India and later the Huns in Europe. The Turks, after their heyday as a power in the east in the seventh century, broke up into several rival groups, some of whom moved west. From the mid-eighth to the mid-tenth century Turks were living on the borders of Abbasid Persia. By the mid- to late tenth century many were serving in the Abbasid armies. By the eleventh century they had gained the upper hand, and in 1055 the Abbasid caliph recognized the Turk Tughril Beg as the sultan (see page 252). From there Turkish power was extended into Syria, Palestine, and other parts of the realm. (Asia Minor is now called Turkey because Turks migrated there by the thousands over several centuries.) Another Turkish confederation had established itself in Afghanistan and extended its control into north India. Thus by the twelfth century separate groups of Turks controlled much of Central Asia and the adjoining lands from Syria to north India and into Chinese Turkestan, then occupied by Uighur Turks. There was, however, no single political unit uniting all of these Turkish forces. Such a unified empire was put together briefly by the next major power on the grasslands, the Mongols.

In Mongolia in the twelfth century ambitious Mongols did not aspire to match the Turks or other groups that had migrated west, but the groups that had stayed in the east had mastered ways to extract resources from China, the largest and richest country in the region. In the tenth and eleventh centuries the Khitans had accomplished this; in the twelfth century the Jurchens had overthrown the Khitans and extended their reach even deeper into China. The Khitans and Jurchens formed hybrid nomadic-urban states, with northern sections where tribesmen continued to live in the traditional way, and southern sections politically controlled by the non-Chinese rulers but settled largely by Chinese (in much the same fashion as the Turks in north India). The Khitans and Jurchens had scripts created to record their languages and adopted many Chinese governing practices. They built cities in pastoral areas as centers of consumption and trade. In both cases, their elite became culturally dual, adept in Chinese ways as well as their own traditions.

The Mongols lived north of these hybrid nomadic-settled societies and maintained their traditional ways. Chinese, Persian, and European observers have all left descriptions of the daily life of the Mongols, which they found strikingly different from their own. The daily life of the peasants of China, India, Vietnam, and Japan had much more in common with each other than with the Mongol pastoralists. Before considering the military conquests of the Mongols, it is useful to look more closely at their way of life.

## Daily Life of the Mongols

Before their great conquests the Mongols did not have cities, towns, or villages. Rather, they moved with their animals between winter and summer pastures. They had to keep their belongings to a minimum because they had to be able to pack up and move everything they owned when it was time to move.

Because they needed to be able to move their settlements, the Mongols lived in portable tents called **yurts** rather than in houses. The yurts, about twelve to fifteen feet in diameter, were constructed of light wooden frames covered by layers of wool felt, greased to make them waterproof. The yurts were always round, since this shape held up better against the strong winds that blew across the treeless grasslands. The yurts could be dismantled and loaded onto pack animals or carts in a short time. The floor of the yurt would be covered with dried grass or straw, then felt, skins, or rugs. In the center would be the hearth, directly under the smoke hole. Usually the yurt was set up with the entrance facing south. The master's bed would be on the north. Goat horns would be attached to the frame of the yurt and used as hooks to hang joints of meat, cooking utensils, bows, quivers of arrows, and the like. A group of families traveling together would set up their yurts in a circle open to the south and draw up their wagons in a circle around the yurts for protection.

For food the Mongols ate mostly animal products. The most common meat was mutton, supplemented with wild game. The Mongols milked sheep, goats, cows, and horses and made cheese and fermented alcoholic drinks from the milk. When grain or vegetables could be obtained through trade with agricultural regions, they were added to the diet. Wood was scarce, so the common fuel for the cook fires was dried animal dung or grasses. Without granaries to store food for years of famine, the Mongols' survival was endangered whenever weather or diseases of their animals threatened their food supply.

Because of the intense cold of the grasslands in the winter, the Mongols made much use of furs and skins for clothing. Both men and women usually wore silk trousers and tunics (the silk obtained from China). Over this they wore robes of fur, for the very coldest times in two layers—an inner layer with the hair on the inside and an outer layer with the hair on the outside. Hats were of felt or fur, boots of felt or leather. Women's clothing differed from men's in that it had more pleats and tucks to make it more formfitting. Men wore leather belts to which their bows and quivers could be attached. Women of high rank wore elaborate headdresses decorated with feathers.

Mongol women had to work very hard and had to be able to care for the animals when the men were away hunting or fighting. They normally drove the carts and set up and dismantled the yurts. They were also the ones who milked the sheep, goats, and cows and made the butter and cheese. In addition, they made the felt, prepared the skins, and sewed the clothes. Because water was scarce, clothes were not washed with water, nor were dishes. Women, like men, had to be expert riders, and many also learned to shoot. Women participated actively in family decisions, especially as wives and mothers. In *The Secret History of the Mongols*, a work written in Mongolian in the mid-thirteenth century, Chinggis Khan's mother and wife frequently make impassioned speeches on the importance of family loyalty.

Mongol men kept as busy as the women. They made carts and wagons and the frames for the yurts. They also made harnesses for the horses and oxen, leather saddles, and the equipment needed for hunting and war, such as bows and arrows. Men also had charge of the horses, and they milked the mares. Young horses were allowed to run wild until it was time to break them in. Catching them took great skill in the use of a long springy pole with a noose at the end. One specialist among the nomads was

**Mongol Yurt** A Chinese artist has captured the essential features of a Mongol yurt to illustrate the story of a Chinese woman who married a nomad. *(The Metropolitan Museum of Art, Gift of The Dillon Fund, 1973 [1973.120.3]. Photograph © 1994 The Metropolitan Museum of Art)*

the blacksmith, who made stirrups, knives, and other metal tools.

Kinship underlay most social relationships. Normally each family occupied a yurt, and groups of families camping together were usually related along the male line (brothers, uncles and nephews, and so on). More distant patrilineal relatives were recognized as members of the same clan and could call on each other for aid. People from the same clan could not marry each other, so clans had to cooperate to provide brides. When a woman's husband died, she would be inherited by another male in the family, such as her husband's brother or his son by another woman. Tribes were groups of clans, often distantly related. Both clans and tribes had recognized chiefs who would make decisions on where to graze and when to retaliate against another tribe that had stolen animals or people. Women were sometimes abducted for brides. When tribes stole men from each other, they normally made them into slaves, and slaves were forced to do much of the heavy work. They would not necessarily remain slaves their entire lives, however, as their original tribes might be able to recapture them or make exchanges for them, or their masters might free them.

Even though population was sparse in the regions where the Mongols lived, conflict over resources was endemic, and each camp had to be on the alert for attacks. Defending against attacks and retaliating against raids was as much a part of the Mongols' daily life as caring for their herds and trading with nearby settlements.

Mongol children learned to ride at a young age, first riding on goats. The horses they later rode were short and stocky, almost like ponies, but nimble and able to endure long journeys and bitter cold. Even in the winter they survived by grazing, foraging beneath the snow. The prime weapon boys had to learn to use was the compound bow, which had a pull of about 160 pounds and a range of more than 200 yards. Other commonly used weapons were small battle-axes and lances fitted with hooks to pull enemies off their saddles.

From their teenage years Mongol men participated in battles, and among the Mongols courage in battle was essential to male self-esteem. Hunting was a common form of military training. Each year there would be one big hunt when mounted hunters would form a vast ring perhaps ten or more miles in circumference, then gradually shrink it down, trapping all the animals before killing them. On military campaigns a Mongol soldier had to be able to ride for days without stopping to cook food; he had to carry a supply of dried milk curd and cured meat, which could be supplemented by blood let from the neck of his horse. When time permitted, the soldiers would pause to hunt, adding to their food dogs, wolves, foxes, mice, and rats.

A common specialist among the Mongols was the shaman, a religious expert able to communicate with the gods. The high god of the Mongols was Heaven, but they recognized many other gods as well. Some groups of Mongols, especially those closer to settled communities, converted to Buddhism, Nestorian Christianity, or Manichaeism.

## Chinggis Khan and the Creation of the Mongol Empire

In the mid-twelfth century, the Mongols were just one of many peoples in the eastern grasslands, neither particularly numerous nor especially advanced. Why did the Mongols suddenly emerge on the historical stage? One explanation is ecological. A drop in the mean annual temperature created a subsistence crisis. As pastures shrank, the Mongols and other nomads had to get more of their food from the agricultural world.

But the Mongols ended up getting much more than just enough to eat. A second reason for their sudden rise has to do with the appearance of a single individual, the brilliant but utterly ruthless Temujin (r. ca 1162–1227), later called Chinggis.

Chinggis's early career was recorded in *The Secret History of the Mongols*, written within a few decades of his death in 1227. In Chinggis's youth the Mongol tribes were in competition with the Tartar tribes, a situation encouraged by the strongest power in the region, the Jurchens. Chinggis's father had built up a modest following and had arranged for his future marriage to the daughter of a more powerful Mongol leader. When Chinggis's father was poisoned by a rival, his followers, not ready to follow a boy of twelve, drifted away, leaving Chinggis and his mother and brothers in a vulnerable position. In 1182 Chinggis was captured and carried in a cage to a rival's camp. After a daring midnight escape, he led his followers to join a stronger chieftain whom his father had once aided. With the chieftain's help, Chinggis began avenging the insults he had received.

As Chinggis subdued the Tartars, Kereyids, Naimans, Merkids, and other Mongol and Turkish tribes, he built up an army of loyal followers. He mastered the art of winning allies through displays of personal courage in battle and generosity to his followers. He also was willing to turn against former allies who proved troublesome. To those who opposed him, he could be merciless. He once asserted that nothing gave more pleasure than massacring one's enemies, seizing their horses and cattle, and

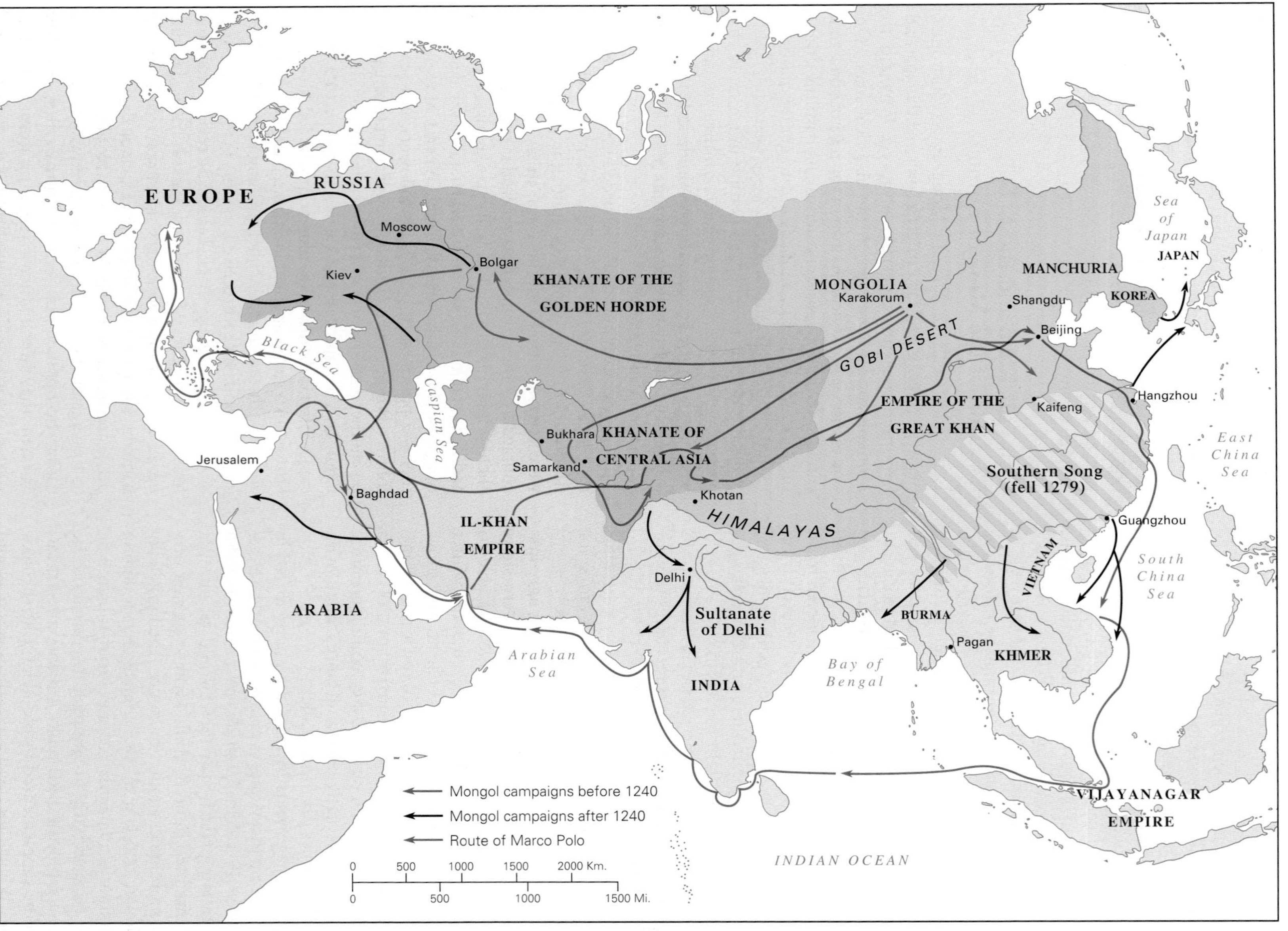


**MAP 11.2 The Mongol Empire** The creation of the vast Mongol Empire facilitated communication across Eurasia and led to both the spread of deadly plagues and the transfer of technical and scientific knowledge. After the death of Chinggis in 1227, the empire was divided into four khanates, ruled by different lines of his successors. In the 1270s, the Mongols conquered southern China, but most of their subsequent campaigns did not lead to further territorial gains.

ravishing their women. Sometimes Chinggis would kill all the men in a defeated tribe to prevent any later vendettas. At other times he would take them on as soldiers in his own armies. Courage impressed him. One of his leading generals, Jebe, first attracted his attention when he held his ground against overwhelming opposition and shot Chinggis's horse out from under him.

In 1206, at a great gathering of tribal leaders, Chinggis was proclaimed the **Great Khan.** He decreed that Mongol, until then an unwritten language, be written down in a script used by the Uighur Turks. With this script a record was made of the Mongol laws and customs, ranging from the rules for the annual hunt to punishments of death for robbery and adultery. Another measure adopted at this assembly was a postal relay system to send messages rapidly by mounted courier.

With the tribes of Mongolia united, the energies previously devoted to infighting and vendettas were redirected to exacting tribute from the settled populations nearby, starting with the Jurchen (Jin) state that extended into north China (see Map 11.2). In this Chinggis was following the precedent of the Jurchens, who had defeated the Khitans to get access to China's wealth a century earlier.

After Chinggis subjugated a city, he would send envoys to cities farther out to demand submission and threaten destruction. Those who opened their city gates and submitted without fighting could become allies and retain local power, but those who resisted faced the prospect of mass slaughter. He despised city dwellers and would sometimes use them as living shields in the next battle. After the Mongol armies swept across north China in 1212–1213, ninety-odd cities lay in rubble. Beijing, captured in 1215, burned for more than a month. Not surprisingly many governors of cities and rulers of small states hastened to offer submission.

Chinggis preferred conquest to administration and did not stay in north China to set up an administrative structure like that used by earlier nomadic conquerors. He left that to subordinates and turned his attention westward, to Central Asia and Persia, then in the hands of the Turks. In 1218 Chinggis proposed to the Khwarazm shah of Persia that he accept Mongol overlordship and establish trade relations. The shah, to show his determination to resist, ordered the envoy and the merchants who had accompanied him killed. The next year Chinggis led an army of 100,000 soldiers west to retaliate. Mongol forces not only destroyed the shah's army but also pursued the shah to an island in the Caspian Sea, where he died. To complete the conquest, Chinggis sacked one Persian city after another, demolishing buildings and massacring hundreds of thousands of people. The irrigation systems that were needed for agriculture in this dry region were destroyed as well.

On his return from Central Asia in 1226, Chinggis turned his attention to the Tanguts, who ruled the Xia state in northwest China. They had earlier declined to join forces with the Mongols and now suffered the consequences. The following years, during the siege of their capital, Chinggis died of illness. Before he died, he instructed his sons not to fall out among themselves but instead to divide the spoils.

## Chinggis's Successors

Although Mongol tribal leaders traditionally had had to win their positions, after Chinggis died the empire was divided into four **khanates,** with one of the lines of his descendants taking charge of each one. Chinggis's third son, Ogodei, became Great Khan, and he directed the next round of invasions.

In 1237 representatives of all four lines led 150,000 Mongol, Turkish, and Persian troops into Europe. During the next five years they gained control of Moscow and Kievan Russia and looted cities in Poland and Hungary. They were poised to attack deeper into Europe when they learned of the death of Ogodei in 1241. To participate in the election of a new khan, the army returned to the Mongols' new capital city, Karakorum.

Once Ogodei's son was certified as his successor, the Mongols turned their attention to Persia and the Middle East. In 1256 a Mongol army took northwest Iran, then pushed on to the Abbasid capital of Baghdad. When it fell in 1258, the last Abbasid caliph was murdered, and the population was put to the sword. The Mongol onslaught was successfully resisted, however, by both the Delhi sultanate (see page 313) and the Mamluk rulers in Egypt (see page 282).

Under Chinggis's grandson Khubilai (r. 1260–1294) the Mongols completed their conquest of Korea and China. Mongol troops poured across the Yalu River in 1231, but Korea did not fully surrender until 1258. By then the Mongols were ready to concentrate on China. South China had never been captured by non-Chinese, in large part because horses were of no strategic advantage in a land of rivers and canals. Perhaps because they were entering a very different type of terrain, the Mongols proceeded deliberately. First they surrounded the Song empire by taking its westernmost province in 1252, destroying the Nanzhao kingdom in modern Yunnan in 1254, and then continuing south and taking Annam (northern Vietnam) in 1257. A surrendered

## MONGOL CONQUESTS

| | |
|---|---|
| 1206 | Chinggis made Great Khan |
| 1215 | Fall of Beijing (Jurchens) |
| 1220 | Fall of Bukhara and Samarkand in Central Asia |
| 1227 | Death of Chinggis |
| 1237–1241 | Raids into eastern Europe |
| 1257 | Conquest of Annam (northern Vietnam) |
| 1258 | Conquest of Abassid capital of Baghdad<br>Conquest of Korea |
| 1260 | Accession of Khubilai |
| 1274 | First attempt at invading Japan |
| 1276 | Surrender of Song Dynasty (China) |
| 1281 | Second attempt at invading Japan |
| 1293 | Expedition to Java |
| **mid-14th century** | Decline of Mongol power; ouster or absorption |

Song commander advised them to build a navy to attack the great Song cities located on rivers. During the five-year siege of a central Chinese river port, both sides used thousands of boats and tens of thousands of troops. The Mongols employed experts in naval and siege warfare from all over their empire—Chinese, Korean, Jurchen, Uighur, and Persian. Catapults designed by Muslim engineers launched a barrage of rocks weighing up to a hundred pounds each. During their advance toward the Chinese capital of Hangzhou, the Mongols ordered the total slaughter of the people of the major city of Changzhou, and in 1276 the Chinese empress dowager surrendered in hopes of sparing the people of the capital a similar fate.

Having overrun China and Korea, Khubilai turned his eyes toward Japan. In 1274 a force of 30,000 soldiers and support personnel sailed from Korea to Japan. In 1281 a combined Mongol and Chinese fleet of about 150,000 made a second attempt to conquer Japan. On both occasions the Mongols managed to land but were beaten back by Japanese samurai armies. The decisive factor was two fierce storms that destroyed the Mongol fleets. The Italian traveler Marco Polo (see page 330) recounted what he heard about one invasion force:

> *It happened, after some time, that a north wind began to blow with great force, and the ships of the Tartars, which lay near the shore of the island, were driven foul of each other. . . . The gale, however, increased to so violent a degree that a number of vessels foundered. The people belonging to them, by floating upon the pieces of the wreck, saved themselves upon an island lying about four miles from the coast of Zipangu [Japan].*[9]

The Japanese claimed that they had been saved by the *kamikaze,* the "divine wind" (which later lent its name to the thousands of Japanese aviators who crashed their airplanes into American warships during World War II).

A decade later, in 1293, Khubilai tried sending a fleet to the islands of Southeast Asia, including Java, but it met with no more success than the fleets sent to Japan.

Why were the Mongols so successful against so many different types of enemies? Even though their population was tiny compared to that of the large agricultural

**Gold-decorated Saddle** The Mongols, like earlier nomads, prized fine metalwork. The gold panels that decorate this saddle were found in the tomb of a Mongol girl of about eighteen. The central motif of the front arch is a reclining deer; surrounding it are peonies. *(Collection of Inner Mongolia Museum, Huhehaote)*

societies they conquered, their tactics, their weapons, and their organization all gave them advantages. Like other nomads before them, they were superb horsemen and excellent archers. Their horses were extremely nimble, able to change direction quickly, thus allowing the Mongols to maneuver easily and ride through infantry forces armed with swords, lances, and javelins. Usually the only armies that could stand up well against the Mongols were other nomadic ones.

Marco Polo left a vivid description of the Mongol soldiers' endurance and military skill:

*They are brave in battle, almost to desperation, setting little value upon their lives, and exposing themselves without hesitation to all manner of danger. Their disposition is cruel. They are capable of supporting every kind of privation, and when there is a necessity for it, can live for a month on the milk of their mares, and upon such wild animals as they may chance to catch. The men are habituated to remain on horseback during two days and two nights, without dismounting, sleeping in that situation whilst their horses graze. No people on earth can surpass them in fortitude under difficulties, nor show greater patience under wants of every kind.*[10]

The Mongols were also open to new military technologies and did not insist on fighting in their traditional ways. To attack walled cities, they learned how to use catapults and other engines of war. At first they employed Chinese catapults, but when they later learned that those used by the Turks in Afghanistan were half again as powerful, they quickly adopted the better model. The Mongols also used exploding arrows and gunpowder projectiles developed by the Chinese.

Because of his early experiences with intertribal feuding, Chinggis mistrusted traditional Mongol tribal loyalties, and as he fashioned a new army, he gave it a new, nontribal structure. Chinggis also created an elite bodyguard of ten thousand sons and brothers of commanders, which served directly under him. Chinggis allowed commanders to pass their posts to their sons, but he could remove them at will. Marco Polo explained the decimal hierarchy of his armies this way:

*When one of the great Tartar chiefs proceeds on an expedition, he puts himself at the head of an army of a hundred thousand horse, and organizes them in the following manner. He appoints an officer to the command of every ten men, and others to command a hundred, a thousand, and ten thousand men, respectively. Thus ten of the officers commanding ten men take their orders from him who commands a hundred; of these, each ten, from him who commands a thousand; and each ten of these latter, from him who commands ten thousand. By this arrangement each officer has only to attend to the management of ten men or ten bodies of men.*[11]

The Mongols also made good use of intelligence and tried to exploit internal divisions in the countries they attacked. Thus, when attacking the Jurchens in north China, they appealed to the Khitans, who had been defeated by the Jurchens a century earlier, to join them. In Syria they exploited the resentment of Christians against their Muslim rulers.

## The Mongols as Rulers

The success of the Mongols in ruling vast territories was due in large part to their willingness to incorporate other ethnic groups into their armies and governments. Whatever their nationality, those who served the Mongols loyally were rewarded and given important posts. (See the feature "Individuals in Society: Mukhali.") Uighurs, Tibetans, Persians, Chinese, and Russians came to hold powerful positions in the Mongol government. Chinese helped breach the walls of Baghdad in the 1250s, and Muslims operated the catapults that helped reduce Chinese cities in the 1270s.

Since, in Mongol eyes, the purpose of fighting was to gain riches, they regularly would loot the settlements they conquered, taking whatever they wanted, including the residents. Land would be granted to military commanders, nobles, and army units, to be governed and exploited as the recipients wished. Those who had worked on the land would be given to them as serfs. The Mongols built a capital city in modern Mongolia, called Karakorum, and to bring it up to the level of the cities they conquered, they transported skilled workers from those cities. For instance, after Bukhara and Samarkand were captured in 1219–1220, some thirty thousand artisans were seized and transported to Mongolia. Sometimes these slaves gradually improved their status. A French goldsmith working in Budapest named Guillaume Boucher was captured by the Mongols in 1242 and taken to Karakorum, where he lived for at least the next fifteen years. He gradually won favor and was put in charge of fifty workers to make gold and silver vessels for the Mongol court.

The traditional nomad disdain for farmers led some commanders to suggest turning north China into a gigantic pasture after it was conquered. In time, though, the Mongols came to realize that simply appropriating the wealth and human resources of the settled lands was not as good as extracting regular revenue from them. A Sinified Khitan who had been working for the Jurchens in China explained to the Mongols that collecting taxes from farmers would be highly profitable: they could extract a revenue of 500,000 ounces of silver, 80,000 bolts of silk, and more than 20,000 tons of grain from the region by taxing it. The Mongols gave this a try, but soon political rivals convinced the khan that he would gain even more by letting Central Asian Muslim merchants bid against each other for licenses to collect taxes any way they could, a system called **tax-farming.** Ordinary Chinese found this method of tax collecting much more oppressive than traditional Chinese methods, since there was little to keep the tax collectors from seizing everything they could.

By the second half of the thirteenth century there was no longer a genuine pan-Asian Mongol Empire. Much of Asia was in the hands of Mongol successor states, but these were generally hostile to each other. Khubilai was often at war with the khanate of Central Asia, then held by his cousin Khaidu, and he had little contact with the khanate of the Golden Horde in south Russia. The Mongols adapted their methods of government to the existing traditions of each place they ruled, and the regions now went their separate ways.

In China the Mongols resisted assimilation and purposely avoided many Chinese social and political practices. The rulers conducted their business in the Mongol language and spent their summers in Mongolia. Khubilai discouraged Mongols from marrying Chinese and took only Mongol women into the palace. Some Mongol princes preferred to live in yurts erected on the palace grounds rather than in the grand palaces constructed at Beijing. Chinese were treated as legally inferior not only to the Mongols but also to all other non-Chinese.

In Central Asia, Persia, and Russia the Mongols tended to merge with the Turkish nomads already there and like them converted to Islam. Russia in the thirteenth century was not a strongly centralized state, and the Mongols were satisfied to see Russian princes and lords continue to rule their territories as long as they turned over adequate tribute (which, of course, added to the burden on peasants). The city of Moscow became the center of Mongol tribute collection and grew in importance at the expense of Kiev. In the Middle East the Mongol Il-khans were more active as rulers, again continuing the traditions of the caliphate. In Mongolia itself Mongol traditions were maintained, though more and more of the

# INDIVIDUALS IN SOCIETY

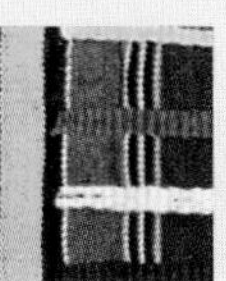

## MUKHALI

The Mongol conquests were carried out in large part by those who had been vanquished by Chinggis. If members of defeated tribes proved their loyalty to Chinggis, they could rise to the highest ranks in his organization.

Mukhali was born in 1170 into the "White" clan of the Jalair tribe, hereditary serfs of the Jurkins, a Mongol tribe. When the Jurkins were defeated by Chinggis in 1197, Mukhali's father gave him and his brother to Chinggis as personal hereditary slaves.

Within a couple of years Mukhali was leading campaigns. In the final battle against the Kereyids, Mukhali led his picked troops into the camp of Chinggis's former patron, the Ong Khan. At the assembly of 1206, when Chinggis was made Great Khan, Mukhali was appointed myriarch of the left wing of the newly reorganized army and granted immunity for up to nine breaches of the law. The first thousand-man corps under his command was made up of his own Jalair tribesmen, who were given to him as his personal property.

In his capacity as commander in chief of the left wing, Mukhali played a leading role in the 1211 campaigns against the Jurchens. He was as ruthless as Chinggis. In 1213, when Chinggis was attacking north China, Mukhali seized the town of Mizhou and ordered all the inhabitants massacred. Perhaps not surprisingly, several Chinese generals serving the Jurchens soon defected to him. In his campaigns in Liaodong in 1214, Mukhali had under his campaign a newly formed Khitan-Chinese army and a special corps of twelve thousand Chinese auxiliary troops.

In 1217 Mukhali was back in Chinggis's camp in Mongolia, where he was given new honors, including the hereditary title of prince, a golden seal, and a white standard with nine tails and a black crescent in the middle. In addition, he was appointed commander in chief of operations in north China. Of the sixty-two thousand troops under his command, about twenty-three thousand were Mongols or Onguts, the rest Chinese and Khitan auxiliaries.

Mukhali spent the next six years of his life campaigning in north China. He regularly reappointed defeated generals and officials and listened to their advice. An envoy from the Chinese who met him in 1221–1222 described him as very tall with curly whiskers and a dark complexion. He was also reported to have had four Mongol and four Jurchen secondary wives.

*Mongol soldiers, as depicted in a Persian history of the Mongols.*
(Bibliothèque nationale de France)

*The Secret History of the Mongols,* a work written in Mongolian in the mid-thirteenth century, portrays Mukhali as one of Chinggis's closest followers, one of the few men able to exert any real influence on him. For instance, when Chinggis was getting ready to begin his campaign against the shah of Khwarazm in Central Asia, one of his wives urged him first to name his heir. When Chinggis asked his first son, Jochi, what he thought of the idea, before he could speak the second son, Chagadai, called Jochi a bastard son of a Merkid, and the two brothers were soon wrestling. At this tense moment it was Mukhali who pulled the brothers apart.

A soldier to the end, Mukhali was still leading troops into battle at age fifty-three, when he died in north China in 1223.

### QUESTIONS FOR ANALYSIS

1. What does Mukhali's life indicate about the nature of slavery in Mongol society?
2. Why would Mukhali have incorporated defeated Jurchens and Chinese into his armies?

**Puppet Show** The performing arts, including both opera and puppet shows, flourished in Chinese cities during Mongol occupation. In this fourteenth-century anonymous painting, men, women, and children are watching a puppet show. Among the most popular types of stories for the theater were farces, love stories, moral tales, and war stories. *(Zhu Yu [Junbi], Chinese, 1293–1365,* Street Scenes in Times of Peace. *Handscroll, ink and colors on paper, 26 × 790 cm. Kate S. Buckingham Fund, 1952.8 [detail]. Photograph © 1988, The Art Institute of Chicago)*

Mongols converted to Lamaist Buddhism (the form of Buddhism common in Tibet).

Mongol control in each of the khanates lasted about a century. In the mid-fourteenth century the Mongol dynasty in China deteriorated into civil war, and in the 1360s the Mongols withdrew back to Mongolia. There was a similar loss of Mongol power in Persia and Central Asia. Only on the south Russian steppe was the Golden Horde able to maintain its hold for another century. As Mongol rule in Central Asia declined, a new conqueror emerged, known as Tamerlane (Timur the Lame). Not a nomad but a highly civilized Turkish noble, Tamerlane in the 1360s struck out from his base in Samarkand into Persia, north India, southern Russia, and beyond. His armies used the terror tactics that the Mongols had perfected, massacring the citizens of cities that resisted. With his death in 1405, however, Tamerlane's empire fell apart.

## EAST-WEST COMMUNICATION DURING THE MONGOL ERA

The Mongols did more to encourage the movement of people and goods across Eurasia than any earlier political entity. They had never looked down on merchants, the way the elites of many traditional states did, and they welcomed the arrival of merchants from distant lands. Even when different groups of Mongols were fighting among themselves, they usually allowed caravans to pass unharassed.

The Mongol practice of transporting skilled people from the lands they conquered also brought people into contact with each other in new ways. Besides those forced to move, the Mongols recruited administrators from all over. Chinese, Persians, and Arabs served the Mongols, and the Mongols often sent them far from home. Especially prominent were the Uighur Turks of Chinese Central Asia, whose familiarity with Chinese civilization and fluency in Turkish were extremely valuable in facilitating communication. Literate Uighurs provided many of the clerks and administrators running the Mongol administration.

One of the most interesting of those who served the Mongols was Rashid al-Din (ca 1247–1318). A Jew from Persia and the son of an apothecary, Rashid al-Din converted to Islam at the age of thirty and entered the service of the Mongol khan of Persia as a physician. He rose in government service, traveling widely, and eventually became prime minister. Rashid al-Din became friends with the ambassador from China, and together they arranged for translations of Chinese works on medicine, agronomy, and statecraft. He had ideas on economic management that he communicated to Mongol officials in Central Asia and China. Aware of the great differences between cultures, he believed that the Mongols should try to rule in accord with the moral principles of the majority in each land. On that basis he convinced the Mongol khan of Persia to convert to Islam. Rashid al-Din undertook to explain the great variety of cultures by writing a history of the world that was much more comprehensive than any previously written. The parts on Europe were based on information he obtained from European

**Depictions of Europeans** The Mongol Empire, by facilitating travel across Asia, increased knowledge of faraway lands. Rashid al-Din's *History of the World* included a history of the Franks, illustrated here with images of Western popes (*left*) conferring with Byzantine emperors (*right*). *(Topkapi Saray Museum, Ms.H.1653, fol 303)*

**Marco Polo Meeting Khubilai Khan** Illustrated European versions of Marco Polo's book show that it was just as difficult for Europeans to imagine what Mongols looked like as it was for Persians to imagine Europeans. *(Bibliothèque nationale de France)*

monks. The sections on China seem to be based on Chinese informants and perhaps Chinese Buddhist narratives. This book was often richly illustrated, with depictions of Europeans based on European paintings and depictions of Chinese based on Chinese paintings, leading to the spread of artistic styles as well.

The Mongols were remarkably open to religious experts from all the lands they encountered. Khubilai, for instance, welcomed Buddhist, Daoist, Islamic, and Christian clergymen to his court and gave tax exemptions to clerics of all religions. More Europeans made their way as far as Mongolia and China in the Mongol period than ever before. Popes and kings sent envoys to the Mongol court in the hope of enlisting the Mongols on their side in their long-standing conflict with Muslim forces over the Holy Land. These and other European visitors were especially interested in finding Christians who had been cut off from the West by the spread of Islam, and in fact there were considerable numbers of Nestorian Christians in Central Asia. Those who left written records of their trips often mention meeting other Europeans in China or Mongolia. There were enough Europeans in Beijing to build a cathedral and appoint a bishop.

The most famous European visitor to the Mongol lands was Marco Polo. The Western world learned of the wealth and sophistication of China when Marco Polo returned from a long sojourn in Asia to dictate his famous *Travels.* Marco Polo described his warm reception by Khubilai and all the lands under the khan's control. He was enormously impressed with the Mongol ruler and awed by the wealth and splendor of Chinese cities. There have always been skeptics who do not believe Marco Polo's tale, and even today some scholars think that he may have learned about China from Persian merchants he met in the Middle East. But most of what he wrote about China tallies well with Chinese sources. The great popularity of his book in Europe contributed enormously to familiarizing Europeans with the notion of Asia as a land of riches.

The more rapid transfer of people and goods across Central Asia spread more than ideas and inventions. It also spread diseases, the most deadly of which was the plague known in Europe as the Black Death. Europe had not had an outbreak of the plague since about 700 and the Middle East since 1200. There was a pocket of active plague in the southwestern mountains of modern Yunnan province in China, the area that had been the independent Nanzhao kingdom of Thai peoples and relatively isolated until the Mongols invaded it in the mid-thirteenth century. Once the Mongols established a garrison there, flea-invested rats carrying plague were transported to central China, then northwest China, and from there to Central Asia and beyond. When caravans carrying goods stopped at oasis towns, the rats and fleas would move from the heavily loaded camels and carts, soon infecting local rats, dogs, and people. Between the oases, desert rodents were infected, and they also passed the disease to dogs and people. By the time the Mongols were assaulting the city of Kaffa in the Crimea in 1346, they themselves were infected by the plague and had to withdraw. But the disease did not retreat and was carried throughout the Mediterranean by the rats on ships. The Black Death of Europe thus was initiated through breaching of the isolation of a remote region in southwest China. The confusion of the mid-fourteenth century that led to the loss of Mongol power in China, Iran, and Central Asia probably owes something to the effect of the spread of the plague and other diseases.

Traditionally, the historians of each of the countries conquered by the Mongols portrayed them as a scourge. Russian historians, for instance, saw this as a period of bondage that set Russia back and cut it off from western Europe. Today it is more common to celebrate the genius of the Mongol military machine and treat the spread of ideas and inventions as an obvious good, probably because we see global communication as a good in our own world. There is no reason to assume, however, that every person or every society benefited equally from the improved communications and the new political institutions of the Mongol era. Merchants involved in long-distance trade prospered, but those enslaved and transported hundreds or thousands of miles from home would not have seen themselves as the beneficiaries of opportunities to encounter cultures different from their own, but rather as the most pitiable of victims.

The places that were ruled by Mongol government for a century or more—China, Central Asia, Persia, and Russia—do not seem to have advanced at a more rapid rate during that century than they did in earlier centuries, either economically or culturally. Indeed, judged by the record of earlier centuries, the Mongol period was generally one of setbacks. By Chinese standards Mongol imposition of hereditary status distinctions was a step backward from a much more mobile and open society, and placing Persians, Arabs, or Tibetans over Chinese did not arouse interest in foreign cultures. Much more in the way of foreign music and foreign styles in clothing, art, and furnishings was integrated into Chinese civilization in Tang times than in Mongol times.

In terms of the spread of technological and scientific ideas, Europe seems to have been by far the main beneficiary of increased communication, largely because in 1200 it lagged farther behind than the other areas. Chinese inventions such as printing, gunpowder, and the compass spread westward. Persian expertise in astronomy and mathematics also spread. In terms of the spread of religions, Islam probably gained the most. It spread into Chinese Central Asia, which had previously been Buddhist, and into Anatolia as Turks pushed out by the Mongols moved west, putting pressure on the Byzantine Empire.

Perhaps because it was not invaded itself, Europe also seems to have been energized by the Mongol-imposed peace in ways that the other major civilizations were not. The goods from China and elsewhere in the East brought by merchants like Marco Polo to Europe whetted the appetites of Europeans for increased contacts with the East, and the demand for Asian goods eventually culminated in the great age of European exploration and expansion. By comparison, in areas the Mongols had directly attacked, protecting their own civilization became a higher priority than drawing from the outside to enrich or enlarge it.

## SUMMARY

The Gupta period is often called India's classical age, but in less than two centuries India reverted to its more typical pattern of regional states. Over the next several centuries Arab and Turkish armies brought Islam to India. Although Buddhism declined, Hinduism continued to flourish. In these developments lay the origins of the modern nations of India, Pakistan, and Bangladesh. Throughout the medieval period India continued to be the center of a very active seaborne trade, and this trade helped carry Indian ideas and practices to Southeast Asia. Local rulers used experts from India to establish strong states.

The nomadic pastoral societies of Central Asia differed in fundamental ways from the settled agricultural societies that lay to their south. Their mastery of the horse and mounted warfare gave them a military advantage that they repeatedly used to overawe or conquer their neighbors. This was carried to the farthest extreme by Chinggis Khan, who through his charismatic leadership and military genius was able to conquer an enormous empire in the early thirteenth century. For a century Mongol hegemony fostered unprecedented East-West trade and contact. More Europeans made their way east than ever before, and Chinese inventions such as printing and the compass made their way west. The Mongols did not try to change the cultures of the countries they conquered, but they still had an enormous impact on them.

## KEY TERMS

| | |
|---|---|
| protected people | nomads |
| jati | grasslands |
| sati | yurts |
| Funan | Great Khan |
| Sanskrit | khanates |
| Srivijaya | tax-farming |

## NOTES

1. Hermann Kulke and Dietmar Rothermund, *A History of India* (London: Routledge, 1990), pp. 86–87.
2. Quoted in A. L. Basham, *The Wonder That Was India,* 2d ed. (New York: Grove Press, 1959), p. 420.
3. Edward C. Sachau, *Alberuni's India*, vol. 1 (London: Kegan Paul, 1910), pp. 19–20, slightly modified.
4. H. A. R. Gibb, *The Travels of Ibn Battuta* (Cambridge: Cambridge University Press for the Hukluyt Society, 1971), pp. 700–701.
5. Guy le Strang, trans., *Clavijo, Embassy to Tamerlane, 1403–1406* (London: Routledge, 1928), pp. 265–266.
6. Quoted in Basham, *The Wonder That Was India*, p. 161.
7. G. Buhler, trans., *The Sacred Laws of the Aryas*. Part 2: *Vasishtha and Baudhayana* (Oxford: Clarendon Press, 1882), p. 31.
8. Quoted in Basham, *The Wonder That Was India,* pp. 459–460.
9. *The Travels of Marco Polo, the Venetian,* ed. Manuel Komroff (New York: Boni and Liveright, 1926), p. 265.
10. Ibid., p. 93.
11. Ibid., pp. 93–94.

## SUGGESTED READING

For Indian history, see the general histories listed in the Suggested Reading for Chapter 3, to which should be added S. A. A. Rizvi, *The Wonder That Was India.* Vol. 2: *1200–1700* (1987). An extensive survey of the Islamic invasions of India is provided in J. F. Richards, "The Islamic Frontier in the East: Expansion into South Asia," *South Asia* 4 (1974):90–109, in which Richards makes the point that many Indian princes put up stiff resistance to the invaders. R. Eaton, *The Rise of Islam and the Bengal Frontier* (1993), offers a major reinterpretation of the spread of Islam. A good treatment of early Islam in India is K. A. Nizami, *Some Aspects of Religion and Politics in India During the Thirteenth Century* (reprint 1970). In *Islam in the Indian Subcontinent* (1980), A. Schimmel surveys many aspects of Islam, including architecture, life, art, and traditions. K. N. Chaudhuri, *Asia Before Europe* (1990), discusses the economy and civilization of cultures within the basin of the Indian Ocean. Two works concentrate on the sultanate of Delhi: M. Habib and K. A. Nizami, eds., *Comprehensive History of India.* Vol. 5: *Delhi Sultanate* (1970); and P. Hardy, "The Growth of Authority over a Conquered Political Elite: The Early Delhi Sultanate as a Possible Case Study," in J. F. Richards, ed., *Kingship and Authority in South Asia* (1998). The *Kamasutra* is now available in a modern translation by M. Vatsyayana and W. Doniger (2002).

General histories of Southeast Asia include D. G. E. Hall, *A History of South-East Asia* (1966); J. F. Cady, *Southeast Asia: Its Historical Development* (1964); and D. R. SarDesai, *Southeast Asia: Past and Present* (1989). More specifically on the early stages of Southeast Asian history are G. Coedes, *The Making of Southeast Asia* (1966); O. W. Wolters, *Early Indonesian Commerce: A Study of the Origins of Sri Vijaya* (1967); and L. Shaffer, *Maritime Southeast Asia to 1500* (1996). The connections between India and early Southeast Asia are treated in two books by H. G. Q. Wales: *The Indianization of China and of South-East Asia* (1967) and *The Making of Greater India,* 3d ed. (1974).

For the early history of Central Asia, see P. B. Golden, *An Introduction to the History of the Turkic Peoples* (1992), which covers the spread of the Turks through Central Asia and the Middle East. D. Simon, ed., *The Cambridge History of Early Inner Asia* (1990), is an ambitious collection that ranges in time from prehistory to the early thirteenth century and in space from the Near East to India and China. S. A. M. Adshead, *Central Asia in World History* (1993), places Central Asia in a larger historical context. A. Kessler, *Empires Beyond the Great Wall: The Heritage of Genghis Khan* (1993), is a well-illustrated volume on the steppe societies from the Xiongnu to the Mongols. T. Barfield, *The Perilous Frontier: Nomadic Empires and China* (1989), offers an explanation of the recurrent confederations of nomadic tribes near China in terms of the benefits they could derive when China had a strong state. The Khitan state is the subject of the large and fully documented study by K. Wittfogel and C. Feng, *History of Chinese Society: Liao (907–1125)* (1946). On the Jurchens, see J. Tao, *The Jurchen in Twelfth-Century China: A Study of Sinicization* (1976). On these states as well as the Mongols, see H. Franke and D. Twitchett, ed., *The Cambridge History of China,* vol. 6 (1994).

E. D. Phillips, *The Mongols* (1969), covers both their history and their way of life. For the founding of the Mongol Empire, see H. D. Martin, *The Rise of Chinghis Khan and His Conquest of North China* (1950), or P. Ratchnevsky, *Genghis Khan: His Life and Legacy* (1992). Overviews of the Mongol conquests include J. J. Saunders, *The History of the Mongol Conquests* (2001), and T. Allsen, *Culture and Conquest in Mongol Eurasia* (2001). P. Kahn, *The Secret History of the Mongols: The Origin of Chinghis Khan* (1984), is a readable version of and the best source for Mongol social practices and values. M. Rossabi provides a lively account of the life of one of the most important Yuan rulers in *Khubilai Khan: His Life and Times* (1988).

For Marco Polo, see L. Olschki, *Marco Polo's Asia* (1960); F. Wood, *Did Marco Polo Go to China?* (1995), which assembles the evidence against believing that Marco Polo saw everything he said he did; and J. Larner, *Marco Polo and the Discovery of the World* (1999), which takes the opposite stance. On Ibn Battuta, see R. E. Dunn, *The Adventures of Ibn Battuta, A Muslim Traveler of the 14th Century* (1986). On other East-West travelers during the period of Mongol domination, see I. de Rachewiltz, *Papal Envoys to the Great Khans* (1971). On the links between the Mongol conquest and the spread of bubonic plague, see W. McNeill, *Plagues and Peoples* (1976). Juivaini's Persian account of the Mongols has been translated by J. A. Boyle, *The History of the World Conquerer* (1958). J. L. Abu-Lughod, *Before European Hegemony: The World System A.D. 1250–1350* (1989), examines the period of Mongol domination from a global perspective.

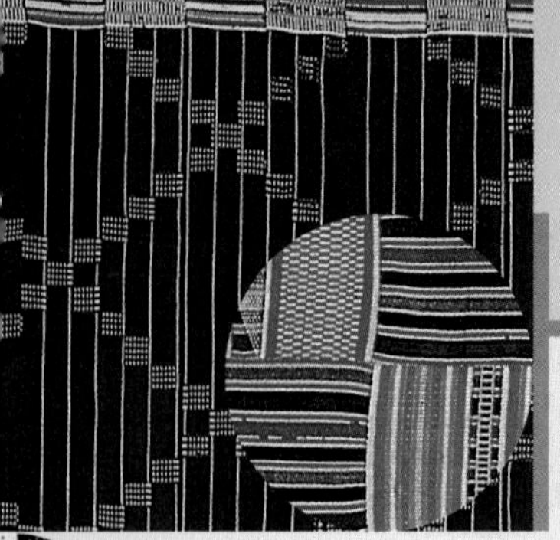

# LISTENING TO THE PAST

## To Commemorate Building a Well

*Much of what we know of medieval India comes from inscriptions carved in stone. Inscribed stones record the genealogies and victories of kings, the establishment of temples, and the construction of bridges, wells, and charitable works. The inscription translated in part below, written in Sanskrit, is dated 1276. It was found twelve miles southwest of modern Delhi.*

*Before commending the donor of the well, the author of this inscription praises the god Shiva and the rulers of the region. A list of earlier rulers comes next, followed by lengthy praise for the military accomplishments of the current sultan, and even for the charms of courtesans, who "proudly dressed in many coloured raiments moved about without fear, filling the air with the tinkle of their bracelets, produced by the wanton movements of their hands." Next comes praise for the sultan's capital city:*

The metropolis of the lord of many hundreds of cities, the charming great city called Delhi, flourishes like a crescent-headed arrow on the side of his enemies. Like the earth, it is the storehouse of innumerable jewels; like the sky, a source of delight; like the nether regions, the abode of many Daityas; like Maya herself, the most bewitching.

In that city of Delhi, renowned under the name Yoganipura, there was a householder who was the wealthy abode of innumerable good qualities, devoid of blemishes, wise, noble-minded, given to meritorious acts, named Uddhara.

Where the clear Candrabhaga joined the beautiful Vitasta, the Vipasa and Satadru; opposite is situated the Indus (Sindhu), the good friend with its tributaries, without high waves. Honey is useless, sugar cane juice is useless, so is the nectar in Heaven. If one drinks the nectar of the Indus, even his nectar of knowledge becomes insipid. In this northernly region, in which the earth is washed by the divine nectar of Sindhu, which removes all kinds of distress, there is Uccapuri, which laughs at the city of gods that is situated on the banks of the heavenly Ganga.

In that city lived his father Haripala, whose father was Yasoraja. His father was Dallahara, whose father was Kipu. This is his genealogy on the father's side. Uddhara's mother was Candi, the daughter of Prthu, whose father was Hasiscandra; his father was Utshahana, the son of Sahadeva, who was the son of Tola. Tola's father was Vyagharahara, who was the son of Singha and grandson of Gaura. In the work entitled *Vamsavali*, the two genealogies have been given in detail; here in this record, the names have been taken to the extent desired to recall them to memory.

He had three wives, embodiments, as it were, of will, wisdom, and energy. The eldest wife, Jajala, was accompanied by Rajasri and Katandevi. Her son was named Hariraja, pure in body, speech, and mind, renowned, the abode of the sixty-four arts, apparently like Vishnu, the sole protector of the universe. His two younger brothers, named Sthiraraja and Jaitra, shine forth along with a sister, Virada. The second wife also had at first a daughter, the liberal-minded Dhanavati. After her, Ratandevi had two sons, Gunaraja and Bhupati. There was also a son, Haradeva, known as Natha, and also another girl. She had also another son, Uttamaraja, and a daughter named Sadali. Thus, we have here the root, stem, branches, fruits, and flowers of this Wishing Tree.

Numerous and extensive free inns were established in different places by this performer of

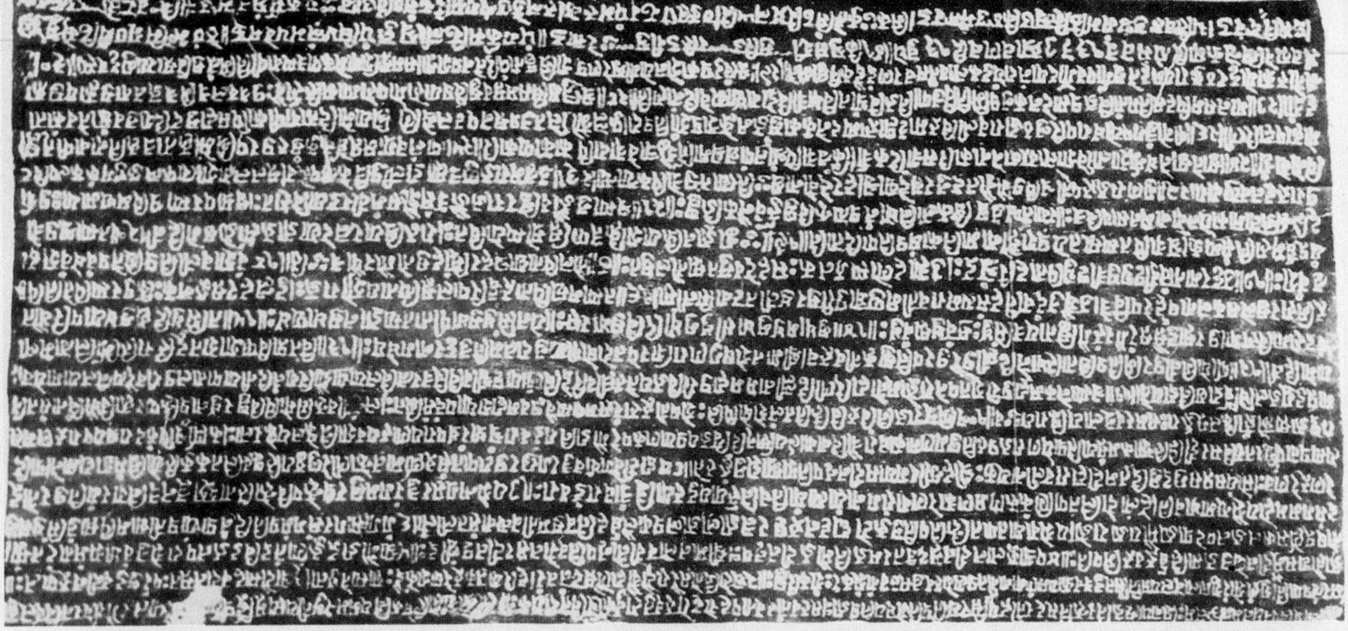

The text, in the Nagari script of Sanskrit, was engraved on a slab of black stone 1 foot, 3 inches, by 3 feet, 11 inches. (From Pushpa Prasad, *Sanskrit Inscriptions of Delhi Sultanate, 1191–1526 [Delhi: Oxford University Press, 1990]*)

sacrifice. But here, this wise one, with a view to relieving the exhaustion of tired travelers, had a well excavated. To the east of the village Palamba and to the west of Kusumbhapura, he made a well which quenches thirst and removes fatigue.

May this well, like a lovely woman with rotund, heaving breasts, gorgeous with undulating necklaces, be the assuager of the thirst of many a lovesick swain and perfumed with the mass of petals from the flowery trees. This well, being very clear, laughs at the minds of good people taking it as turbid. Like the supreme knowledge of philosophers, it shines, causing restfulness to the self.

May this devout and noble Lord Uddhara, whose pleasure rests in the final salvation in Heaven, who is a devotee of Siva, accompanied by sons, wives, friends, and dependents, have the good fortune to enjoy all the worldly pleasures.

This praiseworthy eulogy has been composed by Pandit Yogisvara of eternal fame, to record the construction of this well of Uddhara, the sole receptacle of all blessings.

## QUESTIONS FOR ANALYSIS

1. Why would an inscription for a well praise the ruler before the actual donor?
2. What can you infer about Uddhara's social status?
3. What sorts of imagery does the author use? Why compare a well to a woman?

*Source:* Adapted from Pushpa Prasad, ed., *Sanskrit Inscriptions of Delhi Sultanate, 1191–1526,* pp. 12–15. 

The scholar depicted in this small painting (a little under a foot square) appreciates books, paintings, music, and warmed wine. He is seated in front of a freestanding painted screen on which is hung a portrait of himself. His servant boy pours wine for him as he looks up from his book. Other books and scrolls are laid on a nearby table, along with the lute scholars had been playing since the time of Confucius. *(National Palace Museum, Taipei, Taiwan, Republic of China)*

CHAPTER

# 12 EAST ASIA, CA 800–1400

## CHAPTER OUTLINE



During the six centuries between 800 and 1400, East Asia was the most advanced region of the world. At least that is what the Venetian Marco Polo thought when he got there in the late thirteenth century after traveling through much of Asia. For several centuries the Chinese economy had grown spectacularly, and in fields as diverse as rice cultivation, the production of iron and steel, and the printing of books, China's methods of production were highly advanced. Its system of government was also advanced for its time. In the Song period the principle that the government should be in the hands of highly educated scholar-officials, selected through the competitive written civil service examinations, became well established.

During the previous millennium basic elements of Chinese culture had spread beyond China's borders, creating a large cultural sphere centered on the use of Chinese as the language of civilization. Beginning around 800, however, in East Asia the pendulum shifted toward cultural differentiation, as Japan and Korea developed in distinctive ways. This process is particularly evident in Japan, which by 1200 had developed into a feudal society dominated by samurai quite unlike China's literati elite. Yet none of these countries was ever cut off from the others. China and Korea both had to deal with the same menacing neighbors to the north, the Khitans, the Jurchens, and finally the Mongols. Even Japan had to mobilize its resources to fend off two Mongol attacks.

- What allowed China to take the lead economically and intellectually in this period?
- How did the competition between civilian control and military control fare in each of these countries?
- In what ways did changes beyond their borders shape the developments in these countries?
- How could China, Korea, and Japan have all drawn on both Confucian and Buddhist teachings and yet ended up with elites as distinct as the Chinese scholar-official, the Korean aristocrat, and the Japanese samurai?

This chapter will explore these questions.

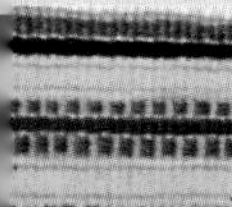

## CHINA (800–CA 1400)

Chinese historians traditionally viewed dynasties as following a typical cycle. Founders were vigorous men able to recruit able followers to serve as officials and generals. Externally they would extend China's borders; internally they would bring peace. They would collect low but fairly assessed taxes. Over time, however, emperors born in the palace would be used to luxury and lack the founder's strength and wisdom. Entrenched interests would find ways to avoid taxes, forcing the government to impose heavier taxes on the poor. Impoverished peasants would flee, the morale of those in the government and armies would decline, and the dynasty would find itself able neither to maintain internal peace nor to defend its borders.

Viewed in terms of this theory of the dynastic cycle, by 800 the Tang Dynasty was in decline. It had ruled China for nearly two centuries, but its high point was in the past. A massive rebellion had wracked it in the mid-eighth century, and the Uighur Turks and Tibetans were menacing its borders. Many of the centralizing features of the government had been abandoned, with power falling more and more to regional military governors.

Chinese political theorists always made the assumption that a strong, centralized government was better than a weak one or political division, but if anything the late Tang period seems to have been both intellectually and economically more vibrant than the early Tang. Less control from the central government seems to have stimulated trade and economic growth. And among educated men, analyzing the problems the country faced was one of the first stages in a major revitalization of Confucianism. For several centuries Buddhism seemed more vital than Confucianism. Beginning in the late Tang period Confucian teachers began claiming that the teachings of the Confucian sages contained all the wisdom one needed and a true Confucian would reject Buddhist teachings.

Nevertheless, the increasing power of non-Chinese peoples in the north did pose long-term problems for the Chinese. When in the tenth century China broke up into separate contending states, several in the north had non-Chinese rulers. Two of these states eventually proved to be long-lasting: the Song, which came to control almost all of China proper south of the Great Wall, and the Liao, whose ruling house was Khitan and who held the territory of modern Beijing and areas north (see Map 12.1). Although the Song Dynasty had a much larger population, the Liao was militarily the stronger of the two.

### The Song Dynasty (960–1279)

The founder of the Song Dynasty, Taizu (r. 960–976), was a general whose troops elevated him to emperor when the previous ruler was succeeded by a young child. Taizu worked to make sure that such an act could not happen in the future by placing the armies under central government control. He retired or rotated his own generals and assigned civil officials to supervise them. In time civil bureaucrats came to dominate every aspect of Song government and society. The civil service examination system was greatly expanded to provide the dynasty with a constant flow of men trained in the Confucian classics.

Curbing the generals ended warlordism but did not solve the military problem of defending against the Khitans to the north. After several attempts to push them back beyond the Great Wall, the Song concluded a peace treaty with them. The Song agreed to make huge annual payments of gold and silk to the Khitans, in a sense paying them not to invade. Even so, the Song rulers had to maintain a standing army of more than a million men. By the middle of the eleventh century military expenses consumed half the government's revenues. China produced swords, armor, and arrowheads in huge quantities but had difficulty maintaining enough horses and well-trained horsemen. Even though China was the economic powerhouse of the region, with by far the largest population, in this period when the horse was a major weapon of war, it was not easy to convert wealth to military advantage.

In the early twelfth century the military situation rapidly worsened when the Khitan state was destroyed by another tribal confederation, led by the Jurchens. Although the Song allied with the Jurchens, the Jurchens quickly realized how easy it would be to defeat the Song. When they marched into the Song capital in 1126, they captured the emperor and took him and his entire court hostage. Song forces rallied around a prince, who reestablished a Song court in the south at Hangzhou (see Map 12.2). This Southern Song Dynasty controlled only about two-thirds of the former Song territories, but the social, cultural, and intellectual life there remained vibrant until the Song fell to the Mongols in 1279.

### The Scholar-Officials and Neo-Confucianism

The Song period saw the full flowering of one of the most distinctive features of Chinese civilization, the scholar-official class certified through highly competitive civil service examinations. This elite was both broader and better

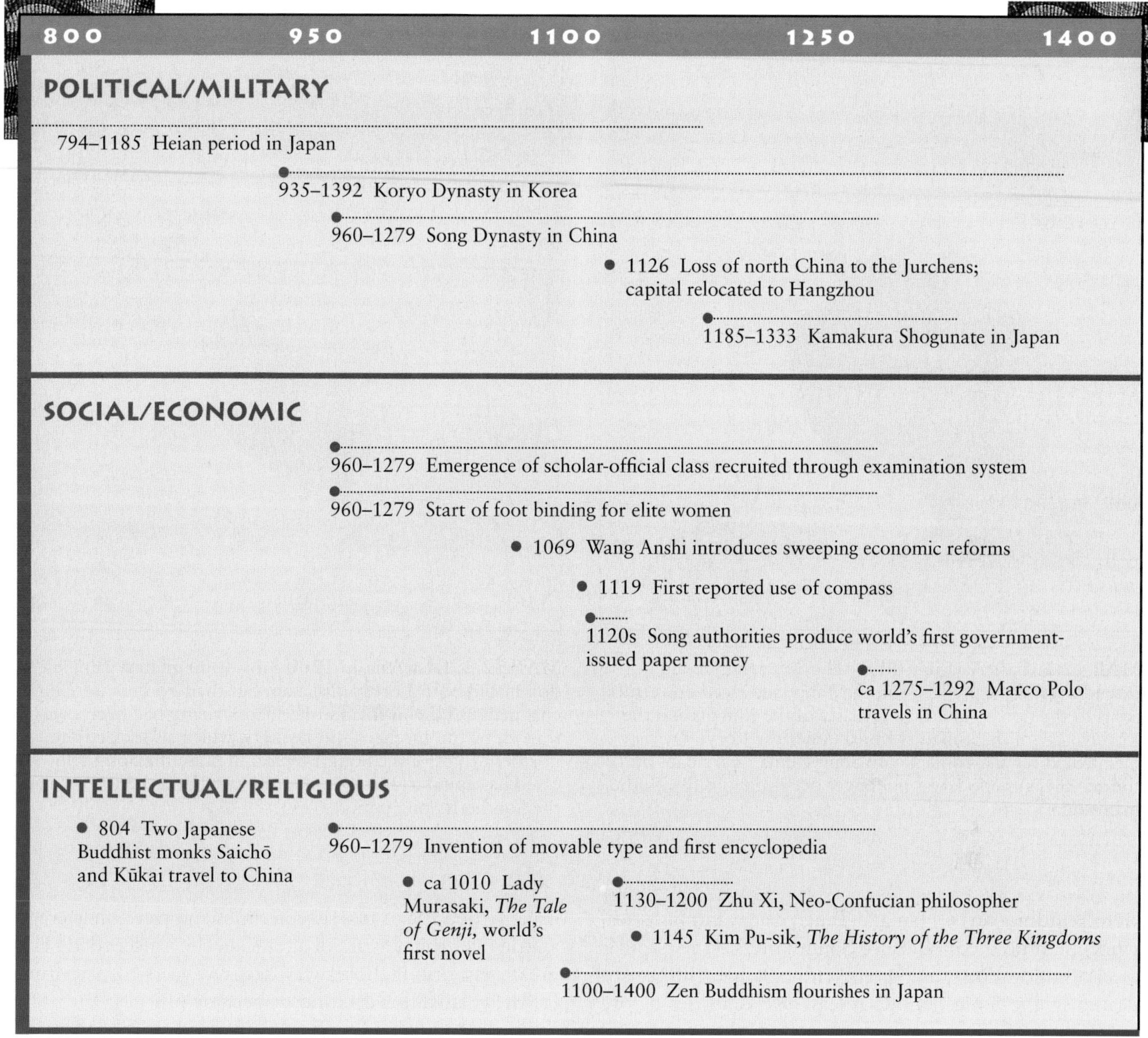


educated than the elites of earlier periods in Chinese history. Once the **examination system** was fully developed, aristocratic habits and prejudices largely disappeared.

The invention of printing should be given some credit for this development. Tang craftsmen developed the art of carving words and pictures into wooden blocks, inking them, and then pressing paper onto the blocks. Each block consisted of an entire page of text and illustrations. Such whole-page blocks were used for printing as early as the middle of the ninth century, and in the eleventh century **movable type** (one piece of type for each character) was invented. Movable type was never widely used in China because whole-block printing was more efficient, but when movable type reached Europe in the fifteenth century, it revolutionized the communication of ideas. In China as in Europe, the introduction of printing dramatically lowered the price of books, thus aiding the spread of literacy.

Among the upper class the availability of cheaper books enabled scholars to amass their own libraries. Song publishers printed the classics of Chinese literature in huge editions to satisfy scholarly appetites. Works on philosophy, science, and medicine also were avidly consumed, as

**MAP 12.1 East Asia in 1000** The Song Empire did not extend as far as its predecessor, the Tang, and faced powerful rivals to the north—the Liao Dynasty of the Khitans and the Xia Dynasty of the Tanguts. Korea under the Koryo Dynasty maintained regular contact with Song China, but Japan, by the late Heian period, was no longer deeply involved with the mainland.

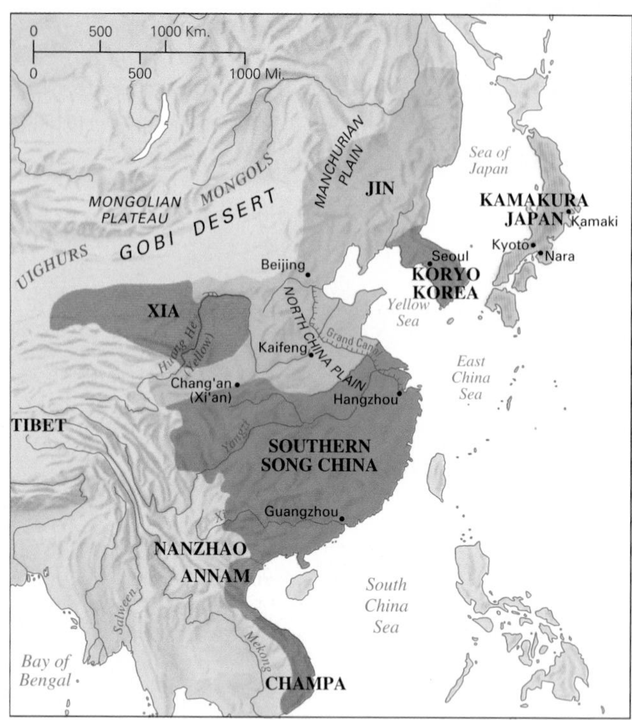


**MAP 12.2 East Asia in 1200** By 1200 military families dominated both Korea and Japan, but their borders were little changed. On the mainland, the Liao Dynasty had been overthrown by the Jurchens' Jin Dynasty, which also seized the northern third of the Song Empire. Because the Song relocated its capital to Hangzhou in the south, this period is called the Southern Song period.

were Buddhist texts. Han and Tang poetry and historical works became the models for Song writers. One popular literary innovation was the encyclopedia, which first appeared in the Song period, at least five centuries before publication of a European encyclopedia.

Not only did the examination system annually recruit four to five times the number of scholars it had in Tang times, but it also came to carry such prestige that the number of scholars entering each competition escalated rapidly, from fewer than 30,000 early in the eleventh century, to nearly 80,000 by the end of that century, to about 400,000 by the dynasty's end. To prepare for the examinations, men had to memorize the classics in order to be able to recognize even the most obscure passages. They also had to master specific forms of composition, including poetic genres. Candidates were usually asked to discuss policy issues, but the examinations tested general education more than knowledge of government laws and regulations. Those who became officials this way had usually tried the exams several times and were on average a little over thirty years of age when they succeeded. The great majority of those who devoted years to preparing for the exams, however, never became officials.

The life of the educated man involved more than study for the civil service examinations. Many took to refined pursuits such as collecting antiques or old books and practicing the arts—especially poetry writing, calligraphy, and painting. For many individuals these interests overshadowed any philosophical, political, or economic concerns; others found in them occasional outlets for creative activity and aesthetic pleasure. In the Song period the engagement of the elite with the arts led to extraordinary achievement in calligraphy and painting, especially landscape painting. But even more people were involved as connoisseurs. A large share of the informal social life of upper-class men was centered on these refined pastimes, as they gathered to compose or criticize poetry, to view each other's treasures, and to patronize young talents.

This new scholar-official elite produced some extraordinary men, able to hold high court offices while pursuing diverse intellectual interests. Ouyang Xiu spared time in his busy official career to write love songs, histories viewed as models of prose style, and the first analytical catalogue of rubbings of ancient stone and bronze inscriptions. Sima Guang, besides serving as prime minister, wrote a narrative history of China from the Warring States Period (403–221 B.C.E.) to the founding of the Song Dynasty. Su Shi wrote more than twenty-seven hundred poems and eight hundred letters while active in opposition politics. He was also an esteemed painter and calligrapher and theorist of the arts. Su Song, another high official, constructed an eighty-foot-tall mechanical clock. He adapted the water-powered clock invented in the Tang period by adding a chain-driven mechanism. The clock told not only the time of day but also the day of the month, the phase of the moon, and the position of certain stars and planets in the sky. At the top was a mechanically rotated armillary sphere. (See also the feature "Individuals in Society: Shen Gua.")

These highly educated men accepted the Confucian responsibility to aid the ruler in the governing of the country. In this period, however, this commitment tended to embroil them in unpleasant factional politics. The main dispute originated in the need to raise revenues to support the army. In 1069 the young Song emperor Shenzong (r. 1067–1085) appointed Wang Anshi as his chief counselor. Wang proposed a series of sweeping reforms. Realizing that government income was ultimately linked to the prosperity of the individual peasant taxpayer, he instituted measures he thought would help them, such as low-cost loans and replacing labor service with a tax. To raise revenues, he also expanded state monopolies on tea, salt, and wine. Many well-respected scholars and officials, led by the statesman-historian Sima Guang, thought that Wang's policies would do more harm than good and resisted enforcing them. Wang, with the emperor's support, responded by transferring them out of the capital, in effect banishing them. When the emperor died, his mother took over as regent for his son and brought back the opponents, who were quick to retaliate against the reformers. When she died, the young emperor reversed her decisions, and there was another round of demotions and banishments.

Politics was not the only issue scholars in this period debated. During the eleventh century many Confucian teachers gathered around them students preparing to take the civil service examinations. The most inspiring of these teachers urged their disciples to set their sights on the higher goals of attaining the wisdom of the sages.

**Landscape Painting** Centuries before Western artists began to see natural scenery as anything more than background, Chinese artists had made landscape painting into a great art. Mountains had long been sacred places, and artists of the tenth and eleventh centuries developed ways to convey their majesty and associations with immortality. In this painting by Fan Kuan (active ca 990–1020), a towering central peak dwarfs the mule train in the foreground. Like many other Chinese paintings, this one was done with ink on silk, using very little color. The scroll could be hung on a wall or rolled up for storage. *(National Palace Museum, Taipei, Taiwan, Republic of China)*

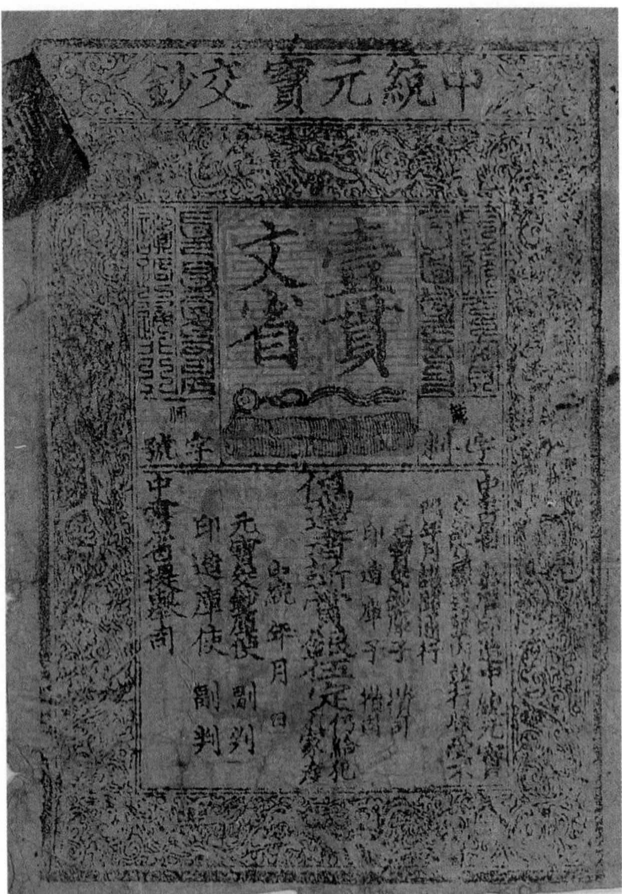


**Chinese Paper Money** Chinese paper currency indicated the unit of currency and the date and place of issue. The Mongols continued the use of paper money, and this note dates from the Mongol period. *(© Cultural Relics Data Center of China)*

Metaphysical theories about the workings of the cosmos in terms of *li* (principle) and *qi* (vital energy) were developed in response to the challenge of the sophisticated metaphysics of Buddhism.

**Neo-Confucianism,** as this movement is generally termed, was more fully developed in the twelfth century by the immensely learned Zhu Xi. Besides serving in office, he wrote, compiled, or edited almost a hundred books, corresponded with dozens of other scholars, and still regularly taught groups of disciples, many of whom stayed with him for years at a time. Although he was treated as a political threat during his lifetime, within decades of his death his writings came to be considered orthodox, and in subsequent centuries candidates for the examinations had to be familiar with his commentaries on the classics.

## The Medieval Chinese Economic Revolution (800–1100)

In 742 China's population was still approximately 50 million, very close to what it had been in 2 C.E. Over the next three centuries, with the expansion of rice cultivation in central and south China, the country's food supply steadily increased, and so did its population, which reached 100 million by 1100. China was certainly the largest country in the world at the time; its population probably exceeded that of all of Europe (as it has ever since).

Agricultural prosperity and denser settlement patterns aided commercialization of the economy. Peasants in Song China did not aim at self-sufficiency. They had found that producing for the market made possible a better life. Peasants in more densely populated regions with numerous markets sold their surpluses and bought charcoal, tea, oil, and wine. In many places, farmers specialized in commercial crops, such as sugar, oranges, cotton, silk, and tea. (See the feature "Global Trade: Tea" on pages 344–345.) The need to transport the products of interregional trade stimulated the inland and coastal shipping industries, providing employment for shipbuilders and sailors and business opportunities for enterprising families with enough capital to purchase a boat. Marco Polo, the Venetian merchant who wrote of his visit to China in the late thirteenth century, was astounded at the boat traffic on the Yangzi River. He claimed to have seen no less than fifteen thousand vessels at one city on the river, "and yet there are other towns where the number is still greater."[1]

As marketing increased, demand for money grew enormously, leading eventually to the creation of the world's first **paper money.** The late Tang government had abandoned the use of bolts of silk as supplementary currency, which increased the demand for copper coins. By 1085 the output of coins had increased tenfold to more than 6 billion coins a year. To avoid the weight and bulk of coins for large transactions, local merchants in late Tang times started trading receipts from deposit shops where they had left money or goods. The early Song authorities awarded a small set of shops a monopoly on the issuing of these certificates of deposit, and in the 1120s the government took over the system, producing the world's first government-issued paper money. Marco Polo wrote one of the earliest descriptions of how Chinese paper money was issued:

*The coinage of this paper money is authenticated with as much form and ceremony as if it were actually of pure gold or silver; for to each note a number of officers, specially*

## INDIVIDUALS IN SOCIETY

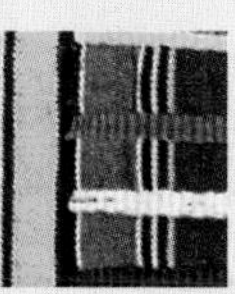

### SHEN GUA

In the eleventh century it was not rare for Chinese men of letters to have broad interests, but few could compare to Shen Gua (1031–1095), a man who tried his hand at everything from mathematics, geography, economics, engineering, medicine, divination, and archaeology to military strategy and diplomacy.

In his youth Shen Gua traveled widely with his father, who served as a provincial official. His own career as an official, which started when he was only twenty, also took him to many places, adding to his knowledge of geography. He received a post in the capital in 1066, just before Wang Anshi's rise to power, and he generally sided with Wang in the political disputes of the day. He eventually held high astronomical, ritual, and financial posts, but he also became involved in waterworks and the construction of defense walls. He was sent as an envoy to the Khitans in 1075 to try to settle a boundary dispute. When a military campaign that he advised failed in 1082, he was demoted and later retired to write.

It is from his book of notes that we know the breadth of his interests. In one note Shen describes how, on assignment to inspect the frontier, he made a relief map of wood and glue-soaked sawdust to show the mountains, roads, rivers, and passes. The emperor was so impressed when he saw it that he ordered all the border prefectures to make relief maps. Elsewhere Shen describes the use of petroleum and explains how to make movable type from clay. Shen Gua often applied a mathematical approach to issues that his contemporaries did not think of in those terms. He once computed the total number of possible situations on a go board, and another time he calculated the longest possible military campaign given the limits of human carriers who had to carry their own food as well as food for the soldiers.

Shen Gua is especially known for what might be called scientific explanations. In one place, he explains the deflection of the compass from due south. In another note he identifies petrified bamboo and from its existence argues that the region where it was found must have been much warmer and more humid in ancient times. He argued against the theory that tides are caused by the rising and setting of the sun, demonstrating that they correlate rather with the cycles of the moon. He proposed switching from a lunar calendar to a solar one of 365 days, saying that even though his contemporaries would reject his idea,

*Among the advances of the Song period was the development of gunpowder. An eleventh-century manual on military technology illustrated this "thunderbolt ball," filled with gunpowder and iron scraps and hurled at the enemy with a catapult.*
(Zeng Gongliang and Ding Du, *Wujing zongyao* [Zhongguo bingshu jicheng, 1988 ed.], 12:59 [p. 640])

"surely in the future some will use my theory." To convince his readers that the sun and the moon were spherical, not flat, he suggested that they cover a ball with fine powder on one side and then look at it obliquely. The powder was the part of the moon illuminated by the sun, and as one looks at it obliquely, the white part would be crescent shaped, like a waxing moon. He did not, however, realize that the sun and moon had entirely different orbits and explained why they did not collide by positing that they were both composed of *qi* (vital energy) and had form but not substance.

Shen Gua also wrote on medicine and criticized his contemporaries for paying more attention to old treatises than to clinical experience. Yet he also was sometimes stronger on theory than on observation. In one note he argues that longevity pills could be made from cinnabar. He reasoned that if cinnabar could be transformed in one direction, it ought to be susceptible to transformation in the opposite direction as well. Therefore, since melted cinnabar causes death, solid cinnabar should prevent death.

#### QUESTIONS FOR ANALYSIS

1. Do you think Shen Gua's wide travels added to his curiosity about the material world?
2. In what ways could Shen Gua have used his scientific interests in his work as an official?
3. How does Shen Gua's understanding of the natural world compare to that of the early Greeks?

# GLOBAL TRADE

## TEA

Tea is made from the young leaves and leaf buds of *Camellia sinensis,* a plant native to the hills of southwest China.

As an item of trade, tea has a very long history. Already by Han times (206 B.C.E.–220 C.E.), tea was being grown and drunk in southwest China, and for several centuries thereafter it was looked on as a local product of the region with useful pharmacologic properties, such as countering the effects of wine. By Tang times (608–907) it was being widely cultivated in the Yangzi River valley and was a major item of interregional trade. Tea was common enough in Tang life that poets often mentioned it in their poems. In the eighth century Lu Yu wrote an entire treatise on the wonders of tea.

During the Tang Dynasty tea was a major commercial crop, especially in the southeast. The most intensive time for tea production was the harvest season, since young leaves were of much more value than mature ones. Women, mobilized for about a month each year, would come out to help pick the tea. Not only were tea merchants among the wealthiest merchants, but from the late eighth century on, taxes on tea became a major item of government revenue.

Tea circulated in several forms, loose and compressed (brick), powder and leaf. The cost of tea varied both by

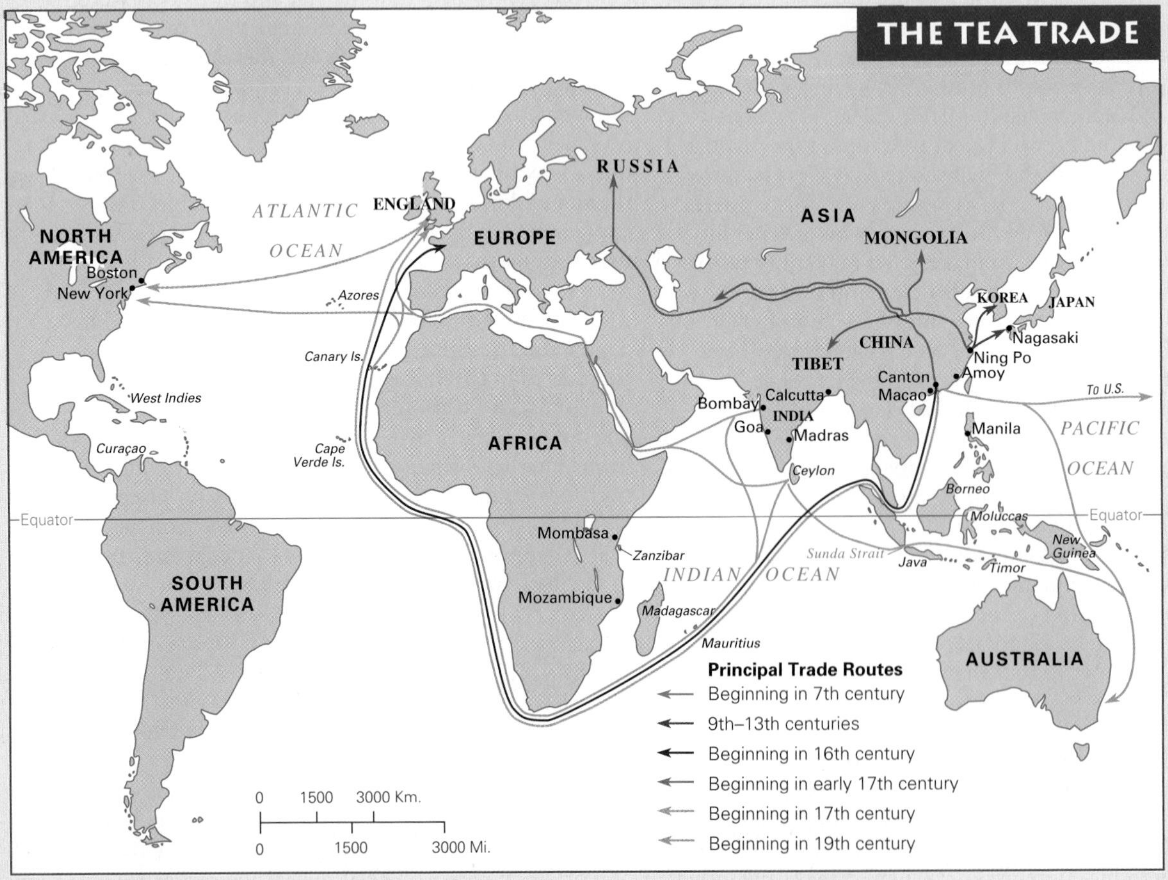

THE TEA TRADE

Principal Trade Routes
Beginning in 7th century
9th–13th centuries
Beginning in 16th century
Beginning in early 17th century
Beginning in 17th century
Beginning in 19th century

*Tea-leaf jar, fourteenth century, south China. This 42-centimeter-tall jar was imported to Japan, where it was treasured as an art object and used by tea masters. In the sixteenth century it came into the possession of the first Tokugawa shogun, Ieyasu.* (The Tokugawa Reimeikai Foundation)

form and by region of origin. In Song times (960–1279), the cheapest tea could cost as little as 18 cash per catty, the most expensive 275. In Kaifeng in the 1070s the most popular type of tea was loose tea powdered at water mills. The tea exported from Sichuan to Tibet, however, was formed into solid bricks.

The Song Dynasty established a government monopoly on tea. Only those who purchased government licenses could legally trade in tea. The dynasty also used its control of tea to ensure a supply of horses, needed for military purposes. The government could do this because the countries on its borders that produced the best horses—Tibet, Central Asia, Mongolia, and so on—were not suitable for cultivating tea. Thus the Song government insisted on horses for tea.

Tea reached Korea and Japan as a part of Buddhist culture. Buddhist monks drank it to help them stay awake during long hours of recitation or meditation. The priest Saichō, patriarch of Tendai Buddhism, visited China in 804–805 and reportedly brought back tea seeds. Tea drinking did not become widespread in Japan, however, until the twelfth century, when Zen monasteries popularized its use. By the fourteenth century tea imported from China was still prized, but the Japanese had already begun to appreciate the distinctive flavors of teas from different regions of Japan.

With the development of the tea ceremony, tea drinking became an art in Japan, with much attention to the selection and handling of tea utensils. In both Japan and Korea, offerings of tea became a regular part of offerings to ancestors.

Tea did not become important in Europe until the seventeenth century. Tea first reached Russia in 1618, when a Chinese embassy presented some to the tsar. Under agreements between the Chinese and Russian governments, camel trains would arrive in China laden with furs and return carrying tea, taking about a year for the return trip. By 1700 Russia was receiving more than 600 camel loads of tea annually. By 1800 it was receiving more than 6,000 loads, amounting to more than 3.5 million pounds. Tea reached western Europe in the sixteenth century, both via Arabs and via Jesuit priests traveling on Portuguese ships.

In Britain, where tea drinking would become a national institution, tea was first drunk in coffeehouses. Samuel Pepys recorded in his famous diary having his first cup of tea in 1660. By the end of the seventeenth century tea made up more than 90 percent of China's exports to England. In the eighteenth century, tea drinking spread to homes and tea gardens. Queen Anne (r. 1702–1714) was credited with starting the custom of drinking tea instead of ale for breakfast. In the nineteenth century afternoon tea became a central feature of British social life.

Already by the end of the eighteenth century Britain imported so much tea from China that it worried about the outflow of silver to pay for it. Efforts to balance trade with China involved promoting the sale of Indian opium to China and efforts to grow tea in British colonies. Using tea seeds collected in China and a tea plant indigenous to India's Assam province, tea was eventually grown successfully in both India and Sri Lanka. By the end of the nineteenth century huge tea plantations had been established in India, and India surpassed China as an exporter of tea.

The spread of the popularity of drinking tea also stimulated the desire for fine cups to drink it from. Importation of Chinese ceramics, therefore, often accompanied adoption of its tea customs.

*appointed, not only subscribe their names, but affix their signets also; and when this has been regularly done by the whole of them, the principal officer . . . having dipped into vermilion the royal seal committed to his custody, stamps with it the piece of paper, so that the form of the seal tinged with the vermilion remains impressed upon it.*[2]

To this day U.S. paper money carries the signatures of federal officials, the seals of the Federal Reserve Bank, and the Great Seal of the United States; only the vermilion is absent.

With the intensification of trade, merchants became progressively more specialized and organized. They set up partnerships and joint stock companies, with a separation of owners (shareholders) and managers. In the large cities merchants were organized into guilds according to the type of product sold, and they arranged sales from wholesalers to shopowners and periodically set prices. When the government wanted to requisition supplies or assess taxes, they dealt with the guild heads.

Foreign trade also flourished in the Song period. The government sent missions to Southeast Asian countries to encourage their traders to come to China. Chinese merchants sailing Chinese ships began to displace Indian and Arab merchants in the South Seas. Ship design was improved in several ways. Watertight bulkheads improved buoyancy and protected cargo. Stern-mounted rudders improved steering. Some of these ships were powered by both oars and sails and large enough to hold several hundred men.

Also important to oceangoing travel was the perfection of the **compass.** The way a magnetic needle would point north had been known for some time, but in Song times it was reduced in size and attached to a fixed stem (rather than floating in water). In some cases it was put in a small protective case with a glass top, making it suitable for sea travel. The first reports of a compass used in this way date to 1119.

The Song also witnessed many advances in industrial techniques. Traditional industries such as silk, lacquer, porcelain, and paper reached very high levels of technical perfection. Papermaking flourished with the demand for paper for books, documents, money, and wrapping paper. Heavy industry, especially iron, also grew astoundingly.

**City Life** In Song times many cities in China grew to 50,000 or more people, and the capital, Kaifeng, reached over a million. The bustle of a commercial city is shown here in a detail from a seventeen-foot-long handscroll painted in the twelfth century. This scene shows draymen and porters, peddlers and shopkeepers, monks and scholars, a storyteller, a fortuneteller, a scribe, a woman in a sedan chair. *(The Palace Museum, Beijing)*

With advances in metallurgy, iron production reached around 125,000 tons per year in 1078, a sixfold increase over the output in 800. At first charcoal was used in the production process, leading to deforestation of parts of north China. By the end of the eleventh century, however, bituminous coke had largely taken the place of charcoal. Much of this iron was put to military purposes. Mass-production methods were used to make iron armor in small, medium, and large sizes. High-quality steel for swords was made through high-temperature metallurgy. Huge bellows, often driven by water wheels, were used to superheat the molten ore. The needs of the army also brought Chinese engineers to experiment with the use of gunpowder. In the wars against the Jurchens, those defending a besieged city used gunpowder to propel projectiles at the enemy.

The quickening of the economy fueled the growth of cities. Dozens of cities had 50,000 or more residents, and quite a few had more than 100,000. Both the capitals are estimated to have had in the vicinity of a million residents. Marco Polo described Hangzhou as the finest and most splendid city in the world. He reported that it had ten marketplaces, each half a mile long, where forty thousand to fifty thousand people would go to shop on any given day. There were also bathhouses; permanent shops selling things such as spices, drugs, and pearls; and innumerable courtesans—"adorned in much finery, highly perfumed, occupying well-furnished houses, and attended by many female domestics"—who were able to intoxicate the visitor with their "wanton arts."[3]

The medieval economic revolution shifted the economic center of China south to the Yangzi River drainage area. This area had many advantages over the north China plain. Rice, which grew in the south, provides more calories per unit of land, and therefore allows denser settlements. The milder temperatures often allowed two crops to be grown on the same plot of land, a summer and a winter crop. The abundance of rivers and streams facilitated shipping, which reduced the cost of transportation and thus made regional specialization economically more feasible. In the first half of the Song Dynasty, the capital was still in the north, but on the Grand Canal, which linked it to the rich south.

The economic revolution of Song times cannot be attributed to intellectual change, as Confucian scholars did not reinterpret the classics to defend the morality of commerce. But neither did scholar-officials take a unified stand against economic development. As officials they had to work to produce revenue to cover government expenses such as defense, and this was much easier to do when commerce was thriving.

**Transplanting Rice** To get the maximum yield per plot and to make it possible to grow two crops in the same field, Chinese farmers grew rice seedlings in a seed bed and then, when a field was free, transplanted the seedlings into the flooded field. Because the Song government wanted to promote up-to-date agricultural technology, in the twelfth century it commissioned a set of twelve illustrations of the steps to be followed. This painting comes from a later version of those illustrations. *(Courtesy of the Freer Gallery of Art, Smithsonian Institution, Washington, D.C. [54.21])*

Ordinary people benefited from the Song economic revolution in many ways. There were more opportunities for the sons of farmers to leave agriculture and find work in cities. Those who stayed in agriculture had a better chance to improve their situations by taking up sideline production of wine, charcoal, paper, or textiles. Energetic farmers who grew cash crops such as sugar, tea, mulberry leaves (for silk), and cotton (recently introduced from India) could grow rich. Greater interregional trade led to the availability of more goods at the rural markets held every five to ten days.

Of course not everyone grew rich. Poor farmers who fell into debt had to sell their land, and if they still owed money, they could be forced to sell their daughters as maids, concubines, or prostitutes. The prosperity of the cities created a huge demand for women to serve the rich in these ways, and Song sources mention that criminals would kidnap girls and women to sell in distant cities at huge profits.

**Draw Loom** Weaving was women's work, even when it required large and complex draw looms, needed to make multicolor brocades. This illustration of a woman at a draw loom, with a child perched above to handle the different yarns, is from a set of pictures of the stages in textile production issued by the Song government to encourage the use of up-to-date techniques. *(Courtesy of the Freer Gallery of Art, Smithsonian Institution, Washington, D.C. [54.20])*

## Women's Lives

With the spread of printing, more books and more types of books survive from the Song period than from earlier periods, letting us catch more glimpses of women's lives. Song stories, documents, and legal cases show us widows who ran inns, maids sent out by their mistresses to do errands, midwives who delivered babies, pious women who spent their days chanting sutras, nuns who called on such women to explain Buddhist doctrine, girls who learned to read with their brothers, farmers' daughters who made money by weaving mats, childless widows who accused their nephews of depriving them of their property, wives who were jealous of the concubines their husbands brought home, and women with large dowries who used part of them to help their husbands' sisters marry well.

Families who could afford it tried to keep their wives and daughters at home, where there was plenty for them to do. Not only was there the work of tending children and preparing meals, but spinning, weaving, and sewing also were considered women's work and took a great deal of time. Families that raised silkworms also needed women to do much of the work of coddling the worms and getting them to spin their cocoons. Within the home women generally had considerable say and took an active interest in issues such as the selection of marriage partners for their children.

Women tended to marry between the ages of sixteen and twenty. The husbands were, on average, a couple of years older than they were. The marriage would have been arranged by their parents, who would have either called on a professional matchmaker (usually an older woman) or turned to a friend or relative for suggestions. Before the wedding took place, written agreements would be exchanged, which would list the prospective bride's and groom's birth dates, parents, and grandparents; the gifts that would be exchanged; and the dowry the bride would bring. The idea was to match families of approximately equal status, but a young man who had just passed the civil service exams would be considered a good prospect even if his family had little wealth or rank.

A few days before the wedding the bride's family would send to the groom's family her dowry, which at a minimum would contain boxes full of clothes and bedding but in better-off families also would include items of substantial value, such as gold jewelry or deeds to land. On the day of the wedding the groom and some of his friends and relatives would go to the bride's home to get her. She would be elaborately dressed and would tearfully bid farewell to everyone in her family. She would be carried to her new home in a fancy sedan chair to the sound of music, alerting everyone on the street that a wedding was taking place. Meanwhile the groom's family's friends and relatives would have gathered at his home, and when the bridal party arrived, they would be there to greet them. The bride would have to kneel and bow to her new parents-in-law and later also to the tablets representing the family's ancestors. Other ceremonies symbolized her new tie to her husband, whom she was meeting for the first time. A classical ritual still practiced was for the new couple to drink wine from the same cup. A ritual that had become popular in Song times was to attach a string to both of them, literally tying them together. Later they would be shown to their new bedroom, where the bride's dowry had already been placed, and people would toss beans or rice on the bed, symbolizing the desired fertility. After teasing them, the guests would finally leave them alone and go out to the courtyard for a wedding feast.

The young bride's first priority was to try to win over her mother-in-law, since everyone knew that mothers-in-law were hard to please. One way to do this was to quickly bear a son for the family. Within the patrilineal system, a woman fully secured her position in the family by becoming the mother of one of the men. Every community had older women skilled in midwifery who could be called to help when she went into labor. If the family was well-to-do, they might also arrange for a wet nurse to help her take care of the newborn, though some Song scholars disapproved of depriving another child for the sake of one's own child.

Women frequently had four, five, or six children, but likely one or more would die in infancy or early childhood. If a son reached adulthood and married before the woman herself was widowed, she would be considered fortunate, for she would have always had an adult man who could take care of business for her—first her husband, then her grown son. But in the days when infectious diseases took many people in their twenties and thirties, it was not uncommon for a woman to be widowed while in her twenties, when her children were still very young. If her husband had brothers and they had not yet divided their households, she would simply stay with them, assuming they were not so poor that they could not afford a few more mouths to feed. Otherwise, she could try to return to her natal family, to her brothers if her parents were no longer living. Taking another husband was also a possibility, though it was considered an inferior alternative from a moral point of view.

A woman with a healthy and prosperous husband faced another challenge in middle age: her husband could bring home a **concubine** (more than one if he could afford it). Moralists insisted that it was wrong for a wife to be jealous of her husband's concubines, but many could not get used to their husbands paying so much attention to another woman. Wives outranked concubines and could give them orders in the house, but a concubine had her own ways of getting back, especially if she was twenty and the wife was forty and no longer very attractive. The children born to a concubine were considered just as much children of the family as the wife's children, and if the wife had had only daughters and the concubine had a son, the wife would find herself in her old age dependent on the concubine's son.

As a woman's children grew up, she would start thinking of suitable marriage partners. Many women liked the idea of bringing another woman from their natal family—perhaps a brother's daughter—to be a daughter-in-law. But there were those who thought such marriages just resulted in relatives falling out with each other.

Women whose sons and daughters were all married could take it easy. They had daughters-in-law to do the cooking and cleaning. They could enjoy their grandchildren and help with their education. Many found more time for religious devotions at this stage of their lives. Their sons, still living with them, were often devoted to them and did their best to make their late years comfortable.

Neo-Confucianism is sometimes blamed for a decline in the status of women in Song times, largely because one of the best known of the Neo-Confucian teachers, Cheng Yi, once told a follower that it would be better for a widow to die of starvation than to lose her virtue by remarrying. In later centuries this saying was often quoted to justify pressuring widows, even very young ones, to stay with their husbands' families and not remarry. In Song times, however, widows frequently remarried.

It is true that **foot binding** began during the Song Dynasty, but it was not recommended by Neo-Confucian teachers; rather it was associated with the pleasure quarters and with women's efforts to beautify themselves. Mothers bound the feet of girls aged five to eight with long strips of cloth to keep them from growing and to bend the four smaller toes under to make the foot narrow and arched. The hope was that the girl would be judged more beautiful. Foot binding spread gradually during Song times but was probably still largely an elite practice. In later centuries it became extremely common in north and central China, eventually spreading to all classes. Women with bound feet were less mobile than women with natural feet, but only those who could afford servants bound their feet so tightly that walking was difficult.

## KOREA (780–1392)

As discussed in Chapter 7, during the Silla period Korea was strongly tied to Tang China and avidly copied China's model. This changed along with so much else in North Asia during the centuries between 800 and 1400. In this period Korea lived more in the shadows of the powerful nomad states of the Khitans, Jurchens, and Mongols than of the Chinese.

The Silla Dynasty began to decline after the king was killed in a revolt in 780. For the next 155 years the kings were selected from several collateral lines, and the majority of them met violent deaths. Rebellions and coups d'état followed one after the other, as different groups of nobles placed their candidates on the throne and killed as many of their opponents as they could. As conditions deteriorated, serfs absconded in large numbers, and independent merchants and seamen of humble origins came to dominate the three-way trade between China, Korea, and Japan.

The dynasty that emerged from this confusion was called Koryo (935–1392). (The English word *Korea* derives from the name of this dynasty.) During this time Korea developed more independently of the China model than it had in Silla times, just as contemporary Japan was doing (see the next section). This was not because the Chinese model was rejected—indeed the Koryo capital was laid out on the Chinese model, and the government was closely patterned on the Tang system. Measures such as these did nothing to alter the fundamentally aristocratic structure of Korean society.

The founder of the dynasty, Wang Kon, was a man of relatively obscure maritime background, but he needed the support of the old aristocracy to maintain his control. His successors introduced civil service examinations on the Chinese model, as well as examinations for Buddhist clergy, but since the aristocrats were the best educated and government schools admitted only sons of aristocrats, this system served primarily to solidify their control. Politics was largely the competition among aristocratic clans for influence at court and marriage of their daughters to the royal princes. Like the Heian aristocrats in Japan, the Koryo aristocrats wanted to stay in the capital and only reluctantly accepted posts in the provinces.

At the other end of the social scale, the serf/slave stratum seems to have increased in size. This lowborn stratum included not only privately held slaves but also large numbers of government slaves, as well as government workers in mines, porcelain factories, and other government industries. Sometimes entire villages or groups of villages were considered lowborn. There were occasional slave revolts, and some manumitted slaves did rise in status, but prejudice against anyone with slave ancestors was so strong that the law provided that "only if there is no evidence of lowborn status for eight generations in one's official household registration may one receive a position in the government."[4] In China and Japan, by contrast, slavery was a much more minor element in the social landscape.

The commercial economy declined in Korea during this period, showing that it was not closely linked to China's economy, then booming. Except for the capital, there were no cities of commercial importance, and in the countryside the use of money decreased. One industry that did flourish was ceramics. Connoisseurs have long appreciated the elegance of the pale green Koryo celadon pottery, decorated with designs executed in inlaid white or gray clay.

Buddhism remained strong throughout Korea, and monasteries became major centers of art and learning. As in Song China and Kamakura Japan, Chan (Zen) and Tiantai (Tendai) were the leading Buddhist teachings. The founder of the Koryo Dynasty attributed the dynasty's success to the Buddha's protection, and he and his successors were ardent patrons of the church. The entire Buddhist canon was printed in the eleventh century and again in the thirteenth. (The 81,258 individual woodblocks used to print it still survive in a monastery in southern Korea.) As in medieval Europe, aristocrats who entered the church occupied the major abbacies. Monasteries played the same roles as they did in China and Japan, such as engaging in money lending and charitable works. Like Japan (but not China), some monasteries accumulated military power.

The most important literary work of the Koryo period is *The History of the Three Kingdoms,* compiled in 1145 in Chinese by Kim Pu-sik. Modeled on Chinese histories, it is the best source of information on early Korean history.

The Koryo Dynasty was preserved in name long after the ruling family had lost most of its power. In 1170 the palace guards massacred the civil officials at court and placed a new king on the throne. The coup leaders scrapped the privileges that had kept the aristocrats in power and appointed themselves to the top posts. After incessant infighting among the generals and a series of coups, in 1196 the general Ch'oe Ch'ung-hon took control. Ch'oe had a private army of about three thousand warrior-retainers and an even larger number of slaves. The domination of Korea by the Ch'oe family was much like the contemporary situation in Japan, where warrior bands were seizing power. Moreover, because the Ch'oe were content to dominate the government while leaving the Koryo king on the throne, they had much in common with the Japanese shoguns, who followed a similar strategy.

Although Korea adopted many ideas from China, it could not so easily adopt the Chinese assumption that it was the largest, most powerful, and most advanced society in the world. Korea, from early times, recognized China as in many ways senior to it, but when strong states emerged to its north in Manchuria, Korea was ready to accommodate them as well. Koryo's first neighbor to the north was the Khitan state of Liao, which in 1010 invaded and sacked the capital. Koryo acceded to vassal status, but Liao invaded again in 1018. This time Koryo was able to repel the Khitans. Afterward a defensive wall was built across the Korean peninsula south of the Yalu River. When the Jurchens supplanted the Khitans, Koryo agreed to send them tribute as well. As mentioned in Chapter 11, Korea was conquered by the Mongols and the figurehead Koryo kings were moved to Beijing, where they married Mongol princesses, their descendants becoming more Mongol than Korean. This was a time of hardship for the Korean people. In the year 1254 alone, the Mongols enslaved 200,000 Koreans and took them away. Ordinary people in Korea suffered grievously when their land was used as a launching pad for the huge Mongol invasions of Japan, as nine hundred ships and the provisions for the soldiers on them had to be procured from the Korean countryside. In this period Korea also suffered from frequent attacks by Japanese pirates, somewhat like the depredations of the Norsemen in Europe a little earlier (see page 370). The Mongol overlords did little to provide protection, and the harried coastal people had little choice but to retreat inland. Korean scholars, familiar with the Neo-Confucian learning of Song and Yuan China, began demanding major reforms such as reallocation of land.

When Mongol rule in China fell apart in the mid-fourteenth century, it declined in Korea as well. Chinese rebels opposing the Mongols entered Korea and even briefly captured the capital in 1361. When the Ming Dynasty was established in 1368, the Koryo court was unsure how to respond. In 1388 a general, Yi Song-gye, was sent to oppose a Ming army at the northwest frontier. When he saw the strength of the Ming, he concluded that making an alliance was more sensible than fighting and led his troops back to the capital, where in 1392 he usurped the throne, founding the Yi Dynasty.

**Celadon Vase** Korea is justly famous for the quality of its ceramics, especially its celadons (ceramics with a grayish blue-green glaze). This early-twelfth-century ewer, probably used for warmed wine, is shaped to resemble a bamboo shoot. *(Courtesy of the Trustees of the Victoria & Albert Museum/Photographer: Ian Thomas)*

## JAPAN IN THE HEIAN AND KAMAKURA ERAS (794–1333)

As discussed in Chapter 7, during the seventh and eighth centuries the Japanese ruling house pursued a vigorous policy of adopting useful ideas, techniques, and policies from the more advanced civilization of China. The rulers built a splendid capital along Chinese lines in Nara and fostered the growth of Buddhism.

### The Heian Period (794–1185)

After less than a century Nara was abandoned and the Japanese imperial court moved the capital to Heian (modern Kyoto). This new capital was, like Nara, modeled on the Tang capital of Chang'an (although neither of the Japanese capitals had walls, a major feature of Chinese cities), and for the first century at Heian the government continued to follow Chinese models. With the decline of the Tang Dynasty in the late ninth century, the Japanese stopped sending embassies to China

## JAPAN, CA 800–1400

| | |
|---|---|
| 794–1185 | Heian era and aristocratic court culture |
| 804–806 | Saichō and Kūkai go to China and return with new Buddhist teachings |
| 894 | Last official embassy to China |
| 995–1027 | Fujiwara Michinaga is dominant |
| ca 1010 | Lady Murasaki writes *The Tale of Genji* |
| 1185–1333 | Kamakura Shogunate and Japanese feudalism |
| 12th–13th centuries | Eisai and Dogen introduce Zen from China |

and rejected dependence on Chinese models. Japan's intellectual and cultural childhood had come to an end, and it was ready to go its own way.

Only the first two Heian emperors were activists. Thereafter political management was taken over by a series of regents from the Fujiwara family, who supplied most of the empresses in this period. The emperors continued to be honored, even venerated, because of their presumed divine descent, but it was the Fujiwaras who ruled. Fujiwara dominance represented the privatization of political power and a reversion to clan politics within an ostensibly bureaucratic system of rule. The bureaucracy built on the Chinese model was not abolished, but it became merely ceremonial. Japanese government took a very different course than that in China, where political contenders sought the throne and successful contenders deposed the old emperor and founded new dynasties. In Japan, for the next thousand years, political contenders sought to manipulate the emperor but not to supplant him.

The Fujiwaras reached the apogee of their glory under Fujiwara Michinaga (966–1027), who dominated the court for more than thirty years. He was the father of four empresses, the uncle of two emperors, and the grandfather of three emperors. He acquired great landholdings and built fine palaces for himself and his family. After ensuring that his sons could continue to rule, he retired to a Buddhist monastery, all the while continuing to exercise most of the control himself. Like many aristocrats of the period, he was learned in music, poetry, Chinese literature and history, and Buddhism.

By the end of the eleventh century several emperors who did not have Fujiwara mothers found a device to counter Fujiwara control: they abdicated but continued to exercise power by controlling their young sons on the throne. This system of rule has been called **cloistered government,** because the retired emperors took Buddhist orders. Thus for a time the imperial house was a contender for political power along with other aristocratic groups.

The rise of a warrior elite finally brought an end to the domination of the Fujiwaras and other Heian aristocratic families. In 1156 civil war broke out, fed by declining central power, feuds among the great families, and the ambitions of local lords. The two most powerful contenders in the struggle were the Taira and Minamoto clans, who quickly outstripped both the emperor and the Fujiwaras. Both clans relied on **samurai,** skilled warriors who were rapidly becoming a new social class. By 1192 the Minamoto clan had vanquished all opposition, and their leader, Yoritomo (1147–1199), became **shogun,** or general-in-chief. With him began the Kamakura Shogunate, which lasted until 1333. This period is often referred to as Japan's feudal period because it was dominated by a military class tied to their superiors by bonds of loyalty and supported by landed estates rather than salaries.

## The Samurai

The emergence of the samurai was made possible by the development of private landed estates. The equal-field system of allotting land in standard amounts to all adult males, copied from Tang China, began breaking down in the eighth century (much as it did in China) because the government failed to keep accurate records and reallocate land. Those who brought new land into cultivation could hold it as private land, as could monasteries, the imperial

**Samurai Armor** A member of the Taira clan once wore this twelfth-century set of armor. Armor had to serve the practical purpose of defense, but as in medieval Europe and medieval Islam, it was often embellished, turning armor into works of art. *(Courtesy of Suzanne Perrin)*

family, and certain high-ranking officials. By the ninth century local lords began escaping imperial taxes and control by formally giving (commending) their land to these tax-exempt entities. The local lord then received his land back as a tenant and paid his protector a small rent. The monastery or privileged individual received a steady income from the land, and the local lord was thereafter free of imperial taxes and control. By the end of the thirteenth century most land seems to have been taken off the tax rolls in this way. Each plot of land could thus have several people with rights to shares of its produce, ranging from the cultivator, to a local lord, to an estate manager working for him, to a regional strongman, to a noble or temple in the capital. Unlike peasants in medieval Europe, where similar practices of commendation occurred, the cultivators in Japan never became serfs.

In spite of his legal status as a tenant, the local lord continued to exercise actual authority over the land—all the more so, in fact, since imperial officials could no longer touch him. To keep order local lords organized private armies of samurai. A samurai and his lord had a double bond: in return for the samurai's loyalty and service, the lord granted him land or income. Each samurai entered into his lord's service in a formal ceremony that included a religious element. The samurai had their own military and social code of conduct, later called **Bushido,** or "Way of the Warrior." Loyalty to the lord came before anything else. In addition, samurai were expected to respect the gods, keep honorable company, be fair and even generous to others, and be sympathetic to the weak and helpless. Honor was so important that a samurai would commit the act of ritual suicide by disemboweling himself rather than face dishonor.

The symbols of the samurai were their swords, with which they were expected to be expert, and the cherry blossom, which falls with the spring wind, signifying the way in which samurai willingly gave their lives for their lords. Like knights in Europe, samurai went into battle in armor and often on horseback. Like the ancient Spartans, samurai were expected to make do with little and like it. Physical hardship became routine, and soft living was despised as weak and unworthy. The life of the samurai was a far cry from the sensitive, poetry-writing aristocrat so admired in Heian court society.

## The Kamakura Shogunate (1185–1333)

The Kamakura Shogunate derives its name from Kamakura, a city near modern Tokyo that was the seat of the Minamoto clan. Yoritomo's victory meant that the emperor was once again an ornament, honored but powerless. It was the military commander, or shogun, who actually ruled.

Yoritomo's rule was an extension of the way in which he ran his own estate. Having established his government at Kamakura, Yoritomo created three bodies, staffed by his retainers, to handle political and legal matters. His administrative board drafted government policy; another board regulated lords and samurai; and a board of inquiry served as the court of the land.

For administration at the local level, Yoritomo created two groups of officials: military land stewards and military governors. To cope with the emergence of hard-to-tax estates, **military land stewards** were put in charge of seeing to the estates' proper operation and maintaining law and order in return for a share of the produce. **Military governors** oversaw the military and police protection of the provinces. They supervised the conduct of the land stewards in peacetime and commanded the provincial samurai in war.

The process of reducing power holders to figureheads went one step further in 1219 when the Hojo family, powerful vassals of the shogun, reduced the shogun to a figurehead. Until 1333 the Hojo family held the reins of power by serving as regents, and the shogun joined the emperor as a political ornament.

The Mongols' massive seaborne invasion (see page 324) rudely interrupted Japan's self-imposed isolation in the thirteenth century. Although the Hojo regents rebuffed the Mongols, they were unable to reward their vassals in the traditional way because little booty was found among the wreckage of the Mongol fleets. Discontent grew among the samurai, and by the fourteenth century the entire political system was breaking down. Both the imperial and the shogunate families were fighting among themselves. Many samurai were becoming impoverished as land grants were divided. Poverty created a pool of warriors ready for plunder, and the samurai shifted their loyalty to local officials who could offer them adequate maintenance.

The factional disputes among Japan's leading families remained explosive until 1331, when the emperor Go-Daigo tried to recapture real power. His attempt sparked an uprising by the great families, local lords, samurai, and even Buddhist monasteries, which commanded the allegiance of thousands of samurai. Go-Daigo destroyed the Kamakura Shogunate in 1333 but soon lost the loyalty of his followers. By 1338 one of his most important military supporters, Ashikaga Takauji, had turned on him and established the Ashikaga Shogunate, which lasted until 1573. Takauji's victory was also a victory for the samurai, who took over civil authority throughout Japan.

## Culture During the Heian and Kamakura Periods

The brilliant aristocratic culture of the Heian period was strongly focused on the capital. It was there that nobles, palace ladies, and imperial family members lived a highly refined and leisured life. Their society was one in which niceties of birth, rank, and breeding counted for everything. From their diaries we know of the pains aristocratic women took in selecting the color combinations of the twelve layers of kimonos they wore. Even among men, knowing how to dress tastefully was more important than skill with a horse or sword. The elegance of one's calligraphy and the allusions in one's poems were matters of intense concern to both men and women at court. Courtiers did not like to leave the capital, and some shuddered at the sight of ordinary working people. The court lady Sei Shonagon recorded in her *Pillow Book* encountering a group of commoners on a pilgrimage: "They looked like so many basket-worms as they crowded together in their hideous clothes, leaving hardly an inch of space between themselves and me. I really felt like pushing them all over sideways."[5] (See the feature "Listening to the Past: The Pillow Book of Sei Shonagon" on pages 358–359.)

In this period a new script was developed for writing Japanese phonetically. Each symbol, based on a simplified Chinese character, represented one of the syllables used in Japanese (such as *ka, ha,* and *ta*). Although "serious" essays, histories, and government documents continued to be written in Chinese, less formal works such as poetry and memoirs were written in Japanese. Mastering the new writing system took much less time than mastering writing in Chinese and aided the spread of literacy, especially among women.

The literary masterpiece of this period is ***The Tale of Genji,*** written in Japanese by Lady Murasaki in about 1010. This long work, the first novel ever written in any language, depicts court life, with close attention to dialogue and personality. The world it depicts is one where taste mattered above all, and people spent time assessing the color combinations of the robes the women wore and the choice of stationery a man or woman selected to write a note. Murasaki also wrote a diary that is similarly revealing of aristocratic culture. In one passage she tells of an occasion when word got out that she had read the Chinese classics:

*Worried what people would think if they heard such rumors, I pretended to be unable to read even the inscriptions on the screens. Then Her Majesty asked me to read to her here and there from the collected works of [the Tang Chinese poet] Bo Juyi, and, because she evinced a desire to know much more about such things, we carefully chose a time when other women would not be present and, amateur that I was, I read with her the two books of Bo Juyi's* New Ballads *in secret; we started the summer before last.*[6]

Apparently even in Heian Japan, the great age of women writers, a woman was wise to hide her erudition.

During the Kamakura period the tradition of long narrative works was continued with the war tale. *The Tale of the Heike,* written by a courtier in the early thirteenth century, tells the story of the fall of the Taira family and the rise of the Minamoto clan. The tale reached a large audience because blind minstrels would chant sections of the tale to the accompaniment of the lute for popular audiences. The story is suffused with the Buddhist idea of the transience of life and the illusory nature of glory. Yet it also celebrates strength, courage, loyalty, and pride. The Minamoto warriors from the east are portrayed as the toughest. In one scene one of them dismissed his own prowess with the bow, claiming that other warriors from his region could pierce three sets of armor with their arrows. He then bragged about the martial spirit of warriors from the east:

**Genji** In *The Tale of Genji* the prince was depicted as artistic and sensitive. Here, in a detail from a twelfth-century handscroll illustrating the great novel, Genji is depicted cradling the child born of his wife's liaison with another man. *(The Tokugawa Art Museum, Nagoya)*

*They are bold horsemen who never fall, nor do they let their horses stumble on the roughest road. When they fight they do not care if even their parents or children are killed; they ride over their bodies and continue the battle.*

*The warriors of the western provinces are quite different. If their parents are killed they retire from the battle and perform Buddhist rites to console the souls of the dead. Only after the mourning is over will they fight again. If their children are slain, their grief is so deep that they cease fighting altogether. When their rations are given out, they plant rice in the fields and go out to fight only after reaping it. They dislike the heat of summer. They grumble at the severe cold of winter. This is not the way of the soldiers of the eastern provinces.*[7]

Both within aristocratic circles and outside them Buddhism remained very strong throughout this period. A mission sent to China in 804 included two monks in search of new texts. Saichō spent time at Mount Tiantai and brought back Tendai (Chinese Tiantai) teachings. Tendai's basic message is that all living beings share the Buddha nature and can be brought to salvation. In addition, the Buddhas and bodhisattvas are always at work helping people to achieve salvation. Tendai practices include strict monastic discipline, prayer, textual study, and meditation. Once back in Japan, Saichō established a monastery on Mount Hiei, outside Kyoto, which grew to be one of the most important monasteries in Japan. By the twelfth century this monastery and its many branch temples had vast lands and a powerful army of monk-soldiers to protect its interests. Whenever the monastery felt that its interests were at risk, it sent the monk-soldiers into the capital to carry its sacred symbols in an attempt to intimidate the civil authorities.

Kūkai, the other monk on the 804 mission to China, came back with texts from another school of Buddhism—Shingon, or **Esoteric Buddhism.** Esoteric Buddhism is based on the idea that teachings containing the secrets of enlightenment have been secretly transmitted from the Buddha. An adept can gain access to these mysteries through initiation into the mandalas (cosmic diagrams), mudras (gestures), and mantras (verbal formulas). The popularity of Esoteric Buddhism proved a great stimulus to art. On his return to Japan, Kūkai attracted many followers and was allowed to establish a monastery at Mount Koya, south of Osaka.

Only later, during the Kamakura period, did Buddhism begin a vigorous proselytizing phase. Honen propagated the Pure Land teaching (see pages 197–198), preaching

**Zen Rock Garden** Rock gardens, such as this one at Ryoanji in Kyoto, capture the austere aesthetic of Zen Buddhism. *(Photo courtesy of the International Society for Educational Information)*

that paradise could be reached through simple faith in the Buddha and repeating the name of the Buddha Amitabha. Neither philosophical understanding of Buddhist scriptures nor devotion to rituals was necessary. Nichiren, a fiery and intolerant preacher, proclaimed that to be saved people had only to invoke sincerely the Lotus Sutra. These lay versions of Buddhism found a receptive audience among ordinary people in the countryside.

It was also during the Kamakura period that Zen (Chan) came to flourish in Japan. As mentioned in Chapter 7, Zen teachings originated in Tang China. Rejecting the authority of the sutras, Zen teachers claimed the superiority of mind-to-mind transmission of Buddhist truth and monastic discipline. When Japanese monks went to China in the twelfth century looking for ways to revitalize Japanese Buddhism, they were impressed by the rigorous monastic life of the Chan/Zen monasteries. Eisai introduced Rinzai Zen, which held that enlightenment could be achieved suddenly through insight into one's own true nature, and he practiced rigorous meditation. This teaching found eager patrons among the samurai, who were attracted to its discipline. Soto Zen teachings, introduced a century later from China by Dogen, focused specifically on seated meditation, which Dogen believed held the secret of enlightenment. After Dogen's death, Soto Zen incorporated elements of Esoteric Buddhism and popular practices such as prayers for material benefit, which gave it wide popular appeal.

Buddhist sentiments pervade much of Japanese literature from this period. For instance, Kamo no Chōmei (1153–1216) wrote a memoir describing the world he knew before and after becoming a monk and settling into a ten-foot-square hut. He stressed the disasters he had personally witnessed, such as a tornado and an earthquake, a fire that had destroyed huge sections of the city, and a two-year famine that resulted in tens of thousands of bodies abandoned in the city. Social circumstances also made life difficult to endure:

*The poor man who is the neighbor of a wealthy family is always ashamed of his wretched appearance, and makes his entrances and exits in bursts of flattery. And when he sees how envious his wife and children and his servants are, or hears how the rich family despises him, his mind is incessantly torn by an agitation that leaves not a moment's peace. If a man's house stands in a crowded place and a fire breaks out in the neighborhood, he cannot escape the danger. If it stands in a remote situation, he must put up with the nuisance of going back and forth to the city, and there is always a danger of robbers.*[8]

In the Ashikaga period Zen temples served as literary salons where monks, nobles, and warriors could mingle. An aesthetic style marked by restraint came to supplant the aristocratic style of the Heian period. The rock gardens of the major Zen temples of Heian offer an example of this aesthetic, as do some of the minimalist ink paintings of the period.

## SUMMARY

In the period from 800 to 1400, China was probably the most advanced society in the world, with a booming economy, a highly developed material culture, and a sophisticated form of government that recruited officials on the basis of their education rather than their birth or military prowess. Philosophy and the arts all flourished. The other principal countries of East Asia, particularly Korea and Japan, were developing in other directions in this period. In both Korea and Japan, after a period in which court aristocrats were dominant both politically and culturally, generals and military interests gained dominance. In the case of Japan, this proved to be a long-term development, and the samurai developed a very distinct ethos. All three countries were affected by the rise of the Mongols. Neither China nor Korea was able to repel the Mongols, though they spent decades trying. Japan marshaled its resources to repulse two seaborne attempts at invasion.

## KEY TERMS

| | |
|---|---|
| examination system | samurai |
| movable type | shogun |
| Neo-Confucianism | Bushido |
| paper money | military land stewards |
| compass | military governors |
| concubine | *The Tale of Genji* |
| foot binding | Esoteric Buddhism |
| cloistered government | |

## NOTES

1. *The Travels of Marco Polo, the Venetian*, ed. Manuel Komroff (New York: Boni and Liveright, 1926), p. 227.
2. Ibid., p. 159.
3. Ibid., p. 235.

*(continued on page 360)*

# LISTENING TO THE PAST

## The Pillow Book of Sei Shonagon

*Beginning in the late tenth century, Japan produced a series of great women writers. At the time women were much freer than men to write in vernacular Japanese, giving them a large advantage. Lady Murasaki, author of the novel* The Tale of Genji, *is the most famous of the women writers of the period, but her contemporary Sei Shonagon is equally noteworthy. Sei Shonagon served as a lady in waiting to Empress Sadako during the last decade of the tenth century (990–1000). Her only known work is* The Pillow Book, *a collection of notes, character sketches, anecdotes, descriptions of nature, and eccentric lists such as boring things, awkward things, hateful things, and things that have lost their power.*

The Pillow Book *portrays the lovemaking/marriage system among the aristocracy more or less as it is depicted in* The Tale of Genji. *Marriages were arranged for family interests, and men could have more than one wife. Wives and their children commonly stayed in their own homes, where their husbands and fathers would visit them. But once a man had an heir by his wife, there was nothing to prevent him from establishing relations with other women. Some relationships were long-term, but many were brief, and men often had several lovers at the same time. Some women became known for their amorous conquests, others as abandoned women whose husbands ignored them. The following passage from* The Pillow Book *looks on this lovemaking system with amused detachment.*

It is so stiflingly hot in the Seventh Month that even at night one keeps all the doors and lattices open. At such times it is delightful to wake up when the moon is shining and to look outside. I enjoy it even when there is no moon. But to wake up at dawn and see a pale sliver of a moon in the sky—well, I need hardly say how perfect that is.

I like to see a bright new straw mat that has just been spread out on a well-polished floor. The best place for one's three-foot curtain of state is in the front of the room near the veranda. It is pointless to put it in the rear of the room, as it is most unlikely that anyone will peer in from that direction.

It is dawn and a woman is lying in bed after her lover has taken his leave. She is covered up to her head with a light mauve robe that has a lining of dark violet; the colour of both the outside and the lining is fresh and glossy. The woman, who appears to be asleep, wears an unlined orange robe and a dark crimson skirt of stiff silk whose cords hang loosely by her side, as if they have been left untied. Her thick tresses tumble over each other in cascades, and one can imagine how long her hair must be when it falls freely down her back.

Nearby another woman's lover is making his way home in the misty dawn. He is wearing loose violet trousers, an orange hunting costume, so lightly coloured that one can hardly tell whether it has been dyed or not, a white robe of still silk, and a scarlet robe of glossy, beaten silk. His clothes, which are damp from the mist, hang loosely about him. From the dishevelment of his side locks one can tell how negligently he must have tucked his hair into the black lacquered head-dress when he got up. He wants to return and write his next-morning letter before the dew on the morning glories has had time to vanish; but the path seems endless, and to divert himself he hums "the sprouts in the flax fields."

As he walks along, he passes a house with an open lattice. He is on his way to report for official duty, but cannot help stopping to lift up the blind and peep into the room. It amuses him to think that a man has probably been spending the night here and has only recently got up to leave, just as

During the Heian period, noblewomen were fashion-conscious. Wearing numerous layers of clothing gave women the opportunity to choose different designs and colors for their robes. The layers also kept them warm in drafty homes. *(The Museum Yamato Bunkakan)*

happened to himself. Perhaps that man too had felt the charm of the dew.

Looking around the room, he notices near the woman's pillow an open fan with a magnolia frame and purple paper; and at the foot of her curtain of state he sees some narrow strips of Michinoku paper and also some other paper of a faded colour, either orange-red or maple.

The woman senses that someone is watching her and, looking up from under her bedclothes, sees a gentleman leaning against the wall by the threshold, a smile on his face. She can tell at once that he is the sort of man with whom she need feel no reserve. All the same, she does not want to enter into any familiar relations with him, and she is annoyed that he should have seen her asleep.

"Well, well, Madam," says the man, leaning forward so that the upper part of his body comes behind her curtains, "what a long nap you're having after your morning adieu! You really are a lie-abed!"

"You call me that, Sir," she replied, "only because you're annoyed at having had to get up before the dew had time to settle."

Their conversation may be commonplace, yet I find there is something delightful about the scene.

Now the gentleman leans further forward and, using his own fan, tries to get hold of the fan by the woman's pillow. Fearing his closeness, she moves further back into her curtain enclosure, her heart pounding. The gentleman picks up the magnolia fan and, while examining it, says in a slightly bitter tone, "How standoffish you are!"

But now it is growing light; there is a sound of people's voices, and it looks as if the sun will soon be up. Only a short while ago this same man was hurrying home to write his next-morning letter before the mists had time to clear. Alas, how easily his intentions have been forgotten!

While all this is afoot, the woman's original lover has been busy with his own next-morning letter, and now, quite unexpectedly, the messenger arrives at her house. The letter is attached to a spray of bush-clover, still damp with dew, and the paper gives off a delicious aroma of incense. Because of the new visitor, however, the woman's servants cannot deliver it to her.

Finally it becomes unseemly for the gentleman to stay any longer. As he goes, he is amused to think that a similar scene may be taking place in the house he left earlier that morning.

## QUESTIONS FOR ANALYSIS

1. What sorts of images does Sei Shonagon evoke to convey an impression of a scene?
2. What can you learn from this passage about the material culture of Japan in this period?
3. Why do you think Sei Shonagon was highly esteemed as a writer?

*Source:* Ivan Morris, trans., *The Pillow Book of Sei Shonagon* (New York: Penguin Books, 1970), pp. 60–62. 

4. Peter H. Lee, ed., *Sourcebook of Korean Civilization* (New York: Columbia University Press, 1993), p. 327.
5. Ivan Morris, trans., *The Pillow Book of Sei Shonagon* (New York: Penguin Books, 1970), p. 258.
6. Quoted in M. Collcott, M. Jansen, and I. Kumakura, *Cultural Atlas of Japan* (New York: Facts on File, 1988), p. 82, slightly modified.
7. Ibid., p. 101.
8. Donald Keene, ed., *Anthology of Japanese Literature* (New York: Grove Press, 1960), p. 205.

## SUGGESTED READING

General histories of China are listed in Chapter 4. Probably the best general introduction to the Song period is J. Gernet, *Daily Life in China on the Eve of the Mongol Invasion, 1250–76* (1962). The flourishing economy of the Song is analyzed in Y. Shiba, *Commerce and Society in Sung China* (1970). Song foreign relations are covered in the symposium volume edited by M. Rossabi, *China Among Equals: The Middle Kingdom and Its Neighbors* (1983). On Song government, see J. Chaffee's study of the examination system, *The Thorny Gates of Learning in Sung China: A Social History of Examinations* (1985); J. Liu on Wang Anshi, *Reform in Sung China: Wang An-Shih (1021–1086) and His New Policies* (1957); and B. McKnight, *Law and Order in Sung China* (1992).

On Neo-Confucianism and the scholar-official elite, see A. C. Graham, *Two Chinese Philosophers: Ch'eng Ming-tao and Ch'eng Yi-ch'uan* (1958); P. Bol, *"This Culture of Ours": Intellectual Transitions in T'ang and Sung China* (1992); and R. Hymes, *Statesmen and Gentlemen: The Elite of Fu-chou, Chiang-hsi, in Northern and Southern Sung* (1986). On popular religion, see V. Hansen, *Changing the Gods in Medieval China, 1127–1276* (1990); E. Davis, *Society and the Supernatural in Song China* (2001); and R. Hymes, *Way and Byway: Taoism, Local Religion, and Models of Divinity in Sung and Modern China* (2002). For a study of women's lives, see P. Ebrey, *The Inner Quarters: Marriage and the Lives of Chinese Women in the Sung Period* (1993).

General histories of Korea and Japan are listed in Chapter 7. R. Lancaster et al., *Buddhism in Koryo: A Royal Religion* (2002), deals with an important issue in Korean history. I. Morris, *The World of the Shining Prince: Court Life in Ancient Japan* (1964), provides an engaging portrait of Heian culture. Lady Murasaki's *The Tale of Genji* has been translated by E. G. Seidensticker (1976); I. Morris has translated *The Pillow Book of Sei Shonagon,* 2 vols. (1967).

Japanese feudalism, like its medieval European counterpart, continues to inspire discussion and disagreement. Some provocative works include P. Duus, *Feudalism in Japan,* 2d ed. (1976); E. O. Reischauer, "Japanese Feudalism," in R. Coulborn, ed., *Feudalism in History* (1956), pp. 26–48; and T. Keirstead, *The Geography of Power in Medieval Japan* (1992), which attempts to determine the cultural framework of the feudal land system. For military affairs, see W. W. Farris, *Heavenly Warriors* (1992), which argues against Western analogies in explaining the dominance of the samurai, and K. F. Friday, *Hired Swords* (1992), which treats the evolution of state military development in connection with the emergence of the samurai. P. Varley, *Warriors of Japan* (1994), draws on war tales to examine samurai culture. A good sense of the world-view of the samurai also can be found by reading literary works of the period in translation, such as *The Tale of the Heike,* trans. H. Kitagawa and B. Tsuchida (1976), and *Yoshitsune,* trans. H. McCullough (1971). On Zen Buddhism in the medieval era, see M. Collcutt, *Five Mountains, the Rinzai Zen Monastic Institution in Medieval Japan* (1981), and H. Dumoulin, *A History of Zen Buddhism* (1963).

Allegorical harvesting scenes from a German manuscript, *Speculum Virginum,* ca 1190. *(Rheinisches Landesmuseum, Bonn)*

CHAPTER

# 13 EUROPE IN THE MIDDLE AGES

## CHAPTER OUTLINE

- The Frankish Kingdom
- Feudalism and Manorialism
- Crisis and Recovery
- Revival and Reform in the Christian Church
- The Crusades
- The Expansion of Latin Christendom
- Medieval Origins of the Modern Western State
- Economic Revival
- Universities, Gothic Art, and Poetry
- Life in Christian Europe in the Central Middle Ages
- Crises of the Later Middle Ages
- Race and Ethnicity on the Frontiers

Historians commonly divide long eras into shorter time periods, according to the features they believe characteristic of those periods. Historians do this as a tool or hypothesis for dealing with vast amounts of material. The Italian Renaissance humanist Francesco Petrarch (1304–1374) coined the term *Middle Ages* to describe the period in European history from about 500 to 1350. Petrarch believed that his own age was a golden age marked by an intellectual and cultural brilliance that recaptured the cultural splendor of ancient Roman civilization. Between the Roman world and the Renaissance, Petrarch believed, there were "the Middle Ages," a time of gothic barbarism and intellectual stagnation (see page 452).

Scholars have adopted Petrarch's terminology and time divisions when studying the postclassical European world before about 1350. But Petrarch had it wrong about barbarism and stagnation. When urban life declined and Roman political institutions decayed in western Europe, Europeans developed new political and economic devices to serve their social needs. Between about 1050 and 1350, Europeans displayed enormous intellectual energy and creative vitality. That later period witnessed the beginnings of ideas and institutions that not only shaped the Western world but subsequently influenced societies around the world.

During the millennium from about 500 to 1500, Europe was not isolated from contacts with other peoples. A small volume of trade trickled across Central Asia to Europe on routes commonly called the Silk Road. In the early eighth century, Muslim forces from North Africa conquered Spain. Later, the Arabs overran Sicily and penetrated southern Italy. They attacked Naples and, in 839, pillaged Ancona in central Italy. In subsequent centuries, Islamic learning profoundly affected European culture in areas such as architecture, medicine, philosophy, and poetry. In the late eighth century, pagan Northmen, or Vikings, from Scandinavia made deep incursions into Europe, from Iceland and Ireland to Russia. The Vikings also influenced Europeans' political, economic, and social institutions. After 1095, Europeans' own imperialistic expansion in the Middle East during the crusading movement, the first large-scale colonizing action beyond the geographical boundaries of the European continent, helped shape the identity of the West. The evidence of medieval art suggests that in the twelfth and thirteenth centuries a few sub-Saharan African people lived in western Europe, although this subject

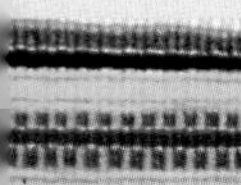

remains to be adequately explored. The period we call the European Middle Ages witnessed many such intercontinental links.

- How did Charlemagne acquire and govern his empire? What Merovingian institutions did he utilize? What is meant by the term *Carolingian Renaissance?*
- In the period from about 900 to 1350, was feudalism—as a method of government, a social "system," and a cultural force—possible without manorialism?
- How did the Christian church and civil governments influence one another during the Middle Ages?
- How did medieval rulers work to solve their problems of government, thereby laying the foundations of modern states?
- How did medieval towns originate, and how do they reveal the beginnings of radical change in European society?
- What were the salient marks of creativity in the central Middle Ages?
- What factors precipitated crises in the later Middle Ages, and how were these crises interrelated?
- In the period from about 800 to 1350, how did Islam and Christian Europe affect each other militarily? What cultural influences did Islam exert on Europe, including artistic, philosophical, and literary elements?

These are among the questions this chapter will explore.

## THE FRANKISH KINGDOM

The Frankish kingdom that had emerged under Clovis (see page 223) by the early sixth century included most of what is now France and a large section of southwestern Germany. Clovis's baptism into Orthodox Christianity won him church support against other Germanic tribes. Although his family, the Merovingians, continued to lead France for two centuries after his death, they were troubled years. Then a new dynasty—the Carolingians—moved to the throne.

Clovis's descendant Charles Martel defeated Muslim invaders in 732 at the Battle of Tours in central France.[1] Muslims and Christians have interpreted the battle differently. Muslims considered it a minor skirmish and attributed the Frankish victory to Muslim difficulties in maintaining supply lines over long distances and to ethnic conflicts and unrest in Islamic Spain. Christians considered the Frankish victory one of the great battles of history because it halted Muslim expansion in Europe. A century later, in 843, Charles Martel's three great-great-grandsons, after a bitter war, concluded the Treaty of Verdun, which divided the European continent among them. Civil disorder and foreign invasion then wracked Europe for about the next 150 years.

Between 732 and 843, a distinctly European society emerged. A new kind of social and political organization, later called feudalism, appeared. And for the first time since the collapse of the Roman Empire, most of western Europe was united under one government, which reached its peak under Charles Martel's grandson, Charlemagne. Christian missionary activity among the Germanic peoples continued, and strong ties were forged with the Roman papacy. A revival of study and learning—the Carolingian Renaissance—occurred during the reign of Charlemagne.

### The Merovingians and the Rise of the Carolingians

When Clovis died, following Frankish custom, he divided his kingdom among his four sons. For the next two centuries, the land was often wracked by civil war. These wars had several causes. Lacking a clear principle of succession, any male of Merovingian blood could claim the throne, and within the family there were always many possibilities. In addition, members of the royal family and their followers hoped to win land, booty, and plunder. So brutal were these wars that historians used the term *Dark Ages* to apply to the entire Merovingian period. Yet recent research has presented a more complex picture, suggesting that the wars did not fundamentally threaten the kingdom and even served as "a unifying part of the structure of the Frankish state."[2]

Merovingian kings based their administration on the *civitas,* the city and the surrounding territory over which a *count* presided. The count raised troops, collected royal revenues, and provided justice on the basis of local, not royal, law. At the king's court—that is, wherever he was present—an official called the *mayor of the palace* supervised legal, financial, and household officials; the mayor of the palace also governed in the king's absence. That position, combined with advantageous marriages, a well-earned reputation for military strength, and the help of the church, paved the way for the rise to power of one family, the Carolingians.[3]

In the eighth century, Irish, Frankish, and Anglo-Saxon missionaries were active throughout the Frankish kingdom. The Englishman Boniface (680–754) is the most famous of these, and his achievements were remarkable. He helped shape the structure of the Frankish church, held

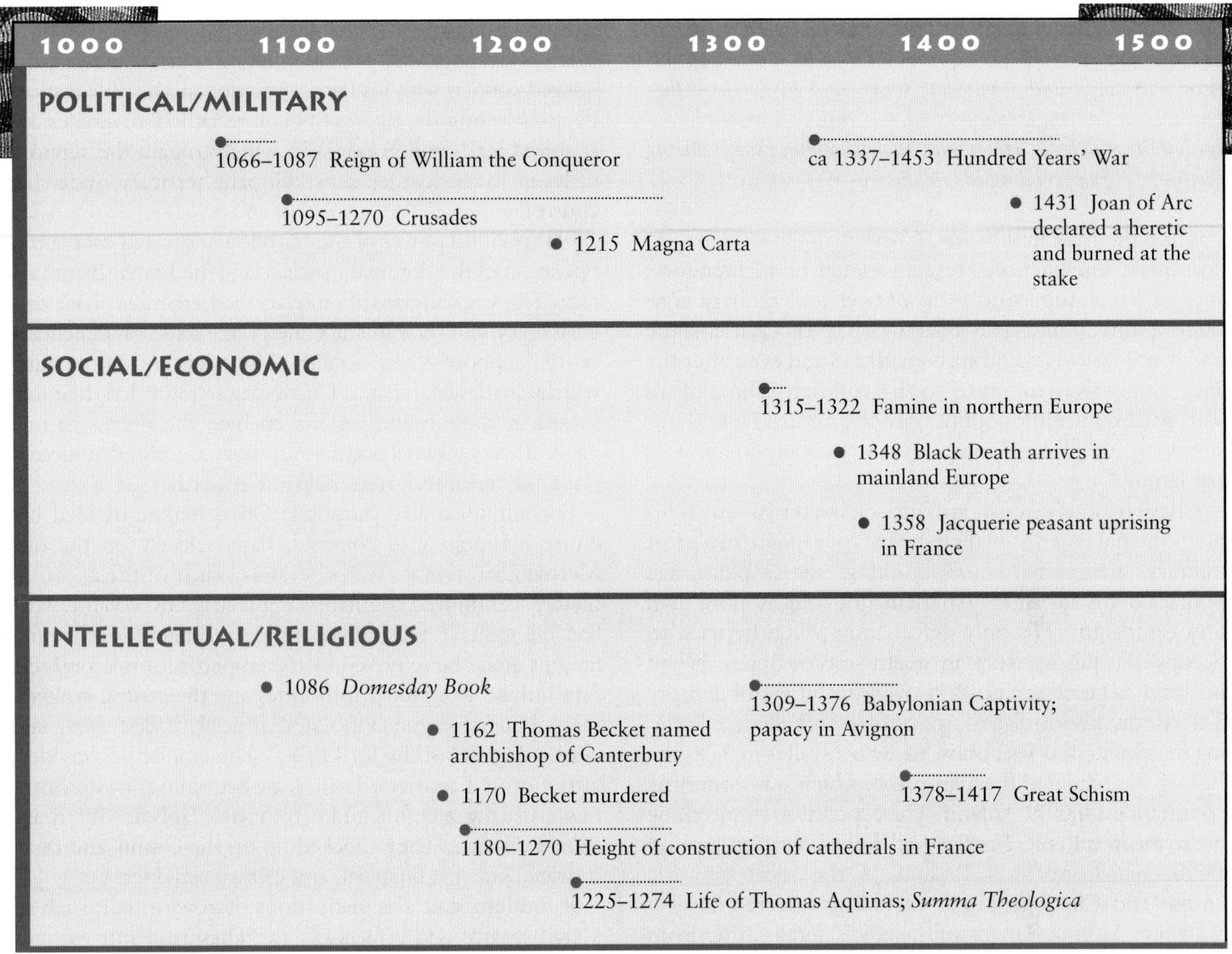


councils to reform it, and tried to establish *The Rule of Saint Benedict* in all the monasteries he founded. The Carolingian mayors Charles Martel (r. 714–741) and Pippin III (r. 751–768) backed these efforts, as missionaries also preached obedience to secular authority. Their support of the church had dividends for the family.

Charles Martel had exercised the power of the king of the Franks. His son Pippin III aspired to the title as well. Pippin did not want to murder the ineffectual Merovingian king, but he wanted the kingship. He consulted Pope Zacharias, who condoned the removal of the king and Pippin's assumption of the throne.

When Pippin died, his son Charles the Great (r. 768–814), generally known as Charlemagne, succeeded him. In the autumn of the year 800, Charlemagne visited Rome, where on Christmas Day Pope Leo III crowned him Holy Roman emperor. The event had momentous consequences. In taking as his motto *Renovatio romani imperi* (Revival of the Roman Empire), Charlemagne was deliberately perpetuating old Roman imperial ideas, while identifying with the new Rome of the Christian church.[4] Charlemagne and his government represented a fusion of Frankish practices and Christian ideals, the two basic elements of medieval European society.

## The Empire of Charlemagne

Charlemagne built on the military and diplomatic foundations of his ancestors. Einhard, his secretary and biographer, wrote a lengthy idealization of the warrior-ruler. It has serious flaws but is the earliest medieval biography of a layman, and historians consider it generally accurate:

*Charles was large and strong, and of lofty stature, though not disproportionately tall . . . the upper part of his head was round, his eyes very large and animated, nose a little long, hair fair, and face laughing and merry. Thus his appearance was always stately and dignified . . . although his neck was thick and somewhat short, and his belly rather prominent; but the symmetry of the rest of his body concealed these defects. His health was excellent, except during the four years preceding his death.*[5]

Though crude and brutal, Charlemagne was a man of enormous intelligence. He appreciated good literature, such as Saint Augustine's *City of God,* and Einhard considered him an unusually effective speaker. Charlemagne had four legal wives and six concubines and even after the age of sixty-five continued to sire children. Three of his sons reached adulthood, but only one outlived him. Four surviving grandsons, however, ensured perpetuation of the family.[6]

Charlemagne's most striking characteristic was his phenomenal energy, which helps to explain his great military achievements. Continuing the expansionist policies of his ancestors, Charlemagne fought more than fifty campaigns. His only defeat came when he tried to occupy Basque territory in northwestern Spain. When his long siege of Saragossa proved unsuccessful and the Saxons on his northeastern borders rebelled, Charlemagne decided to withdraw. At Roncesvalles in 778, the Basques annihilated his rear guard, which was under the command of Count Roland. The expedition inspired the great medieval epic *The Song of Roland,* written around 1100, which portrays Roland as the ideal chivalric knight and Charlemagne as exercising a sacred kind of kingship. Although many of the epic's details differ from the historical evidence, *The Song of Roland* is important because it reveals the popular image of Charlemagne in later centuries.

By around 805, the Frankish kingdom included all of continental Europe except Spain, Scandinavia, southern Italy, and the Slavic fringes of the East (see Map 13.1). The Muslims in northeastern Spain were checked by the establishment of strongly fortified areas known both as *marches* and as *marks.* Not since the third century C.E. had any ruler controlled so much of the Western world.

Charlemagne ruled a vast rural world dotted with isolated estates and characterized by constant petty violence. His empire was not a state as people today understand that term; it was a collection of peoples and semibarbaric tribes. Apart from a small class of warrior-aristocrats and clergy, almost everyone engaged in agriculture. Trade and commerce played only a small part in the economy. Cities served as the headquarters of bishops and as ecclesiastical centers.

By constant travel, personal appearances, and the sheer force of his personality, Charlemagne sought to awe conquered peoples with his fierce presence and terrible justice. By confiscating the estates of great territorial magnates, he acquired lands and goods with which to gain the support of lesser lords, further expanding the territory under his control.

The political power of the Carolingians rested on the cooperation of the dominant social class, the Frankish aristocracy. The Carolingians themselves had emerged from this aristocracy, and their military and political success depended on the support of the nobility. The lands and booty with which Charles Martel and Charlemagne rewarded their followers in these noble families enabled the nobles to improve their economic position. In short, Carolingian success was a matter of reciprocal help and reward.[7]

For administrative purposes, Charlemagne divided his entire kingdom into counties, based closely on the old Merovingian civitas (see page 364). Each of the approximately six hundred counties was governed by a count, who had full military and judicial power and held his office for life but could be removed by the emperor for misconduct. As a link between local authorities and the central government, Charlemagne appointed officials called *missi dominici,* "agents of the lord king." The empire was divided into visitorial districts. Each year, beginning in 802, two missi, usually a count and a bishop or abbot, visited assigned districts. They checked up on the counts and their districts' judicial, financial, and clerical activities.

A modern state has institutions of government such as a civil service and courts of law. These did not exist in Charlemagne's empire. Instead, dependent relationships cemented by oaths promising faith and loyalty held society together. Nevertheless, although the empire lacked viable institutions, Carolingian abbots and bishops who served as Charlemagne's advisers worked out what was for their time a sophisticated political ideology.

In letters and treatises, churchmen set before their ruler high standards of behavior and of government. They wrote that although a ruler holds power from God, the ruler is obliged to respect the law just as all subjects of the empire were required to obey the ruler. The abbots and bishops envisioned a unified Christian society presided over by a king who was responsible for maintaining peace, law, and order and dispensing justice, without which, they pointed out, neither the ruler nor the kingdom had any justification. These views derived largely from Saint Augustine's theories of kingship. Inevitably, they could not be realized in an illiterate, preindustrial society. But they were the seeds from which medieval and even modern ideas of government were to develop.

**MAP 13.1 The Carolingian World** The extent of Charlemagne's nominal jurisdiction was extraordinary. It was not equaled until the nineteenth century.

## The Carolingian Intellectual Revival

It is ironic that Charlemagne's most enduring legacy was the stimulus he gave to scholarship and learning. Barely literate, preoccupied with the control of vast territories, much more a warrior than a thinker, Charlemagne nevertheless set in motion a cultural revival that had widespread and long-lasting consequences.

The revival of learning associated with Charlemagne and his court at Aachen drew its greatest inspiration from seventh- and eighth-century intellectual developments in the Anglo-Saxon kingdom of Northumbria, situated at the northernmost tip of the old Roman world (see Map 13.1). Northumbrian monasteries produced scores of religious books, commentaries on the Scriptures, illuminated manuscripts, law codes, and collections of letters and sermons.

The finest representative of Northumbrian and indeed all Anglo-Saxon scholarship is the Venerable Bede (ca 673–735). The author of learned commentaries on the Scriptures, Bede also produced the *Ecclesiastical History of the English Nation,* our chief source of information about early Britain. He discussed the validity of his evidence, compared various sources, and exercised a rare critical judgment. For these reasons, he has been called "the first scientific intellect among the Germanic peoples of Europe."[8]

At his court at Aachen, Charlemagne assembled learned men from all over Europe. The most important scholar and the leader of the palace school was the Northumbrian Alcuin (ca 735–804). From 781 until his death, Alcuin was the emperor's chief adviser on religious and educational matters. He prepared some of the emperor's official documents and wrote many moral *exempla,* or "models," which set high standards for royal behavior and constitute a treatise on kingship. Alcuin's letters to Charlemagne set forth political theories on the authority, power, and responsibilities of a Christian ruler.

Scholars at Charlemagne's court copied books and manuscripts and built up libraries. They used the beautifully clear handwriting now known as Carolingian minuscule, from which modern Roman type is derived. This script is called "minuscule" because it has lowercase as well as capital letters; the script that the Romans used had only capitals. Because lowercase letters are smaller than capitals, scribes using Carolingian minuscule could put more words on each sheet of vellum and could increase the number of texts they copied.

Scholars established schools all across Europe, attaching them to monasteries and cathedrals. They placed great emphasis on the education of priests, trying to make all priests at least able to read, write, and do simple arithmetic. The greatest contribution of the scholars at Aachen was not so much the originality of their ideas as their hard work of salvaging and preserving the thought and writings of the ancients. The Carolingian Renaissance was a rebirth of interest in, study of, and preservation of the language, ideas, and achievements of classical Greece and Rome.

Once basic literacy was established, monastic and other scholars went on to more difficult work. By the middle of the ninth century, there was a great outpouring of more sophisticated books. Ecclesiastical writers, imbued with the legal ideas of ancient Rome and the theocratic ideals of Saint Augustine, instructed the semi-barbaric rulers of the West. And it is no accident that medical study in the West began, at Salerno in southern Italy, in the late ninth century, *after* the Carolingian Renaissance. By the tenth century, the patterns of thought and lifestyles of educated western Europeans were those of Rome and Latin Christianity. Even the violence and destruction of the great invasions of the late ninth and tenth centuries could not destroy the strong foundations laid by Alcuin and his colleagues.

### Aristocratic Resurgence

Charlemagne left his vast empire to his sole surviving son, Louis the Pious (r. 814–840). Initially, the new king proved as tough as his father, banishing from his court real and supposed conspirators, crushing rebellions, and punishing his enemies. In 821, though, Louis seems to have undergone a change and began to pardon some rebels and allow exiles to return. The emperor underestimated the magnates; they stirred jealousy among his sons and plotted to augment their own wealth and power.

Between 817 and his death, Louis made several divisions of the empire. Dissatisfied with their portions and hoping to win the imperial title, his three sons—Lothar, Louis the German, and Charles the Bald—fought bitterly among themselves. Finally, in the Treaty of Verdun of 843, they agreed to divide the empire.

In the past, historians accounted for the collapse of the Carolingian Empire by stressing the fratricidal wars among Charlemagne's three grandsons. Recent work, however, emphasizes the conspiracies and revolts of the magnates. Charlemagne had tried to prevent the office of count from becoming hereditary in one family, but that is precisely what happened in the ninth century. In addition, some nobles acquired several counties. As they gained power, they could effectively block the king's authority in their lands. The administrative system built by Pippin III and Charlemagne survived, but imperial control weakened. The local magnates held the power.[9]

## FEUDALISM AND MANORIALISM

*Feudalism,* long used to describe medieval society, was a term invented in the seventeenth century and popularized in the eighteenth by political philosophers who disparaged it as a symbol of entrenched aristocratic privilege. Scholars have struggled to work out a definition of feudalism that can apply to the entire Middle Ages (ca 500–1500), but they have not succeeded.

Two main explanations for the rise of feudalism have emerged. According to the older explanation, the eighth-century Carolingian kings and magnates needed armed retainers who could fight on horseback. Around this time, a new Chinese technology, the stirrup, arrived in Europe and was adopted by riders, who could use it to gain leverage and thus use the force of the galloping horse to impale an enemy with a spear. It took time and money to equip and train these riders, so the king and magnates bound their retainers by oaths of loyalty. The second approach dismisses the stirrup, pointing out that most warfare was conducted by infantry. In this view, feudal relationships arose as kings and magnates purchased the support and loyalty of followers with lands or estates confiscated from the church.

Whatever the exact causes, the weakening of central power within the Carolingian Empire led to an increase in the power of local authorities, the counts. They governed virtually independent territories in which weak and distant kings could not interfere. "Political power had become a private, heritable property for great counts and lords."[10] This was feudalism as a form of government.

Feudalism concerned the rights, powers, and lifestyles of the military elite. *Manorialism* involved the services of the peasant class. The two were linked. The economic power of the warrior class rested on landed estates, which were worked by peasants. Peasants needed protection, and lords demanded something in return for that protection. Free farmers surrendered themselves and their land to the lord's jurisdiction. The land was given back to them to farm, but they were tied to the land by various payments and services. Those obligations varied from place to place, but certain practices became common everywhere. The peasant had to give the lord a percentage of the annual harvest, pay a fine to marry someone from outside the lord's estate, and pay a fine—usually the best sheep or cow owned—to inherit property. Most significant, the peasant lost his freedom and became a *serf,* part of the lord's permanent labor force, bound to the land and unable to leave it without the lord's permission. With large tracts of land and a small pool of labor, the most profitable form of capital was not land but laborers.

The transition from freedom to serfdom was slow, depending on the degree of political order in a given region. By the year 800, though, perhaps 60 percent of the population of western Europe had been reduced to serfdom. While there were many economic levels within this serf class, from the highly prosperous to the desperately poor, all had lost their freedom.

**Homage and Fealty** Although the rite of entering a feudal relationship varied widely across Europe and sometimes was entirely verbal, we have a few illustrations of it. Here the vassal kneels before the lord, places his clasped hands between those of the lord, and declares, "I become your man." Sometimes the lord handed over a clump of earth, representing the fief, and the ceremony concluded with a kiss, symbolizing peace between them. *(Osterreichische Nationalbibliothek)*

## CRISIS AND RECOVERY

After the Treaty of Verdun and the division of Charlemagne's empire among his grandsons, continental Europe presented an easy target for foreign invaders. All three kingdoms were torn by domestic dissension and disorder. No European political power was strong enough to put up effective resistance to external attacks.

### Assaults on Western Europe

From the moors of Scotland to the mountains of Sicily, there arose in the ninth century the Christian prayer, "Save us, O God, from the violence of the Northmen." The Northmen, also known as Normans or Vikings, were pagan Germanic peoples from Norway, Sweden, and Denmark who had remained beyond the sway of the Christianizing and civilizing influences of the Carolingian Empire. Some scholars believe that the name *Viking* derives from the Old Norse word *vik,* meaning "creek." A Viking, then, was a pirate who waited in a creek or bay to attack passing vessels.

Viking assaults began around 787, and by the mid-tenth century the Vikings had brought large sections of continental Europe and Britain under their sway. In the east, they pierced the rivers of Russia as far as the Black Sea. In the west, they sailed as far as Iceland, Greenland, and even the coast of North America, perhaps as far south as Long Island Sound, New York.

The Vikings were superb seamen with advanced methods of boatbuilding. Propelled either by oars or by sails, deckless, and about sixty-five feet long, a Viking ship could carry between forty and sixty men—quite enough to harass an isolated monastery or village. Against these ships navigated by thoroughly experienced and utterly fearless sailors, the Carolingian Empire, with no navy, was helpless. The Vikings moved swiftly, attacked, and escaped to return again.

Scholars disagree about the reasons for Viking attacks and migrations. Some maintain that overpopulation forced the Vikings to emigrate. Others argue that climatic conditions and crop failures forced migration. Still others insist that the Vikings were looking for trade and new commercial contacts, along with targets for plunder. At first they attacked and sailed off laden with booty. Later, on returning, they settled down and colonized the areas they had conquered. Between 876 and 954, Viking control extended from Dublin across the Irish Sea to Britain, then across northern Britain and the North Sea to the Vikings' Scandinavian homelands. These invaders also overran a large part of northwestern France and called the territory Norsemanland, from which the word *Normandy* derives.

Scarcely had the savagery of the Viking assaults begun to subside when Europe was hit from the east and south. Beginning about 890, Magyar tribes crossed the Danube and pushed steadily westward. (People thought of them as returning Huns, so the Magyars came to be known as Hungarians.) They subdued northern Italy, compelled Bavaria and Saxony to pay tribute, and penetrated even into the Rhineland and Burgundy. These roving bandits attacked isolated villages and monasteries, taking prisoners and selling them in the Eastern slave markets. The Magyars were not colonizers; their sole object was booty and plunder.

From the south, the Muslims also began new encroachments, concentrating on the two southern peninsulas, Italy and Spain. Seventh- and early-eighth-century Islamic movements had been for conquest and colonization, but the goal of ninth- and tenth-century incursions was plunder. In Italy the Muslims drove northward and sacked Rome in 846. Most of Spain had remained under their domination since the eighth century. Expert seamen, they sailed around the Iberian Peninsula and braved the dangerous shoals and winds of the Atlantic coast. They also attacked Mediterranean settlements along the coast of Provence. But Muslim attacks on the European continent in the ninth and tenth centuries were less destructive than the assaults of the more primitive Vikings and Magyars.

What was the effect of these invasions on the structure of European society? Viking, Magyar, and Muslim attacks accelerated the development of feudalism. Lords capable of rallying fighting men, supporting them, and putting up resistance to the invaders did so. They also assumed political power in their territories. Weak and defenseless people sought the protection of local strongmen. Free peasants sank to the level of serfs. Consequently, European society became further fragmented. Public power became increasingly decentralized.

The ninth-century invaders left significant traces of their own cultures. The Muslims made an important contribution to European agriculture, primarily through their influence in Spain. The Vikings, too, made positive contributions to the areas they settled. They carried everywhere their unrivaled knowledge of shipbuilding and seamanship. The northeastern and central parts of England where the Vikings settled became known as the Danelaw because Danish law and customs, not English, prevailed there. York in northern England, once a Roman army camp and then an Anglo-Saxon town, became a thriving center of Viking trade with Scandinavia. At

Dublin on the east coast of Ireland, Viking ironworkers, steelworkers, and combmakers established a center for trade with the Hebrides, Iceland, and Norway. The Irish cities of Limerick, Cork, Wexford, and Waterford trace their origins to Viking trading centers.

### The Restoration of Order

The eleventh century witnessed the beginnings of political stability in western Europe. Foreign invasions gradually declined, and domestic disorder subsided. This development gave people security in their persons and property. Political order and security provided the foundation for economic recovery and contributed to a slow increase in population.

In the tenth century, Charlemagne's descendants continued to hold the royal title in the West Frankish kingdom, but they exercised no effective control over the magnates. Throughout what is now France, regional differences abounded. Northern French society, for example, had strong feudal elements, but in the south vassalage was almost unknown. Southern territories used Roman law, but the northern counties and duchies relied on unwritten customary law that was not codified until the thirteenth century.

Normandy gradually emerged as the strongest territory with the greatest level of peace. In 911, the West Frankish ruler Charles the Simple, unable to oust the Vikings, officially recognized their leader, Rollo, and later invested him with lands. The Vikings were baptized and pledged their support to Charles. Viking raids ended, and the late tenth and early eleventh centuries saw the assimilation of Norman and French.

After the death of the last Carolingian ruler in 987, an assembly of nobles elected Hugh Capet, the head of a powerful clan of the West Frankish kingdom, as king. The history of France as a separate kingdom begins with this event. The first Capetian kings were weak compared to the duke of Normandy, but by hanging on to what they had, they laid the foundation for later political stability.

In Anglo-Saxon England, recovery followed a different pattern. The Vikings had made a concerted effort to conquer and rule the whole island, and perhaps no part of Europe suffered more. The victory of the remarkable Alfred, king of the West Saxons, over Guthrun the Dane at Edington in 878 inaugurated a great political revival. Alfred and his immediate successors built a system of local defenses and slowly extended royal rule beyond Wessex (the area controlled by the West Saxons) to other Anglo-Saxon peoples until one law—royal law—replaced local custom. Alfred and his successors also laid the foundations for a system of local government responsible directly to the king. Under the pressure of the Vikings, the seven kingdoms of England were gradually united under one ruler.

In the east, the German king Otto I (r. 936–973) inflicted a crushing defeat on the Magyars in 955 at Lechfeld, halting their westward expansion, ending the threat to Germany, and making himself a hero to the Germans. Otto's victory revived the German monarchy. To symbolize his intention to continue the tradition of Charlemagne, Otto selected Aachen as the site of his coronation.

The basis of Otto's power was an alliance with and control of the church. Otto asserted the right to control church appointments. Bishops and abbots had to perform feudal homage for the lands that accompanied the church office. This practice, later called **lay investiture,** led to a grave crisis in the eleventh century (see pages 372–373). Otto's coronation by the pope in 962 revived the imperial dignity and laid the foundation for the Holy Roman Empire. He also filled a power vacuum in northern Italy and brought peace and stability to the region. Here, too, were the seeds of future conflict.

Plague, climatic changes, and invasions had drastically reduced the population in northern Italy, though the cities there survived. By the ninth century, some cities, especially Venice, showed economic recovery. Through privileged access to Byzantine markets, Venice imported silk, textiles, cosmetics, and Crimean slaves, which it sold to Padua and other cities. Its commerce stimulated the growth of Lombard cities such as Milan and Cremona, which, along with Sicily, fed Venice in exchange for luxury goods. The rising economic importance of Venice, Genoa, Pisa, and other Italian cities became a central factor in the struggle between the pope and the Holy Roman emperor.

## REVIVAL AND REFORM IN THE CHRISTIAN CHURCH

The eleventh century witnessed the beginnings of a remarkable religious revival. Monasteries, always the leaders in ecclesiastical reform, remodeled themselves under the leadership of the Burgundian abbey of Cluny. Subsequently, new religious orders, such as the Cistercians, were founded and became a broad spiritual movement.

The papacy itself, after a century of corruption and decadence, was cleaned up. The popes worked to clarify church doctrine and codify church law. They and their officials sought to communicate with all the clergy and peoples of Europe through a clearly defined, obedient hierarchy of bishops. Pope Gregory VII's strong assertion of papal power led to profound changes and serious conflict with secular authorities. The revival of the church manifested itself in the crusading movement.

## Monastic Revival

The Viking, Magyar, and Muslim invaders attacked and ransacked many monasteries across Europe. Some religious communities fled and dispersed. In the period of political disorder that followed the disintegration of the Carolingian Empire, many religious houses fell under the control and domination of local feudal lords. Powerful laymen appointed themselves as abbots but kept their wives or mistresses. They took for themselves the lands and goods of monasteries, spending monastic revenues and selling monastic offices. The level of spiritual observance and intellectual activity declined.

In 909 William the Pious, duke of Aquitaine, established the abbey of Cluny near Macon in Burgundy. In his charter of endowment, Duke William declared that Cluny was to enjoy complete independence from all feudal (or secular) and episcopal lordship. The new monastery was to be subordinate only to the authority of Saints Peter and Paul as represented by the pope.

This monastery and its foundation charter came to exert vast religious influence. The first two abbots of Cluny set very high standards of religious behavior and stressed strict observance of *The Rule of Saint Benedict.* Cluny gradually came to stand for clerical celibacy and the suppression of *simony* (the sale of church offices). In the eleventh century, a series of highly able abbots ruled Cluny for a long time. These abbots paid careful attention to sound economic management. In a disorderly world, Cluny represented religious and political stability. Laypersons placed lands under Cluny's custody and monastic houses under its jurisdiction for reform. Benefactors wanted to be associated with Cluniac piety. Moreover, properties and monasteries under Cluny's jurisdiction enjoyed special protection, at least theoretically, from violence. In this way, hundreds of monasteries, primarily in France and Spain, came under Cluny's authority.

Deeply impressed laypeople showered gifts on monasteries with good reputations. Jewelry, rich vestments, elaborately carved sacred vessels, and lands and properties poured into some houses. But with this wealth came lay influence. And as the monasteries became richer, the lifestyle of the monks grew increasingly luxurious. Monastic observance and spiritual fervor declined. Soon fresh demands for reform were heard. The result was the founding of new religious orders in the late eleventh and early twelfth centuries.

The best representative of the new reforming spirit was the Cistercian order. The Cistercians combined a very simple liturgical life, a radical rejection of the traditional feudal sources of income (such as the possession of mills and serfs), and many innovative economic practices. The Cistercians' dynamic growth and rapid expansion had a profound impact on European society.

## Reform of the Papacy

In the tenth century, the papacy provided little leadership to the Christian peoples of western Europe. Factions in Rome sought to control the papacy for their own material gain. Popes were appointed to advance the political ambitions of their families—the great aristocratic families of Rome—and not because of special spiritual qualifications.

Serious efforts at reform began under Pope Leo IX (r. 1049–1054). He traveled widely, holding councils that issued decrees against violence, simony, and clerical marriage. Although celibacy had been an obligation for ordination since the fourth century, in the tenth and eleventh centuries probably a majority of European priests were married or living with a woman.

A church council produced another reform—removing the influence of Roman aristocratic factions in papal elections. Since the eighth century, the priests of the major churches around Rome had constituted a special group, called a "college," that advised the pope. They were called "cardinals," from the Latin *cardo,* or "hinge." They were the hinges on which the church turned. The Lateran Synod of 1059 decreed that these cardinals had the sole authority and power to elect the pope and that they would govern the church when the office was vacant. By 1073 the reform movement was well advanced. That year, Cardinal Hildebrand was elected as Pope Gregory VII, and reform took on a political character.

Cardinal Hildebrand believed that the pope, as the successor of Saint Peter, was the vicar of God on earth and that papal orders were the orders of God. Once Hildebrand became pope, he and his assistants began to insist on the "freedom of the church." By this they meant the freedom of churchmen to obey canon law and their freedom from control and interference by laypeople.

"Freedom of the church" pointed to the end of lay investiture, the selection and appointment of church officials by lay authorities. When bishops or abbots received the symbols of their office from lay officials, those officials seemed to be distributing spiritual authority. Papal opposition to this practice was not new in the eleventh century, but Gregory's attempt to end lay investiture was a radical departure. Feudal monarchs depended on the literacy and administrative skills of church officials to operate their governments. Gregory's new stand seemed to spell disaster for royal administration and provoked a crisis.

In February 1075, Pope Gregory held a council that published a decree against lay investiture. According to this ruling, clerics who accepted investiture from laymen were to be deposed, and laymen who invested clerics were to be *excommunicated*—cut off from the sacraments and the Christian community. Henry IV of the Holy Roman Empire, William the Conqueror of England, and Philip I of France, however, all immediately protested.

The strongest reaction came from Henry IV. In two basic ways, the relationship of the emperor to the papacy differed from that of other monarchs: the pope crowned the emperor, and both emperor and pope claimed northern Italy. Of course, beneath the question of lay investiture, a more fundamental issue was at stake. Gregory's decree raised the question of the proper rule of the monarch in a Christian society. Did a king have ultimate jurisdiction over all his subjects, including the clergy? For centuries, the answer had been yes.

In January 1076, the German bishops who had been invested by Henry withdrew their allegiance from the pope. Gregory excommunicated them and suspended Henry from the kingship—delighting German nobles, who now did not need to obey the king's commands. By Christmas, ironically, the clergy supported the emperor, while the great nobles favored the pope.

In January 1077, Henry arrived at the pope's residence in Canossa in northern Italy and, according to legend, stood outside in the snow for three days seeking forgiveness. As a priest, Gregory was obliged to grant absolution and readmit the emperor into the Christian community. Although the emperor, the most powerful ruler in Europe, bowed before the pope, Henry actually won a victory—albeit a temporary one. He regained the kingship and authority over his subjects, but for the next two hundred years, rulers in Germany and elsewhere were reluctant to challenge the pope.

The lay investiture issue itself remained unresolved until 1122, when a compromise was forged. Bishops were to be chosen by the clergy in the presence of the emperor or his delegate. The papacy technically won, as the ruler could no longer invest. But lay rulers retained an effective veto power, since they could be present at the election.

**The Countess Matilda** A staunch supporter of the reforming ideals of the papacy, the Countess Matilda of Tuscany (ca 1046–1115) arranged the dramatic meeting of the pope and emperor at her castle at Canossa near Reggio Emilia in the Apennines. The arrangement of the figures—with Henry IV kneeling, Gregory lecturing, and Matilda persuading—suggests contemporary understanding of the scene where Henry received absolution. Matilda's vast estates in northern Italy and her political contacts in Rome made her a powerful figure in the late eleventh century *(Biblioteca Apostolica Vaticana)*

The long controversy had tremendous social and political consequences in Germany. From 1075 to 1125, civil war raged in the land, and the emperors—preoccupied with their struggle with the pope—could do little to stop it. The nobles gained power, subordinating knights and reducing free men and serfs to servile status. When the investiture issue was finally settled in 1122, the nobility held the balance of power in Germany.

Eleventh- and twelfth-century popes pressed reform. They expanded the papal chancery (writing office) and the papal chapel, which, with the college of cardinals, constituted the Roman curia, or papal court. The curia formulated laws for all of Christendom. Papal legates published those laws at councils, or assemblies of clergy and people. The papal curia, with its administrative, financial, and legal bureaucracies, became the first well-organized institution of monarchical authority in medieval Europe.

# THE CRUSADES

**Crusades** in the late eleventh and early twelfth centuries were holy wars sponsored by the papacy for the recovery of the Holy Land from the Muslims. They grew out of the long conflict between Christians and Muslims in Spain (see page 377). Although people of all ages and classes participated in the Crusades, so many knights did so that crusading became a distinctive feature of the upper-class lifestyle. In an aristocratic, military society, men coveted reputations as Crusaders; the Christian knight who had been to the Holy Land enjoyed great prestige. The Crusades manifested the religious and chivalric ideals—as well as the tremendous vitality—of medieval society.

## Background of the Crusades

The Roman papacy supported the holy war in Spain and by the late eleventh century had strong reasons for wanting to launch an expedition against Muslims in the East as well. The papacy had been involved in the bitter struggle over investiture with the German emperors. If the pope could muster a large army against the enemies of Christianity, his claim to be leader of Christian society in the West would be strengthened. Moreover, in 1054 a serious theological disagreement had split the Greek church of Byzantium and the Roman church of the West. The pope believed that a crusade would lead to strong Roman influence in Greek territories and eventually the reunion of the two churches.

In 1071 at Manzikert in eastern Anatolia, Turkish soldiers defeated a Greek army and occupied much of Asia Minor. The emperor at Constantinople appealed to the West for support. Shortly afterward, the city of Jerusalem, the scene of Christ's preaching and burial, fell to the Turks. Pilgrimages to holy places in the Middle East became very dangerous, and the papacy claimed to be outraged that the holy city was in the hands of unbelievers. Since the Muslims had held Palestine since the eighth century, the papacy actually feared that the Seljuk Turks would be less accommodating to Christian pilgrims than the previous Muslim rulers had been.

In 1095 Pope Urban II journeyed to Clermont in France and on November 27 called for a great Christian holy war against the infidels. Urban's appeal at Clermont represents his policy of *rapprochement,* or reconciliation, with Byzantium, with church union his ultimate goal. (Mutual ill will, quarrels, and the plundering of Byzantine property by undisciplined westerners were to frustrate this hope.) He urged Christian knights who had been fighting one another to direct their energies against the true enemies of God, the Muslims. Urban proclaimed an *indulgence,* or remission of the temporal penalties imposed by the church for sin, to those who would fight for and regain Jerusalem.

Encouraged by popular preachers such as Peter the Hermit, great lords from northern France and thousands of people of all classes joined the crusade. Although most of the Crusaders were French, pilgrims from many regions streamed southward from the Rhineland, through Germany and the Balkans. Of all of the developments of the central Middle Ages, none better reveals Europeans' religious and emotional fervor and the influence of the reformed papacy than the extraordinary outpouring of support for the First Crusade. (See the feature "Listening to the Past: An Arab View of the Crusades" on pages 414–415.)

## Motives and Course of the Crusades

The Crusades also brought to the surface latent Christian prejudice against the Jews. Between the sixth and tenth centuries, descendants of **Sephardic** (from the modern Hebrew word *Separaddi,* meaning Spanish or Portuguese) **Jews** had settled along the trade routes of western Europe; in the eleventh century, they played a major role in the international trade between the Muslim Middle East and the West. Jews also lent money to peasants, townspeople, and nobles. When the First Crusade was launched, many poor knights had to borrow from Jews to equip themselves for the expedition. Debt bred resentment.

The experience of the Rhineland Jews illustrates how the Crusades, launched against Muslims in the Middle East, often affected minorities within Europe. Beginning in the late tenth century Jews had trickled into the city of Speyer—partly through Jewish perception of opportunity and partly because of the direct invitation of the bishop of Speyer. The bishop's charter meant that Jews could openly practice their religion, could not be assaulted, and could buy and sell goods.

But Christians resented Jews as newcomers, outsiders, and aliens; for enjoying the special protection of the bishop; and for providing economic competition. Anti-Semitic ideology had received enormous impetus from the virulent anti-Semitic writings of Christian apologists in the first six centuries C.E. Jews, they argued, were *deicides* (Christ-killers). By the eleventh century, anti-Semitism was an old and deeply rooted element in Western society.

Late in April 1096, a large band of Crusaders approached Speyer and randomly murdered eleven Jews. The bishop took the entire Jewish community into his castle, arrested some of the burghers, and cut off their hands. News of these events raced up the Rhine to Worms, creating confusion in the Jewish community. Some took refuge with Christian friends; others sought the bishop's protection. A combination of Crusaders and burghers killed a large number of Jews, looted and burned synagogues and desecrated the Torah (see page 39) and other books. Proceeding on to the old and prosperous city of Mainz, Crusaders continued attacking Jews. Facing overwhelming odds, eleven hundred Jews killed their families and themselves. The Jews were never passive; everywhere they put up resistance. If the Crusades had begun as opposition to Islam, after 1096 that hostility extended to those Christians saw as enemies of society—lepers, Jews, and homosexuals (see pages 383–384).

The First Crusade was successful, mostly because of the dynamic enthusiasm of the participants. The Crusaders had little more than religious zeal. They knew little of the geography or climate of the Middle East. Although there were several counts with military experience, the Crusaders could never agree on a leader, and the entire expedition was marked by disputes among the great lords. Lines of supply were never set up. Starvation and disease wracked the army, and the Turks slaughtered hundreds of noncombatants. Nevertheless, convinced that "God wills it," the war cry of the Crusaders, the army pressed on and in 1099 captured Jerusalem. Although the Crusaders fought bravely, Arab disunity was a chief reason for their victory. At Jerusalem, Edessa, Tripoli, and Antioch, Crusader kingdoms were founded on the Western feudal model (see Map 13.2).

Between 1096 and 1270, the crusading ideal was expressed in eight papally approved expeditions to the East. Despite the success of the First Crusade, none of the later ones accomplished very much. During the Fourth Crusade (1202–1204), careless preparation and inadequate financing had disastrous consequences for Latin-Byzantine relations. In April 1204, the Crusaders and Venetians stormed Constantinople; sacked the city, destroying its magnificent library; and grabbed thousands of relics, which were later sold in Europe. The Byzantine Empire, as a political unit, never recovered from this destruction.

**MAP 13.2 The Routes of the Crusades** The Crusades led to a major cultural encounter between Muslim and Christian values. What significant intellectual and economic effects resulted?

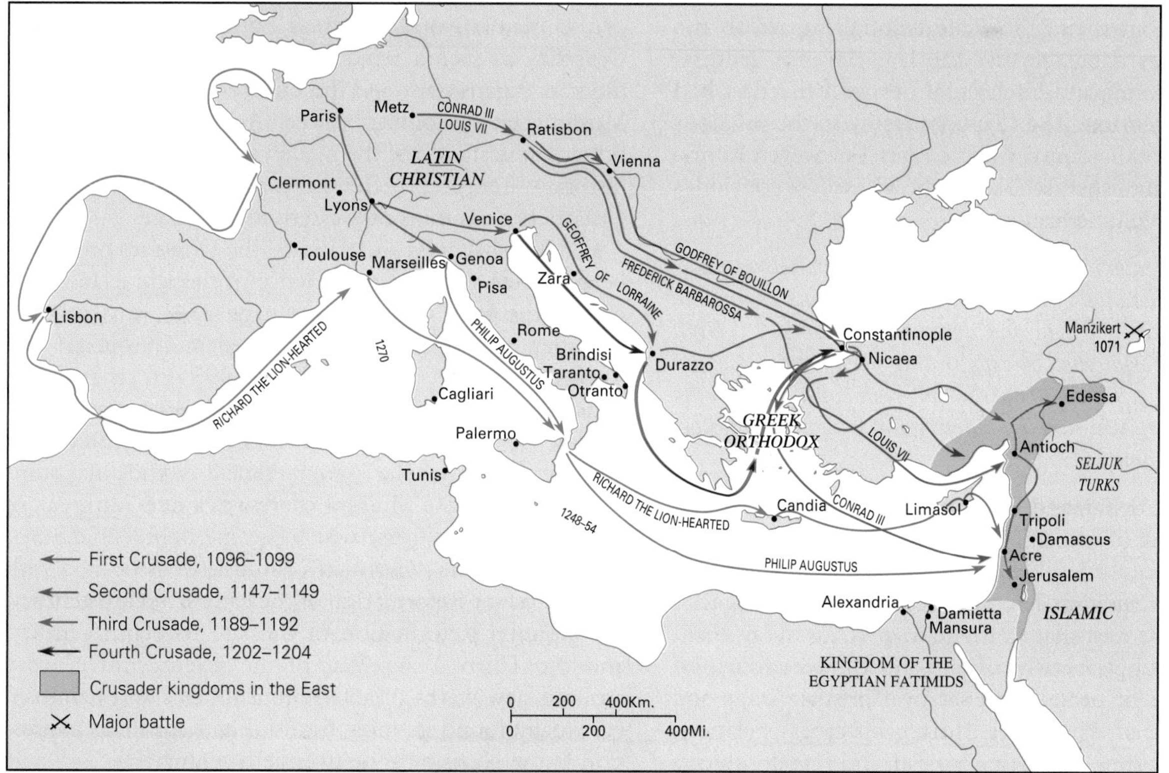

The empire splintered into three parts and soon consisted of little more than the city of Constantinople. Moreover, the assault of one Christian people on another—when one of the goals of the crusade was reunion of the Greek and Latin churches—made the split between the churches permanent.

In the entire crusading movement, fewer women than men participated directly, since the Crusades were primarily military expeditions. Eleanor of Aquitaine (1122?–1204) accompanied her husband, King Louis VII, on the Second Crusade (1147–1149), and the thirteenth-century English chronicler Matthew Paris says that large numbers of women went on the Seventh Crusade (1248–1254) so that they could obtain the crusading indulgence. Women who stayed home assumed their husbands' responsibilities in the management of estates, the dispensation of justice to vassals and serfs, and the protection of property from attack. The many women who operated inns and shops in the towns through which crusading armies passed profited from the rental of lodgings and the sale of foodstuffs, clothing, arms, and fodder for animals. For prostitutes, also, crusading armies offered business opportunities.

## Cultural Consequences

The Crusades introduced some Europeans to Eastern luxury goods, but their immediate cultural impact on the West remains debatable. By the late eleventh century, strong economic and intellectual ties with the East had already been made. The Crusades testify to the religious enthusiasm of the central Middle Ages, but Steven Runciman, a distinguished scholar of the Crusades, concludes in his three-volume history:

> *In the long sequence of interaction and fusion between orient and occident out of which our civilization has grown, the Crusades were a tragic and destructive episode. . . . High ideals were besmirched by cruelty and greed, enterprise and endurance by a blind and narrow self-righteousness; and the Holy War itself was nothing more than a long act of intolerance in the name of God.*[11]

Along the Syrian and Palestinian coasts, the Crusaders set up a string of feudal states that managed to survive for about two centuries before the Muslims reconquered them. The Crusaders left two more permanent legacies in the Middle East that continue to affect us today. First, the long struggle between Islam and Christendom, and the example of persecution set by Christian kings and prelates, left an inheritance of deep bitterness; relations between Muslims and their Christian and Jewish subjects worsened. Second, European merchants, primarily Italians, had established communities in the Crusader states. After those kingdoms collapsed, Muslim rulers still encouraged trade with European businessmen. Commerce with the West benefited both Muslims and Europeans, and it continued to flourish.[12]

The European Crusades represent the first great colonizing movement beyond the geographical boundaries of the European continent. The ideal of a sacred mission to conquer or convert Muslim peoples entered Europeans' consciousness and became a continuing goal. When, in 1492, Christopher Columbus sailed west hoping to reach India, he used the language of the Crusades in his diaries, which show that he was preoccupied with the conquest of Jerusalem (see Chapter 6). Columbus wanted to establish a Christian base in India from which a new crusade could be launched against Islam.

But most medieval and early modern Europeans knew very little about Islam or its adherents. As the crusading goal of conquest and conversion persisted through the centuries, Europeans adopted a strategy that served as a central feature of Western thought and warfare: the dehumanization of the enemy. They described Muslims as "filth." In turn, Muslims called Europeans "infidels" (unbelievers) and considered them "barbarians" because of the unsophisticated level of European medical, philosophical, and mathematical knowledge in comparison to that of the Islamic world. Whereas Europeans perceived the Crusades as sacred religious movements, Muslims saw them as expansionist and imperialistic. Even today, some Muslims see the conflict between Arab and Jew as just another manifestation of the medieval Crusades. Some Arab historians interpret the Jews and the state of Israel as new Crusaders or as tools of Western imperialism.

For Jewish-Christian relations, the Crusades proved to be a disaster. After the experience of the Rhineland Jews during the First Crusade (see page 374), any burst of Christian zeal or enthusiasm evoked in European Jews suspicion, unease, and fear. From 1095 on, most Christians did not regard Jews (or Muslims) as normal human beings, viewing them instead as inhuman monsters. According to one scholar, "Every time a crusade was summoned against the Muslims there was a new outbreak of anti-Semitism in Europe which became an indelible European habit." The "Christian" enthusiasm associated with the Protestant Reformation of the early sixteenth century, the Counter-Reformation of the late sixteenth century, and the Thirty Years' War of the seventeenth century aroused new waves of anti-Semitism. This anti-Semitism eventually found its most frightful and appalling expression in the Nazism of the twentieth century.[13]

Although the legal position of Jews in European society deteriorated after the First Crusade, and despite the pervasive anti-Semitism of the time, Jewish culture flourished. In the period from about 1000 to 1400, Jews worked as tradesmen, craftsmen, moneychangers, and long-distance business people. They established schools for education in the Torah (the body of Hebraic religious law) and the Talmud (rabbinic commentary on the Torah) and produced beautifully illuminated manuscripts. Scholars enjoyed great respect in Jewish communities, and Christian and Muslim nobles sought Jewish physicians. Although both Jewish and Christian law banned Jews from the emerging universities (see pages 389–390), Jews flocked to university towns. In spite of harassment and humiliation—at Pisa on the Feast of Saint Catherine (November 25) students seized the stoutest Jew they could find, put him on scales, and fined the Jewish community his weight in sweets—Jews became students and professors. In 1300 Jacob ben Machir was even appointed dean of the medical school at Montpellier. Andalusian Spain, the safest place for Jews in the Latin West until the fifteenth century, witnessed a "golden age" of Jewish culture in science, music, medicine, philosophy, and especially Hebrew poetry.

## THE EXPANSION OF LATIN CHRISTENDOM

The period after the millennial year 1000 witnessed great migrations and cross-regional contacts. The movement of peoples and ideas from western France, the heartland of Christendom, and from western Germany into frontier regions—Ireland, Scandinavia, the Baltic lands, eastern Europe, and Spain—had, by about 1300, profound cultural consequences for those fringe territories. Wars of expansion, the establishment of new Christian bishoprics, and the vast migration of colonists, together with the papal emphasis on a unified Christian world, brought about the gradual Europeanization of the frontier.

### Northern and Eastern Europe

Beginning in 1177, Norman knights from England began to seize land and build themselves estates in Ireland. Ireland had been technically Christian since the days of Saint Patrick (see page 213), but the coming of the Normans transformed the Irish church from a monastic structure to an episcopal one. The Normans also brought the fief and feudal cavalry to Ireland, as they did to Scotland beginning about the same time.

Latin Christian influences entered Scandinavia and the Baltic lands primarily through the creation of dioceses. This took place in Denmark in the tenth and eleventh centuries, and the institutional church spread rather quickly due to the support offered by the strong throne. Dioceses were established in Norway and Sweden in the eleventh century, and in 1164 Uppsala, long the center of the pagan cults of Odin and Thor, became a Catholic archdiocese.

Otto I (see page 371) planted a string of dioceses along his northern and eastern frontiers, hoping to pacify the newly conquered Slavs in eastern Europe. Frequent Slavic revolts illustrate the people's resentment of German lords and clerics and indicate that the church did not easily penetrate the region. In 1157, though, Albert the Bear (d. 1170) began a ruthless program to pacify the region. He built several castles, which he filled with knights recruited from the Rhineland and used as bases to crush any revolt.

The church also moved into central Europe, first in Bohemia in the tenth century and from there into Poland and Hungary in the eleventh century. In the twelfth and thirteenth centuries, thousands of settlers poured into eastern Europe. They settled in Silesia, Mecklenburg, Bohemia, Poland, Hungary, and Transylvania. New immigrants were German in descent, name, language, and law. Hundreds of small market towns populated by these newcomers supplied the needs of the rural countryside. Larger towns such as Cracow and Riga engaged in long-distance trade and gradually grew into large urban centers.[14]

### Spain

About 950 Caliph Abd al-Rahman III (912–961) of the Umayyad Dynasty of Córdoba ruled most of the Iberian Peninsula, from Gibraltar in the south to the Ebro River in the north (see Map 13.3). Christian Spain consisted of the small kingdoms of Castile, León, Catalonia, Aragon, Navarre, and Portugal. When civil wars erupted among Rahman's descendants, though, Muslim lands were split among several small kingdoms, and the Christian reconquest was made easier.

Fourteenth-century clerics used the term **reconquista** (reconquest) to describe what they called a sacred and patriotic crusade to wrest Spain from "alien" Muslim hands. This religious myth became part of Spanish national psychology. The reconquest took several centuries, however. In 1085 Alfonso VI of Castile and León captured Toledo and invited French knights to settle the central plateau of Spain. In 1233 James the Conqueror of Aragon took Valencia, and in 1236 Ferdinand of Castile and León captured the Muslim intellectual and

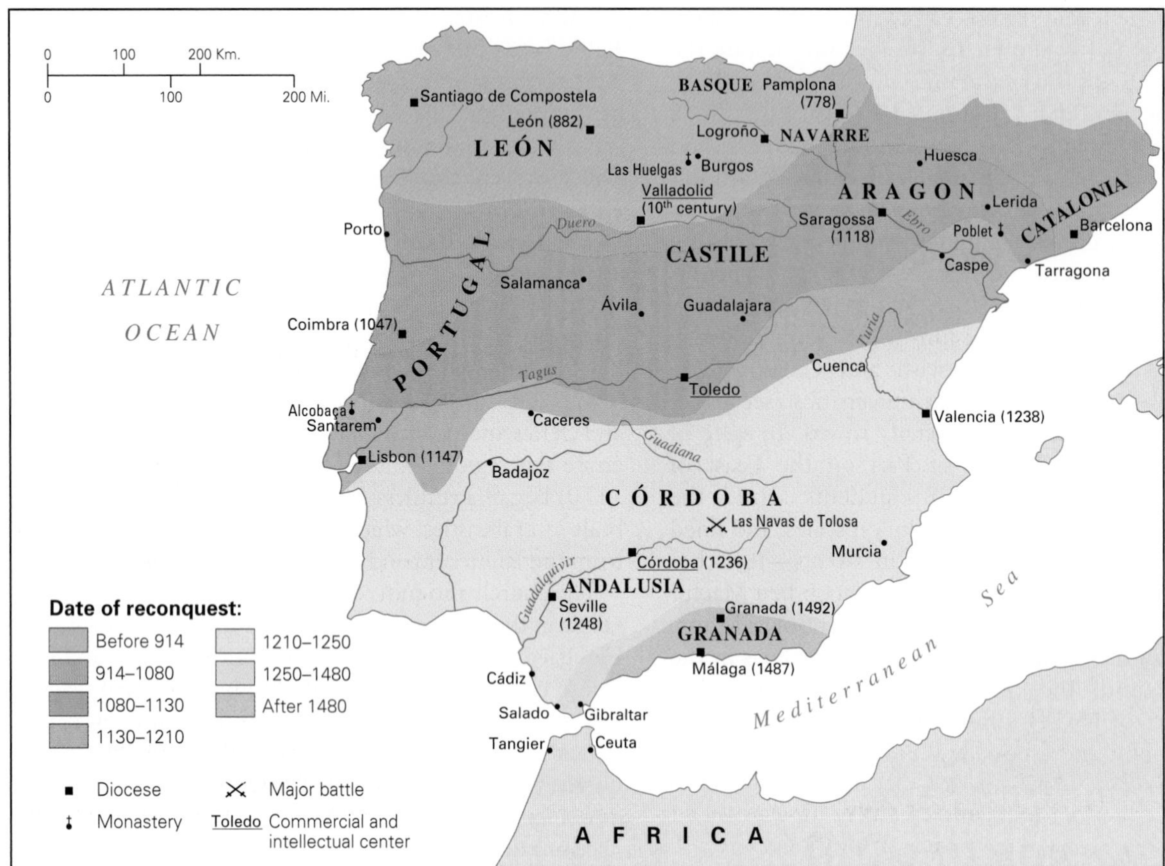


**MAP 13.3 The Reconquista** The Christian conquest of Muslim Spain was followed by ecclesiastical reorganization, with the establishment of dioceses, monasteries, and the Latin liturgy, which gradually tied the peninsula to the heartland of Christian Europe and to the Roman papacy. *(Source: Adapted from David Nicholas,* The Evolution of the Medieval World. *© Longman Group UK Limited 1993. Reprinted by permission of Pearson Education Limited.)*

industrial center of Córdoba. When Seville fell to Ferdinand's forces in 1248, Christians held all of the peninsula save for the small state of Granada.

As the Christians advanced, they changed the face of Spanish cities, transforming mosques into cathedrals and, in the process, destroying Muslim art—just as the Muslims, in the eighth century, had destroyed the pagan temples they found. The reconquista also meant the establishment of the Roman institutional church throughout Spain. There were fifty-one bishoprics in the region by 1300. Spanish rulers also established several Cistercian monasteries, which exercised a broad cultural, military, political, and economic influence as well as a religious one.

Behind the advancing Christian armies came settlers. Most settlers came from within the peninsula, as the Christian kings recruited immigrants from Catalonia, Castile, and León. Many of these immigrants settled in the cities that were depopulated with the expulsion of Muslims. Muslim Spain had had more cities than any other country in Europe, and foreign business people flocked to these urban areas as well.[15]

## Toward a Christian Society

By about 1300, these frontier areas of northern and eastern Europe and Spain shared a broad cultural uniformity with the core regions of western Christendom: France, Germany, England, and Italy. The papal reform movement of the eleventh century had increased the prestige of the papacy and loyalty to it. Loyalty meant, on the

**Almohad Banner** At Las Navas de Tolosa in 1212, King Alfonso VIII of Castile won a decisive victory over the Almohads, a puritanical Muslim sect from North Africa that had ruled most of Spain in the twelfth century. The Spanish victory marked the beginning of Muslim decline. *(Institut Amatller d'Art Hispanic)*

local level, following the Roman liturgy, which led to a broad uniformity of religious practice across Europe.

During the reign of Pope Innocent III (1198–1216), papal directives and legates flowed to all parts of Europe, and twelve hundred prelates obediently left their homes from across Europe to come to Rome for the Fourth Lateran Council in 1215. The papacy was recognized as the nerve center of a homogeneous Christian society. Europeans identified themselves as Christians and even described themselves as belonging to "the Christian race." As in the Islamic world, religion had replaced tribal, political, and ethnic structures as the essence of culture.[16]

## Medieval Origins of the Modern Western State

Rome's great legacy to Western civilization had been the concepts of the state and the law. But for almost five hundred years after the disintegration of the Roman Empire in the West, the state as a reality did not exist. Political authority was completely decentralized. Power was spread among many feudal lords, who gave their localities such protection and security as their strength allowed and whose laws affected a relative few. In the mid-eleventh century, many overlapping layers of authority—earls, counts, barons, knights—existed between a king and the ordinary people.

In these circumstances, medieval rulers had common goals. To increase public order, they wanted to establish an effective means of communication with all peoples. They also wanted more revenue and efficient bureaucracies. The solutions they found to these problems laid the foundations for modern national states.

The modern state is an organized territory with definite geographical boundaries that are recognized by other states. It has a body of law and institutions of government. If the state claims to govern according to law, it is guided in its actions by the law. The modern national state counts on the loyalty of its citizens, or at least of a majority of them. In return, it provides order so that citizens can go about their daily work and other activities. It protects its citizens in their persons and property. The state tries to prevent violence and to apprehend and punish those who commit it. It supplies a currency or medium of exchange that permits financial and commercial transactions. The state conducts relations with foreign governments. In order to accomplish even these minimal functions, the state must have officials, bureaucracies, laws, courts of law, soldiers, information, and money. States with these attributes are relatively recent developments.

### Unification and Communication

Political developments in England, France, and Germany provide good examples of the beginnings of the national state in the central Middle Ages. Under the pressure of the Viking invasions of the ninth and tenth centuries, the seven kingdoms of Anglo-Saxon England united under one king. At the same time, for reasons historians still

**The Bayeux Tapestry** Measuring 231 feet by 19½ inches, the Bayeux Tapestry gives a narrative description of the events surrounding the Norman Conquest of England. The tapestry provides an important historical source for the clothing, armor, and lifestyles of the Norman and Anglo-Saxon warrior class. *(Tapisserie de Bayeux et avec autorisation spéciale de la Ville de Bayeux)*

cannot fully explain, England was divided into local *shires,* or counties, each under the jurisdiction of a sheriff appointed by the king. The kingdom of England, therefore, had a political head start on the rest of Europe.

When Edward the Confessor (r. 1042–1066) died, his cousin Duke William of Normandy claimed the English throne and won it by defeating his Anglo-Saxon rival at the Battle of Hastings. As William the Conqueror (r. 1066–1087) subdued the rest of the country, he distributed land to his Norman followers and required all feudal lords to swear an oath of allegiance to him as king. He retained the Anglo-Saxon institution of sheriff but replaced Anglo-Saxons with Normans in this office. The sheriff had the responsibility of catching criminals, collecting taxes, and raising soldiers for the king when ordered.

In 1085 William decided to conduct a systematic survey of the entire country to determine how much wealth there was in his new kingdom and who had it. Groups of royal officials or judges were sent to every part of England. A priest and six local people swore an oath to answer truthfully. Because they swore (Latin, *juror*), they were called *jurors,* and from this small body of local people, the jury system in English-speaking countries gradually evolved. The records collected from the entire country, called ***Domesday Book,*** provided William and his descendants vital information for governing the country.

In 1128 William's granddaughter Matilda married Geoffrey of Anjou. Their son, who became Henry II of England, inherited the French provinces of Normandy, Anjou, and Touraine in northwestern France. When Henry married the great heiress Eleanor of Aquitaine in 1152, he claimed lordship over Aquitaine, Poitou, and Gascony in southwestern France as well. The histories of England and France were thus closely intertwined in the central Middle Ages.

In the early twelfth century, France consisted of a number of virtually independent provinces, each governed by its local ruler. Unlike the king of England, the king of France had jurisdiction over a very small area. Chroniclers called King Louis VI (r. 1108–1137) *roi de Saint-Denis,* king of Saint-Denis, because the territory he controlled was limited to Paris and the Saint-Denis area surrounding the city. This region, the Île-de-France or royal domain, became the nucleus of the French state. The clear goal of the medieval French king was to increase the royal domain and extend his authority.

The work of unifying France began under Louis VI's grandson Philip II (r. 1180–1223), called "Augustus" because he vastly enlarged the territory of the kingdom. By the end of his reign, Philip was effectively master of northern France. His descendants acquired important holdings in southern France, and by 1300 most of the provinces of modern France had been added to the royal domain through diplomacy, marriage, war, and inheritance. The king of France was stronger than any group of nobles who might try to challenge his authority.

Philip Augustus also devised a method of governing the provinces and building communication between the central government in Paris and local communities. He let each province retain its own institutions and laws, but he dispatched royal agents to each province with the authority to act for the king. These agents were appointed by, paid by, and responsible to the king. This policy reflected the fundamental principle of French administration: royal interests superseded local interests. At the same time, the French system was characterized by a high degree of centralization from Paris and a great variety of customs, laws, and provincial institutions at the local level. The system occasionally fell into disrepair, but it lasted until the Revolution of 1789.

The political problems of Germany differed from those of France and England. The eleventh-century investiture controversy between the German emperor and the Roman papacy left Germany shattered and divided (see pages 372–373). In the twelfth and thirteenth centuries, Germany was split into hundreds of independent provinces, principalities, bishoprics, duchies, and free cities.

There were several barriers to the development of a strong central government. Unlike the French kings, the German rulers lacked a strong royal domain to use as a source of revenue and a base from which to expand royal power. No accepted principle of succession to the throne existed; as a result, the death of the Holy Roman emperor was often followed by civil war and anarchy. Moreover, German rulers were continually attracted south by the wealth of the northern Italian cities or by dreams of restoring the imperial glory of Charlemagne. Time after time, the German kings got involved in Italian affairs, and in turn the papacy, fearful of a strong German power in northern Italy, interfered in German affairs. Consequently, in contrast to France and England, the German Empire witnessed little royal centralization.

Instead, Germany evolved in the direction of *territorial lordships*. From about 1050 to 1400, and down to 1871, German history is regional history. The great duchies—Saxony, Swabia, Bavaria, and Thuringia—emerged as defensive units against Magyar and Slavic invaders, while the great archbishoprics—Salzburg, Mainz, Trier, and Cologne—were established as missionary centers for Scandinavia and eastern Europe. Under Otto I and his successors, a sort of confederacy (a weak union of strong principalities) developed in which the emperor shared power with princes, dukes, counts, archbishops, and bishops. Regionally based authority became the German pattern.[17]

Frederick Barbarossa (r. 1152–1190) of the house of Hohenstaufen tried valiantly to unify the empire. Just as the French rulers branched out from the Île-de-France, Frederick tried to do so from his family duchy of Swabia in southwestern Germany. Outside Swabia, Frederick tried to make feudalism work as a system of government. He made alliances with the great lay princes, who acknowledged that their lands were fiefs of the emperor in return for Frederick's recognition of their military and

**The Chancellery at Palermo** Reflecting the fact that Vandals, Ostrogoths, Greeks, Muslims, and Normans had left their imprint on Sicily, the imperial court bureaucracy kept official records in Greek, Arabic, and Latin, as this manuscript illustration shows. *(Burgerbibliothek Bern)*

political jurisdiction over those lands. He even compelled the great churchmen to become his vassals, so that when they died, he could control their estates.

Unfortunately, Frederick did not concentrate his efforts and resources in one area. He, too, became embroiled in the affairs of Italy, hoping to cash in on the wealth Italian cities had gained through trade. He led six expeditions into Italy, but his brutal methods provoked revolts, and the cities, allied with the papacy, defeated him in 1176. Frederick was forced to recognize the autonomy of the cities. Meanwhile, back in Germany, Frederick's absence allowed the princes and magnates to consolidate their power.

## Law and Justice

Throughout Europe in the twelfth and thirteenth centuries, the law was a hodgepodge of Germanic customs, feudal rights, and provincial practices. Kings wanted to blend these elements into a uniform system of rules acceptable and applicable to all their peoples. In France and England, kings successfully contributed to the development of national states through the administration of their laws.

The French king Louis IX (r. 1226–1270) was famous in his time for his concern for justice. Each French province, even after being made part of the kingdom of France, retained its unique laws and procedures, but Louis IX created a royal judicial system. He established the Parlement of Paris, a kind of supreme court that welcomed appeals from local administrators and from the courts of feudal lords throughout France.

Louis was also the first French monarch to publish laws for the entire kingdom. The Parlement of Paris registered (or announced) these laws, which forbade private warfare, judicial duels, gambling, blaspheming, and prostitution. Louis sought to identify justice with the kingship, and gradually royal justice touched all parts of the kingdom.

Under Henry II (r. 1154–1189), England developed and extended a **common law**—a law common to and accepted by the entire country. No other country in medieval Europe did so. Each year Henry sent out *circuit judges* (royal officials who traveled in a given circuit or district) to hear civil and criminal cases. Wherever the king's judges sat, there sat the king's court. Slowly, the king's court gained jurisdiction over all property disputes and criminal actions.

Proving guilt or innocence in criminal cases could pose a problem. Where there was no specific accuser, the court sought witnesses, then looked for written evidence. If the judges found neither and the suspect had a bad reputation in the community, the person went to trial by ordeal. He or she was bound hand and foot and dropped into a lake or river. Because water was supposed to be a pure substance, it would reject anything foul or unclean. Thus the innocent person would sink and the guilty person float. Because God determined guilt or innocence, a priest had to be present to bless the water. Henry disliked the system because the clergy controlled the procedure and because many suspicious people seemed to beat the system and escape punishment, but he had no alternative. Then in 1215 the church's Fourth Lateran Council forbade priests' participation in such trials, effectively ending them. Royal justice was desacralized.[18] In the course of the thirteenth century, the king's judges adopted the practice of calling on twelve people to decide the accused's guilt or innocence. Trial by jury was only gradually accepted; medieval people had more confidence in the judgment of God than in that of ordinary people.

One aspect of Henry's judicial reform failed, doomed by the dispute between secular and religious authority. In the 1160s, many literate people accused of crimes claimed "benefit of clergy." Although they were not clerics and had no intention of being ordained, the claim gave them the right to be tried in church courts, which meted out punishments far milder than those handed down in secular courts. In 1164 Henry insisted that everyone in the kingdom, including clerics, be subject to the royal courts. Thomas Becket, Henry's friend and former chief adviser and now archbishop of Canterbury, vigorously protested. Their quarrel dragged on for years until, in 1170, a raging Henry wished aloud that Becket were destroyed. Four knights obliged, killing him.

Becket's murder—in his own cathedral during the Christmas season—turned public opinion across Europe against the king. He was forced to abandon his attempts to bring clerics under the authority of the royal courts. Meanwhile, miracles were recorded at Becket's tomb, and Canterbury Cathedral became a major pilgrimage and tourist site.

Henry's son John (r. 1199–1216) also met with disappointment. He lost the French province of Normandy to Philip Augustus in 1204 and spent the rest of his reign trying to win it back. Saddled with heavy debt from his father and brother Richard (r. 1189–1199), John alienated his barons by squeezing as much money as possible from them. Still in need of funds, he infuriated town dwellers by extorting money from them and threatening to revoke the towns' charters of self-government. Then he rejected the pope's choice as archbishop of Canterbury, angering the church.

When John's military campaign failed in 1214, it was clear that the French lands that had once belonged to the English king were lost for good. His ineptitude as a soldier in a culture that idealized military glory turned the people against him. The barons revolted and in 1215 forced him to attach his seal to Magna Carta—the "Great Charter," which became the cornerstone of English justice and law. Magna Carta signifies the principle that the king and the government shall be under the law and that everyone, including the king, must obey the law. Some clauses contain the germ of the ideas of due process of law and the right to a fair and speedy trial. Every English king in the Middle Ages reissued Magna Carta as evidence of his promise to observe the law.

In the later Middle Ages, English common law developed features that differed strikingly from the system of Roman law operative in continental Europe. Common law relied on precedents: a decision in an important case served as an authority for deciding similar cases. By contrast, continental judges, trained in Roman law, used the fixed legal maxims of the sixth-century text known as the Justinian *Code* to decide their cases. Thus the common-law system evolved and reflected the changing experience of the people, while the Roman-law tradition tended toward an absolutist approach. In countries influenced by common law, such as Canada and the United States, the court is open to the public; in countries with Roman-law traditions, such as France and the Latin American nations, courts need not be public. Under common law, people accused in criminal cases have a right to see the evidence against them; under the other system, they do not.

The extension of law and justice led to a phenomenal amount of legal codification all over Europe. Legal texts and encyclopedias exalted royal authority, consolidated royal power, and emphasized political and social uniformity. The pressure for social conformity in turn contributed to a rising hostility toward minorities, Jews, and homosexuals.

By the late eleventh century, many towns in western Europe had small Jewish populations. The laws of most countries forbade Jews to own land, though they could hold land pledged to them for debts. By the twelfth century, many Jews were usurers: they lent to consumers, but primarily to new business enterprises. Like other business people, the Jews preferred to live near their work; they also settled close to their synagogues or schools. Thus originated the Jews' street or quarter or ghetto. Such neighborhoods gradually became legally defined sections where Jews were required to live.

Jews had been generally tolerated and had become important parts of the urban economies through trade and finance. Some Jews had risen to positions of power and prominence. Through the twelfth century, for example, Jews managed the papal household. The later twelfth and entire thirteenth centuries, however, witnessed increasingly ugly anti-Semitism. Why? Present scholarship does not provide completely satisfactory answers, but we have some clues. Shifting agricultural and economic patterns aggravated social tensions. The indebtedness of peasants and nobles to Jews in an increasingly cash-based economy; the xenophobia that accompanied and followed the Crusades; Christian merchants' and financiers' resentment of Jewish business competition; the spread of vicious accusations of ritual murders or sacrileges against Christian property and persons; royal and papal legislation aimed at social conformity—these factors all contributed to rising anti-Semitism. Philip Augustus of France used hostility toward Jews as an excuse to imprison them and then to demand heavy ransom for their release. The Fourth Lateran Council of 1215 forbade Jews to hold public office and restricted their financial activities. In 1290 Edward I of England capitalized on mercantile and other resentment of Jews to expel them from the country in return for a large financial grant. In 1302 Philip IV of France followed suit and confiscated their property. Fear, ignorance, greed, stupidity, and the pressure for social conformity all played a part in anti-Semitism of the central Middle Ages.

Early Christians displayed no special prejudice against homosexuals. Some of the church fathers, such as Saint John Chrysostom (347–407), preached against them, but a general indifference toward homosexual activity prevailed throughout the early Middle Ages. In the early twelfth century, a large body of homosexual literature circulated.

Beginning in the late twelfth century, however, a profound change occurred in public attitudes toward homosexual behavior. Scholars have only begun to investigate why this occurred, and the root cause of intolerance rarely yields to easy analysis. In the thirteenth century, a fear of foreigners, especially Muslims, became associated with the crusading movement. Heretics were the most despised minority in an age that stressed religious and social uniformity. The notion spread that both Muslims and heretics, the great foreign and domestic menaces to the security of Christian Europe, were inclined toward homosexual relations. In addition, the systematization of law and the rising strength of the state made any religious or sexual distinctiveness increasingly unacceptable. Whatever the precise cause, "between 1250 and 1300 homosexual

**The Jews Demonized** The Fourth Lateran Council of 1215 required that Jews wear distinctive clothing—special caps and the Star of David—so that they could be distinguished from Christians. In this caricature from an English treasury record for 1233, Isaac of Norwich (*top center*), reputedly the richest Jew in England, wears a crown implying his enormous influence and power. The figure at left (holding scales) suggests the Jewish occupation of money lending. At right Satan leads Jews to Hell. *(Crown copyright material in the Public Record Office is reproduced by permission of the Controller of the Britannic Majesty's Stationery Office [E 3721])*

activity passed from being completely legal in most of Europe to incurring the death penalty in all but a few legal compilations."[19] Spain, France, England, Norway, and several Italian city-states adopted laws condemning homosexual acts. Most of these laws remained on statute books until the twentieth century. Anti-Semitism and hostility toward homosexuals were at odds with the general creativity and vitality of the period.

## ECONOMIC REVIVAL

A salient manifestation of Europe's recovery after the tenth-century disorders and of the vitality of the central Middle Ages was the rise of towns and the growth of a new business and commercial class. These developments laid the foundations for Europe's transformation, centuries later, from a rural agricultural society into an industrial urban society—a change with global implications.

Why and how did these developments occur when they did? Part of the answer has already been given. Without increased agricultural output, there would not have been an adequate food supply for new town dwellers. Without a rise in population, there would have been no one to people the towns. Without a minimum of peace and political stability, merchants could not have transported and sold goods.

### The Rise of Towns

Early medieval society was traditional, agricultural, and rural. The emergence of a new class that was none of these constituted a social revolution. The new class—artisans and merchants—came from the peasantry. They were landless younger sons of large families, driven away by land shortages. Or they were forced by war and famine to seek new possibilities. Or they were unusually enterprising and adventurous, curious and willing to take a chance.

Some medieval towns that had become flourishing centers of trade by the mid-twelfth century had originally been Roman army camps, or perhaps forts erected during the ninth-century Viking invasions. York in northern England, Bordeaux in west-central France, and Cologne in west-central Germany are good examples of ancient towns that underwent revitalization in the eleventh century. Great cathedrals and monasteries, which represented a demand for goods and services, also attracted concentrations of people. The restoration of order and political stability promoted rebirth and new development. Medieval towns had a few characteristics in common. Walls enclosed the town. (The terms *burgher* and *bourgeois* derive from the Old English and Old German words *burg, burgh, borg,* and *borough* for "a walled or fortified place.") The town had a marketplace. It often had a mint for the coining of money and a court to settle disputes.

In each town, many people inhabited a small, cramped area. As population increased, towns rebuilt their walls, expanding the living space to accommodate growing numbers. Through an archaeological investigation of the amount of land gradually enclosed by walls, historians have gained a rough estimate of medieval town populations. For example, the walled area of the German city of Cologne equaled 100 hectares in the tenth century (1 hectare = 2.471 acres), about 185 hectares in 1106, about 320 in 1180, and 397 in the fourteenth century. In 1180 Cologne's population was at least 32,000; in the mid-fourteenth century, perhaps 40,000.[20]

The aristocratic nobility glanced down with contempt and derision at the moneygrubbing townspeople but were not above borrowing from them. The rural peasantry peered up with suspicion and fear at the town dwellers. Some farmers fled to the towns seeking wealth and freedom. But most farmers wondered what the point of making money was. They believed that only land had real permanence. Nor did the new commercial class make much sense initially to churchmen. The immediate goal of the middle class was obviously not salvation. It would be a long while before churchmen developed a theological justification for the new class.

## Town Liberties and Town Life

The history of towns in the eleventh through thirteenth centuries consists largely of merchants' efforts to acquire liberties. In the Middle Ages, *liberties* meant special privileges. For the town dweller, liberties included the privilege of living and trading on the lord's land. The most important privilege a medieval townsperson could gain was personal freedom. It gradually developed that an individual who lived in a town for a year and a day, and was accepted by the townspeople, was free of servile obligations and servile status. More than anything else, perhaps, the personal freedom that came with residence in a town contributed to the emancipation of the serfs in the central Middle Ages. Liberty meant citizenship, and, unlike foreigners and outsiders of any kind, a full citizen of a town did not have to pay taxes and tolls in the market. Obviously, this exemption increased profits.

In the twelfth and thirteenth centuries, towns fought for, and slowly gained, legal and political rights. Gradually, towns across Europe acquired the right to hold municipal courts that alone could judge members of the town. In effect, this right gave them judicial independence.[21]

In the acquisition of full rights of self-government, the **merchant guilds** played a large role. Medieval people were long accustomed to communal enterprises. In the late tenth and early eleventh centuries, those who were engaged in foreign trade joined together in merchant guilds; united enterprise provided them greater security and less risk of losses than did individual action. At about the same time, the artisans and craftsmen of particular trades formed their own guilds. These were the butchers, bakers, and candlestick makers. Members of the *craft guilds* determined the quality, quantity, and price of the goods produced and the number of apprentices and journeymen affiliated with the guild.

Research indicates that, by the fifteenth century, women composed the majority of the adult urban population. Many women were heads of households.[22] They engaged in every kind of urban commercial activity, both as helpmates to their husbands and independently. In many manufacturing trades women predominated, and in some places women were a large percentage of the labor force. In fourteenth-century Frankfurt, for example, about 33 percent of the crafts and trades were entirely female, about 40 percent wholly male, and the remaining crafts roughly divided between the sexes. Craft guilds provided greater opportunity for women than did merchant guilds. Most members of the Paris silk and woolen trades were women, and some achieved the mastership. Widows frequently followed their late husbands' professions.

Recent research demonstrates that women with ready access to cash—such as female innkeepers, alewives, and women in trade—"extended credit on purchases, gave cash advances to good customers or accepted articles on pawn . . . and many widows supplemented their earnings from their late husbands' businesses or homesteads by putting out cash at interest." Likewise, Christian noblewomen, nuns, and Jewish businesswomen participated in moneylending. Wherever Jews lived, Jewish women were active moneylenders.[23]

By the late eleventh century, especially in the towns of the Low Countries and northern Italy, the leaders of the merchant guilds were quite rich and powerful. They constituted an oligarchy in their towns, controlling economic life and bargaining with kings and lords for political independence. Full rights of self-government included the right to hold a town court, the right to select the mayor and other municipal officials, and the right to tax and collect taxes.

A charter that King Henry II of England granted to the merchants of Lincoln around 1157 nicely illustrates the town's rights. The passages quoted clearly suggest that the merchant guild had been the governing body in the city for almost a century and that anyone who lived in Lincoln for a year and a day was considered free:

*Henry, by the grace of God, etc. . . . Know that I have granted to my citizens of Lincoln all their liberties and customs and laws which they had in the time of Edward [King Edward the Confessor] and William and Henry, kings of England. And I have granted them their gild-merchant, comprising men of the city and other merchants of the shire, as well and freely as they had it in the time of our aforesaid predecessors. . . . I also confirm to them that if anyone has lived in Lincoln for a year and a day without dispute from any claimant, and has paid the customs [tax levied by the king] . . . then let the defendant remain in peace in my city of Lincoln as my citizen, without [having to defend his] right.*[24]

Kings and lords discovered that towns attracted increasing numbers of people—people whom the lords could tax. Moreover, when burghers bargained for a town's political independence, they offered sizable amounts of ready cash. Consequently, feudal lords ultimately agreed to self-government.

Medieval cities served, above all else, as markets. In some respects the entire city was a marketplace. The place where a product was made and sold was also typically the merchant's residence. Usually the ground floor was the scene of production. A window or door opened from the main workroom directly onto the street, and passersby could look in and see the goods being produced. The merchant's family lived above the business on the second or third floor. As the business and the family expanded, the merchant built additional stories on top of the house.

Because space within the town walls was limited, expansion occurred upward. Second and third stories were built jutting out over the ground floor and thus over the street. Since the streets were narrow to begin with, houses lacked fresh air and light. Initially, houses were made of wood and thatched with straw. Fire was a constant danger and spread rapidly. Municipal governments consequently urged construction in stone or brick.

Most medieval cities developed haphazardly. There was little town planning. Air and water pollution presented serious problems. Many families raised pigs for household consumption in sties next to their houses. Horses and oxen, the chief means of transportation and power, dropped tons of dung on the streets every year. It was universal practice in the early towns to dump household waste, both animal and human, into the road in front of

**Spanish Apothecary** Town life meant variety—of peoples and products. Within the town walls, a Spanish pharmacist, seated outside his shop, describes the merits of his goods to a crowd of Christians and Muslims. *(From the* Cantigas *of Alfonso X, ca 1283. El Escorial/Laurie Platt Winfrey, Inc.)*

one's house. The stench must have been abominable. Lack of space, air pollution, and sanitation problems bedeviled urban people in medieval times, as they do today. Still, people wanted to get into medieval cities because they represented opportunities for economic advancement, social mobility, and improvement in legal status.

## The Revival of Long-Distance Trade

The eleventh century witnessed a remarkable revival of trade, as artisans and craftsmen manufactured goods for local and foreign consumption (see Map 13.4). Most trade centered in towns and was controlled by professional traders. The transportation of goods involved serious risks. Shipwrecks were common. Pirates infested the sea-lanes, and robbers and thieves roamed virtually all of the land routes. Since the risks were so great, merchants preferred to share them. A group of people would thus pool some of their capital to finance an expedition to a distant place. When the ship or caravan returned and the goods brought back were sold, the investors would share the profits. If disaster struck the caravan, an investor's loss was limited to the amount of that individual's investment.

The Italian cities, especially Venice, led the West in trade in general and completely dominated the Asian market. Ships carried salt from the Venetian lagoon; pepper and other spices from North Africa; and slaves, silks, and purple textiles from the East to northern and western Europe. Lombard and Tuscan merchants exchanged those goods at the town markets and regional fairs of France, Flanders, and England. (Fairs were periodic gatherings that attracted buyers, sellers, and goods from all over Europe.) Flanders controlled the cloth industry: the towns of Bruges, Ghent, and Ypres built up a vast industry in the manufacture of cloth. Italian merchants exchanged their products for Flemish tapestries, fine broadcloth, and other textiles.

Two circumstances help to explain the lead Venice and the Flemish towns gained in long-distance trade. Both enjoyed a high degree of peace and political stability, but geographical factors were equally, if not more, important (see Map 13.4). Venice was ideally located at the northwestern end of the Adriatic Sea, with easy access to the transalpine land routes as well as the Adriatic and Mediterranean sea-lanes. The markets of North Africa, Byzantium, and Russia and the great fairs of Ghent in Flanders and Champagne in France provided commercial opportunities that Venice quickly seized. The geographical situation of Flanders also offered unusual possibilities. Just across the Channel from England, Flanders had easy access to English wool. Indeed, Flanders and England developed a very close economic relationship.

Wool was the cornerstone of the English medieval economy. Scholars have estimated that, by the end of the twelfth century, roughly 6 million sheep grazed on the English moors and downs.[25] Population growth in the twelfth century and the success of the Flemish and Italian textile industries created foreign demand for English wool. The production of English wool stimulated Flemish manufacturing, and the expansion of the Flemish cloth industry in turn spurred the production of English wool. The availability of raw wool also encouraged the development of domestic cloth manufacture within England. The port cities of London, Hull, Boston, and Bristol thrived on the wool trade. In the thirteenth century, commercial families in these towns grew fabulously rich.

## The Commercial Revolution

A steadily expanding volume of international trade from the late eleventh through the thirteenth century was a sign of the great economic surge, but it was not the only one. In cities all across Europe, trading and transportation firms opened branch offices. Credit was widely extended, considerably facilitating exchange. Merchants devised the letter of credit, which made unnecessary the slow and dangerous shipment of coin for payment.

A new capitalistic spirit developed. Professional merchants were always on the lookout for new markets and opportunities. They invested surplus capital in new enterprises. They became involved in a wide variety of operations. The typical prosperous merchant in the later thirteenth century might well have been involved in buying and selling, shipping, lending some capital at interest, and other types of banking. Medieval merchants were fiercely competitive. Some scholars consider capitalism a modern phenomenon, beginning in the fifteenth or sixteenth century. But in their use of capital to make more money, in their speculative pursuits and willingness to gamble, in their competitive spirit, and in the variety of their interests and operations, medieval businessmen displayed the traits of capitalists.

The ventures of the German Hanseatic League illustrate these impulses. The **Hanseatic League** was a mercantile association of towns formed to achieve mutual security and exclusive trading rights. During the thirteenth century, perhaps two hundred cities from Holland to Poland joined the league, but Lübeck always remained the dominant member. From the thirteenth to the sixteenth century, the Hanseatic League controlled trade over a Novgorod-Reval-Lübeck-Hamburg-Bruges-London axis—that is, the trade

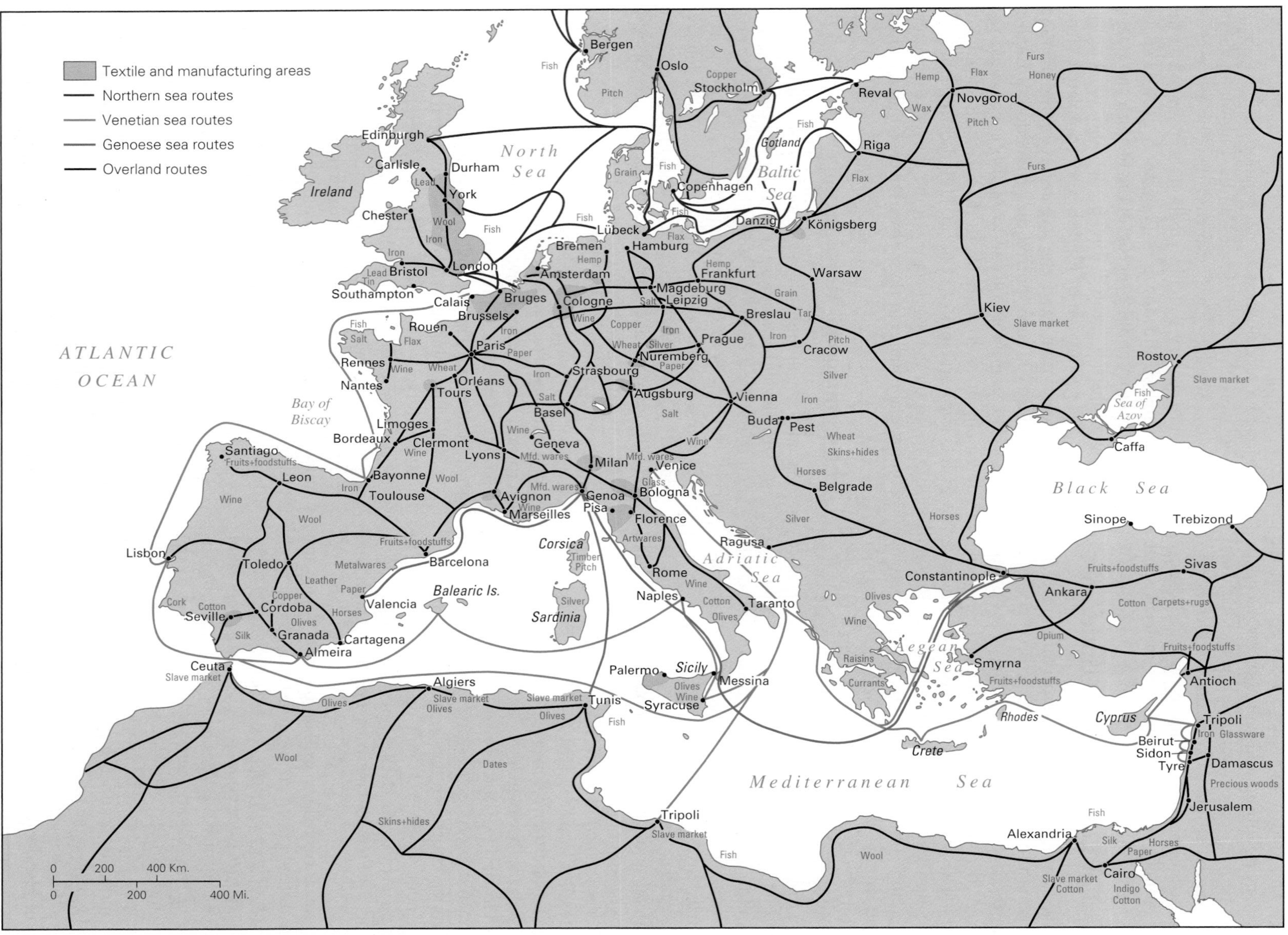


**MAP 13.4 Trade and Manufacturing in Medieval Europe** Note the number of cities and the sources of silver, iron, copper, lead, paper, wool, carpets and rugs, and slaves.

of northern Europe (see Map 13.4). In the fourteenth century, Hanseatic merchants branched out into southern Germany and Italy by land and into French, Spanish, and Portuguese ports by sea.

The ships of league cities carried furs, wax, copper, fish, grain, timber, and wine. These goods were exchanged for finished products, mainly cloth and salt, from western cities. At cities such as Bruges and London, Hanseatic merchants secured special trading concessions exempting them from all tolls and allowing them to trade at local fairs. Hanseatic merchants established foreign trading centers called "factories." (The term *factory* was used in the seventeenth and eighteenth centuries to mean business offices and places in Asia and Africa where goods were stored and slaves held before being shipped to Europe or the Americas; see page 288.) The most famous factory was the London Steelyard, a walled community with warehouses, offices, a church, and residential quarters for company representatives.[26]

By the late thirteenth century, Hanseatic merchants had developed an important business tool, the business register. Merchants publicly recorded their debts and contracts and received a league guarantee for them. This device proved a decisive factor in the later development of credit and commerce in northern Europe. These activities required capital, risk taking, and aggressive pursuit of opportunities—the essential ingredients of capitalism. They also yielded fat profits.

These developments added up to what one modern scholar has called "a commercial revolution, . . . probably the greatest turning point in the history of our civilization."[27] The commercial revolution created a great deal of new wealth. Wealth meant a higher standard of living. The new availability of something as simple as spices, for example, allowed for variety in food. Dietary habits gradually changed. Tastes became more sophisticated. Contact with Eastern civilizations introduced Europeans to eating utensils, and table manners improved. Nobles learned to eat with forks and knives instead of tearing the meat from a roast with their fingers. They began to use napkins instead of wiping their greasy fingers on the dogs lying under the table.

The existence of wealth did not escape the attention of kings and other rulers. Wealth could be taxed, and through taxation kings could create strong and centralized states. In the years to come, alliances with the middle classes were to enable kings to defeat feudal powers and aristocratic interests and to build the states that came to be called "modern."

The commercial revolution also provided the opportunity for thousands of serfs to improve their social position. The slow but steady transformation of European society from almost completely rural and isolated to a relatively more sophisticated one constituted the greatest effect of the commercial revolution that began in the eleventh century. The commercial changes of the eleventh through thirteenth centuries laid the economic foundations for the later development of urban life and culture.

## UNIVERSITIES, GOTHIC ART, AND POETRY

Just as the first strong secular states emerged in the thirteenth century, so did the first universities. This was no coincidence. The new bureaucratic states and the church needed educated administrators, and universities were a response to this need.

Since the time of the Carolingian Empire, monasteries and cathedral schools had offered the only formal instruction available. Monasteries were located in rural environments and geared to religious concerns. They wished to maintain an atmosphere of seclusion and silence and were unwilling to accept large numbers of noisy lay students. In contrast, schools attached to cathedrals and run by the bishop and his clergy were frequently situated in bustling cities, and in the eleventh century in Bologna and other Italian cities wealthy businessmen established municipal schools. Inhabited by people of many backgrounds and "nationalities," cities stimulated the growth and exchange of ideas. In the course of the twelfth century, cathedral schools in France and municipal schools in Italy developed into universities.

The growth of the University of Bologna coincided with a revival of interest in Roman law. The study of Roman law as embodied in Justinian's *Code* had never completely died out in the West, but this sudden burst of interest seems to have been inspired by Irnerius (d. 1125), a great teacher at Bologna. Irnerius not only explained the Roman law of Justinian's *Code* but applied it to difficult practical situations.

At Salerno, interest in medicine had persisted for centuries. Greek and Muslim physicians there had studied the use of herbs as cures and experimented with surgery. The twelfth century ushered in a new interest in Greek medical texts and in the work of Arab and Greek doctors. Students of medicine poured into Salerno and soon attracted royal attention. In 1140, when King Roger II (r. 1130–1154) of Sicily took the practice of medicine under royal control, his ordinance stated: "Who, from now on, wishes to practice medicine, has to present himself before our officials and examiners, in order to pass their judgment. . . . In this way we are taking care that our subjects are not endangered by the inexperience of the physicians."[28]

In the first decades of the twelfth century, students converged on Paris. They crowded into the cathedral school of Notre Dame and spilled over into the area later called the Latin Quarter—whose name probably reflects the Italian origin of many of the students. The cathedral school's international reputation had already drawn to Paris scholars from all over Europe. One of the most famous of them was Peter Abélard (1079–1142).

Fascinated by logic, which he believed could be used to solve most problems, Abélard used a method of systematic doubting in his writing and teaching. As he put it, "By doubting we come to questioning, and by questioning we perceive the truth." Other scholars merely asserted theological principles; Abélard discussed and analyzed them.

The influx of students eager for learning and the presence of dedicated and imaginative teachers created the atmosphere in which universities grew. In northern Europe—at Paris and later at Oxford and Cambridge in England—associations or guilds of professors organized universities. They established the curriculum, set the length of time for study, and determined the form and content of examinations. University faculties grouped themselves according to academic disciplines, or schools—law, medicine, arts, and theology. The professors, known as schoolmen or **Scholastics,** developed a method of thinking, reasoning, and writing in which questions were raised and authorities cited on both sides of a question. The goal of the Scholastic method was to arrive at definitive answers and to provide a rational explanation for what was believed on faith.

The Scholastic approach rested on the recovery of classical philosophical texts and on ancient Greek and Arabic texts that had entered Europe in the early twelfth century. Thirteenth-century philosophers relied on Latin translations of these texts, especially translations of Aristotle. The Scholastics reinterpreted Aristotelian texts in a Christian sense.

Thirteenth-century Scholastics devoted an enormous amount of time to collecting and organizing knowledge on all topics. These collections were published as *summa,* or reference books. There were summa on law, philosophy, vegetation, animal life, and theology. Saint Thomas Aquinas (1225–1274), a professor at Paris, produced the most famous collection, the *Summa Theologica,* which deals with a vast number of theological questions.

Aquinas drew an important distinction between faith and reason. He maintained that, although reason can demonstrate many basic Christian principles such as the existence of God, other fundamental teachings such as the Trinity and original sin cannot be proved by logic. That reason cannot establish them does not, however, mean they are contrary to reason. Rather, people understand such doctrines through revelation embodied in Scripture. Scripture cannot contradict reason, nor reason Scripture:

> *The light of faith that is freely infused into us does not destroy the light of natural knowledge [reason] implanted in us naturally. . . . Indeed, were that the case, one or the other would have to be false, and, since both are given to us by God, God would have to be the author of untruth, which is impossible.*[29]

Thomas Aquinas and all medieval intellectuals held that the end of both faith and reason was the knowledge of, and union with, God. His work later became the fundamental text of Roman Catholic doctrine.

At all universities, the standard method of teaching was the *lecture*—that is, a reading. The professor read a passage from the Bible, Justinian's *Code,* or one of Aristotle's treatises. He then explained and interpreted the passage; his interpretation was called a *gloss.* Students wrote down everything. Because books had to be copied by hand, they were extremely expensive, and few students could afford them. Examinations were given after three, four, or five years of study, when the student applied for a degree. The professors determined the amount of material students had to know for each degree, and students frequently insisted that the professors specify precisely what that material was. Examinations were oral and very difficult. If the candidate passed, he was awarded the first, or bachelor's, degree. Further study, about as long, arduous, and expensive as it is today, enabled the graduate to try for the master's and doctor's degrees. Degrees were technically licenses to teach. Most students, however, did not become teachers. They staffed the expanding royal and papal administrations.

## From Romanesque Gloom to "Uninterrupted Light"

Between 1180 and 1270 in France alone, eighty cathedrals, about five hundred abbey churches, and tens of thousands of parish churches were constructed. All these churches displayed a new architectual style. Fifteenth-century critics called the new style **Gothic** because they mistakenly believed the fifth-century Goths had invented it. It actually developed partly in reaction to the earlier Romanesque style, which resembled ancient Roman architecture. Cathedrals, abbeys, and village churches testify to the deep religious faith and piety of medieval people.

The inspiration for the Gothic style originated in the brain of Suger, abbot of Saint-Denis, who had decided to

**Notre Dame Cathedral, Paris (begun 1163), View from the South** This view offers a fine example of the twin towers (*left*), the spire, the great rose window over the south portal, and the flying buttresses that support the walls and the vaults. Like hundreds of other churches in medieval Europe, it was dedicated to the Virgin. With a nave rising 226 feet, Notre Dame was the tallest building in Europe. *(David R. Frazier/Photo Researchers)*

reconstruct the old Carolingian church at his monastery. The basic features of Gothic architecture—the pointed arch, the ribbed vault, and the flying buttress—allowed unprecedented interior lightness. From Muslim Spain, Islamic methods of ribbed vaulting seem to have heavily influenced the building of Gothic churches. Although architectural historians cannot absolutely prove the connection, "it does not seem pure accident that . . . the first systematic experiments in rib-vaulting started within ten years (1085) of the capture of Toledo," which "contained the finest examples of Islamic rib-vaults."[30] Since the ceiling of a Gothic church weighed less than that of a Romanesque church, the walls could be thinner. Stained-glass windows were cut into the stone, so that the interior, Suger exulted, "would shine with the wonderful and uninterrupted light of most sacred windows, pervading the interior beauty."[31]

The construction of a Gothic cathedral represented a gigantic investment of time, money, and corporate effort. The bishop and the clergy of the cathedral made the decision to build, but they depended on the support of all social classes. Bishops raised revenue from kings, the nobility, the clergy, and those with the greatest amount of ready cash—the commercial classes.

Cathedrals served secular as well as religious purposes. The sanctuary containing the altar and the bishop's chair belonged to the clergy, but the rest of the church belonged to the people. In addition to marriages, baptisms, and funerals, there were scores of feast days on which the entire town gathered in the cathedral for festivities. Local guilds met in the cathedrals to arrange business deals and to plan recreational events and the support of disabled members. Magistrates and municipal officials held political meetings there. Pilgrims slept there, lovers courted there, and traveling actors staged plays there. First and foremost, however, the cathedral was intended to teach the people the doctrines of Christian faith through visual images. Architecture became the servant of theology.

As Gothic churches became more skeletal and had more windows, stained glass replaced manuscript illumination as the leading kind of painting. Thousands of scenes in the cathedral celebrate nature, country life, and the activities of ordinary people.

### Troubadour Poetry

The word *troubadour* comes from the Provençal word *trobar,* which in turn derives from the Arabic *taraba,* meaning "to sing" or "to sing poetry." A troubadour was a poet of Provence who wrote lyric verse in his or her native language and sang it at one of the noble courts. Troubadour songs had a variety of themes. Men sang about "courtly love," the pure love a knight felt for his lady, whom he sought to win by military prowess and patience; about the love a knight felt for the wife of his feudal lord; or about carnal desires seeking satisfaction. Some poems exalted the married state, and others idealized adulterous relationships; some were earthy and bawdy, and others advised young girls to remain chaste in preparation for marriage. The married Countess Beatrice of Dia (1150–1200?) expresses the hurt she felt after being jilted by a young knight:

*Lovely lover, gracious, kind,*
*When will I overcome your fight?*
*O if I could lie with you one night!*
*Feel those loving lips on mine!*
*Listen, one thing sets me afire:*
*Here in my husband's place I want you,*
*If you'll just keep your promise true:*
*Give me everything I desire.*[32]

Troubadours certainly felt Hispano-Arabic influences. In the eleventh century, Christians of southern France were in intimate contact with the Arabized world of Andalusia, where reverence for the lady in a "courtly" tradition had long existed. Troubadour poetry represents another facet of the strong Muslim influence on European culture and life.[33]

The songs of the troubadours were widely imitated in Italy, England, and Germany, and they spurred the development of vernacular languages. Most of the troubadours came from and wrote for the aristocratic classes, and their poetry suggests the interests and values of noble culture in the central Middle Ages.

## LIFE IN CHRISTIAN EUROPE IN THE CENTRAL MIDDLE AGES

In the late ninth century, medieval intellectuals described Christian society as composed of those who pray (the monks), those who fight (the nobles), and those who work (the peasants). According to this image of social structure, function determined social classification.[34] Reality, however, was somewhat different. The division of society into fighters, monks, and peasants presents too static a view of a world in which there was considerable social mobility. Moreover, such a social scheme does not take into consideration townspeople and the emerging commercial classes. That omission, however, is easy to understand. Traders and other city dwellers were not typical members of medieval society. Medieval people were usually contemptuous (at least officially) of profitmaking activities, and even after the appearance of urban commercial groups, the ideological view of medieval Christian society remained the one formulated in the ninth century: the three-part division among peasants, nobles, and monks.

### Those Who Work

According to one modern scholar, "Peasants are rural dwellers who possess (if they do not own) the means of agricultural production."[35] Some peasants worked continuously on the land. Others supplemented their ordinary work as brewers, carpenters, tailors, or housemaids with wage labor in the field. In either case, all peasants supported lords, clergy, townspeople, and themselves. The men and women who worked the land in the twelfth and thirteenth centuries made up the overwhelming majority of the population, probably more than 90 percent. Yet it is difficult to form a coherent picture of them. First, the medieval records that serve as our sources were written by and for the aristocratic classes; they do not give the peasants' perspective. Second, peasants' conditions varied widely across Europe: geography, climate, and individual initiative determined the quality of life in any particular area.[36] Third, although we tend to lump all people who worked the land into one category, the peasantry, there were in fact many kinds of peasants, from complete slaves to very rich farmers. The status of rural workers fluctuated widely, and the period from about 1050 to 1300 saw considerable social mobility.

Slaves were found in western Europe in the central Middle Ages, but in steadily declining numbers. That the word *slave* derives from *Slav* attests to the widespread trade in men and women from the Slavic areas. Legal language differed considerably from place to place, and the distinction between slave and serf was not always clear. Both lacked freedom—the power to do as one wished—and both were subject to the arbitrary will of one person, the lord. A serf, however, could not be bought and sold like an animal or an inanimate object, as a slave could.

The serf was required to perform labor services on the lord's land. The number of workdays varied, but it was usually three days a week except in the planting or harvest seasons, when it increased. Serfs frequently had to pay arbitrary levies, as for marriage or inheritance. The precise amounts of tax paid to the lord depended on local custom and tradition. A free person had to do none of these things. For his or her landholding, rent had to be paid to the lord, and that was often the sole obligation. A free person could move and live as he or she wished.

Serfs were tied to the land, and serfdom was a hereditary condition. A person born a serf was likely to die a serf, though many did secure their freedom. About 1187 Glanvill, an official of King Henry II and an expert on English law, described how **villeins** (literally, "inhabitants of small villages")—as English serfs were called—could be made free:

*No person of villein status can seek his freedom with his own money, . . . because all the chattels of a villein are deemed to be the property of his lord. If, however, a third party provides the money and buys the villein in order to free him, then he can maintain himself for ever in a state of freedom as against his lord who sold him. . . . If any villein stays peaceably for a year and a day in a privileged town and is admitted as a citizen into their commune, that is to say, their gild, he is thereby freed from villeinage.*[37]

Thus, with the advent of a money economy, serfs could save money and, through a third-person intermediary, buy their freedom. (See the feature "Individuals in Society: Jean Mouflet of Sens.")

The economic revival that began in the eleventh century (see pages 384–387) advanced the cause of individual liberty. Hundreds of new towns arose in Ireland, in eastern Europe, and in reconquest Spain; their settlers often came from long distances. The thirteenth century witnessed enormous immigration to many parts of Europe that previously had been sparsely settled. Immigration and colonization provided the opportunity for freedom and social mobility.[38]

Another opportunity for increased personal freedom, or at least for a reduction in traditional manorial obligations and dues, was provided by the reclamation of waste- and forestland in the eleventh and twelfth centuries. Marshes and fens were drained and slowly made arable. This type of agricultural advancement frequently improved the peasants' social and legal condition.

**The Three Classes** Medieval people believed that their society was divided among clerics, warriors, and workers, here represented by a monk, a knight, and a peasant. The new commercial class had no recognized place in the agrarian military world. *(The British Library)*

In the central Middle Ages, most European peasants, free and unfree, lived on a **manor,** the estate of a lord. The manor was the basic unit of medieval rural organization and the center of rural life. The arable land of the manor was divided into two sections. The *demesne,* or home farm, was cultivated by the peasants for the lord. The other, usually larger section was held by the peasantry. All the arable land, both the lord's and the peasants', was divided into strips, and the strips belonging to any given individual were scattered throughout the manor. All peasants cooperated in the cultivation of the land, working it as a group. All shared in any disaster as well as in any large harvest.

The fundamental objective of all medieval agriculture was the production of an adequate food supply. Using the method that historians have called the *open-field system,* peasants divided the arable land of a manor into two or three fields without hedges or fences to mark the individual holdings of the lord, serfs, and freemen. Beginning in the eleventh century in parts of France, England, and Germany, peasants divided all the arable land into three large fields. In any one year, two of the fields were cultivated and one lay fallow. One part of the land was sown with winter cereals such as rye and wheat, the other with spring crops such as peas, beans, and barley. Each year the crop was rotated. Local needs, the fertility of the soil, and dietary customs determined what was planted and the method of crop rotation.

The plow and the harrow (a cultivating instrument with heavy teeth that breaks up and smoothes the soil) were increasingly drawn by horses. The development of the padded horse collar, resting on the horse's shoulders and attached to the load by shafts, led to an agricultural revolution. The horse collar let the animal put its entire weight into the task of pulling. In the twelfth century, the use of horses, rather than oxen, spread because horses' greater strength brought greater efficiency to farming. Horses, however, were an enormous investment, perhaps comparable to a modern tractor. They had to be shod (another indication of increased iron production), and the oats they ate were costly.

The thirteenth century witnessed a tremendous spurt in the use of horses to haul carts to market. Farmers increasingly relied on horses to pull wagons because they could travel much faster than oxen. Consequently, goods reached market faster, and the number of markets within an area to which the peasant had access increased. The opportunities and temptations for consumer spending on nonagricultural goods multiplied.[39]

Agricultural yields varied widely from place to place and from year to year. By twentieth-century standards, they were very low. Inadequate soil preparation, poor seed selection, lack of manure—all made low yields virtually inevitable. And, like farmers of all times and places, medieval peasants were at the mercy of the weather. Yet there was striking improvement over time. Researchers have tentatively concluded that between the ninth and early thirteenth centuries, yields of cereals approximately doubled, and on the best-managed estates farmers harvested five bushels of grain for every bushel of seed planted.

For most people in medieval Europe, life meant country life. A person's horizons were not likely to extend beyond the manor on which he or she was born. Most people rarely traveled more than twenty-five miles beyond their villages. Their world was small, narrow, and provincial: limited by the boundaries of the province.

Scholars have recently spent much energy investigating the structure of medieval peasant households. Because little concrete evidence survives, conclusions are very tentative. It appears, however, that a peasant household consisted of a simple nuclear family: a married couple alone, a couple of children, or a widow or widower with children. Peasant households were *not* extended families containing grandparents or married sons and daughters and their children. Before the first appearance of the Black Death (see pages 399–401), perhaps 94 percent of peasant farmers married, and both bride and groom were in their early twenties. The typical household numbered about five people—the parents and three children.[40]

Women played a significant role in the agricultural life of medieval Europe. Women worked with men in wheat and grain cultivation, in the vineyards, and in the harvest and preparation of crops needed by the textile industry—flax and plants used for dyeing cloth, such as madder (which produces shades of red) and woad (which yields blue dye). Especially at harvest time, women shared with their fathers and husbands the backbreaking labor in the fields, work that was especially difficult for them because of weaker muscular development and frequent pregnancies. Lords of great estates commonly hired female day laborers to shear sheep, pick hops (used in the manufacture of beer and ale), tend gardens, and do household chores such as cleaning, laundry, and baking. Servant girls in the country considered their hired status as temporary, until they married. Thrifty farm wives contributed to the family income by selling for cash the produce of their gardens or kitchens: butter, cheese, eggs, fruit, soap, mustard, cucumbers. In a year of crisis, careful management was often all that separated a household from starvation. And starvation was a very real danger to the peasantry down to the eighteenth century.

Women managed the house. The size and quality of peasants' houses varied according to their relative prosperity and usually depended on the amount of land held. The poorest peasants lived in windowless cottages built of wood and clay or wattle and thatched with straw. These cottages consisted of one large room that served as the kitchen and living quarters for all. The house had an earthen floor and a fireplace. The lack of windows meant that the room was very sooty. A trestle table, several stools, one or two beds, and a chest for storing clothes constituted the furniture. A shed attached to the house provided storage for tools and shelter for animals. Prosperous peasants added rooms and furniture as they could be afforded, and some wealthy peasants in the early fourteenth century had two-story houses with separate bedrooms for parents and children.

Women dominated in the production of ale for the community market. They had to know how to mix the correct proportions of barley, water, yeast, and hops in twelve-gallon vats of hot liquid. Brewing was hard and

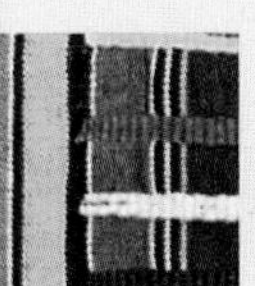

## JEAN MOUFLET OF SENS

*The customary form of manumission,* not *the manner in which Jean Mouflet gained his freedom.* (British Library)

Throughout most of Western history, the vast majority of people left little behind that identifies them as individuals. Baptismal, marriage, and death records; wills; grants for memorial masses; and, after the eighteenth century, brief census information collected by governments—these forms of evidence provide exciting information about groups of people but little about individuals. Before the nineteenth century, most people were illiterate; the relative few who could write, such as business people, used such literary skills as they had in matters connected with their work. The historian, therefore, has great difficulty reconstructing the life of an "ordinary" person. An exception occurs when a person committed a crime in a society that kept judicial records or when he or she made a legal agreement that was preserved. Such is the case of Jean Mouflet of Sens.*

We know little about him except what is revealed in a document granting what was probably the central desire of his life—his personal freedom. His ancestors had been serfs on the lands of the abbey of Saint-Pierre-le-Vif in the Sénonais region of France. There a serf was subject to legal disabilities that debased his dignity and implied inferior status. Work required on the lord's land bred resentment, because work was simultaneously needed on the rustic's own land. At death a peasant gave the lord a token, or not so token, gift—his best beast. Marriage presented another disability, first because one partner had to change dwelling and to do so had to gain the lord's permission; second because it raised the question of children: whose dependents did they become? Special "gifts" to the lord "encouraged" him to resolve these issues. Again, an unfree person, even if he or she possessed the expected dowry, could not become a monk or nun or enter holy orders without the lord's permission, because the lord stood to lose labor services. Finally, residence in a town for a year and a day did not always ensure freedom; years after the person settled there, the lord could claim him or her as a dependent.

In 1249 Jean Mouflet made an agreement with the abbot: in return for an annual payment, the monastery would recognize Jean as a "citizen of Sens." With a stroke of his quill, the abbot manumitted Jean and his heirs, ending centuries of servile obligations.

The agreement describes Jean as a leather merchant. Other evidence reveals that he had a large leather shop in the leather goods section of town† that he leased for the very high rent of fifty shillings a year. If not "rich," Jean was certainly well-to-do. Circumstantial evidence suggests that Jean's father had originally left the land to become a leatherworker and taught his son the trade. The agreement was witnessed by Jean's wife, Douce, daughter of a wealthy and prominent citizen of Sens, Félis Charpentier. To have been a suitable candidate for Douce, Jean would have to have been extremely industrious, very lucky, and accepted as a "rising young man" by the grudging burghers of the town. Such a giant step upward in one generation seems unlikely.

In addition to viticulture (the cultivation of grapes), the Sénonais was well suited for cereal production and for animal grazing. Jean undoubtedly bought hides from local herders and manufactured boots and shoes; saddles, bridles, and reins for horses; and belts and purses. He may also have made wineskins for local vintners or for those of Champagne. It is also fair to assume that the wealthy cathedral clergy, the townspeople, and, if his goods were of sufficiently high quality, the merchants of the nearby fairs of Champagne were his customers.

By private agreements with lords, servile peasants gained the most basic of human rights—freedom.

### QUESTIONS FOR ANALYSIS

1. What is human freedom?
2. How did trade and commerce contribute to the development of individual liberty?

*This essay rests on the fine study of W. C. Jordan, *From Servitude to Freedom: Manumission in the Sénonais in the Thirteenth Century* (Philadelphia: University of Pennsylvania Press, 1986).

†As in all medieval towns, merchants in particular trades—butchers, bakers, leatherworkers—had shops in one area. Sens is still a major French leather-tanning center.

**Saint Maurice** The cult of Saint Maurice (d. 287), a soldier executed by the Romans for refusing to renounce his Christian faith, presents a paradox. Although no solid evidence for him has survived, his cult spread widely in the Carolingian period. Later, he was held up as a model knight and declared a patron of the Holy Roman Empire and protector of the imperial (German) army in wars against the pagan Slavs. His image was used on coins, and his cult was promoted by the archbishops of Magdeburg. Always, until 1240, he was portrayed as a white man. Then, from 1240 to the sixteenth century, he was represented as a black man, as in this sandstone statue from Magdeburg Cathedral (ca 1240–1250). Who commissioned this statue? Who carved it? What black man served as the model? Only further research can answer these questions, as well as the question of his race. *(Image of the Black Project, Harvard University/Hickey-Robertson, Houston)*

dangerous work. Records of the English coroners' courts reveal that 5 percent of women who died lost their lives in brewing accidents, falling into the vats of boiling liquid.[41] Ale was the universal drink of the common people in northern Europe. By modern American standards, the rate of consumption was heroic. Each monk of Abingdon Abbey in twelfth-century England was allotted three gallons a day, and a man working in the fields for ten hours probably drank much more.[42]

The mainstay of the diet for peasants everywhere—and for all other classes—was bread. It was a hard, black substance made of barley, millet, and oats, rarely of expensive wheat flour. The housewife usually baked the household supply once a week. If sheep, cows, or goats were raised, she also made cheese.

The diet of those living in an area with access to a river, lake, or stream was supplemented with fish, which could be preserved by salting. In many places, severe laws against hunting and trapping in the forests restricted deer and other game to the king and nobility. These laws were flagrantly violated, however, and stolen rabbits often found their way to the peasants' tables.

Except for the rare chicken or illegally caught wild game, meat appeared on the table only on the great feast days of the Christian year: Christmas, Easter, and Pentecost. Then the meat was likely to be pork from the pig slaughtered in the fall and salted for the rest of the year. Some scholars believe that by the mid-thirteenth century, there was a great increase in the consumption of meat generally. If so, this improvement in diet is further evidence of an improved standard of living.

## Those Who Fight

The nobility, though a small fraction of the total population, strongly influenced all aspects of medieval culture—political, economic, religious, educational, and artistic. For that reason, European society in the twelfth and thirteenth centuries may be termed aristocratic.

Members of the nobility enjoyed a special legal status. A nobleman was free personally and in his possessions. He was limited only by his military obligation to king, duke, or prince. As the result of his liberty, he had certain rights and responsibilities. He raised troops and commanded them in the field. He held courts that dispensed a sort of justice. Sometimes he coined money for use within his territories. As lord of the people who settled on his lands, he made political decisions affecting them, resolved disputes among them, and protected them in time of attack. The liberty and privileges of the noble were inheritable, perpetuated by blood and not by wealth alone.

The nobleman was a professional fighter. His social function, as churchmen described it, was to protect the weak, the poor, and the churches by arms. He possessed a horse and a sword. These, and the leisure time in which to learn how to use them in combat, were the visible signs of his nobility. He was encouraged to display chivalric virtues—courtesy, loyalty to his commander, and generosity.

The responsibilities of a noble in the central Middle Ages depended on the size and extent of his estates, the number of his dependents, and his position in his territory relative to others of his class and to the king. As a vassal a noble was required to fight for his lord or for the king when called on to do so. By the mid-twelfth century, this service was limited in most parts of western Europe to forty days a year. The noble was obliged to attend his lord's court on important occasions when the lord wanted to put on great displays, such as at Easter, Pentecost, and Christmas. When the lord knighted his eldest son or married off his eldest daughter, he called his vassals to his court. They were expected to attend and to present a contribution known as a "gracious aid."

Until the late thirteenth century, when royal authority intervened, a noble in France or England had great power over the knights and peasants on his estates. He maintained order among them and dispensed justice to them. The quality of life on the manor and its productivity were related in no small way to the temperament and decency of the lord—and his lady.

Women played a large and important role in the functioning of the estate. They were responsible for the practical management of the household's "inner economy"—cooking, brewing, spinning, weaving, caring for yard animals. The lifestyle of the medieval warrior-nobles required constant travel, both for purposes of war and for the supervision of distant properties. When the lord was away for long periods—on crusade, for instance, the lord could be gone from two to five years, if he returned at all—his wife often became the sole manager of the family properties. Between 1060 and 1080, the lady Hersendis was the sole manager of her family's properties in northern France while her husband was on crusade in the Holy Land.

Medieval warfare was largely a matter of brief skirmishes, and few men were killed in any single encounter. But altogether the number slain ran high, and there were many widows. Aristocratic widows frequently controlled family properties and fortunes and exercised great authority. Although the evidence is scattered and sketchy, there are indications that women performed many of the functions of men. In Spain, France, and Germany they bought, sold, and otherwise transferred property.

## Those Who Pray

Monasticism represented some of the finest aspirations of medieval civilization. The monasteries were devoted to prayer, and their standards of Christian behavior influenced the entire church. The monasteries produced the educated elite that was continually drawn into the administrative service of kings and great lords. Monks kept alive the remains of classical culture and experimented with new styles of architecture and art. They introduced new techniques of estate management and land reclamation. Although relatively few in number in the central Middle Ages, the monks played a significant role in medieval society.

Toward the end of his *Ecclesiastical History of England and Normandy,* when he was well into his sixties, Orderic Vitalis (ca 1075–ca 1140), a monk of the Norman abbey of Saint Evroul, interrupted his narrative to explain movingly how he happened to become a monk:

> *And so, O glorious God, you didst inspire my father Odeleric to renounce me utterly and . . . weeping, he gave me, a weeping child, into the care of the monk Reginald, and sent me away into exile for love of thee, and never saw me again. . . . [H]e promised me for his part that if I became a monk I should taste of the joys of Heaven. . . . And so, a boy of ten, I crossed the English channel and came into Normandy as an exile, unknown to all, knowing no one.*[43]

Orderic was the third son of a knight who held lands in western England. Concern for the provision of his two older sons probably led the knight to give his youngest boy to the monastery.

Medieval monasteries were religious institutions whose organization and structure fulfilled the social needs of the feudal nobility. The monasteries provided noble children with both an honorable and aristocratic life and opportunities for ecclesiastical careers.[44] As medieval society changed economically, and as European society ever so slowly developed middle-class traits, the monasteries almost inevitably drew their manpower, when they were able, from the middle classes. Until that time, they were preserves of the aristocratic nobility.

Through the Middle Ages, social class also defined the kinds of religious life open to women. Kings and nobles usually established convents for their daughters, sisters, aunts, or aging mothers. Entrance was restricted to women of the founder's class. Since a wellborn lady could not honorably be apprenticed to a tradesperson or do any kind of manual labor, the sole alternative to life at home was the religious life.

Although the level of intellectual life in the women's houses varied widely, the career of Hildegard of Bingen suggests the activities of some nuns in the central Middle Ages. The tenth child of a lesser noble family, Hildegard (1098–1179) was given when eight years old as an oblate to an abbey in the Rhineland, where she learned Latin and received a good education. In 1147 Hildegard founded the convent of Rupertsberg near Bingen. There she produced a body of writings including the *Scivias* (Know the Ways), a record of her mystical visions that incorporates vast theological learning; the *Physica* (On the Physical Elements), a classification of the natural elements, such as plants, animals, metals, and the movements of the heavenly bodies; a mystery play; and a medical work that led a distinguished twentieth-century historian of science to describe Hildegard as "one of the most original writers of the Latin West in the twelfth century."[45] An exceptionally gifted person, Hildegard represents the Benedictine ideal of great learning combined with a devoted monastic life. Like intellectual monks, however, intellectual nuns were not typical of the era.

In medieval Europe, the monasteries of men greatly outnumbered those of women. The pattern of life within individual monasteries varied widely from house to house and from region to region. One central activity, however—the work of God—was performed everywhere. Daily life centered on the liturgy.

Seven times a day and once during the night, the monks went to choir to chant the psalms and other prayers prescribed by Saint Benedict. Prayers were offered for peace, rain, good harvests, the civil authorities, the monks' families, and their benefactors. Monastic patrons in turn lavished gifts on the monasteries, which often became very wealthy. Through their prayers, the monks performed a valuable service for the rest of society.

Monks and nuns engaged in virtually every aspect of medieval European economic life. Taking advantage of local opportunities, they worked in agriculture, of course, and in sheep farming (for wool production), in viticulture (the cultivation of grapes for wine production), in beekeeping (for the production of honey, the universal sweetener), in coal and iron mining, in horse breeding, and even in banking, where, as one reliable scholar puts it, "it was clerics and ecclesiastical institutions (monasteries and nunneries) that constituted the main providers of credit."[46] Profits from these enterprises supported a variety of social services. Schools for the education of the young; homes for orphaned children, unwed mothers, and the elderly; hospitals for the sick; and inns for travelers were often associated with monasteries and nunneries. In an age when there was no conception of social welfare or public responsibility for the poor, the sick, and the unfortunate, monasteries fulfilled important social needs.

## CRISES OF THE LATER MIDDLE AGES

In the later years of the thirteenth century, Europeans seemed to run out of steam. The crusading movement gradually fizzled out. Few new cathedrals were constructed, and if a cathedral had not been completed by 1300, the chances were high that it never would be. The strong rulers of England and France, building on the foundations of their predecessors, increased their authority and gained the loyalty of all their subjects. The vigor of those kings, however, did not pass to their immediate descendants. Meanwhile, the church, which for two centuries had guided Christian society, began to face grave difficulties. A violent dispute between the papacy and the kings of England and France badly damaged the prestige of the pope. But religious struggle was only one of the crises that would face European society in the fourteenth century.

### A Challenge to Religious Authority

In 1294 King Edward I of England and Philip the Fair of France declared war on each other. To finance this war, both kings laid taxes on the clergy. Kings had been taxing the church for decades. Pope Boniface VIII (r. 1294–1303), arguing from precedent, insisted that kings gain papal consent for taxation of the clergy and forbade churchmen to pay the taxes. Edward and Philip refused to accept this decree. Edward immediately denied the clergy the protection of the law, an action that meant its members could be attacked with impunity. Philip halted the shipment of all ecclesiastical revenue to Rome. Boniface had to back down.

Philip the Fair and his ministers continued their attack on all powers in France outside royal authority. Philip arrested a French bishop. When Boniface protested, Philip replied with the trumped-up charge that the pope was a heretic. The papacy and the French monarchy waged a bitter war of propaganda. Finally, in 1302, in a letter titled *Unam Sanctam* (because its opening sentence spoke of one holy Catholic church), Boniface insisted that all Christians, including kings, are subject to the pope. Philip's university-trained advisers, with an argument drawn from Roman law, maintained that the king of France was completely sovereign in his kingdom and responsible to God alone. French mercenary troops went to Italy and arrested the aged pope. Although Boniface was soon freed, he died shortly afterward.

## The Great Famine and the Black Death

Economic difficulties originating in the later thirteenth century were fully manifest by the start of the fourteenth. In the first decade, the countries of northern Europe experienced considerable price inflation. The costs of grain, livestock, and dairy products rose sharply. Severe weather, which historical geographers label the Little Ice Age, made a serious situation frightful. An unusual number of storms brought torrential rains, ruining the wheat, oat, and hay crops on which people and animals almost everywhere depended. Population had steadily increased in the twelfth and thirteenth centuries. The amount of food yielded, however, did not match the level of population growth. Bad weather had disastrous results. Poor harvests—one in four was likely to be poor—led to scarcity and starvation. Almost all of northern Europe suffered a terrible famine in the years 1315 to 1317. Then in 1318 disease hit cattle and sheep, drastically reducing the herds and flocks. Another bad harvest in 1321 brought famine, starvation, and death. Famine had dire social consequences: rustics were forced to sell or mortgage their lands for money to buy food; the number of vagabonds, or homeless people, greatly increased, as did petty crime; and the dispossessed and starving focused their bitterness on land speculators and Jews. An undernourished population was ripe for the Grim Reaper, who appeared in 1348 in the form of the **Black Death** (see Map 13.5).[47]

In October 1347, Genoese ships traveling from the Crimea in southern Russia brought the bubonic plague to Messina, from which it spread across Sicily and up into Italy. By late spring of 1348, southern Germany was attacked.

**MAP 13.5 The Course of the Black Death in Fourteenth-Century Europe** Note the routes that the bubonic plague took across Europe. How do you account for the fact that several regions were spared the "dreadful death"?

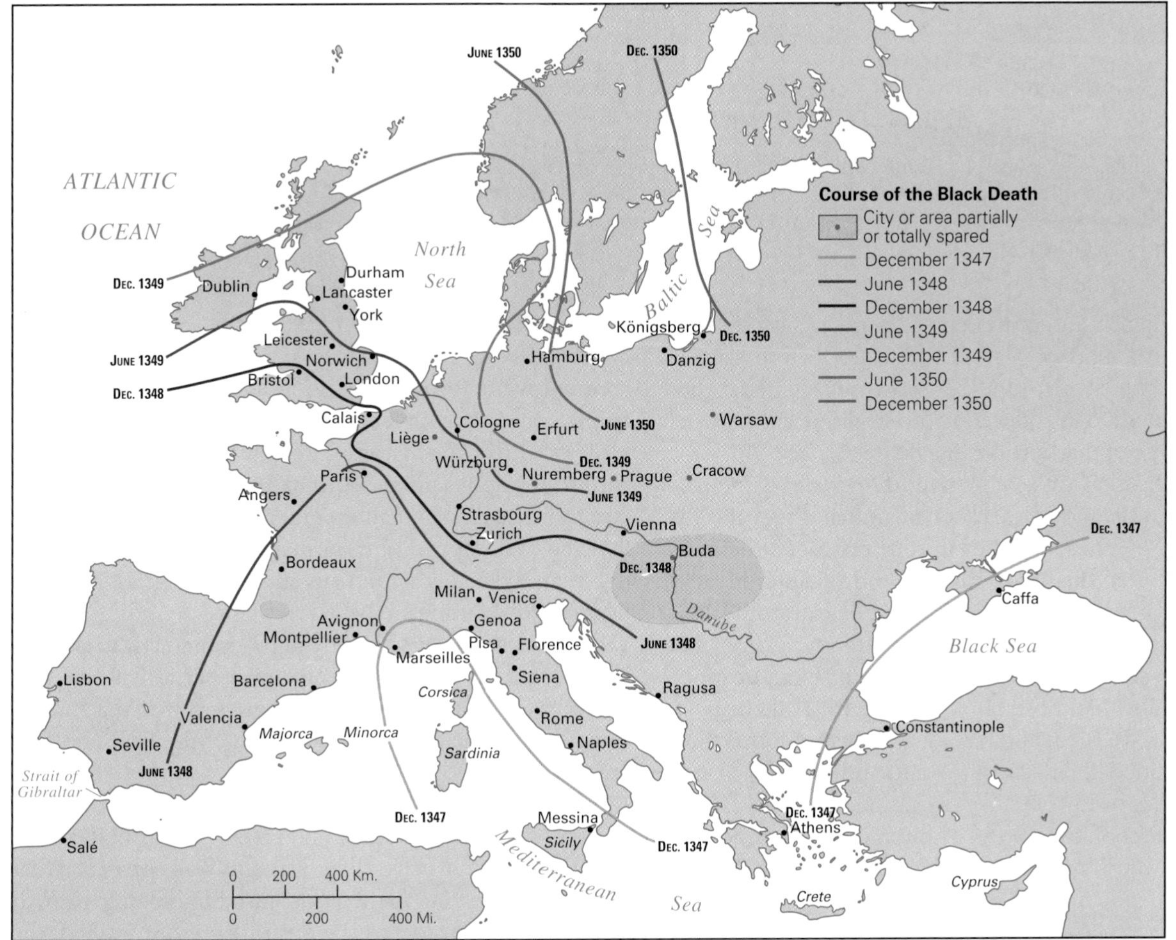

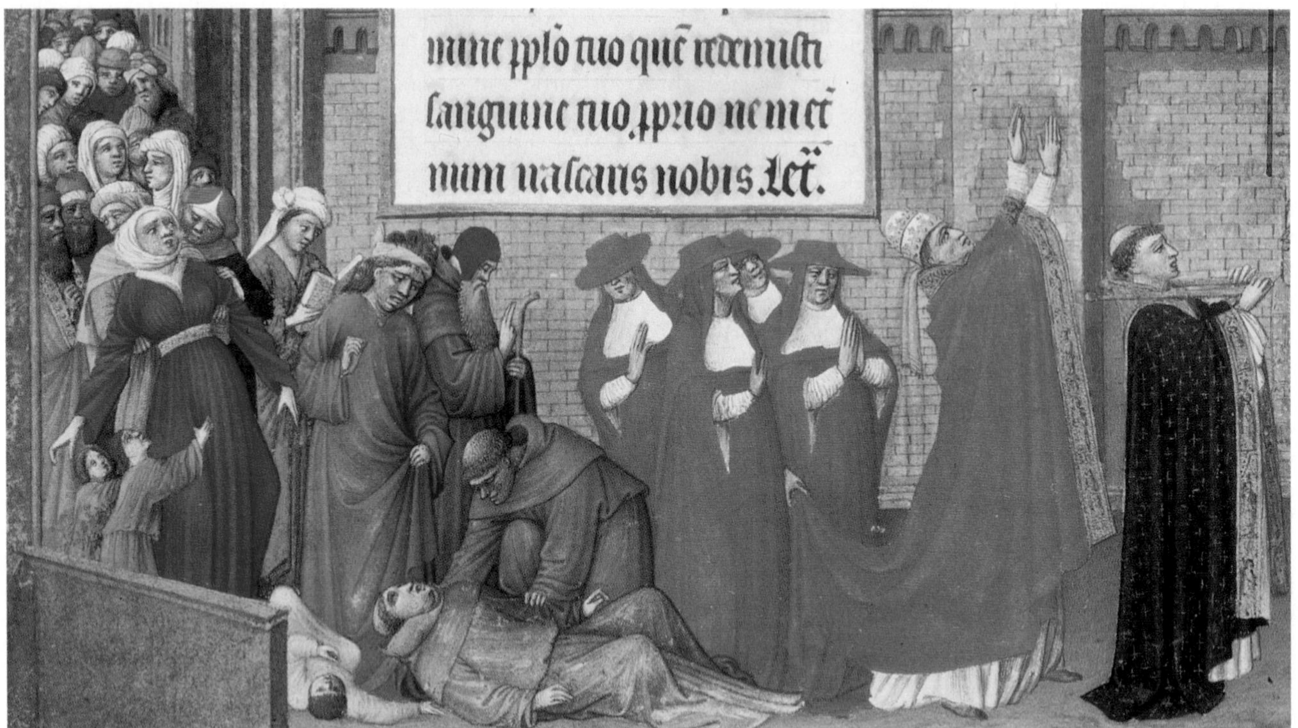

**Procession of Saint Gregory** According to the *Golden Legend,* a thirteenth-century collection of saints' lives, the bubonic plague ravaged Rome when Gregory I was elected pope (r. 590–604). He immediately ordered special prayers and processions around the city. Here, as people circle the walls, new victims fall (*center*). The architecture, the cardinals, and the friars all indicate that this painting dates from the fourteenth, not the sixth, century. *(Musée Condé, Chantilly/Art Resource, NY)*

Frightened French authorities chased a galley bearing the disease from the port of Marseilles, but not before plague had infected the city. In June 1348 two ships entered the Bristol Channel and introduced it into England. All Europe felt the scourge of this horrible disease.

The bacillus that causes the plague, *Pasteurella pestis,* likes to live in the bloodstream of an animal or, ideally, in the stomach of a flea. The flea in turn resides in the hair of a rodent, often the hardy, nimble, and vagabond black rat. In the fourteenth century, the host black rat traveled by ship, where it could feast for months on a cargo of grain or live snugly among bales of cloth. Fleas bearing the bacillus also had no trouble nesting in saddlebags.[48] Comfortable, well-fed, and having greatly multiplied, the black rats ended their ocean voyage and descended on the great cities of Europe.

The plague took two forms—bubonic and pneumonic. The rat was the transmitter of the bubonic form of the disease. The pneumonic form was communicated directly from one person to another.

Urban conditions were ideal for the spread of disease. Narrow streets filled with mud, refuse, and human excrement were as much cesspools as thoroughfares. Dead animals and sore-covered beggars greeted the traveler. Houses whose upper stories projected over the lower ones eliminated light and air. And extreme overcrowding was commonplace. When all members of an aristocratic family lived and slept in one room, it should not be surprising that six or eight persons in a middle-class or poor household slept in one bed.

Standards of personal hygiene remained frightfully low. Fleas and body lice were universal afflictions: one more bite did not cause much alarm. But if that nibble came from a bacillus-bearing flea, an entire household or area was doomed.

The symptoms of the bubonic plague started with a growth the size of a nut or an apple in the armpit, in the groin, or on the neck. This was the boil, or *buba,* that gave the disease its name and caused agonizing pain. If the buba was lanced and the pus thoroughly drained, the victim had a chance of recovery. The secondary stage was the appearance of black spots or blotches caused by bleeding under the skin. Finally, the victim began to cough violently and spit blood. This stage, indicating the presence of thousands of bacilli in the bloodstream, signaled the end, and death followed in two or three days. Rather than evoking compassion for the victim, a French scientist has written, everything about the bubonic plague provoked horror and disgust: "All the matter which exuded from their bodies let off an unbearable stench; sweat, excrement, spittle, breath, so fetid as to be overpowering; urine turbid, thick, black or red."[49]

Physicians could sometimes ease the pain but had no cure. Most people—lay, scholarly, and medical—believed that the Black Death was caused by some "vicious property in the air" that carried the disease from place to place. When ignorance was joined to fear and ancient bigotry, savage cruelty sometimes resulted. Many people believed that the Jews had poisoned the wells of Christian communities and thereby infected the drinking water. This charge led to the murder of thousands of Jews across Europe. According to one chronicler, sixteen thousand were killed at the imperial city of Strasbourg alone in 1349. That this figure is probably a typically medieval numerical exaggeration does not lessen the horror of the massacre.

The Italian writer Giovanni Boccaccio (1313–1375), describing the course of the disease in Florence in the preface to his book of tales, *The Decameron,* pinpointed the cause of the spread:

*Moreover, the virulence of the pest was the greater by reason that intercourse was apt to convey it from the sick to the whole, just as fire devours things dry or greasy when they are brought close to it. Nay, the evil went yet further, for not merely by speech or association with the sick was the malady communicated to the healthy with consequent peril of common death, but any that touched the clothes of the sick or aught else that had been touched or used by them, seemed thereby to contract the disease.*[50]

Because population figures for the period before the arrival of the plague do not exist for most countries and cities, only educated guesses can be made about mortality rates. Of a total English population of perhaps 4.2 million, probably 1.4 million died of the Black Death in its several visits.[51] Densely populated Italian cities endured incredible losses. Florence lost between one-half and two-thirds of its 1347 population of 85,000 when the plague visited in 1348. The disease recurred intermittently in the 1360s and 1370s and reappeared many times down to 1700. Population losses in Bohemia and Poland seem to have been much less. Historians of medicine have postulated that people with blood type O are immune to the bubonic disease; since this blood type predominated in Hungary, that region would have been slightly affected. No estimates of population losses have ever been attempted for Russia and the Balkans.

The traditional thesis of a rat-based bubonic plague has recently been strongly challenged. Using comparative evidence from later visits from the plague in medieval Europe (after 1347–1348), from early modern Europe, from India and China in the late nineteenth century, and from Manchuria in the early twentieth century, one scholar has reached interesting conclusions. He argues that later European visits of the plague were not the same disease as that of 1347 and that, while humans possess no natural immunity to the rat-based disease, the steady decline in the mortality rate in later medieval plagues indicates that humans adapted to it. This historian also claims that later visits of the plague did not provoke the same social, psychological, and political reactions as the initial attack had.[52] A consensus awaits.

Economic historians and demographers sharply dispute the impact of the plague on the economy in the late fourteenth century. The traditional view that the plague had a disastrous effect has been greatly modified. In England it appears that by about 1375, most landlords enjoyed revenues near those of the pre-plague years. By the early fifteenth century, seigneurial prosperity reached a medieval peak. Why? The answer appears to lie in the fact that England and many parts of Europe suffered from overpopulation in the early fourteenth century. Population losses caused by the Black Death "led to increased productivity by restoring a more efficient balance between labour, land, and capital."[53] Population decline meant a sharp increase in per capita wealth. Increased demand for labor meant greater mobility among peasant and working classes. Wages rose, providing better distribution of income. The shortage of labor and steady requests for higher wages put landlords on the defensive. Some places, such as Florence, experienced economic prosperity as a long-term consequence of the plague.

Even more significant than the social effects were the psychological consequences. The knowledge that the disease meant almost certain death provoked the most profound pessimism. It is not surprising that some sought release in orgies and gross sensuality, while others turned to the severest forms of asceticism and frenzied religious fervor. Groups of *flagellants,* men and women who whipped and scourged themselves as penance for their and society's sins, believed that the Black Death was God's punishment for humanity's wickedness.

## The Hundred Years' War (ca 1337–1453)

The centuries-old struggle between the English and French monarchies, the Hundred Years' War, fought intermittently from 1337 to 1453, represents a serious political crisis. Its causes were both distant and immediate. The English claimed Aquitaine as an ancient feudal inheritance. In 1329 England's King Edward III (r. 1327–1377) paid homage to Philip VI (r. 1328–1350) for Aquitaine. French policy, however, was strongly expansionist, and in 1337 Philip, determined to exercise full jurisdiction there, confiscated the duchy. This action was the immediate cause of the war. Edward III maintained that the only way he could exercise his rightful sovereignty over Aquitaine was by assuming the title of king of France.[54] As the grandson and eldest surviving male descendant of Philip the Fair, he believed he could rightfully make this claim.

For centuries, economic factors involving the wool trade and the control of Flemish towns had served as justifications for war between France and England. The wool trade between England and Flanders was the cornerstone of both countries' economies; they were closely interdependent. Flanders was a fief of the French crown, and the Flemish aristocracy was highly sympathetic to the monarchy in Paris. But the wealth of Flemish merchants and cloth manufacturers depended on English wool, and Flemish burghers strongly supported the claims of Edward III.

The Hundred Years' War was popular because it presented unusual opportunities for wealth and advancement. Poor knights and knights who were unemployed were promised regular wages. Great nobles expected to be rewarded with estates. Royal exhortations to the troops before battles repeatedly stressed that, if victorious, the men might keep whatever they seized. The French chronicler Jean Froissart wrote that, at the time of Edward III's military expedition of 1359 to France, men of all ranks flocked to the English king's banner. Some came to acquire honor, but many came in order "to loot and pillage the fair and plenteous land of France."[55]

The period of the Hundred Years' War witnessed the final flowering of the aristocratic code of medieval chivalry. War was considered an ennobling experience: there was something elevating, manly, fine, and beautiful about it.

The chivalric code applied only to the aristocratic military elite. English knights fought French ones as social equals fighting according to a mutually accepted code of behavior. The infantry troops were looked on as inferior beings. When a peasant force at Longueil destroyed a contingent of English knights, their comrades mourned them because "it was too much that so many good fighters had been killed by mere peasants."[56]

The war, fought almost entirely in France and the Low Countries (see Map 13.6), consisted mainly of a series of random sieges and cavalry raids. During the war's early stages, England was highly successful. At Crécy in northern France in 1346, English longbowmen scored a great victory over French knights and crossbowmen. Although the fire of the longbow was not very accurate, it allowed for rapid reloading, and English archers could send off three arrows to the French crossbowmen's one. The result was a blinding shower of arrows that unhorsed the French knights and caused mass confusion. The firing of cannon—probably the first use of artillery in the West—created further panic. Thereupon the English horsemen charged and butchered the French.

Ten years later, Edward the Black Prince, using the same tactics as at Crécy, smashed the French at Poitiers, captured the French king, and held him for ransom. Again, at Agincourt near Arras in 1415, the chivalric English soldier-king Henry V (r. 1413–1422) gained the field over vastly superior numbers. By 1419 the English had advanced to the walls of Paris. But the French cause was not lost. Though England scored the initial victories, France won the war.

The ultimate French success rests heavily on the actions of an obscure French peasant girl, Joan of Arc, whose vision and work revived French fortunes and led to victory. Born in 1412 to well-to-do peasants in the village of Domrémy in Champagne, Joan of Arc grew up in a pious household. During adolescence she began to hear voices, which she later said belonged to Saint Michael, Saint Catherine, and Saint Margaret. In 1428 these voices told her that the dauphin (the uncrowned King Charles VII) had to be crowned and the English expelled from France. Joan went to the French court, persuaded the king to reject the rumor that he was illegitimate, and secured his support for her relief of the besieged city of Orléans (see Map 13.6).

Joan arrived before Orléans on April 28, 1429. Seventeen years old, she knew little of warfare and believed that if she could keep the French troops from swearing and frequenting brothels, victory would be theirs. On May 8 the English, weakened by disease and lack of supplies, withdrew from Orléans. Ten days later, Charles VII was crowned king at Reims. These two events marked the turning point in the war.

In 1430 England's allies, the Burgundians, captured Joan and sold her to the English. When the English handed her over to the ecclesiastical authorities for trial, the French court did not intervene. The English wanted Joan eliminated for obvious political reasons, but sorcery (witchcraft) was the charge at her trial. Witch persecution

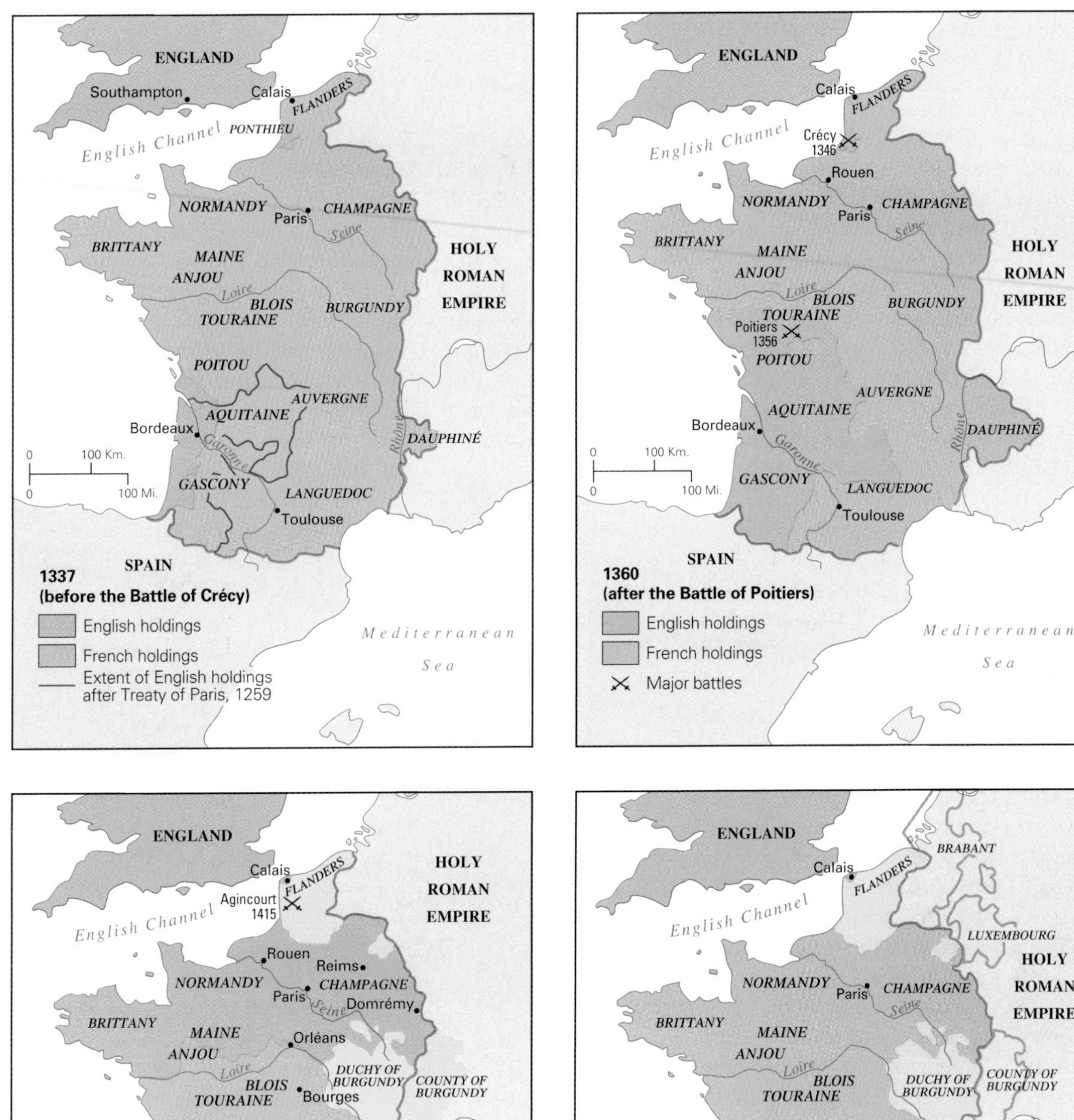


**MAP 13.6 English Holdings in France During the Hundred Years' War** The year 1429 marked the greatest extent of English holdings in France. Why is it unlikely that England could have held these territories permanently?

was increasing in the fifteenth century, and Joan's wearing of men's clothes appeared not only aberrant but indicative of contact with the Devil. In 1431 the court condemned her as a heretic. Her claim of direct inspiration from God, thereby denying the authority of church officials, constituted heresy. She was burned at the stake in the marketplace at Rouen. A new trial in 1456 rehabilitated her name. In 1920 she was canonized, and today she is revered as the second patron saint of France.

The relief of Orléans stimulated French pride and rallied French resources. As the war dragged on, loss of life mounted, and money appeared to be flowing into a bottomless pit, demands for an end increased in England. The clergy and intellectuals pressed for peace. Parliamentary opposition to additional war grants stiffened. Slowly the French reconquered Normandy and finally ejected the English from Aquitaine. At the war's end in 1453, only the town of Calais remained in English hands (see Map 13.6).

For both France and England, the war proved a disaster. In France the English had slaughtered thousands of soldiers and civilians. In the years after the Black Death, this additional killing meant a grave loss of population. Destruction of hundreds of thousands of acres of rich farmland left the rural economy of many parts of France a shambles. The war had disrupted trade and the great fairs, resulting in the drastic reduction of French participation in international commerce. Defeat in battle and heavy taxation contributed to widespread dissatisfaction and aggravated peasant grievances.

The long war had a profound impact on the political and cultural lives of the two countries. Most notably, it stimulated the development of the English Parliament. Between 1250 and 1450, representative assemblies from several classes of society flourished in many European countries. In the English Parliament, French Estates, German diets, and Spanish cortes, deliberative practices developed that laid the foundations for the representative institutions of modern liberal-democratic nations. Representative assemblies declined in most countries after the fifteenth century, but the English Parliament endured. Edward III's constant need for money to pay for the war compelled him to summon not only the great barons and bishops but knights of the shires and burgesses from the towns as well. Between the outbreak of the war in 1337 and the king's death in 1377, parliamentary assemblies met twenty-seven times. Parliament met in thirty-seven of the fifty years of Edward's reign.[57]

In England theoretical consent to taxation and legislation was given in one assembly for the entire country. France had no such single assembly; instead, there were many regional or provincial assemblies. Why did a national representative assembly fail to develop in France? The initiative for convening assemblies rested with the king, who needed revenue almost as much as the English ruler.

No one in France wanted a national assembly. Linguistic, geographical, economic, legal, and political differences were very strong. People tended to think of themselves as Breton, Norman, Burgundian, or whatever, rather than French. Through much of the fourteenth and early fifteenth centuries, weak monarchs lacked the power to call a national assembly. Provincial assemblies, highly jealous of their independence, did not want a national assembly. The costs of sending delegates to it would be high, and the result was likely to be increased taxation.

In both countries, however, the war did promote *nationalism*—the feeling of unity and identity that binds together a people who speak the same language, have a common ancestry and customs, and live in the same area. In the fourteenth century, nationalism largely took the form of hostility toward foreigners. Both Philip VI and Edward III drummed up support for the war by portraying the enemy as an alien, evil people. Perhaps no one expressed this national consciousness better than Joan of Arc, when she exulted that the enemy had been "driven out of *France*."

## Religious Crisis

In times of crisis or disaster, people of all faiths have sought the consolation of religion. In the fourteenth century, however, Christian church leaders offered little solace. In fact, those leaders of the church added to the sorrow and misery of the times.

From 1309 to 1376, the popes lived in the city of Avignon in southeastern France. In order to control the church and its policies, Philip the Fair of France pressured Pope Clement V to settle in Avignon. Critically ill with cancer, Clement lacked the will to resist Philip. This period in church history is often called the **Babylonian Captivity** (referring to the seventy years the ancient Hebrews were held captive in Mesopotamian Babylon).

The Avignon papacy reformed its financial administration and centralized its government. But the seven popes at Avignon concentrated on bureaucratic matters to the exclusion of spiritual objectives. In 1377 Pope Gregory XI (r. 1370–1378) brought the papal court back to Rome. At Gregory's death, Roman citizens demanded an Italian pope who would remain in Rome.

Urban VI (r. 1378–1389), Gregory's successor, had excellent intentions for church reform. He wanted to abolish simony, pluralism (holding several church offices at the same time), absenteeism, clerical extravagance, and ostentation, but he went about the work of reform in a tactless, arrogant, and bullheaded manner. Urban's quick temper and irrational behavior have led scholars to question his sanity. His actions brought disaster.

The cardinals slipped away from Rome, met at Anagni, and declared Urban's election invalid because it had come about under threats from the Roman mob. The cardinals elected Cardinal Robert of Geneva, the cousin of King Charles V of France, as pope. Cardinal Robert took the name Clement VII (r. 1378–1394) and set himself up at Avignon in opposition to the legally elected Urban. So began the **Great Schism,** which divided Western Christendom until 1417.

The powers of Europe aligned themselves with Urban or Clement along strictly political lines. France recognized the Frenchman, Clement; England, France's historic enemy, recognized Urban. The scandal provoked horror and vigorous cries for reform. The common people—hard-pressed by inflation, wars, and plague—were thoroughly confused about which pope was legitimate. The schism weakened the religious faith of many Christians and gave rise to instability and religious excesses. At a time when ordinary Christians needed the consolation of religion and confidence in religious leaders, church officials were fighting among themselves for power.

The English reformer John Wyclif (1329–1384) wrote that papal claims of temporal power had no foundation in the Scriptures and that the church should be stripped of its property. He argued that the Scriptures alone should be the standard of Christian belief and practice and not pious practices such as pilgrimages and the veneration of the saints. Sincere Christians, said Wyclif, should read the Scriptures for themselves. These views had broad social and economic significance. Wyclif's idea that every Christian free of sin possessed lordship was seized by the peasants during a revolt in 1381 and used to justify their goals.

Although Wyclif's ideas were vigorously condemned by ecclesiastical authorities, they were widely disseminated by humble clerics and enjoyed great popularity in the early fifteenth century. The teachings of Wyclif's followers, called Lollards, allowed women to preach and to consecrate the Eucharist. Women, some well educated, played a significant role in the movement. After Anne, sister of Wenceslaus, king of Germany and Bohemia, married Richard II of England, members of Queen Anne's household carried Lollard principles back to Bohemia, where they were read by Jan Hus, rector of the University of Prague.

In response to continued calls throughout Europe for a council, the two colleges of cardinals—one at Rome, the other at Avignon—summoned a council at Pisa in 1409. This gathering deposed both popes and selected another, but neither the Avignon pope nor the Roman pope would resign, and the appalling result was the creation of a threefold schism.

Finally, because of the pressure of the German emperor Sigismund, a great council met at Constance (1414–1418). It had three objectives: to end the schism, to reform the church "in head and members" (from top to bottom), and to wipe out heresy. The council condemned Jan Hus as a Wycliffite, and he was burned at the stake. The council eventually deposed the three schismatic popes and elected a new leader, the Roman cardinal Colonna, who took the name Martin V (1417–1431).

Martin proceeded to dissolve the council. Nothing was done about reform. The schism was over, and though councils subsequently met at Basel and at Ferrara-Florence, in 1450 the papacy held a jubilee, celebrating its triumph over the conciliar movement. In the later fifteenth century, the papacy concentrated on Italian problems to the exclusion of universal Christian interests. The schism and the conciliar movement, however, had exposed the crying need for ecclesiastical reform, thus laying the foundations for the great reform efforts of the sixteenth century.

## Peasant Revolts

Early in the thirteenth century, the French preacher Jacques de Vitry asked rhetorically, "How many serfs have killed their lords or burnt their castles?"[58] In the fourteenth and fifteenth centuries, social and economic conditions caused a great increase in peasant uprisings.

In 1358, when French taxation for the Hundred Years' War fell heavily on the poor, the frustrations of the French peasantry exploded in a massive uprising called the **Jacquerie,** after a supposedly happy agricultural laborer, Jacques Bonhomme (Good Fellow). Two years earlier, the English had captured the French king John and many nobles and held them for ransom. The peasants resented paying for their lords' release. Recently hit by plague, experiencing famine in some areas, and harassed by "fur-collar criminals," peasants erupted in anger and frustration in Picardy, Champagne, and the area around Paris. Crowds swept through the countryside, slashing the throats of nobles, burning their castles, raping their wives and daughters, and killing or maiming their horses and cattle. Artisans, small merchants, and parish priests joined the peasants. Urban and rural groups committed terrible destruction, and for several weeks the nobles were on the defensive. Then the upper class united to repress the revolt with merciless ferocity. Thousands of the "Jacques," innocent as well as guilty, were cut down.

The Peasants' Revolt in England in 1381, involving perhaps a hundred thousand people, was probably the largest single uprising of the entire Middle Ages. The causes of the rebellion were complex and varied from place to place. In general, though, the thirteenth century had witnessed the steady commutation of labor services for cash rents, and the Black Death had drastically cut the labor supply. As a result, peasants demanded higher wages and fewer manorial obligations. Thirty years earlier, the parliamentary Statute of Laborers of 1351 had declared:

*Whereas to curb the malice of servants who after the pestilence were idle and unwilling to serve without securing excessive wages, it was recently ordained . . . that such servants, both men and women, shall be bound to serve in return for salaries and wages that were customary . . . five or six years earlier.*[59]

This attempt by landlords to freeze wages and social mobility could not be enforced. As a matter of fact, the condition of the English peasantry steadily improved in the course of the fourteenth century. Why then was the outburst in 1381 so serious? It was provoked by a crisis of rising expectations.

The relative prosperity of the laboring classes led to demands that the upper classes were unwilling to grant. Unable to climb higher, the peasants found release for their economic frustrations in revolt. But economic grievances combined with other factors. The south of England, where the revolt broke out, had been subjected to frequent and destructive French raids. The English government did little to protect the south, and villages grew increasingly scared and insecure. Moreover, decades of aristocratic violence, much of it perpetrated against the weak peasantry, had bred hostility and bitterness. In France frustration over the lack of permanent victory increased. In England the social and religious agitation of the popular preacher John Ball fanned the embers of discontent. Sayings such as Ball's famous couplet "When Adam delved and Eve span; Who was then the gentleman?" reflect real revolutionary sentiment.

The straw that broke the camel's back in England was the reimposition of a head tax on all adult males. Beginning with assaults on the tax collectors, the uprising in England followed much the same course as had the Jacquerie in France. Castles and manors were sacked; manorial records were destroyed. Many nobles, including the archbishop of Canterbury, who had ordered the collection of the tax, were murdered. Urban discontent merged with rural violence. Apprentices and journeymen, frustrated because the highest positions in the guilds were closed to them, rioted.

The boy-king Richard II (r. 1377–1399) met the leaders of the revolt, agreed to charters ensuring the peasants' freedom, tricked them with false promises, and then proceeded to crush the uprising with terrible ferocity. Although the nobility tried to restore ancient duties of serfdom, virtually a century of freedom had elapsed, and the

**Prostitute Invites a Traveling Merchant** Poverty and male violence drove women into prostitution, which, though denounced by moralists, was accepted as a normal part of the medieval social fabric. In the cities and larger towns where prostitution flourished, public officials passed laws requiring prostitutes to wear a special mark on their clothing, regulated hours of business, forbade women to drag men into their houses, and denied business to women with the "burning sickness," gonorrhea. *(Bodleian Library, University of Oxford, MS. Bodl. 264, fol. 245V)*

commutation of manorial services continued. Rural serfdom had disappeared in England by 1550.

Conditions in England and France were not unique. In Florence in 1378, the *ciompi,* or poor propertyless workers, revolted. Serious social trouble occurred in Lübeck, Brunswick, and other German cities. In Spain in 1391, massive uprisings in Seville and Barcelona took the form of vicious attacks on Jewish communities. Rebellions and uprisings everywhere reveal deep peasant and working-class frustration and the general socioeconomic crisis of the time.

**Spanish Bullfight** Muslims introduced bullfighting to Spain in the eleventh century. The sport takes place in a large outdoor arena, the object being for the bullfighter or matador (*torero*) to kill a wild bull (*toro*) with a sword. Here unsporting spectators goad the bull with whips. *(From the* Cantigas *of Alfonso X, ca 1283. El Escorial/Laurie Platt Winfrey, Inc.)*

## RACE AND ETHNICITY ON THE FRONTIERS

In the twelfth and thirteenth centuries, many people migrated from one part of Europe to another: the English into Scotland and Ireland; Germans, French, and Flemings into Poland, Bohemia, and Hungary; the French into Spain. In the fourteenth century, many Germans moved into eastern Europe, fleeing the Black Death. The colonization of frontier regions meant that peoples of different ethnic or racial backgrounds lived side by side. Race relations became a basic factor in the lives of those living in frontier areas.

Racial categories rest on socially constructed beliefs and customs, not on any biological or anthropological classification. When late medieval chroniclers used the language of race—words such as *gens* (race or clan) and *natio* (species, stock, or kind)—they meant cultural differences. Medieval scholars held that peoples differed according to descent, language, customs, and laws. Descent or blood, basic to the color racism of the United States, played an insignificant part in medieval ideas about race and ethnicity. Rather, the chief marks of an ethnic group were language (which could be learned), customs (for example, dietary practices, dance, marriage and death rituals, clothing, and hairstyles, all of which could be adopted), and laws (which could be changed or modified). What role did race and ethnicity play in relations between native peoples and settlers in the later Middle Ages?

In the early periods of conquest and colonization, and in all frontier regions, a legal dualism existed: native peoples remained subject to their traditional laws; newcomers brought and were subject to the laws of the countries from which they came. On the Prussian and Polish frontier, for example, the law was that "men who come there . . . should be judged on account of any crime or contract engaged in there according to Polish custom if they are Poles and according to German custom if they are Germans."[60] The same dualism operated in Spain with respect to Muslims and Christians. Subject peoples experienced some disabilities, but the broad trend was toward a legal pluralism.

The great exception to this pattern was Ireland, where the English practiced an extreme form of racial discrimination toward the native Irish. The English distinguished between the free and the unfree, and the entire Irish population, simply by the fact of Irish birth, was unfree. A legal structure modeled on that of England, with county courts, itinerant justices, and the common law (see pages 382–383), was set up. But the Irish had no access to the common-law courts. In civil (property) disputes, an English defendant need not respond to his Irish plaintiff; no Irish person could make a will; and an Irish widow could not claim her dower rights (enjoyment of part of the estate during her lifetime). In criminal procedures, the murder of an Irishman was not considered a felony. An English defendant in the criminal matter would claim "that he is not held to answer . . . since he [the plaintiff] is Irish and not of free blood."[61] This emphasis on blood descent naturally provoked bitterness, but only in the Tudor period (see Chapter 15) was the English common law opened to the subject Irish population.

**English View of the Irish** Depicting a subject or colonial people as barbaric and uncivilized has long been a way of denigrating and dehumanizing the enemy. In this thirteenth-century miniature, a king (in a bath) and his courtiers devour horseflesh with their hands, without plates or eating utensils. The viewer is supposed to think that this is how Irish kingship was conferred. *(Bodleian Library, University of Oxford, MS. Laud. Misc. 720f. 226R)*

The later Middle Ages witnessed a movement away from legal pluralism or dualism and toward a legal homogeneity and an emphasis on blood descent. Competition for ecclesiastical offices and the cultural divisions between town and country people became arenas for ethnic tension and racial conflict. Since bishoprics and abbacies carried religious authority, spiritual charisma, and often rights of appointment to subordinate positions, they were natural objects of ambition. When prelates of a language or "nationality" different from that of the local people gained church positions, the latter felt a loss of influence. Bishops were supposed to be pastors. Their pastoral work involved preaching, teaching, and comforting, duties that could be performed effectively only when the bishop (or priest) could communicate with the people. Ideally in a pluralistic society, he should be bilingual; often he was not.

In the late thirteenth century, as waves of Germans migrated into Danzig on the Baltic, into Silesia, and into the Polish countryside and towns, they encountered Jakub Swinka, archbishop of Gniezno (1283–1314), whose jurisdiction included these areas of settlement. The bishop hated Germans and referred to them as "dog heads." His German contemporary, Bishop John of Cracow, detested the Poles, wanted to expel all Polish people, and refused to appoint Poles to any church office. In Ireland, English colonists and the native Irish competed for ecclesiastical offices until 1217, when the English government in London decreed:

> *Since the election of Irishmen in our land of Ireland has often disturbed the peace of that land, we command you . . . that henceforth you allow no Irishman to be elected . . . or preferred in any cathedral . . . (and) you should seek by all means to procure election and promotion to vacant bishoprics of . . . honest Englishmen.*[62]

Although criticized by the pope and not totally enforceable, this law remained in effect in many dioceses for centuries.

Likewise, the arrival of Cistercians and mendicants (Franciscans and Dominicans) from France and Germany in Baltic and Slavic lands provoked racial and "national" hostilities. In the fourteenth and fifteenth centuries, in contrast to earlier centuries, racial or ethnic prejudices became conspicuous. Slavic prelates and princes saw the German mendicants as "instruments of cultural colonization," and Slavs were strongly discouraged from becoming members. In 1333, when John of Drazic, bishop of Prague, founded a friary at Roudnice (Raudnitz), he specified that "we shall admit no one to this convent or monastery of any nation except a Bohemian [Czech], born of two Czech-speaking parents."[63]

Everywhere in Europe, towns recruited people from the countryside (see pages 384–387). In frontier regions, townspeople were usually long-distance immigrants and, in eastern Europe, Ireland, and Scotland, ethnically different from the surrounding rural population. In eastern

Europe, German was the language of the towns; in Ireland, French, the tongue of noble Norman or English settlers, predominated. In fourteenth-century Prague, between 63 percent and 80 percent of new burgesses bore identifiable German names, as did almost all city council members. Towns in eastern Europe "had the character of German islands in Slav, Baltic, Estonian, or Magyar seas."[64] Although native peoples commonly held humbler positions, both immigrant and native townspeople prospered during the expanding economy of the thirteenth century. When economic recession hit during the fourteenth century, ethnic tensions multiplied.

Just as the social and legal status of the Jews in western Europe worsened in the wake of the great famine and the Black Death (see pages 399–401), on the frontiers of Latin Europe discrimination, ghettoization, and racism—now based on blood descent—characterized the attitudes of colonists toward native peoples. But the latter also could express racial savagery. Regulations drawn up by various guilds were explicitly racist, with protectionist bars for some groups and exclusionist laws for others. One set of laws applicable to parts of eastern Europe required that applicants for guild membership be of German descent and sometimes prove it. Cobblers in fourteenth-century Beeskow, a town close to the large Slavic population of Lausitz in Silesia, required that "an apprentice who comes to learn his craft should be brought before the master and guild members. . . . We forbid the sons of barbers, linen workers, shepherds, Slavs."[65]

Intermarriage was forbidden in many places, such as Riga on the Baltic (now the capital of Latvia), where legislation for the bakers guild stipulated that "whoever wishes to have the privilege of membership in our company shall not take as a wife any woman who is ill-famed . . . or non-German; if he does marry such a woman, he must leave the company and office." The most extensive attempt to prevent intermarriage and protect racial purity is embodied in Ireland's Statute of Kilkenny (1366), which stated that

*there were to be no marriages between those of immigrant and native stock; that the English inhabitants of Ireland must employ the English language and bear English names; that they must ride in the English way (i.e., with saddles) and have English apparel; that no Irishmen were to be granted ecclesiastical benefices or admitted to monasteries in the English parts of Ireland; and that the Irish game of hurling and the maintenance of Irish minstrels were forbidden to English settlers.*[66]

Rulers of the Christian kingdoms of Spain drew up comparable legislation discriminating against the Mudéjars.

All these laws had an economic basis: to protect the financial interests of the privileged German, English, or Spanish colonial minorities. The laws also reflect a racism that not only pervaded the lives of frontier peoples at the end of the Middle Ages but also sowed the seeds of difficulties still unresolved in the twenty-first century.

## SUMMARY

The culture that emerged in Europe between 732 and 843 has justifiably been called the "first" European civilization. That civilization was Christian, feudal, and infused with Latin ideas and models. Almost all people were baptized Christians. Latin was the common language—written as well as spoken—of educated people everywhere. This culture resulted from the mutual cooperation of civil and ecclesiastical authorities. Kings and church leaders supported each other's goals and utilized each other's prestige and power. Kings encouraged preaching and publicized church doctrines, such as the stress on monogamous marriage. In return, church officials urged obedience to royal authority. The support that Charlemagne gave to education and learning, the intellectual movement known as the Carolingian Renaissance, proved his most enduring legacy.

The enormous size of Charlemagne's empire, the domestic squabbles among his descendants, the resurgence of aristocratic power, and the invasions of the Vikings, Magyars, and Muslims—these factors all contributed to the empire's disintegration. As the empire broke down, a new form of decentralized government, later known as feudalism, emerged. In a feudal society, public and political power was held by a small group of military leaders. No civil or religious authority could maintain a stable government over a very wide area. Local strongmen provided what little security existed. Commerce and long-distance trade were drastically reduced. Because of their agricultural and commercial impact, the Viking and Muslim invaders were the most dynamic and creative forces of the period.

In the eleventh century, rulers and local authorities gradually imposed some degree of order within their territories. Peace and domestic security contributed to a rise in population, bringing larger crops for the peasants and improving trading conditions for the townspeople. The church overthrew the domination of lay influences, and the spread of the Cluniac and Cistercian orders marked the ascendancy of monasticism. The Gregorian reform movement, with its stress on the "freedom of the church," led to a grave conflict with kings over lay investiture. The papacy achieved a technical success on the religious issue, but in Germany the greatly increased power of the nobility, at the expense of the emperor, represents the significant social consequence. Having put its own house in order, the Roman papacy in the twelfth and thirteenth centuries built the first strong government bureaucracy. In the central Middle Ages, the church exercised general leadership of European society. The Crusades exhibit that leadership, though their consequences for Byzantine-Western and for Christian-Muslim relations proved disastrous.

Through the instruments of justice and finance, the kings of England and France attacked feudal rights and provincial practices, built centralized bureaucracies, and gradually came in contact with all their subjects. In so doing, these rulers laid the foundations for modern national states. The German emperors shared power with territorial lordships. Medieval cities recruited people from the countryside and brought into being a new social class: the middle class. Cities provided economic opportunity, which, together with the revival of long-distance trade and a new capitalistic spirit, led to greater wealth, a higher standard of living, and upward social mobility.

In the twelfth and thirteenth centuries, universities—institutions of higher learning unique to the West—emerged from cathedral and municipal schools and provided trained officials for the new government bureaucracies. The soaring Gothic cathedrals that medieval towns erected demonstrated civic pride, deep religious faith, and economic vitality.

The performance of agricultural services and the payment of rents preoccupied peasants throughout the Middle Ages. Though peasants led hard lives, the reclamation of waste- and forestlands, migration to frontier territory, or flight to a town offered a means of social mobility. The Christian faith, though perhaps not understood on an intellectual level, provided emotional and spiritual solace. Aristocratic values and attitudes shaded all aspects of medieval culture. Trained for war, nobles often devoted considerable time to fighting, yet a noble might shoulder heavy judicial, political, and economic responsibilities, depending on the size of his estates. In their prayers, monks and nuns battled for the Lord. In their chants and rich ceremonials, in their architecture and literary productions, and in the examples of many monks' lives, the monasteries inspired Christian peoples. As the crucibles of sacred art, the monasteries became the cultural centers of Christian Europe.

Late medieval preachers likened the crises of their times to the Four Horsemen of the Apocalypse in the Book of Revelation, who brought famine, war, disease, and death. The crises of the fourteenth and fifteenth centuries were acids that burned deeply into the fabric of traditional medieval European society. Bad weather—beyond human control—brought poor harvests, which contributed to the international economic depression. Disease fostered widespread depression and dissatisfaction. Population losses caused by the Black Death and the Hundred Years' War encouraged the working classes to try to profit from the labor shortage by selling their services for a higher price. When peasant frustrations exploded in uprisings, the frightened nobility and upper middle class joined to crush the revolts. But events had heightened social consciousness among the poor.

The migration of peoples from the European heartland to the frontier regions of Iberia, Ireland, the Baltic, and eastern Europe led to ethnic friction between native peoples and new settlers. Economic difficulties heightened ethnic consciousness and spawned a vicious racism.

Religion held society together. European culture was a Christian culture. But the Great Schism weakened the prestige of the church and people's faith in papal authority. The conciliar movement, by denying the church's universal sovereignty, strengthened the claims of secular governments to jurisdiction over all their peoples. The later Middle Ages witnessed a steady shift of loyalty away from the church and toward the emerging national states.

## KEY TERMS

lay investiture
Crusades
Sephardic Jews
reconquista
*Domesday Book*
common law
merchant guilds
Hanseatic League
Scholastics
Gothic
villeins
manor
Black Death
Babylonian Captivity
Great Schism
Jacquerie

## NOTES

1. The sources, both Muslim and Christian, dispute the date (732 or 733) and the place (Poitiers or Tours) of this battle. I. Wood, *The Merovingian Kingdoms, 450–751* (New York: Longman, 1994), pp. 283–286, offers a careful analysis of all the evidence.
2. Ibid., p. 101.
3. Ibid., pp. 60–66; and E. James, *The Franks* (New York: Basil Blackwell, 1988), pp. 191–194.
4. See P. Geary, "Carolingians and the Carolingian Empire," in *Dictionary of the Middle Ages,* vol. 3, ed. J. R. Strayer (New York: Charles Scribner's Sons, 1983), p. 110.

5. Einhard, *The Life of Charlemagne,* with a foreword by S. Painter (Ann Arbor: University of Michigan Press, 1960), pp. 50–51.
6. P. Stafford, *Queens, Concubines, and Dowagers: The King's Wife in the Early Middle Ages* (Athens: University of Georgia Press, 1983), pp. 60–62.
7. See R. McKitterick, *The Frankish Kingdoms and the Early Carolingians, 751–987* (New York: Longman, 1983), pp. 30–37.
8. R. W. Southern, *Medieval Humanism and Other Studies* (Oxford: Basil Blackwell, 1970), p. 3.
9. McKitterick, *The Frankish Kingdoms,* pp. 134–136, 169.
10. On the thorny issue of feudalism, see S. Reynolds, *Fiefs and Vassals: The Medieval Evidence Reconsidered* (Oxford: Clarendon Press, 1996), pp. 2–3; E. A. R. Brown, "The Tyranny of a Construct: Feudalism and Historians of Medieval Europe," *American Historical Review* 79 (1974): 1060–1088; and J. R. Strayer, "The Two Levels of Feudalism," in *Medieval Statecraft and the Perspectives of History* (Princeton, N.J.: Princeton University Press, 1971), pp. 63–71; the quotation is on page 71.
11. S. Runciman, *A History of the Crusades.* Vol. 3: *The Kingdom of Acre* (Cambridge: Cambridge University Press, 1955), p. 480.
12. See B. Lewis, *The Muslim Discovery of Europe* (New York: W. W. Norton, 1982), pp. 23–25.
13. K. Armstrong, *Holy War: The Crusades and Their Impact on Today's World* (New York: Doubleday, 1991), pp. 373–375.
14. R. Bartlett, *The Making of Europe: Conquest, Colonization and Cultural Change, 950–1350* (Princeton, N.J.: Princeton University Press, 1993), pp. 8, 24, 34–35.
15. Ibid., pp. 11–15.
16. Ibid., pp. 250–255.
17. B. Arnold, *Princes and Territories in Medieval Germany* (New York: Cambridge University Press, 1991), pp. 65–72.
18. R. Bartlett, *Trial by Fire and Water: The Medieval Judicial Ordeal* (Oxford: Clarendon Press, 1986), pp. 25–27, Chap. 3.
19. J. Boswell, *Christianity, Social Tolerance, and Homosexuality: Gay People in Western Europe from the Beginning of the Christian Era to the Fourteenth Century* (Chicago: University of Chicago Press, 1980), pp. 270–293; the quotation is from page 293. For alternative interpretations, see K. Thomas, "Rescuing Homosexual History," *New York Review of Books,* December 4, 1980, pp. 26ff.; and J. DuQ. Adams, *Speculum* 56 (April 1981): 350ff. For the French monarchy's persecution of the Jews, see J. W. Baldwin, *The Government of Philip Augustus: Foundations of French Royal Power in the Middle Ages* (Berkeley: University of California Press, 1986), pp. 51–52, and W. C. Jordan, *The French Monarchy and the Jews* (Philadelphia: University of Pennsylvania Press, 1989).
20. J. C. Russell, *Medieval Regions and Their Cities* (Bloomington: University of Indiana Press, 1972), p. 91.
21. H. Pirenne, *Economic and Social History of Medieval Europe* (New York: Harcourt, Brace, 1956), p. 53.
22. See D. Herlihy, *Medieval and Renaissance Pistoia: The Social History of an Italian Town, 1200–1430* (New Haven, Conn.: Yale University Press, 1967), p. 257.
23. W. C. Jordan, *Women and Credit in Pre-Industrial and Developing Societies* (Philadelphia: University of Pennsylvania Press, 1993), pp. 20 et seq.
24. D. C. Douglas and G. W. Greenaway, eds., *English Historical Documents,* vol. 2 (London: Eyre and Spottiswode, 1961), pp. 969–970.
25. M. M. Postan, *The Medieval Economy and Society: An Economic History of Britain in the Middle Ages* (Baltimore: Penguin Books, 1975), pp. 213–214.
26. See P. Dollinger, *The German Hansa,* trans. and ed. D. S. Ault and S. H. Steinberg (Stanford, Calif.: Stanford University Press, 1970).
27. R. S. Lopez, "The Trade of Medieval Europe: The South," in *The Cambridge Economic History of Europe,* vol. 2, ed. M. M. Postan and E. E. Rich (Cambridge: Cambridge University Press, 1952), p. 289.
28. Quoted in H. E. Sigerist, *Civilization and Disease* (Chicago: University of Chicago Press, 1943), p. 102.
29. Quoted in J. H. Mundy, *Europe in the High Middle Ages, 1150–1309* (New York: Basic Books, 1973), pp. 474–475.
30. J. Bony, *French Gothic Architecture of the Twelfth and Thirteenth Centuries* (Berkeley: University of California Press, 1983), p. 13.
31. E. Panofsky, trans. and ed., *Abbot Suger on the Abbey Church of St.-Denis and Its Art Treasures* (Princeton, N.J.: Princeton University Press, 1946), p. 101.
32. Quoted in J. J. Wilhelm, ed., *Lyrics of the Middle Ages: An Anthology* (New York: Garland Publishers, 1993), pp. 94–95.
33. I have leaned on the very persuasive interpretation of M. R. Menocal, *The Arabic Role in Medieval Literary History* (Philadelphia: University of Pennsylvania Press, 1990), pp. ix–xv, 27–33.
34. G. Duby, *The Chivalrous Society,* trans. C. Postan (Berkeley: University of California Press, 1977), pp. 90–93.
35. B. A. Hanawalt, *The Ties That Bound: Peasant Families in Medieval England* (New York: Oxford University Press, 1986), p. 5.
36. E. Power, "Peasant Life and Rural Conditions," in J. R. Tanner et al., *The Cambridge Medieval History,* vol. 7 (Cambridge: Cambridge University Press, 1958), p. 716.
37. Glanvill, "De Legibus Angliae," bk. 5, chap. 5, in *Social Life in Britain from the Conquest to the Reformation,* ed. G. G. Coulton (London: Cambridge University Press, 1956), pp. 338–339.
38. See R. Bartlett, "Colonial Towns and Colonial Traders," in *The Making of Europe: Conquest, Colonization and Cultural Change, 950–1350* (Princeton, N.J.: Princeton University Press, 1993), pp. 167–196.
39. See John L. Langdon, *Horses, Oxen, and Technological Innovation: The Use of Draught Animals in English Farming, 1066–1500* (New York: Cambridge University Press, 1986), esp. pp. 254–270.
40. See Hanawalt, *The Ties That Bound,* pp. 90–100.
41. Ibid., p. 149.
42. On this quantity and medieval measurements, see D. Knowles, "The Measures of Monastic Beverages," in *The Monastic Order in England* (Cambridge: Cambridge University Press, 1962), p. 717.
43. M. Chibnall, ed. and trans., *The Ecclesiastical History of Orderic Vitalis* (Oxford: Oxford University Press, 1972), 2.xiii.
44. R. W. Southern, *Western Society and the Church in the Middle Ages* (Baltimore: Penguin Books, 1970), pp. 224–230, esp. p. 228.
45. See M. W. Labarge, *A Small Sound of the Trumpet: Women in Medieval Life* (Boston: Beacon Press, 1986), pp. 104–105.
46. Jordan, *Women and Credit in Pre-Industrial and Developing Societies,* p. 61.
47. See W. C. Jordan, *The Great Famine: Northern Europe in the Early Fourteenth Century* (Princeton, N.J.: Princeton University Press, 1996), pp. 97–102.
48. W. H. McNeill, *Plagues and Peoples* (New York: Doubleday, 1976), pp. 151–168.
49. Quoted in P. Ziegler, *The Black Death* (Harmondsworth, Eng.: Pelican Books, 1969), p. 20.
50. J. M. Rigg, trans., *The Decameron of Giovanni Boccaccio* (London: J. M. Dent & Sons, 1903), p. 6.
51. Ziegler, *The Black Death,* pp. 232–239.
52. J. Hatcher, *Plague, Population and the English Economy, 1348–1530* (London: Macmillan Education, 1986), p. 33.

53. See S. K. Cohn, Jr., "The Black Death: End of the Paradigm," *American Historical Review,* 107 (June 2002): 703–738.
54. See G. P. Cuttino, "Historical Revision: The Causes of the Hundred Years' War," *Speculum* 31 (July 1956): 463–472.
55. J. Barnie, *War in Medieval English Society: Social Values and the Hundred Years' War* (Ithaca, N.Y.: Cornell University Press, 1974), p. 34.
56. Ibid., pp. 72–73.
57. See G. O. Sayles, *The King's Parliament of England* (New York: W. W. Norton, 1974), app., pp. 137–141.
58. Quoted in M. Bloch, *French Rural History,* trans. J. Sondeimer (Berkeley: University of California Press, 1966), p. 169.
59. C. Stephenson and G. F. Marcham, eds., *Sources of English Constitutional History,* rev. ed. (New York: Harper & Row, 1972), p. 225.
60. Quoted in Bartlett, *The Making of Europe,* p. 205.
61. Quoted ibid., p. 215.
62. Quoted ibid., p. 224.
63. Quoted ibid., p. 228.
64. Ibid., p. 233.
65. Ibid., p. 238.
66. Quoted ibid., p. 239.

## SUGGESTED READING

For further exploration of the social, religious, political, and economic issues raised in this chapter, the curious student should begin with the titles by Arnold, Baldwin, Bartlett, Boswell, Dollinger, Herlihy, Jordan, McKitterick, Reynolds, Strayer, and Wood listed in the Notes. R. McKitterick, *The Carolingians and the Written Word* (1989), and P. Riche, *Education and Culture in the Barbarian West,* trans. J. Contreni (1976), should prove useful for study of the Carolingian Renaissance.

I. S. Robinson, *The Papacy, 1073–1198: Continuity and Innovation* (1990), treats the changing role of the papacy and the development of papal government, as does C. Morris, *The Papal Monarchy: The Western Church, 1050–1250* (1989).

The following studies provide exciting and highly readable general accounts of the Crusades: J. Riley-Smith, *What Were the Crusades?* (1977), and R. C. Finucane, *Soldiers of the Faith: Crusaders and Muslims at War* (1983). There are excellent articles on many facets of the Crusades in J. R. Strayer, ed., *Dictionary of the Middle Ages,* vol. 4 (1984). For the Fourth Crusade, see the excellent study of D. E. Queller, *The Fourth Crusade: The Capture of Constantinople* (1977), which gives an important revisionist interpretation. B. Lewis, *The Muslim Discovery of Europe* (1982), gives the Muslim view of the Crusades.

G. O. Sayles, *The Medieval Foundations of England* (1961), traces political and social conditions to the end of the twelfth century. For the Becket controversy, see F. Barlow, *Thomas Becket* (1986). J. C. Holt, *Magna Carta* (1969), remains the best modern treatment of the document.

For Spain, R. Fletcher, *The Quest for El Cid* (1990), provides an excellent introduction to Spanish social and political conditions through a study of Rodrigo Dias, the eleventh-century soldier of fortune who became the Spanish national hero. Fletcher's *Moorish Spain* (1992) provides a highly readable sketch of the history of Islamic Spain from the eighth to the seventeenth century. For the developing social and economic importance of the Flemish towns, see D. Nicholas, *Medieval Flanders* (1992).

For France, E. Hallam, *The Capetian Kings of France, 987–1328* (1980), is a readable introduction. Advanced students of medieval French administrative history should see J. Baldwin, *The Government of Philip Augustus: Foundations of French Royal Power in the Middle Ages* (1986), and J. R. Strayer, *The Reign of Philip the Fair* (1980). On Germany, see H. Furhman, *Germany in the High Middle Ages,* trans. T. Reuther (1986), and M. Pacaut, *Frederick Barbarossa,* trans. A. J. Pomerans (1980), perhaps the best one-volume treatment of that important ruler.

For the economic revival of Europe, see P. Spufford, *Money and Its Use in Medieval Europe* (Cambridge: Cambridge University Press, 1988), an exciting and valuable study of how money changed not only commerce but also society. T. H. Lloyd, *England and the German Hanse, 1157–1611: A Study in Their Trade and Commercial Diplomacy* (1992), is essential for northern European commercial development.

For women, see C. Klapisch-Zuber, ed., *A History of Women.* Vol. 2: *Silences of the Middle Ages* (1992), which contains useful essays on many aspects of women's lives and status; and S. Shahar, *The Fourth Estate: Women in the Middle Ages* (1983), a provocative work. J. M. Bennett, *Women in the Medieval English Countryside: Gender and Household in Brigstock Before the Plague* (1987), is a fascinating case study.

Those interested in the origins of medieval towns and cities will learn how historians use the evidence of coins, archaeology, tax records, geography, and laws in J. F. Benton, ed., *Town Origins: The Evidence of Medieval England* (1968). S. Reynolds, *An Introduction to the History of English Medieval Towns* (1982), explores the social structure, political organization, and economic livelihood of English towns. R. H. Hilton, *English and French Towns in Feudal Society* (1992), is an exciting comparative study.

For the new currents of thought in the central Middle Ages, see M. T. Clanchy, *Abelard: A Medieval Life* (1997), which incorporates recent international research. For the development of literacy among laypeople and the formation of a literate mentality, the advanced student should see M. T. Clanchy, *From Memory to Written Record: England, 1066–1307,* 2d ed. (1992). Written by outstanding scholars in a variety of fields, R. L. Benson and G. Constable with C. D. Lanham, eds., *Renaissance and Renewal in the Twelfth Century* (1982), contains an invaluable collection of articles.

On the medieval universities, H. De Ridder-Symoens, ed., *A History of the University in Europe.* Vol. 1: *Universities in the Middle Ages* (1991), offers good interpretations by leading scholars. For the beginnings of Scholasticism and humanism, see the essential R. W. Southern, *Scholastic Humanism and the Unification of Western Europe,* vol. 1 (1994).

F. and J. Gies, *Cathedral, Forge, and Waterwheel* (1993), provides an illustrated survey of medieval technological achievements. The following studies are valuable for the evolution and development of the Gothic style: J. Harvey, *The Master Builders* (1971); J. Bony, *French Gothic Architecture of the Twelfth and Thirteenth Centuries* (1983). C. A. Bruzelius, *The Thirteenth-Century Church at St. Denis* (1985), traces later reconstruction of the church. J. Gimpel, *The Medieval Machine: The Industrial Revolution of the Middle Ages* (1977), discusses the mechanical and scientific problems involved in early industrialization.

On troubadour poetry, see, in addition to the title by Wilhelm cited in the Notes, M. Bogin, *The Women Troubadours* (1980).

The conflict between Pope Boniface VIII and the kings of France and England is well treated in J. R. Strayer, *The Reign of Philip the Fair* (1980), and M. Prestwich, *Edward I* (1988), both sound and important biographies.

For a broad treatment of frontier regions, see R. Bartlett, *The Making of Europe: Conquest, Colonization and Cultural Change, 950–1350* (1993).

The student interested in aspects of medieval slavery, serfdom, or the peasantry should see P. Bonnassie, *From Slavery to Feudalism* (1991); P. Freedman, *The Origins of Peasant Servitude in Medieval Catalonia* (1991); and the highly important work of W. C. Jordan, *From Servitude to Freedom: Manumission in the Sénonais in the Thirteenth Century* (1986).

For the origins and status of the nobility in the central Middle Ages, students are strongly urged to see the study by Duby cited in the Notes. Social mobility among both aristocracy and peasantry is discussed in T. Evergates, *Feudal Society in the Bailliage of Troyes Under the Counts of Champagne, 1152–1284* (1976).

On the monks, see the titles listed in the Suggested Reading for Chapter 8. B. D. Hill's articles "Benedictines" and "Cistercian Order," in J. R. Strayer, ed., *Dictionary of the Middle Ages,* vols. 2 and 3 (1982 and 1983), are broad surveys of the premier monastic orders with useful bibliographies. B. Harvey, *Living and Dying in England: The Monastic Experience, 1100–1540* (1993), has valuable material on monastic diet, clothing, routine, sickness, and death. L. J. Lekai, *The Cistercians: Ideals and Reality* (1977), synthesizes research on the white monks and carries their story down to the twentieth century. Both W. Braunfels, *Monasteries of Western Europe: The Architecture of the Orders* (1972), and C. Brooke, *The Monastic World* (1974), have splendid illustrations and good bibliographies. The best study of medieval English Cistercian architecture is P. Fergusson, *Architecture of Solitude: Cistercian Abbeys in Twelfth Century England* (1984).

For women and children, see B. Hanawalt, *Growing Up in Medieval London: The Experience of Childhood in History* (1993), which has exciting material on class and gender, apprenticeship, and the culture of matrimony; and C. Brooke, *The Medieval Idea of Marriage* (1991), which answers his question, "What is marriage and what sets it apart from other human relationships?" J. M. Bennett, *Women in the Medieval English Countryside* (1987), is an important and pioneering study of women in rural, preindustrial society.

For further treatment of nuns, see J. K. McNamara, *Sisters in Arms* (1996), a broad survey tracing the lives of religious women, from the mothers of the Egyptian desert to the twentieth century; B. Newman, *Sister of Wisdom: St. Hildegard's Theology of the Feminine* (1987), a learned and lucidly written study; S. Elkins, *Holy Women in Twelfth-Century England* (1985); and C. Bynum, *Jesus as Mother: Studies in the Spirituality of the High Middle Ages* (1984), which contains valuable articles on facets of women's religious history and an excellent contrast of the differing spirituality of monks and nuns.

The best starting point for study of the great epidemic that swept the European continent is D. Herlihy, *The Black Death and the Transformation of the West* (1997), a fine treatment of the causes and cultural consequences of the disease. For the social implications of the Black Death, see L. Poos, *A Rural Society After the Black Death: Essex, 1350–1525* (1991); G. Huppert, *After the Black Death: A Social History of Early Modern Europe* (1986); and W. H. McNeill, *Plagues and Peoples* (1976). For the economic effects of the plague, see J. Hatcher, *Plague, Population, and the English Economy, ca. 1300–1450* (1977). The older study of P. Ziegler, *The Black Death* (1969), remains important.

For the background and early part of the long military conflicts of the fourteenth and fifteenth centuries, see the provocative M. M. Vale, *The Origins of the Hundred Years War: The Angevin Legacy, 1250–1340* (1996). See also C. Allmand, *The Hundred Years War: England and France at War, ca 1300–1450* (1988). The broad survey of J. Keegan, *A History of Warfare* (1993), contains a useful summary of significant changes in military technology during the war. J. Keegan, *The Face of Battle* (1977), Chap. 2: "Agincourt," describes what war meant to the ordinary soldier. For strategy, tactics, armaments, and costumes of war, see H. W. Koch, *Medieval Warfare* (1978), a beautifully illustrated book.

T. F. Glick, *From Muslim Fortress to Christian Castle: Social and Cultural Change in Medieval Spain* (1995), explores the reorganization of Spanish society after the reconquest, bringing considerable cultural change. P. C. Maddern, *Violence and Social Order: East Anglia, 1422–1442* (1991), deals with social disorder in eastern England. I. M. W. Harvey, *Jack Cade's Rebellion of 1450* (1991), is an important work in local history. Students are especially encouraged to consult the brilliant work of E. L. Ladurie, *The Peasants of Languedoc,* trans. J. Day (1976). J. C. Holt, *Robin Hood* (1982), is a soundly researched and highly readable study of the famous outlaw.

D. Herlihy, *Women, Family and Society in Medieval Europe: Historical Essays, 1978–1991* (1995), contains several valuable articles dealing with the later Middle Ages, while the exciting study by B. Gottlieb, *The Family in the Western World from the Black Death to the Industrial Age* (1993), explores the family's political, emotional, and cultural roles. For prostitution, see L. L. Otis, *Prostitution in Medieval Society: The History of an Urban Institution in Languedoc* (1987), and J. Rossiaud, *Medieval Prostitution* (1995), a very good treatment of prostitution's social and cultural significance.

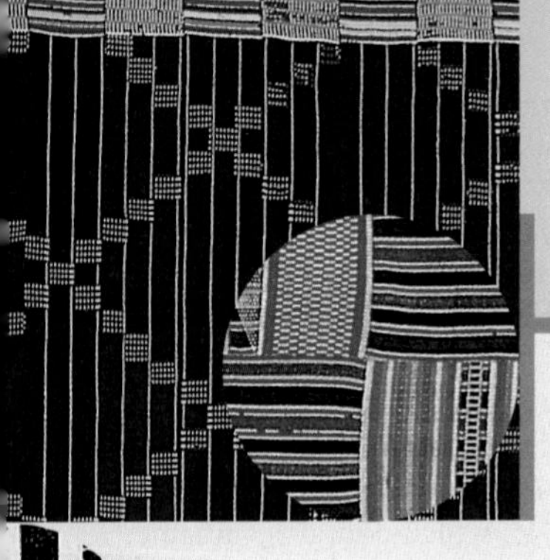

# LISTENING TO THE PAST

## An Arab View of the Crusades

*The Crusades helped shape the understanding that Arabs and Europeans had of each other and all subsequent relations between the Christian West and the Arab world. To medieval Christians, the Crusades were papally approved military expeditions for the recovery of holy places in Palestine; to the Arabs, these campaigns were "Frankish wars" or "Frankish invasions" for the acquisition of territory.*

*Early in the thirteenth century, Ibn Al-Athir (1160–1223), a native of Mosul, an important economic and cultural center in northern Mesopotamia (modern Iraq), wrote a history of the First Crusade. He relied on Arab sources for the events he described. Here is his account of the Crusaders' capture of Antioch.*

The power of the Franks first became apparent when in the year 478/1085–86* they invaded the territories of Islam and took Toledo and other parts of Andalusia [in Spain]. Then in 484/1091 they attacked and conquered the island of Sicily and turned their attention to the African coast. Certain of their conquests there were won back again but they had other successes, as you will see.

In 490/1097 the Franks attacked Syria. This is how it all began: Baldwin, their King, a kinsman of Roger the Frank who had conquered Sicily, assembled a great army and sent word to Roger saying: "I have assembled a great army and now I am on my way to you, to use your bases for my conquest of the African coast. Thus you and I shall become neighbors."

Roger called together his companions and consulted them about these proposals. "This will be a fine thing for them and for us!" they declared, "for by this means these lands will be converted to the Faith!" At this Roger raised one leg and farted loudly, and swore that it was of more use than their advice. "Why?" "Because if this army comes here it will need quantities of provisions and fleets of ships to transport it to Africa, as well as reinforcements from my own troops. Then, if the Franks succeed in conquering this territory they will take it over and will need provisioning from Sicily. This will cost me my annual profit from the harvest. If they fail they will return here and be an embarrassment to me here in my own domain." . . .

He summoned Baldwin's messenger and said to him: "If you have decided to make war on the Muslims your best course will be to free Jerusalem from their rule and thereby win great honor. I am bound by certain promises and treaties of allegiance with the ruler of Africa." So the Franks made ready to set out to attack Syria.

Another story is that the Fatimids of Egypt were afraid when they saw the Seljuqids extending their empire through Syria as far as Gaza, until they reached the Egyptian border and Atsiz invaded Egypt itself. They therefore sent to invite the Franks to invade Syria and so protect Egypt from the Muslims.† But God knows best.

When the Franks decided to attack Syria they marched east to Constantinople, so that they could cross the straits and advance into Muslim territory by the easier, land route. When they reached Constantinople, the Emperor of the East refused them permission to pass through his domains. He said: "Unless you first promise me Antioch, I shall not allow you to cross into the

*Muslims traditionally date events from Muhammad's hegira, or emigration, to Medina, which occurred in 622 according to the Christian calendar.

†Although Muslims, Fatimids were related doctrinally to the Shi'ites, but the dominant Sunni Muslims considered the Fatimids heretics.

Muslim empire." His real intention was to incite them to attack the Muslims, for he was convinced that the Turks, whose invincible control over Asia Minor he had observed, would exterminate every one of them. They accepted his conditions and in 490/1097 they crossed the Bosphorus at Constantinople. . . . They . . . reached Antioch, which they besieged.

When Yaghi Siyan, the ruler of Antioch, heard of their approach, he was not sure how the Christian people of the city would react, so he made the Muslims go outside the city on their own to dig trenches, and the next day sent the Christians out alone to continue the task. When they were ready to return home at the end of the day he refused to allow them. "Antioch is yours," he said, "but you will have to leave it to me until I see what happens between us and the Franks." "Who will protect our children and our wives?" they said. "I shall look after them for you." So they resigned themselves to their fate, and lived in the Frankish camp for nine months, while the city was under siege.

Yaghi Siyan showed unparalleled courage and wisdom, strength and judgment. If all the Franks who died had survived they would have overrun all the lands of Islam. He protected the families of the Christians in Antioch and would not allow a hair of their heads to be touched.

After the siege had been going on for a long time the Franks made a deal with . . . a cuirass-maker called Ruzbih whom they bribed with a fortune in money and lands. He worked in the tower that stood over the riverbed, where the river flowed out of the city into the valley. The Franks sealed their pact with the cuirass-maker, God damn him! and made their way to the water-gate. They opened it and entered the city. Another gang of them climbed the tower with their ropes. At dawn, when more than 500 of them were in the city and the defenders were worn out after the night watch, they sounded their trumpets. . . . Panic seized Yaghi Siyan and he opened the city gates and fled in terror, with an escort of thirty pages. His army commander arrived, but when he discovered on enquiry that Yaghi Siyan had fled, he made his escape by another gate. This was of great help to the Franks, for if he had stood firm for an hour, they would have been wiped out. They entered the city by the gates and sacked it, slaughtering all the Muslims they found there. This happened in jumada I (491/April/May 1098). . . .

It was the discord between the Muslim princes . . . that enabled the Franks to overrun the country.

Miniature showing heavily armored knights fighting Muslims. *(Bibliothèque nationale de France)*

## QUESTIONS FOR ANALYSIS

1. From the Arab perspective, when did the crusade begin?
2. How did Ibn Al-Athir explain the Crusaders' expedition to Syria?
3. Why did Antioch fall to the Crusaders?
4. The use of dialogue in historical narrative is a very old device dating from the Greek historian Thucydides (fifth century B.C.E.). Assess the value of Ibn Al-Athir's dialogues for the modern historian.

*Sources:* P. J. Geary, ed., *Readings in Medieval History* (Peterborough, Ontario: Broadview Press, 1991), pp. 443–444; E. J. Costello, trans., *Arab Historians of the Crusades* (Berkeley and Los Angeles: University of California Press, 1969).

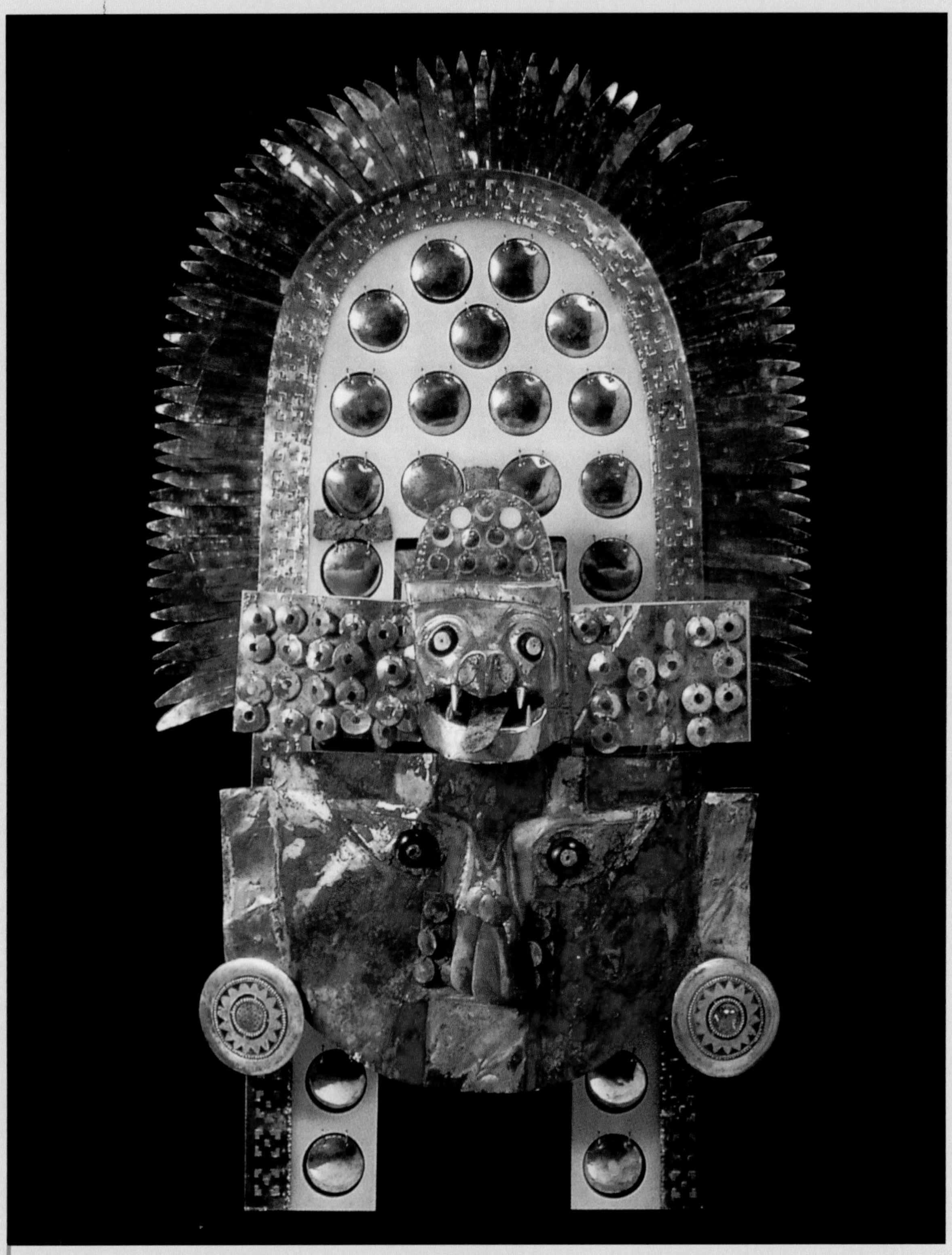

Gold mask assemblage, at least thirteen hundred years old. Excavated from an ancient Peruvian tomb in the town of Sipán. *(© Walter Alva. Photo provided by the Department of Anthropology, UCLA)*

CHAPTER

# 14 CIVILIZATIONS OF THE AMERICAS, CA 400–1500

## CHAPTER OUTLINE

- The Geography and Peoples of the Americas
- Mesoamerican Civilizations from the Olmecs to the Toltecs
- Aztec Society: Religion and War
- The Incas of Peru
- North America and the Mound Builders

Between approximately 300 B.C.E. and 1500 C.E., sophisticated civilizations developed in the Western Hemisphere. But unlike most other societies in the world, which felt the influences of other cultures—sub-Saharan Africa, for example, experienced the impact of Muslims, Asians, and Europeans—American societies grew in almost total isolation from other peoples. Then, in 1501–1502, the Florentine explorer Amerigo Vespucci (1451–1512) sailed down the eastern coast of South America to Brazil. Convinced that he had found a new world, Vespucci published an account of his voyage. Shortly thereafter the German geographer Martin Waldseemüller proposed that this new world be called "America" to preserve Vespucci's memory. Initially applied only to South America, by the end of the sixteenth century the term *America* was used for both continents in the Western Hemisphere.

Our use of the word **Indian** for the indigenous peoples of the Americas stems from early European explorers' geographical misconceptions of where they were—they believed they were near the East Indies (see page 510). South America contained a great diversity of peoples, cultures, and linguistic groups. Modern scholars estimate that around 1500 there were 350 tribal groups, 15 distinct cultural centers, and 150 linguistic stocks. Historians and anthropologists have tended to focus attention on the Maya, Incas, and Aztecs, but the inhabitants of those three empires represent a minority of the total indigenous population; they lived in geographical regions that covered a small percentage of Mesoamerica and South America. Other native peoples included the Aymaras, Caribs, Chibchas, Chichimecas, Ge, Guaranis, Mapuches, Otonis, Pueblos, Quibayas, Tupis, and Zapotecs (see Map 14.1). In North America, aboriginal peoples represent comparable diversity. These peoples shared no unified sense of themselves as "Indians." None of their languages had the word *Indian.* Nor was there any tendency among these peoples to unite in a common resistance to the foreign invaders.[1] Rather, when confronting Europeans, each group or polity sought the most advantageous situation for itself alone. Of course, the idea of "discovery" meant nothing to them. Because much more is known about the Aztecs, Maya, and Incas than about other native peoples, the focus of this chapter is on them. The central feature of early American societies, however, is their great indigenous and cultural diversity.

- What is the geography of the Americas, and how did it shape the lives of the native peoples?
- What patterns of social and political organization did the Maya, Aztecs, and Incas display?
- What were the significant cultural achievements of the Maya, Aztecs, and Incas?
- Who were the North American mound builders, and what do the material remains of their culture tell us about them?

This chapter will consider these questions.

## THE GEOGRAPHY AND PEOPLES OF THE AMERICAS

The distance from the Bering Strait, which separates Asia from North America, to the southern tip of South America is about eleven thousand miles. A mountain range extends all the way from Alaska to the tip of South America, crossing Central America from northwest to southeast and making for rugged country along virtually the entire western coast of both continents.

Scholars use the term **Mesoamerica** to designate the area of present-day Mexico and Central America. Mexico is dominated by high plateaus bounded by coastal plains. Geographers have labeled the plateau regions "cold lands," the valleys between the plateaus "temperate lands," and the Gulf and Pacific coastal regions "hot lands." The Caribbean coast of Central America—modern Belize, Guatemala, Honduras, Nicaragua, El Salvador, Costa Rica, and Panama—is characterized by thick jungle lowlands, heavy rainfall, and torrid heat; it is an area generally unhealthy for humans. Central America's western uplands, with their more temperate climate and good agricultural land, support the densest population in the region.

Like Africa, South America is a continent of extremely varied terrain (see Map 14.4). The entire western coast is edged by the Andes, the highest mountain range in the Western Hemisphere. On the east coast, another mountain range—the Brazilian Highlands—accounts for one-fourth of the area of modern-day Brazil. Three-fourths of South America—almost the entire interior of the continent—is lowland plains. The Amazon River, at 4,000 miles the second-longest river in the world, bisects the north-central part of the continent, draining 2.7 million square miles of land. Tropical lowland rain forests with dense growth and annual rainfall in excess of 80 inches extend from the Amazon and Orinoco River basins northward all the way to southern Mexico.

Most scholars believe that people began crossing the Bering Strait from Russian Siberia between fifty thousand and twenty thousand years ago, when the strait was narrower than it is today. Skeletal finds indicate that these immigrants belonged to several ethnic groups now known collectively as American Indians, or Amerindians. Amerindians were nomadic peoples who lived by hunting small animals, fishing, and gathering wild fruits. As soon as an area had been exploited and a group had grown too large for the land to support, some families broke off from the group and moved on, usually southward. Gradually the newcomers spread throughout the Americas, losing contact with one another.

By the late fifteenth century, three kinds of Amerindian societies had emerged. First, largely nomadic groups depended on hunting, fishing, and gathering for subsistence; they had changed little from their ancestors who had crossed the Bering Strait thousands of years before. A second group of Amerindians, whom historians label sedentary or semi-sedentary, relied primarily on the domestication of plants for food; they led a settled or semi-settled farming life. A third group lived in large, sometimes densely populated settlements supported by agricultural surpluses; specialization of labor, large-scale construction projects, and different social classes characterized this group. These complex cultures existed only in Mesoamerica and western South America. In 1492 the polities of the Anáhuacs (Aztecs), Maya, and Tahuantinsuyas (Incas) were perhaps the best representatives of the third group.[2]

Amerindians in central Mexico built *chinampas,* floating gardens. They dredged soil from the bottom of a lake or pond, placed the soil on mats of woven twigs, and then planted crops in the soil. Chinampas were enormously productive, yielding up to three harvests a year. So extensive was this method of agriculture that central Mexico became known as the chinampas region. In Peru, meanwhile, people terraced the slopes of the Andes with stone retaining walls to keep the hillsides from sliding. Both chinampas and terraced slopes required the large labor force that became available with stable settlement.

Agricultural advancement had definitive social and political consequences. Careful cultivation of the land brought a reliable and steady food supply, which contributed to a relatively high fertility rate and in turn to a population boom. Because corn and potatoes require much less labor than does grain, Amerindian civilizations had a large pool of people who were not involved in agriculture and thus were available to construct religious and political buildings and serve in standing armies.[3]

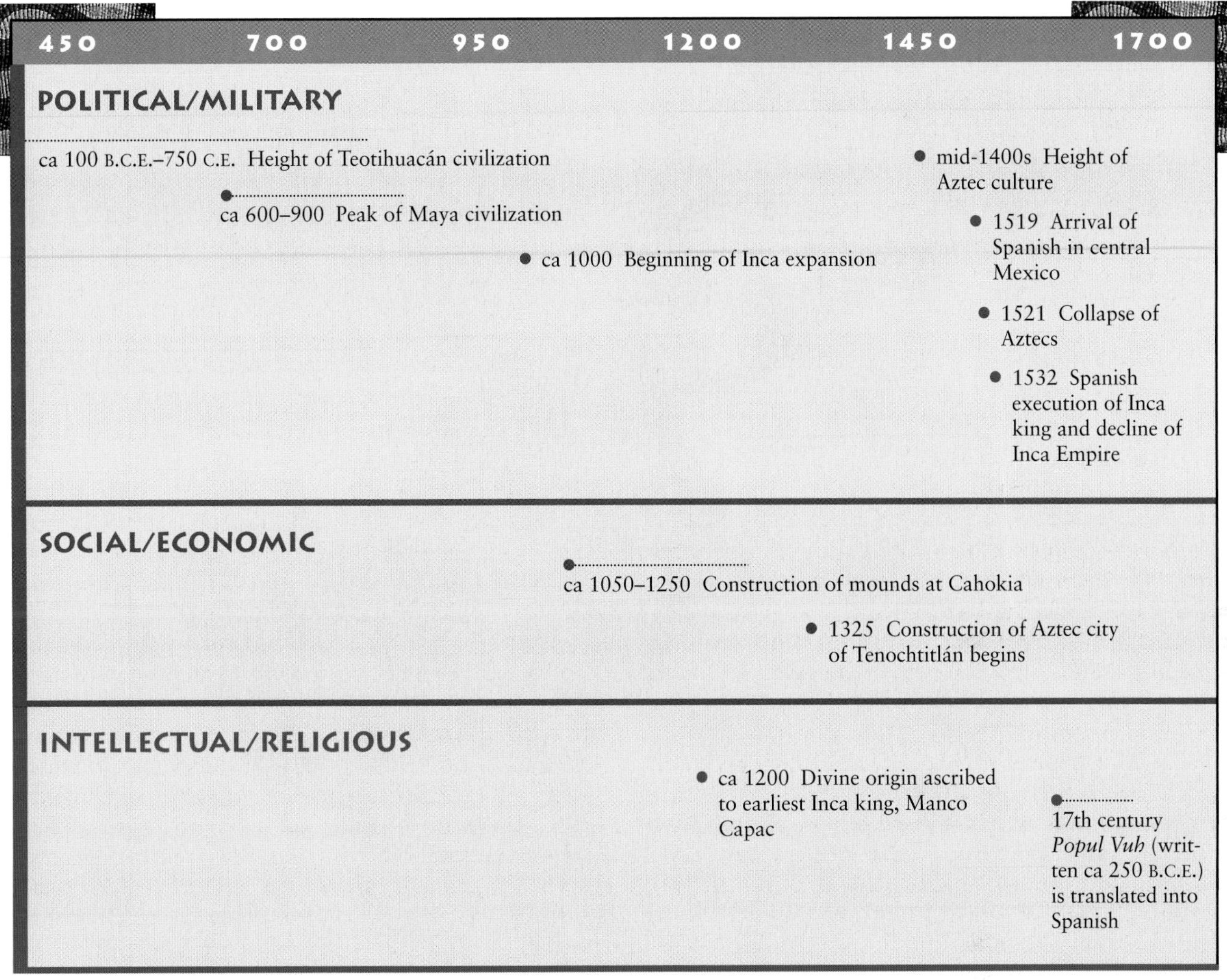


## MESOAMERICAN CIVILIZATIONS FROM THE OLMECS TO THE TOLTECS

Several American civilizations arose between roughly 1500 B.C.E. and 900 C.E.: the civilizations of the Olmecs, the Maya, Teotihuacán, and the Toltecs. Scholars believe that the Olmec civilization is the oldest of the early advanced Amerindian civilizations. Olmec culture, based on agriculture, spread over regions in central Mexico that lie thousands of miles apart. The Olmec practice of building scattered ceremonial centers found its highest cultural expression in the civilization of the Maya. The Maya occupied the area of present-day Yucatán, the highland crescent of eastern Chiapas in Mexico, and much of modern Guatemala and western Honduras. In the central plateau of Mexico, an "empire" centered at Teotihuacán arose. Scholars hotly debate whether the Teotihuacán territory constituted an empire, but they agree that Teotihuacán society was heavily stratified and that it exercised military, religious, and political power over a wide area. The Toltecs, whose culture adopted many features of the Teotihuacán and Olmec civilizations, were the last advanced Amerindian civilization before the rise of the Aztecs.

### The Olmecs

The word **Olmec** comes from an Aztec term for the peoples living in southern Veracruz and western Tabasco, Mexico, between about 1500 and 300 B.C.E. They did not call themselves Olmecs or consider themselves a unified group, but their culture penetrated and influenced

**MAP 14.1 The Peoples of South America** The major indigenous peoples of South America represented a great variety of languages and cultures. *(Source: Adapted from* The Times Atlas of World History, *3d ed. © Times Books. Reproduced by permission of HarperCollins Publishers Ltd.)*

all parts of Mesoamerica. All later Mesoamerican cultures derived from the Olmecs. Modern knowledge of the Olmecs rests entirely on archaeological evidence—pyramids, jade objects, axes, figurines, and stone monuments.

The Olmecs cultivated maize, squash, beans, and other plants and supplemented that diet with wild game and fish. Originally they lived in egalitarian societies that had no distinctions based on status or wealth. After 1500 B.C.E., more complex, hierarchical societies evolved. Anthropologists call these societies chieftains. Most peoples continued to live in small hamlets, villages, and towns along the rivers of the region, while the leaders of the societies resided in the large cities today known as San Lorenzo, La Venta, Tres Zapotes, and Laguna de los Cerros. These cities contained palaces (large private houses) for the elite, large plazas, temples (ritual centers), ball courts, water reservoirs, and carved stone drains for the disposal of wastes. The Olmecs developed a sophisticated system of symbols, as shown in their art; this system clearly influenced the Maya (see page 423). They invented monumental stone sculptures, a characteristic of every subsequent Mesoamerican civilization. In starting a tradition of ruler portraits in stone, the Olmecs also laid the foundations for a practice adopted by the Maya and other peoples. They had sacred ceremonial sites where they sometimes practiced human sacrifice. They erected special courts on which men played a game with a hard rubber ball that was both religious ritual and sport. Finally, the Olmecs engaged in long-distance trade, exchanging rubber, cacao (from which chocolate is made), pottery, figurines, jaguar pelts, and the services of painters and sculptors for obsidian (a hard, black volcanic glass from which paddle-shaped weapons were made), basalt, iron ore, shells, and various perishable goods. Commercial networks extended as far away as central and western Mexico and the Pacific coast.[4]

Around 900 B.C.E. San Lorenzo, the center of early Olmec culture, was destroyed, probably by migrating peoples from the north, and power passed to La Venta in Tabasco. Archaeological excavation at La Venta has uncovered a huge volcano-shaped pyramid. Standing 110 feet high at an inaccessible site on an island in the Tonala River, the so-called Great Pyramid was the center of the Olmec religion. The upward thrust of this monument, like that of the cathedrals of medieval Europe, may have represented the human effort to get closer to the gods. Built of huge stone slabs, the Great Pyramid required, scholars estimated, some 800,000 man-hours of labor. It testifies to the region's bumper harvests, which were able to support a labor force large enough to build such a monument. Around 300 B.C.E. La Venta fell, and Tres Zapotes, 100 miles to the northwest, became the leading Olmec site.

Olmec ceremonialism, magnificent sculpture, skillful stonework, social organization, and writing were important cultural advances that paved the way for the developments of the Classic period (300–900 C.E.), the golden age of Mesoamerican civilization. Just as the ancient Sumerians laid the foundations for later Mesopotamian cultures (see Chapter 1), so the Olmecs heavily influenced subsequent Mesoamerican societies.

## The Maya of Central America

In the Classic period, the Maya attained a level of intellectual and artistic achievement equaled by no other Amerindian people and by few peoples anywhere. The Maya developed a sophisticated system of writing, perhaps derived partly from the Olmecs. They invented a calendar more accurate than the European Gregorian calendar. And they made advances in mathematics that Europeans did not match for several centuries.

Who were the Maya, and where did they come from? What was the basis of their culture? What is the significance of their intellectual and artistic achievement? The word *Maya* seems to derive from *Zamna,* the name of a Maya god. Linguistic evidence leads scholars to believe that the first Maya were a small North American Indian group that emigrated from southern Oregon and northern California to the western highlands of Guatemala. Between the third and second millennia B.C.E., various groups, including the Cholans and Tzeltalans, broke away from the parent group and moved north and east into the Yucatán peninsula. The Cholan-speaking Maya, who occupied the area during the time of great cultural achievement, apparently created the culture.

Maya culture rested on agriculture. The staple crop in Mesoamerica was maize (corn). In 1972 a geographer and an aerial photographer studying the Campeche region of the Yucatán peninsula (see Map 14.2) proved that the Maya practiced intensive agriculture in raised, narrow, rectangular plots that they built above the low-lying, seasonally flooded land bordering rivers. Because of poor soil caused by heavy tropical rainfall and the fierce sun, farmers may also have relied on *milpa* for growing maize. Using this method, farmers cut down the trees in a patch of forest and set the wood and brush afire. They then used a stick to poke holes through the ash and planted maize seeds in the holes. A milpa (the word refers to both the area and the method) produced for only two years, after which it had to lie fallow for between four and seven years. Throughout the Yucatán

**MAP 14.2 The Maya World, 300–900 C.E.** Archaeologists have discovered the ruins of dozens of Maya city-states. Only the largest of them are shown here. Called the "Greeks of the New World," the Maya perfected the only written language in the Western Hemisphere, developed a sophisticated political system and a flourishing trade network, and created elegant art.

**Palace Doorway Lintel at Yaxchilan, Mexico** Lady Xoc, principal wife of King Shield-Jaguar, who holds a torch over her, pulls a thorn-lined rope through her tongue to sanctify with her blood the birth of a younger wife's child—reflecting the importance of blood sacrifice in Maya culture. The elaborate headdresses and clothes of the couple show their royal status. *(© Justin Kerr 1985)*

peninsula, the method of burning and planting in the fertile ashes, known as *swidden agriculture,* remains the typical farming practice today.

In addition to maize, the Maya grew beans, squash, chili peppers, some root crops, and fruit trees. The raised-field and milpa systems of intensive agriculture yielded food sufficient to support large population centers. The entire Maya region could have had as many as 14 million inhabitants. At Uxmal, Uaxactún, Copán, Piedras Negras, Tikal, Palenque, and Chichén Itzá (see Map 14.2), archaeologists have uncovered the palaces of nobles, elaborate pyramids where nobles were buried, engraved *steles* (stone-slab monuments), masonry temples, altars, sophisticated polychrome pottery, and courts for games played with a rubber ball. The largest site, Tikal, may have had forty thousand people. Since these centers lacked industrial activities, scholars avoid calling them cities. Rather they were religious and ceremonial centers.

Public fairs accompanying important religious festivals in population centers seem to have been the major Maya economic institutions. Jade, obsidian, beads of red spiny oyster shell, lengths of cloth, and cacao (chocolate) beans—all in high demand in the Mesoamerican world—served as the medium of exchange. The extensive trade among Maya communities, plus a common language, promoted the union of the peoples of the region and gave them a common sense of identity. Merchants trading beyond Maya regions, such as with the Zapotecs of the Valley of Oaxaca and the Teotihuacanos of the central valley of Mexico, were considered state ambassadors bearing "gifts" to royal neighbors, who reciprocated with their own "gifts." Since this long-distance trade played an important part in international relations, the merchants

**After a Maya Battle** Richly dressed Maya victors lead captives from the battlefield, probably to their fate—sacrifice. *(© Justin Kerr)*

conducting it were high nobles or even members of the royal family.

Lacking iron tools until a few centuries before the Spanish conquest and beasts of burden until after the conquest, how were goods transported to distant regions? The extensive networks of rivers and swamps were the main arteries of transportation; over them large canoes carved out of hardwood trees carried cargoes of cloth and maize. Wide roads also linked Maya centers; on the roads merchants and lords were borne in litters, goods and produce on human backs. Trade produced considerable wealth that seems to have been concentrated in a noble class, for the Maya had no distinctly mercantile class. They did have a sharply defined hierarchical society. A hereditary elite owned private land, defended society, carried on commercial activities, exercised political power, and directed religious rituals. The intellectual class also belonged to the ruling nobility. The rest of the people were free workers, serfs, and slaves.

A fierce and warlike people, the Maya fought wars "for land, for slaves, to avenge insults and punish theft, and to control trade routes and the sources of various valued products, particularly salt." Long periods without rain caused crop failure, which led to famine and then war with other centers for food. Within the same communities, domestic strife between factions over the succession to the kingship, property, or perceived insults seems to have been common.[5]

Yet the Maya also cultivated the arts of peace. They developed a system of hieroglyphic writing with 850 characters and used it to record chronology, religion, and astronomy in books made of bark paper and deerskin. The recent deciphering of this writing has demonstrated that inscriptions on steles are actually historical documents recording the births, accessions, marriages, wars, and deaths of Maya kings. An understanding of the civilization's dynastic history allows scholars to interpret more accurately Maya pictorial imagery and to detect patterns in Maya art. They are finding that the imagery explicitly portrays the text in pictorial scenes and on stelar carvings.[6]

In the sixteenth century, Spanish friars taught Maya students to write their language in the Roman script so that the friars could understand Maya culture. Maya deities and sacrificial customs, however, provoked Spanish outrage. To hasten Maya conversion to Christianity, the priests tried to extirpate all native religion by destroying Maya sculpture and books. Only one Maya hieroglyphic book survived: the *Popul Vuh,* or Book of Council, which was written in European script by a young Quiché noble. Scholars call this document the Maya "Bible," meaning that like the Judeo-Christian Scriptures, the *Popul Vuh* gives the Maya view of the creation of the world, concepts of good and evil, and the entire nature and purpose of the living experience.

From careful observation of the earth's movements around the sun, the Maya invented a calendar of eighteen 20-day months and one 5-day month, for a total of 365 days. Using a system of bars (— = 5) and dots (◦ = 1), the Maya devised a form of mathematics based on the vigesimal (20) rather than the decimal (10) system. They proved themselves masters of abstract knowledge—notably in astronomy, mathematics, calendric development, and the recording of history.

Maya civilization lasted about a thousand years, reaching its peak between approximately 600 and 900 C.E., the period when the Tang Dynasty was flourishing in China,

**Maya Burial Urn** After tightly wrapping the bodies of royal and noble persons in cloth, the K'iché Maya people of Guatemala placed them in urns and buried them in pyramids or sacred caves. The lid represents a divine being through whose mouth gifts may have been offered the deceased. The figure on top of the lid with corncobs stands for the maize-god. The size of this object, fifty-two inches, suggests that the Maya people were very short. *(Museum of Fine Arts, Boston, Gift of Landon T. Clay [1988. 1290a–b]. © 2002 Museum of Fine Arts, Boston)*

Islam was spreading in the Middle East, and Carolingian rulers were extending their sway in Europe. Between the eighth and tenth centuries, the Maya abandoned their cultural and ceremonial centers, and Maya civilization collapsed. Archaeologists and historians attribute the decline to a combination of agricultural failures due to land exhaustion and drought; overpopulation; disease; and constant wars fought as an extension of economic and political goals. These wars brought widespread destruction, which aggravated agrarian problems. Maya royal ideology also played a role in their decline: just as in good times kings attributed moral authority and prosperity to themselves, so in bad times, when military, economic, and social conditions deteriorated, they became the objects of blame.[7]

In 1527 the Spaniards faced a formidable task when they attempted to conquer the Yucatán. The Maya polity did not involve a single political entity, as that of the Aztecs and Incas did; instead the Maya had several cultural centers. The Spaniards had great trouble imposing a centralized government on a divided people using guerrilla and hit-and-run tactics. Although the Spaniards established some degree of control in 1545, only in 1697 did the last independent Maya group fall to the Europeans.

## Teotihuacán and Toltec Civilizations

During the Classic period, **Teotihuacán** in central Mexico witnessed the flowering of a remarkable civilization built by a new people from regions east and south of the Valley of Mexico. The city of Teotihuacán had a population of over 200,000—larger than any European city at the time. The inhabitants were stratified into distinct social classes. The rich and powerful resided in a special precinct, in houses of palatial splendor. Ordinary working people, tradespeople, artisans, and obsidian craftsmen lived in apartment compounds, or *barrios,* on the edge of the city. Agricultural laborers lived outside the city. Teotihuacán was a great commercial center, the entrepôt for trade and culture for all of Mesoamerica. It was also the ceremonial center, a capital filled with artworks, a mecca that attracted thousands of pilgrims a year.

In the center of the city stood the Pyramids of the Sun and the Moon. The Pyramid of the Sun is built of sun-dried bricks and faced with stone. Each of its sides is seven hundred feet long and two hundred feet high. The smaller Pyramid of the Moon is similar in construction. In lesser temples, natives and outlanders worshiped the rain-god and the feathered serpent later called Quetzalcoatl. These gods were associated with the production of corn, the staple of the people's diet.

Although Teotihuacán dominated Mesoamerican civilization during the Classic period, other centers also flourished. In the isolated valley of Oaxaca at modern-day Monte Albán (see Map 14.3), for example, Zapotecan-speaking peoples established a great religious center whose temples and elaborately decorated tombs testify to the wealth of the nobility. The art—and probably the entire culture—of Monte Albán and other centers derived from Teotihuacán.

As had happened to San Lorenzo and La Venta, Teotihuacán collapsed before invaders. Around 700 B.C.E. less-developed peoples from the southwest burned Teotihuacán; Monte Albán fell shortly afterward. By 900 the golden age of Mesoamerica had ended. There followed an interregnum known as the "Time of Troubles" (ca 800–1000), characterized by disorder and extreme militarism. Whereas nature gods and their priests seem to have governed the great cities of the earlier period, militant gods and warriors dominated the petty states that now arose. Among these states, the most powerful heir to Teotihuacán was the Toltec confederation, a weak union of strong states. The **Toltecs** admired the culture of their predecessors and sought to absorb and preserve it. Through intermarriage, they assimilated with the Teotihuacán people. In fact, every new Mesoamerican confederation became the cultural successor of earlier confederations.

Under Topiltzin (r. ca 980–1000), the Toltecs extended their hegemony over most of central Mexico. Topiltzin established his capital at Tula. Its splendor and power became legendary during his reign. (See the feature "Individuals in Society: Quetzalcoatl.")

After the reign of Topiltzin, troubles beset the Toltec state. Drought led to crop failure. Northern peoples, the Chichimecas, attacked the borders in waves. Weak, incompetent rulers could not quell domestic uprisings. When the last Toltec king committed suicide in 1174, the Toltec state collapsed. In 1224 the Chichimecas captured Tula.

The last of the Chichimecas to arrive in central Mexico were the Aztecs. As before, the vanquished strongly influenced the victors: the Aztecs absorbed the cultural achievements of the Toltecs. The Aztecs—building on Olmec, Maya, Teotihuacán, and Toltec antecedents—created the last unifying civilization in Mexico before the arrival of the Europeans.

## AZTEC SOCIETY: RELIGION AND WAR

Although the terms *Aztec* and *Mexica* are used interchangeably here, **Mexica** is actually the more accurate word because it is a pre-Columbian term designating the dominant ethnic people of the island capital of Tenochtitlán-Tlalelolco. **Aztec** derives from *Aztlan,* the legendary homeland of the Mexica people before their migration into the Valley of Mexico, is *not* a pre-Columbian word, and was popularized by nineteenth-century historians.[8]

The Aztecs who appeared in the Valley of Mexico spoke the same **Nahuatl** language as the Toltecs but otherwise had nothing in common with them. Poor, unwelcome, looked on as foreign barbarians, the Aztecs had to settle on a few swampy islands in Lake Texcoco. From these unpromising beginnings, they rapidly assimilated the culture of the Toltecs and in 1428 embarked on a policy of territorial expansion. By the time Cortés arrived in 1519, the Aztec confederation encompassed all of central Mexico from the Gulf of Mexico to the Pacific as far south as Guatemala (see Map 14.3). Thirty-eight subordinate provinces paid tribute to the Aztec king.

**MAP 14.3 The Aztec Empire, 1519** The Aztecs controlled much of central Mexico. The Maya survived in the Yucatán peninsula and some of present-day Guatemala. Notice the number of cities.

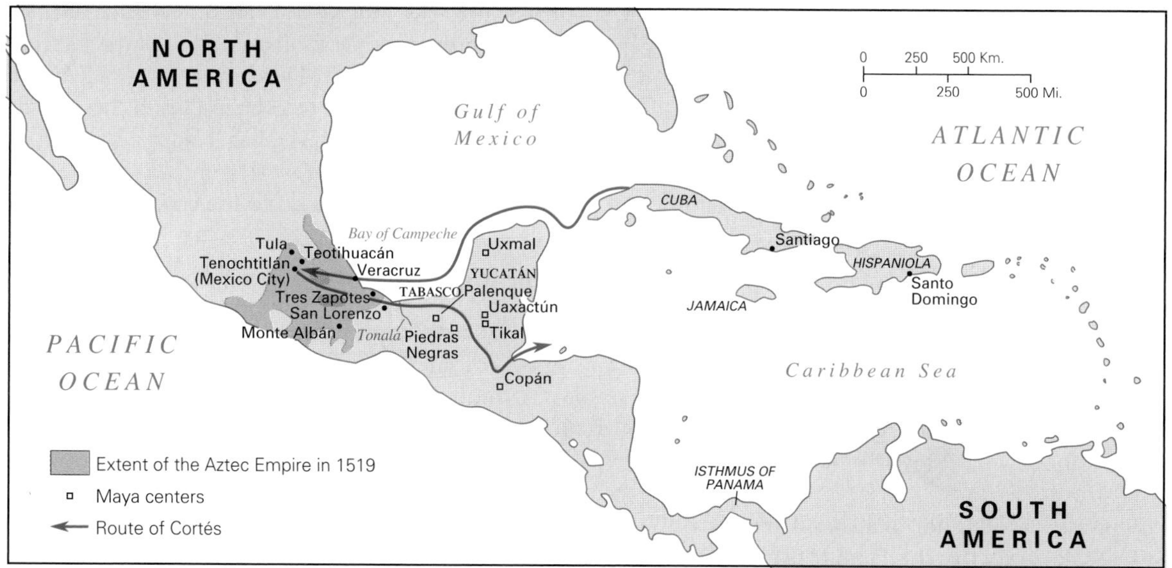

The growth of a strong mercantile class led to an influx of tropical wares and luxury goods: cotton, feathers, cocoa, skins, turquoise jewelry, and gold. The upper classes enjoyed an elegant and extravagant lifestyle; the court of Emperor Montezuma II (r. 1502–1520) was more magnificent than anything in western Europe. How, in less than two hundred years, had the Mexicans (from the Aztec word *mizquitl,* meaning "desolate land," or from *Mixitli,* the Aztec god of war) grown from an insignificant tribe of wandering nomads to a people of vast power and fabulous wealth?

The Aztecs' pictorial records attribute their success to the power of their war-god Huitzilopochtli and to their own drive and willpower. Will and determination they unquestionably had, but there is another explanation for their success: the Aztec state was geared for war.

War was inextricably woven into the fabric of Mexica society. Rather than depending on professional soldiers or foreign mercenaries, as some European princes and city-states did (see pages 544 and 550), the Aztecs relied on their own citizens, and all levels of society were involved. Kings ordered war to acquire tribute for state use and captives for religious sacrifices. Nobles fought to win greater wealth. Commoners fought as a means of social advancement: the ordinary warrior who distinguished himself in battle could earn the status of meritocratic noble (*cuahpipiltin*), a Mexica rank comparable to that of European knight. This status brought the right to own land, to be supported by the king, to share in future war booty, and to hold civic and military office.

War required considerable advance planning by the king. He ordered the calling up of men from the city wards on a rotating basis so that military service was equitably shared. Men fought as ward units bound together by neighborhood and kinship ties. The king determined the route, the number of days the army would march, and the battle plans once the target was reached. The lack of wheeled carts or wagons and of draft animals meant that all food and supplies had to be carried by porters. Scholars project that there was one porter for every two men, each porter carrying fifty pounds of maize. This meant that an "army could carry food for only eight days, giving an effective combat radius of about thirty-six miles—three days going, one day fighting, one day recuperating, and three days returning." To solve this logistical problem, an army might live on the passing countryside, and already-subject peoples would be warned about what they should be prepared to supply.[9]

Preceded by priests carrying on their backs images or statues of the gods, an army marched about twelve miles per day. Aztec messengers went ahead and warned the enemy city that attack was imminent. If it promptly surrendered, the amount of tribute would be modest. If not, battle followed shortly after the Aztec army reached its target.

The beat of the commander's drum, usually at dawn, signaled the start of battle. First, archers and slingers released a hail of arrows and stones. When soldiers—wearing armor consisting of thick sleeveless jackets of unspun cotton quilted between two layers of cloth, which an arrow could not penetrate—advanced, the real barrage began. Each man carried a shield twenty-eight inches in diameter, a spear, and a broadsword made of oak and obsidian (an extremely hard, black volcanic glass, which the Spaniards later saw could slice the head off a horse with a single blow). As opposing armies approached each other, spear throwers cast darts that, though lacking the distance of arrows, could penetrate the cotton armor of front-rank soldiers.

Then combatants switched to obsidian broadswords. Only the front ranks engaged the enemy in close combat, but with their numerical superiority the Aztecs could extend the frontline and encircle the enemy. Units were rotated in and out of battle about every fifteen minutes, bringing up fresh troops. A crippling blow to a foe's knees or to one of the muscles in the back of the thigh enabled the Aztec warrior to bring his enemy to the ground. Once the captive was subdued, men with ropes tied him up and took him to the rear of the battlefield. The goal was not to kill the enemy but to turn him into a tribute producer or to take him to Tenochtitlán as a sacrificial victim. Wounded Aztecs also were taken to the rear, where medical specialists tended them. Runners carried the news of victory or defeat to the king. (Thus an Aztec ruler did not personally command operations on the battlefield, as many European princes did.) Dead Aztecs were identified so that their families could be recompensed and their wards instructed to replace them. If the battle occurred far from home, the bodies of the dead were cremated on the battlefield. Then the army returned to the capital.[10]

## Religion and Culture

In Mexica society, religion was the dynamic factor that transformed other aspects of the culture: economic security, social mobility, education, and especially war. War was an article of religious faith. The state religion of the Aztecs initially gave them powerful advantages over other groups in central Mexico; it inspired them to conquer vast territories in a remarkably short time.[11] But that religion also created economic and political stresses

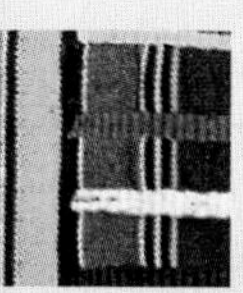

## QUETZALCOATL

Legends are popular beliefs about someone or something that are handed down from the past. They often lack a basis in historical—that is, verifiable—evidence, but they are generally believed to embody the ideals of a people or society. When legends become involved in religious faith, they acquire an established quality and become part of a people's core beliefs. Faith has been defined as "the confident assurance of what we hope for, and conviction of what we do not see" (Hebrews 11:1). How can we be confident of hopes and dreams, certain of what we do not see? Religious faith always presents a paradox, and belief systems have played a powerful part in historical events, as the Mexica god Quetzalcoatl illustrates.

Quetzalcoatl (pronounced kat-sal-koat-al), meaning "feathered serpent," was an important figure in Aztec culture. Students of the history of religions trace his origins either to an ancient deity of the Toltecs or to a historical Toltec ruler credited with the discovery of the cereal maize. He is believed to have been a great supporter of the arts, sciences, and calendar; he was also associated with peace. We do not know whether the historical ruler took his name from the god or, as a successful king, he was revered and deified. Considered the god of civilization, Quetzalcoatl represented to the Mexica the forces of good and light. He was pitted against the Toltecs' original tribal god, Tezcatlipoca, who stood for evil, darkness, and war. When the Aztecs absorbed Toltec culture, they adopted Quetzalcoatl and linked him with the worship of Huitzilopochtli, their war-god.

We may plausibly assume that the Toltec king Topiltzin (see page 425) took the name Quetzalcoatl. According to the "Song of Quetzalcoatl," a long Aztec glorification of Topiltzin,

> *He was very rich and had everything necessary to eat and drink, and the corn under his reign was in abundance. . . . And more than that the said Quetzalcoatl had all the wealth of the world, gold and silver and green stones, jade and other precious things.**

Whatever reality lies behind this legend, it became a cornerstone of Aztec tradition; it also played a profound role in Mexica history. Later Aztec legends describe a powerful struggle between Tezcatlipoca, who required human sacrifices, and Quetzalcoatl. Tezcatlipoca won this battle, and the priest-king Topiltzin-Quetzalcoatl was driven into exile. As he departed, he promised to return and regain his kingdom. By a remarkable coincidence, Quetzalcoatl promised to return in 1519, the year the Spanish explorer Hernando Cortés landed in Mexico. Cortés learned the legend and exploited it for his own purposes. Native and Spanish accounts tell us that Montezuma identified Cortés with the god Quetzalcoatl. Cortés took it as his right that Montezuma should house him in the imperial palace close to the shrine of the Aztec gods (and near the imperial treasury). When, on a tour of the city, Montezuma led Cortés up the many steps of the sacred temple, the emperor stopped and said to Cortés that he must be tired with all those steps. No, Cortés replied, "we" are never tired (as all mortals, but not gods, become). When Montezuma told Cortés that he would share all that he possessed with the Spaniards and that they "must truly be the men whom his ancestors had long ago prophesized, saying that they would come from the direction of the sunrise to rule over these lands," Cortés replied that "he did indeed come from the direction of the sunrise" and that he brought the message of the one true God, Jesus Christ. The conquistador knew that Montezuma would interpret his words as meaning that he was Quetzalcoatl.

*Quetzalcoatl, or Precious Feather Snake.*
(© Musée de l'Homme)

### QUESTIONS FOR ANALYSIS

1. Assess the role of Quetzalcoatl in the fall of the Aztec Empire.
2. What is reality—what we believe or what can be scientifically demonstrated?

*Quoted in I. Bernal, *Mexico Before Cortez: Art, History, and Legend,* rev. ed., trans. W. Barnstone (New York: Anchor Books, 1975), p. 68.

*Sources:* Bernal Díaz, *The Conquest of New Spain,* trans. J. M. Cohen (New York: Penguin Books, 1978); T. Todorov, *The Conquest of America,* trans. R. Howard (New York: Harper & Row, 1984).

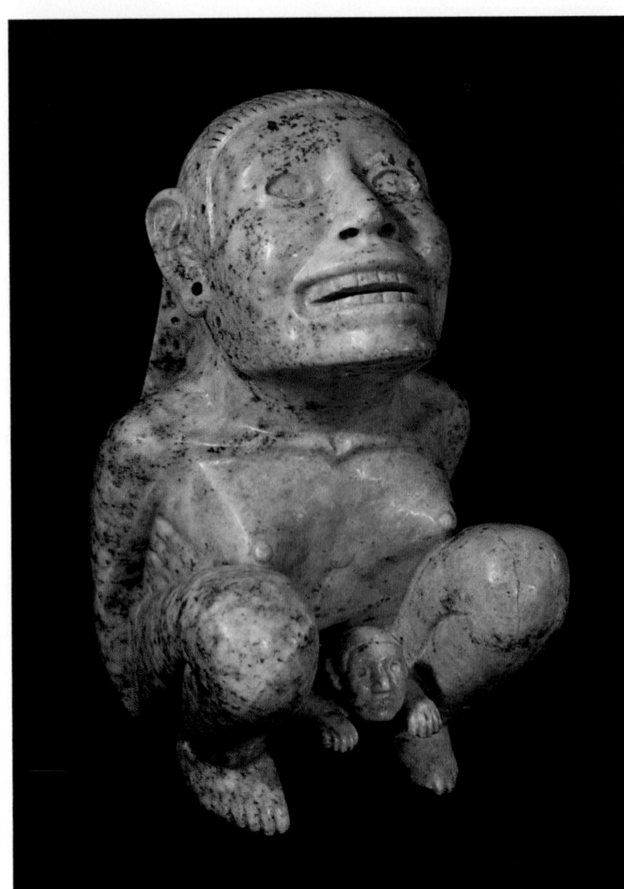

**The Goddess Tlazolteotl** The Aztecs believed that Tlazolteotl (sometimes called "Mother of the Gods") consumed the sins of humankind by eating refuse. As the goddess of childbirth, Tlazolteotl was extensively worshiped. Notice the squatting position for childbirth, then common all over the world. *(Dumbarton Oaks, Pre-Columbian Collection, Washington, D.C.)*

that could not easily be resolved and that ultimately contributed heavily to the society's collapse.

Chief among the Aztecs' many gods was **Huitzilopochtli,** who symbolized the sun blazing at high noon. The sun, the source of all life, had to be kept moving in its orbit if darkness was not to overtake the world. To keep it moving, Aztecs believed, the sun had to be fed frequently precious fluids—that is, human blood. Human sacrifice was a sacred duty, essential for the preservation and prosperity of humankind. Black-robed priests carried out the ritual:

*The victim was stretched out on his back on a slightly convex stone with his arms and legs held by four priests, while a fifth ripped him open with a flint knife and tore out his heart. The sacrifice also often took place in a manner which the Spanish described as gladiatorio: the captive was tied to a huge disk of stone . . . by a rope that left him free to move; he was armed with wooden weapons, and he had to fight several normally-armed Aztec warriors in turn. If, by an extraordinary chance, he did not succumb to their attacks, he was spared; but nearly always the "gladiator" fell, gravely wounded, and a few moments later he died on the stone, with his body opened by the black-robed, long-haired priests.*[12]

Mass sacrifice was also practiced:

*Mass sacrifices involving hundreds and thousands of victims could be carried out to commemorate special events. The Spanish chroniclers were told, for example, that at the dedication in 1487 of the great pyramid of Tenochtitlán, four lines of prisoners of war stretching for two miles each were sacrificed by a team of executioners who worked night and day for four days. Allotting two minutes for sacrifice, the demographer and historian Sherbourne Cook estimated that the number of victims associated with that single event was 14,100. The scale of these rituals could be dismissed as exaggerations were it not for the encounters of Spanish explorers with . . . rows of human skulls in the plazas of the Aztec cities. . . . In the plaza of Xocotlan "there were . . . more than one hundred thousand of them."*[13]

The Mexica did not invent human sacrifice; it seems to have been practiced by many Mesoamerican peoples. The Maya, for example, dedicated their temples with the blood of freshly executed victims. Anthropologists have proposed several explanations—none of them completely satisfactory—for the Aztecs' practice of human sacrifice and the cannibalism that often accompanied it. Some suggest that human sacrifice served to regulate population growth. Yet ritual slaughter had been practiced by earlier peoples—the Olmecs, the Maya, the dwellers of Teotihuacán, and the Toltecs—in all likelihood before population density had reached the point of threatening the food supply. Moreover, almost all the victims were men, instead of women of childbearing age, whose deaths would have had more of an effect on population growth.

According to a second hypothesis, the ordinary people were given victims' bodies as a source of protein.[14] These people lived on a diet of corn, beans, squash, tomatoes, and peppers. Wildlife was scarce, and dog meat, chicken, turkey, and fish were virtually restricted to the upper classes. The testimony of modern nutritionists that beans supply ample protein, and the evidence that, in an area teeming with wild game, the Huron Indians of North America ritually executed captives and feasted on their stewed bodies, weaken the validity of this theory.

A third, more plausible, theory holds that ritual human sacrifice was an instrument of state terrorism—that the Aztec rulers crushed dissent with terror. The Aztecs controlled a large confederation of city-states by sacrificing prisoners seized in battle; by taking hostages from among defeated peoples as ransom against future revolt; and by demanding from subject states an annual tribute of people to be sacrificed to Huitzilopochtli. Unsuccessful generals, corrupt judges, and careless public officials, even people who accidentally entered forbidden precincts of the royal palaces, were routinely sacrificed. When the supply of such victims ran out, slaves, plebeians, and even infants suffered ritual execution. The emperor Montezuma II, who celebrated his coronation with the sacrifice of fifty-one hundred people, could be said to have ruled by sacrifice. Trumpets blasted and drums beat all day long announcing the sacrifice of yet another victim.

How can we at the start of the twenty-first century understand such a terrifying and nightmarish daily ritual? First, we have to remember that in the middle of the twentieth century, as millions of human beings were marched to their deaths, most of the world said nothing (or very little) and went about their daily tasks. Five hundred years ago, as priests performed the actual sacrifices, "the average person" watched. All persons were involved in or complicit in the sacrifices by various means: by the pleasure and satisfaction a household took when one of its warriors brought back a victim for sacrifice; by members of the *calpullis,* the basic civic or local unit, taking their turns in duties at the sacrificial temples; by these groups presenting a sacrificial victim to a temple (much as European medieval guilds donated windows to the local church or cathedral); by the care in feeding, clothing, parading to the temples, and, if necessary, drugging victims for their sacrifice; and by the popular celebrations at mass executions. The Nahuatl-speaking people accepted the ritual sacrifices because the victims, whether captives from hostile tribes or social outcasts from within, represented outsiders, foreigners, "the other."[15]

The Mexica state religion required constant warfare for two basic reasons. One was to meet the gods' needs for human sacrifice; the other was to acquire warriors for the next phase of imperial expansion. "The sacred campaigns of Huitzilopochtli were synchronized with the political and economic needs of the Mexica nation as a whole."[16] Moreover, defeated peoples had to pay tribute in foodstuffs to support rulers, nobles, warriors, and the imperial bureaucracy. The vanquished supplied laborers for agriculture, the economic basis of Mexica society. Likewise, conquered peoples had to produce workers for the construction and maintenance of the entire Aztec infrastructure—roads, dike systems, aqueducts, causeways, and the royal palaces. Finally, merchants also benefited, for war opened new markets for traders' goods in subject territories.

**Aztec Standard-Bearer** The wide stairways leading from Aztec plazas to temple sanctuaries at the top held pairs of sculptures in the form of standard-bearers. This twenty-five-inch seated figure from the late fifteenth or early sixteenth century is clothed in only a loincloth and would have held a banner in its cupped right hand (now damaged). *(The Metropolitan Museum of Art, Harris Brisbane Dick Fund, 1962 [62.47]. Photograph © 1993 The Metropolitan Museum of Art)*

When the Spaniards under Hernando Cortés (1485–1547) arrived in central Mexico in 1519, the sacred cult of Huitzilopochtli had created a combination of interrelated problems for the emperor Montezuma II. The thirty-eight provinces of the empire, never really assimilated into the Mexica state and usually governed by members of the defeated dynasty, seethed with rebellion. Population increases at the capital, Tenochtitlán, had forced the emperor to lay increasingly heavier tribute on conquered provinces, which in turn murdered the tribute collectors. Invasion and reconquest followed. "The provinces were being crushed beneath a cycle of imperial oppression: increases in tribute, revolt, reconquest, retribution, higher tribute, resentment, and repeated revolt."[17] By causing death in battle and by sacrifice of thousands of food producers, Mexica religion destroyed the very economic basis of the empire.

Faced with grave crisis, Montezuma attempted to solve the problem by freezing social positions. He purged the court of many officials, drastically modified the dress and behavior of the merchant class, and severely limited the honors given to lowborn warriors and all but the highest nobility. These reforms provoked great resentment, reduced incentive, and virtually ended social mobility. Scholars have traditionally portrayed Montezuma as weak-willed and indecisive when faced with the Spaniards. But recent research has shown that he was a very determined, even autocratic, ruler. Terrible domestic problems whose roots lay in a religious cult requiring appalling human slaughter offer the fundamental explanation for the Mexica collapse.[18]

## The Life of the People

A wealth of information has survived about fifteenth- and sixteenth-century Mexico. The Aztecs wrote many books recounting their history, geography, and religious practices. They loved making speeches, which scribes copied down. The Aztecs also preserved records of their legal disputes, which alone amounted to vast files. The Spanish conquerors subsequently destroyed much of this material. But enough documents remain to construct a picture of the Mexica people at the time of the Spanish intrusion.

No sharp social distinctions existed among the Aztecs during their early migrations. All were equally poor. The head of a family was both provider and warrior, and a sort of tribal democracy prevailed in which all adult males participated in important decision making. By the early sixteenth century, however, Aztec society had changed. A stratified social structure had come into being, and the warrior aristocracy exercised great authority.

Scholars do not yet understand precisely how this change evolved. According to Aztec legend, the Mexica admired the Toltecs and chose their first king, Acamapichti, from among them. The many children he fathered with Mexica women formed the nucleus of the noble class. At the time of the Spanish intrusion into Mexico, men who had distinguished themselves in war occupied the highest military and social positions in the state. Generals, judges, and governors of provinces were appointed by the emperor from among his servants who had earned reputations as war heroes. These great lords, or **tecuhtli,** dressed luxuriously and lived in palaces. The provincial governors exercised full political, judicial, and military authority on the emperor's behalf. In their territories they maintained order, settled disputes, and judged legal cases; oversaw the cultivation of land; and made sure that tribute—in food or gold—was paid. The governors also led troops in wartime. These functions resembled those of feudal lords in western Europe during the Middle Ages (see pages 396–397). Just as only nobles in France and England could wear fur and carry a sword, just as gold jewelry and elaborate hairstyles for women distinguished royal and noble classes in African kingdoms, so in Mexica societies only the tecuhtli could wear jewelry and embroidered cloaks.

Beneath the great nobility of soldiers and imperial officials was the class of warriors. Theoretically every freeman could be a warrior, and parents dedicated their male children to war, burying a male child's umbilical cord with some arrows and a shield on the day of his birth. In actuality the sons of nobles enjoyed advantages deriving from their fathers' position and influence in the state. At the age of six, boys entered a school that trained them for war. Future warriors were taught to fight with a *macana,* a paddle-shaped wooden club edged with bits of obsidian. Youths were also trained in the use of spears, bows and arrows, and lances fitted with obsidian points. They learned to live on little food and sleep and to accept pain without complaint. At about age eighteen, a warrior fought his first campaign. If he captured a prisoner for ritual sacrifice, he acquired the title *iyac,* or warrior. If in later campaigns he succeeded in killing or capturing four of the enemy, he became a *tequiua*—one who shared in the booty and thus was a member of the nobility. If a young man failed in several campaigns to capture the required four prisoners, he joined the **maceualtin,** the plebeian or working class.

The maceualtin were the ordinary citizens—the backbone of Aztec society and the vast majority of the population. The word *maceualti* means "worker" and implied boorish speech and vulgar behavior. Members of this class performed all sorts of agricultural, military, and domestic services and carried heavy public burdens not required of noble warriors. Government officials assigned the maceualtin work on the temples, roads, and bridges. Army officers called them up for military duty, but Mexica

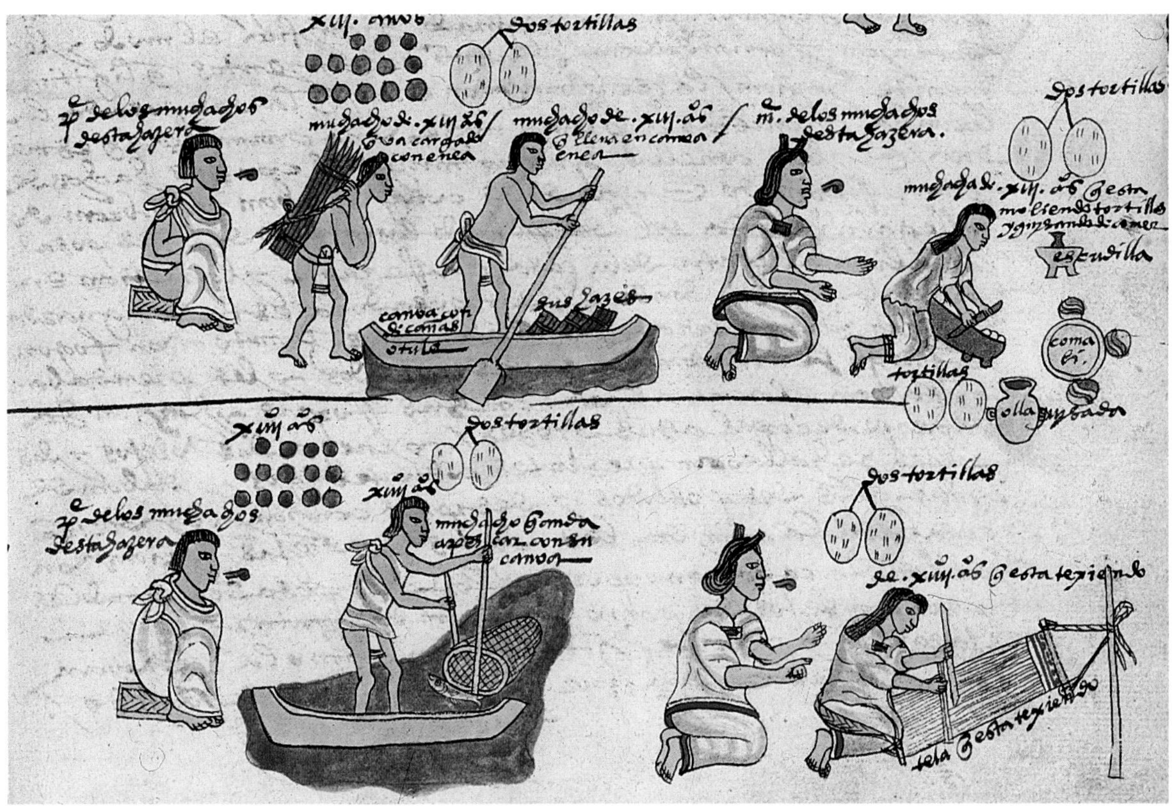


**Aztec Youth** As shown in this codex, Aztec society had basic learning requirements for each age (indicated by dots) of childhood and youth. In the upper panel, boys of age thirteen gather firewood and collect reeds and herbs in a boat, while girls learn to make tortillas on a terra-cotta grill. At fourteen (*lower panel*), boys learn to fish from a boat, and girls are taught to weave. *(The Bodleian Library, University of Oxford, MS Arch. Selden. A.1, fol. 60r)*

considered this an honor and a religious rite, not a burden. Unlike nobles, priests, orphans, and slaves, maceualtin paid taxes. Maceualtin in the capital, however, possessed certain rights: they held their plots of land for life, and they received a small share of the tribute paid by the provinces to the emperor.

Beneath the maceualtin were the *tlalmaitl,* the landless workers or serfs. Some social historians speculate that this class originated during the "Time of Troubles," a period of migrations and upheavals in which weak and defenseless people placed themselves under the protection of strong warriors (see page 425). The tlalmaitl provided agricultural labor, paid rents in kind, and were bound to the soil—they could not move off the land. The tlalmaitl resembled in many ways the serfs of western Europe, but unlike serfs they performed military service when called on to do so. They enjoyed some rights as citizens and generally were accorded more respect than slaves.

Slaves were the lowest social class. Like Asian, European, and African slaves, most were prisoners captured in war or kidnapped from enemy tribes. But Aztecs who stole from a temple or private house or plotted against the emperor could also be enslaved, and people in serious debt sometimes voluntarily sold themselves into slavery. Female slaves often became their masters' concubines. Mexica slaves, however, differed fundamentally from European ones: "Tlatlocotin slaves could possess goods, save money, buy land and houses and even slaves for their own service."[19] Slaves could purchase their freedom. If a male slave married a free woman, their offspring were free, and a slave who escaped and managed to enter the emperor's palace was automatically free. Most slaves eventually gained their freedom. Mexica slavery, therefore, had some humane qualities and resembled slavery in Islamic societies (see pages 255–257).

Women of all social classes played important roles in Mexica society, but those roles were restricted entirely to the domestic sphere. As the little hands of the newborn male child were closed around a tiny bow and arrow indicating his warrior destiny, so the infant female's hands were wrapped around miniature weaving instruments and a small broom: weaving was a sacred and exclusively female art; the broom signaled a female's responsibility for the household shrines and for keeping the household swept and free of contamination. Almost all of the Mexica people married, a man at about twenty when he had secured one or two captives, a woman a couple of years earlier. As in pre-modern Asian and European societies, parents selected their children's spouses, using neighborhood women as go-betweens. Save for the few women vowed to the service of the temple, marriage and the household were a woman's fate; marriage represented social maturity for both sexes. Pregnancy became the occasion for family and neighborhood feasts, and a successful birth launched celebrations lasting from ten to twenty days.

Women took no part in public affairs—with a few notable exceptions. As the bearing of children was both a social duty and a sacred act, midwives enjoyed great respect. The number of midwives at a birth indicated rank: a noblewoman often had two or three midwives. As in the medieval European West, in a very difficult birth midwives sacrificed the life of the child for that of the mother. Mexica society also awarded high status and authority to female physicians and herbalists. They treated men as well as women, setting broken bones and prescribing herbal remedies for a variety of ailments. The sources, though limited, imply that a few women skilled at market trading achieved economic independence. The woman weaver capable of executing complicated designs also had the community's esteem. Prostitutes in the state brothels, not local Mexica but tribute girls from the provinces given to successful warriors as part of their rewards, probably did not enjoy esteem.[20]

Alongside the secular social classes stood the temple priests. Huitzilopochtli and each of the numerous lesser gods had many priests to oversee the upkeep of the temple, assist at religious ceremonies, and perform ritual sacrifices. The priests also did a brisk business in foretelling the future from signs and omens. Aztecs consulted priests on the selection of wives and husbands, on the future careers of newborn babies, and before leaving on journeys or for war. Temples possessed enormous wealth in gold and silver ceremonial vessels, statues, buildings, and land. Fifteen provincial villages had to provide food for the temple at Texcoco and wood for its eternal fires. The priests who had custody of all this property did not marry and were expected to live moral and upright lives. From the temple revenues and resources, the priests supported schools, aided the poor, and maintained hospitals. The chief priests had the ear of the emperor and often exercised great power and influence.

At the peak of the social pyramid stood the emperor. The various Aztec historians contradict one another about the origin of the imperial dynasty, but modern scholars tend to accept the verdict of one sixteenth-century authority that the "custom has always been preserved among the Mexicans (that) the sons of kings have not ruled by right of inheritance, but by election."[21] A small oligarchy of the chief priests, warriors, and state officials made the selection. If none of the sons proved satisfactory, a brother or nephew of the emperor was chosen, but election was always restricted to the royal family.

The Aztec emperor was expected to be a great warrior who had led Mexica and allied armies into battle. All his other duties pertained to the welfare of his people. It was up to the emperor to see that justice was done—he was the final court of appeal. He also held ultimate responsibility for ensuring an adequate food supply. The emperor Montezuma I (r. 1440–1467) distributed twenty thousand loads of stockpiled grain when a flood hit Tenochtitlán. The records show that the Aztec emperors took their public duties seriously.

## Gender, Culture, and Power

In 1519 the council of the newly established port city of Veracruz on the Gulf of Mexico wrote to the emperor Charles V, "In addition to . . . children and men and women being killed and offered in sacrifices, we have learned and have been informed that they (the native peoples of Mexico) are doubtless all sodomites and engage in that abominable sin."[22] The sin the councilors referred to was sexual relations between males. The councilors wanted imperial and papal permission to punish "evil and rebellious natives."

What appalled the Spaniards were the **berdaches,** biological males dressed as women who performed the domestic tasks of women—cooking, cleaning, housekeeping, weaving, and embroidering. Berdaches were not trained in military skills and did not go to war. According to information an Aztec elder provided the Franciscan missionary-ethnographer Bernardino de Sahagûn, evidence that has been confirmed by many other sources, parents chose the gender roles of their male children. When a mother had produced four or five consecutive sons, the next son was dressed in women's clothes and taught to act like a woman. Customarily, men (and boys) did not do women's work. Once made a transvestite, however, a male child played the female role for the rest of his life and never again assumed the dress or conduct of a male. Tribal customs and laws throughout the Americas fully sanctioned this practice.

At about the onset of puberty, the berdache began to serve the sexual needs of the young men of the community. In the Mexica world *caciques* (chieftains or powerful lords), and in the Inca world (see pages 435–441) *oregones* (nobles), used berdaches for their personal pleasure or established them in brothels as prostitutes. In exchange for some service or price, the caciques and oregones supplied the berdaches to their friends and men of their class. The possession of large numbers of women or berdaches enhanced a lord's status and prestige. Berdaches, moreover, were stronger than women and could carry heftier burdens and perform heavier work.

In addition to the peoples of Mexico, Central America, and the Andes, evidence of berdaches survives among many indigenous peoples of North America, including the Timucua tribe of what is now northern Florida, the Mohicans of New York and Connecticut, the Tulelos of Virginia, the Sioux of the Dakotas, and the tribes of the Iroquois Confederacy of upper New York State.

How are we to interpret this phenomenon of socially institutionalized homosexuality among American indigenous peoples? The sources pose a major difficulty. Most information comes to us filtered through sixteenth- and seventeenth-century Iberian and French mentalities. That information, therefore, carries Christian moral and theological values. It also bears Spanish and French political, social, and cultural values. The conquistadors used charges of sodomy as a weapon with which to justify the forcible conquest of New World peoples. Europeans described the native peoples as "barbaric," and they came to Mexico, the Caribbean, and South America, they claimed, "to

**George Catlin: Dance to the Berdache** Determined to study and paint the Indians, Catlin (1796–1872) lived among the Sioux in the Dakota Territory from 1832 to 1836. His paintings not only do not romanticize the Indians but also portray them as individuals and display none of the racist contempt typical of his time. The social role of the berdache shocked him, however, as it had sixteenth-century Spaniards. Observing the dance and sexual activities, Catlin commented that the berdache "is driven to the most servile and degrading duties. . . . This is one of the most disgusting customs I have ever seen in Indian country." The warriors seem to mock the berdache; why, since they have used him sexually? *(National Museum of American Art, Washington, D.C./Art Resource, NY)*

bring civilization" and "to extirpate the evil of sodomitical behavior." Europeans knew of homosexual activity in their own societies (see pages 383–384), but they had never seen the permanent transvestism of the berdaches. Such American practices demonstrated to Europeans the peoples' "barbarism."

At the same time, the Nahuatl-speaking peoples of central and southern Mexico, the Incas of Peru, and the native Americans of North America did not have twentieth-century Western concepts of homosexuals and homosexuality. The Indians did not consider homosexual relations as sin or vice. They made no laws against it. Rather, chieftains used berdaches as instruments of pleasure and symbols of power.[23]

## The Cities of the Aztecs

When the Spanish entered **Tenochtitlán** (which they called Mexico City) in November 1519, they could not believe their eyes. According to Bernal Díaz, one of Cortés's companions,

*when we saw all those cities and villages built in the water, and other great towns on dry land, and that straight and level causeway leading to Mexico, we were astounded. These great towns and cues (temples) and buildings rising from the water, all made of stone, seemed like an enchanted vision. . . . Indeed, some of our soldiers asked whether it was not all a dream.*[24]

**Tenochtitlán** The great Mexican archaeologist Ignacio Marquina designed this reconstruction of the central plaza of the Mexica city as it looked in 1519. The temple precinct, an area about five hundred square yards, contained more than eighty structures, pyramids, pools, and homes of gods and of the men and women who served them. Accustomed to the clutter and filth of Spanish cities, the elegance and cleanliness of Tenochtitlán amazed the Spaniards. *(Enrique Franco-Torrijos)*

Tenochtitlán had about 60,000 households. The upper class practiced polygamy and had many children, and many households included servants and slaves. The total population probably numbered around 250,000. At the time, no European city and few Asian ones could boast a population even half that size. The total Aztec Empire has been estimated at around 5 million inhabitants.

Originally built on salt marshes, Tenochtitlán was approached by four great highways that connected it with the mainland. Bridges stood at intervals (comparable to modern Paris). Stone and adobe walls surrounded the city itself, making it (somewhat like medieval Constantinople; see page 233) highly defensible and capable of resisting a prolonged siege. Wide, straight streets and canals crisscrossed the city. Boats and canoes plied the canals. Lining the roads and canals stood thousands of rectangular one-story houses of mortar faced with stucco. Although space was limited, many small gardens and parks were alive with the colors and scents of flowers. The Mexica loved flowers and used them in ritual ceremonies.

A large aqueduct whose sophisticated engineering astounded Cortés carried pure water from distant springs and supplied fountains in the parks. Streets and canals opened onto public squares and marketplaces. Tradespeople offered every kind of merchandise. Butchers hawked turkeys, ducks, chickens, rabbits, and deer; grocers sold kidney beans, squash, avocados, corn, and all kinds of peppers. Artisans sold intricately designed gold, silver, and feathered jewelry. Seamstresses offered sandals, loincloths and cloaks for men, and blouses and long skirts for women—the clothing customarily worn by ordinary people—and embroidered robes and cloaks for the rich. Slaves for domestic service, wood for building, herbs for seasoning and medicine, honey and sweets, knives, jars, smoking tobacco, even human excrement used to cure animal skins—all these wares made a dazzling spectacle.

At one side of the central square of Tenochtitlán stood the great temple of Huitzilopochtli. Built as a pyramid and approached by three flights of 120 steps each, the temple was about 100 feet high and dominated the city's skyline. According to Cortés, it was "so large that within the precincts, which are surrounded by a very high wall, a town of some five hundred inhabitants could easily be built. All round inside this wall there are very elegant quarters with very large rooms and corridors where their priests live."[25]

Travelers, perhaps inevitably, compare what they see abroad with what is familiar to them at home. Tenochtitlán thoroughly astounded Cortés, and in his letter to the emperor Charles V, he describes the city in comparison to his homeland: "the market square," where 60,000 people a day came to buy and sell, "was twice as big as Salamanca"; the beautifully constructed "towers," as the Spaniards called the pyramids, rose higher "than the cathedral at Seville"; Montezuma's palace was "so marvelous that it seems to me to be impossible to describe its excellence and grandeur[;] . . . in Spain there is nothing to compare with it." Accustomed to the squalor and filth of Spanish cities, the cleanliness of Tenochtitlán dumbfounded the Spaniards, as did all the evidence of its ordered and elegant planning.[26]

Describing the Aztec way of life for the emperor, Cortés concluded, "Considering that they are barbarous and so far from the knowledge of God and cut off from all civilized nations, it is truly remarkable to see what they have achieved in all things."[27] Certainly Cortés's views reflect his own culture and outlook, but it is undeniable that Mexica culture was remarkable.

## THE INCAS OF PERU

In the late 1980s, archaeologists working in the river valleys on the west coast of present-day Peru uncovered stunning evidence of complex societies that flourished between five thousand and three thousand years ago—roughly the same period as the great pyramids of Egypt. In spite of the altitude and dryness of the semidesert region, scores of settlements existed (see Map 14.4). Perhaps the most spectacular was the one at Pampa de las Llamas-Moxeke in the Casma Valley. Stepped pyramids and U-shaped buildings, some more than ten stories high, dominated these settlements. Were these structures cultic temples? places for food storage? centers for such commercial activity that we can call them cities? Why did the inhabitants abandon these settlements and move into the Andean highlands? Scholars have only begun to process these vast remains, but radiocarbon dating has already demonstrated that the settlements are older than the Maya and Aztec structures.[28]

Another archaeological discovery is providing scholars with rich information about pre-Columbian society. For some time, the villagers of Sipán in northern Peru supplemented their meager incomes by plundering ancient cemeteries and pyramids. One night in 1987, while digging deep in a pyramid, they broke into one of the richest funerary chambers ever located, and they filled their sacks with ceramic, gold, and silver objects. A dispute about the distribution of the loot led one dissatisfied thief to go to the police. When archaeologists from Lima and the United States arrived, they ranked the discoveries at Sipán with those at Tutankhamen's tomb in Egypt

**MAP 14.4 The Inca Empire, 1532** South America, which extends 4,750 miles in length and 3,300 miles from east to west at its widest point, contains every climatic zone and probably the richest variety of vegetation on earth. Roads built by the Incas linked most of the Andean region.

and the terra-cotta statues of the Qin Dynasty warriors near Xian, China.

The treasures from the royal tombs at Sipán derive from the Moche civilization, which flourished along a 250-mile stretch of Peru's northern coast between 100 and 800 C.E. Rivers that flowed out of the Andes into the valleys allowed the Moche people to develop complex irrigation systems for agricultural development. Each Moche valley contained a large ceremonial center with palaces and pyramids surrounded by settlements of up to ten thousand people. The dazzling gold and silver artifacts, elaborate headdresses, and ceramic vessels display a remarkable skill in metalwork. Much of later Inca technology seems clearly based on the work of the Moche.[29]

Like the Aztecs, the **Incas** were "a small militaristic group that came to power late, conquered surrounding groups, and established one of the most extraordinary empires in the world."[30] Gradually, Inca culture spread throughout Peru. Modern knowledge of the Incas is concentrated in the last century before Spanish intrusion (1438–1532); today's scholars know far less about earlier developments.

In the center of Peru rise the cold highlands of the Andes. Six valleys of fertile and wooded land at altitudes ranging from eight thousand to eleven thousand feet punctuate highland Peru. The largest of these valleys are the Huaylas, Cuzco, and Titicaca. It was there that Inca civilization developed and flourished.

Archaeologists still do not understand how people of the Andean region acquired a knowledge of agriculture. Around 2500 B.C.E. they were relying on fish and mussels for food. Textiles found in gravesites indicate the cultivation of cotton for ordinary clothing, ceremonial dress, and fishnets. Andean geography—with towering mountains, isolated valleys, and little arable land—posed an almost insurmountable barrier to agriculture. What land there was had to be irrigated, and human beings needed warm clothing to work in the cold climate. They also required a diet that included some meat and fat. Coca (the dried leaves of a plant native to the Andes and from which cocaine is derived), chewed in moderation as a dietary supplement, enhanced their stamina and their ability to withstand the cold.

Around 200 B.C.E. the Andean peoples displayed an enormous burst of creative energy. High-altitude valleys were connected to mountain life and vegetation to form a single interdependent agricultural system called "vertical archipelagoes," capable of supporting large communities. Such vertical archipelagoes often extended more than thirty-seven miles from top to bottom.[31] These terraces were shored up with earthen walls to retain moisture, enabling the production of bumper crops of white potatoes.

Potatoes ordinarily cannot be stored for long periods, but Andean peoples developed a product called *chuñu,* freeze-dried potatoes made by subjecting potatoes alternately to nightly frosts and daily sun. Chuñu will keep unspoiled for several years. The construction of irrigation channels also facilitated the cultivation of corn. Potatoes and corn required far less labor and time than did the cultivation of wheat in Europe or rice in China. By the fifteenth century, enough food was harvested to feed not only the farmers themselves but also massive armies and administrative bureaucracies and thousands of industrial workers.

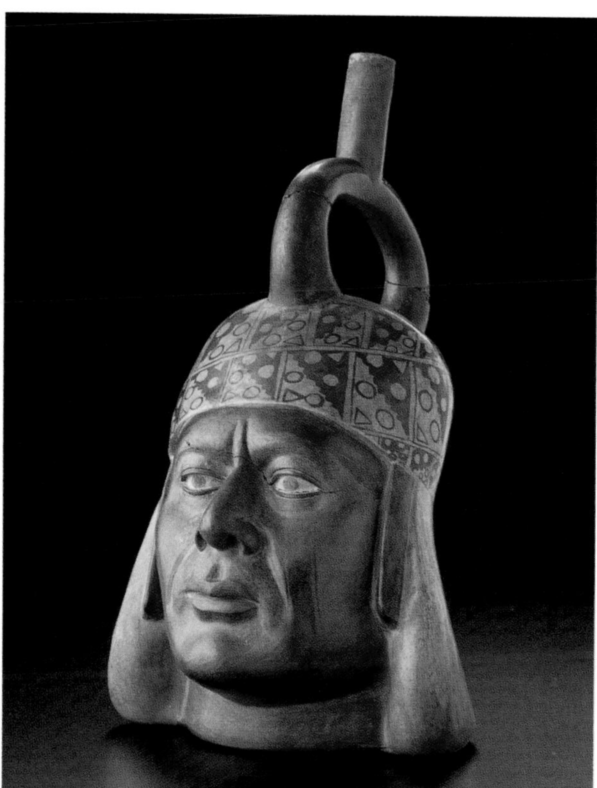

**Portrait Vessel of a Ruler** Artisans of the Moche culture on the northern coast of Peru produced objects representing many aspects of their world, including this flat-bottomed stirrup-spout jar with a ruler's face. The commanding expression conveys a strong sense of power, as does the elaborate headdress with the geometric designs of Moche textiles worn only by elite persons. *(South America, Peru, North Coast, Moche Culture, Portrait Vessel of a Ruler, earthenware with pigmented clay slip, 300–700, 35.6 × 24.1, Kate S. Buckingham Endowment, 1955.2338, ¾ view. Photograph by Robert Hashimoto. Photograph © 1999, The Art Institute of Chicago)*

**Colombian Lime Container** The use of coca in rituals is an ancient tradition in South America. Pieces of coca leaves were placed in the mouth with small amounts of powdered lime made from calcined seashells. The lime helped release the hallucinogens in the coca. This nine-inch gold bottle for holding lime, typical of the rich paraphernalia made in the Quimbaya region of Colombia, shows a seated nude figure with rings in the ears and beads across the forehead and at the neck, wrists, knees, and ankles. A tiny spatula would be used to secure the lime through the bottle's narrow neck. *(The Metropolitan Museum of Art, Jan Mitchell and Sons Collection, Gift of Jan Mitchell, 1991 [1991.419.22]. Photograph © 1992 The Metropolitan Museum of Art)*

## Inca Imperialism

Who were the Incas? *Inca* was originally the name of the governing family of an Amerindian group that settled in the basin of Cuzco (see Map 14.4). From that family, the name was gradually extended to all peoples living in the Andes valleys. The Incas themselves used the word to identify their ruler or emperor. Here the term is used for both the ruler and the people.

As with the Aztecs, so with the Incas: religious ideology was the force that transformed the culture. Religious concepts created pressure for imperialist expansion—with fatal consequences.

The Incas believed their ruler descended from the sun-god and that the health and prosperity of the state depended on him. Dead rulers were thought to link the people to the sun-god. When the ruler died, his corpse was preserved as a mummy in elaborate clothing and housed in a sacred and magnificent chamber. The mummy was brought in procession to all important state ceremonies, his advice was sought in times of crisis, and hundreds of human beings were sacrificed to him. In ordinary times, the dead ruler was carried to visit his friends, and his heirs and relatives came to dine with him. Some scholars call this behavior the "cult of the royal mummies" because it was a kind of ancestor worship.

The mummies were also a powerful dynamic force in Inca society. According to the principle of the "split inheritance," when an Inca ruler died, the imperial office, insignia, and rights and duties of the monarchy passed to the new king. The dead ruler, however, retained full and complete ownership of all his estates and properties. His royal descendants as a group managed his lands and sources of income for him and used the revenues to care for his mummy and to maintain his cult. Thus a new ruler came to the throne land- or property-poor. In order to live in the royal style, strengthen his administration, and reward his supporters, he had to win his own possessions by means of war and imperial expansion.[32]

Around 1000 C.E. the Incas were one of many small groups fighting among themselves for land and water. As they began to conquer their neighbors, a body of religious lore came into being that ascribed divine origin to their earliest king, Manco Capac (ca 1200), and promised warriors the gods' favor and protection. Strong historical evidence, however, dates only from the reign of Pachacuti Inca (1438–1471), who launched the imperialist phase of Inca civilization. (See the feature "Listening to the Past: The Death of Inca Yupanque [Pachacuti Inca] in 1471" on pages 446–447.)

If the cult of ancestor or mummy worship satisfied some Inca social needs, in time it also created serious problems. The desire for conquest provided incentives for courageous (or ambitious) nobles: those who were victorious in battle and gained new territories for the state could expect lands, additional wives, servants, herds of llamas, gold, silver, fine clothes, and other symbols of high status. And even common soldiers who distinguished themselves in battle could be rewarded with booty and raised to noble status. The imperial interests of the emperor paralleled those of other social groups. Thus, under Pachacuti Inca and his successors, Topa Inca (r. 1471–1493) and Huayna Capac (r. 1493–1525), Inca domination was gradually extended by warfare to the frontier of present-day Ecuador and Colombia in the north and to the Maule River in present-day Chile in the south (see Map 14.4), an area of about 350,000 square miles. Eighty provinces, scores of ethnic groups, and 16 million people came under Inca control. A remarkable system of roads held the empire together.

Before Inca civilization, each group that entered the Andes valleys had its own distinct language. These languages were not written and have become extinct. Scholars will probably never understand the linguistic condition of Peru before the fifteenth century when Pachacuti made **Quechua** (pronounced "keshwa") the official language of his people and administration. Conquered peoples were forced to adopt the language, and Quechua spread the Inca way of life throughout the Andes. Though not written until the Spanish in Peru adopted it as a second official language, Quechua had replaced local languages by the seventeenth and eighteenth centuries and is still spoken by most Peruvians today.

Both the Aztecs and the Incas ruled very ethnically diverse peoples. Whereas the Aztecs tended to control their subject peoples through terror, the Incas governed by means of imperial unification. They imposed not only their language but also their entire panoply of gods. Magnificent temples scattered throughout the expanding empire housed idols of these gods. Priests led prayers and elaborate rituals, and on such occasions as a terrible natural disaster or a great military victory, they sacrificed human beings to the gods. Subject peoples were required to worship the state gods. Imperial unification was also achieved through the forced participation of local chieftains in the central bureaucracy and through a policy of colonization called **mitima.** To prevent rebellion in newly conquered territories, Pachacuti transferred all their inhabitants to other parts of the empire, replacing them with workers who had lived longer under Inca rule and whose independent spirit had been broken.[33] An excellent system of roads—averaging three feet in width, some paved and others not—facilitated the transportation of armies and the rapid communication of royal orders by runners. The roads followed straight lines wherever possible but also crossed pontoon bridges and tunneled through hills. This great feat of Inca engineering bears striking comparison with ancient Roman roads, which also linked an empire.

Rapid Inca expansion, however, produced stresses. Although the pressure for growth remained unabated, in the reign of Topa Inca open lands began to be scarce. Topa Inca's attempts to penetrate the tropical Amazon forest east of the Andes led to repeated military disasters. The Incas waged wars with highly trained armies drawn up in massed formation and fought pitched battles on level ground, often engaging in hand-to-hand combat. But in dense jungles, the troops could not maneuver or maintain order against enemies using guerrilla tactics and sniping at them with deadly blowguns. Another source of stress was revolts among subject peoples in conquered territories. It took Huayna Capac several years to put down a revolt in Ecuador. Even the system of roads and trained runners eventually caused administrative prob-

**Machu Picchu** The citadel of Machu Picchu, surrounded by mountains in the clouds, clings to a spectacular crag in upland Peru. It was discovered in 1911 by the young American explorer Hiram Bingham. Its origin and the reason for its abandonment remain unknown. *(W. McIntyre/Photo Researchers, Inc.)*

lems. The average runner could cover about 50 leagues, or 175 miles, per day—a remarkable feat of physical endurance, especially at high altitude—but the larger the empire became, the greater the distances to be covered. The roundtrip from the capital at Cuzco to Quito in Ecuador, for example, took from ten to twelve days, so that an emperor might have to base urgent decisions on incomplete or out-of-date information. The empire was overextended. "In short, the cult of the royal mummies helped to drive the Inca expansion, but it also linked economic stress, administrative problems, and political instabilities in a cyclical relationship."[34]

When the Inca Huayna Capac died in 1525, his throne was bitterly contested by two of his sons, Huascar and Atauhualpa. Inca law called for a dying emperor to assign the throne to his most competent son by his principal wife, who had to be the ruler's full sister. Huascar, unlike Atauhualpa, was the result of such an incestuous union and thus had a legitimate claim to the throne. Atauhualpa, who had fought with Huayna Capac in his last campaign, tried to convince Huascar that their father had divided the kingdom and had given him (Atauhualpa) the northern part. Huascar bitterly rejected his half brother's claim.

When Huascar came to the throne, the problems facing the Inca Empire had become critical: the dead rulers controlled too much of Peru's land and resources. Huascar proposed a radical solution: "Annoyed one day with these dead (his ancestors), [he] said that he ought to order them all buried and take from them all that they had, and that there should not be dead men but living ones, because (the dead) had all that was best in the country."[35]

Although Atauhualpa had the grave liability of being born of a nonincestuous union, to the great nobility responsible for the cult of the royal mummies, Huascar's proposal represented a grave threat to the established order: Huascar intended to insult the mummies who linked the Inca people to the gods, and if his proposals were enacted, the anger of the mummies would ensure a disastrous future. (The nobility did not say the obvious—that if Huascar buried the dead and took their vast properties, the nobles would be deprived of wealth and power.) Not surprisingly, the nobles threw their support behind Atauhualpa.

In the civil war that began in 1532, Atauhualpa's veteran warriors easily defeated Huascar's green recruits. On his way to his coronation at Cuzco, Atauhualpa encountered Pizarro and 168 Spaniards who had recently entered the kingdom. The Spaniards quickly became the real victors in the Inca kingdom (see pages 516–517). The cult of the royal mummies had brought, or at least contributed heavily to, the Inca collapse.

## Inca Society

The **ayllu,** or clan, served as the fundamental social unit of Inca society. All members of the ayllu owed allegiance to the **curacas,** or headman, who conducted relations with outsiders. The ayllu held specific lands, granted it by hamlet or provincial authorities on a long-term basis, and individual families tended to work the same plots for generations. Cooperation in the cultivation of the land and intermarriage among members of the ayllu wove people there into a tight web of connections.

In return for the land, all men had to perform public duties and pay tribute to the authorities. Their duties included building and maintaining palaces, temples, roads, and irrigation systems. Tribute consisted of potatoes, corn, and other vegetables paid to the hamlet head, who in turn paid them to the provincial governor. A draft rotary system called **mita** (turn) determined when men of a particular hamlet performed public works; this responsibility rotated from ward to ward (divisions of the hamlet).

As the Inca Empire expanded, this pattern of social and labor organization was imposed on other, newly conquered indigenous peoples. Regional states had a distinct ethnic identity, and by the time of the Spanish intrusion, the Incas had well-established mechanisms for public labor drafts and tribute collection. Discontent among subject peoples, however, helps to explain the quick fragmentation of imperial authority and the relative swiftness of the Spanish conquest. After the conquest, the Spaniards adopted and utilized the indigenous organization as the basis for Spanish civil and ecclesiastical administration, just as the imperial Incas (and, in Mesoamerica, the Aztecs) had done.[36]

In the fifteenth century, Pachacuti Inca and Topa Inca superimposed imperial institutions on those of kinship. They ordered allegiance to be paid to the ruler at Cuzco rather than to the curacas. They drafted local men for distant wars and relocated the entire populations of certain regions through the mitima system. Entirely new ayllus were formed, based on residence rather than kinship.

The emperors sometimes gave newly acquired lands to victorious generals, distinguished civil servants, and favorite nobles. These lords subsequently exercised authority previously held by the native curacas. Whether long-time residents or new colonists, common people had the status of peasant farmers, which entailed heavy agricultural or other obligations. Just as in medieval Europe peasants worked several days each week on their lord's lands, so the Inca people had to work on state lands (that is, the emperor's lands) or on lands assigned to the temple. Peasants also labored on roads and bridges; terraced and irrigated new arable land; served on construction crews for royal palaces, temples, and public buildings such as fortresses; acted as runners on the post roads; and excavated in the imperial gold, silver, and copper mines. The imperial government annually determined the number of laborers needed for these various undertakings, and each district had to supply an assigned quota. The government also made an ayllu responsible for the state-owned granaries and for the production of cloth for army uniforms.

The state required everyone to marry and even decided when and sometimes whom a person should marry. Men married around the age of twenty, women a little younger. The Incas did not especially prize virginity; premarital sex was common. The marriage ceremony consisted of the joining of hands and the exchange of a pair of sandals. This ritual was followed by a large wedding feast, at which the state presented the bride and groom with two sets of clothing, one for everyday wear and one for festive occasions. If a man or woman did not find a satisfactory mate, the provincial governor selected one for him or her. Travel was forbidden, so couples necessarily came from the same region. Like most warring so-

**Mochica Earring** Elites of the Moche period (ca 100 B.C.E.–500 C.E.) on the northern coast of Peru commissioned vast quantities of jewelry. This gold and turquoise earring depicts a warrior-priest wearing an owl-head necklace, holding a removable war club (right hand) and shield (left hand), and flanked by attendants. Peanuts had recently been domesticated in the area, and the peanut beading around the edge suggests the leader's power over natural fertility in an agriculturally marginal region. The reverse side is of silver. *(Photograph by Susan Einstein, courtesy of UCLA Fowler Museum of Cultural History)*

cieties with high male death rates, the Incas practiced polygamy, though the cost of supporting many wives restricted it largely to the upper classes.

The Incas relied heavily on local authorities and cultural norms for day-to-day matters. In some ways, however, the common people were denied choice and initiative and led regimented lives. The Incas did, however, take care of the poor and aged, distribute grain in times of shortage and famine, and supply assistance in natural disasters. Scholars have debated whether Inca society was socialistic, totalitarian, or a forerunner of the welfare state; it may be merely a matter of definition. Although the Inca economy was strictly regulated, there certainly was not an equal distribution of wealth. Everything above and beyond the masses' basic needs went to the emperor and the nobility.

The backbreaking labor of ordinary people in the fields and mines made possible the luxurious lifestyle of the great Inca nobility. The nobles—called *oregones*, or "big ears," by the Spanish because they pierced their ears and distended the lobes with heavy jewelry—were the ruling Inca's kinsmen. Lesser nobles included the curacas, royal household servants, public officials, and entertainers. As the empire expanded in the fifteenth century, there arose a noble class of warriors, governors, and local officials, whose support the ruling Inca secured with gifts of land, precious metals, and llamas and alpacas (llamas were used as beasts of burden; alpacas were raised for their long fine wool). The nobility was exempt from agricultural work and from other kinds of public service.

## NORTH AMERICA AND THE MOUND BUILDERS

As in South America and Mesoamerica, so in the fifteenth century North America contained hundreds of different societies. Excluding the Inuit people of the Arctic region, anthropologists classify six major cultural areas in North America: the Northwest Coast peoples living along the Pacific coast from southern Alaska to northern California; the Plains peoples inhabiting the region from north of the Canadian border south to Texas and from the Mississippi River west to the Rocky Mountains; the Plateau peoples of the area extending from above the Canadian border through the plateau and mountain region of the Rocky Mountains to the Southwest and including much of California; the Eastern Woodlands peoples inhabiting much of the eastern United States from the Atlantic Ocean to the Mississippi River and including the Great Lakes region; the Northern peoples of the area covering most of Canada; and the Southwest peoples of the region comprising all or parts of the present states of Arizona, New Mexico, Colorado, and Utah. In 1492, between 1 million and 2 million people lived on this vast continent of 9,400,000 square miles (the third largest continent, after Asia and Africa). Some peoples formed sedentary agricultural societies; others led a nomadic existence.

Whereas the agricultural regions of Mesoamerica and South America had dense populations at that time, North America was very sparsely settled, perhaps one person for every square mile. Forests and woodlands covered most of what is now the eastern United States—hence the label "Eastern Woodlands." The peoples of this area lived in villages and practiced agriculture, growing corn, pumpkins, squash, beans, sunflowers, and tobacco. They also hunted wild game and fished in the numerous streams and rivers.

Around 1300 B.C.E., some of these peoples began to build massive earthworks, mounds of earth and stone. The mounds differed in shape, size, and purpose: some

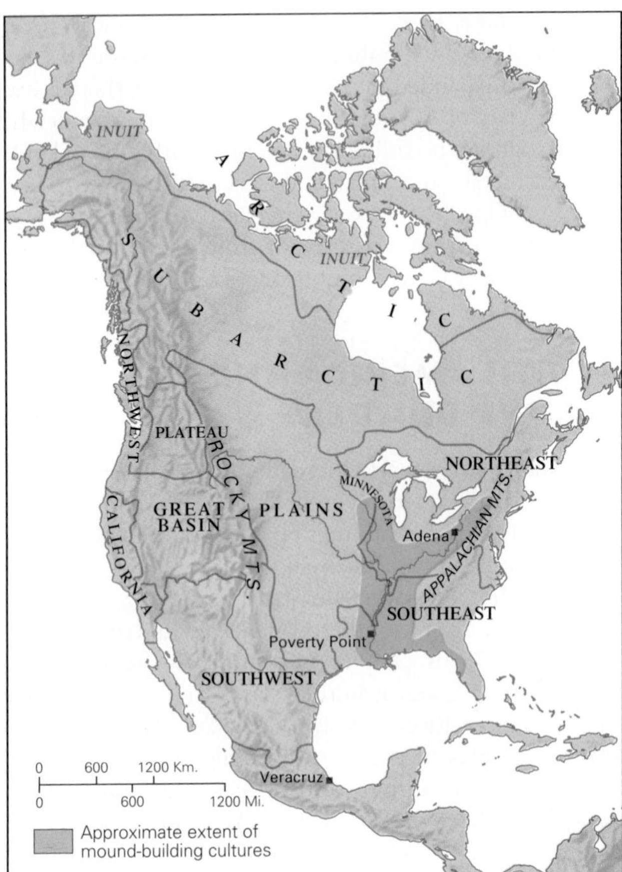


**MAP 14.5 The Mound-Building Cultures** Mound-building peoples, while concentrated in the Ohio Valley, had extensive trading contacts with peoples in the Great Plains, the Northeast, the Southeast, and the Caribbean regions.

were conical, others elongated or wall-like, others pyramidical, and still others, called effigy mounds, in serpentine, bird, or animal form. The Ohio and Mississippi Valleys contain the richest concentration of mounds, but they have been found from the Great Lakes down to the Gulf of Mexico (see Map 14.5). The earliest mound, at Poverty Point, Louisiana, dates from about 1300 B.C.E. and consists of six octagonal ramparts, one within the other, that measure 6 feet high and more than 400 yards across. It seems to belong more to the Olmec culture of Veracruz (see page 419) than to North America and may have served as a defensive fortress. Another mound, near the town of Adena, Ohio, was probably built between 600 B.C.E. and 200 C.E. It is serpentine in shape, 1,254 feet long and 20 feet wide; hence it is called the Great Serpent Mound.

At Cahokia, near East St. Louis, Illinois, archaeologists have uncovered the largest mound of all. Begun about 1050 C.E. and completed about 1250 C.E., the complex at Cahokia covered 5½ square miles and was the ceremonial center for perhaps 38,000 people. A fence of wooden posts surrounded the core. More than 500 rectangular mounds or houses, inside and outside the fence, served as tombs and as the bases for temples and palaces. Within the fence, the largest mound rose in four stages to a height of 100 feet. At its top, a small conical platform supported a wooden fence and a rectangular temple. The mounds at Cahokia represent the culture of the Mississippian **mound builders.**

What do the mounds tell us about the societies of these indigenous peoples? All of our evidence derives from the mounds and their contents. The largest mounds served as burial chambers for chieftains and, in many cases, the women and retainers who were sacrificed in order to assist the chief in the afterlife. Mounds also contain valuable artifacts, such as jewelry made from copper from Michigan, mica (a mineral used in building) from the Appalachians, obsidian from the Rocky Mountains, conch shells from the Caribbean, and pipestone from Minnesota.

From these burial items, archaeologists have deduced that mound culture was hierarchial, governed by a chieftain. The chief had religious responsibilities, such as managing long-distance trade and gift-giving. As with the Chinese, the exchange of goods was not perceived as a form of commerce, but as a means of showing respect and of establishing bonds among diverse groups. Chiefs governed large towns of several thousand inhabitants. The towns served as political and ceremonial centers, and they controlled surrounding villages of a few hundred people. Burial items suggest trade over a wide area of central North America; since the indigenous peoples lacked the wheel and pack animals, such as horses, goods must have been transported by canoe or by human porters.

Pottery in the form of bowls, jars, bottles, and effigy pipes in various shapes best reveals Mississippian peoples' art. Designs showing eagles, plumed serpents, warriors decapitating victims, and ceremonially ornamented priests suggest a strong Mexican influence. The symbolism of Mississippian art deals so strongly with death that scholars speak of a "Death Cult" or a "Vulture Cult."[37]

Cahokia mound culture reached its peak before 1300 C.E. When the first white men uncovered the mounds, they had long been deserted. Why? Crop failure? overpopulation? war, as the fence around Cahokia implies? Additional research of archaeologists may answer these questions.

**Great Serpent Mound, Adams County, Ohio** This 1,254-foot-long Adena mound in the form of a writhing snake has its "head" at the highest point, suggesting an open mouth ready to swallow a huge egg formed by a heap of stones. *(Georg Gerster/Photo Researchers, Inc.)*

**Two-Faced Pipe Bowl** Also called a calumet, the peace pipe was a sacred object to Amerindians. Important in all religious, war, and peace ceremonies, pipes were made from a red stone taken from the Pipestone quarry in southwestern Minnesota. The material was also named catlinite for the Philadelphia traveler and artist George Catlin (see page 433). The bowl of this beautiful pipe contains two human faces, one facing the smoker, the other on the back of the bowl. The carver, Running Cloud, gave it to a Dr. Jarvis in payment for some medical service in the 1830s. *(United States, Plains; Sioux [Sisseton], early 19th century, catlinite or red pipestone, lead inlay, 5¼ [13.3] long. Brooklyn Museum of Art, Frank Sherman Benson Fund and the Henry L. Batterman Fund, 50.67.104)*

## SUMMARY

Several strong Amerindian civilizations flourished in the Western Hemisphere in the years between 300 B.C.E. and 1500 C.E. The Maya are justly renowned for their art and their accomplishments in abstract thought, especially mathematics. The Aztecs built a unified culture based heavily on the Toltec heritage and distinguished by achievements in engineering, sculpture, and architecture. The Incas revealed a genius for organization, and their state was virtually unique in its time for assuming responsibility for all its people. In both the Mexica and the Inca societies, religious ideology shaped other facets of the culture. The Mexica cult of war and human sacrifice and the Inca cult of the royal mummies posed serious dilemmas and contributed to the weakening of those societies.

Inca culture did not die with the Spaniard Pizarro's strangulation of Atauhualpa (see page 517). In May 1536 his successor, Inca Mancu Yupanque, led a massive revolt against the Spanish and then led his people to Machu Picchu deep in the Valcahamba range of the Andes. Inca military resistance to Spanish domination continued throughout the sixteenth to eighteenth centuries. In 1780 Jose Gabriel Kunturkanki, a highly educated businessman and landowner, proclaimed himself Inca Tupac Amaru II and launched a native independence movement that the Spanish put down with the greatest difficulty.

Between about 1300 B.C.E. and 1300 C.E., in the region extending from the Great Lakes south to the Gulf of Mexico, and from the Atlantic Ocean west to the Mississippi River, people erected large earthworks reflecting complex societies. Some of these mounds served as burial tombs for their leaders; others functioned as defensive fortresses. The mound builders were not isolated. Artifacts suggest that they had cultural contacts with the Olmecs and Mexica of Mesoamerica, as well as with peoples throughout central North America.

## KEY TERMS

| | |
|---|---|
| Indian | maceualtin |
| Mesoamerica | berdaches |
| Olmec | Tenochtitlán |
| Teotihuacán | Incas |
| Toltecs | Quechua |
| Mexica | mitima |
| Aztec | ayllu |
| Nahuatl | curacas |
| Huitzilopochtli | mita |
| tecuhtli | mound builders |

## NOTES

1. See J. Lockhart and S. B. Schwartz, *Early Latin America: A History of Colonial Spanish America and Brazil* (Cambridge: Cambridge University Press, 1983), pp. 31–33; M. A. Burkholder and L. Johnson, *Colonial Latin America* (New York: Oxford University Press, 1998), pp. 1–5.
2. Lockhart and Schwartz, *Early Latin America,* pp. 33–49.
3. F. Braudel, *The Structures of Everyday Life: Civilization and Capitalism, 15th–18th Century,* vol. 1, trans. S. Reynolds (New York: Harper & Row, 1981), pp. 160–161.
4. R. A. Diehl and M. A. Coe, "Olmec Archeology," in *The Olmec World: Ritual and Rulership* (Princeton, N.J.: Princeton University Press, 1996), pp. 11–25.
5. D. Webster, *The Fall of the Ancient Maya: Solving the Mystery of the Maya Collapse* (New York: Thames & Hudson, 2002), pp. 98–99. The same scholar's article "Ancient Maya Warfare," in *War and Society in the Ancient and Medieval Worlds: Asia, the Mediterranean, and Mesoamerica,* eds. K. Raaflaub and N. Rosenstein (Cambridge, Mass.: Harvard University Press, 1999), pp. 333–360, argues that the Maya went to war frequently and that warfare was an essential ingredient of their society.
6. L. Schele and M. E. Miller, *The Blood of Kings: Dynasty and Ritual in Maya Art* (New York: Braziller, 1986), pp. 14–15, passim.
7. Webster, *The Fall of the Ancient Maya,* pp. 327–347.
8. G. W. Conrad and A. A. Demarest, *Religion and Empire: The Dynamics of Aztec and Inca Expansionism* (New York: Cambridge University Press, 1993), p. 71.
9. R. Hassig, "The Aztec World," in *War and Society in the Ancient and Medieval Worlds: Asia, the Mediterranean, and Mesoamerica,* eds. K. Raaflaub and N. Rosenstein (Cambridge, Mass.: Harvard University Press, 1999), pp. 375–377.
10. Ibid., pp. 377–378.
11. J. Soustelle, *Daily Life of the Aztecs on the Eve of the Spanish Conquest,* trans. P. O'Brian (Stanford, Calif.: Stanford University Press, 1970), p. 97.
12. M. Harris, *Cannibals and Kings* (New York: Random House, 1977), pp. 99–110; the quotation is from p. 106.
13. Ibid., pp. 109–110.
14. R. Padden, *The Hummingbird and the Hawk* (Columbus: Ohio State University Press, 1967), pp. 76–99.
15. I. Clendinnen, *Aztecs: An Interpretation* (New York: Cambridge University Press, 1992), pp. 88–115.
16. Conrad and Demarest, *Religion and Empire,* p. 49.
17. Ibid., p. 57.
18. Ibid., pp. 66–70.
19. Soustelle, *Daily Life of the Aztecs,* p. 74.
20. Clendinnen, *Aztecs,* pp. 153–173.
21. Quoted in Soustelle, *Daily Life of the Aztecs,* p. 89.
22. Quoted in R. Trexler, *Sex and Conquest: Gendered Violence, Political Order, and the European Conquest of the Americas* (Ithaca, N.Y.: Cornell University Press, 1995), p. 1. This section leans on Trexler's important and provocative study.
23. Ibid., Chaps. 1, 4, 5, and passim.
24. B. Díaz, *The Conquest of New Spain,* trans. J. M. Cohen (New York: Penguin Books, 1978), p. 214.
25. Quoted in J. H. Perry, *The Discovery of South America* (New York: Taplinger, 1979), pp. 161–163.
26. Quoted in Clendinnen, *Aztecs,* pp. 16–17.
27. Quoted in Perry, *The Discovery of South America,* p. 163.

28. William K. Stevens, "Andean Culture Found to Be as Old as the Great Pyramids," *New York Times*, October 3, 1989, p. C1.
29. John Noble Wilford, "Lost Civilization Yields Its Riches as Thieves Fall Out," *New York Times*, July 29, 1994, pp. C1, C28.
30. J. A. Mason, *The Ancient Civilizations of Peru* (New York: Penguin Books, 1978), p. 108.
31. W. Sullivan, *The Secret of the Incas: Myth, Astronomy, and the War Against Time* (New York: Crown Publishers, 1996), pp. 22–24.
32. Conrad and Demarest, *Religion and Empire*, pp. 91–94.
33. Mason, *The Ancient Civilizations of Peru*, p. 123.
34. Ibid., p. 132.
35. Ibid., p. 136.
36. Lockhart and Schwartz, *Early Latin America*, pp. 37–48.
37. See M. Stokstad, *Art History* (New York: Prentice Hall and H. N. Abrams, 1995), pp. 444, 460–462; Paul Carlson, *The Plains Indians* (College Station: Texas A&M Press, 1998), pp. 25–27.


## SUGGESTED READING

The titles by Clendinnen, Diehl and Coe, Conrad and Demarest, Hassig, Lockhart and Schwartz, Schele and Miller, Sullivan, Trexler, and Webster cited in the Notes represent some of the most exciting research on pre-Columbian Mesoamerican and Andean societies. For the Maya, students should also see D. Freidel, *A Forest of Kings: The Untold Story of the Ancient Maya* (1990), a splendidly illustrated work providing expert treatment of many facets of the Maya world; R. Wright, *Time Among the Mayas* (1989), which gives a highly readable account of Maya agricultural and religious calendars; M. D. Coe, *The Maya*, 4th ed. (1987), a sound and well-illustrated survey; the same scholar's *Breaking the Maya Code* (1992); and R. J. Sharer, *Daily Life in Maya Civilization* (1996).

For the gradually expanding literature on the Aztecs, see J. Lockhart, *The Nahuas After the Conquest: A Social and Cultural History of the Indians of Central America, Sixteenth Through Eighteenth Centuries* (1992), and the same author's edition and translation of *We People Here: Nahuatl Accounts of the Conquest of Mexico* (1993). R. F. Townsend, *The Aztecs* (1992), discusses the various classes of Mexica society, as well as expansion, education, and religious ritual in a clearly illustrated study. M. León-Portilla, *The Aztec Image of Self and Society: An Introduction to Nahua Culture* (1992), is perhaps the best appreciation of Aztec religious ritual and symbolism. For warfare, R. Hassig, *Aztec Warfare: Imperial Expansion and Political Control* (1988), is probably the standard work.

J. de Batanzos, *Narrative of the Incas*, trans. and ed. R. Hamilton and D. Buchanan (1996), is an invaluable source for the Incas; it was written by a Spaniard married to an Inca princess, offers fascinating information about Inca customs, and reflects a female oral tradition. W. Sullivan, *The Secret of the Incas: Myth, Astronomy, and the War Against Time* (1996), explains the role of myth and astronomy in the rise and fall of the Inca Empire. For a fine survey of the best literature on preconquest Andean civilization, see B. Larson, "Andean Communities, Political Cultures, and Markets: The Changing Contours of a Field," in *Ethnicity, Markets, and Migration in the Andes: At the Crossroads of History and Anthropology*, ed. B. Larson and O. Harris (1995).

Students wanting to explore aspects of the entire hemisphere before the arrival of Columbus might begin with J. E. Kicza, "The People and Civilizations of the Americas Before Contact," in *Essays in Global and Comparative History*, ed. M. Adas (1998); J. E. Kicza, "Introduction," in *The Indian in Latin American History: Resistance, Resilience, and Acculturation* (1993); B. Fagan, *Kingdoms of Gold, Kingdoms of Jade* (1991), a fine work in comparative anthropology; and *America in 1492*, ed. A. M. Josephy (1992), an interesting collection of essays, many written by leading scholars. For the impact of the Spanish on Mesoamerican peoples, see I. Clendinnen, *Ambivalent Conquests: Maya and Spanish in Yucatan, 1517–1570* (1987), a profoundly sensitive, learned, and important study; R. Wright, *Stolen Continents: The Americas Through Indian Eyes Since 1492* (1992), which emphasizes the persistence and survival of native American cultures and peoples; and *In the Wake of Contact: Biological Responses to Conquest*, ed. C. S. Larsen and G. Milner (1994), a useful collection of articles dealing with many parts of the world.

The following older studies may also prove helpful for particular topics: S. Masuda, I. Shimada, and C. Morris, eds., *Andean Ecology and Civilization* (1985), and E. R. Wolfe, ed., *The Valley of Mexico: Studies in Pre-Hispanic Ecology and Society* (1976), are important for environmental research; L. Baudin, *A Socialist Empire: The Incas of Peru* (1961), gives a provocative interpretation of the Incas; V. W. Van Hagen, *Realm of the Incas* (1961), offers a popular account; F. Katz, *The Ancient American Civilisations* (1972), is a standard anthropological work that surveys all the major Mesoamerican cultures; and T. Todorov, *The Conquest of America*, trans. R. Howard (1984), is an important but difficult study of cross-cultural perceptions.

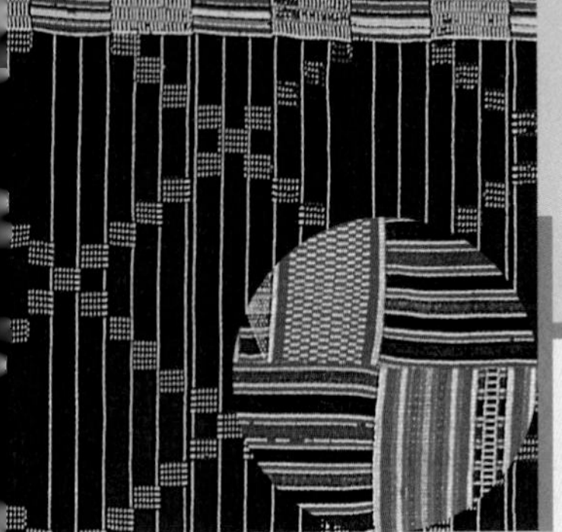

# LISTENING TO THE PAST

## The Death of Inca Yupanque (Pachacuti Inca) in 1471

*In 1551 the Spaniard Juan de Betanzos began to write* Narrative of the Incas. *Although Betanzos had only the Spanish equivalent of a grade school education when he arrived in Peru, and although he lacked dictionaries and grammar books, he had two powerful assets. First, he learned Quechua and earned a reputation for being the best interpreter and translator in postconquest Peru. Second, Betanzos had married Angelina Yupanque, an Inca princess (her Inca name was Cuxirimay Ocllo) who was the widow of Atauhualpa and who also had been Pizarro's mistress. Through her, Betanzos gained immediate and firsthand access to the Inca oral tradition. When he finished his book six years later, modern scholars believe he had produced "the most authentic chronicle that we have."*

Narrative of the Incas *provides a mine of information about Inca customs and social history. There is so much description of marriage, childbirth, weaning, coming-of-age ceremonies, and death that the work shows a strong female experience, undoubtedly the influence of Betanzos's wife. Here is his account of the death of Inca Yupanque (Pachacuti Inca) in 1471.*

Since there were instructions for the idolatries and activities that you have heard about, Inca Yupanque ordered that immediately after he died these activities and sacrifices should be done. In addition, as soon as this was done, word should be sent to all the land, and from all the provinces and towns they should bring again all that was necessary for the service of the new lord, including gold, silver, livestock, clothing, and the rest of the things needed to replenish all the storehouses that, because of his death, had been emptied for the sacrifices and things he ordered to be done, and it should be so abundant because he realized that the state of the one who was thus Inca was growing greater.

While Inca Yupanque was talking and ordering what was to be done after he died, he raised his voice in a song that is still sung today in his memory by those of his generation. This song went as follows: "Since I bloomed like the flower of the garden, up to now I have given order and justice in this life and world as long as my strength lasted. Now I have turned into earth." Saying these words of his song, Inca Yupanque Pachacuti expired, leaving in all the land justice and order, as already stated. And his people were well supplied with idols, idolatries, and activities. After he was dead, he was taken to a town named Patallacta, where he had ordered some houses built in which his body was to be entombed. He was buried by putting his body in the earth in a large new clay urn, with him very well dressed. Inca Yupanque ordered that a golden image made to resemble him be placed on top of his tomb. And it was to be worshiped in place of him by the people who went there. Soon it was placed there. He ordered that a statue be made of his fingernails and hair that had been cut in his lifetime. It was made in that town where his body was kept. They very ceremoniously brought this statue on a litter to the city of Cuzco for the fiestas in the city. This statue was placed in the houses of Topa Inca Yupanque. When there were fiestas in the city, they brought it out for them with the rest of the statues. What is more laughable about this lord Inca Yupanque is that, when he wanted to make some idol, he entered the house of the Sun and acted as though the Sun spoke to him, and he himself answered the Sun to make his people believe that the Sun ordered him to make those idols and *guacas** and so that they would worship them as such.

When the statue was in the city, Topa Inca Yupanque ordered those of his own lineage to bring this statue out for the feasts that were held in Cuzco. When they brought it out like this, they sang about the things that the Inca did in his life, both in the wars and in his city. Thus they served and revered him, changing its garments as he used to do, and serving it as he was served when he was alive. All of which was done thus.

This statue, along with the gold image that was on top of his tomb, was taken by Manco Inca from the city when he revolted. On the advice that Doña Angelina Yupanque gave to the Marquis Don Francisco Pizarro, he got it and the rest of the wealth with it. Only the body is in Patallacta at this time, and judging by it, in his lifetime he seems to have been a tall man. They say that he died at the age of one hundred twenty years. After his father's death, Topa Inca Yupanque ordered that none of the descendants of his father, Inca Yupanque, were to settle the area beyond the rivers of Cuzco. From that time until today the descendants of Inca Yupanque were called *Capacaillo Ynga Yupangue haguaynin,* which means "lineage of kings," "descendants and grandchildren of Inca Yupanque." These are the most highly regarded of all the lineages of Cuzco. These are the ones who were ordered to wear two feathers on their heads.

As time passed, this generation of *orejones* [*oregones*]† multiplied. There were and are today many who became heads of families and renowned as firstborn. Because they married women who were not of their lineage, they took a variety of family names. Seeing this, those of Inca Yupanque ordered that those who had mixed with other people's blood should take new family names and extra names so that those of his lineage could clearly be called *Capacaillo* and descendants of Inca Yupanque. When the Spaniards came, all of this diminished, to the point where they all say they are from that lineage.

* Any object, place, or person worshiped as a deity.
† Nobles.

Revered as a great conqueror and lawgiver, Pachacuti Inca here wears the sacred fringed headband symbolizing his royal authority, and the large earrings of the *oregones,* the nobility. *(Pachacuti Inca, from* Nueva Coronica & Buen Gobierno, *by Guaman Poma de Ayala. Courtesy, Institut d'Ethnologie, Paris. © Musée de l'Homme)*

## QUESTIONS FOR ANALYSIS

1. How does this account of the Inca's death and burial relate to the "cult of the royal mummies" described on page 438?
2. Does Juan de Betanzos show any sign of disapproval, contempt, or "cultural limitation" for Inca funeral practices?

*Source: Narrative of the Incas by Juan de Betanzos,* trans. and ed. Roland Hamilton and Dana Buchanan from the Palma de Mallorca manuscript (Austin: University of Texas Press, 1996), pp. 138–139. Copyright © 1996. Used by permission of the University of Texas Press.

Josse Lieferinxe, *Pilgrims in a Sanctuary.* Christians, especially those who were ill or handicapped, flocked to the shrines of saints in hopes of a cure. *(Scala/Art Resource, NY)*

CHAPTER

# 15 EUROPE IN THE RENAISSANCE AND REFORMATION

## CHAPTER OUTLINE

- Economic and Political Origins of the Italian Renaissance
- Intellectual Hallmarks of the Renaissance
- Social Change During the Renaissance
- Politics and the State in the Renaissance (ca 1450–1521)
- The Condition of the Church (ca 1400–1517)
- Martin Luther and the Birth of Protestantism
- The Growth of the Protestant Reformation
- The Catholic Reformation and the Counter-Reformation
- Politics, Religion, and War
- Changing Attitudes
- Literature, Art, and Music

While the Four Horsemen of the Apocalypse were carrying war, plague, famine, and death across the continent of Europe, a new culture was emerging in southern Europe. The fourteenth century witnessed the beginnings of remarkable changes in many aspects of Italian society. In the fifteenth century, these phenomena spread beyond Italy and gradually influenced society in northern Europe. These cultural changes have collectively been labeled the Renaissance. Cultural change led to religious reform.

The idea of reform is as old as Christianity itself: the need for reform of the individual Christian and of the institutional church is central to the Christian faith. Christian thinkers of the late fifteenth and early sixteenth centuries called for reform of the church on the pattern of the early church, primarily through educational and social change. These cries for reformation were not new. Men and women of every period believed the early Christian church represented a golden age. What was new were the criticisms of educated laypeople whose religious needs were not being met. In the sixteenth century, demands for religious reform became so strong that they became enmeshed with social, political, and economic factors.

- What does the term *Renaissance* mean?
- How did the Renaissance manifest itself in politics, government, art, and social organization?
- Why did the theological ideas of Martin Luther trigger political, social, and economic reactions?
- What response did the Catholic church make to the movements for reform?

This chapter will explore these questions.

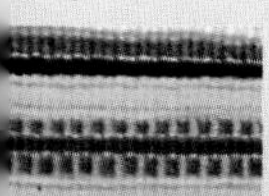

## ECONOMIC AND POLITICAL ORIGINS OF THE ITALIAN RENAISSANCE

The period extending roughly from 1050 to 1300 witnessed phenomenal commercial and financial development, the growing political power of self-governing cities in northern Italy, and great population expansion. The period from the late thirteenth to the late sixteenth century was characterized by an amazing flowering of artistic energies.[1] Scholars commonly use the term **Renaissance** to describe the cultural achievements of the fourteenth through sixteenth centuries. Those achievements rested on the economic and political developments of earlier centuries.

In the great commercial revival of the eleventh century, northern Italian cities led the way. By the middle of the twelfth century, Venice, supported by a huge merchant marine, had grown enormously rich from overseas trade. It profited tremendously from the diversion of the Fourth Crusade to Constantinople (see page 375). Genoa and Milan enjoyed the benefits of a large volume of trade with the Middle East and northern Europe. These cities fully exploited their geographical positions as natural crossroads for mercantile exchange between East and West.

**A Bank Scene, Florence** Originally a "bank" was just a counter; if covered with a carpet like this Ottoman geometric rug with a kufic border, it became a bank of distinction. Money-changers who sat behind the counter became "bankers," exchanging different currencies and holding deposits for merchants and business people. *(Prato, San Francesco/Scala/Art Resource, NY)*

Florence too possessed enormous wealth despite geographical constraints. It was an inland city without easy access to water transportation. But toward the end of the thirteenth century, Florentine merchants and bankers acquired control of papal banking. From their position as tax collectors for the papacy, Florentine mercantile families began to dominate European banking on both sides of the Alps. The profits from loans, investments, and money exchanges that poured back to Florence were pumped into urban industries, such as the Florentine wool industry, which was the major factor in the city's financial expansion and population increase.

In the course of the twelfth century, Milan, Florence, Genoa, Siena, and Pisa fought for and won political and economic independence from surrounding feudal nobles. The nobles, attracted by the opportunities for long-distance and maritime trade, the rising value of urban real estate, the new public offices available in the expanding cities, and the chances for advantageous marriages into rich commercial families, frequently settled within the cities. Marriage vows often sealed business contracts between the rural nobility and the mercantile aristocracy. This merger of the northern Italian feudal nobility and the commercial aristocracy brought into being a new social class—an urban nobility.

This new class made citizenship and political participation in the city-states dependent on a property qualification, years of residence within the city, and social connections. Only a tiny percentage of the male population possessed these qualifications. A new group, called the **pòpolo,** disenfranchised and heavily taxed, bitterly resented its exclusion from power. Throughout most of the thirteenth century, in city after city, the pòpolo used armed force and violence to take over the city governments. Members of the pòpolo could not establish civil order within their cities, however. Consequently, these movements for republican government—government in which political power theoretically resides in the people and is exercised by their chosen representatives—failed. By the year 1300, *signori* (despots, or one-man rulers) or *oligarchies* (the rule of merchant aristocracies) had triumphed everywhere.[2]

Thus in 1422 Venice had a population of 84,000, but 200 men held all the power; Florence had about 40,000 people, but 600 men ruled. Oligarchic regimes maintained only a façade of republican government. Nostalgia for the Roman form of government, combined with calculating shrewdness, prompted the leaders of Venice, Milan, and Florence to use the old forms.

In the fifteenth century, political power and elite culture centered at the princely courts of despots and oligarchs. "A

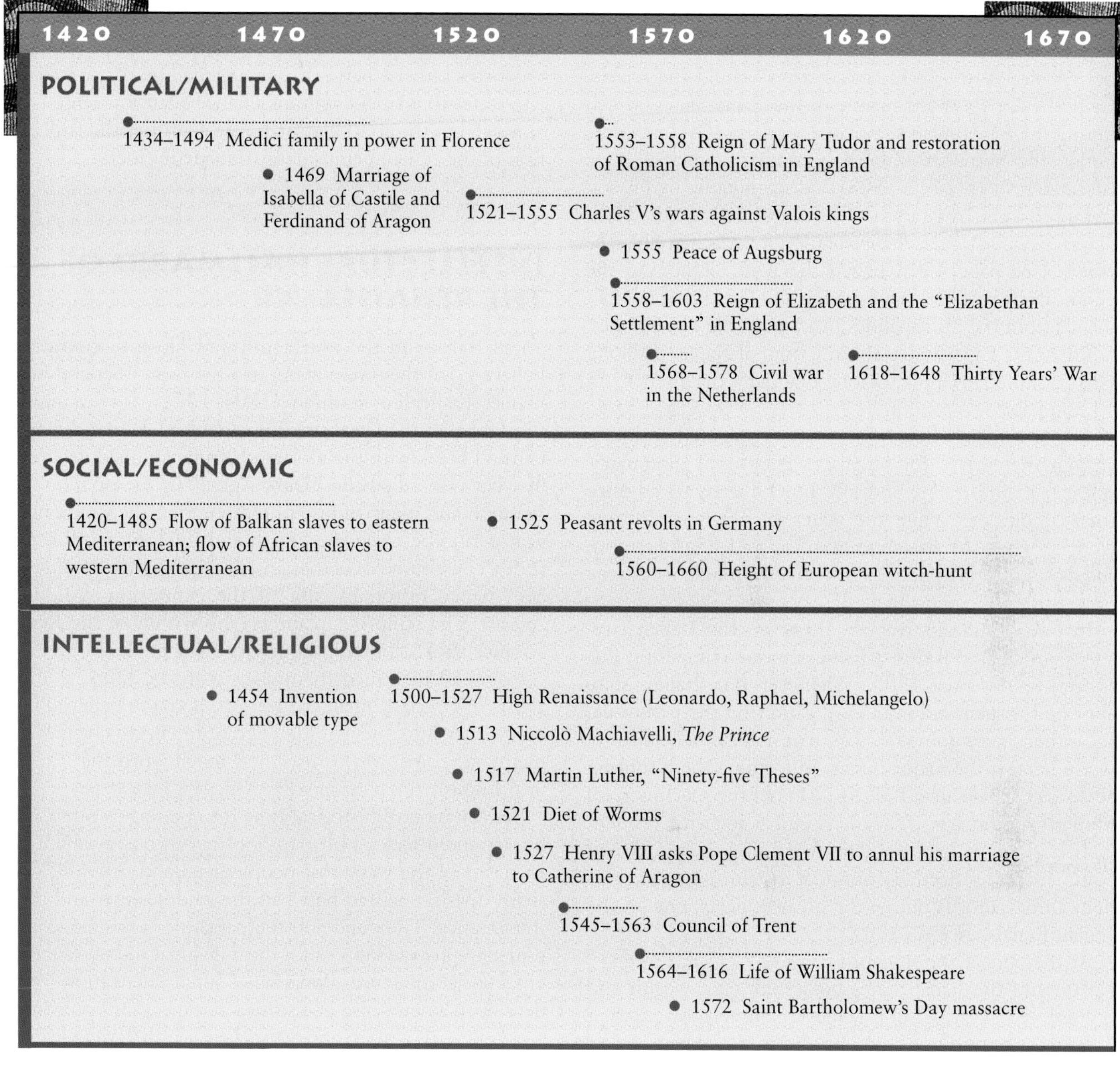


court was the space and personnel around a prince as he made laws, received ambassadors, made appointments, took his meals, and proceeded through the streets."[3] The princely court afforded the despots or oligarchs the opportunity to display and assert their wealth and power. They flaunted their patronage of learning and the arts by munificent gifts to writers, philosophers, and artists, and they promoted occasions for magnificent pageantry and elaborate ritual—all designed to assert their wealth and power. The rulers of the city-states governed as monarchs. They crushed urban revolts, levied taxes, and killed their enemies. And they used massive building programs to employ, and the arts to overawe, the masses.

In the fifteenth century, five powers dominated the Italian peninsula: Venice, Milan, Florence, the Papal States, and the kingdom of Naples. Venice had a sophisticated constitution and was a republic in name, but an oligarchy of merchant-aristocrats actually ran the city. Milan was also called a republic, but despots of the Sforza family ruled harshly and dominated the smaller cities of the north. Likewise in Florence the form of government was republican, but between 1434 and 1494 power in Florence was held by the great Medici banking family. Though not public officers, Cosimo de' Medici (1434–1464) and Lorenzo de' Medici (1469–1492) ruled from behind the scenes. Central Italy consisted mainly of the Papal States, which during the Babylonian Captivity (see page 404) had come under the sway of important Roman families. Pope Alexander VI (r. 1492–1503), aided militarily by his son Cesare Borgia, reasserted papal authority in the Papal States. Cesare Borgia, the inspiration for Machiavelli's *The Prince* (see page 459), began the work of uniting the peninsula by ruthlessly conquering and exacting total obedience from the principalities making up the Papal States. South of the Papal States, the kingdom of Naples had long been disputed by the Aragonese and by the French. In 1435 it passed to Aragon.

The five major Italian city-states competed furiously among themselves for territory. They used diplomacy, spies, paid informers, and any other means to advance their ambitions. While the states of northern Europe were moving toward centralization and consolidation, the world of Italian politics resembled a jungle where the powerful dominated the weak.

In one significant respect, however, the Italian city-states anticipated future relations among competing European states after 1500. Whenever one Italian state appeared to gain a dominant position on the peninsula, the other states joined forces to establish a *balance of power* against the major threat. In forming these shifting alliances, Renaissance Italians invented the machinery of modern diplomacy: permanent embassies with resident ambassadors in capitals where political relations and commercial ties needed continual monitoring. The resident ambassador is one of the great achievements of the Italian Renaissance.

At the end of the fifteenth century, Venice, Florence, Milan, and the Papal States possessed great wealth and represented high cultural achievement. However, their imperialistic ambitions at one another's expense, and their resulting inability to form a common alliance against potential foreign enemies, made Italy an inviting target for invasion. When Florence and Naples entered into an agreement to acquire Milanese territories, Milan called on France for support.

The invasion of Italy in 1494 by the French king Charles VIII (r. 1483–1498) inaugurated a new period in Italian and European power politics. Italy became the focus of international ambitions and the battleground of foreign armies. Charles swept the peninsula with little opposition.

In the sixteenth century, the political and social life of Italy was upset by the relentless competition for dominance between France and the Holy Roman Empire. The Italian cities suffered severely from the continual warfare, especially in the frightful sack of Rome in 1527 by imperial forces under Charles V. Thus the failure of the Italian city-states to form a common alliance against foreign enemies led to the continuation of the centuries-old subjection of the Italian peninsula by outside invaders.

## INTELLECTUAL HALLMARKS OF THE RENAISSANCE

Some Italians in the fourteenth and fifteenth centuries believed that they were living in a new era. Poet and humanist Francesco Petrarch (1304–1374), for example, thought that the Germanic invasions had caused a sharp cultural break with the glories of Rome and had ushered in what was called the "Dark Ages." In the opinion of Petrarch and many of his contemporaries, the thousand-year period between the fourth and the fourteenth centuries constituted a barbarian (or Gothic) or "middle" age (hence historians' use of the expression "Middle Ages"). The sculptors, painters, and writers of the Renaissance spoke contemptuously of their medieval predecessors and identified themselves with the thinkers and artists of Greco-Roman civilization. Petrarch believed he was witnessing a new golden age of intellectual achievement—a rebirth, or, to use the French word that came into English, a *renaissance.*

The division of historical time into periods is often arbitrary and done by historians for their own convenience. In terms of the way most people lived and thought, no sharp division existed between the Middle Ages and the Renaissance. The guild and the parish, for example, continued to provide support for the individual and to exercise great social influence. Renaissance intellectuals, however, developed a new sense of historical distance, and some important poets, writers, and artists believed they were living in a new age.

The Renaissance also manifested itself in new attitudes toward individuals, learning, and the world at large. There was a renewal of belief in the importance of the individual, a rebirth of interest in the Latin classics and in antique lifestyles, and a restoration of interest in the material world.

### Individualism

Though the Middle Ages had seen the appearance of remarkable individuals, recognition of such persons was limited. Christian humility discouraged self-absorption.

In the fourteenth and fifteenth centuries, however, a large literature presenting a distinctly Renaissance individualism emerged.

Many distinctive individuals gloried in their uniqueness. Italians of unusual abilities were self-consciously aware of their singularity and unafraid to be different from their neighbors; they had enormous confidence in their ability to achieve great things. The Florentine goldsmith and sculptor Benvenuto Cellini (1500–1574) prefaced his *Autobiography* with a sonnet that declares:

*My cruel fate hath warr'd with me in vain:*
*Life, glory, worth, and all unmeasur'd skill,*
*Beauty and grace, themselves in me fulfill*
*That many I surpass, and to the best attain.*[4]

Certain of his genius, Cellini wrote so that the whole world might appreciate it.

**Individualism** stressed personality, uniqueness, and the full development of capabilities and talents. Artist, athlete, painter, scholar, sculptor, whatever—a person's abilities should be stretched until fully realized.

**Benvenuto Cellini: Saltcellar of Francis I (ca 1539–1543)** In gold and enamel, Cellini depicts the Roman sea god, Neptune (with trident, or three-pronged spear), sitting beside a small boat-shaped container holding salt from the sea. Opposite him, a female figure personifying Earth guards pepper, which derives from a plant. Portrayed on the base are the four seasons and the times of day, symbolizing seasonal festivities and daily meal schedules. The grace, poise, and elegance of the figures reflect Mannerism, an artistic style popular during the Italian High Renaissance (1520–1600). *(Kunsthistorisches Museum, Vienna/The Bridgeman Art Library International Ltd)*

## Humanism

In the cities of Italy, especially Rome, civic leaders and the wealthy populace showed great archaeological zeal for the recovery of manuscripts, statues, and monuments. The Vatican Library, planned in the fifteenth century to house the nine thousand manuscripts collected by Pope Nicholas V (r. 1447–1455), remains one of the richest repositories of ancient and medieval documents. Patrician Italians consciously copied the lifestyle of the ancients and tried to trace their genealogies back to ancient Rome.

The revival of interest in antiquity was also apparent in the serious study of the Latin classics. This feature of the Renaissance became known as the "new learning," or simply **humanism,** the term used by the Florentine rhetorician and historian Leonardo Bruni (1370–1444). The words *humanism* and *humanist* derive from the Latin *humanitas,* which Cicero used to refer to the literary culture needed by anyone who wanted to be considered educated and civilized. Humanism focused on human beings—their achievements, interests, and capabilities. Although churchmen supported the new learning, by the later fifteenth century Italian humanism was increasingly a lay phenomenon.

Appreciation of the literary culture of the Romans had never died in the West, but medieval writers had accepted pagan and classical authors uncritically. Renaissance humanists, in contrast, were skeptical of their authority, conscious of the historical distance separating themselves from the ancients, and fully aware that classical writers often disagreed among themselves. Medieval writers looked to the classics to reveal God. Renaissance humanists studied the classics to understand human nature, though from a strongly Christian perspective. For example, in a remarkable essay, *On the Dignity of Man,* the Florentine writer Pico della Mirandola (1463–1494) stressed that man possesses great dignity because he was made in the image of God before the Fall and as Christ after the Resurrection. According to Pico, man's place in the universe is somewhere between the beasts and the angels, but, because of the divine image planted in him, there are no limits to what man can accomplish.

The leading humanists of the early Renaissance were rhetoricians, seeking effective and eloquent communication, both oral and written. They loved the language of the classics and scorned the corrupt, "barbaric" Latin of the medieval schoolmen.

## Secular Spirit

**Secularism** is a basic concern with the material world instead of with eternal and spiritual matters. A secular way of thinking tends to find the ultimate explanation of everything and the final end of human beings within the limits of what the senses can discover. Medieval business people ruthlessly pursued profits, while medieval monks fought fiercely over property. But the dominant ideals focused on the otherworldly, on life after death. Renaissance people often held strong and deep spiritual beliefs. But Renaissance society was secular: attention was concentrated on the here and now, often on the acquisition of material things. The fourteenth and fifteenth centuries witnessed the slow but steady growth of secularism in Italy.

The economic changes and rising prosperity of the Italian cities in the thirteenth century worked a fundamental change in social and intellectual attitudes and values. Worries about shifting rates of interest, shipping routes, personnel costs, and employee relations did not leave much time for thoughts about penance and purgatory. Wealth made possible greater material pleasures, a more comfortable life, the leisure time to appreciate and patronize the arts. Money could buy many sensual gratifications, and the rich, social-climbing bankers and merchants of the Italian cities came to see life more as an opportunity to be enjoyed than as a painful pilgrimage to the City of God.

In *On Pleasure,* the humanist Lorenzo Valla (1406–1457) defends the pleasures of the senses as the highest good. Scholars praise Valla as a father of modern historical criticism. His study *On the False Donation of Constantine* (1444) demonstrates by careful textual examination that an anonymous eighth-century document supposedly giving the papacy jurisdiction over vast territories in western Europe was a forgery. The proof that the Donation was a forgery weakened papal claims to temporal authority. Lorenzo Valla's work exemplifies the application of critical scholarship to old and almost sacred writings, as well as the new secular spirit of the Renaissance.

Renaissance writers justified the accumulation and enjoyment of wealth with references to ancient authors, and church leaders did little to combat the new secular spirit. Renaissance popes beautified the city of Rome, patronized artists and men of letters, and expended enormous enthusiasm and huge sums of money. Pope Julius II (r. 1503–1513) tore down the old Saint Peter's Basilica and began work on the present structure in 1506. Michelangelo's dome for Saint Peter's is still considered his greatest work.

Although papal interests fostered the new worldly attitude, the broad mass of the people and the intellectuals and leaders of society remained faithful to the Christian church. Few questioned the basic tenets of the Christian religion. The thousands of pious paintings, sculptures, processions, and pilgrimages of the Renaissance period prove that strong religious feeling persisted.

## Art and the Artist

No feature of the Renaissance evokes greater admiration than its artistic masterpieces. The 1400s (called *quattrocento* in Italian) and 1500s (*cinquecento*) bore witness to a dazzling creativity in painting, architecture, and sculpture. In all the arts, the city of Florence led the way. In the period art historians describe as the High Renaissance (1500–1527), Rome took the lead. The main characteristics of High Renaissance art—classical balance, harmony, and restraint—are revealed in the masterpieces of Leonardo da Vinci (1452–1519), Raphael (1483–1520), and Michelangelo (1475–1564), all of whom worked in Rome. (See the feature "Individuals in Society: Leonardo da Vinci.")

In early Renaissance Italy, art manifested corporate power. Powerful urban groups such as guilds and religious confraternities commissioned works of art. The Florentine cloth merchants, for example, delegated Filippo Brunelleschi (1377–1446) to build the magnificent dome on the cathedral of Florence and selected Lorenzo Ghiberti (1378–1455) to design the bronze doors of the Baptistry. These works were signs of the merchants' dominant influence in the community. The subject matter of art through the early fifteenth century, as in the Middle Ages, remained overwhelmingly religious.

Increasingly in the later quattrocento, individuals and oligarchs, rather than corporate groups, sponsored works of art. Merchants, bankers, popes, and princes supported the arts as a means of glorifying themselves, their families, and their power. Vast sums were spent on family chapels, frescoes, religious panels, and tombs.

As the fifteenth century advanced, the subject matter of art became steadily more secular. Religious topics, such as the Annunciation of the Virgin, remained popular among both patrons and artists, but classical themes and motifs, such as the lives and loves of pagan gods and goddesses, figured increasingly in painting and sculpture. The individual portrait emerged as a distinct artistic genre. Rather than reflecting a spiritual ideal, as medieval painting and sculpture tended to do, Renaissance portraits mirrored reality.

The Florentine painter Giotto (1276–1337) led the way in the use of realism; his treatment of the human body and face replaced the formal stiffness and artificiality that had for so long characterized the representation

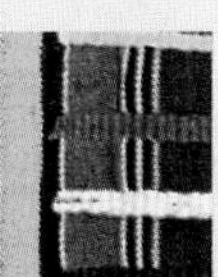

## LEONARDO DA VINCI

What makes a genius? An infinite capacity for taking pains? A deep curiosity about an extensive variety of subjects? A divine spark as manifested by talents that far exceed the norm? Or is it just "one percent inspiration and ninety-nine percent perspiration," as Thomas Edison said? By whatever criteria, Leonardo da Vinci was one of the greatest geniuses in the history of the Western world.

He was born in Vinci, near Florence, the illegitimate son of Caterina, a local peasant girl, and Ser Piero da Vinci, a notary public. Caterina later married another native of Vinci. When Ser Piero's marriage to Donna Albrussia produced no children, they took in Leonardo, who remained with them until Ser Piero secured Leonardo's apprenticeship with the painter and sculptor Andrea del Verrocchio. In 1472, when Leonardo was just twenty years old, he was listed as a master in Florence's "Company of Artists."

Leonardo contributed to the modern concept of the artist as an original thinker and as a special kind of human being: an isolated figure with exceptional creative powers. Leonardo's portrait *Ginevra de' Benci* anticipates his most famous portrait, *Mona Lisa,* with the enigmatic smile that Giorgio Vasari described as "so pleasing that it seemed divine rather than human." Leonardo's experimental method of fresco painting of *The Last Supper* caused the picture to deteriorate rapidly, but it has been called "the most revered painting in the world." To the annoyance of his patrons, none of these paintings was ever completed to Leonardo's satisfaction. For example, *The Last Supper* was left unfinished because he could not find a model for the face of Christ that would evoke the spiritual depth he felt it deserved.

Leonardo once said that "a painter is not admirable unless he is universal." He left notes and plans on drawing, painting, sculpture, music, architecture, town planning, optics, astronomy, biology, zoology, mathematics, and various branches of engineering, such as a model for a submarine, designs for tank warfare, and cranes for dredging. These drafts suggest the astonishing versatility of his mind. One authority has said that Leonardo "saw art from the scientific point of view and science from the artist's point of view."

Vasari described Leonardo as a handsome man with a large body and physical grace, a "sparkling conversationalist" talented at singing while accompanying himself on the lyre. According to Vasari, "his genius was so wonderfully inspired by God, his powers of expression so powerfully fed by a willing memory and intellect . . . that his arguments confounded the most formidable critics."

*Leonardo da Vinci,* Lady with an Ermine. *The whiteness of the ermine's fur symbolizes purity.* (Czartoryski Museum, Krakow/ The Bridgeman Art Library International Ltd)

In a famous essay, the Viennese psychiatrist Sigmund Freud argued that Leonardo was a homosexual who sublimated, pouring his sexual energy into his art. Freud wrote that it is doubtful that Leonardo ever touched a woman or even had an intimate spiritual relationship with one. Although as a master artist he surrounded himself with handsome young men and even had a long emotional relationship with one, Francesco Melzi, the evidence suggests that his male relationships never resulted in sexual activity. On a page of his *Codex Atlanticus,* which includes his sketch of the Florentine navigator Amerigo Vespucci, Leonardo wrote, "Intellectual passion drives out sensuality." For Freud, Leonardo transferred his psychic energy into artistic and scientific study. This thesis has attracted much attention, but no one has refuted it.

Leonardo worked in Milan for the despot Ludovico Sforza, planning a gigantic equestrian statue in honor of Ludovico's father, Duke Francesco Sforza. The clay model collapsed, and only notes survived. Leonardo also worked as a military engineer for Cesare Borgia (see page 452). In 1516 he accepted King Francis I's invitation to France. At the French court and in the presence of his faithful companion Francesco Melzi, Leonardo died in the arms of the king.

### QUESTIONS FOR ANALYSIS

1. How would you explain Leonardo's genius?
2. Consider sublimation as a source of artistic and scientific creativity.

*Sources:* Giorgio Vasari, *Lives of the Artists,* vol. 1, trans. G. Bull (London: Penguin Books, 1965); S. B. Nuland, *Leonardo da Vinci* (New York: Lipper/Viking, 2000); Sigmund Freud, *Leonardo da Vinci: A Study in Psychosexuality* (New York: Random House, 1947).

**Andrea Mantegna: Adoration of the Magi (ca 1495–1505)** Applying his study of ancient Roman relief sculpture, and elaborating on a famous scriptural text (Matthew 2:1), Mantegna painted for the private devotion of the Gonzaga family of Mantua this scene of the Three Kings coming to recognize the divinity of Christ. The Three Kings represent the entire world—that is, the three continents known to medieval Europeans: Europe, Asia, and Africa. They also symbolize the three stages of life: youth, maturity, and old age. Here Melchior, the oldest, his large cranium symbolizing wisdom, personifies Europe. He offers gold in a Chinese porcelain cup from the Ming Dynasty. Balthazar, with an olive complexion and dark beard, stands for Asia and maturity. He presents frankincense in a stunning vessel of Turkish tombac ware. Caspar, representing Africa and youth, gives myrrh in an urn of striped marble. The child responds with a blessing. The black background brings out the rich colors. *(The J. Paul Getty Museum, Los Angeles. Mantegna, Andrea,* Adoration of the Magi, *ca 1495–1505, distemper on linen, 54.6 × 70.7 cm [85.PA.417])*

of the human body. The sculptor Donatello's (1386–1466) many statues express an appreciation of the incredible variety of human nature. He revived the classical figure with its balance and self-awareness. The short-lived Florentine Masaccio (1401–1428), sometimes called the father of modern painting, inspired a new style characterized by great realism, narrative power, and effective use of light and dark.

As important as realism was the new "international style," so called because of the wandering careers of influential artists, the close communications and rivalry of princely courts, and the increased trade in works of art. Rich color, decorative detail, curvilinear rhythms, and swaying forms characterized the international style. As the term *international* implies, this style was European, not merely Italian.

The growing secular influences on art are reflected in the improved social status of the artist in the Renaissance. The lower-middle-class medieval master mason had been viewed in the same light as a mechanic. The artist in the Renaissance was considered a free intellectual worker. Artists did not produce unsolicited pictures or statues for the general public; that could mean loss of status. They usually worked on commission from a powerful prince. The artist's reputation depended on the support of powerful patrons, and through them some artists and architects achieved not only economic security but great wealth. All aspiring artists received a practical (not theoretical) education in a recognized master's workshop.

Renaissance society respected and rewarded the distinguished artist. At a time when a person could live in a princely fashion on 300 ducats a year, Leonardo da Vinci was making 2,000 ducats annually. Michelangelo was paid 3,000 ducats for painting the ceiling of the Sistine Chapel.

The Renaissance witnessed the birth of the concept of the artist as genius. In the Middle Ages, people believed that only God created, albeit through individuals; the medieval conception recognized no particular value in artistic originality. Boastful Renaissance artists and humanists came to think that a work of art was the deliberate creation of a unique personality, of an individual who transcended traditions, rules, and theories. A genius had a peculiar gift, which ordinary laws should not inhibit. Cosimo de' Medici described a painter, because of his genius, as "divine," implying that the artist shared in the powers of God. Others applied the word *divine* to Michelangelo.

But the student must remember that Italian Renaissance culture was that of a small mercantile elite, a business patriciate with aristocratic pretensions. Renaissance culture did not directly affect the broad middle classes, let alone the vast urban proletariat. Renaissance humanists were a smaller and narrower group than the medieval clergy had ever been. In the Middle Ages, high churchmen had commissioned the construction of the Gothic cathedrals, but, once finished, the buildings were for all to enjoy. Nothing comparable was built in the Renaissance. A small, highly educated group of literary humanists and artists created the culture of and for an exclusive elite. They cared little for ordinary people.[5]

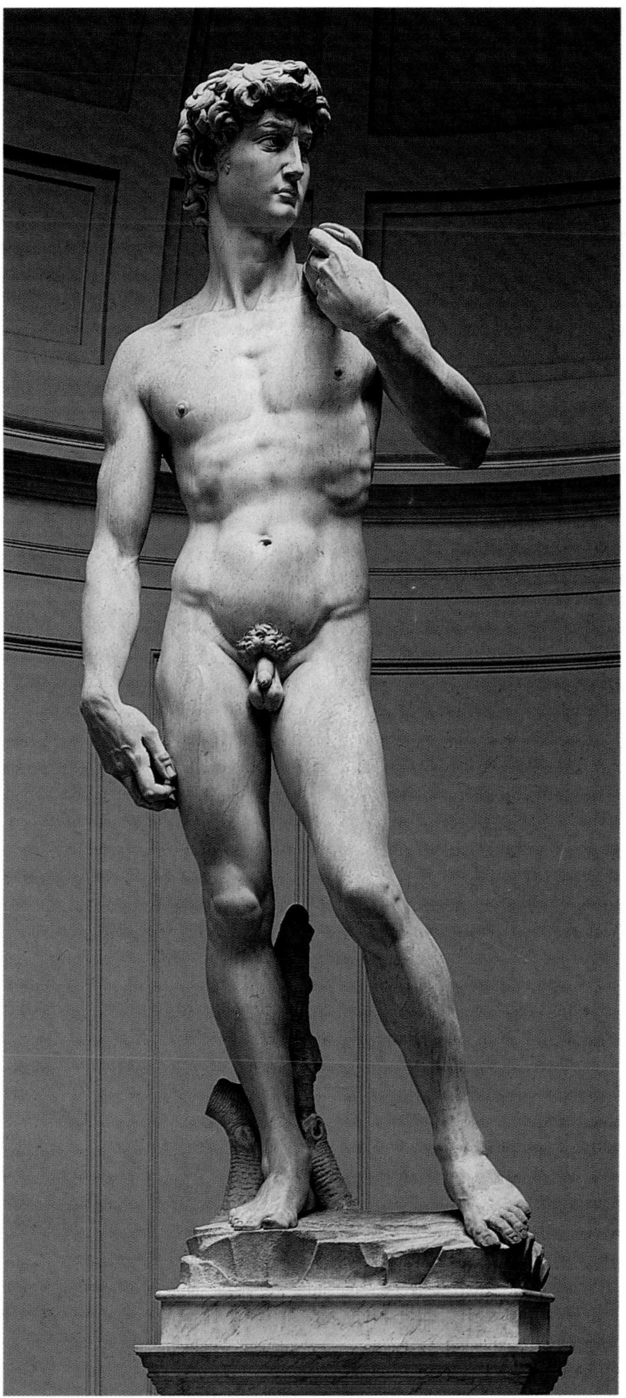

**Michelangelo: David** In 1501 the new republican government of Florence commissioned the twenty-six-year-old Michelangelo to carve David as a symbol of civic independence and resistance to oligarchical tyranny. Tensed in anticipation of action but certain of victory over his unseen enemy Goliath (1 Samuel 17), this male nude represents the ideal of youthful physical perfection. *(Scala/Art Resource, NY)*

## The Renaissance in the North

In the last quarter of the fifteenth century, Italian Renaissance thought and ideals penetrated northern Europe. Students from the Low Countries, France, Germany, and England flocked to Italy, imbibed the "new learning," and carried it back to their countries. However, cultural traditions of northern Europe tended to remain more distinctly Christian, or at least pietistic, than those of Italy. What fundamentally distinguished Italian humanists from northern ones is that the latter had a program for broad social reform based on Christian ideals.

Christian humanists in northern Europe were interested in the development of an ethical way of life. To achieve it, they believed, the best elements of classical and Christian cultures should be combined. For example, the classical ideals of calmness, stoical patience, and broad-mindedness should be joined in human conduct with the Christian virtues of love, faith, and hope. Christian humanists had a profound faith in the power of human intellect to bring about moral and institutional reform. They believed that human nature had been corrupted by sin but nevertheless was fundamentally good and capable of improvement through education, which would lead to piety and an ethical way of life.

The Englishman Thomas More (1478–1535) towers above other figures in sixteenth-century English social and intellectual history. More, who practiced law, entered government service during the reign of Henry VIII and was sent as ambassador to Flanders. There More found the time to write *Utopia* (1516), which presents a revolutionary view of society.

*Utopia,* which literally means "nowhere," describes an ideal socialistic community on an island somewhere off the mainland of the New World. All its children receive a good education, and since the goal of all education is to develop rational faculties, adults divide their days equally between manual labor or business pursuits and various intellectual activities. The profits from business and property are held strictly in common, so there is absolute social equality. The Utopians use gold and silver both to make chamber pots and to prevent wars by buying off their enemies. By this casual use of precious metals, More meant to suggest that the basic problems in society are caused by greed. Utopian law exalts mercy above justice. Citizens of Utopia lead a nearly perfect existence because they live by reason. More punned on the word *Utopia,* which he termed "a good place. A good place which is no place."

More's ideas were profoundly original in the sixteenth century. The long-prevailing view was that vice and violence exist because women and men are basically corrupt. But More maintained that acquisitiveness and private property promote all sorts of vices and civil disorders and that because society protects private property, *society's* flawed institutions are responsible for corruption and war. Today people take this view so much for granted that it is difficult to appreciate how radical it was in the sixteenth century. According to More, the key to improvement and reform of the individual is reform of the social institutions that mold the individual.

Better known by contemporaries than Thomas More was the Dutch humanist Desiderius Erasmus of Rotterdam (1466?–1536), whose lifework became the application of the best humanistic learning to the study and explanation of the Bible.

Erasmus's long list of publications includes *The Education of a Christian Prince* (1504), which combines idealistic and practical suggestions for the formation of a ruler's character; *The Praise of Folly* (1509), a satire on worldly wisdom and a plea for the simple and spontaneous Christian faith of children; and, most important of all, a critical edition of the Greek New Testament (1516). In the preface to the New Testament, Erasmus explains the purpose of his great work:

> *For I utterly dissent from those who are unwilling that the sacred Scriptures should be read by the unlearned translated into their vulgar tongue, as though Christ had taught such subtleties that they can scarcely be understood even by a few theologians. . . . Christ wished his mysteries to be published as openly as possible.*[6]

Two fundamental themes run through all of Erasmus's scholarly work. First, education—study of the Bible and the classics—is the means to reform, the key to moral and intellectual improvement. Second, the essence of Erasmus's thought is, in his own phrase, "the philosophy of Christ." By this Erasmus meant that Christianity is an inner attitude of the heart or spirit. Christianity is not formalism, special ceremonies, or law; Christianity is Christ—his life and what he said and did, not what theologians have written about him.

The distinctly religious orientation of the literary works of the Renaissance in the north also characterized northern art and architecture. Some Flemish painters, notably Rogier van der Weyden (1399/1400–1464) and Jan van Eyck (1366–1441), were considered the artistic equals of Italian painters, were much admired in Italy, and worked a generation before Leonardo and Michelangelo. One of the earliest artists successfully to use oil-based paints, van Eyck, in paintings such as *Ghent Altarpiece* and the portrait *Giovanni Arnolfini and His Bride,* shows the Flemish love for detail; the effect is great realism and remarkable attention to human personality.

A quasi-spiritual aura infuses architectural monuments in the north. The city halls of wealthy Flemish towns such as Bruges, Brussels, Louvain, and Ghent strike the viewer more as shrines to house the bones of saints than as settings for the mundane decisions of politicians and business people. Northern architecture was little influenced by the classical revival so obvious in Renaissance Rome and Florence.

## SOCIAL CHANGE DURING THE RENAISSANCE

The Renaissance changed many aspects of Italian and, subsequently, European society. The new developments brought about real breaks with the medieval past in education and political thought, through new printing technology, and in the experiences of women and blacks.

## Education and Political Thought

Education and moral behavior were central preoccupations of the humanists. Humanists poured out treatises, often in the form of letters, on the structure and goals of education and the training of rulers. In one of the earliest systematic programs for the young, Peter Paul Vergerio (1370–1444) wrote Ubertinus, the ruler of Carrara:

*For the education of children is a matter of more than private interest; it concerns the State, which indeed regards the right training of the young as, in certain aspects, within its proper sphere. . . . Above all, respect for Divine ordinances is of the deepest importance; it should be inculcated from the earliest years. Reverence towards elders and parents is an obligation closely akin.*

*We call those studies liberal which are worthy of a free man; those studies by which we attain and practice virtue and wisdom.*[7]

No book on education had broader influence than Baldassare Castiglione's *The Courtier* (1528). This treatise sought to train, discipline, and fashion the young man into the courtly ideal, the gentleman. According to Castiglione (1478–1529), the educated man of the upper class should have a broad background in many academic subjects, and his spiritual and physical, as well as intellectual, capabilities should be trained. The courtier should have easy familiarity with dance, music, and the arts. Castiglione envisioned a man who could compose a sonnet, wrestle, sing a song and accompany himself on an instrument, ride expertly, solve difficult mathematical problems, and above all speak and write eloquently. In the sixteenth and seventeenth centuries, the courtier envisioned by Castiglione became the model of the European gentleman.

No Renaissance book on any topic has been more widely read and studied in all the centuries since its publication in 1513 than the short political treatise ***The Prince,*** by Niccolò Machiavelli (1469–1527). The subject of *The Prince* is political power: how the ruler should gain, maintain, and increase it. A good humanist, Machiavelli explored the problems of human nature and concluded that human beings are selfish and out to advance their own interests. This pessimistic view of humanity led him to maintain that the prince may have to manipulate the people in any way he finds necessary:

*For a man who, in all respects, will carry out only his professions of good, will be apt to be ruined amongst so many who are evil. A prince therefore who desires to maintain himself must learn to be not always good, but to be so or not as necessity may require.*[8]

The prince should combine the cunning of a fox with the ferocity of a lion to achieve his goals. Pondering the question of whether it is better for a ruler to be loved or feared, Machiavelli wrote:

*It will naturally be answered that it would be desirable to be both the one and the other; but as it is difficult to be both at the same time, it is much more safe to be feared than to be loved, when you have to choose between the two. For it may be said of men in general that they are ungrateful and fickle, dissemblers, avoiders of danger, and greedy of gain. So long as you shower benefits upon them, they are all yours.*[9]

Medieval political theorists and theologians had stressed the way government *ought* to be. They had set high moral and Christian standards for the ruler's conduct. In their opinion, the test of good government is whether it provides justice, law, and order. Machiavelli maintained that the ruler should be concerned not with the way things ought to be but with the way things actually are. The sole test of whether a government is "good" is whether it is effective, whether the ruler increases his power. Machiavelli believed that political action cannot be restricted by moral considerations, but he did not advocate amoral behavior. On the basis of a simplistic interpretation of *The Prince,* the adjective *Machiavellian* entered the language as a synonym for devious, corrupt, and crafty politics in which the end justifies the means. Machiavelli's ultimate significance rests on two ideas: that one permanent social order reflecting God's will cannot be established and that politics has its own laws and ought to be considered a science.[10]

## Movable Type and the Spread of Literacy

Sometime in the thirteenth century, paper money and playing cards from China reached the West. They were *block-printed*—that is, each word, phrase, or picture was carved on a separate wooden block to be inked and used for printing. This method of reproduction was extraordinarily expensive and slow. By the middle of the fifteenth century, Europeans had mastered paper manufacture, which also originated in China and was introduced by the Arabs to the West in the twelfth century. Then around 1454, probably through the combined efforts of three men—Johann Gutenberg, Johann Fust, and Peter Schöffer, all experimenting at Mainz—movable type came into being in the West. The mirror image of each letter (rather than entire words or phrases) was carved in relief on a small block. Individual letters, easily movable, were put together to form words in lines of type that made up a page. An infinite variety of texts could be printed by reusing and rearranging pieces of type.

The effects of the invention of movable-type printing were not obvious overnight. But within a half century of the publication of Gutenberg's Bible of 1456, printing from movable type brought about radical changes. It transformed both the private and the public lives of Europeans. Governments that "had employed the cumbersome methods of manuscripts to communicate with their subjects switched quickly to print to announce declarations of war, publish battle accounts, promulgate treaties or argue disputed points in pamphlet form. Theirs was an effort 'to win the psychological war.'" Printing made propaganda possible, emphasizing differences between opposing groups such as Crown and nobility, church and state. These differences laid the basis for the formation of distinct political parties.

Printing also stimulated the literacy of laypeople and eventually came to have a deep effect on their private lives. Most of the earliest books and pamphlets dealt with religious subjects, but students, housewives, businessmen, and upper- and middle-class people sought books on all subjects. Broadsides and flysheets allowed great public festivals, religious ceremonies, and political events to be experienced vicariously by the stay-at-home. Since books and other printed materials were read aloud to illiterate listeners, print bridged the gap between written and oral cultures.[11]

Besides printing, early modern Europe witnessed other technological advances, such as mechanical clocks. The Arabs knew that the length of daylight, caused by the changing distance between the earth and the sun as the earth moves in orbit, varies with the seasons. Europeans probably learned this from the Arabs. In the fourteenth century, mechanical clocks came into general use, usually installed on a cathedral or town church.

Clocks contributed to the development of a mentality that conceived of the universe in visual and quantitative terms. Measuring the world brought not only understanding of it but the urge to control it. The mechanical clock enabled Europeans to divide time into equal hours, allowing the working day to be fixed in both winter and summer. The Maya in Central America and the Chinese had theoretical knowledge of time, but Europeans put that knowledge to practical use. Along with cannon and printing, clocks gave Europeans technological advantages over other peoples.[12]

## Women and Work

We know relatively little about the lives of individual women of the middle and working classes in the period from about 1300 to 1600. Most women married and thus carried all the domestic responsibilities of the home. They also frequently worked outside the home.

**The Print Shop** Sixteenth-century printing involved a division of labor. Two persons (*left*) at separate benches set the pieces of type. Another (*center, rear*) inks the chase (or locked plate containing the set type). Yet another (*right*) operates the press, which prints the sheets. The boy removes the printed pages and sets them to dry. Meanwhile, a man carries in fresh paper on his head. *(Giraudon/Art Resource, NY)*

**Working Women** Women did virtually every kind of work in Renaissance Europe. They often sold food, cloth, handmade jewelry, trinkets, and other merchandise in the town marketplace, just as many women in developing countries do today. *(Scala/Art Resource, NY)*

In the Venetian Arsenal, the state-controlled dock and shipbuilding area (the largest single industrial plant in Europe and the builder of the biggest fleet), women made the ships' sails. Women were heavily involved in the Florentine textile industry, weaving cloth and reeling and winding silk. In the 1560s, a woman named Suzanne Erkur managed the imperial silver mint at Kutná Hora in Bohemia. Women conducted the ferry service across the Rhône River at Lyons. Throughout Europe rural women assisted fathers and husbands in the many agricultural tasks, and urban women helped in shops and businesses. Widows often ran their husbands' establishments. Tens of thousands of women worked as midwives, maids, cooks, laundresses, and household servants. From the port city of Dubrovnik (formerly Ragusa) on the Dalmatian coast came tens of thousands of female slaves to enter domestic service in upper-class households throughout Italy[13] (see page 463).

What of women of the upper classes? During the Renaissance, the status of upper-class women declined. In terms of the kind of work they performed, their access to property and political power, and their role in shaping the outlook of their society, women in the Renaissance ruling classes generally had less power than comparable women in the feudal age. Well-to-do girls generally received an education, but even so, men everywhere held the conviction that a woman's attention should be focused on the domestic affairs of family life. The Italian humanist and polymath Leon Battista Alberti (1404–1472), discussing morality in his *On the Family,* stressed that a wife's role should be restricted to the orderliness of the household, food and the serving of meals, the education of children, and the supervision of servants. The English statesman Sir Thomas Smith (1513–1577) wrote in *The English Commonwealth* that women were "those whom nature hath made to keepe home and to nourish the familie and children, and not to meddle with affairs abroad."[14] Wealthy women might support charitable organizations, but men denied them any sort of political or legal activity.

Excluded from the public arena, the noblewoman or spouse of a rich merchant managed the household or court (see page 451), where the husband displayed his wealth and power (the larger the number of servants and retainers, the greater his prestige). Households depended on domestic servants, and the lady of the house had to have the shrewdness and managerial prudence to employ capable cooks, maids, tailors and seamstresses, laundresses, gardeners, coachmen, stable hands, nurses, and handymen. If a prosperous Florentine or Venetian merchant's household had fifteen to twenty servants, a great lord or a Medici banker could easily employ four

**Artemesia Gentileschi: Judith Slaying Holofernes** The Old Testament Book of Judith tells the tale of the beautiful widow Judith, who first charms and then decapitates the Assyrian general Holofernes, thus saving Israel. The message is that trust in God will bring deliverance. The talented Roman artist Artemesia Gentileschi (1593–1652/3), elected to the Florentine Academy of Design at age twenty-three, rendered the story in this dramatic and gruesome painting, whose light and gushing blood give it great power. Some scholars hold that the painting is Gentileschi's pictorial revenge for her alleged rape by the decorative artist Agostino Tassi. *(Uffizi, Florence/Alinari/Art Resource, NY)*

times that number. The lady of the house had to make sure that all these people were adequately fed and clothed; to maintain harmony among them; to tend anyone who fell ill, meaning that she must have at least a rudimentary knowledge of medications; and to look after the girl who "accidentally" became pregnant and then her child. Custom also laid on the lady the responsibility for providing the servants with religious instruction. Then there was the education of her own children and possibly the care of aged or infirm in-laws. Her husband expected her to entertain (which, depending on his position, could be an elaborate and complicated undertaking) and preside over each occasion with grace and, if possible, charm. All of these burdens, in addition to her own pregnancies, added up to an enormous responsibility.

## Slavery and Ethnicity

In a famous essay, the French historian Marc Bloch observed that "Western and Central Europe, taken as a whole, were never free of slaves during the High Middle Ages."[15] In central and eastern Europe, where political conditions were unstable and permitted the enslavement of pagans, slavery allowed strong lords to satisfy cheaply the needs of their estates; slaves also offered merchants a commodity for profitable exchange with foreigners. Thus, in the period of eastward expansion (see Chapter 13), German lords seized Polish and Bohemian peoples; used them as agricultural laborers, domestics, and concubines; and sold the rest. In the thirteenth century, Prague was a large slave market. The word *slave* always carried a definite ethnic connotation: it meant an unfree person of Slavic background.[16]

In the fourteenth century, Genoa and Venice dominated the Mediterranean slave trade. The labor shortage caused by the Black Death led to the flow of Russians, Tartars, and Circassian slaves from Azov in the Crimea and of Serbs, Albanians, Greeks, and Hungarians from the Balkans. Venetian control of the northern regions of the Dalmatian coast enabled Venetian slavers to import large numbers of female slaves from the port city of Dubrovnik.[17] All of these people, Slavic but of different ethnic backgrounds, gradually intermingled with the native Italian population.

Ever since the time of the Roman republic, a few black people had lived in western Europe. They had come, along with white slaves, as the spoils of war. Even after the collapse of the Roman Empire, Muslim and Christian merchants continued to import them. The evidence of medieval art attests to the presence of Africans in Europe and to Europeans' awareness of them.

As in Slavic regions, unstable political conditions in many parts of Africa enabled enterprising merchants to seize people and sell them into slavery. Local authorities afforded them no protection. Long tradition, moreover, sanctioned the practice of slavery. Beginning in the fifteenth century, sizable numbers of black slaves entered Europe. Portuguese explorers imported perhaps a thousand a year and sold them at the markets of Seville, Barcelona, Marseilles, and Genoa. By the mid-sixteenth century, blacks, slave and free, constituted about 10 percent of the populations of the Portuguese cities of Lisbon and Évora; other cities had smaller percentages. In all, blacks made up roughly 3 percent of the Portuguese population. The Venetians specialized in the importation of white slaves, but blacks were so greatly in demand at the Renaissance courts of northern Italy that the Venetians defied papal threats of excommunication to secure them. Although blacks were concentrated in the Iberian Peninsula, there must have been some Africans in northern Europe as well. In the 1580s, for example, Queen Elizabeth I of England complained that there were too many "blackamoores" competing with needy English people for places as domestic servants.[18]

What roles did blacks play in Renaissance society? Although few written records survive, obviously black slaves in Europe hated the loss of their freedom, separation from their societal roots, and forced labor without compensation. No doubt, too, they disliked the alien culture, the cold climate, and the strange foods. But so far as we know, few who managed to secure their freedom through manumission or escape chose to return to Africa. The lack of black slave revolts in Europe, so common in South and North America and in Africa under colonial rule, attests to the small numbers and wide dispersion of blacks and to a relatively benign pattern of slavery. Moreover, the legal definition of *slave* never took on the rigid character in Europe that it did in the United States.

Westerners tend to lump all sub-Saharan Africans into one category: black. However, Africans, like Europeans and Asians, belonged to and identified themselves by ethnic groups. In Africa, the world's second-largest continent, there were (and are) more than six hundred distinct ethnic groups. In addition, African slaves in the Iberian Peninsula (and elsewhere in Europe), like Slavic ones in Italy, intermingled with the people they lived among, and their offspring were, in fact, biracial.

However Africans may have been defined in Europe, black servants were much sought after, as the medieval interest in curiosities, the exotic, and the marvelous continued into the Renaissance. In the late fifteenth century, Isabella, the wife of Gian Galazzo Sforza, took pride in the fact that she owned ten blacks, seven of them females. A black lady's maid was both a curiosity and a symbol of wealth. In 1491 Isabella of Este, duchess of Mantua, instructed her agent to secure a black girl between four and eight years old, "shapely and as black as possible." The duchess saw the child as a source of entertainment: "We shall make her very happy and shall have great fun with her." She hoped the girl would become "the best buffoon in the world,"[19] as the cruel ancient practice of a noble household retaining a professional "fool" for the family's amusement persisted through the Renaissance—and even down to the twentieth century.

Adult black slaves served as maids, valets, and domestic servants. Italian aristocrats such as Marchesa Elena Grimaldi had their portraits painted with their black pageboys to indicate their wealth. The Venetians employed blacks—slave and free—as gondoliers and stevedores on the docks. In Portugal kings, nobles, laborers, monasteries and convents, and prostitutes owned slaves. They supplemented the labor force in virtually all occupations—as agricultural laborers, craftsmen, and seamen on ships going to Lisbon and Africa.[20] Tradition, stretching back at least as far as the thirteenth century, connected blacks with music and dance. In Renaissance Spain and Italy, blacks performed as dancers, as actors and actresses in courtly dramas, and as musicians, sometimes making up full orchestras.[21] Slavery during the Renaissance foreshadowed the American, especially the later Brazilian, pattern.

Before the sixteenth-century "discoveries" of the non-European world, Europeans had little concrete

**Drummer** In the early sixteenth century, blacks—such as this drummer in the court of the Emperor Charles V—were highly visible in Portuguese, Spanish, and Italian societies. *(Photographs and Prints Division, Schomburg Center for Research in Black Culture, The New York Public Library, Astor, Lenox, and Tilden Foundations)*

knowledge of Africans and their cultures. What Europeans did know was based on biblical accounts. The European attitude toward Africans was ambivalent. On the one hand, Europeans perceived Africa as a remote place, the home of strange people isolated by heresy and Islam from superior European civilization. Africans' contact, even as slaves, with Christian Europeans could only "improve" the blacks. Most Europeans' knowledge of the black as a racial type was based entirely on theological speculation. Theologians taught that God was light. Blackness, the opposite of light, therefore represented the hostile forces of the underworld: evil, sin, and the Devil. Thus the Devil was commonly represented as a black man in medieval and early Renaissance art. On the other hand, blackness also possessed positive qualities. It symbolized the emptiness of worldly goods, the humility of the monastic way of life. Black clothes permitted a conservative and discreet display of wealth. Black vestments and funeral trappings indicated grief, and Christ had said that those who mourn are blessed. Until the exploration and observation of the sixteenth, seventeenth, and nineteenth centuries allowed, ever so slowly, for the development of more scientific knowledge, the Western conception of black people remained bound up with religious notions.[22] As for the sterile and meaningless concept of race, recent scholarship stresses that it emerged only in the late seventeenth century.[23] In Renaissance society, blacks, like women, were signs of wealth; both were used for display.

## POLITICS AND THE STATE IN THE RENAISSANCE (CA 1450–1521)

The central Middle Ages witnessed the beginnings of many of the basic institutions of the modern state. The linchpin for the development of states was strong monarchy, and during the period of the Hundred Years' War, no ruler in western Europe was able to provide effective leadership. The resurgent power of feudal nobilities weakened the centralizing work begun earlier.

Beginning in the fifteenth century, rulers utilized the aggressive methods implied by Renaissance political ideas to rebuild their governments. First in Italy (see page 451), then in France, England, and Spain, rulers began the work of reducing violence, curbing unruly nobles and troublesome elements, and establishing domestic order. The Holy Roman Empire of Germany, however, remained divided into scores of independent principalities.

The despots and oligarchs of the Italian city-states, together with Louis XI of France, Henry VII of England, and Ferdinand of Aragon, were tough, cynical, calculating rulers. In their ruthless push for power and strong governments, they subordinated morality to hard results. They preferred to be secure and feared rather than loved. They could not have read Machiavelli's *The Prince,* but their actions were in harmony with its ideas.

Some historians have called Louis XI (r. 1461–1483), Henry VII (r. 1485–1509), and Ferdinand and Isabella in Spain (r. 1474–1516) "new monarchs" because they invested kingship with a strong sense of royal authority and national purpose. They stressed that the monarchy was the one institution that linked all classes and peoples within definite territorial boundaries. They insisted on the respect and loyalty of all subjects and ruthlessly suppressed opposition and rebellion, especially from the nobility. And they loved the business of kingship and worked hard at it.

In other respects, however, the methods of these rulers, which varied from country to country, were not so new. They reasserted long-standing ideas and practices of strong monarchs in the Middle Ages. To advance their authority, they seized on the maxim of the Justinian *Code*: "What pleases the prince has the force of law." Like medieval rulers, Renaissance rulers tended to rely on middle-class civil servants. Using tax revenues, medieval rulers had built armies to crush feudal anarchy. Renaissance townspeople with commercial and business interests wanted a reduction of violence, and usually they were willing to pay taxes in order to achieve it.

## France

The Hundred Years' War left France drastically depopulated, commercially ruined, and agriculturally weak. Nonetheless, the ruler whom Joan of Arc had seen crowned at Reims, Charles VII (r. 1422–1461), revived the monarchy and France. He seemed an unlikely person to do so. Frail, indecisive, and burdened with questions about his paternity (his father was deranged, his mother notoriously promiscuous), Charles VII nevertheless began France's long recovery.

Charles reorganized the royal council, giving increased influence to middle-class men, and strengthened royal finances through taxes such as the *gabelle* (on salt) and the *taille* (on land). By establishing regular companies of cavalry and archers—recruited, paid, and inspected by the state—Charles created the first permanent royal army. In 1438 he published the Pragmatic Sanction of Bourges, giving the French crown major control over the appointment of bishops and depriving the pope of French ecclesiastical revenues. The Pragmatic Sanction affirmed the special rights of the French crown over the French church.

Charles's son Louis XI (r. 1461–1483), called the "Spider King" by his subjects because of his treacherous and cruel character, was very much a Renaissance prince. Facing the perpetual French problems of unification of the realm and reduction of feudal disorder, he saw money as the answer. Louis promoted new industries, such as silk weaving at Lyons and Tours, and entered into commercial treaties with other countries. The revenues raised through these economic activities and severe taxation were used to improve the army. With the army, Louis stopped aristocratic brigandage and slowly cut into urban independence. He was also able to gain territory that furthered his goal of expanding royal authority and unifying the kingdom. Some scholars have credited Louis XI with laying the foundations for later French royal absolutism.

## England

English society suffered severely from the disorders of the fifteenth century. The aristocracy dominated the government and indulged in mischievous violence at the local level. Population, decimated by the Black Death, continued to decline. Then between 1455 and 1471, supporters of the ducal houses of York and Lancaster waged civil war, commonly called the Wars of the Roses because the symbol of the Yorkists was a white rose and that of the Lancastrians a red one. The chronic disorder hurt trade, agriculture, and domestic industry, and the authority of the monarchy sank lower than it had been in centuries.

The Yorkist Edward IV (r. 1461–1483) began reestablishing domestic tranquillity. He defeated the Lancastrian forces and after 1471 began to reconstruct the monarchy and consolidate royal power. Henry VII (r. 1485–1509) of the Welsh house of Tudor advanced the work of restoring royal prestige by crushing the power of the nobility and establishing order and law at the local level.

The Hundred Years' War had cost the nation dearly, and the money to finance it had been raised by Parliament, the arena where the nobility exerted its power. As long as the monarchy was dependent on the Lords and the Commons for revenue, the king had to call Parliament. Thus Edward IV, and subsequently the Tudors except for Henry VIII, conducted foreign policy by means of diplomacy and avoided expensive wars. Unlike the continental countries of Spain and France, England had no standing army or professional civil service bureaucracy. The Tudors relied on the support of unpaid local justices of the peace—influential landowners in the shires—to handle the work of local government. From the royal point of view, they were an inexpensive method of government. Thus for a time, the English monarchy did not depend on Parliament for money, and the Crown undercut that source of aristocratic influence.

The center of royal authority under Henry VII was the royal council, which governed at the national level. The royal council handled any business the king put before it—executive, legislative, judicial. It also dealt with real or potential aristocratic threats through a judicial offshoot, the **Court of Star Chamber,** so called because of the stars painted on the ceiling of the room in which it met. The court applied principles of Roman law, a system that exalted the power of the Crown as the embodiment of the state. The court's methods were sometimes terrifying: evidence and proceedings were secret, torture could be applied, and juries were not called. These procedures ran directly counter to English common-law precedents, but they effectively reduced aristocratic troublemaking.

The Tudors won the support of the influential upper middle class because the Crown linked government policy with the interests of that class. A commercial or agricultural upper class fears and dislikes few things more than disorder and violence. Grave, secretive, cautious, and always thrifty, Henry VII promoted peace and social order, and the gentry did not object to arbitrary methods, like those used by the Court of Star Chamber, because the government had ended the long period of anarchy. At the same time, both English exports of wool and the royal export tax on that wool steadily increased. When Henry VII died in 1509, he left a country at peace both domestically and internationally, a substantially augmented treasury, and the dignity and role of the royal majesty much enhanced.

## Spain

The central theme in the history of medieval Spain's separate kingdoms was disunity and plurality. Different languages, laws, and religious communities made for a rich cultural diversity shaped by Hispanic, Roman, Visigothic, Muslim, and Jewish traditions.

By the middle of the fifteenth century, the centuries-long *reconquista*—the attempts of the northern Christian kingdoms to control the entire peninsula—was nearing completion. The kingdoms of Castile and Aragon dominated weaker kingdoms, and with the exception of Granada, the Iberian Peninsula had been won for Christianity. The wedding in 1469 of the dynamic and aggressive Isabella, heiress of Castile, and the crafty and persistent Ferdinand, heir of Aragon, was the final major step in the unification and Christianization of Spain.

Ferdinand and Isabella pursued a common foreign policy. Under their rule Spain remained a loose confederation of separate states, but they determined to strengthen royal authority. In the towns, popular groups called **hermandades,** or brotherhoods, were given the authority to act both as local police forces and as judicial tribunals. The hermandades repressed violence with such savage punishments that by 1498 they could be disbanded. The decisive step that Ferdinand and Isabella took to curb aristocratic power was the restructuring of the royal council. The king and queen appointed to the council only people of middle-class background; they rigorously excluded aristocrats and great territorial magnates. The council and various government boards recruited men trained in Roman law.

In the extension of royal authority and the consolidation of the territories of Spain, the church was the linchpin. Through a diplomatic alliance with the Spanish pope Alexander VI, the Spanish monarchs secured the right to appoint bishops in Spain and in the Hispanic territories in America. This power enabled the "Most Catholic Kings of Spain," a title that the pope granted to Ferdinand and Isabella, to establish, in effect, a national church.[24] Revenues from ecclesiastical estates provided the means to raise an army to continue the reconquista. The victorious entry of Ferdinand and Isabella into Granada on January 6, 1492, signaled the conclusion of eight centuries of Spanish struggle against the Arabs in southern Spain. In 1512 Ferdinand conquered Navarre in the north.

Although the Muslims had been defeated, there still remained a sizable and, in the view of the Catholic sovereigns, potentially dangerous minority, the Jews. In the late fourteenth century, anti-Semitic riots and pogroms led many Spanish Jews to convert to Christianity; such people were called *conversos.*

By the middle of the fifteenth century, many conversos held high positions in Spanish society as financiers, physicians, merchants, tax collectors, and even officials of the church hierarchy. Numbering perhaps 200,000 in a total population of about 7.5 million, Jews exercised an influence quite disproportionate to their numbers. Aristocratic grandees who borrowed heavily from Jews resented their financial dependence, and churchmen questioned the sincerity of Jewish conversions. At first Isabella and Ferdinand continued the policy of royal toleration—Ferdinand himself had inherited Jewish blood from his mother. But public hostility to Jews in the form of urban rioting prompted Ferdinand and Isabella in 1478 to secure Rome's permission to revive the Inquisition, a medieval judicial procedure for the punishment of heretics.

Although the Inquisition was a religious institution established to safeguard the Catholic faith, in Spain it was controlled by the Crown and served primarily as a political unifying force. Because the Spanish Inquisition commonly applied torture to extract confessions—first from lapsed conversos, then from Muslims, and later from Protestants—it gained a notorious reputation. Thus the word *inquisition,* meaning "any judicial inquiry conducted with ruthless severity," came into the English language.

In 1492 Isabella and Ferdinand took a further dire and drastic step against backsliding conversos. They issued an edict expelling all practicing Jews from Spain. Of the community of perhaps 200,000 Jews, 150,000 fled. (Efforts were made, through last-minute conversions, to retain good Jewish physicians.) Absolute religious orthodoxy and purity of blood (untainted by Jews or Muslims) became the theoretical foundation of the Spanish national state.

**Felipe Bigarny: Ferdinand the Catholic and Isabella the Catholic** All governments try to cultivate a popular image. For Ferdinand and Isabella, it was the appearance of piety. Contemporaries, such as the Burgundian sculptor Bigarny, portrayed them as paragons of Christian piety, as shown in these polychrome wooden statues. If Isabella's piety was perhaps more genuine, she used it—together with rich ceremony, elaborate dress, and a fierce determination—to assert royal authority. *(Capilla Real, Granada/ Laurie Platt Winfrey, Inc.)*

The diplomacy of the Catholic rulers of Spain achieved a success they never anticipated. Partly out of hatred for the French and partly to gain international recognition for their new dynasty, Ferdinand and Isabella in 1496 married their second daughter, Joanna, heiress to Castile, to the archduke Philip, heir through his mother to the Burgundian Netherlands and through his father to the Holy Roman Empire.

## Germany and the Habsburg Dynasty

The marriage in 1477 of Maximilian I of the house of Habsburg and Mary of Burgundy was a decisive event in early modern European history. Burgundy consisted of two parts: the French duchy with its capital at Dijon, and the Burgundian Netherlands with its capital at Brussels. Through this union with the rich and powerful duchy of Burgundy, the Austrian house of Habsburg, the strongest ruling family in the empire, started to become an international power.

The Habsburg-Burgundian marriage angered the French, who considered Burgundy part of French territory. Within the empire, German principalities that resented Austria's pre-eminence began to see that they shared interests with France. The marriage of Maximilian and Mary inaugurated centuries of conflict between the Austrian house of Habsburg and the kings of France. Germany was to be the chief arena of the struggle.

The heir of Mary and Maximilian, Philip of Burgundy, married Joanna of Castile, daughter of Ferdinand and Isabella of Spain. Philip and Joanna's son Charles V (1500–1558) fell heir to a vast conglomeration of territories. Through a series of accidents and unexpected deaths, Charles inherited Spain from his mother, together with her possessions in the Americas and the Spanish dominions in Italy, Sicily, Sardinia, and Naples. From his father he inherited the Habsburg lands in Austria, southern Germany, the Low Countries, and Franche-Comté in east-central France.

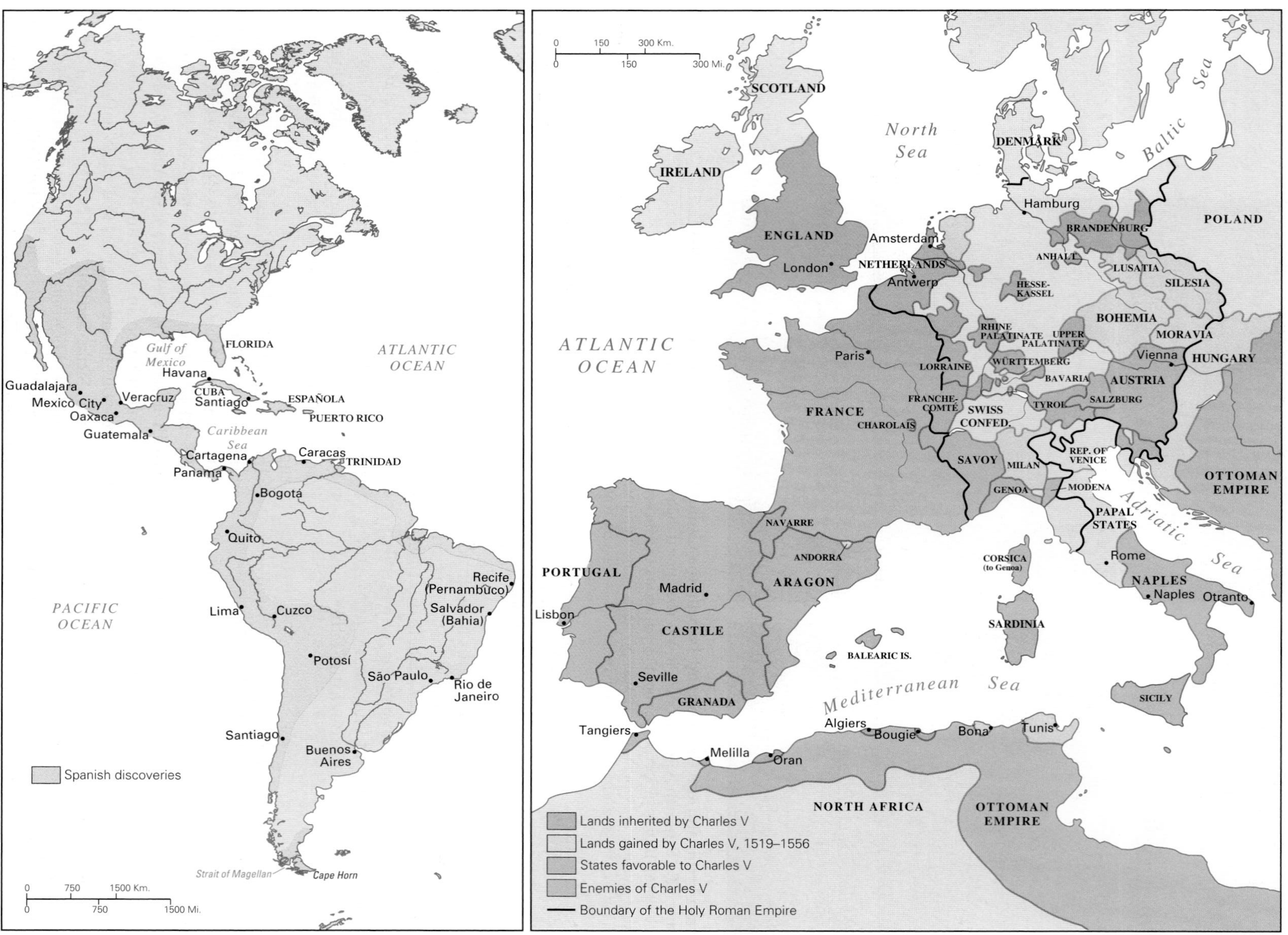


**MAP 15.1 The Global Empire of Charles V** Charles V exercised theoretical jurisdiction over more European territory than anyone since Charlemagne. He also claimed authority over large parts of North and South America.

Charles's inheritance was an incredibly diverse collection of states and peoples, each governed in a different manner and held together only by the person of the emperor (see Map 15.1). Charles was convinced that it was his duty to maintain the political and religious unity of Western Christendom. In this respect, Charles V was the last medieval emperor.

Charles needed and in 1519 secured the imperial title from the electors. Forward-thinking Germans proposed government reforms, but Charles continued the Burgundian policy of his grandfather Maximilian. German revenues and German troops were subordinated to the needs of other parts of the empire, first Burgundy and then Spain. Habsburg international interests came before the need for reform in Germany.

## THE CONDITION OF THE CHURCH (CA 1400–1517)

The papal conflict with the German emperor Frederick II in the thirteenth century, followed by the Babylonian Captivity and then the Great Schism (see pages 404–405), badly damaged the prestige of church leaders. In the fourteenth and fifteenth centuries, leaders of the conciliar movement reflected educated public opinion when they called for the reform of the church "in head and members." The humanists of Italy and the Christian humanists of northern Europe denounced corruption in the church. In *The Praise of Folly,* for example, Erasmus condemned the absurd superstitions of the parish clergy and the excessive rituals of the monks.

In the early sixteenth century, critics of the church concentrated their attacks on three disorders: clerical immorality, clerical ignorance, and clerical pluralism. There was little pressure for doctrinal change; the emphasis was on moral and administrative reform.

Since the fourth century, church law had required candidates for the priesthood to accept absolute celibacy. The requirement had always been difficult to enforce. Many priests, especially those ministering to country people, had concubines, and reports of neglect of the rule of celibacy were common. Immorality, of course, included more than sexual transgressions. Clerical drunkenness, gambling, and indulgence in fancy dress were frequent charges. There is no way of knowing how many priests were guilty of such behavior. But because such conduct was so much at odds with the church's rules and moral standards, it scandalized the educated faithful.

The bishops casually enforced regulations regarding the education of priests. As a result, standards for ordination were shockingly low. Predictably, Christian humanists, with their concern for learning, condemned the ignorance or low educational level of the clergy. Many priests could barely read and write, and critics laughed at the illiterate priest mumbling Latin words to the Mass that he could not understand.

Pluralism and absenteeism constituted the third major abuse. Many clerics, especially higher ecclesiastics, held several *benefices,* or offices, simultaneously but seldom visited them, let alone performed the spiritual responsibilities those offices entailed. Instead, they collected revenues from each benefice and paid a poor priest a fraction of the income to fulfill the spiritual duties of a particular local church. The French king Louis XII's diplomat Antoine du Prat is perhaps the most notorious example of absenteeism. He was archbishop of Sens, but the first time he entered his cathedral was in his own funeral procession.

The Christian church, with its dioceses and abbeys, possessed a large proportion of the wealth of the countries of Europe. What better way for a ruler to reward government officials, who were usually clerics, than with bishoprics and other high church offices? Thus churchmen who served as royal councilors, diplomats, treasury officials, chancellors, viceroys, and judges were paid by the church for their services to the state.

In most countries except England, members of the nobility occupied the highest church positions. The spectacle of proud, aristocratic prelates living in magnificent splendor contrasted very unfavorably with the simple fishermen who were Christ's disciples. Nor did the popes of the period 1450 to 1550 set much of an example.

The court of the Spanish pope Rodrigo Borgia, Alexander VI (r. 1492–1503), who publicly acknowledged his mistress and children, reached new heights of impropriety. Pope Julius II (r. 1503–1513) donned military armor and personally led papal troops against the French invaders of Italy in 1506. After him, Giovanni de' Medici, the son of Lorenzo de' Medici, carried on as Pope Leo X (r. 1513–1521) the Medicean tradition of being a great patron of the arts.

Calls for reform testify to the spiritual vitality of the church as well as to its problems. In the late fifteenth and early sixteenth centuries, both individuals and groups within the church were working actively for reform. In Spain, for example, Cardinal Francisco Jiménez (1436–1517) visited religious houses, encouraged the monks and friars to obey their rules and constitutions, and set high standards for the training of the diocesan clergy.

In Holland, beginning in the late fourteenth century, a group of pious laypeople called Brethren of the Common

Life sought to make religion a personal, inner experience. They lived in stark simplicity while daily carrying out the Gospel teaching of feeding the hungry, clothing the naked, and visiting the sick. The Brethren also taught in local schools to prepare devout candidates for the priesthood. The spirituality of the Brethren of the Common Life found its finest expression in the classic *The Imitation of Christ* by Thomas à Kempis, which urges Christians to take Christ as their model and seek perfection in a simple way of life. In the mid-fifteenth century, the movement had houses in the Netherlands, in central Germany, and in the Rhineland; it was a true religious revival.[25]

The papacy also expressed concern for reform. Pope Julius II summoned an ecumenical, or universal, council, which met in the church of Saint John Lateran in Rome from 1512 to 1517. The bishops and theologians who attended the Lateran Council strove earnestly to reform the church. The council recommended higher standards for education of the clergy and instruction of the common people. The bishops placed the responsibility for eliminating bureaucratic corruption squarely on the papacy and suggested significant doctrinal reforms. But many obstacles stood in the way of ecclesiastical change. Nor did the actions of an obscure German friar immediately force the issue.

## MARTIN LUTHER AND THE BIRTH OF PROTESTANTISM

As a result of a personal religious struggle, a German Augustinian friar, Martin Luther (1483–1546), launched the Protestant Reformation of the sixteenth century. Luther articulated the widespread desire for reform of the Christian church and the deep yearning for salvation that were typical of his time.

Martin Luther was born at Eisleben in Saxony, the second son of a copper miner who later became a mine owner. At considerable sacrifice, his father sent him to school and then to the University of Erfurt. Hans Luther intended his son to study law and have a legal career, which for centuries had been the steppingstone to public office and material success. Badly frightened during a thunderstorm, however, young Luther vowed to become a friar. Without consulting his father, he entered a monastery at Erfurt in 1505. Luther was ordained a priest in 1507 and after additional study earned a doctorate of theology. From 1512 until his death, he served as professor of Scripture at the new University of Wittenberg.

Martin Luther was exceedingly scrupulous in his monastic observances and was devoted to prayer, penance, and fasting. But the doubts and conflicts that trouble any sensitive young person who has just taken a grave step were especially intense in young Luther. He had terrible anxiety about sin, and he worried continually about his salvation. Luther intensified his monastic observances but still found no peace of mind.

Luther's wise and kindly confessor, John Staupitz, directed him to the study of Saint Paul's letters. Gradually, Luther arrived at a new understanding of the Pauline letters and of all Christian doctrine. He came to believe that salvation comes not through external observances and penance but through a simple faith in Christ. Faith is the means by which God sends humanity his grace, and faith is a free gift that cannot be earned.

### Luther's Theology

An incident illustrative of the condition of the church in the early sixteenth century propelled Martin Luther onto the stage of history and brought about the Reformation in Germany. The University of Wittenberg lay within the archdiocese of Magdeburg. The archbishop of Magdeburg, Albert, held two other high ecclesiastical offices. To hold all three offices simultaneously—blatant pluralism—required papal dispensation. Archbishop Albert borrowed money from the Fuggers, a wealthy banking family of Augsburg, to pay Pope Leo X for the dispensation (the pope wanted the money to complete work on Saint Peter's Basilica). Leo X then authorized Archbishop Albert to sell indulgences in Germany to repay the Fuggers.

Wittenberg was in the political jurisdiction of the elector Frederick of Saxony. When Frederick forbade the sale of indulgences within his duchy, the people of Wittenberg, including some of Professor Luther's students, streamed across the border from Saxony into Jütenborg in Thuringia to buy them.

What exactly was an **indulgence?** According to Catholic theology, individuals who sin alienate themselves from God and his love. In order to be reconciled to God, the sinner must confess his or her sins to a priest and do the penance that the priest assigns. The doctrine of indulgence rested on three principles. First, God is merciful, but he is also just. Second, Christ and the saints, through their infinite virtue, established a "treasury of merits" on which the church, because of its special relationship with Christ and the saints, can draw. Third, the church has the authority to grant sinners the spiritual benefits of those merits. Originally, an indulgence was a remission of the temporal (priest-imposed) penalties for sin. Beginning in the twelfth century, the papacy and bishops had given

Crusaders such indulgences. By the later Middle Ages, people widely believed that an indulgence secured total remission of penalties for sin—on earth or in purgatory—and ensured swift entry into Heaven.

Archbishop Albert hired the Dominican friar John Tetzel to sell the indulgences. Tetzel mounted an advertising blitz. One of his slogans—"As soon as coin in coffer rings, the soul from purgatory springs"—brought phenomenal success. Men and women bought indulgences not only for themselves but also for deceased parents, relatives, or friends.

Luther was severely troubled that ignorant people believed they had no further need for repentance once they had purchased an indulgence. Thus, according to historical tradition, in the academic fashion of the times, on the eve of All Saints' Day (October 31), 1517, he attached to the door of the church at Wittenberg Castle a list of ninety-five theses (or propositions) on indulgences. By this act, Luther intended only to start a theological discussion of the subject and to defend the theses publicly.

Luther's theses were soon translated from Latin into German, printed, and read throughout the empire. Immediately, broad theological issues were raised. When questioned, Luther rested his fundamental argument on the principle that there was no biblical basis for indulgences. But, replied Luther's opponents, to deny the legality of indulgences was to deny the authority of the pope who had authorized them. The issue was drawn: where did authority lie in the Christian church?

The papacy responded with a letter condemning some of Luther's propositions, ordering that his books be burned, and giving him two months to recant or be excommunicated. Luther retaliated by publicly burning the letter. By January 3, 1521, when the excommunication was supposed to become final, the controversy involved more than theological issues. The papal legate wrote, "All Germany is in revolution. Nine-tenths shout 'Luther' as their war cry; and the other tenth cares nothing about Luther, and cries 'Death to the court of Rome.'"[26]

In this highly charged atmosphere, the twenty-one-year-old emperor Charles V held his first diet at Worms and summoned Luther to appear before it. When ordered to recant, Luther replied in language that rang all over Europe:

*Unless I am convinced by the evidence of Scripture or by plain reason—for I do not accept the authority of the Pope or the councils alone, since it is established that they have often*

**Lucas Cranach: The Ten Commandments (early sixteenth century)** Protestants condemned images of all kinds but recognized their value for instructional purposes. Here Cranach, an early adherent of Luther's Reformation, illustrates the Ten Commandments. Can you name the commandments? Is it unfair to say that the painting has a misogynistic tinge, given the female devil in number 5 and the wife in number 9? The semicircular rainbow running through the ten scenes symbolizes the covenant between God and humankind. *(Lutherhalle, Wittenberg/The Bridgeman Art Library International Ltd)*

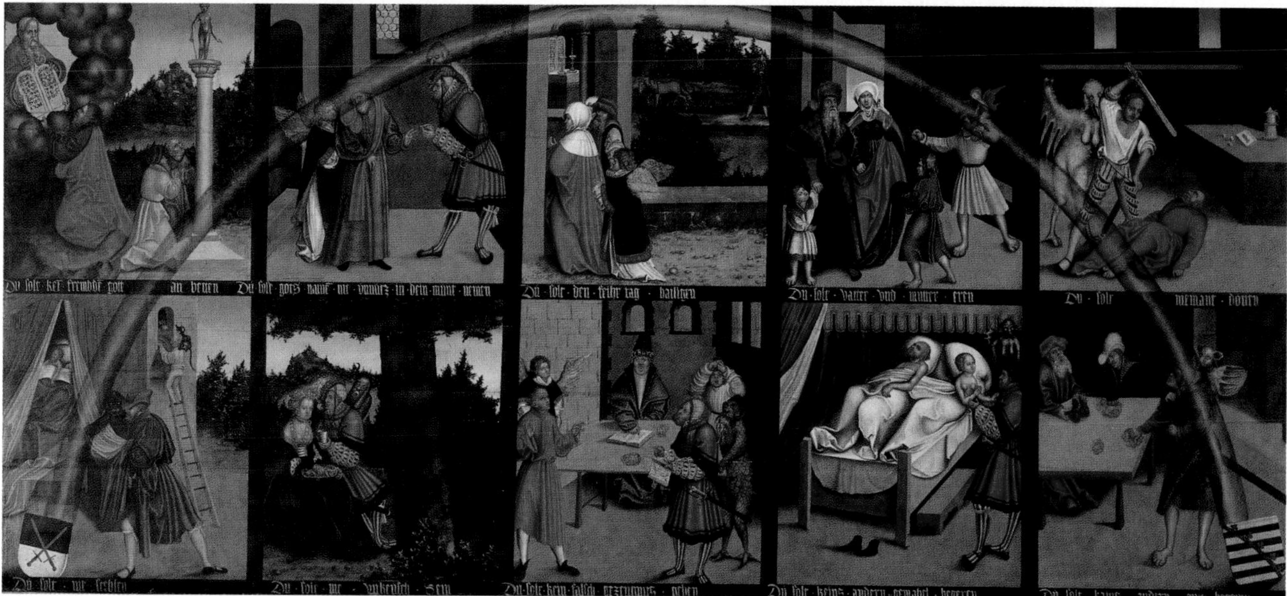

*erred and contradicted themselves—I am bound by the Scriptures I have cited and my conscience is captive to the Word of God. I cannot and will not recant anything, for it is neither safe nor right to go against conscience. God help me. Amen.*[27]

The emperor declared Luther an outlaw of the empire and denied him legal protection. Duke Frederick of Saxony, however, protected him.

Between 1520 and 1530, Luther worked out the basic theological tenets that became the articles of faith for his new church and subsequently for all Protestant groups. At first the word **Protestant** meant "Lutheran," but with the appearance of many protesting sects, it became a general term applied to all non-Catholic Christians. Ernst Troeltsch, a German student of the sociology of religion, has defined *Protestantism* as a "modification of Catholicism, in which the Catholic formulation of questions was retained, while a different answer was given to them." Luther provided new answers to four old, basic theological issues.[28]

First, how is a person to be saved? Traditional Catholic teaching held that salvation was achieved by both faith and good works. Luther held that salvation comes by faith alone. Women and men are saved, said Luther, by the arbitrary decision of God, irrespective of good works or the sacraments. God, not people, initiates salvation.

Second, where does religious authority reside? Christian doctrine had long maintained that authority rests both in the Bible and in the traditional teaching of the church. Luther maintained that authority rests in the Word of God as revealed in the Bible alone and as interpreted by an individual's conscience. He urged that each person read and reflect on the Scriptures.

Third, what is the church? Medieval churchmen had tended to identify the church with the clergy. Luther reemphasized the Catholic teaching that the church consists of the entire community of Christian believers.

Finally, what is the highest form of Christian life? The medieval church had stressed the superiority of the monastic and religious life over the secular. Luther argued that all vocations, whether ecclesiastical or secular, have equal merit and that every person should serve God according to his or her individual calling. Protestantism, in sum, represented a reformulation of the Christian heritage.

## The Social Impact of Luther's Beliefs

By the time of his death in 1546, people of all social classes had become Lutheran. Two significant late medieval developments prepared the way for Luther's ideas. First, since the fifteenth century, city governments had expressed resentment at clerical exemption from taxes and from civic responsibilities such as defending the city. Second, critics of the late medieval church, especially informed and intelligent townspeople, had condemned the irregularity and poor quality of sermons. As a result, prosperous burghers in many towns had established preacherships. Preachers were men of superior education who were required to deliver about a hundred sermons a year. Luther's ideas attracted many preachers, and in many towns preachers became Protestant leaders. Preacherships also encouraged the Protestant form of worship, in which the sermon, not the Eucharist, is the central part of the service.[29]

In the countryside, the attraction of the German peasants to Lutheran beliefs was almost predictable. Luther himself came from a peasant background and admired the peasants' ceaseless toil. Peasants thrilled to the words Luther used in his treatise *On Christian Liberty* (1520): "A Christian man is the most free lord of all and subject to none." Taken out of context, these words easily stirred social unrest. (See the feature "Listening to the Past: Martin Luther, *On Christian Liberty*" on pages 494–495.)

In the early sixteenth century, the economic condition of the peasantry varied from place to place but was generally worse than it had been in the fifteenth century and was deteriorating. The peasants believed their demands conformed to Scripture and cited Luther as a theologian who could prove that they did.

Luther wanted to prevent rebellion. At first he sided with the peasants and in his tract *An Admonition to Peace* blasted the nobles:

*We have no one on earth to thank for this mischievous rebellion, except you lords and princes, especially you blind bishops and mad priests and monks. . . . In your government you do nothing but flay and rob your subjects in order that you may lead a life of splendor and pride, until the poor common folk can bear it no longer.*[30]

But nothing justified the use of armed force, he warned: "The fact that rulers are unjust and wicked does not excuse tumult and rebellion; to punish wickedness does not belong to everybody, but to the worldly rulers who bear the sword."[31] As for biblical support for the peasants' demands, he maintained that Scripture had nothing to do with earthly justice or material gain.

Massive revolts first broke out near the Swiss frontier and then swept through Swabia, Thuringia, the Rhineland, and Saxony. The crowds' slogans came directly from Luther's writings. "God's righteousness" and the "Word of God" were invoked in the effort to secure social and economic justice. The peasants who expected Luther's support were soon disillusioned. He had written of the "freedom" of the Christian, but he had meant the freedom to obey the Word of God, for in sin men and women lose their freedom and break their relationship with God. To Luther, freedom meant independence from the authority of the Roman church; it did *not* mean opposition to legally established secular powers. Firmly convinced that rebellion hastened the end of civilized society, he wrote a tract *Against the Murderous, Thieving Hordes of the Peasants:* "Let everyone who can smite, slay, and stab [the peasants], secretly and openly, remembering that nothing can be more poisonous, hurtful or devilish than a rebel."[32] The nobility ferociously crushed the revolt. Historians estimate that over seventy-five thousand peasants were killed in 1525.

Luther took literally these words in Saint Paul's Letter to the Romans: "Let every soul be subject to the higher powers. For there is no power but of God: the powers that be are established by God. Whosoever resists the power, resists the ordinance of God: and they that resist shall receive to themselves damnation" (Romans 13:1–2). As it developed, Lutheran theology exalted the state, subordinated the church to the state, and everywhere championed "the powers that be." The revolt of 1525 strengthened the authority of lay rulers. Peasant economic conditions, however, moderately improved. For example, in many parts of Germany, enclosed fields, meadows, and forests were returned to common use.

Luther's linguistic skill, together with his translation of the New Testament in 1523, led to the acceptance of his dialect as the standard version of German. His insistence that everyone should read and reflect on the Scriptures attracted the literate and thoughtful middle classes partly because he appealed to their intelligence. Moreover, the business classes, preoccupied with making money, envied the church's wealth, disapproved of the luxurious lifestyle of some churchmen, and resented tithes and ecclesiastical taxation. Luther's doctrines of salvation by faith and the priesthood of all believers not only raised the religious status of the commercial classes but protected their pocketbooks as well.

Hymns, psalms, and Luther's two *Catechisms* (1529)—compendiums of basic religious knowledge—also show the power of language in spreading the ideals of the Reformation. Lutheran hymns such as "A Mighty Fortress Is Our God" expressed deep feelings, were easily remembered, and imprinted on the mind central points of doctrine. Though originally intended for the instruction of pastors, Luther's *Catechisms* became powerful tools for the indoctrination of men and women of all ages, especially the young.[33]

What appeal did Luther's message have for women? Luther's argument that all vocations have equal merit in the sight of God gave dignity to those who performed ordinary, routine, domestic tasks. The abolition of monasticism in Protestant territories led to the exaltation of the home, which Luther and other reformers stressed as the special domain of the wife. Protestants established schools where girls, as well as boys, became literate in the catechism and the Bible. The reformers stressed marriage as the cure for clerical concupiscence. Protestantism thus proved attractive to the many women who had been priests' concubines and mistresses: they became legal and honorable wives.[34]

For his time, Luther held enlightened views on matters of sexuality and marriage. He wrote to a young man, "Dear lad, be not ashamed that you desire a girl, nor you my maid, the boy. Just let it lead you into matrimony and not into promiscuity, and it is no more cause for shame than eating and drinking."[35] He believed that marriage was a woman's career. A happy marriage to the former nun Katharine von Bora mellowed him, and a student quoted him as saying, "Next to God's Word there is no more precious treasure than holy matrimony. God's highest gift on earth is a pious, cheerful, God-fearing, home-keeping wife, with whom you may live peacefully, to whom you may entrust your goods, and body and life."[36] Though Luther deeply loved his "dear Katie," he believed that women's principal concerns were children, the kitchen, and the church.

## The Political Impact of Luther's Beliefs

In the sixteenth century, the practice of religion remained a public matter. Everyone participated in the religious life of the community, just as almost everyone shared in the local agricultural work. Whatever spiritual convictions individuals held in the privacy of their consciences, the emperor, king, prince, magistrate, or other civil authority determined the official form of public religious practice within his jurisdiction. Almost everyone believed that the presence of a faith different from that of the majority represented a political threat to the security of the state. Only a tiny minority, and certainly none of the princes, believed in religious liberty.

The religious storm launched by Martin Luther swept across Germany. Several elements in his religious reformation stirred patriotic feelings. Anti-Roman sentiment ran high. Humanists lent eloquent intellectual support. And Luther's translation of the New Testament into German evoked national pride.

For decades devout laypeople and churchmen had called on the German princes to reform the church. In 1520 Luther took up the cry in his *Appeal to the Christian Nobility of the German Nation.* Unless the princes destroyed papal power in Germany, Luther argued, reform was impossible. He urged the princes to confiscate ecclesiastical wealth and to abolish indulgences, dispensations, pardons, and clerical celibacy. He told them that it was their public duty to bring about the moral reform of the church. Luther based his argument in part on the papacy's financial exploitation of Germany: "How comes it that we Germans must put up with such robbery and such extortion of our property at the hands of the pope? Why do we Germans let them make such fools and apes of us?"[37] These words fell on welcome ears and itchy fingers. Luther's appeal to German patriotism gained him strong support, and national feeling influenced many princes otherwise confused by or indifferent to the complexities of the religious issues.

The church in Germany possessed great wealth. And unlike other countries, Germany had no strong central government to check the flow of gold to Rome. Rejection of Roman Catholicism and adoption of Protestantism would mean the legal confiscation of lush farmlands, rich monasteries, and wealthy shrines. Some German princes were sincerely attracted to Lutheranism, but many civil authorities realized that they had a great deal to gain by embracing the new faith. A steady stream of duchies, margraviates, free cities, and bishoprics did so and secularized church property. Many princes used the religious issue to extend their financial and political independence. The results were unfortunate for the improvement of German government. The Protestant movement ultimately proved a political disaster for Germany.

Charles V must share blame with the German princes for the disintegration of imperial authority in the empire. He neither understood nor took an interest in the constitutional problems of Germany, and he lacked the material resources to oppose Protestantism effectively there. Throughout his reign, he was preoccupied with his Flemish, Spanish, Italian, and American territories. Moreover, the Turkish threat prevented him from acting effectively against the Protestants; Charles's brother Ferdinand needed Protestant support against the Turks who besieged Vienna in 1529.

Five times between 1521 and 1555, Charles V went to war with the Valois kings of France. The issue each time was the Habsburg lands acquired by the marriage of Maximilian and Mary of Burgundy. Much of the fighting occurred in Germany. The cornerstone of French foreign policy in the sixteenth and seventeenth centuries was the desire to keep the German states divided. Thus Europe witnessed the paradox of the Catholic king of France supporting the Lutheran princes in their challenge to his fellow Catholic, Charles V. The Habsburg-Valois Wars advanced the cause of Protestantism and promoted the political fragmentation of the German Empire.

Finally, in 1555, Charles agreed to the Peace of Augsburg, which officially recognized Lutheranism. Each prince was permitted to determine the religion of his territory. Most of northern and central Germany became Lutheran; the south remained Roman Catholic. There was no freedom of religion, however. Princes or town councils established state churches to which all subjects of the area had to belong. Dissidents, whether Lutheran or Catholic, had to convert or leave. The political difficulties Germany inherited from the Middle Ages had been compounded by the religious crisis of the sixteenth century.

## THE GROWTH OF THE PROTESTANT REFORMATION

By 1555 much of northern Europe had broken with the Roman Catholic church. All of Scandinavia, England (except during the reign of Mary Tudor), and Scotland, and large parts of Switzerland, Germany, and France, had rejected the religious authority of Rome and adopted new faiths (see Map 15.2). Because a common religious faith had been the one element uniting all of Europe for almost a thousand years, the fragmentation of belief led to profound changes in European life and society. The most significant new form of Protestantism was Calvinism, of which the Peace of Augsburg had made no mention at all.

### Calvinism

In 1509, while Luther was studying for a doctorate at Wittenberg, John Calvin (1509–1564) was born in Noyon in northwestern France. Luther inadvertently launched the Protestant Reformation. Calvin, however, had the greater impact on future generations. In 1533 he experienced a religious crisis, as a result of which he converted to Protestantism. His theological writings profoundly influenced the social thought and attitudes of Europeans and English-speaking peoples all over the world, especially in Canada and the United States.

Convinced that God selects certain people to do his work, Calvin believed that God had specifically called him to reform the church. Accordingly, he accepted an invitation to assist in the reformation of the city of Geneva. There, beginning in 1541, Calvin worked assiduously to establish a Christian society ruled by God through civil magistrates and reformed ministers. Geneva, "a city that was a Church," became the model of a Christian community for sixteenth-century Protestant reformers.

To understand Calvin's Geneva, it is necessary to understand Calvin's ideas. These he embodied in *The Institutes of the Christian Religion,* first published in 1536 and definitively issued in 1559. The cornerstone of Calvin's theology was his belief in the absolute sovereignty and omnipotence of God and the total weakness of humanity. Before the infinite power of God, he asserted, men and women are as insignificant as grains of sand.

Calvin did not ascribe free will to human beings, because that would detract from the sovereignty of God. Men and women cannot actively work to achieve salvation; rather, God in his infinite wisdom decided at the beginning of time who would be saved and who damned. This viewpoint constitutes the theological principle called **predestination:**

*Predestination we call the eternal decree of God, by which he has determined in himself, what he would have become of every individual of mankind. . . . God has once for all determined, both whom he would admit to salvation, and whom he would condemn to destruction. We affirm that this counsel, as far as concerns the elect, is founded on his gratuitous mercy, totally irrespective of human merit. . . . How exceedingly presumptuous it is only to inquire into the causes of the Divine will.*[38]

"This terrible decree," as even Calvin called it, did not lead to pessimism or fatalism. Rather, the Calvinist believed in the redemptive work of Christ and was confident that God had elected (saved) him or her. Predestination served as an energizing dynamic, forcing a person to undergo hardships in the constant struggle against evil.

Calvin aroused Genevans to a high standard of morality. Using his sermons and a program of religious education, God's laws and man's were enforced in Geneva.

The Genevan Consistory, made up of prominent laymen and pastors, exercised a powerful civic role. The duties of the Consistory were "to keep watch over every man's life [and] to admonish amiably those whom they see leading a disorderly life." Calvin emphasized that the Consistory's activities should be thorough and "its eyes may be everywhere," but corrections were only "medicine to turn sinners to the Lord."[39]

Although all municipal governments in early modern Europe regulated citizens' conduct, none did so with the severity of Geneva's Consistory under Calvin's leadership. Nor did it make any distinction between what we would consider crimes against society and simple un-Christian conduct. The Consistory investigated and punished absence from sermons, criticism of ministers, dancing, playing cards, family quarrels, and heavy drinking. The civil authorities handled serious crimes and heresy and, with the Consistory's approval, sometimes used torture to extract confessions. Between 1542 and 1546 alone, seventy-six persons were banished from Geneva and fifty-eight executed for heresy, adultery, blasphemy, and witchcraft.

To many sixteenth-century Europeans, Calvin's Geneva seemed "the most perfect school of Christ since the days of the Apostles." Religious refugees from France, England, Spain, Scotland, and Italy visited the city. Subsequently, the Reformed church of Calvin served as the model for the Presbyterian church in Scotland, the Huguenot church in France, and the Puritan churches in England and New England. The Calvinist provision for congregational participation and vernacular liturgy helped to satisfy women's desire to belong to and participate in a meaningful church organization. The Calvinist ethic of the "calling" dignified all work with a religious aspect: hard work, well done, was said to be pleasing to God. This doctrine encouraged an aggressive, vigorous activism. In the *Institutes* Calvin provided a systematic theology for Protestantism. The Reformed church of Calvin had a strong and well-organized machinery of government. These factors, together with the social and economic applications of Calvin's theology, made Calvinism the most dynamic force in sixteenth- and seventeenth-century Protestantism.

## The Anabaptists

The name **Anabaptist** derives from a Greek word meaning "to baptize again." The Anabaptists, sometimes described as the "left wing" of the Reformation, believed that only adults could make a free choice about religious faith, baptism, and entry into the Christian community. Thus they considered the practice of baptizing infants and children preposterous and wanted to rebaptize believers who had been baptized as children. Anabaptists took the Gospel and, at first, Luther's teachings absolutely literally and favored a return to the kind of church that had existed among the earliest Christians—a voluntary association of believers who had experienced an inner light.

Anabaptists maintained that only a few people would receive the inner light. This position meant that the Christian community and the Christian state were not

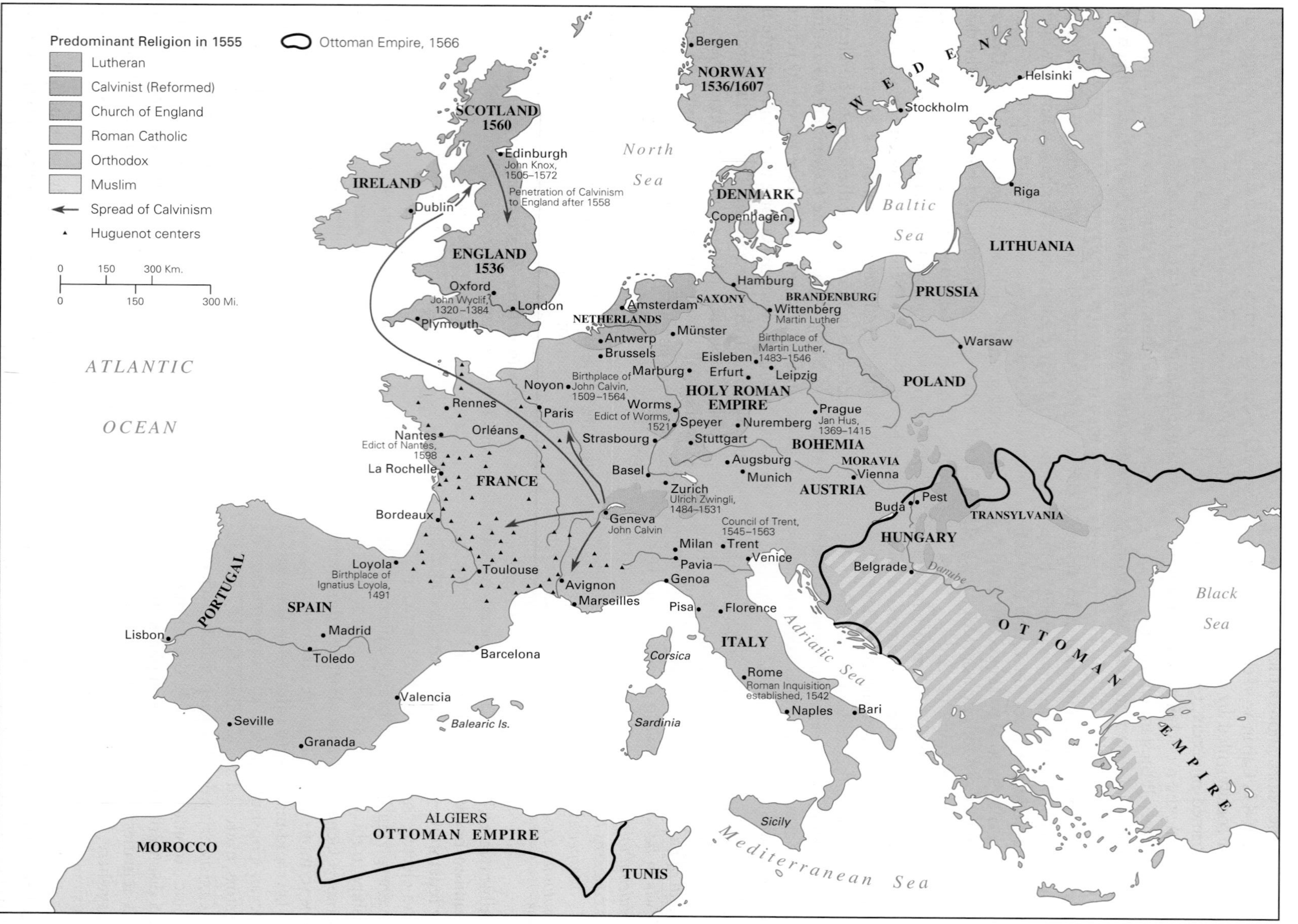


**MAP 15.2 The Protestant and the Catholic Reformations** The Reformations shattered the religious unity of Western Christendom. What common cultural traits predominated in regions where a particular branch of the Christian faith was maintained or took root?

identical. In other words, Anabaptists believed in the separation of church and state and in religious tolerance. They almost never tried to force their values on others. In an age that believed in the necessity of state-established churches, Anabaptist views on religious liberty were thought to undermine that concept.

Each Anabaptist community or church was entirely independent; it selected its own ministers and ran its own affairs. Anabaptists admitted women to the ministry. They shared goods as the early Christians had done, refused all public offices, and would not serve in the armed forces. In fact, they laid great stress on pacifism.

Ideas such as absolute pacifism and the distinction between the Christian community and the state brought down on these unfortunate people fanatical hatred and bitter persecution. Luther, Calvin, and Catholics all saw—quite correctly—the separation of church and state as leading ultimately to the complete secularization of society. The Quakers with their gentle pacifism, the Baptists with their emphasis on an inner spiritual light, the Congregationalists with their democratic church organization, and, in 1787, the authors of the U.S. Constitution with their concern for the separation of church and state—all trace their origins in part to the Anabaptists of the sixteenth century.

## The English Reformation

As on the continent of Europe, the Reformation in England had social and economic causes as well as religious ones. As elsewhere, too, Christian humanists had for decades been calling for the purification of the church. When the personal matter of the divorce of King Henry VIII (r. 1509–1547) became enmeshed with political issues, a complete break with Rome resulted.

Traditional Catholicism exerted an enormously strong, diverse, and vigorous hold over the imagination and loyalty of the people. The teachings of Christianity were graphically represented in the liturgy, constantly reiterated in sermons, enacted in plays, and carved and printed on walls, screens, and the windows of parish churches. A zealous clergy, increasingly better educated, engaged in a "massive catechetical enterprise." No substantial gulf existed between the religion of the clergy and educated elite and the broad mass of the English people.[40] The Reformation in England was an act of state, initiated by the king's emotional life.

In 1527, after eighteen years of marriage, Henry's wife, Catherine of Aragon, had failed to produce a male child, and Henry claimed that only a male child could prevent a disputed succession. Henry had also fallen in love with a lady at court, Anne Boleyn. So Henry petitioned Pope Clement VII for an annulment of his marriage to Catherine. When the pope procrastinated in granting the annulment, Henry decided to remove the English church from papal authority.

Henry used Parliament to legalize the Reformation in England. The Act in Restraint of Appeals (1533) declared the king to be the supreme sovereign in England and forbade judicial appeals to the papacy, thus establishing the Crown as the highest legal authority in the land. The Act for the Submission of the Clergy (1534) required churchmen to submit to the king and forbade the publication of ecclesiastical laws without royal permission. The Supremacy Act of 1534 declared the king the supreme head of the Church of England. In January 1533, Henry and Anne quietly married, but when she failed twice to produce a male heir, Henry had her beheaded.

Between 1535 and 1539, under the influence of his chief minister, Thomas Cromwell, Henry decided to dissolve the English monasteries because he wanted their wealth. The closing of the monasteries did not achieve a more equitable distribution of land and wealth. Rather, redistribution of land strengthened the upper classes and tied them to the Tudor dynasty.

Henry retained such traditional Catholic practices and doctrines as auricular confession, clerical celibacy, and **transubstantiation** (the doctrine that the bread and wine of the Eucharist are transformed into the body and blood of Christ although their appearance does not change). But Protestant literature circulated, and Henry approved the selection of men of Protestant sympathies as tutors for his son.

Did the religious changes have broad popular support? The surviving evidence does not allow us to gauge the degree of opposition to or support for Henry's break with Rome. Certainly, many laypeople wrote to the king, begging him to spare the monasteries. "Most laypeople acquiesced in the Reformation because they hardly knew what was going on, were understandably reluctant to jeopardise life or limb, a career or the family's good name."[41] But not all quietly acquiesced. In 1536 popular opposition in the north to the religious changes led to the Pilgrimage of Grace, a massive multiclass rebellion that proved the largest in English history. In 1546 serious rebellions in East Anglia and in the west, despite possessing economic and Protestant components, reflected considerable public opposition to the state-ordered religious changes.[42]

After Henry's death, the English church shifted left and right. In the short reign of Henry's sickly son Edward VI (r. 1547–1553), strongly Protestant ideas exerted a

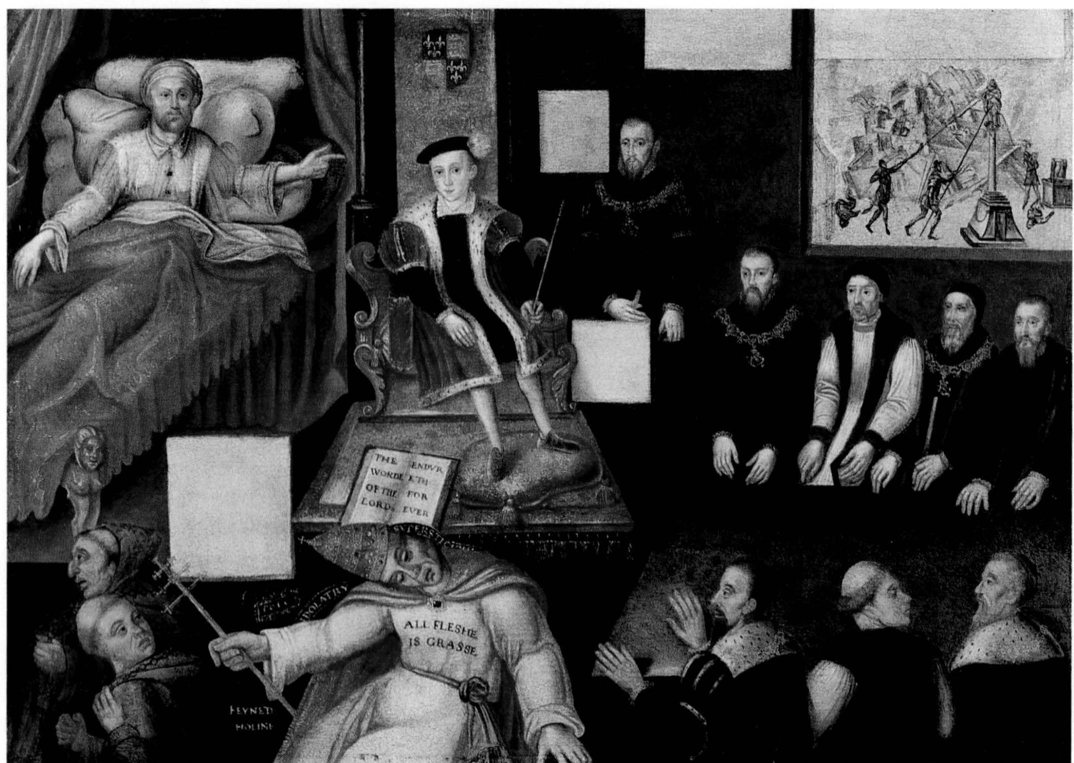


**Allegorical Painting, ca 1548** Henry VIII on his deathbed points to his heir, Edward, surrounded by Protestant worthies, as the wave of the future. The pope collapses, monks flee, and through the window iconoclasts knock down statues, symbolizing error and superstition; stressing Protestantism's focus on Scripture, the Bible is open to 1 Peter 1:24: "The word of the Lord endures forever." Since the new order lacked broad popular support, propagandistic paintings like this and the printing press had to be mobilized to sway public opinion. *(Reproduced by courtesy of the Trustees, National Portrait Gallery, London)*

significant influence on the religious life of the country. Archbishop Thomas Cranmer simplified the liturgy, invited Protestant theologians to England, and prepared the first *Book of Common Prayer* (1549). The equally brief reign of Mary Tudor (r. 1553–1558) witnessed a sharp move back to Catholicism. The devoutly Catholic daughter of Catherine of Aragon and Henry, Mary rescinded the Reformation legislation of her father's reign and fully restored Roman Catholicism. Mary's marriage to her cousin Philip of Spain, son of the emperor Charles V, proved highly unpopular in England, and her persecution and execution of several hundred Protestants further alienated her subjects. Mary's death raised to the throne her sister Elizabeth (r. 1558–1603) and inaugurated the beginnings of religious stability.

Elizabeth had been raised a Protestant, but at the start of her reign sharp differences existed in England. Catholics wanted a Roman Catholic ruler, but a vocal number of returning exiles wanted all Catholic elements in the Church of England eliminated. Members of the latter group were called Puritans because they wanted to "purify" the church. Probably one of the shrewdest politicians in English history, Elizabeth chose a middle course between Catholic and Puritan extremes. She insisted on dignity in church services and political order in the land, and she avoided precise doctrinal definitions.

The parliamentary legislation of the early years of Elizabeth's reign—laws sometimes labeled the "Elizabethan Settlement"—required outward conformity to the Church of England and uniformity in all ceremonies. Everyone had to attend Church of England services; those who refused were fined. During Elizabeth's reign, the Anglican church (from the Latin *Ecclesia Anglicana*), as the Church of England was called, moved in a moderately Protestant direction. Services were conducted in English, monasteries were not re-established, and the clergy were allowed to marry. But the bishops remained as church officials, and apart from language, the services were quite traditional.

## THE CATHOLIC REFORMATION AND THE COUNTER-REFORMATION

Between 1517 and 1547, the reformed versions of Christianity known as Protestantism made remarkable advances. Still, the Roman Catholic church made a significant comeback. After about 1540, no new large areas of Europe, except for the Netherlands, accepted Protestant beliefs (see Map 15.2).

Why did the popes, spiritual leaders of the Western church, move so slowly in reforming the church? The answers lie in the personalities of the popes themselves, in their preoccupation with political affairs in Italy, and in the awesome difficulty of reforming so complicated a bureaucracy as the Roman curia. Clement VII, a true Medici, was far more interested in elegant tapestries and Michelangelo's painting of the Last Judgment than in theological disputes in barbaric Germany or far-off England.

The idea of reform was closely linked to the idea of a general council representing the entire church. Popes such as Clement VII, remembering fifteenth-century conciliar attempts to limit papal authority, resisted calls for a council, fearing loss of power, revenue, and prestige.

### The Council of Trent

Pope Paul III (r. 1534–1549), a Roman aristocrat, humanist, and astrologer, seemed an unlikely person to undertake serious reform. Yet Paul III appointed as cardinals several learned and reform-minded men; established the Inquisition in the Papal States; and called a council, which finally met at Trent, an imperial city close to Italy (see Map 15.2).

The Council of Trent met intermittently from 1545 to 1563. It was called not only to reform the church but also to secure reconciliation with the Protestants. Lutherans and Calvinists were invited to participate, but their insistence that the Scriptures be the sole basis for discussion made reconciliation impossible. International politics repeatedly cast a shadow over the theological debates. Charles V opposed discussions on any matter that might further alienate his Lutheran subjects. The French kings worked against any reconciliation of Roman Catholicism and Lutheranism, wanting the German states to remain divided.

Another problem was the persistence of the conciliar theory of church government. Some bishops wanted a concrete statement asserting the supremacy of a church council over the papacy. The bishops had a provincial and national outlook; only the papacy possessed an international religious perspective. The centralizing tenet was established that all acts of the council required papal approval.

In spite of the obstacles, the achievements of the Council of Trent are impressive. It dealt with both doctrinal and disciplinary matters. The council gave equal validity to the Scriptures and to tradition as sources of religious truth and authority. It reaffirmed the seven sacraments and the traditional Catholic teaching on transubstantiation, rejecting Lutheran and Calvinist positions.

The council tackled the problems arising from ancient abuses by strengthening ecclesiastical discipline. Decrees required bishops to reside in their own dioceses, suppressed pluralism and simony, and forbade the sale of indulgences. Clerics who kept concubines were to give them up. In a highly original canon, the council required every diocese to establish a seminary for the education and training of the clergy and insisted that preference for admission be given to sons of the poor. Seminary professors were to determine whether candidates for ordination had *vocations*—genuine callings as evidenced by purity of life, detachment from the broader secular culture, and a steady inclination toward the priesthood. This was a novel idea, since from the time of the early church, parents had determined their sons' (and daughters') religious careers. Also, great emphasis was laid on preaching and instructing the laity, especially the uneducated.

One decision had especially important social consequences for laypeople. Since the time of the Roman Empire, many couples had treated marriage as a completely personal matter, exchanged vows privately without witnesses, and thus formed clandestine (secret) unions. This widespread practice frequently led later to denials by one party that a marriage had taken place, to conflicts over property, and to disputes in the ecclesiastical courts that had jurisdiction over marriage. The decree *Tametsi* (1563) stipulated that for a marriage to be valid, consent (the essence of marriage) as expressed in the vows had to be given publicly before witnesses, one of whom had to be the parish priest. Trent thereby ended secret marriages in Catholic countries.

The Council of Trent did not bring about reform immediately. But the decrees laid a solid basis for the spiritual renewal of the church and for the enforcement of correction. For four centuries, the doctrinal and disciplinary legislation of Trent served as the basis for Roman Catholic faith, organization, and practice. Church leaders' attention focused on pastoral and missionary matters.

## New Religious Orders and the Inquisition

The establishment of new religious orders within the church reveals a central feature of the Catholic Reformation. These new orders developed in response to the need to raise the moral and intellectual level of the clergy and people. Education was a major goal of them all.

The Ursuline order of nuns, founded by Angela Merici (1474–1540), attained enormous prestige for the education of women. Angela Merici worked for many years among the poor, sick, and uneducated around her native Brescia in northern Italy. In 1535 she established the Ursuline order to combat heresy through Christian education of young girls. The Ursulines sought to re-Christianize society by training future wives and mothers. Approved as a religious community by Paul III in 1544, the Ursulines rapidly grew and spread to France and the New World. Their schools in North America, stretching from Quebec to New Orleans, provided superior education for young women and inculcated the spiritual ideals of the Catholic Reformation.

The Society of Jesus, founded by Ignatius Loyola (1491–1556), a former Spanish soldier, played a powerful international role in resisting the spread of Protestantism, converting Asians and Latin American Indians to Catholicism, and spreading Christian education all over Europe. While recuperating from a severe battle wound to his legs, Loyola studied a life of Christ and other religious books and decided to give up his military career and become a soldier of Christ. His great classic, *Spiritual Exercises,* directed the individual imagination and will to the reform of life and a new spiritual piety.

Loyola was apparently a man of considerable personal magnetism. After study at the universities in Salamanca and Paris, he gathered a group of six companions and in 1540 secured papal approval of the new Society of Jesus, whose members were called **Jesuits.** The first Jesuits were recruited primarily from the wealthy merchant and professional classes. They saw the Reformation as a pastoral problem, its causes and cures related not to doctrinal issues but to people's spiritual condition. Reform of the church as Luther and Calvin understood the word *reform* played no role in the future the Jesuits planned for themselves. Their goal was "to help souls." Loyola also possessed a gift for leadership that consisted of spotting talent and of "the ability to see how at a given juncture change is more consistent with one's scope than staying the course."[43]

The Society of Jesus developed into a highly centralized, tightly knit organization. Candidates underwent a two-year novitiate, in contrast to the usual one-year probation required by older religious orders. Professed members vowed "special obedience to the sovereign pontiff regarding missions."[44] Thus, as stability—the promise to live one's life in the monastery—was what made a monk, so mobility—the commitment to go anywhere—was the defining characteristic of a Jesuit. Flexibility and the willingness to respond to the needs of time and circumstance formed the Jesuit tradition. In this respect, they were very modern, and they attracted many recruits.

The Society of Jesus achieved phenomenal success for the papacy and the reformed Catholic church. Jesuit schools adopted the modern humanist curricula and methods. They first concentrated on the children of the poor but soon were educating the sons of the nobility. As confessors and spiritual directors to kings, Jesuits exerted great political influence. Operating on the principle that the end sometimes justifies the means, they were not above spying. Indifferent to physical comfort and personal safety, they carried Christianity to India and Japan before 1550 and to Brazil, North America, and the Congo in the seventeenth century. Within Europe, the Jesuits brought southern Germany and much of eastern Europe back to Catholicism.

In 1542 Pope Paul III established the **Holy Office** with jurisdiction over the Roman Inquisition, a powerful instrument of the Counter-Reformation. A committee of six cardinals, the Roman Inquisition had judicial authority over all Catholics and the power to arrest, imprison, and execute. Under the fanatical Cardinal Caraffa, it vigorously attacked heresy. The Holy Office published the *Index of Prohibited Books,* a catalogue of forbidden reading. Within the Papal States, the Roman Inquisition effectively destroyed heresy (and some heretics). Outside the papal territories, its influence was slight. Governments had their own judicial systems for the suppression of treasonable activities, as religious heresy was then considered.[45]

# POLITICS, RELIGION, AND WAR

In 1559 France and Spain signed the Treaty of Cateau-Cambrésis, which ended the long conflict known as the Habsburg-Valois Wars. This event marks a watershed in early modern European history. Spain (the Habsburg side) was the victor. France, exhausted by the struggle, had to acknowledge Spanish dominance in Italy, where much of the war had been fought. Spanish governors ruled in Sicily, Naples, and Milan, and Spanish influence was strong in the Papal States and Tuscany. The Treaty of Cateau-Cambrésis ended an era of strictly dynastic wars and initiated a period of conflicts in which politics and religion played the dominant roles.

The wars of the late sixteenth century differed considerably from earlier wars. Sixteenth- and seventeenth-century armies were bigger than medieval ones; some forces numbered as many as fifty thousand men. Because large armies were expensive, governments had to reorganize their administrations to finance them. The use of gunpowder altered both the nature of warfare and popular attitudes toward it. Guns and cannon killed and wounded from a distance, indiscriminately. Writers scorned gunpowder as a coward's weapon that allowed a common soldier to kill a gentleman. Gunpowder weakened the notion, common during the Hundred Years' War (1337–1453), that warfare was an ennobling experience. Governments utilized propaganda, pulpits, and the printing press to arouse public opinion to support war.[46]

Late-sixteenth-century conflicts fundamentally tested the medieval ideal of a unified Christian society governed by one political ruler—the emperor—to whom all rulers were theoretically subordinate, and one church, to which all people belonged. The Protestant Reformation had killed this ideal, but few people recognized it as dead. Catholics continued to believe that Calvinists and Lutherans could be reconverted; Protestants persisted in thinking that the Roman church should be destroyed. Most people believed that a state could survive only if its members shared the same faith. The settlement finally achieved in 1648, known as the Peace of Westphalia, signaled the end of the medieval ideal.

**Primaticcio: Duchess of Etampes's Chamber** In spite of the enormous financial burdens that continuous war placed on his resources, Francis I lavished money on architecture and the arts. To "modernize" the royal residence at Fontainebleau, he summoned the Italian architect and designer Francesco Primaticcio (1504/5–1570), who spent decades on the bedchamber of the king's mistress, Diana, ornamenting it with garlands, woodworking, mythological figures, fresco paintings, and, according to Vasari, the first stucco works in France. Primaticcio inaugurated what was called the School of Fontainebleau. *(Foto Marburg/Art Resource, NY)*

## The Origins of Difficulties in France (1515–1559)

In the first half of the sixteenth century, France continued the recovery begun during the reign of Louis XI (r. 1461–1483). The population losses caused by the plague and the disorders accompanying the Hundred Years' War had created such a labor shortage that serfdom virtually disappeared. Cash rents replaced feudal rents and servile obligations. This development clearly benefited the peasantry. Meanwhile, the declining buying power of money hurt the nobility. Domestic and foreign trade picked up; mercantile centers expanded.

The charming and cultivated Francis I (r. 1515–1547) and his athletic, emotional son Henry II (r. 1547–1559) governed through a small, efficient council. In 1539 Francis issued an ordinance that placed the whole of France under the jurisdiction of the royal law courts and made French the language of those courts. This act had a powerful centralizing impact. The *taille,* a tax on land, provided what strength the monarchy had and supported a strong standing army. Unfortunately, the tax base was too narrow to support France's extravagant promotion of the arts and ambitious foreign policy.

The Habsburg-Valois Wars, which had begun in 1522, cost more than the government could afford. In addition to the time-honored practices of increasing taxes and heavy borrowing, Francis I tried two new devices to raise revenue: the sale of public offices and a treaty with the papacy. The former proved to be only a temporary source of money. The offices sold tended to become hereditary within a family, and once a man bought an office, he and his heirs were tax-exempt. The sale of public offices thus created a tax-exempt class known as the "nobility of the robe."

The treaty with the papacy was the Concordat of Bologna (1516), in which Francis agreed to recognize the supremacy of the papacy over a universal council, thereby accepting a monarchical, rather than a conciliar, view of church government. In return, the French crown gained the right to appoint all French bishops and abbots. This understanding gave the monarchy a rich supplement of money and offices, as well as power over ecclesiastical organization that lasted until the Revolution of 1789. The Concordat of Bologna helps to explain why France did not later become Protestant: in effect, it established Catholicism as the state religion.

After the publication of Calvin's *Institutes of the Christian Religion* in 1536, sizable numbers of French people were attracted to the "reformed religion," as Calvinism was called. Because Calvin wrote in French rather than Latin, his ideas gained wide circulation. At first Calvinism drew converts from among reform-minded members of the Catholic clergy, the industrious middle classes, and artisan groups. Most Calvinists lived in Paris, Lyons, Meaux, Grenoble, and other major cities.

In spite of condemnation by the universities, government bans, and massive burnings at the stake, the numbers of Protestants in France grew steadily. When Henry II died in 1559, perhaps one-tenth of the population had become Calvinist.

## Religious Riots and Civil War in France (1559–1589)

The three weak sons of Henry II could not provide adequate leadership, and the French nobility took advantage of this monarchical weakness. In the second half of the sixteenth century, between two-fifths and one-half of the nobility at one time or another became Calvinist, frequently adopting the "reformed religion" as a religious cloak for their independence from the monarchy. Armed clashes between Catholic royalist lords and Calvinist antimonarchical lords occurred in many parts of France.

Among the upper classes, the fundamental object of the struggle was power. At lower social levels, however, religious concerns were paramount. Working-class crowds composed of skilled craftsmen and the poor wreaked terrible violence on people and property. Both Calvinists and Catholics believed that the others' books, services, and ministers polluted the community. Preachers incited violence, and ceremonies like baptisms, marriages, and funerals triggered it.

In earlier centuries, attacks on great nobles and rich prelates had expressed economic grievances. In contrast, religious rioters of the sixteenth century believed that they could assume the power of public magistrates and rid the community of corruption. Municipal officials criticized the crowds' actions, but the participation of pastors and priests in these riots lent them some legitimacy.[47]

A savage Catholic attack on Calvinists in Paris on August 24, 1572 (Saint Bartholomew's Day), followed the usual pattern. The occasion was a religious ceremony—the marriage of the king's sister Margaret of Valois to the Protestant Henry of Navarre—that was intended to help reconcile Catholics and Huguenots, as French Calvinists were called. The night before the wedding, the leader of the Catholic aristocracy, Henry of Guise, had Gaspard de Coligny, leader of the Huguenot party, attacked. Rioting and slaughter followed. The Huguenot gentry in Paris was massacred, and religious violence spread to the provinces. Between August 25 and October 3, perhaps twelve thousand Huguenots perished at Meaux, Lyons, Orléans, and Paris.

The **Saint Bartholomew's Day massacre** led to the War of the Three Henrys, a civil conflict among factions led by the Protestant Henry of Navarre, by King Henry III (who succeeded the tubercular Charles IX), and by the Catholic Henry of Guise. The Guises wanted not only to destroy Calvinism but to replace Henry III with a member of the Guise family. France suffered fifteen more years of religious rioting and domestic anarchy. Agriculture in many areas was destroyed; commercial life declined severely; starvation and death haunted the land.

What ultimately saved France was a small group of moderates of both faiths called *politiques.* They believed that no religious creed was worth the incessant disorder and destruction and that only the restoration of a strong monarchy could reverse the trend toward collapse. The assassinations of Henry of Guise and King Henry III paved the way for the accession of Henry of Navarre, a politique who ascended the throne as Henry IV (r. 1589–1610).

This glamorous prince, "who knew how to fight, to make love, and to drink," as a contemporary remarked, knew that the majority of the French were Roman Catholics. Declaring "Paris is worth a Mass," Henry knelt before the archbishop of Bourges and was received into the Roman Catholic church. Henry's willingness to sacrifice religious principles in the interest of a strong monarchy saved France. The Edict of Nantes, which Henry published in 1598, granted to Huguenots liberty of conscience and liberty of public worship in two hundred fortified towns, such as La Rochelle. The reign of Henry IV and the Edict of Nantes prepared the way for French absolutism in the seventeenth century (see pages 538–540) by helping to restore internal peace in France.

## The Revolt of the Netherlands and the Spanish Armada

In the last quarter of the sixteenth century, the political stability of England, the international prestige of Spain, and the moral influence of the Roman papacy all became mixed up with a religious crisis in the Low Countries. By this time, the Netherlands was the pivot around which European money, diplomacy, and war revolved. What began as a movement for the reformation of the Catholic church developed into a struggle for Dutch independence from Spanish rule.

The Habsburg emperor Charles V (r. 1519–1556) had inherited the seventeen provinces that compose present-day Belgium and Holland. The French-speaking southern towns produced fine linens and woolens; the wealth of the Dutch-speaking northern cities rested on fishing, shipping, and international banking. In the cities of both regions of the Low Countries, trade and commerce had produced a vibrant cosmopolitan atmosphere.

In the Low Countries, as elsewhere, corruption in the Roman church and the critical spirit of the Renaissance provoked pressure for reform. But Charles's Flemish loyalty checked the spread of Lutheranism. Charles had been born in Ghent and raised in the Netherlands; he was Flemish in language and culture. He identified with the Flemish and they with him. In 1556, however, Charles V abdicated and divided his territories. His younger brother Ferdinand received Austria and the Holy Roman Empire and ruled as Ferdinand I (r. 1558–1564). His son Philip inherited Spain, the Low Countries, Milan and the kingdom of Sicily, and the Spanish possessions in America and ruled as Philip II (r. 1556–1598).

The spread of Calvinism in the Low Countries upset the apple cart. By the 1560s, there was a strong, militant minority of Calvinists to whom Calvinism appealed because of its intellectual seriousness, moral gravity, and approval of any form of labor well done. Many working-class people converted because Calvinist employers would hire only fellow Calvinists. Well organized and with the backing of rich merchants, Calvinists quickly gained a wide following and encouraged opposition to "illegal" civil authorities.

In August 1566, a year of very high grain prices, fanatical Calvinists, primarily of the poorest classes, embarked on a rampage of frightful destruction. As in France, Calvinist destruction in the Low Countries was incited by popular preaching, and attacks were aimed at religious images as symbols of false doctrines, not at people. The cathedral of Notre Dame at Antwerp—which stood as a monument to the commercial prosperity of Flanders, the piety of the business classes, and the artistic genius of centuries—was the first target. Crowds swept through the nave, attacking altars, paintings, books, ecclesiastical vestments, stained-glass windows, and sculptures. Before the havoc was over, thirty more churches had been sacked and irreplaceable libraries burned. From Antwerp the destruction spread to Brussels and Ghent and north to the provinces of Holland and Zeeland.

From Madrid Philip II sent twenty thousand Spanish troops led by the duke of Alva to pacify the Low Countries. Alva interpreted "pacification" to mean the ruthless extermination of religious and political dissidents. His repressive measures and heavy taxation triggered widespread revolt.

For ten years, between 1568 and 1578, civil war raged in the Netherlands between Catholics and Protestants and between the seventeen provinces and Spain. Spanish generals could not halt the fighting. In 1576 the seventeen provinces united under the leadership of Prince William of Orange, called "the Silent" because of his remarkable discretion. In 1578 Philip II sent his nephew Alexander Farnese, duke of Parma, with an army of German mercenaries to crush the revolt once and for all. Avoiding pitched battles, Farnese fought by patient sieges. One by one, the cities of the south fell, and finally Antwerp, the financial capital of northern Europe, also succumbed.

Antwerp marked the farthest extent of Spanish jurisdiction and ultimately the religious division of the Netherlands. The ten southern provinces, the Spanish Netherlands (the future Belgium), remained Catholic and under the control of the Spanish Habsburgs. The seven northern provinces were Protestant and, led by Holland, formed the Union of Utrecht and in 1581 declared their independence from Spain. Thus was born the United Provinces of the Netherlands (see Map 15.3).

Geography and sociopolitical structure differentiated the two countries. The northern provinces were ribboned with sluices and canals and therefore were highly defensible. Several times the Dutch had broken the dikes and flooded the countryside to halt the advancing Farnese. In the southern provinces, the Ardennes mountains interrupt the otherwise flat terrain. In the north, the commercial aristocracy possessed the predominant power; in the south, the landed nobility had the greater influence.

Philip II and Alexander Farnese did not accept the division of the Low Countries, and the struggle continued after 1581. The Protestant United Provinces repeatedly asked the Protestant Queen Elizabeth of England for assistance, but she was reluctant to antagonize Philip II by supporting the Dutch.

**MAP 15.3 The Netherlands, 1559–1609** Some provinces were overwhelmingly agricultural, some involved in manufacturing, others heavily commercial. Each of the seventeen was tied to the Spanish crown in a different way.

Three developments forced Elizabeth's hand. First, the wars in the Low Countries—the chief market for English woolens—badly hurt the English economy. When wool was not exported, the Crown lost valuable customs revenues. Second, the murder of William the Silent in July 1584 eliminated not only a great Protestant leader but also the chief military check on the Farnese advance. Third, the collapse of Antwerp appeared to signal a Catholic sweep through the Netherlands. The next step, the English feared, would be a Spanish invasion of their island. For these reasons, Elizabeth pumped £250,000 and two thousand troops into the Protestant cause in the Low Countries between 1585 and 1587.

Philip of Spain considered himself the international defender of Catholicism and heir to the medieval imperial power. When Pope Sixtus V (r. 1585–1590) heard of the death of the Catholic Mary, Queen of Scots (which Elizabeth had ordered), he promised to pay Philip a million gold ducats the moment Spanish troops landed in England. In addition, Alexander Farnese had repeatedly warned that, to subdue the Dutch, he would have to conquer England and cut off the source of Dutch support.

In these circumstances, Philip prepared a vast armada to sail from Lisbon to Flanders, fight off Elizabeth's navy if it attacked, rendezvous with Farnese, and escort his barges across the English Channel. The expedition's purpose was to transport the Flemish army for a cross-Channel assault. Philip expected to receive the support of English Catholics and anticipated a great victory for Spain.

On May 9, 1588, the 130 vessels of *la felicissima armada*—"the most fortunate fleet," as it was called in official documents—sailed from Lisbon harbor. An English fleet of about 150 ships—smaller, faster, and more maneuverable than the Spanish ships, and many having greater firepower—met the Spanish fleet in the Channel. A combination of storms and squalls, spoiled food and rank water aboard the Spanish ships, inadequate Spanish ammunition, and, to a lesser extent, English fire ships that caused the Spanish to scatter gave England the victory. Many Spanish ships sank on the journey home around Ireland; perhaps 65 managed to reach home ports.

The battle in the Channel had mixed consequences. Spain soon rebuilt its navy, and after 1588 the quality of the Spanish fleet improved. The war between England and Spain dragged on for years. But the defeat of the Spanish Armada did prevent Philip II from reimposing unity on western Europe by force. He did not conquer England, and Elizabeth continued her financial and military support of the Dutch. In the Netherlands, neither side gained significant territory. The borders of 1581 tended to become permanent. In 1609 Philip III of Spain (r. 1598–1621) agreed to a truce, in effect recognizing the independence of the United Provinces. In seventeenth-century Spain, the memory of the loss of the Armada contributed to a spirit of defeatism. In England the victory gave rise to a David and Goliath legend that enhanced English national sentiment.

## The Thirty Years' War (1618–1648)

Meanwhile, the political-religious situation in central Europe deteriorated. An uneasy truce had prevailed in the Holy Roman Empire since the Peace of Augsburg of 1555 (see page 474). Later in the century, Catholics grew alarmed because Lutherans, in violation of the Peace of Augsburg, were steadily acquiring German bishoprics. And Protestants were not pleased by militant Jesuits' success in reconverting Lutheran princes to Catholicism. The spread of Calvinism further confused the issue. Lutherans feared that Catholic and Calvinist gains would totally undermine the Augsburg principles. In an increasingly tense situation, Lutheran princes formed the Protestant Union (1608). Catholics retaliated with the Catholic League (1609). The Holy Roman Empire was divided into two armed camps.

Dynastic interests were also at stake. The Spanish Habsburgs strongly supported the goals of the Austrian Habsburgs: the unity of the empire under Habsburg rule and the preservation of Catholicism within the empire.

Violence erupted first in Bohemia (see Map 15.4), where in 1617 Ferdinand of Styria, the new Catholic king of Bohemia, closed some Protestant churches. In retaliation, on May 23, 1618, Protestants hurled two of Ferdinand's officials from a castle window in Prague. They fell seventy feet but survived: Catholics claimed that angels had caught them; Protestants said the officials fell on a heap of soft horse manure. Called the "defenestration of Prague," this event marked the beginning of the Thirty Years' War (1618–1648).

Historians traditionally divide the war into four phases. The first, or Bohemian, phase (1618–1625) was characterized by civil war in Bohemia, as Bohemians fought for religious liberty and independence from Austrian Habsburg rule. In 1620 Ferdinand, newly elected Holy Roman emperor Ferdinand II (r. 1619–1637), totally defeated Protestant forces at the Battle of the White Mountain and followed up his victories by wiping out Protestantism in Bohemia.

The second, or Danish, phase of the war (1625–1629)—so called because of the participation of King Christian IV of Denmark (r. 1588–1648), the ineffective leader of the Protestant cause—witnessed additional Catholic victories. The year 1629 marked the peak of

**Soldiers Pillage a Farmhouse** Billeting troops on civilian populations caused untold hardships. In this late seventeenth-century Dutch illustration, brawling soldiers take over a peasant's home, eat his food, steal his possessions, and insult his family. Peasant retaliation sometimes proved swift and bloody. *(Rijksmuseum-Stichting Amsterdam)*

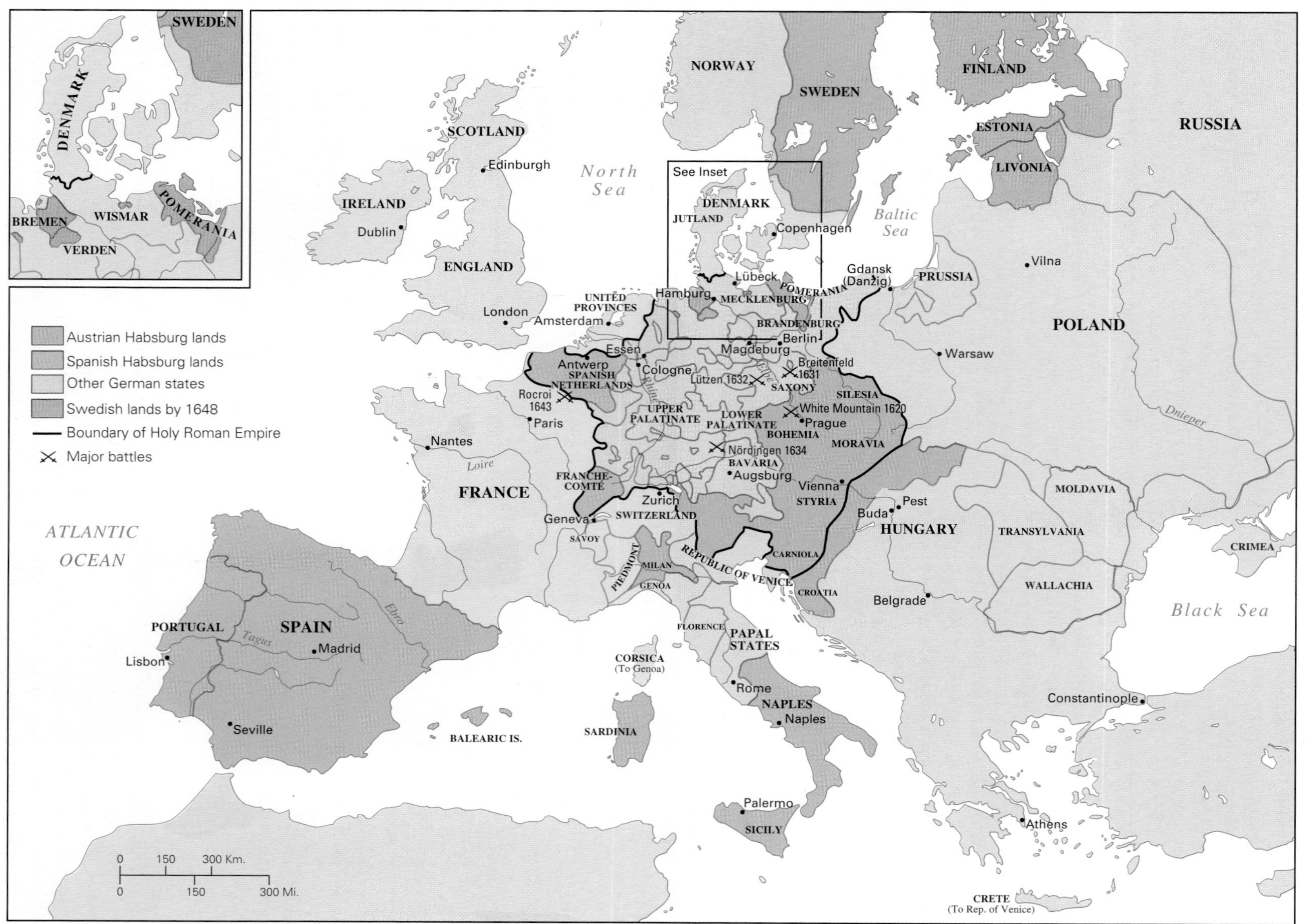


**MAP 15.4 Europe in 1648** Which country emerged from the Thirty Years' War as the strongest European power? What dynastic house was that country's major rival in the early modern period?

Habsburg power. The Jesuits persuaded Ferdinand to issue the Edict of Restitution. It specified that all Catholic properties lost to Protestantism since 1552 were to be restored and only Catholics and Lutherans (*not* Calvinists, Hussites, or other sects) were to be allowed to practice their faiths. Ferdinand appeared to be embarked on a policy to unify the empire. Protestants throughout Europe feared collapse of the balance of power in north-central Europe.

The third, or Swedish, phase of the war (1630–1635) began when Swedish king Gustavus Adolphus (r. 1594–1632) intervened to support the Protestant cause within the empire. The participation of the Swedes in the Thirty Years' War proved decisive for the future of Protestantism and later German history. The Swedish victories ended the Habsburg ambition of uniting all the German states under imperial authority.

The death of Gustavus Adolphus, followed by the defeat of the Swedes at the Battle of Nördlingen in 1634, prompted the French to enter the war on the side of the Protestants. Thus began the French, or international, phase of the Thirty Years' War (1635–1648). For almost a century, French foreign policy had been based on opposition to the Habsburgs, because a weak Holy Roman Empire enhanced France's international stature. Now, in 1635, France declared war on Spain and again sent financial and military assistance to the Swedes and the German Protestant princes. The war dragged on; neither side had the resources to win a decisive victory. French, Dutch, and Swedes, supported by Scots, Finns, and German mercenaries, burned, looted, and destroyed German agriculture and commerce.

Finally, in October 1648, peace was achieved. The treaties signed at Münster and Osnabrück—the **Peace of Westphalia**—mark a turning point in European political, religious, and social history. The treaties recognized the sovereign, independent authority of the German princes. Since the thirteenth century, Germany had followed a pattern of state building different from that of France and England: the imperial authority (the emperor) had shared authority with the princes. After the Peace of Westphalia, central authority in Germany was weak, but the Holy Roman Empire continued to function as a federation.

The independence of the United Provinces of the Netherlands was acknowledged. The political divisions within the Holy Roman Empire and the acquisition of the province of Alsace increased France's size and prestige, and the treaties allowed France to intervene at will in German affairs. Sweden achieved a powerful presence in northeastern Germany (see Map 15.4). The treaties also denied the papacy the right to participate in German religious affairs—a restriction symbolizing the reduced role of the church in European politics.

The Westphalian treaties stipulated that the Augsburg religious agreement of 1555 should stand permanently. The sole modification made Calvinism, along with Catholicism and Lutheranism, a legally permissible creed. In practice, the north German states remained Protestant, the south German states Catholic.

The Thirty Years' War settled little and was a disaster for the German economy and society—probably the most destructive event in German history before the twentieth century. Population losses were frightful. Perhaps one-third of the urban residents and two-fifths of the inhabitants of rural areas died.

In Germany the European-wide economic crisis caused primarily by the influx of silver from South America was badly aggravated by the war. Scholars still cannot estimate the value of losses in agriculture and in trade and commerce, which, compounded by the flood of Spanish silver, brought on severe inflation that was worse in Germany than anywhere else in Europe (see page 530).

The population decline caused a rise in the value of labor. Owners of great estates had to pay more for agricultural workers. Farmers who needed only small amounts of capital to restore their lands started over again. Many small farmers, however, lacked the revenue to rework their holdings and became day laborers. Nobles and landlords were able to buy up many small holdings and amass great estates. In some parts of Germany, especially east of the Elbe River in areas like Mecklenburg and Pomerania, peasants' loss of land led to a new serfdom.[48] The Thirty Years' War contributed to the legal and economic decline of the largest segment of German society.

## CHANGING ATTITUDES

The age of religious wars revealed extreme and violent contrasts. It was a deeply religious period in which men fought passionately for their beliefs; 70 percent of the books printed dealt with religious subjects. Yet the times saw the beginnings of religious skepticism. Europeans explored new continents, partly with the missionary aim of Christianizing the peoples they encountered. Yet the Spanish, Portuguese, Dutch, and English proceeded to dominate and enslave the Indians and blacks they encountered. While Europeans indulged in gross sensuality, the social status of women declined. The exploration of new continents reflects deep curiosity and broad intelligence. Yet Europeans believed in witches and burned thousands at the stake. Sexism, racism, and skepticism had all originated in ancient times. But late in the sixteenth century they began to take on their familiar modern forms.

## The Status of Women

Did new ideas about women appear in this period? Theological and popular literature on marriage published in Reformation Europe helps to answer this question. Manuals emphasized the qualities expected of each partner. A husband was obliged to provide for the material welfare of his wife and children, to protect his family while remaining steady and self-controlled. He was to rule his household firmly but justly; he was not to behave like a tyrant—a guideline that counselors repeated frequently. A wife was to be mature, a good household manager, and subservient and faithful to her spouse. The husband also owed fidelity. Both Protestant and Catholic moralists rejected the double standard of sexual morality, considering it a threat to family unity. Counselors believed that marriage should be based on mutual respect and trust. Although they discouraged impersonal unions arranged by parents, they did not think romantic attachments—based on physical attraction and love—a sound basis for an enduring relationship.

A woman might assist in her own or her husband's business and do charitable work. But moralists held that involvement in social or public activities was inappropriate because it distracted the wife from her primary responsibility: her household. If a woman suffered under her husband's yoke, writers explained, her submission, like the pain of childbearing, was a punishment inherited from Eve, penance for man's fall. Moreover, they said, a woman's lot was no worse than a man's: he had to earn the family's bread by the sweat of his brow.[49]

Catholics viewed marriage as a sacramental union; validly entered into, it could not be dissolved. Protestants stressed the contractual nature of marriage: each partner promised the other support, companionship, and the sharing of mutual property. Protestants recognized the right of both parties to divorce and remarry for various reasons, including adultery and irreparable breakdown.[50]

Society in the early modern period was patriarchal. Women neither lost their identity nor lacked meaningful work, but the all-pervasive assumption was that men ruled. Leading students of the Lutherans, Catholics, French Calvinists, and English Puritans tend to agree that there was no improvement in women's long-standing subordinate status.

Artists' drawings of plump, voluptuous women and massive, muscular men reveal the contemporary standards of physical beauty. It was a sensual age that gloried in the delights of the flesh. Some people, such as the humanist poet Pietro Aretino (1492–1556), found sexual satisfaction with people of either sex. Reformers and public officials simultaneously condemned and condoned sexual "sins."

Prostitution was common because desperate poverty forced women and young men into it. Since the later Middle Ages, licensed houses of prostitution had been common in urban centers. When in 1566 Pope Pius IV (r. 1559–1565) expelled all the prostitutes from Rome, so many people left and the city suffered such a loss of revenue that in less than a month the pope was forced to rescind the order. Scholars debated Saint Augustine's notion that prostitutes serve a useful social function by preventing worse sins. Civil authorities in both Catholic and Protestant countries licensed houses of public prostitution. These establishments were intended for the convenience of single men, and some Protestant cities, such as Geneva and Zurich, installed officials in the brothels with the express purpose of preventing married men from patronizing them.

Single women of the middle and working classes in the sixteenth and seventeenth centuries worked in many occupations and professions—as butchers, shopkeepers, nurses, goldsmiths, and midwives and in the weaving and printing industries. Most women who were married assisted in their husbands' businesses. What became of the thousands of women who left convents and nunneries during the Reformation? This question pertains primarily to women of the upper classes, who formed the dominant social group in the religious houses of late medieval Europe. Luther and the Protestant reformers believed that celibacy had no scriptural basis and that young girls were forced by their parents into convents and, once there, were bullied by men into staying. Therefore, reformers favored the suppression of women's religious houses and encouraged former nuns to marry. Marriage, the reformers maintained, not only gave women emotional and sexual satisfaction but also freed them from clerical domination, cultural deprivation, and sexual repression.[51] It appears that these women passed from clerical domination to subservience to husbands.

Some nuns in the Middle Ages probably did lack a genuine religious vocation, and some religious houses did witness financial mismanagement and moral laxness. Nevertheless, convents had provided women of the upper classes with an outlet for their literary, artistic, medical, or administrative talents if they could not or would not marry. When the convents were closed, marriage became virtually the only occupation available to upper-class Protestant women.

## Witches

The great European witch scare reveals more about contemporary attitudes toward women. The period of the religious wars witnessed a startling increase in the phenomenon of witch-hunting, whose prior history was long but sporadic. "A witch," according to Chief Justice Edward Coke of England (1552–1634), "was a person who hath conference with the Devil to consult with him or to do some act." This definition by the highest legal authority in England demonstrates that educated people, as well as the ignorant, believed in witches. Witches were thought to mysteriously injure other people or animals—by causing a person to become blind or impotent, for instance, or by preventing a cow from giving milk.

Religious reformers' extreme notions of the Devil's powers and the insecurity created by the religious wars contributed to the growth of belief in witches. The idea developed that witches made pacts with the Devil in return for the power to work mischief on their enemies. Since pacts with the Devil meant the renunciation of God, witchcraft was considered heresy, and persecution for it had actually begun in the later fourteenth century when it was so declared. Persecution reached its most virulent stage in the late sixteenth and seventeenth centuries.

Fear of witches took a terrible toll on innocent lives in several parts of Europe. In southwestern Germany, 3,229 witches were executed between 1561 and 1670, most by burning. The communities of the Swiss Confederation in central Europe tried 8,888 persons between 1470 and

**Hans Baldung Grien (1484/5–1545): Witches' Sabbat (1510)** Trained by the great German graphic artist and painter Albrecht Dürer at Nuremberg, Baldung (as he was known) in this woodcut combines learned and stereotypical beliefs about witches: they traveled at night on broomsticks, met at sabbats (assemblies), feasted on infants (in dish held high), concocted strange potions, and possessed an aged and debauched sensuality. *(Germanisches Nationalmuseum Nürnberg)*

1700 and executed 5,417 of them as witches. In all the centuries before 1500, witches in England had been suspected of causing perhaps "three deaths, a broken leg, several destructive storms and some bewitched genitals." Yet between 1559 and 1736, almost 1,000 witches were executed in England.[52]

Some scholars maintain that charges of witchcraft were a means of accounting for inexplicable misfortunes. Other scholars think that in small communities, which typically insisted on strict social conformity, charges of witchcraft were a means of attacking and eliminating the nonconformist; witches, in other words, served the collective need for scapegoats. The evidence of witches' trials, some writers suggest, shows that women were not accused because they harmed or threatened their neighbors; rather, people believed such women worshiped the Devil, engaged in wild sexual activities with him, and ate infants. Other writers argue the exact opposite: that people were tried and executed as witches because their neighbors feared their evil powers. According to still another theory, the unbridled sexuality attributed to witches was a figment of their accusers' imagination—a psychological projection by their accusers resulting from Christianity's repression of sexuality. Despite an abundance of hypotheses, scholars cannot fully understand the phenomenon. The most important capital crime for women in early modern times, witchcraft has considerable significance for the history and status of women.[53]

## LITERATURE, ART, AND MUSIC

The age of religious wars witnessed extraordinary intellectual and artistic ferment. This effervescence can be seen in prose, poetry, and drama, in art, and in music. In many ways, the literature, visual arts, music, and drama of the period mirrored the social and cultural conditions that gave rise to them.

### Literature

Decades of religious fanaticism brought famine, civil anarchy, and death and led both Catholics and Protestants to doubt that any one faith contained absolute truth. The late sixteenth and seventeenth centuries witnessed the beginning of modern *skepticism,* a school of thought founded on doubt that total certainty or definitive knowledge is ever attainable. The skeptic is cautious and critical and suspends judgment. Perhaps the finest representative of early modern skepticism is the Frenchman Michel de Montaigne (1533–1592).

Montaigne developed a new literary genre, the essay—from the French word *essayer,* meaning "to test or try"—to express his thoughts and ideas. His *Essays* provide insight into the mind of a remarkably humane, tolerant, and civilized man. "On Cannibals" reflects the impact of overseas discoveries on Europeans' consciousness. Montaigne's tolerant mind rejected the notion that one culture is superior to another:

> *I long had a man in my house that lived ten or twelve years in the New World, discovered in these latter days, and in that part of it where Villegaignon landed [Brazil]. . . .*
>
> *I find that there is nothing barbarous and savage in [that] nation, by anything that I can gather, excepting, that every one gives the title of barbarism to everything that is not in use in his own country.*[54]

In his belief in the nobility of human beings in the state of nature, uncorrupted by organized society, and in his cosmopolitan attitude toward different civilizations, Montaigne anticipated many eighteenth-century thinkers.

The thought of Michel de Montaigne marks a sharp break with the past. Faith and religious certainty had characterized the intellectual attitudes of Western society for a millennium. Montaigne's rejection of any kind of dogmatism, his secularism, and his skepticism thus represent a basic change.

The period fostered remarkable creativity in other branches of literature. England, especially in the latter part of Elizabeth's reign and in the first years of her successor, James I (r. 1603–1625), witnessed unparalleled brilliance. The immortal dramas of William Shakespeare (1564–1616) and the stately prose of the Authorized, or King James, Bible mark the Elizabethan and Jacobean periods as the golden age of English literature.

Shakespeare's genius lies in the originality of his characterizations, the diversity of his plots, his understanding of human psychology, and his unexcelled gift for language. Shakespeare was a Renaissance man in his deep appreciation for classical culture, individualism, and humanism. Such plays as *Julius Caesar, Pericles,* and *Antony and Cleopatra* deal with classical subjects and figures. Several of his comedies have Italian Renaissance settings. His nine history plays, including *Richard II, Richard III,* and *Henry IV,* enjoyed the greatest popularity among his contemporaries. Written during the decade after the defeat of the Spanish Armada, the history plays express English national consciousness.

Shakespeare's later plays, above all the tragedies *Hamlet, Othello,* and *Macbeth,* explore an enormous range of human problems and are open to an almost infinite variety of interpretations. The central figure in *Hamlet,* a play suffused with individuality, wrestles with moral problems connected with revenge and with man's relationship to life and death. The soliloquy in which Hamlet debates suicide is perhaps the most widely quoted passage in English literature:

*To be, or not to be: that is the question:*
*Whether 'tis nobler in the mind to suffer*
*The slings and arrows of outrageous fortune,*
*Or to take arms against a sea of troubles,*
*And by opposing end them?*

Hamlet's sad cry, "There is nothing either good or bad but thinking makes it so," expresses the anguish and uncertainty of modern man. *Hamlet* has always enjoyed great popularity, because in his many-faceted personality people have seen an aspect of themselves.

The other great masterpiece of the Jacobean period was the Authorized, or King James, Bible (1611). Based on the best scriptural research of the time and divided into chapters and verses, the Authorized Bible is actually a revision of earlier versions rather than an original work. Yet it provides a superb expression of the mature English vernacular in the early seventeenth century. Consider Psalm 37:

*Fret not thy selfe because of evill doers, neither bee thou envious against the workers of iniquitie.*
*For they shall soone be cut downe like the grasse; and wither as the greene herbe.*
*Trust in the Lord, and do good, so shalt thou dwell in the land, and verely thou shalt be fed.*

The Authorized Bible, so called because it was produced under royal sponsorship—it had no official ecclesiastical endorsement—represented the Anglican and Puritan desire to encourage laypeople to read the Scriptures. It quickly achieved great popularity and displaced all earlier versions. British settlers carried this Bible to the North American colonies, where it became known as the King James Bible. For centuries this version of the Bible has had a profound influence on the language and lives of English-speaking peoples.

**Velázquez: Juan de Pareja** This portrait (1650) of the Spanish painter Velázquez's one-time assistant, a black man of obvious intellectual and sensual power and himself a renowned religious painter, suggests the integration of some blacks in seventeenth-century society. The elegant lace collar attests to his middle-class status. *(The Metropolitan Museum of Art, Fletcher Fund, Rogers Fund, and Bequest of Miss Adelaide Milton de Groot [1876–1967], by exchange, supplemented by gifts from friends of the Museum, 1971 [1971.86]. Photograph © 1986 The Metropolitan Museum of Art)*

## Baroque Art and Music

Throughout European history, the cultural tastes of one age have often seemed quite unsatisfactory to the next. So it was with the **baroque**. Late-eighteenth-century art critics used the word as an expression of scorn for what they considered an overblown, unbalanced style. The hostility of these critics has long since passed, and modern specialists agree that the triumphs of the baroque mark one of the high points in the history of Western culture.

The early development of the baroque is complex. Most scholars stress the influence of Rome and the revitalized Catholic church of the later sixteenth century. The papacy and the Jesuits encouraged the growth of an intensely emotional, exuberant art. These patrons wanted artists to go beyond the Renaissance focus on pleasing a small, wealthy cultural elite. They wanted artists to appeal to the senses and thereby touch the souls and kindle the faith of ordinary churchgoers while proclaiming the power and confidence of the reformed Catholic church. In addition to this underlying religious emotionalism, the baroque drew its sense of drama, motion, and ceaseless striving from the Catholic

Reformation. The interior of the famous Jesuit Church of Jesus in Rome—the Gesù—combined all these characteristics in its lavish, shimmering, wildly active decorations and frescoes.

Taking definite shape in Italy after 1600, the baroque style in the visual arts developed with exceptional vigor in Catholic countries—in Spain and Latin America, Austria, southern Germany, and Poland. Yet baroque art was more than just "Catholic art" in the seventeenth century and the first half of the eighteenth. True, neither Protestant England nor the Netherlands ever came fully under the spell of the baroque, but neither did Catholic France. And Protestants accounted for some of the finest examples of baroque style, especially in music. The baroque style spread partly because its tension and bombast spoke to an agitated age, which was experiencing great violence and controversy in politics and religion.

In painting, the baroque reached maturity early in the work of Peter Paul Rubens (1577–1640), the most outstanding and representative of baroque painters. Rubens developed a rich, sensuous, colorful style, characterized by animated figures, melodramatic contrasts, and monumental size.

In music, the baroque style reached its culmination almost a century later in the dynamic, soaring lines of the endlessly inventive Johann Sebastian Bach (1685–1750), one of the greatest composers of the Western world. Organist and choirmaster of several Lutheran churches across Germany, Bach was equally at home writing secular concertos and sublime religious cantatas. Bach's organ music, the greatest ever written, combines the baroque spirit of invention, tension, and emotion in an unforgettable striving toward the infinite. Unlike Rubens, Bach was not fully appreciated in his lifetime, but since the early nineteenth century his reputation has grown steadily.

## SUMMARY

From about 1050 to 1300, a new economy emerged in Italy, based on Venetian and Genoese shipping and long-distance trade and on Florentine banking and cloth manufacture. The combination of these commercial activities and the struggle of urban communities for political independence from surrounding feudal lords led to the appearance of a new wealthy aristocratic class. With this foundation, Italy was the scene of a remarkable intellectual and artistic flowering. Based on renewed interest in the Greco-Roman world, the Renaissance had a classicizing influence on many facets of culture. Despots or oligarchs ruled the city-states of fifteenth- and sixteenth-century Italy and manipulated Renaissance culture to enhance their personal power. Moving beyond Italy, the individualism, humanism, and secular spirit characteristic of the Italian Renaissance affected the culture of all Europe.

In northern Europe, city merchants and rural gentry allied with rising monarchies. Using taxes provided by business people, kings provided a greater degree of domestic peace and order, conditions essential for trade. In Spain, France, and England, rulers also emphasized royal dignity and authority. Except in the Holy Roman Empire, feudal monarchies gradually evolved in the direction of nation-states.

In the sixteenth and seventeenth centuries, religion and religious issues continued to play a major role in the lives of individuals, in rising national consciousness, and in the policies of governments. The break with Rome and the rise of Lutheran, Calvinist, Anglican, and other faiths destroyed European unity as an organic Christian society. Europeans used religious doctrine to explain what they did politically and economically. Religious ideology served as justification for the French nobles' opposition to the Crown, the Dutch struggle for independence from Spain, and the political fragmentation of Germany during and after the Thirty Years' War. The age of Reformation and religious wars marks a decisive watershed between the religious culture of the Middle Ages and the pluralism characteristic of modern times. Though a period of incredible literary and artistic achievement, the age of religious conflict also witnessed the beginnings of skepticism, sexism, and secularism in their modern forms.

## KEY TERMS

Renaissance
pòpolo
individualism
humanism
secularism
*The Prince*
Court of Star Chamber
hermandades
indulgence
Protestant
predestination
Anabaptist
transubstantiation
Jesuits
Holy Office
Saint Bartholomew's Day massacre
Peace of Westphalia
baroque

## NOTES

1. See L. Martines, *Power and Imagination: City-States in Renaissance Italy* (New York: Vintage Books, 1980), esp. pp. 332–333.
2. Ibid., pp. 22–61.
3. Ibid., pp. 221–237, esp. p. 221.
4. *Memoirs of Benvenuto Cellini; A Florentine Artist; Written by Himself* (London: J. M. Dent & Sons, 1927), p. 2.

5. A. Hauser, *The Social History of Art,* vol. 2 (New York: Vintage Books, 1959), pp. 48–49.
6. Quoted in F. Seebohm, *The Oxford Reformers* (London: J. M. Dent & Sons, 1867), p. 256.
7. Quoted in W. H. Woodward, *Vittorino da Feltre and Other Humanist Educators* (Cambridge: Cambridge University Press, 1897), pp. 96–97.
8. C. E. Detmold, trans., *The Historical, Political and Diplomatic Writings of Niccolò Machiavelli* (Boston: J. R. Osgood, 1882), pp. 51–52.
9. Ibid., pp. 54–55.
10. See F. Gilbert, *Machiavelli and Guicciardini: Politics and History in Sixteenth Century Florence* (New York: W. W. Norton, 1984), pp. 197–200.
11. E. L. Eisenstein, *The Printing Press as an Agent of Change: Communications and Cultural Transformations in Early Modern Europe,* vol. 1 (New York: Cambridge University Press, 1979), p. 135; for an overall discussion, see pp. 126–159.
12. See A. W. Crosby, *The Measure of Reality: Quantification and Western Society* (New York: Cambridge University Press, 1997), pp. 49–74.
13. See S. M. Mosher Stuard, "Ancillary Evidence for the Decline of Medieval Slavery," *Past and Present* 149 (November 1995): pp. 3–28.
14. Quoted in J. Hale, *The Civilization of Europe in the Renaissance* (New York: Atheneum, 1994), p. 270.
15. Marc Bloch, *Slavery and Serfdom in the Middle Ages,* trans. William R. Beer (Berkeley: University of California Press, 1975), p. 30.
16. Ibid., p. 28.
17. See Stuard, "Ancillary Evidence," pp. 3–28.
18. Hale, *The Civilization of Europe,* p. 44.
19. Quoted in J. Devisse and M. Mollat, *The Image of the Black in Western Art,* vol. 2, trans. W. G. Ryan (New York: William Morrow, 1979), pt. 2, pp. 187–188.
20. See A. C. DE. C. M. Saunders, *A Social History of Black Slaves and Freedmen in Portugal, 1441–1555* (New York: Cambridge University Press, 1982), pp. 59, 62–88, 176–179.
21. Ibid., pp. 190–194.
22. Ibid., pp. 255–258.
23. See I. Hannaford, *Race: The History of an Idea in the West* (Washington, D.C.: Woodrow Wilson Center Press, 1996), pp. 3–182 passim, 182–187.
24. See J. H. Elliott, *Imperial Spain, 1469–1716* (New York: Mentor Books, 1963), esp. pp. 75, 97–108.
25. See R. R. Post, *The Modern Devotion: Confrontation with Reformation and Humanism* (Leiden: E. J. Brill, 1968), esp. pp. 237–238, 255, 323–348.
26. Quoted in O. Chadwick, *The Reformation* (Baltimore: Penguin Books, 1976), p. 55.
27. Quoted in E. H. Harbison, *The Age of Reformation* (Ithaca, N.Y.: Cornell University Press, 1963), p. 52.
28. This discussion is based heavily on ibid., pp. 52–55.
29. See S. E. Ozment, *The Reformation in the Cities: The Appeal of Protestantism to Sixteenth-Century Germany and Switzerland* (New Haven, Conn.: Yale University Press, 1975), pp. 32–45.
30. S. E. Ozment, *The Age of Reform, 1250–1550: An Intellectual and Religious History of Late Medieval and Reformation Europe* (New Haven, Conn.: Yale University Press, 1980), p. 280.
31. Quoted ibid., p. 281.
32. Quoted ibid., p. 284.
33. G. Strauss, *Luther's House of Learning: Indoctrination of the Young in the German Reformation* (Baltimore: Johns Hopkins University Press, 1978), esp. pp. 159–162, 231–233.
34. See R. H. Bainton, *Women of the Reformation in Germany and Italy* (Minneapolis: Augsburg, 1971), pp. 9–10; Ozment, *The Reformation in the Cities,* pp. 53–54, 171–172.
35. Quoted in H. G. Haile, *Luther: An Experiment in Biography* (Garden City, N.Y.: Doubleday, 1980), p. 272.
36. Quoted in J. Atkinson, *Martin Luther and the Birth of Protestantism* (Baltimore: Penguin Books, 1968), pp. 247–248.
37. *Martin Luther: Three Treatises* (Philadelphia: Muhlenberg Press, 1947), pp. 28–31.
38. J. Allen, trans., *John Calvin: The Institutes of the Christian Religion* (Philadelphia: Westminster Press, 1930), bk. 3, chap. 21, paras. 5, 7.
39. E. W. Monter, *Calvin's Geneva* (New York: Wiley, 1967), p. 137.
40. E. Duffy, *The Stripping of the Altars: Traditional Religion in England, 1400–1580* (New Haven, Conn.: Yale University Press, 1992), pp. 2–6 and passim.
41. J. J. Scarisbrick, *The Reformation and the English People* (Oxford: Basil Blackwell, 1984), pp. 81–84, esp. p. 81.
42. Ibid.
43. See J. W. O'Malley, *The First Jesuits* (Cambridge, Mass.: Harvard University Press, 1993), p. 376.
44. Ibid., p. 298.
45. See P. Grendler, *The Roman Inquisition and the Venetian Press, 1540–1605* (Princeton, N.J.: Princeton University Press, 1977).
46. See J. Hale, "War and Public Opinion in the Fifteenth and Sixteenth Centuries," *Past and Present* 22 (July 1962): 29.
47. See N. Z. Davis, "The Rites of Violence: Religious Riot in Sixteenth Century France," *Past and Present* 59 (May 1973): 51–91.
48. H. Kamen, "The Economic and Social Consequences of the Thirty Years' War," *Past and Present* 39 (April 1968): 44–61.
49. This passage is based heavily on S. E. Ozment, *When Fathers Ruled: Family Life in Reformation Europe* (Cambridge, Mass.: Harvard University Press, 1983), pp. 50–99.
50. Ibid., pp. 85–92.
51. Ibid., pp. 9–14.
52. N. Cohn, *Europe's Inner Demons: An Enquiry Inspired by the Great Witch-Hunt* (New York: Basic Books, 1975), pp. 253–254; K. Thomas, *Religion and the Decline of Magic* (New York: Charles Scribner's Sons, 1971), pp. 450–455.
53. See E. W. Monter, "The Pedestal and the Stake: Courtly Love and Witchcraft," in *Becoming Visible: Women in European History,* ed. R. Bridenthal and C. Koonz (Boston: Houghton Mifflin, 1977), pp. 132–135; A. Fraser, *The Weaker Vessel* (New York: Random House, 1985), pp. 100–103.
54. C. Cotton, trans., *The Essays of Michel de Montaigne* (New York: A. L. Burt, 1893), pp. 207, 210.


## SUGGESTED READING

There are exciting studies available on virtually all aspects of the Renaissance. The curious student might begin with M. Mallett, "Politics and Society in Italy, 1250–1600," a lucid sketch of political change in the various cities, and G. Holmes, "Renaissance Culture," a fine appreciation of the conflict of secular and religious values in art and literature. These articles appear in G. Holmes, ed., *The Oxford History of Italy* (1997). G. Chittolini, "Cities, 'City-States,' and Regional States in North-Central Italy," in *Cities and the Rise of States*

*(continued on page 496)*

# LISTENING TO THE PAST

## MARTIN LUTHER, ON CHRISTIAN LIBERTY

*The idea of liberty has played a powerful role in the history of Western society and culture; that idea is unique to the European world. But the meaning and understanding of liberty has undergone continual change and interpretation. In the Roman world, where slavery was a basic institution, liberty meant the condition of being a free person, independent of obligations to a master. In the Middle Ages, possessing liberty meant having special privileges or rights that other persons or institutions did not have. A lord or a monastery, for example, might speak of his or its liberties. Likewise, the first chapter of Magna Carta (1215), often called the "Charter of Liberties," states: "Holy Church shall be free and have its rights entire and its liberties inviolate," meaning that the English church was independent of the authority of the king.*

*The idea of liberty also has a religious dimension, and the reformer Martin Luther formulated a classic interpretation of liberty in his treatise* On Christian Liberty, *arguably his finest piece. It contains the main themes of Luther's theology: the importance of faith, the relationship of Christian faith and good works, the dual nature of human beings, and the fundamental importance of Scripture in Christian life.*

Christian faith has appeared to many an easy thing; nay, not a few even reckon it among the social virtues, as it were; and this they do because they have not made proof of it experimentally, and have never tasted of what efficacy it is. For it is not possible for any man to write well about it, or to understand well what is rightly written, who has not at some time tasted of its spirit, under the pressure of tribulation; while he who has tasted of it, even to a very small extent, can never write, speak, think, or hear about it sufficiently. . . .

I hope that . . . I have attained some little drop of faith, and that I can speak of this matter, if not with more elegance, certainly with more solidity. . . .

A Christian man is the most free lord of all, and subject to none; a Christian man is the most dutiful servant of all, and subject to everyone.

Although these statements appear contradictory, yet, when they are found to agree together, they will do excellently for my purpose. They are both the statements of Paul himself, who says, "Though I be free from all men, yet have I made myself a servant unto all" (I Cor. 9:19), and "Owe no man anything but to love one another" (Rom. 13:8). Now love is by its own nature dutiful and obedient to the beloved object. Thus even Christ, though Lord of all things, was yet made of a woman; made under the law; at once free and a servant; at once in the form of God and in the form of a servant.

Let us examine the subject on a deeper and less simple principle. Man is composed of a twofold nature, a spiritual and a bodily. As regards the spiritual nature, which they name the soul, he is called the spiritual, inward, new man; as regards the bodily nature, which they name the flesh, he is called the fleshly, outward, old man. The Apostle speaks of this: "Though our outward man perish, yet the inward man is renewed day by day" (II Cor. 4:16). The result of this diversity is that in the Scriptures opposing statements are made concerning the same man, the fact being that in the same man these two men are opposed to one another; the flesh lusting against the spirit, and the spirit against the flesh (Gal. 5:17).

We first approach the subject of the inward man, that we may see by what means a man becomes justified, free, and a true Christian; that is, a spiritual, new, and inward man. It is certain that absolutely none among outward things, under whatever name they may be reckoned, has any influence in producing Christian righteousness or liberty, nor, on the other hand, unrighteousness or slavery. This can be shown by an easy argument.

What can it profit to the soul that the body should be in good condition, free, and full of life, that it should eat, drink, and act according to its pleasure, when even the most impious slaves of every kind of vice are prosperous in these matters? Again, what harm can ill health, bondage, hunger, thirst, or any other outward evil, do to the soul, when even the most pious of men, and the freest in the purity of their conscience, are harassed by these things? Neither of these states of things has to do with the liberty or the slavery of the soul.

And so it will profit nothing that the body should be adorned with sacred vestment, or dwell in holy places, or be occupied in sacred offices, or pray, fast, and abstain from certain meats, or do whatever works can be done through the body and in the body. Something widely different will be necessary for the justification and liberty of the soul, since the things I have spoken of can be done by an impious person, and only hypocrites are produced by devotion to these things. On the other hand, it will not at all injure the soul that the body should be clothed in profane raiment, should dwell in profane places, should eat and drink in the ordinary fashion, should not pray aloud, and should leave undone all the things above mentioned, which may be done by hypocrites.

. . . One thing, and one alone, is necessary for life, justification, and Christian liberty; and that is the most Holy Word of God, the Gospel of Christ, as He says, "I am the resurrection and the life; he that believeth in me shall not die eternally" (John 9:25), and also, "If the Son shall make you free, ye shall be free indeed" (John 8:36), and "Man shall not live by bread alone, but by every word that proceedeth out of the mouth of God" (Matt. 4:4).

Let us therefore hold it for certain and firmly established that the soul can do without everything except the Word of God, without which none at all of its wants is provided for. But, having the Word, it is rich and wants for nothing, since that is the Word of life, of truth, of light, of peace, of justification, of salvation, of joy, of liberty, of wisdom, of virtue, of grace, of glory, and of every good thing. . . .

But you will ask, "What is this Word, and by what means is it to be used, since there are so many words of God?" I answer, "The Apostle Paul (Rom. 1) explains what it is, namely the Gospel of God, concerning His Son, incarnate, suffering, risen, and glorified through the Spirit, the Sanctifier." To preach Christ is to feed the soul, to justify it, to set it free, and to save it, if it believes the preaching. For faith alone, and the efficacious use of the Word of God, bring salvation. "If thou shalt confess with thy mouth the Lord Jesus, and shalt believe in thine heart that God hath raised Him from the dead, thou shalt be saved"; "The just shall live by faith" (Rom. 1:17). . . .

On effective preaching, especially to the uneducated, Luther urged the minister "to keep it simple for the simple." *(Church of St. Marien, Wittenberg/The Bridgeman Art Library International Ltd)*

But this faith cannot consist of all with works; that is, if you imagine that you can be justified by those works, whatever they are, along with it. . . . Therefore, when you begin to believe, you learn at the same time that all that is in you is utterly guilty, sinful, and damnable, according to that saying, "All have sinned, and come short of the glory of God" (Rom. 3:23). . . . When you have learned this, you will know that Christ is necessary for you, since He has suffered and risen again for you, that, believing on Him, you might by this faith become another man, all your sins being remitted, and you being justified by the merits of another, namely Christ alone.

. . . [A]nd since it [faith] alone justifies, it is evident that by no outward work or labour can the inward man be at all justified, made free, and saved; and that no works whatever have any relation to him. . . . Therefore the first care of every Christian ought to be to lay aside all reliance on works, and strengthen his faith alone more and more, and by it grow in knowledge, not of works, but of Christ Jesus, who has suffered and risen again for him, as Peter teaches (I Peter 5).

## QUESTIONS FOR ANALYSIS

1. What did Luther mean by liberty?
2. Why, for Luther, was Scripture basic to Christian life?

*Source: Luther's Primary Works,* ed. H. Wace and C. A. Buchheim (London: Holder and Stoughton, 1896). Reprinted in *The Portable Renaissance Reader,* ed. James Bruce Ross and Mary Martin McLaughlin (New York: Penguin Books, 1981), pp. 721–726.

*in Europe, A.D. 1000 to 1800,* eds. C. Tilly and W. P. Blockmans (1994), provides a good explanation of why Italy lagged in developing a national state, while P. Burke, *The Italian Renaissance: Culture and Society in Italy* (1986), offers an important sociological interpretation. P. Burke, *The Historical Anthropology of Early Modern Italy* (1987), contains many useful essays on Italian cultural history in a comparative European framework, while G. Holmes, ed., *Art and Politics in Renaissance Italy* (1993), treats the art of Florence and Rome against a political background. For the Renaissance court, see the splendid achievement of G. Lubkin, *A Renaissance Court: Milan Under Galeazzo Maria Sforza* (1994). The sophisticated intellectual biography by S. de Grazia, *Machiavelli in Hell* (1989), is based on Machiavelli's literary as well as political writing.

J. Huizinga, *The Waning of the Middle Ages: A Study of the Forms of Life, Thought, and Art in France and the Netherlands in the Dawn of the Renaissance* (1954), challenges the whole idea of the Renaissance. R. J. Knecht, *Renaissance Warrior and Patron: The Reign of Francis I* (1994), is the standard study of Francis. W. Blockmans and W. Prevenier, *The Burgundian Netherlands* (1986), is essential for the culture of Burgundy. The sophisticated study of J. D. Tracy, *Erasmus of the Low Countries* (1996), is probably the best recent work on the great northern humanist, while P. Ackroyd, *The Life of Thomas More* (1997), is a superb appreciation of the English lawyer, statesman, and saint.

For the status of women, see C. Klapisch-Zuper, ed., *A History of Women,* vol. 3 (1994); R. Chartier, ed., *A History of Private Life.* Vol. 3: *Passions of the Renaissance* (1990); and I. Maclean, *The Renaissance Notion of Women* (1980).

The following studies should be helpful to students interested in the political and religious history of Spain: N. Rubin, *Isabella of Castile: The First Renaissance Queen* (1991); P. Lis, *Isabel the Queen: Life and Times* (1992); J. S. Gerber, *The Jews of Spain: A History of the Sephardic Experience* (1992); H. Kamen, *Inquisition and Society in Spain in the Sixteenth and Seventeenth Centuries* (1985); P. F. Albaladejo, "Cities and the State in Spain," in *Cities and the Rise of States in Europe, A.D. 1000 to 1800,* eds. C. Tilly and W. P. Blockmans (1994); and B. Netanyahu, *The Origins of the Inquisition in Fifteenth Century Spain* (1995).

The best reference work on the Reformation is H. J. Hillerbrand, ed., *The Oxford Encyclopedia of the Reformation,* 4 vols. (New York: Oxford University Press, 1996). A. Pettegree, ed., *The Early Reformation in Europe* (1992), explores the Reformation as an international movement and compares developments in different parts of Europe. L. W. Spitz, *The Protestant Reformation, 1517–1559* (1985), provides a comprehensive survey.

For Martin Luther, students should see Atkinson and Haile in the Notes; G. Brendler, *Martin Luther: Theology and Revolution* (1991), a response to the Marxist view of Luther as a tool of the aristocracy who sold out the peasantry; and H. Boehmer, *Martin Luther: Road to Reformation* (1960), a well-balanced work treating Luther's formative years.

The best study of John Calvin is W. J. Bouwsma, *John Calvin: A Sixteenth-Century Portrait* (1988), which puts Calvin within Renaissance culture. D. C. Steinmetz, *Calvin in Context* (1995), treats Calvin as an interpreter of the Bible. W. E. Monter, *Calvin's Geneva* (1967), shows the effect of his reforms on the social life of that city. For the "left wing" of the Reformation, see the profound, though difficult, work of G. H. Williams, *The Radical Reformers* (1962).

For various aspects of the social history of the period, see, in addition to Bainton and Ozment cited in the Notes, S. Ozment, *Magdalena and Balthasar* (1987), which reveals social life through the letters of a Nuremberg couple. For women, see M. E. Wiesner, *Women and Gender in Early Modern Europe* (1993); L. Roper, *The Holy Household: Women and Morals in Reformation Augsburg* (1991), an important study in local religious history as well as the history of gender; and M. Wiesner, *Women in the Sixteenth Century: A Bibliography* (1983), a useful reference tool. The best treatment of marriage and the family is S. Ozment, *When Fathers Ruled: Family Life in Reformation Europe* (1983).

The legal implications of Henry VIII's divorces have been well analyzed in J. J. Scarisbrick, *Henry VIII* (1968), an almost definitive biography. On the dissolution of the English monasteries, see D. Knowles, *The Religious Orders in England,* vol. 3 (1959), a fine example of historical prose.

The definitive study of the Council of Trent was written by H. Jedin, *A History of the Council of Trent,* 3 vols. (1957–1961). For the Jesuits, see W. W. Meissner, *Ignatius of Loyola: The Psychology of a Saint* (1993), and J. W. O'Malley, *The First Jesuits* (1993). These books refute many myths. Perhaps the best recent work on the Spanish Inquisition is W. Monter, *Frontiers of Heresy: The Spanish Inquisition from the Basque Lands to Sicily* (1990). For the impact of the Counter-Reformation on ordinary Spanish people, see H. Kamen, *The Phoenix and the Flame: Catalonia and the Counter Reformation* (New Haven, Conn.: Yale University Press, 1993).

For the religious wars, see M. P. Holt, *The French Wars of Religion, 1562–1629* (1995), and J. B. Collins, *The State in Early Modern France* (1995). For the two major monarchs of the age, see W. MacCaffrey, *Elizabeth I* (1993), and H. Kamen, *Philip of Spain* (1997), both excellent revisionist portraits of rulers at the center of international affairs.

For the Thirty Years' War, R. G. Asch, *The Thirty Years' War: The Holy Roman Empire and Europe* (1997), is an important revisionist study. The titles by Cohn and Monter cited in the Notes are helpful for the study of witchcraft.

Chinese vase of the Ming period. With underglaze of cobalt blue—likely introduced from Mesopotamia and Persia. *(© The Board of Trustees of the Victoria & Albert Museum)*

# CHAPTER 16 THE ACCELERATION OF GLOBAL CONTACT

## CHAPTER OUTLINE

- The World of the Indian Ocean
- European Discovery, Reconnaissance, and Expansion
- Global Trade Networks
- The Chinese and Japanese Discovery of the West
- The Impact of Contact

Between about 1400 and 1700, almost all parts of the world for the first time came into contact with each other. The European search for Southeast Asian spices led to the accidental discovery of the Western Hemisphere. Within a short time, South and North America were joined in a worldwide economic web. The fundamental instrument of globalization was trade and commerce. Islam, originating in and expanding out of the Middle East, had always placed a high premium on mercantile activity (see pages 261–263). In early modern times, merchants and sailors sought new opportunities in East Africa and Southeast Asia. When artisans, scholars, teachers, soldiers, and mercenaries from Arabia and Anatolia followed, a Muslim diaspora resulted. Elite classes everywhere prized Chinese porcelains and silks, while wealthy members of the Celestial Kingdom, as China called itself, wanted ivory, black slaves from East Africa, and exotic goods and peacocks from India. African peoples wanted textiles from India and cowrie shells from the Maldive Islands. Europeans craved spices.

In the fifteenth to seventeenth centuries, the locus of all these desires and commercial exchanges was the Indian Ocean. Arab, Persian, Turkish, Indian, black African, Chinese, and European merchants and adventurers fought each other for the trade that brought great wealth. They also jostled with Muslim scholars, Buddhist teachers, and Christian missionaries, who competed for the religious adherence of the peoples of the Malay Archipelago, Sumatra, Java, Borneo, and the Philippine Islands. The ancient civilizations of Africa, the Americas, Asia, and Southeast Asia confronted each other, and those confrontations sometimes led to conquest, exploitation, and profound social change.

- What were the distinctive features of Southeast Asian cultures? Compare the status of women in Southeast Asia to that of women in other premodern cultures in Africa, East Asia, and Europe.
- What was the impact of Islam and Christianity on Southeast Asian peoples?
- Why and how did Europeans, rather than the Chinese with their superior maritime knowledge and experience, gain control of the major sea-lanes of the world and establish economic and political hegemony on distant continents?

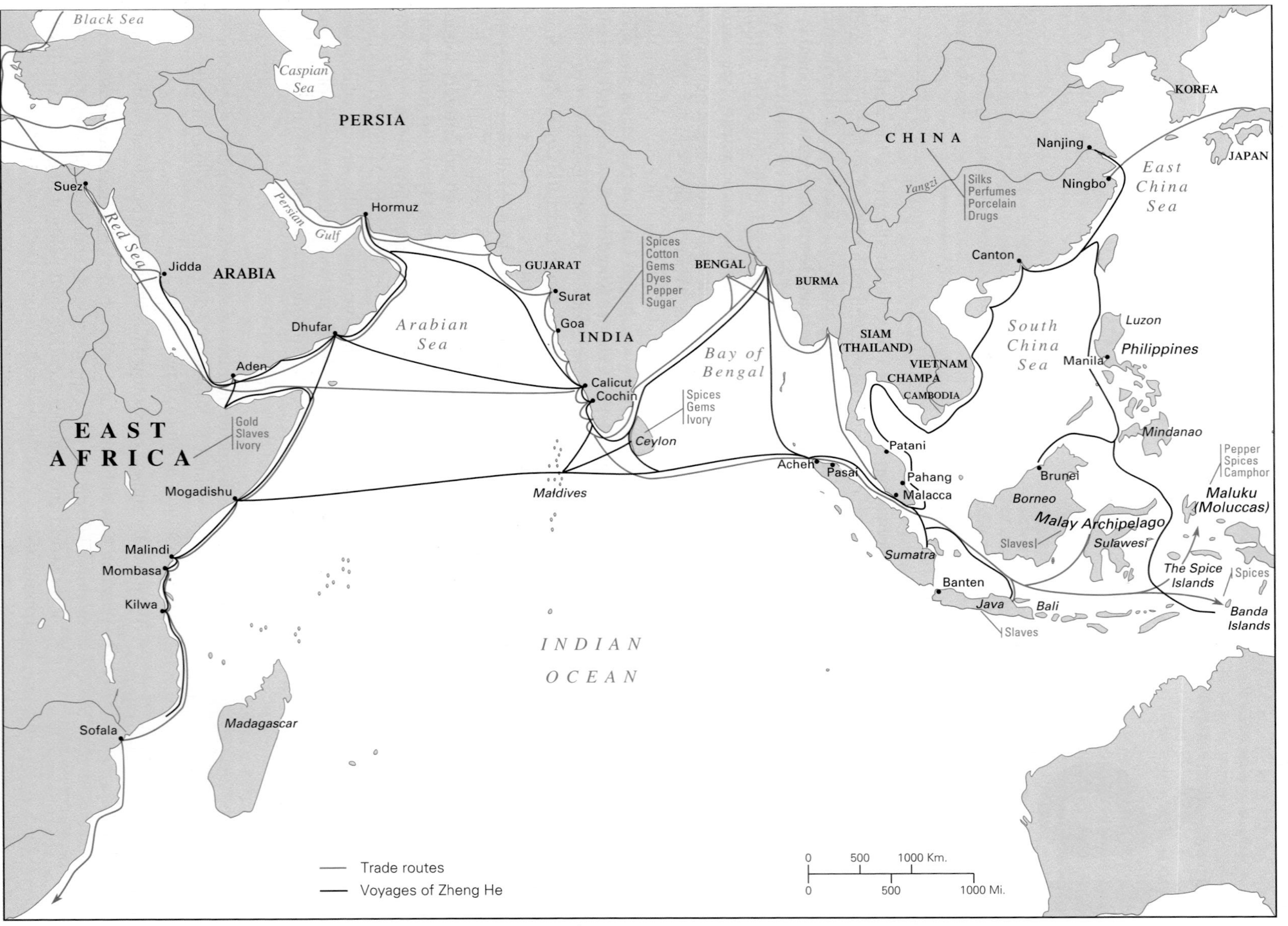


**MAP 16.1 Indian Ocean Trade Routes** The faith of Islam took strong root on the east coast of Africa and in northern India, Sumatra, the Malay Archipelago, and the southern Philippines. In the sixteenth and seventeenth centuries, Christianity competed with Islam for the adherence of peoples on all the Indian Ocean islands. *(Source: Some data from* The Times Atlas of World History, *3d ed., page 146.)*

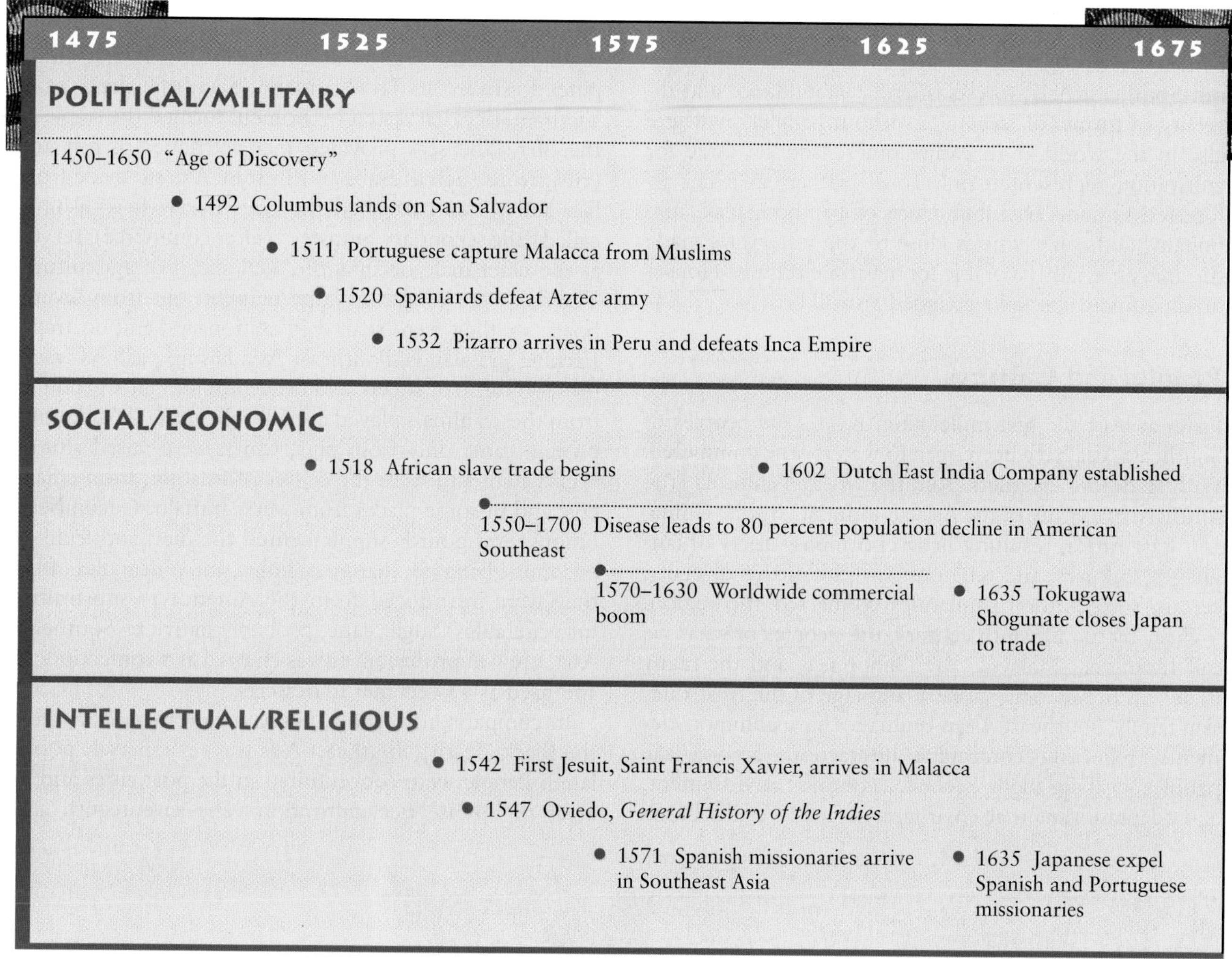

1475
1525
1575
1625
1675
POLITICAL/MILITARY
1450–1650 "Age of Discovery"
1492 Columbus lands on San Salvador
1511 Portuguese capture Malacca from Muslims
1520 Spaniards defeat Aztec army
1532 Pizarro arrives in Peru and defeats Inca Empire
SOCIAL/ECONOMIC
1518 African slave trade begins
1602 Dutch East India Company established
1550–1700 Disease leads to 80 percent population decline in American Southeast
1570–1630 Worldwide commercial boom
1635 Tokugawa Shogunate closes Japan to trade
INTELLECTUAL/RELIGIOUS
1542 First Jesuit, Saint Francis Xavier, arrives in Malacca
1547 Oviedo, General History of the Indies
1571 Spanish missionaries arrive in Southeast Asia
1635 Japanese expel Spanish and Portuguese missionaries


- How did a few Spaniards, fighting far from home, overcome the powerful Aztec and Inca Empires in America?
- How and why did African slave labor become the dominant form of labor organization in America?
- What effect did overseas expansion have on Europe and on conquered societies?

This chapter will address these questions.

## THE WORLD OF THE INDIAN OCEAN

Extending over 28,350,000 square miles, measuring 4,000 miles wide at the equator, and covering 20 percent of the earth's total ocean area, the Indian Ocean is the globe's third-largest (after the Atlantic and Pacific) waterway. To the west, its arms reach into the Red and Arabian Seas, through the former up to the Mediterranean Sea, and through the latter into the Persian Gulf and southwestern Asia. To the north the Indian Ocean joins the Bay of Bengal, to the east the Pacific, to the south the west coast of Australia (see Map 16.1). The Chinese called this vast region the Southern Ocean. Arabs, Indians, and Persians described it as "the lands below the winds," meaning the seasonal monsoons that carried ships across the ocean. Moderate and predictable, the monsoon winds blow from the west or south between April and August, from the northwest or northeast between December and March. Only in the eastern periphery, near the Philippine Islands, is there a dangerous typhoon belt—whirlwinds bringing tremendous rains and possible tornadoes.

High temperatures and abundant rainfall all year round contribute to a heavily forested environment. Throughout Southeast Asia, forests offer "an abundance and diversity of forms (of trees) . . . without parallel anywhere else in the world."[1] In earlier times, land set aside for cultivation represented only small pockets in a heavily forested region. The abundance of bamboo, teak, mahogany, and other woods close to the waterways made the area especially favorable for maritime activity. Household equipment usually included a small boat.

## Peoples and Cultures

From at least the first millennium B.C.E., the peoples of Southeast Asia have been open to waterborne commerce. With trade came settlers from the Malay Peninsula (the southern extremity of the Asian continent), India, China, and East Africa, resulting in an enormous variety of languages, cultures, and religions. In spite of this diversity, certain sociocultural similarities connected the region.

First, by the fifteenth century, the peoples of what we call Indonesia, Malaysia, the Philippines, and the many islands in between all spoke a language of the Austronesian family. Southeast Asian languages have common elements, reflecting continuing interactions among the peoples speaking them. Second, a common environment, and adaptation to that environment, led to a diet based on rice, fish, palms, and palm wine. Rice is probably indigenous to the region, and from Luzon in the Philippines westward to Java, Sumatra, Siam (Thailand), and Vietnam, rice, harvested by women, formed the staple of the diet. The seas provided many varieties of fish and crustaceans such as crabs and shrimp. A paste made from fish and spices garnished the rice. Everywhere fishing, called "the secondary industry" (after commerce), served as the chief male occupation, well ahead of agriculture. The fish were caught in large nets put out from several boats, or they were snared in stationary bamboo traps. Lacking grasslands, Southeast Asia has no pastoral tradition, no cattle or sheep, and thus meat and milk products from these animals played a small role in the diet. Animal protein came only from pigs, which were raised almost everywhere and were the center of feasting; from chickens; and in some places from water buffalo. Cucumbers, onions, and gourds supplemented the diet, and fruits—coconuts, bananas, mangoes, limes, and pineapples (after they were introduced from the Americas)—substituted for vegetables. Sugar cane, probably native to Southeast Asia, grew in profusion. It was chewed as a confectionery and used as a sweetener in desserts.[2]

In comparison to India, China, or even Europe (after the Black Death), Southeast Asia was very sparsely populated. People were concentrated in the port cities and in areas of intense rice cultivation. The seventeenth and

**Agricultural Work in Southeast Asia** Using a water buffalo (a common draft animal in Southeast Asia), a man plows a rice field, while a woman husks rice in this Filipino scene from the early eighteenth century. Their house is on stilts as protection against floods. *(Bibliothèque nationale de France)*

**Woman Offering Betel** In Southeast Asia, betel served as *the* basic social lubricant. A combination of the betel nut, leaf, and lime, betel sweetened the breath and relaxed the mind; it was central to the rituals of lovemaking; and it was offered on all important social occasions, such as birth, marriage, and death. *(Universiteit Leiden Lor 8655)*

eighteenth centuries witnessed slow but steady population growth, while the nineteenth century, under European colonial rule, witnessed very rapid expansion. Almost all Southeast Asian people married at a young age (about twenty). Marriage practices varied greatly from Indian, Chinese, and European ones, reflecting marked differences in the status of women.

The important role played by women in planting and harvesting rice gave them authority and economic power. Because of women's reproductive role, daughters had a high value. In contrast to India, China, the Middle East, and Europe, in Southeast Asia the more daughters a man had, the richer he was. At marriage the groom paid the bride (or sometimes her family) a sum of money, called **bride wealth,** which remained under her control. This practice was in sharp contrast to the Chinese, Indian, and European dowry, which was provided by the wife's family and came under the husband's control. Unlike the Chinese practice, married couples usually resided in the wife's village. Southeast Asian law codes stipulated that all property should be administered jointly, in contrast to the Chinese principle and Indian practice that wives had no say in the disposal of family property. All children, regardless of gender, inherited equally, and when Islam eventually took root in parts of the region, the rule that sons receive double the inheritance of daughters was never implemented.

Likewise, in sexual matters Southeast Asian custom stressed the satisfaction of the woman. Literature shows that women took an unusually active role in courtship and lovemaking and that they expected sexual and emotional satisfaction. Men sometimes underwent painful penile surgery to increase a woman's erotic pleasure, a practice that has no counterpart anywhere in the world. This practice also reveals the strong sociocultural position of women.

Although rulers commonly had multiple wives or concubines for status or diplomatic reasons, the vast majority of ordinary people were monogamous. In contrast to most parts of the world except Africa, Southeast Asian peoples regarded premarital sexual activity with indulgence, and no premium was placed on virginity at marriage. Once couples were married, however, their "fidelity and devotedness . . . appears to have surpassed [that of] Europeans." Foreign observers seemed astonished at the affection married couples showed each other. Still, divorce was very easy if a pair proved incompatible; common property and children were divided. Divorce carried no social stigma, and either the woman or the man could initiate it. Even after Islam was introduced to the region, a woman's status and livelihood were not diminished by divorce.[3]

## Religious Revolutions

Diversity—by district, community, village, and even individual—characterized religious practice in Southeast Asia. No distinction existed between the religious and material spheres. Rather, people held that spiritual forces suffused the material world. They practiced a kind of animism, believing that spiritual powers inhabited natural objects. To survive and prosper, a person had to know how to please, appease, and manipulate those forces. To ensure human fertility, cure sickness, produce a good harvest, safeguard the living, and help the dead attain a contented afterlife, the individual propitiated the forces by providing the appropriate sacrificial offerings or feasts. For example, in the Philippines and eastern Indonesia, certain activities were forbidden during the period of mourning following death, but great feasting then followed. Exquisite clothing, pottery, and jewelry were buried with the corpse to ensure his or her status in the afterlife. In Borneo, Cambodia, Burma, and the Philippines, slaves were sometimes killed to serve their deceased owners. Death rituals, like life rituals, had enormous variation in Southeast Asia.

Throughout the first millennium C.E., Hindu and Buddhist cults; Confucianists; and Jewish, Christian, and Muslim traders and travelers carried their beliefs to Southeast Asia. Rulers tolerated them because they did not expect those beliefs to have much impact. Beginning in the late thirteenth century, Muslim merchants established sizable trading colonies in the ports of northern Sumatra, eastern Java, Champa, and the east coast of the Malay Peninsula (see Map 16.1). Once the ruler of Malacca, the largest port city in Indonesia, accepted Islam, Muslim businessmen controlled all business transactions there; the saying went that these transactions were "sealed with a handshake and a glance at heaven." The very name *Malacca* derives from the Arabic *malakat,* meaning "market," an apt description for this center of Indian Ocean trade. Islamic success continued from 1400 to 1650. Rulers of the port states on the spice route to northern Java and the Moluccas (Maluku), and those on the trading route to Brunei in Borneo and Manila in the Philippines, adhered to the faith of Allah.

With the arrival of the Portuguese in 1498 (see page 510) and their capture of Malacca in 1511, fierce competition ensued between Muslims and Christians for the religious affiliation of Southeast Asian peoples. The middle years of the sixteenth century witnessed the galvanized energy of the Counter-Reformation in Europe (see pages 479–480) and the expansion of the Ottoman Empire through southwestern Asia and southeastern Europe. From Rome the first Jesuit, Saint Francis Xavier (1506–1552), reached Malacca in 1542. Likewise, Suleiman the Magnificent and his successors sent proselytizers. After the Spanish occupation of Manila in the Philippines in 1571, the Spanish crown flooded Southeast Asia with missionaries. Unlike Southeast Asian animism, the two prophetic faiths, Islam and Christianity, insisted on an exclusive path to salvation: the renunciation of paganism and some outward sign of membership in the new faith.

What was the reaction of Southeast Asian peoples to these religions? How did adherents of the Middle Eastern religions spread their faiths? What impact did they have on people's lives in the sixteenth and seventeenth centuries? Southeast Asians saw Muslims and Christians as wealthy, powerful traders and warriors. Thus native peoples believed that the foreigners must possess some secret ability to manipulate the spirit world. A contemporary Spaniard wrote that Southeast Asians believed "that paradise and successful (business) enterprises are reserved for those who submit to the religion of the Moros (Muslims) of Brunei[;] . . . they are the richer people." Southeast Asians also were impressed by Muslim and European ships, and especially by their firearms. The foreigners seemed to have a more ruthless view of war (perhaps because they had no place to retreat to) than the natives. As the Muslims and Christians fought for commercial superiority throughout the sixteenth century, the indigenous peoples watched closely, "partly for reasons of self-preservation, partly that they might adopt the spiritual and practical techniques of the winners."[4]

Christian priests and Muslim teachers rested their authority on the ability to read and explain the Bible and the Qur'an. They quickly learned the locals' languages and translated their Scriptures into those languages. The instruction of rulers and the educated into either faith was by memorization of the catechism, or sacred texts; teaching the masses was oral—they were expected to learn the basic prayers and customs of the new faiths. The Muslims and Christians differed in one fundamental strategy: whereas the Christians relied on a celibate clergy that defined the new community through baptism, the Muslims often married locally and accepted Southeast Asian cultures much more readily than did Spanish priests. Since no Asian was ordained a priest or served as catechist before 1700, European and Iberian terms defined Christian boundaries in Southeast Asia. By contrast, the Muslims showed little of the iconoclastic zeal for the destruction of pagan idols, statues, and temples that the Christians did. The Muslims did face a major obstacle, however: the indigenous peoples' attachment to pork, the main meat source and the central dish in all feasting.

**Minaret at Kudus in Central Java** More than one-third of all Muslims live east of India, in China or Southeast Asia. When Islam spread in the Malay Archipelago, Muslims adapted indigenous building styles to the needs of the mosque. Although most minarets were built of wood and bamboo, this red brick one has the form of the traditional Hindu temple and is similar to Balinese towers, where drums are sounded to summon people to prayer. (In Arabia before loudspeakers, the muezzin chanted the *adban,* or summons to prayer.) *(From A. J. Bernet Kempers,* Ancient Indonesian Art *[Amsterdam, 1959])*

Acceptance of one of the prophetic religions varied with time and place. Recent scholars speak of the "adherence" of peoples in the sixteenth century to Islam, rather than their "conversion." The coastal port cities on major trade routes had "substantial" numbers of Muslims, and rulers of the port states of Sumatra, the Malay Peninsula, northern Java, and the Moluccas identified themselves as Muslims. Because of scanty evidence, we do not know how deeply Islam penetrated the rural hinterland. By 1700, however, most rural and urban people had abandoned pork and pagan practices, adopted Islamic dress, submitted to circumcision, and considered themselves part of the international Muslim community. In Java in 1700, the distinction between Javanese tradition and acceptable Muslim behavior remained perceptible. In the Philippines, Islam achieved some success, especially in the south. But Magellan's military conquest, the enormous enthusiasm of the Jesuit missionaries, and the vigorous support of the Spanish crown led to the Christianization of most of the islands. As elsewhere, whether individuals conformed to Muslim or Christian standards was another matter. The official acceptance of one of the two Scripture-based religions by more than half the people of Southeast Asia has had lasting importance. Today Indonesia has the largest Muslim population in the world.

## Trade and Commerce

Since Han and Roman times (see page 169), seaborne trade between China (always the biggest market for Southeast Asian goods), India, the Middle East, and Europe had flowed across the Indian Ocean. From the seventh through the thirteenth centuries, the volume of this trade steadily increased. In the late fourteenth century, with the European and West Asian populations recovering from the Black Death, demand for Southeast Asian goods accelerated.

Other developments stimulated the market for Southeast Asian goods. The collapse of the Central Asian overland caravan route, the famous Silk Road, gave a boost to the traffic originating in the Indian Ocean and flowing up the Red Sea to Damascus, Beirut, Cairo, and Alexandria. Chinese expansion into Vietnam and Burma increased the population of the Celestial Kingdom and the demand for exotic goods. Above all, the seven voyages of the Chinese admiral Zheng He in 1405 launched for Southeast Asia the "age of commerce." (See the feature "Individuals in Society: Zheng He.")

In the fifteenth century, Malacca became the great commercial entrepôt on the Indian Ocean. To Malacca came Chinese porcelains, silks, and camphor (used in the manufacture of many medications, including those to reduce fevers); pepper, cloves, nutmeg, and raw materials such as sappanwood and sandalwood from the Moluccas; sugar from the Philippines; and Indian printed cotton and woven tapestries, copper weapons, incense, dyes, and opium (which already had a sizable market in China). Muslim merchants in other port cities, such as Patani on the Malay Peninsula, Pasai in Sumatra, and Demak in Java, shared in this trade. They also exchanged cowrie shells from the Maldive Islands. These shells were in enormous demand throughout Africa as symbols of

**Palepai or Ship Cloth (woven cotton textile, Sumatra, nineteenth century)** In southeast Asian society, where the sea permeated so many aspects of life and culture, it is natural that the sea would influence art. Produced for millennia, ship cloths—depicting fabulous sailing vessels with multiple decks, birds, and animals—signified the transition from one social or spiritual state to another. They were displayed by the aristocracy only on important occasions, such as weddings or the presentation of a first grandchild to maternal grandparents. *(Museum of Fine Arts, Boston, The William E. Nickerson Fund No. 2 [1980.172]. © 2002 Museum of Fine Arts, Boston)*

wealth and status, as decoration, and as a medium of currency in African trade. Muslim businessmen in Southeast Asia thus had dealings with their coreligionists in the East African ports of Mogadishu, Kilwa, and Sofala.

Merchants at Malacca stockpiled goods in fortified warehouses while waiting for the next monsoon. Whereas the wealth of cities in Mughal India rested mainly on agriculture, that of Malacca and other Southeast Asian cities depended on commerce. In all of Asia, Malacca, with its many mosques and elegant homes, enjoyed the reputation of being a sophisticated city, full of "music, ballads, and poetry."[5]

## EUROPEAN DISCOVERY, RECONNAISSANCE, AND EXPANSION

Historians of Europe have called the period from 1450 to 1650 the "Age of Discovery," "Age of Reconnaissance," and "Age of Expansion." "Age of Discovery" refers to the era's phenomenal advances in geographical knowledge and technology, often achieved through trial and error. In 1350 it took as long to sail from the eastern end of the Mediterranean to the western end as it had taken a thousand years earlier. Even in the fifteenth century, Europeans knew little more about the earth's surface than the Romans had known. Europeans' geographical knowledge was confined largely to the Mediterranean and southwestern Asia. By 1650, however, Europeans had made an extensive reconnaissance—or preliminary exploration—and had sketched fairly accurately the physical outline of the earth. Much of the geographical information they had gathered was tentative and not fully understood—hence the appropriateness of "Age of Reconnaissance."

The designation "Age of Expansion" refers to the migration of Europeans to other parts of the world. This colonization resulted in political control of much of South and North America; coastal regions of Africa, India, China, and Japan; and many Pacific islands. Political hegemony was accompanied by economic exploitation, religious domination, and the introduction of European patterns of social and intellectual life. The sixteenth-century expansion of European society launched a new age in world history. None of the three "Age" labels reflects the experiences of non-European peoples. Africans, Asians, and native Americans had known the geographies of their regions for centuries. They made no "discoveries" and, with the notable exception of the Chinese, undertook no reconnaissance.

# INDIVIDUALS IN SOCIETY

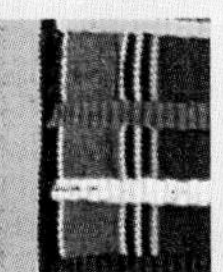

## ZHENG HE

*Zheng He: voyager to India, Persia, Arabia, and Africa.* (From Lo Mon-teng, *The Western Sea Cruises of Eunuch San Pao, 1597)*

In 1403 the Chinese emperor Yongle ordered his coastal provinces to build a vast fleet of ships, with construction centered at Longjiang near Nanjing; the inland provinces were to provide wood and float it down the Yangzi River. Thirty thousand shipwrights, carpenters, sailmakers, ropers, and caulkers worked in a frenzy. As work progressed, Yongle selected a commander for the fleet. Although the emperor feared he was too old (thirty-five) for so politically important an expedition, he chose Zheng He (1373?–1435). The decision rested on Zheng He's unquestioned loyalty, strength of character, energy, ability, and eloquence. These qualities apparently were expected to compensate for Zheng He's lack of seamanship.

The southwestern province of Yunnan had a large Muslim population, and Zheng He was born into that group. When the then Prince Zhi Di defeated the Mongols in Yunnan, Zheng He's father was killed in the related disorder. The young boy was taken prisoner and, as was the custom, castrated. Raised in Zhi Di's household, he learned to read and write, studied Confucian writings, and accompanied the prince on all military expeditions. By age twenty, Zheng He was not the soft, effeminate stereotype of the eunuch; rather he was "seven feet tall and had a waist five feet in circumference. His cheeks and forehead were high . . . [and] he had glaring eyes . . . [and] a voice loud as a bell. . . . He was accustomed to battle." Zheng He must have made an imposing impression. A devout Muslim, he persuaded the emperor to place mosques under imperial protection after a period of persecution. On his travels, he prayed at mosques at Malacca and Hormuz. Unable to sire sons, he adopted a nephew. In Chinese history, he was the first eunuch to hold such an important command.

The first fleet, composed of 317 junks, 100 supply ships, water tankers, warships, transports for horses, and patrol boats, and carrying 28,000 sailors and soldiers, represents the largest naval force in world history before World War I. Because it bore tons of beautiful porcelains, elegant silks, lacquer ware, and exquisite artifacts to be exchanged for goods abroad, it was called the "treasure fleet." Zheng He may have been appointed commander because as a Muslim he could more easily negotiate with Muslim merchants on the Indian Ocean.

Between 1405 and 1433, Zheng He led seven voyages, which combined the emperor's diplomatic, political, geographical, and commercial goals. Yongle wanted to secure China's hegemony over tributary states and collect pledges of loyalty from them. To gain information on winds, tides, distant lands, and rare plants and animals, Zheng He sailed as far west as Egypt. Smallpox epidemics had recently hit China, and one purpose of his voyages was to gather pharmacological products; an Arab text on drugs and therapies was secured and translated into Chinese. He also brought back a giraffe and mahogany, a wood ideal for ships' rudders because of its hardness. Chinese emperors had long found Korean women especially attractive. In 1408 Zheng He delivered 300 virgins to the emperor. The next year, the emperor wanted more.

Just before his death, Zheng He recorded his accomplishments on stone tablets. The expeditions had unified "seas and continents . . . the countries beyond the horizon from the ends of the earth have all become subjects . . . and the distances and routes between distant lands may be calculated," implying that China had accumulated considerable geographical information. From around the Indian Ocean, official tribute flowed to the Ming court. A vast immigration of Chinese people to Southeast Asia, sometimes called the Chinese diaspora, followed the expeditions. Immigrants carried with them Chinese culture, including social customs, diet, and practical objects of Chinese technology—calendars, books, scales for weights and measures, and musical instruments. With legends collected about him and monuments erected to him, Zheng He became a great cult hero.

### QUESTIONS FOR ANALYSIS

1. What do the voyages of the treasure fleet tell us about China in the fifteenth century?
2. What was Zheng He's legacy?

*Source:* Louise Levathes, *When China Ruled the Seas: The Treasure Fleet of the Dragon Throne, 1405–1433* (New York: Oxford University Press, 1996).

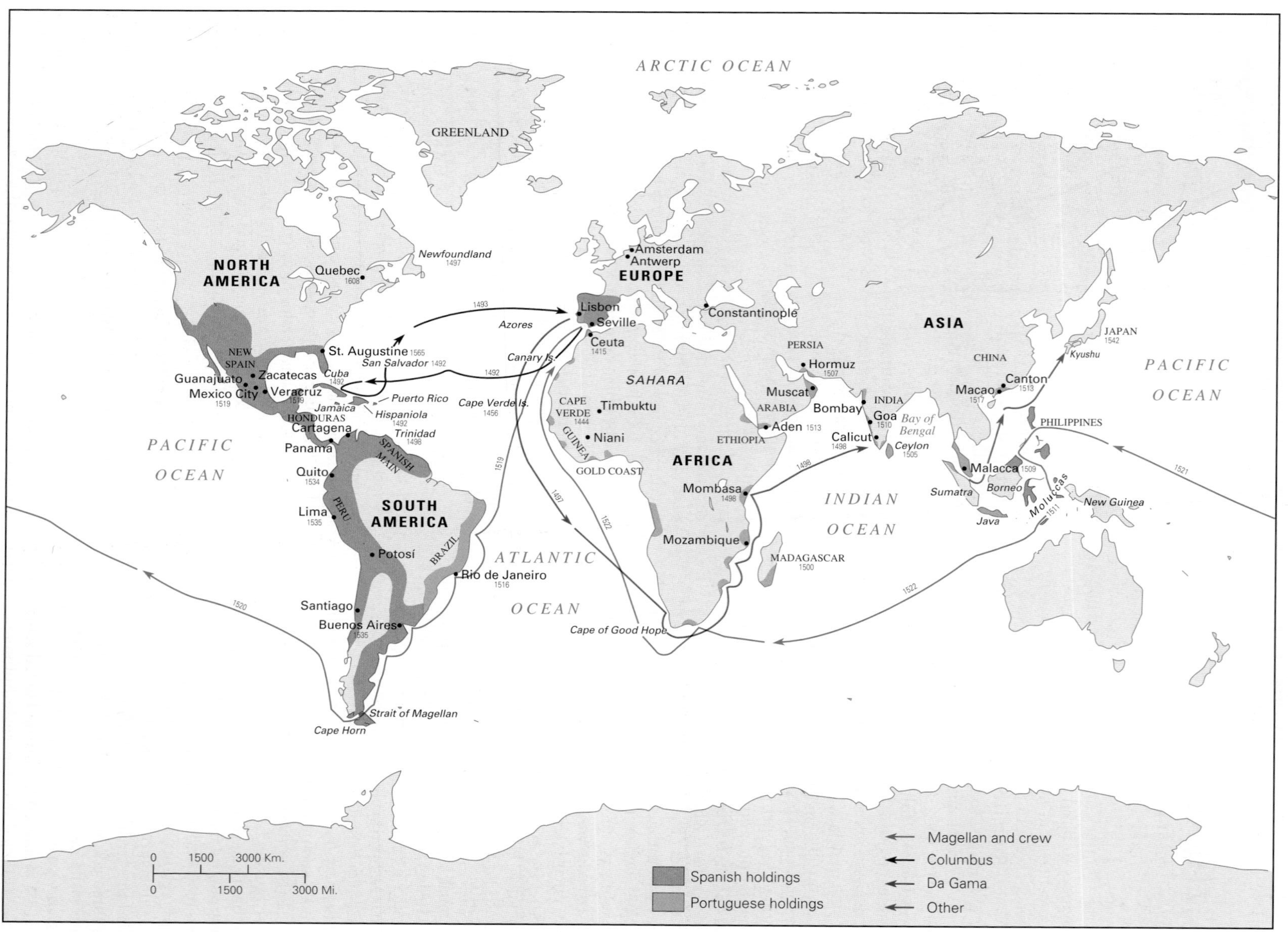


**MAP 16.2 European Exploration and Conquest, Fifteenth and Sixteenth Centuries** The voyages of discovery marked another phase in the centuries-old migrations of European peoples. Consider the major contemporary significance of each of the three voyages depicted on the map.

## Overseas Exploration and Conquest

Migration is a constant theme in the history of world societies. The outward expansion of Europe began with the Viking voyages across the Atlantic in the ninth and tenth centuries. Under Eric the Red and Leif Ericson, the Vikings discovered Greenland and the eastern coast of North America. They made permanent settlements in, and a legal imprint on, Iceland, Ireland, England, Normandy, and Sicily. The Crusades of the eleventh through thirteenth centuries were another phase in Europe's attempt to explore and exploit peoples on the periphery of the continent. But the lack of a strong territorial base, superior Muslim military strength, and sheer misrule combined to make the Crusader kingdoms short-lived. In the mid-fifteenth century, Europe seemed ill prepared for further international ventures. Europeans, however, saw Ottoman Turkish expansion as a grave threat.

Combining excellent military strategy with efficient administration of their conquered territories, the Turks had subdued most of Asia Minor and begun to settle on the western side of the Bosporus. The Muslim Ottoman Turks under Sultan Mohammed II (r. 1451–1481) captured Constantinople in 1453, pressed northwest into the Balkans, and by the early sixteenth century controlled the eastern Mediterranean. The Turkish menace badly frightened Europeans. In France in the sixteenth century, twice as many books were printed about the Turkish threat as about the American discoveries. Yet the fifteenth and sixteenth centuries witnessed a fantastic continuation, on a global scale, of European expansion.

Political centralization in Spain, France, and England helps to explain those countries' outward push. In the fifteenth century, Isabella and Ferdinand had consolidated their several kingdoms to achieve a more united Spain. The Catholic rulers revamped the Spanish bureaucracy and humbled dissident elements, notably the Muslims and the Jews. The Spanish monarchy was stronger than ever before and in a position to support foreign ventures; it could bear the costs and dangers of exploration. But Portugal, situated on the extreme southwestern edge of the European continent, got the start on the rest of Europe. Still insignificant as a European land power despite its recently secured frontiers, Portugal sought greatness in the unknown world overseas.

Portugal's taking of Ceuta, an Arab city in northern Morocco, in 1415 marked the beginning of European exploration and control of overseas territory (see Map 16.2). The objectives of Portuguese policy included the historic Iberian crusade to Christianize Muslims and the search for gold, for an overseas route to the spice markets of India, and for the mythical Christian ruler of Ethiopia, Prester John.

In the early phases of Portuguese exploration, Prince Henry (1394–1460), called "the Navigator" because of the annual expeditions he sent down the western coast of Africa, played the leading role. In the fifteenth century, most of the gold that reached Europe came from the Sudan in West Africa and from the Akan peoples living near the area of present-day Ghana. Muslim caravans brought the gold from the African cities of Niani and Timbuktu and carried it north across the Sahara to Mediterranean ports. Then the Portuguese muscled in on this commerce in gold. Prince Henry's carefully planned expeditions succeeded in reaching Guinea, and under King John II (r. 1481–1495) the Portuguese established trading posts and forts on the Guinea coast and penetrated into the continent all the way to Timbuktu (see Map 16.2). Portuguese ships transported gold to Lisbon, and by 1500 Portugal controlled the flow of gold to Europe. The golden century of Portuguese prosperity had begun.

The Portuguese pushed farther south down the west coast of Africa. In 1487 Bartholomew Diaz rounded the Cape of Good Hope at the southern tip, but storms and a threatened mutiny forced him to turn back. On a second expedition (1497–1499), the Portuguese mariner Vasco da Gama reached India and returned to Lisbon loaded with samples of Indian wares. King Manuel (r. 1495–1521) promptly dispatched thirteen ships under the command of Pedro Alvares Cabral, assisted by Diaz, to set up trading posts in India. On April 22, 1500, the coast of Brazil in South America was sighted and claimed for the crown of Portugal. Cabral then proceeded south and east around the Cape of Good Hope and reached India. Half of the fleet was lost on the return voyage, but the six spice-laden vessels that dropped anchor in Lisbon harbor in July 1501 more than paid for the entire expedition. Thereafter, convoys were sent out every March. Lisbon became the entrance port for Asian goods into Europe.

Black pepper originally derived from the Malabar Coast of southwestern India between Goa and Cochin—"the pepper country" to medieval European and Middle Eastern travelers. In 1500 this region supplied the European demand for pepper. In the next sixty years, pepper production spread in India, as well as to the Malay Peninsula, Sumatra, and Java. Nutmeg and cloves, well known to the Chinese but extremely rare and expensive for Europeans before the sixteenth century, grew in the Moluccas. From the Southeast Asian perspective, rice, salt, pickled or dried fish, and metal ware represented the major items for trade; spices originally were minor. With the arrival of Europeans, however, spices brought the larger profits.

As we have seen (see pages 504–505), Muslims (of Middle Eastern, Indian, Southeast Asian, and Chinese ethnic backgrounds) had controlled the Indian Ocean trade for centuries. They did not surrender it willingly. With the Portuguese entry into the region in 1498, the brisk Muslim trade was drastically disrupted, as the Portuguese sank or plundered every Muslim spice ship they met. Between 1502 and 1520, no Moluccan spices reached Mediterranean ports via the Red Sea. Portuguese ships sailing around the Cape of Good Hope carried about one-fourth the goods the Muslims had transported through southwestern Asia. Then, in 1511, Alfonso de Albuquerque, whom the Portuguese crown had named governor of India (1509–1515), captured Malacca, the great Indian Ocean trading entrepôt. Thereafter Portuguese commercial wealth gradually increased; the Portuguese dominated the European market by delivering on average thirty tons of cloves and ten tons of nutmeg each year. The Middle Eastern route declined. Albuquerque's bombardment of Goa, Calicut, and Malacca laid the foundations for Portuguese imperialism in the sixteenth and seventeenth centuries—a strange way to bring Christianity to "those who were in darkness." As one scholar wrote about the opening of China to the West, "while Buddha came to China on white elephants, Christ was borne on cannon balls."[6]

In March 1493, between the voyages of Diaz and da Gama, Spanish ships entered Lisbon harbor bearing a triumphant Italian explorer in the service of the Spanish monarchy. Christopher Columbus (1451–1506), a Genoese mariner, had secured Spanish support for an expedition to the East. He sailed from Palos, Spain, to the Canary Islands and crossed the Atlantic to the Bahamas, landing in October 1492 on an island that he named San Salvador and believed to be the coast of India. (See the feature "Listening to the Past: Columbus Describes His First Voyage" on pages 534–535.)

**Pepper Harvest** To break the monotony of their bland diet, Europeans had a passion for pepper, which—along with cinnamon, cloves, nutmeg, and ginger—was the main object of the Asian trade. Since one kilo of pepper cost 2 grams of silver at the place of production in the East Indies and from 10 to 14 grams of silver in Alexandria, Egypt, 14 to 18 grams in Venice, and 20 to 30 grams at the markets of northern Europe, we can appreciate the fifteenth-century expression "as dear as pepper." Here natives fill vats, and the dealer tastes a peppercorn for pungency. *(Bibliothèque nationale de France)*

## Technological Stimuli to Exploration

Technological developments were the key to Europe's remarkable outreach. By 1350 cannon made of iron or bronze and able to fire iron or stone balls had been fully developed in western Europe. This artillery emitted frightening noises and great flashes of fire and could batter down fortresses and even city walls. Sultan Mohammed II's siege of Constantinople in 1453 provides a classic illustration of the effectiveness of cannon fire.

Constantinople had very strong walled fortifications. The sultan secured the services of a Western technician, who built fifty-six small cannon and a gigantic gun that could hurl stone balls weighing about eight hundred pounds. The gun had to be moved by several hundred oxen and could be loaded and fired only by about a hundred men working together. Reloading took two hours. This awkward but powerful weapon breached the walls of Constantinople before it cracked on the second day of the bombardment. Lesser cannon finished the job.

Although early cannon posed serious technical difficulties for land warfare, they could be used at sea. The mounting of cannon on ships and improved techniques of shipbuilding gave impetus to European expansion. Since ancient times, most seagoing vessels had been narrow, open boats called *galleys,* propelled largely by oarsmen: slaves or convicts who had been sentenced to the galleys manned the oars of the cargo ships and warships that sailed the Mediterranean (both types of ships carried soldiers for defense). Well suited to the calm and thoroughly explored waters of the Mediterranean, galleys could not withstand the rough winds and uncharted shoals of the Atlantic. The need for sturdier craft, as well as population losses caused by the Black Death, forced the development of a new style of ship that did not require soldiers for defense or a large crew of oarsmen.

In the course of the fifteenth century, the Portuguese developed the *caravel,* a small, light, three-masted sailing ship. Though somewhat slower than the galley, the caravel held more cargo and was highly maneuverable. When fitted with cannon, it could dominate larger vessels, such as the round ships commonly used in commerce. The substitution of wind power for manpower, and artillery fire for soldiers, signaled a great technological advance and gave Europeans navigational and fighting ascendancy over the rest of the world.[7]

Other fifteenth-century developments in navigation helped make possible the conquest of the Atlantic. The

**Nocturnal** An instrument for determining the hour of night at sea by finding the progress of certain stars around the polestar (center aperture). *(National Maritime Museum, London)*

**magnetic compass** enabled sailors to determine their direction and position at sea. The **astrolabe,** an instrument developed by Muslim navigators in the twelfth century and used to determine the altitude of the sun and other celestial bodies, permitted mariners to plot their latitude, or position north or south of the equator. Steadily improved maps and sea charts provided information about distances, sea depths, and geography.

## The Explorers' Motives

The expansion of Europe was not motivated by demographic pressures. The Black Death had caused serious population losses from which Europe had not recovered in 1500. Few Europeans immigrated to North or South America in the sixteenth century. Half of those who did sail to begin a new life in America died en route; half of those who reached what they regarded as the New World eventually returned to their homeland. Why, then, did explorers brave the Atlantic, Pacific, and Indian Oceans?

The reasons are varied and complex. People of the sixteenth century were still basically medieval: their attitudes and values were shaped by religion and expressed in religious terms. In the late fifteenth century, crusading fervor remained a basic part of the Portuguese and Spanish national ideals. The desire to Christianize Muslims and pagan peoples played a central role in European expansion. Queen Isabella of Spain, for example, showed a fanatical zeal for converting the Muslims to Christianity and concentrated her efforts on the Muslims in Granada. But after the abortive crusading attempts of the thirteenth century, Isabella and other rulers realized full well that they lacked the material resources to mount the full-scale assault on Islam necessary for victory. Crusading impulses thus shifted from the Muslims to the pagan peoples of other continents.

Moreover, after the *reconquista*—the Christian reconquest of Muslim areas—enterprising young men of the Spanish upper classes found economic and political opportunities severely limited. As a study of the Castilian city Ciudad Real shows, the traditional aristocracy controlled the best agricultural land and monopolized urban administrative posts. Great merchants and a few nobles (surprisingly, since Spanish law forbade nobles' participation in commercial ventures) dominated the textile and leather-glove manufacturing industries. Thus many ambitious men immigrated to the Americas to seek their fortunes.[8]

Government sponsorship and encouragement of exploration also help to account for the results of the various voyages. Individual mariners and explorers could not afford the massive sums needed to explore mysterious oceans and to control remote continents. The strong financial support of Prince Henry the Navigator led to Portugal's success in the spice trade. Even the grudging and modest assistance of Isabella and Ferdinand eventually brought untold riches—and complicated problems—to Spain. The Dutch in the seventeenth century, through such government-sponsored trading companies as the Dutch East India Company, reaped enormous wealth, and although the Netherlands was a small country, it dominated the European economy in 1650.

Scholars have frequently described the European discoveries as a manifestation of Renaissance curiosity about the physical universe—the desire to know more about the geography and peoples of the world. There is truth to this explanation. Cosmography, natural history, and geography aroused enormous interest among educated people in the fifteenth and sixteenth centuries. Just as science fiction and speculation about life on other planets excite readers today, quasi-scientific literature about Africa, Asia, and the Americas captured the imaginations of Europeans. Oviedo's ***General History of the Indies*** (1547), a detailed eyewitness account of plants, animals, and peoples, was widely read.

Spices were another important incentive to voyages of discovery. Introduced into western Europe by the Crusaders in the twelfth century, pepper, nutmeg, ginger, mace, cinnamon, and cloves added flavor and variety to the monotonous diet of Europeans. Spices, which evoked the scent of the Garden of Eden, seemed a marvel and a mystery. Take, for example, cloves, for which Europeans found many uses. If picked green and sugared, the buds could be transformed into conserve (a kind of jam); if salted and pickled, cloves became a flavoring for vinegar. Cloves sweetened the breath. When added to food or drink, cloves were thought to stimulate the appetite and clear the intestines and bladder. When crushed and powdered, they served as a medicine—rubbed on the forehead to relieve head colds, applied to the eyes to strengthen vision. Taken with milk, cloves were believed to enhance the pleasures of sexual intercourse. In the late thirteenth century, the Venetian Marco Polo (1254?–1324?), the greatest of medieval travelers, visited the court of the Chinese emperor (see page 330). His widely publicized account, *Travels,* stimulated the trade in spices between Asia and Italy. Venice, through its trade with Arab merchants in Cairo and Constantinople, controlled the flow of spices to Europe and grew fabulously rich on it. The Portuguese appreciated the contemporary adage "Whoever is lord of Malacca has his hand on the throat of Venice."[9]

Spices were grown in the Spice Islands, India, and China; shipped across the Indian Ocean to ports on the Persian Gulf; and then transported by Arabs across the Arabian Desert to Mediterranean ports. But the rise of the Ming Dynasty in China in the late fourteenth century resulted in the expulsion of foreigners. And the steady penetration of the Ottoman Turks into the eastern Mediterranean and of Muslims across North Africa forced Europeans to seek a new route to the Asian spice markets.

The basic reason for European exploration and expansion, however, was the quest for material profit. Mariners and explorers frankly admitted this. As Bartholomew Diaz put it, his motives were "to serve God and His Majesty, to give light to those who were in darkness and to grow rich as all men desire to do." When Vasco da Gama reached the port of Calicut, India, in 1498, a native asked what the Portuguese wanted. Da Gama replied, "Christians and spices."[10] The bluntest of the Spanish conquistadors, Hernando Cortés, announced as he prepared to conquer Mexico, "I have come to win gold, not to plow the fields like a peasant."[11]

A sixteenth-century diplomat, Ogier Gheselin de Busbecq, summed up explorers' paradoxical attitude: in expeditions to the Indies and the Antipodes, he said, "religion supplies the pretext and gold the motive."[12]

**Ca' d'Oro (1421–1433)** Travel and long-term residence in the Muslim East gave Venetian merchants familiarity with Islamic architecture. Inspired by what they saw, and using Islamic motifs, Venetian merchants built palaces that served both as headquarters for their businesses and as family homes. The Contarini family, whose colossal fortune rested on banking and commerce, built this palace using the Muslim ogee arch on the Grand Canal. *Ca* is an abbreviation of *casa* (house), a term of modesty to distinguish it from *palazzo* (palace), a word reserved for the doge's residence. Because the exterior was gilded, it was called the House of Gold. *(Scala/Art Resource, NY)*

## The Problem of Christopher Columbus

The year 1992, which marked the quincentenary of Columbus's first voyages to the Americas, spawned an enormous amount of discussion about the significance of his voyages. Journalists, scholars, amateurs, and polemicists debated Columbus's accomplishments and failures. Until the 1980s, most writers generally would have agreed with the Harvard historian Samuel Eliot Morison in his 1942 biography of Columbus:

> *The whole history of the Americas stems from the Four Voyages of Columbus; and as the Greek city-states looked back to the deathless gods as their founders, so today a score of independent nations and dominions unite in homage to Columbus, the stouthearted son of Genoa, who carried Christian civilization across the Ocean Sea.*[13]

In 1942, we must remember, the Western Powers believed they were engaged in a life-and-death struggle to defend "Christian civilization" against the evil forces of fascism. As the five hundredth anniversary of his famous voyage approached, however, Columbus underwent severe criticism.

Critics charged that he enslaved and sometimes killed the Indians and was a cruel and ineffective governor of Spain's Caribbean colony. Moreover, they said, he did not discover a previously unknown continent: Africans and other Europeans had been to the Western Hemisphere before him. And not only did he not discover a "new" continent, he did not realize what he had found. In short, according to his harshest critics, he was a fool who didn't know what was going on around him. Some claim that he was the originator of European exploitation of the non-European world and destroyed the paradise that had been the New World.[14]

Because those judgments rest on social and ethical standards that did not exist in Columbus's world, responsible scholars consider them ahistorical. Instead, using the evidence of his *Journal* (sea log) and letters, let us ask three basic questions: (1) What kind of man was Columbus, and what forces or influences shaped him? (2) In sailing westward from Europe, what were his goals? (3) Did he achieve his goals, and what did he make of his discoveries?

The central feature in the character of Christopher Columbus is that he was a deeply religious man. He began the *Journal* of his voyage to the Americas, written as a letter to Ferdinand and Isabella of Spain, with this recollection:

*On 2 January in the year 1492, when your Highnesses had concluded their war with the Moors who reigned in Europe, I saw your Highnesses' banners victoriously raised on the towers of the Alhambra, the citadel of the city, and the Moorish king come out of the city gates and kiss the hands of your Highnesses and the prince, My Lord. And later in that same month, on the grounds of information I had given your Highnesses concerning the lands of India . . . your Highnesses decided to send me, Christopher Columbus, to see these parts of India and the princes and peoples of those lands and consider the best means for their conversion.*[15]

He had witnessed the Spanish reconquest of Granada and shared fully in the religious and nationalistic fervor surrounding that event. Just seven months separated Isabella and Ferdinand's entry into Granada on January 6 and Columbus's departure westward on August 3, 1492. In his mind, the two events were clearly linked. Long after Europeans knew something of Columbus's discoveries in the Caribbean, they considered the restoration of Muslim Granada to Christian hands as Ferdinand and Isabella's greatest achievements; for the conquest, in 1494 the Spanish pope Alexander VI (r. 1492–1503) rewarded them with the title "Most Catholic Kings." Like the Spanish rulers and most Europeans of his age, Columbus understood Christianity as a missionary religion that should be carried to places and peoples where it did not exist. Although Columbus's character certainly included material and secular qualities, first and foremost, as he wrote in 1498, he believed he was a divine agent: "God made me the messenger of the new heaven and the new earth of which he spoke in the Apocalypse of St. John . . . and he showed me the post where to find it."[16]

A second and fundamental facet of Columbus the man is that he was very knowledgeable about the sea. He was familiar with fifteenth-century Portuguese navigational aids such as **portolans**—written descriptions of routes showing bays, coves, capes, ports, and the distances between these places—and the magnetic compass. He had spent years consulting geographers, mapmakers, and navigators. And, as he implies in his *Journal,* he had acquired not only theoretical but practical experience: "I have spent twenty-three years at sea and have not left it for any length of time worth mentioning, and I have seen everything from east to west [meaning he had been to England] and I have been to Guinea [North and West Africa]."[17] Some of Columbus's calculations, such as his measurement of the distance from Portugal to Japan as 2,760 miles (it is actually 12,000), proved inaccurate. But his successful thirty-three-day voyage to the Caribbean owed a great deal to his seamanship and his knowledge and skillful use of instruments.

What was the object of his first voyage? What did Columbus set out to do? The name of his expedition, "The Enterprise of the Indies," reveals his object. He wanted to find a direct ocean route to Asia, which would provide the opportunity for a greatly expanded trade, a trade in which the European economy, and especially Spain, would participate. Two scholars have written, "If Columbus had not sailed westward in search of Asia, someone else would have done so. The time was right for such a bold undertaking."[18] Someone else might have done so, but the fact remains that Columbus, displaying a characteristic Renaissance curiosity and restless drive, actually accepted the challenge.

How did Columbus interpret what he had found, and did he think he had achieved what he set out to do? His mind had been formed by the Bible and the geographical writings of classical authors, as were the minds of most educated people of his time. Thus, as people in every age have often done, Columbus ignored the evidence of his eyes; he described what he saw in the Caribbean as an idyllic paradise, a peaceful Garden of Eden. When accounts of his travels were published, Europeans' immediate fascination with this image of the New World meant that Columbus's propaganda created an instant myth.

We do not know whether Columbus ever read Marco Polo's *Travels;* if he did, it was not until after his second voyage.[19] But when he sensed that he had not found the spice markets and bazaars of Asia that popular legend described, his goal changed from establishing trade with the (East) Indians and Chinese to establishing the kind of trade the Portuguese were then conducting with Africa and with Cape Verde and other islands in the Atlantic (see Map 16.2). That meant setting up some form of government in the Caribbean islands, even though Columbus had little interest in, or capacity for, governing. In 1496 he forcibly subjugated the island of Hispaniola, enslaved the Amerindians, and laid the basis for a system of land grants tied to the Amerindians' labor service. Borrowing practices and institutions from reconquest Spain and the Canary Islands, Columbus laid the foundation for Spanish imperial administration. In all of this, Columbus was very much a man of his times. He never understood, however, that the scale of his discoveries created problems of trade, settlers, relations with the Amerindians, and, above all, government bureaucracy.[20]

## The Conquest of Aztec Mexico and Inca Peru

The strange end of the Aztec nation remains one of the most fascinating events in the annals of human societies. The Spanish adventurer Hernando Cortés (1485–1547) landed at Veracruz in February 1519. In November he entered Tenochtitlán (Mexico City) and soon had the emperor Montezuma II (r. 1502–1520) in custody. In less than two years, Cortés destroyed the monarchy, gained complete control of the Mexica capital, and extended his jurisdiction over much of the Aztec Empire. Why did a strong people defending its own territory succumb so quickly to a handful of Spaniards fighting in dangerous and completely unfamiliar circumstances? How indeed, since Montezuma's scouts sent him detailed reports of the Spaniards' movements? The answers to these questions lie in the fact that at the time of the Spanish arrival, the Aztec and Inca Empires faced grave internal difficulties brought on by their religious ideologies; by the Spaniards' boldness, timing, and technology; and by Aztec and Inca psychology and attitudes toward war.

The Spaniards arrived in late summer, when the Aztecs were preoccupied with harvesting their crops and not thinking of war. From the Spaniards' perspective, their timing was ideal. A series of natural phenomena, signs, and portents seemed to augur disaster for the Aztecs. A comet was seen in daytime, and two temples were suddenly destroyed, one by lightning unaccompanied by thunder. These and other apparently inexplicable events seemed to presage the return of the Aztec god Quetzalcoatl (see page 427) and had an unnerving effect on the Aztecs. They looked on the Europeans riding "wild beasts" as extraterrestrial forces coming to establish a new social order. Defeatism swept the nation and paralyzed its will.

The Aztec state religion, the sacred cult of Huitzilopochtli, necessitated constant warfare against neighboring peoples to secure captives for religious sacrifice and laborers for agricultural and infrastructural work. Lacking an effective method of governing subject peoples, the Aztecs controlled thirty-eight provinces in central Mexico through terror. When Cortés landed, the provinces were being crushed under a cycle of imperial oppression: increases in tribute provoked revolt, which led to reconquest, retribution, and demands for higher tribute, which in turn sparked greater resentment and fresh revolt. When the Spaniards appeared, the Totonacs greeted them as liberators, and other subject peoples joined them against the Aztecs. Even before the coming of the Spaniards, Montezuma's attempts to resolve the problem of constant warfare by freezing social positions—thereby ending the social mobility that war provided—aroused the resentment of his elite, mercantile, and lowborn classes. Montezuma faced terrible external and internal difficulties.[21] (See page 430.)

Montezuma refrained from attacking the Spaniards as they advanced toward his capital and welcomed Cortés and his men into Tenochtitlán. Historians have often condemned the Aztec ruler for vacillation and weakness. But he relied on the advice of his state council, itself divided, and on the dubious loyalty of tributary communities. When Cortés—with incredible boldness—took Montezuma hostage, the emperor's influence over his people crumbled.

The major explanation for the collapse of the Aztec Empire to six hundred Spaniards lies in the Aztecs' notion of warfare and their level of technology. Forced to leave Tenochtitlán to settle a conflict elsewhere, Cortés placed his lieutenant, Alvarado, in charge. Alvarado's harsh rule drove the Aztecs to revolt, and they almost succeeded in destroying the Spanish garrison. When Cortés returned just in time, the Aztecs allowed his reinforcements to join Alvarado's besieged force. No threatened European or

**Mexica-Spaniard Encounter** The Mexica are armed with spears, the Spaniards with firearms and longbows. The colorful dress of the Mexica—indicating that war was a ceremonial rite for them—contrasts with the dull metallic gray of the Spaniards' armor. *(Institut Amatller d'Art Hispanic)*

Asian state would have conceived of doing such a thing: dividing an enemy's army and destroying the separate parts was basic to their military tactics. But for the Aztecs, warfare was a ceremonial act in which "divide and conquer" had no place.

Having allowed the Spanish forces to reunite, the entire population of Tenochtitlán attacked the invaders. The Aztecs killed many Spaniards. In retaliation, the Spaniards executed Montezuma. The Spaniards escaped from the city and inflicted a crushing defeat on the Aztec army at Otumba near Lake Texcoco on July 7, 1520. The Spaniards won because "the simple Indian methods of mass warfare were of little avail against the manoeuvring of a well-drilled force."[22] Aztec weapons proved no match for the terrifyingly noisy and lethal Spanish cannon, muskets, crossbows, and steel swords. European technology decided the battle. Cortés began the systematic conquest of Mexico.

From 1493 to 1525, the Inca Huayna Capac ruled as a benevolent despot (the word *Inca* refers both to the ruler of the Andeans who lived in the valleys of the Andes in present-day Peru and to the people themselves). His power was limited only by custom. His millions of subjects considered him a god, firm but just to his people, merciless to his enemies. Only a few of the Inca's closest relatives dared look at his divine face. Nobles approached him on their knees, and the masses kissed the dirt as he was carried by in his litter. The borders of his vast empire were well fortified and threatened by no foreign invaders. Grain was plentiful, and apart from an outbreak of smallpox in a distant province—introduced by the Spaniards—no natural disaster upset the general peace. An army of fifty thousand loyal troops stood at the Inca's disposal. Why did this powerful empire fall so easily to Francisco Pizarro and his band of 175 men armed with one small, ineffective cannon?

The Incas were totally isolated. They had no contact with other Amerindian cultures and knew nothing at all of Aztec civilization or its collapse to the Spaniards in 1521. Since about the year 1500, Inca scouts had reported "floating houses" on the seas, manned by white men with beards. Tradesmen told of strange large animals with feet of silver (as horseshoes appeared in the brilliant sunshine). Having observed a border skirmish between Indians and white men, intelligence sources advised Huayna Capac that the Europeans' swords were as harmless as women's weaving battens. A coastal chieftain had poured chicha, the native beer, down the barrel of a gun to appease the god of thunder. These incidents suggest that Inca culture provided no basis for understanding the Spaniards and the significance of their arrival. Moreover, even if the strange pale men planned war, there were very few of them, and the Incas believed that they could not be reinforced from the sea.[23]

At first the Incas did not think that the strangers intended trouble. They believed the old Inca legend that the creator-god **Virocha**—who had brought civilization to them, become displeased, and sailed away promising to return someday—had indeed returned. Belief in a legend prevented the Incas, like the Aztecs, from taking prompt action.

Religious ideology contributed to grave domestic crisis within the empire. When the ruler died, his corpse was preserved as a mummy. The mummy was both a holy object and a dynamic force in Inca society. It was housed in a sacred chamber and dressed in fine clothing. It was carried in procession to state ceremonies and was asked for advice in times of trouble. This cult of the royal mummies left a new Inca (ruler) with the title and insignia of his office but little else. Because each dead Inca retained possession of the estates and properties he had held in life, each new Inca lacked land. Thus, to strengthen his administration, secure the means to live in the royal style, and reward his supporters, a new Inca had to engage in warfare to acquire land.

In 1525 Huascar succeeded his father, Huayna Capac, as Inca and was crowned at Cuzco, the Incas' capital city, with the fringed headband symbolizing his imperial office. By this time, the dead rulers controlled most of Peru's land and resources. The nobility managed the estates of the dead Inca rulers. Needing land and other possessions, Huascar proposed burying the mummies of all the dead Incas and using the profits from their estates for the living. (See page 440.)

According to Inca law, the successor of a dead Inca had to be a son by the ruler's principal wife, who had to be the ruler's full sister. Huascar was the result of such an incestuous union. His half brother Atauhualpa was not. Atauhualpa tried to persuade Huascar to split the kingdom with him, claiming that their father's dying wish was for both sons to rule. Huascar rejected this claim. The great nobles responsible for the cult of the royal mummies, however, were alarmed and outraged by Huascar's proposal to bury the mummies. Not only would Huascar be insulting the dead mummies and thus provoke their anger and retaliation, but the nobility would be deprived of the wealth and power they enjoyed as custodians of the cult. Willing to ignore the fact that Atauhualpa had not been born of an incestuous union, the nobles supported Atauhualpa's claim to rule. Civil war ensued, and Atauhualpa emerged victorious.[24] The five-year struggle may have exhausted him and damaged his judgment.

Francisco Pizarro (ca 1475–1541) landed on the northern coast of Peru on May 13, 1532, the very day Atauhualpa won the decisive battle against his brother. The Spaniard soon learned about the war and its outcome. As Pizarro advanced across the steep Andes toward Cuzco, Atauhualpa was proceeding to the capital for his coronation. Atauhualpa stopped at the provincial town of Cajamarca. He, like Montezuma in Mexico, was kept fully informed of the Spaniards' movements. His plan was to lure the Spaniards into a trap, seize their horses and ablest men for his army, and execute the rest. What had the Inca, surrounded by his thousands of troops, to fear? Atauhualpa thus accepted Pizarro's invitation to meet in the central plaza of Cajamarca with his bodyguards "unarmed so as not to give offense." He rode right into the Spaniard's trap. Pizarro knew that if he could capture that Inca, from whom all power devolved, he would have the "Kingdom of Gold" for which he had come to the New World.

The Inca's litter arrived in the ominously quiet town square. One cannon blast terrified the Andeans. The Spaniards rushed out of hiding and slaughtered them. Atauhualpa's fringed headband was instantly torn from his head. He offered to purchase his freedom with a roomful of gold. Pizarro agreed to this ransom, and an appropriate document was drawn up and signed. But after the gold had been gathered from all parts of the empire to fill the room—its dimensions were seventeen by twenty-two by nine feet—the Spaniards trumped up charges against Atauhualpa and strangled him. The Inca Empire lay at Pizarro's feet.

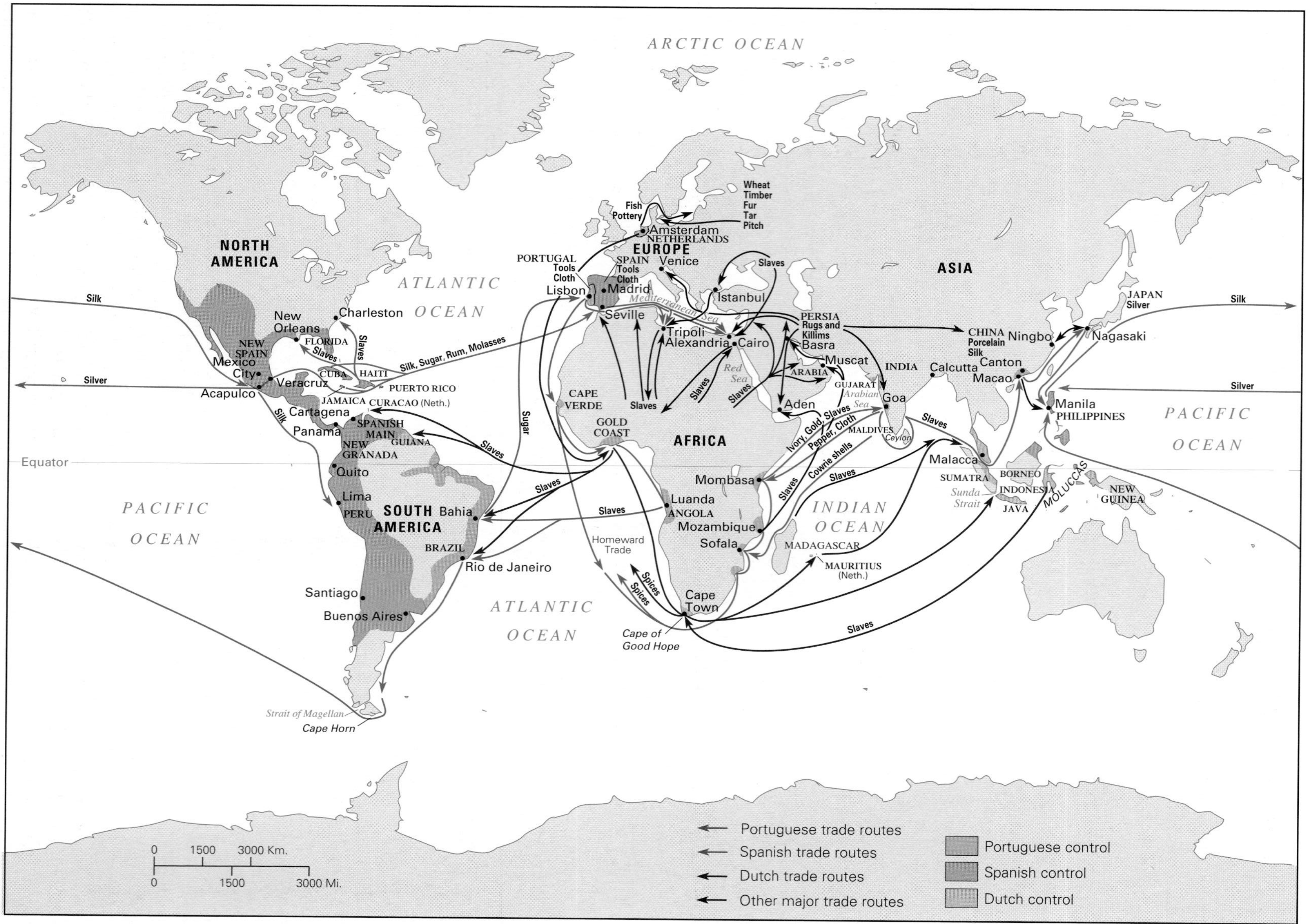


**MAP 16.3 Seaborne Trading Empires in the Sixteenth and Seventeenth Centuries** By the mid-seventeenth century, trade linked all parts of the world, except for Australia. Notice that trade in slaves was not confined to the Atlantic but involved almost all parts of the world.

## GLOBAL TRADE NETWORKS

The Europeans' discovery of the Americas and their exploration of the Pacific for the first time linked the entire world by intercontinental seaborne trade. That trade brought into being three successive commercial empires: the Portuguese, the Spanish, and the Dutch.

In the sixteenth century, naval power and shipborne artillery gave Portugal hegemony over the sea route to India. To Lisbon the Portuguese fleet brought spices, which the Portuguese paid for with textiles produced at Gujarat and Coromandel in India and with gold and ivory from East Africa (see Map 16.3). From their fortified bases at Goa on the Arabian Sea and at Malacca on the Malay Peninsula, ships of Malabar teak carried goods to the Portuguese settlement at Macao in the South China Sea. From Macao, loaded with Chinese silks and porcelains, Portuguese ships sailed to the Japanese port of Nagasaki and to the Philippine port of Manila, where Chinese goods were exchanged for Spanish (that is, Latin American) silver. Throughout Asia, the Portuguese traded in slaves—black Africans, Chinese, and Japanese. The Portuguese exported to India horses from Mesopotamia and copper from Arabia; from India they exported hawks and peacocks for the Chinese and Japanese markets.

Across the Atlantic, Portuguese Brazil provided most of the sugar consumed in Europe in the sixteenth and early seventeenth centuries. African slave labor produced the sugar on the plantations of Brazil, and Portuguese merchants controlled both the slave trade between West Africa and Brazil and the commerce in sugar between Brazil and Portugal. The Portuguese were the first worldwide traders, and Portuguese was the language of the Asian maritime trade.

Spanish possessions in the New World constituted basically a land empire, and in the sixteenth century the Spaniards devised a method of governing that empire (see page 527). But across the Pacific, the Spaniards also built a seaborne empire, centered at Manila in the Philippines, which had been "discovered" by Ferdinand Magellan in 1521. Between 1564 and 1571, the Spanish navigator Miguel Lopez de Legazpi sailed from Mexico and through a swift and almost bloodless conquest took over the Philippine Islands. Legazpi founded Manila, which served as the transpacific bridge between Spanish America and the extreme Eastern trade.

Chinese silk, sold by the Portuguese in Manila for American silver, was transported to Acapulco in Mexico, from which it was carried overland to Veracruz for re-export to Spain. Because hostile Pacific winds prohibited direct passage from the Philippines to Peru, large shipments of silk also went south from Acapulco to Peru (see Map 16.3). Spanish merchants could never satisfy the European demand for silk, so huge amounts of bullion went from Acapulco to Manila. For example, in 1597, 12 million pesos of silver, almost the total value of the transatlantic trade, crossed the Pacific. After about 1640, the Spanish silk trade declined because it could not compete with Dutch imports.

Stimulated by a large demand for goods in Europe, India, China, and Japan, a worldwide commercial boom occurred from about 1570 to 1630. In Japan the gradual decline of violence, unification, and the development of marketing networks led to a leap in orders for foreign products: textiles from India, silks and porcelains from China, raw materials and spices from Southeast Asia. The Japanese navy expanded, and Japanese mines poured out vast quantities of silver that paid for those wares. Then, in 1635, maritime trade stopped when the Tokugawa Shogunate closed the islands to trade and forbade merchants to travel abroad under penalty of death.

China, with a population increase, urban growth, and a rare period of government-approved foreign trade, also underwent international commercial expansion. China wanted raw materials, sugar, and spices from Southeast Asia; ivory and slaves from Africa; and cotton cloth from India. Merchants in Mughal India conducted a huge long-distance trade extending as far north as Poland and Russia. India also sought spices from the Moluccas, sugar from Vietnam and the Philippines, and rice and raw materials from Southeast Asia. In this early modern **age of commerce,** Southeast Asia exchanged its pepper, spices, woods, resin, pearls, and sugar for textiles from India; silver from the Americas and Japan; and silk, ceramics, and manufactures from China. The Southeast Asian merchant marine also expanded. The European demand for Indian pepper, Southeast Asian nutmeg and cloves, and Chinese silks and porcelains was virtually insatiable. But Europeans offered nothing that Asian peoples wanted. Therefore, Europeans had to pay for their purchases with silver or gold—hence the steady flow of specie from Mexico and South America to Asia.

Throughout the world, many people profited: capitalists who advanced money for voyages, captains and crews of ships, and port officials. As spices moved westward or northward, as silks and porcelains moved southward and westward, and as cloth moved eastward and westward, these various goods grew more valuable in the boom of long-distance trade.[25]

In the latter half of the seventeenth century, the worldwide Dutch seaborne trade predominated. The Dutch

Empire was built on spices. In 1599 a Dutch fleet returned to Amsterdam carrying 600,000 pounds of pepper and 250,000 pounds of cloves and nutmeg. Those who had invested in the expedition received a 100 percent profit. The voyage led to the establishment in 1602 of the Dutch East India Company, founded with the stated intention of capturing the spice trade from the Portuguese.

The Dutch fleet, sailing from the Cape of Good Hope and avoiding the Portuguese forts in India, steered directly for the Sunda Strait in Indonesia (see Map 16.3). The Dutch wanted direct access to and control of the Indonesian sources of spices. In return for assisting Indonesian princes in local squabbles and disputes with the Portuguese, the Dutch won broad commercial concessions. Through agreements, seizures, and outright war, they gained control of the western access to the Indonesian archipelago. Gradually, they acquired political domination over the archipelago itself. Exchanging European manufactured goods—armor, firearms, linens, and toys—the Dutch soon had a monopoly on the very lucrative spice trade.[26] The seaborne empires of Portugal, Spain, and Holland paved the way for the eighteenth-century mercantilist empires of France and Great Britain.

**Kangnido Map (1684)** Diplomatic relations between Korea and the Ming Chinese court brought Korean scholars in touch with Chinese thought. This Korean map of the world is probably based on a Chinese model. *(British Library. From Lee Chan,* Hanguk ui ko chido/Yi Chan cho *[Old Maps of Korea], 1997)*

## THE CHINESE AND JAPANESE DISCOVERY OF THE WEST

Why did Europeans, rather than Chinese, take the lead in exploring parts of the globe distant from their native countries? In the fifteenth century, China was obviously the largest geographical power in Asia. Chinese sailors had both the theoretical maritime knowledge and the practical experience of long-distance ocean travel (see page 507). In 1435, the Chinese knew some of the Pacific Ocean, all of the Indian Ocean, the Arabian Sea, and the Red Sea. Europeans knew little more than the Mediterranean Sea and the Atlantic Ocean along the northwestern coast of Africa. About 1500, China had a population between 65 million and 80 million, whereas the population of Spain was only about 6.5 million, barely one-tenth of China's. Although the wealth of the Ottoman sultans may have exceeded that of the Chinese emperors, the emperors' wealth was more than double that of the kings of Spain and France combined.

Europeans, as we have seen, sailed to the Americas and Asia seeking spices, gold, and trade. Was Chinese culture hostile to trade and foreign commerce? According to traditional scholarship, Chinese Confucian teaching disparaged commerce and merchants. In the orthodox Confucian ordering of social classes—scholars, farmers, artisans, and merchants—merchants ranked lowest. Moreover, Confucian belief held that trade encouraged competition, competition led to social mobility and change, and change promoted disorder in society. But whatever theoretical ideas the Chinese literati may have had about merchants, Western observers took a different view. One later expert on China wrote that the Chinese had "a singular penchant for trade"; another writer commented that the Chinese were "a race of traders than whom there has not been in the world a shrewder and a keener." Following Zheng He's voyages (see page 507), tens of thousands of Chinese emigrated to the Philippines, and the dominant position many of them acquired in business in Luzon by 1600 would bear out the observation of a distinguished historian that "a powerful materialistic streak runs through the Chinese psyche."[27] Thus hostility to trade and commerce does not explain China's failure to expand.

Rather, internal and domestic difficulties offer better explanations. In the fifteenth century, Mongol pressures on China's northern border forced the emperors to focus on domestic security rather than foreign exploration. The emperor Zhengtong (r. 1436–1449 and 1457–1464) held that overseas expeditions brought little visible return. At a time when he was forced to conserve resources for the army, he stopped maritime expeditions, closed China's borders, and forbade foreign travel (the last law was widely flouted). Administrative disorder also aggravated imperial financial difficulties. Eunuchs controlled the palace guard, the imperial workshops, and foreign tribute or trade (the Chinese did not distinguish between the two). In the imperial administration, eunuchs' numbers were legion and their greed proverbial, and their corruption and use of blackmail paralyzed the government.[28] Hence, at the time when "the new monarchs" of Europe (see page 464) were reducing disorderly elements in their societies and centralizing their administrations, Chinese emperors were losing domestic control and threatened by strong foreign invaders. The failure to utilize rich maritime knowledge opened China's vast coastline first to Japanese pirates and then to persistent and aggressive European traders.

The desire to Christianize pagan peoples was a major motive in Europeans' overseas expansion. In 1582 the Jesuit Matteo Ricci (1552–1610) settled at Macao on the mouth of the Canton River. Like the Christian monks who had converted the Germanic tribes of early medieval Europe, Ricci sought first to convert the emperor and elite groups and then, through gradual assimilation, to win the throngs of Chinese. He tried to present Christianity to the Chinese in Chinese terms. He understood the Chinese respect for learning and worked to win converts among the scholarly class. When Ricci was admitted to the Imperial City at Beijing (Peking), he addressed the emperor Wan-li:

> *Li Ma-tou [Ricci's name transliterated into Chinese], your Majesty's servant, comes from the Far West, addresses himself to Your Majesty with respect, in order to offer gifts from his country. Despite the distance, fame told me of the remarkable teaching and fine institutions with which the imperial court has endowed all its peoples. I desired to share these advantages and live out my life as one of Your Majesty's subjects, hoping in return to be of some small use.*[29]

Ricci presented the emperor with two clocks, one of them decorated with dragons and eagles in the Chinese style. The emperor's growing fascination with clocks gave Ricci the opportunity to display other examples of Western technology. He instructed court scholars about astronomical equipment and the manufacture of cannon and drew for them a map of the world—with China at its center. These inventions greatly impressed the Chinese intelligentsia. Over a century later, a Jesuit wrote, "The Imperial Palace is stuffed with clocks, . . . watches, carillons, repeaters, organs, spheres, and astronomical clocks of all kinds—there are more than four thousand pieces from the best masters of Paris and London."[30] The Chinese first learned about Europe from the Jesuits.

But the Christians and the Chinese did not understand one another. Because the Jesuits served the imperial court as mathematicians, astronomers, and cartographers, the Chinese emperors allowed them to remain in Beijing. The Jesuits, however, were primarily interested in converting the Chinese to Christianity. The missionaries thought that by showing the pre-eminence of Western science, they were demonstrating the superiority of Western religion. This was a relationship that the Chinese did not acknowledge. They could not accept a religion that required total commitment and taught the existence of an absolute. Only a small number of the highly educated, convinced of a link between ancient Chinese tradition and Christianity, became Christians. Most Chinese were hostile to the Western faith. They accused Christians of corrupting Chinese morals because they forbade people to honor their ancestors—and corruption of morals translated into disturbing the public order. They also accused Christians of destroying Chinese sanctuaries, of revering a man (Christ) who had been executed as a public criminal, and of spying on behalf of the Japanese.

The **Rites Controversy,** a dispute over ritual between the Jesuits and other Roman Catholic religious orders, sparked a crisis. The Jesuits supported the celebration of the Mass in Chinese and the performance of other ceremonies in terms understandable to the Chinese. The Franciscans and other missionaries felt that the Jesuits had sold out the essentials of the Christian faith in order to win converts.

One burning issue was whether Chinese reverence for ancestors was homage to the good that the dead had done during their lives or an act of worship. The Franciscans secured the support of Roman authorities, who decided against the Jesuits. In 1704 and again in 1742, Rome decreed that Roman ceremonial practice in Latin (not in Chinese) was to be the law for Chinese missions. Papal letters also forbade Chinese Christians from participating in the rites of ancestor worship. The emperor in turn banned Christianity in China, and the missionaries were forced to flee.

The Christian West and the Chinese world learned a great deal from each other. The Jesuits probably were "responsible for the rebirth of Chinese mathematics in the seventeenth and eighteenth centuries," and Western contributions stimulated the Chinese development of other sciences.[31] From the Chinese, Europeans got the idea of building bridges suspended by chains. The first Western experiments in electrostatics and magnetism in the seventeenth century derived from Chinese models. Travel accounts about Chinese society and customs had a profound impact on Europeans, making them more sensitive to the beautiful diversity of peoples and manners.

Initial Japanese contacts with Europeans paralleled those of the Chinese. In 1542 Portuguese merchants arrived in Japan. They vigorously supported Christian missionary activity, and in 1547 the Jesuit missionary Saint Francis Xavier landed at Kagoshima, preached widely, and in two years won many converts. From the beginning, however, the Japanese government feared that native converts might have conflicting political loyalties. Divided allegiance could encourage European invasion of the islands—the Japanese authorities had the example of the Philippines, where Spanish conquest followed missionary activity.

Convinced that European merchants and missionaries had contributed to the civil disorder, which the regime was trying to eradicate, the Japanese government decided to expel the Spanish and Portuguese and to close Japan to all foreign influence. A decree of 1635 was directed at the commissioners of the port of Nagasaki, a center of Japanese Christianity:

> *If there is any place where the teachings of the padres (Catholic priests) is practiced, the two of you must order a thorough investigation. . . . If there are any Southern Barbarians (Westerners) who propagate the teachings of the padres, or otherwise commit crimes, they may be incarcerated in the prison.*[32]

In 1639 an imperial memorandum decreed, "Hereafter entry by the Portuguese galeota [galleon or large ocean-going warship] is forbidden. If they insist on coming [to Japan], the ships must be destroyed and anyone aboard those ships must be beheaded."[33]

When tens of thousands of Japanese Christians made a stand on the peninsula of Shimabara, the Dutch lent the Japanese government cannon. The Protestant Dutch hated Catholicism, and as businessmen they hated the Portuguese, their great commercial rivals. Convinced that the Dutch had come only for trade and did not want to proselytize, the imperial government allowed them to remain. But Japanese authorities ordered them to remove their factory-station from Hirado on the western tip of Kyushu to the tiny island of Deshima, which covered just 2,100 square feet. The government limited Dutch trade to one ship a year, watched the Dutch very closely, and required Dutch officials to pay an annual visit to the capital to renew their loyalty. The Japanese also compelled the Dutch mer-

**Arrival of the Nanbanjin or "Southern Barbarians"** Just as wealthy eighteenth-century Europeans craved Chinese silken wallpaper because of its "exotic" quality, so rich Japanese decorated their homes with screens depicting the "strange" Westerners; the gold leaf suggests the screen's great value. In the central panel, a Portuguese ship captain (shaded by a parasol carried by a black servant) arrives in the port of Nagasaki. Black porters carry boxes of goods and rare animals as gifts "to sweeten up" Japanese merchants. They are received by tall, black-robed Jesuits. Europeans were called "barbarians" because of what the Japanese perceived as their terrible manners and the stench they emitted from lack of bathing. *(Michael Holford)*

chants to perform servile acts that other Europeans considered humiliating.

Long after Christianity ceased to be a possible threat to the Japanese government, the fear of Christianity sustained a policy of banning Western books on science or religion. Until well into the eighteenth century, Japanese intellectuals were effectively cut off from Western developments. The Japanese opinion of Westerners was not high. What little the Japanese knew derived from the few Dutch businessmen at Deshima. Very few Japanese people ever saw Europeans. If they did, they considered them "a special variety of goblin that bore only a superficial resemblance to a normal human being." The widespread rumor was that when Dutchmen urinated, they raised one leg like dogs.[34]

## THE IMPACT OF CONTACT

In the sixteenth and seventeenth centuries, following Columbus's voyages, substantial numbers of Spaniards crossed the Atlantic for ports in the Caribbean, the Spanish Main, and present-day Argentina. Thousands of Portuguese sailed for Brazil. The ships on which they traveled were not as large as the so-called Indiamen going to the Indian Ocean; the latter had larger carrying capacities and were expected to return with tons of spices, pepper, sugar, and gold. Only half the migrants, merchants, missionaries, royal officials, soldiers, wives, concubines, and slaves reached American (or Indian Ocean) ports. Poor health, poor shipboard hygiene, climatic extremes, rancid food, and putrid water killed the other half.[35] Those who reached America, however, eventually had an enormous impact, not only there but also on the whole world.

### The Columbian Exchange

Nearly thirty years ago, a historian asserted that "the most important changes brought on by the Columbian voyages were biological in nature."[36] His book explored on a global scale the biosocial consequences of 1492. The migration of peoples led to the exchange of flora and fauna, of animals and diseases. Settlers launched an agricultural revolution with worldwide implications.

When people travel to another country, they often want to eat the foods with which they are familiar. They want to re-create the circumstances they know at home. What Iberian settlers considered essential—wheat for bread, grapes for wine, olive oil for both culinary and sacramental purposes—were not grown in America. So the migrants sought to turn the New World into the Old: they searched for climatic zones favorable to those crops. Everywhere they settled, they raised wheat: in the highlands of Mexico, the Rio de la Plata, New Granada (in northern South America), and Chile. By 1535 Mexico was exporting wheat. Grapes did well in parts of Peru and Chile. It took the Spanish longer to discover areas where suitable soil and adequate rainfall would nourish olive trees, but by the 1560s the coastal valleys of Peru and Chile were dotted with olive groves. Columbus had brought sugar plants on his second voyage; Spaniards also introduced rice and bananas from the Canary Islands, and the Portuguese carried these items to Brazil. All plants and trees had to be brought from Europe, but not all plants arrived intentionally. In clumps of mud on shoes and the folds of textiles came immigrant grasses such as Kentucky bluegrass, daisies, and the common dandelion.

Apart from wild turkeys and game, native Americans had no animals for food; apart from alpacas and llamas, they had no animals for travel or to use as beasts of burden. (Human power had moved the huge stones needed to build the monumental Aztec temples.) On his second voyage in 1493, Columbus introduced horses, cattle, sheep, dogs, pigs, chickens, and goats. The multiplication of these animals proved spectacular. By the 1550s, when the Spaniards explored, they took herds of swine. The horse enabled the Spanish conquerors and the Amerindians to travel faster and farther and to transport heavy loads.

In return, the Spanish and Portuguese took back to Europe the main American cereal, maize (corn), from Mexico; white potatoes from Peru; and many varieties of beans, squash, pumpkins, avocados, and tomatoes (which Europeans distrusted, fearing that they were sexually stimulating). Maize was the great gift of the Amerindians to all the peoples of the world as food for humans and livestock. Because maize grows in climates too dry for rice and too wet for wheat, gives a high yield per unit of land, and has a short growing season, it proved an especially important crop for Europeans. Initially they looked on the white potato with contempt, but they gradually recognized its nutritional value. Its cultivation slowly spread from west to east—to Ireland, England, and France in the seventeenth century; to Germany, Poland, Hungary, and Russia in the eighteenth. Ironically, the white potato reached New England from old England in 1718.

Africa and Asia also shared in the Columbian Exchange. Merchants took maize to West Africa before the mid-sixteenth century, and its cultivation spread rapidly to the Gold Coast, the Congo, Angola, and southern Africa. Perhaps more important than maize for Africans was the South American plant manioc, or cassava, which Americans know as the dessert tapioca. It grows in almost any kind of soil, is resistant to African pests, and yields bumper crops in Africa. In the island countries of the Indian Ocean such as Java, Amerindian food products arrived with Europeans. By the seventeenth century, sweet potatoes, beans, and maize were all raised there; by 1800 maize was the most important crop after rice. The Chinese adopted American foods faster than any other Old World people: peanuts introduced by the Portuguese in Brazil, maize and manioc, and sweet and white potatoes, all of which flourished in China by 1550.

**Indians Harvesting Wheat** Sixteenth-century Spaniards introduced wheat into Latin America, where it competed with the native corn and manioc. By the nineteenth century, wheat enjoyed great success in Argentina, Chile, Mexico, the Canadian prairies, the Midwest of the United States, South Africa, and northern China. It is a symbol of the Columbian Exchange and of European expansion. *(Institut d'Amatller d'Art Hispanic)*

So far as limited evidence allows scholars to estimate, between the mid-seventeenth and early nineteenth centuries, every region of the world except Africa experienced considerable population growth. Whatever political, medical, or hygienic reasons there may have been for this growth in different parts of the globe, there can be no doubt that the spread of American agricultural products contributed heavily to demographic change. Around 1500 to 1800, Europe underwent a population explosion, solved partly by immigration to the Americas. The transfer of Old World animals enhanced the Americas' ability to feed their growing population.

The Columbian Exchange had a negative side. While Spaniards brought smallpox, measles, and other European diseases to the Americas (see below), the Amerindians gave the Spaniards the venereal disease syphilis. Sailors and settlers probably carried it back to Europe in 1493. Medical researchers trying to find the origins of the "pox" have examined bones of the dead; they have found no evidence of it before 1493 but have unequivocal proof of syphilitic damage after that date. Whatever its precise origins, this horrible disease raced across Europe, then spread into Asia.[37]

## The Native American Population Decline

In the sixteenth century, perhaps 200,000 Spaniards immigrated to the New World. Mostly soldiers demobilized from the Spanish and Italian campaigns and adventurers and drifters unable to find work in Spain, they did not intend to work in the New World. After assisting in the conquest of the Aztecs and the subjugation of the Incas, these drifters wanted to settle down and become a ruling class. In temperate grazing areas, they carved out vast estates and imported Spanish sheep, cattle, and horses for the kinds of ranching with which they were familiar. In the coastal tropics, unsuited for grazing, the Spanish erected huge sugar plantations. Columbus had introduced sugar into the West Indies; Cortés had introduced it into Mexico. Sugar was a great luxury in Europe, and demand for it was high. Around 1550 the discovery of silver at Zacatecas and Guanajuato in Mexico and Potosí in present-day Bolivia stimulated silver rushes. How were the cattle ranches, sugar plantations, and silver mines to be worked? Obviously, by the Amerindians.

The Spanish quickly established the **encomienda system,** whereby the Crown granted the conquerors the right to employ groups of Amerindians in a town or area as agricultural or mining laborers or as tribute payers. Theoretically, the Spanish were forbidden to enslave the natives; in actuality, the encomiendas were a legalized form of slavery. The European demand for sugar, tobacco, and silver prompted the colonists to exploit the Amerindians mercilessly. Unaccustomed to forced labor, especially in the blistering heat of tropical cane fields or the dark, dank, and dangerous mines, they died like flies. Recently scholars have tried to reckon the death rate of the Amerindians in the sixteenth century. Some historians maintain that the Andean population of Peru fell from 1.3 million in 1570 to 600,000 in 1620; central Mexico had 25.3 million Amerindians in 1519 and 1 million in 1605.[38] Some demographers dispute these figures, but all agree that the decline of the native population in all of Spanish-occupied America amounted to a catastrophe greater in scale than any that occurred even in the twentieth century.

What were the causes of this devastating slump in population? Students of the history of medicine have suggested the best explanation: disease. The major cause of widespread epidemics is migration, and those peoples isolated longest from other societies suffer most. Contact with disease builds up bodily resistance. At the beginning of the sixteenth century, Amerindians probably had the unfortunate distinction of longer isolation from the rest of humankind than any other people on earth. Crowded concentrations of laborers in the mining camps bred infection, which the miners carried to their home villages. With little or no resistance to diseases brought from the Old World, the inhabitants of the highlands of Mexico and Peru, especially, fell victim to smallpox. According to one expert, smallpox caused "in all likelihood the most severe single loss of aboriginal population that ever occurred."[39]

Although disease was the prime cause of the Amerindian population decline, the Spaniards themselves contributed heavily to the natives' death rate.[40] According to the Franciscan missionary Bartolomé de Las Casas (1474–1566), the Spanish maliciously murdered thousands:

> *This infinite multitude of people [the Indians] was . . . without fraud, without subtilty or malice . . . toward the Spaniards whom they serve, patient, meek and peaceful. . . .*
>
> *To these quiet Lambs . . . came the Spaniards like most c(r)uel Tygres, Wolves and Lions, enrag'd with a sharp and tedious hunger; for these forty years past, minding nothing else but the slaughter of these unfortunate wretches, whom with divers kinds of torments neither seen nor heard of before, they have so cruelly and inhumanely butchered, that of three millions of people which Hispaniola itself did contain, there are left remaining alive scarce three hundred persons.*[41]

Las Casas's remarks concentrate on the tropical lowlands, but the death rate in the highlands was also staggering.

The Christian missionaries who accompanied the conquistadors and settlers—Franciscans, Dominicans, and Jesuits—played an important role in converting the Amerindians to Christianity, teaching them European methods of agriculture, and inculcating loyalty to the Spanish crown. In terms of numbers of people baptized, missionaries enjoyed phenomenal success, though the depth of the Amerindians' understanding of Christianity remains debatable. Missionaries, especially Las Casas, asserted that the Amerindians had human rights, and through Las Casas's persistent pressure, the emperor Charles V in 1531 abolished the worst abuses of the encomienda system.

Some scholars offer a psychological explanation for the colossal death rate of the Amerindians, suggesting that they simply lost the will to survive because their gods appeared to have abandoned them to a world over which they had no control. Hopelessness, combined with abusive treatment and overwork, pushed many men to suicide, many women to abortion or infanticide.

Whatever its precise causes, the astronomically high death rate created a severe labor shortage in Spanish America. As early as 1511, King Ferdinand of Spain observed that the Amerindians seemed to be "very frail" and that "one black could do the work of four Indians."[42] Thus was born an absurd myth and the massive importation of black slaves from Africa.

South American conditions were not unique; the same patterns of epidemic disease struck the indigenous peoples of North America. Between 1539 and 1543, the Spanish explorer Hernando de Soto (ca 1500–1542), who had served under Pizarro in Peru, led an expedition from northern Florida to the Mississippi River in search of silver and gold. Everywhere the Spaniards went, they introduced germs that had a devastating effect on native societies. Historians estimate that between 1550 and 1700, the aboriginal peoples of the Southeast suffered an 80 percent population loss from disease. In the mid-seventeenth century in his book *Of Plymouth Plantation,* William Bradford (1590–1657), who had crossed the Atlantic on the *Mayflower* and become governor of Plymouth Colony in Massachusetts, expressed horror at the effects of smallpox and tuberculosis on the Amerindians of New England. Although Spanish and English immigrants to the Americas did not plan or intend these disasters, the term *holocaust* suggests their magnitude.

## Colonial Administration

Having seized the great Amerindian and Andean ceremonial centers in Mexico and Peru, the Spanish conquistadors proceeded to subdue the main areas of native American civilization in the New World. Columbus, Cortés, and Pizarro claimed the lands they had "discovered" for the Spanish crown. How were these lands to be governed?

According to the Spanish theory of absolutism, the Crown was entitled to exercise full authority over all imperial lands. In the sixteenth century, the Crown divided Spain's New World territories into four **viceroyalties,** or administrative divisions. New Spain, with its capital at Mexico City, consisted of Mexico, Central America, and present-day California, Arizona, New Mexico, and Texas. Peru, with its viceregal seat at Lima, originally consisted of all the lands in continental South America but later was reduced to the territory of modern Peru, Chile, Bolivia, and Ecuador. New Granada, with Bogotá as its administrative center, included present-day Venezuela, Colombia, Panama, and, after 1739, Ecuador. La Plata, with Buenos Aires as its capital, consisted of Argentina, Uruguay, and Paraguay. Within each territory a *viceroy,* or imperial governor, had broad military and civil authority as the Spanish sovereign's direct representative. The viceroy presided over the **audiencia,** twelve to fifteen judges who served as advisory council and as the highest judicial body.

From the early sixteenth century to the beginning of the nineteenth, the Spanish monarchy acted on the mercantilist principle that the colonies existed for the financial benefit of the mother country. The mining of gold and silver was always the most important industry in the colonies. The Crown claimed the **quinto,** one-fifth of all precious metals mined in the Americas. Gold and silver yielded the Spanish monarchy 25 percent of its total income. In return, Spain shipped manufactured goods to the New World and discouraged the development of native industries.

The Portuguese governed their colony of Brazil in a similar manner. After the union of the Portuguese and Spanish crowns in 1580, Spanish administrative forms were introduced. Local officials called *corregidores* held judicial and military powers. Mercantilist policies placed severe restrictions on Brazilian industries that might compete with those of Portugal. In the seventeenth century, the use of black slave labor made possible the cultivation of coffee, cotton, and sugar. In the eighteenth century, Brazil led the world in the production of sugar.

## Slavery and the Origins of American Racism

Americans commonly link the words *slavery* and *Africa.* It is true that from the early sixteenth to the late nineteenth century, Africa was the great source of slave labor for South and North America. From a global perspective, however, the Atlantic slave trade represents only one aspect of a worldwide phenomenon. The Indian Ocean has served as a major conduit for slaves down to the present. China and India imported slaves from East Africa, Madagascar, and Southeast Asia. Portuguese, Spanish, and Dutch merchants enslaved thousands of Malayan, Filipino, and Japanese people.[43] Muslims of the Ottoman and Safavid Empires brought slaves from western and central Africa (as they had done for centuries) and from the Circassian region of what is today southern Russia. Slavery took different forms in different places according to perceived economic, social, and cultural needs, but everywhere slaves lacked the freedom to move about as they wished. Slavery remains pervasive in parts of Africa today. In December 1998, grade school children in Aurora, Colorado, saved their dimes, nickels, and pennies to purchase and free slave children in the Sudan. The $35,000 these American children raised was expected to obtain the freedom of more than six hundred people (at about $50 per person) from chattel slavery.[44]

Except for the Aborigines of Australia, almost all peoples in the world have engaged in the enslavement of other human beings at some time in their histories. Since ancient times, victors in battle have enslaved conquered peoples. In the later Middle Ages, slavery was deeply entrenched in southern Italy, Sicily, Crete, and Mediterranean Spain. The bubonic plague, famines, and other epidemics created a severe shortage of agricultural and domestic workers throughout Europe, encouraging Italian merchants to buy slaves from the Balkans, Thrace, southern Russia, and central Anatolia for sale in the West. The slave trade was a lucrative business enterprise in Italy during the Renaissance (see page 463). Where profits were high, papal threats of excommunication failed to stop it. Genoese slave traders set up colonial stations in the Crimea and along the Black Sea, and according to an international authority on slavery, these outposts were "virtual laboratories" for the development of slave plantation agriculture in the New World.[45] This form of slavery had nothing to do with race; almost all of these slaves were white. How, then, did black African slavery enter the picture and take root in the New World?

**African Slave and Indian Woman** A black slave approaches an Indian prostitute. Unable to explain what he wants, he points with his finger; she eagerly grasps for the coin. The Spanish caption above moralizes on the black man using stolen money—yet the Spaniards ruthlessly expropriated all South American mineral wealth. *(New York Public Library)*

The capture of Constantinople by the Ottoman Turks in 1453 halted the flow of white slaves from the Black Sea region and the Balkans. Mediterranean Europe, cut off from its traditional source of slaves, had no alternative source for slave labor but sub-Saharan Africa. The centuries-old trans-Saharan trade in slaves was greatly stimulated by the existence of a ready market for slaves in the vineyards and sugar plantations of Sicily and Majorca. By the later fifteenth century, before the discovery of America, the Mediterranean had developed an "American" form of slavery.

Meanwhile, the Genoese and other Italians had colonized the Canary Islands in the western Atlantic. And sailors working for Portugal's Prince Henry the Navigator (see page 509) discovered the Madeira Islands and made settlements there. In this stage of European expansion, "the history of slavery became inextricably tied up with the history of sugar."[46] Population increases and monetary expansion in the fifteenth century led to an increasing demand for sugar even though it was an expensive luxury that only the affluent could afford. Between 1490 and 1530, three hundred to two thousand black slaves arrived annually at the port of Lisbon (see Map 16.4). From Lisbon, where African slaves performed much of the manual labor and constituted 10 percent of the city's population, slaves were transported to the sugar plantations of Madeira, the Azores, the Cape Verde Islands, and then Brazil. Sugar and those small Atlantic islands gave slavery in the Americas its distinctive shape. Columbus himself spent a decade in Madeira and took sugar plants on his voyages to "the Indies."

As European economic exploitation of the Americas proceeded, the major problem settlers faced was a shortage of labor. As early as 1495, the Spanish solved the problem by enslaving the native Amerindians. In the next two centuries, the Portuguese, Dutch, and English followed suit.

Unaccustomed to any form of forced labor, certainly not to panning for gold for more than twelve hours a day in the broiling sun, the Amerindians died "like fish in a bucket," one Spanish settler reported.[47] In 1515 the Spanish missionary Bartolomé de Las Casas (see page 526), who had seen the evils of Amerindian slavery, urged the future emperor Charles V to end such slavery in his American dominions. Las Casas recommended the importation of blacks from Africa, both because church law did not strictly forbid black slavery and because he thought blacks could better survive under South American conditions. Charles agreed, and in 1518 the African

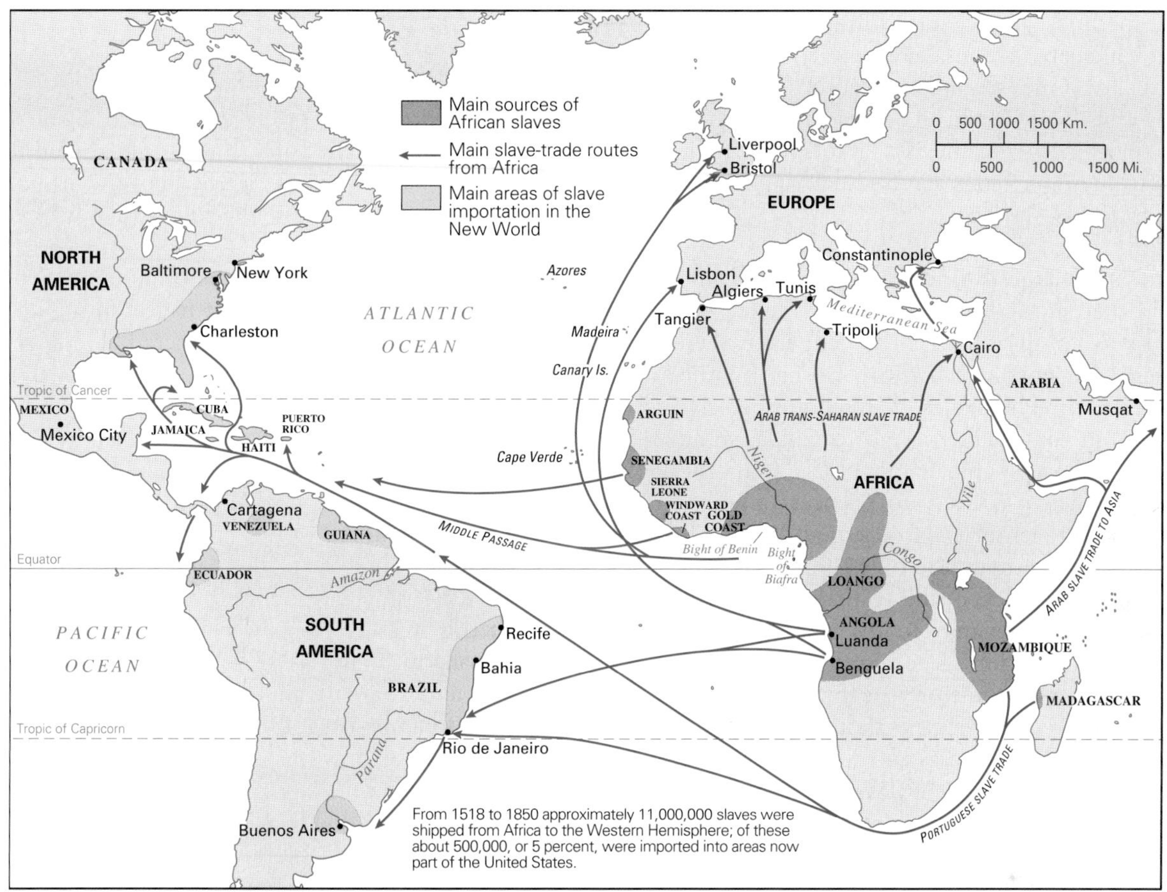


**MAP 16.4 The African Slave Trade** Decades before the discovery of America, Greek, Russian, Bulgarian, Armenian, and then black slaves worked the plantation economies of southern Italy, Sicily, Portugal, and Mediterranean Spain—thereby serving as models for the American form of slavery.

slave trade began. (When the blacks arrived, Las Casas immediately regretted his suggestion.) Columbus's introduction of sugar plants, moreover, stimulated the need for black slaves, and the experience and model of plantation slavery in Portugal and on the Atlantic islands encouraged the establishment of a similar agricultural pattern in the New World.

Portugal brought the first slaves to Brazil; by 1600, 4,000 were being imported annually. After its founding in 1621, the Dutch West India Company, with the full support of the government of the United Provinces, transported thousands of Africans to Brazil and the Caribbean. Only in the late seventeenth century, with the chartering of the Royal African Company, did the English get involved. Thereafter, large numbers of African blacks poured into the West Indies and North America. In 1790 there were 757,181 blacks in a total U.S. population of 3,929,625. When the first census was taken in Brazil in 1798, blacks numbered about 2 million in a total population of 3.25 million.

European settlers brought to the Americas the racial attitudes they had absorbed in Europe. Their beliefs and attitudes toward blacks derived from two basic sources: Christian theological speculation (see page 464), and Muslim ideas. In the sixteenth and seventeenth centuries, the English, for example, were extremely curious about Africans' lives and customs, and slavers' accounts were extraordinarily popular. Travel literature depicted Africans as savages because of their eating habits, morals, clothing, and social customs; as barbarians because of their language and methods of war; and as heathens because they were not Christian. Africans were believed to possess a potent sexuality. One seventeenth-century observer considered Africans "very lustful and impudent, . . . their members' extraordinary greatness is a token of their lust." African women were considered sexually aggressive with a "temper hot and lascivious."[48]

"At the time when Columbus sailed to the New World, Islam was the largest world religion, and the only world religion that showed itself capable of expanding rapidly in areas as far apart and as different from each other as Senegal [in northwest Africa], Bosnia [in the Balkans], Java, and the Philippines."[49] In contrast to civilized peoples from the Mediterranean to China, some Muslim writers claimed, sub-Saharan blacks were the only peoples who had produced no sciences or stable states. The fourteenth-century Arab historian Ibn Khaldun (1332–1406) wrote that "the only people who accept slavery are the Negroes, owing to their low degree of humanity and their proximity to the animal stage." Though black kings, Khaldun alleged, sold their subjects without even a pretext of crime or war, the victims bore no resentment because they gave no thought to the future and had "by nature few cares and worries; dancing and rhythm are for them inborn."[50] It is easy to see how such absurd images developed into the classic stereotypes used to justify black slavery in South and North America in the seventeenth, eighteenth, and nineteenth centuries. Perhaps centuries of commercial contacts between Muslim and Mediterranean peoples had familiarized the latter with Muslim racial attitudes. The racial beliefs that the Portuguese, Spanish, Dutch, and English brought to the New World, however, derive primarily from Christian theological speculation.

Europeans had no monopoly on ridiculous racist notions. The Chinese, for example, had used enslavement as a form of punishment since the Han Dynasty. Records from the tenth century show that the Chinese greatly prized slaves from Africa for their physical differences. A customs official noted in his private diary that "(in the West) there is an island in the sea (Madagascar?) in which there are many savages. Their bodies are as black as lacquer and they have frizzled hair. They are enticed by (offers of) food and then captured and sold as slaves to Arabic countries where they fetch a high price." In China Africans worked as gatekeepers at private estates and as divers to repair leaky boats (because they "swam without blinking their eyes"). They were forced to carry heavy loads and generally treated as beasts of burden. Wealthy people in the city of Guangzhou (Canton) "kept devil slaves," as the Chinese described them.[51]

## The Economic Effects of Spain's Discoveries

The sixteenth century has often been called Spain's golden century. The influence of Spanish armies, Spanish Catholicism, and Spanish wealth was felt all over Europe. This greatness rested largely on the influx of precious metals from the Americas.

At an altitude of 15,000 feet, where nothing grew because of the cold, and after a two-and-a-half-month journey by pack animal from Lima, Peru, an incredible source of silver was discovered at Potosí (in present-day Bolivia) in 1545. The place had no population. By 1600, 160,000 people lived there, making it smaller than Nanjing or Delhi but about the size of London. In the second half of the sixteenth century, Potosí yielded perhaps 60 percent of all the silver mined in the world. From Potosí and the mines at Zacatecas and Guanajuato in Mexico, huge quantities of precious metals poured forth.

To protect this treasure from French and English pirates, armed convoys transported it each year to Spain. Between 1503 and 1650, 16 million kilograms of silver and 185,000 kilograms of gold entered Seville's port. Spanish predominance, however, proved temporary.

In the sixteenth century, Spain experienced a steady population increase, creating a sharp rise in the demand for food and goods. Spanish colonies in the Americas also represented a demand for products. Since Spain had expelled some of the best farmers and businessmen—the Muslims and Jews—in the fifteenth century, the Spanish economy was suffering and could not meet the new demands. Prices rose. Because the cost of manufacturing cloth and other goods increased, Spanish products could not compete in the international market with cheaper products made elsewhere. The textile industry was badly hurt. Prices spiraled upward faster than the government could levy taxes to dampen the economy. (Higher taxes would have cut the public's buying power; with fewer goods sold, prices would have come down.)

Did the flood of silver bullion from America cause the inflation? Prices rose most steeply before 1565, but bullion imports reached their peak between 1580 and 1620. Thus there is no direct correlation between silver imports and the inflation rate. Did the substantial population growth accelerate the inflation rate? It may have done so. After 1600, when the population pressure declined, prices gradually stabilized. One fact is certain: the price revolution severely strained government budgets. Several times between 1557 and 1647, Spain's King Philip II and his successors repudiated the state debt, thereby undermining confidence in the government and leading the economy into a shambles.

As Philip II paid his armies and foreign debts with silver bullion, Spanish inflation was transmitted to the rest of Europe. Between 1560 and 1600, much of Europe experienced large price increases. Prices doubled and in some cases quadrupled. Spain suffered most severely, but all European countries were affected. People who lived on fixed incomes, such as the continental nobles, were badly hurt because their money bought less. Those who owed fixed sums of money, such as the middle class, prospered: in a time of rising prices, debts had less value each year. Food costs rose most sharply, and the poor fared worst of all.

And what of Asia? What economic impact did the Spanish and Portuguese discoveries have on Asian societies and on world trade? Some recent scholars argue that the key to understanding world trade in the sixteenth and early seventeenth centuries is not Europe, where hitherto most research has focused, but China. They also claim that the silver market explains the emergence of world trade. China was the main buyer of world silver—that is, China exchanged its silks and porcelains for silver. While the mines of South America and Mexico poured out silver, so too did Japanese mines, shipping to Manila and Macao perhaps two hundred tons a year. "When silver from Mexico and Japan entered the Ming empire in great quantity, the value of silver began to decline and inflation set in, for as the metal became more abundant its buying power diminished."[52] This inflationary trend affected the values of all commodities. Europeans were only the middlemen in the trade between Europe, the New World, and China.

China demanded silver for its products, and the value of silver was initially very high. As the heart of world trade was China, so the center of early modern trade was not Europe, but China. The silver market drove world trade, with the Americas and Japan being the mainstays on the supply side and China dominating the demand side.

Within China the overissue of paper money had by 1450 reduced the value of that medium of currency to virtually nothing. Gold was too valuable for ordinary transactions. So the Ming government shifted to a silver-based currency. American and Japanese silver had a profound impact on China. On the one hand, it contributed to the rise of a merchant class that converted to a silver zone. On the other hand, the Ming Dynasty, by allowing the payment of taxes in silver instead of the traditional rice, weakened its financial basis. As the purchasing power of silver declined in China, so did the value of silver taxes. This development led to a fiscal crisis that helped bring down the Ming Dynasty and lead to the rise of the Qing. From a global perspective, however, the economic impact of China on the West was far greater than any European influence on China or the rest of Asia.[53]

## SUMMARY

From the late fifteenth through the early seventeenth centuries, Indian Ocean trade and commerce attracted the attention and pecuniary ambitions of countries in all parts of the world. Merchants and business people in China, Japan, India, and the Middle East fought for shares in that rich trade. The trade also drew the attention of Europeans, who, in their search for a direct route to "the Indies," inadvertently "discovered" the continents of the Western Hemisphere. Within a short time, South America was joined to a worldwide commercial network.

This Age of Reconnaissance and Age of Discovery had profound global consequences. In Southeast Asia, it stimulated the production of pepper and spices and led to the arrival of Christian missionaries and Muslim teachers, who competed for the adherence of native peoples. In China the lure of international trade encouraged the development of the porcelain and silk industries, as well as the immigration of thousands of Chinese people to Southeast Asia. In Japan the Indian Ocean trade in spices, silks, and Indian cotton prompted the greater exploitation of Japanese silver mines to yield the ore with which to pay for foreign goods. European intrusion into the Americas led to the forcible subjugation of native peoples for use in American silver and gold mines, along with the establishment of political and ecclesiastical administrations to govern the new territories. For mining and even more for agricultural purposes, Europeans introduced African slaves into the Americas, thereby intensifying the ancient African tradition of slave labor. The spread of American plants, especially maize and potatoes, improved the diets of Asian, African, and European peoples and contributed to an almost worldwide population boom beginning in the mid-seventeenth century. Europeans carried smallpox and other diseases to the Americas, causing a holocaust among native American peoples. Europeans returned home with syphilis, which rapidly spread across Europe and went with the thousands of migrants from Europe to Asia and Africa.

## KEY TERMS

bride wealth
magnetic compass
astrolabe
*General History of the Indies*
portolans
Virocha
"age of commerce"
Rites Controversy
encomienda system
viceroyalties
audiencia
quinto

## NOTES

1. A. Reid, *Southeast Asia in the Age of Commerce, 1450–1680.* Vol. 1: *The Land Under the Winds* (New Haven, Conn.: Yale University Press, 1988), p. 2.
2. Ibid., pp. 3–20.
3. Ibid., pp. 146–155.
4. A. Reid, *Southeast Asia in the Age of Commerce, 1450–1680.* Vol. 2: *Expansion and Crisis* (New Haven, Conn.: Yale University Press, 1993), pp. 133–192; the quotation is on p. 151.
5. Ibid., Chaps. 1 and 2, pp. 1–131.
6. Quoted in C. M. Cipolla, *Guns, Sails, and Empires: Technological Innovation and the Early Phases of European Expansion, 1400–1700* (New York: Minerva Press, 1965), pp. 115–116.
7. J. H. Parry, *The Age of Reconnaissance* (New York: Mentor Books, 1963), Chaps. 3 and 5.
8. C. R. Phillips, *Ciudad Real, 1500–1750: Growth, Crisis, and Readjustment in the Spanish Economy* (Cambridge, Mass.: Harvard University Press, 1979), pp. 103–104, 115.
9. See C. Corn, *The Scents of Eden: A History of the Spice Trade* (New York: Kodansha International, 1999), pp. 4, xix.
10. Quoted in Cipolla, *Guns, Sails, and Empires,* p. 132.
11. Quoted in F. H. Littell, *The Macmillan Atlas History of Christianity* (New York: Macmillan, 1976), p. 75.
12. Quoted in Cipolla, *Guns, Sails, and Empires,* p. 133.
13. S. E. Morison, *Admiral of the Ocean Sea: A Life of Christopher Columbus* (Boston: Little, Brown, 1942), p. 339.
14. T. K. Rabb, "Columbus: Villain or Hero?" *Princeton Alumni Weekly,* October 14, 1992, pp. 12–17.
15. J. M. Cohen, ed. and trans., *The Four Voyages of Christopher Columbus* (New York: Penguin Books, 1969), p. 37.
16. Quoted in R. L. Kagan, "The Spain of Ferdinand and Isabella," in *Circa 1492: Art in the Age of Exploration,* ed. J. A. Levenson (Washington, D.C.: National Gallery of Art, 1991), p. 60.
17. Quoted in F. Maddison, "Tradition and Innovation: Columbus' First Voyage and Portuguese Navigation in the Fifteenth Century," in *Circa 1492: Art in the Age of Exploration,* ed. J. A. Levenson (Washington, D.C.: National Gallery of Art, 1991), p. 69.
18. W. D. Phillips and C. R. Phillips, *The Worlds of Christopher Columbus* (Cambridge: Cambridge University Press, 1992), p. 273.
19. J. Larner, *Marco Polo and the Discovery of the World* (New Haven, Conn.: Yale University Press, 2001), pp. 155–159.
20. Phillips and Phillips, *The Worlds of Christopher Columbus*, p. 273.
21. G. W. Conrad and A. A. Demarest, *Religion and Empire: The Dynamics of Aztec and Inca Expansionism* (New York: Cambridge University Press, 1993), pp. 67–69.
22. G. C. Vaillant, *Aztecs of Mexico* (New York: Penguin Books, 1979), p. 241. Chapter 15, on which this section leans, is fascinating.
23. V. W. Von Hagen, *Realm of the Incas* (New York: New American Library, 1961), pp. 204–207.
24. Conrad and Demarest, *Religion and Empire,* pp. 135–139.
25. Reid, *Southeast Asia,* vol. 2, pp. 10–26.
26. Parry, *The Age of Reconnaissance,* Chaps. 12, 14, and 15.
27. L. E. Eastman, *Family, Fields, and Ancestors: Constancy and Change in China's Social and Economic History, 1550–1949* (New York: Oxford University Press, 1988), pp. 101–102.
28. A. Paludan, *Chronicle of the Chinese Emperors* (London: Thames and Hudson, 1998), pp. 166, 170–172.
29. Quoted in S. Neill, *A History of Christian Missions* (New York: Penguin Books, 1977), p. 163.
30. Quoted in C. M. Cipolla, *Clocks and Culture: 1300–1700* (New York: W. W. Norton, 1978), p. 86.
31. J. Gernet, *A History of Chinese Civilization* (New York: Cambridge University Press, 1982), p. 458.
32. Quoted in A. J. Andrea and J. H. Overfield, *The Human Record,* vol. 1 (Boston: Houghton Mifflin, 1990), pp. 406–407.
33. Quoted ibid., p. 408.
34. D. Keene, *The Japanese Discovery of Europe,* rev. ed. (Stanford, Calif.: Stanford University Press, 1969), pp. 1–17; the quotation is on p. 16.
35. A. J. R. Russell-Wood, *The Portuguese Empire, 1415–1808: A World on the Move* (Baltimore: Johns Hopkins University Press, 1998), pp. 58–59.
36. A. W. Crosby, *The Columbian Exchange: Biological and Cultural Consequences of 1492* (Westport, Conn.: Greenwood, 1972), p. xiv.
37. Ibid., passim. This section rests on Crosby's fascinating book.
38. N. Sanchez-Albornoz, *The Population of Latin America: A History,* trans. W. A. R. Richardson (Berkeley: University of California Press, 1974), p. 41.
39. Quoted in Crosby, *The Columbian Exchange,* p. 39.
40. Ibid., pp. 35–59.
41. Quoted in C. Gibson, ed., *The Black Legend: Anti-Spanish Attitudes in the Old World and the New* (New York: Knopf, 1971), pp. 74–75.
42. Quoted in L. B. Rout, Jr., *The African Experience in Spanish America* (New York: Cambridge University Press, 1976), p. 23.
43. For slavery in the Spice Islands, see Reid, *Southeast Asia,* vol. 2, pp. 35, 86, 108.
44. M. Sink, "Schoolchildren Set Out to Liberate Slaves in the Sudan," *New York Times,* December 2, 1998, p. B14.
45. C. Verlinden, *The Beginnings of Modern Colonization,* trans. Y. Freccero (Ithaca, N.Y.: Cornell University Press, 1970), pp. 5–6, 80–97.
46. This section leans heavily on D. B. Davis, *Slavery and Human Progress* (New York: Oxford University Press, 1984), pp. 54–62.
47. Quoted in D. P. Mannix with M. Cowley, *Black Cargoes: A History of the Atlantic Slave Trade* (New York: Viking Press, 1968), p. 5.
48. Quoted ibid., p. 19.
49. P. Brown, "Understanding Islam," *New York Review of Books,* February 22, 1979, pp. 30–33.
50. Davis, *Slavery and Human Progress,* pp. 43–44.
51. L. Levathes, *When China Ruled the Seas: The Treasure Fleet of the Dragon Throne, 1405–1433* (New York: Oxford University Press, 1996), pp. 37–38.
52. Quoted in D. O. Flynn and A. Giráldez, "Born with a 'Silver Spoon': The Origin of World Trade in 1571," *Journal of World History* 6 (Fall 1985): 203.
53. Ibid., pp. 217–218.

## SUGGESTED READING

Many of the titles listed in the Notes should prove helpful to students interested in exploring specific topics related to the acceleration of global contacts. Reid's two-volume work provides a broad, detailed, and fascinating study of many facets of Southeast Asian cultures and of the changes brought by Chinese and European intrusion. These books might be supplemented by K. McPherson, *The Indian Ocean: A History of People and the Sea* (1993), which stresses that regional history is the foundation of global history. A useful anthology for all the Chinese emperors and their interests is A. Paludan, *Chronicle of the Chinese Emperors: The Reign-by-Reign Record of the Rulers of Imperial China* (1998), which has many illustrations and charts. Russell-Wood's book, cited in the Notes, describes the geographical, navigational, and human factors involved in the rise and decline of that empire. For the Spanish, Dutch, and English Empires, see the Suggested Reading for Chapters 15 and 17. Crosby's book, cited in the Notes, is now a standard and stimulating account of the biological implications of global contact. His *Measure of Reality: Quantification and Western Society, 1250–1600* (1997) shows how Europeans' shift from a qualitative to a quantitative method of perception helped them to become world leaders in business practices, navigation, and technology.

Perhaps the best starting point for the study of European society in the age of exploration is Parry's book, cited in the Notes, which treats the causes and consequences of the voyages of discovery. His splendidly illustrated *The Discovery of South America* (1979) examines Europeans' reactions to the maritime discoveries and treats the entire concept of new discoveries. For the earliest European reaction to the Japanese, see D. Massarella, *A World Elsewhere: Europe's Encounter with Japan in the Sixteenth and Seventeenth Centuries* (1990). The urbane studies of C. M. Cipolla present fascinating material on technological and sociological developments written in a lucid style. In addition to the titles cited in the Notes, see *Cristofano and the Plague: A Study in the History of Public Health in the Age of Galileo* (1973) and *Public Health and the Medical Profession in the Renaissance* (1976). Morison's work, cited in the Notes, is the standard biography of Columbus. The advanced student should consult F. Braudel, *Civilization and Capitalism, 15th–18th Century,* trans. S. Reynolds. Vol. 1: *The Structures of Everyday Life* (1981); vol. 2: *The Wheels of Commerce* (1982); and vol. 3: *The Perspective of the World* (1984). These three fat volumes combine vast erudition, a global perspective, and remarkable illustrations. For the political ideas that formed the background of the first Spanish overseas empire, see A. Pagden, *Spanish Imperialism and the Political Imagination* (1990).

For the medieval and early modern background to European and American racial attitudes, see G. M. Fredrickson, *Racism. A Short History,* chapter 1 (2002). As background to issues of racism and slavery in North and South America, students should see J. L. Watson, ed., *Asian and African Systems of Slavery* (1980), a valuable collection of essays. Davis's *Slavery and Human Progress,* cited in the Notes, shows how slavery was viewed as a progressive force in the expansion of the Western world. For North American conditions, interested students should consult W. D. Jordan, *The White Man's Burden: Historical Origins of Racism in the United States* (1974), and the title by Mannix and Cowley listed in the Notes, a hideously fascinating account. For Caribbean and South American developments, see F. P. Bowser, *The African Slave in Colonial Peru* (1974); J. S. Handler and F. W. Lange, *Plantation Slavery in Barbados: An Archeological and Historical Investigation* (1978); and R. E. Conrad, *Children of God's Fire: A Documentary History of Black Slavery in Brazil* (1983).

# LISTENING TO THE PAST

## Columbus Describes His First Voyage

*On his return voyage to Spain in January 1493, Christopher Columbus composed a letter intended for wide circulation and had copies of it sent ahead to Isabella and Ferdinand and others when the ship docked at Lisbon. Because the letter sums up Columbus's understanding of his achievements, it is considered the most important document of his first voyage.*

Since I know that you will be pleased at the great success with which the Lord has crowned my voyage, I write to inform you how in thirty-three days I crossed from the Canary Islands to the Indies, with the fleet which our most illustrious sovereigns gave me. I found very many islands with large populations and took possession of them all for their Highnesses; this I did by proclamation and unfurled the royal standard. No opposition was offered.

I named the first island that I found "San Salvador," in honour of our Lord and Saviour who has granted me this miracle. . . . When I reached Cuba, I followed its north coast westwards, and found it so extensive that I thought this must be the mainland, the province of Cathay.* . . . From there I saw another island eighteen leagues eastwards which I then named "Hispaniola."† . . .

*Cathay is the old name for China. In the log-book and later in this letter Columbus accepts the native story that Cuba is an island that they can circumnavigate in something more than twenty-one days, yet he insists here and later, during the second voyage, that it is in fact part of the Asiatic mainland.

†Hispaniola is the second largest island of the West Indies; Haiti occupies the western third of the island, the Dominican Republic the rest.

Hispaniola is a wonder. The mountains and hills, the plains and meadow lands are both fertile and beautiful. They are most suitable for planting crops and for raising cattle of all kinds, and there are good sites for building towns and villages. The harbours are incredibly fine and there are many great rivers with broad channels and the majority contain gold.‡ The trees, fruits and plants are very different from those of Cuba. In Hispaniola there are many spices and large mines of gold and other metals. . . . §

The inhabitants of this island, and all the rest that I discovered or heard of, go naked, as their mothers bore them, men and women alike. A few of the women, however, cover a single place with a leaf of a plant or piece of cotton which they weave for the purpose. They have no iron or steel or arms and are not capable of using them, not because they are not strong and well built but because they are amazingly timid. All the weapons they have are canes cut at seeding time, at the end of which they fix a sharpened stick, but they have not the courage to make use of these, for very often when I have sent two or three men to a village to have conversation with them a great number of them have come out. But as soon as they saw my men all fled immediately, a father not even waiting for his son. And this is not because we have harmed any of them; on the contrary, wherever I have gone and been able to have conversation with them, I have given them some of the various things I had, a cloth and other articles, and received nothing in exchange. But they have still remained incurably timid. True, when they have been reassured and lost their fear, they are so ingenuous and so liberal with all their possessions that no one who has not seen them

‡This did not prove to be true.

§These statements are also inaccurate.

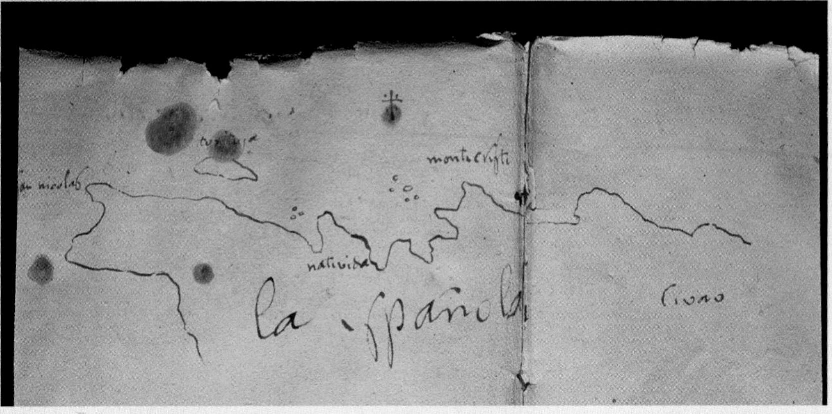

Columbus's map of Hispaniola. Would this small, vague sketch of Hispaniola (now Haiti and the Dominican Republic) have been of much use to explorers after Columbus? *(Col. Duke of Alba, Madrid/Institut Amatller d'Art Hispanic)*

would believe it. If one asks for anything they have they never say no. On the contrary, they offer a share to anyone with demonstrations of heartfelt affection, and they are immediately content with any small thing, valuable or valueless, that is given them. I forbade the men to give them bits of broken crockery, fragments of glass or tags of laces, though if they could get them they fancied them the finest jewels in the world.

I hoped to win them to the love and service of their Highnesses and of the whole Spanish nation and to persuade them to collect and give us of the things which they possessed in abundance and which we needed. They have no religion and are not idolaters; but all believe that power and goodness dwell in the sky and they are firmly convinced that I have come from the sky with these ships and people. In this belief they gave me a good reception everywhere, once they had overcome their fear; and this is not because they are stupid—far from it, they are men of great intelligence, for they navigate all those seas, and give a marvellously good account of everything—but because they have never before seen men clothed or ships like these. . . .

In all these islands the men are seemingly content with one woman, but their chief or king is allowed more than twenty. The women appear to work more than the men and I have not been able to find out if they have private property. As far as I could see whatever a man had was shared among all the rest and this particularly applies to food. . . . In another island, which I am told is larger than Hispaniola, the people have no hair. Here there is a vast quantity of gold, and from here and the other islands I bring Indians as evidence.

In conclusion, to speak only of the results of this very hasty voyage, their Highnesses can see that I will give them as much gold as they require, if they will render me some very slight assistance; also I will give them all the spices and cotton they want. . . . I will also bring them as much aloes as they ask and as many slaves, who will be taken from the idolaters. I believe also that I have found rhubarb and cinnamon and there will be countless other things in addition. . . .

So all Christendom will be delighted that our Redeemer has given victory to our most illustrious King and Queen and their renowned kingdoms, in this great matter. They should hold great celebrations and render solemn thanks to the Holy Trinity with many solemn prayers, for the great triumph which they will have, by the conversion of so many peoples to our holy faith and for the temporal benefits which will follow, for not only Spain, but all Christendom will receive encouragement and profit.

This is a brief account of the facts.

Written in the caravel off the Canary Islands.[||]

15 February 1493

At your orders
THE ADMIRAL

## QUESTIONS FOR ANALYSIS

1. How did Columbus explain the success of his voyage?
2. What was Columbus's view of the native Americans he met?
3. Evaluate his statements that the Caribbean islands possessed gold, cotton, and spices.
4. Why did Columbus cling to the idea that he had reached Asia?

[||]Actually, Columbus was off Santa Maria in the Azores.

*Source:* J. M. Cohen, ed. and trans., *The Four Voyages of Christopher Columbus* (Penguin Classics, 1958), pp. 115–123. 

Peter the Great's magnificent new crown, created for his coronation in 1682 with his half-brother Ivan. *(State Historical-Cultural Museum, Kremlin, Moscow)*

CHAPTER

# 17 ABSOLUTISM AND CONSTITUTIONALISM IN EUROPE, CA 1589–1725

## CHAPTER OUTLINE

- France: The Model of Absolute Monarchy
- The Decline of Absolutist Spain in the Seventeenth Century
- Absolutism in Eastern Europe: Austria, Prussia, and Russia
- England: The Triumph of Constitutional Monarchy
- The Dutch Republic in the Seventeenth Century

The seventeenth century in Europe was an age of intense conflict and crisis. The crisis had many causes, but the era's almost continuous savage warfare was probably the most important factor. War drove governments to build enormous armies and levy ever higher taxes on an already hard-pressed, predominately peasant population. Deteriorating economic conditions also played a major role. Europe as a whole experienced an unusually cold and wet climate over many years—a "little ice age" that brought small harvests, periodic food shortages, and even starvation. Not least, the combination of war, increased taxation, and economic suffering triggered social unrest and widespread peasant revolts, which were both a cause and an effect of profound dislocation.

The many-sided crisis of the seventeenth century posed a grave challenge to European governments: how were they to maintain order? The most common response of monarchical governments was to seek more power to deal with the problems and the threats that they perceived. Thus at the same time that powerful governments were emerging and evolving in Asia—such as the Qing Dynasty in China, the Tokugawa Shogunate in Japan, and the Mughal Empire in India—European rulers generally sought to attain *absolute,* or complete, power and build absolutist states. Under **absolutism** monarchs regulated religious sects and abolished the liberties long held by certain areas, groups, or provinces. Absolutist rulers also created new state bureaucracies to enhance their power and to direct the economic life of the country in the interest of the monarch. Above all, monarchs fought to free themselves from the restrictions of custom, competing institutions, and powerful social groups. In doing so, they sought freedom from the nobility and from traditional representative bodies—most commonly known as Estates or Parliament—that were usually dominated by the nobility.

The monarchical demand for freedom of action upset the status quo and led to bitter political battles. Nobles and townspeople sought to maintain their traditional rights, claiming that monarchs could not rule at will but rather had to respect representative bodies and follow established constitutional practices. Thus opponents of absolutism argued for **constitutionalism**—the limitation of the state by law. In seventeenth-century Europe, however, advocates of constitutionalism generally lost out, and would-be absolutists triumphed in most countries.

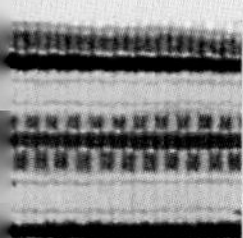

Thus in the period between roughly 1589 and 1725 two basic patterns of government emerged in Europe: absolute monarchy and the constitutional state. Almost all subsequent governments in the West have been modeled on one of these patterns, which have also influenced greatly the rest of the world in the past three centuries.

- How and why did Louis XIV of France lead the way in forging the absolute state?
- How did Austrian, Prussian, and Russian rulers in eastern Europe build absolute monarchies—monarchies that proved even more durable than that of Louis XIV?
- How did the absolute monarchs' interaction with artists, architects, and writers contribute to the splendid cultural achievements of both western and eastern Europe in this period?
- How and why did the constitutional state triumph in Holland and England?

This chapter will explore these questions.

## FRANCE: THE MODEL OF ABSOLUTE MONARCHY

France had a long history of unifying and centralizing monarchy, although the actual power and effectiveness of the French kings had varied enormously over time. Passing through a time of troubles and civil war after the death of Henry II in 1559, both France and the monarchy recovered under Henry IV and Cardinal Richelieu in the early seventeenth century. They laid the foundations for fully developed French absolutism under the "Great Monarch," Louis XIV. Providing inspiration for rulers all across Europe, Louis XIV and the mighty machine he fashioned deserve special attention.

### The Foundations of French Absolutism

Henry IV, the ingenious Huguenot-turned-Catholic, ended the French religious wars with the Edict of Nantes in 1598 (see page 482). The first of the Bourbon dynasty, Henry IV and his great minister Maximilian de Béthune, duke of Sully (1560–1641), then laid the foundations of later French absolutism.

Henry denied influence on the royal council to the nobility, which had harassed the countryside for half a century. Maintaining that "if we are without compassion for the people, they must succumb and we all perish with them," Henry also lowered taxes paid by the overburdened peasantry. Sully reduced the crushing royal debt accumulated during the era of religious conflict, encouraged French trade, and started a countrywide highway system. Within twelve years Henry IV and his minister had restored public order in France and laid the foundation for economic prosperity. Unfortunately, the murder of Henry IV in 1610 by a crazed fanatic led to a severe crisis.

After the death of Henry IV, the queen-regent Marie de' Medici led the government for the child-king Louis XIII (r. 1610–1643), but feudal nobles and princes of the blood dominated the political scene. In 1624 Marie de' Medici secured the appointment of Armand Jean du Plessis—Cardinal Richelieu (1585–1642)—to the council of ministers. It was a remarkable appointment. The next year Richelieu became president of the council, and after 1628 he was first minister of the French crown. Richelieu used his strong influence over King Louis XIII to exalt the French monarchy as the embodiment of the French state.

Richelieu's aim was the total subordination of all groups, individuals, and institutions to the monarchy. He ruthlessly crushed conspiracies staged by the nobility—long the greatest threat to the centralizing efforts of the monarchy—and refused to call the Estates General, which was dominated by the nobility. To impose monarchical policy in the provinces, he installed royal commissioners (*intendants*) in charge of each of France's thirty-two districts. Members of the upper middle class or minor nobility, they owed their position to the king; they had the power to "decide, order, and execute all they see good to do." They recruited soldiers for the army, collected taxes, kept tabs on the local nobility, administered the law, and regulated the local economy. Finally, Richelieu broke the power of Protestantism, which had often served as a cloak for the political ambitions of the nobles. After the Huguenot revolt of 1625 was suppressed, Richelieu abolished fortified cities. No longer would Huguenots have the means to be an independent party.

French foreign policy under Richelieu was aimed at the destruction of the fence of Habsburg territories that surrounded France. Consequently, in the Thirty Years' War Richelieu supported the Habsburgs' enemies, like the Lutheran king Gustavus Adolphus (see page 487). French influence became an important factor in the political future of the German Empire.

These new policies, especially war, cost money. Richelieu fully realized the need for greater revenues through increased taxation. But seventeenth-century France remained "a collection of local economies and local societies dominated by local elites." The rights of assemblies

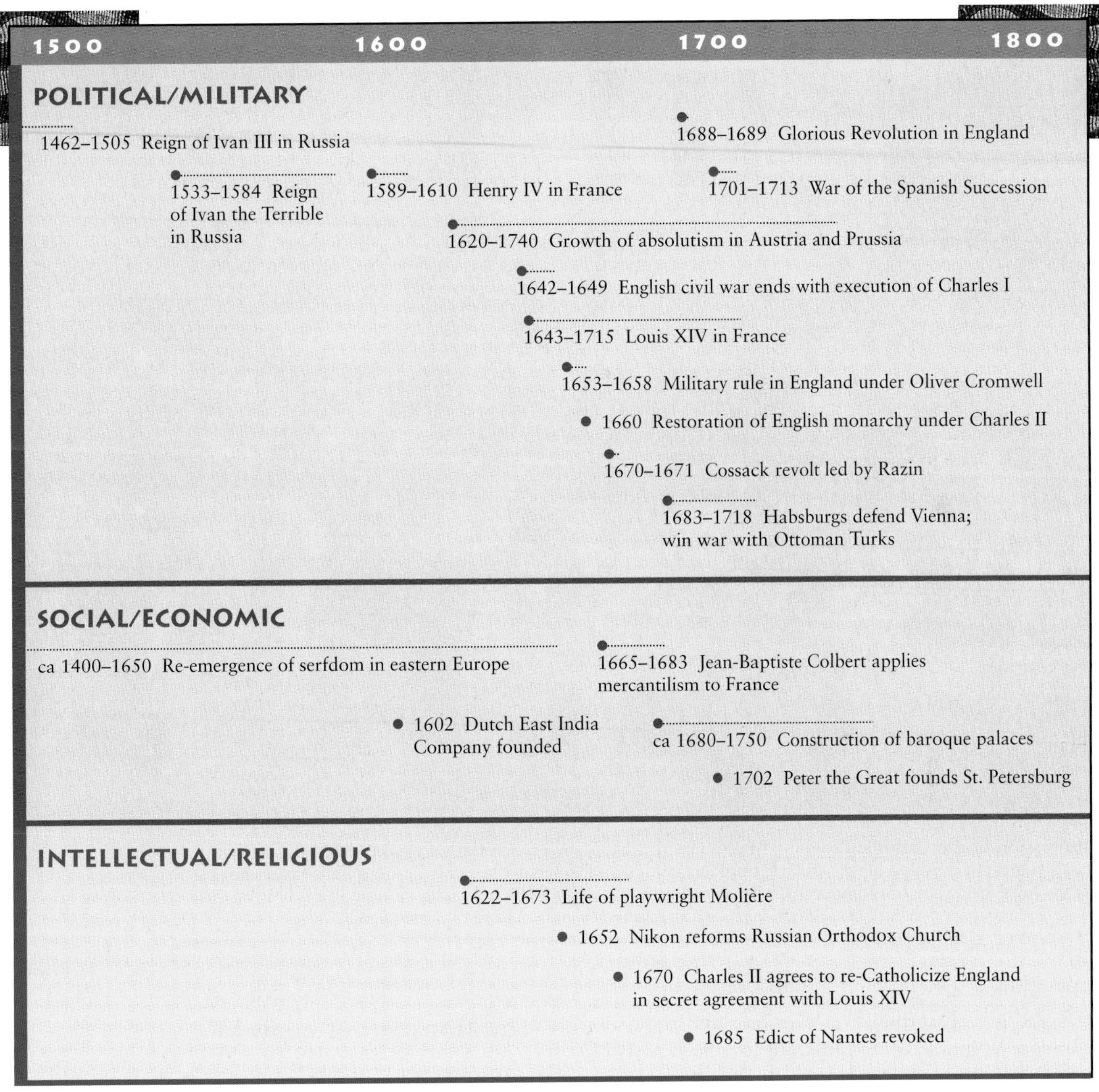


in some provinces to vote their own taxes; the hereditary exemption from taxation of many wealthy members of the nobility and the middle class; and the royal pension system drastically limited the government's power to tax. Richelieu—and later Louis XIV—temporarily solved his financial problems by securing the cooperation of local elites. Even in France royal absolutism was restrained by its need to compromise with the financial interests of well-entrenched groups.[1]

Richelieu persuaded Louis XIII to appoint his protégé Jules Mazarin (1602–1661) as his successor. Governing for the child-king Louis XIV, Mazarin became the dominant power in the government. He continued the centralizing policies of Richelieu, but in 1648 his unpopular attempts to increase royal revenues and expand the state bureaucracy resulted in a widespread rebellion known as the **Fronde.** Bitter civil war ensued between the monarchy and the opposition, led by the nobility and middle

**Procession of the Catholic League** In response to what many French Catholics considered the monarchy's laxness in crushing heresy, nobles, burghers, and friars formed groups or leagues to fight Protestantism at the local level. The resulting chaos, with armed private citizens indiscriminately firing guns, is illustrated in this scene, probably in Paris. *(Musée des Beaux-Arts, Valenciennes/Giraudon/Art Resource, NY)*

class. Riots and turmoil wracked Paris and the nation. Violence continued intermittently for the next twelve years.

Conflicts during the Fronde had a traumatic effect on the young Louis XIV. The king and his mother were frequently threatened and sometimes treated as prisoners by aristocratic factions. This period formed the cornerstone of Louis's political education and of his conviction that the sole alternative to anarchy was to concentrate as much power as possible in his own hands. Yet Louis XIV also realized that he would have to compromise with the bureaucrats and social elites who controlled local institutions and constituted the state bureaucracy. And he did so.

## The Monarchy of Louis XIV

In the reign of Louis XIV (1643–1715), the longest in European history, the French monarchy reached the peak of its absolutist development. In the magnificence of his court, in the brilliance of the culture over which he presided and which permeated all of Europe, and in his remarkably long life, the "Sun King" dominated his age. It was said that when Louis sneezed, all Europe caught cold.

Born in 1638, king at the age of five, Louis entered into personal, or independent, rule in 1661. Always a devout Catholic, Louis believed that God had established kings as his rulers on earth. The royal coronation conse-

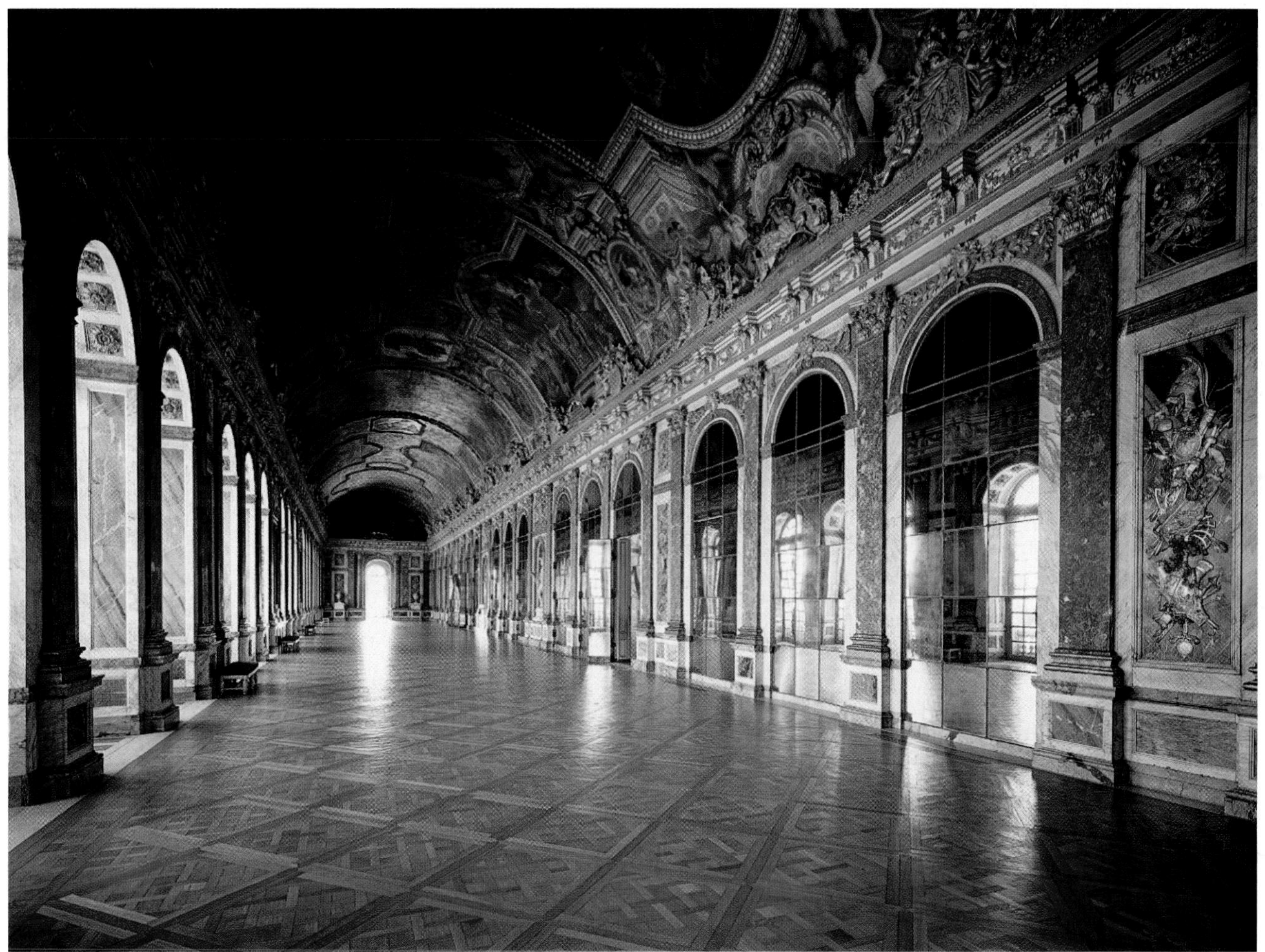

**Hall of Mirrors, Versailles** The grandeur and elegance of the Sun King's reign are reflected in the Hall of Mirrors, where the king's victories were celebrated in paintings on the domed ceiling. Hundreds of candles lit up the dome. *(Michael Holford)*

crated Louis to God's service, and he was certain that although kings were a race apart, they had to obey God's laws and rule for the good of the people.

Louis's education was more practical than formal. He learned statecraft by direct experience. The misery he suffered during the Fronde gave him an eternal distrust of the nobility and a profound sense of his own isolation. Accordingly, silence, caution, and secrecy became political tools for the achievement of his goals. His characteristic answer to requests of all kinds became the enigmatic *"Je verrai"* (I shall see).

Louis XIV installed his royal court at Versailles, an old hunting lodge ten miles from Paris. His architects, Le Nôtre and Le Vau, turned what the duke of Saint-Simon called "the most dismal and thankless of sights" into a veritable paradise. Louis XIV required all the great nobility of France—at the peril of social, political, and sometimes economic disaster—to live at Versailles for at least part of the year. Versailles became a model of rational order, the center of France, and the perfect symbol of the king's power. In the gigantic Hall of Mirrors hundreds of candles illuminated the domed ceiling, where allegorical paintings celebrated the king's victories. Louis skillfully used the art and architecture of Versailles to overawe his subjects and visitors and reinforce his power. (See the feature "Listening to the Past: The Court at Versailles" on pages 566–567.) Many monarchs subsequently imitated Louis XIV's example, and French became the language of diplomatic exchange and of royal courts all across Europe.

Historians have often said that Louis XIV was able to control completely the nobility, which historically had opposed the centralizing goals of the French monarchy. The duke of Saint-Simon, a high-ranking noble and fierce critic of the king, wrote in his memoirs that Louis XIV

*reduced everyone to subjection, and brought to his court those very persons he cared least about. Whoever was old enough to serve did not dare demur. It was still another device to ruin the nobles by accustoming them to equality and forcing them to mingle with everyone indiscriminately.*[2]

As Saint-Simon suggests, the king did use court ceremonial to curb the great nobility. By excluding the highest nobles from his councils, he also weakened their ancient right to advise the king and to participate in government. They became mere instruments of policy, their time and attention occupied with operas, balls, gossip, and trivia.

Recent research, however, has suggested that Louis XIV actually secured the active collaboration of the nobility. For example, Louis persuaded the nobles of Languedoc to support an ambitious canal project, with increased taxation, in return for royal support of local industries and oppressive measures against Huguenots in the region. Thus Louis separated power from status and grandeur at Versailles: he secured the nobles' cooperation, and the nobility enjoyed their status and the grandeur in which they lived. The nobility agreed to participate in projects that both exalted the monarchy and reinforced their own ancient aristocratic prestige. Thus French government in the seventeenth century rested on a social and political structure in which the nobility continued to exercise great influence.[3]

In day-to-day government Louis utilized several councils of state, which he personally attended, and the intendants, who acted for the councils throughout France. A stream of questions and instructions flowed between local districts and Versailles, and under Louis XIV a uniform and centralized administration was imposed on the country. The councilors of state came from the upper middle class or from the recently ennobled, who were popularly known as "nobility of the robe" (because of the long judicial robes many of them wore). These ambitious professional bureaucrats served the state in the person of the king.

Throughout Louis's long reign and despite increasing financial problems, he never called a meeting of the Estates General. Thus his critics had no means of united action. French government remained highly structured, bureaucratic, centered at Versailles, and responsible to Louis XIV.

## Economic Management and Religious Policy

Louis XIV's bureaucracy, court, and army cost a great amount of money, and the French method of collecting taxes consistently failed to produce the necessary revenue. An old agreement between the Crown and the nobility permitted the king to tax the common people if he did not tax the nobles. The nobility thereby relinquished a role in government: since nobles did not pay taxes, they could not legitimately claim a say in how taxes were spent. Because many among the rich and prosperous classes were exempt, the tax burden fell heavily on those least able to pay: the poor peasants.

The king named Jean-Baptiste Colbert (1619–1683), the son of a wealthy merchant-financier, as controller general of finances. Colbert came to manage the entire royal administration and proved himself a financial genius. His central principle was that the French economy should serve the state, and he rigorously applied to France the system called mercantilism.

**Mercantilism** is a collection of government policies for the regulation of economic activities, especially commercial activities, by and for the state. In the seventeenth and eighteenth centuries a nation's international power was thought to be based on its wealth—specifically on the gold so necessary for fighting wars. To accumulate gold, economic theory suggested, a country should always sell more goods abroad than it bought. Colbert insisted that France should be self-sufficient, able to produce within its borders everything needed by the subjects of the French king. If France were self-sufficient, the outflow of gold would be halted, debtor states would pay in bullion, and, with the wealth of the nation increased, France's power and prestige would be enhanced.

Colbert attempted to accomplish self-sufficiency through state support for both old industries and newly created ones. New factories in Paris manufactured mirrors to replace Venetian imports, for example. To ensure a high-quality finished product, Colbert set up a system of state inspection and regulation. He compelled all craftsmen to organize into guilds, and he encouraged skilled foreign craftsmen and manufacturers to immigrate to France. To improve communications, he built roads and canals. To protect French products, he placed high tariffs on foreign goods. His most important accomplishment was the creation of a powerful merchant marine to transport

French goods. This merchant marine would then closely connect France with its colonial holdings in North America. Colbert tried to organize and regulate the entire French economy for the glory of the French state as embodied in the king.

Colbert's achievement in the development of manufacturing was prodigious. The commercial classes prospered, and between 1660 and 1700 their position steadily improved. The national economy, however, rested on agriculture. Although French peasants were not serfs, as were the peasants of eastern Europe, they were mercilessly taxed. After 1685 other hardships afflicted them: savage warfare, poor harvests, continuing deflation of the currency, and fluctuation in the price of grain. Many peasants emigrated. A totally inadequate tax base and heavy expenditure for war in the later years of Louis's reign made Colbert's goals unattainable.

Economic policy was complicated in 1685 by Louis XIV's revocation of the Edict of Nantes. The new law ordered the destruction of churches, the closing of schools, the Catholic baptism of Huguenots, and the exile of Huguenot pastors who refused to renounce their faith. Why did Louis, by revoking the edict, persecute some of his most loyal and industrially skilled subjects?

Recent scholarship has convincingly shown that Louis XIV was basically tolerant. He insisted on religious unity not for religious but for political reasons. His goal was "one king, one law, one faith." He hated division within the realm and insisted that religious unity was essential to his royal dignity and to the security of the state. Thus after permitting religious liberty in the early years of his reign, Louis finally decided to crack down on Protestants.

Although France's large Catholic majority applauded Louis XIV, writers in the eighteenth century and later damned him for intolerance and for the adverse impact that revocation of the Edict of Nantes had on the economy and foreign affairs. They claimed that tens of thousands of Huguenot craftsmen, soldiers, and business

**The Spider and the Fly** In reference to the insect symbolism (*upper left*), the caption on the lower left side of this illustration states, "The noble is the spider, the peasant the fly." The other caption (*upper right*) notes, "The more people have, the more they want. The poor man brings everything—wheat, fruit, money, vegetables. The greedy lord sitting there ready to take everything will not even give him the favor of a glance." This satirical print summarizes peasant grievances. *(New York Public Library)*

people emigrated, depriving France of their skills and tax revenues and carrying their bitterness to Holland, England, and Prussia. Although the claims of economic damage were exaggerated, the revocation certainly aggravated Protestant hatred for Louis and for his armies.

## French Classicism

Artists and writers of the age of Louis XIV deliberately imitated the subject matter and style of classical antiquity, for which their work is called **French classicism.** French art of this period possesses the classical qualities of discipline, balance, and restraint. The principles of absolutism molded these artistic ideals. Individualism was not allowed, and artists glorified the state, personified by the king. Precise rules governed all aspects of culture.

Contemporaries said that Louis never ceased playing the role of grand monarch on the stage of his court, and he used music and theater as a backdrop for court ceremonial. He favored the works of Jean-Baptiste Lully (1632–1687), whose orchestral works, ballets, and operatic productions attained wide influence. French classicism also achieved heights in plays, an art form the king loved. Playwright, stage manager, director, and actor Jean-Baptiste Poquelin, known as Molière (1622–1673), produced satirical comedies that exposed the hypocrisies and follies of society, being careful to attack only the bourgeoisie and never the nobility. One of his contemporaries, Jean Racine (1639–1699), wrote restrained, balanced tragedies that used classical settings to explore the power of love and the conflict of good and evil.

## The Wars of Louis XIV

Visualizing himself as a great military hero, Louis XIV used almost endless war to exalt himself above the other rulers of Europe. His secretary of war created a professional army, which was modern in the sense that the French state, rather than nobles, employed the soldiers. The army was equipped with standardized weapons and uniforms. With this new military machine, one national state, France, was able to dominate the politics of Europe for the first time.

In 1667 Louis used a dynastic excuse to invade Flanders, part of the Spanish Netherlands, and Franche-Comté. He gained twelve towns, including important commercial centers (see Map 17.1). Another war gained him more Flemish towns and all of Franche-Comté, and

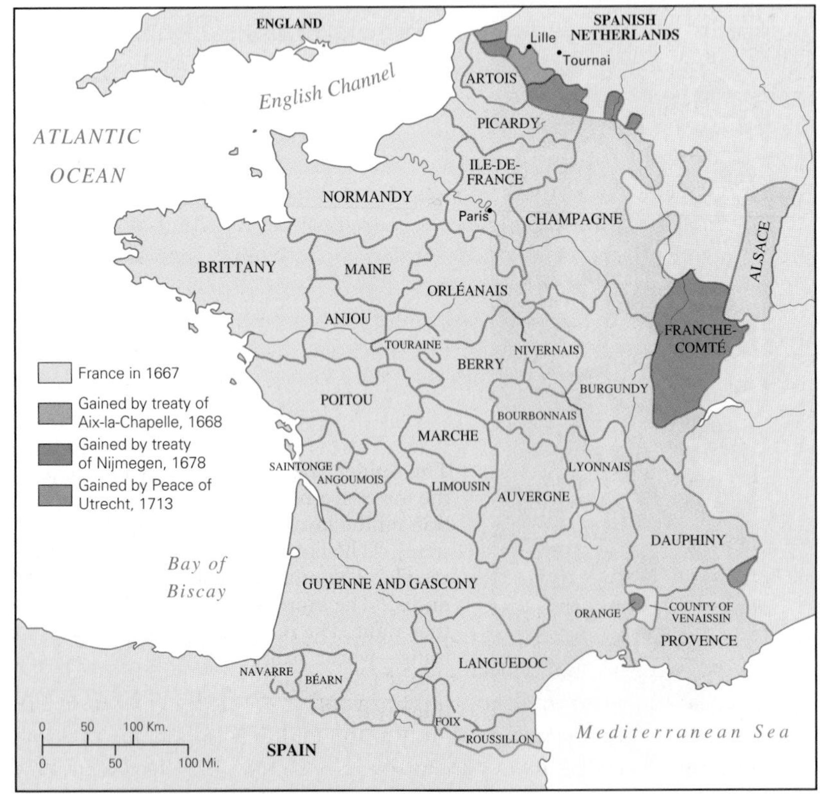


**MAP 17.1 The Acquisitions of Louis XIV, 1668–1713** The desire for glory and the weakness of his German neighbors encouraged Louis's expansionist policy, but he paid a high price for his acquisitions.

in 1681 he seized the city of Strasbourg. After that victory Louis's military fortunes faded. The wars of the 1680s and 1690s brought no new territorial gains. The Habsburg emperor; the kings of England, Spain, and Sweden; and the electors of Bavaria, Saxony, and the Palatinate united against Louis in the League of Augsburg to check his advance. By the end of the War of the League of Augsburg, fought to a draw, France was financially exhausted.

At the same time a series of bad harvests between 1688 and 1694 brought catastrophe. Cold, wet summers reduced the harvests by an estimated one-third to two-thirds, and in many provinces the death rate rose to several times the normal figure. Rising grain prices, new taxes, a slump in manufacturing, and the constant nuisance of pillaging troops—all these meant great suffering for the French people. France wanted peace at any price. Louis XIV granted a respite for five years while he prepared for the conflict later known as the War of the Spanish Succession.

This struggle (1701–1713) involved the dynastic question of the succession to the Spanish throne. When Charles II (r. 1665–1700) died in 1700, his will left the Spanish crown and the worldwide Spanish Empire to Philip of Anjou, Louis XIV's grandson. By accepting this will, Louis obviously would gain power in Spain; he would also be reneging on an earlier treaty to divide the vast Spanish possessions between himself and the Holy Roman emperor. He accepted the will, thereby provoking a great war.

The Dutch and the English would not accept French acquisition of the Spanish Netherlands and of the rich trade with the Spanish colonies, which would make France too strong in Europe and in North America. Thus in 1701 they joined with the Austrians and Prussians in the Grand Alliance. In the ensuing series of conflicts, Louis suffered major defeats and finally sued for peace.

The war was concluded at Utrecht in 1713, where the principle of partition was applied. Louis's grandson Philip remained the first Bourbon king of Spain on the understanding that the French and Spanish crowns would never be united. France surrendered Newfoundland, Nova Scotia, and the Hudson Bay territory to England, which also acquired Gibraltar, Minorca, and control of the African slave trade from Spain. The Dutch gained little because Austria received the former Spanish Netherlands (see Map 17.2).

The **Peace of Utrecht** represented the balance-of-power principle in operation, setting limits on the extent to which any one power, in this case France, could expand. The treaty completed the decline of Spain as a Great Power. It expanded the British Empire. The Peace of Utrecht also marked the end of French expansionist policy. In Louis's thirty-five-year quest for military glory, his main territorial acquisition after 1678 was Strasbourg. Even revisionist historians sympathetic to Louis acknowledge "that the widespread misery in France during the period was in part due to royal policies, especially the incessant wars."[4] The news of Louis's death in 1715 brought rejoicing throughout France.

## The Decline of Absolutist Spain in the Seventeenth Century

Spanish absolutism and greatness had preceded that of the French. In the sixteenth century Spain (or, more precisely, the kingdom of Castile) had developed the standard features of absolute monarchy: a permanent professional bureaucracy, a standing army, and national taxes that fell most heavily on the poor. Spanish absolutism was based on silver bullion extracted from its colonial possessions, especially Peru. But by the 1590s the seeds of disaster were sprouting, and in the seventeenth century Spain experienced a steady decline. The lack of a strong middle class, agricultural crisis and population decline, failure to invest in productive enterprises, intellectual isolation and psychological malaise—by 1715 all combined to reduce Spain to a second-rate power.

The fabulous flow of silver from Mexico and Peru had led Philip II to assume the role of defender of Roman Catholicism in Europe (see page 484). But when the "Invincible Armada" went down in 1588, a century of Spanish pride and power went with it. After 1590 a spirit of defeatism and disillusionment crippled most reform efforts.

Philip II's Catholic crusade had been financed by the revenues of the Spanish-Atlantic economy. In the early seventeenth century the Dutch and English began to trade with the Spanish colonies, and Mexico and Peru developed local industries. Between 1610 and 1650 Spanish trade with the colonies fell 60 percent, and the American silver lodes started to run dry. Yet in Madrid royal expenditures remained high. The result was chronic deficits and frequent cancellations of Spain's national debt. These brutal cancellations—a form of bankruptcy—shook public confidence in the state.

Spain, in contrast to the other countries of western Europe, developed only a tiny middle class. Public opinion, taking its cue from the aristocracy, condemned moneymaking as vulgar and undignified. Those with influence

**MAP 17.2 Europe in 1715** The series of treaties commonly called the Peace of Utrecht (April 1713–November 1715) ended the War of the Spanish Succession and redrew the map of Europe. A French Bourbon king succeeded to the Spanish throne on the understanding that the French not attempt to unite the French and Spanish crowns. France surrendered to Austria the Spanish Netherlands (later Belgium), then in French hands, and France recognized the Hohenzollern rulers of Prussia. Spain ceded Gibraltar to Great Britain, for which it has been a strategic naval station ever since. Spain also granted to Britain the *asiento,* the contract for supplying African slaves to America.

or connections sought titles of nobility and social prestige, or they became priests, monks, and nuns. The flood of gold and silver had produced severe inflation, and many businessmen found so many obstacles in the way of profitable enterprise that they simply gave up. The expulsion of the Jews and Moors had also deprived Spanish society of a significant proportion of middle-class people.

Spanish aristocrats, attempting to maintain an extravagant lifestyle that they could no longer afford, increased the rents on their estates. High rents and heavy taxes in turn drove the peasants from the land. Agricultural production suffered, and the peasants departed for the large cities, where they swelled the ranks of beggars.

Their most Catholic majesties, the kings of Spain, had no solutions to these dire problems. Philip IV (r. 1622–1665) left the management of his several kingdoms to Count Olivares. An able administrator, the count devised new sources of revenue, but he clung to the grandiose belief that the solution to Spain's difficulties rested in a return to the imperial tradition. Unfortunately, the imperial tradition demanded the revival of war with the Dutch in 1622 and a long war with France over Mantua (1628–1659). These conflicts, on top of an empty treasury, brought disaster. The Treaty of the Pyrenees of 1659, which ended the French-Spanish wars, compelled Spain to surrender extensive territories to France. After this treaty, Spain's decline as a Great Power became irreversible.

In the brilliant novel ***Don Quixote,*** the Spanish writer Miguel de Cervantes (1547–1616) produced one of the masterpieces of world literature. *Don Quixote* delineates the whole fabric of sixteenth-century Spanish society. The main character, Don Quixote, lives in a dream world, traveling about the countryside seeking military glory. A leading scholar wrote, "The Spaniard convinced himself that reality was what he felt, believed, imagined. He filled the world with heroic reverberations. Don Quixote was born and grew."[5]

## ABSOLUTISM IN EASTERN EUROPE: AUSTRIA, PRUSSIA, AND RUSSIA

The rulers of eastern Europe also labored to build strong absolutist states in the seventeenth century. But they built on social and economic foundations different from those in western Europe. These foundations were laid between 1400 and 1650, when the princes and the landed nobility of eastern Europe rolled back the gains made by the peasantry during the High Middle Ages and reimposed serfdom on the rural masses. The nobility also enhanced its power as the primary social force by reducing the importance of the towns and the middle classes.

Despite the strength of the nobility, strong kings did begin to emerge in many eastern European lands in the course of the seventeenth century. There were endless wars, and in this atmosphere of continuous military emergency monarchs found ways to reduce the political power of the landlord nobility. Cautiously leaving the nobles the unchallenged masters of their peasants, eastern monarchs gradually monopolized political power in three key areas. They taxed without consent; maintained permanent standing armies, which policed their subjects in addition to fighting abroad; and conducted relations with other states as they pleased.

There were important variations on the absolutist theme in eastern Europe. The royal absolutism created in Prussia was stronger and more effective than that established in Austria. As for Russia, it developed its own form of absolutism, which was quite different from that of France or even Prussia.

### Lords and Peasants

Lords and peasants were the basic social groups in eastern Europe, a vast region including Bohemia, Silesia, Hungary, eastern Germany, Poland, Lithuania, and Russia. Peasants in eastern Europe had done relatively well in the period from roughly 1050 to 1300, a time of gradual economic expansion and population growth. Eager to attract German settlers to their sparsely populated lands, the rulers and nobles of eastern Europe had offered potential newcomers economic and legal incentives. Large numbers of incoming settlers had obtained land on excellent terms and gained much personal freedom. These benefits were gradually extended to the local Slavic populations, even those of central Russia. Thus by 1300 serfdom had all but disappeared in eastern Europe. Peasants were able to bargain freely with their landlords and move about as they pleased.

After about 1300, however, as Europe's population and economy declined grievously, mainly because of the Black Death, noble landlords sought to solve their tough economic problems by more heavily exploiting the peasantry. In western Europe this attempt generally failed, but in the vast region east of the Elbe River in Germany the landlords were successful in degrading peasants. By 1500 eastern peasants were on their way to becoming serfs again.

Eastern lords triumphed because they made their kings and princes issue laws that restricted the right of their

**Estonia in the 1660s** The Estonians were conquered by German military nobility in the Middle Ages and reduced to serfdom. The German-speaking nobles ruled the Estonian peasants with an iron hand, and Peter the Great reaffirmed their domination when Russia annexed Estonia (see Map 17.4 on page 553). *(Mansell/TimePix)*

peasants to move to take advantage of better opportunities elsewhere. In Prussian territories by 1500, the law required that runaway peasants be hunted down and returned to their lords, and a runaway servant was to be nailed to a post by one ear and given a knife to cut himself loose. Moreover, lords steadily took more and more of their peasants' land and arbitrarily imposed heavier and heavier labor obligations. By the early 1500s lords in many territories could command their peasants to work for them without pay for as many as six days a week.

The gradual erosion of the peasantry's economic position was bound up with manipulation of the legal system. The local lord was also the local prosecutor, judge, and jailer. There were no independent royal officials to provide justice or uphold the common law.

Between 1500 and 1650 the consolidation of serfdom in eastern Europe was accompanied by the growth of estate agriculture, particularly in Poland and eastern Germany. As economic expansion and population growth resumed after 1500, Eastern lords had powerful economic incentives to increase the production of their estates, and they succeeded in squeezing sizable surpluses out of the impoverished peasants. These surpluses were sold to foreign merchants, who exported them to the growing cities of wealthier western Europe.

The re-emergence of serfdom in eastern Europe in the early modern period was a momentous human development. Above all, it reflected the fact that eastern lords enjoyed much greater political power than their western counterparts. In the late Middle Ages, when much of eastern Europe was experiencing innumerable wars and general political chaos, the noble landlord class had greatly increased its political power at the expense of the ruling monarchs. Moreover, the Western concept and reality of sovereignty, as embodied in a king who protected the interests of all his people, were not well developed in eastern Europe before 1650.

Finally, with the approval of weak kings, the landlords systematically undermined the medieval privileges of the towns and the power of the urban classes. For example, eastern towns also lost their medieval right of refuge and were compelled to return runaways to their lords. The population of the towns and the urban middle classes declined greatly. This development both reflected and promoted the supremacy of noble landlords in most of eastern Europe in the sixteenth century.

## Austria and the Ottoman Turks

The Habsburgs of Austria emerged from the Thirty Years' War impoverished and exhausted. The effort to root out Protestantism in the German lands had failed, and the authority of the Holy Roman Empire and its emperors had declined drastically. Yet defeat in central Europe opened new vistas. The Habsburg monarchs were forced to turn inward and eastward in an attempt to fuse their diverse holdings into a strong, unified state.

An important step in this direction had actually been taken in Bohemia during the Thirty Years' War. Protestantism had been strong among the Czechs, a Slavic people concentrated in Bohemia. In 1618 the Czech nobles who controlled the Bohemian Estates—the representative body of the different legal orders—had risen up against their Habsburg king. This revolt was crushed, and then the Czech nobility was totally restructured to ensure its loyalty to the monarchy. The condition of the enserfed peasantry worsened, Protestantism was stamped out, and religious unity began to emerge. The reorganization of Bohemia was a giant step toward royal absolutism.

After the Thirty Years' War, Ferdinand III (r. 1637–1657) centralized the government in the hereditary German-speaking provinces, most notably Austria, Styria, and the Tyrol. The king created a permanent standing army ready to put down any internal opposition. The Habsburg monarchy was then ready to turn toward the vast plains of Hungary, in opposition to the Ottoman Turks.

The Ottomans had come out of Anatolia, in present-day Turkey, to create one of history's greatest military empires. Their armies had almost captured Vienna in 1529, and for more than 150 years thereafter the Ottomans ruled all of the Balkan territories, almost all of Hungary, and part of southern Russia. In the late seventeenth century, under vigorous reforming leadership, the Ottoman Empire succeeded in marshaling its forces for one last mighty blow at Christian Europe. A huge Turkish army surrounded Vienna and laid siege to it in 1683. After holding out against great odds for two months, the city was relieved at the last minute, and the Ottomans were forced to retreat. The Habsburgs then conquered all of Hungary and Transylvania (part of present-day Romania) by 1699 (see Map 17.3).

The Turkish wars and this great expansion strengthened the Habsburg army and promoted some sense of unity in the Habsburg lands. But Habsburg efforts to create a fully developed, highly centralized, absolutist

**MAP 17.3 The Growth of Austria and Brandenburg-Prussia to 1748** Austria expanded to the southwest into Hungary and Transylvania at the expense of the Ottoman Empire. It was unable to hold the rich German province of Silesia, however, which was conquered by Brandenburg-Prussia.

state were only partly successful. The Habsburg state remained a composite of three separate and distinct territories: the old "hereditary provinces" of Austria, the kingdom of Bohemia, and the kingdom of Hungary. Each part had its own laws, culture, and political life, for the noble-dominated Estates continued to exist, though with reduced powers. Above all, the Hungarian nobility effectively thwarted the full development of Habsburg absolutism. Time and again throughout the seventeenth century, Hungarian nobles rose in revolt against the attempts of Vienna to impose absolute rule. They never triumphed decisively, but neither were they ever crushed.

The Hungarians resisted because many of them were Protestants, especially in the area long ruled by the more tolerant Turks, and they hated the heavy-handed attempts of the Habsburgs to re-Catholicize everyone. Moreover, the lords of Hungary were determined to maintain as much independence and local control as possible. Thus when the Habsburgs were bogged down in the War of the Spanish Succession (see page 545), the Hungarians rose in one last patriotic rebellion under Prince Francis Rákóczy in 1703. Rákóczy and his forces were eventually defeated, but this time the Habsburgs had to accept many of the traditional privileges of the Hungarian aristocracy in return for Hungarian acceptance of hereditary Habsburg rule. Thus Hungary, unlike Austria or Bohemia, never came close to being fully integrated into a centralized, absolute Habsburg state.

## The Emergence of Prussia

As the status of east German peasants declined steadily after 1400, local princes lost political power, and a revitalized landed nobility became the undisputed ruling class. The Hohenzollern family, which ruled through different branches as the electors of Brandenburg and the dukes of Prussia, were little more than the largest landowners in a landlord society. Nothing suggested that the Hohenzollerns and their territories would ever play an important role in European or even German affairs.

Brandenburg was a helpless spectator in the Thirty Years' War, its territory alternately ravaged by Swedish and Habsburg armies. Yet the country's devastation prepared the way for Hohenzollern absolutism, because foreign armies dramatically weakened the political power of the Estates. The weakening of the Estates helped the very talented young elector Frederick William (r. 1640–1688), later known as the "Great Elector," to ride roughshod over traditional constitutional liberties and to take a giant step toward royal absolutism.

When Frederick William came to power in 1640, the twenty-year-old ruler was determined to unify his three quite separate provinces and to add to them by diplomacy and war. These provinces were Brandenburg itself, the area around Berlin; Prussia, inherited in 1618 when the junior branch of the Hohenzollern family died out; and scattered holdings along the Rhine in western Germany (see Map 17.3). Each province was inhabited by Germans, but each had its own Estates.

The struggle between the Great Elector and the provincial Estates was long, complicated, and intense. After the Thirty Years' War the representatives of the nobility zealously defended the right of the Estates to vote taxes, but Frederick William eventually forced the Estates to accept permanent taxation without consent, in order to pay for the permanent standing army that the king first established in 1660. The soldiers doubled as tax collectors and policemen, becoming the core of the expanding state bureaucracy. The power of the Estates declined rapidly thereafter, and the Great Elector turned the screws of taxation. State revenue tripled and the size of the army leaped about tenfold during his reign.

In accounting for the Great Elector's fateful triumph, two factors appear central. First, as in the formation of every absolutist state, war was a decisive factor. The ongoing struggle between Sweden and Poland for control of the Baltic after 1648 and the wars of Louis XIV in western Europe created an atmosphere of permanent crisis. It was no accident that, except in commercially minded Holland, constitutionalism won out only in England, the only major country to escape devastating foreign invasions in the seventeenth century.

Second, the nobility had long dominated the government through the Estates, but only for its own narrow self-interest. When, therefore, the Great Elector reconfirmed the nobility's freedom from taxation and its unlimited control over the peasants in 1653 and after, the nobility accepted a self-serving compromise. While Frederick William reduced the nobility's political power, the bulk of the Great Elector's new taxes fell on towns, and royal authority stopped at the landlords' gates.

By the time of his death in 1688, the Great Elector had created a single state out of scattered principalities. But his new creation was still small and fragile. It was Frederick William I, the "Soldiers' King" (r. 1713–1740), who truly established Prussian absolutism and gave it its unique character. A dangerous psychoneurotic as well as a talented reformer, Frederick William I created the best army in Europe, for its size, and he infused military values into a whole society.

Frederick William's attachment to the army and military life was intensely emotional. He had, for example, a bizarre, almost pathological love for tall soldiers, whom he credited with superior strength and endurance. Like some fanatical modern-day basketball coach in search of a championship team, he sent his agents throughout both Prussia and all of Europe, tricking, buying, and kidnapping top recruits. Neighboring princes sent him their giants as gifts to win his gratitude. Prussian mothers told their sons, "Stop growing or the recruiting agents will get you."[6] Frederick William's love of the army was also based on a hardheaded conception of the struggle for power and a dog-eat-dog view of international politics. He never wavered in his conviction that the welfare of king and state depended above all else on the army.

As in France, the cult of military power provided the rationale for a great expansion of royal absolutism. As the ruthless king himself put it, "I must be served with life and limb, with house and wealth, with honour and conscience, everything must be committed except eternal salvation—that belongs to God, but all else is mine."[7] To make good these extraordinary demands, Frederick William created a strong and exceptionally honest bureaucracy, which administered the country and tried to develop it economically. The last traces of the parliamentary Estates and local self-government vanished.

The king's grab for power brought him into considerable conflict with the noble landowners, the Junkers. In the end the Prussian nobility responded to a combination of threats and opportunities and became the officer caste. By 1739 all but 5 of 245 officers with the rank of major or above were aristocrats. A new compromise had been worked out: the nobility imperiously commanded the peasantry in the army as well as on its estates.

Coarse and crude, penny-pinching and hard-working, Frederick William achieved results. Above all, he built a first-rate army out of third-rate resources. Twelfth in Europe in population, Prussia had the fourth-largest army by 1740, behind France, Russia, and Austria. Soldier for soldier the Prussian army became the best in Europe, astonishing foreign observers with its precision, skill, and discipline. Curiously, the king loved his "blue boys" so much that he hated to "spend" them. This most militaristic of kings was, paradoxically, almost always at peace.

Nevertheless, the Prussian people paid a heavy and lasting price for the obsessions of the royal drillmaster. Civil society became rigid and highly disciplined. Prussia became the "Sparta of the North"; unquestioning obedience was the highest virtue. As a Prussian minister later

**A Prussian Giant Grenadier** Frederick William I wanted tall, handsome soldiers. He dressed them in tight bright uniforms to distinguish them from the peasant population from which most soldiers came. He also ordered several portraits of his favorites from his court painter, J. C. Merk. Grenadiers wore the miter cap instead of an ordinary hat so that they could hurl their heavy grenades unimpeded by a broad brim. *(The Royal Collection © 2002, Her Majesty Queen Elizabeth II)*

summed up, "To keep quiet is the first civic duty."[8] Thus the absolutism of Frederick William I combined with harsh peasant bondage and Junker tyranny to lay the foundations for probably the most militaristic country of modern times.

## The Rise of Moscow

After the death of Prince Iaroslav the Wise in 1054, the Kievan state disintegrated into competing units until the Mongol conquest. Nomadic tribes from present-day Mongolia, the Mongols were temporarily unified in the thirteenth century by Chinggis Khan (1162–1227), one of history's greatest conquerors. In five years his armies subdued all of China (see Chapter 11). His successors then wheeled westward and reached the plains of Hungary before they pulled back in 1242. The Mongols ruled the eastern Slavs for more than two hundred years. They forced all the bickering Slavic princes to submit to their rule, and they were quick to punish rebellion with death and destruction.

Beginning with Alexander Nevsky in 1252, the previously insignificant princes of Moscow became particularly adept at serving the Mongols. They loyally put down popular uprisings and collected the khan's harsh taxes. By way of reward, the princes of Moscow emerged as hereditary great princes. Eventually the Muscovite princes were able to destroy their princely rivals and even to replace the khan as supreme ruler.

Ivan III (r. 1462–1505) completed the process of consolidating power around Moscow and won Novgorod, gaining access to the Baltic Sea (see Map 17.4). In his reign the prince of Moscow became an absolute ruler: the **tsar,** the Slavic word for "caesar." This imperious conception of absolute power was reinforced by two developments. In about 1480 Ivan III stopped acknowledging the Mongol khan as a supreme ruler, but he and his successors assimilated the Mongol concept of kingship as the exercise of unrestrained and unpredictable power. Moreover, after the fall of Constantinople to the Turks in 1453, the tsars saw themselves as the heirs of both the caesars and Orthodox Christianity, the one true faith. This idea was promoted by Orthodox clergy, who spoke of "holy Russia" as the "third Rome."

As the peasants had begun losing their freedom of movement in the fifteenth century, so had the nobles, or boyars, begun losing power and influence. After Ivan III conquered the principality of Novgorod in the 1480s, he seized much of the land for himself and distributed the remainder to members of a newly emerging service nobility, who held the tsar's land on the explicit condition that they serve in the tsar's army.

The rise of the new service nobility accelerated under Ivan IV (r. 1533–1584), the famous "Ivan the Terrible." Having ascended the throne at age three, Ivan suffered insults and neglect at the hands of the haughty boyars after his mother died. But at age sixteen he suddenly pushed aside his hated boyar advisers and soon declared war on the remnants of Mongol power. He defeated the faltering khanates of Kazan and Astrakhan between 1552 and 1556, adding vast new territories to Russia. In the course of these wars Ivan decreed that all nobles, old and new, had to serve the tsar in order to hold any land.

This transformation was completed in the second part of Ivan the Terrible's reign. In 1557 Ivan began an exhausting, unsuccessful twenty-five-year war primarily with the large Polish-Lithuanian state. Quarreling with the boyars, Ivan reduced the ancient Muscovite boyar families with a reign of terror and execution. Large estates were confiscated and reapportioned to the lower service nobility.

Ivan also took giant strides toward making all commoners servants of the tsar. As the service nobles demanded more from their peasants, more and more peasants fled toward the wild, recently conquered territories to the east and south. There they formed free groups and outlaw armies known as **Cossacks.** Ivan's solution to peasant flight was to complete the tying of the peasants to the land, making them serfs perpetually bound to serve the noble landholders.

In the time of Ivan the Terrible, urban traders and artisans were also bound to their towns and jobs so that the tsar could tax them more heavily. The urban classes had no security in their work or property and remained weak and divided. Even the wealthiest merchants were basically dependent agents of the tsar.

The death of the ironfisted tyrant ushered in an era of confusion and violent struggles for power. Events were particularly chaotic from 1598 to 1613, a period that is aptly called the Time of Troubles.

Close relatives of the deceased tsar intrigued against and murdered each other, alternately fighting and welcoming the invading Swedes and Poles, who even occupied Moscow. There was also a great social upheaval as Cossacks marched northward, rallying peasants and slaughtering nobles and officials. This social explosion from below brought the nobles to their senses. In 1613 they elected Ivan's sixteen-year-old grandnephew, Michael Romanov, the new hereditary tsar and rallied around him.

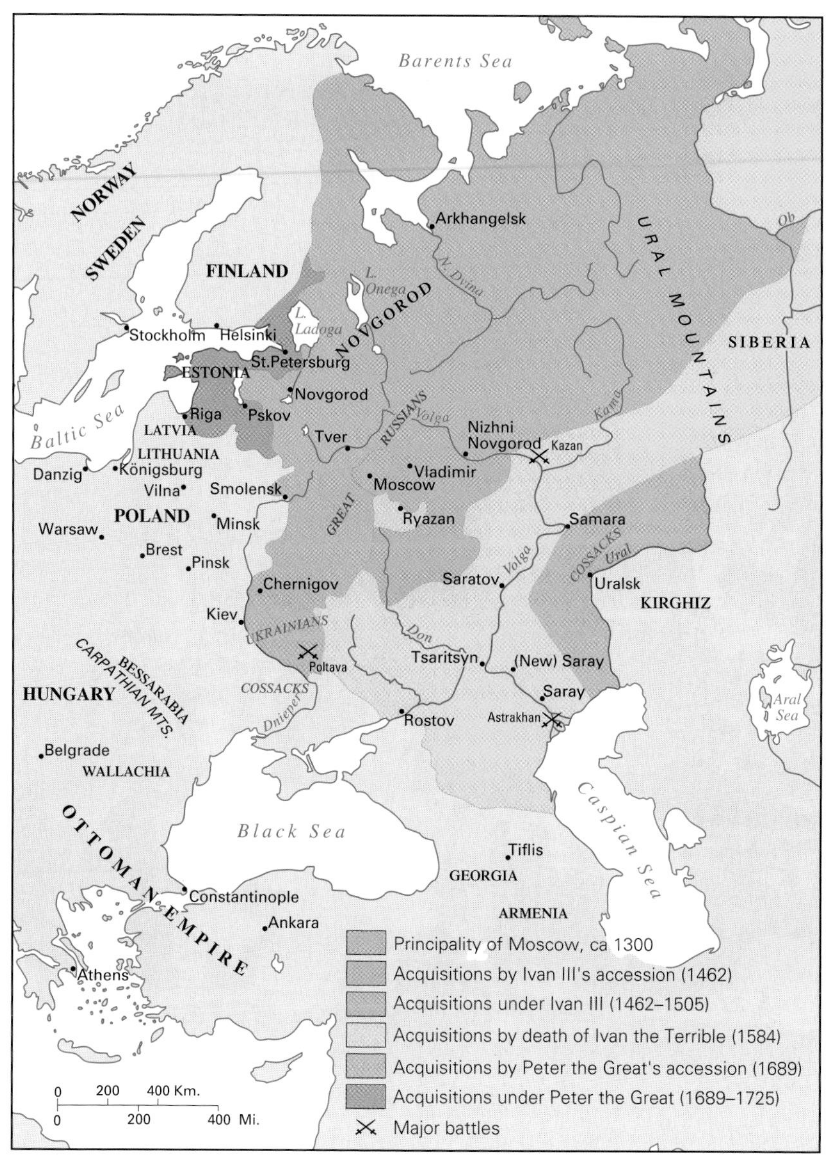


**MAP 17.4 The Expansion of Russia to 1725** After the disintegration of the Kievan state and the Mongol conquest, the princes of Moscow and their descendants gradually extended their rule over an enormous territory. Ivan the Terrible acquired more territory than Peter the Great.

Michael's reign saw the gradual re-establishment of tsarist autocracy. The recently rebellious peasants were ground down further, while Ivan's heavy military obligations on the nobility were relaxed considerably. The result was a second round of mass upheaval and protest.

In the mid-seventeenth century the unity of the Russian Orthodox church was torn apart by the religious reforms of the patriarch Nikon, a dogmatic purist who wished to bring "corrupted" Russian practices of worship into line with the Greek Orthodox model. The self-serving church hierarchy quickly went along, but the intensely religious common people resisted. Great numbers left the church and formed illegal communities of "Old Believers," who were hunted down and persecuted. The established church became totally dependent on the state for its authority.

Again the Cossacks revolted against the state, which was doggedly trying to catch up with them on the frontiers and reduce them to serfdom. Under the leadership of Stenka Razin they moved up the Volga River in 1670 and 1671, attracting a great undisciplined army of peasants, murdering landlords and high church officials, and proclaiming freedom from oppression. This rebellion

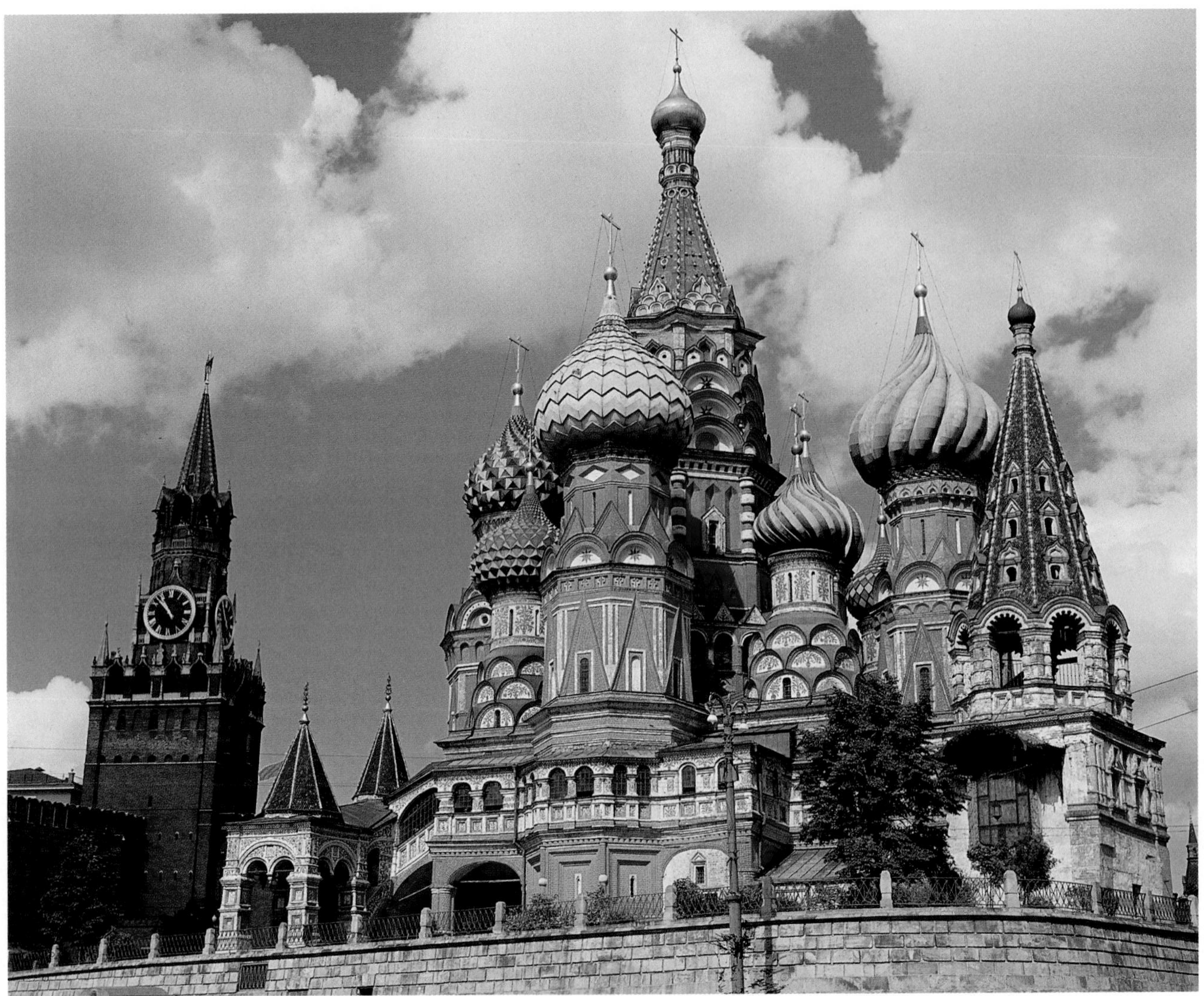

**Saint Basil's Cathedral, Moscow** With its sloping roofs and colorful onion-shaped domes, Saint Basil's is a striking example of powerful Byzantine influences on Russian culture. According to tradition, an enchanted Ivan the Terrible blinded the cathedral's architects to ensure that they would never duplicate their fantastic achievement, which still dazzles the beholder in today's Red Square. *(George Holton/Photo Researchers)*

was finally defeated by the government. (See the feature "Individuals in Society: Stenka Razin, Russian Rebel.") In response the thoroughly scared upper classes tightened the screws of serfdom even further.

## The Reforms of Peter the Great

It is now possible to understand the reforms of Peter the Great (r. 1682–1725) and his kind of monarchical absolutism. Contrary to some historians' assertions, Peter was interested primarily in military power and not in some grandiose westernization plan. A giant for his time, at six feet seven inches, and possessing enormous energy and determination, Peter was determined to increase Russia's power and to continue the territorial expansion that had gained a large part of Ukraine in 1667 and had completed the conquest of Siberia in the seventeenth century. Little wonder that the forty-three years of Peter's rule knew only one year of peace.

When Peter took full control in 1689, the heart of his part-time army still consisted of cavalry made up of boyars

# INDIVIDUALS IN SOCIETY

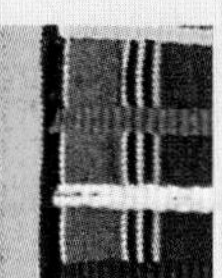

## STENKA RAZIN, RUSSIAN REBEL

The Don Cossack Stenka Razin led the largest peasant rebellion in Europe in the seventeenth century, a century rich in peasant revolt. Who was this Cossack leader who challenged Moscow, this outlaw who grew into a social revolutionary?

Descended from fugitives who fled to the turbulent southern frontier in search of freedom, Razin epitomized the old Cossack spirit of liberty and self-rule. Sharing the Cossack love of fighting and adventure, Razin also felt great sympathy for northern "have-nots" who had lost out and could not escape their fate. Why this was so remains a mystery. His family belonged to the Cossack establishment, which had settled the lower Don Valley long ago and received annual payments from the tsar in return for friendship and defense. One folk story tells of a hatred kindled by a Russian prince who unjustly hanged an older brother leading a Cossack detachment in Poland. True or not, rebel leaders like Razin have often come from comfortable backgrounds. As Paul Avrich notes, "Seldom have the oppressed themselves led the way, but rather those who have been aroused by their suffering and degradation."*

Whatever his motivation, Stenka Razin was a born leader. A striking personality with violent emotions, he was also shrewd and generous. He understood the lower classes and how to move them. The crowds called him a magician—a magician who hated the privileged and whom they felt compelled to follow.

Razin was a seasoned warrior of about forty years of age when in 1667 he led his first campaign. With an armed band of poor and rootless Cossacks, recent fugitives living upstream from the well-settled Cossacks, Razin sailed down the Volga River and seized a rich convoy of Russian merchant ships. He reportedly told survivors they were free to go or join him as free Cossacks. "I have come to fight only the boyars and the wealthy lords. As for the poor and the plain folk, I shall treat them as brothers."† Moving on to plunder Persian commerce on the Caspian Sea, Razin's forces returned home loaded with booty, which they divided equally according to Cossack custom. Gaining immense popularity and responding to threats from Moscow, Razin and his movement changed. The gang of outlaws became a rebel army.

In early 1670, Razin marched north with seven thousand Don Cossacks. His leaflets proclaimed that he was entering Russia "to establish the Cossack way, so that all men will be equal." Shrewdly blaming treacherous nobles and officials, and not the divinely appointed tsar, for the exploitation of the people, Razin's agents infiltrated the fortified towns along the Volga. Some towns resisted, but many threw open their gates, as the urban poor rose up against the "traitors and bloodsuckers." Peasants joined the revolt, killing lords and burning manor houses.

*Stenka Razin in Cossack dress, from a contemporary engraving.* (Novosti)

Frightened but unified, Russia's tiny elite mobilized all its strength. In late 1670, crack cavalry units of service nobility finally repulsed the swollen, ill-equipped army of the poor at Simbirsk on the upper Volga. The insurgents had to retreat. Fighting until the end, Razin was captured, hideously tortured, and chopped into pieces on the execution block. His followers and sympathizers were slaughtered with ferocious cruelty.

A fearless leader in the struggle against tsarist absolutism, Stenka Razin nurtured a myth of rebellion that would inspire future generations with dreams of freedom. He became Russia's most celebrated folk hero. He lived in story and song, an immortal superman who would someday ride out of the forest and deliver the people from oppression.

### QUESTIONS FOR ANALYSIS

1. What did Stenka Razin do? Why did his rebellion inspire future generations?
2. How would you interpret Razin? Was he a great hero, a common criminal, or something else?

*Paul Avrich, *Russian Rebels, 1600–1800* (New York: Schocken Books, 1972), p. 67. This account is based on Avrich's masterful study.

†Quoted ibid., p. 70.

and service nobility. The Russian army was lagging behind the professional standing armies being formed in Europe in the seventeenth century. The core of such armies was a highly disciplined infantry—an infantry that fired and refired rifles as it fearlessly advanced, before charging with fixed bayonets. Such a large, permanent army was enormously expensive. Given Peter's desire to conquer more territory, his military problem was serious.

Peter's solution was, in essence, to tighten up Muscovy's old service system and really make it work. He put the nobility back in harness with a vengeance. Every nobleman, great or small, was once again required to serve in the army or in the civil administration—for life. Since a more modern army and government required skilled technicians and experts, Peter created schools and even universities. One of his most hated reforms required five years of compulsory education away from home for every young nobleman. Peter established a merit-based military-civilian bureaucracy in which some people of non-noble origin rose to high positions. He also searched out talented foreigners—twice in his reign he went abroad to study and observe—and placed them in his service. These measures combined to make the army and government more powerful and efficient.

Peter also greatly increased the service requirements of the commoners. He established a regular standing army of more than 200,000 soldiers. The departure of a drafted peasant boy was regarded by his family and village as almost like a funeral, as indeed it was, since the recruit was drafted for life. The peasantry also served with its taxes, which increased threefold during Peter's reign. Serfs were arbitrarily assigned to work in the growing number of factories and mines.

The constant warfare of Peter's reign consumed from 80 to 85 percent of all revenues but brought only modest territorial expansion. Yet after initial losses in the Great Northern War with Sweden, which lasted from 1700 to 1721, Peter's new war machine crushed Sweden's smaller army in Ukraine at Poltava in 1709, one of the most significant battles in Russian history. Sweden never really regained the offensive. Annexing Estonia and much of present-day Latvia (see Map 17.4), Russia became the dominant power on the Baltic Sea and very much a European Great Power. If victory or defeat is the ultimate historical criterion, Peter's reforms were a success.

There were other important consequences of Peter's reign. Because of his feverish desire to use modern technology to strengthen the army, many Westerners and Western ideas flowed into Russia for the first time. A new class of educated Russians began to emerge. At the same time, vast numbers of Russians, especially among the poor and weak, hated Peter's massive changes. The split between the enserfed peasantry and the educated nobility thus widened, even though all were caught up in the endless demands of the sovereign.

In sum, Peter built primarily on the service obligations of old Muscovy. His monarchical absolutism was truly the culmination of the long development of a unique Russian civilization. Yet the creation of a more modern army and state introduced much that was new and Western to that civilization. This development paved the way for Russia to move much closer to the European mainstream in its thought and institutions during the Enlightenment under Catherine the Great.

## Absolutism and Baroque Architecture

The rise of royal absolutism in eastern Europe had major cultural consequences. Inspired in part by Louis XIV of France, the great and not-so-great rulers called on the artistic talent of the age to glorify their power and magnificence. This exaltation of despotic rule was particularly striking in architecture and city planning.

As soaring Gothic cathedrals expressed the idealized spirit of the High Middle Ages, so dramatic baroque palaces symbolized the age of absolutist power. By 1700 palace building had become an obsession for the rulers of central and eastern Europe. Their baroque palaces were clearly intended to overawe the people with the monarch's strength. One such palace was Schönbrunn, an enormous Viennese Versailles begun in 1695 by Emperor Leopold I to celebrate Austrian military victories and Habsburg might.

Petty princes and important nobles also contributed mightily to the mania of palace building. Palaces like Schönbrunn and the Belvedere (see the accompanying illustration) were magnificent examples of the baroque style. They expressed the baroque delight in bold, sweeping statements intended to provide a dramatic emotional experience. To create this experience, baroque masters dissolved the usual artistic frontiers: the architect permitted the painter and the artisan to cover the undulating surfaces with wildly colorful paintings, graceful sculptures, and fanciful carvings. Space was used in a highly original way, to blend everything together in a total environment.

Not content with fashioning ostentatious palaces, absolute monarchs and baroque architects remodeled existing capital cities or built new ones to reflect royal magnificence and the centralization of political power. Karlsruhe, founded in 1715 as the capital city of a small German principality, is one extreme example. There broad, straight avenues radiated out from the palace, so that all roads—like all power—were focused on the ruler. More typically, the monarch's architects added new urban areas alongside the old city, and these areas became the real heart of the expanding capital.

The distinctive features of the new additions were their broad avenues, their imposing government buildings, and their rigorous mathematical layout. Along major thoroughfares the nobles built elaborate townhouses; stables and servants' quarters were built on the alleys behind. Under arcades along the avenues appeared smart and expensive shops, the first department stores, with plate-glass windows and fancy displays. The additions brought reckless speed to the European city. Whereas everyone had walked through the narrow, twisting streets of the medieval town, the high and mighty raced down the broad boulevards in elegant carriages. A social gap opened between the wealthy riders and the gaping, dodging pedestrians.

No city illustrates better than St. Petersburg the close ties among politics, architecture, and urban development in this period. In 1702 Peter the Great's armies seized a desolate Swedish fortress on one of the waterlogged islands at the mouth of the Neva River on the Baltic Sea. Within a year the tsar had decided to build a new city there and to make it, rather than ancient Moscow, his capital. The land was swampy and inhospitable. But for Peter it was a future metropolis gloriously bearing his name. After the decisive Russian victory at Poltava in 1709, he moved into high gear. In one imperious decree after another, he ordered his people to build a new city, his "window on Europe."

Peter believed that it would be easier to reform the country militarily and administratively from such a city than from Moscow, and his political goals were reflected in his architectural ideas. First Peter wanted a comfortable, "modern" city. Modernity meant broad, straight, stone-paved avenues, houses built in a uniform line, large parks, canals for drainage, stone bridges, and street lighting. Second, all building had to conform strictly to detailed architectural regulations set down by the government. Finally, each social group—the nobility, the merchants, the artisans, and so on—was to live in a certain section of town. In short, the city and its population were to conform to a carefully defined urban plan of the baroque type.

Peter used the methods of Russian autocracy to build his modern capital. The creation of St. Petersburg was

**Prince Eugene's Summer Palace, Vienna** The prince's summer residence featured two baroque gems, the Lower Belvedere and the lovely Upper Belvedere, completed in 1722 and shown here. The building's interior is equally stunning, with crouching giants serving as pillars and a magnificent great staircase. Art and beauty convey a feeling of immense prestige and power. *(Erich Lessing/Art Resource, NY)*

just one of the heavy obligations he dictatorially imposed on all social groups in Russia. The peasants bore the heaviest burdens. Just as the government drafted peasants for the army, it also drafted from twenty-five thousand to forty thousand men each summer to labor in St. Petersburg for three months, without pay. Peasants hated forced labor in the capital, and each year from one-fourth to one-third of those sent risked brutal punishment and ran away. Many peasant construction workers died each summer from hunger, sickness, and accidents. Beautiful St. Petersburg was built on the shoveling, carting, and paving of a mass of conscripted serfs.

Peter also drafted more privileged groups to his city, but on a permanent basis. Nobles were summarily ordered to build costly stone houses and palaces in St. Petersburg and to live in them most of the year. Merchants and artisans were also commanded to settle and build in St. Petersburg. These nobles and merchants were then required to pay for the city's avenues, parks, canals, embankments, pilings, and bridges. The building of St. Petersburg was, in truth, an enormous direct tax levied on the wealthy, who in turn forced the peasantry to do most of the work. No wonder so many Russians hated Peter's new city.

Yet the tsar had his way. By the time of his death in 1725, there were at least six thousand houses and numerous impressive government buildings in St. Petersburg. Under the remarkable women who ruled Russia throughout most of the eighteenth century, St. Petersburg blossomed as a majestic and well-organized city, at least in its wealthy showpiece sections. Chief architect Bartolomeo Rastrelli combined Italian and Russian traditions into a unique, wildly colorful St. Petersburg style in many noble palaces and government buildings. All the while St. Petersburg grew rapidly, and its almost 300,000 inhabitants in 1782 made it one of the world's largest cities. A magnificent and harmonious royal city, St. Petersburg proclaimed the power of Russia's rulers and the creative potential of the absolutist state.

## ENGLAND: THE TRIUMPH OF CONSTITUTIONAL MONARCHY

In 1588 Queen Elizabeth I of England exercised great personal power, but by 1689 the power of the English monarchy was severely limited. Change in England was anything but orderly. Yet out of this tumultuous century England built the foundations for a strong and enduring constitutional monarchy.

In the middle years of the seventeenth century, the problem of sovereignty was vigorously debated. In *Leviathan* the English philosopher and political theorist Thomas Hobbes (1588–1679) maintained that sovereignty is ultimately derived from the people, who transfer it to the monarchy by implicit contract. The power of the ruler is absolute, Hobbes said, but kings do not hold their power by divine right. This abstract theory pleased no one in the seventeenth century, but it did stimulate fruitful thinking about England's great seventeenth-century problem—the problem of order and political power.

### The Decline of Absolutism in England (1603–1660)

Elizabeth I's extraordinary success was the result of her political shrewdness and flexibility, her careful management of finances, her wise selection of ministers, her clever manipulation of Parliament, and her sense of royal dignity and devotion to hard work. After her Scottish cousin James Stuart succeeded her as James I (r. 1603–1625), Elizabeth's strengths seemed even greater.

King James was learned and, with thirty-five years' experience as king of Scotland, politically shrewd. But he was not as interested in displaying the majesty and mystique of monarchy as Elizabeth had been, and he lacked the common touch. Moreover, James was a dogmatic proponent of the theory of divine right of kings. "There are no privileges and immunities," said James, "which can stand against a divinely appointed King." This absolutist notion implied total royal jurisdiction over the liberties, persons, and properties of English men and women. Such a view ran directly counter to many long-standing English ideas, including the belief that a person's property could not be taken away without due process of law. And in the House of Commons the English had a strong representative body to question these absolutist pretensions.

The House of Commons guarded the state's pocketbook, and James and later Stuart kings badly needed to open that pocketbook. James I looked on all revenues as a windfall to be squandered on a lavish court and favorite courtiers. The extravagance displayed in James's court, as well as the public flaunting of his male lovers, weakened respect for the monarchy. These actions also stimulated the knights and burgesses who sat in the House of Commons at Westminster to press for a thorough discussion of royal expenditures, religious reform, and foreign affairs. In short, the Commons aspired to sovereignty—the ultimate political power in the realm.

During the reigns of James I and his son Charles I (r. 1625–1649) the English House of Commons was very different from the assembly that Henry VIII had manipulated into passing his Reformation legislation. The class that dominated the Commons during the Stuarts' reign wanted political power corresponding to its economic strength. A social revolution had brought about this change. The dissolution of the monasteries and the sale of monastic land had enriched many people. Agricultural techniques like the draining of wasteland had improved the land and increased its yield. In the seventeenth century old manorial common land was enclosed and profitably turned into sheep runs. Many invested in commercial ventures at home, such as the expanding cloth industry, and in foreign trade. Many also made prudent marriages. These developments increased social mobility. The typical pattern was for the commercially successful to set themselves up as country gentry. This elite group possessed a far greater proportion of the land and of the nation's wealth in 1640 than in 1540. Increased wealth resulted in a better-educated and more articulate House of Commons.

In England, unlike France, no social stigma was attached to paying taxes, although the House of Commons wanted some say in state spending and state policies. The Stuart kings, however, considered such ambitions intolerable presumption and a threat to their divine-right prerogative. Consequently, at every Parliament between 1603 and 1640, bitter squabbles erupted between Crown and Commons. Like the Great Elector in Prussia, Charles I tried to govern without Parliament (1629–1640) and to finance his government by arbitrary levies, measures that brought intense political conflict.

Religion was another source of conflict. In the early seventeenth century increasing numbers of English people felt dissatisfied with the Church of England established by Henry VIII. Many **Puritans** remained committed to "purifying" the Anglican church of Roman Catholic elements—elaborate vestments and ceremonies, even the giving and wearing of wedding rings.

Many Puritans were also attracted by the socioeconomic implications of John Calvin's theology. Calvinism emphasized hard work, sobriety, thrift, competition, and postponement of pleasure, and it tended to link sin and poverty with weakness and moral corruption. These attitudes, which have frequently been called the "Protestant ethic," "middle-class ethic," or "capitalist ethic," fit in precisely with the economic approaches and practices of many (successful) business people and farmers. These "Protestant virtues" represented the prevailing values of members of the House of Commons.

James I and Charles I both gave the impression of being highly sympathetic to Roman Catholicism. Charles supported the policies of Archbishop of Canterbury William Laud (1573–1645), who tried to impose elaborate ritual and rich ceremonial on all churches. In 1637 Laud attempted to impose Anglican organization and a new prayer book in Scotland. The Scots revolted. To finance an army to put down the Scots, King Charles was compelled to summon Parliament in November 1640. It was a fatal decision.

For eleven years Charles I had ruled without Parliament, financing his government through extraordinary stopgap levies considered illegal by most English people. Most members of Parliament believed that such taxation without consent amounted to absolutist despotism. Accordingly, the Parliament summoned in November 1640 (commonly called the Long Parliament because it sat from 1640 to 1660) enacted legislation that limited the power of the monarch and made arbitrary government impossible.

In 1641 the Commons passed the Triennial Act, which compelled the king to summon Parliament every three years. The Commons also impeached Archbishop Laud and abolished the House of Lords and the ecclesiastical Court of High Commission. King Charles reluctantly accepted these measures. But understanding and peace were not achieved, and an uprising in Ireland precipitated civil war.

Ever since Henry II had conquered Ireland in 1171, English governors had mercilessly ruled the land, and English landlords had ruthlessly exploited the Irish people. The English Reformation had made a bad situation worse: because the Irish remained Catholic, religious differences united with economic and political oppression. Without an army Charles I could neither come to terms with the Scots nor put down the Irish rebellion, and the Long Parliament remained unwilling to place an army under a king it did not trust. Charles thus recruited an army drawn from the nobility, the rural gentry, and mercenaries. The parliamentary army that rose in opposition was composed of the militia of the city of London, country squires with business connections, and men with a firm belief that serving was their spiritual duty.

The English civil war (1642–1649) tested whether ultimate political power in England was to reside in the king or in Parliament. The civil war did not resolve that problem, although it ended in 1649 with the execution of King Charles on the charge of high treason and thus dealt a severe blow to the theory of divine-right, absolute monarchy in England. Kingship was abolished in England, and a **commonwealth,** or republican form of government, was proclaimed.

In fact, the army that had defeated the royal forces controlled the government, and Oliver Cromwell controlled the army. Indeed, the period from 1649 to 1660,

**Cartoon of 1649: "The Royall Oake of Brittayne"** Chopping down this tree signifies the end of royal authority, stability, the Magna Carta (see page 383), and the rule of law. As pigs graze (representing the unconcerned common people), being fattened for slaughter, Oliver Cromwell, with his feet in Hell, quotes Scripture. This is a royalist view of the collapse of Charles I's government and the rule of Cromwell. *(Courtesy of the Trustees of the British Museum)*

known as the Interregnum because it separated two monarchical periods, was a transitional time of military dictatorship, and for most of that time Cromwell was head of state.

Oliver Cromwell (1599–1658) came from the country gentry, and he was a member of the Long Parliament. Cromwell rose in the parliamentary army and achieved nationwide fame by infusing the army with his Puritan convictions and molding it into a highly effective military machine, called the New Model Army. In 1653 the army prepared a constitution that invested executive power in a lord protector (Cromwell) and a council of state. The instrument gave Parliament the sole power to raise taxes. But after repeated disputes Cromwell tore up the document and proclaimed quasi-martial law.

On the issue of religion Cromwell favored broad toleration, and the Instrument of Government gave all Christians, except Roman Catholics, the right to practice their faith. In 1649 he crushed rebellion in Ireland with merciless savagery, leaving a legacy of Irish hatred for England. He also rigorously censored the press, forbade sports, and kept the theaters closed in England.

Cromwell pursued mercantilist economic policies. He enforced a navigation act requiring that English goods be transported on English ships, which was a great boost to the development of an English merchant marine.

Military government collapsed when Cromwell died in 1658. The English longed for a return to civilian government, restoration of the common law, and social and religious stability. Government by military dictatorship was an experiment in absolutism that the English never forgot or repeated. By 1660 they were ready to try a restoration of monarchy.

## The Restoration of the English Monarchy

The Restoration of 1660 re-established the monarchy in the person of Charles II (r. 1660–1685), eldest son of Charles I. At the same time both houses of Parliament were also restored, together with the established Anglican church. The Restoration failed to resolve two serious problems. What was to be the attitude of the state toward Puritans, Catholics, and dissenters from the established church? And what was to be the constitutional relationship between the king and Parliament?

Charles II, a relaxed, easygoing, and sensual man, was not much interested in religious issues. But the new members of Parliament were, and they proceeded to enact a body of laws that sought to compel religious uniformity. Those who refused to receive the sacrament of the Church of England could not vote, hold public office, preach, teach, attend the universities, or even assemble for meetings, according to the Test Act of 1673.

In politics Charles II was at first determined to get along with Parliament and share power with it. His method for doing so had profound importance for later constitutional development. The king appointed a council of five men who served both as his major advisers and as members of Parliament, thus acting as liaison agents between the executive and the legislature. It gradually came to be accepted that the council of five was answerable in Parliament for the decisions of the king.

Harmony between the Crown and Parliament rested on the understanding that Charles would summon Parliament frequently and Parliament would vote him sufficient revenues. But Parliament did not grant him an adequate income. Accordingly, in 1670 Charles entered into a secret agreement with Louis XIV. The French king would give Charles £200,000 annually. In return Charles would relax the laws against Catholics, gradually re-Catholicize England, support French policy against the Dutch, and convert to Catholicism himself.

When the details of this secret treaty leaked out, a wave of anti-Catholic fear swept England. Charles had produced only bastards, and therefore it appeared that his brother and heir, James, duke of York, an avowed Catholic, would inaugurate a Catholic dynasty. The combination of hatred for the French absolutism embodied in Louis XIV and hostility to Roman Catholicism led the Commons to pass an exclusion bill denying the succession to a Roman Catholic. But Charles quickly dissolved Parliament, and the bill never became law.

James II (r. 1685–1688) succeeded his brother. Almost at once the worst English anti-Catholic fears, already aroused by Louis XIV's recent revocation of the Edict of Nantes, were realized. In direct violation of the Test Act, James appointed Roman Catholics to positions in the army, the universities, and local government. The king appeared to be reviving the absolutism of his father (Charles I) and grandfather (James I). He went further. Attempting to broaden his base of support with Protestant dissenters and nonconformists, James issued a declaration of indulgence granting religious freedom to all.

Two events gave the signals for revolution. First, seven bishops of the Church of England petitioned the king that they not be forced to read the declaration of indulgence because of their belief that it was an illegal act. They were imprisoned in the Tower of London but subsequently acquitted amid great public enthusiasm. Second, in June 1688 James's second wife produced a male heir. A Catholic dynasty seemed assured. The fear of a Roman Catholic monarchy, supported by France and ruling outside the law, prompted a group of eminent persons to offer the English throne to James's Protestant daughter, Mary, and her Dutch husband, Prince William of Orange. In December 1688 James II, his queen, and their infant son fled to France. In 1689 William and Mary were crowned king and queen of England.

The English call the events of 1688 to 1689 the "Glorious Revolution." It replaced one king with another with a minimum of bloodshed, and it represented the destruction, once and for all, of the idea of divine-right absolutism in England. William and Mary accepted the English throne from Parliament and in so doing explicitly recognized the supremacy of Parliament.

The men who brought about the revolution quickly framed their intentions in the Bill of Rights, the cornerstone of the modern British constitution. The basic principles of the Bill of Rights were formulated in direct response to Stuart absolutism. Law was to be made in Parliament; once made, it could not be suspended by the Crown. Parliament had to be called at least every three years. Both elections to and debate in Parliament were to be free, in the sense that the Crown was not to interfere in them. Judges would hold their offices "during good behavior," a provision that assured judicial independence.

In striking contrast to the states of continental Europe, there was to be no standing army that could be used against the English population in peacetime. Moreover, the Bill of Rights granted Protestants the right to possess firearms. Additional legislation granted freedom of worship to Protestant dissenters and nonconformists and required that the English monarch always be Protestant.

The Glorious Revolution found its best defense in John Locke's ***Second Treatise of Civil Government*** (1690). The political philosopher Locke (1632–1704) maintained that people set up civil governments in order to protect life, liberty, and property. A government that oversteps its proper function—protecting the natural rights of life, liberty, and property—becomes a tyranny. (By "natural" rights, Locke meant rights basic to all men because all have the ability to reason.) Under a tyrannical government the people have the natural right to rebellion. Recognizing the close relationship between economic and political freedom, Locke linked economic liberty and private property with political freedom.

Locke served as the great spokesman for the liberal English revolution of 1688 to 1689 and for representative government. His idea—that there are natural or universal rights equally valid for all peoples and societies—played a powerful role in eighteenth-century Enlightenment thought.

The events of 1688 to 1689 did not constitute a *democratic* revolution. The revolution formalized Parliament's power, and Parliament represented the upper classes. The great majority of English people had little say in their government. The English revolution established a constitutional monarchy; it also inaugurated an age of aristocratic government.

In the course of the eighteenth century the **cabinet system** of government evolved out of Charles II's old council-of-five system. The term *cabinet* derives from the small private room in which English rulers consulted their chief ministers. In a cabinet system, the leading ministers formulate common policy and conduct the business of the country. During the administration of one royal minister, Sir Robert Walpole, who led the Cabinet from 1721 to 1742, the idea developed that the Cabinet was responsible to the House of Commons. Walpole enjoyed the favor of the monarchy and of the House of Commons and came to be called the king's first, or "prime," minister. In the English cabinet system, both legislative and executive powers are held by the leading ministers, who form the government.

## THE DUTCH REPUBLIC IN THE SEVENTEENTH CENTURY

In the late sixteenth century the seven northern provinces of the Netherlands, of which Holland and Zeeland were the most prosperous, had thrown off Spanish domination (see pages 483–484). The seventeenth century then witnessed an unparalleled flowering of Dutch scientific, artistic, and literary achievement. In this period, often called the golden age of the Netherlands, Dutch ideas and attitudes played a profound role in shaping a new and modern world-view.

The Republic of the United Provinces of the Netherlands represents a variation in the development of the modern constitutional state. Within each province an oligarchy of wealthy merchants called regents handled domestic affairs in the local Estates. A federal assembly, or **States General,** handled matters of foreign affairs, such as war, but all issues had to be referred back to the local Estates for approval. The regents in each province jealously guarded local independence and resisted efforts at centralization. Nevertheless, Holland, which had the largest navy and the most wealth, dominated the republic and the States General.

The government of the United Provinces was not monarchical but fiercely republican. The government was controlled by wealthy merchants and financiers. Though rich, their values were not aristocratic but strongly middle class. The moral and ethical bases of that commercial wealth were thrift, hard work, and simplicity in living.

John Calvin had written, "From where do the merchant's profits come except from his own diligence and industry." This attitude undoubtedly encouraged a sturdy people who had waged a centuries-old struggle against the sea. Louis XIV's hatred of the Dutch was proverbial. They represented all that he despised—middle-class values, religious toleration, and independent political institutions.

Alone of all European peoples in the seventeenth century, the Dutch practiced religious toleration. Peoples of all faiths were welcome within their borders. Jews enjoyed a level of acceptance and absorption in Dutch business and general culture unique in early modern Europe.

Toleration paid off. It attracted a great amount of foreign capital and business expertise. The Bank of Amsterdam became Europe's best source of cheap credit and commercial intelligence and the main clearing-house for bills of exchange. People of all races and creeds traded in Amsterdam, at whose docks on the Amstel River five thousand ships were berthed. Joost van den Vondel, the poet of Dutch imperialism, exulted:

*God, God, the Lord of Amstel cried, hold every conscience free;*
*And Liberty ride, on Holland's tide, with billowing sails to sea,*
*And run our Amstel out and in; let freedom gird the bold,*
*And merchant in his counting house stand elbow deep in gold.*[9]

The fishing industry was a cornerstone of the Dutch economy. For half of the year, from June to December,

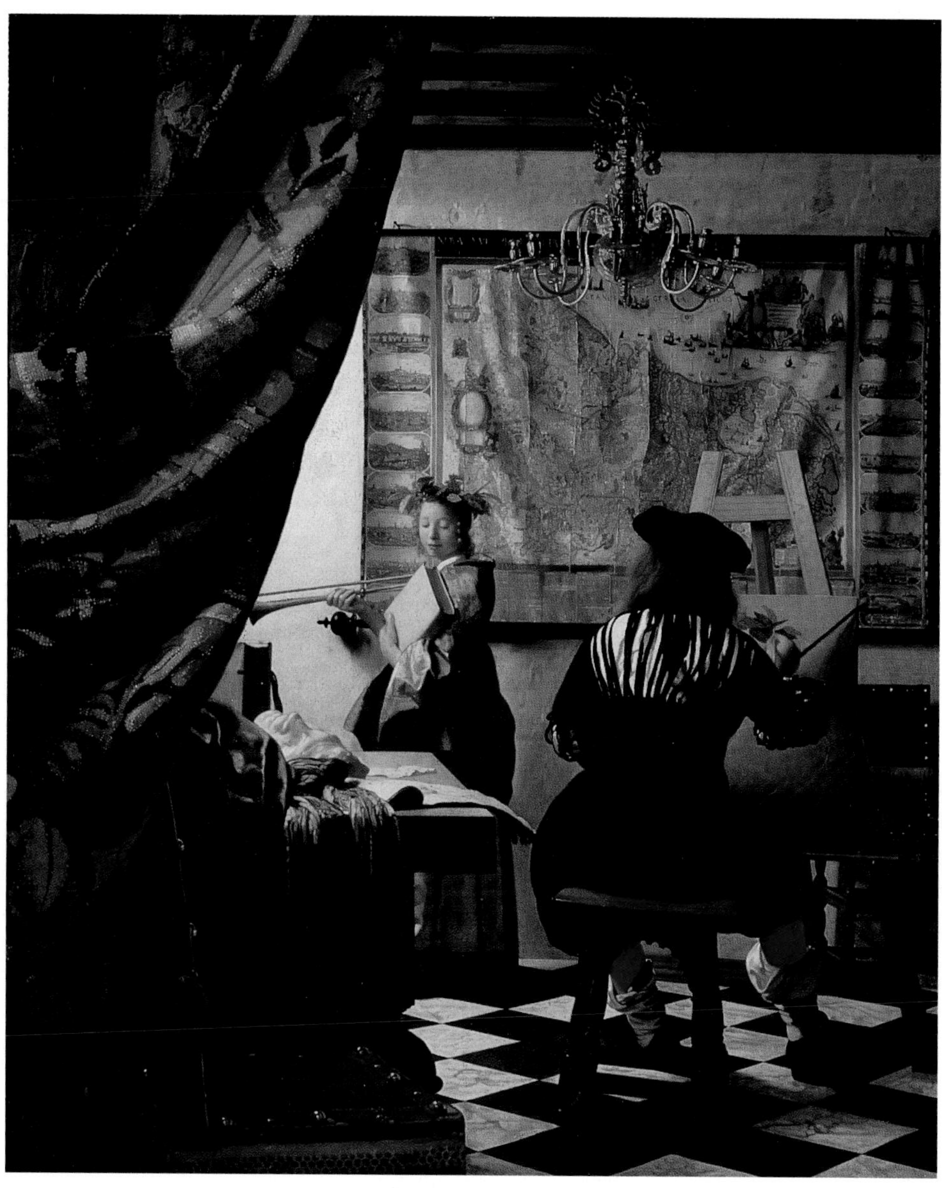

**Jan Vermeer: The Art of Painting or The Artist's Studio** In a typically Dutch interior—black and white marble floor, brass chandelier, map of Holland on the wall—an artist paints an allegory of Clio, the Muse of History (often shown holding a book and a trumpet). The Muses, nine goddesses of Greek mythology, were thought to inspire the arts. Considered the second-greatest Dutch painter (after Rembrandt), Vermeer (1632–1675) was a master of scenes of everyday life, but he probably meant his work to be understood on more than one level. *(Kunsthistorisches Museum, Vienna/Art Resource, NY)*

fishing fleets combed the dangerous English coast and the North Sea, raking in tiny herring. Profits from herring stimulated shipbuilding, and even before 1600 the Dutch were offering the lowest shipping rates in Europe. In 1650 the Dutch merchant marine was the largest in Europe, accounting for roughly half of the European total. Dutch merchants controlled the Baltic grain trade, buying wheat and rye in Poland, east Prussia, and Swedish Pomerania. Foreign merchants coming to Amsterdam could buy anything from precision lenses for the newly invented microscope to muskets for an army of five thousand.

In 1602 a group of the regents of Holland formed the **Dutch East India Company,** a joint stock company. Within a half century, the Dutch East India Company had cut heavily into Portuguese trading in East Asia. The Dutch seized the Cape of Good Hope, Ceylon, and Malacca and established trading posts in each place. In the 1630s the Dutch East India Company was paying its investors about a 35 percent annual return on their investments. The Dutch West India Company traded extensively with Latin America and Africa (see Map 17.5).

Trade and commerce brought the Dutch prodigious wealth. In the seventeenth century the Dutch enjoyed

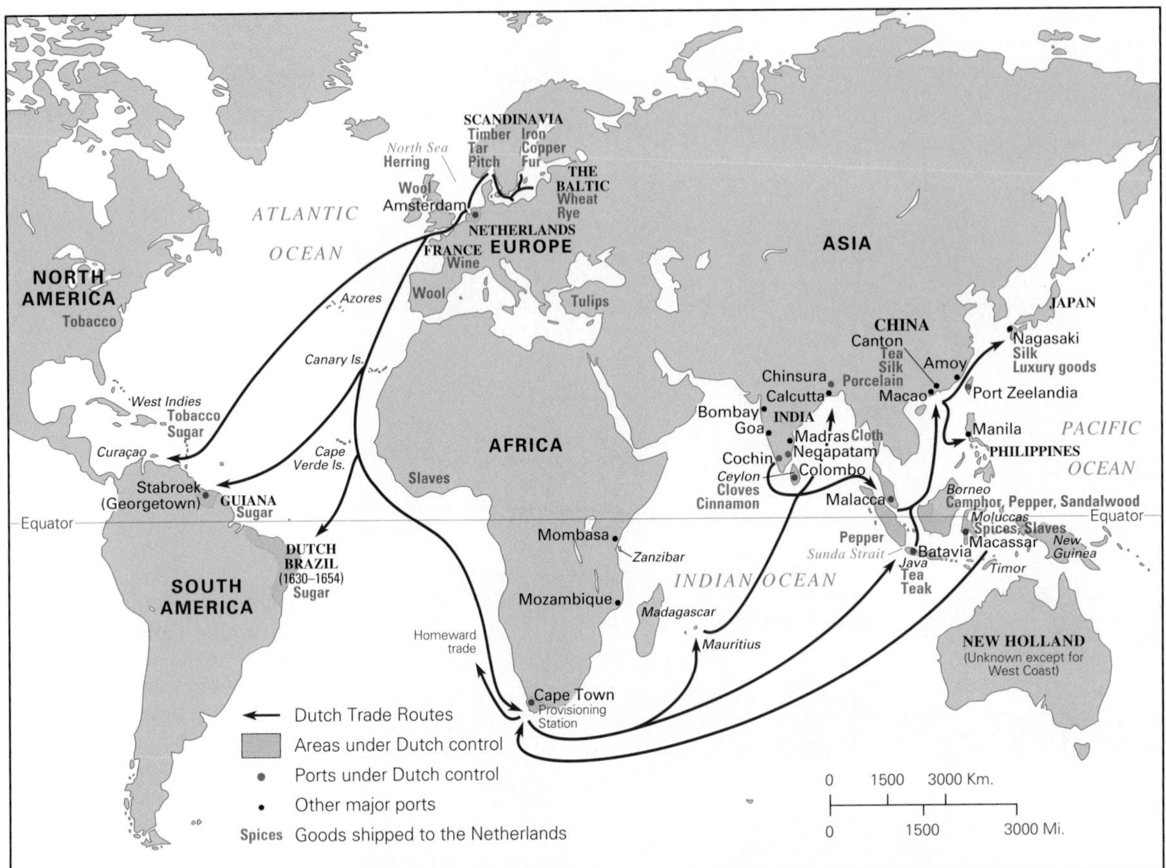


**MAP 17.5 Seventeenth-Century Dutch Commerce** Dutch wealth rested on commerce, and commerce depended on the huge Dutch merchant marine, manned by perhaps forty-eight thousand sailors. The fleet carried goods from all parts of the globe to the port of Amsterdam.

the highest standard of living in Europe, perhaps in the world. By the standards of Cologne, Paris, or London, salaries were high for all workers, except women. All classes of society, including unskilled laborers, ate well. The low price of bread meant that, compared with other places in Europe, a higher percentage of a worker's income could be spent on fish, cheese, butter, vegetables, even meat. A leading scholar has described the Netherlands as "an island of plenty in a sea of want."[10]

Dutch economic leadership was eventually sapped by wars, beginning with those with France and England in the 1670s. The long War of the Spanish Succession, in which the Dutch supported England against France, was a costly drain on Dutch manpower and financial resources. The peace signed in 1713 to end that war marked the beginning of Dutch economic decline.

## SUMMARY

War, religious strife, economic depression, and peasant revolts were all aspects of a deep crisis in seventeenth-century Europe. Rulers responded by aggressively seeking to expand their power, which they claimed was essential to meet emergencies and quell disorders. Claiming also that they ruled by divine right, monarchs sought the freedom to wage war, levy taxes, and generally make law as they saw fit. Although they were limited by technology and inadequate financial resources, monarchical governments on the European continent succeeded to a large extent, overpowering organized opposition and curbing the power of the nobility and the traditional representative institutions.

The France of Louis XIV led the way to royal absolutism. France developed a centralized bureaucracy, a professional army, and a state-directed economy, all of which Louis personally supervised. The king saw himself as the representative of God on earth and accountable to no one here below. His majestic bearing and sumptuous court dazzled contemporaries. Yet behind the grand façade of unchallenged personal rule and obedient bureaucrats working his will there stood major limitations on Louis XIV's power. Most notable were the financial independence of some provinces and the nobility's traditional freedom from taxation, which Louis himself was compelled to reaffirm.

Within a framework of resurgent serfdom and entrenched nobility, Austrian and Prussian monarchs also fashioned absolutist states in the seventeenth and early eighteenth centuries. These monarchs won absolutist control over standing armies, permanent taxes, and legislative bodies. But they did not question the underlying social and economic relationships. Indeed, they enhanced the privileges of the nobility, which furnished the leading servitors for enlarged armies and growing government bureaucracies.

In Russia social and economic trends were similar to those in Austria and Prussia. Unlike those two states, however, Russia had a long history of powerful princes. Tsar Peter the Great succeeded in tightening up Russia's traditional absolutism and modernizing it by reforming the army, the bureaucracy, and the defense industry. In Russia and throughout eastern Europe war and the needs of the state in times of war weighed heavily in the triumph of absolutism.

Triumphant absolutism interacted spectacularly with the arts. It molded the ideals of French classicism, which glorified the state as personified by Louis XIV. Baroque art, which had grown out of the Catholic Reformation's desire to move the faithful and exalt the faith, admirably suited the secular aspirations of eastern European rulers. Thus baroque art attained magnificent heights in eastern Europe, symbolizing the ideal and harmonizing with the reality of imperious royal absolutism.

Holland and England defied the general trend toward absolute monarchy. While Holland prospered under a unique republican confederation of separate provinces, England—fortunately shielded from continental armies and military emergencies by its navy and the English Channel—evolved into the first modern constitutional state. The bitter conflicts between Parliament and the first two Stuart rulers, James I and Charles I, tested where supreme power would rest in the state. The resulting civil war deposed the king, but it did not settle the question. A revival of absolutist tendencies under James II brought on the Glorious Revolution of 1688, and the people who made that revolution settled three basic issues. Power was divided between king and Parliament, with Parliament enjoying the greater share. Government was to be based on the rule of law. And the liberties of English people were to be made explicit in written form, in the Bill of Rights. This constitutional settlement marked an important milestone in world history, although the framers left to later generations the task of making constitutional government work.

## KEY TERMS

absolutism
constitutionalism
Fronde
mercantilism
French classicism
Peace of Utrecht
*Don Quixote*
tsar
Cossacks
Puritans
commonwealth
*Second Treatise of Civil Government*
cabinet system
States General
Dutch East India Company

## NOTES

1. J. B. Collins, *Fiscal Limits of Absolutism: Direct Taxation in Early Seventeenth Century France* (Berkeley: University of California Press, 1988), pp. 1, 3–4, 215–222.
2. S. de Gramont, ed., *The Age of Magnificence: Memoirs of the Court of Louis XIV by the Duc de Saint Simon* (New York: Capricorn Books, 1964), pp. 141–145.
3. W. Beik, *Absolutism and Society in Seventeenth Century France: State Power and Provincial Aristocracy in Languedoc* (Cambridge: Cambridge University Press, 1985), pp. 279–302.
4. W. F. Church, *Louis XIV in Historical Thought: From Voltaire to the Annales School* (New York: W. W. Norton, 1976), p. 92.
5. B. Bennassar, *The Spanish Character: Attitudes and Mentalities from the Sixteenth to the Nineteenth Century,* trans. B. Keen (Berkeley: University of California Press, 1979), p. 125.
6. Quoted in R. Ergang, *The Potsdam Fuhrer: Frederick William I, Father of Prussian Militarism* (New York: Octagon Books, 1972), pp. 85, 87.
7. Quoted in R. A. Dorwart, *The Administrative Reforms of Frederick William I of Prussia* (Cambridge, Mass.: Harvard University Press, 1953), p. 226.
8. Quoted in H. Rosenberg, *Bureaucracy, Aristocracy, and Autocracy: The Prussian Experience, 1660–1815* (Boston: Beacon Press, 1966), p. 38.
9. Quoted in D. Maland, *Europe in the Seventeenth Century* (New York: Macmillan, 1967), pp. 198–199.
10. S. Schama, *The Embarrassment of Riches: An Interpretation of Dutch Culture in the Golden Age* (New York: Knopf, 1987), pp. 165–170.

*(continued on page 568)*

# LISTENING TO THE PAST

## THE COURT AT VERSAILLES

*Although the Duc de Saint-Simon (1675–1755) was a soldier, courtier, and diplomat, his enduring reputation rests on his* Memoirs *(1788), an eyewitness account of the personality and court of Louis XIV. A nobleman of ancient lineage, Saint-Simon resented Louis's "domestication" of the nobility and his promotion of the bourgeoisie.* The Memoirs, *excerpted here, remains a monument of French literature and an indispensable historical source, partly for its portrait of the court at Versailles.*

Very early in the reign of Louis XIV the Court was removed from Paris, never to return. The troubles of the minority had given him a dislike to that city; his enforced and surreptitious flight from it still rankled in his memory; he did not consider himself safe there, and thought cabals would be more easily detected if the Court was in the country, where the movements and temporary absences of any of its members would be more easily noticed. . . . No doubt that he was also influenced by the feeling that he would be regarded with greater awe and veneration when no longer exposed every day to the gaze of the multitude.

His love-affair with Mademoiselle de la Vallière, which at first was covered as far as possible with a veil of mystery, was the cause of frequent excursions to Versailles. . . . The visits of Louis XIV becoming more frequent, he enlarged the *château* by degrees till its immense buildings afforded better accommodation for the Court than was to be found at St. Germain, where most of the courtiers had to put up with uncomfortable lodgings in the town. The Court was therefore removed to Versailles in 1682, not long before the Queen's death. The new building contained an infinite number of rooms for courtiers, and the King liked the grant of these rooms to be regarded as a coveted privilege.

He availed himself of the frequent festivities at Versailles, and his excursions to other places, as a means of making the courtiers assiduous in their attendance and anxious to please him; for he nominated beforehand those who were to take part in them, and could thus gratify some and inflict a snub on others. He was conscious that the substantial favours he had to bestow were not nearly sufficient to produce a continual effect; he had therefore to invent imaginary ones, and no one was so clever in devising petty distinctions and preferences which aroused jealousy and emulation. The visits to Marly later on were very useful to him in this way; also those to Trianon [Marly and Trianon were small country houses], where certain ladies, chosen beforehand, were admitted to his table. It was another distinction to hold his candlestick at his *coucher;* as soon as he had finished his prayers he used to name the courtier to whom it was to be handed, always choosing one of the highest rank among those present. . . .

Not only did he expect all persons of distinction to be in continual attendance at Court, but he was quick to notice the absence of those of inferior degree; at his *lever* [formal rising from bed in the morning], his *coucher* [preparations for going to bed], his meals, in the gardens of Versailles (the only place where the courtiers in general were allowed to follow him), he used to cast his eyes to right and left; nothing escaped him, he saw everybody. If any one habitually living at Court absented himself he insisted on knowing the reason; those who came there only for flying visits had also to give a satisfactory explanation; any one who seldom or never appeared there was certain to incur his displea-

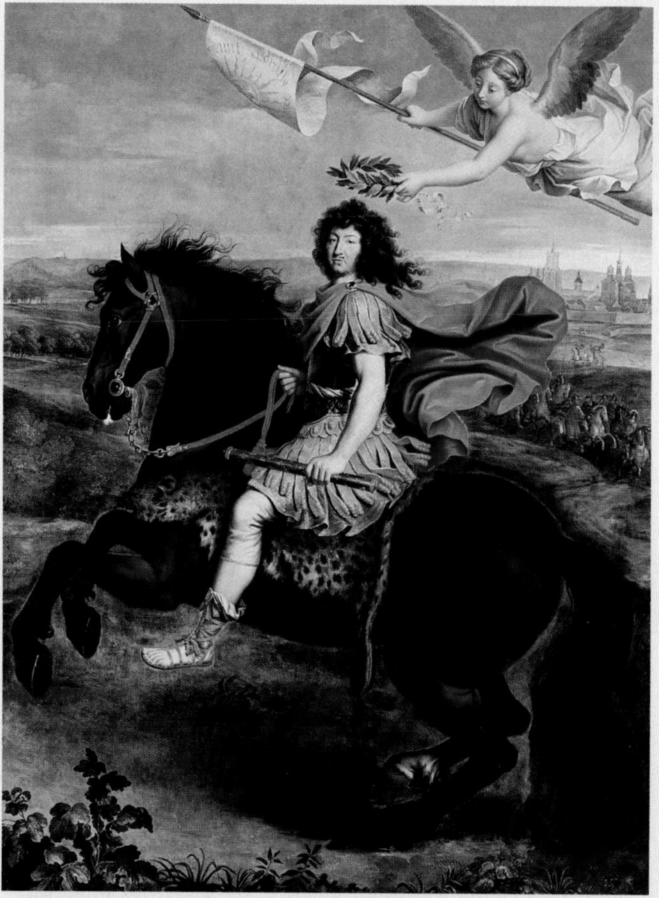

Painting of Louis XIV by Mignard Pierre (1612–1695). *(Galleria Sabauda, Turin/Scala/Art Resource, NY)*

sure. If asked to bestow a favour on such persons he would reply haughtily: "I do not know him"; of such as rarely presented themselves he would say, "He is a man I never see"; and from these judgements there was no appeal.

He always took great pains to find out what was going on in public places, in society, in private houses, even family secrets, and maintained an immense number of spies and tale-bearers. These were of all sorts; some did not know that their reports were carried to him; others did know it; there were others, again, who used to write to him directly, through channels which he prescribed; others who were admitted by the backstairs and saw him in his private room. Many a man in all ranks of life was ruined by these methods, often very unjustly, without ever being able to discover the reason; and when the King had once taken a prejudice against a man, he hardly ever got over it. . . .

No one understood better than Louis XIV the art of enhancing the value of a favour by his manner of bestowing it; he knew how to make the most of a word, a smile, even of a glance. If he addressed any one, were it but to ask a trifling question or make some commonplace remark, all eyes were turned on the person so honored; it was a mark of favour which always gave rise to comment. . . .

He loved splendour, magnificence, and profusion in all things, and encouraged similar tastes in his Court; to spend money freely on equipages [the king's horse carriages] and buildings, on feasting and at cards, was a sure way to gain his favour, perhaps to obtain the honour of a word from him. Motives of policy had something to do with this; by making expensive habits the fashion, and, for people in a certain position, a necessity, he compelled his courtiers to live beyond their income, and gradually reduced them to depend on his bounty for the means of subsistence. This was a plague which, once introduced, became a scourge to the whole country, for it did not take long to spread to Paris, and thence to the armies and the provinces; so that a man of any position is now estimated entirely according to his expenditure on his table and other luxuries. This folly, sustained by pride and ostentation, has already produced widespread confusion; it threatens to end in nothing short of ruin and a general overthrow.

## QUESTIONS FOR ANALYSIS

1. How would you define the French court? Why did Louis XIV move it to Versailles?
2. By what means did Louis control the nobility at Versailles? Why did he use those particular means?
3. Consider the role of ritual and ceremony in some modern governments, such as the U.S. government. How does it compare to Louis XIV's use of ceremony, as portrayed by Saint-Simon?
4. Saint-Simon faulted Louis for encouraging the nobles' extravagance. Is that a justifiable criticism?

*Source:* F. Arkwright, ed., *The Memoirs of the Duke de Saint-Simon,* vol. 5 (New York: Brentano's, n.d.), pp. 271–274, 276–278.

## SUGGESTED READING

Students who wish to explore the problems presented in this chapter will find a rich and exciting literature. G. Parker, *Europe in Crisis, 1598–1618* (1980), provides a sound introduction to the social, economic, and religious tensions of the period, as does R. S. Dunn, *The Age of Religious Wars, 1559–1715,* 2d ed. (1979). P. K. Monod, *The Power of Kings: Monarchy and Religion in Europe, 1589–1715* (1999), is an important comparative study, while P. Anderson, *Lineages of the Absolutist State* (1974), offers a stimulating Marxist interpretation of European absolutism.

Louis XIV and his age have attracted the attention of many scholars. J. Wolf, *Louis XIV* (1968), remains the best available biography. P. Burke, *The Fabrication of Louis XIV* (1992), explores the representations of the Sun King. The advanced student will want to consult the excellent historiographical analysis by Church mentioned in the Notes, *Louis XIV in Historical Thought.* P. Goubert's heavily detailed *The Ancien Régime: French Society, 1600–1750,* 2 vols. (1969–1973), contains invaluable material on the lives and work of ordinary people. R. Bonney, *The King's Debts: Finance and Politics in France, 1589–1661* (1981), and A. Trout, *Jean-Baptiste Colbert* (1978), consider economic and financial conditions. R. Hatton, *Europe in the Age of Louis XIV* (1979), is a splendidly illustrated survey of many aspects of seventeenth-century European culture.

For Spain, M. Defourneaux, *Daily Life in Spain in the Golden Age* (1976), is extremely useful. See also C. R. Phillips, *Ciudad Real, 1500–1750: Growth, Crisis, and Readjustment in the Spanish Economy* (1979), a significant case study. A. Pagden, *Spanish Imperialism and the Political Imagination* (1990), explores Spanish ideas of empire. V. L. Tapie, *The Age of Grandeur: Baroque Art and Architecture* (1960), emphasizes the relationship between art and politics with excellent illustrations. Art and architecture are also treated admirably in E. Hempel, *Baroque Art and Architecture in Central Europe* (1965), and R. Harbison, *Reflections on the Baroque* (2001), is a well-illustrated integration of ideas and the arts.

The best study on early Prussian history is still F. L. Carsten, *The Origin of Prussia* (1954). Rosenberg, *Bureaucracy, Aristocracy, and Autocracy,* cited in the Notes, is a masterful analysis of the social context of Prussian absolutism. Ergang, *The Potsdam Fuhrer,* also cited in the Notes, is an exciting and critical biography of ramrod Frederick William I. G. Craig, *The Politics of the Prussian Army, 1640–1945* (1964), expertly traces the great influence of the military on the Prussian state over three hundred years. R. J. Evans, *The Making of the Habsburg Empire, 1550–1770* (1979), analyzes the development of absolutism in Austria, as does A. Wandruszka, *The House of Habsburg* (1964). D. McKay and H. Scott, *The Rise of the Great Powers, 1648–1815* (1983), is a good general account. R. Vierhaus, *Germany in the Age of Absolutism* (1988), offers a thorough survey of the different German states.

On eastern European peasants and serfdom, D. Chirot, ed., *The Origins of Backwardness in Eastern Europe: Economics and Politics from the Middle Ages Until the Twentieth Century* (1989), is a wide-ranging introduction. E. Levin, *Sex and Society in the World of the Orthodox Slavs, 900–1700* (1989), carries family history to eastern Europe. J. Blum, *Lord and Peasant in Russia from the Ninth to the Nineteenth Century* (1961), provides a good look at conditions in rural Russia, and P. Avrich, *Russian Rebels, 1600–1800* (1972), treats some of the violent peasant upheavals that those conditions produced. In addition to the fine survey by N. V. Riasanovsky, *A History of Russia* (1963), J. Billington, *The Icon and the Axe* (1970), is a stimulating history of early Russian intellectual and cultural developments. B. H. Sumner, *Peter the Great and the Emergence of Russia* (1962), is a good brief introduction, while B. Lincoln, *Sunlight at Midnight: St. Petersburg and the Rise of Modern Russia* (2001), captures the spirit of Peter's new northern capital.

English political and social issues of the seventeenth century are considered by M. Ashley, *The House of Stuart: Its Rise and Fall* (1980); C. Hill, *A Century of Revolution* (1961); and K. Wrightson, *English Society, 1580–1680* (1982). Comprehensive treatments of Parliament include C. Russell, *Crisis of Parliaments, 1509–1660* (1971). L. Stone, *The Causes of the English Revolution* (1972), and B. Manning, *The English People and the English Revolution* (1976), are recommended. D. Underdown, *Revel, Riot, and Rebellion* (1985), discusses the extent of popular involvement. For English intellectual currents, see J. O. Appleby, *Economic Thought and Ideology in Seventeenth Century England* (1978). Other recommended works include P. Collinson, *The Religion of Protestants* (1982); R. Thompson, *Women in Stuart England and America* (1974); and A. Fraser, *The Weaker Vessel* (1985). For Cromwell and the Interregnum, A. Fraser, *Cromwell, the Lord Protector* (1973), is valuable. C. Hill, *The World Turned Upside Down* (1972), discusses radical thought during the period. For the Restoration and the Glorious Revolution, see R. Hutton, *Charles II: King of England, Scotland and Ireland* (1989); J. Childs, *The Army, James II, and the Glorious Revolution* (1980); and L. G. Schwoerer, *The Declaration of Rights, 1689* (1981), a fine assessment of that fundamental document. The ideas of John Locke are analyzed by J. P. Kenyon, *Revolution Principles: The Politics of Party, 1689–1720* (1977).

On Holland, K. H. D. Haley, *The Dutch Republic in the Seventeenth Century* (1972), is a splendidly illustrated appreciation of Dutch commercial and artistic achievements, and Schama, *The Embarrassment of Riches,* cited in the Notes, is a lively synthesis. R. Boxer, *The Dutch Seaborne Empire* (1980), is useful for Dutch overseas expansion. V. Barbour, *Capitalism in Amsterdam in the Seventeenth Century* (1950), and D. Regin, *Traders, Artists, Burghers: A Cultural History of Amsterdam in the Seventeenth Century* (1977), focus on the leading Dutch city. The leading statesmen of the period may be studied in these biographies: H. H. Rowen, *John de Witt, Grand Pensionary of Holland, 1625–1672* (1978); S. B. Baxter, *William the III and the Defense of European Liberty, 1650–1702* (1966); and J. den Tex, *Oldenbarnevelt,* 2 vols. (1973).

Voltaire, the renowned Enlightenment thinker, leans forward on the left to exchange ideas and witty conversation with Frederick the Great, king of Prussia. *(Bildarchiv Preussischer Kulturbesitz)*

CHAPTER

# 18 TOWARD A NEW WORLD-VIEW IN THE WEST

## CHAPTER OUTLINE

- The Scientific Revolution
- The Enlightenment
- The Enlightenment and Absolutism

Most people are not philosophers, but they nevertheless have a basic outlook on life, a more or less coherent **world-view.** At the risk of oversimplification, one may say that the world-view of medieval and early modern Europe was primarily religious and theological. Not only did Christian or Jewish teachings form the core of people's spiritual and philosophical beliefs, but religious teachings also permeated all the rest of human thought and activity. Political theory relied on the divine right of kings, for example, and activities ranging from marriage and divorce to eating habits and hours of business were regulated by churches and religious doctrines.

In the course of the eighteenth century, this religious and theological world-view underwent a fundamental transformation among the European upper and comfortable classes. Economically secure and increasingly well educated, these privileged groups of preindustrial Europe often came to see the world primarily in secular and scientific terms. And while few individuals abandoned religious beliefs altogether, the role of churches and religious thinking in earthly affairs and in the pursuit of knowledge was substantially reduced. Among many in the aristocracy and solid middle classes, a new critical, scientific, and very modern world-view took shape.

- Why did this momentous change occur?
- How did this new world-view affect the way people thought about society and human relations?
- What impact did this new way of thinking have on political developments and monarchical absolutism?

This chapter will focus on these questions.

## THE SCIENTIFIC REVOLUTION

The foremost cause of the change in world-view was the scientific revolution. Modern science—precise knowledge of the physical world based on the union of experimental observations with sophisticated mathematics—crystallized in the seventeenth century. Whereas science had been secondary and subordinate in medieval intellectual life, it became independent and

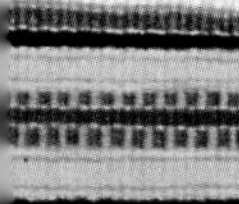

even primary for many educated people in the eighteenth century.

To be sure, other civilizations developed early forms of scientific inquiry. For example, the West did not have a monopoly on the study of astronomy, which played a key role in scientific development, as we shall see. Many other cultures collected data on the heavens. The Maya of Central America constructed exceptionally accurate calendars based on astronomical observations and maintained a view of the universe not substantially different from that of Ptolemy. Ulugh Beg (r. 1447–1449), grandson of the famous Tamerlane, was a Central Asian astronomer-king who ordered the creation of the Samarkand Tables, the most accurate compilation of astronomical data ever made, based on the evidence collected at his huge observatory. Yet although other cultures conducted extensive observations of the heavens, it was only in the West that such observations became part of a systematic approach to the study of the physical universe, the scientific method.

The emergence of modern science was a development of tremendous long-term significance. A noted historian has even said that the scientific revolution of the late sixteenth and seventeenth centuries "outshines everything since the rise of Christianity" and was "the real origin both of the modern world and the modern mentality."[1] This statement is an exaggeration, but not much of one. Of all the great civilizations, only that of the West developed modern science. Let us examine the milestones on this fateful march toward modern science first and then search for the nonscientific influences along the route.

## Scientific Thought in 1500

Since developments in astronomy and physics were at the heart of the scientific revolution, one must begin with the traditional European conception of the universe and movement within it. In the early 1500s traditional European ideas about the universe were still based primarily on the ideas of Aristotle, the great Greek philosopher of the fourth century B.C.E. These ideas had been recovered gradually during the Middle Ages and then brought into harmony with Christian doctrines by medieval theologians. According to this revised Aristotelian view, a motionless earth was fixed at the center of the universe. Around it moved ten separate transparent crystal spheres. In the first eight spheres were embedded, in turn, the moon, the sun, the five known planets, and the fixed stars. Then followed two spheres that theologians added during the Middle Ages to account for slight changes in the positions of the stars over the centuries. Beyond the tenth sphere was Heaven, with the throne of God and the souls of the saved. Angels kept these perfect spheres moving in perfect circles.

Aristotle's views also dominated thinking about physics and motion on earth—the sublunar world. The sublunar world was made up of four imperfect, changeable elements. The "light" elements (air and fire) naturally moved upward; the "heavy" elements (water and earth) naturally moved downward. These natural directions of motion did not always prevail, however, for elements were often mixed together and could be affected by an outside force such as a human being. Aristotle and his followers also believed that a uniform force moved an object at a constant speed and that the object would stop as soon as that force was removed.

Aristotle's science as interpreted by Christian theologians fit neatly with Christian doctrines. It established a home for God and a place for Christian souls. It put human beings at the center of the universe and made them the critical link in a "great chain of being" that stretched from the throne of God to the most lowly insect on earth. Thus science was primarily a branch of theology, and it reinforced religious thought.

## The Copernican Hypothesis

The desire to explain and thereby glorify God's handiwork led to the first great departure from the medieval system. This departure was the work of the Polish clergyman and astronomer Nicolaus Copernicus (1473–1543). As a young student Copernicus saw how professional astronomers still depended for their most accurate calculations on the work of Ptolemy, the last great ancient astronomer, who had lived in Alexandria in the second century C.E. Ptolemy's achievement had been to work out complicated rules to help stargazers and astrologers to track the planets with greater precision.

The young Copernicus was uninterested in astrology and felt that Ptolemy's cumbersome and occasionally inaccurate rules detracted from the majesty of a perfect Creator. He preferred an old Greek idea being discussed in Renaissance Italy—the idea that the sun, rather than the earth, was at the center of the universe. Working on his hypothesis from 1506 to 1530, Copernicus indeed theorized that the stars and planets, including the earth, revolve around a fixed sun. Yet Copernicus was a cautious man. Fearing the ridicule of other astronomers, he did not publish his *On the Revolutions of the Heavenly Spheres* until 1543, the year of his death.

The **Copernican theory** had enormous scientific and religious implications. Perhaps most significant from a religious standpoint, Copernicus destroyed the basic idea

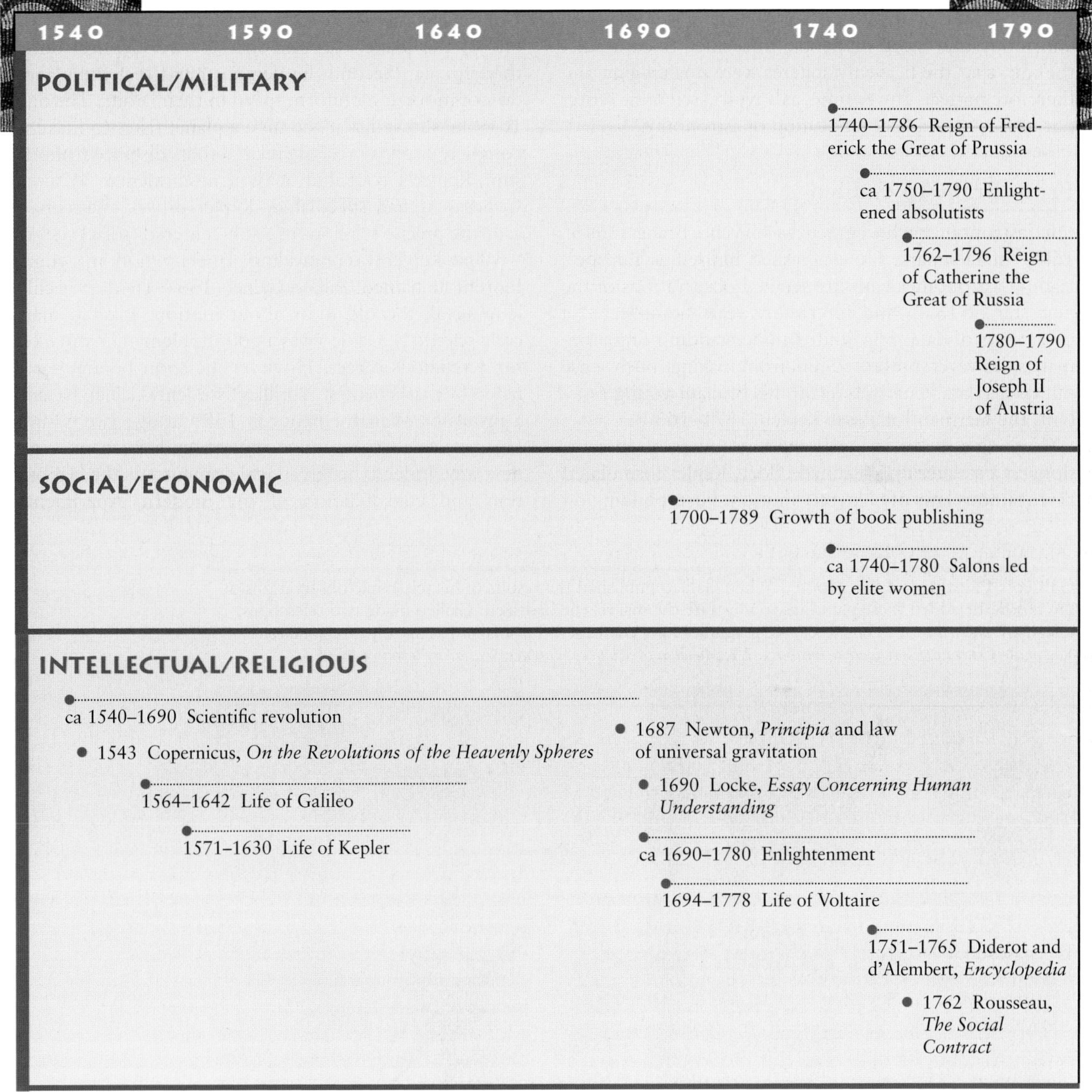


of Aristotelian physics—the idea that the earthly world was quite different from the heavenly one. Where were Heaven and the throne of God?

The Copernican theory quickly brought sharp attacks from religious leaders, especially Protestants. Hearing of Copernicus's work even before it was published, Martin Luther spoke of him as the "new astrologer who wants to prove that the earth moves and goes round. . . . The fool wants to turn the whole art of astronomy upside down." Luther noted that "as the Holy Scripture tells us, so did Joshua bid the sun stand still and not the earth."[2] Catholic reaction was milder at first, but in 1616 the church officially declared the Copernican theory false.

Astronomical phenomena also cast doubts on traditional astronomical ideas. In 1572 a new star appeared and shone very brightly for almost two years. The new star, which was actually a distant exploding star, made an enormous impression on people. It seemed to contradict the idea that the heavenly spheres were unchanging and therefore perfect. It was time, as a typical scientific writer put it, for "the radical renovation of astronomy."[3]

## From Brahe to Galileo

One astronomer who agreed was Tycho Brahe (1546–1601) of Denmark. He established himself as Europe's leading astronomer with his detailed observations of the new star of 1572, and for twenty years he collected a great mass of data. His limited understanding of mathematics, however, prevented him from making much sense out of his data. That was left to his brilliant young assistant, the German Johannes Kepler (1571–1630).

Working and reworking Brahe's mountain of observations in a staggering sustained effort, Kepler formulated three famous laws of planetary motion. First, building on Copernican theory, he demonstrated in 1609 that the orbits of the planets around the sun are elliptical rather than circular. Second, he demonstrated that the planets do not move at a uniform speed in their orbits. Third, in 1619 he showed that the time a planet takes to make its complete orbit is precisely related to its distance from the sun. Kepler's contribution was monumental. Whereas Copernicus had speculated, Kepler proved mathematically the precise relations of a sun-centered (solar) system.

While Kepler was unraveling planetary motion, a young Florentine named Galileo Galilei (1564–1642) was challenging all the old ideas about motion. Like so many early scientists, Galileo was a poor nobleman first marked for a religious career. However, he soon became fascinated by mathematics. A brilliant student, Galileo became a professor of mathematics in 1589 at age twenty-five. He proceeded to examine motion and mechanics in a new way. Indeed, his great achievement was the elaboration and consolidation of the modern experimental

**Galileo's Paintings of the Moon** When Galileo published the results of his telescopic observations of the moon, he added these paintings to illustrate the marvels he had seen. Galileo made two telescopes, which are shown here. The larger one magnifies fourteen times, the smaller twenty times. *(Biblioteca Nazionale Centrale, Florence/Art Resource, NY; Museum of Science, Florence/Scala/Art Resource, NY)*

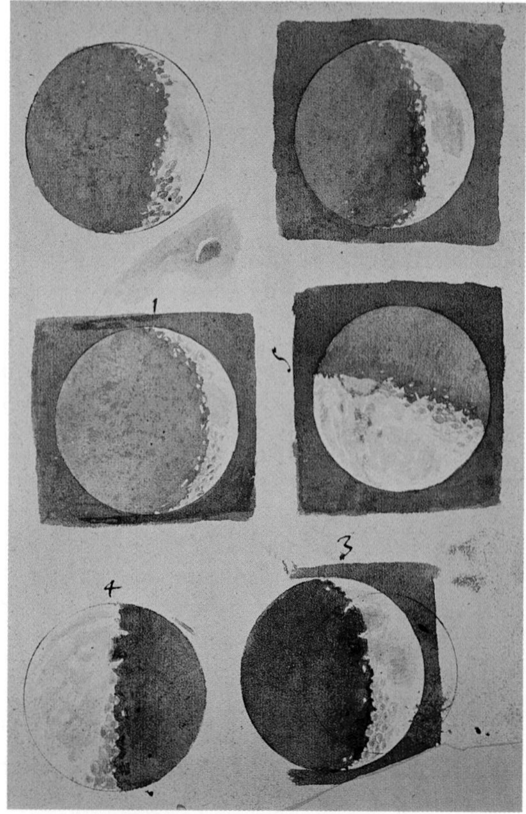


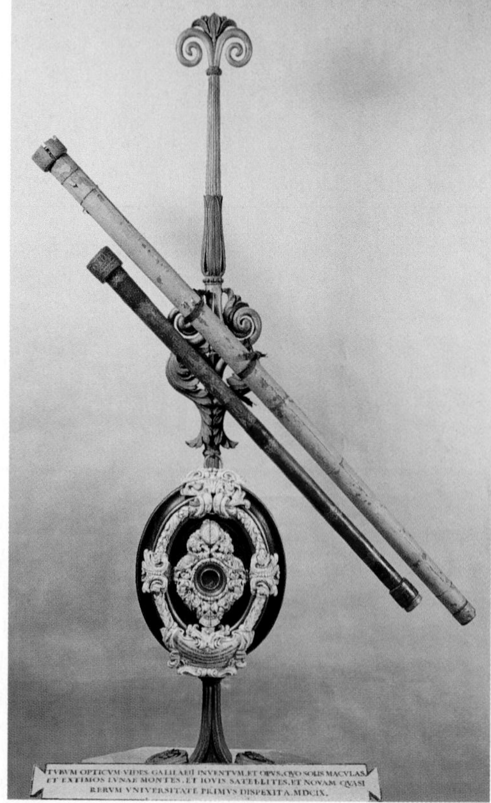

method: rather than speculate about what might or should happen, Galileo conducted controlled experiments to find out what actually *did* happen.

In his famous acceleration experiment, by rolling brass balls down an inclined plane, he showed that a uniform force—in this case, gravity—produces a uniform acceleration. With this and other experiments, Galileo went on to formulate the **law of inertia:** rather than rest being the natural state of objects, an object continues in motion forever unless stopped by some external force. Aristotelian physics was in a shambles.

On hearing details about the invention of the telescope in Holland, Galileo made one for himself and soon trained it on the moon. He wrote in 1610 in *Siderus Nuncius:*

*I feel sure that the moon is not perfectly smooth, free from inequalities, and exactly spherical, as a large school of philosophers considers with regard to the moon and the other heavenly bodies. On the contrary, it is full of inequalities, uneven, full of hollows and protuberances, just like the surface of the earth itself. . . . The next object which I have observed is the essence or substance of the Milky Way. By the aid of a telescope anyone may behold this in a manner which so distinctly appeals to the senses that all the disputes which have tormented philosophers through so many ages are exploded by the irrefutable evidence of our eyes. . . . For the galaxy is nothing else but a mass of innumerable stars planted together in clusters.*[4]

Reading these famous lines, one feels a crucial corner in Western civilization being turned. The traditional religious and theological world-view, which rested on identifying and accepting the proper established authority, was beginning to give way in certain fields to a critical, scientific method. This new method of learning and investigating was the greatest accomplishment of the entire scientific revolution, for it proved capable of great extension.

Openly lampooning the traditional views of Aristotle and Ptolemy and defending those of Copernicus, Galileo was tried for heresy by the papal Inquisition in 1633. Imprisoned and threatened with torture, the aging Galileo recanted, "renouncing and cursing" his Copernican errors. Galileo's trial later became for some writers the perfect symbol of the inherent conflict between religious belief and scientific knowledge.

## Newton's Synthesis

The accomplishments of Kepler, Galileo, and other scientists had taken effect by about 1640. The old astronomy and physics were in ruins, and several fundamental breakthroughs had been made. The fusion of the new findings in a new synthesis, a single explanatory system that would comprehend motion both on earth and in the skies, was the work of Isaac Newton (1642–1727).

Newton was born into lower English gentry and attended Cambridge University. Fascinated by alchemy, Newton was also intensely religious. He was far from being the perfect rationalist so endlessly eulogized by later writers.

Of his intellectual genius there can be no doubt, however. Arriving at some of his most basic ideas about physics in 1666 at age twenty-four, but unable to prove these theories mathematically, he attained a professorship and studied optics for many years. In 1684 Newton returned to physics for eighteen extraordinarily successful months. In his immortal *Principia,* published in Latin in 1687, he proposed to lay down "the laws of certain motions, and powers or forces" and "demonstrate the frame of the System of the World."

Newton made good his grandiose plan. He integrated the astronomy of Copernicus, as corrected by Kepler's laws, with the physics of Galileo and his predecessors. Newton did this by means of a set of mathematical laws that explain motion and mechanics. These laws of dynamics are complex, and it took scientists and engineers two hundred years to work out all their implications. The key feature of the Newtonian synthesis was the **law of universal gravitation.** According to this law, every body in the universe attracts every other body in the universe in a precise mathematical relationship, based on mass and distance. The whole universe—from Kepler's elliptical orbits to Galileo's rolling balls—was unified in one majestic system.

## Causes of the Scientific Revolution

With a charming combination of modesty and self-congratulation, Newton once wrote, "If I have seen further [than others], it is by standing on the shoulders of Giants."[5] Surely the path from Copernicus to Newton confirms the "internal" view of the scientific revolution as the product of towering individual genius. Yet there were certainly broader causes as well.

First, the long-term contribution of medieval intellectual life and medieval universities to the scientific revolution was considerable. By 1300 philosophy had taken its place in universities alongside law, medicine, and theology. Medieval philosophers developed a limited but real independence from theologians and a sense of free inquiry. They nobly pursued a body of knowledge and tried to arrange it meaningfully by means of abstract theories.

**Descartes in Sweden** Queen Christina of Sweden encouraged art and science, and she invited many foreign artists and scholars to visit her court. She speaks here with French mathematician and philosopher René Descartes in 1649. The daughter of Protestant hero Gustavus Adolphus, Christina rejected marriage, abdicated in 1654, converted to Catholicism, and died in Rome. *(Réunion des Musées Nationaux/Art Resource, NY)*

Within this framework science was able to emerge as a minor but distinct branch of philosophy, as leading universities established new professorships of mathematics, astronomy, and physics (natural philosophy) within their faculties of philosophy. An outlet existed for the talents of a Galileo or a Newton: all the great pathfinders either studied or taught at universities.

Second, the Renaissance also stimulated scientific progress. The recovery of the finest works of Greek mathematics—a byproduct of Renaissance humanism's ceaseless search for the knowledge of antiquity—greatly improved European mathematics well into the early seventeenth century. In the Renaissance pattern of patronage, especially in Italy, various rulers and wealthy business people supported scientific investigations, as the Medicis of Florence did those of Galileo.

The navigational problems of long sea voyages in the age of overseas expansion were a third factor in the scientific revolution. As early as 1484 the king of Portugal appointed a commission of mathematicians to perfect tables to help seamen find their latitude. This resulted in the first European navigation manual. The problem of fixing longitude was much more difficult, but a union of leading merchants and top scientists, who were sponsored by the English government through the Royal Navy, was able to solve it. This collaborative effort led to the establishment in 1662 of the Royal Society of London, which published scientific papers and sponsored scientific meetings.

Navigational problems were also critical in the development of many new scientific instruments, such as the telescope, barometer, thermometer, pendulum clock, microscope, and air pump. Better instruments, which permitted more accurate observations, were part of a fourth factor in the scientific revolution, the development of better ways of obtaining knowledge about the world. Two important thinkers, Francis Bacon (1561–1626) and René Descartes (1596–1650), represented key aspects of this improvement in scientific methodology.

The English politician, writer, and courtier Francis Bacon was the greatest early propagandist for the new experimental method. He argued that new knowledge had to be pursued through empirical, experimental research. A researcher who wants to learn more about rocks should not speculate but collect a multitude of specimens and compare and analyze them, he said. General principles will then emerge. Bacon formalized Brahe's and Galileo's empirical method into the general theory of inductive reasoning known as **empiricism.** He claimed that the empirical method would produce highly practical, useful knowledge, giving a new and effective justification for the pursuit of science.

French philosopher René Descartes began as a mathematician and remained more systematic and mathematical than Bacon. Descartes decided it was necessary to doubt everything that could reasonably be doubted and then, as in geometry, use deductive reasoning from self-evident principles to ascertain scientific laws. Bacon's inductive experimentalism and Descartes's deductive, mathematical rationalism are combined in the modern scientific method, which began to crystallize in the late seventeenth century and which relies on both these intellectual approaches.

Finally, there is the question of the role of religion in the development of science. Just as some historians have argued that Protestantism led to the rise of capitalism, others have concluded that Protestantism, by supposedly making scientific inquiry a question of individual conscience and not of religious doctrine, was a fundamental factor in the rise of modern science. However, all religious authorities in the West—Catholic, Protestant, and Jewish—opposed the Copernican system to a greater or lesser extent until about 1630, by which time the scientific revolution was definitely in progress. The Catholic church was initially less hostile than Protestant and Jewish religious leaders, and Italian scientists played a crucial role in scientific progress right up to the trial of Galileo in 1633. Thereafter, the Counter-Reformation church became more hostile to science in Italy (but not in Catholic France). At the same time, some Protestant countries became quite proscience, especially if the country lacked a strong religious authority capable of imposing religious orthodoxy on scientific questions, as did Protestant England after 1630. Neutral and useful, science became an accepted part of life and developed rapidly in England after about 1640.

### Some Consequences of the Scientific Revolution

The rise of modern science had many consequences, some of which are still unfolding. First, it went hand in hand with the rise of a new and expanding social group—the international scientific community. Members of this community were linked together by common interests and shared values as well as by journals and the learned scientific societies founded in many countries in the later seventeenth and eighteenth centuries. Expansion of knowledge was the primary goal of this community, and scientists' material and psychological rewards depended on their success in this endeavor. Thus science became quite competitive, and even more scientific advance was inevitable.

Second, the revolutionary modern scientific method, in addition to being both theoretical and experimental, was highly critical, and it differed profoundly from the old way of getting knowledge about nature. It refused to base its conclusions on tradition and established sources, on ancient authorities and sacred texts.

The scientific revolution had few consequences for economic life and the living standards of the masses until the late eighteenth century at the very earliest. True, improvements in the techniques of navigation facilitated overseas trade and helped enrich leading merchants, but science had relatively few practical economic applications. The close link between theoretical, or pure, science and applied technology, which we take for granted today, simply did not exist before the nineteenth century. Thus the scientific revolution of the seventeenth century was first and foremost an intellectual revolution. For more than a hundred years its greatest impact was on how people thought and believed.

## THE ENLIGHTENMENT

The scientific revolution was the single most important factor in the creation of the new world-view of the eighteenth-century **Enlightenment.** This world-view, which played a large role in shaping the modern mind, grew out of a rich mix of ideas. These ideas were diverse and often conflicting, for the talented (and not-so-talented) writers who espoused them competed vigorously for the attention of a growing public of well-educated but fickle readers, who remained a small minority of the population. Despite this diversity, three central concepts stand at the core of Enlightenment thinking.

The most important and original idea of the Enlightenment was that the methods of natural science could and should be used to examine and understand all aspects of life. This was what intellectuals meant by *reason,* a favorite word of Enlightenment thinkers. Nothing was to be accepted on faith. Everything was to be submitted to the rational, critical, scientific way of thinking. This approach often brought the Enlightenment into a head-on conflict with established churches, which rested their beliefs on the special authority of the Bible and Christian theology. A second important Enlightenment concept was that the scientific method was capable of discovering the laws of human society as well as those of nature. Thus was social science born. Its birth led to the third key idea, that of **progress.** Armed with the proper method of discovering the laws of human existence, Enlightenment thinkers believed it was at least possible for human beings to create better societies and better people. Their belief was strengthened by some modest improvements in economic and social life during the eighteenth century.

The Enlightenment was therefore thoroughly secular. It revived and expanded the Renaissance concentration on worldly explanations. In the course of the eighteenth century the Enlightenment had a profound impact on the thought and culture of the urban middle classes and the aristocracy. It did not, however, have much appeal for the urban poor and the peasants, who were preoccupied with the struggle for survival and who often resented the Enlightenment attack on traditional popular beliefs.

### The Emergence of the Enlightenment

Loosely united by certain key ideas, the European Enlightenment was a broad intellectual and cultural movement that gained strength gradually and did not reach its maturity until about 1750. Yet it was the generation that came of age between the publication of Newton's *Principia* in 1687 and the death of Louis XIV in 1715 that tied the crucial knot between the scientific revolution and a new outlook on life. Talented writers of that generation popularized hard-to-understand scientific achievements for the educated elite.

The most famous and influential popularizer was a versatile French man of letters, Bernard de Fontenelle (1657–1757). He set out to make science witty and entertaining for a broad nonscientific audience—as easy to read as a novel. This was a tall order, but Fontenelle largely succeeded. His most famous work, *Conversations on the Plurality of Worlds* (1686), begins with two elegant figures walking in the gathering shadows of a large park. One is a woman, a sophisticated aristocrat, and the other is her friend, perhaps even her lover. They gaze at the stars, and their talk turns to a passionate discussion of . . . astronomy! He confides that "each star may well be a different world," then gently stresses how error is giving way to truth. At one point he explains:

> *There came on the scene . . . one Copernicus, who made short work of all those various circles, all those solid skies, which the ancients had pictured to themselves. . . . Fired with the noble zeal of a true astronomer, he took the earth and spun it very far away from the center of the universe, where it had been installed, and in that center he put the sun, which had a far better title to the honor.*[6]

**Popularizing Science** The frontispiece illustration of Fontenelle's *Conversations on the Plurality of Worlds* invites the reader to share the pleasures of astronomy with an elegant lady and an entertaining teacher. The drawing shows the planets revolving around the sun. *(By permission of the Syndics of Cambridge University Library)*

Rather than despair at this dismissal of traditional understanding, Fontenelle's lady rejoices in the knowledge that the human mind is capable of making great progress. The concept of progress was a late-seventeenth-century creation. Unlike their medieval and Renaissance predecessors, Fontenelle and like-minded writers had come to believe that progress was very possible.

Fontenelle and other writers of his generation were instrumental in bringing science into conflict with religion. Many seventeenth-century scientists, both Catholic and Protestant, believed that their work exalted God. Fontenelle, in contrast, was skeptical about absolute truth and cynical about the claims of organized religion. His antireligious ideas, drawn from the scientific revolution, reflected a crisis in European thought that had its roots in several intellectual uncertainties. The nature of religious truth was one such uncertainty, highlighted by the destructive wars of religion fought in early-seventeenth-century Europe. Both Catholics and Protestants had believed that religious truth was absolute and that a strong state required unity of religious faith. Yet the disastrous results of the many attempts to impose such religious unity led some to ask if it was really necessary and others to doubt that religious truth could ever be known with absolute certainty.

The most famous of these **skeptics** was Pierre Bayle (1647–1706), a French Huguenot refugee who despised Louis XIV. Bayle concluded that nothing can ever be known beyond all doubt and that in religion, as in philosophy, humanity's best hope is open-minded toleration. Bayle's skeptical views were very influential.

The rapidly growing travel literature on non-European lands and cultures was another cause of uncertainty. Europeans were learning that the peoples of China, India, Africa, and the Americas all had their own very different beliefs and customs. Europeans shaved their faces and let their hair grow. Turks shaved their heads and let their beards grow. In Europe a man bowed before a woman to show respect. In Siam a man turned his back on a woman when he met her because it was disrespectful to look directly at her. Countless similar examples discussed in the travel accounts helped change the perspective of educated Europeans. They began to look at truth and morality in relative, rather than absolute, terms. If anything was possible, who could say what was right or wrong?

A third cause and manifestation of European intellectual turmoil was John Locke's epoch-making *Essay Concerning Human Understanding.* Published in 1690—the same year Locke published his *Second Treatise of Civil Government* (see page 561)—Locke's essay brilliantly set forth a new theory about how human beings learn and form their ideas. In doing so, he rejected the prevailing view of Descartes, who had held that all people are born with certain basic ideas and ways of thinking. Locke insisted that all ideas are derived from experience. The human mind at birth is like a blank tablet, or **tabula rasa,** on which the environment writes the individual's understanding and beliefs. Human development is therefore determined by education and social institutions, for good or for evil. Locke's *Essay* was, along with Newton's *Principia,* one of the dominant intellectual inspirations of the Enlightenment.

## The Philosophes and the Public

By the time Louis XIV died in 1715, many of the ideas that would soon coalesce into the new world-view had been assembled. Yet Christian Europe was still strongly attached to its traditional beliefs, and there was a powerful revival of religious orthodoxy in the first half of the eighteenth century. By the outbreak of the American Revolution in 1775, however, a substantial portion of western Europe's educated elite had embraced many of the new ideas. This acceptance was the work of one of history's most influential groups of intellectuals, the **philosophes.** It was the philosophes who proudly and effectively proclaimed that they, at long last, were bringing the light of knowledge to their ignorant fellow creatures in an Age of Enlightenment.

*Philosophe* is the French word for "philosopher," and it was in France that the Enlightenment reached its highest development. The French philosophes were indeed philosophers, asking fundamental philosophical questions about the meaning of life, God, human nature, good and evil, and cause and effect. Not content with abstract arguments or ivory-tower speculations, they were determined to reach and influence all the economic and social elites, whom they perceived as the educated or enlightened public, or simply **the public.**

As a wealth of recent scholarship has shown, this public was quite different from the great majority of the population, which was known as the common people, or simply *the people.* French philosophe Jean le Rond d'Alembert (1717–1783) characteristically made a sharp distinction between "the truly enlightened public" and "the blind and noisy multitude."[7] The philosophes believed that the great majority of the common people were doomed to superstition and confusion because they lacked the money and leisure to look beyond their bitter struggle with grinding poverty.

The great philosophes and their imitators were not free to write as they wished, for it was illegal in France to criticize openly either church or state. Their most radical works had to circulate in manuscript form. Knowing that direct attacks would probably be banned or burned, the philosophes wrote novels and plays, histories and philosophies, dictionaries and encyclopedias, all filled with satire and double meanings to spread their message to the public.

One of the greatest philosophes, the baron de Montesquieu (1689–1755), brilliantly pioneered this approach in *The Persian Letters,* an extremely influential social satire published in 1721. Montesquieu's work consisted of amusing letters supposedly written by Persian travelers, who see European customs in unique ways and thereby cleverly criticize existing practices and beliefs. Having gained fame by using wit as a weapon against cruelty and superstition, Montesquieu settled down on his family estate to study history and politics. Inspired by the example of the physical sciences, he set out to apply the critical method to the problem of government in *The Spirit of Laws* (1748). The result was a complex comparative study of republics, monarchies, and despotisms.

**Madame du Châtelet** Fascinated by the new world system of Isaac Newton, Madame du Châtelet helped to spread Newton's ideas in France by translating his *Principia* and by influencing Voltaire, her companion for fifteen years until her death. *(Giraudon/Art Resource, NY)*

Dismayed by the triumph of royal absolutism under Louis XIV, Montesquieu focused on the conditions that would promote liberty and prevent tyranny. He argued that despotism could be avoided if political power was divided and shared by a variety of classes and legal orders holding unequal rights and privileges. Apprehensive about the uneducated poor, Montesquieu was clearly no democrat, but his theory of separation of powers had a great impact on France's wealthy, well-educated elite. The constitutions of the young United States in 1789 and of France in 1791 were based in large part on this theory.

The most famous and in many ways most representative philosophe was François Marie Arouet, who was known by the pen name Voltaire (1694–1778). The early career of this son of a comfortable middle-class family was turbulent. In 1717 Voltaire was imprisoned for eleven months in the Bastille in Paris for insulting the regent of France. In 1726 a barb from his sharp tongue led a great French nobleman to have him beaten and arrested. This experience made a deep impression on Voltaire. All his life he struggled against legal injustice and unequal treatment before the law.

After being exiled to England for three years and then returning to France, Voltaire had the great fortune of meeting Gabrielle-Emilie Le Tonnelier de Breteuil, marquise du Châtelet (1706–1749), an intellectually gifted woman from the high aristocracy with a passion for science. Inviting Voltaire to live in her country house at Cirey in Lorraine, Madame du Châtelet studied physics and mathematics and published scientific articles and translations.

Perhaps the finest representative of a small number of elite French women and their scientific accomplishments during the Enlightenment, Madame du Châtelet suffered nonetheless because of her gender. Excluded on principle from the Royal Academy of Sciences and depending on private tutors for instruction, she became uncertain of her ability to do research. Madame du Châtelet therefore concentrated on spreading the ideas of others, and her translation of Newton's *Principia* into French was her greatest work. But she had no doubt that women's limited scientific contributions in the past were due to limited and unequal education. If she were a ruler, Madame du Châtelet wrote, she "would make women participate in all the rights of humankind, and above all in those of the intellect."[8]

While living at Cirey, Voltaire wrote various works praising England and popularizing English scientific progress. Typical of the Enlightenment, Voltaire mixed the glorification of science and reason with an appeal for better individuals and institutions. Yet like almost all of the philosophes, Voltaire was a reformer, not a revolutionary, in social and political matters.

Unlike Montesquieu, Voltaire pessimistically concluded that the best one could hope for in the way of government was a good monarch since human beings "are very rarely worthy to govern themselves." Nor did he believe in social and economic equality in human affairs, which he considered "absurd and impossible." The only realizable equality, Voltaire thought, was that "by which the citizen only depends on the laws which protect the freedom of the feeble against the ambitions of the strong."[9]

Voltaire's philosophical and religious positions were much more radical. In the tradition of Bayle, Voltaire's voluminous writings challenged, often indirectly, the Catholic church and Christian theology at almost every point. Though he was considered by many devout Christians to be a shallow blasphemer, Voltaire's religious views were influential and quite typical of the mature Enlightenment. Voltaire clearly believed in a God, but his was a distant, deistic God, a great Clockmaker who built an orderly universe and then stepped aside and let it run. Above all, Voltaire and most of the philosophes hated all forms of religious intolerance, which, they believed, often led to fanaticism and savage, inhuman action. Simple piety and human kindness—as embodied in Christ's great commandments to "love God and your neighbor as yourself"—were religion enough, even Christianity enough.

The philosophes' greatest and most representative intellectual achievement was, quite fittingly, a group effort—the seventeen-volume *Encyclopedia: The Rational Dictionary of the Sciences, the Arts, and the Crafts,* edited by Denis Diderot (1713–1784) and Jean le Rond d'Alembert. Diderot and d'Alembert set out to teach people how to think critically and objectively about all matters. As Diderot said, he wanted the *Encyclopedia* to "change the general way of thinking."[10]

**Illustrating the *Encyclopedia:* "The Print Shop"** Diderot wanted to present all valid knowledge—that is, knowledge based on reason and the senses and not on tradition and authority. This plate, one of 3,000 detailed illustrations accompanying the 70,000 essays in the *Encyclopedia,* shows (*from left to right*) compositors setting type, arranging lines, and blocking down completed forms. Printed sheets dry above. *(Division of Rare & Manuscript Collections, Cornell University Library)*

The editors of the *Encyclopedia* had to conquer innumerable obstacles. After the appearance in 1751 of the first volume, which dealt with such controversial subjects as atheism, the soul, and blind people, the government temporarily banned publication. The work was placed on the Catholic church's index of banned books. Later the timid publisher watered down some of the articles in the last ten volumes without the editors' consent. Yet Diderot's unwavering belief in the importance of his mission held the encyclopedists together for fifteen years, and the enormous work was completed in 1765. Hundreds of thousands of articles by leading scientists, famous writers, skilled workers, and progressive priests treated every aspect of life and knowledge.

Not every article was daring or original, but the overall effect was little short of revolutionary. Science and the industrial arts were exalted, religion and immortality questioned. Intolerance, legal injustice, and out-of-date social institutions were openly criticized. The encyclopedists were convinced that greater knowledge would result in greater human happiness, for knowledge was useful and made possible economic, social, and political progress. The *Encyclopedia,* widely read and extremely influential throughout western Europe, summed up the new world-view of the Enlightenment.

## The Later Enlightenment

After about 1770 the harmonious unity of the philosophers and their thought began to break down. As the new world-view became increasingly accepted by the educated public, some thinkers sought originality by exaggerating certain Enlightenment ideas to the exclusion of others. These latter-day philosophes often built rigid, dogmatic systems.

In his *System of Nature* (1770) the wealthy German-born but French-educated Baron Paul d'Holbach (1723–1789) argued that human beings were machines completely determined by outside forces. Free will, God, and immortality of the soul, he claimed, were foolish myths. D'Holbach's atheism and determinism dealt the unity of the Enlightenment movement a severe blow.

One of d'Holbach's associates whose carefully argued skepticism had a powerful long-term influence was the Scottish philosopher David Hume (1711–1776). Building on Locke's teachings on learning, Hume argued that the human mind is only a bundle of impressions. These impressions originate only in sense experiences and our habits of joining these experiences together. Reason, therefore, cannot tell us anything about questions that cannot be verified by sense experience (in the form of controlled experiments or mathematics), such as the origin of the universe or the existence of God. Paradoxically, Hume's rationalistic inquiry ended up undermining the Enlightenment's faith in the power of reason.

Other thinkers and writers after about 1770 began to attack the Enlightenment's faith in reason, progress, and moderation. The most famous of these was the Swiss Jean-Jacques Rousseau (1712–1778), a brilliant but difficult thinker, an appealing but neurotic individual. Born into a poor family of watchmakers in Geneva, Rousseau went to Paris and was greatly influenced by Diderot and Voltaire. Always extraordinarily sensitive and suspicious, Rousseau came to believe that his philosophe friends and the women of the Parisian salons were plotting against him. In the mid-1750s he broke with them personally and intellectually, living thereafter as a lonely outsider with his uneducated common-law wife and going in his own highly original direction.

Like other Enlightenment thinkers, Rousseau was passionately committed to individual freedom. Unlike them, however, he attacked rationalism and civilization as destroying, rather than liberating, the individual. Warm, spontaneous feeling had to complement and correct cold intellect, he believed. Moreover, the basic goodness of the individual and the unspoiled child had to be protected from the cruel refinements of civilization. These ideas greatly influenced the early romantic movement (see Chapter 24), which rebelled against the culture of the Enlightenment. Rousseau's ideas also had a powerful impact on the development of child psychology and modern education. (See the feature "Listening to the Past: Gender Constructions and Education for Girls" on pages 594–595.)

Rousseau's contribution to political theory in *The Social Contract* (1762) was equally significant. It was based on two fundamental concepts: the general will and popular sovereignty. According to Rousseau, the general will is sacred and absolute, reflecting the common interests of all the people, who have displaced the monarch as the holder of sovereign power. The general will is not necessarily the will of the majority, however. At times the general will may be the authentic, long-term needs of the people as correctly interpreted by a farseeing minority. Little noticed before the French Revolution, Rousseau's concept of the general will appealed greatly to democrats and nationalists after 1789. The concept has also been used since 1789 by many dictators claiming that they, rather than some momentary majority of the voters, represent the general will and thus the true interests of democracy and the sovereign masses.

## Urban Culture and Public Opinion

The writings and press campaigns of the philosophes were part of a profound cultural transformation. The object of impressive ongoing research and scholarly debate in recent years, this transformation had several interrelated aspects.

Of great importance, the European market for books grew dramatically in the eighteenth century. In Germany the number of new titles appearing annually grew fourfold from 1700 to 1780. France witnessed an explosive growth in book consumption. While a modest increase in literacy among the popular classes had some impact, the solid and upper middle classes, the clergy, and the aristocracy accounted for most of the change in book ownership. Moreover, the number of religious and devotional books published legally in Paris declined precipitously, while the proportion of legally published books treating the arts and sciences surged.

In addition, France's unpredictable but pervasive censorship caused many books to be printed abroad and then smuggled back into the country for "under-the-cloak" sale. Experts believe that perhaps the majority of French books produced between 1750 and 1789 came from publishing companies located outside France. These publishers also smuggled forbidden books in French and other languages into the absolutist states of central, southern, and eastern Europe. The recently discovered catalogues of some of these foreign publishers reveal a massive presence of the famous French philosophes, reaffirming the philosophes' central role in the spread of critical secular attitudes.

Reading more books on many more subjects, the educated public in France and throughout Europe increasingly approached reading in a new way. The result was what some German scholars have called a "reading revolution." The old style of reading in Europe had been centered on sacred texts read aloud slowly with the audience reverently savoring each word. Now reading involved many texts, which were constantly changing and commanded no special respect. Reading became individual, silent, and rapid. The well-educated classes were reading insatiably, skeptically, and carelessly. Subtle but profound, the reading revolution was closely linked to the rise of a critical world-view.

As the reading public developed, it joined forces with the philosophes to call for the autonomy of the printed word. Outside Prussia, the Netherlands, and Great Britain, however, censorship was the rule. And the philosophes and the public resorted to discussion and social interchange in order to circumvent censorship and create an autonomous cultural sphere. Indeed, sparkling conversation in private homes spread Enlightenment ideas to Europe's upper middle class and aristocracy. Paris set the

**Selling Books, Promoting Ideas** This appealing bookshop with its intriguing ads for the latest works offers to put customers "Under the Protection of Minerva," the Roman goddess of wisdom. Large packets of books sit ready for shipment to foreign countries. Book consumption surged in the eighteenth century. *(Musée des Beaux-Arts, Dijon/Art Resource, NY)*

example, and other French and European cities followed. In Paris a number of talented and often rich women presided over regular social gatherings in their elegant drawing rooms, or **salons.** There they encouraged the exchange of witty, uncensored observations on literature, science, and philosophy.

Elite women also exercised an unprecedented feminine influence on artistic taste. Soft pastels, ornate interiors, sentimental portraits, and starry-eyed lovers protected by hovering Cupids were all hallmarks of the style they favored. This style, known as the rococo, was popular throughout Europe in the eighteenth century. Some philosophes championed greater rights and expanded education for women, claiming that the position and treatment of women were the best indicators of a society's level of civilization and decency.[11] To be sure, to these male philosophes greater rights for women did not mean equal rights, and the philosophes were not particularly disturbed by the fact that elite women remained legally subordinate to men in economic and political affairs. Elite women lacked many rights, but so did most men.

The salons created an independent cultural realm free from religious dogma and political censorship. There educated members of the intellectual, economic, and social elites could debate issues and form their own ideas, their own *public opinion.* In this gracious atmosphere the public of philosophes, the French nobility, and the prosperous middle classes intermingled and increasingly influenced one another. Critical thinking about almost any question became fashionable and flourished with hopes for human progress through greater knowledge and enlightened public opinion.

## The Enlightenment and the Common People

In recent years historians have delved into the collective attitudes of the common people—the peasants and urban workers—and compared them with those of the upper and middle classes in the Enlightenment. These studies have often focused on popular reading habits and recreation, and they have produced important insights.

A remarkable growth in basic literacy between 1600 and 1800, especially after 1700, certainly promoted an increase in popular reading. Yet it seems clear that the major philosophical works of the Enlightenment had little impact on peasants and workers, who could neither afford nor understand them.

Although the Bible remained the overwhelming favorite, especially in Protestant countries, the staple of popular literature was short pamphlets known as chapbooks. Many chapbooks dealt with Bible stories, prayers, devo-

**A Peasant Family Reading the Bible** Praised by the philosophe Diderot for its moralistic message, this engraving of a painting by Jean-Baptiste Greuze (1725–1805) does capture the power of sacred texts and the spoken word. The peasant patriarch reads aloud from the massive family Bible and the close-knit circle of absorbed listeners concentrates on every word. Only the baby is distracted. *(Bibliothèque nationale de France/Giraudon/Art Resource, NY)*

tions, and the lives of saints. Promising happiness after death, devotional literature gave the believer moral teachings and a confidence in God that helped in daily living.

Entertaining stories formed a second element of popular literature. Fairy tales, medieval romances, fictionalized history, and fantastic adventures were favorites. Some popular literature was highly practical, dealing with rural crafts, household repairs, useful plants, and similar matters. Much of such lore was stored in almanacs, which were highly appreciated. In short, the reading of the common people was simple, practical, and escapist.

These characteristics fit well with the modest educational objectives of rulers and educated elites. They believed that limited instruction stressing religion and practical problems was useful to the masses but that too much study would only disorient them and foster discontent.

Improved training for midwives was one example. Initially, the typical midwife was an older, often widowed woman of modest social origins who was trained by another woman practitioner. The midwife orchestrated labor and birth in a woman's world, where friends and relatives offered the pregnant woman assistance in her own home. During the eighteenth century, however, male surgeon-physicians began to attack midwives as ignorant and dangerous, and they persuaded some wealthy women of the superiority of their services. Yet women practitioners successfully defended most of their practice, in part because they received better training. In France, for example, one enterprising Parisian midwife secured royal financing for her campaign to teach better birthing techniques to village midwives, which reinforced the position of women practitioners. (See the feature "Individuals in Society: Madame du Coudray, the Nation's Midwife.")

Though the critical spirit of the Enlightenment spread among the educated elite in the eighteenth century, the majority of ordinary men and women remained firmly committed to the Christian religion, especially in rural areas. Religious faith promised salvation and eternal life, and it was usually embedded in local traditions, everyday social experience, and recreation.

The usual pattern of leisure and recreation featured socializing in groups. Women would gather together in someone's cottage to chat, sew, spin, and laugh. Men loved to drink and talk with buddies in public places.

Towns and cities offered a wide range of amusements, which attracted a variety of social classes. Old-fashioned **blood sports,** such as bullbaiting and cockfighting, remained popular with the masses. In bullbaiting, for example, the bull, usually staked on a chain in the courtyard of an inn, was attacked by ferocious dogs for the amusement of the innkeeper's clients.

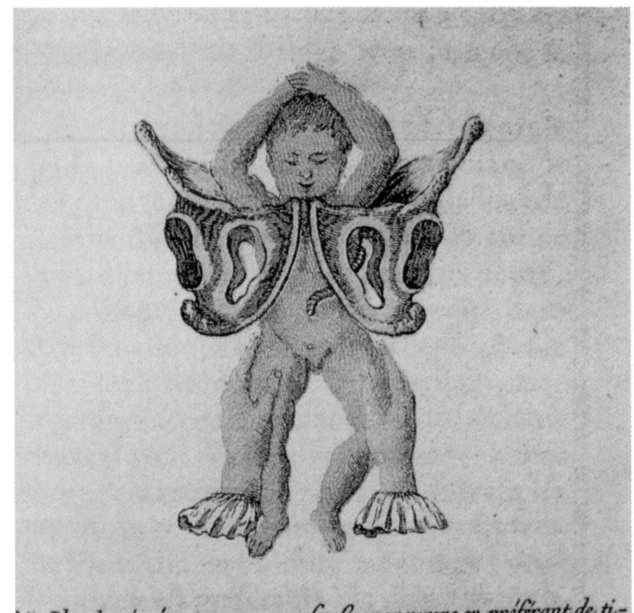


**Teaching Midwives** This plate from Madame du Coudray's text for midwives, *Manual on the Art of Childbirth,* illustrates "another incorrect method of delivery." The caption tells the midwife that she should have rotated the baby within the womb to face the mother's back, so that the chin does not catch on the pubis bone and dislocate the jaw. *(Rare Books Division, Countway [Francis A.] Library of Medicine)*

Generally, as the educated elites embraced the critical world-view of the Enlightenment, they levied a growing criticism against the popular culture. These elites had previously shared the popular enthusiasm for religious festivals, drinking in taverns, blood sports, and the like, but now they tended to see only superstition, sin, disorder, and vulgarity.[12] This shift in cultural attitudes drove a wedge between the common people and the educated public, and it played an important role in the emergence of sharp class conflict in the era of the French and Industrial Revolutions.

**Cockfighting in England** This engraving by William Hogarth (1697–1764) satirizes the popular taste for blood sports, which Hogarth despised and lampooned in his famous *Four Stages of Cruelty*. The central figure in the wildly excited gathering is a blind nobleman, who actually existed and seldom missed a fight. Note the steel spurs on the birds' legs. *(Courtesy of Trustees of the British Museum)*

## THE ENLIGHTENMENT AND ABSOLUTISM

How did the Enlightenment influence political developments? To this important question there is no easy answer. On the one hand, the French philosophes and kindred spirits in most European countries were primarily interested in converting people to critical, scientific thinking and were not particularly concerned with politics. On the other hand, such thinking naturally led to political criticism and interest in political reform as both possible and desirable.

Some Enlightenment thinkers, led by the nobleman Montesquieu, argued for curbs on monarchical power in order to promote liberty. Until the American Revolution, however, most Enlightenment thinkers outside England and the Netherlands believed that political change could best come from above—from the ruler—rather than from below, especially in central and eastern Europe. Royal absolutism was a fact of life, and the kings and queens of Europe's leading states clearly had no intention of giving up their great power. Therefore, the philosophes and their sympathizers realistically concluded that a benevolent absolutism offered the best opportunities for improving society. Critical thinking was turning the art of good government into an exact science. It was necessary only to educate and "enlighten" the monarch, who could then make good laws and promote human happiness. Enlightenment thinkers also turned toward rulers because rulers seemed to be listening, treating them with respect, and seeking their advice. Finally, the philosophes distrusted "the people," who they believed were deluded by superstitions and driven by violent passions, little children in need of firm parental guidance.

Encouraged and instructed by the philosophes, many absolutist rulers of the later eighteenth century tried to govern in an "enlightened" manner. Yet the actual programs and accomplishments of these rulers varied greatly. It is necessary, therefore, to examine the evolution of monarchical absolutism at close range before trying to form any overall judgment about the Enlightenment's effect on it.

Enlightenment teachings inspired European rulers in small as well as large states in the second half of the eighteenth century. Yet by far the most influential of the new-style monarchs were in Prussia, Russia, and Austria, and they deserve primary attention.

# INDIVIDUALS IN SOCIETY

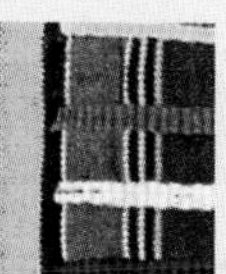

## MADAME DU COUDRAY, THE NATION'S MIDWIFE

In 1751 a highly esteemed Parisian midwife left the capital for a market town in central France. Having accepted an invitation to instruct local women in the skills of childbirth, Madame Angelique Marguerite Le Boursier du Coudray soon demonstrated a marvelous ability to teach students and win their respect. The thirty-six-year-old midwife found her mission: she would become the nation's midwife.

For eight years Madame du Coudray taught young women from the impoverished villages of Auvergne. In doing so, she entered into the world of unschooled midwives, typically solid matrons with several children who relied on traditional birthing practices and folk superstitions. Trained in Paris through a rigorous three-year apprenticeship and imbued with an Enlightenment faith in the power of knowledge, du Coudray had little sympathy for these village midwives. Many peasant mothers told her about their difficult deliveries and their many uterine "infirmities," which they attributed to "the ignorance of the women to whom they had recourse, or to that of some inexperienced village [male] surgeons."* Du Coudray agreed. Botched deliveries by incompetents resulted in horrible deformities and unnecessary deaths.

Determined to raise standards, Madame du Coudray saw that her unlettered pupils learned through the senses, not through books. Thus she made, possibly for the first time in history, a life-size obstetrical model—a "machine"—out of fabric and stuffing for use in her classes. "I had . . . the students maneuver in front of me on a machine . . . which represented the pelvis of a woman, the womb, its opening, its ligaments, the conduit called the vagina, the bladder, and *rectum intestine*. I added a [toy] child of natural size, whose joints were flexible enough to be able to be put in different positions." Now du Coudray could demonstrate the problems of childbirth, and each student could practice on the model in the "lab session."

As her reputation grew, Madame du Coudray sought to reach a national audience. In 1757 she wrote and had published the first of several editions of her *Manual on the Art of Childbirth*. Handsomely and effectively illustrated (see page 585), the *Manual* incorporated her hands-on teaching method and served as a text and reference for students and graduates. In 1759 the government authorized Madame du Coudray to carry her instruction "throughout the realm" and promised financial support. Her reception was not always warm, for she was a self-assured and demanding woman, who could anger old midwives, male surgeons, and skeptical officials. But aided by servants, a niece, and her husband, this inspired and indefatigable woman took her course from town to town until her retirement in 1784. Typically her students were young peasant women on tiny stipends, who came into town from surrounding villages for two to three months of instruction. Classes met mornings and afternoons six days a week, with ample time to practice on the mannequin. After a recuperative break, Madame du Coudray and her entourage moved on.

*Madame du Coudray in 1769, at the height of her importance.* (From Elizabeth C. Goldsmith, *Going Public: Women and Publishing in Early Modern France* [Ithaca, N.Y.: Cornell University Press, 1995]. Reproduced with permission)

Teaching thousands of fledgling midwives, Madame du Coudray may well have contributed to the decline in infant mortality and to the increase in population occurring in France in the eighteenth century—an increase she and her royal supporters fervently desired. Certainly she spread better knowledge about childbirth from the educated elite to the common people.

### QUESTIONS FOR ANALYSIS

1. How do you account for Madame du Coudray's remarkable success?
2. Does Madame du Coudray's career reflect tensions between educated elites and the common people? If so, how?

*Quotes are from Nina Gelbart, *The King's Midwife: A History and Mystery of Madame du Coudray* (Berkeley: University of California Press, 1998), pp. 60–61. This definitive biography is excellent.

## Frederick the Great of Prussia

Frederick II (r. 1740–1786), commonly known as Frederick the Great, built masterfully on the work of his father, Frederick William I (see pages 550–551). This was somewhat surprising, for like many children with tyrannical parents, he rebelled against his family's wishes in his early years. Rejecting the crude life of the barracks, Frederick embraced culture, literature, and the French language. Yet like many other rebellious youths, Frederick eventually reached a reconciliation with his father, and when he came to the throne in 1740, he was determined to use the splendid army that his father had left him.

Therefore, when the ruler of Austria, Charles VI, also died in 1740 and his young and charismatic daughter, Maria Theresa, inherited the Habsburg dominions, Frederick suddenly and without warning invaded her rich, mainly German province of Silesia. This action defied solemn Prussian promises to respect the Pragmatic Sanction, which guaranteed Maria Theresa's succession. Maria Theresa's ethnically diverse army was no match for Prussian precision. In 1742, as other greedy powers were falling on her lands in the general European War of the Austrian Succession (1740–1748), she was forced to cede almost all of Silesia to Prussia (see Map 17.3 on page 549). In one stroke Prussia doubled its population to 6 million people. Now Prussia unquestionably towered above all the other German states and stood as a European Great Power.

Though successful in 1742, Frederick had to spend much of his reign fighting against great odds to save Prussia from total destruction. Maria Theresa was determined to regain Silesia, and during the Seven Years' War (1756–1763) Austria fashioned an aggressive alliance with France and Russia to conquer Prussia and divide up its territory. Frederick led his army brilliantly, striking repeatedly at vastly superior forces invading from all sides. In the end he was miraculously saved: Peter III came to the Russian throne in 1762 and called off the attack against Frederick, whom he greatly admired.

In the early years of his reign Frederick II had kept his enthusiasm for Enlightenment culture strictly separated from a brutal concept of international politics. He wrote that states always sought to expand their territories and that "the passions of rulers have no other curb but the limits of their power. Those are the fixed laws of European politics to which every politician submits."[13] But the terrible struggle of the Seven Years' War tempered Frederick and brought him to consider how more humane policies for his subjects might also strengthen the state.

Thus Frederick went beyond a superficial commitment to Enlightenment culture for himself and his circle. He tolerantly allowed his subjects to believe as they wished in religious and philosophical matters. He promoted the advancement of knowledge, improving his country's schools and permitting scholars to publish their findings. Moreover, Frederick tried to improve the lives of his subjects more directly. He energetically promoted the reconstruction of agriculture and industry following the Seven Years' War. Prussia's laws were simplified, torture of prisoners was abolished, and judges decided cases quickly and impartially. Prussian officials became famous for their hard work and honesty. Frederick himself set a good example. He worked hard and lived modestly, claiming that he was "only the first servant of the state." Thus Frederick justified monarchy in terms of practical results and said nothing of the divine right of kings.

Frederick's dedication to high-minded government went only so far, however. He never tried to change Prussia's existing social structure. True, he condemned serfdom in the abstract, but he accepted it in practice. He accepted and extended the privileges of the nobility, which he saw as his primary ally in the defense and extension of his realm. The Junker nobility remained the backbone of the army and the entire Prussian state.

Nor did Frederick listen to thinkers such as Moses Mendelssohn (1729–1786), who urged that Jews be given freedom and civil rights. As in other German states, Jews in Prussia remained an oppressed group. Frederick opposed steadfastly any general emancipation for the Jews, as he did for the serfs.

## Catherine the Great of Russia

Catherine the Great of Russia (r. 1762–1796) was one of the most remarkable rulers who ever lived, and the French philosophes adored her. Catherine was a German princess from an insignificant German principality, but her mother was related to the Romanovs of Russia, and that relationship proved to be Catherine's chance.

Peter the Great had abolished the hereditary succession of tsars so that he could name his successor and thus preserve his policies. Peter's youngest daughter, Elizabeth, came to the Russian throne in 1741, named her nephew Peter heir to the throne, and chose Catherine to be his wife in 1744. It was a mismatch from the beginning. The fifteen-year-old Catherine was intelligent and attractive; her husband was stupid and ugly. Ignored by her childish husband, Catherine carefully studied Russian, endlessly read writers such as Bayle and Voltaire, and made friends at court. Soon she knew what she wanted. "I did not care about Peter," she wrote in her *Memoirs,* "but I did care about the crown."[14]

As the old empress Elizabeth approached death, Catherine plotted against her unpopular husband. She selected as her new lover a tall, dashing young officer named Gregory Orlov, who with his four officer brothers commanded considerable support among the soldiers stationed in St. Petersburg. When Peter came to the throne in 1762, his decision to withdraw Russian troops from the coalition against Prussia alienated the army. At the end of six months Catherine and her military conspirators deposed Peter III in a palace revolution. Then the Orlov brothers murdered him. The German princess became empress of Russia.

Catherine had drunk deeply at the Enlightenment well. Never questioning the common assumption that absolute monarchy was the best form of government, she set out to rule in an enlightened manner. She had three main goals. First, she worked hard to bring the sophisticated culture of western Europe to backward Russia. To do so, she imported Western architects, sculptors, musicians, and intellectuals. She bought masterpieces of Western art in wholesale lots and patronized the philosophes. An enthusiastic letter writer, she corresponded extensively with Voltaire and praised him as the "champion of the human race." When the French government banned the *Encyclopedia,* she offered to publish it in St. Petersburg. She sent money to Diderot when he needed it. With these and countless similar actions, Catherine won good press in the West for herself and for her country. Moreover, this intellectual ruler, who wrote plays and loved good talk, set the tone for the entire Russian nobility. Peter the Great westernized Russian armies, but it was Catherine who westernized the thinking of the Russian nobility.

Catherine's second goal was domestic reform, and she began her reign with sincere and ambitious projects. Better laws were a major concern. She appointed a special legislative commission to prepare a new law code. No new unified code was ever produced, but Catherine did restrict the practice of torture and allowed limited religious toleration. She also tried to improve education and strengthen local government. The philosophes applauded these measures and hoped more would follow.

Such was not the case. In 1773 a Cossack soldier named Emelian Pugachev ignited a violent and bloody revolt of the serfs. Catherine's noble-led army was able to suppress it, but the event was a turning point in the empress's domestic policy. On taking the throne she had condemned serfdom, but the revolt put an end to any thoughts she may have had of reforming society. The peasants were dangerous, and the nobles were her allies. After 1775 she gave the nobles absolute control over their serfs. Ten years later she freed nobles forever from taxes and state service.

**Pugachev and Catherine** This haunting portrait of Pugachev was painted over an existing portrait of Catherine the Great, who seems to be peeking over the rebel leader's head. Painting from life in 1773, the artist may have wanted to represent Pugachev's legitimacy as Catherine's rightful successor. *(From* Pamiatniki Kul'tury, *No. 32, 1961)*

Catherine's third goal was territorial expansion, and in this she was extremely successful. Her armies subjugated the last descendants of the Mongols, the Crimean Tartars, and began the conquest of the Caucasus. Her greatest coup by far was the partitioning of Poland, whose fate in the late eighteenth century demonstrated the dangers of failing to build a strong absolutist state. All important decisions continued to require the unanimous agreement of all nobles elected to the Polish Diet, which meant that nothing could ever be done to strengthen the state. When Frederick of Prussia proposed that Prussia, Austria, and Russia each take a gigantic slice of Polish territory, Catherine jumped at the chance. The first partition of Poland took place in 1772. Two more partitions, in 1793 and 1795, gave all three powers more Polish territory, and the ancient republic of Poland simply vanished from the map.

## The Austrian Habsburgs

In Austria two talented rulers did manage to introduce major reforms, although traditional power politics was more important than Enlightenment teachings. One was Joseph II (r. 1780–1790), a fascinating individual. For an earlier generation of historians he was the "revolutionary emperor," a tragic hero whose lofty reforms were undone by the landowning nobility he challenged. More recent scholarship has revised this romantic interpretation and stressed how Joseph II continued the state-building work of his mother, the empress Maria Theresa (r. 1740–1780), a remarkable but old-fashioned absolutist.

Emerging from the long War of the Austrian Succession in 1748 with only the serious loss of Silesia, Maria Theresa and her closest ministers were determined to introduce reforms that would make the state stronger and more efficient. Three aspects of these reforms were most important. First, Maria Theresa introduced measures aimed at limiting the papacy's political influence in her realm. Second, a whole series of administrative reforms strengthened the central bureaucracy, smoothed out some provincial differences, and revamped the tax system, taxing even the lands of nobles without special exemptions. Third, the government sought to improve the lot of the agricultural population, cautiously reducing the power of lords over their hereditary serfs and their partially free peasant tenants.

Coregent with his mother from 1765 onward and a strong supporter of change, Joseph II moved forward rapidly when he came to the throne in 1780. He controlled the established Catholic church even more closely and granted religious toleration and civic rights to Protestants and Jews. In even more spectacular peasant reforms, Joseph abolished serfdom in 1781, and in 1789 he decreed that all peasant labor obligations be converted into cash payments. This ill-conceived measure was violently rejected not only by the nobility but also by the peasants it was intended to help, for their primitive barter econ-

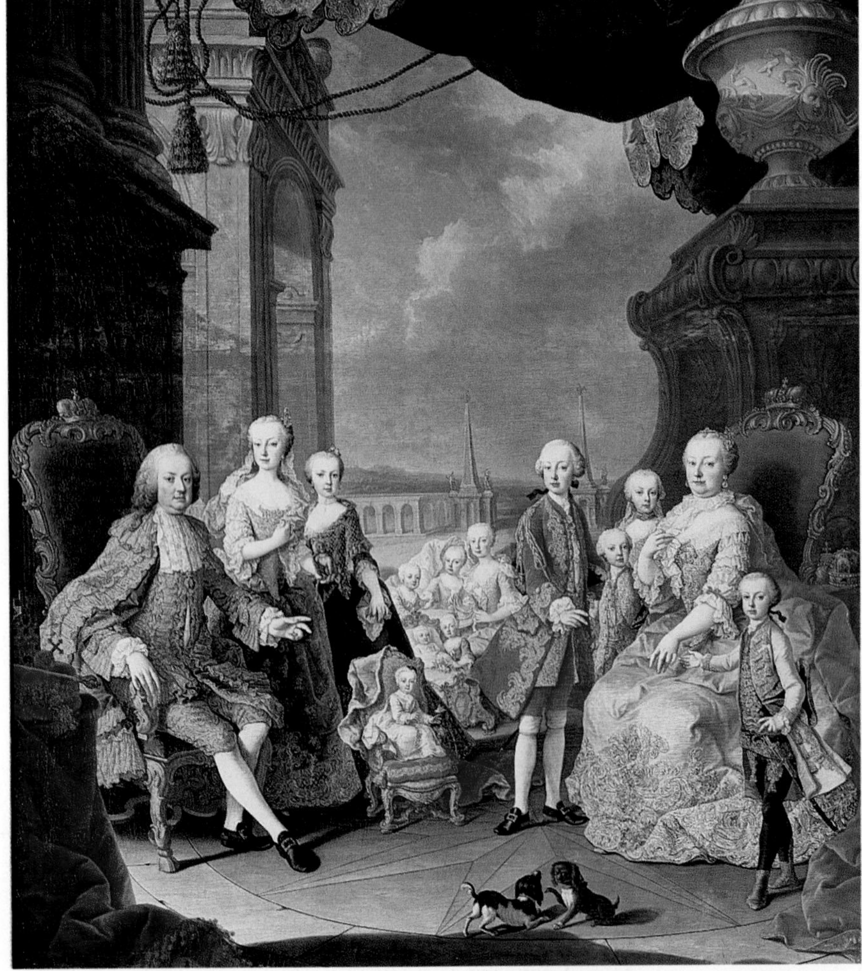

**Maria Theresa** The empress and her husband pose with eleven of their sixteen children at Schönbrunn palace in this family portrait by court painter Martin Meytens (1695–1770). Joseph, the heir to the throne, stands at the center of the star pattern. Wealthy women often had very large families, in part because they seldom nursed their babies as poor women usually did. *(Réunion des Musées Nationaux/Art Resource, NY)*

omy was woefully lacking in money. When a disillusioned Joseph died prematurely at forty-nine, the entire Habsburg empire was in turmoil. His brother Leopold II (r. 1790–1792) was forced to cancel Joseph's radical edicts in order to re-establish order. Peasants once again were required to do forced labor for their lords.

## Absolutism in France

The Enlightenment's influence on political developments in France was complex. The monarchy maintained its absolutist claims, and some philosophes, such as Voltaire, believed that the king was still the best source of needed reform. At the same time, discontented nobles and learned judges drew on thinkers such as Montesquieu for liberal arguments. They sought with some success to limit the king's power, as France diverged from the absolutist states just considered.

When Louis XIV finally died in 1715, to be succeeded by his five-year-old great-grandson, Louis XV (r. 1715–1774), the Sun King's elaborate system of absolutist rule was challenged in a general reaction. Favored by the duke of Orléans (1674–1723), who governed as regent until 1723, the nobility made a strong comeback.

Most important, in 1715 the duke restored to the high court of Paris—the Parlement—the ancient right to evaluate royal decrees publicly before they were given the force of law. The restoration of this right, which had been suspended under Louis XIV, was a fateful step. The judges of the Parlement of Paris had originally come from the middle class. By the eighteenth century, however, these middle-class judges had risen to become hereditary nobles, which conferred much-desired social status on them. Moreover, the judicial positions became essentially private property, passed down from father to son. By allowing this well-entrenched and increasingly aristocratic group to evaluate the king's decrees, the duke of Orléans sanctioned a counterweight to absolute power.

These implications became clear when the heavy expenses of the War of the Austrian Succession plunged France into financial crisis. In 1748 Louis XV authorized a 5 percent income tax on every individual regardless of social status. The result was a vigorous protest from many sides, led by the Parlement of Paris. The monarchy retreated; the new tax was dropped.

After the disastrously expensive Seven Years' War, the conflict re-emerged. The government tried to maintain emergency taxes after the war ended. The Parlement of Paris protested and even challenged the basis of royal authority, claiming that the king's power had to be limited to protect liberty. Once again the government caved in and withdrew the wartime taxes in 1764.

Indolent and sensual by nature, more interested in his many mistresses than in affairs of state, Louis XV finally roused himself for a determined defense of his absolutist inheritance. "The magistrates," he angrily told the Parlement of Paris in a famous face-to-face confrontation, "are my officers. . . . In my person only does the sovereign power rest."[15] In 1768 Louis appointed a tough career official named René de Maupeou as chancellor and ordered him to crush the judicial opposition.

Maupeou abolished the Parlement of Paris and exiled its members to the provinces. He created a new and docile Parlement of royal officials, and he began once again to tax the privileged groups. Most philosophes and educated public opinion as a whole sided with the old Parlement, however, and there was widespread criticism of "royal despotism." The illegal stream of scandalmongering attacks on the king and his court became a torrent. Yet Maupeou and Louis XV would probably have prevailed—if the king had lived to a very ripe old age.

But Louis XV died in 1774. The new king, Louis XVI (r. 1774–1792), was a shy twenty-year-old with good intentions. Upon taking the throne, he is reported to have said, "What I should like most is to be loved."[16] The eager-to-please monarch decided to yield in the face of such strong criticism from so much of France's educated elite. He dismissed Maupeou and repudiated the strong-willed minister's work. The old Parlement of Paris was reinstated as enlightened public opinion cheered and anticipated moves toward more representative government. But such moves were not forthcoming. Increasingly locked in stalemate, the country was drifting toward renewed financial crisis and political upheaval.

## The Overall Influence of the Enlightenment

Having examined the evolution of monarchical absolutism in four leading states, we can begin to look for meaningful generalizations and evaluate the overall influence of Enlightenment thought on politics.

France clearly diverged from its eastern neighbors in its political development in the eighteenth century. The capacity of the French monarch to govern in a truly absolutist manner declined substantially. The political resurgence of the French nobility after 1715 and the growth of judicial opposition drew crucial support from educated public opinion.

The situation in eastern and east-central Europe was different. The liberal critique of absolute monarchy remained an intellectual curiosity, and proponents of reform from above held sway. Moreover, despite differences, the leading eastern European monarchs of the later eighteenth century all claimed that they were acting on the principles of the Enlightenment. The philosophes generally agreed with this assessment and cheered them on. Beginning in the mid-nineteenth century historians developed the idea of a common "enlightened despotism" or "enlightened absolutism," and they canonized Frederick, Catherine, and Joseph as its most outstanding examples. More recent research has raised doubts about this old interpretation and has led to a fundamental re-evaluation.

There is general agreement that these absolutists, especially Catherine and Frederick, did encourage and spread the cultural values of the Enlightenment. They were proud of their intellectual accomplishments and good taste, and they supported knowledge, education, and the arts. Historians also agree that the absolutists believed in change from above and tried to enact needed reforms. Yet the results of these efforts brought only very modest improvements, and the life of the peasantry remained very hard. Thus some historians have concluded that these monarchs were not really sincere in their reform efforts. Others disagree, arguing that powerful nobilities blocked the absolutists' genuine commitment to reform. (The old interpretation of Joseph II as the tragic revolutionary emperor forms part of this argument.)

The emerging answer to this controversy is that the later eastern absolutists were indeed committed to reform but that humanitarian objectives were of quite secondary importance. Above all, the absolutists wanted reforms that would strengthen the state and allow them to compete militarily with their neighbors. Modern scholarship has therefore stressed how Catherine, Frederick, and Joseph were in many ways simply continuing the state building of their predecessors, reorganizing armies and expanding bureaucracies to raise more taxes and troops. The reason for this continuation was simple. The international political struggle was brutal, and the stakes were high. First Austria under Maria Theresa and then Prussia under Frederick the Great had to engage in bitter fighting to escape dismemberment. Decentralized Poland was coldly divided and eventually liquidated.

Yet in this drive for more state power, the later absolutists were also innovators, and the idea of an era of enlightened absolutism retains a certain validity. Sharing the Enlightenment faith in critical thinking and believing that knowledge meant power, these absolutists really were more enlightened than their predecessors because they put state-building reforms in a new, broader perspective. Above all, the later absolutists considered how more humane laws and practices could help their populations become more productive and satisfied and thus able to contribute more substantially to the welfare of the state. It was from this perspective that they introduced many of their most progressive reforms, tolerating religious minorities, simplifying legal codes, and promoting practical education. Nevertheless, reforms had to be grafted onto existing political and social structures. Thus each enlightened absolutist sought greater state power, but each believed a different policy would attain it.

The eastern European absolutists of the later eighteenth century combined old-fashioned state building with the culture and critical thinking of the Enlightenment. In doing so, they succeeded in expanding the role of the state in the life of society. Unlike the successors of Louis XIV, they perfected bureaucratic machines that were to prove surprisingly adaptive and capable of enduring into the twentieth century.

## SUMMARY

This chapter has focused on the complex development of a new world-view in Western civilization. This new view was essentially critical and secular, drawing its inspiration from the scientific revolution and crystallizing in the Enlightenment.

Decisive breakthroughs in astronomy and physics in the seventeenth century, which demolished the imposing medieval synthesis of Aristotelian philosophy and Christian theology, had only limited practical consequences despite the expectations of scientific enthusiasts. Yet the impact of new scientific knowledge on intellectual life became great. Interpreting scientific findings and Newtonian laws in an antitraditional, antireligious manner, the French philosophes of the Enlightenment extolled the superiority of rational, critical thinking. This new method, they believed, promised not just increased knowledge but even the discovery of the fundamental laws of human society. Although they reached different conclusions when they turned to social and political realities, they did stimulate absolute monarchs to apply reason to statecraft and the search for useful reforms. Above all, the philosophes succeeded in shaping an emerging public opinion and spreading their radically new world-view. These were momentous accomplishments.

## KEY TERMS

world-view
Copernican theory
law of inertia
law of universal gravitation
empiricism
Enlightenment
progress
skeptics
tabula rasa
philosophes
the public
salons
blood sports

## NOTES

1. H. Butterfield, *The Origins of Modern Science* (New York: Macmillan, 1951), p. viii.
2. Quoted in A. G. R. Smith, *Science and Society in the Sixteenth and Seventeenth Centuries* (New York: Harcourt Brace Jovanovich, 1972), p. 97.
3. Quoted in Butterfield, *The Origins of Modern Science,* p. 47.
4. Quoted in Smith, *Science and Society in the Sixteenth and Seventeenth Centuries,* p. 120.
5. Quoted in A. R. Hall, *From Galileo to Newton, 1630–1720* (New York: Harper & Row, 1963), p. 290.
6. Quoted in P. Hazard, *The European Mind, 1680–1715* (Cleveland: Meridian Books, 1963), pp. 304–305.
7. Quoted in R. Chartier, *The Cultural Origins of the French Revolution* (Durham, N.C.: Duke University Press, 1991), p. 27.
8. Quoted in L. Schiebinger, *The Mind Has No Sex? Women in the Origins of Modern Science* (Cambridge, Mass.: Harvard University Press, 1989), p. 64.
9. Quoted in G. L. Mosse et al., eds., *Europe in Review* (Chicago: Rand McNally, 1964), p. 156.
10. Quoted in P. Gay, "The Unity of the Enlightenment," *History* 3 (1960): 25.
11. E. Fox-Genovese, "Women in the Enlightenment," in *Becoming Visible: Women in European History,* 2d ed., ed. R. Bridenthal, C. Koonz, and S. Stuard (Boston: Houghton Mifflin, 1987), esp. pp. 252–259, 263–265.
12. I. Woloch, *Eighteenth-Century Europe: Tradition and Progress, 1715–1789* (New York: W. W. Norton, 1982), pp. 220–221.
13. Quoted in L. Krieger, *Kings and Philosophers, 1689–1789* (New York: W. W. Norton, 1970), p. 257.
14. Quoted in G. P. Gooch, *Catherine the Great and Other Studies* (Hamden, Conn.: Archon Books, 1966), p. 15.
15. Quoted in R. R. Palmer, *The Age of Democratic Revolution,* vol. 1 (Princeton, N.J.: Princeton University Press, 1959), pp. 95–96.
16. Quoted in G. Wright, *France in Modern Times,* 4th ed. (New York: W. W. Norton, 1987), p. 34.

## SUGGESTED READING

The first three authors cited in the Notes—Butterfield, Smith, and Hall—have written excellent general interpretations of the scientific revolution. These may be compared with S. Shapin, *The Scientific Revolution* (2001), which is concise and dramatic, and M. Jacob, *The Cultural Meaning of the Scientific Revolution* (1988). A. Debus, *Man and Nature in the Renaissance* (1978), is good on the Copernican revolution. S. Drake, *Galileo* (1980), is a good short biography. E. Andrade, *Sir Isaac Newton* (1958), is a good brief biography, which may be compared with F. Manuel, *The Religion of Isaac Newton* (1974), and R. Westfall, *Never at Rest: A Biography of Isaac Newton* (1993).

Hazard, listed in the Notes, is a classic study of the formative years of Enlightenment thought. R. Reill and E. Wilson, *Encyclopedia of the Enlightenment* (1996), is particularly helpful on culture and the leading philosophes. M. Jacob, *The Enlightenment: A Brief History with Documents* (2000), is also recommended. Important works from a cultural perspective include D. Goodman, *The Republic of Letters: A Cultural History of the Enlightenment* (1994), and A. Farge, *Subversive Worlds: Public Opinion in Eighteenth Century France* (1994). P. Gay has written several studies on the Enlightenment: *Voltaire's Politics* (1959) and *The Party of Humanity* (1971) are two of the best. J. Sklar, *Montesquieu* (1987), is an engaging biography. F. Baumer, *Religion and the Rise of Skepticism* (1969); H. Payne, *The Philosophes and the People* (1976); and H. Chisick, *The Limits of Reform in the Enlightenment: Attitudes Toward the Education of the Lower Classes in Eighteenth-Century France* (1981), are interesting studies of important aspects of Enlightenment thought. D. van Kley, *The Religious Origins of the French Revolution* (1996), is a stimulating interpretation. On women, see the study by Fox-Genovese cited in the Notes, as well as E. Goldsmith and D. Goodman, eds., *Going Public: Women and Publishing in Early Modern France* (1995), and K. Rogers, *Feminism in Eighteenth-Century England* (1982). J. Landes, *Women and the Public Sphere in the Age of the French Revolution* (1988), is a fascinating and controversial study of women and politics. Above all, one should read some of the philosophes themselves. Two good anthologies are C. Brinton, ed., *The Portable Age of Reason* (1956), and F. Manuel, ed., *The Enlightenment* (1951). Voltaire's famous novel *Candide* is highly recommended, as is S. Gendzier, ed., *Denis Diderot: The Encyclopedia: Selections* (1967).

In addition to the works mentioned in the Suggested Reading for Chapter 17, the monarchies of Europe are carefully analyzed in H. Scott, *Enlightened Absolutism* (1990); C. Tilly, ed., *The Formation of National States in Western Europe* (1975); and J. Gagliardo, *Enlightened Despotism* (1967), all of which have useful bibliographies. M. Anderson, *Historians and Eighteenth-Century Europe* (1979), is a valuable introduction to modern scholarship, and C. Behrens, *Society, Government, and the Enlightenment: The Experience of Eighteenth-Century France and Prussia* (1985), is a stimulating comparative study. E. Le Roy Ladurie, *The Ancien Régime* (1996), is an excellent synthesis by a leading French historian. J. Lynch, *Bourbon Spain, 1700–1808* (1989), and R. Herr, *The Eighteenth-Century Revolution in Spain* (1958), skillfully analyze the impact of Enlightenment thought in Spain. Important works on Austria include C. Macartney, *Maria Theresa and the House of Austria* (1970), and T. Blanning, *Joseph II and Enlightened Absolutism* (1970). There are several fine works on Russia. J. Alexander, *Catherine the Great: Life and Legend* (1989), is the best biography of the famous ruler. I. de Madariaga, *Russia in the Age of Catherine the Great* (1981), is strongly recommended.

The culture of the time may be approached through A. Cobban, ed., *The Eighteenth Century* (1969), a richly illustrated work with excellent essays, and C. B. Behrens, *The Ancien Régime* (1967). T. Crow, *Painters and Public Life in Eighteenth-Century Paris* (1985), examines artists and cultural politics. C. Rosen, *The Classical Style: Haydn, Mozart, Beethoven* (1972), brilliantly synthesizes music and society, as did Mozart himself in his great opera *The Marriage of Figaro,* where the count is the buffoon and his servant the hero.

# LISTENING TO THE PAST

## GENDER CONSTRUCTIONS AND EDUCATION FOR GIRLS

*Emile, or On Education (1762), by Jean-Jacques Rousseau, is one of history's most original and influential books. Sometimes called a declaration of rights for children, it pleads for the humane treatment of children and lambasts widespread indifference and harsh discipline.*

*Rousseau's long, rambling work, part novel and part philosophical treatise, also had a powerful impact on theories of education.* Emile *argues that education must shield the unspoiled child from the corrupting influences of civilization and allow the child to develop naturally and spontaneously. Children should learn what they—not their teachers—find interesting and useful.*

*As this selection shows, Rousseau constructed sharp gender divisions. Girls and boys were basically equal as human beings, but sex made them both similar and different, intended by their natures for different occupations. Whereas Emile would eventually tackle academic subjects, Sophie, his future wife, would receive only lessons in household management, good mothering, and wifely obedience. The idea of educating girls and boys to operate "naturally" in their "separate spheres" would flourish in the nineteenth century.*

Sophie ought to be a woman as Emile is a man—that is to say, she ought to have everything which suits the constitution of her species and her sex in order to fill her place in the physical and moral order. Let us begin, then, by examining the similarities and the differences of her sex and ours.

In everything not connected with sex, woman is man. She has the same organs, the same needs, the same faculties. The machine is constructed in the same way; its parts are the same; the one functions as does the other; the form is similar; and in whatever respect one considers them, the difference between them is only one of more or less.

In everything connected with sex, woman and man are in every respect related and in every respect different. The difficulty of comparing them comes from the difficulty of determining what in their constitutions is due to sex and what is not. . . .

There is no parity between the two sexes in regard to the consequences of sex. The male is male only at certain moments. The female is female her whole life or at least during her whole youth. Everything constantly recalls her sex to her; and, to fulfill its functions well, she needs a constitution which corresponds to it. She needs care during her pregnancy; she needs rest at the time of childbirth; she needs a soft and sedentary life to suckle her children; she needs patience and gentleness, a zeal and an affection that nothing can rebuff in order to raise her children. She serves as the link between them and their father; she alone makes him love them and give them the confidence to call them his own. How much tenderness and care is required to maintain the union of the whole family! . . .

Once it is demonstrated that man and woman are not and ought not to be constituted in the same way in either character or temperament, it follows that they ought not to have the same education. In following nature's directions, man and woman ought to act in concert, but they ought not to do the same things. The goal of their labors is common, but their labors themselves are different, and consequently so are the tastes directing them. . . .

All the faculties common to the two sexes are not equally distributed between them; but taken together, they balance out. Woman is worth more as woman and less as man. Wherever she makes use of her rights, she has the advantage. Wherever she wants to usurp ours, she remains beneath us. . . .

To cultivate man's qualities in women and to neglect those which are proper to them is obviously to work to their detriment. . . . Believe me, judicious mother, do not make a decent man of your daughter, as though you would give

Jean-Jacques Rousseau (1712–1778), portrayed as a gentle teacher and a pensive philosopher. *(The Granger Collection, New York)*

nature the lie. Make a decent woman of her, and be sure that as a result she will be worth more for herself and for us.

Does it follow that she ought to be raised in ignorance of everything and limited to the housekeeping functions alone? Will man turn his companion into his servant? . . . Surely not. It is not thus that nature has spoken in giving women such agreeable and nimble minds. On the contrary, nature wants them to think, to judge, to love, to know, to cultivate their minds as well as their looks. These are the weapons nature gives them to take the place of the strength they lack and to direct others. They ought to learn many things but only those that are suitable for them to know. . . .

The children of both sexes have many common entertainments, and that ought to be so. Is this not also the case when they are grown up? They also have particular tastes which distinguish them. Boys seek movement and noise: drums, boots, little carriages. Girls prefer what presents itself to sight and is useful for ornamentation: mirrors, jewels, dresses, particularly dolls. The doll is the special entertainment of this sex. . . .

Observe a little girl spending the day around her doll. . . . [S]he puts all her coquetry into it. She will not always leave it there. She awaits the moment when she will be her own doll.

This is a very definite primary taste. You have only to follow and regulate it. It is certain that the little girl would want with all her heart to know how to adorn her doll, to make its bracelets, its scarf, its flounce, its lace. . . . In this way there emerges the reason for the first lessons she is given. They are not tasks prescribed to her, they are kindnesses done for her. In fact, almost all little girls learn to read and write with repugnance. But as for holding a needle, that they always learn gladly. They imagine themselves to be grown up and think with pleasure that these talents will one day be useful for adorning themselves.

Once this first path is opened, it is easy to follow. Sewing, embroidery, and lacemaking come by themselves. Tapestry is not much to their taste. . . .

Whatever humorists may say, good sense belongs equally to the two sexes. Girls are generally more docile than boys, and one should even use more authority with them, as I shall say a little later. But it does not follow that anything ought to be demanded from them whose utility they cannot see. The art of mothers is to show them the utility of everything they prescribe to them, and that is all the easier since intelligence is more precocious in girls than in boys. This rule banishes—for their sex as well as for ours—not only idle studies which lead to no good and do not even make those who have pursued them more attractive to others, but even those which are not useful at their age and whose usefulness for a more advanced age the child cannot foresee. If I do not want to push a boy to learn to read, all the more I do not want to force girls to before making them well aware of what the use of reading is. In the way this utility is ordinarily showed to them, we follow our own idea far more than theirs. After all, where is the necessity for a girl to know how to read and write so early? Will she so soon have a household to govern? There are very few girls who do abuse this fatal science more than they make good use of it. And all of them have too much curiosity not to learn it—without our forcing them to do so—when they have the leisure and the occasion. Perhaps girls ought to learn to do arithmetic before anything, for nothing presents a more palpable utility at all times, requires longer practice, and is so exposed to error as calculation. If the little girl were to get cherries for her snack only by doing an arithmetical operation, I assure you that she would soon know how to calculate.

## QUESTIONS FOR ANALYSIS

1. What similarities and differences between women/girls and men/boys does Rousseau see? In your opinion, which appear more important to Rousseau? Why?
2. Were Rousseau's views on gender differences and education reactionary or progressive?

*Source:* Jean-Jacques Rousseau, *Emile, or On Education,* trans. Alan Bloom. 

Waist pendant of Benin, Edo peoples, Nigeria, 16th–19th centuries. The facial features, the beard, and the ruffled collar are clearly Portuguese, but the braided hair is distinctly African, probably signifying royalty. *(The Metropolitan Museum of Art, Gift of Mr. and Mrs. Klaus G. Perls, 1991 [1991.162.9]. Photograph © 1991 The Metropolitan Museum of Art)*

CHAPTER

# 19 AFRICA AND THE WORLD, CA 1400–1800

## CHAPTER OUTLINE



African states and societies of the fifteenth through eighteenth centuries comprised hundreds of ethnic groups and a wide variety of languages, cultures, and kinds of economic and political development. Modern European intrusion into Africa beginning in the fifteenth century led to the transatlantic slave trade, one of the great forced migrations in world history. Africa made a substantial, though involuntary, contribution to the building of the West's industrial civilization. In the seventeenth century, an increasing desire for sugar in Europe resulted in an increasing demand for slave labor in South America and the West Indies. In the eighteenth century, Western technological changes created a demand for cotton and other crops that required extensive human labor. As a result, the West's "need" for slaves from Africa increased dramatically.

Africa's relationship with Asia, the Islamic world, and the West stretches back a very long time, but only recently have anthropologists, economists, and historians begun to ask critical questions about African societies in early modern times.

- What kinds of economic and social structures did African societies have?
- What impact did Islam have on African societies?
- What role did slavery play in African societies before European intrusion?
- Why, in the seventeenth and eighteenth centuries, did slavery in the Americas become exclusively African?
- What were the geographical and societal origins of the slaves involuntarily shipped to America and to Asia?

This chapter will explore these questions.

## SENEGAMBIA AND BENIN

In Africa in the mid-fifteenth century, there were societies held together by family or kinship ties, and there were kingdoms and states ruled by princes who governed defined areas through bureaucratic hierarchies. Along the two-thousand-mile west coast between Senegambia and the northeastern shore of the Gulf of Guinea, a number of kingdoms flourished. Because much

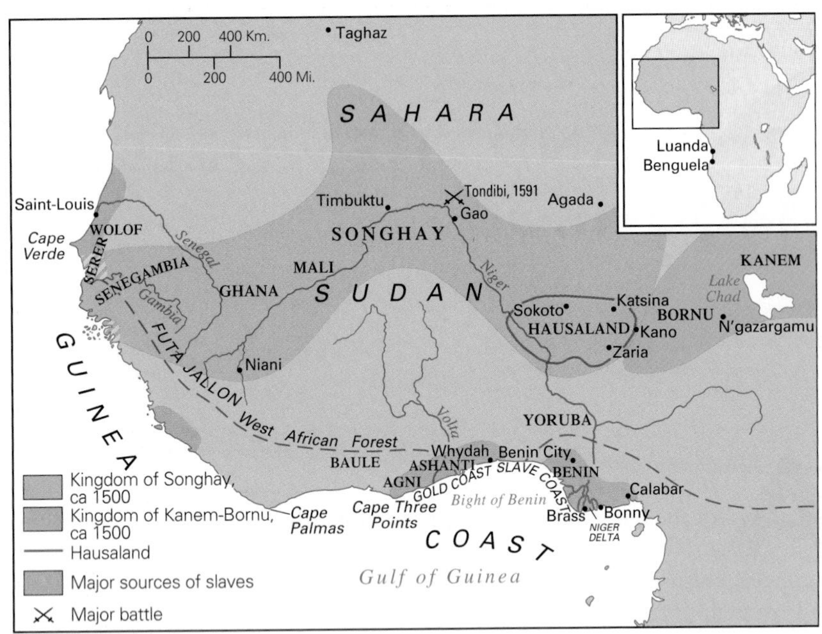


**MAP 19.1 West African Kingdoms and the Slave Trade, ca 1500 to 1800** Consider the role that rivers and other geographical factors played in the development of the West African slave trade. Why were Luanda and Benguela the logical Portuguese sources for slaves?

of that coastal region is covered by tropical rain forest, in contrast to the western Sudan, it is called the West African Forest Region (see Map 19.1). The Senegambian states in the north possessed a homogeneous culture and a common history. For centuries Senegambia—named for the Senegal and Gambia Rivers—had served as an important entrepôt for desert caravan contact with the Islamic civilizations of North Africa and the Middle East. Through the transatlantic slave trade, Senegambia contributed heavily to New World population in the early seventeenth century. That trade brought Senegambia into contact with the Americas and Europe. Thus Senegambia felt the impact of Islamic culture to the north and of European influences from the maritime West.

In the thirteenth century, the kingdoms of Ghana and Mali had incorporated parts of Senegambia. Mali's influence disintegrated after 1450, and successor kingdoms that were independent but connected to one another through family ties emerged. Stronger states rose and temporarily exercised power over weaker ones.

Scholars are still exploring the social and political structures of the various Senegambian states. The peoples of Senegambia spoke Wolof, Serer, and Pulaar, which all belong to the West African language group. Both the Wolof-speakers and the Serer-speakers had clearly defined social classes: royalty, nobility, warriors, peasants, low-caste artisans such as blacksmiths and leatherworkers, and slaves. Slaves were individuals who were pawned for debt, house servants who could not be sold, and people who were acquired through war or purchase. Senegambian slavery varied from society to society but generally was not a benign institution. In some places, the treatment of slaves was as harsh as treatment in the Western world later would be. However, many Senegambian slaves were not considered property to be bought and sold, and some served as royal advisers and enjoyed great power and prestige.[1]

The king of the Wolof was elected by the nobility. After his election, the king immediately acquired authority and a special religious charisma. He commanded contingents of soldier-slaves and appointed village chiefs. The king gained his revenue from the chiefs, from merchants, and from taxes levied on defeated peoples.[2] The Wolof had a well-defined government hierarchy.

Among the stateless societies of Senegambia, where kinship and lineage groups tended to fragment communities, **age-grade systems** evolved. Age-grades were groups of men and women whom the society initiated into adulthood at the same time. Age-grades cut across family ties, created community-wide loyalties, and provided a means of local law enforcement, because the group was responsible for the behavior of all its members.

The typical Senegambian community was a small self-supporting agricultural village of closely related families. Custom assigned a high value to cultivation of the land—the shared objective of the group. Fields were cut from the surrounding forest, and the average farm of six to eight

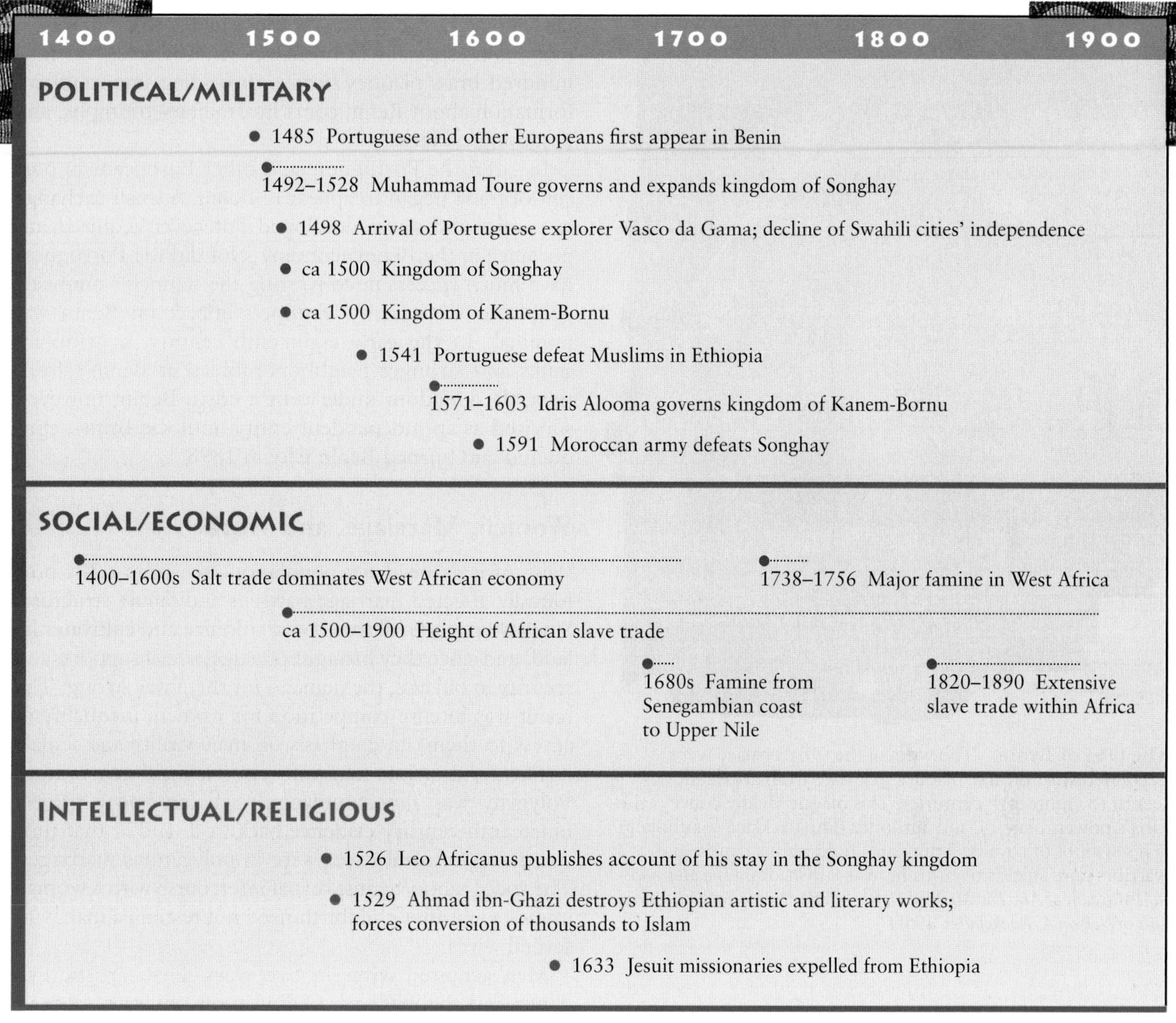


acres supported a moderate-size family. Often the family worked the land for a common harvest; sometimes individuals had their own private fields. Millet and sorghum were the staple grains in northern Senegambia; farther south, forest dwellers cultivated yams as a staple. Senegambians supplemented their diet with plantains, beans, bananas, fish, oysters, and small game such as rabbits and monkeys. Along the Guinea coast, rice was the basic cereal, and okra, onions, melons, and pepper spiced the regular diet. Frequent fairs in neighboring villages served as markets for the exchange of produce and opportunities for receiving outside news and social diversion. As one scholar has put it, "Life was simple, government largely limited to the settlement of disputes by family heads or elders . . . social life centered on the ceremony accompanying birth, death, and family alliance."[3]

The fifteenth and sixteenth centuries saw the emergence of the great forest kingdom of Benin (see Map 19.1) in what is now southern Nigeria. Although scholars still know little about Benin's origins, its history seems to have been characterized by power struggles between the king and the nobility that neither side ever completely won. An elaborate court ceremonial exalted the position of the **oba,** or king, and brought stability to the state. In the later fifteenth century, the oba Ewuare played off his palace chiefs against the village chiefs and thereby maintained a balance of power. A great warrior, Ewuare strengthened his army and pushed Benin's borders as far

**The Oba of Benin** The walls of the Oba's palace were decorated with bronze plaques that date from about the sixteenth to eighteenth centuries. This plaque vividly conveys the Oba's power, majesty, and authority. The necklace (or choker) is his symbol of royalty. Attendants hold up his hands, and warriors raise shields over his head as sunshades. *(The Metropolitan Museum of Art, The Michael C. Rockefeller Memorial Collection, Gift of Nelson A. Rockefeller, 1965)*

as the Niger River in the east, westward into Yoruba country, and south to the Gulf of Guinea. During the late sixteenth and seventeenth centuries, the office of the oba evolved from a warrior-kingship to a position of spiritual leadership.

At its height in the late sixteenth century, Benin controlled a vast territory, and European visitors described a sophisticated society. According to a modern historian, the capital, Benin City, "was a stronghold twenty-five miles in circumference, protected by walls and natural defenses, containing an elaborate royal palace and neatly laid-out houses with verandas and balustrades, and divided by broad avenues and smaller intersecting streets."[4] Visitors also noted that Benin City was kept scrupulously clean and had no beggars and that public security was so effective that theft was unknown. The period also witnessed remarkable artistic creativity in ironwork, in carved ivory, and especially in bronze portrait busts. Over nine hundred brass plaques survive, providing important information about Benin court life, military triumphs, and cosmological ideas.

In 1485 the Portuguese and other Europeans in pursuit of trade began to appear in Benin. A small exchange in pepper and slaves developed but never acquired importance in the Benin economy. Nor did the Portuguese have much success in converting the staunchly animistic people to Christianity. Europe's impact on Benin was minimal. In the early eighteenth century, as tributary states and stronger neighbors nibbled at Benin's frontiers, the kingdom underwent a crisis. Benin, however, survived as an independent entity until the British conquered and burned Benin City in 1898.

## Women, Marriage, and Work

West Africa's need for population (see page 620) profoundly affected marriage patterns and family structure. Since wives and children could colonize and cultivate the land, and since they brought prestige, social support, and security in old age, the demand for them was strong. The result was intense competition for women, inequality of access to them, an emphasis on male virility and female fertility, and serious tension between male generations. Polygyny was almost universal; scholars today project nineteenth-century evidence backward, and at that time two-thirds of rural wives were in polygynous marriages. The social taboo against sexual intercourse with a woman immediately after childbirth need not restrain a man with several wives.

Men acquired wives in two ways. First, artistic evidence and the evidence of European observers suggest that groups of young men formed subcultures that emphasized dress and personal adornment, virility, and aggression to attract girls' attention. Convinced of her interest, a young man abducted a girl, and they eloped and began a union. The second method was by bride wealth, in which a man's family paid the bride's family for the loss of her labor and fertility. Since it took time for a young man to acquire the bride wealth, most men married at an older age. Whereas women married at about the onset of puberty, all but the richest men delayed marriage until about age thirty, although that need not mean they were celibate.

The easy availability of land in Africa reduced the kinds of generational conflict that occurred in western Europe, where land was scarce. The competition for wives between male generations, however, became "one of the most dynamic and enduring forces in African history."[5] On the one hand, myth and folklore stressed respect for the elderly, and the older men in a community imposed their authority over the younger ones by conducting painful rites of initiation into adulthood, such as circumcision. On the other hand, West African societies were not gerontocracies, as few people lived much beyond forty, and young men possessed the powerful asset of their labor, which could easily be turned into independence where so much land was available.

"Without children you are naked" goes a Yoruba proverb, and the production of children was the primary goal of marriage. Just as a man's virility determined his honor, so barrenness damaged a woman's status. A wife's infidelity was considered a less serious problem than her infertility. A woman might have six widely spaced pregnancies in her fertile years; the universal practice of breast-feeding infants for two, three, or even four years may have inhibited conception. Long intervals between births due to food shortages also may have limited pregnancies and checked population growth. Although little reliable evidence survives before the nineteenth century, scholars assume a very high infant mortality rate due to climate, poor nutrition, and infectious diseases.

Both extended and nuclear families seem to have been common in West Africa. The household of a Big Man (a man of power in the locality) included his wives, married and unmarried sons, unmarried daughters, poor relations, dependents, and scores of children. Extended families were common among the Hausa and Malinke peoples (see pages 602–604) and were the main colonizing groups in equatorial Africa. On the Gold Coast in the seventeenth century, a well-to-do man's household might number 150 people, in the Kongo region several hundred. Where one family cultivated extensive land, a large household of young adults, children, and slaves probably proved most efficient. Most families elsewhere, however, seemed to number only five or six people.

In agriculture men did the heavy work of felling trees and clearing the land; women performed the tedious chores of planting and weeding. All cooperated. Between 1000 and 1400, cassava (manioc), bananas, and plantains came to West Africa from Asia, leading to a reliance on cassava as the staple food. Cassava required little effort to grow, the tubers could be left unharvested for years, and they stored well, but they also had little nutritional value. In the sixteenth century, the Portuguese introduced maize (corn), sweet potatoes, and new varieties of yams from the Americas.[6] Fish supplemented the diet of people living in a region near a river or stream. Describing the food of his Ibo people in Benin in the mid-eighteenth century, Olaudah Equiano lists plantains, yams, beans, and Indian corn, along with stewed poultry, goat, or bullock (castrated steer) seasoned with peppers. Such a protein-rich diet was probably exceptional. Equiano also writes, "When our women are not employed with the men in tillage, their usual occupation is spinning and weaving cloth which they afterwards dye and make into garments."[7]

Disease posed perhaps the biggest obstacle to population growth. Malaria, spread by mosquitoes and rampant in West Africa (except in cool, dry Cameroon), was the greatest killer, especially of infants. West Africans developed a relatively high degree of immunity to malaria and other parasitic diseases, including hookworm (which enters the body through shoeless feet and attaches itself to the intestines); yaws (contracted by nonsexual contact

**Queen Mother and Attendants** As in Ottoman, Chinese, and European societies, so the mothers of rulers in Africa sometimes exercised considerable political power because of their influence on their sons. African kings granted the title "Queen Mother" as a badge of honor. In this figure, the long beaded cap, called "chicken's beak," symbolizes the mother's rank as do her elaborate neck jewelry and attendants. *(Metropolitan Museum of Art. Gift of Mr. and Mrs. Klaus G. Perls, 1991 [1991.17.111]. Photograph © 1991 The Metropolitan Museum of Art)*

and recognized by ulcerating lesions); sleeping sickness (the parasite enters the blood through the bite of the tsetse fly; symptoms are enlarged lymph nodes and, at the end, a comatose state); and a mild nonsexual form of syphilis. As in Chinese and European communities in the early modern period, the sick depended on folk medicine. The Hausa people had several kinds of medical specialists: midwives, bone setters, exorcists using religious methods, and herbalists. Medical treatment consisted of herbal medication: salves, ointments, and purgatives. Modern anthropologists have great respect for African folk medicine, but disease was common where the diet was poor and lacked adequate vitamins. Slaves taken to the Americas grew much taller and broader than their African ancestors.

The devastating effects of famine, often mentioned in West African oral traditions, represent another major check on population growth. Drought, excessive rain, swarms of locusts, and rural wars that prevented the cultivation of land all meant later food shortages. In the 1680s, famine extended from the Senegambian coast to the Upper Nile, and many people sold themselves into slavery for food. In the eighteenth century, "slave exports" (see pages 608–615) "peaked during famines, and one ship obtained a full cargo merely by offering food." The worst disaster occurred from 1738 to 1756, when, according to one chronicler, the poor were reduced to cannibalism, an African metaphor for the complete collapse of civilization. The acute strains of smallpox introduced by Europeans certainly did not help population growth, nor did venereal syphilis, which originated in Latin America.[8]

## Trade and Industry

As in all premodern societies, the West African economies rested on agriculture and the production of adequate food for local needs. There was some trade and industry, but population shortages encouraged local self-sufficiency, slowed transportation, and hindered exchange. There were very few large markets, and their relative isolation from the outside world and their failure to attract large numbers of foreign merchants limited technological innovation.

For centuries, black Africans had exchanged goods with North African merchants in centers such as Goa, Djenné, and Timbuktu. That long-distance trade was conducted and controlled by Muslim Berber merchants. Except as servants or slaves, black Africans did not make the long trek across the Sahara.

As elsewhere, the cheapest method of transportation was by water, and many small dugout canoes and larger trading canoes plied the Niger and its delta region (see Map 19.1). On land West African peoples used pack animals (camels or donkeys) rather than wheeled vehicles; south of the Sahara, only a narrow belt of land was suitable for animal-drawn carts. When traders reached an area infested with tsetse flies (see page 602), they transferred each animal's load to two human porters. Such difficulties in transport severely restricted long-distance trade, so most people relied on the regional exchange of local specialties.

West African communities had a well-organized market system. At informal markets on riverbanks, fishermen bartered fish for local specialties. More formal markets existed within towns and villages or on neutral ground between them. Markets also rotated among neighboring villages on certain days. People exchanged cotton cloth, thread, palm oil, millet, vegetables, and small articles for daily living. Olaudah Equiano says that foods constituted the main articles of commercial exchange. Local sellers were usually women; traders from afar were men.

Between the fifteenth and seventeenth centuries, salt represented West Africa's chief mineral product, its value worth more than the entire trans-Saharan trade. Salt is essential to human health; the Hausa language has more than fifty words for it. The main salt-mining center was at **Taghaz** (see Map 19.1) in the western Sahara, a desolate settlement about which the fourteenth-century traveler Ibn Battuta says, "This is a village with nothing good about it." In the most wretched conditions, slaves dug the salt from desiccated lakes and loaded heavy blocks onto camels' backs. The camels sometimes traveled in caravans of twenty thousand to thirty thousand stretching over many miles. **Tuareg** warriors and later Moors (peoples of Berber and Arab descent) controlled the north-south trade; they traded their salt for gold, grain, slaves, and kola nuts, which were used by Muslims as stimulants or aphrodisiacs. **Cowrie shells,** imported from the Maldive Islands in the Indian Ocean by way of Gujarat (see page 647) and North Africa, served as the medium of exchange. (Shell money continued as a medium long after European intrusion.) Gold continued to be mined and shipped from Mali until South American bullion flooded Europe in the sixteenth century. Thereafter, its production in Africa steadily declined.

West African peoples engaged in many crafts, such as weaving various types of baskets. Ironworking, a specialized skill producing articles useful to hunters, farmers, and warriors, became hereditary in individual families; such expertise was regarded as family property. The textile industry had the greatest level of specialization. The earliest fabric in West Africa was made of vegetable fiber.

Muslim traders introduced cotton and its weaving in the ninth century, as the fine-quality fabrics found in Mali reveal. By the fifteenth century, the Wolof and Malinke regions had professional weavers producing beautiful cloth, but this cloth was too expensive to compete in the Atlantic and Indian Ocean markets after 1500. Women who spun cotton used only a spindle and not a wheel, which slowed output. Women wove on inefficient broadlooms, men on less clumsy but unproductive narrow looms. These were the only machines that West Africans had.[9]

## THE SUDAN: SONGHAY, KANEM-BORNU, AND HAUSALAND

The kingdom of Songhay, a successor state of Ghana and Mali, dominated the whole Niger region of the western and central Sudan (see Map 19.1). Muhammad Toure (r. 1492–1528) completed the expansionist and administrative consolidation begun by his predecessors. Muhammad Toure's power rested on his successful military expeditions. From his capital at Gao, he extended his lordship as far north as the salt-mining center at Taghaz in the western Sahara and as far east as Agada and Kano. A convert to Islam, Muhammad made a pilgrimage to Mecca. Impressed by what he saw there, he tried to bring about greater centralization in his own territories. In addition to building a strong army and improving taxation procedures, he replaced local Songhay officials with more efficient Arab ones in an effort to substitute royal institutions for ancient kinship ties.

What kind of economy existed in the Songhay Empire? What social structures? What role did women play in Songhay society? What is known of Songhay education and culture? The paucity of written records and of surviving artifacts prevents scholars from satisfactorily exploring these questions. Some information is provided by Leo Africanus (ca 1465–1550), a Moroccan captured by pirates and given as a slave to Pope Leo X. Leo Africanus became a Christian, taught Arabic in Rome, and in 1526 published an account of his many travels, including a stay in the Songhay kingdom.

As a scholar, Leo was naturally impressed by Timbuktu, the second city of the empire, which he visited in 1513. "Here [is] a great store of doctors, judges, priests, and other learned men, that are bountifully maintained at the King's court," Leo reported.[10] Many of these Islamic scholars had studied in Cairo and other centers of Muslim learning. They gave Timbuktu a reputation for intellectual sophistication, religious piety, and moral justice.

Songhay under Muhammad Toure seems to have enjoyed economic prosperity. Leo Africanus noted the abundant food supply, which was produced in the southern Savanna and carried to Timbuktu by a large fleet of canoes controlled by the king. The Sudanese had large amounts of money to spend, and expensive North African and European luxuries were much in demand: clothes, copperware, glass and stone beads, perfumes, and horses. The existence of many shops and markets implies the development of an urban culture. At Timbuktu merchants, scholars, judges, and artisans constituted a distinctive bourgeoisie. The presence of many foreign merchants, including Jews and Italians, gave the city a cosmopolitan atmosphere. Jews largely controlled the working of gold.

Slaves played a very important part in the economy of Songhay. On the royal farms scattered throughout the kingdom, slaves produced rice—the staple crop—for the royal granaries. Although slaves could possess their own slaves, land, and cattle, they could not bequeath any of this property; the king inherited all of it. Muhammad Toure greatly increased the number of royal slaves through raids on the pagans (non-Muslims). He gave slaves to favorite Muslim scholars, who thus gained a steady source of income. Or the slaves were sold at the large market at Gao. Traders from North Africa bought them for sale in Cairo, Constantinople, Lisbon, Naples, Genoa, and Venice.

The kingdom of Songhay had considerable economic and cultural strengths, but it also had serious internal problems. Islamic institutions never took root in the countryside, and Muslim officials alienated the king from his people. Muhammad Toure's reforms were a failure. He governed a diverse group of peoples—Tuareg, Malinke, Fulani, as well as Songhay—who were often hostile to one another, and no cohesive element united them. Finally, the Songhay never developed an effective method of transferring power. Revolts, conspiracies, and palace intrigues followed the deaths of every king, and only three of the nine rulers in the dynasty begun by Muhammad Toure died natural deaths. Muhammad himself was murdered by one of his sons. His death began a period of political instability that led to the slow disintegration of the kingdom.[11]

In 1582 the sultanate of Morocco began to press southward in search of a greater share of the trans-Saharan trade. The people of Songhay, lacking effective leadership and believing the desert to be a sure protection against invasion, took no defensive precautions. In 1591 a Moroccan army of three thousand soldiers—many of whom were slaves of European origin equipped with

European muskets—crossed the Sahara and inflicted a crushing defeat on the Songhay at Tondibi. This battle spelled the end of the Songhay Empire. Although a moderate-size kingdom lingered on in the south for a century or so and weak political units arose, not until the eighteenth century did kingdoms able to exercise wide authority emerge again.

To the east of Songhay lay the kingdoms of Kanem-Bornu and Hausaland (see Map 19.1). Under the dynamic military leader Idris Alooma (1571–1603), Kanem-Bornu subdued weaker peoples and gained jurisdiction over an extensive area. Well drilled and equipped with firearms, camel-mounted cavalry and a standing army decimated warriors fighting with spears and arrows. Idris Alooma perpetuated the feudal pattern of government in which lands were granted to able fighters in return for loyalty and the promise of future military assistance. Meanwhile, agriculture occupied most people, peasants and slaves alike. Kanem-Bornu shared in the trans-Saharan trade, shipping eunuchs and young girls to North Africa in return for horses and firearms. A devout Muslim, Idris Alooma elicited high praise from ibn Fartura, who wrote a history of his reign called *The Kanem Wars:*

> *So he made the pilgrimage and visited Medina with delight. . . . Among the benefits which God . . . conferred upon the Sultan Idris Alooma was the acquisition of Turkish musketeers and numerous household slaves who became skilled in firing muskets. . . .*
>
> *Among the most surprising of his acts was the stand he took against obscenity and adultery, so that no such thing took place openly in his time. Formerly the people had been indifferent to such offences. . . . In fact he was a power among his people and from him came their strength.*
>
> *The Sultan was intent on the clear path laid down by the Qur'an . . . in all his affairs and actions.*[12]

Idris Alooma built mosques at his capital city of N'gazargamu and substituted Muslim courts and Islamic law for African tribunals and ancient customary law. His eighteenth-century successors lacked his vitality and military skills, however, and the empire declined.

Between Songhay and Kanem-Bornu were the lands of the Hausa. An agricultural people living in small villages, the Hausa grew millet, sorghum, barley, rice, cotton, and citrus fruit and raised livestock. Some Hausa merchants carried on a heavy trade in slaves and kola nuts with North African communities across the Sahara. Obscure trading posts evolved into important Hausa city-states like Kano and Katsina, through which Islamic influences entered the region. Kano and Katsina became Muslim intellectual centers and in the fifteenth century attracted scholars from Timbuktu. The Muslim chronicler of the reign of King Muhammad Rimfa of Kano (r. 1463–1499) records that Muhammad introduced the Muslim practices of *purdah,* or seclusion of women; of the *idal-fitr,* or festival after the fast of Ramadan; and of assigning eunuchs to the high offices of state.[13] As in Songhay and Kanem-Bornu, however, Islam made no strong imprint on the mass of the Hausa people until the nineteenth century.

## ETHIOPIA

At the beginning of the sixteenth century, the powerful East African Christian kingdom of Ethiopia extended from Massawa in the north to several tributary states in the south (see Map 19.2). The ruling Solomonid Dynasty, however, faced serious troubles. Adal, a Muslim state along the southern base of the Red Sea, began incursions into Ethiopia, and in 1529 the Adal general Ahmad ibn-Ghazi inflicted a disastrous defeat on the Ethiopian emperor Lebna Dengel (r. 1508–1540). Ahmad followed up his victory with systematic devastation of the land, destruction of many Ethiopian artistic and literary works, and the forced conversion of thousands to Islam. Lebna Dengel fled to the mountains and appealed to Portugal for assistance.

In the late twelfth century, tales of Prester John, a powerful Christian monarch who ruled a vast and wealthy empire in Africa, reached western Europe. Letters he had supposedly written circulated widely. The search for Prester John, as well as for gold and spices, spurred the Portuguese to undertake a series of trans-African expeditions. In the 1480s they reached Timbuktu and Mali. By 1508 Portuguese emissaries had reached the Ethiopian capital and identified the king as Prester John. This contact led to the exchange of gifts and priests between the Ethiopian and Portuguese courts.[14]

Interested in the conversion of Ethiopia from Coptic Christianity to Roman Catholicism, the Portuguese responded to Lebna Dengel's request for help with a force of musketeers. In 1541 they decisively defeated the Muslims near Lake Tana.

No sooner had the Muslim threat ended than Ethiopia encountered three more dangers. The Galla, Cushitic-speaking peoples, moved northward in great numbers, occupying portions of Harar, Shoa, and Amhara. The Ethiopians could not defeat them militarily, and the Galla were not interested in assimilation. For the next two centuries, the two peoples lived together in an uneasy truce. Simultaneous with the Galla migrations was the Ottoman Turks' seizure of Massawa and other coastal cities. Then

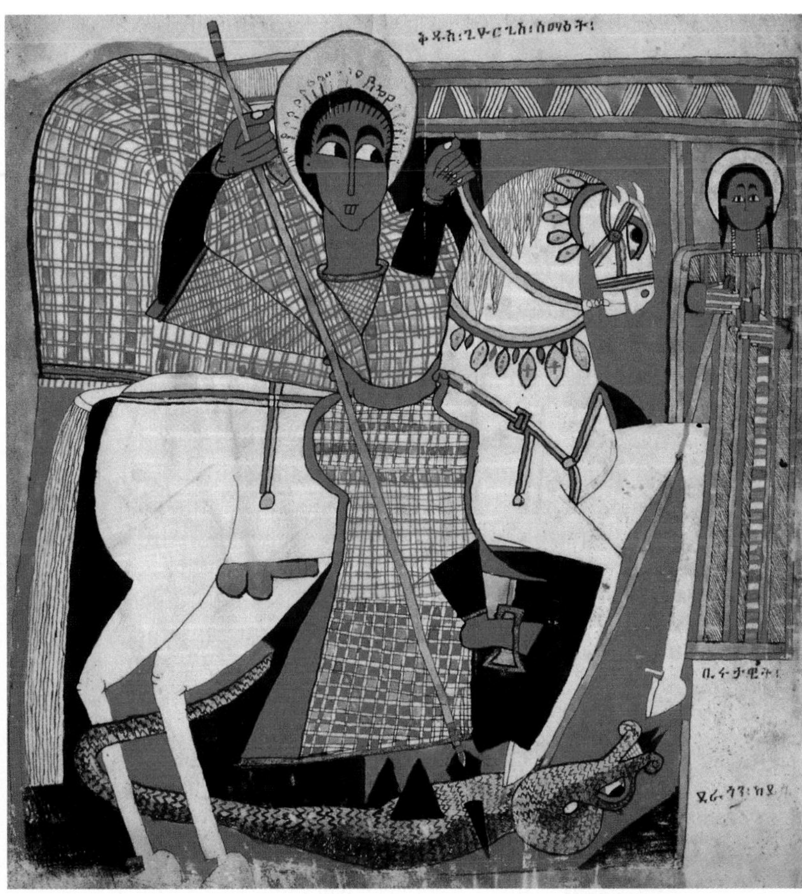

**Saint George in Ethiopian Art** This image of a black Saint George slaying a dragon, from a seventeenth-century Ethiopian manuscript, attests to the powerful and pervasive Christian influence in Ethiopian culture. *(The British Library)*

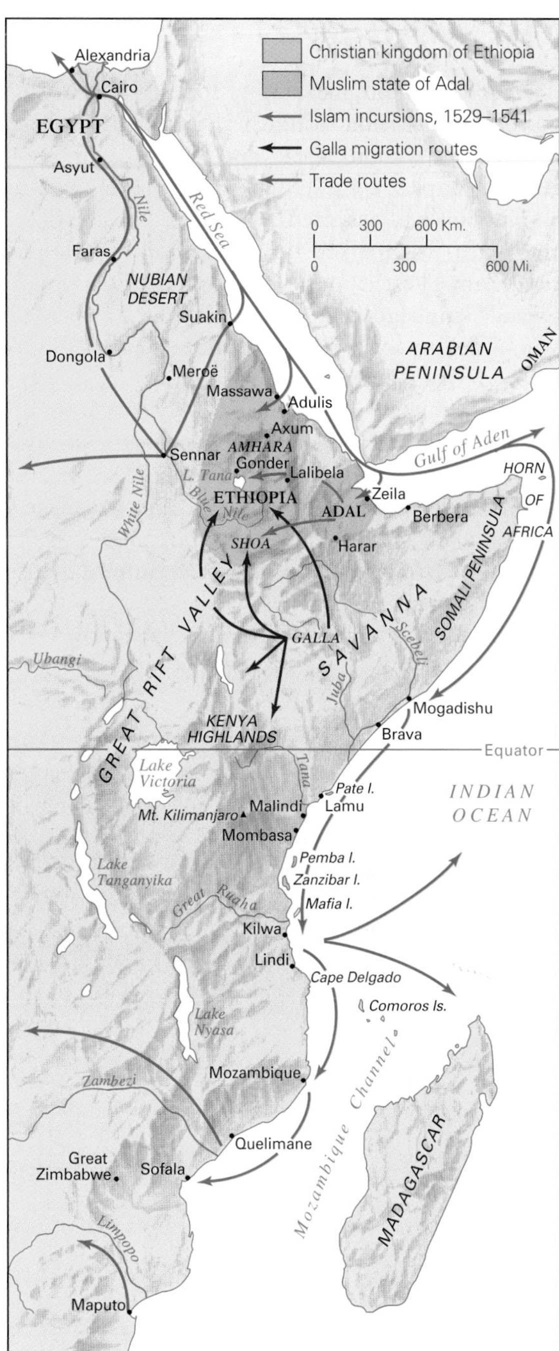


**MAP 19.2 East Africa in the Sixteenth Century** In early modern times, the Christian kingdom of Ethiopia, first isolated and then subjected to Muslim and European pressures, played an insignificant role in world affairs. But the East African city-states, which stretched from Sofala in the south to Mogadishu in the north, had powerfully important commercial relations with Mughal India, China, the Ottoman world, and southern Europe.

the Jesuits arrived, eager to capitalize on earlier Portuguese support, and attempted to force Roman Catholicism on a proud people whose Coptic form of Christianity long antedated the European version. The overzealous Jesuit missionary Alphonse Mendez tried to revamp the Ethiopian liturgy, rebaptize the people, and replace ancient Ethiopian customs and practices with Roman ones. Since Ethiopian national sentiment was closely tied to Coptic Christianity, violent rebellion and anarchy ensued.

In 1633 the Jesuit missionaries were expelled. For the next two centuries, hostility to foreigners, weak political leadership, and regionalism characterized Ethiopia. Civil conflicts between the Galla and the Ethiopians erupted continually. The Coptic church, though lacking strong authority, survived as the cornerstone of Ethiopian national identity.

## THE SWAHILI CITY-STATES

The word **Swahili,** meaning "People of the Coast," refers to the people living along the East African coast and on the nearby islands. Their history, unlike that of most African peoples, exists in writing. By the eleventh century, the Swahili had accepted Islam, and "its acceptance was the factor that marked the acquisition of 'Swahili' identity: Islam gave the society coherent cultural form."[15] The Swahili language is studied today by North Americans who want to explore their African ancestry, but slaves shipped from East Africa came from inland, not from Swahili-speaking coastal, peoples; virtually no Swahili people went to North America. As a people living on the shores of the Indian Ocean, the Swahili felt the influences of Indians, Indonesians, Persians, and especially Arabs.

Swahili civilization was overwhelmingly maritime. A fertile, well-watered, and intensely cultivated stretch of land no more than ten miles wide extends down the coast: it yielded rice, grains, citrus fruit, and cloves. The sea provided fish. But the considerable prosperity of the region rested on trade and commerce. The Swahili acted as middlemen in an Indian Ocean–East African protocapitalism, exchanging ivory, rhinoceros horn, tortoise shells, inlaid ebony chairs, copra (dried coconut meat that yields coconut oil), and inland slaves for Arabian and Persian perfumes, toilet articles, ink, and paper and for Indian textiles, beads, and iron tools. In the fifteenth century, the city-states of Mogadishu, Pate, Lamu, Mombasa, and especially Kilwa enjoyed a worldwide reputation for commercial prosperity.[16] These cities were cosmopolitan, and their standard of living was very high.

The arrival of the Portuguese explorer Vasco da Gama (see Map 16.2 on page 508) in 1498 spelled the end of the Swahili cities' independence. Da Gama, lured by the spice trade, wanted to build a Portuguese maritime empire in the Indian Ocean. The rulers of the East African city-states responded in different ways to Portuguese intrusion. Some, such as the sultan of Malindi, quickly agreed to a trading alliance with the Portuguese. Others,

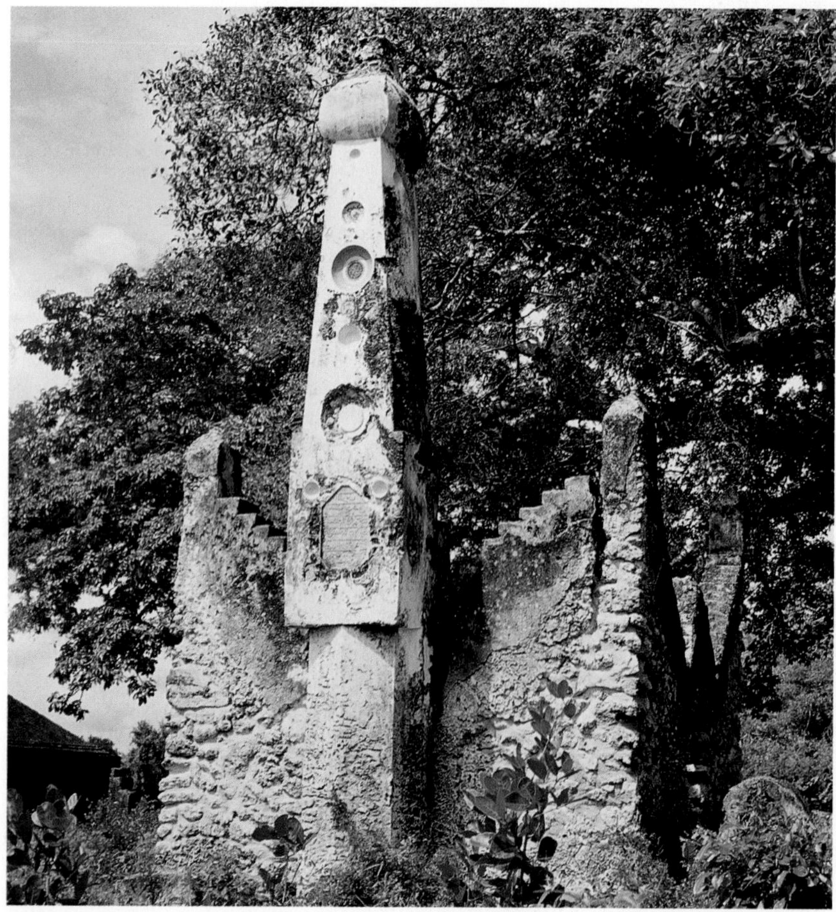

**Chinese Porcelain Plates** Embedded in an eighteenth-century Kunduchi pillar tomb, these Chinese plates testify to the enormous Asian-African trade that flourished in the fourteenth to sixteenth centuries. Kunduchi, whose ruins lie north of Dar es Salaam in present-day Tanzania, was one of the Swahili city-states. Why would a Muslim-African want a Chinese plate embedded in his tomb? To indicate that he was involved in the porcelain trade? *(WernerForman/Art Resource, NY)*

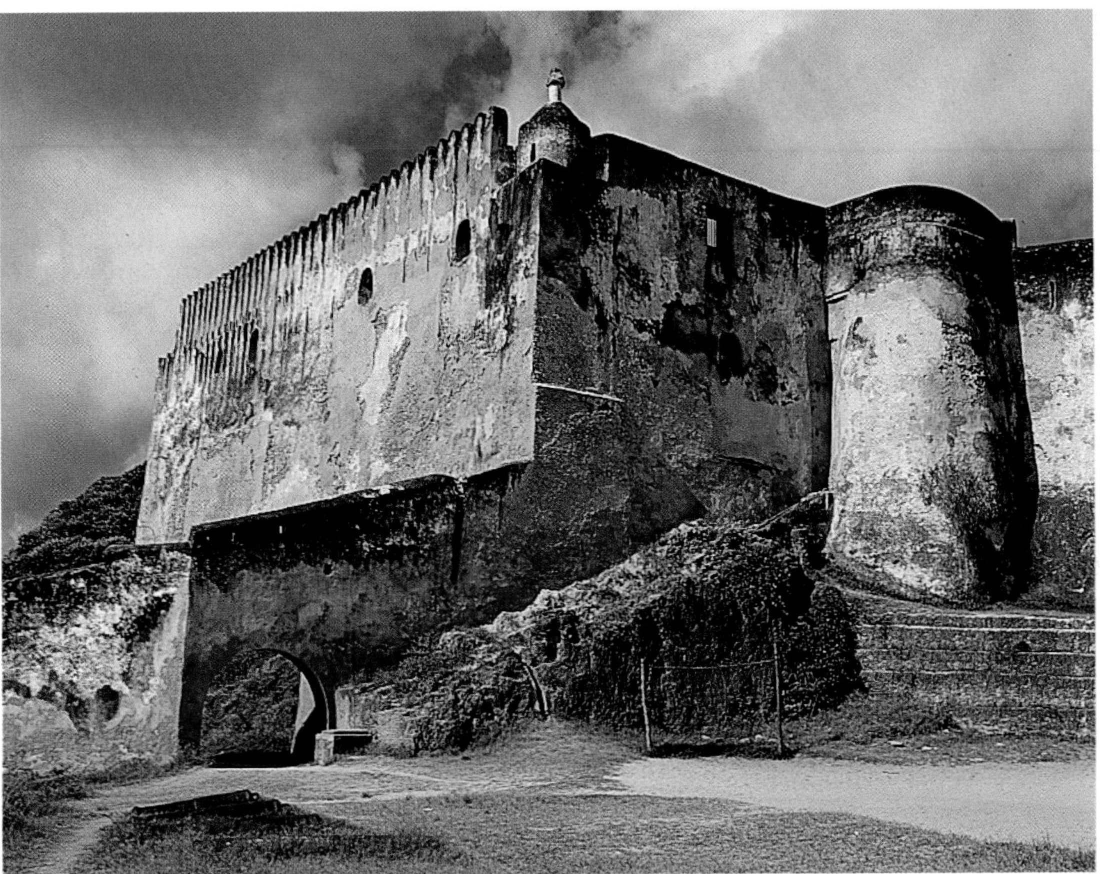

**Fort Jesus, Mombasa** Designed by the Milanese military architect Joao Batista Cairato in traditional European style, and built between 1593 and 1594, this great fortress still stands as a symbol of Portuguese military and commercial power in East Africa and the Indian Ocean in the sixteenth and seventeenth centuries. *(Wolfgang Kaehler/Getty Images)*

such as the sultan of Mombasa, were tricked into commercial agreements. Still other Swahili rulers totally rejected Portuguese overtures and were subjected to bombardment. In any case, the Portuguese backed up alliances made between 1502 and 1507 with the erection of forts at the southern port cities of Sofala, Kilwa, Zanzibar, and Mozambique. These forts—fortified markets and trading posts—served as the foundation of Portuguese commercial power on the Swahili coast.[17] (See the feature "Listening to the Past: Duarte Barbosa on the Swahili City-States" on pages 624–625.) The better-fortified northern cities, such as Mogadishu, survived as important entrepôts for goods to India.

The Portuguese victory in the south proved hollow, however. Rather than accept Portuguese commercial restrictions, the residents deserted the towns, and the town economies crumbled. Large numbers of Kilwa's people, for example, immigrated to northern cities. The flow of gold from inland mines to Sofala slowed to a trickle. Swahili passive resistance successfully prevented the Portuguese from gaining control of the local coastal trade.

After the intermittent bombardment of several cities, Portugal finally won an administrative stronghold near Mombasa in 1589. Called Fort Jesus, it remained a Portuguese base for over a century. In the late seventeenth century, pressures from the northern European maritime powers—the Dutch, French, and English—aided greatly by the Arabs of Oman, combined with local African rebellions to bring about the collapse of Portuguese influence in Africa. A Portuguese presence remained only at Mozambique in the far south.

The Portuguese had no religious or cultural impact on the Swahili cities. Their sole effect was the cities' economic decline.

## THE AFRICAN SLAVE TRADE

Slavery had a long tradition within Africa. The exchange of peoples captured in ethnic and tribal wars within sub-Saharan Africa, the trans-Saharan **slave** trade with the Mediterranean Islamic world beginning in the seventh century, and the slave traffic across the Indian Ocean going back centuries before European intrusion all testify to the continental dimensions of the trade. "Slavery was . . . fundamental to the social, political, and economic order of parts of the northern savanna, Ethiopia and the East African coast. . . . Enslavement was an organized activity, sanctioned by law and custom. Slaves were a principal commodity in trade, including the export sector, and slaves were important in the domestic sphere" as concubines, servants, soldiers, and ordinary laborers.[18]

**Below Stairs** The prints and cartoons of Thomas Rowlandson (1756–1827) testify to the sizable numbers of blacks in eighteenth-century London, where they worked in naval and military, as well as domestic, service. Here the household cook, maid, and footman relax before the kitchen fire. Interracial marriages were not uncommon. *(Courtesy of the Trustees of the British Museum)*

Islam had heavily influenced African slavery. African rulers justified enslavement with the Muslim argument that prisoners of war could be sold; and since captured peoples were considered chattel, they could be used in the same positions that prevailed in the Muslim world. Between 650 and 1600, black as well as white Muslims transported perhaps as many as 4.82 million black slaves across the trans-Saharan trade route.[19] In the fourteenth and fifteenth centuries, the rulers and elites of Mali and Benin imported thousands of white slave women who had originally come from the eastern Mediterranean.[20] These women were signs of wealth and status symbols. In 1444, when Portuguese caravels landed 235 slaves at Algarve in southern Portugal, a contemporary observed that they seemed "a marvelous (extraordinary) sight, for, amongst them, were some white enough, fair enough, and well-proportioned; others were less white, like mulattoes; others again were black as Ethiops."[21]

Meanwhile, the flow of black people to Europe, begun during the Renaissance, continued. In the seventeenth and eighteenth centuries, perhaps as many as two hundred thousand Africans entered European societies. Some arrived as slaves, others as servants; the legal distinction was not always clear. Eighteenth-century London, for example, had more than ten thousand blacks, most of whom arrived as sailors on Atlantic crossings or as personal servants brought from the West Indies. In England most were free, not slaves. Initially, a handsome black was a fashionable accessory, a rare status symbol. Later, English aristocrats considered black servants too ordinary. The duchess of Devonshire offered her mother an eleven-year-old boy, explaining that the duke did not want a Negro servant because "it was more original to have a Chinese page than to have a black one; everybody had a black one."[22] London's black population constituted a well-organized, self-conscious subculture, with black pubs, black churches, and black social groups assisting the black poor and unemployed. Some black people attained wealth and position, the most famous being Francis Barber, the literary giant Samuel Johnson's servant, who inherited Johnson's sizable fortune.

Beginning in 1658, the Dutch in the Cape Colony of southern Africa imported large numbers of slaves, initially from India and Southeast Asia, then from Madagascar. By the late eighteenth century, Mozambique in East Africa (see Map 19.2) had become the largest supplier of slaves for the Cape Colony. They labored as domestic servants or field workers, producing wheat and wine. In 1780 only one farmer in the colony admitted to possessing one hundred slaves, a small number by South or North American standards, but half of all white men there had at least one slave. That created a strong sense of racial and economic solidarity in the white master class.

Modern scholars consider slavery in the Cape Colony far more oppressive than that in the Americas or the Muslim world. Because male slaves greatly outnumbered female slaves in the Cape Colony, marriage and family life were almost nonexistent. There were few occupations requiring special skills, thus denying slaves a chance to earn manumission. In contrast to Muslim society, where the offspring of a freeman and a slave woman were free, in southern Africa such children were slaves. And in contrast to North and South America and Muslim societies, only a very tiny number of slaves in the Cape Colony won manumission. Most were women, suggesting a sexual or close personal relationship with their owners. While seventeenth- and eighteenth-century Holland enjoyed a European-wide reputation for its religious toleration and intellectual freedom (see page 562), in the Cape Colony the Dutch used a strict racial hierarchy and heavy paternalism to maintain control over native peoples and foreign-born slaves.[23]

The Savanna and Horn regions of East Africa experienced a great expansion of the slave trade in the late eighteenth century, and in the first half of the nineteenth century, slave exports from these areas and from the eastern coast amounted to perhaps thirty thousand a year. Why this demand? Merchants and planters wanted slaves to work the sugar plantations on the Mascarene Islands, located east of Madagascar, the clove plantations on Zanzibar and Pemba, and the food plantations along the Kenyan coast. The eastern coast also exported slaves to the Americas when Brazilian businessmen significantly increased their purchases. In the late eighteenth and early nineteenth centuries, precisely when the slave trade to North America and the Caribbean declined, the Eastern and Asian markets expanded. Only with colonial conquest by Great Britain, Germany, and Italy after 1870 did suppression of the trade begin. Slavery, of course, persists even today. (See the feature "Global Trade: Slaves" on pages 610–611.)

**Charles Davidson Bell (1813–1882): Schoolmaster Reading** In this watercolor print, a schoolmaster reads and explains the newspaper *Zuid Afrikaan* (The South African) to the (probably illiterate) household, while black servants cook and fan. Chickens peck for crumbs on the floor. *(William Fehr Collection, Cape Town)*

# GLOBAL TRADE

## SLAVES

The history of the global slave trade is rife with ironies. The traffic in human persons bought and sold for the profits of their labor cannot decently be compared with that in other commodities; people are not goods. But most societies, with the remarkable exception of the Aborigines in Australia, have treated people as goods and engaged in the slave trade. Those who are enslaved include captives in war, persons convicted of crimes, persons sold for debt, and persons bought and sold for sex. The ancient Greek philosophers, notably Aristotle, justified slavery as "natural." The Middle Eastern monotheistic faiths—Judaism, Christianity, and Islam—while professing the sacred dignity of each individual, and the Asian religious and sociopolitical ideologies of Buddhism and Confucianism, while stressing an ordered and harmonious society, all tolerated slavery and urged slaves' obedience to established authorities. Until the Enlightenment of the eighteenth century, most people, everywhere, accepted slavery as a "natural phenomenon." Nor is it without irony that the Thirteenth Amendment to the U.S. Constitution (ratified in 1865), popularly interpreted as abolishing slavery, allows slavery "as a punishment for crime whereof the party shall have been duly convicted."

Between 1500 and 1900, the transatlantic African slave trade accounted for the largest number of people

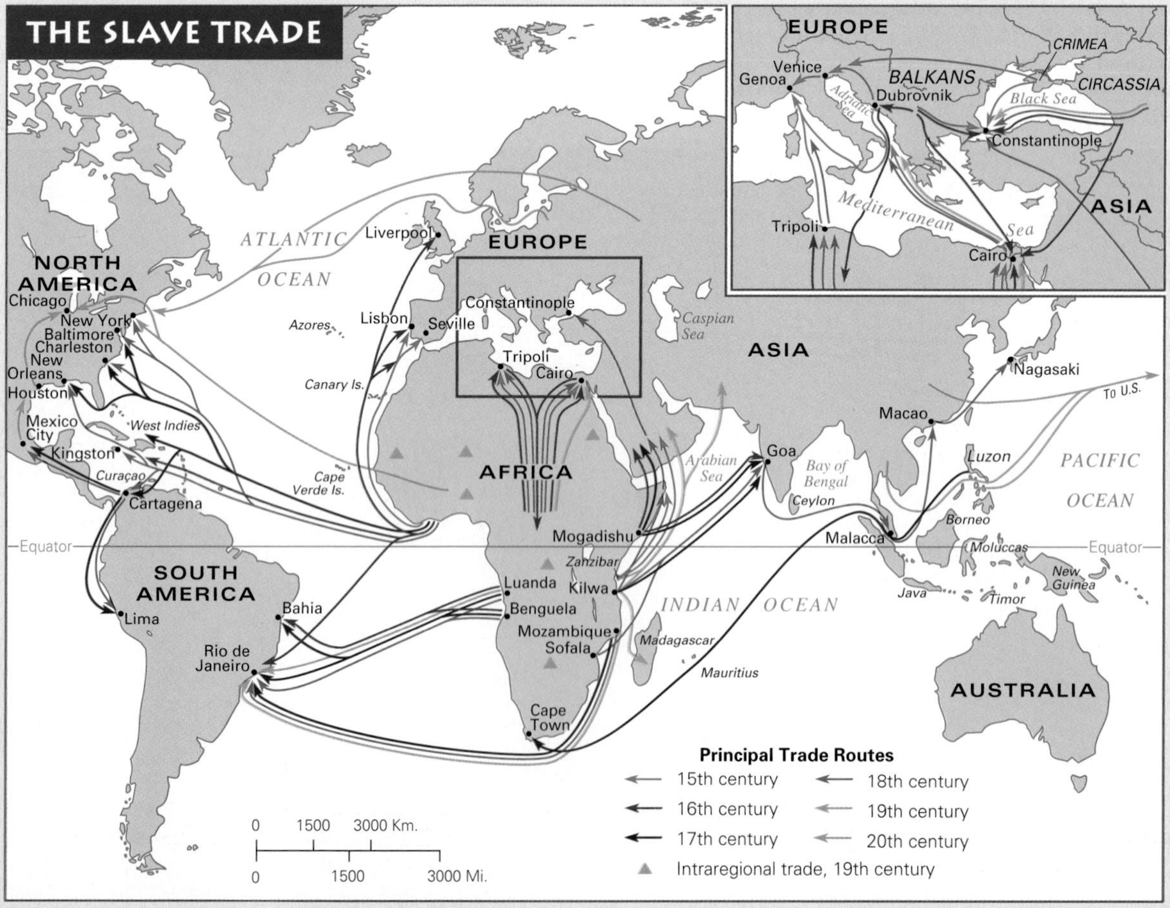

THE SLAVE TRADE

EUROPE
CRIMEA
Venice
Genoa
BALKANS
Dubrovnik
Adriatic Sea
Black Sea
CIRCASSIA
Constantinople
Mediterranean Sea
Tripoli
Cairo
ASIA

ATLANTIC OCEAN
Liverpool
EUROPE
NORTH AMERICA
Chicago
New York
Baltimore
Charleston
New Orleans
Houston
Mexico City
Kingston
Curaçao
Cartagena
West Indies
Azores
Lisbon
Seville
Constantinople
Caspian Sea
Tripoli
Cairo
Canary Is.
Cape Verde Is.
AFRICA
ASIA
Nagasaki
To U.S.
Macao
Goa
Arabian Sea
Bay of Bengal
Ceylon
Luzon
PACIFIC OCEAN
Borneo
Malacca
Mogadishu
Equator
Zanzibar
Luanda
Kilwa
Benguela
Mozambique
Sofala
Madagascar
Mauritius
INDIAN OCEAN
Moluccas
New Guinea
Java
Timor
SOUTH AMERICA
Lima
Bahia
Rio de Janeiro
Cape Town
AUSTRALIA

Principal Trade Routes
15th century
16th century
17th century
18th century
19th century
20th century
Intraregional trade, 19th century

0 1500 3000 Km.
0 1500 3000 Mi.

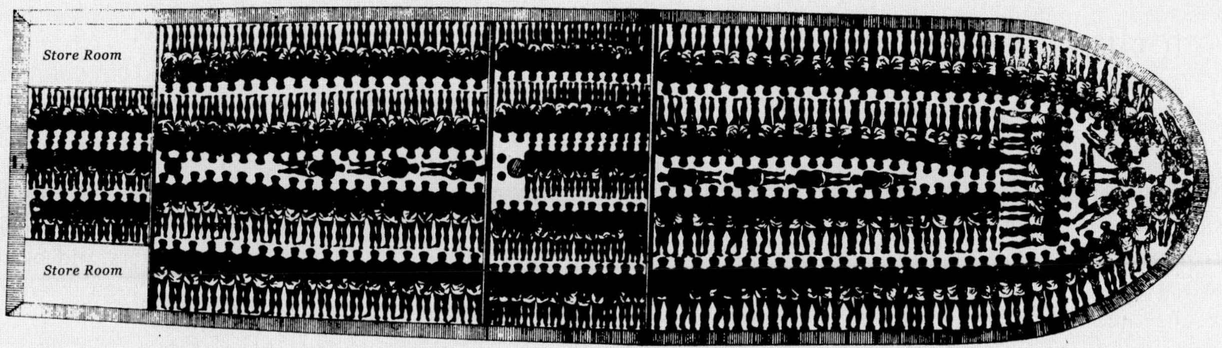


*The revolting conditions on slave ships sailing to Caribbean and North American ports pale in barbarity beside conditions on the southern route to Brazil, where slaves were literally packed like sardines in a can.*

bought and sold. As such, and because of ample documentation, it has attracted much of the attention of scholars; it also has tended to identify the institution of slavery with African blacks. From a global perspective, however, the trade was far broader. Indeed, hundreds of thousands of slaves were white or Asian. The steady flow of women and children from the Crimea, the Caucasus, and the Balkans in the fourteenth to eighteenth centuries for domestic, military, or sexual services in Ottoman lands, Italy, and sub-Saharan Africa; the use of convicts as galley slaves in the Venetian, French, Spanish, and Turkish navies (after the Battle of Lepanto in 1571, ten thousand Christian galley slaves in Turkish service were freed); the enslavement of peoples defeated in war by Aztec, Inca, Sioux, Navajo, and other indigenous peoples of the Americas; the various forms of debt slavery in China and in Russia (where the legal distinction between serf and slave before 1861 was very hazy indeed); the traffic of Indonesian and Pacific Island peoples for slave labor in Dutch South Africa; and the trans-Saharan stream of Africans to Mediterranean ports that continued at medieval rates into the late nineteenth century—all these were different forms of a worldwide practice. Although these forms sometimes had little in common with one another (such as the domestic and military slavery of the Islamic world and the plantation slavery of the Americas), they all involved the buying and selling of human beings who could not move about freely or enjoy the fruits of their labor.

The price of slaves varied widely over time and from market to market, according to age, sex, physical appearance, and buyers' perceptions of the social characteristics of each slave's ethnic background. The Mediterranean and Indian Ocean markets preferred women for domestic service; the Atlantic markets wanted strong young men for mine and plantation work. Changes in supply and demand could lead to great price fluctuations: the arrival of a very large number of slaves in a particular market or the failure of a dealer to appear when expected could drive prices down. We have little solid information on prices for slaves in the Balkans, Caucasus, or Indian Ocean region. Even in the Atlantic trade, it is difficult to determine, over several centuries, the value of currencies such as the Dutch guilder and the British pound; the cost and insurance on transported slaves; and the cost of goods exchanged for slaves. Yet the grand palazzi of Venice, the gold-encrusted cathedrals of Spain, and the elegant plantation houses of the Southern United States stand as testimony to the vast fortunes made in the slave trade. But how is the human toll measured?

Transformations within societies occurred not only because of local developments but also because of interactions among regions. For example, the virulent racism that in so many ways defines the American experience resulted partly from medieval European habits of dehumanizing the enemy (English vs. Irish, German vs. Slav, Christian vs. Jew and Muslim) and partly from the movement of peoples and ideas all over the globe. American gold prospectors in the 1850s carried the bigotry they had heaped on blacks in the Americas to Australia (see page 928), where it conditioned attitudes toward Asians and other peoples of color. Racism, like the slave trade, is a global phenomenon.

A final irony exists in the fact that for all the cries for human rights today, the slave trade continues on a broad scale. The ancient Indian Ocean traffic in Indian girls and boys for "service" in the Persian Gulf oil kingdoms and the sale of African children for work in Asia persist. Well-verified British, American, and United Nations reports prove that each year between 1998 and 2000, "criminal elements" brought more than fifty thousand women and children from Latvia, Nigeria, the Philippines, Thailand, China, Russia, and Mexico into the United States to work as sex slaves. They were bought, sold, tricked, and held in captivity, and their labor was exploited for the financial benefit of masters in a global enterprise.

## The Atlantic Slave Trade

Although the trade in African people was a worldwide phenomenon, the Atlantic slave trade was probably the most extensive aspect of it. This trade, extending from the early sixteenth to the late nineteenth century and involving the forced migration of millions of human beings, represents one of the most inhumane, unjust, and tragic blots on the history of human societies. The African diaspora immediately provokes a host of questions. First, why Africa? Why, in the seventeenth and eighteenth centuries, did slavery in the Americas become exclusively African? Why didn't Europeans raise the crops and secure the minerals they wanted for export to Europe right in Africa rather than employ enslaved Africans in the mines and plantations of the Americas? Why didn't Europeans bring to the Americas slaves from Asia, which did not have the demographic shortages of Africa and where, in the eighteenth century, population was greatly expanding?

As we have seen (see page 526), Europeans first used indigenous peoples, the Amerindians, to mine the silver and gold found in Mexico. When these peoples proved ill-suited to the harsh rigors of mining, the Spaniards brought in Africans. Although the Dutch had transported Indonesian peoples to the Cape Colony in South Africa, the cost of transporting Chinese or Pacific island peoples to the Americas was far too great.

One student has recently argued that across Europe, a pan-European insider/outsider ideology prevailed. This cultural attitude permitted the enslavement of outsiders but made the enslavement of white Europeans taboo. Europeans could not bear the sight of other Europeans doing plantation slave labor. According to this theory, a similar pan-African ideology did not exist, as Africans had no problem with selling Africans to Europeans.[24] Several facts argue against the validity of this theory. The merciless severity with which English landlords exploited their Irish peasants, the cold contempt with which French aristocrats often looked on their peasantry, and the casual indifference and harsh brutality with which Russian boyars treated their serfs all contradict the existence of a pan-European ideology or culture that opposed the enslavement of white Europeans. Moreover, the flow of white Slavic slaves from the Balkans into the eastern Mediterranean continued.

According to another theory, in the Muslim and Arab worlds by the tenth century, an association had developed between blackness and menial slavery. The Arab word *abd,* or "black," had become synonymous with *slave.* Although the great majority of slaves in the Islamic world were white, a racial element existed in Muslim slavery: not all slaves were black, but blacks were identified with slavery. In Europe, after the arrival of tens of thousands of sub-Saharan Africans in the Iberian Peninsula during the fifteenth century, Christian Europeans began to make a strong association between slavery and black Africans. Therefore, Africans seemed the "logical" solution to the labor shortage in the Americas.[25]

Another important question provoked by the African diaspora concerns the lack of economic development in Africa during the sixteenth through eighteenth centuries. Beginning in the late nineteenth century and continuing to the present, European entrepreneurs invested in African-owned and African-managed plantations and mines within Africa. Africans developed African products for export abroad. Why didn't this occur in the sixteenth century? Once Europeans realized the potential in the Americas for the production of goods such as sugar, tobacco, coffee, and cotton, the expansion of America took precedence over economic development within Africa. Moreover, plantations and mines in the Americas required a steady flow of cheap labor, which was provided by African captives.

Some scholars have argued that political conditions in parts of West Africa help to explain why that region was a major source of slaves. Like the Balkans in southern Europe and the Caucasus in southeastern Russia, West Africa suffered from a relatively high degree of political fragmentation. The lack of strong political authority and the frequency of destructive domestic warfare that generated captives encouraged the slave trade. Portuguese, Spanish, and then English traders cultivated special relationships with rulers of African coastal states. The captives that Europeans bought had been the subjects of other rulers and thus came from territories unknown to the traders. Europeans' willingness to purchase large numbers of captives from African traders stimulated slave raiding and aggravated political disorder in the continent's interior.[26]

The development of the Atlantic slave trade suggests many other questions. What regions of Africa were the sources of slaves? What goods and business procedures were involved in the exchange of slaves? What were the economic, social, political, and demographic effects of the slave trades on African societies? In a period when serfdom was declining in western Europe, why were African peoples enslaved, when land was so widely available and much of the African continent had a labor shortage?

The answer to the last question seems to lie in a technical problem related to African agriculture. Partly because of the tsetse fly, which causes sleeping sickness and other diseases, and partly because of easily leached lateritic soils (containing high concentrations of oxides), farmers had great difficulty using draft animals. Tropical soils responded poorly to plowing, and most work had to be done with the hoe. Productivity, therefore, was low. Economists maintain that in most societies, the value of a worker's productivity determines the value of his or her labor. In precolonial Africa, the individual's agricultural productivity was low, so his or her economic value to society was less than the economic value of a European peasant in Europe. Slaves in the Americas were more productive than free producers in Africa. And European slave dealers were very willing to pay a price higher than the value of an African's productivity in Africa.

The incidence of disease in the Americas also helps to explain the enslavement of Africans. Smallpox took a terrible toll on Native Americans (see page 526), and between 30 and 50 percent of Europeans exposed to malaria succumbed to that sickness. Africans had developed some immunity to both diseases, and in the New World they experienced the lowest mortality rate of any people. Europeans wanted workers for mines and sugar cane plantations. A coerced (or slave) labor force proved easier to exploit than a wage labor force.[27] As the demand for sugar increased, and as the technology for sugar production improved and shipping rates declined, the pressure for slave labor accelerated.

**TABLE 19.1 ESTIMATED SLAVE IMPORTS BY DESTINATION, 1451–1870**

| DESTINATION | ESTIMATED TOTAL SLAVE IMPORTS |
|---|---|
| British North America | 399,000 |
| Spanish America | 1,552,100 |
| British Caribbean | 1,665,000 |
| French Caribbean | 1,600,200 |
| Dutch Caribbean | 500,000 |
| Danish Caribbean | 28,000 |
| Brazil | 3,646,800 |
| Old World | 175,000 |
| | 9,566,100 |

*Source: P. D. Curtin,* The Atlantic Slave Trade: A Census *(Madison: University of Wisconsin Press, 1969), p. 268. Used with permission of The University of Wisconsin Press.*

The search for a sea route to India led the Portuguese in the fifteenth century to explore the West African coast. Having "discovered" Brazil in 1500, the Portuguese founded a sugar colony at Bahia in 1551. Between 1551 and 1575, before the traffic to North America had gotten under way, the Portuguese delivered more African slaves to Brazil than would ever reach British North America (see Table 19.1). Portugal essentially monopolized the slave trade until 1600 and continued to play a large role in the seventeenth century, though it was increasingly threatened by the Dutch, French, and English. From 1690 until the House of Commons abolished the slave trade in 1807, England was the leading carrier of African slaves.

Population density and supply conditions along the West African coast and the sailing time to New World markets determined the sources of slaves. As the demand for slaves rose, slavers moved down the West African coast from Senegambia to the more densely populated hinterlands of the Bight of Benin and the Bight of Biafra (see Map 16.4 on page 529). In the sixteenth and early seventeenth centuries, the Senegambian coast and the area near the mouth of the Congo River yielded the greatest numbers. By the late seventeenth century, the British found the Ivory Coast region the most profitable territory. A century later, the Bight of Benin and the Gold Coast had become the largest suppliers. The abundant supply of slaves in Angola, the region south of the Congo River, and the quick passage from Angola to Brazil and the Caribbean established that region as the major coast for Portuguese slavers.

Transatlantic wind patterns partly determined the routes of exchange. Shippers naturally preferred the swiftest crossing—that is, from the African port nearest the latitude of the intended American destination. Thus Portuguese shippers carried their cargoes from Angola to Brazil, and British merchants sailed from the Bight of Benin to the Caribbean. The great majority of slaves were intended for the sugar and coffee plantations extending from the Caribbean islands to Brazil.[28]

Angola produced 26 percent of all African slaves and 70 percent of all Portuguese slaves. Trading networks extending deep into the interior culminated at two major ports on the Angolan coast, Luanda and Benguela (see inset to Map 19.1). Between the 1730s and 1770s, Luanda shipped between 8,000 and 10,000 slaves each year; at the end of the eighteenth century, Benguela's numbers equaled those of Luanda. In 1820, the peak year, 18,957 blacks left Luanda. The Portuguese acquired a few slaves through warfare but secured the vast majority through trade with African dealers. Whites did not participate in the inland markets.

**City of Luanda, Angola** Founded by the Portuguese in 1575, Luanda was a center of the huge slave trade to Brazil. In this eighteenth-century print, offices and warehouses line the streets, and (right foreground) slaves are dragged to the ships for transportation to America. *(New York Public Library, Astor, Lenox, and Tilden Foundations)*

Almost all Portuguese shipments went to satisfy the virtually insatiable Brazilian demand for slaves.[29] The transatlantic slave trade lasted for almost four centuries and involved the brutalization and exploitation of millions of human beings. Here is an excerpt from a Portuguese doctor's 1793 report on conditions in Luanda before the voyage across the Atlantic had begun:

*Here takes place the second round of hardships that these unlucky people are forced to suffer . . . their human nature entirely overlooked. The dwelling place of the slave is simply the dirt floor of the compound, and he remains there exposed to harsh conditions and bad weather, and at night there are only a lean-to and some sheds . . . which they are herded into like cattle.*

*Their food continues scarce as before . . . limited at times to badly cooked beans, at other times to corn. . . .*

*And when they reach a port . . . , they are branded on the right breast with the coat of arms of the king and nation, of whom they have become vassals. . . . This mark is made with a hot silver instrument in the act of paying the king's duties, and this brand mark is called a* carimbo. . . .

*In this miserable and deprived condition the terrified slaves remain for weeks and months, and the great number of them who die is unspeakable. With some ten or twelve thousand arriving at Luanda each year, it often happens that only six or seven thousand are finally transported to Brazil.*[30]

Olaudah Equiano (see the feature "Individuals in Society: Olaudah Equiano") describes the experience of his voyage from Benin to Barbados in the Caribbean:

*At last, when the ship we were in had got in all her cargo [of slaves], they made ready with many fearful noises, and we were all put under deck so that we could not see how they managed the vessel. . . . The stench of the hold while we were on the coast was so intolerably loathsome that it was dangerous to remain there for any time, and some of us had been permitted to stay on the deck for the fresh air; but now that the whole ship's cargo were confined together it became absolutely pestilential. The closeness of the place and the*

# INDIVIDUALS IN SOCIETY

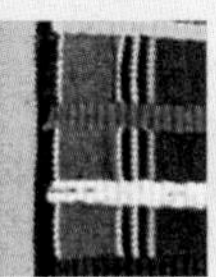

## OLAUDAH EQUIANO

The transatlantic slave trade was a mass movement involving millions of human beings. It was also the sum of individual lives spent partly or entirely in slavery. Most of those lives remain hidden to us. Olaudah Equiano (1745–1797) represents a rare ray of light into the slaves' obscurity; he is probably the best-known African slave.

Equiano was born in Benin (modern Nigeria) of Ibo ethnicity. His father, one of the village elders (or chieftains), presided over a large household that included "many slaves," prisoners captured in local wars. All people, slave and free, shared in the cultivation of family lands. One day, when all the adults were in the fields, two strange men and a woman broke into the family compound, kidnapped the eleven-year-old Olaudah and his sister, tied them up, and dragged them into the woods. Brother and sister were separated, and Olaudah was sold several times to various dealers before reaching the coast. As it took six months to walk there, his home must have been far inland. The sea, the slave ship, and the strange appearance of the white crew terrified the boy (see page 616). Equiano's master took him to Jamaica, Virginia, and then to England, where he placed him in the custody of a kind family. They gave him the rudiments of an education, and he was baptized a Christian.

Equiano soon went to sea as a captain's boy (servant), serving in the Royal Navy during the Seven Years' War. On shore at Portsmouth, England, after one battle, Equiano's master urged him to read, study, and learn basic mathematics. This education served him well, for after a voyage to the West Indies, his master sold him to a Philadelphia Quaker, Robert King, who was a rum and sugar merchant. Equiano worked as a clerk in King's warehouse, as a longshoreman loading and unloading cargo ships, and at sea where he developed good navigational skills; for his work, King paid him. Equiano became an entrepreneur himself, buying and selling small goods in the islands and mainland ports. Determined to buy his freedom, Equiano had amassed enough money by 1766, and King signed the deed of manumission. Equiano was twenty-one years old; he had been a slave for ten.

He returned to London and used his remaining money to hire tutors to teach him hairdressing, mathematics, and how to play the French horn. When money was scarce, he found work as a merchant seaman, traveling to Portugal, Nice, Genoa, Naples, and Turkey. He participated in an Arctic expedition.

*Olaudah Equiano, 1789, dressed as an elegant Englishman, his Bible open to the Book of Acts.* (New York Public Library, Schomburg Center for Research in Black Culture)

Equiano's *Travels** (1788) reveals a complex and sophisticated man. He had a strong constitution and an equally strong character. His Christian faith undoubtedly sustained him. On the title page of his book, he cited a verse from Isaiah (12:2): "The Lord Jehovah is my strength and my song." The very first thought that came to his mind the day he was freed was a passage from Psalm 126: "I glorified God in my heart, in whom I trusted."

Equiano loathed the brutal slavery he saw in the West Indies and the vicious racism he experienced in the North American colonies. He respected the fairness of Robert King, admired British navigational and industrial technologies, and had many close white friends. He once described himself as "almost an Englishman." He was also involved in the black communities in the West Indies and in London. *Travels* is a well-documented argument for the abolition of slavery and a literary classic that went through nine editions before his death.

Olaudah Equiano spoke to large crowds in the industrial cities of Manchester and Birmingham, arguing that it was in the business interests of manufacturers to support abolition, as Africa was a huge, virtually untapped market for English cloth.

### QUESTIONS FOR ANALYSIS

1. How typical was Olaudah Equiano's life as a slave? How atypical?
2. Describe his culture and his sense of himself.

*Subjected to critical textual analysis, Equiano's *Travels* has recently been treated as an example of the "noble savage" ideal, a rags-to-riches story, a spiritual autobiography, a publicist's argument against the slave trade, and a composite of oral history and contemporary journalism by authors other than Equiano. The jury is out.

*Source: Equiano's Travels: The Interesting Narrative of the Life of Olaudah Equiano,* ed. Paul Edwards (Portsmouth, N.H.: Heinemann, 1996).

> *heat of the climate, added to the number in the ship, which was so crowded that each had scarcely room to turn himself, almost suffocated us. This produced copious perspirations, so that the air soon became unfit for respiration from a variety of loathsome smells, and brought on a sickness among the slaves, of which many died, thus falling victims to the improvident avarice, as I may call it, of their purchasers. This wretched situation was again aggravated by the galling of the chains, now become insupportable, and the filth of the necessary tubs [of human waste], into which the children often fell and were almost suffocated. The shrieks of the women and the groans of the dying rendered the whole a scene of horror almost inconceivable. Happily perhaps for myself I was soon reduced so low here that it was thought necessary to keep me almost always on deck, and from my extreme youth I was not put in fetters. . . . Two of my wearied countrymen who were chained together (I was near them at the time), preferring death to such a life of misery, somehow made through the nettings and jumped into the sea: immediately another quite dejected fellow, who on account of his illness was suffered to be out of irons, also followed their example. . . . Two of the wretches were drowned, but they got the other and afterwards flogged him unmercifully. . . . The want of fresh air, . . . and the stench of the necessary tubs carried off many. . . . At last we came in sight of the island of Barbados, at which the whites on board gave a great shout and made many signs of joy to us. . . . We soon anchored amongst them off Bridgetown. Many merchants and planters now came on board, though it was in the evening. They put us in separate parcels and examined us attentively. They also made us jump, and pointed to the land, signifying we were to go there. We thought by this we should be eaten by these ugly men, as they appeared to us. . . . They told us we were not to be eaten but to work, and were soon to go on land where we should see many of our country people. This report eased us much; and sure enough soon after we were landed there came to us Africans of all languages.*[31]

Unlike Great Britain, France, and the Netherlands, Portugal did not have a strong mercantile class involved in slaving in the eighteenth century. Instead, the Portuguese colony of Brazil provided the ships, capital, and goods for the slave trade. Credit played a major role in the trade: Brazilian-controlled firms in Luanda extended credit to African operators, who had to make payments in slaves six or eight months later. Portuguese ironware and wine; Brazilian tobacco and brandies; and European and Asian textiles, firearms, and beads were the main goods exchanged for slaves. All commodities entered Angola from Brazil. The Luandan (or Benguelan) merchants

**Queen Njiga (also Nzinga) Mbandi Ana de Sousa (1582–1633)** Njiga of Ndongo (r. 1624–1629) is the most important female political figure in the history of early modern Angola. She used military force in her expansionist policy and participated fully in the slave trade, but she fiercely resisted Portuguese attempts to control that trade. Here she sits enthroned, wearing her crown (the cross a sign of her Christian baptism) and bracelets, giving an order. She has become a symbol of African resistance to colonial rule. *(Courtesy, Ezio Bassani)*

**Pedlars, Rio de Janeiro (early nineteenth century)** A British army officer sketched this scene of everyday life in Rio de Janeiro, Brazil. The ability to balance large burdens on the head meant that the hands were free for other use. Note the player (*third from right*) of a musical instrument originating in the Congo. We do not know whether the pedlars were free and self-employed or were selling for their owners. *(From "Views and Costumes of the City and Neighborhood of Rio de Janeiro, Brazil," in Drawings Taken by Lieutenant Chamberlain, During the Years 1819 and 1820 [London: Columbian Press, 1822])*

pegged the value of the goods to the value of prime young slaves but then undervalued the worth of the slaves and overpriced the goods. As a result, the African operators frequently ended up in debt to the merchants.

Although the demand was great, Portuguese merchants in Angola and Brazil sought to maintain only a steady trickle of slaves from the African interior to Luanda and across the ocean to Bahia and Rio de Janeiro: a flood of slaves would have depressed the American market. Rio, the port capital through which most slaves passed, commanded the Brazilian trade. Planters and mine operators from the provinces traveled to Rio to buy slaves. Between 1795 and 1808, approximately 10,000 Angolans per year stood in the Rio slave market. In 1810 the figure rose to 18,000; in 1828 it reached 32,000.[32]

The English ports of London, Bristol, and particularly Liverpool dominated the British slave trade. In the eighteenth century, Liverpool was the world's greatest slave-trading port. In all three cities, small and cohesive merchant classes exercised great public influence. The cities also had huge stores of industrial products for export, growing shipping industries, and large amounts of ready cash for investment abroad. Merchants generally formed partnerships to raise capital and to share the risks; each voyage was a separate enterprise or venture.

Slaving ships from Bristol searched the Gold Coast, the Bight of Benin, Bonny, and Calabar. The ships of Liverpool drew slaves from Gambia, the Windward Coast, and the Gold Coast. To Africa, British ships carried textiles, gunpowder and flint, beer and spirits, British and Irish linens, and woolen cloth. A collection of goods was grouped together into what was called the **sorting.** An English sorting might include bolts of cloth, firearms, alcohol, tobacco, and hardware; this batch of goods would be traded for an individual slave or a quantity of gold, ivory, or dyewood. When Europeans added a markup for profit, Africans followed suit. Currency was not exchanged; it served as a standard of value and a means of keeping accounts.[33]

European traders had two systems for exchange. First, especially on the Gold Coast, they established **factory-forts.** These fortified trading posts were expensive to maintain but proved useful for fending off rival Europeans. Second, they used **shore trading,** in which European ships sent boats ashore or invited African dealers to bring traders and slaves out to the ships. The English captain John Adams, who made ten voyages to Africa between 1786 and 1800, described the shore method of trading at Bonny:

*This place is the wholesale market for slaves, as not fewer than 20,000 are annually sold here; 16,000 of whom are natives of one nation called Ibo. . . . Fairs where the slaves of the Ibo nation are obtained are held every five or six weeks at several villages, which are situated on the banks of the rivers and creeks in the interior, and to which the African traders of Bonny resort to purchase them.*

*. . . The traders augment the quantity of their merchandise, by obtaining from their friends, the captains of the slave ships, a considerable quantity of goods on credit. . . . Evening is the period chosen for the time of departure, when they proceed in a body, accompanied by the noise of drums, horns, and gongs. At the expiration of the sixth day, they generally return bringing with them 1,500 or 2,000 slaves, who are sold to Europeans the evening after their arrival, and taken on board the ships. . . .*

*It is expected that every vessel, on her arrival at Bonny, will fire a salute the instant the anchor is let go, as a compliment to the black monarch who soon afterwards makes his appearance in a large canoe, at which time, all those natives who happen to be alongside the vessel are compelled to proceed in their canoes to a respectful distance, and make way for his Majesty's barge. After a few compliments to the captain, he usually enquires after brother George, meaning the King of England, George III, and hopes he and his family are well. He is not pleased unless he is regaled with the best the ship affords. . . . His power is absolute; and the surrounding country, to a considerable distance, is subject to his dominion.*[34]

The shore method of buying slaves allowed the ship to move easily from market to market. The final prices of the slaves depended on their ethnic origin, their availability when the shipper arrived, and their physical health when offered for sale in the West Indies or the North or South American colonies.

Meanwhile, according to one scholar, the northbound trade in slaves across the Sahara "continued without serious disruption until the late nineteenth century, and in a clandestine way and on a much reduced scale it survived well into the twentieth century."[35] The present scholarly consensus is that the trans-Saharan slave trade in the seventeenth and eighteenth centuries was never as important as the transatlantic trade.

Supplying slaves for the foreign market was in the hands of a small, wealthy merchant class, or it was a state monopoly. Gathering a band of raiders and the capital for equipment, guides, tolls, and supplies involved considerable expense. By contemporary standards, slave raiding was a costly operation. Only black entrepreneurs with sizable capital and labor could afford to finance and direct raiding drives. They exported slaves because the profits on exports were greater than the profits to be made from using labor in the domestic economy:

*The export price of slaves never rose to the point where it became cheaper for Europeans to turn to alternative sources of supply, and it never fell to the point where it caused more than a temporary check to the trade. . . . The remarkable expansion of the slave trade in the eighteenth century provides a horrific illustration of the rapid response of producers in an underdeveloped economy to price incentives.*[36]

African peoples, captured and forcibly brought to the Americas, played an integral part in the formation of the Atlantic world. They had an enormous impact on the economics of the Portuguese and Spanish colonies of South America and in the Dutch, French, and British colonies of the Caribbean and North America. For example, on the sugar plantations of Mexico and the Caribbean; on the cotton, rice, and tobacco plantations of North America; and in the silver and gold mines of Peru and Mexico, slaves of African descent not only worked in the mines and fields but also filled skilled, supervisory, and administrative positions, as well as performed domestic service.

But the importance of the slave trade extended beyond the Atlantic world. The expansion of capitalism, as well as the industrialization of Western societies, Egypt, and the nations of West, Central, and South Africa—all of these related in one way or another to the traffic in African peoples. In the United States, African slaves and their descendants influenced many facets of American culture, such as language ("it's cool"), music (ragtime and jazz), dance, and diet. Even the U.S. Capitol building, where Congress meets, was built partly by slave labor.[37]

## Consequences Within Africa

What economic impact did European trade have on African societies? Africans possessed technology well suited to their environment. Over the centuries, they had cultivated a wide variety of plant foods; developed plant and animal husbandry techniques; and mined, smelted, and otherwise worked a great variety of metals. Apart from firearms, American tobacco and rum, and the cheap brandy brought by the Portuguese, European goods presented no novelty to Africans. What made foreign products desirable to Africans was their price. Traders of handwoven Indian cotton textiles, Venetian imitations of African beads, and iron bars from European smelters could undersell African manufacturers. Africans exchanged slaves, ivory, gold, pepper, and animal skins for those goods. Their earnings usually did not remain in Africa. African states eager to expand or to control commerce bought European firearms, although the difficulty of maintaining guns often gave gun owners only marginal superiority over skilled bowmen.[38] The kingdom of Dahomey, however, built its power on the effective use of firearms.

The African merchants who controlled the production of exports gained from foreign trade. The king of Dahomey, for example, had a gross income in 1750 of £250,000 from the overseas export of slaves. A portion of his profit was spent on goods that improved the living standard of his people. Slave-trading entrepôts, which provided opportunities for traders and for farmers who supplied foodstuffs to towns, caravans, and slave ships, prospered. But such economic returns did not spread very far.[39] International trade did not lead to the economic development of Africa. Neither technological growth nor the gradual spread of economic benefits occurred in Africa in early modern times.

As in the Islamic world (see page 634), women in sub-Saharan Africa also engaged in the slave trade. In Guinea the *signeres,* women slave merchants, acquired considerable riches in the business. One of them, Mae Correia, led a life famous in her region for its wealth and elegance.

The arrival of Europeans caused basic social changes in some West African societies. In Senegambia chattel slavery seems to have been unknown before the growth of the transatlantic trade. By the late eighteenth century, however, chiefs were using the slave labor of craftsmen, sailors, and farm workers. If the price was right, they were sold off. Those who committed crimes had traditionally paid fines, but because of the urgent demand for slaves, many misdemeanors became punishable by sale to slave dealers. Europeans introduced corn, pineapples, cassava, and sweet potatoes to West Africa, which had important consequences for population growth.

The intermarriage of French traders and Wolof women in Senegambia created a *métis,* or mulatto, class. In the emerging urban centers at Saint-Louis, this small class adopted the French language, the Roman Catholic faith, and a French manner of life. The métis exercised consid-

**Sapi-Portuguese Saltcellar** Contact with the Sapi people of present-day Sierra Leone in West Africa led sixteenth-century Portuguese traders to commission this ivory saltcellar, for which they brought Portuguese designs. But the object's basic features—a spherical container and separate lid on a flat base, with men, women, and supporting beams below—are distinctly African. An executioner, holding an ax with which he has beheaded five men, stands on the lid. This piece was probably intended as an example of Sapi artistic virtuosity, rather than for practical table use. *(Courtesy, Museo Preistorico Etnografico, Rome)*

**TABLE 19.2 THE TRANSATLANTIC SLAVE TRADE, 1450–1900**

| PERIOD | VOLUME | PERCENT |
|---|---|---|
| 1450–1600 | 367,000 | 3.1 |
| 1601–1700 | 1,868,000 | 16.0 |
| 1701–1800 | 6,133,000 | 52.4 |
| 1801–1900 | 3,330,000 | 28.5 |
| Total | 11,698,000 | 100.0 |

*Source: P. E. Lovejoy,* Transformations in Slavery: A History of Slavery in Africa *(Cambridge: Cambridge University Press, 1983), p. 19. Used with permission.*

erable political and economic power. When granted French citizenship in the late eighteenth century, its members sent Senegalese grievances to the Estates General of 1789.[40] However, European cultural influences did not penetrate West African society beyond the seacoast.

The political consequences of the slave trade varied from place to place. The trade enhanced the power and wealth of some kings and warlords in the short run but promoted conditions of instability and collapse over the long run. In the kingdom of the Congo, the perpetual Portuguese search for slaves undermined the monarchy, destroyed political unity, and led to constant disorder and warfare; power passed to the village chiefs. Likewise in Angola, which became a Portuguese proprietary colony, the slave trade decimated and scattered the population and destroyed the local economy. By contrast, the military kingdom of Dahomey, which entered into the slave trade in the eighteenth century and made it a royal monopoly, prospered enormously from trading in slaves. The economic strength of the state rested on the slave trade. The royal army raided deep into the interior, and in the late eighteenth century Dahomey became one of the major West African sources of slaves. When slaving expeditions failed to yield sizable catches, and when European demands declined, the resulting depression in the Dahomean economy caused serious political unrest. Iboland, inland from the Niger Delta, from whose great port cities of Bonny and Brass the British drained tens of thousands of slaves, experienced minimal political effects and suffered no permanent population loss. A high birthrate kept pace with the incursions of the slave trade, and Ibo societies remained demographically and economically strong.

What demographic impact did the slave trade have on Africa? In all, between approximately 1500 and 1900, about 12 million Africans were exported to the Americas, 6 million were exported to Asia, and 8 million were retained within Africa. Tables 19.1 and 19.2 report the somewhat divergent findings of two careful scholars on the number of slaves shipped to the New World. Export figures do not include the approximately 10 to 15 percent who died during procurement or in transit.

The early modern slave trade involved a worldwide web of relationships among markets in Cairo, Istanbul, Kilwa, Luanda, Malacca, Goa, Rio de Janeiro, and Kingston. But Africa was the crucible of the trade. There is no small irony in the fact that the continent most desperately in need of population, Africa, lost so many millions to the slave trade. Although the British Parliament abolished the slave trade in 1807 and traffic in Africans to Brazil and Cuba gradually declined, *within* Africa the trade continued at the levels of the peak years of the transatlantic trade, 1780–1820. In the later nineteenth century, developing African industries, using slave labor, produced a variety of products for domestic consumption and export. Again, there is irony in the fact that in the eighteenth century, European demand for slaves expanded the trade (and wars) within Africa, yet in the nineteenth century, European imperialists defended territorial aggrandizement by arguing that they were "civilizing" Africans by abolishing slavery. But after 1880, European businessmen (and African governments) did not push abolition; they wanted cheap labor.

Western and American markets wanted young male slaves. Asian and African markets preferred young females. Women were sought for their reproductive value, as sex objects, and because their economic productivity was not threatened by the possibility of physical rebellion, as might be the case with young men. Consequently, two-thirds of those exported to the Americas were male, one-third female. The population on the western coast of Africa became predominantly female; the population in the East African Savanna and Horn regions was predominantly male. The slave trade therefore had significant consequences for the institutions of marriage, slavery itself, and the sexual division of labor—topics scholars have yet to explore. Although overall population may have shown modest growth from roughly 1650 to 1900, that growth was offset by declines in the Horn and on the eastern and western coasts. While Europe and Asia experienced considerable demographic and economic expansion in the eighteenth century, Africa suffered a decline.[41]

## SUMMARY

In the early modern world, African kingdoms and societies represented considerable economic and political diversity. The communities of Wolof-, Serer-, and Pulaar-speaking peoples in Senegambia had long known the trans-Saharan caravan trade, which along with goods brought Islamic, and later French, culture to the region. The West African kingdoms of Benin, Kanem-Bornu, and Hausaland maintained their separate existences for centuries. They also experienced strong Islamic influences, although Muslim culture affected primarily the royal and elite classes and seldom penetrated into the broad masses of people. In eastern Africa, Ethiopia had accepted Christianity long before northern and eastern Europe; Ethiopians practiced Coptic Christianity, which shaped their identity, and Jesuit attempts to substitute Roman liturgical forms met with fierce resistance. The wealthy Swahili city-states on the southeastern coast of Africa possessed a Muslim and mercantile culture. Cities such as Mogadishu, Kilwa, and Sofala used Arabic as the language of communication, and their commercial economies were tied to the trade of the Indian Ocean. The arrival of Europeans proved disastrous for those cities.

It is a brutal historical irony that Africa, so desperate for population, exported people in exchange for goods that chiefly benefited a small royal and commercial elite. The slave trade across the Atlantic and Indian Oceans greatly delayed population growth. We do not know how many Africans were exported to India, China, and Southeast Asia. Despite the export of as many as 12 million human beings to meet the labor needs of South and North America, European influences scarcely penetrated the African interior. The overall impact of the slave trade on Africa was devastating for some regions and societies but marginal for others.

But the Atlantic slave trade had another effect. When it declined after 1810, the search for slaves within Africa accelerated, and traders pressed ever deeper into the interior. Slaves were one part of the overall economy, which remained overwhelmingly agricultural. As the demand for workers to cultivate land rose, regions that possessed firearms traded them for slaves. In most places, such as Senegambia, the slaves went into agriculture. Thus the slave trade led to a wider use of slaves within Africa itself, and rather than promoting technological development in sub-Saharan Africa, slavery delayed it.

## KEY TERMS

age-grade systems
oba
Taghaz
Tuareg
cowrie shells
Swahili
slave
sorting
factory-forts
shore trading

## NOTES

1. P. D. Curtin, *Economic Change in Precolonial Africa: Senegambia in the Era of the Slave Trade* (Madison: University of Wisconsin Press, 1975), pp. 34–35; J. A. Rawley, *The Transatlantic Slave Trade: A History* (New York: W. W. Norton, 1981), p. 12.
2. R. W. July, *A History of the African People,* 3d ed. (New York: Scribner's, 1980), pp. 128–129.
3. R. W. July, *Precolonial Africa: An Economic and Social History* (New York: Scribner's, 1975), p. 99.
4. July, *A History of the African People,* p. 141.
5. J. Iliffe, *Africans: The History of a Continent* (Cambridge: Cambridge University Press, 1995), p. 95.
6. Ibid., pp. 66–67, 93–94.
7. *Equiano's Travels: The Interesting Narrative of the Life of Olaudah Equiano,* ed. P. Edwards (Portsmouth, N.H.: Heinemann, 1996), p. 4.
8. Iliffe, *Africans,* pp. 66–67.
9. Ibid., pp. 81–85.
10. Quoted in R. Hallett, *Africa to 1875* (Ann Arbor: University of Michigan Press, 1970), p. 151.
11. *The Cambridge History of Africa.* Vol. 3: *Ca 1050 to 1600,* ed. R. Oliver (Cambridge: Cambridge University Press, 1977), pp. 427–435.
12. A. ibn-Fartura, "The Kanem Wars," in *Nigerian Perspectives,* ed. T. Hodgkin (London: Oxford University Press, 1966), pp. 111–115.

13. "The Kano Chronicle," quoted in T. Hodgkin, ed., *Nigerian Perspectives* (London: Oxford University Press, 1966), pp. 89–90.
14. See A. J. R. Russell-Wood, *The Portuguese Empire: A World on the Move* (Baltimore: Johns Hopkins University Press, 1998), pp. 11–13.
15. J. Middleton, *The World of Swahili: An African Mercantile Civilization* (New Haven, Conn.: Yale University Press, 1992), p. 27.
16. Ibid., pp. 35–38.
17. Russell-Wood, *The Portuguese Empire,* pp. 43–44.
18. P. E. Lovejoy, *Transformations in Slavery: A History of Slavery in Africa* (Cambridge: Cambridge University Press, 1983), p. 19. This section leans heavily on Lovejoy's work.
19. See Table 2.1, "Trans-Saharan Slave Trade, 650–1600," ibid., p. 25.
20. Iliffe, *Africans,* p. 75.
21. Quoted in H. Thomas, *The Slave Trade* (New York: Simon and Schuster, 1997), p. 21.
22. G. Gerzina, *Black London: Life Before Emancipation* (New Brunswick, N.J.: Rutgers University Press, 1995), pp. 29–66, passim; the quotation is on p. 53.
23. Iliffe, *Africans,* pp. 121–126.
24. See D. Eltis, *The Rise of African Slavery in the Americas* (Cambridge: Cambridge University Press, 2000), Chap. 3; and the review/commentary by J. E. Inikori, *American Historical Review* 106, no. 5 (December 2001): 1751–1753.
25. R. Blackburn, *The Making of New World Slavery: From the Baroque to the Modern, 1492–1800* (New York: Verso, 1998), pp. 79–80.
26. Ibid., pp. 81–83.
27. P. Manning, *Slavery and African Life: Occidental, Oriental, and African Slave Trades* (New York: Cambridge University Press, 1990), pp. 31–37.
28. Rawley, *The Transatlantic Slave Trade,* p. 45.
29. Ibid., pp. 41–47.
30. R. E. Conrad, *Children of God's Fire: A Documentary History of Black Slavery in Brazil* (Princeton, N.J.: Princeton University Press, 1983), pp. 20–23.
31. *Equiano's Travels,* pp. 23–26.
32. Rawley, *The Transatlantic Slave Trade,* pp. 45–47.
33. July, *A History of the African People,* p. 208.
34. J. Adams, "Remarks on the Country Extending from Cape Palmas to the River Congo," in T. Hodgkin, ed., *Nigerian Perspectives* (London: Oxford University Press, 1966), pp. 178–180.
35. A. G. Hopkins, *An Economic History of West Africa* (New York: Columbia University Press, 1973), p. 83.
36. Ibid., p. 105.
37. J. Thornton, *Africa and Africans in the Making of the Atlantic World* (New York: Cambridge University Press, 1992), pp. 138–142.
38. July, *Precolonial Africa,* pp. 269–270.
39. Hopkins, *An Economic History of West Africa,* p. 119.
40. July, *A History of the African People,* pp. 201–202.
41. Manning, *Slavery and African Life,* pp. 22–23 and Chap. 3, pp. 38–59.

## SUGGESTED READING

Perhaps the best general survey of African history is the title by Iliffe cited in the Notes; it is soundly researched, and it takes the history of population as its theme. Students wishing to explore more fully some of the issues raised in this chapter might begin with *African History: Text and Readings.* Vol. 1: *Western African History;* Vol. 2: *Eastern African History;* and Vol. 3: *Central and Southern African History* (1990), all edited by R. O. Collins. This work gives a useful introduction to the geography and history of the continent and brings together a solid collection of primary documents and scholarly commentaries. B. Davidson, ed., *African Civilization Revisited* (1991), also contains interesting source readings on many facets of African history and cultures from antiquity to the present. K. Shillington, *History of Africa* (1989), provides a soundly researched, highly readable, and well-illustrated survey, while R. Oliver, *The African Experience* (1991), traces African history through particular historical problems. Although many of the articles in *The Cambridge History of Africa.* Vol. 4: *From 1600–1790,* ed. R. Gray (1975), are now dated, the following articles are still useful: "The Central Sahara and Sudan," "North-West Africa," and "Southern Africa and Madagascar." V. B. Thompson, *Africa and Unity* (1969), offers an African and African-American response to the traditional Eurocentric interpretation of African history and culture.

J. Thornton, *Africa and Africans in the Making of the Atlantic World, 1400–1680* (1992), places African developments in an Atlantic context. Likewise, both A. L. Karras and J. R. McNeill, eds., *Atlantic American Societies: From Columbus Through Abolition, 1492–1888* (1992), and B. Solow, ed., *Slavery and the Rise of the Atlantic System* (1991), contain important and valuable articles on many of the economic and cultural factors that linked Africa and the Western Hemisphere. For Ethiopia, see H. G. Marcus, *A History of Ethiopia* (1994), a concise but highly readable study. The standard study of the Savanna is probably J. Vansina, *Kingdoms of the Savanna* (1966). For East Africa and the Horn region, see J. Middleton, *The World of Swahili: An African Mercantile Civilization* (1992), which provides an expert synthesis of recent scholarly literature by a social anthropologist. The older study by C. S. Nicholls, *The Swahili Coast* (1971), is still useful. J. Knappert, *Four Centuries of Swahili Verse: A Literary History and Anthology* (1979), is a most interesting celebration of literary manifestations of Swahili culture.

The literature on slavery continues to grow. D. Eltis, *The Rise of African Slavery in the Americas* (2000), is a most important, if sometimes provocative, work. G. M. Fredrickson, *Racism: A Short History* (2002), contains probably the best recent study of the connection between African slavery and Western racism.

The slave trade represents tropical Africa's first extensive relationship with the outside world. P. D. Curtin, *The Rise and Fall of the Plantation Complex: Essays in Atlantic History,* 2d ed. (1998), is broader in scope than the title implies, for in a series of stimulating articles, it treats most aspects of slavery in Europe and in the Americas from about 1300 to 1888. R. Segal, *The Black Diaspora: Five Centuries of the*

*Black Experience Outside Africa* (1995), is narrower in scope than its title suggests, for it ignores the black experience in Asia and Europe. R. Blackburn, *The Making of New World Slavery: From the Baroque to the Modern, 1492–1800* (1998), describes the ways slavery in the Americas differed from earlier patterns, reflected distinctly modern business techniques, and contributed to a destructive pattern of human conduct. H. Thomas, *The Slave Trade* (1997), contains a mine of exciting information. Students seeking an understanding of African slave women and their reactions to slavery, work, and domestic situations might consult M. Morissey, *Slave Women in the New World: Gender Stratification in the Caribbean* (1989). In addition to the titles by Manning and Middleton cited in the Notes, see P. Manning, *Slavery, Colonialism and Economic Growth in Dahomey, 1640–1960* (1982), an in-depth study of the kingdom of Dahomey, which, after Angola, was the largest exporter of slaves to the Americas. J. F. Searing, *West African Slavery and Atlantic Commerce, 1700–1860* (1993), explores the effects of the Atlantic slave trade on the societies of the Senegal River valley. The theme of R. L. Stein's *The French Slave Trade in the Eighteenth Century: An Old Regime Business* (1979) is indicated by its title.

Although the emphasis in J. E. Harris, ed., *Global Dimensions of African Diaspora* (1982), is heavy on the United States and the Caribbean, with very little on South America, East Asia, or South Asia, some of the articles are very important: see especially those by J. E. Harris, L. W. Levine, and S. C. Drake. The highly important role of black sailors is treated in W. J. Bolster, *Black Jacks: African American Seamen in the Age of Sail* (1997). For the black experience in eighteenth- and early-nineteenth-century England, see Gerzina's work, cited in the Notes.

# LISTENING TO THE PAST

## DUARTE BARBOSA ON THE SWAHILI CITY-STATES

*The Portuguese linguist Duarte Barbosa made two voyages to India. Arriving first in 1500, he acted for five years as interpreter and translator in Cochin and Cananor in Kerala (in southwestern India on the Malabar Coast) and returned to Lisbon in 1506. On his second visit, in 1511, he served the Portuguese government as chief scribe in the factory of Cananor (a factory was a warehouse for the storage of goods, not a manufacturing center) and as the liaison with the local Indian rajah (prince). When Afonso de Albuquerque dismissed Barbosa, he went to Calicut. He returned to Cananor about 1520 and died there in 1545.*

*On the basis of his trips around the Indian Ocean in 1518, Barbosa completed his* Libro des Coisas da India, *a geographical and ethnographic survey of peoples, lands, and commerce from the Cape of Good Hope to China. It was based largely on his personal observations. First published in Italian, the book won wide acclaim in Europe, and modern scholars consider the geographical information in it very accurate.*

### Sofala

And the manner of their traffic was this: they came in small vessels named *zambucos* from the kingdoms of Kilwa, Mombasa, and Malindi, bringing many cotton cloths, some spotted and others white and blue, also some of silk, and many small beads, gray, red, and yellow, which things come to the said kingdoms from the great kingdom of Cambay [in Northwest India] in other greater ships. And these wares the said Moors who came from Malindi and Mombasa [purchased from others who bring them hither and] paid for in gold at such a price that those merchants departed well pleased; which gold they gave by weight.

The Moors of Sofala kept these wares and sold them afterwards to the heathen of the Kingdom of Benametapa, who came thither laden with gold which they gave in exchange for the said cloths without weighing it. These Moors collect also great store of ivory which they find hard by Sofala, and this also they sell in the Kingdom of Cambay at five or six cruzados the quintal. They also sell some ambergris, which is brought to them from the Hucicas, and is exceeding good. These Moors are black, and some of them tawny; some of them speak Arabic, but the more part use the language of the country. They clothe themselves from the waist down with cotton and silk cloths, and other cloths they wear over their shoulders like capes, and turbans on their heads. Some of them wear small caps dyed in grain in chequers and other woolen clothes in many tints, also camlets and other silks.

Their food is millet, rice, flesh and fish. In this river as far as the sea are many sea horses, which come out on the land to graze, which horses always move in the sea like fishes; they have tusks like those of small elephants, being whiter and harder, and it never loses color. In the country near Sofala are many wild elephants, exceeding great (which the country-folk know not how to tame), ounces, lions, deer and many other wild beasts. It is a land of plains and hills with many streams of sweet water. . . .

### Kilwa

Going along the coast from [the] town of Mozambique, there is an island hard by the mainland which is called Kilwa, in which is a Moorish town with many fair houses of stones and mortar, with many windows after our fashion, very well arranged in streets, with many flat roofs. The doors are of wood, well carved, with excellent joinery. Around it are streams and orchards and fruit-gardens with many channels of sweet water. It has a Moorish king over it. From this place they trade with Sofala, whence they bring back gold, and from here they spread all over . . . the seacoast [which] is well peopled with villages and abodes of Moors.

Before the King our Lord sent out his expedition to discover India the Moors of Sofala, Cuama, Angoya and Mozambique were all subject to the king of Kilwa, who was the most mighty king among them. And in this town was great plenty of gold, as no ships passed towards Sofala without first coming to this island. . . .

This town was taken by force from its king by the Portuguese, as, moved by arrogance, he refused to obey the King our Lord. There they took many prisoners and the king fled from the island, and His Highness ordered that a fort should be built there, and kept it under his rule and governance. Afterwards he ordered that it should be pulled down, as its maintenance was of no value nor profit to him, and it was destroyed by Antonio de Saldanha. . . .

### Malindi

. . . Journeying along the coast towards India, there is a fair town on the mainland lying along a strand, which is named Malindi. It pertains to the Moors and has a Moorish king over it; the which place has many fair stone and mortar houses of many stories, with great plenty of windows and flat roofs, after our fashion. The place is well laid out in streets. The folk are both black and white; they go naked, covering only their private parts with cotton and silk cloths. Others of them wear cloths folded like cloaks and waistbands, and turbans of many rich stuffs on their heads.

They are great barterers, and deal in cloth, gold, ivory, and divers other wares with the Moors and heathen of the great kingdom of Cambay; and to their haven come every year many ships with cargoes of merchandise, from which they get great store of gold, ivory and wax. In this traffic the Cambay merchants make great profits, and thus, on one side and the other, they earn much money. There is great plenty of food in this city, rice, millet, and some wheat which they bring from Cambay, and divers sorts of fruit, inasmuch as there is here abundance of fruit-gardens and orchards. Here too are plenty of round-tailed sheep, cows and other cattle and great store of oranges, also of hens.

The king and people of this place ever were and are friends of the King of Portugal, and the Portuguese always find in them great comfort and friendship and perfect peace, and there the ships, when they chance to pass that way, obtain supplies in plenty.

Husuni Kubwa at Kilwa combined a royal palace, a resting place for caravans, and an enclosure for slaves held for later sale. *(From Peter S. Garlake,* The Early Islamic Architecture of the East African Coast, *Memoir 1 of the British Institute in Eastern Africa, Nairobi, 1966. Original drawing by Peter S. Garlake. Copyright, British Institute in Eastern Africa. Reproduced with permission of BIEA)*

## QUESTIONS FOR ANALYSIS

1. Locate on a map the city-states that Barbosa discusses.
2. What seems to have impressed Barbosa? What was his attitude toward the various peoples he saw? What Portuguese or Western prejudices do you discern?
3. What was the Portuguese relationship to the Swahili city-states at the time Barbosa saw them?
4. What was the source of Sofala's gold? Of Sofala's and Malindi's ivory? What did Cambay (that is, India) use ivory for?

*Source:* Basil Davidson, *The African Past: Chronicles from Antiquity to Modern Times* (Boston: Little, Brown, 1964). 

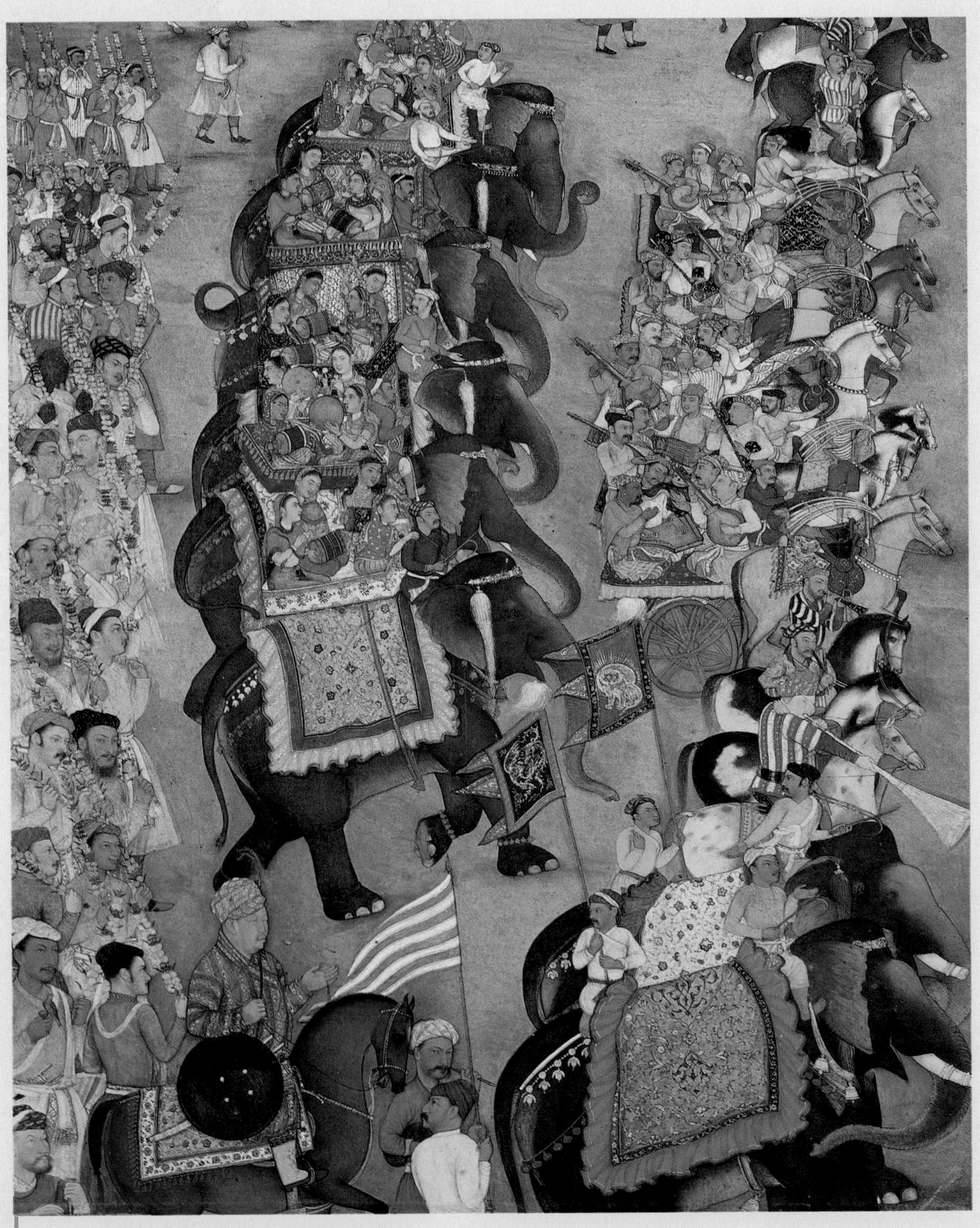

Female musicians ride atop elephants in *Wedding Procession of Prince Dara-Shikoh,* Agra, February 1633. *(The Royal Collection © Her Majesty Queen Elizabeth II)*

CHAPTER

# 20 WEST AND SOUTH ASIA: THE ISLAMIC WORLD POWERS, CA 1450–1800

## CHAPTER OUTLINE

- The Ottoman Turkish Empire
- The Persian Theocratic State
- India, from Mughal Domination to British Dominion (ca 1498–1805)

Around 1450 the spiritual descendants of the Prophet Muhammad controlled three vast and powerful empires: the Ottoman Empire centered in Anatolia, the Safavid Empire of Persia, and the Mughal Empire of India. From West Africa to Central Asia, from the Balkans to Southeast Asia, Muslim armies pursued policies of territorial expansion. Between 1450 and 1800, these powerful Muslim kingdoms reached the zenith of their territorial extension and their intellectual and artistic vitality. With the conquest of Constantinople in 1453, the Ottoman Turks gained a nearly impregnable capital and the respect of all Islam. The Ottomans soon overran much of Anatolia, North Africa, and the Balkans. Lasting almost five hundred years (1453–1918), the Ottoman Empire was one of the largest, best-organized, and most enduring political entities in world history. In Persia the Safavid Dynasty created a theocracy and presided over a brilliant culture. A theological dispute between the Ottomans and the Safavids brought bitter division in the Islamic world and weakened both powers. Meanwhile, the Mughal leader Babur and his successors conquered the Indian subcontinent, and Mughal rule inaugurated a period of radical administrative reorganization in India and the flowering of intellectual and architectural creativity.

In 1450 all the great highways of international trade were in Muslim hands, and the wealth of the Muslim states derived largely from commerce. By 1750 the Muslims had lost that control, and the Muslim states were declining economically, politically, and culturally.

- What military and religious factors gave rise to the Ottoman, Safavid, and Mughal Empires? How were they governed?
- To what extent were these empires world powers?
- What intellectual developments characterized the Ottoman and Safavid Empires?
- How did Ottoman-Safavid relations affect Turkish diplomacy with Westerners in Europe and in Asia?
- How did Muslim government reform and artistic inspiration affect the dominant Hindu population in India?
- What domestic and external difficulties caused the decline of Ottoman Turkey, Safavid Persia, and Mughal India?

These are the questions this chapter will explore.

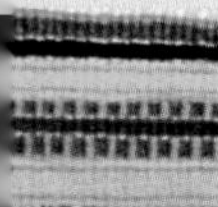

# THE OTTOMAN TURKISH EMPIRE

The **Ottomans** took their name from Osman (r. 1280–1324), the ruler of a Turkish-speaking people in western **Anatolia** who began expansionist moves in the fourteenth century. The Ottomans gradually absorbed other peoples on the Anatolian peninsula, and the Ottoman state emerged as one of many small Turkish states during the breakup of the empire of the Seljuk Turks. The first Ottoman state thus occupied the border between Islam and Byzantine Christendom. The Ottoman ruler called himself "border chief," or leader of the *gazis,* frontier fighters in the *jihad,* or holy war. The earliest Ottoman historical source, a fourteenth-century saga, describes the gazis as the "instrument of God's religion . . . God's scourge who cleanses the earth from the filth of polytheism . . . God's pure sword."[1]

## Evolution of the Ottoman State

The holy war was intended to subdue, not destroy. The Ottomans built their empire by absorbing the Muslims of Anatolia and by becoming the protector of the Orthodox church and of the millions of Greek Christians in Anatolia and the Balkans. On the promise of obedience and the payment of a poll tax, the Muslims guaranteed the lives and property of Christians and Jews. Thus Serbs, Bosnians, Croats, and other Orthodox peoples submitted to the Ottoman rulers for the religious toleration, better administration (than the Byzantines), and tax breaks the Turks promised. Muslims had long practiced a religious toleration unknown in Christian Europe, and the Ottomans, preferring the voluntary submission of Christians to war against them, continued that policy. But when faced with determined opposition, the Ottomans could prove ruthless. The Ottoman Empire became a "frontier empire," a cosmopolitan state binding different ethnic groups and religious creeds in a single unified entity.[2] In 1389 at Kosovo, in what is today the former Yugoslavia, the Ottomans defeated a combined force of Serbs and Bosnians. In 1396, on the Danube River in modern Bulgaria, they crushed King Sigismund of Hungary, who was supported by French, German, and English knights.

The reign of Sultan Mehmet II (r. 1451–1481) saw the end of all Turkish dynasties in Anatolia and the Ottoman conquest of Constantinople, capital of the Byzantine Empire, which had lasted a thousand years. The six-week siege of Constantinople in 1453 remains one of the dramatic events in world history, because Constantinople symbolized the continuation of imperial Rome. The Byzantine emperor Constantine IX Palaeologus (r. 1449–1453), with only about ten thousand men, relied on the magnificent system of circular walls and stone fortifications that had protected the city for a thousand years. Mehmet II had more than one hundred thousand men and a large fleet, but iron chains spanning the harbor kept him out of the Golden Horn, the inlet of the Bosporus Strait that connects the Black and Marmora Seas and forms the harbor of Istanbul. Turkish ingenuity and Western technology eventually decided the battle. Mehmet's army carried boats over the steep hills to come in behind the chains blocking the harbor, then bombarded the city from the rear. A Transylvanian cannon founder who deserted the Greeks for the Turks cast huge bronze cannon on the spot (bringing raw materials to the scene of military action was easier than moving guns long distances).[3] When cannon shots shattered a city gate, the Turks entered the city. Mounting the dome of the church of Hagia Sophia and observing the ruined buildings, Mehmet recited poetic lines lamenting the glories of the past:

*The spider serves as gatekeeper in the halls of Khosrau's dome,*
*The owl plays martial music in the palace of Afrasiyab.*[4]

Victorious troops looted the city for three days, as was customary when a city did not surrender voluntarily. The Muslim historian Oruc describes the conquest:

*Sultan Mehmet, the son of Sultan Murad, inspired by zeal, said "in the cause of God" and commanded plunder. The gazis, entering by force on every side, found a way in through the breaches in the fortress made by the guns and put the infidels in the fortress to the sword. . . . They looted and plundered. They seized their money and possessions and made their sons and daughters slaves. The Muslims took so much booty that the wealth gathered in Istanbul (Constantinople) since it was built 2400 years before became the portion of the gazis. They plundered for three days, and after three days plunder was forbidden.*[5]

The conquest of Constantinople inaugurated the imperial phase of the Ottoman state. The Ottoman sultans considered themselves successors of both the Byzantine and Seljuk emperors, as their title **Sultan-i-Rum** (Sultan of Rome) attests. The Arabic word **sultan,** originally used by the Seljuk Turks to mean "authority" or "dominion," was used by the Ottomans to connote political and military supremacy; it was carried by all members of the dynasty to stress that sovereign power was a family prerogative. The Ottomans renamed the city Istanbul.

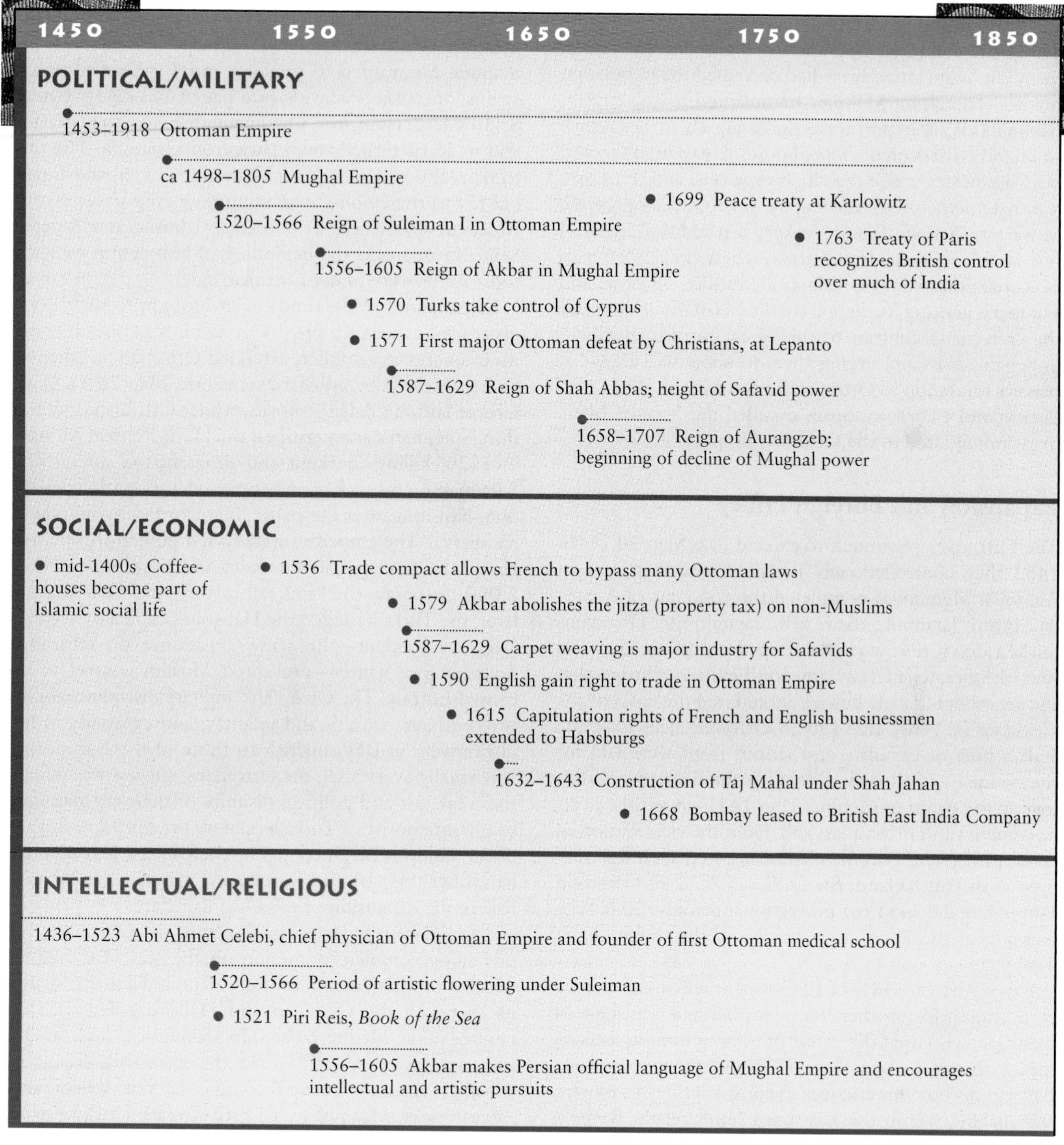

1450
1550
1650
1750
1850
POLITICAL/MILITARY
1453–1918 Ottoman Empire
ca 1498–1805 Mughal Empire
1520–1566 Reign of Suleiman I in Ottoman Empire
1556–1605 Reign of Akbar in Mughal Empire
1570 Turks take control of Cyprus
1571 First major Ottoman defeat by Christians, at Lepanto
1587–1629 Reign of Shah Abbas; height of Safavid power
1658–1707 Reign of Aurangzeb; beginning of decline of Mughal power
1699 Peace treaty at Karlowitz
1763 Treaty of Paris recognizes British control over much of India
SOCIAL/ECONOMIC
mid-1400s Coffee-houses become part of Islamic social life
1536 Trade compact allows French to bypass many Ottoman laws
1579 Akbar abolishes the jitza (property tax) on non-Muslims
1587–1629 Carpet weaving is major industry for Safavids
1590 English gain right to trade in Ottoman Empire
1615 Capitulation rights of French and English businessmen extended to Habsburgs
1632–1643 Construction of Taj Mahal under Shah Jahan
1668 Bombay leased to British East India Company
INTELLECTUAL/RELIGIOUS
1436–1523 Abi Ahmet Celebi, chief physician of Ottoman Empire and founder of first Ottoman medical school
1520–1566 Period of artistic flowering under Suleiman
1521 Piri Reis, Book of the Sea
1556–1605 Akbar makes Persian official language of Mughal Empire and encourages intellectual and artistic pursuits


Mehmet began the transformation of the city into an imperial Ottoman capital. He ordered Istanbul cleaned up and the walls repaired. He appointed officials to adapt the city administration to Ottoman ways and ordered wealthy Ottomans to participate in building mosques, markets, water fountains, baths, and other public facilities. He nominated the Greek patriarch as official representative of the Greek population, giving them protection and freedom of religion as long as they paid the **jitza,** a tax on non-Muslims. These appointments recognized non-Muslims as functioning parts of Ottoman society and economy, with all but a few posts within it open to them.

The population of Istanbul had declined in the decades before the conquest, and warfare, flight, and the sale of many survivors into slavery had decreased the population further. Therefore, Mehmet transplanted to the city inhabitants of other territories, granting them tax remissions and possession of empty houses. He wanted them to start businesses, make the city prosperous, and transform it into a microcosm of the empire. Jews cruelly oppressed in western Europe found Turkey "a paradise." In 1454 one Jewish resident, Isaac Sarfati, sent a circular letter to his coreligionists in the Rhineland, Swabia, Moravia, and Hungary, praising the happy conditions of the Jews under the crescent in contrast to the "great torture chamber" under the cross and urging them to come to Turkey.[6] A massive migration to Ottoman lands followed. When Ferdinand and Isabella of Spain expelled the Jews in 1492, many immigrated to the Ottoman Empire.

## Expansion and Foreign Policy

The Ottomans continued to expand (see Map 20.1). In 1453 they controlled only the northwest quadrant of Anatolia. Mehmet II completed the conquest of Anatolia. From Istanbul, their new capital, the Ottomans pushed down the Aegean and up the Adriatic. They so severely threatened Italy and southeastern Europe that the aged Pope Pius II himself shouldered the cross of the Crusader in 1464. In 1480 an Ottoman fleet took the Italian port of Otranto, and serious plans were laid for the conquest of all Italy. Only a disputed succession following the death of Mehmet II in 1481 caused the postponement of that conquest and, later, the cancellation of those plans. The Ottoman Turks inspired such fear that even in distant Iceland, the Lutheran Book of Common Prayer begged God for protection not only from "the cunning of the Pope" but also from "the terror of the Turk."

Bayezid II (r. 1481–1512) won the Ottoman throne by defeating his brother, Jem. Jem became a hostage of the pope, who used the threat of putting him on the Ottoman throne to keep Bayezid from attacking Europe. Bayezid devoted his energies to consolidating the empire and making war in the East until Jem's death. Bayezid also strengthened the Ottoman navy, enabling it to play a major role in the Mediterranean. In the first half of the sixteenth century, the Ottomans gained control of shipping in the eastern Mediterranean, eliminated the Portuguese from the Red Sea and Persian Gulf, and supported Andalusian and North African Muslims in their fight against the Spanish *reconquista*. Selim I (r. 1512–1520) gained the title "the Grim" because he forced his father, Bayezid, to abdicate; executed his brother; and pursued inhumane policies. Selim was, however, a superb military commander. He wanted to pursue a more aggressive policy against the rising Safavids (see pages 642–644). Under Selim's leadership, the Ottomans defeated the Safavids and in 1514 turned them back from Anatolia. The Ottomans also added Syria and Palestine (1516) and Egypt (1517) to the empire, extending their rule across North Africa to Cyrenaica, Tripolitania, Tunisia, and Algeria. Selim's rule marks the beginning of four centuries when most Arabs were under Ottoman rule.

Suleiman (r. 1520–1566), who brought to the throne great experience as a provincial administrator and enormous energy as a soldier, extended Ottoman jurisdiction to its widest geographical extent (see Map 20.1). With Greece and the Balkans already under Ottoman domination, Suleiman's army crushed the Hungarians at Mohács in 1526, killing the king and thousands of his nobles. Suleiman seems to have taken this victory entirely as his due. Not long after the battle, he recorded laconically in his diary, "The emperor, seated on a golden throne, receives the homage of the vizirs and beys: massacre of 2,000 prisoners: the rains fall in torrents." Three years later, the Turks besieged the Habsburg capital of Vienna. Only an accident—the army's insistence on returning home before winter—prevented Muslim control of all central Europe. The Ottomans' military discipline, ability to coordinate cavalry and infantry, and capability in logistics were usually superior to those of the Europeans. In virtually every area, the Ottomans' success was due to the weakness and political disunity of their enemies and to the superiority of Turkish military organization and artillery. Gunpowder, invented by the Chinese and adapted to artillery use by the Europeans, played an influential role in the expansion of the Ottoman state.

Though usually victorious on land, the Ottomans did not enjoy complete dominion on the seas. The middle decades of the sixteenth century witnessed a titanic struggle between the Ottoman and Habsburg Empires for control of the Mediterranean. In September 1538, an Ottoman naval victory at Preveze, the chief Turkish port in Albania, ensured Turkish control of the Ionian and Aegean Seas. Meanwhile, Christian pirates' attacks from the island of Cyprus on Ottoman shipping in the eastern Mediterranean provoked the sultan to conquer Cyprus in 1570. He introduced Ottoman administration and settled thousands of Turks from Anatolia there. (Thus began the large Turkish presence on Cyprus that continues to the present day.) In response, Pope Pius V organized a Holy League against the Turks. Only an accident—the arrival of the Holy League's fleet so late that the Ottomans had

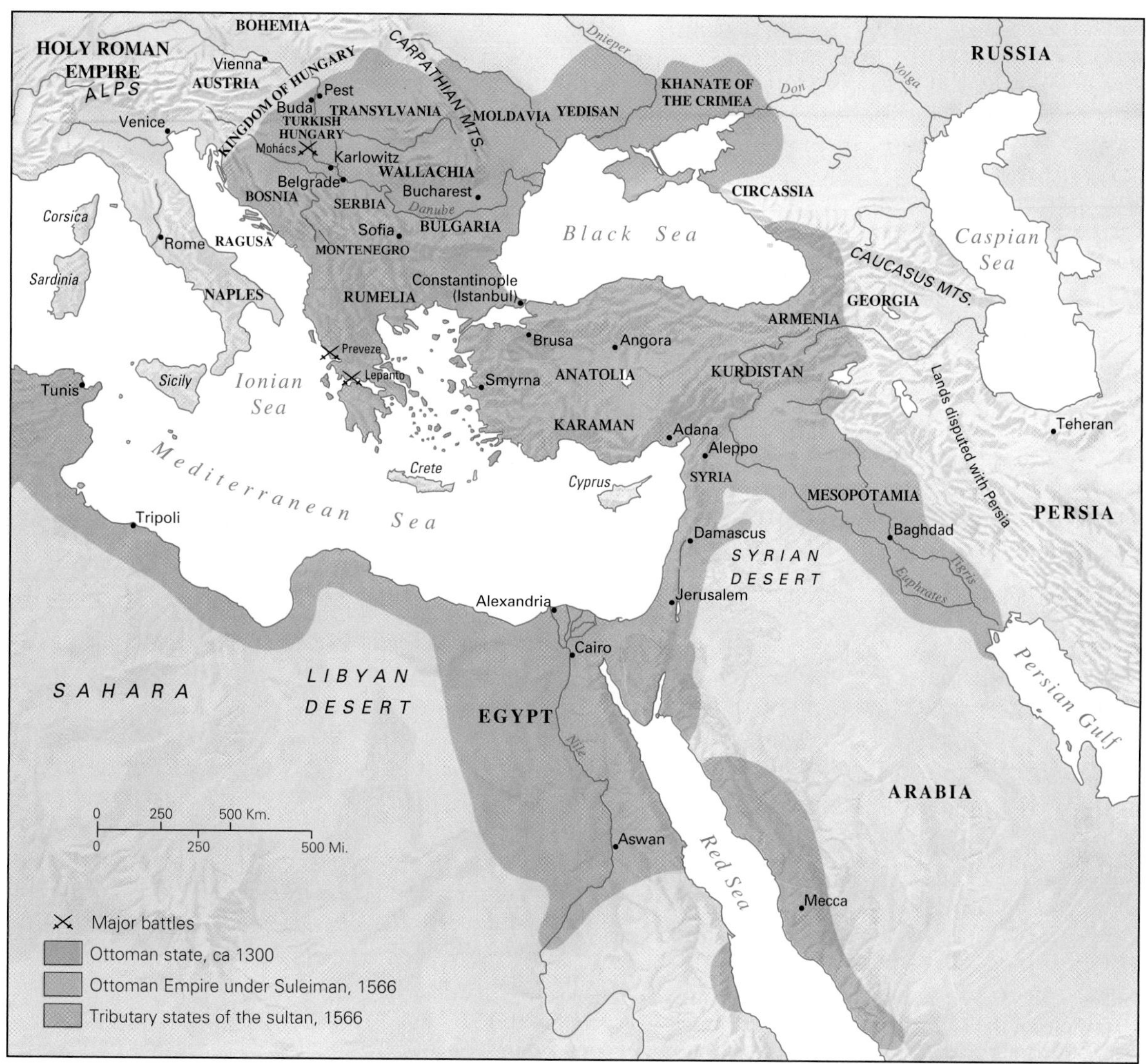


**MAP 20.1 The Ottoman Empire at Its Height, 1566** The Ottomans, like their great rivals the Habsburgs, rose to rule a vast dynastic empire encompassing many different peoples and ethnic groups. The army and the bureaucracy served to unite the disparate territories into a single state.

already gone into port for the winter—brought temporary defeat. On October 7, 1571, a squadron of more than 200 Spanish, Venetian, and papal galleys smashed the Turks at Lepanto at the mouth of the Gulf of Patras in Greece (see Map 20.1). The victors lost about 7,000 men, the Turks lost about 15,000, and 10,000 Christian galley slaves were freed. Across western Europe, church bells signaled the victory, the first major Ottoman defeat by Christian forces. But Lepanto marked no decisive change in Turkish hegemony: the Turks remained supreme on land and quickly rebuilt their entire fleet.

From the late fourteenth to the early seventeenth century, from the Atlantic to the Indian Ocean, the Ottoman Empire exercised a decisive influence in world affairs. In western Europe, the Habsburg-Valois Wars worked to Ottoman advantage: they kept Europe divided. In 1525 Francis I of France and Suleiman struck an alliance; both believed that only their collaboration could prevent Habsburg hegemony in Europe. Suleiman's invasion of Hungary, culminating in his victory over the Habsburgs at Mohács in 1526, terrified Europe. The Habsburg emperor Charles V retaliated by seeking

**Battle of Mohács** The *Süleymanname* (Book of Suleiman), a biography, contains these wonderful illustrations of the battle that took place in Hungary on August 29, 1526. In the right panel, Suleiman in a white turban sits on a black horse surrounded by his personal guard, while janissaries fire cannon at the enemy. In the left panel, the Europeans are in disarray, in contrast to the Turks' discipline and order. Suleiman inflicted a crushing defeat and absorbed Hungary into the Ottoman Empire. The artist attempted to show the terrain and battle tactics. *(Topkapi Saray Museum, Istanbul)*

an alliance with Safavid Persia. Suleiman renewed the French agreement with Francis's son, Henry II (r. 1547–1559), and the French entente became the cornerstone of Ottoman policy in western Europe. Suleiman also allied with the German Protestant princes, forcing the Catholic Habsburgs to grant concessions to the Protestants. Ottoman pressure proved an important factor in the official recognition of Lutheran Protestants at the Peace of Augsburg in 1555. In addition to the rising tide of Protestantism, the Ottoman threat strengthened the growth of national monarchy in France.

In eastern Europe to the north of Ottoman lands stood the Grand Duchy of Moscow. In the fifteenth century, Ottoman rulers did not regard it as a threat; in 1497 they even gave Russian merchants freedom of trade within the empire. But in 1547 Grand Prince Ivan IV (the Terrible) assumed the title of tsar, or emperor, and after conquering the Muslim khanates of Kazan and Astrakhan from the Tartars (1552–1556), he brought under Russian control the entire Volga region (see Map 20.1). In 1557 Ivan's ally, the Cossack chieftain Dimitrash, tried to take Azov, the northernmost Ottoman fortress. Russian influence thus entered Ottoman territories in the Caucasus and Black Sea regions.

Preoccupied with war against the Habsburgs, Suleiman delayed action. Grand Vizier Sokullu Mehmet prepared a large expedition to retake Astrakhan, use it as the center of a fortified defense system in the area, and build a canal between the Volga and the Don that would unite the Black and Caspian Seas. The object of this plan was to drive the Russians from the Volga basin and to encircle Persia (see Map 20.1). The proposal only succeeded in uniting Russia, Persia, and the pope against the Turks. Field commanders failed to receive adequate supplies, and the scheme failed. But Sokullu did expand Turkish influence in Moldavia, Wallachia, and Poland, thereby blocking Russian influence east of the Black Sea.

To the east, war with Persia occupied the sultans' attention throughout the sixteenth century. Several issues lay at the root of the long and exhausting conflicts: religious antagonism between the Sunni Ottomans and the Shi'ite Persians; disputes over territories south and west of the Caspian Sea; the Ottoman goal of controlling the international trade routes bringing silks from Persia and spices from the East, which yielded huge customs revenues to the Ottoman treasury; and Persian diplomatic alliances with the Habsburgs while the Ottomans supported the French. The Balkan conflicts and declining revenues prevented the sultans from winning a decisive victory. Finally, in 1638, Sultan Merad IV captured Baghdad, and the treaty of Kasr-I-Shirim established a permanent border between the two powers.

Meanwhile, in South Asia the Ottomans fought the Portuguese and Spanish for control of the Indian Ocean trade. An Ottoman fleet secured from some cities on the East African coast, such as Mombasa, recognition of Ottoman supremacy. In the face of tough Iberian naval power, however, Ottoman influence collapsed, and in the early seventeenth century the Dutch and the English came to dominate the Indian Ocean. Loss of supremacy on the seas and the sharp decline in customs duties contributed to Ottoman economic decline.[7]

## Ottoman Society

The Ottoman social and administrative systems reached their classic form under Suleiman I. The seventeenth-century Ottoman historian Mustafa Naima divided Muslim society into producers of wealth, Muslim and non-Muslim, and the military. In Naima's view, there could be no state without the military, wealth was needed to support the military, the state's subjects raised the wealth, subjects could prosper only through justice, and without the state there could be no justice.[8]

All authority flowed from the sultan to his public servants: provincial governors, police officers, military generals, heads of treasuries, viziers. Under Suleiman I, the Ottoman ruling class consisted in part of descendants of Turkish families that had formerly ruled parts of Anatolia and in part people of varied ethnic origins who rose through the bureaucratic and military ranks. All were committed to the Ottoman way: Islamic in faith, loyal to the sultan, and well versed in the Turkish language and the culture of the imperial court. In return for their services to the sultan, they held *timars* (landed estates) for the duration of their lives. The ruling class had the legal right to use and enjoy the profits, but not the ownership, of the land. Since all property belonged to the sultan and reverted to him on the holder's death, Turkish nobles, unlike their European counterparts, could not put down roots. The absence of a hereditary nobility and private property on agricultural land differentiates the Ottoman system from European feudalism.[9]

Modern scholarship has provided little information about the lives and public activities of ordinary women in the Ottoman world, but we know a fair amount about royal and wealthy women. Royal women resided in seclusion in the harem. In Muslim culture, the Arabic word *harem* means a sacred place; a sanctuary; a place of honor, respect, and religious purity. The word was often applied to the holy cities of Mecca and Medina. Just as the sultan's private quarters in the imperial palace were a kind of harem, so in the fifteenth century another set of chambers for his mother, wife, **concubines,** unmarried sisters, and royal children gained the same name. (In the seventeenth century, as absolute monarchy evolved in Europe, Europeans developed the myth of Muslim tyranny, and the sultan's harem was the crux of that tyranny. In the Western imagination, "orgiastic sex became a metaphor for power corrupted."[10]) The Ottoman harem was *not* a stable of sexual partners for the sultan.

Because Muslim "histories rarely mention women" and "virtually ignore concubinage,"[11] it is difficult for students to penetrate the walled harem to get at the personalities and activities of the royal ladies. In the fourteenth and early fifteenth centuries, marriage served as a tool of diplomacy. Ottoman marriages were arranged as part of the negotiations ending a war to symbolize the defeated party's acceptance of subordinate status. After the conquest of Constantinople and the Ottoman claim to world empire, no foreigner was seen as worthy of so intimate a bond as marriage; the sultan had to occupy a position of visible superiority. By the reign of Selim I, the principle was established that the sultan did not contract legal marriage but perpetuated himself through concubinage. Slave concubinage served as the central element of Ottoman reproductive policy. Since according to Muslim law, a child held the legal status of its father, the sons of a slave concubine were just as eligible for the throne as those of a free woman. With a notable exception (see the feature "Individuals in Society: Hürrem"), the sultans preferred to continue the dynasty through concubines. They could have none of the political aspirations or leverage that a native or foreign-born noblewoman had. Nor could a slave concubine press legal claims on the sultan, as a legal wife could. The latter also could demand a ceremonial deference, which a concubine could not.[12]

Other Muslim dynasties, such as the Abbasids, had practiced slave concubinage, but the Ottomans carried the institution beyond anything that had previously existed. Slave concubinage paralleled the Ottoman development of the janissary system (see page 636), whereby slave boys were trained for imperial service. Slave viziers, slave generals, and slave concubines held positions entirely at the sultan's pleasure, owed loyalty solely to him, and thus were more reliable than a hereditary nobility, as existed in Europe. Great social prestige, as well as the opportunity to acquire power and wealth, was attached to being a slave of the imperial household. Being a slave in the Ottoman world did not carry the demeaning social connotations connected with slavery in the Western Hemisphere.

When one of the sultan's concubines became pregnant, her status and her salary increased. If she delivered a boy, she raised the child until the age of ten or eleven. Then the child was given a province to govern under his mother's supervision. She accompanied him there, was responsible for his good behavior, and worked through imperial officials and the janissary corps to promote his interests. Since succession to the throne was open to all the sultan's sons, at his death fratricide often resulted, and the losers were blinded or executed. If a woman produced a girl, she raised her daughter until the girl married. Within the Ottoman dynasty, motherhood was the source of female power.[13]

Ottoman women of wealth and property—acquired through dowries, inheritance, gifts, salaries, and divorce—also possessed economic and social power. As society expected of them, wealthy women made charitable contributions by endowing religious foundations, freeing slaves (which the Qur'an called a meritorious act), and helping paupers, prisoners, and prostitutes. As in the Byzantine world, and as with rich Protestant women, Muslim women's assistance seems to have gone primarily to other women.

Evidence of women's charitable and business activities in the eighteenth and nineteenth centuries is more plentiful. For example, we know that in 1881 eighteen of the forty-two slave dealers in Istanbul (almost one-half) were women. Wealthy upper-class women in large harems bought Circassian girls, trained them in proper etiquette, and later sold them to the imperial harem or other large harems. These women dealers enjoyed financial profit in a society where the demand for slaves remained strong, as it did well into the twentieth century (although slavery was theoretically abolished).[14]

In the mid-fifteenth century, a new social convention spread throughout the Islamic world—drinking coffee. Arab writers trace the origins of coffee to Yemen, where the mystical Sikhs drank coffee in their *dhiks,* or "devotional services." Sikhs sought a trancelike concentration on God to the exclusion of everything else, and the use of coffee helped them to stay awake. Most Sikhs were not professional holy men but were employed as tradesmen and merchants. Therefore, the use of coffee for pious purposes led to its use as a business lubricant—an extension of hospitality to a potential buyer in a shop. Merchants carried the Yemenite practice to Mecca, in Arabia, about 1490. From Mecca (where pilgrims were introduced to it), drinking coffee spread to Egypt and Syria. In 1555 two Syrians opened a coffeehouse in Istanbul.

Coffeehouses provided a place for conversation and male sociability; there a man could entertain his friends cheaply and more informally than at home. But coffeehouses encountered religious and governmental opposition, which are indistinguishable under the *shari'a,* or holy law. Opponents of coffeehouses rested their arguments on four grounds: (1) because of its chemical composition, coffee is intoxicating and physically harmful; (2) coffee drinking was an innovation, and therefore a violation of Islamic law; (3) the coffeehouse encouraged political discussions that could be dangerous to the sultan; and (4) patrons of coffeehouses tended to be low types who engaged in immoral behavior, such as gambling, using drugs, soliciting prostitutes, and engaging in sodomy. The musical entertainment that coffeehouses provided, critics said, lent an atmosphere of debauchery. Thus coffeehouses drew the attention of government officials, who were also the guardians of public morality.

Although debate over the morality of coffeehouses continued through the sixteenth century, the acceptance of them represented a revolution in Islamic life: socializing was no longer confined to the home. Since the medical profession remained divided on coffee's harmful

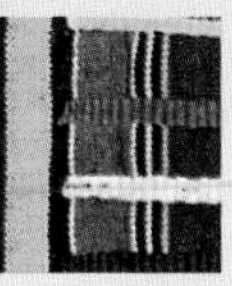

## HÜRREM

She was born in the western Ukraine (then part of Poland), the daughter of a Ruthenian priest, and given the Polish name Aleksandra Lisowska. After she acquired fame, Europeans called her Roxelana, the Polish term for "Ruthenian maiden." When Tartar raiders took Rogatin, a town on the Dniester River near Lvov, they captured and enslaved her. The next documented incident in her life dates from September 1520, when she was given as a gift to Suleiman on the occasion of his accession to the throne. The Venetian ambassador (probably relying on second- or third-hand information) described her as "young, graceful, petite, but not beautiful." She was given the Turkish name Hürrem, meaning "joyful."

Hürrem (1505?–1558) apparently brought joy to Suleiman. Their first child was born in 1521; by 1525 they had five children (four sons), and sources note that by that year Suleiman visited no other woman. But he waited eight or nine years before breaking Ottoman dynastic tradition. In 1533 or 1534, he made Hürrem his legal wife, the first slave concubine so honored. For the rest of her life, Hürrem played a highly influential role in the political, diplomatic, and philanthropic life of the Ottoman state. First, great power flowed from her position as mother of the prince, the future sultan Selim II (r. 1566–1574). Then, as the intimate and most trusted adviser of the sultan, she was Suleiman's closest confidant. He was frequently away in the far-flung corners of his multiethnic empire. Hürrem wrote him long letters filled with her love and longing for him, her prayers for his safety in battle, and political information about affairs in Istanbul, the activities of the grand vizier, and the attitudes of the janissaries. At a time when some people believed that the sultan's absence from the capital endangered his hold on the throne, Hürrem acted as his eyes and ears for potential threats.

Hürrem was the sultan's contact with her native Poland, which sent more embassies to Istanbul than any other power. Through her correspondence with King Sigismund I, peace between Poland and the Ottomans was maintained. When Sigismund II succeeded his father in 1548, Hürrem sent congratulations on his accession, along with two pairs of pajamas (originally a Hindu garment, but commonly worn in southwestern Asia) and six handkerchiefs. By sending the shah of Persia gold-embroidered sheets and shirts she had sewn herself, Hürrem sought to display the wealth of the sultanate and to keep peace between the Ottomans and the Safavids.

*Hürrem and her ladies in the harem.* (Bibliothèque nationale de France)

The enormous stipend that Suleiman gave Hürrem permitted her to participate in his vast building program. In Jerusalem (in the Ottoman province of Palestine), she founded a hospice for fifty-five pilgrims that included a soup kitchen that fed four hundred pilgrims a day. In Istanbul Suleiman built and Hürrem endowed the Haseki (meaning "royal favorite concubine") mosque complex and a public bath for women near the Women's Market. We do not know whether these charitable benefactions reflected genuine concern for the poor, were intended to show the interests of the dynasty, or were meant to court favorable public opinion, for contemporaries hated and reviled Hürrem and thought she had bewitched Suleiman.

Perhaps Hürrem tried to fulfill two functions hitherto distinct in Ottoman political theory: those of the sultan's favorite and mother of the prince. She also performed the conflicting roles of slave concubine and imperial wife.

### QUESTIONS FOR ANALYSIS

1. Compare Hürrem to other powerful fifteenth- or sixteenth-century women, such as Isabella of Castile, Catherine de' Medici of France, Elizabeth of England, and Mary Queen of Scots.
2. What was Hürrem's "nationality"? What role did it play in her life?

*Source:* Leslie P. Pierce, *The Imperial Harem: Women and Sovereignty in the Ottoman Empire* (New York: Oxford University Press, 1993).

**Turkish Coffeehouse** This sixteenth-century miniature depicts many activities typical of coffeehouses: patrons enter (*upper left*); some sit drinking coffee in small porcelain cups (*center*); the manager makes fresh coffee (*right*). In the center, on a low sofa, men sit reading and talking. At bottom appear activities considered disreputable: musicians playing instruments, others playing games such as backgammon, a board game where moves are determined by rolls of dice. *(Reproduced by kind permission of the Trustees of the Chester Beatty Library, Dublin, Ms 439, folio 9)*

effects, and since the religious authorities could not prove that coffeehouses violated the shari'a, drinking coffee could not be forbidden.[15] In the seventeenth century, coffee and coffeehouses spread to Europe.

Recent scholars have demonstrated what European ambassadors and tourists had long speculated about: the prevalence of homosexual activity in the imperial palace, the janissary corps, and Ottoman society in general. Selected for "their bodily perfection, muscular strength, and intellectual ability," palace pages commonly had intimate relationships with court officials and the sultan himself.[16] Ibrahim Pasa ascended the chain of offices—grand falconer, governor of Ruyelia, vizier, grand vizier (1523–1536)—through his mental acumen and relationship with Suleiman. His marriage to the daughter of Selim I suggests his prestige. Accused of aspiring to the sultanate, Ibrahim was executed by strangulation, an event that marked the ascendancy of Hürrem (see page 635). Ibrahim's successor as grand vizier, the Croatian-born page Rustem, won considerable wealth because of his relationship with Suleiman. A slave himself, he owned seventeen hundred slaves at his death. Earlier, in 1475, the Genoese visitor Jacopo de Promontoria ascribed the low birthrate among noble Turks in Anatolia to "the infinite lechery of various slaves and young boys to whom they give themselves."[17] With the prevalence of homosexuality in Genoa,[18] Jacopo was in no position to criticize. Moreover, in the fifteenth and sixteenth centuries, the Turkish population vastly increased,[19] rather than declined. Other writers at the time and through the nineteenth century, however, confirmed Jacopo's impression of sodomitical activity.

Slaves who had been purchased from Spain, North Africa, and Venice; captured in battle; or acquired through the system known as **devshirme**—by which the sultan's agents swept the provinces for Christian youths—were recruited for the imperial civil service and the standing army. Southern Europeans did not shrink from selling Christians into slavery, and as the Ottoman frontier advanced in the fifteenth and sixteenth centuries, Albanian, Bosnian, Wallachian, and Hungarian slave boys filled Ottoman imperial needs. Moreover, because devshirme recruitment often meant social advancement, some Christian parents bribed government officials to accept their children. All these children were converted to Islam. The brightest 10 percent entered the palace school. There they learned to read and write Arabic, Ottoman Turkish, and Persian; received special religious instruction; and were trained for the civil service. Other boys were sent to Turkish farms, where they acquired physical toughness in preparation for military service. Known as **janissaries** (Turkish for "recruits"), they formed the elite army corps. Thoroughly indoctrinated and absolutely loyal to the sultan, the janissary slave corps eliminated the influence of old Turkish families and played the central role in Ottoman military affairs in the sixteenth century.

## Cultural Flowering

The reign of Suleiman I witnessed an extraordinary artistic flowering and represents the peak of Ottoman influence and culture. In Turkish history, Suleiman is known as **Kanuni** (Lawgiver) because of his profound influence on the civil law. He ordered Lütfi Paşa (d. 1562), a poet and juridical scholar of slave origin, to draw up a new general code of laws. Published in Suleiman's name, this sultanic legal code prescribed penalties for routine criminal acts such as robbery, adultery, and murder. It also sought to reform bureaucratic and financial corruption in areas such as harem intervention in administrative affairs, foreign merchants' payment of bribes to avoid customs duties, imprisonment without trial, and promotion in the provincial administration because of favoritism rather than ability. The legal code also introduced the idea of balanced financial budgets. The head of the religious establishment, Hoja Sadeddin Efendi, was given the task of reconciling sultanic law with Islamic law. Suleiman's legal acts influenced many legal codes, including that of the United States. Today, Suleiman's image, along with the images of Solon, Moses, and Thomas Jefferson, appears in the chamber of the U.S. House of Representatives.

Europeans called Suleiman "the Magnificent" because of the grandeur of his court. With annual state revenues of about $80 million (at a time when Elizabeth I of England could expect $150,000 and Francis I of France perhaps $1 million), with thousands of servants to cater to his whims, and with a lifestyle no European monarch could begin to rival, Suleiman was indeed magnificent. He used his fabulous wealth to adorn Istanbul with palaces, mosques, schools, and libraries. The building of hospitals, roads, and bridges and the reconstruction of the water systems of the great pilgrimage sites at Mecca and Jerusalem benefited his subjects.

The Ottomans under Suleiman demonstrated splendid creativity in carpet weaving, textiles, ceramics, and, above all, architecture. In the buildings of Pasha Sinan (1491–1588), a Greek-born devshirme recruit who rose to become imperial architect, the Ottoman spirit is powerfully expressed. A contemporary of Michelangelo,

**Suleimaniye Mosque** Designed and built (1548–1557) by Sinan, a janissary who became the greatest architect in Ottoman history, surrounded by madrasah, hospital, and shops, this mosque asserts the dynasty's power, religious orthodoxy, and the sultan's position as "God's shadow on earth." Suleiman, who financed it, is buried here. *(Robert Frerck/Woodfin Camp & Associates)*

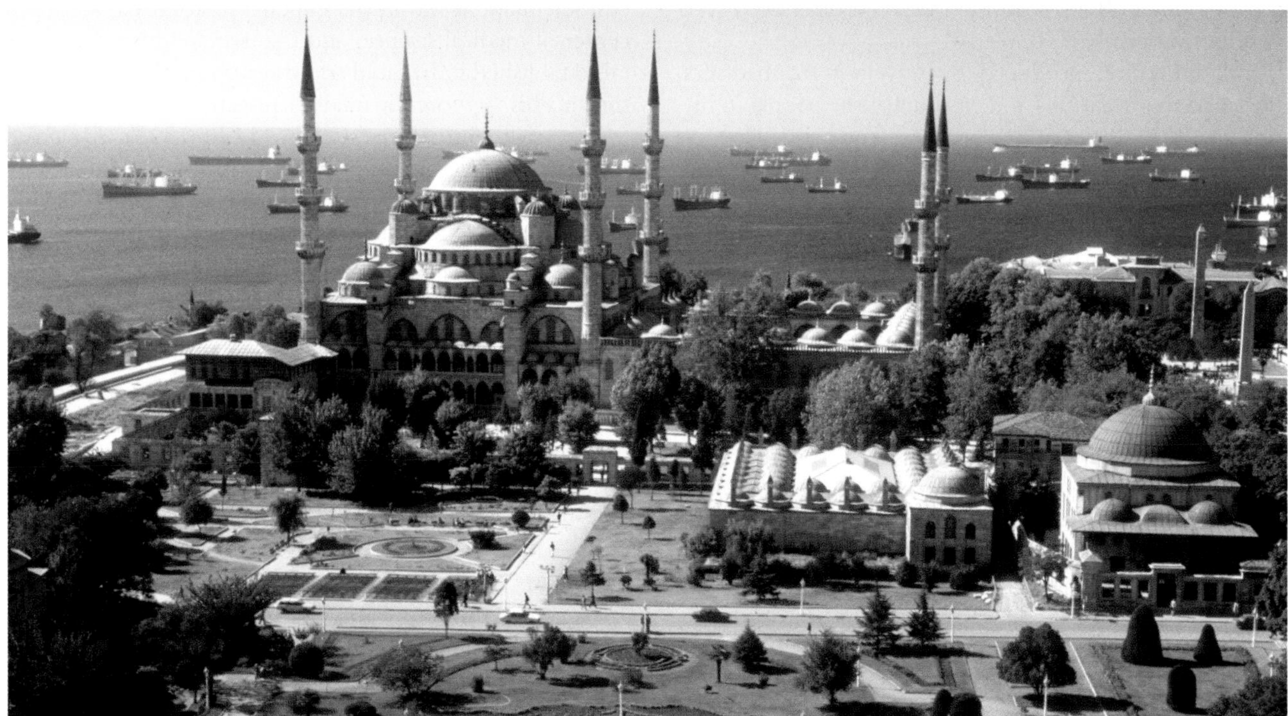

Sinan designed 312 public buildings—mosques, schools, hospitals, public baths, palaces, and burial chapels. His masterpieces, the Shehzade and Suleimaniye mosques in Istanbul, which rivaled the Byzantine church of Hagia Sophia, represented solutions to spatial problems unique to domed buildings and expressed the discipline, power, and devotion to Islam that characterized the Ottoman Empire under Suleiman. With pardonable exaggeration, Suleiman began a letter to the king of France, with whom he was allied, by saying, "I who am the sultan of sultans, the sovereign of sovereigns, the dispenser of crowns to the monarchs on the face of the earth . . . to thee who are Francis, King of the land of France."[20]

The cultural explosion of Suleiman's reign rivaled the artistic and literary achievements of the European Renaissance. In addition to architecture, Ottoman scholars and artists showed great distinction in poetry, painting, history, mathematics, geographical literature, astronomy, medicine, and the religious sciences.

Poetry, rather than prose, was the main vehicle of Ottoman literary expression. *Diwan* poetry, so called because it consisted of collections of poems, though written by intellectuals in Turkish, followed classical Islamic (Arabic) forms and rules and addressed the ruling class. Modern scholars consider Bursah Ahmet Pasa, an imperial judge and confidential adviser to the sultan Mehmet II, to be the greatest Ottoman poet of the fifteenth century. Bursah Ahmet Pasa's beautiful odes and diversified style won him widespread popularity.

Folk literature, produced by traveling troubadours, described the traditions and wisdom of the people in humorous short stories and anecdotes. The folk collection of Dede Korkut, set down in Turkish prose, includes tribal epics describing the conflicts with the Georgians, Circassians, and Byzantines and serves as a source for the history of the fourteenth century. Just as Western historical writing in the early modern period often served to justify the rights of ruling dynasties, so Ottoman historical scholarship under Mehmet II and Suleiman promoted the claims of the family of Osman. Perhaps the greatest historian of the early sixteenth century was Ahmet Semseddin ibn-I-Kemal, or Kemalpasazêde (d. 1526), the Muslim judge and administrator whose *History of the House of Osman* gives original source material for the reigns through which he himself lived. Building on the knowledge of earlier Islamic writers and stimulated by Ottoman naval power, the geographer and cartographer Piri Reis produced a map incorporating Islamic and Western knowledge that showed all the known world (1513); another of his maps detailed Columbus's third voyage to the New World. Piri Reis's *Book of the Sea* (1521) contained 129 chapters, each with a map incorporating all Islamic (and Western) knowledge of the seas and navigation and describing harbors, tides, dangerous rocks and shores, and storm areas. Takiyuddin Mehmet (1521–1585), who served as the sultan's chief astronomer, built an observatory at Istanbul. His *Instruments of the Observatory* catalogued astronomical instruments and described an astronomical clock that fixed the location of heavenly bodies with greater precision than ever before.

What medical treatment or health care was available to the sick in the Ottoman world? Muslim medical education was practical, not theoretical: students received their training not in the *madrasas,* or mosque schools, but by apprenticeship to experienced physicians or in the **bimaristans,** or hospitals. Under a senior's supervision, medical students studied the course of various diseases, learned the techniques of surgery, and especially mastered pharmacology—the preparation of drugs from plants. The Muslim knowledge of pharmacology derived from centuries-old traditions, and modern students of the history of medicine believe that pharmacology as an institution is an Islamic invention.

By the fifteenth century, Muslims knew the value of quarantine. Yet when devastating epidemics such as the bubonic plague struck the empire during Mehmet II's reign, he and the court fled to the mountains of the Balkans, and the imperial government did little to fight the plague. Under Suleiman, however, the imperial palace itself became a center of medical science, and the large number of hospitals established in Istanbul and throughout the empire testifies to his support for medical research and his concern for the sick. Abi Ahmet Celebi (1436–1523), the chief physician of the empire, produced a study on kidney and bladder stones and supported the research of the Jewish doctor Musa Colinus ul-Israil on the application of drugs. Celebi founded the first Ottoman medical school, which served as a training institution for physicians of the empire.[21] The sultans and the imperial court relied on a cadre of elite Jewish physicians.

To fight smallpox, the Chinese had successfully practiced inoculation in the sixteenth century, and the procedure spread to Turkey in the seventeenth. Lady Mary Wortley Montagu, wife of the British ambassador to Istanbul, had her son inoculated in 1717. Here is her description of the method:

> *The smallpox, so fatal and so general amongst us (in England), is here entirely harmless by the invention of engrafting. . . . Every autumn . . . people send one another to know if any of their family has a mind to have the smallpox (get inoculated). . . . An old woman comes with a nutshell full of*

*the matter of the best sort of smallpox and asks what veins you please (want) to have opened. She immediately rips open what you offer to her with a large needle (which gives you no more pain than a common scratch) and puts into the vein as much venom as can lie upon the head of the needle, and after binds up the little wound. . . . The children or young patients play together all the rest of the day and are in perfect health till the eighth. Then the fever begins to seize 'em and they keep their beds two days, very seldom three. They have very rarely twenty or thirty (pockmarks) in their faces, which never mark (leave a permanent scar), and in eight days' time they are as well as before their illness. . . . Every year thousands undergo this operation. . . . There is no example of anyone that has died in it.*[22]

This was eighty years before the English physician Edward Jenner tried the procedure using cowpox in England.

Lady Mary Wortley Montagu marveled at the splendor of Ottoman culture. Remarkably intelligent and fluent in several languages, Lady Mary, a pioneer feminist, also had a mind exceptionally open to different cultures. As an aristocrat, the wife of an official foreign representative, and a woman, she had access to people and places (such as the imperial *seraglio,* or harem) that were off-limits to ordinary tourists. Her many letters to relatives and friends in England provide a wealth of information about upper-class Ottoman society.

On January 19, 1718, Lady Mary gave birth to a daughter and described the experience in a letter to an English friend:

*I was brought to bed of a daughter. . . . I must own that it was not half so mortifying here as in England, there being as much difference as there is between a little cold in the head, which sometimes happens here, and the consumptive coughs so common in London.*[23]

The naturalness of childbirth in Turkey, Lady Mary suggests, may have been because Turkish women had much more experience of it than Englishwomen:

*In this country 'tis more despicable to be married and not fruitful than 'tis with us to be fruitful before marriage. They have a notion that whenever a woman leaves off bearing children, 'tis because she is too old for that business, whatever her face says to the contrary, and this opinion makes the ladies here so ready to make proofs of their youth. . . . Without any exaggeration, all the women of my acquaintance that have been married ten years have twelve or thirteen children, and the old ones boast of having had five and twenty or thirty apiece and are respected according to the number they have produced.*[24]

**Lady Mary Wortley Montagu** Famous in her own time for her letters from Constantinople and, after her return to England, for her efforts to educate the English public about inoculation against smallpox, Lady Mary is praised by modern scholars as a brilliant and urbane woman struggling for emancipation. *(Boston Athenaeum)*

Turkish women's sense of self-worth seems to have been closely tied to their production of children, as was common in many cultures at the time. As for Turkish morality, "'Tis just as 'tis with you; and the Turkish ladies don't commit one sin the less for not being Christians." In other words, Turkish women were neither better nor worse than European ones. Moreover,

*'tis very easy to see that they have more liberty than we have, . . . and their shapes are wholly concealed by a thing they call a ferigee, which no woman of any sort (class) appears without. . . . You may guess how effectively this disguises them, that there is no distinguishing the great lady from her slave, and 'tis impossible for the most jealous husband to know his wife when he meets her, and no man dare either touch or follow a woman in the street. . . . The most usual method of intrigue is to send an appointment to the*

*lover to meet the lady at a Jew's shop, which are as notoriously convenient as our Indian houses. . . .*

*You may easily imagine the number of faithful wives very small in a country where they have nothing to fear from their lovers' indiscretion. . . . Neither have they much to apprehend from the resentment of their husbands, those ladies that are rich having all their money in their own hands, which they take with 'em upon a divorce with an addition which he is obliged to give 'em. Upon the whole, I look upon the Turkish women as the only free people in the empire.*[25]

In short, in spite of the legal restrictions of the harem, upper-class ladies found ways to go out.

## The Decline of Ottoman Power

In the fifteenth and early sixteenth centuries, government depended heavily on the sultan, and the matter of the dynastic succession posed a major political problem. Heirs to the throne had gained administrative experience as governors of provinces and military experience on the battlefield as part of their education. After Suleiman's reign, however, this tradition was abandoned. To prevent threats of usurpation, heirs were brought up in the harem and were denied a role in government. By the time a prince succeeded his father, years of dissipation were likely to have rendered the prince alcoholic, insane, or exhausted from excessive sexual activity. Selim II (r. 1566–1574), whom the Turks called "Selim the Drunkard," left the conduct of public affairs to his vizier while he pursued the pleasures of the harem. Turkish sources attribute his death to a fall in his bath caused by dizziness when he tried to stop drinking. A series of rulers who were incompetent or minor children left power in the hands of leading bureaucratic officials and the mothers of the heirs. Instead of a fight for the throne among the surviving sons of the dead sultan, the practice arose of granting the throne to the eldest male member of the dynasty. Political factions formed around viziers, military leaders, and palace women. In the contest for political favor, the devshirme was abandoned, and political and military ranks were filled by Muslims.

Under the competent vizier Mehmet Köprülü (r. 1656–1661), imperial fortunes revived. Köprülü abolished corruption, maintained domestic peace, and conducted a vigorous war with Venice. His son Ahmet succeeded as vizier and continued these policies. Ahmet's ambitious brother-in-law and successor, Kara Mustafa, pursued a more aggressive foreign policy: his objective was an attack on the Habsburg capital, Vienna. When battle came on September 12, 1683, the combination of a strong allied Christian force (see page 549) and Habsburg heavy artillery, which the Turks lacked, gave the Europeans the victory. The Ottomans rallied again, but defeat at Vienna and domestic disorders led to the decline of Ottoman power in the Balkans. In the words of one historian, "The Ottoman state was predicated upon, committed to, and organized for conquest. . . . An end to significant and sustained conquest rocked the entire state structure and sent aftershocks through all its institutions."[26]

The peace treaty signed at Karlowitz (1699) marks a watershed in Ottoman history. By its terms, the empire lost (to Austria) the major European provinces of Hungary and Transylvania, along with the tax revenues they had provided. Karlowitz also shattered Ottoman morale. Eighteenth-century wars against European powers—Venice (1714–1718), Austria and Russia (1736–1739), and Russia alone (1768–1774 and 1787–1792)—proved indecisive but contributed to general Ottoman internal disintegration.

As in parts of Europe, rising population without corresponding economic growth caused serious social problems. A long period of peace in the later sixteenth century and again in the mid-eighteenth century—while the War of the Austrian Succession (1740–1748) and the Seven Years' War (1756–1763) were preoccupying the European powers (see page 579)—and a decline in the frequency of visits of the plague led to a doubling of the population. The land could not sustain so many people, nor could the towns provide jobs for the thousands of agricultural workers who fled to them. The return of demobilized soldiers aggravated the problem. Inflation, famine, and widespread revolts resulted. The economic center of gravity shifted from the capital to the provinces, and politically the empire began to decentralize as well. Local notables and military men, rather than central officials, exercised political power. Scholars regard this provincial autonomy as the precursor of nationalism.

European colonialism and worldwide economic changes isolated the Ottomans from the centers of growth in the Western Hemisphere and the East Indies. European trade with the Americas, Africa, and Asia by means of the Atlantic also meant that the old southwestern Asian trade routes were bypassed. Ottoman trade turned more to regional and local markets, where profits were lower and there was little growth. Meanwhile, Ottoman guilds set the prices of commodities such as wheat, wool, copper, and precious metals, and European willingness to pay high prices pulled those commodities out of the Ottoman Empire. The result was scarcity, which led to a decline in Turkish industrial production. Likewise in the craft industries, Europeans bought Ottoman raw materi-

**Nur al-Din Room** (Damascus, Syria, 1707, Ottoman period) This reception room's marble floors, wooden panels painted with Arabic poetic inscriptions and geometric designs, stained glass windows, and open niches (*far end*) holding books and prized porcelain reflect an elegant Islamic simplicity in the home of a well-to-do merchant or official. A low cushioned bench runs around the three walls. *(The Metropolitan Museum of Art, Gift of The Hagop Kevorkian Fund, 1970 [1970.170]. Photography by Schecter Lee. Photograph © 1986 The Metropolitan Museum of Art)*

als, used them to manufacture textiles and metallurgical goods, and sold them in Turkish lands, thereby disrupting Ottoman craft industries in the early nineteenth century. Prices rose, inflation increased, and the government devalued the currency, causing new financial crises.

More than any other single factor, a series of agreements known as **capitulations,** which the Ottoman government signed with European powers, contributed to the Ottoman decline. A trade compact signed in 1536 and renewed in 1569 virtually exempted French merchants from Ottoman law and allowed them to travel and buy and sell throughout the sultan's dominions and to pay low customs duties on French imports and exports. In 1590, in spite of strong French opposition, a group of English merchants gained the right to trade in Ottoman territory in return for supplying the sultan with iron, steel, brass, and tin for his war with Persia. In 1615, as part of a twenty-year peace treaty, the capitulation rights already given to French and English businessmen were extended to the Habsburgs. These capitulations progressively gave European merchants an economic stranglehold on Ottoman trade and commerce; Europeans had greater military power. In the nineteenth century, the Ottoman Empire was beset by the loss of territory, the pressures of European capitalistic imperialism, and unresolved internal problems; Tsar Nicholas I of Russia (r. 1825–1855) called it "the sick man of Europe."[27]

## THE PERSIAN THEOCRATIC STATE

Describing the Mongol destruction of Persia in the thirteenth century, the Persian historian Juvaini wrote, "With one stroke, a world which billowed with fertility was laid desolate, and the regions thereof became a desert, and the greater part of the living dead, and their skin and bones crumbling dust."[28] Pursuing a scorched-earth policy toward the land and a psychological reign of terror over the people, the Mongols, so modern demographers estimate, reduced the population of Persia, Khurasan,

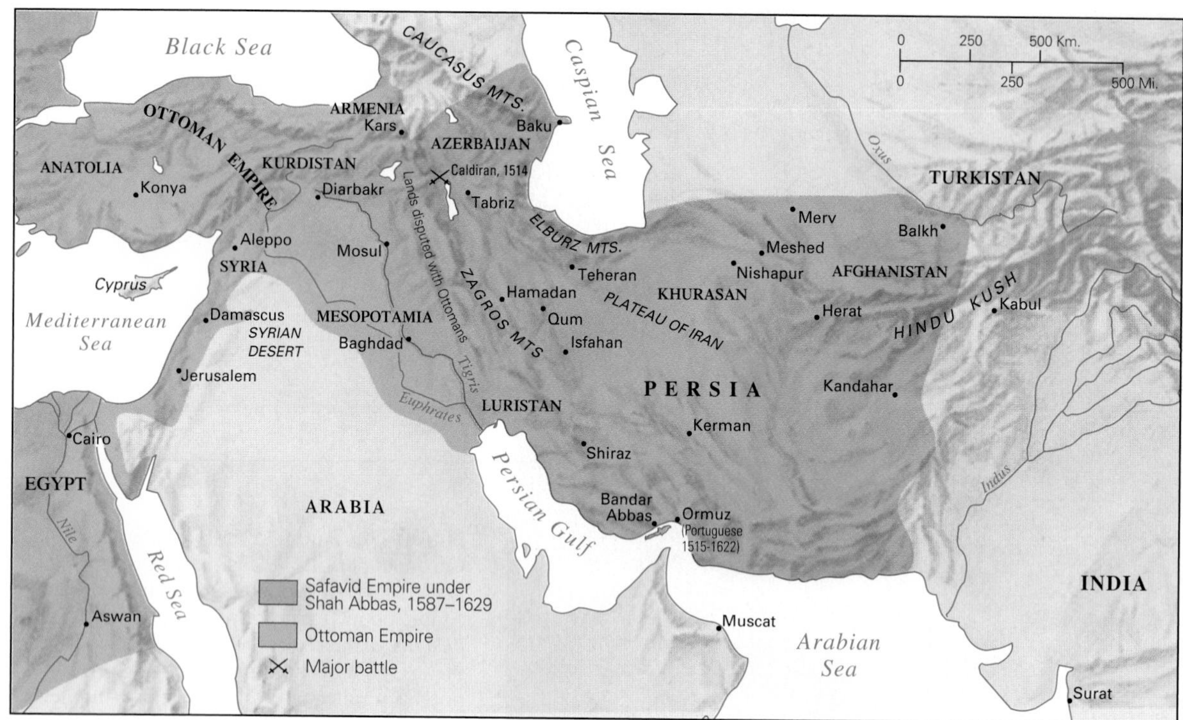


**MAP 20.2 The Safavid Empire** In the late sixteenth century, the power of the Safavid kingdom of Persia rested on its strong military force, its Shi'ite Muslim faith, and its extraordinarily rich trade in rugs and pottery. Many of the cities on the map, such as Tabriz, Qum, and Shiraz, were great rug-weaving centers.

Iraq, and Azerbaijan (see Map 20.2) from 2.5 million to 250,000. Mongol devastation represents the last great sweep of Turkish steppe nomads from Central Asia into the European and Islamic heartlands. Turkish tribes in Central Asia far outnumbered the ethnic Mongols. The Turks joined Chinggis Khan partly because he had defeated them and partly because westward expansion with the Mongols offered adventure and rich pasturelands for their herds of sheep and horses.[29]

The rehabilitation of Persia began under Ghazan (r. 1295–1304), the **Ilkhan,** as the Mongol rulers of Persia were called. A descendant of Chinggis Khan, Ghazan reduced peasants' taxes and thereby encouraged their will to produce. He also worked to improve the fiscal and administrative systems. His declaration of Islam as the state religion had profound political and cultural consequences: native (and Muslim) Persians willingly served the state government; they alone had the literacy needed to run a bureaucracy. Turkish-Mongol soldiers adapted to Persian ways. The court patronized Persian art. The rehabilitation of Persia under Ghazan legitimated the Mongols as a Persian dynasty. Across the Central Asian heartlands, hundreds of Chinese doctors, engineers, artists, and potterymakers came seeking opportunity in the Persian-Mongol-Turkish capital at Tabriz. Chinese artistic influences left a permanent mark on Persian miniature painting, calligraphy, and pottery design.

But Mongol rule of Persia did not last long. While Mehmet II was extending Ottoman jurisdiction through eastern Anatolia, the **Safavid** movement advanced in Persia. The Safavid Dynasty, which takes its name from Safi al-Din (1252–1334), a supposed descendant of Ali (the fourth caliph), began as leaders of a contemplative Sufi sect. Gradually the dynasty evolved into a militant and (to the Sunni Muslims) heretical Shi'ite regime. The attraction of the masses to Shi'ism perhaps reflects the role of religion as a vehicle for the expression of political feeling—in this case, opposition to Mongol domination. It also shows the organizational role played by Sufi orders such as the Safavids in a society disrupted by conquest. In the early sixteenth century, Persia emerged as a powerful Muslim state under the Safavids. (Since 1935

**The Prodigal Son** The court of the Safavid shahs of Isfahan attracted artists from China and Europe and supported their many styles and motifs. Based on the woodcut of a German printmaker, a Persian artist depicts the prodigal son (Luke 15:11–24), who, while his brother stayed home and worked, squandered his inheritance on wine and women and was forced to care for the pigs, an especially despicable animal in Muslim culture. *(San Diego Museum of Art, Gift of Dr. and Mrs. Edwin Binney 3d)*

Persia has been known as Iran.) Between 1502 and 1510, Ismail (r. 1502–1524) defeated petty Turkish leaders, united Persia under his sovereignty, and proclaimed himself **shah,** or king.

The strength of the early Safavid state rested on three crucial features. First, it had the loyalty and military support of **Qizilbash** nomadic tribesmen, many from Anatolia. (*Qizilbash,* a Turkish word meaning "redheads," was applied to these people because of the red hats they wore.) The shah secured the loyalty of the Qizilbash by granting them vast grazing lands, especially on the troublesome Ottoman frontier. In return, the Qizilbash supplied him with troops. Second, the Safavid state utilized the skills of urban bureaucrats and made them an essential part of the civil machinery of government. The third source of Safavid strength was the Shi'ite faith. The Shi'ites claimed descent from Ali, Muhammad's cousin and son-in-law, and believed that leadership among Muslims rightfully belonged to them as the Prophet's descendants. Ismail claimed descent from a line of twelve infallible *imams* (leaders) beginning with Ali and was officially regarded as their representative on earth. When Ismail conquered Tabriz in 1501, he declared Shi'ism the official and compulsory religion of his new empire under penalty of death. In the early twenty-first century, Iran remained the only Muslim state in which Shi'ism was the official religion.

Shi'ism gradually shaped the cultural and political identity of Persia (and later Iran). Recent scholarship asserts that Ismail was not "motivated by cynical notions of political manipulation."[30] He imported Shi'ite *ulama* (scholars outstanding in learning and piety) from other Arab lands to instruct and guide his people, and he persecuted and exiled Sunni ulama. With its puritanical emphasis on the holy law and on self-flagellation in penance for any disloyalty to Ali, the Safavid state represented theocracy triumphant throughout the first half century of its existence.

Safavid power reached its height under Shah Abbas (r. 1587–1629), whose military achievements, support for trade and commerce, and endowment of the arts earned him the epithet "the Great." The Persian army had hitherto consisted of tribal units under tribal leadership. Using the Ottoman model, Shah Abbas built a national army composed of Armenian and Georgian recruits paid by and loyal to himself. Shah Abbas campaigned against the Turks and captured Baghdad, Mosul, and Diarbakr in Mesopotamia (see Map 20.2).

Military victories account for only part of Shah Abbas's claim to greatness. Determined to improve his country's

**Polo** Two teams of four on horseback ride back and forth on a grass field measuring 200 by 400 yards, trying to hit a 4½-ounce wooden ball with a 4-foot mallet through the opponents' goal. Because a typical match involves many high-speed collisions among the horses, each player has to maintain a string of expensive ponies in order to change mounts several times during the game. Students of the history of sports believe the game originated in Persia, as shown in this eighteenth-century miniature, whence it spread to India, China, and Japan. Brought from India to England, where it became very popular among the aristocracy in the nineteenth century, polo is a fine example of cross-cultural influences. *(Private Collection)*

export trade, he built the small cottage business of carpet weaving into a national industry. In the capital city of Isfahan alone, factories employed more than twenty-five thousand weavers, who produced woolen carpets, brocades, and silks of brilliant color, design, and quality. Armenians controlled the carpet industry; the Safavids had brought them to Isfahan to protect them from Turkish military attacks. Three hundred Chinese potters were imported to make glazed building tiles, which adorned the great Safavid buildings. They captured much of the European tile market.

The jewel of the empire was Isfahan, whose prosperity and beauty rested on trade and industry. A seventeenth-century English visitor described Isfahan's bazaar as "the surprisingest piece of Greatness in Honour of commerce the world can boast of." Besides splendid rugs, stalls displayed pottery and fine china, metalwork of exceptionally high quality, and silks and velvets of stunning weave and design. A city of perhaps 750,000 people, Isfahan contained 162 mosques, 48 schools where future members of the ulama learned the sacred Muslim sciences, 273 public baths, and the vast imperial palace. Private houses had their own garden courts, and public gardens, pools, and parks adorned the wide streets. Tales of the beauty of Isfahan circulated worldwide, attracting thousands of tourists annually in the seventeenth and eighteenth centuries.

Flowers represent a distinctive and highly developed feature of Persian culture. From the second century, and with the model of the biblical account of the Garden of Eden (Genesis 2 and 3), a continuous tradition of gardening had existed in Persia. A garden was a walled area with a pool in the center and geometrically laid-out flowering plants, especially roses. "In Arabic, paradise is sim-

**Isfahan Tiles** The embellishment of Isfahan under Shah Abbas I created an unprecedented need for tiles—as had the rebuilding of imperial Istanbul after 1453, the vast building program of Suleiman the Magnificent, and a huge European demand. Persian potters learned their skills from the Chinese. By the late sixteenth century, Italian and Austrian potters had imitated the Persian and Ottoman tilemakers. *(Courtesy of the Trustees of the Victoria & Albert Museum)*

ply *al janna*, the garden,"[31] and often as much attention was given to flowers as to food crops. First limited to the ruler's court, gardening soon spread among the wealthy citizens. Gardens served not only as centers of prayer and meditation but also as places of revelry and sensuality. A ruler might lounge near his pool as he watched the ladies of his harem bathe in it.

After the Abbasid conquest of Persia in 636–637, formal gardening spread west and east through the Islamic world, as illustrated by the magnificent gardens of Muslim Spain, southern Italy, and later southeastern Europe. The Mongol followers of Tamerlane took landscape architects from Persia back to Samarkand and adopted their designs to nomad encampments. In 1396 Tamerlane ordered the construction of a garden in a meadow, called House of Flowers. When Tamerlane's descendant Babur established the Mughal Dynasty in India (see next section), he adapted the Persian garden to the warmer southern climate. Gardens were laid out near palaces, mosques, shrines, and mausoleums, the most famous being the Taj Mahal at Agra (see page 651).

Because it represented paradise, the garden played a large role in Muslim literature. Some scholars hold that to understand Arabic poetry, one must study Arabic gardening. The literary genres of flowers and gardens provided basic themes for Hispano-Arab poets and a model for medieval Christian Europe. The secular literature of Muslim Spain, rife with references such as "a garland of verses," influenced the lyric poetry of southern France, the troubadours, and the courtly love tradition.[32]

Gardens, of course, are seasonal. To remind themselves of "paradise" during the cold winter months, rulers, city people, and nomads ordered Persian carpets, which flower all year. Most Persian carpets of all periods use floral patterns and have a formal garden design. Because Islamic teaching holds that only God can create perfection, every carpet has some flaw or imperfection. Although Turkish, Caucasian, Indian, and other peoples produced carpets with their own local designs, motifs, patterns, and colors, so powerful was the Persian influence that Westerners came to label all carpets as "Persian." Carpets are always knotted; usually the smaller the knot, the more valuable the rug. Because the small hands of women and children can tie tinier knots than the large hands of men, women and children have often been used (and exploited) in the manufacture of expensive rugs. *Kilims,* floor or wall coverings or bags used on camels or horses, were woven.

The fifteenth century witnessed the acceleration of Eastern, especially Chinese, influences on West Asian art and culture. The naturalistic reproduction of lotus blossoms, peonies, chrysanthemums, birds, and even dragons, as well as tulips and carnations, appear in many carpets. The role of flowers and gardens in literature and life took on central significance. The Persian culture of flowers spread from the Islamic world to early modern Europe.[33]

Shah Abbas was succeeded by inept rulers whose heavy indulgence in wine and the pleasures of the harem weakened the monarchy and fed the slow disintegration of the state. Internal weakness encouraged increased foreign aggression. In the eighteenth century, the Turks, Afghans, and Russians invaded and divided Persia among themselves, and political anarchy and social chaos characterized Persian life.

## INDIA, FROM MUGHAL DOMINATION TO BRITISH DOMINION (CA 1498–1805)

Of the three great Islamic empires of the early modern world, the Mughal Empire of India was the largest, wealthiest, and most populous. Extending over 1.2 million square miles at the end of the seventeenth century, with a population between 100 million and 150 million, and with fabulous wealth and resources, the Mughal Empire surpassed Safavid Persia and Ottoman Turkey. Among the Mughal ruler's world contemporaries, only the Ming emperor of China could compare with him.[34]

In 1504 Babur (r. 1483–1530), the Turkish ruler of a small territory in Central Asia, captured Kabul and established the kingdom of Afghanistan. From Kabul he moved southward into India. In 1526, with a force of only twelve thousand men, Babur defeated the decrepit sultan of Delhi at Panipat. Babur's capture of the cities of Agra and Delhi, key fortresses of the north, paved the way for further conquests in northern India. Babur and his son and successor, Humayun, after a bitter struggle with the Afghans, laid the foundations of the Mughal Empire. The center of their power rested in the Ganges plain of north India. Mughal rule lasted until the eighteenth century, when domestic disorder and incompetent government opened the door to European intervention on the subcontinent. The term **Mughal,** a variant of *Mogul,* is often used to refer to the Muslim empire of India, but the founders of Mughal India were primarily Turks, Afghans, and Persians, though Babur claimed remote descent from the Mongol conquerors Tamerlane and Chinggis Khan.

### The Rule of the Mughals

Muslims first invaded India in the eighth century. The Turkish general Mahmud raided the Punjab (see Map 20.3) in the early eleventh century, and in the late twelfth century Turkish Muslim cavalry under Muhammad Bakhtiyar gained entrance to the royal city of Nudiya and overthrew the Hindu ruler of Bengal. In 1398 Central Asian forces under Tamerlane (Timur the Lame) swept down from the northwest, looted Delhi, and took thousands of slaves as booty. A contemporary wrote that he left Delhi completely destroyed, with "not a bird moving," and all India politically fragmented.

Babur's son Humayun reigned from 1530 to 1540 and from 1555 to 1556. When the Afghans of northern India rebelled, he lost most of the territories that his father had acquired. Humayun went into temporary exile in Persia, where he developed a deep appreciation for Persian art and literature. This interest led to a remarkable flowering of Mughal art under his son Akbar.

The reign of Akbar (r. 1556–1605) may well have been the greatest in the history of India. Under his dynamic leadership, the Mughal state took definite form. A boy of thirteen when he became **badshah,** or imperial ruler, Akbar was ably assisted during his early years by his father's friend Bairam Khan, a superb military leader. In 1555 Bairam Khan defeated Hindu forces at Panipat and

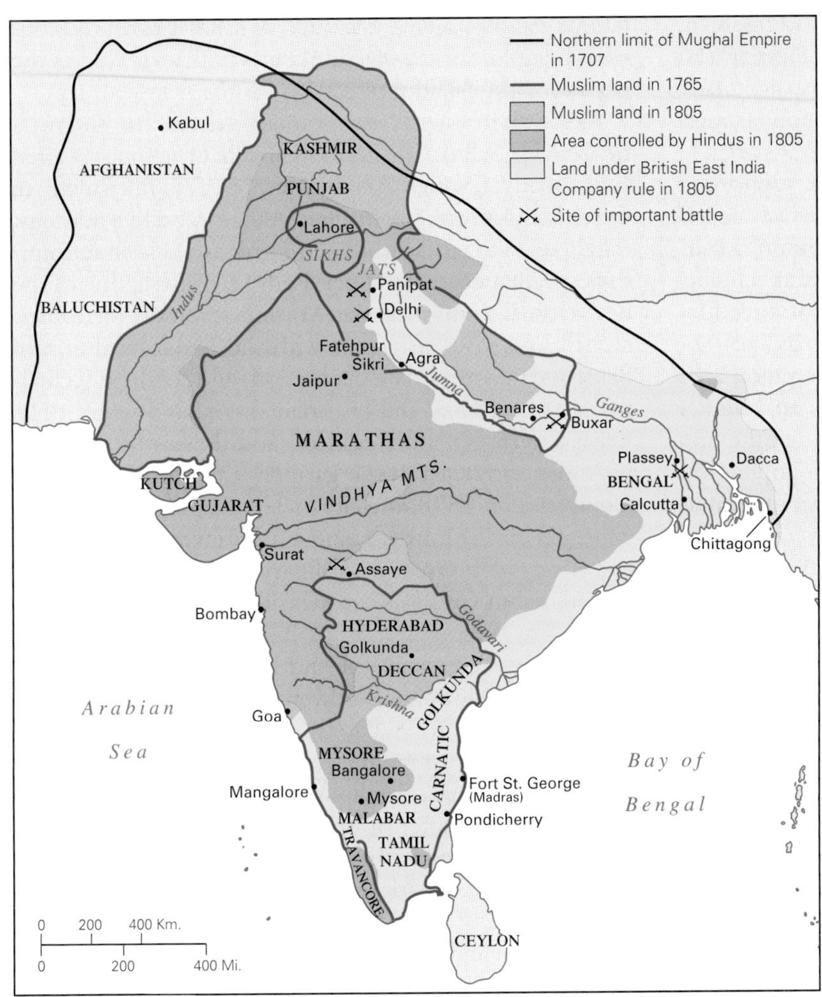


**MAP 20.3 India, 1707–1805** In the eighteenth century, Mughal power gradually yielded to the Hindu Marathas and to the British East India Company.

shortly afterward recaptured Delhi and Agra. Before falling from power in 1560, Bairam Khan took the great fortress of Gwalior, annexed the rich city of Jaunpur, and prepared for war against Malwa. Akbar continued this expansionist policy throughout this time, gradually adding the territories of Malwa, Gondwana, and Gujarat. Because the Afghan tribesmen put up tremendous resistance, it took Akbar several years to acquire Bengal. The Mughal Empire under Akbar eventually included most of the subcontinent north of the Godavari River (see Map 20.3). No kingdom, or coalition of kingdoms, could long resist Akbar's armies. The once independent states of northern India were forced into a centralized political system under the sole authority of the Mughal emperor.

To govern this vast region, Akbar developed an administrative bureaucracy centered on four co-equal ministers: for finance and revenue; the army and intelligence; the judiciary and religious patronage; and the imperial household, which included roads, bridges, and infrastructure throughout the empire. Under Akbar's finance minister, Raja Todar Mal (a Hindu), a *diwan* (bureau of finance) and royal mint came into existence. Raja Todar Mal devised methods for the assessment and collection of taxes that were applied everywhere. In the provinces, imperial governors, appointed by and responsible solely to the emperor, presided over administrative branches modeled on those of the central government. The government, however, rarely interfered in the life of village communities. Whereas the Ottoman sultans recruited and utilized Balkan slaves (converted from Orthodox Christianity to Islam) for military and administrative positions, Akbar used the services of royal princes, **amirs** (nobles), and *mansabdars* (warrior-aristocrats). Initially these men were Muslims from Central Asia, but to reduce their influence, Akbar vigorously recruited Persians and Hindus. The Mughal nobility and the administration of the empire rested on a heterogeneous body of freemen, not slaves "who rose as their talents and the emperor's favor permitted."[35] Most were Sunni Muslims, but many also were Hindus. No single ethnic or religious faction could challenge the emperor.

How could a Muslim ruler win the active support of millions of Hindu subjects, representing the vast majority of the population? Conversion to any religion is usually a gradual and complex process, and recent scholars agree that the possibility of mass conversion, or forced Islamization, in India in the sixteenth century did not exist.[36] Moreover, the Ganges Plain, the geographical area of the subcontinent most intensely exposed to Mughal rule and for the longest span of time, had, when the first reliable census was taken in 1901, a Muslim population of only 10 to 15 percent. In fact, "in the subcontinent as a whole there is an inverse relationship between the degree of Muslim political penetration and the degree of Islamization."[37]

Scholars disagree about Mughal religious policy. One scholar writes that it was one "of not interfering with Hindu society," of maintaining a "hands-off policy towards non-Muslim religions."[38] Another holds that "the cultural and religious climate of [late] sixteenth-century India was more open and tolerant of change"; that Akbar took a personal interest in religious questions and theological speculation; and that the emperor's greatest difficulties came not from Hindus but from Muslim ulama, the scholars learned in Islamic law. The ulama argued that the emperor should lead a pious and devout life and ensure that all Muslims could live according to the shari'a, or Islamic law.[39]

Akbar acted according to the principle of **sulahkul**, universal tolerance: the emperor was responsible for all his people, regardless of their religion. He celebrated important Hindu festivals, such as Diwali, the festival of lights. He wore his uncut hair in a turban "as a concession to Indian usage and to please his Indian subjects."[40] Twice Akbar married Hindu princesses, one of whom became the mother of his heir, Jahangir. He appointed the Spanish Jesuit Antonio Monserrate (1536–1600) as tutor to his second son, Prince Murad. Hindus eventually totaled 30 percent of the imperial bureaucracy. In 1579 Akbar abolished the jitza, the property tax on non-Muslims. These actions, especially the abolition of the jitza, infuriated the ulama, and serious conflict erupted between them and the emperor. Ultimately, Akbar issued an imperial decree declaring that the Mughal emperor had supreme authority, even above the ulama, in all religious matters. This statement, resting on a policy of benign toleration, represented a severe defeat for the Muslim religious establishment. Although Muslim-Hindu tensions were by no means resolved, Akbar's policies served as the basis for Mughal administration for the next century.

Akbar often sought the spiritual advice of the Sufi mystic Shaykh Salim Chishti. The birth of a long-awaited son, Jahangir, which Akbar interpreted as fulfillment of the shaykh's prophecy, inspired Akbar to build a new city, Fatehpur-Sikri, to symbolize the regime's Islamic foundations. He personally supervised the construction of the new city. It combined the Muslim tradition of domes, arches, and spacious courts with the Hindu tradition of flat stone beams, ornate decoration, and solidity. According to Abu-l-Fazl, the historian of Akbar's reign, "His majesty plans splendid edifices, and dresses the work of his mind and heart in the garment of stone and clay."[41] Completed in 1578, the city included an imperial palace, a mosque, lavish gardens, and a hall of worship, as well as thousands of houses for ordinary people. Akbar placed Shaykh Salim Chishti's tomb inside the great mosque to draw on its presumed sanctity. Just as medieval European rulers such as Charlemagne and Philip the Fair sought to strengthen their political power through association with Christian saints, so Akbar tried to identify Mughal authority with a Muslim saint. Along with the ancient cities of Delhi and Agra, Fatehpur-Sikri served as an imperial capital and the center of Akbar's lavish court.

Akbar was gifted with a creative intellect and imagination. He replaced Barlas Turkish with Persian as the official language of the Mughal Empire. Persian remained the official language until the British replaced it with English in 1835. Akbar enthusiastically supported artists who produced magnificent paintings and books in the Indo-Persian style. In Mughal India, as throughout the Muslim world, books were regarded as precious objects. Time, talent, and expensive materials went into their production, and they were highly coveted because they reflected wealth, learning, and power. Akbar reportedly possessed twenty-four thousand books when he died. Abu-l-Fazl describes the library and Akbar's love of books:

*His Majesty's library is divided into several parts. . . . Prose works, poetical works, Hindi, Persian, Greek, Kashmirian, Arabic, are all separately placed. In this order they are also inspected. Experienced people bring them daily and read them before His Majesty, who hears every book from beginning to end . . . and rewards the readers with presents of cash either in gold or silver, according to the number of leaves read out by them. . . . There are no historical facts of past ages, or curiosities of science, or interesting points of philosophy, with which His Majesty, a leader of impartial sages, is unacquainted.*[42]

Akbar's son Jahangir (r. 1605–1628) lacked his father's military abilities and administrative genius, but he did succeed in consolidating Mughal rule in Bengal. His patronage of the arts and lavish court have led scholars to characterize his reign as an "age of splendor."

Jahangir's son Shah Jahan (r. 1628–1658) launched fresh territorial expansion. Faced with dangerous revolts by the Muslims in Ahmadnagar and the resistance of the newly arrived Portuguese in Bengal, Shah Jahan not only crushed them but also strengthened his northwestern frontier. He reasserted Mughal authority in the Deccan and Golkunda.

All the Mughal emperors did some building, but Shah Jahan had the most sophisticated interest in architecture. The buildings in his capital at Agra suffered erosion, and its streets were too narrow for the large crowds that flocked there for festivals. In 1639 Shah Jahan, to distinguish himself from his predecessors and to leave a permanent mark on his era, decided to found a new capital city in the region of Delhi. Hindus considered the area especially sacred, and the site reflects their influence. In the design and layout of the buildings, however, Persian ideas predominated, an indication of the numbers of Persian architects and engineers who had flocked to the subcontinent. The walled palace-fortress alone extended over 125 acres. Built partly of red sandstone, partly of marble, it included private chambers for the emperor; mansions for the wives, widows, and concubines of the imperial

**City of Fatehpur-Sikri** In 1569 Akbar founded the city of Fatehpur-Sikri to honor the Muslim holy man Shaykh Salim Chishti, who had foretold the birth of Akbar's son and heir, Jahangir. The red sandstone city, probably the finest example of Mughal architecture still intact, was Akbar's capital for fifteen years. *(Nrupen Madhvani/Dinodia Picture Agency, Bombay)*

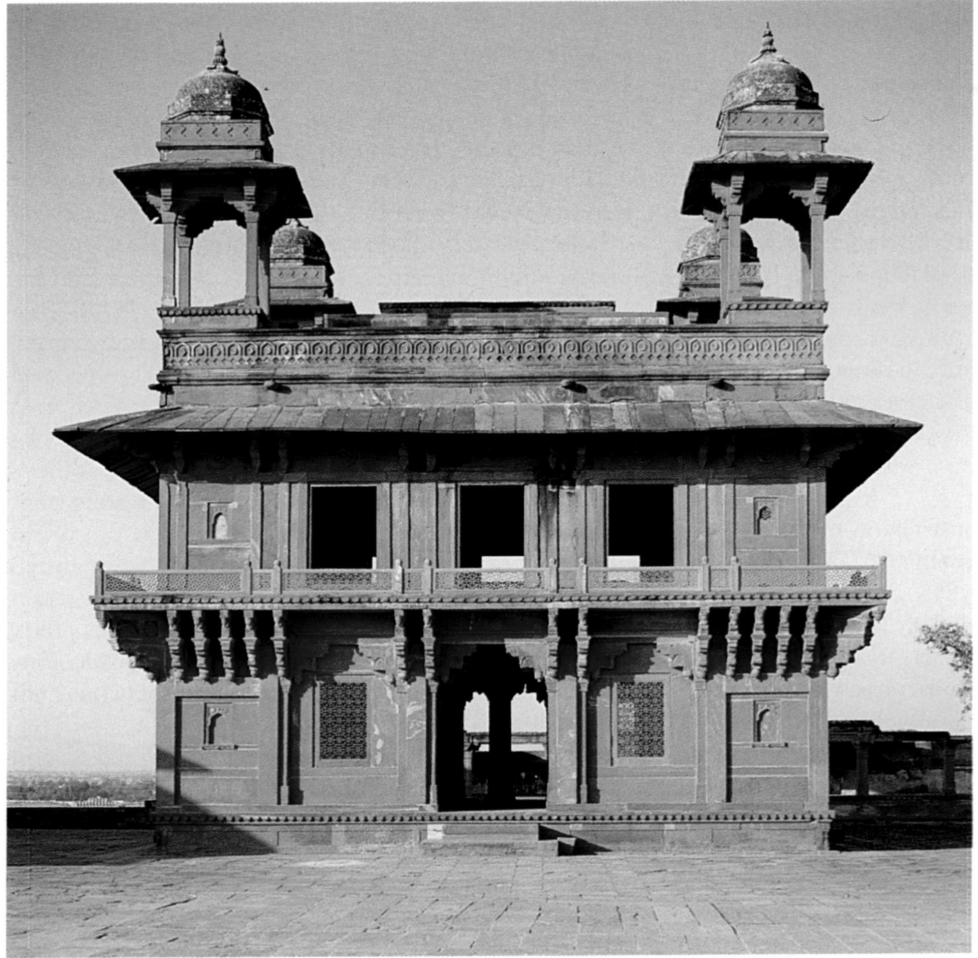

household; huge audience rooms for the conduct of public business (treasury, arsenal, and military); baths; and vast gardens filled with flowers, trees, and thirty silver fountains spraying water. In 1650, with living quarters for guards, military officials, merchants, dancing girls, scholars, and hordes of cooks and servants, the palace-fortress housed 57,000 people. It also boasted a covered public bazaar (comparable to a modern mall), 270 feet long and 27 feet wide, with arcaded shops. It was probably the first roofed shopping center in India, although such centers were common in western Asia. The sight of the magnificent palace left contemporaries speechless, and the words of an earlier poet were inscribed on the walls:

*If there is a paradise on the face of the earth,*
*It is this, it is this.*

Beyond the walls, princes and aristocrats built mansions and mosques on a smaller scale. Muslim visitors called the Juma Masjid mosque one of the finest in Islam. They marveled at the broad thoroughfares. With a population between 375,000 and 400,000, Delhi gained the reputation of being one of the great cities of the Muslim world.[43]

But Delhi (also called Shahjahanabad) and cities in general were not typical of Indian society. As everywhere in the premodern world, most people lived in rural villages and engaged in some form of agriculture, especially rice and cotton production. Based on the evidence of one typical late-seventeenth-century tax roll from northern India, scholars believe that rural populations were divided roughly into three groups: perhaps 7 percent were wealthy grain or cotton merchants who controlled village society; about 19 percent were peasants tilling large amounts of land; and the largest group, roughly 74 percent, farmed small plots. Artisans, weavers, water carriers, and landless rustics worked on a seasonal or piecemeal basis and served the others.

Shah Jahan ordered the construction of the Peacock Throne. (See the feature "Listening to the Past: The Weighing of Shah Jahan on His Forty-Second Lunar Birthday" on pages 658–659.) This famous piece, actually a cot resting on golden legs, was encrusted with emeralds, diamonds, pearls, and rubies. It took seven years to fashion and cost the equivalent of $5 million. It served as the imperial throne of India until 1739, when the Persian warrior Nadir Shah seized it as plunder and carried it to Persia.

Shah Jahan's most enduring monument is the Taj Mahal, the supreme example of a garden tomb. The Mughals sought to bring their vision of paradise alive in the walled garden tombs in which they buried their dead. Twenty thousand workers toiled eighteen years to build this memorial in Agra to Shah Jahan's favorite wife, Mumtaz Mahal, who died giving birth to their fifteenth child. One of the most beautiful structures in the world, the Taj Mahal is both an expression of love and a superb architectural blending of Islamic and Indian culture. It also asserted the power of the Mughal Dynasty.

The Mughal state never developed a formal procedure for the imperial succession, and a crisis occurred toward the end of Shah Jahan's reign. Competition among his sons ended with the victory of Aurangzeb, who executed his elder brother and locked his father away until his death in 1666. A puritanically devout and strictly orthodox Muslim, a skillful general and a clever diplomat, Aurangzeb (r. 1658–1707) ruled more of India than did any previous badshah. His reign witnessed the culmination of Mughal power and the beginning of its decline (see Map 20.3).

A combination of religious zeal and financial necessity seems to have prompted Aurangzeb to introduce a number of reforms. He appointed censors of public morals in important cities to enforce Islamic laws against gambling, prostitution, drinking, and the use of narcotics. He forbade *sati*—the self-immolation of widows on their husbands' funeral pyres—and the castration of boys to be sold as eunuchs. He also abolished all taxes not authorized by Islamic law. This measure led to a serious loss of state revenues. To replace them, Aurangzeb in 1679 reimposed the jitza, the tax on non-Muslims. It fell mostly on the Hindu majority.

Regulating Indian society according to Islamic law meant modifying the religious toleration and cultural cosmopolitanism instituted by Akbar. Aurangzeb ordered the destruction of some Hindu temples. He required Hindus to pay higher customs duties than Muslims. Out of fidelity to Islamic law, he even criticized his mother's tomb, the Taj Mahal: "The lawfulness of a solid construction over a grave is doubtful, and there can be no doubt about the extravagance involved."[44] Aurangzeb employed more Hindus in the imperial administration than any previous Mughal ruler, but his religious policy proved highly unpopular with the majority of his subjects and created problems that weaker successors could not handle.

Aurangzeb's military ventures also had mixed results. A tireless general, he pushed the conquest of the south and annexed the Golkunda and Bijapur sultanates. The stiffest opposition came from the Marathas, a militant Hindu group centered in the western Deccan. From 1681 until his death in 1707 at the age of ninety, Aurangzeb led repeated sorties through the Deccan. He

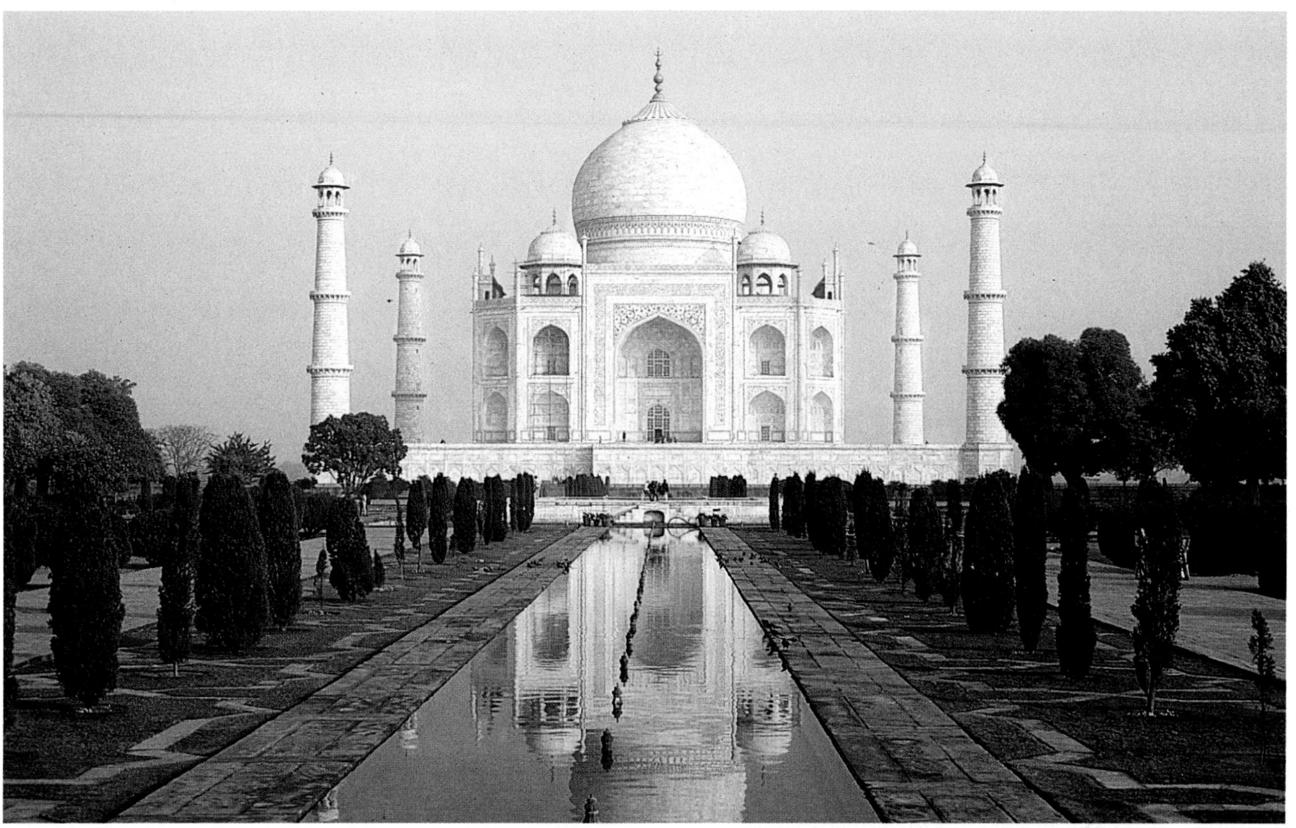

**Taj Mahal at Agra** This tomb is the finest example of Muslim architecture in India. Its white marble exterior is inlaid with semiprecious stones in Arabic inscriptions and floral designs. The oblong pool reflects the building, which asserts the power of the Mughal Dynasty. *(John Elk/Stock, Boston)*

took many forts and won several battles, but total destruction of the Maratha guerrilla bands eluded him. After his death, they played an important role in the collapse of the Mughal Empire.

Aurangzeb's eighteenth-century successors faced formidable problems. They were less successful than the Ottomans at making the dynasty the focus of loyalty. Repeated disputes over the succession undermined the stability of the monarchy. Court intrigues replaced the battlefield as the testing ground for the nobility. Mughal provincial governors began to rule independently, giving only minimal allegiance to the badshah at Delhi. The Marathas, who revolted and pressed steadily northward, constituted the gravest threat to Mughal authority. No ruler could defeat them.

In 1739 the Persian adventurer Nadir Shah invaded India, defeated the Mughal army, looted Delhi, and after a savage massacre carried off a huge amount of treasure, including the Peacock Throne. When Nadir Shah withdrew to Afghanistan, he took with him the Mughal government's prestige. Constant skirmishes between the Afghans and the Marathas for control of the Punjab and northern India ended in 1761 at Panipat, where the Marathas were crushed by the Afghans. At that point, India no longer had any power capable of imposing order on the subcontinent or checking the penetration of the rapacious Europeans.

## Trade and Commerce

The Mughal period witnessed the growth of a thriving capitalist commercial economy on the Indian subcontinent. Although most people were involved in agriculture, from which most imperial revenue was derived, a manufacturing industry supported by a money economy and mercantile capitalism expanded.

Block-printed cotton cloth, produced by artisans working at home, was the chief export. Through an Islamic

**Textile from Kalamkari** Containing a rich variety of Persian, Hindu, Muslim, and Christian motifs, this superb example of seventeenth-century painted cotton suggests the beauty and complexity of Indian textile manufacture, as well as the diversity of influences in Indian culture itself. *(The Metropolitan Museum of Art, Gift of Mrs. Albert Blum, 1920 [20.79]. Photograph © 1985 The Metropolitan Museum of Art)*

business device called the **sillim**, "contracts invoking prompt payment in return for a distant (future) delivery,"[45] banker-brokers supplied the material for production and the money that the artisans could live on while they worked; the cloth brokers specified the quality, quantity, and design of the finished product. This procedure resembles the later English "domestic" or "putting-out" system (see page 735), for the very good reason that the English took the idea from the Indians. In and around the cities of Surat, Ahmedabad, Pattan, Baroda, and Broach, varieties of cloth were produced and shipped to Gujarat. Within India, the demand for cotton cloth, as well as for food crops, was so great that Akbar had to launch a wide-scale road-building campaign. From Gujarat, Indian merchant bankers shipped their cloth worldwide: across the Indian Ocean to Aden and the Muslim-controlled cities on the east coast of Africa; across the Arabian Sea to Muscat and Hormuz and up the Persian Gulf to the cities of Persia; up the Red Sea to the Mediterranean; by sea also to Malacca, Indonesia, China, and Japan; by land across Africa to Ghana on the west coast; and to Astrakhan, Poland, Moscow, and even the Russian cities on the distant Volga River. In many of these places, Indian businessmen had branch offices. All this activity represented enormous trade, which produced fabulous wealth for some Indian merchants. Some scholars have contrasted India's "international" trade in the sixteenth century with that of Italian firms, such as the Medici. The Indian trade actually extended over a far wider area. Since Indian merchants were often devout Hindus, Muslims, Buddhists, or Jains, the argument of some Western writers, notably Karl Marx (see page 770), that religion "retarded" Asia's economic development is patently false.[46]

## European Rivalry for the Indian Trade

Shortly before Babur's invasion of India, the Portuguese under the navigator Pedro Alvares Cabral had opened the subcontinent to Portuguese trade. In 1510 they established the port of Goa on the Arabian Sea as their headquarters and through a policy of piracy and terrorism took control of Muslim shipping in the Indian and Arabian Oceans (see Map 20.3), charging high fees for passage. The Portuguese historian Barrões attempted to justify Portugal's seizure of commercial traffic that the Muslims had long dominated:

*It is true that there does exist a common right to all to navigate the seas and in Europe we recognize the rights which others hold against us; but the right does not extend beyond Europe and therefore the Portuguese as Lords of the Sea are justified in confiscating the goods of all those who navigate the seas without their permission.*[47]

In short, Western principles of international law did not apply in Asia. For almost a century, the Portuguese controlled the spice trade over the Indian Ocean.

In 1602 the Dutch formed the Dutch East India Company with the stated goal of wresting the enormously lucrative spice trade from the Portuguese. The scent of fabulous profits also attracted the English. With a charter signed by Queen Elizabeth, eighty London merchants organized the British East India Company. In 1619 Emperor Jahangir granted a British mission important commercial concessions at Surat on the west coast of India. Gifts, medical services, and bribes to Indian rulers enabled the British to set up twenty-seven other coastal forts. Fort St. George on the east coast became the modern city of Madras. In 1668 the city of Bombay—given to England when the Portuguese princess Catherine of Braganza married King Charles II—was leased to the company, marking the virtually total British absorption of Portuguese power in India. In 1690 the company founded a fort that became the city of Calcutta. Thus the three places that later became centers of British economic and political imperialism—Madras, Bombay, and Calcutta—existed before 1700. The Dutch concentrated their efforts in Indonesia.

## Factory-Fort Societies

The British called their trading post at Surat a **factory-fort** and the term was later used for all European settlements in India. The term did not signify manufacturing; it designated the walled compound containing the residences, gardens, and offices of British East India Company officials and the warehouses where goods were stored before being shipped to Europe. The company president exercised political authority over all residents.

Factory-forts existed to make profits from the Asian-European trade, and they evolved into flourishing centers of economic profit. The British East India Company sold silver, copper, zinc, lead, and fabrics to the Indians and bought cotton goods, silks, pepper and other spices, sugar, and opium from them. By the late seventeenth century, the company was earning substantial profits. Profitability increased after 1700, when the company began to trade with China. Some Indian merchants in Calcutta and Bombay made gigantic fortunes from trade within Asia.

Because the directors of the British East India Company in London discouraged all unnecessary expenses and financial risks, they opposed any interference in local Indian politics and even missionary activities. Conditions in India, however, brought about a fundamental change in the nature of the company's factories. The violent disorders and political instability that wracked India during Aurangzeb's reign and in the early eighteenth century caused the factories to evolve into defensive installations manned by small garrisons of native troops. When warlords appeared or an uprising occurred, people from the surrounding countryside flocked into the fort, and the company factory-forts gradually came to exercise political authority over the territories around them.

Indian and Chinese wares enjoyed great popularity in England and on the European continent in the late seventeenth and early eighteenth centuries. The middle classes wanted Indian textiles, which were colorful, durable, cheap, and washable. The upper classes desired Chinese wallpaper and porcelains and Indian silks and brocades. In the European economies, however, Asian goods created serious problems. As early as 1695, English manufacturers called for an embargo on Indian cloth, and silk weavers picketed the House of Commons.

Trade with Asia was one-way: Asians had little interest in European manufactured articles. Finding the Siamese (Thai) completely uninterested in traditional Dutch goods, the Dutch East India Company tried to interest them in collections of pornography. Europeans had to pay for everything they bought from Asia with precious metals.

**English Factory-Fort at Surat** The factory-fort began as a storage place for goods before they were bought and transported abroad; it gradually expanded to include merchants' residences and some sort of fortification. By 1650 the English had twenty-three factory-forts in India. Surat, in the Gujarat region on the Gulf of Cambay, was the busiest factory-fort and port until it was sacked by the Marathas in 1664. *(Mansell Collection/TimePix)*

Thus there was insistent pressure in England, France, and the Netherlands against the importation of Asian goods. As one authority explains: "The root of the argument from which grew a tree of many branches was the old fear of the drain of gold."[48]

## The Rise of the British East India Company

The French were the last to arrive in India. Louis XIV's financial wizard Colbert (see page 542) planned the French East India Company for trade in the Eastern Hemisphere, and in the 1670s the company established factories at Chandernagore in Bengal, Pondicherry, and elsewhere. Joseph Dupleix (1697–1764), who was appointed governor general at Pondicherry in 1742, made allies of Indian princes and built an army of native troops, called **sepoys,** who were trained as infantrymen. The British likewise built an army with Indian surrogates trained in Western military drill and tactics. War broke out at midcentury.

From 1740 to 1763, Britain and France were almost continually engaged in a tremendous global struggle. India, like North America in the Seven Years' War, became a battlefield and a prize. The French won land battles, but English sea power decided the first phase of the war. Then a series of brilliant victories destroyed French power in southern India. By preventing French reinforcements from arriving, British sea power again proved to be the determining factor, and British jurisdiction soon extended over the important northern province of Bengal. The Treaty of Paris of 1763 recognized British control of much of India, and scholars acknowledge the treaty as the beginning of the British Empire in India.

How was the vast subcontinent to be governed? Parliament believed that the British East India Company had too much power and considered the company responsible for the political disorders in India, which were bad for business. Parliament attempted to solve Indian problems with special legislation. The Regulating Act of 1773 created the office of governor general, with an advisory council, to exercise political authority over the territory controlled by the company. The India Act of 1784 required that the governor general be chosen from outside the company, and it made company directors subject to parliamentary supervision.

Implementation of these reforms fell to Warren Hastings, the governor of Bengal and first governor general (r. 1774–1785), with jurisdiction over Bombay and Madras. Hastings tried to build an effective administrative system and to turn the British East India Company into a government. He laid the foundations for the first Indian civil service, abolished tolls to facilitate internal trade, placed the salt and opium trades under government control, and planned a codification of Muslim and Hindu laws. He sought allies among Indian princes. The biggest problem facing Hastings's administration was a coalition of the rulers of Mysore and the Marathas aimed at the expulsion of the British. Hastings's skillful diplomacy offset this alliance temporarily.

Hastings's successor, Lord Charles Cornwallis, served as governor general of India from 1786 to 1794. Cornwallis continued the work of building a civil service and the war against Mysore. His introduction of the British style of property relations in effect converted a motley collection of former Mughal officers, tax collectors, and others into English-style landlords. The result was a new system of landholding, in which the rents of tenant farmers supported the landlords.

The third governor general, the marquess Richard Wellesley (r. 1797–1805), defeated Mysore in 1799 and four years later crushed the Marathas at the Battle of Assaye (see Map 20.3). Building on the work of his predecessors, he vastly extended British influence in India. Like most nineteenth-century British governors of India, Wellesley believed that British rule strongly benefited the Indians. With supreme condescension, he wrote that British power should be established over the Indian princes in order

*to deprive them of the means of prosecuting any measure or of forming any confederacy hazardous to the security of the British empire, and to enable us to preserve the tranquility of India by exercising a general control over the restless spirit of ambition and violence which is characteristic of every Asiatic government.*[49]

By the beginning of the nineteenth century, the authority and power of the British East India Company had yielded to the government in London. Subsequent British rule of India rested on three foundations: the support of puppet Indian princes who exercised the trappings but not the reality of power; a large army of sepoys of dubious loyalty; and an increasingly effective civil service, staffed largely by Englishmen, with Hindus and Muslims in minor positions.

## SUMMARY

Pursuing a policy of territorial expansion, the Muslim Ottoman Turks captured the ancient Byzantine capital of Constantinople in May 1453. Renamed Istanbul, the city under Suleiman the Magnificent served as the administrative center of a vast multiethnic empire extending from the Atlantic to the Indian Ocean. Strong military organization and their enemies' disunity gave the Ottomans superiority. The wealth of the empire, based largely on commerce, provided the material basis for a great cultural efflorescence. In architecture, as shown in the many mosques, markets, schools, hospitals, and public baths; in poetry, folk literature, and historical writing; in ceramics, textiles, and carpet weaving; and in medical pharmacology, the splendid creativity of the early Ottomans is revealed. In the seventeenth century, economic, demographic, and political issues connected with the imperial succession all contributed to the weakening of Ottoman power.

Meanwhile, Shi'ite Persia under Safavid rule recovered from Mongol devastation. Under Shah Abbas, military success, strong domestic industry based on carpet weaving, and the talents of hundreds of Chinese immigrants from Central Asia led to a brilliant period of prosperity and artistic creativity.

For size of population, fabulous wealth, and sheer geographical extent, the Mughal Empire on the Indian subcontinent was the grandest of the three Muslim polities. The Turkish leader Babur's conquest of Delhi in the early sixteenth century laid the foundation for an enduring Muslim presence. Babur's grandson Akbar continued the policy of expansion, built a sound administrative bureaucracy, and conciliated his millions of Hindu subjects through a policy of universal religious toleration. Akbar's grandson left two powerful and enduring monuments—a new capital city in the region of Delhi and the Taj Mahal, a garden tomb in Agra in honor of his favorite wife. Indian textiles, much desired in Southeast Asia, China, and Europe, developed into a large industry. Manufacturing, in turn, attracted European businessmen. The inability of Indian leaders in the eighteenth century to resolve their domestic differences led first to British intervention and then to full British rule. Bitter hostility between Hindus and Muslims persisted as a dominant theme of Indian life and culture.

## KEY TERMS

Ottomans
Anatolia
Sultan-i-Rum
sultan
jitza
concubines
devshirme
janissaries
Kanuni
bimaristans
capitulations
Ilkhan
Safavid
shah
Qizilbash
Mughal
badshah
amirs
sulahkul
sillim
factory-fort
sepoys

## NOTES

1. Quoted in B. Lewis, *The Muslim Discovery of Europe* (New York: W. W. Norton, 1982), p. 29.
2. H. Inalcik, *The Ottoman Empire: The Classical Age, 1300–1600,* trans. N. Itzkowitz and C. Imber (London: Weidenfeld and Nicolson, 1975), pp. 6–7.
3. W. H. McNeill, *The Pursuit of Power: Technology, Armed Force, and Society Since A.D. 1000* (Chicago: University of Chicago Press, 1982), p. 87.
4. Quoted in P. Mansel, *Constantinople: City of the World's Desire, 1453–1924* (New York: St. Martin's Griffin, 1996), p. 4.
5. Quoted in Lewis, *The Muslim Discovery of Europe,* p. 30.
6. F. Babinger, *Mehmed the Conqueror and His Times,* trans. R. Manheim (Princeton, N.J.: Princeton University Press, 1978), p. 107.
7. Inalcik, *The Ottoman Empire,* Chap. 5.
8. F. Robinson, *Atlas of the Islamic World Since 1500* (New York: Facts on File, 1982), p. 72.
9. S. J. Shaw, *History of the Ottoman Empire and Modern Turkey.* Vol. 1: *Empire of the Gazis: The Rise and Decline of the Ottoman Empire, 1208–1808* (Cambridge: Cambridge University Press, 1988), pp. 139–151.
10. L. Pierce, *The Imperial Harem: Women and Sovereignty in the Ottoman Empire* (New York: Oxford University Press, 1993), p. 3.
11. Ibid., p. 31.
12. Ibid., pp. 32–47.
13. Ibid., pp. 47–72.
14. E. R. Tolendano, *The Ottoman Slave Trade and Its Suppression* (Princeton, N.J.: Princeton University Press, 1982), pp. 59–61.
15. See R. S. Hattox, *Coffee and Coffeehouses: The Origins of a Social Beverage in the Medieval Near East* (Seattle: University of Washington Press, 1996), Chaps. 2 and 3, pp. 11–60.
16. S. O. Murray and W. Roscoe, *Islamic Homosexualities: Culture, History, and Literature* (New York: New York University Press, 1997), pp. 174–186; the quotation is on p. 175.
17. Ibid., footnote 10, p. 183.
18. See M. Rocke, *Forbidden Friendships: Homosexuality and Male Culture in Renaissance Florence* (New York: Oxford University Press, 1996), Chap. 1.
19. On the Ottoman Turkish population, see H. Inalcik and D. Quataert, *An Economic and Social History of the Ottoman Empire.* Vol. 1: *1300–1600* (Cambridge: Cambridge University Press, 1994), pp. 25–43. Although we lack data for the Muslim population of Andalusian Spain before 1520, between 1520 and 1580 the Muslim and non-Muslim population of western Asia Minor grew by 41.7 percent.
20. Quoted in P. K. Hitti, *The Near East in History* (Princeton, N.J.: Van Nostrand, 1961), p. 336.
21. Shaw, *History of the Ottoman Empire,* p. 148.
22. *The Selected Letters of Lady Mary Wortley Montagu,* ed. R. Halsband (London: Longman Group, 1970), pp. 98–99.
23. Ibid., p. 106.
24. Ibid., p. 105.
25. Ibid., pp. 96–97.
26. N. Itzkowitz, *Ottoman Empire and Islamic Tradition* (Chicago: University of Chicago Press, 1980), p. 95.
27. Shaw, *History of the Ottoman Empire,* pp. 171–175, 225, 246–247; V. H. Parry, H. Inalcik, A. N. Kurat, and J. S. Bromley, *A History of the Ottoman Empire to 1715* (New York: Cambridge University Press, 1976), pp. 126, 139–140.
28. Quoted in R. E. Dunn, *The Adventures of Ibn Battuta: A Muslim Traveler of the 14th Century* (Berkeley: University of California Press, 1986), p. 81.
29. Ibid., pp. 83–87. On population losses in Persia, see D. Morgan, *The Mongols* (Oxford: Basil Blackwell, 1987), pp. 149–151.
30. D. Morgan, *Medieval Persia, 1040–1797* (New York: Longman, 1988), pp. 112–113.
31. J. Goody, *The Culture of Flowers* (Cambridge: Cambridge University Press, 1993), p. 103.
32. Ibid., pp. 106–110.
33. Ibid., pp. 111–115.
34. J. F. Richards, *The New Cambridge History of India: The Mughal Empire* (Cambridge: Cambridge University Press, 1995), pp. 19–30.
35. Ibid., pp. 19–30, 59–60.
36. R. M. Eaton, *The Rise of Islam and the Bengal Frontier, 1204–1760* (Berkeley: University of California Press, 1993), Chap. 5; Richards, *The New Cambridge History of India,* p. 36.
37. Eaton, *The Rise of Islam,* p. 115.
38. Ibid., pp. 177–179.
39. Richards, *The New Cambridge History of India,* pp. 34–36; the quotation is on p. 34.
40. Quoted ibid., p. 45.
41. Quoted in V. A. Smith, *The Oxford History of India* (Oxford: Oxford University Press, 1967), p. 398.
42. Quoted in M. C. Beach, *The Imperial Image: Paintings for the Mughal Court* (Washington, D.C.: Freer Gallery of Art, Smithsonian Institution, 1981), pp. 9–10.
43. S. P. Blake, *Shahjahanabad: The Sovereign City in Mughal India,* 1639–1739 (Cambridge: Cambridge University Press, 1991), Chaps. 1 and 2, pp. 1–82; the quotation is on p. 44.
44. Quoted in S. K. Ikram, *Muslim Civilization in India* (New York: Columbia University Press, 1964), p. 202.
45. J. Goody, *The East in the West* (Cambridge: Cambridge University Press, 1996), p. 93.
46. Ibid., pp. 91–96, 104 et seq.
47. Quoted in K. M. Panikkar, *Asia and Western Domination* (London: George Allen & Unwin, 1965), p. 35.
48. Quoted ibid., p. 53.
49. Quoted in W. Bingham, H. Conroy, and F. W. Iklé, *A History of Asia,* vol. 2 (Boston: Allyn and Bacon, 1967), p. 74.

## Suggested Reading

The curious student interested in the Ottoman world might begin with A. Wheatcroft, *The Ottomans* (1993), an excitingly written and beautifully illustrated popular account of many facets of Ottoman culture that separates Western myths from Turkish reality. P. Mansel, *Constantinople: City of the World's Desire, 1453–1924* (1995), is another broad popular survey, but better informed. In addition to the titles by Babinger, Inalcik, Itzkowitz, Pierce, and Shaw cited in the Notes, Chapters 13, 14, and 15 of A. Hourani, *A History of the Arab Peoples* (1991), should also prove helpful. Perhaps the best broad general studies of the material in this chapter are M. G. S. Hodgson, *The Venture of Islam*. Vol. 3: *The Gunpowder Empires and Modern Times* (1974), and Part 2 of I. M. Lapidus, *A History of Islamic Societies* (1989). For Suleiman the Magnificent, E. Atil, *The Age of Sultan Suleyman the Magnificent* (1987), is a splendidly illustrated celebration of the man and his times, while G. Necipoglu, *Architecture, Ceremonial and Power: The Topkapi Palace in the Fifteenth and Sixteenth Centuries* (1991), is broader than the title might imply and is valuable for many aspects of Ottoman culture. A. Stratton, *Sinan* (1972), is a highly informative biography of the great Ottoman architect. For the later empire, see R. Dankoff, *The Intimate Life of an Ottoman Statesman* (1991), the memoirs of a seventeenth-century traveler; B. Masters, *The Origins of Western Economic Dominance in the Middle East* (1988); and S. J. Shaw, *Between Old and New: The Ottoman Empire Under Sultan Selim III, 1789–1807* (1971).

The literature on women is growing, though still largely restricted to the upper classes. In addition to the important work by Pierce cited in the Notes, see, for general background, L. Ahmed, ed., *Women and Gender in Islam* (1992), which is especially useful for Mamluk Egypt; F. Davis, *The Ottoman Lady: A Social History from 1718 to 1918* (1986); A. L. Croutier, *The World Behind the Veil* (1989); and *The Selected Letters of Lady Mary Wortley Montagu,* cited in the Notes. J. Freely, *Inside the Seraglio: Private Lives of the Sultans in Istanbul* (2000), surveys the role of the harem in Ottoman political and public life from the rise of the dynasty to 1921.

For slavery and race, see B. Lewis, *Race and Slavery in the Middle East* (1990); E. R. Toledano, *The Ottoman Slave Trade and Its Suppression: 1840–1890* (1982), which, although dealing with a period later than this chapter, offers useful references to earlier centuries; and E. R. Toledano, ed., *Slavery and Abolition in the Ottoman Middle East* (1998), which has valuable source materials. The superb achievement of D. B. Davis, *Slavery and Human Progress* (1984), is the only work that explores slavery in a world context.

For Safavid Persia, see P. Jackson and L. Lockhart, eds., *The Cambridge History of Iran*. Vol. 6: *The Timurid and Safavid Periods* (1986), a standard reference work; C. Melville, ed., *Safavid Persia*, which contains useful source readings; and L. Lockhart, *Nadir Shah, a Critical Study* (1973), an interesting, if somewhat dated, political biography. Students interested in understanding Persian culture through its remarkable art should study A. Soudawar and M. C. Beach, *The Art of the Persian Courts* (1992), and Y. A. Petrosyan et al., *Pages of Perfection: Islamic Painting and Calligraphy from the Russian Academy of Sciences* (1995); these volumes are magnificently illustrated.

Perhaps the best general introduction to the history and civilization of India is S. Wolpert's elegant appreciation *India* (1990), but see also P. Spears, *A History of India,* vol. 2 (1986). The books by Blake, Eaton, and Richards cited in the Notes have sound material and are highly recommended. The titles by Smith and Ikram cited in the Notes provide broad general treatments, as do P. M. Holt et al., eds., *The Cambridge History of India,* 2 vols. (1970); M. Mujeeb, *The Indian Muslims* (1967); and I. Habib, *The Agrarian System of Mughal India, 1556–1707* (1963), whose theme and scope are indicated by the title. Many of the essays in J. F. Richards, *Power, Administration and Finance in Mughal India* (1993), are useful and authoritative. For the decline of imperial authority in eighteenth-century India, see the important study of M. Alam, *The Crisis of Empire in Mughal North India: Awadh and the Punjab, 1707–48* (1986). Students wishing to study Indian culture through its architecture should consult two splendid achievements: C. Tadgell, *The History of Architecture in India: From the Dawn of Civilization to the End of the Raj* (1995), and G. Mitchell, *The Royal Palaces of India* (1995). E. B. Findly, *Nur Jahan: Empress of Mughal India* (1993), provides a vivid picture of one powerful and influential woman. For Babur, see *The Baburnama: Memoirs of Babur, Prince and Emperor*, trans. and ed. by W. M. Thackston (1996), the well-annotated and beautifully illustrated diary of the founder of the Mughal Dynasty; and M. C. Beach and E. Koch, eds., *King of the World: The Padshahnama* (1997), a supremely elegant, learned, and splendidly illustrated study of the reign of Jahangir. E. Maclagan, *The Jesuits and the Great Mogul* (1932), discusses the Jesuits at the courts of Akbar, Jahangir, and Shah Jahan. B. Gascoigne, *The Great Moghuls* (1971), and G. Hambly, *The Cities of Mughal India: Delhi, Agra, and Fatehpur Sikri* (1968), are well illustrated and highly readable. For the impact of Portuguese, Dutch, and English mercantile activities in India, see M. N. Pearson, *Merchants and Rulers in Gujarat: The Response to the Portuguese in the Sixteenth Century* (1976). For Asian influences on European economic ideas and institutions, see J. Goody, *The East in the West* (1996).

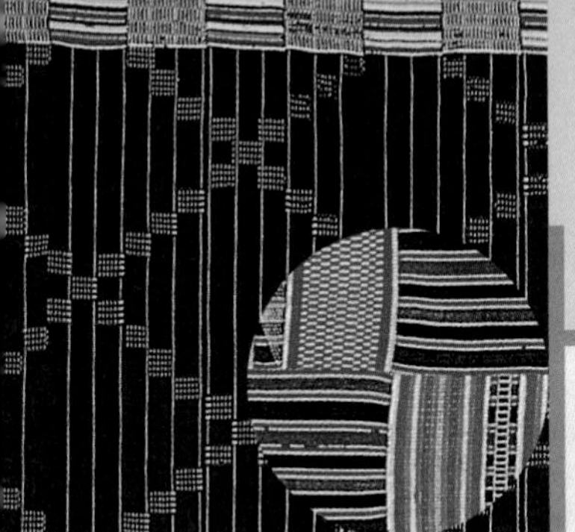

# LISTENING TO THE PAST

## THE WEIGHING OF SHAH JAHAN ON HIS FORTY-SECOND LUNAR BIRTHDAY*

*In 1799 the nawab (provincial governor) of Oudh in northern India sent to King George III of Great Britain the* Padshahnama, *or official history of the reign of Shah Jahan. A volume composed of 239 folios on very high quality gold-flecked tan paper, with forty-four stunningly beautiful paintings illustrating the text, the* Padshahnama *represents both a major historical chronicle of a Mughal emperor's reign and an extraordinary artistic achievement. One of the great art treasures of the world, it now rests in the Royal Library at Windsor.*

*All the Mughal emperors had a strong historical sense and the desire to preserve records of their reigns. They brought to India the traditional Muslim respect for books as sources of secular and religious knowledge and as images of their wealth and power. The* Padshahnama, *in stressing Shah Jahan's descent from Tamerlane and his right to the throne, in celebrating his bravery and military prowess, and in magnifying his virtues, is one long glorification of Jahan's rule. The Persian scholar and calligrapher Abdul-Hamid Lahawri wrote the text. Many Persian artists painted the illustrations with detailed precision and an exactitude that art historians consider sensitive and faithful to the original.*

Since alms are beneficial for repelling bodily and psychic harm and for attracting spiritual and corporeal benefits, as all peoples, religions, and nations are agreed, His Majesty Arsh-Ashyani [Akbar] established the custom of weighing and had himself weighed twice [a year], once after the end of the solar year and the other after the end of the lunar year. In the solar weighing he was

The "Weighing of Shah Jahan," who sits cross-legged on one plate of the scales, as bags of gold and silver wait to be placed on the other side. *(The Royal Collection © Her Majesty Queen Elizabeth II)*

*A solar year is the time required for the earth to make one complete revolution around the sun (365 days). A lunar year equals 12 lunar months.

weighed twelve times, first against gold and then eleven other items, while in the lunar weighing he was weighed eight times, first against silver and then seven other items. . . . The amounts from the weighings were given away in alms.

. . . Inasmuch as it benefited the needy, His Majesty Jahanbani [Shah Jahan] has his perfect self weighed twice, and in his generosity he has ordered that gold and silver be used each time. . . .

. . . The lunar weighing ceremony for the end of the forty-third year of the Emperor's life was held. The Emperor, surrounded by a divine aura, was weighed against gold and the other usual things, and the skirt of the world was held out in expectation of gold and silver. On this auspicious day Muhammad-Ali Beg, the ambassador of Iran, was awarded a gold-embroidered robe of honor, a jeweled belt, an elephant, a female elephant, and four large ashrafis, one weighing 400 tolas [a measure of weight, slightly more than two mithcals], the second 300 tolas, the third 200 tolas, and the fourth 100 tolas, and four rupees also of the weights given above, and he was given leave to depart. From the time he paid homage until the time he set out to return he had been given 316,000 rupees in cash and nearly a lac of rupees in goods.

An earlier weighing ceremony of the Emperor Jahangir, on 1 September 1617, was described by the always observant, and usually skeptical, first English ambassador to the Mughal court, Sir Thomas Roe: "Was the Kings Birth-day, and the solemnitie of his weighing, to which I went, and was carryed into a very large and beautifull Garden; the square within all water; on the sides flowres and trees. . . . Here attended the Nobilitie, all sitting about it on Carpets, vntill the King came; who at last appeared clothed, or rather loden with Diamonds, Rubies, Pearles, and other precious vanities, so great, so glorious! . . . Suddenly hee entered into the scales, sate like a woman on his legges, and there was put against him many bagges to fit his weight, which were changed sixe times, and they say was siluer, and that I vnderstood his weight to be nine thousand *Rupias,* which are almost one thousand pound sterling."

*Another official history of Shah Jahan's reign, the 'Amal-i-Salih, describes the ceremonial weighing that took place another year.*

Since it is His Majesty's custom and habit to have beggars sought out, and his generous nature is always looking for a pretext to relieve those who are in need, therefore twice a year he sits, like the orient sun in majesty, in the pan of the scale of auspiciousness in the solar and lunar weighing ceremonies. Twice a year by solar and lunar calculation a magnificent celebration and a large-scale banquet is arranged by order of His Majesty. An amount equal to his weight in gold and silver is distributed among the destitute and the poor according to their deservedness and merits. Although this type of alms is not mentioned in the religious law, nonetheless since scholars of this country are all in agreement that such alms are the most perfect type of alms for repelling corporeal and spiritual catastrophes and calamities, therefore this pleasing method was chosen and established by His Majesty Arsh-Ashyani, whose personality was, like the world-illuminating sun, based upon pure effulgence. By this means the poor attained their wishes, and in truth the custom of *aqiqa*—which is an established custom in the law of the Prophet and his Companions, and in which on the seventh day after birth the equivalent weight of an infant's shaven hair in silver is given in alms, and a sacrificial animal is divided and distributed among the poor—has opened the way to making this custom permissible.

## QUESTIONS FOR ANALYSIS

1. Consider Shah Jahan's motives for the practice of ceremonial weighing. Does it have any theological basis?
2. Compare the Mughal practice to something similar in Ottoman, European, and South American societies.

*Source: King of the World. The Padshahnama. An Imperial Mughal Manuscript from the Royal Library, Windsor Castle,* ed. Milo Cleveland Beach and Ebba Koch, trans. Wheeler Thackston (Washington, D.C.: Azimuth Editions—Sackler Gallery, 1997, pp. 39–43). Courtesy of the Arthur M. Sackler Gallery, Smithsonian Institution, Washington, D.C.

Women prepare for cotton spinning, using a tool called a *kinuta,* while a man (*at right*) carries bundles of refined cotton fiber. *(Freer Gallery of Art, Smithsonian Institution, Washington, D.C., Gift of Charles Lanng Freer, F1902.48)*

CHAPTER

# 21 CONTINUITY AND CHANGE IN EAST ASIA, CA 1400–1800

## CHAPTER OUTLINE

- China, from the Ming to the Mid-Qing (ca 1368–1795)
- Korea (ca 1400–1800)
- Japan (ca 1400–1800)

The period from about 1400 to 1800 witnessed growth and dynamic change in East Asia. In China, the native Ming Dynasty (1368–1644) replaced the Mongol Yuan Dynasty (1271–1368). Under the Ming, China saw agricultural reconstruction, commercial expansion, remarkable maritime expeditions abroad, and the production of magnificent porcelain, which was in high demand throughout Asia. By the later fifteenth century, however, incompetent emperors allowed corrupt and grasping eunuchs to gain control of commercial wealth and military power; friction between court factions paralyzed the state bureaucracy. The flood of Japanese and South American silver to China compounded a fiscal crisis. Meanwhile, the Manchus pressed along the northern frontier. In 1644, the Ming Dynasty collapsed and was replaced by the Qing.

The Manchus inaugurated a long period of peace, relative prosperity, and population expansion. In the Manchu, or Qing, period, the Chinese empire reached its greatest territorial extent, and literary and artistic creativity reached an apogee.

In the same centuries, the Korean peninsula saw the establishment of a new dynasty. Korea achieved agricultural and commercial expansion that led to considerable social change. Korean culture was heavily influenced by the Chinese, and Korea several times felt the effects of Japanese aggression.

In the Japanese islands, united by Nobunaga and later the Tokugawa Shogunate (1600–1867), the feudal military aristocracy continued to evolve. Although Japan developed largely in isolation from outside influences, its sociopolitical system bore striking similarities to medieval European feudalism. The period of the Tokugawa Shogunate, like that of the Ming Dynasty in China, was marked by remarkable agricultural productivity and industrial growth.

- What features characterized the governments of the Ming and Qing Dynasties in China and the Tokugawa Shogunate?
- How did agricultural and commercial developments affect Chinese and Japanese societies?
- What significant political, economic, and cultural changes did Korea undergo?
- What developments occurred in literature, art, and drama in China and Japan under the Ming and Qing Dynasties and the Tokugawa Shogunate?

This chapter will explore these questions.

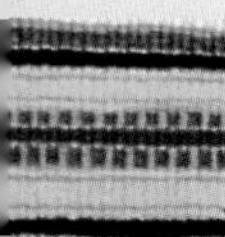

## CHINA, FROM THE MING TO THE MID-QING (CA 1368–1795)

In the fourteenth century, a combination of military, natural, and epidemiological disasters dramatically weakened Yuan (Mongol) rule in China. Factions of local warlords fought among themselves; they, rather than the emperor, held real power. The flooding of the Yellow River did great damage and caused widespread famine. Beginning in 1353–1354, disease hit an already weak population. Modern scholars strongly suspect that this epidemic was the Black Death (bubonic plague), which spread to western Europe from Mongol territory. Revolts against Mongol rule in the southern provinces disrupted the transportation of rice on the Grand Canal from Beijing (Peking) to Nanjing (Nanking). Food shortages, which were aggravated by the issue of paper money, provoked terrible inflation. Still, the Mongols spent more time fighting each other for control of the central government than suppressing the large-scale revolts in the south. One rebel leader, Zhu Yuanzhang, leader of the Red Turbans, eventually emerged as master of all the others. His military skill and administrative ability won wide popular support. By 1359 he controlled the Nanjing region. In 1368 he proclaimed himself founder of the **Ming Dynasty,** taking the regnal name Hongwu (meaning "vast military power"). The Ming Dynasty (1368–1644) was the only dynasty that originated south of the Yangzi River (see Map 21.1 on page 673).

Under the Ming, China experienced dynamic change. Agricultural and commercial reconstruction followed a long period of chaos and disorder. Hongwu revised social and political institutions. By the middle of the fifteenth century, however, his administrative framework had begun to decay. Externally, defeats in Mongolia in the later fifteenth century led to a long period of Chinese withdrawal. Nevertheless, the Ming period stands out because of its social and cultural achievements.

The Qing were not Chinese but Manchus from the north. Never more than 2 percent of the population, the Qing developed a centralized and authoritarian government, retaining the Ming administrative system but under Manchu supervision. Initially, this continuity brought prosperity and peace. By the mid-eighteenth century, however, the maintenance of the traditional Chinese position toward foreign "barbarians" and the refusal to trade with Westerners and to adopt Western technology weakened imperial rule. It also left China at the mercy of European mercantile and imperialistic ambitions.

### Ming Government

The character of Hongwu presents interesting paradoxes and odd contradictions. He was the youngest of six children, his father an itinerant laborer who fled Nanjing for defaulting on his taxes, his mother the daughter of a popular sorcerer. When most of the family died during a famine in 1344, the boy Zhu took refuge in a monastery, where he learned to read and write. At twenty-five, he joined the Red Turbans, a secret society contesting Mongol rule. He proved an excellent soldier and eventually married the leader's daughter.

As emperor, Hongwu displayed many qualities of a good political and military leader: he selected able officials, paid attention to detail, was decisive, and encouraged Confucian filial piety. He controlled the army, forbidding looting and rape under penalty of death. By contrast, he also seems to have been highly insecure. His family name, Zhu, means "pig," and Hongwu was reported to have had an ugly, porcine face. This feature,

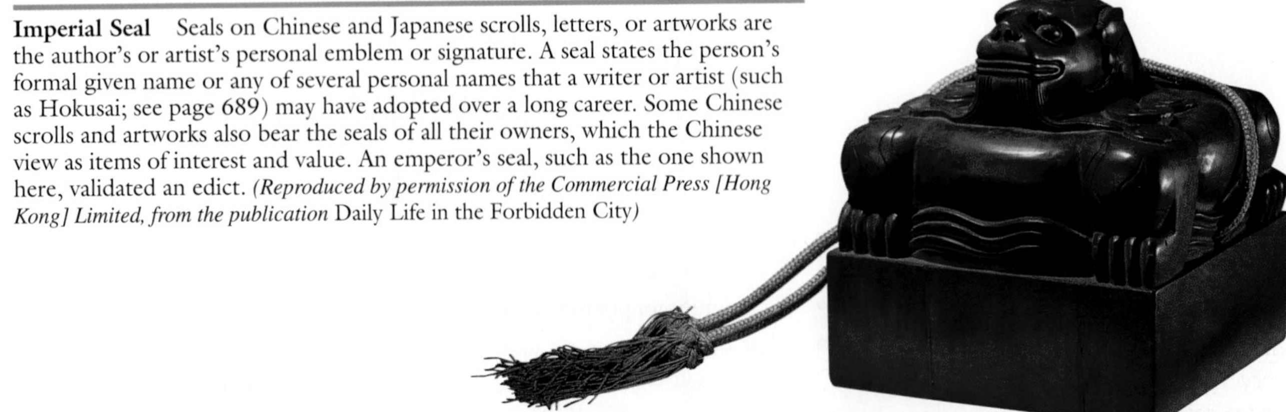

**Imperial Seal** Seals on Chinese and Japanese scrolls, letters, or artworks are the author's or artist's personal emblem or signature. A seal states the person's formal given name or any of several personal names that a writer or artist (such as Hokusai; see page 689) may have adopted over a long career. Some Chinese scrolls and artworks also bear the seals of all their owners, which the Chinese view as items of interest and value. An emperor's seal, such as the one shown here, validated an edict. *(Reproduced by permission of the Commercial Press [Hong Kong] Limited, from the publication* Daily Life in the Forbidden City*)*

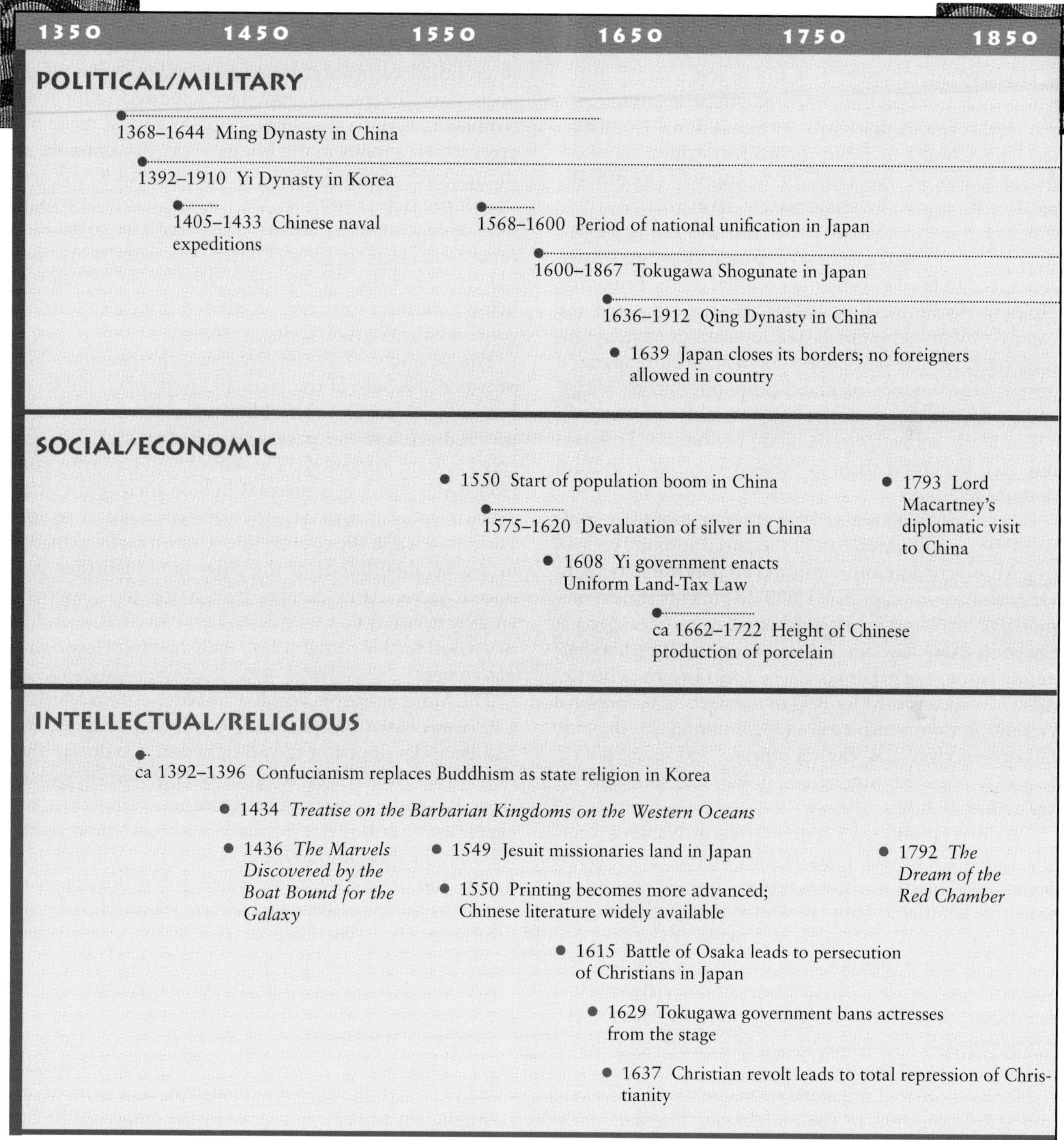


together with his humble background, made him extremely suspicious, especially of those he perceived to be of a higher station—the gentry and scholarly class. For all his pious and legal homilies (see below), Hongwu was a very violent man. For example, when he discovered his prime minister plotting against him, he had the man beheaded, together with his entire extended family—forty thousand people. Hongwu was the father of thirty-six sons and eighteen daughters, suggesting that he was also a very sensual man. When he died, thirty-eight concubines were sacrificed and buried with him, in the Mongol tradition. A leading student of Chinese history writes that Hongwu's personality was a "disaster" for China and that his character shaped that of the entire dynasty.[1]

Hongwu attempted to rule the largest country in the world—a land of enormous geographical, economic, social, and religious diversity—with traditional Confucian teachings: loyalty to authority in a hierarchical social order; agriculture as the source of the country's wealth; the ideal of economically self-sufficient farm villages where frugality was the greatest virtue and the gentry helped the needy; commerce as base, as parasitic, and to be discouraged; and taxes as an unfair burden on the peasantry. Holding rigidly to these beliefs, Hongwu flooded the country "with admonitions and regulations to guide his subjects' conduct—law codes, commandments, ancestral instructions, a series of grand pronouncements, village and government statutes and commercial regulations."[2] These ideals derive from the Song period, but Hongwu intended to enforce them in a society very different from that of the Song.

When Hongwu executed his prime minister, he abolished the central secretariat. He acquired absolute control of government administration and an impossible burden. One scholar estimates that 1,600 documents (called memorials), involving 3,391 issues to be resolved, arrived at the court every day. No one could cope with such a staggering amount of paperwork. The court became a bottleneck. Hongwu turned for help to members of his personal entourage, from which evolved the Embroidered Brocade Guards—bodyguards, clerical officials, and secret police. In 1382 the guards numbered 16,000; they gradually increased to 75,000.

Hongwu established China's capital at Nanjing (literally, "southern capital"), his old base on the Yangzi River. He stripped many wealthy people of their estates and divided the lands among the peasantry. Although Hongwu had been a monk, he confiscated many of the temples' tax-exempt lands, thereby increasing the proceeds of the state treasury. In the Song period, commercial taxes had fed the treasury. In the Ming and, later, the Manchu periods, imperial revenues came mainly from agriculture: farmers produced the state's resources.

Hongwu ordered a general survey of all China's land and several censuses of the population. The data gathered were recorded in official registers, which provided valuable information about the taxes that landlords, temples, and peasants owed. According to the registers, the capital was owed 8 million **shih,** or 160,000 tons, of rice per year. Such thorough fiscal information contributed to the efficient operation of the state.

To secure soldiers for the army and personnel for his administration and to generate revenue, Hongwu adopted the Yuan practice of requiring service to the state. Theoretically, the entire Chinese population was divided into three broad categories: peasants, artisans, and soldiers. Such a social structure may have appeared rational according to Confucian theory, but in reality there was great social mobility in the Ming period. For example, although each artisan household had to provide one artisan for the state workshops, the large majority of artisans were independent capitalists who were free to take on other work, as were their children. Ordinary people had the chance to rise through the examination system (see below). Farmers were not prohibited from trying to become scholars or merchants.

The Ministry of Finance oversaw the peasants, who provided the bulk of the taxes and performed public labor services (corvée). The Ministry of Public Works supervised artisans and people who had special skills and crafts in state workshops. The Ministry of the Army controlled the standing army of 2 million men. Each social category prevailed in a particular geographical region. Peasants lived in the countryside. Craftsmen lived mainly in the neighborhoods of the cities for which they produced goods. Army families lived along the coasts and lengthy frontiers that they defended. When a soldier died or proved unable to fight, his family had to provide a replacement.

The Ming emperors wielded absolute power, which in China was based on traditional Confucian teaching as it had been developed in the Song period. Confucian theory stresses that to achieve order and harmony in society, there has to be a hierarchical gradation of inferiors and superiors, that duties are more important than rights, and that the most important duty is loyalty. As a son owes loyalty and obedience to his father, public officials owed loyalty to the emperor, who was the Son of Heaven, the central divinity of the Chinese state and society. The emperor had to maintain political control over subordinate processes, such as economic growth and cultural diversification.

Access to the emperor's personal favor was the only means of acquiring privilege or some limited derivative power. The complex ceremonial and court ritual surrounding any public appearance by the emperor, the vast imperial palace staffed only by servile women and eunuchs, and the precise procedures of the imperial bureaucracy, which blamed any difficulties on the emperor's advisers—all lent the throne a rarefied aura and exalted the emperor's authority. In addition, Hongwu demanded that the military nobles (his old rebel comrades-in-arms) live at his court in Nanjing, where he could keep an eye on them. He raised many generals to the nobility, a posi-

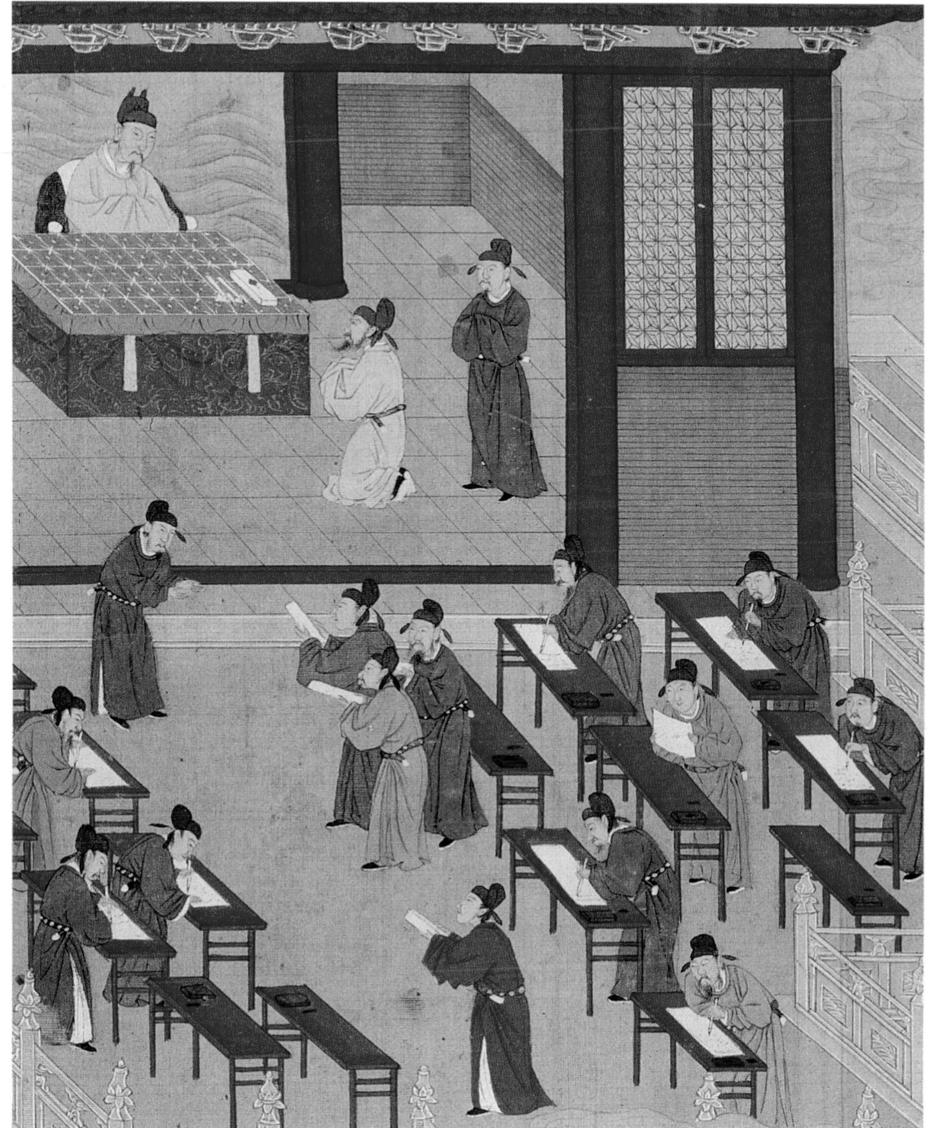

**Civil Services Examinations** The examinations tested candidates' knowledge of the Confucian canon: rituals, history, poetry, cosmology— all believed to provide the basis for a moral life—and calligraphy. By the eighteenth century, the system was under attack because it failed to select the ablest scholars, the number of candidates had not increased in proportion to population, degrees were sold to the rich, and frequently even successful candidates could not find positions. *(Bibliothèque nationale de France)*

tion that bestowed honor and financial benefits but no political power whatsoever.

Late in his reign, Hongwu divided China into fifteen principalities, putting one of his sons in charge of each. Suspicious even of his sons' loyalty, he checked their power over the bureaucracy by filling positions in it through the **civil service examinations,** a system that Hongwu reinstituted and that lasted until 1905.

The imperial civil service examination system provides insight into many aspects of Ming, and later Qing, society and culture. The imperial examinations, which became the sole channel of official recruitment and produced the gentry class of scholar-officials, reveal China's method of social mobility. These examinations also help explain why China, in spite of considerable technological knowledge in the early modern period, failed to begin industrialization, as Western countries did.

The examinations were given every three years at the district, provincial, and state (imperial) levels. Candidates had to pass the lower levels before trying for the imperial level, where the success rate in the late nineteenth century was between 1 and 2 percent. All men, except for beggars, slaves, police, and the sons of prostitutes, were eligible. The examinations required a minute and precise knowledge of the ancient Chinese classics, knowledge of and conformity to the commentaries on the Four Books by the Song Neo-Confucian scholar Zhu Xi, and a formal literary style. (Neo-Confucianism centered on the family and involved an entire ethical, social, and political system. As harmony and order in an individual family depended on the obedience of children to their father, so good government depended on the moral character of the ruler, who was expected to display benevolence, righteousness, reverence, and wisdom. Neo-Confucianism as stated in Zhu Xi's Four Books became the accepted political philosophy of the Ming and Qing periods.)

Candidates who earned the **jinshi,** the highest degree, were eligible for appointment to the highest offices in the imperial bureaucracy. One part of that bureaucracy functioned at Beijing, advised the emperor, served him in an elaborate hierarchy in one of six state ministries, looked after his personal needs, and worked with the enormous palace staff of guards, grooms, cooks, concubines, maids, nurses, and the imperial children. The other part of the Chinese bureaucracy, also organized in a complicated hierarchy, staffed the many positions in the fifteen provinces and acted as prefects in the larger cities and as magistrates in the counties. Below these local officials were the police, soldiers, and tax collectors. An office in any part of the imperial bureaucracy provided the holder's basic salary. But, as in any pre-modern government (and in some modern governments in Africa and Asia), the officeholder expected to augment his income through "gifts" and through his patronage power—that is, his ability to appoint to subordinate positions. To prevent nepotism, corruption, and officials from using their positions to form a family base that could threaten the throne, civil service positions were filled according to the "Rule of Avoidance": a candidate could not be appointed to a place in his native province, nor could two members of the same family serve in the same province.

Poor boys could, and did, rise. The civil service examinations provided mobility into the **gentry** of scholar-officials who ran the imperial bureaucracy; it bridged the gap between the state—as embodied by the emperor—and the hordes of commoners. The gentry enjoyed enormous prestige and behaved in an elitist, paternalistic, and authoritarian manner toward the masses, who were expected to be orderly and obedient and to pay their taxes.

Whereas in western European society, law, medicine, and the priesthood were the usual paths to social status, or at least to modest affluence, such was not the case in China. The goal of any ambitious Chinese was entry into the gentry class, for which success on the examinations was an absolute prerequisite. Did wealth bring status? In the West since the Middle Ages, and certainly since the nineteenth century, wealth derived from commerce or trade has often brought prestige, political power, and social affluence. In China, prestige was attached to scholar-official status: "as soon as a merchant or manufacturer became reasonably well-off, he attempted to attain literati status for himself or his sons, either by procuring the necessary education or by purchasing an academic degree or bureaucratic post." Successful businessmen used their wealth to buy land, acquire libraries (symbolizing the lifestyle of the scholar-official), and patronize scholarship.[3]

China's social structure, with the gentry class at its core, had significant implications for the country's failure to industrialize. The Chinese invented paper, printing, gunpowder, the magnet, iron and steel technology, and the suspension bridge. In the Middle Ages they displayed enormous technological creativity. But they valued social stability and harmony higher than change and domination—which the military use of gunpowder, for example, could have brought. Also, the diversion of wealth into the purchase of land and the hiring of tutors for an education leading to a jinshi, rather than investing capital in manufacturing, retarded the invention of new mechanical devices. Likewise, the examination system concentrated the attention of the educated on literature and the Confucian classics. The great social prestige related to literary study directed the educated away from scientific and technological interests and into a narrow literary scholarship. The scholar's soft hands and long fingernails were proof that he never did any kind of manual labor, which was looked upon with contempt. Thus social values and the social structure diverted the money, time, and interests of China's elite from all pursuits that could have promoted technological and industrial change.[4]

After 1426 the eunuch-dominated secret police controlled the palace guards and the imperial workshops, infiltrated the civil service, and headed all foreign missions. Through blackmail, espionage, and corruption, the secret police exercised enormous domestic power. How did eunuchs acquire such power? Often drawn from the lowest classes of society and viewed with distaste by respectable people, eunuchs had no hope of gaining status except by satisfying every whim of the emperor. Because they had access to the emperor's personal quarters, they had access to the emperor. By appearing to be totally submissive to the emperor, they won his absolute trust; thus they controlled many emperors and hence the machinery of government. Some eunuchs had been castrated by their families so that they could gain positions in the imperial palace. Some eunuchs married, adopted children, and had extended families. Several eunuchs—Wang Zhi in the 1500s and Zhongxian in the 1620s—gained dictatorial power when their emperors lost interest in affairs of state.

Fiscal disorders were the biggest problem of the Ming Dynasty. The imperial court made no distinction between the private household revenue of the emperor and public or state funds. Although Hongwu was a frugal man, under eunuch management the size of the imperial household steadily rose, and with it the costs to maintain the household. Imperial income derived largely from a 10 percent land tax—not a heavy burden. Most governments in the early modern world, such as those of France and England, had all state income delivered to a central treasury, and from there bills were paid. Because of the immense size of the Chinese empire, however, revenue was collected from specific sources and carried to the places of approved expenditure. A complex network of clerks and runners developed, and this network gradually "hardened into inflexible precedent." Because no single official or office had responsibility for the imperial finances, the considerable bribery and corruption that occurred along the financial road could not be policed and corrected. Fragmentation of revenue and expenditure drastically weakened the central government.[5]

A secondary problem, as in most governments in the early modern world, was that the maintenance of public infrastructure—roads, bridges, and canals—fell to local corvée service, not to the central government. This was true of the Grand Canal in China. Begun in the Sui period (518–618), the 1,250-mile-long Grand Canal was actually a series of canals from Hangzhou in the southwest to Yangzhou on the Yangzi River and northwest to Luoyang. Khubilai, with the labor of 2.5 million workers, extended it north to the Beijing region (see Map 21.1). The Grand Canal's purpose was to connect "the southern rice bowl" to the northern plains. In the fifteenth century, local soldiers had responsibility for its upkeep and for the transportation of grain. But because the soldiers were seldom paid, the troops depended for support on transporting private rice barges. Sections of the canal fell into disrepair. Any emergency, such as a flood, required crisis management.

A third problem was the steady decline of the value of the currency. Unaware that the unlimited printing of paper money produces inflation, Hongwu's government continued issuing it. By 1425 paper money had less than one-fortieth of its original value and gradually went out of use. Although trade expanded and the need for copper coins increased, the Ming issued very few coins. Counterfeiters forged tons of coins, with the result that the value of copper coins steadily declined.

In the sixteenth century, China became part of the worldwide trade network (see pages 519–520). Demand for Chinese porcelain, silk, and later tea led to the massive flow of Japanese and South American silver into China. This potential wealth, however, did not lead to currency reform or fiscal stability. As silver entered the empire in vast quantities, its value declined and its buying power diminished, compounding inflation. Taxes customarily paid in rice were converted to payments of a fixed amount of silver. People owing local corvée services bought substitutes with silver. Between about 1575 and 1620, silver lost two-thirds of its value. The fiscal foundation of the Ming Dynasty eroded as China's tax revenues continually declined. Domestic price inflation in the late sixteenth and early seventeenth centuries destroyed the Ming's financial basis.

## Economic, Social, and Cultural Change

China had experienced an agricultural revolution during the Song period. The civil wars that accompanied the breakdown of Yuan rule—with vast stretches of farmland laid waste or entirely abandoned and dikes, bridges, and canals rendered unusable—necessitated reconstruction. At the heart of this reconstruction was a radical improvement in methods of rice production.

More than bread in Europe, rice supplied almost the total nourishment of the population in central and south China. (In north China, wheat, made into steamed or baked bread or into noodles, served as the staple of the diet.) Terracing and irrigation of mountain slopes, introduced in the eleventh century, had increased rice harvests. The introduction of drought-resistant Indochinese, or Champa, rice proved an even greater boon. Although Champa rice was of lower nutritional quality than the native rice, it considerably increased the total output of food. Ming farmers experimented with Champa rice that required only sixty days from planting to harvesting instead of the usual hundred days. Peasants soon reaped two harvests a year, an enormous increase in production.

Other innovations also brought good results. Ming era peasants introduced irrigation pumps worked by pedals. Farmers began to stock the rice paddies with fish, which continuously fertilized the rice fields, destroyed malaria-bearing mosquitoes, and enriched the diet. Fish farming in the paddies eventually enabled large, previously uninhabitable parts of southern China to be brought under cultivation. Farmers discovered the possibilities of commercial cropping in cotton, sugar cane, and indigo. And new methods of crop rotation allowed for continuous cultivation and for more than one harvest per year from a single field.

The Ming rulers promoted the repopulation and colonization of devastated regions through massive transfers

### TABLE 21.1 LAND RECLAMATION IN EARLY MING CHINA

| YEAR | RECLAIMED LAND (IN HECTARES; 1 HECTARE = 2.5 ACRES) |
|---|---|
| 1371 | 576,000 |
| 1373 | 1,912,000 |
| 1374 | 4,974,000 |
| 1379 | 1,486,000 |

*Source: J. Gernet,* A History of Chinese Civilization, *trans. J. R. Foster (Cambridge: Cambridge University Press, 1982), p. 391. Used with permission.*

of people. Immigrants received large plots of land and exemption from taxation for many years. Table 21.1, based on fourteenth-century records of newly reclaimed land, helps tell the story.[6]

Reforestation was a dramatic aspect of the agricultural revolution. In 1391 the Ming government ordered 50 million trees planted in the Nanjing area. Lumber from the trees was intended for the construction of a maritime fleet. In 1392 each family holding colonized land in Anhui province had to plant 200 each of mulberry, jujube, and persimmon trees. In 1396 peasants in the present-day provinces of Hunan and Hupeh in the east planted 84 million fruit trees. Historians have estimated that 1 billion trees were planted during Hongwu's reign.[7]

What were the social consequences of agricultural development? Increased food production led to steady population growth. Demographers date the start of the Chinese population boom at about 1550, as a direct result of improved methods of rice production. Increases in total yields differed fundamentally, however, from comparable agricultural growth in Europe: Chinese grain harvests were improved through intensification of peasant labor. This meant lower income per capita.

Population increase led to the multiplication of towns and small cities. Urbanization in the Ming era (and, later, in the Manchu period) meant the proliferation of market centers and small towns rather than the growth of "large" cities like those in Europe in the central Middle Ages and China in the Song period. Most people lived in tiny hamlets or villages that had no markets. What distinguished a village from a town was the existence of a market in the town.

The population density of a particular region determined the frequency of the markets there. In cities and larger towns, shops were open all the time, but not all on the same schedule. Smaller towns had periodic markets—some every five days, some every ten days, some only once a month. Town markets usually consisted of little open-air shops that sold essential goods—pins, matches, oil for lamps, candles, paper, incense, tobacco (after it was introduced from the Americas)—to country people from the surrounding hamlets. The market usually included a tearoom, sometimes a wine shop where tea and rice wine were sold, entertainers, and moneylenders and pawnbrokers. Sometimes the tearooms served the function of banks.

Tradesmen, who carried their wares on their backs, and craftsmen—carpenters, barbers, joiners, locksmiths—moved constantly from market to market. Itinerant salesmen depended on the city market for their wares. In large towns and cities, foodstuffs from the countryside and rare and precious goods from distant places were offered for sale. Cities gradually became islands of sophistication in the highly localized Chinese economy. Nanjing, for example, spread out enormously because the presence of the imperial court and bureaucracy generated a great demand for goods. The concentration of people in turn created a greater demand for goods and services. Industrial development was stimulated. Small businesses manufactured textiles, paper, and luxury goods such as silks and porcelains. Nanjing and Shanghai became centers for the production of cotton and silks; Xiangtan specialized in the grain and salt trade and in silver. Small towns remained embedded in peasant culture, but large towns and cities pursued contacts with the wider world.

Some cities in the late Ming period were large commercial centers where trade set the pattern of daily life. Some merchants accumulated vast fortunes and had elegant and luxurious lifestyles. Other cities were bureaucratic centers where busy officials carried out their tax-gathering and administrative duties. All cities had a bustling, energetic, thriving air.

In spite of grave political weakness and financial instability, commercial wealth in the later Ming period supported a remarkable flowering of artistic creativity. In novels, drama, short stories, poetry, landscape painting, and historical and medical works, Chinese artists and scholars produced some of the masterpieces of the world. The plays of the dramatist Tang Xianzu, for example, have been compared for richness and complexity of character and plot to those of Shakespeare. China's classic novel of adventure and religious quest, *The Journey to the West,* which describes the experiences of a clever monkey

**Transport of Chinese Porcelain** Chinese blue and white porcelain, especially the large covered jars shown here, enjoyed enormous popularity in southwestern Asia. This Turkish miniature painting depicts several such pieces, carried for public display in a filigreed cart in a wedding procession; the porcelain was probably part of the bride's dowry. *(Topkapi Saray Museum, Istanbul)*

on his travels to India in search of Buddhist scriptures, was written in the 1590s. The tensions within an elite Chinese family are explored in the socially complex and sexually explicit anonymous novel *The Golden Lotus,* which can be analyzed on several levels. Printing, originally a Chinese invention using woodblocks (ca 1040) and then advanced by Koreans using movable type from metal molds in the early thirteenth century, achieved technical excellence around 1550. This advance, plus Chinese expertise in paper manufacture, made cheap copies of classical, educational, and popular literature widely available.[8]

The better Ming porcelain dates from the fifteenth century, when ceramic factories at Jingdezhen in Jiangxi province, subsidized by the imperial treasury, poured out dishes, flasks, vases, and other objects with the underglaze blue decoration. Or they had green or red enamel ornamentations of flowers and dragons. When, in the late sixteenth and early seventeenth centuries, the imperial court spent what revenue it had on frontier defense against the Manchus, support for the porcelain factories ceased. Roughly potted from poorly prepared paste, Chinese ceramics declined in quality. This had no effect on the imperial court and elite classes, which continued to dine on gold, silver, or jade plates.[9]

## Foreign Relations

Throughout the Ming period, Mongol nomads raided along China's northern frontier. Initially, Hongwu adopted a defensive strategy, absorbing thousands of Mongols into the Chinese army. By such recruitment, and by enlisting men from military households in southern China, the entire military force in 1392 totaled 1.2 million men, with 531,000 on the northern frontier. To supply this enormous force, Hongwu intended that the soldiers, under the officers' supervision, should raise their own food in peacetime. Hongwu boasted that he "had supported an army of one million men without using as much as one kernel of peasant-produced grain."[10] He spoke too soon. Because the land along the northern frontier was only partially arable, the soldiers were not interested in farming and were very inefficient, and the officers acted as landlords working soldier-tenants, the system failed. A self-supporting Chinese army did not work. The imperial government refused to allocate resources for it permanently, and Mongol attacks continued.

In the fifteenth century, an alternative solution arose. The Chinese could maintain a peaceful equilibrium on the frontier through extensive trade with the Mongols. Diplomatic ties with selected Mongol groups could be developed, the goal being the promotion of trade. But Ming emperors refused such commercial negotiations. Rather, they attempted to organize commercial relations with the Mongols of the steppe region according to the Chinese concept of the **tribute system.** In return for elaborate gifts delivered to the Ming court and presented with the traditional acts of ritual subordination (the **kowtow**), the emperor would allow a limited amount of trade at specified times and places. This was the pattern of relations with Burma, Korea (see page 681), and Vietnam. But the Ming had never conquered Mongolia and really could not insist on tribute. Nor were the Mongols under such circumstances willing to pay it.

Thus, unable to defeat the Mongols militarily and unwilling to trade with them, the Ming in the sixteenth century tried to keep the nomads out by building walls. The Chinese had built border walls or fortifications since the seventh century B.C.E. Ming chroniclers called the fortifications that became China's great modern tourist attraction, the Great Wall, "border garrisons." In response to the path of nomad migrations, Ming wall building began in the west and moved eastward. Building was in brick and stone, which meant that masons had to be recruited; a network of brick kilns, quarries, and transportation routes had to be developed; and the dynasty had to finance this barrier. Towers, not for combat but for signaling by fire, smoke, or cannon blast, pierced the several thousand miles of fortifications. These fortifications slowed but never completely thwarted determined advance. Construction of them continued even as the dynasty fell. Today the Great Wall stands as China's symbol of patriotism and pride, but in the seventeenth century it represented futility and failure.[11]

Another dramatic development of the Ming period was the series of naval expeditions sent out between 1405 and 1433 under Yongle (r. 1403–1424) and his successors. China had a strong maritime history stretching back to the eleventh century, and these early-fifteenth-century voyages were a continuation of that tradition. The Ming expeditions established China as the greatest maritime power in the world—considerably ahead of Portugal, whose major seafaring reconnaissances began a half century later.

In contrast to Hongwu, Yongle broadened diplomatic and commercial contacts within the tribute system. He had two basic motives for launching overseas voyages. First, he sent them in search of Jian Wen, a serious contender for the throne whom he had defeated but who, rumor claimed, had escaped to Southeast Asia. Second, he launched the expeditions to explore and to expand the tribute system. Led by the Muslim eunuch admiral Zheng He and navigating by compass, seven fleets sailed to East and South Asia.

These voyages had important consequences. They extended the prestige of the Ming Dynasty throughout Asia. Trade, in the form of tribute from as far as the west coast of southern India, greatly increased. Diplomatic contacts with the distant Middle East led to the arrival in Nanjing of embassies from Egypt. The maritime expeditions also led to the publication of geographical works such as the *Treatise on the Barbarian Kingdoms on the Western Oceans* (1434) and *The Marvels Discovered by the Boat Bound for the Galaxy* (1436). The information acquired from the voyages served as the basis of Chinese knowledge of the maritime world until the nineteenth century. Finally, these expeditions resulted in Chinese immigration to the countries of Southeast Asia and the ports of southern India. The voyages were terminated because Confucian court intellectuals persuaded the emperor that his quest for strange and exotic things signaled the collapse of the dynasty. After 1435 China returned to a policy of isolation. Xenophobia and anticommercialism triumphed.

## Ming Decline

In the middle of the sixteenth century, China showed many signs of developing into an urban mercantile society. Merchants and businessmen had large amounts of capital, and a few invested it not in land, as in the past, but in commercial and craft industries. Silkmaking, cotton weaving, porcelain manufacture, printing, and steel production assumed a definite industrial character. So many peasants seeking employment migrated to the towns that agriculture declined. Some businesses employed several hundred workers, many of them women. According to a French scholar, "Peasant women took jobs at Sung-chiang, southwest of Shanghai in the cotton mills. According to contemporary descriptions, in the big workshops the employees were already the anonymous labor force that we regard as characteristic of the industrial age."[12]

Technical treatises reveal considerable progress in manufacturing procedures. Silk looms had three or four shuttle winders. Printers could produce a sheet of paper with three or four different colors, similar to the page of a modern magazine. Chinese ceramics displayed astonishing technology—which helps explain the huge demand for them. Likewise, agricultural treatises described new machines for working the soil, sowing seed, and irrigation. Population, which stood at roughly 70 million at the start of the Ming period, increased to about 130 million by 1600.

In Confucian theory, wealth is thought to be based on agriculture, and from agriculture the state derived its taxes and the ruling class its income. Also, according to Confucian philosophy, any promotion of trade would encourage people to aspire to a different lifestyle and to a higher social status, and such aspirations would bring change and social disorder. Moreover, Chinese thinkers held that merchants produced nothing: they bought something from its grower or maker and sold it at a higher price than they had paid; thus they were parasites living off the labor of others. In addition, the proliferation of luxury goods, which people did not really need, would lead to extravagance and excessive consumption and in turn to moral decay.

Believing that virtue lies in frugality, vice in extravagance, the Ming emperors issued sumptuary laws restricting or prohibiting certain styles of clothing and tableware, means of conveyance, and articles of household decoration. The effect of these laws, however, was *increased* social stratification: the rich became richer, the poor poorer. Nevertheless, the Confucian ideal remained intact: a "successful merchant" was, by definition, one who had stopped trading and had invested his wealth in agriculture. Theory did not square with social reality.

Between about 1575 and 1625, a combination of problems led to the collapse of the Ming. The entire imperial administration revolved around the emperor, who was expected to carry out certain duties. Often he did not. The emperor Wanli (r. 1573–1620), for example, refused after 1589 to appear at imperial audiences; declined to see his eunuch grand secretaries, who gradually assumed his responsibilities; ignored issues he found unpleasant; and eventually refused to consider even pressing matters of defense and finance. Offices were left vacant for decades. The imperial bureaucracy slowed to a halt.

Military and defensive difficulties multiplied. In 1560 the Mongols invaded and occupied Qinghai. Between 1593 and 1598, China supported its tributary state, Korea, against Japanese invasion. And in 1599–1600, Chinese troops entered another tributary country, Burma, to quell rebels from southwestern China. To pay for these expensive campaigns, Wanli reopened Chinese silver mines and imposed new taxes on trade. From both these potential sources of income, greedy eunuch tax officials siphoned off much of the revenue. Likewise, the eunuchs skimmed off huge sums when the emperor tried to provide relief for areas hit by famines, floods, or earthquakes. As partisan factionalism divided court eunuchs, a desperate population resorted to banditry or rebellion.

As we have seen, the influx of Japanese and South American silver destabilized the currency. The extravagance of the imperial court aggravated a terrible financial situation. Sensual, vain, and self-indulgent, Wanli spent ninety thousand ounces of silver on his wedding clothes. Prodigious sums were spent on palaces and tombs: the

**Pirates Attacking Ship** Beginning in the fifteenth century, the Chinese demand for cloves, pepper, and sappanwood (a wood that yields a red dye) from Southeast Asia stimulated great competition among Chinese merchants, smugglers, and pirates. The arrival of Portuguese and Japanese traders in the sixteenth century led to increased conflict, the identification of trade with violence, and eventually imperial bans on foreign commerce. *(Shuihu zhuan, 1610)*

Jesuit Matteo Ricci saw a convoy of wood two miles long, pulled by tens of thousands of workers, on the Grand Canal; the wood was brought from the southwest to Beijing to rebuild two palaces, and Ricci was told it would take four years to deliver it all.

As the Ming weakened, the Manchus from southeastern Manchuria grew stronger. In 1636 they occupied the Liaoning region in north China, selected Shenyang (Mukden) as their capital, and proclaimed a new dynasty with the Chinese name Qing (meaning "pure"). Helped by rebel opposition to the Ming, the Manchus captured Beijing in 1644. The entry of the Manchus' imperial armies into Yunnan in 1681 marked their complete military triumph.

## Qing Rule

By purging the civil service of the old court eunuchs and troublesome factions, and by offering Chinese intellectuals positions in the bureaucracy, the Manchus gained the support of the influential academic and intellectual classes. Chinese scholars flocked to Beijing. The Manchu government, staffed by able and honest Chinese, became much more efficient than the Ming.

The **Qing Dynasty** ruled until 1912. In its heyday in the eighteenth century, the Qing Empire covered much of Asia—China proper, Manchuria, Mongolia, Tibet, and Xinjiang (Sinkiang)—and enjoyed tribute from Burma, Nepal, Laos, Siam, Annam, and Korea (see Map 21.1). China had the largest population on earth and achieved an unprecedented degree of prosperity.

How did a million Manchus govern 350 million Chinese? The Qing Dynasty retained the basic structures of Ming and Confucian government. The emperor, possessor of the Mandate of Heaven, governed as a supreme and autocratic ruler. The bureaucracies continued as they had in Ming and earlier times: the imperial household bureaucracy managed the emperor's palaces and households; the central bureaucracy administered his vast empire. Most positions in the empire were assigned on the basis of candidates' performances on the civil service examinations in the Confucian classics. The highest positions in Beijing and in the provinces of China were open to Chinese as well as to Manchus. These measures pacified the Chinese economic and intellectual elites. The Manchus, however, maintained a privileged status in society. They wore distinctive clothes, did not practice foot binding, retained their own language and alphabet, and maintained ethnic separatism by forbidding intermarriage with the Chinese. The Manchus required Chinese males to wear their hair in a pigtail as a sign of subservience.

Along with the agricultural improvements begun in the Ming period, internal peace, relative prosperity, and

**The Scholar-Bureaucrat's Study, Qing Period** The study was located in the most private part of the scholar's house. Notice the carved rosewood desk with brass-edged corners (*rear left*); the small stove for preparing tea for guests; the cushioned couch (*rear right*); the rich carpet; the long narrow table for painting or studying scrolls, some of which stand in a holder on the tiled floor; and the birdcage on the window wall. The immaculate order, restrained elegance, and sense of calm tranquillity of this room incorporate the loftiest Confucian ideals for the highest class, the scholars. *(Philadelphia Museum of Art. Gift of Wright S. Ludington in memory of his father, Charles H. Ludington, 1929-30-1)*

engineering methods that prevented flooding of the countryside contributed to a population explosion in the eighteenth century, as the statistics in Table 21.2 illustrate. But in the late eighteenth century, growth without increased agricultural output led to rebellions and uprisings that eventually weakened the Qing Dynasty.

The reign of the emperor Kangxi (1662–1722) launched a period of great achievement. A contemporary of the Indian ruler Aurangzeb, the French king Louis XIV, and the Russian tsar Peter the Great, Kangxi demonstrated exceptional intelligence, energy, and concern for the welfare of his people. He also enjoyed much greater freedom of action than had the Ming emperor Wanli a century earlier. Whereas Wanli had been a captive of precedent, incapable of making changes, Kangxi cut both court expenses and taxes and traveled extensively throughout his domain. On these trips, he investigated the conduct of local bureaucrats in an effort to prevent them from oppressing the people. Kangxi squarely faced and thoroughly crushed a massive rebellion in southern China in 1678. He personally led an army into Mongolia and smashed the forces of the Mongol leader Galdan. This victory permanently eliminated the danger of a reinvigorated Mongolian empire on China's borders.

Kangxi also cultivated the arts of peace. He invited scholars to his court and subsidized the compilation of a huge encyclopedia and two monumental dictionaries. *The Complete Library of the Four Treasuries,* a collection of all of Chinese literature, required the work of 15,000 calligraphers and 361 editors. It preserved the Chinese literary tradition. Kangxi's contributions to literature hold a distinguished place in the long history of Chinese culture. Europeans and Americans, however, appreciate this period primarily for its excellent porcelain. An imperial

**MAP 21.1 The Qing Empire, 1759** The sheer size of the Qing Empire in China almost inevitably led to its profound cultural influence on the rest of Asia. What geographical and political factors limited the extent of the empire?

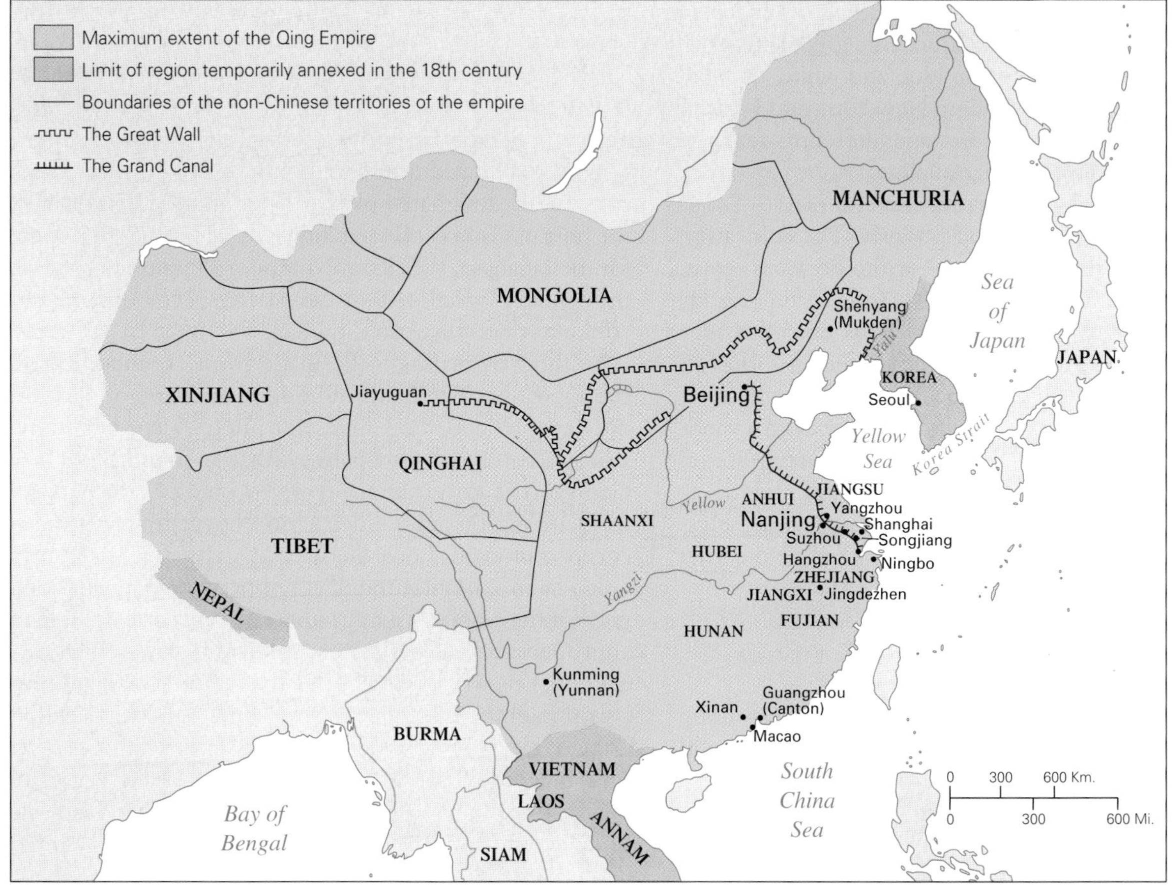

**TABLE 21.2 POPULATION OF CHINA, CA 1390–1790**

| | |
|---|---|
| ca 1390 | 150,000,000 |
| ca 1585 | 100,000,000* |
| ca 1749 | 177,495,000 |
| 1767 | 209,840,000 |
| 1776 | 268,238,000 |
| 1790 | 301,487,000 |

*The catastrophic drop in China's overall population from the time of the Ming-Qing transition to the end of Kangxi's wars with three powerful rebels in 1681 was due to civil wars, foreign invasions, bandit actions, natural disasters, virulent epidemics, and the failure of irrigation systems.

*Source: J. D. Spence,* The Search for Modern China *(New York: W. W. Norton, 1991), pp. 93–95.*

factory at Jiangxi (Kiangsi), directly controlled by Kangxi's court, produced porcelain masterpieces. Monochrome vases, bowls, and dishes in oxblood, pale green, and dark blue, and polychrome pieces in blue and white, enjoyed great popularity in Paris, London, New York, and Boston, although modern art collectors and museums rate the early Ming porcelain of higher quality.

The long reign of the Qianlong emperor (1736–1795) marked the zenith of the Qing Dynasty. The cultivation of new crops from the Americas—white potatoes, corn, peanuts—on marginal lands helped to support the steadily expanding population. Chinese rule was extended into Central Asia. The imperial court continued to support arts and letters. In the last two decades of his reign, however, Qianlong showered titles, gifts, and offices on a handsome young Manchu named Heshen. Contemporaries considered Heshen uncultured, greedy, and ambitious. The corruption of the imperial civil service under Heshen, combined with heavy taxation, sparked revolts that continued to the end of the dynasty in 1912.

## External Pressures

By the middle years of the eighteenth century, Qianlong also faced increasing foreign pressures. In the north and northwest, the region from which invaders had historically entered China, Mongols, Russians, and ethnic minority peoples pressed the borders. Christian missionaries, notably the Jesuits, wanted greater scope for their proselytizing activities. Nearby Asian countries that had many cultural affinities with China—Korea, Burma, Siam, Vietnam—desired greater trade with China. So, too, did European merchants: the European demand for Chinese silk, porcelain, and tea was enormous. The British East India Company, for example, had by 1740 become an international corporation with global activities, backed by eager investors in Great Britain. What was the response of the imperial government to these increasing foreign pressures?

The Qing government had no ministry of foreign affairs. Chinese relations with all foreign countries reflected the Chinese belief that China was the "central kingdom" and that all other countries were "peripheral" and removed from the cultural center of the universe. The Office of Border Affairs conducted relations with peoples in the northwest crescent (Mongols and Russians). It took police action when necessary and used the marriages of imperial daughters as the means of making alliances and maintaining peace in the north. Acting on the theory that religious evangelization by foreigners reflected on the prestige of the emperor, the imperial household itself supervised the activities of Jesuit missionaries. The Ministry of Rituals managed commercial relations with the nations of East Asia. Business delegations from Korea, Burma, and Siam were termed "tribute missions." As long as they used a language of subservience to the emperor and his ministers and made the ritual prostrations, they were allowed limited amounts of trade with China in precisely designated places and times—for Europeans, the port of Canton (Guangzhou) from October to March; for the Japanese, the city of Ningbo. As mentioned above, the Chinese value system did not respect business and commerce and distrusted traders.

Sniffing fat profits to be made from expanded trade, the aggressive merchants of London and Liverpool could not comprehend the Chinese attitude. Accordingly, the British East India Company, with the support of King George III's government, resolved on a personal appeal to Qianlong through a delegation headed by an experienced diplomat, Lord George Macartney. Three ships sailed from Portsmouth in September 1792 carrying rich gifts for the emperor: a huge imperial state coach fashioned after George III's own vehicle; a variety of heavily jeweled pocket, wrist, and neck watches; and a planetarium, a working model of the entire solar system. The dazzling array of gifts was intended to show that England was the most scientifically advanced and economically powerful nation on earth. Delivered in a diamond-encrusted gift box, George III's respectful letter to the emperor stated in part:

**Tea Fields** When tea became England's national drink in the eighteenth century, tea imported from China cost the English a staggering £20,000,000 per year—all paid for in silver, because the Chinese did not want to accept English goods in exchange. China also exported huge quantities of porcelain and cotton textiles to Europe and the Americas, leading to a net drain from the West to China of 3,000,000 ounces of silver in 1760 and 16,000,000 ounces in 1780. These figures suggest the urgency of the Macartney mission (see pages 674–676). *(Private Collection. From Ann Paluda,* Chronicle of the Chinese Emperors *[New York: Thames & Hudson])*

*His Most Sacred Majesty George III . . . to the Supreme Emperor of China Qianlong, worthy to live tens of thousands and tens of thousands thousand years, sendeth*

*Greeting . . .*

*We have been still more anxious to inquire into the arts and manners of countries where civilization has been perfected by the wise ordinances and virtuous examples of their Sovereigns thro a long series of ages; and, above all, Our ardent wish had been to become acquainted with those celebrated institutions of Your Majesty's populous and extensive Empire which have carried its prosperity to such a height as to be the admiration of all surrounding nations. . . .*

*We have the happiness of being at peace with all the World. . . . Many of our subjects have also frequented for a long time past a remote part of your Majesty's dominions for the purpose of Trade. No doubt the interchange of commodities between Nations distantly situated tends to their mutual convenience, industry, and wealth.*[13]

The letter went on to ask for the establishment of permanent Chinese-British diplomatic relations; broader trade, including the opening of new ports for international commerce; and a fair system of tariffs or customs duties.

The mission that reached Canton in June 1793 (the long journey is an indication of the time involved in eighteenth-century travel) almost foundered over the issue of ritual and procedure. Court officials agreed that Macartney might see the emperor at his summer palace, if the British emissaries acknowledged that they came as a "tributary nation" and performed the *kowtow*—kneeling and striking their heads on the ground nine times in front of the emperor. Macartney protested that he was not required to show such obeisance even to George III. A compromise was finally reached when Macartney agreed to bow on one knee as he would bow to his English sovereign. Qianlong, however, was not pleased. The ruler of China considered himself supreme and all other kings his subordinates. Though thoroughly courteous to his guests, he denied all their requests. (See the feature "Listening to the Past: The Qianlong Emperor Responds to King George III" on pages 694–695.)

The Macartney mission represented the clash of two different cultures. On the one side was China, "an immobile empire," convinced of its superiority, opposed to all innovation, and certain that the ancient Confucian texts contained the answers to all problems. On the other side was Great Britain, equally convinced of its superiority "because it was modern: founded on science, the free exchange of ideas, and the mastery of commercial exchange."[14] Understanding and communication proved impossible.

## The Life of the People

The family is the fundamental unit of every society. In Ming and Qing China, however, the family probably exercised greater social influence than it did anywhere else—and far more than in Western societies. The family directed the moral education of the child, the economic advancement and marriage of the young, and religious life through ceremonial rites honoring family ancestors. The Chinese family discharged many of the roles that the Christian church performed in Europe in the Middle Ages and that the state carries out today. It assumed total responsibility for the sick, the indigent, and the aged. The family expected and almost invariably received the full devotion and loyalty of its members. A person without a family had no material or psychological support.

Poor families tended to be nuclear: couples established their own households and raised their own children. The educated, the middle class, and the wealthy frequently resided in extended families: several generations of patrilineal relatives and their wives lived together in one large house or compound, individual families occupying different sections. In both kinds of families, the paternal head of the family held autocratic power over all members of the household. Apart from crimes against the emperor and his family, the worst crimes were those committed by children against their parents. Fathers who harmed their sons received lighter punishment than sons who harmed (or even insulted) their fathers. In one instance, the Ministry of Punishments reviewed a local governor's sentence that a father be beaten for burying his son alive. The son had used foul language to his father. The ministry concluded that "although the killing (by the father) was done intentionally, it was the killing of a son who had committed a capital crime by reviling his father. The father was acquitted."[15] When a father died, his authority over the household passed to his eldest son.

The father led the family in the ancient Confucian rites honoring the family ancestors. If these ceremonies were not continued by the next generation, the family suffered social disgrace and, it was believed, the dead endured great misery. Thus marriage and childbearing were extremely important.

Although women in the Han and Tang periods had enjoyed a fair degree of freedom—to mingle socially with men and even, in the Song period, to inherit, if they had no brothers, a father's property—the Ming period stressed puritanical Neo-Confucian ideals of womanhood. A woman should be humble, diligent in her work, serene, and polite in serving her husband. Ming and Qing ideals emphasized female virginity and chastity, and a woman who had been raped could best prove her morality by committing suicide, thereby ensuring her fidelity to her husband. To what extent social reality conformed to these ideals, we do not know. Much evidence suggests that widows did commonly remarry, but was it from economic necessity, because in-laws pressured them to remarry so that they could claim the original dowry and their sons' property? We do not yet have definitive answers. One able scholar writes that "women were one of the most disparaged and exploited segments of society."[16]

Almost everyone married. Marriage was not intended to satisfy emotional longings or personal pleasures. Marriage promoted familial interests. Reverence for one's parents, maintenance of the family, and perpetuation of the line required that sons marry shortly after reaching puberty. The father and family elders discussed the possibilities and employed a local go-between to negotiate with the prospective bride's family. The go-between drew up a marriage contract specifying the property, furniture, clothing, and gifts that the two young people would bring to the union. As elsewhere, parents wanted to make the most economically and socially advantageous union for their children. The couple had no part in these arrangements. Often they did not meet each other until the groom lifted the bride's veil on their wedding day. But they were brought up to accept this custom.

A Chinese bride became part of her husband's family, subject to him and to her in-laws. Her first duty was to bear sons. If she did not, he might adopt a son. Failure to provide heirs gave her husband grounds for divorce, which brought great disgrace on her family. A woman, however, could not divorce her husband for any reason. Divorce was extremely rare in Chinese society, but a wealthy man with a "nonproductive" wife might bring concubines to live in the house along with his wife.

Men held a much higher position in society than did women. The desperately poor often killed girl babies or sold their daughters as servants or concubines. Young brides came under the direct control of their mothers-in-law, whose severity and cruelty are a common theme in Chinese literature. Once a strong-willed woman had sons, she gained increasing respect as the years went by. The Chinese deeply respected age. Some women of the wealthy classes, with servants to do the household chores, spent their days in semiseclusion nibbling dainties, smoking opium, and gambling. Women who brought large dowries to their marriages could dispose of part of those dowries as they wished. Some invested in profitable business activities. Poor women worked in the fields beside their husbands, in addition to bearing children and managing the household.

The educational system during the Ming and Qing periods had both virtues and weaknesses. Most villages and all towns and cities operated schools that prepared boys for the all-important civil service examinations. Boys learned to write with a brush the approximately three thousand commonly used characters of literary Chinese, and they learned the standard texts of Confucian philosophy, ethics, and history. The curriculum was very limited, and the instructional method stressed memorization and discouraged imagination. The civil service aspirant received no practical training in the work of government. But the system yielded a high percentage of literate men (relative to Europe at the same time) and gave Chinese society cohesion and stability. All educated Chinese shared the same basic ethical and literary culture, much as medieval Europeans were formed by Latin Christian culture.

In China, as in medieval Europe, educational opportunities for girls were limited. Rich men occasionally hired tutors for their daughters, and a few women achieved exceptional knowledge. Most women of all classes received training that prepared them for their roles as wives and mothers: courteous behavior, submission to their husbands, and the administration of a household.

In the late sixteenth century, when book publishing and educational facilities increased, women began to share in these opportunities. A few upper-class women, such as the poet/painter Lin Yiu (1618–1664) and the painter Ch'en Shu (1660–1736), gained considerable public recognition. We know of Ch'en Shu's life only because her eldest son, the prominent scholar-official Ch'ien Ch'en-ch'un, wrote her biography, casting her as a model of Confucian virtue.[17] Even in the early nineteenth century, only 1 to 10 percent of women were literate. By the criterion of education, the status of women in the Qing period may have fallen lower than at any other time in China's long history.[18]

What of health and medical care in imperial China? The Chinese medical tradition is the oldest continuing

**Ch'en Shu: The White Cockatoo** Like Italy and France in the early modern period, China and Japan can boast of distinguished women artists. This painting in ink and color on a hanging scroll depicts a highly prized species of parrot. The work of Ch'en Shu is very much in the Chinese artistic tradition. *(The Metropolitan Museum of Art, John Stewart Kennedy Fund, 1913 [13.220.31]. Photograph © 1987 The Metropolitan Museum of Art)*

usage in the world. Chinese medical theory deriving from the Han period (from the third century B.C.E. to the third century C.E.) attributed all ailments to a lack of harmony in the body; cure, then, rested on restoring harmony. Diagnosis of disease depended on visual observation, studying the case history, auditory symptoms, and taking the pulse. Physicians held that three spots along the wrist gave the pulse readings of different organs, and the experienced physician could diagnose the malfunction of any internal organ by checking the pulse. Two basic forms of therapy (treatment) existed. Medicinal therapy was based on the curative effects of herbs. This treatment entailed taking pills or powders in a boiled broth. The other therapy was acupuncture, the insertion of needles into specific parts of the body.

The theory behind acupuncture is that twelve channels run over the body close to the skin, each channel is related to a specific organ, and the needle stimulates a sluggish or pacifies an overactive organ. The early acupuncturist used fine needles and avoided vital organs. Certainly acupuncture was no more dangerous than the widespread European practice of bleeding.

Reliance on acupuncture and the Confucian principle that the body is the sacred gift of parents to child made dissection a terrible violation of filial piety and thus strongly discouraged serious surgery. Another factor militating against surgery was the Chinese culture's disdain for manual work of any kind. A "wise" doctor mastered a body of classical texts, prescribed medicine for treatment, and "did not lower himself to perform manual, surgical operations."[19] Nor should a doctor accept fees for service.

Several emperors decreed that medical colleges should be established, but these orders were never implemented. As a result, although the idea of state-supported hospitals was an ancient one in China, the first institutions to provide medical care for the sick of a community were established by Christian medical missionaries in the nineteenth century.

In sharp contrast to Europe, China had few social barriers. The emperors fought the development of a hereditary aristocracy that could have undermined their absolute monarchy, and they granted very few titles of nobility in perpetuity. Though China had no legally defined aristocracy, it did have an "upper class" based on a *combination* of wealth, education, lineage, and bureaucratic position. Agricultural land remained the most highly prized form of wealth, but silver ingots, jade, libraries of classical works, porcelain, and urban real estate also indicated status. China did not develop a politically articulate bourgeoisie. Because everyone accepted the Confucian principle that the learned and civilized should rule the state, scholars ranked highest in the social order. They, along with Heaven, Earth, the emperor, and parents, deserved special veneration. With the possible exception of the Jewish people, no people have respected learning as much as the Chinese. Merchants tried to marry into the scholar class in order to rise in the world. At the bottom of society were actors, prostitutes, and beggars.

The Chinese found recreation and relaxation in many ways. All classes gambled at cards and simple numbers games. The teahouse served as the local meeting place for exchanging news and gossip and listening to the tales

**Chinese Cookery** Everywhere in the world, until very recently, meat was scarce and thus a luxury. In China, the shortage of meat encouraged great sophistication in the preparation of foods, especially vegetables. Although European travelers interpreted the frequent servings of vegetables and fish as a sign of poverty, the Chinese, if we can trust modern nutritionists, probably had a healthier diet than that of Europeans. Notice the variety of dishes. Women obviously ate separately from men. *(Roger-Viollet/Getty Images)*

of professional storytellers, who enjoyed great popularity. The affluent indulged in an alcoholic drink made from fermented and distilled rice, and both men and women liked pipes and tobacco. Everyone who could afford to do so went to the theater. The actors, like their ancient Greek counterparts, wore happy and sad masks, and their gestures were formal and stylized. The plays typically dramatized episodes from Chinese history and literature. The Chinese associated athletics, riding, and horse racing with soldiers, at best a necessary evil, and regarded the active life as the direct antithesis of the scholarly contemplation they most valued.

The Qianlong emperor's reign saw the publication of China's greatest novel, ***The Dream of the Red Chamber.*** In 120 chapters with hundreds of characters, several levels of meaning, and echoes of the great Ming plays and novels, the author Cao Xuepin tells a tale of a wealthy extended family: its complex business dealings, varied religions, involvement in the imperial civil service, and loves and sexual liaisons, both heterosexual and homosexual. *The Dream of the Red Chamber* is both a love story and an account of one man's quest for identity and the meaning of life. Cao had not finished the book when he died in 1763; only in 1792 did a completed version appear. It achieved immediate success among all literate social classes and remains today one of the world's great literary classics.[20]

## KOREA (CA 1400–1800)

The peninsula of Korea juts out of the East Asian landmass, dividing the Yellow Sea to the west from the Sea of Japan to the east. Korea is bounded on the south by the Korea Strait and on the north by other natural barriers—the Yalu River and the Changpai Mountains, which separate Korea from China and Russia. With a highly indented coastline, Korea measures 600 miles in length and 135 miles in width. Because of a mountainous and rocky terrain, only about 20 percent of the soil is arable, and half of that arable land is given to the chief crop, rice. Surrounded on three sides by water, encompassing some of the best fishing areas in the world, Koreans have depended heavily on fish as their chief source of protein.

### Political and Cultural Foundations

Korea was united as a kingdom in the seventh century B.C.E., but much of its history shows strong Chinese influences. From China, Buddhism entered Korea in the fourth century C.E. and became the official state religion. Likewise, in the tenth century, Confucianism came to Korea, and although Buddhism remained the state religion, Confucianism controlled the model of government. In 1231 Mongol forces from China invaded Korea, leading to thirty years of war and domestic turmoil. Only when the ruling Koryo Dynasty accepted Mongol rule and made an alliance with it did peace come.

Throughout the fourteenth century, Japanese marauders raided Korea's east coast and penetrated deep into the interior; towns in southern Korea especially felt the brunt of Japanese assault. In this crisis, a soldier from the northeastern frontier, Yi Song-gye (1335–1408) saved the country. His successive victories over the Japanese won him a national following. In 1392, with the support of the Ming rulers of China, who had just overthrown the Mongols (see page 662), Yi Song-gye staged a coup: he overthrew the Koryo and seized the throne. Yi Song-gye (r. 1392–1396) founded the **Yi Dynasty** (also known as the Choson Dynasty), which lasted until 1910, the longest dynasty of East Asian history.

The reign of Yi Song-gye launched a broad movement of Neo-Confucian reform. Confucianism replaced Buddhism as the state religion. Neo-Confucian ideals of the Chinese philosopher Zhu Xi (1130–1200) determined state policy in land reform, educational reconstruction, and cultural development. For example, the government confiscated the tax-exempt monastic lands, laicized the monks and nuns, and redistributed the lands to the peasants, whose produce (mainly rice) yielded revenue for the state. Scholars rewrote the law codes and redesigned government institutions along Confucian lines. A Korean phonetic alphabet and printing with movable metal type were developed. A system of state examinations for civil service positions, similar to the Chinese system, was set up. In 1392 Yi Song-gye turned the fortress and trade center at Seoul, on the Han River, into his capital.

In 1592 the Japanese military leader Hideyoshi (see page 683) attacked Korea. After broad devastation and destruction, the Koreans, with Chinese help, repulsed the invaders. Then, in 1637, the Manchus assailed Korea, and after the Ming collapse in 1644, Korea became a vassal state of the Manchus.

Although Koreans form a distinct ethnic people, Korean culture reflects strong Chinese cultural models. In the seventeenth and eighteenth centuries, Korea had a Chinese-style calendrical system, a script for writing adapted from Chinese models, similar dress and food, the practice of Buddhism and Confucianism, and a governmental administration similar to the Chinese. China held to the fixed assumption that it was "the central kingdom," the cultural center of the universe. It followed, by

**Korean Man (*left*) by Rubens and Portrait of the Monk Sa-Myong Taesa (*right*)** The great Flemish master Peter Paul Rubens sketched the drawing on the left (ca 1617–1618) with black chalk and a little red chalk on the face. Scholars consider it one of the earliest representations of a Korean in the West and one of Rubens's most meticulous portraits. It is a fine example of cross-cultural interests. We do not know the name of the Korean or what he was doing in Antwerp, where Rubens encountered him. Roughly contemporaneous with the Rubens piece is this portrait of a Korean monk, painted in ink and colors on silk and mounted on a hanging scroll. Taesa had organized an army of monks to fight the Japanese invaders, and after their defeat he negotiated the peace treaty. Rubens relied on stark simplicity for effect, and the man's face on the left has a direct, inquiring expression. In contrast, the Korean artist used rich colors and details, such as the chair panels. Taesa's facial expression is idealized, denoting his spirituality. *(Left: The J. Paul Getty Museum, Los Angeles. Accession number: 83.GB.384; Right: 17th-century Korea, Choson Dynasty. Museum of Fine Arts, Boston, Denman Waldo Ross Collection)*

Chinese logic, that all other countries were marginal, removed from the center (see page 674). Thus Korea (along with Siam, renamed Thailand in 1938; Burma; and Annam) was a subordinate, or "tributary," state that had to acknowledge China's cultural and political preeminence. Korean diplomats, emissaries, and merchants had to use a language of submission and to kowtow when received by the Chinese emperors in imperial audiences. On a fixed annual schedule, Korea sent emissaries to Beijing and were allowed limited rights of trade. From the Chinese perspective, these were "tribute missions." The Chinese government had, as we have seen, no foreign office or department of state. Rather, the Ministry of Rituals had authority over all diplomatic and commercial relations with Korea, and that ministry stressed Korea's cultural inferiority.

## Economic and Social Change

The Yi government relied for revenue on "tribute taxes" on many locally produced items. Inequitably levied and collected, these taxes imposed a heavy burden on all peasants and drove some off the land. The establishment of the Uniform Land-Tax Law—requiring payment of 1 percent of the harvest of each unit of land, payable in rice, cotton, or corn—effectively abolished the tribute system. First imposed in 1608, the Uniform Land-Tax Law was enforced throughout the country a century later.

The law had significant consequences. It reduced the tax burden on the peasantry; allowed government-designated merchants (*kongin*), who purchased goods for the government, to accumulate capital; and led to the emergence of independent artisans who manufactured goods for the kongin.

Beginning in the seventeenth century, advances in farming technology led to a great increase in agricultural yields. Farmers used a new technique for starting rice seedlings: they were first planted in a small seedbed. A winter barley crop went into the fields. After the barley was harvested, the fields were flooded and the rice seedlings were transferred to the paddy. This "double-cropping" method required large amounts of water, and reservoirs were constructed to supply it. By the late eighteenth century, six thousand reservoirs dotted the Korean countryside. These improvements reduced the amount of labor needed, and one farmer could cultivate a larger amount of land. "Enlarged-scale farming," as the new method was called, became widespread. The condition of tenant farmers, the great majority of Yi rustics, also improved. Their labor was more valuable, and rather than working under the supervision of the landowner, they could farm as they chose. Payment in cash gradually replaced payment in kind.[21]

The seventeenth and eighteenth centuries also witnessed a great expansion of commercial farming: the raising of specialized crops for (distant) domestic and foreign sale. Tobacco, introduced from the Americas in the early seventeenth century, had a big market in China, as well as in Korea; tobacco proved even more profitable than rice. Ginseng, a family of tropical herbs, was in great demand in China, both as a cure for various ailments and for use in the manufacture of fine rice paper. The acreage given to cotton production also expanded.

Korean rural society underwent considerable change. A new-rich class of peasant farmers, whose wealth derived from crops grown for distant commercial markets, appeared. Below them, the ranks of successful tenant farmers increased. At the bottom were the unemployed; some became wage laborers, and others joined roving bands of robbers.

Economic and social change accelerated in the eighteenth century. The kongin emerged as a class of specialized merchants, each dealing in a specific product. Private merchants—some transporting goods by boat, others by overland routes—extended their operations throughout the country. The capital city, Seoul, especially enjoyed the advantages of more and greatly varied goods. As Seoul's population grew, more than one thousand local markets also sprang up throughout the Korean countryside.

In 1976 deep-sea divers at Sinan off the Korean coast uncovered a Chinese ship. Dated about 1323, it had sailed from Ningbo in Zhejiang province in China to Japan with a stop in Korea. The wreck, containing a huge cargo of Chinese ceramics, provides valuable evidence about Korean trade in the early modern world.

Since at least the Song period of Chinese history, Koreans had shown a strong interest in Chinese porcelain and had imported large quantities of it. Ceramic dishes and jars for everyday use, together with perfume bottles, jugs, ink pots, vases, candlesticks, teapots, and bowls, arrived in Korean markets for sale to the elite and scholarly classes. Just as Persian, Turkish, and later English potters did, Korean craftsmen quickly copied Chinese porcelain figures, styles, and colors. Throughout the Ming and Qing periods, Koreans also bought ceramic building and roofing tiles from China, as well as silks. In return, Korea exported tobacco, paper—ordinary paper for business uses and printing, heavy writing paper for scholars—brushes, ginseng, and cotton. The large forests that constituted one of Korea's great natural resources supplied the wood for paper manufacture.

# JAPAN (CA 1400–1800)

The Ashikaga Shogunate lasted from the middle of the fourteenth to the late sixteenth century. During this period, Japanese society experienced almost continual violence and civil war. Weak central governments could not maintain order. Throughout the islands, local strongmen took charge. Around 1450, 250 **daimyos,** or lords, held power; by 1600 only 12 survivors could claim descent from daimyo families of the earlier date. Successful military leaders carved out large territories and governed them as independent rulers. Political and social conditions in fifteenth- and sixteenth-century Japan strongly resembled conditions in western Europe in the tenth and eleventh centuries. Political power was in the hands of a small group of military leaders. Historians often use the same term—*feudalism*—to describe the Japanese and the European experiences. As in medieval Europe, feudalism paved the way for the rise of a strong centralized state in seventeenth-century Japan.

## Feudalism in Japan

Feudalism played a powerful role in Japanese culture until the nineteenth century. The similarities between feudalism in Japan and that in medieval Europe have fascinated scholars, as have the very significant differences. In Europe, feudalism emerged out of the fusion of Germanic and Roman social institutions and flowered under the impact of Muslim and Viking invasions. In Japan, feudalism evolved from a combination of the native warrior tradition and Chinese Confucian ethics. Japanese society had adopted the Confucian emphasis on filial respect for the head of the family, for the local civil authorities, and for the supreme authority of the head of state.

The two constituent elements of Japanese feudalism appeared between the eighth and twelfth centuries: (1) the **shoen** (private land outside imperial control) with its **shiki** (rights) and (2) the **samurai** (military warrior clique). Some scholars have equated the shoen with the European manor or estate, but the comparison needs very careful qualification. Most shoen were tracts of agricultural land granted by imperial charter that delineated the boundaries of the land, the holder's tax liability for it, and the extent of his administrative authority over it. Within the shoen were fields, forests, and rice paddies that belonged to others. A Japanese lord ordinarily did not live on his shoen (unlike the French or English lord, who did reside on his estate), and his lands were usually scattered over much of central Japan. Those who held shoen possessed the shiki there—that is, the right to the income or rice produced on the land. But just as several persons might hold rights—judicial, military, grazing—on a medieval European manor and all those rights yielded income, so several persons could hold shiki rights on a Japanese estate.

By the sixteenth century, only a small proportion of samurai had attained the rank of daimyo and possessed a shoen. Most warriors were salaried fighters with no connection to land. From their daimyos, they received stipends in rice, not in land; and in this respect they resembled those European knights who were supported by cash or money fiefs.

The Japanese samurai warrior resembled the knight of twelfth-century France in other ways as well. Both were armed with expensive weapons, and both fought on horseback. Just as the knight was supposed to live according to the chivalric code, so Japanese samurai were expected to live according to **Bushido,** or "Way of the Warrior," a code that stressed military honor, courage, stoic acceptance of hardship, and, above all, loyalty. Disloyalty brought social disgrace, which the samurai could avoid only through *seppuku,* ritual suicide by slashing his belly. Both samurai and knights were highly conscious of themselves as aristocrats. But knights fought as groups, and samurai fought as individuals.

By the middle of the sixteenth century, Japanese feudalism had taken on other distinctive features. As the number of shoen decreased and the powerful daimyos consolidated their territories, the practice of *primogeniture,* keeping an estate intact under the eldest or ablest son, became common. Around 1540 the introduction of the musket from Europe made infantrymen effective against mounted samurai, and the use of Western cannon required more elaborately fortified castles. Thus, in addition to armed cavalrymen, daimyos began to employ large numbers of foot soldiers equipped with spears, and they constructed new castles. These military and social developments occurred during a century of turbulence and chronic disorder, out of which emerged a leader who ended the chaos and began the process of unification, laying the foundation of the modern Japanese national state.

## Nobunaga and National Unification

Oda Nobunaga (1534–1582), a samurai of the lesser daimyo class, won control of his native province of Owari in 1559. He began immediately to extend his power, defeating a powerful daimyo in 1560 and eight years later seizing Kyoto, the capital city, where the emperor and his court resided. As a result, Nobunaga became the virtual ruler of central Japan.

Scholars have called the years from 1568 to 1600 the period of "national unification." During this time, Japan underwent aggressive and dynamic change. Adopting the motto "Rule the empire by force," Nobunaga set out to subdue all real and potential rivals and to replace them with his vassals. With the support of Toyotomi Hideyoshi (1537–1598), a brilliant general, he subdued first western and then eastern and northern Japan.

The great Buddhist temple-fortresses proved to be Nobunaga's biggest problem. Some of these monasteries possessed vast wealth and armed retainers. During the civil wars, the Buddhists had supported various daimyos in their private wars, but Nobunaga would tolerate no such interference. The strategically located monastery on Mount Hiei near Kyoto had long provided sanctuary for political factions. Previous daimyos had refused to attack it because it was sacred. Nobunaga, however, used fire to reduce it, and his men slaughtered thousands of its fleeing occupants.

Although Nobunaga won control of most of Japan by the sword, he backed up his conquests with government machinery and a policy of conciliation. He gave lands and subordinate positions in the army to his defeated enemies. Trusted daimyos received complete civil jurisdiction over entire provinces. At strategic points, such as Nijo near Kyoto and Azuchi on the shores of Lake Biwa, Nobunaga built castles to serve as key administrative and defensive centers for the surrounding territories. He opened the little fishing village of Nagasaki to foreign commerce; it soon grew into the nation's largest port. He standardized the currency, eliminated customs barriers, and encouraged the development of trade and industry. In 1582, when Nobunaga was murdered by one of his vassals, his general and staunchest adherent, Hideyoshi, carried on his work.

A peasant's son who had risen to power by his military service, Hideyoshi advanced the unification and centralization of Japan in two important ways. First, in 1582 he attacked the great fortress at Takamatsu. When direct assault failed, his troops flooded the castle and forced its surrender. When Takamatsu fell, so did the large province of Mori. A successful siege of the town of Kagoshima then brought the southern island of Kyushu under his domination. Hideyoshi soothed the vanquished daimyos as Nobunaga had done—with lands and military positions—but he also required them to swear allegiance and to obey him "down to the smallest particular."

Having reduced his most dangerous adversaries, Hideyoshi ordered a survey of the entire country. The military power of the unified Japanese state depended on a strong agricultural base, and Hideyoshi wanted to exploit the peasantry fully. His agents collected detailed information about the daimyos' lands and about towns, villages, agricultural produce, and industrial output all over Japan. This material enabled Hideyoshi to assess military quotas and taxable property. His surveys tied the peasant population to the land and tightened the collection of the land tax. With the country pacified, Hideyoshi embarked on an ill-fated attempt to conquer Korea and China. The expedition failed amid great bloodshed and devastation; it was the last Japanese medieval involvement in continental Asia. When Hideyoshi died in 1598, he left a strong centralized state. Brute force had created a unified Japan.

On his deathbed, the old soldier set up a council of regents to govern during the minority of his infant son. The strongest regent was Hideyoshi's long-time supporter Tokugawa Ieyasu (1543–1616), who ruled vast territories around Edo (modern-day Tokyo). Ieyasu quickly eliminated the young ruler and in 1600 at Sekigahara smashed a coalition of daimyo defenders of the heir. This battle was the beginning of the Tokugawa regime.

## The Tokugawa Regime

Japanese children are taught that "Ieyasu ate the pie that Nobunaga made and Hideyoshi baked." As the aphorism suggests, Ieyasu took over and completed the work begun by his able predecessors. He took decisive steps to solidify his dynasty and control the feudal nobility and to maintain peace and prosperity in Japan. The Tokugawa regime that Ieyasu fashioned worked remarkably well, lasting until 1867.

Ieyasu obtained from the emperor the ancient title of *shogun,* or general-in-chief. Constitutionally, the emperor exercised sovereign authority. In practice, authority and power—both the legal right and the physical means—were held by the Tokugawa shogun. Ieyasu declared the emperor and his court at Kyoto "very precious and decorative, like gold and silver," and surrounded the imperial court with all the ceremonial trappings but none of the realities of power.

In the course of the seventeenth century, the **Tokugawa Shogunate** worked to consolidate relations between the **bakufu** (imperial government) and the daimyos. In a scheme resembling the later residency requirement imposed by Louis XIV in France (see page 541) and Peter the Great in Russia (see page 556), Ieyasu set up the **sankin kōtai,** or alternate residence, system, whereby the feudal lords were compelled to live in the capital, Edo, every other year and to leave their wives and sons there—

**Daimyo Procession** Sankin kōtai, or system of alternate residence, meant that some daimyos were always on the road. Travel with retinues between the daimyos' residences and Edo, the shogun's residence, stimulated construction of roads, inns, and castle towns. As administrative headquarters, Edo functioned as a major consumer center; other castle towns such as Osaka developed as banking and manufacturing centers. *(Tokugawa Art Museum, Nagoya/Tokugawa Reimeikai Foundation)*

essentially as hostages. This arrangement had obvious advantages: the shogun could keep tabs on the daimyos, control them through their children, and weaken them financially with the burden of maintaining two residences. Ieyasu justified this course of action by invoking the Bushido code, with its emphasis on loyalty. He forbade members of the nobility to marry without his consent, thus preventing the formation of dangerous alliances.

As the daimyos accustomed themselves to the sankin kōtai system, the bakufu routinely approved the succession of each surviving heir to his predecessor's domain. The daimyos swore loyalty to the regime; the bakufu assured the daimyos of their privileged status. The bakufu also limited the number of vassals a daimyo could have. The end of civil disorder led to the demobilization of tens of thousands of samurai. The resulting loss of employment and social mobility in turn led to discontent among the military class. Gradually, the bakufu found employment for some of the former samurai in the fiscal and civil bureaucracy, while others were absorbed into the mercantile class (see page 685).[22]

The early Tokugawa shoguns also restricted the construction of castles—symbols, in Japan as in medieval Europe, of feudal independence. Later, the practice of alternate residence led to considerable castle building—castles that represented demands for goods and services. The Tokugawa regime also enforced a policy of complete separation of samurai and peasants. Samurai were defined as those who could bear swords; peasants could not bear swords. Samurai had to live in castles (which evolved into castle-towns), and they depended on stipends from their lords, the daimyos. Samurai were effectively prevented from establishing ties to the land, so they could not become landholders. Likewise, merchants and artisans had to live in towns and could not own land. Japanese castle-towns evolved into bustling, sophisticated urban centers. Peasants had to live in villages and till the land. According to the Neo-Confucian theory of the Tokugawa regime, society had four strata: samurai, peasants, artisans, and merchants.[23]

As in medieval Europe and early modern China, the agricultural class held a respected position because its members provided Japanese society with sustenance. Even so, farmers had to mind their betters, and they bore a disproportionate share of the tax load. According to the survey made by Hideyoshi, taxes were imposed on villages, not on individuals; the tax varied between 30 and 40 percent of the rice crop. Also as in Europe and China, the commercial classes in Japan theoretically occupied the lowest rungs on the social ladder because they profited from the toil of others.

## Urbanization and Commercialization

In the early seventeenth century, Japanese society rested on agriculture—a rice-based economy. Peasants paid their taxes in rice. Both the bakufu and the daimyos needed to exchange their rice for cash. This need led to the growth of central markets where quantities of rice could be exchanged and cash received for the purchase of other goods and services. Osaka came to manage most of

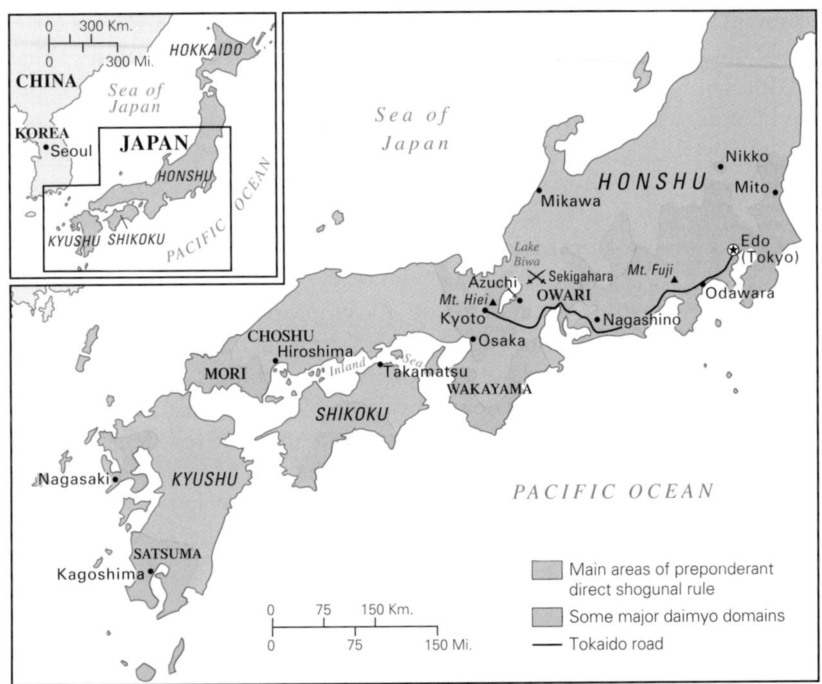


**MAP 21.2 Tokugawa Japan** Consider the cultural and political significance of the fact that Japan is an island. How did the concentration of shogunate lands affect the shogunate's government of Japan?

this rice trade. Other goods—cotton cloth, oil, sugar, salt, paper, and iron ore—also flowed into Osaka. Granted special privileges by the government, and with the facilities for large commodity exchange, Osaka became the commercial center of Japan. Wholesalers and brokers were concentrated there. The city was also closely tied to Kyoto, where the emperor and his court resided and which also represented a big demand for goods and services. Thus Osaka, "the kitchen of Japan," developed as the central market for the entire country. By the mid-eighteenth century, Osaka's population numbered about 1 million, Kyoto's 400,000. Edo, the center of government and the city where daimyos and their retainers had to spend part of each year according to the system of alternate residence, also expanded to about 400,000.

Other towns and cities sprang up. In contrast to western and eastern Europe, where cities grew out of religious centers (cathedrals), military camps (fortifications), or small marketplaces in the Middle Ages, Japanese towns in the seventeenth century trace their origins to a *political* factor: the daimyos' requirement that their vassals live at their castles. The concentration of vassals-in-residence, representing a consumer class and joined by commoners providing services, gave rise to castle-towns in Tokugawa Japan (see Map 21.2). Two hundred fifty towns, most ranging in size from 3,000 to 20,000 people—but a few, such as Hiroshima, Kagoshima, and Nagoya, that had populations between 65,000 and 100,000 people—came into being. In most places, half of the people had samurai status; the other half were commoners. In addition, perhaps 200 transit towns along the roads and highways emerged to service the needs of men traveling on the alternate residence system. In the eighteenth century, perhaps 4 million people, 15 percent of the Japanese population, resided in cities or towns.

In most cities, merchant families with special privileges from the government controlled the urban economy. The founders of businesses had entered the cities as samurai and changed their status to merchants. Frequently, a particular family dominated the trade of a particular product; then that family branched out into other businesses. The family of Kōnoike Shinroku provides a typical example.

In 1600 he established a sake brewery in the village of Kōnoike (sake is an alcoholic beverage made from fermented rice). By 1604 he had opened a branch office in Edo, and in 1615 he opened an office in Osaka; that same year, he began shipping tax-rice (taxes paid in rice) from western Japan to Osaka. One of Shinroku's sons, Kōnoike Zen'amon (remember that the Japanese put the surname before the individual name), in 1656 founded a banking or money-changing business in Osaka. Forty years later, the Kōnoike family was doing business in thirty-two daimyo domains. Eventually, the Kōnoike banking house made loans to and handled the tax-rice for 110 daimyo families. The Kōnoike continued to expand their businesses. In 1705, with the interest paid from daimyo loans, the Kōnoike bought a tract of ponds and swampland, turned the land into rice paddies, and settled 480 households numbering perhaps 2,880 peasants on the land. Land reclamation under merchant supervision became a typical feature of Tokugawa business practices. Involved in five or six business enterprises, the "house of Kōnoike" had come a long way from brewing sake.

Recent scholarship demonstrates that the Tokugawa regime witnessed the foundations of modern Japanese capitalism: the development of a cash economy, the use of money to make more money, the accumulation of large amounts of capital available for investment in factory or technological enterprises, and the growth of business ventures operating over a national network of roads. That these developments occurred simultaneously with, but entirely independent of, similar changes in Europe fascinates and challenges historians.

Japanese merchant families also devised distinct patterns and procedures for their business operations. What today is called "Family Style Management Principles" determined the age of appointment or apprenticeship (between eleven and thirteen); the employee's detachment from past social relations and adherence to the norms of a particular family business; salaries; seniority as the basis of promotion—though job performance at the middle rungs determined who reached the higher ranks; and the time for retirement. All employees in a family business were imbued with the "cardinal tenets" of Tokugawa business law: frugality, resourcefulness, and careful accounting. The successful employee also learned appropriate business behavior and a spirit of self-denial. These values formed the basis of what has been called the Japanese "industrious revolution." They help to explain how, after the Meiji Restoration of 1867 (see page 874), Japan

**Whaling** Island peoples often depend on the sea for much of their food. In Japan, where whaling is an old and dangerous pursuit, fishermen first snared the whale in huge nets and then harpooned it. Here the banners tell that a whale has been caught. A Japanese proverb holds that "when one whale is caught, it makes seven villages prosperous." The yellowish oil obtained from whale blubber was used for lighting and for the manufacture of soap and candles. *(Local History Archives, Ministry of Education, Tokyo/Photo courtesy of the International Society for Educational Information)*

was able to industrialize rapidly and to compete successfully with the West.[24]

The peace that the Tokugawa Shogunate imposed brought a steady rise in population and prosperity. As demand for goods grew, so did the numbers of merchants. To maintain stability, the early Tokugawa shoguns froze the four ancient social categories: imperial court nobility, samurai, peasants, and merchants. Laws rigidly prescribed what each class could and could not do. Nobles, for example, were "strictly forbidden, whether by day or by night, to go sauntering through the streets or lanes in places where they have no business to be." Daimyos were prohibited from moving troops outside their frontiers, making alliances, and coining money. Designated dress and stiff rules of etiquette distinguished one class from another. As intended, this stratification protected the Tokugawa shoguns from daimyo attack and inaugurated a long era of peace.

In the interests of stability and peace, Ieyasu's descendants also imposed measures called *sakoku.* This "closed country policy" sealed Japan's borders around 1639. Japanese were forbidden to leave the country. Foreigners were excluded.

In 1549 the Jesuit missionary Francis Xavier landed at Kagoshima. He soon made many converts among the poor and even some among the daimyos. By 1600 there were 300,000 baptized Christians in Japan. Most of them lived on Kyushu, the southernmost island (see Map 21.2), where the shogun's power was weakest and the loyalty of the daimyos most doubtful. In 1615 bands of Christian samurai supported Ieyasu's enemies at the fierce Battle of Osaka. In 1637, 30,000 peasants in the heavily Catholic area of northern Kyushu revolted. The shoguns thus came to associate Christianity with domestic disorder and feudal rebellion. Accordingly, what had been mild persecution of Christians became ruthless repression after 1639. Foreign priests were expelled or tortured, and thousands of Japanese Christians suffered crucifixion. The "closed country policy" remained in force for almost two centuries. The shogunate kept Japan isolated—but not totally.

Through the Dutch factory on the tiny island of Deshima in Nagasaki harbor (see page 685), a stream of Western ideas and inventions trickled into Japan in the eighteenth century. Western writings, architectural illustrations, calendars, watches, medicine, and paintings deeply impressed the Japanese. Western portraits and other paintings introduced the Japanese to perspective and shading. When the Swedish scientist C. P. Thunberg, physician to the Dutch at Deshima, visited Nagasaki and Edo, the Japanese looked on him as a scientific oracle and plied him with questions. Japanese scholars believed that Western inventions were more efficient than their Japanese equivalents and that these inventions contributed to the prosperity of European nations. Japanese curiosity about things Western gave rise to an intellectual movement known as *rangaku,* foreign studies, which urged that these Western ideas and inventions be adopted by the Japanese.

Japanese understanding of the West was severely limited and often fanciful, as was Western knowledge of Asian civilizations. Like eighteenth-century Europeans who praised Chinese and Persian customs to call attention to shortcomings at home, Japanese scholars idealized Western conditions. Both peoples wanted to create within their countries the desire for reform and progress.[25]

## The Life of the People

The Tokugawa Shogunate subdued the nobility by emasculating it politically. Stripped of power and required to spend alternate years at Edo, the daimyos and samurai passed their lives pursuing pleasure. They spent frantically on fine silks, paintings, concubines, boys, the theater, and the redecoration of their castles. Around 1700 one scholar observed that the entire military class was living "as in an inn, that is, consuming now and paying later."[26] Eighteenth-century Japanese novels, plays, and histories portray the samurai engrossed in tavern brawls and sexual orgies. These frivolities, plus more sophisticated pleasures and the heavy costs of maintaining an alternate residence at Edo, gradually ruined the warrior class.

In traditional Japanese society, women were subordinate to men, and the civil disorders of the sixteenth century strengthened male domination. Parents in the samurai class arranged their daughters' marriages to advance family interests. Once a woman married, her life centered on her children and domestic chores. The management of a large household with several children and many servants imposed heavy responsibilities on women. An upper-class wife rarely left home unchaperoned. "Middle-class" women, however, began to emerge from the home. The development of an urban commercial culture in the cities (see page 685) in the Tokugawa period led to the employment of women in silk and textile manufacture, in publishing, in restaurants and various shops, and especially in entertainment.

All major cities contained places of amusement for men—teahouses, theaters, restaurants, houses of prostitution. Desperately poor parents sometimes sold their daughters to entertainment houses (as they did in medieval Europe), and the most attractive or talented girls, trained in singing, dancing, and conversational arts, became courtesans, called *geishas,* or "accomplished persons," in modern

**Interior View of a Theater** Complex kabuki plays, which dealt with heroes, loyalty, and tragedy, and which included music and dance, became the most popular form of entertainment in Tokugawa Japan for all classes. Movable scenery and lighting effects made possible the staging of storms, fires, and hurricanes. *(Tokyo National Museum)*

times. The Tokugawa period saw the beginnings for men of the separation of family and business life on the one hand, and leisure and amusement on the other. That separation is still evident in Japanese society.[27]

The samurai spent heavily on kabuki theater. (See the feature "Individuals in Society: Katsushika Hokusai.") An art form created by townspeople, kabuki consisted of crude, bawdy skits dealing with love and romance or aspects of prostitution, an occupation in which many actors and actresses had professional experience. Performances featured elaborate costumes, song, dance, and poetry. Because actresses were thought to be corrupting the public morals, the Tokugawa government banned them from the stage in 1629. From that time on, men played all the parts. Male actors in female dress and makeup performed as seductively as possible to entice the burly samurai who thronged the theaters. Homosexuality, long accepted in Japan, was widely practiced among the samurai, who pursued the actors and spent profligately on them. According to one seventeenth-century writer, "'Youth's kabuki' began with beautiful youths being made to sing and dance, whereupon droll fools . . . had their hearts captivated and their souls stolen. . . . There were many of these men who soon had run through their fortunes."[28] Some moralists and bureaucrats complained from time to time, but the Tokugawa government decided to accept kabuki and prostitution as necessary evils. The practices provided employment, gratified the tastes of samurai and townspeople, and diverted former warriors from potential criminal and political mischief.[29] The samurai paid for their costly pleasures in the way their European counterparts did—by fleecing the peasants and borrowing from the merchants.

# INDIVIDUALS IN SOCIETY

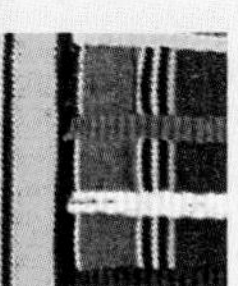

## KATSUSHIKA HOKUSAI

Today some of Katsushika Hokusai's paintings and prints sell for hundreds of thousands of dollars; in his lifetime, he knew mainly want and poverty. In spite of a very long and often tragic life, his art is filled with wit and humor. Although he wanted to be an artist from age six, he realized his potential and produced his greatest art only after age eighty. When dying in his eighty-ninth year, he prayed that God would give him just five more years to perfect his art.

Hokusai (1760–1849) was born to a lower-middle-class family in Edo, but probably because he was an expendable younger child, he was put out for adoption and taken in by an important artisan family. As a boy, he did all kinds of work: running errands; engraving the backs of metal mirrors, which he later adapted to cutting woodblocks; peddling wood, books, and calendars; selling red peppers and hot sweet potatoes on the streets. A long apprenticeship in the workshop of a famous Edo woodblock artist, Katsukawa Shunsho (1726–1792), launched Hokusai's artistic career. Following Japanese tradition, he was given the formal art name Katsukawa Shunro, but he used more than fifty names before settling on the one by which we know him.

Hokusai married twice and had five children, but they brought him slight consolation. A son and a grandson implicated him in financial difficulties from which he was never able to extricate himself. As an old man at the height of his powers, when he should have been an honored citizen of Edo, he lived in a rural hovel and had to walk miles into the city, "sneaking into his publishers after dark to check upon the prints which were later to bedazzle the world." Hokusai's youngest daughter, Oci, was his only solace. An able artist herself, Oci took care of him in his long old age.

Hokusai belonged to the *ukiyo-e* ("pictures of the floating world") movement, a seventeenth- to nineteenth-century art movement devoted to recording transient everyday life, with an emphasis on leisure pursuits. He produced thousands of street scenes, as well as scenes from Japanese history, legend, and kabuki theater and scenes of the culture of rice; of women—tending children, as prostitutes, and as nuns; of sports and games; of erotic situations; of fat, thin, and blind people; and of fauna—real and fantastic—and flora. He illustrated many novels and short stories, and his thirteen-volume *Manga* (sketches or drawings) represents a rich collection of cartoons, figure studies, and fabulous beasts. His most famous landscapes are the dramatic *Thirty-six Views of Mount Fuji,* showing the volcanic mountain in Honshu province in a wide range of seasonal and weather conditions. The richness of his imagination and the quality of his humor appealed to the Japanese bourgeoisie who bought his works. (Most people could afford his inexpensive woodblock prints.)

*Hokusai self-portrait. In his later years Hokusai often used the pen name Gakyojin, "old man mad about drawing."* (Réunion des Musées Nationaux/Art Resource, NY)

Hokusai's unsentimental love for animals and the natural world inspired the Victorian illustrator Beatrix Potter (*The Tale of Peter Rabbit*). His technical excellence and careful representation of ordinary life influenced the French artists Edouard Manet and Edgar Degas, and they in turn influenced Toulouse-Lautrec and Picasso. Hokusai was not just a great Japanese artist; with Michelangelo and Titian, his nearest rivals for longevity, he was one of the great artists of the world.

### QUESTIONS FOR ANALYSIS

1. Where did Hokusai find the models for his art?
2. Consider Hokusai's art in light of Charlie Chaplin's remark, "There are more valid facts and details in works of art than there are in history books."

*Sources:* James A. Michener, *The Hokusai Sketch-Books: Selections from the Manga* (Rutland, Vt., and Tokyo: Charles E. Tuttle, 1989); *The Random House Library of Painting and Sculpture,* vol. 4: *Dictionary of Artists and Art Terms* (New York: Random House, 1981).

**Hokusai Manga** Hokusai produced fifteen fat volumes of *manga* (random sketches or cartoons), testimony to his incredible energy and vitality. They have been called "a record of the people of Japan" and "a major art treasure." This charming scene of children playing with toys gives the lie to the view that Hokusai was a crusty, irascible old man. *(Private collection)*

According to Japanese tradition, farmers deserved respect. In practice, peasants were sometimes severely oppressed and led miserable lives. It was government policy to tax them to the level of bare subsistence, and official legislation repeatedly redefined their duties. In 1649 every village in Japan received these regulations:

*Peasants are people without sense or forethought. Therefore they must not give rice to their wives and children at harvest time, but must save food for the future. They should eat millet, vegetables, and other coarse food instead of rice. Even the fallen leaves of plants should be saved as food against famine. . . . During the seasons of planting and harvesting, however, when the labor is arduous, the food taken may be a little better. . . .*

*They must not buy tea or sake [a fermented liquor made from rice] to drink nor must their wives.*

*The husband must work in the fields, the wife must work at the loom. Both must do night work. However good-looking a wife may be, if she neglects her household duties by drinking tea or sightseeing or rambling on the hillsides, she must be divorced.*

*Peasants must wear only cotton or hemp—no silk. They may not smoke tobacco. It is harmful to health, it takes up time, and costs money. It also creates a risk of fire.*[30]

The conspicuous consumption of the upper classes led them during the seventeenth and eighteenth centuries to increase taxes from 30 or 40 percent of the rice crop to 50 percent. Merchants who bought farm produce fixed the price of rice so low that it seemed to farmers that the more they produced, the less they earned. They found release only by flight or revolt.

After 1704 peasant rebellions were chronic. Oppressive taxation provoked eighty-four thousand farmers in the province of Iwaki to revolt in 1739. After widespread burning and destruction, their demands were met. In other instances, the shoguns ordered savage repression.

Natural disasters also added to the peasants' misery. In the 1770s fires, floods, and volcanic eruptions hit all parts of Japan. Drought and torrential rain led to terrible famines between 1783 and 1788 and again between 1832 and 1836. Taxation, disaster, and oppression often combined to make the lot of peasants one of unrelieved wretchedness.

This picture of the Japanese peasantry tells only part of the story, however. Scholarship has demonstrated that in the Tokugawa period, peasant society was "a pyramid of wealth and power . . . that rose from the tenant farmer at the bottom through small landholders to wealthy peasants at the top."[31] Agricultural productivity increased substantially, and assessed taxes were fixed, though they remained high. Peasants who improved their lands and increased their yields continued to pay the same assessed tax and could pocket the surplus as profit. Their social situation accordingly improved. By the early nineteenth century, there existed a large class of relatively wealthy, educated, and ambitious peasant families who resembled the middle ranks of the warrior class.

Likewise, local economic conditions and family social status shaped the lives of Japanese women. The existence of a rich peasant's wife, daughter, or sister differed considerably from that of poor peasant women. The well-to-do seem to have made few distinctions in the early upbringing of male and female children. Regional prosperity determined the amounts of money spent on the education of both sexes in their early years. In the early nineteenth century, the regions around flourishing Edo and Kyoto spent far more than the poor Tohoku region, and parents in thriving areas devoted considerable sums to their daughters' education. Girls from middle-level peasant families may have had from two to five years of formal schooling, but they were thought incapable of learning the difficult Chinese characters, so their education focused on moral instruction intended to instill the virtue of obedience. Daughters of wealthy peasant families learned penmanship, the Chinese classics, poetry, and the proper forms of correspondence, and they rounded out their education with travel.[32]

Scholars of the Japanese family, like students of the late medieval and early modern European family, have explored the extent of premarital sex, the age at which people married, the frequency with which they married someone from another village, and the level of divorce. For Tokugawa Japan, considerable regional variations make broad generalizations dangerous; research continues. It is clear, however, that marriage linked families of equal status and class; Japanese marriages, therefore, strengthened economic and social divisions.

On the Japanese bride fell the responsibility of bringing harmony to the household. Harmony "meant that she had to refrain from quarreling with the members of her new household, do the work expected of her position, and conform to family custom."[33] Both samurai and peasant teachings stressed that "the married couple was the foundation of morality" and that the basis for harmony in the couple rested on good connubial relations. Once, the author of *Observations of Agricultural Practices,* a study of rural life, stayed overnight at a farmhouse. Newlyweds in the family went to bed early and, separated from the others by only a screen, began noisy lovemaking. "Outrageous," exclaimed the guest, whereupon the old woman of the family got angry. "Harmony between husband and

**A Male Prostitute** A male prostitute writes a poem as a female prostitute massages their patron's back. Notice the elaborate hairstyles, the rich material of the kimonos, and the boxes of writing instruments. *(The Fine Arts Museum of San Francisco. Achenbach Foundation for Graphic Arts purchase, 1969, 32.20)*

wife is the basis for prosperity for the descendants. . . . I permit this coupling day and night. People who laugh at their passion are themselves outrageous. Get out!"[34] Domestic harmony and social necessity were closely linked.

A peasant wife shared with her husband responsibility for the family's economic well-being. If of poor or middling status, she worked alongside her husband in the fields, doing the routine work while he did the heavy work. If they were farm hands and worked for salaries, the wife invariably earned half or a third less than her husband. Wives of prosperous farmers never worked in the fields, but they spun silk, wove cloth, helped in any family business, and supervised the maids. Whatever their economic status, Japanese women, like women everywhere in the world, tended the children; children were women's special responsibility. The production of children, especially sons, strengthened a wife's prestige, but among well-to-do Japanese farmwomen, the bride's skill in prudent household management was the most desired talent.

How was divorce initiated, and how frequent was it? Customs among the noble class differed considerably from peasant practices. Widows and divorcées of the samurai aristocracy—where female chastity was the core of fidelity—were not expected to remarry. The husband alone could initiate divorce by ordering his wife to leave or by sending her possessions to her natal home. The wife could not prevent divorce or ensure access to her children.

Among the peasant classes, divorce seems to have been fairly common—at least 15 percent in the villages near Osaka in the eighteenth century. Women as well as men could begin the procedure. Wives' reasons were husbands' drunkenness, physical abuse, or failure to support the family. Many women secured divorce from temples whose function was to dissolve marriages: if a married woman entered the temple and performed its rites for three years, her marriage bond was dissolved. Sometimes Buddhist temple priests served as divorce brokers: they went to the village headman and had him force the husband to agree to a divorce. News of the coming of temple officials was usually enough to produce a letter of separation. A poor woman wanting a divorce simply left her husband's home. Opportunities for remarriage were severely limited. Divorce in samurai society carried a social stigma; it did not among the peasantry.[35]

The Tokugawa period witnessed a major transformation of agriculture, a great leap in productivity and specialization. The rural population increased, but the agricultural population did not; surplus labor was drawn to other employment and to the cities. In fact, Japan suffered an acute shortage of farm labor from 1720 to 1868. In some villages, industry became almost as important as agriculture. At Hirano near Osaka, for example, 61.7 percent of all arable land was sown in cotton. The peasants had a thriving industry: they ginned the cotton locally before transporting it to wholesalers in Osaka. In many rural places, as many peasants worked in the manufacture of silk, cotton, or vegetable oil as in the production of rice.[36] In theory, the urban commercial classes, scorned for benefiting from the misery of the peasants and the appetites of the samurai, occupied the bottom rung of the social ladder. Merchants had no political power, but they accumulated wealth, sometimes great wealth. They also demonstrated the possibility of social mobility and thus the inherent weakness of the regime's system of strict social stratification.

The commercial class grew in response to the phenomenal development of urban life. In the seventeenth century, the surplus rural population, together with underemployed samurai and the ambitious and adventurous, thronged to the cities. All wanted a better way of life than could be found in the dull farming villages. Japan's cities grew tremendously: Kyoto, home to the emperor and his pleasure-loving court; Edo (modern Tokyo), the political capital, with its multitudes of government bureaucrats, daimyos in alternate residence, intellectuals, and police; and Osaka, by this time the greatest commercial city in Japan, with its huge grain exchange and commercial banks. In the eighteenth century, Edo's population of almost a million represented the largest demand for goods and services in the world.

The Tokugawa shoguns turned the samurai into urban consumers by denying them military opportunities. Merchants stood ready to serve them. Towns offered all kinds of luxury goods and catered to every extravagant and exotic taste. By marketing the daimyos' grain, town merchants gave the aristocrats the cash they needed to support their rich establishments. Merchants formed guilds and banks and lent money to the samurai. Those who defaulted on their debts found themselves cut off from further credit.[37]

As the ruling samurai with their fixed stipends became increasingly poorer, the despised merchants grew steadily wealthier. By contemporary standards anywhere in the world, the Japanese "middle" class lived very well. In 1705 the shogunate confiscated the property of a merchant in Osaka "for conduct unbecoming a member of the commercial class." In fact, the confiscation was at the urging of influential daimyos and samurai who owed the merchant gigantic debts. The government seized 50 pairs of gold screens, 360 carpets, several mansions, 48 granaries and warehouses scattered around the country, and hundreds of thousands of gold pieces. This merchant possessed fabulous wealth, but other merchants also enjoyed a rich lifestyle.[38]

## SUMMARY

In the eighteenth century, China experienced a rapid increase in both prosperity and population. The Qing rulers were not Chinese but Manchus from the north. Never more than 2 percent of the population, the Qing developed a centralized and authoritarian government, retaining the Ming administrative system but under Manchu supervision. Initially, this continuity brought peace and relative affluence. Over the centuries, however, the maintenance of the traditional Chinese position toward foreign "barbarians" and the refusal to trade with Westerners and to adopt Western technology weakened imperial rule and left China, in the nineteenth century, at the mercy of European mercantile and imperialistic ambitions.

In Korea, commercial expansion brought into being a new class of wealthy peasants. Chinese culture influenced the Koreans in many ways.

In 1800 Tokugawa Japan was reaping the rewards of two centuries of peace and social order. Steady economic growth and improved agricultural technology had swelled the population. The samurai had been transformed into peaceful city dwellers and civil bureaucrats. The wealth of the business classes grew, and the samurai, dependent on fixed agricultural rents or stipends in rice in a time of rising standards of living, fell into debt. The Tokugawa regime formed submissive citizens whose discipline is apparent even today.

Although the shogunate maintained a policy of national isolation and no foreign power influenced Japan's political or social life, Japan was not really cut off from outside cultural contacts. Through the port of Nagasaki, Western scientific ideas and some Western technology entered Japan in response to the persistent interest of Japanese scholars. The Japanese readily absorbed foreign technological ideas.

## KEY TERMS

Ming Dynasty
shih
civil service examinations
jinshi
gentry
tribute system
kowtow
Qing Dynasty
*The Dream of the Red Chamber*
Yi Dynasty
daimyos
shoen
shiki
samurai
Bushido
Tokugawa Shogunate
bakufu
sankin kōtai

## NOTES


1. J. K. Fairbank, *China: A New History* (Cambridge, Mass.: Harvard University Press, 1992), p. 128.
2. Ibid., p. 129.
3. See L. E. Eastman, *Family, Fields, and Ancestors: Constancy and Change in China's Social and Economic History, 1550–1949* (New York: Oxford University Press, 1988), p. 153.
4. Ibid., pp. 153–154.
5. Fairbank, *China,* p. 133.
6. J. Gernet, *A History of Chinese Civilization,* trans. J. R. Foster (New York: Cambridge University Press, 1982), p. 391.
7. Ibid.
8. J. D. Spence, *The Search for Modern China* (New York: W. W. Norton, 1991), pp. 9–10.
9. S. J. Vainker, *Chinese Pottery and Porcelain: From Prehistory to the Present* (New York: G. Braziller, 1991), Chap. 5, pp. 134–159.
10. A. Waldron, *The Great Wall of China: From History to Myth* (New York: Cambridge University Press, 1990), p. 83.
11. Ibid., pp. 140–164.
12. Gernet, *A History of Chinese Civilization,* pp. 425–426.
13. Quoted in A. Peyrefitte, *The Immobile Empire,* trans. J. Rothschild (New York: Knopf, 1992), pp. 195–196.
14. Ibid., p. 539.
15. Quoted in Spence, *The Search for Modern China,* p. 125.
16. Eastman, *Family, Fields, and Ancestors,* p. 20.
17. M. Weidner, ed., *Flowering in the Shadows: Women in the History of Chinese and Japanese Painting* (Honolulu: University of Hawaii Press, 1990), pp. 123–154.
18. Eastman, *Family, Fields, and Ancestors,* p. 20.
19. See R. C. Croizier, *Traditional Medicine in Modern China* (Cambridge, Mass.: Harvard University Press, 1968), pp. 19–27.
20. Spence, *The Search for Modern China,* pp. 106–110.
21. C. J. Eckert et al., *Korea, Old and New: A History* (Cambridge, Mass.: Harvard University Press, 1980), pp. 155–164.
22. See C. Totman, *Japan Before Perry: A Short History* (Berkeley: University of California Press, 1981), pp. 142–148.
23. C. Nakane, "Tokugawa Society," in *Tokugawa Japan: The Social and Economic Antecedents of Modern Japan,* ed. C. Nakane and S. Ōishi (Tokyo: University of Tokyo Press, 1991), pp. 213–214.
24. Y. Sakudo, "The Management Practices of Family Business," in *Tokugawa Japan: The Social and Economic Antecedents of Modern Japan,* ed. C. Nakane and S. Ōishi (Tokyo: University of Tokyo Press, 1991), pp. 147–166.
25. D. Keene, *The Japanese Discovery of Europe, 1720–1830* (Stanford, Calif.: Stanford University Press, 1969), pp. 24–25, Chap. 4, and passim.
26. Quoted in D. H. Shively, "Bakufu Versus Kabuki," in *Studies in the Institutional History of Early Modern Japan,* ed. J. W. Hall (Princeton, N.J.: Princeton University Press, 1970), p. 236.
27. E. O. Reischauer and A. M. Craig, *Japan: Tradition and Transformation,* rev. ed. (Boston: Houghton Mifflin, 1989), pp. 104–105.
28. Quoted in Shively, "Bakufu Versus Kabuki," pp. 241–242.
29. Ibid.
30. Quoted in G. B. Sansom, *A History of Japan, 1615–1867,* vol. 3 (Stanford, Calif.: Stanford University Press, 1978), p. 99.
31. T. C. Smith, "The Japanese Village in the Seventeenth Century," in *Studies in the Institutional History of Early Modern Japan,* ed. J. W. Hall (Princeton, N.J.: Princeton University Press, 1970), p. 280.


*(continued on page 696)*

# LISTENING TO THE PAST

## The Qianlong Emperor Responds to King George III

*Lord George Macartney's embassy to China (1792–1794) sought to establish permanent diplomatic relations between China and Great Britain and to expand trade between the two countries. The mission failed when the emperor rejected the British proposals for the reasons that he states in the letter that follows. Although Macartney later wrote, "Nothing could be more fallacious than to judge of China by any European standard," the British refused to recognize the right of Chinese civilization to be different. The Macartney mission thus serves as a parading of the cultural clashes between the West and Asia that marked the next two centuries.*

You, O King, from afar have yearned after the blessings of our civilization, and in your eagerness to come into touch with our converting influence have sent an Embassy across the sea bearing a memorial.* I have already taken note of your respectful spirit of submission, have treated your mission with extreme favor and loaded it with gifts. . . .

Yesterday your Ambassador petitioned my Ministers to memorialize me regarding your trade with China, but his proposal is not consistent with our dynastic usage and cannot be entertained. Hitherto, all European nations, including your own country's barbarian merchants, have carried on their trade with our Celestial Empire at Canton. Such has been the procedure for many years, although our Celestial Empire possesses all things in prolific abundance and lacks no product within its own borders. There was therefore no need to import the manufactures of outside barbarians in exchange for our own produce. But as the tea, silk and porcelain which the Celestial Empire produces, are absolute necessities to European nations and to yourselves, we have permitted, as a signal mark of favor, that foreign *hongs*† should be established at Canton, so that your wants might be supplied and your country thus participate in our beneficence. But your Ambassador has now put forward new requests which completely fail to recognize the Throne's principle to "treat strangers from afar with indulgence," and to exercise a pacifying control over barbarian tribes, the world over. Moreover, our dynasty, swaying the myriad races of the globe, extends the same benevolence towards all. Your England is not the only nation trading at Canton. If other nations, following your bad example, wrongfully importune my ear with further impossible requests, how will it be possible for me to treat them with easy indulgence? Nevertheless, I do not forget the lonely remoteness of your island, cut off from the world by intervening wastes of sea, nor do I overlook your excusable ignorance of the usages of our Celestial Empire. I have consequently commanded my Ministers to enlighten your Ambassador on the subject, and have ordered the departure of the mission. . . .

Your request for a small island near Chusan,‡ where your merchants may reside and goods be warehoused, arises from your desire to develop trade. As there are neither foreign *hongs* nor interpreters in or near Chusan, where none of your ships have ever called, such an island would be utterly useless for your purposes. Every inch of the territory of our Empire is marked on the map and the strictest vigilance is exercised over it all:

*Memorandum.

†Groups of merchants.

‡A group of islands in the East China Sea at the entrance to Hangzhou Bay.

even tiny islets and far-lying sand-banks are clearly defined as part of the provinces to which they belong. Consider, moreover, that England is not the only barbarian land which wishes to establish . . . trade with our Empire. . . .

The next request, for a small site in the vicinity of Canton city, where your barbarian merchants may lodge or, alternatively, that there be no longer any restrictions over their movements at Aomen,[§] has arisen from the following causes. Hitherto, the barbarian merchants of Europe have had a definite locality assigned to them at Aomen for residence and trade, and have been forbidden to encroach an inch beyond the limits assigned to that locality. . . . If these restrictions were withdrawn, friction would inevitably occur between the Chinese and your barbarian subjects, and the results would militate against the benevolent regard that I feel towards you. From every point of view, therefore, it is best that the regulations now in force should continue unchanged. . . .

Regarding your nation's worship of the Lord of Heaven, it is the same religion as that of other European nations. Ever since the beginning of history, sage Emperors and wise rulers have bestowed on China a moral system and inculcated a code, which from time immemorial has been religiously observed by the myriads of my subjects.[||] There has been no hankering after heterodox doctrines. Even the European (missionary) officials in my capital are forbidden to hold intercourse with Chinese subjects; they are restricted within the limits of their appointed residences, and may not go about propagating their religion. The distinction between Chinese and barbarian is most strict, and your Ambassador's request that barbarians shall be given full liberty to disseminate their religion is utterly unreasonable.

It may be, O King, that the above proposals have been wantonly made by your Ambassador on his own responsibility, or peradventure you yourself are ignorant of our dynastic regulations and had no intention of transgressing them when you expressed these wild ideas and hopes. . . . If, after the receipt of this explicit decree, you lightly give ear to the representations of your subordinates and allow your barbarian merchants to proceed to Chêkiang and Tientsin,** with the object of landing and trading there, the ordinances of my Celestial Empire are strict in the extreme, and the local officials, both civil and military, are bound reverently to obey the law of the land. Should your vessels touch the shore, your merchants will assuredly never be permitted to land or to reside there, but will be subject to instant expulsion. In that event your barbarian merchants will have had a long journey for nothing. Do not say that you were not warned in due time! Tremblingly obey and show no negligence! A special mandate!

§A city some forty-five miles to the south of Canton, at the lower end of the Pearl (Zhu) River delta.

||The reference is to Confucianism.

Lord Macartney tries to impress the Qianlong emperor with an array of expensive presents. *(National Maritime Museum, London)*

## QUESTIONS FOR ANALYSIS

1. Consider the basic premises of eighteenth-century European Enlightenment culture and the premises of Chinese culture.
2. What reasons does the emperor give for denying Britain's requests? What is the basis for the emperor's position?
3. How does the emperor view China's economic and cultural position in the world?

**Two Chinese port cities.

*Source:* A. J. Andrea and J. H. Overfield, eds., *The Human Record: Sources of Global History*, vol. 2 (Boston: Houghton Mifflin, 1990), pp. 262–264. Reprinted from E. Backhouse and J. O. P. Brand, *Annals and Memoirs of the Court of Peking* (Boston: Houghton Mifflin, 1914), pp. 325–331.

32. A. Walthall, "The Life Cycle of Farm Women in Tokugawa Japan," in *Recreating Japanese Women, 1600–1945,* ed. G. L. Bernstein (Berkeley: University of California Press, 1991), pp. 46–47.
33. Ibid., pp. 55–56.
34. Quoted ibid., p. 56.
35. Ibid., pp. 60–62.
36. Smith, "The Japanese Village."
37. Nakane, "Tokugawa Society."
38. G. B. Sansom, *Japan: A Cultural History,* rev. ed. (New York: Appleton-Century-Crofts, 1962), p. 472.

## SUGGESTED READING

All the titles cited in the Notes represent solid scholarship; the books by Eastman, Fairbank, Spence, Totman, and Waldron are especially recommended. Fairbank was probably the most distinguished American Sinologist of the past half century. The many works of J. D. Spence also include *The Chan's Great Continent: China in Western Minds* (1998), a fascinating study of how Europeans and Americans have perceived China; *Chinese Roundabout* (1992), a collection of excellent essays on such diverse topics as Matteo Ricci, Ming life, food, medicine, and gambling, and the great scholars who shaped the study of Chinese history in North America; and *Emperor of China: Self-Portrait of Kang-Hsi* (1988), described as a "masterpiece." For Ming government, the enterprising student should also see C. Hucker, ed., *Chinese Government in Ming Times* (1969); R. Huang, *1587, A Year of No Significance: The Ming Dynasty in Decline* (1981); and *The Cambridge History of China,* vol. 7: *The Ming Dynasty, 1368–1644* (1988). J. Spence and J. Wills, eds., *From Ming to Ch'ing: Conquest, Region, and Continuity in Seventeenth Century China* (1979), is also valuable. For the importance of commercialization in the social and economic history of the period, see T. Brook, *The Confusions of Pleasure: Commerce and Culture in Ming China* (1998). M. Elwin, *The Pattern of the Chinese Past* (1973), offers a broad but difficult survey of premodern China, with particular attention to China's failure to maintain its technological superiority.

The following titles should prove useful for serious study of the Qing period: B. S. Bartlett, *Monarchs and Ministers: The Grand Council in Mid-Ch'ing China, 1723–1820* (1991); S. Naquin and E. Rawski, *Chinese Society in the Eighteenth Century* (1987); W. Yeh-Chien, "The Sprouts of Capitalism," in *Ming and Qing Historical Studies in the People's Republic of China,* ed. F. Wakeman (1981); and S. Min-hsiung, *The Silk Industry in Ch'ing China* (1976). The latter two works are very helpful for understanding China's economic development.

For aspects of everyday life, see K. C. Chang, ed., *Food in Chinese Culture: Anthropological and Historical Perspectives* (1977); C. Clunas, *Superfluous Things: Material Culture and Social Status in Early Modern China* (1991); and P. Huard and M. Wong, *Chinese Medicine* (1972).

The literature on the history of women steadily expands. S. Mann, *Precious Records: Women in China's Long Eighteenth Century* (1997), discusses many aspects of gender relations in the period 1683–1839 and revises traditional interpretations of women in China's patriarchial society. F. Bray, *Technology and Gender: Fabrics of Power in Late Imperial China* (1997), explores the everyday life of women in the history of technology, as well as intimate aspects of women's lives such as childbearing and child rearing. J. D. Spence, *The Death of Woman Wang* (1978), is a masterpiece of historical reconstruction. P. B. Ebrey, "Women, Marriage, and the Family in Chinese History," in *Heritage of China: Contemporary Perspectives on Chinese Civilization,* ed. P. S. Ropp (1990); C. Furth, "Rethinking van Gulik: Sexuality and Reproduction in Traditional Chinese Medicine," in *Engendering China: Women, Culture, and the State,* eds. C. K. Gilmartin, G. Hershatter, L. Rofel, and T. White (1994); and V. Ng, "Ideology and Sexuality: Rape Laws in Qing China," *Journal of Asian Studies* 46 (1987): 57–70, should also prove helpful.

For Korea, R. Tennant, *A History of Korea* (1996), is an informed and highly readable survey, helpful to the tourist as well as the student. C. J. Eckert et al., *Korea, Old and New: A History* (1990), focuses on the political-cultural background from which modern Korea emerged, while Ki-baik Lee, *A New History of Korea,* trans. E. W. Wagner (1984), is a very detailed political history.

The titles by Reischauer and Craig, Sansom, and Smith cited in the Notes are highly recommended for Japan. P. Duus, *Feudalism in Japan* (1976), contrasts Japanese and European feudalism and explores the political-social background of the Tokugawa regime. H. Ooms, *Tokugawa Ideology: Early Constructs, 1570–1680* (1985), treats the Buddhist, Shinto, and Neo-Confucian intellectual foundations of the Tokugawa regime. R. P. Toby, *State and Diplomacy in Early Modern Japan: Asia in the Development of the Tokugawa Bakufu* (1983), revises the standard interpretation that Tokugawa Japan existed in virtual isolation from the rest of the world, arguing that Japan's foreign policy sought to maintain the nation's security in a hostile world. For the Japanese understanding of the West, see D. Keene, *The Japanese Discovery of Europe, 1720–1830,* rev. ed. (1969), and for the West's early perception of Japan, see D. Massarella, *A World Elsewhere: Europe's Encounter with Japan in the Sixteenth and Seventeenth Centuries* (1990). An important work of social history, H. P. Bix, *Peasant Protest in Japan, 1590–1884* (1986), discusses concepts of class, status, and exploitation and the different forms of peasant protest. The essays in C. Nakane and S. Ōishi, eds., *Tokugawa Japan: The Social and Economic Antecedents of Modern Japan,* trans. C. Totman (1991), are invaluable for the study of the beginnings of Japanese capitalism. G. Bernstein, ed., *Recreating Japanese Women, 1600–1945* (1991), contains exciting, informed, and very readable essays on many aspects of women's lives.

*The Planting of a Liberty Tree,* by Pierre Antoine Leseur.
*(Giraudon/Art Resource, NY)*

# CHAPTER 22 THE REVOLUTION IN WESTERN POLITICS, 1775–1815

## CHAPTER OUTLINE

- Liberty and Equality
- The American Revolutionary Era (1775–1789)
- The French Revolution (1789–1791)
- World War and Republican France (1791–1799)
- The Napoleonic Era (1799–1815)

The last years of the eighteenth century were a time of great upheaval in the West. A series of revolutions and revolutionary wars challenged the old order of monarchs and aristocrats. The ideas of freedom and equality, ideas that have not stopped shaping the world since that era, flourished and spread. The revolutionary era began in North America in 1775. Then in 1789 France, the most influential country in Europe, became the leading revolutionary nation. It established first a constitutional monarchy, then a radical republic, and finally a new empire under Napoleon. The armies of France also joined forces with patriots and radicals abroad in an effort to establish throughout much of Europe new governments based on new principles.

The French and American Revolutions were in many ways world-historical events, for their impact was felt far beyond Europe. The universal nature of the aspirations of the French revolutionaries in particular soon inspired revolutionary movements, such as the Haitian Revolution in the Caribbean and the independence struggles in Latin America in the early nineteenth century. And in the course of the nineteenth century the revolutionary ideals of individual liberty, representative government, and nationalism would find adherents around the world, contributing eventually to the emergence of independence movements in Asia and Africa. The modern pattern of domestic and international politics was born.

- What caused this era of revolution?
- What were the ideas and objectives of the men and women who rose up violently to undo the established system?
- What were the gains and losses for privileged groups and for ordinary people in a generation of war and upheaval?

These are the questions underlying this chapter's examination of the revolutionary era.

## LIBERTY AND EQUALITY

While the economic distress of the French laboring classes and France's outdated social hierarchy played a significant role in determining the course of events in France, certain concepts associated with the new world-view of the Enlightenment were also critical. Indeed, two ideas fueled the revolutionary period in both America and Europe: liberty and equality. What did eighteenth-century politicians and other people mean by liberty and equality, and why were those ideas so radical and revolutionary in their day?

The call for liberty was first of all a call for individual human rights. Even the most enlightened monarchs customarily claimed that it was their duty to regulate what people wrote and believed. Liberals of the revolutionary era protested such controls. They demanded freedom to worship, an end to censorship, and freedom from arbitrary laws and from judges who simply obeyed orders from the government. The Declaration of the Rights of Man, issued at the beginning of the French Revolution, proclaimed, "Liberty consists in being able to do anything that does not harm another person." In the context of the monarchical and absolutist forms of government then dominating Europe, this was a truly radical idea.

The call for liberty was also a call for a new kind of government. Revolutionary liberals believed that the people were **sovereign**—that is, that the people alone had the authority to make laws limiting an individual's freedom of action. In practice this system of government meant choosing legislators who represented the people and were accountable to them.

Equality was a more ambiguous idea. Eighteenth-century liberals argued that, in theory, *all* citizens should have identical rights and civil liberties, regardless of birth. However, liberals accepted some well-established distinctions.

First, most eighteenth-century liberals were *men* of their times, and they generally shared with other men the belief that equality between men and women was neither practical nor desirable. Women played an important political role in the French Revolution at several points, but the men of the French Revolution limited formal political rights—the right to vote, to run for office, to participate in government—to men.

Second, liberals never believed that everyone should be equal economically. Quite the contrary. As Thomas Jefferson wrote in an early draft of the American Declaration of Independence (before he changed "property" to the more noble-sounding "happiness"), everyone was equal in "the pursuit of property." Jefferson and other liberals certainly did not expect equal success in that pursuit. Great differences in wealth and income between rich and poor were perfectly acceptable to liberals. The essential point was that everyone should legally have an equal chance.

In eighteenth-century Europe, however, such equality of opportunity was a truly revolutionary idea. Society was still legally divided into groups with special privileges, such as the nobility and the clergy, and groups with special burdens, such as the peasantry. And in most countries, various middle-class groups—professionals, business people, townspeople, and craftsmen—enjoyed privileges that allowed them to monopolize all sorts of economic activity. Liberals criticized not economic inequality itself but this kind of economic inequality based on legal distinctions among different social groups.

Although the ideas of liberty and equality—the central ideas of classical liberalism—had firm roots in Western history dating back to ancient Greece and the Judeo-Christian tradition, classical liberalism first crystallized at the end of the seventeenth century and during the Enlightenment. Liberal ideas reflected the Enlightenment's stress on human dignity, personal liberty, and human happiness on earth and its faith in science, rationality, and progress.

Certain English and French thinkers were mainly responsible for joining the Enlightenment's concern for personal freedom and legal equality to a theoretical justification of liberal self-government. The two most important were John Locke and the baron de Montesquieu. Locke maintained that England's long political tradition rested on "the rights of Englishmen" and on representative government through Parliament. He argued that if a government oversteps its proper function of protecting the natural rights of life, liberty, and private property, it becomes a tyranny. Montesquieu was also inspired by English constitutional history. He, too, believed that powerful "intermediary groups"—such as the judicial nobility of which he was a proud member—offered the best defense of liberty against despotism.

The belief that representative institutions could defend their liberty and interests appealed powerfully to well-educated, prosperous, middle-class groups, which historians have traditionally labeled as the **bourgeoisie.** Yet liberal ideas about individual rights and political freedom also appealed to much of the hereditary nobility, at least in western Europe. **Representative government** did not mean democracy, which liberal thinkers tended to equate with mob rule. Rather, they envisioned voting for representatives as being restricted to those who owned property—those with "a stake in society." England had shown the way. After 1688 it had combined a parliamentary system and considerable individual liberty with a restricted franchise and unquestionable aristocratic pre-eminence. In the course of the eighteenth century, many leading

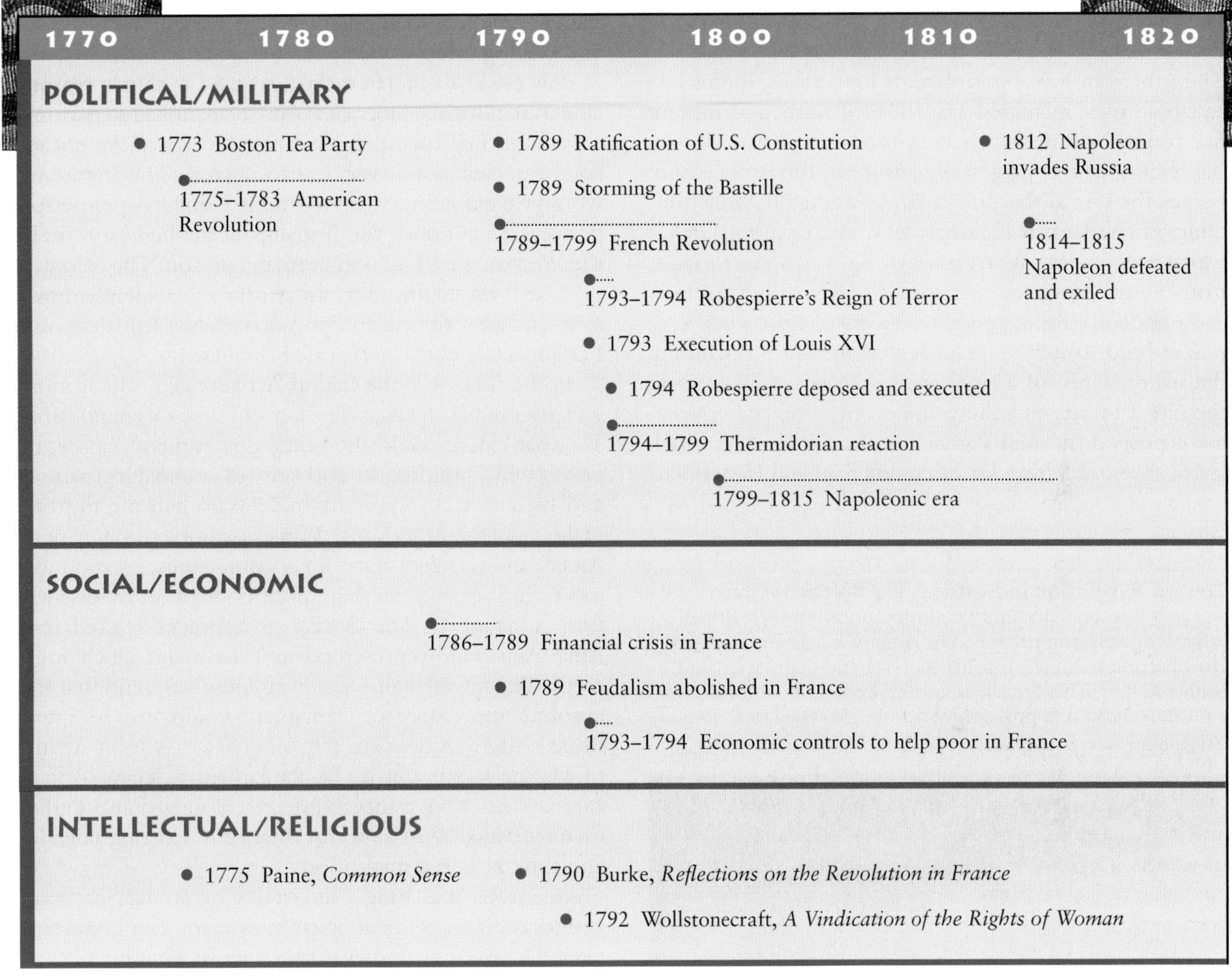


French nobles, led by a judicial nobility inspired by the doctrines of Montesquieu, were increasingly eager to follow the English example. Thus eighteenth-century liberalism in western Europe found broad support among the prosperous, well-educated elites in both the nobility and the bourgeoisie.

What liberalism lacked from the beginning was strong popular support. At least two reasons account for the people's wary attitude. First, for common people the great questions were not theoretical and political but immediate and economic; getting enough to eat was a crucial challenge. Moreover, some of the traditional practices and institutions that liberals wanted to abolish were dear to peasants and urban workers, such as the regulation of food prices. These differences in outlook and well-being led to misunderstandings and conflicts for both groups in the revolutionary era.

## THE AMERICAN REVOLUTIONARY ERA (1775–1789)

The era of liberal political revolution began in the New World. The thirteen mainland colonies of British North America revolted against their home country and then succeeded in establishing a new unified government.

The American revolutionaries believed that they were demanding only the traditional rights of English men and women. But those traditional rights were liberal rights, and in the American context they had very strong democratic and popular overtones that made them quite radical. In founding a government firmly based on liberal principles, the Americans set an example that had a forceful impact on Europe and sped up political development there.

## The Origins of the Revolution

The American Revolution had its immediate origins in a squabble over increased taxes. The British government had fought and decisively won the Seven Years' War on the strength of its professional army and navy. The high cost of the war to the British, however, had led to a doubling of the British national debt. Anticipating further expense defending its recently conquered western lands from Native American uprisings, the British government in London set about reorganizing the empire with a series of bold, largely unprecedented measures, including the maintenance of a large army in North America and the direct taxation of the colonies. In 1765 the government pushed through Parliament the Stamp Act, which levied taxes on a long list of commercial and legal documents, diplomas, pamphlets, newspapers, almanacs, dice, and playing cards.

**Toward Revolution in Boston** The Boston Tea Party was only one of many angry confrontations between British officials and Boston patriots. On January 27, 1774, an angry crowd seized a British customs collector and then tarred and feathered him. This French engraving from 1784 commemorates the defiant and provocative action. *(The Granger Collection, New York)*

This effort to increase taxes seemed perfectly reasonable to the British. Americans were being asked to pay only a share of their own defense costs. Moreover, Americans had been paying only very low local taxes. The Stamp Act would have doubled taxes to about 2 shillings per person per year. In contrast, the British paid the highest taxes in the Western world—26 shillings per person. The colonists protested the Stamp Act vigorously and violently, however, and after rioting and boycotts against British goods, Parliament reluctantly repealed the new tax.

As the fury over the Stamp Act revealed, much more was involved than taxes. The key questions were political. To what extent could the home government reassert its power while limiting the authority of colonial legislatures and their elected representatives? Who had the right to make laws for Americans? While a troubled majority of Americans searched hard for a compromise, some radicals began to proclaim that "taxation without representation is tyranny." The British government replied that Americans were represented in Parliament, albeit indirectly (like most English people themselves), and that the absolute supremacy of Parliament could not be questioned. Many Americans felt otherwise. As John Adams of Massachusetts put it, "A Parliament of Great Britain can have no more rights to tax the colonies than a Parliament of Paris." At risk were Americans' existing liberties and time-honored institutions.

Americans had long exercised a great deal of independence. The colonial assemblies made the important laws. The right to vote was much more widespread than in England. In many parts of colonial Massachusetts, for example, as many as 95 percent of the adult males could vote. Moreover, greater political equality was matched by greater social and economic equality. Neither a hereditary nobility nor a hereditary serf population existed, though the slavery of the Americas consigned blacks to a legally oppressed caste. Independent farmers were the largest group in the country and set much of its tone. In short, the colonial experience had slowly formed a people who felt themselves separate and distinct from the home country, and the controversies over taxation intensified those feelings.

The efforts of Britain to restructure its empire and increase direct control were mirrored in Latin America. There the Spanish monarchy tightened control over its colonies, exacerbating tensions between *peninsulares* (Spaniards), who monopolized the imperial bureaucracy, and *creoles* (people of Spanish blood born in the New World). These tensions set the stage for the indepen-

**The Signing of the Declaration of Independence, July 4, 1776** John Trumbull's famous painting shows the dignity and determination of America's revolutionary leaders. An extraordinarily talented group, they succeeded in rallying popular support without losing power to more radical forces in the process. *(The Granger Collection, New York)*

dence movements of the early nineteenth century (see Chapter 28).

In 1773 the dispute over taxes and representation flared up again. The British government had given the financially hard-pressed East India Company a monopoly on the tea trade, which excluded colonial merchants. The colonists were quick to protest.

In Boston men disguised as Indians had a rowdy "tea party" and threw the company's tea into the harbor. Parliament responded by closing the port of Boston and greatly expanding the royal governor's power. County conventions in Massachusetts protested vehemently, and other colonial assemblies joined in the denunciations. In September 1774 the First Continental Congress met in Philadelphia, where the more radical members argued successfully against concessions to the Crown. Compromise was also rejected by the British Parliament, and in April 1775 fighting began in Massachusetts, at Lexington and Concord.

## Independence

The fighting spread, and the colonists moved slowly but inevitably toward open rebellion and a declaration of independence. The uncompromising attitude of the British government and its use of German mercenaries went a long way toward dissolving long-standing loyalties to the home country and rivalries among the separate colonies. *Common Sense* (1775), a brilliant attack by the recently arrived English radical Thomas Paine (1737–1809), also mobilized public opinion in favor of independence. A runaway bestseller, Paine's tract ridiculed the idea of a small island ruling a great continent and called for freedom and republican government.

On July 4, 1776, the Second Continental Congress adopted the Declaration of Independence, which boldly listed the tyrannical acts committed by King George III (r. 1760–1820) and confidently proclaimed the natural rights of mankind and the sovereignty of the American states. Sometimes called the world's greatest political editorial, the Declaration of Independence in effect universalized the traditional rights of English people and made them the rights of all mankind. It stated "that all men are created equal; that they are endowed by their Creator with certain unalienable rights; that among these are life, liberty, and the pursuit of happiness." No other American political document has ever caused such excitement, either at home or abroad.

Many American families remained loyal to Britain; many others divided bitterly. After the Declaration of Independence, the conflict often took the form of a civil war pitting patriots against those who remained loyal to the king. The Loyalists tended to be wealthy and politically moderate. Many patriots, too, were wealthy—individuals such as John Hancock and George Washington—but willingly allied themselves with farmers and artisans in a broad coalition. The broad social base of the revolutionaries tended to make the liberal revolution democratic. State governments extended the right to vote to many more men in the course of the war and re-established themselves as republics.

On the international scene the French sympathized with the rebels and supplied guns and gunpowder from the beginning. They wanted revenge for the humiliating defeats of the Seven Years' War. By 1777 French volunteers were arriving in Virginia, and a dashing young nobleman, the marquis de Lafayette (1757–1834), quickly became one of Washington's most trusted generals. In 1778 the French government offered a formal alliance, and in 1779 and 1780 the Spanish and Dutch declared war on Britain.

Thus by 1780 Great Britain was engaged in an imperial war against most of Europe as well as the thirteen colonies. In these circumstances, and in the face of severe reverses in India, in the West Indies, and at Yorktown in Virginia, a new British government decided to cut its losses. American negotiators in Paris were receptive. They feared that France wanted a treaty that would bottle up the new United States east of the Allegheny Mountains and give British holdings west of the Alleghenies to France's ally, Spain. Thus the American negotiators separated themselves from their French allies and accepted the extraordinarily favorable terms Britain offered.

By the Treaty of Paris of 1783 Britain recognized the independence of the thirteen colonies and ceded all its territory between the Allegheny Mountains and the Mississippi River to the Americans. Out of the bitter rivalries of the Old World, the Americans snatched dominion over almost half a continent.

## Framing the Constitution

The liberal program of the American Revolution was consolidated by the federal Constitution, the Bill of Rights, and the creation of a national republic. Assembling in Philadelphia in the summer of 1787, the delegates to the Constitutional Convention were determined to end the period of economic depression, social uncertainty, and very weak central government that had followed independence. In secret deliberations the delegates decided to grant the federal, or central, government important powers: regulation of domestic and foreign trade, the right to levy taxes, and the means to enforce its laws.

Strong rule would be placed squarely in the context of representative self-government. Senators and congressmen would be the lawmaking delegates of the voters, and the president of the republic would be an elected official. The central government would operate in Montesquieu's framework of **checks and balances.** The executive, legislative, and judicial branches would systematically balance one another. The power of the federal government would in turn be checked by the powers of the individual states.

When the draft constitution was presented to the states for ratification, a great public debate began. The opponents of the proposed constitution—the Antifederalists—charged that the new document took too much power from the individual states, made the federal government too strong, and endangered the personal liberties and individual freedoms for which they had just fought. In order to overcome these objections, the Federalists solemnly promised to spell out these basic freedoms as soon as the new Constitution was adopted. The result was the first ten amendments to the Constitution, the Bill of Rights, passed in March 1789. These amendments formed an effective safeguard for the individual. Most of them—trial by jury, due process of law, right to assemble, freedom from unreasonable search—had their origins in English law and the English Bill of Rights of 1689. Others—the freedoms of speech, the press, and religion—reflected natural-law theory and the American experience.

The American Constitution and the Bill of Rights exemplified the great strengths and the limits of what came to be called **classical liberalism.** Liberty meant individual freedoms and political safeguards. Liberty also meant representative government but did not necessarily mean democracy, with its principle of one person, one vote. Equality—slaves excepted—meant equality before the law, not equality of political participation or wealth. The radicalism of liberal revolution in America was primarily legal and political, *not* economic or social.

# THE FRENCH REVOLUTION (1789–1791)

No country felt the consequences of the American Revolution more directly than France. Hundreds of French officers served in America and were inspired by the experience. The most famous of these, the young and impressionable marquis de Lafayette, left home as a great aristocrat determined to fight only France's traditional foe, England. He returned with a love of liberty and firm republican convictions. French intellectuals and publicists engaged in passionate analysis of the federal and state constitutions. The American Revolution undeniably hastened upheaval in France.

Yet the French Revolution did not mirror the American example. It was more radical and more complex, more influential and more controversial, more loved and more hated. For Europeans and most of the rest of the world, it was the great revolution of the eighteenth century, *the* revolution that opened the modern era in politics.

## The Breakdown of the Old Order

Like the American Revolution, the French Revolution had its immediate origins in the financial difficulties of the government. With both the high court of Paris—the Parlement—and public opinion successfully resisting increased taxes, the government was forced to finance all of its enormous expenditures during the American war with borrowed money. As a result, the national debt and the annual budget deficit soared. By the 1780s fully 50 percent of France's annual budget went for interest on the ever-increasing debt. Another 25 percent went to maintain the military, while 6 percent was absorbed by the costly and extravagant king and his court at Versailles. Less than 20 percent of the entire national budget was available for the productive functions of the state, such as transportation and general administration. This was an impossible financial situation.

One way out would have been for the government to declare partial bankruptcy, forcing its creditors to accept greatly reduced payments on the debt. Both the Spanish and the French monarchies had done this in earlier times. By the 1780s, however, the French debt was being held by an army of aristocratic and bourgeois creditors, and the French monarchy, though absolute in theory, had become far too weak for such a drastic and unpopular action.

Nor could the king and his ministers, unlike modern governments, print money and create inflation to cover their deficits. Unlike England and Holland, which had far larger national debts relative to their populations, France had no central bank, no paper currency, and no means of creating credit. French money was good gold coin. Therefore, when a depressed economy and a lack of public confidence made it increasingly difficult for the government to obtain new gold loans in 1786, it had no alternative but to try increasing taxes. But since France's tax system was unfair and out-of-date, increased revenues were possible only through fundamental reforms. Such reforms, which would affect all groups in France's complex and fragmented society, opened a Pandora's box of social and political demands.

## Legal Orders and Social Realities

As in the Middle Ages, France's 25 million inhabitants were still legally divided into three orders, or **estates**—the Roman Catholic clergy, the nobility, and everyone else. As the nation's first estate, the clergy numbered about 100,000 and had important privileges. It owned about 10 percent of the land and paid only a "voluntary gift," rather than regular taxes, to the government every five years. Moreover, the church levied a tax (the tithe) on landowners, which averaged somewhat less than 10 percent. Much of the church's income was actually drained away from local parishes by political appointees and worldly aristocrats at the top of the church hierarchy—to the intense dissatisfaction of the poor parish priests.

The second legally defined estate consisted of some 400,000 noblemen and noblewomen. The nobles owned outright about 25 percent of the land and were taxed very lightly. Moreover, nobles continued to enjoy certain **manorial rights,** or privileges of lordship, that dated back to medieval times and allowed them to tax the peasantry for their own profit. They did this by means of exclusive rights to hunt and fish, village monopolies on baking bread and pressing grapes for wine, fees for justice, and a host of other "useful privileges." In addition, nobles had "honorific privileges," such as the right to precedence on public occasions and the right to wear a sword. These rights conspicuously proclaimed the nobility's legal superiority and exalted social position.

Everyone else was a commoner, legally a member of the third estate. A few commoners—prosperous merchants or lawyers and officials—were well educated and rich, and might even buy up manorial rights as profitable investments. Many more commoners were urban artisans and unskilled day laborers. The vast majority of the third estate consisted of the peasants and agricultural workers in the countryside. Thus the third estate was a conglomeration of vastly different social groups united only by their shared legal status as distinct from the nobility and clergy.

In discussing the long-term origins of the French Revolution, historians have long focused on growing tensions between the nobility and the comfortable members of the third estate, usually known as the bourgeoisie, or middle class. A dominant historical interpretation, which held sway for at least two generations, maintained that the bourgeoisie was basically united by economic position and class interest. Aided by a general economic expansion, the middle class grew rapidly in the eighteenth century, tripling to about 2.3 million persons, or about 8 percent of France's population. Increasing in size, wealth, culture, and self-confidence, this rising bourgeoisie became progressively exasperated by archaic "feudal" laws and customs that restrained the economy and their needs and aspirations. As a result, the French bourgeoisie eventually rose up to lead the entire third estate in a great social revolution, a revolution that destroyed feudal privileges and established a capitalist order based on individualism and a market economy.

In recent years a flood of new research has challenged these accepted views. Above all, revisionist historians have questioned the existence of a growing social conflict between a progressive capitalistic bourgeoisie and a reactionary feudal nobility in eighteenth-century France. Rather than standing as unified blocs against each other, nobility and bourgeoisie—both fragmented and ridden with internal rivalries—formed two parallel social ladders increasingly linked together at the top by wealth, marriage, and Enlightenment culture.

Revisionist historians stress three developments in particular. First, the nobility remained a fluid and relatively open order. Throughout the eighteenth century substantial numbers of successful commoners continued to seek and obtain noble status through government service and purchase of expensive positions conferring nobility. Second, key sections of the nobility were no less liberal than the middle class, and both groups generally supported the judicial opposition to the government. Third, the nobility and the bourgeoisie were not really at odds in the economic sphere. Both looked to investment in land and to government service as their preferred activities, and the goal of the merchant capitalist was to gain enough wealth to live nobly as a large landowner. At the same time, wealthy nobles often acted as aggressive capitalists, investing especially in mining, metallurgy, and foreign trade.

The revisionists have clearly shaken the interpretation of the bourgeoisie and the nobility as inevitably locked in growing conflict before the French Revolution. But in stressing the similarities between the two groups, especially at the top, revisionists have also reinforced the view, long maintained by historians, that the Old Regime had ceased to correspond with social reality by the 1780s. Legally, society was still based on rigid orders inherited from the Middle Ages. But France had moved far toward being a society based on wealth and education, where an emerging elite that included both aristocratic and bourgeois notables was frustrated by a bureaucratic monarchy that continued to claim the right to absolute power.

## The Formation of the National Assembly

The Revolution was under way by 1787, though no one could have realized what was to follow. Spurred by a depressed economy and falling tax receipts, Louis XVI's minister of finance convinced the king to call an assembly of notables to gain support for a general tax on all landed property. The assembled notables, mainly important noblemen and high-ranking clergy, responded that such sweeping tax changes required the approval of the Estates General, the representative body of all three estates, which had not met since 1614.

Facing imminent bankruptcy, the king tried to reassert his authority. He dismissed the notables and established new taxes by decree. In stirring language the Parlement of Paris promptly declared the royal initiative null and void. When the king tried to exile the judges, a tremendous wave of protest swept the country. Frightened investors also refused to advance more loans to the state. Finally, in July 1788, a beaten Louis XVI bowed to public opinion and called for a spring session of the Estates General. Absolute monarchy was collapsing.

What would replace it? Throughout the unprecedented election campaign of 1788 and 1789 that question excited France. All across the country clergy, nobles, and commoners met together in their respective orders to draft petitions for change and to elect their respective delegates to the Estates General. The local assemblies of the clergy chose two-thirds of the delegates from among the poorer parish priests, who were commoners by birth. Among the nobles, already badly split by wealth and education, a conservative majority was drawn from the poorer and more numerous provincial nobility. But fully one-third of the nobility's representatives were liberals committed to major changes.

As for the third estate, there was great popular participation in the elections. Almost all male commoners ages twenty-five years and older had the right to vote. Still, most of the representatives finally selected were well-educated, prosperous lawyers and government officials. There were no delegates elected from the great mass of laboring poor—the peasants and also the urban artisans.

The petitions for change coming from the three estates showed a surprising degree of consensus on most issues. There was general agreement that royal absolutism should give way to constitutional monarchy, in which the Estates General, meeting regularly, should pass all laws and taxes; that individual liberties should be guaranteed by law; and that general reforms, such as the abolition of internal tariffs, should be introduced to promote economic development. The striking similarities in the grievance petitions of the clergy, nobility, and third estate reflected the broad commitment of France's educated elite to liberalism.

Yet an increasingly bitter quarrel undermined this consensus during the intense electoral campaign. *How* would the Estates General vote, and precisely *who* would lead in the political reorganization that was generally desired? The Estates General of 1614 had sat as three separate houses. Any action had required the agreement of at least two branches, a requirement that had virtually guaranteed control by the nobility and the clergy. The aristocratic Parlement of Paris ruled that the Estates General should once again sit separately. Certain middle-class intellectuals and some liberal nobles demanded instead a single assembly dominated by representatives of the third estate. The government agreed that the third estate should have as many delegates as the clergy and the nobility combined. When it then rendered this act meaningless by upholding voting by separate order, middle-class leaders saw fresh evidence of an aristocratic conspiracy.

The Estates General opened in May 1789 at Versailles with twelve hundred delegates. The estates were almost immediately deadlocked. Delegates of the third estate refused to transact any business until the king ordered the clergy and nobility to sit with them in a single body. Finally, after a six-week war of nerves, the third estate on June 17 voted to call itself the National Assembly. On June 20 the delegates of the third estate, excluded from their hall because of "repairs," moved to a large indoor tennis court. There they swore the Oath of the Tennis Court, pledging not to disband until they had written a new constitution.

**The Oath of the Tennis Court** This painting, based on an unfinished work by Jacques-Louis David (1748–1825), enthusiastically celebrates the revolutionary rupture of June 20, 1789. Locked out of their assembly hall at Versailles and joined by some sympathetic priests, the delegates of the third estate have moved to an indoor tennis court and are swearing never to disband until they have written a new constitution and put France on a firm foundation. *(Réunion des Musées Nationaux/Art Resource, NY)*

The indecisive king's actions were then somewhat contradictory. On June 23 he made a conciliatory speech urging reforms to a joint session and ordered the three estates to meet together. Then, apparently following the advice of relatives and court nobles that he dissolve the Estates General by force, the king called an army of eighteen thousand troops toward Versailles. On July 11 he dismissed his finance minister and his other more liberal ministers. Having resigned himself to bankruptcy, Louis XVI belatedly sought to reassert his historic "divine right" to rule. The middle-class delegates and their allies from the liberal nobility had done their best, but they were resigned to being disbanded at bayonet point. One third-estate delegate reassured a worried colleague, "You won't hang—you'll only have to go back home."[1]

## The Revolt of the Poor and the Oppressed

While the delegates of the third estate pressed for symbolic equality with the nobility and clergy in a single legislative body at Versailles, economic hardship gripped the common people of France in a tightening vise. Grain was the basis of the diet of ordinary people in the eighteenth century, and in 1788 the harvest had been extremely poor. The price of bread began to soar. By July 1789 it had climbed as high as 8 sous per pound in the provinces. In Paris, where bread was regularly subsidized by the government in an attempt to prevent popular unrest, the price rose to 4 sous, a price at which a laborer with a wife and three children had to spend most of his wages to buy the family's bread.

Harvest failure and high bread prices unleashed a classic economic depression of the preindustrial age. With food so expensive and with so much uncertainty, the demand for manufactured goods collapsed, resulting in thousands of artisans and small traders being thrown out of work. By the end of 1789 almost half of the French people were in need of relief. In Paris perhaps 150,000 of the city's 600,000 people were without work in July 1789.

Against this background of poverty and ongoing political crisis, the people of Paris entered decisively onto the revolutionary stage. They believed in a general, though ill-defined, way that the economic distress had human causes. They believed that they should have steady work and enough bread at fair prices to survive. Specifically, they feared that the dismissal of the king's moderate finance minister would put them at the mercy of aristocratic landowners and grain speculators. Rumors that the king's troops would sack the city began to fill the air. Angry crowds formed, and passionate voices urged action. On July 13 the people began to seize arms for the defense of the city, and on July 14 several hundred people marched to the Bastille to search for gunpowder.

The governor of the medieval fortress-prison refused to hand over the powder, panicked, and ordered his men to fire, killing ninety-eight people attempting to enter. Cannon were brought to batter the main gate, and fighting continued until the prison surrendered. The governor of the prison was later hacked to death, and his head was stuck on a pike and paraded through the streets. The next day a committee of citizens appointed the marquis de Lafayette commander of the city's armed forces. Paris was lost to the king, who was forced to recall the finance minister and disperse his troops. The popular uprising had saved the National Assembly.

As the delegates resumed their long-winded and inconclusive debates at Versailles, the people in the countryside sent them a radical and unmistakable message. Sparked by rumors of vagabonds and outlaws roaming the countryside, called the **Great Fear** by contemporaries, peasants all across France began to rise in spontaneous, violent, and effective insurrection against their lords. Neither middle-class landowners nor the larger, more prosperous farmers were spared. Peasants seized forests, and taxes went unpaid. Rebellion raced through the countryside.

Faced with chaos yet afraid to call on the king to restore order, some liberal nobles and middle-class delegates at Versailles responded to peasant demands with a surprise maneuver on the night of August 4, 1789. The duke of Aiguillon, one of France's greatest noble landowners, declared that

> *in several provinces the whole people forms a kind of league for the destruction of the manor houses, the ravaging of the lands, and especially for the seizure of the archives where the title deeds to feudal properties are kept. It seeks to throw off at last a yoke that has for many centuries weighted it down.*[2]

He urged equality in taxation and the elimination of feudal dues. In the end, all the old exactions imposed on the peasants—serfdom where it still existed, village monopolies, the right to make peasants work on the roads, and a host of other dues—were abolished. They never paid feudal dues again. Thus the French peasantry, which already owned about 30 percent of all the land, achieved a great and unprecedented victory in the early days of revolutionary upheaval. Henceforth, the French peasants would seek mainly to protect and consolidate their triumph, becoming a force for order and stability.

**Storming the Bastille** This representation by an untrained contemporary artist shows civilians and members of the Paris militia—the "conquerors of the Bastille"—on the attack. This successful action had enormous practical and symbolic significance, and July 14 has long been France's most important national holiday. *(Photos12.com—ARJ)*

## A Limited Monarchy

The National Assembly moved forward. On August 27, 1789, it issued the Declaration of the Rights of Man, which stated, "Men are born and remain free and equal in rights." The declaration also maintained that mankind's natural rights are "liberty, property, security, and resistance to oppression." As for law, "it is an expression of the general will; all citizens have the right to concur personally or through their representatives in its formation. . . . Free expression of thoughts and opinions is one of the most precious rights of mankind: every citizen may therefore speak, write, and publish freely." In short, this clarion call of the liberal revolutionary ideal guaranteed equality before the law, representative government for a sovereign people, and individual freedom. This revolutionary credo, only two pages long, was propagandized throughout France and the rest of Europe and around the world.

Moving beyond general principles to draft a constitution proved difficult. The questions of how much power the king should retain led to another deadlock. Once again the decisive answer came from the poor—in this instance, the poor women of Paris.

Women customarily bought the food and managed the poor family's slender resources. In Paris great numbers of women also worked for wages. In the general economic crisis, increasing unemployment and hunger put tremendous pressure on household managers, and the result was another popular explosion.

On October 5 some seven thousand desperate women marched the twelve miles from Paris to Versailles to demand action. This great crowd invaded the National

Assembly, "armed with scythes, sticks and pikes." One tough old woman directing a large group of younger women defiantly shouted into the debate, "Who's that talking down there? Make the chatterbox shut up. That's not the point: the point is that we want bread."[3] Hers was the genuine voice of the people, essential to any understanding of the French Revolution.

The women invaded the royal apartments, slaughtered some of the royal bodyguards, and furiously searched for the queen, Marie Antoinette, who was widely despised for her lavish spending and supposedly immoral behavior. "We are going to cut off her head, tear out her heart, fry her liver, and that won't be the end of it," they shouted, surging through the palace in a frenzy. It seems likely that only the intervention of Lafayette and the National Guard saved the royal family. But the only way to calm the disorder was for the king to go and live in Paris, as the crowd demanded. With this victory the women clearly emerged as a major and enduring element in the Parisian revolutionary crowd.[4]

The National Assembly followed the king to Paris, and the next two years, until September 1791, saw the consolidation of the liberal revolution. Under middle-class leadership, the National Assembly abolished the French nobility as a legal order and pushed forward with the creation of a constitutional monarchy, which Louis XVI reluctantly agreed to accept in July 1790. In the final constitution the king remained the head of state, but all lawmaking power was placed in the hands of the National Assembly, elected by the economic upper half of French males.

New laws broadened women's rights to seek divorce, to inherit property, and to obtain financial support from fathers for illegitimate children. But women were not allowed to vote or hold political office. The great majority of comfortable, well-educated males in the National Assembly believed that women should be limited to child raising and domestic duties and should leave politics and most public activities to men. The delegates to the National Assembly also believed that excluding women from politics would free the political system from the harmful effects of the sexual intrigue common at court; and pure, home-focused wives would raise the high-minded sons needed to govern and defend the nation.

The National Assembly replaced the complicated patchwork of historic provinces with eighty-three departments of approximately equal size. It replaced the jumble of weights and measures that varied from province to province with the simple, rational metric system in 1793. It prohibited monopolies, guilds, and workers' combinations, and it abolished barriers to trade within France in the name of economic liberty. Thus the National Assembly applied the critical spirit of the Enlightenment to reform France's laws and institutions completely.

The National Assembly also nationalized the Catholic church's property and abolished monasteries as useless relics of a distant past. The government sold all former church property in an attempt to put the state's finances on a solid footing. Peasants eventually purchased much of this land when it was subdivided. The purchases strengthened their attachment to the revolutionary state. These actions, however, brought the new government into conflict with the Catholic church and with many sincere Christians, especially in the countryside.

Many delegates to the National Assembly, imbued with the rationalism and skepticism of the eighteenth-century philosophes, harbored a deep distrust of popular piety and "superstitious religion." Thus they established a national church and a Civil Constitution of the Clergy, requiring priests to be chosen by voters. In the face of widespread resistance, the National Assembly then required the clergy to take a loyalty oath to the new government. The Catholic clergy became just so many more employees of the state. The pope formally condemned this attempt to subjugate the church. Only half of the priests of France took the oath of allegiance, and confusion and hostility among French Catholics were pervasive. The attempt to remake the Catholic church, like the National Assembly's abolition of guilds and workers' combinations, sharpened the division between the educated classes and the common people that had been emerging in the eighteenth century. This policy toward the church was the revolutionary government's first important failure.

## WORLD WAR AND REPUBLICAN FRANCE (1791–1799)

When Louis XVI accepted the final version of the completed constitution in September 1791, a young and still obscure provincial lawyer and member of the National Assembly named Maximilien Robespierre (1758–1794) evaluated the work of two years and concluded, "The Revolution is over." Robespierre was both right and wrong. He was right in the sense that the most constructive and lasting reforms were in place, but he was wrong in the sense that a much more radical stage lay ahead. New heroes and new ideologies were to emerge in revolutionary wars and international conflict.

## Foreign Reactions and the Beginning of War

The outbreak and progress of the French Revolution produced great excitement and a sharp division of opinion in Europe and the United States. Liberals and radicals saw a mighty triumph of liberty over despotism. In Great Britain especially, they hoped that the French example would lead to a fundamental reordering of the political system that had placed Parliament in the hands of the aristocracy and a few wealthy merchants, with the great majority of people having little say in the government. Conservative leaders such as Edmund Burke (1729–1797) were deeply troubled by the aroused spirit of reform. In 1790 Burke published *Reflections on the Revolution in France,* one of the great intellectual defenses of European conservatism. Defending inherited privileges, he glorified the unrepresentative Parliament and predicted that thoroughgoing reform like that occurring in France would lead only to chaos and tyranny. Burke's work sparked vigorous debate.

One passionate rebuttal came from a young writer in London, Mary Wollstonecraft (1759–1797). Born into the middle class, Wollstonecraft was schooled in adversity by a mean-spirited father who beat his wife and squandered his inherited fortune. Determined to be independent in a society that generally expected women of her class to become homebodies and obedient wives, she struggled for years to earn her living as a governess and teacher—practically the only acceptable careers for single, educated women—before attaining success as a translator and author. Incensed by Burke's book, Wollstonecraft immediately wrote a blistering, widely read attack, *A Vindication of the Rights of Man* (1790).

Then she made a daring intellectual leap. She developed for the first time the logical implications of natural-law philosophy in her masterpiece, *A Vindication of the Rights of Woman* (1792). To fulfill the still-unrealized potential of the French Revolution and to eliminate the sexual inequality she had felt so keenly, she demanded that

> *the Rights of Women be respected . . . [and] JUSTICE for one-half of the human race. . . . It is time to effect a revolution in female manners, time to restore to them their lost dignity, and make them, as part of the human species, labor, by reforming themselves, to reform the world.*

Setting high standards for women, Wollstonecraft advocated rigorous coeducation, which would make women better wives and mothers, good citizens, and even economically independent people. Women could manage businesses and enter politics if only men would give them the chance. Men themselves would benefit from women's rights, for Wollstonecraft believed that "the two sexes mutually corrupt and improve each other."[5] Wollstonecraft's analysis testified to the power of the Revolution to excite and inspire outside France. Paralleling ideas put forth independently in France by Olympe de Gouges (1748–1793), a self-taught writer and woman of the people (see the feature "Listening to the Past: Revolution and Women's Rights" on pages 726–727), Wollstonecraft's work marked the birth of the modern women's movement for equal rights, and it was ultimately very influential.

The kings and nobles of continental Europe, who had at first welcomed the Revolution in France as weakening a competing power, began to feel threatened. At their courts they listened to the diatribes of great court nobles who had fled France and were urging intervention in France's affairs. When Louis XVI and Marie Antoinette were arrested and returned to Paris after trying unsuccessfully to slip out of France in June 1791, the monarchs of Austria and Prussia, in the Declaration of Pillnitz, declared their willingness to intervene in France in certain circumstances.

But the crowned heads of Europe did not deter the revolutionary spirit in France. When the National Assembly disbanded, it decreed that none of its members would be eligible for election to the new Legislative Assembly. This meant that when the new representative body convened in October 1791, it had a different character. The great majority of the legislators were still prosperous, well-educated, middle-class men, but they were younger and less cautious than their predecessors. Loosely allied and known as **Jacobins,** after the name of their political club, the representatives to the Legislative Assembly were passionately committed to liberal revolution.

The Jacobins increasingly lumped "useless aristocrats" and "despotic monarchs" together and easily whipped themselves into a patriotic fury with bombastic oratory. If the courts of Europe were attempting to incite a war of kings against France, then "we will incite a war of people against kings. . . . Ten million Frenchmen, kindled by the fire of liberty, armed with the sword, with reason, with eloquence would be able to change the face of the world and make the tyrants tremble on their thrones."[6] In April 1792 France declared war on Francis II, the Habsburg monarch.

France's crusade against tyranny went poorly at first. Prussia joined Austria in the Austrian Netherlands (present-day Belgium), and French forces broke and fled at their

FRENCH DEMOCRATS surprizing the Royal Runaways.

**The Capture of Louis XVI, June 1791** This English cartoon satirizes the royal family's disastrous attempt to sneak out of France. Recognized and arrested only a few miles from safety across the Belgian border, Louis XVI appeared guilty of treason to many of the French. The radicalization of the Revolution accelerated. *(Courtesy of the Trustees of the British Museum)*

first encounter with armies of this First Coalition. The road to Paris lay open, and it is possible that only conflict between the eastern monarchs over the division of Poland saved France from defeat.

Military reversals and Austro-Prussian threats caused a wave of patriotic fervor to sweep France. In this supercharged wartime atmosphere rumors of treason by the king and queen spread in Paris. On August 10, 1792, a revolutionary crowd captured the royal palace at the Tuileries after heavy fighting. The king and his family fled for their lives to the nearby Legislative Assembly, which suspended the king from all his functions, imprisoned him, and called for a new National Convention to be elected by universal male suffrage. Monarchy in France was on its deathbed, mortally wounded by war and popular upheaval.

## The Second Revolution

The fall of the monarchy marked a rapid radicalization of the Revolution, a phase that historians often call the **second revolution.** Louis's imprisonment was followed by the September Massacres. Wild stories seized the city that imprisoned counter-revolutionary aristocrats and priests were plotting with the allied invaders. As a result, angry crowds invaded the prisons of Paris and summarily slaughtered half of the men and women they found. In late September 1792 the new, popularly elected National Convention proclaimed France a republic.

The republic sought to create a new popular culture, fashioning compelling symbols that broke with the past and glorified the new order. It adopted a brand-new revolutionary calendar, which eliminated saints' days and renamed the days and the months after the seasons of the year. The republic energetically promoted broad, open-air, democratic festivals that sought to redirect the people's traditional enthusiasm for Catholic religious celebrations to secular holidays. Instilling republican virtue and a love of nation, these spectacles were less successful in villages than in cities, where popular interest in politics was greater and Catholicism was weaker.

All of the members of the National Convention were Jacobins and republicans, and the great majority continued to come from the well-educated middle class. But the Convention was increasingly divided into two bitterly competitive groups—the **Girondists,** named after a department in southwestern France, and **the Mountain,** led by Robespierre and another young lawyer, Georges Jacques Danton. The Mountain was so called because its members sat on the uppermost left-hand benches of the assembly hall.

This division was clearly apparent after the National Convention overwhelmingly convicted Louis XVI of treason. By a narrow majority the Convention then unconditionally sentenced him to death in January 1793. Louis died with tranquil dignity on the newly invented guillotine.

Both the Girondists and the Mountain were determined to continue the "war against tyranny." After

## THE FRENCH REVOLUTION

| | |
|---|---|
| **May 5, 1789** | Estates General convene at Versailles. |
| **June 17, 1789** | Third estate declares itself the National Assembly. |
| **June 20, 1789** | Oath of the Tennis Court is sworn. |
| **July 14, 1789** | Storming of the Bastille occurs. |
| **July–August 1789** | Great Fear ravages the countryside. |
| **August 4, 1789** | National Assembly abolishes feudal privileges. |
| **August 27, 1789** | National Assembly issues Declaration of the Rights of Man. |
| **October 5, 1789** | Women march on Versailles and force royal family to return to Paris. |
| **November 1789** | National Assembly confiscates church lands. |
| **July 1790** | Civil Constitution of the Clergy establishes a national church.<br>Louis XVI reluctantly agrees to accept a constitutional monarchy. |
| **June 1791** | Royal family is arrested while attempting to flee France. |
| **August 1791** | Austria and Prussia issue the Declaration of Pillnitz. |
| **April 1792** | France declares war on Austria. |
| **August 1792** | Parisian mob attacks the palace and takes Louis XVI prisoner. |
| **September 1792** | September Massacres occur.<br>National Convention declares France a republic and abolishes monarchy. |
| **January 1793** | Louis XVI is executed. |
| **February 1793** | France declares war on Britain, Holland, and Spain.<br>Revolts take place in some provincial cities. |
| **March 1793** | Bitter struggle occurs in the National Convention between Girondists and the Mountain. |
| **April–June 1793** | Robespierre and the Mountain organize the Committee of Public Safety and arrest Girondist leaders. |
| **September 1793** | Price controls are instituted to aid the sans-culottes and mobilize the war effort. |
| **1793–1794** | Reign of Terror darkens Paris and the provinces. |
| **Spring 1794** | French armies are victorious on all fronts. |
| **July 1794** | Robespierre is executed.<br>Thermidorian reaction begins. |
| **1795–1799** | Directory rules. |
| **1795** | Economic controls are abolished, and suppression of the sans-culottes begins. |
| **1797** | Napoleon defeats Austrian armies in Italy and returns triumphant to Paris. |
| **1798** | Austria, Great Britain, and Russia form the Second Coalition against France. |
| **1799** | Napoleon overthrows the Directory and seizes power. |

stopping the Prussians at the indecisive Battle of Valmy on September 20, 1792, republican armies successfully invaded Savoy and the German Rhineland. To the north the revolutionary armies won their first major battle at Jemappes and by November 1792 were occupying the entire Austrian Netherlands. Everywhere they went, French armies of occupation chased the princes, "abolished feudalism," and found support among some peasants and middle-class people.

But the French armies also lived off the land, requisitioning food and supplies and plundering local treasures. The liberators looked increasingly like foreign invaders. In February 1793 the National Convention, at war with Austria and Prussia, declared war on Britain, Holland, and Spain as well. Republican France was now at war with almost all of Europe, a great war that would last almost without interruption until 1815.

As the forces of the First Coalition drove the French from the Austrian Netherlands, peasants in western France revolted against being drafted into the army. They were supported and encouraged in their resistance by devout Catholics, royalists, and foreign agents.

In Paris the quarrelsome National Convention found itself locked in a life-and-death political struggle between the Girondists and the Mountain. Both groups hated privilege and wanted to temper economic liberalism with social concern. Yet personal hatreds ran deep. The Girondists feared a bloody dictatorship by the Mountain, and the Mountain was no less convinced that the more moderate Girondists would turn to conservatives and even royalists in order to retain power. With the middle-class delegates so bitterly divided, the laboring poor of Paris emerged as the decisive political factor.

The laboring men and women of Paris always constituted—along with the peasantry in the summer of 1789—the elemental force that drove the Revolution forward. It was they who had stormed the Bastille, marched on Versailles, driven the king from the Tuileries, and carried out the September Massacres. The petty traders and laboring poor were often known as the **sans-culottes,** "without breeches," because the men wore trousers instead of the knee breeches of the aristocracy and the solid middle class. The immediate interests of the sans-culottes were mainly economic, and in the spring of 1793 rapid inflation, un-

**Contrasting Visions of the Sans-Culottes** The woman on the left, with her playful cat and calm simplicity, suggests how the French sans-culottes saw themselves as democrats and virtuous citizens. The ferocious sans-culotte harpy on the right, a creation of wartime England's vivid counter-revolutionary imagination, screams for more blood, more death: "I am the Goddess of Liberty! Long live the guillotine!" *(Bibliothèque nationale de France)*

employment, and food shortages were again weighing heavily on poor families. Sans-culottes men and women, encouraged by the so-called angry men, were demanding radical political action to guarantee them their daily bread. At first the Mountain joined the Girondists in violently rejecting these demands. But in the face of military defeat, peasant revolt, and hatred of the Girondists, Robespierre's group joined with sans-culottes activists in the city government to engineer a popular uprising, which forced the Convention to arrest thirty-one Girondist deputies for treason on June 2. All power passed to the Mountain.

Robespierre and others from the Mountain joined the recently formed Committee of Public Safety, to which the Convention had given dictatorial power to deal with the national emergency. These developments in Paris triggered revolt in leading provincial cities, such as Lyons and Marseilles, where moderates denounced Paris and demanded a decentralized government. The peasant revolt spread, and the republic's armies were driven back on all fronts. By July 1793 defeat appeared imminent.

## Total War and the Terror

A year later, in July 1794, the Austrian Netherlands and the Rhineland were once again in the hands of conquering French armies, and the First Coalition was falling apart. This remarkable change of fortune was due to the revolutionary government's success in harnessing, for perhaps the first time in history, the explosive forces of a planned economy, revolutionary terror, and modern nationalism in a total war effort.

Robespierre and the Committee of Public Safety advanced with implacable resolution on several fronts in 1793 and 1794. First, they continued to collaborate with the fiercely patriotic and democratic sans-culottes, who retained the common people's traditional faith in fair prices and a moral economic order, distrusting wealthy capitalists and all aristocrats. Thus Robespierre and his coworkers established, as best they could, a **planned economy** with egalitarian social overtones. Rather than let supply and demand determine prices, the government set maximum allowable prices for a host of key products. Though the state was too weak to enforce all its price regulations, it did fix the price of bread in Paris at levels the poor could afford. Bakers were permitted to make only the "bread of equality"—a brown bread made of a mixture of all available flours. White bread and pastries were outlawed as frivolous luxuries. The poor of Paris may not have eaten well, but at least they ate.

They also worked, mainly to produce arms and munitions for the war effort. The government told craftsmen what to produce, nationalized many small workshops, and requisitioned raw materials and grain from the peasants. Seldom if ever before had a government attempted to manage an economy so thoroughly. The second revolution and the ascendancy of the sans-culottes had produced an embryonic emergency socialism, which thoroughly frightened Europe's propertied classes and had great influence on the subsequent development of socialist ideology.

Second, while radical economic measures supplied the poor with bread and the armies with weapons, the Reign of Terror (1793–1794) used revolutionary terror to solidify the home front. Special revolutionary courts responsible only to Robespierre's Committee of Public Safety tried rebels and "enemies of the nation" for political crimes. Drawing on popular, sans-culottes support, these local courts ignored normal legal procedures and judged severely. Some 40,000 French men and women were executed or died in prison. Another 300,000 suspects crowded the prisons.

Robespierre's Reign of Terror was one of the most controversial phases of the French Revolution. Most historians now believe that the Reign of Terror was not directed against any single class but was a political weapon directed impartially against all who might oppose the revolutionary government. For many Europeans of the time, however, the Reign of Terror represented a terrifying perversion of the generous ideals that had existed in 1789.

The third and perhaps most decisive element in the French republic's victory over the First Coalition was its ability to continue drawing on the explosive power of patriotic dedication to a national state and a national mission. This is the essence of modern nationalism, and it was something new in history. With a common language and a common tradition newly reinforced by the ideas of popular sovereignty and democracy, large numbers of French people were stirred by a common loyalty. They developed an intense emotional commitment to the heroic defense of the nation, and they imagined the nation as a great loving family that included all good patriots. Everyone had to participate in the national effort. According to a famous decree of August 23, 1793:

*The young men shall go to battle and the married men shall forge arms. The women shall make tents and clothes, and shall serve in the hospitals; children shall tear rags into lint. The old men will be guided to the public places of the cities to kindle the courage of the young warriors and to preach the unity of the Republic and the hatred of kings.*

Like the wars of religion, war in 1793 was a crusade, a life-and-death struggle between good and evil. This war, however, was fought for a secular, rather than a religious, ideology.

**The Last Roll Call** Prisoners sentenced to death by revolutionary courts listen to an official solemnly reading the names of those selected for immediate execution. After being bound, the prisoners will ride standing up in a small cart through the streets of Paris to the nearby guillotine. As this painting highlights, both women and men were executed for political crimes under the Terror. *(Mansell/TimePix)*

Because all unmarried young men were subject to the draft, the French armed forces swelled to a million men in fourteen armies. A force of this size was unprecedented in the history of European warfare. The soldiers were led by young, impetuous generals who had often risen rapidly from the ranks and personified the opportunities the Revolution seemed to offer gifted sons of the people. These generals used mass attacks at bayonet point by their highly motivated forces to overwhelm the enemy. By the spring of 1794 French armies were victorious on all fronts. The republic was saved.

## The Thermidorian Reaction and the Directory (1794–1799)

The success of the French armies led Robespierre and the Committee of Public Safety to relax the emergency economic controls, but they extended the political Reign of Terror. Their lofty goal was increasingly an ideal democratic republic where justice would reign and there would be neither rich nor poor. Their lowly means were unrestrained despotism and the guillotine, which struck down any who might seriously question the new order. In March 1794, to the horror of many sans-culottes, Robespierre's Terror wiped out many of the angry men, who had been criticizing Robespierre for being soft on the wealthy. Two weeks later several of Robespierre's long-standing collaborators, led by the famous orator Danton, marched up the steps to the guillotine. A strange assortment of radicals and moderates in the Convention, knowing that they might be next, organized a conspiracy. They howled down Robespierre when he tried to speak to the National Convention on 9 Thermidor (July 27, 1794). On the following day, it was Robespierre's turn to be shaved by the revolutionary razor.

As Robespierre's closest supporters followed their leader, France unexpectedly experienced a thorough reaction to the despotism of the Reign of Terror. In a general way this

**Thermidorian reaction** recalled the early days of the Revolution. The respectable middle-class lawyers and professionals who had led the liberal revolution of 1789 reasserted their authority, drawing support from their own class, the provincial cities, and the better-off peasants. The National Convention abolished many economic controls and let prices rise sharply. And all the while wealthy bankers and newly rich speculators celebrated the sudden end of the Terror with an orgy of self-indulgence and ostentatious luxury, an orgy symbolized by the shockingly low-cut gowns that quickly became the rage among their wives and mistresses.

The collapse of economic controls, coupled with runaway inflation, hit the working poor very hard. The gaudy extravagance of the rich wounded their pride. The sans-culottes accepted private property, but they believed passionately in small business, decent wages, and economic justice. Increasingly disorganized after Robespierre purged radical leaders, the common people of Paris finally revolted against the emerging new order in early 1795. The Convention quickly used the army to suppress these insurrections and made no concessions to the poor. In the face of all these catastrophes, the revolutionary fervor of the laboring poor in Paris finally subsided.

In villages and small towns there arose a great cry for peace and a turning toward religion, especially from women, who had seldom experienced the political radicalization of sans-culottes women in the big cities. Instead, these women had tenaciously defended their culture and religious beliefs. As the frustrated government began to retreat on the religious question from 1796 to 1801, the women of rural France brought back the Catholic church and the open worship of God. In the words of a leading historian, these women worked for a return to a normal and structured lifestyle:

*Peacefully but purposefully, they sought to re-establish a pattern of life punctuated by a pealing bell and one in which the rites of passage—birth, marriage, and death—were respected and hallowed. The state had intruded too far and women entered the public arena to push it back and won. It was one of the most resounding political statements made by the populace in the entire history of the Revolution.*[7]

As for the middle-class members of the National Convention, in 1795 they wrote yet another constitution, which they believed would guarantee their economic position and political supremacy. The mass of the population voted only for electors, who were men of means. Electors then elected the members of a reorganized Legislative Assembly, as well as key officials throughout France. The new assembly also chose a five-man executive—the Directory.

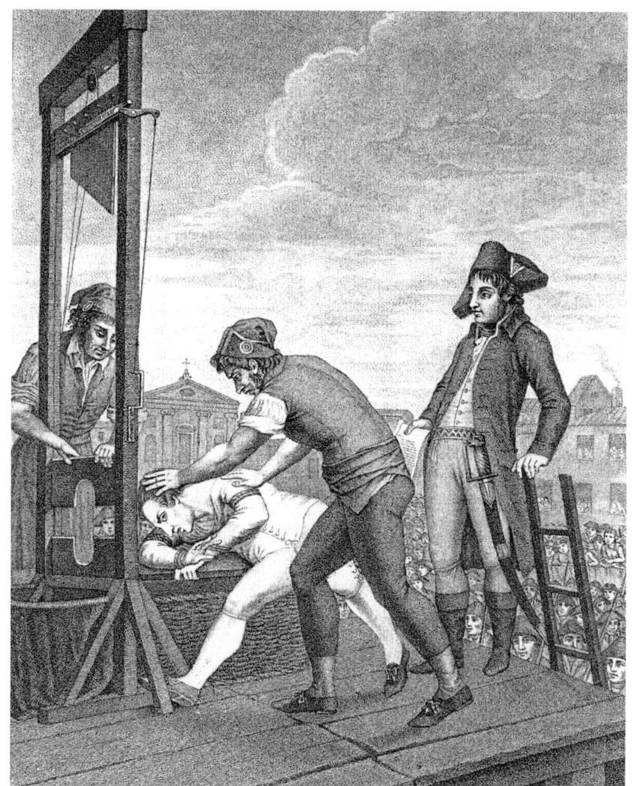

**The Execution of Robespierre** The guillotine was painted red and completely wooden except for the heavy iron blade. Large crowds witnessed the executions in a majestic public square in central Paris, then known as the Place de la Revolution and now called the Place de la Concorde (Harmony Square). *(Musée Carnavalet/Edimedia)*

The Directory continued to support French military expansion abroad. War was no longer so much a crusade as a means to meet ever-present, ever-unsolved economic problems. Large, victorious French armies reduced unemployment at home and were able to live off the territories they conquered and plundered.

The unprincipled action of the Directory reinforced widespread disgust with war and starvation, and the national elections of 1797 returned a large number of conservative and even monarchist deputies who favored peace at almost any price. The members of the Directory, fearing for their skins, used the army to nullify the elections and began to govern dictatorially. Two years later Napoleon Bonaparte ended the Directory in a coup d'état and substituted a strong dictatorship for a weak one. The effort to establish stable representative government had failed.

**MAP 22.1 Napoleonic Europe in 1810** Only Great Britain remained at war with Napoleon at the height of the Grand Empire. Many British goods were smuggled through Helgoland, a tiny but strategic British possession off the German coast.

## THE NAPOLEONIC ERA (1799–1815)

For almost fifteen years, from 1799 to 1814, France was in the hands of a keen-minded military dictator of exceptional ability. One of history's most fascinating leaders, Napoleon Bonaparte (1769–1821) realized the need to put an end to civil strife in France in order to create unity and consolidate his rule (see Map 22.1). And he did. But Napoleon saw himself as a man of destiny, and the glory of war and the dream of universal empire proved irresistible.

### Napoleon's Rule of France

In 1799 when he seized power, young General Napoleon Bonaparte was a national hero. Born in Corsica into an impoverished noble family in 1769, Napoleon left home and became a lieutenant in the French artillery in 1785. After a brief and unsuccessful adventure fighting for Corsican independence in 1789, he returned to France as a French patriot and a dedicated revolutionary. Rising rapidly in the new army, Napoleon was placed in command of French forces in Italy and won brilliant victories there in 1796 and 1797. His next campaign, in Egypt, was a failure, but Napoleon returned to France before the fiasco was generally known. His reputation remained intact.

Napoleon soon learned that some prominent members of the Legislative Assembly were plotting against the Directory. These plotters wanted a stronger dictatorship, because ten years of upheaval and uncertainty had made firm rule much more appealing than liberty and popular politics to these disillusioned revolutionaries. They wanted a strong military ruler, and the flamboyant thirty-year-old Napoleon was ideal. Thus the conspirators and Napoleon organized a takeover. On November 9, 1799, they ousted the Directors, and the following day soldiers disbanded the Legislative Assembly at bayonet point. Napoleon was named first consul of the republic, and a new constitution consolidating his position was overwhelmingly approved in a plebiscite in December 1799. Republican appearances were maintained, but Napoleon was already the real ruler of France.

The essence of Napoleon's domestic policy was to use his great and highly personal powers to maintain order and end civil strife. He worked out unwritten agreements with powerful groups whereby these groups received favors in return for loyal service. Napoleon's bargain with the solid middle class was codified in the Civil Code of 1804, which reasserted two of the fundamental principles of the liberal and essentially moderate revolution of 1789: equality of all male citizens before the law and absolute security of wealth and private property. Napoleon's defense of the new economic order also appealed successfully to the peasants, who had gained both land and status from the revolutionary changes.

At the same time, Napoleon accepted and strengthened the power of the French bureaucracy and perfected the centralized state. A network of officials depended on him and served him well. Napoleon also granted amnesty to émigrés on the condition that they return to France and take a loyalty oath. Members of this returning elite soon ably occupied many high posts in the expanding centralized state. In addition, Napoleon created a new imperial nobility in order to reward his most talented generals and officials.

Napoleon's skill in gaining support from important and potentially hostile groups is illustrated by his treatment of the Catholic church in France. Personally uninterested in religion, Napoleon wanted to heal the religious division so that a united Catholic church could serve as a bulwark of order and social peace. After long and arduous negotiations, Napoleon and Pope Pius VII (r. 1800–1823) signed the Concordat of 1801. The pope gained for French Catholics the precious right to practice their religion freely, but Napoleon gained political power: his government now nominated bishops, paid the clergy, and exerted great influence over the church in France.

The domestic reforms of Napoleon's early years were his greatest achievement. Much of his legal and administrative reorganization has survived in France to this day. More generally, Napoleon's domestic initiatives gave the great majority of French people a welcome sense of order and stability.

Order and unity had their price: Napoleon's authoritarian rule. Women, who had often participated in revolutionary politics, lost many of the gains they had made in the 1790s under the new Napoleonic Code. Under the law women were dependents of either their fathers or their husbands. Indeed, Napoleon and his advisers aimed at re-establishing a **family monarch,** where the power of the husband and father was as absolute over the wife and the children as that of Napoleon was over his subjects.

Free speech and freedom of the press were continually violated. By 1811 only four newspapers were left, and they were little more than organs of government propaganda. The occasional elections were a farce.

These changes in the law were part of the creation of a police state in France. Since Napoleon was usually busy making war, this task was largely left to Joseph Fouché, an unscrupulous opportunist who had earned a reputation for brutality during the Reign of Terror. As minister

## THE NAPOLEONIC ERA

| | |
|---|---|
| November 1799 | Napoleon overthrows the Directory. |
| December 1799 | French voters overwhelmingly approve Napoleon's new constitution. |
| 1801 | France defeats Austria and acquires Italian and German territories. Napoleon signs the Concordat with the pope. |
| 1802 | France signs the Treaty of Amiens with Britain. |
| December 1804 | Napoleon crowns himself emperor. |
| October 1805 | Britain defeats the French and Spanish fleet at the Battle of Trafalgar. |
| December 1805 | Napoleon defeats Austria and Russia at the Battle of Austerlitz. |
| 1807 | Napoleon redraws the map of Europe in the treaties of Tilsit. |
| 1810 | The Grand Empire is at its height. |
| June 1812 | Napoleon invades Russia with 600,000 men. |
| Fall–Winter 1812 | Napoleon makes a disastrous retreat from Russia. |
| March 1814 | Russia, Prussia, Austria, and Britain form the Quadruple Alliance to defeat France. |
| April 1814 | Napoleon abdicates and is exiled to Elba. |
| February–June 1815 | Napoleon escapes from Elba and rules France until he is defeated at the Battle of Waterloo. |

of police, Fouché organized a ruthlessly efficient spy system, which kept thousands of citizens under continual police surveillance. People suspected of subversive activities were arbitrarily detained, placed under house arrest, or even consigned to insane asylums. After 1810 political suspects were held in state prisons, as they had been during the Terror. There were about twenty-five hundred such political prisoners in 1814.

## Napoleon's Wars and Foreign Policy

Napoleon was above all a military man, and a great one. After coming to power in 1799, he sent peace feelers to Austria and Great Britain, the two remaining members of the Second Coalition, which had been formed against France in 1798. When these overtures were rejected, French armies led by Napoleon decisively defeated the Austrians. Once more, as in 1797, the British were alone—and war-weary, like the French. Still seeking to consolidate his regime domestically, Napoleon concluded the Treaty of Amiens with Great Britain in 1802. France remained in control of Holland, the Austrian Netherlands, the west bank of the Rhine, and most of the Italian peninsula. The Treaty of Amiens was clearly a diplomatic triumph for Napoleon, and peace with honor and profit increased his popularity at home.

In 1802 Napoleon was secure but unsatisfied. Ever a romantic gambler as well as a brilliant administrator, he could not contain his power drive. He aggressively threatened British interests in the eastern Mediterranean and tried to restrict British trade with all of Europe. Deciding to renew war with Britain in May 1803, Napoleon began making preparations to invade England. But Great Britain remained dominant on the seas. When Napoleon tried to bring his Mediterranean fleet around Gibraltar to northern France, a combined French and Spanish fleet was, after a series of mishaps, virtually annihilated by Lord Nelson at the Battle of Trafalgar on October 21, 1805. A cross-Channel invasion of England was henceforth impossible. Renewed fighting had its advantages, however, for the

**The Coronation of Napoleon, 1804 (detail)** In this grandiose painting by Jacques-Louis David, Napoleon prepares to crown his beautiful wife, Josephine, in an elaborate ceremony in Notre Dame Cathedral. Napoleon, the ultimate upstart, also crowned himself. Pope Pius VII, seated glumly behind the emperor, is reduced to being a spectator. *(Louvre/Réunion des Musées Nationaux/Art Resource, NY)*

first consul used the wartime atmosphere to have himself proclaimed emperor in late 1804.

Austria, Russia, and Sweden joined with Britain to form the Third Coalition against France shortly before the Battle of Trafalgar. Both Alexander I of Russia and Francis II of Austria were convinced that Napoleon was a threat to their interests and to the European balance of power. Yet the Austrians and the Russians were no match for Napoleon, who scored a brilliant victory over them at the Battle of Austerlitz in December 1805. Alexander I decided to pull back, and Austria accepted large territorial losses in return for peace as the Third Coalition collapsed.

Victorious at Austerlitz, Napoleon proceeded to reorganize the German states to his liking. He established by decree the German Confederation of the Rhine, a union of fifteen German states minus Austria, Prussia, and Saxony. Naming himself "protector" of the confederation, Napoleon firmly controlled western Germany. His intervention in German affairs alarmed the Prussians, who mobilized their armies after more than a decade of peace with France. Napoleon attacked and won two more brilliant victories in October 1806, at Jena and Auerstädt. The war with Prussia, now joined by Russia, continued into the spring. After Napoleon's larger armies won another victory, Alexander I of Russia wanted peace. In the subsequent treaties of Tilsit in 1807, Prussia lost half of its population, while Russia accepted Napoleon's reorganization of western and central Europe. Alexander also promised to enforce Napoleon's recently decreed economic blockade against British goods.

Napoleon now saw himself as the emperor of Europe and not just of France. The so-called Grand Empire he built had three parts. The core, or first part, was an ever-expanding France, which by 1810 included Belgium, Holland, parts of northern Italy, and much German territory on the east bank of the Rhine. Beyond French borders were a number of dependent satellite kingdoms, on the thrones of which Napoleon placed (and replaced) the members of his large family. The third part comprised the independent but allied states of Austria, Prussia, and Russia. Both satellites and allies were expected after 1806 to support Napoleon's continental system and cease trade with Britain.

The impact of the Grand Empire on the peoples of Europe was considerable. In the areas incorporated into France and in the satellites, Napoleon introduced many French laws, abolishing feudal dues and serfdom where French revolutionary armies had not already done so. Some of the peasants and middle class benefited from these reforms. Yet while he extended progressive measures to his cosmopolitan empire, Napoleon had to put the prosperity and special interests of France first in order to safeguard his power base. Levying heavy taxes in money and men for his armies, Napoleon came to be regarded more as a conquering tyrant than as an enlightened liberator. Thus French rule sparked patriotic upheavals and encouraged the growth of reactive nationalisms, for individuals in different lands learned to identify with their own embattled families, as the French had done earlier.

The first great revolt occurred in Spain. In 1808 a coalition of Catholics, monarchists, and patriots rebelled against Napoleon's attempts to make Spain a French satellite with a Bonaparte as its king. French armies occupied Madrid, but the foes of Napoleon fled to the hills and waged uncompromising guerrilla warfare. Resistance to French imperialism was growing. Yet Napoleon pushed on, determined to hold his empire together.

In 1810, when the Grand Empire was at its height, Britain still remained at war with France, helping the guerrillas in Spain and Portugal. Napoleon's continental system, organized to exclude British goods from the European continent and force that "nation of shopkeepers" to its knees, was a failure. Instead, it was France that suffered from Britain's counter-blockade, which created hard times for French artisans and the middle class. Perhaps looking for a scapegoat, Napoleon turned on Alexander I of Russia, who had been giving only lukewarm support to Napoleon's war of prohibitions against British goods.

Napoleon's invasion of Russia began in June 1812 with a force that eventually numbered 600,000, probably the largest force yet assembled in a single army. Only one-third of this force was French, however; nationals of all the satellites and allies were drafted into the operation. (See the feature "Individuals in Society: Jakob Walter, German Draftee with Napoleon.") Originally planning to winter in the Russian city of Smolensk if Alexander did not sue for peace, Napoleon reached Smolensk and recklessly pressed

**The War in Spain** This unforgettable etching by the Spanish painter Francisco Goya (1746–1828) comes from his famous collection "The Disasters of the War." A French firing squad executes captured Spanish rebels almost as soon as they are captured, an everyday event in a war of atrocities on both sides. Do you think these rebels are "terrorists," or "freedom fighters"? *(Foto Marburg/Art Resource, NY)*

# INDIVIDUALS IN SOCIETY

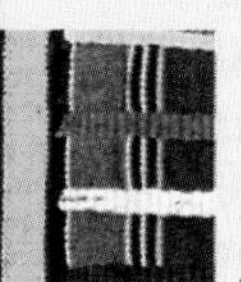

## JAKOB WALTER, GERMAN DRAFTEE WITH NAPOLEON

In January 1812, a young German named Jakob Walter (1788–1864) was recalled to active duty in the army of Württemberg, a Napoleonic satellite in the Confederation of the Rhine. Stonemason and common draftee, Walter later wrote a rare enlisted man's account of the Russian campaign, a personal history that testifies to the terrible price paid by the common people for a generation of war.

Napoleon's invasion of Russia was a desperate gamble from the beginning. French armies were accustomed to living off well-developed local economies, but this strategy did not work well in poor, sparsely populated eastern Europe. Scrounging for food dominated Walter's recollection of earlier fighting in Poland, and now, in 1812, the food situation was much worse. Crossing into Russia, Walter and his buddies found the nearby villages half-burned and stripped of food. Running down an occasional hog, they greedily tore it to pieces and ate it raw. Strangled by dust and thirst and then pelted for days by cold rain, the Great Army raced to catch the retreating Russians and force them into battle. When the famished troops stopped, the desperate search for food began.

In mid-August Walter's company helped storm the city of Smolensk in heavy fighting. From there onward, the road was littered with men, horses, and wagons, and all the towns and villages had been burned by the Russians to deprive the enemy of supplies. Surrounded by all these horrors, Walter almost lost his nerve, but he drew on his Catholic faith and found the courage "to go on trustingly to meet my fate."* Fighting at the great Battle of Borodino, "where the death cries and the shattering gunfire seemed a hell," he and the allied troops entered a deserted and fire-damaged Moscow in mid-September. But food, liquor, and fancy silks were there for the taking, and the weather was warm.

On October 18, the reprieve was over, and the retreating allied infantrymen re-entered Hell. Yet Walter, "still alert and spirited," was asked by an officer to be his attendant and received for his services a horse to ride. The horse proved a lifesaver. It allowed Walter to forage for food farther off the highway, to flee from approaching Cossacks, and to conserve his strength as vicious freezing winter weather set in. Yet food found at great peril could be quickly lost. Once Walter fought off some French soldiers with the help of some nearby Germans, who then robbed him of his bread. But what, he reflected later, could one expect? The starving men had simply lost their humanity. "I myself could look cold-bloodedly into the lamenting faces of the wounded, the freezing, and the burned," he wrote. When his horse was stolen as he slept, he silently stole someone else's. Struggling on in this brutal every-man-for-himself environment, Walter reached Poland in late December and hobbled home, a rare survivor. He went on to recover, marry, and have ten children.

*The retreat from Moscow; detail of an engraving by G. Küstler. Soldiers strip the sick of their blankets and boots, leaving them to die in the cold.* (Slavic and Baltic Division, The New York Public Library, Astor, Lenox and Tilden Foundation)

Why did Jakob Walter survive? Pure chance surely played a large part. So did his robust constitution and street smarts. His faith in God also provided strength to meet each day's challenges. The beautiful vision of returning home and seeing his family offered equal encouragement. Finally, he lacked hatred and animosity, whether toward the Russians, the French, or whomever. He accepted the things he could not change and concentrated on those he could.

### QUESTIONS FOR ANALYSIS

1. Why was obtaining food such a problem for Jakob Walter and his fellow soldiers?
2. What impresses you most about Walter's account of the Russian campaign?

*Jakob Walter, *The Diary of a Napoleonic Foot Soldier,* ed. with an introduction by M. Raeff (New York: Penguin Books, 1993), p. 53. Also pp. 54, 66.

on toward Moscow. The great Battle of Borodino that followed was a draw, and the Russians retreated in good order. Alexander ordered the evacuation of Moscow, which then burned, and he refused to negotiate. Finally, after five weeks in the burned-out city, Napoleon ordered a retreat. That retreat was one of the great military disasters in history. The Russian army and the Russian winter cut Napoleon's army to pieces. When the frozen remnants staggered into Poland and Prussia in December, 370,000 men had died, and another 200,000 had been taken prisoner.[8]

Leaving his troops to their fate, Napoleon raced to Paris to raise yet another army. When he refused to accept a France reduced to its historical size—the proposal offered by Austria's foreign minister, Prince Klemens von Metternich—Austria and Prussia deserted Napoleon and joined with Russia and Great Britain in forming the Quadruple Alliance. All across Europe patriots called for a "war of liberation" against Napoleon's oppression, and the well-disciplined regular armies of Napoleon's enemies closed in for the kill. Less than a month later, on April 4, 1814, a defeated Napoleon abdicated his throne. After this unconditional abdication, the victorious allies granted Napoleon the island of Elba off the coast of Italy as his own tiny state.

The allies also agreed to the restoration of the Bourbon dynasty. The new monarch, Louis XVIII (r. 1814–1824), issued the Constitutional Charter, which accepted many of France's revolutionary changes and guaranteed civil liberties. Indeed, the Charter gave France a constitutional monarchy roughly similar to that established in 1791, although far fewer people had the right to vote for representatives to the resurrected Chamber of Deputies. Moreover, in an attempt to strengthen popular support for Louis XVIII's new government, France was treated leniently by the allies, who agreed to meet in Vienna to work out a general peace settlement (see pages 763–764).

Louis XVIII—old, ugly, and crippled by gout—totally lacked the glory and magic of Napoleon. Hearing of political unrest in France and diplomatic tensions in Vienna, Napoleon staged a daring escape from Elba in February 1815. Landing in France, he issued appeals for support and marched on Paris with a small band of followers. Many veterans responded to the call. Louis XVIII fled, and once more Napoleon took command. But Napoleon's gamble was a desperate long shot, for the allies were united against him. At the end of a frantic period known as the Hundred Days, they crushed his forces at Waterloo on June 18, 1815, and imprisoned him on the rocky island of St. Helena, far off the western coast of Africa. Old Louis XVIII returned again—"in the baggage of the allies," as his detractors scornfully put it—and recommenced his reign. The allies now dealt more harshly with the apparently incorrigible French. As for Napoleon, he took revenge by writing his memoirs, skillfully nurturing the myth that he had been Europe's revolutionary liberator, a romantic hero whose lofty work had been undone by oppressive reactionaries. An era had ended.

## SUMMARY

The French Revolution left a compelling and many-sided political legacy. This legacy included, most notably, liberalism, assertive nationalism, radical democratic republicanism, embryonic socialism, and self-conscious conservatism. It also left a rich and turbulent history of electoral competition, legislative assemblies, and even mass politics. Thus the French Revolution and conflicting interpretations of its significance presented a whole range of political options and alternative visions of the future. For this reason it was truly *the* revolution in modern European politics.

The revolution that began in America and spread to France was a liberal revolution. Revolutionaries on both sides of the Atlantic wanted to establish civil liberties and equality before the law within the framework of representative government, and they succeeded. In France liberal nobles and an increasingly class-conscious middle class overwhelmed declining monarchical absolutism and feudal privilege, thanks to the intervention of the common people—the sans-culottes and the peasants. France's new political system reflected a social structure based increasingly on wealth and achievement rather than on tradition and legal privileges.

After the establishment of the republic, the radical phase of the Revolution during the Terror, and the fall of Robespierre, the educated elites and the solid middle class reasserted themselves under the Directory. And though Napoleon sharply curtailed representative institutions and individual rights, he effectively promoted the reconciliation of old and new, of centralized bureaucracy and careers open to talent, of noble and bourgeois in a restructured property-owning elite. Louis XVIII had to accept the commanding position of this restructured elite, and in granting representative government and civil liberties to facilitate his restoration to the throne in 1814, he submitted to the rest of the liberal triumph of 1789 to 1791. The liberal core of the French Revolution had successfully survived a generation of war and dictatorship.

The lived experience of the French Revolution and the wars that went with it exercised a pervasive influence on politics and the political imagination in the nineteenth century, not only in France but also throughout Europe and even the rest of the world. The radical legacy of the embattled republic of 1793 and 1794, with its sans-culottes democratic republicanism and its egalitarian ideology and embryonic socialism, would inspire republicans, democrats, and early socialists. Indeed, revolutionary upheaval encouraged generations of radicals to believe that political revolution might remake society and even create a new humanity. At the same time, there was a legacy of a powerful and continuing reaction to the French Revolution and to aggressive French nationalism. Monarchists and traditionalists believed that 1789 had been a tragic mistake. They concluded that democratic republicanism and sans-culottes activism led only to war, class conflict, and savage dictatorship. Conservatives and many comfortable moderates were profoundly disillusioned by the revolutionary era. They looked with nostalgia toward the supposedly ordered world of benevolent monarchy, firm government, and respectful common people.

## KEY TERMS

sovereign
bourgeoisie
representative government
checks and balances
classical liberalism
estates
manorial rights
Great Fear
Jacobins
second revolution
Girondists
the Mountain
sans-culottes
planned economy
Thermidorian reaction
family monarch

## NOTES

1. Quoted in G. Lefebvre, *The Coming of the French Revolution* (New York: Vintage Books, 1947), p. 81.
2. P. H. Beik, ed., *The French Revolution* (New York: Walker, 1970), p. 89.
3. G. Pernoud and S. Flaisser, eds., *The French Revolution* (Greenwich, Conn.: Fawcett, 1960), p. 61.
4. O. Hufton, *Women and the Limits of Citizenship in the French Revolution* (Toronto: University of Toronto Press, 1992), pp. 3–22.
5. Quotations from Wollstonecraft are drawn from E. W. Sunstein, *A Different Face: The Life of Mary Wollstonecraft* (New York: Harper & Row, 1975), pp. 208, 211; and H. R. James, *Mary Wollstonecraft: A Sketch* (London: Oxford University Press, 1932), pp. 60, 62, 69.
6. Quoted in L. Gershoy, *The Era of the French Revolution, 1789–1799* (New York: Van Nostrand, 1957), p. 150.
7. Hufton, *Women and the Limits of Citizenship in the French Revolution,* p. 130.
8. D. Sutherland, *France, 1789–1815: Revolution and Counterrevolution* (New York: Oxford University Press, 1986), p. 420.

## SUGGESTED READING

For fascinating eyewitness reports on the French Revolution, see the edited works by Beik and by Pernoud and Flaisser mentioned in the Notes. In addition, A. Young, *Travels in France During the Years 1787, 1788 and 1789* (1969), offers an engrossing contemporary description of France and Paris on the eve of revolution. E. Burke, *Reflections on the Revolution in France,* first published in 1790, is the classic conservative indictment. The intense passions the French Revolution has generated may be seen in nineteenth-century French historians, notably the enthusiastic J. Michelet, *History of the French Revolution;* the hostile H. Taine; and the judicious A. de Tocqueville, whose masterpiece, *The Old Regime and the French Revolution,* was first published in 1856. Important general studies on the entire period include R. R. Palmer, *The Age of the Democratic Revolution* (1959), which paints a comparative international picture; E. J. Hobsbawm, *The Age of Revolution, 1789–1848* (1962); C. Breunig, *The Age of Revolution and Reaction, 1789–1850* (1970); O. Connelly, *French Revolution—Napoleonic Era* (1979); and L. Dehio, *The Precarious Balance: Four Centuries of the European Power Struggle* (1962).

Revisionist study has created a wealth of new scholarship and interpretation. A. Cobban, *The Social Interpretation of the French Revolution* (1964), and F. Furet, *Interpreting the French Revolution* (1981), are major reassessments of long-dominant ideas, which are admirably presented in N. Hampson, *A Social History of the French Revolution* (1963), and in the volume by Lefebvre listed in the Notes. E. Kennedy, *A Cultural History of the French Revolution* (1989), beautifully written and handsomely illustrated, and W. Doyle, *Origins of the French Revolution,* 3d ed. (1988), are excellent on long-term developments. P. Jones, ed., *The French Revolution in Social and Political Perspective* (1996), offers a representative sampling of recent scholarship, while T. Tackett, *Becoming a Revolutionary* (1996), is an important attempt at a new synthesis. Among studies that are often quite critical of revolutionary developments, several are noteworthy: J. Bosher, *The French Revolution* (1988); S. Schama, *Citizens: A Chronicle of the French Revolution* (1989); W. Doyle, *The Oxford History of the French Revolution* (1989); and D. Sutherland, *France, 1789–1815: Revolution and Counterrevolution* (1986).

Two valuable anthologies concisely presenting a range of interpretations are F. Kafker and J. Laux, eds., *The French Revolutions: Conflicting Interpretations,* 4th ed. (1989), and G. Best, ed., *The Permanent Revolution: The French Revolution and Its Legacy, 1789–1989* (1988). G. Rudé makes the men and women of the great days of upheaval come alive in *The Crowd in the French Revolution* (1959), whereas R. R. Palmer studies sympathetically the leaders of the Terror in *Twelve Who Ruled* (1941). Four other particularly interesting, detailed works are B. Shapiro, *Revolutionary Justice in*

*(continued on page 728)*

# LISTENING TO THE PAST

## REVOLUTION AND WOMEN'S RIGHTS

*The 1789 Declaration of the Rights of Man was a revolutionary call for legal equality, representative government, and individual freedom. But the new rights were strictly limited to men; Napoleon tightened further the subordination of French women.*

*Among those who saw the contradiction in granting supposedly universal rights to only half the population was Marie Gouze (1748–1793), known to history as Olympe de Gouges. The daughter of a provincial butcher and peddler, she pursued a literary career in Paris after the death of her husband. Between 1790 and 1793, she wrote more than two dozen political pamphlets under her new name. De Gouges's great work was her "Declaration of the Rights of Woman" (1791). Excerpted here, de Gouges's manifesto went beyond the 1789 Rights of Man. It called on males to end their oppression of women and give women equal rights. A radical on women's issues, de Gouges sympathized with the monarchy and criticized Robespierre in print. Convicted of sedition, she was guillotined in November 1793.*

. . . Man, are you capable of being just? . . . Tell me, what gives you sovereign empire to oppress my sex? Your strength? Your talents? Observe the Creator in his wisdom . . . and give me, if you dare, an example of this tyrannical empire. Go back to animals, consult the elements, study plants . . . and distinguish, if you can, the sexes in the administration of nature. Everywhere you will find them mingled; everywhere they cooperate in harmonious togetherness in this immortal masterpiece.

Man alone has raised his exceptional circumstances to a principle. . . . [H]e wants to command as a despot a sex which is in full possession of its intellectual faculties; he pretends to enjoy the Revolution and to claim his rights to equality in order to say nothing more about it.

### DECLARATION OF THE RIGHTS OF WOMAN AND THE FEMALE CITIZEN

For the National Assembly to decree in its last sessions, or in those of the next legislature:

Preamble

Mothers, daughters, sisters and representatives of the nation demand to be constituted into a national assembly. Believing that ignorance, omission, or scorn for the rights of woman are the only causes of public misfortunes and of the corruption of governments, [the women] have resolved to set forth in a solemn declaration the natural, inalienable, and sacred rights of woman. . . .

. . . the sex that is as superior in beauty as it is in courage during the sufferings of maternity recognizes and declares in the presence and under the auspices of the Supreme Being, the following Rights of Woman and of Female Citizens:

I. Woman is born free and lives equal to man in her rights. Social distinctions can be based only on the common utility.

II. The purpose of any political association is the conservation of the natural and imprescriptible rights of woman and man; these rights are liberty, property, security, and especially resistance to oppression.

III. The principle of all sovereignty rests essentially with the nation, which is nothing but the union of woman and man. . . .

IV. Liberty and justice consist of restoring all that belongs to others; thus, the only limits on the exercise of the natural rights of woman are perpetual male tyranny; these limits are to be reformed by the laws of nature and reason.

V. Laws of nature and reason proscribe all acts harmful to society. . . .

VI. The law must be the expression of the general will; all female and male citizens must contribute either personally or through their representatives to its formation; it must be the same for all: male and female citizens, being equal in the eyes of the law, must be equally admitted to all honors, positions, and public employment according to their capacity and without other distinctions besides those of their virtues and talents.

VII. No woman is an exception; she is accused, arrested, and detained in cases determined by law. Women, like men, obey this rigorous law.

VIII. The law must establish only those penalties that are strictly and obviously necessary. . . .

IX. Once any woman is declared guilty, complete rigor is [to be] exercised by the law.

X. No one is to be disquieted for his very basic opinions; woman has the right to mount the scaffold; she must equally have the right to mount the rostrum, provided that her demonstrations do not disturb the legally established public order.

XI. The free communication of thoughts and opinions is one of the most precious rights of woman, since that liberty assures the recognition of children by their fathers. Any female citizen thus may say freely, I am the mother of a child which belongs to you, without being forced by a barbarous prejudice to hide the truth. . . .

XIII. For the support of the public force and the expenses of administration, the contributions of woman and man are equal; she shares all the duties . . . and all the painful tasks; therefore, she must have the same share in the distribution of positions, employment, offices, honors, and jobs. . . .

XIV. Female and male citizens have the right to verify, either by themselves or through their representatives, the necessity of the public contribution. This can only apply to women if they are granted an equal share, not only of wealth, but also of public administration. . . .

XV. The collectivity of women, joined for tax purposes to the aggregate of men, has the right to demand an accounting of his administration from any public agent.

XVI. No society has a constitution without the guarantee of rights and the separation of powers; the constitution is null if the majority of individuals comprising the nation have not cooperated in drafting it.

The late-eighteenth-century French painting *La Liberté*. *(Giraudon/Art Resource, NY)*

XVII. Property belongs to both sexes whether united or separate; for each it is an inviolable and sacred right. . . .

Postscript

Women, wake up. . . . Discover your rights. . . . Oh, women, women! When will you cease to be blind? What advantage have you received from the Revolution? A more pronounced scorn, a more marked disdain. . . . [If men persist in contradicting their revolutionary principles,] courageously oppose the force of reason to the empty pretensions of superiority . . . and you will soon see these haughty men, not groveling at your feet as servile adorers, but proud to share with you the treasure of the Supreme Being. Regardless of what barriers confront you; it is in your power to free yourselves; you have only to want to. . . .

## QUESTIONS FOR ANALYSIS

1. On what basis did de Gouges argue for gender equality? Did she believe in natural law?
2. What consequences did "scorn for the rights of woman" have for France, according to de Gouges?
3. Did de Gouges stress political rights at the expense of social and economic rights? If so, why?

*Source: Women in Revolutionary Paris, 1789–1795: Selected Documents Translated with Notes and Commentary.* Translated with notes and commentary by Darline Gay Levy, Harriet Branson Applewhite, and Mary Durham Johnson. 

*Paris, 1789–1790* (1993); D. Jordan, *The Revolutionary Career of Maximilien Robespierre* (1985); J. P. Bertaud, *The Army of the French Revolution: From Citizen-Soldier to Instrument of Power* (1988); and C. L. R. James, *The Black Jacobins* (1938, 1980), on black slave revolt in Haiti. Other significant studies on aspects of revolutionary France include P. Jones's pathbreaking *The Peasantry in the French Revolution* (1979) and L. Hunt's innovative *Politics, Culture, and Class in the French Revolution* (1984). Two major reinterpretations of the era's continuous wars are T. Blanning, *The French Revolutionary Wars, 1787–1802* (1996), and O. Connelly, *Blundering to Glory: Napoleon's Military Campaigns* (1987).

Studies on women in the French Revolution are increasing knowledge and raising conflicting interpretations. These developments may be seen by comparing two particularly important works: J. Landes, *Women and the Public Sphere in the Age of the French Revolution* (1988), and Hufton's work, listed in the Notes. D. Outram, *The Body and the French Revolution: Sex, Class and Political Culture* (1989), and L. Hunt, *The Family Romance of the French Revolution* (1992), also provide analyses of gender-related questions. D. Levy, H. Applewhite, and M. Johnson, eds., *Women in Revolutionary Paris, 1789–1795* (1979), is a valuable collection of contemporary documents with helpful commentaries. Mary Wollstonecraft's dramatic life is the subject of several good biographies, including those by Sunstein and James cited in the Notes.

Two important works placing political developments in a comparative perspective are P. Higonnet, *Sister Republics: The Origins of French and American Republicanism* (1988), and E. Morgan, *Inventing the People: The Rise of Popular Sovereignty in England and America* (1988). B. Bailyn, *The Ideological Origins of the American Revolution* (1967), is also noteworthy.

The best synthesis on Napoleonic France is L. Bergeron, *France Under Napoleon* (1981). E. Arnold, Jr., ed., *A Documentary Survey of Napoleonic France* (1944), includes political and cultural selections. K. Kafker and J. Laux, eds., *Napoleon and His Times: Selected Interpretations* (1989), is an interesting collection of articles, which may be compared with R. Jones, *Napoleon: Man and Myth* (1977). Good biographies are J. Thompson, *Napoleon Bonaparte: His Rise and Fall* (1952); F. Markham, *Napoleon* (1964); and V. Cronin, *Napoleon Bonaparte* (1972). Wonderful novels inspired by the period include Raphael Sabatini's *Scaramouche,* a swashbuckler of revolutionary intrigue with accurate historical details; Charles Dickens's fanciful *Tale of Two Cities;* and Leo Tolstoy's monumental saga of Napoleon's invasion of Russia (and much more), *War and Peace.*

A colored engraving by J. C. Bourne of the Great Western Railway emerging from a tunnel. *(Science & Society Picture Library, London)*

CHAPTER

# 23 THE INDUSTRIAL REVOLUTION IN EUROPE

## CHAPTER OUTLINE



While the Revolution in France was opening a new political era, another revolution was transforming economic and social life. The Industrial Revolution, which began in England around the 1780s, started to influence continental Europe and the rest of the world after 1815. Because the Industrial Revolution was less dramatic than the French Revolution, some historians see industrial development as basically moderate and evolutionary. From a long perspective, however, it was rapid and brought about radical changes. Perhaps only the development of agriculture during Neolithic times had a similar impact and significance.

The Industrial Revolution profoundly modified much of human experience. It changed patterns of work, transformed the social class structure, and even altered the international balance of political and military power, giving added impetus to ongoing Western expansion into non-Western lands. The Industrial Revolution also helped ordinary people gain a higher standard of living.

Unfortunately, improvement in the European standard of living was quite limited until about 1850, for at least two reasons. First, even in England only a few key industries experienced a technological revolution. Many more industries continued to use old methods, especially on the European continent, and this held down the increase in total production. Second, the increase in Europe's total population, which began in the eighteenth century, continued as the era of the Industrial Revolution unfolded. As a result, the rapid growth in population threatened—quite literally—to eat up the growth in production and to leave individuals poorer than ever.

- What was the Industrial Revolution?
- What were the origins of the Industrial Revolution, and how did it develop?
- How did the changes brought by the Industrial Revolution affect people and society in an era of continued rapid population growth?

These are the questions that this chapter will seek to answer. Chapter 25 will examine in detail the emergence of accompanying changes in urban civilization, and Chapters 26 and 27 will probe the consequences of industrialization in Europe for world history.

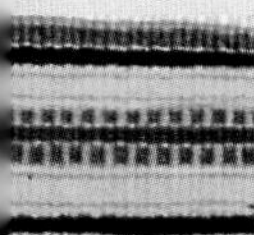

# THE INITIAL BREAKTHROUGH IN ENGLAND

The Industrial Revolution began in England. It was something new in history, and it was quite unplanned. With no models to copy and no idea of what to expect, England had to pioneer not only in industrial technology but also in social relations and urban living. Between 1793 and 1815 almost constant war with France complicated these formidable tasks.

## Eighteenth-Century Origins

Although many aspects of the Industrial Revolution are still matters for scholarly debate, it is generally agreed that the industrial changes that did occur grew out of a complex combination of factors. These factors came together in eighteenth-century England and initiated a decisive breakthrough that many place in the 1780s.

**MAP 23.1 Cottage Industry and Transportation in Eighteenth-Century England** England had an unusually good system of navigable rivers. From about 1770 to 1800 a canal-building boom linked these rivers together and greatly improved inland transportation.

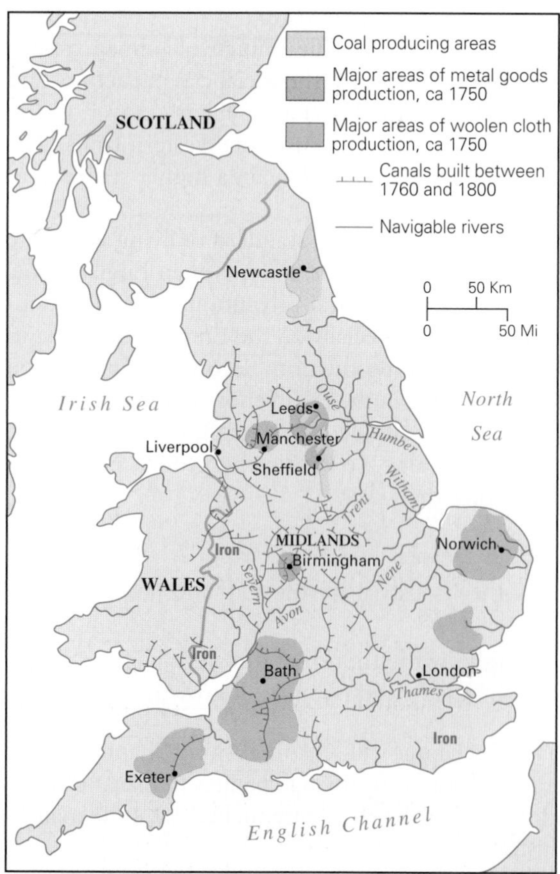


In analyzing the causes of the late-eighteenth-century acceleration in the English economy, historians have paid particular attention to dramatic changes in agriculture, foreign trade, technology, energy supplies, and transportation. Although this chapter focuses on those issues, one must first understand that England had other, less conspicuous assets that favored the long process of development that culminated in industrial breakthrough.

Relatively good government was one such asset. The monarchy and the aristocratic oligarchy, which jointly ruled the country after the constitutional settlement of 1688, provided stable and predictable government. Neither civil strife nor invading armies threatened peace. Thus the government let the domestic economy operate fairly freely and with few controls, encouraging personal initiative, technological change, and a free market.

A related asset was an experienced business class with very modern characteristics. This business class, which traced its origins to the High Middle Ages, eagerly sought to make profits and to accumulate capital. England also had a large class of hired agricultural laborers. These rural wage earners were relatively mobile—compared with village-bound peasants in France and western Germany, for example—and along with cottage workers they formed a potential labor force for capitalist entrepreneurs.

Several other assets supporting English economic growth stand out. First, unlike France and most other countries, England had an effective central bank and well-developed credit institutions. Second, although England may seem a rather small country today, it undoubtedly enjoyed the largest effective domestic market in eighteenth-century Europe. In an age when shipping goods by water was much cheaper than shipping goods by land, no part of England was more than twenty miles from navigable water. Beginning in the 1770s a canal-building boom greatly enhanced this natural advantage (see Map 23.1). Nor were there any tariffs within the country to hinder trade, as there were in France before 1789 and in politically fragmented Germany and Italy. Finally, only in Holland did the lower classes appear to live as well as in England. The ordinary English family did not have to spend almost everything it earned just to buy bread. It could spend more on other items, thereby adding significantly to the growing demand for manufactured goods that was a critical factor in initiating England's industrial breakthrough.

All these factors combined to bring about the **Industrial Revolution,** a term coined in the 1830s by awed contemporaries to describe the burst of major inventions

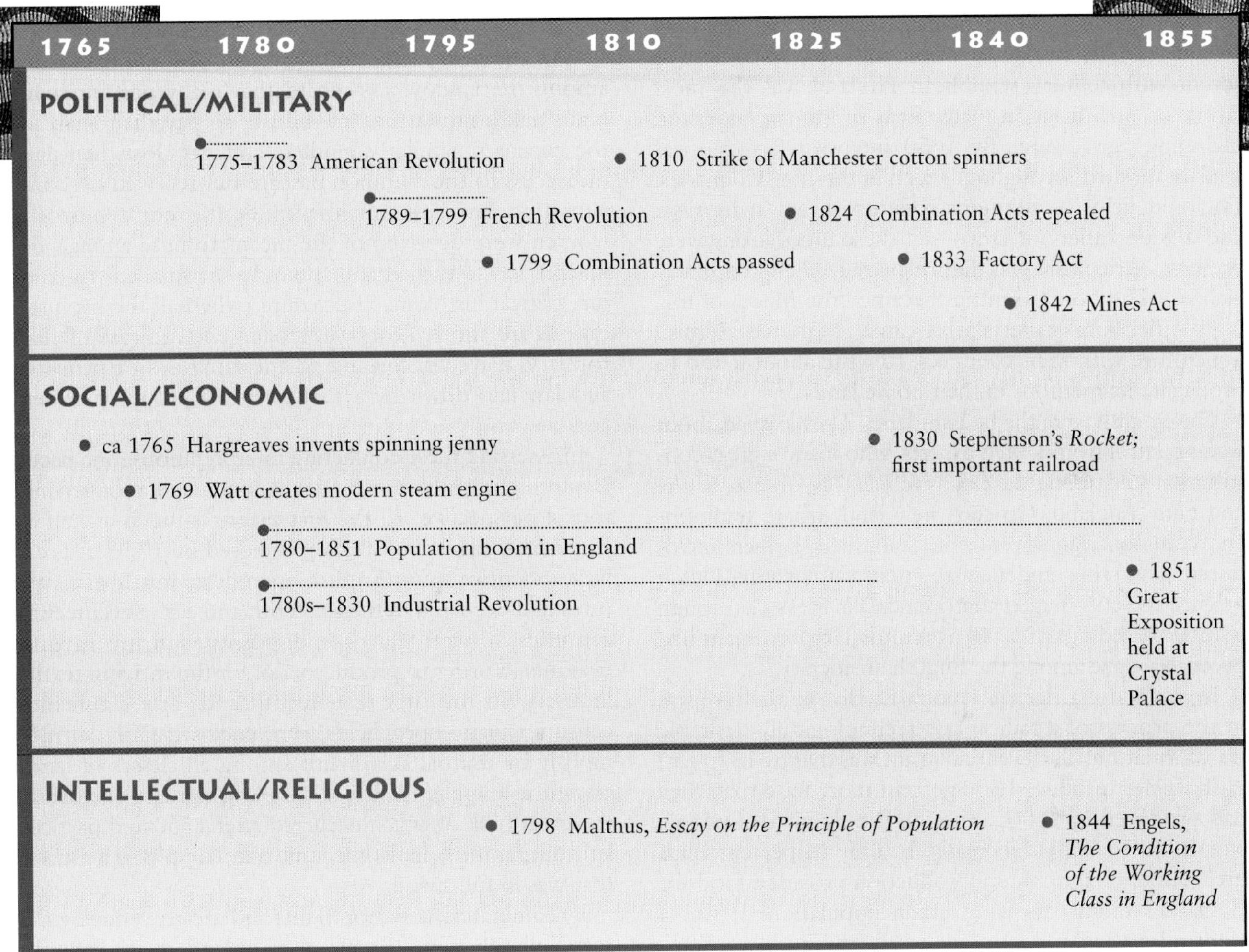


and technical changes that they had witnessed in certain industries. This technical revolution went hand in hand with an impressive quickening in the annual rate of industrial growth in England. Thus industry grew at only 0.7 percent per year between 1700 and 1760—before the Industrial Revolution—but it grew at the much higher rate of 3 percent between 1801 and 1831, when industrial transformation was in full swing.[1] The decisive quickening of growth probably came in the 1780s, after the American War of Independence and just before the French Revolution.

The great economic and political revolutions that shaped the modern world occurred almost simultaneously. The Industrial Revolution, however, was a longer process. It was not complete in England until 1830 at the earliest, and it had no real impact on continental European countries until after the Congress of Vienna (see page 763) ended the era of revolutionary wars in 1815.

## The Agricultural Revolution

Although scholars no longer believe that radical agricultural change was a necessary precondition for the industrial breakthrough, a gradual but profound revolution in agricultural methods did promote accelerated economic growth. In essence, the **agricultural revolution** eliminated the traditional pattern of village agriculture found in northern and central Europe. It replaced the medieval **open-field system** and the annual fallowing of some fields with a new system of continuous rotation that resulted in more food for humans and their animals. The new agricultural system had profound implications, for it eliminated long-standing **common rights** as well as the fallow. But whereas peasants and rural laborers checked the spread of the new system on the continent of Europe in the eighteenth century, large landowners and powerful market forces overcame such opposition in England.

The new methods of agriculture originated in the Low Countries. The vibrant, dynamic middle-class society of seventeenth-century republican Holland was the most advanced in Europe in many areas of human endeavor, including agriculture. By 1650 intensive farming was well established throughout much of the Low Countries. Enclosed fields, continuous rotation, heavy manuring, and a wide variety of crops—all these innovations were present. Agriculture was highly specialized and commercialized. The Low Countries became "the Mecca of foreign agricultural experts who came . . . to see Flemish agriculture with their own eyes, to write about it and to propagate its methods in their home lands."[2]

The English were the best students. They learned about water control from Dutch experts, who made a great contribution to draining the extensive marshes, or fens, of wet and rainy England. On such new land, where traditions and common rights were not established, farmers introduced new crops and new rotations fairly easily. Dutch practice also encouraged improvements in livestock through selective breeding. By 1740 agricultural improvement had become a craze among the English aristocracy.

By the mid-eighteenth century English agriculture was in the process of a radical and technologically desirable transformation. The eventual result was that by 1870 English farmers produced 300 percent more food than they had produced in 1700, although the number of people working the land had increased by only 14 percent. This great surge of agricultural production provided food for England's rapidly growing urban population. It was a tremendous achievement.

## The Cost of Enclosure

What was the cost of technological progress in England, and to what extent did its payment result in social injustice? Scholars agree that the impetus for enclosing the fields came mainly from the powerful ruling class—the English landowning aristocracy, who benefited directly from higher yields that could support higher rents. Beyond these certainties there are important differences of interpretation among historians.

Many historians assert that the open fields were enclosed fairly and that both large and small owners received their fair share after the strips were surveyed and consolidated. Other historians argue that fairness was more apparent than real. These historians point out that the large landowners controlled Parliament, which made the laws. They had Parliament pass hundreds of "enclosure acts," each of which authorized the fencing of open fields in a given village and the division of the common in proportion to one's property in the open fields. The division of the heavy legal and surveying costs of **enclosure** among the landowners meant that many peasants who had small holdings had to sell out to pay their share of the expenses. Similarly, landless cottagers lost their age-old access to the common pasture but received no compensation. Landless families were dealt a serious blow, for women were deprived of the means to raise animals for market and to earn vital income. In the spirited words of one critical historian, "Enclosure (when all the sophistications are allowed for) was a plain enough case of class robbery, played according to the fair rules of property and law laid down by a Parliament of property-owners and lawyers."[3]

In assessing these conflicting interpretations, one needs to put eighteenth-century developments in a longer historical perspective. In the first place, as much as half of English farmland was already enclosed by 1750. A great wave of enclosure of English open fields into sheep pastures had occurred in the sixteenth and early seventeenth centuries, a wave that had dispossessed many English peasants in order to produce wool for the thriving textile industry. In the later seventeenth and early eighteenth centuries many open fields were enclosed fairly harmoniously by mutual agreement among all classes of landowners in English villages. Thus parliamentary enclosure, the great bulk of which occurred after 1760 and particularly during the Napoleonic wars, only completed a process that was in full swing.

By eliminating common rights and greatly reducing the access of poor men and women to the land, the eighteenth-century enclosure movement marked the completion of two major historical developments in England: the rise of market-oriented estate agriculture and the emergence of a landless proletariat. By 1815 a tiny minority of wealthy English (and Scottish) landowners held most of the land and pursued profits aggressively, leasing their holdings through agents to middle-size farmers at competitive prices. These farmers produced mainly for cash markets and relied on landless laborers for their workforce. In strictly economic terms these landless laborers may have lived as well in 1800 as in 1700, but they had lost that bit of independence and self-respect that common rights had provided. They had become completely dependent on cash wages. In no other European country had this **proletarianization**—this transformation of large numbers of small peasant farmers into landless rural wage earners—gone so far as it had in England by the late eighteenth century. And, as in the earlier English enclosure movement, the village poor found the cost of economic change and technological progress heavy and unjust.

## The Growth of Foreign Trade

In the eighteenth century Great Britain (formed in 1707 by the union of England and Scotland into a single kingdom) also became the leading maritime power, dominating long-distance trade, particularly intercontinental trade across the Atlantic. This foreign trade stimulated the economy.

Britain's commercial leadership in the eighteenth century had its origins in the mercantilism of the seventeenth century. European **mercantilism** was a system of economic regulations aimed at increasing the power of the state. What distinguished English mercantilism was the unusual idea that government economic regulations could and should serve the private interests of individuals and groups as well as the public needs of the state.

The seventeenth-century Navigation Acts reflected the desire of Great Britain to increase both its military power and its private wealth. The initial target of these instruments of economic warfare was the Dutch, who were far ahead of the English in shipping and foreign trade in the mid-seventeenth century. By the later seventeenth century, after three Anglo-Dutch wars, the Netherlands was falling behind England in shipping, trade, and colonies. France then stood clearly as England's most serious rival in the competition for overseas empire. Rich in natural resources and endowed with a population three or four times that of England, continental Europe's leading military power was already building a powerful fleet and a worldwide system of rigidly monopolized colonial trade. Thus from 1701 to 1763 Britain and France were locked in a series of wars to decide, in part, which nation would become the leading maritime power and claim the lion's share of the profits of Europe's overseas expansion.

The first round was the War of the Spanish Succession, which resulted in major gains for Great Britain in the Peace of Utrecht (1713). France ceded Newfoundland, Nova Scotia, and the Hudson Bay territory to Britain. Spain was compelled to give Britain control of the lucrative West African slave trade—the so-called *asiento*—and to let Britain send one ship of merchandise into the Spanish colonies annually.

The Seven Years' War (1756–1763) was the decisive round in the Franco-British competition for colonial empire. With the Treaty of Paris (1763) France lost all its possessions on the mainland of North America and gave up most of its holdings in India as well. By 1763 Britain had realized its goal of monopolizing a vast trade and colonial empire for its benefit.

This interconnected expansion of trade and empire marked a major step toward the Industrial Revolution, although people could not know it at the time. Protected colonial markets provided a great stimulus for many branches of English manufacturing. The value of the sales of manufactured products to the Atlantic economy—primarily the mainland colonies of North America and the West Indian sugar islands, with an important assist from West Africa and Latin America—soared from £475,000 in 1700 to £3.9 million in 1773. English exports of manufactured goods to continental Europe grew hardly at all in these years, as states there adopted protectionist policies to help develop their own industries.

English exports became much more balanced and diversified. To America and Africa went large quantities of metal items—axes to frontiersmen, firearms, chains for slave owners. Also exported were clocks and coaches, buttons and saddles, china and furniture, musical instruments and scientific equipment, and a host of other things. Thus the mercantile system established in the seventeenth century continued to shape trade in the eighteenth century, and the English concentrated in their hands much of the demand for manufactured goods from the growing Atlantic economy. Sales to other "colonies"—Ireland and India—also rose substantially in the eighteenth century. Nor was this all. Demand from the well-integrated home market was also rising. The English were relatively well-off, and their population was growing. Lower food prices meant ordinary people could buy more manufactured goods. Rising demand from home and abroad put intense pressure on the whole system of production.

## The First Factories

The pressure to produce more goods for a growing market was directly related to the first decisive breakthrough of the Industrial Revolution—the creation of the world's first large factories in the English cotton textile industry. Technological innovations in the manufacture of cloth led to a whole new pattern of production and social relationships. No other industry experienced such a rapid or complete transformation before 1830.

Although merchant-capitalists "put out" raw materials to cottage workers for processing and payment all across Europe before the Industrial Revolution at the end of the eighteenth century, this pattern of rural industry was most fully developed in England. Thus it was in England, under the pressure of growing demand, that the putting-out system's shortcomings first began to outweigh its advantages—especially in the cottage textile industry after about 1760.

There was always a serious imbalance in this family enterprise: the work of four or five spinners was needed to keep one weaver steadily employed. The wife and the husband had constantly to try to find more thread and more spinners. Widows and unmarried women—"spinsters" who spun for their living—were recruited by the wife. Or perhaps the weaver's son went off on horseback to seek thread.

Deep-seated conflict between workers and employers complicated increased production. In "The Clothier's Delight, or the Rich Men's Joy and the Poor Men's Sorrow," an English popular song written about 1700, a merchant boasts of his countless tricks used to "beat down wages":

*We heapeth up riches and treasure great store*
*Which we get by griping and grinding the poor.*
*And this is a way for to fill up our purse*
*Although we do get it with many a curse.*[4]

There were constant disputes over the weights of materials and the quality of the cloth. Merchants accused workers of stealing raw materials, and weavers complained that merchants delivered underweight bales. Both were right; each tried to cheat the other, even if only in self-defense.

There was another problem, at least from the merchant-capitalist's point of view. Scattered rural labor was cheap but hard to control. Cottage workers tended to work in spurts. After they got paid on Saturday afternoon, the men in particular tended to drink and carouse for two or three days. By the end of the week the weaver was probably working feverishly to make his quota. But if he did not succeed, there was little the merchant could do. The merchant-capitalist's search for more efficient methods of production intensified.

Attention focused on ways of improving spinning. Many a tinkering worker knew that a better spinning wheel promised rich rewards. It proved hard to spin the traditional raw materials—wool and flax—with improved machines, but cotton was different. Cotton textiles had first been imported into England from India by the East India Company, and by 1760 there was a tiny domestic industry in northern England. After many experiments over a generation, a gifted carpenter and jack-of-all-trades, James Hargreaves, invented his cotton-spinning jenny about 1765. At almost the same moment a barber-turned-manufacturer named Richard Arkwright invented (or possibly pirated) another kind of spinning machine, the water frame. These breakthroughs produced an explosion in the infant cotton textile industry in the 1780s. By 1790 the new machines were producing ten times as much cotton yarn as had been made in 1770.

Hargreaves's **spinning jenny** was simple and inexpensive. It was also hand operated. In early models from six to twenty-four spindles were mounted on a sliding carriage, and each spindle spun a fine, slender thread. The woman moved the carriage back and forth with one hand

**Woman Working a Hargreaves's Spinning Jenny** The loose cotton strands on the slanted bobbins passed up to the sliding carriage and then on to the spindles in back for fine spinning. The worker, almost always a woman, regulated the sliding carriage with one hand and with the other she turned the crank on the wheel to supply power. By 1783 one woman could spin by hand a hundred threads at a time on an improved model. *(Mary Evans Picture Library)*

and turned a wheel to supply power with the other. Now it was the male weaver who could not keep up with the vastly more efficient female spinner.

Arkwright's **water frame** employed a different principle. It quickly acquired a capacity of several hundred spindles and demanded much more power—waterpower. The water frame thus required large specialized mills, factories that employed as many as one thousand workers from the very beginning. The water frame could spin only coarse, strong thread, which was then put out for respinning on hand-powered cottage jennies. After about 1790, all cotton spinning was gradually concentrated in factories.

The first consequences of these revolutionary developments were more beneficial than is generally believed. Cotton goods became much cheaper, and they were bought and treasured by all classes. In the past only the wealthy could afford the comfort and cleanliness of underwear, which was called **body linen** because it was made from expensive linen cloth. Now millions of poor people, who had earlier worn nothing underneath their coarse, filthy outer garments, could afford to wear cotton slips and underpants as well as cotton dresses and shirts.

Families using cotton in cottage industry were freed from their constant search for adequate yarn from scattered, part-time spinners, for all the thread needed could be spun in the cottage on the jenny or obtained from a nearby factory. The wages of weavers, now hard-pressed to keep up with the spinners, rose markedly until about 1792. Weavers were among the best-paid workers in England. As a result, large numbers of agricultural laborers became hand-loom weavers, while mechanics and capitalists soon sought to invent a power loom to save on labor costs. This Edmund Cartwright achieved in 1785. But the power looms of the factories worked poorly at first, and hand-loom weavers continued to receive good wages until at least 1800.

Until the late 1780s most English factories were in rural areas, where they had access to waterpower. These factories employed a relatively small percentage of all cotton textile workers. Working conditions in the early factories were less satisfactory than the conditions of cottage weavers and spinners, and people were reluctant to work in them. Therefore, factory owners turned to young children who had been abandoned by their parents and put in the care of local parishes. Parish officers often "apprenticed" such unfortunate orphans to factory owners, who gained over them almost the authority of slave owners.

Both symbolically and substantially, the big new cotton mills marked the beginning of the Industrial Revolution in England. By 1831 the largely mechanized cotton textile industry towered above all others, accounting for fully 22 percent of the country's entire industrial production.

## ENERGY AND TRANSPORTATION

The growth of the cotton textile industry might have been stunted or cut short if water from rivers and streams had remained the primary source of power for the new factories. But this did not occur. Instead, an epoch-making solution was found to the age-old problem of energy and power. It was this solution to the energy problem (a problem that reappeared in recent times) that permitted continued rapid development in cotton textiles, the gradual generalization of the factory system, and the triumph of the Industrial Revolution in England and Scotland.

### The Problem of Energy

Human beings, like all living organisms, require energy. Adult men and women need two thousand to four thousand calories (units of energy) daily simply to fuel their bodies, work, and survive. Prehistoric people relied on plants and plant-eating animals as their sources of energy. With the development of agriculture, early civilizations were able to increase the number of useful plants and thus the supply of energy. Some plants could be fed to domesticated animals, such as the horse. Stronger than human beings, these animals converted the energy in the plants into work.

Human beings have used their toolmaking abilities to construct machines that convert one form of energy into another for their own benefit. In the common era people began to develop water mills to grind their grain and windmills to pump water and drain swamps. More efficient use of water and wind in the sixteenth and seventeenth centuries enabled human beings, especially Europeans, to accomplish more; intercontinental sailing ships were a prime example. Nevertheless, European society continued to rely mainly on plants for energy, and human beings and animals continued to perform most work. This dependence meant that Western civilization remained poor in energy and power.

Lack of power lay at the heart of the poverty that afflicted the large majority of people. The man behind the plow and the woman at the spinning wheel could employ only horsepower and human muscle in their labor. No matter how hard they worked, they could not produce very much.

The shortage of energy had become particularly severe in England by the eighteenth century. Because of the growth of population, most of the great forests of medieval England had long ago been replaced by fields of grain and hay. Wood was in ever-shorter supply, yet it remained tremendously important. In addition to serving as the primary source of heat for homes and industries and as a basic raw material, processed wood (charcoal)

**Manchester, England, 1851** The development of the steam engine enabled industry to concentrate in towns and cities. Manchester mushroomed from a town of 20,000 in 1750 into "Cottonopolis," cotton city, with 400,000 inhabitants in 1850. In this painting the artist contrasts the smoky city and its awesome power with the idealized beauty of the suburbs, where the new rich settled and built their mansions. *(The Royal Collection, © 2002 Her Majesty Queen Elizabeth II)*

was the fuel that was mixed with iron ore in the blast furnace to produce pig iron. The iron industry's appetite for wood was enormous, and by 1740 the English iron industry was stagnating. Vast forests enabled Russia in the eighteenth century to become the world's leading producer of iron, much of which was exported to England. But Russia's potential for growth was limited, too, and in a few decades Russia would reach the barrier of inadequate energy that was already holding England back.

## The Steam Engine Breakthrough

As this early energy crisis grew worse, England looked toward its abundant and widely scattered reserves of coal as an alternative to its vanishing wood. Coal was first used in England in the late Middle Ages as a source of heat. By 1640 most homes in London were heated with it, and it also provided heat for making beer, glass, soap, and other products. Coal, however, was not used to make iron, to produce mechanical energy, or to power machinery. It was there that coal's potential was enormous, as a simple example shows.

A hard-working miner can dig out five hundred pounds of coal a day using hand tools, producing about one horsepower-hour in the course of his labor. Even an extremely inefficient converter, which transforms only 1 percent of the heat energy in coal into mechanical energy, will produce twenty-seven horsepower-hours of work from that five hundred pounds of coal. Early steam engines were just such inefficient converters.

As more coal was produced, mines were dug deeper and deeper and were constantly filling with water. Mechanical pumps, usually powered by animals walking in circles at the surface, had to be installed. At one mine fully five hundred horses were used in pumping. Such power was expensive and bothersome. In an attempt to overcome these disadvantages Thomas Savery in 1698 and Thomas Newcomen in 1705 invented the first primitive **steam engines.** Both engines burned coal to produce steam, which was then used to operate a pump.

Both engines were extremely inefficient, but by the early 1770s many of the Savery engines and hundreds of the Newcomen engines were operating successfully in English and Scottish mines.

In the early 1760s a gifted young Scot named James Watt (1736–1819) was drawn to a critical study of the steam engine. Watt was employed at the time by the University of Glasgow as a skilled craftsman making scientific instruments. The Scottish universities were pioneers in practical technical education, and in 1763 Watt was called on to repair a Newcomen engine being used in a physics course. After a series of observations Watt saw that the Newcomen engine's great waste of energy could be reduced by adding a separate condenser. This splendid invention, patented in 1769, greatly increased the efficiency of the steam engine.

To invent something in a laboratory is one thing; to make it a practical success is quite another. Watt needed skilled workers, precision parts, and capital, and the relatively advanced nature of the English economy proved essential. A partnership with a wealthy, progressive toymaker provided risk capital and a manufacturing plant. In the craft tradition of locksmiths, tinsmiths, and millwrights, Watt found skilled mechanics who could install, regulate, and repair his sophisticated engines. From ingenious manufacturers such as the cannonmaker John Wilkinson, Watt was gradually able to purchase precision parts. This support and more than twenty years of constant effort allowed him to create and regulate a complex engine. By the late 1780s the steam engine had become a practical and commercial success in England.

The steam engine of Watt and his followers was the Industrial Revolution's most fundamental advance in technology. For the first time in history, humanity had, at least for a few generations, almost unlimited power at its disposal. For the first time inventors and engineers could devise and implement all kinds of power equipment to aid people in their work. For the first time abundance was at least a possibility for ordinary men and women.

The steam engine was quickly put to use in several industries in England. It drained mines and made possible the production of ever more coal to feed steam engines elsewhere. The steam-power plant began to replace waterpower in the cotton-spinning mills during the 1780s, contributing greatly to that industry's phenomenal rise. Steam also took the place of waterpower in flour mills, in the malt mills used in breweries, in the flint mills supplying the china industry, and in the mills exported by England to the West Indies to crush sugar cane.

Steam power promoted important breakthroughs in other industries. The English iron industry was radically transformed. The use of powerful, steam-driven bellows in blast furnaces helped ironmakers switch over rapidly from limited charcoal to unlimited **coke** (which is made

**James Nasmyth's Mighty Steam Hammer** Nasmyth's invention was the forerunner of the modern pile driver, and its successful introduction in 1832 epitomized the rapid development of steam power technology in Britain. In this painting by the inventor himself, workers manipulate a massive iron shaft being hammered into shape at Nasmyth's foundry near Manchester. *(Science & Society Picture Library, London)*

from coal) in the smelting of pig iron after 1770. In the 1780s Henry Cort developed the puddling furnace, which allowed pig iron to be refined in turn with coke. Strong, skilled ironworkers—the puddlers—"cooked" molten pig iron in a great vat, raking off globs of refined iron for further processing. Cort also developed heavy-duty, steam-powered rolling mills, which were capable of spewing out finished iron in every shape and form.

The economic consequence of these technical innovations was a great boom in the English iron industry. In 1740 annual British iron production was only 17,000 tons. With the spread of coke smelting and the first impact of Cort's inventions, production reached 68,000 tons in 1788, 125,000 tons in 1796, and 260,000 tons in 1806. In 1844 Britain produced 3 million tons of iron. This was a truly amazing expansion. Once scarce and expensive, iron became the cheap, basic, indispensable building block of the economy.

## The Coming of the Railroads

The second half of the eighteenth century saw extensive construction of hard and relatively smooth roads, particularly in France before the Revolution. Yet it was passenger traffic that benefited most from this construction. Overland shipment of freight, relying solely on horsepower, was still quite limited and frightfully expensive. Shippers used rivers and canals for heavy freight whenever possible. It was logical, therefore, that inventors would try to apply steam power to transportation.

As early as 1800 an American ran a "steamer on wheels" through city streets. Other experiments followed. In the 1820s English engineers created steam cars capable of carrying fourteen passengers at ten miles an hour—as fast as the mail coach. But the noisy, heavy steam automobiles frightened passing horses and damaged themselves as well as the roads with their vibrations. For the rest of the century horses continued to reign on highways and city streets.

The coal industry had long been using plank roads and rails to move coal wagons within mines and at the surface. Rails reduced friction and allowed a horse or a human being to pull a heavier load. Thus once a rail capable of supporting a heavy locomotive was developed in 1816, all sorts of experiments with steam engines on rails went forward. In 1825 after ten years of work, George Stephenson built an effective locomotive. In 1830 his *Rocket* sped down the track of the just-completed Liverpool and Manchester Railway at sixteen miles per hour. This was the world's first important railroad, fittingly steaming in the heart of industrial England. The line from Liverpool to Manchester was a financial as well as a technical success, and many private companies were quickly organized to build more rail lines. Within twenty years these companies had completed the main trunk lines of Great Britain. Other countries were quick to follow.

The significance of the railroad was tremendous. The railroad dramatically reduced the cost and uncertainty of shipping freight overland. This advance had many economic consequences. Previously, markets had tended to be small and local. As the barrier of high transportation costs was lowered, markets became larger and even nationwide. These larger markets encouraged larger factories with more sophisticated machinery in a growing number of industries. Such factories could make goods more cheaply, and they gradually subjected most cottage workers and many urban artisans to severe competitive pressures.

In all countries the construction of railroads created a strong demand for unskilled labor and contributed to the growth of a class of urban workers. Many landless farm laborers and poor peasants, long accustomed to leaving their villages for temporary employment, went to build railroads. By the time the work was finished, life back home in the village often seemed dull and unappealing, and many men drifted to towns in search of work. By the time they sent for their wives and sweethearts to join them, they had become urban workers.

The railroad changed the outlook and values of the entire society. The last and culminating invention of the Industrial Revolution, the railroad dramatically revealed the power and increased the speed of the new age. Racing down a track at sixteen miles per hour or, by 1850, at a phenomenal fifty miles per hour was a new and awesome experience. As a French economist put it after a ride on the Liverpool and Manchester in 1833, "There are certain impressions that one cannot put into words!"

Some great painters, notably Joseph M. W. Turner (1775–1851) and Claude Monet (1840–1926), succeeded in expressing this sense of power and awe. So did the massive new train stations, the cathedrals of the industrial age. Leading railway engineers, whose tunnels pierced mountains and whose bridges spanned valleys, became public idols—the astronauts of their day. Everyday speech absorbed the images of railroading. After you got up a "full head of steam," you "highballed" along. And if you didn't "go off the track," you might "toot your own whistle." The railroad fired the imagination.

**The Saltash Bridge** Railroad construction presented innumerable challenges, such as the building of bridges to span rivers and gorges. Civil engineers responded with impressive feats, and their profession bounded ahead. This painting portrays the inauguration of I. K. Brunel's Saltash Bridge, where the railroad crosses the Tamar River into Cornwall in southwest England. The high spans allow large ships to pass underneath. *(Elton Collection, Ironbridge Gorge Museum Trust)*

## Industry and Population

In 1851 London was the site of a famous industrial fair. This Great Exhibition was held in the newly built **Crystal Palace,** an architectural masterpiece made entirely of glass and iron, both of which were now cheap and abundant. For the millions who visited, one fact stood out: the little island of Britain—England, Wales, and Scotland—was the "workshop of the world." It alone produced two-thirds of the world's coal and more than one-half of its iron and cotton cloth. More generally, it has been estimated that in 1860 Britain produced 20 percent of the entire world's output of industrial goods, whereas it had produced only about 2 percent of the world total in 1750.[5] Experiencing revolutionary industrial change, Britain became the first industrial nation (see Map 23.2).

As the British economy significantly increased its production of manufactured goods, the gross national product (GNP) rose roughly fourfold at constant prices between 1780 and 1851. In other words, the British people as a whole increased their wealth and their national income dramatically. At the same time, the population of Great Britain boomed, growing from about 9 million in 1780 to almost 21 million in 1851. Thus average consumption per person increased by only 75 percent between 1780 and 1851, as the growth in the total population ate up a large part of the fourfold increase in GNP in those years.[6]

Many economic historians now believe that rapid population growth in Great Britain was not harmful because it facilitated industrial expansion. More people meant a more mobile labor force, with many young workers in need of employment and ready to go where the jobs were. Contemporaries were much less optimistic. In his famous and influential *Essay on the Principle of Population* (1798), Thomas Malthus (1766–1834) argued that population

**The Crystal Palace** The Great Exhibition of 1851 attracted more than six million visitors, many of whom journeyed to London on the newly built railroads. Companies and countries displayed their products and juries awarded prizes in the strikingly modern Crystal Palace. Are today's malls really that different? *(Guildhall Library, Corporation of London/The Bridgeman Art Library International Ltd)*

would always tend to grow faster than the food supply. In Malthus's opinion the only hope of warding off "positive checks" to population growth such as war, famine, and disease was "prudential restraint": young men and women had to limit the growth of population by the old tried-and-true means of marrying late in life. But Malthus was not optimistic about this possibility. The powerful attraction of the sexes would cause most people to marry early and have many children.

Wealthy English stockbroker and leading economist David Ricardo (1772–1823) coldly spelled out the pessimistic implications of Malthus's thought. Ricardo's depressing **iron law of wages** posited that because of the pressure of population growth, wages would always sink to subsistence level—that is, wages would be just high enough to keep workers from starving. With Malthus and Ricardo setting the tone, economics was soon dubbed "the dismal science."

Malthus, Ricardo, and their many followers were proved wrong—in the long run. However, until the 1820s, or even the 1840s, contemporary observers might reasonably have concluded that the economy and the total population were racing neck and neck, with the outcome very much in doubt. The closeness of the race added to the difficulties inherent in the unprecedented journey toward industrial civilization.

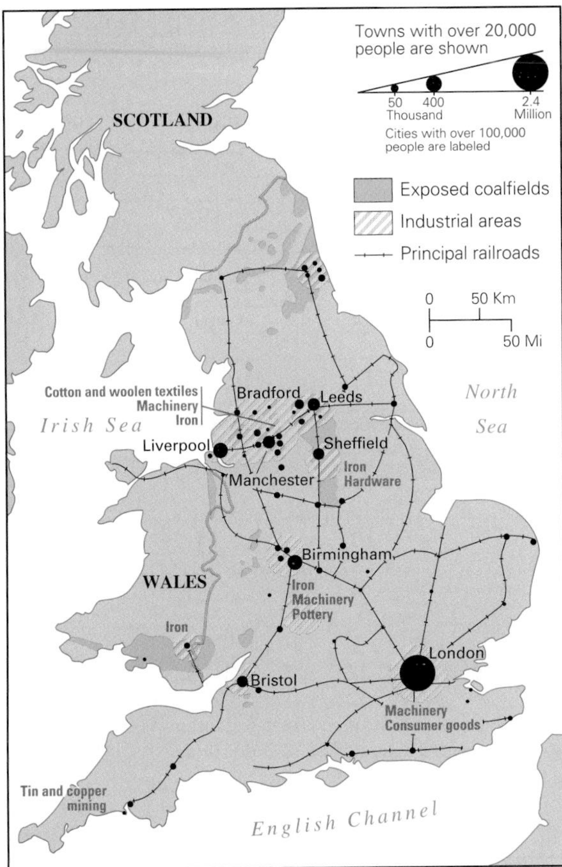


**MAP 23.2 The Industrial Revolution in England, ca 1850** Industry concentrated in the rapidly growing cities of the north and the Midlands, where rich coal and iron deposits were in close proximity.

There was another problem as well. Perhaps workers, farmers, and ordinary people did not get their rightful share of the new wealth. Perhaps only the rich got richer while the poor got poorer or made no progress. We will turn to this great issue after looking at the process of industrialization in continental European countries in the nineteenth century.

# INDUSTRIALIZATION IN CONTINENTAL EUROPE

The new technologies developed in the British Industrial Revolution were adopted rather slowly by businesses in continental Europe, and there were uneven jerks and national (and regional) variations. Scholars are still struggling to explain these variations, especially since good answers may offer valuable lessons in our own time for poor countries seeking to improve their material condition through industrialization and economic development. The latest findings on the Western experience are encouraging. They suggest that there were alternative paths to the industrial world in the nineteenth century and that there was (and is) no need to follow a rigid, predetermined British model.

## National Variations

European industrialization, like most economic developments, requires some statistical analysis as part of the effort to understand it. One set of data, the work of a Swiss scholar, compares the level of industrialization on a per capita basis in several countries from 1750 to 1913. These data are presented in Table 23.1 for closer study.

The table is a comparison of how much industrial product was available, on average, to each person in a given country in a given year. Therefore, all the numbers in Table 23.1 are expressed in terms of a single index number of 100, which equals the per capita level of industrial goods in Great Britain (and Ireland) in 1900. Every number is thus a percentage of the 1900 level in Great Britain and is directly comparable. The countries are listed in roughly the order in which they began to use large-scale, power-driven technology.

This quantitative overview of European industrialization confirms the primacy and relative rapidity of Britain's Industrial Revolution. In 1750 all countries were fairly close together. But by 1800 Britain had opened up a noticeable lead, and that gap progressively widened as the British Industrial Revolution accelerated to full maturity by 1860. The British level of per capita industrialization was twice the French level in 1830, for example, and more than three times the French level in 1860. All other large countries (except the United States) had fallen even further behind Britain than France had at both dates.

Second, variations in the timing and in the extent of industrialization in the continental powers and the United States are also apparent. Belgium, independent in 1831 and rich in iron and coal, led in adopting Britain's new technology. France developed factory production more gradually, and most historians now detect no burst in French mechanization and industrial output that may accurately be called revolutionary. They stress instead France's relatively good pattern of early industrial growth, which was unjustly tarnished by the spectacular rise of Germany and the United States after 1860. By 1913 Germany was rapidly closing in on Britain, and the United States had already passed Britain in per capita production.

**TABLE 23.1 PER CAPITA LEVELS OF INDUSTRIALIZATION, 1750–1913**

| | 1750 | 1800 | 1830 | 1860 | 1880 | 1900 | 1913 |
|---|---|---|---|---|---|---|---|
| Great Britain | 10 | 16 | 25 | 64 | 87 | 100 | 115 |
| Belgium | 9 | 10 | 14 | 28 | 43 | 56 | 88 |
| United States | 4 | 9 | 14 | 21 | 38 | 69 | 126 |
| France | 9 | 9 | 12 | 20 | 28 | 39 | 59 |
| Germany | 8 | 8 | 9 | 15 | 25 | 52 | 85 |
| Austria-Hungary | 7 | 7 | 8 | 11 | 15 | 23 | 32 |
| Italy | 8 | 8 | 8 | 10 | 12 | 17 | 26 |
| Russia | 6 | 6 | 7 | 8 | 10 | 15 | 20 |
| China | 8 | 6 | 6 | 4 | 4 | 3 | 3 |
| India | 7 | 6 | 6 | 3 | 2 | 1 | 2 |

*Note:* All entries are based on an index value of 100, equal to the per capita level of industrialization in Great Britain in 1900. Data for Great Britain are actually for the United Kingdom, thereby including Ireland with England, Wales, and Scotland.

*Source:* P. Bairoch, "International Industrialization Levels from 1750 to 1980," *Journal of European Economic History* 11 (Fall 1982): 294. Reprinted with permission.

Finally, all European states (as well as the United States, Canada, and Japan) managed to raise per capita industrial levels in the nineteenth century. These continent-wide increases stood in stark contrast to the large decreases that occurred at the same time in most non-Western countries, most notably in China and India. European countries industrialized to a greater or lesser extent even as most of the non-Western world *de*-industrialized. Thus differential rates of wealth- and power-creating industrial development, which heightened disparities within Europe, also greatly magnified existing inequalities between Europe and the rest of the world. We shall return to this momentous change in Chapters 26 and 27.

## The Challenge of Industrialization

The different patterns of industrial development suggest that the process of industrialization was far from automatic. Indeed, building modern industry was an awesome challenge. When the pace of English industry began to accelerate in the 1780s, continental businesses began to adopt the new methods as they proved their profitability. English industry enjoyed clear superiority, but at first continental Europe was close behind. By 1815, however, the situation was quite different. In spite of wartime difficulties, English industry maintained the momentum of the 1780s and continued to grow and improve between 1789 and 1815. On the continent, the unending political and economic upheavals that began with the French Revolution disrupted trade, created runaway inflation, and impeded continental efforts to use new British machinery and technology. Thus economically and industrially France and the rest of Europe were further behind Britain in 1815 than in 1789.

This widening gap made it more difficult, if not impossible, for other countries to follow the British pattern in energy and industry after peace was restored in 1815. Above all, in the newly mechanized industries British goods were being produced very economically, and these goods had come to dominate world markets completely. Continental European firms had little hope of competing with mass-produced British goods in foreign markets for

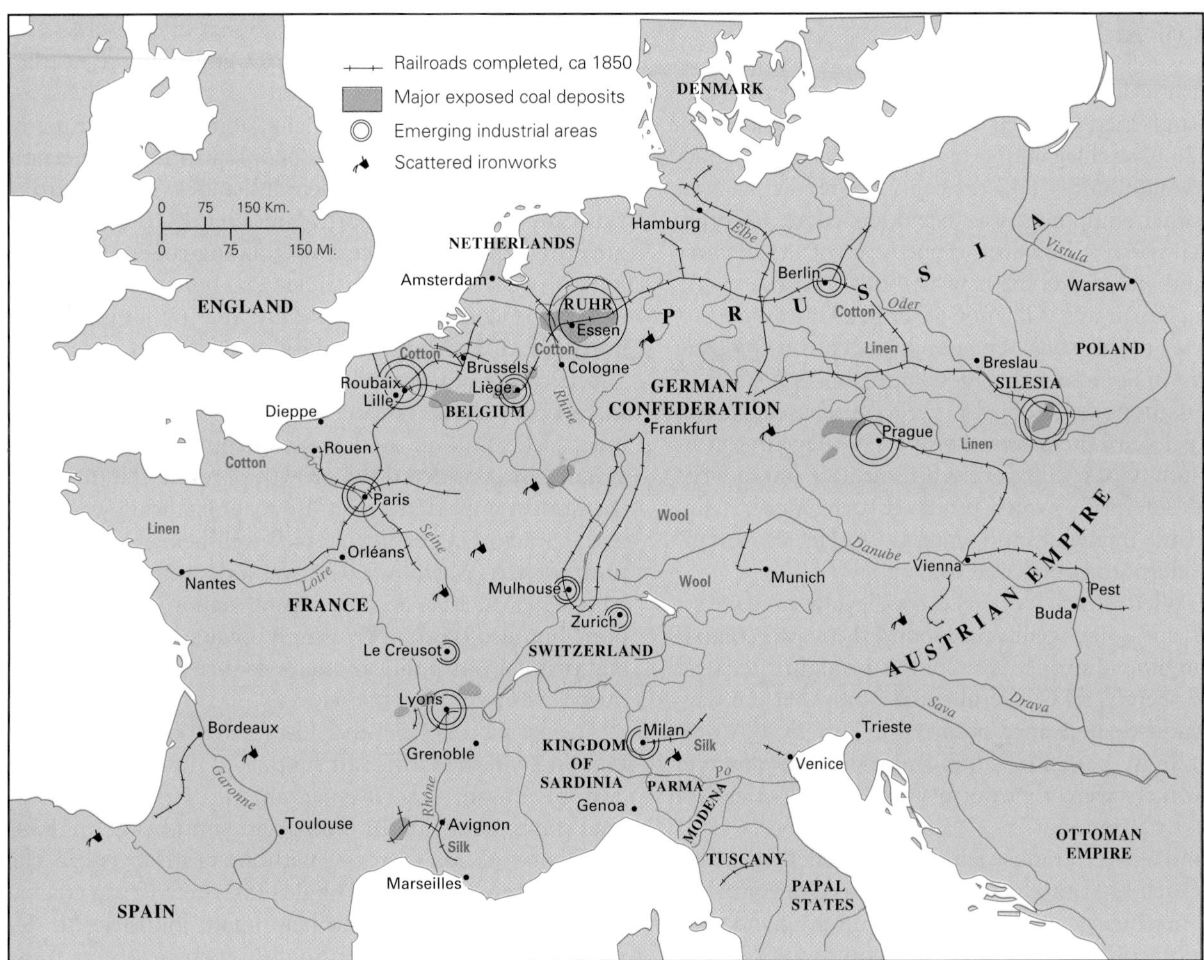


**MAP 23.3 Continental European Industrialization, ca 1850** Although continental countries were beginning to make progress by 1850, they still lagged far behind Britain. For example, continental railroad building was still in an early stage, whereas the British rail system was essentially complete.

a long time. In addition, British technology had become so advanced and complicated that very few engineers or skilled technicians outside England understood it. Moreover, the technology of steam power had grown much more expensive. It involved large investments in the iron and coal industries and, after 1830, required the existence of railroads, which were very costly. Continental business people had great difficulty finding the large sums of money the new methods demanded, and there was a shortage of laborers accustomed to working in factories. Landowners and government officials were often so suspicious of the new form of industry and the changes it brought that they did little at first to encourage it. All these disadvantages slowed the spread of modern industry (see Map 23.3).

After 1815, however, continental countries also had at least three important advantages. First, most had a rich tradition of putting-out enterprise, merchant capitalists, and skilled urban artisans. Such a tradition gave continental firms the ability to adapt and survive in the face of new market conditions. Second, continental capitalists could simply "borrow" the advanced technology already developed in Great Britain, as well as engineers and some of the financial resources these countries lacked. European countries had a third asset that many non-Western areas lacked in the nineteenth century. They had strong independent governments, which did not fall under foreign political control. These governments could fashion economic policies to serve their own interests.

## Agents of Industrialization

The British realized the great value of their technical discoveries and tried to keep their secrets to themselves. Until 1825 it was illegal for artisans and skilled mechanics to leave Britain; until 1843 the export of textile machinery and other equipment was forbidden. Many talented, ambitious workers, however, slipped out of the country illegally and introduced the new methods abroad.

One such man was William Cockerill, a Lancashire carpenter. He and his sons began building cotton-spinning equipment in French-occupied Belgium in 1799. In 1817 the most famous son, John Cockerill, purchased the old summer palace of the deposed bishops of Liège in southern Belgium. Cockerill converted the palace into a large industrial enterprise, which produced machinery, steam engines, and then railway locomotives. He also established modern ironworks and coal mines.

Many skilled British workers came illegally to work for Cockerill, and some went on to found their own companies throughout Europe. Newcomers brought the latest plans and secrets, so Cockerill could boast that ten days after an industrial advance occurred in Britain, he knew all about it in Belgium. Thus British technicians and skilled workers were a powerful force in the spread of early industrialization.

A second agent of industrialization was talented entrepreneurs such as Fritz Harkort, a business pioneer in the German machinery industry. Serving in England as a Prussian army officer during the Napoleonic wars, Harkort concluded that Germany had to match English achievements as quickly as possible. Setting up shop in an abandoned castle in the still-tranquil Ruhr Valley, he felt an almost religious calling to build steam engines and become the "Watt of Germany."

Harkort's basic idea was simple but enormously difficult to carry out. Lacking skilled laborers to do the job, Harkort turned to England for experienced, though expensive, mechanics. He had to import from England the thick iron boilers that he needed at great cost. In spite of these problems, Harkort built and sold engines, winning fame and praise. His ambitious efforts over sixteen years also resulted in large financial losses for himself and his partners, and in 1832 his financial backers forced him out of his company and cut back operations to reduce losses. Harkort's career illustrates both the great efforts of a few important business leaders to duplicate the British achievement and the difficulty of the task.

Less famous entrepreneurs adopted factory technology slowly, and handicraft methods lived on. In France, for example, artisan production of luxury items grew, as the rising income of the international middle class created foreign demand for silk scarfs, embroidered needlework, perfumes, and fine wines.

A third force for industrialization was government, which often helped business people in European countries to overcome some of their difficulties. **Tariff protection** was one such support. And after 1815 continental governments bore the cost of building roads and canals to improve transportation. They also bore to a significant extent the cost of building railroads, the all-important leading sector in continental industrialization.

The career of German journalist and thinker Friedrich List (1789–1846) reflects government's greater role in industrialization on the European continent than in England. List considered the growth of modern industry of the utmost importance because manufacturing was a primary means of increasing people's well-being and relieving their poverty. Moreover, List was a dedicated nationalist who believed that an agricultural nation was not only poor but also weak, increasingly unable to defend itself and maintain its political independence. To promote industry was to defend the nation.

The practical policies that List focused on were railroad building and the tariff. List supported the formation of a customs union, or *Zollverein,* among the separate German states. Such a tariff union came into being in 1834. It allowed goods to move without tariffs between the German member states. A single uniform tariff was erected against all other nations to help infant industries to develop. List denounced the English doctrine of free trade as little more than England's attempt "to make the rest of the world, like the Hindus, its serfs in all industrial and commercial relations." By the 1840s List's **economic nationalism** had become increasingly popular in Germany and elsewhere.

Banks, like governments, also played a larger and more creative role in Europe than in England. Previously, almost all banks in Europe had been private partnerships. All the active partners were liable for all the debts of the firm. This unlimited liability meant that in the event of a disastrous bankruptcy each partner could lose all of his or her personal wealth. Such banks were content to deal with a few rich clients and a few big merchants. They generally avoided industrial investment as being too risky.

In the 1830s two important Belgian banks pioneered in a new direction, establishing themselves as corporations enjoying limited liability. A stockholder in these two banks could lose only his or her original investment in the bank's common stock. Able to attract many shareholders, large and small, because of the reduced risk, these Belgian banks mobilized impressive resources for

**A German Ironworks, 1850** This big business enterprise has mastered the new British method of smelting iron with coke. Germany, and especially the state of Prussia, was well endowed with both iron and coal, and the rapid exploitation of these resources after 1840 transformed a poor agricultural country into an industrial powerhouse. *(Deutsches Museum Munich)*

investment in big industrial companies. They became industrial banks and successfully promoted industrial development.

Similar corporate banks became important in France and Germany in the 1850s and 1860s. Usually working in collaboration with governments, they established and developed many railroads and many companies working in heavy industry, which were increasingly organized as limited-liability corporations.

The combined efforts of skilled workers, entrepreneurs, governments, and industrial banks meshed successfully between 1850 and the financial crash of 1873. In Belgium, Germany, and France, key indicators of modern industrial development—railway mileage, iron and coal production, and steam-engine capacity—increased at average annual rates ranging from 5 to 10 percent compounded. In the early 1870s Britain was still Europe's most industrial nation, but a select handful of countries was closing the gap that had been opened up by the Industrial Revolution.

## Capital and Labor

Industrial development brought new social relations and intensified long-standing problems between capital and labor. A new group of factory owners and industrial capitalists arose. These men and women and their families strengthened the wealth and size of the middle class, which had previously been made up mainly of merchants and professional people. The nineteenth century became the golden age of the middle class. Modern industry also created a much larger group: the factory workers. For the first time large numbers of men, women, and children

**Ford Maddox Brown: Work** This mid-century painting provides a rich visual representation of the new concepts of social class that became common by 1850. The central figures are the colorful laborers, endowed by the artist with strength and nobility. Close by, a poor girl minds her brother and sister for her working mother. On the right, a middle-class minister and a social critic observe and do intellectual work. What work does the couple on horseback perform? *(Birmingham Museums and Art Gallery/The Bridgeman Art Library International Ltd)*

came together under one roof to work with complicated machinery for a single owner or a few partners in large companies.

The growth of new occupational groups in industry stimulated new thinking about social relations. It was argued, with considerable success, that individuals were members of economically determined classes that had conflicting interests. Accordingly, the comfortable, well-educated "public" of the eighteenth century came increasingly to see itself as the backbone of the middle class (or the middle classes), and the "people" gradually transformed themselves into the modern working class (or working classes). The new class interpretation appealed to many because it seemed to explain what was happening. Thus conflicting classes came into being in part because many individuals came to believe that they existed and developed an appropriate sense of class feeling—what Marxists call **class consciousness.**

## The New Class of Factory Owners

Early industrialists operated in a highly competitive economic system in which success and large profits were by no means certain. Manufacturers waged a constant battle to cut their production costs and stay afloat. Much of the profit had to go back into the business for new and better machinery. "Dragged on by the frenzy of this terrible life," according to one of the dismayed critics, the struggling manufacturer had "no time for niceties. He must conquer or die, make a fortune or drown himself."[7]

The early industrialists came from a variety of backgrounds. Many, such as Harkort, were from well-established merchant families, but artisans and skilled workers of exceptional ability had unparalleled opportunities. The ethnic and religious groups that had been discriminated against in the traditional occupations controlled by the landed aristocracy jumped at the new chances. Quakers and Scots were tremendously important in England; Protestants and Jews dominated banking in Catholic France. Many of the industrialists were newly rich and, not surprisingly, very proud and self-satisfied.

As factories grew larger, opportunities declined, at least in well-developed industries. It became considerably harder for a gifted but poor young mechanic to end up as a wealthy manufacturer. Formal education became more important as a means of advancement, and formal education at the advanced level was expensive. In England by 1830 and in France and Germany by 1860, leading industrialists were more likely to have inherited their well-established enterprises, and they were financially much more secure than their fathers and grandfathers had been. They also had a greater sense of class consciousness, fully aware that ongoing industrial development had widened the gap between themselves and their workers.

The wives and daughters of successful businessmen also found fewer opportunities for active participation in Europe's increasingly complex business world. Rather than contributing as vital partners in a family-owned enterprise, as so many middle-class women such as Elizabeth Strutt had done (see the feature "Individuals in Society: The Strutt Family"), these women were increasingly valued for their ladylike gentility. By 1850 some influential women writers and most businessmen assumed that middle-class wives and daughters should steer clear of undignified work in offices and factories. Rather, a middle-class lady should protect and enhance her femininity, concentrating on her proper role as wife and mother.

## The New Factory Workers

The social consequences of the Industrial Revolution have long been hotly debated. The condition of English workers during the transformation has always generated the most controversy among historians because England was the first country to industrialize and because the social consequences seemed harshest there. Before 1850 other countries had not proceeded very far with industrialization, and almost everyone agrees that the economic conditions of European workers improved after 1850. Thus the experience of English workers to about 1850 deserves special attention. (Industrial growth also promoted rapid urbanization, with its own awesome problems, as will be shown in Chapter 25.)

From the beginning the Industrial Revolution in England had its critics. Among the first were the romantic poets. William Blake (1757–1827) called the early factories "satanic mills" and protested against the hard life of the London poor. William Wordsworth (1770–1850) lamented the destruction of the rural way of life and the pollution of the land and water. Some handicraft workers—notably the **Luddites,** who attacked whole factories in northern England in 1812 and after—smashed the new machines, which they believed were putting them out of work. Doctors and reformers wrote eloquently of problems in the factories and new towns, and Malthus and Ricardo concluded that workers would earn only enough to stay alive.

Friedrich Engels (1820–1895), the future revolutionary and colleague of Karl Marx, accepted and reinforced this pessimistic view. After studying conditions in northern England, this young middle-class German published in 1844 *The Condition of the Working Class in England.* "At the bar of world opinion," he wrote, "I charge the English middle classes with mass murder, wholesale robbery, and all the other crimes in the calendar."[8] The new poverty of industrial workers was worse than the old poverty of cottage workers and agricultural laborers, according to Engels, and the culprit was industrial capitalism. Engels's extremely influential charge of middle-class exploitation and increasing worker poverty was embellished by Marx and later socialists.

Meanwhile, other observers believed that conditions were improving for the working people. Edwin Chadwick, a great and conscientious government official well acquainted with the problems of the working population, concluded that the "whole mass of the laboring community" was increasingly able "to buy more of the necessities and minor luxuries of life."[9] Nevertheless, if all the contemporary assessments had been counted up, those who thought conditions were getting worse for working people would probably have been the majority.

Scholarly statistical studies have weakened the idea that the condition of the working class got much worse with industrialization. But recent studies also confirm the view that the early years of the Industrial Revolution were hard ones for British workers. From about 1780 to about 1820 there was little or no increase in the purchasing power of the average British worker's wages. The years from 1792 to 1815, a period of almost constant warfare with France, were particularly difficult. Food prices rose faster than wages, and the living conditions of the laboring poor declined. Only after 1820, and especially after 1840, did real wages rise substantially. The average worker earned and consumed roughly 50 percent more in real terms in 1850 than in 1770.[10] In short, there was considerable economic improvement for workers throughout Great Britain by 1850, but that improvement was hard won and slow in coming.

This important conclusion must be qualified, however. Increased purchasing power meant more goods but not necessarily greater happiness. More goods may have provided meager compensation for work that was dangerous and monotonous, for example. Also, statistical studies do not say anything about how the level of unemployment may have risen, for the simple reason that there are no good unemployment statistics from this period. Furthermore, the hours in the average workweek increased; to an unknown extent, workers earned more simply because they worked more. Finally, notwithstanding what came afterward, the difficult wartime years colored the early experience of modern industrial life in somber tones.

Another way to consider the workers' standard of living is to look at the goods they purchased. Again the evidence is somewhat contradictory. Speaking generally, workers ate somewhat more food of higher nutritional quality as the Industrial Revolution progressed, except during wartime, and diets became more varied. Clothing improved, but housing for working people probably deteriorated somewhat. In short, per capita use of specific goods supports the position that the standard of living of the working classes rose, at least moderately, after the long wars with France.

## Conditions of Work

What about working conditions? Did workers eventually earn more only at the cost of working longer and harder? Were workers exploited harshly by the new factory owners?

The first factories were cotton mills, which began functioning along rivers and streams in the 1770s. Cottage workers were reluctant to work in factories even when they received relatively good wages. In the factory, workers had to keep up with the machine and follow its tempo. They had to show up every day and work long, monotonous hours, adjusting their daily lives to the shrill call of the factory whistle. Cottage workers were not used to that kind of life and discipline. All members of the family worked hard and long, but in spurts, setting their own pace. They could interrupt their work when they wanted to. Women and children could break up their long hours of spinning with other tasks.

Also, early factories resembled English poorhouses, where totally destitute people went to live at public expense. Some poorhouses were industrial prisons where the inmates had to work in order to receive their food and lodging. The similarity between large brick factories and large stone poorhouses increased the cottage workers' fear of factories and their hatred of factory discipline.

It was cottage workers' reluctance to work in factories that prompted the early cotton mill owners to turn to abandoned and pauper children for their labor. These owners contracted with local officials to employ large numbers of these children, who were apprenticed as young as five or six years of age and who were forced by law to labor for their "master" for as many as fourteen years. Housed, fed, and locked up nightly in factory dormitories, the young workers received little or no pay. Hours were appalling—commonly thirteen or fourteen hours a day, six days a week. Harsh physical punishment maintained strict discipline. To be sure, poor children typically worked long hours from an early age in the eighteenth century, but this unprecedented wholesale exploitation ultimately stirred the conscience of reformers and encouraged more humanitarian attitudes toward children and their labor.

By 1790 the early pattern was rapidly changing. The use of pauper apprentices was in decline, and in 1802 it was forbidden by Parliament. Many more factories were being built, mainly in urban areas, where they could use steam power rather than waterpower and attract a workforce more easily than in the countryside. People came from near and far to work in the cities, both as factory workers and as laborers, builders, and domestic servants. Yet as they took these new jobs, working people did not simply give in to a system of labor that had formerly repelled them. Rather, they helped modify the system by carrying over old, familiar working traditions.

For one thing, they often came to the mills and the mines as family units. This was how they had worked on farms and in cottage industry. The mill or mine owner paid the head of the family for the work of the whole family. In the cotton mills children worked for their mothers or fathers, collecting wastes and "piecing" broken threads together. In the mines children sorted coal, mothers pulled coal wagons through narrow tunnels, and fathers hewed with pick and shovel at the face of the seam.

The preservation of the family as an economic unit in the factories from the 1790s on made the new surroundings more tolerable, both in Great Britain and in other

# INDIVIDUALS IN SOCIETY

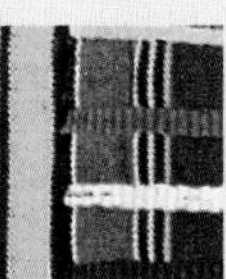

## THE STRUTT FAMILY

For centuries economic life in Europe revolved around hundreds of thousands of small family enterprises. These family enterprises worked farms, crafted products, and traded goods. They built and operated the firms and factories of the early industrial era, with the notable exceptions of the capital-hungry railroads and a few big banks. Indeed, until late in the nineteenth century, close-knit family groups continued to control most successful businesses, including those organized as corporations.

One successful and fairly well-documented family enterprise began with the marriage of Jedediah Strutt (1726–1797) and Elizabeth Woollat (1729–1774) in Derbyshire in northern England in 1755. The son of a farmer, Jedediah fell in love with Elizabeth when he was apprenticed away from home as a wheelwright and lodged with her parents. Both young people grew up in the close-knit dissenting Protestant community, which did not accept the doctrines of the state-sponsored Church of England, and the well-educated Elizabeth worked in a local school for dissenters and then for a dissenter minister in London. Indecisive and self-absorbed, Jedediah inherited in 1754 a small stock of animals from an uncle and finally married Elizabeth the following year.

Aided by Elizabeth, who was "obviously a very capable woman" and who supplied some of the drive her husband had previously lacked, Jedediah embarked on a new career.* He invented a machine to make handsome, neat-fitting ribbed silk stockings, which had previously been made by hand. He secured a patent, despite strong opposition from competitors, and went into production. Elizabeth helped constantly in the enterprise, which was nothing less than an informal partnership between husband and wife.†

In 1757, for example, when Jedediah was fighting to uphold his patent in the local court, Elizabeth left her son of nine months and journeyed to London to seek a badly needed loan from her former employer. She also canvassed her London relatives and dissenter friends for orders for stockings and looked for sales agents and sources of capital. Elizabeth's letters reveal a detailed knowledge of ribbed stockings and the prices and quality of different kinds of thread. The family biographers, old-line economic historians writing without a trace of feminist concerns, conclude that her husband "owed much of his success to her energy and counsel." Elizabeth was always "active in the business—a partner in herself."‡ Historians have often overlooked such invaluable contributions from wives like Elizabeth, partly because the legal rights and consequences of partnership were denied to married women in Britain and Europe in the eighteenth and nineteenth centuries.

*Jedediah Strutt (ca 1790), by Joseph Wright of Derby.* (Derby Museum & Art Gallery/ The Bridgeman Art Library International Ltd)

The Strutt enterprise grew and gradually prospered, but it always retained its family character. The firm built a large silk mill and then went into cotton spinning in partnership with Richard Arkwright, the inventor of the water frame (see page 736). The brothers of both Jedediah and Elizabeth worked for the firm, and their eldest daughter worked long hours in the warehouse. Bearing three sons, Elizabeth fulfilled yet another vital task because the typical family firm looked to its own members for managers and continued success. All three sons entered the business and became cotton textile magnates. Elizabeth never saw these triumphs. The loyal and talented wife in the family partnership died suddenly at age forty-five while in London with Jedediah on a business trip.

### QUESTIONS FOR ANALYSIS

1. How and why did the Strutts succeed?
2. What does Elizabeth's life tell us about the role of British women in the early Industrial Revolution?

*R. Fitton and A. Wadsworth, *The Strutts and the Arkwrights, 1758–1830: A Study of the Early Factory System* (Manchester, England: Manchester University Press, 1958), p. 23.

†See the excellent discussion by C. Hall, "Strains in the 'Firm of Wife, Children and Friends'? Middle-Class Women and Employment in Early Nineteenth-Century England," in P. Hudson and W. Lee, eds., *Women's Work and the Family Economy in Historical Perspective* (Manchester, England: Manchester University Press, 1990), pp. 106–132.

‡Fitton and Wadsworth, *The Strutts,* pp. 110–111.

countries. Parents disciplined their children and directed their upbringing. The presence of the whole family meant that children and adults worked the same long hours (twelve-hour shifts were normal in cotton mills in 1800). Only when technical changes threatened to place control and discipline in the hands of impersonal managers and foremen did adult workers protest against inhuman conditions in the name of their children.

Some enlightened employers and social reformers in Parliament definitely felt otherwise. They argued that more humane standards were necessary, and they used widely circulated parliamentary reports to influence public opinion. (See the feature "Listening to the Past: The Testimony of Young Mine Workers" on pages 758–759.) For example, Robert Owen (1771–1858), a very successful manufacturer in Scotland, testified in 1816 before an investigating committee on the basis of his experience. He stated that "very strong facts" demonstrated that employing children under ten years of age as factory workers was "injurious to the children, and not beneficial to the proprietors."[11] Workers also provided graphic testimony at such hearings as the reformers pressed Parliament to pass corrective laws. They scored some important successes.

Their first major accomplishment was the **Factory Act of 1833.** It limited the factory workday for children between the ages of nine and thirteen to eight hours and that of adolescents between fourteen and eighteen to twelve hours, although the act made no effort to regulate the hours of work for children at home or in small businesses. The law also prohibited the factory employment of children under nine; they were to be enrolled in the elementary schools that factory owners were required to establish. The employment of children declined rapidly. Thus the Factory Act broke the pattern of whole families working together in the factory.

**Cotton Mill Workers** Family members often worked side by side in early British factories, and the child on the left is quite possibly the daughter of the woman nearby. They are combing raw cotton and drawing it into loose strands called rovings, which will be spun into fine thread on the machines to the right. *(Mary Evans Picture Library)*

## The Sexual Division of Labor

The era of the Industrial Revolution witnessed major changes in the sexual division of labor. In preindustrial Europe certain jobs were traditionally defined by gender—women and girls for milking and spinning, men and boys for plowing and weaving—but many tasks might go to either sex as particular circumstances dictated. Family employment carried over into early factories and subcontracting, but it collapsed as child labor was restricted and new attitudes emerged. A different sexual division of labor gradually arose to take its place. The man emerged as the family's primary wage earner, and the woman found only limited job opportunities. Generally denied good jobs at good wages in the growing urban economy, women were expected to concentrate on unpaid housework, child care, and craftwork at home.

This new pattern of "separate spheres" had several aspects. First, all studies agree that married women were much less likely to work full-time for wages outside the house after the first child arrived, although they often earned small amounts doing putting-out handicrafts at home and taking in boarders. Second, married women who did work for wages outside the house usually came from the poorest families, where the husbands were poorly paid, sick, unemployed, or missing. Third, these poor married (or widowed) women were joined by legions of young unmarried women, who worked full-time but only in certain jobs. Fourth, all women were generally confined to low-paying, dead-end jobs. Virtually no occupation open to women paid a wage sufficient for a person to live independently. Evolving gradually but largely in place by 1850, the new sexual division of labor in Britain constituted a major development in the history of women and of the family.

Although the reorganization of paid work along gender lines is widely recognized, there is as yet no agreement on its causes. One school of scholars sees little connection with industrialization and finds the answer in the deeply ingrained sexist attitudes of a "patriarchal tradition," which predated the economic transformation. These scholars stress the role of male-dominated craft unions in denying women access to good jobs and relegating them to unpaid housework. Other scholars, stressing that the gender roles of women and men can vary enormously with time and culture, look more to a combination of economic and biological factors to explain the emergence of a sex-segregated division of labor.

Three ideas stand out in this more recent interpretation. First, the new and unfamiliar discipline of the clock and the machine was especially hard on married women. Above all, relentless factory discipline conflicted with child care in a way that labor on the farm or in the cottage had not done. A woman operating ear-splitting spinning machinery could mind a child of seven or eight working beside her (until such work was outlawed), but she could no longer pace herself through pregnancy or breast-feed her baby on the job. Thus a working-class woman had strong incentives to concentrate on child care within her home if her family could afford for her to do so.

Second, running a household in conditions of primitive urban poverty was an extremely demanding job in its own right. There were no supermarkets or public transportation. Everything had to be done on foot. Shopping and feeding the family constituted a never-ending challenge. The woman marched from one tiny shop to another, dragging her tired children (for who was to watch them?) and struggling valiantly with heavy sacks and tricky shopkeepers. Yet another brutal job outside the house—a "second shift"—had limited appeal for the average married woman. Thus women might well have accepted the emerging division of labor as the best available strategy for family survival in the industrializing society.[12]

Third, why were the women who did work for wages outside the home segregated and confined to certain "women's jobs"? No doubt the desire of men to monopolize the best opportunities and hold women down provides part of the answer. But as some feminist scholars have argued, sex-segregated employment was also a collective response to the new industrial system. The growth of factories and mines brought unheard-of opportunities for girls and boys to mix on the job, free of familial supervision. Continuing to mix after work, they were "more likely to form liaisons, initiate courtships, and respond to advances."[13] Such intimacy also led to more unplanned pregnancies and fueled the illegitimacy explosion that had begun in the late eighteenth century and that gathered force until at least 1850. Thus segregation of jobs by gender was partly an effort by older people to help control the sexuality of working-class youths.

Investigations into the British coal industry before 1842 provide a graphic example of this concern (see pages 758–759). The middle-class men leading the inquiry often failed to appreciate the physical effort of the girls and women who dragged the carts of coal along narrow underground passages. But they professed horror at the sight of girls and women working without shirts, which was a common practice because of the heat, and they quickly assumed the prevalence of licentious sex with the male miners, who also wore very little clothing. In fact, most girls and married women worked for related males in a family unit that provided considerable protection and restraint. Yet many witnesses from the working class also believed that "blackguardism and debauchery" were common and that "they are best out of the pits, the lasses." Some miners stressed particularly the danger of sexual aggression in letting girls work past puberty. As one explained, "I consider it a scandal for girls to work in the pits. Till they are 12 or 14 they may work very well but after that it's an abomination. . . . The work of the pit does not hurt them, it is the effect on their morals that I complain of."[14] The **Mines Act of 1842** prohibited underground work for all women as well as for boys under ten.

Some women who had to support themselves protested against being excluded from coal mining, which paid higher wages than most other jobs open to women. But the girls and the women who had worked underground were generally pleased with the law if they were part of families that could manage economically. In explaining her satisfaction in 1844, one mother of four provided a real insight into why many women accepted the emerging sexual division of labor:

> *While working in the pit I was worth to my [miner] husband seven shillings a week, out of which we had to pay 2½ shillings to a woman for looking after the younger children. I used to take them to her house at 4 o'clock in the morning, out of their own beds, to put them into hers. Then there was one shilling a week for washing; besides, there was mending to pay for, and other things. The house was not guided. The other children broke things; they did not go to school when they were sent; they would be playing about, and get ill-used by other children, and their clothes torn. Then when I came home in the evening, everything was to do after the day's labor, and I was so tired I had no heart for it; no fire lit, nothing cooked, no water fetched, the house dirty, and nothing comfortable for my husband. It is all far better now, and I wouldn't go down again.*[15]

## The Early Labor Movement

Many kinds of employment changed slowly during and after the Industrial Revolution in Great Britain. In 1850 more British people still worked on farms than in any other occupation. The second largest occupation was domestic service, with more than a million household servants, 90 percent of whom were women. Thus many old, familiar jobs outside industry lived on and provided alternatives for individual workers. This helped ease the transition to industrial civilization.

Within industry itself the pattern of artisans working with hand tools in small shops remained unchanged in many trades, even as technological change revolutionized some others. For example, as in the case of cotton and coal, large-scale capitalist firms completely dominated the British iron industry by 1850. Yet the firms that fashioned iron into small metal goods—such as tools, tableware, and toys—employed on average fewer than ten wage workers, who used time-honored handicraft skills. The survival of small workshops in some handicraft industries gave many workers an alternative to factory employment.

In Great Britain and in other countries later on, workers gradually built a labor movement to improve working conditions and to serve their needs. In 1799, partly in panicked reaction to the French Revolution, Parliament had passed the Combination Acts outlawing unions and strikes. These acts were widely disregarded by workers. Societies of skilled factory workers organized unions, as printers, papermakers, carpenters, and other such craftsmen had long since done. The unions sought to control the number of skilled workers, limit apprenticeship to members' own children, and bargain with owners over wages. They were not afraid to strike; there was, for example, a general strike of adult cotton spinners in Manchester in 1810. In the face of widespread union activity Parliament repealed the Combination Acts in 1824, and unions were tolerated though not fully accepted after 1825.

The next stage in the development of the British trade-union movement was the attempt to create a single large national union. This effort was led not so much by working people as by social reformers such as Robert Owen. Owen, the self-made cotton manufacturer quoted earlier, had pioneered in industrial relations by combining firm discipline with concern for the health, safety, and hours of his workers. After 1815 he experimented with cooperative and socialist communities, including one at New Harmony, Indiana. Then in 1834 Owen organized one of the largest and most visionary of the early national unions, the **Grand National Consolidated Trades Union.** When this and other grandiose schemes collapsed, the British labor movement moved once again after 1851 in the direction of craft unions. The most famous of these "new model unions" was the Amalgamated Society of Engineers. These unions won real benefits for members by fairly conservative means and thus became an accepted part of the industrial scene.

British workers also engaged in direct political activity in defense of their own interests. After the collapse of Owen's national trade union, many working people went into the Chartist movement, whose goal was political democracy. The key Chartist demand—that all men be given the right to vote—became the great hope of mil-

No. 11. VOL. III.] SATURDAY, NOVEMBER 9, 1833. [Price 1½d.

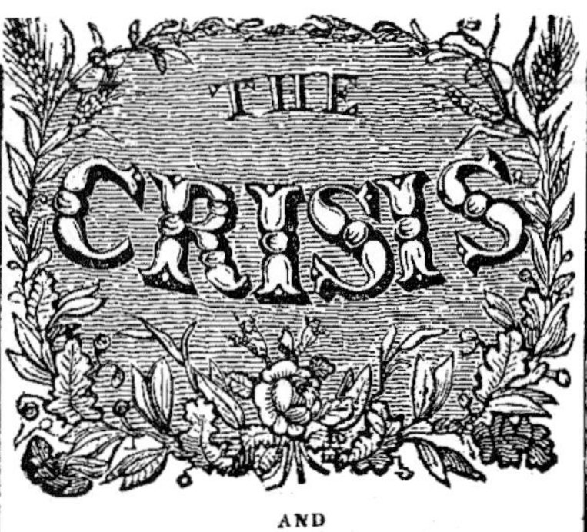

AND

NATIONAL CO-OPERATIVE TRADES' UNION AND EQUITABLE LABOUR EXCHANGE GAZETTE

"THE CHARACTER OF EVERY HUMAN BEING IS FORMED FOR, AND NOT BY, THE INDIVIDUAL."—*Owen.*

**Weekly Proceedings.**

INSTITUTION, CHARLOTTE-STREET.

SUNDAY EVENING.

Mr. *Smith* lectured on "CIRCUMSTANCES—INFLUENCE OF CLIMATE ON RELIGION."

In hot climates men have always considered themselves entitled to as many wives as they chose. The Jews were not restricted to any number. Solomon had a thousand, and the chaste and more just than those of Moses himself, who by the authority of God went much further, in respect to women at least, than either Owen or St. Simon. These changes are entirely to be accounted for by a change of circumstances; there is no particular system or form of manners or customs either good or bad in themselves; but those which conduce to the greatest amount of happiness to the public at large, and the individual in particular, ought other replies,—"Every day as soon as they have dressed themselves they take up their arms, and, entering the lists, they fight till they cut each other in pieces. This is their diversion. But no sooner does the hour of repast approach, than they remount their steeds, all safe and whole again, and return to drink in the palace of Odin." But the hell of these cold climates is the very opposite of the hells that come from the tropics. The hell of these northern

**The Working-Class Press** *The Crisis,* an influential newspaper inspired by the teachings of Robert Owen, summed up its analysis of Britain's problems with two images at the top of the first page. Degrading poverty for the many and superfluous wealth for the few equaled national crisis. Newspapers helped to strengthen and channel the British labor movement. *(Private Collection/The Bridgeman Art Library International Ltd)*

lions of aroused people. Workers were also active in campaigns to limit the workday in factories to ten hours and to permit duty-free importation of wheat into Great Britain to secure cheap bread. Thus working people developed a sense of their own identity and played an active role in shaping the new industrial system. Clearly, they were neither helpless victims nor passive beneficiaries.

## SUMMARY

Western society's industrial breakthrough grew out of a long process of economic and social change in which the rise of capitalism, overseas expansion, and the growth of rural industry stood out as critical preparatory developments. Eventually taking the lead in all of these developments, and also profiting from stable government, abundant natural resources, and a flexible labor force, England experienced between the 1780s and the 1850s an epoch-making transformation, one that is still aptly termed the Industrial Revolution. Building on technological breakthroughs, power-driven equipment, and large-scale enterprise, Great Britain became the first industrial nation. By 1850 the level of British per capita industrial production was surpassing levels on the European continent by a growing margin, and Britain savored a near monopoly in world markets for mass-produced goods.

Continental European countries inevitably took rather different paths to the urban industrial society. They relied more on handicraft production in both towns and villages. Only in the 1840s did railroad construction begin to create the strong demand for iron, coal, and railway equipment that speeded up the process of industrialization in the 1850s and 1860s.

The rise of modern industry had a profound impact on people and their lives. In the early stages Britain again led the way, experiencing in a striking manner the long-term social changes accompanying the economic transformation. Factory discipline and Britain's stern capitalist economy weighed heavily on working people, who, however, actively fashioned their destinies and refused to be passive victims. Improvements in the standard of living came slowly, but they were substantial by 1850. The era of industrialization fostered new attitudes toward child labor, encouraged protective factory legislation, and called forth a new sense of class feeling and an assertive labor movement. It also promoted within the family a more rigid division of roles and responsibilities that severely restricted women socially and economically, another gradual but profound change of revolutionary proportions.

## KEY TERMS

Industrial Revolution
agricultural revolution
open-field system
common rights
enclosure
proletarianization
mercantilism
spinning jenny
water frame
body linen
steam engines
coke
Crystal Palace
iron law of wages
tariff protection
economic nationalism
class consciousness
Luddites
Factory Act of 1833
Mines Act of 1842
Grand National Consolidated Trades Union

## NOTES

1. N. F. R. Crafts, *British Economic Growth During the Industrial Revolution* (Oxford: Oxford University Press, 1985), p. 32. These estimates are for Great Britain as a whole.
2. B. H. Slicher van Bath, *The Agrarian History of Western Europe, A.D. 500–1850* (New York: St. Martin's Press, 1963), p. 240.
3. E. P. Thompson, *The Making of the English Working Class* (New York: Vintage Books, 1966), p. 218.
4. Quoted in P. Mantoux, *The Industrial Revolution in the Eighteenth Century* (New York: Harper & Row, 1961), p. 75.
5. P. Bairoch, "International Industrialization Levels from 1750 to 1980," *Journal of European Economic History* 11 (Spring 1982): 269–333.
6. Crafts, *British Economic Growth During the Industrial Revolution,* pp. 45, 95–102.
7. J. Michelet, *The People,* trans. with an introduction by J. P. McKay (Urbana: University of Illinois Press, 1973; original publication, 1846), p. 64.
8. F. Engels, *The Condition of the Working Class in England,* trans. and ed. W. O. Henderson and W. H. Chaloner (Stanford, Calif.: Stanford University Press, 1968), p. xxiii.
9. Quoted in W. A. Hayek, ed., *Capitalism and the Historians* (Chicago: University of Chicago Press, 1954), p. 126.
10. Crafts, *British Economic Growth During the Industrial Revolution,* p. 95.
11. Quoted in E. R. Pike, *"Hard Times": Human Documents of the Industrial Revolution* (New York: Praeger, 1966), p. 109.
12. See especially J. Brenner and M. Rama, "Rethinking Women's Oppression," *New Left Review* 144 (March–April 1984): 33–71, and sources cited there.
13. J. Humphries, ". . . 'The Most Free from Objection' . . . : The Sexual Division of Labor and Women's Work in Nineteenth-Century England," *Journal of Economic History* 47 (December 1987): 948.
14. Ibid., p. 941; Pike, *"Hard Times,"* p. 266.
15. Quoted in Pike, *"Hard Times,"* p. 208.

## SUGGESTED READING

There is a vast and exciting literature on the Industrial Revolution. R. Cameron, *A Concise Economic History of the World* (1989), provides an introduction to the issues and has a carefully annotated bibliography. J. Goodman and K. Honeyman, *Gainful Pursuits: The Making of Industrial Europe, 1600–1914* (1988); D. S. Landes, *The Unbound Prometheus: Technological Change and Industrial Development in Western Europe from 1750 to the Present* (1969); and S. Pollard, *Peaceful Conquest: The Industrialization of Europe* (1981), are excellent general treatments of European industrial growth. T. Kemp, *Industrialization in Europe,* 2d ed. (1985), is also useful. M. Berg, *The Age of Manufactures: Industry, Innovation and Work in Britain, 1700–1820* (1985), and P. Mathias, *The First Industrial Nation: An Economic History of Britain, 1700–1914* (1969), admirably discuss the various aspects of the English breakthrough and offer good bibliographies, as do the works by Mantoux and Crafts mentioned in the Notes. W. Rostow, *The Stages of Economic Growth: A Non-Communist Manifesto* (1960), was a popular, influential study.

W. Walton, *France and the Crystal Palace: Bourgeois Taste and Artisan Manufacture in the 19th Century* (1992), and H. Kirsh, *From Domestic Manufacturing to Industrial Revolution: The Case of the Rhineland Textile Districts* (1989), examine the persistence and gradual transformation of handicraft techniques. The works of A. S. Milward and S. B. Saul, *The Economic Development of Continental Europe, 1780–1870* (1973) and *The Development of the Economies of Continental Europe, 1850–1914* (1977), may be compared with J. Clapham's classic, *Economic Development of France and Germany* (1963). C. Tortella, *The Development of Modern Spain* (2000); M. Wintle, *An Economic and Social History of the Netherlands: Demographic, Economic, and Social Transitions* (2000); and L. Magnusson, *An Economic History of Sweden* (2000), are excellent recent surveys of three smaller countries. L. Moch, *Paths to the City: Regional Migration in Nineteenth-Century France* (1983), and W. Schivelbusch, *Disenchanted Night: The Industrialization of Light in the Nineteenth Century* (1983), imaginatively analyze quite different aspects of industrialization's many consequences.

The debate between "optimists" and "pessimists" about the consequences of industrialization in England goes on.

Two excellent studies with a gender perspective revitalize the debate: D. Valenze, *The First Industrial Woman* (1995), and P. Hudson and W. Lee, eds., *Women's Work and the Family Economy in Historical Perspective* (1990). P. Taylor, ed., *The Industrial Revolution: Triumph or Disaster?* (1970), is a useful introduction to different viewpoints. It is also fascinating to compare F. Engels's classic condemnation, cited in the Notes, with Andrew Ure's optimistic defense, *The Philosophy of Manufactures,* first published in 1835 and reprinted recently. J. Rule, *The Labouring Classes in Early Industrial England, 1750–1850* (1987), is a recommended synthesis, whereas E. P. Thompson continues and enriches the Engels tradition in *The Making of the English Working Class* (1963). E. R. Pike's documentary collection, cited in the Notes, provides fascinating insights into the lives of working people. An unorthodox but moving account of a doomed group is D. Bythell, *The Handloom Weavers* (1969). F. Klingender, *Art and the Industrial Revolution,* rev. ed. (1968), is justly famous, and D. S. Landes, *Revolution in Time: Clocks and the Making of the Modern World* (1983), is a brilliant integration of industrial and cultural history.

Among general studies, G. S. R. Kitson Clark, *The Making of Victorian England* (1967), is particularly imaginative. A. Briggs, *Victorian People* (1955), provides an engrossing series of brief biographies. H. Ausubel discusses a major reformer in *John Bright* (1966), and B. Harrison skillfully illuminates the problem of heavy drinking in *Drink and the Victorians* (1971). The most famous contemporary novel dealing with the new industrial society is Charles Dickens's *Hard Times,* an entertaining but exaggerated story. *Mary Barton* and *North and South* by Elizabeth Gaskell are more realistic portrayals, and both are highly recommended.

# LISTENING TO THE PAST

## The Testimony of Young Mine Workers

*The use of child labor in British industrialization quickly attracted the attention of humanitarians and social reformers. This interest led to investigations by parliamentary commissions, which resulted in laws limiting the hours and the ages of children working in large factories. Designed to build a case for remedial legislation, parliamentary inquiries gave large numbers of workers a rare chance to speak directly to contemporaries and to historians.*

*The moving passages that follow are taken from testimony gathered in 1841 and 1842 by the Ashley Mines Commission. Interviewing employers and many male and female workers, the commissioners focused on the physical condition of the youth and on the sexual behavior of workers far underground. The subsequent Mines Act of 1842 sought to reduce immoral behavior and sexual bullying by prohibiting underground work for all women (and for boys younger than ten).*

**Mr. Payne, coal master:**

That children are employed generally at nine years old in the coal pits and sometimes at eight. In fact, the smaller the vein of coal is in height, the younger and smaller are the children required; the work occupies from six to seven hours per day in the pits; they are not ill-used or worked beyond their strength; a good deal of depravity exists but they are certainly not worse in morals than in other branches of the Sheffield trade, but upon the whole superior; the morals of this district are materially improving; Mr. Bruce, the clergyman, has been zealous and active in endeavoring to ameliorate their moral and religious education. . . .

**Ann Eggley, hurrier, 18 years old:**

I'm sure I don't know how to spell my name. We go at four in the morning, and sometimes at half-past four. We begin to work as soon as we get down. We get out after four, sometimes at five, in the evening. We work the whole time except an hour for dinner, and sometimes we haven't time to eat. I hurry [move coal wagons underground] by myself, and have done so for long. I know the corves [small coal wagons] are very heavy, they are the biggest corves anywhere about. The work is far too hard for me; the sweat runs off me all over sometimes. I am very tired at night. Sometimes when we get home at night we have not power to wash us, and then we go to bed. Sometimes we fall asleep in the chair. Father said last night it was both a shame and a disgrace for girls to work as we do, but there was naught else for us to do. I began to hurry when I was seven and I have been hurrying ever since. I have been 11 years in the pits. The girls are always tired. I was poorly twice this winter; it was with headache. I hurry for Robert Wiggins; he is not akin to me. . . . We don't always get enough to eat and drink, but we get a good supper. I have known my father go at two in the morning to work . . . and he didn't come out till four. I am quite sure that we work constantly 12 hours except on Saturdays. We wear trousers and our shifts in the pit and great big shoes clinkered and nailed. The girls never work naked to the waist in our pit. The men don't insult us in the pit. The conduct of the girls in the pit is good enough sometimes and sometimes bad enough. I never went to a day-school. I went a little to a Sunday-school, but I soon gave it over. I thought it too bad to be confined both Sundays and week-days. I walk about and get the fresh air on Sundays. I have not learnt to read. I don't know my letters. I never

This illustration of a girl dragging a coal wagon was one of several that shocked public opinion and contributed to the Mines Act of 1842. *(The British Library)*

learnt naught. I never go to church or chapel; there is no church or chapel at Gawber, there is none nearer than a mile. . . . I have never heard that a good man came into the world who was God's son to save sinners. I never heard of Christ at all. Nobody has ever told me about him, nor have my father and mother ever taught me to pray. I know no prayer; I never pray.

**Patience Kershaw, aged 17:**

My father has been dead about a year; my mother is living and has ten children, five lads and five lasses; the oldest is about thirty, the youngest is four; three lasses go to mill; all the lads are colliers, two getters and three hurriers; one lives at home and does nothing; mother does nought but look after home.

All my sisters have been hurriers, but three went to the mill. Alice went because her legs swelled from hurrying in cold water when she was hot. I never went to day-school; I go to Sunday-school, but I cannot read or write; I go to pit at five o'clock in the morning and come out at five in the evening; I get my breakfast of porridge and milk first; I take my dinner with me, a cake, and eat it as I go; I do not stop or rest any time for the purpose; I get nothing else until I get home, and then have potatoes and meat, not every day meat. I hurry in the clothes I have now got on, trousers and ragged jacket; the bald place upon my head is made by thrusting the corves; my legs have never swelled, but sisters' did when they went to mill; I hurry the corves a mile and more under ground and back; they weigh 300; I hurry 11 a day; I wear a belt and chain at the workings to get the corves out; the putters [miners] that I work for are *naked* except their caps; they pull off all their clothes; I see them at work when I go up; sometimes they beat me, if I am not quick enough, with their hands; they strike me upon my back; the boys take liberties with me, sometimes, they pull me about; I am the only girl in the pit; there are about 20 boys and 15 men; all the men are naked; I would rather work in mill than in coal-pit.

**Isabel Wilson, 38 years old, coal putter:**

When women have children thick [fast] they are compelled to take them down early. I have been married 19 years and have had 10 bairns [children]; seven are in life. When on Sir John's work was a carrier of coals, which caused me to miscarry five times from the strains, and was gai [very] ill after each. Putting is no so oppressive; last child was born on Saturday morning, and I was at work on the Friday night.

Once met with an accident; a coal brake my cheek-bone, which kept me idle some weeks.

I have wrought below 30 years, and so has the guid man; he is getting touched in the breath now.

None of the children read, as the work is no regular. I did read once, but no able to attend to it now; when I go below lassie 10 years of age keeps house and makes the broth or stir-about.

## QUESTIONS FOR ANALYSIS

1. To what extent are the testimonies of Ann Eggley and Patience Kershaw in harmony with that of Payne?
2. Describe the work of Eggley and Kershaw. What do you think of their work? Why?
3. What strikes you most about the lives of these workers?
4. The witnesses were responding to questions from middle-class commissioners. What did the commissioners seem interested in? Why?

*Source:* J. Bowditch and C. Ramsland, eds., *Voices of the Industrial Revolution*. Copyright © 1961, 1989 by the University of Michigan. Reprinted by permission.

*Revolutionaries in Transylvania.* Ana Ipatescu was a member of the first group of revolutionaries in Transylvania against Russia, 1848. *(National Historical Museum, Bucharest/The Art Archive)*

CHAPTER

# 24 IDEOLOGIES AND UPHEAVALS, 1815–1871

## CHAPTER OUTLINE

- The Peace Settlement
- Radical Ideas and Early Socialism
- Romanticism
- Reforms and Revolutions (1815–1850)
- Nation Building in France, Italy, and Germany

The momentous economic and political transformation of modern times began in the late eighteenth century with the Industrial Revolution in England and then the French Revolution. Until about 1815 these economic and political revolutions were separate, involving different countries and activities and proceeding at very different paces. After peace returned in 1815, the situation changed. Economic and political changes tended to fuse, reinforcing each other and bringing about what historian Eric Hobsbawm has incisively called the **dual revolution.** For instance, the growth of the industrial middle class encouraged the drive for representative government, and the demands of the French sans-culottes in 1793 and 1794 inspired many socialist thinkers. Gathering strength, the dual revolution rushed on to alter completely first Europe and then the rest of the world. Much of world history in the past two centuries can be seen as the progressive unfolding of the dual revolution.

In Europe in the nineteenth century, as in Asia and Africa in more recent times, the interrelated economic and political transformation was built on complicated histories, strong traditions, and highly diverse cultures. Radical change was eventually a constant, but the particular results varied enormously. In central and eastern Europe especially, the traditional elites—the monarchs, noble landowners, and bureaucrats—proved capable of defending their privileges and eventually using the nationalism of the dual revolution to serve their interests.

The dual revolution posed a tremendous intellectual challenge. The changes that were occurring fascinated observers and stimulated the growth of new ideas and powerful ideologies. The most important of these were conservatism, liberalism, nationalism, and socialism.

- How did thinkers develop these ideas?
- How did the artists and writers of the romantic movement reflect and influence changes in this era?
- How did popular political revolution well up again after 1815, and why did it fail almost completely in 1848 after a moment of victory?
- How did strong leaders and the power of nationalism combine to redraw the map of Europe in the 1860s and provide a fateful answer to the challenge of the dual revolution?

These are the questions this chapter will explore.

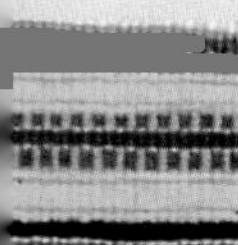

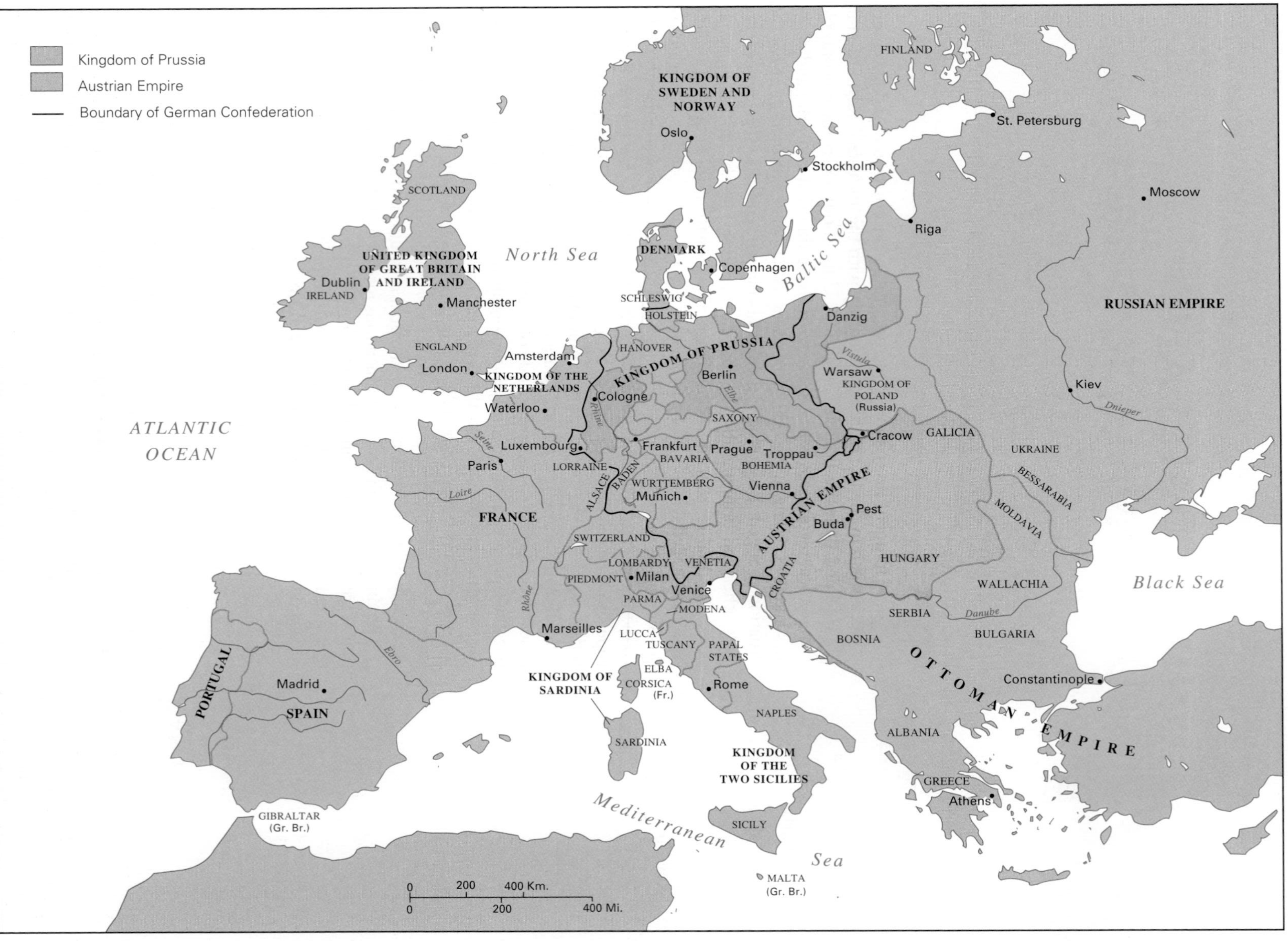


**MAP 24.1 Europe in 1815** Europe's leaders re-established a balance of political power after the defeat of Napoleon. Prussia gained territory on the Rhine and in Saxony and consolidated its position as a Great Power.

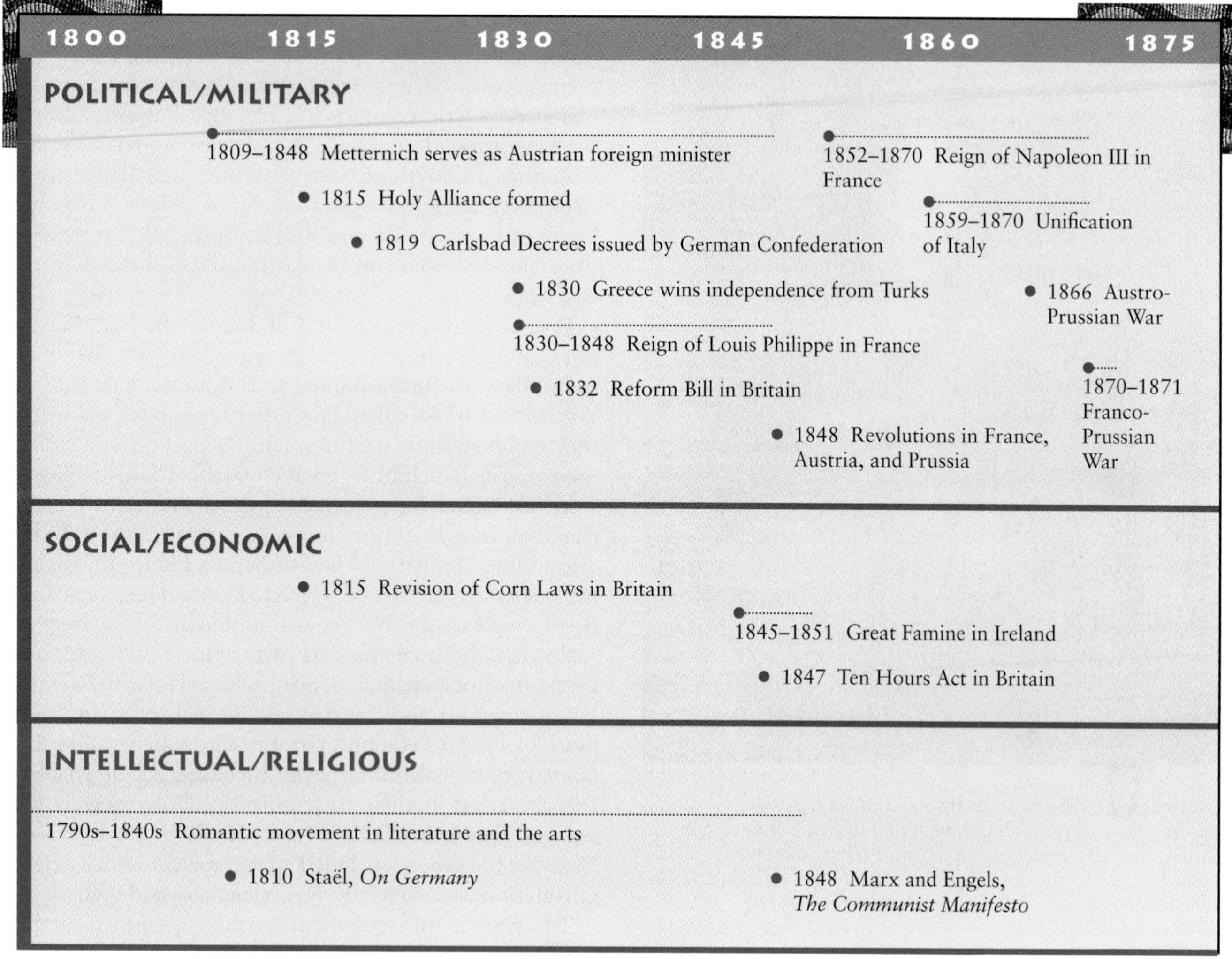

1800
1815
1830
1845
1860
1875
POLITICAL/MILITARY
1809–1848 Metternich serves as Austrian foreign minister
1815 Holy Alliance formed
1819 Carlsbad Decrees issued by German Confederation
1830 Greece wins independence from Turks
1830–1848 Reign of Louis Philippe in France
1832 Reform Bill in Britain
1848 Revolutions in France, Austria, and Prussia
1852–1870 Reign of Napoleon III in France
1859–1870 Unification of Italy
1866 Austro-Prussian War
1870–1871 Franco-Prussian War
SOCIAL/ECONOMIC
1815 Revision of Corn Laws in Britain
1845–1851 Great Famine in Ireland
1847 Ten Hours Act in Britain
INTELLECTUAL/RELIGIOUS
1790s–1840s Romantic movement in literature and the arts
1810 Staël, On Germany
1848 Marx and Engels, The Communist Manifesto


## THE PEACE SETTLEMENT

The eventual triumph of revolutionary economic and political forces was by no means certain as the Napoleonic era ended. Quite the contrary. The conservative, aristocratic monarchies of Russia, Prussia, Austria, and Great Britain had finally defeated France and reaffirmed their determination to hold France in line. But many other international questions were outstanding, and the allies agreed to meet at the **Congress of Vienna** to fashion a general peace settlement.

Most people felt a profound longing for peace. The great challenge for political leaders in 1814 was to construct a settlement that would last and not sow the seeds of another war. Their efforts were largely successful and contributed to a century unmarred by destructive, generalized war in Europe (see Map 24.1).

### The European Balance of Power

The allied powers were concerned first and foremost with the defeated enemy, France. Agreeing to the restoration of the Bourbon dynasty (see page 724), the allies were quite lenient toward France after Napoleon's abdication. France was given the boundaries it possessed in 1792, and France did not have to pay any war reparations. Thus the victorious powers did not foment a spirit of injustice and revenge in the defeated country.

When the four allies of the Quadruple Alliance—Austria, Britain, Prussia, and Russia—met together at the Congress of Vienna, assisted in a minor way by a host of delegates from the smaller European states, they also agreed to raise a number of formidable barriers against renewed French aggression. The Low Countries—Belgium and Holland—were united under an enlarged Dutch monarchy capable of

**Metternich** This portrait by Sir Thomas Lawrence reveals much about Metternich the man. Handsome, refined, and intelligent, Metternich was a great aristocrat who was passionately devoted to the defense of his class and its interests. *(The Royal Collection © Her Majesty Queen Elizabeth II)*

opposing France more effectively. Moreover, Prussia received considerably more territory on France's eastern border so as to stand as the "sentinel on the Rhine" against France. In these ways the Quadruple Alliance combined leniency toward France with strong defensive measures.

In their moderation toward France, the allies were motivated by self-interest and traditional ideas about the balance of power. To Klemens von Metternich and Robert Castlereagh, the foreign ministers of Austria and Great Britain, respectively, as well as their French counterpart, Charles Talleyrand, the balance of power meant an international equilibrium of political and military forces that would discourage aggression by any combination of states or, worse, the domination of Europe by any single state.

The Great Powers—Austria, Britain, Prussia, Russia, and France—used the balance of power to settle their own dangerous disputes at the Congress of Vienna. There was general agreement among the victors that each of them should receive compensation in the form of territory for their successful struggle against the French. Great Britain had already won colonies and strategic outposts during the long wars. Metternich's Austria gave up territories in Belgium and southern Germany but expanded greatly elsewhere, taking the rich provinces of Venetia and Lombardy in northern Italy as well as former Polish possessions and new lands on the eastern coast of the Adriatic (see Map 24.1).

One ticklish question almost led to renewed war in January 1815, however. The vaguely progressive Tsar Alexander I of Russia wanted to restore the kingdom of Poland and be its ruler. The Prussians agreed, provided they could swallow up the wealthy kingdom of Saxony, their German neighbor to the south. These demands were too much for Castlereagh and Metternich, who feared an unbalancing of forces in central Europe. In an astonishing about-face, they turned to France for diplomatic support and signed a secret alliance directed against Russia and Prussia. War seemed imminent.

But the threat of war caused the rulers of Russia and Prussia to moderate their demands. Russia accepted a small Polish kingdom, and Prussia took only part of Saxony (see Map 24.1). This compromise was very much within the framework of balance-of-power ideology, and it enabled France to end its diplomatic isolation. Unfortunately for France, Napoleon suddenly escaped from the island of Elba. Yet the peace concluded after Napoleon's final defeat at Waterloo was still relatively moderate toward France.

The rest of the settlement already concluded at the Congress of Vienna was left intact. The members of the Quadruple Alliance, however, did agree to meet periodically to discuss their common interests and to consider appropriate measures for the maintenance of peace in Europe. This agreement marked the beginning of the European "congress system," which lasted long into the nineteenth century and settled many international crises through international conferences and balance-of-power diplomacy.

## Intervention and Repression

There was also a domestic political side to the re-establishment of peace. Within their own countries the leaders of the victorious states were much less flexible. In 1815 under Metternich's leadership, Austria, Prussia, and Russia embarked on a crusade against the ideas and politics of the dual revolution. This crusade lasted until 1848. The first step was the **Holy Alliance,** formed by Austria, Prussia, and Russia in September 1815. First proposed by Russia's Alexander I, the alliance soon became a symbol of the repression of liberal and revolutionary movements all over Europe.

In 1820 revolutionaries succeeded in forcing the monarchs of Spain and the southern Italian kingdom of the Two Sicilies to grant liberal constitutions against their wills. Metternich was horrified: revolution was rising once again. Calling a conference at Troppau in Austria under the provisions of the Quadruple Alliance, he and Alexander I proclaimed the principle of active intervention to maintain all autocratic regimes whenever they were threatened. Austrian forces then marched into Naples in 1821 and restored Ferdinand I to the throne of the Two Sicilies, while French armies likewise restored the Spanish regime.

In the following years Metternich continued to battle against liberal political change. Sometimes he could do little, as in the case of the new Latin American republics that broke away from Spain. Nor could he undo the dynastic changes of 1830 and 1831 in France and Belgium. Nonetheless, until 1848 Metternich's system proved quite effective in central Europe, where his power was the greatest.

Metternich's policies dominated not only Austria and the Italian peninsula but also the entire German Confederation, which the peace settlement of Vienna had called into being. The confederation was composed of thirty-eight independent German states and was dominated by Austria, with Prussia a willing junior partner in the planning and execution of repressive measures.

It was through the German Confederation that Metternich had the infamous **Carlsbad Decrees** issued in 1819. These decrees required the thirty-eight German member states to root out subversive ideas in their universities and newspapers. The decrees also established a permanent committee with spies and informers to investigate and punish any liberal or radical organizations.

## Metternich and Conservatism

Metternich's determined defense of the status quo made him a villain in the eyes of most progressive, optimistic historians of the nineteenth century. Yet rather than denounce the man, we can try to understand him and the general conservatism he represented.

Born into the middle ranks of the landed nobility of the Rhineland, Prince Klemens von Metternich (1773–1859) was an internationally oriented aristocrat who made a brilliant diplomatic career in Austria. Austrian foreign minister from 1809 to 1848, the cosmopolitan Metternich always remained loyal to his class and jealously defended its rights and privileges to the day he died. Like most other conservatives of his time, he did so with a clear conscience. The nobility was one of Europe's most ancient institutions, and conservatives regarded tradition as the basic source of human institutions. In their view the proper state and society remained those of pre-1789 Europe, which rested on a judicious blend of monarchy, bureaucracy, aristocracy, and respectful commoners.

Metternich firmly believed that liberalism, as embodied in revolutionary America and France, had been responsible for a generation of war with untold bloodshed and suffering. Like many other conservatives then and since, Metternich blamed liberal revolutionaries for stirring up the lower classes, which he believed desired nothing more than peace and quiet.

The threat of liberalism appeared doubly dangerous to Metternich because it generally went with national aspirations. Liberals believed that each people, each national group, had a right to establish its own independent government and seek to fulfill its own destiny. The idea of national self-determination was repellent to Metternich. It not only threatened the existence of the aristocracy but also threatened to destroy the Austrian Empire and revolutionize central Europe.

The vast Austrian Empire of the Habsburgs was a great dynastic state made up of many peoples (see Map 24.2). The Germans had long dominated the empire, yet they accounted for only one-fourth of the population. The Magyars (Hungarians), a substantially smaller group, dominated the kingdom of Hungary, though even they did not account for a majority of the population in that part of the Austrian Empire.

The Czechs, the third major group, were concentrated in Bohemia and Moravia. There were also large numbers of Italians, Poles, and Ukrainians as well as smaller groups of Slovenes, Croats, Serbs, Ruthenians, and Romanians. The various Slavic peoples, together with the Italians and the Romanians, represented a widely scattered and completely divided majority in an empire dominated by Germans and Hungarians. Different ethnic groups often lived in the same provinces and even in the same villages. Thus the parts and provinces of the empire differed in languages, customs, and institutions.

The multinational state that Metternich served was both strong and weak. It was strong because of its large population and vast territories; it was weak because of its many and potentially dissatisfied nationalities. In these circumstances, Metternich virtually had to oppose liberalism and nationalism, for Austria was simply unable to accommodate those ideologies of the dual revolution.

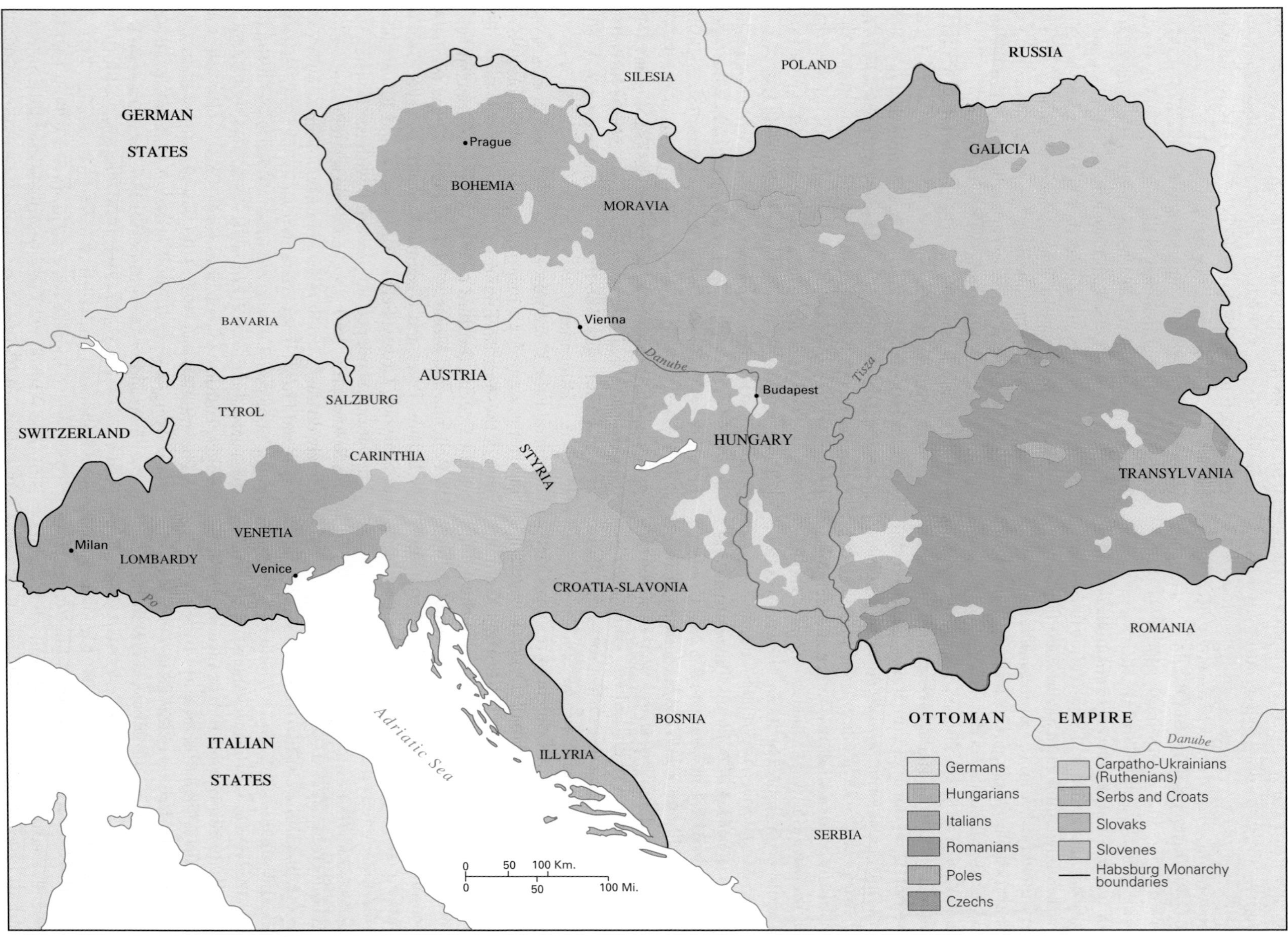


**MAP 24.2 Peoples of the Habsburg Monarchy, 1815** The old dynastic state was a patchwork of nationalities. Note the widely scattered pockets of Germans and Hungarians.

## Radical Ideas and Early Socialism

In the years following the peace settlement of 1815 intellectuals and social observers sought to understand the revolutionary changes taking place. These efforts led to ideas that still motivate the world.

Almost all of these basic ideas were radical. In one way or another they rejected the old, deeply felt conservatism, with its stress on tradition, a hereditary monarchy, a strong and privileged landowning aristocracy, and an official church. Instead, radicals developed and refined alternative visions—alternative ideologies—and tried to convince society to act on them. With time, they were very successful.

### Liberalism

The principal ideas of liberalism—liberty and equality—were by no means defeated in 1815. Liberalism demanded representative government as opposed to autocratic monarchy, equality before the law as opposed to legally separate classes. The idea of liberty also continued to mean specific individual freedoms: freedom of the press, freedom of speech, freedom of assembly, and freedom from arbitrary arrest. In Europe only France with Louis XVIII's Constitutional Charter and Great Britain with its Parliament and historic rights of English men and women had realized much of the liberal program in 1815. Even in those countries, liberalism had not fully succeeded.

Although liberalism retained its cutting edge, many considered it a somewhat duller tool than it had been. The reasons for this opinion were that liberalism faced more radical ideological competitors in the early nineteenth century. Opponents of classical liberalism especially criticized its economic principles, which called for unrestricted private enterprise and no government interference in the economy. This philosophy was popularly known as the doctrine of **laissez faire.** (This form of liberalism is often called "classical" liberalism in the United States to distinguish it sharply from modern American liberalism, which usually favors more government programs to meet social needs and to regulate the economy.)

The idea of a free economy had first been persuasively formulated by Scottish philosophy professor Adam Smith, whose *Inquiry into the Nature and Causes of the Wealth of Nations* (1776) founded modern economics. Smith was highly critical of eighteenth-century mercantilism and its attempt to regulate trade and economic activity. Far preferable, he believed, were free competition and the "invisible hand" of the self-regulating market, which would give all citizens a fair and equal opportunity to do what they did best. Smith argued effectively that freely competitive private enterprise would result in greater income for everyone, not just the rich.

In the early nineteenth century in Britain this economic liberalism, which promoted economic growth in the Industrial Revolution, was embraced most enthusiastically by business groups and became a doctrine associated with business interests. Businessmen used the doctrine to defend their right to do as they wished in their factories. Labor unions were outlawed because they supposedly restricted free competition and the individual's "right to work."

In the early nineteenth century liberal political ideals also became more closely associated with narrow class interests. Early-nineteenth-century liberals favored representative government, but they generally wanted property qualifications attached to the right to vote. In practice this meant limiting the vote to well-to-do aristocratic landowners, substantial businessmen, and successful members of the professions. Workers and peasants as well as the lower middle class of shopkeepers, clerks, and artisans did not own the necessary property and so could not vote.

As liberalism became increasingly identified with the middle class after 1815, some intellectuals and foes of conservatism felt that liberalism did not go nearly far enough. Inspired by memories of the French Revolution and the young American republic, they called for universal voting rights, at least for males, and for democracy. These democrats and republicans were more radical than the liberals, and they were more willing than most liberals to endorse violent upheaval to achieve goals. All of this meant that liberals and radical, democratic republicans could join forces against conservatives only up to a point.

### Nationalism

Nationalism was a second radical idea in the years after 1815—an idea destined to have an enormous influence in the modern world. Early advocates of the "national idea" argued that each people had its own genius and its own *cultural* unity, which manifested itself especially in a common language, history, and territory. In fact, in the early nineteenth century such cultural unity was more a dream than a reality in Europe. Within each ethnic grouping only an elite spoke a standardized written language, and a variety of ethnic groups shared the territory of most states.

Nevertheless, European nationalists usually sought to turn the cultural unity that they perceived into a *political* reality, so that each people lived in an independent

**Creating Nationalism** Festivals and patriotic celebrations helped build a feeling of belonging to a large invisible community. This illustration from May 1848 depicts "the Solemn Entry of Archduke Johann of Austria into Frankfurt," when cannon sounded and dignitaries proclaimed the opening of a new era. The revolutionary assembly in Frankfurt had named Johann regent of the unified Germany that it was hoping to establish. In May 1849 the assembly offered the imperial crown to the king of Prussia. *(Germanisches Nationalmuseum, Nürnberg)*

nation-state. It was this political goal that made nationalism so explosive in central and eastern Europe after 1815, when there were either too few states (Austria, Russia, and the Ottoman Empire) or too many (the Italian peninsula and the German Confederation) and when different peoples overlapped and intermingled.

The nationalist vision, often fitting poorly with existing conditions and promising so much upheaval, triumphed in the long run partly because the epoch-making development of complex industrial and urban society required much better communication between individuals and groups.[1] These communication needs promoted the use of a standardized national language within many countries, creating at least a superficial cultural unity as it eventually encompassed the entire population through mass education.

Nation-states also emerged because those who believed in the new ideology wanted to create "imagined communities," communities seeking to bind millions of strangers together around the abstract concept of an all-embracing national identity. Thus nationalist intellectuals and leaders brought citizens together with emotionally charged symbols and ceremonies, such as ethnic festivals and flag-waving parades, which celebrated the imagined nation of spiritual equals.[2]

Between 1815 and 1850 most people who believed in nationalism also believed in either liberalism or radical, democratic republicanism. A common faith in the creativity and nobility of the people was perhaps the single most important reason for the linking of these two concepts. Liberals and especially democrats saw the people as the ultimate source of all good government. Yet the benefits of self-government were possible only if the people were united by common loyalties and language that transcended local interests and even class differences.

Early nationalists usually believed that every nation, like every citizen, had the right to exist in freedom and to develop its character and spirit. They were confident that a symphony of free nations would promote the harmony and ultimate unity of all peoples. The great Italian patriot Giuseppe Mazzini believed that "in laboring according to the true principles of our country we are laboring for Humanity." (See the feature "Listening to the Past: Faith in Democratic Nationalism" on pages 790–791.) Thus the liberty of the individual and the love of a free nation overlapped greatly in the early nineteenth century.

Yet even as early nationalists talked of serving the cause of humanity, they stressed the differences among peoples. Even early nationalism developed a strong sense of "we" and "they." To this "we-they" outlook, it was all too easy for nationalists to add a sense of national mission and superiority. In 1846 the French historian Jules Michelet believed, for example, that the principles espoused in the French Revolution had made France the "salvation of mankind."

German and Spanish nationalists had a very different opinion of France. To them, the French often seemed oppressive, as the Germans did to the Czechs and as the Russians did to the Poles. Thus "they" were often the enemy.

Early nationalism was ambiguous. Its main thrust was liberal and democratic. But below the surface lurked ideas of national superiority and national mission that could lead to aggression and conflict.

## French Utopian Socialism

**Socialism,** the new radical doctrine after 1815, began in France, despite the fact that France trailed Great Britain in developing modern industry. These French thinkers were acutely aware that the political revolution in France, the rise of laissez faire, and the emergence of factory industry in England were transforming society. They were disturbed because they saw these trends as fomenting selfish individualism and splitting the community into isolated fragments. There was, they believed, an urgent need for a further reorganization of society to establish cooperation and a new sense of community.

Early French socialists believed in economic planning. Inspired by the emergency measures of 1793 and 1794 in France, they argued that the government should rationally organize the economy and not depend on destructive competition to do the job. Early socialists also shared an intense desire to help the poor, and they preached that the rich and the poor should be more nearly equal economically. Finally, socialists believed that private property should be strictly regulated by the government or that it should be abolished and replaced by state or community ownership. Planning, greater economic equality, and state control of property—these were the key ideas of early French socialism and of all socialism since.

One of the most influential early socialist thinkers was a nobleman, Count Henri de Saint-Simon (1760–1825). Saint-Simon optimistically proclaimed the tremendous possibilities of industrial development: "The age of gold is before us!" The key to progress was proper social organization. Such an arrangement of society required the **parasites**—the court, the aristocracy, lawyers, churchmen—to give way, once and for all, to the **doers**—the leading scientists, engineers, and industrialists. The doers would carefully plan the economy and guide it forward. Saint-Simon also stressed in highly moralistic terms that every social institution ought to have as its main goal improved conditions for the poor.

After 1830 the socialist critique of capitalism became sharper. Charles Fourier (1772–1837), a lonely, saintly man with a tenuous hold on reality, envisaged a socialist utopia of mathematically precise, self-sufficient communities, each made up of 1,620 people.

Fourier was also an early proponent of the total emancipation of women. Extremely critical of middle-class family life, Fourier believed that most marriages were only another kind of prostitution. According to Fourier, young single women were shamelessly "sold" to their future husbands for dowries and other financial considerations. Fourier called for the abolition of marriage, free unions based only on love, and sexual freedom. To many middle-class men and women, these ideas were shocking and immoral. The suggested liberation of women as well as workers made the socialist program appear to them as doubly dangerous and revolutionary.

Of great importance, the message of French utopian socialists interacted with the experiences of French urban workers. Workers cherished the memory of the French Revolution, and they became violently opposed to laissez-faire laws that denied workers the right to organize. Developing a sense of class in the process, workers favored collective action and government intervention in economic life. Thus the aspirations of workers and utopian theorists reinforced each other, and a genuine socialist movement emerged in Paris in the 1830s and 1840s. To Karl Marx was left the task of establishing firm foundations for modern socialism.

## The Birth of Marxian Socialism

In 1848 the thirty-year-old Karl Marx (1818–1883) and the twenty-eight-year-old Friedrich Engels (1820–1895) published *The Communist Manifesto,* which became the bible of socialism. The son of a Jewish lawyer who had converted to Christianity, the atheistic young Marx had studied philosophy at the University of Berlin before turning to journalism and economics. He read widely in French socialist thought and then developed his own socialist ideas.

**Karl Marx** Active in the revolution of 1848, Marx fled from Germany in 1849 and settled in London. There he wrote *Capital,* the weighty exposition of his socialist theories, and worked to organize the working class. Marx earned a modest living as a journalist, supplemented by financial support from his coauthor, Friedrich Engels. *(The Granger Collection, New York)*

Early French socialists often appealed to the middle class and the state to help the poor. Marx ridiculed such appeals as naive. He argued that the interests of the middle class and those of the industrial working class were inevitably opposed to each other. Indeed, according to the *Manifesto,* the "history of all previously existing society is the history of class struggles." In Marx's view one class had always exploited the other, and with the advent of modern industry society was split more clearly than ever before: between the middle class (the **bourgeoisie**) and the modern working class (the **proletariat**).

Just as the bourgeoisie had triumphed over the feudal aristocracy, the proletariat, Marx predicted, would conquer the bourgeoisie in a violent revolution. While a tiny minority owned the means of production and grew richer, the ever-poorer proletariat was constantly growing in size and in class consciousness. The critical moment, Marx thought, was very near. "Let the ruling classes tremble at a Communist revolution. The proletarians have nothing to lose but their chains. They have a world to win. WORKING MEN OF ALL COUNTRIES, UNITE!" So ends *The Communist Manifesto.*

Marx's ideas united sociology, economics, and all human history in a vast and imposing edifice. He synthesized in his socialism not only French utopian schemes but also English classical economics and German philosophy—the major intellectual currents of his day.

Marx's debt to England was great. He was the last of the classical economists. Following David Ricardo, who had taught that labor was the source of all value, Marx went on to argue that profits were really wages stolen from the workers. Moreover, Marx incorporated Engels's account of the terrible oppression of the new class of factory workers in England; thus Marx's doctrines seemed to be based on hard facts.

Marx's theory of historical evolution was built on the philosophy of the German Georg Hegel (1770–1831). Hegel believed that each age in history is characterized by a dominant set of ideas, which produces opposing ideas and eventually a new synthesis. Thus history has pattern and purpose. Marx retained Hegel's view of history as a dialectic process of change but made economic relationships between classes the driving force. This dialectic explained the decline of agrarian feudalism and the rise of industrial capitalism. Marx's idea, that it was now the bourgeoisie's turn to give way to the socialism of revolutionary workers, appeared to many as a brilliant interpretation of humanity's long development. Thus Marx pulled together powerful insights to create one of the great secular religions of modern times.

**Nature and the Meaning of Life** Caspar David Friedrich (1774–1840) was Germany's greatest romantic painter, and his *Traveler Looking over a Sea of Fog* (1815) is a representative masterpiece. Friedrich's paintings often focus on dark silhouetted figures, silently contemplating an eerie landscape. Friedrich came to believe that humans were only an insignificant part of an all-embracing higher unity. *(Hamburger Kunsthalle/Bildarchiv Preussischer Kulturbesitz. Photo: Elke Walford)*

## ROMANTICISM

Radical concepts of politics and society were accompanied by comparable changes in literature and other arts during the dual revolution. The early nineteenth century marked the acme of the romantic movement, which profoundly influenced the arts and enriched European culture immeasurably.

The romantic movement was in part a revolt against classicism and the Enlightenment. The classicists believed that the ancient Greeks and Romans had discovered eternally valid aesthetic rules; that these rules fit with the Enlightenment's belief in rationality, order, and restraint; and that playwrights and painters should continue to follow them.

Forerunners of the romantic movement appeared from about 1750 on. Of these, Rousseau—the passionate advocate of feeling, freedom, and natural goodness—was the most influential. Romanticism then crystallized fully in the 1790s, primarily in England and Germany. The French Revolution kindled the belief that radical reconstruction was also possible in cultural and artistic life, and romanticism gained strength until the 1840s.

Romanticism was characterized by a belief in emotional exuberance, unrestrained imagination, and spontaneity in both art and personal life. In Germany early romantics of the 1770s and 1780s called themselves the **Sturm und Drang** (Storm and Stress), and many romantic artists of the early nineteenth century lived lives of tremendous emotional intensity. Suicide, duels to the death, madness, and strange illnesses were not uncommon among leading romantics. Great individualists, they believed the full development of one's unique human potential to be the supreme purpose in life.

Eugène Delacroix (1798–1863) was a master of dramatic, colorful scenes that stirred the emotions. He was fascinated with remote and exotic subjects, whether lion hunts in Morocco or the languishing, sensuous women of a sultan's harem. He was also a passionate spokesman for freedom. His masterpiece, *Liberty Leading the People,* celebrated the nobility of popular revolution in general and revolution in France in particular.

It was in music that romanticism realized most fully and permanently its goals of free expression and emotional intensity. Whereas the composers of the eighteenth century had remained true to well-defined structures, the great romantics used a great range of forms. Romantic composers also transformed the small classical orchestra, tripling its size by adding wind instruments, percussion, and more brass and strings. The crashing chords evoking the surge of the masses in Chopin's Revolutionary Etude, the bottomless despair of the funeral march in Beethoven's Third Symphony—such were the musical paintings that plumbed the depths of human feeling.

Though romanticism dominated music until late in the nineteenth century, no composer ever surpassed its first great master, Ludwig van Beethoven (1770–1827). As the contemporary German novelist Ernst Hoffmann (1776–1822) wrote, "Beethoven's music sets in motion the lever of fear, of awe, of horror, of suffering, and awakens just that infinite longing which is the essence of Romanticism." Beethoven's range was tremendous, and he continued to pour out immortal music until his death. But he never heard much of his later work, including the unforgettable choral finale to the Ninth Symphony, for his last years were spent in total deafness.

Nowhere was the break with classicism more apparent than in romanticism's general conception of nature. Classicism was not particularly interested in nature. In the words of eighteenth-century English author Samuel Johnson, "A blade of grass is always a blade of grass; men and women are my subjects of inquiry." The romantics, in contrast, were enchanted by nature. Sometimes fascinated by its awesome and tempestuous side, at other times they saw nature as a source of spiritual inspiration. As the great English landscape artist John Constable declared, "Nature is Spirit visible."

Most romantics saw the growth of modern industry as an ugly, brutal attack on their beloved nature and on the human personality. They sought escape—in the unspoiled Lake District of northern England, in exotic North Africa, in an idealized Middle Ages.

Fascinated by color and diversity, the romantic imagination turned toward history with a passion. For romantics, history was beautiful and exciting. And it was the art of change over time—the key to a universe that was now perceived to be organic and dynamic. Historical studies supported the development of national aspirations and encouraged entire peoples to seek in the past their special destinies.

Born in Edinburgh, Walter Scott (1771–1832) personified the romantic movement's fascination with history. Raised on his grandfather's farm, Scott fell under the spell of the old ballads and tales of the Scottish border. He was also deeply influenced by German romanticism, particularly by the immortal poet and dramatist Johann Wolfgang von Goethe (1749–1832). A natural storyteller, Scott composed long narrative poems and a series of historical novels. He excelled in faithfully recreating the spirit of bygone ages and great historical events, especially those of Scotland.

Classicism remained strong in France under Napoleon and inhibited the growth of romanticism there. In 1813 Germaine de Staël (1766–1817), a Franco-Swiss writer living in exile, urged the French to throw away their worn-out classical models. Her study *On Germany* (1810) extolled the spontaneity and enthusiasm of German writers and thinkers, and it had a powerful impact on the post-1815 generation in France. (See the feature "Individuals in Society: Germaine de Staël.") Between 1820 and 1850 the romantic impulse broke through in poetry and prose. In both of these Victor Hugo (1802–1885) was the greatest French master.

Son of a Napoleonic general, Hugo achieved an amazing range of rhythm, language, and image in his lyric poetry. His powerful novels exemplified the romantic fascination with fantastic characters, strange settings, and human emotions. The hero of Hugo's famous *Hunchback of Notre Dame* (1831) is the great cathedral's deformed bellringer, a "human gargoyle" overlooking the teeming life of fifteenth-century Paris.

In central and eastern Europe, literary romanticism and early nationalism often reinforced each other. Seeking a unique greatness in every people, well-educated romantics plumbed their own histories and cultures. Like modern anthropologists, they turned their attention to peasant life and transcribed the folk songs, tales, and proverbs that the cosmopolitan Enlightenment had disdained. The brothers Jacob and Wilhelm Grimm were particularly successful at rescuing German fairy tales from oblivion. In the Slavic lands romantics played a decisive

# INDIVIDUALS IN SOCIETY

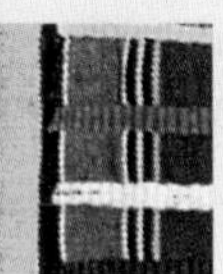

## GERMAINE DE STAËL

Rich, intellectual, passionate, and assertive, Germaine Necker de Staël (1766–1817) astonished contemporaries and still fascinates historians. She was strongly influenced by her parents, poor Swiss Protestants who soared to the top of prerevolutionary Parisian society. Her brilliant but rigid mother filled Germaine's head with knowledge, and each week the precocious child listened, wide-eyed and attentive, to illustrious writers and philosophers performing at her mother's salon. At age twelve, she suffered a physical and mental breakdown. Only then was she allowed to have a playmate and romp and run on the family estate. Her adoring father was Jacques Necker, a banker who made an enormous fortune and became France's reform-minded minister of finance before the Revolution. Worshiping her father in adolescence, Germaine also came to love politics.

Accepting at nineteen an arranged marriage with Baron de Staël-Holstein, a womanizing Swedish diplomat bewitched by her dowry, Germaine began her life's work. She opened an intellectual salon and began to write and publish. Her wit and exuberance attracted foreigners and liberal French aristocrats, one of whom became the first of many lovers as her marriage soured and she searched unsuccessfully for the happiness of her parents' union. Fleeing Paris in 1792 and returning after the Thermidorian reaction, she subsequently angered Napoleon by criticizing his dictatorial rule. In 1803 he permanently banished her from Paris.

Retiring again to her isolated estate in Switzerland and skillfully managing her inherited wealth, Staël fought insomnia with opium and boredom with parties that attracted luminaries from all over Europe. Always seeking stimulation for her restless mind, she traveled widely in Italy and Germany and drew upon these experiences in her novel *Corinne* (1807) and her study *On Germany* (1810). Both works summed up her romantic faith and enjoyed enormous success.

Staël urged creative individuals to abandon traditional rules and classical models. She encouraged them to embrace experimentation, emotion, and enthusiasm. Enthusiasm, which she had in abundance, was the key, the royal road to creativity, personal fulfillment, and human improvement. Thrilling to music, for example, she felt that only an enthusiastic person could really appreciate this gift of God, this wordless message that "unifies our dual nature and blends senses and spirit in a common rapture."*

*Germaine de Staël, by J.-B. Isabey.*
(Réunion des Musées Nationaux/ Art Resource, NY)

Yet a profound sadness runs through her writing. This sadness, so characteristic of the romantic temperament, grew in part out of disappointments in love and prolonged exile. But it also grew out of the insoluble predicament of being an enormously gifted woman in an age of intense male chauvinism. Little wonder that uneasy male competitors and literary critics took delight in ridiculing and defaming her as a neurotic and masculine woman, a mediocre and unnatural talent who had foolishly dared to enter the male world of serious thought and action. Even her supporters could not accept her for what she was. The admiring poet Lord Byron recognized her genius and called her "the most eminent woman author of this, or perhaps of any century." But he quickly added that "she should have been born a man."†

Buffeted and saddened by scorn and condescension because of her gender, Staël advocated equal rights for women throughout her life. Only with equal rights and duties—in education and careers, in love and marital relations—could an exceptional woman like herself, or indeed any woman, ever hope to realize her intellectual and emotional potential. Practicing what she preached as best she could, Germaine de Staël was a trailblazer in the struggle for women's rights.

### QUESTIONS FOR ANALYSIS

1. In what ways did Germaine de Staël's life and thought reflect basic elements of the romantic movement?
2. Why did male critics often attack Staël? What do these criticisms tell us about gender relations in the early nineteenth century?

*Quoted in G. R. Besser, *Germaine de Staël Revisited* (New York: Twayne Publishers, 1994), p. 106. Enhanced by a feminist perspective, this is the best recent study.
†Quoted ibid., p. 139.

role in converting spoken peasant languages into modern written languages. The greatest of all Russian poets, Aleksander Pushkin (1799–1837), used his lyric genius to mold the modern literary language of Russia.

## REFORMS AND REVOLUTIONS (1815–1850)

While the romantic movement was developing, liberal, national, and socialist forces battered against the conservatism of 1815. In a few countries change occurred gradually and peacefully. Elsewhere pressure built up like steam in a pressure cooker without a safety valve. Then in 1848 revolutionary political and social ideologies combined with economic crisis and the romantic impulse to produce a vast upheaval. National independence, liberal-democratic constitutions, and social reform: the lofty aspirations of a generation seemed at hand. Yet in the end the revolutions failed, and the lofty aspirations were shattered.

### National Liberation in Greece

National, liberal revolution, frustrated in Italy and Spain by conservative statesmen, succeeded first after 1815 in Greece. Since the fifteenth century the Greeks had been living under the domination of the Ottoman Turks. It was perfectly natural that the general growth of national aspirations and a desire for independence would inspire some Greeks in the early nineteenth century. This rising national movement led to revolt in 1821.

The Great Powers, particularly Metternich, were opposed to all revolution, even revolution against the Islamic Turks, and they supported the Ottoman Empire. Yet for many Europeans the Greek cause became a holy one. Educated Americans and Europeans were in love with the culture of classical Greece; Russians were stirred by the piety of their Orthodox brethren. Turkish atrocities toward the rebels fanned the fires of European outrage and Greek determination.

In 1827 Great Britain, France, and Russia responded to popular demands at home and directed Turkey to ac-

**Delacroix: Massacre at Chios** The Greek struggle for freedom and independence won the enthusiastic support of liberals, nationalists, and romantics. The Ottoman Turks were portrayed as cruel oppressors who were holding back the course of history, as in this moving masterpiece by Delacroix. *(Réunion des Musées Nationaux/Art Resource, NY)*

cept an armistice. When the Turks refused, the navies of these three powers trapped the Turkish fleet at Navarino and destroyed it. Russia then declared another of its periodic wars of expansion against the Turks. This led to the establishment of a Russian protectorate over much of present-day Romania, which had also been under Turkish rule. Great Britain, France, and Russia finally declared Greece independent in 1830. In the end the Greeks had won: a small nation had gained its independence in a heroic war against a foreign empire.

## Liberal Reform in Great Britain

Eighteenth-century British society had been both flexible and remarkably stable. It was dominated by the landowning aristocracy, but that class was neither closed nor rigidly defined. Basic civil rights for all were balanced by a tradition of deference to one's social superiors. Parliament was manipulated by the king and was thoroughly undemocratic. Only about 8 percent of the population could vote for representatives to Parliament, and by the 1780s there was growing interest in some kind of political reform. But the French Revolution threw the British aristocracy into a panic for a generation. The Tory party, completely controlled by the landed aristocracy, was particularly fearful of radical movements at home and abroad. After 1815 the aristocracy energetically defended its ruling position.

The first step in this direction began in 1815 with revision of the **Corn Laws** restricting foreign grain imports. During a generation of war with France the British had been unable to import cheap grain from eastern Europe. As shortages occurred and agricultural prices skyrocketed, a great deal of marginal land had been brought under cultivation, fattening the landed aristocracy's rent rolls. Peace meant that grain could be imported again and that the price of wheat and bread would go down, benefiting almost everyone except the aristocracy. The aristocracy, however, rammed through Parliament a new law that prohibited the importation of foreign grain unless the price at home rose to improbable levels. Seldom has a class legislated more selfishly for its own narrow economic advantage or done more to promote a class-based interpretation of political action.

The change in the Corn Laws, coming at a time of widespread unemployment and postwar adjustment, led to protests and demonstrations by urban laborers, supported by radical intellectuals. At the same time, the new manufacturing and commercial groups insisted on a place for their new wealth alongside the landed wealth of the aristocracy in the framework of political power and social prestige. They called for many kinds of liberal reform and pressed especially for reform of Parliament. The House of Lords successfully blocked this reform until 1832, when a surge of popular protest helped convince the king and lords to give in.

The Reform Bill of 1832 had profound significance. First, the House of Commons had emerged as the all-important legislative body. Second, the new industrial areas of the country gained representation in the Commons. Third, the number of voters increased by about 50 percent. Comfortable middle-class groups in the urban population, as well as some substantial farmers who leased their land, received the vote. Thus the pressures building in Great Britain were temporarily released without revolution or civil war.

The principal radical program was embodied in the "People's Charter" of 1838 and the Chartist movement (see page 754), with its core demand for universal male (but not female) suffrage. In three separate campaigns hundreds of thousands of people signed gigantic petitions calling on Parliament to grant all men the right to vote. Parliament rejected the petitions, but the working poor learned a valuable lesson in mass politics.

While calling for universal male suffrage, many working-class people joined with middle-class manufacturers in the Anti–Corn Law League, founded in Manchester in 1839. Mass participation made possible a popular crusade led by fighting liberals, who argued that lower food prices and more jobs in industry depended on repeal of the Corn Laws. When Ireland's potato crop failed in 1845, famine prices for food and even famine itself also seemed likely in England. To avert the impending catastrophe, Tory prime minister Robert Peel joined with the Whigs and a minority of his own party to repeal the Corn Laws in 1846 and allow free imports of grain. England escaped famine. Thereafter the liberal doctrine of free trade became almost sacred dogma in Great Britain.

The following year the Tories passed a bill designed to help the working classes. The Ten Hours Act of 1847 limited the workday for women and young people in factories to ten hours. Tory aristocrats continued to champion legislation regulating factory conditions. They were competing vigorously with the middle class for the support of the working class. This healthy competition between a still-vigorous aristocracy and a strong middle class was a crucial factor in Great Britain's peaceful evolution. The working classes could make temporary alliances with either competitor to better their own conditions.

The people of Ireland did not benefit from this political competition. Long ruled as a conquered people, the great mass of the population (outside the northern

**Daniel McDonald: The Discovery of the Potato Blight** Although the leaves of diseased plants usually shriveled and died, they could also look deceptively healthy. This Irish family has dug up its potato harvest and just discovered to its horror that the blight has rotted the crop. Like thousands of Irish families, this family now faces the starvation and the mass epidemics of the Great Famine. *(Department of Irish Folklore, University College, Dublin)*

counties of Ulster, which were partly Presbyterian) were Irish Catholic peasants who rented their land from a tiny minority of Church of England Protestants, many of whom lived in England. Ruthlessly exploited and growing rapidly in numbers, Irish peasants had come to depend on the potato crop.

The potato crop failed in 1845, 1846, 1848, and 1851 in Ireland and throughout much of Europe. Blight attacked the young plants, and the tubers rotted. The general result was high food prices, widespread suffering, and, frequently, social upheaval. In Ireland the result was widespread starvation and mass fever epidemics. Total losses of population were staggering. Fully 1 million emigrants fled the famine between 1845 and 1851, going primarily to the United States and Great Britain, and at least 1.5 million people died or went unborn because of the disaster.

## Revolutions in France

Louis XVIII's Constitutional Charter of 1814—theoretically a gift from the king but actually a response to political pressures—was basically a liberal constitution (see page 724). The economic and social gains made by sections of the middle class and the peasantry in the French Revolution were fully protected, great intellectual and artistic freedom was permitted, and a real parliament with upper and lower houses was created.

Louis XVIII's charter was anything but democratic. Only about 100,000 of the wealthiest people out of a total population of 30 million had the right to vote for the deputies, who, with the king and his ministers, made the laws of the nation. Nonetheless, the "notable people" who did vote came from very different backgrounds. There were wealthy businessmen, war profiteers, successful professionals, former revolutionaries, large landowners from the old aristocracy and the middle class, Bourbons, and Bonapartists.

The old aristocracy, with its pre-1789 mentality, was a minority within the voting population. It was this situation that Louis's successor, his brother Charles X (r. 1824–1830), could not abide. Crowned in a lavish, utterly medieval ceremony in 1824, Charles was a true reactionary who wanted to re-establish the old order in France. Finally repudiating the Constitutional Charter in an attempted coup in July 1830, Charles issued decrees stripping much of the wealthy middle class of its voting rights, and he censored the press. The immediate reaction, encouraged by journalists and lawyers, was an insurrection in the capital by printers, other artisans, and small traders. In "three glorious days" the revolution of 1830 brought down the government. Charles fled. Then the upper middle class, which had encouraged the revolt, skillfully seated Charles's cousin, Louis Philippe, duke of Orléans, on the vacant throne.

Louis Philippe (r. 1830–1848) accepted the Constitutional Charter of 1814; adopted the red, white, and blue flag of the French Revolution; and admitted that he was merely the "king of the French people." In spite of such symbolic actions, the situation in France remained fundamentally unchanged. The vote was extended only from 100,000 to 170,000 citizens. Republicans, democrats, social reformers, and the poor of Paris were bitterly disappointed.

These disappointments in France grew in the 1840s, which were economically hard and politically tense throughout Europe. The government's stubborn refusal to consider electoral reform heightened a sense of class injustice among shopkeepers and urban working people, and it eventually touched off a popular revolt in Paris. Barricades went up on the night of February 22, 1848, and by February 24 Louis Philippe had abdicated.

The revolutionaries were firmly committed to a republic (as opposed to any form of constitutional monarchy), and they immediately set about drafting a constitution for France's Second Republic. Moreover, they wanted a truly popular and democratic republic so that the healthy, life-giving forces of the common people—the peasants and the workers—could reform society with wise legislation. In practice, building such a republic meant giving the right to vote to every adult male, and this was quickly done. Revolutionary compassion and sympathy

**The Triumph of Democratic Republics** This French illustration constructs a joyous, optimistic vision of the initial revolutionary breakthrough in 1848. The peoples of Europe, joined together around their respective national banners, are achieving republican freedom, which is symbolized by the statue of liberty and the discarded crowns. The woman wearing pants (*front left*)—very radical attire—represents feminist hopes for liberation. *(Archive of Arnoldo Mondadori Editore, Milan)*

for freedom were expressed in the freeing of all slaves in French colonies, the abolition of the death penalty, and the establishment of **national workshops** in Paris.

Yet there were profound differences within the revolutionary coalition in Paris. The moderate, liberal republicans of the middle class viewed universal male suffrage as the ultimate concession to be made to popular forces, and they strongly opposed any further radical social measures. The radical republicans, influenced by a generation of utopian socialists, were committed to some kind of socialism.

Worsening depression and rising unemployment brought these conflicting goals to the fore. The French masses went to the election polls in late April. Voting in most cases for the first time, the people elected a majority of moderate republicans to the new Constituent Assembly. The socialism that seemed the most characteristic aspect of the revolution in Paris was evoking a violent reaction not only among the frightened middle and upper classes but also among the peasants. Many French peasants owned land, and they had been seized with a universal hatred of radical Paris. A majority of the Constituent Assembly members were thus firmly committed to the republic and strongly opposed to the socialists.

This clash of ideologies—of liberal capitalism and socialism—became a clash of classes and arms after the elections. As the national workshops continued to fill and grow more radical, the fearful but powerful propertied classes in the Assembly took the offensive. On June 22 the government dissolved the national workshops in Paris, giving the workers the choice of joining the army or going to workshops in the provinces.

The result was a spontaneous and violent uprising. Frustrated in attempts to create a socialist society, masses of desperate people were now losing even their life-sustaining relief. When the famous astronomer François Arago counseled patience, a voice from the crowd cried out, "Ah, Monsieur Arago, you have never been hungry!"[3] Barricades sprang up in the narrow streets of Paris, and a terrible class war began. Working people fought with the courage of utter desperation, but the government had the army and the support of peasant France. After three terrible "June Days" and the death or injury of more than ten thousand people, the republican army stood triumphant in a sea of working-class blood and hatred.

The revolution in France thus ended in spectacular failure. The February coalition of the middle and working classes had in four short months become locked in mortal combat. In place of a generous democratic republic, the Constituent Assembly completed a constitution featuring a strong executive. This allowed Louis Napoleon, nephew of Napoleon Bonaparte, to win a landslide victory in the election of December 1848.

## The Austrian Empire in 1848

Throughout central Europe news of the upheaval in France evoked feverish excitement and eventually revolution. Liberals demanded written constitutions, representative government, and greater civil liberties from authoritarian regimes. When governments hesitated, popular revolts followed. Urban workers and students served as the shock troops, but they were allied with middle-class liberals and peasants. In the face of this united front, monarchs collapsed and granted almost everything. The popular revolutionary coalition, having secured great and easy victories, then broke down as it had in France. The traditional forces—the monarchy, the aristocracy, and the regular army—recovered their nerve, reasserted their authority, and took back many, though not all, of the concessions. Reaction was everywhere victorious.

The revolution in the Austrian Empire began in Hungary, where nationalistic Hungarians demanded national autonomy, full civil liberties, and universal suffrage. When the monarchy in Vienna hesitated, Viennese students and workers took to the streets, and peasant disorders broke out in parts of the empire. The Habsburg emperor Ferdinand I (r. 1835–1848) capitulated and promised reforms and a liberal constitution. Metternich fled in disguise toward London. The old absolutist order seemed to be collapsing with unbelievable rapidity.

The coalition of revolutionaries was not stable, however. The Austrian Empire was overwhelmingly agricultural, and serfdom still existed. On March 20, as part of its capitulation before upheaval, the monarchy abolished serfdom, with its degrading forced labor and feudal services. Feeling they had won a victory reminiscent of that in France in 1789, newly free men and women of the land then lost interest in the political and social questions agitating the cities. Meanwhile, the coalition of urban revolutionaries also broke down. When the urban poor rose in arms and presented their own demands for socialist workshops and universal voting rights for men, the prosperous middle classes recoiled in alarm.

The coalition of March was also weakened, and ultimately destroyed, by conflicting national aspirations. In March the Hungarian revolutionary leaders pushed through an extremely liberal, almost democratic, constitution. But the Hungarian revolutionaries also sought to transform the mosaic of provinces and peoples that was the kingdom of Hungary into a unified, centralized Hungarian nation. To the minority groups that formed half of the population—the Croats, Serbs, and Romanians—such unification was completely unacceptable. Each felt entitled to political autonomy and cultural independence. The Habsburg monarchy in Vienna exploited the fears of the minority groups, and they were soon locked in armed combat with the new Hungarian government. In a somewhat similar way Czech nationalists based in Bohemia and the city of Prague came into conflict with German nationalists. Thus the national aspirations within the Austrian Empire enabled the monarchy to play one group off against the other.

Finally, the conservative aristocratic forces gathered around Emperor Ferdinand I regained their nerve and reasserted their great strength. The archduchess Sophia, a conservative but intelligent and courageous Bavarian princess married to the emperor's brother, provided a rallying point. Deeply ashamed of the emperor's collapse before a "mess of students," she insisted that Ferdinand, who had no heir, abdicate in favor of her son, Francis Joseph.[4] Powerful nobles who held high positions in the government, the army, and the church agreed completely. They organized around Sophia in a secret conspiracy to reverse and crush the revolution.

Their first breakthrough came when the army bombarded Prague and savagely crushed a working-class revolt there on June 17. Other Austrian officials and nobles began to lead the minority nationalities of Hungary against the revolutionary government proclaimed by the Hungarian patriots. At the end of October the well-equipped, predominantly peasant troops of the regular Austrian army attacked the student and working-class radicals in Vienna and retook the city at the cost of more than four thousand casualties. Thus the determination of the Austrian aristocracy and the loyalty of its army were the final ingredients in the triumph of reaction and the defeat of revolution.

When Francis Joseph (r. 1848–1916) was crowned emperor of Austria immediately after his eighteenth birthday in December 1848, only Hungary had yet to be brought under control. But another determined conservative, Nicholas I of Russia (r. 1825–1855), obligingly lent his iron hand. On June 6, 1849, 130,000 Russian troops poured into Hungary and subdued the country after bitter fighting. For a number of years the Habsburgs ruled Hungary as a conquered territory.

## Prussia and the Frankfurt Assembly

After Austria, Prussia was the largest and most influential German kingdom. Prior to 1848, the goal of middle-class Prussian liberals had been to transform absolutist Prussia into a liberal constitutional monarchy, which would lead the thirty-eight states of the German Confederation into a unified nation. Following the fall of Louis Philippe in France, artisans and factory workers in Berlin exploded in March 1848 and joined with the middle-class liberals in the struggle against the monarchy. The autocratic yet paternalistic Frederick William IV (r. 1840–1861) caved in, and on March 21 he promised to grant Prussia a liberal constitution and to merge Prussia into a new national German state. But urban workers wanted much more, and they issued a series of democratic and vaguely socialist demands that troubled their middle-class allies. The conservative clique gathered around the king to urge counter-revolution.

As an elected Prussian Constituent Assembly met in Berlin to write a constitution for the Prussian state, a self-appointed committee of liberals from various German states successfully called for a national assembly to begin writing a federal constitution for a unified German state. Meeting in Frankfurt in May, the National Assembly was a curious revolutionary body. It was really a serious middle-class body of lawyers, professors, doctors, officials, and businessmen.

The learned body was soon absorbed in a battle with Denmark over the provinces of **Schleswig and Holstein.** The provinces were inhabited primarily by Germans but were ruled by the king of Denmark, although Holstein was a member of the German Confederation. When Frederick VII, the new nationalistic king of Denmark, tried to integrate both provinces into the rest of his state, the Germans in these provinces revolted. Hypnotized by this conflict, the National Assembly at Frankfurt debated ponderously and finally called on the Prussian army to oppose Denmark in the name of the German nation. Prussia responded and began war with Denmark. As the Schleswig-Holstein issue demonstrated, the national ideal was a crucial factor motivating the German middle classes in 1848.

In March 1849 the National Assembly finally completed its drafting of a liberal constitution and elected King Frederick William of Prussia emperor of the new German national state. By early 1849, however, reaction had been successful almost everywhere. Frederick William had reasserted his royal authority, disbanded the Prussian Constituent Assembly, and granted his subjects a conservative constitution. Reasserting that he ruled by divine right, Frederick William contemptuously refused to accept the "crown from the gutter." Bogged down by their preoccupation with nationalist issues, the reluctant revolutionaries in Frankfurt had waited too long and acted too timidly.

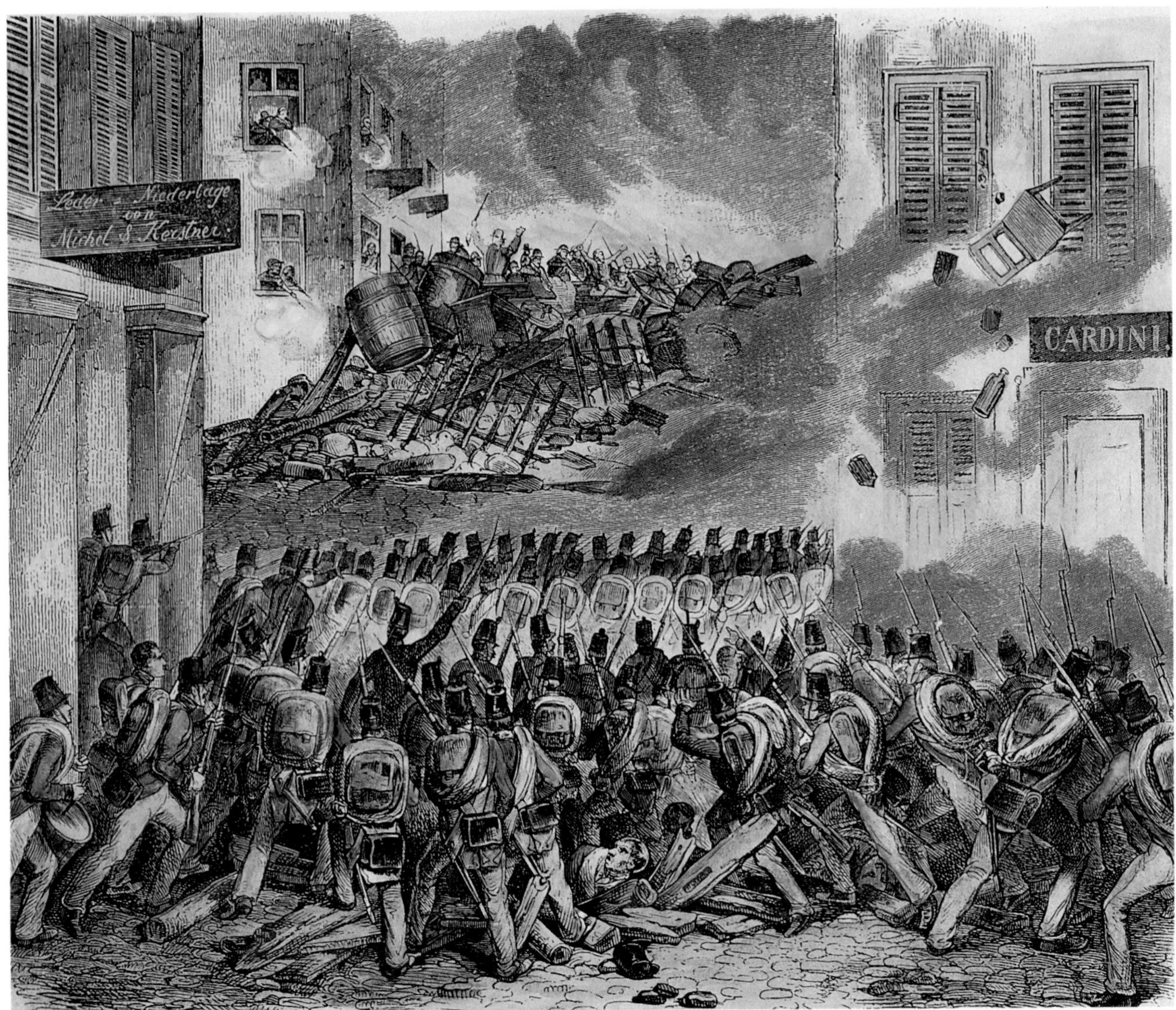


**Street Fighting in Frankfurt, 1848** Workers and students could tear up the cobblestones, barricade a street, and make it into a fortress. But urban revolutionaries were untrained and poorly armed. They were no match for professional soldiers led by tough officers who were sent against them after frightened rulers had recovered their nerve. *(The Granger Collection, New York)*

When Frederick William, who really wanted to be emperor but only on his own authoritarian terms, tried to get the small monarchs of Germany to elect him emperor, Austria balked. Supported by Russia, Austria forced Prussia to renounce all its schemes of unification in late 1850. The German Confederation was re-established. Attempts to unite the Germans—first in a liberal national state and then in a conservative Prussian empire—had failed completely.

## NATION BUILDING IN FRANCE, ITALY, AND GERMANY

Political, economic, and social pressures building up after 1815 exploded dramatically in 1848. But the upheavals were abortive, and very few revolutionary goals were realized. The moderate, nationalistic middle classes were unable to consolidate their initial victories in France or elsewhere in Europe. Instead, they drew back when artisans, factory workers, and radical socialists rose up to present their own much more revolutionary demands. This retreat made possible the crushing of Parisian workers by a coalition of solid bourgeoisie and landowning peasantry in France, and it facilitated the efforts of dedicated aristocrats in central Europe. A sea of blood and disillusion had washed away the lofty ideals and utopian visions of a generation. Thus the revolutions of 1848 closed one era in the West and opened another.

In thought and culture exuberant romanticism gave way to hardheaded realism. In the Atlantic economy the hard years of the 1840s were followed by good times and prosperity throughout most of the 1850s and 1860s. In international politics the repressive peace and diplomatic stability of Metternich's time were replaced by a period of war and rapid change. Perhaps most important of all, Western society progressively found, for better or worse, a new and effective organizing principle capable of coping with the many-sided challenges of the dual revolution and the emerging urban civilization. That principle was nationalism—dedication to and identification with the nation-state.

The triumph of modern nationalism was an enormously significant historical development. A powerful force since at least 1789, nationalism became an almost universal faith in Western society after 1850, evolving away from a narrow appeal to predominately middle-class liberals to an intoxicating creed moving the broad masses. Leaders of the entire world eventually embraced large parts of the doctrine of nationalism and the nation-state.

## Louis Napoleon in France

France was representative of the general trend. Early nationalism in France was at least liberal and idealistic and often democratic and radical as well. The ideas of nationhood and popular sovereignty, so seductive in France, posed an awesome threat to conservatives like Metternich. Yet from the vantage point of the twentieth century, it is clear that nationalism can flourish in dictatorial states that are conservative, fascist, or communist. In France Napoleon I had already combined national devotion with authoritarian rule. Significantly, it was Napoleon's nephew, Louis Napoleon, who revived and extended this merger. He showed how governments could reconcile popular and conservative forces in an authoritarian nationalism. In doing so, he provided a model for political leaders elsewhere.

Although Louis Napoleon Bonaparte had played no part in French politics before 1848, universal male suffrage gave him three times as many votes as the four other presidential candidates combined in the French presidential election of December 1848. Not only had Louis Napoleon the great name of his uncle, but middle-class and peasant property owners feared socialism and wanted a tough ruler to provide protection. Moreover, Louis Napoleon had a positive "program" for France, which he had elaborated in widely circulated pamphlets and which was to guide him throughout most of his long reign.

Above all, Louis Napoleon believed that the government should represent the people and that it should try hard to help them economically. But how were these tasks to be done? Parliaments and political parties were not the answer, according to Louis Napoleon. French politicians represented special-interest groups, particularly middle-class ones. The answer was a strong, even authoritarian, national leader, like the first Napoleon, who would serve all the people, rich and poor. This leader would be linked to the people by direct democracy, his sovereignty uncorrupted by politicians and legislative bodies. These political ideas went hand in hand with Louis Napoleon's vision of national unity and social progress. The state and its leader had a sacred duty to provide jobs and stimulate the economy. All classes would benefit by such action.

Louis Napoleon's political and social ideas were at least vaguely understood by large numbers of French peasants and workers in December 1848. To many common people he appeared to be a strong man *and* a forward-looking champion of their interests, and that is why they voted for him.

Elected to a four-year term, President Louis Napoleon at first shared power with a conservative National Assembly. But in 1851, after the Assembly failed to change the constitution so he could run for a second term, Louis Napoleon began to organize a conspiracy with key army officers. On December 2, 1851, he illegally dismissed the Assembly and seized power in a coup d'état. Armed resistance in Paris and widespread insurrection in the countryside in southern France were quickly crushed by the army. Louis Napoleon called on the French, as his uncle had done, to legalize his actions. They did: 92 percent voted to make him a strong president for ten years. A year later 97 percent agreed in a national plebiscite to make him hereditary emperor.

Louis Napoleon—now proclaimed Emperor Napoleon III—experienced both success and failure between 1852 and 1870. His greatest success was with the economy, particularly in the 1850s. His government encouraged the new investment banks and massive railroad construction that were at the heart of the Industrial

Revolution in Europe. The government also fostered general economic expansion through an ambitious program of public works, which included the rebuilding of Paris to improve the urban environment. The profits of business people soared with prosperity, and unemployment declined greatly.

Louis Napoleon always hoped that economic progress would reduce social and political tensions. This hope was at least partially realized. Until the mid-1860s there was considerable support for his government from France's most dissatisfied group, the urban workers. In the 1860s Napoleon III granted workers the right to form unions and the right to strike—important economic rights denied by earlier governments.

At first political power remained in the hands of the emperor and his ministers. At the same time, Napoleon III restricted but did not abolish the Assembly. Members were elected by universal male suffrage every six years, and Louis Napoleon and his government took the parliamentary elections very seriously. They tried to entice notable people, even those who had opposed the regime, to stand as government candidates in order to expand the government's base of support. Moreover, the government used its officials and appointed mayors to spread the word that the election of the government's candidates—and the defeat of the opposition—was the key to roads, schools, tax rebates, and a thousand other local concerns.

In 1857 and again in 1863 Louis Napoleon's system worked brilliantly and produced overwhelming electoral victories. Yet in the 1860s Napoleon III's electoral system gradually disintegrated. France's problems in Italy and the rising power of Prussia led to increasing criticism at home from his Catholic and nationalist supporters. With growing effectiveness the middle-class liberals who had always wanted a less authoritarian regime continued to denounce his rule.

Napoleon was always sensitive to the public mood. Public opinion, he once said, always wins the last victory. Thus in the 1860s he progressively liberalized his empire. He gave the Assembly greater powers and the opposition candidates greater freedom, which they used to good advantage. In 1869 the opposition, consisting of republicans, monarchists, and liberals, polled almost 45 percent of the vote.

The next year a sick and weary Louis Napoleon again granted France a new constitution, which combined a basically parliamentary regime with a hereditary emperor as chief of state. In a final great plebiscite on the eve of a disastrous war with Prussia, 7.5 million Frenchmen voted in favor of the new constitution, and only 1.5 million opposed it. Napoleon III's attempt to reconcile a strong national state with universal male suffrage was still evolving and was doing so in a democratic direction.

## Cavour, Garibaldi, and the Unification of Italy

Italy had never been a united nation prior to 1860. Part of Rome's great empire in ancient times, the Italian peninsula was divided in the Middle Ages into competing city-states, and it became a battleground for Great Powers after 1494. Italy was reorganized in 1815 at the Congress of Vienna. The rich northern provinces of Lombardy and Venetia were taken by Metternich's Austria. Sardinia and Piedmont were under the rule of an Italian monarch, and Tuscany shared north-central Italy with several smaller states. Central Italy and Rome were ruled by the papacy. Naples and Sicily were ruled by a branch of the Bourbons. Metternich was not wrong in dismissing Italy as "a geographical expression" (see Map 24.3).

Between 1815 and 1848 the goal of a unified Italian nation captured the imaginations of increasing numbers of Italians. There were three basic approaches. The first was the radical program of the idealistic patriot Giuseppe Mazzini, who preached a centralized democratic republic based on universal suffrage and the will of the people (see pages 790–791). The second was that of Vincenzo Gioberti, a Catholic priest who called for a federation of existing states under the presidency of a progressive pope. The third was the program of those who looked for leadership toward the autocratic kingdom of Sardinia-Piedmont, much as many Germans looked toward Prussia.

The third alternative was strengthened by the failures of 1848, when an Austrian army smashed Italian revolutionaries in Austria's possessions in northern Italy. Almost by accident, independent Sardinia's monarch, Victor Emmanuel, retained the moderate liberal constitution granted under duress in March 1848. To the Italian middle classes Sardinia appeared to be a liberal, progressive state ideally suited to achieve the goal of national unification. By contrast, Mazzini's brand of democratic republicanism seemed quixotic and too radical. As for the papacy, the initial cautious support for unification by Pope Pius IX (r. 1846–1878) had given way to fear and hostility after he was temporarily driven from Rome during the upheavals of 1848. For a long generation, the papacy would stand opposed to most modern trends. In 1864 in the *Syllabus of Errors,* Pius IX strongly denounced rationalism, socialism, separation of church and state, and religious liberty, denying that "the Roman pontiff can and ought to reconcile and align himself with progress, liberalism, and modern civilization."

**MAP 24.3 The Unification of Italy, 1859–1870** The leadership of Sardinia-Piedmont and nationalist fervor were decisive factors in the unification of Italy.

Sardinia had the good fortune of being led by a brilliant statesman, Count Camillo Benso di Cavour. Indicative of the coming tacit alliance between the aristocracy and the solid middle class under the banner of the strong nation-state, Cavour came from a noble family and embraced the economic doctrines and business activities associated with the prosperous middle class. Cavour's national goals were limited and realistic. Until 1859 he sought unity only for the states of northern and perhaps central Italy in a greatly expanded kingdom of Sardinia.

In the 1850s Cavour worked to consolidate Sardinia as a liberal constitutional state capable of leading northern Italy. His program of highways and railroads, of civil liberties and opposition to clerical privilege, increased support for Sardinia throughout northern Italy. Yet Cavour realized that Sardinia could not drive Austria out of Lombardy and Venetia, and thus he worked for a secret diplomatic alliance with Napoleon III. Finally, in July 1858, Cavour succeeded and goaded Austria into attacking Sardinia. Napoleon III came to Sardinia's defense. Then after the victory of the combined Franco-Sardinian forces, Napoleon III did a complete about-face. Criticized by French Catholics for supporting the pope's declared enemy, Napoleon III abandoned Cavour. He made a compromise peace with the Austrians in July 1859. Sardinia would receive only Lombardy, the area around Milan. Cavour resigned in a rage.

Popular revolts and Italian nationalism salvaged Cavour's plans. While the war against Austria had raged in the north, dedicated nationalists in central Italy had risen and driven out their rulers. Nationalist fervor seized the urban masses, and the leaders of the nationalist movement called for fusion with Sardinia. This was not at all what France and the other Great Powers wanted, but the nationalists held firm and eventually had their way. Cavour returned to power in early 1860, and the people of central Italy voted overwhelmingly to join a greatly enlarged kingdom of Sardinia. Cavour had achieved his original goal of a north Italian state (see Map 24.3).

For superpatriots such as Giuseppe Garibaldi (1807–1882), the job of unification was still only half done. The son of a poor sailor, Garibaldi personified the romantic, revolutionary nationalism of Mazzini and 1848. Leading a corps of volunteers against Austria in 1859, Garibaldi emerged in 1860 as a powerful independent force in Italian politics.

Partly to use him and partly to get rid of him, Cavour secretly supported Garibaldi's bold plan to "liberate" the kingdom of the Two Sicilies. Landing on the shores of Sicily in May 1860, Garibaldi's guerrilla band of a thou-

**Garibaldi and Victor Emmanuel** The historic meeting in Naples between the leader of Italy's revolutionary nationalists and the king of Sardinia sealed the unification of northern and southern Italy in a unitary state. With only the sleeve of his red shirt showing, Garibaldi offers his hand—and his conquests—to the uniformed king and his moderate monarchical government. *(Scala/Art Resource, NY)*

sand **Red Shirts** captured the imagination of the Sicilian peasantry. Outwitting the twenty-thousand-man royal army, the guerrilla leader took Palermo. Then he and his men crossed to the mainland and prepared to attack Rome and the pope. But the wily Cavour quickly sent Sardinian forces to occupy most of the Papal States (but not Rome) and to intercept Garibaldi.

Cavour realized that an attack on Rome would bring about war with France, and he also feared Garibaldi's popular appeal. Thus he immediately organized a plebiscite in the conquered territories. Despite the urging of some more radical supporters, the patriotic Garibaldi did not oppose Cavour, and the people of the south voted to join Sardinia. When Garibaldi and Victor Emmanuel rode through Naples to cheering crowds, they symbolically sealed the union of north and south, of monarch and people.

Cavour had succeeded. He had controlled Garibaldi and had turned popular nationalism in a conservative direction. The new kingdom of Italy, which did not include Venice until 1866 or Rome until 1870, was a parliamentary monarchy under Victor Emmanuel, neither radical nor democratic. Only a small minority of Italian males had the right to vote. Despite political unity, the propertied classes and the common people were divided. A great and growing social and cultural gap separated the progressive, industrializing north from the stagnant, agrarian south.

## Bismarck and German Unification

In the aftermath of 1848 the German states were locked in a political stalemate. After Austria and Russia had blocked Frederick William's attempt to unify Germany "from above," tension grew between Austria and Prussia as each power sought to block the other within the German Confederation. Stalemate and reaction also prevailed in the domestic politics of the individual German states in the 1850s.

At the same time, powerful economic forces were undermining the political status quo. Modern industry grew rapidly within the German customs union (*Zollverein*), founded officially in 1834 to stimulate trade and increase the revenues of member states. By the end of 1853 all the German states except Austria had joined the customs union, and a new Germany excluding Austria was becoming an economic reality.

The national uprising in Italy in 1859 made a profound impression in Prussia. Great political change and war—perhaps with Austria, perhaps with France—seemed quite possible. Along with his top military advisers, the tough-minded William I of Prussia (r. 1861–1888), who had replaced the unstable Frederick William IV as regent in 1858 and become king himself in 1861, was convinced of the need for major army reforms and wanted to double the size of the regular army. Army reforms meant a bigger defense budget and higher taxes.

Prussia had emerged from 1848 with a parliament of sorts, the Prussian Assembly, which was in the hands of the liberal middle class by 1859. The wealthy middle class wanted society to be less, not more, militaristic. Above all, middle-class representatives wanted to establish once and for all that the parliament, not the king, had the ultimate political power and that the army was responsible to Prussia's elected representatives. These demands were popular. The parliament rejected the military budget in 1862, and the liberals triumphed completely. King William then called on Count Otto von Bismarck to head a new ministry and defy the parliament. This was a momentous choice.

The most important figure in German history between Luther and Hitler, Otto von Bismarck (1815–1898) was above all a master of politics. Born into the Prussian landowning aristocracy, the young Bismarck was a wild and tempestuous student given to duels and drinking. Proud of his Junker heritage and always devoted to his Prussian sovereign, Bismarck had a strong personality and an unbounded desire for power. Yet he was also extraordinarily flexible and pragmatic. "One must always have two irons in the fire," he once said. He kept his options open, pursuing one policy and then another as he moved with skill and cunning toward his goal.

When Bismarck took office as chief minister in 1862, his appointment made a strong but unfavorable impression. Declaring that the government would rule without parliamentary consent, Bismarck lashed out at the middle-class opposition: "The great questions of the day will not be decided by speeches and resolutions—that was the blunder of 1848 and 1849—but by blood and iron." Denounced for this view that "might makes right," Bismarck had the Prussian bureaucracy go right on collecting taxes even though the parliament refused to approve the budget. Bismarck reorganized the army. And for four years, from 1862 to 1866, the voters of Prussia supported the opposition and sent large liberal majorities to the parliament.

Opposition at home spurred the search for success abroad. When the Danish king tried again, as in 1848, to bring the provinces of Schleswig and Holstein into a centralized Danish state, Prussia joined Austria in a short and successful war against Denmark in 1864. Then, convinced that Prussia had to control completely the northern, predominantly Protestant part of the German Confederation, Bismarck worked to expell Austria from

**Otto von Bismarck** The commanding presence and the haughty pride of the Prussian statesman are clearly evident in this photo taken shortly before he came to power. Dressed in formal diplomatic attire as Prussia's ambassador in Paris, Bismarck is perhaps on his way to see Emperor Louis Napoleon and size up his future adversary once again. *(AKG London)*

German affairs. By skillfully neutralizing Russia and France, Bismarck was in a position to engage in a war of his own making.

The Austro-Prussian War of 1866 lasted only seven weeks. Utilizing railroads to mass troops, the reorganized Prussian army overran northern Germany and defeated Austria decisively at the Battle of Sadowa in Bohemia. Anticipating Prussia's future needs, Bismarck offered Austria realistic, even generous, peace terms. Austria paid no reparations and lost no territory to Prussia, although Venice was ceded to Italy. But the German Confederation was dissolved, and Austria agreed to withdraw from German affairs. The states north of the Main River were grouped in the new North German Confederation, led by an expanded Prussia. The mainly Catholic states of the south remained independent while forming alliances with Prussia. Bismarck's fundamental goal of Prussian expansion was being realized (see Map 24.4).

Bismarck had long been convinced that the old order he so ardently defended should make peace, on its own conservative terms, with the liberal middle class and the nationalist movement. Moreover, Bismarck believed that because of the events of 1848, the German middle class could eventually be led to prefer the reality of national unity under conservative leadership to a long, uncertain battle for truly liberal institutions. Thus during the attack on Austria in 1866, he increasingly identified Prussia's fate with the "national development of Germany."

In the aftermath of victory Bismarck fashioned a federal constitution for the new **North German Confederation.** Each state retained its own local government, but the king of Prussia became president of the Confederation, and the chancellor—Bismarck—was responsible only to the president. The federal government—William I and Bismarck—controlled the army and foreign affairs. There was also a legislature consisting of two houses that shared equally in the making of laws. Delegates to the lower house were elected by universal male suffrage. With this radical innovation, Bismarck opened the door to popular participation and the possibility of going over the head of the middle class directly to the people, much as Napoleon III had done in France. All the while, however, ultimate power rested as securely as ever in the hands of Prussia and its king and army.

In Prussia itself Bismarck held out an olive branch to the parliamentary opposition. Marshaling all his diplomatic skill, he asked the parliament to pass a special indemnity bill to approve after the fact all of the government's "illegal" spending between 1862 and 1866. Most of the liberals snatched at the chance to cooperate. With German unity in sight, they repented their "sins." The constitutional struggle was over, and the German middle class was accepting respectfully the monarchical authority and aristocratic superiority that Bismarck represented.

The final act in the drama of German unification followed quickly. Bismarck realized that a patriotic war with France would drive the south German states into his arms. The French obligingly played their part. The apparent issue—whether a distant relative of Prussia's William I (and France's Napoleon III) might become king of Spain—was only a diplomatic pretext. By 1870

**MAP 24.4 The Unification of Germany, 1866–1871** This map deserves careful study. Note how Prussian expansion, Austrian expulsion from the old German Confederation, and the creation of a new German Empire went hand in hand. Austria lost no territory, but Prussia's neighbors in the north suffered grievously or simply disappeared. The annexation of Alsace-Lorraine turned France into a lasting enemy of Germany before 1914.

the French leaders of the Second Empire, alarmed by their powerful new neighbor on the Rhine, had decided on a war to teach Prussia a lesson.

As soon as war against France began in 1870, Bismarck had the wholehearted support of the south German states. With other governments standing still—Bismarck's generosity to Austria in 1866 was paying big dividends—German forces under Prussian leadership decisively defeated Louis Napoleon's armies at Sedan on September 1, 1870. Three days later French patriots in Paris proclaimed yet another French republic (the third) and vowed to continue fighting. But after five months, in January 1871, a starving Paris surrendered, and France went on to accept Bismarck's harsh peace terms. By this time the south German states had agreed to join a new German Empire. The victorious William I was proclaimed emperor of Germany in the Hall of Mirrors in the palace of Versailles. Europe had a nineteenth-century German "sun king." As in the 1866 constitution, the king of Prussia and his ministers had ultimate power in the new German Empire, and the lower house of the legislature was elected by universal male suffrage.

The Franco-Prussian War, which Europeans generally saw as a test of nations in a pitiless Darwinian struggle for existence, released an enormous surge of patriotic feeling in Germany. Bismarck's genius, the invincible Prussian army, the solidarity of king and people in a unified nation—these and similar themes were trumpeted endlessly during and after the war. The weakest of the Great Powers in 1862 (after Austria, Britain, France, and Russia), Prussia had become the most powerful state in Europe in less than a decade. Most Germans were enormously proud, blissfully imagining themselves the fittest and best of the European species. Semi-authoritarian nationalism and a "new conservatism," which was based on an alliance of the propertied classes and sought the active support of the working classes, had triumphed in Germany.

## SUMMARY

In 1814 the victorious allied powers sought to restore peace and stability in Europe. Dealing moderately with France and wisely settling their own differences, the allies laid the foundations for beneficial international cooperation throughout much of the nineteenth century. Led by Metternich, the conservative powers also sought to prevent the spread of subversive ideas and radical changes in domestic politics. Yet European thought has seldom been more powerfully creative than after 1815, and ideologies of liberalism, nationalism, and socialism all developed to challenge the existing order. The romantic movement, breaking decisively with the dictates of classicism, reinforced the spirit of change and revolutionary anticipation.

All of these forces culminated in the liberal and nationalistic revolutions of 1848. Political, economic, and social pressures that had been building since 1815 exploded dramatically. Yet the failed upheavals of 1848 realized very few revolutionary goals. The moderate middle classes were unable to consolidate their initial victories. Instead, they drew back in fear when artisans, factory workers, and radical socialists rose up to present their own much more revolutionary demands.

This retreat facilitated a resurgence of conservative forces that crushed revolution all across Europe. These conservative forces then took the lead in refashioning politics after 1850, relying on strong rule that was fortified by popular nationalism at critical moments. Thus larger, more unified, and more popular states emerged in the West, and support for the nation appeared to provide the basis for a stabilizing response to the profoundly unsettling challenges of the dual revolution.

## KEY TERMS

dual revolution
Congress of Vienna
Holy Alliance
Carlsbad Decrees
laissez faire
socialism
parasites
doers
bourgeoisie
proletariat
Sturm und Drang
Corn Laws
national workshops
Schleswig and Holstein
"Red Shirts"
North German Confederation

## NOTES

1. E. Gellner, *Nations and Nationalism* (Oxford: Basil Blackwell, 1983), pp. 19–39.
2. B. Anderson, *Imagined Communities: Reflections on the Origins and Spread of Nationalism,* rev. ed. (London/New York: Verso, 1991).
3. M. Agulhon, *1848* (Paris: Éditions du Seuil, 1973), pp. 68–69.
4. Quoted in W. L. Langer, *Political and Social Upheaval, 1832–1852* (New York: Harper & Row, 1969), p. 361.

## SUGGESTED READING

The works cited in the Notes are highly recommended. Langer's book is a balanced synthesis with an excellent bibliography, and those by Gellner and Anderson are influential reconsiderations of nationalism. Among general studies, R. Gildea, *Barricades and Borders: Europe, 1800–1914,* 2d ed. (1996), is recommended. C. Morazé, *The Triumph of the Middle Classes* (1968), a wide-ranging procapitalist interpretation, may be compared with E. J. Hobsbawm's flexible Marxism in *The Age of Revolution, 1789–1848* (1962). R. Brubaker, *Citizenship and Nationhood in France* (1992), is an important comparative study. E. Kedourie, *Nationalism* (1960), is an influential historical critique of the new faith. H. Nicolson, *The Congress of Vienna* (1946), is entertaining. On 1848, J. Sperber, *The European Revolutions, 1848–1851* (1993), is a solid synthesis. I. Deak, *The Lawful Revolution: Louis Kossuth and the Hungarians, 1848–49* (1979), is a noteworthy study of an interesting figure.

On early socialism and Marxism, see A. Lindemann's stimulating survey, *A History of European Socialism* (1983), and W. Sewell, Jr.'s *Work and Revolution in France: The Language of Labor from the Old Regime to 1848* (1980), as well as G. Lichtheim's high-powered *Marxism* (1961) and *Short History of Socialism* (1970). J. Seigel, *Marx's Fate: The Shape of a Life* (1978), is an outstanding biography. Fourier is treated sympathetically in J. Beecher, *Charles Fourier* (1986). J. Schumpeter, *Capitalism, Socialism and Democracy* (1947), is important but challenging, a real mind-stretcher. Also highly recommended is B. Taylor, *Eve and the New Jerusalem: Socialism and Feminism in the Nineteenth Century* (1983), which explores fascinating English attempts to emancipate workers and women at the same time. On liberalism, see R. Heilbroner's entertaining *The Worldly Philosophers* (1967) and G. de Ruggiero's classic *History of European Liberalism* (1959). J. Barzun, *Classic, Romantic and Modern* (1961), skillfully discusses the emergence of romanticism, and J. Seigel, *Bohemian Paris: Culture, Politics, and the Boundaries of Bourgeois Life* (1986), imaginatively places romantic aspirations in a broad cultural framework. R. Stromberg, *An Intellectual History of Modern Europe,* 3d ed. (1981), is a valuable survey. The important place of religion in nineteenth-century thought is considered from different perspectives in H. McLeod, *Religion and the People of Western Europe* (1981), and O. Chadwick, *The Secularization of the European Mind in the Nineteenth Century* (1976). Two good church histories with useful bibliographies are J. Altholz, *The Churches in the Nineteenth Century* (1967), and A. Vidler, *The Church in an Age of Revolution: 1789 to the Present Day* (1961).

For English history, A. Briggs's socially oriented *The Making of Modern England, 1784–1867* (1967) and D. Thomson's *England in the Nineteenth Century, 1815–1914* (1951) are excellent. C. Ó Gráda, *Black '47 and Beyond: The Irish Famine in History, Economy, and Memory* (1999), is an outstanding reconsideration of the Great Famine. Restoration France is sympathetically portrayed by G. de Bertier de Sauvigny in *The Bourbon Restoration* (1967), whereas R. Price, *A Social History of Nineteenth-Century France* (1987), is a fine synthesis incorporating modern research. D. Harvey, *Napoleon III and His Comic Empire* (1988), brings the world of Napoleon III vibrantly alive. Émile Zola's novel *The Debacle* treats the Franco-Prussian War realistically. D. M. Smith has written widely on Italy, and his *Garibaldi* (1956) and *Italy: A Modern History,* rev. ed. (1969), are recommended. Two stimulating general histories of Germany are H. James, *A German Identity, 1770–1990* (1989), and J. Sheehan, *Germany, 1770–1866* (1989), which may be compared with H. Treitschke's bombastic pro-Prussian *History of Germany in the Nineteenth Century* (1915–1919), a classic of nationalistic history. O. Pflanze, *Bismarck and the Development of Germany* (1963), and E. Eyck, *Bismarck and the German Empire* (1964), are excellent biographies. H. Glasser, ed., *The German Mind in the Nineteenth Century* (1981), is an outstanding anthology, as is R. E. Joeres and M. Maynes, eds., *German Women in the Eighteenth and Nineteenth Centuries* (1986). A. Sked, *The Decline and Fall of the Habsburg Empire, 1815–1918* (1989), and R. Kann, *The Multinational Empire,* 2 vols. (1950, 1964), probe the intricacies of the nationality problem in Austria-Hungary.

The thoughtful reader is strongly advised to delve into the rich writing of contemporaries. J. Bowditch and C. Ramsland, eds., *Voices of the Industrial Revolution* (1961), is an excellent starting point, with well-chosen selections from leading economic thinkers and early socialists. H. Hugo, ed., *The Romantic Reader,* is another fine anthology. Mary Shelley's *Frankenstein,* a great romantic novel, draws an almost lovable picture of the famous monster and is highly recommended. Jules Michelet's compassionate masterpiece *The People* is a famous historian's anguished examination of French social divisions on the eve of 1848. Alexis de Tocqueville covers some of the same ground less romantically in his *Recollections,* which may be compared with Karl Marx's white-hot "instant history," *Class Struggles in France, 1848–1850* (1850). Great novels that accurately portray aspects of the times are Victor Hugo, *Les Misérables,* an exciting story of crime and passion among France's poor; Honoré de Balzac, *La Cousine Bette* and *Le Père Goriot*; and Thomas Mann, *Buddenbrooks,* a wonderful historical novel that traces the rise and fall of a prosperous German family over three generations during the nineteenth century.

# LISTENING TO THE PAST

## FAITH IN DEMOCRATIC NATIONALISM

*Early advocates of the national ideal usually believed that progress for one people would also contribute to the progress of all humanity. They believed that a Europe of independent nation-states would provide the proper framework for securing freedom, democracy, social justice, and even international peace.*

*This optimistic faith guided Giuseppe Mazzini (1805–1872), the leading prophet of Italian nationalism and unification. Banished from Italy in 1830, the exiled Mazzini founded a secret society called Young Italy to fight for Italian unification and a democratic republic. Mazzini's group inspired numerous local insurrections and then led Italy's radicals in the unsuccessful revolutions of 1848. Italy was united a decade later, but by other means.*

*Mazzini's best-known work was* The Duties of Man, *a collection of essays. The following famous selection, titled "Duties Towards Your Country," was written in 1858 and addressed to Italian workingmen.*

Your first Duties . . . are to Humanity. . . . But what can each of you, with his isolated powers, do for the moral improvement, for the progress of Humanity? . . .

God gave you the means of multiplying your forces and your powers of action indefinitely when he gave you a Country, when, like a wise overseer of labor, who distributes the different parts of the work according to the capacity of the workmen, he divided Humanity into distinct groups upon the face of our globe, and thus planted the seeds of nations. Evil governments have disfigured the design of God, which you may see clearly marked out, as far, at least, as regards Europe, by the courses of the great rivers, by the lines of the lofty mountains, and by other geographical conditions; they have disfigured it by conquest, by greed, by jealousy of the just sovereignty of others; disfigured it so much that today there is perhaps no nation except England and France whose confines correspond to this design.

[These evil governments] did not, and they do not, recognize any country except their own families and dynasties, the egoism of caste. But the divine design will infallibly be fulfilled. Natural divisions, the innate spontaneous tendencies of the peoples will replace the arbitrary divisions sanctioned by evil governments. The map of Europe will be remade. The Countries of the People will rise, defined by the voice of the free, upon the ruins of the Countries of Kings and privileged castes. Between these Countries there will be harmony and brotherhood. And then the work of Humanity for the general amelioration, for the discovery and application of the real law of life, carried on in association and distributed according to local capacities, will be accomplished by peaceful and progressive development.

Then each of you, strong in the affections and in the aid of many millions of men speaking the same language, endowed with the same tendencies, and educated by the same historic tradition, may hope by your personal effort to benefit the whole of Humanity.

Without Country you have neither name, voice, nor rights, no admission as brothers into the fellowship of the Peoples. You are the bastards of Humanity. Soldiers without a banner, . . . you will find neither faith nor protection. . . . Do not beguile yourselves with the hope of emancipation from unjust social conditions if you do not first conquer a Country for yourselves; where there is no Country there is no common agreement to which you can appeal; the egoism of self-interest rules alone, and he who has the upper hand keeps it, since there is no common safeguard for the interests of all. . . .

Portrait of Giuseppe Mazzini, from the Museo del Risorgimento, Milan. *(Museo del Risorgimento/ Scala/ Art Resource, NY)*

O my Brothers! love your Country. Our Country is our home, the home which God has given us, placing therein a numerous family which we love and are loved by. . . . In labouring according to true principles for our Country we are labouring for Humanity; our Country is the fulcrum of the lever which we have to wield for the common good. If we give up this fulcrum we run the risk of becoming useless to our Country and to Humanity. . . .

There is no true Country without a uniform law. There is no true Country where the uniformity of that law is violated by the existence of caste, privilege, and inequality, where the powers and faculties of a large number of individuals are suppressed or dormant, where there is no common principle accepted, recognized, and developed by all. In such a state of things there can be no Nation, no People, but only a multitude, a fortuitous agglomeration of men whom circumstances have brought together and different circumstances will separate. In the name of your love for your Country you must combat without truce the existence of every privilege, every inequality, upon the soil which has given you birth. . . .

Your Country should be your Temple. God at the summit, a People of equals at the base. Do not accept any other formula, any other moral law, if you do not want to dishonour your Country and yourselves. Let the secondary laws for the gradual regulation of your existence be the progressive application of this supreme law.

And in order that they should be so, it is necessary that *all* should contribute to the making of them. The laws made by one fraction of the citizens only can never by the nature of things and men do otherwise than reflect the thoughts and aspirations and desires of that fraction; they represent, not the whole Country, but a third, a fourth part, a class, a zone of the Country. The law must express the general aspiration, promote the good of all, respond to a beat of the nation's heart. The whole nation therefore should be, directly or indirectly, the legislator. By yielding this mission to a few men, you put the egoism of one class in the place of the Country, which is the union of *all* the classes.

A Country is not a mere territory; the particular territory is only its foundation. The Country is the idea which rises upon that foundation; it is the sentiment of love, the sense of fellowship which binds together all the sons of that territory.

So long as a single one of your brothers is not represented by his own vote in the development of the national life—so long as a single one vegetates uneducated among the educated—so long as a single one able and willing to work languishes in poverty for want of work—you have not got a Country such as it ought to be, the Country of all and for all.

*Votes, education, work* are the three main pillars of the nation; do not rest until your hands have solidly erected them.

## QUESTIONS FOR ANALYSIS

1. What did Mazzini mean by "evil governments"? Why are they evil?
2. What are the characteristics of the "true Country"?
3. What form of government is best? Why?
4. Why, according to Mazzini, should poor workingmen have been interested in the political unification of Italy?
5. How might a woman today criticize Mazzini's program? Debate how Mazzini might respond to such criticism.

*Source:* Slightly adapted from J. Mazzini, *The Duties of Man and Other Essays* (London: J. M. Dent and Sons, 1907), pp. 51–57.

John Perry, *A Bill-poster's Fantasy* (1855), explores the endless diversity of big-city entertainment. *(dunhill Museum & Archive, 48 Germyn Street, St. James's, London)*

CHAPTER

# 25 EUROPEAN LIFE IN THE AGE OF NATIONALISM

## CHAPTER OUTLINE

- Cities and Social Classes
- The Changing Family
- Science and Culture
- The Responsive National State (1871–1914)
- Marxism and the Socialist Movement

After 1848, as identification with the nation-state was becoming one of the basic organizing principles of Western society, the growth of towns and cities rushed forward with undiminished force. In 1900 Western society was urban and industrial as surely as it had been rural and agrarian in 1800. This rapid urbanization, both a result of the Industrial Revolution and a key element in its enormous long-term impact, posed pressing practical problems that governments had to deal with. Eventual success with urban problems encouraged people to look to government as a problem solver and put their faith in a responsive national state. Even socialists forming international alliances were not exempt from the trend.

- How did life in cities change?
- What did the emergence of urban industrial society mean for rich and poor and those in between?
- How did families change as they coped with the developing urban civilization?
- What changes in science and culture reflected and influenced this new civilization?
- How did governments respond to problems and try to win the support of politically active citizens?

These are the questions this chapter will investigate.

## CITIES AND SOCIAL CLASSES

The growth of industry posed enormous challenges for all elements of Western society, from young factory workers confronting relentless discipline to aristocratic elites maneuvering to retain political power. As we saw in Chapter 22, the early consequences of economic transformation were mixed and far-reaching and by no means wholly negative. By 1850 at the latest, working conditions were improving and real wages were rising for the mass of the population, and they continued to do so until 1914. Given the poverty and uncertainty of preindustrial life, some historians maintain that the history of

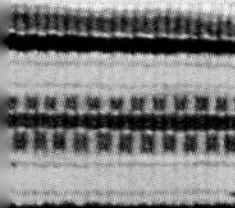

European industrialization in the nineteenth century is probably better written in terms of increasing opportunities than of greater hardships. Critics of this relatively optimistic view of industrialization claim that it neglects the quality of life in urban areas, where poor people especially suffered from bad housing, lack of sanitation, and a sense of hopelessness. Did not these drawbacks more than cancel out higher wages and greater opportunity? An examination of cities in the nineteenth century provides some answers to this complex question.

## Industry and the Growth of Cities

Since the Middle Ages European cities had been centers of government, culture, and large-scale commerce. They had also been congested, dirty, and unhealthy. People were packed together almost as tightly as possible within the city limits. The typical city was a "walking city": for all but the wealthiest classes, walking was the only available form of transportation. Infectious disease spread with deadly speed in cities, and people were always more likely to die in the city than in the countryside.

Clearly, deplorable urban conditions did not originate with the Industrial Revolution. What the Industrial Revolution did was to reveal those conditions more nakedly than ever before. The steam engine freed industrialists from dependence on the energy of fast-flowing streams and rivers, so by 1800 there was every incentive to build new factories in urban areas. Cities had better shipping facilities than the countryside and thus better supplies of coal and raw materials. There were also many hands wanting work in the cities, for cities drew people like a magnet. Therefore, as industry grew, there was also a rapid expansion of already overcrowded and unhealthy cities.

The challenge of the urban environment was felt first and most acutely in Great Britain. The number of people living in cities of 20,000 or more in England and Wales jumped from 1.5 million in 1801 to 6.3 million in 1851 and reached 15.6 million in 1891. Such cities accounted for 17 percent of the total English population in 1801, 35 percent as early as 1851, and fully 54 percent in 1891. Other countries gradually duplicated the English pattern as they industrialized (see Map 25.1).

In the 1820s and 1830s people in Britain and France began to worry about the condition of their cities. With urban areas expanding at such previously undreamed-of rates, people's fatalistic acceptance of overcrowded, unsanitary urban living conditions began to give way to active concern.

On one point everyone could agree: except on the outskirts, each town or city was using every scrap of land to the full extent. Parks and open areas for exercise and recreation were almost nonexistent. Buildings were erected on the smallest possible lots in order to pack the maximum

**MAP 25.1 European Cities of 100,000 or More, 1800 and 1900** There were more large cities in Great Britain in 1900 than in all of Europe in 1800. Northwestern Europe was the most urbanized area.

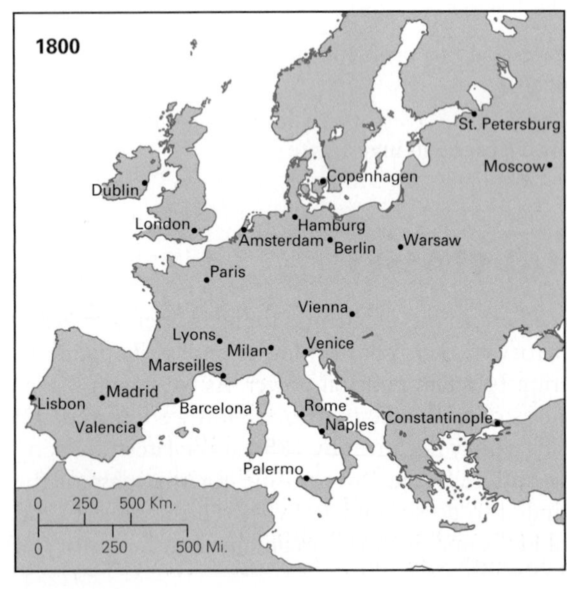


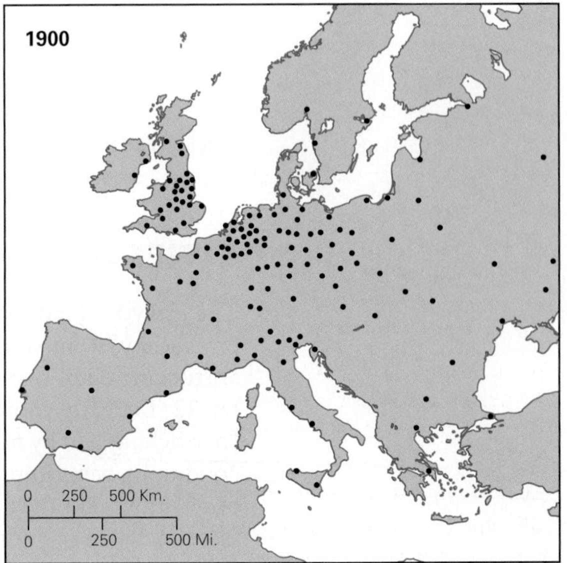

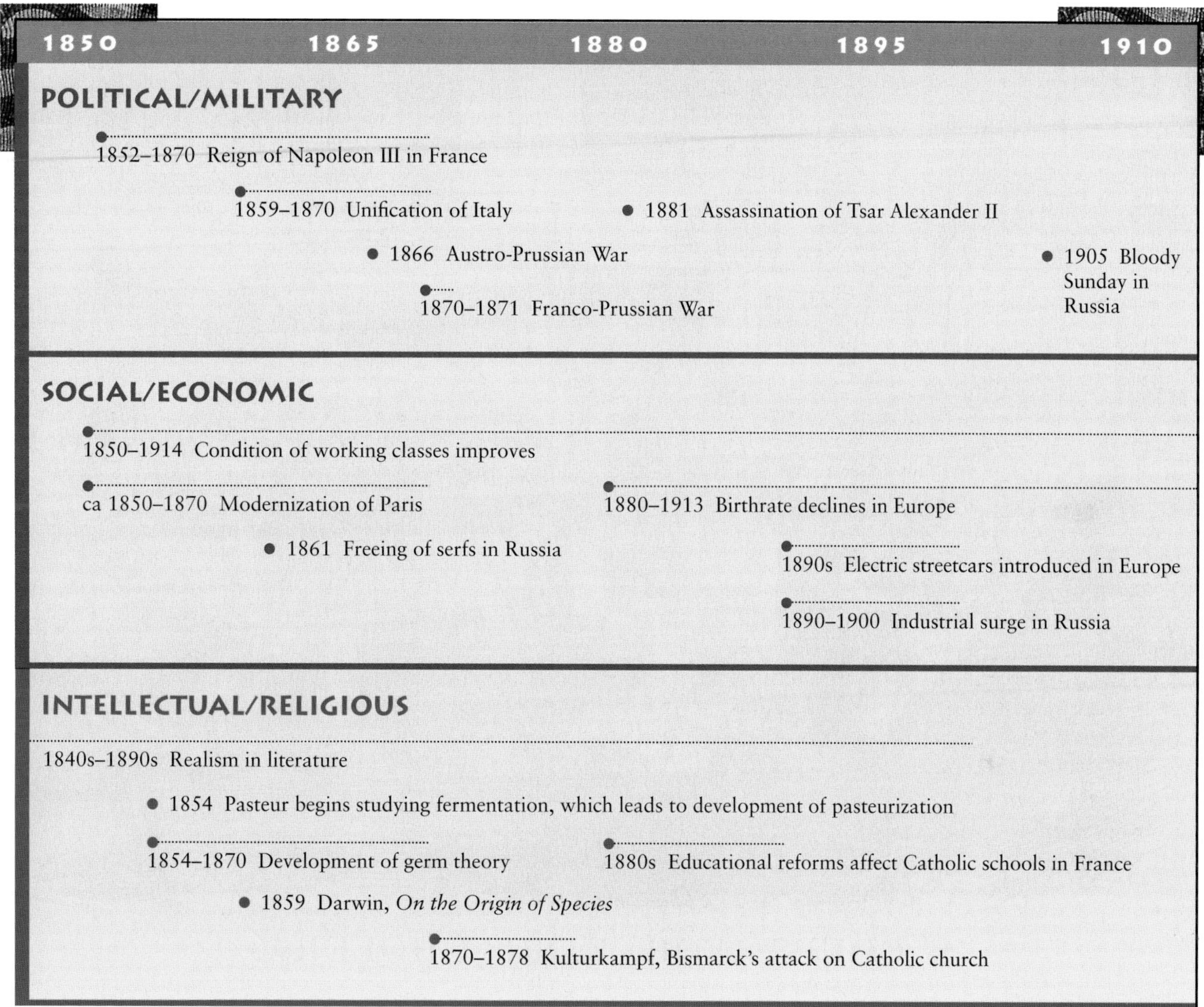


number of people into a given space. Narrow houses were built wall to wall in long rows. Or buildings were built around tiny courtyards completely enclosed on all four sides. "Six, eight, and even ten occupying one room is anything but uncommon," wrote a doctor from Aberdeen in Scotland for a government investigation in 1842.

These highly concentrated urban populations lived in extremely unsanitary and unhealthy conditions. Open drains and sewers flowed alongside or down the middle of unpaved streets. Toilet facilities were primitive in the extreme. In parts of Manchester as many as two hundred people shared a single outhouse. Such privies filled up rapidly, and sewage often overflowed and seeped into cellar dwellings. By the 1840s there was among the better-off classes a growing, shocking "realization that, to put it as mildly as possible, millions of English men, women, and children were living in shit."[1]

Who or what was responsible for these awful conditions? The crucial factors were the tremendous pressure of more people and the total absence of public transportation. People simply had to jam themselves together if they were to be able to walk to shops and factories. Another factor was that government, often uncertain how best to approach the problems, was slow to provide sanitary facilities and establish adequate building codes. Even many continental cities with strong traditions of municipal regulation were beset by overcrowded and unhealthy conditions. Also responsible was the sad legacy of rural housing conditions in preindustrial society. As one authority concludes, "the decent cottage was

**Filth and Disease** This 1852 drawing from *Punch* tells volumes about the unhealthy living conditions of the urban poor. In the foreground children play with a dead rat and a woman scavenges a dungheap. Cheap rooming houses provide shelter for the frightfully overcrowded population. *(The British Library)*

the exception, the hovel the rule."[2] Thus housing was far down on the newcomer's list of priorities, and ordinary people generally took dirt and dung for granted.

## Public Health and the Bacterial Revolution

Although cleanliness was not next to godliness in most people's eyes, it was becoming so for some reformers. The most famous of these was Edwin Chadwick, one of the commissioners charged with the administration of relief to paupers under Britain's revised Poor Law of 1834. Chadwick was a good **Benthamite**—that is, a follower of radical philosopher Jeremy Bentham (1748–1832). Bentham had taught that public problems ought to be dealt with on a rational, scientific basis and according to the "greatest good for the greatest number." Applying these principles, Chadwick soon became convinced that disease and death actually caused poverty simply because a sick worker was an unemployed worker and orphaned children were poor children. Most important, Chadwick believed that disease could be prevented by cleaning up the urban environment. That was his "sanitary idea."

Collecting detailed reports from local Poor Law officials and publishing his hard-hitting findings in 1842,

Chadwick correctly believed that the stinking excrement of communal outhouses could be carried off by water through sewers at less than one-twentieth the cost of removing it by hand. The cheap iron pipes and tile drains of the industrial age would provide running water and sewerage for all sections of town, not just the wealthy ones. In 1848, with the cause strengthened by the cholera epidemic of 1846, Chadwick's report became the basis of Great Britain's first public health law, which created a national health board and gave cities broad authority to build modern sanitary systems. The public health movement won dedicated supporters in the United States, France, and Germany from the 1840s on. By the 1860s and 1870s European cities were making real progress toward adequate water supplies and sewerage systems, and city dwellers were beginning to reap the reward of better health.

Early reformers were seriously handicapped by the prevailing **miasmatic theory** of disease—the belief that people contract disease when they breathe the bad odors of decay and putrefying excrement. Keen observation by doctors and public health officials in the 1840s and 1850s pinpointed the role of bad drinking water in the transmission of disease and suggested that contagion was *spread through* filth and not caused by it, thus weakening the miasmatic idea.

The theoretical breakthrough was the development of the **germ theory** of disease by Louis Pasteur (1822–1895), a French chemist who began studying fermentation in 1854 at the request of brewers. Using his microscope to develop a simple test that brewers could use to monitor the fermentation process and avoid spoilage, Pasteur found that fermentation depended on the growth of living organisms and that the activity of these organisms could be suppressed by heating the beverage—by **pasteurization.** The breathtaking implication was that specific diseases were caused by specific living organisms—germs—and that those organisms could be controlled in people as well as in beer, wine, and milk.

By 1870 the work of Pasteur and others had demonstrated the general connection between germs and disease. When, in the middle of the 1870s, German country doctor Robert Koch and his coworkers developed pure cultures of harmful bacteria and described their life cycles, the dam broke. Over the next twenty years researchers—mainly Germans—identified the organisms responsible for disease after disease. These discoveries led to the development of a number of effective vaccines.

Acceptance of the germ theory brought about dramatic improvements in the deadly environment of hospitals and surgery. In 1865, when Pasteur showed that the air was full of bacteria, English surgeon Joseph Lister (1827–1912) immediately grasped the connection between aerial bacteria and the problem of wound infection. He reasoned that a chemical disinfectant applied to a wound dressing would "destroy the life of the floating particles." Lister's **antiseptic principle** worked wonders. In the 1880s German surgeons developed the more sophisticated practice of sterilizing not only the wound but also everything—hands, instruments, clothing—that entered the operating room.

The achievements of the bacterial revolution coupled with the ever-more-sophisticated public health movement saved millions of lives, particularly after about 1890. In England, France, and Germany death rates declined dramatically from a range of twenty-one to twenty-seven per thousand inhabitants in the 1860s to a range of fourteen to eighteen per thousand in 1913. The awful death sentences of the past—diphtheria, typhoid, typhus, cholera, yellow fever—became vanishing diseases.

## Urban Planning and Public Transportation

More effective urban planning also improved the quality of urban life. Urban planning was in decline by the early nineteenth century, but after 1850 its practice was revived and extended. France took the lead during the rule of Napoleon III (1848–1870), who believed that rebuilding much of Paris would provide employment, improve living conditions, and glorify his empire. In the baron Georges Haussmann (1809–1884), an aggressive, impatient Alsatian whom he placed in charge of Paris, Napoleon III found an authoritarian planner capable of bulldozing both buildings and opposition. In twenty years Paris was transformed (see Map 25.2).

The Paris of 1850 was a labyrinth of narrow, dark streets, the results of desperate overcrowding. Terrible slum conditions and extremely high death rates were facts of life.

Haussmann and his fellow planners proceeded on many interrelated fronts. With a bold energy that often shocked their contemporaries, they razed old buildings in order to cut broad, straight, tree-lined boulevards through the center of the city as well as in new quarters on the outskirts. These boulevards, designed in part to prevent the easy construction and defense of barricades by revolutionary crowds, permitted traffic to flow freely and also afforded impressive vistas. Their creation also demolished some of the worst slums. New streets stimulated the construction of better housing, especially for the middle classes. Small neighborhood parks and open spaces were created throughout the city, and two very large parks suitable for all kinds of holiday activities were developed—one on the wealthy west side and one on the poor east side of the city (see Map 25.2). The city also improved its sewers and doubled the supply of good fresh water. Rebuilding Paris provided a new model for urban planning and stimulated modern urbanism throughout Europe, particularly after 1870.

The development of mass public transportation was also of great importance in the improvement of urban living conditions. In the 1870s many European cities authorized private companies to operate horse-drawn streetcars, which had been developed in the United States. Then in the 1890s the real revolution occurred: European countries adopted another American transit innovation, the electric streetcar.

Electric streetcars were cheaper, faster, more dependable, and more comfortable than their horse-drawn counterparts. Service improved dramatically. Millions of Europeans—workers, shoppers, schoolchildren—hopped on board during the workweek. And on weekends and holidays, streetcars carried millions on happy outings to

**MAP 25.2 The Modernization of Paris, ca 1850–1870** Broad boulevards, large parks, and grandiose train stations transformed Paris. The cutting of the new north-south axis—known as the Boulevard Saint-Michel—was one of Haussmann's most controversial projects. It razed much of Paris's medieval core and filled the Île de la Cité with massive government buildings.

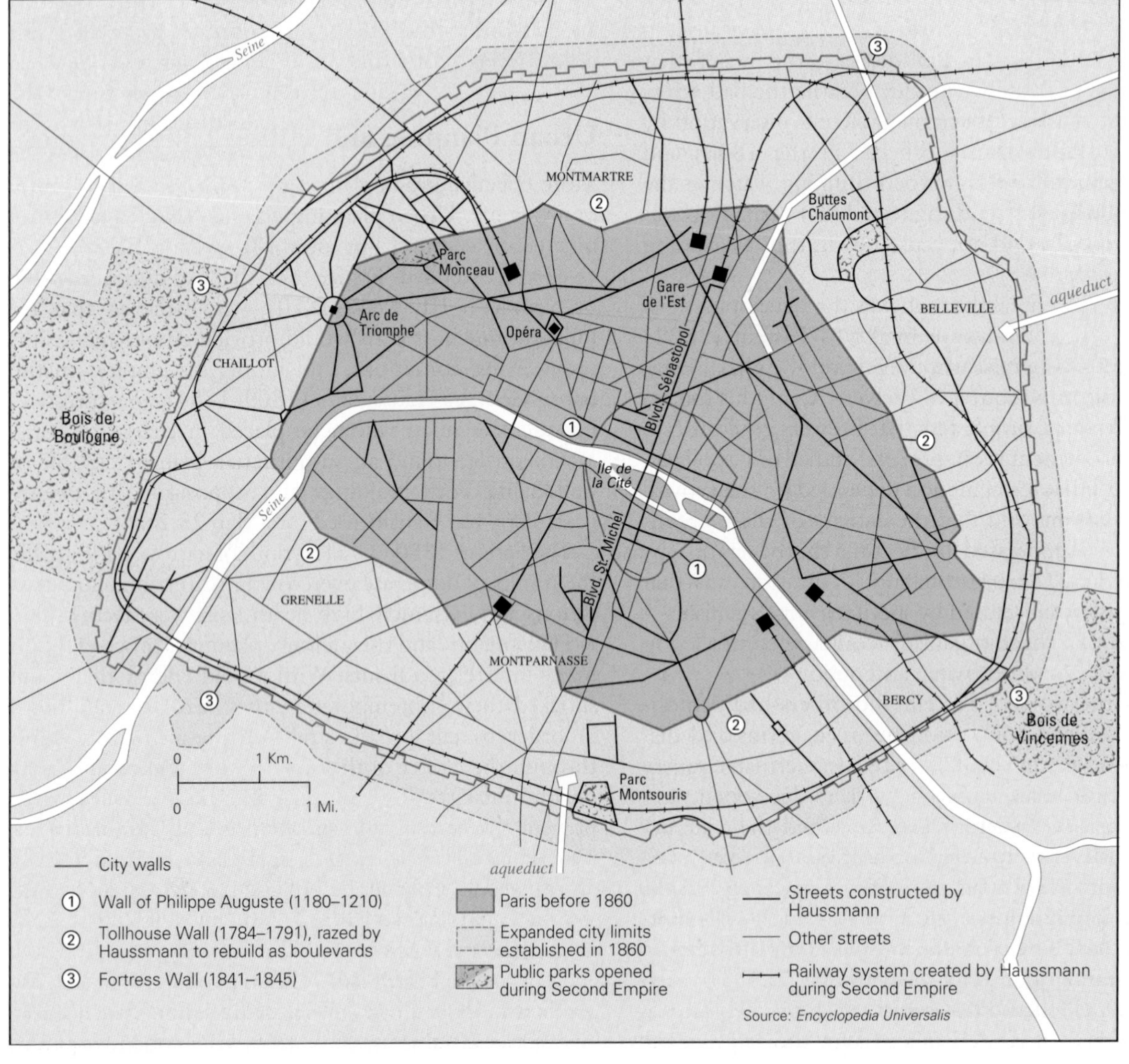

parks and the countryside, racetracks and music halls. In 1886 the horse-drawn streetcars of Austria-Hungary, France, Germany, and Great Britain were carrying about 900 million riders. By 1910 electric streetcars in the four countries were carrying 6.7 billion riders.[3] Each person was using public transportation four times as often in 1910 as in 1886.

Good mass transit helped greatly in the struggle for decent housing. The new boulevards and horse-drawn streetcars had facilitated a middle-class move to better housing in the 1860s and 1870s; after 1890 electric streetcars gave people of modest means access to new, improved housing. The still-crowded city was able to expand and become less congested. In England in 1901, only 9 percent of the urban population was "overcrowded" in terms of the official definition of more than two persons per room.

## Urbanization and Social Structure

With general improvements in health and in the urban environment, the almost-completed journey to an urban industrialized world was bringing beneficial consequences for all kinds of people. The first great change was a substantial increase in the standard of living for the average person. The real wages of British workers, for example, which had already risen by 1850, almost doubled between 1850 and 1906. Similar increases occurred in continental European countries as industrial development quickened after 1850. Ordinary people took a major step forward in the centuries-old battle against poverty, reinforcing efforts to improve many aspects of human existence.

There is another side to the income coin, however. Greater economic rewards for the average person did *not* eliminate hardship and poverty, nor did they make the wealth and income of the rich and the poor significantly more equal. In almost every advanced country around 1900 the richest 20 percent of households received anywhere from 50 to 60 percent of all national income, and the bottom 30 percent of households received 10 percent or less of all income (see Figure 25.1). The middle classes, which were smaller than they are today, accounted for less than 20 percent of the population; thus the statistics show that the upper and middle classes alone received more than 50 percent of all income. The poorest 80 percent—the working classes, including peasants and agricultural laborers—received less altogether than the two richest classes. Moreover, income taxes on the wealthy were light or nonexistent. Thus the gap between rich and poor remained enormous. It was probably almost as great in 1900 as it had been in the age of agriculture and aristocracy before the Industrial Revolution.

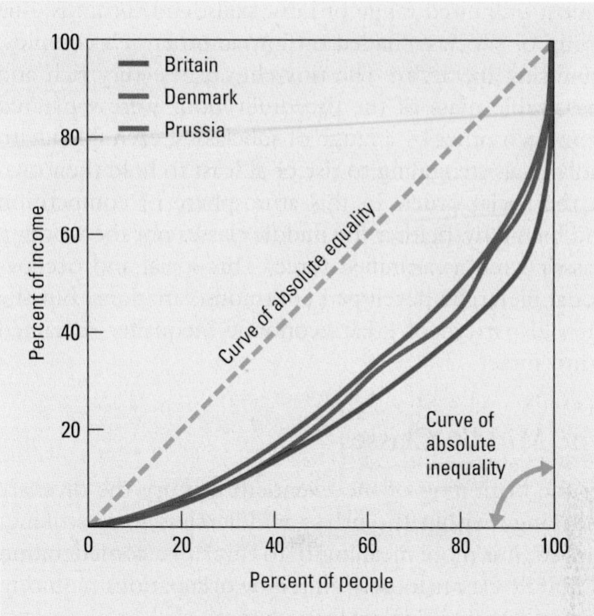


**Distribution of Income**

| | Richest 5% | Richest 10% | Richest 20% | Poorest 60% |
|---|---|---|---|---|
| Britain | 43% | | 59% | |
| Denmark | 30% | 39% | 55% | 31% |
| Prussia | 30% | | 50% | 33% |

**FIGURE 25.1 The Distribution of Income in Britain, Denmark, and Prussia in 1913** The so-called Lorenz curve is useful for showing the degree of economic inequality in a given society. The closer the actual distribution of income lies to the (theoretical) curve of absolute equality, where each 20 percent of the population receives 20 percent of all income, the more incomes are nearly equal. European society was very far from any such equality before World War I. Notice that incomes in Prussia were somewhat more equal than those in Britain. *(Source: S. Kuznets,* Modern Economic Growth, *pp. 208–209. Copyright © 1966 by Yale University Press. Reprinted by permission of Yale University Press.)*

The great gap between rich and poor endured, in part, because industrial and urban development made society more diverse and less unified. By no means did society split into two sharply defined opposing classes, as Marx had predicted. Instead, economic specialization created more new social groups than it destroyed. There developed an almost unlimited range of jobs, skills, and earnings; one group or subclass shaded off into another in a complex, confusing hierarchy. The tiny elite of the very rich and the sizable mass of the dreadfully poor were separated from each other by a range of subclasses, each filled with individuals struggling to rise or at least to hold their own in the social order. In this atmosphere of competition and hierarchy, neither the middle classes nor the working classes acted as a unified force. This social and occupational hierarchy developed enormous variations, but the age-old pattern of great economic inequality remained firmly intact.

## The Middle Classes

By the beginning of the twentieth century the diversity and range within the urban middle class were striking. Indeed, it is more meaningful to think of a confederation of middle classes loosely united by occupations requiring primarily mental, rather than physical, skill.

At the top stood the upper middle class, composed mainly of the most successful business families from banking, industry, and large-scale commerce. As people in the upper middle class gained in income and progressively lost all traces of radicalism after the trauma of 1848, they were almost irresistibly drawn toward the aristocratic lifestyle. And although the genuine hereditary aristocracy constituted only a tiny minority in every European country, it retained imposing wealth, unrivaled social prestige, and substantial political influence, especially in central and eastern Europe.

As the aristocracy had long divided the year between palatial country estates and lavish townhouses during "the season," so the upper middle class purchased country places or built beach houses for weekend and summer use. The number of servants was an important indicator of wealth and standing for the middle class, as it had always been for the aristocracy. Private coaches and carriages, ever expensive items in the city, were also signs of rising social status.

The topmost reaches of the upper middle class tended to shade off into the old aristocracy to form a new upper class of at most 5 percent of the population. Much of the aristocracy welcomed this development. Having experienced a sharp decline in its relative income in the course of industrialization, the landed aristocracy had met big business coming up the staircase and was often delighted to trade titles, country homes, and snobbish elegance for good hard cash. Some of the best bargains were made through marriages to American heiresses. Correspondingly, wealthy aristocrats tended increasingly to exploit their agricultural and mineral resources as if they were business people.

Below the wealthy upper middle class were much larger, much less wealthy, and increasingly diversified middle-class groups. Here one found the moderately successful industrialists and merchants as well as professionals in law and medicine. This was the middle middle class, solid and quite comfortable but lacking great wealth. Below it were independent shopkeepers, small traders, and tiny manufacturers—the lower middle class. Both of these traditional elements of the middle class expanded modestly in size with economic development.

Meanwhile, the traditional middle class was gaining two particularly important additions. The expansion of industry and technology created a growing demand for experts with specialized knowledge. The most valuable of the specialties became solid middle-class professions. Engineering, for example, emerged from the world of skilled labor as a full-fledged profession of great importance, considerable prestige, and many branches. Architects, chemists, accountants, and surveyors, to name only a few, first achieved professional standing in this period. They established criteria for advanced training and certification and banded together in organizations to promote and defend their interests.

Management of large public and private institutions also emerged as a kind of profession as governments provided more services and as very large corporations such as railroads came into being. Government officials and many private executives did not own business enterprises, but they had specialized knowledge, and they shared most of the values of the business-owning entrepreneurs and the older professionals.

Industrialization and urbanization also expanded and diversified the lower middle class. The number of shopkeepers and small business people grew, and so did the number of white-collar employees—a mixed group of traveling salesmen, bookkeepers, store managers, and clerks who staffed the offices and branch stores of large corporations. White-collar employees were propertyless and often earned no more than the better-paid workers. Yet white-collar workers were fiercely committed to the middle class and to the ideal of moving up in society. In the Balkans, for example, clerks let their fingernails grow very long to distinguish themselves from people who worked with their hands.

In spite of growing occupational diversity and conflicting interests, the middle classes were loosely united by a certain style of life. Food was the largest item in the household budget, for middle-class people liked to eat very well. The European middle classes consumed meat

**"The German Theater, Munich"** This happy, vibrant poster advertisement calls the passerby to come and savor the treats of a popular music hall. Many music halls and vaudeville theaters attracted a mixed urban clientele, which included white-collar employees and better-paid workers. *(Barbara Singer/The Bridgeman Art Library International Ltd)*

in abundance; a well-off family might spend 10 percent of its substantial earnings on meat and fully 25 percent of its income on food and drink. Spending on food was also great because the dinner party was this class's favored social occasion. A wealthy family might give a lavish party for eight to twelve almost every week, whereas more modest households would settle for once a month.

The middle-class wife could cope with this endless procession of meals, courses, and dishes because she had both servants and money at her disposal. Indeed, the employment of at least one enormously helpful full-time maid to cook and clean was the best single sign that a family had crossed the cultural divide separating the working classes from what some contemporary observers called the "servant-keeping classes."

Well-fed and well served, the middle classes were also well housed by 1900. By 1900 the middle classes were also quite clothes conscious. The factory, the sewing machine, and the department store had all helped reduce the cost and expand the variety of clothing. Middle-class women were particularly attentive to the fickle dictates of fashion.

Education was another growing expense, as middle-class parents tried to provide their children with ever-more-crucial advanced education. The keystones of culture and leisure were books, music, and travel.

Finally, the middle classes were loosely united by a shared code of expected behavior and morality. This code was strict and demanding. It laid great stress on hard work, self-discipline, and personal achievement. Men and women who fell into crime or poverty were generally assumed to be responsible for their own circumstances. Traditional Christian morality was reaffirmed by this code and was preached tirelessly by middle-class people. Drinking and gambling were denounced as vices; sexual purity and fidelity were celebrated as virtues. In short, the middle-class person was supposed to know right from wrong and to act accordingly.

## The Working Classes

About four out of five people belonged to the working classes at the turn of the century. Many members of the working classes—that is, people whose livelihoods depended on physical labor and who did not employ domestic servants—were still small landowning peasants and hired farm hands. This was especially true in eastern Europe. In western and central Europe, however, the typical worker had left the land. In Great Britain less than 8 percent of the people worked in agriculture, and in rapidly industrializing Germany only 25 percent were employed in agriculture and forestry.

The urban working classes were even less unified and homogeneous than the middle classes. In the first place, economic development and increased specialization expanded the traditional range of working-class skills, earnings, and experiences. Meanwhile, the old sharp distinction between highly skilled artisans and unskilled manual workers gradually broke down.

In the second place, skilled, semiskilled, and unskilled workers developed widely divergent lifestyles and cultural values, and their differences contributed to a keen sense of social status and hierarchy within the working classes. The result was great variety and limited class unity.

Highly skilled workers, who made up about 15 percent of the working classes, became a real **labor aristocracy.**

These workers earned only about two-thirds of the income of the bottom ranks of the servant-keeping classes, but that was fully twice as much as the earnings of unskilled workers. The most "aristocratic" of the highly skilled workers were construction bosses and factory foremen, men who had often risen from the ranks and were fiercely proud of their achievement. The labor aristocracy also included members of the traditional highly skilled handicraft trades that had not been mechanized or placed in factories, like cabinetmakers, jewelers, and printers.

This group as a whole was under constant long-term pressure. Irregularly but inexorably, factory methods were being extended to more crafts, and many skilled artisans were being replaced by lower-paid semiskilled factory workers. At the same time, the labor aristocracy was consistently being enlarged by new kinds of skilled workers such as shipbuilders and railway locomotive engineers. Thus the labor elite remained in a state of flux as individuals and whole crafts moved in and out of it.

To maintain this precarious standing, the upper working class adopted distinctive values and strait-laced, almost puritanical behavior. Like the middle classes, the labor aristocracy was strongly committed to the family and to economic improvement. Yet skilled workers viewed themselves primarily not as aspirants to the middle class but as the pacesetters and natural leaders of all the working classes. They practiced self-discipline and generally frowned on heavy drinking and sexual permissiveness.

Below the labor aristocracy stood semiskilled and unskilled urban workers. The enormous complexity of this sector of the world of labor is not easily summarized. Workers in the established crafts—carpenters, bricklayers, pipe fitters—stood near the top of the semiskilled hierarchy, often flirting with (or sliding back from) the labor elite. A large number of the semiskilled were factory workers who earned highly variable but relatively good wages and whose relative importance in the labor force was increasing.

Below the semiskilled workers was a larger group of unskilled workers that included day laborers such as longshoremen, wagon-driving teamsters, teenagers, and every kind of "helper." Many of these people had real skills and performed valuable services, but they were unorganized and divided, united only by the common fate of meager earnings. The same lack of unity characterized street vendors and market people—self-employed workers who competed savagely with each other and with the established shopkeepers of the lower middle class.

One of the largest components of the unskilled group was domestic servants, whose numbers grew steadily in the nineteenth century. In advanced Great Britain, for example, one out of every seven employed persons was a domestic servant in 1911. The great majority were women, many of whom were recent migrants from rural areas. Domestic service was still hard work at low pay, but it had real attractions for "rough country girls" with strong hands and few specialized skills. Marriage prospects were more varied in the city, and though wages were low, they were higher and more regular than in hard agricultural work.

Many a poor wife and mother eventually joined the broad ranks of working women in the "sweated industries." These industries flowered after 1850 and resembled the old putting-out and cottage industries of earlier times. The women normally worked at home, paid by the piece and not by the hour. By 1900 only a few highly skilled male tailors lingered on in high-priced "tailor-made" shops. An army of poor women accounted for the bulk of the inexpensive "ready-made" clothes displayed on department store racks and in tiny shops.

Notwithstanding the rise and fall of groups and individuals, the urban working classes sought fun and recreation, and they found both. Across the face of Europe drinking remained unquestionably the favorite leisure-time activity of working people. Generally, however, heavy "problem" drinking declined in the late nineteenth century as it became less and less socially acceptable. This decline reflected in part the moral leadership of the upper working class. At the same time, drinking became more public and social. Cafés and pubs became increasingly bright, friendly places. Working-class political activities, both moderate and radical, were also concentrated in taverns and pubs. Moreover, social drinking in public places by married couples and sweethearts became an accepted and widespread practice for the first time. This greater participation by women undoubtedly helped civilize the world of drink and hard liquor.

The two other leisure-time passions of the working classes were sports and music halls. A great decline in "cruel sports," such as bullbaiting and cockfighting, had occurred throughout Europe by the late nineteenth century. Their place was filled by modern spectator sports, of which racing and soccer were the most popular. There was a great deal of gambling on sports events, and for many a working person a desire to decipher racing forms provided a powerful incentive toward literacy. Music halls and vaudeville theaters, the working-class counterparts of middle-class opera and classical theater, were enormously popular throughout Europe.

Did religion and Christian churches continue to provide working people with solace and meaning? Although many historians see the early nineteenth century as an age of religious revival, they also recognize that in the late nineteenth century a considerable decline in both church attendance and church donations was occurring in most European countries. And it seems clear that this decline was greater for the urban working classes than for their rural counterparts or for the middle classes. Yet most working-class families still baptized their children and considered themselves Christians. Although more research is necessary, it appears that the urban working classes in Europe did become more secular and less religious in the late nineteenth and early twentieth centuries.

One reason was that throughout the nineteenth century both Catholic and Protestant churches were normally seen as they saw themselves—as conservative institutions defending social order and custom. Therefore, as the European working classes became more politically conscious, they tended to see the church as the defender of what they wished to change and as the ally of their political opponents.

## THE CHANGING FAMILY

Urban life wrought many fundamental changes in the family. Although much is still unknown, it seems clear that in the second half of the nineteenth century the family had stabilized considerably after the disruption of the late eighteenth and early nineteenth centuries. The home became more important for both men and women. The role of women and attitudes toward children underwent substantial change, and the concept of adolescence as a distinct stage of life emerged. These are but a few of the transformations that affected all social classes in varying degrees.

### Premarital Sex and Marriage

By 1850 the preindustrial pattern of lengthy courtship and mercenary marriage was pretty well dead among the working classes. In its place the ideal of romantic love had triumphed. Couples were ever more likely to come from different, even distant, towns and to be more nearly the same age, as romantic sentiment replaced tradition and financial considerations.

Economic considerations in marriage remained more important to the middle classes after 1850. In France dowries and elaborate legal marriage contracts were common practice among the middle classes in the later nineteenth century, and marriage was for many families one of life's most crucial financial transactions.

A young woman of the middle class found her romantic life carefully supervised by her well-meaning mother, who schemed for a proper marriage and guarded her daughter's virginity like the family's credit. (See the feature "Listening to the Past: Middle-Class Youth and Sexuality" on pages 822–823.) After marriage middle-class morality sternly demanded fidelity.

Middle-class boys were watched, too, but not as vigilantly. By the time they reached late adolescence, they had usually attained considerable sexual experience with maids or prostitutes.

In Paris alone 155,000 women were registered as prostitutes between 1871 and 1903, and 750,000 others were suspected of prostitution in the same years. Men of all classes visited prostitutes, but the middle and upper classes supplied much of the motivating cash. Although many middle-class men abided by the publicly professed code of stern puritanical morality, others indulged their appetites for prostitutes and sexual promiscuity.

In the early nineteenth century among the working classes, sexual experimentation before marriage also triumphed, as did illegitimacy. By the 1840s as many as one birth in three was occurring outside of wedlock in many large cities. In the second half of the century, however, the rising rate of illegitimacy was reversed: more babies were born to married mothers. Some have argued that this shift reflected the growth of puritanism and a lessening of sexual permissiveness among the unmarried. This explanation, however, is unconvincing.

The percentage of brides who were pregnant continued to be high and showed little or no tendency to decline after 1850. In many parts of urban Europe around 1900, as many as one woman in three was going to the altar an expectant mother. Moreover, unmarried people almost certainly used the cheap condoms and diaphragms the industrial age had made available to prevent pregnancy, at least in predominately Protestant countries. Unmarried young people were probably engaging in just as much sexual activity as their parents and grandparents who had created the **illegitimacy explosion** of 1750 to 1850. But in the later nineteenth century pregnancy for a young single woman led increasingly to marriage and the establishment of a two-parent household.

### Gender Roles and Family Life

Industrialization and the growth of modern cities brought great changes to the lives of European women. These changes were particularly consequential for married women, and most women did marry in the nineteenth century.

After 1850 the work of most wives continued to become increasingly distinct and separate from that of their husbands (see pages 753–754). Husbands became wage earners in factories and offices; wives tended to stay home and manage households and care for children. As economic conditions improved, only married women in poor families tended more and more to work outside the home. One old English worker recalled that "the boy wanted to get into a position that would enable him to keep a wife and family, as it was considered a thoroughly unsatisfactory state of affairs if the wife had to work to help maintain the home."[4] The ideal became a strict division of labor by sex: the wife as mother and homemaker, the husband as wage earner.

This rigid division of labor meant that married women faced great injustice if they tried to move into the man's world of employment outside the home. Husbands were unsympathetic or hostile. Well-paying jobs were off-limits to women, and a woman's wage was almost always less than a man's, even for the same work. Moreover, married women were subordinated to their husbands by law and lacked many basic legal rights.

With middle-class women suffering, sometimes severely, from a lack of legal rights and with all women facing discrimination in education and employment, there is little wonder that some women rebelled and began the long-continuing fight for equality of the sexes and the rights of women. Their struggle proceeded on two main fronts. First, following in the steps of women such as Mary Wollstonecraft (see page 711), organizations founded by middle-class feminists campaigned for equal legal rights for women as well as access to higher education and professional employment. In the later nineteenth century middle-class women scored some significant victories, such as the 1882 law giving English married women full property rights. In the years before 1914 middle-class feminists increasingly shifted their attention to securing the right to vote for women.

Women inspired by utopian and especially Marxian socialism blazed a second path. Often scorning the programs of middle-class feminists, socialist women leaders argued that the liberation of working-class women would come only with the liberation of the entire working class through revolution. In the meantime they championed the cause of working women and won some practical improvements, especially in Germany, where the socialist movement was most effectively organized. In a general way these different approaches to women's issues reflected the diversity of classes in urban society.

If the ideology and practice of rigidly **separate spheres** undoubtedly narrowed women's horizons and caused some women to rebel, there was a brighter side to the same coin. As home and children became the typical wife's main concerns in the later nineteenth century, her control and influence there apparently became increasingly strong throughout Europe. Among the English working classes it was the wife who generally determined how the family's money was spent. All the major domestic decisions, from the children's schooling and religious instruction to the selection of new furniture or a new apartment, were hers. In France women had even greater power in their assigned domain. One English feminist noted in 1908 that "though legally women occupy a much inferior status than men [in France], in practice they constitute the superior sex. They are the power behind the throne."[5]

Women ruled at home partly because running the urban household was a complicated, demanding, and valuable task. Twice-a-day food shopping, penny-pinching, economizing, and the growing crusade against dirt—not to mention child rearing—were a full-time occupation. Nor were there any laborsaving appliances to help.

The woman's guidance of the household went hand in hand with the increased emotional importance of home and family. The home she ran was idealized as a warm shelter in a hard and impersonal urban world. In England, songs about its beauties were ever on people's lips. "Home, Sweet Home," first heard in the 1870s, had become "almost a second national anthem." Wall hangings like "HOME IS THE NEST WHERE ALL IS BEST" attested to domestic joys.[6]

Married couples also developed stronger emotional ties to each other. Even in the comfortable classes, marriages in the late nineteenth century were increasingly based on sentiment and sexual attraction as money and financial calculation gradually declined in importance. Affection and eroticism became more central to the couple after marriage.

Many French marriage manuals of the late 1800s stressed that women had legitimate sexual needs, such as the "right to orgasm." The rise of public socializing by couples in cafés and music halls as well as franker affection within the family suggests a more erotic, pleasurable intimate life for women throughout Western society.

## Child Rearing

One of the most striking signs of deepening emotional ties within the family was the growing love and concern that mothers gave their tiny infants. This was a sharp break with the past. Although it may seem hard to believe today, the typical mother in preindustrial Western society was frequently indifferent toward her baby. This indifference—an unwillingness to make real sacrifices for the welfare of the infant—was beginning to give way among the comfortable classes by the end of the eighteenth century, but the ordinary mother of modest means adopted new attitudes only as the nineteenth century progressed. The baby became more important, and women became better mothers.

Mothers increasingly breast-fed their infants, for example, rather than paying wet nurses to do so. Breast-feeding involved sacrifice—a temporary loss of freedom, if nothing else. Yet in an age when there was no good alternative to mother's milk, it saved lives. The surge of maternal feeling also gave rise to a wave of specialized books on child rearing and infant hygiene.

The loving care lavished on infants was matched by greater concern for older children and adolescents. They, too, were wrapped in the strong emotional ties of a more intimate and protective family. For one thing, European women began to limit the number of children they bore in order to care adequately for those they had. By the late nineteenth century the birthrate was declining across Europe, and it continued to do so until after World War II.

The most important reason for this revolutionary reduction in family size, in which the comfortable and well-educated classes took the lead, was parents' desire to improve their economic and social position and that of their children by having fewer youngsters. Indeed, many parents, especially in the middle classes, probably became *too* concerned about their children, unwittingly subjecting them to an emotional pressure cooker of almost unbearable intensity. The result was that many children and especially adolescents came to feel trapped and in desperate need of greater independence.

The working classes probably had more avenues of escape from such tensions than did the middle classes. Unlike their middle-class counterparts, who remained economically dependent on their families until a long education was finished or a proper marriage secured, working-class boys and girls went to work when they reached adolescence. Earning wages on their own, they could bargain with their parents for greater independence within the household by the time they were sixteen or

**A Working-Class Home, 1875** Emotional ties within ordinary families grew stronger in the nineteenth century. Parents gave their children more love and better care. *(Illustrated London News Library)*

seventeen. If they were unsuccessful, they could and did leave home to live cheaply as paying lodgers in other working-class homes. Thus the young person from the working classes broke away from the family more easily when emotional ties became oppressive. In the twentieth century middle-class youths would follow this lead.

## SCIENCE AND CULTURE

Major changes in Western thought and culture accompanied the emergence of urban society. Two aspects of these complex developments stand out as especially significant. Scientific knowledge expanded rapidly and came to influence the Western world-view even more profoundly than it had since the scientific revolution and the early Enlightenment. And between about the 1840s and the 1890s, European literature underwent a shift from soaring romanticism to tough-minded realism.

### The Triumph of Science

The intellectual achievements of the scientific revolution had resulted in few practical benefits, and theoretical knowledge had also played a relatively small role in the Industrial Revolution in England. But breakthroughs in industrial technology enormously stimulated basic scientific inquiry, as researchers sought to explain theoretically how such things as steam engines and blast furnaces actually worked. The result was an explosive growth of fundamental scientific discoveries from the 1830s onward, which were increasingly transformed into material improvements for the general population.

A perfect example of the translation of better scientific knowledge into practical human benefits was the work of Louis Pasteur and his followers in biology and the medical sciences (see page 797). Another was the development of the branch of physics known as **thermodynamics,** the relationship between heat and mechanical energy. By mid-century physicists had formulated the fundamental laws of thermodynamics, which were then applied to mechanical engineering, chemical processes, and many other fields.

Chemistry and electricity were two other fields characterized by extremely rapid scientific progress. Chemists devised ways of measuring the atomic weight of different elements, and in 1869 the Russian chemist Dmitri Mendeleev (1834–1907) codified the rules of chemistry in the periodic law and the periodic table. Applying theoretical insights gleaned from the new field of **organic chemistry,** researchers in large German chemical companies discovered ways of transforming the dirty, useless coal tar that accumulated in coke ovens into beautiful, expensive synthetic dyes for the world of fashion. The basic discoveries of Michael Faraday (1791–1867) in electromagnetism during the 1830s and 1840s resulted in the first dynamo (generator) and opened the way for the subsequent development of electric motors, electric lights, and electric streetcars. The rapid development of the electrical and organic chemical industries spurred European economic growth between 1880 and 1913.

The triumph of science and technology had at least three significant consequences. First, though ordinary citizens continued to lack detailed scientific knowledge, everyday experience and innumerable popularizers impressed the importance of science on the popular mind.

Second, as science became more prominent in popular thinking, the philosophical implications of science formulated in the Enlightenment spread to broad sections of the population. Natural processes appeared to be determined by rigid laws, leaving little room for either divine intervention or human will.

Third, the methods of science acquired unrivaled prestige after 1850. For many the union of careful experiment and abstract theory was the only reliable route to truth and objective reality. Thus many thinkers tried to apply the objective methods of science to the study of society from the 1830s onward. Leading nineteenth-century social scientists resembled the eighteenth-century philosophes, but their systems were more all-encompassing and dogmatic. Marx was a prime example (see page 770).

Another extremely influential system builder was French philosopher Auguste Comte (1798–1857). Initially a disciple of the utopian socialist Saint-Simon (see page 769), Comte wrote the six-volume *System of Positive Philosophy* (1830–1842), which came into its own after 1850. By applying the **positivist,** or scientific, **method,** Comte believed, his new discipline of sociology would soon discover the eternal laws of human relations, which would enable expert social scientists to impose a disciplined harmony and well-being on less enlightened citizens.

Comte's stages of knowledge exemplify the nineteenth-century fascination with the idea of **evolution** and dynamic development. Thinkers in many fields, such as the romantic historians and "scientific" Marxists, shared and applied this basic concept. The most influential of all nineteenth-century evolutionary thinkers was Charles Darwin (1809–1882). Darwin came to doubt the general belief in a special divine creation of each species of animal. Instead, he concluded, all life had gradually evolved from a common ancestral origin in an unending "struggle for survival." After long hesitation Darwin published his research, which immediately attracted wide attention.

SOCIETY FOR THE PREVENTION OF CRUELTY TO ANIMALS. PRES. BERGH
THE ORIGIN OF SPECIES BY DARWIN
Th. Nast
MR. BERGH TO THE RESCUE.
THE DEFRAUDED GORILLA. "That *Man* wants to claim my Pedigree. He says he is one of my Descendants."
MR. BERGH. "Now, Mr. DARWIN, how could you insult him so?"

**Satirizing Darwin's Ideas** The heated controversies over Darwin's theory of evolution also spawned innumerable jokes and cartoons. This cartoon is by Darwin's contemporary, the American Thomas Nast. *(Culver Pictures)*

Darwin's theory is summarized in the title of his work *On the Origin of Species by the Means of Natural Selection* (1859). Darwin argued that chance differences among the members of a given species help some survive while others die. Thus the variations that prove useful in the struggle for survival are selected naturally and spread gradually to the entire species through reproduction.

Darwin's theory had a powerful and many-sided influence on European thought and the European middle classes. His findings reinforced the teachings of secularists such as Comte and Marx, who scornfully dismissed religious belief in favor of agnostic or atheistic materialism. Many writers also applied the theory of biological evolution to human affairs. Herbert Spencer (1820–1903), an English disciple of Auguste Comte, saw the human race as driven forward to ever-greater specialization and progress by the brutal economic struggle that efficiently determines the "survival of the fittest." The poor are the ill-fated weak, the prosperous the chosen strong. Understandably, Spencer and other **Social Darwinists,** as they were called, were especially popular with the upper middle class.

## Realism in Literature

In 1868 Émile Zola (1840–1902), the giant of the realist movement in literature, defended his violently criticized first novel against charges of pornography and corruption of morals. Such accusations were meaningless, Zola claimed: he was only a purely objective scientist using "the modern method, the universal instrument of inquiry of which this age makes such ardent use to open

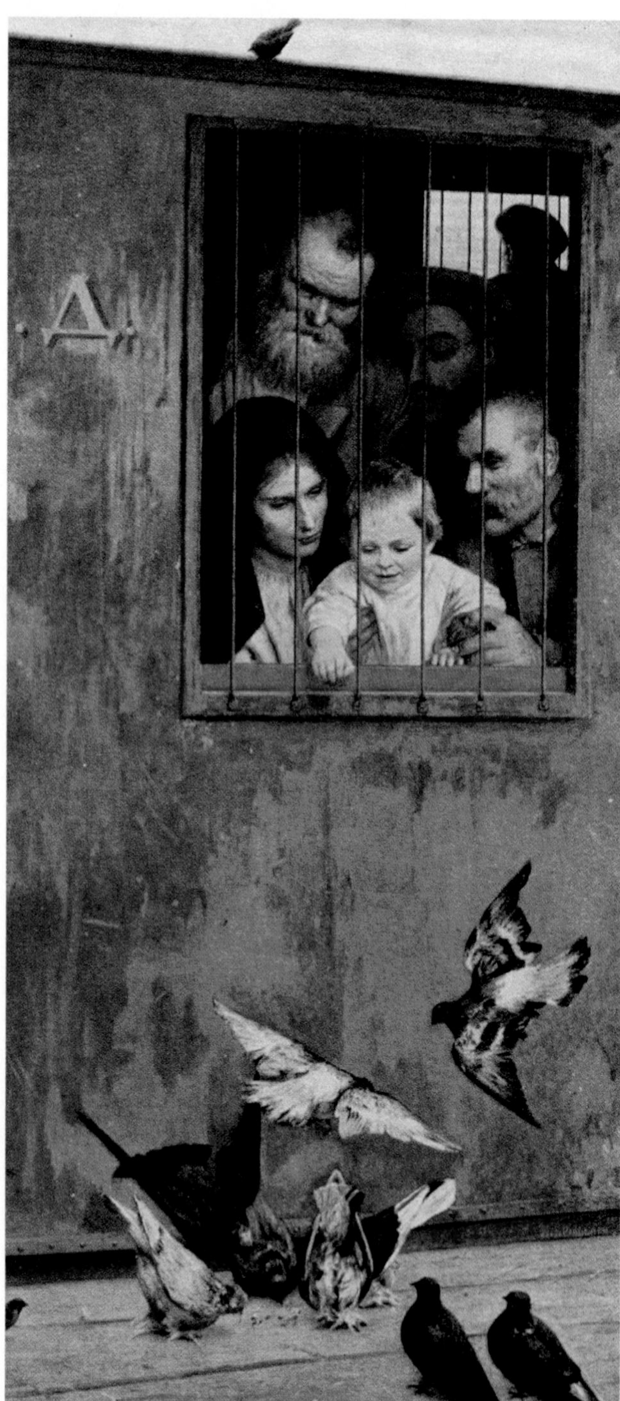

**"Life Is Everywhere"** The simple but profound joys of everyday life infuse this outstanding example of Russia's powerful realist tradition. Painted in 1888 by N. A. Yaroshenko, this representation of the mother and child and adoring men also draws on the classic theme of the infant Jesus and the holy family. *(Sovfoto)*

up the future. . . . I chose characters completely dominated by their nerves and their blood, deprived of free-will, pushed to each action of their lives by the fatality of their flesh."[7]

Zola's literary manifesto articulated the key themes of realism, which had emerged in the 1840s and continued to dominate Western culture and style until the 1890s. Realist writers believed that literature should depict life exactly as it is. Forsaking poetry for prose and the personal, emotional viewpoint of the romantics for strict, scientific objectivity, the realists simply observed and recorded—content to let the facts speak for themselves.

The major realist writers focused their extraordinary powers of observation on contemporary everyday life. Emphatically rejecting the romantic search for the exotic and the sublime, they energetically pursued the typical and the commonplace. Beginning with a dissection of the middle classes, from which most of them sprang, many realists eventually focused on the working classes, especially the urban working classes, which had been neglected in imaginative literature before this time. The realists put a microscope to many unexplored and taboo subjects—sex, strikes, violence, alcoholism—and hastened to report that slums and factories teemed with savage behavior. Many shocked middle-class critics denounced realism as ugly sensationalism wrapped provocatively in pseudoscientific declarations and crude language.

The realists' claims of objectivity did not prevent the elaboration of a definite world-view. Unlike the romantics, who had gloried in individual freedom and an unlimited universe, realists such as Zola were strict determinists. They believed that human beings, like atoms, are components of the physical world and all human actions are caused by unalterable natural laws. Heredity and environment determine human behavior; good and evil are merely social conventions.

The greatest Russian realist, Count Leo Tolstoy (1828–1910), combined realism in description and character development with an atypical moralizing, which came to dominate his later work. Tolstoy's greatest work is *War and Peace,* a monumental novel set against the historical background of Napoleon's invasion of Russia in 1812. Tolstoy went to great pains to develop his fatalistic theory of history, which regards free will as an illusion and the achievements of even the greatest leaders as only the channeling of historical necessity. Yet Tolstoy's central message is one that most of the people discussed in this chapter would have readily accepted: human love, trust, and everyday family ties are life's enduring values.

## THE RESPONSIVE NATIONAL STATE (1871–1914)

After 1871 the heartland of Europe was organized into strong national states, and the common themes within that framework were the emergence of mass politics and growing mass loyalty toward the national state. On the borders of Europe—in Ireland and Russia, in Austria-Hungary and the Balkans—the dynamics were different. Subject peoples there were still striving for political unity and independence. National aspirations created tensions, and mass politics often undermined existing states.

There were good reasons why ordinary people—the masses of an industrializing, urbanizing society—felt increasing loyalty to their governments in central and western Europe. More people could vote. By 1914 universal male suffrage had become the rule rather than the exception. This development had as much psychological as political significance. Ordinary men felt that they were becoming "part of the system."

Women also began to demand the right to vote. The women's suffrage movement achieved its first success in the western United States, and by 1913 women could vote in twelve states. Europe, too, moved slowly in this direction. In 1914 Norway gave the vote to most women. Elsewhere women such as the English Emmeline Pankhurst were militant in their demands. They heckled politicians and held public demonstrations. These efforts generally failed before 1914, but they prepared the way for the triumph of the women's suffrage movement in many countries immediately after World War I.

As the right to vote spread, politicians and parties in national parliaments represented the people more responsively. The multiparty system prevailing in most countries meant that parliamentary majorities were built on shifting coalitions, which gave parties leverage to obtain benefits for their supporters. Governments also passed laws to alleviate general problems, thereby acquiring greater legitimacy and appearing more worthy of support.

Less positively, governments found that they could manipulate national feeling to create a sense of unity and to divert attention away from underlying class conflicts. Therefore, governing elites frequently channeled national sentiment in an antiliberal and militaristic direction after 1871. This policy helped manage domestic conflicts, but only at the expense of increasing the international tensions that erupted in 1914 in cataclysmic war and revolution (see Chapter 29).

### The German Empire

Politics in Germany after 1871 reflected many of the general developments. The new German Empire was a federal union of Prussia and twenty-four smaller states. Much of the everyday business of government was conducted by the separate states, but there was a strong national government with a chancellor—until 1890 Bismarck—and a popularly elected parliament, called the **Reichstag.** Although Bismarck refused to be bound by a parliamentary majority, he tried nonetheless to maintain one. This situation gave the political parties opportunities. Until 1878 Bismarck relied mainly on the National Liberals, who had rallied to him after 1866. They supported legislation useful for further economic and legal unification of the country.

Less wisely, they backed Bismarck's attack on the Catholic church, the so-called **Kulturkampf,** or "struggle for civilization." Like Bismarck, the middle-class National Liberals were particularly alarmed by Pius IX's declaration of papal infallibility in 1870. That dogma seemed to ask German Catholics to put loyalty to their church above loyalty to their nation. Only in Protestant Prussia did the Kulturkampf have even limited success. Catholics throughout the country generally voted for the Catholic Center party, which blocked passage of national laws hostile to the church. Finally, in 1878 Bismarck abandoned his attack. Indeed, he and the Catholic Center party entered into an uneasy but mutually advantageous alliance. Their reasons for doing so were largely economic.

Bismarck moved to enact high tariffs on cheap grain from the United States, Canada, and Russia, against which less efficient European producers could not compete. This won over not only the Catholic Center, whose supporters were small farmers in western and southern Germany, but also the Protestant Junkers, who had large landholdings in the east. With the tariffs, then, Bismarck won Catholic and conservative support. His use of tariffs was typical of other governments of the late 1800s, which tried to protect national industries. The general rise of protectionism in this period was an outstanding example of the dangers of self-centered nationalism: high tariffs led to international name-calling and nasty trade wars.

As for socialism, Bismarck tried to stop its growth in Germany, and in 1878 he forced through a law outlawing the Social Democrats. He genuinely feared its revolutionary language and allegiance to a movement transcending the nation-state. Unable to force socialism out of existence, Bismarck's essentially conservative nation-state pioneered social measures designed to win the

## THE AGE OF NATIONALISM IN EUROPE, 1871–1914

| | |
|---|---|
| 1871–1914 | Third Republic in France |
| 1878 | Suppression of Social Democrats in Germany |
| 1881 | Assassination of Tsar Alexander II |
| 1883–1889 | Enactment of social security laws in Germany |
| 1884 | Third Reform Bill passed by British Parliament |
| 1889–1914 | Second International of socialists |
| 1890 | Repeal of anti–Social Democrat law in Germany |
| 1892–1903 | Witte directs modernization of Russian economy |
| 1904–1905 | Japan wins decisive victory in Russo-Japanese War |
| 1905 | Revolution in Russia: Tsar Nicholas II forced to issue the October Manifesto promising a popularly elected Duma |
| 1906–1914 | Liberal reform in Great Britain |
| 1907–1912 | Stolypin's agrarian reforms in Russia |
| 1912 | German Social Democratic party is largest party in the German Reichstag |
| 1914 | Irish home-rule bill passed by British Parliament but immediately suspended with outbreak of First World War |

support of working-class people. In 1883 he pushed through the Reichstag the first of several modern social security laws to help wage earners. Henceforth sick, injured, and retired workers could look forward to some regular benefits from the state. This national social security system, paid for through compulsory contributions by wage earners and employers as well as grants from the state, was the first of its kind anywhere.

In 1890 the new emperor, the young, idealistic, and unstable William II (r. 1888–1918), opposed Bismarck's attempt to renew the law outlawing the Social Democratic party. Eager to rule in his own right and to earn the support of the workers, William II forced Bismarck to resign. The government did pass new laws to aid workers and to legalize socialist political activity, but German foreign policy changed profoundly and mostly for the worse.

Yet William II was no more successful than Bismarck in getting workers to renounce socialism. Indeed, socialist ideas spread rapidly, and more and more Social Democrats were elected to the Reichstag in the 1890s. Yet the "revolutionary" socialists were actually becoming less and less revolutionary in Germany. In the years before World War I, as the Social Democratic party broadened its base and adopted a more patriotic tone, German socialists identified increasingly with the German state, and they concentrated on gradual social and political reform.

## Republican France

Although Napoleon III's reign made some progress in reducing antagonisms between classes, the war with Prussia undid these efforts, and in 1871 France seemed hopelessly divided once again. The patriotic republicans who proclaimed the Third Republic in Paris after the military disaster at Sedan refused to admit defeat. They defended Paris with great heroism for weeks, living off rats and zoo animals until they were starved into submission by German armies in January 1871. When national elections then sent a large majority of conservatives and monarchists to the National Assembly, the traumatized

Parisians exploded in patriotic frustration and proclaimed the Paris Commune in March 1871. Vaguely radical, the leaders of the Commune wanted to govern Paris without interference from the conservative French countryside. The National Assembly, led by aging politician Adolphe Thiers, would hear none of it. The Assembly ordered the French army into Paris and brutally crushed the Commune. Twenty thousand people died in the fighting. As in June 1848, it was Paris against the provinces, French against French.

Out of this tragedy France slowly formed a new national unity, achieving considerable stability before 1914. How is one to account for this? Luck played a part. Until 1875 the monarchists in the "republican" National Assembly had a majority but could not agree about who should be king. Thiers's destruction of the radical Commune and his other firm measures showed the fearful provinces and the middle class that the Third Republic might be moderate and socially conservative. France therefore retained the republic, though reluctantly. As President Thiers cautiously said, this was "the government which divides us least."

Another stabilizing factor was the skill and determination of the moderate republican leaders in the early years. The most famous of these was Léon Gambetta, the son of an Italian grocer, a warm, easygoing lawyer who had turned professional politician. By 1879 the great majority of members of both the upper and lower houses of the National Assembly were republicans, and the Third Republic had firm foundations after almost a decade.

The moderate republicans sought to preserve their creation by winning the hearts and minds of the next generation. Trade unions were fully legalized, and France acquired a colonial empire. More important, a series of laws between 1879 and 1886 established free compulsory elementary education for both girls and boys. At the same time, the state system of public tax-supported schools was expanded. In France and elsewhere the general expansion of public education served as a critical nation-building tool in the late nineteenth century. In France most elementary and much secondary education had traditionally been in the parochial schools of the Catholic church, which had long been hostile to republics and to much of secular life. Free compulsory elementary education in France became secular republican education. The pledge of allegiance and the national anthem replaced the catechism and the "Ave Maria."

Although the educational reforms of the 1880s disturbed French Catholics, many of them rallied to the republic in the 1890s, and tensions between church and state eased. Unfortunately, the **Dreyfus affair** changed all that. Alfred Dreyfus, a Jewish captain in the French army, was falsely accused and convicted of treason. His family never doubted his innocence and fought to reopen the case, enlisting the support of prominent republicans and intellectuals such as novelist Émile Zola. In 1898 and 1899 the case split France apart. On one side was the army, which had manufactured evidence against Dreyfus, joined by anti-Semites and most of the

**Captain Alfred Dreyfus** Leaving an 1899 reconsideration of his original court martial, Dreyfus receives an insulting "guard of dishonor" from soldiers whose backs are turned. Top army leaders were determined to brand Dreyfus as a traitor. *(Roger-Viollet/Getty Images)*

Catholic establishment. On the other side stood the civil libertarians and most of the more radical republicans.

This battle, which eventually led to Dreyfus's being declared innocent, revived republican feeling against the church. Between 1901 and 1905 the government severed all ties between the state and the Catholic church after centuries of close relations. The salaries of priests and bishops were no longer paid by the government. Catholic schools were put completely on their own financially, and in a short time they lost a third of their students. The state school system's power of indoctrination was greatly strengthened. In France only the growing socialist movement, with its very different but thoroughly secular ideology, stood in opposition to patriotic, republican nationalism.

## Great Britain and Ireland

Britain in the late nineteenth century has often been seen as a shining example of peaceful and successful political evolution, where an effective two-party parliament skillfully guided the country from classical liberalism to full-fledged democracy with hardly a misstep. This view of Great Britain is not so much wrong as incomplete. After the right to vote was granted to males of the solid middle class in 1832, opinion leaders and politicians wrestled with the uncertainties of a further extension of the franchise. In 1867 Benjamin Disraeli and the Conservatives extended the vote to all middle-class males and the best-paid workers in the Second Reform bill, in order to broaden the Conservative party's traditional base of aristocratic and landed support. After 1867 English political parties and electoral campaigns became more modern, and the "lower orders" appeared to vote as responsibly as their "betters." Hence the Third Reform Bill of 1884 gave the vote to almost every adult male.

While the House of Commons was drifting toward democracy, the House of Lords, between 1901 and 1910, tried and ultimately failed to reassert itself. Aristocratic conservatism yielded to popular democracy once and for all. The result was that extensive social welfare measures, slow to come to Great Britain, were passed in a spectacular rush between 1906 and 1914. During those years the Liberal party, inspired by the fiery Welshman David Lloyd George (1863–1945), substantially raised taxes on the rich as part of the so-called People's Budget. This income helped the government pay for national health insurance, unemployment benefits, old-age pensions, and a host of other social measures. The state was integrating the urban masses socially as well as politically.

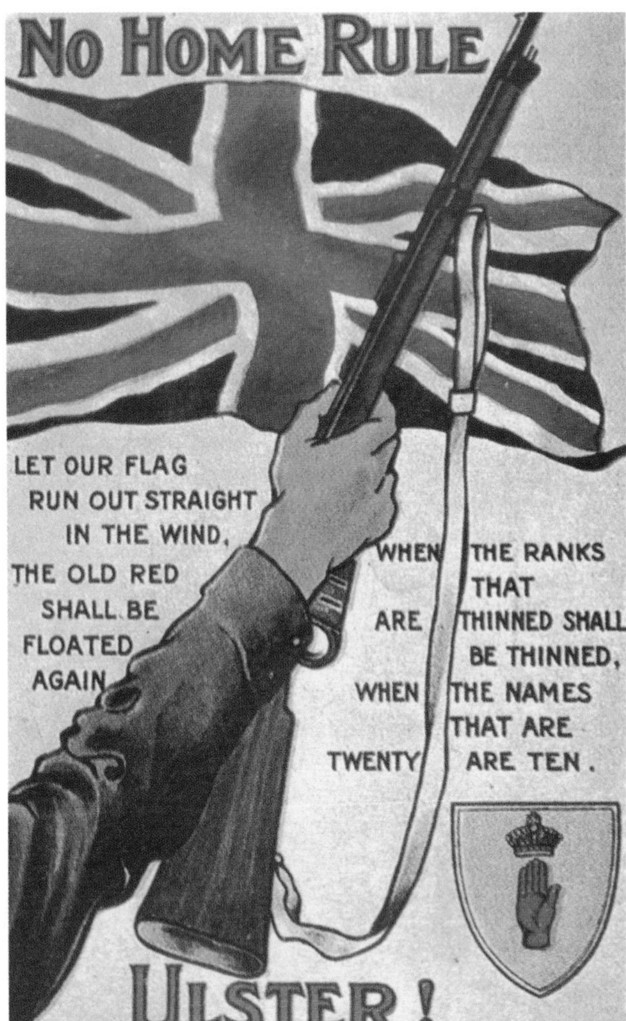


**"No Home Rule"** Posters like this one helped to foment pro-British, anti-Catholic sentiment in the northern Irish counties of Ulster before the First World War. The rifle raised defiantly and the accompanying rhyme are a thinly veiled threat of armed rebellion and civil war. *(Reproduced with the kind permission of the Trustees of the National Museums & Galleries of Northern Ireland)*

This record of accomplishment was only part of the story, however. On the eve of World War I the question of Ireland brought Great Britain to the brink of civil war. The Irish famine in the 1840s (see page 776) fueled an Irish revolutionary movement. Thereafter the English slowly granted concessions, such as the abolition of the privileges of the Anglican church and rights for Irish peasants. Liberal prime minister William Gladstone (1809–1898) introduced bills to give Ireland self-government in

1886 and in 1893, but they failed to pass. After two decades of relative quiet, Irish nationalists in the British Parliament saw their chance. They supported the Liberals in their battle for the People's Budget and in 1913 received a home-rule bill for Ireland in return.

Ireland, however, was composed of two peoples. As much as the Irish Catholic majority in the southern counties wanted home rule, precisely that much did the Irish Protestants in the northern counties of Ulster come to oppose it. Motivated by the accumulated fears and hostilities of generations, the Ulsterites vowed to resist home rule in northern Ireland. By December 1913 they had raised a hundred thousand armed volunteers, and they were supported by much of English public opinion. Thus in 1914 the Liberals in the House of Lords introduced a compromise home-rule bill that did not apply to the northern counties. This bill, which openly betrayed promises made to Irish nationalists, was rejected, and in September the original home-rule bill was passed but simultaneously suspended for the duration of the hostilities. The momentous Irish question was overtaken by an earth-shattering world war in August 1914.

Similarly, progressive Sweden was powerless to stop the growth of the Norwegian national movement, which culminated in Norway's breaking away from Sweden and becoming a fully independent nation in 1905. In this light one can also see how hopeless was the case of the Ottoman Empire in Europe in the later nineteenth century. It was only a matter of time before the Serbs, Bulgarians, and Romanians would break away, and they did.

## The Austro-Hungarian Empire

The dilemma of conflicting nationalisms in Ireland also helps one appreciate how desperate the situation in the Austro-Hungarian Empire had become by the early twentieth century. In 1849 Magyar nationalism had driven Hungarian patriots to declare an independent Hungarian republic, which was savagely crushed by Russian and Austrian armies (see pages 778–779). Throughout the 1850s Hungary was ruled as a conquered territory, and Emperor Francis Joseph and his bureaucracy tried hard to centralize the state and Germanize the language and culture of the different nationalities.

Then in the wake of defeat by Prussia in 1866, a weakened Austria was forced to strike a compromise and establish the so-called dual monarchy. The empire was divided in two, and the nationalistic Magyars gained virtual independence for Hungary. The two states were joined only by a shared monarch and common ministries for finance, defense, and foreign affairs. After 1867 the disintegrating force of competing nationalisms continued unabated, for both Austria and Hungary had several "Irelands" within their borders.

Another aspect of growing national antagonisms in the Austro-Hungarian Empire was virulent anti-Semitism, which emerged in the late nineteenth century and called into question the entire process of Jewish emancipation throughout western and central Europe (see pages 815–816).

In Hungary the Magyar nobility in 1867 restored the constitution of 1848 and used it to dominate both the Magyar peasantry and the minority populations until 1914. Only the wealthiest one-fourth of adult males had the right to vote, making the parliament the creature of the Magyar elite. Laws promoting use of the Magyar (Hungarian) language in schools and government were rammed through and bitterly resented, especially by the Croatians and Romanians. While Magyar extremists campaigned loudly for total separation from Austria, the radical leaders of the subject nationalities dreamed in turn of independence from Hungary. Unlike most major countries, which harnessed nationalism to strengthen the state after 1871, the Austro-Hungarian Empire was progressively weakened and destroyed by nationalism.

## The Modernization of Russia

The Russian empire was also an enormous multinational state, containing all the ethnic Russians and many other nationalities as well. After 1853 Russia's leaders found themselves in serious trouble. It became clear that they had to embrace the process of **modernization,** defined narrowly as the changes that enable a country to compete effectively with the leading countries at a given time.

In the 1850s Russia was a poor agrarian society with backward agricultural techniques. Serfdom was still the basic social institution, but it had become the great moral and political issue for the government by the 1840s. Then the Crimean War of 1853 to 1856, arising out of a dispute with France over who should protect certain Christian shrines in the Ottoman Empire, brought crisis. France and Great Britain, aided by Sardinia and the Ottoman Empire, inflicted a humiliating defeat on Russia.

Military defeat marked a turning point in Russian history because it clearly demonstrated that Russia had fallen behind the rapidly industrializing nations of western Europe in many areas. At the very least, Russia needed railroads, better armaments, and reorganization of the army if it was to maintain its international position. Moreover, the disastrous war had caused hardship and raised the specter of massive peasant rebellion. Reform of serfdom was imperative. Military disaster thus forced the new tsar, Alexander II (r. 1855–1881), and his ministers along the path of rapid social change and general modernization.

The first and greatest of the reforms was the freeing of the serfs in 1861. Human bondage was abolished forever, and the emancipated peasants received, on average, about half of the land. But the peasants had to pay fairly high prices for their land, which was owned collectively. High land prices and collective ownership made it difficult for individual peasants to improve agricultural methods, and thus the effects of the reform were limited.

Most of the later reforms were also halfway measures. More successful was reform of the legal system, which established independent courts and equality before the law. Education was also liberalized somewhat, and censorship was relaxed but not removed.

Until 1905 Russia's greatest strides toward modernization were economic rather than political. Industry and transport were transformed in two industrial surges. In 1860 the empire had only about 1,250 miles of railroads; by 1880 it had about 15,500 miles. The railroads enabled agricultural Russia to export grain and thus earn money for further industrialization. Industrial suburbs grew up around Moscow and St. Petersburg, and a class of modern factory workers began to take shape. Industrial development contributed mightily to the spread of Marxian thought and the transformation of the Russian revolutionary movement after 1890.

In 1881 a small group of terrorists assassinated Alexander II. The era of reform came to an abrupt end, for the new tsar, Alexander III (r. 1881–1894), was a determined reactionary. Political modernization remained frozen until 1905, but economic modernization sped forward in the massive industrial surge of the 1890s. Nationalism played a decisive role, as it had after the Crimean War. The key leader was Sergei Witte, the energetic minister of finance, who believed that industrial backwardness was threatening Russia's power and greatness. Under Witte's leadership the government built state-owned railroads rapidly, promoted Russian industry with high protective tariffs, and put Russia on the gold standard of the "civilized world" to strengthen its finances.

Witte's greatest innovation, however, was to use the West to catch up with the West. He encouraged foreigners to use their capital and technology to build great factories in backward Russia, telling the tsar that this was "the only way by which our industry will be able to supply our country quickly with abundant and cheap products."[8] This policy was brilliantly successful, especially in southern Russia. There, in eastern Ukraine, foreign capitalists and their engineers built an enormous and very modern steel and coal industry almost from scratch in little more than a decade. By 1900 only the United States, Germany, and Great Britain were producing more steel than Russia. A fiercely autocratic and independent Russia was catching up with the advanced nations of the West.

Catching up partly meant vigorous territorial expansion, for this was the age of Western imperialism. By 1903 Russia had established a sphere of influence in Chinese Manchuria and was casting greedy eyes on northern Korea. When the diplomatic protests of equally imperialistic Japan were ignored, the Japanese launched a surprise attack in February 1904. To the amazement of self-confident Europeans, Japan scored repeated victories, and Russia was forced in August 1905 to accept a humiliating defeat.

As is often the case, military disaster abroad brought political upheaval at home. The business and professional classes had long wanted a representative government, and factory workers and peasants suffered from poverty and overpopulation. With the army pinned down in Manchuria, all these currents of discontent converged in the revolution of 1905.

The beginning of the revolution pointed out the incompetence of the government. On a Sunday in January 1905, a massive crowd of workers and their families converged peacefully on the Winter Palace in St. Petersburg to present a petition to the tsar. Suddenly troops opened fire, killing and wounding hundreds. The **Bloody Sunday** massacre turned ordinary workers against the tsar and produced a wave of general indignation.

Outlawed political parties came out into the open, and by the summer of 1905 strikes, peasant uprisings, revolts among minority nationalities, and troop mutinies were sweeping the country. The revolutionary surge culminated in October 1905 in a great paralyzing general strike, which forced the government to capitulate. The tsar issued the **October Manifesto,** which granted full civil rights and promised a popularly elected *Duma* (parliament) with real legislative power.

On the eve of the opening of the first Duma in May 1906, the government issued the new constitution, the Fundamental Laws. The tsar retained great powers. The Duma, elected indirectly by universal male suffrage, and a largely appointive upper house could debate and pass laws, but the tsar had an absolute veto.

The new constitution disappointed the middle-class liberals, the largest group in the newly elected Duma, and efforts to cooperate with the tsar's ministers soon broke down. After a hostile Duma was elected in 1907, the tsar and his reactionary advisers rewrote the electoral law to increase greatly the weight of the wealthy classes at

**"Freedom!"** So reads the red "socialist" banner of this peasant woman, who appears as the symbol of radical demands in the Russian countryside in the revolution of 1905. This vibrant drawing is on the first page of a new review featuring political cartoons from the rapidly growing popular press. *(New York Public Library, Slavonic Division)*

the expense of workers, peasants, national minorities, and middle-class professionals.

The new law had the intended effect. With landowners assured half of the seats in the Duma, the government secured a loyal majority in 1907. Thus armed, the tough chief minister, Peter Stolypin, pursued a policy seeking to broaden support for the state. He pushed through important agrarian reforms designed to break down collective village ownership of land and to encourage the more enterprising peasants—a strategy known as the "wager on the strong." On the eve of World War I, Russia was partially modernized, a conservative constitutional monarchy with a peasant-based but industrializing economy.

## Jewish Emancipation and Modern Anti-Semitism

Revolutionary changes in political principles and the triumph of the nation-state brought equally revolutionary changes in Jewish life in western and central Europe. Beginning in France in 1791, Jews gradually gained their civil rights, although the process was slow and uneven. In the revolution of 1848, the Frankfurt Assembly called for full rights for German Jews, and throughout the 1850s and 1860s liberals in Austria, Italy, and Prussia pressed successfully for legal equality. In 1871 the constitution of the new German Empire consolidated the process of

Jewish emancipation in central Europe. It abolished all restrictions on Jewish marriage, choice of occupation, place of residence, and property ownership. Exclusion from government employment and discrimination in social relations remained. However, according to one leading historian, by 1871 "it was widely accepted in Central Europe that the gradual disappearance of anti-Jewish prejudice was inevitable."[9]

The process of emancipation presented Jews with challenges and opportunities. Traditional Jewish occupations, such as court financial agent, village moneylender, and peddler, were undermined by free-market reforms, but careers in business, the professions, and the arts were opening to Jewish talent. Many Jews responded energetically and successfully. By 1871 a majority of Jewish people in western and central Europe had improved their economic situation and entered the middle classes. Most Jewish people also identified strongly with their respective nation-states and with good reason saw themselves as patriotic citizens.

Vicious anti-Semitism reappeared after the stock market crash of 1873, beginning in central Europe. Drawing on long traditions of religious intolerance, ghetto exclusion, and periodic anti-Jewish riots and expulsions, this anti-Semitism was also a modern development. It built on the general reaction against liberalism and its economic and political policies. Modern anti-Semitism whipped up resentment against Jewish achievement and Jewish "financial control," while fanatics claimed that the Jewish race (rather than the Jewish religion) posed a biological threat to the German people. Anti-Semitic beliefs were particularly popular among conservatives, extremist nationalists, and people who felt threatened by Jewish competition.

Anti-Semites also created modern political parties to attack and degrade Jews. In 1893, the prewar electoral high point in Germany, small anti-Semitic parties secured 2.9 percent of the votes cast. However, in Austrian Vienna in the early 1890s, Karl Lueger and his "Christian socialists" won striking electoral victories, spurring Theodor Herzl to turn from German nationalism and advocate political **Zionism** and the creation of a Jewish state. (See the feature "Individuals in Society: Theodor Herzl.") Lueger, the popular mayor of Vienna from 1897 to 1910, combined fierce anti-Semitic rhetoric with municipal ownership of basic services, and he appealed especially to the German-speaking lower middle class—and an unsuccessful young artist named Adolf Hitler.

Before 1914 anti-Semitism was most oppressive in eastern Europe, where Jews also suffered from terrible poverty. In the Russian empire, where there was no Jewish emancipation and 4 million of Europe's 7 million Jewish people lived in 1880, officials used anti-Semitism to channel popular discontent away from the government and onto the Jewish minority. Russian Jews were denounced as foreign exploiters, and in 1881–1882 a wave of violent pogroms commenced in southern Russia. The police and the army stood aside for days while peasants looted and destroyed Jewish property. Official harassment continued in the following decades, and quotas were placed on Jewish residency, education, and participation in the professions. As a result, some Russian Jews turned toward self-emancipation and the vision of a Zionist settlement in Palestine. Large numbers also emigrated to western Europe and the United States. About 2.75 million Jews left eastern Europe between 1881 and 1914.

## MARXISM AND THE SOCIALIST MOVEMENT

Nationalism served, for better or worse, as a new unifying principle. But what about socialism? Did the rapid growth of socialist parties, which were generally Marxian parties dedicated to an international proletarian revolution, mean that national states had failed to gain the support of workers? This question requires close examination.

### The Socialist International

Certainly socialism appealed to large numbers of working men and women in the late nineteenth century, and the growth of socialist parties after 1871 was phenomenal. Neither Bismarck's antisocialist laws nor his extensive social security system checked the growth of the German Social Democratic party, which espoused the Marxian ideology. By 1912 it had millions of followers and was the largest party in the Reichstag. Socialist parties also grew in other countries, though nowhere else with such success. Marxian socialist parties were eventually linked together in an international organization.

The bookish Marx showed a rare flair for combining theorization with both lively popular writing and organizational ability. In 1864 he played an important role in founding the First International of socialists—the International Working Men's Association. In the following years he battled successfully to control the organization, and he used its annual meetings as a means of spreading his realistic, "scientific" doctrines of inevitable socialist revolution. When Marx enthusiastically embraced the passionate, vaguely radical patriot-

# INDIVIDUALS IN SOCIETY

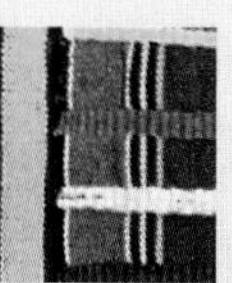

## THEODOR HERZL

In September 1897, only days after his vision and energy had called into being the First Zionist Congress in Basel, Switzerland, Theodor Herzl (1860–1904) assessed the results in his diary: "If I were to sum up the Congress in a word—which I shall take care not to publish—it would be this: At Basel I founded the Jewish state. If I said this out loud today I would be greeted by universal laughter. In five years perhaps, and certainly in fifty years, everyone will perceive it."* Herzl's buoyant optimism, which so often carried him forward, was prophetic. Leading the Zionist movement until his death at age forty-four in 1904, Herzl guided the first historic steps toward modern Jewish political nationhood and the creation of Israel in 1948.

Theodor Herzl was born in Budapest, Hungary, into an upper-middle-class German-speaking Jewish family. When Herzl was eighteen, his family moved to Vienna, where he studied law. As a university student, he soaked up the liberal beliefs of most well-to-do Viennese Jews, who also championed the assimilation of German culture. Wrestling with his nonreligious Jewishness and his strong pro-German feeling, Herzl embraced German nationalism and joined a German dueling fraternity. There he discovered that full acceptance required openly anti-Semitic attitudes and a repudiation of all things Jewish. This Herzl could not tolerate, and he resigned. After receiving his law degree, he embarked on a literary career. In 1889 Herzl married into a wealthy Viennese Jewish family, but he and his socialite wife were mismatched and never happy together.

Herzl achieved considerable success as both a journalist and a playwright. His witty comedies focused on the bourgeoisie, including Jewish millionaires trying to live like aristocrats. Accepting many German stereotypes, Herzl sometimes depicted eastern Jews as uneducated and grasping. But as a dedicated, highly educated liberal, he mainly believed that the Jewish shortcomings he perceived were the results of age-old persecution and would disappear through education and assimilation. Herzl also took a growing pride in Jewish steadfastness in the face of victimization and suffering. He savored memories of his early Jewish education and going with his father to the synagogue.

The emergence of modern anti-Semitism shocked Herzl, as it did many acculturated Jewish Germans. Moving to Paris in 1891 as the correspondent for Vienna's leading liberal newspaper, Herzl studied politics and pondered recent historical developments. He then came to a bold conclusion, published in 1896 as *The Jewish State: An Attempt at a Modern Solution to the Jewish Question.* According to Herzl, Jewish assimilation had failed, and attempts to combat anti-Semitism would never succeed. Only by building an independent Jewish state could the Jewish people achieve dignity and renewal. As recent scholarship shows, Herzl developed his political nationalism, or Zionism, before the anti-Jewish agitation accompanying the Dreyfus affair, which only strengthened his faith in his analysis.

*Theodor Herzl, ca 1900.* (AKG London)

Generally rebuffed by skeptical Jewish elites in western and central Europe, Herzl turned for support to youthful idealists and the poor Jewish masses. He became an inspiring man of action, rallying the delegates to the annual Zionist congresses, directing the growth of the worldwide Zionist organization, and working himself to death. Herzl also understood that national consciousness required powerful emotions and symbols, such as a Jewish flag. Flags build nations, he said, because people "live and die for a flag."

Putting the Zionist vision before non-Jews and world public opinion, Herzl believed in international diplomacy and political agreements. He traveled constantly to negotiate with European rulers and top officials, seeking their support in securing territory for a Jewish state, usually in the Ottoman Empire. Aptly described by an admiring contemporary as "the first Jewish statesman since the destruction of Jerusalem," Herzl proved most successful in Britain. He paved the way for the 1917 Balfour Declaration, which solemnly pledged British support for a "Jewish homeland" in Palestine.

### QUESTIONS FOR ANALYSIS

1. Describe Theodor Herzl's background and early beliefs. Do you see a link between Herzl's early German nationalism and his later Zionism?
2. How did Herzl work as a leader to turn his Zionist vision into a reality?

*Quotes are from Theodor Herzl, *The Diaries of Theodor Herzl,* trans. and ed. with an introduction by Marvin Lowenthal (New York: Grosset & Dunlap, 1962), pp. 224, 22, xxi.

**"Greetings from the May Day Festival"** Workers participated enthusiastically in the annual one-day strike on May 1 to honor internationalist socialist solidarity, as this postcard from a happy woman visitor to her cousin suggests. Speeches, picnics, and parades were the order of the day, and workers celebrated their respectability and independent culture. Picture postcards developed with railroads and mass travel. *(AKG London)*

ism of the Paris Commune, he frightened the more moderate British labor leaders, and the First International collapsed.

Yet international proletarian solidarity remained an important objective for Marxists. In 1889 socialist leaders came together to form the Second International, which lasted until 1914. The International was only a federation of national socialist parties, but it had great psychological impact. Every three years delegates from the different parties met to interpret Marxian doctrines and plan coordinated action. May 1 (May Day) was declared an annual international one-day strike, a day of marches and demonstrations. A permanent executive for the International was established. Many feared and many others rejoiced in the growing power of socialism and the Second International.

## Unions and Revisionism

Was socialism really radical and revolutionary in these years? On the whole, it was not. Indeed, as socialist parties grew and attracted large numbers of members, they looked more and more toward gradual change and steady improvement for the working class and less and less toward revolution.

Workers themselves were progressively less inclined to follow radical programs. There were several reasons for this. As workers gained the right to vote and won real benefits, their attention focused more on elections than on revolutions. Workers were also not immune to patriotic education, drum-beating parades, and aggressive foreign policy as they loyally voted for socialists. Nor were workers a unified social group. Perhaps most important of all, workers' standard of living rose gradually but substantially after 1850 as the promise of the Industrial Revolution was at least partially realized. The quality of life also improved dramatically in urban areas. Thus workers tended more and more to become militantly moderate: they demanded gains, but they were less likely to take to the barricades in pursuit of them.

The growth of labor unions reinforced this trend toward moderation. In the early stages of industrialization modern unions were considered subversive bodies and were generally prohibited by law. From this sad position workers struggled to escape. Great Britain led the way in 1824 and 1825 when unions won the right to exist but (generally) not the right to strike. After the collapse of Robert Owen's attempt to form one big union in the 1830s (see page 754), new and more practical kinds of unions appeared. Limited primarily to highly skilled workers such as machinists and carpenters, the "new model unions" avoided radical politics and concentrated on winning better wages and hours for their members through collective bargaining and compromise. After 1890 unions for unskilled workers developed, and between 1901 and 1906 the legal position of British unions was further strengthened.

Germany was the most industrialized, socialized, and unionized country in continental Europe by 1914. German unions were not granted important rights until 1869, and until the antisocialist law was repealed in 1890, the government frequently harassed them as socialist fronts. With German industrialization still storming ahead and almost all legal harassment eliminated, union membership skyrocketed from only about 270,000 in 1895 to roughly 3 million in 1912. Genuine collective bargaining, long opposed by socialist intellectuals as a "sellout," was officially recognized as desirable by the German Trade Union Congress in 1899. Gradual improvement, not revolution, was becoming the primary goal of the German trade-union movement.

The German trade unions and their leaders were in fact, if not in name, thoroughgoing revisionists. **Revisionism** was an effort by various socialists to update Marxian doctrines to reflect the realities of the time. The socialist Edward Bernstein (1850–1932) argued in 1899 in his *Evolutionary Socialism* that Marx's predictions of ever-greater poverty for workers had been proved false. Therefore, Bernstein suggested, socialists should reform their doctrines and tactics. They should combine with other progressive forces to win gradual evolutionary gains for workers through legislation, unions, and further economic development. The Second International denounced these views as heresy. Yet the revisionist, gradualist approach continued to gain the tacit acceptance of many German socialists, particularly in the trade unions.

Moderation found followers elsewhere. In France the great socialist leader Jean Jaurès (1859–1914) formally repudiated revisionist doctrines in order to establish a unified socialist party, but he remained at heart a gradualist. Questions of revolutionary versus gradualist policies split Russian Marxists.

Socialist parties before 1914 had clear-cut national characteristics. Russians and socialists in the Austro-Hungarian Empire tended to be the most radical. The German party talked revolution and practiced reformism, greatly influenced by its enormous trade-union movement. The French party talked revolution and tried to practice it, unrestrained by a trade-union movement that was both very weak and very radical. In England the socialist but non-Marxian Labour party, reflecting the well-established union movement, was formally committed to gradual reform. In Spain and Italy Marxian socialism was very weak. There anarchism, seeking to smash the state rather than the bourgeoisie, dominated radical thought and action.

In short, socialist policies and doctrines varied from country to country. Socialism itself was to a large extent "nationalized" behind the imposing façade of international unity. This helps explain why almost all socialist leaders supported their governments when war came in 1914.

## SUMMARY

The Industrial Revolution had a decisive influence on the urban environment. As the populations of towns and cities grew rapidly, long-standing overcrowding and unhealthy living conditions worsened alarmingly. Eventually government leaders, city planners, reformers, scientists, and ordinary citizens responded to this frightening challenge. They took effective action in public health, developed badly needed urban services, and gradually tamed the savagery of the traditional city.

As urban civilization came to prevail, there were major changes in family life. Especially among the working classes, family life became more stable, more loving, and less mercenary. These improvements exacted a price, however. Sex roles for men and women became sharply defined and rigidly separate. Women tended to be locked into a subordinate and stereotypical role. Nonetheless, on balance, the quality of family life improved. Better, more stable family relations reinforced the benefits for the masses of higher real wages, increased social security, political participation, and education.

While the quality of urban and family life improved, the class structure became more complex and diversified than before. Urban society featured many distinct social groups, and the gap between rich and poor remained enormous. Large numbers of poor women in particular continued to labor as workers in sweated industries and as domestic servants and prostitutes, meeting the demands of the servant-keeping classes. Small wonder then that inequality was a favorite theme of realist novelists such as Balzac and Zola. More generally, literary realism reflected Western society's growing faith in science, material progress, and evolutionary thinking. The emergence of urban, industrial civilization accelerated the secularization of the Western world-view.

Finally, Western society became increasingly nationalistic as well as urban and industrial. Nation-states enlisted widespread support and gave men and women a greater sense of belonging. Even socialism became increasingly national in orientation, gathering strength as a champion of working-class interests in domestic politics. Yet even though nationalism served to unite peoples, it also drove them apart—not only in Austria-Hungary and Ireland but also throughout Europe and the rest of the world. The national faith, which reduced social tensions within states, promoted a bitter, almost Darwinian competition between states and thus threatened the progress and unity it had helped to build, as we shall see in Chapter 29.

## KEY TERMS

Benthamite
miasmatic theory
germ theory
pasteurization
antiseptic principle
labor aristocracy
illegitimacy explosion
separate spheres
thermodynamics
organic chemistry
positivist method
evolution
Social Darwinists
Reichstag
Kulturkampf
Dreyfus affair
modernization
Bloody Sunday
October Manifesto
Zionism
revisionism

## NOTES

1. S. Marcus, "Reading the Illegible," in *The Victorian City: Images and Realities,* vol. 1, ed. H. J. Dyos and Michael Wolff (London: Routledge & Kegan Paul, 1973), p. 266.
2. E. Gauldie, *Cruel Habitations: A History of Working-Class Housing, 1780–1918* (London: George Allen & Unwin, 1974), p. 21.
3. J. P. McKay, *Tramways and Trolleys: The Rise of Urban Mass Transport in Europe* (Princeton, N.J.: Princeton University Press, 1976), p. 81.
4. Quoted in G. S. Jones, "Working-Class Culture and Working-Class Politics in London, 1870–1900: Notes on the Remaking of a Working Class," *Journal of Social History* 7 (Summer 1974): 486.
5. Quoted in T. Zeldin, *France, 1848–1945,* vol. 1 (Oxford: Clarendon Press, 1973), p. 346.
6. Quoted in R. Roberts, *The Classic Slum: Salford Life in the First Quarter of the Century* (Manchester, Eng.: University of Manchester Press, 1971), p. 35.
7. Quoted in G. J. Becker, ed., *Documents of Modern Literary Realism* (Princeton, N.J.: Princeton University Press, 1963), p. 159.
8. Quoted in J. P. McKay, *Pioneers for Profit: Foreign Entrepreneurship and Russian Industrialization, 1885–1913* (Chicago: University of Chicago Press, 1970), p. 11.
9. R. Seltzer, *Jewish People, Jewish Thought: The Jewish Experience in History* (New York: Macmillan, 1980), p. 533.

## SUGGESTED READING

All of the books and articles cited in the Notes are highly recommended. Zeldin's work is a fascinating social history. T. Hamerow, *The Birth of a New Europe: State and Society in the Nineteenth Century* (1983), is an ambitious synthesis, and P. Pillbeam, *The Middle Classes in Europe, 1789–1914: France, Germany, Italy, and Russia* (1990), is a stimulating introduction. Aristocratic strength and survival is the theme of A. Mayer, *Persistence of the Old Regime: Europe to the Great War* (1981).

On the European city, D. Harvey, *Consciousness and the Urban Experience* (1985), is provocative. D. Silverman, *Art Nouveau in Fin-de-Siècle France: Politics, Psychology, and Style* (1989), and N. Evenson's beautifully illustrated *Paris: A Century of Change, 1878–1978* (1979), are fascinating, as are G. Masur, *Imperial Berlin* (1970); M. Hamm, ed., *The City in Russian History* (1976); and D. Grew's authoritative *Town in the Ruhr: A Social History of Bochum, 1860–1914* (1979). J. Merriman, *Margins of City Life: Explorations on the French Urban Frontier* (1991), is an important work on France. The outstanding study by J. Schmiechen, *Sweated Industries and Sweated Labor: The London Clothing Trades* (1984), complements H. Mayhew's wonderful contemporary study, *London Labour and the Labouring Poor* (1861), reprinted recently. Michael Crichton's realistic historical novel on organized crime, *The Great Train Robbery* (1976), is excellent. J. P. Goubert, *The Conquest of Water: The Advent of Health in the Industrial Age* (1989), and G. Rosen, *History of Public Health* (1958), offer a fine introduction to sanitary and medical developments.

For society as a whole, J. Burnett, *History of the Cost of Living* (1969), cleverly shows how different classes spent their money, and B. Tuchman, *The Proud Tower* (1966), draws an unforgettable portrait of people and classes before 1914. B. Gottlieb, *The Family in the Western World* (1993), is a wide-ranging synthesis. Sexual attitudes are examined in J. Walkowitz, *Prostitution and Victorian Society: Women, Class and State* (1980); J. Phayer, *Sexual Liberation and Religion in Nineteenth-Century Europe* (1977); and L. Engelstein, *The Key to Happiness: Sex and the Search for Modernity in Fin-de-Siècle Russia* (1992). G. Alter, *Family and Female Life Course: The Women of Verviers, Belgium, 1849–1880* (1988), and A. McLaren, *Sexuality and Social Order: Birth Control in Nineteenth-Century France* (1982), explore attitudes toward family planning.

Women have come into their own in historical studies. Among general works, L. Tilly and J. Scott, *Women, Work and Family* (1978), is especially recommended. Eye-opening specialized investigations include L. Davidoff, *The Best Circles* (1973), and P. Jalland, *Women, Marriage and Politics, 1860–1914* (1986), on upper-class society types. M. J. Peterson, *Love and Work in the Lives of Victorian Gentlewomen* (1989), and M. Vicinus, *Independent Women: Work and Community for Single Women, 1850–1920* (1985), examine women at work. L. Tiersten, *Marianne in the Market: Envisioning Consumer Society in Fin-de-Siècle France* (2001), and D. Crane, *Fashion and Its Social Agendas: Class, Gender, and Identity* (2000), are valuable, innovative studies. M. Vicinus, ed., *Suffer and Be Still* (1972) and *A Widening Sphere* (1981), are far-ranging collections of essays on women's history, as is R. Bridenthal, S. Stuard, and M. Wiesner, eds., *Becoming Visible: Women in European History,* 3d ed. (1998). Feminism is treated perceptively in R. Evans, *The Feminists: Women's Emancipation in Europe, America, and Australia* (1979), and in C. Moses, *French Feminism in the Nineteenth Century* (1984). L. Tickner, *The Spectacle of Women: Imagery of the Suffrage Campaign, 1907–1914* (1988), perceptively discusses Britain. J. Gillis, *Youth and History* (1974), is a good introduction.

Among studies of special groups, J. R. Wegs, *Growing Up Working Class: Continuity and Change Among Viennese Youth, 1890–1938* (1989), and W. S. Haine, *The World of the Paris Café: Sociability Among the French Working Class, 1789–1914* (1996), are recommended. Servants and their employers receive excellent treatment in T. McBride, *The Domestic Revolution: The Modernization of Household Service in England and France, 1820–1920* (1976), and B. Smith, *Ladies of the Leisure Class: The Bourgeoises of Northern France in the Nineteenth Century* (1981).

On Darwin, M. Ruse, *The Darwinian Revolution* (1979), and P. Bowler, *Evolution: The History of an Idea,* rev. ed. (1989), are good starting points. O. Chadwick, *The Secularization of the European Mind in the Nineteenth Century* (1976), analyzes the impact of science (and other factors) on religious belief. The masterpieces of the great realist social novelists remain one of the best and most memorable introductions to nineteenth-century culture and thought. In addition to the novels discussed in this chapter and those cited in the Suggested Reading for Chapters 23 and 24, Ivan Turgenev's *Fathers and Sons* and Émile Zola's *The Dram-Shop* are especially recommended.

For individual countries, in addition to the general works mentioned in the Suggested Reading for Chapter 24, G. Craig, *Germany, 1866–1945* (1980), and B. Moore, *Social Origins of Dictatorship and Democracy* (1966), are outstanding. R. Anderson, *France, 1870–1914* (1977), provides a good introduction and has a useful bibliography. E. Weber, *France, Fin de Siècle* (1986), captures the spirit of Paris at the end of the century. E. Cahm, *The Dreyfus Affair in French Society and Politics* (1996), and G. Chapman, *The Dreyfus Case: A Reassessment* (1955), are careful examinations of the famous case. In *Jean Barois,* Nobel Prize winner Roger Du Gard accurately re-creates in novel form the Dreyfus affair. D. M. Smith has written widely on Italy, and his *Garibaldi* (1956) and *Italy: A Modern History,* rev. ed. (1969), are recommended.

H. Wehler, *The German Empire, 1871–1918* (1985), stresses the strength of the landed nobility and the weakness of the middle class in an influential synthesis, which is challenged by D. Blackbourn and G. Eley, *The Peculiarities of German History: Bourgeois Society and Politics in 19th-Century Germany* (1984). L. Cecil, *Wilhelm II: Prince and Emperor, 1859–1900* (1989), probes the character and politics of Germany's ruler. C. Schorske, *Fin de Siècle Vienna: Politics and Culture* (1980), is brilliant on aspects of modern culture.

On Russia, in addition to McKay cited in the Notes, see T. von Laue, *Sergei Witte and the Industrialization of Russia* (1970); A. Rieber, *Merchants and Entrepreneurs in Imperial Russia* (1982); and H. Rogger, *Russia in the Age of Modernization and Revolution, 1881–1917* (1983), which has an excellent bibliography. H. Troyat, *Daily Life in Russia Under the Last Tsar* (1962), is lively and recommended. T. Friedgut, *Iuzovka and Revolution: Life and Work in Russia's Donbass, 1869–1924* (1989), and R. Zelnik, *Labor and Society in Tsarist Russia, 1855–1870* (1971), skillfully treat different aspects of working-class life and politics. W. E. Mosse, *Alexander II and the Modernization of Russia* (1958), discusses midcentury reforms. D. Boyce, *Nationalism in Ireland,* 2d ed. (1991), provides an excellent account of the Irish struggle for nationhood.

J. Seigel, *Marx's Fate: The Shape of a Life* (1978), is an outstanding biography. C. Schorske, *German Social Democracy, 1905–1917* (1955), is a modern classic. V. Lidtke, *The Alternative Culture: Socialist Labor in Imperial Germany* (1985), and J. Quataert, *Reluctant Feminists in German Social Democracy, 1885–1917* (1979), are also recommended for the study of the German socialists. Two excellent collections by specialists are L. Berlanstein, ed., *Rethinking Labor History* (1993), and D. Geary, ed., *Labour and Socialist Movements in Europe Before 1914* (1989), which examines several different countries and has valuable references.

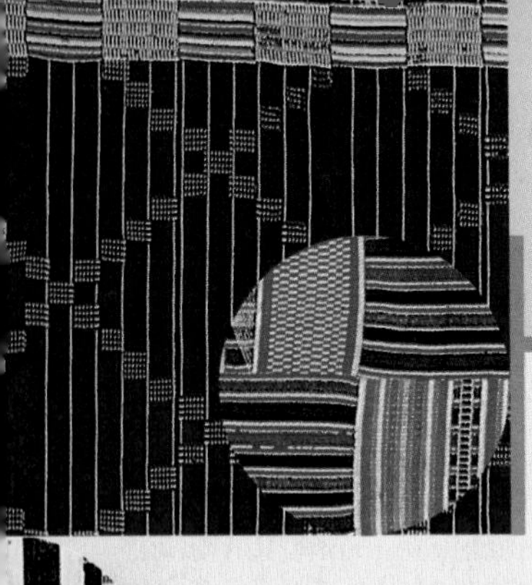

# LISTENING TO THE PAST

## Middle-Class Youth and Sexuality

*Growing up in Vienna in a prosperous Jewish family, Stephan Zweig (1881–1942) became an influential voice calling for humanitarian values and international culture in early-twentieth-century Europe. Passionately opposed to the First World War, Zweig wrote poetry, plays, and novels. But he was most famous for many outstanding biographies, which featured shrewd psychological portraits of intriguing historical figures such as Magellan and Marie Antoinette. After Hitler came to power in Germany in 1933, Zweig lived in exile until his death in 1942.*

*Zweig's last work was* The World of Yesterday *(1943), one of the truly fascinating autobiographies of the twentieth century. In the following passage taken from that work, Zweig recalls and also interprets the romantic experiences and the sexual separation of middle-class youth before the First World War.*

During the eight years of our higher schooling [beyond grade school], something had occurred which was of great importance to each one of us: we ten-year-olds had grown into virile young men of sixteen, seventeen, and eighteen, and Nature began to assert its rights. . . . It did not take us long to discover that those authorities in whom we had previously confided—school, family, and public morals—manifested an astonishing insincerity in this matter of sex. But what is more, they also demanded secrecy and reserve from us in this connection. . . .

This "social morality," which on the one hand privately presupposed the existence of sexuality and its natural course, but on the other would not recognize it openly at any price, was doubly deceitful. While it winked one eye at a young man and even encouraged him with the other "to sow his wild oats," as the kindly language of the home put it, in the case of a woman it studiously shut both eyes and acted as if it were blind. That a man could experience desires, and was permitted to experience them, was silently admitted by custom. But to admit frankly that a woman could be subject to similar desires, or that creation for its eternal purposes also required a female polarity, would have transgressed the conception of the "sanctity of womanhood." In the pre-Freudian era, therefore, the axiom was agreed upon that a female person could have no physical desires as long as they had not been awakened by man, and that, obviously, was officially permitted only in marriage. But even in those moral times, in Vienna in particular, the air was full of dangerous erotic infection, and a girl of good family had to live in a completely sterilized atmosphere, from the day of her birth until the day when she left the altar on her husband's arm. In order to protect young girls, they were not left alone for a single moment. . . . Every book which they read was inspected, and above all else, young girls were constantly kept busy to divert their attention from any possible dangerous thoughts. They had to practise the piano, learn singing and drawing, foreign languages, and the history of literature and art. They were educated and overeducated. But while the aim was to make them as educated and as socially correct as possible, at the same time society anxiously took great pains that they should remain innocent of all natural things to a degree unthinkable today. A young girl of good family was not allowed to have any idea of how the male body was formed, or to know how children came into the world, for the angel was to enter into matrimony not only physically untouched, but completely "pure" spiritually as well. "Good breeding," for a young girl of that time, was identical with ignorance of life; and this ignorance ofttimes lasted for the rest of their lives. . . .

What possibilities actually existed for a young man of the middle-class world? In all the others, in the so-called lower classes, the problem was no problem at all. . . . In most of our Alpine villages the number of natural children greatly exceeded the legitimate ones. Among the proletariat, the worker, before he could get married, lived with another worker in free love. . . . It was only in our middle-class society that such a remedy as an early marriage was scorned. . . . And so there was an artificial interval of six, eight, or ten years between actual manhood and manhood as society accepted it; and in this interval the young man had to take care of his own "affairs" or adventures.

Those days did not give him too many opportunities. Only a very few particularly rich young men could afford the luxury of keeping a mistress, that is, taking an apartment and paying her expenses. And only a very few fortunate young men achieved the literary ideal of love of the times—the only one which it was permitted to describe in novels—an affair with a married woman. The others helped themselves for the most part with shopgirls and waitresses, and this offered little inner satisfaction. . . . But, generally speaking, prostitution was still the foundation of the erotic life outside of marriage; in a certain sense it constituted a dark underground vault over which rose the gorgeous structure of middle-class society with its faultless, radiant façade.

The present generation has hardly any idea of the gigantic extent of prostitution in Europe before the [First] World War. Whereas today it is as rare to meet a prostitute on the streets of a big city as it is to meet a wagon in the road, then the sidewalks were so sprinkled with women for sale that it was more difficult to avoid than to find them. To this was added the countless number of "closed houses," the night clubs, the cabarets, the dance parlours with their dancers and singers, and the bars with their "come-on" girls. At that time female wares were offered for sale at every hour and at every price. . . . And this was the same city, the same society, the same morality, that was indignant when young girls rode bicycles, and declared it a disgrace to the dignity of science when Freud in his calm, clear, and penetrating manner established truths that they did not wish to be true. The same world that so pathetically defended the purity of womanhood allowed this cruel sale of women, organized it, and even profited thereby.

Nineteenth-century illustration depicting socializing in Vienna. *(Österreichische Nationalbibliothek)*

We should not permit ourselves to be misled by sentimental novels or stories of that epoch. It was a bad time for youth. The young girls were hermetically locked up under the control of the family, hindered in their free bodily as well as intellectual development. The young men were forced to secrecy and reticence by a morality which fundamentally no one believed or obeyed. Unhampered, honest relationships—in other words, all that could have made youth happy and joyous according to the laws of Nature—were permitted only to the very few.

## QUESTIONS FOR ANALYSIS

1. According to Zweig, how did the sex lives of young middle-class women and young middle-class men differ? What accounted for these differences?
2. Was there nonetheless a basic underlying unity in the way society treated both the young men and the young women of the comfortable middle class? If so, what was that unity?
3. Zweig ends this passage with a value judgment: "It was a bad time for youth." Do you agree or disagree? Why?

*Source: The World of Yesterday* by Stephan Zweig, translated by Helmut Ripperger. 

Ottoman sultan Abdulaziz (r. 1861–1876), supporter of vigorous modernizing reform.
*(Topkapi Saray Museum/Dagli Orti/The Art Archive)*

CHAPTER

# 26 AFRICA, WEST ASIA, AND WESTERN IMPERIALISM, 1800–1914

## CHAPTER OUTLINE

- Industrialization and the World Economy
- Western Imperialism, 1880–1914
- The Islamic Heartland Under Pressure
- Sub-Saharan Africa: From the Slave Trade to European Rule

While industrialization and nationalism were transforming urban life and Western society, Western society itself opened a new era in world history. An ever-growing stream of products, people, and ideas flowed out of Europe at this time. The most spectacular manifestation of this many-sided Western expansion came in the late nineteenth century when the leading European nations established or enlarged their far-flung political empires.

Western industrialization and imperialism posed a profound challenge to the many, highly diverse peoples of Africa and Asia. Economic relationships changed, as Europe consolidated its industrial lead and urged Africa and Asia to sell more commodities and raw materials. Political independence and established cultural and religious values also were threatened by Western penetration. It is little wonder, therefore, that African and Asian states and peoples often tried to repel the foreigners with military force and that they searched for other methods when they were defeated. Stretching over two centuries, the timing of these encounters with the West certainly contributed to the great diversity of historical experiences in Africa and Asia in the years before World War I. This chapter will consider the Islamic heartland and Africa, and Chapter 27 will turn to East Asia.

The Western challenge in the land of Islam emerged in the late seventeenth century, when the Ottoman Empire began to suffer military reversals. The Ottomans eventually responded with a series of reforms designed to modernize the army and protect the empire, but these efforts were only partly successful. The Ottoman Empire continued to lose territory throughout the nineteenth century. Its Egyptian province became increasingly independent and launched its own campaign of westernization until it went bankrupt and was conquered by Britain. Yet both the Ottoman Empire and Egypt also made real progress and laid the foundations of modern Turkey and Egypt.

In sub-Saharan Africa the slow decline of the transatlantic slave trade in the nineteenth century accompanied a great expansion of commodity exports, a shift that marked the beginning of modern economic development in this vast and diverse region. At the same time, powerful movements of Islamic revival extended the sway of Islam in West and central Africa and made Islam a more important part of everyday life and culture. In southern Africa competing groups of white settlers pressed northward and eastward after 1800, foreshadowing European conquest and empire building in the whole continent after 1880. In short, in the nineteenth century Africa experienced greater and more far-reaching changes than ever before.

- How and why did the West's many-sided, epoch-making expansion occur in the nineteenth century?
- How did the Ottoman Empire and its Egyptian province try to revitalize themselves, and what were the most important results?
- In what ways did African economies and societies change as the Atlantic slave trade declined, and what were the consequences of European conquest and empire building in Africa?

These are the questions this chapter will examine.

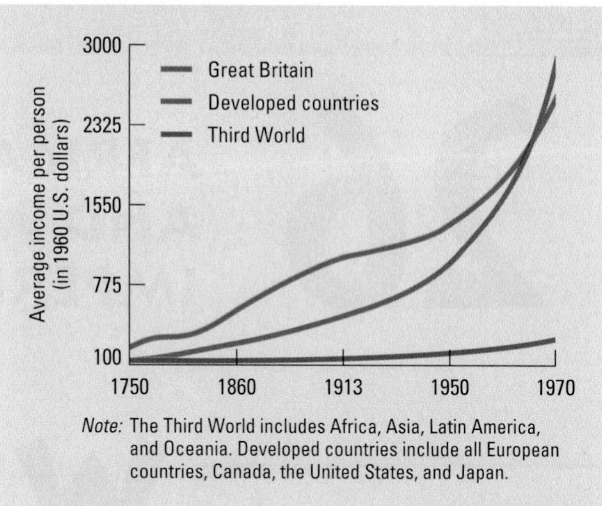


**FIGURE 26.1 The Growth of Average Income per Person in the Third World, Developed Countries, and Great Britain, 1750–1970** *(Source: P. Bairoch and M. Lévy-Leboyer, eds.,* Disparities in Economic Development Since the Industrial Revolution. *Copyright © 1981 by P. Bairoch and M. Lévy-Leboyer. Reprinted with permission of Palgrave Macmillan.)*

## INDUSTRIALIZATION AND THE WORLD ECONOMY

The Industrial Revolution created, first in Great Britain and then in continental Europe and North America, a growing and dynamic economic system. In the course of the nineteenth century that system expanded and transformed economic relations across the face of the earth. Some of this global extension was peaceful and beneficial for all concerned, for the West had products and techniques that the rest of the world desired. If peaceful methods failed, however, Europeans used their superior military power to force non-Western nations to open their doors to Western economic interests. Moreover, Westerners fashioned the global economic system so that the largest share of the ever-increasing gains from trade, technology, and migration flowed to the West and its propertied classes. Thus Western industrialization had profound consequences for the world economy and for Africa and Asia.

### The Rise of Global Inequality

The Industrial Revolution in Europe marked a momentous turning point in human history. Indeed, only by placing Europe's economic breakthrough in a global perspective can one truly appreciate its revolutionary implications and consequences.

From such a global perspective, the ultimate significance of the Industrial Revolution was that it allowed those regions of the world that industrialized in the nineteenth century to increase their wealth and power enormously in comparison to those that did not. As a result, a gap between the industrializing regions (mainly Europe and North America) and the nonindustrializing ones (mainly Africa, Asia, and Latin America) opened up and grew steadily throughout the nineteenth century. Moreover, this pattern of uneven global development became institutionalized, or built into the structure of the world economy, and the **lopsided world**—a world of rich lands and poor—evolved.

In recent years historical economists have begun to chart the long-term evolution of this gap. Figure 26.1 summarizes the important findings of one such study. It compares the long-term evolution of average income per person in today's "developed" (or industrialized) regions with average income per person in the developing regions of Africa, Asia, and South America, also often known as the Third World (see page 1138). To get these individual income figures, researchers estimate a country's gross national product (GNP) at different points in time, convert those estimates to some common currency, and divide by the total population.

Figure 26.1 highlights three main points. First, in 1750 the average standard of living was no higher in Europe as a whole than in the rest of the world. In 1750 Europe as a whole was still a poor agricultural society. By 1970, however, the average person in the wealthiest countries had an income fully twenty-five times as great as the in-

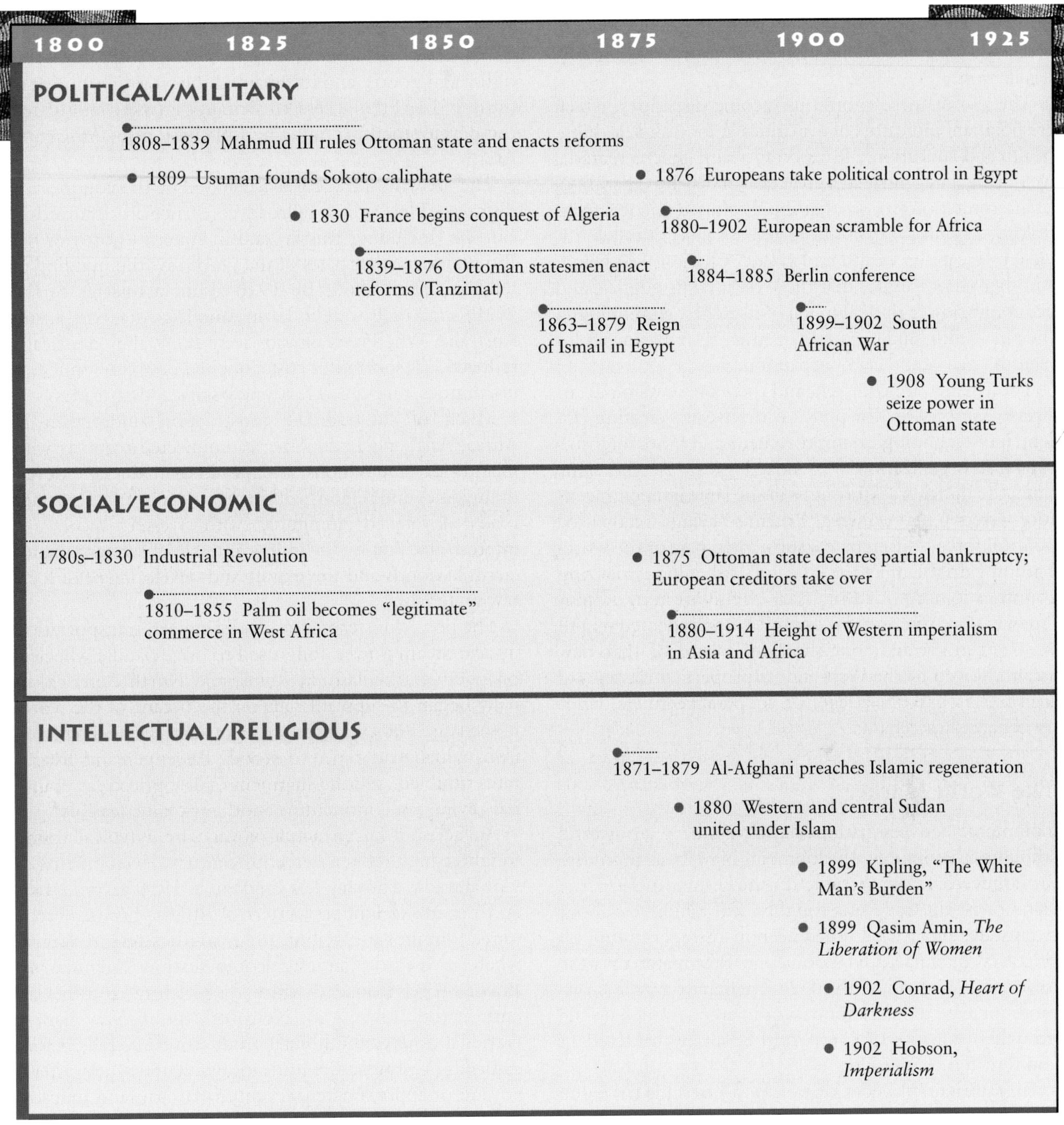


come received by the average person in the poorest countries of Africa and Asia.

Second, it was industrialization that opened the gaps in average wealth and well-being among countries and regions. Great Britain had jumped well above the developed countries' average by 1830. But as the developed countries successfully industrialized in the course of the nineteenth century, Great Britain's lead gradually narrowed, although the gap between the industrializing West and the undeveloped nations continued to grow.

Third, income per person stagnated in the Third World before 1913, in striking contrast to the industrializing regions. Only after 1945, in the era of political independence and decolonization, did the developing countries of Africa, Asia, and Latin America finally make some real economic progress, beginning the critical process of industrialization.

The rise of these enormous income disparities, which are poignant indicators of disparities in food and clothing, health and education, life expectancy and general material well-being, has generated a great deal of debate. One school of interpretation stresses that the West used science, technology, capitalist organization, and even its critical worldview to create its wealth and greater physical well-being. Another school argues that the West used its political and economic power to steal much of its riches, continuing in the nineteenth (and twentieth) century the rapacious colonialism born of the era of expansion.

These issues are complex, and there are few simple answers. As noted in Chapter 24, the wealth-creating potential of technological improvement and more intensive capitalist organization was indeed great. At the same time, the initial breakthroughs in the late eighteenth century rested in part on Great Britain's having already used political force to dominate a substantial part of the world economy. In the nineteenth century other industrializing countries joined with Britain to extend Western dominion over the entire world economy. Unprecedented wealth was indeed created, but the lion's share of that new wealth flowed to the West and its propertied classes and to a tiny non-Western elite of cooperative rulers, landowners, and merchants.

## The World Market

Commerce between nations has always been a powerful stimulus to economic development. Never was this more pronounced than in the nineteenth century. In 1913 the value of world trade was roughly $38 billion, or about twenty-five times what it had been in 1800, even though prices of manufactured goods and raw materials were lower in 1913 than in 1800. In a general way, the enormous increase in international commerce summed up the growth of an interlocking world economy centered in and directed by Europe.

Great Britain played a key role in using trade to tie the world together economically. In 1815 Britain already had a colonial empire, for India, Canada, Australia, and other scattered areas remained British possessions after American independence. The technological breakthroughs of the Industrial Revolution allowed Britain to manufacture cotton textiles, iron, and other goods more cheaply and to far outstrip domestic demand for such products. Thus British manufacturers sought export markets first in Europe and then around the world.

After the repeal of the Corn Laws in 1846 (see page 775), Britain also became the world's leading importer of foreign goods, and it remained the world's emporium until 1914. Free access to Britain's market stimulated the development of mines and plantations in Africa and Asia.

The growth of trade was facilitated by the conquest of distance. The earliest railroad construction occurred in Europe (including Russia) and in America north of the Rio Grande; other parts of the globe saw the building of rail lines after 1860. By 1920 about a quarter of the world's railroads were in Latin America, Asia, Africa, and Australia. Wherever railroads were built, they drastically reduced transportation costs, opened new economic opportunities, and called forth new skills and attitudes.

Much of the railroad construction undertaken in Africa, Asia, and Latin America connected seaports with inland cities and regions, as opposed to linking and developing cities and regions within a given country. Thus railroads dovetailed admirably with Western economic interests, facilitating the inflow and sale of Western manufactured goods and the export and development of local raw materials.

The power of steam also revolutionized transportation by sea. Steam power, long used to drive paddle wheelers on rivers, particularly in Russia and North America, finally began to supplant sails on the oceans of the world in the late 1860s. Lighter, stronger, cheaper steel replaced iron, which had replaced wood. Passenger and freight rates tumbled, and the shipment of low-priced raw materials from one continent to another became feasible.

An account of an actual voyage by a typical tramp freighter highlights nineteenth-century developments in global trade. The ship left England in 1910 carrying rails and general freight to western Australia. From there it carried lumber to Melbourne in southeastern Australia, where it took on harvester combines for Argentina. In Buenos Aires it loaded wheat for Calcutta, and in Calcutta it took on jute for New York. From New York it carried a variety of industrial products to Australia before returning to England with lead, wool, and wheat after a voyage of approximately seventy-two thousand miles to six continents in seventeen months.

The revolution in land and sea transportation helped European settlers take vast, thinly populated territories and produce agricultural products and raw materials there for sale in Europe. Improved transportation enabled Asia, Africa, and Latin America to export not only the traditional tropical products—spices, tea, sugar, coffee—but also new raw materials for industry, such as jute, rubber, cotton, and coconut oil.

**The Uganda Railroad** Begun in 1895 and completed in 1901, the Uganda railroad linked the port of Mombasa with Lake Victoria, the source of the Nile. The railroad brought great changes, projecting British strength into east-central Africa and opening Kenya's temperate highlands to European settlement and plantation agriculture. Many construction workers were recruited in India, and some stayed on as small traders. *(Laurie Platt Winfrey)*

Intercontinental trade was enormously facilitated by the Suez and Panama Canals. Of great importance, too, was large and continual investment in modern port facilities, which made loading and unloading cheaper, faster, and more dependable. Finally, transoceanic telegraph cables inaugurated rapid communications among the financial centers of the world and linked world commodity prices in a global network.

The growth of trade and the conquest of distance encouraged the expanding European economy to make massive foreign investments beginning about 1840. By the outbreak of the First World War in 1914, Europeans had invested more than $40 billion abroad. In the decade before 1914, Great Britain was investing 7 percent of its annual national income abroad, or slightly more than it was investing in its entire domestic economy. The great gap in income between rich and poor within Europe meant that the wealthy and moderately well-to-do could and did send great sums abroad in search of interest and dividends.

Most of the capital exported did not go to European colonies or protectorates in Asia and Africa. About three-quarters of total European investment went to other European countries, the United States and Canada, Australia and New Zealand, and Latin America. Europe found its most profitable opportunities for investment in construction of the railroads, ports, and utilities that were necessary to settle and develop the lands of extensive European settlement. Much of this investment was peaceful and mutually beneficial for lenders and borrowers. The victims were Native American Indians and Australian Aborigines, who were displaced and decimated by the diseases, liquor, and weapons of an aggressively expanding Western society (see Chapter 28).

## The Great Migration

A poignant human drama was interwoven with economic expansion: millions of people pulled up stakes and left their ancestral lands in the course of history's greatest migration. For millions of ordinary people this great movement was the central experience in the saga of Western expansion.

In the early eighteenth century the world's population entered a period of rapid growth, which continued unabated through the nineteenth and twentieth centuries,

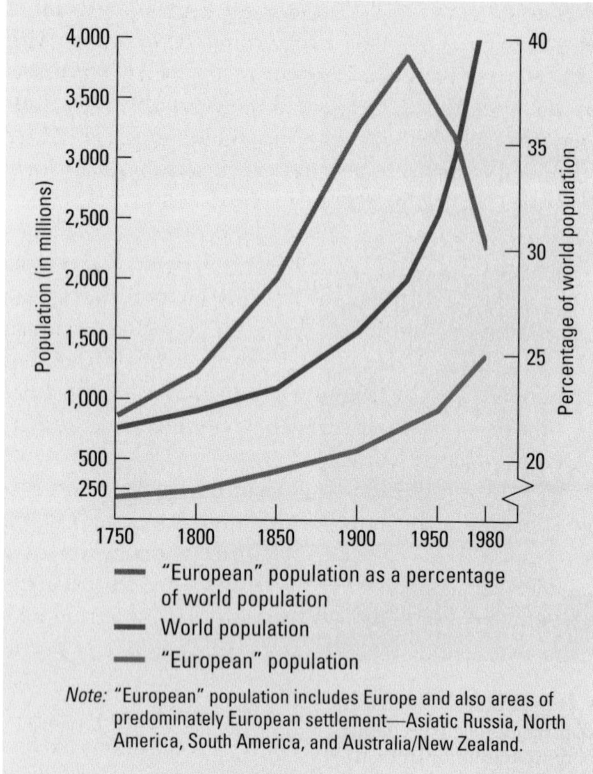


**FIGURE 26.2 The Increase of European and World Populations, 1750–1980** *(Sources: W. Woodruff,* Impact of Western Man: A Study of Europe's Role in the World Economy. *St. Martin's Press, New York, 1967, p. 103; United Nations,* Statistical Yearbook, 1982, *pp. 2–3.)*

as Figure 26.2 shows. The population of Europe (including Asiatic Russia) more than doubled, from approximately 188 million in 1800 to roughly 432 million in 1900. These figures actually understate Europe's population explosion, for between 1815 and 1932 more than 60 million people left Europe, primarily for the rapidly growing "areas of European settlement"—North and South America, Australia, New Zealand, and Siberia (see Chapter 28). North America (the United States and Canada) alone grew from 6 million to 81 million between 1800 and 1900 because of continual immigration and high fertility rates.

Between 1750 and 1900 the population of Asia followed the same general trend, as scholars now realize. China, by far the world's most populous country in the middle of the eighteenth century, increased from about 143 million in 1741 to a little more than 400 million in the 1840s, although total numbers grew more slowly in the turbulent late nineteenth century. Since population increased more slowly in Africa and Asia than in Europe, Europeans and people of European origin jumped from about 22 percent of the world's total in 1850 to about 38 percent in 1930, as Figure 26.2 shows.

The growing number of Europeans was a driving force behind emigration and Western expansion. The rapid increase in numbers led to relative overpopulation in area after area in Europe. Thus millions of country folk went abroad as well as to nearby cities in search of work and economic opportunity.

European emigration crested in the first decade of the twentieth century, when more than five times as many men and women departed as in the 1850s. The United States absorbed the largest number of European migrants, but slightly more than half of all migrants went to Asiatic Russia, Canada, Argentina, Brazil, and Australia. The common American assumption that European migration meant migration to the United States is quite inaccurate.

What kind of people left Europe, and what were their reasons for leaving? The European migrant was most often a small peasant landowner or a village craftsman whose traditional way of life was threatened by too little land, estate agriculture, and cheap factory-made goods. Thus the European migrant was generally an energetic small farmer or skilled artisan trying hard to stay ahead of poverty, not a desperately impoverished landless peasant or urban proletarian. Determined to maintain or improve their status, the vast majority of migrants were young and very often unmarried. They came in the prime of life and were ready to work hard in their new lands, at least for a time. Many Europeans were truly migrants as opposed to immigrants—that is, they returned home after some time abroad. One in two migrants to Argentina and probably one in three to the United States eventually returned to their native land.

Ties of family and friendship played a crucial role in the movement of peoples. Many people from a given province or village settled together in rural enclaves or tightly knit urban neighborhoods thousands of miles away. Very often a strong individual—a businessman, a religious leader—would blaze the way and others would follow, forming a **migration chain.**

Many young European men and women were spurred to leave by a spirit of revolt and independence. In Sweden and Norway, in Jewish Russia and Italy, these young people felt frustrated by the small privileged classes that often controlled both church and government and resisted demands for change and greater opportunity. Many a young Norwegian seconded the passionate cry of Norway's national poet, Bjørnstjerne Bjørnson (1832–1910): "Forth will I! Forth! I will be crushed and consumed if I stay."[1] Thus migration was also a radical way to "get out from under." Migration slowed when people won basic political and social reforms, such as the right to vote and social security.

A substantial number of Asians—especially Chinese, Japanese, Indians, and Filipinos—also responded to population pressure and rural hardship with temporary or permanent migration. At least 3 million Asians (as opposed to more than 60 million Europeans) moved abroad before 1920. Most went as indentured laborers to work under incredibly difficult conditions on the plantations or in the gold mines of Latin America, southern Asia, Africa, California, Hawaii, and Australia (see Chapter 27). White estate owners very often used Asians to replace or supplement blacks after the suppression of the Atlantic slave trade.

Such migration from Asia would undoubtedly have grown to much greater proportions if planters and mine owners in search of cheap labor had had their way. But usually they did not. Asians fled the plantations and gold mines as soon as possible, seeking greater opportunities in trade and towns. There they came into conflict with white settlers in areas of European settlement. These settlers demanded a halt to Asian immigration. By the 1880s Americans and Australians were building **great white walls**—discriminatory laws designed to keep Asians out.

A critical factor in the migrations before 1914 was, therefore, the general policy of "whites only" in the lands of large-scale European settlement. Europeans and people of European ancestry reaped the main benefits of the great migration. By 1913 people in Australia, Canada, and the United States all had higher average incomes than people in Great Britain, still Europe's wealthiest nation. This, too, was part of Western dominance in the increasingly lopsided world.

Within Asia and Africa the situation was different. Migrants from south China frequently settled in Dutch, British, and French colonies of Southeast Asia, where they established themselves as peddlers and small shopkeepers (see Chapter 27). These "overseas Chinese" gradually

**Vaccinating Migrants Bound for Hawaii, 1904** First Chinese, then Japanese, and finally Koreans and Filipinos went in large numbers across the Pacific to labor in Hawaii on American-owned sugar plantations in the late nineteenth century. The native Hawaiians had been decimated by disease, preparing the way for the annexation of Hawaii by the United States in 1898. *(Corbis)*

**Splitting Up Africa** Beginning with Britain's seizure of Egypt in 1882, France and Britain competed furiously for African territory. This 1904 cartoon summarizes some of this battle. France and Britain pull the continent apart, as France (*on the left*) grabs Algeria and Morocco and Britain tears off Egypt and East Africa. *(The Granger Collection, New York)*

emerged as a new class of entrepreneurs and officeworkers. Traders from India and modern-day Lebanon performed the same function in much of sub-Saharan Africa after the European seizure in the late nineteenth century. Thus in some parts of Asia and Africa the business class was both Asian and foreign, protected and tolerated by Western imperialists who found them useful.

While migration from Europe, and to a lesser extent Asia, increased in the nineteenth century, the total flow of enslaved men and women out of Africa declined only moderately in these years. The decline began in the 1830s and continued at an accelerating pace until the 1890s, when the export of African slaves had been greatly reduced. The gradual passing of the long-standing and massive forced migration of Africans to the Americas had many far-reaching consequences for African societies, as we shall see.

## WESTERN IMPERIALISM, 1880–1914

Western expansion into Asia and Africa reached its apex between about 1880 and 1914. In those years the leading European nations continued to send streams of money and manufactured goods to both continents, and they also rushed to create or enlarge vast political empires abroad. This frantic political empire building contrasted sharply with the economic penetration of non-Western territories between 1816 and 1880, which, albeit by naked military force, had left a China or a Japan "opened" but politically independent. By contrast, the empires of the late nineteenth century recalled the old European colonial empires of the seventeenth and eighteenth centuries and led contemporaries to speak of the "new imperialism."

The most spectacular manifestation of the new imperialism was the seizure of Africa, which broke sharply with previous patterns and fascinated contemporary Europeans and Americans. As late as 1878 European nations controlled less than 10 percent of the African continent, and their possessions were hardly increasing (see Map 26.1). In addition to French conquests in Algeria and Dutch and British settlers in southern Africa, European trading posts and forts dating back to the Age of Discovery and the slave trade dotted the coast of West Africa. The Portuguese proudly but ineffectively held their old possessions in Angola and Mozambique. Elsewhere over the great mass of the continent, Europeans did not rule.

Between 1880 and 1900 the situation changed drastically, and by 1900 nearly the whole African continent had been carved up and placed under European rule. In the years before 1914 the European powers tightened their control and established colonial governments to rule their gigantic empires (see Map 26.2 on page 848).

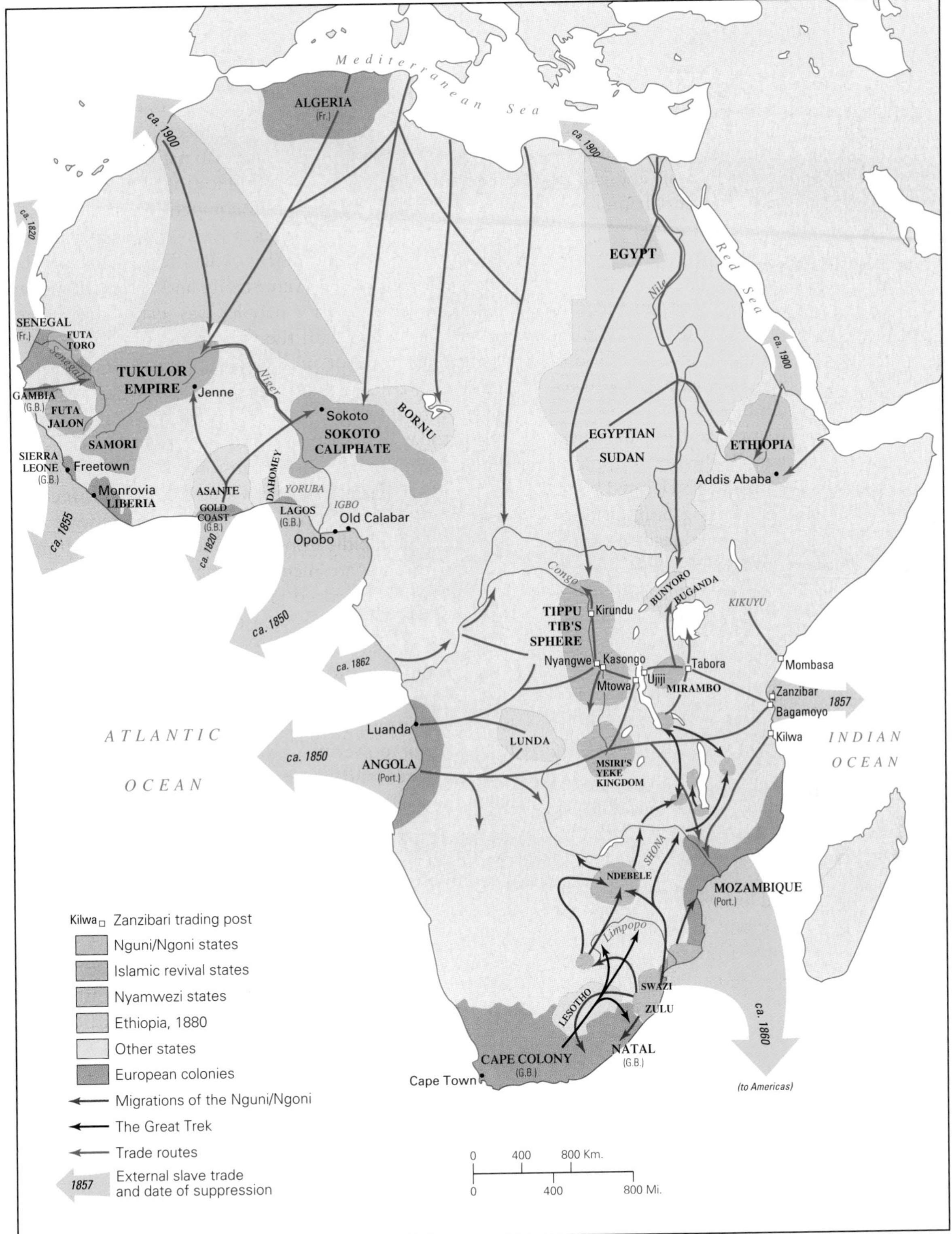


**MAP 26.1 Africa, 1800–1878** The export of African slaves declined gradually in the early nineteenth century and by 1860 it was greatly reduced. Islamic reformers forged stronger states in West Africa, and Arab traders and Nyamwezi elites built informal empires in central Africa. In 1878 European settlement was limited to Algeria, southern Africa, and a few scattered outposts on the Atlantic coast.

Although the sudden division of Africa was more spectacular, Europeans also extended their political control in Asia. The British expanded from their base in India, and in the 1880s the French took Indochina (modern Vietnam, Cambodia, and Laos). India and China also experienced a profound imperialist impact (see Chapter 27).

## Causes of the New Imperialism

Many factors contributed to the West's late-nineteenth-century rush for territory and empire, and it is little wonder that controversies have raged over interpretation of the new imperialism. But despite complexity and controversy, basic causes are clearly identifiable.

Economic motives played an important role in the extension of political empires, especially the British Empire. By the late 1870s France, Germany, and the United States were industrializing rapidly behind rising tariff barriers. Great Britain was losing its early lead and facing increasingly tough competition in foreign markets. In this new economic situation Britain came to value more highly its old possessions, especially its vast colony in India, which it had exploited most profitably for more than a century. When European continental powers began to grab any and all unclaimed territory in the 1880s, the British followed suit immediately. They feared that France and Germany would seal off their empires with high tariffs and restrictions and that future economic opportunities would be lost forever.

Actually, the overall economic gains of the new imperialism proved quite limited before 1914. The new colonies were simply too poor to buy much, and they offered few immediately profitable investments. Nonetheless, colonies became important for political and diplomatic reasons. Each leading European country saw colonies as crucial to national security, military power, and international prestige. For instance, safeguarding the Suez Canal played a key role in the British occupation of Egypt, and protecting Egypt in turn led to the bloody conquest of the Sudan, as we shall see. Far-flung possessions guaranteed ever-growing navies the safe havens and the dependable coaling stations they needed in times of crisis or war.

Many people convinced themselves that colonies were essential to great nations. "There has never been a great power without great colonies," wrote one French publicist in 1877. "Every virile people has established colonial power," echoed the famous nationalist historian of Germany, Heinrich von Treitschke. "All great nations in the fullness of their strength have desired to set their mark upon barbarian lands and those who fail to participate in this great rivalry will play a pitiable role in time to come."[2]

Treitschke's harsh statement reflects not only the increasing aggressiveness of European nationalism after Bismarck's wars of German unification but also Social Darwinian theories of brutal competition among races. Thus European nations, which were seen as racially distinct parts of the dominant white race, had to seize colonies to show they were strong and virile. Moreover, the conquest of inferior peoples was just. "The path of progress is strewn with the wreck . . . of inferior races," wrote one professor in 1900. "Yet these dead peoples are, in very truth, the stepping stones on which mankind has risen to the higher intellectual and deeper emotional life of today."[3] Social Darwinism and harsh racial doctrines fostered imperialist expansion.

So did the industrial world's unprecedented technological and military superiority. Three aspects were crucial. First, the rapidly firing machine gun was an ultimate weapon in many an unequal battle. Second, newly discovered **quinine** proved effective in controlling attacks of malaria, which had previously decimated Europeans in the tropics whenever they left breezy coastal enclaves and dared to venture into mosquito-infested interiors. Third, the combination of the steamship and the international telegraph permitted Western powers to quickly concentrate their firepower in a given area when it was needed. Never before—and never again after 1914—would the technological gap between the West and non-Western regions of the world be so great.

Social tensions and domestic political conflicts also contributed mightily to overseas expansion, according to a prominent interpretation of recent years. In Germany, Russia, and other countries to a lesser extent, conservative political leaders were charged with manipulating colonial issues in order to divert popular attention from the class struggle at home and to create a false sense of national unity. Therefore, imperial propagandists relentlessly stressed that colonies benefited workers as well as capitalists, providing jobs and cheap raw materials that raised workers' standard of living. Government leaders and their allies in the tabloid press successfully encouraged the masses to savor foreign triumphs and glory in the supposed increase in national prestige.

Finally, certain special-interest groups in each country were powerful agents of expansion. Shipping companies wanted lucrative subsidies. White settlers on turbulent frontiers constantly demanded more land and greater protection. Missionaries and humanitarians wanted to

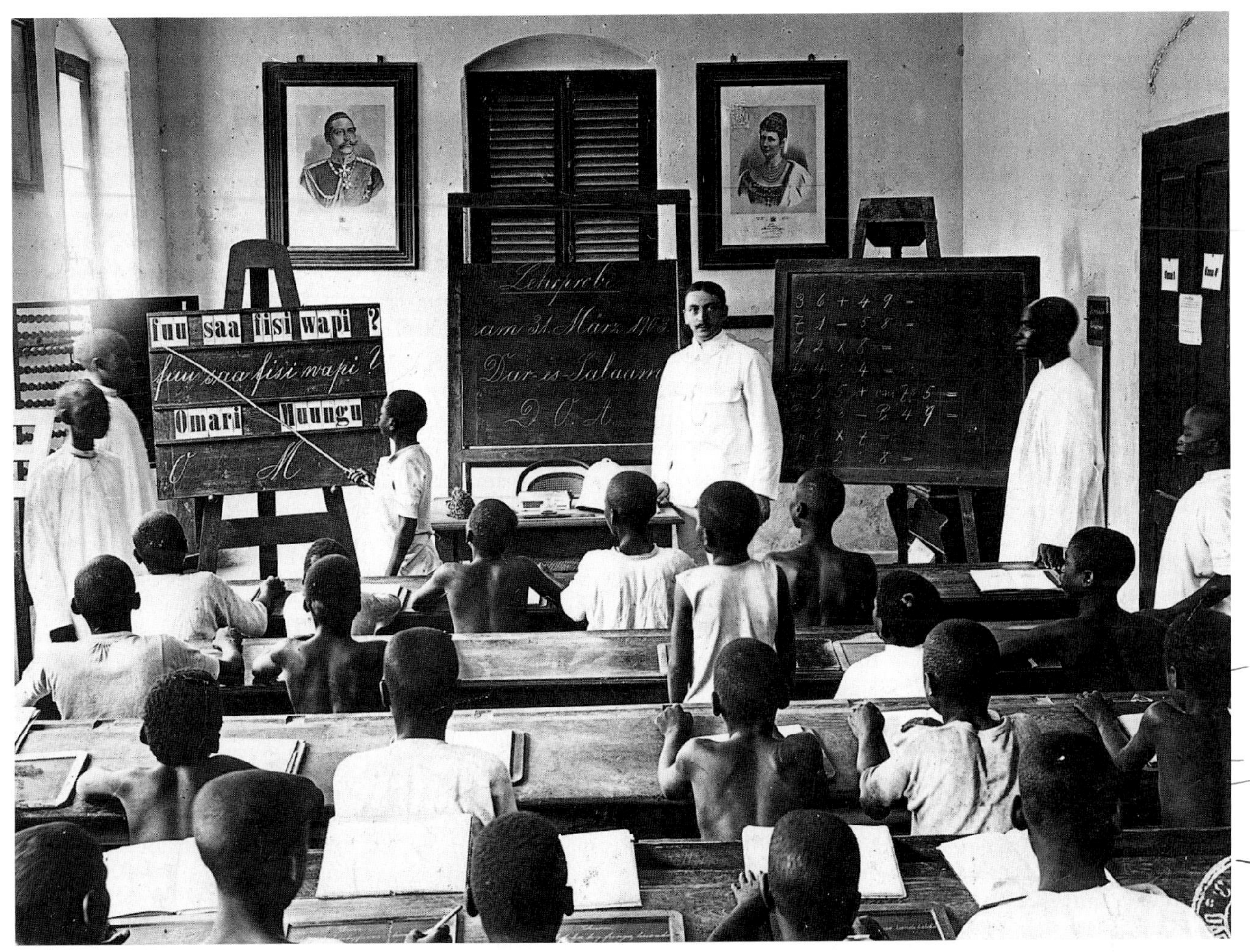


**A Missionary School** A Swahili schoolboy leads his classmates in a reading lesson in Dar es Salaam in German East Africa before 1914, as portraits of Emperor William II and his wife look down on the classroom. Europeans argued that they were spreading the benefits of a superior civilization with schools like this one, which is unusually solid because of its strategic location in the capital city. *(Ullstein Bilderdienst)*

spread Christianity and stop the slave trade. Military men and colonial officials foresaw rapid advancement and high-paid positions in growing empires. The actions of such groups and the determined individuals who led them thrust the course of empire forward.

Western society did not rest the case for empire solely on naked conquest and a Darwinian racial struggle or on power politics and the need for naval bases on every ocean. Imperialists developed additional arguments to satisfy their consciences and answer their critics. A favorite idea was that Europeans and Americans could and should "civilize" supposedly primitive, non-Western peoples. According to this view, Africans and Asians would receive the benefits of modern economies, cities, advanced medicine, and higher standards of living and eventually might be ready for self-government and Western democracy.

Another argument was that imperial government protected colonized peoples from ethnic warfare and the slave trade within Africa, as well as from cruder forms of exploitation by white settlers and business people. Thus the French spoke of their sacred "civilizing mission." Rudyard Kipling (1865–1936), who wrote extensively on Anglo-Indian life and was perhaps the most influential

British writer of the 1890s, exhorted Europeans to unselfish service in distant lands:

*Take up the White Man's Burden—*
*Send forth the best ye breed—*
*Go bind your sons to exile*
*To serve your captives' need,*
*To wait in heavy harness,*
*On fluttered folk and wild—*
*Your new-caught, sullen peoples*
*Half-devil and half-child.*[4]

Another rationalization for the new imperialism was that peace and stability under European control would permit the spread of Christianity. In Africa Catholic and Protestant missionaries competed with Islam south of the Sahara, seeking converts and building schools to spread the Gospel. Many Africans' first real contact with Europeans and Americans was in mission schools. Some peoples, such as the Ibo in Nigeria, became highly Christianized. Such occasional successes in black Africa contrasted with the general failure of missionary efforts in the Islamic world and in much of Asia.

## Western Critics of Imperialism

The expansion of empire aroused sharp, even bitter, Western critics. A forceful attack was delivered in 1902, after the unpopular South African War, by radical English economist J. A. Hobson (1858–1940) in his *Imperialism,* a work that influenced Lenin and others. Hobson contended that the rush to acquire colonies was due to the economic needs of unregulated capitalism, particularly the need of the rich to find outlets for their surplus capital. Yet, Hobson argued, imperial possessions did not pay off economically for the home country as a whole. Only unscrupulous special-interest groups profited from them, at the expense of both the European taxpayer and the natives. Moreover, Hobson argued, the quest for empire diverted popular attention away from domestic reform and the need to reduce the great gap between rich and poor at home. These and similar arguments did not appeal to a wide audience, however. Most people then (and now) were sold on the idea that imperialism was economically profitable for the homeland, and a broad and genuine enthusiasm for empire developed among the masses.

Hobson and many Western critics struck home, however, with their moral condemnation of whites imperiously ruling nonwhites. They rebelled against crude Social Darwinian thought. "O Evolution, what crimes are committed in thy name!" cried one foe. Another sardonically coined a new beatitude: "Blessed are the strong, for they shall prey on the weak."[5] Kipling and his kind were lampooned as racist bullies whose rule rested on brutality, racial contempt, and the Maxim machine gun. Polish-born novelist Joseph Conrad (1857–1924), in *Heart of Darkness,* castigated the "pure selfishness" of Europeans in "civilizing" Africa. The main character in the novel, once a liberal European scholar, is corrupted by power in Africa and turns into a savage brute.

Critics charged Europeans with applying a degrading double standard and failing to live up to their own noble ideals. At home Europeans had won or were winning representative government, individual liberties, and a certain equality of opportunity. In their empires Europeans imposed military dictatorships on Africans and Asians; forced them to work involuntarily, almost like slaves; and discriminated against them shamelessly. Only by renouncing imperialism, critics insisted, and giving captive peoples the freedoms idealized in Western society would Europeans be worthy of their traditions. Europeans who denounced the imperialist tide provided colonial peoples with a Western ideology of liberation.

## African and Asian Resistance

To peoples in Africa and Asia, Western expansion represented a disruptive, many-sided assault. Everywhere it threatened traditional ruling classes, economies, and ways of life. Christian missionaries and European secular ideologies challenged established beliefs and values. African and Asian societies experienced a crisis of identity and a general pattern of reassertion, although the details of each people's story varied substantially.

Often the initial response of African and Asian rulers was to try driving the unwelcome foreigners away, as in China and Japan (see Chapter 27). Violent antiforeign reactions exploded elsewhere again and again, but the superior military technology of the industrialized West almost invariably prevailed. Beaten in battle, many Africans and Asians concentrated on preserving their cultural traditions at all costs. Others found themselves forced to reconsider their initial hostility. Some concluded that the West was indeed superior in certain ways and that it was therefore necessary to reform their societies and copy some European achievements. Thus it is possible to think of responses to the Western impact as a spectrum, with **traditionalists** at one end, westernizers or **modernizers** at the other, and many shades of opinion in between. The struggles among these groups were often intense.

With time, however, the modernizers tended to gain the upper hand.

When armed resistance to European domination was thoroughly shattered by superior force, the great majority of Asians and Africans accepted imperial rule. Political participation in non-Western lands was historically limited to small elites, and the masses were used to doing what their rulers told them. In these circumstances Europeans, clothed in power and convinced of their righteousness, governed effectively. They received considerable support from both traditionalists (local chiefs, landowners, and religious leaders) and modernizers (Western-educated professional classes and civil servants).

Nevertheless, imperial rule was in many ways an imposing edifice built on sand. Support for European rule among the conforming and accepting millions was shallow and weak. Thus the conforming masses came to follow with greater or lesser enthusiasm a few determined personalities who came to oppose the Europeans. Such leaders always arose, both when Europeans ruled directly and when they manipulated native governments, for at least two basic reasons.

First, the nonconformists—the eventual anti-imperialist leaders—developed a burning desire for human dignity. They came to feel that such dignity was incompatible with foreign rule, with its smirks and smiles, its paternalism and condescension. Second, potential leaders found in the Western world the ideologies and justification for their protest. Thus they discovered liberalism, with its credo of civil liberty and political self-determination. They echoed the demands of anti-imperialists in Europe and America that the West live up to its own ideals.

More important, they found themselves attracted to the nineteenth-century Western ideology of nationalism, which asserted that every people—or at least every European people—had the right to control its own destiny. After 1917 anti-imperialist revolt would find another weapon in Lenin's version of Marxian socialism. Thus the anti-imperialist quest for dignity and equality eventually drew strength from Western culture.

## THE ISLAMIC HEARTLAND UNDER PRESSURE

Stretching from West Africa into southeastern Europe and across West Asia all the way to the East Indies, Islamic civilization competed successfully and continuously with western Europe for centuries. Thus from the seventh to the seventeenth centuries, Muslim forces conquered and ruled many lands, while Muslim economies generally equaled or surpassed those in Europe. Of critical importance, Muslim societies were proud and self-confident because they believed in the truth and the superiority of their faith. Muslims acknowledged that the ancient Hebrews and the Christians had experienced divine but imperfect revelations about monotheism and the one God. But only Muhammad had received the final, complete revelation from God, thereby making the true nature of the one God accessible to the community of the Muslim faithful. This self-confidence in their faith helps explain why Muslim rulers generally tolerated their Christian and Jewish subjects and permitted them both to practice their religions, albeit at the cost of moderate discrimination in taxation and economic opportunity. Only animists who believed in many gods and spirits were forced to convert to Islam.

Beginning in the late seventeenth century, the rising absolutist states of Austria and Russia began to challenge the greatest Muslim state, the vast Ottoman Empire, and gradually reverse Ottoman rule in southeastern Europe. In the nineteenth century European industrialization and nation building further altered the long-standing balance of power, and Western expansion eventually posed a serious challenge to Muslims everywhere. In the words of Albert Hourani, a leading historian, "Muslim states and societies could no longer live in a stable and self-sufficient system of inherited culture; their need was now to generate the strength to survive in a world dominated by others."[6]

In close contact with Europe and under constant European pressure, the ruling elites both in the Ottoman Empire and in Egypt, a largely independent Ottoman province, led the way in trying to generate the strength to survive. The ongoing military crisis required, first of all, wrenching army reforms on Western lines in order to defend and preserve the state. These military reforms then snowballed into a series of innovations in education, which created modern schools and skilled specialists as well as army officers and had a powerful cultural impact on Ottoman and Egyptian elites. Western interests and governments also pushed for the adoption of the entire Western liberal creed—that is, the West demanded free trade, constitutional government, civil liberties, and equal rights for all religious groups. Western ideas challenged the superiority of Islam and undermined the traditional Muslim self-confidence.

The results of all these pressures and the momentous changes they brought were profound and paradoxical. On the one hand, the Ottoman Empire and Egypt did

**Pasha Halim Receiving Archduke Maximilian of Austria** As this painting suggests, Ottoman leaders became well versed in European languages and culture. They also mastered the game of power politics, playing one European state off against another and securing the Ottoman Empire's survival. The black servants on the right may be slaves from the Sudan. *(Miramare Palace Trieste/Dagli Orti/The Art Archive)*

achieve considerable modernization on Western lines. On the other hand, these impressive accomplishments never came fast enough to offset the growing power and appetite of the West. The Islamic heartland in West Asia and North Africa fell increasingly under foreign control. Only in the twentieth century did parts of the Islamic world escape Western economic and political domination.

## Decline and Reform in the Ottoman Empire

Although the Ottoman Empire began to decline slowly after reaching its high point of development under Suleiman the Magnificent in the sixteenth century (see pages 628–641), the relationship between the Ottomans and the Europeans in about 1750 was still one of roughly equal strength. However, in the later eighteenth century this situation began to change quickly and radically. The Ottomans fell behind western Europe in science, industrial skill, and military technology, thereby opening up a gap that would increase throughout the nineteenth century. At the same time, absolutist Russia and its powerful westernized army pushed southward between 1768 and 1774, overrunning and occupying Ottoman provinces on the Danube River and inflicting a decisive defeat on the sultan's once mighty forces. Ottoman weakness was clear. The danger that the Great Powers of Europe would gradually conquer the Ottoman Empire and divide up its vast territories was real.

Caught up in the Napoleonic wars and losing more territory to Russia, the Ottomans were forced in 1816 to grant Serbia local autonomy. In 1821 the Greeks revolted against Ottoman rule, and in 1830 they won their national independence. Facing uprisings by their Christian subjects in Europe, the Ottomans also failed to defend their Islamic provinces in North Africa. In 1830

French armies began their long and bloody conquest of the Arabic-speaking province of Algeria. By 1860, 200,000 French, Italian, and Spanish colonists had settled among the Muslim majority, which had been reduced to about 2.5 million by the war against the French and related famines and epidemics. The European immigrants wanted Algeria to become entirely French. They even argued that there was "no longer an Arab people," but only men and women "who talk a different language than ours."[7] French efforts to strip Algerians of their culture and identity were brutal and persistent, eventually resulting in one of Africa's most bitter anticolonial struggles after 1945.

Ottoman weakness reflected the decline of the sultan's "slave army," the so-called **janissary corps.** In the sixteenth century the Ottoman sultans levied an annual slave tax of one thousand to three thousand male children on the conquered Christian provinces in the Balkans. The boys and other slaves were raised in Turkey as Muslims, trained to fight and administer, and joined the elite corps of the Ottoman infantry. With time, however, the janissaries became a corrupt and privileged hereditary caste. They zealously pursued their own interests and refused any military innovations that might undermine their high status.

A transformation of the army was absolutely necessary to battle the Europeans more effectively, as well as to enhance the sultanate's authority within the empire. The empire was no longer a centralized military state with provincial governors firmly controlled from the capital. Instead, local governors were becoming increasingly independent, pursuing their own interests and even seeking to establish their own governments and hereditary dynasties.

The energetic sultan Selim III (r. 1789–1807) understood these realities, but when he tried to reorganize the army, the janissaries refused to use any "Christian" equipment. In 1807 they revolted, and Selim was quickly executed in a palace revolution, one of many that plagued the Ottoman state. The reform-minded Mahmud III (r. 1808–1839) proceeded cautiously, picking loyal officers and building up his dependable artillery corps. In 1826 his council ordered the janissaries to drill in the European manner. As expected, the janissaries revolted and charged the palace, where they were mowed down by the waiting artillery corps.

The destruction and abolition of the janissaries cleared the way for building a new army, but it came too late to stop the rise of Muhammad Ali, the Ottoman governor in Egypt (see the next section). In 1831 his French-trained forces occupied the Ottoman province of Syria and appeared ready to depose Mahmud II. The Ottoman sultan survived, but only by begging Europe for help. Britain, Russia, and Austria responded and forced Muhammad Ali to stop his military campaign. Succeeding in reestablishing direct rule over the province of Iraq, the overconfident Ottomans were saved again in 1839 after their forces were routed trying to drive Muhammad Ali from Syria. Britain, backed by Russia and Austria, compelled France to abandon its Egyptian ally, and it forced Muhammad Ali to return Syria and Arabia to the Ottomans. The European powers, minus France, preferred a weak and dependent Ottoman state to a strong and revitalized Muslim entity under a dynamic leader such as Muhammad Ali.

Realizing their precarious position, liberal Ottoman statesmen launched in 1839 an era of radical reforms, which lasted with fits and starts until 1876 and culminated in a constitution and a short-lived parliament. Known as the **Tanzimat** (literally, regulations or orders), these reforms were designed to remake the empire on a western European model. The new decrees called for the equality of Muslims, Christians, and Jews before the law and in business, security of life and property, and a modernized administration and military. New commercial laws allowed free importation of foreign goods, as British advisers demanded, and permitted foreign merchants to operate freely throughout an economically dependent empire. Under heavy British pressure, slavery in the empire was drastically curtailed, though not abolished completely.

Of great importance for later developments, the reform era brought profound cultural changes, which gathered speed until World War I. Growing numbers among the elite and the upwardly mobile embraced Western education, adopted Western manners and artistic styles, and accepted secular values to some extent.

Intended to bring revolutionary modernization such as that experienced by Russia under Peter the Great (see pages 554–556) and Japan in the Meiji era (see pages 874–878), the Tanzimat permitted partial recovery. Yet the Ottoman state and society failed to regain its earlier strength, for several reasons. First, implementation of the reforms required a new generation of well-trained and trustworthy officials, and that generation did not exist. Second, the liberal reforms failed to halt the growth of nationalism among Christian subjects in the Balkans (see Chapter 29), which resulted in crises and defeats that undermined all reform efforts. Third, the Ottoman initiatives did not curtail the appetite of Western imperialism. For example, European bankers gained a usurious stranglehold on Ottoman finances. In 1875 the Ottoman state had to declare partial bankruptcy and place its finances in the hands of European creditors.

Finally, the elaboration—at least on paper—of equal rights for citizens and religious communities did not create greater unity within the state. Indeed, religious disputes increased, worsened by the relentless interference of the Great Powers. This development embittered relations between the religious communities, distracted the government from its reform mission, and split Muslims into secularists and religious conservatives. Many conservative Muslims detested the religious reforms, which they saw as an impious departure from Islamic tradition and holy law. These Islamic conservatives became the most dependable support of Sultan Abdülhamid (r. 1876–1909), who abandoned the model of European liberalism in his long and repressive reign.

The combination of declining international power and conservative tyranny eventually led to a powerful resurgence of the modernizing impulse among idealistic Turkish exiles in Europe and young army officers in Istanbul. These fervent patriots, the so-called **Young Turks,** seized power in the revolution of 1908, and they forced the sultan to implement reforms. Failing to stop the rising tide of anti-Ottoman nationalism in the Balkans, the Young Turks helped to prepare the way for the birth of modern secular Turkey after the defeat and collapse of the Ottoman Empire in World War I (see pages 974–976).

## Egypt: From Reform to British Occupation

Of great importance in African and Middle Eastern history, the ancient land of the pharaohs had been ruled by a succession of foreigners since 525 B.C.E., most recently conquered by the Ottoman Turks in the early sixteenth century. In 1798 French armies under the young General Napoleon Bonaparte invaded the Egyptian part of the Ottoman Empire and occupied the territory for three years as part of the war with Britain. Into the power vacuum left by the French withdrawal stepped an extraordinary Albanian-born Turkish general, **Muhammad Ali** (1769–1849).

First appointed governor of Egypt by the Turkish sultan, Muhammad Ali set out to build his own state on the strength of a large, powerful army organized along European lines. In 1820–1822 the Egyptian leader conquered much of the Sudan to secure slaves for his army, and thousands of African slaves were brought to Egypt during his reign. Because many slaves died in Egyptian captivity, Muhammad Ali turned to drafting Egyptian peasants. He also reformed the government and energetically promoted modern industry. (See the feature "Individuals in Society: Muhammad Ali: Egyptian Hero or Ottoman Adventurer?") For a time Muhammad Ali's ambitious strategy seemed to work, but it eventually floundered when he was defeated by his Ottoman overlords and their British allies. Nevertheless, by the time of his death in 1849, Muhammad Ali had established a strong and virtually independent Egyptian state to be ruled by his family on a hereditary basis within the Turkish empire.

To pay for a modern army and the industrialization effort, Muhammad Ali encouraged the development of commercial agriculture geared to the European market. This development had profound social implications. Egyptian peasants had been poor but largely self-sufficient, growing food on state-owned land allotted to them by tradition. Offered the possibility of profits from export agriculture, high-ranking officials and members of Muhammad Ali's family began carving large private landholdings out of the state domain, and they forced the peasants to grow cash crops for European markets. Ownership of land became very unequal. By 1913, 12,600 large estates owned 44 percent of the land and 1.4 million peasants owned only 27 percent. Egyptian estate owners "modernized" agriculture, but to the detriment of peasant well-being.

Muhammad Ali's policies of modernization attracted growing numbers of Europeans to the banks of the Nile. As one Arab sheik of the Ottoman Empire remarked in the 1830s, "Englishmen are like ants; if one finds a bit of meat, hundreds follow."[8] By 1863, when Muhammad Ali's grandson Ismail began his sixteen-year rule as Egypt's *khedive,* or prince, the port city of Alexandria had more than fifty thousand Europeans. Europeans served not only as army officers but also as engineers, doctors, high government officials, and police officers. Others found their "meat" in trade, finance, and shipping. Above all, Europeans living in Egypt combined with landlords and officials to continue the development of commercial agriculture geared to the needs of Europe. By the early twentieth century about 200,000 Europeans lived in Egypt and accounted for 2 percent of the population. As throughout the Ottoman Empire, Europeans enjoyed important commercial and legal privileges and formed an economic elite.

Educated at France's leading military academy, Ismail (r. 1863–1879) was a westernizing autocrat. Although his grandfather's efforts to industrialize Egypt had failed, Ismail still dreamed of using European technology and capital to modernize Egypt and build a vast empire in northeast Africa. He concentrated on agriculture, and the large irrigation networks he promoted caused cotton production and exports to Europe to boom. Ismail also borrowed large sums to install modern communications,

# INDIVIDUALS IN SOCIETY

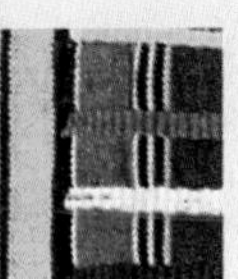

## MUHAMMAD ALI: EGYPTIAN HERO OR OTTOMAN ADVENTURER?

The dynamic leader Muhammad Ali (1769–1849) stands across the history of modern Egypt like a colossus. Yet the essence of the man remains a mystery, and historians vary greatly in their interpretations of him.

Sent by the Ottomans, with Albanian troops, to oppose the French occupation of Egypt in 1799, Muhammad Ali maneuvered skillfully after the French withdrawal in 1802. In 1805 he was named *pasha,* or Ottoman governor, of Egypt. Only the Mamluks remained as rivals. Originally an elite corps of Turkish slave-soldiers, the Mamluks had become a semifeudal military ruling class living off the Egyptian peasantry. In 1811 Muhammad Ali offered to make peace, and he invited the Mamluk chiefs and their retainers to a banquet in Cairo's Citadel. As the unsuspecting guests processed through a narrow passage, his troops opened fire, slaughtering all the Mamluk leaders.

After eliminating his foes, Muhammad Ali embarked on a program of radical reforms. He reorganized agriculture and commerce, reclaiming most of the cultivated land for the state domain, which he controlled. He also established state agencies to monopolize, for his own profit, the sale of agricultural goods. Commercial agriculture geared to exports to Europe developed rapidly, especially after the successful introduction of high-quality cotton in 1821. Canals and irrigation systems along the Nile were rebuilt and expanded.

Muhammad Ali used his growing revenues to recast his army along European lines. He recruited French officers to train the soldiers. As the military grew, so did the need for hospitals, schools of medicine and languages, and secular education. Young Turks and some Egyptians were sent to Europe for advanced study. The ruler boldly financed factories to produce uniforms and weapons, and he prohibited the importation of European goods so as to protect Egypt's infant industries. In the 1830s state factories were making one-fourth of Egypt's cotton into cloth. Above all, Muhammad Ali drafted Egyptian peasants into the military for the first time, thereby expanding his army to 100,000 men. It was this force that conquered the Ottoman province of Syria, threatened the sultan in Istanbul, and triggered European intervention. Grudgingly recognized by his Ottoman overlord as Egypt's hereditary ruler in 1841, Muhammad Ali nevertheless had to accept European and Ottoman demands to give up Syria and abolish his monopolies and protective tariffs. The old ruler then lost heart; his reforms languished, and his factories disappeared.

*Muhammad Ali, the Albanian-born ruler of Egypt, in 1839.* (Aldus Archive/Mirror Syndication International)

In the attempt to understand Muhammad Ali and his significance, many historians have concluded that he was a national hero, the "founder of modern Egypt." His ambitious state-building projects—hospitals, schools, factories, and the army—were the basis for an Egyptian reawakening and eventual independence from the Ottomans' oppressive foreign rule. Similarly, state-sponsored industrialization promised an escape from poverty and Western domination, which was foiled only by European intervention and British insistence on free trade.

A growing minority of historians question these views. They see Muhammad Ali primarily as an Ottoman adventurer. This disobedient Turkish general, they say, did not aim for national independence for Egypt, but rather "intended to carve out a small empire for himself and for his children after him."* Paradoxically, his success, which depended on heavy taxes and brutal army service, did lead to Egyptian nationalism among the Arabic-speaking masses, but that new nationalism was directed *against* Muhammad Ali and his Turkish-speaking entourage. Continuing research into this leader's life will help to resolve these conflicting interpretations.

### QUESTIONS FOR ANALYSIS

1. Which of Muhammad Ali's actions support the interpretation that he was the founder of modern Egypt? Which actions support the opposing view?
2. After you have studied this chapter, compare Muhammad Ali and the Meiji reformers in Japan. What accounts for the similarities and differences?

*K. Fahmy, *All the Pasha's Men: Mehmed Ali, His Army, and the Making of Modern Egypt* (Cambridge: Cambridge University Press, 1997), p. 310.

and with his support the Suez Canal was completed by a French company in 1869. The canal shortened the voyage from Europe to Asia by thousands of miles. Traffic boomed, and the French company became very successful. Like Napoleon III whom he admired, Ismail wanted an impressive, up-to-date capital city. A new Cairo with long straight boulevards, apartment buildings, Western hotels, and an opera house grew up to the west, alongside the medieval maze of twisting lanes, tiny shops, and beautiful historic mosques. Ismail proudly declared, "My country is no longer in Africa, we now form part of Europe."[9]

Major cultural and intellectual changes accompanied the political and economic ones. The Arabic of the masses, rather than the Turkish of the conquerors, became the official language, and young Egyptians educated in Europe helped spread new skills and ideas in the bureaucracy. A host of writers, intellectuals, and religious thinkers responded to the novel conditions with innovative ideas that had a powerful impact in Egypt and in other Muslim societies.

Three influential figures, who represented broad families of thought, were especially significant. The teacher and writer Jamal al-Din al-Afghani (1838/39–1897), who lived in Cairo from 1871 to 1879, preached Islamic regeneration and defense against Western/Christian aggression. Regeneration, he argued, required the purification of religious belief, the unity of all Muslim peoples, and a revolutionary overthrow of corrupt Muslim rulers and foreign exploiters. An inspiring radical, al-Afghani also confidently believed that Islam embodied modern rationalism, and he said that everyone could find self-worth and a sense of equality in Islam.

The more moderate Muhammad Abduh (1849–1905) also searched for Muslim rejuvenation and launched the modern Islamic reform movement, which became very

**British Rule in Egypt** In this 1900 photo, a group of British soldiers enters Cairo's old fortress, the Citadel, with its graceful minarets and Ottoman military architecture. British armies occupied Egypt in 1882, and Egypt lost its political and economic independence. *(Billie Love)*

important in the twentieth century. Abduh concluded that Muslims should return to the purity of the earliest, most essential doctrines of Islam and reject later additions that could limit Muslim creativity. This would permit a flexible, reasoned approach to change, social questions, and foreign ideas.

Finally, the writer Qasim Amin (1863–1908) represented those who found inspiration in the West in the late nineteenth century. In his influential book *The Liberation of Women* (1899), Amin argued forcefully that superior education for European women had contributed greatly to the Islamic world's falling far behind the West. The rejuvenation of Muslim societies required greater equality for women.

Egypt changed more rapidly during Ismail's rule than it had in centuries. But Ismail was too impatient, and his projects were reckless and enormously expensive. By 1876 Egypt owed foreign bondholders a colossal $450 million and could not pay the interest on its debt. Rather than let Egypt go bankrupt and repudiate its loans, as some Latin American countries had done, France and Great Britain intervened politically to protect the European bankers who held the Egyptian bonds. They forced Ismail to appoint French and British commissioners to oversee Egyptian finances so that the Egyptian debt would be paid in full. This was a momentous decision. It implied direct European political control: Europeans were going to determine the state budget and in effect rule Egypt.

Foreign financial control evoked a violent nationalistic reaction among Egyptian religious leaders, young intellectuals, and army officers. In 1879, under the leadership of Colonel Ahmed Arabi, they formed the Egyptian Nationalist party. Continuing diplomatic pressure, which forced Ismail to abdicate in favor of his weak son, Tewfiq (r. 1879–1892), resulted in bloody anti-European riots in Alexandria in 1882. A number of Europeans were killed, and Tewfiq and his court had to flee to British ships for safety. When the British fleet bombarded Alexandria, more riots swept the country, and Colonel Arabi declared that "an irreconcilable war existed between the Egyptians and the English." A British expeditionary force decimated Arabi's forces and occupied all of Egypt.

The British said that their occupation was temporary, but British armies remained in Egypt until 1956. They maintained the façade of the khedive's government as an autonomous province of the Ottoman Empire, but the khedive was a mere puppet. The able British consul, General Evelyn Baring, later Lord Cromer, ruled the country after 1883. Once a vocal opponent of involvement in Egypt, Baring was a paternalistic reformer who had come to believe that "without European interference and initiative reform is impossible here." Baring's rule did result in tax reforms and better conditions for peasants, while foreign bondholders tranquilly received their interest payments and Egyptian nationalists nursed their injured pride.

In Egypt Baring and the British abandoned what some scholars have called the "imperialism of free trade," which was based on economic penetration and indirect rule. Reluctantly but spectacularly, they accepted a new model for European expansion in the densely populated lands of Africa and Asia. Such expansion was based on military force, political domination, and a self-justifying ideology of beneficial reform. This model was to predominate from the 1880s until 1914. Thus did Europe's Industrial Revolution lead to tremendous political as well as economic expansion throughout the world.

## SUB-SAHARAN AFRICA: FROM THE SLAVE TRADE TO EUROPEAN RULE

From the beginning of the nineteenth century to the global depression of the 1930s, the different regions of sub-Saharan Africa experienced gradual but monumental change. The long-standing transatlantic slave trade declined and practically disappeared by the late 1860s. In the early nineteenth century Islam expanded its influence in a long belt south of the Sahara, but Africa generally remained free of European political control. After about 1880 further Islamic expansion to the south stopped, but the pace of change accelerated as France and Britain led European nations in the "scramble for Africa." Africa was divided and largely conquered by Europeans, and by 1900 the foreigners were building imperial systems to consolidate their authoritarian rule. Only in the 1930s did powerful nationalist movements arise, and following World War II African peoples regained their political independence.

### African Trade and Social Change (1800–1880)

The most important development in West Africa before the European conquest was the decline of the Atlantic slave trade and the simultaneous rise of the export of palm oil and other commodities. A major break with the past, the shift in African foreign trade marked the beginning of modern economic development in sub-Saharan Africa.[10]

Although the trade in African people was a worldwide phenomenon, the Atlantic slave trade became the most extensive and significant portion of it. The forced migration of millions of Africans—so cruel, unjust, and tragic—intensified after 1700, and especially after 1750. By the 1780s, shipments of black men and women averaged 80,000 a year, in an attempt to satisfy the constantly rising demand for labor—and slave owner profits—in the Americas. Increasing demand resulted in rising prices for African slaves in the eighteenth century. Some African merchants and rulers who controlled exports profited, and some Africans secured foreign products that they found appealing because of price or quantity. But the negative consequences of the expanding trade predominated in Africa, because warfare increased and enslavement spread.

Until 1700, and perhaps even 1750, almost all Europeans considered the African slave trade a legitimate business activity. Even so, shiploads of African slaves were never landed in northwestern Europe, although blacks did arrive in Britain (and France) as personal slaves. If a slave ran away, the poor and the courts often supported the slave, and many runaways merged into London's growing population of free and escaped blacks. In 1772 a high court ruling "clearly doomed the slave status in England."[11]

After 1775 a much broader campaign to abolish slavery developed in Britain. This campaign grew into one of the first peaceful mass political movements based on the mobilization of public opinion in British history. British women played a critical role in this movement, denouncing the immorality of human bondage and stressing the cruel treatment of female slaves and slave families. In 1807 Parliament declared the slave trade illegal, and Britain began pressuring other nations to do the same. Britain then used its navy to seize the ships of the slave runners, liberating the captives and settling them in the British port of Freetown, in Sierra Leone.

British action had a limited impact at first. The transatlantic slave trade regained its previous massive level after peace returned to Europe in 1815, and it declined only gradually. Britain's African squadron intercepted less than 10 percent of all slave ships, and the demand for slaves remained high on the expanding sugar and coffee plantations of Cuba and Brazil until the 1850s and 1860s. (The United States prohibited the importation of slaves in 1808, and natural increase accounted mainly for the subsequent growth of the African American slave population there before the Civil War.) Strong incentives remained for Portuguese slave traders, as well as for those African rulers who relied on profits from the trade for power and influence.

As the abolitionist movement broadened and more nations joined Britain in outlawing the slave trade, the shipment of human cargo slackened along the West African coast. The decline began on the long stretch from Guinea and Senegal to the Gold Coast and present-day Nigeria by the 1830s and occurred thereafter in west-central Africa, in present-day Congo and Angola (see Map 26.1). At the same time, as a generation of research has shown, the ancient but limited shipment of slaves across the Sahara and from the East African coast into the Indian Ocean and through the Red Sea expanded dramatically. Only in the 1860s did this expanding trade begin to decline rapidly. As a result of these shifting currents, exports of slaves from all of West Africa across the Atlantic declined from an estimated 5.6 million persons in the eighteenth century to 3.5 million in the nineteenth century, a drop of 37.5 percent. Yet total exports of slaves from all regions of sub-Saharan Africa declined less than half as fast in the same years, from 7.4 million to 6.1 million.[12] The abolitionist vision of "legitimate" commerce in tropical products quickly replacing illegal slave exports was not realized.

Nevertheless, beginning in West Africa, trade in tropical products did make steady progress, for several reasons. First, the oil and kernels of naturally growing palm trees already provided food for coastal populations. With Britain encouraging palm tree cultivation as an alternative to the slave trade, **palm oil** sales from West Africa to Britain surged from only 1,000 tons in 1810 to more than 40,000 tons in 1855. Second, the sale of palm oil admirably served the self-interest of industrializing Europe. From palm oil, manufacturers made the first good, cheap soap that ordinary people used in their newfound pursuit of cleanliness, and they mass-produced candles to light people's homes. Third, the production of peanuts for export from West Africa also grew rapidly, in part because small, independent African farmers and their families could compete effectively with large-scale producers in growing peanuts but not in producing palm oil and kernels.

Finally, powerful West African rulers and warlords who had benefited from the Atlantic slave trade succeeded in redirecting some of their slaves into the production of "legitimate" goods for world markets. This was possible because slavery and slave markets remained strong in sub-Saharan Africa, as local warfare and slave raiding continued to enslave large numbers of men, women, and

**Palm Oil for Soap and Power** Europeans, led by the British, encouraged West Africans to stop exporting slaves and start selling palm oil from naturally growing palm trees, as seen on the left. In Europe palm oil was made into soap, which was heavily advertised and endowed with symbols and hidden messages. In this 1890s ad (*right*), the Lifebuoy soap given to British travelers becomes a lifesaving charm warding off danger in foreign lands. *(Left: Corbis; Right: Mary Evans Picture Library)*

children for many uses. Enslaved captives were sold abroad, and they became wives, concubines, and servants. They transported goods, mined gold, grew crops for both African and European markets, and served in slave armies. For example, after the collapse of the Oyo empire, which included the large Yoruba ethnic grouping in present-day Nigeria, Yoruba warlords fought to re-establish a centralized state and enslaved their enemies. By the 1840s the Yoruba elite was developing palm oil plantations worked by slaves, and in some areas of Yorubaland and neighboring Dahomey, slaves became a majority of the population. One Yoruba warlord named Kurumi seized a town, and by 1859 he had 300 wives and a slave army of 1,000 men. By the 1860s and 1870s, 104 families in the city of Ibadan owned 50,000 slaves, an average of 500 per family.[13] As the experience of the Yoruba suggests, the slow decline of the transatlantic slave trade coincided with the most intensive use of slaves within Africa.

At the same time, a new group of African merchants—often liberated slaves from Freetown who had received some Western education—did rise to handle legitimate trade, and some grew rich. By the 1850s and 1860s legitimate African traders, flanked by Western-educated African lawyers, teachers, and journalists, formed an emerging middle class in the coastal towns of West Africa. Standing in clear contrast to African rulers and aristocracies who thrived on slavery, this tiny middle class provided new leadership that augured well for the region's future. Unfortunately for West Africans, in the 1870s big European companies redoubled their efforts to control West Africa's foreign trade. European firms also pressured their governments for support in their dealings with African rulers, which played a small but significant role in the

European seizure of African territory in the 1880s and 1890s. African business leadership then gave way to imperial subordination.

## Islamic Revival and Expansion

In the early eighteenth century Islam had been practiced throughout the Sudanic Savanna—that vast belt of flat grasslands that stretches across Africa below the southern fringe of the Sahara from Senegal and Gambia in the west to the mountains of Ethiopia in the east—for five hundred to a thousand years, depending on the area. The cities, political rulers, and merchants in many small states were Muslim. Yet the peasant farmers and migratory cattle raisers—the vast majority of the population—generally remained true to traditional animist practices, worshiping ancestors, local shrines, and protective spirits. Many Muslim rulers shared some of these beliefs and did not try to convert their subjects in the countryside or enforce Islamic law.

Beginning in the eighteenth century and gathering strength in the early nineteenth century, a powerful Is-

**Islamic Influence in Northern Nigeria** The striking ornamentation on the cement façade of this house is inspired by abstract Arabic handwriting. It attests to the powerful expansion of Islam in sub-Saharan Africa in the nineteenth century. The man's cap and white robe are those of the Hausa, who are predominantly Muslim. *(M & E Bernheim/Woodfin Camp & Associates)*

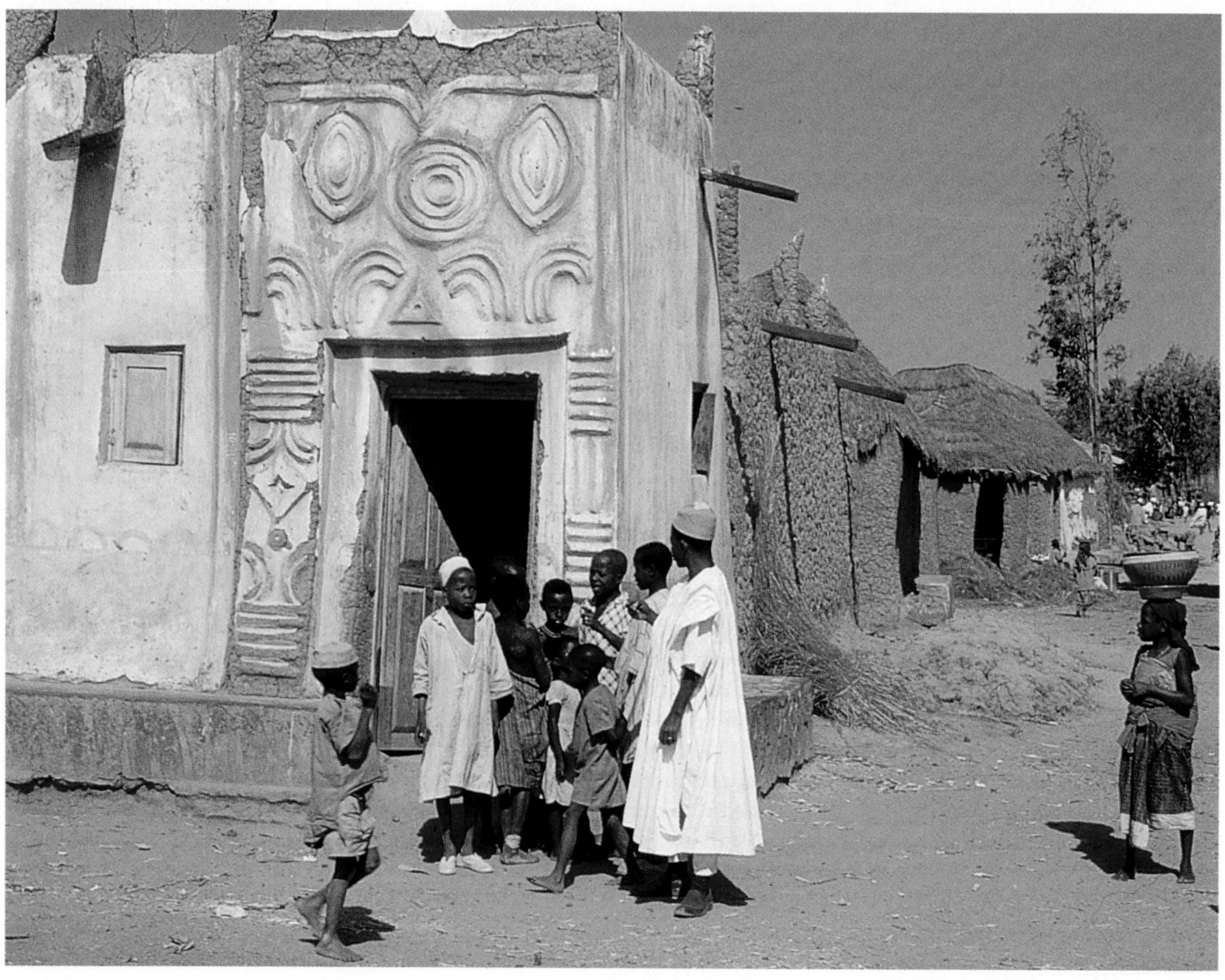

lamic revival brought reform and revolutionary change from within to the western and eastern Sudan, until this process was halted by European military conquest at the end of the nineteenth century. In essence, Muslim scholars and fervent religious leaders arose to wage successful **jihads**, or religious wars, against both animist rulers and Islamic states that they deemed corrupt. The new reformist rulers believed that African cults and religious practice could no longer be tolerated, and they often effected mass conversions of animists to Islam.

The most important of these revivalist states, the enormous **Sokoto caliphate,** illustrates the general pattern. It was founded by Usuman dan Fodio (1754–1817), an inspiring Muslim teacher who first won zealous followers among both the Fulani herders and the Hausa peasants in the Muslim state of Gobir in the northern Sudan. After his religious community was attacked by Gobir's rulers, Usuman launched the jihad of 1804, one of the most important events in nineteenth-century West Africa. Usuman claimed that the Hausa rulers of Muslim Gobir "worshipped many places of idols, and trees, and rocks, and sacrificed to them," killing and plundering their subjects without any regard for Islamic law.[14] Young religious students and discontented Fulani cattle raisers formed the backbone of the fighters, who succeeded in overthrowing the Hausa rulers and inspired more jihads in the Sudan. In 1809 Usuman founded the new Sokoto caliphate, which was ably consolidated by his son Muhammad Bello as a vast and enduring decentralized state.

The triumph of the Sokoto caliphate had profound consequences for Africa and the Sudan. First, the caliphate was based on Islamic history and law, which gave sub-Saharan Africa a sophisticated written constitution that earlier preliterate states had never achieved. This government of laws, not men, provided stability and made Sokoto one of the most prosperous regions in tropical Africa. Second, because of Sokoto and other revivalist states, Islam became much more widely and deeply rooted in sub-Saharan Africa than ever before. By 1880 the entire western and central Sudan was united in Islam. In this vast expanse Islam became an unquestioned part of everyday life and culture. Women gained greater access to education, even as veiling and seclusion became more common. Finally, Islam had always approved of slavery for non-Muslims and Muslim heretics, and "the *jihads* created a new slaving frontier on the basis of rejuvenated Islam."[15] In 1900 the Sokoto caliphate had 1 million and perhaps as many as 2.5 million slaves. Of all modern slave societies, only the American South had more, about 4 million in 1860.

**Tippu Tip, Merchant and Ruler** The most famous of the Arab and Swahili traders from Zanzibar, Tippu Tip acquired great wealth and influence. Raiding for slaves and trading for ivory, he established an informal empire in the eastern Congo. There he and his men assembled large caravans of slaves to carry huge ivory elephant tusks hundreds of miles to Zanzibar, from where the ivory was exported to Asia and Europe. *(Hulton/Getty Images)*

Islam also expanded in East Africa, in large part because of the efforts of Sayyid Said (r. 1804–1856), the energetic imam of Oman. Reviving his family's lordship of the African island of Zanzibar and eventually moving his capital from southern Arabia to Zanzibar in 1840, Said and his Baluchi mercenaries (from present-day Pakistan) gained control of most of the Swahili-speaking East African coast. Said concentrated the shipment of slaves to the Ottoman Empire and Arabia through Zanzibar. In addition, he successfully encouraged Indian merchants to develop slave-based clove plantations in his territories. Thus from the 1820s on, Arab merchants and

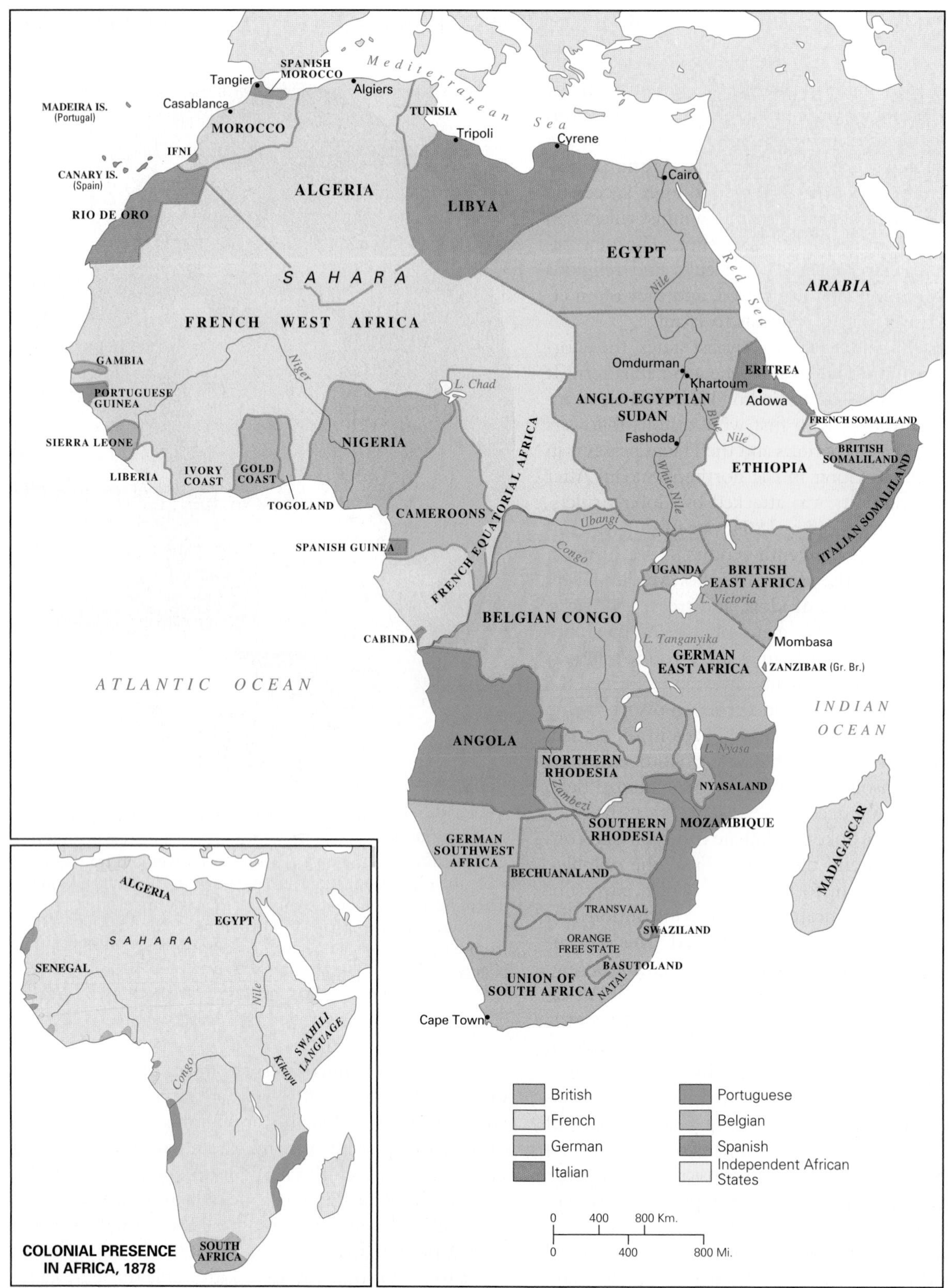


**MAP 26.2 Africa in 1878 and 1914** European nations carved up Africa after 1878 and built vast political empires. Britain and France took the most territory. What African states remained independent?

adventurers pressed far into the interior in search of slaves and ivory, converting and intermarrying with local Nyamwezi elites and establishing small Muslim states. The Arab immigrants brought literacy, administrative skills, and increased trade and international contact, as well as the intensification of slavery, to East Africa. In 1870, before Christian missionaries and Western armies began to arrive in force, it appeared that most of the East African population would accept Islam within a generation.[16]

## The Seizure of Africa (1880–1902)

Between 1880 and 1900 Britain, France, Germany, and Italy scrambled for African possessions as if their national livelihoods were at stake. By 1902 only Ethiopia in northeast Africa and Liberia on the West African coast remained independent (see Map 26.2).

In the complexity of the European seizure of Africa, certain events and individuals stand out. First, as the antislavery movement succeeded in almost completely shutting down the Atlantic slave trade by the late 1860s, the persistence of slavery elsewhere attracted growing attention in Europe. Through the publications of Protestant missionaries such as David Livingstone and the fiery preaching of the Catholic White Fathers, Europeans learned of the horrors of slave raids and the suffering of thousands of innocent victims sold within Africa and through East African ports. The public was led to believe that European rule would end this human tragedy, as well-meaning Protestants and Catholics "provided a moral justification for the conquest of Africa."[17]

Second, **Leopold II** of Belgium (r. 1865–1909), an energetic, strong-willed monarch with a lust for distant territory, played a crucial rule. "The sea bathes our coast, the world lies before us," he had exclaimed in 1861. "Steam and electricity have annihilated distance, and all the non-appropriated lands on the surface of the globe can become the field of our operations and of our success."[18] By 1876 Leopold was focusing on central Africa. Subsequently, he formed a financial syndicate under his personal control to send Henry M. Stanley, a sensation-seeking journalist and part-time explorer, to the Congo basin. Stanley was able to establish trading stations, sign "treaties" with African chiefs, and plant Leopold's flag. Leopold's actions alarmed the French, who quickly sent out an expedition under Pierre de Brazza. In 1880 de Brazza signed a treaty of protection with the chief of the large Teke tribe and began to establish a French protectorate on the north bank of the Congo River. Leopold's buccaneering intrusion into the Congo area raised the question of the political fate of Africa south of the Sahara.

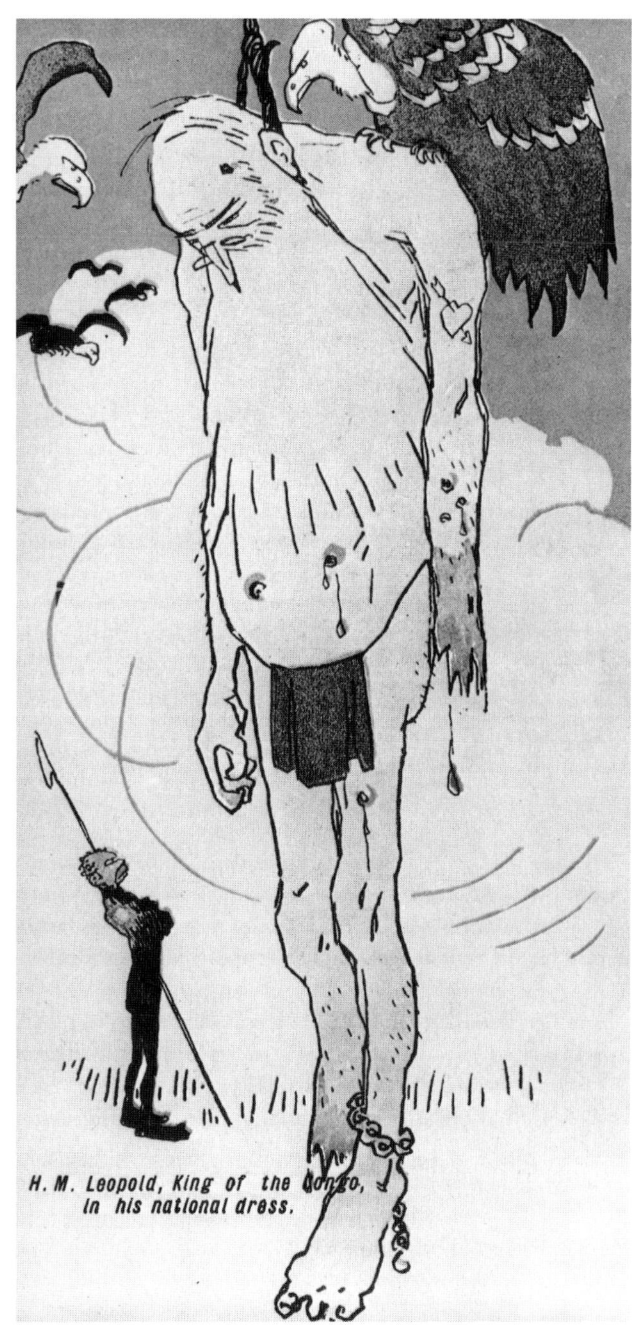

H. M. Leopold, King of the Congo,
in his national dress.


**European Imperialism at Its Worst** This 1908 English cartoon, "Leopold, King of the Congo, in his native dress," focuses on the barbaric practice of cutting off the hands and feet of Africans who refused to gather as much rubber as Leopold's company demanded. In 1908 an international human rights campaign forced the Belgian king to cede his personal fief to the Belgian state. *(Archive of Arnoldo Mondadori Editore, Milan)*

Third, the British invasion and occupation of Egypt in 1882 had enormous importance. It established a new model of imperial conquest and formal political control. By 1883 Europe had caught "African fever." There was a gold-rush mentality, and the race for territory was on.

To lay down some basic rules for this new and dangerous game of imperialist competition, Premier Jules Ferry of France and Chancellor Otto von Bismarck of Germany arranged an international conference on Africa in Berlin in 1884–1885. The **Berlin conference,** at which no Africans were present (nor had any even been invited), established the principle that European claims to African territory had to rest on "effective occupation" in order to be recognized by other states. This principle was very important. It meant that Europeans would push relentlessly into interior regions from all sides and that no single European power would be able to claim the entire continent. The conference recognized Leopold's personal rule over a neutral Congo free state and declared all of the Congo basin a free-trade zone. The conference also agreed to work to stop slavery and the slave trade in Africa.

The Berlin conference coincided with Germany's sudden emergence as an imperial power. Prior to about 1880 Bismarck, like many other European leaders at the time, had seen little value in colonies. Colonies reminded him, he said, of a poor but proud nobleman who wore a fur coat when he could not afford a shirt underneath. Then in 1884 and 1885, as political agitation for expansion increased, Bismarck did an abrupt about-face, and Germany established protectorates over a number of small African kingdoms and societies in Togo, Cameroons, southwest Africa, and, later, East Africa. In acquiring

**Omdurman, 1898** European machine guns cut down the charging Muslim tribesmen again and again. "It was not a battle but an execution," said one witness. Thus the Sudan was conquered and one million square miles were added to the British Empire. *(E.T. Archive)*

colonies, Bismarck cooperated with France's Ferry, who was an ardent and influential imperialist, against the British. (See the feature "Listening to the Past: A French Leader Defends Imperialism" on pages 858–859.) With Bismarck's tacit approval, the French pressed vigorously southward from Algeria, eastward from their old forts on the Senegal coast, and northward from de Brazza's newly formed protectorate on the Congo River.

Meanwhile, the British began enlarging their West African enclaves and forcefully pushing northward from the Cape Colony and westward from the East African coast. Their thrust southward from Egypt was blocked in the eastern Sudan by fiercely independent Muslims, who had felt the full force of Islamic revival. In 1881 a pious local leader, Muhammad Ahmad (1844–1885), declared himself the Mahdi, the expected savior. The Mahdi called for restoration of uncorrupted Islam, and he led a revolt against foreign control of Egypt. In 1885 the Mahdi's army massacred a British force and took the city of Khartoum. The Mahdi himself died in 1885, but his followers maintained the Islamic state that had been established, and the British retreated to Cairo. The Sudanese people were deeply committed to Islam. For them the struggle to preserve Islam and the struggle for freedom were one and the same thing.

The invaders bided their time, and in 1896 a British force under General Horatio H. Kitchener moved cautiously and more successfully up the Nile River, building a railroad to supply arms and reinforcements as it went. Finally, in 1898, these troops met their foe at Omdurman, where Sudanese Muslims armed with spears charged time and time again, only to be cut down by the recently invented machine gun. For one smug participant, the young British officer Winston Churchill, it was "like a pantomime scene" in a play. "These extraordinary foreign figures . . . march up one by one from the darkness of Barbarism to the footlights of civilization . . . and their conquerors, taking their possessions, forget even their names. Nor will history record such trash." For another, more somber English observer, "it was not a battle but an execution. The bodies were not in heaps . . . but they spread evenly over acres and acres."[19] In the end eleven thousand brave but poorly armed Muslim tribesmen lay dead. Only twenty-eight Britons had been killed.

The British conquest of the Sudan exemplified the general process of empire building in Africa. The fate of the Muslim force at Omdurman was eventually inflicted on all colonized peoples who resisted European rule: they were crushed by vastly superior military force. But however much the European powers squabbled for territory and privilege around the world, they always had the sense to stop short of actually fighting each other. Imperial ambitions were not worth a great European war.

## Southern Africa in the Nineteenth Century

The development of southern Africa diverged from the rest of sub-Saharan Africa in important ways. Whites settled in large numbers, modern capitalist industry took off, and British imperialists had to wage all-out war.

In 1652 the Dutch East India Company established a supply station at Cape Town for Dutch ships sailing between Amsterdam and Indonesia. The healthy, temperate climate and the sparse Nguni population near the Cape resulted in the colony's gradual expansion. When the British took possession in the Napoleonic wars, the Cape Colony included about twenty thousand free Dutch citizens and twenty-five thousand African slaves, with substantial mixed-race communities on the northern frontier of white settlement.

After 1815 powerful African chiefdoms, Dutch settlers—first known as Boers, and then as **Afrikaners**—and British colonial forces waged a complicated, three-cornered battle to build strong states in southern Africa. Of great importance, the talented Zulu leader Shaka (r. 1818–1828) revolutionized African warfare between 1818 and his death in 1828, and he managed to create "the largest and most powerful African society in southern Africa in the nineteenth century."[20] Drafted by age groups until they were forty years old and placed in highly disciplined regiments, Shaka's warriors perfected the use of a new, short stabbing spear in deadly hand-to-hand combat. Shaka's Zulu armies often destroyed their African enemies completely, sowing chaos and sending refugees fleeing in all directions. Shaka's wars also led to the consolidation of the Zulu, Swazi, and Sotho peoples into stronger states in southern Africa. By 1880 these states were largely subdued by Dutch and British invaders, but only after many hard-fought frontier wars.

Beginning in 1834, the British gradually abolished slavery in the Cape Colony and introduced colorblind legislation to protect African labor. In 1836 these measures led about ten thousand Afrikaner cattle ranchers and farmers to make their so-called Great Trek northward into the interior. Another group of Afrikaners moved eastward into Natal, defeated a Zulu army, and declared an independent republic. But Britain refused to recognize Afrikaner rule and annexed Natal in 1845, causing most Afrikaners there to join the other trekkers north of the Orange River. Over the next thirty years

**Diamond Mining in South Africa** At first, both black and white miners could own and work claims at the diamond diggings, as this early photo suggests. However, as the industry expanded and was monopolized by European financial interests, white workers claimed the supervisory jobs and blacks were limited to dangerous, low-wage labor. Mining revolutionized the South African economy. *(Royal Commonwealth Society. By permission of the Syndics of Cambridge University Library)*

Afrikaner and British settlers, who often fought and usually detested each other, reached a mutually advantageous division of southern Africa. The British ruled strategically valuable coastal colonies, and the Afrikaners controlled their ranch-land republics in the interior. The Zulu, Xhosa, and other African peoples lost much of their land but remained the majority—albeit an exploited majority. The Afrikaners treated Africans as racial inferiors, destined by God for forced labor, while the British relied on literacy tests and property qualifications to subordinate Africans.

The discovery of incredibly rich deposits of diamonds in 1867 and later gold revolutionized the economy of southern Africa, making possible large-scale industrial capitalism and transforming the lives of all its peoples. Small white and black diamond diggers soon gave way to Cecil Rhodes and the powerful financiers behind his De Beers mining company, which reaped fabulous profits monopolizing the world's diamond industry. The regular, deep-level gold deposits discovered in 1886 in the Afrikaners' Transvaal republic required big foreign investment, European engineering expertise, and an enormous labor force. The "color bar" system of the diamond fields gave whites—often English-speaking immigrants—the well-paid skilled positions and put black Africans in the dangerous, low-wage jobs far below the surface. Whites lived with their families in subsidized housing. African workers lived in all-male dormitories like men in prison, closely watched by company guards. As the demand for labor soared and southern Africa became the world's leading gold producer by a wide margin, the industrializing economy pulled in migratory workers from all over the region.

The mining bonanza whetted the appetite of British imperialists led by the powerful Rhodes, who believed that "we [English] are the finest race in the world and the more of the world we inhabit the better it is for the human race."[21] Between 1889 and 1893 he used missionaries and a front company chartered by the British government to force African chiefs to accept British protectorates and managed to add Southern and Northern Rhodesia (modern-day Zimbabwe and Zambia) to the British Empire (see Map 26.2). Rhodes and the imperialist clique then succeeded in starting the South African War of 1899–1902 (also known as the Anglo-Boer War), Britain's greatest imperial campaign on African soil. British armies defeated the smaller Afrikaner forces within a year, but they needed 450,000 soldiers from all over the empire and a savage "total war" of burned farms and deadly concentration camps for Afrikaner women and children to crush 80,000 Afrikaner commandos after they turned to guerrilla warfare. The long and bitter war divided whites and sapped the imperial spirit in Britain.

South Africa's blacks, however, were the biggest losers. The British had promised the Afrikaners representative government in return for surrender in 1902, and they made good on their pledge. In 1910 the Cape Colony, Natal, and the two Afrikaner republics formed a new self-governing Union of South Africa. Because whites—21.5 percent of the total population in 1910—held almost all political power and because the Afrikaners outnumbered the English speakers, following the peace settlement the Afrikaners began to regain what they had lost on the battlefield. South Africa, under a joint British-Afrikaner government within the British Empire, began the creation of a modern, segregated society that culminated in an even harsher system of racial separation, or apartheid, after World War II.

## The Imperial System (1900–1930)

By 1900 most of black Africa had been conquered—or, as Europeans preferred to say, "pacified"—and a system of imperial administration was taking shape.

In general, this system weakened or shattered the traditional social order and challenged accepted values. Yet this generalization must be qualified. For one thing, sub-Saharan Africa consisted of an astonishing diversity of peoples and cultures prior to the European invasion. There were, for example, more than eight hundred distinct languages and thousands of previously independent political units. The effects of imperialism varied accordingly.

European powers also took rather different approaches to colonial rule. The British tended to exercise indirect rule through existing leaders. The French believed in direct rule by appointed officials, both black and white. Moreover, the number of white settlers varied greatly from region to region, and their presence had important consequences. In light of these qualifications, how did imperial systems generally operate in sub-Saharan Africa?

The self-proclaimed political goal of the French and the British—the principal foreign powers—was to provide good government for their African subjects, especially after World War I. "Good government" meant, above all, law and order. It meant strong, authoritarian government, which maintained a small army and built up an African police force to put down rebellion, suppress ethnic warfare, and protect life and property. Good government required a modern bureaucracy capable of taxing and governing the population. Many African leaders and their peoples had chosen not to resist the invaders' superior force, and most others had stopped fighting after experiencing crushing military defeat. Thus the goal of law and order was widely achieved.

Colonial governments demonstrated much less interest in providing basic social services. Expenditures on education, public health, hospitals, and other social services increased after the First World War but still remained small. Europeans feared the political implications of mass education and typically relied instead on the modest efforts of state-subsidized mission schools. Moreover, they tried to make even their poorest colonies pay for themselves. Thus salaries for government workers normally absorbed nearly all tax revenues.

Economically, the imperialist goal was to draw the African interior into the world economy on terms favorable to the dominant Europeans. The key was railroads linking coastal trading centers to outposts hundreds of miles in the interior. Cheap, dependable transportation facilitated easy shipment of raw materials out and manufactured goods in. Most African railroads were built after 1900; fifty-two hundred miles were in operation by 1926, when attention turned to road building for trucks. Railroads and roads had two other important outcomes: they allowed the quick movement of troops to put down any local unrest, and they allowed many African peasants to earn wages for the first time.

The focus on economic development and low-cost rule explained why colonial governments were reluctant to move decisively against slavery within Africa. Officials feared that an abrupt abolition of slavery where it existed would disrupt production and lead to costly revolts by powerful slaveholding elites, especially in Muslim areas. Thus colonial regimes settled for halfway measures designed to satisfy humanitarian groups in Europe and also make all Africans, free or slave, participate in a market economy and work for wages. Even this cautious policy was enough for many slaves to boldly free themselves by running away, and it facilitated a rapid decline of slavery within Africa. At the same time, colonial governments often imposed head taxes, payable in money or labor, to compel Africans to work for their white overlords. No aspect of imperialism was more despised by Africans than forced labor, widespread until about 1920. In some regions, particularly in West Africa, African peasants continued to respond freely to the new economic opportunities by voluntarily shifting to export crops on their own farms. Overall, the result of these developments was an increase in wage work and production geared to the world market and a decline in traditional self-sufficient farming and nomadic herding.

In sum, the imposition of bureaucratic Western rule and the gradual growth of a world-oriented cash economy between 1900 and 1930 had a revolutionary impact on large parts of Africa. The experiences of Ghana and Kenya, two very different African countries, dramatically illustrate variations on the general pattern.

**The Governor's Arrival** This painting by an African artist depicts the landing of a high British official at a port on the East African coast. African soldiers stand at attention, ready to do the governor's bidding and maintain imperial order. *(National Museums, Tanzania)*

Present-day Ghana (see Map 34.2 on page 1112), which takes its name from one of West Africa's famous early kingdoms, had a fairly complex economy well before British armies smashed the powerful Asante kingdom in 1873 and established the crown colony that they called the Gold Coast. Precolonial local trade was vigorous and varied, and palm oil exports were expanding. Into this sophisticated economy British colonists subsequently introduced the production of cocoa beans for the world's chocolate. Output rose spectacularly, from a few hundred tons in the 1890s to 305,000 tons in 1936.

Independent peasants and energetic African business people (many of the traders were women) were mainly responsible for the spectacular success of cocoa-bean production. Creative African entrepreneurs even went so far as to build their own roads, and they sometimes reaped big profits. During the boom of 1920 "motor cars were purchased right and left, champagne flowed freely, and expensive cigars scented the air."[22]

The Gold Coast also showed the way politically and culturally. The westernized elite—relatively prosperous and well-educated lawyers, professionals, and journalists—and business people took full advantage of opportunities provided by the fairly enlightened colonial regime. The black elite was the main presence in the limited local elections permitted by the British, for few permanent white settlers ventured to hot and densely populated West Africa.

Across the continent in the British East African colony of Kenya, events unfolded differently. Before the arrival of Western imperialists, East African peoples were more self-sufficient, less numerous, and less advanced commercially and politically than Africans in the Gold Coast. Once the British had built their strategic railroad from the Indian Ocean across Kenya to Uganda, foreigners from Great Britain and India moved in to exploit the situation. Indian settlers became shopkeepers, clerks, and laborers in the towns. British settlers dreamed of turning the cool, beautiful, and fertile Kenyan highlands into a "white man's country" like Southern Rhodesia or the Union of South Africa. They dismissed the local population of peasant farmers as "barbarians," fit only to toil as cheap labor on their large estates and plantations. By 1929 two thousand white settlers were producing a variety of crops for export. The white settlers in Kenya manipulated the colonial government for their own interests and imposed rigorous segregation on the black and Indian populations. Kenya's Africans thus experienced much harsher colonial rule than did their fellow Africans in the Gold Coast.

## SUMMARY

In the nineteenth century the industrializing West subordinated non-Western lands to its economic interests, sent forth millions of emigrants, and built vast empires in Africa and Asia. The reasons were many, but the economic thrust of robust industrial capitalism, an ever-growing lead in technology, and the competitive pressures of European nationalism were particularly important.

In the Muslim heartland both the Ottoman Empire and Egypt introduced reforms to improve the military, provide technical and secular education, and expand personal liberties. In so doing, both countries prepared the way for modern nation-states in the twentieth century, but they failed to defend themselves from Western imperialism. The Ottoman Empire survived as an economic colony and groped for unity. Egypt went bankrupt and was conquered and ruled by Britain. Western domination was particularly bitter for most Muslims because they saw it profaning their religion as well as taking away their political independence.

Sub-Saharan Africa also experienced epoch-making changes before 1914. Constant European pressure contributed to the reorientation of the economy, which gradually turned from a focus on the Atlantic slave trade to the production of commodities for export, frequently on the basis of slave labor. The European conquest of Africa then led to colonial empires that improved internal security and built bureaucracies, but also treated Africans as racial inferiors. Government based on racial discrimination, which was most thoroughly developed in southern Africa, set the stage for an anti-imperialist struggle for equality and genuine independence. This struggle would emerge as a central drama of world history after the great European civil war of 1914 to 1918, which reduced the West's technological advantage and shattered its self-confidence and complacent moral superiority.

## KEY TERMS

lopsided world
migration chain
great white walls
quinine
traditionalists
modernizers
janissary corps
Tanzimat
Young Turks
Muhammad Ali
palm oil
jihads
Sokoto caliphate
Leopold II
Berlin conference
Afrikaners

## NOTES

1. Quoted in T. Blegen, *Norwegian Migration to America,* vol. 2 (Northfield, Minn.: Norwegian-American Historical Association, 1940), p. 468.
2. Quoted in G. H. Nadel and P. Curtis, eds., *Imperialism and Colonialism* (New York: Macmillan, 1964), p. 94.
3. Quoted in W. L. Langer, *The Diplomacy of Imperialism,* 2d ed. (New York: Knopf, 1951), pp. 86, 88.
4. Rudyard Kipling, *The Five Nations* (London, 1903).
5. Quoted in Langer, *The Diplomacy of Imperialism,* p. 88.
6. A. Hourani, *A History of the Arab Peoples* (Cambridge, Mass.: Harvard University Press, 1991), p. 263.
7. Quoted ibid.
8. Quoted in R. Hallett, *Africa to 1875* (Ann Arbor: University of Michigan Press, 1970), p. 109.
9. Quoted in Earl of Cromer, *Modern Egypt* (London, 1911), p. 48.
10. A. Hopkins, *An Economic History of West Africa* (New York: Columbia University Press, 1973), p. 124.
11. S. Drescher, *Capitalism and Slavery: British Mobilization in Comparative Perspective* (London: Macmillan, 1986), p. 38.
12. P. Lovejoy, *Transformations in Slavery: A History of Slavery in Africa,* 2d ed. (Cambridge: Cambridge University Press, 2000), p. 142.
13. Ibid., p. 179.
14. Quoted in J. Iliffe, *Africans: The History of a Continent* (Cambridge: Cambridge University Press, 1995), p. 169.
15. Lovejoy, *Transformations in Slavery,* p. 15.
16. R. Oliver, *The African Experience* (New York: Icon Editions, 1991), pp. 164–166.
17. S. Miers and R. Roberts, eds., *The End of Slavery in Africa* (Madison: University of Wisconsin Press, 1988), p. 16.
18. Quoted in W. L. Langer, *European Alliances and Alignments, 1871–1890* (New York: Vintage Books, 1931), p. 290.
19. Quoted in J. Ellis, *The Social History of the Machine Gun* (New York: Pantheon Books, 1975), pp. 86, 101.
20. R. Beck, *The History of South Africa* (Westport, Conn.: Greenwood Press, 2000), p. 63.
21. Quoted by R. Rothberg, *The Founder: Cecil Rhodes and the Pursuit of Power* (New York: Oxford University Press, 1988), p. 150.
22. G. B. Kay, ed., *The Political Economy of Colonialism in Ghana: A Collection of Documents and Statistics* (Cambridge: Cambridge University Press, 1972), p. 48.

## SUGGESTED READING

General interpretations of European expansion in a broad perspective include P. Curtin, *The World and the West: The European Challenge and the Overseas Response in the Age of Empire* (2000); J. Blaut, *The Colonizer's Model of the World* (1993); A. Thornton, *Imperialism in the Twentieth Century* (1977); and W. Woodruff, *Impact of Western Man* (1967). P. Stearns, *The Industrial Revolution in World History* (1993), examines industrialization in comparative perspective. D. K. Fieldhouse has written two fine surveys, *Economics and Empire, 1830–1914* (1970) and *Colonialism, 1870–1945* (1981). J. A. Hobson's classic *Imperialism* (1902) is readily available, and the Marxist-Leninist case is effectively presented in V. G. Kieran, *Imperialism and Its Contradictions* (1996). H. Wright, ed., *The "New Imperialism,"* rev. ed. (1975), is an excellent anthology. K. M. Panikkar, *Asia and Western Dominance: A Survey of the Vasco da Gama Epoch of Asian History* (1959), is a classic study of Western expansion from an Indian viewpoint.

G. Stocking, *Victorian Anthropology* (1987), is a brilliant analysis of the cultural and racial implications of Western expansion. Britain's leading position in European imperialism is examined in a lively way by B. Porter, *The Lion's Share* (1976); J. Morris, *Pax Britannica* (1968); and D. Judd, *The Victorian Empire* (1970), a stunning pictorial history. B. Semmel, *The Rise of Free Trade Imperialism* (1970); H. Brunschwig, *French Colonialism, 1871–1914* (1966); and W. Baumgart, *Imperialism: The Idea and Reality of British and French Colonial Expansion* (1982), are well-balanced studies. A. Moorehead, *The White Nile* (1971), tells the story of European exploration of the mysterious Upper Nile. D. Ralston, *Importing the European Army: Military Techniques and Institutions in the Extra-European World, 1600–1914* (1990), compares the experiences of Egypt, Japan, China, and others, while D. Headrick, *Tools of Empire* (1981), highlights Western technological superiority. C. Erikson, *Emigration from Europe, 1815–1914* (1976), and R. Vecoli and S. Sinke, eds., *A Century of European Migrations, 1830–1930* (1991), are valuable studies.

E. Wolf, *Europe and the People Without History* (1982), considers, with skill and compassion, the impact of imperialism on non-Western peoples. Two unusual and provocative studies on personal relations between European rulers and non-European subjects are D. Mannoni, *Prospero and Caliban: The Psychology of Colonialization* (1964), and F. Fanon, *Wretched of the Earth* (1965), a bitter attack on white racism by a black psychologist active in the Algerian revolution. V. Ware, *Beyond the Pale: White Women, Racism and History* (1992), examines the complex role of European women in imperialism. Novels also bring the psychological and human dimensions of imperialism alive. H. Rider Haggard, *King Solomon's Mines,* portrays the powerful appeal of adventure in exotic lands. Rudyard Kipling, the most popular advocate of European expansion, is at his best in *Kim* and *Soldiers Three.* Joseph Conrad unforgettably probes European motives in *Heart of Darkness.* William Boyd, *An Ice-Cream War,* a good story of British and Germans fighting each other in Africa during the First World War, is a favorite of students.

I. Lapidus, *A History of Islamic Societies* (1988), is an excellent introduction to nineteenth-century developments. Hourani, cited in the Notes, is also recommended. B. Lewis, *What Went Wrong? Western Impact and Middle Eastern Response* (2002), is a provocative analysis of Middle Eastern efforts to catch up with the West. J. Freely, *Istanbul: The Imperial City* (1996), is a lively account of Ottoman grandeur and decline. Two important specialized studies on Egypt are K. Cuno, *The Pasha's Peasants: Land, Society, and Economics in Lower Egypt, 1740–1858* (1992), and J. Tucker, *Women in Nineteenth-Century Egypt* (1985). The history of Cairo, one of the world's truly great cities, comes alive in A. Raymond, *Cairo* (2000), and M. Rodenbeck, *Cairo: The City Victorious* (1998). H. Mahfouz, *Palace of Desire* (1991), is a great novelist's unforgettable portrait of an Egyptian middle-class family and its social setting before 1914. T. Mitchell, *Colonizing Egypt* (1988); E. Toledano, *State and Society in Mid-Nineteenth Century Egypt* (1990); and A. Palmer, *The Decline and Fall of the Ottoman Empire* (1992), are useful and engaging studies.

Iliffe, cited in the Notes, is a brilliant and unusual history of Africa stressing environmental factors. J. Reader, *A Biography of the Continent* (1998), is a big, exciting book with a wealth of insight. Oliver and Hallett, both cited in the Notes, and R. July, *A History of the African People* (1970), contain excellent introductions to Africa in the age of imperialism. Hopkins, cited in the Notes, is a pioneering work stressing African successes before imperialism. Lovejoy's revised study on slavery, cited in the Notes, is outstanding on nineteenth-century developments. Important specialized studies on slavery include Miers and Roberts, cited in the Notes; P. Lovejoy and J. Hogendon, *Slow Death for Slavery: The Course of Abolition in Northern Nigeria, 1897–1936* (1993); and S. Miers and M. Klein, eds., *Slavery and Colonial Rule in Africa* (1999). Also strongly recommended are A. Sheriff, *Spices and Ivory in Zanzibar* (1987); C. Midgley, *Women Against Slavery: The British Campaign, 1780–1870* (1992); and A. Hochschild, *King Leopold's Ghost* (1998), which tells the chilling story of Belgian atrocities in the Congo and the international outcry that followed.

# LISTENING TO THE PAST

## A French Leader Defends Imperialism

*Although Jules Ferry (1832–1893) first gained political prominence as an ardent champion of secular public education, he was most famous for his empire building. While he was French premier in 1880–1881 and again in 1883–1885, France occupied Tunisia, extended its rule in Indonesia, seized Madagascar, and penetrated the Congo. Criticized by conservatives, socialists, and some left-wing republicans for his colonial expansion, Ferry defended his policies before the French National Assembly and also elaborated a philosophy of imperialism in his writings.*

*In a speech to the Assembly on July 28, 1883, portions of which follow, Ferry answered his critics and summarized his three main arguments with brutal honesty. Note that Ferry adamantly insisted that imperial expansion did not weaken France in its European struggle with Germany, as some opponents charged, but rather that it increased French grandeur and power. Imperialists needed the language of patriotic nationalism to be effective.*

*M. Jules Ferry:* Gentlemen, . . . I believe that there is some benefit in summarizing and condensing, in the form of arguments, the principles, the motives, and the various interests by which a policy of colonial expansion may be justified; it goes without saying that I will try to remain reasonable, moderate, and never lose sight of the major continental interests which are the primary concern of this country. What I wish to say, to support this proposition, is that in fact, just as in word, the policy of colonial expansion is a political and economic system; I wish to say that one can relate this system to three orders of ideas: economic ideas, ideas of civilization in its highest sense, and ideas of politics and patriotism.

In the area of economics, I will allow myself to place before you, with the support of some figures, the considerations which justify a policy of colonial expansion from the point of view of that need, felt more and more strongly by the industrial populations of Europe and particularly those of our own rich and hard working country: the need for export markets. Is this some kind of chimera? Is this a view of the future or is it not rather a pressing need, and, we could say, the cry of our industrial population? I will formulate only in a general way what each of you, in the different parts of France, is in a position to confirm. Yes, what is lacking for our great industry, drawn irrevocably on to the path of exportation by the [free trade] treaties of 1860, what it lacks more and more is export markets. Why? Because next door to us Germany is surrounded by barriers, because beyond the ocean, the United States of America has become protectionist, protectionist in the most extreme sense. . . .

Gentlemen, there is a second point, . . . the humanitarian and civilizing side of the question. On this point the honorable M. Camille Pellatan has jeered in his own refined and clever manner; he jeers, he condemns, and he says "What is this civilization which you impose with cannonballs? What is it but another form of barbarism? Don't these populations, these inferior races, have the same rights as you? Aren't they masters of their own houses? Have they called upon you? You come to them against their will, you offer them violence, but not civilization." There, gentlemen, is the thesis; I do not hesitate to say that this is not politics, nor is it history: it is political metaphysics. ("Ah, Ah" *on far left.*)

. . . Gentlemen, I must speak from a higher and more truthful plane. It must be stated openly that, in effect, superior races have rights over inferior races. *(Movement on many benches on the far left.)*

*M. Jules Maigne:* Oh! You dare to say this in the country which has proclaimed the rights of man!

Jules Ferry, French politician and ardent imperialist. *(Corbis)*

*M. de Guilloutet:* This is a justification of slavery and the slave trade! . . .

*M. Jules Ferry:* I repeat that superior races have a right, because they have a duty. They have the duty to civilize inferior races. . . . *(Approval from the left. New interruptions from the extreme left and from the right.)*

. . . M. Pelletan . . . then touched upon a third point, more delicate, more serious, and upon which I ask your permission to express myself quite frankly. It is the political side of the question. The honorable M. Pelletan, who is a distinguished writer, always comes up with remarkably precise formulations. I will borrow from him the one which he applied the other day to this aspect of colonial policy.

"It is a system," he says, "which consists of seeking out compensations in the Orient with a circumspect and peaceful seclusion which is actually imposed upon us in Europe."

I would like to explain myself in regard to this. I do not like this word, "compensation," and, in effect, not here but elsewhere it has often been used in a treacherous way. If what is being said or insinuated is that any government in this country, any Republican minister could possibly believe that there are in any part of the world compensations for the disasters which we have experienced [in connection with our defeat in the Franco-Prussian War of 1870–1871], an injury is being inflicted . . . and an injury undeserved by that government. *(Applause at the center and left.)* I will ward off this injury with all the force of my patriotism! *(New applause and bravos from the same benches.)*

Gentlemen, there are certain considerations which merit the attention of all patriots. The conditions of naval warfare have been profoundly altered. ("Very true! Very true!")

At this time, as you know, a warship cannot carry more than fourteen days' worth of coal, no matter how perfectly it is organized, and a ship which is out of coal is a derelict on the surface of the sea, abandoned to the first person who comes along. Thence the necessity of having on the oceans provision stations, shelters, ports for defense and revictualling. *(Applause at the center and left. Various interruptions.)* And it is for this that we needed Tunisia, for this that we needed Saigon and the Mekong Delta, for this that we need Madagascar, that we are at Diégo-Suarez and Vohemar [two Madagascar ports] and will never leave them! *(Applause from a great number of benches.)* Gentlemen, in Europe as it is today, in this competition of so many rivals which we see growing around us, some by perfecting their military or maritime forces, others by the prodigious development of an ever growing population; in a Europe, or rather in a universe of this sort, a policy of peaceful seclusion or abstention is simply the highway to decadence! Nations are great in our times only by means of the activities which they develop; it is not simply "by the peaceful shining forth of institutions" (*interruptions on the extreme left and right*) that they are great at this hour.

. . . [The Republican Party] has shown that it is quite aware that one cannot impose upon France a political ideal conforming to that of nations like independent Belgium and the Swiss Republic; that something else is needed for France: that she cannot be merely a free country, that she must also be a great country, exercizing all of her rightful influence over the destiny of Europe, that she ought to propagate this influence throughout the world and carry everywhere that she can her language, her customs, her flag, her arms, and her genius. *(Applause at center and left.)*

## QUESTIONS FOR ANALYSIS

1. What was Jules Ferry's economic argument for imperial expansion? Why had colonies recently gained greater economic value?
2. How did Ferry's critics attack the morality of foreign expansion? How did Ferry try to claim the moral high ground in his response?
3. What political arguments did Ferry advance? How would you characterize his philosophy of politics and national development?

*Source:* Speech before the French National Assembly, July 28, 1883. Reprinted in R. A. Austen, ed., *Modern Imperialism: Western Overseas Expansion and Its Aftermath, 1776–1965* (Lexington, Mass.: D. C. Heath, 1969), pp. 70–73.

Western warehouses and offices in Canton Harbor, nineteenth century (detail).
*(Peabody Essex Museum)*

CHAPTER

# 27 ASIA IN THE ERA OF WESTERN IMPERIALISM, 1800–1914

## CHAPTER OUTLINE

- Europeans See Opportunities
- South and Southeast Asia: The Consolidation of European Colonial Control
- East Asia: Pressure to Conform to a Western-Dominated International Order
- The Movement of Peoples

Western commercial expansion and imperialism posed profound challenges to the peoples of Asia during the nineteenth century. As Europe consolidated its industrial lead, it pressured the countries of Asia to sell more raw materials and buy more manufactured goods. Moreover, as had been the case since Vasco da Gama and Christopher Columbus, Western nations were prepared to use force to aid their merchants, defining commercial profit as a national goal. But Westerners were not interested solely in commercial and industrial penetration. Missionary ventures picked up in the nineteenth century as Protestants came to compete with the long-established Catholic missions. Teachers, translators, and journalists also were involved in adding to and shaping both Asian knowledge of the West and Western knowledge of Asia.

The societies of Asia varied enormously at the beginning of the century, but the common encounter with the expanding West gradually gave them more in common. Colonial rule became the fate of most of those in tropical Asia, from India on the west to the islands of Indonesia and the Philippines on the east. Even in temperate East Asia, where China and Japan retained their political independence, the commercial, industrial, and military might of Europe created crises that profoundly shaped the policies they adopted. Japan came out of this crisis stronger than any other Asian nation. It became the first non-Western country to industrialize successfully and by the end of this period had become an imperialist power itself, making Korea and Taiwan its colonies.

Throughout Asia intellectuals had to rethink central political, religious, and cultural tenets in the face of these new challenges. Responses varied from outright rejection of all things foreign to eager imitation, but in the long run the most common response involved appropriating key elements of Western culture toward national goals of independence and strength. In India agitation for independence was well established by the 1880s.

- Why were some Asian societies reduced to colonies and others not?
- What choices did the traditional elites of the various societies see open to them?
- In what ways did the societies of Asia benefit from Western penetration?

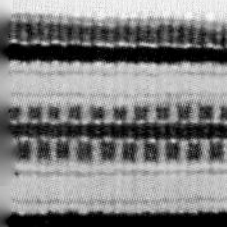

- What other factors affected the course of development in Asia during the nineteenth century?

These are the questions this chapter will examine.

## EUROPEANS SEE OPPORTUNITIES

Ever since Marco Polo, Asia had evoked wonder in Europeans: it was vast, populous, and produced all sorts of marvelous products. From the fifteenth through the seventeenth centuries, European traders penetrated markets in Asia. Spain, the Netherlands, and Portugal acquired territory—Spain in the Philippines, the Netherlands in the East Indies (Indonesia), and Portugal in the ports of Goa, Malacca, and Macao on the coasts of India, Malaysia, and China, respectively. Catholic missionaries were active in India, China, Japan, the Philippines, and elsewhere. But the primary engine behind these ventures was the profits to be had from trade, especially the importation of porcelain and tea from China, spices from the Indies, and cotton and jute from India.

Half the people of the world lived in the region from India east to the Pacific Ocean, but they were very unevenly distributed. In the temperate zones of East Asia the old established monarchies of China, Japan, and Korea were all densely populated and boasted long literary traditions. India was just as densely populated but politically and culturally more diverse, with several major languages and dozens of independent rulers reigning in kingdoms large and small. What Britain and later the other Western powers initially wanted from the more developed Asian societies was to refashion trading relations to the West's benefit. At the other extreme were thinly populated and relatively primitive areas without literate cultures and sometimes even without agriculture. These areas included some of the islands of the Philippines and Indonesia as well as Australia and New Zealand. They could not provide manufactured goods such as porcelain or silk, but they offered opportunities for Western development, much as the Americas had earlier.

Communication between Europe and Asia became much faster, safer, and more predictable in this period, which facilitated a greater movement of people and goods than ever before. Sailing ships in the eighteenth century rarely carried more than three hundred tons, but after 1850 tall-masted clipper ships, whose timbers were fastened with iron, frequently held two thousand tons, and their huge sails cut the voyage from Europe to India from six to three months, greatly reducing shipping costs. By the 1850s steamships were competing with clipper ships, and they made ocean travel more predictable. After the Suez Canal was opened in 1869, one could travel by steamship from England to India in three weeks. In the 1860s cables were laid on the ocean floor, allowing telegrams to be sent from England to India. Whereas at the beginning of the nineteenth century one had to wait a year or more to get an answer to a letter sent to India, by 1870 it took only a couple of months—or, if the matter was urgent, only a few hours by telegraph.

The economics of industrialization and the political rivalries among the European powers all shaped the steps taken by Western nations to gain power in Asia, and these influences changed over the course of the century. Western science and technology were making rapid advances, which gave European armies progressively greater advantages in weaponry. The Industrial Revolution made it possible for early industrializers such as Britain to produce huge surpluses of goods for which they had to find markets, shifting their interest in Asia from a place to buy goods to a place to sell goods. Britain had been able to profit from its colonization of India, and this profit both encouraged it to consolidate its rule and invited its European rivals to look for their own colonies. After 1880 rivalries among the Western powers—Britain, France, Germany, Russia, and the United States especially—led them to compete for territories or spheres of influence in Asia. Although the sudden division of Africa was more spectacular (see Chapter 26), Europeans also set about carving up Asia. Even though economic motivations underlay the new imperialism, the actual economic gains proved quite limited before 1914. Yet the leading European countries saw colonies as crucial to national security, military power, and international prestige. Far-flung possessions guaranteed ever-growing navies the safe havens and dependable coaling stations they needed in times of crisis or war.

Westerners who participated in the imperialist enterprise saw themselves not as bringing harm to the people of Asia but as bringing progress. Missionaries believed that all people would be better off if they converted to Christianity and generally saw European political penetration as paving the way for their efforts. Colonial civil servants believed that Western government and culture would bring peace, prosperity, and modern science and technology to Asia. Colonial governments, some asserted, protected natives from tribal warfare and from cruder forms of exploitation by white settlers and business people. Thus the French spoke of their sacred "civilizing mission," and Rudyard Kipling (1865–1936), perhaps the most influential British writer of the 1890s, exhorted Europeans to "take up the white man's burden" and serve the needs of

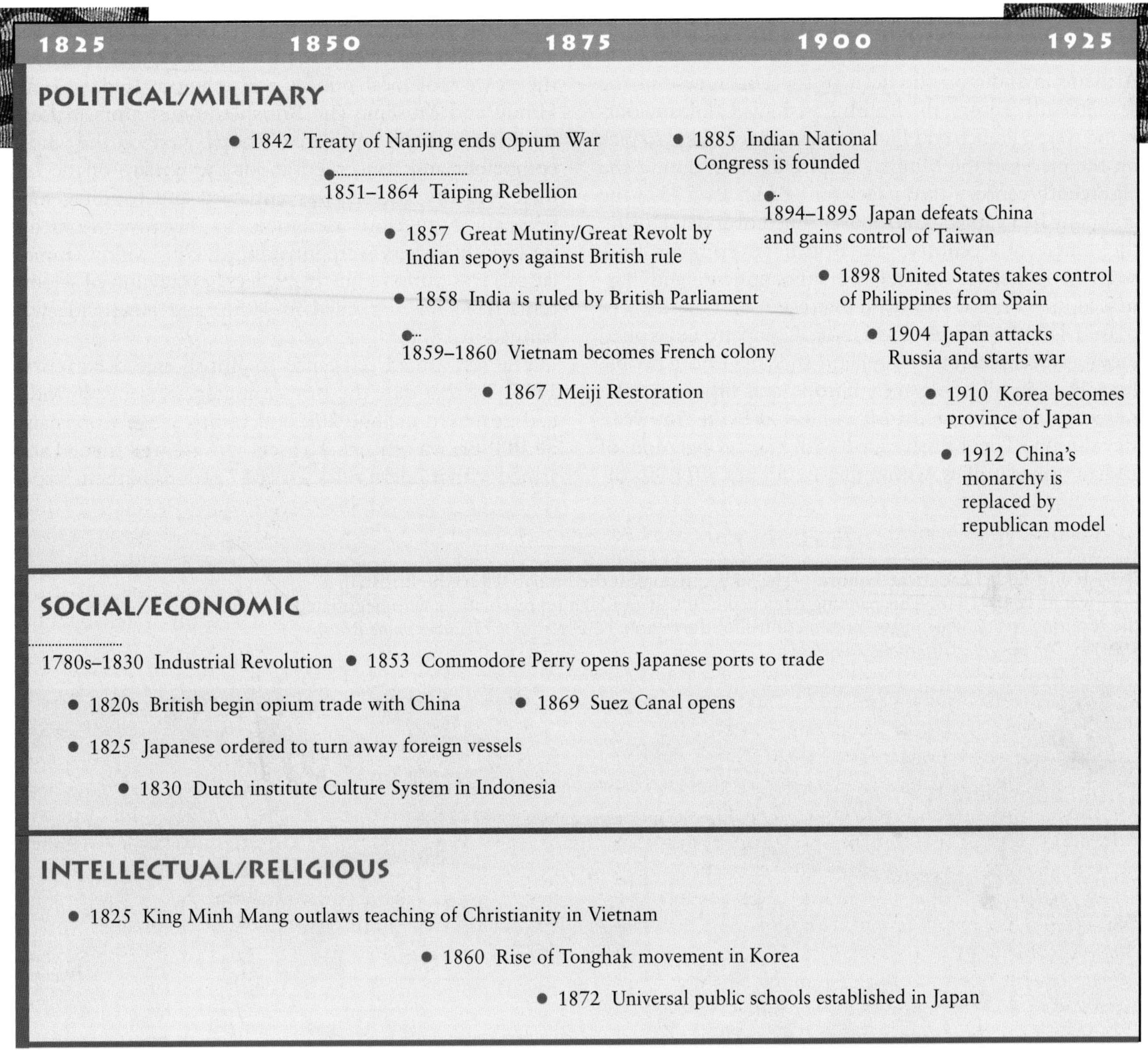


the less civilized, even when the natives did not appreciate their sacrifice.

1825
1850
1875
1900
1925
POLITICAL/MILITARY
1842 Treaty of Nanjing ends Opium War
1851–1864 Taiping Rebellion
1857 Great Mutiny/Great Revolt by Indian sepoys against British rule
1858 India is ruled by British Parliament
1859–1860 Vietnam becomes French colony
1867 Meiji Restoration
1885 Indian National Congress is founded
1894–1895 Japan defeats China and gains control of Taiwan
1898 United States takes control of Philippines from Spain
1904 Japan attacks Russia and starts war
1910 Korea becomes province of Japan
1912 China's monarchy is replaced by republican model
SOCIAL/ECONOMIC
1780s–1830 Industrial Revolution
1853 Commodore Perry opens Japanese ports to trade
1820s British begin opium trade with China
1869 Suez Canal opens
1825 Japanese ordered to turn away foreign vessels
1830 Dutch institute Culture System in Indonesia
INTELLECTUAL/RELIGIOUS
1825 King Minh Mang outlaws teaching of Christianity in Vietnam
1860 Rise of Tonghak movement in Korea
1872 Universal public schools established in Japan

The evolution of European ambitions toward Asia helps account for the forces the societies of Asia had to contend with in the nineteenth century, but the main focus of this chapter is on those societies themselves. Incorporation into a world order in which Europe played a more and more dominant role had wide-ranging effects on their historical development. This chapter looks at imperialism and colonialism more from the perspective of the colonized than the colonizers.

## SOUTH AND SOUTHEAST ASIA: THE CONSOLIDATION OF EUROPEAN COLONIAL CONTROL

At the beginning of the nineteenth century, only a small part of the population of South and Southeast Asia was under direct European control. Spain administered the Philippines, the Dutch controlled Java, and the British, through the offices of the East India Company, held a patchwork of territories in India. By the end of the century, most of the region would be in foreign hands.

## India and the British Empire in Asia

Arriving in India on the heels of the Portuguese in the seventeenth century, the British East India Company outmaneuvered French and Dutch rivals and was there to pick up the pieces as the Mughal Empire decayed during the eighteenth century (see pages 650–651). By 1757, the company had gained control over much of India. During the nineteenth century, the British government took over, progressively unified the subcontinent, and harnessed its economy to British interests.

In 1818 the British East India Company controlled territory occupied by 180 million Indians—more people than lived in all of western Europe and fifty times the number of people the British had lost after the American Revolution. The British ruled with the cooperation of Indian princely allies, whom they could not afford to offend. Still, the British disbanded and disarmed local armies, introduced simpler private property laws, and enhanced the powers of local princes and religious leaders, both Hindu and Muslim. The British administrators, backed by British officers and native troops, were on the whole competent and concerned about the welfare of the Indian peasants. Slavery was outlawed and banditry suppressed. New laws designed to improve women's position in society were introduced. Sati (widow immolation) was outlawed in 1829, legal protection of widow remarriage was extended in 1856, and infanticide was banned in 1870.

The last armed resistance to British rule occurred in 1857. By that date the British military presence in India had grown to include 200,000 Indian sepoy troops and 38,000 British officers. The sepoys were well trained and armed with modern rifles. In 1857 groups of them, espe-

**British and Sikh Leaders at Lahore** The Sikh kingdom in the Punjab fell to the British in a brief war in 1845–1846. This painting depicts the British and Sikh representatives who negotiated the resulting treaty, which gave Britain control of the region. *(Courtesy of the Trustees of the British Museum, Department of Prints and Drawings)*

cially around Delhi, revolted in what the British called the **Great Mutiny** and the Indians called the **Great Revolt.** Their grievances were many, ranging from the use of animal grease on their rifles to the incorporation of low-caste soldiers into the army to high tax rates. The insurrection spread rapidly throughout northern and central India before it was finally crushed, primarily by native troops from other parts of India loyal to the British. Thereafter, although princely states were allowed to continue, Britain ruled India much more tightly. Moreover, the British in India were more aware that they were an occupying power and mixed less with the Indian elite.

After 1858 India was ruled by the British Parliament in London and administered by a civil service in India, the upper echelons of which were all white. In 1900 this elite consisted of fewer than 3,500 top officials for a population of 300 million. In 1877 Queen Victoria adopted the title **Empress of India,** and her image became a common sight in India.

The impact of British rule on the Indian economy was multi-faceted. In the early stages, the British East India Company expanded agricultural production, creating large plantations. Early crops were opium to export to China (see page 870) and tea to substitute for imports from China. India replaced China as the leading exporter of tea to Europe. During the nineteenth century India also exported agricultural commodities to be processed elsewhere, such as cotton fiber, silk, sugar, jute, and coffee. Clearing land for tea and coffee plantations, along with massive commercial logging operations, led to extensive deforestation.

Britain invested heavily in India's infrastructure. By 1855 India's major cities had all been linked by telegraph and railroads, and postal service was being extended to local villages. By 1870 India had the fifth largest rail network in the world—4,775 miles, carrying more than 18 million passengers a year. By 1900 the rail network had increased fivefold to 25,000 miles, and the number of passengers had increased tenfold to 188 million. Irrigation also received attention, and by 1900 India had the world's most extensive irrigation system. Efforts to industrialize India lagged, but some progress had been made by the end of the nineteenth century. Local Gujaratis set up textile mills in Bombay, the Tata family started the first steel mill in Bihar in 1911, and coal mines were opened in many places. By 1914 about 1 million Indians worked in factories.

Development of this sort did not lead to much improvement in the standard of living of the poor. Tenancy and landlessness increased with the growth in plantation agriculture. Britain imported India's raw cotton but exported machine-spun yarn and machine-woven cloth, displacing millions of Indian hand-spinners and hand-weavers. Increases in production were eaten up by increases in population, which reached approximately 300 million by 1900. There was also a negative side to improved communication. As Indians traveled more widely on the convenient trains, disease spread, especially cholera, which is transmitted by exposure to contaminated water. The practice of pilgrims bathing in and drinking from sacred pools and rivers exacerbated this problem. New sewage and water supply systems were installed in Calcutta in the late 1860s, and the death rate there decreased, but in 1900 four out of every one thousand residents of British India still died of cholera each year.

The Indian middle class probably gained more from British rule than the poor. The British built a large educational establishment in India with instruction in English to form, in Thomas Macaulay's words, "a class of persons Indian in blood and color, but English in taste, in opinions, in morals, and in intellect."[1] Missionaries also established schools with Western curricula, and by 1870, 790,000 Indians were attending some 24,000 schools. Three universities were established in 1857. High-caste Hindus came to form a new elite profoundly influenced by Western thought and culture.

By creating a well-educated, English-speaking Indian elite and a bureaucracy based on a modern communication system, the British laid the groundwork for a unified, powerful state. Britain placed under the same general system of law and administration the various Hindu and Muslim peoples of the subcontinent who had resisted one another for centuries. It was as if Europe, with its many states and varieties of Christianity, had been conquered and united in a single great empire. University graduates tended to look on themselves as Indians more than as residents of the separate states and kingdoms, a necessary step for the development of Indian nationalism.

In spite of these achievements, British rule rankled the educated elite. Some Indian intellectuals sought to reconcile the values of the modern West and their own traditions. Rammohun Roy (1772–1833), who had risen to the top of the native ranks in the British East India Company, founded the Hindu College in Calcutta in 1816, offering instruction in Western languages and subjects. A few years later he founded a society to reform certain Hindu customs, especially child marriage, the caste system, and restrictions on widows. He espoused a modern Hinduism founded on the *Upanishads,* the ancient sacred texts of Hinduism.

The more that Western-style education was developed in India, the more the inequalities of the system became apparent to educated Indians. Indians were eligible to

**Imperial Complexities in India** Britain permitted many native princes to continue their rule, if they accepted British domination. This photo shows a road-building project designed to facilitate famine relief in a southern native state. Officials of the local Muslim prince and their British "advisers" watch over workers drawn from the Hindu majority. *(Nizam's Good Works Project–Famine Relief: Road Building, Aurangabad 1895–1902, from Judith Mara Gutman,* Through Indian Eyes. *Courtesy, Private Collection)*

take the examinations for entry into the elite Indian Civil Service, but the exams were given in England, and in 1870 only 1 of the 916 members of the service was Indian. In other words, no matter how Anglicized the educated classes became, they could never become the white rulers' equals. The top jobs, the best clubs, the modern hotels, and even certain railroad compartments were sealed off to brown-skinned men and women. Most of the British elite considered the jumble of Indian peoples and castes to be racially inferior. For example, when the British Parliament in 1883 was considering a major bill to allow Indian judges to try white Europeans in India, the British community rose in protest and defeated the measure. The idea of being judged by Indians was inconceivable to the Europeans, for it was clear to them that the empire in India rested squarely on racial inequality. As Lord Kitchener, one of the most distinguished military commanders of India, stated:

> *It is this consciousness of the inherent superiority of the European which has won for us India. However well educated and clever a native may be, and however brave he may prove himself, I believe that no rank we can bestow on him would cause him to be considered an equal of the British officer.*[2]

The peasant masses might accept such inequality as the latest version of age-old class and caste hierarchies, but the well-educated, English-speaking elite eventually could not. They had studied not only Milton and Shakespeare but also English traditions of democracy, liberty, and national pride.

In the late nineteenth century the colonial ports of Calcutta, Bombay, and Madras, now all linked by railroads, became centers of intellectual ferment. In these and other cities, newspapers in English and regional languages gained influence. Lawyers trained in English law began agitating for Indian independence. By 1885, when educated Indians came together to found the **Indian National Congress,** demands were increasing for the equality and self-government that Britain enjoyed and had already granted white-settler colonies such as Canada and Australia. Members of the congress called for more opportunities for Indians in the Indian Civil Service and reallocation of the government budget from military expenditures to the alleviation of poverty. They advocated unity across religious and caste lines, but most members were upper-caste, Western-educated Hindus.

By 1907, emboldened in part by Japan's military and diplomatic success (see pages 875–878), the radicals in the Indian National Congress were calling for complete independence. Even the moderates were demanding home rule for India through an elected parliament. Although there were sharp divisions between Hindus and Muslims, the common experience of British rule and exposure to Western ideals had created a genuine movement for national independence.

Defending its possessions in India became a key element of British foreign policy during the nineteenth century and led to steady expansion of the territory Britain controlled in Asia. Not far from India's northern borders, Russia was extending its control, and Britain kept a wary eye on it. Twice Britain sent armies into Afghanistan and made it a protectorate. The kingdom of Burma, to India's east, also was trying to expand, which led the British to annex Assam (located between India and Burma) in 1826, then all of Burma by 1852. Burma was then administered as a province of India. British trade between India and China went through the Strait of Malacca, making that region strategically important. Britain had taken over several Dutch territories in this region during the Napoleonic occupation of the Netherlands, including Java. After returning them to the Netherlands in 1814, Britain created its own base in the area at Singapore, later expanding into Malaya (now Malaysia) in the 1870s and 1880s. In both Burma and Malaya, Britain tried to foster economic development. Railroads were built and trade promoted. Burma became a major exporter of timber and rice, Malaya of tin and rubber. So many laborers were brought into Malaya for the expanding mines and plantations that its population came to be approximately one-third Malay, one-third Chinese, and one-third Indian.

## The Dutch East Indies

Although Dutch forts and trading posts in the East Indies dated back to the seventeenth century, in 1816 the Dutch ruled little more than the island of Java. Thereafter they gradually brought almost all of the 3,000-mile-long archipelago under their political authority, although, in good imperialist fashion, they had to share some of the spoils with Britain. In extending their rule, the Dutch, like the British in India, brought diverse peoples with different languages and distinct cultural traditions into a single political entity (see Map 27.1). Thus they inadvertently created the foundations of modern-day Indonesia—the world's fourth most populous nation.

Taking over the Dutch East India Company in 1799, the Dutch government modified the company's loose control of Java and gradually built a modern bureaucratic state. The extension of Dutch control was bitterly resisted by the Javanese. In 1825 war broke out when the Dutch disturbed a Muslim saint's grave to build a highway. In the five years of brutal combat that ensued (known as the **Java War,** 1825–1830), more than 200,000 people, including 8,000 Dutch soldiers, died of war or the diseases that accompanied it. After the war the Dutch abolished the combination of tribute from rulers and forced labor from peasants that they had used to obtain spices, and they established instead a particularly exploitive policy called the **Culture System.** Indonesian peasants were forced to plant a fifth of their land in export crops, especially coffee and sugar, to turn over to the Dutch as their taxes. The Culture System proved highly profitable for the Dutch and brought Dutch shipping and intercontinental commerce back to life. In 1870 Dutch liberals succeeded in eliminating some of the system's most coercive elements, but the practical effects were limited because Dutch and Javanese officials still worked together to make sure the flow of goods continued.

At the end of the nineteenth century the Dutch encouraged Western education in the East Indies for the first time. This decision, inspired in part by a newfound sense of a "civilizing mission" and European racial superiority, had far-reaching consequences. Above all, the children of local rulers and privileged elites, much like their counterparts in India, encountered new ideas in Dutch-speaking schools. They began to question the long-standing cooperation of local elites with Dutch colonialism, and they searched for a new identity. Thus anticolonial nationalism

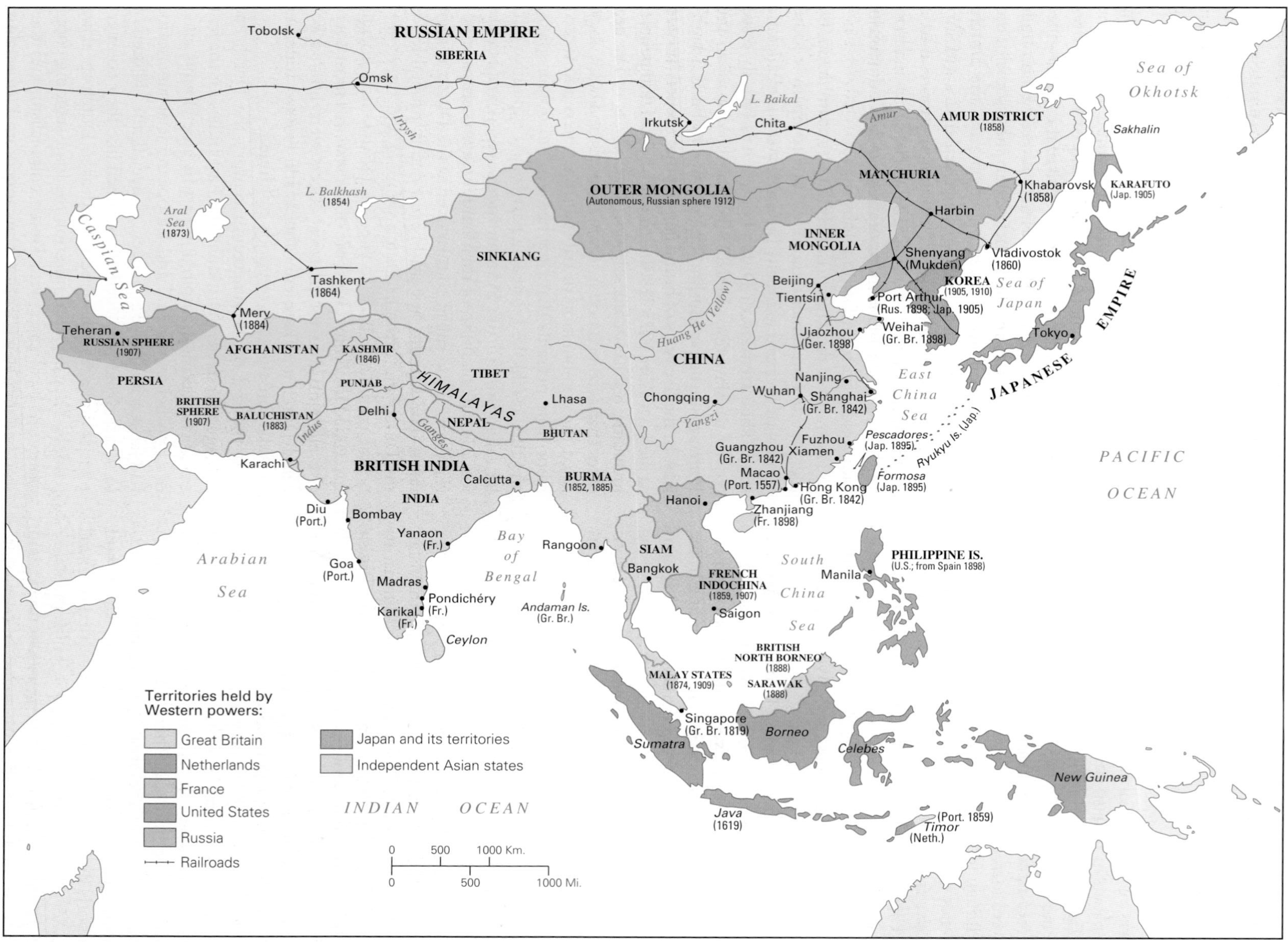


**MAP 27.1 Asia in 1914** India remained under British rule, while China precariously preserved its political independence. The Dutch empire in modern-day Indonesia was old, but French control of Indochina was a product of the new imperialism.

began to take shape in the East Indies in the early twentieth century, and it would blossom after World War I.

## Mainland Southeast Asia

Unlike India and Java, mainland Southeast Asia had escaped European rule through the eighteenth century. In 1802 the new Nguyen Dynasty came to power in Vietnam, putting an end to thirty years of peasant rebellion and civil war. For the first time in the country's history, a single Vietnamese monarchy ruled the entire country, and Vietnam's future appeared bright. Working through a centralizing scholar bureaucracy fashioned on the Chinese model, the dynasty energetically built irrigation canals, roads and bridges, and high walls and impressive palaces in Hue, the new capital city. In 1821 a European who had lived in India, Java, and Siam (Thailand) wrote that Hue had a "neatness, magnitude, and perfection" that made other Asian achievements look "like the works of children."[3] Yet construction placed a heavy burden on the peasants drafted to do the work, and it contributed to a resurgence of peasant uprisings.

Roman Catholic missionaries from France posed a second, more dangerous threat to Vietnam's Confucian ruling elite. The king and his advisers believed that Christianity would undermine Confucian moral values and the unity of the Vietnamese state. Therefore, following a logic that France's Louis XIV would have understood completely (see page 543), in 1825 King Minh Mang (r. 1820–1841) outlawed the teaching of Christianity. In the 1830s his government began executing Catholic missionaries and Vietnamese converts. But Christianity continued to spread, appealing particularly to peasants and leading to the execution of as many as thirty thousand Vietnamese Christians in the 1850s. In response, in 1859–1860 a French naval force seized Saigon and three surrounding provinces in southern Vietnam, making it a French colony. In 1884–1885 France launched a second war against Vietnam and conquered the rest of the country. Laos and Cambodia were added to French Indochina in 1887. In all three countries the local rulers were left on their thrones, but France dominated and tried to promote French culture.

After the French conquest, Vietnamese patriots continued to resist with a combination of loyalty to Confucian values and an intense hatred of foreign rule. Following Japan's victory over Russia in 1905 (see page 876), a new generation of more modern nationalists saw Japan as a model for Vietnamese revitalization and freedom. They went to Japan to study and planned for anticolonial revolution in Vietnam.

In all of Southeast Asia, only Siam succeeded in preserving its independence. Siam was sandwiched between the British in Burma (and India) and the French in Indochina, which enabled its very able King Chulalongkorn (r. 1868–1910) to balance the two competitors against each other and to escape the smothering embrace of both.

**Ready for the Final?** A panel of Vietnamese scholar-bureaucrats sits ready in 1890 to give the "make-or-break" oral examination to degree candidates in liberal arts. As this photo suggests, Vietnamese education for government employment and cultural leadership was still heavily influenced by traditional Chinese models, although the study of French and Western thought was of growing importance. *(Roger-Viollet/Getty Images)*

Chulalongkorn also implemented modernizing reforms, building a stronger, centralized government that could assert effective control over outlying provinces coveted by the imperialists. Thus independent Siam gradually developed a modern centralizing state similar to those constructed by Western imperialists in their Asian possessions.

## The Philippines

The United States became one of the imperialist powers in Asia when it took the Philippines from Spain in 1898.

When the Spanish established rule in the Philippines in the sixteenth century, the islands had no central government or literate culture, but rather were ruled by village units dominated by local chiefs. Under the Spanish, Roman Catholic churches were established, and Spanish priests became the most common intermediaries between the local population, who rarely could speak Spanish, and the new rulers. Spaniards were encouraged to colonize the Philippines through the **encomienda system,** by which Spaniards who had served the Crown were rewarded with grants of the exclusive right to control public affairs in a locality, including collecting taxes in it. A local elite also developed, aided by the Spanish introduction of private ownership of land. Given the great distance between Madrid and Manila, the governor general, appointed by Spain, had almost unlimited powers over the courts and the military. Manila developed into an important entrepôt in the galleon trade between Mexico and China, and this trade also attracted a large Chinese community, which handled much of the trade in the country.

Spain did not do much to promote education in the Philippines, and few Filipinos could read, write, or speak Spanish. In the late nineteenth century, however, wealthy Filipinos began to send their sons to study abroad, and a movement to press Spain for reforms was established. When the Spanish cracked down on critics, a rebellion erupted in 1896. It was settled in 1897 with Spanish promises to reform. In 1898, however, war between Spain and the United States broke out on the coast of Cuba (see page 907), and in May the American naval officer Commodore George Dewey sailed into Manila Bay and sank the Spanish fleet there. Dewey called on the Philippine rebels to help defeat the Spanish forces, but when the rebels declared independence, the Americans refused to recognize them, despite protests by American anti-imperialists. U.S. forces fought the Philippine rebels, and by the end of the insurrection in 1902, the war had cost the lives of 5,000 Americans and about 200,000 Filipinos. In the following years, the United States introduced a more advanced form of colonial rule that included more public works and economic development projects, improved education and medicine, and, in 1907, an elected legislative assembly.

# EAST ASIA: PRESSURE TO CONFORM TO A WESTERN-DOMINATED INTERNATIONAL ORDER

At the beginning of the nineteenth century, long-established ruling houses controlled the major states of East Asia. The Qing Dynasty (Manchus) had ruled in China for a century and a half, the Yi Dynasty had been on the throne in Korea since the fourteenth century, and the military government of the Tokugawa shoguns had maintained peace in the more feudally organized Japan for nearly two centuries. These three countries had been in frequent contact with one another for well over a thousand years and shared key elements of their cultures. In responding to the new challenges of the expanding West, they learned from one another's successes and failures.

## China

In 1800 most Chinese had no reason to question the conception of China as the central kingdom: no other country had so many people, Chinese products were in great demand in foreign countries, and the borders had recently been expanded. A century later, all that had changed. In 1900 foreign troops marched into China's capital, and more and more Chinese had come to think that their government, society, and cultural values needed radical alteration.

The Manchu emperors, who had been ruling China since 1644 (see pages 672–674), seeing little to gain from trade with European countries, permitted foreign trade only at the port of Guangzhou (Canton) and only through licensed Chinese merchants. Initially, the balance of trade was in China's favor, as Great Britain and the other Western nations used silver to pay for tea. By the 1820s, however, the British had found something the Chinese would buy—**opium.** Grown legally in British-occupied India, opium was smuggled into China, where its use and sale were illegal. Like illegal drugs today, huge profits and the cravings of addicts led to rapid increases in sales, from 4,500 chests a year in 1810 to 10,000 in 1830 to 40,000 in 1838. At this point it was China that suffered a drain of silver.

To deal with this crisis, the Chinese government dispatched Lin Zexu to Guangzhou in 1839. He dealt harshly with Chinese who purchased opium and seized the opium stores of British merchants. When he pressured the Portuguese to expel the uncooperative British from their trading post at Macao, the British settled on the barren island of Hong Kong. Lin even wrote to Queen Victoria, "Suppose there were people from another country who carried opium for sale to England and seduced your people into buying and smoking it; certainly your honorable ruler would deeply hate it and be bitterly aroused."[4]

Although for years the little community of foreign merchants had accepted Chinese rules, by this date the British, the dominant group, were ready to flex their muscles. British merchants wanted to create a market for their goods in China and get tea cheaper by trading closer to its source in central China. They also wanted a diplomatic system more on the European model, with envoys and ambassadors, commercial treaties and published tariffs. With the encouragement of their merchants in China, the British sent an expeditionary force from India with forty-two warships, many of them leased from the major opium trader, Jardine, Matheson, and Company.

With its control of the seas, the British easily shut down key Chinese ports and forced the Chinese to negotiate. Dissatisfied with the resulting agreement, the British sent a second, larger force, which took even more coastal cities, including Shanghai. This Opium War was settled at gunpoint in 1842. The resulting **Treaty of Nanjing** (Nanking) opened five ports to international trade, fixed the tariff on imported goods at 5 percent, imposed an indemnity of 21 million ounces of silver on China to cover Britain's war expenses, and ceded the island of Hong Kong to Britain. Through the clause on "extraterritoriality," British subjects in China were answerable only to British law, even in disputes with Chinese. The treaty also had a "most-favored nation" clause, which meant that whenever one nation extracted a new privilege from China, it was extended automatically to Britain.

This treaty satisfied neither side. China continued to refuse to accept foreign diplomats at its capital in Beijing (Peking), and its compliance with the commercial clauses regarding the expansion of trade fell far short of Western expectations. Between 1856 and 1860 Britain and France renewed hostilities with China. Seventeen thousand British and French troops occupied Beijing and set the emperor's summer palace on fire. Another round of harsh treaties gave European merchants and missionaries greater privileges and forced the Chinese to open several more cities to foreign trade. Large areas in some of the treaty ports were leased in perpetuity to foreign powers; these were known as **concessions.** Since the foreigners who lived there did not have to obey Chinese laws, these concessions, especially in Shanghai, came to resemble international cities attached to the Chinese mainland.

China's problems in the nineteenth century were not all of foreign origin, however. By 1850 China, for centuries the world's most populous country, had more than 400 million people. As the population grew, farm size shrank, forests were put to the plow, and surplus labor suppressed wages. Social relations suffered from the strain.

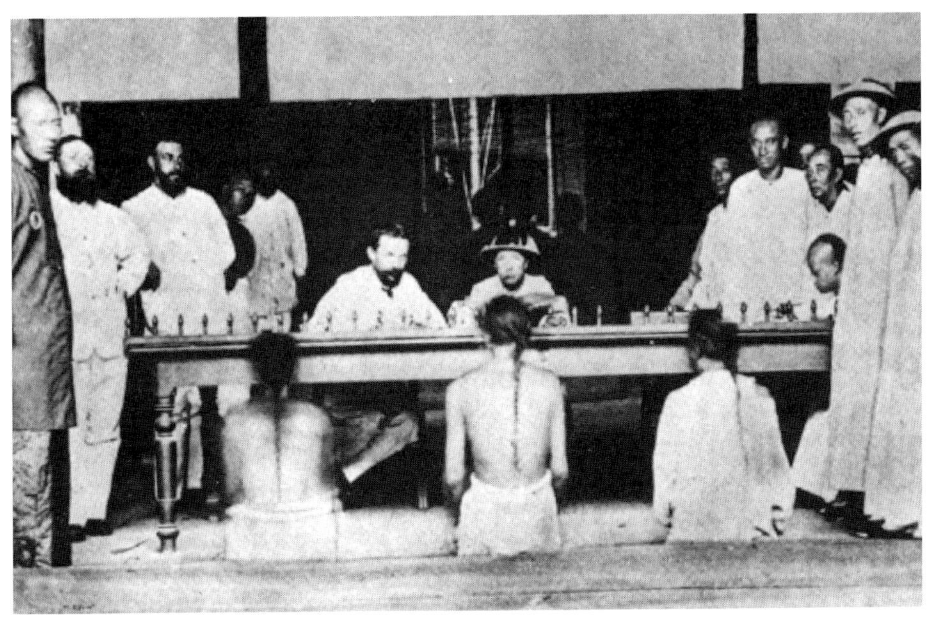

**Mixed Court** In the treaty ports, beginning in 1864, disputes between Chinese and Westerners were heard by two judges, one Chinese and one representing the Western powers. These "mixed courts" applied Western law for offenses that occurred within the concessions. *(John Hillelson Agency)*

When the best parcels of land were all occupied, conflicts over rights to water or tenancy increased. Hard times also led to increased female infanticide, as families felt that they could not afford to raise more than two or three children and saw sons as necessities. A shortage of marriageable women resulted, reducing the incentive for young men to stay near home and do as their elders told them. Some became bandits, others boatmen, carters, sedan-chair carriers, or, by the end of the century, rickshaw pullers. These economic and demographic circumstances led to some of the most destructive rebellions in China's history. The worst was the **Taiping Rebellion** (1851–1864), in which some 20 million people lost their lives, making it one of the bloodiest wars in world history.

This rebellion was initiated by Hong Xiuquan (1814–1864), a man from South China who had studied for the civil service examinations but never passed. His career as a religious leader began with visions of a golden-bearded old man and a middle-aged man who addressed him as younger brother and told him to annihilate devils. After reading a Christian tract given to him by a missionary, Hong interpreted his visions to mean he was Jesus' younger brother. He soon gathered followers, whom he instructed to destroy idols and ancestral temples, give up opium and alcohol, and renounce foot binding and prostitution. In 1851 he declared himself king of the Heavenly Kingdom of Great Peace (Taiping), an act of open insurrection. By 1853 the Taipings had moved north and established their capital at the major city of Nanjing. From this base they set about creating a utopian society based on the equalization of landholdings and the equality of men and women. Christian missionaries quickly concluded that the Christian elements in Taiping doctrines were heretical and did not help them, but the Taiping rebels held on in Nanjing for a decade. To suppress the Taipings, the Manchus had to turn to Chinese scholar-officials, who raised armies on their own, revealing that the Manchus were no longer the mighty warriors they had been when they had conquered China two centuries earlier.

After the various rebellions were suppressed, forward-looking reformers began addressing the Western threat. They set about modernizing the military along Western lines. Arsenals and dockyards were established, mines and factories were opened, and envoys were sent abroad. Recognizing that guns and ships were merely the surface manifestations of the Western powers' economic strength, some of the most progressive reformers also initiated new industries, which in the 1870s and 1880s included railway lines, steam navigation companies, coal mines, telegraph lines, and cotton spinning and weaving factories. These were the same sorts of initiatives that the British were introducing in India, but China lagged behind, especially in railroads.

**China's First Railroad** Soon after this railroad was constructed near Shanghai in 1876, the provincial governor bought it in order to tear it out. Many Chinese of the period saw railroads as harmful not only to the balance of nature but also to people's livelihoods, since the railroads eliminated jobs in transport like dragging boats along canals or driving pack horses. *(Peabody Essex Museum)*

**Slaying the Chinese Dragon** This *Puck* cartoon from August 1900 shows Japan and the European powers fighting over the prostrate Chinese dragon. As the others get ready to carve off their share, the American eagle, in the upper left, merely watches. *(The Granger Collection, New York)*

These measures drew resistance from conservatives, who thought copying Western practices was compounding defeat. The highly placed Manchu official Woren objected to the establishment of an interpreters college on the grounds that "from ancient down to modern times," there had never been "anyone who could use mathematics to raise a nation from a state of decline or to strengthen it in times of weakness."[5] Yet knowledge of the West gradually improved with more translation and travel in both directions. Newspapers covering world affairs began publication in Shanghai and Hong Kong. By 1880 China had embassies in London, Paris, Berlin, Madrid, Washington, Tokyo, and St. Petersburg.

Despite the enormous effort put into trying to catch up, China was humiliated yet again at the end of the nineteenth century. First came the discovery that Japan had so successfully modernized that it posed a threat to China (see pages 875–876). In 1894 Japanese efforts to separate Korea from Chinese influence led to a brief naval war in which China was decisively defeated, even though much of its navy had been purchased abroad at great expense. In the peace negotiations, China ceded territory (including Taiwan) to Japan, agreed to a huge indemnity, and gave Japan the right to open factories in China. China's helplessness in the face of aggression led to a scramble among the European powers for concessions and protectorates in China. At the high point of this rush in 1898, it appeared that the European powers might actually divide China among themselves, the way they had recently divided Africa. Probably only the jealousy each nation felt toward its imperialist competitors saved China from partition, although the U.S. Open Door policy, which opposed formal annexation of Chinese territory, may have helped tip the balance.

China's humiliating defeat led to a renewed drive for reform. In 1898 a group of educated young reformers gained access to the twenty-seven-year-old emperor Guangxu. They warned the emperor of the fate of Poland (divided by the European powers in the eighteenth century) and regaled him with the triumphs of the Meiji reformers in Japan. They proposed redesigning China as a constitutional monarchy with modern financial and educational systems. The Manchu establishment and the empress dowager, who had dominated the court for the past quarter century, felt threatened and not only suppressed the reform movement but imprisoned the emperor. Hope for reform from the top was dashed.

A period of violent reaction swept the country, reaching its peak in 1900 with the uprising of a secret society foreigners dubbed the **Boxers.** These Boxers blamed

China's ills on foreigners, especially the missionaries who traveled throughout China telling the Chinese that their beliefs were wrong and their practices backward. The empress dowager, deluding herself into thinking that the Boxers might solve the foreign problem for her, declared war. After the Boxers laid siege to the legation quarter in Beijing, a dozen nations including Japan sent twenty thousand troops to lift the siege. In the negotiations that followed, China had to accept a long list of penalties, including canceling the civil service examinations for five years (punishment for gentry collaboration) and a staggering indemnity of 450 million ounces of silver, almost twice the government's annual revenues.

After this defeat the Manchu court adopted its own plans to establish a limited constitutional government on the Japanese model, but gradual reform had lost its appeal. More and more Chinese were studying abroad and learning about Western political ideas, including democracy and revolution. The most famous of these was Sun Yatsen (1866–1925). Sent by his peasant family to Hawaii, he learned English there and continued his education in Hong Kong. From 1894 on, he spent his time abroad organizing revolutionary societies and seeking financial support from overseas Chinese. He later joined forces with Chinese student revolutionaries studying in Japan, and together they attempted several times to spark rebellion. In 1911 one of their plots finally triggered the collapse of China's imperial system. Army officers fearful that their connections to the revolutionaries would be exposed staged a coup and persuaded the provincial governments to secede. The powers behind the child emperor (who had ascended to the throne at the age of three in 1908) agreed to his abdication, and at the beginning of 1912 China's long history of monarchy came to an end, to be replaced by a republic modeled on Western political ideas. China had escaped direct foreign rule but would never be the same again.

## Japan

During the nineteenth century, while China's standing in the world was falling, Japan's was rising.

European traders and missionaries first arrived in Japan in the sixteenth century, but by the early seventeenth century, due in part to the remarkable success of Catholic missionaries, the Japanese government ejected them. During the eighteenth century, Japan had much more effectively than China kept foreign merchants and missionaries at bay. Because Japan's land and population were so much smaller than China's, the Western powers had never expected much from it as a trading partner and did not press it as urgently. Equally important, Japan's government decided to seal off the country from European influences; limited trade to a single port (Nagasaki), where only the Dutch came; and prohibited Japanese to travel abroad. When American and British whaling ships began to appear off Japanese coasts almost two hundred years later, the policy of exclusion was still in effect. An order of 1825 commanded Japanese officials to "drive away foreign vessels without second thought."[6]

The United States, wanting to play a greater role in the Pacific, decided it would force the Japanese to share their ports and behave as a "civilized" nation. In 1853 Commodore Matthew Perry steamed into Edo (now Tokyo) Bay and demanded diplomatic negotiations with the emperor. Some Japanese warriors urged resistance, but senior officials realized how defenseless their cities were against naval bombardment. Shocked and humiliated, they reluctantly signed a treaty with the United States that opened two ports and permitted trade.

When Japan was "opened" by gunboat diplomacy, it was a complex feudal society. The emperor in Kyoto had no effective powers. For more than two hundred years real power had been in the hands of the Tokugawa shogun in Edo (see pages 683–684). The country was divided into numerous domains, each under a lord (*daimyo*) who had full control of that area. Each lord had under him **samurai** (warriors), who had hereditary stipends and privileges, such as the right to wear a sword. Peasants and merchants were also legally distinct classes, and in theory social mobility from peasant to merchant or merchant to samurai was impossible. After two centuries of peace, there were many more samurai than were needed to administer or defend the country, and many lived very modestly. They were proud, however, and felt humiliated by the sudden American intrusion and the unequal trade treaties that the Western countries imposed.

When foreign diplomats and merchants began to settle in Yokohama after 1858, radical samurai reacted with a wave of antiforeign terrorism and antigovernment assassinations. The Western imperialist response was swift and unambiguous. Much as the Western powers had sent troops to Beijing a few years before, they now sent an allied fleet of American, British, Dutch, and French warships to demolish key Japanese forts, further weakening the power and prestige of the shogun's government.

In 1867 a coalition of reform-minded domains led a coup that ousted the Tokugawa shogunate. The samurai who led this coup declared a return to direct rule by the emperor, not practiced in Japan for more than six hundred years. This was the **Meiji Restoration,** a great turning point in Japanese development.

**East Meets West** This painting gives a Japanese view of the first audience of the American consul and his staff with the shogun, Japan's hereditary military governor, in 1859. The Americans appear strange and ill at ease. *(Laurie Platt Winfrey, Inc.)*

The domain leaders who had organized the coup, called the Meiji oligarchs, moved the boy emperor to Tokyo castle (previously the seat of the shogun, now the imperial palace). They used the young sovereign to win over both the lords and the commoners. During the emperor's first decade on the throne, the leaders carried him around in hundreds of grand imperial processions so that he could see his subjects and they him. The emerging press also worked to keep its readers informed of the young emperor's actions and aware of their obligations to him. Real power, however, remained in the hands of the oligarchs.

The battle cry of the Meiji reformers had been "Enrich the state and strengthen the armed forces." But how were these tasks to be accomplished? In an about-face that is one of history's most remarkable chapters, the idealistic but flexible leaders of Meiji Japan dropped their antiforeign attacks. Convinced that they could not beat the West until they mastered the secrets of its military and industrial might, they initiated a series of measures to reform Japan along modern, Western lines. Some proposed that "Japan must be reborn with America its mother and France its father."[7]

In 1868 the political leaders behind the emperor issued in his name a five-point charter that promised representative government and stated that "knowledge shall be sought throughout the world so as to strengthen the foundations of imperial rule." Within four years a delegation was traveling the world studying what made the Western powers strong, from the U.S. Constitution to the factories, shipyards, and railroads that made the European landscape so different from Japan's.

Japan under the shoguns had been decentralized, with most of the power over the population in the hands of the daimyos. By elevating the emperor, the oligarchs were able to centralize the government. In 1871 they merged the domain armies and abolished the domains themselves. Following the example of the French Revolution, they dismantled the four-class legal system and declared everyone equal. This amounted to stripping the samurai (7 to 8 percent of the population) of its privileges. First the samurai's stipends were reduced, then in 1876 the stipends were replaced by one-time grants of income-bearing bonds. Most samurai soon had to find work or start businesses, as the value of the bonds declined with inflation. Samurai

**A Japanese View of America** Japanese publishers memorialized the opening of Japan to foreign trade with popular woodblock prints. An 1860 American newspaper illustration showing the visit of the Japanese embassy to the sewing and laundry rooms of the Willard Hotel in Washington, D.C., inspired this print. The Americans pose with symbols of their technology—a pocket watch and a sewing machine. The Japanese text celebrates American wealth, power, and technological superiority, which the Japanese admired and soon imitated. *(Private Collection)*

no longer were to wear their swords, long the symbols of their status. Even their monopoly on the use of force was eliminated: the new army would recruit commoners along with samurai. Not surprisingly, some samurai rose to protest their loss of privileges. In one extreme case, the samurai rebels refused to use guns in a futile effort to retain the mystique of the sword. None of these uncoordinated uprisings had much effect.

Several leaders of the Meiji Restoration, in France on a fact-finding mission during the Franco-Prussian War of 1870–1871, were impressed by the active participation of French citizens in the defense of Paris. This contrasted with the indifference of most Japanese peasants during the wars that led to the Meiji Restoration. For Japan to survive in the hostile international environment, they concluded, ordinary people had to be trained to fight. A conscription law, modeled on the French version, was issued in 1872. Like French law, it exempted first sons. (See the feature "Listening to the Past: A Japanese Plan for a Modern Army" on pages 886–887.) The new War College was organized along German lines, and German instructors were recruited to teach there. Young samurai were trained to form the new professional officer corps.

The success of this approach was demonstrated first in 1877, when the professionally led army of draftees crushed a major rebellion by feudal elements protesting the loss of their privileges. Much more convincing were its victories over foreign countries. Having "opened" Korea with the gunboat diplomacy of imperialism in 1876 (see page 878), Japan decisively defeated China in 1894–1895 and gained Taiwan. In 1900 Japan participated with the European powers in occupying Beijing to suppress the Boxer Rebellion. In this period Japan was competing aggressively with the leading European powers for influence and territory in China, particularly in the northeast (Manchuria). There Japanese and Russian imperialism met and collided. In 1904 Japan attacked Russia without warning, and after a bloody war Japan emerged with a valuable foothold in China—Russia's former protectorate over Port Arthur (see Map 27.1). By 1910, with the annexation of Korea, Japan had become a full-fledged imperialist power, ruling colonies in Taiwan and Korea. These victories changed the way European nations looked at Japan. Through negotiations Japan was able to get rid of extraterritoriality in 1899 and gain control of its own tariffs in 1911. Within Japan the success of the military in raising Japan's international reputation added greatly to its political influence.

Many of the new institutions established in the Meiji period reached down to the local level. Universal public schools were called for in 1872, and progress in establishing them was remarkably rapid. Teachers were trained in newly established normal schools, where they learned to inculcate discipline, patriotism, and morality. Another modern institution that reached down to the local level was a national police force. In 1884 police training schools were established in every prefecture, and within a few years one- or two-man police stations were set up throughout the country. These policemen came to act as local agents of the central government. They not only dealt with crime but also enforced public health rules, conscription laws, and codes of behavior.

In 1889 Japan became the first non-Western country to adopt the constitutional form of government. Prefectural assemblies, set up in the 1870s and 1880s, gave local elites some experience in debating political issues. The constitution, however, was handed down from above, drafted by the top political leaders and issued in the name of the emperor. A commission had been sent abroad to study European constitutional governments and had come to the conclusion that the German constitutional monarchy provided the best model for Japan, rather than the more democratic British, French, and American ones. The new government had a two-house parliament, called the Diet, with an upper house of lords, drawn largely from former lords and nobles, and a lower house elected by a limited electorate (only about 5 percent of the adult male population in 1890). Although Japan was now a government based on laws, it was an authoritarian, rather than a democratic, one. The emperor was declared "sacred and inviolable," and he was sovereign. He had the right to appoint the prime minister and cabinet. He did not have to ask the Diet for funds, as the wealth assigned to the imperial house was entrusted to the Imperial Household Ministry, which was outside the government's control. The power of the lower house was very limited, and much of the population was not even enfranchised.

Cultural change during the Meiji period was just as profound as political change. For more than a thousand years China had provided the major source of ideas and technologies introduced into Japan, ranging from the writing system to Confucianism and Buddhism, tea and silk, chopsticks and soy sauce. But in the late nineteenth century China, beset by Western pressure, had become an object lesson in the dangers of stagnation rather than a model to follow. In the 1880s the influential author Fukuzawa Yukichi warned the Japanese that they should not let foreigners confuse them with the Chinese and even asserted that Japan should get out of Asia. Fukuzawa advocated learning Western languages and encouraged Japan to learn from the West in order to catch up with it. Fukuzawa admired not only the West's technology but also its restless spirit. Not all Japanese intellectual leaders were as avidly pro-Western as Fukuzawa, however, and by the end of the century the wholesale borrowing of the early Meiji period had given way to a more selective emphasis on those things foreign that fit best with Japanese tradition.

The leaders of the Meiji Restoration had visions of Japan becoming an industrial nation. They wanted Japan to adapt the West's science and modern technology, particularly in industry, medicine, and education. Japanese were encouraged to study abroad, and the government

**Japan's First Skyscraper** Meiji Japan's fascination with things Western led to the construction of Western-style buildings. Japan's first elevator made possible this twelve-story tower built in Tokyo in 1890. Built in the entertainment district, it was filled with shops, theaters, bars, and restaurants. *(Department of Historical Documents, National Institute of Japanese Literature. Photo courtesy of the International Society for Educational Information, Japan)*

paid large salaries to attract foreign experts. The government also played an active role in getting railroads, mines, and factories started. The oligarchs felt hampered by Japan's lack of natural resources other than coal and by the imposition of fixed tariffs under the unequal treaties with the West. Early on they decided to compete with China in the export of tea and silk to the West. Introducing the mechanical reeling of silk gave Japan a strong advantage there. The next stage was to develop heavy industry. The huge indemnity exacted from China in 1895 was used to establish the Yawata Iron and Steel Works, a major step in that direction. A third step would today be called import substitution. Factories such as cotton mills were set up to help cut the importation of Western consumer goods. By 1912 factory output accounted for 13 percent of the national product, even though only 3 percent of the labor force worked in factories, mostly small ones with fewer than fifty workers. Most of the great Japanese industrial combines, known as zaibatsu, got their start in this period.

As in Europe, the early stages of industrialization brought hardship to the countryside. Farmers often rioted as their incomes did not keep up with prices or their tax burdens were raised. Still, rice production increased, death rates dropped as public health was improved, and population grew from about 30 million in 1868 to about 45 million in 1900.

Japan became the first non-Western country to use an ancient love of country to transform itself and thereby meet the many-sided challenge of Western expansion. Moreover, Japan demonstrated convincingly that a modern Asian nation could defeat and humble a great Western power. Japan provided patriots in Asia and Africa with an inspiring example of national recovery and liberation.

## Korea

One country that was not inspired by Japan's progress was Korea, since it became a victim of Japan's success.

The Yi Dynasty had been on the throne in Korea since 1392. Chinese influence had grown over this period as the Korean elite enthusiastically embraced Confucian teachings and studied for Chinese-style civil service examinations.

By the second half of the nineteenth century Korea found itself caught between China, Japan, and Russia, each trying to protect or extend its sphere of influence. Added to this, Westerners also began demanding that Korea be "opened." Korea's first response was to try to keep out all but the Chinese, since it viewed itself as a vassal of China and insisted that its foreign relations be handled through Beijing. Matters were complicated by the rise of a religious cult in the 1860s that had strong xenophobic elements. Although the government executed the cult founder in 1864, this **Tonghak movement** continued to gain support, especially among impoverished peasants. Thus, like China in the same period, the Korean government faced simultaneous internal and external threats.

In 1871 the U.S. minister to China took five warships to try to "open" Korea but left after exchanges of fire resulted in 250 Koreans dead and the Korean government still unwilling to make concessions. Japan tried next, bringing a fleet to Inchon, the port of Seoul, in 1876. The Japanese forced the Korean government to sign an unequal treaty, open three ports to Japanese trade, and

**Queen Min of Korea** An ambitious and successful politician, Queen Min promoted the dominance of her family clan. She also led the effort to resist Japan and maintain Korean independence. In 1895 Japanese troops, acting under orders, stormed the palace, murdered Queen Min, and burned her body. Japanese pressure on Korea was relentless until the end of World War II. *(Courtesy, Yushin Yoo)*

cease considering itself a tributary of China. On China's urging, Korea also signed treaties with the European powers in an effort to counterbalance Japan.

Over the next couple of decades reformers in China tried to encourage Korea to adopt its own "self-strengthening" movement, but Korean conservatives, including the queen (regent for the child king), did their best to undo reform efforts. Reformers in Korea who admired the Meiji Restoration in Japan staged a coup in 1884 with Japan's help. China intervened to rescue the king and help suppress the rebels. Afterward both China and Japan agreed to withdraw their troops and military advisers. Nevertheless, in 1894, when peasant unrest erupted in a massive revolt of followers of the Tonghak movement, both China and Japan sent military forces, claiming to come to the Korean government's aid. They ended up fighting each other instead.

With Japan's decisive victory, Korea became a protectorate of Japan. The Japanese encouraged a plot to assassinate the queen in 1895. Twelve years later, when the king proved less than fully compliant, the Japanese forced him to abdicate in favor of his feeble-minded son. Korean resistance was suppressed in bloody fighting, and in 1910 Korea was formally annexed as a province of Japan. It would remain under Japanese occupation until the end of World War II.

## THE MOVEMENT OF PEOPLES

With Western imperialism came the extensive movement of people into, across, and out of Asia throughout the nineteenth century. In no earlier period had so many Europeans lived in Asia or so many Asians taken up residence in other countries. This vast migration both resulted from and helped accelerate the increasing integration of the world economy. Improvements in shipping and the digging of the Suez and Panama Canals made crossing the oceans faster and safer. Knowledge of foreign languages improved dramatically, and translations of works from Western to Asian languages and vice versa made understanding of alien cultures much easier to acquire, at least for the literate.

### Westerners to Asia

Imperialism brought Europeans to Asia in unprecedented numbers. There were significant expatriate communities of Europeans and Americans in most of the countries of Asia by the early 1900s. These communities consisted of businessmen, missionaries, and colonial civil servants. The most extreme case was India. By 1863 there were already sixty-five thousand British troops in India and many more British in the civil service and commercial companies. The higher levels of the Indian Civil Service and the Indian army were staffed by British men, including, over time, many who had been born in India. Especially after the opening of the Suez Canal in 1869, British working in India were accompanied by their wives and children, who would return to Britain every few years on leave. By the eve of World War I, hundreds of thousands of expatriates lived in India.

Beginning in 1809 British recruits to the British East India Company and subsequently to the Indian Civil Service were required to learn at least one Indian language fluently, but the trend, especially after the Great Revolt of 1857, was for the British to live separately from the Indians in their own enclaves. Houses were adapted to the local climate, with wide, well-shaded porches and large lawns. Houses and grounds were tended by Indian servants, who also minded the colonists' children, did their shopping, and handled most of their dealings with local Indians. Thus British women had little need to interact with Indians other than as servants. British colonists who were curious about India and wanted to make Indian friends found social intercourse difficult, especially with Muslims and higher-caste Hindus, whose social contact with outsiders was restricted by traditional rules.

China was not under colonial occupation and so did not have so many foreign civil servants and soldiers in its cities, but it did attract more missionaries than any other Asian country. Queen Victoria had discouraged missionaries from trying to convert her Indian subjects, who were guaranteed the right to practice their own religions freely, but she had no objection to their trying to convert the Chinese. After 1860, when China agreed in an unequal treaty imposed on it to allow missionaries to proselytize throughout the country, missionaries came in large numbers. By 1900 there were 886 Catholic and about 3,000 Protestant missionaries in China, more than half of them women. Unlike the British civil servants in India, missionaries had no choice but to mix with the local population, finding the best opportunities for conversion among ordinary, poor Chinese. Although the majority of missionaries devoted themselves to preaching, over the course of the nineteenth century more and more missionaries worked in medicine or education. By 1905 there were about 300 fully qualified physicians doing medical missionary work, and the 250 mission hospitals and dispensaries served about 2 million patients. Missionary hospitals in Hong Kong also ran a medical school, which trained hundreds of Chinese as physicians.

**Missionary Orphanage** The Chinese often were suspicious of Christian missionaries, even when they devoted themselves to charitable activities such as caring for orphans. In the scene depicted here, from about 1891, a Roman Catholic nun in an inland city along the Yangzi River is organizing the transfer of a group of babies. They have been placed in baskets so that they can be carried on shoulder poles. *(Harvard-Yenching Library)*

Missionaries helped spread Western learning at their schools. For their elementary schools, missionaries produced textbooks in Chinese on a full range of subjects. They also translated dozens of standard works into Chinese, especially in the natural sciences, mathematics, history, and international law. By 1906 nearly 60,000 Chinese students were attending 2,400 Christian schools. Most of this activity was supported by contributions sent from America and Britain.

Most missionaries were critical of elements of Chinese culture and society—such as the treatment of women, foot binding, opium smoking, and work habits—and this arrogant attitude offended many Chinese of all social classes. In addition, the sheer strangeness of the Westerners made many Chinese suspicious of them. For instance, missionaries often ran orphanages, a "good work" that also helped produce converts, but some Chinese suspected that they were buying babies for nefarious purposes. By the 1890s, however, educated Chinese reformers often adopted some of the goals that the missionaries had been advocating, such as the elimination of foot binding.

Missionaries in China had more success in spreading Western learning than in gaining converts. By 1900 fewer than a million Chinese were Christians. Ironically, although Western missionaries paid much less attention to Korea—the first missionary arrived there in 1884—Christianity took much stronger root there, and today about 25 percent of the Korean population is Christian. Missionaries also had some success in Vietnam, where Catholic missionaries were protected by the French government.

## Asian Emigration

The nineteenth century was also a period when Asians left their native countries in unprecedented numbers. Like the tens of millions of Europeans who moved to the Americas or Australia in search of economic opportunities (see Chapter 28), millions of Asians emigrated as well. As in Europe, both push and pull factors prompted people to leave home. Between 1750 and 1900 world population grew rapidly, in many places tripling. China and India were extremely densely populated countries—China with about 400 million people in the mid-nineteenth century, India with more than 200 million. Not surprisingly, these two giants were the leading exporters of people. On the pull side were the new opportunities created in part by the flow of development capital into previously underdeveloped areas. In many of the European colonies in Asia and Africa the business class came to consist of both Asian and European migrants, the Asians protected and tolerated by the Western imperialists who found them useful.

In China voluntary migration in search of opportunity had been going on for centuries. Young men who learned of opportunities abroad would borrow money from friends or relatives to try their luck there. If successful, they would send for their families later. Chinese from the southern coastal regions had formed key components of the mercantile communities throughout Southeast Asia, from Siam south to Java and east to the Philippines. Chinese often assimilated in Siam and Vietnam, but they rarely did so in Muslim areas such as Java, Catholic areas such as the Philippines, and primitive tribal areas such as northern Borneo. In these places, distinct Chinese communities emerged, usually dominated by speakers of one Chinese dialect.

With the growth in trade that accompanied the European expansion, Chinese began to settle in insular Southeast Asia in larger numbers. After Singapore was founded by the British in 1819, Chinese rapidly poured in, soon to become its dominant ethnic group. Many Chinese pros-

**Chinese Street Opera in Singapore** In Singapore there were so many Chinese people that they were able to maintain their traditional forms of entertainment, such as the opera shown here in a photograph from the 1890s. Although most of the men were still wearing the Manchu-imposed queue hairstyle, many concealed them under Western-style hats. *(National Archives of Singapore)*

pered as these areas developed. In British-controlled Malaya, some Chinese built great fortunes in the tin business, while others worked in the mines. There the Chinese community included both old overseas families long settled in the Portuguese city of Malacca, who spoke Malay, and a much larger number of more recent immigrants, most of whom spoke Cantonese. In the Spanish-controlled Philippines and Dutch-controlled Indonesia, however, the Chinese suffered repeated persecutions. Early in the nineteenth century in Borneo, the Dutch expropriated the mines that the Chinese had worked for generations. Elsewhere, however, the Dutch made use of the Chinese. In Java, for instance, Chinese merchants were used as tax collectors. Moreover, after the Dutch conquered southern Sumatra in 1864, Chinese were recruited to work in the sugar and tobacco plantations. By 1900 more than 500,000 Chinese were living in the Dutch East Indies.

Discovery of gold in California in 1848, Australia in 1851, and Canada in 1858 encouraged many Chinese to book passage to those places. In California few arrived soon enough to strike gold, but they found other work. Thousands worked laying railroads, and others took up mining in Wyoming and Idaho. In 1880 more than 100,000 Chinese men and 3,000 Chinese women were living in the western United States. (See the feature "Individuals in Society: Chin Gee-hee.")

Indian entrepreneurs were attracted by the burgeoning commerce of Southeast Asia, though not in quite so large numbers as Chinese. In many communities, such as Malaya, Indian business communities became sizeable. Indian migrants also moved outside Asia, especially to areas under British control.

The bulk of Indian emigrants were indentured laborers, recruited under contract. The rise of indentured labor from Asia was a direct result of the outlawing of the African slave trade in the early nineteenth century (see pages 620–621). Sugar plantations in the Caribbean and elsewhere needed new sources of workers. In the British colonies, planters discovered that they could recruit Indian laborers to replace blacks. By 1870 more than half a million Indians had migrated to Mauritius (in the southern Indian Ocean, east of Madagascar) and the British Caribbean, especially Trinidad. After the French abolished slavery in 1848, they recruited workers from India as well, with nearly 80,000 Indians making the trip to the French Caribbean over the next half-century. Later in the century, many Indians emigrated to British colonies in Africa, the largest numbers to South Africa. Indentured Indian laborers also built the railroad in East Africa. Malaya, Singapore, and Fiji also received many emigrants from India.

Indentured laborers secured as substitutes for slaves were often treated little better than slaves, both on the ships that delivered them and on the plantations and mines where they worked. After abuses of this sort were exposed, the Indian government established regulations stipulating a maximum period of five years' indenture, after which the migrant would be entitled to passage home. Even though government "protectors" were appointed at the ports of embarkation, exploitation of indentured workers continued largely unchecked. Few of the indentured workers were women, so the community failed to reproduce itself, and emigration had to be continued to maintain the workforce. Still, many of the migrants stayed on after their indenture.

In areas outside the British Empire, China offered the largest supply of ready labor for plantations and mines. Starting in the 1840s, contractors arrived at Chinese ports to recruit labor for plantations and mines in Cuba, Peru, Hawaii, Sumatra, and elsewhere. In the 1840s, for example, the Spanish government actively recruited Chinese laborers for the plantations of Cuba. They came under eight-year contracts, were paid about twenty-five cents a day, and were fed potatoes and salted beef. Between 1853 and 1873 more than 130,000 Chinese laborers came to Cuba, the majority spending their lives as virtual slaves.

Chinese laborers did not have the British government to protect them and seem to have suffered even more than Indian workers. Some of the worst abuses were in Peru, where nearly 100,000 Chinese had arrived by 1875, lured by promoters who had promised them easy riches. Instead, they were set to laying railroads or working on cotton plantations or in dangerous guano pits. Those who tried to flee were forced to work in chains. In Hawaii sugar planters brought over the first Chinese laborers in 1852 on three- or five-year contracts, giving them three dollars per month plus room and board for working a twelve-hour day, six days a week. After they finished their contracts, many stayed in Hawaii, where they set up small businesses. These Chinese became an important part of Hawaii's business community, although land remained almost entirely in the hands of white families. By 1900 there were about 25,000 Chinese in Hawaii.

India and China sent more people abroad than any other Asian countries during this period, but they were not alone. As Japan started to industrialize, its cities could not absorb all those forced off the farms, and people began emigrating in significant numbers, many to Hawaii and later to South America. Emigration from the Philippines also was substantial, especially after it became a U.S. territory in 1898.

# INDIVIDUALS IN SOCIETY

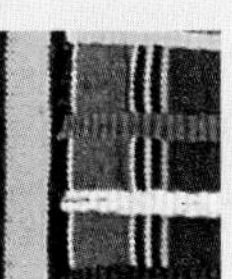

## CHIN GEE-HEE

Chin Gee-hee was one of the earliest and most successful of the tens of thousands of Chinese who emigrated from China in the nineteenth century. He was born in 1840, the son of a poor potter in southern China. As a boy, he carried his father's wares to market using a shoulder pole—a perilous undertaking on foot with a precious, fragile cargo. When he fell one day and all his father's pots shattered, an onlooker took pity on him and offered to take him to America.

By 1858, when he was eighteen, Chin Gee-hee was working in Port Gamble, Washington, moving from job to job as a laborer, a launderer, and finally a cook at the local lumber mill. He learned English, and when he moved to Seattle in 1873, he joined the Wah Chong Company as a junior partner. Soon Chin had saved enough money to send for a wife from China. The couple had a son in 1875.

The Wah Chong Company provided a variety of services, including tailoring, manufacturing cigars, and selling of tea and other Chinese merchandise. Chin became involved in the company's labor contracting business, which advertised that they could secure Chinese workers on short notice. Chin negotiated contracts with local enterprises such as lumber camps, mines, railroad companies, and farms, then organized the men arriving in steady streams off the boats from China. His company became a center of social contact for the Chinese, providing food, accommodations, banking, and writing and translation services. As Chin developed his company into the largest labor contractor in the Seattle area, he made influential friends among business leaders.

During the depression that lasted from 1883 to 1886, the Chinese who had been eagerly sought to assist in the area's development were pressured to leave, and over the next few years local white citizens became more vocal in their anti-Chinese sentiments. A group called the Committee of Fifteen tried to expel all remaining Chinese from the Puget Sound area in 1885. When Chin heard that Chinese in Tacoma had been driven out by armed white men, he sent a telegram to the Chinese consul in San Francisco requesting assistance. Meanwhile, the mayor of Seattle, who had known Chin since his beginnings in Port Gamble, tried to protect the Chinese. The next year, however, all of the remaining Chinese were herded together to await deportation. Although most of them were deported, the mayor, and other sympathetic citizens managed to protect Chin and a few others. On behalf of his countrymen, Chin compiled a detailed account of their loss of property, sending the list of damages to the Chinese consul. Eventually, his efforts secured more than $700,000 in compensation for the Chinese.

*Chin at work in his office. Although Chin helped well-to-do Seattle residents acquire Chinese furnishings, his own office was strictly business.* (Corbis)

Chinese laborers returned slowly to the Seattle area, where they were soon in demand again. Chin started his own business, the Quong Tuck Company, in 1888. His laborers built the Burke Building, and his company helped Thomas Burke decorate his judicial chambers with Chinese furnishings.

Back in China, Chin became best known for the railroad he had built. Dreaming of a railroad that would connect China to Europe, Chin traveled throughout North America selling shares to overseas Chinese in his railroad company. By 1904 he had raised $1.4 million, and he continued to raise money for another fifteen years. All that ever got built was one line in his home province, which proved a great boon to the local economy. In the late 1930s the railroad was dismantled to deter Japanese invaders. Sometime after it was destroyed, a statue of Chin was erected in Toishan, in a park near the former station.

### QUESTIONS FOR ANALYSIS

1. What types of ties did Chin maintain with China?
2. Did China gain anything from the flow of emigrants like Chin out of China?

Based on Ruthanne Lum McCunn, *Chinese American Portraits: Personal Histories 1828–1988* (San Francisco: Chronicle Books, 1988), pp. 47–55.

Asian migration to the United States, Canada, and Australia—the primary destinations of European emigrants—would undoubtedly have been greater if it had not been so vigorously resisted by the white settlers in those regions. On the West Coast of the United States, friction between Chinese and white settlers was fed by racist rhetoric that depicted Chinese as opium-smoking heathens. In 1882 Chinese were barred from becoming American citizens, and the immigration of Chinese laborers was suspended. In 1888 President Grover Cleveland declared the Chinese "impossible of assimilation with our people, and dangerous to our peace and welfare."[8] One Australian brutally summed up the typical view of Chinese in that country: "The Chinaman knows nothing about Caucasian civilization. It would be less objectionable to drive a flock of sheep to the poll than to allow Chinamen to vote."[9] Thus the "great migration" to the United States, Canada, and Australia (see pages 903–904) primarily benefited Europeans.

Most of the Asian migrants discussed so far were illiterate peasants or business people, not members of the traditional educated elites. By the beginning of the twentieth century, however, another group of Asians was going abroad in significant numbers: students. Indians and others in the British colonies usually went to Britain, Vietnamese and others in the French colonies to France, and so on. Chinese eager to master modern learning most commonly went to Japan, but others went to Europe and the United States. Most of these students traveled abroad to learn about Western science, law, and government in the hope of strengthening their own countries. On their return they contributed enormously to the intellectual life of their societies, increasing understanding of the modern Western world but also becoming the most vocal advocates of overthrowing the old order and driving out the colonial masters.

## SUMMARY

During the nineteenth century, the societies of Asia underwent enormous changes—the results of population growth, social unrest, and the looming presence of Western imperialist powers. Although Western powers arrived at Asian shores at different times and with different aims, the ruling classes of these Asian societies responded to Western expansion in similar ways.

Often the initial response was to try to drive the unwelcome foreigners away. This was seen in China, Japan, and Korea in particular. Violent antiforeign reactions exploded again and again, but the superior military technology of the industrialized West almost invariably prevailed. After suffering humiliating defeats, some Asians insisted on the need to preserve their cultural traditions at all costs. Others came to the opposite conclusion that the West was indeed superior in some ways and that they would have to adopt European ideas or techniques for their own purposes. The struggles between the traditionalists and the westernizers were often intense.

By the end of the nineteenth century, most of the southern tier of Asia, from India to the Philippines, had been made colonies of Western powers. Many of these areas became major exporters of agricultural products or raw materials, including timber, rubber, tin, sugar, tea, cotton, and jute. New knowledge and new technologies spread rapidly. Railroads, telegraphs, modern sanitation, and a wider supply of inexpensive manufactured goods brought fundamental changes in everyday life. To a much greater extent than in any earlier time, Europeans were living in Asia and learning its languages and cultures, and Asians were studying Western languages or emigrating abroad. Still, cultural barriers between the colonizers and the colonized were huge. The West relied on force to conquer and rule, and it treated non-Western peoples as racial inferiors.

Throughout Asia, Western domination was resented by the beginning of the twentieth century. The more Asian intellectual elites learned about the West, the more justification they found for resistance. They echoed the demands of anti-imperialists in Europe and America that the West live up to its own ideals of civil liberty and political self-determination. As nationalism took hold in the West (see Chapter 24), it found a receptive audience among the educated elites in Asia. How could the assertion that every people had the right to control its own destiny not appeal to the colonized?

## KEY TERMS

Great Mutiny/Great Revolt
Empress of India
Indian National Congress
Java War
Culture System
encomienda system
opium
Treaty of Nanjing
concessions
Taiping Rebellion
Boxers
samurai
Meiji Restoration
Tonghak movement

## NOTES

1. Quoted in Stanley Wolpert, *A New History of India* (New York: Oxford University Press, 1993), p. 215.
2. Quoted in K. M. Panikkar, *Asia and Western Dominance: A Survey of the Vasco da Gama Epoch of Asian History* (London: George Allen & Unwin, 1959), p. 116.
3. Quoted in D. Steinberg, ed., *In Search of Southeast Asia: A Modern History*, rev. ed. (Honolulu: University of Hawaii Press, 1987), p. 129.
4. S. Teng and J. K. Fairbank, *China's Response to the West: A Documentary Survey* (New York: Atheneum, 1971), p. 26.
5. Ibid., p. 76, modified.
6. Quoted in J. W. Hall, *Japan, from Prehistory to Modern Times* (New York: Delacorte Press, 1970), p. 250.
7. Quoted ibid., p. 289.
8. Quoted in J. D. Spence, *The Search for Modern China* (New York: W. W. Norton, 1990), p. 215.
9. Quoted in C. A. Price, *The Great White Walls Are Built: Restrictive Immigration to North America and Australia, 1836–1888* (Canberra: Australian National University Press, 1974), p. 175.

## SUGGESTED READING

General studies of imperialism, colonialism, and the global impact of the Industrial Revolution help put the histories of the various societies of Asia in the nineteenth century into context. See, for instance, W. Baumgart, *Imperialism* (1982); M. Doyle, *Empires* (1986); and B. Porter, *The Lion's Share: A Short History of British Imperialism, 1850–1970* (1976). E. Wolf, *Europe and the People Without History* (1982), traces the impact of imperialism on non-Western peoples. D. Northrup, *Indentured Labor in the Age of Imperialism, 1834–1922* (1995), discusses the vast movement of peoples during this period. D. Headrick, *The Tools of Empire: Technology and European Imperialism in the Nineteenth Century* (1981), analyzes the connection between technological innovation and the ease with which Europeans established control over huge areas of the world. See also M. Adas, *Machines as the Measure of Man* (1989).

On India under British control, see C. Bayly, *Indian Society and the Making of the British Empire* (1990), and T. Metcalf, *Ideologies of the Raj* (1997), both part of *The New Cambridge History of India.* On Indian nationalism, see B. Chandra, *Nationalism and Colonialism in Modern India* (1989), and J. Masselos, *Indian Nationalism: A History* (1998). S. Bose and A. Jalal, *Modern South Asia: History, Culture, Political Economy* (1998), incorporates recent scholarship with a postcolonial perspective in a wide-ranging study. P. Mitter, *Art and Nationalism in Colonial India, 1850–1922* (1994), is insightful and richly illustrated. R. Guha, ed., *A Subaltern Studies Reader 1986–1995* (1997), provides articles that look at Indian society from the perspective of those outside the elite.

Steinberg, cited in the Notes, is an impressive work on Southeast Asia by seven specialists. See also the authoritative N. Tarling, ed., *The Cambridge History of Southeast Asia: From c. 1800 to the 1930s* (2000). On America's rule of the Philippines, see S. Karnow, *In Our Image: America's Empire in the Philippines* (1989).

Hall, cited in the Notes, is a good introduction to the history of Japan. E. Reischauer's topical survey, *Japan: The Story of a Nation* (1981), is recommended, as are T. Huber, *The Revolutionary Origins of Modern Japan* (1981), and Y. Fukuzawa, *Autobiography* (1966), the personal account of a leading intellectual who witnessed the emergence of modern Japan. M. Weiner, *Race and Migration in Imperial Japan* (1994); W. Beasley, *The Meiji Restoration* (1972); and G. Wilson, *Patriots and Redeemers in Japan: Motives in the Meiji Restoration* (1992), are important works. M. Jansen, ed., *The Cambridge History of Japan: The Nineteenth Century* (1989), provides excellent reference. On Japan's conquest of Korea, see P. Duus, *The Abacus and the Sword: The Japanese Penetration of Korea, 1895–1910* (1995).

For overviews of China in the nineteenth century, see F. Wakeman, *The Fall of Imperial China* (1975); J. Fairbank, *The Great Chinese Revolution* (1987); J. Spence, *The Search for Modern China,* 2d ed. (2000); and I. Hsü, *The Rise of Modern China*, 6th ed. (1999). J. Spence, *God's Chinese Son* (1997), tells the story of the Taiping rebels. For the beginning of the treaty port system, see P. Ward, *The Opium War, 1840–1842* (1975). On the relationship between the Chinese and Christian missionaries, see P. Cohen, *China and Christianity: The Missionary Movement and Growth of Chinese Anti-Foreignism, 1860–1870* (1963), and J. Hunter, *The Gospel of Gentility: American Missionary Women in Turn-of-the-Century China* (1984). The concerns of leading intellectuals at the end of the nineteenth century and beginning of the twentieth are analyzed in H. Chang, *Chinese Intellectuals in Crisis: Search for Order and Meaning (1890–1911)* (1987). On the Boxers, see J. Esherick, *The Origins of the Boxer Uprising* (1987). On the end of the monarchical system, see H. Schiffrin, *Sun Yat-sen: Reluctant Revolutionary* (1980). I. Pruitt, *A Daughter of Han: The Autobiography of a Chinese Working Woman* (1967), offers the reader a glimpse of a segment of Chinese society rarely depicted in books.

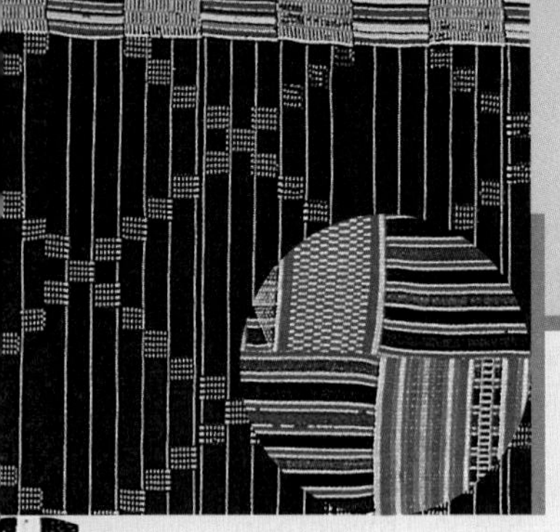

# LISTENING TO THE PAST

## A JAPANESE PLAN FOR A MODERN ARMY

*Japan responded to the imperialist West by adopting Western methods and technologies. Aritomo Yamagata (1838–1922) contributed significantly to that approach and its successes. Born into the military nobility known as samurai, Yamagata joined in the movement to restore the power of the emperor. To him fell the task of strengthening the armed forces. After traveling for more than a year to study Europe's armies and navies, he wrote the memorandum reprinted here, "Opinion on Military Affairs and Conscription." The next year, he helped overturn traditional Japanese society by writing a law calling for a Japanese army drafted from the whole male population, on the Western pattern. No longer would fighting be the province of samurai alone.*

A military force is required to defend the country and protect its people. Previous laws of this country inculcated in the minds of the samurai these basic functions, and there was no separation between the civilian and military affairs. Nowadays civilian officials and military officials have separate functions, and the practice of having the samurai serve both functions has been abandoned. It is now necessary to select and train those who can serve the military functions, and herein lies the change in our military system. . . .

The status of our armed forces today is as follows: We have the so-called Imperial Guards whose functions are nothing more than to protect the sacred person of His Majesty and to guard the Imperial Palace. We have altogether more than twenty battalions manning the four military garrisons who are deployed to maintain domestic tranquility, and are not equipped to fight against any foreign threat. As to our navy, we have a few battleships yet to be completed. How can they be sufficient to counteract foreign threats? . . .

The first concern of the Ministry of Military Affairs is to set up a system to defend our homeland. For this purpose two categories of soldiers are required: a standing army and those on the reserve list. The number of troops differ from country to country. Of the major countries, Russia maintains the largest number of troops and the United States the smallest. The reason for this discrepancy comes from the fact that the governmental system differs from one country to another. Consequently the regulations governing each of the countries also differ. The Netherlands and Belgium are among the smallest countries, but they are located between large countries, and in order to avoid contempt and scorn from their neighbors, they diligently go about the business of defending their countries. Even though one of these countries has a total area not exceeding one-third of the area of our country, it maintains a standing army numbering not less than forty to fifty thousand. . . .

. . . The creation of a standing army for our country is a task which cannot be delayed. It is recommended that a certain number of strong and courageous young men be selected from each of the prefectures in accordance with the size of the prefectures, and that such young men be trained in the Western-type military science and placed under rigorous drills, so that they may be deployed as occasion demands.

The so-called reservists do not normally remain within the military barracks. During peacetime they remain in their homes, and in an emergency they are called to service. All of the countries in Europe have reservists, and amongst them Prussia has most of them. There is not a single able-bodied man in Prussia who is not trained in military affairs. Recently Prussia and France fought each other and the former won handily. . . .

It is recommended that our country adopt a system under which any able-bodied man twenty years of age be drafted into military service, unless his absence from home will create undue hardship for his family. There shall be no distinction made

The new Japanese army, with Western uniforms, ca 1870. *(Tsuneo Tamba Collection, Yokohama, Japan/ Laurie Platt Winfrey, Inc.)*

between the common man and those who are of the samurai class. They shall all be formed into ranks, and after completion of a period of service, they shall be returned to their homes. In this way every man will become a soldier, and not a single region in the country will be without defense. Thus our defense will become complete.

The second concern of the Ministry is coastal defense. This includes building of warships and constructing coastal batteries. Actually, battleships are movable batteries. Our country has thousands of miles of coastline, and any mobile corner of our country can become the advance post of our enemy. . . .

The third concern of the Military is to create resources for the navy and the army. There are three items under consideration, namely military academies, a bureau of military supplies, and a bureau of munitions depots. It is not difficult to have one million soldiers in a short time, but it is difficult to gain one good officer during the same span of time. Military academies are intended to train officers for these two services. If we pay little attention to this need today, we shall not be able to have the services of capable officers for another day. Therefore, without delay military academies must be created and be allowed to prosper. . . . The bureau of military supplies shall be in charge of procuring military provisions and manufacturing weapons of war for the two services. The bureau of munitions depots shall store such provisions and munitions. If we lack military provisions and weapons and our munitions depots are empty, what good will the million soldiers in the army or thousands of warships do? . . .

Some people may argue that while they are aware of the urgency in the need for the Ministry of Military Affairs, they cannot permit the entire national resources to be committed to the need of one ministry alone. They further aver that from the larger perspective of the imperial government, there are so many other projects covering a wide range of things which require governmental attention. . . . This argument fails to discern the fundamental issues. The recommendations herein presented by the Ministry of Military Affairs in no way asks for the stoppage of all governmental activities or for the monopolization of all government revenues. But in a national emergency, a new set of priorities must be established. Those of us who are given the task of governing must learn from the past, discern the present, and weigh all matters carefully. . . .

Those of us who govern must first of all discern the conditions prevailing in the world, set up priorities and take appropriate measures. In our opinion Russia has been acting very arrogantly. Previously, contrary to the provisions of the Treaty of Sevastopol, she placed her warships in the Black Sea. Southward, she has shown her aggressive intent toward Muslim countries and toward India. Westward, she has crossed the borders of Manchuria and has been navigating the Amur River. Her intents being thus, it is inevitable that she will move eastward sooner or later by sending troops to Hokkaido, and then taking advantage of the seasonal wind move to the warmer areas.

At a time like this it is very clear where the priority of this country must lie. We must now have a well-trained standing army supplemented by a large number of reservists. We must build warships and construct batteries. We must train officers and soldiers. We must manufacture and store weapons and ammunitions. The nation may consider that it cannot bear the expenses. However, even if we wish to ignore it, this important matter cannot disappear from us. Even if we prefer to enter into this type of defense undertaking, we cannot do without our defense for a single day.

## QUESTIONS FOR ANALYSIS

1. What aspects of military modernization are highlighted here? What goals was Aritomo trying to achieve with each proposal?
2. How does Aritomo use the examples of European countries to reach conclusions?

*Source:* David John Lu, *Japan: A Documentary History* (Armonk, N.Y.: M. E. Sharpe, 1997), pp. 315–318. Excerpted with permission.

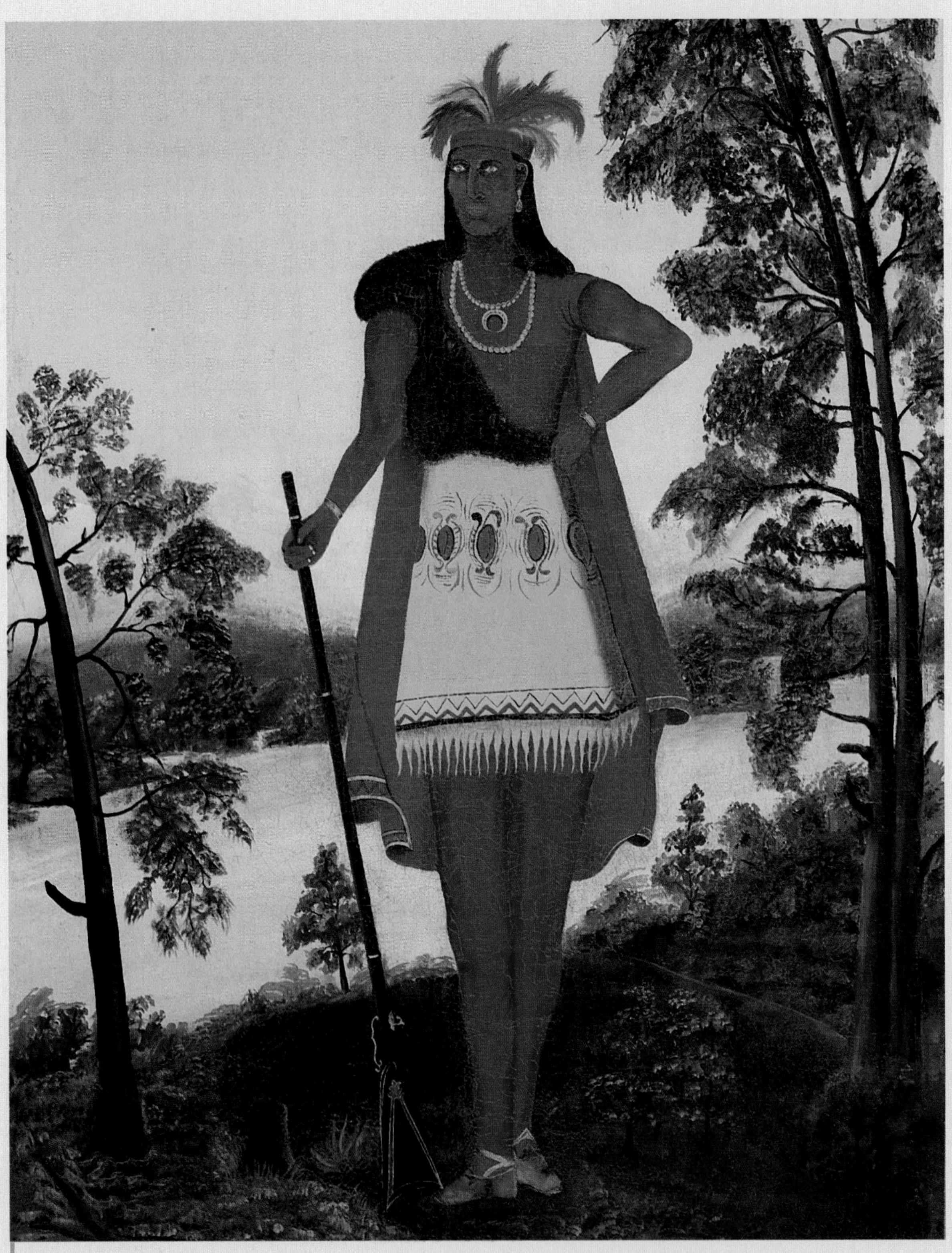

Portrait of Skikellany. The clothing worn by this important Oneida Indian of upstate New York identifies him as a member of the Northeast Woodlands Indians. *(Unknown artist, American, Portrait of a Native American Man of the Northeast Woodlands. Philadelphia Museum of Art, The Collection of Edgar William Bernice Chrysler Garbisch, 1966 [1966-219-3])*

CHAPTER

# 28 NATION BUILDING IN THE WESTERN HEMISPHERE AND AUSTRALIA

## CHAPTER OUTLINE



In the Western Hemisphere and in Australia, as in Europe, the nineteenth century was a period of nation building, geographical expansion, and industrial and commercial growth. Waves of emigrants moved from Europe and Asia to the Americas and to Australia. The millions who braved the oceans populated and built new nations and linked the Western Hemisphere and Australia with the rest of the globe.

The countries of North and South America became highly diverse ethnically and culturally, and the issue of race created serious tensions throughout the hemisphere. In the United States, it helped to bring on the Civil War. In the late nineteenth and early twentieth centuries, European immigration directly affected the ways in which the United States and the Latin American nations coped with racial situations.

Today North America consists of Canada, the United States, Mexico, and the countries of Central America north of the Isthmus of Panama; South America comprises the twelve independent nations south of that isthmus. Thus the United States is not synonymous with North America, nor is Latin America synonymous with South America.

At the end of the eighteenth century, Canada and the countries of South America remained colonies. Their European mother countries looked on the democratic experiment of the infant United States with suspicion and scorn. The island continent of Australia, remote from Europe and economically undeveloped, served as a dumping ground for English criminals. By 1914 the Latin American states, Canada, and Australia were enjoying political independence and playing a crucial role in the world economy. The United States had become a colossus on which the Old World depended in the First World War.

- Why and how did the Spanish and Portuguese colonies of North and South America shake off European domination and develop into national states?
- What role did the concept of manifest destiny play in the evolution of the United States?
- How did the experience of slavery and racism affect blacks in the United States?
- How did the Americas and Australia absorb new peoples, and what was the social impact of the immigrants?

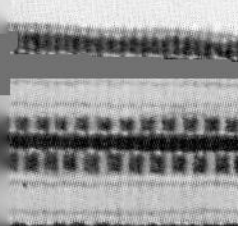

- What geographical, economic, and political conditions shaped the development of Canada?
- What factors aided the economic growth of Australia?

These are among the questions that this chapter will address.

## LATIN AMERICA (1800–1929)

In 1800 the Spanish Empire in the Western Hemisphere stretched from the headwaters of the Mississippi River in present-day Minnesota to the tip of Cape Horn in the Antarctic (see Map 28.1). According to the Kentucky statesman Henry Clay (1777–1852), "Within this vast region, we behold the most sublime and interesting objects of creation: the loftiest mountains, the most majestic rivers in the world; the richest mines of precious metals, the choicest productions of the earth."[1] Spanish and Portuguese America was vast; British America was tiny. In addition to large regions of South America (the world's fourth-largest continent), the Spanish Empire included large parts of southwestern sections of the present-day United States, including California. Geographical barriers alone posed tremendous obstacles to political unity. Spain believed that the great wealth of the Americas existed for its benefit, and Spanish policies fostered bitterness and the desire for independence in the colonies. Between 1806 and 1825, the Spanish colonies in Latin America were convulsed by upheavals that ultimately resulted in their separation from Spain.

The Latin American wars were *revolutions* because the colonists were revolting against the domination of Spain and fighting for direct self-government. They were *wars of independence* because the colonies were seeking economic liberation and management of their own commercial affairs. They were *civil wars* because social and racial groups were fighting one another. The **Creoles**—people of Spanish descent born in America—resented the economic and political dominance of the **peninsulares,** as natives of Spain or Portugal were called. Peninsulares controlled the rich export-import trade, intercolonial trade, and mining industries. At the same time, *mestizos* of mixed Spanish and Indian background and *mulattos* of mixed Spanish and African heritage sought an end to their systematic subordination.

Between 1850 and the worldwide depression of 1929, the countries of Latin America developed into national states. The predominant factors in this evolution were the heritage of colonial exploitation, a neocolonial economic structure, massive emigration from Europe and Asia, and the fusion of Amerindian, Caucasian, African, and Asian peoples.

**Don Juan Joachin Gutierrez Altamirano Velasco, ca 1752** In this painting by Miguel Cabrera, the pleated cuffs on Velasco's shirt, the richly embroidered and very expensive coat, the knee breeches, the tricorn hat, and the coat of arms on the wall all attest to the proud status of this member of the peninsulares, the most powerful element in colonial Mexican society. *(Brooklyn Museum of Art)*

### The Origins of the Revolutions

Because of regional, geographical, and racial differences, the Latin American movements for independence took different forms in different places. Everywhere, however, they grew out of recent colonial grievances. By the late seventeenth century, the Spanish colonies had achieved a high degree of economic diversity and independence. The Spanish crown, however, determined to control colonial trade for its financial benefit. Thus the Casa de Contratacion, or Board of Trade, set up in Cádiz in 1717, worked

1765 | 1805 | 1845 | 1885 | 1925

## POLITICAL/MILITARY

- 1770 Cook lands in Australia; claims land for British crown
- 1780–1781 Rebellion led by Tupac Amaru II in Peru
- 1786 British government establishes a penal colony at Botany Bay, Australia
- 1791 Constitution Act in Canada
- 1803 Louisiana Purchase by U.S. President Jefferson
- 1810–1825 Wars of independence in South America
- 1812–1814 War of 1812 with Great Britain
- 1840–1905 Age of confederation in Canada
- 1845 Texas and Florida are admitted into United States
- 1861–1865 U.S. Civil War
- 1865–1877 U.S. Reconstruction
- 1898 Spanish-American War
- 1901 Commonwealth of Australia formed
- 1914–1918 World War I

## SOCIAL/ECONOMIC

- 1778–1788 Height of Spain's trade with colonies
- 1796 Spanish government lifts restrictions against neutrals trading with colonies
- 1860–1900 Surge in immigration to United States
- 1865 Thirteenth Amendment to U.S. Constitution frees all slaves
- 1865–1910 Rapid industrialization in United States
- 1880–1965 Jim Crow laws in United States
- 1882 Chinese Exclusion Act in United States
- 1883–1894 Mexican land laws put most land into the hands of a few individuals
- 1904 United States takes control of Panama Canal

## INTELLECTUAL/RELIGIOUS

- 1774 Quebec Act grants religious freedom to French Canadians
- 1794 Colombian Antonio Nariño translates and publishes French Declaration of the Rights of Man and the Citizen
- 1831 De Tocqueville, *Democracy in America*
- 1845 Origin of term "manifest destiny" in United States
- 1890 Riis, *How the Other Half Lives*

to strengthen Spain through greater commercial exploitation of the empire. The colonies, meanwhile, had become self-sufficient producers of foodstuffs, wine, textiles, and consumer goods. What was not produced domestically was secured through a healthy intercolonial trade that had developed independently of Spain, despite formidable geographical obstacles and colonial policies designed to restrict it.

In Peru, for example, domestic agriculture supported the large mining settlements, and the colony did not have to import food. Craft workshops owned by the state or by private individuals produced consumer goods for the working class; what was not manufactured locally was bought from Mexico and transported by the Peruvian merchant marine. By 1700 Mexico and Peru were sending shrinking percentages of their revenues to Spain and retaining more for public works, defense, and administration. The colonies lived for themselves, not for Spain.

The reforms of the Spanish Bourbons radically reversed this economic independence. Spain's humiliating defeat in the War of the Spanish Succession (1701–1713) prompted demands for sweeping reform of all of Spain's institutions, including colonial policies and practices. To improve administrative efficiency, the enlightened monarch Charles III (r. 1759–1788) carved the region of modern Colombia, Venezuela, and Ecuador out of the vast viceroyalty of Peru; it became the new viceroyalty of New Granada with its capital at Bogotá. The Crown also created the viceroyalty of Rio de la Plata (present-day Argentina) with its capital at Buenos Aires (see Map 28.1).

Far more momentous was Charles III's radical overhaul of colonial trade policies, to enable Spain to compete with Great Britain and Holland in the great eighteenth-century struggle for empire. The Spanish crown intended the colonies to serve as sources of raw materials and as markets for Spanish manufactured goods. Charles III's free-trade policies cut duties and restrictions drastically for Spanish merchants. In Latin America, these actions stimulated the production of crops in demand in Europe: coffee in Venezuela; sugar in Cuba and throughout the Caribbean; hides, leather, and salted beef in the Rio de la Plata viceroyalty. In Mexico and Peru, production of silver climbed steadily in the last quarter of the century. The volume of Spain's trade with the colonies soared, possibly as much as 700 percent between 1778 and 1788.[2]

Colonial manufacturing, which had been growing steadily, suffered severely. Better-made and cheaper European goods drove colonial goods out of the marketplace. Colonial textiles, china, and wine, for example, could not compete with cheap Spanish products. For one thing, Latin American free laborers were paid more than European workers in the eighteenth century; this disparity helps explain the great numbers of immigrants to the colonies. Also, intercolonial transportation costs were higher than transatlantic costs. In the Rio de la Plata region, for example, heavy export taxes and light import duties shattered the wine industry. Geographical obstacles—mountains, deserts, jungles, and inadequate natural harbors—also frustrated colonial efforts to promote economic integration.

Having made the colonies dependent on essential Spanish goods, however, Spain found that it could not keep the sea routes open. After 1789 the French Revolution and Napoleonic wars isolated Spain from Latin America. Foreign traders, especially from the United States, swarmed into Spanish-American ports. In 1796 the Madrid government lifted the restrictions against neutrals trading with the colonies, thus acknowledging Spain's inability to supply the colonies with needed goods and markets.[3] All these difficulties spelled disaster for colonial trade and industry.

At the end of the eighteenth century, colonists also complained bitterly that only peninsulares were appointed to the **audiencias**—the colonies' highest judicial bodies, which also served as councils to the viceroys—and to other positions in the colonial governments. According to the nineteenth-century Mexican statesman and historian Lucas Alamán (1792–1853),

> *This preference shown to Spaniards in political offices and ecclesiastical benefices has been the principal cause of the rivalry between the two classes; add to this the fact that Europeans possessed great wealth, which although it may have been the just reward of effort and industry, excited the envy of Americans and was considered as so much usurpation from them; consider that for all these reasons the Spaniards had obtained a decided preponderance over those born in the country; and it will not be difficult to explain the increasing jealousy and rivalry between the two groups which culminated in hatred and enmity.*[4]

From 1751 to 1775, only 13 percent of appointees to the audiencias were Creoles.[5] To the Creole elite of Spanish America, the world seemed "upside down."[6] Creoles hungered for political office and resented their successful Spanish rivals.

Madrid's tax reforms also aggravated discontent. In the 1770s and 1780s, the Spanish crown needed income to finance imperial defense. Colonial ports had to

**MAP 28.1 Latin America Before Independence**
Consider the factors that led to the boundaries of the various Spanish and Portuguese colonies in North and South America.

NEW FRANCE
ENGLISH COLONIES (Independence declared, 1776)
Mississippi
Colorado
Effective frontier of Spanish settlement
San Antonio
Rio Grande
COAHUILA
St. Augustine
FLORIDA (Ceded to England, 1763–1783)
ATLANTIC OCEAN
Gulf of Mexico
VICEROYALTY OF NEW SPAIN (1535)
Zacatecas
BAJIO LEÓN
Guadalajara
Guanajuato
Mexico City
Veracruz
Havana
HAITI [SAINT DOMINGUE] (Ceded to France, 1697)
PUERTO RICO
SANTO DOMINGO
BRITISH HONDURAS
JAMAICA (Conquered by England, 1655)
Guatemala
Caribbean Sea
Cartagena
Caracas
Magdalena
Suarez
Bogotá
GUIANA
VICEROYALTY OF NEW GRANADA (Separated from Viceroyalty of Peru, 1717, 1739)
Quito
ANDES
Amazon
PACIFIC OCEAN
VICEROYALTY OF PERU (1590s)
VICEROYALTY OF BRAZIL (1720)
Pernambuco
Lima
Cuzco
Bahia
La Paz
Chuquisaca (La Plata; Sucre)
Potosí
Paraná
São Paulo
Rio de Janeiro (Capital, 1763)
VICEROYALTY OF LA PLATA (Separated from Viceroyalty of Peru, 1776)
Santiago
Buenos Aires
Montevideo
AUDIENCIA OF CHILE (Retained by Viceroyalty of Peru, 1776)
Claimed but not settled by Spain
Islas Malvinas (Falkland Islands)
Cape Horn
Spanish Colonies
Viceroyalty of New Spain
Viceroyalty of New Granada
Viceroyalty of Peru and Audiencia of Chile
Viceroyalty of La Plata
Portuguese Colonies
Viceroyalty of Brazil
Mine
0 500 1000 Km.
0 500 1000 Mi.

be fortified and standing armies built. Like Great Britain, Spain believed its colonies should bear some of the costs of their own defense. Accordingly, Madrid raised the prices of tobacco and liquor and increased the *alcabala* (a sales tax of Arabic origin) on many items. Improved government administration made tax collection more efficient. Creole business and agricultural interests resented the Crown's monopoly of the tobacco industry and opposed new taxes.

As in the thirteen North American colonies a decade earlier, protest movements in Latin America claimed that the colonies were being taxed unconstitutionally. Merchants in Boston and Philadelphia had protested taxation without representation; the Spanish colonies, however, had no tradition of legislative approval of taxes. Creole mercantile leaders argued instead that relations between imperial authorities and colonial interests stayed on an even keel through consultation and compromise and that when the Crown imposed taxes without consultation, it violated ancient constitutional practice.

The imperial government recognized the potential danger of the North American example. Although Spain had joined France on the side of the rebel colonies against Great Britain during the American Revolution, the Madrid government refused in 1783 to grant diplomatic recognition to the new United States. North American ships calling at South American ports had introduced the subversive writings of Thomas Paine and Thomas Jefferson. For decades the ideas of Voltaire, Rousseau, and Montesquieu had been trickling into Latin America. In 1794 the Colombian Antonio Nariño translated and published the French Declaration of the Rights of Man and the Citizen (Spanish authorities sentenced him to ten years in an African prison, but he lived to become the father of Colombian independence). By 1800 the Creole elite throughout Latin America was familiar with liberal Enlightenment political thought.[7] The Creoles assumed, however, that the "rights of man" were limited, and they did not share such rights with Indians and blacks.

## Race in the Colonial Period

The racial complexion of Latin American societies is one of the most complicated in the world. Because few European women immigrated to the colonies, Spanish men had relations with Indian and African women. African men deprived of black women sought Indian women. The result was a population composed of every possible combination of Indian, Spanish, and African blood.

Spanish theories of racial purity rejected people of mixed blood, particularly those of African descent. A person's social status depended on the degree of European blood he or she possessed or appeared to possess. Peninsulares and Creoles reinforced their privileged status by showing contempt for people who were not white. As the great nineteenth-century German scientist Alexander von Humboldt put it, having spent five years traveling throughout South America, "Any white person, although he rides his horse barefoot, imagines himself to be of the nobility of the country."[8] Coupled with the Spaniards' aristocratic disdain for manual labor, a three-hundred-year tradition had instilled in the minds of Latin Americans the notion that dark skin and manual labor went together. Owners of mines, plantations, and factories had a vested interest in keeping blacks and Indians in servile positions. Racism and discrimination pervaded all the Latin American colonies.

Demographers estimate that Indians still accounted for between three-fifths and three-fourths of the total population of Latin America at the end of the colonial period, in spite of the tremendous population losses caused by the introduction of diseases in the sixteenth and seventeenth centuries. The colonies that became Peru and Bolivia had Indian majorities; the regions that became Argentina and Chile had European majorities. Indians and black slaves toiled in the silver and gold mines of Mexico, Colombia, and Peru; in the wheat fields of Chile; in the humid, mosquito-ridden canebrakes of Mexico and the Caribbean; and in the diamond mines and coffee and sugar plantations of Brazil.

Nevertheless, nonwhites in Latin America did experience some social mobility in the colonial period, certainly more than nonwhites in North America experienced. In Mexico, decreasing reliance on slaves led to a great increase in manumissions. Once freed, however, Negroes (the Spanish term for "black persons" coined in 1555) immediately became subject to the payment of a money tribute, as were Indians. Freedmen also incurred the obligation of military service. A few mulattos rose in the army, some as high as the rank of colonel. The army and the church seem to have offered the greatest opportunities for social mobility. Many black slaves gained their freedom by fleeing to the jungles or mountains, where they established self-governing communities. Around the year 1800, Venezuela counted twenty-four thousand fugitive slaves in a total population of eighty-seven thousand.

Many Indians were still subject to the *mit'a* and the *repartimiento*. *Mit'a* means a turn or rotation. The practice was that every seventh household in the region between Huancavelica and Potosí in the Andes took a turn working in the silver mines, with the duration of service varying. Some historians have called this forced labor.

But the Indians took their wives and other family members, who pilfered on the side, usually were not caught, and often made a tidy income for themselves.[9] The law of repartimiento required Indians to buy goods solely from local *corregidores,* officials who collected taxes. The new taxes of the 1770s and 1780s fell particularly heavily on the Indians. When Indian opposition to these taxes and to oppressive conditions exploded into violence, the Creoles organized the protest movements and assumed leadership of them.

## Resistance and Rebellion

The middle years of the eighteenth century witnessed frequent Andean Indian rebellions against the Spaniards' harsh exploitation. Five uprisings occurred in the 1740s, eleven in the 1750s, twenty in the 1760s, and twenty in the 1770s. In 1780, under the leadership of José Gabriel Condorcanqui (1742–1781), who claimed descent from the Inca rulers and took the name Tupac Amaru II, a massive insurrection exploded. The *kurakas,* Indian chieftains from the Cuzco region, gathered a powerful force of Indians and *castas,* people of mixed race, including those of African ancestry. They wanted the redress of long-standing grievances. Rebellion swept across highland Peru, and many Spanish officials were executed. In 1781 an army sent from Lima put down the rebellions and captured and savagely executed Tupac Amaru II. Violent rebellion continued, however, and before peace was restored two years later, a hundred thousand people lay dead and vast amounts of property were destroyed. Although these movements failed militarily, the government abolished the repartimiento system and established an audiencia in Cuzco. By raising elite fears of racial and class warfare, these revolts served to buttress Creole loyalty to the Spanish crown, which delayed the drive for Peru's independence.

News of the rebellion of Tupac Amaru II trickled northward, where it helped stimulate revolution in the New Granada viceroyalty. Disorders occurred first at Socorro in modern Colombia (see Map 28.2). Throughout the eighteenth century, Socorro had prospered. Sugar cane, corn, and cattle flourished because of its exceptionally fertile soil. Large cotton crops stimulated the production of textiles, mostly in a primitive cottage industry worked by women. Socorro's location on the Suarez River made it an agricultural and manufacturing center and an entrepôt for trade with the hinterland. Hard-working Spanish immigrants had prospered and often intermarried with the Indians.

When the viceroy published new taxes on tobacco and liquor and reorganized the alcabala, riots broke out in Socorro in March 1781 and spread to other towns. Representatives of peasants and artisan groups from many towns elected a *comun,* or central committee, to lead the insurrection. Each town elected its local comun and the captain of its militia. Known as the Comunero Revolution, the insurrection in New Granada enjoyed broad-based support and good organization.

An Indian peasant army commanded by Creole captains marched on Bogotá. Government officials, lacking adequate military resources, sent a commission to play for time by negotiating with the comuneros. On June 4, the commission agreed to the rebels' terms: reduction of the alcabala and of the Indians' forced tribute, abolition of the new taxes on tobacco, and preference for Creoles over peninsulares in government positions. The joyful Indian army disbanded and went home. What the Indians did not know was that the commission had already secretly disclaimed the agreement with the rebels on the grounds that it had been achieved by force. Having succeeded in dispersing the Indians, the government at Bogotá won over the Creole leaders with a promise of pardons and then moved in reserve troops, who captured large numbers of rebels. When the last rebel base—that of José Antonio Galan—had been captured, a kangaroo court tried Galan and condemned him

> *to be taken out of jail, dragged and taken to the place of execution where he will be hung until dead, that his head be removed from his dead body, that the rest of his body be quartered, that his torso be committed to flames for which purpose a fire shall be lit in front of the platform. . . . All his descendants shall be declared infamous, all his property shall be confiscated by the royal treasury, his home shall be burnt, and the ground salted, so that in this fashion his infamous name may be forgotten.*[10]

Thus ended the revolt of the comuneros in New Granada. They failed to win self-rule, but they forced the authorities to act in accordance with the spirit of the "unwritten constitution," whose guiding principle was consultation and compromise.

Much more than the Peruvian and Colombian revolts, the successful revolution led by Toussaint L'Ouverture (ca 1744–1803) in Haiti aroused elite fears of black revolt and class warfare. The Arawaks, native Americans of the region, gave the name "Haiti" (land of mountains) to the western third of the island of Hispaniola, because most of it is mountainous. Haiti was a haven for French and English pirates in the seventeenth century, but in the eighteenth century, French settlers established sugar plantations there and imported African slaves to work them. Haiti soon became France's most prosperous

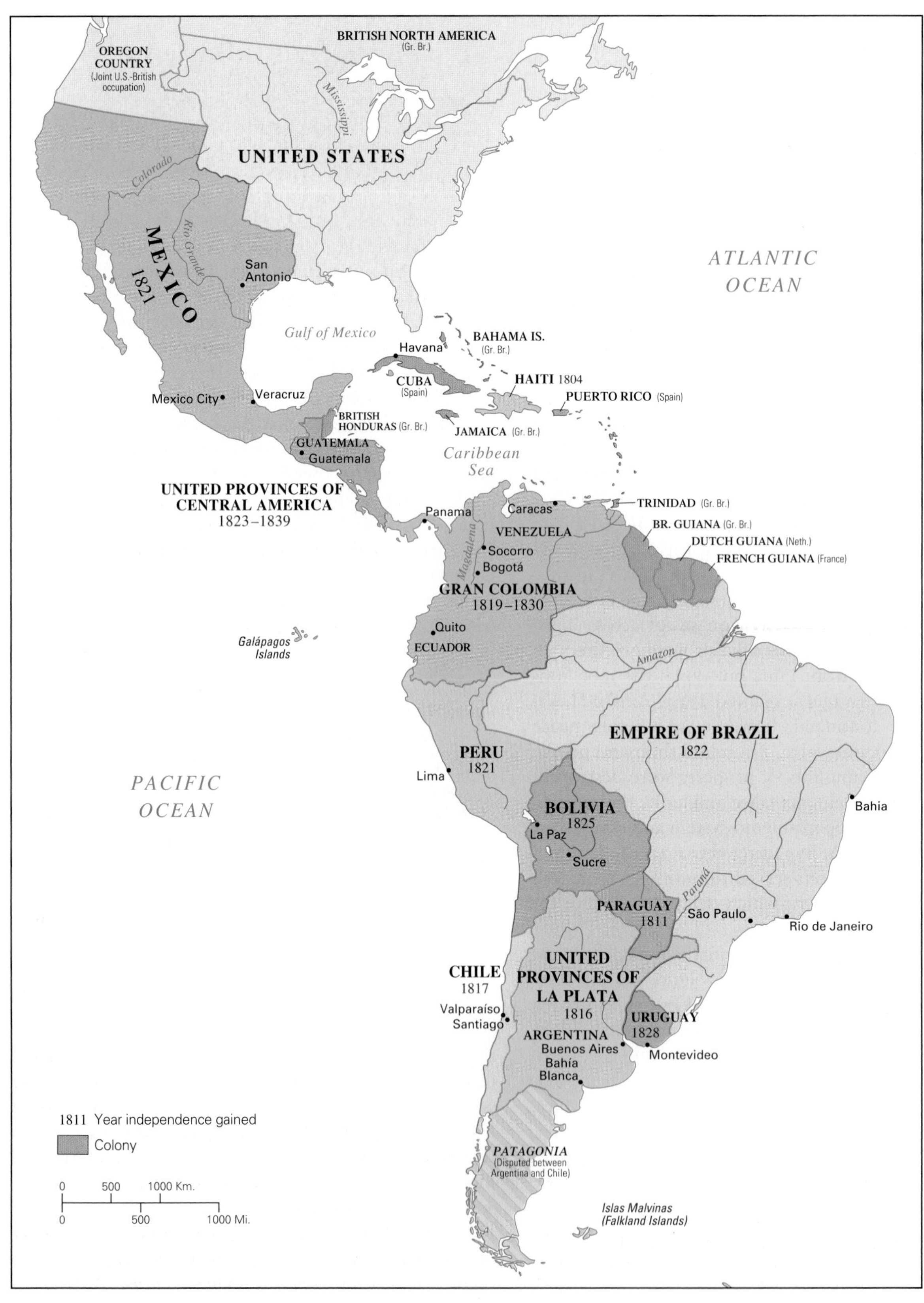
BRITISH NORTH AMERICA (Gr. Br.)
OREGON COUNTRY (Joint U.S.-British occupation)
Mississippi
UNITED STATES
Colorado
Rio Grande
MEXICO 1821
San Antonio
ATLANTIC OCEAN
Gulf of Mexico
Havana
BAHAMA IS. (Gr. Br.)
CUBA (Spain)
HAITI 1804
PUERTO RICO (Spain)
Mexico City
Veracruz
BRITISH HONDURAS (Gr. Br.)
JAMAICA (Gr. Br.)
GUATEMALA
Guatemala
Caribbean Sea
UNITED PROVINCES OF CENTRAL AMERICA 1823–1839
Panama
Caracas
TRINIDAD (Gr. Br.)
BR. GUIANA (Gr. Br.)
DUTCH GUIANA (Neth.)
FRENCH GUIANA (France)
VENEZUELA
Magdalena
Socorro
Bogotá
GRAN COLOMBIA 1819–1830
Quito
ECUADOR
Galápagos Islands
Amazon
EMPIRE OF BRAZIL 1822
PERU 1821
Lima
PACIFIC OCEAN
BOLIVIA 1825
La Paz
Sucre
Bahia
Paraná
PARAGUAY 1811
São Paulo
Rio de Janeiro
CHILE 1817
UNITED PROVINCES OF LA PLATA 1816
Valparaíso
Santiago
URUGUAY 1828
ARGENTINA
Buenos Aires
Montevideo
Bahía Blanca
PATAGONIA (Disputed between Argentina and Chile)
Islas Malvinas (Falkland Islands)
1811 Year independence gained
Colony
0 500 1000 Km.
0 500 1000 Mi.

colony and the world's chief producer of sugar and coffee. Unable to maintain its claim to the region, Spain ceded Haiti to France.

The French maintained a rigid social stratification of French, Creoles, freed blacks, and black slaves. When the Creoles refused the mulattos representation in the local assemblies and in the French National Assembly of 1789, the mulattos revolted. Blacks formed guerrilla bands under the self-educated freed slave Toussaint L'Ouverture. In 1793, as part of their campaign against Napoleon, the British invaded Haiti and took all of its coastal cities. As the recognized leader of the revolt, L'Ouverture had widespread support and retook the cities. In 1801 he also conquered Santo Domingo (which Spain had also ceded to France), declared himself emperor of the entire island of Hispaniola, abolished slavery, and instituted reforms. Napoleon dispatched a large army to restore French control, but the French could not take the interior. U.S. president Thomas Jefferson, fearing that the French would use the island to invade Louisiana, aided the rebels. Weakened by yellow fever, the French withdrew. L'Ouverture negotiated peace with France, but French officials tricked him and took him to France, where he died in prison. In 1804 Haiti became the second nation (after the United States) in the Western Hemisphere to achieve independence. The revolt was also the first successful uprising of a non-European people against a colonial power. The establishment of a legitimate black nation in Latin America sent waves of fear through the upper classes.

**François Bonneville: Toussaint L'Ouverture** The French engraver Bonneville usually worked from paintings; lacking one for L'Ouverture, he used his imagination. Thus this quizzical face lacks the strength and determination for which L'Ouverture was famous. He inspired great enthusiasm among liberal contemporaries, such as the English romantic poet William Wordsworth, who concluded a sonnet dedicated to L'Ouverture: "There's not a breathing of the common wind / That will forget thee; thou hast great allies; / Thy friends are exultations, agonies, / And love, and man's unconquerable mind." *(Menil Foundation/Hickey and Robertson, Houston)*

## Independence

In 1808, as part of his effort to rule Europe, Napoleon Bonaparte deposed the Spanish king Ferdinand VII and placed his own brother on the Spanish throne (see page 722). In Latin America, the Creoles subsequently seized the opportunity. Since everything in Spanish America was done in the name of the king, the Creoles argued that the removal of the legitimate king shifted sovereignty to the people—that is, to themselves. In 1810 the small, wealthy Creole aristocracy used the removal of the Spanish king as justification for their seizure of political power and their preservation of that power.

**MAP 28.2 Latin America in 1830** By 1830 almost all of Central America, South America, and the Caribbean islands had won independence. Note that the many nations that Central America now make up were unified when they first won independence from Mexico. Similarly, modern Venezuela, Colombia, and Ecuador were still joined in Gran Colombia.

The Creoles who led the various movements for independence did not intend a radical redistribution of property or reconstruction of society. They merely rejected the authority of the Spanish crown. A distinguished scholar has described the war for independence as

> *a prolonged, confused, and in many ways contradictory movement. In Mexico it began as a popular social movement and ended many years later as a conservative uprising against a liberal Spanish constitution. In Venezuela it came to be a war unto the death; in other places it was a war between a small Creole minority and the Spanish authorities. It was not an organized movement with a central revolutionary directorate. It had no Continental Congress. . . . If there was no central direction, no centrally recognized leadership, likewise there was no formally accepted political doctrine. . . .*

*In Latin America each separate area went its own way. Central America broke way from Mexico and then splintered into five separate nations. Uruguay, Paraguay, and Bolivia separated themselves from Argentina, Chile from Peru, and [Simón] Bolívar's attempt to federate the state of Greater Colombia (Venezuela, Colombia, and Ecuador) with Peru and Bolivia under a centralized government broke down.*[11]

The great hero of the movement for independence was Simón Bolívar (1783–1830), a very able general who is considered the Latin American George Washington. (See the feature "Listening to the Past: Simón Bolívar's Speculation on Latin America" on pages 932–933.) Bolívar's victories over the royalist armies won him the presidency of Gran (Greater) Colombia in 1819. He dreamed of a continental union and in 1826 summoned a conference of the American republics at Panama. The meeting achieved little. Bolívar organized the government of Bolivia and became the head of the new state of Peru. The territories of Gran Colombia splintered, however, and a sadly disillusioned Bolívar went into exile, saying, "America is ungovernable. Those who served the revolution plowed the seas." The failure of Pan-Americanism isolated individual countries, prevented collective action, and later paved the way for the political and economic intrusion of the United States and other powers.

Brazil's quest for independence from Portugal was unique: Brazil won its independence without violent upheaval. When Napoleon's troops entered Portugal, the royal family fled to Brazil and made Rio de Janeiro the capital of the Portuguese Empire. The new government immediately lifted the old mercantilist restrictions and opened Brazilian ports to the ships of all friendly nations. Under popular pressure, King Pedro I (r. 1822–1831) proclaimed Brazil's independence in 1822 and published a constitution. Pedro's administration was wracked by factional disputes between Portuguese courtiers and Brazilian Creoles, a separatist movement in the Rio Grande do Sul region, and provincial revolts. His successor, Pedro II (r. 1831–1889), restored order and laid the foundations of the modern Brazilian state. The reign of Pedro II witnessed the expansion of the coffee industry, the beginnings of the rubber industry, and massive immigration.

**Departure of the Emperor Pedro II** In 1889, the Brazilian army overthrew the emperor Pedro II, forced him into exile, and proclaimed a republic. In this allegorical painting Pedro, holding the crown in his right hand, passes the staff of state to the seated female figure personifying the republic. *(Courtesy of Fundacao Maria Luisa e Oscar Americano, São Paulo)*

## The Consequences of Independence

The wars of independence ended around 1825. What effects did they have on Latin American societies, governments, and national development? Because the movements for independence differed in character and course in different regions and countries, generalizations are likely to be misleading. Significant changes did occur, however, throughout Latin America.

The newly independent nations did not achieve immediate political stability when the wars of independence ended. The Spanish crown had served as a unifying symbol, and its disappearance left a power vacuum. Civil disorder typically followed. The Creole leaders of the revolutions had no experience in government, and the wars left a legacy of military, not civilian, leadership. Throughout the continent, idealistic but impractical leaders proclaimed republics governed by representative assemblies. In practice, the generals ruled.

In Argentina, Juan Manuel de Rosas (r. 1835–1852) assumed power amid widespread public disorder and ruled as dictator. In Mexico, liberals declared a federal republic, but incessant civil strife led to the rise of the dictator Antonio López de Santa Anna in the mid-nineteenth century. Likewise in Venezuela, strongmen, dictators, and petty aristocratic oligarchs governed from 1830 to 1892. Some countries suffered constant coups d'état. In the course of the century, Bolivia had sixty and Venezuela fifty-two. The rule of force prevailed almost everywhere. Enlightened dictatorship was the typical form of government.

Although isolated territories such as Paraguay and much of Central America suffered little damage, the wars of liberation disrupted the economic life of most Latin American countries. The prosperity that many areas had achieved toward the end of the colonial period was destroyed. Mexico and Venezuela in particular lost large percentages of their populations and suffered great destruction of farmland and animals. Even areas that saw relatively little violence, such as Chile and New Granada, experienced a weakening of economic life. Armies were frequently recruited by force, and when the men were demobilized, many did not return home. The consequent population dislocation hurt agriculture and mining. Guerrilla warfare disrupted trade and communications. Forced loans and the seizure of private property for military use ruined many people.

Brazil, which had a large slave population, did not free its slaves until 1888. Spain abolished slavery in its Cuban colony in a series of measures between 1870 and 1886; Cuba itself became independent in 1903, a consequence of the Spanish-American War. Elsewhere, however, independence accelerated the abolition of slavery. The destruction of agriculture in countries such as Mexico and Venezuela caused the collapse of the plantation system, and fugitive slaves could not be recaptured. Also, the royalists and patriot generals such as Bolívar offered slaves their freedom in exchange for military service. Most of the new independent states adopted republican constitutions declaring the legal equality of all men. For Indians and blacks, however, these noble words were meaningless, for the revolution brought about no redistribution of property, nor could long-standing racist attitudes be eliminated by the stroke of a pen.

Although the edifice of racism persisted in the nineteenth century, Latin America experienced much more assimilation and offered Negroes greater economic and social mobility than did the United States. As a direct result of their heroic military service in the wars of independence, a substantial number of Negroes improved their social status. Some even attained political heights: the Mexican revolutionary Vicente Guerrero served as president of his country in 1829; Antonio Guzmán governed Venezuela as a benevolent dictator (r. 1870–1888); Ramón Castilla, a mestizo, served as president of Peru (r. 1845–1851 and 1855–1862) and made great improvements in state financing.

What accounts for the relative racial permeability of Latin America in contrast with the severe segregation in the United States? The Creole elite in Latin America had a "whitening" ideology—that is, they viewed race mixture as a civilizing process that diminished and absorbed the dark and "barbarous" blood of Africans and Indians. Legally and socially, Latin American societies classified people as white, mestizo, mulatto, Negro, *indigena* (native), and *asiatico* (Asiatic). Supposedly, this system measured bloodlines and racial origins. When linked to social class, lightness of skin helped social mobility, but a nonwhite person could not completely shed the absence of *pureza de sangre,* "purity of blood." Although skin color proved a major part of the Latin American system of classification, we have to guard against using United States–centric methods of racial definition when studying Latin American societies. Moreover, racism in Latin America aggressively attacked the indigenous peoples (the Indians). The United States, according to the Dutch scholar H. Hoetink, evolved a simple two-tiered racial edifice. Anyone who was not "pure" white was classified as Negro or black (see pages 915–917).

Hoetink explains the problem partly in terms of the large population of poor whites in the United States: "Nowhere, but in the North American mainland, did the number of extremely poor whites always exceed the

## LATIN AMERICA, CA 1760–1900

| | |
|---|---|
| 1764–1780 | Charles III of Spain's administrative and economic reforms |
| 1781 | Comunero Revolution in New Granada |
| 1810–1825 | Latin American wars of independence against Spain |
| 1822 | Proclamation of Brazil's independence by Portugal |
| 1825–ca 1870 | Political instability in most Latin American nations |
| 1826 | Call by Simón Bolívar for Panama conference on Latin American union |
| ca 1870–1929 | Latin American neocolonialism |
| 1876–1911 | Porfirio Díaz's control of Mexico |
| 1880–1914 | Massive emigration from Europe and Asia to Latin America |
| 1888 | Emancipation of slaves in Brazil; final abolition of slavery in Western Hemisphere |
| 1898 | Spanish-American War<br>End of Spanish control over Cuba<br>Transfer of Puerto Rico and the Philippines to the United States |

number of slaves. Nowhere, but in the U.S. South, were special police forces predominantly manned by poor whites."[12] Also, Latin American elites' definition of *whiteness* and perception of physical beauty seem to have been broader than the definition and perception of the white majority in the United States.

Nevertheless, the advantages of assimilation did not (and do not) apply to dark-skinned people in Latin America. Substantial numbers of light-skinned colored people rose economically and socially, but the great mass of dark-skinned blacks continued to experience all the consequences of systematic and insistent racism.

## Neocolonialism

At first, political instability and the preoccupation of European and North American financiers with industrial expansion in their own countries discouraged foreign investment in Latin America's newly independent nations. The advent of stable dictatorships, however, eventually paved the way for economic growth. After 1870 capital began to flow south and across the Atlantic. In Mexico, North American capital supported the production of hemp (used in the United States for grain harvesting), sugar, bananas, and rubber, frequently on American-owned plantations. British and American interests backed the development of tin, copper, and gold mining in Mexico. By 1911 Mexico had taken third place among the world's oil producers. British financiers built Argentina's railroads, meatpacking industry, and utilities. British businessmen in Chile developed the copper and nitrate industries (nitrate is used in the production of pharmaceuticals and fertilizers). Likewise in Brazil, foreign capital—primarily British—flowed into coffee, cotton, and sugar production and manufacturing. By 1904 Brazil produced 76 percent of the world's coffee. When massive overproduction of coffee led to a sharp drop in prices in 1906, a commission of British, American, German, and French bankers rescued the Brazilian government from near disaster.

The price that Latin America paid for economic development at the end of the nineteenth century was a new form of economic domination. Foreign investors acquired control of the railroads, mineral resources, and banking, and they made heavy inroads into real estate. British investments led all others. But beginning in 1898, the United States flexed its imperialistic muscles and sent gunboats and troops to defend its dollars in the Caribbean and Central America. By the turn of the century, the Latin American nations were active participants in the international economic order, but foreigners controlled most of

**Picking Coffee, Colombia, 1900** The coffee tree, a small evergreen, grows at high altitudes in cool, frost-free climates. Both adults and children pick the red fruits containing the coffee beans, which are prepared by roasting—the longer the roasting, the stronger the coffee. Coffee was, and still is, Colombia's major export crop. *(Col. Archivo fotogràfico de la Kunsthaus, Zurich)*

their industries. Between 1904 and 1929, for example, the United States intervened in Latin American affairs whenever it felt its economic interests threatened. Americans secured control of the Panama Canal in 1904 on their own terms; in 1912 and 1926 U.S. Marines interfered in Nicaragua to bolster conservative governments; and the Marines who were sent to Haiti in 1915 to protect American property stayed until 1934. The result has been a bitter legacy of anti-American feeling throughout Latin America. Only with the launching of President Franklin Roosevelt's Good Neighbor Policy did relations between the United States and Latin America begin to improve.

Another distinctive feature of **neocolonialism** was that each country's economy revolved around only one or two products: sugar in Cuba, nitrates and copper in Chile, meat in Argentina, coffee in Brazil. A sharp drop in the world market demand for a product could destroy the industry and with it the nation's economic structure. The outbreak of the First World War in 1914 drastically reduced exports of Latin American raw materials and imports of European manufactured goods, provoking a general economic crisis.[13]

Throughout the eighteenth century, the Spanish-owned **haciendas**—large landed estates—and plantations had continued to expand to meet the needs of commercial agriculture: wheat for the cities, corn for the Indians' consumption, sugar for export to Europe and North America. By means of purchase, forced removal of Indians, and outright seizure, the Spanish continued to take Indian land, as they had done in the seventeenth century. Some land was acquired merely to eliminate competition by depriving Indians of their fields, which were then left fallow.

The late nineteenth century witnessed ever-greater concentrations of land in ever fewer hands. In places like the Valley of Mexico in southern Mexico, a few large haciendas controlled all the land. Under the dictatorship of General Porfirio Díaz, the Mexican government in 1883 passed a law allowing real estate companies (controlled by Díaz's political cronies) to survey public and "vacant" lands and to retain one-third of the land they surveyed. An 1894 law provided that land could be declared vacant if legal title to it could not be produced. Since few Indians had deeds to the land that their ancestors had worked for centuries, the door swung open to wholesale expropriation of small landowners and entire villages. Shrewd speculators tricked illiterate Indians into selling their lands for trifling sums. Thousands of litigants clogged the courts. Indians who dared armed resistance were crushed by

**Rivera: Sugar Cane** Diego Rivera's art often carries a strong social message. Here Indians and blacks labor in the sugar-cane fields, while a white man relaxes in a hammock. *(Diego Rivera,* Sugar Cane, *1931. Philadelphia Museum of Art, Gift of Mr. and Mrs. Herbert Cameron Morris [1943-46-2])*

government troops and carried off to virtual slave labor. Vast stretches of land came into the hands of private individuals—in one case, 12 million acres. Stripped of their lands, the Indians were a ready labor supply. They were mercilessly exploited. Debt peonage became common: landowners paid their laborers not in cash but in vouchers redeemable only at the company store, whose high prices and tricky bookkeeping kept the **peons** permanently in debt.

Some scholars maintain that the hacienda owners usually let their land lie fallow until it rose in value or attracted American investors. The lack of cultivation, they assert, kept the prices of corn and other crops artificially high. The owners themselves, supported by rents, passed indolent lives in extravagant luxury in Mexico City and other cities.

Other scholars argue that the haciendas were efficient enterprises whose owners sought to maximize profits on invested capital. The Sanchez Navarro family of northwestern Mexico, for instance, engaged in a wide variety of agricultural and commercial pursuits, exploiting their lands and resources as fully as possible. Ultimately, their *latifundio*—a large landed estate—was about the size of West Virginia. Along with vast cattle ranches and sheep runs containing as many as 250,000 sheep, the Sanchez Navarros cultivated maize, wheat, and cotton. They invested heavily and profitably in silver mining and manufacturing and lent sizable sums at high interest. Although they brutally exploited their peons and practiced debt peonage, the Sanchez Navarros lived very modestly on their own estates rather than luxuriating in Mexico City.[14] A final determination of whether the Sanchez Navarros' work ethic and frugal lifestyle were unique or representative must await further investigation.

## The Impact of Immigration

In 1852 the Argentine political philosopher Juan Bautista Alberdi published *Bases and Points of Departure for Argentine Political Organization,* arguing that "to govern is to populate." Alberdi meant that the development of his country—and, by extension, all of Latin America—depended on immigration. Argentina had an adequate labor supply, but it was unevenly distributed throughout the country. Moreover, Alberdi maintained, Indians and blacks lacked basic skills, and it would take too long to train them. Thus he pressed for massive immigration from the "advanced" countries of northern Europe and the United States. Alberdi's ideas won immediate acceptance and were even incorporated into the Argentine constitution, which declared that "the Federal government will encourage European immigration." Other Latin American countries adopted similar policies promoting immigration.[15]

European needs coincided perfectly with those of Latin America. After 1880, Ireland, Great Britain, Germany, Italy, Spain, and the central European nations experienced greater population growth than their labor markets could absorb. Meanwhile, the growing industries of Europe needed South American raw materials and markets for their finished goods, and South American countries wanted European markets for their minerals, coffee, sugar, beef, and manufactured goods. Italian, Spanish, and Portuguese people poured into Latin America.

Immigrants from South, East, and southwestern Asia also flowed into South America and the Caribbean islands. For example, in the late nineteenth and early twentieth centuries, large numbers of Japanese arrived in Brazil, most settling in urban areas, especially in São Paulo. By 1920 Brazil had the largest Japanese community in the world outside of Japan. From the Middle East, Lebanese, Turks, and Syrians also entered Brazil. Peru and Argentina received small numbers of immigrants from Japan and China. Between 1850 and 1880, 144,000 East Indian laborers went to Trinidad, 39,000 to Jamaica, and smaller numbers to the islands of St. Lucia, Grenada, and St. Vincent. They all arrived as indentured servants under five-year contracts. Perhaps one-third returned to India, but the rest stayed, saved money, and bought small businesses or land. These people formed tightly knit communities, intermarried only within their group, and maintained their distinct ethnic identity. So, too, did the 8,000 Chinese, who arrived in Trinidad before 1893, bought out the last years of their indentured service contracts, and established businesses. Cuba, the largest of the Caribbean islands (about the size of Pennsylvania), had received 500,000 African slaves between 1808 and 1865. When slavery was abolished in 1886, some of their work in the sugar-cane fields was done by Chinese indentured servants, who followed the same pattern as those who had gone to Trinidad. Likewise, the abolition of slavery in Mexico led to the arrival of thousands of Chinese bonded servants. Worldwide migration knit together all parts of the globe (see pages 880–882), and the migrants helped build the nations where they settled.

Immigration also led to rapid urbanization, which meant Europeanization and industrialization. By 1900 Buenos Aires and Rio de Janeiro had populations of more than 500,000 people; Mexico City, Montevideo, Santiago, and Havana also experienced spectacular growth. Portuguese, Italian, French, Chinese, and Japanese immigrants gave an international flavor to the cities, and a more vigorous tempo replaced the somnolent Spanish atmosphere.

By 1914 Buenos Aires had emerged as one of the most cosmopolitan cities in the world. In less than a half century, the population of the city and its province had grown from 500,000 to 3.6 million. As Argentina's political capital, the city housed all its government bureaucracies and agencies. The meatpacking, food-processing, flour-milling, and wool industries were concentrated in Buenos Aires. Half of all overseas tonnage passed through the city, which was also the heart of the nation's railroad network. The University of Buenos Aires was the intellectual hub of the nation. Elegant shops near the Plaza de Mayo catered to the expensive tastes of the elite upper classes, who constituted about 5 percent of the population. But the thousands of immigrants who toiled twelve hours a day, six days a week, on docks and construction sites and in meatpacking plants crowded into the city's *conventillos,* or tenements:

> *The one-room dwelling . . . served a family with two to five children or a group of four or five single men. At the door to each room stood a pile of wooden boxes. One generally held a basin for washing; another a charcoal brazier on which to cook the daily watery stew, or puchero; and garbage accumulated in a third. Two or three iron cots, a pine table, a few wooden chairs, an old trunk, perhaps a sewing machine, and more boxes completed the furnishings. Light came from the open door and one window, from an oil or gas lamp, or occasionally from a bare electric light bulb. On the once-whitewashed walls were tacked pictures of popular heroes, generals, or kings torn from magazines, an image of the Madonna and a couple of saints, perhaps a faded photograph of family members in Europe. The women often eked out miserable incomes by taking in laundry and washing and drying it in the patios. Others ironed or sewed on a piecework basis. Some men worked here: in one corner a shoemaker might ply his trade, in another a man might bend over a small table repairing watches.*[16]

Immigrants dreamed of rapid economic success in the New World, and there was in fact plenty of upward social mobility. The first generation almost always did manual labor, but its sons often advanced to upper-blue-collar or white-collar jobs. The rare Genoese or Neapolitan immigrant whose labor and thrift made his son a millionaire quickly learned the meaning of assimilation: the son typically imitated the dress, style, and values of the Spanish elite. Hispanic attitudes toward class, manual labor, and egalitarianism prevailed.[17]

Europeans and Asians gave an enormous boost to the development of industry and commerce. Italian and Spanish settlers in Argentina stimulated the expansion of the cattle industry and the development of the wheat and shoe industries. In Brazil, Swiss immigrants built the cheese business, Italians gained a leading role in the coffee industry, and Japanese pioneered the development of the cotton industry. In Peru, Italians became influential in banking and in part of the restaurant business, while the French dominated jewelry, dressmaking, and pharmaceuticals. Chinese laborers built the railroads, and in sections of large cities such as Lima, the Chinese came to dominate the ownership of shops and restaurants. The North American Henry Meiggs ("Yankee Pizarro") long remained the largest railroad contractor in Peru. When the country went bankrupt after a war with Chile (1879–1884), the Peruvian government had to cede control of the railroads to the British shareholders in exchange for their assumption of the national debt. Indeed, the arrival of millions of immigrants changed the entire commercial structure of South America.

Immigration promoted further ethnic integration. The vast majority of migrants were unmarried males; seven out of ten people who landed in Argentina between 1857 and 1924 were single males between thirteen and forty years old. There, as in other South American countries, many of those who stayed sought out Indian or other low-status women. Male settlers from eastern Europe and women of all nationalities preferred to marry within their own ethnic groups. But men greatly outnumbered women, and a man who chose to marry usually had to marry an Indian.[18] Immigration, then, furthered the racial mixture of Europeans, Asians, and native South Americans.

For Latin America's sizable black population, immigration proved a calamity. The abolition of slavery in Spanish America had scarcely changed the economic and social status of the Negro population. Accustomed to cutting sugar cane and working the rural coffee plantations, blacks sometimes had little preparation for urban living. Many former slaves had skills, even for factory work, but racism explains the greater presence of white immigrants in factories. In 1893, 71.2 percent of the working population of São Paulo was foreign-born. Anxious to adapt to America and to climb the economic ladder, immigrants quickly learned the traditional racial prejudices. Negro women usually found work as domestics, but employers excluded black males from good jobs.

**Business District in Mexico, 1921** Business signs in several languages—such as those here in Spanish, English, and Chinese—indicate the pluralistic, multicultural character of many Latin American cities in the early twentieth century. *(Courtesy of the photographer, C. B. Williams)*

Racial prejudice kept the vast bulk of the South American black population in a wretched socioeconomic position until the Second World War.

Recent research has greatly challenged the traditional view that independence did little to change the basic social, economic, and political structure of Latin American countries. The Spanish crown was gone, and *caudillismo* (dictatorial or authoritarian rule), militarism, and standing armies filled the power vacuum. The old colonial caste system with two social classes, Spanish and Indian, dissolved, and social categories shifted. Property changed hands and haciendas expanded, reflecting the concentration of wealth and greater Creole social mobility, often at the expense of the Indians. Some Spanish and Portuguese merchants returned to the Iberian Peninsula, to be replaced by British and U.S. businessmen. As happened in the United States, Latin American nations extended their borders in the later nineteenth century. Just as the United States waged wars against the Indians (see page 908) and pushed its frontier westward, so Brazil, Venezuela, Ecuador, Peru, and Bolivia expanded into the Amazonian frontier, at the expense of indigenous peoples. Likewise, Mexico, Chile, and Argentina had their "Indian wars" and frontier expansion. Neocolonialism's modernizing influence on commerce and industry strengthened the position of the elite and allowed it to use capitalistic values and ideals as a shield against demands for fundamental socioeconomic reforms. European styles in art, clothing, housing, and literature became highly popular, particularly among members of the elite as they sought acceptance and approval by their economic masters.

# THE UNITED STATES (1789–1929)

The victory of the North American colonies and the founding of the United States seemed to validate the Enlightenment idea that a better life on earth was possible. Americans carried over into the nineteenth and twentieth centuries an unbounded optimism about the future. Although most eastern states retained a property or taxpaying qualification for the vote down to 1860, suffrage was gradually expanded to include most adult white males; New Jersey alone gave (propertied) women the vote for a time. The movement toward popular democracy accelerated as the young nation, confident of its "manifest destiny," pushed relentlessly across the continent. Westward movement, however, threatened to extend black slavery, which generated increasing disagreement between the industrialized North and the agricultural South. The ensuing Civil War cost more American lives than any other war the nation has fought. The victory of the North did not resolve the racial issue that had led to war, but it did preserve the federal system.

The years between 1865 and 1917 witnessed the building of a new industrialized nation. Immigrants settled much of the West, provided the labor to exploit the country's mineral resources, turned small provincial towns into sophisticated centers of ethnic and cultural diversity, and built the railroads that tied the country together. The ideology of manifest destiny lived on after the frontier closed and considerably affected relations between the United States and Latin America. In the First World War, American aid and American troops were the deciding factor in the Allied victory. After the war, "normalcy" and the façade of prosperity supported a persistent optimism.

## Manifest Destiny

In an 1845 issue of the *United States Magazine and Democratic Review,* editor John L. O'Sullivan boldly declared that foreign powers were trying to prevent American annexation of Texas in order to impede "the fulfillment of our manifest destiny to overspread the continent allotted by Providence for the free development of our yearly multiplying millions." O'Sullivan was articulating a sentiment prevalent in the United States since early in its history: that God had foreordained the nation to cover the entire continent. After a large-circulation newspaper picked up the phrase **manifest destiny,** it was used on the floor of Congress and soon entered the language as a catchword for and justification of expansion. The concept of manifest destiny played an important role in some basic developments in American history: the settlement of peoples of diverse nationalities, the issue of slavery, and the conflict over whether the United States was to remain agrarian or become a commercial and industrial society.

Two other concepts also played a powerful role in the formation of the young republic: social equality, by which was meant equality of opportunity, and optimism about the future. After a visit to the United States in 1831, the French nobleman Alexis de Tocqueville wrote in *Democracy in America,* a classic analysis of American civilization, "No novelty in the United States struck me more visibly during my stay there than the equality of conditions." By equality Tocqueville meant the relative fluidity of American society, and he attributed this to Americans' mobility. Unlike Europe, where family and inherited wealth meant a great deal and people typically lived all their lives in the regions where they were born, geographical mobility in America provided enormous opportunity. A deeply rooted work ethic taught that everyone could advance through

**Christian Mayr: Kitchen Ball at White Sulphur Springs, 1838** The German artist who painted this picture shortly after his arrival in the United States apparently had no preconceived racial views; he portrayed blacks without the insulting caricatures, marginalized situations, or political formulas typical of many mid-century representations. Rather, African Americans are shown here as graceful, dignified, and in a social scene of their own creation. Light-skinned and dark-skinned, old and young, plain and beautiful celebrate and reveal an individual and a group dignity. White Sulphur Springs was (and is) a fashionable resort. *(North Carolina Museum of Art, Raleigh. Purchased with funds from the state of North Carolina)*

thrift and hard work. Americans also had an unbounded faith in the future. This belief that America offered golden and limitless opportunities is epitomized in the letter an immigrant Englishman wrote home to his wife:

*I do not repent coming, for you know that there was nothing but poverty before me, and to see you and the dear children want was more than I could bear. I would rather cross the Atlantic ten times than hear my children cry for victuals. . . . There is plenty of room yet, and will be for a thousand years to come.*[19]

When George Washington took office in 1789, fewer than 4 million people inhabited the thirteen states on the eastern seaboard. By the time Abraham Lincoln became the sixteenth president in 1861, the United States stretched across the continent and had 31 million inhabitants.

During the colonial period, pioneers had pushed westward to the Appalachian Mountains. After independence, westward movement accelerated. The eastern states claimed all the land from the Atlantic Ocean to the Mississippi River, but two forces blocked immediate expansion. The Indians, trying to save their lands, allied with the British in Canada to prevent further American encroachment. In 1794, however, Britain agreed to evacuate border forts in the Northwest Territory, roughly the area north of the Ohio River and east of the Mississippi, and thereby end British support for the Indians. A similar treaty with Spain paved the way for southeastern expansion.

Events in Europe and the Caribbean led to a massive increase in American territory. In 1800 Spain ceded the Louisiana Territory—the land between the Mississippi River and the Rocky Mountains—to France. Napoleon planned a war with Great Britain, and on the day he opened hostilities, his foreign minister, Talleyrand, casually asked Robert Livingston, the American minister to Paris, "What would you give us for the whole of Louisiana?" The astonished American proposed $4 million. "Too low!" said Talleyrand. "Reflect and see me tomorrow." Less than three weeks later, the deed of sale was signed. The United States paid only $12 million for millions of acres of some of the world's richest farmland.

Scarcely was the ink dry on the agreement when pressure rose for war with England. Repeated British attacks on American vessels on the high seas and British interference in American trade provided diplomatic justification for the War of 1812. Western "war hawks" wanted further expansion and believed that a war with Britain would yield Canada, permanently end Indian troubles, and open up vast forestlands for settlement. The Treaty of Ghent (1814) ended the conflict but left the prewar boundaries unchanged.

After the restoration of peace, settlers poured into the Northwest Territory and the Gulf Plains (the Gulf Coast region of Georgia, Alabama, and Mississippi). Congress sold land in lots of 160 acres at $2 an acre; only $80 was needed as a down payment. Irish and German immigrants rapidly put the black earth of Indiana and Illinois under cultivation. Pioneers of American stock planted cotton in the lush delta of the Gulf Plains. Scandinavian and German settlers found the softly rolling hills of the Wisconsin country ideal for cattle.

Spain, preoccupied with rebellions in South America, sold the Florida Territory to the U.S. government, and beginning in 1821 American settlers poured into the Mexican territory of Texas, whose soil proved excellent for the production of cotton and sugar. Contemptuous of the government of the Mexican president Santa Anna, the Texans rebelled and proclaimed Texas an independent republic in 1836. Southern politicians, fearing that Texas would become a refuge for fugitive slaves, pressured President John Tyler to admit Texas to the United States. A joint resolution of Congress, hastily signed by Tyler, did so in 1845. The admission of Texas as the twenty-eighth state and Florida as the twenty-seventh state (also in 1845) meant the absorption of large numbers of Hispanic people into the United States. Many of them had lived in those regions since the sixteenth century, long before Anglo immigration.

The acquisition of Texas's 267,339 square miles (France, by comparison, covers 211,200 square miles) whetted American appetites for the rest of the old Spanish Empire in North America. Some expansionists even dreamed of taking Cuba and Central America.

Exploiting Mexico's political instability, President James Polk goaded Mexico into war. Mexico suffered total defeat and in the **Treaty of Guadalupe Hidalgo (1848)** surrendered its remaining claims to Texas, yielded New Mexico and California, and recognized the Rio Grande as the international border. A treaty with Great Britain in 1846 had already recognized the American settlement in the Oregon Territory. The continent had been acquired. Then, in 1898, a revolt in Cuba against an incompetent Spanish administration had consequences beyond "manifest destiny." Inflamed by press reports of Spanish atrocities, public opinion swept the United States into war. The Spanish-American War—the "splendid little war," as Secretary of State John Hay called it—lasted just ten weeks and brought U.S. control over Cuba, the Philippine Islands, and Puerto Rico. Denying imperialistic ambitions, President William McKinley justified the U.S. acquisition of Cuba and the Philippines with a classic imperialistic argument: the nation wanted only "to take them all and educate the Filipinos and uplift and civilize and Christianize them." McKinley, like most other Americans, did not know that the Filipinos had an old, sophisticated culture and that they had been Christians for three hundred years. The nation's "manifest destiny," originally achieved at the expense of Native Americans, had evolved into worldwide imperialism.

How did the only people who were native to this vast continent fare under manifest destiny? The Indians faithfully observed their treaties with the United States, but "white pioneers in the Northwest committed the most wanton and cruel murders of them, for which it was almost impossible to obtain a conviction from a pioneer jury."[20] Government officials sometimes manipulated the Indians by gathering a few chiefs, plying them with cheap whiskey, then inducing them to hand over the tribes' hunting grounds. Sometimes officials exploited rivalries among tribes or used bribes. By these methods, William Henry Harrison, superintendent of the Indians of the Northwest Territory and a future president, got some native Americans to cede 48 million acres (see Map 28.3). He had the full backing of President Jefferson.

The policy of pushing the Indians westward across the Mississippi, which President James Monroe's administration adopted early in the century, accelerated during Andrew Jackson's presidency (1829–1837). Thousands of Delawares, Shawnees, and Wyandots, tricked into moving from the Northwest Territory to reservations west of Missouri, died of cholera and measles during the journey. The survivors found themselves hopelessly in debt for supplies and farming equipment. The state of Georgia, meanwhile, was nibbling away at Cherokee lands, which were theoretically protected by treaty with the U.S. government. Then gold was discovered on the Cherokee lands, and a gold rush took place. A Vermont missionary, the Reverend Samuel C. Worcester, carried the Indians' case to the Supreme Court. Chief Justice John Marshall ruled that the laws of Georgia had no force within the Cherokee territory and that white settlers and gold rustlers had to leave. President Jackson retorted, "John Marshall has made his decision. Now let him enforce it." The Creek, Cherokee, and other tribes were rounded up, expelled, and sent beyond the western boundaries of Missouri and Arkansas.[21]

The two decades before and after the Civil War saw a steady flow of white settlers westward. The U.S. Army sought to protect the migrants by warfare against the Indians, the destruction of their lodges and horses, and the slaughter of the buffalo on which the Indians depended for food, shelter, and clothing. The federal government's policy was to confine indigenous people to reservations, where malnutrition and disease took a terrible toll. Railroad expansion, new discoveries of gold and silver, and continuing white pressure for land aggravated old conflicts.

Two issues reflect the great cultural differences between white and Native Americans. First, Indians did not understand the concept of land ownership—the idea that a person could possess legal title to a piece of land and use and exploit it as he or she saw fit. Indians believed that land, like other resources such as air and water, belonged to everyone, that individuals or groups might hold temporary stewardship over the land but that it should be respected and treasured for future generations. Second, because Americans had a commander in chief (the president) who could give orders and expect them to be carried out, they assumed that a respected Native Ameri-

**MAP 28.3 Indian Cession of Lands to the United States** Forced removal of the Creek, Cherokee, and Chickasaw Indians led to the deaths of thousands on the Trail of Tears to reservations in Oklahoma, as well as to the destruction of their cultures.

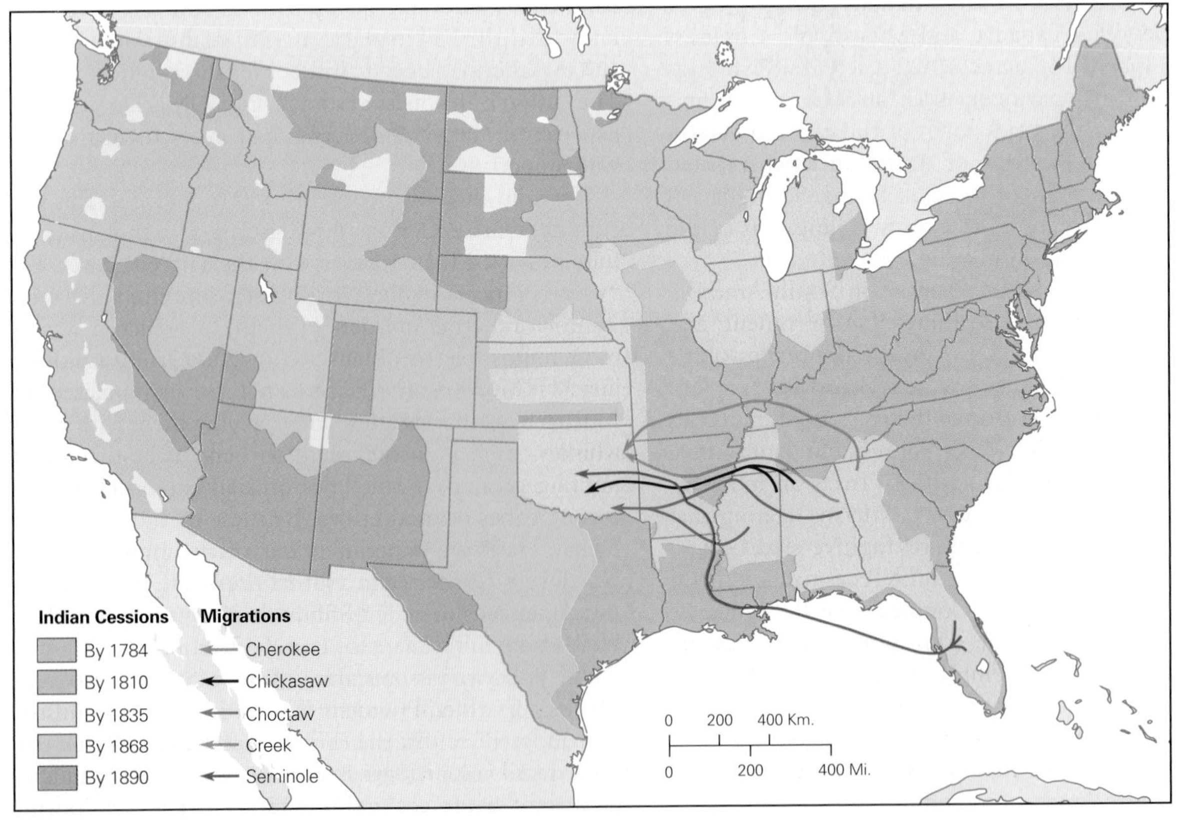

**The Army Attacks an Indian Village** Knowing that white armies possessed better rifles, Indians avoided armed conflict. To force action, army units attacked Indian settlements, often with terrible results for noncombatants. At Little Bighorn, however, when the Indians chose to stand and fight, the army suffered a disastrous loss. This artist's sketch is labeled "Indian Warfare," although it is obvious that the U.S. Army is attacking the Indians. *("Indian Warfare,"* Harper's Weekly, *October 31, 1885)*

can chief could make agreements binding all tribes. But no chief could command all the Sioux, let alone all the Plains Indians. If, however, a chief seemed willing to deal with whites, they would negotiate with him. When a tribe or group of tribes opposed or disregarded a treaty made by such a chief, the whites then claimed that the Indians as a whole had broken the treaty.

In 1868, after pursuing a policy of total war on the Plains Indians, General W. T. Sherman brokered the Treaty of Fort Laramie. This treaty promised that the United States would close western forts and grant the Sioux and Cheyenne their ancestral lands in the Dakotas, the Black Hills, as well as the area between the Platte River and the Bighorn Mountains forever. A few chiefs signed; many did not. In 1874 gold was discovered in the Black Hills. Prospectors flooded the area. By 1875 there were more whites than Indians there. Disaster ensued. (See the feature "Individuals in Society: Crazy Horse" on page 911.)

## Black Slavery in the South

Dutch traders brought the first black people as prisoners to Virginia in 1619 as one solution to the chronic shortage of labor in North America (white indentured servants who worked for a term of years was another solution). The first black arrivals, however, were not slaves. In the seventeenth century, a system of racial servitude and discrimination did not exist. Some blacks themselves acquired property and indentured servants.

In the early eighteenth century, as rice cultivation expanded in the Carolinas and tobacco in the Chesapeake Bay colonies of Virginia and Maryland, planters demanded more laborers. Between 1720 and 1770, black prisoners poured into the Southern colonies. In South Carolina, they came to outnumber whites by almost two to one. In the decades 1730 through 1760, white fears of black revolts pushed colonial legislatures to pass laws that established tight white control and blacks' legal position as slaves, enshrining the slave system in law. Economic demands led to the legal and social institutionalization of black slavery in North America. Racist arguments of blacks' supposed inferiority were used to justify that institutionalization.

Slavery and race relations have posed a serious dilemma for the American majority for more than two centuries. One scholar posed the question in this way:

*How did the slave-holding class, which was molded by the same forces that shaped the nation, which fought America's wars and helped inspire its Revolution, a class which boasted of its patriotism, its devotion to freedom, its adherence to the major tenets of liberalism—how did such a class justify its continuing commitment to slavery?*[22]

The answer can be given in two words: *profit* and *status.*

Many slave owners realized reasonable, sometimes handsome, profits in the decades before the Civil War. For white planters and farmers, slavery proved lucrative, and ownership of slaves was a status symbol as well as a means of social control. Slavery "was at the center of a well-established way of life to which [slave owners] were accustomed and attached, and the disruption or demise of which they feared above all else."[23] Millions of whites, whether or not they owned many slaves, would have agreed with the South Carolina planter who wrote, "Slavery informs all our modes of life, all our habits of thought, lies at the basis of our social existence, and of our political faith." Since the possession of slaves brought financial profit *and* conferred social status and prestige, struggling small farmers had a material and psychological interest in maintaining black bondage. Slavery provided the means by which they might rise and the floor beneath which they could not fall. The issue of slavery is further complicated. In 1840 the U.S. Census Bureau reported six thousand free Negroes holding slaves in the nation. Six thousand black slave owners, most of whom probably held few slaves, constitute a small percentage of all slaveholders, but that number is not insignificant. The slave-owning class cannot be identified entirely with whites.

Between 1820 and 1860, as new lands in the South and West—in Arkansas, Mississippi, Texas, and Louisiana—were put to the production of cotton and sugar, the demand for labor skyrocketed. The upper South—Maryland and Virginia—where decades of tobacco farming had reduced the fertility of the soil, supplied the slaves. Slave traders worked either independently or from firms in Charleston, Natchez, or New Orleans, the largest slave market in the United States. Dealers bought slaves in the upper South, then either transported them overland in coffles (from an Arabic word for a group of prisoners shackled together with chains) several hundred miles or shipped them by boat down the Mississippi to New Orleans. This period witnessed the forced migration of about 650,000 people, in many cases causing the breakup of slave families.[24]

American society subsequently paid a high price in guilt and psychological conflict. Some slaveholders, like President George Washington, found the subject of slavery too uncomfortable even to talk about: "I shall frankly declare to you that I do not like even to think, much less talk of it."[25] In the half century before the Civil War, most slave owners were deeply religious. On the one hand, they taught their children to get rich by the accumulation of land and slaves; on the other hand, they taught that God would punish the greedy with eternal damnation. Slaveholders justified slavery by dismissing blacks as inferior, but religion preached that in the eyes of God, black and white were equal and would ultimately be judged on that basis.

Perhaps to an even greater extent than men, women of the planter class felt troubled by slavery. The South Carolina aristocrat Mary Boykin Chesnut confided to her diary in 1861:

*I wonder if it be a sin to think slavery a curse to any land. . . . God forgive us, but ours is a monstrous system and wrong and iniquity. Perhaps the rest of the world is as bad—this only I see. Like the patriarchs of old our men live all in one house with their wives and their concubines, and the mulattoes one sees in every family exactly resemble the white children—and every lady tells you who is the father of all the mulatto children in everybody's household, but those in her own she seems to think drop from the clouds, or pretends so to think.*[26]

Mary Chesnut believed that most white women of the South were abolitionists in their hearts. She enjoyed the attentions and services of her slaves, but when Lincoln issued the Emancipation Proclamation, she welcomed it with "an unholy joy."[27]

What impact did slavery have on the black family? Herbert G. Gutman's authoritative *The Black Family in Slavery and Freedom, 1750–1925* has demonstrated that, in spite of the destructive effects of slavery, African Americans established strong family units. Most slave couples had long marriages. A study of the entire adult slave population of North Carolina in 1860 has shown that 25 percent of slave marriages lasted between ten and nineteen years, 20 percent lasted at least twenty years, and almost 10 percent endured thirty years or more. Most slave women spent their entire adult lives in settled unions with the same husband. Planters encouraged slave marriages, because, as one owner put it, "marriage adds to

# INDIVIDUALS IN SOCIETY

## CRAZY HORSE

On June 25, 1876, in the valley of the Little Bighorn in southern Montana, Colonel George Armstrong Custer attacked an encampment of Sioux Indians. Custer had been warned that his regiment of 647 men faced a superior force of perhaps 2,500 Sioux warriors; he was specifically ordered not to attack until reinforcements arrived. Nevertheless, Custer recklessly divided his men, sending one group to scout along the left side of the valley while he led troops along the right side. In the ensuing battle Custer and his greatly outnumbered soldiers were surrounded and slaughtered by the Indians under the Sioux leader Crazy Horse (1842?–1877).

Our only verifiable evidence about Crazy Horse derives from two sources: the 1906–1907 interviews by Nebraska judge Eli Ricker of about fifty people (only ten of them Indians) and the 1930–1931 interviews by journalist Eleanor Hinman and Nebraska writer Mari Sandoz of Crazy Horse's lifelong friend, He Dog, a man then in his nineties. In both sets of interviews, most of the questions related to the last four months of Crazy Horse's life, meaning that we know nothing of his first thirty-four years. But an enormous legend has grown up around him, reflecting "a broken people's need to remember and believe in unbroken heroes . . . who remained true to the precepts of their fathers and to the ways of the culture and traditions which bred them."

The Sioux people, one of many Plains Indian tribes, scarcely knew Crazy Horse; they called him "Our Strange Man" and "Our Mystery." Short Buffalo described him as of medium build and height, with hair and complexion lighter than that of other Indians. Legend held him to be a genius at war but a lover of peace, a dreamer and a mystic who spent long periods alone on the plains. He avoided people, especially white men, and detested reservations. His people respected and loved him as much for the charity he showed the poor and oppressed as for his courage in battle.

When the Indians realized that the U.S. government intended to take back the Black Hills (see page 909), they knew that their old ways of life were ending and that they would have to yield to the white men's plans for them (life on reservations) or die opposing them. In the spring of 1876 vast numbers of Indians moved north to an encampment of the Sioux chief Sitting Bull in the region of the Little Bighorn River, creating the last great gathering of native peoples on the Great Plains. The U.S. Army followed.

*Crazy Horse refused to be photographed, so this portrait is probably an idealization.* (Corbis)

Precisely what happened at Little Bighorn we will never know. With at least two thousand horses milling and charging, the battleground would have been a hell of dust and gunsmoke, making visibility very poor. Custer received wounds in the chest and head, either of which would have been fatal. But his head was not scalped nor his body mutilated. Crazy Horse survived; the huge force of Indians melted away on the plains.

Though not a traditional chief, Crazy Horse had about nine hundred followers who looked to him for protection and provision. The long winter of 1876–1877, with bitter cold and little food, wore them down. For their sake, having been promised the army's respect, his own agency, and a buffalo hunt for his people, Crazy Horse laid down his arms at Fort Robinson, Nebraska, in May 1877. He still enjoyed the respect of his people and had moral authority over them. That influence provoked jealousy among other Indians at Fort Robinson. For their part, whites feared that he would become a symbol of resistance and lead another war.

The fort's commander ordered Crazy Horse's arrest. The moment he saw, or smelled, the filthy cells where chained Indians were held, he tried to escape. In a brief melee, his Sioux enemies shouted, "Kill the son of a bitch." A white private, William Gentles, bayoneted him twice, one thrust piercing his kidneys. Crazy Horse fell to the ground, mortally wounded. Receiving no medical attention, he died that night, September 6, 1877.

### QUESTIONS FOR ANALYSIS

1. Being such a "loner" all his life, was Crazy Horse an "individual in society"?
2. Consider one scholar's assessment that the Sioux Indians' insistence on holding on to lands greater in area than France and Spain combined, thus denying the lands' use to millions of immigrants, is an example of the selfishness of the rich.

*Sources:* L. McMurtry, *Crazy Horse* (New York: Penguin Books, 1999); J. Keegan, *Fields of Battle: The Wars for North America* (New York: Vintage Books, 1997).

the comfort, happiness, and health of those entering upon it, besides insuring a greater increase."[28] Large slave families advanced owners' economic interests, and planters rewarded slave women who had many children. Forcible separation due to the sale of one partner proved the greatest threat to the permanence of slave marriages. Evidence from all parts of the South reveals that, in spite of illiteracy, separated spouses tried to remain in touch with one another and, once slavery had been abolished, went to enormous lengths to reunite their families.

Women often had to resist the attentions of the slave owners. In addition, owners not infrequently supplied slave women with black men who had reputations for sexual prowess. Slave women, however, made choices: they tried to select their own husbands, rejecting—up to the point of risking being sold—mates chosen by their owners.

Typically, slave women had their first child around the age of nineteen. On the Good Hope plantation in South Carolina, 80 percent of slave couples had at least four children. Almost all women had all their children by one husband, and most children grew to their teens in households with both parents present. Although premarital intercourse was common among slaves—though not as common as among young American adults during the 1970s—the weight of the evidence shows that women rarely engaged in extramarital sexual activity.

The South had no monopoly on racism, which was equally prevalent in the North. In spite of the dehumanization that characterized a racist society, there are some notable "success" stories. James Forten, a free black man (d. 1842) from Philadelphia, built a large sailmaking business that employed an integrated workforce. He had a

**Slave Auction, 1850s** In a scene outside a country tavern near a river with a Mississippi-type steamer on it, an auctioneer extols a biracial girl's qualities to a group of planters (*center*), while another dealer with a whip (*at left*) brutally separates a mother from her children. The picture was intended to send an abolitionist message. *(Carnegie Museum of Art, Pittsburgh. Gift of Mrs. W. Fitch Ingersoll)*

reputation as a businessman of integrity and acquired considerable wealth. But most whites of the city refused to accept him as a citizen and subjected him to verbal and physical assaults.[29] When, in 1857, the Supreme Court issued the Dred Scot decision saying that a black slave could not be an American citizen (the decision avoided the issue of free blacks), it institutionalized popular social attitudes into formal law.

## Westward Expansion and Civil War

Cotton was king in the mid-nineteenth century, and cotton carried slavery westward. It was westward expansion, not moral outrage, that brought the controversy over slavery to a head. As Congress created new territories, the question of whether slavery would be extended arose again and again (see Map 28.4). For years elaborate compromises were worked out, but the North increasingly feared that the South was intent on controlling the nation. The South was afraid that free territories would harbor fugitive slaves. Issues of sectional political power became more and more heated.

In the 1850s, the question of the further expansion of slavery agitated the nation. Accepting the Republican party nomination for a seat in the U.S. Senate in 1858, Abraham Lincoln predicted the tragic events ahead:

*A house divided against itself cannot stand.*

*I believe this government cannot endure, permanently half* slave *and half free.*

*I do not expect the Union to be* dissolved*—I do not expect the house to fall—but I* do *expect it will cease to be divided.*

*It will become all one thing, or all the other.*

*Either the opponents of slavery will arrest the further spread of it, and place it where the public mind shall rest in the belief that it is in the course of ultimate extinction; or its advocates will push it forward, till it shall become alike lawful in* all *the States, old as well as new—North as well as South.*[30]

In this and every other speech that Lincoln made between 1854 and his election to the presidency in 1860, he argued against slavery less on moral or legal grounds and more in terms of free labor's self-interest.

**MAP 28.4 Slavery in the United States, 1861** This map illustrates the nation on the eve of the Civil War. Although many issues contributed to the developing tensions between North and South, slavery was the fundamental, enduring force that underlay all others. Lincoln's prediction, "I believe this government cannot endure, permanently half *slave* and half free," tragically proved correct.

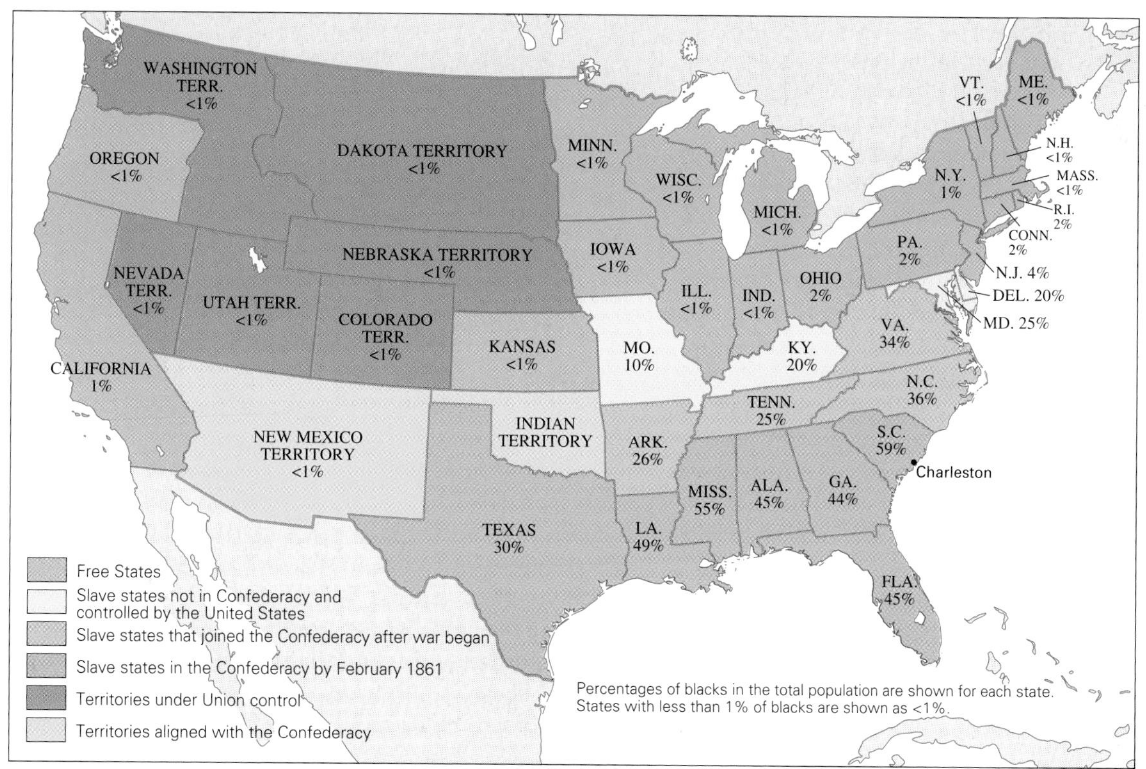

To protest Lincoln's victory in the presidential election of 1860, South Carolina seceded from the Union in December 1860. Ten Southern states soon followed South Carolina's example and formed the **Confederacy.** Its capital was at Richmond, Virginia.

The Civil War began in 1861. Lincoln fought it to preserve the Union and to maintain the free labor system; the abolition of slavery was a secondary outcome, which he in fact tried to avoid. When a Union general in the field declared the slaves of South Carolina and Georgia free, Lincoln overruled the order. He wanted to bring the seceding states back into the Union with their institutions intact. To many people it seemed absurd to fight the Confederacy, which depended on slavery to wage the war, without abolishing slavery. In the words of one historian, Lincoln wanted "to conduct the war for the preservation of *status quo,* which had produced the war."[31] Only after the war had dragged on and the slaughter had become frightful on both sides, and only when it had been proved that the Southern war effort benefited considerably from slave labor, did Lincoln, reluctantly, resolve on emancipation.

The Emancipation Proclamation became effective on January 1, 1863. It expressed no moral indignation. It freed slaves only in states and areas that were in rebellion against the United States. It preserved slavery in states that were loyal to the United States or under military jurisdiction. It allowed slavery for convicted felons. The *London Spectator* sneered, "The principle is not that a human being cannot justly own another, but that he cannot own him unless he is loyal to the United States."[32] The Emancipation Proclamation nevertheless spelled the doom of North American slavery. It transformed the Civil War from a political struggle to preserve the Union into a moral crusade for the liberty of more Americans.

European and English liberals greeted the proclamation with joy. A gathering of working people in Manchester, England, wrote President Lincoln: "The erasure of that foul blot upon civilization and Christianity—**chattel slavery**—during your Presidency will cause the name of Abraham Lincoln to be honoured and revered by posterity."[33] As Lincoln acknowledged, this was a magnanimous statement, for the Civil War hurt working people in Manchester. In fact, it had a worldwide impact socially and economically.

By 1862, deprived of cotton from the American South because of the Union blockade of Confederate ports, the mills of Lancashire in England had closed. Tens of thousands of workers were thrown out of work and nearly starved. Many emigrated to the United States. Between 1862 and 1864, efforts to alleviate the terrible suffering severely taxed the resources of the British government. English manufacturers looked for new suppliers and found them in Egypt, India, and Brazil, where cotton production had been stimulated by the Union blockade. The demands of English industry for Egyptian and Indian cotton played a significant role in the expansion of the English merchant marine fleet. Although England initially opposed construction of the Suez Canal, it later became a major shareholder. The canal was the swiftest route to Indian cotton.

The war also had important political consequences in Europe. In 1861 British and European opinion had divided along class lines. The upper classes sympathized with the American South; the commercial classes and working people sided with the North. The English people interpreted the Northern victory as a triumph of the democratic experiment over aristocratic oligarchy. Thus the United States gave a powerful stimulus to those in Britain and elsewhere who supported the cause of political democracy. When parliaments debated the extension of suffrage, the American example was frequently cited.

Military historians describe the American Civil War as the first modern war:

> *It was the first conflict in which the massive productive capacities of the Industrial Revolution were placed at the disposal of the military machine. It witnessed the first prominent use of mass production of goods to sustain mass armies, mass transportation on railroads, and telegraphic communication between different theaters and on the battlefield. It saw also the first use of such devices of the future as armored warships, breech-loading and repeating rifles, rifled artillery, land and sea mines, submarines, balloons, precursors of the machine gun, and trench warfare. . . . In its material manifestations alone, in its application of the resources of technology to the business of killing, the Civil War presaged the later world wars.*[34]

In April 1865, the Confederate general Robert E. Lee surrendered his army at Appomattox Court House in Virginia, ending the war. Lincoln had called for "malice toward none and charity for all" in his second inaugural address in 1864 and planned a generous policy toward the defeated South. The bullet that killed him brought on a different kind of reconstruction, the central figure in which was the Negro.

During the period called Reconstruction (1865–1877), the vanquished South adjusted to a new social and economic order without slavery, and the eleven Confederate states rejoined the Union. For former slaves, Reconstruction meant the reunion of black families separated before emancipation. Reconstruction also represented an opportunity for blacks to exercise their new freedom, though Southerners detested the very notion of social equality and Northerners were ambivalent on the subject.

Blacks wanted land to farm, but, lacking cash, they soon accepted the sharecropping system: farmers paid landowners about half of a year's crops at harvest time in return for a cabin, food, mules, seed, and tools the rest of the year. Believing that education was the key to economic advancement, blacks flocked to country schools and to colleges supported by Northern religious groups. Although the Fifteenth Amendment to the U.S. Constitution forbade states to deny anyone the vote "on account of race, color, or previous condition of servitude," whites used violence, terror, and, between 1880 and 1920, so-called Jim Crow laws to prevent blacks from voting and to enforce rigid racial segregation. Lacking strong Northern support, blacks did not gain legal equality or suffrage in many parts of the old Confederacy until the 1960s. Racist assumptions and attitudes thwarted their legal, social, and economic advance.

In the construction of a black community, no institution played a larger role than the black Protestant churches. Local black churches provided hope, education, and a forum for the spread of political ideas and platforms. During Reconstruction, black preachers esteemed for their oratorical skill, organizational ability, and practical judgment held important positions in black politics. In a racist and exploitative society, the black church gave support, security, and a sense of solidarity.

## Who Is Black? The Racial Debate

In the summer of 1925, Abraham Lincoln's aging son, Robert Todd Lincoln, visited a resort in Manchester, Vermont. Lincoln hated blacks and refused to allow them to wait on him, and if a black man touched his luggage, car, or possessions, he whacked him with his cane. Lincoln selected the fair, blue-eyed, blond-haired Adam Clayton Powell (1908–1972) as his servant. Powell was an undergraduate at Colgate University working as a bellhop for the summer. The other bellhops were very amused because Powell, by the peculiarity of American society, was "black." Powell went on to represent Harlem in the U.S. Congress (1945–1970).

Millions of other biracial Americans could tell a similar tale. From the seventeenth century to the present, the issue of race has permeated virtually every aspect of American life and culture. Although Americans rarely explore the terms they use when discussing race, a critical analysis of racial concepts is as important to the study of U.S. history as the analysis of the concepts of gender and class.[35] Who is black? How have Americans come to make racial classifications? Why are millions of people whose genetic origins are more European than African defined by custom, by law, and by even themselves as black? Why is there a tremendous disparity between the scientific definition of who is black and the sociocultural one?

Words can mean anything a community wants them to mean. The use of "black" as a racial category in the United States is actually of recent origin. Until the 1960s, persons with some African ancestry were described in the United States as "Negro" or sometimes "colored"; neither the federal government nor people of some African ancestry described themselves as "black." In the late 1960s, leaders of the Black Power movement, which emphasized racial pride and insisted on self-definition, demanded the substitution of the Old English word *black* for the traditional Spanish or Portuguese term *negro*. The broader American society accepted the word. The recent adoption of the expression *African American* suggests blacks' conscious desire to preserve a link with Africa. Some research shows that in the nineteenth century, however, no one tried to preserve an African culture in the United States and free people of color strongly rejected any hint of an African connection.

Since the arrival of the first Africans, sexual contacts have taken place between whites and blacks. The colonies and later the young American republic, with some hesitations and variation, defined all children born of such unions, regardless of their personal appearance, as Negro. In the American South, this manner of definition became known as the "one drop rule," meaning that a single drop of "African blood" made a person "black." Anthropologists call this the "hypo descent rule": racially mixed persons are arbitrarily assigned the status of the subordinate group. Before 1865 Southern society accepted sexual liaisons between white men and black women with general permissiveness. Recent research demonstrates that Southern communities also tacitly accepted relationships between white women and black men. White concerns for the preservation of slave property sometimes checked owners' violence against their human chattels for such sexual activity. After 1865 and the abolition of slavery, however, property rights ended, whites insisted on a total separation of the races—or at least of white women and black men—and restraints against physical violence disappeared. During Reconstruction, whites resorted to lynching in order to maintain the ideology of superiority.[36]

The U.S. census of 1850 showed that 11.2 percent of the population classed as Negro were of mixed race; the 1910 census put the figure at 20.9 percent. Because these counts were based solely on the census takers' perception of racial visibility, the estimates were probably gross undercounts of all Negroes with some white ancestry. Today, according to reliable estimates, between 75 and 90 percent of all American blacks have some white ancestry, and millions of white Americans have at least small amounts of black genetic heritage. A central theme in *Light in August* and other novels by Mississippi writer William Faulkner is the anxiety that thousands of white Southerners feel about their racial purity.

Before the Civil War, many parts of the South, but especially Charleston and New Orleans, had sizable populations of mulattos (persons with one Negro parent), quadroons (one Negro grandparent), and octoroons (one Negro great-grandparent). These persons were the results of liaisons (some of long, sometimes lifelong, duration) between persons of European and at least some African ancestry. Louisiana and South Carolina did not apply the "one drop rule" to these mixed-race people, and in 1835 Judge William Harper of South Carolina ruled that a person's acceptance as white, not the proportion of white and black "blood," determined a person's race. In short, the local community determined an individual's race. But as the South came under increasing abolitionist pressure to defend slavery, and as fears of slave revolts increased, attitudes hardened. Custom became law that defined as Negro all persons with any perceptible African ancestry.

Southerners encouraged the "one drop rule" as a way of enlarging the slave population. Likewise, after 1865, when native-born whites feared and resented blacks' economic and political potential, and between 1880 and 1910, when floods of poor immigrants from southern and eastern Europe competed with former slaves for jobs, the physical contrast between blacks and whites (in terms of skin pigmentation) proved useful to whites in justifying and legitimating their economic interests. After 1920, because there were so many mixed-race persons, and because so many Americans with some black ancestry appeared white, the U.S. census stopped counting mixed-race peoples, and the "one drop rule" became the national legal standard. Scorned and rejected by whites, biracial persons allied with "pure" blacks and in the twentieth century began to lead the struggle for racial equality.[37] The great advocate of nonviolent social action and perhaps the greatest leader of the civil rights movement, Martin Luther King, Jr. (see page 1080), had an Irish grandmother.

Racial categories rest on socially constructed beliefs and on custom backed by law, not on any biological or anthropological classification. While a great amount of myth and folklore surrounds issues of race—myth that cannot stand up to scientific scrutiny—still, an ideology based on

**Harlem Hellfighters** Returning to New York in 1919 aboard the USS *Stockholm*, these black men of the famed U.S. 369th Division had fought in the bloody battle of the Meuse-Argonne during the First World War. The French government awarded 150 of them the coveted Croix de Guerre. Since the United States practiced strict racial segregation, God help them if they tried to be served in a restaurant south of Philadelphia. *(Corbis)*

myth has had significant effects on people's lives.[38] Race and culture are not the same thing. *Culture* is defined as patterns of behavior, life, and beliefs. Peoples of the same race often have vastly different cultures—as, for example, Chinese culture differs from Japanese culture though both the Chinese and the Japanese are Asian, or as Italian culture differs from Russian culture though both peoples are Caucasian. So with African Americans, among whom different cultures also exist.

The accelerated immigration of huge numbers of Latin Americans and Asians to the United States since 1975 has complicated these issues. In preparation for the federal census of the year 2000, government agencies modified customary racial categories and questioned whether it was even proper for the national government to classify people according to the arbitrary and nonscientific criteria of race. The federal Office of Management and Budget, which sets racial and ethnic standards on all governmental forms on the basis of census results, provided rules that will influence the size and shape of congressional districts, college and business affirmative action programs, university scholarships, and loans and mortgages. As one congressman put it, "The numbers drive the dollars."

The racial makeup of the United States is changing. More Native Americans marry outside their group than within it. In the 1980s black men married white women at a rate of 10 percent (black women married whites at half that rate). Immigration also means cultural change. Large numbers of Asian women are today marrying white, Hispanic, and black men.

Hispanic people pose the greatest racial complexity. According to the Latin American concept of race, skin color is an individual variable, not a group marker; thus within a given family, one child might be considered white, another black. The 1960 census listed all people from Latin America as white—blacks from the Dominican Republic, European whites from Argentina, and Mexicans who resembled Native Americans (Indians). In neither the state of Hawaii nor the commonwealth of Puerto Rico does the term *race* carry the connotation it does on the U.S. mainland.

Three broad currents of opinion about racial classification are emerging. One group urges doing away with all racial classifications because they are meaningless and unscientific and have been the historical means of exploiting persons perceived as "inferior." Other thinkers, primarily African American scholars, agree that the notion of race is a cruel hoax but insist that the racial idea of "black" makes an important political statement. They argue that racial categories are needed to correct injustices and that the U.S. relinquishing of the racial idea of "black" would amount to the abandonment of a poor underclass. These writers have not so far addressed the situations of Hispanics, Asians, and Native Americans. The third group consists of increasing numbers of biracial and multiracial persons who resent being assigned to any single category—persons who feel strong ethnic and cultural ties to two or more groups.[39] Should their feelings and pain be ignored? What do racial categories mean, anyway? Should people be discriminated against, or rewarded, on the basis of others' perceptions of who they are? Should the federal government continue its pattern of defining race in order to support the dominant race's economic goals? What if the dominant race is Hispanic? In 2003 the U.S. Census Bureau announced that with 37 million, Hispanics constitute the largest minority in the United States (compared with 36 million African Americans); what effect will that have? Should "the numbers drive the dollars"?

## Industrialization and Immigration

After the Civil War, the United States underwent an industrial boom powered by exploitation of the country's natural resources. The federal government turned over vast amounts of land and mineral resources to industry for development. In particular, the railroads—the foundation of industrial expansion—received 130 million acres. By 1900 the U.S. railroad system was 193,000 miles long, connected every part of the nation, and represented 40 percent of the railroad mileage of the entire world. Immigrant workers built it.

The late nineteenth and early twentieth centuries witnessed the immigration of unprecedented numbers of Europeans and Asians to the United States. Between 1860 and 1900, 14 million immigrants came, and during the peak years between 1900 and 1914, another 14 million immigrants passed through the U.S. customs inspection station at Ellis Island in New York City. All sought a better life and a higher standard of living.

The immigrants' ambitions precisely matched the labor needs of the times. Chinese, Scandinavian, and Irish immigrants laid 30,000 miles of railroad tracks between 1867 and 1873 and another 73,000 miles in the 1880s. At the Carnegie Steel Corporation (later USX), Slavs and Italians produced one-third of the world's total steel supply in 1900. Lithuanians, Poles, Croats, Scandinavians, Irish, and blacks entered the Chicago stockyards and built the meatpacking industry. Irish immigrants continued to operate the spinning frames and knitting machines of New England's textile mills. Industrial America developed on the sweat and brawn—the cheap labor—of its immigrant millions.

As industrial expansion transformed the eastern half of the United States, thousands of land-hungry farmers moved westward, where land was still only $1.25 an acre. In the final third of the nineteenth century, pioneers put 225 million acres under cultivation.

The West also held precious metals. The discovery of gold and silver in California, Colorado, Arizona, and Montana, and on the reservations of the Sioux Indians of South Dakota (see page 909), precipitated huge rushes. Even before 1900, miners had extracted $1.24 billion in gold and $901 million in silver from western mines. Many miners settled down to farm and help their territories toward statehood. By 1912 the West had been won.

Generally speaking, the settlers' life blurred sex roles. Women commonly did the same dawn-to-dusk back-breaking agricultural work as men. In addition, it fell to women to make a home out of crude log cabins that had no windows or doors or out of tarpaper shacks that had mud floors. One "gently reared" bride of seventeen took one look at her mud roof and dirt floor and indignantly announced, "My father had a much better house for his hogs!"[40] Lacking cookstoves, they prepared food over open fireplaces, using all kinds of substitutes for ingredients easily available back east. Before they could wash clothes, women had to make soap out of lye and carefully saved household ashes.

Considered the carriers of "high culture," women organized whatever educational, religious, musical, and recreational activities the settlers' society possessed. Women also had to defend their homes against prairie fires and Indian attacks. These burdens were accompanied by frequent pregnancies and, often, the need to give birth without medical help or even the support of other women. Many women settlers used such contraceptive devices as spermicides, condoms, and, after 1864, vaginal diaphragms. The death rate for infants and young children ran as high as 30 percent in the mid-nineteenth century. Even so, these women had large families.

As in South America, immigration led to rapid urbanization. In 1790 only 5.1 percent of Americans were living in centers of twenty-five hundred or more people. By 1860 this figure had risen to 19.9 percent, and by 1900 almost 40 percent were living in cities. The overwhelming majority of the southern and eastern Europeans who came to North America at the turn of the century became urban industrial workers, their entire existence framed by the factory and the tenement. Newly uprooted from rural Europe, Italians, Greeks, Croats, Hungarians, Czechs, Poles, Russians, and Jews contrasted sharply with their urban neighbors and with each other. Older residents saw only "a sea of strange faces, babbling in alien tongues and framed by freakish clothes. Walking through these multitudes now was really like a voyage round the globe."[41]

Between 1880 and 1920, industrial production soared. New inventions such as the steam engine, the dynamo (generator), and the electric light were given industrial and agricultural applications. Large factories replaced small ones. Large factories could buy large machines, operate them at full capacity, and take advantage of railroad discount rates. In the automobile industry, Henry Ford of Detroit set up assembly lines. Each person working on the line performed only one task instead of assembling an entire car. In 1910 Ford sold 10,000 cars; in 1914, a year after he inaugurated the first moving assembly line, he sold 248,000 cars. Such developments changed the face of American society. Sewing machines made cheap, varied, mass-produced clothing available to city people in department stores and to country people through mail-order catalogues. The automobile increased opportunities for travel, general mobility, and change.

As elsewhere, by the 1890s U.S. factory managers were stressing industrial efficiency and the importance of time. Management engineers wanted to produce more at lower costs. They aimed to reduce labor costs by eliminating unnecessary workers. As quantity rather than quality became the measure of acceptability, workers' skills were less valued. Assembly-line workers more and more performed only monotonous and time-determined work; in effect they became interchangeable parts of the machines they operated.

Despite accelerated production, and perhaps because of overproduction, the national economy experienced repeated cycles of boom and bust in the late nineteenth century. Serious depressions in 1873, 1884, and 1893 slashed prices and threw many people out of work. Leading industrialists responded by establishing larger corporations and consolidated companies into huge conglomerates. As a result of the merger of several small oil companies, John D. Rockefeller's Standard Oil Company controlled 84 percent of the nation's oil and most American pipelines in 1898. J. P. Morgan's United States Steel monopolized the iron and steel industries, and Swift & Co. of Chicago controlled the meat-processing industry.

Industrialization led to the creation of a vast class of wage workers who depended totally on their employers for work. Corporate managers, however, were always preoccupied with cutting labor costs. Thus employers paid workers piecemeal for the number of articles produced, to encourage the use of the new machines; managers hired more women and children and paid them much less than they paid men. Most women worked in the textile industry. Some earned as little as $1.56 for seventy hours of work, while men received from $7 to $9 for the same work. Employers reduced wages, forcing workers to toil longer and harder to maintain a certain level of income. Owners fought in legislatures and courts against the installation of costly safety devices, so working conditions in mines and mills were frightful. In 1913, even after some safety measures had been taken, 25,000 people died in industrial accidents. Between 1900 and 1917, 72,000 railroad worker deaths occurred. Workers responded with strikes, violence, and, gradually, unionization.

Urbanization brought serious problems. In *How the Other Half Lives* (1890), Jacob Riis, a newspaper reporter and recent immigrant from Denmark, drew national attention to what he called "the foul core of New York's slums." Riis estimated that 300,000 people inhabited a single square mile on New York's Lower East Side. Overcrowding, poor sanitation, and lack of health services caused frequent epidemics. The blight of slums increased crime, prostitution, alcoholism, and other drug-related addictions. Riis attacked the vicious economic exploitation of the poor.

New York City was not unique; slums and the social problems resulting from them existed in all large American cities. Reformers fought for slum clearance, but public apathy and vested economic interests delayed massive urban renewal until after the Second World War. In spite of all these industrial and urban difficulties, immigrants continued to come.

European and Asian immigrants aroused nativist sentiments—that is, intense hostility to foreign and "un-American" looks, behavior, and loyalties—in native-born Americans. Some of this antagonism sprang from the deep-rooted Anglo-Saxon racism of many Americans. Some grew out of old Protestant suspicions of Roman Catholicism, the faith of most of the new arrivals. A great deal of the dislike of the foreign-born sprang from

**Racism Rampant** Nineteenth-century immigrants encountered terrible prejudice, as "respectable" magazines and newspapers spewed out racism, such as this cartoon from an 1869 issue of *Harper's Weekly.* The Irishman (identifiable by the shillelagh or blackthorn club, supposedly a sign of his tendency toward violence) and the Chinese man (identifiable by the pigtail, supposedly a sign of his devious obsequiousness) are both satirized as "barbarians." Well into the twentieth century, being "American" meant being of Anglo-Saxon descent. (Harper's Weekly, *August 28, 1869. Private Collection)*

CASTLE GARDEN
GOLDEN GATE
Hunk. E. Doré
THE COMING MAN—JOHN CHINAMAN.
Uncle Sam introduces Eastern Barbarism to Western Civilization.

fear of economic competition. To most Americans, the Chinese with their exotic looks and willingness to work for very little seemed the most dangerous. Increasingly violent agitation against Asians led to race riots in California and finally culminated in the Chinese Exclusion Act of 1882, which denied Chinese laborers entrance to the country.

Immigrants from Europe seized on white racism as a way to compensate for their immigrant status by claiming superiority to former slaves and their descendants. The arrival of millions of Italians and Slavs between 1880 and 1914 aggravated an already bad situation. What the German scientist Alexander von Humboldt wrote about the attitude of peninsulares toward Creoles in Latin America in the early nineteenth century—"the lowest, least educated, and uncultivated European believes himself superior to the white born in the New World"[42]—precisely applies to the outlook of Italian or Slavic immigrants to the United States at the turn of this century if one merely substitutes *black* for *white.* The social status of blacks remained the lowest, while that of immigrants rose. As the United States underwent expansion and industrialization during the nineteenth century, blacks remained the worst off *because of immigration.*[43]

In the 1890s, the nation experienced a severe economic depression. Faced with overproduction, the rich and politically powerful owners of mines, mills, and factories fought the organization of labor unions, laid off thousands, slashed wages, and ruthlessly exploited their workers. Workers in turn feared that immigrant labor would drive salaries lower. The frustrations provoked during the depression boiled over into savage attacks on the foreign-born. One of the bloodiest incidents took place in western Pennsylvania in 1897, when about 150 unarmed Polish and Hungarian coal miners persuaded others to join their walkout. The mine owners convinced the local sheriff that the strike was illegal. He panicked and ordered his deputies to shoot at the strikers. Twenty-one immigrants died, and forty were wounded. The sheriff declared that the miners were only "infuriated foreigners . . . like wild beasts." Local people agreed that if the strikers had been American-born, no blood would have been shed.[44]

After the First World War, labor leaders lobbied Congress for restrictions on immigration because they feared losing the wage gains achieved during the war. In the 1920s, Congress responded with laws that set severe quotas—2 percent of resident nationals as of the 1890 census—on immigration from southern and eastern Europe. The Japanese were completely excluded. These racist laws remained on the books until 1965.

## CANADA, FROM FRENCH COLONY TO NATION

In 1608 the French explorer Samuel de Champlain (1567–1635) sailed down the St. Lawrence River and established a trading post on the site of present-day Quebec. Thus began the permanent colony of New France. The fur-trading monopolies subsequently granted to Champlain by the French crown attracted settlers, and Jesuit missionaries to the Indians further increased the French population. The British, however, vigorously challenged French control of the lucrative fur trade, and the long mid-eighteenth-century global struggle for empire between the British and the French, known in North America as the French and Indian Wars because of Indian border warfare, tested French control. In 1759, on the Plains of Abraham, a field next to the city of Quebec, the English under General James Wolfe defeated the French under General Louis Montcalm. This battle ended the French empire in North America. By the Treaty of Paris of 1763, France ceded Canada to Great Britain.

### British Colony (1763–1839)

For the French Canadians, who in 1763 numbered about ninety thousand, the British conquest was a tragedy and the central event in their history. British governors replaced the French; English-speaking merchants from Britain and the thirteen American colonies to the south took over the colony's economic affairs. The Roman Catholic church remained and until about 1960 played a powerful role in the political and cultural, as well as the religious, life of French Canadians. Most of the French Canadians engaged in agriculture, though a small merchant class sold furs and imported manufactured goods.

Intending to establish a permanent administration for Canada, in 1774 the British Parliament passed the Quebec Act. This law granted religious freedom to French Canadians and recognized French law in civil matters, but it denied Canadians a legislative assembly, a traditional feature of British colonial government. Parliament placed power in the hands of an appointed governor and an appointed council; the latter, however, was composed of French Canadians as well as English-speaking members. English Canadian businessmen protested that they were being denied a basic right of Englishmen—representation.

During the American Revolution, about forty thousand Americans demonstrated their loyalty to Great Britain and its empire by immigrating to Canada. These "loyalists" not only altered the French-English ratio in

**George Heriot: Quebec City** Founded at the confluence of the St. Lawrence and the St. Charles Rivers as a French colony in 1608, making it the second oldest city in North America (after St. Augustine, Florida, founded in 1565), Quebec City has always been the ideological heart of French Canada. Although this scene seems derivative of many Dutch waterfront paintings, it has a certain charm and suggests the excitement of winter sports. *(Royal Ontario Museum, Canadiana Department, Toronto)*

the population but also pressed for a representative assembly. In 1791 Parliament responded with the Constitution Act, which divided the province of Quebec at the Ottawa River into Lower Canada (present-day Quebec, predominantly French and Catholic) and Upper Canada (present-day Ontario, primarily English and Protestant). The act also provided for an elective assembly in each of the two provinces. Because the assemblies' decisions could be vetoed by an appointed upper house or by the governor and his council, general discontent continued. Finally, in 1837, disputes over control of revenue, the judiciary, and the established churches erupted into open rebellion in both Upper and Lower Canada. The British government, fearful of a repetition of the American events of 1776, decided on a full investigation and appointed Lord Durham, a prominent liberal reformer, to make recommendations. Lord Durham published his *Report on the Affairs of British North America,* later called the "Magna Carta" of British colonial administration, in 1839.

## The Age of Confederation (1840–1905)

Acting on Lord Durham's recommendations, Parliament in 1840 passed the Union Act, which united Ontario and Quebec under one government composed of a governor, an appointed legislative council, and an elective assembly in which the two provinces had equal representation. The imperial government in London was to retain control over trade, foreign affairs, public lands, and the colonial constitution. The Union Act marks an important milestone toward **confederation.** When Lord Durham's son-in-law, Lord Elgin, was appointed governor in 1847, he made it clear that his cabinet (council) would be chosen from the party with the majority in the elected assembly; following the British model, the cabinet had to retain the support of that majority in order to stay in office.

The idea of a union or confederation of the other Canadian provinces persisted in the 1860s. During the American Civil War, English-American relations were

**MAP 28.5 The Dominion of Canada, 1871** Shortly after Canada became a dominion in 1867, new provinces were added (the year that appears near each province's name is the date the province joined the dominion). Still, vast areas of present-day Canada were too sparsely populated to achieve that status. Alberta and Saskatchewan did not become part of the Dominion until 1905, Newfoundland only in 1949.

severely strained, and according to one historian, "Canada found herself in the centre of the storm. The resulting fear of American aggression was a powerful factor in bringing confederation to completion."[45] Parliament's passage of the British North America Act in 1867 brought the Canadian constitution to its modern form. By the act, the traditional British parliamentary system was adapted to the needs of the new North American nation. The provinces of New Brunswick and Nova Scotia joined Ontario and Quebec to form the Dominion of Canada (see Map 28.5). A governor general, who represented the British crown and fulfilled ceremonial functions, governed through the Dominion Cabinet, which, like the British Cabinet, was composed of members selected from the lower house of the legislature, to which it was responsible.

Legislative power rested in a Parliament of two houses: a Senate, whose members were appointed for life by the governor general, and a House of Commons, whose members were elected by adult males. (Canadian women won the right to vote in national elections in 1917, shortly before women in the United States and Great Britain but after women in Australia.) In theory, the two houses had equal power, though money bills had to originate in the House of Commons. In practice, the Senate came to serve only as a deliberative check on hasty legislation and as a means of rewarding elder statesmen for their party services.

The Dominion Cabinet received complete jurisdiction over internal affairs. Britain retained control over foreign policy. (In 1931 the British Statute of Westminster officially recognized Canadian autonomy in foreign affairs.)

Believing that the American system of the division of powers between the states and the federal government left the states too strong and helped to bring on the Civil War, the framers of the Canadian constitution intended to create a powerful central government. Thus provincial legislatures were assigned powers explicitly stated and applicable only to local conditions. With the implementation of the British North America Act, John A. Macdonald (1815–1891), the strongest advocate of confederation, became the Dominion's first prime minister.

Macdonald vigorously pushed Canada's "manifest destiny" to absorb all the northern part of the continent. In 1869 his government purchased for $1.5 million the vast Northwest Territories of the Hudson's Bay Company. From this territory, the province of Manitoba emerged to become part of the Dominion in 1870. Fearful that the sparsely settled colony of British Columbia would join the United States, Macdonald lured British Columbia into the confederation with a subsidy to pay its debts and the promise of a transcontinental railroad. Likewise, the debt-ridden little maritime province of Prince Edward Island was drawn into confederation with a large subsidy. In five short years, between 1868 and 1873, through Macdonald's imagination and drive, Canadian sovereignty stretched from coast to coast.

Believing that a transcontinental railroad was essential to Canada's survival as a nation, Macdonald declared that "until this great work is completed our Dominion is little more than a 'geographical expression.' We have as much interest in British Columbia as in Australia, and no more. The railroad . . . finished, we [will] become a great united country with a large interprovincial trade and a common interest."[46] On November 7, 1885, Macdonald received a telegram announcing that the first train from Montreal in Quebec was approaching the Pacific; traveling at twenty-four miles per hour, the train had made the coast-to-coast trip in a little over five days. The completion of the railroad led to the formation of two new prairie provinces, Alberta and Saskatchewan, which in 1905 entered the Dominion. (Only in 1949 did the island of Newfoundland renounce colonial status and join the Dominion.) The **Canadian Pacific Railroad** was Macdonald's greatest achievement.

## Growth, Development, and National Maturity

Macdonald's hopes for large numbers of immigrants to people the thinly populated country did not immediately materialize. Between 1897 and 1912, however, 961,000 people entered Canada from the British Isles, 594,000 from Europe, and 784,000 from the United States. Some immigrants went to work in the urban factories of Hamilton, Toronto, and Montreal. Most immigrants from continental Europe—Poles, Germans, Scandinavians, and Russians—flooded the midwestern plains and soon transformed the prairies into one of the world's greatest grain-growing regions.

Because of Canada's small population, most of which in the early twentieth century was concentrated in Ontario and Quebec, the assimilation of the immigrants to the older English-Canadian culture occurred more slowly than in the pluralistic United States. French Canadians remained the largest minority in the population. Distinctively different in language, law, and religion, and fiercely proud of their culture, they resisted assimilation. Since the 1950s, Italian and Hungarian immigration has contributed to the evolution of a more cosmopolitan culture.

Supported by population growth, Canada experienced an agricultural and industrial boom between 1891 and 1914. In those years, wheat production rocketed from 2 million bushels per year to 150 million bushels. The discovery of gold, silver, copper, and nickel in northern Ontario led to the full exploitation of those mineral resources. British Columbia, Ontario, and Quebec produced large quantities of wood pulp, much of it sold to the United States. Canada's great rivers were harnessed to supply hydroelectric power for industrial and domestic use. Meanwhile, the government erected tariffs to protect industry, established a national civil service, and built a sound banking system.

Canada's powerful support of the Allied cause in the First World War demonstrated its full maturity as a nation. In 1914 the British government still controlled the foreign policy of all parts of the empire. When Britain declared war on Germany, Canada unhesitatingly followed. More than 600,000 Canadian soldiers served with distinction in the army, some of them in the bloodiest battles in France. The 60,661 Canadians killed represent a greater loss than that experienced by the more populous United States. Canadian grain and foodstuffs supplied much of the food of the Allied troops, and Canadian metals were in demand for guns and shells. Canadian resentment, therefore, over lack of voice in the formulation of Allied war policies was understandable.

In 1917 the British government established the Imperial War Cabinet, a body composed of the chief British ministers and the prime ministers of the Dominions (Australia, Canada, New Zealand, and South Africa) to set policy. In 1918 Canada demanded and received—over the initial opposition of Britain, France, and the United States—the right to participate in the Versailles Peace Conference and in the League of Nations. Canada had become a respected and independent nation. Since 1939 Canada has been a member of the British Commonwealth of Nations. The constitution of 1982 abolished the power of the London Parliament to amend Canada's constitution and ended all appeals from the provinces to London. Quebec did not sign the 1982 document, and the strong separatist movement within Quebec continues to articulate the desire of French-speaking Canadians for independence from English Canada and sovereignty as a separate nation.

## AUSTRALIA, FROM PENAL COLONY TO NATION

In April 1770, James Cook, the English explorer, navigator, and captain of H.M.S. *Endeavor,* dropped anchor in a wide bay about ten miles south of the present city of Sydney on the coast of eastern Australia. Because the young botanist on board the ship, Joseph Banks, subsequently discovered 30,000 specimens of plant life in the bay, 1,600 of them unknown to European science, Captain Cook called the place **Botany Bay.** Totally unimpressed by the flat landscape and its few naked inhabitants—the Aborigines, or native people—Cook sailed north along the coast. Finally, the ship rounded Cape York Peninsula, the northernmost point of Australia (see Map 28.6). On August 21, on a rock later named Possession Island, Cook formally claimed the entire land south of where he stood for King George III, 16,000 miles away. Cook called the land **New South Wales.** In accepting possession, the British crown acted on the legal fiction that Australia was *Terra Nullius,* completely unoccupied, thus entirely ignoring the native people.

The world's smallest continent, Australia is located southeast of Asia between the Pacific and Indian Oceans.

**MAP 28.6 Australia** The vast deserts in western Australia meant that cities and industries would develop mainly in the east. Australia's early geographical and cultural isolation bred a sense of inferiority. Air travel, the communications revolution, and the massive importation of Japanese products and American popular culture have changed that.

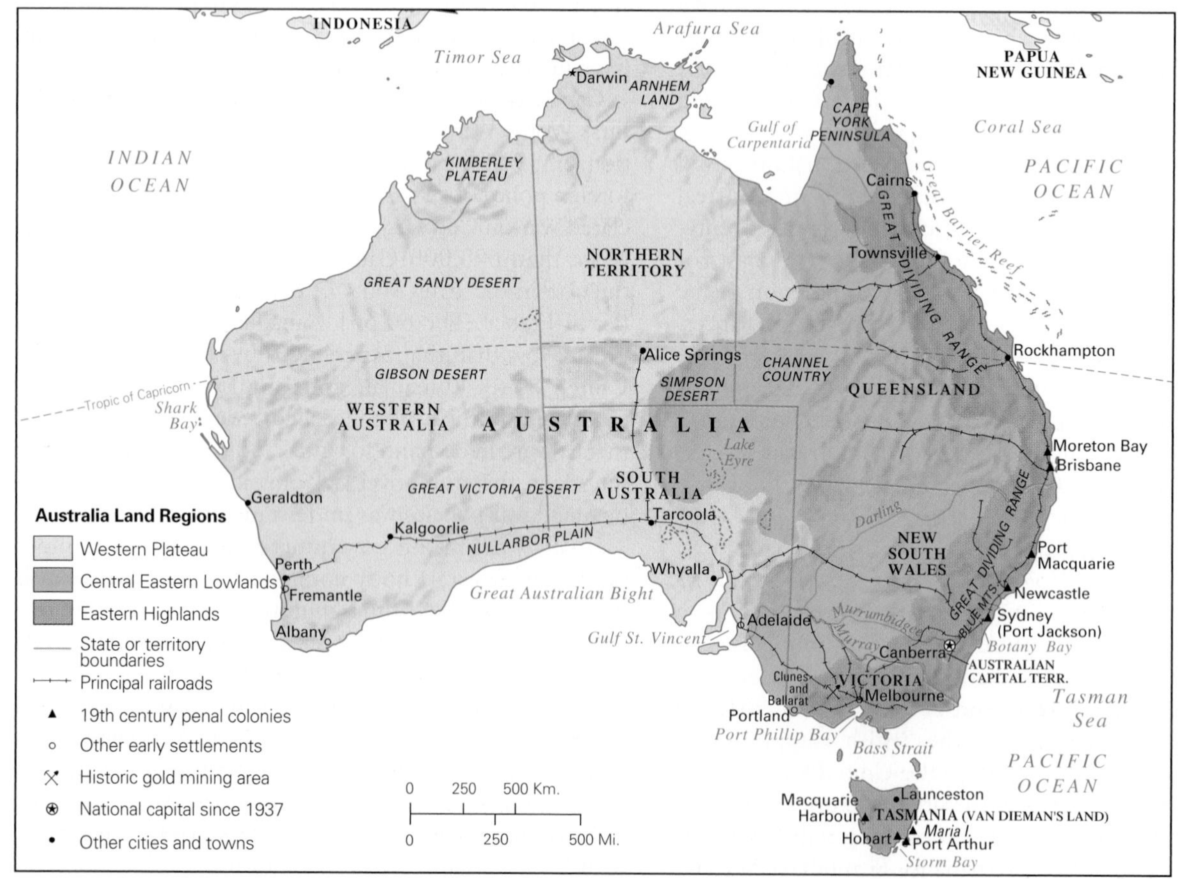

It is about half the size of Europe and almost as large as the United States (excluding Alaska and Hawaii). Three topographical zones roughly divide the continent. The Western Plateau, a vast desert and semidesert region, covers almost two-thirds of the continent. The Central Eastern Lowlands extend from the Gulf of Carpentaria in the north to western Victoria in the south. The Eastern Highlands are a complex belt of tablelands. Australia is one of the world's driest continents. It has a temperate climate and little intense cold.

When Cook arrived in Australia, about three hundred thousand Aborigines inhabited the continent. A peaceful and nomadic people who had emigrated from southern Asia millennia before, the Aborigines lived entirely by food gathering, fishing, and hunting. They had no domestic agriculture. Tribal customs governed their lives. Although they used spears and bows and arrows in hunting, they never practiced warfare as it was understood by more technologically advanced peoples such as the Aztecs of Mexico or the Mandinke of West Africa. When white settlers arrived, they occupied the Aborigines' lands unopposed. According to one Australian scholar, from 1788 to the present, "Australian governments have been much more concerned with protecting the Aborigines than with fighting them."[47] Nevertheless, like the Indians of Central and South America, the Aborigines fell victim to the white peoples' diseases and to a spiritual malaise caused by the breakdown of their tribal life. Today only about forty-five thousand pureblood Aborigines survive.

## Penal Colony

The victory of the thirteen North American colonies in 1783 inadvertently contributed to the establishment of a colony in Australia five years later. Before 1775 the British government had shipped about one thousand convicts annually to Georgia. Crime in England was increasing in the 1770s and 1780s, and the transportation of felons "beyond the seas" seemed the answer to the problem of overcrowded prisons. Moreover, the establishment of a colony in Australia would provide a home for dispossessed loyalists who had fled America during the American Revolution.

In England, the prisons were so full that old transport ships in southern naval ports were being used to house criminals, and pressure on the government to do something was intense. Finally, in August 1786, the British Cabinet approved the establishment of a penal colony at Botany Bay to serve as "a remedy for the evils likely to result from the late alarming and numerous increase of felons in this country, and more particularly in the metropolis (London)."[48] The name "Botany Bay" became a byword for the forced and permanent exile of criminals. In May 1787, a fleet of eleven ships packed with one thousand felons and their jailers sailed for Australia. After an eight-month voyage, it landed in Sydney Cove on January 28, 1788.

Mere survival in an alien world was the first challenge. Because the land at Botany Bay proved completely unsuited for agriculture and lacked decent water, the first governor, Arthur Phillip, moved the colony ten miles north to Port Jackson, later called Sydney. Announcing that those who did not work would not eat, Phillip set the prisoners to planting seeds. Coming from the slums of London, the convicts knew nothing of agriculture, and some were too ill or old to work. The colony lacked draft animals and plows. The troop detachments sent to guard the prisoners considered it below their dignity to work the land. For years the colony of New South Wales tottered on the brink of starvation.

For the first thirty years, men far outnumbered women. Because the British government refused to allow wives to accompany their convict-husbands, prostitution flourished. Many women convicts, if not professional prostitutes when they left England, became such during the long voyage south. Army officers, government officials, and free immigrants chose favorite convicts as mistresses.

Recent research provides useful information about the official attitude toward women. On May 3, 1791, Lieutenant Ralph Clark recorded in his diary that he had ordered three women convicts flogged. Catherine White fainted after the first 15 lashes, Mary Teut after 22. When Mary Higgins had received 26 lashes, Lieutenant Clark "forgave her the remainder [he had ordered 50] because she was an old woman." From other sources we know that another woman convict was six months' pregnant at the time with Clark's child.[49] This incident shows the brutality of power and the hypocrisy of an administration that simultaneously savagely punished and sexually exploited women. The vast majority of children born in the colony were illegitimate.

Officers and jailers, though descended from the middle and lower middle classes, tried to establish a colonial gentry and to impose the rigid class distinctions that they had known in England. Known as **exclusionists,** this self-appointed colonial gentry tried to exclude from polite society all freed or emancipated persons, called **emancipists.** Deep and bitter class feeling took root.

**Departure of Convicts for New South Wales** Prisoners are marched from Newgate Prison in London to the dock at Blackfriars, from which they will begin the five-month voyage to Australia. Some had committed serious crimes, such as armed robbery; others had merely stolen a loaf of bread. *(From Sian Rees,* The Floating Brothel *[New York: Hyperion, 2002]. Reproduced with permission)*

## Economic Development

For eighty long years after 1787, Britain continued to transport convicts to New South Wales. Transportation rested on two premises: that criminals should be punished and that they should not be a financial burden on the state. Convicts became free when their sentences expired or were remitted. Few returned to England.

Governor Phillip and his successors urged the Colonial Office to send free settlers. The Napoleonic wars slowed emigration before 1815, but thereafter a steady stream of people relocated. The end of the European wars also released capital for potential investment. But investment in what? What commodity could be developed and exported to England?

Immigrants explored several economic enterprises. In the last decade of the eighteenth century, for example, sealing seemed a likely possibility. Sealing merchants hired Aborigine women to swim out to the seal rocks, lie down among the seals until their suspicions were dulled, and then at a signal rise up and club the seals to death. In 1815 a single ship carried sixty thousand sealskins to London (a normal cargo contained at least ten thousand skins). Such destruction rapidly depleted the seals.

Credit for the development of the product that was to be Australia's staple commodity for export—wool—goes to John Macarthur (1767–1834). Granted a large tract of Crown lands and assigned thirty convicts to work for him, Macarthur conducted experiments in the production of fine merino wool. In 1800 he sent sample fleeces to England to determine their quality. He also worked to change the government's penal view of New South Wales to a commercial one and to attract the financial support of British manufacturers.

The report of J. T. Bigge, an able lawyer sent out in 1819 to evaluate the colony, proved decisive. Persuaded by large landowners like Macarthur, Bigge reported that wool was the country's future staple. He recommended that convicts be removed from the temptations of towns and seaports and dispersed to work on the estates of men of capital. He also urged that British duties on colonial wool be suspended. The Colonial Office accepted this advice, and the pastoral economy of Australia, as the continent was beginning to be called, began.

Australia's temperate though capricious climate is ideally suited to sheep farming. Moreover, wool production requires much land and little labor—precisely the situation in Australia. In 1820 the sheep population was 120,000; by 1830 it reached a half million. After 1820 the commercial importance of Australia exceeded its significance as a penal colony, and wool exports steadily increased, from 75,400 pounds in 1821, to 2 million pounds in 1830, to 24 million pounds in 1845.

Settlers also experimented with wheat farming. Soil deficiencies and the dry climate slowed early production, but farmers eventually developed a successful white-grained winter variety. By 1900 wheat proved Australia's second most valuable crop.

Population shortage remained a problem. In this area, the development of Australia owes something to the vision of Edward Gibbon Wakefield (1769–1862), a theorist of colonization. Between 1825 and 1850, 3 million people emigrated from Great Britain. In the quest for immigrants, Australia could not really compete with North America. The 12,000-mile journey to Australia cost between £20 and £25 and could take five weary months. By contrast, the trip to Canada or the United States cost only £5 and lasted just ten weeks. Wakefield proposed that Australian land be sold relatively cheaply and that proceeds from the sale be used to pay the passages of free laborers and mechanics. That eliminated the disadvantage of cost. Although over 2.5 million British immigrants went to North America, 223,000 industrious English and Irish people chose Australia.

Population in the early nineteenth century concentrated on the eastern coast of the continent. The growth of sheep farming stimulated exploration and led to the opening of the interior. In 1813 explorers discovered a route over the Blue Mountains. New settlements were made in Hobart, Tasmania, in 1813; in Queensland on the Brisbane River in 1824; and on the Swan River in western Australia in 1829. Melbourne was established on Port Phillip Bay in 1835 and Adelaide on Gulf St. Vincent in 1836. These settlements served as the bases for further exploration and settlement. Population continued to grow with the arrival of more convicts (a total of 161,000 when the system was finally abolished in 1868). The Ripon Land Regulation Act of 1831, which provided land grants, attracted free settlers. By 1850 Australia had 500,000 inhabitants. The discovery of gold in Victoria in 1851 quadrupled that number in a few years.

## From Colony to Nation

On February 12, 1851, Edward Hargraves, an Australian-born prospector who had returned to Australia after unsuccessful digging in the California gold rush of 1849, discovered gold in a creek on the western slopes of the Blue Mountains. Hargraves gave the district the biblical name Ophir (Job 22:24), and the newspapers said the region was "one vast gold field." In July a miner found gold at Clunes, one hundred miles west of Melbourne, and in September gold was found in what proved to be the richest field of all, Ballarat, just seventy-five miles west of Melbourne. Gold fever convulsed Australia. Although the government charged prospectors a very high license fee, men and women from all parts of the globe flocked to Australia to share in the fabulous wealth.

Contemporaries agreed with explorer and politician W. C. Wentworth, who said that the gold rush opened in Australia a new era, "which must in a very few years precipitate us from a colony to a nation."[50] Although recent scholars have disputed Wentworth, there is much truth to his viewpoint. The gold rush led to an enormous improvement in transportation within Australia. People customarily traveled by horseback or on foot and used two-wheel ox-drawn carts to bring wool from inland ranches to coastal cities. Then two newly arrived Americans, Freeman Cobb and James Rutherford, built sturdy four-wheel coaches capable of carrying heavy cargo and of negotiating the bush tracks. Carrying passengers and mail up to 80 miles a day, a week's work for ox-drawn vehicles, Cobb and Co. coaches covered 28,000 miles per week by 1870. Railroad construction began in the 1870s, and by 1890, 9,000 miles of track were laid. Railroad construction, financed by British investors, stimulated agricultural growth.

The gold rush also provided the financial means for the promotion of education and culture. The 1850s witnessed the establishment of universities at Sydney and Melbourne and later at Adelaide and Hobart. Public libraries, museums, art galleries, and schools opened in the thirty years after 1851. In keeping with the overwhelmingly British ethnic origin of most immigrants to Australia, these institutions dispensed a distinctly British culture, though a remote and provincial version.

On the negative side, the large numbers of Asians in the goldfields—in Victoria in 1857, one adult male in seven was Chinese—sparked bitter racial prejudice. Scholars date the "white Australia policy" to the hostility, resentment, and fear that whites showed the Chinese.

Although Americans numbered only about five thousand in Victoria and Asians forty thousand, Americans with their California gold-rush experience, aggressive ways, and "democratic" frontier outlook, exercised an influence on Australian society far out of proportion to their numbers. "There was evidence to suggest that some Americans, bringing with them their pre–Civil War racist attitudes, had an appreciable influence on the growth of color prejudice in Australia."[51] On the Fourth of July in 1852, 1854, and 1857 (anniversaries of the American Declaration of Independence), anti-Chinese riots occurred in the goldfields of Victoria. After the gold-rush decade, public pressure for the exclusion of all colored peoples increased. Nevertheless, Asian peoples continued to arrive. Chinese and Japanese built the railroads and ran the market gardens near, and the shops in, the towns. Filipinos and Pacific Islanders did the hard work in the sugar-cane fields. Afghanis and their camels controlled the carrying trade in some areas.

"Colored peoples" (as all nonwhites were called in Australia) adapted more easily than the British to the warm climate and worked for lower wages. Thus they proved essential to the country's economic development in the nineteenth century. But fear that colored labor would lower living standards and undermine Australia's distinctly British culture triumphed. The Commonwealth Immigration Restriction Act of 1901 closed immigration to Asians and established the "white Australia policy." Australia achieved racial and cultural unity only at the price of Asian resentment at discrimination and retarded economic development in the northern colonies, which desperately needed labor. The laws of 1901 remained on the books until the 1970s.

The gold rush had a considerable political impact. In 1850 the British Parliament had passed the Australian Colonies Government Act, which allowed the four most populous colonies—New South Wales, Tasmania, Victoria, and South Australia—to establish colonial legislatures, determine the franchise, and frame their own constitutions. The gold rush, vastly increasing population, accelerated the movement for self-government. Acknowledging this demand, the colonial secretary in London wrote that the gold discoveries "imparted new and unforeseen features to (Australia's) political and social condition." Western Australia's decision to remain a penal colony delayed responsible government there, but by 1859 all other colonies were self-governing. The provincial parliament of South Australia was probably the most democratic in the world, since it was elected by universal manhood suffrage and by secret ballot. Other colonies soon adopted the secret ballot. In 1902 Australia became one of the first countries in the world to adopt woman suffrage.

The government of Australia combines features of the British and American systems. In the later nineteenth century, pressure for continental federation culminated in meetings of the premiers (governors) of the colonies. They drafted a constitution that the British Parliament approved in 1900. The Commonwealth of Australia came into existence on January 1, 1901. From the British model, Australia adopted the parliamentary form of government in which a cabinet is responsible to the House of Commons. From the American system, Australia took the concept of decentralized government, whereby the states and the federal government share power. The states in Australia, as in the United States, retain considerable power, especially in local or domestic affairs.

Deep loyalty to the mother country led Australia to send 329,000 men and vast economic aid to Britain in the First World War. The issue of conscription, however, bitterly divided the country, partly along religious lines. About one-fourth of Australia's population was (and is) Irish and Roman Catholic. Although the Catholic population, like the dominant Anglican one, split over conscription, the powerful, influential, and long-lived Catholic archbishop of Melbourne, Daniel Mannix (r. 1917–1963), publicly supported Sinn Fein—the Irish nationalist (and later terrorist) movement. Mannix also denounced the English and the European war.

Twice submitted to public referendum, conscription twice failed. When the Australian poet Frank Wilmot (1881–1942) wrote, "The fumes of ancient hells have invaded your spirit," he meant that English wrongs in Ireland had become part of Australian culture.

Australian troops fought valiantly in the Dardanelles campaign, where more than 10,000 died. During the long nightmare of trench warfare on the western front, Australian soldiers were brilliantly led by Sir John Monash, a Jewish Australian whose planning led to the Allied breakthrough and the ultimate defeat of Germany. Australia's staggering 213,850 casualties, however, exerted a traumatic effect on Australian life and society. With the young men died the illusion that remote Australia could escape the problems and sins of the Old World. But the experience of the Great War forged a sense of national identity among the states of Australia.

At the Paris Peace Conference in 1919, Australian delegates succeeded in excluding recognition of the principle of racial equality in the League of Nations Covenant. Australians did not want Asian immigrants. The treaties that followed the war allowed Australia a mandate over German New Guinea and the equatorial island of Nauru. Nauru had vast quantities of phosphates that Australian wheat fields needed as fertilizer. The former penal colony had become a colonial power.

## SUMMARY

Between 1788 and 1931, the United States, Canada, and Australia developed from weak, agricultural colonies of Great Britain into powerful industrial and commercial nations, and the countries of Latin America first secured independence from Spain and then began the process of nation building. Inspired by notions of social equality and manifest destiny, galvanized by the optimism of millions of immigrants who came seeking a better life, Americans subdued the continent, linked it with railroads, and built gigantic steel, oil, textile, food-processing, and automobile industries. The North's victory in the bloody Civil War, fought largely over the issue of black slavery, proved the permanence of the Union, but the unresolved ideal of equality remains the American dilemma. Industrialization and the assimilation of foreign peoples also preoccupied the nations of Latin America, but political instability and economies often dominated by the United States or Great Britain slowed growth.

Canada and Australia followed the path of the United States, though at a slower pace. Adopting the British model of cabinet government under John A. Macdonald and utilizing rich natural resources, the provinces of Canada formed a strong federation with close economic ties to the United States; each is the other's major trading partner. French separatism, centered in Quebec, remains the Canadian dilemma. Australia utilized political features of both the British and the American systems. Immigrant production of wool, wheat, and now wine has transformed Australia from a remote penal colony into the great democratic nation of the Pacific.

## KEY TERMS

Creoles
peninsulares
audiencias
neocolonialism
haciendas
peons
manifest destiny
Treaty of Guadalupe Hidalgo (1848)
Confederacy
chattel slavery
confederation
Canadian Pacific Railroad
Botany Bay
New South Wales
exclusionists
emancipists

## NOTES

1. Quoted in W. S. Robertson, *Rise of the Spanish American Republics* (New York: Free Press, 1965), p. 19.
2. See B. Keen and M. Wasserman, *A Short History of Latin America* (Boston: Houghton Mifflin, 1980), pp. 109–115.
3. J. Lynch, *The Spanish-American Revolutions, 1808–1826* (New York: Norton, 1973), pp. 13–14; Keen and Wasserman, *A Short History of Latin America,* pp. 145–146.
4. Quoted in Lynch, *The Spanish-American Revolutions, 1808–1826,* p. 18.
5. M. Burkholder and D. S. Chandler, *From Impotence to Authority: The Spanish Crown and the American Audiencias, 1687–1808* (Columbia: University of Missouri Press, 1977), p. 145.
6. Ibid., p. 141.
7. Keen and Wasserman, *A Short History of Latin America,* p. 146.
8. Quoted in J. L. Phelan, *The People and the King: The Comunero Revolution in Colombia, 1781* (Madison: University of Wisconsin Press, 1978), p. 62; see also L. B. Rout, *The African Experience in Spanish America* (New York: Cambridge University Press, 1977), p. 165.
9. See S. J. Stern, *Resistance, Rebellion, and Consciousness in the Andean Peasant World* (Madison: University of Wisconsin Press, 1987).
10. Quoted in Phelan, *The People and the King,* pp. 206–207.
11. F. Tannenbaum, *Ten Keys to Latin America* (New York: Random House, 1962), pp. 69–71.
12. H. Hoetink, *Slavery and Race Relations in the Americas* (New York: Harper & Row, 1973), p. 14.
13. Keen and Wasserman, *A Short History of Latin America,* pp. 201–204.
14. See C. H. Harris, *A Mexican Family Empire: The Latifundio of the Sanchez Navarros, 1765–1867* (Austin: University of Texas Press, 1975).
15. N. Sanchez-Albornoz, *The Population of Latin America: A History,* trans. W. A. R. Richardson (Berkeley: University of California Press, 1974), pp. 151–152.
16. J. R. Scobie, "Buenos Aires as a Commercial-Bureaucratic City, 1880–1910: Characteristics of a City's Orientation," *American Historical Review* 77 (October 1972): 1046.
17. Ibid., p. 1064.
18. See M. Morner, ed., *Race and Class in Latin America.* Part II: *Immigration, Stratification, and Race Relations* (New York: Columbia University Press, 1971), pp. 73–122; Sanchez-Albornoz, *The Population of Latin America,* pp. 160–167.
19. Quoted in M. B. Norton et al., *A People and a Nation: A History of the United States,* 4th ed. (Boston: Houghton Mifflin, 1994), p. 351.
20. S. E. Morison, *The Oxford History of the American People* (New York: Oxford University Press, 1965), pp. 380–381.
21. Ibid., pp. 446–452.
22. J. Oakes, *The Ruling Race: A History of American Slaveholders* (New York: Knopf, 1982), pp. x–xi.
23. See P. J. Parish, *Slavery: History and Historians* (New York: Harper & Row, 1989), pp. 45–46.
24. See W. Johnson, *Soul by Soul: Life Inside the Antebellum Slave Market* (Cambridge, Mass.: Harvard University Press, 1999), pp. 78–134 and passim.
25. Quoted in Oakes, *The Ruling Race,* p. 120.
26. C. V. Woodward, ed., *Mary Chesnut's Civil War* (New Haven, Conn.: Yale University Press, 1981), p. 29.
27. Ibid., pp. xlix–l.
28. H. G. Gutman, *The Black Family in Slavery and Freedom, 1750–1925* (New York: Random House, 1977).

29. See J. Winch, *A Gentleman of Color: The Life of James Forten* (New York: Oxford University Press, 2002), passim.
30. R. P. Basler, ed., *The Collected Works of Abraham Lincoln*, vol. 2 (New Brunswick, N.J.: Rutgers University Press, 1953), pp. 255–256, 271.
31. R. Hofstadter, *The American Political Tradition* (New York: Random House, 1948), p. 114.
32. Quoted ibid., pp. 128–129.
33. Quoted in Morison, *The Oxford History of the American People*, p. 654.
34. T. H. Williams, *The History of American Wars: From Colonial Times to World War I* (New York: Knopf, 1981), p. 202.
35. Report of the University Committee on Diversity and Liberal Education to President Harold Shapiro of Princeton University, cited in *Princeton Today* 7, no. 2 (Summer 1994): 7.
36. See M. Hodes, *White Women, Black Men: Illicit Sex in the 19th-Century South* (New Haven, Conn.: Yale University Press, 1997), pp. 3–9 and passim.
37. F. J. Davis, *Who Is Black? One Nation's Definition* (University Park: Pennsylvania State University Press, 1991), passim, but esp. Chaps. 2 and 3, pp. 31–80.
38. Hodes, *White Women, Black Men*, p. 9.
39. See Lawrence Wright, "One Drop of Blood," *The New Yorker*, July 25, 1994, pp. 46–55.
40. S. L. Myres, *Westering Women and the Frontier Experience, 1800–1915* (Albuquerque: University of New Mexico Press, 1982), Chaps. 6 and 7.
41. G. Barth, *City People: The Rise of Modern City Culture in the Nineteenth Century* (New York: Oxford University Press, 1980), p. 15.
42. Quoted in Lynch, *The Spanish-American Revolutions, 1808–1826*, p. 18.
43. Hoetink, *Slavery and Race Relations in the Americas*, p. 18.
44. Quoted in J. Higham, *Strangers in the Land: Patterns of American Nativism, 1860–1925* (New York: Atheneum, 1971), pp. 89–90.
45. Quoted in R. Cook, *Canada: A Modern Study* (Toronto: Clarke, Irwin, 1971), p. 89.
46. Quoted ibid., p. 127.
47. R. Ward, *Australia* (Englewood Cliffs, N.J.: Prentice-Hall, 1965), p. 21.
48. Quoted in R. Hughes, *The Fatal Shore* (New York: Knopf, 1987), p. 66.
49. J. Kociumbas, *The Oxford History of Australia*. Vol. 2: *Colonial Australia, 1770–1860* (New York: Oxford University Press, 1992), p. 1.
50. Quoted in Ward, *Australia*, p. 60.
51. Ibid., p. 59.

## SUGGESTED READING

For the colonial period, both J. Lockhart and S. B. Schwartz, *Early Latin America: A History of Colonial Spanish America and Brazil* (1983), and M. A. Burkholder and L. Johnson, *Colonial Latin America*, 3d ed. (1998), are important and sound studies of the colonial period. J. E. Rodriguez O., *The Independence of Spanish America* (1998), represents an up-to-date treatment of that subject; it is also clearly written and focuses on nation building. The older work of R. Graham, *The Independence of Latin America* (1975), is still valuable. For the Indians in the seventeenth and eighteenth centuries, S. J. Stern, *Peru's Indian Peoples and the Challenge of the Spanish Conquest*, 2d ed. (1993), and J. Kicza, ed., *The Indian in Latin America* (1993), are recommended. Brazilian economic developments and religious and cultural changes are well treated in A. J. R. Russell-Wood, *The Portuguese Empire, 1415–1808: A World on the Move* (1998), and in the essays in his older study, *From Colony to Nation: Essays on the Independence of Brazil* (1975). The most useful biographies of Simón Bolívar are those of G. Masur, *Simón Bolívar*, 2d ed. (1969), and J. J. Johnson and D. M. Ladd, *Simón Bolívar and Spanish American Independence, 1783–1830* (1968). J. Rogoziński, *A Brief History of the Caribbean: From the Arawak to the Carib* (1992), contains helpful information on the island societies. For the North American reaction to Latin American independence, A. P. Whitaker, *The United States and the Independence of Latin America, 1800–1830* (1941), remains the standard.

For Mexico, see J. Tutino, *From Insurrection to Revolution in Mexico: Social Bases of Agrarian Violence, 1750–1940* (1986), an important study treating a broad span of time; C. C. Griffin, "Economic and Social Aspects of the Era of Spanish-American Independence," *Hispanic American Historical Review* 29 (1949); and J. Lafaye, *Quetzalcoatl and Guadalupe: The Formation of Mexican National Consciousness, 1531–1813*, rev. ed. (1987), a very exciting ethnohistorical study.

For issues of race and ethnicity, W. Wright, *Café con Leche: Race, Class, and National Image in Venezuela* (1993), is an excellent starting point. J. C. Miller, *Slavery and Slaving in World History: A Bibliography, 1900–1901* (1993), is a useful reference tool with material comparing slavery in North and South America. Some important comparative studies are I. Berlin and P. Morgan, eds., *Cultivation and Culture: Labor and the Shaping of Slave Life in the Americas* (1991); H. Klein, *Slavery in the Americas: A Comparative Study of Virginia and Cuba* (1967); and C. Degler, *Neither Black Nor White: Slavery and Race Relations in Brazil and the United States* (1971). For South American labor and conditions of slavery, see S. Schwartz, *Sugar Plantations in the Formation of Brazilian Society* (1985), and the same author's *Slaves, Peasants, and Rebels: Reconsidering Brazilian Society* (1992); C. E. Martin, *Rural Society in Colonial Morelos* (1985); and P. J. Carroll, *Blacks in Colonial Veracruz* (1991). The elegant study by Parish, cited in the Notes, surveys a large body of scholarship.

For social and economic developments and the triumph of neocolonialism, the following titles are useful: J. Bazant, *A Concise History of Mexico from Hidalgo to Cardenas, 1805–1940* (1978); R. Knowlton, *Church Property and the Mexican Reform, 1856–1910* (1976); and D. Rock, *Politics in Argentina, 1890–1930: The Rise and Fall of Radicalism* (1975).

The major themes in U.S. history have been extensively treated by many able scholars, and students will have no difficulty finding a wealth of material. J. M. Burns, *The Vineyard of Liberty* (1982), traces the origins and development of American society, politics, and culture from the 1780s to 1863, emphasizing the growth of liberty. The standard study of manifest destiny remains F. Merk, *Manifest Destiny and Mission in American History: A Reinterpretation* (1963), but see also K. Jack Bauer, *The Mexican-American War, 1846–1848* (1976). In *The Only Land They Knew: The Tragic Story of the American Indians in the Old South* (1981), J. Leitch Wright recounts the interaction of Native Americans, Africans, and Europeans in the American South.

The literature on the Indians of North America is vast. As an introduction, the curious student should find the following titles helpful: F. E. Hoxie, ed., *Encyclopedia of North American Indians: Native American History, Culture, and Life from Paleo-Indians to the Present* (1996), an excellent reference tool; G. Catlin, *North American Indians,* ed. P. Matthiessen (1989), the work of a famous nineteenth-century artist who lived among Indian peoples for many years; and J. Ehle, *Trail of Tears: The Rise and Fall of the Cherokee Nation* (1988).

The best recent studies of colonial slavery in North America are I. Berlin, *Many Thousands Gone: The First Two Centuries of Slavery in North America* (1998), and P. D. Morgan, *Slave Counterpoint: Black Culture in the Eighteenth-Century Chesapeake and Low Country* (1998).

On black women and the family, see J. Jones, *Labor of Love, Labor of Sorrow: Black Women, Work, and the Family from Slavery to the Present* (1985), and C. Neverdon-Morton, *Afro-American Women of the South and the Advancement of the Race, 1895–1925* (1989). See also W. S. McFeely, *Frederick Douglass* (1991), and I. Berlin et al., eds., *Freedom: A Documentary History of Emancipation* (1990). For the powerful influence of the black church, see E. Lincoln and C. H. Mamiya, *The Black Church in the African American Experience* (1990), and J. T. McGreevy, *Parish Boundaries: The Catholic Encounter with Race in the Twentieth Century Urban North* (1996).

M. Hodes, "The Mercurial Nature and Abiding Power of Race: A Transnational Family Story," in *The American Historical Review,* vol. 108, no. 1, Feb. 2003, pp. 84–118, discusses the complexities and difficulties of racial classifications in the United States and in the West Indies, while W. Sollors, *Neither Black Nor White Yet Both* (1997), explores interracial relationships in literature. There is also excellent material on race-related issues in the titles in the Notes by Hodes, Johnson, and Winch, and in K. Fischer, *Sex, Race, and Resistance in Colonial North Carolina* (2002); A. Bontemps, *The Punished Self: Surviving Slavery in the Colonial South* (2001); and M. Ellis, *Race, War, and Surveillance: African Americans and the United States Government During World War I* (2001).

The literature on the Civil War and Reconstruction is mammoth. The best comprehensive treatment of the pre–Civil War years is K. M. Stampp, *America in 1857: A Nation on the Brink* (1990). The following titles should also prove useful to students: J. M. McPherson, *Battle Cry of Freedom: The Era of the Civil War* (1988), and E. Foner, *Reconstruction: America's Unfinished Revolution, 1863–1877* (1988).

On the lives of Jews and other immigrants in American cities, see I. Howe's brilliant achievement, *World of Our Fathers* (1976), which is splendidly illustrated and contains a good bibliography, and S. S. Weinberg, *The World of Our Mothers: The Lives of Jewish Immigrant Women* (1988).

For developments in Canada, see, in addition to the highly readable sketch by Cook, cited in the Notes, K. McNaught, *The Pelican History of Canada* (1976), a sound survey that emphasizes those cultural traits that are distinctly Canadian. For the age of confederation, J. M. S. Careless, *The Union of the Canadas, 1841–1857* (1967), is a solid treatment by a distinguished scholar. D. G. Creighton, *John A. Macdonald,* 2 vols. (1952, 1955), is probably the best study of the great prime minister. The critical years of expansion and development are discussed in the full accounts of R. C. Brown and G. R. Cook, *Canada, 1896–1921* (1974), and R. Graham, *Canada, 1922–1939* (1979).

Perhaps the best starting point for the study of Australian history is the title by Hughes, cited in the Notes. M. Clark, *A Short History of Australia* (1987), is a highly readable general sketch. C. M. H. Clark, *A History of Australia,* 6 vols. (1962–1987), is the standard political history. R. Terrill, *The Australians* (1987), offers an attractive appreciation of the Australian people and the society they made, from the first settlers to the present.

# LISTENING TO THE PAST

## Simón Bolívar's Speculation on Latin America

*Descended from a wealthy Venezuelan family, Simón Bolívar (1783–1830) was educated privately by tutors, who instilled in him the liberal and republican ideals of the French Enlightenment. He traveled to Europe and in 1805, while in Rome, dedicated himself to liberating his country from Spanish rule. Returning to Venezuela, Bolívar worked as a diplomat, a statesman, and, above all, the general who defeated the Spaniards and liberated northern regions of the continent. When he entered Caracas, the citizens called him "the Liberator," and the name stuck.*

*Almost two generations earlier, on July 4, 1776, the Second Continental Congress (an anachronism and misnomer, since the men in Philadelphia hardly represented the entire "continent") had adopted Virginia planter Thomas Jefferson's Declaration of Independence, justifying the thirteen colonies' independence and appealing for European support with a long diatribe against King George III's supposedly tyrannical acts. It was a document of propaganda. In 1815 Simón Bolívar addressed a letter to the governor of Jamaica, responding to the latter's request for Bolívar's views on prospects for Latin American liberation and the establishment of one unified nation. Bolívar's "Letter from Jamaica" expresses Latin American ideals and came to serve purposes comparable to those served by the Declaration of Independence. Excerpts from this letter follow.*

Kingston, Jamaica, September 6, 1815.

My dear Sir:

. . . With what a feeling of gratitude I read that passage in your letter in which you say to me: "I hope that the success which then followed Spanish arms may now turn in favor of their adversaries, the badly oppressed people of South America." I take this hope as a prediction. . . . The hatred that the Peninsula* has inspired in us is greater than the ocean between us. . . .

Europe could do Spain a service by dissuading her from her rash obstinacy, thereby at least sparing her the costs she is incurring and the blood she is expending. And if she will fix her attention on her own precincts she can build her prosperity and power upon more solid foundations than doubtful conquests, precarious commerce, and forceful exactions from remote and powerful peoples. Europe herself, as a matter of common sense policy, should have prepared and executed the project of American independence, not alone because the world balance of power so necessitated, but also because this is the legitimate and certain means through which Europe can acquire overseas commercial establishments. . . .

It is even more difficult to foresee the future fate of the New World, to set down its political principles, or to prophesy what manner of government it will adopt. Every conjecture relative to America's future is, I feel, pure speculation. . . . We are a young people. We inhabit a world apart, separated by broad seas. We are young in the ways of almost all the arts and sciences, although, in a certain manner, we are old in the ways of civilized society. . . . We are, moreover, neither Indian nor European, but a species midway between the legitimate proprietors of this country and the Spanish usurpers. In short, though Americans by birth we derive our rights from Europe, and we have to assert these rights against the rights of the natives, and at the same time we must defend ourselves against the invaders. This places us in a most extraordinary and involved situation. Notwithstanding that it is a type of divination to predict the result of the political course which America is pursuing, I shall

*The Iberian Peninsula—Spain and Portugal.

The Liberator: Simón Bolívar. *(ARCHIVO CENIDIAP-INBA, Mexico City. Collection of Fernando Leal Audirac)*

venture some conjectures which, of course, are colored by my enthusiasm and dictated by rational desires rather than by reasoned calculations. . . .

. . . We have been harassed by a conduct which has not only deprived us of our rights but has kept us in a sort of permanent infancy with regard to public affairs. If we could at least have managed our domestic affairs and our internal administration, we could have acquainted ourselves with the processes and mechanics of public affairs. We should also have enjoyed a personal consideration, thereby commanding a certain unconscious respect from the people, which is so necessary to preserve amidst revolutions. That is why I say we have even been deprived of an active tyranny, since we have not been permitted to exercise its functions.

Americans today, and perhaps to a greater extent than ever before, who live within the Spanish system occupy a position in society no better than that of serfs destined for labor, or at best they have no more status than that of mere consumers. Yet even this status is surrounded with galling restrictions, such as being forbidden to grow European crops, or to store products which are royal monopolies, or to establish factories of a type the Peninsula itself does not possess. To this add the exclusive trading privileges, even in articles of prime necessity, and the barriers between American provinces, designed to prevent all exchange of trade, traffic, and understanding. In short, do you wish to know what our future held?—simply the cultivation of the fields of indigo, grain, coffee, sugar cane, cacao, and cotton; cattle raising on the broad plains; hunting wild game in the jungles; digging in the earth to mine its gold—but even these limitations could never satisfy the greed of Spain. . . .

More than anyone, I desire to see America fashioned into the greatest nation in the world, greatest not so much by virtue of her area and wealth as by her freedom and glory. Although I seek perfection for the government of my country, I cannot persuade myself that the New World can, at the moment, be organized as a great republic. Since it is impossible, I dare not desire it; yet much less do I desire to have all America a monarchy because this plan is not only impracticable but also impossible. Wrongs now existing could not be righted, and our emancipation would be fruitless. The American states need the care of paternal governments to heal the sores and wounds of despotism and war. . . .

From the foregoing, we can draw these conclusions: The American provinces are fighting for their freedom, and they will ultimately succeed. Some provinces as a matter of course will form federal and some central republics; the larger areas will inevitably establish monarchies, some of which will fare so badly that they will disintegrate in either present or future revolutions. To consolidate a great monarchy will be no easy task, but it will be utterly impossible to consolidate a great republic.

It is a grandiose idea to think of consolidating the New World into a single nation, united by pacts into a single bond. It is reasoned that, as these parts have a common origin, language, customs, and religion, they ought to have a single government to permit the newly formed states to unite in a confederation. But this is not possible. . . . Would to God that some day we may have the good fortune to convene . . . an august assembly of representatives of republics, kingdoms, and empires to deliberate upon the high interests of peace and war with the nations of the other three-quarters of the globe. This type of organization may come to pass in some happier period of our regeneration. But any other plan . . . would be meaningless.

When success is not assured, when the state is weak, and when results are distantly seen, all men hesitate; opinion is divided, passions rage, and the enemy fans these passions in order to win an easy victory because of them. As soon as we are strong and under the guidance of a liberal nation which will lend us her protection, we will achieve accord in cultivating the virtues and talents that lead to glory. Then will we march majestically toward that great prosperity for which South America is destined. . . .

## QUESTIONS FOR ANALYSIS

1. Compare the arguments in the Declaration of Independence (see page 703) and the "Letter from Jamaica."
2. For Bolívar, what are the prospects for Latin American unity as one nation?

*Source:* A. J. Andrea and J. H. Overfield, eds., *The Human Record,* vol. 2, rev. ed. (Boston: Houghton Mifflin, 1994).

John Singer Sargent's World War I painting *Gassed* (detail). *(By courtesy of the Trustees of the Imperial War Museum)*

CHAPTER

# 29 THE GREAT BREAK: WAR AND REVOLUTION

## CHAPTER OUTLINE

- The First World War
- The Home Front
- The Russian Revolution
- The Peace Settlement

In the summer of 1914 the nations of Europe went willingly to war. They believed they had no other choice. Moreover, both peoples and governments confidently expected a short war leading to a decisive victory. Such a war, they believed, would "clear the air," and then European society would be able to go on as before.

These expectations were largely mistaken. The First World War was long, indecisive, and tremendously destructive. To the shell-shocked generation of survivors, it was known simply as the Great War: the war of unprecedented scope and intensity. From today's perspective it is clear that the First World War marked a great break in the course of world historical development. The war accelerated the growth of nationalism in Asia (see Chapter 30), and it consolidated the position of the United States as a global power. Yet the war's greatest impact was on Europe, the focus of this chapter. A noted British political scientist has gone so far as to say that even in victorious and relatively fortunate Great Britain, the First World War was *the* great turning point in government and society, "as in everything else in modern British history. . . . There's a much greater difference between the Britain of 1914 and, say, 1920, than between the Britain of 1920 and today."[1] This strong statement contains a great amount of truth, for all Europe as well as for Britain.

- What caused the Great War?
- How did the war lead to revolution and the fall of empires?
- How and why did war and revolution have such enormous and destructive consequences?
- How did the years of trauma and bloodshed form elements of today's world, many of which people now accept and even cherish?

These are the questions this chapter will try to answer.

## THE FIRST WORLD WAR

The First World War was so long and destructive because it involved all the Great Powers and because it quickly degenerated into a senseless military stalemate. Like evenly matched boxers in a championship bout, the two sides

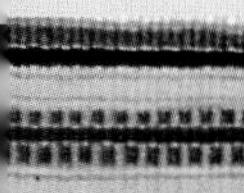

tried to wear each other down. But there was no referee to call a draw, only the blind hammering of a life-or-death struggle.

## The Bismarckian System of Alliances

The defeat of France in 1871 (see page 810) and the founding of the German Empire opened a new era in international relations. In just ten years, from 1862 to 1871, Bismarck had made Prussia-Germany—traditionally the weakest of the Great Powers—the most powerful nation in Europe. Yet, as Bismarck never tired of repeating after 1871, Germany was a "satisfied" power. Within Europe Germany had no territorial ambitions and wanted only peace.

But how was peace to be preserved? Bismarck's first concern was to keep an embittered France diplomatically isolated and without military allies. His second concern was the threat to peace posed by Austria-Hungary and Russia. Those two enormous multinational empires had many conflicting interests, particularly in the Balkans, where the Ottoman Empire was losing its grip despite many efforts to recapture its former power. There was a real threat that Germany might be dragged into a great war between the two rival empires. Bismarck's solution was a system of alliances to restrain both Russia and Austria-Hungary, to prevent conflict between them, and to isolate a hostile France.

A first step was the creation during 1873 of the **Three Emperors' League,** which linked the conservative monarchs of Austria-Hungary, Germany, and Russia in an alliance against radical movements. In 1877 and 1878, when Russia's victories over the Ottoman Empire threatened the balance of Austrian and Russian interests in the Balkans and the balance of British and Russian interests in the Middle East, Bismarck played the role of sincere peacemaker at the Congress of Berlin in 1878 (see page 939). But his balancing efforts at the congress infuriated Russian nationalists, and their anger led Bismarck to conclude a defensive military alliance with Austria against Russia in 1879. This alliance lasted until 1918 and the end of World War I. Motivated by tensions with France, Italy joined Germany and Austria in 1882, thereby forming what became known as the Triple Alliance.

Bismarck continued to work for peace in eastern Europe, seeking to neutralize tensions between Austria-Hungary and Russia. In 1881 he cajoled them both into a secret alliance with Germany. This Alliance of the Three Emperors lasted until 1887.

Bismarck also maintained good relations with Britain and Italy, while encouraging France in Africa but keeping France isolated in Europe. In 1887 Russia declined to renew the Alliance of the Three Emperors because of new tensions in the Balkans. Bismarck craftily substituted the Russian-German Reinsurance Treaty, by which both states promised neutrality if the other was attacked.

Bismarck's accomplishments in foreign policy after 1871 were great. For almost a generation he maintained German leadership in international affairs, and he worked successfully for peace by managing conflicts and by restraining Austria-Hungary and Russia with defensive alliances.

## The Rival Blocs

In 1890 the young, impetuous German emperor William II forced Bismarck to resign, in part because of the chancellor's friendly policy toward Russia since the 1870s. William then adamantly refused to renew the Russian-German Reinsurance Treaty, in spite of Russian willingness to do so. This fateful departure in foreign affairs prompted long-isolated republican France to court absolutist Russia, offering loans, arms, and friendship. After a preliminary agreement was reached in 1891, France and Russia became military allies in 1894, pledging to remain so as long as the Triple Alliance of Austria, Germany, and Italy existed. As a result, continental Europe was dangerously divided into two rival blocs.

Great Britain's foreign policy became increasingly crucial. Long content with "splendid isolation" and no permanent alliances, Britain after 1891 was the only uncommitted Great Power. Could Britain afford to remain isolated, or would it feel compelled to take sides? Alliance with France or Russia certainly seemed highly unlikely. With a vast and rapidly expanding empire, Britain was often in serious conflict with these countries around the world.

Britain also squabbled with Germany, but many Germans and some Britons felt that a "natural alliance" united the advanced, racially related Germanic and Anglo-Saxon peoples. However, the generally good relations that had prevailed between Prussia and Great Britain ever since the mid-eighteenth century, and certainly under Bismarck, gave way to a bitter Anglo-German rivalry.

There were several reasons for this tragic development. Commercial rivalry in world markets between Germany and Great Britain increased sharply in the 1890s, and William II's tactless public statements and Germany's pursuit of world power unsettled the British. Above all, Germany's decision in 1900 to expand greatly its battle fleet posed a challenge to Britain's long-standing naval supremacy. This decision coincided with the hard-fought South African War (1899–1902) between the British and

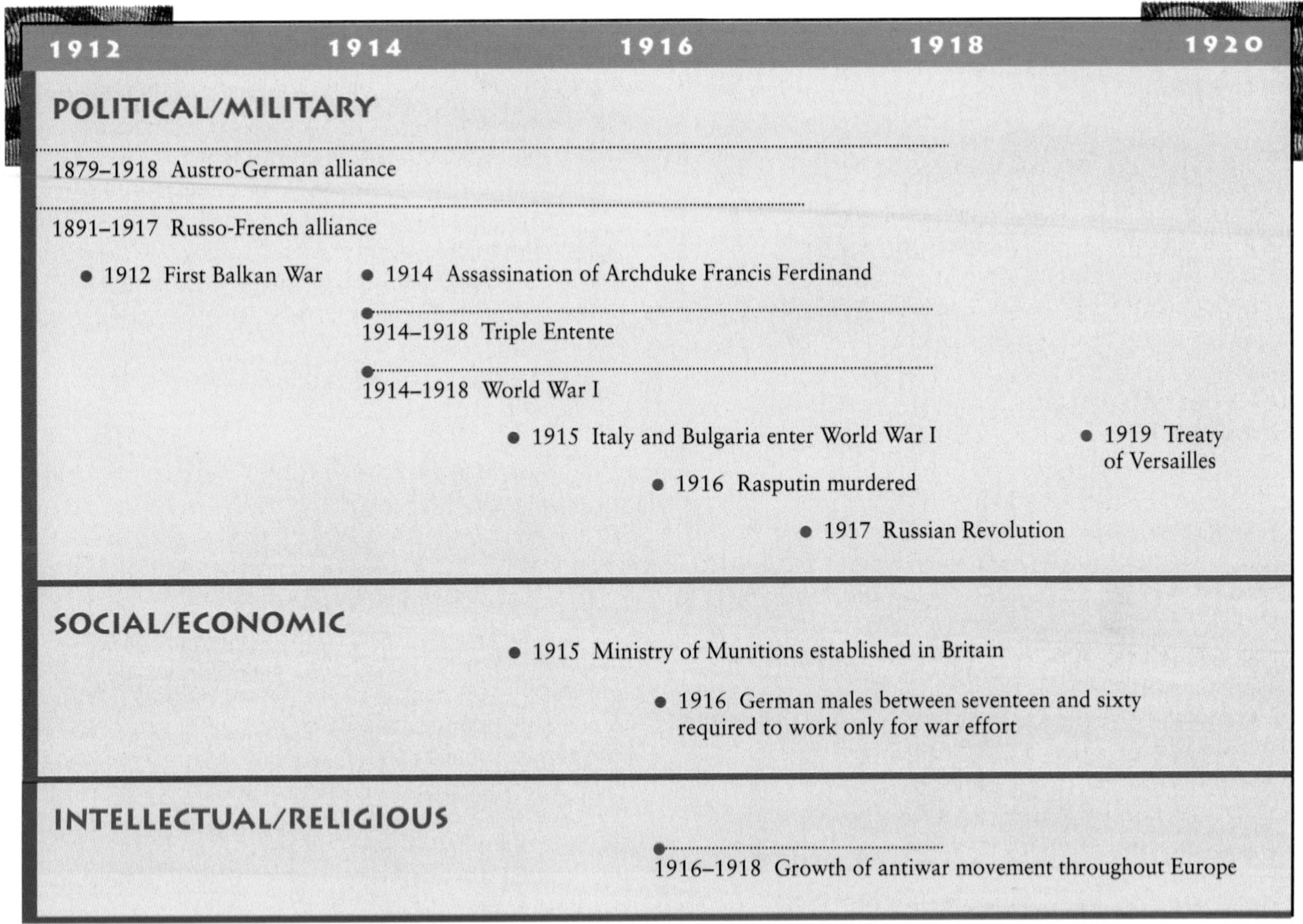


Afrikaner republics of South Africa, which convinced British leaders that Britain was overextended around the world. The South African War also brought into the open widespread anti-British feeling, and there was even talk of Germany, Austria, France, and Russia forming a grand alliance against the bloated but insatiable British Empire. Thus British leaders prudently set about shoring up their exposed position with alliances and agreements.

1912
1914
1916
1918
1920
POLITICAL/MILITARY
1879–1918 Austro-German alliance
1891–1917 Russo-French alliance
1912 First Balkan War
1914 Assassination of Archduke Francis Ferdinand
1914–1918 Triple Entente
1914–1918 World War I
1915 Italy and Bulgaria enter World War I
1919 Treaty of Versailles
1916 Rasputin murdered
1917 Russian Revolution
SOCIAL/ECONOMIC
1915 Ministry of Munitions established in Britain
1916 German males between seventeen and sixty required to work only for war effort
INTELLECTUAL/RELIGIOUS
1916–1918 Growth of antiwar movement throughout Europe

Britain improved its often-strained relations with the United States and in 1902 concluded a formal alliance with Japan, which lasted until 1915. Britain then responded favorably to the advances of France's skillful foreign minister Théophile Delcassé, who wanted better relations with Britain and was willing to accept British rule in Egypt in return for British support of French plans to dominate Morocco. The resulting Anglo-French Entente of 1904 settled all outstanding colonial disputes between Britain and France.

Frustrated by Britain's turn toward France in 1904, Germany's leaders decided to test the strength of the entente. Rather than accept the typical territorial payoff of imperial competition—a slice of French jungle somewhere in Africa or a port in Morocco—in return for French primacy in Morocco, the Germans foolishly rattled their swords by insisting in 1905 on an international conference on the whole Moroccan question. Germany's crude bullying forced France and Britain closer together, and Germany left the resulting Algeciras Conference of 1906 empty-handed and isolated (except for Austria-Hungary).

The result of the Moroccan crisis and the Algeciras Conference was something of a diplomatic revolution. Britain, France, Russia, and even the United States began to see Germany as a potential threat, a would-be intimidator that might seek to dominate all Europe. At the same time, German leaders began to see sinister plots to "encircle" Germany and block its development as a world power. In 1907 Russia, battered by its disastrous war with Japan and the revolution of 1905, agreed to settle its quarrels with Great Britain in Persia and Central

**German Warships Under Full Steam** As these impressive ships engaged in battle exercises in 1907 suggest, Germany did succeed in building a large modern navy. But Britain was equally determined to maintain its naval superiority, and the spiraling arms race helped poison relations between the two countries. *(Bibliothèque des Arts Décoratifs/Jean-Loup Charmet/The Bridgeman Art Library International Ltd)*

Asia with a special Anglo-Russian Agreement. As a result of that agreement, Germany's blustering paranoia increased, as did Britain's thinly disguised hostility.

Germany's decision to add an enormously expensive fleet of big-gun battleships to its already expanding navy also heightened tensions after 1907. German nationalists saw a large navy as the legitimate mark of a great world power and as a source of pride and patriotic unity. But British leaders such as David Lloyd George saw it as a detestable military challenge that forced them to spend the "People's Budget" (see page 812) on battleships rather than social welfare. Ongoing economic rivalry, portrayed by journalists as a form of economic warfare, also contributed to distrust and hostility between the two nations, while nationalists in both countries simultaneously admired and feared the power and accomplishments of their nearly equal rival. In 1909 the mass-circulation *London Daily Mail* hysterically informed its readers in a series of reports that "Germany is deliberately preparing to destroy the British Empire."[2] By then Britain was psychologically, if not officially, in the Franco-Russian camp. The leading nations of Europe were divided into two hostile blocs, both ill-prepared to deal with upheaval on Europe's southeastern frontier.

## The Outbreak of War

In the early years of the twentieth century, war in the Balkans was as inevitable as anything can be in human history. The reason was simple: nationalism was destroying the Ottoman Empire in Europe and threatening to break up the Austro-Hungarian Empire. The only ques-

**MAP 29.1 The Balkans After the Congress of Berlin, 1878** The Ottoman Empire suffered large territorial losses but remained a power in the Balkans.

**MAP 29.2 The Balkans in 1914** Ethnic boundaries did not follow political boundaries, and Serbian national aspirations threatened Austria-Hungary.

tions were what kinds of wars would occur and where would they lead.

Greece had long before led the struggle for national liberation, winning its independence in 1830. In 1875 widespread nationalist rebellion in the Ottoman Empire had resulted in Turkish repression, Russian intervention, and Great Power tensions. Bismarck had helped resolve this crisis at the 1878 Congress of Berlin, which worked out the partial division of Turkish possessions in Europe. Austria-Hungary obtained the right to "occupy and administer" Bosnia and Herzegovina. Serbia and Romania won independence, and a part of Bulgaria won local autonomy. But the Ottoman Empire retained important Balkan holdings (see Map 29.1).

By 1903 Balkan nationalism was asserting itself once again. Serbia led the way, becoming openly hostile toward both Austria-Hungary and the Ottoman Empire. The Serbs, a Slavic people, looked to Slavic Russia for support of their national aspirations. To block Serbian expansion and to take advantage of Russia's weakness after the revolution of 1905, Austria in 1908 formally annexed Bosnia and Herzegovina, with their large Serbian, Croatian, and Muslim populations. The kingdom of Serbia erupted in rage but could do nothing without Russian support.

Then in 1912, in the First Balkan War, Serbia joined with Greece and Bulgaria to attack the Ottoman Empire and then quarreled with Bulgaria over the spoils of victory—a dispute that led in 1913 to the Second Balkan War. Austria intervened in 1913 and forced Serbia to give up Albania. After centuries, nationalism had finally destroyed the Ottoman Empire in Europe (see Map 29.2).

This sudden but long-awaited event elated the Balkan nationalists and dismayed the leaders of multinational Austria-Hungary. The former hoped and the latter feared that Austria might be next to be broken apart.

Within this tense context Archduke Francis Ferdinand, heir to the Austrian and Hungarian thrones, and his wife, Sophie, were assassinated by ultranationalist Serbian revolutionaries on June 28, 1914, during a state visit to the Bosnian capital of Sarajevo. After some hesitation the leaders of Austria-Hungary concluded that Serbia was implicated and had to be severely punished once and for all. On July 23 Austria-Hungary finally presented Serbia with an unconditional ultimatum. The Serbian government had just forty-eight hours in which to agree to demands that would amount to Austrian control of the Serbian state. When Serbia replied moderately but evasively, Austria began to mobilize and then declared war on Serbia on July 28. Thus a desperate multinational Austria-Hungary deliberately chose war in a last-ditch attempt to stem the rising tide of hostile nationalism within its borders and save the existing state. The "Third Balkan War" had begun.

Of prime importance in Austria-Hungary's fateful decision was Germany's unconditional support. Emperor William II and his chancellor, Theobald von Bethmann-Hollweg, gave Austria-Hungary a "blank check" and urged aggressive measures in early July, even though they realized that war between Austria and Russia was the most probable result. A resurgent Russia could not stand by, as in the Bosnian crisis, and simply watch the Serbs be crushed. Yet Bethmann-Hollweg apparently hoped that while Russia (and therefore France) would go to war, Great Britain would remain neutral, unwilling to fight for "Russian aggression" in the distant Balkans.

**Nationalist Opposition in the Balkans** This band of well-armed and determined guerrillas from northern Albania was typical of groups fighting against Ottoman rule in the Balkans. Balkan nationalists succeeded in driving the Ottoman Turks out of most of Europe, but their victory increased tensions with Austria-Hungary and among the Great Powers. *(Roger-Viollet/Getty Images)*

In fact, the diplomatic situation was already out of control. Military plans and timetables began to dictate policy. On July 28, as Austrian armies bombarded Belgrade, Tsar Nicholas II ordered a partial mobilization against Austria-Hungary. Almost immediately he found that this was impossible. All the complicated mobilization plans of the Russian general staff had assumed a war with both Austria and Germany: Russia could not mobilize against one without mobilizing against the other. Therefore, on July 29 Russia ordered full mobilization and in effect declared general war.

The same tragic subordination of political considerations to military strategy shaped events in Germany. The German general staff had also thought only in terms of a two-front war. The staff's plan for war called for knocking out France first with a lightning attack through neutral Belgium before turning on Russia. So on August 2, 1914, General Helmuth von Moltke, "acting under a dictate of self-preservation," demanded that Belgium permit German armies to pass through its territory. Belgium, whose neutrality had been solemnly guaranteed in 1839 by all the great states including Prussia, refused. Germany attacked. Thus Germany's terrible, politically disastrous response to a war in the Balkans was an all-out invasion of France by way of the plains of neutral Belgium on August 3. In the face of this act of aggression, Great Britain joined France and declared war on Germany the following day. The First World War had begun.

In reflecting on the origins of the First World War, it seems clear that Austria-Hungary deliberately started the conflict. A war for the right to survive was Austria-Hungary's desperate response to the revolutionary drive of Serbian nationalists to unify their people in a single state. Moreover, in spite of Russian intervention in the quarrel, it is also clear that Germany was most responsible for turning a third war in the Balkans into the Great War by its attack on Belgium and France. Why Germany was so aggressive in 1914 is less certain.

Diplomatic historians stress that German leaders lost control of the international system after Bismarck's resignation in 1890. They felt increasingly that Germany's status as a world power was declining, while the status of Britain, France, Russia, and the United States was growing. Indeed, the powers of what officially became in August 1914 the **Triple Entente**—Great Britain, France, and Russia—were checking Germany's vague but real aspirations as well as working to strangle Austria-Hungary, Germany's only real ally. Germany's aggression in 1914 reflected the failure of all European leaders, not just those in Germany, to incorporate Bismarck's mighty empire permanently and peacefully into the international system.

**"Never Forget!"** This 1915 French poster with its passionate headline dramatizes Germany's brutal invasion of Belgium in 1914. Neutral Belgium is personified as a traumatized mother, assaulted and ravished by savage outlaws. The "rape of Belgium" featured prominently—and effectively—in anti-German propaganda. *(Mary Evans Picture Library)*

A more controversial interpretation argues that domestic conflicts and social tensions lay at the root of German aggression. While Germany industrialized and urbanized rapidly after 1870 and had a popularly elected parliament, political power remained concentrated in the hands of the monarchy, army, and nobility. Determined to hold on to power and frightened by the socialist movement and a wave of strikes in 1914, the German ruling class was willing to take a gamble on a diplomatic victory or even war as the means of rallying the masses to its side and preserving the existing system. Historians have also discerned similar, if less clear-cut, behavior in

**MAP 29.3 The First World War in Europe** The trench war on the western front was concentrated in Belgium and northern France, while the war in the east encompassed an enormous territory.

Great Britain, where leaders faced civil war in northern Ireland, and in Russia, where the revolution of 1905 had brought tsardom to its knees.

This debate over social tensions and domestic political factors correctly suggests that the triumph of nationalism was a crucial underlying precondition of the Great War. Nationalism was at the heart of the Balkan wars, and it drove the spiraling international arms race. Broad popular commitment to "my country right or wrong" weakened groups that thought in terms of international communities and consequences. Thus the big international bankers, who were frightened by the prospect of war in July 1914, and the extreme-left socialists, who believed that the enemy was at home and not abroad, were equally out of step with national feeling. In each country the great majority of the population enthusiastically embraced the outbreak of war in August 1914. The people rallied to defend their nation, and patriotic nationalism brought unity in the short run.

In all of this, Europe's governing classes underestimated the risk of war to themselves in 1914. They had forgotten that great wars and great social revolutions very often go hand in hand. Metternich's alliance of conservative forces in support of international peace and the social status quo had become a distant memory.

## Stalemate and Slaughter

When the Germans invaded Belgium in August 1914, they and everyone else believed that the war would be short, for urban society rested on the food and raw materials of the world economy: "The boys will be home by Christmas." The Belgian army heroically defended its homeland, however, and fell back in good order to join a rapidly landed British army corps near the Franco-Belgian border. Instead of quickly capturing Paris in a vast encircling movement, by the end of August dead-tired German soldiers were advancing along an enormous front in the scorching summer heat. On September 6 the French attacked a gap in the German line at the Battle of the Marne. For three days France threw everything into the attack. At one point the French government desperately requisitioned all the taxis of Paris to rush reserves to the troops at the front. Finally, the Germans fell back. Paris and France had been miraculously saved (see Map 29.3).

Soon, with the armies stalled, both sides began to dig trenches to protect themselves from machine-gun fire. By November 1914 an unbroken line of trenches extended from the Belgian ports through northern France past the fortress of Verdun and on to the Swiss frontier. In the face of this unexpected stalemate, slaughter on the western front began in earnest. The defenders on both sides dug in behind rows of trenches, mines, and barbed wire. For days and even weeks ceaseless shelling by heavy artillery supposedly "softened up" the enemy in a given area (and also signaled the coming attack). Then young draftees and their junior officers went "over the top" of the trenches in frontal attacks on the enemy's line.

The cost in lives was staggering; the gains in territory were minuscule. The massive French and British offensives during 1915 never gained more than three miles of blood-soaked earth from the enemy. In the Battle of the Somme in the summer of 1916, the British and French gained an insignificant 125 square miles at the cost of 600,000 dead or wounded, and the Germans lost 500,000 men. In that same year the unsuccessful German campaign against Verdun cost 700,000 lives on both sides. British poet Siegfried Sassoon (1886–1967) wrote of the Somme offensive, "I am staring at a sunlit picture of Hell."

The year 1917 was equally terrible. The hero of Erich Remarque's great novel *All Quiet on the Western Front* (1929) describes a typical attack:

*We see men living with their skulls blown open; we see soldiers run with their two feet cut off. . . . Still the little piece of convulsed earth in which we lie is held. We have yielded no more than a few hundred yards of it as a prize to the enemy. But on every yard there lies a dead man.*

Such was war on the western front.

**Trench warfare** shattered an entire generation of young men. Millions who could have provided political creativity and leadership after the war were forever missing. Moreover, those who lived through the holocaust were maimed, shell-shocked, embittered, and profoundly disillusioned. The young soldiers went to war believing in the world of their leaders and elders—the pre-1914 world of order, progress, and patriotism. Then, in Remarque's words, the "first bombardment showed us our mistake, and under it the world as they had taught it to us broke in pieces."

## The Widening War

On the eastern front slaughter did not degenerate into suicidal trench warfare. With the outbreak of the war, the "Russian steamroller" immediately moved into eastern Germany. Very badly damaged by the Germans under General Paul von Hindenburg and General Erich Ludendorff at the Battle of Tannenberg and the Battle of the

**The Tragic Absurdity of Trench Warfare** Soldiers charge across a scarred battlefield and overrun an enemy trench. The dead defender on the right will fire no more. But this is only another futile charge that will yield much blood and little land. A whole generation is being decimated by the slaughter. *(By courtesy of the Trustees of the Imperial War Museum)*

Masurian Lakes in August and September 1914, Russia never threatened Germany again (see Map 29.3). On the Austrian front enormous armies seesawed back and forth, suffering enormous losses. Austro-Hungarian armies were repulsed twice by little Serbia in bitter fighting. But with the help of German forces, they reversed the Russian advances of 1914 and forced the Russians to retreat deep into their own territory in the eastern campaign of 1915. A staggering 2.5 million Russians were killed, wounded, or taken prisoner that year.

These changing tides of victory and hopes of territorial gains brought neutral countries into the war. Italy, a member of the Triple Alliance since 1882, had declared its neutrality in 1914 on the grounds that Austria had launched a war of aggression. Then, in May 1915, Italy joined the Triple Entente of Great Britain, France, and Russia in return for promises of Austrian territory. In October 1914 the Ottoman Empire joined with Austria and Germany, by then known as the Central Powers. The following September Bulgaria decided to follow the

**Otto Dix: War (detail)** Returning to Germany after the war, Dix was haunted by the horrors he had seen. This vivid expressionist masterpiece, part of a triptych painted in 1929–1932, probes the tormented memory of endless days in muddy trenches and dugouts, living with rats and lice and the constant danger of exploding shells, snipers, and all-out attack. Many who escaped death or dismemberment were mentally wounded forever by their experiences. *(Staatliche Kunstsammlungen Dresden. © 2002 Artists Rights Society [ARS], New York/VG Bild-Kunst, Bonn)*

Ottoman Empire's lead in order to settle old scores with Serbia (see Map 29.3).

The entry of the Ottoman Turks carried the war into the Middle East, a momentous development. Heavy fighting between the Ottomans and Russia saw bloody battle lines seesawing back and forth. In 1915 British forces tried to take the Dardanelles and Constantinople from Turkey but were badly defeated. The British were more successful at inciting the Arabs to revolt against their Turkish overlords. An enigmatic British colonel, soon known to millions as Lawrence of Arabia, helped lead the Arab revolt in early 1917. In 1918 British armies totally smashed the old Ottoman state, drawing primarily on imperial forces from Egypt, India, Australia, and New Zealand. Thus war brought revolutionary change to the Middle East (see pages 971–978).

War also spread to some parts of East Asia and Africa. Instead of revolting as the Germans hoped, the colonial

**Indian Soldiers** from the so-called warrior castes had long been a critical factor in imperial Britain's global power. These Indian troops, preparing for the Battle of the Somme in 1916, ironically appear to be out for a pleasant bicycling excursion. Dispatched to France in October 1914, most Indian soldiers were moved to western Asia in 1915 to fight against the Ottoman Empire. *(By courtesy of the Trustees of the Imperial War Museum)*

subjects of the British and French supported their foreign masters, providing critical supplies and fighting in armies in Europe and in the Ottoman Empire. They also helped local British and French commanders seize Germany's colonies around the globe. The Japanese, allied in Asia with the British since 1902, similarly used the war to grab German outposts in the Pacific Ocean and on the Chinese mainland, infuriating Chinese patriots and heightening long-standing tensions between China and Japan. More than a million Africans served in the various armies of the warring powers, with more than double that number serving as porters to carry equipment. The French, facing a shortage of young men, made especially heavy use of colonial troops. The spectacle of Europeans fighting each other to protect their nations' freedom and their individual rights had a profound impact on the minds of these soldiers. African American soldiers serving in France also were affected by their experiences in the war.

Another crucial development in the expanding conflict came in April 1917 when the United States declared war on Germany. American intervention grew out of the war at sea, sympathy for the Triple Entente, and the increasing desperation of total war. At the beginning of the war Britain and France had established a total naval blockade to strangle the Central Powers. No neutral ship was permitted to sail to Germany with any cargo. The blockade annoyed Americans, but effective propaganda about German atrocities in occupied Belgium as well as lush profits from selling war supplies to Britain and France blunted American indignation.

Moreover, in early 1915 Germany launched a counter-blockade using the murderously effective submarine, a new weapon that sank ships without the traditional niceties of fair warning under international law. In May 1915 a German submarine sank the British passenger liner ***Lusitania,*** which was also carrying arms and munitions. More than a thousand lives, including 139 Americans, were lost. President Woodrow Wilson protested vigorously. Germany was forced to relax its submarine warfare for almost two years; the alternative was almost certain war with the United States.

Early in 1917 the German military command—confident that improved submarines could starve Britain into submission before the United States could come to its rescue—resumed unrestricted submarine warfare. Like the invasion of Belgium, this was a reckless gamble. "German submarine warfare against commerce," President Wilson told a sympathetic Congress and people, "is a warfare against mankind." Thus the last uncommitted great nation, as fresh and enthusiastic as Europe had been in 1914, entered the world war in April 1917, almost three years after it began. Eventually the United States was to tip the balance in favor of the Triple Entente and its allies.

## THE HOME FRONT

Before looking at the last year of the Great War, let us turn our attention to the people on the home front. They were tremendously involved in the titanic struggle. War's impact on them was no less massive than on the men crouched in the trenches.

### Mobilizing for Total War

In August 1914 most people had greeted the outbreak of hostilities enthusiastically. In every country the masses believed that their nation was in the right and was defending itself from aggression. With the exception of a few extreme left-wingers, even socialists supported the war. Everywhere the support of the masses and working class contributed to national unity and an energetic war effort.

By mid-October generals and politicians had begun to realize that more than patriotism would be needed to win the war, whose end was not in sight. Each country experienced a relentless, desperate demand for men and weapons. In each country economic life and organization had to change, and change fast, to keep the war machine from sputtering to a stop. And change they did.

In each country a government of national unity began to plan and control economic and social life in order to wage **total war.** Government planning boards established priorities and decided what was to be produced and consumed. Rationing, price and wage controls, and even restrictions on workers' freedom of movement were imposed by government. Thus, though there were national variations, the great nations all moved toward planned economies commanded by the established political leadership.

The economy of total war blurred the old distinction between soldiers on the battlefield and civilians at home. The war was a war of whole peoples and entire populations. Based on tremendously productive industrial economies not confined to a single nation, total war yielded an effective—and therefore destructive—war effort on all sides. (See the feature "Listening to the Past: The Experience of War" on pages 964–965.)

However awful the war was, the ability of governments to manage and control highly complicated economies strengthened the cause of socialism. With the First World War socialism became for the first time a realistic economic blueprint rather than a utopian program. Germany illustrates the general trend. It also went furthest in developing a planned economy to wage total war.

As soon as war began, the talented Jewish industrialist Walter Rathenau convinced the German government to set up the **War Raw Materials Board** to ration and distribute raw materials. Under Rathenau's direction every useful material from foreign oil to barnyard manure was inventoried and rationed. Moreover, the board launched successful attempts to produce substitutes, such as synthetic rubber and synthetic nitrates, needed to make explosives and essential to the blockaded German war machine. An aggressive recycling campaign, including everything from fruit peels to women's hair, augmented these efforts. Food was also rationed in accordance with physical need. Men and women doing hard manual work were given extra rations. During the last two years of the war only children and expectant mothers received milk rations. At the same time, Germany failed to tax the war profits of private firms heavily enough. This failure contributed to massive deficit financing, inflation, the growth of a black market, and the eventual re-emergence of class conflict.

Following the terrible Battles of Verdun and the Somme in 1916, Chancellor Bethmann-Hollweg was driven from office in 1917 by military leaders Hindenburg and Ludendorff, who became the real rulers of Germany. They decreed the ultimate mobilization for total war: all agriculture, industry, and labor must be "used exclusively for the conduct of War."[3] In December 1916 military leaders rammed through the Reichstag the Auxiliary Service Law, which required all males between seventeen and sixty to work only at jobs considered critical to the war effort.

With the passage of the **Auxiliary Service Law,** many more women followed those already working in war factories, mines, and steel mills. Potatoes gave way to turnips, and people averaged little more than a thousand calories a day. Thus in Germany total war led to the establishment of history's first "totalitarian" society, and war production increased while some people starved to death.

Great Britain mobilized for total war less rapidly and less completely than Germany, for it could import materials from its empire and from the United States. By 1915, however, a serious shortage of shells had led to the establishment of the Ministry of Munitions under David Lloyd George. The ministry organized private industry to produce for the war, controlled profits, allocated labor, fixed wage rates, and settled labor disputes. By December 1916 the British economy was largely planned and regulated directly by the state. Great Britain had followed successfully in Germany's footsteps.

## The Social Impact

The social impact of total war was no less profound than the economic impact, though again there were important national variations. The insatiable needs of the military created a tremendous demand for workers. Jobs were available for everyone. This situation—seldom, if ever, seen before 1914, when unemployment and poverty had been facts of urban life—brought about momentous changes.

One such change was greater power and prestige for labor unions. Having proved their loyalty in August 1914, labor unions cooperated with war governments on work

**Waging Total War** A British war plant strains to meet the insatiable demand for trench-smashing heavy artillery shells. Quite typically, many of these defense workers are women. *(By courtesy of the Trustees of the Imperial War Museum)*

rules, wages, and production schedules in return for real participation in important decisions. This entry of labor leaders into policymaking councils paralleled the entry of socialist leaders into the war governments.

The role of women changed dramatically. In every country large numbers of women left home and domestic service to work in industry, transportation, and offices. Moreover, women became highly visible—not only as munitions workers but as bank tellers, mail carriers, even police officers. Women also served as nurses and doctors at the front. In general, the war greatly expanded the range of women's activities and changed attitudes toward women. As a direct result of women's many-sided war effort, Britain, Germany, and Austria granted women the right to vote immediately after the war. Women also showed a growing spirit of independence during the war, as they started to bob their hair, shorten their skirts, and smoke in public.

War promoted greater social equality, blurring class distinctions and lessening the gap between rich and poor. This blurring was most apparent in Great Britain, where wartime hardship was never extreme. In fact, the bottom third of the population generally lived better than they ever had, for the poorest gained most from the severe shortage of labor. English writer Robert Roberts recalled how his parents' tiny grocery store in the slums of Manchester thrived during the war as never before—when people who had scrimped to buy bread and soup bones were able to afford fancy cakes and thick steaks. In continental European countries greater equality was reflected in full employment, rationing according to physical needs, and a sharing of hardships. There, too, society became more uniform and more egalitarian, in spite of some war profiteering.

Finally, death itself had no respect for traditional social distinctions. It savagely decimated both the young aristocratic officers who led the charge and the mass of drafted peasants and unskilled workers who followed. Death, however, often spared the aristocrats of labor—the skilled workers and foremen. Their lives were too valuable to squander at the front, for they were needed to train the newly recruited women and older unskilled men laboring valiantly in war plants at home.

## Growing Political Tensions

During the first two years of war most soldiers and civilians supported their governments. Even in Austria-Hungary—the most vulnerable of the belligerents, with its competing nationalities—loyalty to the state and monarchy remained astonishingly strong through 1916. Belief in a just cause, patriotic nationalism, the planned economy, and a sharing of burdens united peoples behind their various national leaders.

Each government employed rigorous censorship to control public opinion, and each used both crude and subtle propaganda to maintain popular support. German propaganda hysterically pictured black soldiers from France's African empire raping German women. The French and British ceaselessly recounted and exaggerated German atrocities in Belgium and elsewhere. Patriotic posters and slogans, slanted news, and biased editorials inflamed national hatreds and helped sustain superhuman efforts.

By the spring of 1916, however, people were beginning to crack under the strain of total war. In April 1916 Irish nationalists in Dublin tried to take advantage of this situation and rose up against British rule in their great Easter Rebellion. A week of bitter fighting passed before the rebels were crushed and their leaders executed. Strikes and protest marches over inadequate food began to flare up on every home front. Soldiers' morale began to decline. Italian troops mutinied. Numerous French units refused to fight for a time after General Robert Nivelle's disastrous offensive of May 1917. A rising tide of war-weariness and defeatism also swept France's civilian population before Georges Clemenceau emerged as a ruthless and effective wartime leader in November 1917. Clemenceau (1841–1929) established a virtual dictatorship, pouncing on strikers and jailing without trial journalists and politicians who dared to suggest a compromise peace with Germany.

The strains were worse for the Central Powers. In October 1916 the chief minister of Austria was assassinated by a young socialist crying, "Down with Absolutism! We want peace!"[4] The following month, when feeble old Emperor Francis Joseph died, a symbol of unity disappeared. In spite of absolute censorship, political dissatisfaction and conflicts among nationalities grew. Both Czech and Yugoslav leaders demanded autonomous democratic states for their peoples. In April 1917 Austria's new chief minister summed up the situation in the gloomiest possible terms. The country and army were exhausted. Another winter of war would bring revolution and disintegration.

The strain of total war and of the Auxiliary Service Law was also evident in Germany. By 1917 the national political unity of the first two years of war was collapsing as the social conflict of prewar Germany re-emerged. A growing minority of socialists in the Reichstag began to vote against war credits. In July 1917 a coalition of socialists and Catholics passed a resolution in the Reichstag calling for a compromise "peace without annexations or reparations." Such a peace was unthinkable for conservatives and military leaders. So also was the surge in revolutionary agitation and strikes by war-weary workers that occurred in early 1917. When the bread ration was further reduced in April, more than 200,000 workers struck and demonstrated for a week in Berlin, returning to work only under the threat of prison and military discipline. Thus militaristic Germany, like its ally Austria-Hungary (and its enemy France), was beginning to crack in 1917. But it was Russia that collapsed first and saved the Central Powers—for a time.

## THE RUSSIAN REVOLUTION

The Russian Revolution of 1917, directly related to the growing tensions of World War I, had a significance far beyond the wartime agonies of a single European nation. The Russian Revolution opened a new era. For some it was Marx's socialist vision come true; for others it was the triumph of dictatorship. To all it presented a radically new prototype of state and society.

### The Fall of Imperial Russia

Like its allies and its enemies, Russia embraced war with patriotic enthusiasm in 1914. At the Winter Palace, while throngs of people knelt and sang "God Save the Tsar," Tsar Nicholas II (r. 1894–1917) repeated the oath Alexander I had sworn in 1812 and vowed never to make peace as long as the enemy stood on Russian soil. Russia's lower house, the Duma, voted war credits. Conservatives anticipated expansion in the Balkans. Liberals and most socialists believed alliance with Britain and France would bring democratic reforms. For a moment Russia was united. But soon the strains of war began to take their toll.

Unprecedented artillery barrages used up Russia's supplies of shells and ammunition, and better-equipped German armies inflicted terrible losses. In 1915 substantial numbers of Russian soldiers were sent to the front without rifles; they were told to find their arms among the dead. There were 2 million Russian casualties in 1915 alone. Nevertheless, Russia's battered peasant army continued to fight courageously, and Russia moved toward full mobilization on the home front. The Duma and organs of local government took the lead, setting up special committees to coordinate defense, industry, transportation, and agriculture. These efforts improved the military situation. Yet there were many failures, and Russia mobilized less effectively for total war than the other warring nations.

The great problem was leadership. Under the constitution resulting from the revolution of 1905 (see pages 814–815), the tsar had retained complete control over the bureaucracy and the army. Legislation proposed by the Duma, which was weighted in favor of the wealthy and conservative classes, was subject to the tsar's veto. Moreover, Nicholas II fervently wished to maintain the sacred inheritance of supreme royal power, which, with the Orthodox church, was for him the key to Russia's greatness. A kindly, slightly stupid man, of whom a friend said he "would have been an ideal country gentleman, devoting his life to wife and children, his farms and his sport," Nicholas failed to form a close partnership with his citizens in order to fight the war more effectively. He relied instead on the old bureaucratic apparatus, distrusting the moderate Duma, rejecting popular involvement, and resisting calls to share power.

As a result, the Duma, the educated middle classes, and the masses became increasingly critical of the tsar's leadership. Demands for more democratic and responsive government exploded in the Duma in the summer of 1915. In September parties ranging from conservative to moderate socialist formed the Progressive bloc, which called for a completely new government responsible to the Duma instead of to the tsar. In answer, Nicholas temporarily adjourned the Duma and announced that he was traveling to the front in order to lead and rally Russia's armies.

His departure was a fatal turning point. With the tsar in the field with the troops, control of the government was taken over by the hysterical empress, Tsarina Alexandra, and a debauched adventurer, the monk Rasputin. A minor German princess and granddaughter of England's Queen Victoria, Nicholas's wife was a devoted mother with a sick child, a strong-willed woman with a hatred of parliaments. Having constantly urged her husband to rule absolutely, Alexandra herself tried to do so in his absence. She seated and unseated the top ministers. Her most trusted adviser was "our Friend Grigori," an uneducated Siberian preacher who was appropriately nicknamed "Rasputin"—the "Degenerate."

Rasputin began his career with a sect noted for mixing sexual orgies with religious ecstasies, and his influence rested on mysterious healing powers. Alexis, Alexandra's fifth child and heir to the throne, suffered from a rare disease, hemophilia. The tiniest cut meant uncontrollable bleeding, terrible pain, and possible death. Medical science could do nothing. Only Rasputin could miraculously stop the bleeding, perhaps through hypnosis. The empress's faith in Rasputin was limitless. "Believe more in our Friend," she wrote her husband in 1916. "He lives for you and Russia." In this atmosphere of unreality the government slid steadily toward revolution.

In a desperate attempt to right the situation and end unfounded rumors that Rasputin was the empress's lover, three members of the high aristocracy murdered Rasputin in December 1916. The empress went into semipermanent shock, her mind haunted by the dead man's prophecy: "If I die or you desert me, in six months you will lose your son and your throne."[5] Food shortages in the cities worsened; morale declined. On March 8 women calling for bread in Petrograd (formerly St. Petersburg) started riots, which spontaneously spread throughout the city. From the front the tsar ordered troops to restore order, but discipline broke down, and the soldiers joined the revolutionary crowd. The Duma responded by declaring a provisional government on March 12, 1917. Three days later Nicholas abdicated.

**"The Russian Ruling House"** This wartime cartoon captures the ominous, spellbinding power of Rasputin over Tsar Nicholas II and his wife, Alexandra. Rasputin's manipulations disgusted Russian public opinion and contributed to the monarchy's collapse. *(Stock Montage)*

## The Provisional Government

The March revolution was joyfully accepted throughout the country. The patriotic upper and middle classes rejoiced at the prospect of a more determined and effective war effort. Workers happily anticipated better wages and more food. All classes and political parties called for liberty and democracy. They were not disappointed. After generations of arbitrary authoritarianism, the provisional government quickly established equality before the law; freedom of religion, speech, and assembly; the right of unions to organize and strike; and the rest of the classic liberal program.

But both the liberal and the moderate socialist leaders of the provisional government rejected social revolution. The reorganized government formed in May 1917, which included the fiery agrarian socialist Alexander Kerensky, who became prime minister in July, refused to confiscate large landholdings and give them to peasants, fearing that such drastic action in the countryside would only complete the disintegration of Russia's peasant army. For the patriotic Kerensky, as for other moderate socialists, the continuation of war was still the all-important national duty. There would be plenty of time for land reform later, and thus all the government's efforts were directed toward a last offensive in July. Human suffering and war-weariness grew, sapping the limited strength of the provisional government.

From its first day the provisional government had to share power with a formidable rival—the **Petrograd Soviet** (or council) of Workers' and Soldiers' Deputies. Modeled on the revolutionary soviets of 1905, the Petrograd Soviet was a huge, fluctuating mass meeting of two thousand to three thousand workers, soldiers, and socialist intellectuals. This counter- or half-government issued its own radical orders, further weakening the provisional government. Most famous of these was **Army Order No. 1,** which stripped officers of their authority and placed power in the hands of elected committees of common soldiers.

Army Order No. 1 led to a total collapse of army discipline. Many an officer was hanged for his sins. Meanwhile, following the foolhardy summer offensive, masses of peasant soldiers began "voting with their feet," to use Lenin's graphic phrase. They began returning to their

**Mass Demonstrations in Petrograd, June 1917** The protests showed a surge of working-class support for the Bolsheviks. In this photo a few banners of the Mensheviks and other moderate socialists are drowned in a sea of Bolshevik slogans. *(Sovfoto)*

villages to help their families get a share of the land, which peasants were simply seizing as they settled old scores in a great agrarian upheaval. All across the country liberty was turning into anarchy in the summer of 1917. It was an unparalleled opportunity for the most radical and most talented of Russia's many socialist leaders, Vladimir Ilyich Lenin (1870–1924).

## Lenin and the Bolshevik Revolution

From his youth Lenin's whole life had been dedicated to the cause of revolution. Born into the middle class, Lenin became an implacable enemy of imperial Russia when his older brother was executed for plotting to kill the tsar in 1887. As a law student Lenin began searching for a revolutionary faith. He found it in Marxian socialism. Exiled to Siberia for three years because of socialist agitation, Lenin studied Marxian doctrines with religious intensity. After his release this young priest of socialism joined fellow believers in western Europe. There he lived for seventeen years and developed his own revolutionary interpretations of the body of Marxian thought.

Three interrelated ideas were central for Lenin. First, turning to the early fire-breathing Marx of 1848 and *The Communist Manifesto* for inspiration, Lenin stressed that capitalism could be destroyed only by violent revolution. He tirelessly denounced all revisionist theories of a peaceful evolution to socialism as a betrayal of Marx's revolutionary message. Lenin's second, more original idea was that a socialist revolution was possible even in a country like Russia, where capitalism was not fully developed. There the industrial working class was small, but the peasants were poor and thus potential revolutionaries.

Lenin believed that at a given moment revolution was determined more by human leadership than by vast historical laws. Thus was born his third basic idea: the necessity of a highly disciplined workers' party, strictly controlled by a dedicated elite of intellectuals and full-time revolutionaries like Lenin himself. Unlike ordinary workers and trade-union officials, this elite would never be seduced by short-term gains. It would not stop until revolution brought it to power.

Lenin's theories and methods did not go unchallenged by other Russian Marxists. At meetings of the Russian Social Democratic Labor party in London in 1903, matters came to a head. Lenin demanded a small, disciplined, elitist party; his opponents wanted a more democratic party with mass membership. The Russian party of Marxian socialism promptly split into two rival factions. Lenin's camp was called **Bolsheviks,** or "majority group"; his opponents were *Mensheviks,* or "minority group." Lenin's majority did not last, but Lenin did not care. He kept the fine-sounding name Bolshevik and developed the party he wanted: tough, disciplined, revolutionary.

Lenin, from neutral Switzerland, saw the war as a product of imperialistic rivalries and as a marvelous opportunity for class war and socialist upheaval. After the March revolution the German government provided the impatient Lenin, his wife, and about twenty trusted colleagues with safe passage across Germany and back into Russia in April 1917. The Germans hoped that Lenin would undermine Russia's sagging war effort. They were not disappointed.

Arriving triumphantly at Petrograd's Finland Station on April 3, Lenin attacked at once. To the great astonishment of the local Bolsheviks, he rejected all cooperation with the "bourgeois" provisional government of the liberals and moderate socialists. His slogans were radical in the extreme: "All power to the soviets"; "All land to the peasants"; "Stop the war now." Never a slave to Marxian determinism, the brilliant but not unduly intellectual Lenin was a superb tactician. The moment was now.

Yet Lenin almost overplayed his hand. An attempt by the Bolsheviks to seize power in July collapsed, and Lenin fled and went into hiding. He was charged with being a German agent, and indeed he and the Bolsheviks were getting money from Germany.[6] But no matter. In September commander in chief General Lavr Kornilov, a popular war hero "with the heart of a lion and the brains of a sheep," led a feeble attack against the provisional government. In the face of this rightist "counter-revolutionary" threat, the Bolsheviks were rearmed and redeemed. Kornilov's forces disintegrated, but Prime Minister Kerensky lost all credit with the army, the only force that might have saved him and democratic government in Russia.

Throughout the summer the Bolsheviks markedly increased their popular support, and in October they gained a fragile majority in the Petrograd Soviet. It was now Lenin's supporter Leon Trotsky (1879–1940), a spellbinding revolutionary orator and independent radical Marxist, who brilliantly executed the Bolshevik seizure of power.

Painting a vivid but untruthful picture of German and counter-revolutionary plots, Trotsky first convinced the Petrograd Soviet to form a special military-revolutionary committee in October and make him its leader. Military power in the capital passed into Bolshevik hands. Trotsky then insisted that the Bolsheviks take power in the name not of the Bolsheviks but of the more popular and democratic soviets, which were meeting in Petrograd from all over Russia in early November. On the night of November 6, militants from Trotsky's committee joined with trusty Bolshevik soldiers to seize government buildings and pounce on members of the provisional government.

**Lenin Rallies Worker and Soldier Delegates** At a midnight meeting of the Petrograd Soviet, the Bolsheviks rise up and seize power on November 6, 1917. This painting from the 1940s idealizes Lenin, but his great talents as a revolutionary leader are undeniable. In this re-creation Stalin, who actually played only a small role in the uprising, is standing behind Lenin, already his trusty right-hand man. *(Sovfoto)*

## THE RUSSIAN REVOLUTION

| | |
|---|---|
| 1914 | Russia enthusiastically enters the First World War. |
| 1915 | Russia suffers 2 million casualties.<br>Progressive bloc calls for a new government responsible to the Duma rather than to the tsar.<br>Tsar Nicholas adjourns the Duma and departs for the front; Alexandra and Rasputin exert a strong influence on the government. |
| December 1916 | Rasputin is murdered. |
| March 8, 1917 | Bread riots take place in Petrograd (St. Petersburg). |
| March 12, 1917 | Duma declares a provisional government. |
| March 15, 1917 | Tsar Nicholas abdicates without protest. |
| April 3, 1917 | Lenin returns from exile and denounces the provisional government. |
| May 1917 | Reorganized provisional government, including Kerensky, continues the war.<br>Petrograd Soviet issues Army Order No. 1, granting military power to committees of common soldiers. |
| Summer 1917 | Agrarian upheavals: peasants seize estates; peasant soldiers desert the army to participate. |
| October 1917 | Bolsheviks gain a majority in the Petrograd Soviet. |
| November 6, 1917 | Bolsheviks seize power; Lenin heads the new "provisional workers' and peasants' government." |
| November 1917 | Lenin accepts peasant seizure of land and worker control of factories; all banks are nationalized. |
| January 1918 | Lenin permanently disbands the Constituent Assembly. |
| February 1918 | Lenin convinces the Bolshevik Central Committee to accept a humiliating peace with Germany in order to safeguard the revolution. |
| March 1918 | Treaty of Brest-Litovsk: Russia loses one-third of its population.<br>Trotsky as war commissar begins to rebuild the Russian army. |
| Summer 1918 | White armies oppose the Bolshevik Revolution. |
| 1918–1920 | Great civil war takes place. |
| 1919 | White armies are on the offensive but divided politically; they receive little benefit from Allied intervention. |
| 1920 | Lenin and the Red Army are victorious. |

Then they went on to the congress of soviets. There a Bolshevik majority—roughly 390 of 650 turbulent delegates—declared that all power had passed to the soviets and named Lenin head of the new government.

The Bolsheviks came to power for three key reasons. First, by late 1917 democracy had given way to anarchy: power was there for those who would take it. Second, in Lenin and Trotsky the Bolsheviks had an utterly determined and truly superior leadership. Third, in 1917 the Bolsheviks succeeded in appealing to many soldiers and urban workers, people who were exhausted by war and eager for socialism. With time many workers would become bitterly disappointed, but for the moment they had good reason to believe that they had won what they wanted.

## Dictatorship and Civil War

History is full of short-lived coups and unsuccessful revolutions. The truly monumental accomplishment of Lenin, Trotsky, and the rest of the Bolsheviks was not taking power but keeping it and conquering the chaos they had helped create. How was this done?

Lenin had the genius to profit from developments over which he and the Bolsheviks had no control. Since summer a peasant revolution had been sweeping across Russia as the tillers of the soil invaded and divided among themselves the estates of the landlords and the church. Peasant seizure of the land was not very Marxian, but it was unstoppable in 1917. Thus Lenin's first law, which supposedly gave land to the peasants, actually merely approved what peasants were already doing. Urban workers' great demand in November was direct control of individual factories by local workers' committees. This, too, Lenin rectified with a decree in November 1917.

Lenin also acknowledged that Russia had lost the war with Germany and that the only realistic goal was peace at any price. That price was very high. Germany demanded in December 1917 that the Soviet government give up all its western territories. These areas were inhabited by Poles, Finns, Lithuanians, and other non-Russians—all those people who had been conquered by the tsars over three centuries and put into the "prisonhouse of nationalities," as Lenin had earlier called the Russian empire.

At first Lenin's fellow Bolsheviks would not accept such great territorial losses. But when German armies resumed their unopposed march into Russia in February 1918, Lenin had his way in a very close vote in the Central Committee of the party. A third of old Russia's population was sliced away by the German meat ax in the Treaty of Brest-Litovsk in March 1918. With peace Lenin had escaped the certain disaster of continued war and could pursue his goal of absolute political power for the Bolsheviks—now renamed Communists—within Russia.

In November 1917 the Bolsheviks had cleverly proclaimed their regime only a "provisional workers' and peasants' government," promising that a freely elected **Constituent Assembly** would draw up a new constitution. But after the Bolsheviks won less than one-fourth of the elected delegates, the Constituent Assembly met for only one day, on January 18, 1918. It was then permanently disbanded by Bolshevik soldiers acting under Lenin's orders.

With the destruction of the democratically elected Constituent Assembly, people who had risen up for self-rule in November saw that once again they were getting dictatorship from the capital. For the next three years "Long live the [democratic] soviets; down with the Bolsheviks" was a popular slogan. The officers of the old army took the lead in organizing the so-called White opposition to the Bolsheviks in southern Russia, Ukraine, Siberia, and west of Petrograd. The Whites came from many social groups and were united only by their hatred of the Bolsheviks—the Reds. By the end of 1918 White armies were on the attack. In October 1919 it appeared they might triumph, as they closed in on Lenin's government from three sides. Yet they did not. By the spring of 1920 the White armies had been almost completely defeated, and by the following year the civil war was over. Lenin had won.

Lenin and the Bolsheviks won for several reasons. Strategically, they controlled the center, while the Whites were always on the fringes and disunited. Moreover, the poorly defined political program of the Whites was vaguely conservative, and it did not unite all the foes of the Bolsheviks under a progressive, democratic banner. Most important, the Communists quickly developed a better army, an army for which the divided Whites were no match.

Once again Trotsky's leadership was decisive. Named war commissar, in March 1918 Trotsky re-established the draft and the most drastic discipline for the newly formed Red Army. Soldiers deserting or disobeying an order were summarily shot. Moreover, Trotsky effectively recruited former tsarist army officers. In short, he formed a disciplined and effective fighting force.

The Bolsheviks also mobilized the home front. Establishing **war communism**—the application of the total-war concept to a civil conflict—they seized grain from peasants, introduced rationing, nationalized all banks and industry, and required everyone to work. Although these measures contributed to a breakdown of normal economic activity, they also served to maintain labor discipline and to keep the Red Army supplied.

"Revolutionary terror" also contributed to the Communist victory. The old tsarist secret police was reestablished as the **Cheka,** which hunted down and executed thousands of real or supposed foes, such as the tsar and his family and other "class enemies." Moreover, people were shot or threatened with being shot for minor nonpolitical failures. The terror caused by the secret police became a tool of the government. The Cheka sowed fear, and fear silenced opposition.

Finally, foreign military intervention in the civil war ended up helping the Communists. The Allies (the Americans, British, and Japanese) sent troops to Archangel and Vladivostok to prevent war materiel that they had sent to the provisional government from being captured by the Germans. After the Soviet government nationalized all foreign-owned factories without compensation and refused to pay all of Russia's foreign debts, Western governments, particularly that of France, began to support White armies. Yet these efforts were small and halfhearted. Allied intervention in the civil war did not aid the Whites effectively, though it did permit the Communists to appeal to the patriotic nationalism of ethnic Russians, in particular former tsarist army officers.

Together, the Russian Revolution and the Bolshevik triumph were one of the reasons why the First World War was such a great turning point in modern history. A radically new government, based on socialism and one-party dictatorship, came to power in a great European state, maintained power, and eagerly encouraged worldwide revolution. Although Russia was undoubtedly headed for some kind of political crisis before 1914, it is hard to imagine the triumph of the most radical proponents of change and reform except in a situation of total collapse. That was precisely what happened to Russia in the First World War.

## THE PEACE SETTLEMENT

Victory over revolutionary Russia boosted sagging German morale, and in the spring of 1918 the Germans launched their last major attack against France. This offensive, just like those before it, failed. With breathtaking rapidity, the United States, Great Britain, and France decisively defeated Germany militarily. Austria-Hungary and the Ottoman Empire broke apart and ceased to exist. The guns of world war finally fell silent. Then as civil war spread in Russia and as chaos engulfed much of eastern Europe, the victorious Western Allies came together in Paris to establish a lasting peace.

Expectations were high; optimism was almost unlimited. The Allies labored intensively and soon worked out terms for peace with Germany and for the creation of the peacekeeping **League of Nations.** Nevertheless, the hopes of peoples and politicians were soon disappointed, for the peace settlement of 1919 turned out to be a failure. Rather than creating conditions for peace, it sowed the seeds of another war. Surely this was the ultimate tragedy of the Great War, a war that directly and indirectly cost $332 billion and left 10 million people dead and another 20 million wounded. How did this tragedy happen? Why was the peace settlement unsuccessful?

### The End of the War

In early 1917 the strain of total war was showing everywhere. After the Russian Revolution in March, there were major strikes in Germany. In July a coalition of moderates passed a "peace resolution" in the Reichstag, calling for peace without territorial annexations. To counter this moderation born of war-weariness, the German military established a virtual dictatorship. The military also aggressively exploited the collapse of Russian armies, winning great concessions in the Treaty of Brest-Litovsk.

With victory in the east quieting German moderates, General Ludendorff and company fell on France once more in the great spring offensive of 1918. For a time German armies pushed forward, coming within thirty-five miles of Paris. But Ludendorff's exhausted, over-extended forces never broke through. They were decisively stopped in July at the second Battle of the Marne, where 140,000 fresh American soldiers saw action. Adding 2 million men in arms to the war effort by August, the late but massive American intervention decisively tipped the scales in favor of Allied victory.

By September British, French, and American armies were advancing steadily on all fronts, and on October 4 the emperor formed a new, more liberal German government to sue for peace. As negotiations over an armistice dragged on, an angry and frustrated German people finally rose up. On November 3 sailors in Kiel mutinied, and throughout northern Germany soldiers and workers began to establish revolutionary councils on the Russian soviet model. The same day Austria-Hungary surrendered to the Allies and began breaking apart. With army discipline collapsing, the German emperor abdicated and fled to Holland. Socialist leaders in Berlin proclaimed a German republic on November 9 and simultaneously agreed to tough Allied terms of surrender. The armistice went into effect on November 11, 1918. The war was over.

The German Revolution of November 1918 resembled the Russian Revolution of March 1917. In both countries a popular uprising toppled an authoritarian monarchy, and moderate socialists took control of the government. But when Germany's radical socialists, headed by Karl Liebknecht and Rosa Luxemburg, tried to seize power, the moderate socialists called on the army to crush the attempted coup. Liebknecht and Luxemburg were arrested and murdered by army leaders. Thus Germany had a political revolution, but without a communist second installment. It was Russia without Lenin's Bolshevik triumph. (See the feature "Individuals in Society: Rosa Luxemburg.")

Military defeat brought political revolution to Austria-Hungary, as it had to Germany, Russia, and the Ottoman Empire (see pages 971–974). In Austria-Hungary the revolution was primarily nationalistic and republican in character. Independent Austrian, Hungarian, and Czechoslovak republics were proclaimed, and a greatly expanded Serbian monarchy united the South Slavs and took the name Yugoslavia. The prospect of firmly establishing the new national states overrode class considerations for most people in east-central Europe.

## The Treaty of Versailles

The peace conference opened in Paris in January 1919 with seventy delegates representing twenty-seven victorious nations. There were great expectations. A young British diplomat later wrote that the victors "believed in nationalism, we believed in the self-determination of peoples." Indeed, "we were journeying to Paris . . . to found a new order in Europe. We were preparing not Peace only, but Eternal Peace."[7] This general optimism and idealism had been greatly strengthened by President Wilson's January 1918 peace proposal, the Fourteen Points, which stressed national self-determination and the rights of small countries.

The real powers at the conference were the United States, Great Britain, and France, for Germany was not allowed to participate and Russia was locked in civil war and did not attend. Italy was considered one of the Big Four, but its role was quite limited. Almost immediately the three great Allies began to quarrel. President Wilson was almost obsessed with creating the League of Nations. He insisted that this question come first, for he passionately believed that only a permanent international organization could protect member states from aggression and avert future wars. Wilson had his way, although Lloyd George of Great Britain and especially Clemenceau of France were unenthusiastic. They were primarily concerned with punishing Germany.

Playing on British nationalism, Lloyd George had already won a smashing electoral victory in December on the popular platform of making Germany pay for the war. "We shall," the British prime minister promised, "squeeze the orange until the pips squeak." Personally inclined to make a somewhat moderate peace with Germany, Lloyd George was to a considerable extent a captive of demands for a total victory worthy of the sacrifices of total war against a totally depraved enemy. As Rudyard Kipling summed up the general British feeling at the end of the war, the Germans were "a people with the heart of beasts."[8]

France's Georges Clemenceau, "the Tiger" who had broken wartime defeatism and led his country to victory, wholeheartedly agreed. Like most French people, Clemenceau wanted old-fashioned revenge. He also wanted lasting security for France. This, he believed, required the creation of a buffer state between France and Germany, the permanent demilitarization of Germany, and vast German reparations. He feared that sooner or later Germany with its 60 million people would attack France with its 40 million unless the Germans were permanently weakened. Moreover, France had no English Channel (or Atlantic Ocean) as a reassuring barrier against German aggression. Wilson, supported by Lloyd George, would hear none of this. Clemenceau's demands seemed vindictive, violating morality and the principle of national self-determination. By April the conference was deadlocked on the German question, and Wilson packed his bags to go home.

In the end, convinced that France should not break with its allies because France could not afford to face Germany alone in the future, Clemenceau agreed to a compromise. He gave up the French demand for a Rhineland buffer state in return for a formal defensive alliance with the United States and Great Britain. Under the terms of this alliance both Wilson and Lloyd George promised that their countries would come to France's aid in the event of a German attack. Thus Clemenceau appeared to win his goal of French security, as Wilson had won his of a permanent international organization. The Allies moved quickly to finish the settlement, believing that any adjustments would later be possible within the dual framework of a strong Western alliance and the League of Nations.

The **Treaty of Versailles** between the Allies and Germany was the key to the settlement, and the terms were not unreasonable as a first step toward re-establishing international order. Had Germany won, it seems certain that France and Belgium would have been treated with greater severity, as Russia had been at Brest-Litovsk. Germany's colonies were given to France, Britain, and Japan as League of Nations mandates. Germany's territorial losses within Europe were minor, thanks to Wilson. Alsace-Lorraine was returned to France. Parts of Germany inhabited primarily by Poles were ceded to the new Polish state, in keeping with the principle of national self-determination. Germany had to limit its army to 100,000 men and agree to build no military fortifications in the Rhineland (see Map 29.4).

More harshly, the Allies declared that Germany (with Austria) was responsible for the war and had therefore to pay reparations equal to all civilian damages caused by the war. This unfortunate and much-criticized clause expressed inescapable popular demands for German blood, but the actual figure was not set, and there was the clear possibility that reparations might be set at a reasonable level in the future when tempers had cooled.

When presented with the treaty, the German government protested vigorously. But there was no alternative, especially considering that Germany was still starving because the Allies had not yet lifted their naval blockade. On June 28, 1919, German representatives of the ruling moderate Social Democrats and the Catholic party signed the treaty in the Sun King's Hall of Mirrors at Versailles, where Bismarck's empire had been joyously proclaimed almost fifty years before.

**The Allied Leaders at Versailles** The old tiger, Clemenceau of France, gestures with his walking stick to the scholarly Woodrow Wilson, as the strong-willed Lloyd George strides forward on the left. The negotiations at Versailles were difficult and often bitter, but the Allies reached a compromise agreement and imposed it on Germany. *(Corbis)*

# INDIVIDUALS IN SOCIETY

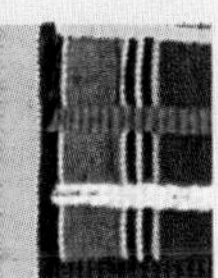

## ROSA LUXEMBURG

When Rosa Luxemburg (1870–1919) was arrested and then clubbed down and murdered by soldiers while being taken to jail, the left wing of European socialism lost a leading thinker and a passionate activist. But it gained an icon, a revolutionary saint.

Luxemburg grew up in Warsaw, the fifth child in a loving, nonreligious Jewish family. Speaking Polish and German at home, the mature Luxemburg identified "indignantly with Polish victims of linguistic oppression far more easily than with her fellow Jews."* But recent research also suggests that she was profoundly affected by the 1881 anti-Jewish riots and massacres in Russia and tsarist Poland, when middle-class Jewish families like hers huddled in terror until the Russian government decided the riots had gone far enough. These pogroms of 1881 led many Jewish intellectuals to turn to socialism. So it was with Luxemburg. She found in Marxism the promise of liberation for *all* oppressed groups and thus an end to terrible ethnic hatreds.

Smuggled out of Poland in 1889 and studying economics and socialism in Zurich with like-minded Polish exiles, one of whom became her lover and lifelong companion in revolution, Luxemburg settled in 1898 in Germany, the heartland of Marxian socialism. Small, foreign-born, and walking with a limp because of a childhood accident, she relentlessly attacked all revisions of Marxism (see page 819) and emerged in Germany as the "most prominent and influential of the party's radicals." She denounced any compromise with capitalism and stressed the absolute necessity of revolution.

Luxemburg also played a leading role in the outlawed Polish Socialist party. She thrilled to the revolution of 1905 in the tsarist empire and worked feverishly for the cause in Warsaw—"the happiest months of my life." Strengthened in her revolutionary convictions, she fought to radicalize Germany's socialists. When senior party and trade-union leaders opposed her ideas and tried to marginalize her, she went over their heads to the rank and file. A popular speaker who lectured tirelessly to enthusiastic working-class audiences, "Red Rosa" even challenged army discipline and the emperor as she condemned militarism as well as capitalism. In 1913 she told a large meeting, "If they think we are going to lift the weapons of murder against our French and other brethren, then we shall shout: 'We will not do it!'"† Arrested and tried for sedition, she was sentenced to prison.

*Rosa Luxemburg, addressing a meeting of the Socialist International in 1907.*
(AKG London)

The outbreak of war put existing trends in fast-forward. Luxemburg was heartbroken when the Second International stood by impotently in all countries and Germany's Social Democrats rallied to the government. From prison she denounced her former coworkers as working-class traitors and cheered on Karl Liebknecht's tiny group of radical socialists (see page 957). After her release in November 1918, she embraced the Bolshevik Revolution and worked with heart and soul for a replay of radical revolution in Germany until her martyr's death two months later.

Rosa Luxemburg's legacy is complex, but two points seem clear. First, she personified brilliantly the resurgent radical minority in Marxian socialism after 1905, which eventually triumphed in Russia and was rejected in Germany. Second, brave and ever multinational, Luxemburg embodied the strongest element in prewar socialism's hostility toward militarism and national hatreds, an idealistic vision tragically shattered in the great break of World War I.

### QUESTIONS FOR ANALYSIS

1. In what ways did Rosa Luxemburg's career reflect tensions and divisions in the Marxian socialist movement in Germany and throughout Europe before and during the First World War?
2. Evaluate Luxemburg's life. Was she a success or a failure? Or was she both? Defend your conclusions in a class debate.

*Richard Abraham, *Rosa Luxemburg: A Life for the International* (Oxford and New York: Berg, 1989), p. 20; also pp. 75, 80. This brief study is excellent.

†J. P. Nettl, *Rosa Luxemburg,* abr. ed. (New York: Schocken Books, 1969), p. 321.

**MAP 29.4 Territorial Changes in Europe After World War I** The Great War brought tremendous changes to eastern Europe. Empires were shattered, and new nations were established. A dangerous power vacuum was created between Germany and Soviet Russia.

Separate peace treaties were concluded with the other defeated powers—Austria, Hungary, Bulgaria, and Turkey. For the most part these treaties merely ratified the existing situation in east-central Europe following the breakup of the Austro-Hungarian Empire (see Map 29.4). Like Austria, Hungary was a particularly big loser, as its "captive" nationalities (and some interspersed Hungarians) were ceded to Romania, Czechoslovakia, Poland, and Yugoslavia. Italy got some Austrian territory. The Turkish empire was broken up. France received Lebanon and Syria. Britain took Iraq and Palestine, which was to include a Jewish national homeland first promised by Britain in 1917. Officially League of Nations mandates, these acquisitions of the Western Powers were one of the most imperialistic elements of the peace settlement. Another was mandating Germany's holdings in China to Japan (see page 984). The age of Western imperialism lived on. National self-determination remained a reality only for Europeans and their offspring.

## American Rejection of the Versailles Treaty

The rapidly concluded peace settlement of early 1919 was not perfect, but within the context of war-shattered Europe it was an acceptable beginning. The principle of national self-determination, which had played such a large role in starting the war, was accepted and served as an organizing framework. Germany had been punished but not dismembered. A new world organization complemented a traditional defensive alliance of satisfied powers. The serious remaining problems could be worked out in the future. Moreover, Allied leaders had seen speed as essential for another reason: they detested Lenin and feared that his Bolshevik Revolution might spread. They realized that their best answer to Lenin's unending calls for worldwide upheaval was peace and tranquillity for war-weary peoples.

There were, however, two great interrelated obstacles to such peace: Germany and the United States. Plagued by communist uprisings, reactionary plots, and popular disillusionment with losing the war at the last minute, Germany's moderate socialists and their liberal and Catholic supporters faced an enormous challenge. Like French republicans after 1871, they needed time (and luck) if they were to establish firmly a peaceful and democratic republic. Progress in this direction required understanding yet firm treatment of Germany by the victorious Western Allies, particularly by the United States.

However, the U.S. Senate and, to a lesser extent, the American people rejected Wilson's handiwork. Republican senators led by Henry Cabot Lodge refused to ratify the Treaty of Versailles without changes in the articles creating the League of Nations. The key issue was the League's power—more apparent than real—to require member states to take collective action against aggression. Lodge and others believed that this requirement gave away Congress's constitutional right to declare war. In failing health Wilson, with narrow-minded self-righteousness, rejected all attempts at compromise. In doing so, he ensured that the treaty would never be ratified by the United States in any form and that the United States would never join the League of Nations. Moreover, the Senate refused to ratify Wilson's defensive alliance with France and Great Britain. America turned its back on Europe.

The Wilson-Lodge fiasco and the newfound gospel of isolationism represented a tragic and cowardly renunciation of America's responsibility. Using America's action as an excuse, Great Britain, too, refused to ratify its defensive alliance with France. Betrayed by its allies, France stood alone. Very shortly France was to take actions against Germany that would feed the fires of German resentment and seriously undermine democratic forces in the new German republic. The great hopes of early 1919 had turned to ashes by the end of the year. The Western alliance had collapsed, and a grandiose plan for permanent peace had given way to a fragile truce. For this and for what came later, the United States must share a large part of the blame.

# SUMMARY

Why did World War I have such revolutionary consequences? Why was it such a great break with the past? World War I was, first of all, a war of committed peoples. In France, Britain, and Germany in particular, governments drew on genuine popular support. This support reflected not only the diplomatic origins of the war but also the way western European society had been unified under the nationalist banner in the later nineteenth century, despite the fears that the growing socialist movement aroused in conservatives. The relentlessness of total war helps explain why so many died, why so many were crippled physically and psychologically, and why Western civilization would in so many ways never be the same again. More concretely, the war swept away monarchs and multinational empires. National self-determination apparently triumphed, not only in Austria-Hungary but also in many of Russia's western borderlands. Except in Ireland and parts of Soviet Russia, the revolutionary dream of national unity, born of the French Revolution, had finally come true.

Two other revolutions were products of the war. In Russia the Bolsheviks established a radical regime, smashed existing capitalist institutions, and stayed in power with a new kind of authoritarian rule. Whether the new Russian regime was truly Marxian or socialist was questionable, but it indisputably posed a powerful, ongoing revolutionary challenge to Europe and its colonial empires.

More subtle but quite universal in its impact was an administrative revolution. This revolution, born of the need to mobilize entire societies and economies for total war, greatly increased the power of government in the West. And after the guns grew still, government planning and wholesale involvement in economic and social life did not disappear in Europe. Liberal market capitalism and a well-integrated world economy were among the many casualties of the administrative revolution, and greater social equality was everywhere one of its results. Thus even in European countries where a communist takeover never came close to occurring, society still experienced a great revolution.

Finally, the "war to end war" brought not peace but only a fragile truce. In the West the Allies failed to maintain their wartime solidarity. Germany remained unrepentant and would soon have more grievances to nurse. Moreover, the victory of national self-determination in eastern Europe created a power vacuum between a still-powerful Germany and a potentially mighty communist Russia. A vast area lay open to military aggression from two sides.

## KEY TERMS

| | |
|---|---|
| Three Emperors' League | Army Order No. 1 |
| Triple Entente | Bolsheviks |
| trench warfare | Constituent Assembly |
| *Lusitania* | war communism |
| total war | Cheka |
| War Raw Materials Board | League of Nations |
| Auxiliary Service Law | Treaty of Versailles |
| Petrograd Soviet | |

## NOTES

1. M. Beloff, quoted in *U.S. News & World Report,* March 8, 1976, p. 53.
2. Quoted in J. Remak, *The Origins of World War I* (New York: Holt, Rinehart & Winston, 1967), p. 84.
3. Quoted in F. P. Chambers, *The War Behind the War, 1914–1918* (London: Faber & Faber, 1939), p. 168.
4. Quoted in R. O. Paxton, *Europe in the Twentieth Century* (New York: Harcourt Brace Jovanovich, 1975), p. 109.
5. Quoted in Chambers, *The War Behind the War, 1914–1918,* pp. 302, 304.
6. A. B. Ulam, *The Bolsheviks* (New York: Collier Books, 1968), p. 349.
7. H. Nicolson, *Peacemaking 1919* (New York: Grosset & Dunlap Universal Library, 1965), pp. 8, 31–32.
8. Quoted ibid., p. 24.

## SUGGESTED READING

E. Hobsbawm, *The Age of Extremes: A History of the World, 1914–1991* (1996), offers a provocative interpretation of the "short twentieth century," with a good description of war and revolution. O. Hale, *The Great Illusion, 1900–1914* (1971), is a thorough account of the prewar era. Remak's volume, cited in the Notes; J. Joll, *The Origins of the First World War* (1992); and L. Lafore, *The Long Fuse* (1971), are recommended studies of the causes of the First World War. E. Brose, *The Kaiser's Army, 1870–1914: Technological, Tactical, and Operational Dilemmas in Germany During the Machine Age* (2001); V. Steiner, *Britain and the Origins of the First World War* (1978); and G. Kennan, *The Decline of Bismarck's European Order: Franco-Russian Relations, 1875–1890* (1979), are also major contributions. K. Jarausch's *The Enigmatic Chancellor* (1973) is an important study on Bethmann-Hollweg and German policy in 1914. M. Gilbert, *The First World War: A Complete History* (1994), is comprehensive. C. Falls, *The Great War* (1961), is the best brief introduction to military aspects of the war. B. Tuchman, *The Guns of August* (1962), is a marvelous account of the dramatic first month of the war and the beginning of military stalemate. G. Ritter provides an able study in *The Schlieffen Plan* (1958). J. Winter, *The Experience of World War I* (1988), is a strikingly illustrated history of the war, and A. Horne, *The Price of Glory: Verdun 1916* (1979), is a moving account of the famous siege. J. Ellis, *Eye-Deep in Hell* (1976), is a vivid account of trench warfare, whereas J. Keegan's fascinating *Face of Battle* (1976) examines soldiers and warfare in a long-term perspective. V. Brittain's *Testament of Youth,* the moving autobiography of an English nurse in wartime, shows lives buffeted by new ideas and personal tragedies.

F. L. Carsten, *War Against War* (1982), considers radical movements in Britain and Germany. The best single volume on the home fronts is still the one by Chambers mentioned in the Notes. M. Higonnet, J. Jensen, and M. Weitz, eds., *Behind the Lines: Gender and the Two World Wars* (1987), examines the changes that the war brought for women and for relations between the sexes. A. Marwick, *War and Change in Twentieth-Century Europe* (1990), is a useful synthesis. Three excellent collections of essays—R. Wall and J. Winter, eds., *The Upheaval of War: Family, Work, and Welfare in Europe, 1914–1918* (1988); J. Roth, ed., *World War I* (1967); and R. Albrecht-Carrié, ed., *The Meaning of the First World War* (1965)—probe the enormous consequences of the war for people and society. The debate over Germany's guilt and aggression may be best approached through G. Feldman, ed., *German Imperialism, 1914–1918* (1972), and A. Hillgruber, *Germany and the Two World Wars* (1981). In addition to Erich Maria Remarque's great novel *All Quiet on the Western Front,* Henri Barbusse, *Under Fire* (1917), and Jules Romains, *Verdun* (1939), are highly recommended for their fictional yet realistic re-creations of the war. P. Fussell, *The Great War and Modern Memory* (1975), probes all the powerful literature inspired by the war. M. Eckstein, *Rites of Spring: The Great War and the Birth of the Modern Age* (1989), is an imaginative cultural investigation that has won critical acclaim. C. Read, *From Tsar to Soviets: The Russian People and Their Revolution, 1917–1921* (1996), is highly recommended.

R. Suny and A. Adams, eds., *The Russian Revolution and Bolshevik Victory* (1990), presents a wide range of old and new interpretations. Ulam's work, cited in the Notes, which focuses on Lenin, is a masterful introduction to the Russian Revolution, whereas S. Fitzpatrick, *The Russian Revolution* (1982), provides a provocative reconsideration. B. Wolfe, *Three Who Made a Revolution* (1955), a collective biography of Lenin, Trotsky, and Stalin, and R. Conquest, *V. I. Lenin* (1972), are recommended. D. Volkogonov, *Lenin: A New Biography* (1994), is a lively study with some new revelations by a well-known postcommunist Russian historian. L. Trotsky wrote the colorful and exciting *History of the Russian Revolution* (1932), which may be compared with the classic eyewitness account of the young, pro-Bolshevik American J. Reed, *Ten Days That Shook the World* (1919). R. Daniels, *Red October* (1969), provides a clear account of the Bolshevik seizure of power, and R. Pipes, *The Formation of the Soviet Union* (1968), is recommended for its excellent treatment of the nationality problem during the revolution. D. Koenker, W. Rosenberg, and R. Suny, eds., *Party, State and Society in the Russian Civil War* (1989), probes the social foundations of Bolshevik victory. A. Wildman, *The End of the Russian Imperial Army* (1980), is a fine account of the soldiers' revolt, and G. Leggett, *The Cheka: Lenin's Secret Police* (1981), shows revolutionary terror in action. Boris Pasternak's justly celebrated *Doctor Zhivago* is a great historical novel of the revolutionary era. R. Massie, *Nicholas and Alexandra* (1971), is a moving popular biography of Russia's last royal family and the terrible health problem of the heir to the throne. Nicolson's study, listed in the Notes, captures the spirit of the Versailles settlement. T. Bailey, *Woodrow Wilson and the Lost Peace* (1963), and W. Widenor, *Henry Cabot Lodge and the Search for an American Foreign Policy* (1981), are also highly recommended.

# LISTENING TO THE PAST

## THE EXPERIENCE OF WAR

*World War I was a "total" war: it enlisted the efforts of men, women, adults, and children, both at home and on the battlefield. It was a terrifying and painful experience for all those involved. To be sure, it was not the romantic endeavor it was purported to be. The documents below offer two different wartime experiences. The first excerpt is from a letter written by a German soldier fighting in the trenches. The second is from the diary of a Viennese woman. As you read both passages, think about the different ways war and its consequences were made real for these two people.*

### A German Soldier Writes from the Trenches, March 1915

*Souchez, March 11th, 1915*

"So fare you well, for we must now be parting," so run the first lines of a soldier-song which we often sang through the streets of the capital. These words are truer than ever now, and these lines are to bid farewell to you, to all my nearest and dearest, to all who wish me well or ill, and to all that I value and prize.

Our regiment has been transferred to this dangerous spot, Souchez. No end of blood has already flowed down this hill. A week ago the 142nd attacked and took four trenches from the French. It is to hold these trenches that we have been brought here. There is something uncanny about this hill-position. Already, times without number, other battalions of our regiment have been ordered here in support, and each time the company came back with a loss of twenty, thirty or more men. In the days when we had to stick it out here before, we had 22 killed and 27 wounded. Shells roar, bullets whistle; no dug-outs, or very bad ones; mud, clay, filth, shell-holes so deep that one could bathe in them.

This letter has been interrupted no end of times. Shells began to pitch close to us—great English 12-inch ones—and we had to take refuge in a cellar. One such shell struck the next house and buried four men, who were got out from the ruins horribly mutilated. I saw them and it was ghastly!

Everybody must be prepared now for death in some form or other. Two cemeteries have been made up here, the losses have been so great. I ought not to write that to you, but I do so all the same, because the newspapers have probably given you quite a different impression. They tell only of our gains and say nothing about the blood that has been shed, of the cries of agony that never cease. The newspaper doesn't give any description either of *how* the "heroes" are laid to rest, though it talks about "heroes' graves" and writes poems and such-like about them. Certainly in Lens I have attended funeral-parades where a number of dead were buried in one large grave with pomp and circumstance. But up here it is pitiful the way one throws the dead bodies out of the trench and lets them lie there, or scatters dirt over the remains of those which have been torn to pieces by shells.

I look upon death and call upon life. I have not accomplished much in my short life, which has been chiefly occupied with study. I have commended my soul to the Lord God. It bears His seal and is altogether His. Now I am free to dare anything. My future life belongs to God, my present one to the Fatherland, and I myself still possess happiness and strength.

### A Viennese Woman Remembers Home Front Life

Ten dekagrammes [3½ ounces] of horse-flesh per head are to be given out to-day for the week. The cavalry horses held in reserve by the military authorities are being slaughtered for lack of fodder, and the people of Vienna are for a change

Germans wait in line for their meager rations in Berlin in 1916. *(Corbis)*

to get a few mouthfuls of meat of which they have so long been deprived. Horse-flesh! I should like to know whether my instinctive repugnance to horse-flesh as food is personal, or whether my dislike is shared by many other housewives. My loathing of it is based, I believe, not on a physical but on a psychological prejudice.

I overcame my repugnance, rebuked myself for being sentimental, and left the house. A soft, steady rain was falling, from which I tried to protect myself with galoshes, waterproof, and umbrella. As I left the house before seven o'clock and the meat distribution did not begin until nine o'clock, I hoped to get well to the front of the queue.

No sooner had I reached the neighbourhood of the big market hall than I was instructed by the police to take a certain direction. I estimated the crowd waiting here for a meagre midday meal at two thousand at least. Hundreds of women had spent the night here in order to be among the first and make sure of getting their bit of meat. Many had brought with them improvised seats—a little box or a bucket turned upside down. No one seemed to mind the rain, although many were already wet through. They passed the time chattering, and the theme was the familiar one: What have you had to eat? What are you going to eat? One could scent an atmosphere of mistrust in these conversations: they were all careful not to say too much or to betray anything that might get them into trouble.

At length the sale began. Slowly, infinitely slowly, we moved forward. The most determined, who had spent the night outside the gates of the hall, displayed their booty to the waiting crowd: a ragged, quite freshly slaughtered piece of meat with the characteristic yellow fat. [Others] alarmed those standing at the back by telling them that there was only a very small supply of meat and that not half the people waiting would get a share of it. The crowd became very uneasy and impatient, and before the police on guard could prevent it, those standing in front organized an attack on the hall which the salesmen inside were powerless to repel. Everyone seized whatever he could lay his hands on, and in a few moments all the eatables had vanished. In the confusion stands were overturned, and the police forced back the aggressors and closed the gates. The crowds waiting outside, many of whom had been there all night and were soaked through, angrily demanded their due, whereupon the mounted police made a little charge, provoking a wild panic and much screaming and cursing. At length I reached home, depressed and disgusted, with a broken umbrella and only one galosh.

We housewives have during the last four years grown accustomed to standing in queues; we have also grown accustomed to being obliged to go home with empty hands and still emptier stomachs. Only very rarely do those who are sent away disappointed give cause for police intervention. On the other hand, it happens more and more frequently that one of the pale, tired women who have been waiting for hours collapses from exhaustion. The turbulent scenes which occurred to-day inside and outside the large market hall seemed to me perfectly natural. In my dejected mood the patient apathy with which we housewives endure seemed to me blameworthy and incomprehensible.

## QUESTIONS FOR ANALYSIS

1. How does the soldier see the war he is in? Is it a grand patriotic effort? Or is it a story of senseless bloodshed and loss of life?
2. How did the soldiers cope with the reality of war in the trenches?
3. How does the experience of the Viennese woman differ from the soldier's?
4. Were the women who pillaged the food hall "blameworthy" or "incomprehensible," as the Viennese woman says?

*Sources:* Alfons Ankenbrand, in *German Students' War Letters,* ed. A. F. Wedd (London: Methuen, 1929), pp. 72–73; *Blockade: The Diary of an Austrian Middle-Class Woman, 1914–1924,* trans. Winifred Ray (New York: Ray Long & Richard Smith, 1932), pp. 63–68.

Turks celebrating victory at Smyrna, October 1922. *(Liaison/Getty Images)*

CHAPTER

# 30 NATIONALISM IN ASIA, 1914–1939

## CHAPTER OUTLINE

- The First World War and Western Imperialism
- The Middle East
- Toward Self-Rule in India
- Turmoil in East Asia

From Asia's perspective the First World War was largely a European civil war that shattered the united front of Western imperialism and convulsed prewar relationships throughout Asia. Most crucially, the war speeded the development of modern nationalism in Asia. Before 1914, the nationalist gospel of anti-imperialist political freedom and racial equality had already won converts among Asia's westernized, educated elites. In the 1920s and 1930s it increasingly won the allegiance of the masses. As in Europe in the nineteenth century, nationalism in Asia between 1914 and 1939 became a mass movement with potentially awesome power.

There were at least three reasons for the upsurge of nationalism in Asia. First and foremost, nationalism provided the most effective means of organizing the anti-imperialist resistance both to direct foreign rule and to indirect Western domination. Second, nationalism called for fundamental changes and challenged old political and social practices and beliefs. Thus modernizers used it as a weapon in their ongoing contest for influence and power with conservative traditionalists. Third, nationalism spread because it gave both leaders and followers a vision of a shining future for a rejuvenated people. Thus nationalism provided an ideology to ennoble the sacrifices that the struggle for rejuvenation would require.

The spread of nationalism also had its dark side. As in Europe (see page 767), nationalists in Asia developed a strong sense of "we" and "they." "They" were often the enemy—the oppressor. White-skinned European imperialists were just such a "they," and nationalist feeling generated the power to destroy European empires and challenge foreign economic domination. But, as in Europe, nationalism in Asia also stimulated bitter conflicts and wars between peoples, in two different ways.

First, it stimulated conflicts between relatively homogeneous peoples in large states, rallying, for example, Chinese against Japanese and vice versa. Second, nationalism often heightened tensions between ethnic (or religious) groups within states, especially states with a variety of peoples, like British India or the Ottoman Empire. Such states had been formed by authoritarian rulers and their armies and bureaucracies, very much like the Austro-Hungarian and Russian empires before 1914. When their rigid rule declined or snapped, increasingly self-conscious and nationalistic peoples might easily quarrel, seeking to divide the existing state or to dominate the enemy "they" within its borders.

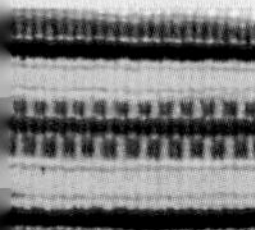

Although modern nationalism has everywhere exhibited certain shared characteristics, it has never been monolithic. In Asia especially, the range of historical experience has been enormous, and the new and often narrow ideology of nationalism was grafted onto old, rich, and complex civilizations. Between the outbreak of the First and Second World Wars each Asian country developed a distinctive national movement, rooted in its unique culture and history. Each nation's people created its own national reawakening, which renovated thought and culture as well as politics and economics.

- How did modern nationalism—the dominant force in most of the world in the twentieth century—develop in Asia between the First and Second World Wars?
- How did national movements arise in different countries, and how did some of these parallel movements come into brutal conflict?

These are the questions that this chapter will seek to answer.

## THE FIRST WORLD WAR AND WESTERN IMPERIALISM

Every Asian national movement shared a burning desire for genuine freedom from foreign imperialism. The First World War had a profound effect on these aspirations by altering relations between Asia and Europe.

In the words of a distinguished Indian historian, "the Great War of 1914–1918 was from the Asian point of view a civil war within the European community of nations."[1] For four years Asians watched the haughty bearers of what Kipling had called "the White Man's Burden" (see page 836) vilifying and destroying each other. Far from standing united and supremely self-confident, the Western nations were clawing at each other in total disarray. The impact of this spectacle was enormous. Japan's defeat of imperial Russia in 1904 (see page 876) had shown that an Asian power could beat a European Great Power; now for the first time Asians saw the entire West as divided and vulnerable.

In the East Asian countries of China and Japan few people particularly cared who won the vicious family quarrel in distant Europe. In India and French Indochina enthusiasm was also limited, but the impact of the war was unavoidably greater. The British and the French were driven by the harsh logic of total war to draft their colonial subjects into the conflict. They uprooted hundreds of thousands of Asians to fight the Germans and the Ottoman Turks. This too had major consequences. An Indian or Vietnamese soldier who fought in France and came in contact there with democratic and republican ideas was likely to be less willing to accept foreign rule when he returned home.

The British and the French also made rash promises to gain the support of colonial peoples during the war. British leaders promised Jewish nationalists in Europe a homeland in Palestine, even as they promised Arab nationalists independence from the Ottoman Empire. In India the British were forced in 1917 to announce a new policy of self-governing institutions in order to counteract Indian popular unrest fanned by wartime inflation and heavy taxation. After the war the nationalist genie that the colonial powers had called on refused to slip meekly back into the bottle.

The war aims of President Wilson also raised the hopes of peoples under imperial rule. In January 1918 Wilson proposed to make peace on the basis of his Fourteen Points (see page 957), whose key idea was national self-determination for the peoples of Europe and the Ottoman Empire. Wilson also proposed that in all colonial questions "the interests of native populations be given equal weight with the desires of European governments," and he seemed to call for national self-rule. This subversive message had enormous appeal for educated Asians, fueling their hopes of freedom.

Military service and Wilsonian self-determination also fired the hopes of some Africans and some visionary American black supporters of African freedom. The First World War, however, had less impact on European imperialism in sub-Saharan Africa than in Asia and the Arab world. For sub-Saharan Africa, the Great Depression and the Second World War were to prove much more influential in the growth of nationalist movements (see pages 1122–1125).

Once the Allies had won the war, they tried to shift gears and re-establish or increase their political and economic domination in Asia and Africa. Although fatally weakened, Western imperialism remained very much alive in 1918. Part of the reason for its survival was that President Wilson was certainly no revolutionary. At the Versailles Peace Conference he proved willing to compromise on colonial questions in order to achieve some of his European goals and the creation of the League of Nations. Also, Allied statesmen and ordinary French and British citizens quite rightly believed that their colonial empires had contributed to their ultimate victory over the Central Powers. They were in no mood to give up such valuable possessions voluntarily. Finally, the victors remained convinced of the

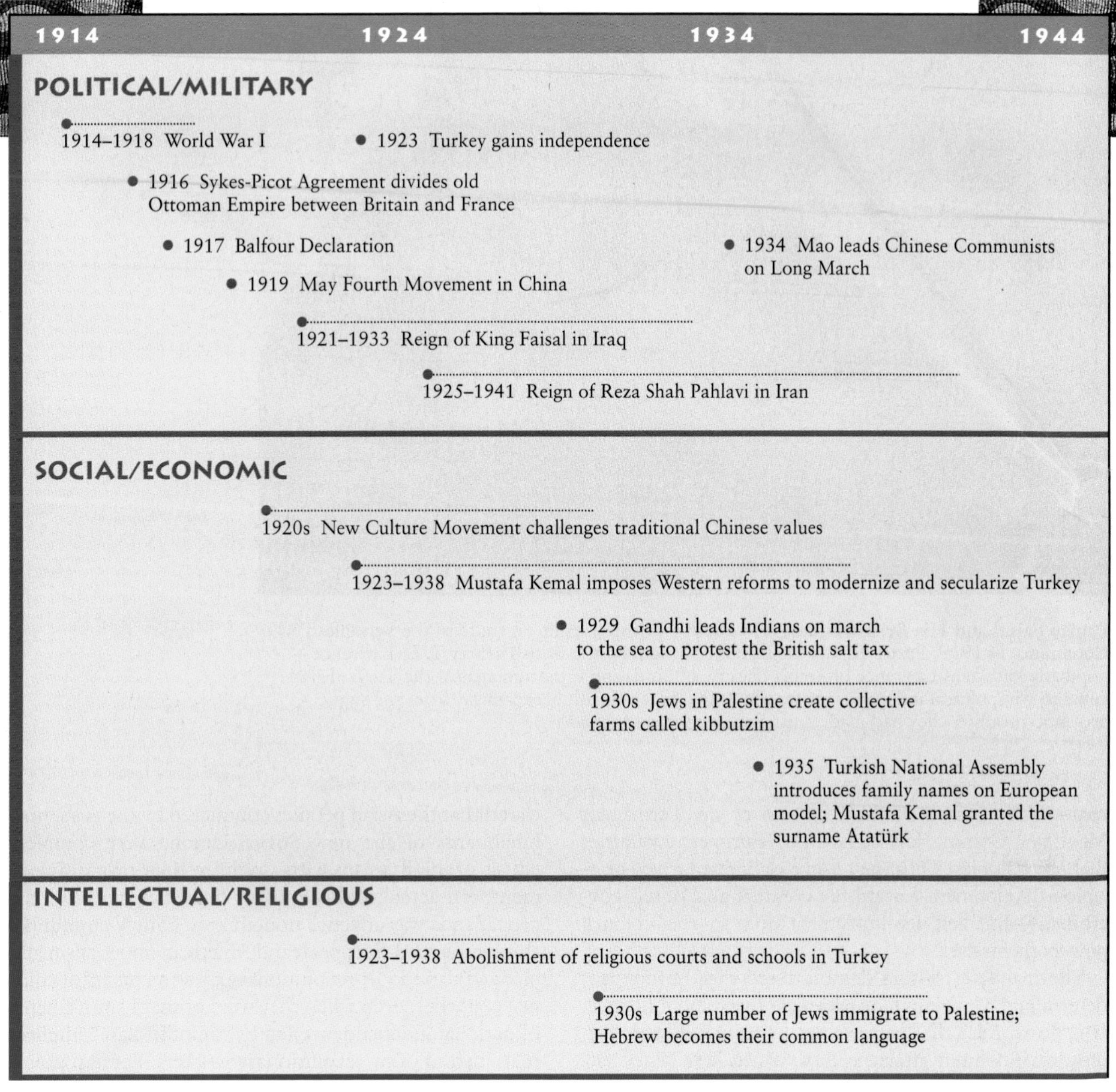


superiority of their civilization. They believed that their rule was best for colonial peoples. A few "discontented" Asian or African intellectuals might agitate for self-rule, but Europeans generally believed that the "humble masses" were grateful for the law and order brought by the white man's administration. If pressed, Europeans said that such administration was preparing colonial subjects for eventual self-rule, but only in the distant future.

1914
1924
1934
1944
POLITICAL/MILITARY
1914–1918 World War I
1923 Turkey gains independence
1916 Sykes-Picot Agreement divides old Ottoman Empire between Britain and France
1917 Balfour Declaration
1934 Mao leads Chinese Communists on Long March
1919 May Fourth Movement in China
1921–1933 Reign of King Faisal in Iraq
1925–1941 Reign of Reza Shah Pahlavi in Iran
SOCIAL/ECONOMIC
1920s New Culture Movement challenges traditional Chinese values
1923–1938 Mustafa Kemal imposes Western reforms to modernize and secularize Turkey
1929 Gandhi leads Indians on march to the sea to protest the British salt tax
1930s Jews in Palestine create collective farms called kibbutzim
1935 Turkish National Assembly introduces family names on European model; Mustafa Kemal granted the surname Atatürk
INTELLECTUAL/RELIGIOUS
1923–1938 Abolishment of religious courts and schools in Turkey
1930s Large number of Jews immigrate to Palestine; Hebrew becomes their common language

The compromise at Versailles between Wilson's vague, moralistic idealism and the European preoccupation with "good administration" was the establishment of a system of League of Nations mandates over Germany's former colonies and the old Ottoman Empire. Article 22 of the League of Nations Covenant, which was part of the Treaty of Versailles, assigned territories "inhabited by peoples incapable of governing themselves" to various "developed nations." "The well-being and development of such peoples" was declared "a sacred trust of civilization." The **Permanent Mandates Commission** was created to oversee the developed nations' fulfillment of their international

**Prince Faisal and His British Allies** On board a British warship en route to the Versailles Peace Conference in 1919, Prince Faisal is flanked on his right by the British officer T. E. Lawrence—popularly known as Lawrence of Arabia because of his daring campaign against the Turks. Faisal failed to win political independence for the Arabs, as the British backed away from the vague pro-Arab promises they had made during the war. *(Rowley Atterbury)*

responsibility; most of the members of the Permanent Mandates Commission came from European countries that had colonies. Thus the League elaborated a new principle—development toward the eventual goal of self-government—but left its implementation to the colonial powers themselves.

The mandates system demonstrated that Europe was determined to maintain its imperial power and influence. It is no wonder that patriots throughout Asia were bitterly disappointed after the First World War. They saw France, Great Britain, and other nations—industrialized Japan was the only Asian state to obtain mandates—grabbing Germany's colonies as spoils of war and extending the existing system of colonial rule in Muslim North Africa into the territories of the old Ottoman Empire. Yet Asian patriots were not about to give up. They preached national self-determination and struggled to build mass movements capable of achieving freedom and independence.

In this struggle they were encouraged and sometimes inspired by Soviet communism. Immediately after seizing power in 1917, Lenin and his fellow Bolsheviks declared that the Asian peoples conquered by the tsars, now inhabitants of the new Soviet Union, were complete equals of the Russians with a right to their own development. (In actuality this equality hardly existed, but the propaganda was effective nonetheless.) The Communists also denounced European and American imperialism and pledged to support revolutionary movements in all colonial countries, even when they were primarily movements of national independence led by "middle-class" intellectuals instead of by revolutionary workers. Foreign political and economic exploitation was the immediate enemy, they said, and socialist revolution could wait until after Western imperialism had been defeated.

The example, ideology, and support of Soviet communism exerted a powerful influence in the 1920s and 1930s, particularly in China and French Indochina. A nationalistic young Vietnamese man who had pleaded the cause of Vietnamese independence unsuccessfully at the Versailles Peace Conference described his feelings when he read Lenin's statement on national self-determination for colonial peoples, adopted by the Communist Third International in 1920:

*These resolutions filled me with great emotion, enthusiasm, and faith. They helped me see the problem clearly. My joy was so great I began to cry. Alone in my room I wrote the following words, as if I were addressing a great crowd: "My dear compatriots, so miserable and oppressed, here is what we need. Here is the path to our liberation."*[2]

The young nationalist was Ho Chi Minh (1890–1969), who was to fight a lifetime to create an independent, communist Vietnam.

The appeal of nationalism in Asia was not confined to territories under direct European rule. The extraordinary growth of international trade after 1850 had drawn millions of peasants and shopkeepers throughout Asia into the Western-dominated world economy, disrupting local markets and often creating hostility toward European businessmen. Moreover, Europe and the United States had forced even the most solid Asian states, China and Japan, to accept unequal treaties and humiliating limitations on their sovereignty. Thus the nationalist promise of genuine economic independence and true political equality with the West appealed as powerfully in old but weak states like China as in colonial territories like British India.

Finally, as in Russia after the Crimean War or in Japan after the Meiji Restoration, the nationalist creed went hand in hand with acceptance of modernization by the educated elites. Modernization promised changes that would enable old societies to compete effectively with the world's leading nations.

## THE MIDDLE EAST

The most flagrant attempt to expand the scope of Western imperialism occurred in what is usually called the Middle East but is perhaps more accurately termed West Asia—that vast expanse that stretches eastward from the Suez Canal and Turkey's Mediterranean shores across the Tigris-Euphrates Valley and the Iranian Plateau to the Arabian Sea and the Indus Valley. There the British and the French successfully encouraged an Arab revolt in 1916 and destroyed the Ottoman Empire. The conquering Europeans then sought to replace the Turks as principal rulers throughout the region, even in Turkey itself. Turkish, Arab, and Iranian nationalists, as well as Jewish nationalists arriving from Europe, reacted violently. They struggled to win dignity and nationhood, and as the Europeans were forced to make concessions, they sometimes came into sharp conflict with each other, most notably in Palestine.

### The First World War and the Arab Revolt

Long subject to European pressure, the Ottoman Empire fell short in its efforts to reform and modernize its rule in the late nineteenth century (see pages 837–840). The combination of declining international stature and domestic tyranny eventually led to an upsurge of revolutionary activity among idealistic exiles and young army officers who wanted to seize power and save the Ottoman state. These patriots, the so-called **Young Turks,** succeeded in the revolution of 1908, and subsequently they were determined to hold together the remnants of the vast multiethnic empire. Defeated by Bulgaria, Serbia, and Greece in the Balkan War of 1912, and stripped of practically all territory in Europe, the Young Turks redoubled their efforts in Asia. The most important of their Asian possessions were Syria—consisting of modern-day Lebanon, Syria, Israel, and Jordan—and Iraq. The Ottoman Turks also claimed the Arabian peninsula but exercised only loose control there.

For centuries the largely Arabic populations of Syria and Iraq had been tied to their Ottoman rulers by their common faith in Islam (though there were Christian Arabs as well). Yet beneath the surface, ethnic and linguistic tensions simmered between Turks and Arabs, who were as different as Chinese and Japanese or French and Germans.

The actions of the Young Turks after 1908 made the embryonic "Arab movement" a reality. Although some Turkish reformers argued for an Ottoman federalism that would give equal political rights to all ethnic and religious groups within the empire, the majority successfully insisted on a narrow Turkish nationalism. They further centralized the Ottoman Empire and extended the sway of the Turkish language, culture, and race. In 1909 the Turkish government brutally slaughtered thousands of Armenian Christians, a prelude to the wholesale destruction of more than a million Armenians during the heavy fighting with Russia in the First World War. Meanwhile, Arab discontent grew. By 1914 some Arab leaders believed that armed conflict with their Turkish masters was inevitable.

In close contact with Europeans for centuries, the Turks willingly joined forces with Germany and Austria-Hungary in late 1914. The Young Turks were pro-German because the Germans had helped reform the Ottoman armies before the war and had built important railroads, like the one to Baghdad. Alliance with Germany permitted the Turks to renounce immediately the limitations on Ottoman sovereignty that the Europeans had imposed in the nineteenth century, and it offered the prospect of settling old scores with Russia, the Turks' historic enemy.

**The Armenian Atrocities** When in 1915 some Armenians welcomed Russian armies as liberators after years of persecution, the Ottoman government ordered a genocidal mass deportation of its Armenian citizens from their homeland in the empire's eastern provinces. This photo, taken in Kharpert in 1915 by a German businessman from his hotel window, shows Turkish guards marching Armenian men off to a prison, where they will be tortured to death. A million Armenians died from murder, starvation, and disease during World War I. *(Courtesy of the Armenian Library & Museum of America, Watertown, Mass.)*

The Young Turks' fatal decision to side with the Central Powers pulled the entire Middle East into the European civil war and made it truly a world conflict. While Russia attacked the Ottomans in the Caucasus, the British had to protect their rule in Egypt and the Suez Canal, the lifeline to India. Thus Arab leaders opposed to Ottoman rule suddenly found an unexpected ally in Great Britain. The foremost Arab leader was Hussein ibn-Ali (1856–1931), a direct descendant of the prophet Muhammad through the house of Quraysh. As the **sharif,** or chief magistrate, of Mecca, the holiest city in the Muslim world, Hussein governed much of the Ottoman Empire's territory along the Red Sea, an area known as the Hejaz (see Map 30.1). Basically anti-Turkish, Hussein refused to second the Turkish sultan's call for a holy war against the Triple Entente. His refusal pleased the British, who feared that such calls would trigger a Muslim revolt in India.

In 1915 Hussein managed to win vague British commitments for an independent Arab kingdom. The British attempt to take the Dardanelles and capture Constantinople in 1915 failed miserably, and Britain (and Russia) badly needed a new ally on the Ottoman front. Thus in 1916 Hussein revolted against the Turks, proclaiming

**MAP 30.1 The Partition of the Ottoman Empire, 1914–1923** The decline of the mighty Ottoman Empire began in 1699, when the Habsburgs conquered Hungary, and it accelerated after 1805, when Egypt became virtually independent. By 1914 the Ottoman Turks had been pushed out of the Balkans, and their Arab provinces were on the edge of revolt; that revolt erupted in the First World War and contributed greatly to the Ottomans' defeat. When the Allies then attempted to implement their plans, including independence for the Armenian people, Mustafa Kemal arose to forge in battle the modern Turkish state.

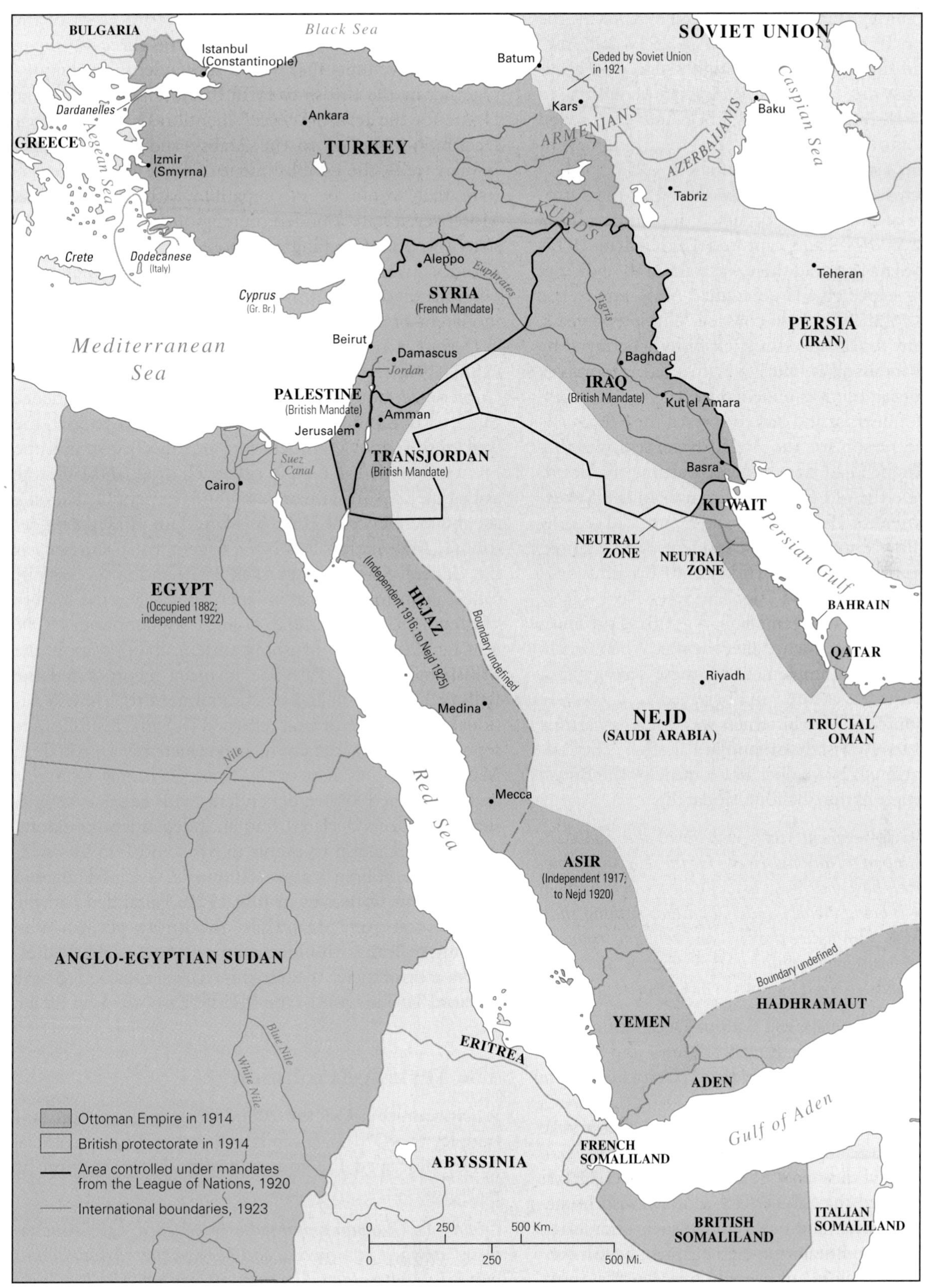
BULGARIA
Black Sea
SOVIET UNION
Istanbul
(Constantinople)
Batum
Ceded by Soviet Union
in 1921
Kars
Dardanelles
Ankara
ARMENIANS
Baku
Caspian Sea
GREECE
Aegean Sea
TURKEY
AZERBAIJANIS
Izmir
(Smyrna)
Tabriz
KURDS
Crete
Dodecanese
(Italy)
Aleppo
Euphrates
Teheran
Cyprus
(Gr. Br.)
SYRIA
(French Mandate)
Tigris
PERSIA
(IRAN)
Mediterranean
Sea
Beirut
Damascus
Baghdad
Jordan
PALESTINE
(British Mandate)
IRAQ
(British Mandate)
Kut el Amara
Amman
Jerusalem
Suez
Canal
TRANSJORDAN
(British Mandate)
Basra
Cairo
KUWAIT
NEUTRAL
ZONE
NEUTRAL
ZONE
Persian Gulf
EGYPT
(Occupied 1882;
independent 1922)
HEJAZ
(Independent 1916; to Nejd 1925)
Boundary undefined
BAHRAIN
QATAR
Riyadh
Medina
NEJD
(SAUDI ARABIA)
TRUCIAL
OMAN
Nile
Red Sea
Mecca
ASIR
(Independent 1917;
to Nejd 1920)
ANGLO-EGYPTIAN SUDAN
Boundary undefined
HADHRAMAUT
YEMEN
ERITREA
Blue Nile
White Nile
ADEN
Gulf of Aden
Ottoman Empire in 1914
British protectorate in 1914
Area controlled under mandates
from the League of Nations, 1920
International boundaries, 1923
FRENCH
SOMALILAND
ABYSSINIA
0
250
500 Km.
0
250
500 Mi.
BRITISH
SOMALILAND
ITALIAN
SOMALILAND

himself king of the Arabs. Hussein joined forces with the British under T. E. Lawrence, who in 1917 led Arab tribesmen and Indian soldiers in a highly successful guerrilla war against the Turks on the Arabian peninsula. In September 1918 British armies and their Arab allies rolled into Syria. This offensive culminated in the triumphal entry of Hussein's son Faisal into Damascus.

Similar victories were eventually scored in the Ottoman province of Iraq. Britain occupied the southern Iraqi city of Basra in 1914 and captured Baghdad in 1917. Throughout Syria and Iraq there was wild Arab rejoicing. Many patriots expected a large, unified Arab state to rise from the dust of the Ottoman collapse. Within two years, however, many Arab nationalists felt bitterly betrayed by Great Britain and its allies. The issues involved are complex and controversial, but it is undeniable that this bitterness left a legacy of distrust and hatred toward the West.

Part of the reason for the Arabs' bitterness was that Britain and France had signed secret wartime treaties to divide and rule the old Ottoman Empire. In the **Sykes-Picot Agreement** of 1916, Britain and France had secretly agreed that France would receive modern-day Lebanon, Syria, and much of southern Turkey, and Britain would receive Palestine, Jordan, and Iraq. The Sykes-Picot Agreement contradicted British (and later Wilsonian) promises concerning Arab independence after the war. When Britain and France set about implementing these secret plans, Arab nationalists felt cheated and betrayed.

A related source of Arab bitterness was Britain's wartime commitment to a Jewish homeland in Palestine. The **Balfour Declaration** of November 1917, made by the British foreign secretary Arthur Balfour, declared:

*His Majesty's Government views with favor the establishment in Palestine of a National Home for the Jewish People, and will use their best endeavors to facilitate the achievement of this object, it being clearly understood that nothing shall be done which may prejudice the civil and religious rights of existing non-Jewish communities in Palestine, or the rights and political status enjoyed by Jews in any other country.*

As careful reading reveals, the Balfour Declaration made contradictory promises to European Jews and Middle Eastern Arabs. It has been a subject of passionate debate ever since 1917.

Some British Cabinet members apparently believed such a declaration would appeal to German, Austrian, and American Jews and thus help the British war effort. Others sincerely supported the Zionist vision of a Jewish homeland. These supporters also believed that such a homeland would be grateful to Britain and help maintain British control of the Suez Canal. In any event, Arabs were dismayed.

In 1914 Jews accounted for about 11 percent of the predominantly Arab population in the three Ottoman administrative units that would subsequently be lumped together by the British to form Palestine. The "National Home for the Jewish People" mentioned in the Balfour Declaration implied to the Arabs—and to the Zionist Jews as well—the establishment of some kind of Jewish state that would be incompatible with majority rule. Moreover, a state founded on religious and ethnic exclusivity was out of keeping with both Islamic and Ottoman tradition, which had historically been more tolerant of religious diversity and minorities than had the Christian monarchs or nation-states in Europe.

Despite strong French objections, Hussein's son Faisal (1885–1933) was allowed to attend the Versailles Peace Conference, but his efforts to secure Arab independence came to nothing. President Wilson wanted to give the Arab case serious consideration, but the British and the French were determined to rule Syria, Iraq, and Palestine as League of Nations mandates, and they confirmed only the independence of Hussein's kingdom of Hejaz. In response, Arab nationalists came together in Damascus as the General Syrian Congress in 1919 and unsuccessfully called again for political independence. (See the feature "Listening to the Past: Arab Political Aspirations in 1919" on pages 996–997.) Brushing aside Arab opposition, the British mandate in Palestine formally incorporated the Balfour Declaration and its commitment to a Jewish national home. When Faisal returned to Syria, his followers repudiated the agreement he had reluctantly accepted. In March 1920 they met as the Syrian National Congress and proclaimed Syria independent, with Faisal as king. A similar congress declared Iraq an independent kingdom.

Western reaction to events in Syria and Iraq was swift and decisive. A French army stationed in Lebanon attacked Syria, taking Damascus in July 1920. Faisal fled and the French took over. Meanwhile, the British put down an uprising in Iraq with bloody fighting and established effective control there. Western imperialism appeared to have replaced Turkish rule in the Middle East (see Map 30.1).

## The Turkish Revolution

In November 1918 the Allied fleet entered Constantinople, the Ottoman capital. A young English official vividly described the strange and pathetic situation he encountered:

*I found the Ottoman Empire utterly smashed, her vast territories stripped into pieces, and her conquered populations blinded and bewildered by their sudden release. The Turks were worn out, dead-tired, and without bitterness awaited their fate. . . . The debris of the old order waited to be constructed into a new system.*[3]

The Allies' "new system" was blatant imperialism, and it proved harsher for the defeated Turks than for the "liberated" Arabs. A treaty forced on the helpless sultan dismembered Turkey and reduced it to a puppet state. Great Britain and France occupied parts of Turkey, and Italy and Greece claimed shares as well. There was a sizable Greek minority in western Turkey, and Greek nationalists cherished the "Great Idea" of incorporating this territory into a modern Greek empire modeled on long-dead Christian Byzantium. In 1919 Greek armies carried by British ships landed on the Turkish coast at Smyrna. The sultan ordered his exhausted troops not to resist, and Greek armies advanced into the interior. Turkey seemed finished.

But Turkey produced a great leader and revived to become an inspiration to the entire Middle East. Mustafa Kemal (1881–1938), the father of modern Turkey, was a military man. The son of a petty government official and sympathetic to the Young Turk movement, Kemal had distinguished himself in the Great War by directing the successful defense of the Dardanelles against British attack. After the armistice, Mustafa Kemal watched with anguish the Allies' aggression and the sultan's cowardice. In early 1919 he moved from Constantinople to central Turkey and began working to unify the Turkish resistance.

The sultan, bowing to Allied pressure, initially denounced Kemal, but the cause of national liberation proved more powerful. The catalyst was the Greek invasion and attempted annexation of much of western Turkey. A young woman who was to play a major role in the Turkish revolution describes feelings she shared with countless others:

*After I learned about the details of the Smyrna occupation by Greek armies, I hardly opened my mouth on any subject except when it concerned the sacred struggle. . . . I suddenly ceased to exist as an individual. I worked, wrote and lived as a unit of that magnificent national madness.*[4]

Refusing to acknowledge the Allied dismemberment of their country, the Turks battled on through 1920 despite staggering defeats. The next year the Greeks, egged on by the British, advanced almost to Ankara, the nationalist stronghold in central Turkey. There Mustafa Kemal's forces took the offensive and won a great victory. The Greeks and their British allies sued for peace. After long negotiations the resulting **Treaty of Lausanne** (1923) solemnly abolished the hated Capitulations, which the European powers had imposed in the nineteenth century to give their citizens special privileges in the Ottoman Empire, and recognized the territorial integrity of a truly independent Turkey. Turkey lost only its former Arab provinces.

**Mustafa Kemal** The father of modern Turkey explains his radical reform of the written Turkish language. Impeccably elegant European dress symbolizes Kemal's conception of a modernized Turkey. *(Stock Montage)*

Mustafa Kemal, a nationalist without religious faith, believed that Turkey should modernize and secularize along Western lines. His first moves were political. Drawing on his prestige as a war hero, Kemal called on the somewhat reluctant National Assembly to depose the sultan and establish a republic. He had himself elected president and moved the capital from cosmopolitan Constantinople (soon to be renamed Istanbul) to Ankara in the Turkish heartland. Kemal savagely crushed the demands for independence of ethnic minorities like the Armenians and the Kurds, but he realistically abandoned all thought of winning back lost Arab territories. He focused instead on internal affairs, creating a one-party system—partly inspired by the Bolshevik example—in order to work his will.

## THE MIDDLE EAST, 1914–1939

| | |
|---|---|
| 1914 | Ottoman Empire enters First World War on Germany's side. |
| 1916 | Allies agree secretly to partition Ottoman Empire. |
| 1916–1917 | Arab revolt against Turkish rule grows. |
| November 1917 | Balfour Declaration pledges British support for a Jewish homeland in Palestine. |
| October 1918 | Arabs and British triumph as Ottoman Empire collapses. |
| 1919 | Treaty of Versailles divides old Ottoman Empire into League of Nations mandates. |
| 1919 | Mustafa Kemal mounts nationalist struggle against foreign occupation of Turkey. |
| 1920 | Faisal proclaimed king of Syria but quickly deposed by the French, who establish their mandate in Syria. |
| early 1920s | Tide of Jewish immigration surges into British mandate of Palestine. |
| 1923 | Treaty of Lausanne recognizes independent Turkey.<br>Mustafa Kemal begins to secularize Turkish society. |
| 1925 | Reza Shah Pahlavi takes power in Iran and rules until 1941. |
| 1932 | Iraq gains independence in return for military alliance with Great Britain. |
| 1936 | Syrian nationalists sign treaty with France in return for promises of independence. |
| late 1930s | Tensions mount between Arabs and Jews in Palestine. |

The most radical of Kemal's changes pertained to religion and culture. For centuries most of the intellectual and social activities of believers had been regulated by Islamic religious authorities. Profoundly influenced by the example of western Europe, Mustafa Kemal set out, like the philosophes of the Enlightenment, to limit the place of religion and religious leaders in daily affairs. Like Russia's Peter the Great, he employed dictatorial measures rather than reason to reach his goal. Kemal and his followers simply decreed a revolutionary separation of church and state. Religious courts were abolished, replaced by secular law codes that were inspired by European models. Religious schools gave way to state schools that taught such secular subjects as science, mathematics, and social sciences.

To dramatize the break with the past, Mustafa Kemal struck down many entrenched patterns of behavior. Women, traditionally secluded and inferior to males in Islamic society, received the right to vote. Marriage was now governed by civil law on a European model, rather than by the Islamic code. Women were allowed to seek divorces, and no man could have more than one wife at a time. Men were forbidden to wear the tall red fez of the Ottoman era as headgear; government employees were ordered to wear business suits and felt hats, erasing the visible differences between Muslims and "infidel" Europeans. The old Arabic script was replaced with a new Turkish alphabet based on Roman letters, which moved the written language closer to the spoken vernacular and facilitated massive government efforts to spread literacy after 1928. Finally, in 1935, family names on the European model were introduced. The National Assembly granted Mustafa Kemal the surname **Atatürk,** which means "father of the Turks."

By the time of his death in 1938, Atatürk and his supporters had consolidated their revolution. Government-sponsored industrialization was fostering urban growth and new attitudes, encouraging Turks to embrace business and science. Poverty persisted in rural areas, as did some religious discontent among devout Muslims. But like the Japanese after the Meiji Restoration, the Turkish people had rallied around the nationalist banner to repulse European imperialism and were building a modern secular nation-state.

## Iran and Afghanistan

In Persia (renamed Iran in 1935), strong-arm efforts to build a unified modern nation ultimately proved less successful than in Turkey.

In the late nineteenth century Iran was also subject to extreme foreign pressure, which stimulated efforts to reform the government as a means of reviving Islamic civilization. In 1906 a nationalistic coalition of merchants, religious leaders, and intellectuals revolted. The despotic shah was forced to grant a constitution and establish a national assembly, the **Majlis.** Nationalist hopes ran high.

Yet the Iranian revolution of 1906 was doomed to failure, largely because of European imperialism. Without consulting Iran, Britain and Russia in 1907 simply divided the country into spheres of influence. Britain's sphere ran along the Persian Gulf; the Russian sphere encompassed the whole northern half of Iran (see Map 30.1). Thereafter Russia intervened constantly. It blocked reforms, occupied cities, and completely dominated the country by 1912. When Russian power temporarily collapsed in the Bolshevik Revolution, British armies rushed into the power vacuum. By bribing corrupt Iranians liberally, Great Britain in 1919 negotiated a treaty allowing the installation of British "advisers" in every department of the government.

The Majlis refused to ratify the treaty, and the blatant attempt to make Iran a British satellite aroused the national spirit. In 1921 reaction against the British brought to power a military dictator, Reza Shah Pahlavi (1877–1944), who proclaimed himself shah in 1925 and ruled until 1941.

Inspired throughout his reign by the example of Turkey's Mustafa Kemal, the patriotic, religiously indifferent Reza Shah had three basic goals: to build a modern nation, to free Iran from foreign domination, and to rule with an iron fist. The challenge was enormous. Iran was a vast, backward country of deserts, mountain barriers, and rudimentary communications. Most of the rural population was poor and illiterate, and among the Persian majority were sizable ethnic minorities with their own aspirations. Furthermore, Iran's powerful religious leaders hated Western (Christian) domination but were no less opposed to a more secular, less Islamic society.

To realize his vision of a strong Iran, the energetic shah created a modern army, built railroads, and encouraged commerce and industry. He won control over ethnic minorities such as the Kurds in the north and Arab tribesmen on the border with Iraq. He withdrew many of the privileges granted to foreigners and raised taxes on the powerful Anglo-Persian Oil Company, which had been founded in 1909 to exploit the first great oil strike in the Middle East. Yet Reza Shah was less successful than Atatürk.

Because the European-educated elite in Iran was smaller than the comparable group in Turkey, the idea of recreating Persian greatness on the basis of a secularized society attracted relatively few determined supporters. Many powerful religious leaders turned against Reza Shah, and he became increasingly brutal, greedy, and tyrannical, murdering his enemies and lining his pockets. His support of Hitler's Nazi Germany also exposed Iran's tenuous and fragile independence to the impact of European conflicts.

Afghanistan, meanwhile, was nominally independent in the nineteenth century, but the British imposed political restrictions and constantly meddled in the country's affairs. In 1919 the new, violently anti-British amir Amanullah (1892–1960) declared a holy war on the British government in India and won complete independence for the first time. Amanullah then decreed revolutionary reforms designed to hurl his primitive country into the twentieth century. The result was tribal and religious revolt, civil war, and retreat from reform. Islam remained both religion and law. A powerful but primitive patriotism had enabled Afghanistan to win political independence from the West, but modest efforts to build a modern society met with little success.

## The Arab States and Palestine

The establishment of French and British mandates at gunpoint forced Arab nationalists to seek independence by gradual means after 1920. Arab nationalists were indirectly aided by Western taxpayers, who wanted cheap—that is, peaceful—empires. As a result, Arabs won considerable control over local affairs in the mandated states, except Palestine, though the mandates remained European satellites in international and economic affairs.

The wily British chose Faisal, whom the French had so recently deposed in Syria, as king of Iraq. Faisal obligingly signed an alliance giving British advisers broad behind-the-scenes control. The king also accepted British ownership of Iraq's oil fields, consequently giving the West a stranglehold on the Iraqi economy. Given the severe limitations imposed on him, Faisal (r. 1921–1933) proved to be an able ruler, gaining the support of his people and encouraging moderate reforms. In 1932 he secured Iraqi independence at the price of a restrictive long-term military alliance with Great Britain.

Egypt, occupied by Great Britain ever since 1882 (see page 843) and a British protectorate since 1914, pursued a similar path. Following intense nationalist agitation after the Great War, Great Britain in 1922 proclaimed Egypt formally independent but continued to occupy the country militarily and control its politics. In 1936, the British agreed to a treaty restricting their troops to their big bases in the Suez Canal Zone.

The French were less compromising in Syria. They practiced a policy of divide-and-rule, carving out a second mandate in Lebanon and generally playing off ethnic and religious minorities against each other. Lebanon eventually became a republic, dominated by a very slender Christian majority and under French protection. Arab nationalists in Syria finally won promises of Syrian independence in 1936 in return for a treaty of friendship with France.

In short, the Arab states gradually freed themselves from Western political mandates but not from the Western military threat or from pervasive Western influence. Of great importance, large Arab landowners and urban merchants increased their wealth and political power after 1918, and they often supported the Western hegemony, from which they benefited greatly. Western control of the newly discovered oil fields in Arab lands helped to convince radical nationalists that economic independence and genuine freedom had not yet been achieved.

Relations between the Arabs and the West were complicated by the tense situation in the British mandate of Palestine, and that situation deteriorated in the interwar years. Both Arabs and Jews denounced the British, who tried unsuccessfully to compromise with both sides. The anger of Arab nationalists, however, was aimed primarily at Jewish settlers. The key issue was Jewish migration from Europe to Palestine.

A small Jewish community had survived in Palestine ever since the destruction of Jerusalem and the dispersal of the Jews in Roman times. But Jewish nationalism, known as **Zionism,** took shape in Europe in the late nineteenth century under the leadership of Theodore Herzl (see pages 816–817). Herzl believed that only the re-creation of a Jewish state could guarantee Jews dignity and security. The Zionist movement encouraged Jews from all over the world to settle in the Palestine region, but until 1921 the great majority of Jewish emigrants preferred the United States.

After 1921 the situation changed radically. An isolationist United States drastically limited immigration from eastern Europe, where war and revolution had kindled anti-Semitism. Moreover, the British began honoring the Balfour Declaration despite Arab protests. Thus the number of Jewish immigrants to Palestine from turbulent Europe grew rapidly. In the 1930s German and Polish persecution created a mass of Jewish refugees. By 1939 the Jewish population of Palestine had increased almost fivefold since 1914 and accounted for about 30 percent of all inhabitants.

Jewish settlers in Palestine faced formidable difficulties. Much of the land purchased by the Jewish National Fund was productive. But many of the sellers of such land were wealthy absentee Arab landowners who had little interest in the welfare of their Arab tenants. When the new Jewish owners subsequently replaced those age-old Arab tenants with Jewish settlers, Arab farmers and intellectuals burned with a sense of injustice. Moreover, most Jewish immigrants came from urban backgrounds and preferred to establish new cities like Tel Aviv or to live in existing towns, where they competed with the Arabs. The land issue combined with economic and cultural friction to harden Arab protest into hatred. Anti-Jewish riots and even massacres ensued.

The British gradually responded to Arab pressure and tried to slow Jewish immigration. This effort satisfied neither Jews nor Arabs, and by 1938 the two communities were engaged in an undeclared civil war. On the eve of the Second World War, the frustrated British proposed an independent Palestine in which the number of Jews would be permanently limited to only about one-third of the total population. Zionists felt themselves in grave danger.

In the face of adversity Jewish settlers from many different countries gradually succeeded in forging a cohesive community. Hebrew, which for centuries had been used only in religious worship, was revived as a living language to bind the Jews in Palestine together. Despite its slow beginnings, rural development achieved often remarkable results. The key unit of agricultural organization was the **kibbutz,** a collective farm on which each member shared equally in the work, rewards, and defense of the farm. Men and women labored side by side, a nursery cared for the children, and a common dining hall served meals. An egalitarian socialist ideology also characterized industry, which grew rapidly and was owned largely by the Jewish trade unions. By 1939 a new but old nation was emerging in the Middle East.

**Reuven Rubin: First Fruits (or First Pioneers) (1923)** Whereas Jerusalem was the center of Jewish religious culture and conservative art in the 1920s, the new coastal city of Tel Aviv sprang up secular, and it gloried in avant-garde modern art (see pages 1006–1008). In this painting Rubin, a leader of Tel Aviv's modernist school, depicts Jewish pioneers in a stark, two-dimensional landscape and conveys an exotic "Garden of Eden" flavor. Arriving from Romania, Rubin was bowled over by Palestine. "The world about me became clear and pure: life was formless, blurred, primitive." *(Reuven Rubin,* First Fruits, *1922, Coll. Rubin Museum, Tel-Aviv, Israel)*

## TOWARD SELF-RULE IN INDIA

The national movement in British India grew out of two interconnected cultures, Hindu and Muslim, which came to see themselves as fundamentally different in rising to challenge British rule. Nowhere has the power of modern nationalism, both to unify and to divide, been more strikingly demonstrated than in India.

### Promises and Repression (1914–1919)

Indian nationalism had emerged in the late nineteenth century (see page 865), and when the First World War began, the British feared revolt. Instead, somewhat like Europe's equally mistrusted socialist workers, Indians supported the war effort. About 1.2 million Indian soldiers and laborers volunteered for duty and served in Europe, Africa, and the Middle East. The British government in India and the native Indian princes sent large supplies of food, money, and ammunition. In return, the British opened more good government jobs to Indians and made other minor concessions.

As the war in distant Europe ground on, however, inflation, high taxes, food shortages, and a terrible influenza epidemic created widespread suffering and discontent. The prewar nationalist movement revived, stronger than ever, and the moderate and radical wings of the Indian National Congress joined forces. Moreover, in 1916 the Hindus leading the Congress party hammered out an alliance—the **Lucknow Pact**—with India's Muslim League. Founded in 1906 to uphold Muslim interests, the league had grown out of fears arising from the fact that under British rule the once-dominant Muslim minority had fallen behind the Hindu majority, especially in the Western education necessary to secure good jobs in the government. The Lucknow Pact forged a powerful united front of Hindus and Muslims and called for putting India on equal footing with self-governing white British dominions like Canada, Australia, and New Zealand.

The British response was contradictory. On the one hand, the secretary of state for India made the unprecedented announcement in August 1917 that British policy in India called for the "gradual development of self-governing institutions and the progressive realization of responsible government." The means of achieving this great step forward were spelled out in late 1919 in the **Government of India Act,** which established a dual administration: part Indian and elected, part British and authoritarian. Such noncontroversial activities as agriculture, health, and education were transferred from British to Indian officials who were accountable to elected provincial assemblies. More sensitive matters like taxes, police, and the courts remained solely in British hands.

The positive impact of this reform, so typical of the British tradition of gradual political change, was seriously undermined by old-fashioned authoritarian rule. Despite the unanimous opposition of the elected Indian members, the British in 1919 rammed the repressive Rowlatt Acts through India's Imperial Legislative Council. These acts indefinitely extended wartime "emergency measures" designed to curb unrest and root out "conspiracy." The result was a wave of rioting across India.

Under these tense conditions an unsuspecting crowd of some ten thousand gathered to celebrate a Hindu religious festival in an enclosed square in Amritsar, a city in the northern province of Punjab. Without the knowledge of the crowd, the local English commander, General Reginald Dyer, had banned all public meetings that very day. Dyer marched his native Gurkha troops onto the field and, without warning, ordered them to fire into the unarmed mass at point-blank range until the ammunition ran out. The Amritsar Massacre, killing 379 and wounding 1,137, shattered wartime hopes in a frenzy of postwar reaction. India seemed to stand on the verge of more violence and repression and, sooner or later, terrorism and guerrilla war. That India took a different path to national liberation was due largely to Mohandas "Mahatma" Gandhi (1869–1948), who became the most fascinating and influential Indian of modern times.

## The Roots of Militant Nonviolence

By the time of Gandhi's birth in 1869, the Indian subcontinent was firmly controlled by the British. Part of the country was ruled directly by British (and subordinate Indian) officials, answerable to the British Parliament in London. In each of the so-called protected states, the native prince—usually known as the *maharaja*—remained the titular ruler, although he was bound to the British by unequal treaties and had to accept the "advice" of the British resident assigned to his court.

Gandhi grew up in one of the small protected states north of Bombay, where his father served as hereditary prime minister. Gandhi's father was the well-to-do head

**British Repression** After the Amritsar Massacre of 1919, British repression in northern India was harsh and sadistic. Assisted by obedient native policemen wielding heavy clubs, these British officers are inflicting the kind of pain and humiliation that would soon fuel Gandhi's nationalist movement. *(J. C. Allen)*

of a large extended family, which included five brothers and their wives, children, and children's children. The big three-story ancestral home swarmed with relatives. In such a communal atmosphere, patience, kindness, and a good-natured love of people were essential virtues. Gandhi's mother was very devoted but undogmatic in religious matters, and she exercised a strong influence on her precocious son.

After his father's death, Gandhi decided to study law in England. To win over his wife and anxious mother, who feared he would abandon Hindu practices, Gandhi swore that he would not touch meat, women, or wine in the foreign land. He kept his word. After passing the English bar and returning to India, Gandhi decided in 1893 to try his luck as a lawyer for wealthy Indian merchants in South Africa. It was a momentous decision.

As Gandhi's law practice flourished, he began to examine the plight of the Indian community in South Africa. Plantation owners there imported desperately poor Indians as indentured laborers on five-year renewable contracts. When some Indians completed their terms and remained in South Africa as free persons and economic competitors, the Dutch and British settlers passed brutally discriminatory laws. Poor Indians had to work on white-owned plantations or return to India; rich Indians lost the vote. Gandhi undertook the legal defense of his countrymen, infuriating the whites. In 1896 a mob almost lynched the "coolie lawyer."

Meanwhile, Gandhi was searching for a spiritual theory of social action. Identifying with South Africa's black majority as well as with his own countrymen, he meditated on the Hindu pursuit of spiritual strength through fasting, sexual abstinence, devotion to duty, and reincarnation. He also studied Christian teachings. Gradually Gandhi developed and articulated a weapon for the weak that he called **Satyagraha.** Gandhi conceived of Satyagraha, loosely translated as "Soul Force," as a means of striving for truth and social justice through love, suffering, and conversion of the oppressor. Its tactic is courageous nonviolent resistance.

As the undisputed leader of South Africa's Indians before the First World War, Gandhi put his philosophy into action. When the white government of South Africa severely restricted Asians' immigration and internal freedom of movement, he led a campaign of mass resistance. Thousands of Indian men and women marched across forbidden borders and peacefully withstood beatings, arrest, and imprisonment.

In 1914, South Africa's exasperated whites agreed to many of the Indians' demands. A law was passed abolishing discriminatory taxes on Indian traders, recognizing the legality of non-Christian marriages, and permitting the continued immigration of free Indians. Satyagraha—militant nonviolence in pursuit of social justice—had proved itself a powerful force in Gandhi's hands.

## Gandhi Leads the Way

In 1915 Gandhi returned to India. His reputation had preceded him: the masses hailed him as a *Mahatma,* or "Great Soul"—a Hindu title of veneration for a man of great knowledge and humanity. Feeling his way into Indian affairs, Gandhi, dressed in peasant garb, crisscrossed India on third-class trains, listening to common folk and talking to Congress party leaders in the aftermath of the Amritsar Massacre.

Drawing on his South African experience, Gandhi in 1920 launched a national campaign of nonviolent resistance to British rule. Denouncing British injustice, he urged his countrymen to boycott British goods, jobs, and honors. He told peasants not to pay taxes or buy heavily taxed liquor. Gandhi electrified the people. The result was nothing less than a revolution in Indian politics.

The nationalist movement had previously touched only the tiny, prosperous, Western-educated elite. Now both the illiterate masses of village India and the educated classes heard a voice that seemed to be in harmony with their profoundest values. Gandhi's call for militant nonviolence was particularly appealing to the masses of Hindus who were not members of the warrior caste or the so-called military races and who were traditionally passive and nonviolent. The British had regarded ordinary Hindus as cowards. Gandhi told them that they could be courageous and even morally superior:

> *What do you think? Wherein is courage required—in blowing others to pieces from behind a cannon, or with a smiling face to approach a cannon and be blown to pieces? Who is the true warrior—he who keeps death always as a bosom-friend, or he who controls the death of others? Believe me that a man devoid of courage and manhood can never be a passive resister.*[5]

Gandhi made Congress into a mass political party, welcoming members from every ethnic group and cooperating closely with the Muslim minority.

In 1922 some Indian resisters turned to violence. A mob murdered twenty-two policemen, and savage riots broke out. Gandhi abruptly called off his campaign. Arrested for fomenting rebellion, Gandhi told the British judge that he had committed "a Himalayan blunder to believe that India had accepted nonviolence."[6] Released from prison after two years, Gandhi set up a commune,

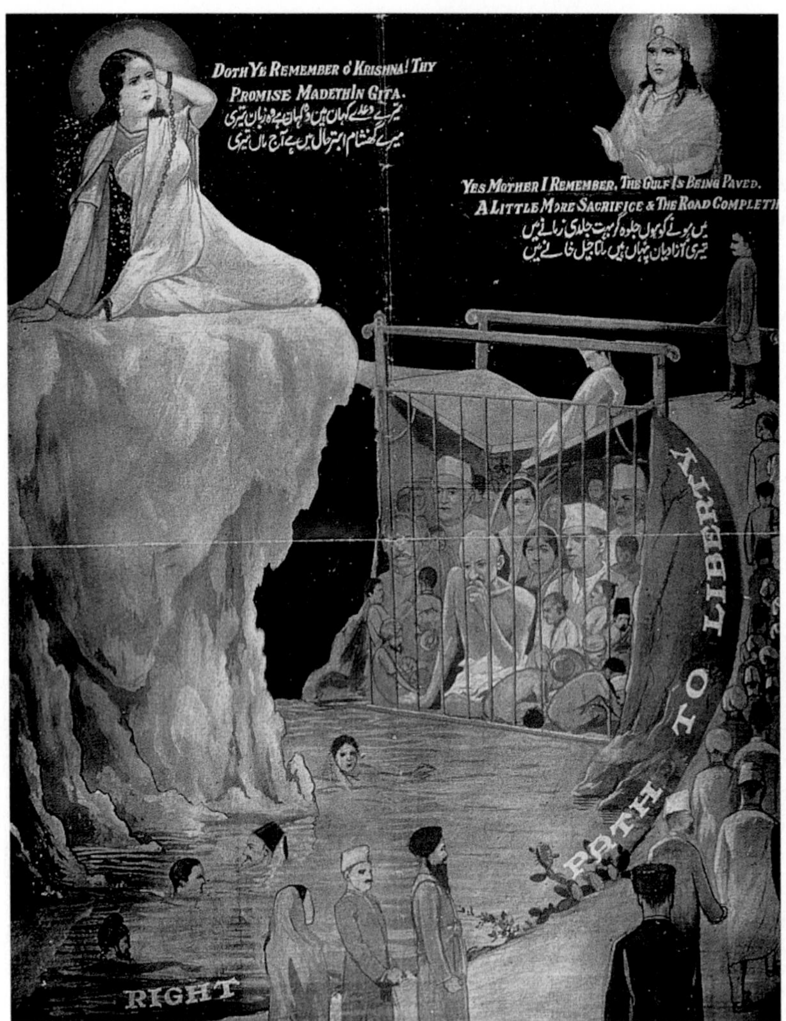


**"The Right Path to Liberty"** This Indian National Congress poster draws upon Indian culture to build support for nationalism. All Indian communities are marching toward freedom, but Gandhi, Nehru, and others are in prison and a bridge has collapsed. Yet the Hindu deity Krishna reassures anxious Mother India: with a little more sacrifice the journey will be complete. *(British Library)*

established a national newspaper, and set out to reform Indian society and improve the lot of the poor. He welcomed the outcaste untouchables, worked to help child widows, and promoted native cottage industry producers. For Gandhi moral improvement, social progress, and the national movement went hand in hand.

The resistance campaign of 1920–1922 left the British severely shaken, but the commission formed in 1927 to consider further steps toward self-rule included no Indian members. Indian resentment was intense. In 1929 the radical nationalists, led by the able and aristocratic Jawaharlal Nehru (1889–1964), pushed through the National Congress a resolution calling for virtual independence within a year. The British stiffened, and Indian radicals talked of a bloody showdown.

In this tense situation Gandhi masterfully reasserted his leadership. He took a hard line toward the British, but he insisted on nonviolent methods. He organized a massive resistance campaign against the hated salt tax, which affected every Indian family. Gandhi himself led fifty thousand people in a spectacular march to the sea to make salt without paying a tax, in defiance of the law. Gandhi was arrested, but his followers continued the march to the sea. Demonstrating peacefully at the salt pans, they were beaten senseless by policemen in a brutal and well-publicized encounter. The marchers did not even raise their arms to protect themselves.

Over the next few months sixty thousand protesters followed Gandhi to jail. But this time there was very little rioting. In 1931 the frustrated and unnerved British released Gandhi from jail and sat down to negotiate with him, as an equal, over self-rule for India. Finally, in 1935 the negotiations resulted in a new constitution, which greatly strengthened India's parliamentary repre-

**Gandhi Arrives in Delhi, October 1939** A small frail man, Gandhi possessed enormous courage and determination. His campaign of nonviolent resistance to British rule inspired the Indian masses and mobilized a nation. Here he arrives for talks with the British viceroy after the outbreak of World War II. *(Corbis)*

sentative institutions. It was virtually a blueprint for independence, which would come quickly after World War II.

Gandhi inspired people far beyond India's borders. Martin Luther King, Jr., was later to be deeply influenced by his tactics and philosophy of nonviolent social action. Gandhi did much to transform the elitist nationalism of Indian intellectuals into a mighty mass movement with social as well as political concerns. Above all, Gandhi nurtured national identity and self-respect. As Nehru summed it up, Gandhi "instilled courage and manhood in India's people; . . . courage is the one sure foundation of character, he had said; without courage there is no morality, no religion, no love."[7]

Despite his best efforts, Gandhi failed to heal a widening split between Hindus and Muslims. The development of an Indian nationalism based largely on Hindu symbols and customs increasingly disturbed the Muslim minority. Tempers mounted, and atrocities were committed by both sides. By the late 1930s the leaders of the Muslim League were calling for the creation of a Muslim nation in British India, a "Pakistan" or "land of the pure." As in Palestine, the rise of conflicting nationalisms in India would lead to tragedy (see pages 1108–1109).

## TURMOIL IN EAST ASIA

Because of the efforts of the Meiji reformers, nationalism and modernization were well developed in Japan by 1914. Not only was Japan capable of competing politically and economically with the world's leading nations, but it had already begun building its own empire and proclaiming its special mission in Asia. China lagged far behind, but after 1912 the pace of nationalist development there began to quicken.

In the 1920s the Chinese nationalist movement managed to win a large measure of political independence from the imperialist West and promoted extensive modernization. But these achievements were soon undermined by internal conflict and war with an expanding Japan. Nationalism also flourished elsewhere in Asia, scoring a major victory in the Philippine Islands.

### The Rise of Nationalist China

The revolution of 1911–1912, which overthrew the Qing Dynasty (see page 874), opened an era of unprecedented change for Chinese society. Before the revolution many progressive Chinese had realized that fundamental technological and political reforms were necessary to save the Chinese state and to meet the many-sided Western challenge. Most had hoped, however, to preserve the traditional core of Chinese civilization and culture. The fall of the two-thousand-year-old dynastic system shattered such hopes. If the emperor himself was no longer sacred, what was? Everything was open to question and to alteration.

The central figure in the revolution was a crafty old military man, Yuan Shigai (Yüan Shih-k'ai). Called out of retirement to save the dynasty, Yuan (1859–1916) betrayed the Manchus and convinced the revolutionaries that he was a strong man who could unite the country peacefully and prevent foreign intervention. Once elected president of the republic, however, Yuan concentrated on building his own power. In 1913 he used military force to dissolve China's parliament and ruled as a dictator. China's first modern revolution had failed.

The extent of the failure became apparent only after Yuan's death in 1916. The central government in Beijing (Peking) almost disintegrated. For more than a decade power resided in a multitude of local military leaders, the so-called warlords. Most warlords were men of strong, flamboyant personality, capable of building armies by preying on the peasantry and of winning Beijing's recognition of them as local governors. Their wars, taxes, and corruption created only terrible suffering.

Foreign imperialism intensified the agony of warlordism. Although China declared its neutrality in 1914, Japan used the Great War in Europe as an opportunity to seize Germany's holdings on the Shandong (Shantung) Peninsula and in 1915 forced China to accept Japanese control of Shandong and southern Manchuria (see Map 30.2). Japan's expansion angered China's growing middle class and enraged China's young patriots. On May 4, 1919, five thousand students in Beijing exploded against the decision of the Versailles Peace Conference to leave the Shandong Peninsula in Japanese hands. This famous incident launched the **May Fourth Movement,** which opposed both foreign domination and warlord government.

The May Fourth Movement and the anti-imperialism of Bolshevik Russia renewed the hopes of Chinese nationalists. Struggling for a foothold in southern China, Sun Yatsen (1866–1925) decided in 1923 to ally his Nationalist party, or Guomindang (Kuomintang), with the Communist Third International and the newly formed Chinese Communist party. The result was the first of many so-called national liberation fronts, in keeping with Lenin's blueprint for (temporarily) uniting all anticonservative, anti-imperialist forces in a common revolutionary struggle. In an effort to develop a disciplined party apparatus and a well-indoctrinated party army, Sun reorganized the Nationalist party along Bolshevik lines.

Sun, however, was no Communist. In his *Three Principles of the People,* elaborating on the official Nationalist party ideology—nationalism, democracy, and people's livelihood—nationalism remained of prime importance:

> *Compared to the other peoples of the world we have the greatest population and our civilization is four thousand years old; we should be advancing in the front rank with the nations of Europe and America. But the Chinese people have only family and clan solidarity, they do not have national spirit. Therefore even though we have four hundred million people gathered together in one China, in reality they are just a heap of loose sand. Today we are the poorest and weakest nation in the world, and occupy the lowest position in international affairs. . . . If we do not earnestly espouse nationalism and weld together our four hundred million people into a strong nation, there is a danger of China's being lost and our people being destroyed. If we wish to avert this catastrophe, we must espouse nationalism and bring this national spirit to the salvation of the country.*[8]

Democracy, in contrast, had a less exalted meaning. Sun equated it with firm rule by the Nationalists, who would promote the people's livelihood through land reform and welfare measures. Sun was in some ways a traditional

**Students Demonstrating in Tiananmen Square, Beijing, Summer 1919** The news that the Versailles Peace Conference left China's Shandong Peninsula in Japanese hands brought an explosion of student protest on May 4, 1919. Student demonstrations in the capital's historic Tiananmen Square continued through June, as the May Fourth Movement against foreign domination took root and grew. *(YMCA Archives of the USA and the Kautz Family YMCA Archives, University of Minnesota Libraries)*

Chinese rebel and reformer who wanted to re-establish order and protect the peasants.

Sun's plan was to use the Nationalist party's revolutionary army to crush the warlords and reunite China under a strong central government. When Sun unexpectedly died in 1925, this task was assumed by Jiang Jieshi (Chiang Kai-shek), the young Japanese-educated director of the party's army training school. In 1926 and 1927 Jiang (1887–1975) led enthusiastic Nationalist armies in a highly successful attack on warlord governments in central and northern China. Preceded by teams of party propagandists, the well-disciplined Nationalist armies were welcomed by the people. In a series of complicated moves, the Nationalists consolidated their rule in 1928 and established a new capital at Nanjing (Nanking). Foreign states recognized the Nanjing government, and superficial observers believed China to be truly reunified.

In fact, national unification was only skin-deep. China remained a vast agricultural country plagued by foreign concessions, regional differences, and a lack of modern communications. Moreover, the uneasy alliance between the Nationalist party and the Chinese Communist party had turned into a bitter, deadly rivalry. Justifiably fearful of Communist subversion of the Nationalist government and encouraged by his military success and by wealthy Chinese capitalists, Jiang decided in April 1927 to liquidate his left-wing "allies" in a bloody purge. Secret agents raided Communist cells without warning, and soldiers gunned down suspects on sight. Chinese Communists went into hiding and vowed revenge.

**EAST ASIA, 1911–1939**

| | |
|---|---|
| 1911–1912 | Revolution in China overthrows Manchu (Qing) Dynasty and establishes republic. |
| 1915 | Japan seizes German holdings in China and expands into southern Manchuria. |
| May 4, 1919 | Demonstration by Chinese students against Versailles Peace Conference and Japan sparks broad nationalist movement. |
| 1920s | New Culture Movement challenges traditional Chinese values. |
| 1922 | Japan signs naval agreement with Western powers. |
| 1923 | Sun Yatsen allies the Nationalist party with Chinese Communists.<br>Kita Ikki advocates ultranationalism in Japan. |
| 1925–1928 | Jiang Jieshi, leader of the Nationalist party, attacks warlord government and seeks to unify China. |
| 1927 | Jiang Jieshi purges his Communist allies.<br>Mao Zedong recognizes the revolutionary potential of the Chinese peasantry. |
| 1930–1934 | Nationalists campaign continually against the Chinese Communists. |
| 1931 | Mukden incident leads to Japanese occupation of Manchuria. |
| 1932 | Japan proclaims Manchuria an independent state. |
| 1934 | Mao leads Communists on Long March to new base in northwestern China.<br>The Philippines gain self-governing commonwealth status from United States. |
| 1936 | Japan allies with Germany in anticommunist pact. |
| 1937 | Japanese militarists launch general attack on China. |

## China's Intellectual Revolution

Nationalism was the most powerful idea in China between 1911 and 1929, but it was only one aspect of a complex intellectual revolution that hammered at traditional Chinese thought and custom, advocated cultural renaissance, and pushed China into the modern world. Two other currents in that intellectual revolution, generally known as the **New Culture Movement,** were significant.

The New Culture Movement was founded by young Western-oriented intellectuals in Beijing during the May Fourth era. These intellectuals fiercely attacked China's ancient Confucian ethics, which subordinated subjects to rulers, sons to fathers, and wives to husbands. In such widely read magazines as *New Youth* and *New Tide,* the modernists provocatively advocated new and anti-Confucian virtues: individualism, democratic equality, and the critical scientific method. They also promoted the use of simple, understandable written language as a means to clear thinking and mass education. China, they said, needed a whole new culture, a radically different world-view.

The most influential of these intellectuals championing liberalism was Hu Shi (1891–1962). Educated on a scholarship in the United States, the mature Hu Shi envisioned a vague and uninspiring future. The liberation and reconstruction of China was possible, he said, but it would have to occur gradually, "bit by bit, drop by drop." Hu personified the limitations of the Western liberal tradition in China.

The other major current growing out of the New Culture Movement was Marxian socialism. It too was Western in origin, "scientific" in approach, and materialist in its denial of religious belief and Confucian family ethics. But while liberalism and individualism reflected the bewildering range of Western thought since the Enlightenment, Marxian socialism offered Chinese intellectuals the certainty of a single all-encompassing creed. As one young Communist exclaimed: "I am now able to impose order on all the ideas which I could not reconcile; I have found the key to all the problems which appeared to me self-contradictory and insoluble."[9]

Marxism was undeniably Western and therefore modern. But it also provided a means of criticizing Western dominance, thereby salving Chinese pride. Chinese Communists could blame China's pitiful weakness on rapacious foreign capitalistic imperialism. Thus Marxism, as modified by Lenin and applied by the Bolsheviks in the Soviet Union, appeared as a means of catching up with the hated but envied West. For Chinese believers, it promised salvation soon.

Chinese Communists could and did interpret Marxism-Leninism to appeal to the masses—the peasants. Mao Zedong (Mao Tse-tung) in particular recognized quickly the enormous revolutionary potential of the impoverished Chinese peasantry. A member of a prosperous, hard-working peasant family, Mao (1893–1976) converted to Marxian socialism in 1918 while employed as an assistant librarian at Beijing University. He began his revolutionary career as an urban labor organizer. In 1925 protest strikes by Chinese textile workers against their Japanese employers unexpectedly spread from the big coastal cities to rural China, prompting Mao to reconsider the peasants. Investigating the rapid growth of radical peasant associations in Hunan province, Mao argued passionately in a 1927 report that

*the force of the peasantry is like that of the raging winds and driving rain. It is rapidly increasing in violence. No force can stand in its way. The peasantry will tear apart all nets which bind it and hasten along the road to liberation. They will bury beneath them all forces of imperialism, militarism, corrupt officialdom, village bosses and evil gentry.*[10]

The task of Communists was to harness the peasant hurricane and use its elemental force to destroy the existing order and take power. Mao's first experiment in peasant revolt—the Autumn Harvest Uprising of September 1927—was no more successful than the abortive insurrections of urban workers launched by his more orthodox comrades. But Mao learned quickly. He advocated equal distribution of land and broke up his forces into small guerrilla groups. After 1928 he and his supporters built up a self-governing Communist soviet, centered at Ruijin (Juichin) in southeastern China, and dug in against Nationalist attacks.

**Mao Zedong** Adapting Marxian theory to Chinese reality, Mao concentrated on the revolutionary potential of the peasantry. Here the forty-year-old Mao is preaching his gospel to representatives of poor peasants in southern China in 1933. *(Wide World Photos)*

China's intellectual revolution stimulated profound changes in popular culture and family life. For many centuries Confucian reverence for the family and family ties had helped to stabilize traditional Chinese society and had given life meaning. The Confucian principle of subordination had suffused family life—subordination of the individual to the group, of the young to the old, of the wife to the husband.

After the revolution of 1911 there was an accelerating trend toward greater freedom and equality for Chinese women. Foot binding was outlawed and attacked in public campaigns as cruel and uncivilized. Arranged marriages and polygamy declined. Marriage for love became increasingly common, and unprecedented educational and economic opportunities gradually opened up for women.

Thus rising nationalism and the intellectual revolution interacted with monumental changes in Chinese family life. (See the feature "Individuals in Society: Ning Lao: A Chinese Working Woman.")

## From Liberalism to Ultranationalism in Japan

The efforts of the Meiji reformers (see page 874) to build a powerful nationalistic state and resist Western imperialism were spectacularly successful and deeply impressive to Japan's fellow Asians. The Japanese, alone among the peoples of Asia, had mastered modern industrial technology by 1910 and fought victorious wars against both China and Russia. The First World War brought more triumphs. Japan easily seized Germany's Asian holdings and held on to most of them as League of Nations mandates. The Japanese economy expanded enormously. Profits soared as Japan won new markets that wartime Europe could no longer supply.

In the early 1920s Japan seemed to make further progress on all fronts. Most Japanese nationalists believed that Japan had a semidivine mission to enlighten and protect Asia, but some were convinced that they could achieve their goal peacefully. In 1922 Japan signed a naval arms limitation treaty with the Western powers and returned some of its control over the Shandong Peninsula to China. These conciliatory moves reduced tensions in East Asia. At home Japan seemed headed toward genuine democracy. The electorate expanded twelvefold between 1918 and 1925 as all males over twenty-five won the vote. Two-party competition was intense, and cabinet ministers were made responsible to the lower house. Japanese living standards were the highest in Asia. Literacy was universal.

**Japanese Suffragists** In the 1920s Japanese women pressed for political emancipation in demonstrations like this one, but they did not receive the right to vote until 1946. Like these suffragists, some young women adopted Western fashions. Most workers in modern Japanese textile factories were also women. *(Mansell/TimePix)*

## INDIVIDUALS IN SOCIETY

# NING LAO: A CHINESE WORKING WOMAN

The voice of the poor and uneducated is often muffled in history. Thus *A Daughter of Han*, a rare autobiography of an illiterate working woman as told to an American friend, offers unforgettable insights into the evolution of ordinary Chinese life and family relations.

Ning Lao was born in 1867 to poor parents in the northern city of Penglai on the Shandong Peninsula. Her foot binding was delayed to age nine, "since I loved so much to run and play." When the bandages were finally drawn tight, "my feet hurt so much that for two years I had to crawl on my knees."* Her arranged marriage at age fourteen was a disaster. She found that her husband was a drug addict ("in those days everyone took opium to some extent") who sold everything to pay for his habit. Yet "there was no freedom then for women," and "it was no light thing for a woman to leave her house" and husband. Thus Ning Lao endured her situation until her husband sold their four-year-old daughter to buy opium. Taking her remaining baby daughter, she fled.

Taking off her foot bandages, Ning Lao became a beggar. Her feet began to spread, quite improperly, but she walked without pain. And the beggar's life was "not the hardest one," she thought, for a beggar woman could go where she pleased. To care better for her child, Ning Lao became a servant and a cook in prosperous households. Some of her mistresses were concubines (secondary wives taken by rich men in middle age), and she concluded that concubinage resulted in nothing but quarrels and heartache. Hot tempered and quick to take offense and leave an employer, the hard-working woman always found a new job quickly. In time she became a peddler of luxury goods to wealthy women confined to their homes.

The two unshakable values that buoyed Ning Lao were a tough, fatalistic acceptance of life—"Only fortune that comes of itself will come. There is no use to seek for it"—and devotion to her family. She eventually returned to her husband, who had mellowed, seldom took opium, and was "good" in those years. "But I did not miss him when he died. I had my newborn son and I was happy. My house was established. . . . Truly all my life I spent thinking of my family." Her lifelong devotion was reciprocated by her son and granddaughter, who cared for her well in her old age.

Ning Lao's remarkable life story encompasses both old and new Chinese attitudes toward family life. Her son moved to the capital city of Beijing, worked in an office, and had only one wife. Her granddaughter, Su Teh, studied in missionary schools and became a college teacher and a determined foe of arranged marriages. She personified the trend toward greater freedom for Chinese women.

*The tough and resilient Ning Lao (right) with Ida Pruitt.*
(From Ida Pruitt, *A Daughter of Han*. Reproduced by permission)

Generational differences also highlighted changing political attitudes. When the Japanese invaded China and occupied Beijing in 1937, Ning Lao thought that "perhaps the Mandate of Heaven had passed to the Japanese . . . and we should listen to them as our new masters." Her nationalistic granddaughter disagreed. She urged resistance and the creation of a new China, where the people governed themselves. Leaving to join the guerrillas in 1938, Su Teh gave her savings to her family and promised to continue to help them. One must be good to one's family, she said, but one must also work for the country.

### QUESTIONS FOR ANALYSIS

1. Compare the lives of Ning Lao and her granddaughter. In what ways were they different and similar?
2. In a broader historical perspective, what do you find most significant about Ning Lao's account of her life? Why?

*Ida Pruitt, *A Daughter of Han: The Autobiography of a Chinese Working Woman* (New Haven, Conn.: Yale University Press, 1945), p. 22. Other quotations are from pages 83, 62, 71, 182, 166, 235, and 246.

Japan's remarkable rise, however, was accompanied by serious problems. Japan had a rapidly growing population, but natural resources were scarce. As early as the 1920s Japan was exporting manufactured goods in order to pay for imports of food and essential raw materials. Deeply enmeshed in world trade, Japan was vulnerable to every boom and bust. These conditions reinforced the widespread belief that colonies and foreign expansion were matters of life and death for Japan.

Also, rapid industrial development had created an imbalanced "dualistic" economy. The modern sector consisted of a handful of giant conglomerate firms, the **zaibatsu**, or "financial combines." A zaibatsu firm like Mitsubishi employed thousands of workers and owned banks, mines, steel mills, cotton factories, shipyards, and trading companies, all of which were closely interrelated. Zaibatsu firms had enormous economic power and dominated the other sector of the economy, which consisted of an unorganized multitude of peasant farmers and craftsmen. The result was financial oligarchy, corruption of government officials, and a weak middle class.

Behind the façade of party politics, the old and new elites—the emperor, high government officials, big businessmen, and military leaders—were jockeying savagely for the real power. Cohesive leadership, which had played such an important role in Japan's modernization by the Meiji reformers, had ceased to exist. By far the most serious challenge to peaceful progress, however, was fanatical nationalism. As in Europe, ultranationalism first emerged in Japan in the late nineteenth century but did not flower fully until the First World War and the 1930s.

Though often vague, Japan's ultranationalists shared several fundamental beliefs. They were violently anti-Western. They rejected democracy, big business, and Marxian socialism, which they blamed for destroying the older, superior Japanese practices that they wanted to restore. Reviving old myths, they stressed the emperor's godlike qualities and the samurai warrior's code of honor and obedience. Despising party politics, they assassinated moderate leaders and plotted armed uprisings to achieve their goals. Above all else, the ultranationalists preached foreign expansion. Like Western imperialists shouldering "the White Man's Burden," Japanese ultranationalists thought their mission was a noble one. "Asia for the Asians" was their self-satisfied rallying cry. As the famous ultranationalist Kita Ikki wrote in 1923, "Our seven hundred million brothers in China and India have no other path to independence than that offered by our guidance and protection."[11]

The ultranationalists were noisy and violent in the 1920s, but it took the Great Depression of the 1930s to tip the scales decisively in their favor. The worldwide depression hit Japan like a tidal wave in 1930. Exports and wages collapsed; unemployment and raw suffering soared. Starving peasants ate the bark off trees and sold their daughters to brothels. The ultranationalists blamed the system, and people listened.

## Japan Against China

Among those who listened with particular care were young Japanese army officers in Manchuria, the underpopulated, resource-rich province of northeastern China, controlled by the Japanese army since its victory over Russia in 1905. Many junior Japanese officers in Manchuria came from the peasantry and were distressed by the stories of rural suffering they heard from home. They also knew that the budget and prestige of the Japanese army had declined in the prosperous 1920s.

Most worrisome of all to the young officers was the rise of Chinese nationalism. This new political force challenged the control that Japan exercised over Manchuria through Chinese warlords that they controlled. In response, junior Japanese officers in Manchuria, in cooperation with top generals in Tokyo, secretly manufactured an excuse for aggression in late 1931. They blew up some tracks on a Japanese-owned railroad near the city of Mukden and then quickly occupied all of Manchuria in "self-defense."

In 1932 Japan proclaimed Manchuria an independent state and installed a member of the old Manchu Dynasty as puppet emperor. When the League of Nations condemned its aggression in Manchuria, Japan resigned in protest. Politics in Japan became increasingly chaotic. The army, though reporting directly to the emperor of Japan, was clearly an independent force subject to no outside control.

For China the Japanese conquest of Manchuria was disastrous. Japanese aggression in Manchuria drew attention away from modernizing efforts. The Nationalist government promoted a massive boycott of Japanese goods but lost interest in social reform. Above all, the Nationalist government after 1931 completely neglected land reform and the grinding poverty of the Chinese peasants. As in many poor agricultural societies throughout history, Chinese peasants paid roughly half of their crops to their landlords as rent. Ownership of land was very unequal. One careful study estimated that fully half of the land was owned by a mere 4 percent of the families, usually absentee landlords living in cities. Poor peasants and farm laborers—70 percent of the rural population—owned only one-sixth of the land.

As a result, peasants were heavily in debt and chronically underfed. Eggs and meat accounted for only 2 percent of the food consumed by poor and middle-income peasants. A contemporary Chinese economist spelled out the revolutionary implications: "It seems clear that the land problem in China today is as acute as that of eighteenth-century France or nineteenth-century Russia."[12] Mao Zedong certainly agreed.

Having abandoned land reform, partly because they themselves were often landowners, the Nationalists under Jiang Jieshi devoted their energies between 1930 and 1934 to five great campaigns of encirclement and extermination against the Communists' rural power base in southeastern China. In 1934 they closed in for the kill, only to miss again. In one of the most incredible sagas of modern times, the main Communist army broke out of the Nationalist encirclement, beat off attacks, and retreated 6,000 miles in twelve months to a remote region on the northwestern border (see Map 30.2). Of the estimated 100,000 men and women who began the **Long March,** only 8,000 to 10,000 reached the final destination. There Mao built up his forces once again, established a new territorial base, and won the support of local peasants by undertaking land reform.

In 1937 the Japanese military and the ultranationalists were in command and decided to use a minor incident near Beijing as a pretext for a general attack. The Nationalist government, which had just formed a united front with the Communists in response to the demands of Chinese patriots, fought hard but could not halt the Japanese. By late 1938 Japanese armies occupied sizable portions of coastal China (see Map 30.2). But the Nationalists and

**Japanese Soldiers Celebrating Victory** Shanghai, China's leading port, fell to the invading Japanese in November 1937. These jubilant infantry troops have successfully stormed the city's North Station. In China, the Japanese won the battles but they could not win the war. *(Ullstein Bilderdienst)*

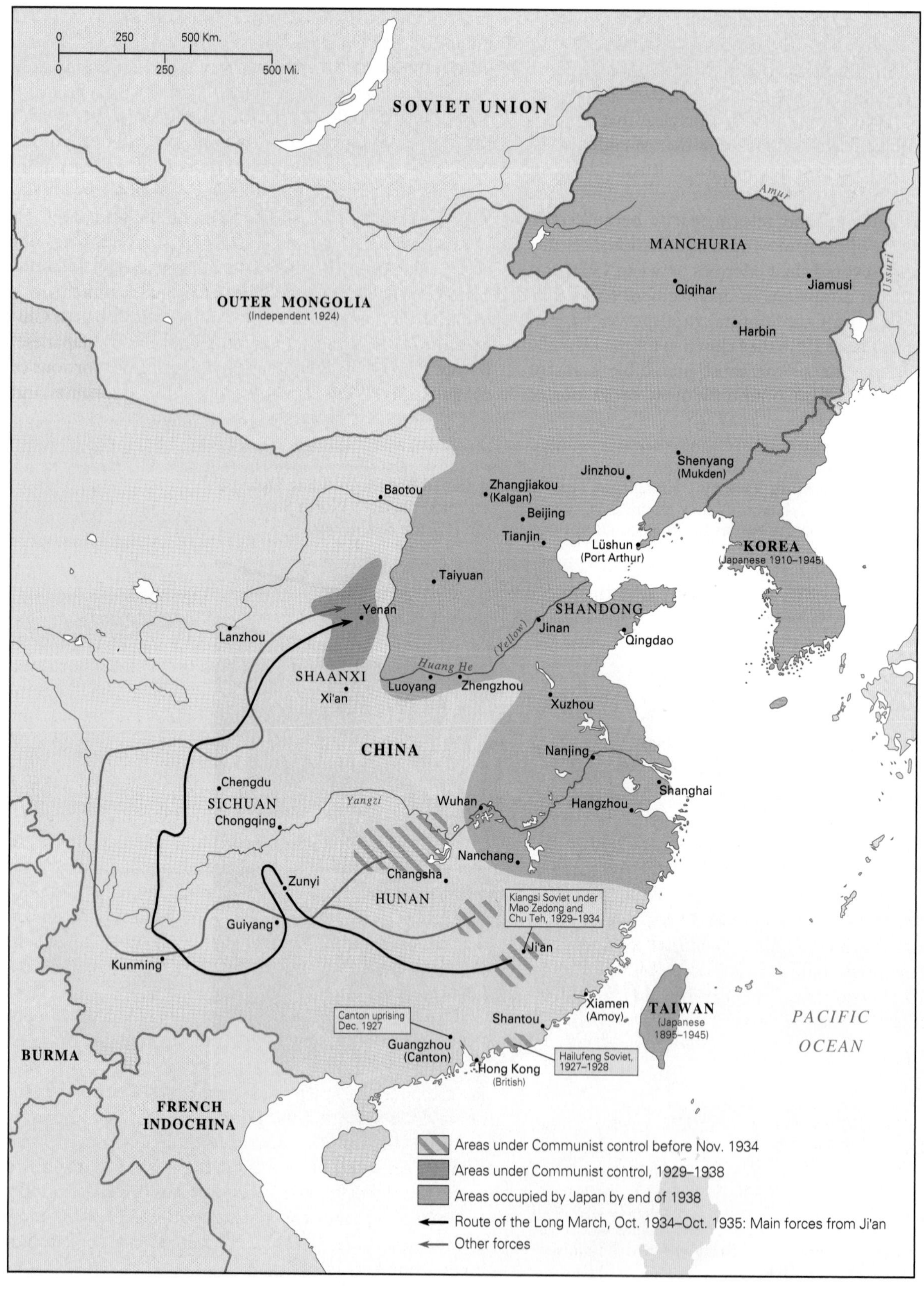
0
250
500 Km.
0
250
500 Mi.
SOVIET UNION
Amur
Ussuri
MANCHURIA
Qiqihar
Jiamusi
Harbin
OUTER MONGOLIA
(Independent 1924)
Shenyang
(Mukden)
Jinzhou
Zhangjiakou
(Kalgan)
Baotou
Beijing
Tianjin
Lüshun
(Port Arthur)
KOREA
(Japanese 1910–1945)
Taiyuan
Yenan
SHANDONG
Jinan
Qingdao
Lanzhou
(Yellow)
Huang He
SHAANXI
Xi'an
Luoyang
Zhengzhou
Xuzhou
CHINA
Nanjing
Shanghai
Chengdu
SICHUAN
Chongqing
Yangzi
Wuhan
Hangzhou
Nanchang
Changsha
Zunyi
HUNAN
Kiangsi Soviet under Mao Zedong and Chu Teh, 1929–1934
Guiyang
Ji'an
Kunming
Xiamen
(Amoy)
TAIWAN
(Japanese 1895–1945)
PACIFIC
OCEAN
Shantou
Canton uprising Dec. 1927
Guangzhou
(Canton)
Hong Kong
(British)
Hailufeng Soviet, 1927–1928
BURMA
FRENCH
INDOCHINA
Areas under Communist control before Nov. 1934
Areas under Communist control, 1929–1938
Areas occupied by Japan by end of 1938
Route of the Long March, Oct. 1934–Oct. 1935: Main forces from Ji'an
Other forces

the Communists had retreated to the interior, and both refused to accept defeat. The determination of the Communist guerrillas equaled that of the Nationalists, and their political skill would prove superior. In 1939, as Europe edged toward another great war, the undeclared war between China and Japan bogged down in a savage stalemate. The bloody undeclared war provided a spectacular example of conflicting nationalisms, convulsing China and setting the stage for further Japanese aggression in South Asia.

## Southeast Asia

The tide of nationalism was also rising in Southeast Asia. Like their counterparts in India, China, and Japan, nationalists in Southeast Asia urgently wanted genuine political independence and freedom from foreign rule. In both French Indochina and the Dutch East Indies, local nationalists, inspired by events elsewhere in Asia, pressed their own demands. In both cases they ran up against an imperialist stone wall.

In the words of one historian, "Indochina was governed by Frenchmen for Frenchmen, and the great liberal slogans of liberty, equality, and fraternity were not considered to be export goods for overseas dominions."[13] This uncompromising attitude stimulated the growth of an equally stubborn communist opposition under Ho Chi Minh, which despite ruthless repression emerged as the dominant anti-French force.

In the East Indies—modern Indonesia—the Dutch made some concessions after the First World War, establishing a people's council with very limited lawmaking power. But in the 1930s the Dutch cracked down hard, jailing all the important nationalist leaders. Like the French, the Dutch were determined to hold on.

In the Philippines, however, a well-established nationalist movement achieved greater success. As in colonial Latin America, the Spanish in the Philippines had been indefatigable missionaries. By the late nineteenth century 80 percent of the Filipino population was Catholic. Filipinos shared a common cultural heritage as well as a common racial origin. Education, especially for girls, was quite advanced for Southeast Asia, and in 1843 a higher percentage of people could read in the Philippines than in Spain itself. Economic development helped to create a westernized elite, which turned first to reform and then to revolution in the 1890s. As in Egypt or Turkey, long-standing intimate contact with Western civilization created a strong nationalist movement at an early date.

Filipino nationalists were bitterly disillusioned when the United States, having taken the Philippines from Spain in the Spanish-American War of 1898, ruthlessly beat down a patriotic revolt and denied the universal Filipino desire for independence. The Americans claimed that the Philippines were not ready and might be seized by Germany or Britain. As the imperialist power in the Philippines, the United States encouraged education and promoted capitalistic economic development. As in British India, an elected legislature was given some real powers. In 1919 President Wilson even promised eventual independence, though subsequent Republican administrations saw it as a distant goal.

As in India and French Indochina, demands for independence grew. One important contributing factor was American racial attitudes. Americans treated Filipinos as inferiors and introduced segregationist practices borrowed from the American South. American racism made passionate nationalists of many Filipinos. However, it was the Great Depression that had the most radical impact on the Philippines.

As the United States collapsed economically, the Philippines suddenly appeared to be a liability rather than an asset. American farm groups lobbied for protection from cheap Filipino sugar. To protect American jobs, labor unions demanded an end to Filipino immigration. In 1934 Congress made the Philippines a self-governing commonwealth and scheduled independence for 1944. Sugar imports were reduced, and immigration was limited to only fifty Filipinos per year.

Like Britain and France in the Middle East, the United States was determined to hold on to its big military bases in the Philippines as it permitted increased local self-government and promised eventual political independence. Some Filipino nationalists denounced the continued presence of U.S. fleets and armies. Others were less certain that the American presence was the immediate problem. Japan was fighting in China and expanding economically into the Philippines and throughout Southeast Asia. By 1939 a new threat to Filipino independence appeared to come from Asia itself.

**MAP 30.2 The Chinese Communist Movement and the War with Japan, 1927–1938** After urban uprisings ordered by Stalin failed in 1927, Mao Zedong succeeded in forming a self-governing Communist soviet in mountainous southern China. Relentless Nationalist attacks between 1930 and 1934 finally forced the Long March to Yenan, where the Communists were well positioned for guerrilla war against the Japanese.

## SUMMARY

The Asian revolt against the West began before the First World War. But only after 1914 did Asian nationalist movements broaden their bases and become capable of challenging Western domination effectively. These mass movements sought human dignity as well as political freedom. Generally speaking, Asian nationalists favored modernization and adopted Western techniques and ideas even as they rejected Western rule. Everywhere Asian nationalists had to fight long and hard, though their struggle gained momentum from growing popular support and the encouragement of the Soviet Union.

Asia's nationalist movements arose out of separate historical experiences and distinct cultures. Variations on the common theme of nationalism were evident in Turkey, the Arab world, India, China, Japan, and the Philippines. This diversity helps explain why Asian peoples became defensive in their relations with one another while rising against Western rule. Like earlier nationalists in Europe, Asian nationalists developed a strong sense of "we" and "they"; "they" included other Asians as well as Europeans. Nationalism meant freedom, modernization, and cultural renaissance, but it nonetheless proved a mixed blessing.

## KEY TERMS

Permanent Mandates Commission
Young Turks
sharif
Sykes-Picot Agreement
Balfour Declaration
Treaty of Lausanne
Atatürk
Majlis
Zionism
kibbutz
Lucknow Pact
Government of India Act
Satyagraha
May Fourth Movement
New Culture Movement
zaibatsu
Long March

## NOTES

1. K. M. Panikkar, *Asia and Western Dominance: A Survey of the Vasco da Gama Epoch of Asian History* (London: George Allen & Unwin, 1959), p. 197.
2. Quoted in H. Grimal, *La Décolonisation, 1919–1965* (Paris: Armand Colin, 1965), p. 100.
3. H. Armstrong, *Turkey in Travail: The Birth of a New Nation* (London: John Lane, 1925), p. 75.
4. Quoted in Lord Kinross, *Atatürk: A Biography of Mustafa Kemal, Father of Modern Turkey* (New York: Morrow, 1965), p. 181.
5. Quoted in E. Erikson, *Gandhi's Truth: On the Origins of Militant Nonviolence* (New York: W. W. Norton, 1969), p. 225.
6. Quoted in W. Bingham, H. Conroy, and F. Iklé, *A History of Asia*, vol. 1, 2d ed. (Boston: Allyn and Bacon, 1974), p. 447.
7. Quoted in L. Rudolph and S. Rudolph, *The Modernity of Tradition: Political Development in India* (Chicago: University of Chicago Press, 1967), p. 248.
8. Quoted in W. T. deBary, W. Chan, and B. Watson, *Sources of Chinese Tradition* (New York: Columbia University Press, 1964), pp. 768–769.
9. Quoted in J. F. Fairbank, E. O. Reischauer, and A. M. Craig, *East Asia: Tradition and Transformation* (Boston: Houghton Mifflin, 1973), p. 774.
10. Quoted in B. I. Schwartz, *Chinese Communism and the Rise of Mao* (Cambridge, Mass.: Harvard University Press, 1951), p. 74.
11. Quoted in W. T. deBary, R. Tsunoda, and D. Keene, *Sources of Japanese Tradition*, vol. 2 (New York: Columbia University Press, 1958), p. 269.
12. Quoted in O. Lang, *Chinese Family and Society* (New Haven, Conn.: Yale University Press, 1946), p. 70.
13. Quoted in W. Bingham, H. Conroy, and F. Iklé, *A History of Asia*, vol. 2, 2d ed. (Boston: Allyn and Bacon, 1974), p. 480.

## SUGGESTED READING

All of the works cited in the Notes are highly recommended. Two important general interpretations of nationalism and independence movements are P. Chatterjee, *Nationalist Thought and the Colonial World: A Derivative Discourse* (1986), and R. Emerson, *From Empire to Nation: The Rise to Self-Assertion of Asian and African Peoples* (1960). These may be compared with the provocative works of E. Kedourie, including *Nationalism in Asia and Africa* (1970), and with an influential global history of the twentieth century by G. Barraclough, *An Introduction to Contemporary History* (1975). B. Lewis, *The Shaping of the Modern Middle East* (1993), is a reflective work by a leading historian, which complements A. Hourani, *History of the Arab Peoples* (1991). On Turkey, in addition to Lord Kinross's *Atatürk* (1965), see D. Kushner, *The Rise of Turkish Nationalism, 1876–1908* (1977). Peter Mansfield, *The Arab World: A Comprehensive History* (1976), and S. G. Haim, ed., *Arab Nationalism: An Anthology* (1964), provide engaging general coverage and important source materials. W. Lacqueur, *A History of Zionism* (1972), and A. Eban, *My People* (1968), discuss the Jewish homeland in Palestine. The Arab viewpoint is presented by G. Antonius, *The Arab Awakening: The Story of the Arab National Movement* (1946). R. Cottam, *Nationalism in Iran*, rev. ed. (1979), is recommended.

The historical literature on modern India is very rich. S. Wolpert, *A New History of India*, 5th ed. (1997), is an excellent introduction. Also see P. Chatterjee, *The Nation and Its Fragments: Colonial and Postcolonial Histories* (1993), and the handsomely illustrated volume by F. Watson, *A Concise History of India* (1975). In addition to the biography by Erikson cited in the Notes, L. Fischer, *Gandhi: His Life and Message for the World* (1954), is fascinating. J. Brown, *Gandhi: Prisoner of Hope* (1989), and V. Mehta, *Mahatma Gandhi and His Apostles* (1977), are major studies. Developments in the Muslim community are considered in P. Hardy, *The Muslims of British India* (1972); B. Metcalf, *Islamic Revival in British India: Deoband, 1860–1900* (1982); and F. Robinson, *Atlas of the Islamic World Since 1500* (1982), a beautifully illustrated survey encompassing far more than India.

Studies of China in the twentieth century are also numerous. J. Spence, *The Search for Modern China* (1990), and I. Hsü, *The Rise of Modern China,* 5th ed. (1995), are comprehensive studies with extensive bibliographies, which may be supplemented by the documentary collection of F. Schurmann and O. Schell, eds., *Republican China: Nationalism, War and the Rise of Communism, 1911–1949* (1967). J. Spence, *The Gate of Heavenly Peace: The Chinese and Their Revolution, 1895–1980* (1981), skillfully focuses on leading literary figures. T. Chow, *The May Fourth Movement: Intellectual Revolution in Modern China* (1960), examines a critical time period. Other important studies of China in this period include A. Dirlik, *The Origins of Chinese Communism* (1989); S. Schram, *Mao Tse-tung* (1966); and H. Schriffrin, *Sun Yat-sen and the Origins of the Chinese Revolution* (1970). L. Eastman, *Family, Consistency and Change in China's Social and Economic History, 1550–1949* (1974), is a masterful synthesis. P. Ebrey, ed., *Chinese Civilization: A Sourcebook,* 2d ed. (1993), complements the classic study of the Chinese family by Lang, cited in the Notes, which may be compared with M. J. Levy, *The Family Revolution in Modern China* (1949).

E. Reischauer, *Japan: The Story of a Nation,* rev. ed. (1970), and P. Duus, *The Rise of Modern Japan* (1976), are excellent interpretations of the island nation. W. Lockwood, *The Economic Development of Japan, 1868–1938* (1954), and R. Storry, *The Double Patriots: A Story of Japanese Nationalism* (1973), are valuable specialized works. M. Hane, *Peasants, Rebels, and Outcasts: The Underside of Modern Japan* (1982), sees few benefits for the poor before 1945. S. Garon, *The State and Labor in Modern Japan* (1988), skillfully analyzes the history of Japanese labor relations. Two edited collections, J. Morley, *The China Quagmire* (1983), and R. Myers and M. Peattie, *The Japanese Colonial Expansion, 1895–1945* (1984), probe Japan's imperial expansion.

For Southeast Asia, see D. G. E. Hall, *A History of South-East Asia,* 4th ed. (1981); J. Pluvier, *South-East Asia from Colonialism to Independence* (1974); and the Suggested Reading for Chapter 34. Two more recommended works are M. Osborne, *Southeast Asia: An Illustrated History,* expanded ed. (1988), and D. R. Sardesa, *Southeast Past and Present,* 2d ed. (1989).

# LISTENING TO THE PAST

## Arab Political Aspirations in 1919

*Great Britain and France had agreed to divide up the Arab lands, and the British also had made conflicting promises to Arab and Jewish nationalists. However, President Wilson insisted at Versailles that the right of self-determination should be applied to the conquered Ottoman territories, and he sent an American commission of inquiry to Syria, even though the British and French refused to participate. The commission canvassed political views throughout greater Syria, and its long report with many documents reflected public opinion in the region in 1919.*

*To present their view to the Americans, Arab nationalists from present-day Syria, Lebanon, Israel, and Jordan came together in Damascus as the General Syrian Congress, and they passed the following resolution on July 2, 1919. In addition to the Arab call for political independence, the delegates addressed the possibility of French rule under a League of Nations mandate and the establishment of a Jewish national home.*

We the undersigned members of the General Syrian Congress, meeting in Damascus on Wednesday, July 2nd, 1919, . . . provided with credentials and authorizations by the inhabitants of our various districts, Moslems, Christians, and Jews, have agreed upon the following statement of the desires of the people of the country who have elected us to present them to the American Section of the International Commission; the fifth article was passed by a very large majority; all the other articles were accepted unanimously.

1. We ask absolutely complete political independence for Syria within these boundaries. [Describes the area including the present-day states of Syria, Lebanon, Israel, and Jordan.]

2. We ask that the Government of this Syrian country should be a democratic civil constitutional Monarchy on broad decentralization principles, safeguarding the rights of minorities, and that the King be the Emir Faisal, who carried on a glorious struggle in the cause of our liberation and merited our full confidence and entire reliance.

3. Considering the fact that the Arabs inhabiting the Syrian area are not naturally less gifted than other more advanced races and that they are by no means less developed than the Bulgarians, Serbians, Greeks, and Roumanians at the beginning of their independence, we protest against Article 22 of the Covenant of the League of Nations, placing us among the nations in their middle stage of development which stand in need of a mandatory power.

4. In the event of the rejection by the Peace Conference of this just protest for certain considerations that we may not understand, we, relying on the declarations of President Wilson that his object in waging war was to put an end to the ambition of conquest and colonization, can only regard the mandate mentioned in the Covenant of the League of Nations as equivalent to the rendering of economical and technical assistance that does not prejudice our complete independence. And desiring that our country should not fall a prey to colonization and believing that the American Nation is farthest from any thought of colonization and has no political ambition in our country, we will seek the technical and economical assistance from the United States of America, provided that such assistance does not exceed 20 years.

5. In the event of America not finding herself in a position to accept our desire for assistance, we will seek this assistance from Great Britain, also

provided that such assistance does not infringe the complete independence and unity of our country and that the duration of such assistance does not exceed that mentioned in the previous article.

6. We do not acknowledge any right claimed by the French Government in any part whatever of our Syrian country and refuse that she should assist us or have a hand in our country under any circumstances and in any place.

7. We oppose the pretensions of the Zionists to create a Jewish commonwealth in the southern part of Syria, known as Palestine, and oppose Zionist migration to any part of our country; for we do not acknowledge their title but consider them a grave peril to our people from the national, economical, and political points of view. Our Jewish compatriots shall enjoy our common rights and assume the common responsibilities.

8. We ask that there should be no separation of the southern part of Syria, known as Palestine, nor of the littoral western zone, which includes Lebanon, from the Syrian country. We desire that the unity of the country should be guaranteed against partition under whatever circumstances.

9. We ask complete independence for emancipated Mesopotamia [today's Iraq] and that there should be no economical barriers between the two countries.

10. The fundamental principles laid down by President Wilson in condemnation of secret treaties impel us to protest most emphatically against any treaty that stipulates the partition of our Syria country and against any private engagement aiming at the establishment of Zionism in the southern part of Syria; therefore we ask the complete annulment of these conventions and agreements.

The noble principles enunciated by President Wilson strengthen our confidence that our desires emanating from the depths of our hearts, shall be the decisive factor in determining our future; and that President Wilson and the free American people will be our supporters for the realization of our hopes, thereby proving their sincerity and noble sympathy with the aspiration of the weaker nations in general and our Arab people in particular.

We also have the fullest confidence that the Peace Conference will realize that we would not have risen against the Turks, with whom we had participated in all civil, political, and representative privileges, but for their violation of our national rights, and so will grant us our desires in full in order that our political rights may not be less after the war than they were before, since we have shed so much blood in the cause of our liberty and independence.

We request to be allowed to send a delegation to represent us at the Peace Conference to defend our rights and secure the realization of our aspirations.

Palestinian Arabs protest against large-scale Jewish migration into Palestine. *(Roger-Viollet/Getty Images)*

## QUESTIONS FOR ANALYSIS

1. What kind of state did the delegates want?
2. How would the delegates modify an unwanted League of Nations mandate to make it less objectionable?
3. Did the delegates view their "Jewish compatriots" and the Zionists in different ways? Why?

*Source:* "Resolution of the General Syrian Congress at Damascus, 2 July 1919," from the King-Crane Commission Report, in *Foreign Relations of the United States: Paris Peace Conference, 1919,* 12: 780–781.

This detail of George Grosz's *Draussen und Drinnen* (Outside and Inside) captures the uncertainty and anxiety of the 1920s. *(AKG London)*

CHAPTER

# 31 THE AGE OF ANXIETY IN THE WEST

## CHAPTER OUTLINE

- Uncertainty in Modern Thought
- Modern Art and Music
- Movies and Radio
- The Search for Peace and Political Stability
- The Great Depression (1929–1939)

When Allied diplomats met in Paris in early 1919 with their optimistic plans for building a lasting peace, most looked forward to happier times. They hoped that life would return to normal after the terrible trauma of total war. They hoped that once again life would make sense in the familiar prewar terms of peace, prosperity, and progress. These hopes were in vain. The Great Break—the First World War and the Russian Revolution—had mangled too many things beyond repair. Life would no longer fit neatly into the old molds. Thus in the 1920s and 1930s, as Asians developed renewed self-confidence and forged powerful nationalist movements directed against Western domination (see Chapter 30), great numbers of men and women in the West felt themselves increasingly adrift in a strange, uncertain, and uncontrollable world. They saw themselves living in an age of anxiety, an age of continual crisis (which would last until the early 1950s). In almost every area of human experience, they went searching for ways to put meaning back into life.

- What did such doubts and searching mean for Western thought, art, and culture?
- How did leaders deal with the political dimensions of uncertainty and try to re-establish real peace and prosperity between 1919 and 1939?
- Why did those leaders fail?

These are the questions this chapter will explore.

## UNCERTAINTY IN MODERN THOUGHT

A complex revolution in thought and ideas was under way in Western society before the First World War, but only small, unusual groups were aware of it. After the war new and upsetting ideas began to spread through the entire population. Western society began to question and even abandon many cherished values and beliefs that had guided it since the eighteenth-century Enlightenment and the nineteenth-century triumph of industrial development, scientific advances, and evolutionary thought.

Before 1914 most people in the West still believed in progress, reason, and the rights of the individual. Progress was a daily reality, apparent in the rising

**"The War, As I Saw It"** This was the title of a series of grotesque drawings that appeared in 1920 in *Simplicissimus,* Germany's leading satirical magazine. Nothing shows better the terrible impact of World War I than this profoundly disturbing example of expressionist art. *(Caroline Buckler)*

standard of living, the taming of the city, and the steady increase in popular education. Such developments also encouraged the comforting belief in the logical universe of Newtonian physics as well as faith in the ability of a rational human mind to understand that universe through intellectual investigation. And just as there were laws of science, so were there laws of society that rational human beings could discover and then wisely act on. At the same time, the rights of the individual were not just taken for granted; they were actually increasing. Well-established rights were gradually spreading to women and workers, and new "social rights," such as old-age pensions, were emerging. In short, before World War I most Europeans and North Americans had a moderately optimistic view of the world, and with good reason.

Nevertheless, since the 1880s a small band of serious thinkers and creative writers had been attacking these well-worn optimistic ideas. These critics rejected the general faith in progress and the power of the rational human mind. An expanding chorus of thinkers echoed and enlarged their views after the experience of history's most destructive war—a war that suggested to many that human beings were a pack of violent, irrational animals quite capable of tearing the individual and his or her rights to shreds. Disorientation and pessimism were particularly acute in the 1930s, when the rapid rise of harsh dictatorships and the Great Depression transformed old certainties into bitter illusions.

No one expressed this state of uncertainty better than French poet and critic Paul Valéry (1871–1945) in the

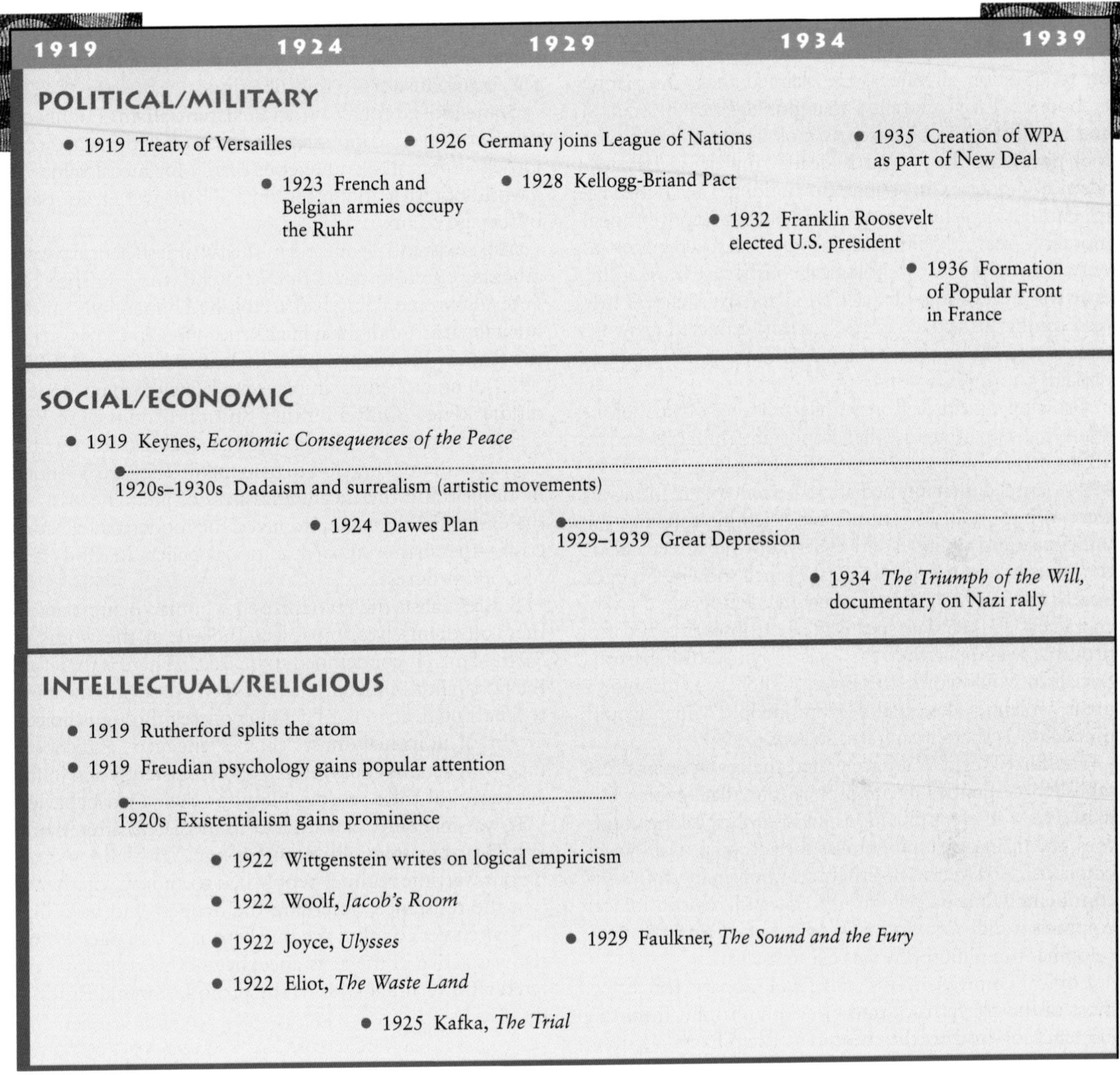


early 1920s. Valéry wrote, "We think of what has disappeared, and we are almost destroyed by what has been destroyed; we do not know what will be born, and we fear the future, not without reason."[1] Above all, Valéry saw the "cruelly injured mind," besieged by doubts and suffering from anxieties. In this general intellectual crisis of the twentieth century, the implications of new ideas and discoveries in philosophy, physics, psychology, and literature played a central role.

1919
1924
1929
1934
1939
POLITICAL/MILITARY
1919 Treaty of Versailles
1923 French and Belgian armies occupy the Ruhr
1926 Germany joins League of Nations
1928 Kellogg-Briand Pact
1932 Franklin Roosevelt elected U.S. president
1935 Creation of WPA as part of New Deal
1936 Formation of Popular Front in France
SOCIAL/ECONOMIC
1919 Keynes, *Economic Consequences of the Peace*
1920s–1930s Dadaism and surrealism (artistic movements)
1924 Dawes Plan
1929–1939 Great Depression
1934 *The Triumph of the Will*, documentary on Nazi rally
INTELLECTUAL/RELIGIOUS
1919 Rutherford splits the atom
1919 Freudian psychology gains popular attention
1920s Existentialism gains prominence
1922 Wittgenstein writes on logical empiricism
1922 Woolf, *Jacob's Room*
1922 Joyce, *Ulysses*
1922 Eliot, *The Waste Land*
1925 Kafka, *The Trial*
1929 Faulkner, *The Sound and the Fury*

## Modern Philosophy

Among those thinkers in the late nineteenth century who challenged the belief in progress and the general faith in the rational human mind, German philosopher Friedrich Nietzsche (1844–1900) was particularly influential. The son of a Lutheran minister, Nietzsche utterly rejected Christianity. In 1872 in his first great work he argued that ever since classical Athens, the West had overemphasized rationality and stifled the passion and animal instinct that drive human activity and true creativity. Nietzsche went on to question all values. He claimed that Christianity embodied a "slave morality" that glorified weakness, envy, and mediocrity. In Nietzsche's most famous line, a wise fool proclaims that "God is dead," murdered by lackadaisical modern Christians who no longer really believe in Him. Nietzsche viewed the pillars of conventional morality—reason, democracy, progress, respectability—as outworn social and psychological constructs whose influence was suffocating self-realization and excellence. Little read during his active years, Nietzsche attracted growing attention in the early twentieth century, and his influence remains enormous to this day.

Growing dissatisfaction with established ideas before 1914 was apparent in other important thinkers. In the 1890s French philosophy professor Henri Bergson (1859–1941) argued that immediate experience and intuition were as important as rational and scientific thinking for understanding reality. Another thinker who agreed about the limits of rational thinking was French socialist Georges Sorel (1847–1922). Sorel, rejecting democracy, frankly characterized Marxian socialism as an inspiring but unprovable religion rather than a rational scientific truth. Socialism would come to power, he believed, through a great, violent strike of all working people, which would miraculously shatter capitalist society.

The First World War accelerated the revolt against established certainties in philosophy, but that revolt went in two very different directions. In English-speaking countries, the main development was the acceptance of logical empiricism (or logical positivism) in university circles. In continental Europe, where esoteric and remote logical empiricism did not win many converts, the primary development in philosophy was existentialism.

**Logical empiricism** was truly revolutionary. It rejected most of the concerns of traditional philosophy, from the existence of God to the meaning of happiness, as nonsense and hot air. This outlook began primarily with Austrian philosopher Ludwig Wittgenstein (1889–1951), who later immigrated to England, where he trained numerous disciples.

Wittgenstein argued in his pugnacious *Tractatus Logico-Philosophicus* (Essay on Logical Philosophy) in 1922 that philosophy is only the logical clarification of thoughts and that it therefore becomes the study of language, which expresses thoughts. In Wittgenstein's opinion the great philosophical issues of the ages—God, freedom, morality, and so on—are quite literally senseless, a great waste of time, for statements about them can be neither tested by scientific experiments nor demonstrated by the logic of mathematics. Logical empiricism drastically reduced the scope of philosophical inquiry. Anxious people could find few, if any, answers in this direction.

Some looked for answers in **existentialism.** Highly diverse and even contradictory, existential thinkers were loosely united in a courageous search for moral values in a world of terror and uncertainty. Theirs were true voices of the age of anxiety.

Most existential thinkers in the twentieth century were atheists. Often inspired by Nietzsche, they did not believe a Supreme Being had established humanity's fundamental nature and given life its meaning. In the words of the famous French existentialist Jean-Paul Sartre (1905–1980), human beings simply exist: "They turn up, appear on the scene." Only after they "turn up" do they seek to define themselves. Honest human beings are terribly alone, for there is no God to help them. They are hounded by despair and the meaninglessness of life. The crisis of the existential thinker epitomized the modern intellectual crisis—the shattering of traditional beliefs in God, reason, and progress.

Existentialists did recognize that human beings, unless they kill themselves, must act. Indeed, in the words of Sartre, "man is condemned to be free." There is therefore the possibility—indeed, the necessity—of giving meaning to life through actions, of defining oneself through choices. To do so, individuals must become "engaged" and choose their own actions courageously and consistently and in full awareness of their responsibility for their own behavior.

It was in France during and immediately after World War II that existentialism came of age. With Hitler's barbarous wartime regime, people had to choose whether to join the resistance, accepting the dangers and hardships of that choice, or abet the murderous Nazis. Sartre himself was active in the resistance; he and his colleagues offered a powerful answer to the profound moral issues of the day.

## The Revival of Christianity

The loss of faith in human reason and in continual progress also led to a renewed interest in the Christian view of the world. Christianity and religion in general had been on the defensive in intellectual circles since the Enlightenment. In the years before 1914 some theologians, especially Protestant ones, had felt the need to interpret Christian doctrine and the Bible so that they did not seem to contradict science, evolution, and common sense. Christ was therefore seen primarily as the greatest moral teacher, and the "supernatural" aspects of his divinity were strenuously played down.

Especially after World War I, a number of thinkers and theologians began to revitalize the fundamentals of Christianity. Sometimes described as Christian existentialists because they shared the loneliness and despair of atheistic existentialists, they stressed human beings' sinful nature, the need for faith, and the mystery of God's forgiveness. The revival of fundamental Christian belief was fed by rediscovery of the work of nineteenth-century Danish religious philosopher Søren Kierkegaard (1813–1855). Having rejected formalistic religion, Kierkegaard had eventually resolved his personal anguish over his imperfect nature by making a total religious commitment to a remote and majestic God.

Similar ideas were brilliantly developed by Swiss Protestant theologian Karl Barth (1886–1968). Barth maintained that religious truth is made known to human beings only through God's grace. Sinful creatures whose reason and will are hopelessly flawed, people have to accept God's Word and the supernatural revelation of Jesus Christ with awe, trust, and obedience. Lowly mortals should not expect to "reason out" God and his ways.

Among Catholics the leading existential Christian thinker was Gabriel Marcel (1887–1973), who found in the Catholic church an answer to what he called the postwar "broken world." Catholicism and religious belief provided the hope, humanity, honesty, and piety for which he hungered. Flexible and gentle, Marcel and his countryman Jacques Maritain (1882–1973) denounced anti-Semitism and supported closer ties with non-Catholics.

After 1914 religion became much more relevant and meaningful to thinking people than it had been before the Great War. Many illustrious individuals turned to religion between about 1920 and 1950. Poets T. S. Eliot and W. H. Auden, novelists Evelyn Waugh and Aldous Huxley, historian Arnold Toynbee, Oxford professor C. S. Lewis, psychoanalyst Karl Stern, physicist Max Planck, and philosopher Cyril Joad were all either converted to religion or attracted to it for the first time. Religion, often of a despairing, existential variety, was one meaningful answer to terror and anxiety. In the words of another famous Roman Catholic convert, English novelist Graham Greene, "One began to believe in heaven because one believed in hell."[2]

## The New Physics

Ever since the scientific revolution of the seventeenth century, scientific advances and their implications had greatly influenced the beliefs of thinking people. By the late nineteenth century science was one of the main pillars supporting Western society's optimistic and rationalistic view of the world. Darwin's concept of evolution had been accepted and assimilated in most intellectual circles. Progressive minds believed that science was based on hard facts and controlled experiments. Science seemed to have achieved an unerring and almost completed picture of reality. Unchanging natural laws seemed to determine physical processes and permit useful solutions to more and more problems. All this was comforting, especially to people who were no longer committed to traditional religious beliefs. And all this was challenged by the new physics.

An important first step toward the new physics was the discovery at the end of the nineteenth century that atoms were not like hard, permanent little billiard balls. They were actually composed of many far-smaller, fast-moving particles, such as electrons and protons. Polish-born physicist Marie Curie (1867–1934) and her French husband discovered that radium constantly emits subatomic particles and thus does not have a constant atomic weight. Building on this and other work in radiation, German physicist Max Planck (1858–1947) showed in 1900 that subatomic energy is emitted in uneven little spurts, which Planck called "quanta," and not in a steady stream, as previously believed. Planck's discovery called into question the old sharp distinction between matter and energy and challenged the old view of atoms as the stable, basic building blocks of nature.

In 1905 German-born Jewish genius Albert Einstein (1879–1955) went further in undermining Newtonian physics. His famous theory of special relativity postulated that time and space are relative to the viewpoint of the observer and that only the speed of light is constant for all frames of reference in the universe. In order to make his revolutionary and paradoxical idea somewhat comprehensible to the nonmathematical layperson, Einstein later used analogies involving moving trains. For example, if a woman in the middle of a moving car gets up and walks forward to the door, she has moved relative to the train, a half car length. But relative to an observer on the embankment, she has moved farther. The closed framework of Newtonian physics was quite limited compared to that of Einsteinian physics, which unified an apparently infinite universe with the incredibly small, fast-moving subatomic world. Moreover, Einstein's theory stated clearly that matter and energy are interchangeable and that even a particle of matter contains enormous levels of potential energy.

The 1920s opened the "heroic age of physics," in the apt words of one of its leading pioneers, Ernest Rutherford (1871–1937). Breakthrough followed breakthrough. In 1919 Rutherford showed that the atom could be split. By 1944 seven subatomic particles had been identified, of which the most important was the **neutron.** The neutron's capacity to pass through other atoms allowed for even more intense experimental bombardment of matter, leading to chain reactions of unbelievable force. This was the road to the atomic bomb.

Although few nonscientists understood this revolution in physics, the implications of the new theories and discoveries, as presented by newspapers and popular writers, were disturbing to millions of men and women in the 1920s and 1930s. The new universe was strange and troubling. It seemed to lack any absolute objective reality. Everything was said to be "relative"—that is, dependent on the observer's frame of reference. Moreover, science seemed to have little to do with human experience and human problems. When, for example, Planck was asked what science could contribute to resolving conflicts of values, his response was simple: "Science is not qualified to speak to this question."

## Freudian Psychology

With physics presenting an uncertain universe so unrelated to ordinary human experience, questions about the power and potential of the human mind assumed special significance. The findings and speculations of leading psychologist Sigmund Freud were particularly disturbing.

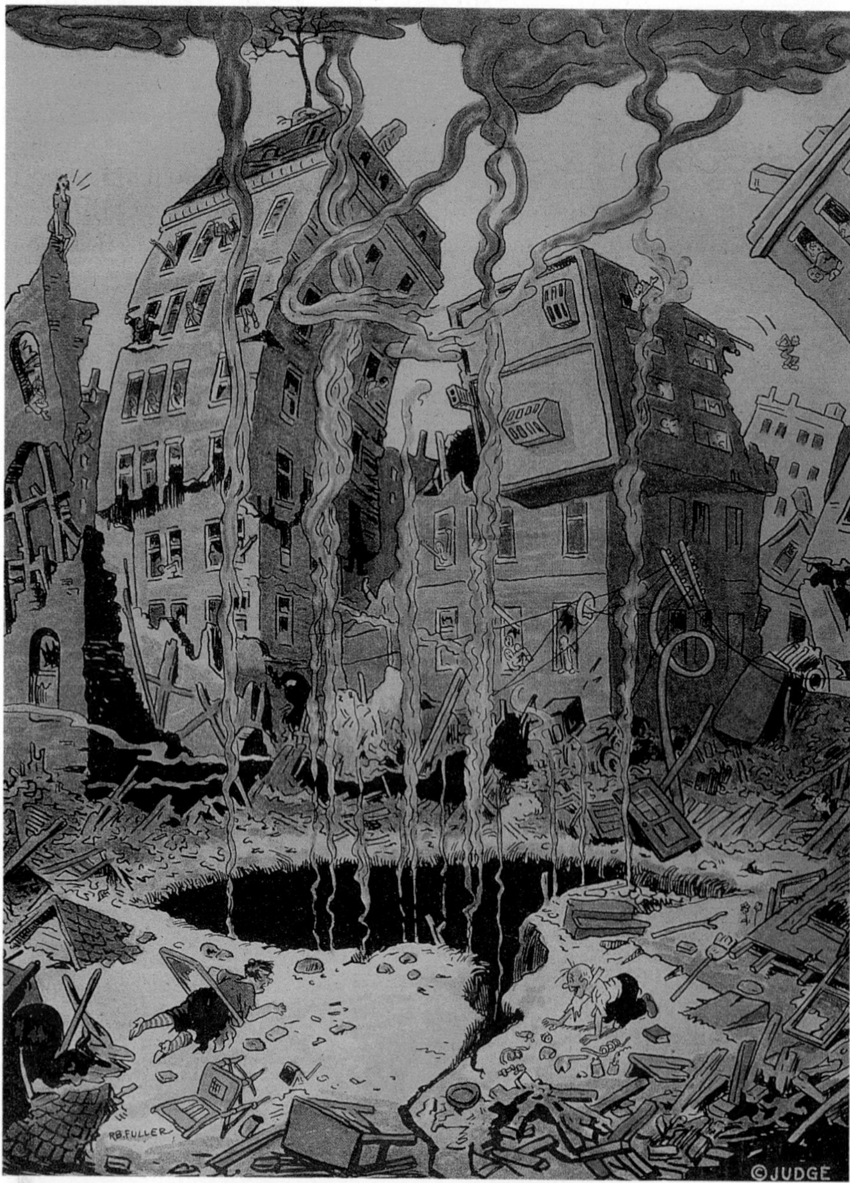


**Unlocking the Power of the Atom** Many of the fanciful visions of science fiction came true in the twentieth century, although not exactly as first imagined. This 1927 cartoon satirizes a professor who has split the atom and unwittingly destroyed his building and neighborhood in the process. In the Second World War the professors harnessed the atom in bombs and decimated faraway cities and foreign civilians. *(Mary Evans Picture Library)*

Before Freud, poets and mystics had probed the unconscious and irrational aspects of human behavior. But most professional, "scientific" psychologists assumed that human behavior was the result of rational calculation—of "thinking"—by the single, unified conscious mind. Basing his insights on the analysis of dreams and of hysteria, Freud developed a very different view of the human psyche beginning in the late 1880s.

According to Freud, human behavior is basically irrational. The key to understanding the mind is the primitive, irrational unconscious, which he called the **id.** The unconscious is driven by sexual, aggressive, and pleasure-seeking desires and is locked in a constant battle with the other parts of the mind: the rationalizing conscious (the *ego*), which mediates what a person *can* do, and ingrained moral values (the **superego**), which specify what a person *should* do. Human behavior is a product of a fragile compromise between instinctual drives and the controls of rational thinking and moral values. Since the instinctual drives are extremely powerful, the ever-present danger for individuals and whole societies is that unacknowledged drives will overwhelm the control mechanisms in a violent, distorted way. Yet Freud also agreed with Nietzsche that the mechanisms of rational thinking and traditional moral values can be too strong. They can repress sexual desires too effectively, crippling individuals and entire peoples with guilt and neurotic fears.

Freudian psychology and clinical psychiatry had become an international movement by 1910, but only after 1918 did they receive popular attention, especially in the Protestant countries of northern Europe and in the United States. Many interpreted Freud as saying that the first requirement for mental health is an uninhibited sex life. This popular interpretation reflected and encouraged growing sexual experimentation, particularly among middle-class women. For more serious students the psychology of Freud and his followers drastically undermined the old, easy optimism about the rational and progressive nature of the human mind.

**Virginia Woolf** Her novels captured sensations like impressionist paintings, and her home attracted a circle of artists and writers known as the Bloomsbury Group. Many of Woolf's essays dealt with women's issues and urged greater opportunity for women's creativity. *(Gisèle Freund/Photo Researchers, Inc.)*

## Twentieth-Century Literature

The general intellectual climate of pessimism, relativism, and alienation was also articulated in literature. Novelists developed new techniques to express new realities. The great nineteenth-century novelists had typically written as all-knowing narrators, describing realistic characters and their relationship to an understandable, if sometimes harsh, society. In the twentieth century most major writers adopted the limited, often confused viewpoint of a single individual. Like Freud, these novelists focused their attention on the complexity and irrationality of the human mind, where feelings, memories, and desires are forever scrambled. The great French novelist Marcel Proust (1871–1922), in his semi-autobiographical *Remembrance of Things Past* (1913–1927), recalled bittersweet memories of childhood and youthful love and tried to discover their innermost meaning as he withdrew from the present to dwell on the past.

Serious novelists also used the **stream-of-consciousness technique** to explore the psyche. In *Jacob's Room* (1922) Virginia Woolf (1882–1941) created a novel made up of a series of internal monologues, in which ideas and emotions from different periods of time bubble up as randomly as from a patient on a psychoanalyst's couch. William Faulkner (1897–1962), perhaps America's greatest twentieth-century novelist, used the same technique in *The Sound and the Fury* (1929), much of whose intense drama is confusedly seen through the eyes of an idiot. The most famous stream-of-consciousness novel—and surely the most disturbing novel of its generation—is *Ulysses,* which Irish novelist James Joyce (1882–1941) published in 1922. Into an account of an ordinary day in the life of an ordinary man, Joyce weaves an extended ironic parallel between his hero's aimless wanderings through the streets and pubs of Dublin and the adventures of Homer's hero Ulysses on his way home from Troy. Abandoning conventional grammar and blending foreign words, puns, bits of knowledge, and scraps of memory together in bewildering confusion, the language of *Ulysses* is intended to mirror modern life itself: a gigantic riddle waiting to be unraveled.

As creative writers turned their attention from society to the individual and from realism to psychological relativity, they rejected the idea of progress. Some even described "anti-utopias," nightmare visions of things to come. In 1918 an obscure German high school teacher named Oswald Spengler (1880–1936) published *The Decline of the West,* which quickly became an international sensation. According to Spengler, every culture experiences a life cycle of growth and decline. Western civilization, in Spengler's opinion, was in its old age, and death was approaching in the form of conquest by the yellow race. T. S. Eliot (1888–1965), in his famous poem *The Waste Land* (1922), depicts a world of growing desolation, although after his conversion to Anglo-Catholicism in 1927 Eliot came to hope cautiously for humanity's salvation. No such hope appeared in the work of Franz Kafka (1883–1924), whose novels *The Trial* (1925) and *The Castle* (1926) as well as several of his greatest short stories portray helpless individuals crushed by inexplicably hostile forces.

Englishman George Orwell (1903–1950) had seen the nightmarish reality of the Nazi state and its Stalinist counterpart by 1949 when he wrote perhaps the ultimate in anti-utopian literature: *1984.* Orwell set the action in the future. Big Brother—the dictator—and his totalitarian state use a new kind of language, sophisticated technology, and psychological terror to strip a weak individual of his last shred of human dignity. The supremely self-confident chief of the Thought Police tells the tortured, broken, and framed Winston Smith, "If you want a picture of the future, imagine a boot stamping on a human face—forever."[3] A phenomenal bestseller, *1984* spoke to millions of people in the closing years of the age of anxiety.

## MODERN ART AND MUSIC

Throughout the twentieth and early twenty-first centuries, there has been considerable unity in the arts. The "modernism" of the immediate prewar years and the 1920s is still strikingly modern. Like the scientists who were partaking of the same culture, creative artists rejected old forms and old values. Modernism in art and music meant constant experimentation and a search for new kinds of expression. And though many people find the many and varied modern visions of the arts strange, disturbing, and even ugly, the twentieth century, so dismal in many respects, will probably stand as one of Western civilization's great artistic eras.

### Architecture and Design

Modernism in the arts was loosely unified by a revolution in architecture. This revolution intended nothing less than a transformation of the physical framework of urban society according to a new principle: **functionalism.** Buildings, like industrial products, should be useful and "functional"—that is, they should serve, as well as possible, the purpose for which they were made. Thus architects and designers had to work with engineers, town planners, and even sanitation experts. Moreover, they had to throw away useless ornamentation and find beauty and aesthetic pleasure in the clean lines of practical constructions and efficient machinery. Franco-Swiss genius Le Corbusier (1887–1965) insisted that "a house is a machine for living in."[4]

The United States, with its rapid urban growth and lack of rigid building traditions, pioneered in the new architecture. In the 1890s the Chicago school of architects, led by Louis H. Sullivan (1856–1924), used cheap steel, reinforced concrete, and electric elevators to build skyscrapers and office buildings lacking almost any exterior ornamentation. Europeans were inspired by these and other American examples of functional construction, like the massive, unadorned grain elevators of the Midwest.

In Europe architectural leadership centered in German-speaking countries until Hitler took power in 1933. In 1911 twenty-eight-year-old Walter Gropius (1883–1969) broke sharply with the past in his design of the Fagus shoe factory at Alfeld, Germany—a clean, light, elegant building of glass and iron. After the First World War Gropius merged the schools of fine and applied arts at Weimar into a single, interdisciplinary school, the Bauhaus. The Bauhaus brought together many leading modern architects, artists, designers, and theatrical innovators. Working as an effective, inspired team, they combined the study of fine art, such as painting and sculpture, with the study of applied art in the crafts of printing, weaving, and furniture making. Throughout the 1920s the Bauhaus, with its stress on functionalism and good design for everyday life, attracted enthusiastic students from all over the world. It had a great and continuing impact.

## Modern Painting and Music

Modern painting grew out of a revolt against French impressionism. The *impressionism* of such French painters as Claude Monet (1840–1926), Pierre Auguste Renoir (1841–1919), and Camille Pissarro (1830–1903) was, in part, a kind of "superrealism." Leaving exact copying of objects to photography, these artists sought to capture the momentary overall feeling, or impression, of light falling on a real-life scene before their eyes. By 1890, when impressionism was finally established, a few artists known as *postimpressionists,* or sometimes as *expressionists,* were already striking out in new directions. After 1905 art increasingly took on a nonrepresentational, abstract character, a development that reached its high point after World War II.

Though individualistic in their styles, postimpressionists were united in their desire to know and depict unseen, inner worlds of emotion and imagination. Like modern novelists, they wanted to express a complicated psychological view of reality as well as an overwhelming emotional intensity. In *The Starry Night* (1889), for example, the great Dutch expressionist Vincent van Gogh (1853–1890) painted the moving vision of his mind's eye. Paul

**Van Gogh: The Starry Night** Van Gogh absorbed impressionism in Paris, but under the burning sun of southern France he went beyond the portrayal of external reality. In *The Starry Night* (1889) flaming cypress trees, exploding stars, and a comet-like Milky Way swirl together in one great cosmic rhythm. Painting an inner world of intense emotion and wild imagination, van Gogh contributed greatly to the rise of expressionism in modern art. *(© MoMA/Scala/Art Resource, NY)*

**Picasso: Guernica** In this rich, complex work a shrieking woman falls from a burning house on the far right. On the left a woman holds a dead child, while toward the center are fragments of a warrior and a screaming horse pierced by a spear. Picasso has used only the mournful colors of black, white, and gray. *(Museo del Prado/Giraudon/Art Resource, NY. © Artists Rights Society [ARS], New York/ADAGP, Paris)*

Gauguin (1848–1903), the French stockbroker-turned-painter, pioneered in expressionist techniques, though he used them to infuse his work with tranquillity and mysticism. In 1891 he fled to the South Pacific in search of unspoiled beauty and a primitive life. Gauguin believed that the form and design of a picture were important in themselves and that the painter need not try to represent objects on canvas as the eye actually saw them.

Fascination with form, as opposed to light, was characteristic of postimpressionism and expressionism. Paul Cézanne (1839–1906), who had a profound influence on twentieth-century painting, was particularly committed to form and ordered design. He told a young painter, "You must see in nature the cylinder, the sphere, and the cone."[5] As Cézanne's later work became increasingly abstract and nonrepresentational, it also moved away from the traditional three-dimensional perspective toward the two-dimensional plane, which has characterized much of modern art.

In 1907 a young Spaniard in Paris, Pablo Picasso (1881–1973), founded another movement—*cubism.* Cubism concentrated on a complex geometry of zigzagging lines and sharply angled, overlapping planes. About three years later came the ultimate stage in the development of abstract, nonrepresentational art. Artists such as the Russian-born Wassily Kandinsky (1866–1944) turned away from nature completely. "The observer," said Kandinsky, "must learn to look at [my] pictures . . . as form and color combinations . . . as a representation of mood and not as a representation of *objects.*"[6]

In the 1920s and 1930s the artistic movements of the prewar years were extended and consolidated. The most notable new developments were *dadaism* and *surrealism.* Dadaism attacked all accepted standards of art and behavior, delighting in outrageous conduct. A famous example of dadaism is a reproduction of Leonardo da Vinci's *Mona Lisa* in which the famous woman with the mysterious smile sports a mustache and is ridiculed with an obscene inscription. After 1924 many dadaists were attracted to surrealism, which became very influential in art in the late 1920s and 1930s. Surrealists painted a fantastic world of wild dreams and complex symbols, where watches melted and giant metronomes beat time in precisely drawn but impossible alien landscapes.

Refusing to depict ordinary visual reality, surrealist painters made powerful statements about the age of anxiety. Picasso's 26-foot-long mural *Guernica* (see the illustration above) masterfully unites several powerful strands in twentieth-century art. Inspired by the Spanish civil war (see page 1043), the painting commemorates the bombing of the ancient Spanish town of Guernica by fascist planes, which took the lives of a thousand people in a single night of terror. Combining the free distortion of expressionism, the overlapping planes of cubism, and the surrealist fascination with grotesque subject matter, *Guernica* is what Picasso meant it to be: an unforgettable attack on "brutality and darkness."

Developments in modern music were strikingly parallel to those in painting. Composers, too, were attracted by the emotional intensity of expressionism. The ballet *The Rite of Spring* by composer Igor Stravinsky (1882–1971) practically caused a riot when it was first performed in Paris in 1913 by Sergei Diaghilev's famous Russian dance company. The combination of pulsating, dissonant rhythms from the orchestra pit and an earthy representation of lovemaking by the dancers on the stage seemed a shocking, almost pornographic enactment of a primitive fertility rite.

After the experience of the First World War, when irrationality and violence seemed to pervade the human experience, expressionism in opera and ballet flourished. Some composers turned their backs on long-established musical conventions. As abstract painters arranged lines and color but did not draw identifiable objects, so modern composers arranged sounds without creating recognizable harmonies. Accustomed to the harmonies of classical and romantic music, audiences generally resisted modern atonal music.

## MOVIES AND RADIO

Until after World War II at the earliest, these revolutionary changes in art and music appealed mainly to a minority of "highbrows" and not to the general public. That public was primarily and enthusiastically wrapped up in movies, radio, and advertising. The long-declining traditional arts and amusements of people in villages and small towns almost vanished, replaced by standardized, commercial entertainment.

Moving pictures were first shown as a popular novelty in naughty peepshows—"What the Butler Saw"—and penny arcades in the 1890s, especially in Paris. The first movie houses date from an experiment in Los Angeles in 1902. They quickly attracted large audiences and led to the production of short, silent action films such as the eight-minute *Great Train Robbery* of 1903. American directors and business people then set up "movie factories," at first in the New York area and then after 1910 in Los Angeles. These factories churned out two short films each week. On the eve of the First World War, full-length feature films such as the Italian *Quo Vadis* and the American *Birth of a Nation,* coupled with improvements in the quality of pictures, suggested the screen's vast possibilities.

During the First World War the United States became the dominant force in the rapidly expanding silent-film industry. In the 1920s Mack Sennett (1884–1960) and his zany Keystone Kops specialized in short, slapstick comedies noted for frantic automobile chases, custard-pie battles, and gorgeous bathing beauties. Screen stars such as Mary Pickford and Lillian Gish, Douglas Fairbanks and Rudolf Valentino, had their own "fan clubs" and became household names. But in the 1920s Charlie Chaplin (1889–1978), a funny little Englishman working in Hollywood, was unquestionably the king of the "silver screen." In his enormously popular role as a lonely tramp, complete with baggy trousers, battered derby, and an awkward, shuffling walk, Chaplin symbolized the "gay spirit of laughter in a cruel, crazy world."[7] Chaplin also demonstrated that in the hands of a genius the new

**The Great Dictator** In 1940 the renowned actor and director Charlie Chaplin abandoned the little tramp to satirize the "great dictator," Adolf Hitler. Chaplin had strong political views and made a number of films with political themes as the escapist fare of the Great Depression gave way to the reality of the Second World War. *(The Museum of Modern Art/Still Film Archives)*

medium could combine mass entertainment and artistic accomplishment.

The early 1920s were also the great age of German films. Protected and developed during the war, the large German studios excelled in bizarre expressionist dramas, beginning with *The Cabinet of Dr. Caligari* in 1919. Unfortunately, their period of creativity was short-lived. By 1926 American money was drawing the leading German talents to Hollywood and consolidating America's international domination. Film making was big business, and European theater owners were forced to book whole blocks of American films to get the few pictures they really wanted. This system put European producers at a great disadvantage until "talkies" permitted a revival of national film industries in the 1930s, particularly in France.

Whether foreign or domestic, motion pictures became the main entertainment of the masses until after the Second World War. The greatest appeal of motion pictures was that they offered ordinary people a temporary escape from the hard realities of international tensions, uncertainty, unemployment, and personal frustrations. The appeal of escapist entertainment was especially strong during the Great Depression. Millions flocked to musical comedies featuring glittering stars such as Ginger Rogers and Fred Astaire and to the fanciful cartoons of Mickey Mouse and his friends.

Radio became possible with the transatlantic "wireless" communication of Guglielmo Marconi (1874–1937) in 1901 and the development of the vacuum tube in 1904, which permitted the transmission of speech and music. But only in 1920 were the first major public broadcasts of special events made in Great Britain and the United States. Singing from London in English, Italian, and French, "the world's very best, the soprano Nellie Melba,"[8] was heard simultaneously all over Europe on June 16, 1920. This historic event captured the public's imagination. The meteoric career of radio was launched.

Every major country quickly established national broadcasting networks. In the United States such networks were privately owned and were financed by advertising. In Great Britain Parliament set up an independent, public corporation, the British Broadcasting Corporation (BBC), supported by licensing fees. Elsewhere in Europe the typical pattern was direct control by the government. Whatever the institutional framework, radio became popular and influential. By the late 1930s more than three out of every four households in both democratic Great Britain and dictatorial Germany had at least one cheap, mass-produced radio.

Radio was particularly well suited for political propaganda. Dictators such as Mussolini and Hitler controlled the airwaves and could reach enormous national audiences with their frequent, dramatic speeches. In democratic countries politicians such as President Franklin Roosevelt and Prime Minister Stanley Baldwin effectively used informal "fireside chats" to bolster their support.

Motion pictures also became powerful tools of indoctrination, especially in countries with dictatorial regimes. Lenin encouraged the development of Soviet film making, believing that the new medium was essential to the social and ideological transformation of the country. Beginning in the mid-1920s a series of epic films, the most famous of which were directed by Sergei Eisenstein (1898–1948), brilliantly dramatized the communist view of Russian history.

In Germany Hitler turned to a young and immensely talented woman film maker, Leni Riefenstahl (b. 1902), for a masterpiece of documentary propaganda, *The Triumph of the Will,* based on the Nazi party rally at Nuremberg in 1934. Riefenstahl combined stunning aerial photography, joyful crowds welcoming Hitler, and mass processions of young Nazi fanatics. Her film was a brilliant and all-too-powerful documentary of Germany's "Nazi rebirth." The new media of mass culture were potentially dangerous instruments of political manipulation.

## THE SEARCH FOR PEACE AND POLITICAL STABILITY

As established patterns of thought and culture were challenged and mangled by the ferocious impact of World War I, so also was the political fabric stretched and torn by the consequences of the great conflict. The Versailles settlement had established a shaky truce, not a solid peace. Thus national leaders faced a gigantic task as they struggled with uncertainty and sought to create a stable international order within the general context of intellectual crisis and revolutionary artistic experimentation.

The pursuit of real and lasting peace proved difficult for many reasons. Germany hated the Treaty of Versailles. France was fearful and isolated. Britain was undependable, and the United States had turned its back on European problems. Eastern Europe was in ferment, and no one could predict the future of communist Russia. In addition, the international economic situation was poor and greatly complicated by war debts and disrupted patterns of trade. Yet for a time, from 1925 to late 1929, it appeared that peace and stability were within reach. When the subsequent collapse of the 1930s mocked these hopes, the disillusionment of liberals in the democracies was intensified.

## Germany and the Western Powers

Germany was the key to lasting peace. Yet to Germans of all political parties, the Treaty of Versailles represented a harsh, dictated peace, to be revised or repudiated as soon as possible. The treaty had neither broken nor reduced Germany, which was potentially still the strongest country in Europe. Thus the treaty had fallen between two stools: too harsh for a peace of reconciliation, too soft for a peace of conquest.

Moreover, France and Great Britain did not see eye to eye on Germany. By the end of 1919 France wanted to stress the harsh elements in the Treaty of Versailles. Most of the war in the West had been fought on French soil, and the expected costs of reconstruction, as well as repaying war debts to the United States, were staggering. Thus French politicians believed that massive reparations from Germany were a vital economic necessity. America's failure to ratify the treaty left many French leaders believing that strict implementation of all provisions of the Treaty of Versailles was France's last best hope. Large reparation payments could hold Germany down indefinitely, and France would realize its goal of security.

The British soon felt differently. Prewar Germany had been Great Britain's second-best market in the entire world, and after the war a healthy, prosperous Germany appeared to be essential to the British economy. Indeed, many English people agreed with the analysis of the young English economist John Maynard Keynes (1883–1946). In his famous *Economic Consequences of the Peace* (1919) Keynes argued that astronomical reparations and harsh economic measures would impoverish Germany and increase economic hardship in all countries. Only a complete revision of the foolish treaty could save Germany—and Europe. Keynes's attack stirred deep guilt feelings about Germany in the English-speaking world, feelings that often paralyzed English and American leaders in their relations with Germany and its leaders between the First and Second World Wars.

The British were suspicious of France's army—the largest in Europe and authorized at Versailles to occupy the German Rhineland until 1935—and the British and French were also on cool terms because of conflicts relating to their League of Nations mandates in the Middle East (see page 970). While French and British leaders drifted in different directions, the Allied reparations commission completed its work. In April 1921 it announced that Germany had to pay the enormous sum of 132 billion gold marks ($33 billion) in annual installments of 2.5 billion gold marks. Facing possible occupation of more of its territory, the young German republic—known as the Weimar Republic—made its first payment in 1921. Then in 1922, wracked by rapid inflation and political assassinations and motivated by hostility and arrogance as well, the Weimar Republic announced its inability to pay more and proposed a moratorium on reparations for three years.

**"Hands Off the Ruhr"** The French occupation of the Ruhr to collect reparations payments raised a storm of patriotic protest in Germany. This anti-French poster of 1923 turns Marianne, the personification of French republican virtue, into a vicious harpy. *(International Instituut voor Sociale Geschiedenis)*

The British were willing to accept a moratorium on reparations, but the French were not. Led by their tough-minded, legalistic prime minister, Raymond Poincaré (1860–1934), they decided they had to either call Germany's bluff or see the entire peace settlement dissolve to France's great disadvantage. So, despite strong British protests, in early January 1923, armies of France and its ally Belgium began to occupy the Ruhr district, the heartland of industrial Germany, creating the most serious international crisis of the 1920s.

Strengthened by a wave of patriotism, the German government ordered the people of the Ruhr to stop working and start passively resisting the French occupation. The coal mines and steel mills of the Ruhr grew silent, leaving 10 percent of Germany's total population in need of relief. The French answer to passive resistance was to seal off not only the Ruhr but also the entire Rhineland from the rest of Germany, letting in only enough food to prevent starvation.

By the summer of 1923 France and Germany were engaged in a great test of wills. French armies could not collect reparations from striking workers at gunpoint. But French occupation was paralyzing Germany and its economy and had turned rapid German inflation into runaway inflation. Faced with the need to support the striking Ruhr workers and their employers, the German government began to print money to pay its bills. Prices soared. People went to the store with a big bag of paper money; they returned home with a handful of groceries. German money rapidly lost all value, and so did anything else with a stated fixed value.

Runaway inflation brought about a social revolution. The accumulated savings of many retired and middle-class people were wiped out. Catastrophic inflation cruelly mocked the old middle-class virtues of thrift, caution, and self-reliance. Many Germans felt betrayed. They hated and blamed the Western governments, their own government, big business, the Jews, the workers, and the communists for their misfortune. They were psychologically prepared to follow radical leaders in a crisis.

In August 1923, as the mark fell and political unrest grew throughout Germany, Gustav Stresemann (1878–1929) assumed leadership of the government. Stresemann adopted a compromising attitude. He called off passive resistance in the Ruhr and in October agreed in principle to pay reparations but asked for a re-examination of Germany's ability to pay. Poincaré accepted. His hard line was becoming increasingly unpopular with French citizens, and it was hated in Britain and the United States. (See the feature "Individuals in Society: Gustav Stresemann.")

More generally, in both Germany and France power was finally passing to the moderates, who realized that continued confrontation was a destructive, no-win situation. Thus after five years of hostility and tension, culminating in a kind of undeclared war in the Ruhr in 1923, Germany and France decided to give compromise and cooperation a try. The British, and even the Americans, were willing to help. The first step was a reasonable compromise on the reparations question.

## Hope in Foreign Affairs (1924–1929)

The reparations commission appointed an international committee of financial experts headed by American banker Charles G. Dawes to re-examine reparations from a broad perspective. The resulting **Dawes Plan** (1924) was accepted by France, Germany, and Britain. Germany's yearly reparations were reduced and depended on the level of German economic prosperity. Germany would also receive large loans from the United States to promote German recovery. In short, Germany would get private loans from the United States and pay reparations to France and Britain, thus enabling those countries to repay the large sums they owed the United States.

This circular flow of international payments was complicated and risky, but for a while it worked. The German republic experienced a spectacular economic recovery. By 1929 Germany's wealth and income were 50 percent greater than in 1913. With prosperity and large, continual inflows of American capital, Germany easily paid about $1.3 billion in reparations in 1927 and 1928, enabling France and Britain to pay the United States. In this way the Americans belatedly played a part in the general economic settlement that, though far from ideal, facilitated the worldwide recovery of the late 1920s.

This economic settlement was matched by a political settlement. In 1925 the leaders of Europe signed a number of agreements at Locarno, Switzerland. Germany and France solemnly pledged to accept their common border, and both Britain and Italy agreed to fight either France or Germany if one invaded the other. Stresemann also agreed to settle boundary disputes with Poland and Czechoslovakia by peaceful means, and France promised those countries military aid if Germany attacked them. For years a "spirit of Locarno" gave Europeans a sense of growing security and stability in international affairs.

Other developments also strengthened hopes. In 1926 Germany joined the League of Nations, where Stresemann continued his "peace offensive." In 1928 fifteen countries signed the Kellogg-Briand Pact, initiated by French prime minister Aristide Briand and U.S. secretary of state Frank B. Kellogg. This multinational pact "condemned and renounced war as an instrument of national policy." The signing states agreed to settle international disputes peacefully. The pact fostered the cautious optimism of the late 1920s and also encouraged the hope that the United States would accept its international responsibilities.

Domestic politics also offered reason to hope. During the occupation of the Ruhr and the great inflation, republican government in Germany had appeared on the

# INDIVIDUALS IN SOCIETY

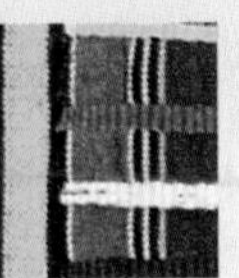

## GUSTAV STRESEMANN

The German foreign minister Gustav Stresemann (1878–1929) is a controversial historical figure. Hailed by many as a hero of peace, he was denounced as a traitor by radical German nationalists and then by Hitler's Nazis. After World War II, revisionist historians stressed Stresemann's persistent nationalism and cast doubt on his peaceful intentions. Weimar Germany's most renowned leader is a fascinating example of the restless quest for convincing historical interpretation.

Stresemann's origins were modest. His parents were Berlin innkeepers and retailers of bottled beer, and only Gustav of their five children was able to attend high school. Attracted first to literature and history, Stresemann later turned to economics, earned a doctoral degree, and quickly reached the top as a manager and director of German trade associations. A highly intelligent extrovert with a knack for negotiation, Stresemann entered the Reichstag in 1907 as a business-oriented liberal and nationalist. When World War I erupted, he believed, like most Germans, that Germany had acted defensively and was not at fault. He emerged as a strident nationalist and urged German annexation of conquered foreign territories. Germany's collapse in defeat and revolution devastated Stresemann. He seemed a prime candidate for the hateful extremism of the far right.

Yet although Stresemann opposed the Treaty of Versailles as an unjust and unrealistic imposition, he turned back toward the center. He accepted the new Weimar Republic and played a growing role in the Reichstag as the leader of his own small probusiness party. His hour came in the Ruhr crisis, when French and Belgian troops occupied the district. Named chancellor in August 1923, he called off passive resistance and began talks with the French. His government also quelled communist uprisings; put down rebellions in Bavaria, including Hitler's attempted coup; and ended runaway inflation with a new currency. Stresemann fought to preserve German unity, and he succeeded.

Voted out as chancellor in November 1923, Stresemann remained as foreign minister in every government until his death in 1929. Proclaiming a policy of peace and agreeing to pay reparations, he achieved his greatest triumph in the Locarno agreements of 1925 (see page 1012). But the interlocking guarantees of existing French and German borders (and the related agreements to resolve peacefully all disputes with Poland and Czechoslovakia) did not lead the French to make any further concessions that might have disarmed Stresemann's extremist foes. Working himself to death, he made little additional progress in achieving international reconciliation and sovereign equality for Germany.

*Foreign Minister Gustav Stresemann of Germany (right) leaves a meeting with Aristide Briand, his French counterpart.* (Corbis)

Stresemann was no fuzzy pacifist. Historians debunking his "legend" are right in seeing an enduring love of nation in his defense of German interests. But Stresemann, like his French counterpart Aristide Briand, was a statesman of goodwill who wanted peace through mutually advantageous compromise. A realist trained by business and politics in the art of the possible, Stresemann also reasoned that Germany had to be a satisfied and equal partner if peace was to be secure. His unwillingness to guarantee Germany's eastern borders (see Map 29.4 on page 960), which is often criticized, reflects his conviction that keeping some Germans under Polish and Czechoslovak rule created a ticking time bomb in Europe. Stresemann was no less convinced that war on Poland would almost certainly re-create the Allied coalition that had crushed Germany in 1918.* His insistence on the necessity of peace in the east as well as the west was prophetic. Hitler's 1939 invasion of Poland resulted in an even mightier coalition that almost annihilated Germany in 1945.

### QUESTIONS FOR ANALYSIS

1. What did Gustav Stresemann do to promote reconciliation in Europe? How did his policy toward France differ from that toward Poland and Czechoslovakia?
2. What is your interpretation of Stresemann? Does he arouse your sympathy or your suspicion and hostility? Why?

*Robert Grathwol, "Stresemann: Reflections on His Foreign Policy," *Journal of Modern History* 45 (March 1973): 52–70.

verge of collapse. In 1923 communists momentarily entered provincial governments, and in November an obscure nobody named Adolf Hitler leaped onto a table in a beer hall in Munich and proclaimed a "national socialist revolution." But Hitler's plot to seize control of the government was poorly organized and easily crushed, and Hitler was sentenced to prison, where he outlined his theories and program in his book ***Mein Kampf*** (My Struggle). Throughout the 1920s, Hitler's National Socialist party attracted support only from a few fanatical anti-Semites, ultranationalists, and disgruntled former servicemen.

The moderate businessmen who tended to dominate the various German coalition governments believed that economic prosperity demanded good relations with the Western Powers, and they supported parliamentary government at home. Elections were held regularly, and as the economy boomed, republican democracy appeared to have growing support among a majority of Germans.

**American Jazz in Paris** This woodcut from a 1928 French book on cafés and nightclubs suggests how black musicians took Europe by storm, although the blacks are represented stereotypically. One French critic concluded that American blacks had attained a "pre-eminent" place in music since the war, "for they have impressed the entire world with their vibrating or melancholy rhythms." *(AKG London)*

There were, however, sharp political divisions in the country. Many unrepentant nationalists and monarchists populated the right and the army. Members of Germany's Communist party were directed from Moscow, and they endlessly accused the Social Democrats of betraying the revolution. The working classes were divided politically, but most supported the nonrevolutionary but socialist Social Democrats.

The situation in France had numerous similarities to that in Germany. Communists and socialists battled for the support of the workers. After 1924 the democratically elected government rested mainly in the hands of coalitions of moderates, and business interests were well represented. France's great accomplishment was rapid rebuilding of its war-torn northern region, and good times prevailed until 1930.

France attracted artists and writers from all over the world in the 1920s. Much of the intellectual and artistic ferment of the times flourished in Paris. As writer Gertrude Stein (1874–1946), a leader of the large colony of American expatriates living in Paris, later recalled, "Paris was where the twentieth century was."[9] More generally, France appealed to foreigners and to the French as a harmonious combination of small businesses and family farms, of bold innovation and solid traditions.

Britain, too, faced challenges after 1920. The wartime trend toward greater social equality continued, however, helping maintain social harmony. The great problem was unemployment, which throughout the 1920s hovered around 12 percent. The state provided unemployment benefits and supplemented those payments with subsidized housing, medical aid, and increased old-age pensions. These and other measures kept living standards from seriously declining, defused class tensions, and pointed the way toward the welfare state that Britain established after World War II.

Relative social harmony was accompanied by the rise of the Labour party as a determined champion of the working classes and of greater social equality. Committed to moderate, "revisionist" socialism, the Labour party under Ramsay MacDonald (1866–1937) governed the country in 1924 and 1929 with the support of the declining Liberal party. Yet Labour moved toward socialism gradually and democratically, so that the middle classes were not overly frightened as the working classes won new benefits.

The Conservatives under Stanley Baldwin (1867–1947) showed the same compromising spirit on social issues. In spite of such conflicts as the 1926 strike by hard-pressed coal miners, which ended in an unsuccessful general strike, social unrest in Britain was limited in the 1920s and 1930s. In 1922 Britain granted southern, Catholic Ireland full autonomy after a bitter guerrilla war, thereby removing another source of prewar friction. Thus developments in both international relations and in the domestic politics of the leading democracies gave cause for cautious optimism in the late 1920s.

## THE GREAT DEPRESSION (1929–1939)

Like the Great War, the Great Depression must be spelled with capital letters. Economic depressions occurred regularly throughout the nineteenth century, but this depression was exceptionally long and severe. It struck the entire world with ever-greater intensity from 1929 to 1933, and recovery was uneven and slow. Only with the Second World War did the depression disappear in much of the world.

The social and political consequences of prolonged economic collapse were enormous all around the world. Subsequent military expansion in Japan has already been described (see page 876), and later chapters will examine a similarly powerful impact on Latin America and Africa. In Europe and the United States the depression shattered the fragile optimism of political leaders in the late 1920s. Mass unemployment made insecurity a reality for millions of ordinary people, who had paid little attention to the intellectual crisis or to new directions in art and ideas. In desperation, people looked for leaders who would "do something." They were willing to support radical attempts to deal with the crisis by both democratic leaders and dictators.

### The Economic Crisis

Though economic activity was already declining moderately in many countries by early 1929, the crash of the stock market in the United States in October of that year really started the Great Depression. The American stock market boom, which had seen stock prices double between early 1928 and September 1929, was built on borrowed money. Many wealthy investors, speculators, and people of modest means had bought stocks by paying only a small fraction of the total purchase price and borrowing the remainder from their stockbrokers. Such buying "on margin" was extremely dangerous. When prices started falling, the hard-pressed margin buyers started selling to pay their debts. The result was a financial panic. Countless investors and speculators were wiped out in a matter of days or weeks.

The financial panic in the United States triggered a worldwide financial crisis, and that crisis resulted in a drastic decline in production in country after country. Throughout the 1920s American bankers and investors had lent large sums to many countries, and as panic broke, New York bankers began recalling their short-term loans. The panicky European public began to withdraw its savings from the banks, leading to general financial chaos. The recall of American loans also accelerated the collapse in world prices, as business people around the world dumped goods in a frantic attempt to get cash to pay what they owed.

The financial chaos led to a general crisis of production. Between 1929 and 1933 world output of goods fell by an estimated 38 percent. As this happened, each country turned inward and tried to go it alone. Country after country followed the example of the United States when it raised protective tariffs to their highest levels ever in 1930 and tried to seal off shrinking national markets for American producers only. Within this context of fragmented and destructive economic nationalism, recovery finally began in 1933.

Although opinions differ, two factors probably best explain the relentless slide to the bottom from 1929 to early 1933. First, the international economy lacked a leadership able to maintain stability when the crisis came. The seriously weakened British, the traditional leaders of the world economy, "couldn't and the United States wouldn't" stabilize the international economic system in 1929.[10] The United States, which had momentarily played a positive role after the occupation of the Ruhr, cut back its international lending and erected high tariffs.

The second factor was poor national economic policy in almost every country. Governments generally cut their budgets and reduced spending when they should have run large deficits in an attempt to stimulate their economies. After World War II such a "counter-cyclical policy," advocated by John Maynard Keynes, became a well-established weapon against depression. But in the 1930s orthodox economists generally regarded Keynes's prescription with horror.

### Mass Unemployment

The need for large-scale government spending was tied to mass unemployment. As the financial crisis led to cuts in production, workers lost their jobs and had little money to buy goods. This led to still more cuts in production

**Isaac Soyer: Employment Agency (1937)** The frustration and agony of looking for work against long odds are painfully evident in this American masterpiece. The time-killing, pensive resignation, and dejection seen in the three figures are only aspects of the larger problem. One of three talented brothers born in Russia and trained as artists in New York, Isaac Soyer worked in the tradition of American realism and concentrated on people and the influence of their environment. *(Oil on canvas, 34¼ × 45 in. Whitney Museum of American Art, New York, Purchase 37.44)*

and still more unemployment, until millions were out of work. In Britain unemployment had averaged 12 percent in the 1920s; between 1930 and 1935 it averaged more than 18 percent. In Japan 3 million people were out of work. Far worse was the case of the United States. In the 1920s unemployment there had averaged only 5 percent; in 1932 it soared to about 33 percent of the entire labor force: 14 million people were out of work. Only by pumping new money into the economy could the government increase demand and break the vicious cycle of decline.

Along with economic effects, mass unemployment posed a great social problem. Poverty increased dramatically, although in most industrialized countries unemployed workers generally received some kind of meager unemployment benefits or public aid that prevented starvation. (See the feature "Listening to the Past: Life on the Dole in Great Britain" on pages 1022–1023.) Millions of people lost their spirit, condemned to an apparently hopeless search for work or idle boredom. Homes and ways of life were disrupted in millions of personal tragedies. In 1932 the workers of Manchester, England, appealed to their city officials—a typical appeal echoed throughout the Western world:

> *We tell you that thousands of people . . . are in desperate straits. We tell you that men, women, and children are going hungry. . . . We tell you that great numbers are being rendered distraught through the stress and worry of trying to exist without work. . . .*
>
> *If you do not do this—if you do not provide useful work for the unemployed—what, we ask, is your alternative? Do not imagine that this colossal tragedy of unemployment is going on endlessly without some fateful catastrophe. Hungry men are angry men.*[11]

Only strong government action could deal with mass unemployment, a social powder keg preparing to explode.

## The New Deal in the United States

Of all the major industrial countries, only Germany was harder hit by the Great Depression, or reacted more radically to it, than the United States. Depression was so traumatic in the United States because the 1920s had been a period of complacent prosperity. The Great Depression and the response to it marked a major turning point in American history.

President Herbert Hoover (1874–1964) and his administration initially reacted to the stock market crash and economic decline with dogged optimism and limited action. But when the full force of the financial crisis struck Europe in the summer of 1931 and boomeranged back to the United States, people's worst fears became reality. Banks failed; unemployment soared. In 1932 industrial production fell to about 50 percent of its 1929 level. In these tragic circumstances Franklin Delano Roosevelt (1882–1945), an inspiring wheelchair-bound aristocrat previously crippled by polio, won a landslide electoral victory in 1932 with grand but vague promises of a "**New Deal** for the forgotten man."

Roosevelt's basic goal was to reform capitalism in order to preserve it. Roosevelt rejected socialism and government ownership of industry in 1933. To right the situation he chose forceful government intervention in the economy. In this choice Roosevelt was flexible, pragmatic, and willing to experiment. Roosevelt and his "brain trust" of advisers adopted policies echoing the American experience in World War I, when the American economy had been thoroughly planned and regulated.

Innovative programs promoted agricultural recovery, a top priority. As in Asia, Africa, and Latin America, American farmers were hard hit by the Depression. Roosevelt's decision to leave the gold standard and devalue the dollar was designed to raise American prices and save farmers. The Agricultural Adjustment Act (1933) aimed at raising prices and farm income by limiting production. These measures worked for a while, and farmers overwhelmingly supported Roosevelt in the 1936 election.

The most ambitious attempt to control and plan the economy was the National Recovery Administration (NRA). Intended to reduce competition and fix prices and wages for everyone's benefit, the NRA broke with the cherished American tradition of free competition and aroused conflicts among business people, consumers, and bureaucrats. It did not work well and was declared unconstitutional in 1935.

Roosevelt and his advisers then attacked the key problem of mass unemployment. The federal government accepted the responsibility of employing directly as many people as financially possible. New agencies were created to undertake a vast range of public works projects. The most famous of these was the **Works Progress Administration (WPA),** set up in 1935. One-fifth of the entire labor force worked for the WPA at some point in the 1930s, constructing public buildings, bridges, and highways. The WPA was enormously popular, and the hope of a job with the government helped check the threat of social revolution in the United States.

Such relief programs were part of the New Deal's fundamental commitment to use the federal government to provide for the welfare of all Americans. This commitment marked a profound shift from the traditional stress on family support and community responsibility. Embraced by a large majority in the 1930s, this shift proved to be one of the New Deal's most enduring legacies.

Other social measures aimed in the same direction. Following the path blazed by Germany's Bismarck in the 1880s (see page 810), the U.S. government in 1935 established a national social security system, with old-age pensions and unemployment benefits, to protect many workers against some of life's uncertainties. The National Labor Relations Act of 1935 gave union organizers the green light by declaring collective bargaining to be the policy of the United States. Union membership more than doubled, from 4 million in 1935 to 9 million in 1940. In general, between 1935 and 1938 government rulings and social reforms chipped away at the privileges of the wealthy and tried to help ordinary people.

Yet despite undeniable accomplishments in social reform, the New Deal was only partly successful as a response to the Great Depression. At the height of the recovery in May 1937, 7 million workers were still unemployed, as opposed to a high of 15 million in 1933. The economic situation then worsened seriously in the recession of 1937 and 1938, and unemployment was still a staggering 10 million when war broke out in Europe in September 1939. The New Deal brought fundamental reform, but it never did pull the United States out of the depression.

## The Scandinavian Response to the Depression

Of all the Western democracies, the Scandinavian countries under socialist leadership responded most successfully to the challenge of the Great Depression. Having grown steadily in number in the late nineteenth century, the socialists became the largest political party in Sweden and then in Norway after the First World War. In the 1920s they passed important social reform legislation for both peasants and workers, gained practical administrative experience, and developed a unique kind of socialism. Flexible and nonrevolutionary, Scandinavian socialism grew out of a strong tradition of cooperative community action. Even before 1900, Scandinavian agricultural cooperatives had shown how individual peasant families could join together for everyone's benefit. Labor leaders and capitalists were also inclined to work together.

When the economic crisis struck in 1929, socialist governments in Scandinavia built on this pattern of cooperative social action. Sweden in particular pioneered in the use of large-scale deficits to finance public works and thereby maintain production and employment. Scandinavian governments also increased social welfare benefits, from old-age pensions and unemployment insurance to subsidized housing and maternity allowances. All this spending required a large bureaucracy and high taxes, first on the rich and then on practically everyone. Yet

**Oslo Breakfast** Scandinavian socialism championed cooperation and practical welfare measures, playing down strident rhetoric and theories of class conflict. The Oslo Breakfast exemplified the Scandinavian approach. It provided every schoolchild in the Norwegian capital with a good breakfast free of charge. *(Universitets-biblioteket i Oslo)*

both private and cooperative enterprise thrived, as did democracy. Some observers saw Scandinavia's welfare socialism as an appealing "middle way" between sick capitalism and cruel communism or fascism.

## Recovery and Reform in Britain and France

In Britain MacDonald's Labour government and then, after 1931, the Conservative-dominated coalition government followed orthodox economic theory. The budget was balanced, but unemployed workers received barely enough welfare to live. Despite government lethargy, the economy recovered considerably after 1932. By 1937 total production was about 20 percent higher than in 1929. In fact, for Britain the years after 1932 were actually somewhat better than the 1920s had been, quite the opposite of the situation in the United States and France.

This good but by no means brilliant performance reflected the gradual reorientation of the British economy. After going off the gold standard in 1931 and establishing protective tariffs in 1932, Britain concentrated increasingly on the national, rather than the international, market. The old export industries of the Industrial Revolution, such as textiles and coal, continued to decline, but new industries, such as automobiles and electrical appliances, grew in response to British home demand. Moreover, low interest rates encouraged a housing boom. These developments encouraged Britain to look inward and avoid unpleasant foreign questions.

Because France was relatively less industrialized and more isolated from the world economy, the Great Depression came there late. But once the depression hit France, it stayed and stayed. Decline was steady until 1935, and a short-lived recovery never brought production or employment back up to predepression levels. Economic stagnation both reflected and heightened an ongoing political crisis. There was no stability in government. As before 1914, the French parliament was made up of many political parties, which could never cooperate for very long. In 1933, for example, five coalition cabinets formed and fell in rapid succession.

The French lost the underlying unity that had made government instability bearable before 1914. Fascist-type organizations agitated against parliamentary democracy and looked to Mussolini's Italy and Hitler's Germany for inspiration. In February 1934 French fascists and semifascists rioted and threatened to overturn the republic. At the same time, the Communist party and many workers looked to Stalin's Russia for guidance. The vital center of moderate republicanism was sapped from both sides.

Frightened by the growing strength of the fascists at home and abroad, the Communists, the Socialists, and the Radicals formed an alliance—the **Popular Front**—for the national elections of May 1936. Their clear victory reflected the trend toward polarization. The number of Communists in the parliament jumped dramatically from 10 to 72, and the Socialists, led by Léon Blum, became the strongest party in France, with 146 seats. The really quite moderate Radicals slipped badly, and the conservatives lost ground to the semifascists.

In the next few months Blum's Popular Front government made the first and only real attempt to deal with the social and economic problems of the 1930s in France. Inspired by Roosevelt's New Deal, the Popular Front encouraged the union movement and launched a far-reaching program of social reform, complete with paid vacations and a forty-hour workweek. Popular with workers and the lower middle class, these measures were quickly sabotaged by rapid inflation and cries of revolution from fascists and frightened conservatives. Wealthy people sneaked their money out of the country, labor unrest grew, and France entered a severe financial crisis. Blum was forced to announce a "breathing spell" in social reform.

The fires of political dissension were also fanned by civil war in Spain. Communists demanded that France support the Spanish republicans, while many French conservatives would gladly have joined Hitler and Mussolini in aiding the attack of Spanish fascists. Extremism grew, and France itself was within sight of civil war. Blum was forced to resign in June 1937, and the Popular Front quickly collapsed. An anxious and divided France drifted aimlessly once again, preoccupied by Hitler and German rearmament.

# SUMMARY

After the First World War Western society entered a complex and difficult era—truly an age of anxiety. Intellectual life underwent a crisis marked by pessimism, uncertainty, and fascination with irrational forces. Ceaseless experimentation and rejection of old forms characterized art and music, while motion pictures and radio provided a new, standardized entertainment for the masses. Intellectual and artistic developments that before 1914 had been confined to small avant-garde groups gained wider currency, as did the insecure state of mind they expressed.

Politics and economics were similarly disrupted. In the 1920s political leaders groped to create an enduring peace and rebuild the prewar prosperity, and for a brief period late in the decade they seemed to have succeeded. Then the Great Depression shattered that fragile stability. Uncertainty returned with redoubled force in the 1930s. The international economy collapsed, and unemployment struck millions worldwide. The democracies turned inward as they sought to cope with massive domestic problems and widespread disillusionment. Generally speaking, they were not very successful. The old liberal ideals of individual rights and responsibilities, elected government, and economic freedom, even when they managed to survive, seemed ineffective and outmoded to many. And in many countries these ideals were abandoned completely.

## KEY TERMS

| | |
|---|---|
| logical empiricism | functionalism |
| existentialism | Dawes Plan |
| neutron | *Mein Kampf* |
| id | New Deal |
| superego | Works Progress Administration (WPA) |
| stream-of-consciousness technique | Popular Front |

## NOTES

1. P. Valéry, *Variety*, trans. M. Cowley (New York: Harcourt Brace, 1927), pp. 27–28.
2. G. Greene, *Another Mexico* (New York: Viking Press, 1939), p. 3.
3. G. Orwell, *1984* (New York: New American Library, 1950), p. 220.
4. C. E. Jeanneret-Gris (Le Corbusier), *Towards a New Architecture* (London: J. Rodker, 1931), p. 15.
5. Quoted in A. H. Barr, Jr., *What Is Modern Painting?* 9th ed. (New York: Museum of Modern Art, 1966), p. 27.
6. Quoted ibid., p. 25.
7. R. Graves and A. Hodge, *The Long Week End: A Social History of Great Britain, 1918–1939* (New York: Macmillan, 1941), p. 131.
8. Quoted in A. Briggs, *The Birth of Broadcasting*, vol. 1 (London: Oxford University Press, 1961), p. 47.
9. Quoted in R. J. Sontag, *A Broken World, 1919–1939* (New York: Harper & Row, 1971), p. 129.
10. C. P. Kindleberger, *The World in Depression, 1929–1939* (Berkeley: University of California Press, 1973), p. 292.
11. Quoted in S. B. Clough et al., eds., *Economic History of Europe: Twentieth Century* (New York: Harper & Row, 1968), pp. 243–245.

## SUGGESTED READING

Among general works, E. Wiskemann's *Europe of the Dictators, 1919–1945* (1966), and Sontag's study cited in the Notes are particularly recommended. The latter has an excellent bibliography. A. Bullock, ed., *The Twentieth Century* (1971), is a lavish visual feast combined with penetrating essays on major developments since 1900. Two excellent accounts of contemporary history—one with a liberal and the other with a conservative point of view—are R. Paxton, *Europe in the Twentieth Century*, 3d ed. (1997), and P. Johnson, *Modern Times: The World from the Twenties to the Eighties* (1983). Crucial changes in thought before and after World War I are discussed in three rewarding intellectual histories: S. Kern, *The Culture of Time and Space, 1880–1918;* M. Berman, *All That Is Solid Melts into Air: The Experience of Modernity* (1982); and G. Masur, *Prophets of Yesterday* (1961). R. Stromberg, *European Intellectual History Since 1789* (1986), and F. Baumer, *Modern European Thought: Continuity and Change in Ideas, 1600–1950* (1970), are recommended general surveys. W. Kaufmann, *Nietzsche* (1974), is a sympathetic and justly famous study, and S. Aschheim, *The Nietzsche Legacy in Germany, 1890–1990* (1992), considers the range of responses to the pioneering philosopher.

N. Cantor, *The American Century: Varieties of Culture in Modern Times* (1997), is a pugnacious and stimulating survey. J. Rewald's *The History of Impressionism* (1961) and *Post-Impressionism* (1956) are excellent, as is the work by Barr cited in the Notes. P. Collaer, *A History of Modern Music* (1961), and H. R. Hitchcock, *Architecture: Nineteenth and Twentieth Centuries* (1958), are good introductions. T. Wolfe, *From Bauhaus to My House* (1981), is a lively critique of modern architecture. L. Barnett, *The Universe and Dr. Einstein* (1952), is a fascinating study of the new physics. A. Storr, *Freud* (1989), and P. Rieff, *Freud* (1956), consider the man and how his theories have stood the test of time. In *Civilization and Its Discontents* (1930), which is highly recommended, S. Freud explores his theory of instinct and repression, arguing that society's necessary repression of instinctual drives will always leave people unhappy. M. White, ed., *The Age of Analysis* (1955), opens up basic questions of twentieth-century psychology and philosophy. H. Liebersohn, *Fate and Utopia in German Sociology* (1988), analyzes developments in German social science. T. Judt, *The Burden of Responsibility: Blum, Camus, Aron, and the French Twentieth Century* (1998), probes the moral and intellectual issues of the modern age. J. Willett, *The New Sobriety: Art and Politics in the Weimar Period, 1917–1933* (1978), and P. Gay, *Weimar Culture* (1970), consider the artistic renaissance and the political culture in Germany in the 1920s. H. Daniels-Rops, *A Fight for God*, 2 vols. (1966), is a sympathetic history of the Catholic church between 1870 and 1939.

G. Ambrosius and W. Hibbard, *A Social and Economic History of Twentieth-Century Europe* (1989), provides a good survey; C. Maier, *Recasting Bourgeois Europe* (1975), is an ambitious comparative study of social classes and conflicts in France, Germany, and Italy after World War I. R. Wohl, *The Generation of 1914* (1979), and R. Kuisel, *Capi-*

*tal and State in Modern France: Renovation and Economic Management* (1982), are important studies on aspects of the postwar challenge. J. Jacobson, *Locarno Diplomacy: Germany and the West, 1925–1927* (1972), is a superb study of Stresemann and enduring tensions after the Locarno breakthrough. B. Martin, *France and the Après Guerre: Illusions and Disillusionments* (1999), is a solid work with masterful portraits of key figures. S. Reynolds, *France Between the Wars: Gender and Politics* (1996), and J. Keiger, *Raymond Poincaré* (1996), are major reconsiderations of French politics from different perspectives. H. James, *The German Slump: Politics and Economics, 1924–1936* (1986), is an excellent analysis of economic recovery and subsequent collapse. M. Childs, *Sweden: The Middle Way* (1961), applauds Sweden's efforts at social reform. In addition to the contemporary works discussed in the text, the crisis of the interwar period comes alive in R. Crossman, ed., *The God That Failed* (1950), in which famous Western writers tell why they were attracted to and later repelled by communism; J. Ortega y Gasset's renowned *The Revolt of the Masses* (1932); and F. A. Hayek's *The Road to Serfdom* (1944), a famous warning of the dangers to democratic freedoms.

In addition to Kindleberger's excellent study of the Great Depression cited in the Notes, there is J. Galbraith's very lively and understandable account of the stock market collapse, *The Great Crash* (1955). P. Temin, *Lessons from the Great Depression* (1987), is an excellent evaluation. J. Garraty, *Unemployment in History* (1978), is noteworthy, though novels best portray the human tragedy of economic decline. Winifred Holtby, *South Riding* (1936), and Walter Greenwood, *Love on the Dole* (1933), are moving stories of the Great Depression in England; Hans Fallada, *Little Man, What Now?* (1932), is the classic counterpart for Germany. Also highly recommended as commentaries on English life between the wars are N. Gray, *The Worst of Times: An Oral History of the Great Depression in Britain* (1985), and George Orwell, *The Road to Wigan Pier* (1972). Among French novelists, André Gide painstakingly examines the French middle class and its values in *The Counterfeiters,* and the great existentialist Albert Camus is at his unforgettable best in *The Stranger* (1942) and *The Plague* (1947).

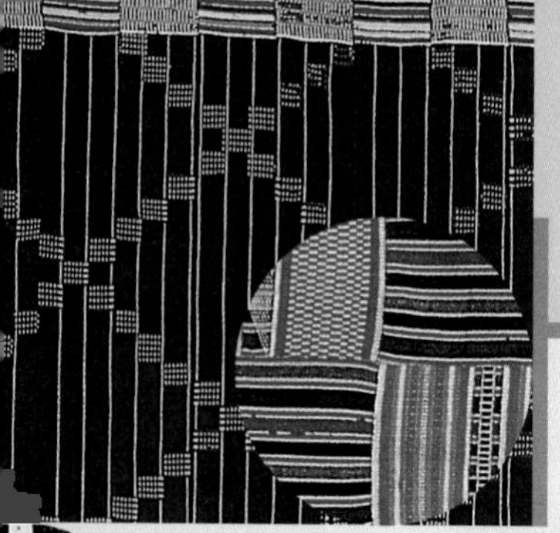

# LISTENING TO THE PAST

## Life on the Dole in Great Britain

*Periodic surges in unemployment were an old story in capitalist economies, but the long-term joblessness of millions in the Great Depression was something new and unexpected. In Britain especially, where the depression followed a weak postwar recovery, large numbers suffered involuntary idleness for years at a time. Whole families lived "on the dole," the weekly welfare benefits paid by the government.*

*One of the most insightful accounts of unemployed workers was written by the British journalist and novelist George Orwell (1903–1950), who studied the conditions in northern England and wrote* The Road to Wigan Pier *(1937). An independent socialist who distrusted rigid Marxism, Orwell believed that socialism could triumph in Britain if it came to mean "justice and liberty" for a commonsense majority. Orwell's disillusionment with authoritarian socialism and communism pervades his most famous work,* 1984 *(1949).*

When you see the unemployment figures quoted at two millions, it is fatally easy to take this as meaning that two million people are out of work and the rest of the population is comparatively comfortable. . . . [Adding in the destitute,] you might take the number of underfed people in England (for *everyone* on the dole or thereabouts is underfed) as being, at the very most, five millions.

This is an enormous under-estimate, because, in the first place, the only people shown on unemployment figures are those actually drawing the dole—that is, in general, heads of families. An unemployed man's dependants do not figure on the list unless they too are drawing a separate allowance. . . . In addition there are great numbers of people who are in work but who, from a financial point of view, might equally be unemployed, because they are not drawing anything that can be described as a living wage. Allow for these and their dependants, throw in as before the old-age pensioners, the destitute and other nondescripts, and you get an *underfed* population of well over ten millions. . . .

Take the figures for Wigan, which is typical enough of the industrial and mining districts. . . . The total population of Wigan is a little under 87,000; so that at any moment more than one person in three out of the whole population—not merely the registered workers—is either drawing or living on the dole. . . .

Nevertheless, in spite of the frightful extent of unemployment, it is a fact that poverty—extreme poverty—is less in evidence in the industrial North than it is in London. Everything is poorer and shabbier, there are fewer motor-cars and fewer well-dressed people; but also there are fewer people who are obviously destitute. . . . In the industrial towns the old communal way of life has not yet broken up, tradition is still strong and almost everyone has a family—potentially, therefore, a home. In a town of 50,000 or 100,000 inhabitants there is no casual and as it were unaccounted-for population; nobody sleeping in the streets, for instance. Moreover, there is just this to be said for the unemployment regulations, that they do not discourage people from marrying. A man and wife on twenty-three shillings a week are not far from the starvation line, but they can make a home of sorts; they are vastly better off than a single man on fifteen shillings. . . .

But there is no doubt about the deadening, debilitating effect of unemployment upon everybody, married or single, and upon men more than upon women. . . . Everyone who saw Greenwood's play *Love on the Dole* must remember that dreadful moment when the poor, good, stupid working man beats on the table and cries out, "O God, send me some work!" This was not dramatic exaggeration, it was a touch from life. That cry must have been uttered, in

Poster used in the election campaign of 1931, when unemployment rose to a new record high. *(Conservative Research Department/ The Bridgeman Art Library International Ltd)*

almost those words, in tens of thousands, perhaps hundreds of thousands of English homes, during the past fifteen years.

But, I think not again—or at least, not so often. . . . When people live on the dole for years at a time they grow used to it, and drawing the dole, though it remains unpleasant, ceases to be shameful. Thus the old, independent, workhouse-fearing tradition is undermined. . . .

So you have whole populations settling down, as it were, to a lifetime of the P.A.C. . . . Take, for instance, the fact that the working class think nothing of getting married on the dole. . . . Life is still fairly normal, more normal than one really has the right to expect. Families are impoverished, but the family-system has not broken up. The people are in effect living a reduced version of their former lives. Instead of raging against their destiny they have made things tolerable by lowering their standards.

But they don't necessarily lower their standards by cutting out luxuries and concentrating on necessities; more often it is the other way about—the more natural way, if you come to think of it. Hence the fact that in a decade of unparalleled depression, the consumption of all cheap luxuries has increased. The two things that have probably made the greatest difference of all are the movies and the mass-production of cheap smart clothes since the war. The youth who leaves school at fourteen and gets a blind-alley job is out of work at twenty, probably for life; but for two pounds ten on the hire-purchase system he can buy himself a suit which, for a little while and at a little distance, looks as though it had been tailored in Saville Row. The girl can look like a fashion plate at an even lower price. . . . You can stand on the street corner, indulging in a private daydream of yourself as Clark Gable or Greta Garbo, which compensates you for a great deal. . . .

Trade since the war has had to adjust itself to meet the demands of underpaid, underfed people, with the result that a luxury is nowadays almost always cheaper than a necessity. One pair of plain solid shoes costs as much as two ultra-smart pairs. . . . And above all there is gambling, the cheapest of all luxuries. Even people on the verge of starvation can buy a few days' hope ("Something to live for," as they call it) by having a penny on a sweepstake. . . . Twenty million people are underfed but literally everyone in England has access to a radio. What we have lost in food we have gained in electricity. Whole sections of the working class who have been plundered of all they really need are being compensated, in part, by cheap luxuries which mitigate the surface of life.

Do you consider all this desirable? No, I don't. But it may be that the psychological adjustment which the working class are visibly making is the best they could make in the circumstances. They have neither turned revolutionary nor lost their self-respect; merely they have kept their tempers and settled down to make the best of things on a fish-and-chip standard. The alternative would be God knows what continued agonies of despair; or it might be attempted insurrections which, in a strongly governed country like England, could only lead to futile massacres and a régime of savage repression.

## QUESTIONS FOR ANALYSIS

1. According to Orwell, "extreme poverty" was less visible in the northern industrial towns than in London. Were family relations important in this regard?
2. What were the consequences of long-term unemployment for English workers? Were some of the consequences surprising?
3. Judging from Orwell's description, did radical revolution seem likely in England in the Great Depression? Why or why not?

*Source:* Excerpts from Chapter V in *The Road to Wigan Pier* by George Orwell, copyright © 1958 and renewed 1986 by the Estate of Sonia B. Orwell. Reprinted by permission of Harcourt, Inc.

Hugo Jager's photograph of a crowd of enthusiastic Hitler supporters. *(Hugo Jager/TimePix)*

CHAPTER

# 32 DICTATORSHIPS AND THE SECOND WORLD WAR

## CHAPTER OUTLINE



The era of anxiety and economic depression was also a time of growing strength for political dictatorship. In Europe, as in Japan and China in the 1930s, popularly elected governments and basic civil liberties declined drastically. On the eve of the Second World War, liberal democratic governments were surviving only in Great Britain, France, the Low Countries, the Scandinavian nations, and neutral Switzerland. Elsewhere in Europe, various kinds of strongmen ruled. Dictatorship seemed the wave of the future. Thus the intellectual and economic crisis discussed in Chapter 31 and the decline in liberal political institutions and the rise of dictatorships to be discussed in this chapter were interrelated elements in the general crisis of European civilization.

The West's era of dictatorship is a highly disturbing chapter in the history of civilization. The key development was not only the resurgence of authoritarian rule but also the rise of a particularly ruthless and dynamic tyranny. This new kind of tyranny reached its full realization in the Soviet Union and Nazi Germany in the 1930s. Stalin and Hitler mobilized their peoples for enormous undertakings and ruled with unprecedented severity. Hitler's mobilization was ultimately directed toward racial aggression and territorial expansion, and his sudden attack on Poland in 1939 started World War II. Hitler's successes then encouraged the Japanese to expand their stalemated campaign in China into a vast war in the Pacific with their attack on Pearl Harbor and their advance into South Asia.

Nazi armies and Japanese imperialists were defeated by a great coalition, and today we want to believe that the era of totalitarian dictatorship was a terrible accident, that Stalin's slave labor camps and Hitler's gas chambers "can't happen again." But the cruel truth is that horrible atrocities continue to plague the world in our time. The Khmer Rouge inflicted genocide on its people in Kampuchea, and civil war in Bosnia and Rwanda led to ethnically motivated atrocities recalling the horrors of the Second World War. And there are other examples. Thus it is vital that we understand Europe's era of brutal dictatorship in order to guard against the possibility of its recurrence.

- What was the nature of twentieth-century dictatorship and authoritarian rule?
- How did people live in the most extreme states: the Soviet Union and Nazi Germany?

- How did the rise of aggressive dictatorships result in another world war?

These are the questions this chapter will seek to answer.

## AUTHORITARIAN STATES

Both conservative and radical dictatorships swept through Europe in the 1920s and the 1930s. Although these two types of dictatorship shared some characteristics and sometimes overlapped in practice, they were in essence profoundly different. Conservative authoritarian regimes were an old story in Europe. Radical, totalitarian dictatorships were a new and frightening development.

### Conservative Authoritarianism

The traditional form of antidemocratic government in European history was conservative authoritarianism. Like Catherine the Great in Russia and Metternich in Austria, the leaders of such governments tried to prevent major changes that would undermine the existing social order. To do so, they relied on obedient bureaucracies, vigilant police departments, and trustworthy armies. They forbade popular participation in government or else severely limited it to natural allies such as landlords, bureaucrats, and high church officials. They persecuted liberals, democrats, and socialists as subversive radicals, often consigning them to jail or exile.

Yet old-fashioned authoritarian governments were limited in their power and in their objectives. They had neither the ability nor the desire to control many aspects of their subjects' lives. Preoccupied with the goal of mere survival, these governments largely limited their demands to taxes, army recruits, and passive acceptance. As long as the people did not try to change the system, they often had considerable personal independence.

After the First World War, this kind of authoritarian government revived, especially in the less-developed eastern part of Europe. There the parliamentary regimes that had been founded on the wreckage of empires in 1918 fell one by one. By early 1938 only economically and socially advanced Czechoslovakia remained true to liberal political ideals. Conservative dictators also took over in Spain and Portugal. There were several reasons for this development.

These lands lacked a strong tradition of self-government, with its necessary restraint and compromise. Moreover, many of these new states, such as Yugoslavia, were torn by ethnic conflicts that threatened their very existence. Dictatorship appealed to nationalists and military leaders as a way to repress such tensions and preserve national unity. Large landowners and the church were still powerful forces in these largely agrarian areas, and they often looked to dictators to save them from progressive land reform or communist agrarian upheaval. So did some members of the middle class, which was small and weak in eastern Europe. Finally, though some kind of democracy managed to stagger through the 1920s in Austria, Bulgaria, Romania, Greece, Estonia, and Latvia, the Great Depression delivered the final blow to those countries in 1936.

Although some of the conservative authoritarian regimes adopted certain Hitlerian and fascist characteristics in the 1930s, their general aims were limited. They were concerned more with maintaining the status quo than with mobilizing the masses or forcing society into rapid change or war. This tradition continued into the late twentieth century, especially in some of the military dictatorships that ruled in Latin America.

### Radical Totalitarian Dictatorships

Conservative authoritarianism predominated in the smaller states of central and eastern Europe by the mid-1930s, but a new kind of radical dictatorship emerged in the Soviet Union, Germany, and, to a lesser extent, Italy. Almost all scholars agree that the leaders of these radical dictatorships violently rejected liberal values and exercised unprecedented control over the masses. However, there has always been controversy over the interpretation of these regimes.

One extremely useful approach relates the radical dictatorships to the rise of modern totalitarianism. The concept of **totalitarianism** emerged in the 1920s and 1930s, although it is frequently and mistakenly seen as developing only after 1945 as part of anti-Soviet propaganda during the cold war. In 1924 Benito Mussolini spoke of the "fierce totalitarian will" of his movement in Italy. In the 1930s more and more British, American, and German exiled writers used the concept of totalitarianism to describe what they saw happening before their eyes. They linked Italian and especially German fascism with Soviet communism in "a 'new kind of state' that could be called totalitarian." With the alliance between Hitler and Stalin in 1939, "all doubts" about the totalitarian nature of both dictatorships "were swept away for most Americans."[1]

Early writers believed that modern totalitarian dictatorship burst on the scene with the revolutionary total war effort of 1914–1918. The war called forth a tendency to subordinate all institutions and all classes to the state in order to achieve one supreme objective: victory.

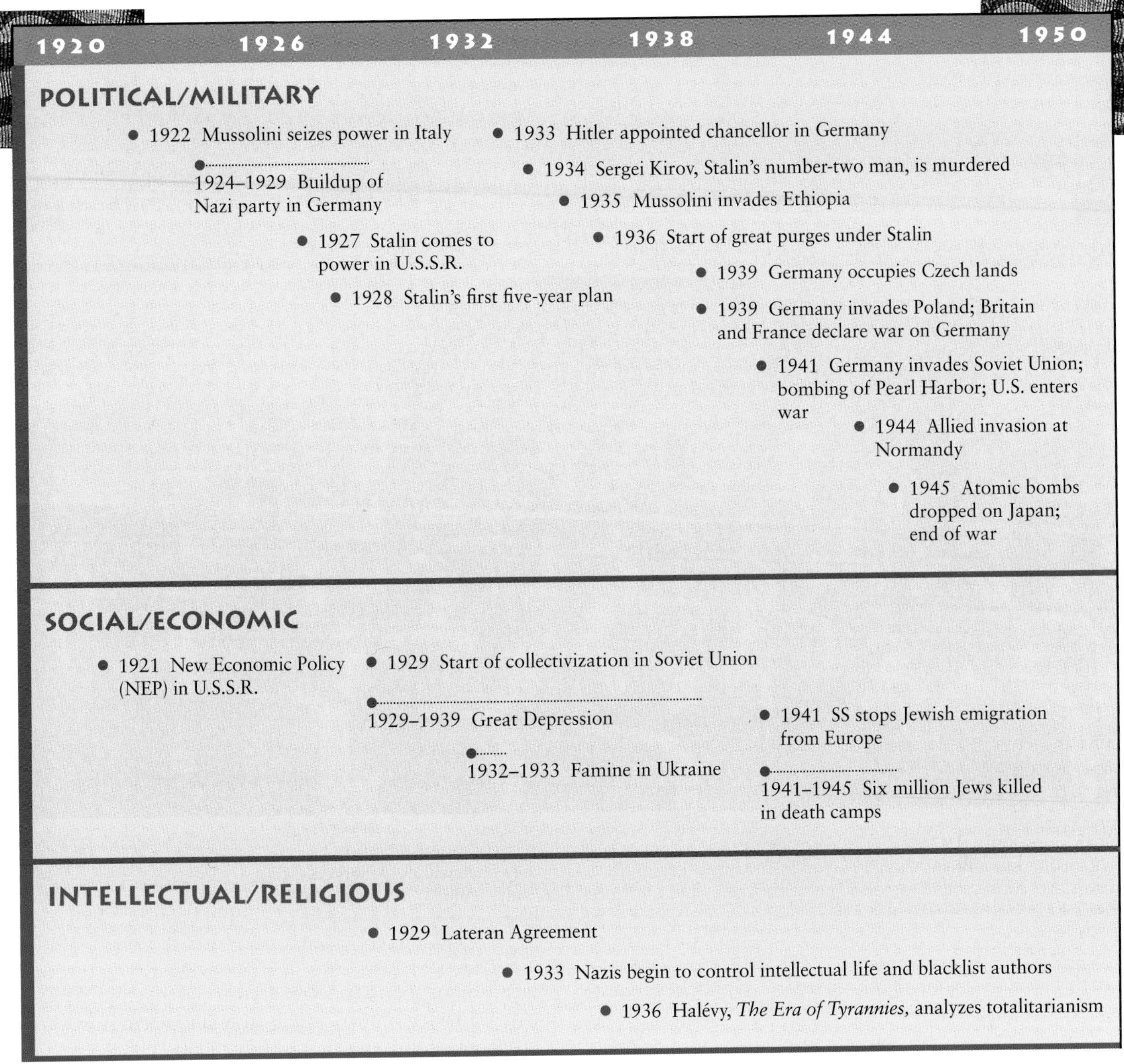

1920
1926
1932
1938
1944
1950
POLITICAL/MILITARY
1922 Mussolini seizes power in Italy
1924–1929 Buildup of Nazi party in Germany
1927 Stalin comes to power in U.S.S.R.
1928 Stalin's first five-year plan
1933 Hitler appointed chancellor in Germany
1934 Sergei Kirov, Stalin's number-two man, is murdered
1935 Mussolini invades Ethiopia
1936 Start of great purges under Stalin
1939 Germany occupies Czech lands
1939 Germany invades Poland; Britain and France declare war on Germany
1941 Germany invades Soviet Union; bombing of Pearl Harbor; U.S. enters war
1944 Allied invasion at Normandy
1945 Atomic bombs dropped on Japan; end of war
SOCIAL/ECONOMIC
1921 New Economic Policy (NEP) in U.S.S.R.
1929 Start of collectivization in Soviet Union
1929–1939 Great Depression
1932–1933 Famine in Ukraine
1941 SS stops Jewish emigration from Europe
1941–1945 Six million Jews killed in death camps
INTELLECTUAL/RELIGIOUS
1929 Lateran Agreement
1933 Nazis begin to control intellectual life and blacklist authors
1936 Halévy, The Era of Tyrannies, analyzes totalitarianism


As the French thinker Elie Halévy put it in 1936 in his influential *The Era of Tyrannies,* the varieties of modern totalitarian tyranny—fascism, Nazism, and communism—could be thought of as "feuding brothers" with a common father: the nature of modern war.[2]

Writers such as Halévy believed that the crucial experience of World War I was carried further by Lenin and the Bolsheviks during the Russian civil war. Lenin showed how a dedicated minority could achieve victory over a less determined majority and subordinate institutions and human rights to the needs of a single group—the Communist party—and its leader. Providing a model for single-party dictatorship, Lenin inspired imitators, including Adolf Hitler. The modern totalitarian state reached maturity in the 1930s in the Stalinist U.S.S.R. and Nazi Germany.

Embellishing on early insights, scholars also argued in the 1950s and 1960s that the totalitarian state used modern technology and communications to exercise complete political power. Increasingly, the state also tried to control just as completely the economic, social, intellectual, and cultural aspects of people's lives. Deviation from the

**Nazi Mass Rally, 1936** This picture captures the essence of the totalitarian interpretation of dynamic modern dictatorship. The uniformed members of the Nazi party have willingly merged themselves into a single force and await the command of the godlike leader. *(Wide World Photos)*

norm, even in art or family behavior, could become a crime.

This vision of total state represented a radical revolt against liberalism. Classical liberalism (see page 767) sought to limit the power of the state and protect the rights of the individual. Moreover, liberals stood for rationality, peaceful progress, economic freedom, and a strong middle class. All of that disgusted totalitarians. They believed in willpower, preached conflict, and worshiped violence. The individual was infinitely less valuable than the state.

Unlike old-fashioned authoritarianism, modern totalitarianism was based not on an elite but on people who had already become engaged in the political process, most notably through commitment to nationalism and socialism. Thus totalitarian societies were fully mobilized societies moving toward some goal and possessing boundless dynamism. As soon as one goal was achieved, another arose at the leader's command. Thus totalitarianism was a *permanent* revolution, an *unfinished* revolution, in which rapid, profound change imposed from on high went on forever.

In developing the concept of totalitarianism, scholars recognized that there were major differences between Stalin's communist U.S.S.R. and Hitler's Nazi Germany. Soviet communism, growing out of Marxian socialism, seized all private property (except personal property) for the state and crushed the middle classes. Nazi Germany, growing out of extreme nationalism and racism, criticized big landowners and industrialists, but both private property and the middle classes survived. This difference in property and class relations led some scholars to speak of "totalitarianism of the left"—Stalinist Russia—and "totalitarianism of the right"—Nazi Germany.

A second group of writers in the 1930s approached radical dictatorships outside the Soviet Union through the concept of **fascism.** A term of pride for Mussolini and Hitler, who used it to describe the supposedly "total" and revolutionary character of their movements, fascism was severely criticized by these writers and linked to decaying capitalism and domestic class conflict. Orthodox Marxists, generally sympathetic to the Soviet Union and the socialism it established, argued that fascism was the way powerful capitalists sought to create a mass movement capable of destroying the revolutionary working class and thus protect their enormous profits.

Comparative studies of fascist movements all across Europe later showed that they shared many characteristics, including extreme nationalism; an antisocialism aimed at destroying working-class movements; alliances with powerful capitalists and landowners; a dynamic and violent leader; and glorification of war and the military. These studies also highlighted how fascist movements generally failed to gain political power.

In recent years, many historians have tended to adopt a third approach, emphasizing the uniqueness of developments in each country. This is especially true for Hitler's Germany, where some elements of the totalitarian interpretation have been nuanced and revised, as we shall see. A similar revaluation of Stalin's U.S.S.R. is in progress now that the fall of communism has opened the former Soviet Union's archives to new research.

In summary, although the concept of totalitarianism has been questioned, it remains a valuable tool for historical understanding. It correctly highlights that both Hitler's Germany and Stalin's Soviet Union made an unprecedented "total claim" on the beliefs and behaviors of their respective citizens, as a noted scholar has recently concluded.[3] As for fascism, antidemocratic, antisocialist fascist movements sprang up all over Europe, but only in Italy and Germany (and some would say Spain) were they able to take power. Studies of fascist movements seeking to gain power identify important common elements, but they do not explain what fascist governments in Italy and Germany actually did. Finally, it is important to remember that the problem of Europe's radical dictatorships is complex and that there are few easy answers.

## STALIN'S SOVIET UNION

Lenin's harshest critics claim that he established the basic outlines of a modern totalitarian dictatorship after the Bolshevik Revolution and during the Russian civil war. If this is so, then Joseph Stalin (1879–1953) certainly finished the job. A master of political infighting, Stalin cautiously consolidated his power and eliminated his enemies in the mid-1920s. Then in 1928, as undisputed leader of the ruling Communist party, he launched the first **five-year plan**—the "revolution from above," as he so aptly termed it.

The five-year plans were extremely ambitious. They marked the beginning of a renewed attempt to mobilize and transform Soviet society along socialist lines. Their ultimate goal was to generate new attitudes, new loyalties, and a new socialist humanity. The means Stalin and the small Communist party elite chose in order to do so were constant propaganda, enormous sacrifice, and unlimited violence and state control. Thus many historians argue that the Soviet Union in the 1930s became a dynamic, modern totalitarian state.

### From Lenin to Stalin

By spring 1921 Lenin and the Bolsheviks had won the civil war, but they ruled a shattered and devastated land. Many farms were in ruins, and food supplies were exhausted. In southern Russia drought combined with the ravages of war to produce the worst famine in generations. Industrial production also broke down completely. The Bolsheviks had destroyed the economy as well as their foes.

In the face of economic disintegration, riots by peasants and workers, and an open rebellion by previously pro-Bolshevik sailors at Kronstadt, the tough but ever-flexible Lenin changed course. In March 1921 he announced the **New Economic Policy (NEP),** which re-established limited economic freedom in an attempt to rebuild agriculture and industry. Peasant producers were permitted to sell their surpluses in free markets, and private traders and small handicraft manufacturers were now allowed to reappear. Heavy industry, railroads, and banks, however, remained wholly nationalized.

The NEP was shrewd and successful both politically and economically. Politically, it was a necessary but temporary compromise with the Soviet Union's overwhelming peasant majority. Realizing that his government was not strong enough to take land from the peasants, Lenin made a deal with the only force capable of overturning his government. Economically, the NEP brought rapid recovery. In 1926 industrial output surpassed the level of 1913, and Soviet peasants were producing almost as much grain as before the war.

As the economy recovered, an intense struggle for power began in the inner circles of the Communist party, for Lenin had left no chosen successor when he died in

1924. The principal contenders were the stolid Stalin and the flamboyant Trotsky.

The son of a shoemaker, Joseph Dzhugashvili—later known as Stalin—studied for the priesthood but was expelled from his theological seminary, probably for rude rebelliousness. By 1903 he was a Bolshevik revolutionary in southern Russia.

Stalin was a good organizer but a poor speaker and writer, with no experience outside Russia. Trotsky, an inspiring leader who had planned the 1917 takeover (see page 953) and created the victorious Red Army, appeared to have all the advantages. Yet it was Stalin who succeeded Lenin. Stalin won because he was more effective at gaining the all-important support of the party, the only genuine source of power in the one-party state. Rising to general secretary of the party's Central Committee just before Lenin's first stroke in 1922, Stalin used his office to win friends and allies with jobs and promises.

The practical Stalin also related Marxian teachings to Soviet realities more effectively than Trotsky. Stalin developed a theory of "socialism in one country," arguing that the Russian-dominated Soviet Union had the ability to build socialism on its own. Trotsky maintained that socialism in the Soviet Union could succeed only if revolution occurred quickly throughout Europe. To many Soviet communists Trotsky's views seemed to sell their country short, whereas Stalin's willingness to push socialism at home appealed to their optimistic idealism.

With cunning skill Stalin gradually achieved absolute power between 1922 and 1927. Stalin used the moderates to crush Trotsky, then he turned against the moderates and destroyed them as well. Stalin's final triumph came at the party congress December 1927, which condemned all "deviation from the general party line" formulated by Stalin. The dictator was then ready to launch his revolution from above—the real revolution for millions of ordinary citizens.

## The Five-Year Plans

The party congress of 1927 marked the end of the NEP and the beginning of the era of socialist five-year plans. The first five-year plan had staggering economic objectives. In just five years, total industrial output was to increase by 250 percent. Agricultural production was slated to increase by 150 percent, and one-fifth of the peasants in the Soviet Union were scheduled to give up their private plots and join socialist collective farms. In spite of warnings from moderate communists that these goals were unrealistic, Stalin raised them higher as the plan got under way. By 1930 economic and social change was sweeping the country.

Stalin unleashed his "second revolution" for a variety of interrelated reasons. There were, first of all, ideological considerations. Like Lenin, Stalin and his militant supporters were deeply committed to socialism as they understood it. Moreover, the economic recovery seemed to have stalled in 1927 and 1928. A new socialist offensive seemed necessary if industry and agriculture were to grow rapidly.

Political considerations were most important. Internationally, there was the old problem of catching up with the advanced and presumably hostile capitalist nations of the West. Stalin said in 1931, when he pressed for ever-greater speed and sacrifice, "We are fifty or a hundred years behind the advanced countries. We must make good this distance in ten years. Either we do it, or we shall go under."[4]

Domestically, there was the problem of the peasants. For centuries the peasants had wanted to own the land, and finally they had it. Sooner or later, the communists reasoned, the peasants would become conservative little capitalists and pose a threat to the regime. Therefore, Stalin decided on a preventive war against the peasantry in order to bring it under the absolute control of the state.

That war was **collectivization**—the forcible consolidation of individual peasant farms into large, state-controlled enterprises. Beginning in 1929 peasants all over the Soviet Union were ordered to give up their land and animals and become members of collective farms, although they continued to live in their own homes. As for the **kulaks,** the better-off peasants, Stalin instructed party workers to "liquidate them as a class." Stripped of land and livestock, the kulaks were generally not even permitted to join the collective farms. Many starved or were deported to forced-labor camps for "re-education."

Since almost all peasants were in fact poor, the term *kulak* soon meant any peasant who opposed the new system. Whole villages were often attacked. One conscience-stricken colonel in the secret police confessed to a foreign journalist,

> *I am an old Bolshevik. I worked in the underground against the Tsar and then I fought in the Civil War. Did I do all that in order that I should now surround villages with machine guns and order my men to fire indiscriminately into crowds of peasants? Oh, no, no!*[5]

Forced collectivization of the peasants led to disaster. Large numbers of peasants slaughtered their animals and burned their crops in sullen, hopeless protest. Between 1929 and 1933 the number of horses, cattle, sheep, and goats in the Soviet Union fell by at least half. Nor were

**Life in a Forced-Labor Camp** This rare photo from about 1933 shows the reality of deported peasants and other political prisoners building the Stalin–White Sea Canal in far northern Russia, with their bare hands and under the most dehumanizing conditions. In books and plays, Stalin's followers praised the project as a model for the regeneration of "reactionaries" and "kulak exploiters" through the joys of socialist work. *(David King Collection)*

the state-controlled collective farms more productive. The output of grain barely increased between 1928 and 1938. Collectivized agriculture was unable to make any substantial financial contribution to Soviet industrial development during the first five-year plan.

The human dimension of the tragedy was absolutely staggering. Stalin himself confided to Winston Churchill at Yalta in 1945 that 10 million people had died in the course of collectivization. In Ukraine the drive against peasants snowballed into a general assault on Ukrainians as reactionary nationalists and enemies of socialism. In 1932 Stalin and his associates set levels of grain deliveries for the Ukrainian collective farms at excessively high levels, and they refused to relax those quotas or even allow food relief when Ukrainian communist leaders reported that starvation was occurring. The result was a terrible man-made famine in Ukraine in 1932 and 1933, which probably claimed 6 million lives.

Collectivization was a cruel but real victory for communist ideologues. By 1938, 93 percent of peasant families had been herded onto collective farms. Regimented as employees of the state and dependent on the state-owned tractor stations, the collectivized peasants were no longer even a potential political threat to the regime.

Yet, as recent research shows, peasants fought back with indirect daily opposition and forced the supposedly all-powerful state to make modest compromises. Peasants secured the right to limit a family's labor on the state-run farms and to cultivate tiny, grudgingly tolerated family plots, which provided them with much of their food. In 1938 these family plots produced 22 percent of all Soviet agricultural produce on only 4 percent of all cultivated land, eloquent testimony to the quiet resistance of the weak in the countryside.

The industrial side of the five-year plans was more successful—indeed, quite spectacular. Soviet industry produced about four times as much in 1937 as it had in 1928. No other major country had ever achieved such rapid industrial growth. Heavy industry led the way; consumer industry grew quite slowly. Urban development accelerated, and more than 25 million people migrated to cities during the 1930s.

The great industrialization drive, concentrated between 1928 and 1937, was an awe-inspiring achievement purchased at enormous sacrifice. The sudden creation of dozens of new factories (and the increasingly voracious military) demanded tremendous resources. The money was collected from the people by means of heavy, hidden sales taxes.

Two other factors contributed importantly to rapid industrialization: firm labor discipline and foreign engineers. Trade unions lost most of their power, and individuals could not move without the permission of the police. When factory managers needed more hands, they called on their counterparts on the collective farms, who sent them millions of "unneeded" peasants over the years.

Foreign engineers were hired to plan and construct many of the new factories. Highly skilled American engineers, hungry for work in the depression years, were particularly important until newly trained Soviet experts began to replace them after 1932. The gigantic mills of the new Siberian steel industry were modeled on America's best. Thus Stalin's planners harnessed even the skill and technology of capitalist countries to promote the surge of socialist industry.

## Life and Culture in Soviet Society

The aim of Stalin's five-year plans was to create a new kind of society and human personality as well as a strong industrial economy and a powerful army. Stalin and his helpers were good Marxian economic determinists. Once everything was owned by the state, they believed, a socialist society and a new kind of human being would inevitably emerge. Their utopian vision of a new humanity floundered, but they did build a new society, whose broad outlines existed into the mid-1980s. Life in this society had both good and bad aspects.

Because consumption was reduced to pay for investment, there was no improvement in the average standard of living. Indeed, the average nonfarm wage fell by 50 percent between 1928 and 1932, and rose only slightly thereafter. Collectivized peasants experienced greater declines.

Life was hard in Stalin's Soviet Union. The masses of people lived primarily on black bread and wore old, shabby clothing. There were constant shortages in the stores, although very heavily taxed vodka was always readily available. A shortage of housing was a particularly serious problem. A relatively lucky family received one room for all its members and shared both a kitchen and a toilet with others on the floor. Less fortunate people built scrap-lumber shacks in shantytowns.

Life was hard but by no means hopeless. Idealism and ideology had real appeal for many communists, who saw themselves heroically building the world's first socialist society while capitalism crumbled and fascism rose in the West. This optimistic belief in the future of the Soviet Union also attracted many disillusioned Westerners to communism in the 1930s.

On a more practical level Soviet workers did receive some important social benefits, such as old-age pensions, free medical services, free education, and day-care centers for children. Unemployment was almost unknown. Finally, there was the possibility of personal advancement.

The keys to improving one's position were specialized skills and technical education. Rapid industrialization

**Adult Education** Illiteracy, especially among women, was a serious problem after the Russian Revolution. This early photo suggests how many adults successfully learned to read and write throughout the Soviet Union. *(Sovfoto)*

required massive numbers of trained experts, such as skilled workers, engineers, and plant managers. Thus the Stalinist state broke with the egalitarian policies of the 1920s and provided tremendous incentives to those who could serve its needs. A growing technical and managerial elite joined with the political and artistic elites in a new upper class, whose members were rich, powerful, and insecure. Thus millions struggled for an education.

The radical transformation of Soviet society had a profound impact on women's lives. Marxists had traditionally believed that both capitalism and the middle-class husband exploited women. The Russian Revolution of 1917 immediately proclaimed complete equality of rights for women. In the 1920s divorce and abortion were made easily available, and women were urged to work outside the home and liberate themselves sexually. After Stalin came to power, sexual and familial liberation was played down, and the most lasting changes for women involved work and education.

Young women were constantly told that they had to be fully equal to men. Peasant women continued to work on farms, and millions of women now toiled in factories and heavy construction. Determined women pursued their studies and entered the ranks of the better-paid specialists in industry and science. Medicine practically became a woman's profession. By 1950, 75 percent of all doctors in the Soviet Union were women.

Soviet society gave women great opportunities, but it demanded great sacrifices as well. The vast majority of women simply *had* to work outside the home. Wages were so low that it was almost impossible for a family or couple to live only on the husband's earnings. Men continued to dominate the very best jobs. In any event, the massive mobilization of women was a striking characteristic of the Soviet state.

Culture lost its autonomy in the 1930s and became thoroughly politicized through constant propaganda and indoctrination. Party activists lectured workers in factories and peasants on collective farms, while newspapers, films, and radio broadcasts endlessly recounted socialist achievements and capitalist plots. Whereas the 1920s had seen considerable experimentation in modern art and theater, writers and artists who could effectively combine genuine creativity and political propaganda became the darlings of the regime. It became increasingly important for the successful writer and artist to glorify Russian nationalism. Russian history was rewritten so that early tsars such as Ivan the Terrible and Peter the Great became worthy forerunners of the greatest Russian leader of all—Stalin.

**Stalin and Soviet Workers, Marching to Victory** Stalin appeared rarely in public, but posters singing his praises were everywhere. Here the mighty ruler is almost one of the boys. "Our program is realistic," Stalin proclaims on the poster, "because it is you and me working together." *(David King Collection)*

## Stalinist Terror and the Great Purges

In the mid-1930s the great offensive to build socialism and a new socialist personality culminated in ruthless police terror and a massive purging of the Communist party. The top members of the party and government publicly supported Stalin's initiatives, but there was some grumbling in the party. In late 1934 Stalin's number two man, Sergei Kirov, was suddenly and mysteriously murdered. Although Stalin himself probably ordered Kirov's murder, he used the incident to launch a reign of terror.

In August 1936 sixteen prominent Old Bolsheviks confessed to all manner of plots against Stalin in spectacular public trials in Moscow. Then in 1937 the secret police arrested a mass of lesser party officials and newer members, also torturing them and extracting more confessions for more show trials. In addition to the party faithful, union officials, managers, intellectuals, army officers, and countless ordinary citizens were struck down. In all at least 8 million people were probably arrested, and millions of these were executed or never returned from prisons and forced-labor camps.

Stalin and the remaining party leadership recruited 1.5 million new members to take the place of those purged. Thus more than half of all Communist party members in 1941 had joined since the purges. "These new men were 'thirty-something' products of the Second Revolution of the 1930s, Stalin's upwardly mobile yuppies, so to speak."[6] Often sons (and daughters) of workers who had studied in the new technical schools, this new generation of Stalin-formed Communists would serve the leader effectively until his death in 1953, and they would govern the Soviet Union until the early 1980s.

Stalin's mass purges remain baffling, for almost all historians believe that those purged posed no threat and confessed to crimes they had not committed. Certainly the highly publicized purges sent a warning to the people: no one was secure; everyone had to serve the party and its leader with redoubled devotion. Some Western scholars have also argued that the terror reflected a fully developed totalitarian state, which must always be fighting real or imaginary enemies.

The long-standing interpretation that puts the blame for the great purges on Stalin's cruelty or madness has been challenged in recent years. Revisionist historians argue that Stalin's fears were exaggerated but genuine and that they were shared by many in the party and in the general population. Bombarded with ideology and political slogans, the population responded energetically to Stalin's directives. Investigations and trials snowballed into a mass hysteria, a new witch-hunt.[7] In short, in this view of the 1930s, a popular but deluded Stalin found large numbers of willing collaborators for crime as well as for achievement.

## MUSSOLINI AND FASCISM IN ITALY

Mussolini's movement and his seizure of power in 1922 were important steps in the rise of dictatorships in Europe between the two world wars. Like all the future dictators, the young Mussolini hated liberalism and wanted to destroy it in Italy. At the same time, he and his supporters were the first to call themselves "fascists"—revolutionaries determined to create a certain kind of totalitarian state. Few scholars today would argue that Mussolini succeeded. His dictatorship was brutal and theatrical, but it remained a halfway house between conservative authoritarianism and modern totalitarianism.

### The Seizure of Power

In the early twentieth century Italy was a liberal state with civil rights and a constitutional monarchy. On the eve of the First World War the parliamentary regime finally granted universal male suffrage. But there were serious problems. Much of the Italian population was still poor, and many peasants were more attached to their villages and local interests than to the national state. Moreover, the papacy, many devout Catholics, conservatives, and landowners remained strongly opposed to the middle-class lawyers and politicians who ran the country largely for their own benefit. Relations between church and state were often tense. Class differences were also extreme, and by 1912 the powerful revolutionary socialist movement was led by the radical wing of the Socialist party.[8]

The war worsened the political situation. Having fought on the side of the Allies almost exclusively for purposes of territorial expansion, the parliamentary government bitterly disappointed Italian nationalists with Italy's modest gains at Versailles. Workers and peasants also felt cheated: to win their support during the war, the government had promised social and land reform, which it did not deliver after the war.

The Russian Revolution inspired and energized Italy's revolutionary socialist movement, and radical workers and peasants began occupying factories and seizing land in 1920. These actions scared and mobilized the property-owning classes. Thus by 1921 revolutionary socialists, antiliberal conservatives, and frightened property owners were all opposed—though for different reasons—to the liberal parliamentary government.

Into these crosscurrents of unrest and fear stepped the blustering, bullying Benito Mussolini (1883–1945). Son of a village schoolteacher and a poor blacksmith, Mussolini began his political career as a Socialist party leader and radical newspaper editor before World War I. Expelled from the Italian Socialist party for supporting the war and wounded in 1917, Mussolini returned home and began organizing bitter war veterans into a band of fascists—from the Italian word for "a union of forces."

At first Mussolini's program was a radical combination of nationalist and socialist demands, including territorial expansion, benefits for workers, and land reform for peasants. It competed directly with the well-organized Socialist party and failed to get off the ground. When Mussolini saw that his violent verbal assaults on rival Socialists won him growing support from conservatives and the frightened middle classes, he shifted gears in 1920. In thought and action Mussolini was a striking example of the turbulent uncertainty of the age of anxiety.

Mussolini and his growing private army of **Black Shirts** began to grow violent. Typically, a band of fascist toughs would roar off in trucks at night and swoop down on a few isolated Socialist organizers, beating them up and force-feeding them almost deadly doses of castor oil. Few people were killed, but Socialist newspapers, union halls, and local Socialist party headquarters were destroyed. Mussolini's toughs pushed Socialists out of the city governments of northern Italy.

A skillful politician, Mussolini allowed his followers to convince themselves that they were not just opposing the "Reds" but also making a real revolution of their own, forging a strong, dynamic movement that would help the little people against the established interests. With the government breaking down in 1922, largely because of the chaos created by his direct-action bands, Mussolini stepped forward as the savior of order and property. Striking a conservative note in his speeches and gaining the sympathetic neutrality of army leaders, Mussolini demanded the resignation of the existing government and his own appointment by the king. In October 1922, to force matters, a large group of fascists marched on Rome to threaten the king and force him to call on Mussolini. The threat worked. Victor Emmanuel III (r. 1900–1946), who had no love for the old liberal politicians, asked Mussolini to form a new cabinet. Thus, after widespread violence and a threat of armed uprising, Mussolini seized power "legally." He was immediately granted dictatorial authority for one year by the king and the parliament.

**Mussolini** A charismatic orator with a sure touch for emotional propaganda, Mussolini loved settings that linked fascist Italy to the glories of imperial Rome. Poised to address a mass rally in Rome shortly after his thugs had murdered the leader of the Socialist opposition, Mussolini then called for 90,000 more volunteers to join his fascist militia. Members of the militia stand as an honor guard in front of the podium. *(Popperfoto)*

## The Regime in Action

Mussolini became dictator on the strength of Italians' rejection of parliamentary government coupled with fears of Soviet-style revolution. At first Mussolini's goals were not clear. But in 1924 he responded to another crisis by declaring his desire to "make the nation Fascist," and he then imposed a series of repressive measures. Freedom of the press was abolished, elections were fixed, and the government ruled by decree. Mussolini arrested his political opponents, disbanded all independent labor unions, and put dedicated Fascists in control of Italy's schools. He created a fascist youth movement, fascist labor unions, and many other fascist organizations. He trumpeted his goal in a famous slogan of 1926: "Everything in the state, nothing outside the state, nothing against the state." By the end of that year Italy was a one-party dictatorship under Mussolini's unquestioned leadership.

Mussolini, however, did not complete the establishment of a modern totalitarian state. His Fascist party never destroyed the old power structure. Interested primarily in personal power, Mussolini was content to compromise with the old conservative classes that controlled the army, the economy, and the state. He never tried to purge these classes or even move very vigorously against them. He controlled and propagandized labor but left big business to regulate itself, profitably and securely. There was no land reform.

Mussolini also drew increasing support from the Catholic church. In the **Lateran Agreement** of 1929, he recognized the Vatican as a tiny independent state, and he agreed to give the church heavy financial support. The pope expressed his satisfaction and urged Italians to support Mussolini's government.

Nothing better illustrates Mussolini's unwillingness to harness everyone and everything for dynamic action than his treatment of women. He abolished divorce and told women to stay at home and produce children. To promote that goal he decreed a special tax on bachelors in 1934. In 1938 women were limited by law to a maximum of 10 percent of the better-paying jobs in industry and government. Italian women appear not to have changed their attitudes or behavior in any important way under fascist rule.

Mussolini's government did not pass racial laws until 1938 and did not persecute Jews savagely until late in the Second World War, when Italy was under Nazi control. Nor did Mussolini establish a truly ruthless police state. Only twenty-three political prisoners were condemned to death between 1926 and 1944. In spite of much pompous posing by the chauvinist leader and in spite of mass meetings, salutes, and a certain copying of Hitler's aggression in foreign policy after 1933, Mussolini's fascist Italy, though repressive and undemocratic, was never really totalitarian.

## HITLER AND NAZISM IN GERMANY

The most frightening dictatorship developed in Nazi Germany. A product of Hitler's evil genius, as well as of Germany's social and political situation and the general attack on liberalism and rationality in the age of anxiety, the Nazi movement shared some of the characteristics of Mussolini's Italian model and was a form of fascism. But the Nazi dictatorship smashed or took over most independent organizations, mobilized the economy, and persecuted the Jewish population. Thus **Nazism** asserted an unlimited claim over German society and proclaimed the ultimate power of its endlessly aggressive leader—Adolf Hitler. The aspirations of Nazism were truly totalitarian.

### The Roots of Nazism

Nazism grew out of many complex developments, of which the most influential were extreme nationalism and racism. These two ideas captured the mind of the young Hitler, and it was he who dominated Nazism for as long as it lasted.

Born the fourth child of a successful Austrian customs official and an indulgent mother, Adolf Hitler (1889–1945) spent his childhood in small towns in Austria. A good student in grade school, Hitler did poorly in high school and dropped out at age fourteen after the death of his father. After four years of unfocused loafing, Hitler finally left for Vienna, where he lived a comfortable, lazy life on his generous orphan's pension and found most of the perverted beliefs that guided his life.

In Vienna Hitler soaked up extreme German nationalism, which was particularly strong there. Austro-German nationalists believed Germans to be a superior people and the natural rulers of central Europe. They often advocated union with Germany and violent expulsion of "inferior" peoples as the means of maintaining German domination of the Austro-Hungarian Empire.

Hitler was deeply impressed by Vienna's mayor, Karl Lueger (1844–1910). With the help of the Catholic trade unions, Lueger had succeeded in winning the support of the little people of Vienna, and he showed Hitler the enormous potential of anticapitalist and antiliberal propaganda.

From Lueger and others Hitler eagerly absorbed virulent anti-Semitism, racism, and hatred of Slavs. He developed an unshakable belief in the crudest, most exaggerated distortions of the Darwinian theory of survival, the superiority of Germanic races, and the inevitability of racial conflict. Anti-Semitism and racism became Hitler's most passionate convictions, his explanation for everything. The Jews, he claimed, directed an international conspiracy of finance capitalism and Marxian socialism against German culture, German unity, and the German race. Hitler's belief was totally irrational, but he never doubted it.

Although he moved to Munich in 1913 to avoid being drafted into the Austrian army, the lonely Hitler greeted the outbreak of the First World War as a salvation. He later wrote in his autobiography, *Mein Kampf,* that, "overcome by passionate enthusiasm, I fell to my knees and thanked heaven out of an overflowing heart." The struggle and discipline of war gave life meaning, and Hitler served bravely as a dispatch carrier on the western front.

When Germany was suddenly defeated in 1918, Hitler's world was shattered. Not only was he a fanatical nationalist, but war was his reason for living. Convinced that Jews and Marxists had "stabbed Germany in the back," he vowed to fight on.

In late 1919 Hitler joined a tiny extremist group in Munich called the German Workers' party, which promised unity under a uniquely German "national socialism" that would abolish the injustices of capitalism and create a mighty "people's community." By 1921 Hitler had gained absolute control of this small but growing party. He was already a master of mass propaganda and political showmanship. His most effective tool was the mass rally, a kind of political revival meeting, where he often worked his audience into a frenzy with wild attacks on the Versailles treaty, the Jews, war profiteers, and Germany's Weimar Republic.

Party membership multiplied tenfold after early 1922. In late 1923 the Weimar Republic seemed on the verge of collapse, and Hitler, inspired by Mussolini's recent easy victory, decided on an armed uprising in Munich. Despite the failure of the poorly organized plot and Hitler's arrest, Nazism had been born.

## Hitler's Road to Power

At his trial Hitler violently denounced the Weimar Republic, and he gained enormous publicity and attention. Moreover, he learned from his unsuccessful revolt. Hitler concluded that he had to undermine, rather than overthrow, the government and come to power legally through electoral competition. He forced his more violent supporters to accept his new strategy. He also used his brief prison term to dictate *Mein Kampf*. There he expounded on his basic themes: "race," with a stress on anti-Semitism; "living space," with a sweeping vision of war and conquered territory; and the leader-dictator (**Führer**), with unlimited, arbitrary power.

In the years of prosperity and relative stability between 1924 and 1929, Hitler concentrated on building his National Socialist German Workers' party, or Nazi party. Yet the Nazis remained a small splinter group in 1928, when they received only 2.6 percent of the vote in the general elections and twelve seats in the Reichstag.

The Great Depression, shattering economic prosperity from 1929 on, presented Hitler with a fabulous opportunity. Unemployment jumped from 1.3 million in 1929 to 5 million in 1930. By the end of 1932 an incredible 43 percent of the labor force was unemployed. Industrial production fell by one-half between 1929 and 1932. No factor contributed more to Hitler's success than the economic crisis. Never very interested in economics before, Hitler began promising German voters economic as well as political and international salvation.

Above all, Hitler rejected free-market capitalism and advocated government programs to bring recovery. Hitler pitched his speeches especially to middle- and lower-middle-class groups—small business people, officeworkers, artisans, and peasants—as well as to skilled workers striving for middle-class status. As the economy collapsed, great numbers of middle- and lower-middle-class people "voted their pocketbooks,"[9] as new research argues convincingly, and deserted the conservative and moderate parties for the Nazis. In the election of 1930 the Nazis won 6.5 million votes and 107 seats, and in July 1932 the Nazis gained 14.5 million votes—38 percent of the total—and became the largest party in the Reichstag.

The appeal to pocketbook interests was particularly effective in the early 1930s because Hitler appeared more mainstream, playing down his anti-Jewish hatred and racist nationalism. A master of mass propaganda and psychology, he had written in *Mein Kampf* that the masses were the "driving force of the most important changes in this world" and were themselves driven by fanaticism and not by knowledge. But now when he harangued vast audiences with wild oratory and simple slogans, he featured "national rebirth" and the "crimes" of the Versailles treaty. And many uncertain individuals, surrounded by thousands of enthralled listeners, found a sense of belonging as well as hope for better times.

Hitler and the Nazis also appealed strongly to German youth. Indeed, in some ways the Nazi movement was a mass movement of young Germans. Hitler himself was only forty in 1929, and he and most of his top aides were much younger than other leading German politicians. "National Socialism is the organized will of the youth," proclaimed the official Nazi slogan, and the battle cry of Gregor Strasser, a leading Nazi organizer, was "Make way, you old ones."[10] In 1931 almost 40 percent of Nazi party members were under thirty, compared with 20 percent of Social Democrats. National recovery, exciting and rapid change, and personal advancement were the appeals of Nazism to millions of German youths.

Another reason Hitler came to power was that normal democratic government broke down as early as May 1930. Unable to gain the support of a majority in the Reichstag, Chancellor (chief minister) Heinrich Brüning convinced the president, the aging war hero General Hindenburg, to authorize rule by decree. Intending to use this emergency measure indefinitely, Brüning was determined to overcome the economic crisis by cutting back government spending and ruthlessly forcing down prices and wages. Brüning's ultraorthodox policies intensified the economic collapse in Germany and convinced many voters that the country's republican leaders were stupid and corrupt, thereby adding to Hitler's appeal.

The continuing struggle between the Social Democrats and the Communists was another aspect of the breakdown of democratic government. The Communists refused to cooperate with the Social Democrats, even

**"The Officers of Tomorrow"** The Nazis tried hard to win the support of young people. After they came to power, the Nazis put boys in the uniform of the Hitler Youth, shown here in a German historical museum. The Hitler Youth preached Nazi values and militarism, the message of the poster and its caption. *(AKG London)*

though the two parties together outnumbered the Nazis in the Reichstag, even after the elections of 1932. German Communists (and the still complacent Stalin) were blinded by hatred of socialists and by ideology: the Communists believed that Hitler's fascism represented the last agonies of monopoly capitalism and that a communist revolution would soon follow his taking power. Disunity on the left was undoubtedly another nail in the republic's coffin.

Finally, Hitler excelled in the dirty, backroom politics of the decaying Weimar Republic. That, in fact, brought him to power. In complicated infighting in 1932, he cleverly succeeded in gaining additional support from key people in the army and big business. These people thought they could use Hitler to their own advantage, and many conservative and nationalistic politicians thought similarly. They thus accepted Hitler's demand that he would join a coalition government only if he became chancellor, believing that they could control him in such a government. On January 30, 1933, Adolf Hitler, leader of the largest party in Germany, was legally appointed chancellor by Hindenburg.

## The Nazi State and Society

Hitler moved rapidly and skillfully to establish an unshakable dictatorship. He immediately called for new elections. When the Reichstag building was partly destroyed by fire, Hitler screamed that the Communist party was responsible, and he convinced President Hindenburg to sign dictatorial emergency acts that practically abolished freedom of speech and assembly as well as most personal liberties.

When the Nazis won only 44 percent of the vote in the elections, Hitler immediately outlawed the Communist party and arrested its parliamentary representatives. Then on March 23, 1933, the Nazis used threats and blackmail to help push through the Reichstag the so-called **Enabling Act,** which gave Hitler absolute dictatorial power for four years. Armed with the Enabling Act, Hitler and the Nazis took over the government bureaucracy intact, installing many Nazis in top positions. At the same time, they created a series of overlapping Nazi party organizations responsible solely to Hitler.

As recent research shows, the resulting system of dual government was riddled with rivalries, contradictions, and inefficiencies. The Nazi state lacked the all-encompassing unity that its propagandists claimed and was sloppy and often disorganized, but this fractured system suited Hitler and his purposes. He could play the established bureaucracy against his private, personal "party government" and maintain his freedom of action. Hitler could concentrate on general principles and the big decisions, which he always made.

One big decision outlawed strikes and abolished independent labor unions, which were replaced by the Nazi Labor Front. Professional people—doctors and lawyers, teachers and engineers—also saw their previously independent organizations swallowed up in Nazi associations. Publishing houses and universities were put under Nazi control, and passionate students and pitiful professors burned forbidden books in public squares. Modern art and architecture were ruthlessly prohibited. Life became violently anti-intellectual. As the cynical Goebbels put it, "When I hear the word 'culture' I reach for my gun."[11] By 1934 a brutal dictatorship characterized by frightening dynamism and obedience to Hitler was already largely in place.

Only the army retained independence, and Hitler moved ruthlessly and skillfully to establish his control there, too. The Nazi storm troopers (the SA), the quasi-military band of 3 million toughs in brown shirts who had fought communists and beaten up Jews before the Nazis took power, expected top positions in the army and even talked of a "second revolution" against capitalism. Needing to preserve good relations with the army and with big business, Hitler decided that the SA leaders had to be eliminated. On the night of June 30, 1934, he struck. Hitler's elite personal guard—the SS—arrested and shot without trial roughly a thousand SA leaders and assorted political enemies. Shortly thereafter army leaders swore a binding oath of "unquestioning obedience . . . to the Leader of the German State and People, Adolf Hitler." The SS grew rapidly. Under its methodical, inhuman leader, Heinrich Himmler (1900–1945), the SS joined with the political police, the Gestapo, to expand its network of special courts and concentration camps. Nobody was safe.

From the beginning Jews were a special object of Nazi persecution. By the end of 1934 most Jewish lawyers, doctors, professors, civil servants, and musicians had lost their jobs and the right to practice their professions. In 1935 the infamous Nuremberg Laws classified as Jewish anyone having one or more Jewish grandparents and deprived Jews of all rights of citizenship. By 1938 roughly one-quarter of Germany's half million Jews had emigrated, sacrificing almost all their property in order to leave Germany.

In late 1938 the attack on the Jews accelerated. A well-organized wave of violence destroyed homes, synagogues, and businesses, after which German Jews were rounded up and made to pay for the damage. It became very difficult for Jews to leave Germany. Some Germans privately opposed these outrages, but most went along or looked the other way. Although this lack of response reflected the individual's helplessness in a totalitarian state, it was more certainly a sign of the strong popular support Hitler's government enjoyed.

## Hitler's Popularity

Hitler had promised the masses economic recovery—"work and bread"—and he delivered. Breaking with Brüning's do-nothing policies, Hitler immediately launched a large public works program to pull Germany out of the depression. Work began on superhighways, offices, gigantic sports stadiums, and public housing. In 1936 Germany turned decisively toward rearmament. Unemployment dropped steadily, and by 1938 everyone had work, while the average standard of living increased moderately. The profits of business rose sharply. For millions of people economic recovery was tangible evidence that Nazi promises were more than show and propaganda.

For the masses of ordinary German citizens who were not Jews, Slavs, Gypsies, Jehovah's Witnesses, communists, or homosexuals, Hitler's government meant greater equality and more opportunities. In 1933 barriers between classes in Germany were generally high. Hitler's rule introduced changes that lowered these barriers. For example, stiff educational requirements, which favored the well-to-do, were relaxed. The new Nazi elite included many young and poorly educated dropouts, rootless lower-middle-class people like Hitler who rose to the top with breathtaking speed. More generally, the Nazis tolerated privilege and wealth only as long as they served the needs of the party.

Yet few historians today believe that Hitler and the Nazis brought about a real social revolution, as an earlier generation of scholars often argued. Quantitative studies show that the well-educated classes held on to most of their advantages and that only a modest social leveling occurred in the Nazi years. It is significant that the Nazis shared with the Italian fascists the stereotypic view of women as housewives and mothers. Only under the relentless pressure of war did they reluctantly mobilize large numbers of German women for work in offices and factories.

Hitler's rabid nationalism, which had helped him gain power, continued to appeal to Germans after 1933. Thus in later years, when Hitler went from one foreign triumph to another and a great German empire seemed within reach, the majority of the population was delighted and kept praising the Führer's actions well into the war.

Not all Germans supported Hitler, however, and a number of German groups actively resisted him after 1933. Tens of thousands of political enemies were imprisoned, and thousands were executed. In the first years of Hitler's rule, the principal resisters were the communists and the socialists in the trade unions. But the expansion of the SS system of terror after 1935 smashed most of these leftists. A second group of opponents arose in the Catholic and Protestant churches. However, their efforts were directed primarily at preserving genuine religious life, not at overthrowing Hitler. Finally in 1938 (and again from 1942 to 1944) some high-ranking army officers, who feared the consequences of Hitler's reckless aggression, plotted against him, unsuccessfully.

## NAZI EXPANSION AND THE SECOND WORLD WAR

Although economic recovery and somewhat greater opportunity for social advancement won Hitler support, they were only byproducts of the Nazi regime. The guiding and unique concepts of Nazism remained space and race—the territorial expansion of the superior German race. As we shall see, German expansion was facilitated by the uncertain, divided, pacific Western democracies, which tried to buy off Hitler to avoid war.

Yet war inevitably broke out, in both western and eastern Europe, for Hitler's ambitions were essentially unlimited. On both war fronts Nazi soldiers scored enormous successes until late 1942, establishing a horrifyingly vast empire of death and destruction. Hitler's victories prompted Japan to attack the United States and overrun much of Southeast Asia. Yet reckless aggression by Germany and Japan also raised a mighty coalition determined to smash the aggressors. Led by Britain, the United States, and the Soviet Union, the Grand Alliance—to use Winston Churchill's favorite term—functioned quite effectively in military terms. Thus the Nazi and Japanese empires proved short-lived.

### Aggression and Appeasement (1933–1939)

Hitler realized that his aggressive policies had to be carefully camouflaged at first, for Germany's army was limited by the Treaty of Versailles to only a hundred thousand men. As he told a group of army commanders in February 1933, the early stages of his policy of "conquest of new living space in the East and its ruthless Germanization" had serious dangers. If France had real leaders, Hitler said, it would "not give us time but attack us, presumably with its eastern satellites."[12] Thus Hitler loudly proclaimed his peaceful intentions, although Germany's withdrawal from the League of Nations in October 1933 indicated its determination to rearm.

Following this action Hitler sought to incorporate independent Austria into a greater Germany. But a worried Mussolini threatened to fight, and Hitler backed down. When in March 1935 Hitler established a general military draft and declared the "unequal" disarmament clauses of the Treaty of Versailles null and void, other countries appeared to understand the danger. With France taking the lead, Italy and Great Britain protested strongly and warned against future aggressive actions.

But the emerging united front against Hitler quickly collapsed. Britain adopted a policy of appeasement, grant-

**Hitler's Success with Aggression** This biting criticism of appeasing leaders by the cartoonist David Low appeared shortly after Hitler remilitarized the Rhineland. Appeasement also appealed to millions of ordinary citizens in Britain and France, who wanted to avoid at any cost another great war. *(Reproduced by permission of London Evening Standard/Solo Syndication)*

ing Hitler everything he could reasonably want (and more) in order to avoid war. The first step was an Anglo-German naval agreement in June 1935 that broke Germany's isolation. The second step came in March 1936 when Hitler suddenly marched his armies into the demilitarized Rhineland, brazenly violating the Treaties of Versailles and Locarno. This was the last good chance to stop the Nazis, for Hitler had ordered his troops to retreat if France resisted militarily. But an uncertain France would not move without British support, and the occupation of German soil by German armies seemed right and just to Britain (see Map 32.1). With a greatly improved strategic position, Germany handed France a tremendous psychological defeat.

British appeasement, which practically dictated French policy, lasted far into 1939. It was motivated by British

**MAP 32.1 The Growth of Nazi Germany, 1933–1939** Until March 1939, Hitler brought ethnic Germans into the Nazi state; then he turned on the Slavic peoples he had always hated. He stripped Czechoslovakia of its independence and prepared for an attack on Poland in September 1939.

## EVENTS LEADING TO WORLD WAR II

| | |
|---|---|
| 1919 | Treaty of Versailles is signed; J. M. Keynes publishes *Economic Consequences of the Peace.* |
| 1919–1920 | U.S. Senate rejects the Treaty of Versailles. |
| 1921 | Germany is billed $33 billion in reparations. |
| 1922 | Mussolini seizes power in Italy; Germany proposes a moratorium on reparations. |
| January 1923 | France and Belgium occupy the Ruhr; Germany orders passive resistance to the occupation. |
| October 1923 | Stresemann agrees to reparations based on Germany's ability to pay. |
| 1924 | Dawes Plan: German reparations are reduced and put on a sliding scale; large U.S. loans to Germany are recommended to promote German recovery; Adolf Hitler dictates *Mein Kampf.* |
| 1924–1929 | Spectacular German economic recovery occurs; circular flow of international funds enables sizable reparations payments. |
| 1925 | Treaties of Locarno promote European security and stability. |
| 1926 | Germany joins the League of Nations. |
| 1928 | Kellogg-Briand Pact renounces war as an instrument of international affairs. |
| 1929 | U.S. stock market crashes. |
| 1929–1939 | Great Depression rages. |
| 1931 | Japan invades Manchuria. |
| 1932 | Nazis become the largest party in the Reichstag. |
| January 1933 | Hitler is appointed chancellor of Germany. |
| March 1933 | Reichstag passes the Enabling Act, granting Hitler absolute dictatorial power. |
| October 1933 | Germany withdraws from the League of Nations. |
| 1935 | Nuremberg Laws deprive Jews of all rights of citizenship. |
| March 1935 | Hitler announces German rearmament. |
| June 1935 | Anglo-German naval agreement is signed. |
| October 1935 | Mussolini invades Ethiopia and receives Hitler's support. |
| March 1936 | German armies move unopposed into the demilitarized Rhineland. |
| July 1936 | Civil war breaks out in Spain. |
| 1937 | Japan invades China; Rome-Berlin Axis in effect. |
| March 1938 | Germany annexes Austria. |
| September 1938 | Munich Conference: Britain and France agree to German seizure of the Sudetenland from Czechoslovakia. |
| March 1939 | Germany occupies the rest of Czechoslovakia; appeasement ends in Britain. |
| August 1939 | Nazi-Soviet nonaggression pact is signed. |
| September 1, 1939 | Germany invades Poland. |
| September 3, 1939 | Britain and France declare war on Germany. |

feelings of guilt toward Germany and the pacifism of a population still horrified by the memory of the First World War. As in Germany, many powerful conservatives in Britain underestimated Hitler. They also believed that Soviet communism was the real danger and that Hitler could be used to stop it. Such strong anticommunist feelings made an alliance between the Western Powers and Stalin unlikely.

As Britain and France opted for appeasement and the Soviet Union watched all developments suspiciously, Hitler found powerful allies. In 1935 the bombastic Mussolini attacked the independent African kingdom of Ethiopia. The Western Powers and the League of Nations piously condemned Italian aggression, but Hitler supported Italy energetically and thereby overcame Mussolini's lingering doubts about the Nazis. The result in 1936 was an agreement on close cooperation between Italy and Germany, the so-called Rome-Berlin Axis. Japan, which had been expanding into Manchuria since 1931, soon joined the Axis alliance.

At the same time, Germany and Italy intervened in the Spanish civil war (1936–1939). Their support eventually helped General Francisco Franco's fascist movement defeat republican Spain. Spain's only official aid came from the Soviet Union, for public opinion in Britain and especially in France was hopelessly divided on the Spanish question.

In late 1937 Hitler moved forward with his plans to crush Austria and Czechoslovakia as the first step in his long-contemplated drive to the east for living space. By threatening Austria with invasion, Hitler forced the Austrian chancellor in March 1938 to put local Nazis in control of the government. The next day German armies moved in unopposed, and Austria became two provinces of Greater Germany (see Map 32.1).

Simultaneously, Hitler began demanding that the pro-Nazi, German-speaking minority of western Czechoslovakia—the Sudetenland—be turned over to Germany. Democratic Czechoslovakia, however, was prepared to defend itself. Moreover, France had been Czechoslovakia's ally since 1924, and if France fought, the Soviet Union was pledged to help. War appeared inevitable, but appeasement triumphed again. In September 1938 Prime Minister Chamberlain flew to Germany three times in fourteen days. In these negotiations, to which the Soviet Union was deliberately not invited, Chamberlain and the French agreed with Hitler that the Sudetenland should be ceded to Germany immediately. Returning to London from the Munich Conference, Chamberlain told cheering crowds that he had secured "peace with honor . . . peace for our time." Sold out by the Western Powers, Czechoslovakia gave in.

Confirmed once again in his opinion of the Western democracies as weak and racially degenerate, Hitler accelerated his aggression. His armies occupied the remainder of Czechoslovakia in March 1939. The effect on Western public opinion was electrifying. For the first time, there was no possible rationale of self-determination for Nazi aggression, because Hitler was treating the Czechs and Slovaks as captive peoples. Thus when Hitler used the question of German minorities in Danzig as a pretext to confront Poland, a suddenly militant Chamberlain declared that Britain and France would fight if Hitler attacked his eastern neighbor. Hitler did not take these warnings seriously and decided to press on.

In an about-face that stunned the world, Hitler offered and Stalin signed a ten-year Nazi-Soviet nonaggression pact in August 1939. Each dictator promised to remain neutral if the other became involved in war. An attached secret protocol ruthlessly divided eastern Europe into German and Soviet zones "in the event of a political territorial reorganization." The nonaggression pact itself was enough to make Britain and France cry treachery, for they, too, had been negotiating with Stalin. But Stalin had remained distrustful of Western intentions, and Hitler had offered territorial gain.

For Hitler, everything was set. He told his generals on the day of the nonaggression pact, "My only fear is that at the last moment some dirty dog will come up with a mediation plan." On September 1, 1939, German armies and warplanes smashed into Poland from three sides. Two days later Britain and France, finally true to their word, declared war on Germany. The Second World War had begun.

## Hitler's Empire (1939–1942)

Using planes, tanks, and trucks in the first example of a **blitzkrieg,** or "lightning war," Hitler's armies crushed Poland in four weeks. The Soviet Union quickly took its part of the booty—the eastern half of Poland and the Baltic states of Lithuania, Estonia, and Latvia. French and British armies dug in in the west; they expected another war of attrition and economic blockade.

In spring 1940 the lightning war struck again. After occupying Denmark, Norway, and Holland, German motorized columns broke through southern Belgium, split the Franco-British forces, and trapped the entire British army on the beaches of Dunkirk. By heroic efforts the British were able to withdraw their troops but not their equipment.

**MAP 32.2 World War II in Europe** The map shows the extent of Hitler's empire at its height, before the Battle of Stalingrad in late 1942 and the subsequent advances of the Allies until Germany surrendered on May 7, 1945.

**London, 1940** Hitler believed that his relentless terror bombing of London—the "blitz"—could break the will of the British people. He was wrong. The blitz caused enormous destruction, but Londoners went about their business with courage and calm determination, as this unforgettable image of a milkman in the rubble suggests. *(Hulton-Deutsch Collection/Corbis)*

France was taken by the Nazis. Aging marshal Henri-Philippe Pétain formed a new French government—the so-called Vichy government—to accept defeat, and German armies occupied most of France. By July 1940 Hitler ruled practically all of western continental Europe; Italy was an ally, the Soviet Union a friendly neutral (see Map 32.2). Only Britain, led by the uncompromising Winston Churchill (1874–1965), remained unconquered.

Germany sought to gain control of the air, the necessary first step for an amphibious invasion of Britain. In the Battle of Britain, up to a thousand German planes attacked British airfields and key factories in a single day, dueling with British defenders high in the skies. Losses were heavy on both sides. Then in September Hitler angrily turned from military objectives to indiscriminate bombing of British cities in an attempt to break British morale. British aircraft factories increased production, and the heavily bombed people of London defiantly dug in. In September and October 1940 Britain was beating Germany three to one in the air war. There was no possibility of immediate German invasion of Britain.

Turning from Britain and moving into the Balkans by April 1941, Hitler now allowed his lifetime obsession with a vast eastern European empire for the "master race" to dictate policy. In June 1941 German armies suddenly attacked the Soviet Union along a vast front. By October Leningrad was practically surrounded, Moscow was besieged, and most of Ukraine had been conquered. But the Soviets did not collapse, and when a severe winter struck German armies that were outfitted in summer uniforms, the invaders were stopped.

Stalled in Russia, Hitler had come to rule a vast European empire stretching from the outskirts of Moscow to the English Channel. He and the top Nazi leadership began building their **New Order,** and they continued their efforts until their final collapse in 1945. In doing so, they showed what Nazi victory would have meant.

Hitler's New Order was based firmly on the guiding principle of Nazi totalitarianism: racial imperialism. Within this New Order the Nordic peoples—the Dutch, Norwegians, and Danes—received preferential treatment, for they were racially related to the Germans. The French, an "inferior" Latin people, occupied the middle position. All the occupied territories of western and northern Europe, however, were to be exploited with increasing intensity.

Slavs in the conquered territories to the east were treated with harsh hatred as "subhumans." At the height of success in 1941 and 1942, Hitler set the tone. He painted for his intimate circle the fantastic vision of a vast eastern colonial empire where Poles, Ukrainians, and Russians would be enslaved and forced to die out, while Germanic peasants resettled the resulting abandoned lands. But he needed countless helpers, and these accomplices came forth. Himmler and the elite corps of SS volunteers, supported (or condoned) by military commanders and German policemen in the occupied territories, pressed relentlessly to implement this program of destruction and to create a "mass settlement space" for Germans.

Finally, the Nazi state condemned all European Jews to extermination, along with many Gypsies, Jehovah's Witnesses, and captured communists. After the fall of Warsaw the Nazis began deporting all German Jews to occupied Poland, and in 1941 expulsion spiraled into extermination on the Russian front. Himmler's special SS killing squads and regular army units forced Soviet Jews to dig giant pits, which became mass graves as the victims were lined up on the edge and cut down by machine guns. Then in late 1941 Hitler and the Nazi leadership, in some still-debated combination, ordered the SS to stop all Jewish emigration from Europe and speeded up planning for mass murder. All over the Nazi empire Jews were systematically arrested, packed like cattle onto freight trains, and dispatched to extermination camps. (See the feature "Listening to the Past: Witness to the Holocaust" on pages 1056–1057.)

There the victims were taken by force or deception to "shower rooms," which were actually gas chambers. For fifteen to twenty minutes came the terrible screams and gasping sobs of men, women, and children choking to death on poison gas. Then, only silence. Special camp workers quickly yanked the victims' gold teeth from their jaws, and the bodies were then cremated, or sometimes boiled for oil to make soap. The extermination of European Jews was the ultimate monstrosity of Nazi racism and racial imperialism. By 1945, 6 million Jews had been murdered.

**Prelude to Murder** This photo captures the terrible inhumanity of Nazi racism. Frightened and bewildered families from the soon-to-be-destroyed Warsaw Ghetto are being forced out of their homes by German soldiers for deportation to concentration camps. There they face murder in the gas chambers. *(Hulton Archive/Getty Images)*

Who was responsible for this terrible crime? An older generation of historians usually laid most of the guilt on Hitler and the Nazi leadership. Ordinary Germans had little knowledge of the extermination camps, it was argued, and those who cooperated had no alternative given the brutality of Nazi terror and totalitarian control. But in recent years many studies have revealed a much broader participation of German people in the Holocaust and popular indifference (or worse) to the fate of the Jews.

Yet in most occupied countries, local non-German officials also cooperated in the arrest and deportation of Jews to a large extent. As in Germany, only a few exceptional bystanders, like those in the French village of Le Chambon, did not turn a blind eye. (See the feature "Individuals in Society: Le Chambon, a Refuge for the Persecuted.") Thus some scholars have concluded that the key for most Germans (and most people in occupied countries) was that they felt no personal responsibility for Jews, and therefore they were not prepared to help them. This meant that many individuals, conditioned by Nazi racist propaganda but also influenced by peer pressure and brutalizing wartime violence, were psychologically prepared to perpetrate ever-greater crimes. They were ready to plumb the depths of evil and to spiral downward from mistreatment to arrest to mass murder.

## The War in the Pacific, 1940–1942

By late 1938, 1.5 million Japanese troops were bogged down in China in a war they could not win (see page 993). Thus Japanese leaders followed events in Europe closely, looking for alliances and actions that might deliver them from their Chinese quagmire. Hitler's victories in 1940 opened unexpected opportunities, as European empires in Southeast Asia appeared vulnerable. In September 1940 Japan signed a formal alliance with Germany and Italy and promptly invaded northern French Indochina.

Japan's invasion of Indochina worsened relations with the United States, which had repeatedly condemned Japanese aggression in China. President Franklin Roosevelt now demanded that Japan withdraw from China, keeping only Manchuria. This was completely unacceptable to Japan, and in July 1941 the Japanese moved into southern Indochina. The United States responded by cutting off the sale of U.S. oil to Japan, thereby reducing Japan's oil supplies by 90 percent. Japanese leaders believed increasingly that war with the United States was inevitable, for Japan's battle fleet would run out of fuel in eighteen months, and its industry would be crippled. After much debate Japanese leaders decided to launch a surprise attack on the United States. They hoped to disable their Pacific rival and gain time to build a defensible Asian empire.

The Japanese attack on the U.S. naval base at Pearl Harbor in the Hawaiian Islands was a complete surprise but a limited success. On December 7, 1941, the Japanese sank or crippled every American battleship, but by chance all the American aircraft carriers were at sea and escaped unharmed. This enabled rapid American recovery, because aircraft carriers quickly dominated the Pacific war. More important, most Americans felt superior to the Japanese, and they were humiliated by this unexpected defeat. Pearl Harbor brought Americans together in a spirit of anger and revenge. Hitler immediately declared war on the United States.

Simultaneously, Japanese armies successfully attacked European and American colonies in Southeast Asia. Japanese armies were small (because most soldiers remained in China), but they were well trained, well led, and highly motivated. In the Netherlands East Indies a Japanese army defeated a Dutch force four times as large, while another outnumbered army took the British colonies of Hong Kong, Malaya, and Singapore. During the attack on Pearl Harbor, the Japanese also attacked the Philippines, although American forces did not surrender until May 1942. By that time Japan held a vast empire in Southeast Asia and the western Pacific (see Map 32.3).

The Japanese claimed that they were freeing Asians from Western imperialism, and they called their empire the Greater Asian Co-prosperity Sphere. Initially they tapped currents of nationalist sentiment, and most local populations were glad to see the Western Powers go. But Asian faith in "co-prosperity" and support for Japan steadily declined, for three interrelated reasons.

First, although the Japanese set up anticolonial governments and promised genuine independence, real power always rested with Japanese military commanders and their superiors in Tokyo. The "independent" governments established in the Philippines, French Indochina, Burma, and the Dutch East Indies were shams. Moreover, the Japanese never treated local populations as equals.

Second, the Japanese occupiers exploited local peoples for Japan's wartime needs. They cut wages, imposed supply quotas on raw materials, and drafted local people for military and labor service. Ships left for Japan laden with rice, oil, and raw materials, but they returned empty.

Finally, the Japanese often exhibited great cruelty toward prisoners of war and civilians, especially the Chinese. After the fall of Hong Kong in December 1941, for example, wounded prisoners were murdered and burned, and there was a mass rape of nurses. Recurring cruel behavior also aroused local populations against the invaders.

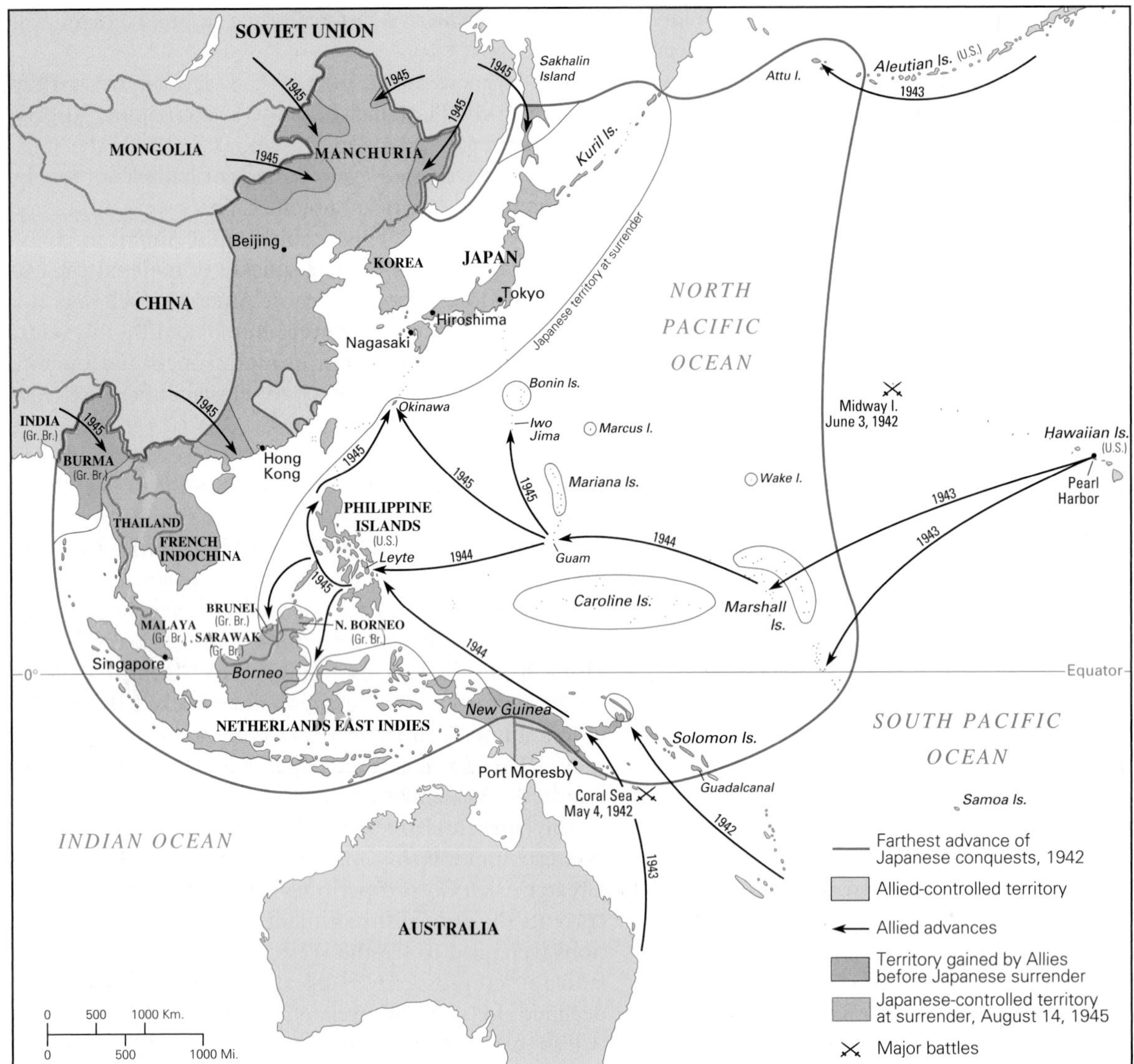


**MAP 32.3 World War II in the Pacific** Japanese forces overran an enormous amount of territory in 1942, which the Allies slowly recaptured in a long, bitter struggle. As this map shows, Japan still held a large Asian empire in August 1945, when the unprecedented devastation of atomic warfare suddenly forced it to surrender.

## The Grand Alliance

While the Nazis and the Japanese built their savage empires, the Allies faced the hard fact that chance, rather than choice, had brought them together. Stalin had been cooperating fully with Hitler between August 1939 and June 1941, and only the Japanese attack on Pearl Harbor in December 1941 had overwhelmed powerful isolationism in the United States. The Allies' first task was to overcome their mutual suspicions and build an unshakable alliance on the quicksand of accident. By means of three interrelated policies they succeeded.

First, U.S. president Franklin D. Roosevelt accepted the contention of Winston Churchill (Chamberlain's successor as British prime minister) that the United States should concentrate first on defeating Hitler. Only after victory in Europe was achieved would the United States turn toward the Pacific for an all-out attack on Japan, the

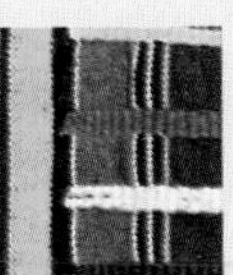

## LE CHAMBON, A REFUGE FOR THE PERSECUTED

*André and Magda Trocmé, resistance leaders at Le Chambon, in a family snapshot taken shortly before 1940.* (Papers of André and Magda Trocmé, Swarthmore College Peace Collection, © Nellie Trocmé Hewett)

On a cold night in February 1943, French officials arrived in Le Chambon-sur-Lignon in southern France. Known as a "nest of Jews in Protestant country," Le Chambon was a mountainous town of three thousand people that hid Jews and openly said so to the government.* Now the officials had finally come to arrest the Protestant minister André Trocmé, the assistant minister Edouard Theis, and the local school principal—the leaders of this defiant cell. Watching silently, the villagers demonstrated their unmistakable solidarity. They lined the streets, sang "A Mighty Fortress Is Our God," and then fell in behind their friends as they passed. As on other occasions, the people of Le Chambon showed the moral courage that would cause others in the region to search their hearts and examine their own conduct toward Jews.

Imprisoned in a camp with communists and resistance fighters, the three men led religious services, discussion groups, and classes that attracted prisoners and even guards. The camp administration, perhaps fearing that its authority was being subverted, offered the three men freedom in return for a signed oath of obedience to the Vichy government, which ruled southern France in collaboration with the Nazi occupiers in the north. Trocmé and his companions refused, but they were mysteriously released the next day. Returning home, Trocmé believed that the village had influential friends in the government.

The strength of the villagers and the quality of their leadership, so clearly evident in these confrontations with the state in early 1943, help explain how Le Chambon became one of the safest places for Jews in Europe in the first two years of the Nazi occupation and how it and the surrounding area successfully sheltered about thirty-five hundred Jewish refugees. Pastors Trocmé and Theis were inspired rebels who wanted to live an active, dangerous Christian love. They conceived of Le Chambon as a city of refuge for the innocent and as a means of overcoming evil with good through nonviolence. Magda Trocmé, André's spirited wife and the mother of four young children, was equally important. Warm and practical, she instinctively aided those in need. She welcomed Jews arriving at the parsonage, housed them, and helped find families to shelter them. She carried on after André himself fled in late 1943 to escape arrest by the Gestapo. Within the village, prayer meetings became conspiracies of goodness. A Jewish refugee printer forged papers and ration cards for the guests, and Theis and the local network helped them escape to Switzerland.

If the how is clear, the why is less so. Certainly a collective memory of persecution helped the Protestants of Le Chambon and nearby villages to identify with the Jews and feel a moral responsibility for their fate. They, too, were a tiny minority in France, the descendants of Protestant refugees who had fled to the mountains and been hounded and executed. But non-Protestants also joined the cause. Above all, the Trocmés, Theis, and the villagers responded because they had a strong moral philosophy rooted in their Christian belief. They believed that they should not obey evil laws but rather abide by God's commandments. They considered it evil to harm anyone, for God had instructed them to love and care for each other. Finally, Le Chambon was broadly representative of other exceptional groups and individuals who worked to help Jews in Nazi Europe. The common experience showed that a sense of moral responsibility was crucial, and that goodness, like evil, is contagious in life-and-death ethical situations.

### QUESTIONS FOR ANALYSIS

1. What did the people of Le Chambon-sur-Lignon do? Why did they do it?
2. What is the larger significance of the town's actions in terms of the Holocaust? Debate the idea that "goodness, like evil, is contagious."

*Philip Hallie, *Lest Innocent Blood Be Shed: The Story of the Village of Le Chambon and How Goodness Happened There* (New York: Harper & Row, 1979), p. 18. In addition to this moving study, see *Weapons of Spirit* (1986), a documentary film by Pierre Sauvage.

lesser threat. The promise of huge military aid under America's policy of **Europe first** helped solidify the anti-Hitler coalition.

Second, within the European framework the Americans and the British put immediate military needs first. They consistently postponed until after the war tough political questions relating to the eventual peace settlement and thereby avoided conflicts that might have split the alliance.

Third, to further encourage mutual trust, the Allies adopted the principle of the "unconditional surrender" of Germany and Japan. This policy cemented the Grand Alliance because it denied Hitler any hope of dividing his foes. Of great importance for the postwar shape of Europe, it meant that Soviet and Anglo-American armies would almost certainly come together to divide all of Germany, and most of the European continent, among the victorious allies. It also meant that Japan would fight to the bitter end.

The military resources of the Grand Alliance were awesome. The strengths of the United States were its mighty industry, its large population, and its national unity. In the course of the war the United States equipped its own armies and also gave its allies about $50 billion in arms and equipment. Gearing up rapidly for all-out war in 1942, the United States acquired a unique capacity to wage global war. In 1943 it outproduced not only Germany, Italy, and Japan but also all of the rest of the world combined.[13]

Too strong to lose and too weak to win standing alone, Britain continued to make a great contribution as well. The British economy was totally and effectively mobilized, and the sharing of burdens through rationing and heavy taxes on war profits maintained social harmony. Moreover, by early 1943 the Americans and the British were combining small aircraft carriers with radar-guided bombers to rid the Atlantic of German submarines. Britain, the impregnable floating fortress, became a gigantic front-line staging area for the decisive blow to the heart of Germany.

As for the Soviet Union, so great was its strength that it might well have defeated Germany without Western help. In the face of the German advance, whole factories and populations were successfully evacuated to eastern Russia and Siberia. There war production was reorganized and expanded, and the Red Army was increasingly well supplied. The Red Army was also well led, for a new generation of talented military leaders quickly arose to replace those so recently purged. Most important of all, Stalin drew on the massive support and heroic determination of the Soviet people, especially those in the central Russian heartland. Broad-based Russian nationalism, as opposed to narrow communist ideology, became the powerful unifying force in what the Soviet people appropriately called the "Great Patriotic War of the Fatherland."

Finally, the United States, Britain, and the Soviet Union were not alone. They had the resources of much of the world at their command. And, to a greater or lesser extent, they were aided by a growing resistance movement against the Nazis throughout Europe, even in Germany. Thus although Ukrainian peasants often welcomed the Germans as liberators, the barbaric occupation policies of the Nazis quickly drove them to join and support behind-the-lines guerrilla forces. More generally, after the Soviet Union was invaded in June 1941, communists throughout Europe took the lead in the underground resistance, joined by a growing number of patriots, Christians, and agents sent by governments-in-exile in London.

## The Tide of Battle

Barely halted at the gates of Moscow and Leningrad in 1941, the Germans renewed their offensive against the Soviet Union in July 1942, driving toward the southern city of Stalingrad and occupying most of the city in a month of incredibly savage house-to-house fighting.

Then in November 1942 Soviet armies counterattacked. They quickly rolled over Romanian and Italian troops to close a trap surrounding the entire German Sixth Army of 300,000 men. By the end of January 1943 only 123,000 soldiers were left to surrender. Hitler, who had refused to allow a retreat, had suffered a catastrophic defeat. In the summer of 1943 the larger, better-equipped Soviet armies took the offensive and began moving forward (see Map 32.2).

In 1942 the tide also turned in the Pacific. In April 1942 the Japanese devised a complicated battle plan to take Port Moresby in New Guinea and also destroy U.S. aircraft carriers in an attack on Midway Island. Well informed of these plans because they had broken the Japanese code, the Americans avoided decoys and skillfully deployed the smaller number of ships at their disposal. The result was a decisive naval victory. First, in the Battle of the Coral Sea in May 1942, an American carrier force fought its Japanese counterpart to a draw, thereby stopping the Japanese advance on Port Moresby and relieving Australia from the threat of invasion. This engagement was followed in June 1942 by the Battle of Midway, in which American carrier-based pilots sank all four of the attacking Japanese aircraft carriers and established overall American equality with Japan in the Pacific. In August

1942 American marines attacked Guadalcanal in the Solomon Islands. Badly hampered by the policy of "Europe first," the Americans and their Australian allies nevertheless began "island hopping" toward Japan. Japanese forces were on the defensive.

The war in the Pacific was extremely brutal—a "war without mercy," in the words of a leading American scholar—and atrocities were committed on both sides.[14] Knowing of Japanese atrocities in China and the Philippines, both the U.S. Marines and army troops seldom took Japanese prisoners after the Battle of Guadalcanal, killing even those rare Japanese soldiers who offered to surrender. American forces moving across the central and western Pacific in 1943 and 1944 faced unyielding resistance on tiny islands such as Tarawa, Kwajalein, and New Britain, and this resistance hardened the hearts of American servicemen and their leaders as American casualties kept rising. A product of spiraling violence, mutual hatred, and dehumanizing racial stereotypes, the war without mercy intensified as it moved toward Japan.

In North Africa the war had been seesawing back and forth since 1940 (see Map 32.2). In the summer of 1942 combined German and Italian armies were finally defeated by British forces at the Battle of El Alamein, only seventy miles from Alexandria. Almost immediately thereafter an Anglo-American force landed in Morocco and Algeria. These French possessions, which were under the control of Pétain's Vichy French government, quickly went over to the side of the Allies.

Having driven the Axis powers from North Africa by the spring of 1943, Allied forces maintained the initiative by invading Sicily and then mainland Italy. Mussolini was deposed by a war-weary people, and the new Italian government publicly accepted unconditional surrender in September 1943. Italy, it seemed, was liberated. But then German commandos in a daring raid rescued Mussolini and put him at the head of a puppet government. German armies seized Rome and all of northern Italy. Fighting continued in Italy.

Indeed, bitter fighting continued in Europe for almost two years. Germany, less fully mobilized for war than

**The Normandy Invasion, Omaha Beach, June 6, 1944** Airborne paratroopers landed behind German coastal fortifications around midnight, and American and British forces hit several beaches at daybreak as Allied ships and bombers provided cover. American troops secured full control of Omaha Beach by nightfall, but at a price of three thousand casualties. Allied air power prevented the Germans from bringing up reserves and counterattacking. *(Corbis)*

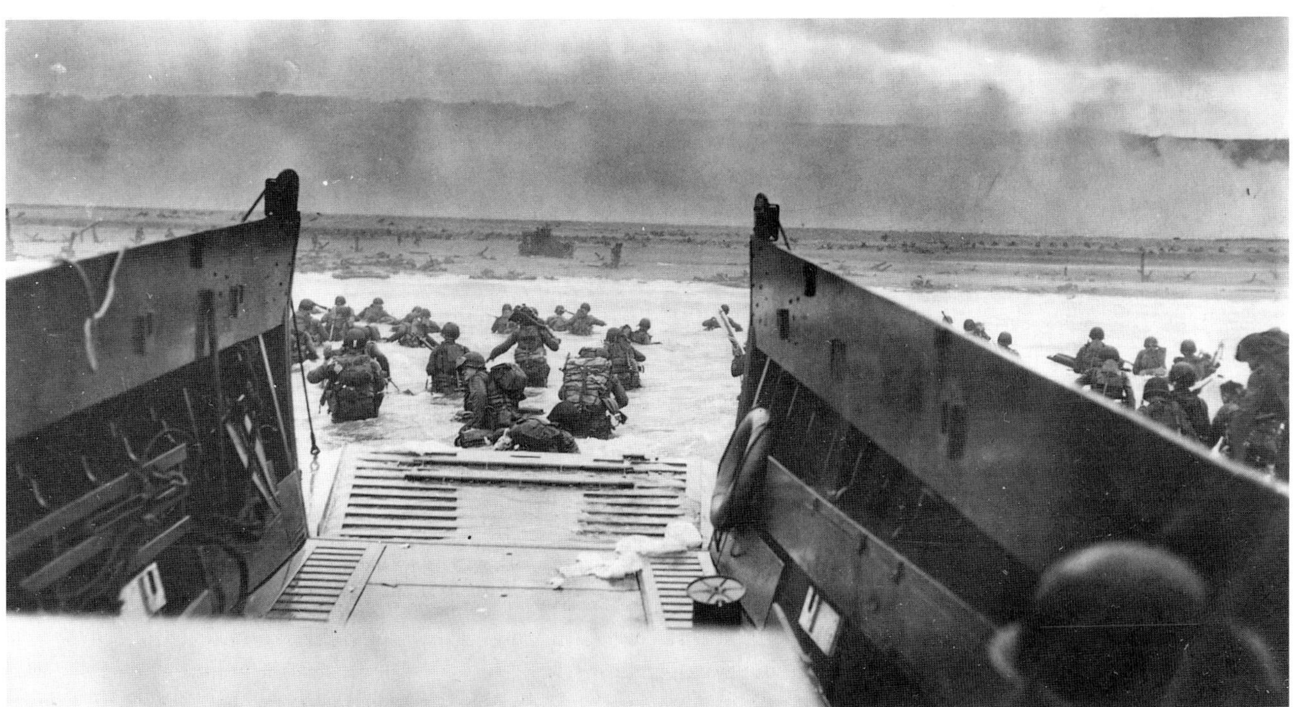

Britain in 1941, applied itself to total war in 1942 and enlisted millions of German women and millions of prisoners of war and slave laborers from all across occupied Europe in that effort. Between early 1942 and July 1944 German war production actually tripled in spite of heavy bombing by the British and American air forces. German resistance against Hitler also failed. After an unsuccessful attempt on Hitler's life in July 1944, SS fanatics brutally liquidated thousands of Germans. Terrorized at home and frightened by the prospect of unconditional surrender, the Germans fought on with suicidal stoicism.

On June 6, 1944, American and British forces under General Dwight Eisenhower landed on the beaches of Normandy, France, in history's greatest naval invasion. In a hundred dramatic days more than 2 million men and almost a half million vehicles pushed inland and broke through German lines. Rejecting proposals to strike straight at Berlin in a massive attack, Eisenhower moved forward cautiously on a broad front. Not until March 1945 did American troops cross the Rhine and enter Germany.

The Soviets, who had been advancing steadily since July 1943, reached the outskirts of Warsaw by August 1944. For the next six months they moved southward into Romania, Hungary, and Yugoslavia. In January 1945 the Red Army again moved westward through Poland, and on April 26 they met American forces on the Elbe River. The Allies had closed their vise on Nazi Germany and overrun Europe. As Soviet forces fought their way into

**"Follow Me!"** This painting by Charles McBarron, Jr., shows the action at Red Beach on October 20, 1944, in the Battle of Leyte Gulf in the Philippine Islands. It captures the danger and courage of U.S. troops, which had to storm well-fortified Japanese positions again and again in their long island-hopping campaign. The officer exhorts his men, and death is all around. *(The Granger Collection, New York)*

Berlin, Hitler committed suicide in his bunker, and on May 7 the remaining German commanders capitulated.

Allied advances in the Pacific paralleled those in Europe. In October 1944 American forces under General Douglas MacArthur landed on the island of Leyte in the Philippines. The Japanese believed that they could destroy MacArthur's troops and transport ships before the main American fleet arrived. The result was the four-day Battle of Leyte Gulf, the greatest battle in naval history, with 282 ships involved. The Japanese lost 13 large warships, including 4 aircraft carriers, while the Americans lost only 3 small ships in their great triumph. The Japanese navy was practically finished.

In spite of all their defeats, Japanese troops continued to fight with enormous courage and determination. Indeed, the bloodiest battles of the Pacific war took place on Iwo Jima in February 1945 and on Okinawa in June 1945. MacArthur believed the conquest of Japan might cost a million American casualties. In fact, Japan was almost helpless, its industry and dense, fragile wooden cities largely destroyed by incendiary bombing and uncontrollable hurricanes of fire. In early 1945 labor discipline broke down and absenteeism soared. Yet the Japanese seemed determined to fight on, if only with bamboo spears, ever ready to die for a hopeless cause.

On August 6 and 9, 1945, the United States dropped atomic bombs on Hiroshima and Nagasaki in Japan. Mass bombing of cities and civilians, one of the terrible new practices of World War II, had ended in the final nightmare—unprecedented human destruction in a single blinding flash. On August 14, 1945, the Japanese announced their surrender. The Second World War, which had claimed the lives of more than 50 million soldiers and civilians, was over.

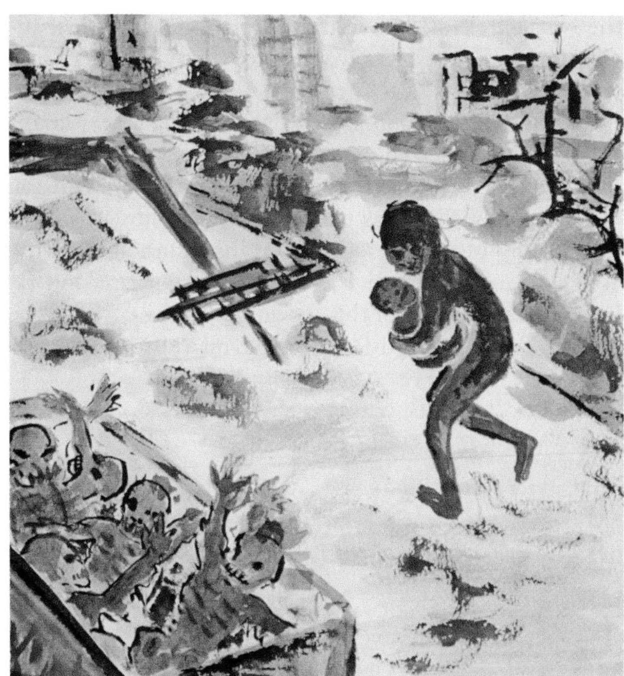

**A Hiroshima Survivor Remembers** Yasuko Yamagata was seventeen when she saw the brilliant blue-white "lightning flash" that became a fiery orange ball consuming everything that would burn. Thirty years later Yamagata painted this scene, her most unforgettable memory of the atomic attack. An incinerated woman, poised as if running with her baby clutched to her breast, lies near a water tank piled high with charred corpses. *(From a public exhibition assembled by the Japan Broadcasting Corporation)*

## SUMMARY

The Second World War marked the climax of the tremendous practical and spiritual maladies of the age of anxiety, which led in many lands to the rise of dictatorships. Many of these dictatorships were variations on conservative authoritarianism, but there was also a fateful innovation—a new kind of radical dictatorship that was exceptionally dynamic and theoretically unlimited in its actions.

When apprehensive middle-class liberals in the West faced the rise of these new dictatorships, they often focused on their perceived similarities. Liberals fastened on the violent, profoundly antiliberal, and apparently totalitarian character of these brutal challengers, linking the one-party socialism of Lenin and Stalin with the one-party fascism of Mussolini and Hitler. In contrast, the political left usually insisted on the differences between the revolutionary socialist tradition—triumphing, however imperfectly, in the Bolsheviks' Soviet Union—and the reactionary and capitalist nature of European fascist movements and fascist governments in Italy and Germany. Concentrating on the specific developments in each regime, historians increasingly see Hitler's Nazism as a uniquely evil and nihilistic system. Nazism had fascist origins, but German fascism in power ultimately presented only superficial similarities with fascism in Italy. As for Hitler's Germany and Stalin's Soviet Union, both asserted a total claim on the lives of their citizens, posed ambitious goals, and demanded popular support. This combination gave both dictatorships their awesome power and dynamism. That dynamism, however, was channeled in quite different directions. Stalin and the Communist party aimed at building their kind of socialism and the new socialist personality at home. Hitler and the Nazi elite aimed at unlimited territorial and racial aggression on behalf of a "master race"; domestic recovery was only a means to that end.

Nazi racism and unlimited aggression made war inevitable, first with the western European democracies, then with hated eastern neighbors, and finally with the United States. Plunging Europe into the ultimate nightmare, unlimited aggression unwittingly forged a mighty coalition that smashed the racist Nazi empire and its leader. In the words of the ancient Greeks, he whom the gods would destroy, they first make mad.

## KEY TERMS

totalitarianism
fascism
five-year plan
New Economic Policy (NEP)
collectivization
kulaks
Black Shirts
Lateran Agreement
Nazism
Führer
Enabling Act
blitzkrieg
New Order
Europe first

## NOTES

1. A. Gleason, *Totalitarianism: The Inner History of the Cold War* (New York: Oxford University Press, 1995), p. 50.
2. E. Halévy, *The Era of Tyrannies* (Garden City, N.Y.: Doubleday, 1965), pp. 265–316, esp. p. 300.
3. I. Kershaw, *The Nazi Dictatorship: Problems and Perspectives of Interpretation,* 2d ed. (London: Edward Arnold, 1989), p. 34.
4. Quoted in A. G. Mazour, *Soviet Economic Development: Operation Outstrip, 1921–1965* (Princeton, N.J.: Van Nostrand, 1967), p. 130.
5. Quoted in I. Deutscher, *Stalin: A Political Biography,* 2d ed. (New York: Oxford University Press, 1967), p. 325.
6. M. Malia, *The Soviet Tragedy: A History of Socialism in Russia* (New York: Free Press, 1994), p. 248.
7. R. Thurston, *Life and Terror in Stalin's Russia, 1934–1941* (New Haven, Conn.: Yale University Press, 1996), esp. pp. 16–106; and Malia, *The Soviet Tragedy,* pp. 227–270.
8. R. Vivarelli, "Interpretations on the Origins of Fascism," *Journal of Modern History* 63 (March 1991): 41.
9. W. Brustein, *The Logic of Evil: The Social Origins of the Nazi Party, 1925–1933* (New Haven, Conn.: Yale University Press, 1996), pp. 52, 182.
10. Quoted in K. D. Bracher, *The German Dictatorship: The Origins, Structure and Effects of National Socialism* (New York: Praeger, 1970), pp. 146–147.
11. Quoted in R. Stromberg, *An Intellectual History of Modern Europe* (New York: Appleton-Century-Crofts, 1966), p. 393.
12. Quoted in Bracher, *The German Dictatorship,* p. 289.
13. H. Willmott, *The Great Crusade: A New Complete History of the Second World War* (New York: Free Press, 1989), p. 255.
14. J. Dower, *War Without Mercy: Race and Power in the Pacific War* (New York: Pantheon, 1986).

## SUGGESTED READING

The historical literature on fascist and totalitarian dictatorships is rich and fascinating. Kershaw's work, cited in the Notes, provides an excellent survey of this literature and is highly recommended. P. Brooker, *Twentieth-Century Dictatorships: The Ideological One-Party State* (1995), compares leading examples throughout the world, and Gleason, cited in the Notes, is an important recent study. H. Arendt, *The Origins of Totalitarianism* (1951), is a classic interpretation. F. L. Carsten, *The Rise of Fascism* (1982), and W. Laqueur, ed., *Fascism* (1976), are also recommended.

Malia's work, cited in the Notes, is a provocative reassessment of Soviet history and an excellent introduction to scholarly debates. It may be compared with the fine synthesis by M. Lewin, *The Making of the Soviet System* (1985). R. Stites, *The Women's Liberation Movement in Russia: Feminism, Nihilism, and Bolshevism, 1860–1930* (1978), is highly recommended. D. Volkogonov, *Autopsy for an Empire: The Seven Leaders Who Built the Soviet Union* (1988), is an engrossing collective biography. R. Conquest, *The Great Terror: A Reassessment* (1990), is an excellent account of Stalin's purges of the 1930s, and A. Solzhenitsyn, *The Gulag Archipelago* (1964), passionately condemns Soviet police terror. Three important reconsiderations of Soviet purges, women, and urban life are Thurston's revisionist work, cited in the Notes; S. Fitzpatrick and Y. Slezkine, eds., *In the Shadow of Revolution: Life Stories of Russian Women from 1917 to the Second World War* (2000); and S. Kotkin, *Magnetic Mountain: Stalinism as Civilization* (1995). Arthur Koestler, *Darkness at Noon* (1956), is a famous fictional account of Stalin's trials of the Old Bolsheviks. R. Conquest, *The Harvest of Sorrow: Soviet Collectivization and the Terror-Famine* (1986), authoritatively recounts Soviet collectivization and the human-made famine. J. Scott, *Behind the Urals* (1973), an eyewitness account of an American steelworker in the Soviet Union in the 1930s, is recommended.

A. De Grand, *Italian Fascism: Its Origins and Development* (1989), and A. Lyttelton, *The Seizure of Power: Fascism in Italy, 1919–1929,* 2d ed. (1987), are excellent studies of Italy under Mussolini. D. Mack Smith, *Mussolini* (1982), is authoritative. I. Silone, *Bread and Wine* (1937), is a moving novel by a famous opponent of dictatorship in Italy. E. Morante, *History* (1978), a fictional account of one family's divergent reactions to Mussolini's rule, is recommended. H. Thomas, *The Spanish Civil War* (1977), is an excellent account. In the area of foreign relations, G. Kennan, *Russia and the West Under Lenin and Stalin* (1961), is justly famous; A. L. Rowse, *Appeasement* (1961), powerfully denounces the policies of the appeasers.

On Germany, F. Stern, *The Politics of Cultural Despair* (1963), and W. Smith, *The Ideological Origins of Nazi Imperialism* (1986), are fine complementary studies on the origins of Nazism. Bracher's work, cited in the Notes, remains an outstanding account of Hitler's Germany. Two major studies by influential German historians are M. Brozat, *The Nazi State* (1981), and H. Mommsen, *From Weimar to Auschwitz* (1991). A. Bullock, *Hitler and Stalin* (1993), is a fascinating comparison by a master biographer. I. Kershaw, *The "Hitler Myth": Image and Reality in the Third Reich* (1987), is a provocative reassessment of the limits of Hitler's power. M. Mayer, *They Thought They Were Free* (1955), probes the minds of ten ordinary Nazis and why they believed that Hitler was their liberator. A. Speer, *Inside the Third Reich* (1970), contains the fascinating recollections of Hitler's wizard of the armaments industry. C. Koonz, *Mothers in the Fatherland: Women, the Family, and Nazi Politics* (1987), and D. Peukert, *Inside Nazi Germany: Conformity, Opposition, and Racism in Everyday Life* (1987), are pioneering forays into the social history of the Nazi era. Moving accounts of the Holocaust include M. Gilbert, *The Holocaust: The History of the Jews During the Second World War* (1985), and R. Hilberg, *The Destruction of the European Jews, 1933–1945*, 3 vols., rev. ed. (1985), a monumental scholarly achievement. M. Marrus, *The Holocaust in History* (1987), is an excellent interpretive survey, and I. Clendinnen, *Reading the Holocaust* (1999), is an imaginative reconsideration of victims and perpetrators. Two brilliant works on German participants are C. Browning, *Ordinary Men: Reserve Police Battalion 101 and the Final Solution in Poland* (1992), and E. Staub, *The Roots of Evil: The Origins of Genocide and Other Group Violence* (1989), a profound study by a noted psychologist. Especially recommended are E. Weisel, *Night* (1961), a brief and compelling autobiographical account of a young Jew in a Nazi concentration camp, and A. Frank, *The Diary of Anne Frank,* a remarkable personal account of a Jewish girl in hiding during the Nazi occupation of Holland. R. Gellately and N. Stolzfus, eds., *Social Outcasts in Nazi Germany* (2000), studies various groups, and A. Fraser, *The Gypsies* (1992), considers a misunderstood people decimated by Nazi terror.

J. Campbell, *The Experience of World War II* (1989), is attractively illustrated and captures the drama of global conflict, as does J. Keegan, *The Second World War* (1990). G. Weinberg, *World at Arms: A Global History of World War II* (1994), is a masterful overview. Willmott's work, cited in the Notes, is a comprehensive overview of military developments. A. Dallin, *German Rule in Russia, 1941–1945* (1981), analyzes the effects of Nazi occupation policies on the Soviet population, and L. Collins and D. La Pierre, *Is Paris Burning?* (1965), is a best-selling account of the liberation of Paris and Hitler's plans to destroy the city. A. Iriye, *The Origins of the Second World War in Asia and the Pacific* (1987), probes relations between Japan and the United States. Dower, cited in the Notes, is a powerful analysis of American attitudes and behavior toward the Japanese, while J. Hsuing and S. Levine, eds., *China's Bitter Victory: The War with Japan, 1937–1945* (1992), investigates various aspects of the long struggle.

# LISTENING TO THE PAST

## WITNESS TO THE HOLOCAUST

*The Second World War brought mass murder to the innocent. The Nazis and their allies slaughtered 6 million Jews in addition to about 5 million Slavs, Gypsies, Jehovah's Witnesses, homosexuals, and mentally ill persons. On the Russian front, some Jews were simply mowed down with machine guns, but most Jews were arrested in their homelands and taken in freight cars to unknown destinations, which were in fact extermination camps. The most infamous camp—really two camps on different sides of a railroad track—was Auschwitz-Birkenau in eastern Poland. There 2 million people were murdered in gas chambers.*

*The testimony of camp survivors helps us comprehend the unspeakable crime known to history as the Holocaust. One eyewitness was Marco Nahon, a Greek Jew and physician who escaped extermination at Auschwitz-Birkenau along with several thousand other slave laborers in the camp. The following passage is taken from* Birkenau: The Camp of Death, *which Nahon wrote in 1945 after his liberation. Conquered by Germany in 1941, Greece was divided into German, Italian, and Bulgarian zones of occupation. The Nahon family lived in Dimotika in the Bulgarian zone.*

Early in March 1943, disturbing news arrives from Salonika [in the German occupation zone]: the Germans are deporting the Jews [of Salonika]. They lock them up in railway cattlecars . . . and send them to an unknown destination—to Poland, it is said. . . . Relatives and friends deliberate. What can be done in the face of this imminent threat? . . . My friend Vitalis Djivré speaks with conviction: "We must flee, cross over into Turkey at once, go to Palestine, Egypt—anywhere at all—but leave immediately." . . . A few friends and I held a completely different opinion. . . . [I say that] I am not going to emigrate. They are going to take us away to Germany or Poland [to work]? If so, I'll work. . . . It is certain that the Allies will be the victors, and once the war is over, we'll go back home. . . .

Until the end we were deaf to all the warnings. . . . [None of the warnings] would be regarded as indicating the seriousness of the drama in preparation. But does not the human mind find inconceivable the total extermination of an innocent population? In this tragic error lay the main cause, the sole cause, of our perdition. . . .

On Monday May 10, 1943, the bugles awaken us at a very early hour. We [have already been arrested and] today we are leaving for Poland. . . . As soon as a freight car has been packed to capacity with people, it is quickly locked up, and immediately the remaining passengers are pushed into the next one. . . .

Every two days the train stops in some meadow in open country. The car doors are flung open, and the whole transport spreads out in the fields. Men and women attend to their natural needs, side by side, without any embarrassment. Necessity and common misfortune have made them part of one and the same family. . . .

We are now in a small station in Austria. Our car door half opens; a Schupo [German police officer] is asking for the doctor. . . . He leads me to the rear of the convoy and shuts me inside the car where the woman is in labor. She is very young; this is her first child. The car, like all the others, is overcrowded. The delivery takes place in deplorable conditions, in front of everybody—men, women, and children. Fortunately, everything turns out well, and a few hours later a baby boy comes into the world. The new mother's family is very happy and passes candy around. Surely no one realizes that two days later the mother and her baby and more than half of the company will pass through the chimney of a crematorium at Birkenau.

It is May 16, 1943. We have reached the end of our journey [and arrived at Auschwitz-Birkenau]. The train stops along a wooden platform. Through the openings of the cars we can see people wearing strange costumes of blue and white stripes [the prisoners who work in the camp]. We immediately notice that they are doing nothing voluntarily but are moving and acting on command. . . . The people in stripes . . . line us up five by five, the women on one side, the men on the other. I lose sight of my wife and little girl in the crowd. I will never see them again.

They make us march, swiftly as always, before a group of [German] officers. One of them, without uttering a word and with the tip of his forefinger, makes a rapid selection. He is, as we know later on, the Lagerarzt, the SS medical doctor of the camp [the notorious Dr. Mengele]. They call him here the "Angel of Death." [Mengele divides the men into two groups: those who are young and sturdy for work in the camp, and those who are old, sick, and children. The women are also divided and only healthy young women without children are assigned to work. All those not selected for work] are immediately loaded on trucks and driven off somewhere. Where? Nobody knows yet. . . .

[After being assigned to a crude windowless barrack,] we must file before the . . . scribes, who are responsible for receiving and registering the transport. Each prisoner must fill out a form in which he relinquishes his identity and becomes a mere number. . . . I am given the number 122274. My son, who is next, gets 122275. This tattoo alarms us terribly. . . . Each one of us now comes to realize in the deepest part of his conscious being, and with a bitter sense of affliction, that from this moment on he is no more than an animal. . . .

After our meal [of watery soup] Léon Yahiel, a veteran among the Lager inmates, . . . gives us this little speech: "My friends, here you must . . . forget your families, your wives, your children. You must live only for yourselves and try to last as long as possible." At these words our spirits plunge into grief and despair. Forget about our families? The hint is unmistakable. Our minds are confused. . . . Our families taken away from us forever? No, it is humanly not conceivable that we should pay such a penalty without having done anything to deserve it, without any provocation.

Jewish victims of Nazism, on the arrival platform at Auschwitz station. *(AKG London)*

What miserable wretches we prisoners are! We have no idea that while we entertain these thoughts, our wives, our children, our mothers and our fathers have already ceased to exist. They have arrived at Auschwitz this morning, healthy and full of life. They have now been reduced to smoke and ashes.

## QUESTIONS FOR ANALYSIS

1. How did the Jews of Dimotika react in early 1943 to the news of Jews being deported? Why?
2. Describe the journey to Auschwitz-Birkenau. Did those on the train know what was awaiting them there?
3. How did the Nazis divide the Jews at Auschwitz-Birkenau? Why?
4. What did you learn from Nahon's account? What parts of his testimony made the greatest impression on you?

*Source:* Slightly adapted from Marco Nahon, *Birkenau: The Camp of Death,* trans. J. Bowers (Tuscaloosa: University of Alabama Press, 1989), pp. 21, 23, 33–39. 

The youth revolution. London, ca 1980. *(Anthea Seiveking/The Wellcome Trust Medical Photographic Library)*

CHAPTER

# 33 RECOVERY AND CRISIS IN EUROPE AND THE AMERICAS

## CHAPTER OUTLINE

- The Division of Europe
- Renaissance and Crisis in Western Europe
- Soviet Eastern Europe, 1945–1991
- The Western Hemisphere
- The Post–Cold War Era, 1991 to the Present

The total defeat of the Nazis and their allies laid the basis for one of Western civilization's most remarkable recoveries. A battered western Europe dug itself out from under the rubble and fashioned a great renaissance. The Western Hemisphere, with its strong European heritage, also made exemplary progress. And the Soviet Union became more humane and less totalitarian after Stalin's death. Yet there was also a tragic setback. Dictatorship settled over eastern Europe, and the Grand Alliance against Hitler gave way to a lengthy cold war that threatened world peace.

During these cold war years the global economic boom of the 1950s and 1960s finally came to an end in the early 1970s. Domestic political stability and social harmony evaporated, and several countries experienced major crises. Serious economic difficulties returned with distressing regularity to Europe and the Americas in the 1980s and early 1990s and threatened again in 1998. These difficulties encompassed much of the globe, a trend that accelerated the knitting together of the world's peoples and regions.

The spectacular collapse of communism in eastern Europe in 1989 and the end of the cold war reinforced the trend toward global integration. Political leaders and opinion makers in the Americas and in Europe embraced visions of free-market capitalism and liberal democracy. The result was monumental change, especially in postcommunist eastern Europe, but a similar if less dramatic transformation occurred in western Europe as it moved toward greater unity in the European Union. Economic and political liberalization brought increased efficiency and more electoral competition, but it also challenged established social benefits and created considerable popular dissatisfaction in some countries.

- What were the causes of the cold war?
- How and why, in spite of the cold war, did western Europe recover so successfully from the ravages of war and Nazism?
- To what extent did communist eastern Europe and the Americas experience a similar recovery?
- Why, after a generation, did the economy shift into reverse gear, and what were some of the social consequences of the reversal?
- Why did a reform movement eventually triumph in eastern Europe in 1989 and bring an end to the cold war?

- What patterns of thought dominated in the 1990s, and how did both eastern and western Europe transform themselves?

These are the questions that this chapter will seek to answer.

## THE DIVISION OF EUROPE

In 1945 triumphant American and Russian soldiers came together and embraced on the banks of the Elbe River in the heart of vanquished Germany. At home, in the United States and in the Soviet Union, the soldiers' loved ones erupted in joyous celebration. Yet victory was flawed. The Allies could not cooperate politically in peacemaking. Motivated by different goals and hounded by misunderstandings, the United States and the Soviet Union soon found themselves at loggerheads. By the end of 1947 Europe was rigidly divided. It was West versus East in a cold war that eventually was waged around the world.

### The Origins of the Cold War

The Soviet Union and the United States began to quarrel almost as soon as the unifying threat of Nazi Germany disappeared. The hostility between the Eastern and Western superpowers was the sad but logical outgrowth of military developments, wartime agreements, and long-standing political and ideological differences.

In the early phases of the Second World War, the Americans and the British made military victory their highest priority. They consistently avoided discussion of Stalin's war aims and the shape of the eventual peace settlement. For example, when Stalin asked the United States and Britain to ratify the gains he had made in Poland from his deal with Hitler in 1939, he received only a military alliance and no postwar commitments. Yet the United States and Britain did not try to take advantage of the Soviet Union's precarious position in 1942, fearing that hard bargaining might encourage Stalin to make a separate peace with Hitler. They focused instead on the policy of unconditional surrender to solidify the alliance.

By late 1943 decisions that would affect the shape of the postwar world could no longer be postponed. The conference that Stalin, Roosevelt, and Churchill held in the Iranian capital of Teheran in November 1943 thus proved of crucial importance in determining subsequent events. There the **Big Three** jovially reaffirmed their determination to crush Germany and searched for the appropriate military strategy. Churchill argued that American and British forces should follow up their Italian campaign with an indirect attack on Germany through the Balkans. Roosevelt, however, agreed with Stalin that an American-British frontal assault through France would be better. This meant that Soviet armies would liberate eastern Europe.

When the Big Three met again in February 1945 at Yalta on the Black Sea in southern Russia, advancing Soviet armies were within a hundred miles of Berlin. The Red Army had occupied not only Poland but also Bulgaria, Romania, Hungary, part of Yugoslavia, and much of Czechoslovakia. The temporarily stalled American-British forces had yet to cross the Rhine into Germany. Moreover, the United States was far from defeating Japan. In short, the Soviet Union's position was strong and America's weak.

There was little the increasingly sick and apprehensive Roosevelt could do but double his bet on Stalin's peaceful intentions. It was agreed at Yalta that Germany would be divided into zones of occupation and would pay heavy reparations to the Soviet Union. At American insistence Stalin agreed to declare war on Japan after Germany was defeated. As for Poland and eastern Europe—"that Pandora's Box of infinite troubles," according to American secretary of state Cordell Hull—the Big Three struggled to reach an ambiguous compromise: eastern European governments were to be freely elected but pro-Russian.

This compromise broke down almost immediately. Even before the Yalta Conference, Bulgaria and Poland were controlled by communists who arrived home with the Red Army. Elsewhere in eastern Europe pro-Soviet "coalition" governments of several parties were formed, but the key ministerial posts were reserved for Moscow-trained communists.

At the postwar Potsdam Conference of July 1945, the long-avoided differences over eastern Europe finally surged to the fore. The compromising Roosevelt had died and been succeeded by the more assertive Harry Truman, who demanded immediate free elections throughout eastern Europe. Stalin refused point-blank. "A freely elected government in any of these East European countries would be anti-Soviet," he admitted simply, "and that we cannot allow."[1]

Here, then, is the key to the much-debated origins of the cold war. American ideals, pumped up by the crusade against Hitler, and American politics, heavily influenced by millions of U.S. voters of eastern European heritage, demanded free elections in Soviet-occupied eastern Europe. Stalin, who had lived through two enormously destructive German invasions, wanted absolute military security from Germany and its potential eastern European allies, once

1945 1955 1965 1975 1985 1995 2004

## POLITICAL/MILITARY

- 1945–1960s Decolonization of Asia and Africa
- 1947 Truman Doctrine
- 1949 Formation of NATO
- 1953–1964 De-Stalinization of Soviet Union
- 1961 Building of Berlin Wall
- 1962 Cuban missile crisis
- 1964–1973 U.S. involvement in Vietnam War
- November 1989 Collapse of Berlin Wall
- 1989–1991 Fall of communism in Soviet Union and eastern Europe
- 1991–2001 Civil war in Yugoslavia
- 1993 Creation of European Union
- Sept. 2001 Attack on United States by al-Qaeda terrorist network
- Nov. 2001 Fall of Taliban in Afghanistan
- March 2003 U.S. invasion of Iraq

## SOCIAL/ECONOMIC

- 1947 Marshall Plan
- 1956–1960 Construction of Brasília, new capital city of Brazil
- 1957 Formation of Common Market
- 1964 Civil Rights Act in United States
- 1973 OPEC oil embargo
- 1991 Maastricht treaty
- 1992–1997 "Shock therapy" in Russia causes decline of economy
- 1994 North American Free Trade Agreement (NAFTA)
- Jan. 2002 New Euro (unified) currency goes into effect in European Union

## INTELLECTUAL/RELIGIOUS

- 1962 Solzhenitsyn, *One Day in the Life of Ivan Denisovich*
- 1985 Glasnost leads to greater freedom of speech and expression in Soviet Union
- 1991–2000 Resurgence of nationalism and ethnic conflict in eastern Europe
- 1992 Fukuyama, *The End of History and the Last Man*

**The Big Three** In 1945 a triumphant Winston Churchill, an ailing Franklin Roosevelt, and a determined Joseph Stalin met at Yalta in southern Russia to plan for peace. Cooperation soon gave way to bitter hostility. *(F.D.R. Library)*

and for all. Suspicious by nature, he believed that only communist states could be truly dependable allies. By the middle of 1945 there was no way short of war that the United States could determine political developments in eastern Europe, and war was out of the question. Stalin was bound to have his way.

## West Versus East

The American response to Stalin's exaggerated conception of security was to "get tough." In May 1945 Truman abruptly cut off all aid to Russia. In October he declared that the United States would never recognize any government established by force against the free will of its people. In March 1946 former British prime minister Churchill ominously informed an American audience that an "iron curtain" had fallen across the European continent, dividing Germany and all of Europe into two antagonistic camps. Emotional, moralistic denunciations of Stalin and communist Russia emerged as part of American political life. Yet the United States also responded to the popular desire to "bring the boys home" and demobilized with great speed. When the war against Japan ended in September 1945, there were 12 million Americans in the armed forces; by 1947 there were only 1.5 million, as opposed to 6 million for the Soviet Union. Some historians have argued that American leaders believed that the atomic bomb gave the United States all the power it needed, but "getting tough" really meant "talking tough."

Stalin's agents quickly reheated what they viewed as the "ideological struggle against capitalist imperialism." The large, well-organized Communist parties of France and Italy challenged their own governments with violent criticisms and large strikes. The Soviet Union also put pressure on Iran, Turkey, and Greece, while a bitter civil war raged in China. By the spring of 1947 it appeared to many Americans that Stalin was determined to export communism by subversion throughout Europe and around the world.

The United States responded to this challenge with the **Truman Doctrine,** which was aimed at "containing" communism in areas already occupied by the Red Army. Truman told Congress in March 1947, "I believe it must be the policy of the United States to support free people who are resisting attempted subjugation by armed minorities or by outside pressure." To begin, Truman asked Congress for military aid to Greece and Turkey. Then, in June, Secretary of State George C. Marshall offered Europe economic aid—the **Marshall Plan**—to help it rebuild.

Stalin refused Marshall Plan assistance for all of eastern Europe. He purged the last remaining noncommunist elements from the coalition governments of eastern Europe and established Soviet-style, one-party communist dictatorships. Thus, when Stalin blocked all traffic through the Soviet zone of Germany to Berlin, the Western allies began flying hundreds of planes over the Soviet roadblocks to supply provisions to the West Berliners. After 324 days the Soviets backed down: containment seemed to work. In 1949, therefore, the United States formed an anti-Soviet military alliance of Western governments: the North Atlantic Treaty Organization (NATO). Stalin countered by tightening his hold on his satellites, later united in the Warsaw Pact. Europe was divided into two hostile blocs.

As tensions rose in Europe, the cold war spread to Asia. In 1945 Korea, like Germany, was divided into Soviet and American zones of occupation as the defeated Japanese surrendered. Plans to unify Korea faded, and in 1948 the country was divided into a communist north and an anticommunist south. In late 1949 the Communists triumphed in China (see page 1102), frightening and angering many Americans, who saw new evidence of a powerful worldwide communist conspiracy. When the Russian-backed communist forces of North Korea invaded South Korea in the spring of 1950, President Truman acted swiftly. American-led United Nations forces under General Douglas MacArthur intervened. The cold war had become very hot.

The Korean War was bitterly fought and extremely bloody. Initially, the well-equipped North Koreans almost conquered the entire peninsula, but the South Koreans and the Americans rallied and drove their foes all the way to the Chinese border. At that point China suddenly intervened, and its armies pushed the South Koreans and Americans back south. The war then seesawed back and forth near where it had begun, as President Truman rejected General MacArthur's call to attack China and fired him instead. In 1953 a fragile truce was finally negotiated, and the fighting stopped. Thus the United States extended its policy of containing communism to Asia but drew back from an invasion of communist China and possible nuclear war.

## RENAISSANCE AND CRISIS IN WESTERN EUROPE

As the cold war divided Europe into two blocs, the future appeared bleak on both sides of the iron curtain. Economic conditions were the worst in generations. Politically, Europe was weak and divided, a battleground for cold war ambitions. Moreover, European empires were crumbling in the face of nationalism in Asia and Africa. Yet western Europe recovered to enjoy unprecedented economic prosperity and peaceful social transformation. Then, in the early 1970s, the cycle turned abruptly. A downturn in the world economy hit western Europe hard with serious social and psychological consequences.

### The Postwar Challenge

After the war economic conditions in western Europe were terrible. Runaway inflation and black markets testified to severe shortages and hardships. Many believed that Europe was simply finished.

Suffering was most intense in defeated Germany. The major territorial change of the war had moved the Soviet Union's border far to the west. Poland was in turn compensated for this loss to the Soviets with land taken from Germany (see Map 33.1). To solidify these changes in boundaries, 13 million people were driven from their homes throughout eastern Europe and forced to resettle in a greatly reduced Germany. Conditions were not much better in the Western zones, for the Western allies also treated the German population with great severity at first. By the spring of 1947 refugee-clogged, hungry, prostrate Germany was on the verge of total collapse and threatening to drag down the rest of Europe.

Yet western Europe was not finished. The Nazi occupation and the war had discredited old ideas and old leaders. All over Europe many people were willing to change and experiment, and new groups and new leaders were coming to the fore to guide these aspirations. Progressive Catholics and their Christian Democrat political parties were particularly influential. In Italy and Germany antifascist Alcide De Gasperi and anti-Nazi Konrad Adenauer took power, steadfastly rejecting totalitarianism and narrow nationalism and placing their faith in democracy and cooperation. The socialists and the communists, active in the resistance against Hitler, also emerged from the war with increased power and prestige, especially in France and Italy. They, too, provided fresh leadership and pushed for social change. In the immediate postwar years welfare measures such as family allowances, health insurance, and increased public housing were enacted throughout much of continental Europe. Social reform complemented political transformation, creating solid foundations for a great European renaissance.

The United States also supplied strong and creative leadership, providing western Europe with both massive economic aid in the Marshall Plan and ongoing military protection through NATO, which featured American troops stationed permanently in Europe and the American nuclear umbrella. As Marshall Plan aid poured in, the battered economies of western Europe began to turn the

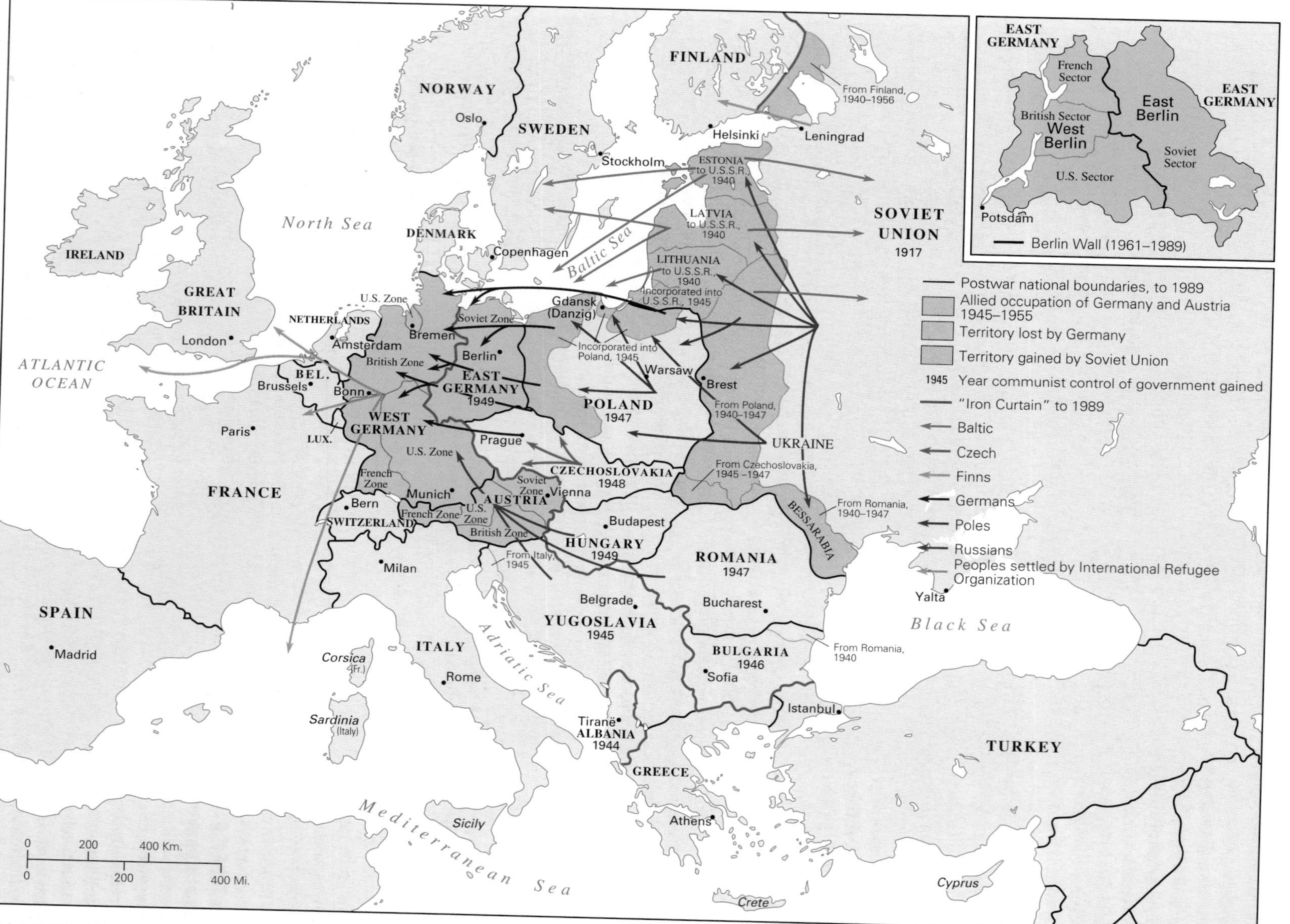


**MAP 33.1 The Results of World War II in Europe** Millions of refugees fled westward because of war and territorial changes. The Soviet Union and Poland took land from Germany, which the Allies partitioned into occupation zones. Those zones subsequently formed the basis of the East and West German states, as the iron curtain fell to divide both Germany and Europe. Austria was detached from Germany, but the Soviets subsequently permitted Austria to reunify as a neutral state.

corner in 1948, and Europe entered a period of unprecedented economic progress that lasted into the late 1960s. There were many reasons for this brilliant economic performance. American aid helped the process get off to a fast start. Moreover, economic growth became a basic objective of all western European governments, eager to avoid a return to the demoralizing stagnation of the 1930s. Thus governments generally accepted Keynesian economics (see page 1011) and sought to stimulate their economies.

The governments also adopted a variety of imaginative and successful strategies. In postwar West Germany, Minister of Economy Ludwig Erhard, a roly-poly, cigar-smoking former professor, broke decisively with the straitjacketed Nazi economy. Erhard bet on the free-market economy while maintaining the extensive social welfare network inherited from the Hitler era. West German success renewed respect for free-market capitalism. The French innovation was a new kind of planning. A planning commission set ambitious but flexible goals for the French economy and used the nationalized banks to funnel money into key industries. France achieved the most rapid economic development in its long history.

Another factor was the workforce, ready to work hard for low wages and the hope of a better future. Moreover, few Europeans had been able to afford many of the new consumer products during the Great Depression. In 1945 the electric refrigerator, the washing machine, and the automobile were rare luxuries. There was great potential demand, which the economic system moved to satisfy. Finally, western European nations abandoned protectionism and gradually created a large, unified market known as the **Common Market.** This historic action, which certainly stimulated the economy, was part of a larger search for European unity.

## "Building Europe" and Decolonization

Western Europe's political recovery was spectacular in the generation after 1945. Republics were re-established in France, West Germany, and Italy. Constitutional monarchs were restored in Belgium, the Netherlands, and Norway. Democratic governments, often within the framework of multiparty politics and shifting parliamentary coalitions, took root again and thrived in an atmosphere of civil liberties and individual freedom.

A similarly extraordinary achievement was the march toward a united Europe. The Christian Democrats, with their common Catholic heritage, were particularly committed to "building Europe," and other groups shared their dedication. Many Europeans believed that only unity could forestall European conflict in the future and that only a new "European nation" could reassert western Europe's influence in world affairs dominated by the United States and the Soviet Union.

The close cooperation among European states required by the Americans for Marshall Plan aid led to the creation of both the Organization of European Economic Cooperation (OEEC) and the Council of Europe in 1948. European federalists hoped that the Council of Europe would quickly evolve into a true European parliament with sovereign rights, but this did not happen. Britain opposed giving real power to the council, and many old-fashioned continental nationalists and communists agreed.

Frustrated in the direct political approach, European federalists turned toward economics as a way of working toward genuine unity. In 1950 French statesmen called for a special international organization to control and integrate all European steel and coal production. West Germany, Italy, Belgium, the Netherlands, and Luxembourg accepted the French idea in 1952; the British would have none of it. The immediate economic goal—a single steel and coal market without national tariffs or quotas—was rapidly realized. The more far-reaching political goal was to bind the six member nations so closely together economically that war among them would become unthinkable and virtually impossible.

In 1957 the six nations of the Coal and Steel Community signed the Treaty of Rome, which created the European Economic Community, generally known as the Common Market. The first goal of the treaty was a gradual reduction of all tariffs among the six in order to create a single market almost as large as that of the United States. Other goals included common economic policies and institutions and the free movement of capital and labor.

The Common Market was a great success, encouraging hopes of rapid progress toward political as well as economic union. In the 1960s, however, these hopes were frustrated by a resurgence of more traditional nationalism. France took the lead once again. Charles de Gaulle, president from 1958 to 1969, was at heart a romantic nationalist, and he labored to re-create a powerful, truly independent France. Viewing the United States as the main threat to genuine French (and European) independence, he withdrew all French military forces from the "American-controlled" NATO command as France developed its own nuclear weapons. Within the Common Market de Gaulle refused to permit the scheduled advent of majority rule. Thus throughout the 1960s the Common Market thrived economically but remained a union of sovereign states.

As Europe moved toward greater economic unity in the postwar era, its long overseas expansion was dramatically reversed. Between 1947 and 1962 almost every colonial

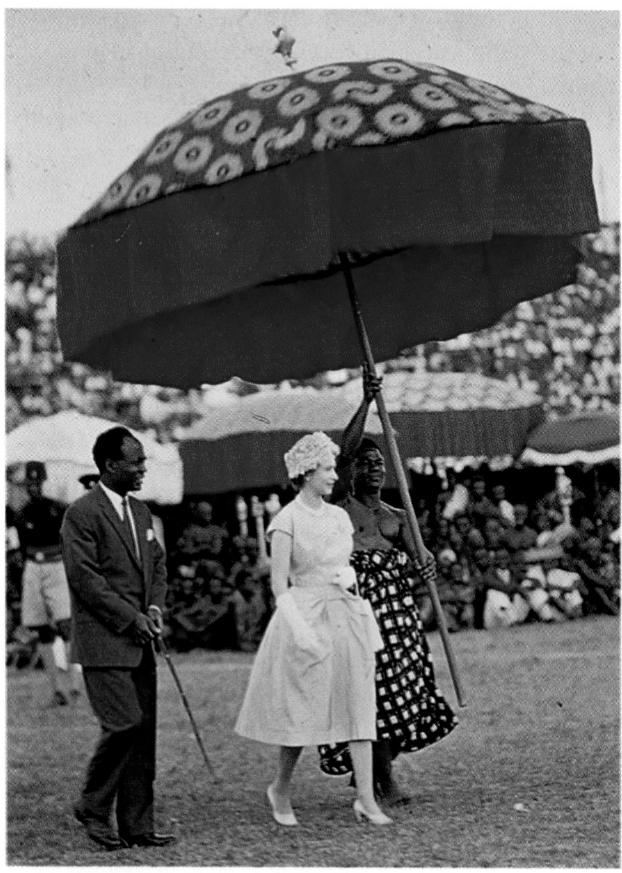

**African Independence** Britain's Queen Elizabeth II pays an official visit in 1961 to Ghana, the former Gold Coast colony. Accompanying the queen at the colorful welcoming ceremony is Ghana's popular Kwame Nkrumah, who was educated in black colleges in the United States and led Ghana's breakthrough to independence in 1957. *(Bettmann/Corbis)*

territory gained formal independence. Future generations will almost certainly see this rolling back of Western expansion as one of world history's great turning points.

The basic cause of imperial collapse—what Europeans called **decolonization**—was the rising demand by Asian and African peoples for national self-determination and racial equality (see Chapter 34). Yet decolonization also involved the imperial powers, and looking at the process from their perspective helps explain why independence came so quickly and why a kind of neocolonialism subsequently took its place in some areas.

European empires had been based on an enormous power differential between the rulers and the ruled, a difference that had almost vanished by 1945. Moreover, most Europeans regarded their empires very differently after 1945 than before 1914. Empire had rested on self-confidence and self-righteousness; Europeans had believed their superiority to be not only technical and military but also spiritual and moral. The horrors of the Second World War destroyed such complacent arrogance and gave opponents of imperialism much greater influence in Europe. After 1945 many Europeans were willing to let go of their colonies more or less voluntarily and to concentrate on rebuilding at home.

They still wanted some ties with the former colonies, however. As a result, western European countries actually managed to increase their economic and cultural ties with their former African colonies in the 1960s and 1970s. They used the lure of special trading privileges with the Common Market and heavy investment in French- and English-language education to enhance a powerful Western presence in the new African states. This situation led a variety of leaders and scholars to charge that western Europe (and the United States) had imposed a system of **neocolonialism** designed to perpetuate Western economic domination and undermine political independence, as the United States had subordinated the new nations of Latin America in the nineteenth century. At the very least, enduring influence in Africa testified to western Europe's resurgent economic and political power in international relations.

## The Changing Class Structure

Rapid economic growth went a long way toward creating a more mobile and more democratic society in Europe after the Second World War. Old class barriers relaxed, and class distinctions became fuzzier.

The structure of the middle class changed. In the nineteenth and early twentieth centuries the model for the middle class had been the independent, self-employed property owner who ran a business or practiced a liberal profession such as law or medicine. After 1945 a new breed of managers and experts required by large corporations and government agencies replaced traditional property owners as the leaders of the middle class. Moreover, the old propertied middle class lost control of many family-owned businesses (including family farms) and joined the ranks of salaried employees. The middle class also became harder to define. The salaried specialists of the new middle class came from all social classes, even the working class. Managers and technocrats passed on the opportunity for all-important advanced education to their children, but only in rare instances could they pass on the positions they had attained. Thus the new middle class, which was based largely on specialized skills and high levels of education, was more open, democratic, and insecure than the old propertied middle class.

The structure of the lower classes also became more flexible and open. There was a mass exodus from farms and the countryside, as one of the most traditional and least mobile groups in European society drastically declined. Meanwhile, the industrial working class ceased to expand, and job opportunities for white-collar and service employees grew rapidly. Such employees bore a greater resemblance to the new middle class of salaried specialists than to industrial workers, who were also better educated and more specialized.

European governments were reducing class tensions with a series of social reforms. Many of these reforms—such as increased unemployment benefits and more extensive old-age pensions—simply strengthened social security measures first pioneered in Bismarck's Germany. Other programs were new, such as comprehensive national health systems directed by the state. Most countries also introduced family allowances—direct government grants to parents to help them raise their children—that helped many poor families make ends meet. Most European governments gave maternity grants and built inexpensive public housing for low-income families and individuals. These and other social reforms provided a humane floor of well-being and promoted greater equality.

The rising standard of living and the spread of standardized consumer goods also worked to level Western society, as the percentage of income spent on food and drink declined substantially. For example, in 1948 there were only 5 million cars in western Europe, but in 1965 there were 44 million. Car ownership was democratized and came within the range of better-paid workers. Europeans also took great pleasure in the products of the "gadget revolution," filling their houses and apartments with washing machines, vacuum cleaners, refrigerators, dishwashers, TVs, and stereos.

The most astonishing leisure-time development in the consumer society was the blossoming of mass travel and tourism. With month-long paid vacations required by law in most European countries and widespread automobile ownership, beaches and ski resorts came within the reach of the middle class and many workers. By the late 1960s packaged tours with cheap group flights and bargain hotel accommodations had made even distant lands easily accessible.

## Economic and Social Dislocation, 1970–1990

For twenty years after 1945 most Europeans were preoccupied with the possibilities of economic progress and consumerism. The more democratic class structure also helped to reduce social tension, and ideological conflict went out of style. In the late 1960s sharp criticism and social conflicts re-emerged, heralding a new era of uncertainty and crisis. Radical college students led this loud but brief protest, demanding reforms in society as well as the university. It was the appearance of economic crisis in the 1970s, however, that brought the most serious challenges for the average person.

That crisis had two main causes. The postwar international monetary system was based on the American dollar, backed by American gold reserves. By early 1971 the United States had only $11 billion in gold left, and Europe had accumulated U.S. $50 billion. Foreigners panicked and raced to exchange their dollars for gold. When President Richard Nixon stopped its sale, the value of the dollar fell sharply, and inflation accelerated worldwide. Fixed rates of exchange were abandoned, and uncertainty replaced predictability in international trade and finance.

Even more damaging was the dramatic reversal in the price and availability of energy. The postwar boom was fueled by cheap oil. (See the feature "Global Trade: Oil" on pages 1068–1069.) By 1971 the Arab-led Organization of Petroleum Exporting Countries (**OPEC**) had watched the price of crude oil decline compared with the rising price of manufactured goods. OPEC decided to reverse that trend by presenting a united front against the oil companies. After the fourth Arab-Israeli war in October 1973 (see page 1117), crude oil prices quadrupled in a year. The rapid price rise was economically destructive, but the world's big powers did nothing. The Soviet Union, itself an oil exporter, benefited directly; the United States was immobilized by the Watergate crisis in politics (see page 1082). Thus governments, companies, and individuals had no choice other than to deal piecemeal with the so-called oil shock—which was really an earthquake.

Coming on the heels of upheaval in the international monetary system, the revolution in energy prices plunged the world into its worst economic decline since the 1930s. Unemployment rose; productivity and living standards declined. By 1976 a modest recovery was in progress, but when Iranian oil production collapsed during Iran's fundamentalist Islamic revolution (see page 1120), the price of crude oil doubled again in 1979. Unemployment and inflation rose dramatically before another uneven recovery began in 1982. But in the summer of 1985 the unemployment rate in western Europe rose again, to its highest levels since the Great Depression. Although unemployment declined somewhat in the late 1980s, the 1990s opened with renewed recession in the United States and Europe, where it was especially severe. Global recovery was painfully slow until late 1993.

# GLOBAL TRADE

## OIL

Crude oil is a liquid hydrocarbon that is located in certain rocks below the earth's crust. Although it is found throughout the world, the Persian Gulf and Caspian Sea areas contain about three-quarters of the world's proven reserves. The uses of crude oil are limited, but it may be refined into valuable products such as kerosene, gasoline, and fuel oil.

Oil has been used throughout history, although it did not become a worldwide commodity until the nineteenth century. In antiquity, the Sumerians and Babylonians mixed evaporated oil from tar pits with sand to make asphalt for waterproofing ships and paving roads. Islamic societies in the Middle East used small quantities of oil for lighting, although cooking fires were probably the main source of light. In Europe lamp oil—from animal fats and plants—was a luxury.

The nineteenth century brought revolutionary changes in lighting—the "industrialization of light." By the 1840s manufacturers in coal-rich Europe were distilling coal into crude oil and gas, which were sold for lighting. North America followed suit. Thus when E. L. Drake drilled the first successful oil well in Pennsylvania in 1859, a growing demand for lamp oil already existed. The production of kerosene, easily distilled from the light oils of Pennsylvania, took off as American consumers accepted the bright, clean-burning, and relatively inexpensive oil for use in their lamps.

The modern oil industry operated on a global scale from the beginning. After the late 1860s the United States exported two-thirds of its kerosene, first in wooden barrels, then in large tin cans, and finally in tankers for bulk distribution. The leading producer was John D. Rockefeller's Standard Oil, which held a monopoly on kerosene until the U.S. government broke it into separate companies in 1911. Most kerosene went

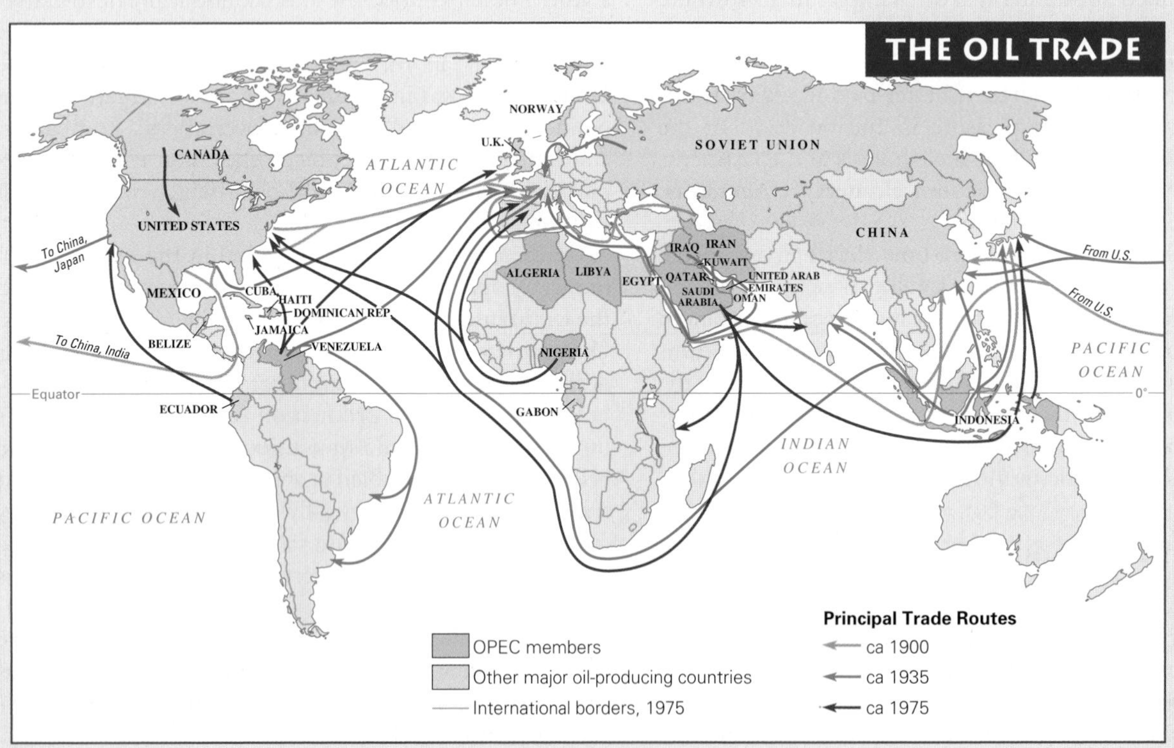

*Following the Iranian revolution in 1979 and the surge in oil prices to all-time highs, most Western consumers viewed OPEC as an unstoppable malignant force, as this American cartoon suggests. OPEC seemed much less threatening when prices came down, even though the world economy still depended heavily on Middle Eastern oil.* (Oliphant © Universal Press Syndicate. Reprinted with permission. All rights reserved)

to Europe at first, but other markets grew rapidly. In the 1870s the Baku region on the Caspian Sea, home of an ancient artisan oil industry, introduced drilling, brought in fabulous gushers, and created a Russian refining industry. Russian capitalists fought well-publicized "oil wars" with Standard Oil for world kerosene markets.

International differences were significant. In the United States and western Europe kerosene appealed especially to farmers and urban working people, who had previously lacked decent lighting. The affluent urban classes generally continued to use coal-distilled gas until the 1880s, when electricity from central power stations began to replace gas in elegant neighborhoods. In China peasants rejected bulk distribution and insisted on kerosene in tin cans, recycling them into valuable all-purpose containers. Russia pioneered in using oil as fuel, as the refining of heavy Baku crude yielded abundant thick "leftovers"—an excellent power source for riverboats, railroads, and factories.

During the twentieth century oil became a major fuel source, as kerosene production declined. Until 1941 the explosive growth of automobiles in the United States was easily outpaced by the development of domestic oil fields, enabling the United States to sell one-third of all the oil consumed beyond its borders. In oil-poor Europe (Russia excepted), fuel oil loomed large as a strategic material. After 1919 the British government took control of the two oil companies in Iran and Iraq to guarantee supplies for its military and industrial needs. Germany distilled coal into synthetic gasoline, and Hitler relentlessly pushed production of this very expensive alternative to free his war machine from dependence on foreign oil.

The international oil trade shifted dramatically after 1945. The United States, previously producing half the world's oil, became the world's largest importer. The Middle East, producing very modestly in the 1920s and 1930s, became the world's leading exporter. At the same time, western Europe and Japan shifted from coal to oil to drive their factories and fuel their automobiles. Nevertheless, the American and British oil companies in the Middle East expanded output so rapidly—sixteen times between 1948 and 1972—that the inflation-adjusted price for Middle Eastern oil actually fell substantially in these years.

Increasingly dissatisfied with their share of the profits, the main exporting countries—Iran, Iraq, Kuwait, Saudi Arabia, and Venezuela—organized OPEC (Organization of Petroleum Exporting Countries) in 1960 to gain control of their oil resources. In 1973, in the fourth Arab-Israeli war, OPEC engineered a fourfold price increase, with enormous global consequences (see page 1067). The exporting states also nationalized their oil industries, reducing foreign companies to simple buyers and transporters. The oil exporters used their financial windfalls to improve health and living standards somewhat, but vast sums went for lavish spending by the elite and overly ambitious development projects. Above all, money went for expensive military hardware from the industrialized countries, which increased tensions and prolonged the terrible war between Iraq and Iran in the 1980s (see Chapter 34).

After the unexpected price revolution of the 1970s came the unexpected price collapse of the 1980s and early 1990s. Conservation, greater efficiency, recession, environmental concerns, and big new discoveries outside the Middle East, such as those in the North Sea, Angola, and Nigeria, eliminated much of the inflation-adjusted price increases between 1973 and 1979. By 2002 some argued that oil was really "just another commodity." Others stressed that one volatile area—the Middle East—held two-thirds of the world's oil reserves and believed that the control of foreign oil remained essential for national security.

**Saudi Riches** Enormous oil reserves make Saudi Arabia one of the most influential members of the Organization of Petroleum Exporting Countries (OPEC) and give it one of the world's highest per capita incomes. Oil has also made rich men of Prince Fahd and King Khalid, shown here considering plans for a new urban development. *(Robert Azzi/Woodfin Camp & Associates)*

The most pervasive consequences of this economic stagnation in Europe were probably psychological and attitudinal. Optimism gave way to pessimism; romantic utopianism yielded to sober realism. This drastic change in mood—a complete surprise only to those who had never studied history—affected states, institutions, and individuals in countless ways.

The welfare system fashioned in the postwar era prevented mass suffering through extended benefits for the unemployed, free medical care and special allowances for the needy, and a host of lesser supports. The responsive, socially concerned national state undoubtedly contributed to the preservation of political stability and democracy in the face of economic difficulties that might have brought revolution and dictatorship in earlier times.

But increased government spending was not matched by higher taxes, causing a rapid growth of budget deficits, national debts, and inflation. By the late 1970s a powerful reaction against government's ever-increasing role had set in. Growing voter dissatisfaction helped bring Conservative Margaret Thatcher (b. 1925) to power in Britain in 1979. Thatcher slowed government spending and privatized industry by selling off state-owned companies to private investors. Of great social significance, Thatcher's government encouraged low- and moderate-income renters in state-owned housing projects to buy their apartments at rock-bottom prices. This step created a whole new class of property owners, thereby eroding the electoral base of Britain's socialist Labour party. Other Western governments introduced austerity measures to slow the seemingly inexorable growth of public spending and the welfare state.

The striking but temporary exception to the trend toward greater frugality was François Mitterrand (1916–1996) of France. After his election as president in 1981, Mitterrand led his Socialist party and communist allies on a lurch to the left, launching a vast program of nationalization and public investment designed to spend France out of economic stagnation. By 1983 this attempt had clearly failed. Mitterrand's Socialist government was then compelled to impose a wide variety of austerity measures, but the French economy continued to limp and sputter through the decade.

Individuals felt the impact of austerity at an early date, for unlike governments, they could not pay their bills by printing money and going ever further into debt. The energy crisis of the 1970s forced them to re-examine not only their fuel bills but also the whole pattern of self-indulgent materialism in the postwar era. The result in both Europe and North America was a leaner, tougher lifestyle, featuring more attention to nutrition and a passion for exercise. There was less blind reliance on medical science for good health and a growing awareness that individuals had to accept a large portion of the responsibility for illness and disease.

Economic troubles strengthened existing trends within the family. Men and women were encouraged to postpone marriage until they had put their careers on a firm foundation, so the age of marriage rose sharply for both sexes in many Western countries. Indeed, the very real threat of unemployment—or "underemployment" in a dead-end job—seemed to shape the outlook of a whole generation. The students of the 1980s were serious, practical, and often conservative. As one young woman at a French university told a reporter in 1985, "Jobs are the big worry now, so everyone wants to learn something practical."[2] In France as elsewhere, the shift away from the romantic visions and political activism of the late 1960s was remarkable.

Harder times also meant that more women entered or remained in the workforce after they married. Although attitudes related to personal fulfillment were one reason for the continuing increase—especially for well-educated, upper-middle-class women—many wives in poor and middle-class families worked outside the home because of economic necessity. As in preindustrial Europe, the wife's earnings provided the margin of survival for millions of hard-pressed families.

## SOVIET EASTERN EUROPE, 1945–1991

While western Europe surged ahead economically after the Second World War, eastern Europe followed a different path. The Soviet Union under Stalin first tightened its grip on the "liberated" nations of eastern Europe and then refused to let go. Thus postwar economic recovery in eastern Europe proceeded along Soviet lines, and changes in the Soviet Union strongly influenced political and social developments. That trend remained true more than forty years later, when radical reform in the Soviet Union opened the door to popular revolution in the eastern European satellites—and ultimately to the collapse of the Soviet Union itself.

### Stalin's Last Years

Americans were not the only ones who felt betrayed by Stalin's postwar actions. The "Great Patriotic War of the Fatherland" had fostered Russian nationalism and a relaxation of totalitarian terror. It also produced a rare but real unity between Soviet rulers and most Russian people. Having made a heroic war effort, the vast majority of the Soviet people hoped in 1945 that a grateful party and government would grant greater freedom and democracy. Such hopes were soon crushed.

Even before the war ended, Stalin was moving his country back toward rigid dictatorship. As early as 1944 the leading members of the Communist party were being given a new motivating slogan: "The war on Fascism ends, the war on capitalism begins."[3] By early 1946 Stalin was publicly singing the old tune that war was inevitable as long as capitalism existed. Stalin's new foreign foe in the West provided an excuse for re-establishing a harsh dictatorship. Thousands of returning soldiers and ordinary civilians were purged in 1945 and 1946, as Stalin revived the terrible forced-labor camps of the 1930s. Culture and art were purged in violent campaigns that reimposed rigid anti-Western ideological conformity. In 1949 Stalin launched a savage verbal attack on Soviet Jews, accusing them of being pro-Western and antisocialist.

In the political realm Stalin reasserted the Communist party's complete control of the government and his absolute mastery of the party. Five-year plans were reintroduced to cope with the enormous task of economic reconstruction. Once again heavy and military industry were given top priority, and consumer goods, housing, and collectivized agriculture were neglected. Everyday life was very hard. In short, it was the 1930s all over again in the Soviet Union, although police terror was less intense.

Stalin's prime postwar innovation was to export the Stalinist system to eastern Europe. Rigid ideological indoctrination, attacks on religion, and a lack of civil liberties were soon facts of life in the one-party states of the region. Industry was nationalized, and the middle class was stripped of its possessions. Economic life was then faithfully recast in the Stalinist mold. Only Josip Tito (1892–1980), the popular resistance leader and Communist party chief of Yugoslavia, could resist Soviet domination successfully, because there was no Russian army in Yugoslavia.

### Limited De-Stalinization and Stagnation

In 1953 the aging Stalin finally died. Even as his heirs struggled for power, they realized that reforms were necessary because of the widespread fear and hatred of Stalin's political terrorism. The power of the secret police was curbed, and gradually many forced-labor camps were closed. Change was also necessary for economic reasons. Agriculture was in bad shape, and shortages of consumer goods were discouraging hard work and initiative. Moreover, Stalin's belligerent foreign policy had led directly to a strong Western alliance, which isolated the Soviet Union.

On just how much change to permit, the Communist party leadership was badly split. Conservatives wanted as few changes as possible. Reformers, led by Nikita Khrushchev (1894–1971), argued for major innovations and won control of the government. Khrushchev launched an all-out attack on Stalin and his crimes. At a closed session of the Twentieth Party Congress in 1956, he described in gory detail to startled delegates how Stalin had tortured and murdered thousands of loyal Communists, bungled the country's defense by trusting Hitler, and "supported the glorification of his own person." Khrushchev's "secret speech," read to Communist party meetings throughout the country, strengthened the reform movement.

The liberalization—or **de-Stalinization,** as it was called in the West—of the Soviet Union was genuine. The Communist party jealously maintained its monopoly on political power, but Khrushchev shook up the party and brought in new members. Some resources were shifted from heavy industry and the military toward consumer goods and agriculture, and controls over workers were relaxed. The Soviet Union's very low standard of living finally began to improve and continued to rise substantially throughout the booming 1960s.

De-Stalinization created great ferment among writers and intellectuals who hungered for cultural freedom. Courageous editors let the sparks fly. The writer Aleksandr Solzhenitsyn (b. 1918) created a sensation when his *One Day in the Life of Ivan Denisovich* was published in the Soviet Union in 1962. Solzhenitsyn's novel portrays in grim detail life in a Stalinist concentration camp and is a damning indictment of the Stalinist past.

Khrushchev also de-Stalinized Soviet foreign policy. "Peaceful coexistence" with capitalism was possible, he argued, and great wars were not inevitable. Between 1955 and 1957 cold war tensions relaxed.

De-Stalinization stimulated rebelliousness in the eastern European satellites, where communist reformers and the masses sought greater liberty and national independence. Poland took the lead in 1956, when extensive rioting brought a new government that managed to win greater autonomy. Hungary experienced a real and tragic revolution. Led by students and workers—the classic urban revolutionaries—the people of Budapest installed a liberal communist reformer as their new chief in October 1956. After the new government promised free elections and renounced Hungary's military alliance with Moscow, Russian leaders ordered an invasion and crushed the revolution. Hungarians had hoped that the United States would come to their aid. When this did not occur, most people in eastern Europe concluded that their only hope was to strive for small domestic gains while following Russia obediently in foreign affairs.

By late 1962 opposition in Soviet party circles to Khrushchev's policies was strong. De-Stalinization seemed a dangerous threat. How could Khrushchev denounce the dead dictator without eventually denouncing and perhaps even arresting his still-powerful henchmen? Moreover, the widening campaign of de-Stalinization posed a clear threat to the authority of the party by producing growing criticism of the whole system. Finally, Khrushchev's policy toward the West was erratic and ultimately unsuccessful. In 1958 he had ordered the Western allies to evacuate West Berlin within six months but backed down in the face of the allies' unity. In 1961 he had forced the Americans to accept the building of a wall between East and West Berlin but stumbled again the following year. When Khrushchev ordered missiles with nuclear warheads installed in Fidel Castro's communist Cuba in 1962, U.S. president John F. Kennedy countered with a naval blockade of Cuba. After a tense diplomatic crisis Khrushchev agreed to remove the missiles. The Soviet leader looked like a bumbling buffoon. Within two years of the Cuban fiasco he was gone in a bloodless palace revolution.

After Leonid Brezhnev (1906–1982) and his supporters took over in 1964, they started talking quietly of Stalin's "good points" and stopped further liberalization. Soviet leaders, determined never to suffer Khrushchev's humiliation in the face of American nuclear superiority, also launched a massive arms buildup.

In the wake of Khrushchev's reforms the 1960s brought modest liberalization and more consumer goods to eastern Europe, as well as somewhat greater national autonomy. In January 1968 the reform elements in the Czechoslovak Communist party gained a majority and replaced a long-time Stalinist leader with Alexander Dubček (1921–1992), whose new government launched dramatic reforms. Although Dubček constantly proclaimed his loyalty to the Warsaw Pact, the determination of the Czech reformers to build what they called "socialism with a human face" frightened hard-line Communists. Thus in August 1968, 500,000 Russian and eastern European troops occupied Czechoslovakia, and the Czech experiment in humanizing communism came to an end. Shortly afterward, Brezhnev declared the so-called **Brezhnev Doctrine,** according to which the Soviet Union and its allies had the right to intervene in any socialist country whenever they saw the need.

The aftermath of intervention in Czechoslovakia also brought a certain re-Stalinization of the U.S.S.R. Free expression and open protest disappeared. Dissidents were blacklisted or quietly imprisoned in jails or mental institutions. Unlike in the Stalinist era, though, dictatorship was collective rather than personal, and coercion replaced uncontrolled terror. This compromise seemed to suit the leaders and a majority of the people, and the Soviet Union appeared stable in the 1970s and early 1980s.

A rising standard of living for ordinary people contributed to stability, although the economic crisis of the 1970s greatly slowed the rate of improvement, and long lines and shortages persisted. The enduring advantages of the elite also reinforced the system. Ambitious individuals still had tremendous incentive to do as the state wished in order to gain access to special, well-stocked stores, attend superior schools, and travel abroad.

Another source of stability was the enduring nationalism of ordinary Russians. Party leaders successfully identified themselves with Russian patriotism, stressing their role in saving the motherland during the Second World War and protecting it now from foreign foes, including eastern European "counter-revolutionaries." Moreover, the politically dominant Great Russians, only half of the total Soviet population, held the top positions in the Soviet Union's non-Russian republics.

Beneath this stability, however, the Soviet Union was experiencing a social revolution. Three aspects of this revolution were particularly significant. First, the growth of the urban population continued rapidly in the 1960s and 1970s. In 1985 two-thirds of all Soviet citizens lived in cities, and one-fourth lived in big cities. This expanding urban population lost its old peasant ways, exchanging them for more education, better job skills, and greater sophistication. Second, the number of highly trained scientists, managers, and specialists expanded prodigiously, jumping fourfold between 1960 and 1985. Third, the education that created expertise also helped foster the growth of Soviet public opinion. Educated people read,

**The Invasion of Czechoslovakia** A Russian soldier holds his assault rifle on a young Czech student, who is greeting the invader with only a sign. In 1968 the Czechs and Slovaks knew that armed resistance would be suicidal. *(Joseph Koudelka/Magnum Photos)*

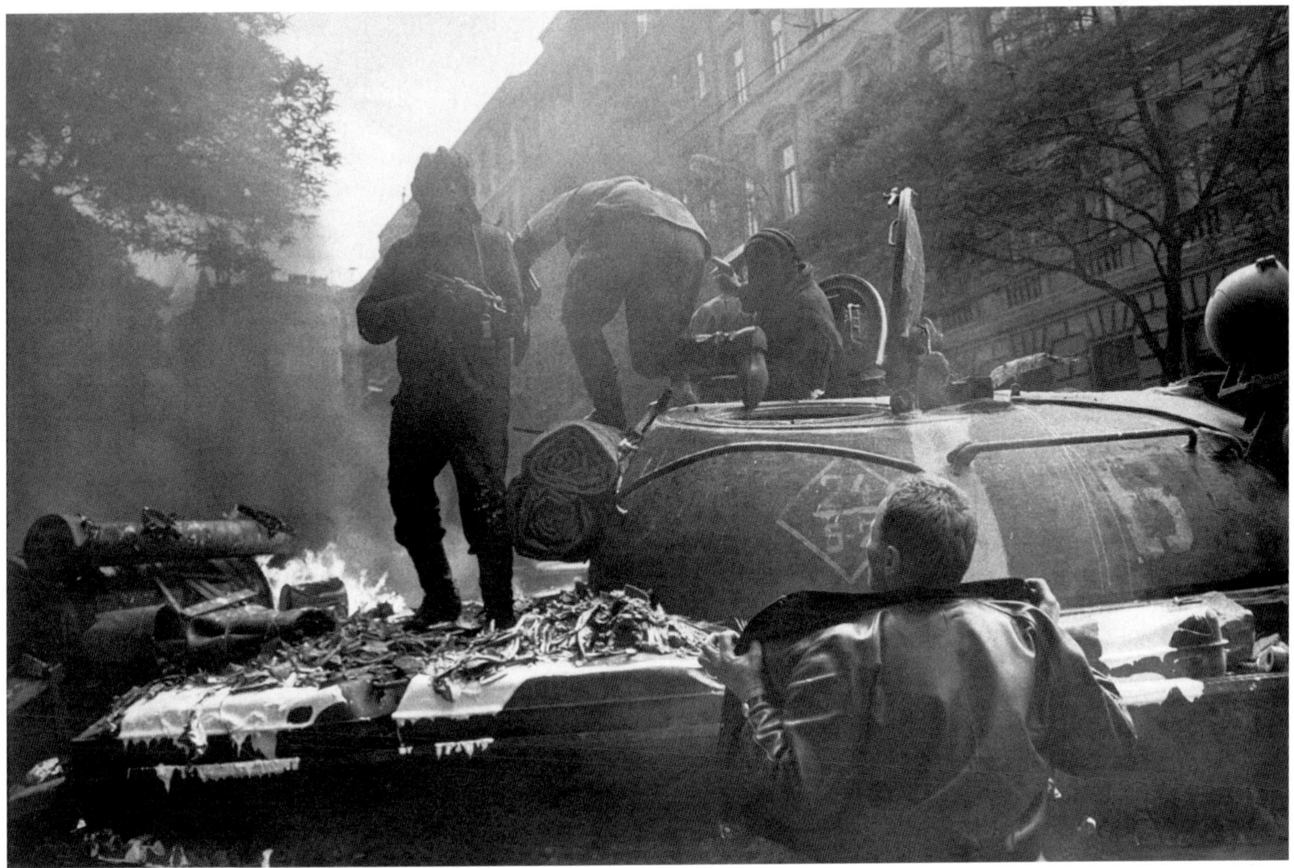

discussed, and formed definite ideas about social questions from environmental pollution to urban transportation. They increasingly saw themselves as worthy of having a voice in society's decisions, even its political decisions. These changes set the stage for the dramatic reforms of the Gorbachev era.

## The Gorbachev Era

Fundamental change in Russian history has often come in short, intensive spurts, which contrast vividly with long periods of immobility. So it was with the era of dramatic change that began with the reforms launched by Mikhail Gorbachev in 1985.

The Soviet Union's Communist party elite seemed safe in the early 1980s from any challenge from below. The party's long-established system of centralized control reached down to factories, neighborhoods, and villages. The party hierarchy continued to manipulate every aspect of national life. Organized opposition was impossible, and average people simply left politics to the bosses.

The country had serious problems, however. The massive state and party bureaucracy discouraged personal initiative and promoted economic inefficiency and apathy among the masses and the rapidly growing class of well-educated urban experts. Therefore, when the ailing Brezhnev died in 1982, efforts were made to improve economic performance and to combat worker absenteeism and high-level corruption. These efforts set the stage for the emergence in 1985 of Mikhail Gorbachev (b. 1931), the most vigorous Soviet leader since Stalin.

Smart, charming, and tough, Gorbachev believed in communism, though he realized it was failing. He (and his intelligent, influential wife, Raisa, a professor of Marxist-Leninist thought) wanted to save the Soviet system by reforming it. And Gorbachev realized full well that success at home required better relations with the West, for the wasteful arms race had had a disastrous impact on living standards in the Soviet Union.

In his first year in office Gorbachev attacked corruption and incompetence in the upper bureaucracy, and he consolidated his power. He also attacked alcoholism and drunkenness, scourges of Soviet society. More basically he elaborated a series of reform policies designed to revive and even remake the vast Soviet Union.

The first set of reforms was designed to transform and restructure the economy. To accomplish this economic restructuring, or **perestroika,** Gorbachev and his supporters permitted freer prices, more independence for state enterprises, and the setting up of some profit-seeking private cooperatives. But the reforms were rather timid, and when the economy stalled, the lack of success gradually eroded Gorbachev's popular support.

Gorbachev's bold and far-reaching campaign of openness, or **glasnost,** was much more successful. Where censorship, dull uniformity, and outright lies had long characterized public discourse, the new frankness of the government and the media led rather quickly to something approaching free speech and free expression, a veritable cultural revolution. A disaster like the Chernobyl nuclear reactor accident, which devastated part of the Ukraine and showered Europe with radioactive fallout, was reported with honesty and thoroughness. The works of long-banned and vilified Russian émigré writers sold millions of copies in new editions, and denunciations of Stalin and his terror became standard fare in plays and movies.

Democratization was the third element of Gorbachev's reform. Beginning as an attack on corruption in the Communist party and as an attempt to bring the class of educated experts into the decision-making process, it led to the first free elections in the Soviet Union since 1917. Gorbachev and the party remained in control, but a minority of critical independents were elected in April 1989 to a revitalized Congress of People's Deputies. Many top-ranking Communists who ran unopposed saw themselves defeated as angry voters struck their names from the ballot.

Democratization also encouraged demands for greater autonomy by non-Russian minorities, especially in the Baltic region and in the Caucasus. These demands certainly went beyond what Gorbachev had envisaged. But whereas China's Communist party leaders brutally massacred similar prodemocracy demonstrators in Beijing (Peking) in June 1989 (see page 1105), Gorbachev drew back from repression. Thus nationalist demands continued to grow.

Finally, the Soviet leader brought "new political thinking" to foreign affairs. He withdrew Soviet troops from Afghanistan and sought to reduce East-West tensions. Of enormous historical importance, Gorbachev pledged to respect the political choices of the peoples of eastern Europe, repudiating the Brezhnev Doctrine. By 1989 it seemed that if Gorbachev held to his word, the tragic Soviet occupation of eastern Europe might gradually wither away.

## The Revolutions of 1989

Instead of gradual change, history accelerated. In 1989 a series of largely peaceful revolutions swept across eastern Europe. These revolutions overturned existing communist regimes and led to the formation of governments dedicated to democratic elections, human rights, and national rejuvenation. The face of eastern Europe changed dramatically almost overnight.

The Polish people led the way. Poland had been an unruly satellite from the beginning, and Stalin said that introducing communism to Poland was like putting a saddle on a cow. After widespread riots in 1956 Polish communists dropped their efforts to impose Soviet-style collectivization on the peasants and to break the Roman Catholic church. With an independent agriculture and a vigorous church, the communists failed to monopolize society.

They also failed to manage the economy effectively and put it into a nosedive by the mid-1970s. Then the "Polish miracle" occurred: Cardinal Karol Wojtyla, archbishop of Cracow, was elected pope, and in June 1979 he returned to his native land to preach the love of Christ and country and the "inalienable rights of man." Pope John Paul II electrified the Polish nation, and the economic crisis became a spiritual crisis as well.

In August 1980 scattered strikes snowballed into a working-class revolt. Led by a feisty electrician and devout Catholic named Lech Walesa, the workers organized an independent trade union that they called **Solidarity.** Solidarity became the union of the nation, and cultural and intellectual freedom blossomed. As economic hardship increased, grassroots radicalism and frustration mounted. In response, Communist party leader General Wojciech Jaruzelski proclaimed martial law in December 1981 and arrested Solidarity's leaders. (See the feature "Listening to the Past: A Solidarity Leader Speaks from Prison" on pages 1098–1099.)

Though outlawed and driven underground, Solidarity maintained its organization, and popular support remained strong and deep. By 1988 widespread labor unrest and raging inflation had brought Poland to the brink of economic collapse. Profiting from Gorbachev's tolerant attitude and skillfully mobilizing its forces, Solidarity pressured Poland's frustrated Communist party leaders into another round of negotiations. The subsequent agreement legalized Solidarity and announced that free elections for some seats in the Polish parliament would be held in June 1989. Solidarity won every contested seat. A month later the editor of Solidarity's weekly newspaper was sworn in as the first noncommunist leader in eastern Europe in a generation. Soon Poland was not alone in its revolution.

In Czechoslovakia communism died in December 1989 in an almost good-humored ousting of Communist party bosses in only ten days. This so-called **Velvet Revolution** grew out of popular demonstrations led by students, intellectuals, and a dissident playwright turned moral revolutionary named Václav Havel. Massive street protests forced the resignation of the communist government, and as 1989 ended, Havel was elected president. (See the feature "Individuals in Society: Václav Havel.")

In Romania revolution was violent and bloody. There the iron-fisted communist dictator Nicolae Ceauşescu, alone among eastern European bosses, ordered his ruthless security forces to slaughter thousands, thereby sparking an armed uprising. After Ceauşescu's forces were defeated, the tyrant and his wife were captured and executed by a military court.

Change swept Hungary as well, when growing popular resistance forced the Communist party to renounce one-party rule and schedule free elections for early 1990. Hungarians gleefully tore down the barbed-wire "iron curtain" that separated Hungary and Austria and opened their border to refugees from East Germany.

As thousands of dissatisfied East Germans began pouring through Hungary on their way to thriving West Germany, a protest movement arose in East Germany. Some people, in huge candlelight demonstrations, tried to promote reforms to create a democratic, independent, but still socialist East Germany. These "stayers" failed to convince the "leavers," however, who continued to flee en masse. Desperately hoping to stabilize the situation, the East German government opened the Berlin Wall in November 1989, and people danced for joy atop that grim symbol of the prison state. East Germany's aging Communist party leaders were swept aside, and a reform government called for general elections in March 1990. In those elections a conservative-liberal "Alliance for Germany" won and quickly negotiated an economic union with West Germany on favorable terms.

Three factors contributed to this rapid reunification. First, the opening of the Berlin Wall had a huge impact. In the first week alone almost 9 million East Germans—roughly half the country's population—poured across the border into West Germany. While almost all returned home, the joy of warm welcomes from long-lost friends and family aroused long-dormant hopes of unity among ordinary citizens. Second, West German chancellor Helmut Kohl and his closest advisers moved skillfully. Kohl reassured American, Soviet, and European leaders that they need not fear a reunified Germany. At the same time, he promised the ordinary people of bankrupt East Germany an immediate economic bonanza—a one-for-one exchange of all East German marks held in savings accounts and pensions into much more valuable West German marks. Finally, the complicated international aspect of German unification was settled when Kohl and Gorbachev signed a historic agreement in July 1990. United Germany

**The Fall of the Berlin Wall** The sudden opening of the Berlin Wall in November 1989 dramatized the spectacular collapse of Communism throughout eastern Europe. Built by the Soviet leader Nikita Khrushchev in 1961, the hated barrier had stopped the flow of refugees from East Germany to West Germany. *(Patrick Piel/Gamma)*

solemnly affirmed its peaceful intentions and pledged never to develop nuclear, biological, or chemical weapons. On October 3, 1990, East Germany merged into West Germany, forming a single nation under the West German constitution and laws.

## Cold War Finale and Soviet Disintegration

The peaceful reunification of Germany accelerated the pace of agreements to reduce armaments and liquidate the cold war. With the Soviet Union's budget deficit rising rapidly in 1990, Gorbachev sought arrangements to justify massive cuts in military spending. Thus in November 1990 delegates from twenty-two European countries joined those from the United States and the Soviet Union in Paris and agreed to a scaling down of all their armed forces. The delegates also solemnly affirmed that all existing borders in Europe—from unified Germany to the Baltic republics of Lithuania, Latvia, and Estonia, which had declared their independence from the Soviet Union that year—were legal and valid. The **Paris Accord** was for all practical purposes a general peace treaty, bringing an end to World War II and the cold war that followed.

The establishment of peace in Europe encouraged the United States and the Soviet Union to scrap a significant portion of their nuclear weapons. In September 1991 a confident President George Bush unilaterally declared another major cut in American nuclear weapons. He also canceled the around-the-clock alert status for American bombers outfitted with atomic bombs. A floundering Gorbachev quickly followed suit. For the first time in four decades Soviet and American nuclear weapons were no longer standing ready to destroy capitalism, communism, and life itself.

# INDIVIDUALS IN SOCIETY

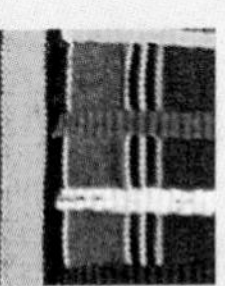

## VÁCLAV HAVEL

On the night of November 24, 1989, the revolution in Czechoslovakia reached its climax. Three hundred thousand people had poured into Prague's historic Wenceslas Square to continue the massive protests that had erupted a week earlier after the police savagely beat student demonstrators. Now all eyes were focused on a high balcony. There an elderly man with a gentle smile and a middle-aged intellectual in jeans and sport jacket stood arm in arm and acknowledged the cheers of the crowd. "Dubček-Havel," the people roared. "Dubček-Havel!" Alexander Dubček, who represented the failed promise of reform communism in the 1960s (see page 1072), was symbolically passing the torch to Václav Havel, who embodied the uncompromising opposition to communism that was sweeping the country. That very evening, the hard-line Communist government resigned, and soon Havel was the unanimous choice to head a new democratic Czechoslovakia. Who was this man to whom the nation turned in 1989?

Born in 1936 into a prosperous, cultured, upper-middle-class family, the young Havel was denied admission to the university because of his class origins. Loving literature and philosophy, he gravitated to the theater, became a stagehand, and emerged in the 1960s as a leading playwright. His plays were set in vague settings, developed existential themes, and poked fun at the absurdities of life and the pretensions of communism. In his private life, Havel thrived on good talk, Prague's lively bar scene, and officially forbidden rock-and-roll.

In 1968 the Soviets rolled into Czechoslovakia, and Havel watched in horror as a tank commander opened fire on a crowd of peaceful protesters in a small town. "That week," he recorded, "was an experience I shall never forget."* The free-spirited artist threw himself into the intellectual opposition to communism and became its leading figure for the next twenty years. The costs of defiance were enormous. Purged and blacklisted, Havel lifted barrels in a brewery and wrote bitter satires that could not be staged. In 1977 he and a few other dissidents publicly protested Czechoslovakian violations of the Helsinki Accord on human rights, and in 1989 this Charter '77 group became the inspiration for Civic Forum, the democratic coalition that toppled communism. Havel spent five years in prison and was constantly harassed by the police.

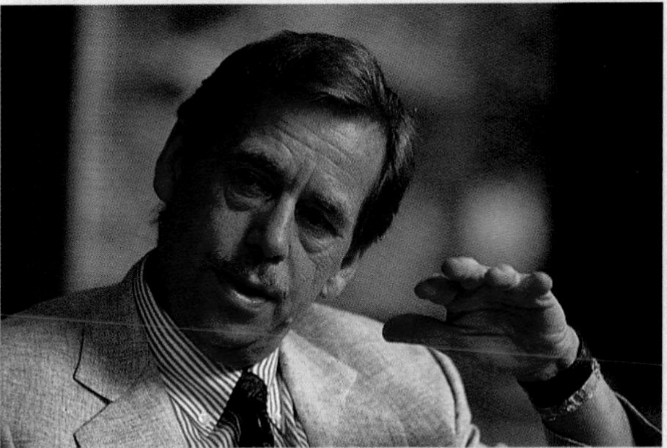

*Václav Havel, playwright, dissident leader, and the first postcommunist president of the Czech Republic.* (Chris Niedenthal/stockphoto.com)

Havel's thoughts and actions focused on truth, decency, and moral regeneration. In 1975, in a famous open letter to Czechoslovakia's Communist boss, Havel wrote that the people were indeed quiet, but only because they were "driven by fear. . . . Everyone has something to lose and so everyone has reason to be afraid." Thus Havel saw lies, hypocrisy, and apathy undermining and poisoning all human relations in his country. "Order has been established—at the price of a paralysis of the spirit, a deadening of the heart, and a spiritual and moral crisis in society."†

Yet Havel saw a way out of the Communist quagmire. He argued that a profound but peaceful revolution in human values was possible. Such a revolution could lead to the moral reconstruction of Czech and Slovak society, where, in his words, "values like trust, openness, responsibility, solidarity and love" might again flourish and nurture the human spirit. Havel was a voice of hope and humanity, a voice who inspired his compatriots with a lofty vision of a moral postcommunist society. As president of his country (1989–2003), Havel continued to speak eloquently on the great questions of our time.

### QUESTIONS FOR ANALYSIS

1. Why did Havel oppose Communist rule? How did his goals differ from those of Dubček and other advocates of reform communism?
2. Havel has been called a "moralist in politics." Is this a good description of him? Why? Can you think of a better one?

*Quoted in M. Simmons, *The Reluctant President: A Political Life of Václav Havel* (London: Methuen, 1991), p. 91.

† Quoted ibid., p. 110.

The great question then became whether the Soviet Union would follow its former satellites in a popular anticommunist revolution. Near–civil war between Armenians and Azerbaijanis in the Caucasus and growing dissatisfaction among the Soviet peoples were part of a fluid, unstable political situation. Increasingly, the reform-minded Gorbachev stood as a moderate, besieged by those who wanted revolutionary changes and by hard-line Communist party members who longed to reverse course and clamp down.

In February 1990 the Communist party suffered a stunning defeat in local elections throughout the country. Democrats and anticommunists won clear majorities in the leading cities of the Russian Federation. When nationalists in Lithuania declared that republic's independence, Gorbachev responded by placing an economic embargo on Lithuania, but he refused to use the army to crush the separatist government. The result was a tense political stalemate, which further undermined Russian support for Gorbachev. Separating himself further from Communist party hard-liners, a hard-pressed Gorbachev asked Soviet citizens to ratify a new constitution, which formally abolished the Communist party's monopoly of political power and expanded the power of the Congress of People's Deputies. Gorbachev then convinced a majority of deputies to elect him president of the Soviet Union.

Gorbachev's eroding power and unwillingness to risk a popular election for the presidency strengthened his rival, Boris Yeltsin (b. 1931). A radical reform communist, Yeltsin was a tough and crafty Siberian who became the most prominent figure in the democratic movement in the Russian Federation. In May 1990, as leader of the Russian parliament, Yeltsin boldly announced that Russia would declare its independence from the multiethnic Soviet Union, a move that broadened the base of the anticommunist movement by skillfully joining the patriotism of ordinary Russians with the democratic aspirations of big-city intellectuals. While nationalists in the Soviet republics continued to agitate for separatism, the country's economic decline accelerated.

Gorbachev was next challenged by the old guard of the Communist party. In August 1991 a gang of hard-

**Celebrating Victory, August 1991** A Russian soldier flashes the victory sign in front of the Russian parliament, as the last-gasp coup attempt of Communist hard-liners is defeated by Boris Yeltsin and an enthusiastic public. The soldier has cut the hammer and sickle out of the Soviet flag, consigning those famous symbols of proletarian revolution to what Trotsky once called the "garbage can of history." *(Filip Horvat/Corbis Saba)*

liners kidnapped him and his family and tried to seize the Soviet government. The attempted coup collapsed in the face of massive popular resistance, which rallied in Moscow around Yeltsin. Gorbachev was rescued and returned to power as head of the Soviet Union.

The leaders of the coup had wanted to preserve Communist party power and the multinational Soviet Union; they succeeded only in destroying both. An anticommunist revolution swept the Russian Federation as the Communist party was outlawed and its property confiscated. Locked in a personal and political duel with Gorbachev, Yeltsin and his liberal allies declared Russia independent and withdrew from the Soviet Union. All the other Soviet republics followed suit; the Soviet Union—and Gorbachev's job as its president—ceased to exist on December 25, 1991 (see Map 33.2).

## THE WESTERN HEMISPHERE

One way to think of what historians used to call the "New World" is as a vigorous offshoot of Western civilization—an offshoot that has gradually developed its own characteristics while retaining European roots. From this perspective can be seen many illuminating parallels and divergences in the histories of Europe and the Americas. After the Second World War the Western Hemisphere experienced a many-faceted recovery, somewhat similar to that of Europe, although it began earlier, especially in Latin America. And after a generation the countries of the New World experienced their own period of turbulence and crisis. The response of many Latin American countries was to establish authoritarian military regimes until, in the late 1980s, Latin America joined with eastern Europe in turning

**MAP 33.2 Russia and the Successor States** After the attempt in August 1991 to depose Gorbachev failed, an anticommunist revolution swept the Soviet Union. Led by Russia and Boris Yeltsin, the republics that formed the Soviet Union declared their sovereignty and independence. Eleven of the fifteen republics then formed a loose confederation called the Commonwealth of Independent States, but the integrated economy of the Soviet Union dissolved into separate national economies, each with its own goals and policies.

toward elected civilian governments and in embracing economic liberalism for the first time since the 1920s.

## America's Civil Rights Revolution

The Second World War ended the Great Depression in the United States and brought about a great economic boom. Unemployment practically vanished, and the well-being of Americans increased dramatically. Despite fears that peace would bring renewed depression, conversion to a peacetime economy went smoothly. As in western Europe, the U.S. economy advanced fairly steadily for a generation.

Prosperity helps explain why postwar domestic politics consisted largely of modest adjustments to the status quo until the 1960s. Truman's upset victory in 1948 demonstrated that Americans had no interest in undoing Roosevelt's social and economic reforms. Congress proceeded to increase Social Security benefits, subsidize middle- and lower-class housing, and raise the minimum wage. These and other liberal measures consolidated the New Deal. In 1952 the Republican party and the voters turned to General Dwight D. Eisenhower (1890–1969), a national hero and self-described moderate. Some Americans came to fear that the United States was becoming a "blocked society," incapable of wholesome change. This feeling contributed in 1960 to the election of the young John F. Kennedy (1917–1963), who captured the popular imagination, revitalized the old Roosevelt coalition, and modestly expanded existing liberal legislation before he was struck down by an assassin's bullet in 1963.

Belatedly and reluctantly, complacent postwar America did experience a genuine social revolution: after a long struggle African Americans (and their white supporters) threw off a deeply entrenched system of segregation and discrimination in the Southern United States. This civil rights movement advanced on several fronts. Eloquent lawyers from the National Association for the Advancement of Colored People (NAACP) challenged school segregation in the courts. In 1954 they won a landmark decision in the Supreme Court, which ruled in *Brown v. Board of Education* that "separate educational facilities are inherently unequal." Blacks effectively challenged institutionalized inequality with bus boycotts, sit-ins, and demonstrations. As civil rights leader Martin Luther King, Jr. (1929–1968), told the white power structure, "We will not hate you, but we will not obey your evil laws."[4]

**The March on Washington, August 1963** The march marked a dramatic climax in the civil rights struggle. More than 200,000 people gathered at the Lincoln Memorial to hear the young Martin Luther King, Jr., deliver his greatest address, the "I have a dream" speech. *(Francis Miller/TimePix)*

In key Northern states African Americans used their growing political power to gain the support of the liberal wing of the Democratic party. In a liberal landslide Lyndon Johnson (1908–1973) won the presidential election in 1964. The **Civil Rights Act** of 1964 prohibited discrimination in public services and on the job. The Voting Rights Act of 1965 firmly guaranteed all blacks the right to vote. By the 1970s substantial numbers of blacks had been elected to public office throughout the Southern states, proof of major changes in American race relations.

African Americans enthusiastically supported new social legislation in the mid-1960s. President Johnson solemnly declared "unconditional war on poverty." Congress and the administration created a host of antipoverty projects, such as medical care for the poor and aged, free preschools for poor children, and community-action programs. Thus the United States promoted in the mid-1960s the kind of fundamental social reform that western Europe had embraced immediately after the Second World War. It became more of a welfare state, as government spending for social benefits rose dramatically and approached European levels.

## Youth and the Counterculture

Economic prosperity and a more democratic class structure had a powerful impact on youth throughout the Western world. The bulging cohort of youth born after World War II developed a distinctive and very international youth culture. Self-consciously different in the late 1950s, this youth culture became increasingly oppositional in the 1960s, interacting with a revival of leftist thought to create a counterculture that rebelled against parents, authority figures, and the status quo.

Young people in the United States took the lead. American college students in the 1950s were docile and often dismissed as the "Silent Generation," but some young people did revolt against the conformity of middle-class suburbs. The "beat" movement of the late 1950s expanded on the theme of revolt, and this subculture quickly spread to major American and western European cities.

Rock music helped tie this international subculture together. Rock grew out of the black music culture of rhythm and blues, which was flavored with country and western to make it more accessible to white teenagers. Artists Elvis Presley and the Beatles became enormously popular, while suggesting a personal and sexual freedom that many older people found disturbing. Then Bob Dylan, a young folksinger turned rock poet, captured the radical aspirations of some youth when he sang that "the times they are a'changing."

Several factors contributed to the emergence of the international youth culture in the 1960s. First, mass communications and youth travel linked countries and continents together. Second, the postwar baby boom meant that young people became an unusually large part of the population and could therefore exercise exceptional influence on society as a whole. Third, postwar prosperity and greater equality gave young people more purchasing power than ever before. This enabled them to set their own trends and fads in everything from music to chemical stimulants to sexual behavior. Common patterns of consumption and behavior fostered generational loyalty. Finally, prosperity meant that good jobs were readily available. Students and young job seekers had little need to fear punishment from strait-laced employers for unconventional behavior.

The youth culture practically fused with the counterculture in opposition to the established order in the late 1960s. Student protesters embraced romanticism and revolutionary idealism, dreaming of complete freedom and simpler, purer societies. The materialistic West was hopelessly rotten, but better societies were being built in the newly independent countries of Asia and Africa, or so many young radicals believed. Thus the Vietnam War took on special significance. Many politically active students in the United States and Europe believed that the older generation in general and American leaders in particular were fighting an immoral and imperialistic war against a small and heroic people that wanted only national unity and human dignity. As the war in Vietnam intensified, so did worldwide student opposition to it.

## The United States in World Affairs, 1964–1991

President Johnson wanted to go down in history as a master reformer and a healer of old wounds. Instead, he opened new ones with the Vietnam War.

American involvement in Vietnam was a product of the cold war and the ideology of containment (see page 1062). After the defeat of the French in Indochina in 1954 (see page 1115), the Eisenhower administration refused to sign the Geneva Accords, which temporarily divided the country into two zones pending national unification by means of free elections. President Eisenhower then acquiesced in the refusal of the anticommunist South Vietnamese government to accept the verdict of elections and provided military aid to help that government resist communist North Vietnam. President Kennedy increased the number of American "military advisers" to sixteen thousand.

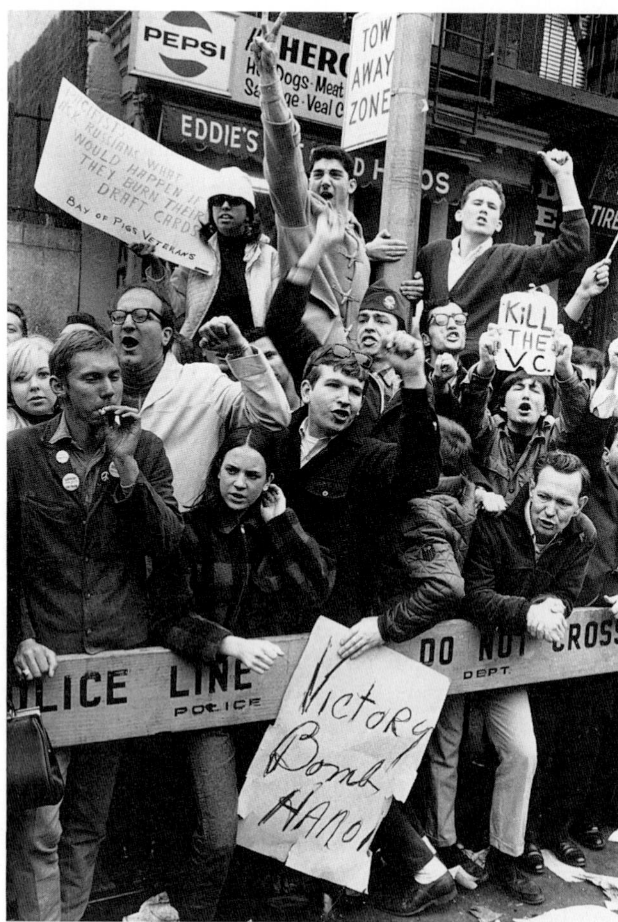


**Anti-Vietcong Protesters** Divisions over the Vietnam War ran deep in the United States. Antiwar protesters captured the public's attention, but anti-Vietcong demonstrations like this one spoke for many Americans. Opinion polls showed that fewer than 20 percent of Americans supported withdrawal from Vietnam until after the November 1968 elections, by which time the decision to get out had been made. *(Burt Glinn/Magnum Photos)*

President Johnson greatly expanded the American role in the Vietnam conflict. As Johnson explained to his ambassador in Saigon, "I am not going to lose Vietnam. I am not going to be the President who saw Southeast Asia go the way China went."[5] American strategy was to "escalate" the war sufficiently to break the will of the North Vietnamese and their southern allies without resorting to "overkill," which might risk war with the entire Communist bloc. Thus South Vietnam received massive military aid, American forces in the South gradually grew to a half million men, and the United States bombed North Vietnam with ever-greater intensity. But there was no invasion of the North or naval blockade. In the end the American strategy of gradual escalation backfired. It was the Americans who grew weary and the American leadership that cracked.

The undeclared war in Vietnam, fought nightly on American television, eventually divided the nation. Initial support was strong. The politicians, the media, and the population as a whole saw the war as part of a legitimate defense against communist totalitarianism in all poor countries. But an antiwar movement quickly emerged on college campuses, where the prospect of being drafted to fight savage battles in Asian jungles made male stomachs churn. In October 1965 student protesters joined forces with old-line socialists, New Left intellectuals, and pacifists in antiwar demonstrations in fifty American cities. By 1967 a growing number of critics denounced the war as a criminal intrusion into a complex and distant civil war.

Criticism reached a crescendo after the Vietcong Tet Offensive against major South Vietnamese cities in January 1968. The attack was a military failure, but it resulted in heavy losses on both sides, and it belied Washington's claims that victory in South Vietnam was in sight. American critics of the Vietnam War quickly interpreted the bloody combat as a decisive defeat. America's leaders lost heart, and in 1968 President Johnson called for negotiations with North Vietnam and announced that he would not stand for re-election.

Elected by a razor-slim margin in 1968, Richard Nixon (1913–1994) sought to disengage America gradually from Vietnam and the accompanying national crisis. Intensifying the continuous bombardment of the enemy while simultaneously pursuing peace talks with the North Vietnamese, President Nixon suspended the draft, so hated on college campuses, and cut American forces in Vietnam from 550,000 to 24,000 in four years. Moreover, he launched a flank attack in diplomacy. He journeyed to China in 1972 and reached a spectacular if limited reconciliation with the People's Republic of China.

Fortified by the overwhelming endorsement of the voters in the 1972 election, Nixon and Secretary of State Henry Kissinger finally reached a peace agreement with North Vietnam in 1973. The agreement allowed remaining American forces to complete their withdrawal, and the United States reserved the right to resume bombing if the accords were broken. Fighting declined markedly in South Vietnam. The storm of crisis in the United States seemed to have passed.

On the contrary, the country reaped the **Watergate** whirlwind. Like some other recent American presidents, Nixon authorized domestic spying activities that went beyond the law. Going further than his predecessors,

Nixon authorized special units to use various illegal means to stop the leaking of government documents to the press. One such group broke into Democratic party headquarters in Washington's Watergate building complex in June 1972 and was promptly arrested. Nixon and many of his assistants tried to hush up the bungled job, but in 1974 a beleaguered Nixon was forced to resign in disgrace.

The renewed political crisis flowing from the Watergate affair had profound consequences. First, Watergate resulted in a major shift of power away from the presidency and toward Congress, especially in foreign affairs. Therefore, as an emboldened North Vietnam launched a general invasion against South Vietnamese armies in early 1974, Congress refused to permit any American military response. After more than thirty-five years of battle, the Vietnamese communists unified their country in 1975 as a harsh dictatorial state—a second consequence of the U.S. crisis. Third, the fall of South Vietnam shook America's postwar confidence and left the country divided and uncertain about its proper role in world affairs.

One alternative to the policy of containing communism was the policy of **détente,** or progressive relaxation of cold war tensions. Détente reached its high point when all European nations (except isolationist Albania), the United States, and Canada signed the Final Act of the Helsinki Conference in 1975. These nations agreed that Europe's existing political frontiers could not be changed by force, and they solemnly accepted numerous provisions guaranteeing the human rights and political freedoms of their citizens.

Optimistic hopes for détente gradually faded in the later 1970s. Brezhnev's Soviet Union ignored the human rights provisions of the Helsinki agreement, and in December 1979 it invaded Afghanistan to save an unpopular Marxist regime. Thus, once again, many alarmed Americans looked to the Western alliance of NATO members to thwart communist expansion.

Jimmy Carter (b. 1924), elected president in 1976, tried to lead the Western alliance beyond verbal condemnation of the Soviet Union, but among the European allies only Great Britain supported the American policy of economic sanctions. Some observers concluded that the alliance had lost its cohesiveness.

Yet the Western alliance endured. The U.S. military buildup launched by Jimmy Carter was greatly accelerated by Ronald Reagan (b. 1911), who was swept into office in 1980 by a wave of patriotism and economic discontent. The Reagan administration concentrated especially on nuclear arms and an expanded navy as keys to American power in the renewed crusade against the Soviet Union—which the president anathematized as the "evil empire"—and its allies.

The broad swing of the historical pendulum toward greater conservatism in the 1980s gave Reagan invaluable allies in Britain's strong-willed Margaret Thatcher (see page 1070) and in West Germany's distinctly pro-American Helmut Kohl (see page 1075). The Western nations also gave indirect support to ongoing efforts to liberalize authoritarian communist eastern Europe and probably helped convince Mikhail Gorbachev that endless cold war conflict was foolish and dangerous. With the collapse of the Soviet Union, the United States emerged as the world's lone superpower.

In 1991 the United States used its military superiority on a grand scale in a quick war in western Asia after Iraq's strongman, Saddam Hussein (b. 1937), invaded Kuwait in August 1990 (see page 1120). Reacting vigorously, the United States called on the United Nations to turn back Iraqi aggression. The five permanent members of the U.N. Security Council—the United States, the Soviet Union, China, the United Kingdom, and France—agreed to impose a strict naval blockade on Iraq, and allied naval forces halted all trade between Iraq and the rest of the world. Receiving the support of ground units from some Arab states as well as from Great Britain and France, the United States eventually put 500,000 American soldiers in Saudi Arabia near the border of Kuwait. When a defiant Saddam Hussein refused to withdraw from Kuwait, the Security Council authorized the U.S.-led military coalition to attack Iraq. The American army and air force then smashed Iraqi forces in a lightning-quick desert campaign.

The Gulf War demonstrated the awesome power of the rebuilt and revitalized U.S. military. In the flush of victory President George H. W. Bush spoke of a "new world order." That order would apparently feature the United States and a cooperative United Nations working together to impose peace and security throughout the world.

## Economic Nationalism in Latin America

Although the countries of Latin America exhibit striking differences, the growth of economic nationalism was a major development throughout the region in much of the twentieth century. As the early nineteenth century saw Spanish and Portuguese colonies win wars of political independence, so was much of recent history a quest for genuine economic independence.

To understand the rise of economic nationalism, one must remember that Latin American countries developed as producers of foodstuffs and raw materials that were exported to Europe and the United States in return for manufactured goods and capital investment. This exchange brought considerable economic development but exacted a heavy price: neocolonialism (see pages 900–902). Latin America became dependent on foreign markets, products, and investments. Industry did not develop, and those who profited most from economic development were large landowners, who used their advantage to enhance their social and political power.

The old international division of labor, badly shaken by World War I, was destroyed by the Great Depression. Prices and exports of Latin American commodities collapsed as Europe and the United States drastically reduced their purchases and raised tariffs to protect domestic products. With their foreign sales plummeting, Latin American countries could not buy the industrial goods they needed from abroad.

Latin America suffered the full force of the global depression. Especially in the largest Latin American countries—Argentina, Brazil, Chile, and Mexico—the result was a profound shift toward economic nationalism after 1930. The most popularly based governments worked to reduce foreign influence and gain control of their own economies and natural resources. They energetically promoted national industry by means of high tariffs, government grants, and even state enterprise. They favored the lower middle and urban working classes with social benefits and higher wages in order to increase their purchasing power and gain their support. These efforts at recovery gathered speed during World War II and were fairly successful. By the late 1940s the factories of Argentina, Brazil, and Chile could generally satisfy domestic consumer demand for the products of light industry. In the 1950s some countries began moving into heavy industry.

Economic nationalism and the rise of industry are particularly striking in the two largest and most influential countries, Mexico and Brazil. These countries account for half of the population of Latin America.

The spasmodic, often-chaotic Mexican Revolution of 1910 overthrew the elitist, upper-class rule of the tyrant Porfirio Díaz and culminated in 1917 in a new constitution. This radical nationalistic document called for universal suffrage, massive land reform, benefits for labor, and strict control of foreign capital. Actual progress was quite modest until 1934, when a charismatic young Indian from a poor family, Lázaro Cárdenas, became president and dramatically revived the languishing revolution. Under Cárdenas many large estates were divided up among small farmers or returned undivided to Indian communities.

Meanwhile, state-supported Mexican businessmen built many small factories to meet domestic needs. In 1938, when Mexican workers became locked in a bitter dispute with British and American oil companies, Cárdenas nationalized the petroleum industry—to the amazement of a world unaccustomed to such bold action. Finally, the 1930s saw the flowering of a distinctive Mexican culture, which proudly embraced its long-despised Indian past and gloried in the modern national revolution.

In 1940 the official, semi-authoritarian party that had governed Mexico continuously after the revolution selected the first of a series of more moderate presidents. These presidents used the power of the state to promote industrialization through a judicious mixture of public, private, and even foreign enterprise. Following the postwar trend in Europe and the United States, the Mexican economy grew rapidly to the late 1960s, although the upper and middle classes reaped the lion's share of the benefits.

In Brazil politics was dominated by the coffee barons and by regional rivalries after the fall of Brazil's monarchy in 1889 (see page 898). Regional rivalries and deteriorating economic conditions allowed a military revolt led by Getúlio Vargas to seize control of the federal government in 1930. Vargas, a consummate politician, established a mild dictatorship that lasted until 1945. His rule was generally popular, combining effective economic nationalism and moderate social reform.

Vargas and his allies set out to industrialize. The government supported Brazilian manufacturers with high tariffs, generous loans, and labor peace encouraged by new social legislation: workers received shorter hours, pensions, health and accident insurance, paid vacations, and other benefits. Finally, Vargas shrewdly upheld the nationalist cause in his relations with the United States.

Modernization continued for the next fifteen years. The economy boomed. Presidential politics was later reestablished, though the military kept a watchful eye for extremism among the civilian politicians. Economic nationalism was especially vigorous under the flamboyant President Juscelino Kubitschek. Between 1956 and 1960 the government borrowed heavily from international bankers to promote industry and build the new capital of Brasília in the midst of a wilderness. Kubitschek's slogan was "Fifty Years' Progress in Five," and he meant it.

The Brazilian and Mexican formula of national economic development, varying degrees of electoral competition, and social reform was shared by some other Latin American countries, notably Argentina and Chile. By the late 1950s optimism was widespread though cautious. Economic and social progress seemed to be bringing less violent, more democratic politics to the region. These expectations were shaken by the Cuban Revolution.

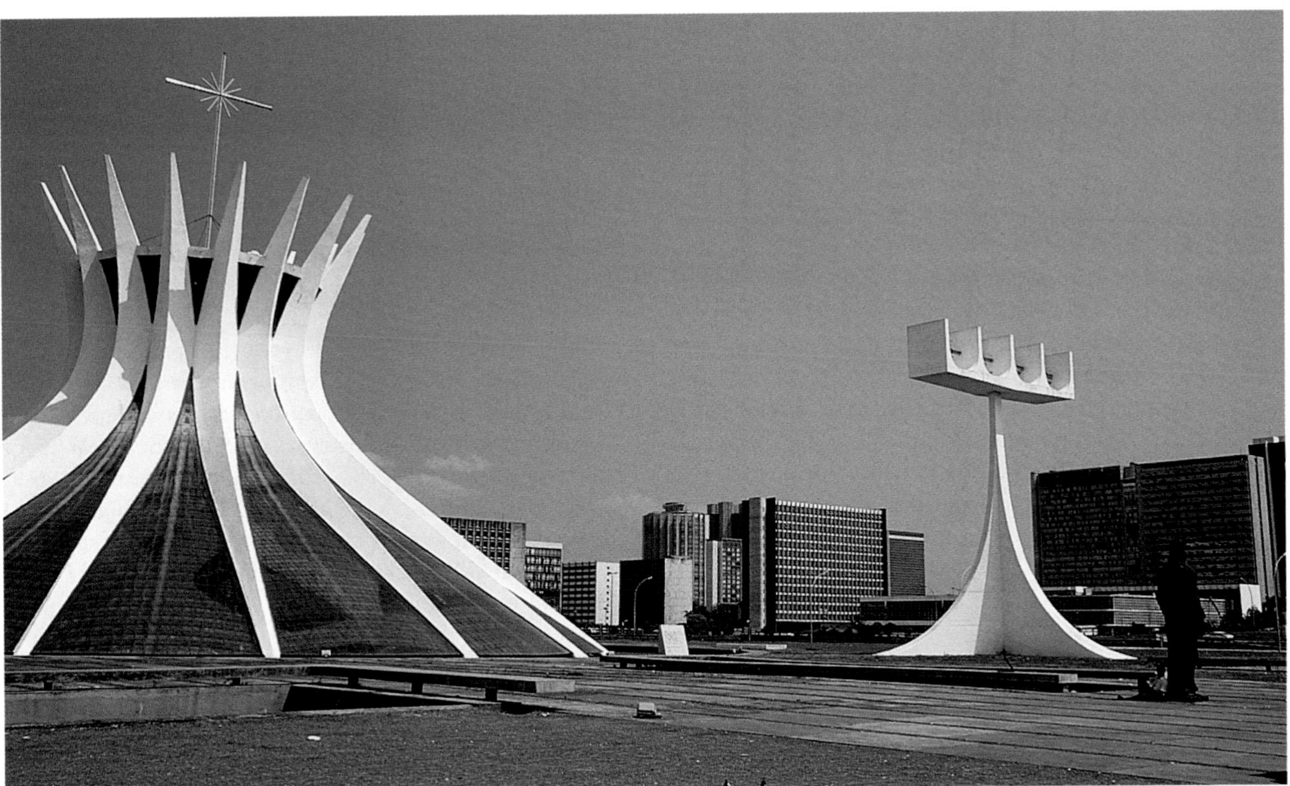

**Brasília, Capital of the Future** Construction of Brazil's ambitious—and controversial—new capital began in 1957 with the airport, for all building materials had to be flown in until roads could be hacked through the wilderness. Laid out like a jet airliner, with the wings for apartments and stores and the fuselage for government buildings, Brasília emerged as a gigantic monument to postwar optimism and extravagance. *(Bernard Boutrit/Woodfin Camp & Associates)*

## Authoritarianism and Democracy in Latin America

Achieving nominal independence in 1898 as a result of the Spanish-American War, Cuba was virtually an American protectorate until the 1930s. Partly because the American army was often the real power on the island, Cuba's political institutions were weak and its politicians corrupt. Yet Cuba was one of Latin America's most prosperous countries by the 1950s, although it displayed the enormous differences between rich and poor that were typical of Latin America.

Fidel Castro (b. 1927), a magnetic leader with the gift of oratory, led his guerrilla forces to triumph in late 1958. Castro had promised a "real" revolution, and it soon became clear that "real" meant "communist." Middle-class Cubans began fleeing to Miami. Cuban relations with the Eisenhower administration deteriorated rapidly. In April 1961 the newly elected U.S. president, John Kennedy, tried to use Cuban exiles to topple Castro, but he abandoned the exiles as soon as they were put ashore at the Bay of Pigs.

After routing the Bay of Pigs forces, Castro proceeded to build his version of an authoritarian communist society. Political life in Cuba featured anti-imperialism, an alliance with the Soviet bloc, a dictatorship of the party, state ownership, and a Castro cult. Revolutionary enthusiasm was genuine among party activists, while prisons and emigration silenced opposition. The Castro regime also pursued social equality and tried to export communist revolutions throughout Latin America. The fear that Castro would succeed led the United States in 1961 to fund the new hemispheric **Alliance for Progress,** intended to promote long-term economic development and social reform.

U.S. aid contributed modestly to continued Latin American economic development in the 1960s, but democratic social reforms—the other half of the Alliance for Progress formula—stalled. A growing conflict between leftist movements and ruling elites developed. In most countries the elites and their military allies won the struggle, but at the cost of imposing a new kind of conservative authoritarianism. By the late 1970s only Costa Rica, Venezuela, Colombia, and Mexico retained some measure of democratic government. Brazil, Argentina, and Chile represented the general trend.

Influential Brazil led the way. Intense political competition in the early 1960s prompted President João Goulart to swing to the left to gain fresh support. Castroism appeared to spread in the impoverished northeast, and mass meetings of leftists were answered by huge demonstrations of conservatives. When Goulart and his followers appeared ready to use force to implement their program of breaking up landed estates and extending the vote to Brazil's many illiterates, army leaders took over in 1964 and ruled by decree. Industrialization and urbanization went forward under right-wing military rule, but social inequalities increased.

In Argentina the military had intervened in 1955 to oust the dictatorial populist and economic nationalist Juan Perón, and it had restored elected democratic government. Then, worried by a Peronist revival and heartened by the Brazilian example, the army took control in 1966 and again in 1976 after a brief civilian interlude. Each military takeover was followed by an escalation of repression. Though culturally and economically advanced, Argentina became a brutal military dictatorship.

Events in Chile were truly tragic. Chile has a long tradition of democracy and moderate reform. Thus when Salvador Allende, a doctor and the Marxist head of a coalition of communists, socialists, and radicals, won a plurality in 1970, he was duly elected president by the Chilean Congress. Allende completed the nationalization of the American-owned copper companies and proceeded to socialize private industry, accelerate the breakup of landed estates, and radicalize the poor. Marxism in action evoked a powerful backlash, and by 1973 Chile seemed headed for civil war. Then, with widespread conservative support and U.S. backing, the traditionally impartial army struck in a well-organized coup. Allende died, probably murdered, and thousands of his supporters were arrested, or worse. As in Argentina, the military imposed a harsh despotism.

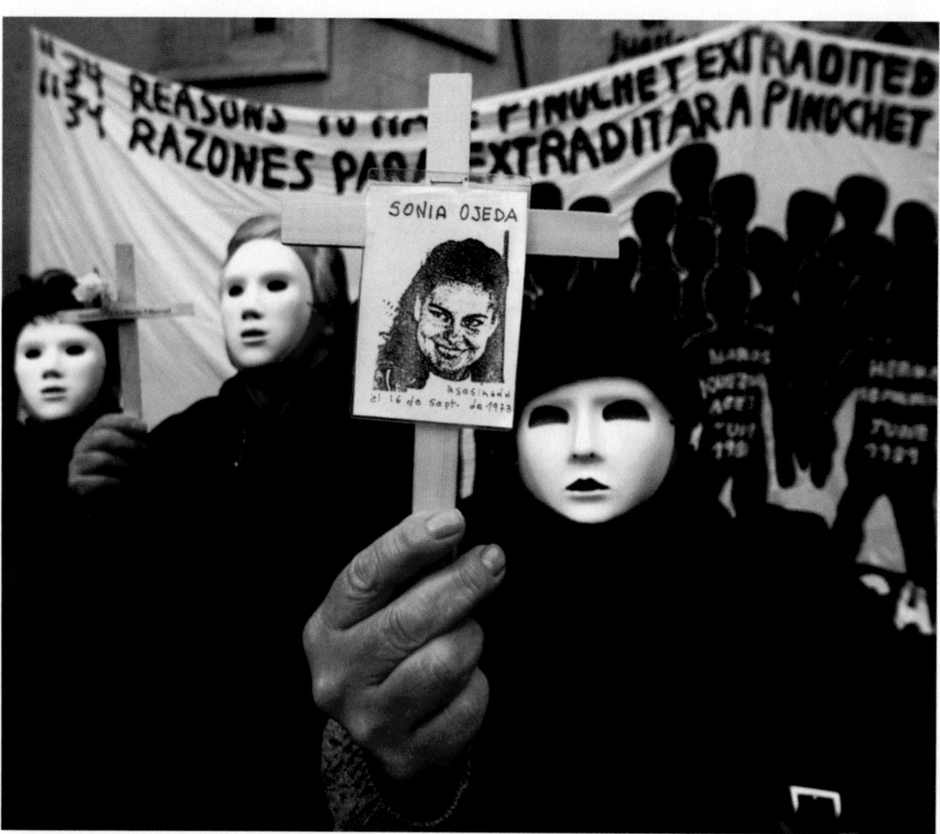


**Justice for the Victims of Chile's General Pinochet** With their faces covered with death masks, demonstrators outside Britain's High Court in 2000 hold up crosses carrying pictures of the "Disappeared"—the thousands kidnapped and allegedly murdered between 1973 and 1988 under the military dictatorship of General Pinochet. The High Court ruled against extraditing Pinochet to Spain to stand trial, but he was finally charged with torture and murder when he returned to Chile. *(Dan Chung/Reuters NewMedia Inc./ Corbis)*

The military governments that revived antidemocratic authoritarianism in Latin America blocked not only the Marxist and socialist program but most liberal and moderate reform as well. Yet the new military governments grew out of political crises that threatened national unity as well as the upper classes and big business. In such circumstances the politically conscious officer corps saw the military as the only institution capable of preventing chaos. Moreover, the new authoritarians were determined modernizers. They were often deeply committed to nationalism, industrialization, technology, and some modest social progress. They even promised free elections in the future.

That time came in the 1980s, when another democratic wave gained momentum throughout Latin America. The three Andean nations—Peru, Bolivia, and Ecuador—led the way with the re-establishment of presidential parties and popularly elected governments committed to some social reform. In Argentina the military government gradually lost almost all popular support because of its "dirty war" against its own citizens, in which it imprisoned, tortured, and murdered thousands whom it arbitrarily accused of opposing the regime. In 1982, in a desperate gamble to rally the people, Argentina's military rulers seized the Falkland (or Malvinas) Islands (see Map 28.2 on page 896) from Great Britain. The British rout of Argentina's poorly led troops forced the humiliated generals to schedule national elections. The democratically elected government prosecuted the former military rulers for their crimes and laid solid foundations for liberty and political democracy.

The Brazilian military was relatively successful in its industrialization effort, but it had proved unable (or unwilling) to improve the social and economic position of the masses. In 1985, after twenty-one years of rule, the military leaders were ready to let civilian politicians have a try. Chile also turned from right-wing military dictatorship to elected government. Thus by the second half of the 1980s, 94 percent of Latin America's population lived under regimes that guaranteed elections and civil liberties.

The most dramatic developments in Central America occurred in Nicaragua. In 1979 a broad coalition of liberals, socialists, and Marxist revolutionaries drove long-time dictator Anastasio Somoza from power. The new leaders, known as the **Sandinistas,** wanted genuine political and economic independence from the United States, as well as thoroughgoing land reform, some state ownership of industry, and friendly ties with communist countries. These policies infuriated the Reagan administration, which tried to undermine the Sandinista government. The Nicaraguan economy collapsed, and the popularity of the Sandinista government eventually declined. Then, after a decade of rule, the Sandinistas accepted free elections and stepped down when they were defeated by a coalition of opposition parties. In 1994 Haiti, one of the last repressive dictatorships in the Americas, also established democratic rule, with the help of U.S. military intervention.

In the 1990s Latin America's popularly elected governments accepted greater freedom in their economic relations with other countries. They moved decisively from tariff protection and economic nationalism toward free markets and international trade, revitalizing their economies and registering solid gains. In 1994 Mexico joined with the United States and Canada in the North American Free Trade Agreement, commonly known as NAFTA. In December 1994, building on NAFTA and the Southern Common Market, which already linked Brazil, Argentina, Paraguay, and Uruguay, a summit meeting of thirty-four governments in Miami agreed to forge a vast free-trade area incorporating every country of the Americas by 2005. Latin American politicians and business leaders generally believed that their countries could compete effectively with their large northern neighbor, the United States.

## THE POST–COLD WAR ERA, 1991 TO THE PRESENT

The collapse of communism in Europe opened a new era in both Western and world history. Yet the dimension and significance of this new era are far from clear. A constant stream of information and events assails us, but what, we wonder, is truly significant? We are so close to what is going on that we lack vital perspective.

Still, the historian must take a stand and find patterns of development and explanation. Thus we will concentrate on two main themes of Western development since the end of the cold war. First, we will examine broad economic, social, and political trends that operated throughout Europe in these years. These trends, which also had a powerful influence on Asia and Africa in an increasingly interconnected age, included national economies caught up in global capitalism, the defense of social achievements under attack, and a powerful resurgence of nationalism, ethnic conflict, and terrorism. Second, we will focus on the massive transformations taking place in eastern and western Europe, as the former Soviet bloc works to rebuild and as western Europe forges an ever-closer economic union.

**MAP 33.3 Contemporary Europe** No longer divided by ideological competition and the cold war, today's Europe features a large number of independent states. Several of these states were previously part of the Soviet Union and Yugoslavia, both of which broke into many different countries. Czechoslovakia also divided on ethnic lines, while a reunited Germany emerged, once again, as the dominant nation in central Europe.

## Common Patterns and Problems

The end of the cold war and the disintegration of the Soviet Union ended the division of Europe into two opposing camps. Thus, although Europe in the 1990s was a collage of diverse peoples with their own politics, cultures, and histories, the entire continent shared an underlying network of beliefs and behaviors (see Map 33.3).

In economic affairs European leaders embraced, or at least accepted, a large part of the neoliberal, free-market vision of capitalist development. This was strikingly the case in eastern Europe, where states such as Poland and Hungary implemented market reforms and sought to create vibrant capitalist economies. Thus postcommunist governments in eastern Europe freed prices, turned state enterprises over to private owners, and sought to move toward strong currencies and balanced budgets. Milder doses of this same free-market medicine were administered by politicians and big business to the lackluster economies of western Europe. These moves marked a considerable modification of western Europe's still-dominant welfare capitalism.

Two factors were particularly important in explaining this shift to tough-minded capitalism. First, Europeans were following practices and ideologies revived and enshrined in the 1980s in the United States and Great Britain (see page 1070). Western Europeans especially took American prescriptions more seriously in the Clinton years because U.S. prestige and power were so high after the cold war ended and because the U.S. economy outperformed its western European counterparts. Second, the deregulation of markets and the privatization of state-controlled enterprises in different European countries were integral parts of the momentous trend toward a wide-open, wheeler-dealer global economy. The rules of this global economy, laid down by powerful Western governments, multinational corporations, and big banks and international financial organizations such as the International Monetary Fund (IMF), called for the free movement of capital and goods and services, low inflation, and limited government deficits. Accepting these rules and attempting to follow them was the price of participating in the global economy.

The freer global economy, which probably speeded up world economic growth, had powerful social consequences. Millions of ordinary citizens in western Europe saw global capitalism and freer markets as challenging hard-won social achievements. As in the United States and Great Britain in the 1980s, the public in other countries generally opposed the unemployment that accompanied corporate downsizing, the efforts to reduce the power of labor unions, and, above all, government plans to reduce social benefits. The reaction was particularly intense in France and Germany, where unions remained strong and socialists championed a minimum of change in social policies.

In the 1990s political developments across the European continent were also loosely unified by common patterns and problems. Most obviously, the demise of European communism brought the apparent triumph of liberal democracy everywhere. All countries embraced genuine electoral competition, with elected presidents and legislatures, and they guaranteed basic civil liberties. For the first time since before the French Revolution almost all of Europe followed the same general political model, although the variations were endless.

The triumph of the liberal-democratic program in Europe (and large parts of Latin America and Asia) led the American scholar Francis Fukuyama to discern the "end of history" in an influential book by that title. According to Fukuyama, first fascism and Nazism and then communism had been bested by liberal-democratic politics and market economics. In fact, as James Cronin perceptively noted, the fall of communism and the end of ideological competition actually marked the return of nationalism and national history.[6] During the cold war the superpowers had generally kept their allies and clients in line throughout the world, either by force or by granting them conditional aid. As soon as the cold war was over, nationalism and ethnic conflict re-emerged, and history, as the story of different peoples, began again.

The resurgence of nationalism after the cold war led to terrible tragedy and bloodshed in parts of eastern Europe, Africa, and Asia. During the civil wars in Yugoslavia, many observers feared that national and ethnic hatreds would spread throughout eastern Europe and infect western Europe in the form of racial hostility toward minorities and immigrants. Although nationalist and racist incidents were a recurring theme after 1991, in Europe they remained limited in the extent of their damage. An important reason was that almost all states wished to become or remain full-fledged members of the European society of nations and to join an ever-expanding economic partnership, whereas Yugoslavia—the state that embraced ethnic warfare—was branded an outlaw and isolated by the international community, as we shall see. The process of checking resurgent nationalism in Europe and generally keeping it from getting out of hand was almost as significant as the resurgence itself.

Generally succeeding in keeping ethnic nationalism under control in the West in the 1990s, many Europeans and most Americans believed that terrorism was primarily a problem for the developing countries of Asia, Africa,

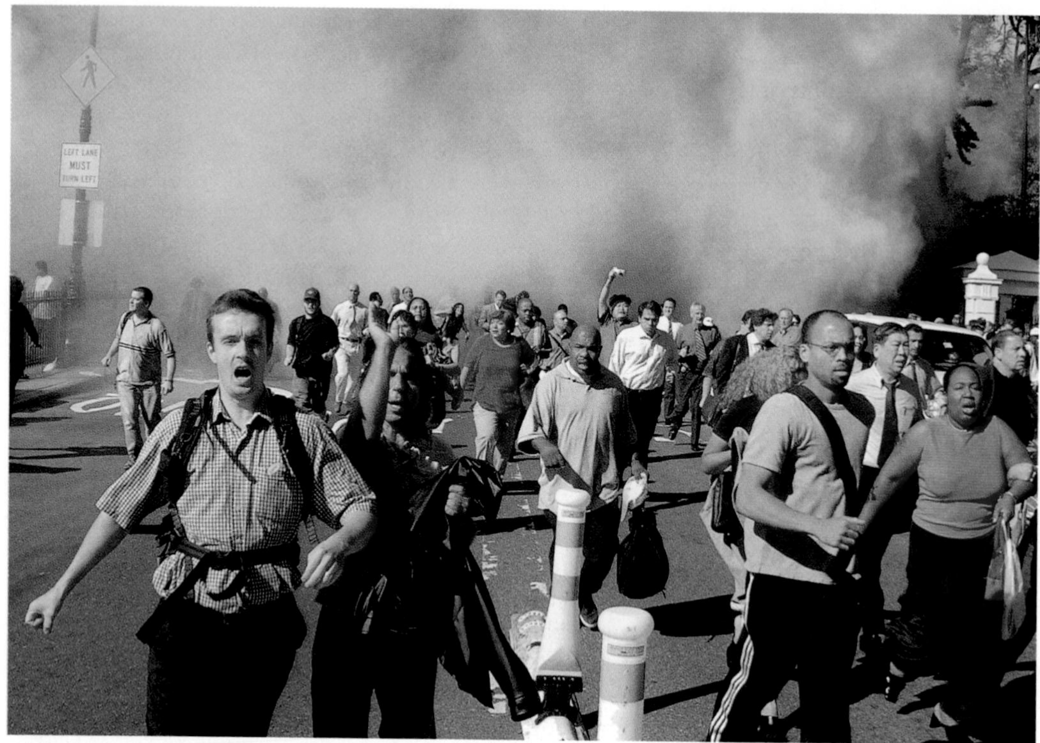


**New York, September 11, 2001** Pedestrians race for safety as the first World Trade Center tower collapses after being hit by a jet airliner. Al-Qaeda terrorists with box cutters hijacked four aircraft and used three of them as suicide missiles to perpetrate their unthinkable crime. Heroic passengers on the fourth plane realized what was happening and forced their hijackers to crash in a field. *(Paul Hawthorne/AP/Wide World Photos)*

and Latin America. In fact, terrorism was part of a complex global pattern of violence and political conflict (see Chapter 36). In northwestern Spain the Basque separatist organization used assassinations and car bombings in its bloody campaign to obtain a breakaway state from the Spanish government. In Northern Ireland Protestant and Catholic extremists turned to bombs and killings in their bitter conflict. As the new century opened, the global dimension of terrorism was revealed most dramatically in the United States.

On the morning of September 11, 2001, two hijacked passenger planes from Boston crashed into and destroyed the World Trade Center in New York City. Shortly thereafter a third plane crashed into the Pentagon, and a fourth, believed to be headed for the White House or the U.S. Capitol, crashed into a field in rural Pennsylvania. These terrorist attacks took the lives of almost three thousand people from many countries.

The United States, led by President George W. Bush, launched a military campaign to destroy the perpetrators of the crime, Saudi-born millionaire Osama bin Laden's al-Qaeda network of terrorists and Afghanistan's reactionary Muslim government, the Taliban. Building a broad international coalition that included western Europe, Russia, and Pakistan, the United States joined its tremendous airpower with the faltering Northern Alliance in Afghanistan, which had been fighting the Taliban for years. American forces devastated Taliban and al-Qaeda troops, and a rejuvenated Northern Alliance took the offensive. In mid-November 2001 the Taliban collapsed, and jubilant crowds in the capital of Kabul welcomed Northern Alliance soldiers as liberators. Afghan opposition leaders and United Nations mediators worked out plans for a new Afghan government, while American planes and tribal fighters searched for bin Laden and his die-hard supporters. In 2002 foreign governments, aid organizations, and the United Nations turned to the arduous task of helping the Afghans get themselves back on their feet. The swift punishment of al-Qaeda and its Afghan supporters reaffirmed the West's commitment to the most basic of all human rights—the right to life itself.

Unfortunately, Western unity in dealing with Afghanistan soon turned into bitter quarreling and international crisis over the prospect of war with Iraq. Building on American fears of renewed terrorism, the Bush administration charged in 2002 that Saddam Hussein was still developing weapons of mass destruction and might give them to anti-American terrorists, although no evidence linking the secular Iraqi dictator with bin Laden or other Islamic extremists was produced. Above all, President George W. Bush and his most influential advisers were determined to overthrow Saddam's government, which, they claimed, would lead to a democratic Iraq and a more peaceful Middle East. Unable to gain United Nations approval for any military action (see pages 1167–1168), the United States and Britain nevertheless attacked Iraq in March 2003 and quickly defeated Saddam's forces. After chaos spread and unchallenged looters stripped Baghdad's museums of their priceless ancient treasures, allied armies gradually established some order. An earthquake in world affairs, the war with Iraq split the West, and it promised to reorient relations between Western and Islamic peoples in new and unpredictable directions.

## Recasting Eastern Europe

With Soviet-style communism in ruins, the peoples of eastern Europe experienced continued rapid change. In Russia politics and economics were closely intertwined after the attempted Communist party coup in 1991 and the dissolution of the Soviet Union. President Boris Yeltsin, his democratic supporters, and his economic ministers wanted to create conditions that would prevent a return to communism and right the faltering economy. Following the example of some postcommunist governments in eastern Europe, the reformers opted in January 1992 for breakneck liberalization. Their shock therapy freed prices on 90 percent of all Russian goods, with the exception of bread, vodka, oil, and public transportation. The government also launched a rapid privatization of industry and turned thousands of factories and mines over to new private companies. However, control of the privatized companies usually remained in the hands of the old bosses.

Yeltsin and his advisers believed that shock therapy would revive production and bring prosperity after a brief period of hardship. The results were quite different. Prices soared and production fell sharply. The expected months of hardship stretched into years. By 1996 the Russian economy produced at least one-third and possibly one-half less than in 1991. In 1998, after stabilizing briefly, the Russian economy resumed its downward spiral.

Rapid economic liberalization worked poorly in Russia for several reasons. With privatization, the powerful state monopolies in industry simply became powerful private monopolies, which cut production and raised prices to limit losses and maximize profits. Powerful managers and bureaucrats forced Yeltsin's government to hand out enormous subsidies and credits to reinforce the positions of big firms or avoid bankruptcies. The managerial elite also combined with criminal elements, which had already been strong in the late Soviet period, to intimidate would-be rivals, preventing the formation of new firms. In addition, many Russians—told for decades that all capitalists were "speculators" and "exploiters"—were not interested in starting new businesses.

Runaway inflation and poorly executed privatization brought a profound social revolution to Russia. A new capitalist elite acquired great wealth and power, while large numbers of people fell into abject poverty, and the majority struggled to make ends meet.

Managers, former officials, and financiers who came out of the privatization process with large shares of the old state monopolies stood at the top of Russian society. This new elite was more highly concentrated in Moscow than ever before, and Westerners who visited only the capital had difficulty believing that there was a national economic decline.

At the other extreme the vast majority saw their savings become practically worthless. Pensions lost much of their value, and people sold personal goods to survive. In 1996, 35 percent of the population was living in poverty. The quality of public services and health care declined precipitously—so far that the life expectancy of the average Russian male dropped from sixty-nine years in 1991 to only fifty-eight years in 1996. In 1997 a respected expert concluded, "Russia has suffered a minimum of five years of travail. . . . It is necessary to acknowledge that the economic reforms in Russia have not been the success so many insisted they were for so long."[7]

Yeltsin and his supporters proved more successful in politics than in economics. In April 1993, 58 percent of the voters approved Yeltsin's new constitution, which gave him strong presidential powers. Although his allies lost ground to the communists and nationalists in two subsequent elections, the president himself won re-election in 1996 in an impressive come-from-behind victory.

Political problems remained. Russian political parties were weak, and Russia still lacked a rule of law and a court system that could deal with crime and corruption. Yet all politicians looked to the ballot box for legitimacy, as the election of President Vladimir Putin, Yeltsin's handpicked

**Russia's New Rich** Members of Moscow's exclusive Chimney Club dine in privacy and extravagance in 1994. Club members paid an annual membership fee of U.S.$1000—an astronomical sum for the vast majority of Russians, who had no opportunity to loot the economy. *(Anthony Suau/Getty Images)*

successor, clearly indicated in 2000. Putin's stress on public order and economic reform was popular.

Russia's moderation in relations with foreign countries also provided a reason for guarded optimism. Military spending continued to decline under Yeltsin, and Russia reluctantly accepted the enlargement of NATO in 1997 to include Poland, Hungary, and the Czech Republic. Moreover, Russia generally respected the independence of the Soviet successor states. The notable exception to this pattern was in Chechnya, a tiny republic of 1 million Muslims in southern Russia, where Yeltsin sent troops to crush a separatist movement. The war was highly unpopular in Russia, and Yeltsin was forced to accept a face-saving truce in 1996—a wily move that helped him win re-election. The brutal war was subsequently resumed, and it continued unabated under Putin.

Developments in the rest of eastern Europe shared important similarities with those in Russia, as many of the problems were the same. First, the postcommunist states worked to replace state planning and socialism with market mechanisms and private property. Second, Western-style electoral politics took hold, and as in Russia these politics were marked by intense battles between presidents and parliaments and by weak political parties. Third, ordinary citizens and the elderly were the big losers, while the young and the former Communist party members were the big winners. Regional inequalities persisted. Capital cities such as Warsaw, Prague, and Budapest concentrated wealth, power, and opportunity while provincial centers stagnated and industrial areas declined.

The postcommunist era saw more than a difficult transition to market economies and freely elected governments in eastern Europe, however. The peoples of eastern Europe had never fully accepted communism, which the rebels of 1989 linked to Russian imperialism and the loss of national independence. The joyous crowds that toppled communist regimes believed that they were liberating the nation as well as the individual. Thus as communism died, nationalism was reborn, as had occurred when authoritarian multinational empires had come crashing down in defeat in World War I.

The response to this opportunity was varied. Most observers agreed that Poland, the Czech Republic, and Hungary were the most successful in making the transition. Reasons for their success included considerable experience with limited market reforms before 1989, flexibility in government policy, and an enthusiastic embrace of capitalism by a rapidly rising entrepreneurial class. These three countries also fared better than Russia in creating new civic institutions, legal systems, and independent broadcasting networks that reinforced political freedom and national revival. They managed to control national and ethnic tensions that might have destroyed their postcommunist reconstruction. Thus, in 1993, when Slovakian nationalists grew dissatisfied with Czech majority rule after Czechoslovakia's 1989 Velvet Revolution and clam-

**MAP 33.4 The Ethnic Composition of Yugoslavia, 1991** Yugoslavia had the most ethnically diverse population in eastern Europe. The Republic of Croatia had substantial Serbian and Muslim minorities. Bosnia-Herzegovina had large Muslim, Serbian, and Croatian populations, none of which had a majority. In June 1991, Serbia's brutal effort to seize territory and unite all Serbs in a single state brought a tragic civil war.

ored for their own state, Václav Havel agreed. He led his country to accept a "velvet divorce" that peacefully split Czechoslovakia into the Czech Republic and Slovakia. The popular goal of "rejoining the West" also was a powerful force toward moderation in Poland, Hungary, and the Czech Republic. These countries hoped to find security in NATO membership, which came in 1997, and prosperity by joining western Europe's ever-tighter economic union (see the next section).

The great postcommunist tragedy was Yugoslavia, which under Josip Tito had been a federation of republics and regions. After Tito's death in 1980 power passed increasingly to the sister republics, which encouraged a revival of regional and ethnic conflicts that were exacerbated by charges of ethnically inspired massacres during World War II and by a dramatic economic decline in the mid-1980s.

The revolutions of 1989 accelerated the breakup of Yugoslavia. Serbian president Slobodan Milosevic intended to grab land from other republics and unite all Serbs in a "greater Serbia." In 1989 Milosevic arbitrarily abolished self-rule in the Serbian province of Kosovo, where Albanian-speaking people constituted the overwhelming majority and the Serbs were only a small minority. Milosevic's moves strengthened the cause of separatism, and in June 1991 Slovenia and Croatia declared their independence. Slovenia repulsed a Serbian attack, but Milosevic's forces were able to take about 30 percent of Croatia. In 1992 the civil war spread to Bosnia-Herzegovina, which had declared its independence. Serbs—about 30 percent of that region's population—refused to live under the more numerous Bosnian Muslims (see Map 33.4). The civil war unleashed ruthless brutality, with murder, rape, the

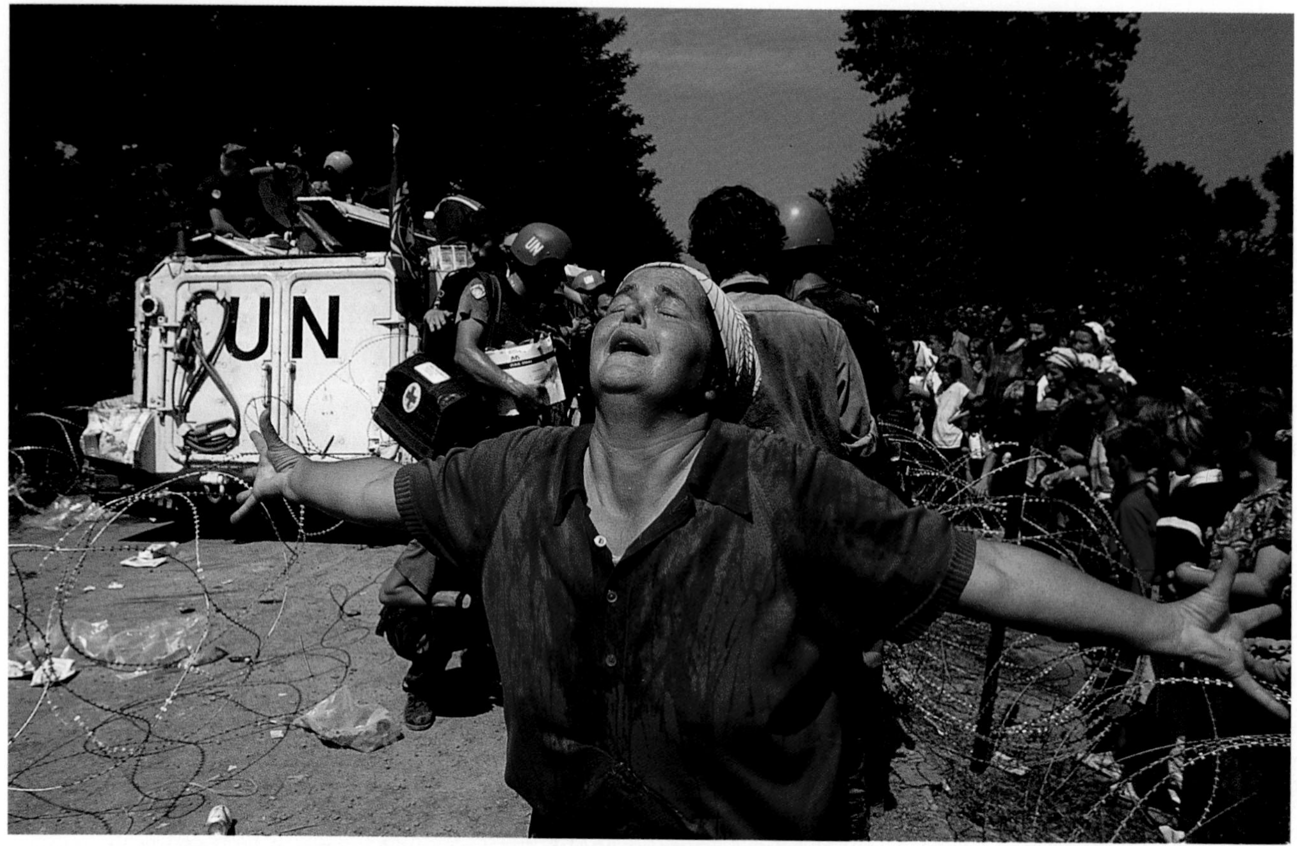


**Escape from Srebrenica** A Bosnian Muslim refugee arrives at the United Nations base in Tuzla and with her anguished screams tells the world of the Serbian atrocities. Several thousand civilians were murdered at Srebrenica, and Western public opinion finally demanded decisive action. Efforts continue to arrest those Serbs believed responsible and to try them for crimes against humanity. *(J. Jones/Corbis SYGMA)*

destruction of villages, and the herding of refugees into concentration camps.

While scenes of cruelty and horror shocked the world, the Western nations had difficulty formulating an effective response. Finally, in July 1995, Bosnian Serbs overran a Muslim city that the United Nations had declared a "safe area" and killed several thousand civilians. World outrage prompted NATO to bomb Bosnian Serb military targets, and the Croatian army drove all the Serbs from Croatia. In November 1995 President Bill Clinton brought the warring sides to Dayton, Ohio, where they hammered out a complicated accord that gave Bosnian Serbs about 49 percent of Bosnia and the Muslim-Croatian peoples the rest. Troops from many NATO countries patrolled Bosnia to try to keep the peace.

The Albanian Muslims of Kosovo—the Kosovars—gained nothing from the Dayton agreement. In early 1998 the militant Kosovars formed the Kosovo Liberation Army, or KLA, and began to fight for independence. Serbian repression increased greatly, displacing 250,000 people within Kosovo.

Serbian aggression appalled the Western nations. By January 1999 the Western powers, led by the United States, were threatening Milosevic with heavy air attacks if he did not withdraw Serbian armies from Kosovo, accept self-government (but not independence) for Kosovo, and permit NATO troops to enter the province to guarantee the agreement. Milosevic refused, and in March NATO began bombing Yugoslavia. Serbian paramilitary forces responded by driving about 780,000 Kosovars into exile. NATO redoubled its highly destructive bombing campaign, which eventually forced Milosevic to withdraw and allowed the joyous Kosovars to regain their homeland.

The impoverished Serbs eventually voted the still-defiant Milosevic out of office, and in July 2001 a new pro-Western Serbian government turned him over to the war crimes tribunal in the Netherlands, to stand trial for crimes against humanity. The civil wars in the former Yugoslavia were a monument to human cruelty. But ongoing efforts to preserve peace, repatriate refugees, and try war criminals also testified to the regenerative power of liberal values and human rights.

## Unity and Identity in Western Europe

The movement toward western European unity, which since the late 1940s had inspired practical politicians hoping to promote economic recovery and idealistic visionaries wanting to construct a genuine European identity, received a powerful second wind in the mid-1980s. The Single Europe Act of 1986 laid down a legal framework for establishing a single market that would add the free flow of labor, capital, and services to the free flow of goods. In 1993 the European Community proudly rechristened itself the **European Union (EU).** Meanwhile, French president François Mitterrand and German chancellor Helmut Kohl took the lead in pushing for monetary union of EU members. After long negotiations the members of the EU reached an agreement in December 1991 in the Dutch town of Maastricht. The Maastricht treaty set strict financial criteria for joining the proposed monetary union, with its single currency, and set January 1, 1999, as the target date for its establishment.

Western European elites and opinion makers generally supported this step toward economic union. They saw monetary union as a means of coping with Europe's ongoing economic problems, imposing financial discipline, cutting costs, and reducing high unemployment. These elites also saw monetary union as a historic, irreversible step toward basic political unity. The Maastricht plan encountered widespread skepticism and considerable opposition from ordinary people, leftist political parties, and nationalists. Ratification votes were close, especially when the public rather than the politicians could vote yes or no on the question.

There were several interrelated reasons for this opposition. Many people resented the unending flow of rules handed down by the EU's growing bureaucracy, which sought to standardize everything from cheeses to day care. Moreover, many people feared that more power in the hands of distant bureaucrats would undermine popular sovereignty and democratic control. Above all, ordinary citizens feared that the new Europe was being made at their expense. Joining the monetary union required governments to meet stringent fiscal standards and impose budget cuts and financial austerity. The resulting reductions in health care and social benefits hit ordinary citizens and did nothing to reduce western Europe's high unemployment rate.

The movement toward union also raised profound questions about the meaning of European unity and identity. Would the EU remain an exclusive Western club, or would it expand to include the postcommunist nations of eastern Europe? If some of them were included, how could Muslim Turkey's long-standing application for membership be ignored? Conversely, how could a union of twenty-five to thirty countries have any real unity?

The merging of East Germany into the German Federal Republic suggested the enormous difficulties of full East-West integration. After 1991 Helmut Kohl pumped massive investments into Germany's new eastern provinces, but Germans in the east still saw closed factories and social dislocation. Unemployment in Germany reached a postwar high of 12.8 percent in 1997, but in the eastern regions it soared to 20 percent. Germany's generous social benefits cushioned the blow, but many ordinary citizens felt hurt and humiliated.

Eastern German women in particular suffered. Before unification the overwhelming majority had worked outside the home, helped by cheap child care, flexible hours, and the prevailing socialist ideology. Now they faced expensive child care and a variety of pressures to stay at home and let men take hard-to-find jobs. Many, who had found autonomy and self-esteem in paid work, felt a keen sense of loss. They helped vote Kohl out of office in 1998.

Instructed by the difficulties of German unification, western Europeans proceeded cautiously at first in considering new requests for EU membership. Sweden, Finland, and Austria were admitted because they had strong capitalist economies and no longer had to maintain the legal neutrality that the Soviet Union had required during the cold war. Of the former communist states, Poland, the Czech Republic, and Hungary had the best prospects in the 1990s, and in late 2000 the EU's fifteen members agreed in principle to admit these three nations by 2006. The highly successful introduction of the Euro as the common currency of all Euro-zone citizens on January 1, 2002, encouraged the EU to accelerate plans for an ambitious enlargement to the east. In late 2002 the member states voted to bring ten eastern European countries into the EU by the end of 2004. A reunifying Europe was moving toward common institutions and groping for a common identity, but the process was far from complete.

## SUMMARY

The postwar recovery of western Europe and the Americas was a memorable achievement in the long, uneven course of Western civilization. The transition from imperialism to decolonization proceeded rapidly, and political democracy gained unprecedented strength in the West. Economic progress and social reforms improved the lives of ordinary citizens.

Postwar developments in eastern Europe displayed both similarities to and differences from developments in western Europe and the Americas. Perhaps the biggest difference was that Stalin imposed harsh one-party rule in the lands occupied by his armies, which led to the long cold war. Nevertheless, the Soviet Union became more liberal and less dictatorial under Khrushchev, and in the 1950s and 1960s the standard of living in the Soviet Union improved markedly.

In the late 1960s and early 1970s Europe and the Americas entered a turbulent time of crisis. Many nations, from France to Czechoslovakia and from Argentina to the United States, experienced major political difficulties, as social conflicts and ideological battles divided peoples and shook governments. Beginning with the oil shocks of the 1970s, severe economic problems added to the turmoil. Yet in western Europe and North America the postwar welfare system held firm, and both democracy and the movement toward European unity successfully passed through the storm.

Elsewhere the response to political and economic crisis sent many countries veering off toward repression. The communist system in eastern Europe was tightened up in the Brezhnev years, and a new kind of conservative authoritarianism arose in most of Latin America. Then, in the 1980s, both regions turned toward free elections and civil liberties, most spectacularly so in the eastern European revolutions of 1989. Like eastern Europe, Latin America also moved toward freer markets and embraced international trade and foreign investment, thereby abandoning its long-standing commitment to economic nationalism.

The remarkable result of all these parallel developments was that differences in political organization, human rights, and economic philosophy became less pronounced in the reuniting Western civilization of the 1990s than at any time since 1914. Eastern Europe especially struggled to rejoin the West and replace the bankrupt communist order with efficient capitalist democracies. Results varied greatly, and ordinary citizens often experienced real hardships in the process. But in the early twenty-first century few Westerners saw attractive alternatives to global liberalism, and no effort was made to restore economic planning or one-party rule. This suggests that the anticommunist revolutions of 1989 marked a major turning point in Western history, and perhaps in world history as well, as we will see in the following chapters.

## KEY TERMS

| | |
|---|---|
| Big Three | glasnost |
| Truman Doctrine | Solidarity |
| Marshall Plan | Velvet Revolution |
| Common Market | Paris Accord |
| decolonization | Civil Rights Act |
| neocolonialism | Watergate |
| OPEC | détente |
| de-Stalinization | Alliance for Progress |
| Brezhnev Doctrine | Sandinistas |
| perestroika | European Union (EU) |

## NOTES

1. Quoted in N. Graebner, *Cold War Diplomacy, 1945–1960* (Princeton, N.J.: Van Nostrand, 1962), p. 17.
2. *Wall Street Journal,* June 25, 1985, p. 1.
3. Quoted in D. Treadgold, *Twentieth Century Russia,* 5th ed. (Boston: Houghton Mifflin, 1981), p. 442.
4. Quoted in S. E. Morison et al., *A Concise History of the American Republic* (New York: Oxford University Press, 1977), p. 697.
5. Quoted ibid., p. 735.
6. F. Fukuyama, *The End of History and the Last Man* (New York: Free Press, 1992); and J. Cronin, *The World the Cold War Made: Order, Chaos and the Return of History* (New York: Routledge, 1996), pp. 267–281.
7. M. Goldman, "Russia's Reform Effort: Is There Growth at the End of the Tunnel?" *Current History* 96 (October 1997): 313.

## SUGGESTED READING

M. Eksteins, *Walking Since Daybreak: A Story of Eastern Europe, World War II, and the Heart of Our Century* (1999), is a powerful, partly autobiographical account that is highly recommended. Three important general studies with extensive bibliographies are W. Laqueur, *Europe in Our Time: A History, 1945–1992* (1992); P. Johnson, *Modern Times: The World from the Twenties to the Eighties* (1983); and C. Black, *Rebirth: A History of Europe Since World War II* (1992). Winston Churchill, Charles de Gaulle, and Dwight Eisenhower all wrote interesting histories of the war in the form of memoirs. Dean Acheson, *Present at the Creation* (1969), is a defense of American foreign policy in the early cold war. W. La Feber, *America, Russia, and the Cold War* (1967), claims, on the contrary, that the United States was primarily responsible for the conflict with the Soviet Union. K. Sainsbury, *Churchill and Roosevelt at War: The War They Fought and the Peace They Hoped to Make* (1994), is an excellent, very readable introduction. A. Winkler, *The Cold War: A Collection of Documents* (2000), and M. Walker, *The Cold War: A History* (1993), are recommended.

D. Urwin, *The Community of Europe,* 2d ed. (1995), focuses on steps toward European unity. Postwar economic and social developments are analyzed in G. Ambrosius and W. Hibbard, *A Social and Economic History of Twentieth-Century Europe* (1989), and F. Tipton and R. Aldrich, *An Economic and Social History of Europe from 1939 to the Present* (1986). I. Unger and D. Unger, *Postwar America: The United States Since 1945* (1989), and W. Leuchtenberg, *In the Shadow of FDR: From Harry Truman to Ronald Reagan* (1989), ably discuss developments in the United States. The culture and politics of protest are provocatively analyzed in H. Hughes, *Sophisticated Rebels: The Political Culture of European Dissent, 1968–1987* (1988), and W. Hampton, *Guerrilla Minstrels: John Lennon, Joe Hill, Woody Guthrie, Bob Dylan* (1986).

Two outstanding works on France are J. Ardagh, *The New French Revolution* (1969), which puts the momentous social changes after 1945 in human terms, and S. Bernstein, *The Republic of de Gaulle, 1958–1969* (1993). On postwar Germany, H. Turner, *The Two Germanies Since 1945: East and West* (1987), is recommended. The spiritual dimension of West German recovery is probed by G. Grass in his world-famous novel *The Tin Drum* (1963). W. Laqueur, *The Germans* (1985), is a journalistic report by a well-known historian. A. Marwick, *British Society Since 1945* (1982), is good on postwar developments, and P. Jenkins, *Mrs. Thatcher's Revolution: The End of the Socialist Era* (1988), is a provocative critique. Two outstanding books on the Vietnam War are N. Sheehan, *A Bright and Shining Lie: John Paul Vann and America in Vietnam* (1988), and A. Short, *The Origins of the Vietnam War* (1989). On the women's movement, see M. Boxer and J. Quartaert, *Connecting Spheres: European Women in a Globalizing World, 1500 to the Present,* 2d ed. (2000), and N. Cott, *The Grounding of Modern Feminism* (1987). J. Lovenduski, *Women and European Politics: Contemporary Feminism and Public Policy* (1986), provides an extremely useful comparative study of similar developments in different countries.

Z. Brzezinski, *The Grand Failure: The Birth and Death of Communism in the Twentieth Century* (1989), is a readable overview by a leading American scholar. L. Johnson, *Central Europe: Enemies, Neighbors, Friends* (1996), ably interprets events before and after 1989. P. Zinner, *Revolution in Hungary* (1962), is excellent on the tragic events of 1956, and Z. Zeman, *Prague Spring* (1969), is good on Czechoslovakia. T. Ash, *The Polish Revolution: Solidarity* (1983), and M. Kaufman, *Mad Dreams, Saving Graces: Poland, a Nation in Conspiracy* (1989), are recommended. A. Amalrik, *Will the Soviet Union Survive Until 1984?* (1970), is a fascinating interpretation of Soviet society and politics in the 1960s by a Russian who paid for his criticism with prison and exile. H. Smith wrote two outstanding journalistic reports, *The Russians* (1976) and *The New Russians* (1990). Gorbachev's reforms are perceptively examined by M. Lewin, *The Gorbachev Phenomenon: A Historical Interpretation* (1988).

M. Chamberlain, *Decolonization: The Fall of European Empires,* 2d ed. (1999), is a clear, up-to-date account. T. von Laue, *The World Revolution of Westernization: The Twentieth Century in Global Perspective* (1987), is a stimulating interpretation. Related economic developments are considered in T. Vadney, *The World Since 1945* (1988). Two excellent general studies on Latin America are J. E. Fagg, *Latin America: A General History,* 3d ed. (1977), and R. J. Shafer, *A History of Latin America* (1978). Both contain detailed suggestions for further reading. A. Lowenthal and G. Treverton, eds., *Latin America in a New World* (1994), analyzes the move toward regional cooperation and market economies. E. Burns, *A History of Brazil* (1970); M. Meyer and W. Sherman, *The Course of Mexican History* (1979); and B. Loveman, *Chile: The Legacy of Hispanic Capitalism* (1979), are recommended studies of postwar developments in three leading nations.

On more recent developments, M. Dobbs, *Down with Big Brother: The Fall of the Soviet Empire* (1997), is a superb account by a journalist who covered eastern Europe, and M. Goldman, *Lost Opportunity: What Has Made Economic Reform in Russia So Difficult?* (1996), is an important work. C. Fink et al., *1968: The World Transformed* (1998), is a stimulating reconsideration. J. Lampe, *Yugoslavia as History: Twice There Was a Country* (1996), considers judiciously the Bosnian tragedy. K. Jarausch, *The Rush to Unity* (1994), discusses German unification, and G. Rose, *Jacques Delors and European Integration* (1995), analyzes the EU in the 1990s. Fukuyama, cited in the Notes, sees the collapse of communism as the victory of democratic capitalism over all its competitors. Cronin, also cited in the Notes, and R. Caplan and J. Feffer, *Europe's New Nationalism: States and Minorities in Conflict* (1996), stress realistically the revival of nationalism.

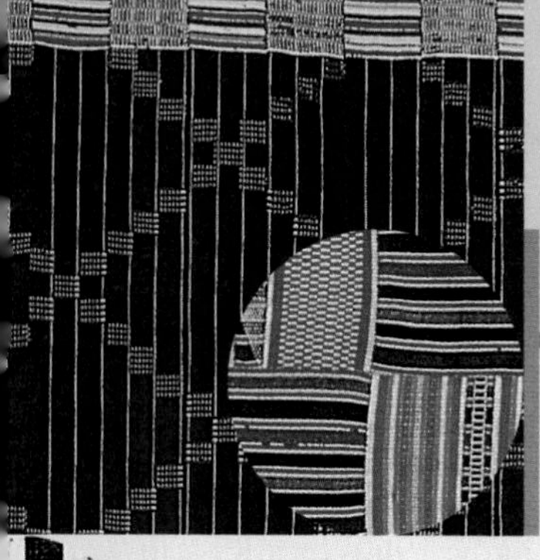

# Listening to the Past

## A Solidarity Leader Speaks from Prison

*Solidarity built a broad-based alliance of intellectuals, workers, and the Catholic church, which was one reason it became such a powerful movement in Poland. Another reason was Solidarity's commitment to social and political change through nonviolent action. This enabled Solidarity to avoid a bloodbath in 1981 and thus maintain its structure after martial law was declared, although at the time foreign observers often criticized Lech Walesa's leadership for being too cautious and unrealistic.*

*One of Walesa's closest coworkers was Adam Michnik. Walesa was a skilled electrician and a devout Catholic, whereas Michnik was an intellectual and disillusioned Communist. But their faith in nonviolence and gradual change bound them together. Trained as a historian but banned from teaching because of his leadership in student strikes in 1968, Michnik earned his living as a factory worker. In 1977 he joined with others to found the Committee for the Defense of Workers (KOR), which supported workers fired for striking. In December 1981, Michnik was arrested with the rest of Solidarity's leadership. While in prison until July 1994, he wrote his influential* Letters from Prison, *from which the following is taken.*

Why did Solidarity renounce violence? This question returned time and again in my conversations with foreign observers. I would like to answer it now. People who claim that the use of force in the struggle for freedom is necessary must first prove that in a given situation it will be effective and that force, when it is used, will not transform the idea of liberty into its opposite.

No one in Poland is able to prove today that violence will help us to dislodge Soviet troops from Poland and to remove the communists from power. The U.S.S.R. has such enormous military power that confrontation is simply unthinkable. In other words, we have no guns. Napoleon, upon hearing a similar reply, gave up asking further questions. However, Napoleon was above all interested in military victories and not building democratic, pluralistic societies. We, by contrast, cannot leave it at that.

In our reasoning, pragmatism is inseparably intertwined with idealism. Taught by history, we suspect that by using force to storm the existing Bastilles we shall unwittingly build new ones. It is true that social change is almost always accompanied by force. But it is not true that social change is merely a result of the violent collision of various forces. Above all, social changes follow from a confrontation of different moralities and visions of social order. Before the violence of rulers clashes with the violence of their subjects, values and systems of ethics clash inside human minds. Only when the old ideas of the rulers lose this moral duel will the subjects reach for force—sometimes. This is what happened in the French Revolution and the Russian Revolution—two examples cited in every debate as proof that revolutionary violence is preceded by a moral breakdown of the old regime. But both examples lose their meaning when they are reduced to such compact notions, in which the Encyclopedists are paired with the destruction of the Bastille, and the success of radical ideologies in Russia is paired with the storming of the Winter Palace. An authentic event is reduced to a sterile scheme.

In order to understand the significance of these revolutions, one must remember Jacobin and Bolshevik terror, the guillotines of the sans-culottes, and the guns of the commissars. Without reflection on the mechanisms in victorious revolutions that gave birth to terror, it is impossible to even pose the fundamental dilemma facing contemporary freedom movements. Historical awareness of the possible consequences of revolutionary violence must be etched into any program of struggle for freedom. The experience of being corrupted by terror must be imprinted

Solidarity activist Adam Michnik in 1984, appearing under police guard in the military court that sentenced him to prison. *(Wide World Photos)*

upon the consciousness of everyone who belongs to a freedom movement. [Or], as Simone Weil wrote, freedom will again become a refugee from the camp of the victors. . . .

Solidarity's program and ethos are inextricably tied to this strategy. Revolutionary terror has always been justified by a vision of an ideal society. In the name of this vision, Jacobin guillotines and Bolshevik execution squads carried out their unceasing, gruesome work. The road to God's Kingdom on Earth led through rivers of blood.

Solidarity has never had a vision of an ideal society. It wants to live and let live. Its ideals are closer to the American Revolution than to the French. . . . The ethics of Solidarity, with its consistent rejection of the use of force, has a lot in common with the idea of nonviolence as espoused by Gandhi and Martin Luther King, Jr. But it is not an ethic representative of pacifist movements.

Pacifism as a mass movement aims to avoid suffering; pacifists often say that no cause is worth suffering or dying for. The ethics of Solidarity are based on an opposite premise: that there are causes worth suffering and dying for. Gandhi and King died for the same cause as the miners in Wujek who rejected the belief that it is better to remain a willing slave than to become a victim of murder [and who were shot down by police for striking against the imposition of martial law in 1981]. . . .

But ethics cannot substitute for a political program. We must therefore think about the future of Polish-Russian relations. Our thinking about this key question must be open; it should consider many different possibilities. . . .

The Soviet state has a new leader; he is a symbol of transition from one generation to the next within the Soviet elite. This change may offer an opportunity, since Mikhail Gorbachev has not yet become a prisoner of his own decisions. No one can rule out the possibility that an impulse for reform will spring from the top of the hierarchy of power. This is exactly what happened in the time of Alexander II and, a hundred years later, under Khrushchev. Reform is always possible, even in the face of resistance by the old apparatus. . . .

So what can now happen [in Poland]?

The "fundamentalists" say, no compromises. Talking about compromise, dialogue, or understanding demobilizes public opinion, pulls the wool over the eyes of the public, spreads illusions. Walesa's declarations about readiness for dialogue were often severely criticized from this point of view. I do not share the fundamentalist point of view. . . . The logic of fundamentalism precludes any attempt to find compromise, even in the future. It harbors not only the belief that communists are ineducable but also a certainty that they are unable to behave rationally, even in critical situations—that, in other words, they are condemned to suicidal obstinacy.

This is not so obvious to me. Historical experience shows that communists were sometimes forced by circumstances to behave rationally and to agree to compromises. Thus the strategy of understanding must not be cast aside. We should not assume that a bloody confrontation is inevitable and, consequently, rule out the possibility of evolutionary, bloodless change. This should be avoided all the more inasmuch as democracy is rarely born from bloody upheavals. We should be clear in our minds about this: The continuing conflict may transform itself into either a dialogue or an explosion. The TKK [the underground Temporary Coordinating Committee of outlawed Solidarity] and [Lech] Walesa are doing everything in their power to make dialogue possible. Their chances of success will be greater if the level of self-organization of independent Polish society increases. For street lynchings, angry crowds are enough; compromise demands an organized society.

## QUESTIONS FOR ANALYSIS

1. What arguments does Michnik present for opposing the government with nonviolent actions? Are his arguments convincing?
2. How did Michnik's study of history influence his thinking? What lessons did he learn?
3. Analyze Michnik's attitudes toward the Soviet Union and Poland's Communist leadership. What policies did he advocate? Why?

*Source:* Adam Michnik, *Letters from Prison and Other Essays,* trans. Maya Latynski (Berkeley and Los Angeles: University of California Press, 1985), pp. 86–89, 92, 95, by permission of the University of California Press. 

Shinto priests perform a ceremony of purification in front of a reactor pressure chamber, Japan.
*(Yoshitaka Nakatani/PLUS ONE, Inc., Tokyo)*

CHAPTER

# 34 ASIA AND AFRICA IN THE CONTEMPORARY WORLD

## CHAPTER OUTLINE

- The Resurgence of East Asia
- New Nations in South Asia
- The Islamic Heartland
- Imperialism and Nationalism in Black Africa
- Sub-Saharan Africa Since 1960

When future historians look back at our era, they are likely to be particularly struck by the epoch-making resurgence of Asia and Africa after the Second World War. They will try to explain the rapid rise of new or radically reorganized Asian and African countries and their increasingly prominent role in world affairs. And they will try to understand the continued development of these countries as they sought to realize the promise of independence and to build strong nations.

- How did Asian and African countries reassert or establish their political independence in the postwar era?
- How, in the postindependence world, did leading states face up to the enormous challenges of nation building?
- To what extent did Asian and African countries choose democratic or authoritarian governments, and why?

These are the questions that this chapter seeks to answer. Chapter 35 will focus on common problems of economic and social development in Asia and Africa.

## THE RESURGENCE OF EAST ASIA

In 1945 Japan and China, the two great powers of East Asia, lay exhausted and devastated. Japanese aggression had sown extreme misery in China and reaped an atomic whirlwind at Hiroshima and Nagasaki. The future looked bleak. Yet both nations recovered even more spectacularly than western Europe. In the course of recovery the two countries went their separate ways. China under Mao Zedong (Mao Tse-tung) transformed itself into a strong, one-party communist state. Japan under American occupation turned from military expansion to democracy and extraordinarily successful economic development until the 1990s. Not until the late 1970s did the reborn giants begin moving closer together, as China retreated from Maoist communism and moved toward capitalism.

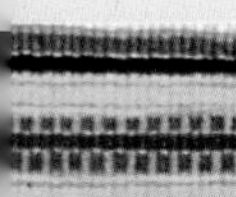

## The Communist Victory in China

There were many reasons for the triumph of communism in China. As a noted historian has forcefully argued, however, "Japanese aggression was . . . the most important single factor in Mao's rise to power."[1] When Japanese armies advanced rapidly in 1938, the Nationalist government of Jiang Jieshi (Chiang Kai-shek) moved its capital to Chongqing (Chungking), deep in the Chinese interior. As the Communists, aided by their uneasy "united front" alliance with the Nationalists, built up their strength in guerrilla bases in the countryside behind Japanese lines, Mao avoided pitched battles and concentrated on winning peasant support and forming a broad anti-Japanese coalition. By reducing rents, promising land redistribution, enticing intellectuals, and spreading propaganda, Mao and the Communists emerged in peasant eyes as the true patriots, the genuine nationalists.

Meanwhile, the long war with Japan was exhausting the established government and its supporters. Half of Japan's overseas armies were pinned down in China in 1945. Jiang Jieshi's Nationalists had mobilized 14 million men, and a staggering 3 million Chinese soldiers had been killed or wounded. The war created massive Chinese deficits and runaway inflation, hurting morale and ruining lives.

When Japan suddenly collapsed in August 1945, Communists and Nationalists both rushed to seize evacuated territory. Heavy fighting broke out in Manchuria, and civil war began in earnest in April 1946. At first Jiang Jieshi's more numerous Nationalists had the upper hand. Soon the better-led, more determined Communists rallied, and by 1948 the demoralized Nationalist forces were disintegrating. The following year Jiang Jieshi and a million mainland Chinese fled to the island of Taiwan, and in October 1949 Mao Zedong proclaimed the People's Republic of China.

Within three years the Communists had succeeded in consolidating their rule. The Communist government seized the holdings of landlords and rich peasants—10 percent of the farm population had owned between 70 and 80 percent of the land—and distributed it to 300 million poor peasants and landless laborers. This revolutionary land reform was extremely popular.

Meanwhile, the Communists were dealing harshly with their foes. Mao admitted in 1957 that 800,000 "class enemies" had been summarily liquidated between 1949 and 1954; the true figure is probably much higher. By means of mass arrests, forced-labor camps, and re-education through relentless propaganda and self-criticism sessions, all visible opposition from the old ruling groups was destroyed.

**Shaming Party Officials** During the Cultural Revolution, Chairman Mao's rebellious Red Guards lashed out at the Chinese establishment, denouncing high-ranking officials and intellectuals for their errors and lack of revolutionary zeal. In this 1967 photo, the minister of railroads and his assistant are paraded through Beijing in a truck, hanging their heads in disgrace and wearing gigantic dunce caps. Many of those shamed were purged and exiled to labor camps. *(AP/Wide World Photos)*

Finally, Mao and the Communists reunited China's 550 million inhabitants in a strong centralized state. They laid claim to a new Mandate of Heaven and demonstrated that China was once again a great power. This was the real significance of China's participation in the Korean War. In 1950, when the American-led United Nations forces in Korea crossed the thirty-eighth parallel and appeared to threaten China's industrial base in Manchuria, the Chinese attacked, advanced swiftly, and fought the Americans to a bloody standstill on the Korean peninsula. This struggle against "American imperialism" mobilized the masses, and military success increased Chinese self-confidence.

## Mao's China

Asserting Chinese power and prestige in world affairs, Mao and the party looked to the Soviet Union for inspiration in the early 1950s. Along with the gradual collectivization of agriculture, China adopted a typical Soviet

1940 1955 1970 1985 2000

## POLITICAL/MILITARY

1946–1964 Decolonization in Africa and Asia

• 1947 Separation of India and Pakistan

• 1948 End of British mandate in Palestine; Jews proclaim state of Israel

• 1949 End of civil war in China; formation of People's Republic of China

• 1952 End of American occupation of Japan

1964–1973 Vietnam War

• 1967 Six-Day War in Israel

• 1978 Islamic revolution in Iran

1980–1988 Iran-Iraq War

• 1991 Gulf War

• 1994 Nelson Mandela becomes president of South Africa

• 1995 Assassination of Israeli prime minister Yitzhak Rabin

## SOCIAL/ECONOMIC

1930s Gold Coast cocoa holdups

1949–1954 Mass arrests, forced-labor camps, and Communist propaganda in China

1950–1990 Rapid growth of Japanese economy

• 1956 Nasser nationalizes Suez Canal Company

1973–1976 Indira Gandhi's sterilization campaign to reduce population growth

• 1976 China implements campaign of the Four Modernizations

1978–1987 Rapid growth of Chinese economy

• 1989 Chinese military puts down student revolt in Tiananmen Square

• 1991 Congress party in India embraces Western capitalist reforms

## INTELLECTUAL/RELIGIOUS

1920s–1930s Black cultural nationalism grows among African intellectuals

1949–present Harsh restrictions against religion and speech in China

• 1965 Cultural Revolution in China; intellectuals are exiled and art is destroyed

Late 1970s–present Growth of Islamic fundamentalism

five-year plan to develop large factories and heavy industry rapidly. Russian specialists built many Chinese plants. Soviet economic aid was also considerable. The first five-year plan was successful, as undeniable economic growth followed the Communists' social revolution.

In the cultural and intellectual realms, too, the Chinese followed the Soviet example. Basic civil and political rights, which had been seriously curtailed by the Nationalists, were simply abolished. Temples and churches were closed, and freedom of the press died. A Soviet-style puritanism took hold. To the astonishment of "old China hands," the Communists quickly eradicated the long-standing scourges of prostitution and drug abuse, which they had long regarded as humiliating marks of exploitation and national decline. The Communists enthusiastically promoted Soviet-Marxian ideas concerning women and the family. Full equality, work outside the home, and state-supported child care became primary goals.

By the mid-1950s the People's Republic of China seemed to be firmly set on the Marxist-Leninist course of development previously perfected in the Soviet Union. In 1958, however, China began to go its own way. Mao had always stressed revolutionary free will and peasant equality. Now he proclaimed a spectacular acceleration of development, a **Great Leap Forward** in which soaring industrial growth was to be based on small-scale backyard workshops run by peasants living in gigantic self-contained communes. Creating a new socialist personality that rejected individualism and traditional family values was a second goal. In extreme cases commune members ate in common dining halls, nurseries cared for children, and fiery crusaders preached the evils of family ties.

The intended great leap past the Soviets to socialist utopia—true communism—produced an economic disaster in the countryside, for frantic efforts with primitive technology often resulted only in chaos. By 1960 only China's efficient rationing system was preventing starvation. But when Soviet premier Nikita Khrushchev criticized Chinese policy, Mao condemned Khrushchev and his Russian colleagues as detestable "modern revisionists"—capitalists and cowards unwilling to risk a world war that would bring communist revolution in the United States. The Russians abruptly cut off economic and military aid. A mood of fear and hostility developed in both China and the Soviet Union in the 1960s as the communist world split apart.

Mao lost influence in the party after the fiasco of the Great Leap Forward and the Sino-Soviet split, but in 1965 the old revolutionary staged a dramatic comeback. Fearing that China was becoming bureaucratic, capitalistic, and "revisionist" like the Soviet Union, Mao launched what he called the Great Proletarian **Cultural Revolution.** Its objective was to purge the party of time-serving bureaucrats and to recapture the revolutionary fervor of his guerrilla struggle (see page 991). The army and the nation's young people, especially students, responded enthusiastically. Encouraged by Mao to organize themselves into radical cadres called **Red Guards,** young people denounced their teachers and practiced rebellion in the name of revolution. One Red Guard manifesto exulted, "Revolution is rebellion, and rebellion is the soul of Mao Tse-tung's thought."[2]

The Red Guards sought to purge China of all traces of "feudal" and "bourgeois" culture and thought. Some ancient monuments and works of art were destroyed. Party officials, professors, and intellectuals were exiled to remote villages to purify themselves with heavy labor. The Red Guards attracted enormous worldwide attention and served as an extreme model for the student rebellions in the West in the late 1960s (see page 1081).

## The Limits of Reform

Mao and the Red Guards succeeded in mobilizing the masses, shaking up the party, and creating greater social equality. But the Cultural Revolution also created growing chaos and a general crisis of confidence, especially in the cities. Persecuted intellectuals, technicians, and purged party officials launched a counterattack on the radicals and regained much of their influence by 1969. Thus China shifted to the right at the same time that Europe and the United States did. This shift in China, coupled with actual fighting between China and the Soviet Union on the northern border in 1969, opened the door to a limited but lasting reconciliation between China and the United States in 1972.

The moderates were led by Deng Xiaoping (1904–1997), a long-time member of the Communist elite who had been branded a dangerous agent of capitalism during the Cultural Revolution. After Mao's death in 1976, Deng and his supporters initiated a series of new policies, embodied in the ongoing campaign of the "Four Modernizations"—agriculture, industry, science and technology, and national defense. The campaign to modernize had a profound effect on China's people, and Deng proudly called it China's "second revolution."

China's 800 million peasants experienced the greatest and most beneficial change from this "second revolution"—a fact that at first glance may seem surprising. The support of the peasantry had played a major role in the Communist victory. After 1949 land reform and rationing undoubtedly improved the diet of poor peasants. Subsequently, literacy campaigns taught rural people how to read, and "barefoot doctors"—local peasants trained to do simple diagnosis and treatment—brought modern medicine to the countryside. But rigid collectivized agriculture failed to provide either the peasants or the country with adequate food. Levels of agricultural production and per capita food consumption were no higher in the mid-1970s than in the mid-1950s, and only slightly higher than in 1937, before the war with Japan.

Determined to prevent a return to Maoist extremism as well as to modernize the economy, Deng and the reformers looked to the peasants as natural allies. They decided to let China's peasants farm the land in small family units rather than in large collectives. Peasants were encouraged to produce what they could produce best and "dare to be rich." Peasants responded enthusiastically, increasing food production by more than 50 percent in just six years after 1978.

The successful use of free markets and family responsibility in agriculture encouraged further economic experimentation. Foreign capitalists were allowed to open factories in southern China, and they successfully exported Chinese products around the world. The private enterprise of Chinese citizens was also permitted in cities. Snack shops, beauty parlors, and a host of small businesses sprang up. The Chinese economy grew rapidly between 1978 and 1987, and the level of per capita income doubled in these years.

Change, however, was also circumscribed. Most large-scale industry remained state owned, and cultural change proceeded slowly. Above all, under Deng's leadership the Communist party zealously preserved its monopoly of political power.

When the worldwide movement for greater democracy and political freedom in the late 1980s also took root in China, the government responded by banning all demonstrations and slowing the trend toward a freer economy. Inflation then soared to more than 30 percent a year. The economic reversal, the continued lack of political freedom, and the conviction that Chinese society was becoming more corrupt led China's idealistic university students to spearhead demonstrations in April 1989.

The students evoked tremendous popular support, and more than a million people streamed into Beijing's central **Tiananmen Square** on May 17 in support of their demands. The government then declared martial law and ordered the army to clear the students. Masses of courageous Chinese citizens blocked the soldiers' entry into the city for two weeks, but in the early hours of June 4, 1989, tanks rolled into Tiananmen Square. At least seven hundred students died as a wave of repression, arrests, and executions descended on China. China's Communist leaders claimed that they had saved the country from plots to destroy socialism and national unity.

**Chinese Students in 1989** These exuberant demonstrators in Tiananmen Square personify the idealism and optimism of China's prodemocracy movement. After some hesitation the Communist government crushed the student leaders and their supporters with tanks and executions, reaffirming its harsh, authoritarian character. *(Erika Lansner/stockphoto.com)*

In the months after Tiananmen Square communism fell in eastern Europe, the Soviet Union broke apart, and China's rulers felt vindicated. They believed that their strong action had preserved Communist power, prevented chaos, and showed the limits of permissible reform. After some hesitation Deng reaffirmed economic liberalization, as did his successor, Jiang Zemin, and private enterprise and foreign investment boomed in the 1990s. Consumerism was encouraged, and the standard of living rose. But the rulers jailed critics of Communist rule, and they made every effort to ensure that the People's Army would again crush the people if called to do so. Thus China coupled growing economic freedom with continued political repression, embracing only one half of the trend toward global liberalization and rejecting the other.

These policies continued in the twenty-first century. After long negotiations China succeeded in joining the World Trade Organization, which gave China all the privileges and obligations of participation in the liberal global economy. In 2002 the Communist leadership smoothly avoided an internal power struggle and chose a technocrat, Hu Jintao, to succeed the aging Jiang Zemin. Hu and his colleagues appeared ready to introduce modest legal reforms and experiment with freer elections for village officials, but they were clearly committed to maintaining a strong authoritarian state.

## Japan's American Revolution

After Japan's surrender in August 1945, American occupation forces began landing in the Tokyo-Yokohama area. Riding through what had been the heart of industrial Japan, they found only smokestacks and giant steel safes standing amid miles of rubble. The bleak landscape manifested Japan's state of mind as the nation lay helpless before its conqueror.

Japan, like Nazi Germany, was formally occupied by all the Allies, but real power resided in American hands. The commander was General Douglas MacArthur (1880–1964), the five-star hero of the Pacific, who with his advisers exercised almost absolute authority.

MacArthur and the Americans had a revolutionary plan for defeated Japan. Convinced that militaristic, antidemocratic forces were responsible for Japanese aggression and had to be destroyed, they introduced fundamental reforms designed to make Japan a free, democratic society along American lines. The exhausted, demoralized Japanese, who had feared a worse fate, accepted passively. Long-suppressed liberal leaders emerged to offer crucial support and help carry the reforms forward.

Japan's sweeping American revolution began with demilitarization and a systematic purge. A special international tribunal tried and convicted as war criminals twenty-five top government leaders and army officers. Other courts sentenced hundreds to death and sent thousands to prison. Over 220,000 politicians, businessmen, and army officers were declared ineligible for office.

Although the American-dictated constitution of 1946 allowed the emperor to remain "the symbol of the State," the new constitution made the government fully responsible to the Japanese Diet, whose members were popularly elected by all adults. A bill of rights granted basic civil liberties and freed all political prisoners, including communists. The constitution also abolished all Japanese armed forces. Japan's resurrected liberals enthusiastically supported this American move to destroy militarism.

The American occupation left Japan's powerful bureaucracy largely intact and used it to implement the fundamental social and economic reforms that were rammed through the Japanese Diet. Many had a New Deal flavor. The occupation promoted the Japanese labor movement and introduced American-style antitrust laws. The American reformers proudly "emancipated" Japanese women, granting them equality before the law.

The occupation also imposed revolutionary land reform. This reform strengthened the small, independent peasant, who became a staunch defender of postwar democracy.

The United States' efforts to remake Japan in its own image were powerful but short-lived. By 1948, when China was going communist, American leaders began to see Japan as a potential ally, not as an object of social reform. The American command began purging leftists and rehabilitating prewar nationalists, many of whom joined the Liberal Democratic party, which became increasingly conservative and emerged as the dominant political organization in postwar Japan. The United States ended the occupation in 1952. Under the treaty terms Japan regained independence, and the United States retained its vast military complex in Japan. With American encouragement Japan also developed an effective "Defense Force," a sophisticated modern army in everything but name.

## "Japan, Inc."

Restricted to satellite status in world politics, the Japanese people applied their creative powers to rebuilding their country. Japan's economic recovery, like Germany's, proceeded painfully slowly immediately after the war. At the time of the Korean War, however, the economy took off and grew with spectacular speed for a whole generation. Between 1950 and 1970 the real growth rate of Japan's economy—adjusted for inflation—averaged a breathtaking 10 percent a year. Even after the shock of much higher energy prices in 1973, the petroleum-poor Japanese did considerably better than most other peoples. In 1986 average per capita income in Japan exceeded that in the United States for the first time.

Japan's emergence as an economic superpower fascinated outsiders. Many Asians and Africans looked to Japan for the secrets of successful modernization, but some of Japan's Asian neighbors again feared Japanese exploitation. And in the 1970s and 1980s some Americans and Europeans bitterly accused "Japan, Inc.," of an unholy alliance between government and business and urged their own governments to retaliate.

In trying to explain Japanese success, most scholars agreed that Japan's remarkable economic surge seemed to have had deep roots in Japanese history, culture, and national character. By the time American and European pressure forced open Japan's gates in the mid-nineteenth century, Japanese agriculture, education, and material well-being were advanced even by European standards. Moreover, a culturally homogeneous Japanese society put the needs of the group before those of the individual. When the Meiji reformers redefined Japan's primary task as catching up with the West, they had the support of a sophisticated and disciplined people (see pages 874–878). Japan's modernization, even including a full share of aggressive imperialism, was extremely rapid.

By the end of the American occupation, this tight-knit, group-centered society had reassessed its future and worked out a new national consensus. Japan's new task was to build its economy and compete efficiently in world markets. Improved living standards emerged as a related goal after the initial successes of the 1950s.

In a system of managed capitalism, government and big business shared leading roles in the drama of economic growth, or so most observers believed at the time. As during the Meiji Restoration, capable, respected bureaucrats directed and aided the efforts of cooperative business leaders. The government decided which industries were important, then made loans and encouraged mergers to create powerful firms in those industries. The antitrust policy introduced by the American occupation was quickly scrapped, and the home market was protected from foreign competition by various measures.

Big business was valued and respected in postwar Japan because it served the national goal and mirrored Japanese society. Big companies traditionally hired workers for life immediately after they finished school, and employees' social lives revolved around the company. (Discrimination against women remained severe: their wages and job security were strikingly inferior to men's.) Most unions became moderate, agreeable company unions. The social and economic distance between salaried managers and workers was slight and often breached. *Efficiency, quality,* and *quantity* were the watchwords.

The 1990s brought a sharp reversal in Japan's economic performance and a decade of frustration. Financial problems were critical. Driven to great heights by excessive optimism, the Japanese stock market dropped by 65 percent from 1990 to 1992, and it hardly recovered thereafter. The bursting of the speculative bubble crippled Japanese banks, stymied economic growth, and led to record postwar unemployment of 4.5 percent in late 1998. Japan also faced increasingly tough competition from its industrializing neighbors in Asia (see Chapter 35), especially in the important American market. In 2001 the economy slid into recession once again.

Japan's stagnation after 1990 was perplexing. Ironically, many observers, especially Americans, did an about-face

**Searching for Work** Japanese young people, who once could expect many first job offers after leaving school, have suffered severely from the recession that began in 2001. These job seekers, like many others, have headed to Young Hellowork in Tokyo, the nation's first employment center designed specifically for young men and women. *(Kazuhiro Nogi/AFP/Corbis)*

and blamed government regulation and unimaginative business leaders for the newly discovered "Japanese disease." They prescribed a radical restructuring of the Japanese economy, in which government officials would step aside and aggressive capitalists would "downsize" big firms with layoffs and consolidations.

Yet postwar Japanese society, with its stress on discipline and cooperation as opposed to individualism and competition, has generally proved well adapted to meet the challenges of modern industrial urban society. For example, Japan, almost alone among industrial nations, has experienced a marked decrease in crime over the past generation. Similarly, since the 1970s the Japanese have addressed themselves effectively to such previously neglected problems as serious industrial pollution and their limited energy resources. Specific reforms are necessary, but on balance Japanese leaders seem justified in proceeding cautiously.

## NEW NATIONS IN SOUTH ASIA

South Asia transformed itself no less spectacularly than China and Japan. The national independence movements, which had been powerful mass campaigns since the 1930s, triumphed decisively over weakened and demoralized European imperialism after the Second World War. Between 1947 and 1962, as decolonization gathered irresistible strength, virtually every colonial territory won its political freedom. The complete reversal of the long process of European expansion was a turning point in world history.

The newly independent nations of South Asia exhibited many variations on the dominant themes of national renaissance and modernization, especially as the struggle for political independence receded into the past. Ethnic rivalries greatly complicated the process of renewal and development.

### The End of British India

After the First World War, Mahatma Gandhi and the Indian Congress party developed the philosophy of militant nonviolence to oppose British rule of India and to lessen oppression of the Indian poor by the Indian rich (see pages 981–983). By 1929 Gandhi had succeeded in transforming the Congress party from a narrow, middle-class party into a mass independence movement. Gradually and grudgingly, Britain's rulers introduced reforms culminating in limited self-government in 1937.

The Second World War accelerated the drive toward independence but also pointed it in a new direction. Congress party leaders, humiliated that Great Britain had declared war against Germany on India's behalf without consulting them, resigned their posts in the Indian government and demanded self-rule as the immediate price of political cooperation. In 1942 Gandhi called on the British to "Quit India" and threatened another civil disobedience campaign. He and the other Congress leaders were quickly arrested and jailed for most of the war. As a result, India's wartime support for hard-pressed Britain was substantial but not always enthusiastic. Meanwhile, the Congress party's prime political rival skillfully seized the opportunity to increase its influence.

That rival was the **Muslim League,** led by the brilliant, elegant, English-educated lawyer Muhammad Ali Jinnah (1876–1948). Jinnah and the other leaders of the Muslim League feared Hindu domination of an independent Indian state led by the Congress party. Asserting in nationalist terms the right of Muslim areas to separate from the Hindu majority, Jinnah described the Muslims of India as "a nation with our distinct culture and civilization, . . . our own distinctive outlook on life and of life."[3] In March 1940 Jinnah told a hundred thousand listeners at the Muslim League's Lahore Conference that the British government should grant the Muslim and Hindu peoples separate homelands by dividing India into autonomous national states.

The Muslim League's insistence on the division of India appalled Gandhi. He regarded Jinnah's two-nation theory as simply untrue and as promising the victory of hate over love. The passionate debate continued unabated during the war as millions argued whether India was one nation or two. By 1945 the subcontinent was intellectually and emotionally divided, though still momentarily held together by British rule.

When Britain's Labour government agreed to speedy independence for India after 1945, conflicting Hindu and Muslim nationalisms and religious hatred became obstacles leading to murderous clashes between the two communities in 1946. In a last attempt to preserve the subcontinent's political unity, the British proposed a federal constitution providing for extensive provincial—and thus religious and cultural—autonomy. When after some hesitation Jinnah and the Muslim League would accept nothing less than an independent Pakistan, India's last viceroy—war hero Lord Louis Mountbatten (1900–1979), Queen Victoria's great-grandson—proposed partition. Both sides accepted. At the stroke of midnight on August 14, 1947, one-fifth of humanity gained political independence.

Yet independence through partition also brought tragedy. In the weeks after independence communal strife exploded into an orgy of massacres and mass expulsions. Perhaps a hundred thousand Hindus and Muslims were

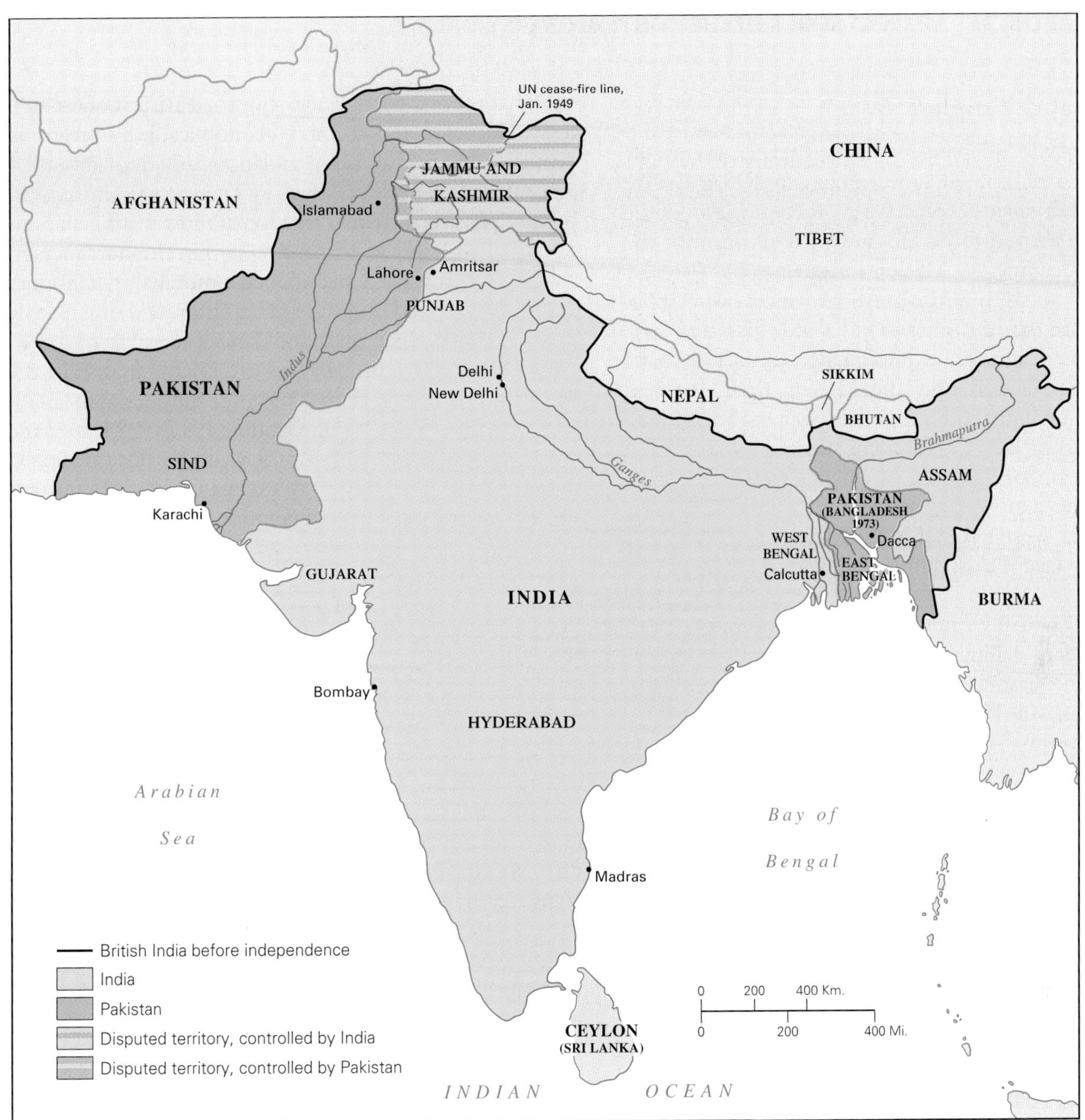


**MAP 34.1 The Partition of British India, 1947** Violence and fighting were most intense where there were large Hindu and Muslim minorities—in Kashmir, the Punjab, and Bengal. The tragic result of partition, which occurred repeatedly throughout the world in the twentieth century, was a forced exchange of populations and greater homogeneity on both sides of the border.

slaughtered, and an estimated 5 million refugees from both communities fled in opposite directions to escape being hacked to death by frenzied mobs.

This wave of violence was a bitter potion for Congress party leaders, who were completely powerless to stop it. "What is there to celebrate?" exclaimed Gandhi. "I see nothing but rivers of blood."[4]

In January 1948, while announcing a fast to protest Hindu persecution of Muslims, Gandhi was gunned down by a Hindu fanatic. As the Mahatma's death tragically testifies, the constructive and liberating forces of modern nationalism have frequently deteriorated into blind hatred.

After the ordeal of independence, relations between India and Pakistan—both members of the British Commonwealth—remained tense. Fighting over the disputed area of Kashmir continued until 1949 and broke out again in 1965–1966 and 1971 (see Map 34.1).

## Pakistan and Bangladesh

Like many newly independent states, Pakistan eventually adopted an authoritarian government in 1958. Unlike most, Pakistan failed to preserve its exceptionally fragile unity, which proved to be the unworkable dream of the intellectuals leading the Muslim League.

Pakistan's western and eastern provinces were separated by more than a thousand miles of Indian territory, as well as by language, ethnic background, and social custom. They shared only the Muslim faith that had temporarily brought them together against the Hindus. The Bengalis of East Pakistan constituted a majority of the population of Pakistan as a whole but were neglected by the central government, which remained in the hands of West Pakistan's elite after Jinnah's death. In essence, East Pakistan remained a colony of West Pakistan.

Tensions gradually came to a head in the late 1960s. Bengali leaders calling for virtual independence were charged with treason, and martial law was proclaimed in East Pakistan. In 1971 the Bengalis revolted. Despite savage repression—10 million Muslim Bengalis fled temporarily to India, which provided some military aid—the Bengalis won their independence as the new nation of Bangladesh in 1973. The world's eighth most populous country, Bangladesh was also one of its poorest.

Emerging as completely separate states, Pakistan and Bangladesh after 1973 exhibited many similarities. Both countries moved erratically from semi-authoritarian one-party rule toward competitive parliamentary systems with open elections. In the process each also experienced a series of military takeovers, restorations of civilian authority, political assassinations, and charges of official corruption. Each achieved some economic improvement but little social progress, especially for women.

## India Since Independence

India was ruled for a generation after 1947 by Jawaharlal Nehru (1889–1964) and the Congress party, which introduced major social reforms. Hindu women and even young girls were granted legal equality, which included the right to vote, to seek a divorce, and to marry outside their caste. The constitution abolished the untouchable caste and, in an effort to compensate for centuries of the most profound discrimination, established "ex-untouchable" quotas for university scholarships and government jobs. In practice attitudes toward women and untouchables evolved slowly—especially in the villages, where 85 percent of the people lived.

The Congress party leadership tried with modest success to develop the country economically by means of democratic socialism. But population growth of about 2.4 percent per year ate up much of the increase in output. Intense poverty remained the lot of most people and encouraged widespread corruption within the bureaucracy.

The Congress party maintained a moralizing neutrality in the cold war and sought to group India and other newly independent states in Asia and Africa into a "third force" of "nonaligned" nations. This effort culminated in the Afro-Asian Conference in Bandung, Indonesia, in 1955.

Nehru's daughter, Indira Gandhi (1917–1984), became prime minister in 1966. Mrs. Gandhi (whose deceased husband was no relation to Mahatma Gandhi) dominated Indian political life for a generation with a combination of charm, tact, and toughness. As it became clear that population growth was frustrating efforts to improve living standards, Mrs. Gandhi's government stepped up measures to promote family planning and birth control measures, including vasectomy for both psychological and religious reasons. In the face of widespread resistance to such measures, Mrs. Gandhi in 1975 subverted parliamentary democracy and proclaimed a state of emergency. Attacking dishonest officials, black-marketeers, and tax evaders, she also threw the weight of the government behind a heavy-handed campaign of mass sterilization to reduce population growth. More than 7 million men were sterilized in 1976.

Many Indian and foreign observers believed that Mrs. Gandhi's emergency measures marked the end of the parliamentary democracy and Western liberties introduced in the last phase of British rule. But Mrs. Gandhi—true to the British tradition—called for free elections. She suffered a spectacular electoral defeat, largely because of the vastly unpopular sterilization campaign and her subversion of democracy. Her successors, however, fell to fighting among themselves, and in 1980 Mrs. Gandhi won an equally stunning electoral victory. Her defeat and re-election undoubtedly strengthened India's democratic tradition.

Mrs. Gandhi's last years in office were plagued by another old political problem—separatist ethnic nationalism. Democratic India remained a patchwork of religions, languages, and peoples. This enduring diversity threatened to further divide the country along ethnic or religious lines, as several peoples began to make political demands—most notably the 15 million Sikhs of the Punjab in northern India (see Map 34.1).

The Sikhs have their own religion—a blend of Islam and Hinduism—and a distinctive culture. Most Sikhs wanted greater autonomy for the Punjab, and by 1984

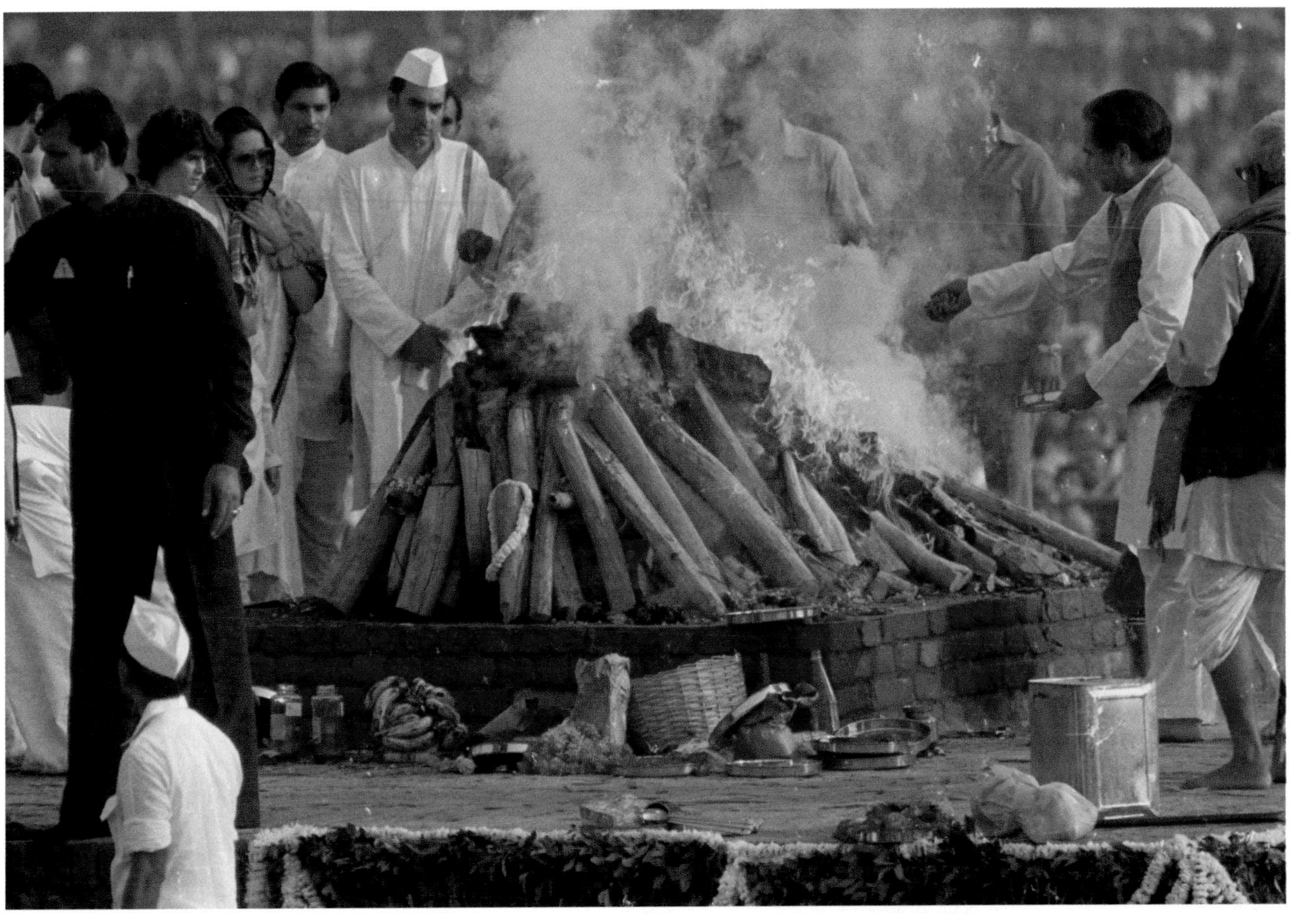

**Indira Gandhi's Funeral** Covered with beautiful flower wreaths and carried to her funeral pyre by devoted friends, the body of the assassinated leader was then cremated in a solemn public ceremony according to Hindu religion and custom. Although the strong-willed Gandhi flirted with dictatorship, she nurtured and strengthened modern India's vibrant democratic tradition. *(David Turnley/Corbis)*

some Sikh radicals were fighting for independence. Mrs. Gandhi cracked down hard and was assassinated by Sikhs in retaliation. Violence followed as Hindu mobs slaughtered over a thousand Sikhs throughout India.

Elected prime minister in 1984 by a landslide sympathy vote, one of Mrs. Gandhi's sons, Rajiv Gandhi (1944–1991), showed considerable skill at effecting a limited reconciliation with a majority of the Sikh population. Under his leadership the Congress party also moved away from the socialism of his mother and grandfather. In 1991 the Congress party wholeheartedly embraced market reforms, capitalist development, and Western technology and investment. These reforms were successful, and in the 1990s India's economy grew rapidly.

Holding power almost continuously from 1947, the Congress party was challenged increasingly by Hindu nationalists in the 1990s. These nationalists argued forcefully that India was based, above all, on Hindu culture and religious tradition and that these values had been badly compromised by the Western secularism of Congress party leaders and by the historical influence of India's Muslims. Campaigning also for a strong Indian military, the Hindu nationalist party finally gained power in 1998. The new government immediately exploded nuclear devices, asserting its vision of a militant Hindu nationalism.

Pakistan also exploded a nuclear weapon in 1998, and relations between Pakistan and India continued to worsen. Pakistan stepped up its support for "freedom fighters" in the disputed territory of Kashmir and for Muslim guerrilla groups operating out of Pakistan. When a terrorist attack on the Indian parliament in New Delhi took fourteen lives in December 2001, India blamed Pakistan and

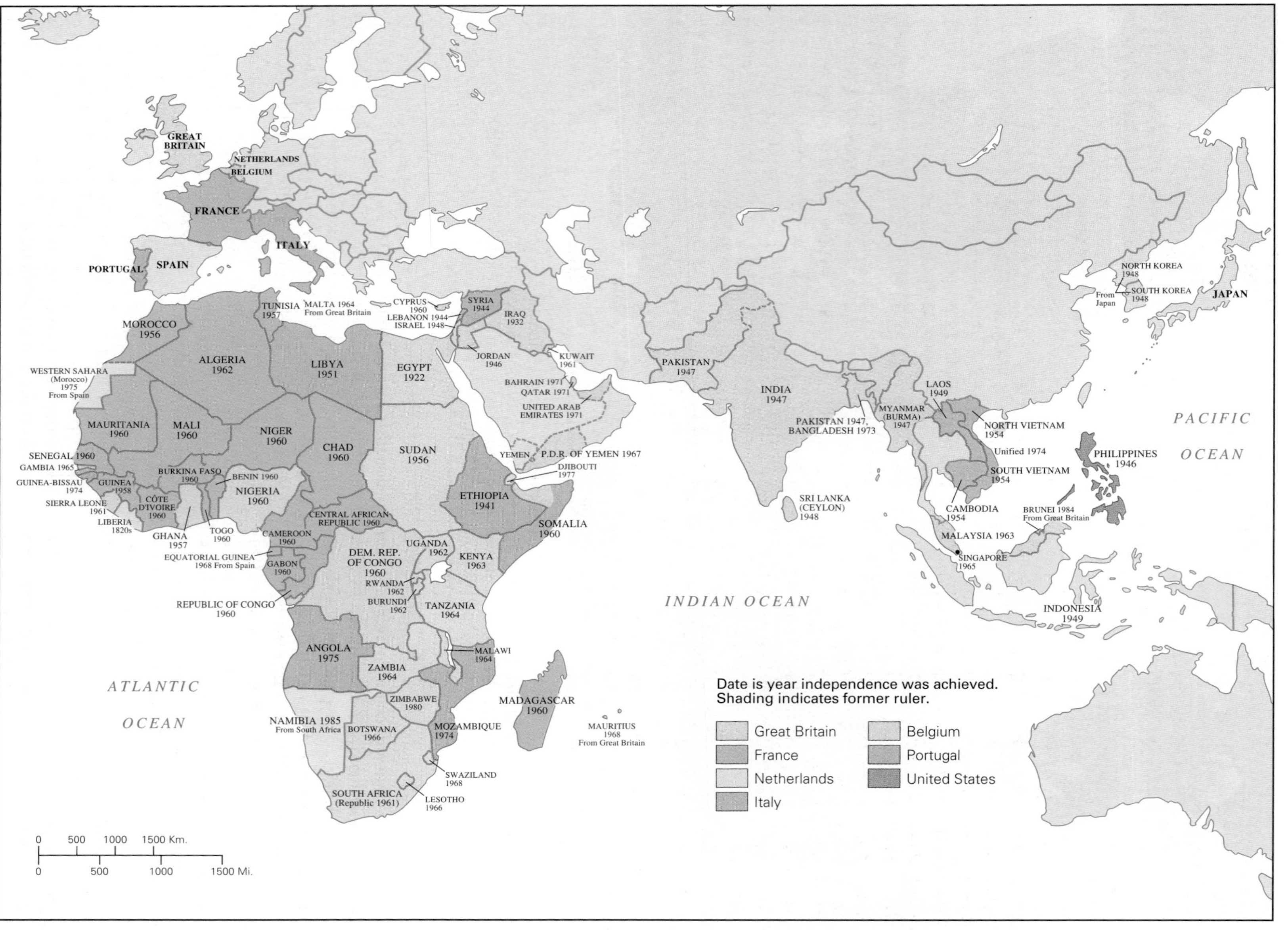


**MAP 34.2 The New States in Africa and Asia** Divided primarily along religious lines into two states, British India led the way to political independence in 1947. Most African territories achieved statehood by the mid-1960s, as European empires passed away, unlamented.

**Facing War in Kashmir** Tension, terrorism, and guerrilla attacks are constants along the India-Pakistan border in Kashmir. When all-out war with atomic weapons threatened in 2002, thousands of Pakistani villagers fled from their homes in trucks. *(K. M. Chaudary/AP/Wide World Photos)*

demanded the surrender of the alleged ringleaders. Pakistan's military ruler, Pervez Musharraf, who had long supported the Taliban in Afghanistan before suddenly joining the Americans after the terrorist attacks on the United States in September 2001, refused. Within days the two nuclear powers had massive armies facing each other and appeared posed for war. After intense diplomatic pressure, they stepped back from the abyss. The conflicting claims of Muslim and Hindu nationalists remained on a collision course, raising again the threat of nuclear catastrophe.

## Malaya, Singapore, and the Philippine Islands

The rest of Southeast Asia gained independence quickly after 1945, but the attainment of stable political democracy proved a more difficult goal (see Map 34.2). Ethnic conflicts and cold war battles could easily divide countries. Thus leaders frequently turned to authoritarian rule and military power in an effort to impose order and unity.

Malaya encountered serious problems not unlike those of British India. The native Malays, an Islamic agricultural people, feared and disliked the Chinese, who had come to the Malay Peninsula as poor migrant workers in the nineteenth century and stayed on to dominate the urban economy. The Malays pressured the British into giving them the dominant voice in a multiethnic federation of Malayan territories. In 1948 local Chinese Communists launched an all-out guerrilla war. They were eventually defeated by the British and the Malays, and Malaya became self-governing in 1957 and independent in 1961.

Yet two peoples soon meant two nations. In 1965 the largely Chinese city of Singapore was pushed out of the Malayan-dominated Federation of Malaysia. The independent city-state of Singapore prospered on the hard work and inventiveness of its largely Chinese population. Singapore's government promoted education, private enterprise, high technology, and affordable housing for all citizens. By the mid-1990s Singapore enjoyed one of the highest per capita incomes in the world. The government,

**Promoting the Chinese Language** The government of Singapore worries that the country's largely Chinese population could gradually turn from Chinese to English, and the Speak Madarin Campaign has become a major annual event. Government campaigns play an important role in developing public opinion and molding social attitudes in the well-disciplined island nation. *(National Archives of Singapore)*

dominated by a single party, continued to push hard for conservative family values and strict social discipline. For example, teenagers convicted of vandalism were often sentenced to a harsh beating with a cane.

The Philippine Islands suffered greatly under Japanese occupation during the Second World War. After the war the United States retained its large military bases but followed through on its earlier promises by granting the Philippines independence in 1946. As in Malaya, communist guerrillas tried unsuccessfully to seize power. The Philippines pursued American-style two-party competition until 1965, when President Ferdinand Marcos (1917–1989) subverted the constitution and ruled as dictator. Abolishing martial law in 1981 but retaining most of his power, Marcos faced growing opposition as the economy crumbled and land-hungry communist guerrillas made striking gains in the countryside. Led by the courageous Corazón Aquino (b. 1933), the opposition won a spectacular electoral victory in 1986 and forced Marcos to flee.

As president, Aquino negotiated a cease-fire with the communist rebels, beat off several attempted takeovers by dissident army officers, and pursued a policy of national reconciliation. Her democratically elected successor continued her policy of reconciliation. In 1996 a final peace agreement granted Muslim separatists an autonomous region in southern Mindinao, thereby ending a long and bloody rebellion and further strengthening the forces of peaceful change.

## Nation Building in Indonesia

The Netherlands East Indies emerged in 1949 as independent Indonesia under the nationalist leader Achmed Sukarno (1901–1970), after successfully resisting stubborn Dutch efforts at reconquest. Like the Philippines, the populous new nation encompassed a variety of peoples, islands, and religions (Islam was predominant; see Map 34.3). Beginning in 1957 Sukarno tried to forge unity by means of his so-called guided democracy. He rejected parliamentary democracy as politically divisive and claimed to replicate at the national level the traditional deliberation and consensus of the Indonesian village. For a time the authoritarian, anti-Western Sukarno seemed to be under the sway of well-organized Indonesian communists, who murdered seven leading army generals as part of an unsuccessful uprising in 1965. The army immediately retaliated, systematically slaughtering a half million or more Indonesian communists, radicals, and noncommunist Chinese. Sukarno was forced to resign.

The military leaders, led by General Suharto, established their own form of authoritarian rule. The government promoted an official five-point ideology stressing belief in one God, nationalism, humanitarianism, democracy, and social justice. But Suharto's New Order concentrated mainly on economic development. Blessed with large oil revenues, it welcomed foreign capital, expanded the Indonesian middle classes, and achieved solid economic growth for a generation. Increasingly tied to the world economy, Indonesia in 1997 was suddenly devastated by financial crisis. In 1998 Suharto was forced to resign as calls for democratic reform swept the country.

After Suharto's fall, freely elected governments had considerable success in dealing with Indonesia's problems. They attacked corruption and reversed the economic decline.

**Burning General Suharto in Effigy, May 1998** Student demonstrations played a decisive role in driving Indonesia's aging president from office. Students are a potent but unpredictable force in domestic politics around the world, as they have been since the early nineteenth century. *(Kees/Sygma)*

In 2000 Indonesia gave East Timor political independence, twenty-five years after Suharto's army conquered the territory. Above all, in a country where 85 percent of the population is Muslim, political and religious leaders worked to protect Islamic culture and maintain the peaceful, tolerant character of Islam in Indonesia.

## The Reunification of Vietnam

The most bitter struggle for independence in Southeast Asia occurred in French Indochina. The French tried to reimpose imperial rule there after the communist and nationalist guerrilla leader Ho Chi Minh (1890–1969) declared an independent republic in 1945, but they were decisively defeated in 1954 in the Battle of Dien Bien Phu. At the subsequent international peace conference, French Indochina gained independence. Laos and Cambodia (later known as Kampuchea) became separate states; Vietnam was "temporarily" divided into two hostile sections at the seventeenth parallel pending elections to select a single unified government within two years.

The elections were never held, and the civil war that soon broke out between the two Vietnamese governments, one communist and one anticommunist, became the hottest cold war conflict in the 1960s. The United States invested tremendous military effort but fought its Vietnam War as a deeply divided country (see pages 1081–1082). The tough, dedicated communists eventually proved victorious in 1975. Thus events in Vietnam roughly replicated those in China, but in a long, drawn-out fashion: After a bitter civil war worsened by cold war hatreds, the communists succeeded in creating a unified Marxist nation. After another generation the Vietnamese communists began to turn from central planning toward freer markets and private initiative, but they zealously guarded their monopoly of political power.

## THE ISLAMIC HEARTLAND

Throughout the vast arc of predominantly Islamic lands that stretches from Iran in West Asia to Senegal in West Africa (see Map 34.3), nationalism remained the primary political force after 1945. Anti-Western and anticommunist in most instances, nationalism in the Muslim world generally combined a strong secular state with a basic loyalty to Islam. Cold war conflicts and enormous oil resources enhanced the region's global standing.

In the Arab countries of North Africa and West Asia, with their shared but highly differentiated language and culture, nationalism wore two faces. The idealistic side focused on the Pan-Arab dream of uniting all Arabs in a single nation that would be strong enough to resist the West, defeat the new state of Israel, and achieve genuine independence. This Pan-Arab vision contributed to political and economic alliances like the Arab League; but no Arab Bismarck appeared, and the vision foundered on intense regional, ideological, and personal rivalries. Thus the practical, down-to-earth side of Arab nationalism focused largely on nation building within the particular states that supplanted former League of Nations mandates and European colonies.

This effort eventually seemed to some to result in one-party dictatorship, corruption, and continued daily hardship. Beginning in the late 1970s some Islamic preachers and devoted laypeople charged that the model of modernizing, Western-inspired nationalism had failed. These critics, generally known in the West as fundamentalists, urged a return to strict Islamic principles and traditional morality. They evoked a sympathetic response among many educated Muslims as well as among villagers and city dwellers, and in Iran they gained power.

**MAP 34.3 Modern Islam, 2002** Although the Islamic heartland remains the Middle East and North Africa, Islam is growing steadily in Africa south of the Sahara and is the faith of heavily populated Indonesia.

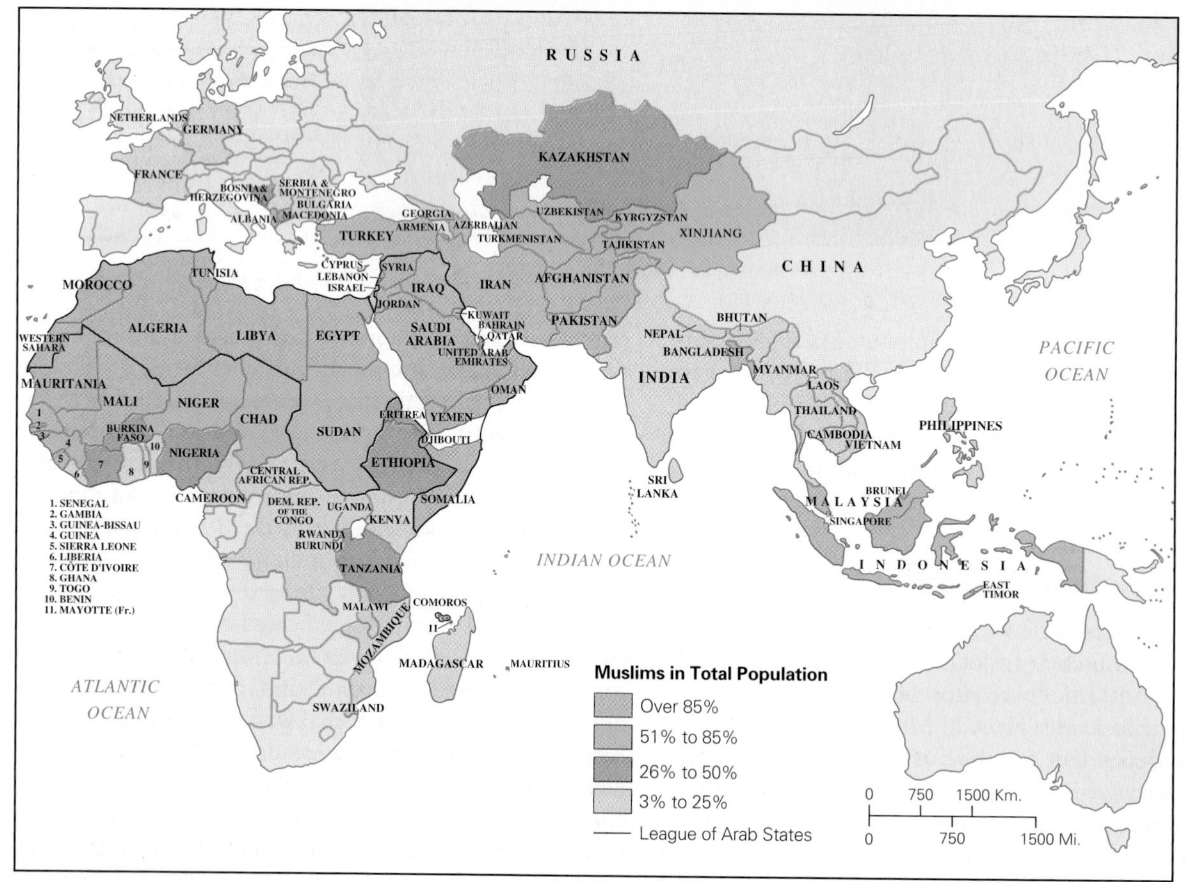

## The Arab-Israeli Conflict

Before the Second World War, Arab nationalists were loosely united in their opposition to the colonial powers and to Jewish migration to Palestine. The French gave up their League of Nations mandates in Syria and Lebanon in 1945, having been forced by popular uprisings to follow the British example in Egypt and Iraq. Attention then focused even more sharply on British-mandated Palestine. The situation was volatile. The Jews' demand that the British permit all survivors of Hitler's death camps to settle in Palestine was strenuously opposed by the Palestinian Arabs and the seven independent states of the newly founded Arab League (Egypt, Iraq, Jordan, Lebanon, Saudi Arabia, Syria, and Yemen). Murder and terrorism flourished, nurtured by bitterly conflicting Arab and Jewish nationalisms.

The British—their occupation policies in Palestine condemned by Arabs and Jews, by Russians and Americans—announced in 1947 their intention to withdraw from Palestine in 1948. The insoluble problem was dumped in the lap of the United Nations. In November 1947 the United Nations General Assembly passed a nonbinding resolution supporting a plan to partition Palestine into two separate states—one Arab and one Jewish (see Map 34.4). The Jews accepted, but the Arabs rejected, partition of Palestine.

By early 1948 an undeclared civil war was raging in Palestine. When the British mandate officially ended on May 14, 1948, the Jews proclaimed the state of Israel. Arab countries immediately launched an attack on the new Jewish state, but the Israelis drove off the invaders and conquered more territory. Roughly 900,000 Arab refugees—the exact number is disputed—fled or were expelled from old Palestine. This war left an enormous legacy of Arab bitterness toward Israel and its political allies, Great Britain and the United States, and it led to the creation of the **Palestine Liberation Organization,** a loose union of Palestinian refugee groups opposed to Israel.

## The Development of Egypt

In Egypt the humiliation of Arab defeat triggered a nationalist revolution. A young army colonel named Gamal Abdel Nasser (1918–1970) drove out the corrupt and pro-Western King Farouk in 1952. A gifted politician and the unchallenged leader of the largest Arab state, Nasser enjoyed powerful influence in the Middle East and throughout Asia and Africa. Perhaps his most successful and widely imitated move was radical land reform: large estates along the Nile were nationalized and divided up among peasants without violence or drastic declines in production.

Nasser preached the gospel of neutralism in the cold war, jailed Egyptian communists, and turned for aid to the Soviet Union to demonstrate Egypt's independence of the West. Relations with Israel and the West worsened, and in 1956 Nasser nationalized the European-owned Suez Canal Company, the last vestige of European power in the Middle East. Outraged, the British and French joined forces with the Israelis and successfully invaded Egypt. But the Americans unexpectedly sided with the Soviets and forced the British, French, and Israelis to withdraw from Egypt.

This great victory for Nasser encouraged anti-Western radicalism, hopes of Pan-Arab political unity, and a vague "Arab socialism." Yet the Arab world remained deeply divided. The only shared goals were bitter opposition to Israel—war recurred in 1967 and in 1973—and support for the right of Palestinian refugees to return to their homeland. In late 1977 President Anwar Sadat of Egypt tried another tack: a pathbreaking official visit to Israel.

Sadat's visit led to direct negotiations between Israel and Egypt, which were effectively mediated by U.S. president Jimmy Carter, and a historic though limited peace settlement. Each country gained: Egypt got back the Sinai Peninsula, which Israel had taken in the 1967 Six-Day War (see Map 34.4), and Israel obtained peace and normal relations with Egypt. Israel also kept the Gaza Strip, taken from Egypt in 1967 and home to about 1 million Palestinians. Some Arab leaders denounced Sadat's initiative as treason.

After Sadat's assassination by Islamic radicals in 1981, Egypt's relations with Israel deteriorated badly. The key dispute involved ever-increasing Israeli settlements in the Gaza Strip and the West Bank—the area west of the Jordan River inhabited by Palestinian Arabs but taken by Israel from Jordan during the 1967 war and occupied by Israel thereafter. Yet Egypt and Israel maintained their fragile peace, and Egypt concentrated on curbing fundamentalism and promoting economic development.

## Israel and the Palestinians

In 1988 young Palestinians in the occupied territories began a prolonged campaign of rock throwing and civil disobedience against Israeli soldiers. Inspired increasingly by Islamic fundamentalists, the Palestinian uprising eventually posed a serious challenge not only to Israel but also to the secular Palestinian liberation movement, long led from abroad by Yasir Arafat. The result was an unexpected and mutually beneficial agreement in 1993

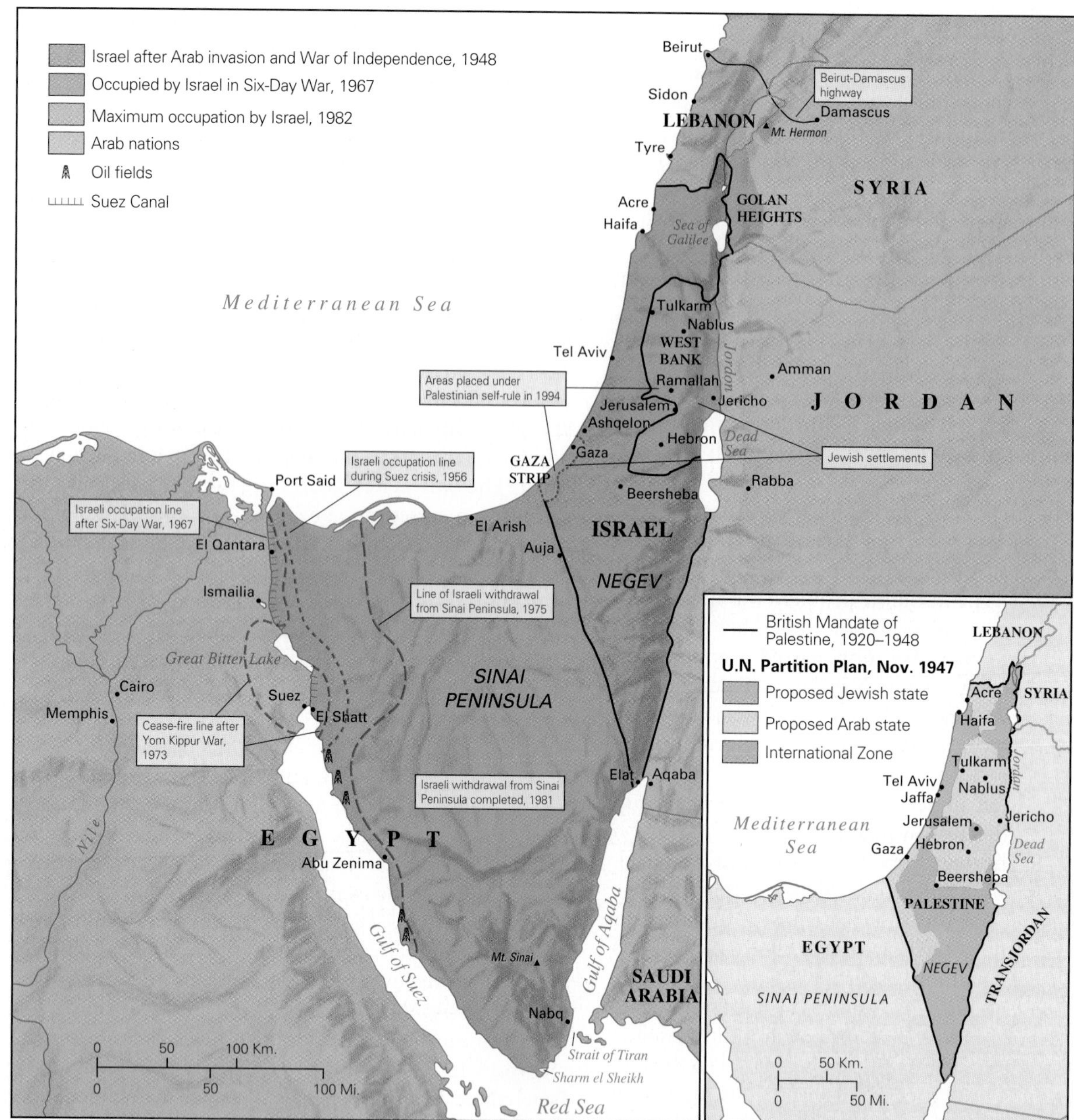


**MAP 34.4 Palestine, Israel, and the Middle East, 1947–2003** Since the British mandate expired on May 14, 1948, there have been five major wars and innumerable armed clashes in what was formerly Palestine. After winning the War of Independence in 1948, Israel achieved spectacular victories in 1967 in the Six-Day War, occupying the Sinai Peninsula, the Golan Heights, and the West Bank. The Yom Kippur War of 1973 eventually led to the Israeli evacuation of the Sinai and peace with Egypt. In 1993 Israel and the Palestine Liberation Organization agreed in principle to self-rule for Palestinian Arabs in the West Bank in five years, and in 1994 the Gaza Strip and Jericho were placed under the administration of the Palestinian Authority. Negotiations in Washington in 2000 failed to reach a final peace agreement, and armed conflict began again. The Israeli army reoccupied much of the West Bank, and the peace process collapsed.

between Israel and the Palestine Liberation Organization. Israel agreed to recognize Arafat's organization and start a "peace process" that granted Palestinian self-rule in Gaza and Jericho and called for self-rule throughout the West Bank in five years. In return, Arafat renounced terrorism and abandoned the long-standing demand that Israel must withdraw from all the land it had occupied in the 1967 war, a demand that the United Nations Security Council had endorsed in Resolution 242.

The 1993 agreement and the peace process were hotly debated in an increasingly divided Israel. In 1995, in this tense atmosphere, a right-wing Jewish extremist assassinated Prime Minister Yitzhak Rabin (r. 1992–1995), thereby following the lead of those Israelis who had denounced the war hero and leader as a traitor to his people. In 1996 a coalition of opposition parties won a slender majority, charging the Palestinian leadership with condoning anti-Jewish terrorism. The new Israeli government limited Palestinian self-rule where it existed and expanded Jewish settlements in the West Bank. On the Palestinian side, dissatisfaction with the peace process grew. Between 1993 and 2000 the number of Jewish settlers in the West Bank doubled to 200,000 and Palestinian per capita income declined by 20 to 25 percent. In addition, many Palestinians came to consider Arafat's administration corrupt and self-serving.

Nevertheless, the peace process inched along. In early 2000 Arafat, Israeli prime minister Ehud Barak, and U.S. president Bill Clinton met in Washington to negotiate a final peace agreement. The key Israeli proposal, strongly endorsed by President Clinton, offered self-rule in five different districts, each separated and surrounded by Israeli roads and territory but covering perhaps 90 percent of the West Bank. In the end, the Palestinians rejected this proposal. They wanted their own state—a sovereign and independent state—not one cut up into separate districts surrounded by Israel and under Israeli control.

The aftermath of the failed negotiations was an explosion of tit-for-tat violence beginning in September 2000 in Israel and in the West Bank and Gaza Strip. Palestinian

**Controlling Palestinian Movement** An Israeli soldier watches Palestinians passing through the Surda checkpoint near the West Bank city of Ramallah in 2002. Israel's military reoccupation of the West Bank since 2000 features severe restrictions on Palestinian travel between and within Palestinian towns and cities, in part to protect growing Israeli settlements in the occupied territories. *(Ammar Avad/Reuters NewMedia Inc./Corbis)*

militants resorted to suicide bombings directed at Israeli civilians, while the Israeli army bulldozed houses, assassinated alleged terrorist leaders, and devastated the Palestinian economy. The deadly suicide bombings infuriated the Israelis and alienated public opinion in the United States, the only country capable of influencing Israel. Lasting peace in the Middle East, which almost certainly can come only with a truly independent Palestinian state in the West Bank and Gaza Strip, appeared unlikely for the foreseeable future.

## Nationalism, Fundamentalism, and Competition

The recent history of the non-Arab states of Turkey and Iran and of the Arab state of Iraq (see Map 34.3) testifies to the diversity of national development in the Muslim world. That history also dramatically illustrates the intense competition between rival states and the growing strength of Islamic revival.

Turkey remained basically true to Atatürk's vision of a thoroughly modernized, secularized, Europeanized state (see pages 975–977). Islam continued to exert less influence in daily life and thought there than it did in other Middle Eastern countries. Turkey still looked toward the West, joining NATO in 1952 and eventually seeking full membership in the European Community (EU). In 2002, however, Turkey was not one of the ten eastern European countries scheduled to join the EU in 2004. Many Europeans questioned Turkey's dedication to the protection of human rights and feared that Turkish membership in the EU would result in a large inflow of unwanted Muslim immigrants.

After 1945 Iran tried again to follow Turkey's example, as it had before 1939 (see page 977). Once again its success was limited. The new shah—Muhammad Reza Pahlavi (r. 1941–1979), the son of Reza Shah Pahlavi—angered Iranian nationalists by courting Western powers and Western oil companies in the course of freeing his country from Soviet influence after the Second World War. In 1953, after leading the effort to nationalize the British-owned Anglo-Iranian Oil Company, the Iranian Majlis and the fiery prime minister Muhammad Mossaddeq forced the shah to flee to Europe. But Mossaddeq's victory was short-lived. Loyal army officers, with the help of the American CIA, quickly restored the shah to his throne.

The shah set out to build a powerful modern nation to ensure his rule. Iran's gigantic oil revenues provided the necessary cash. The shah undermined the power bases of the traditional politicians—large landowners and religious leaders—by means of land reform, secular education, and increased power for the central government. Modernization surged forward, but at the price of ancient values, widespread corruption, and harsh dictatorship. The result was a violent reaction against modernization and secular values: an Islamic revolution in 1978 that aimed at infusing strict Islamic principles into all aspects of personal and public life. Led by religious leaders grouped around the spellbinding Ayatollah Ruholla Khomeini, the fundamentalists deposed the shah and tried to build their vision of a true Islamic state.

Iran's Islamic republic frightened its neighbors. Iraq, especially, feared that Iran—a nation of Shi'ite Muslims—would succeed in getting Iraq's Shi'ite majority to revolt against its Sunni leaders. Thus in September 1980 Iraq's strongman, Saddam Hussein (b. 1937), launched a surprise attack, expecting his well-equipped armies to defeat an increasingly chaotic Iran. Instead, Iraqi aggression galvanized the Iranian revolutionaries in a fanatical determination to defend their homeland and punish Iraq's leader. With their enormous oil revenues and military machines, Iranians and Iraqis—Persians and Arabs—clashed in one of the bloodiest wars in modern times, a savage eight-year conflict that killed hundreds of thousands of soldiers before finally grinding to a halt in 1988.

Emerging from the eight-year war with a big, tough army equipped by Western countries and the Soviet bloc, Saddam Hussein set out to make himself the leader of the entire Arab world. Eyeing the great oil wealth of his tiny southern neighbor, he suddenly ordered his forces to overrun Kuwait in August 1990, and he proclaimed its annexation to Iraq. To Saddam's surprise, his aggression brought a vigorous international response (see page 1083).

In early 1991 his troops were chased out of Kuwait by an American-led, United Nations–sanctioned military coalition. American troops, accompanied by small British, French, and Italian forces, were joined in ground operations against Iraq by some Arab forces from Egypt, Syria, and Saudi Arabia. Thus the Arab peoples, long wracked by bitter rivalries between nation-building states, came to fight a kind of bloody civil war.

Iraq and Iran went in different directions in the 1990s. The United Nations Security Council imposed stringent economic sanctions on Iraq as soon as it invaded Kuwait, and these sanctions were maintained after the Gulf War to force Iraq to destroy its weapons of mass destruction. United Nations inspectors destroyed many such weapons, but the United States charged Iraq with deceit and ongoing weapons development. In December 1998 President Bill Clinton ordered a large-scale bombing campaign of suspected weapons sites, paving the way for the

**Supporting Iran's Reform Movement** Defying threats by the supreme leader of an army crackdown, thousands of students mobilized repeatedly at Teheran University in November 2002 in defense of a popular reform-minded professor sentenced to death for blasphemy. The sentence was later overturned. Iranian women participate actively in politics and the public sphere. *(AFP/Corbis)*

American-led invasion of Iraq in 2003 (see page 1091). Throughout this period the United Nations' economic sanctions caused enormous suffering for the Iraqi people.

As secular Iraq spiraled downward toward collapse and foreign occupation, Iran unexpectedly backed away from fundamentalism. Following the constitution established by the Ayatollah Khomeini, executive power in Iran was divided between a supreme leader elected by leading Islamic clerics and a president and parliament elected by universal male and female suffrage. After 1990 the supreme leader remained a very conservative religious leader, but a growing reform movement pressed for a relaxation of strict Islamic decrees and elected a winsome moderate as president in 1997 and again in 2001. The supreme leader, controlling the army and the courts, vetoed many reform measures and jailed some of his most vocal opponents. But a large majority, led by Iran's youth, continued to press for less religious dogma in everyday life and achieved considerable practical success. One Iranian reform journalist summed up the Iranian experience: "Fundamentalism is good for protest, good for revolution, and good for war, but not so good for development. No country can organize its society on fundamentalism."[5]

## Algeria and Civil War

The important North African country of Algeria also highlighted the development of nationalism and then fundamentalism. Nationalism in the French colony of Algeria was emboldened by Nasser's great triumph in Egypt—and by the defeat of the French in Indochina. But Algeria's large European population was determined to keep Algeria part of France, and the Algerian war for independence was long, bitter, and bloody. Finally, in 1962, Algeria became an independent Arab state. The European population quickly fled.

The victorious anticolonial movement, known as the **National Liberation Front,** or FLN, used the revenues of Algeria's nationalized oil fields to promote state-owned industries, urban growth, and technical education. But the FLN also imposed a one-party state, which crushed dissent and favored a self-serving party elite. In the 1980s increasing numbers of dissatisfied Algerians looked toward Islam for moral and social revival, and in the early 1990s the Islamic opposition swept municipal and national elections. The FLN called on the army to preserve its power, claiming that the fundamentalists would "hijack" democracy and create an Islamic dictatorship. Military rule then led to growing violence and armed struggle between the government and the radical minority in the fundamentalist opposition. The ruthless civil war in Algeria placed in bold relief the cultural and ideological divisions simmering just below the surface in the Muslim world.

## IMPERIALISM AND NATIONALISM IN BLACK AFRICA

Most of sub-Saharan Africa won political independence fairly rapidly after the Second World War. Only Portugal's colonies and white-dominated southern Africa remained beyond the reach of African nationalists by 1964. The rise of independent states in black Africa—a major development in world history—resulted directly from both a reaction against Western imperialism and the growth of African nationalism.

### The Growth of African Nationalism

Western intrusion was the critical factor in the development of African nationalism, as it had been in Asia and the Middle East. But two things were different about Africa. First, because the imperial system and Western education did not solidify in Africa until after 1900 (see pages 853–855), national movements began to come of age only in the 1920s and reached maturity after 1945. Second, Africa's multiplicity of ethnic groups, coupled with imperial boundaries that often bore no resemblance to existing ethnic boundaries, greatly complicated the development of political—as distinct from cultural—nationalism. Was a modern national state to be based on ethnic tribal loyalties (as it had been in France and Germany, in China and Japan)? Was it to be founded on an all-African union of all black peoples? Or would such a state have to be built on the multitribal territories arbitrarily carved out by competing European empires? Only after 1945 did a tentative answer emerge.

A few educated West Africans in British colonies had articulated a kind of black nationalism before 1914. But the first real impetus came from the United States and the British West Indies. American blacks struggling for racial justice took a keen interest in their African origins, and their influence on educated Africans was great.

Of the many persons who participated in this "black nationalism" and in the "Renaissance" of American black literature in the 1920s, the most renowned was W. E. B. Du Bois (1868–1963). The first black to receive a Ph.D. from Harvard, this brilliant writer and historian organized Pan-African congresses in Paris during the Versailles Peace Conference and in Brussels in 1921. The goals of **Pan-Africanists** were solidarity among blacks everywhere and, eventually, a vast self-governing union of all African peoples.

Many educated French and British Africans experienced a strong surge of pride and cultural nationalism in the 1920s, inspired in part by American and West Indian blacks. African students and white intellectuals in Europe marveled at the accomplishments of American blacks in music, art, literature, history, and anthropology.

African intellectuals in Europe formulated and articulated the rich idea of *négritude,* or blackness: racial pride, self-confidence, and joy in black creativity and the black spirit. The powerful cultural nationalism that grew out of the cross-fertilization of African intellectuals and blacks from the United States and the West Indies was an unexpected byproduct of European imperialism.

Black consciousness also emerged in the British colonies in the 1920s, especially in West Africa. The westernized elite pressed for more equal access to government jobs, modest steps toward self-government, and an end to humiliating discrimination. This elite began to claim the right to speak for ordinary Africans and to denounce the government-supported chiefs as "Uncle Toms." Yet the great majority of well-educated British and French Africans remained moderate in their demands.

The Great Depression was the decisive turning point in the development of African nationalism. For the first time unemployment was widespread among educated Africans. Hostility toward well-paid white officials rose sharply. The Western-educated elite became more vocal, and some real radicals appeared.

In the towns educated Africans supplied the leadership for many new organizations, including political parties, trade unions, Christian churches, and agricultural cooperatives. Radical journalists published uncompromising attacks on colonial governments in easy-to-read mass-circulation newspapers.

The Great Depression also produced extreme hardship and profound discontent among the African masses. African peasants and small business people who had been drawn into world trade, and who sometimes profited from booms, felt the agony of the decade-long bust, as did urban workers. In some areas the result was unprecedented mass protest. The Gold Coast **cocoa holdups** of 1930–1931 and 1937–1938 are the most famous examples.

Cocoa completely dominated the Gold Coast's economy. As prices plummeted after 1929, cocoa farmers refused to sell their beans to the large British firms that

## NATIONALISM IN BLACK AFRICA

| | |
|---|---|
| 1919 | Du Bois organizes first Pan-African congress |
| 1920s | Cultural nationalism grows among Africa's educated elites |
| 1929 | Great Depression brings economic hardship and discontent |
| 1930–1931 | Farmers in the Gold Coast organize first "cocoa holdups" |
| 1939–1945 | World War II accelerates political and economic change |
| 1951 | Nkrumah and Convention People's party win national elections in Ghana |
| 1957 | Nkrumah leads Ghana—former Gold Coast—to independence |
| 1958 | De Gaulle offers commonwealth status to France's African territories<br>Guinea alone chooses independence |
| 1960 | Nigeria becomes an independent state |
| 1966 | Ghana's Nkrumah deposed in military coup |
| 1967 | Ibos secede from Nigeria to form state of Biafra |
| 1979 | Nigeria's military rulers permit elected civilian government |
| 1980 | Blacks rule Zimbabwe—formerly Southern Rhodesia—after long civil war with white settlers |
| 1984 | South Africa's whites maintain racial segregation and discrimination |
| 1989–1990 | South African government begins process of reform<br>Black leader Nelson Mandela freed from prison |
| 1994 | Mandela elected president of South Africa |

fixed prices and monopolized the export trade. Instead, the farmers organized cooperatives to cut back production and sell their crops directly to European and American chocolate manufacturers. The cocoa holdups succeeded in mobilizing much of the population against the foreign companies, and it demonstrated that mass organization and mass protest had come to advanced West Africa. Powerful mass movements for national independence would not be far behind.

## Achieving Independence with New Leaders

The repercussions of the Second World War in black Africa greatly accelerated the changes begun in the 1930s. Mines and plantations strained to meet wartime demands. Towns mushroomed into cities, whose tin-can housing, inflation, and shortages of consumer goods created discontent and hardship. Many African soldiers who served in India were powerfully impressed by Indian nationalism.

The attitudes of Western imperialists also changed. Both the British and the French acknowledged the need for rapid social and economic improvement in their colonies; both began sending money and aid on a large scale for the first time. The principle of self-government was written into the United Nations charter and was supported by Great Britain's postwar Labour government. Thus the key question for Great Britain's various African colonies was their rate of progress toward self-government. The British and the French were in no rush. But a new breed of African leader was emerging. Impatient and insistent, these spokesmen for modern African nationalism were remarkably successful: by 1964 almost all of western, eastern, and central Africa had achieved statehood, usually without much bloodshed.

These new postwar African leaders formed an elite by virtue of advanced European or American education, and they were profoundly influenced by Western thought. But compared with the interwar generation of educated Africans, they were more radical and humbler in social origin. Among them were former schoolteachers, union leaders, government clerks, and unemployed students, as well as lawyers and prizewinning poets.

Postwar African leaders accepted prevailing colonial boundaries to avoid border disputes and achieve freedom as soon as possible. Sometimes tribal chiefs became their worst political enemies. Skillfully, the new leaders channeled postwar hope and discontent into support for mass political organizations. These organizations staged gigantic protests and became political parties. Eventually they came to power by winning the general elections that the colonial governments belatedly called to choose their successors.

## Ghana Shows the Way

Perhaps the most charismatic of this generation of African leaders was Kwame Nkrumah (1909–1972). Under his leadership the Gold Coast—which he rechristened "Ghana"—became the first independent African state to emerge from colonialism. Having begun his career as a schoolteacher in the Gold Coast, Nkrumah spent ten years studying in the United States, where he was deeply influenced by European socialists and by the Jamaican-born black leader Marcus Garvey (1887–1940). Nkrumah returned to the Gold Coast immediately after the Second World War and entered politics.

**The Opening of Parliament in Ghana** As part of an ancient ritual, two medicine men pour out sacred oil and call on the gods to bless the work of the Second Parliament and President Kwame Nkrumah, standing on the right. The combination of time-honored customs and modern political institutions was characteristic of African states after they secured independence. *(Wide World Photos)*

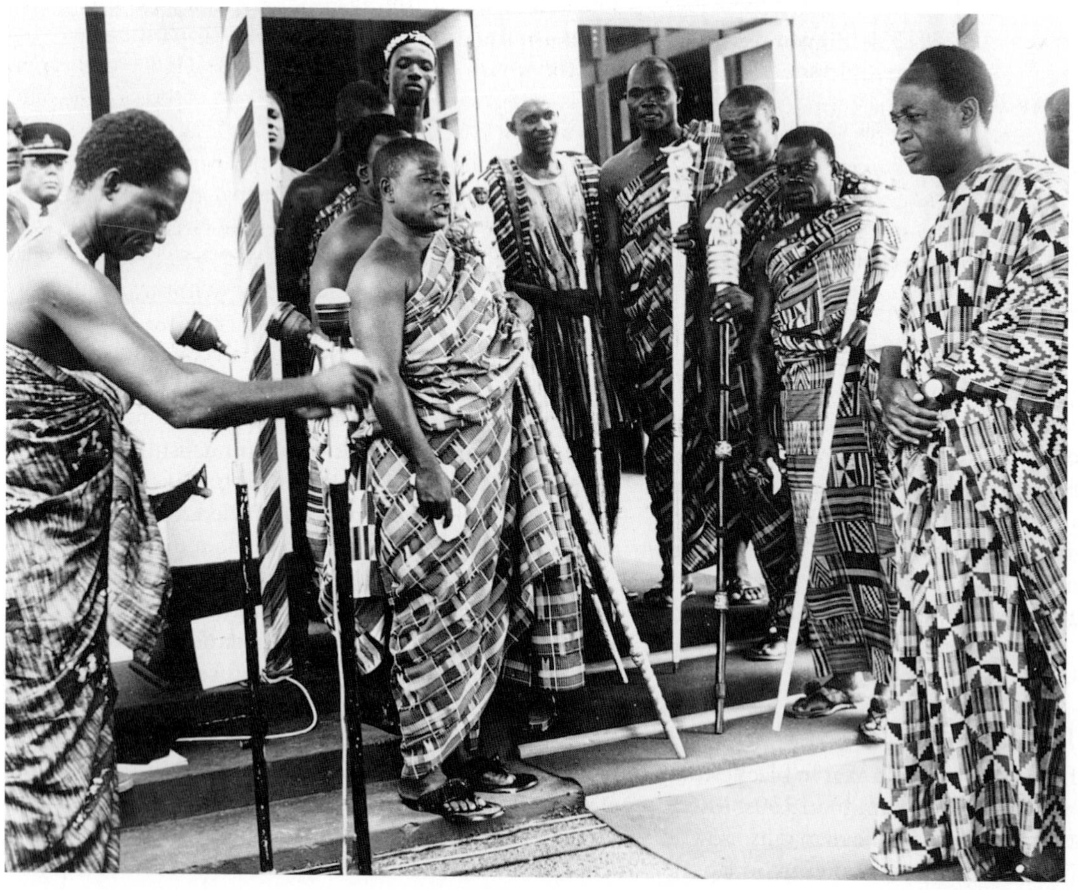

The time was ripe. Economic discontent erupted in rioting in February 1948; angry crowds looted European and Lebanese stores. The British, embarking on their new course, established a new constitution, which gave more power to Africans within the framework of (eventual) parliamentary democracy. Meanwhile, Nkrumah was building a radical mass party appealing particularly to modern elements—former servicemen, market women, union members, urban toughs, and cocoa farmers. He and his party injected the joy and enthusiasm of religious revivals into their rallies and propaganda: "Self-Government Now" was their credo, secular salvation the promise.

Rejecting halfway measures—"We prefer self-government with danger to servitude in tranquillity"—Nkrumah and his Convention People's party staged strikes and riots. Arrested, the "Deliverer of Ghana" campaigned from jail and saw his party win a smashing victory in the national elections of 1951. Called from prison to head the transitional government, Nkrumah and his nationalist party defeated both westernized moderates and more traditional "tribal" rivals in free elections. By 1957 Nkrumah had achieved worldwide fame and influence as Ghana became the first African state to emerge from colonial control.

After Ghana's breakthrough, independence for other African colonies followed rapidly. As in Algeria, the main problem was the permanent white settlers, as distinguished from the colonial officials. Wherever white settlers were at all numerous, as in Kenya, they sought to preserve their privileged position. But only in Southern Rhodesia were whites numerous enough to prevail for long. Southern Rhodesian whites declared independence illegally in 1965 and held out until 1980, when black nationalists won a long guerrilla war and renamed the country Zimbabwe.

### French-Speaking Regions

Decolonization took a somewhat different course in French-speaking Africa. France tried hard to hold on to Indochina and Algeria after 1945. Thus although France upped its aid to its African colonies, independence remained a dirty word until de Gaulle came to power in 1958. Seeking to head off radical nationalists, and receiving the crucial support of moderate black leaders, de Gaulle chose a divide-and-rule strategy. He divided the federations of French West Africa and French Equatorial Africa into thirteen separate governments, thus creating a "French commonwealth." Plebiscites were called in each territory to ratify the new arrangement. An affirmative vote meant continued ties with France; a negative vote signified immediate independence and a complete break with France.

De Gaulle's gamble was shrewd. The educated black elite—as personified by the influential poet-politician Léopold Sédar Senghor, who now led the government of Senegal (see the feature "Individuals in Society: Léopold Sédar Senghor, Poet and Statesman")—loved France and dreaded a sudden divorce. They also wanted French aid to continue. France, in keeping with its ideology of assimilation, had given the vote to the educated elite in its colonies after the Second World War, and about forty Africans held seats in the French parliament after 1946. For both cultural and practical reasons, therefore, French Africa's leaders tended to be moderate and in no rush for independence.

Yet political nationalism was not totally submerged. In Guinea a young radical named Sekou Touré (1922–1984) led his people in overwhelming rejection of the new constitution in 1958. Inspired by Ghana's Nkrumah, Touré laid it out to de Gaulle, face-to-face: "We have to tell you bluntly, Mr. President, what the demands of the people are. . . . We have one prime and essential need: our dignity. But there is no dignity without freedom. . . . We prefer freedom in poverty to opulence in slavery."[6] After some hesitation the leaders of the other French territories followed suit, though the new states retained close ties with France.

Belgium tried belatedly to imitate de Gaulle in its enormous Congo colony, but without success. Long-time practitioners of paternalism coupled with harsh, selfish rule, the Belgians had discouraged the development of an educated elite. In 1959, therefore, when after wild riots they suddenly decided to grant independence, the fabric of government simply broke down. Independence was soon followed by violent ethnic conflict, civil war, and foreign intervention. The Belgian Congo was the great exception to black Africa's generally peaceful and successful transition to independence between 1957 and 1964.

## SUB-SAHARAN AFRICA SINCE 1960

The facility with which most of black Africa achieved independence stimulated buoyant optimism in the early 1960s. As Europeans congratulated themselves on having fulfilled their "civilizing mission," Africans anticipated even more rapid progress. But in the course of a generation the outlook changed. In most former colonies democratic government and civil liberties gave way to one-party rule or military dictatorship. In many countries it became common for the winners in a political power struggle to imprison, exile, or murder the losers. Corruption was widespread.

The rise of authoritarian government in Africa after independence must be viewed in historical perspective. Representative institutions on the eve of independence were an imperial afterthought, and the new African countries faced tremendous challenges. Above all, ethnic divisions threatened civil conflicts that could tear the fragile states apart. Yet this did not happen. Strong leaders used nationalism, first harnessed to throw off foreign rule, to build one-party regimes and promote unity. Unfortunately, nation building by idealistic authoritarians often deteriorated into brutal dictatorships, frequent military coups, and civil strife. Then, in the early 1990s, a powerful reaction to this decline resulted in a surge of democratic protest, which achieved major political gains and rekindled in part the optimism of the independence era.

## Striving for National Unity

The common legacy of imperialism in Africa resulted in certain basic patterns and problems. The legacy of imperialism in Africa was not all bad. One positive outcome was the creation of about forty well-defined states (see Map 34.2). These new states inherited functioning bureaucracies, some elected political leaders, and some modern infrastructure—that is, transportation, schools, hospitals, and the like.

The new African states inherited relatively modern, diversified social structures. Traditional tribal and religious rulers had generally lost out to a dynamic westernized elite whose moderate and radical wings faithfully reproduced the twentieth-century political spectrum. Each new state had the beginnings of an industrial working class and a volatile urban poor. Each country inherited the cornerstone of imperial power—a tough, well-equipped army to maintain order.

Other features of the imperialist legacy served to torment independent Africa. The disruption of traditional life had caused real suffering and resulted in postindependence expectations that could not be met. The prevailing export economies were weak, lopsided, and concentrated in foreign hands. Technical, managerial, and medical skills were in acutely short supply. Above all, the legacy of political boundaries imposed by foreigners without regard to ethnic and cultural groupings weighed heavily on postindependence Africa. Almost all of the new states encompassed a variety of peoples, and these peoples might easily develop conflicting national aspirations.

Great Britain and France had granted their African colonies democratic government as they prepared to depart. Yet belated, Western-style democracy served the new multiethnic states poorly. After freedom from imperialism no longer provided a unifying common objective, political parties often coalesced along regional and ethnic lines. Open political competition often encouraged regional and ethnic conflict, complicated nation building, and promoted political crisis. Many African leaders concluded that democracy threatened to destroy the existing states, which they deemed essential for social and economic progress. Thus these leaders maintained the authoritarian tradition they inherited from the imperialists. They imposed tough measures to hold their countries together, and free elections often gave way to dictators and one-party rule.

After Ghana won its independence, for instance, Nkrumah jailed without trial his main opponents—chiefs, lawyers, and intellectuals—and outlawed opposition parties. Embracing the authoritarian model, Nkrumah worked to build a "revolutionary" one-party state and a socialist economy. By the mid-1960s Nkrumah's grandiose economic projects had almost bankrupted Ghana, and in 1966 the army suddenly seized power while Nkrumah was visiting China. Across the continent in East Africa, Kenya and Tanzania likewise became one-party socialist states with strong leaders.

The French-speaking countries also shifted toward one-party government to promote state unity and develop distinctive characteristics that could serve as the basis for statewide nationalism. Mali followed Guinea into Marxist radicalism. Senegal and the Ivory Coast stressed moderation and close economic and cultural ties with France.

Like Nkrumah, many of the politicians at the helm of one-party states were eventually overthrown by military leaders. The rise of would-be Napoleons was lamented by many Western liberals and African intellectuals, who often failed to note that military rule was also widespread in Latin America, Asia, and the Near East in the 1970s and 1980s.

As elsewhere, military rule in Africa was authoritarian and undemocratic. Sometimes it placed a terrible burden on Africans. In Uganda, for instance, Idi Amin (b. 1925?), a brutal former sergeant, seized power in 1971, packed the army with his tribal supporters, and terrorized the population for a decade. Yet military leaders generally did manage to hold their countries together, and they worked to build viable states. Many military regimes, like their counterparts in Latin America (see pages 1085–1087), were committed to social and economic modernization. Drawing on an educated and motivated elite, they sometimes accomplished a good deal.

African military leaders often claimed that their ultimate goal was free, representative civilian government, which they would restore after surmounting a grave national crisis. They also claimed that they would purge

# INDIVIDUALS IN SOCIETY

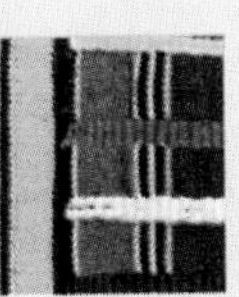

## LÉOPOLD SÉDAR SENGHOR, POET AND STATESMAN

*President Léopold Sédar Senghor in 1965.* (Hulton Archive/Getty Images)

Of all the modern leaders in French-speaking Africa, Léopold Sédar Senghor (1906–2001) was the most famous and the most intriguing. His early years in a dusty village in southern Senegal were happy and varied. Later, in cold and lonely Paris, he would feast on memories of this "kingdom of childhood." Senghor's father, a successful peanut merchant, lived in the port city of Joal and had two dozen children and several wives. His last wife, Senghor's mother, remained in her village, where her extended family taught the boy the legends and mysteries of his people. In a famous poem, Senghor later wrote that his mother's brother, Uncle Waly the shepherd, could hear "what is beyond hearing," and that he lovingly explained to the wondering child "the signs that the Ancestors give in the calm seas of the constellations."*

Islam is Senegal's majority religion and the Wolof its dominant ethnic group. But Senghor's family was staunchly Christian and of the Serer people, and when Sédar was seven, his practical father sent him to a French mission school near Joal. Learning French and Wolof, Senghor made rapid progress. When he was seventeen, his teachers sent him on to the colonial capital of Dakar, where he became the top student in the predominately white lycée. In 1928 he received a rare scholarship for advanced study in Paris. Working hard in elite schools and settling on a university career, Senghor became the first African to win the equivalent of a Ph.D. He then took a position as a classics teacher in a lycée near Paris. It was an extraordinary achievement.

Senghor's chance to pursue advanced education reflected French colonial policy in Africa. The French believed that most Africans deserved only a little practical schooling, but they also wanted to create a tiny elite of "black Frenchmen." This elite would link the French rulers and the African masses, who would need permanent French guidance. In the 1930s the brilliant Senghor seemed a model of elitist assimilation.

In fact, however, Senghor was experiencing a severe identity crisis. Who was he? How could he reconcile his complex African heritage with his French education and culture? Making close friends with other black intellectuals in Paris and strongly influenced by African American music and literature, Senghor concluded that he would never be a "black Frenchman," for in European eyes the most accomplished African always remained exotic and inferior. He then found a new identity in racial pride and the idea of *négritude,* or blackness (see page 1122). Yet Senghor did not repudiate Europe. Instead, he reconciled his identity crisis—his being torn "between the call of the Ancestors and the call of Europe"—by striving to hold his "two sides" in equilibrium and "peaceful accord." He advocated "cross-fertilization" for Africa and Europe, which, he believed, would benefit both continents.†

Serving in the French army in World War II and turning to politics after 1945, Senghor was elected Senegal's deputy to the French National Assembly. Idolized in Senegal, he joined with other African deputies to press for greater autonomy, as well as for harmony between France and Africa. He led Senegal into Charles de Gaulle's "French commonwealth" in 1958 and then on to independence in 1960. All the major political parties in Senegal were merged to form a one-party government, with Senghor as president. Wisely avoiding dictatorship, ethnic conflict, and military rule, he led Senegal until 1980, when he retired voluntarily. Lionized in France as a great poet and statesman, Senghor was increasingly criticized by some young Senegalese, who grumbled that the aging leader had become too cooperative with France—a real "black Frenchman."

### QUESTIONS FOR ANALYSIS

1. What cultural and intellectual forces influenced Senghor's development? Why did he have difficulty reconciling these influences?
2. How did Senghor fit into the whole process of decolonization and African independence?

*Quoted in J. Vaillant, *Black, French, and African: A Life of Léopold Sédar Senghor* (Cambridge: Harvard University Press, 1990), p. 18.

† Ibid., p. 146.

widespread civilian corruption, a promise often warmly welcomed by dissatisfied citizens. Yet the purification of public life and the restoration of elected government became increasingly rare. As economic and social conditions stagnated and often declined in African countries from the mid-1970s to the early 1990s (see Chapter 35), army leaders became more and more greedy and dishonest. By the late 1980s military rule and one-party authoritarian regimes had reached a dead end in Africa.

## Nigeria, Africa's Giant

The history of Nigeria illustrates just how difficult genuine nation building could be after independence was achieved. "Nigeria" was a name coined by the British to designate their nineteenth-century conquests in the Niger River basin, which encompassed many ancient kingdoms and hundreds of ethnic groups. In addition, for administrative convenience, the British consolidated the northern Muslim territories and the southern Christian or animist areas. Despite this diverse population, by 1945 Nigeria had spawned a powerful independence movement, and in the early postwar era Nigeria entered into a period of intense but peaceful negotiation. In 1954 the third constitution in seven years set up the framework within which independence was achieved in 1960.

The key constitutional question was the relationship between the central government and the various regions. Ultimately Nigeria adopted a federal system, whereby the national government at Lagos shared power with three regional or state governments in the north, west, and east. Each region had a dominant tribe and a corresponding political party. The parties were expected to cooperate in the national parliament, and the rights of minorities were protected by law.

After independence Nigerians' bright hopes gradually dimmed because of growing ethnic rivalries. In 1964 minorities in the Western Region began forming their own region in order to escape Yoruba domination, and tribal battles erupted. At this point a group of young army officers seized power and executed the leading politicians in an attempt to end the crisis and preserve the nation.

At first the young officers were popular, but many of them were Ibos. The Muslim northerners had long distrusted the hard-working, clannish, non-Muslim Ibos. When the Ibo-led military council proclaimed a centralized dictatorship, wild mobs in northern cities massacred thousands of Ibos, and the panic-stricken survivors fled. When a group of northern officers then seized the national government in a countercoup, the traumatized Ibos revolted and proclaimed the independent state of Biafra in 1967.

The war in Biafra lasted three years. The Ibos fought with heroic determination, believing that political independence was their only refuge from genocide. Heavily outnumbered, the Ibos were gradually surrounded.

**Mobilizing in Biafra** A Biafran officer, himself only nine years old, drills a column of fresh recruits in 1969 during the Nigerian civil war. The boy soldiers were used for spying and sabotage, as Biafra struggled desperately against encirclement and starvation in its fight for independence. *(Hachette Filipachi)*

Perhaps millions starved to death as Biafra became a symbol of monumental human tragedy.

The bloody civil war in Nigeria showed the world that Africa's "artificial" boundaries and states were remarkably durable. Having preserved the state in the 1960s, Nigeria's military rulers focused on building a nation in the 1970s. Although the federal government held the real power, the country was divided into nineteen small, manageable units to handle local and cultural matters. The defeated Ibos were pardoned, and Iboland was rebuilt with federal oil revenues, as Nigeria became the world's seventh largest oil producer.

In 1979 Nigeria's army leaders returned power to an elected civilian government, but four years later the army again seized control. Combinations of Hausa-Fulani Muslim army officers then ruled until 1998, when the brutal military dictator General Sani Abacha suddenly died and gave Nigeria renewed hope for unity and democracy. In 1999 Nigerians voted in free elections and re-established civilian rule, as "Africa's giant" joined the trend toward greater political freedom in Africa.

## The Struggle in Southern Africa

After the great rush toward political independence in the early 1960s, decolonization stalled. Southern Africa remained under white minority rule, largely because of the numerical strength and determination of its white settlers. In Portuguese Angola and Mozambique, the white population actually increased from 70,000 to 380,000 between 1940 and the mid-1960s, as white settlers using forced native labor established large coffee farms.

As economic exploitation grew, so did resentment. Nationalist liberation movements arose to wage unrelenting guerrilla warfare. After a coup overturned the long-established dictatorship in Portugal, African guerrillas managed to take control in Angola and Mozambique in 1975. Shortly thereafter a coalition of nationalist groups also won in Zimbabwe after a long struggle.

The battle in South Africa threatened to be still worse. The racial conflict in the white-ruled Republic of South Africa could be traced back in part to the outcome of the South African War (see page 853). Although the British finally conquered the inland Afrikaner republics, they had to compromise to avoid a long guerrilla war. Specifically, the British agreed to grant all of South Africa self-government as soon as possible and to let its government decide which nonwhites, if any, should vote. It was to be a tragic compromise.

Defeated on the battlefield, the embittered Afrikaners elaborated a potently racist nationalism. Between 1910—when South Africa became basically a self-governing dominion, like Canada and Australia—and 1948 the Afrikaners gradually won political power from their English-speaking settler rivals. After their decisive electoral victory in 1948, Afrikaner nationalists spoke increasingly for a large majority of South African whites, who supported the political leadership with varying degrees of enthusiasm.

The goals of Afrikaner nationalism in the twentieth century were remarkably consistent: white supremacy and racial segregation. In 1913 the new South African legislature passed the **Native Land Act,** which limited black ownership of land to native reserves encompassing a mere one-seventh of the country. Poor, overpopulated, and too small to feed themselves, the native reserves in the countryside served as a pool of cheap, temporary black labor for white farms, gold mines, and urban factories. A black worker—typically a young single person—could leave the reserve only with special permission. In the eyes of the law he or she was only a temporary migrant who could be returned at will by the employer or the government. The native reserves system, combining racial segregation and indirect forced labor, formed the foundation of white supremacy in South Africa.

After 1948 successive Afrikaner governments wove the somewhat haphazard early racist measures into an authoritarian fabric of racial discrimination and inequality. This system was officially known as **apartheid,** meaning "separation" or "segregation." The population was divided into four legally unequal racial groups: whites, blacks, Asians, and racially mixed "coloureds." Although Afrikaner propagandists claimed to serve the interests of all racial groups by preserving separate cultures and racial purity, most observers saw apartheid as a way of maintaining the lavish privileges of the white minority, which accounted for only one-sixth of the total population.

After 1940 South Africa's cities grew rapidly in conjunction with its emergence as the most highly industrialized country in Africa. Urbanization changed the face of the country, but good jobs in the cities were reserved for whites. Whites lived in luxurious modern central cities. Blacks, legally classified as temporary migrants, were restricted to outlying black townships plagued by poverty, crime, and white policemen. In spite of segregation, the growing cities produced a vibrant urban black culture, largely distinct from that of the tribal reserves.

South Africa's harsh white supremacy elicited many black nationalist protests from the 1920s onward. By the 1950s blacks—and their coloured, white, and Asian allies—were staging large-scale peaceful protests. A high point came in 1960, when police at Sharpeville fired into a crowd of demonstrators and killed sixty-nine blacks.

**Men of Destiny** Nelson Mandela shakes hands with Frederik de Klerk following a televised presidential debate in the 1994 electoral campaign. Mandela won and replaced de Klerk as president of South Africa after 350 years of white supremacy. De Klerk became vice president. Both leaders vowed to build a multiracial democratic society. *(Mark Peters/Sipa Press)*

The main black nationalist organization—the **African National Congress (ANC)**—was outlawed but sent some of its leaders abroad to establish new headquarters. Other members, led by a young black lawyer named Nelson Mandela (b. 1918), stayed in South Africa to set up an underground army to oppose the government. Captured after seventeen months, Mandela was tried for treason and sentenced to life imprisonment. (See the feature "Listening to the Past: The Struggle for Freedom in South Africa" on pages 1134–1135.)

By the late 1970s the white government had apparently destroyed the moderate black opposition within South Africa. Operating out of the sympathetic black states of Zimbabwe and Mozambique to the north, the militant ANC turned increasingly to armed struggle. South Africa struck back hard and forced its neighbors to curtail the ANC's guerrilla activities. Fortified by these successes, South Africa's white leaders launched in 1984 a program of cosmetic "reforms." For the first time, the 3 million coloureds and the 1 million South Africans of Asian descent were granted limited parliamentary representation. But no provision was made for any representation of the country's 22 million blacks, and laws controlling black movement and settlement were maintained.

The government's self-serving reforms provoked black indignation and triggered a massive reaction. In the segregated townships young black militants took to the streets, attacking in particular black civil servants and policemen as agents of white oppression. Heavily armed white security forces clashed repeatedly with black protesters, who turned funerals for fallen comrades into mass demonstrations. Between 1985 and 1989 five thousand died and fifty thousand were jailed without charges because of the political unrest.

By 1989 the white government and the black opposition had reached an impasse. Black protesters had been bloodied but not beaten, and their movement for democracy had gathered worldwide support. The U.S. Congress had applied strong sanctions against South Africa in October 1986, and the Common Market had followed. The white government still held power, but harsh repression of black resistance had failed.

A major step toward breaking the political stalemate came in September 1989 with the election of a new state president, Frederik W. de Klerk, an Afrikaner lawyer and politician. A late-blooming reformer, de Klerk cautiously opened a dialogue with ANC leaders. Negotiating with Nelson Mandela, whose reputation had soared among urban blacks during his long years in prison, de Klerk lifted the state of emergency in most of the country, legalized the ANC, and freed Mandela in February 1990. Emerging from prison as a proud and impressive leader, Mandela courageously suspended the ANC's armed struggle and thereby met de Klerk's condition for serious talks on South Africa's political future. Negotiations were long and difficult, but Mandela and de Klerk persevered. They reached an agreement calling for universal suffrage, which meant black majority rule. They also guaranteed the civil and economic rights of minorities, including job security for white government workers.

Elected president of South Africa by an overwhelming majority in May 1994, Mandela told his jubilant supporters of his "deep pride and joy—pride in the ordinary, humble people of this country. . . . And joy that we can loudly proclaim from the roof tops—free at last!"[7] Heading the new "government of national unity," which included de Klerk as vice president, Mandela and the peoples of South Africa set about building a democratic, multiracial nation. The new constitution guaranteed that all political parties would have some legislative seats until 1998.

Black majority rule under Mandela and his successors worked remarkably well. In an imaginative attempt to heal the wounds of apartheid, the government established the Truth and Reconciliation Commission. This commission let black victims speak out and share their suffering, and it also offered white perpetrators amnesty from prosecution in return for fully confessing their crimes. Mandela's ministers repudiated their earlier socialist beliefs and accepted realistically the liberal order of global capitalism as the only way to develop the economy and reduce widespread black poverty. Social and economic problems persisted in South Africa, but the country's peaceful transition to majority rule was an inspiring achievement.

## Political Reform Since 1990

The triumph of democratic rule in South Africa was part of a broad trend toward elected civilian government that swept through sub-Saharan Africa after 1990. Beginning in late 1989 in the small French-speaking state of Benin, political protesters rose up and forced one-party authoritarian regimes to grant liberalizing reforms and call national conferences, which often led to competitive elections and new constitutions. These changes occurred in almost all African countries, and, in the words of two leading scholars, "they amounted to the most far-reaching shifts in African political life since the political independence of thirty years earlier."[8]

Many factors contributed to this historic watershed. The anticommunist revolutions of 1989 in eastern Europe were extremely important. They showed Africans that even the most well-entrenched one-party regimes—regimes that had often inspired Africa's own authoritarians—could be opposed, punished for prolonged misrule, and replaced with electoral competition and even democracy. The decline of military rule in Latin America and the emerging global trend toward political and economic liberalism worked in the same direction.

The end of the cold war also transformed Africa's relations with Russia and the United States. Both superpowers had viewed Africa as an important cold war battleground, and both had given large-scale military and financial aid to their allies, as well as to "uncommitted" African leaders who could play one side against the other. The failure of reform communism in Europe brought an abrupt end to communist aid to its African clients, which left them weakened and much more willing to compromise with opposition movements.

American involvement in Africa also declined. During the cold war U.S. leaders had generally supported "pro-Western" African dictators, no matter how corrupt or repressive. This interventionist policy gave way to a less intense (and much cheaper) interest in free elections and civil rights in the 1990s. A striking example of this evolution was steadfast U.S. support for the "anticommunist" General Mobutu Sese Seko after he seized power in 1965 in Zaire (the former Belgian Congo, renamed the Democratic Republic of the Congo in 1997). Mobutu looted and impoverished his country for decades before the United States cut off its aid in the early 1990s, which helped an opposition group topple the dying tyrant in 1997.

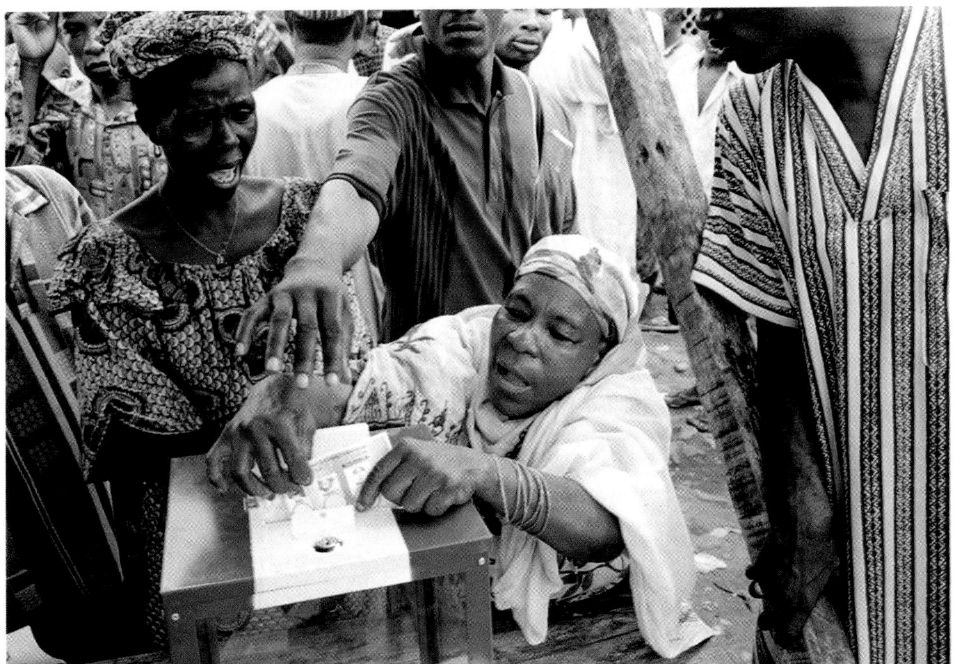

**The Presidential Election in Nigeria** In February 1999 tens of millions of Nigerians enthusiastically went to the polls in a free election, as civilian rule replaced military dictatorship in Africa's largest country. This tiny woman, a domestic servant in the capital city of Lagos, is making her voice heard. *(Ozier Muhammad/NYT Pictures)*

If events outside Africa established conditions favoring political reform, Africans themselves were the principal actors in the shift toward democracy. They demanded reform because long years of mismanagement and repression had delegitimized one-party rule. In many countries the nation-building claims of ruling parties and dictators rang increasingly hollow because a single ethnic group dominated the government, thereby promoting the resentment and the ethnic conflict the ruling group had promised to master. Protests also exploded because governments had failed to improve living conditions in the 1980s (see Chapter 35).

Above all, the strength of the democratic opposition rested on a growing class of educated urban Africans, for postindependence governments had enthusiastically expanded opportunities in education, especially higher education. In the typical West African state of Cameroon, the number of students graduating from the French-speaking national university jumped from a minuscule 213 in 1961 to 10,000 in 1982 and 41,000 in 1992.[9] The growing middle class of educated professionals chafed at the ostentatious privilege of tiny closed elites, and it pressed for political reforms that would democratize social and economic opportunities. Reacting primarily to the excesses of African governments after independence rather than to the legacy of European imperialism, the new leaders of the democratic movement were generally pragmatic, moderate, and open to new ideas.

As the twenty-first century opened, democratic reform in Africa was still in its early stages. Yet African governments were much less authoritarian than a decade earlier. Moreover, civil rights, public debate, and freedom of the press had all been strengthened. Real progress had been made, and a general return to one-party dictatorship appeared unlikely. Thus after 1990 sub-Saharan Africa participated fully in the global trend toward greater democracy and human rights.

## SUMMARY

Asian and African peoples experienced a remarkable resurgence after the Second World War, a resurgence that will almost certainly stand as a decisive turning point in world history. The long-developing nationalist movement in China culminated in a social revolution led by the Communists, who went on to pursue innovative and fiercely independent policies that redeemed China as a great power in world affairs. Japan—defeated, demilitarized, and democratized—took a completely different path to the rank of economic superpower in a no less spectacular renaissance. Elsewhere—in India, Indonesia, and the Philippines—Asian peoples won their freedom and self-confidently charted independent courses. The Muslim world was also rejuvenated, most notably under Nasser in Egypt. In black Africa a generation of nationalist leaders successfully guided colonial territories to self-rule by the middle of the 1960s.

The resurgence and political self-assertion of Asian and African peoples in revitalized or developing nation-states did not proceed without conflict. Serious regional and ethnic confrontations erupted, notably between Hindus and Muslims in India and between Arabs and Israelis in the Middle East, and similar conflicts continued after independence was won. The vestiges of Western colonialism and cold war struggles resulted in atypical but highly destructive conflicts in Algeria, Vietnam, and Zimbabwe. The revitalized peoples of Asia and Africa continued to face tremendous economic and social challenges, as the next chapter will show.

Gaining independence under strong nationalist leaders after 1945, Asian and African peoples joined in the late twentieth century in the worldwide movement toward liberal democracy. In Asia well-entrenched authoritarians, such as Marcos in the Philippines and Suharto in Indonesia, were driven from office, although the Chinese Communist party retained its monopoly of political power. In sub-Saharan Africa the movement toward multiparty electoral competition and greater civil rights achieved striking breakthroughs. Thus the whole world moved, fitfully but unmistakably, in the same political direction—eloquent testimony to the globalization of history as the third millennium began.

## KEY TERMS

Great Leap Forward
Cultural Revolution
Red Guards
Tiananmen Square
Muslim League
Palestine Liberation Organization
National Liberation Front
Pan-Africanists
cocoa holdups
Native Land Act
apartheid
African National Congress (ANC)

## NOTES

1. S. Schram, *Mao Tse-tung* (New York: Simon and Schuster, 1966), p. 151.
2. Quoted in P. B. Ebrey, ed., *Chinese Civilization and Society: A Source Book* (New York: Free Press, 1981), p. 393.

3. Quoted in W. Bingham, H. Conroy, and F. Iklé, *A History of Asia*, vol. 2, 2d ed. (Boston: Allyn and Bacon, 1974), p. 459.
4. Quoted in K. Bhata, *The Ordeal of Nationhood: A Social Study of India Since Independence, 1947–1970* (New York: Atheneum, 1971), p. 9.
5. Quoted in B. Baktiari and H. Vaziri, "Iran's Liberal Revolution?" *Current History*, January 2002, p. 21.
6. Quoted in R. Hallett, *Africa Since 1875: A Modern History* (Ann Arbor: University of Michigan Press, 1974), pp. 378–379.
7. *Chicago Tribune*, May 3, 1994, section 1, p. 5.
8. M. Bratton and N. van de Walle, *Democratic Experiments in Africa: Regime Transitions in Comparative Perspectives* (Cambridge: Cambridge University Press, 1997), p. 3.
9. D. Birmingham and P. Martin, eds., *History of Central Africa: The Contemporary Years Since 1960* (London: Routledge, 1998), p. 59.

## Suggested Reading

Many of the works mentioned in the Suggested Reading for Chapter 30 are also valuable for considering postwar developments in Asia and the Middle East. Two other important studies on developments in China are J. Wasserman, ed., *Twentieth Century China: New Approaches* (2002), and C. Johnson, *Peasant Nationalism and Communist Power: The Emergence of Revolutionary China, 1937–1945* (1962). M. Meisner, *Mao's China: A History of the People's Republic* (1977), is an excellent comprehensive study. Recent developments are ably analyzed by D. Davis, ed., *The Consumer Revolution in Urban China* (2000), and J. Spence, *The Search for Modern China* (1990). T. Yueh and C. Wakeman, *To the Storm: The Odyssey of a Revolutionary Chinese Woman* (1985), and M. Bo, *Blood Red Sunset: A Memoir of the Chinese Cultural Revolution* (1995), are poignant accounts by participants. Important works on Deng's reforms include R. Evans, *Deng Xiaoping and the Making of Modern China* (1994), and M. Meisner, *The Deng Xiaoping Era* (1996). A. and J. Tyson, *Chinese Awakenings: Life Stories from Unofficial China* (1995), is recommended.

K. Kawai, *Japan's American Interlude* (1960), and R. P. Dore, *Land Reform in Japan* (1959), consider key problems of occupation policy. A. Gordon, ed., *Postwar Japan as History* (1993), contains essays by leading scholars and has an extensive bibliography. Two excellent and thought-provoking studies of contemporary Japanese society are E. Reischauer, *The Japanese Today, Change and Continuity* (1989), and F. Gibney, *Japan, the Fragile Superpower* (1977). G. Bernstein, *Haruko's World: A Japanese Farm Woman and Her Community* (1983), probes changing patterns of rural life. A. Iriye, *The Cold War in Asia: A Historical Introduction* (1974), and M. Schaller, *The United States and China in the Twentieth Century* (1979), analyze international conflicts in the postwar Pacific basin.

S. Cohen, *India: Emerging Power* (2001), and G. Adhikari, *India: The First Fifty Years* (1997), a lively survey by a noted Indian journalist, are both recommended. G. Hutchins, *India's Revolution: Gandhi and the Quit India Movement* (1973), is an excellent account of wartime developments in India, which may be compared with J. Nehru, *An Autobiography* (1962). F. Frankel, *India's Political Economy, 1947–1977* (1978), intelligently discusses the economic policies of independent India. There is a good biography of Indira Gandhi by D. Moraes (1980). B. Rubin, *The Fragmentation of Afghanistan* (2002), considers recent developments. H. Tinker, *South Asia: A Short History*, 2d ed. (1990), is a good guide to the states of the Indian subcontinent. C. Dubois, *Social Forces in Southeast Asia* (1967), and R. N. Kearney, *Politics and Modernization in South and Southeast Asia* (1974), are solid general accounts. Two valuable works on specific countries are B. Dahm, *Sukarno and the Struggle for Indonesian Independence* (1969), and T. Friend, *Between Two Empires: The Ordeal of the Philippines, 1929–1946* (1965). F. FitzGerald, *Fire in the Lake* (1973), probes the tragic war in Vietnam.

Recommended studies of the Middle East and Israel include a balanced account by C. Smith, *Palestine and the Arab-Israeli Conflict* (1988), and B. Kimmerling and J. Migdal, *The Palestinians: The Making of a People* (1992). A. Goldschmidt, Jr., *Modern Egypt: The Formation of a Nation-State* (1988), treats the post-Nasser years extensively. Religious fundamentalism is sympathetically analyzed in J. Esposito, *The Islamic Threat: Myth or Reality?* (1992). A. Sidahmed and A. Ehteshami, eds., *Islamic Fundamentalism* (1996), is also useful.

In addition to the study by Hallett cited in the Notes, J. Fage, *A History of Africa*, 3d ed. (1995), is a balanced introduction to modern Africa's rich and complex history. Important works on the colonial era include A. Boahen, *African Perspectives on Colonialism* (1989), and R. O. Collins, *Problems in the History of Modern Africa* (1997). B. Davidson, *The Black Man's Burden: Africa and the Curse of the Nation State* (1993), is a thought-provoking reconsideration by a noted historian. W. E. B. Du Bois, *The World and Africa* (1947), and J. Kenyatta, *Facing Mount Kenya* (1953), are powerful comments on African nationalism by, respectively, the distinguished American black thinker and Kenya's foremost revolutionary and political leader. R. July, *The African Voice: The Role of the Humanities in African Independence* (1987), focuses on intellectuals and artists struggling against cultural imperialism. A. Hopkins, *An Economic History of West Africa* (1973), is a pioneering synthesis. R. Olaniyan, ed., *African History and Culture* (1982), is a valuable collection. M. Crowder, ed., *The Cambridge History of Africa*, vol. 8, examines the struggle for independence. Major works on specific countries include M. Crowder, *The Story of Nigeria*, 4th ed. (1978); L. Thompson, *A History of South Africa*, rev. ed. (1995); and the work by Birmingham and Martin cited in the Notes. F. Willett, *African Art* (1971), is a good introduction. Important studies on more recent political changes include J. Clark and D. Gardinier, eds., *Political Reform in Francophone Africa* (1997), and J. Harbeson and D. Rothchild, eds., *Africa in World Politics: Post–Cold War Challenges*, 2d ed. (1995).

# LISTENING TO THE PAST

## THE STRUGGLE FOR FREEDOM IN SOUTH AFRICA

*Many African territories won political freedom in the mid-1960s, but in South Africa the struggle was long and extremely difficult. Only in 1990 did the white government release Nelson Mandela from prison and begin negotiations with the famous black leader and the African National Congress (ANC). Only in 1994 did Mandela and the ANC finally come to power and establish a new system based on majority rule and racial equality.*

*Born in 1918 into the royal family of the Transkei, Nelson Mandela received an education befitting the son of a tribal chief. But he ran away to escape an arranged tribal marriage, experienced the harsh realities of black life in Johannesburg, studied law, and became an attorney. A born leader with a natural air of authority, Mandela was drawn to politics and the ANC. In the 1950s the white government responded to the growing popularity of Mandela and the ANC with tear gas and repression.*

*In 1960 the ANC called a general strike to protest the shooting of peaceful protesters at Sharpeville. Acts of sabotage then shook South Africa, and Mandela led the underground opposition. Betrayed by an informer, he was convicted of treason in 1964 and sentenced to life imprisonment. Mandela defended all of the accused in the 1964 treason trial. The following selection is taken from Mandela's opening statement.*

At the outset, I want to say that the suggestion made by the State in its opening that the struggle in South Africa is under the influence of foreigners or communists is wholly incorrect. I have done whatever I did, both as an individual and as a leader of my people, because of my experience in South Africa and my own proudly felt African background, and not because of what any outsider might have said.

In my youth in the Transkei I listened to the elders of my tribe telling stories of the old days. Amongst the tales they related to me were those of wars fought by our ancestors in defence of the fatherland. . . . I hoped then that life might offer me the opportunity to serve my people and make my own humble contribution to their freedom struggle. . . .

It is true that there has often been close cooperation between the ANC [African National Congress] and the Communist Party. But cooperation is merely proof of a common goal—in this case the removal of White supremacy—and is not proof of a complete community of interests. . . . What is more, for many decades communists were the only political group in South Africa who were prepared to treat Africans as human beings and their equals; who were prepared to eat with us, talk with us, live with us, and work with us. . . . Because of this, there are many Africans who today tend to equate freedom with communism. . . .

I turn now to my own position. I have denied that I am a communist. . . . [But] I am attracted by the idea of a classless society, an attraction which springs in part from Marxist reading and, in part, from my admiration of the structure and organization of early African societies in this country. The land, then the main means of production, belonged to the tribe. There were no rich or poor and there was no exploitation. . . .

[Unlike communists] I am an admirer of the parliamentary system of the West. . . . [Thus] I have been influenced in my thinking by both West and East. . . . [I believe] I should be absolutely impartial and objective. I should tie myself to no particular system of society other than of socialism. I must leave myself free to borrow the best from the West and from the East. . . .

Nelson Mandela at the time of his imprisonment in 1964. *(Mohamed Lounes/Gamma)*

Our fight is against real, and not imaginary, hardships or, to use the language of the State Prosecutor, "so-called hardships." . . . Basically, we fight against two features which are the hallmarks of African life in South Africa and which are entrenched by legislation which we seek to have repealed. These features are poverty and lack of human dignity, and we do not need communists or so-called "agitators" to teach us about these things.

South Africa is the richest country in Africa, and could be one of the richest countries in the world. But it is a land of extremes and remarkable contrasts. The Whites enjoy what may well be the highest standard of living in the world, while Africans live in poverty and misery. . . .
Poverty goes hand in hand with malnutrition and disease. . . .

The lack of human dignity experienced by Africans is the direct result of the policy of White supremacy. White supremacy implies Black inferiority. Legislation designed to preserve White supremacy entrenches this notion. . . . Because of this sort of attitude, Whites tend to regard Africans as a separate breed. They do not look upon them as people with families of their own; they do not realize that they have emotions. . . .

Africans want to be paid a living wage. Africans want to perform work which they are capable of doing, and not work which the Government declares them to be capable of. . . . Africans want a just share in the whole of South Africa; they want security and a stake in society.

Above all, we want equal political rights, because without them our disabilities will be permanent. I know this sounds revolutionary to the Whites in this country, because the majority of voters will be Africans. This makes the White man fear democracy.

But this fear cannot be allowed to stand in the way of the only solution which will guarantee racial harmony and freedom for all. It is not true that the enfranchisement of all will result in racial domination. Political division, based on color, is entirely artificial and, when it disappears, so will the domination of one color group by another. The ANC has spent half a century fighting against racialism. When it triumphs it will not change that policy.

This then is what the ANC is fighting. Their struggle is a truly national one. It is a struggle of the African people, inspired by their own suffering and their own experience. It is a struggle for the right to live.

During my lifetime I have dedicated myself to this struggle of the African people. I have fought against White domination, and I have fought against Black domination. I have cherished the ideal of a democratic and free society in which all persons live together in harmony and with equal opportunities. It is an ideal which I hope to live for and to achieve. But if need be, it is an ideal for which I am prepared to die.

## QUESTIONS FOR ANALYSIS

1. How does Nelson Mandela respond to the charge that he and the ANC are controlled by communists?
2. What factors influenced Mandela's thinking? In what ways has he been influenced by "both East and West" and by his African background?
3. According to Mandela, what is wrong with South Africa? What needs to be done?
4. What are Mandela's goals for South Africa? Are his goals realistic or idealistic? Or both?

*Source:* Slightly adapted from Nelson Mandela, *No Easy Walk to Freedom: Articles, Speeches and Trial Addresses* (London: Heinemann, 1973), pp. 163, 179–185, 187–189. Reprinted by permission of Heinemann Publishers (Oxford) Ltd.

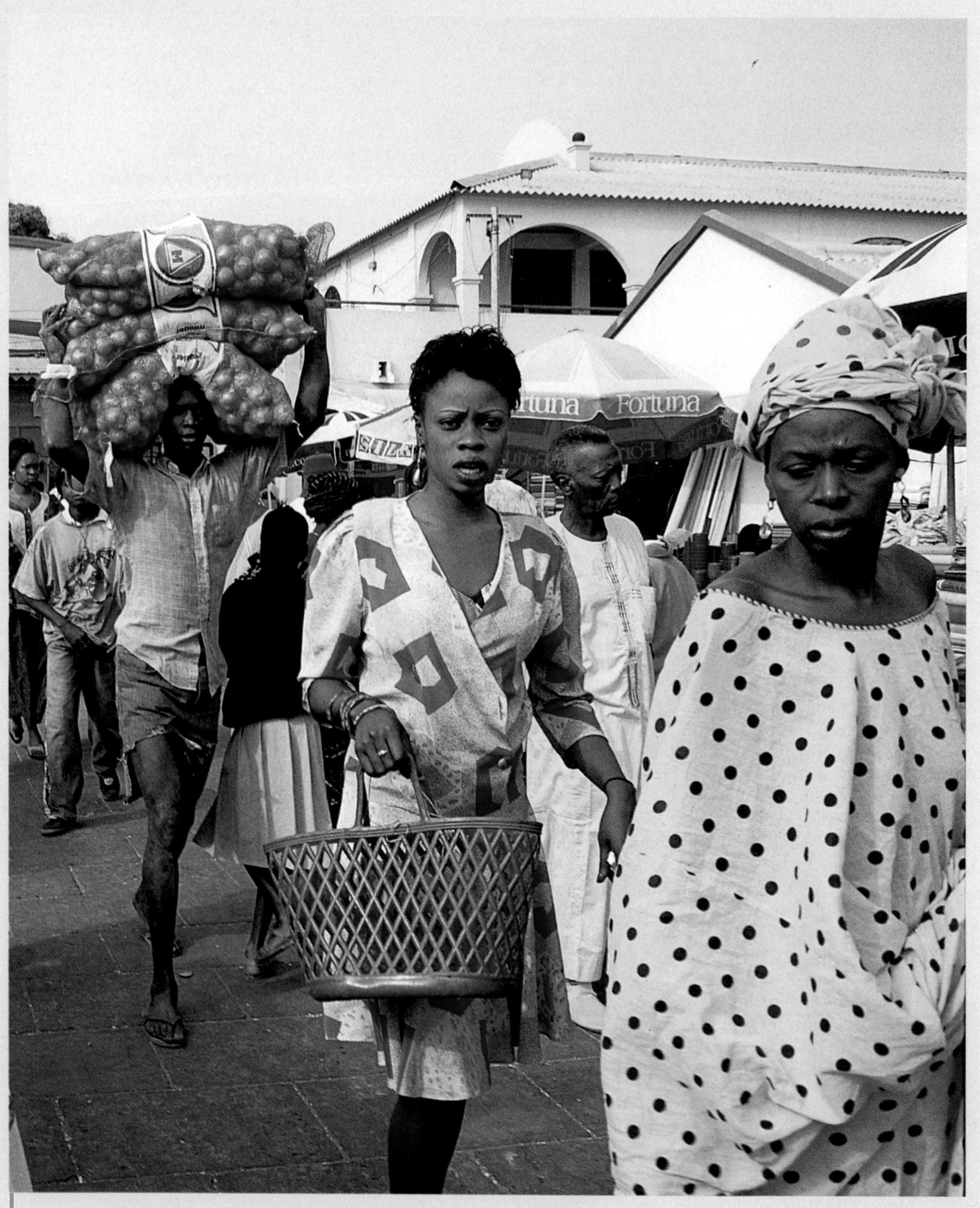


The bustling Albert Market in Banjul, Gambia, reflects the vibrant diversity of modern Africa.
*(Betty Press/Woodfin Camp & Associates)*

# CHAPTER 35 CHANGING LIVES IN THE DEVELOPING COUNTRIES

## CHAPTER OUTLINE

- The Emergence of the Third World
- Economic and Social Challenges
- The Growth of Cities, 1945 to the Present
- Growing Diversity Since 1980
- Mass Culture and Contemporary Thought

After the Second World War everyday life in the emerging nations of Asia and Africa changed dramatically as many peoples struggled to overcome the legacy of imperialism and build effective nation-states. Some of the changes paralleled the experiences of Europe and North America, but most observers stressed the enormous differences in development between the emerging nations and the industrialized nations. The new nations—along with the older states of Latin America—suffered widespread poverty, shared a heritage of foreign domination, and discerned a widening economic gap between themselves and the industrialized nations of Europe and North America. Thus many leaders and intellectuals in Asia, Africa, and Latin America felt that they were all joined together in an underlying unity, which was generally known as the Third World.

From the mid-1970s onward this sense of shared experience and solidarity gradually broke down. Different countries and whole regions went their separate ways. Above all, some countries in East Asia experienced remarkable economic progress and emerged as middle- and lower-middle-income nations. Countries elsewhere were less fortunate. Much of sub-Saharan Africa in particular experienced economic retreat and great hardship. Thus the Third World fragmented increasingly into a wide range of so-called developing countries, and the global class structure became more complicated and diverse.

- How did the emerging nations of the Third World seek to escape from poverty? What were the results of their efforts?
- What caused the prodigious growth of cities in Africa, Asia, and Latin America, and what did this growth mean for their inhabitants?
- How did thinkers and artists in the developing countries interpret the modern world and the experiences of their peoples before, during, and after foreign domination?

These are the questions we will explore in this chapter.

## THE EMERGENCE OF THE THIRD WORLD

Beginning in the 1950s many thinkers, journalists, and politicians viewed Africa, Asia, and Latin America as a single entity—the **Third World.** Or, as some scholars would say today, they imagined and "constructed" Africa, Asia, and Latin America as a unity for effective analysis and action. For a generation, in spite of all these countries' differences in history and culture, they did share many common characteristics. These characteristics linked them together and encouraged a common consciousness and ideology. There are several reasons for this important development.

First, many writers and politicians argued that virtually all the countries of Africa, Asia, and even Latin America had experienced political or economic domination, nationalist reaction, and a struggle for genuine independence. This shared past gave rise to a common consciousness and a widespread feeling of being oppressed and victimized in dealings with the West. A variety of nationalists, Marxists, and anti-imperialist intellectuals nurtured this outlook, and they believed that the Third World countries had to band together to end the ongoing exploitation by the wealthy capitalist nations. Precisely because of their shared sense of past injustice and continued exploitation, many influential Latin Americans identified with the Third World, in spite of their countries' greater affluence. Moreover, the term came into global use during the cold war era as a convenient way of distinguishing Africa, Asia, and Latin America from the "First World" and the "Second World"—the capitalist and communist industrialized nations, respectively.

Second, in the 1950s and 1960s a large majority of men and women in most poor countries lived in the countryside and depended on agriculture for a living. Agricultural goods and raw materials were the primary exports of these countries. By contrast, in Europe, Canada, the United States, and Japan, most people lived in cities and depended mainly on industry and urban services for employment.

Finally, the agricultural countries of Asia, Africa, and most of Latin America were united by a growing awareness of their common poverty. By no means was everyone in the Third World poor; some people were quite wealthy. The average standard of living, however, was low, especially compared with that of people in the wealthy industrialized nations, and massive poverty was ever present.

## ECONOMIC AND SOCIAL CHALLENGES

As postindependence leaders confronted the tough task of preserving political unity and building cohesive nation-states (see Chapter 34), the enormous challenges of poverty, malnutrition, and disease weighed especially heavily on rural people. In the 1950s and 1960s most Third World leaders and their advisers believed that rapid industrialization and "modernization" were the answers to rural poverty and disease. Industrialization and modernization would also kindle popular enthusiasm and thus serve nation building, which in turn promised economic self-sufficiency and cultural renewal. Moreover, having raised people's hopes in the struggle for freedom, these leaders had to start delivering on their promises if they were to maintain trust and stay in power. For all these reasons the leaders and peoples of the newly independent countries set themselves the massive task of building modern factories, roads, and public health services like those in Europe and North America. Their considerable success fueled rapid economic progress.

Yet social problems, complicated by surging population growth, almost dwarfed the accomplishment. Disappointments multiplied. By and large, the poorest rural people in the poorest countries gained the least from industrialization, and industrial expansion provided jobs for only a small segment even of the urban population. By the late 1960s widespread dissatisfaction with policies of all-out industrialization prompted a greater emphasis on rural development.

### Poverty

After World War II the gap in real income—income adjusted for differences in prices—between the industrialized world and the former colonies and dependencies of Africa, Asia, and Latin America was enormous. According to a leading historian, in 1950, when war-scarred Europe was in the early phase of postwar reconstruction,

> *the real income per capita of the Third World was five or six times lower than that of the developed countries. . . . In the developed countries, a century and a half of Industrial Revolution had resulted in a multiplication by more than five of the average standard of living in 1950. . . . For the average Third World countries the 1950s level was practically that of 1800 or, at best, only 10–20 percent above.*[1]

The people of these poor Third World countries were overwhelmingly concentrated in the countryside as small farmers and landless laborers.

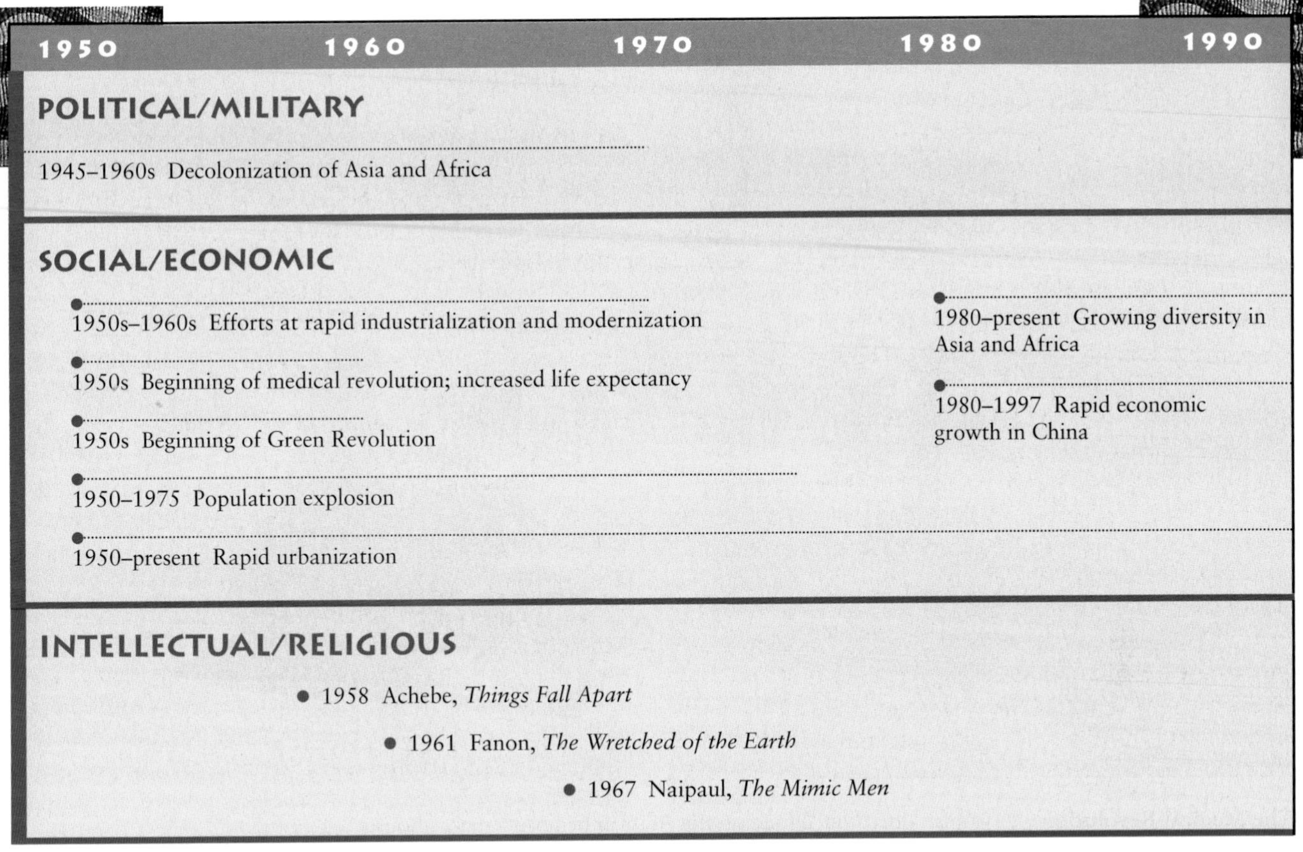

1950
1960
1970
1980
1990
POLITICAL/MILITARY
1945–1960s Decolonization of Asia and Africa
SOCIAL/ECONOMIC
1950s–1960s Efforts at rapid industrialization and modernization
1950s Beginning of medical revolution; increased life expectancy
1950s Beginning of Green Revolution
1950–1975 Population explosion
1950–present Rapid urbanization
1980–present Growing diversity in Asia and Africa
1980–1997 Rapid economic growth in China
INTELLECTUAL/RELIGIOUS
1958 Achebe, Things Fall Apart
1961 Fanon, The Wretched of the Earth
1967 Naipaul, The Mimic Men


Poverty meant, above all, not having enough to eat. For millions hunger and malnutrition were harsh facts of life. In India, Ethiopia, Bolivia, and other extremely poor countries, the average adult ate fewer than two thousand calories a day—only 85 percent of the minimal requirement. Although many poor countries fared better, in the 1960s none but Argentina could match the three thousand or more calories consumed in the more fortunate industrialized world. Even Third World people who consumed enough calories often suffered from the effects of unbalanced high-starch diets and inadequate protein. Severe protein deficiency stunts the brain as well as the body, and many of the poorest children grew up mentally retarded.

Poor housing—crowded, often damp, and exposed to the elements—also contributed significantly to the less-developed world's high incidence of chronic ill health. So too did scanty education and lack of the fundamentals of modern public health: adequate and safe water, sewage disposal, immunizations, prenatal care, and control of communicable diseases. Village women around the world spent much of each day carrying water and searching for firewood or dung to use as fuel, as they must still do in many countries. Infant mortality was savage, and chronic illness weakened and demoralized many adults, making them unfit for the hard labor their lives required. Generally speaking, people's health was better in Asia and Latin America than in the new states of sub-Saharan Africa.

## The Medical Revolution and the Population Explosion

The most thoroughgoing success achieved by the Third World after the Second World War was a spectacular **medical revolution.** Immediately after winning independence, the governments of emerging nations began adopting modern methods of immunology and public health. These methods were often simple and inexpensive but extremely effective. One famous measure was spraying DDT in Southeast Asia to control mosquitoes bearing malaria, one of the deadliest and most debilitating tropical diseases. In Sri Lanka (formerly Ceylon), DDT spraying halved the yearly death toll in the first postwar decade—at a modest cost of $2 per person. According to the United Nations

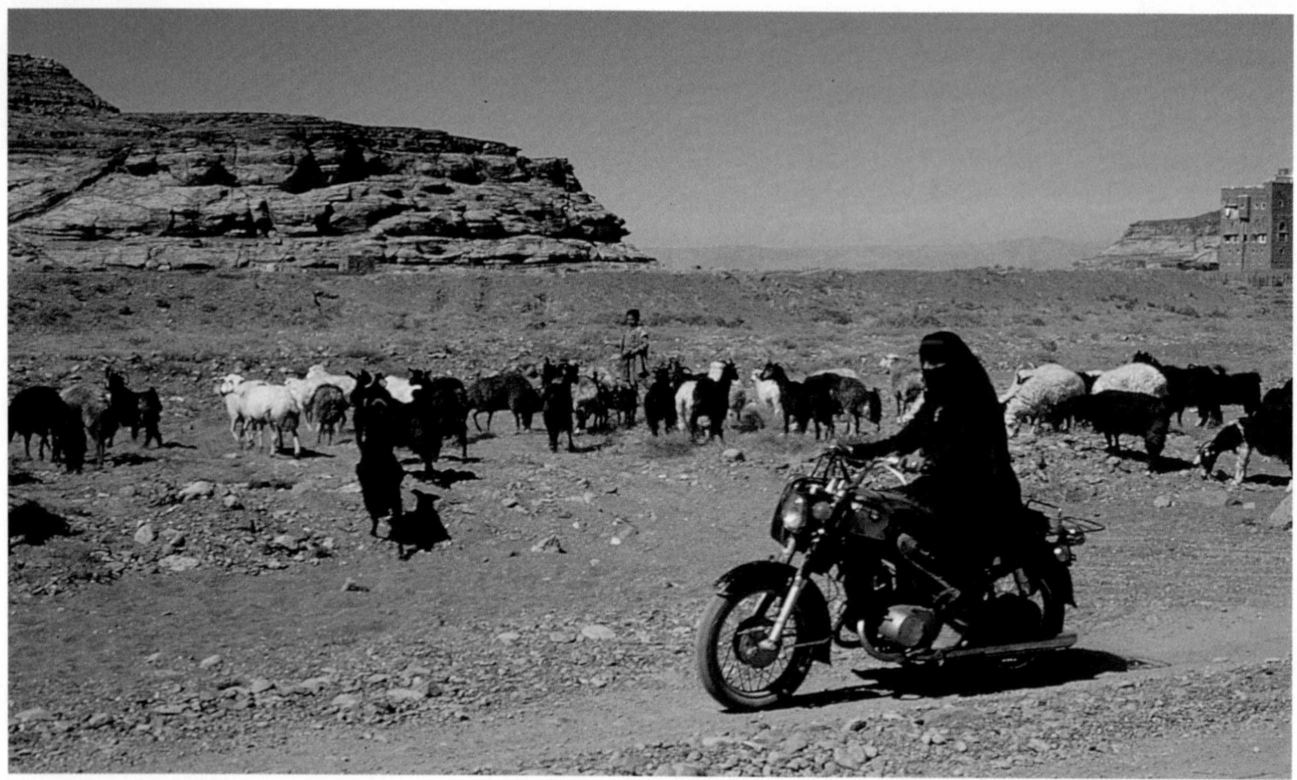

**The Medical Revolution** A woman doctor in Yemen on the Arabian peninsula makes house calls by motorcycle, thereby carrying modern medicine to women in isolated desert communities. The doctor wears the veil traditionally required of women in public throughout parts of the Arab world. *(Hans Bollinger for STERN magazine)*

World Health Organization, which helped provide medical expertise to the new states, deaths from smallpox, cholera, and plague declined by more than 95 percent worldwide between 1951 and 1966.

Asian and African countries increased the small numbers of hospitals, doctors, and nurses that they had inherited from the colonial past. Sophisticated medical facilities became symbols of the commitment to a better life. Some critics, however, maintained that expensive medical technology was an indulgence that the newly independent countries could not afford, for it was ill suited to the pressing health problems of most of the population. Such criticism eventually prompted greater emphasis on delivering medical services to the countryside. Local people were successfully trained as paramedics to staff rural outpatient clinics that offered medical treatment, health education, and prenatal and postnatal care. Many paramedics were women, as many health problems involved childbirth and infancy, and villagers the world over considered it improper for a male to examine a woman's body.

The medical revolution significantly lowered death rates and lengthened life expectancies. In particular, children became increasingly likely to survive their early years, although infant and juvenile mortality remained far higher in poor countries than in rich ones. By 1980 the average inhabitant of the developing countries could expect to live about fifty-four years; life expectancy at birth varied from forty to sixty-four years depending on the country. In industrialized countries life expectancy at birth averaged seventy-one years.

A less favorable consequence of the medical revolution was the acceleration of population growth. As in Europe during the nineteenth century, a rapid decline in death rates was not immediately accompanied by a similar decline in birthrates. Third World women continued to bear five to seven children each, as their mothers and grandmothers had done. The combined populations of Asia, Africa, and Latin America, which had grown relatively modestly from 1925 to 1950, increased between 1950 and 1975 from 1.7 billion to 3 billion. It was an unprecedented explosion, which promised to continue for many years.

The population explosion aroused fears of approaching famine and starvation. Thomas Malthus's gloomy late-eighteenth-century conclusion that population always tends to grow faster than the food supply (see pages 741–742) was revived and updated by **neo-Malthusian** social scientists. Such fears were exaggerated, but they did produce uneasiness in the developing countries, where leaders saw that their people had to run fast just to maintain already low standards of living.

Some governments began pushing family planning and birth control to slow population growth. These measures were not very successful in the 1950s and 1960s. In many countries Islamic and Catholic religious teachings were hostile to birth control. Moreover, widespread cultural attitudes dictated that a "real" man keep his wife pregnant. There were also economic reasons for preferring large families. Farmers needed the help of plenty of children at planting and harvest times, and sons and daughters were a sort of social security system for their elders. Thus a prudent couple wanted several children because some would surely die young.

## The Race to Industrialize (1950–1970)

Throughout the 1950s and most of the 1960s many key leaders in Africa, Asia, and Latin America, pressed on by their European, American, and Soviet advisers, were convinced that a vigorous **industrialization strategy** was the only answer to poverty and population growth. The masses, they concluded, were poor because they were imprisoned in a primitive, inefficient agricultural economy. Only modern factory industry appeared capable of creating wealth quickly enough to outrace the increasing number of people.

The two-century experience of the West, Japan, and the Soviet Union seemed to validate this faith in industrialization. To Third World elites economic history taught the encouraging lesson that the wealthy countries had also been agricultural and "underdeveloped" until the Industrial Revolution had lifted them out of poverty, one by one. According to this view, the uneven progress of industrialization was primarily responsible for the great income gap that existed between rich and poor countries in 1950.

Theories of **modernization,** which were particularly popular in the 1960s, also assumed that all countries were following the path already taken by the industrialized nations and that the task of the elites was to speed the trip. Marxism, with its industrial and urban bias, preached a similar gospel. These ideas reinforced the desire to industrialize in the newly independent countries.

Nationalist leaders believed that a successful industrialization strategy required state action and enterprise. Many were impressed by socialism in general and by Stalin's forced industrialization in particular, which they saw as having won the Soviet Union international power and prominence. In Asia and Africa capitalists and private enterprise were often equated with the old rulers and colonial servitude. The reasoning was practical as well as ideological: socialism meant an expansion of steady government jobs for political and ethnic allies, and modern industry meant ports, roads, schools, and hospitals, as well as factories. Only the state could afford such expensive investments.

The degree of state involvement varied considerably. A few governments, such as communist China, tried to control all aspects of economic life. A few one-party states in Africa, notably Zambia, Ghana, and Ethiopia, mixed Marxist-Leninist ideology and peasant communes in an attempt to construct a special "African socialism." At the other extreme only the British colony of Hong Kong downgraded government control of the economy and emphasized private enterprise and the export of manufactured goods. A large majority of governments assigned the state an important, even leading, role, but they also recognized private property and tolerated native (and foreign) business people. The **mixed economy**—part socialist, part capitalist—became the general rule in Africa and Asia.

Political leaders concentrated state investment in big, highly visible projects that proclaimed the country's independence and stimulated national pride. Enormous dams for irrigation and hydroelectric power were favored undertakings. Nasser's stupendous Aswan Dam harnessed the Nile, demonstrating that modern Egyptians could surpass even the pyramids of their ancient ancestors. The gigantic state-owned steel mill was another favorite project. These big projects testified to the prevailing faith in expensive advanced technology and modernization along European lines.

Nationalist leaders and their economic experts measured overall success by how fast national income grew, and they tended to assume that social problems and income distribution would take care of themselves. For example, after India achieved independence in 1947, Mahatma Gandhi's special brand of nationalism was redirected toward economic and social rebirth through state enterprise and planning. Jawaharlal Nehru and many Congress party leaders believed that unregulated capitalism and free trade under British rule had deepened Indian poverty. Considering themselves democratic socialists, they introduced five-year

**Building the Aswan Dam** Financed and engineered by the Soviet Union, the massive high dam at Aswan was Nasser's dream for Egypt's economic future. Here workers dig the dam that will harness the Nile for irrigation and hydroelectric power. *(Hulton-Deutsch Collection/Corbis)*

plans, built state-owned factories and steel mills, and raised tariffs to protect Indian manufacturers. Quite typically, they neglected agriculture, land reform, and village life.

The Third World's first great industrialization drive was in many ways a success. Industry grew faster than ever before, though from an admittedly low base in Africa and most of Asia. According to the United Nations, industry in the noncommunist developing nations grew at more than 7 percent per year between 1950 and 1970, which meant a per capita rate of about 4.5 percent per year. This matched the fastest rates of industrialization in the United States before 1914 and was double the rates of Britain and France in the same years.

Industrial expansion stimulated the other sectors of Third World economies. National income per capita grew about 2.5 percent per year in the booming world economy of the 1950s and 1960s. This pace was far superior to the very modest increases that had occurred under colonial domination between 1900 and 1950.

Nevertheless, by the late 1960s disillusionment with relatively rapid industrialization was spreading. The countries of Asia, Africa, and Latin America did not as a whole match the "miraculous" concurrent advances of western Europe and Japan, and the great economic gap between the rich and the poor nations continued to widen.

Also, most leaders in the developing countries had genuinely believed that rapid industrial development would help the rural masses. Yet careful studies showed increasingly that the main beneficiaries of industrialization were business people, bureaucrats, skilled workers, and urban professionals. Peasants and agricultural laborers gained little or nothing. Moreover, the poorest countries—such as India and Indonesia in Asia, and Ethiopia and the Sudan in Africa—were growing most slowly in per capita terms. The industrialization prescription appeared least effective where poverty was most intense. Economic dislocations in the global economy after the 1973 oil crisis accentuated this trend, visiting particularly devastating effects on the poorest countries.

Perhaps most serious, industrialization failed to provide the sheer number of jobs needed for the sons and daughters of the population explosion. Statisticians estimated that the growth of manufacturing in the world's developing countries between 1950 and 1970 provided jobs for only about one-fifth of the 200 million young men and women who entered the exploding labor force in the same period. For the foreseeable future, most people in these countries would have to remain on the farm or work in traditional handicrafts and service occupations. All-out modern industrialization had failed as a panacea.

## Agriculture and the Green Revolution (1960–1980)

From the late 1960s onward the limitations of industrial development forced governments in the developing nations to take a renewed interest in rural people and village life. At best this attention meant giving agriculture its due and coordinating rural development with industrialization and urbanization. At worst, especially in the very poorest countries, it deflated the optimistic vision of living standards approaching those of the wealthy industrialized nations.

Nationalist elites had neglected agriculture in the 1950s and 1960s for various reasons. They regarded an agricultural economy as a mark of colonial servitude, which they were symbolically repudiating by embracing industrialization. They wanted to squeeze agriculture and peasant producers in order to provide capital for industry. Thus governments often established artificially low food prices, which also subsidized their volatile urban supporters at the expense of the farmers.

In addition, the obstacles to more productive farming seemed overwhelming to unsympathetic urban elites and condescending foreign experts: farms were too small and fragmented for mechanization, peasants were too stubborn and ignorant to change their ways, and so on. Little wonder that only big farmers and some plantations received much government support. Wherever large estates and absentee landlords predominated—in large parts of Asia and in most of Latin America, excluding Mexico, though not in sub-Saharan Africa—landless laborers and poor peasants who had no choice other than to rent land simply lacked the incentive to work harder. Any increased profits from larger crops went mainly to the absentee landowners.

**Peasants Farming Near Lake Titicaca, Peru** Planting a new crop of potatoes with only the aid of the time-honored Incan plow of their ancestors, this husband and wife can expect only a subsistence living from their backbreaking labor. In many poor countries a high rent to an absentee landlord also weighs heavily on peasant well-being. *(Eric Lawrie/The Hutchison Library)*

Most honest observers were convinced that improved farm performance required land reform. Yet ever since the French Revolution, genuine land reform has been a profoundly radical measure, frequently bringing violence and civil war. Powerful landowners and their allies generally succeeded in blocking or subverting redistribution of land to benefit the poor. Land reform, unlike industrialization, was generally too hot for most politicians to handle.

Governments also neglected agriculture because feeding the masses was deceptively easy in the 1950s and early 1960s. Before 1939 the countries of Asia, Africa, and Latin America had collectively produced more grain than they consumed. But after 1945, as their populations soared, they began importing ever-increasing quantities. Very poor countries received food from the United States at giveaway prices as part of a U.S. effort to dispose of enormous grain surpluses and help American farmers.

Crops might fail in poor countries, but starvation seemed a thing of the past. In 1965, when India was urged to build up its food reserves, one top Indian official expressed a widespread attitude: "Why should we bother? Our reserves are the wheat fields of Kansas."[2] In the short run, the Indian official was right. In 1966 and again in 1967, when the monsoon failed to deliver its life-giving rains to the Indo-Pakistan subcontinent and famine gripped the land, the United States gave India one-fifth of the U.S. wheat crop. More than 60 million Indians lived exclusively on American grain. The effort required a food armada of six hundred ships, the largest fleet assembled since the Normandy invasion of 1944. The famine was ultimately contained, and instead of millions of deaths, there were only a few thousand.

That close brush with mass starvation sent a shiver down the world's spine. Complacency dissolved in Asia and Africa, and neo-Malthusian prophecies of disaster multiplied in wealthy nations. Paul Ehrlich, an American scientist, envisioned a grisly future in his polemical 1968 bestseller *The Population Bomb:*

> *The battle to feed all of humanity is over. In the 1970s the world will undergo famines—hundreds of millions of people are going to starve to death in spite of any crash programs embarked upon now. At this stage nothing can prevent a substantial increase in the world death rate.*[3]

Countering such nightmarish visions was the hope of technological improvements. Plant scientists and agricultural research stations had already set out to develop new hybrid seeds genetically engineered to suit the growing conditions of tropical agriculture. Their model was the extraordinarily productive hybrid corn developed for the American Midwest in the 1940s. The first breakthrough came in Mexico in the 1950s, when an American-led team developed new high-yielding dwarf wheats. These varieties enabled farmers to double their yields, though they demanded greater amounts of fertilizer and water for irrigation. Mexican wheat production soared. Thus began the transformation of agriculture in some poor countries—the so-called **Green Revolution.**

In the 1960s an American-backed team of scientists in the Philippines turned their attention to rice, the Asian staff of life; they quickly developed a "miracle rice." The new hybrid required more fertilizer and water but yielded more and grew much faster. It permitted the revolutionary advent of year-round farming on irrigated land, making possible two, three, or even four crops a year. Asian scientists, financed by their governments, developed similar hybrids to meet local conditions.

Increases in grain production were rapid and dramatic in some Asian countries. In gigantic India farmers upped production more than 60 percent in fifteen years. By 1980 thousands of new grain bins dotted the countryside, symbols of the agricultural revolution in India and the country's newfound ability to feed all its people. China followed with its own highly successful version of the Green Revolution under Deng Xiaoping.

The Green Revolution offered new hope to the developing nations, but it was no cure-all. At first most of its benefits seemed to flow to large landowners and substantial peasant farmers who could afford the necessary investments in irrigation and fertilizer. Subsequent experience in China and other Asian countries showed, however, that even peasant families with tiny farms could gain substantially. Indeed, the Green Revolution's greatest successes occurred in Asian countries with broad-based peasant ownership of land.

The technological revolution shared relatively few of its benefits with the poorest villagers, who gained only slightly more regular employment from the Green Revolution's demand for more labor. Pakistan, the Philippines, and other countries with large numbers of landless peasants and insecure tenant farmers experienced less improvement than did countries such as South Korea and Taiwan, where land was generally owned by peasants. This helps explain why the Green Revolution failed to spread from Mexico throughout Latin America: as long as 3 to 4 percent of the rural population owned 60 to 80 percent of the land, as was still the case in many Latin American countries, the Green Revolution usually remained stillborn.

**Old and New** A fetish statue designed to frighten off evil spirits stands by as the proud owner of a two-acre plot in southern India shows a visiting expert his crop of "miracle rice." As this picture suggests, the acceptance of modern technology does not necessarily require the repudiation of cultural traditions. *(Marc and Evelyne Bernheim/Woodfin Camp & Associates)*

In the early years of the transformation sub-Saharan Africa benefited little from the new agricultural techniques, even though land reform was a serious challenge only in white-ruled South Africa. Poor transportation, inadequate storage facilities, and low government-imposed agricultural prices must bear much of the blame. More generally, the climatic conditions of black Africa encouraged continued adherence to dry farming and root crops, whereas the Green Revolution was almost synonymous with intensive irrigation and grain production.

The Green Revolution, like the medical revolution and first industrialization drive, represented a large but uneven step forward for the developing countries, especially in Asia. Yet even in the best of circumstances, relatively few of its benefits flowed to the poorest groups. These poor, who lacked political influence and had no clear idea about what needed to be done, increasingly longed to escape from ill-paid, irregular work in somebody else's fields. For many of the strongest and most enterprising, life in a nearby town or city seemed a way out.

## THE GROWTH OF CITIES, 1945 TO THE PRESENT

The changing lives of people in the developing countries were marked by violent contrasts, which were most striking in urban areas. Shiny airports, international hotels, and massive government buildings were constructed next to tarpaper slums. Like their counterparts in the industrialized world, these rapidly growing cities were monuments to political independence and ongoing industrial development. They were also testimonials to increasing population, limited opportunities in the countryside, and neocolonial influence. Runaway urban growth became a distinctive feature of the developing countries.

### Rapid Urbanization

The cities of Africa, Asia, and Latin America expanded at an astonishing pace after the Second World War. An **urban explosion** caused many cities to double or even triple

### TABLE 35.1 URBAN POPULATION AS A PERCENTAGE OF TOTAL POPULATION IN THE WORLD AND IN EIGHT MAJOR AREAS, 1925–2025

| AREA | 1925 | 1950 | 1975 | 2000 | 2025 (EST.) |
|---|---|---|---|---|---|
| World total | 21 | 28 | 39 | 50 | 63 |
| North America | 54 | 64 | 77 | 86 | 93 |
| Europe | 48 | 55 | 67 | 79 | 88 |
| Soviet Union | 18 | 39 | 61 | 76 | 87 |
| East Asia | 10 | 15 | 30 | 46 | 63 |
| Latin America | 25 | 41 | 60 | 74 | 85 |
| Africa | 8 | 13 | 24 | 37 | 54 |
| South Asia | 9 | 15 | 23 | 35 | 51 |
| Oceania | 54 | 65 | 71 | 77 | 87 |

Little more than one-fifth of the world's population was urban in 1925. In 2000 the urban proportion in the world total was about 50 percent and, according to United Nations experts, it should reach two-thirds by about 2025. The most rapid urban growth will come in Africa and Asia, where the move to cities is still in its early stages.

in size in a single decade. The Algerian city of Algiers jumped from 300,000 to 900,000 between 1950 and 1960; Accra in Ghana, Lima in Peru, and Nairobi in Kenya grew just as fast. Moreover, rapid urban growth continued. The less-developed countries became far more urbanized in recent times than most people realized. In Latin America three out of five people lived in towns and cities by 1975; in Asia and Africa, as Table 35.1 shows, one in four people lived in an urban area by the same year.

The urban explosion continued in the 1980s and 1990s, so that by 2000 more than 60 percent of the planet's city dwellers lived in the cities of Africa, Asia, and Latin America, according to United Nations estimates. Rapid urbanization in the developing countries represented a tremendous historical change. As recently as 1920, three out of every four of the world's urban inhabitants were concentrated in Europe and North America.

In most of the developing world the largest cities grew fastest. Gigantic **supercities** of 2 million to 10 million persons arose. In 2000 about one-half of the urban population of Africa and Latin America lived in thirty-four very large agglomerations containing more than 5 million people. The capital city often emerged as the all-powerful urban center, encompassing all the important elite groups and dwarfing smaller cities as well as villages. Mexico City, for example, grew from 3 million to 12 million people between 1950 and 1975, and it had an estimated 22 million people in 2000. The pattern of a dominant megalopolis has continued to spread from Latin America to Africa and Asia (though not to Asia's giants, China and India).

In the poorest countries of Africa and Asia the process of urbanization is still in the early stages. Thus if United Nations projections hold true, the urban population will triple from 1.4 billion persons in 1990 to 4.4 billion in 2025. Such rapid urbanization has posed enormous ongoing challenges for peoples and governments.

What caused this urban explosion? First, the general growth of population in the developing nations was critical. Urban residents gained substantially from the medical revolution but only gradually began to reduce the size of their families. At the same time, the pressure of numbers in the countryside encouraged millions to set out for the nearest city. More than half of all urban growth has been due to rural migration.

Another factor was the desire to find jobs. Manufacturing jobs in the developing nations were concentrated in cities. In 1980 half of all the industrial jobs in Mexico were located in Mexico City, and the same kind of extreme concentration of industry occurred in many poor countries. Yet industrialization accounted for only part of the urban explosion. Urbanization without industrialization began to appear in many poor countries, presenting serious problems of urban unemployment and underemployment.

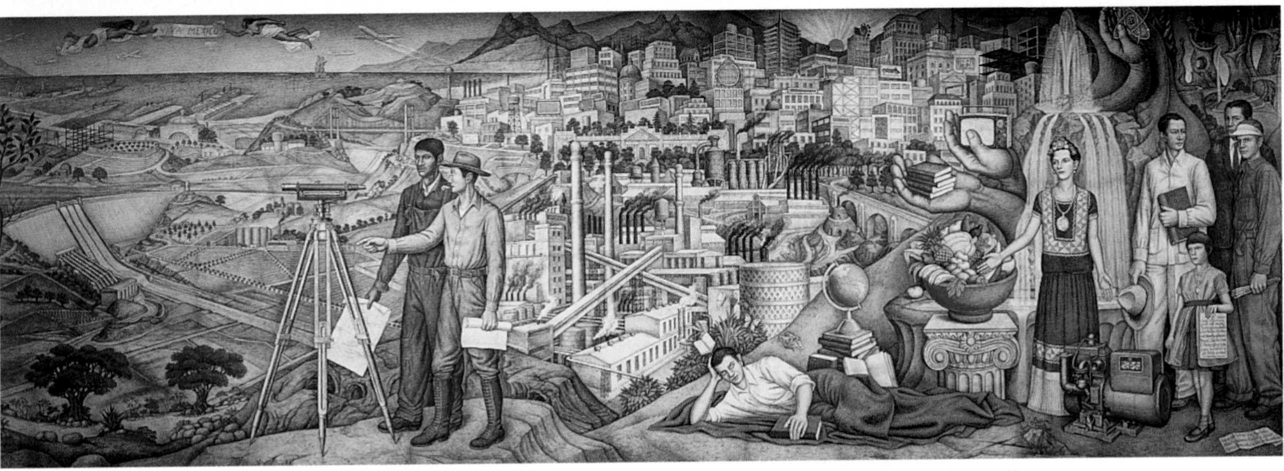

**Juan O'Gorman: Credit Transforms Mexico (1965)** Emerging as an important architect in the 1930s, O'Gorman championed practical buildings and then led the movement to integrate architecture with art in postrevolutionary Mexico. These panels from a fresco for a bank interior combine an optimistic view of economic development with many Mexican motifs. O'Gorman believed that Mexico had to preserve its cultural values in order to preserve its independence. *(Photos: Enrique Franco-Torrijos. Courtesy, Banco Bital, S.A., Mexico City)*

Thus many newcomers streamed to the cities for nonindustrial employment. Many were pushed: they simply lacked enough land to survive. Large landowners found it more profitable to produce export crops, such as sugar or coffee, for wealthy industrialized countries, and their increasingly mechanized operations provided few jobs for agricultural laborers. The push factor was particularly strong in Latin America, with its neocolonial pattern of large landowners and foreign companies exporting food and raw materials. More generally, much migration was seasonal or temporary. Many young people left home for the city to work in construction or serve as maids, expecting higher wages and steadier work and planning to return shortly with a modest nest egg.

Finally, the magnetic attraction of cities was more than economic. Their attraction rested on the services and opportunities they offered, as well as on changing attitudes and the urge to escape from the traditional restraints of village life. Most of the modern hospitals, secondary schools, and transportation systems in less-developed countries were in the cities. So were most banks, libraries, movie houses, and basic conveniences. Safe piped water and processed food, for instance, were rare in rural areas, and village women by necessity spent much of their time carrying water and grinding grain.

The city held a special appeal for rural people who had been exposed to the seductive influence of modern education. One survey from the 1960s in the Ivory Coast found two out of three rural high school graduates planning to move to the city; only one in ten illiterate persons expressed the same intention. Africa was not unique in this. For the young and the ambitious, the allure of the city was the excitement and opportunity of modern life. The village took on the curse of boredom and failure.

## Overcrowding and Shantytowns

Rapid population growth placed great pressure on existing urban social services, and in many cities in the developing countries the local authorities could not keep up with the demand. New neighborhoods often lacked running water, paved streets, electricity, and police and fire protection. As in the early days of Europe's industrialization, sanitation was minimal in poor sections of town. Outdoor toilets were shared by many. Raw sewage often ran in streets and streams.

Faced with a rising human tide, government officials and their well-to-do urban allies sometimes tried to restrict internal migration to preserve the cities. Particularly in Africa, politicians talked of sending newcomers "back to the land" to reduce urban unemployment, crime rates, congestion, and environmental decline. In Africa as elsewhere, these antimigration efforts proved unsuccessful, and frustrated officials often threw up their hands in despair.

Surging population growth had particularly severe consequences for housing. As in western Europe in the early nineteenth century, overcrowding reached staggering proportions in a great many Third World cities. Old buildings were often divided and redivided until population density reached the absolute saturation point.

Makeshift squatter settlements were another striking manifestation of the urban housing problem. These **shantytowns** sprang up continuously, almost overnight, on the worst possible urban land. Typically, a group of urban poor "invaded" unoccupied land and quickly threw up tents or huts. Often beaten off by the police, they invaded again and again until the authorities gave up and a new squatter beachhead had been secured.

Squatter shantytowns, also known more positively as **self-help housing,** grew much faster than more conventional urban areas in most developing countries. In the giant Brazilian city of Rio de Janeiro, for example, the population of the shantytowns grew four times faster

**Self-Help Housing in Mexico City** A hardworking couple adds a second floor to their home in a hilltop barrio. The modern skyscrapers of Mexico's enormous megalopolis rise in the distance. With some skill and lots of sweat labor, a little money can go a long way. *(Mark Henley/Panos Pictures)*

than the population of the rest of the city in the 1950s and 1960s. As a result, the Third World's self-help settlements came to house up to two-fifths of the urban population. The proportion was particularly high in Asia. Such settlements had occasionally grown up in American mining towns and in Europe, but never to the extent they did in Latin America, Asia, and Africa.

The meaning of spontaneous self-help housing has been hotly debated. For a time most observers stressed the miseries of squatter settlements—the lack of the most basic services, the pitiful one-room shacks, the hopelessness of disoriented migrants. However, by the 1970s some excellent studies stressed the vitality of what were seen as real neighborhoods, whose resourceful residents often shared common ethnic origins and kinship ties.

Moreover, the shantytowns themselves evolved. Poor but enterprising inhabitants relied on their own efforts to improve their living conditions. With much sweat labor and a little hard-earned cash, a family replaced its mud walls with concrete blocks and gradually built a real home. Or the community pressured the city to install a central water pump or build a school. Low-paid officeworkers in search of cheap housing sometimes moved in and continued the upgrading process. Nor were people who lived in squatter communities particularly attracted to revolutionary doctrines. In short, when self-help settlers were not threatened by eviction, they showed themselves capable of improving their housing.

Better understanding of spontaneous settlements led most governments to re-evaluate their hostility toward them. Efforts to bulldoze them out of existence in the 1960s and 1970s were generally abandoned. Under pressure from these still primitive neighborhoods and their activists, some governments, particularly in Asia, turned to supporting improvements—gradually installing piped water, public toilets, lighting, and some paved streets. New self-help settlements continued to spring up on the urban fringes, but in the largest cities they became less desirable because poor transportation made getting to and from work a nightmare. As a result, more centrally located slums and old shantytowns became more attractive to government planners and capitalists, who sometimes combined to banish the poor and build new housing for the middle and upper classes.

## Rich and Poor

After the developing countries achieved political independence, massive inequality continued, with few exceptions, to be the reality of life. A monumental gap separated rich and poor. In about 1975 in most developing countries, the top 20 percent of the people took more than 50 percent of all national income, and the poorest 20 percent got about 5 percent of the income. Thus the average household in the top fifth of the population received about ten times as much monetary income as the average household in the bottom fifth in the 1970s. This situation did not change significantly thereafter.

Such differences have been the rule in human history. The distribution of income in the developing countries strongly resembled that of the industrialized countries prior to the First World War, before the movement toward greater equality accelerated sharply (see page 799). It is noteworthy that types of economy—rightist or leftist, capitalist or socialist—had a limited effect on shares of income.

Differences in wealth and well-being were most pronounced in the exploding towns and cities. Few rich or even middle-class people lived in the countryside. Urban squatters may have been better off than landless rural laborers, but they were light-years away from the luxury of the urban elite. In Asia and Africa the rich often moved into the luxurious sections previously reserved for colonial administrators and white business people. Particularly in Latin America, upper-class and upper-middle-class people built fine mansions in exclusive suburbs, where they lived behind high walls, with many servants and protected from intruders by armed guards and fierce dogs.

A lifestyle in the "modern" mold was almost the byword of the Third World's urban elite. From French perfume and Scotch whisky to electronic gadgets and the latest rock music, imported luxuries became the unmistakable signs of wealth and privilege. In Swahili-speaking East Africa, the common folk called the elite *wa Benzi*, "those who ride in a Mercedes-Benz."

Education also distinguished the wealthy from the masses. The children of the elite often attended expensive private schools, where classes were taught in English or French and had little in common with the overcrowded public school classes taught in the national language. Subsequently, they often studied abroad at leading European and North American universities, or they monopolized openings at local universities. While absorbing the latest knowledge in a prestigious field such as civil engineering or economics, they also absorbed foreign customs and values. They mastered the fluent English or French that is indispensable for many top-paying jobs, especially with international agencies and giant multinational corporations. Thus elites in the developing countries often had more in common with the power brokers of the industrialized nations than with their own people, and they seemed willing tools of neocolonial penetration and globalization.

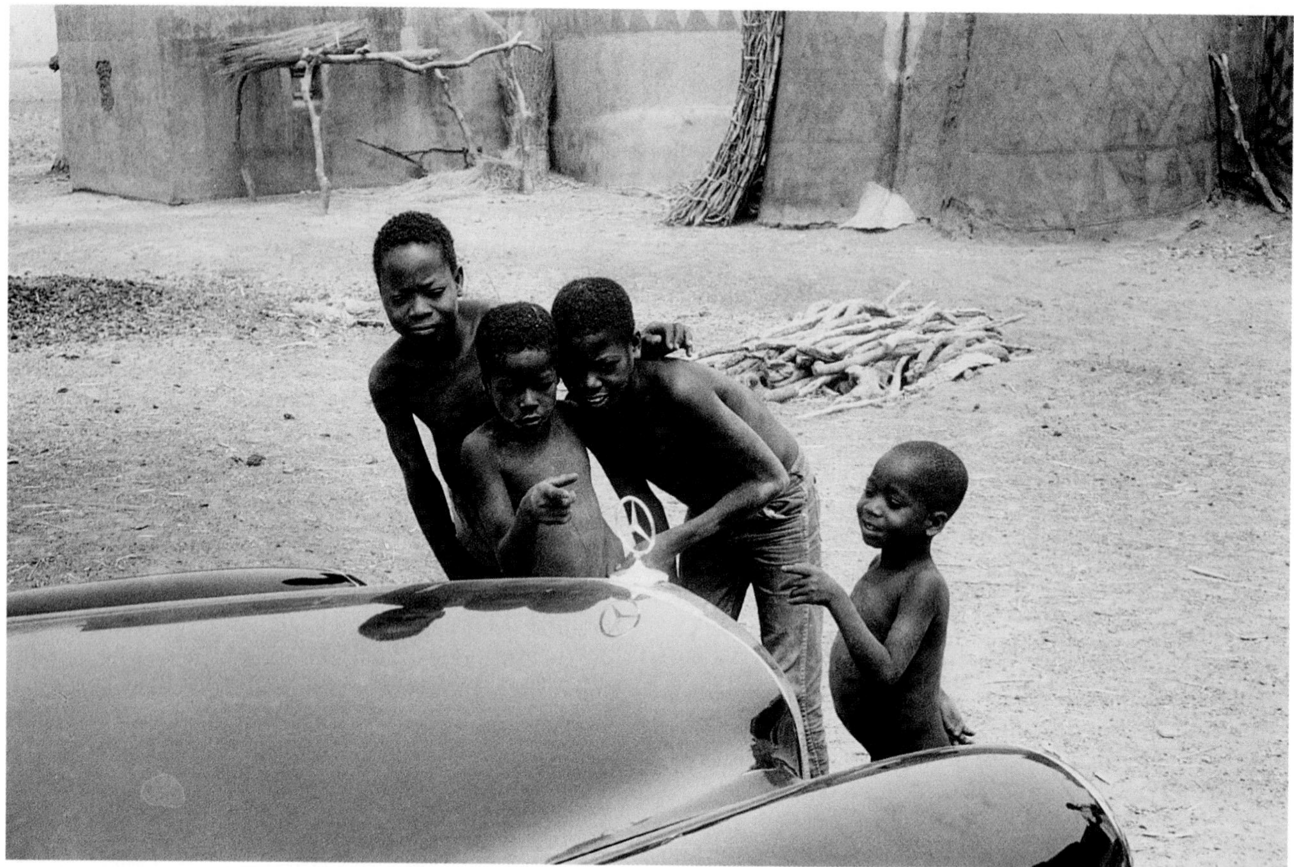

**A Sleek Automobile** The most ambitious of these four boys in an African village may already dream of acquiring power and wealth in the city. *(Marc and Evelyne Bernheim/Woodfin Camp & Associates)*

The middle classes in the developing countries generally remained small relative to the total population in most countries, although some notable exceptions emerged in Asia in the 1980s and 1990s. White-collar workers and government bureaucrats joined the traditional ranks of merchants and professionals in the urban middle class. Their salaries, though modest, were secure and usually carried valuable fringe benefits. An unexpected component of the urban middle class until quite recently was the modern factory proletariat, a privileged segment of the population in many poor countries. Few in number because sophisticated machines required few workers relative to agriculture or traditional crafts, they were often well organized and received high wages for their skilled work.

In the 1980s and 1990s the growth of economic liberalism and global competition tended to undermine the factory worker's relatively privileged position. Many of the plants of the first industrialization drive, like those in Latin America in the 1930s, had grown up with strong unions behind tariff walls that protected them from more sophisticated producers in the wealthy industrialized countries. As barriers to trade came down, these factories had to cut costs in an attempt to survive. Factory workers often encountered lower wages, permanent layoffs, and plant closings.

In general, the majority of the exploding population of urban poor earned precarious livings in a modern yet traditional **bazaar economy** of petty trades and unskilled labor. Here regular salaried jobs were rare and highly prized, and a complex world of tiny, unregulated businesses and service occupations predominated. Peddlers and pushcart operators hawked their wares, and sweatshops and home-based workers manufactured cheap goods for popular consumption. This old-yet-new bazaar economy continued to grow prodigiously as migrants streamed to the cities, as modern industry provided too few jobs, and as the wide gap between rich and poor persisted.

## Migration and the Family

Large-scale urban migration had a massive impact on traditional family patterns in the developing countries. Particularly in Africa and Asia, the great majority of migrants to the city were young men, married and unmarried; women tended to stay in the villages. The result was a sexual imbalance in both places. There were several reasons for this pattern. Much of the movement to cities (and mines) remained temporary or seasonal. At least at first, young men left home to earn hard cash to bring back to their villages. Moreover, the cities were expensive, and prospects there were uncertain. Only after a man secured a genuine foothold did he marry or send for his wife and children.

Kinship and village ties helped ease the rigors of temporary migration. Often a young man could go to the city rather easily because his family had close ties with friends and relatives there. Many city neighborhoods were urban versions of their residents' original villages. Networks of friendship and mutual aid helped young men (and some women, especially brides) move back and forth without being overwhelmed.

For rural women the consequences of male outmigration were mixed. Asian and African women had long been treated as subordinates, if not inferiors, by their fathers and husbands. Rather suddenly, such women found themselves heads of households, faced with managing the farm, feeding the children, and running their own lives. In the East African country of Kenya, for instance, one-third of all rural households were headed by women in the late 1970s. African and Asian village women had to become unprecedentedly self-reliant and independent. As a result, the real beginnings of more equal rights and opportunities, of "women's liberation," became readily visible in Africa and Asia. (See the feature "Listening to the Past: Voices from the Village" on pages 1160–1161.)

In Latin America the pattern of migration was different. Whole families migrated, very often to squatter settlements, much more commonly than in Asia and Africa. These families frequently belonged to the class of landless laborers, which was generally larger in Latin America than in Africa and Asia. Migration was also more likely to be once and for all. Another difference was that single women were as likely as single men to move to the cities, in part because there was a high demand for women as domestic servants. The situation in Mexico in the late 1970s was typical:

> *They [women] leave the village seeking employment, often as domestic servants. When they do not find work in the cities, they have few alternatives. If they are young, they frequently turn to prostitution; if not, they often resort to begging in the streets. Homeless peasant women, often carrying small children, roam every quarter of Mexico City.*[4]

Some women also left to escape the narrow, male-dominated villages. Even so, in Latin America urban migration seemed to have less impact on traditional family patterns and on women's attitudes than it did in Asia and Africa.

# GROWING DIVERSITY SINCE 1980

The ongoing urban explosion was one of several factors promoting growing diversity in the developing world. First, the transformation of modest cities into gigantic agglomerations sharpened the contrast between life in urban areas and life in rural areas. This difference in experiences made individual countries and their citizens less homogeneous. Second, continuing urban expansion diversified further the class structure, expanding especially the middle classes and thereby strengthening the forces of democratic reform. Third, the growth of middle-income people was very uneven. It depended primarily on economic performance, which varied more and more by country and region beginning with the world recession of the early 1980s.

Momentous economic changes occurred in East Asia. The rapid industrial progress that characterized first Japan and then the "Four Dragons"—Taiwan, Hong Kong, Singapore, and South Korea—was replicated in China in the 1980s and most of the 1990s. After Deng Xiaoping took over in 1978 and launched economic reforms (see page 1104), the Chinese economy grew through 1993 at an average annual rate of about 9 percent. Average per capita income in China was doubling every ten years, three to five times faster than in successfully industrializing countries such as the United States and Britain before 1914. According to the World Bank, the number of very poor people in China declined by 60 percent after 1978. The spectacular economic surge of almost one-fourth of the human race helped to vitalize all of East Asia. Starting from low levels, first Indonesia and then India did fairly well among big countries; Malaysia and Thailand led the smaller newly industrializing countries. A vibrant, independent East Asia emerged an economic powerhouse, an event of enormous significance in long-term historical perspective.

One key to China's success was the example of South Korea and Taiwan, which with Hong Kong and Singapore showed the way in East Asia. Both South Korea and

Taiwan were typical underdeveloped countries in the early postwar years—poor, small, agricultural, densely populated, and lacking in natural resources. They also had suffered from Japanese imperialism and from destructive civil wars with communist foes. Yet they managed to make good. How was this possible?

Radical land reform expropriated large landowners, who were mainly Japanese or pro-Japanese, and drew the mass of small farmers into a competitive market economy, which proved an excellent school of self-reliance and initiative. As in Japan, economic development became a national mission in South Korea and Taiwan. Probusiness governments cooperated with capitalists, opposed strikes, and did nothing to improve the long hours and low wages of self-sacrificing workers. These governments protected their own farmers and industrialists from foreign competition, while also securing almost free access to the large American market. And like Japan, both countries succeeded in preserving many fundamentals of their interrelated Korean and Chinese cultures even as they accepted and mastered Western technology. Tough nationalist leaders maintained political stability at the expense of genuine political democracy.

When China turned toward the market in 1979, it could build on the national unity and radical land distribution inherited from Mao. Introducing economic reforms gradually and maintaining many tools of economic regulation, China's Communist party leaders encouraged native entrepreneurs and also drew on the business talent of wealthy "overseas" Chinese in Hong Kong and Taiwan. They knew the world market, needed new sources of cheap labor, and played a key role in the emerging **Greater China.** Authoritarian political rule encouraged

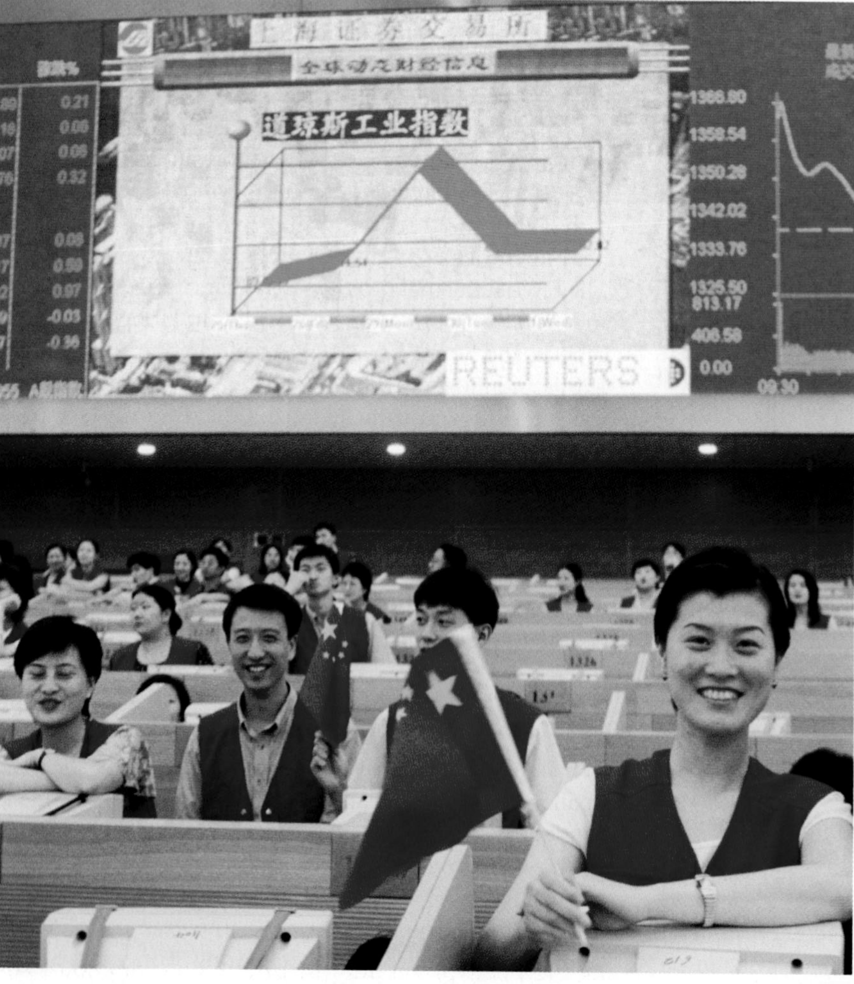


**China's Booming Stock Exchange** The happy faces of these young workers are in harmony with China's dynamic economy and its exuberant stock market. The Chinese exchange relies on modern electronic trading, as this photo suggests, and speculation is intense. *(Wally McNamee/Corbis)*

China's people to focus on "daring to be rich," as Deng advised them.

No other region in Asia, Africa, or Latin America (or in Europe or North America) came close to matching East Asia after 1980. Latin America had some bright spots, most notably Brazil. But West Asia and North Africa, wracked by war, political instability, and low oil prices, experienced spiraling urbanization without much new industrialization or economic development. The situation in sub-Saharan Africa was particularly grave. Severe famines, bitter ethnic conflicts, the AIDS crisis, and low prices for African exports of raw materials weighed heavily on the vast region, vivid testimony to the growing diversity in the developing world.

In the late 1990s lingering visions of underlying Third World unity appeared less fanciful once again. In 1997 the great boom in East Asia came to an end. Indonesia, South Korea, Malaysia, and Thailand experienced financial crashes and industrial decline, which undermined China and worsened conditions in stagnating Japan. In 1998 the financial crisis spread to Russia and threatened Latin America. Frantic efforts to limit the global impact of the Asian economic crisis, which were largely successful, highlighted again the world's interdependency, as we will see in Chapter 36.

## MASS CULTURE AND CONTEMPORARY THOUGHT

Ideas and beliefs continued to change dramatically in the developing nations after independence. Education fostered new attitudes, and mass communications relentlessly spread the sounds and viewpoints of modern life. Intellectuals and writers, in their search for the meanings of their countries' experiences, articulated a wide spectrum of independent opinions in keeping with growing regional and national diversity.

### Education and Mass Communications

In their efforts to modernize and better their societies after securing independence, political leaders in the developing countries became increasingly convinced of the critical importance of education. They realized that **human capital**—skilled and educated workers, managers, and citizens—played a critical role in the development process. Faith in education and "book learning" then spread surprisingly rapidly to the masses, for whom education principally meant jobs. Thus young people in the developing countries headed for schools and universities in unprecedented numbers. There still remained, however, a wide education gap between them and the rich countries, where more than 90 percent of both sexes attended school through age seventeen.

Moreover, the quality of education in the developing countries was often mediocre. African and Asian universities tended to retain the old colonial values, stressing law and liberal arts at the expense of technical and vocational training. As a result, many poor countries found themselves with large numbers of unemployed or underemployed liberal arts graduates. These "generalists" competed for scarce jobs in the already bloated government bureaucracies, while less prestigious technical jobs went begging.

A related problem was the **brain drain** in the developing countries: many gifted students in vital fields such as engineering and medicine ended up pursuing their careers in the rich countries of the developed world. For example, in the early 1980s as many Indian-trained doctors practiced abroad, mainly in advanced countries, as served India's entire rural population of 480 million. The threat represented by the brain drain helped explain why the professional elite received high salaries even in very poor countries.

In recent years many observers have concluded that the education drive, like its forerunner the industrialization drive, served the rural masses poorly. It sometimes seemed that its greatest beneficiaries were schoolteachers, who profited from the elite status provided by a permanent government job. Instruction was often impractical and mind numbing. The children of farmers generally learned little about agriculture, raising animals, or practical mechanics. Instead, students often memorized passages from ancient literary works and religious texts and spewed back cut-and-dried answers. No wonder children stayed away from schools in droves. Village schools succeeded best at identifying the exceptional pupils, who were then shipped off to the city for further study and were lost forever to the village.

Whatever its shortcomings, formal education spread with another influential agent of popular instruction: mass communications. The transistor radio penetrated the most isolated hamlets of the developing world. Governments universally embraced radio broadcasting as a means of power, propaganda, and education. Relentlessly, the transistor radio propagated the outlooks and attitudes of urban elites and in the process challenged old values.

The second communications revolution—the visual one—was reaching rural people everywhere by the beginning of the twenty-first century. Television was bringing the whole planet into the bars and meetinghouses of

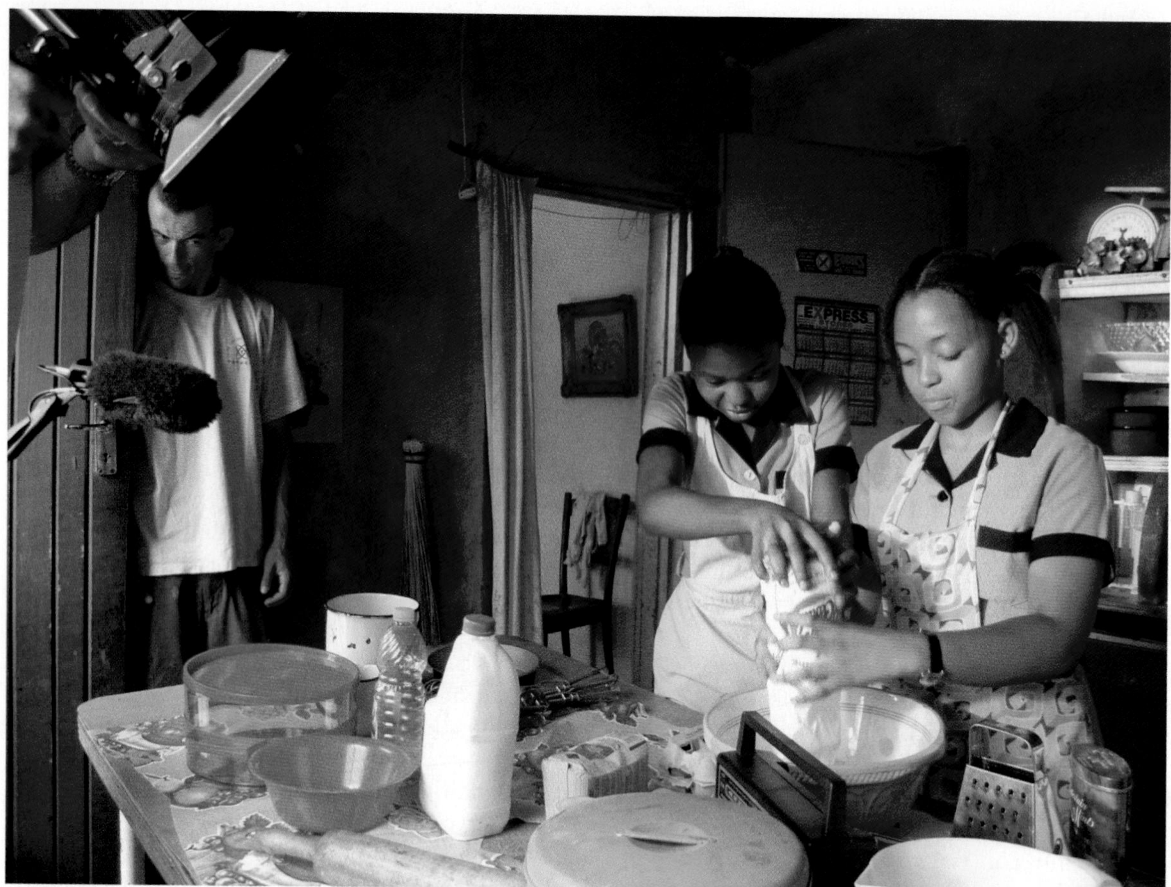


**Educational TV in South Africa** A South African TV crew films *Soul Buddyz,* a popular show for children that grapples honestly with everything from sexuality and AIDS to child abuse and physical disabilities. This show was inspired by *Soul City,* an award-winning soap opera for teenagers and young adults that includes practical information on safe sex and HIV infection. *(Louise Gubb/Corbis Saba)*

the world's villages. Experience elsewhere—in remote French villages, in Eskimo communities above the Arctic Circle—showed that television was having a profound, even revolutionary, impact. At the very least the lure of the city continued to grow.

## Interpreting the Experiences of the Emerging World

Popular education and mass communications compounded the influence of the developing world's writers and thinkers—its purveyors of explanations. Some intellectuals meekly obeyed their employers, whether the ministry of information or a large newspaper. Others simply embellished or reiterated some received ideology, such as Marxism or free-market capitalism. But some intellectuals led in the search for meaning and direction that has accompanied rapid social change and economic struggle.

Having come of age during and after the struggle for political emancipation, numerous intellectuals embraced the vision of Third World solidarity, and some argued that genuine independence and freedom from outside control required a total break with the former colonial powers and a total rejection of Western values. This was the message of Frantz Fanon (1925–1961) in his powerful study of colonial peoples, *The Wretched of the Earth* (1961).

Fanon, a French-trained black psychiatrist from the Caribbean island of Martinique, was assigned to a hospital in Algeria during the bloody war for Algerian independence. He quickly came to sympathize with the guerrillas and probed deeply into the psychology of colonial revolt. According to Fanon, decolonization is always a violent and totally consuming process whereby one "species" of men, the colonizers, is completely replaced by an absolutely different species—the colonized, the wretched of the earth. During decolonization the colonized masses mock colonial values, "insult them, and vomit them up," in a psychic purge.

Fanon believed that the battle for formal independence was only the first step. Throughout Africa and Asia the former imperialists and their local collaborators—the "white men with black faces"—remained the enemy:

*During the colonial period the people are called upon to fight against oppression; after national liberation, they are called upon to fight against poverty, illiteracy, and underdevelopment. The struggle, they say, goes on.*

*. . . We are not blinded by the moral reparation of national independence; nor are we fed by it. The wealth of the imperial countries is our wealth too. . . . Europe is literally the creation of the Third World. The wealth which smothers her is that which was stolen from the underdeveloped peoples.*[5]

For Fanon national independence and Third World solidarity went hand in hand with outrage at the misdeeds and moral posturings of the former colonial powers. Fanon's passionate, angry work became a sacred text for radicals attacking imperialism and struggling for liberation.

As countries gained independence and self-rule, some writers looked beyond wholesale rejection of the industrialized powers. They too were "anti-imperialist," but they saw colonial domination as only one chapter in the life of their peoples. They were often activists and cultural nationalists who applied their talents to celebrating the rich histories and cultures of their peoples. And many did not hesitate to criticize their leaders or fight against oppression and corruption. (See the feature "Individuals in Society: Rigoberta Menchú: Speaking for Her People.")

The Nigerian writer Chinua Achebe (b. 1930) rendered these themes with acute insight and vivid specificity in his short, moving novels. Achebe wrote in English rather than his native Ibo tongue, but he wrote primarily for Africans, seeking to restore his people's self-confidence by reinterpreting the past. For Achebe the "writer in a new nation" had first to embrace the "fundamental theme":

*This theme—quite simply—is that the African people did not hear of culture for the first time from Europeans; that their societies were not mindless but frequently had a philosophy of great depth and volume and beauty; that they had poetry and above all, they had dignity. It is this dignity that many African peoples all but lost in the colonial period, and it is this that they must now regain. The worst thing that can happen to any people is the loss of their dignity and self-respect. The writer's duty is to help them regain it by showing what happened to them, what they lost.*[6]

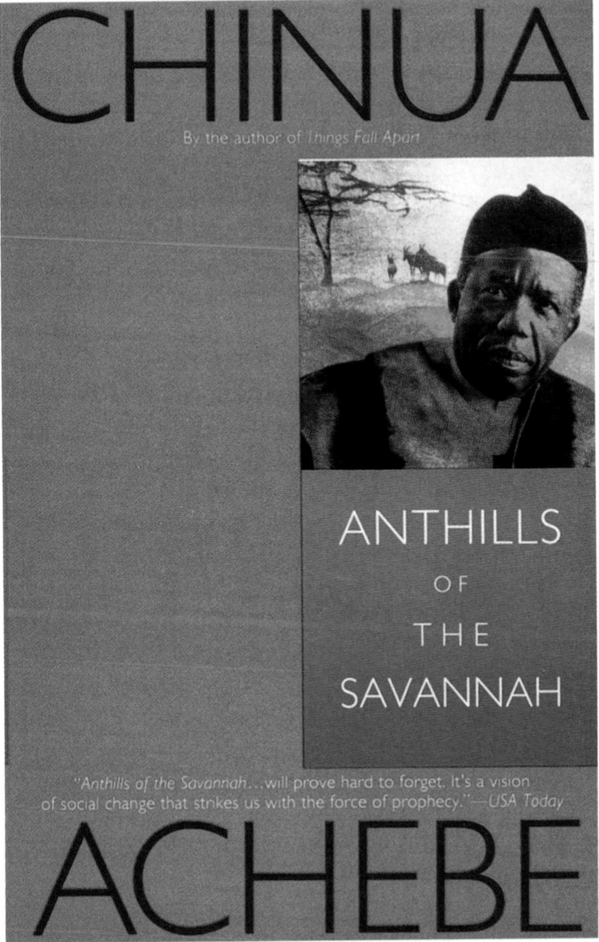


**Nigeria's Conscience** Chinua Achebe's powerful novels focus on complex and believable individuals caught up in the unfolding drama of colonialism, independence, and nation building in Africa. As this book jacket photo suggests, Achebe is an intensely serious writer, a man who speaks for his people and believes in the high moral calling of literature and art. *(Cover of* Anthills of the Savannah *[New York: Anchor Books/Doubleday, 1989]. Reproduced with permission)*

In *Things Fall Apart* (1958) Achebe achieved his goal by vividly bringing to life the men and women of an Ibo village at the beginning of the twentieth century, with all their virtues and frailties. The hero, Okonkwo, is a mighty wrestler and a hard-working, prosperous farmer, but he is stern and easily angered. Enraged at the failure of his people to reject newcomers, and especially at the white missionaries who convert his son to Christianity and provoke the slaying of the sacred python, Okonkwo kills a colonial messenger. When his act fails to spark a tribal revolt, he commits suicide. Okonkwo is destroyed by the general breakdown of tribal authority and his own intransigent recklessness. Woven into the story are the proverbs and wisdom of a sophisticated people and the beauty of a vanishing world.

In later novels Achebe portrays the postindependence disillusionment of many writers and intellectuals. In *A Man of the People* (1966) the villain is Chief The Honorable Nanga, a politician with the popular touch. This "man of the people" lives in luxury, takes bribes to build expensive apartment buildings for foreigners, and flimflams the voters with celebrations and empty words. The hero, an idealistic young schoolteacher, tries to unseat Chief Nanga, with disastrous results. Beaten up and hospitalized, the hero broods that the people "had become even more cynical than their leaders and were apathetic into the bargain."[7] Achebe's harsh but considered judgment reflected trends in many developing nations in the 1960s and 1970s: the rulers seemed increasingly corrupted by Western luxury and estranged from the rural masses.

From the 1970s onward Achebe was active in the struggle for democratic government in Nigeria. In his novel *Anthills of the Savannah* (1989), he calls upon Africa to stand on its own two feet, take responsibility, and realize that widespread corruption is frustrating hopes of progress and genuine independence. Yet in his recent essays and speeches he also returns to his earlier theme of the West's enduring low opinion of Africa—ever the "dark continent," the savage, non-Western "other world." Achebe urges his readers to throw away these old prejudices, which he sees rooted in racism, and fashion instead new, socially beneficial visions that will help both Africans and non-Africans to redefine Africa and its prospects.

**Mariama Bâ** Bâ's first novel, translated from French into English as *So Long a Letter* in 1981, was a literary milestone and an enormous success. For the first time in an African novel, a woman tells her own story. But Bâ's fictional "I" also speaks for all Senegalese women, telling her society that she exists, suffers from injustice, and will now make her own decisions. *(© George Hallett)*

The celebrated novelist V. S. Naipaul, born in Trinidad in 1932 of Indian parents, also castigated governments in the developing countries for corruption, ineptitude, and self-deception. Another of Naipaul's recurring themes is the poignant loneliness and homelessness of people uprooted by colonialism and Western expansion. In *The Mimic Men* (1967) the blacks and whites and the Hindus and Chinese who populate the tiny Caribbean islands are all aliens, thrown together by "shipwreck." As one of the characters says:

*It was my hope in writing to give expression to the restlessness, the deep disorder, which the great exploration, the overthrow in three continents of established social organizations, the unnatural bringing together of peoples who could achieve fulfillment only within the security of their own societies and the landscapes hymned by their ancestors . . . has brought about. The empires of our time were short-lived, but they altered the world forever; their passing away is their least significant feature.*[8]

Most of Naipaul's stories take place in postindependent developing countries, which are struggling to find themselves and to build national identities out of the bewildering legacy of native cultures, colonial experiences, and modern ideologies.

Naipaul and Achebe, like many other talented writers and intellectuals in developing nations, probed memories and experiences in pursuit of understanding and identity.

## INDIVIDUALS IN SOCIETY

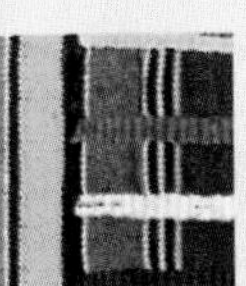

# RIGOBERTA MENCHÚ: SPEAKING FOR HER PEOPLE

*Rigoberta Menchú, activist in the struggle for native rights.* (José Luis Yuste/Corbis Sygma)

In 1992 Rigoberta Menchú became the first person of indigenous origin ever to receive the prestigious Nobel Prize for Peace. In honoring Menchú and placing her alongside such historic figures as Martin Luther King, Jr., and Lech Walesa, the Nobel committee praised her work for social justice and ethnocultural reconciliation. In the midst of the "large-scale oppression of Indian peoples" in Guatemala, she was lauded for playing a "prominent part as an advocate of native rights." And although her actions were not always peaceful, she stood as a "uniquely potent symbol of a just struggle."

Although certain aspects of Menchú's life remain controversial and disputed, Menchú's achievement clearly grew out of a long history of oppression. After almost five hundred years a minority of Ladinos, mostly the descendants of Spanish settlers, still rules over the twenty-three indigenous peoples that make up 60 to 80 percent of Guatemala's population. Long-standing government practices of conferring legal ownership of land mainly on Ladinos, condoning Ladino seizure of Indian communal lands, and refusing to acknowledge community ownership have been particularly devastating. Many Indians cannot earn a living on their meager landholdings, and they must seek seasonal work on coastal plantations, where they receive low pay and brutal treatment. Efforts to hold on to land or gain higher wages are met by repression and assassination.

Born in mountainous northern Guatemala, where the large Menchú family survived mainly on the beans and corn they grew, Rigoberta absorbed a profound love of her culture. Her moving autobiography speaks reverently of ancestors, treasured traditions, and the fierce determination of the Quiché people to maintain their collective identity in the face of scorn and hostility. Thus at their marriage ceremony, a young Quiché couple asks "for help with bringing up their children in Indian ways" and "always remaining true to their race no matter how much trouble, sadness and hunger they endure. And their parents answer: 'Generations and generations will pass but we will always remain Indians.'"*

Menchú's early education included laboring on a coffee plantation from dawn to dusk at the age of eight, but her formative struggle occurred at home. According to Menchú, a brutal landowner and his gun-toting thugs, acting in collusion with the government, sought to terrorize the Menchús' village into either abandoning its land or accepting the status of landless peons.

Rigoberta's father, Vicente, led the resistance, organizing traps for invaders in 1977 and forming a national union of peasants and plantation workers. The whole family followed his lead, and, with tens of thousands of other highland Indians, they paid a frightful price. Rigoberta joined her father on his organizing missions in the mountains and learned the major Indian languages as well as Spanish in order to forge unity and communicate with poor Ladinos and sympathetic Europeans. Her sixteen-year-old brother became an organizer and was kidnapped, mutilated, and publicly burned to death. Branded a communist and repeatedly imprisoned and tortured, Vicente died in 1980 when troops stormed the building that he and others had occupied in the capital. Rigoberta's activist mother was then seized by soldiers and beaten to death. Hunted by security forces, Rigoberta escaped to Mexico in 1981.

Since 1981 Rigoberta Menchú has emerged through her writing and international organizing as a powerful advocate for indigenous peoples and their rights. As in the case of the African writer Chinua Achebe in his recent work, Menchú is an outstanding example of individuals in developing countries who are looking beyond Western imperialism and focusing instead on their own societies and how to improve them.

### QUESTIONS FOR ANALYSIS

1. How has society been divided in Guatemala? How does Rigoberta Menchú's identity relate to these divisions?
2. Is the struggle of the Menchú family an isolated event? Or is it an aspect of larger historical developments? Which developments?

*Rigoberta Menchú, *I . . . Rigoberta Menchú: An Indian Woman in Guatemala,* ed. E. Burgos-Debray (New York: Verso, 1985), p. 67.

A similar soul-searching went on in other creative fields, from art and dance to architecture and social science, and seemed to reflect a growing intellectual maturity and cultural vitality.

## SUMMARY

As Third World leaders and peoples threw off foreign domination after 1945 and reasserted themselves in new or revitalized states, they turned increasingly inward to attack poverty and limited economic development. The collective response was an unparalleled medical revolution and the Third World's first great industrialization drive. Long-neglected agriculture also made progress, and some countries experienced a veritable Green Revolution. Moreover, rapid urbanization, expanding educational opportunities, and greater rights for women were striking evidence of modernization and fundamental human progress. The achievement was great.

But so was the challenge, and results fell far short of aspirations. Deep and enduring rural poverty, overcrowded cities, enormous class differences, and the sharp criticisms of leading writers mocked early hopes of quick solutions. From the late 1960s onward there was growing dissatisfaction and frustration in developing nations, lessened only slightly by the emergence of China and East Asia as economic powerhouses. Thus, as Chapter 36 will show, in recent times many observers came to believe that the developing nations can meet their challenges only by reordering the global system and dissolving the unequal ties that bind them to the rich nations.

## KEY TERMS

Third World
medical revolution
neo-Malthusian
industrialization strategy
modernization
mixed economy
Green Revolution
urban explosion
supercities
shantytowns
self-help housing
bazaar economy
Greater China
human capital
brain drain

## NOTES

1. P. Bairoch, *Economics and World History: Myths and Paradoxes* (Chicago: University of Chicago Press, 1993), p. 95.
2. Quoted in L. R. Brown, *Seeds of Change: The Green Revolution and Development in the 1970s* (New York: Praeger, 1970), p. 16.
3. P. Ehrlich, *The Population Bomb* (New York: Ballantine, 1968), p. 11.
4. P. Huston, *Third World Women Speak Out: Interviews in Six Countries on Change, Development, and Basic Needs* (New York: Praeger, 1979), p. 11.
5. F. Fanon, *The Wretched of the Earth* (New York: Grove Press, 1968), pp. 43, 93–94, 97, 102.
6. C. Achebe, *Morning Yet on Creation Day* (London: Heinemann, 1975), p. 81.
7. C. Achebe, *A Man of the People* (London: Heinemann, 1966), p. 161.
8. V. S. Naipaul, *The Mimic Men* (New York: Macmillan, 1967), p. 38.

## SUGGESTED READING

Many of the works in the Suggested Reading for Chapter 34 discuss themes considered in this chapter. P. Bairoch, *Economics and World History: Myths and Paradoxes* (1993), is a concise summation of a leading specialist's many valuable studies. T. von Laue, *The World Revolution of Westernization: The 20th Century in Global Perspective* (1988), and L. Harrison, *Who Prospers? How Cultural Values Shape Economic and Political Success* (1992), are stimulating interpretations of problems in the developing world. R. Auty, *Patterns of Development: Resources, Policy and Economic Growth* (1995), and J. Mittelman and M. K. Pasha, *Out from Underdevelopment Revisited: Changing Structures and the Remaking of the Third World* (1997), are useful introductions to recent trends and issues. The November 1999 issue of *Current History,* "Rethinking the Third World," is also recommended. R. Gamer, *The Developing Nations: A Comparative Perspective,* 2d ed. (1986), is a useful synthesis. Two excellent works from a non-Western perspective are especially recommended: E. Hermassi, *The Third World Reassessed* (1980), and M. ul Haq, *The Poverty Curtain: Choices for the Third World* (1976). B. Ward, *The Lopsided World* (1968), and G. Myrdal, *Asian Drama: An Inquiry into the Poverty of Nations,* 3 vols. (1968), movingly convey the hopes and frustrations of sympathetic Western economists in the 1960s. Valuable introductions to world agriculture and population are found in various works by L. R. Brown, including the work cited in the Notes and *In the Human Interest: A Strategy to Stabilize World Population* (1974). A. Maddison, *Monitoring the World Economy, 1820–1992* (1995), is a brief but authoritative overview.

Three valuable studies on African questions are R. Austen, *African Economic History: Internal Development and External Dependency* (1987); B. Turner et al., eds., *Population Growth and Agricultural Change in Africa* (1993); and P. Lloyd, ed., *The New Elites of Tropical Africa* (1966). C. Turnbull, *The Lonely African* (1962), provides intimate portraits of Africans caught up in decolonization and rapid social change. J. Iliffe, *The African Poor: A History* (1987), is an original and important work that is highly recommended. Critical aspects of Indian economic development are carefully considered in M. Franda, *India's Rural Development: An Assessment of Alternatives* (1980). E. Vogel, *The Four Little Dragons: The*

*Spread of Industrialization in East Asia* (1991), is an outstanding short study. China's economic and social challenges in the early 1980s are skillfully placed in a broad and somewhat somber perspective by two Chinese-speaking journalists, F. Butterfield, *China: Alive in the Bitter Sea* (1982), and R. Bernstein, *From the Center of the Earth: The Search for the Truth About China* (1982). W. Overholt, *The Rise of China: How Economic Reform Is Creating a Modern Superpower* (1993), is an account of more recent success.

For the prodigious growth of Third World cities, J. Kasarda and A. Parnell, eds., *Third World Cities: Problems, Policies and Prospects* (1993); A. Gilbert and J. Gugler, *Cities, Poverty and Development: Urbanization in the Third World,* 2d ed. (1992); and J. Abu-Lughod and R. Hay, Jr., eds., *Third World Urbanization* (1977), are highly recommended. Similarly recommended is a fascinating investigation of enduring poverty by M. Lipton and J. van der Gaag, eds., *Including the Poor* (1993).

A good introduction to changes within families is Huston, cited in the Notes, a truly remarkable study. C. Johnson-Odim and M. Stroebel, eds., *Expanding the Boundaries of Women's History: Essays on Women in the Third World* (1992), is an important study. Other useful works on Third World women and the changes they have experienced include J. Momsen, *Women and Development in the Third World* (1991); N. Keddie and B. Baron, eds., *Women in Middle Eastern History: Shifting Boundaries in Sex and Gender* (1992); A. de Souza, *Women in Contemporary India and South Asia* (1980); N. J. Hafkin and E. Bay, eds., *Women in Africa* (1977); and M. Wolf, *Revolution Postponed: Women in Contemporary China* (1985).

The reader is especially encouraged to enter into the contemporary Third World with the aid of the gifted writers discussed in this chapter. F. Fanon, *The Wretched of the Earth* (1961), is a particularly strong indictment of colonialism from the 1960s. Chinua Achebe illuminates the proud search for a viable past in his classic novel of precolonial Africa, *Things Fall Apart* (1958), and the disillusionment with unprincipled postindependence leaders in *A Man of the People* (1966). G. Moore and U. Beier, eds., *Modern Poetry from Africa* (1963), is a recommended anthology. In addition to his rich and introspective novels such as *The Mimic Men* (1967), V. S. Naipaul has reported extensively on life in Third World countries. His *India: A Wounded Civilization* (1978), impressions gleaned from a trip to his family's land of origin, and *A Bend in the River* (1980), an investigation of the high price that postcolonial Africa is paying for modernization, are especially original and thought provoking. E. Burke III, ed., *Struggle and Survival in the Modern Middle East, 1700 to the Present* (1993), contains colorful brief biographies of a wide variety of ordinary people and is outstanding. L. Heng and J. Shapiro, *Son of the Revolution* (1983), brilliantly captures the drama of Mao's China through the turbulent real-life story of a young Red Guard.

# LISTENING TO THE PAST

## VOICES FROM THE VILLAGE

*How did social and economic development change women's lives and family relations in the villages of the Third World? How did women and families cope with enormous changes, and how could governments and international agencies better respond to the real needs of rural people? These questions fascinated the American writer Perdita Huston (1936–2001), who worked as a medical-social worker in rural North Africa in the early 1960s. The only literate woman in the area, she served as "nurse, letter-writer, marriage counselor, and midwife." And she learned to respect the wisdom and courage of poor peasant women "who searched ceaselessly for food, firewood, dung, water, and hope."*

*In the mid-1970s, as the critical importance of women in both development and population control was increasingly recognized, Huston received a grant from the United Nations to study the needs of village women in Tunisia, Egypt, Sudan, Kenya, Sri Lanka, and Mexico. Assisted by interpreters and using unstructured interviews, Huston talked first with women in groups and then with volunteers in private, "heart-to-heart" exchanges. In each village she began with a simple but profound question: "How does your life differ from that of your mother or grandmother?" This question brought many answers and opened up further discussion of key issues, such as housing, education, jobs, male-female relationships, and children. The following women were representative.*

A young, high-school educated woman in Sri Lanka, the eldest of nine children:

"My mother's generation did not have all the opportunities we have. They did not have education, health services, or the transportation systems that exist now. But economically, they were better off. The income they got was sufficient to meet all their needs. At the moment, the high cost of living makes life difficult. They find it difficult to have a happy life.

"Today young people have the opportunity to show their capabilities in sports and cultural activities—even in social and public affairs. Earlier generations did not allow girls to leave the home and attend public meetings. Now we have that opportunity. Even without the consent of our parents, we take part in social and public affairs or in political matters.

"That is why I wanted to come and join this [agricultural] cooperative. When I live at home, I have no freedom. Wherever I go, I have to be accompanied by a brother and I have to return home early. I am questioned all the time. . . . But here I can earn my living and have some freedom to move about and make choices about participation in after-work activities.

"Of course, my parents didn't want me to come here. They refused at first. They were concerned about letting a daughter come to a place like this, but the second time I asked—or rather, insisted—they gave their consent.

"You see, my father is a farmer. My parents lived from the land, but when my grandfather died, the land was distributed among his sons. Now my parents' portion is very small. It is not sufficient for them to exist on. They continue to work the land and to search for other jobs.

"I want my children to have a firmer footing—not to have this type of life. They must learn a profession and have a better job than mine. Women in Sri Lanka need employment. They should all have jobs. They must be taught skills so that they can earn a bit for their families.

"I will have only two children: When you have more than two, you have all sorts of problems and expenses to worry about."

A nomadic Bedouin woman in Tunisia:

"I was given in marriage at age thirteen. I hadn't even reached puberty. My father was dead, so my uncle arranged the marriage with a neighbor. Now it is better; there is a law that says girls mustn't marry before the age of seventeen. That is good. You know, I hadn't had my period when I married. A month later it came—and a month after that I was pregnant. I had five children—three girls and two boys—but one daughter was stillborn.

"My children go to school, and I want them, both sons and daughters, to go as far as their ability lets them. I want them to have a good future, a profession, a happy life. I don't want them working in the fields, picking up straws and leftovers as I do. I would like so much to have gone to school. I would like to have opened my mind. I would have taught other people about things. I want to know everything—everything you can learn if you have an education. I won't let my daughters marry earlier than seventeen.

"Men are much better these days than they were before. They respect women more. . . . Before, a woman could be divorced, beaten, and poorly treated. That kind of thing doesn't exist anymore, thanks to President Bourguiba. Thanks to him and the laws, women are much better off today.

"We have family planning now, and you can take better care of your children. That, too, is different. You can't imagine how many things I tried to swallow to prevent myself from having more children. I even used to eat mothballs, thinking that would help. I am only thirty-six years old, and I have planned my family now for five years. I have a loop. I don't want any more children. Life is too difficult." [She paused.] "Before the new laws, all women lived the lives of beasts."

A young Muslim woman in Sudan:

"Mother's life was, and is, very different from my own. She couldn't go out or talk to any men other than her husband. She never even went out into the street with him. She just stays home all the time; that is her life. But I go to market; I go out with my husband; we may even go to a movie. My husband does not mind. Sometimes I don't even put on my tow [veil]. Mother would never go outside without a full veil covering her face and hair.

"These changes are all due to education. Before, women did not go to school. They did not know their husbands. They never saw them until the wedding night, once they were already married. But here in Sudan, women don't have as much access to education as men. It is better for boys, much better. I want my children to have more education than I did; then they will be different from me, just as I am different from my mother. The main thing is education. Schools are very important for girls.

"A girl and a boy must be equal. A woman must work in all areas—doctor, teacher, anything. Any work a man can do, a woman can do also."

Village women and their daughters in a hut in southern Mexico. *(Cindy Karp/stockphoto.com)*

## QUESTIONS FOR ANALYSIS

1. In what ways do these women think their lives are different from their mothers'?
2. What common themes emerge in these responses?
3. What do these women think about education and jobs? About marriage and children?
4. Huston found many women who spoke openly in private but who did not want their names used or their neighbors or husbands informed of their views. How do you explain this?

*Source:* Perdita Huston, *Third World Women Speak Out: Interviews in Six Countries on Change, Development, and Basic Needs* (New York: Praeger, 1979), pp. 25, 27–28.

Highways for the twenty-first century: a new expressway in Singapore supports excellent public transportation, while a telecommunications ground station relays messages from around the world on the Internet superhighway. *(AFP/Corbis)*

CHAPTER

# 36 ONE SMALL PLANET

## CHAPTER OUTLINE

- World Politics
- Global Interdependence
- Patterns of Thought

We live in a global age. One small but telling indicator of our interconnectedness is the surprising similarity of the popular subjects being searched at any given time at Google.com—the world's leading Internet search engine—by people from all over the world in several different languages. Technology accelerates the flow of information and the interaction of countries and cultures. Economic cycles, international organizations, common challenges, and new ideas tie the world's citizens together in complex networks.

As we bring our history of the world's regions and peoples to a close, let us look at our interconnected planet from a truly global perspective. In doing so, we shall look for insight into the world's ongoing development and the prospect for its talented but quarrelsome human race.

- In the early twenty-first century, how did the planet organize itself politically, and how did competing nation-states address common problems?
- How was the human race using its resources to meet its material needs?
- What key ideas guided human behavior as the world moved toward an uncertain future?

## WORLD POLITICS

One of the most astonishing aspects of recent scientific and technological achievements was that no corresponding change occurred in the way the human race governed—or failed to govern—itself. Sovereign nation-states reigned supreme and were reinforced by enormous military power. The embryonic growth of an effective global political organization, of a government that could protect the world's nations from themselves, appeared permanently arrested. Efforts to control universal threats such as weapons of mass destruction sometimes led to global agreements, but the tension generated by powerful, independent nation-states in a fragile and interdependent world was one of the most striking—and dangerous—characteristics of our small planet.

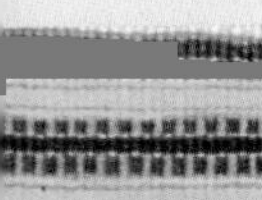

## Nation-States and the United Nations

The rise of the nation-state and the global triumph of nationalism have been a grand theme of modern world history. The independent territorial **nation-state**—sometimes containing separatist ethnic groups striving for nationhood in their own right—remained the fundamental principle of political organization in the early twenty-first century. Yet from a global perspective we must surely question what has been taken for granted.

Has the nation-state system, with its apparently inevitable conflicts, become a threat to life on the planet? Some have thought so. It is one of history's ironies that nationalism was widely condemned in the twentieth century, especially in Europe, just as it triumphed decisively in world politics. In *Mankind and Mother Earth* (1976), his last work, the renowned British historian Arnold Toynbee (1889–1975) poignantly expressed the post-1914 disillusionment of many European and American intellectuals. At the time of his birth, Toynbee wrote, his middle-class countrymen "supposed Earthly Paradise was just around the corner." They also assumed that the national state was "the natural, normal, rightful political unit." Toynbee's generation of Europeans, however, lived through an era of "self-inflicted tribulation," war and genocide, largely due to their "explosive, subversive" faith in national self-determination.

Toynbee borrowed a term from the ancient Greeks to explain that the spread of the western European political idea of the national state, first to eastern Europe and then to Asia and Africa, had created a fatal discrepancy:

*the discrepancy between the political partition of the Oikoumené [the habitat of the human race] into local sovereign states and the global unification of the Oikoumené on technological and economic planes. This misfit is the crux of mankind's present plight. Some form of global government is now needed for keeping the peace . . . and for reestablishing the balance between Man and the rest of the biosphere.*[1]

A small but articulate group of intellectuals and political scientists continued to advocate similar views and gave the "unrealistic" question of world government serious consideration. The history of the **United Nations** is a good place to begin our search for possible signs of the emergence of a global authority transcending sovereign states.

When the United Nations was founded in San Francisco in 1945, the United States was the driving force behind its creation. President Franklin D. Roosevelt and Democrats in the Wilsonian tradition believed that the failure of the United States to join the League of Nations had contributed to the tragic breakdown of "collective security" in the 1930s. A resurrected League, they believed, would facilitate Allied cooperation in the postwar era.

The main purpose of the new organization was "to maintain international peace and security." Thus the United Nations charter prohibited any nation from using armed force except for self-defense. At the same time, the charter gave the organization's **Security Council** the authority to examine any international conflict, impose economic and political penalties on an aggressor, and even "take such action by air, sea, or land forces as may be necessary to restore international peace and security." In short, the Security Council had the power to police the world.

In practice, however, this theoretical power was severely restricted. China, Great Britain, France, the Soviet Union, and the United States were all made permanent members of the Security Council, and all five had to agree on any peacekeeping action. None of the Big Five, and certainly not the United States, was willing to surrender sovereign power to a potential world government.

A second principle of the United Nations affirmed and reinforced the primacy of the national state in world politics. The charter directed the United Nations to pursue "friendly relations between nations based on the principle of equal rights and self-determination of peoples." Every "peace-loving" state was eligible to join and to participate in the **General Assembly,** the United Nations' second main body. Founded with 50 members, the General Assembly reached 122 members in 1965 and 191 in 2002. Each member state, whatever its size, always had one voice and one vote on all resolutions, but the resolutions of the General Assembly became legally binding on states only if all five of the Security Council's permanent members agreed.

The third express purpose of the United Nations testified to the expanded scope of government tasks since the late nineteenth century, as well as to an emerging vision of global interdependence. According to its charter, the United Nations was "to achieve international cooperation in solving international problems of an economic, social, cultural, or humanitarian character, and in promoting and encouraging respect for human rights and for fundamental freedom for all without distinction as to race, sex, language, or religion." This open-ended assignment was the province of a Social and Economic Council, whose eighteen members were to be elected periodically by the General Assembly. The council was also to work with specialized affiliated agencies such as the World Health Organization in Geneva and the Food and Agriculture Organization in Rome.

The scope of its original purposes helps explain the evolution of the United Nations. Hopes of effective

1950 1960 1970 1980 1990 2004

## POLITICAL/MILITARY

- 1952 United States explodes first hydrogen bomb
- 1955 Asian and African nations form a "third force" of nonaligned nations
- 1970 Treaty on the Non-Proliferation of Nuclear Weapons
- 1989 Fall of communism in eastern Europe
- 1991 United Nations Security Council orders Iraq to destroy weapons of mass destruction
- 1998 Bombing of U.S. embassy in Kenya
- 1998 India and Pakistan explode nuclear weapons
- 2001 Al-Qaeda attacks World Trade Center and Pentagon
- 2003 North Korea withdraws from 1970 nonproliferation treaty
- 2003 U.S. invasion of Iraq

## SOCIAL/ECONOMIC

- 1950s–present Growth of multinational corporations
- 1972 *The Limits to Growth* argues that unlimited economic development is impossible
- 1973 OPEC raises price of crude oil and causes panic in industrialized countries
- 1975–present Slower population growth in Asia and Latin America
- 1980s–1990s Drought and famine in Africa
- 1980s–present AIDS epidemic
- 1982 United States refuses to sign new Law of the Sea
- 1982 United States organizes rescue operation to save Mexican economy
- 1997 Asian currencies collapse; International Monetary Fund provides emergency loans

## INTELLECTUAL/RELIGIOUS

- 1970s–present Resurgence of Islamic fundamentalism
- 1973 Schumacher, *Small Is Beautiful*
- 1976 Toynbee, *Mankind and Mother Earth*
- 1977 Revel, *The Totalitarian Temptation*

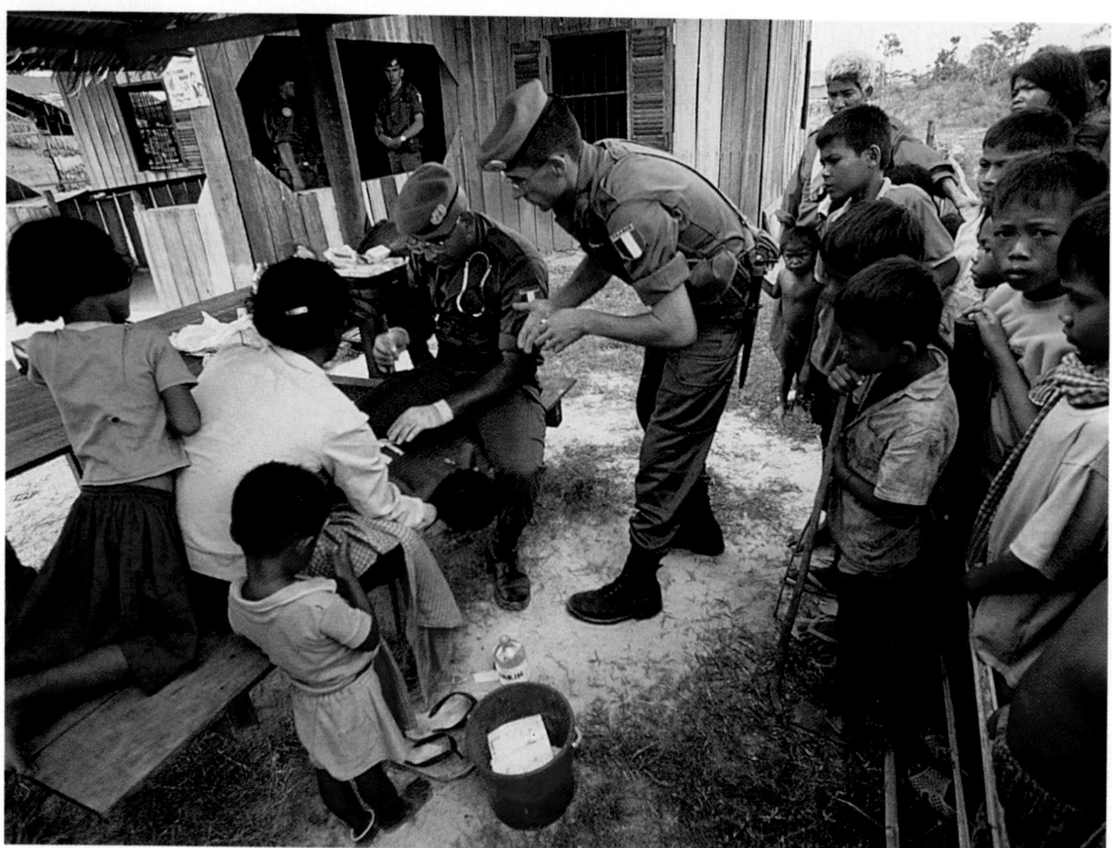

**The United Nations in Action** These soldiers are part of a French battalion serving in a United Nations peacekeeping operation in Cambodia (Kampuchea), a country wracked by war and civil conflict since 1970. United Nations forces usually provide humanitarian aid as they try to preserve fragile cease-fires after warring armies agree to stop fighting. *(J. F. Roussier/Sipa Press)*

Allied cooperation in the Security Council faded in the early cold war, as the outnumbered Soviet Union often used its veto power to paralyze that body. The Security Council proved somewhat more successful at quieting bloody conflicts between smaller states where the interests of the superpowers were not directly involved, such as the dispute between India and Pakistan over Kashmir and that between Greece and Turkey over Cyprus.

With the Security Council often deadlocked, the General Assembly claimed ever greater authority. As decolonization picked up speed and the number of member states grew, a nonaligned, anticolonial Afro-Asian bloc emerged. Reinforced by sympathetic Latin American countries, the bloc succeeded in organizing a Third World majority in the General Assembly by the mid-1960s. This majority concentrated on economic and social issues, while also passing many resolutions often directed against the former colonial powers, the United States, Israel, imperial Portugal, and the white government of South Africa.

The long-term significance of these developments at the United Nations was mixed. On the one hand, the Third World majority, predominantly composed of small and poor countries, mistook the illusion of power at the United Nations for the substance of power in world affairs. By the late 1970s many of the General Assembly's resolutions were ignored. Many critical international issues, such as the Arab-Israeli conflict, were increasingly resolved by resorting to traditional diplomacy or war.

Moreover, the United Nations generated limited popular support around the world. Most people continued to identify with their national states, which may even provide adults with a psychological substitute for the family bonds that nurtured them in childhood. Thus nation-states continued to weave the powerful social bonds necessary for group action. As two American political scientists put it, "The nation-state may all too seldom speak the voice of reason. But it remains the only serious alternative to chaos."[2]

On the other hand, the United Nations proved to be a remarkably hardy institution. With a large numerical majority, the developing nations succeeded in expanding the scope of the organization's economic, social, and cultural mission. By the 1970s an alphabet soup of United Nations committees, specialized agencies, and affiliated international organizations studied and promoted health, labor, agriculture, industrial development, and world trade, not to mention disarmament, control of narcotics, and preservation of the great whales. These agencies and affiliated organizations derived their initial authority from treaties and agreements between sovereign states, but once in operation they took on a life of their own and expanded their activities.

Staffed by a talented international bureaucracy, United Nations agencies worked tenaciously to consolidate their power and to serve their main constituency—the overwhelming majority of developing nations in both the General Assembly and the world's total population. Without directly challenging national sovereignty, they exerted a steady pressure for more international cooperation in dealing with specific global issues, and the world's big powers sometimes went along. The United Nations also emerged as the central forum for the debate on the relations between rich and poor countries. Thus sharp-eyed observers detected a gradual, many-sided enlargement of United Nations involvement in the planet's social and economic affairs.

Throughout the 1970s and 1980s the United Nations also continued to play a role in establishing peace in conflicts that did not directly involve the superpowers. Typically, United Nations negotiators helped weary foes to work out a cease-fire agreement, which was then monitored by a United Nations command drawing its troops from many countries.

Then, as the cold war ended, the United Nations acted on a grand scale to stop aggression and maintain stability. In 1990 the five permanent members of the Security Council agreed to repel the Iraqi invasion of Kuwait, and in 1991 they required a defeated Saddam Hussein to destroy all his weapons of mass destruction. Success in Iraq led some leaders and observers to believe that Great Power cooperation on the Security Council would enable the United Nations to fulfill its original purpose and guarantee peace throughout the world.

One such attempt came in 1992, when armed forces from the United States landed on the East African beaches of Somalia to stop a savage civil war and allow United Nations soldiers to maintain peace thereafter. The operation failed, as some Somali fighters attacked and killed their would-be benefactors. United Nations negotiators also failed to stop the savage civil war in Bosnia, which was eventually resolved by the NATO alliance in the Dayton Accords (see page 1094). In response to these and other setbacks, the United Nations scaled back its peacekeeping ambitions and concentrated on helping warring factions that wanted to make peace. Even this was an awesome task. In 1995 sixty-seven thousand United Nations soldiers were stationed in hot spots around the world. United Nations peacekeeping efforts were imperfect, but they also were indispensable.

In 2002 another grave crisis over Iraq brought the United Nations to the center of the world's political stage. Echoing the Clinton administration, President George W. Bush accused Iraq of rebuilding its weapons of mass destruction and made clear his intention to drive Saddam Hussein from power (see page 1091). However, according to the United Nations charter, the Security Council has the sole authority to use armed force except in self-defense, and Iraq, impoverished by a decade of tough United Nations sanctions, gave no indication of attacking any of its neighbors or the United States. Moreover, large numbers of Americans shared the world's doubts about the legality—and wisdom—of an American attack on Iraq. Thus the Bush administration reluctantly agreed to new Security Council resolutions requiring Iraq to destroy any remaining prohibited weapons and accept the return of United Nations weapons inspectors. Iraq accepted, declaring it had destroyed all prohibited weapons.

As 2002 ended and the inspections resumed, Kofi Annan, the United Nations' widely respected secretary-general, coordinated efforts to achieve the Security Council's stated objectives and avoid war. (See the feature "Individuals in Society: Kofi Annan.") The inspectors operated freely in Iraq and found no weapons of mass destruction. However, the United States and Britain denounced Iraq's lukewarm cooperation, dismissed the inspections as a fraud, moved armies to the Middle East, and lobbied for a new resolution authorizing immediate military action against Iraq. As the world followed the debates in the Security Council with unprecedented interest, France, Russia, China, Germany, and a majority of the smaller states argued instead for continued weapons inspections, and the Security Council deadlocked. Claiming that earlier resolutions provided ample authorization, the United States and Britain invaded

**Weapons Inspections in Iraq** United Nations inspectors search for weapons of mass destruction inside a military complex north of Baghdad. Although United Nations inspections in 2002 and 2003 failed to uncover prohibited weapons, Iraqi cooperation in the disarmament process was incomplete. Asserting that Saddam Hussein was still hiding chemical and biological weapons, the United States and Britain launched a massive invasion of Iraq in March 2003. *(Reuters NewMedia Inc./Corbis)*

Iraq. Thus the Security Council failed to act. Nonetheless, all parties in the crisis recognized the United Nations as a key source of international legality. Fears that the United Nations was becoming irrelevant seemed exaggerated.

## Complexity and Violence

Alongside territorial nation-states and international organizations that focused on specific problems stretched a wide range of alliances, blocs, partnerships, regional rivalries, and local conflicts. It was often difficult to make sense of this tangle of associations for several reasons.

First, the end of the cold war, beginning in 1989, removed one of the planet's most enduring political realities. During the cold war the hostile superpowers dominated and curbed their allies and clients, and both superpowers were in turn restrained by them. The sudden end of the cold war shattered these interlocking restraints, removing a basic principle of global organization and order.

The cold war division had contributed to the ideology of Third World solidarity, long a second organizing force in planetary affairs (see Chapter 35). A critical step was taken in 1955, when Asian and African nations came together in Bandung, Indonesia, to form a **third force** of nonaligned nations. The neutralist leaders of Asia and Africa believed that genuine independence and social justice were the real challenges before them, and with their Latin American counterparts they worked in the United Nations for a restructuring of the world economic system (see page 1174). However, in the 1980s and 1990s big differences in economic performance in countries and regions undermined the whole idea of Third World solidarity. Developing countries increasingly went their own ways.

A striking third development was the growing "multipolar" nature of world politics. Calling on nationalism as a mobilizing force, increasingly assertive **middle powers** jockeyed for regional leadership and sometimes came into conflict. The rise of the middle powers reflected the fact that most of the world's countries were small and

# INDIVIDUALS IN SOCIETY

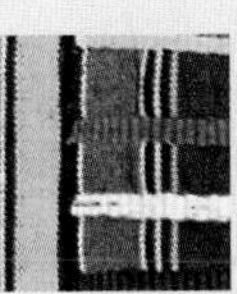

## KOFI ANNAN

*Kofi Annan, secretary-general of the United Nations, discusses his Nobel Peace Prize in 2001.* (Reuters NewMedia Inc./Corbis)

The key role of the Security Council in the Iraqi weapons crisis of 2002–2003 highlighted the renewed prominence of the United Nations in world affairs after the disappointments of the mid-1990s. This revival owed a great deal to Kofi Annan (b. 1938), the confident, compassionate African diplomat who headed the international organization beginning in 1997. Annan offered an inspiring moral vision of a global community committed to peace, democracy, and universal human rights.

Kofi Annan was born into the West African elite. His parents were hereditary nobles of the Fante people in Ghana, and his father was an elected provincial governor and business executive. As a boy, Annan attended excellent private schools, but he also grew up with deep roots in his African heritage. He later recalled, "My family moved in and out all the time from a traditional to a modern urban setting."* Active in student politics and winning a Ford Foundation scholarship for young foreign leaders, the winsome Annan attended Macalester College in St. Paul, Minnesota, where he developed an idealistic commitment to international peace and understanding.

Although he had intended to return to Ghana after graduation, the increasingly authoritarian rule of President Kwame Nkrumah caused him to reconsider. In 1962 Annan took a job as a budget officer with the World Health Organization (WHO), an important United Nations agency based in Geneva, Switzerland. In the following years he gradually worked his way up the ladder in the United Nations, experiencing the world's tragedies and emergencies firsthand and also learning to create budgets and plan programs as a skilled administrator.

In 1992 United Nations secretary-general Boutros Boutros-Ghali put Annan in charge of all United Nations peacekeeping operations. It proved to be a monumental challenge. As the cold war order disappeared, civil war enveloped a host of countries, including Bosnia, Croatia, Somalia, Haiti, Rwanda, Angola, Afghanistan, and Sudan. Annan had to manage an unprecedented explosion in the size, scope, and complexity of peacekeeping efforts. Civilian and military peacekeepers working for the United Nations skyrocketed from about ten thousand in 1992 to almost seventy thousand, from seventy-seven countries, in 1995. Widely praised from many sides for his sensitive and effective leadership, Annan was selected secretary-general for a five-year term beginning in 1997 and began serving a second term in 2002.

Annan's first act as secretary-general was to reform the United Nations. He reduced total spending, as the wealthy nations led by the United States adamantly demanded, but he did so by refocusing the organization's efforts on the welfare of the world's poorest citizens, many of whom were in Annan's native Africa. This focus in turn helped bolster the developing countries' support of United Nations efforts.

Guided by an idealistic, moral view of the world, Annan believed that humanity should know no divisions. As he said when he and the United Nations were jointly awarded the Nobel Peace Prize in December 2001, the "poor and dispossessed are no less deserving of human dignity, fundamental freedoms, security and education than any of us." Moreover, he acted on his beliefs in countless ways, rallying humanitarian organizations, launching initiatives, and setting a moral agenda. His contribution to the global campaign for human rights, called the Annan Doctrine, argues that states must no longer use their rights of sovereignty as a shield for gross violations of human rights and that the global community has at times a "duty to intervene." Annan helped lead the international attack on the HIV/AIDS epidemic, which he called his "personal priority," and said that he tried "to place human beings at the center of everything we do" at the United Nations.

### QUESTIONS FOR ANALYSIS

1. How was Annan able to rise out of the United Nations' bureaucracy and reach the very top as secretary-general? What factors were most important? Why?
2. What is the Annan Doctrine? What, in your opinion, is the proper role of the United Nations in today's world?

*Quoted in J. Tessitore, *Kofi Annan: The Peacekeeper* (New York: Franklin Watts, 2000), p. 18.

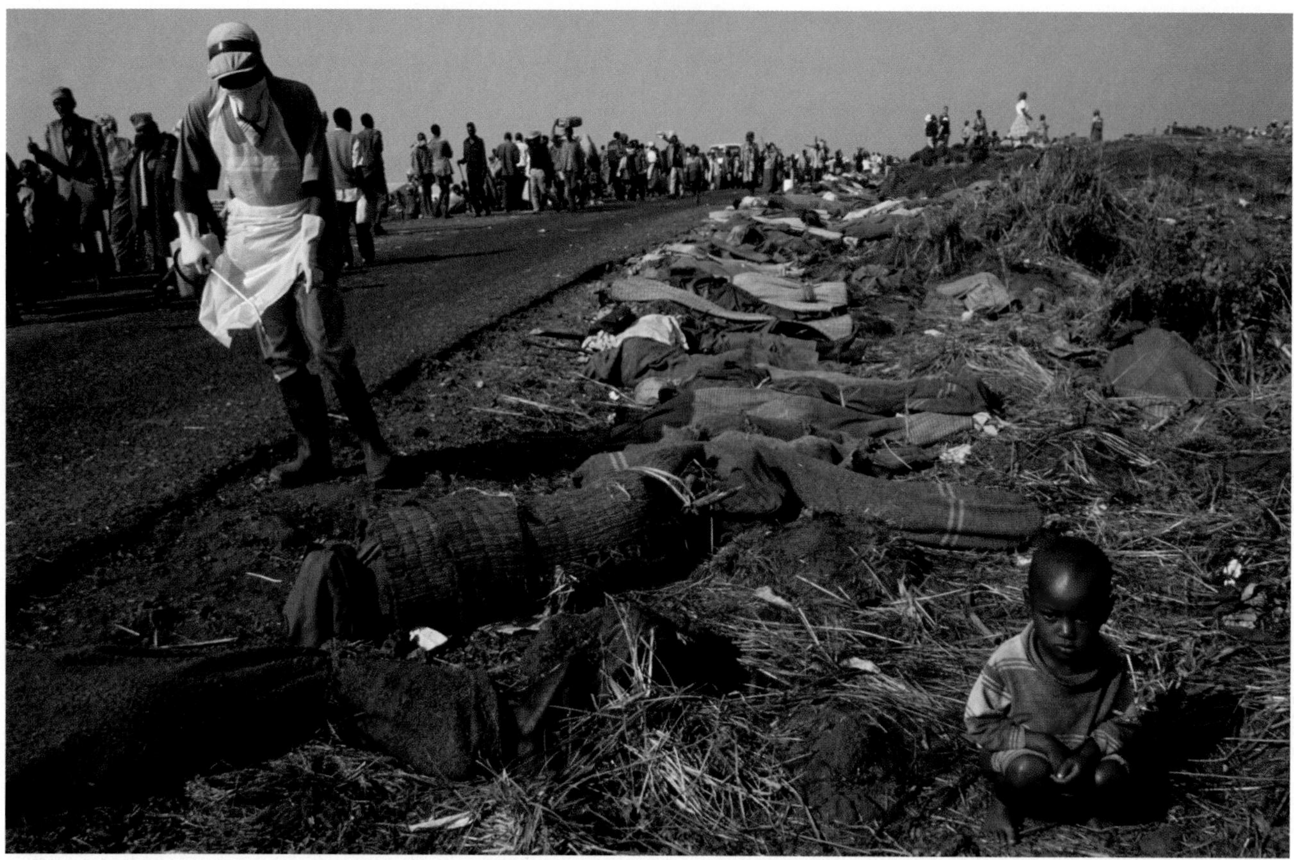

**Civil War in Rwanda** After Hutus and Tutsis slaughtered each other in genocidal ethnic conflict in 1994, thousands of refugees fled to neighboring Zaire, where many died in a cholera epidemic. The bodies of some of the cholera victims lie beside the road, as streams of refugees observe from the other side. Refugee populations, weakened by trauma and hunger, are highly susceptible to epidemic disease. *(Peter Turnley/Corbis)*

weak, with fewer than 20 million people. Few countries had the resources necessary for real power on a regional or global scale.

In South America, Brazil, with more than 140 million people, vast territory and resources, and a rapidly industrializing economy, emerged as the dominant nation-state. Equally impressive was the emergence of Mexico as the natural leader of the Spanish-speaking Americas. Strong regional powers such as France and West Germany had re-emerged in western Europe by the early 1960s. Nigeria and South Africa were unquestionably the leading powers in sub-Saharan Africa. Heavily populated Egypt and much smaller Israel were also regional powerhouses. Iran and Iraq competed and fought for dominance in the Persian Gulf. China, India, and Japan were all leading regional powers, and several other Asian countries—notably Indonesia, Vietnam, and Pakistan—were determined to join them.

Conflict and violence often characterized the emerging multipolar political system, leading to several major wars and many small ones. Some countries were literally torn apart. Lebanon, long considered the most advanced state in the Arab world, was practically destroyed by ethnic struggles and foreign occupation.

The ongoing plague of local wars and battles caused great suffering and millions of refugees. For example, Vietnam's "boat people" fled in desperation after unification under the communists. The war for independence in Bangladesh temporarily created more than 10 million refugees, who fled into India. In 1981 the United Nations commission for emergency relief counted 10 million refugees in Asia and Africa. In the 1990s civil war in Bosnia, Kosovo, Rwanda, and Afghanistan sent many hundreds of thousands of new refugees running for their lives.

Rivalries between ethnic groups were often at the heart of the civil wars that produced so many refugees. Different groups and their politicians competed for power, or they fought to overturn entrenched discrimination and oppression. Ethnic competition could turn violent and lead to **separatism**—radical demands for ethnic autonomy or political independence. Yet only about twenty states, representing about 10 percent of the world's population, were truly homogeneous. Even if common language were the only basis for ethnic identity, which it is not, the number of countries in the world could explode to six thousand.[3] Thus the goal of a separate state for each self-defined people—the classic nationalist goal—could lead to endless battles and tragedy on a global scale. The peaceful reconciliation of existing states with widespread separatist aspirations stood as a mighty challenge in the early twenty-first century.

## The Terrorist Threat

The challenge of separatism appeared even greater in light of the fact that civil war and terrorism often went hand in hand during the twentieth century. Beginning in the 1920s and peaking in the 1960s, many nationalist movements used **terrorism** in their battles to win nationhood and political independence. This was the case in several new states, including Ireland, Israel, Cyprus, Yemen, and Algeria.[4] Those fighting for independence often targeted police forces for assassination campaigns, thereby breaking down confidence in colonial governments and provoking counter-atrocities that generated increased support for the independence movement.

In the Vietnam War era, a second wave of terrorism saw some far-left supporters of the communist Vietcong, such as the American Weathermen, the German Red

**Terrorism in Northern Ireland** In August 1998 a powerful car bomb suddenly devastated the busy shopping district of Omagh, killing twenty-nine persons and maiming two hundred more. The most deadly terrorist act in thirty years of often violent political conflict in Northern Ireland, this bombing by a dissident IRA group sought to derail peace negotiations between Catholic and Protestant leaders. *(Lewis Alan/Corbis Sygma)*

Army Faction, and the Italian Red Brigades, practicing "revolutionary terror" in an effort to cripple the Western heartland. These groups engineered a series of deadly bombings, assassinations, and kidnappings. They also hijacked airplanes—more than a hundred each year in the 1970s—in order to take hostages and blackmail governments into meeting some demand, such as the release of convicted fellow terrorists. Some terrorists trained in the facilities of the Palestine Liberation Organization (PLO) operated international networks and targeted Israel and U.S. installations abroad. This second wave receded in the 1980s as painstaking police work and international cooperation defeated these "revolutionaries" in country after country.

In the late twentieth century a third wave was building, cresting perhaps in the murderous attack by the **al-Qaeda** network on the World Trade Center and Pentagon on September 11, 2001. In trying to understand this third wave, many commentators were quick to stress the role of extreme Islamic fundamentalism as a motivating factor. But the most perceptive scholars noted that recent heinous crimes had been committed by terrorists inspired by several religious faiths and sects and were by no means limited to Islamic extremists.[5] These scholars also noted that different terrorist movements needed to be linked to underlying political conflicts and civil wars for meaningful understanding.

Applying this perspective to Osama bin Laden and al-Qaeda members, two stages of their activities stand out. First, in the long, bitter fighting against the Soviet Union and the local communists in Afghanistan, bin Laden and like-minded "holy warriors" developed terrorist skills and a narrow-minded, fanatical Islamic puritanism. They also developed a hatred of most existing Arab governments, which they viewed as corrupt, un-Islamic, and unresponsive to the needs of ordinary Muslims. The objects of their hostility included the absolute monarchy of oil-rich Saudi Arabia (bin Laden's own country of origin), pro-Western but undemocratic Egypt, and the secular, one-party dictatorship of Saddam Hussein.

Second, when these Islamic extremists returned home and began to organize, they met the fate of many earlier Islamic extremists and were jailed or forced into exile, often in tolerant Europe. There they blamed the United States for being the supporter and corrupter of existing Arab governments and organized murderous plots against the United States—a despised proxy for the Arab rulers they could not reach. Bin Laden's network also blamed the United States for steadfastly supporting Israel and denying the claims of the Palestinians, although attempts to exploit the Israeli-Palestinian tragedy generally came later and operated mainly as a recruiting tool. These developments set the stage for the 1998 bombing of the U.S. embassy in Nairobi, Kenya, which claimed nearly two hundred lives, the September 11 atrocity in 2001, and the U.S.-led decimation of al-Qaeda in Afghanistan.

## Weapons of Mass Destruction

Fears that terrorists might acquire weapons of mass destruction revived global concern about the enduring menace of nuclear proliferation and nuclear war, as well as the danger of chemical and biological attacks. How had this frightening situation arisen? And what was being done to find solutions?

Having let the atomic genie out of the bottle at Hiroshima and Nagasaki in 1945, a troubled United States immediately proposed that it be recaptured through effective international control of all atomic weapons. The Soviets, suspicious that the United States was really trying to preserve its atomic monopoly through its proposal for international control and inspection, rejected the American idea. Instead, the Soviet Union continued its crash program and exploded its first atomic bomb in 1949. The United States exploded its first hydrogen bomb in 1952, and within ten months the Soviet Union did the same. Further American, Soviet, and then British tests aroused worldwide fear that radioactive fallout would enter the food chain and cause leukemia, bone cancer, and genetic damage. Concerned scientists called for an international agreement to stop all testing of atomic bombs.

Partly in response to worldwide public pressure, the United States, the Soviet Union, and Great Britain agreed in 1958 to stop testing for three years. In 1963 these three powers signed an agreement, eventually signed by more than 150 countries, banning nuclear tests in the atmosphere. A second step toward control was the 1970 Treaty on the Non-Proliferation of Nuclear Weapons, designed to halt their spread to non-nuclear states and to reduce stockpiles of existing bombs held by the nuclear powers. It seemed that the nuclear arms race might yet be reversed.

This outcome did not come to pass. De Gaulle's France and Mao's China, seeing themselves as great world powers, simply disregarded the test ban and continued their development of nuclear weapons, although they later signed the nonproliferation treaty. By 1968 they too had hydrogen bombs. Reversing its previous commitment to nuclear arms limitations, India also developed weapons and in 1974 exploded an atomic device. The nuclear arms race between the Soviet Union and the United States surged ahead after 1968. The much-discussed SALT talks in the 1970s confined themselves to limiting the rate at which the Soviet Union and the United States produced more nuclear warheads.

India developed its atomic capability partly out of fear of China, which had manhandled India in a savage border war in 1962. India's nuclear blast in 1974 in turn frightened Pakistan, which after 1947 regarded India as a bitter enemy. Pakistan's president Zulfikar Ali Bhutto (1928–1979) was reported to have said that Pakistan must have the bomb even if its people had to eat grass. In the 1980s Pakistan was close to producing nuclear weapons.

It was also generally believed that Israel had an arsenal of nuclear bombs. Israel's apparent nuclear superiority was profoundly distasteful to the Arabs. Hence Iraq pushed hard, with help from France, to develop nuclear capability. In June 1981 Israel responded suddenly, attacking and destroying the Iraqi nuclear reactor. At the same time, many near–nuclear powers appeared poised to go nuclear by 1980. One expert on nuclear arms warned that the human race was "an endangered species."[6]

Such warnings helped to mobilize the international community and contributed to positive developments. Armed to the teeth with atomic bombs, the United States and the Soviet Union did cooperate successfully in limiting the spread of nuclear weapons to their friends and foes. The international commission monitoring the nonproliferation treaty helped Argentina and Brazil abandon their nuclear weapons program by providing a framework of effective verification. Related agencies monitored exports of nuclear material, technology, and missiles that could carry atomic bombs. These measures encouraged confidence in global cooperation and the nonproliferation treaty, which was extended indefinitely in 1995.

Yet at least four serious challenges remained in the early twenty-first century. First, top-secret efforts by Iraq to build a bomb before the Persian Gulf War had almost succeeded, highlighting the need for better ways to detect cheating. Second, Russia and the United States had promised vaguely to cut their nuclear weapons drastically, but in 2002 they were stalled at about six thousand each, with no hope of quick progress. Third, in 1998 first India and then Pakistan exploded nuclear weapons, dealing a severe blow to long efforts to stop the spread of these weapons. In 2002 India and Pakistan appeared on the brink of war, and the planet shuddered. Finally, in early 2003 long-standing tensions between North Korea and the United States, which had never signed a peace treaty ending the 1950–1953 Korean War, reached crisis proportions over the question of nuclear arms on the Korean peninsula. As both sides accused the other of failing to live up to a 1994 agreement, North Korea announced its intention to withdraw from the 1970 nonproliferation treaty and stood ready to quickly develop a nuclear arsenal. This confrontation, like that between India and Pakistan, showed the danger of atomic war in a multipolar world of intense regional rivalries.

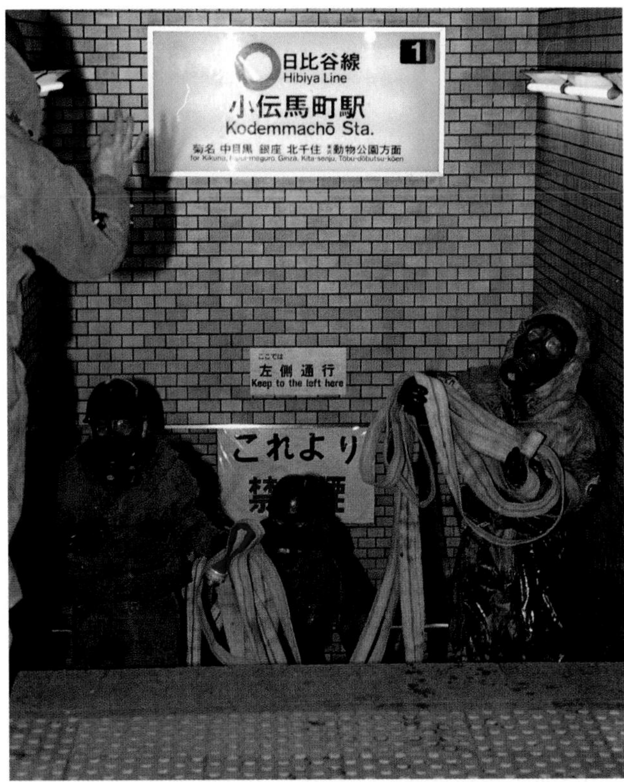


**Killer Gas in Tokyo** A gas attack on the Tokyo subway system by members of a Japanese cult on March 20, 1995, took the lives of a dozen people and left more than 5,500 others sickened and traumatized. Wearing gas masks and protective clothing, these firefighters are emerging after cleaning contaminated cars. The gas attack in Tokyo has reinforced fears of terrorists using chemical weapons. *(Atusushi Tsukada/Wide World Photos)*

Chemical and biological weapons of mass destruction created similar anxieties. For many years the use of chemical weapons had been outlawed by international agreement, but the manufacture of these terrible weapons was nonetheless permitted. In 1997 most of the world's nations signed a convention banning the production of chemical weapons and requiring the destruction of those in existence. Inspectors received the right to make surprise searches "anytime, anywhere." But complex practical questions relating to effective verification remained. Moreover, most Arab countries refused to sign the treaty, pointing to Israel's long-standing refusal to join the nuclear non-proliferation agreement.

Building credible verification was an even greater problem for the experts monitoring the 1972 Biological and Toxin Weapons Convention, which outlawed the production of the tiny quantities sufficient to poison large populations. Iraq's attempts to develop biological weapons, discovered after the Persian Gulf War, gave new urgency to formulating rules for surprise inspections and trade controls. In short, the terrible doomsday scenario of man-made plagues, lethal nerve gases, and mushroom clouds still haunted humanity, which sought in turn to escape the threat of self-inflicted cataclysm.

As far as terrorism was concerned, most weapons experts believed that terrorists were less likely to acquire or use nuclear arms, because of the great complexity of construction and the need for missiles to deliver them, than to get their hands on chemical and biological weapons. This belief prompted expanded efforts in 2002 to develop improved defenses against these nightmarish killers.

## GLOBAL INTERDEPENDENCE

Alongside political competition, war, and civil conflict, a contradictory phenomenon unfolded: as Toynbee suggested, the nations of our small world became increasingly interdependent both economically and technologically. Even the great continental states with the largest landmasses and populations and the richest natural resources found that they could not depend only on themselves. The United States required foreign oil, China needed foreign markets, and Russia needed foreign grain. All countries and peoples had need of each other.

Mutual dependence in economic affairs was often interpreted as a promising sign for the human race. Dependence promoted peaceful cooperation and limited the scope of violence. Yet the existing framework of global interdependence also came under intense attack. The poor countries of the developing world—sometimes called the Third World or the South—charged that the North (the industrialized countries) continued to receive far more than its rightful share from existing economic relationships, which had been forged unjustly to the South's disadvantage in the era of European political domination. The South demanded a new international economic order. (See the feature "Listening to the Past: One World and a Plan for Survival" on pages 1186–1187.) Critics also saw strong evidence of neocolonialism in the growing importance of the North's huge global business corporations—the so-called multinationals—in world economic development. Thus global interdependence was widely acknowledged in principle and hotly debated in practice.

### Pressure on Vital Resources

During the postwar economic boom of the 1950s and 1960s the nations of the world became more dependent on each other for vital resources. Yet resources also seemed abundant, and rapid industrialization was a worldwide article of faith. Only those alarmed by the population explosion predicted grave shortages, and they spoke almost exclusively about food shortages in the Third World.

The situation changed suddenly in the 1970s. Fear that the world was running out of resources was widely voiced. In a famous study aptly titled *The Limits to Growth* (1972), a group of American and European scholars argued that unlimited economic development is impossible on a finite planet. In the early twenty-first century, they predicted, the ever-increasing demands of too many people and factories would exhaust the world's mineral resources and destroy the fragile biosphere with pollution.

Meanwhile, Japan imported 99 percent of its petroleum, western Europe 96 percent. When the Organization of Petroleum Exporting Countries (OPEC) increased the price of crude oil fourfold in 1973, there was panic in many industrial countries. Skyrocketing prices for oil and other raw materials in the 1970s seemed to confirm grim predictions that the world was exhausting its vital resources.

In many developing countries the pressure to grow more food for more people led to piecemeal destruction of forests and increased soil erosion. These countries suffered from what has been called "the other energy crisis"—a severe lack of firewood for cooking and heat. A striking case was the southern edge of the Sahara. Population growth caused the hard-pressed peoples of this region to overgraze the land and denude the forests. As a result, the sterile sand of the Sahara advanced southward as much as thirty miles a year along a three-thousand-mile front. Thus land available for cultivation decreased, leaving Africa all the more exposed to terrible droughts. In the 1980s and 1990s crops shriveled up and famine stalked the land, but an interdependent world mobilized, and international relief prevented mass starvation.

Of all the pressures on global resources, many observers believed that population growth was the most serious. Here recent experience offered room for optimism: population growth in the industrialized countries fell dramatically. In the 1950s women there had 2.8 children on average; in the late 1990s they had only 1.5. This level is not enough to maintain a stable population, and if present trends continue, total numbers in the developed countries will decline in the next generation.

Of much greater importance from a global perspective, the world's poor women began to bear fewer children. Small countries such as Barbados, Chile, Costa Rica, South Korea, Taiwan, and Tunisia led the way. Between 1970 and 1975 China followed, registering the fastest five-year decline in the birthrate in recorded history. Then other big countries, especially in Latin America and East Asia, experienced large declines in fertility. In 1970 the average Brazilian woman had close to 6 children; by 1994 she had slightly more than 2. In 1970 the average woman in Bangladesh had more than 7 children; in 1994 she had 4.5. Overall, the average woman in the developing world had 6.2 children in 1950 and just under 3 in 1998.

There were several reasons for this decline in fertility among women in the developing world. Fewer babies were dying of disease or malnutrition, thus couples needed fewer births to guarantee the survival of the number of children they wanted. As had happened earlier in the industrialized nations, better living conditions, urbanization, and more education encouraged women to have fewer children. No wonder the most rapidly industrializing countries, such as Taiwan and South Korea, led the way in declining birthrates.

Outside East Asia contraception and especially abortion remained controversial. This helps explain why birthrates and population growth remained much higher in Africa and in the Muslim world than in East Asia. In 1985 Africa led the world with a population growth of 3.2 percent per year—enough to double the continent's numbers in only twenty-two years. Yet even in fast-growing Africa the rate of growth began to fall, with the average woman having about six children in 1994 as opposed to eight a few years earlier.

**Five Generations of the Yang Family** This group portrait suggests the enduring Chinese commitment to close family ties. It also puts a human face on social transformation, for the great-great-grandmother has bound feet and the baby she holds will be an only child. In the 1980s the Chinese government prohibited couples from having more than one child, a major factor in China's falling birthrate. *(Dermot Tatlow/Panos Pictures)*

Recent experience suggested that, barring catastrophe, worldwide population growth would continue to decline, primarily as a result of billions of private decisions, which were influenced by government policies supporting contraception. In the early twenty-first century more than half of the world's couples practiced birth control, up from one in eight just forty years earlier, and that proportion continued to rise.

As a result, projections of world population declined sharply. In the 1980s experts calculated that the population would probably not stabilize until the mid-twenty-first century at the earliest, when it was estimated it would reach between 10 billion and 11 billion people. In 1998, when total world population was just under 6 billion, some experts concluded that stabilization could occur by 2040 with "only" 7.7 billion people.

Whatever the case may be, efforts to bring living standards in developing countries to levels approaching those in rich industrialized countries will put tremendous pressure on global resources. Yet even with 11 billion people, the earth would be less densely populated than Europe is today, and only one-fourth as densely populated as small, prosperous countries such as Belgium and the Netherlands, which largely feed themselves. Moreover, the human race has exhibited considerable skill throughout its history in finding new resources and inventing new technologies. An optimist could conclude that, at least from a quantitative and technical point of view, the adequacy of resources is a serious but by no means insolvable problem.

## Relations Between Rich and Poor Countries

The real key to adequate resources is probably global cooperation. Will the world's peoples work together, or will they eventually fight over resources like wild dogs over meat?

After the 1960s there was dissatisfaction in Asia, Africa, and Latin America not only with the fruits of the industrialization drive but also with the world's economic system. Scholars imbued with a Third World perspective and spokesmen for the United Nations majority declared that the international system was unjust and in need of radical change. Mahbub ul Haq, a Pakistani World Bank official and member of the international bureaucratic elite, sympathetically articulated this position in 1976:

*The vastly unequal relationship between the rich and the poor nations is fast becoming the central issue of our time. The poor nations are beginning to question the basic premises of an international order which leads to ever-widening disparities between the rich and the poor countries and to a persistent denial of equality of opportunity to many poor nations. They are, in fact, arguing that in international order—just as much as within national orders—all distribution of benefits, credit, services, and decision-making becomes warped in favor of a privileged minority and that this situation cannot be changed except through fundamental institutional reforms.*[7]

The subsequent demand of the developing nations for a "new international economic order" had many causes, both distant and immediate. Critics of imperialism such as J. A. Hobson (see page 836) and Third World writers on decolonization such as Frantz Fanon (see page 1154) had long charged that the colonial powers grew rich exploiting Asia, Africa, and Latin America. Beginning in the 1950s a number of writers, many of them Latin American Marxists, breathed new life into these ideas with their "theory of dependency."

The poverty and so-called underdevelopment of the South, they argued, were not the starting points, but the deliberate and permanent results of exploitation by the capitalist industrialized nations in the modern era. Poor countries produced cheap raw materials for wealthy, industrialized countries and were conditioned to buy their expensive manufactured goods. As in the case of Latin America since the nineteenth century, the industrialized nations perpetuated this neocolonial pattern after Third World countries gained political independence. Thus the prevailing economic interdependence was the unequal, unjust interdependence of dominant and subordinate, of master and peon. The international order needed a radical restructuring.

The OPEC oil coup of 1973–1974 ignited hopes in the developing countries of actually achieving a new system of economic interdependence. Perhaps 2 percent of all the income of the rich nations was suddenly forwarded to the OPEC countries. Critics of dependence and neocolonialism were euphoric, even if higher oil prices weighed heavily on poor countries that lacked oil. For years the developed countries had gradually been reducing their modest levels of economic aid, but OPEC's success suggested that radical change was possible.

In 1974 a special session of the United Nations General Assembly rammed through two landmark resolutions calling for a "new international economic order" and a "program of action" to attain it. Among the specific demands were each country's firm control of its own natural resources, higher and more stable prices for raw materials, and equal tariff treatment for manufactured goods from the developing countries. As one sympathetic scholar observed in 1980, these demands were subject to "collective bargaining," but the Third World was now "unionized" and vigorously insisted on new terms.[8]

Subsequently, the developing countries did negotiate some victories, notably a Common Fund under United Nations auspices to support the prices of raw materials and a scaling down of their enormous debts to the industrial nations (see below). But generally the industrialized countries, deeply troubled by inflation and by their own economic problems, proved very tough bargainers when it came to basic changes.

For example, in the late 1970s the developing nations laid great hopes on a long, complicated conference to formulate a new **Law of the Sea.** The proposed law was based on the principle that the world's oceans are "a common heritage of mankind" and should be exploited only for the benefit of all nations. In practice this would mean that a United Nations–sponsored authority would regulate and tax use of the sea. Some wealthy countries and their business firms were reluctant to accept such an infringement of their economic sovereignty and scope of action. The United States refused to sign the final draft of the law in 1982.

Increasingly frustrated in their desire to fashion a new international economic order quickly, some leaders in the developing countries predicted more confrontation and perhaps military conflict between a wealthy North and an impoverished South. Some alarmists in the North voiced similar concerns.

In considering these frightening predictions, an impartial observer was initially struck by the great gap between the richest and poorest nations. That gap was built on the coercive power of Western imperialism as well as on the wealth-creating achievements of continuous technological improvement since the Industrial Revolution. In the face of bitter poverty, unbalanced economies, and local elites that often catered to Western interests, people of the developing countries had reason for anger.

But close examination of our small planet hardly suggested two sharply defined economic camps, a "North" and a "South." Rather, by the early 1990s there were several distinct classes of nations in terms of wealth and income, as may be seen in Map 36.1. The former communist countries of eastern Europe formed something of a middle-income group, as did the major oil-exporting states, which still lagged behind the wealthier countries of western Europe and North America. Latin America was much better off than sub-Saharan Africa, but it contained a wide range of national per capita incomes. South and East Asia were equally diverse.

When one added global differences in culture, religion, politics, and historical development, the supposed clear-cut split between the rich North and the poor South broke down further. Moreover, the solidarity of the South had always been fragile, resting largely on the ideas of some Third World intellectuals and their supporters.

Thus a continuation of the global collective bargaining that first emerged in the 1970s seemed more likely than an international class war. The poorer nations will press to reduce international economic differences through trade preferences, redistribution measures, and special aid to the most unfortunate countries. And because global interdependence had become a reality by 2003, they will probably win more concessions, as the working classes have won gains within the wealthy nations since the late nineteenth century.

The recurring international debt crisis illustrates the process of global bargaining. The economic dislocations of the 1970s and early 1980s worsened the problems of many developing countries, especially those that had to import oil. Growing unemployment, unbalanced budgets, and large trade deficits forced many poor countries to borrow rapidly from the wealthy industrialized nations. By the early 1980s much of this debt was short-term and could not be repaid as it came due.

In 1982 Mexico appeared ready to default, and financial chaos seemed at hand. Yet the Reagan administration, consistently opposed to calls from the developing countries for a new international system, quickly organized a gigantic rescue operation to pump new money into Mexico. The reason was simple: Mexico's failure to service its foreign debt would cripple large American banks that had lent Mexico money and possibly cause a global financial panic and depression. Thus a series of international negotiations beginning in the 1980s reduced the debts of developing countries, granted new loans, and encouraged economic liberalization. Lenders and borrowers, rich and poor, North and South, realized that they were bound together in mutual dependence by the international debt challenge.

After the United States again saved Mexico (and American banks) from default in 1995, the world saw a new round of global financial crisis. In 1997 the rapidly growing economies of Thailand, Malaysia, South Korea, and Indonesia experienced a "run on the bank," as previously enthusiastic foreign investors panicked and withdrew their funds. As a result, the currencies of these Asian countries plunged, many Asian banks and companies could not repay their debts, and prices and unemployment soared. As in the 1980s, the industrialized countries and the International Monetary Fund (IMF) tried to stem the crisis with emergency loans and prescriptions for recovery. Yet the "Asian contagion" spread, bringing financial collapse

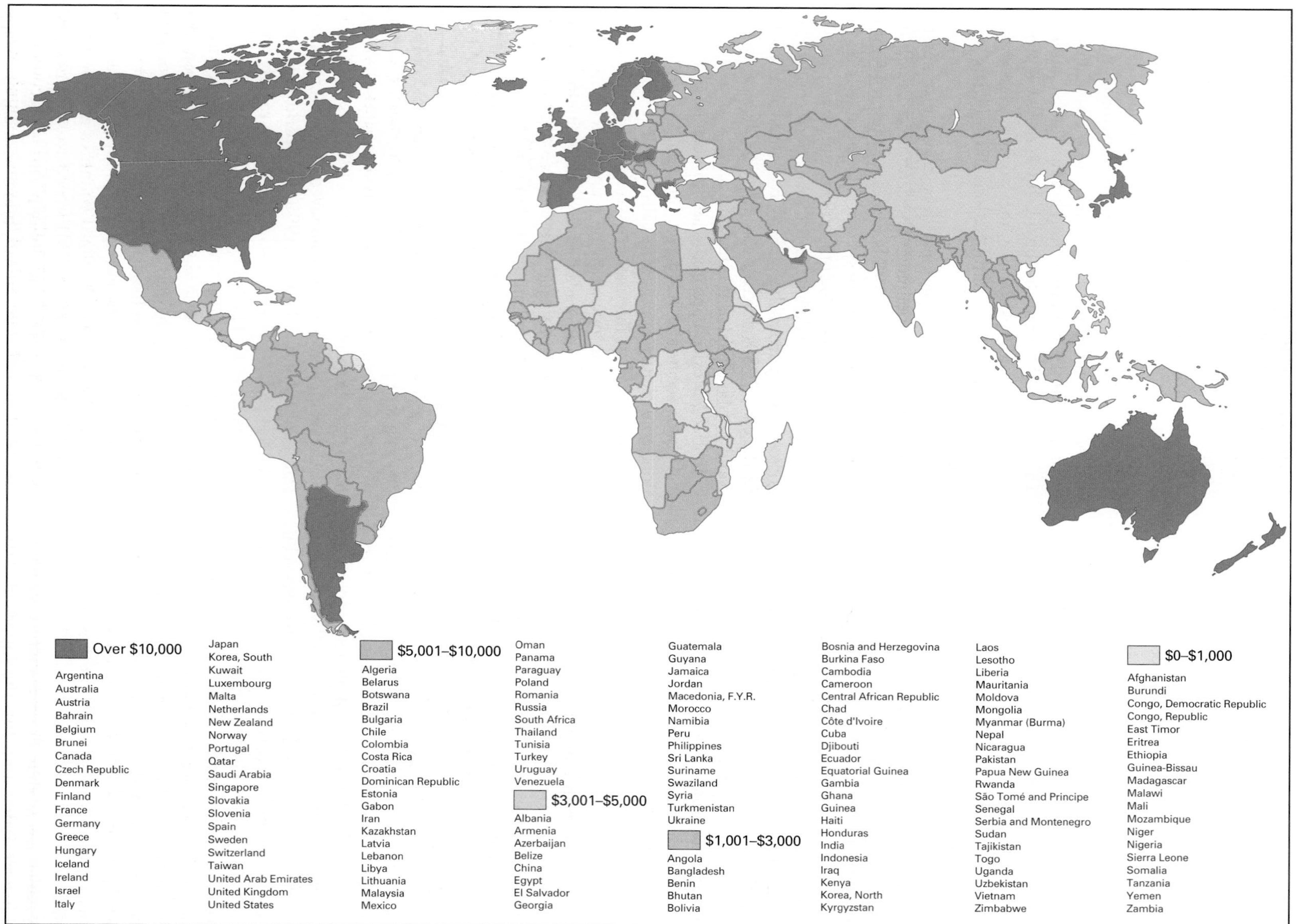
Over $10,000
Argentina
Australia
Austria
Bahrain
Belgium
Brunei
Canada
Czech Republic
Denmark
Finland
France
Germany
Greece
Hungary
Iceland
Ireland
Israel
Italy
Japan
Korea, South
Kuwait
Luxembourg
Malta
Netherlands
New Zealand
Norway
Portugal
Qatar
Saudi Arabia
Singapore
Slovakia
Slovenia
Spain
Sweden
Switzerland
Taiwan
United Arab Emirates
United Kingdom
United States
$5,001–$10,000
Algeria
Belarus
Botswana
Brazil
Bulgaria
Chile
Colombia
Costa Rica
Croatia
Dominican Republic
Estonia
Gabon
Iran
Kazakhstan
Latvia
Lebanon
Libya
Lithuania
Malaysia
Mexico
Oman
Panama
Paraguay
Poland
Romania
Russia
South Africa
Thailand
Tunisia
Turkey
Uruguay
Venezuela
$3,001–$5,000
Albania
Armenia
Azerbaijan
Belize
China
Egypt
El Salvador
Georgia
Guatemala
Guyana
Jamaica
Jordan
Macedonia, F.Y.R.
Morocco
Namibia
Peru
Philippines
Sri Lanka
Suriname
Swaziland
Syria
Turkmenistan
Ukraine
$1,001–$3,000
Angola
Bangladesh
Benin
Bhutan
Bolivia
Bosnia and Herzegovina
Burkina Faso
Cambodia
Cameroon
Central African Republic
Chad
Côte d'Ivoire
Cuba
Djibouti
Ecuador
Equatorial Guinea
Gambia
Ghana
Guinea
Haiti
Honduras
India
Indonesia
Iraq
Kenya
Korea, North
Kyrgyzstan
Laos
Lesotho
Liberia
Mauritania
Moldova
Mongolia
Myanmar (Burma)
Nepal
Nicaragua
Pakistan
Papua New Guinea
Rwanda
São Tomé and Principe
Senegal
Serbia and Montenegro
Sudan
Tajikistan
Togo
Uganda
Uzbekistan
Vietnam
Zimbabwe
$0–$1,000
Afghanistan
Burundi
Congo, Democratic Republic
Congo, Republic
East Timor
Eritrea
Ethiopia
Guinea-Bissau
Madagascar
Malawi
Mali
Mozambique
Niger
Nigeria
Sierra Leone
Somalia
Tanzania
Yemen
Zambia

**MAP 36.1 Estimated Gross Domestic Product (GDP) per Capita, 2002** *(Source: Data from* CIA World Factbook 2002*)*

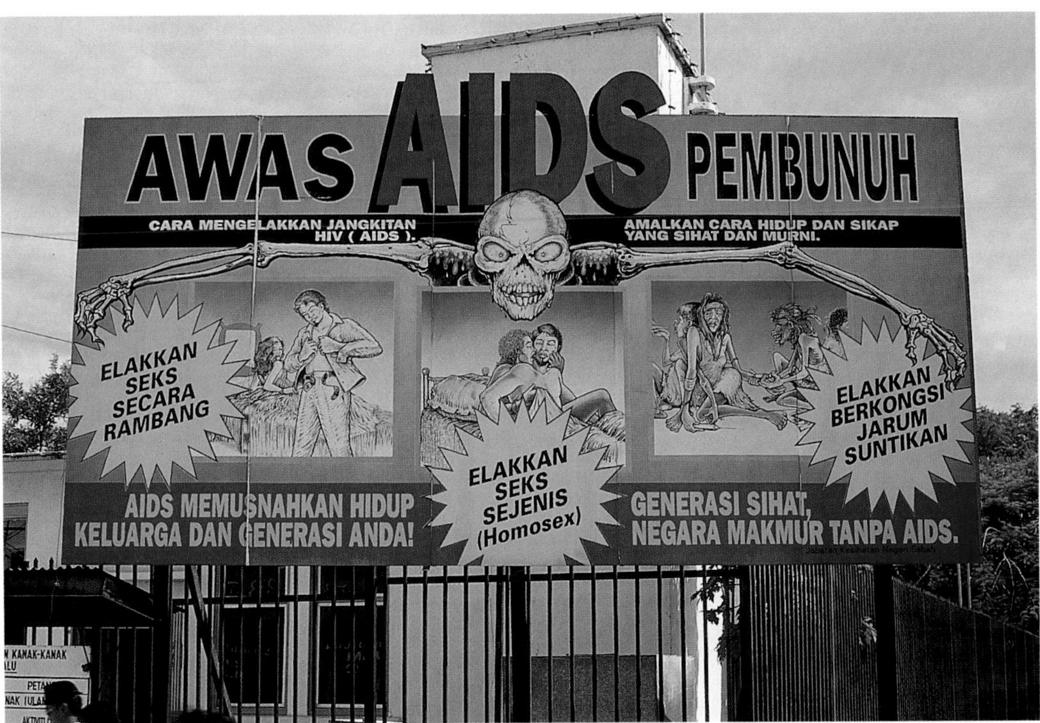


**Fighting the AIDS Epidemic in Asia** A dramatic billboard warns people in Malaysia about the deadly dangers of AIDS. The billboard offers sound advice, focusing on the three primary ways by which the AIDS virus is spread. Can you "read" the three-part message? *(Robert Francis/The Hutchison Library)*

in Russia and threatening to destroy Latin America's hard-won financial stability. Worried increasingly about the fate of their own economies, in late 1998 Japan, the United States, and the European Union, working with the IMF, redoubled their rescue operations and managed to stabilize international finances. The outcome benefited rich and poor countries, and global interdependence was clearly a fact of life.

The terrible **AIDS epidemic** highlighted this situation no less dramatically. In 2002 the Population Division of the United Nations calculated that 40 million persons around the world were infected with HIV, the virus that causes AIDS. AIDS was the fourth leading cause of death in the world.

The distribution of AIDS testified to the existence of a lopsided, unequal world. About 90 percent of all persons who had died from AIDS and 86 percent of those currently infected with HIV lived in sub-Saharan Africa. This was partly because AIDS apparently originated in Africa and had had more time to spread there, and partly because men and women frequently failed to protect themselves against the disease in casual sexual relations. Such risky behavior, based in part on a lack of knowledge about AIDS, led some African and Asian countries, such as Senegal, Uganda, and Malaysia, to launch vigorous campaigns to teach people about how AIDS is spread and how it can be reduced with condoms and clean needles for drug users. Such changes in behavior will be critical to slowing the spread of AIDS in the developing world. Although complicated treatments to contain the epidemic were available in 2003 in the wealthy industrialized countries, these treatments were still too expensive and too complicated for most national health services in the poor countries. Global interdependence increased, but profound inequalities remained.

## The Multinational Corporations

One of the most striking features of global interdependence beginning in the early 1950s was the rapid emergence of **multinational corporations,** business firms that operate in a number of different countries and tend to adopt a global rather than a national perspective. Multinational corporations themselves were not new, but their great importance was. By 1971 multinational corporations accounted for fully one-fifth of the noncommunist world's

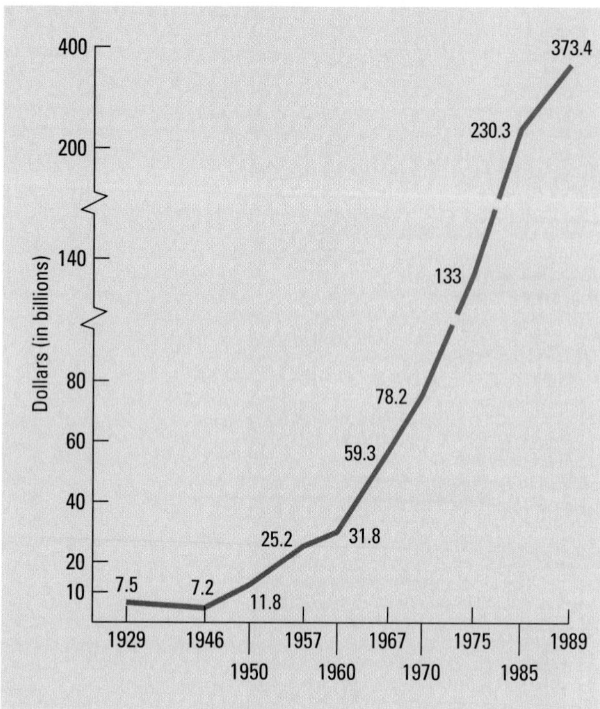


**FIGURE 36.1 Total Investment by American Corporations in Foreign Subsidiaries, 1929–1989** *(Source: Data from U.S. Department of Commerce, Survey of Current Business)*

annual income, and they grew to be even more important in the 1980s and 1990s.

The rise of multinationals aroused a great deal of discussion around the world. Defenders saw the multinational corporations as building an efficient world economic system and transcending narrow national ties. Critics worried precisely that the nation-state was getting the worst of the new arrangement. Provocative book titles portrayed *Frightening Angels* holding *Sovereignty at Bay* while building *Invisible Empires* and extending their nefarious *Global Reach.*

The rise of the multinationals was partly due to the general revival of capitalism after the Second World War, relatively free international economic relations, and the worldwide drive for rapid industrialization. The multinationals also had three specific assets, which they used to their advantage.

First, "pure" scientific knowledge unrelated to the military was freely available, but profitable industrial applications generally remained in the hands of the world's largest business firms. Second, the multinationals knew how to sell, as well as how to innovate and produce. They used modern advertising and marketing skills to push their products. Third, the multinationals developed new techniques to escape from political controls and national policies. They treated the world as one big market, coordinating complex activities across many political boundaries.

In the late nineteenth century U.S. businesses took the lead in building multinational industrial corporations. The United States had a vast, unified market and the world's highest standard of living by 1890, so U.S. firms were positioned to pioneer in the mass production of standardized consumer goods in foreign lands. Famous examples included the cheap automobile (Henry Ford) and standardized food (Coca-Cola, Wrigley's chewing gum).

After 1945 the giant American manufacturing firms surged again. There was continued multinational investment in raw-material production in Latin America (particularly copper, sugar, and bananas) as well as in the Middle East and Africa (primarily oil and gold). By 1967 American corporations—mainly the largest, most familiar household names—had sunk $60 billion into their foreign operations (see Figure 36.1).

A few European companies, notably German chemical and electrical firms, also became multinationals before 1900. Others emerged in the twentieth century. By the 1970s these European multinationals were in hot pursuit. Big Japanese firms such as Sony rushed to catch up and go multinational in the 1960s and 1970s. Japanese firms turned at first to Asia for raw materials and cheap, high-quality factory labor. By the 1970s Japanese subsidiaries in Taiwan, Thailand, Hong Kong, and Malaysia were pouring out a torrent of transistor radios, televisions, cameras, and pocket calculators.

In the 1980s a host of Japanese firms began manufacturing in the United States. The Japanese inflow was so great that by 1989 Japanese multinationals had invested $70 billion in their subsidiaries in the United States, far surpassing the $19 billion that American multinationals had invested in Japan. The emergence of European and Japanese multinational corporations alongside their American forerunners marked the coming of age of global business in an interdependent world.

The impact of multinational corporations, especially on Third World countries, was heatedly debated. From an economic point of view, the effects were mixed. The giant firms provided advanced technology, but the technology was expensive and often inappropriate for poor countries with widespread unemployment.

The social consequences were quite striking. The multinationals helped spread the products and values of consumer society to the elites of the developing world. They fostered the creation of growing islands of Western wealth, management, and consumer culture around the world.

**Children Against Smoking** Students in Thailand urge their elders to kick the habit during a recent World No Smoking Day parade. After a slow start, no smoking campaigns are beginning to gather force in Asia, where 60 percent of men smoke and millions of children are constantly exposed to the dangers of secondhand smoke. *(AFP/Corbis)*

After buying up local companies, multinational corporations often hired local business leaders to manage their operations abroad. Critics considered this practice an integral part of the process of neocolonialism, whereby local elites abandoned the national interest and made themselves willing tools of continued foreign domination. Global corporations often used aggressive techniques of modern marketing to sell products that were not well suited to Third World conditions, and they frequently came into sharp conflict with host countries.

Far from acting helpless in such conflicts, some poor countries found ways to assert their sovereign rights over the foreign multinationals. Many foreign mining companies, such as the extremely profitable U.S. oil companies in the Middle East, were simply nationalized by the host countries. More important, governments in the developing countries learned how to play Americans, Europeans, and Japanese off against each other and to make foreign manufacturing companies conform to some of their plans and desires. Increasingly, multinationals had to share ownership with local investors, hire more local managers, provide technology on better terms, and accept a variety of controls.

## PATTERNS OF THOUGHT

The renowned economist John Maynard Keynes often said that we live by our ideas and by very little else. True or not, a global perspective requires keen attention to patterns of collective thinking. As Keynes saw, ideas shape the uncertain destiny of this small, politically fragmented, economically interdependent planet.

To be sure, human thought can be baffling in its rich profusion. Nevertheless, in the late twentieth century, three distinct patterns on a global scale could be identified: the enduring strength of the modern world's secular ideologies, a vigorous revival of the world's great religions, and a search for mystical experience.

### Secular Ideologies

Most of the modern world's great secular ideologies—liberalism, nationalism, Marxian socialism, as well as faith in scientific and technical progress, industrialism, and democratic republicanism—took form in Europe between the eighteenth-century Enlightenment and the revolutions of 1848. These ideologies continued to evolve with

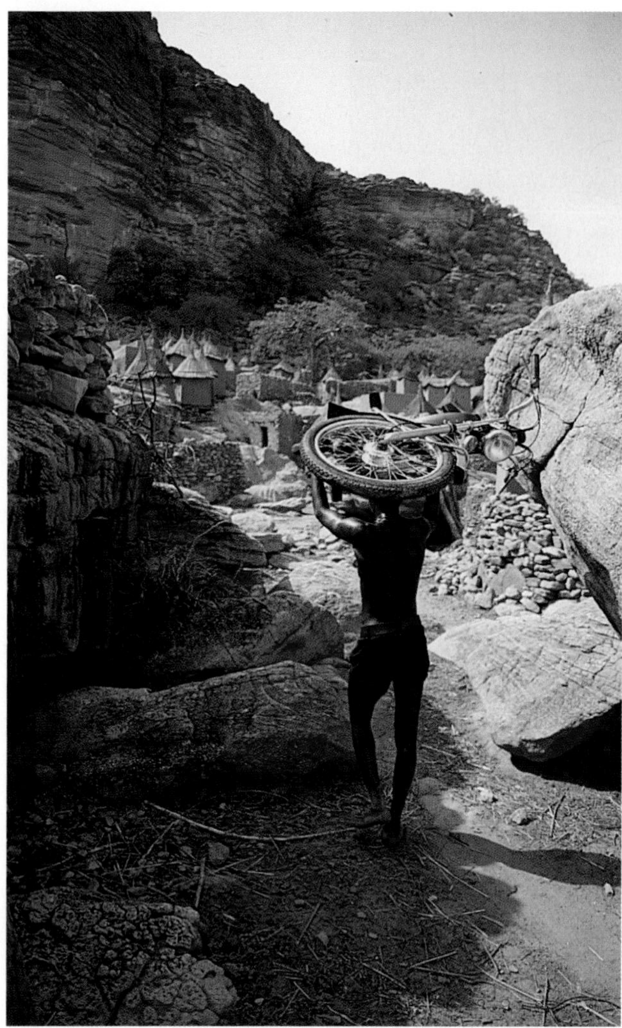

**The Revolution in Communications** Although this young man must carry his motorbike up a rocky path to reach his home, he has gained access to speed and excitement, to roads and cities. The messages of the modern world easily reach remote villages by transistor radio. *(S. Pern/The Hutchison Library)*

the coming of mass society in the late nineteenth century and were exported along with imperialism to the highly diverse societies of Asia and Africa. There they won converts among the local elites, who eventually threw off their imperialist masters in the twentieth century. European ideologies became worldwide ideologies, outgrowing their early, specifically European, character.

All this can be seen as a fundamental aspect of global interdependence. The world came to live, in part, by shared ideas. These ideas continued to develop in a complex global dialogue, and champions of competing views arose from all regions. This was certainly true of nationalist ideology and also of Marxism. Europe, the birthplace of Marxism, made few original intellectual contributions to Marxism after Stalin transformed it into a totalitarian ideology of forced industrialization. After 1945 it was Marxists from the developing countries who injected new meanings into the old ideology, notably with Mao's brand of peasant-based revolution and the Marxist theory of Third World dependency. Leftist intellectuals in Europe cheered and said "me too."

It was primarily as critics that Europeans contributed to world Marxism. Yugoslavs were particularly influential. After breaking with Stalin in 1948, they revived and expanded the ideas of Stalin's vanquished rival, Leon Trotsky. Trotsky claimed that Stalin perverted socialism by introducing "state capitalism" and reactionary bureaucratic dictatorship. According to the influential Yugoslav Milovan Djilas (1911–1995), Lenin's dedicated elite of full-time revolutionaries became Stalin's ruthless bureaucrats, "a new class" that was unprecedented in history. Djilas's powerful impact stemmed from his mastery of the Marxian theory of history and the Marxian dialectic:

> *The social origin of the new class lies in the proletariat just as the aristocracy arose in peasant society, and the bourgeoisie in a commercial and artisans' society. . . .*
>
> *Former sons of the working class are the most steadfast members of the new class. It has always been the fate of slaves to provide for their masters the most clever and gifted representatives. In this case a new exploiting and governing class is born from the exploited class. . . .*
>
> *The communists are . . . a new class.*[9]

Non-Marxian criticism of communism also continued to develop, as in Jean François Revel's provocative *The Totalitarian Temptation* (1977). According to Revel, the application of the Marxist-Leninist-Maoist model brought about phony revolution. Under the guise of supposedly progressive socialism, it built reactionary totalitarian states of the Stalinist variety. Critics of Marxism-Leninism like Revel, Djilas, and Václav Havel (see page 1077) undermined the intellectual appeal of communism and thereby contributed to its being overthrown in eastern Europe in 1989.

As Marxism lost its luster, old-fashioned, long-battered liberalism and democracy survived and flourished as a global ideology. In communist countries small human rights movements bravely demanded the basic liberties, preparing the way for the renewed triumph of liberal revolution in eastern Europe in 1989. And there were always some African and Asian intellectuals, often in exile, calling for similar rights even in the most authoritarian states. The call for human rights and representative government interacted with a renewed faith in economic liberalism as an effective strategy of economic and social development. That countries as highly diverse as Brazil, Russia, China, and Ghana all moved in this direction in recent years was little short of astonishing.

Efforts to combine the best elements of socialism and liberalism in a superior hybrid were also important. The physicist Andrei Sakharov (1921–1990), the father of the Russian atomic bomb who in the 1960s became a fearless advocate of human rights, argued that humanity's best hope lay in an accelerated convergence of liberal capitalism and dictatorial communism on some middle ground of welfare capitalism and democratic socialism. This outlook waned somewhat in the 1990s, but it had deep historical roots and remained a potent force in world thought.

Finally, there was an ongoing global critique of the long-dominant faith in industrialization, consumerism, and unrestrained "modernization." The disillusionment of the developing countries was matched by considerable disillusionment in the industrialized countries and a search for alternative secular visions of the future. There were many advocates of alternative lifestyles and technologies friendly to the environment. E. F. Schumacher, an English disciple of Mahatma Gandhi, in *Small Is Beautiful* (1973) urged the building of solar-heated houses to conserve nonrenewable oil. Many Africans and Asians stressed "appropriate technologies" tailored to village life rather than borrowed from large-scale urban industrialized society—such as small, rugged, three-wheeled motorized carts suited to existing country lanes, rather than large trucks requiring expensive modern highways and imported fuel. Writers from the industrialized countries also reassessed traditional cultures and found nobility and value similar to that championed by the Nigerian novelist Chinua Achebe (see page 1155). Opponents of modern industrial society and defenders of the environment probably remained a minority, but their worldwide presence was a vivid example of the globalization of intellectual life.

## Religious Belief: Christianity and Islam

The questioning of industrialism and consumerism was part of a broader religious response to the dominance of secular ideologies in general. The revival of Christianity among intellectuals after the First World War (see pages 1002–1003) was matched beginning in the 1970s by a surge of popular, often fundamentalist, Christianity in many countries. Judaism, Islam, and Buddhism also experienced a resurgence, and militant Hinduism became a political force in India. The continuing importance of religion in contemporary human thought had to impress the unbiased observer.

Pope John Paul II (r. 1978–) exemplified several aspects of the worldwide Christian revival. A jet-age global evangelist, John Paul journeyed to Africa, Asia, and North and South America, inspiring enthusiastic multitudes with his warm sincerity and unfailing popular touch. John Paul's melding of a liberal social gospel with conservatism in doctrinal matters often seemed to reflect the religious spirit of the age. Thus the pope boldly urged a more equitable distribution of wealth in plutocratic Brazil and more civil liberties in Marcos's authoritarian Philippines while reaffirming the church's long-standing opposition to contraception and women in the priesthood. Many of Christianity's most rapidly growing Protestant churches also espoused theological fundamentalism, based on a literal reading of the Bible.

It was emblematic that the "Polish Pope" came from an officially atheist communist country. Yet after long years of communist rule, Poland was more intensely Catholic than ever before. Poland illustrated the enduring strength of spiritual life in the face of materialistic culture and secular ideologies.

Islam, the religion of one-seventh of the earth's people, also experienced a powerful resurgence from the 1970s onward. Like Orthodox Judaism and fundamentalist Christianity, Islam had been challenged by the self-confident secular ideologies of the West since the early nineteenth century. And although the acids of modern thought did not eat as deeply as in Europe and North America, they etched a seductive alternative to Islam. Moderate Muslim intellectuals advocated religious reforms; radicals wanted drastic surgery. The most famous and successful of the radicals was the twentieth-century Turkish nationalist Mustafa Kemal, or Atatürk (see pages 975–977), who reflected and accelerated the impact of secularism on the Muslim world.

The generation of Muslim intellectual and political leaders born in the interwar years, who reached maturity after the Second World War, agreed that Islam required at least some modernizing. They accepted the attractively simple Muslim creed, "There is no god but God, and Muhammad is his Prophet," but they did not think that the laws of the Qur'an should be taken literally. The prohibition on lending money at interest, the social inferiority of women, even cutting off the hands of thieves and public beheading of murderers, had made sense for the Arabian peninsula in the Middle Ages. But, they argued, such practices did not suit the modern age. It was necessary for Islam to adapt.

These views were still common among educated elites in the 1970s, and they remained dominant in Turkey and probably in Egypt. But throughout much of the Middle East they had to bow before a revival of Islamic fundamentalism, the critical development of recent years. Like some of their Christian and Jewish counterparts, orthodox Muslim believers wanted to return to fundamentals. In taking the Qur'an literally, they demanded that the modern world adapt to the Prophet's teachings, not vice versa. And because the masses remained deeply religious and profoundly disturbed by rapid change, Islamic fundamentalism aroused a heartfelt popular response.

Iran provided the first spectacular manifestation of resurgent Islamic fundamentalism. In 1979 the shah was deposed and an "Islamic Republic" was established to govern according to the sacred laws of the Qur'an. State and church were tightly bound together, until the reforms of the 1990s relaxed the tie somewhat.

Iran's fundamentalism was exceptionally rigid and antimodern, partly because the country adhered to the minority Shi'ite version of Islam. But similar movements developed in every Muslim country. In Algeria in the early 1990s only harsh military rule prevented the fundamentalists from forming a popularly elected government (see page 1121). Even where the fundamentalists were less likely to take power, as in Indonesia or Pakistan, and where they were usually co-opted and neutralized, as in Saudi Arabia, they found enthusiastic support among the masses and revitalized the Muslim faith. Islamic missionary activity also remained extremely vigorous and continued to win converts, especially in sub-Saharan Africa.

**Tahir Square, Cairo** Moderate forms of Islam remain very strong in Egypt, the cultural and intellectual center of the Arab world, and sophisticated technology is readily accepted. In this typical commuter crowd, most men and women wear modern clothing, while the woman in traditional dress follows custom and is not veiled. The blue barrier hides a gigantic excavation, a future stop on another new line for Cairo's ultramodern subway system. The Egyptian Museum, vast treasure-trove of ancient Egypt, stands behind. *(Mark Henley/Panos Pictures)*

Finally, like their Christian, Jewish, and Hindu counterparts, the vast majority of Islamic fundamentalists were peaceful worshipers and not extremists who advocated or practiced terrorism. As previously noted (see page 1172), all religions have at times been twisted by extremists to provide a motivation for terrorist acts in political conflicts and civil wars.

## Searching for Mystical Experience

Alongside continuing secular ideologies and a revival of the world's great religions, the third powerful current of intellectual attraction was an enormous variety of religious sects, cults, and spiritual yearnings. Some of these new outpourings welled up within one or another of the great religions; many more did not. Though widely divergent, these movements seemed to share a common urge toward nonrational experiences such as meditation, spiritual mysteries, and direct communication with supernatural forces.

Not that this was new. Preliterate peoples have always embraced myths, visions, and continuous revelation. So too have the world's main religions, especially those of the ancient East—Taoism, Hinduism, and the Zen form of Buddhism. What was new was the receptiveness of many people in the rationalistic, scientific, industrialized countries (and the well-educated elite in the developing world) to ancient modes of mystical experience. Some of this interest stemmed from the doubt about the power of the rational human mind that blossomed after the First World War. By the 1960s it had struck deep chords in the mass culture of Europe and North America, and it remained strong thereafter.

In this sense the early twenty-first century was reminiscent of the initial encounter of West and East in the Hellenistic Age. Then, the rationalistic, humanistic Greeks encountered the Eastern mystery religions and were profoundly influenced by them. Now, various strains of mystical thought were again appearing from the East and from "preliterate" peoples. It can be said that the non-Western world was providing intellectual repayment for the secular ideologies that it borrowed in the nineteenth century.

Reflecting on this ongoing encounter, the American social scientist Robert Heilbroner was not alone in suggesting startling implications for the future:

*It is therefore possible that a post-industrial society would also turn in the direction of many preindustrial societies—toward the exploration of inner states of experience rather than the outer world of fact and material accomplishment. Tradition and ritual, the pillars of life in virtually all societies other than those of an industrial character, would probably once again assert their ancient claims as the guide to and solace for life.*[10]

Some observers saw the onrush of science and technology as actually reinforcing the search for spiritual experience. Electronic communications and the Internet were demolishing time and distance; information itself was becoming the new global environment. According to the philosopher William Thompson:

*Culture is full of many surprises, because culture is full of the play of opposites. And so there will be scientists and mystics in the New Age. . . . To look at the American counterculture today, one would guess . . . that the East was about to engulf the West. But in fact . . . America is swallowing up and absorbing the traditional Eastern techniques of transformation, because only these are strong enough to humanize its technology. In the days before planetization, when civilization was split between East and West, there were basically two cultural directions. The Westerner went outward to level forests, conquer nations, and walk on the moon; the Easterner went inward and away from the physical into the astral and causal planes. Now . . . we can glimpse the beginnings of a new level of religious experience, neither Eastern nor Western, but planetary.*[11]

Many people may have doubts about the significance of such views. But it seems quite possible that the upsurge of mysticism and religious searching will exert a growing influence in the coming era, especially if political conflict and economic difficulties continue to undermine the old secular faith in endless progress.

# SUMMARY

Whatever does or does not happen, the study of world history puts the future in perspective. Future developments on this small planet will surely build on the many-layered foundations hammered out in the past. Moreover, the study of world history, of mighty struggles and fearsome challenges, of shining achievements and tragic failures, imparts a strong sense of life's essence: the process of change over time. Again and again we have seen how peoples and societies evolve, influenced by ideas, human passions, and material conditions. Armed with the ability to think historically, students of history are prepared to comprehend this inexorable process of change in their own lifetimes, as the world races forward toward an uncertain destiny.

*(continued on page 1188)*

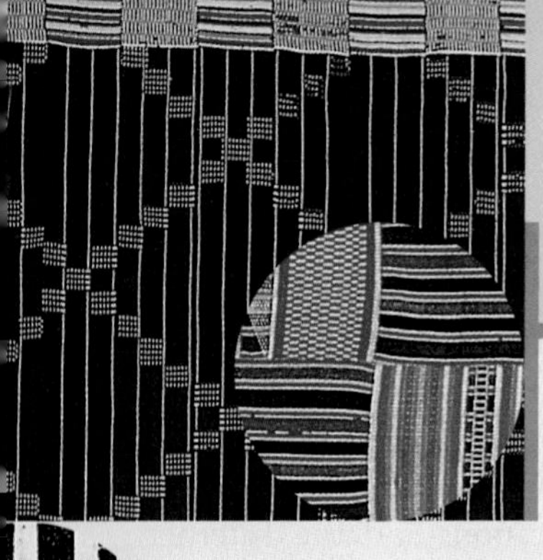

# LISTENING TO THE PAST

## One World and a Plan for Survival

*In the 1970s Third World countries of the South called on the industrialized countries of the North to join with them in establishing a "new international order." Using the United Nations General Assembly as a platform, Third World countries argued that the world economy worked to their disadvantage and that the ominous gap between the wealthy North and the poor South was widening.*

*Third World countries found only limited support from politicians and voters in the North, which was wracked by a deep recession caused in part by an explosion in oil prices. Yet the South did find some sympathy in the North, especially among journalists, professors, and moderate western European socialists.*

*An outstanding example of such support came from the Brandt Commission, an independent, self-appointed international study group chaired by Willy Brandt, the former chancellor of West Germany, a moderate socialist, and a renowned world leader. Brandt's blue-ribbon commission presented its findings and proposals in 1980 as* North-South Relations: A Program for Survival. *The following selection is taken from this influential and widely publicized call to action.*

The crisis through which international relations and the world economy are now passing presents great dangers, and they appear to be growing more serious. We believe that the gap which separates rich and poor countries—a gap so wide that at the extremes people seem to live in different worlds—has not been sufficiently recognized as a major factor in this crisis. It is a great contradiction of our age that these disparities exist—and are in some respects widening—just when human society is beginning to have a clearer perception of how it is interrelated and of how North and South depend on each other in a single world economy. . . .

The nations of the South see themselves as sharing a common predicament. Their solidarity in global negotiations stems from the awareness of being dependent on the North, and unequal to it; and a great many of them are bound together by their common colonial experience. The North including Eastern Europe has a quarter of the world's population and four-fifths of its income; the South including China has three billion people—three-quarters of the world's population but living on one-fifth of the world's income. . . .

Behind these differences lies the fundamental inequality of economic strength. . . . Because of this economic power northern countries dominate the international economic system—its rules and regulations, and international institutions of trade, money and finance. Some developing nations have swum against this tide . . . but most of them find the currents too strong for them. In the world as in nations, economic forces left entirely to themselves tend to produce growing inequality. Within nations public policy has to protect the weaker partners. The time has come to apply this precept to relations between nations within the world community. . . .

The North-South debate is often described as if the rich were being asked to make sacrifices in response to the demands of the poor. We reject this view. The world is now a fragile and interlocking system, whether for its people, its ecology or its resources. Many individual societies have settled their inner conflicts by accommodation, to protect the weak and to promote principles of justice, becoming stronger as a result. The world too can become stronger by becoming a just and humane society. If it fails in this, it will move towards its own destruction. . . .

[In conclusion] mankind already faces basic problems which cannot be solved purely at the national or even regional levels, such as security, protection of the environment, energy, and the control of space and ocean resources. The international community has begun to tackle these problems, though inadequately.

At the beginning of the 1980s the world community faces much greater dangers than at any time since the Second World War. It is clear that the world economy is now functioning so badly that it damages both the immediate and the longer-run interests of all nations. . . . A new international order will take time to achieve. . . . But the present world crisis is so acute that we also feel compelled to draw up an emergency program . . . [and lay out the] tasks for the 80s and 90s. . . .

Priority must be given to the needs of the poorest countries and regions. We call for a major initiative in favor of the poverty belts of Africa and Asia. We recognize that the removal of poverty requires both substantial resource transfers from the developed countries and an increased determination of the developing countries to improve economic management and deal with social and economic inequalities.

The world must aim to abolish hunger and malnutrition by the end of the century through the elimination of absolute poverty. Greater food production, intensified agricultural development, and measures for international food security are essential. These too require both major additional external assistance and revised priorities in many developing countries. . . .

The North should reverse the present trend towards protecting its industries against competition from the Third World. . . .

The objectives we have defined . . . will call for a transfer of funds [from North to South] on a very considerable scale . . . [and] will require sums equal to more than a doubling of the current $20 billion of annual official development assistance, together with substantial additional lending on market terms. . . . The large-scale transfer of resources we call for should be organized in partnership between developed and developing countries. . . .

The global agreement we envisage, with the understanding that must lie behind it, will call for a joint effort of political will and a high degree of trust between the partners, with a common conviction in their mutual interest. . . . [And indeed] whatever their differences and however profound, there is a mutuality of interest between North and South. The fate of both is intimately connected. The search for solutions is not an act of benevolence but a condition of mutual survival. We believe it is dramatically urgent today to start taking concrete steps, without which the world situation can only deteriorate still further, even leading to conflict and catastrophe.

Earth Summit in Rio de Janeiro, 1992.
*(Claus Meyer/stockphoto.com)*

## QUESTIONS FOR ANALYSIS

1. Why do the nations of the South "see themselves as sharing a common predicament"?
2. Why, according to the Brandt Commission, should the North aid the South?
3. What does the Brandt Commission propose? What are the most urgent priorities?
4. "Resolved: the North must help the South to avoid conflict and global catastrophe." What are the arguments for and against this proposition? Take sides, and debate this proposition.
5. Do you think the members of this commission would support steps toward world government? Why or why not?

*Source:* Independent Commission on International Development Issues [Brandt Commission], *North-South Relations: A Program for Survival* (Cambridge, Mass.: MIT Press, 1980), pp. 30–33, 267, 270–273, 280–282.

## KEY TERMS

nation-state
United Nations
Security Council
General Assembly
third force
middle powers
separatism
terrorism
al-Qaeda
Law of the Sea
AIDS epidemic
multinational corporations

## NOTES

1. A. Toynbee, *Mankind and Mother Earth* (New York: Oxford University Press, 1976), pp. 576–577.
2. D. Calleo and B. Rowland, *America and the World Political Economy* (Bloomington: Indiana University Press, 1973), p. 191.
3. B. Barber, *Jihad vs. McWorld* (New York: Times Books, 1995), p. 9.
4. D. Rappaport, "The Fourth Wave: September 11 in the History of Terrorism," *Current History,* December 2001, pp. 419–424.
5. Ibid.
6. W. Epstein, *The Last Chance: Nuclear Proliferation and Arms Control* (New York: Free Press, 1976), p. 274.
7. M. ul Haq, *The Poverty Curtain: Choices for the Third World* (New York: Columbia University Press, 1976), p. 152.
8. E. Hermassi, *The Third World Reassessed* (Berkeley: University of California Press, 1980), p. 76.
9. M. Djilas, *The New Class* (New York: Praeger, 1957), pp. 41–42, 44.
10. R. L. Heilbroner, *An Inquiry into the Human Prospect* (New York: W. W. Norton, 1974), p. 140.
11. W. I. Thompson, *Evil and World Order* (New York: Harper & Row, 1980), p. 53.

## SUGGESTED READING

Many of the books cited in the Suggested Reading for Chapters 34 and 35 pertain to the themes of this chapter. Three helpful and stimulating studies on global politics from different perspectives are M. Juergensmeyer, *The New Cold War? Religious Nationalism Confronts the Secular State* (1993); M. Klare, *Resource Wars: The New Landscape of Global Conflict* (2001); and Barber's work, cited in the Notes. Two wide-ranging appraisals of current trends are found in Z. Brzezinski, *Out of Control: Global Turmoil on the Eve of the 21st Century* (1993), and B. Hoffman, *Inside Terrorism* (1998).

An excellent introduction to early negotiations for the international control of nuclear arms is W. Epstein, *The Last Chance: Nuclear Proliferation and Arms Control* (1976). G. Cameron, *Nuclear Terrorism: A Threat Assessment for the Twenty-first Century* (1999), is a balanced consideration. M. Reiss and R. Litwak, eds., *Nuclear Proliferation After the Cold War* (1994), is a stimulating work.

A. Escobar, *The Making and Unmaking of the Third World* (1995), concentrates on Third World ideology. M. ul Haq's book, cited in the Notes, is an excellent presentation of Third World demands for a new economic order. This position is expanded in J. Tinbergen and A. J. Dolman, eds., *North-South: A Program for Survival* (1980), a report calling for increased help for the South. Such views do not go unchallenged, and P. T. Bauer, *Equality, the Third World, and Economic Delusion* (1981), is a vigorous defense of the industrialized nations and their wealth.

Common problems and aspirations are the focus of E. Laszlo et al., *Goals for Mankind* (1977). *World Development Report,* which the World Bank publishes annually, is an outstanding source of information about current trends. Valuable studies on multinational corporations and global indebtedness include L. Solomon, *Multinational Corporations and the Emerging World Order* (1978), and A. Sampson, *The Money Lenders: The People and Politics of the World Banking Crisis* (1983). Famines, AIDS, and global migration are examined perceptively in V. Smil, *Feeding the World* (2002); W. Rushing, *The AIDS Epidemic: Social Implications of an Infectious Disease* (1995); and S. Castles and M. Miller, *International Population Movements in the Modern World* (1993).

Contemporary thought is so rich and diverse that any selection must be highly arbitrary. G. Blainey, *The Great Seesaw: A New View of the Western World, 1750–2000* (1988), uncovers a cyclical pattern of optimism and pessimism and is recommended as an introduction to the history of ideas. D. H. Meadows and D. L. Meadows, *The Limits of Growth* (1974), argues that the world will soon exhaust its natural resources. R. M. Pirsig, *Zen and the Art of Motorcycle Maintenance: An Inquiry into Values* (1976), is a stimulating exploration of the tie between modern technology and personal development. E. Rice, *Wars of the Third Kind: Conflict in Underdeveloped Countries* (1988), is a thoughtful inquiry into the dynamics of guerrilla movements. T. R. Gurr, *Why Men Rebel* (1970), skillfully reworks the idea that revolutions occur when rising expectations are frustrated. E. Egan, *Such a Vision of the Street: Mother Teresa—The Spirit and the Work* (1985), is highly recommended.

The Islamic revival may be approached through the sympathetic work of E. Gellner, *Muslim Society* (1981), and the reservations of V. S. Naipaul, *Among the Believers: An Islamic Journey* (1981). F. Gerges, *America and Political Islam: Clash of Cultures or Clash of Interests?* (2001), stresses the role of domestic political conflicts in forming Islamic radicals. Muslim writers address issues in the Islamic world in J. Donohue and J. Esposito, eds., *Islam in Transition: Muslim Perspectives* (1982).

Studies of the future are so numerous that M. Marien, *Societal Directions and Alternatives: A Critical Guide to the Literature* (1977), is a useful aid with its annotated bibliography. P. Kennedy, *Preparing for the Twenty-First Century* (1993), is the work of a well-known historian. Also recommended is J. Lukacs, *The End of the Twentieth Century and the End of the Modern Age* (1993).

# INDEX

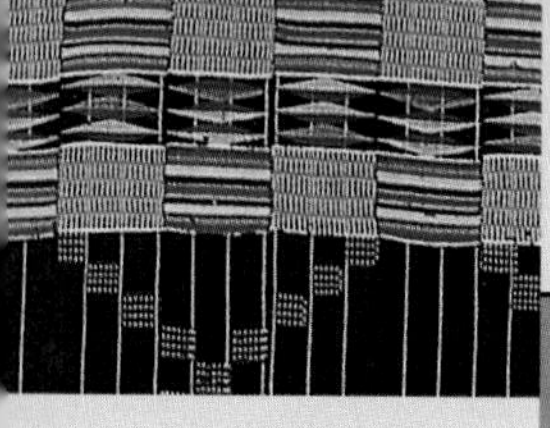

# TIMELINE A HISTORY OF WORLD SOCIETIES

## A BRIEF OVERVIEW

| | AFRICA AND THE MIDDLE EAST | THE AMERICAS |
|---|---|---|
| **10,000 B.C.E.** | New Stone Age culture, ca 10,000–3500 | Migration into Americas begins, ca 20,000 |
| **5000 B.C.E.** | Farming begins in Tigris-Euphrates and Nile River Valleys, ca 6000<br>First writing in Sumeria; city-states emerge, ca 3500<br>Unification of Egypt, 3100–2660 | Maize domesticated in Mexico, ca 5000 |
| **2500 B.C.E.** | Egypt's Old Kingdom, 2660–2180<br>Akkadian empire, ca 2331–2200<br>Egypt's Middle Kingdom, 2080–1640<br>Hyksos "invade" Egypt, 1640–1570<br>Hammurabi, 1792–1750<br>Hebrew monotheism, ca 1700 | First pottery in Americas, Ecuador, ca 3000<br>First metalworking in Peru, ca 2000 |
| **1500 B.C.E.** | Egypt's New Kingdom; Egyptian empire, ca 1570–1075<br>Hittite Empire, ca 1475–1200<br>Akhenaten institutes worship of Aton, ca 1360<br>Moses leads Hebrews out of Egypt, ca 1300–1200<br>Political fragmentation of Egypt; rise of small kingdoms, ca 1100–700<br>United Hebrew kingdom, 1020–922 | Olmec civilization, Mexico, ca 1500 B.C.E.–300 C.E. |
| **1000 B.C.E.** | Ironworking spreads throughout Africa, ca 1000 B.C.E.–300 C.E.<br>Assyrian Empire, 900–612<br>Zoroaster, ca 600<br>Babylonian captivity of Hebrews, 586–539<br>Cyrus the Great founds Persian Empire, 550<br>Persians conquer Egypt, 525<br>Darius and Xerxes complete Persian conquest of Middle East, 521–464 | Chavin civilization in Andes, ca 1000–200 B.C.E.<br>Olmec center at San Lorenzo destroyed, ca 900; power passes to La Venta |
| **500 B.C.E.** | | |
| **400 B.C.E.** | Alexander the Great extends empire, 334–331<br>Death of Alexander (323): Ptolemy conquers Egypt, Seleucus rules Asia | |

| EAST ASIA | INDIA AND SOUTHEAST ASIA | EUROPE |
| --- | --- | --- |
| Farming begins in Yellow River Valley, ca 4000 | Indus River Valley civilization, ca 2800–1800; capitals at Mohenjo-daro and Harappa | |
| Horse domesticated in China, ca 2500 | | Greek Bronze Age, 2000–1100<br>Arrival of Greeks in peninsular Greece<br>Height of Minoan culture, 1700–1450 |
| Shang Dynasty, first writing in China, ca 1500–ca 1050 | Aryans arrive in India; Early Vedic Age, ca 1500–1000<br>Vedas, oldest Hindu sacred texts | Mycenaeans conquer Minoan Crete, ca 1450<br>Mycenaean Age, 1450–1200<br>Trojan War, ca 1180<br>Greek Dark Age, ca 1100–800 |
| Zhou Dynasty, promulgation of the Mandate of Heaven, ca 1027–256<br>Confucius, 551–479<br>First written reference to iron, ca 521 | Later Vedic Age, solidification of caste system, ca 1000–500<br>Upanishads; foundation of Hinduism, 700–500<br>Persians conquer parts of India, 513<br>Maharira, founder of Jainism, 540–486<br>Siddhartha Gautama (Buddha), 528–461 | Greek Lyric Age; rise of Sparta and Athens, 800–500<br>Origin of Greek polis, ca 700<br>Roman Republic founded, 509 |
| | | Persian Wars, 499–479<br>Athenian Empire; flowering of art and philosophy, 5th century<br>Peloponnesian War, 431–404 |
| Warring States Period in China, 403–221<br>Zhuangzi and development of Daoism, 369–268 | Alexander invades India, 327–326<br>Chandragupta founds Mauryan Dynasty, 322–ca 185 | Plato, 426–347<br>Roman expansion, 390–146<br>Conquests of Alexander the Great, 334–323 |

| | AFRICA AND THE MIDDLE EAST | THE AMERICAS |
|---|---|---|
| **300 B.C.E.** | Arsaces of Parthia begins conquest of Persia, ca 250–137<br>Scipio Africanus defeats Hannibal at Zama, 202 | Fall of La Venta, 300; Tres Zapotes becomes leading Olmec site |
| **200 B.C.E.** | | Andean peoples intensify agriculture, ca 200 |
| **100 B.C.E.** | Meroë becomes iron-smelting center, 1st century B.C.E.<br>Dead Sea Scrolls<br>Pompey conquers Syria and Palestine, 63 | |
| **100 C.E.** | Jesus Christ, ca 4 B.C.E.–30 C.E.<br>Bantu migrations begin<br>Jews revolt; Romans destroy temple in Jerusalem: end of Hebrew state, 70 | Moche civilization flourishes in Peru, ca 100–800 |
| **200 C.E.** | Camel first used for trans-Saharan transport, ca 200<br>Expansion of Bantu-speaking peoples, ca 200–900<br>Axum (Ethiopia) controls Red Sea trade, ca 250 | |
| **300 C.E.** | Axum accepts Christianity, ca 4th century | Maya civilization in Central America, ca 300–1500<br>Classic period of Teotihuacán civilization in Mexico, ca 300–900 |
| **500 C.E.** | Political and commercial ascendancy of Axum, ca 6th–7th centuries<br>Muhammad, 570–632; the *hijra,* 622<br>African Mediterranean slave trade, ca 600–1900<br>Umayyad Dynasty, 661–750; continued expansion of Islam | Mayan civilization reaches peak, ca 600–900<br>Tiahuanaco civilization in South America, ca 600–1000 |
| **700 C.E.** | Berbers control trans-Saharan trade, ca 700–900<br>Abbasid Dynasty, 750–1258; Islamic capital moved to Baghdad<br>Decline of Ethiopia, ca 9th century<br>Golden age of Muslim learning, ca 900–1100<br>Kingdom of Ghana, ca 900–1300 | Teotihuacán, Monte Alban destroyed, ca 700<br>"Time of Troubles" in Mesoamerica, 800–1000<br>Toltec hegemony, ca 980–1000 |

| EAST ASIA | INDIA AND SOUTHEAST ASIA | EUROPE |
| --- | --- | --- |
| Development of Legalism, ca 250–208<br>Qin Dynasty unifies China; Great Wall begun, Confucian literature destroyed, 221–210<br>Han Dynasty, 206 B.C.E.–220 C.E. | Ashoka, 269–232 | Punic Wars, destruction of Carthage, 264–146 |
| | Greeks invade India, ca 183–145<br>Mithridates creates Parthian empire, ca 171–131 | Late Roman Republic, 133–27 |
| China expands, ca 111<br>Silk Road opens to Parthia, Rome; Buddhism enters China, ca 104<br>First (Chinese) written reference to Japan, 45 C.E. | First Chinese ambassadors to India and Parthia, ca 140<br>Bhagavad Gita, ca 100 B.C.E.–100 C.E.<br>Shakas and Kushans invade eastern Parthia and India, 1st century C.E. | Julius Caesar killed, 44<br>Octavian seizes power, rules imperial Rome as Augustus, 27 B.C.E.–14 C.E. |
| Chinese invent paper, 105<br>Emperor Wu, 140–186 | Kushan rule in northwestern India, 2d–3d century<br>Roman attacks on Parthian empire, 115–211 | Roman Empire at greatest extent, 117<br>Breakdown of pax Romana, ca 180–284 |
| Creation of Yamato state in Japan, ca 3d century<br>Buddhism gains popularity in China and Japan, ca 220–590<br>Fall of Han Dynasty, 220; Period of Division, 220–589 | Fall of the Parthian empire, rise of the Sassanids, ca 225 | Reforms by Diocletian, 284–305 |
| Three Kingdoms Period in Korea, 313–668<br>China divides into northern, southern regimes, 316 | Chandragupta I founds Gupta Dynasty in India, ca 320–480<br>Gupta expansion, trade with Middle East and China, ca 400<br>Huns invade India, ca 450 | Constantine, 306–337; Edict of Milan, 313; founding of Constantinople, 324; Council of Nicaea, 325<br>Theodosius recognizes Christianity as official state religion, 380<br>Germanic raids on western Europe, 400s<br>Clovis rules Gauls, 481–511 |
| Sui Dynasty restores order in China, 581–618<br>Shotoku's "Constitution" in Japan, 604<br>Tang Dynasty, 618–907; cultural flowering<br>Taika Reforms in Japan, 646<br>Korea unified, 668 | Sanskrit drama, ca 600–1000 | Saint Benedict publishes his *Rule,* 529<br>Code of Justinian, 529<br>Synod of Whitby, 664 |
| Nara era, creation of Japan's first capital, 710–794<br>Heian era in Japan, 794–1185; literary flowering<br>Era of the Five Dynasties in China, 907–960<br>Song Dynasty, 960–1279 | Islam reaches India, 713<br>Khmer Empire (Kampuchea) founded, 802 | Charles Martel defeats Muslims at Tours, 732<br>Charlemagne rules, 768–814<br>Viking, Magyar invasions, 845–900<br>Treaty of Verdun divides Carolingian Empire, 843<br>Cluny monastery founded, 909 |

| | AFRICA AND THE MIDDLE EAST | THE AMERICAS |
|---|---|---|
| **1000** | Seljuk Turks take Baghdad, 1055<br>Islam penetrates sub-Saharan Africa, ca 11th century<br>Great Zimbabwe built, flourishes, ca 1100–1400<br>Kingdom of Benin, ca 1100–1897 | Inca civilization in South America, ca 1000–1500<br>Toltec state collapses, 1174 |
| **1200** | Kingdom of Mali, ca 1200–1450<br>Mongol invasion of Middle East, ca 1220<br>Mongols conquer Baghdad, 1258; fall of Abbasid Dynasty | Manco Capac, first Inca king, ca 1200 |
| **1300** | Rise of Yoruba states, West Africa, ca 1300<br>Height of Swahili (East African) city-states, ca 1300–1500<br>Mansa Musa rules Mali, 1312–1337<br>Ottomans invade Europe, 1356 | Aztecs arrive in Valley of Mexica, found Tenochtitlán (Mexico City), ca 1325 |
| **1400** | Arrival of Portuguese in Benin, ca 1440<br>Songhay Empire, ca 1450–1591<br>Atlantic slave trade, ca 1450–1850<br>Ottoman Empire, 1453–1918<br>Da Gama reaches East Africa, 1498 | Height of Inca Empire, 1438–1493<br>Reign of Montezuma I, 1440–1468; height of Aztec culture<br>Columbus reaches Americas, 1492 |
| **1500** | Portugal dominates East Africa, ca 1500–1650<br>Safavid Empire in Persia, 1501–1722; height of power under Shah Abbas, 1587–1629<br>Peak of Ottoman power under Suleiman, 1520–1566<br>Height of Kanem-Bornu, 1571–1603<br>Battle of Lepanto, 1571, signals Ottoman naval weakness in the eastern Mediterranean | Mesoamerican and South American holocaust, ca 1500–1600<br>First African slaves brought to Americas, ca 1510<br>Cortés arrives in Mexico, 1519; Aztec Empire falls, 1521<br>Pizarro reaches Peru, conquers Incas, 1531 |
| **1600** | Dutch West India Co. supplants Portuguese in West Africa, ca 1630<br>Dutch settle Cape Town, 1651 | British settle Jamestown, 1607<br>Champlain founds Quebec, 1608<br>Dutch found New Amsterdam, 1624<br>Black slave labor allows vast increase in sugar production in the Caribbean; of sugarcane, cotton, and coffee in Brazil; and of rice in the North American Carolinas and tobacco in Virginia |

| EAST ASIA | INDIA AND SOUTHEAST ASIA | EUROPE |
|---|---|---|
| China divided into Song, Jin empires, 1127<br>Kamakura Shogunate, 1185–1333 | Vietnam gains independence from China, ca 1000<br>Construction of Angkor Wat, ca 1100–1150<br>Muslim conquerors end Buddhism in India, 1192 | Yaroslav the Wise, 1019–1054; peak of Kievan Russia<br>Latin, Greek churches split, 1054<br>Norman Conquest of England, 1066<br>Investiture struggle, 1073–1122<br>Crusades, 1096–1270<br>Growth of trade and towns, ca 1100–1400<br>Barbarossa invades Italy, 1154–1158 |
| Mongol conquest of China begins, 1215<br>Yuan (Mongol) Dynasty, 1271–1368<br>Unsuccessful Mongol invasions of Japan, 1274, 1281<br>Marco Polo arrives at Kublai Khan's court, ca 1275 | Peak of Khmer Empire in Southeast Asia, ca 1200<br>Turkish sultanate at Delhi, 1206–1526 | Magna Carta, 1215<br>Aquinas, *Summa Theologica,* 1253<br>Nevsky recognizes Mongol overlordship of Moscow, 1252 |
| Ashikaga Shogunate, 1336–1408<br>Hung Wu defeats Mongols, 1368; founds Ming Dynasty, 1368–1644 | Tamerlame conquers the Punjab, 1398 | Babylonian Captivity of papacy, 1307–1377<br>Tver revolt in Russia, 1327–1328<br>Hundred Years' War, 1337–1453<br>Bubonic plague, 1347–1700<br>Beginnings of representative government, ca 1350–1500 |
| Ming policy encourages foreign trade, ca 15th century<br>Ming maritime expeditions to India, Middle East, Africa, 1405–1433 | Sultan Mehmed II, 1451–1481<br>Da Gama reaches India, 1498 | Italian Renaissance, ca 1400–1530<br>Voyagers of discovery, ca 1450–1600<br>Ottomans capture Constantinople, 1453; end of Byzantine Empire<br>War of the Roses in England, 1453–1471<br>Unification of Spain completed, 1492 |
| Portuguese trade monopoly in East Asia, ca 16th century<br>Christian missionaries active in China and Japan, ca 1550–1650<br>Unification of Japan, 1568–1600 | Babur defeats Delhi sultanate, 1526–1527; founds Mughal Empire<br>Akbar expands Mughal Empire, 1556–1605<br>Spanish conquer the Philippines, 1571 | Luther's Ninety-five Theses, 1517<br>Charles V elected Holy Roman emperor, 1519<br>English Reformation begins, 1532<br>Council of Trent, 1545–1563<br>Dutch declare independence, 1581<br>Spanish Armada, 1588 |
| Tokugawa Shogunate, 1600–1867<br>Japan expels all Europeans, 1637<br>Manchus establish Qing Dynasty, 1644–1911<br>Height of Qing Dynasty under K'ang-hsi, 1662–1722 | Height of Mughal Empire under Shah Jahan, 1628–1658<br>British found Calcutta, 1690 | Romanov Dynasty in Russia, 1613–1917<br>Thirty Years' War, 1618–1648<br>English Civil War, 1642–1649<br>Louis XIV, king of France, 1643–1715<br>Growth of absolutism in central and eastern Europe, ca 1680–1790<br>The Enlightenment, ca 1680–1800<br>Ottomans besiege Vienna, 1683<br>Revocation of Edict of Nantes, 1685<br>Glorious Revolution in England, 1688 |

| | AFRICA AND THE MIDDLE EAST | THE AMERICAS |
|---|---|---|
| **1700** | Rise of Ashanti Empire, ca 1700<br>Decline of Safavid Empire under Nadir Shah, 1737–1747 | Silver production quadruples in Mexico and Peru, ca 1700–1800<br>Spain's defeat in War of the Spanish Succession results in colonial dependence on Spanish goods, 1700s |
| **1750** | Selim III introduces administrative and military reforms, 1761–1808<br>British seize Cape Town, 1795<br>Napoleon's campaign in Egypt, 1798 | "French and Indian Wars," 1756–1763<br>Quebec Act, 1774<br>American Revolution, 1775–1783<br>Comunero revolution, New Granada, 1781 |
| **1800** | Muhammad Ali founds dynasty in Egypt, 1805–1848<br>Slavery abolished in British Empire, 1807<br>Peak year of African transatlantic slave trade, 1820 | Latin American wars of independence, 1806–1825<br>Brazil wins independence, 1822<br>Monroe Doctrine, 1823<br>Political instability in most Latin American countries, 1825–1870<br>U.S.-Mexican War, 1846–1848 |
| **1850** | Crimean War, 1853–1856<br>Suez Canal opens, 1869<br>European "scramble for Africa," 1880–1900<br>Battle of Omdurman, 1898<br>Boer War, 1899–1902 | American Civil War, 1861–1865<br>British North America Act, 1867, for Canada<br>Diaz controls Mexico, 1876–1911<br>United States practices "dollar diplomacy" in Latin America, 1890–1920s<br>Spanish-American War, 1898 |
| **1900** | Union of South Africa formed, 1910<br>French annex Morocco, 1912<br>Ottoman Empire dissolved, 1919; Kemal's nationalist struggle in Turkey | Massive immigration from Europe and Asia to the Americas, 1880–1914<br>Mexican Revolution, 1910<br>Panama Canal opens, 1914<br>Mexico adopts constitution, 1917 |
| **1920** | Cultural nationalism in Africa, 1920s<br>Turkish Republic recognized, 1923<br>Reza Shah leads Iran, 1925–1941 | U.S. "consumer revolution," 1920s<br>Stock market crash in United States; Great Depression begins, 1929 |
| **1930** | African farmers organize first "cocoa holdups," 1930–1931<br>Iraq gains independence, 1932 | Revolutions in six South American countries, 1930<br>New Deal begins in United States, 1933 |
| **1940** | Arabs and Jews at war in Palestine; Israel created, 1948<br>Apartheid system in South Africa, 1948–1991 | Surprise attack by Japan on Pearl Harbor, 1941<br>United Nations established, 1945<br>Perón rules Argentina, 1946–1953 |

| EAST ASIA | ᴉIA AND SOUTHEAST ASIA | EUROPE |
|---|---|---|
| Height of Edo urban cult 1700<br>Height of Qing Dynasty u Ch'ien-lung, 1736–179 | ine of Mughal Empire, ca 1700–1800<br>ian invaders loot Delhi, 1739<br>ch and British fight for control of India, 40–1763 | War of Spanish Succession, 1701–1713<br>Treaty of Utrecht, 1713<br>Cabinet system develops in England, 1714–1742 |
| Maximum extent of Qing | ty of Paris gives French colonies in India Britain, 1763<br>k in Australia, 1768–1771; first British vict-settlers arrive in Australia, 1788<br>India Act, 1784 | Watt produces first steam engine, 1769<br>Outbreak of French Revolution, 1789<br>National Convention declares France a republic, 1792 |
| Anglo-Chinese Opium Wa<br>Treaty of Nanjing, 1842: M Hong Kong to British | h found Singapore, 1819<br>War, 1825–1830<br>h defeat last independent native state in ia, 1848 | Napoleonic Empire, 1804–1814<br>Congress of Vienna, 1814–1815<br>European economic penetration of non-Western countries, ca 1816–1880<br>Greece wins independence, 1830<br>Revolution of 1848 |
| Taiping Rebellion, 1850–1<br>Perry's arrival opens Japan and Europe, 1853<br>Meiji Restoration in Japan,<br>Adoption of constitution in<br>Sino-Japanese War, 1894–1<br>"Hundred Days of Reform" | Rebellion in India, 1857–1858<br>h seize Saigon, 1859<br>n National Congress formed, 1885<br>h acquire Indochina, 1893<br>d States gains Philippines, 1898 | Second Empire and Third Republic in France, 1852–1914<br>Unification of Italy, 1859–1870<br>Bismarck controls Germany, 1862–1890<br>Franco-Prussian War, 1870–1871; foundation of the German Empire<br>Second Reform Bill, Great Britain, 1867<br>Second Socialist International, 1889–1914 |
| Boxer Rebellion in China, 1<br>Russo-Japanese War, 1904–<br>Chinese revolution; fall of Q 1911<br>Chinese Republic, 1912–194 | nonwealth of Australia, 1900<br>n League formed, 1906<br>alls for Indian independence, 1907<br>ar massacre in India, 1919<br>ification of Indian nationalism, 1919– | Revolution in Russia; Tsar Nicholas II issues October Manifesto, 1905<br>Triple Entente (Britain, Russia, France), 1914–1918<br>World War I, 1914–1918<br>Treaty of Versailles, 1919 |
| Kita Ikki advocates ultranatio 1923<br>Jiang Jieshi unites China, 19 | i launches nonviolent resistance cam-, 1920 | Mussolini seizes power in Italy, 1922<br>Stalin takes power in U.S.S.R., 1927<br>Depths of Great Depression, 1929–1933 |
| Japan invades China, 1931<br>Mao Zedong's Long March,<br>Sino-Japanese War, 1937–19 | i's Salt March, 1930<br>onquers Southeast Asia, 1939–1942 | Hitler gains power, 1933<br>Civil War in Spain, 1936–1939<br>World War II, 1939–1945 |
| United States drops atomic b Hiroshima and Nagasaki, 19<br>Chinese civil war, 1945–1949 win | nes gain independence, 1946<br>Hindu) and Pakistan (Muslim) gain endence, 1947 | Marshall Plan, 1947<br>NATO formed, 1949<br>Soviet Union and Red China sign 30-year alliance, 1949 |

| | | |
|---|---|---|
| **1950** | Egypt declared a republic; Nass premier, 1954<br>Morocco, Tunisia, Sudan, and independence, 1956–1957<br>French-British Suez invasion, 1 | es power in Cuba, 1959 |
| **1960** | Mali, Nigeria, and the Congo ence, 1960<br>Biafra declares independence f 1967<br>Arab-Israeli Six-Day War, 1967 | issile crisis, 1962<br>lictatorship in Brazil, 1964–1985<br>tates escalates war in Vietnam, 1964 |
| **1970** | "Yom Kippur War," 1973<br>Islamic revolution in Iran, 197<br>Camp David Accords, 1979 | coup in Chile, 1973<br>ergate scandal, 1974<br>ons in Nicaragua and El Salvador, |
| **1980** | Iran-Iraq War, 1980–1988<br>Reforms in South Africa, 198 | itary buildup, 1980–1988<br>a restores civilian rule, 1983 |
| **1990** | Growth of Islamic fundament present<br>Iraq driven from Kuwait by U allies, 1991<br>Israel and Palestinians sign pe 1993<br>Nelson Mandela elected presi Africa, 1994 | Mexico, and United States form free- rea (NAFTA), 1994<br>ablishes democratic government,<br>ent extension of Treaty on the Non- ration of Nuclear Weapons, 1995 |
| **2000** | End of Taliban regime in Afg | st attack on United States, mber 11, 2001 |

| EAST ASIA | INDIA AND SOUTHEAST ASIA | EUROPE |
| --- | --- | --- |
| Korean War, 1950–1953<br>Japan begins long period of rapid economic growth, 1950<br>Mao Zedong announces Great Leap Forward, 1958 | Vietnamese nationalists defeat French; Vietnam divided, 1954<br>Islamic Republic of Pakistan declared, 1956 | Death of Stalin, 1953<br>Warsaw Pact, 1955<br>Revolution in Hungary, 1956<br>Common Market formed, 1957 |
| Sino-Soviet split becomes apparent, 1960<br>Great Proletarian Cultural Revolution in China, 1965–1969 | Indira Gandhi prime minister of India, 1966–1977, 1980–1984 | Student revolution in France, 1968<br>Soviet invasion of Czechoslovakia, 1968 |
| China pursues modernization, 1976 to present | India-Pakistan war, 1971<br>Communist victory in Vietnam War, 1975<br>Chinese invade Vietnam, 1979 | Brandt's Ostpolitik, 1969–1973<br>Soviet invasion of Afghanistan, 1979 |
| Japanese foreign investment surge, 1980–1992<br>China crushes democracy movement, 1989 | Sikh nationalism in India, 1984 to present<br>Corazón Aquino takes power in Philippines, 1986 | Soviet reform under Gorbachev, 1985–1991<br>Communism falls in eastern Europe, 1989–1990 |
| Birthrates keep falling<br>Economic growth and political repression in China, 1990 to present<br>Hong Kong returns to Chinese rule, 1997 | Vietnam embraces foreign investment, 1990 to present<br>U.S. military bases closed in Philippines, 1991 | Maastricht treaty proposes monetary union, 1990<br>Conservative economic policies, 1990s<br>End of Soviet Union, 1991<br>Civil war in Bosnia, 1991–1995<br>Creation of European Union, 1993 |
|  |  | Euro note enters circulation, 2002 |

# TEXT CREDITS

**Pages 11, 15:** Excerpts from S. N. Kramer, *The Sumerians: Their History, Culture and Character,* University of Chicago Press, Chicago, 1963, page 238. Reprinted by permission. **Page 16:** Poem from *Ancient Near Eastern Texts,* 3d ed., by J. B. Pritchard. Copyright © 1969 by Princeton University Press. Reprinted by permission of Princeton University Press. **Page 62:** Poem reprinted from Juan Mascaro, trans., *The Upanishads* (London: Penguin Books, 1965). Copyright Juan Mascaro, 1965. Reproduced by permission of Penguin Books Ltd. **Page 69:** Excerpt from *The Bhagavad-gita: Krishna's Counsel in Time of War,* trans. by Barbara Stoll Miller, pages 31–32. Copyright © 1986 Columbia University Press. Reprinted with permission of the publisher. **Pages 73–74:** Poem from *Poems of Love and War,* by A. K. Ramanujan, page 115. Copyright © 1985 Columbia University Press. Reprinted with permission of the publisher. **Pages 89, 90, 94, 95, 96, 97, 98:** Extracts reprinted with the permission of The Free Press, an imprint of Simon & Schuster Adult Publishing Group, from *Chinese Civilization: A Sourcebook,* 2d ed., by Patricia Buckley Ebrey. Copyright © 1993 by Patricia Buckley Ebrey. **Page 197:** "A cup of wine" from "Drinking Alone by Moonlight," by Li Bo, translated by Arthur Waley from *More Translations from the Chinese,* George Allen & Unwin Ltd. Reprinted by permission of The Arthur Waley Estate. **Page 197:** "From these high walls" from "After Collecting the Autumn Taxes," by Po-Chui (Bo Juyi), translated by Arthur Waley from *Chinese Poems,* George Allen & Unwin Ltd. Reprinted by permission of The Arthur Waley Estate. **Page 204:** Poem from Martin Collcott, Marius Jansen, and Isao Kumakura, *Cultural Atlas of Japan,* page 65. Reprinted by permission of Andromeda (Oxford) Ltd. **Pages 308, 314, 315:** Poetry from A. L. Basham, trans., *The Wonder That Was India*, 2d ed. (New York: Grove Press, 1959), pp. 420, 161, 459–460. Reprinted with permission. **Page 562:** Poetry by Joost van den Vondel from *Europe in the Seventeenth Century,* by David Ogg, pages 198–199. Reprinted by permission of A&C Black Publishers Ltd. **Pages 614, 616:** Excerpt from *Equiano's Travels: The Interesting Narrative of the Life of Olaudah Equiano,* ed. Paul Edwards (Portsmouth, N.H.: Heineman, 1996).

GREENLAND
(DENMARK)
ICELAND
ALASKA
(U.S.)
CANADA
IRELAND
UNITED STATES
PORTUGAL
Azores
Bermuda
ATLANTIC OCEAN
Midway Is.
WESTERN
SAHARA
(MOROCCO)
BAHAMAS
Hawaiian Is.
MEXICO
DOMINICAN REP.
Virgin Is.
CUBA
JAMAICA
HAITI
ST. KITTS AND NEVIS
ANTIGUA AND BARBUDA
BELIZE
HONDURAS
Puerto Rico
DOMINICA
MAURITANIA
GUATEMALA
BARBADOS
ST. LUCIA
ST. VINCENT AND
THE GRENADINES
CAPE
VERDE
SENEGAL
GAMBIA
GRENADA
NICARAGUA
EL SALVADOR
PACIFIC OCEAN
GUINEA-BISSAU
GUINEA
COSTA RICA
TRINIDAD AND TOBAGO
VENEZUELA
GUYANA
SIERRA
LEONE
IVORY
COAST
PANAMA
FR. GUIANA
LIBERIA
COLOMBIA
Equator
SURINAM
Galapagos Is.
ECUADOR
PERU
BRAZIL
WESTERN
SAMOA
BOLIVIA
TONGA
PARAGUAY
CHILE
Easter Is.
URUGUAY
ARGENTINA
Falkland Is.
160¡W
140¡W
120¡W
100¡W
80¡W
60¡W
40¡W
20¡W
80¡N
60¡N
40¡N
20¡N
0¡
20¡S
40¡S
60¡S
80¡S